THE BIBLE
FOR EVERYONE

THE BIBLE FOR EVERYONE

A new translation

John Goldingay
and
Tom Wright

First published in Great Britain in 2018

Society for Promoting Christian Knowledge
Studio 101, The Record Hall
16-16A Baldwins Gardens, London EC1N 7RJ
www.spckpublishing.co.uk

Old Testament translation, introductory material and glossary
copyright © John Goldingay 2018
New Testament translation originally published in Great Britain in 2011
as *The New Testament for Everyone*. New Testament translation
copyright © Nicholas Thomas Wright 2011, 2018; introductory material and glossary
copyright © Nicholas Thomas Wright 2018

Maps in Genesis to Hosea by Kev Jones <kevdesign@me.com>
Maps in the New Testament by Pantek Arts Ltd, Maidstone, Kent, UK

All rights reserved. No part of this book may be reproduced or transmitted in any form or by any means, electronic or mechanical, including photocopying, recording, or by any information storage and retrieval system, without permission in writing from the publisher.

SPCK does not necessarily endorse the individual views contained
in its publications.

British Library Cataloguing-in-Publication Data
A catalogue record for this book is available from the British Library

ISBN 978–0–281–07401–3
eBook ISBN 978–0–281–07402–0

5 7 9 10 8 6 4

Typeset by Manila Typesetting Company
Printed in China
FT1491901

eBook by Manila Typesetting Company

Produced on paper from sustainable forests

Contents

List of maps   vii

THE OLD TESTAMENT FOR EVERYONE
John Goldingay

Preface to the Old Testament for Everyone	xi	Psalms	526
		Proverbs	604
Introduction to the Old Testament for Everyone	xv	Ecclesiastes	631
		The Song of Songs	641
Genesis	1	Isaiah	648
Exodus	52	Jeremiah	709
Leviticus	94	Lamentations	773
Numbers	125	Ezekiel	780
Deuteronomy	168	Daniel	831
Joshua	206	Hosea	847
Judges	233	Joel	858
Ruth	259	Amos	863
1 Samuel	264	Obadiah	871
2 Samuel	297	Jonah	874
1 Kings	326	Micah	877
2 Kings	359	Nahum	884
1 Chronicles	391	Habakkuk	888
2 Chronicles	422	Zephaniah	892
Ezra	457	Haggai	896
Nehemiah	469	Zechariah	899
Esther	486	Malachi	909
Job	495	*An Old Testament glossary*	913

THE NEW TESTAMENT FOR EVERYONE
Tom Wright

Preface to the New Testament for Everyone	927	1 Corinthians	1132
		2 Corinthians	1148
Introduction to the New Testament for Everyone	931	Galatians	1159
		Ephesians	1165
Matthew	935	Philippians	1172
Mark	971	Colossians	1177
Luke	993	1 Thessalonians	1182
John	1029	2 Thessalonians	1186
The Acts of the Apostles	1059	1 Timothy	1189
Romans	1115	2 Timothy	1194

Titus	1198	1 John	1231
Philemon	1201	2 John	1236
Hebrews	1203	3 John	1238
James	1216	Judah	1240
1 Peter	1221	The Revelation of John	1242
2 Peter	1227	*A New Testament glossary*	1260

Alphabetical listing of the books of the Bible   1269

Maps

Old Testament

Ancient Near East	xix
Ancient Israel	xx
City of Jerusalem	xxi
Genesis 13: Abraham	11
Genesis 25: Yitshaq (Isaac)	23
Genesis 38: Ya'aqob (Jacob)	38
Exodus 1: Mosheh (Moses)	53
Exodus 25: The sanctuary – Yahweh's dwelling	77
Numbers 10: The wilderness	139
Kena'an (Canaan) at the time of Yehoshua (Joshua)	208
Joshua 13: The twelve clans	220
The 'major' judges	236
Yisra'el at the time of Shemu'el (Samuel)	267
1 Samuel 16: Sha'ul (Saul) and David	280
2 Samuel 1: David	299
1 Kings 6: The temple of Shelomoh (Solomon)	334
1 Kings 12: The two nations – Ephrayim and Yehudah (Ephraim and Judah)	344
2 Kings 2: Eliyyahu (Elijah) and Elisha	361
2 Kings 17: The fall of Ephrayim and Yehudah (Ephraim and Judah)	379
1 Chronicles 5: The twelve clans	397
1 Chronicles 12: David	406
Ancient Near East at the time of Ezra	458
Nehemiah 4: Nehemyah's Yerushalaim (Nehemiah's Jerusalem)	473
Isaiah 14: Ancient Near East at the time of Yesha'yahu (Isaiah)	661
Jeremiah 7: Yehudah (Judah) at the time of Yirmeyahu (Jeremiah)	719
Ezekiel 40: The temple in Yehezqe'l's (Ezekiel's) vision	822
Ephrayim (Ephraim) and Yehudah (Judah) at the time of Hoshea (Hosea)	848

New Testament

Galilee, Samaria and Judaea in the first century AD	934
The eastern Mediterranean in the first century AD	1058
Acts 1.6–8	1060
Acts 2.5–13	1062
Acts 3.1–10, 11–16	1064
Acts 6.9	1068
Acts 8.4–25	1071
Acts 8.26–40	1072
Acts 9.1–9	1073
Acts 9.19–26, 30	1074
Acts 9.32, 35, 36	1075
Acts 10.1–16	1076
Acts 11.19–30	1079
Acts 12.20–25	1080
Acts 13.1–6	1081
Acts 13.13–25	1082
Acts 13.51	1084
Acts 14.1–7	1085
Acts 14.21–28	1086
Acts 15.1–11	1087
Acts 15.39–41	1088
Acts 16.1–10	1089

Acts 16.11–12	1090	Acts 21.15–17	1101
Acts 17.1	1091	Acts 23.23–35	1104
Acts 17.10–21	1092	Acts 27.1–12	1109
Acts 18.1	1093	Acts 27.13–32	1110
Acts 18.18–28	1094	Acts 28.11–22	1112
Acts 19.1–10	1096	The destinations of Paul's letters	1114
Acts 20.1–12	1098		
Acts 20.13–27	1099	1 Peter 1.1	1222
Acts 21.1–14	1100	The seven churches of Asia	1244

THE OLD TESTAMENT FOR EVERYONE

JOHN GOLDINGAY

Preface to the Old Testament for Everyone

The idea of an 'Old Testament for Everyone' in English goes back at least to William Tyndale, the first great figure of the English Reformation, who was executed in 1536. A few decades after the printing press came into use in Europe, Tyndale made it his ambition to produce an English translation of the Bible that could be printed and made available to the 'boy that driveth the plough' (so John Foxe's *Book of Martyrs*, published a few decades after Tyndale's death). In other words, it could be made available to 'everyone'. Tyndale completed the New Testament and started on the Old, which Miles Coverdale later completed. The 'Old Testament for Everyone' is thus a long-running project.

The present translation brings together the translation sections from the series of little commentaries called the Old Testament for Everyone, and fills in the gaps in those volumes. I have substantially revised the translation in those commentaries, partly because I hadn't worried about consistency of style and approach between them as I produced them, whereas it seemed necessary to aim at consistency in this complete translation.

There are many ways of going about translation, and sometimes people try to argue that such-and-such an approach is right and others wrong. I don't think that one approach is necessarily better than all others, and there's no such thing as the best translation of the Old Testament. All translations are more or less accurate, but producing a faithful equivalent of any piece of writing in another language is an impossible undertaking; all approaches involve compromise. Translations thus have varying strengths and weaknesses according to the way they choose to prioritize the principles of translation.

I had three or four principles in mind when I began this work, and I formulated three or four more in the course of completing it. There is some tension between these principles, and where my translation is jerky, the jerkiness probably reflects one or other of them. I have finally aimed to produce a translation that as far as possible has the following characteristics.

- It sticks close to the way the Hebrew (and Aramaic) works rather than paraphrasing it, so that readers can get as close as possible to the details of the original text. Sometimes when I've added words to make the meaning clearer, I've put these words in square brackets. Nowadays translations are more inclined to aim at translating sentence by sentence, which has opposite advantages and disadvantages to translating word by word. My translation moves in that older direction, in rendering more word by word. It's consequently more suitable for a slow read than for a quick read, and more suitable for reading on one's own than for reading out loud. And where a sentence may make sense but you're not sure what it refers to or how it fits into the context, it's probably because the text itself doesn't make it clear, and I've left it that way. As a further consequence, although I myself prefer to use gender-inclusive language, I've let the translation stay gendered where inclusivizing it obscures whether the text is using singular or plural – in other words, the translation often uses 'he' when the text refers to a man or a woman and where in my own writing I would thus say 'they' or 'he or she'.

- It stays with the traditional Hebrew text (like the New Jewish Publication Society Version) rather than emending it. When I was making the translation I thus started from that traditional text itself, but I did refer to some existent translations, and sometimes adopted expressions from them. These other translations also occasionally made me see where I had slipped up, by missing out some words or misreading a word, just like an ancient scribe. I noticed, too, that sometimes they had slipped up in similar ways. I expect I have not eliminated all my mistakes, and you are welcome to let me know at johngold@fuller.edu where you notice one. At johngoldingay.com, under OT Introduction – OT for Everyone, I will post any corrections that come to my notice and any other comments I think of regarding my reason for translating particular verses the way I have.

- It uses everyday English in the sense that it often employs abbreviations such as 'I'll' and 'we'll' for 'I will and 'we will'. In addition, for some common Hebrew words it generally avoids traditional English translations such as salvation, holiness, eternity, covenant, justice and righteousness, where these translations don't correspond well to the Hebrew words and/ or where the English words are misleading when used to translate Hebrew words that have different connotations.

- In the poetic sections, I've laid out the lines so that they correspond to the way I think the poetry works. Poetic lines commonly comprise two parts (sometimes three) that link with each other to form a complete sentence. In the translation, the second part (and the third, if there is one) appears indented as a second (or third) line.

- It tries to use the same English word to translate any one Hebrew word, so that one can see points of connection between texts. Translations of Exodus, for instance, commonly use the words slavery, bondage, servant and worship to render forms of the same Hebrew word, and part of the point of the story depends on our being able to see the links between the occurrences of this word. So in this example I try to use 'serve' and related words for all occurrences of the related Hebrew words. This principle is also different from the one taken by modern translations that focus on the meaning of words in individual sentences.

- It uses the name for God that God invited Israel to use, the name Yahweh, rather than replacing it with the expressions 'the LORD' or 'GOD'. 'Yahweh' is the name God gave Moses to share with the Israelites. It's God's personal name. For many centuries within Old Testament times Israelites thus used this name, and it comes very frequently in the Old Testament. But late on in Old Testament times, people were less inclined to use the name, perhaps for two reasons. On one hand, if it's important not to take Yahweh's name in vain, it might be safer not to take it at all. On the other, using this name could give the impression that Israel's God was just a little local god, whereas in reality he's the Creator and Lord of the whole world. So Jews started replacing the name Yahweh by the word for 'Lord' or 'God', and they added marks to the text of the Scriptures to remind people to read out one of those other words in place of the name. When the Bible got translated into other languages, the name was then replaced by the equivalents of those words. The snag is that the alteration often spoils the sense of passages. So I have accepted Yahweh's invitation to call him by his personal name. (People sometimes ask me whether this practice is offensive to Jews. The general answer is that they are not offended by other people using the name. As with prescriptions in the Torah, not to do so is simply their vocation or discipline.)

- It translates some other names rather than just transliterating them, or it provides an equivalent English expression for them. English forenames and place names such as Hope or Grace or Wells or Orange County are ordinary words as well as names, and English-speakers are sometimes aware of the resonance about such a name. Other names such as John and Sheffield also have ordinary words behind them, but English-speakers are less likely to be aware of these. Something similar applies to Hebrew names. So I occasionally translate such names when it seems likely that an Israelite would have been aware of their meaning (e.g. 'The Height' for the place transliterated as Ramah, which has 'the' on the front of it in Hebrew). In some other cases I provide the English meaning of the name in square brackets after the name, especially where the context implies an awareness of the name's meaning (e.g. Adam means 'human being').

- Another consequence of the translation of the Old Testament into Greek, then of the Greek into Latin, then of the Latin into English, was that Mosheh became Moses, Yesha'yahu became Isaiah, Yerushalaim became Jerusalem, and so on (and Yohanan became John). I have left such names in their original form, but sometimes added in square brackets the familiar English form

of a name – especially the first time it occurs. By using more precise transliterations (without being too technical) I hope also to make it a bit easier to work out the pronunciation of names (e.g. 'Jehoiachin' gives the impression that the name includes a 'j' sound and a 'ch' sound, neither of which is true: 'Yehoyakin' is less misleading). I have represented Hebrew letters as follows:
- zayin becomes z (rather than s);
- kaph becomes k (rather than ch);
- qoph becomes q (rather than k);
- tsade becomes ts (rather than z; except that I spell Misrayim rather than Mitsrayim);
- he and het both become h (sorry not to distinguish these);
- sameq and sin both become s (sorry not to distinguish these);
- when aleph or ayin comes in the middle of names, both become ' (sorry not to distinguish these), like an apostrophe in English, so as to help with pronouncing them. But when they come at the beginning or end of names, I ignore them.

- There is one further aspect of the appearance of names that may seem surprising to Western readers. As William Shakespeare had a number of ways of spelling his name, so the Old Testament uses several forms of some names. For instance, Hizqiyyahu, Hizqiyyah and Yehizqiyyahu are all ways of referring to the king who usually appears in English translations as Hezekiah. The place we know as Bethel can be called Bet-el or Bet El. I have preserved these differences rather than smoothed them out, so where such differences appear in the translation, it probably means they are examples of this inherent diversity rather than mistakes.

The Old Testament for Everyone series and this translation were the brainchild of Philip Law, with whom I've worked both at SPCK and at Westminster John Knox. I'm grateful to him for our long-standing and relaxed partnership; as I am to my agent Pieter Kwant, whom I ask for advice about possible projects, and whose enthusiasm for the Old Testament for Everyone commentary series was important to my agreeing to embark on that undertaking. I am also grateful to Mollie Barker for her exceedingly careful editing work, which saved me from many slips.

I've tried to work out how long the translation took, and the nearest I have to an answer is an hour or two a day for about five years, plus the revision time which took me the best part of a year. The commentary took another hour or two a day for about five years.

Introduction to the Old Testament for Everyone

'The Old Testament' is the usual Christian name for the collection of Scriptures dating from before the time of Jesus that Jews and Christians have in common. The actual title 'The Old Testament' comes from two or three centuries after Jesus and links with the fact that by then the Church had acquired some further Scriptures which it came to call 'The New Testament'. As well as pairing the Old Testament Scriptures with the New Testament Scriptures, Christian Bibles have the Old Testament Scriptures in a different order, and that order is the one *The Old Testament for Everyone* follows.

In this order, the Old Testament unfolds as follows:

1. Genesis, Exodus, Leviticus, Numbers, Deuteronomy
    – the 'Pentateuch' or the 'Torah', traditionally 'The Five Books of Moses', telling the story of the world's beginnings and of the beginnings of Israel;
2. Joshua, Judges, Ruth, 1 and 2 Samuel, 1 and 2 Kings
    – the continuation of Genesis to Deuteronomy, relating Israel's story from its arrival in Canaan to the fall of Jerusalem to the Babylonians;
3. Chronicles, Ezra, Nehemiah, Esther
    – a retelling of the entire story in Genesis to Kings followed by a continuation that relates the restoration of Jerusalem, and by a story about Jewish experience in Persia itself;
4. Job, Psalms, Proverbs, Ecclesiastes, Song of Songs
    – books that are nearly all poetry and that relate more directly to everyday life, worship and prayer, sometimes in confident affirmations, sometimes in questions;
5. Isaiah, Jeremiah, Lamentations, Ezekiel, Daniel, the Twelve Shorter Prophets
    – mostly collections of short messages that challenge and encourage Israel about its present life and circumstances and about the future that lies ahead of it.

What was the Old Testament for?

Why is the Old Testament this kind of collection of works? What were they supposed to do for the Israelites for whom they were written and for the Jewish community that first came to recognize them as their Scriptures? And what are they supposed to do for the Christian Church?

Their very nature suggests what they were designed to be for Israel and for the Jewish people. First they tell them the beginning of their story, and they thus help them understand who they are. Then they continue that story into subsequent centuries, which adds to this effect. They collect the expectations regarding their lives that God enabled them to formulate over the centuries, which are also therefore expected to shape their life on an ongoing basis. They speak in the present about how life works, how praise and prayer are designed to be, and how to wrestle with some of life's key problems. And they record some of God's nightmares and dreams about the people's future.

When some Jews came to believe in Jesus and to see his coming as the climax of Israel's own story, they naturally used these resources to help them understand Jesus. The 'New Testament' did not regard the 'Old Testament' as 'old' in the sense of antiquated or out of date; to make that point, I sometimes like to refer to it as the First Testament rather than the Old Testament. For Jesus and the New Testament writers, these Scriptures were a living resource for understanding God, God's ways in the world and God's ways with us. Every part of them was useful 'for teaching, reproving, correcting, and training in righteousness, so that anyone who belongs to God can be proficient, equipped for every good work' (2 Timothy 3.16–17). They were for everyone, in fact. So it's strange that Christians don't read them very much.

1. The first three sequences as the Old Testament unfolds are stories or histories. Calling them histories implies that they are talking about things that happened. They helped Israel understand itself by talking about where it came from. Calling them stories points to the fact that they are not just talking about things that happened; they have lessons written into them. Sometimes they pass on traditional stories that are simply good stories to illustrate a point, but more often they are stories with a basis in things that happened.

   That fact points us to a significant aspect of the significance of these stories for Israel. Christians sometimes assume that the basic thing about their faith is that it is a challenge to live the right kind of life and pursue peace and justice, and that the stories in the Old Testament are there to give us good examples (or warning examples). But the stories themselves rarely have moral evaluations built into them, and people reading the stories may disagree about the moral evaluation we should come to. This points us to the fact that the stories are more about what God has been doing than about what human beings have been doing. God is pursuing a project – to bring into being a world that fulfils his creation purpose. He can sometimes achieve things by means of the human beings he gets involved with; he sometimes has to pursue his objectives despite the actions of the people he gets involved with. But the propriety of their actions is not the main point. The main point is that God is at work.

2. God's expectations of human beings do come into focus within the first sequence, the Torah, which incorporates considerable material telling Israel about how its life is to be lived. It mixes up moral challenges, social policy and instructions for worship. It connects the teaching on these topics to the story by describing the kind of lifestyle that God has a right to expect in light of what he's done for Israel. It also warns Israel of trouble to follow if people take no notice of the teaching.

   Jesus suggests several clues for interpreting this material. One is that the entirety of the Torah and the Prophets depends on the two commands to love God and love one's neighbour. So of any of the commands (especially the puzzling ones) one may ask how it is an outworking of either of these basic commands. Another clue is that sometimes the Torah is expounding God's creation vision, while sometimes it is making allowance for the human stubbornness that resists this creation vision. Paradoxically, even when it is making allowance in this way, it is an expression of love; the particular circumstance that Jesus mentions is the requirement that a man who divorces a wife must provide her with papers that lay out her legal position.

3. The books from Joshua to Kings relate how Israel put the teaching into practice – or more often failed to do so. So by the time you get to the end of Joshua to Kings, what the books are doing is explaining how things went wrong in Israel's life and why Israel ended up being put down by two successive superpowers, Assyria and Babylon. So they draw Israel to face facts and turn back to God.

   The books from Chronicles to Esther then do two things. They retell the story from Genesis to Kings, in a bit the way that (say) Matthew retells the story in Mark. In both cases, the assumption is that a story needs to be told in a way that will help its readers see what it has to say to them. The people for whom Chronicles is written are not under God's judgement like the people for whom Joshua to Kings are written. They need encouragement more than rebuke. So the story is told in a way designed to encourage them.

   Ezra–Nehemiah and Esther then take the story on into the time of people living later, whether in Jerusalem or in the Dispersion. They make explicit some of the reasons why people in their day needed encouragement, and they also thereby indicate something of the ongoing significance of the books from Chronicles to Esther. The Church in the West, at least, lives in discouraging times. And the Church in other parts of the world often lives in dangerous times, the kind of times about which Esther speaks.

4. The books from Job to Song of Songs more explicitly focus on the present. Psalms provides us with 150 examples of things you can say to God in praise, in prayer and in thanksgiving. It's

been said that the book of Psalms used to be where Christians learned to pray, but if it was so in the past, it's isn't so now. We could try reverting to it. Proverbs, Job, Ecclesiastes and Song of Songs all start from everyday life outside the context of worship and share with their readers insights that the writers have gained from their experience of life or through considering the wisdom of other people who have reflected on life. On the whole, Proverbs does so in a positive way, telling people how life works and how to make it work. Job and Ecclesiastes do so in a more questioning way. Job starts from the fact that bad things happen to good people and wrestles with various ways of living with that reality. Ecclesiastes starts from the more general fact that it's hard to make sense of life in the world (especially given that we all die), and seeks to help readers live with that fact. The Song of Songs takes an enthusiastic but realistic look at the wonder of relationships between the sexes and at the pressures that come on those relationships.

5. The background of the Prophets is the time when the great powers start to dominate Israel's life, the time of Assyria and Babylon, then of Persia and Greece. The Prophets seek to get Israel to see how God is involved in this development, initially to bring God's chastisement because of Israel's rebellion and unfaithfulness (in the time of Assyria and Babylon), then to bring God's restoration (by means of Persia), then to bring agents of persecution from which God needs to rescue his people (in the Greek period). They challenge Israel to turn back to God and to live by trust rather than by the assumption that they control their own destinies. The Prophets' messages about the empires provide the Church with ways of thinking about empires and superpowers in the modern world.

A minor theme in the Prophets is the articulation of a hope for a better king to come – the figure later called the Messiah (but the word does not come in this connection in the Old Testament). That promise is part of the broader theme that chastisement and persecution will not be God's last word. There is going to be a new heaven and a new earth in the sense of a new Jerusalem, one characterized by mutual commitment rather than by people taking advantage of one another and by joy and fulfilment, where everyone will be able to sit under their vine or fig tree. Some aspects of the Prophets' promises found fulfilment in Israel's life, some illumine what Jesus was and did, some continue to promise us the fulfilment of God's creation purpose.

How did the Old Testament come into being?

The books in the Old Testament were written in the form that we have them between about the eighth and the second centuries before Christ. (Like most things in this Introduction, there could be arguments about those dates – and the same applies to the translation that follows – but I don't think anything here is an idiosyncratic view of mine.)

Most of the Old Testament is of anonymous authorship, and we don't know who wrote the books or when. The King James Version has some introductions such as 'The First Book of Moses, Called Genesis' or 'The Lamentations of Jeremiah', but these are not part of the text. The first books that give us names and dates are those associated with prophets such as Hosea, Amos and Micah, and these give us dates in the eighth century, which is the reason for mentioning the eighth century. The last event directly referred to is the great crisis in Jerusalem in the 160s BC when a Greek Seleucid king banned proper worship in Jerusalem, which the visions in Daniel refer to, so that's the reason for mentioning the second century. We also don't know much about the process whereby the Jewish community came to accept these books as their Scriptures.

The book of Ezra does speak of a priest-theologian called Ezra bringing 'the Torah' from Babylonia to Jerusalem in 458 BC, and 'The Torah' or 'The Law' is the later name for the books from Genesis to Deuteronomy. It wouldn't be surprising if this story in Ezra tells us when 'The Torah' came to be accepted as Scripture in Jerusalem. Later, again in the second century, the preface to a work variously called Ecclesiasticus or Ben Sira or Sirach refers to 'The Law and the Prophets and the rest of the books', which is quite similar to the later expression 'The Torah, the Prophets and the Writings', a common title in the Jewish community for what Christians call the Old Testament.

And as far as Jesus and the New Testament writers were concerned, these were the Scriptures. In putting it that way, I cut a corner a bit, as the New Testament never gives us a list of these Scriptures, but the body of writings that the Jewish people accept is as near as we can get to identifying the collection that Jesus and the New Testament writers would have worked with.

We don't have any record of a meeting 'deciding' that these books and no others would count as the Scriptures. It wouldn't surprise me if it just happened; nobody exactly decided it. These writings compelled themselves on the Jewish people one by one. And it wouldn't surprise me if the last time something compelled itself on the Jewish people with this kind of force was that crisis in Jerusalem in the 160s when the visions in Daniel promised God's deliverance of his people, and were proved true.

The Church also came to accept some extra books such as Maccabees and the aforementioned Ecclesiasticus. They were traditionally called the 'Apocrypha', the books that were 'hidden away', but that name came to imply 'spurious'. They're now often known as the 'Deutero-canonical Writings', which is more cumbersome but less pejorative. It simply indicates that these books have less authority than the Torah, the Prophets and the Writings. The precise list of them varies among different churches. For the purposes of the series of books that sought to expound the 'Old Testament for Everyone', by the 'Old Testament' we meant the Scriptures accepted by the Jewish community, though in the Jewish Bible they come in that different order as the Torah, the Prophets and the Writings.

An outline of the Old Testament story

Here is an outline of the story that emerges from the Old Testament books (I give no dates for events in Genesis, which involves too much guesswork).

1200s	The Israelites are state serfs in Egypt; God enables them to get out of Egypt under Moses and to settle in Canaan under Joshua
1100s	The 'judges'
1000s	The Israelites decide to become a monarchic state; King Saul, King David
900s	King Solomon; Israel splits into two nations, Ephraim and Judah
800s	Elijah, Elisha
700s	Amos, Hosea, Isaiah, Micah; Assyria the superpower; the Assyrians terminate the life of Ephraim (722)
600s	Jeremiah, King Josiah; Babylon the superpower
500s	Ezekiel; the Babylonians terminate the independent life of Judah (587)
	Persia the superpower; Judahites free to return home (537) and rebuild the temple
400s	Ezra brings the Torah to Jerusalem (458); Nehemiah rebuilds its walls (445)
300s	Alexander (333) puts Jerusalem under the authority of Greece as the superpower
200s	Syria (the Seleucids) and Egypt (the Ptolemies) pull Judah one way or the other
100s	Judah rebels against Seleucid domination and persecution and gains independence (164)
000s	Rome the superpower

© Karla Bohmbach

Genesis

Genesis provides the people of God with two aspects of the back story to its own story. Chapters 1—11 go back to the beginning of the world as a whole. They thus invite the people of God to see their own story against the broadest and longest backcloth. Then chapters 12—50 tell them about their particular prehistory in God's bringing their ancestors from Mesopotamia to Canaan with the intention of settling them there permanently in due course.

By its nature, then, Genesis tells a story about actual events of the past. Yet a reading of the story makes us hesitate to take it as simply historical. Noah putting specimens of every animal species into a giant box in which they survive a worldwide flood? Lot's wife turned into a column of salt? Genesis is like other histories from its world such as the works of the Greek historians Herodotus and Thucydides. They combine reminiscences of historical events, traditional stories and works of imagination, and comment on what it all means and what readers should make of it. In inspiring Genesis, God let its authors write in the way that was natural to them, and used their way of telling a story to instruct Israel and us about ourselves and about him.

Indeed, rather than comparing Genesis with the kind of history that we might try to write, we do better to compare it with Shakespeare or with historical novels or with the kind of Hollywood movie that's 'based on fact'. In understanding such works, we miss the point if we focus too much on what actually happened. What makes them instructive is the way a creative team has turned them into an illuminating story. It's this kind of story that God inspired his team to write.

The plot of the story is as follows. Act One describes how God set the world going but how it soon went wrong, which made God wonder whether the whole thing had been a mistake; that's Scene One. God starts again, but things again go wrong, and you wonder whether there is no way this project can be a success. That's Scene Two.

One can imagine an intermission at chapter 11 before the beginning of Act Two, which occupies the rest of the book. Its three scenes focus on the story of three families. First God summons Abraham and Sarah from Mesopotamia and promises to give them such blessing that the whole world will pray to be blessed as they are blessed. So God is indeed continuing with his original purpose to bless the entire world. Much of the drama of the first scene focuses on whether Abraham and Sarah will ever have a son through whom God's blessing can find fulfilment. This son, Isaac, is the focus of Scene Two. In turn, much of his story focuses on his two sons, and the conflict between them. Scene Three tells of the family of one of these sons, Jacob, which also becomes a story of conflict. By the end of Genesis, Jacob's family has grown to quite a size, so that one element in God's promise has found fulfilment. But because of a famine it has had to take refuge in Egypt, which is not the country that had been promised to it.

So the end of the story is not really the end of the story. It's more like the cliffhanger at the end of the first series in a television drama. We have to read on into Exodus.

Readers often assume that the point of the stories about people such as Abraham and Sarah is to give us examples of how to live or how not to live our lives. This assumption doesn't make sense of the stories. They're more about God and about God as seeking to fulfil his purpose for the world and for his people, which often works despite the actions of human beings rather than via them. They're stories that help us understand who we are rather than stories that tell us what to be.

In the beginning (days one to three)

1 At the beginning of God's creating the heavens and the earth, ²when the earth was an empty void, with darkness over the face of the deep, and God's breath sweeping over the face of the water, ³God said, 'Light!' and light came into being. ⁴God saw that light was good, and God made a distinction between light and darkness. ⁵God called the light 'day'; the darkness he called 'night'. And there was evening and there was morning, day one.

⁶God said, 'A dome in the middle of the water to make water distinct from water!' ⁷And God made the dome and made a distinction between the water that was under the dome and the water that was above the dome. So it came to be. ⁸God called the dome 'heavens'. And there was evening and there was morning, a second day.

⁹God said, 'The water under the heavens is to come together into one place so the dry land may appear!' So it came to be. ¹⁰God called the dry land 'earth'; the coming together of water he called 'seas'. God saw that it was good. ¹¹God said, 'The earth is to put forth vegetation: plants generating seed, fruit trees producing fruit by its species, with its seed in it, on the earth!' So it came to be. ¹²The earth brought forth vegetation, plants generating seed by its species, and trees producing fruit with its seed in it by its species. God saw that it was good. ¹³And there was evening and there was morning, a third day.

Filling in the outline (days four to six)

¹⁴God said, 'Lights in the dome of the heavens to make a distinction between day and night! They'll be for signs and set times and days and years, ¹⁵and they'll be lights in the dome of the heavens to give light on the earth!' So it came to be. ¹⁶God made the two big lights (the bigger light to rule the day and the smaller light to rule the night) and the stars. ¹⁷God put them in the dome of the heavens to give light on the earth, ¹⁸to rule over the day and over the night, and to make a distinction between light and darkness. God saw that it was good. ¹⁹And there was evening and there was morning, a fourth day.

²⁰God said, 'The water is to teem with living creatures, and birds are to fly over the earth, over the face of the dome of the heavens!' ²¹God created the big sea monsters and every living creature that moves, with which the water teems, by their species, and every winged bird by its species. God saw that it was good. ²²God blessed them: 'Be fruitful, be numerous, fill the water in the seas; birds are to be numerous on the earth.' ²³And there was evening and there was morning, a fifth day.

²⁴God said, 'The earth is to bring forth living creatures by their species – animals, moving things and the living things of the earth, by their species!' So it came to be. ²⁵God made the living things of the earth by their species, animals by their species and all the things that move on the ground by their species. God saw that it was good.

The week's work completed

²⁶God said, 'Let's make human beings in our image, as our likeness, so they can hold sway over the fish in the sea, over the birds in the heavens, over the animals, over all the earth and over all the things that move on the earth.' ²⁷So God created human beings in his image. He created them in the image of God. He created them male and female. ²⁸God blessed them, and said to them, 'Be fruitful, be numerous, fill the earth and subjugate it, hold sway over the fish in the sea, over the birds in the heavens and over every creature that moves on the earth.'

²⁹God said, 'Here, I give you all the plants that generate seed that are on the face of all the earth, and every tree with fruit that generates seed. These will be food for you, ³⁰for all the creatures of the earth, for all the birds in the heavens and for all the things that move on the earth that have living breath in them, all the green plants as food.' So it came to be.

³¹God saw all that he had made, and there – it was very good. And there was evening and there was morning, the sixth day.

2 So the heavens and the earth were finished, with all their forces. ²On the seventh day God had finished his work that he had been doing, so on the seventh day he stopped from all his work that he had been doing. ³God blessed the seventh day and made it sacred, because on it God stopped from his entire work of creation that he had been doing.

To put it another way . . .

⁴These are the lines of descent of the heavens and the earth when they were created.

When Yahweh God made the earth and the heavens, ⁵and no bush of the wild was on the earth yet and no plant of the wild had grown yet (because Yahweh God had not made it rain on the earth, and there was no human being to serve the ground, ⁶though a stream would go up from the earth and water the entire face of the ground), ⁷Yahweh God shaped a human person [*adam*] with earth from the ground [*adamah*] and blew into its nostrils living breath, and the human person became a living being.

⁸Yahweh God planted a garden in Eden ['Lavishness'], in the east, and put there the human being he had shaped. ⁹Yahweh God made to grow up from the ground every tree that's desirable to look at and good for food, with the life-tree in the middle of the garden, and the good-and-bad-knowledge tree.

¹⁰There was a river going out of Eden to water the garden, and from there dividing and becoming four headwaters. ¹¹The name of the first was Pishon; it was the one going round the entire Havilah region, where the gold is. (¹²The gold of that region is good; pearl and onyx stone are there.) ¹³The name of the second river was Gihon; it was the one going round the entire Kush [Sudan] region. ¹⁴The name of the third river was Tigris; it was the one going east of Ashshur. The fourth river was the Euphrates.

The helper

¹⁵Yahweh God took the human being and set him down in Eden Garden to serve it and keep it. ¹⁶Yahweh God ordered the human being: 'From every tree in the garden you may definitely eat. ¹⁷But from the good-and-bad-knowledge tree you will not eat, because on the day you eat from it, you will definitely die.'

¹⁸Yahweh God said, 'It's not good for the human being to be on his own. I'll make him a helper suitable for him.' ¹⁹Yahweh God shaped from the ground every creature of the wild and every bird in the heavens, and brought them to the human being to see what he'd call it. Whatever the human being called a living being, that became its name. ²⁰The human being gave names to all the animals, to the birds in the heavens and to all the creatures of the wild. But for a human being he didn't find a helper suitable for him.

²¹So Yahweh God made a coma fall on the human being so he slept, took one of his ribs and closed up its place with flesh. ²²Yahweh God built the rib that he'd taken from the human being into a woman, and brought her to the human being. ²³The human being said: 'This, now, is bone from my bones and flesh from my flesh! This one will be called Woman [*ishshah*], because from a man [*ish*] this one was taken.' ²⁴That's why a man abandons his father and his mother and attaches himself to his woman and they become one flesh.

²⁵The two of them were naked, the man and his woman, but they felt no shame.

Creation asserts itself

3 Now the snake was the shrewdest of all the creatures of the wild that Yahweh God had made. It said to the woman, 'Did God really say you will not eat from any tree in the garden?' ²The woman said to the snake, 'We may eat of the fruit from the trees in the garden, ³but from the fruit of the tree that's in the middle of the garden God said, "You will not eat of it and you will not touch it, so that you don't die."'

⁴The snake said to the woman, 'You won't die at all. ⁵Rather, God knows that on the day you eat of it, your eyes will open and you'll become like gods, knowing good and bad.' ⁶The woman saw that the tree was good to eat and that it was an object of longing to the eyes, and the tree was desirable for giving insight. So she took of its fruit and ate, and also gave some to her man with her, and he ate. ⁷The eyes of the two of them opened and they knew that they were naked, so they sewed fig leaves together and made themselves loincloths.

⁸They heard the sound of Yahweh God walking about in the garden in the breezy time

of the day, so the man and his woman hid from the face of Yahweh God among the trees in the garden. ⁹Yahweh God called to the man and said to him, 'Where are you?' ¹⁰He said, 'I heard the sound of you in the garden, and I was afraid because I was naked, so I hid.' ¹¹He said, 'Who told you that you were naked? Have you eaten from the tree that I ordered you not to eat from?' ¹²The man said, 'The woman you put with me – she gave to me from the tree, and I ate.' ¹³Yahweh God said to the woman, 'What is this that you've done?' The woman said, 'The snake – it deceived me, and I ate.'

The consequences

¹⁴Yahweh God said to the snake, 'Because you've done this, you're cursed, away from all the animals and the creatures of the wild. On your stomach you'll go and soil you'll eat all the days of your life. ¹⁵I shall put enmity between you and the woman, and between your offspring and her offspring. He'll hit you on the head; you'll hit him on the heel.'

¹⁶To the woman he said, 'I shall make very great your pain in connection with pregnancy. In painfulness you'll give birth to children. Towards your man will be your desire, but he – he'll rule over you.'

¹⁷To Adam he said, 'Because you listened to the voice of your woman and ate from the tree I ordered you, "You will not eat from it", the ground is cursed because of you. In pain you'll eat from it all the days of your life. ¹⁸Thorn and thistle it will grow for you and you'll eat plants of the wild. ¹⁹By the sweat of your face you'll eat bread, until you go back to the ground, because you were taken from it. Because you were earth, and you'll go back to earth.'

²⁰The man named his woman Havvah [Eve], because she became the mother of every living person [*hay*]. ²¹Yahweh God made for Adam and his woman leather coats, and clothed them. ²²But Yahweh God said, 'Here, the man has become like one of us in knowing good and bad. So now, he mustn't put out his hand and also take from the life-tree and eat, and live permanently.' ²³So Yahweh God sent him off from Eden Garden to serve the ground from which he'd been taken.

²⁴So Yahweh God drove the man out and made the sphinxes dwell east of Eden Garden, with a sword-like flame whirling, to keep the way to the life-tree.

The first family, the first worship, the first acceptance, the first rejection

4 Now the man slept with his woman, Havvah, she got pregnant, and she gave birth to Qayin [Cain]. She said, 'I've acquired [*qanah*] someone with Yahweh.' ²She went on to give birth to his brother, Hebel ['Breath'; Abel]. Hebel became one who kept sheep, while Qayin became one who served the ground. ³After some time, Qayin brought some of the fruit of the ground as an offering for Yahweh, ⁴while Hebel, too, brought some of the firstborn of his flock, some of the fat parts. Yahweh recognized Hebel and his offering, ⁵but Qayin and his offering Yahweh did not recognize. It really enraged Qayin and he went into a huff. ⁶Yahweh said to Qayin, 'Why does it enrage you? Why have you gone into a huff? ⁷If you do what's good, there'll be honouring, won't there? But if you don't do what's good, wrongdoing is crouching at the entrance. Towards you will be its desire, but you – you're to rule over it.'

⁸Qayin said to Hebel his brother . . . And while they were in the open country, Qayin set upon Hebel his brother and killed him.

⁹Yahweh said to Qayin, 'Where's Hebel, your brother?' He said, 'I don't know – am I the one who keeps my brother?' ¹⁰He said, 'What have you done? A sound! Your brother's spilt blood is crying out to me from the ground. ¹¹There, you are cursed, away from the ground that has opened its mouth to receive your brother's spilt blood from your hand. ¹²When you serve the ground, it will no more give its energy to you. A drifter, a vagrant, you'll be on the earth.'

The protection

¹³Qayin said to Yahweh, 'My waywardness is too big to carry. ¹⁴Here, you've driven me away today from the face of the ground, and from your face I'm to conceal myself, and I'm to be a drifter, a vagrant on the earth – and anyone

who finds me can kill me.' ¹⁵But Yahweh said to him, 'Therefore, anyone who kills Qayin, sevenfold it's to be redressed.' And Yahweh put a mark on Qayin so no one who found him would strike him down. ¹⁶So Qayin went out from being before Yahweh's face and lived in the country of Nod ['Drifting'], east of Eden.

¹⁷Qayin slept with his woman, she got pregnant, and she gave birth to Hanok. He was building a town, and he named the town after his son Hanok. ¹⁸To Hanok was born Irad, Irad fathered Mehuya'el, Mehiya'el fathered Metusa'el, and Metusa'el fathered Lemek. ¹⁹Lemek got himself two women; the name of one was Adah, the name of the second Tsillah. ²⁰Adah gave birth to Yabal; he was the ancestor of everyone who lives with a tent and livestock. ²¹His brother's name was Yubal; he was the ancestor of everyone who plays guitar or pipe. ²²Tsillah, she too gave birth, to Tubal Qayin, forger of all copper and iron. Tubal-qayin's sister was Na'amah.

²³Lemek said to his women,

> Adah and Tsillah, listen to my voice;
>   as Lemek's women, give ear to my word.
> Because I've killed someone for wounding me,
>   a young man for injuring me.
> ²⁴If for Qayin it's to be redressed sevenfold,
>   for Lemek seventy-sevenfold.

²⁵Once more Adam slept with his woman and she gave birth to a son. She named him Set, because 'God has granted me [*sit*] another offspring in place of Hebel, because Qayin killed him'. ²⁶To Set, too, a son was born, and he named him Enosh. At that time a beginning was made to calling in Yahweh's name.

Then he died

5 This is the document with Adam's lines of descent. On the day God created human beings, it was in the likeness of God that he made them. ²Male and female he created them, and he blessed them, and named them 'human beings', on the day he created them. ³When Adam had lived 130 years, he fathered someone in his likeness, as his image, and named him Set. ⁴Adam's days after fathering Set came to 800 years, and he fathered sons and daughters. ⁵So all the days that Adam lived came to 930 years. Then he died.

⁶When Set had lived 105 years, he fathered Enosh. ⁷Set lived 807 years after fathering Enosh, and he fathered sons and daughters. ⁸So all the days of Set came to 912 years. Then he died.

⁹When Enosh had lived 90 years, he fathered Qenan. ¹⁰Enosh lived 815 years after fathering Qenan, and he fathered sons and daughters. ¹¹So all the days of Enosh came to 905 years. Then he died.

¹²When Qenan had lived 70 years, he fathered Mahalal'el. ¹³Qenan lived 840 years after fathering Mahalal'el, and he fathered sons and daughters. ¹⁴So all the days of Qenan came to 910 years. Then he died.

¹⁵When Mahalal'el had lived 65 years, he fathered Yared. ¹⁶Mahalal'el lived 830 years after fathering Yared, and he fathered sons and daughters. ¹⁷So all the days of Mahalal'el came to 895 years. Then he died.

¹⁸When Yared had lived 162 years, he fathered Hanok [Enoch]. ¹⁹Yared lived 800 years after fathering Hanok, and he fathered sons and daughters. ²⁰So all the days of Yared came to 962 years. Then he died.

²¹When Hanok had lived 65 years, he fathered Metushalah. ²²Hanok walked about with God 300 years after fathering Metushalah, and he fathered sons and daughters. ²³So all the days of Hanok came to 365 years. ²⁴Hanok walked about with God, and then he was no more, because God took him.

The need and the promise

²⁵When Metushalah had lived 187 years, he fathered Lemek. ²⁶Metushalah lived 782 years after fathering Lemek, and he fathered sons and daughters. ²⁷So all the days of Metushalah came to 969 years. Then he died.

²⁸When Lemek had lived 182 years, he fathered a son, ²⁹and named him Noah ['Settling Down'], saying: 'This man: he'll relieve us [*niham*] from our work, from

the pain of our hands, from the ground that Yahweh cursed.' ³⁰Lemek lived 595 years after fathering Noah, and he fathered sons and daughters. ³¹So all the days of Lemek came to 777 years. Then he died. ³²When Noah had lived 500 years, Noah fathered Shem, Ham and Yephet.

6 When humanity started to be numerous on the face of the ground and daughters were born to them, ²the sons of the divine beings saw that the daughters of the human beings were good-looking and they took women for themselves, any one that they chose.

³Yahweh said, 'My spirit will not dwell in humanity permanently, because it's flesh. Its time will be 120 years.' ⁴Now the Nephilim ['Fallen'] were on the earth at that time, and also afterwards, when the sons of the divine beings had sex with the daughters of human beings, and they gave birth for them. These were the strong men that were of old, famous men.

⁵Yahweh saw that humanity's bad state on the earth was great. The entire inclination of its mind's intentions was simply bad, all day. ⁶Yahweh regretted that he had made humanity on the earth. It pained his heart. ⁷Yahweh said, 'I shall wipe out the humanity that I created from the face of the ground, from humanity to animals to moving things to birds in the heavens, because I regret that I made them.' ⁸But Noah found grace in Yahweh's eyes.

⁹These are Noah's lines of descent. Now Noah was someone who was faithful and a person of integrity among his generations. It was with God that Noah walked about. ¹⁰Noah fathered three sons, Shem, Ham and Yephet.

Filled with violence

¹¹So the earth had become devastated before God; the earth was full of violence. ¹²God looked at the earth: there, it had become devastated, because all flesh had devastated its way on the earth.

¹³So God said to Noah, 'The end of all flesh has come before me, because the earth is full of violence through them. Here, I'm going to devastate them, with the earth. ¹⁴Make for yourself a chest of gopher wood. With rooms you're to make the chest, and cover it inside and outside with pitch. ¹⁵This is how you're to make it: the length of the chest 150 metres, its width 25 metres and its height 15 metres. ¹⁶You're to make a skylight for the chest, to finish it to half a metre above, and to put the entrance of the chest in its side. You're to make it with bottom, second and third levels.

¹⁷And I: here, I'm bringing a deluge, water on the earth, to devastate all flesh in which there is living breath, from under the heavens. Everything on the earth will breathe its last. ¹⁸But I shall implement my pact with you. You're to come into the chest, you, your sons, your wife and your sons' wives with you. ¹⁹And of everything living, of all flesh, bring two of each into the chest to keep them alive with you. They're to be a male and a female. ²⁰Of the birds of each species, of the animals of each species and of everything that moves on the ground of each species, two of each are to come to you to keep them alive. ²¹And you: get yourself some of all food that's eaten and gather it for yourself. It will be food for you and for them.'

²²Noah acted in accordance with all that God ordered him. So he did.

The great deep breaks out

7 Yahweh said to Noah, 'Go into the chest, you and your entire household, because I've seen that you're a person who is faithful before me in this generation. ²Of every pure animal take with you seven of each, a male and its mate, and of an animal that's not pure, two, a male and its mate, ³also of the birds in the heavens seven of each, male and female, to keep offspring alive on the face of the entire earth. ⁴Because in seven more days I'm going to make it rain on the earth for forty days and forty nights and wipe out everything that exists that I made, from on the face of the ground.' ⁵Noah acted in accordance with all that God ordered him.

⁶Noah was a man of 600 years when the deluge happened, as water on the earth. ⁷Noah, his sons, his wife and his sons' wives with him came into the chest because of the water of the deluge. ⁸Of the pure animals, of the animals that are not pure, of the birds and of everything that moves on the ground, ⁹two

of each came to Noah into the chest, male and female, as God ordered Noah; ¹⁰and after the seven days the water of the deluge came on the earth. ¹¹In the six hundredth year of Noah's life, in the second month, on the seventeenth day of the month, on that day all the springs in the great deep broke out and the apertures in the heavens opened. ¹²The rain came on the earth forty days and forty nights.

And God shut him in

¹³On this particular day Noah, with Shem, Ham and Yephet, Noah's sons, and Noah's wife and his sons' three wives, came into the chest, ¹⁴they and every living thing by its species, every animal by its species, everything that moves on the earth by its species and everything that flies by its species, every bird and every winged creature. ¹⁵They came to Noah into the chest, two each of all flesh in which was living breath. ¹⁶So the ones who came, male and female from all flesh, came as God ordered him. And Yahweh shut him in.

¹⁷The deluge went on for forty days on the earth, and the water increased and lifted the chest, and it rose up from on the earth. ¹⁸The water grew strong and increased greatly on the earth, and the chest moved on the face of the water. ¹⁹When the water grew very, very strong on the earth, all the lofty mountains under the entire heavens were covered. ²⁰Seven metres higher the water grew strong; the mountains were covered. ²¹All flesh moving on the earth breathed its last: birds, animals, living things, all the things teeming on the earth, and all humanity. ²²Everything that had living breath in its nostrils, everything that was on the dry land, died. ²³It wiped out everything that existed that was on the face of the ground, from human beings to animals to moving things to birds in the heavens. They were wiped out from the earth. Only Noah and those with him in the chest remained. ²⁴And the water grew strong on the earth for 150 days.

But God remembered Noah

8 But God was mindful of Noah and all the living things and the animals that were with him in the chest, and God made a wind pass over the earth, and the water abated. ²The springs in the deep and the apertures in the heavens were blocked up, the rain from the heavens held back ³and the water gradually withdrew from on the earth. The water decreased at the end of 150 days, ⁴and the chest came to a stop in the seventh month, on the seventeenth day of the month, on the Ararat mountains. ⁵As the water gradually decreased until the tenth month, in the tenth month on the first day of the month the tops of the mountains appeared.

⁶At the end of forty days, Noah opened the window in the chest that he had made ⁷and sent out a raven. It continued to go out and come back until the water dried up from on the earth. ⁸He sent out a dove from being with him to see if the water had diminished from on the face of the ground, ⁹but the dove didn't find a place to alight for the sole of its foot and it came back to him to the chest, because there was water on the face of the entire earth. So he put out his hand and took it and brought it to him into the chest.

¹⁰He waited again seven more days and once more sent out the dove from the chest. ¹¹The dove came to him at evening time, and there, in its mouth a plucked-off olive leaf. So Noah knew that the water had diminished from on the earth. ¹²He waited again seven more days and sent out the dove, and it didn't come back to him again.

Never again

¹³In the six hundred and first year, in the first month, on the first of the month, the water dried up from on the earth. Noah removed the chest's cover and looked: there, the face of the ground was dry. ¹⁴In the second month, on the twenty-seventh day of the month, the earth was dried out. ¹⁵God spoke to Noah: ¹⁶'Get out of the chest, you, your wife, your sons and your sons' wives with you. ¹⁷Every living thing that's with you from all flesh, birds, animals and everything that moves on the earth: get them out with you, so they may teem on the earth and be fruitful and be numerous on the earth.'

[18] So Noah got out, he, his sons, his wife and his sons' wives with him. [19] Every living thing, everything that moves and every bird, everything that moves on the earth got out of the chest by their families.

[20] Noah built an altar for Yahweh, took some of every pure animal and of every pure bird, and offered up burnt offerings on the altar, [21] and Yahweh smelled the nice smell. Yahweh said to himself, 'I won't ever again slight the ground on account of humanity, because the inclination of the human mind is bad from its youth. I won't ever again strike down everything living, as I did. [22] Never again, for all earth's days, will seedtime and harvest, cold and heat, summer and winter, day and night, stop.'

The renewed creation blessing and the first pact or covenant

9 God blessed Noah and his sons and said to them, 'Be fruitful, be numerous, fill the earth. [2] Reverence towards you and awe towards you will be on all the living things on the earth, on all the birds in the sky, on everything that moves on the ground and on all the fish in the sea; they're given into your hand. [3] Everything that moves, that's alive, will be yours as food. As I gave you green plants, everything is yours. [4] Yet flesh with its life, its blood, you will not eat.

[5] And indeed, your blood, for your life, I shall require. From every living thing I shall require it, and from a human being I shall require a human life, an individual for his brother. [6] One who sheds human blood, by means of a human being his blood will flow, because it was in God's image that he made humanity. [7] But you: be fruitful, be numerous, teem on the earth, be numerous on it.'

[8] And God said to Noah and to his sons with him: [9] 'Here, I myself am going to implement my pact with you, with your offspring after you [10] and with every living being that's with you: birds, animals and every living thing on the earth with you, all that got out of the chest, every living thing on the earth. [11] I shall implement my pact with you and all flesh will not be cut off again by the water of a deluge. Never again will there be a deluge to devastate the earth.'

The bow laid aside (but things go wrong again)

[12] And God said, 'This is the sign of the pact that I'm putting between me and you and every living creature that's with you, to the generations, permanently. [13] I've put my bow in the clouds. It will be a sign of the pact between me and the earth. [14] When I bring clouds on the earth and the bow appears in the clouds, [15] I shall be mindful of my pact that's between me and you and every living creature among all flesh, and the water will never again become a deluge to devastate all flesh. [16] The bow will be in the clouds and I shall see it, being mindful of the permanent pact between God and every living creature among all flesh that's on the earth.' [17] God said to Noah, 'This will be the sign of the pact that I've implemented between me and all flesh that's on the earth.'

[18] Noah's sons who got out of the chest were Shem, Ham and Yephet; Ham was the father of Kena'an [Canaan]. [19] These three were Noah's sons, and from them the entire earth dispersed.

[20] Noah, a man of the ground, as his first act planted a vineyard. [21] He drank some of the wine and got drunk, and exposed himself inside his tent. [22] Ham, Kena'an's father, saw his father's nakedness and told his two brothers outside. [23] Shem and Yephet took a cover, put it on both their shoulders, walked backwards and covered their father's nakedness, with their faces turned backwards so they didn't see their father's nakedness.

[24] Noah woke up from his wine and came to know what his youngest son had done to him. [25] He said, 'Cursed be Kena'an ['Bow Down']: he'll be the lowest servant to his brothers.' [26] And he said, 'Yahweh, the God of Shem, be blessed. May Kena'an be a servant to them. [27] May God extend [*yapht*] Yephet and may he dwell in Shem's tents. May Kena'an be a servant to them.'

[28] Noah lived after the deluge 350 years. [29] So all Noah's days came to 950 years. Then he died.

The nations

10 These are the lines of descent of Noah's sons, Shem, Ham and Yephet. Sons were born to them after the deluge.

²The sons of Yephet: Gomer, Magog, Maday [Media], Yavan [Greece], Tubal, Meshek and Tiras.
³The sons of Gomer: Ashkenaz, Riphat and Togarmah.
⁴The sons of Yavan: Elishah, Tarshish, Kittites and Dodanites.
⁵From these, the nations on far shores parted into their countries, each with its language, by their kin-groups among their nations.

⁶The sons of Ham: Kush [Sudan], Misrayim [Egypt], Put and Kena'an.
⁷The sons of Kush: Seba, Havilah, Sabtah, Ra'mah and Sabteka.
The sons of Ra'mah: Sheba and Dedan.
⁸Kush fathered Nimrod, who was the first to become a strong man on the earth. ⁹He became a strong man as a hunter before Yahweh; that's why it's said, 'Like Nimrod, a strong man as a hunter before Yahweh'. ¹⁰The beginning of his kingdom was Babel, Erek, Akkad and Kalneh, in the region of Shin'ar. ¹¹From that region Ashshur went out and built Nineveh and the town squares, Kalah, ¹²and Resen between Nineveh and Kalah: that's the big town.
¹³Misrayim fathered Ludites, Anamites, Lehabites, Naphtuhites, ¹⁴Patrusites, Kasluhites (from whom the Pelishtites [Philistines] went out) and Kaphtorites.
¹⁵Kena'an fathered Tsidon his firstborn, Het, ¹⁶the Yebusites, the Amorites, the Girgashites, ¹⁷the Hivvites, the Arkites, the Sinites, ¹⁸the Arvadites, the Tsemarites and the Hamatites. Later, the Kena'anite kin-groups dispersed ¹⁹and the Kena'anite border reached from Tsidon until you come to Gerar, near Azzah [Gaza], until you come to Sedom, Amorah, Admah and Tseboyim, near Lasha.
²⁰These are the descendants of Ham by their kin-groups, by their languages, in their countries, by their nations.

Babel becomes Babble-on

²¹Sons were also born to Shem, the ancestor of all the descendants of Eber, and Yephet's older brother. ²²The descendants of Shem: Elam, Ashshur, Arpakshad, Lud and Aram.
²³The descendants of Aram: Uts, Hul, Geter and Mash.
²⁴Arpakshad fathered Shelah; Shelah fathered Eber.
²⁵Two sons were born to Eber: the name of the first was Peleg, because in his time the earth divided [*palag*], and the name of the second was Yoktan.
²⁶Yoktan fathered Almodad, Sheleph, Hatsarmavet, Yerah, ²⁷Hadoram, Uzal, Diklah, ²⁸Obal, Abima'el, Sheba, ²⁹Ophir, Havilah and Yobab. All these were descendants of Yoktan. ³⁰Their settlements went from Mesha until you come to Sephar, the eastern highland.
³¹These are the descendants of Shem by their kin-groups, by their languages, in their countries, by their nations.
³²These are the kin-groups of Noah's sons by their lines of descent according to their nations. From these the nations parted in the earth after the deluge.

11 Now the entire earth was of one language and common words. ²As people moved on in the east they found a valley in the region of Shin'ar and lived there. ³They said, one to his neighbour, 'Come on, let's make bricks and bake them thoroughly'; so they had brick in place of stone, and tar in place of cement. ⁴They said, 'Come on, let's build ourselves a town and a tower with its top in the heavens, and make a name for ourselves, so we don't disperse over the face of the entire earth.'
⁵But Yahweh went down to see the town and the tower that the human beings had made. ⁶Yahweh said, 'Here, one people with one language for all of them, and this is the first thing they do. So now nothing that they may scheme to do is closed off from them. ⁷Come on, let's go down and make a babble of their language there, so one person won't be able to hear his neighbour's language.'
⁸So Yahweh dispersed them from there over the face of the entire earth and they left off from building the town. ⁹That's why it was named Babel, because there Yahweh made a babble of the language of the entire earth, and from there Yahweh dispersed them over the face of the entire earth.

The tragedies of family

¹⁰These are Shem's lines of descent. When Shem had lived 100 years, he fathered Arpakshad, two years after the deluge. ¹¹After fathering Arpakshad, Shem lived 500 years and fathered sons and daughters. ¹²When Arpakshad had lived 35 years, he fathered Shelah. ¹³After fathering Shelah, Arpakshad lived 403 years and fathered sons and daughters. ¹⁴When Shelah had lived 30 years, he fathered Eber. ¹⁵After fathering Eber, Shelah lived 403 years and fathered sons and daughters. ¹⁶When Eber had lived 34 years, he fathered Peleg. ¹⁷After fathering Peleg, Eber lived 430 years and fathered sons and daughters. ¹⁸When Peleg had lived 30 years, he fathered Re'u. ¹⁹After fathering Re'u, Peleg lived 209 years and fathered sons and daughters. ²⁰When Re'u had lived 32 years, he fathered Serug. ²¹After fathering Serug, Re'u lived 207 years and fathered sons and daughters. ²²When Serug had lived 30 years, he fathered Nahor. ²³After fathering Nahor, Serug lived 200 years and fathered sons and daughters. ²⁴When Nahor had lived 29 years, he fathered Terah. ²⁵After fathering Terah, Nahor lived 119 years and fathered sons and daughters. ²⁶When Terah had lived 70 years, he fathered Abram, Nahor and Haran.

²⁷So these are Terah's lines of descent. Terah fathered Abram, Nahor and Haran, and Haran fathered Lot. ²⁸Haran died before Terah his father in the country that was his homeland, Ur of the Kasdites [Babylonians]. ²⁹Abram and Nahor got themselves wives; the name of Abram's wife was Sarai and the name of Nahor's wife was Milkah daughter of Haran, the father of Milkah and of Yiskah. ³⁰But Sarai was infertile; she had no child.

Get yourself out of here

³¹Terah took Abram his son, Lot ben Haran, his grandson, and Sarai his daughter-in-law, the wife of Abram, and they left Ur of the Kasdites together to go to the country of Kena'an, but they came as far as Harran and lived there. ³²Terah's days came to 205 years, and Terah died in Harran.

12 Yahweh said to Abram, 'Get yourself from your country, from your homeland and from your father's household, to the country that I shall enable you to see, ²and I shall make you into a big nation. I shall bless you and make your name big and you'll become a blessing. ³I shall bless the people who bless you, but the person who slights you I shall curse. All the kin-groups on the earth will bless themselves by you.' ⁴Abram went as Yahweh spoke to him, and Lot went with him. Abram was a man of seventy-five years when he left Harran.

⁵So Abram took Sarai his wife, Lot his brother's son, all the property that they had acquired and all the people that they had produced in Harran, and left to go to the country of Kena'an. When they came to the country of Kena'an, ⁶Abram passed through the country as far as the site at Shekem, as far as Moreh Oak. The Kena'anites were then in the country. ⁷Yahweh appeared to Abram and said, 'To your offspring I shall give this country.' He built an altar there for Yahweh who had appeared to him. ⁸He went on from there to the mountain country on the east of Bet-el [Bethel], and spread his tent, Bet-el on the west, Ha'ay [Ai, 'The Ruin'] on the east. He built an altar there for Yahweh and called in Yahweh's name.

⁹Abram moved on, moving on gradually to the Negeb.

The fear and the lie

¹⁰A famine came in the country, and Abram went down to Misrayim to reside there, because the famine was heavy in the country. ¹¹When he was near coming into Misrayim, he said to Sarai his wife, 'Here, please: I know that you're a woman who's attractive in appearance. ¹²When the Misrayimites see you and say, "She's his wife", they may kill me and let you live. ¹³Please say that you're my sister, in order that things may be good for me on account of you and I myself may live on by means of you.' ¹⁴When Abram came to Misrayim, the

Misrayimites saw that the woman was very attractive. [15]The officials of Par'oh [Pharaoh] saw her and praised her to Par'oh, and the woman was taken into Par'oh's household. [16]For Abram things were good because of her; he had flock, herd, male and female donkeys, servants, maidservants and camels.

[17]But Yahweh touched Par'oh and his household with serious epidemics on account of Sarai, Abram's wife. [18]Par'oh called for Abram and said, 'What is this that you've done to me? Why didn't you tell me that she was your wife? [19]Why did you say "She's my sister", so I got her for myself as a wife? Now, here's your wife; take her and go.' [20]Par'oh gave men orders concerning him and sent him off, him and his wife and all that he had.

13

So Abram went up from Misrayim, he and his wife and all that he had, and Lot with him, to the Negeb.

[2]Now Abram was a man of great substance, with livestock, with silver and with gold. [3]In his moving on he went from the Negeb as far as Bet-el, as far as the place where his tent had been formerly, between Bet-el and Ha'ay, [4]the site of the altar that he had made there at first. There Abram called in Yahweh's name.

The implausible promise

[5]Lot, who went with Abram, also had flock and herd and tents, [6]and the region couldn't support them living together, because their property was great. So they couldn't live together. [7]There was argument between the herdsmen of Abram's livestock and the herdsmen of Lot's livestock (and the Kena'anite and the Perizzite were then living in the country). [8]So Abram said to Lot, 'Please, there mustn't be arguing between me and you and between my herdsmen and your herdsmen, because we're brothers. [9]The entire country is before you, isn't it? Part from me, please: if you go north, I'll go south, but if you go south, I'll go north.'

[10]Lot lifted his eyes and looked at the entire plain of the Yarden [Jordan], that it was well-watered, all of it, before Yahweh devastated Sedom and Amorah [Sodom and Gomorrah], like Yahweh's garden, like the country of Misrayim as you come to Tso'ar; [11]and Lot chose for himself the entire Yarden plain.

So Lot moved on east, and they parted, each from his brother. [12]Abram lived in the country of Kena'an, and Lot lived in the towns of the

Genesis 13: Abraham

plain and put up his tents near Sedom. ¹³Now the people of Sedom were bad, wrongdoers in relation to Yahweh, greatly. ¹⁴But Yahweh said to Abram after Lot parted from him, 'Lift your eyes and look, please, from the place where you are, to the north, to the south, to the east and to the west, ¹⁵because the entire country that you're looking at I shall give to you and to your offspring, permanently. ¹⁶I shall make your offspring like the earth's soil, so if a person can count the earth's soil, your offspring will also be counted. ¹⁷Set off, walk about in the country, through its length and its width, because I shall give it to you.'

¹⁸So Abram moved his tents and came and lived by the Mamre oaks, which are at Hebron, and built an altar for Yahweh there.

Sedom not such a safe place

14 In the time of Amraphel king of Shin'ar, Aryok king of Ellasar, Kedorla'omer king of Elam and Tid'al king of Goyim, ²they did battle with Bera king of Sedom, Birsha king of Amorah, Shin'ab king of Admah, Shem'eber king of Tseboyim, and the king of Bela (i.e. Tso'ar). ³All these joined together in Siddim Vale (i.e. the Salt Sea). ⁴For twelve years they had served Kedorla'omer, but in the thirteenth year they rebelled.

⁵In the fourteenth year, Kedorla'omer and the kings who were with him came and struck down the Repha'ites at Ashterot Karnayim, the Zuzites at Ham, the Emim at Qiryatayim Plain ⁶and the Horites in their highland, Se'ir as far as Pa'ran Oak, which is near the wilderness. ⁷They went back and came to Ayin Mishpat (i.e. Qadesh), and struck down the Amaleqites' entire area, and also the Amorites who were living in Hatsatson Tamar.

⁸Then the king of Sedom, the king of Amorah, the king of Admah, the king of Tseboyim and the king of Bela (i.e. Tso'ar) went out, and lined up with them for battle in the Siddim Vale: ⁹Kedorla'omer king of Elam, Tidal king of Goyim, Amraphel king of Shin'ar and Aryok king of Ellasar, four kings against the five. ¹⁰Now the Siddim Vale was pit after pit of bitumen; the kings of Sedom and Amorah fled and fell into them, while the rest fled to the highland.

And a time for war

¹¹They took all the property of Sedom and Amorah and all their food, and went. ¹²So they took Lot, the son of Abram's brother, and his property, and went; he was living in Sedom. ¹³Someone who had escaped came and told Abram the Hebrew. He was dwelling by the oaks of Mamre the Amorite, brother of Eshkol and brother of Aner; these were partners in a pact with Abram.

¹⁴So Abram heard that his brother had been taken captive and mustered his trained men, people born in his household, 318 of them, and went in pursuit as far as Dan. ¹⁵He and his servants split up against them by night, struck them down and pursued them as far as Hobah, which is north of Dammeseq [Damascus]. ¹⁶He took back all the property, and took back both his brother Lot and his property, and also the women and the company. ¹⁷The king of Sedom went out to meet him after he got back from striking down Kedorla'omer and the kings that were with him, in the Shaveh Vale (i.e. the King's Vale), ¹⁸and Melkitsedeq king of Salem brought out bread and wine (he was priest of God On High) ¹⁹and blessed him, saying,

Blessed be Abram by God On High,
   Lord of the heavens and the earth,
²⁰And God On High be blessed,
   who has delivered your attackers into your hand.

He gave him a tenth of everything. ²¹The king of Sedom said to Abram, 'Give me the people but take the property for yourself.' ²²But Abram said to the king of Sedom, 'I raise my hand to Yahweh, God On High, Lord of the heavens and the earth: ²³"From a thread to a bootstrap, if I take anything that's yours . . ." You will not say, "I'm the one who made Abram wealthy." ²⁴Not me. Only what the boys have eaten, and the share of the men who went with me, Aner, Eshkol and Mamre – they are to have their share.'

How can you know?

15 Subsequently, Yahweh's word came to Abram in a vision: 'Don't be afraid,

Abram. I will be your deliverance, and your wages will be very big.' ²Abram said, 'Lord Yahweh, what will you give me, when I'm going to die childless, and the heir to my household will be a man from Dammeseq, Eli'ezer?'

³So Abram said, 'Here, you haven't given me offspring. Here, someone from my household will come into possession from me.' ⁴But here, Yahweh's word came to him: 'This man won't come into possession from you. No, only someone who comes from inside you – he'll come into possession from you.' ⁵He took him outside and said, 'Look at the heavens, please, and count the stars, if you can count them.' He said to him, 'That's what your offspring will be like.'

⁶He trusted in Yahweh, and he deemed it as faithfulness on his part. ⁷He said to him, 'I am Yahweh who brought you out from Ur of the Kasdites to give you this country as a possession.'

⁸But he said, 'Lord Yahweh, how may I know that I shall take possession of it?' ⁹He said to him, 'Get me a heifer of three years, a goat of three years, a ram of three years, a pigeon and a baby bird.' ¹⁰He got him all these, cut them in half and put one half opposite its neighbour, but didn't cut the birds in half. ¹¹Birds of prey came down on the carcases, but Abram drove them away. ¹²As the sun was about to go, a coma fell on Abram, and there, a great dark dread was falling on him.

Yahweh confirms a pact or covenant (but will they believe it?)

¹³He said to Abram, 'You can know for sure that your offspring will be residents in a country not theirs. They will serve them, and they will humble them for 400 years. ¹⁴But the nation that they serve I'm indeed going to judge. After this they will get out with much property. ¹⁵But you: you will go to your ancestors with things being well. You'll be buried in a good old age. ¹⁶In the fourth generation they'll come back here, because the Amorites' waywardness is not yet complete.'

¹⁷The sun went and it was dark, and there, a smoking firepot, a blazing torch, that passed between those pieces. ¹⁸On that day Yahweh solemnized a pact with Abram, saying 'To your offspring I'm giving this country, from the Misrayimite river to the big river (the River Euphrates): ¹⁹the Qenite, the Qenizzite, the Qadmonite, ²⁰the Hittite, the Perizzite, the Repha'ites, ²¹the Amorite, the Kena'anite, the Girgashite and the Yebusite.'

16 Now Sarai, Abram's wife, had not borne children for him. She had a Misrayimite maidservant; her name was Hagar. ²Sarai said to Abram, 'Here, Yahweh has held me back from giving birth to children. You have sex with my maidservant; maybe I can be built up through her.'

Abram listened to Sarai's voice. ³Sarai, Abram's wife, got Hagar the Misrayimite, her maidservant (after Abram had been living in the country of Kena'an for ten years), and gave her to Abram her husband as a wife. ⁴He had sex with Hagar and she got pregnant. When she saw that she was pregnant, her mistress became of slight worth in her eyes.

Hagar names God

⁵Sarai said to Abram, 'The violence done to me rests on you. I myself put my maidservant in your arms, she's seen that she's pregnant, and I've become of slight worth in her eyes. Yahweh decide between me and you!' ⁶Abram said to Sarai, 'Here, your maidservant is in your hand. Do to her what's good in your eyes.' Sarai humbled her, and she took flight from her.

⁷Yahweh's envoy found her by a spring of water in the wilderness, by the spring on the Shur road. ⁸He said, 'Hagar, maidservant of Sarai, where have you come from and where are you going?' She said, 'From Sarai, my mistress – I'm taking flight.' ⁹Yahweh's envoy said to her, 'Go back to your mistress. Let yourself be humbled under her hand.' ¹⁰But Yahweh's envoy said to her, 'I shall make your offspring very numerous; they won't be able to be counted because of the large number.'

¹¹Yahweh's envoy said to her, 'There, you're pregnant and you'll give birth to a son. You're to name him Yishma'e'l [Ishmael], because Yahweh has listened [*shama*] to your humbling. ¹²And he – he'll be a wild donkey of a man, his hand against everyone and everyone's hand against him, and he'll dwell over against all his brothers.'

¹³She named Yahweh who spoke to her, 'You are "God Seeing Me" [El Ro'i]', because (she said), 'Did I really see here, after he was seeing me?' ¹⁴That's why they called the well 'The Well of the Living One Seeing Me' [Be'er Lahay Ro'i]. There, it's between Qedesh and Bered.

¹⁵So Hagar gave birth to a son for Abram, and Abram named his son, to whom Hagar gave birth, Yishma'e'l. ¹⁶Abram was a man of 86 years when Hagar gave birth to Yishma'e'l for Abram.

God renames Abram and Sarai

17 Abram was a man of ninety-nine years. Yahweh appeared to Abram and said to him, 'I am God Shadday. Live your life before me and be a person of integrity. ²I shall make my pact between me and you, and make you very, very numerous.' ³Abram fell on his face.

God spoke with him: ⁴'I myself – here is my pact with you. You'll become the ancestor of a horde of nations. ⁵You'll no longer be named Abram. Your name will be Abraham, because I'm making you the "ancestor of a horde" [ab-hamon] of nations. ⁶I shall enable you to be very, very fruitful and I shall make you into nations. From you kings will come. ⁷I shall implement my pact between me and you and your offspring after you, through their generations, as a permanent pact, to be God for you and for your offspring after you. ⁸I shall give to you, and to your offspring after you, the country in which you're residing, the entire country of Kena'an, as a permanent holding, and I shall be God for them.'

⁹God said to Abraham, 'And you, you're to keep my pact, you and your offspring after you, through their generations. ¹⁰This is my pact that you're to keep, between me and you and your offspring after you: the circumcising of every male you have. ¹¹You're to circumcise the flesh of your foreskin. It will be the sign of a pact between me and you. ¹²As a child of eight days, every male among you is to be circumcised, through your generations. The person born in the household or acquired for silver from any foreigner, who doesn't belong to your offspring: ¹³he's definitely to be circumcised, the one born in your household and the one acquired for silver. My pact in your flesh will be a permanent pact. ¹⁴But a foreskinned male who does not circumcise the flesh of his foreskin: that person will be cut off from his kin. He's contravened my pact.'

¹⁵And God said to Abraham: 'Sarai, your wife: you're not to name her Sarai, because her name is Sarah ['Princess']. ¹⁶I shall bless her. There, I'm giving you a son from her. I shall bless her and she'll become nations; kings of peoples will come from her.'

A promise for Yishma'e'l

¹⁷Abraham fell on his face, laughed and said to himself, 'Can a child be born to a man of a hundred years, or can Sarah give birth to a child as a woman of ninety years?' ¹⁸Abraham said to God, 'If only Yishma'e'l might live before you.' ¹⁹God said, 'Well: Sarah your wife, she's going to give birth to a son for you, and you're to name him Yitshaq [Isaac]. I shall implement my pact for him as a permanent pact for his offspring after him.

²⁰As for Yishma'e'l: I've listened. There, I'm blessing him, and making him fruitful and making him very, very numerous. Twelve leaders he will father, and I shall make him a big nation. ²¹But my pact I shall implement with Yitshaq, to whom Sarah will give birth for you at this set time next year.' ²²When he had finished speaking with him, God went up from Abraham.

²³So Abraham took Yishma'e'l his son and all those born in his household and all those bought with his silver, every male among the people in Abraham's household, and circumcised the flesh of their foreskin, on that very day, as God had spoken with him. ²⁴Abraham was a man of ninety-nine years at the circumcising of the flesh of his foreskin, ²⁵while Yishma'e'l his son was a boy of thirteen years at the circumcising of the flesh of his foreskin. ²⁶On that very day Abraham and Yishma'e'l his son were circumcised, ²⁷and all the men in his household, those born in the household and those acquired with silver from a foreigner, were circumcised with him.

18 Yahweh appeared to him by the Mamre oaks, when he was sitting at the tent entrance as the day grew hot. ²He lifted his eyes and looked, and there, three men were standing opposite him. When he saw them, he ran to meet them from the tent entrance, bowed to the ground, ³and said, 'Sirs, please, if I've found grace in your eyes, don't pass by your servant, please. ⁴May someone please get a little water? Bathe your feet. Rest under the tree. ⁵I shall get a bit of bread. Sustain your heart, then you can pass on, since you've passed near your servant.' They said, 'Yes, you may do as you have spoken.'

Entertaining angels unawares

⁶Abraham hurried to the tent to Sarah and said, 'Hurry, three measures of fine flour, meal, knead it, make bread.' ⁷Abraham ran to the herd, got a nice, tender calf, and gave it to a boy, and he hurried to prepare it. ⁸He got curds and milk and the calf that he'd prepared and set it before them. He stood opposite them under the tree as they ate.

⁹They said to him, 'Where's Sarah your wife?' He said, 'There, in the tent.' ¹⁰He said, 'I shall definitely come back to you at [nature's] reviving time. There, Sarah your wife will have a son.' Sarah was listening at the tent entrance, which was behind him. ¹¹Now Abraham and Sarah were old, going on in years; the way women menstruate had left off from happening for Sarah.

¹²So Sarah laughed to herself, saying 'After I'm withered is there going to be enjoyment for me, with my lord old?' ¹³Yahweh said to Abraham, 'Why did Sarah laugh, saying "Shall I truly give birth, when I'm old?" ¹⁴Is a thing too extraordinary for Yahweh? At this set time I shall come back to you at reviving time and Sarah will have a son.' ¹⁵Sarah lied, saying 'I didn't laugh', because she was afraid. He said, 'No, you laughed.'

¹⁶From there the men set off, and they looked down at Sedom, with Abraham going with them to send them off.

¹⁷Now Yahweh had said, 'Am I going to hide from Abraham what I'm doing, ¹⁸when Abraham is indeed to become a big, numerous nation, and all the nations on the earth are to bless themselves by him? ¹⁹Because I've acknowledged him in order that he may order his children and his household after him so they may keep Yahweh's way by showing faithfulness in the exercise of authority, in order that Yahweh may bring about for Abraham what he's spoken concerning him.'

The cry from and for Sedom

²⁰So Yahweh said, 'The outcry of Sedom and Amorah, it's big. Their wrongdoing, it's very grave. ²¹I must go down and see whether they have acted totally in keeping with the outcry that has come to me. If not, I must acknowledge it.'

²²The men turned their face from there and went to Sedom, while Abraham was still standing before Yahweh. ²³Abraham came up and said, 'Will you really sweep away the faithful with the faithless? ²⁴Maybe there are fifty faithful people within the town. Will you really sweep it away and not bear with the place for the sake of the fifty faithful people within it? ²⁵Far be it from you to do a thing like this, putting to death the faithful with the faithless, so the faithful and the faithless are the same. Far be it from you. Isn't the one who exercises authority over the entire earth to exercise authority?'

²⁶Yahweh said, 'If I find in Sedom fifty faithful people within the town, I shall bear with the entire place on account of them.' ²⁷Abraham answered: 'There, please: I've resolved to speak to my Lord, when I'm soil and ash. ²⁸Maybe the fifty faithful will be five short. Will you devastate the entire town because of five?' He said, 'I won't devastate it if I find there forty-five.'

²⁹He spoke yet again to him: 'Maybe forty will be found there.' He said, 'I won't act, on account of the forty.' ³⁰He said, 'May it please not enrage my Lord, and I shall speak. Maybe thirty will be found there.' He said, 'I won't act if I find there thirty.' ³¹He said, 'There, please: I've resolved to speak with my Lord. Maybe twenty will be found there.' He said, 'I won't devastate it on account of the twenty.' ³²He said, 'May it please not enrage my Lord, and I shall speak one last time. Maybe ten will be found there.' He said, 'I won't devastate it on account of the ten.'

³³Yahweh went when he had finished speaking to Abraham, and Abraham went back to his place.

Sex and violence in Sedom

19 ¹The two envoys came to Sedom in the evening, and Lot was sitting at the gateway of Sedom. Lot saw them, and got up to meet them. He bowed low, his face to the ground. ²He said, 'Here, sirs, please do turn aside to your servant's house so you can stay the night and bathe your feet. Then you can start early and go on your way.' They said, 'No, because we can stay the night in the square.' ³But he pressed them hard, so they turned aside to him and came into his house. He made a banquet for them and baked flatbread, and they ate.

⁴Before they could go to bed, the men of the town, the men of Sedom, surrounded the house, from young right to old, the entire people, from every part. ⁵They called to Lot and said to him, 'Where are the men who came to you tonight? Bring them out so we can have sex with them.' ⁶Lot went out to them at the entrance but shut the door behind him.

⁷He said, 'My brothers, don't do this wrong, please. ⁸So, please: I have two daughters who haven't had sex with a man. Let me bring them out to you and you can do to them whatever is good in your eyes. Only don't do anything to these men, because this is why they've come under the shelter of my roof-beam.'

⁹But they said, 'Get over there.' They said, 'The man came to reside, and he's actually exercising authority. Now we'll deal badly with you, worse than with them.' They pressed hard against the man (against Lot) and came up to break the door. ¹⁰But the men put out their hand and got Lot to come to them, into the house, and they shut the door. ¹¹As for the men who were at the entrance of the house, they struck them down with a daze, from young right to old, so they became weary of trying to find the entrance.

Don't look back

¹²The men said to Lot, 'Who else do you have here, sons-in-law, sons, daughters, anyone who belongs to you in the town? Take them out of the place. ¹³Because we're going to devastate this place, because the outcry before Yahweh against them has become so big that Yahweh has sent us to devastate it.' ¹⁴So Lot went out and spoke to his sons-in-law, who were to get his daughters, and said 'Set off, get out of this place, because Yahweh is going to devastate the town.' But in the eyes of his sons-in-law he was like someone making a joke.

¹⁵As dawn came, the envoys pressed Lot, saying 'Set off, take your wife and your two daughters who are to be found here, so you're not swept away because of the waywardness of the town.' ¹⁶But he delayed, so the men took strong hold of his hand, his wife's hand and his two daughters' hand, by Yahweh's mercy on him, and got him out and set him down outside the town. ¹⁷When they had got them outside, one said, 'Escape for your life, don't gaze behind you, don't halt anywhere in the plain. Escape to the highland, so you're not swept away.'

¹⁸Lot said to them, 'No, please, my Lord! ¹⁹There, please: your servant has found grace in your eyes. You've acted in such great commitment with me in preserving my life. But I – I can't flee to the highland in order that the bad event doesn't attach itself to me and I die. ²⁰Here, please – this town's near for fleeing to, and it's small. I can flee there, it's small, so my life can be preserved.'

²¹He said to him, 'Here, I honour your person in this thing too, in not overthrowing the town that you spoke of. ²²Hurry up and escape there, because I can't do anything till you come there.' That's why the town was named Tso'ar ['Small'].

²³As the sun rose on the earth and Lot arrived at Tso'ar, ²⁴Yahweh rained on Sedom and Amorah burning sulphur from Yahweh, from the heavens. ²⁵He overthrew these towns and the entire plain and all the people living in the towns and what grew in the ground.

A distasteful aftermath

²⁶But his wife gazed behind him and became a salt pilaster.

²⁷Abraham started early in the morning for the place where he had stood before Yahweh ²⁸and looked out over the face of Sedom and Amorah and over the face of the entire plain region. He saw, and there, smoke from the region went up like the smoke from a

furnace. ²⁹So it was that when God devastated the towns of the plain, God was mindful of Abraham and sent Lot out from the middle of the overthrow, when he overthrew the towns in which Lot lived.

³⁰Lot went up from Tso'ar and lived in the highland, his two daughters with him, because he was afraid to live in Tso'ar. He lived in a cave, he and his two daughters. ³¹The firstborn said to the young one, 'Our father is old and there's no one on earth to have sex with us in the way of the entire world. ³²Come on, let's get our father to drink wine so we can sleep with him and get offspring alive through our father.'

³³So they got their father to drink wine that night, and the firstborn went in and slept with her father. He didn't know when she lay down or when she got up. ³⁴Next day the firstborn said to the young one, 'There, I slept with my father last night. Let's get him to drink wine tonight as well, and you come and sleep with him, so we can get offspring alive through our father.' ³⁵So they got their father to drink wine that night as well, and the young one got up and slept with him. He didn't know when she lay down or when she got up.

³⁶So Lot's two daughters got pregnant through their father. ³⁷The firstborn gave birth to a son and named him Mo'ab. He's the ancestor of Mo'ab until today. ³⁸The younger one also gave birth to a son, and named him Ben-ammi. He's the ancestor of the Ammonites until today.

Do we ever learn?

20 Abraham moved on from there to the Negeb region and lived between Qadesh and Shur. When he resided in Gerar, ²Abraham said of Sarah his wife, 'She's my sister.' So Abimelek king of Gerar sent and took Sarah. ³But God came to Abimelek in a dream by night and said to him, 'Here, you're a dead man because of the woman whom you've taken. She's married to someone.'

⁴Now Abimelek had not approached her. He said, 'Lord, would you kill a nation even if it's faithful? ⁵That man said to me, "She's my sister", didn't he. And she herself also said, "He's my brother." It was with integrity in my heart and with freedom of guilt in the palms of my hands that I did this.' ⁶God said to him in the dream, 'I myself both know that you did this with integrity in your heart, and have also held you back from doing wrong in relation
to me. That's why I didn't let you touch her. ⁷So now give the man's wife back. Because he's a prophet, he can intercede for you. Save your life. But if you don't give her back, acknowledge that you will definitely die, you and everything that's yours.'

⁸Abimelek started early in the morning, called for all his servants and spoke all these things in their ears. The men were very frightened. ⁹Abimelek called for Abraham and said to him, 'What have you done to us? How did I do wrong in relation to you that you've brought a big wrong on me and on my entire kingdom? You've done deeds with me that should not be done.'

¹⁰Abimelek said to Abraham, 'What did you see that you did this thing?' ¹¹Abraham said, 'I said, "There's just no awe for God in this place, and they'll kill me on account of my wife." ¹²And also, she truly is my sister, my father's daughter, admittedly not my mother's daughter. So she became my wife, ¹³and when God made me wander from my father's household, I said to her, "This is the commitment with which you're to act towards me: every place we come to, say about me: he's my brother."'

The promise fulfilled

¹⁴Abimelek took flock and herd, servants and maidservants, and gave them to Abraham, and gave his wife Sarah back to him. ¹⁵Abimelek said, 'Here, my country is before you. Live wherever is good in your eyes.' ¹⁶To Sarah he said, 'Here, I'm giving your brother a thousand pieces of silver. Here, it will be cover over the eyes for you and for everyone who is with you and with everyone, and you will be vindicated.'

¹⁷Abraham interceded with God and God healed Abimelek and his wife and his handmaids, and they gave birth (¹⁸because Yahweh had totally held back every womb belonging to Abimelek's household on account of Sarah, Abraham's wife).

21 When Yahweh attended to Sarah as he had said, Yahweh did for Sarah as he had spoken, ²and Sarah got pregnant and gave birth to a son for Abraham in his old age, at the set time of which God had spoken to him. ³Abraham named his son, who had been born to him, whom Sarah had borne to him, Yitshaq ['He Will Laugh']. ⁴Abraham circumcised Yitshaq his son when he was eight days old, as God ordered him, ⁵Abraham being a man of a hundred years when his son Yitshaq was born to him.

⁶Sarah said, 'God has made laughter for me, since everyone who hears will laugh for me', ⁷and said, 'Who would have uttered to Abraham, "Sarah has nursed children"? But I've given birth to a son for his old age.'

On not watching your son die

⁸The child grew and was weaned, and Abraham made a big banquet on the day that Yitshaq was weaned. ⁹But Sarah saw the son of Hagar the Misrayimite, to whom she gave birth for Abraham, laughing. ¹⁰She said to Abraham, 'Drive this handmaid and her son out, because this handmaid's son is not to come into possession with my son, with Yitshaq.'

¹¹The thing was very bad in Abraham's eyes, on account of his son. ¹²But God said to Abraham, 'It isn't to be bad in your eyes about the boy or about your handmaid. Everything that Sarah says to you, listen to her voice, because it's through Yitshaq that offspring will be named for you. ¹³The son of the handmaid: I shall make him into a nation, too, because he's your offspring.'

¹⁴Abraham started early in the morning, got bread and a skin of water, and gave them to Hagar. He put them on her shoulder, and the child, and sent her away. She went, and wandered about in the Be'er Sheba Wilderness. ¹⁵When the water in the skin was finished, she threw the child under one of the bushes ¹⁶and went and sat herself down at a distance, a bowshot away, because (she said), 'I'm not going to watch the child die.'

So she sat down at a distance and lifted up her voice and cried. ¹⁷But God listened to the boy's voice, and God's envoy called to Hagar from the heavens and said to her, 'What's with you, Hagar? Don't be afraid, because God has listened to the voice of the boy where he is. ¹⁸Get up, lift up the boy, take strong hold of him with your hand, because I'm going to make him into a big nation.' ¹⁹And God opened her eyes and she saw a well of water. She went and filled the skin with water, and got the boy to drink.

²⁰God was with the boy. He grew up and lived in the wilderness, and became a bowman. ²¹He lived in the Pa'ran Wilderness. His mother got a wife for him from the country of Misrayim.

Testimony to the blessing fulfilled

²²At that time Abimelek and Phikol, his army officer, said to Abraham: 'God is with you in everything that you do. ²³So now, swear to me here by God: if you deal falsely with me or with my offspring or with my posterity . . . You're to act with me and with the country in which you've resided in accordance with the commitment with which I've acted with you.' ²⁴Abraham said, 'I myself swear.'

²⁵Abraham reproved Abimelek concerning a well of water that Abimelek's servants had seized. ²⁶Abimelek said, 'I don't know who did this thing. You didn't tell me; I hadn't heard of it till today.' ²⁷Abraham took flock and herd and gave them to Abimelek, and the two of them solemnized a pact. ²⁸Abraham put seven ewes from the flock on their own. ²⁹Abimelek said to Abraham, 'What are these seven ewes here that you've put on their own?' ³⁰He said, 'You're to take the seven ewes from my hand so it will be a witness for me that I dug this well [be'er].' ³¹That's why that place was called Be'er Sheba, because the two of them swore [shaba] there. ³²So they solemnized a pact at Be'er Sheba, and Abimelek and Phikol, his army officer, set off and went back to the Pelishtites' country.

³³He planted a tamarisk at Be'er Sheba and called there in the name of Yahweh, God For Ever. ³⁴Abraham resided in the Pelishtites' country for a long time.

The test

22 Subsequently, God tested Abraham. He said to him, 'Abraham!' He said, 'I'm here.' ²He said, 'Please take your son, your only one, the one you love, Yitshaq, get yourself out to the Moriyyah region and offer him up as a burnt offering there, on one of the mountains that I shall say to you.' ³Abraham started early in the morning, saddled his donkey and took two of his boys with him, and Yitshaq his son. He cut the wood for the burnt offering, set off and went to the place that God said to him. ⁴On the third day, Abraham lifted his eyes and saw the place from a distance. ⁵Abraham said to his boys, 'You stay here with the donkey. The boy and I will go over there and bow low, and come back to you.' ⁶Abraham took the wood for the burnt offering and put it on his son Yitshaq, and took in his own hand the fire and the knife, and the two of them walked together.

⁷Yitshaq said to Abraham his father, 'Father!' He said, 'I'm here, son.' He said, 'Here are the fire and the wood, but where's the sheep for the burnt offering?' ⁸Abraham said, 'God will see for himself to the sheep for the burnt offering, son.' The two of them walked together ⁹and came to the place that God had said to him. There Abraham built the altar, laid out the wood, bound his son Yitshaq and placed him on the altar on top of the wood. ¹⁰Abraham put out his hand and got the knife to slaughter his son.

¹¹But Yahweh's envoy called to him from the heavens and said, 'Abraham, Abraham!' He said, 'I'm here.' ¹²He said, 'Don't put out your hand to the boy, don't do anything to him, because now I acknowledge that you live in awe of God; you haven't held back your son, your only son, from me.'

¹³Abraham lifted his eyes and looked: there, a ram caught in a thicket by its horns. Abraham went and got the ram and offered it up as a burnt offering in place of his son. ¹⁴Abraham named that place 'Yahweh Sees' [*Yahweh yir'eh*], so it's said today, 'On Yahweh's mountain it's seen.'

The promise and the loss

¹⁵Yahweh's envoy called to Abraham a second time from the heavens ¹⁶and said, 'By myself I swear (Yahweh's declaration) that since you've done this thing and not held back your son, your only one, ¹⁷I shall bless you abundantly and make your offspring very numerous, like the stars in the heavens and like the sand that's on the seashore; your offspring will take possession of their enemies' gateway. ¹⁸All the nations on the earth will bless themselves by your offspring, on account of the fact that you listened to my voice.'

¹⁹Abraham went back to his boys and they set off and went together to Be'er Sheba. Abraham lived at Be'er Sheba.

²⁰Subsequently, it was told to Abraham: 'Here, Milkah has given birth to children for your brother Nahor, too: ²¹Uts his firstborn, Buz his brother, Qemu'el the father of Aram, ²²Kesed, Hazo, Pildash, Yidlaph and Betu'el'; ²³and Betu'el fathered Ribqah. To these eight Milkah gave birth for Nahor, Abraham's brother. ²⁴His secondary wife – her name was Re'umah – also gave birth to Tebah, Gaham, Tahash and Ma'akah.

23

Sarah's lifetime was 127 years (the years of Sarah's life). ²Sarah died at Arba Township (i.e. Hebron) in the country of Kena'an. Abraham came to lament for Sarah and bewail her.

³Abraham set off from being in the presence of his dead and spoke to the Hittites: ⁴'I'm a resident, a settler, living with you. Give me a burial holding with you, so I may bury my dead away from my presence.' ⁵The Hittites answered Abraham, ⁶'Hear us, sir. You're an almighty leader among us. Bury your dead in the choicest of our burial places. None of us would withhold his burial place from you for burying your dead.'

The polite negotiation

⁷Abraham got up and bowed low to the people of the country, to the Hittites, ⁸and spoke with them: 'If it's your desire that I should bury my dead away from my presence, hear me and intercede for me with Ephron ben Tsohar, ⁹so he may give me the cave at Makpelah which is his and which is at the edge of his field. May he give it to me for the full silver as a burial holding among you.' ¹⁰Ephron was sitting among the Hittites.

Ephron the Hittite answered Abraham in the ears of the Hittites, all who came to the town gateway: ¹¹'No, sir, listen to me. The field – I give it to you, and the cave that's in it. I give it to you, before the eyes of the members of my people I give it to you. Bury your dead.' ¹²Abraham bowed low before the people of the country ¹³and spoke with Ephron in the ears of the people of the country: 'But if you yourself would please listen to me: I give you the silver for the field. Take it from me, so I may bury my dead there.' ¹⁴Ephron answered Abraham, ¹⁵'Sir, listen to me: land worth 400 sheqels – between me and you, what's that? Bury your dead.' ¹⁶Abraham listened to Ephron.

So Abraham weighed out to Ephron the silver that he had spoken of in the ears of the Hittites, 400 sheqels of silver, as current for the merchants. ¹⁷And Ephron's field which is at Makpelah, which is close to Mamre (the field and the cave that was in it and all the trees that were in the field, which were in all its border around) passed ¹⁸to Abraham as his acquisition before the eyes of the Hittites, all who had come to the town gateway.

¹⁹After this Abraham buried his wife Sarah in the cave in the field at Makpelah, close to Mamre (i.e. Hebron) in the country of Kena'an. ²⁰The field and the cave that was in it became the sure possession of Abraham as a burial holding, from the Hittites.

Where to find Yitshaq a wife

24 Abraham was old, going on in years, and Yahweh had blessed Abraham in every way. ²Abraham said to his senior servant in his household, who ruled over everything that he had, 'Please put your hand under my thigh, ³and I'll get you to swear by Yahweh the God of the heavens and the God of the earth that you won't get a wife for my son from the daughters of the Kena'anites among whom I'm living, ⁴but go to my country, to my homeland, and get a wife for my son, for Yitshaq.' ⁵The servant said to him, 'Maybe the woman won't be willing to follow me to this country. Should I actually take your son back to the country that you left?' ⁶Abraham said to him, 'Keep watch so that you don't take my son back there. ⁷Yahweh, the God of the heavens, who took me from my father's household and from the country that is my homeland and spoke to me and swore to me: "To your offspring I shall give this country" – he will send his envoy before you and you'll get a wife for my son from there. ⁸If the woman is not willing to follow you, then you'll be free from this oath to me. Only don't take my son back there.'

⁹The servant put his hand under the thigh of Abraham his lord and swore to him concerning this thing. ¹⁰The servant took ten camels from his lord's camels and went, with all the good things belonging to his lord in his possession. He set off and went to Aram of the Two Rivers, to Nahor's town, ¹¹and got the camels to kneel outside the town at the water well, at evening time, at the time when the women who draw water go out.

Too much of a coincidence

¹²He said, 'Yahweh, God of my lord Abraham, please make things happen for me today. Act with commitment to my lord Abraham. ¹³Here, I'm standing by the water spring, and the daughters of the townspeople are going out to draw water. ¹⁴May the girl to whom I say "Please put down your pitcher so I can drink", and she says "Drink, and I'll also water your camels", may she be the one you've decided on for your servant, for Yitshaq. By this I shall acknowledge that you've acted with commitment to my lord.'

¹⁵Before he had finished speaking, there was Ribqah [Rebekah], who had been born to Betu'el ben Milkah, wife of Nahor, Abraham's brother, coming out with her pitcher on her shoulder. ¹⁶The girl was very good-looking, a young girl that no one had had sex with. She went down to the spring, filled her pitcher and went up.

¹⁷The servant ran to meet her and said, 'Please may I sip a little water from your pitcher.' ¹⁸She said, 'Drink, sir', and hurried and lowered her pitcher onto her hand and let him drink. ¹⁹When she had finished letting him drink, she said, 'I'll draw water for your camels as well, till they've finished drinking.' ²⁰She hurried and emptied her pitcher into the trough, ran back to the well to draw and drew for all his camels, ²¹while the man was looking at her, staying quiet, to know whether or not Yahweh had made his journey successful.

²²When the camels had finished drinking, the man got a gold nose-ring (its weight a half-sheqel) and two gold hand-bracelets (their weight ten sheqels). ²³He said, 'Whose daughter are you? Please tell me, is there room at your father's house for us to stay the night?' ²⁴She said to him, 'I'm the daughter of Betu'el ben Milkah, to whom she gave birth for Nahor.' ²⁵And she said to him, 'There's plenty of both straw and fodder with us, and also a place to stay the night.'

Meet the family

²⁶The man bent his head and bowed low to Yahweh ²⁷and said, 'Yahweh the God of my lord Abraham be blessed, who hasn't abandoned his commitment and his truthfulness with my lord. I myself – Yahweh has led me on the way to the house of my lord's brothers!' ²⁸The girl ran and told her mother's household all these actual words.

²⁹Now Ribqah had a brother; his name was Laban. Laban ran out to the spring to the man. ³⁰When he saw the nose-ring and his sister's two hand-bracelets and heard the words of his sister Ribqah, 'This is how the man spoke to me', he came to the man. There he was, standing by the camels by the spring. ³¹He said, 'Come in, you who are blessed by Yahweh. Why stand outside when I've cleared the house and a place for the camels?'

³²So the man came into the house and unharnessed the camels. He gave the camels straw and fodder, and water to wash his feet and the feet of the men who were with him. ³³Something to eat was set before him, but he said, 'I won't eat until I've spoken my words.' So he said, 'Speak.'

³⁴He said, 'I'm Abraham's servant. ³⁵As Yahweh has greatly blessed my lord, he's become big. He's given him flock and herd, silver and gold, servants and maidservants, camels and donkeys. ³⁶Sarah, my lord's wife, gave birth to a son for my lord in her old age, and he's given him everything that he has. ³⁷My lord got me to swear, saying "You will not get a wife for my son from the daughters of the Kena'anites among whom I'm living in their country. ³⁸No, you are to go to my father's household, to my kin-group, and get a wife for my son."

It's from God

³⁹I said to my lord, "Maybe the woman won't follow me." ⁴⁰He said to me, "Yahweh, before whom I've walked – he will send his envoy with you and he will make your journey successful. You'll get a wife for my son from my kin-group. ⁴¹Then you'll be free from the vow to me if, when you come to my kin-group, they don't give her to you. You'll be free from the vow to me."

⁴²So I came today to the spring and I said, "Yahweh, God of my lord Abraham: if you could please be one who makes my journey that I'm going on successful! ⁴³Here, I'm standing by the water spring. May the girl who goes out to draw and to whom I say 'Please let me drink a little water from your pitcher', ⁴⁴and she says to me 'Drink, and I'll also draw for your camels', may she be the woman whom Yahweh has decided on for my lord's son."

⁴⁵Before I'd finished speaking in my mind, there was Ribqah going out with her pitcher on her shoulder. She went down to the spring and drew. I said to her, "Please give me a drink." ⁴⁶She hurried and lowered her pitcher from on her shoulder and said, "Drink, and I'll water your camels as well." So I drank, and she watered the camels as well. ⁴⁷I asked her, "Whose daughter are you?" and she said, "The daughter of Betu'el ben Nahor, to whom Milkah gave birth for him." I put the nose-ring on her nose and the bracelets on her hands. ⁴⁸I bent my head and bowed low to Yahweh and blessed Yahweh the God of my father Abraham, who had led me on a true way to get the daughter of my lord's brother for his son.

Will you go with this man?

⁴⁹So now: if you're going to act with commitment and truthfulness to my lord, tell me. And if not, tell me, so I may turn my face to the right or to the left.'

⁵⁰Laban and Betu'el answered, 'It's from Yahweh that the thing has issued. We can't speak to you bad or good. ⁵¹Here is Ribqah before you. Take her and go, so she can be a wife for your lord's son, as Yahweh has said.'

⁵²When Abraham's servant heard their words, he bowed low to the ground before Yahweh. ⁵³The servant brought out objects of

silver and objects of gold, and clothes, and gave them to Ribqah, and he gave choice things to her brother and to her mother. ⁵⁴They ate and drank, he and the men who were with him, and stayed the night.

They got up in the morning, and he said, 'Send me off to my lord.' ⁵⁵Her brother and her mother said, 'The girl should stay with us for some days – say ten. Afterwards, she can go.' ⁵⁶He said to them, 'Don't make me delay when Yahweh has made my journey successful. Send me off so I can go to my lord.'

⁵⁷They said, 'Let's call the girl and ask for her bidding.' ⁵⁸They called Ribqah and said to her, 'Will you go with this man?' She said, 'I'll go.' ⁵⁹So they sent Ribqah their sister off, with her nanny and Abraham's servant and his men. ⁶⁰They blessed Ribqah and said to her, 'Our sister, may you become thousands of myriads, and may your offspring take possession of the gateway that belongs to people who are hostile to them.' ⁶¹ᵃRibqah and her girls got up, mounted their camels and followed the man.

The romantic story finds a satisfactory ending

⁶¹ᵇSo the servant took Ribqah and went. ⁶²Now Yitshaq had come from where you come to The Well of the Living One Seeing Me; he was living in the Negeb region. ⁶³Yitshaq had gone out to think in the open country as evening turned its face. He lifted his eyes and saw: there, camels coming.

⁶⁴And Ribqah lifted her eyes and saw Yitshaq. She jumped down from her camel ⁶⁵and said to the servant, 'Who's that man walking in the open country about to meet us?' The servant said, 'That's my lord.' She took her veil and covered herself, ⁶⁶and the servant told Yitshaq all the things that he'd done. ⁶⁷Yitshaq brought her into the tent of Sarah his mother. He took Ribqah and she became his wife, and he loved her. So Yitshaq found consolation after his mother.

25 Abraham again took a wife; her name was Qeturah. ²She gave birth to Zimran, Yoqshan, Medan, Midyan, Yishbaq and Shuah for him. ³Yoqshan fathered Sheba and Dedan, while Dedan's descendants were the Ashshurites, the Letushites and the Le'ummites, ⁴and Midyan's descendants were Ephah, Epher, Hanok, Abida and Elda'ah. All these were Qeturah's descendants.

⁵Abraham gave all that he had to Yitshaq, ⁶but to the sons of Abraham's secondary wives Abraham gave gifts while he was still alive and sent them off away from Yitshaq his son eastward, to the east country.

⁷This is the span of the years in the life that Abraham lived: 175 years. ⁸So he breathed his last. Abraham died at a good age, old and full, and was gathered to his kin. ⁹Yitshaq and Yishma'e'l his sons buried him in the cave at Makpelah in the field of Ephron ben Tsohar the Hittite, which is close to Mamre, ¹⁰the field that Abraham acquired from the Hittites. There Abraham and his wife Sarah were buried.

¹¹After Abraham's death, God blessed Yitshaq his son. Yitshaq lived near The Well of the Living One Seeing Me.

The hand grasping the heel

¹²These are the lines of descent of Yishma'e'l, Abraham's son, to whom Hagar the Misrayimite, Sarah's maidservant, gave birth for Abraham. ¹³These are the names of Yishma'e'l's sons, by their names according to their lines of descent. Yishma'e'l's firstborn, Nebayot, Qedar, Adbe'el, Mibsam, ¹⁴Mishma, Dumah, Massa, ¹⁵Hadad, Tema, Yetur, Naphish and Qedemah. ¹⁶These are Yishma'e'l's sons and these are their names, by their villages and by their enclosures, twelve leaders for their peoples.

¹⁷These are the years of Yishma'e'l's life: 137 years. So he breathed his last and died, and was gathered to his kin.

¹⁸They dwelt from Havilah as far as Shur, which is close to Misrayim, as you come to Ashshur. He fell close to all his brothers.

¹⁹These are the lines of descent of Yitshaq, Abraham's son. Abraham fathered Yitshaq, ²⁰and Yitshaq was a man of forty years when he got himself as wife Ribqah daughter of Betu'el the Aramite of Paddan Aram, sister of Laban the Aramite. ²¹Yitshaq entreated Yahweh on behalf of his wife, because she was infertile. Yahweh let himself be entreated, and Ribqah his wife got pregnant. ²²The children pressed on one another inside her, and she said, 'If this is how it is, why is it that I exist?'

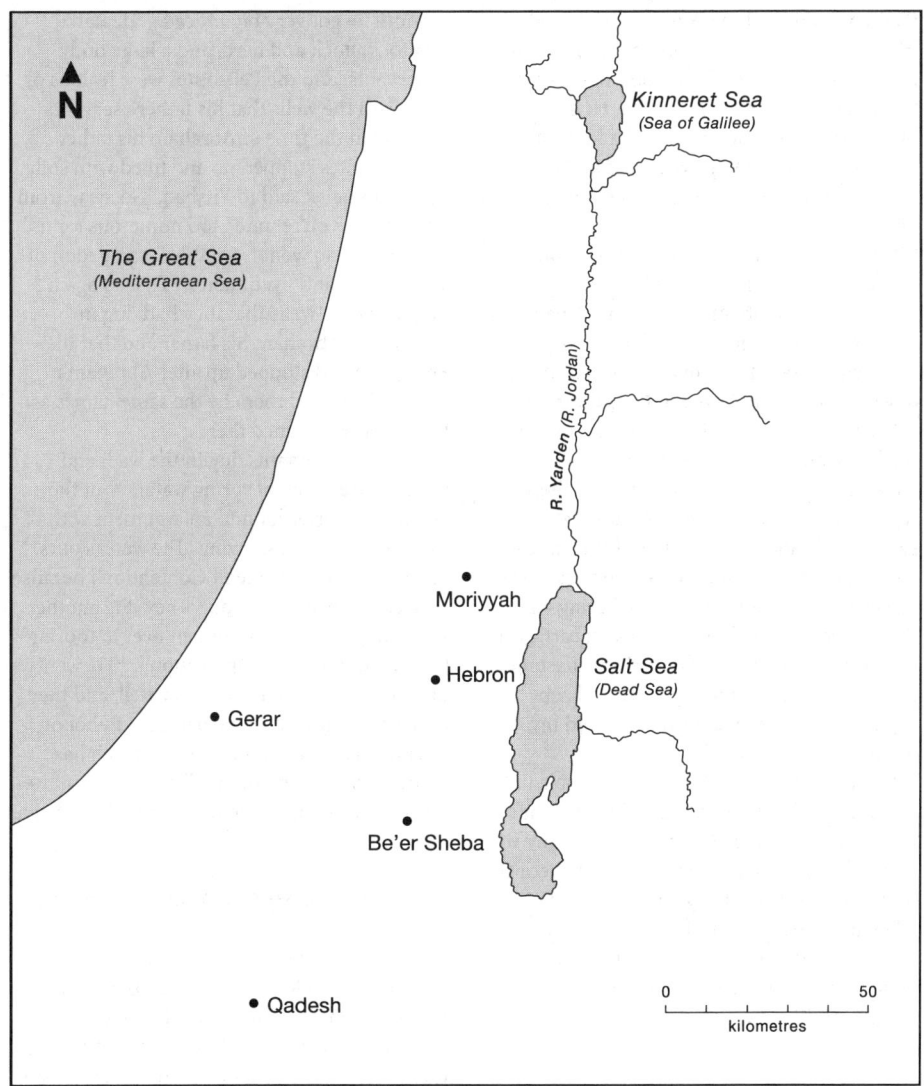

Genesis 25: Yitshaq (Isaac)

She went to enquire of Yahweh [23]and Yahweh said to her, 'Two nations are in your womb; two peoples will divide from your body. One people will be stronger than the other people, and the older one will serve the younger one.'

[24]Her time became full for giving birth, and there, twins were in her womb. [25]The first came out red, all of him, like a garment of hair [*se'ar*]. So they named him Esaw. [26]After that, his brother came out, his hand grasping Esaw's heel [*aqeb*]. They named him Ya'aqob [Jacob]. Yitshaq was a man of sixty years when they were born.

The birthright

[27]The boys grew up and Esaw became a man who knew about hunting, a man of the open country, while Ya'aqob was a regular man, staying at the tents. [28]Yitshaq loved Esaw because there was game in his mouth, while Ribqah loved Ya'aqob.

[29]Ya'aqob cooked stew, and Esaw came in from the open country. He was faint. [30]Esaw said to Ya'aqob, 'Please let me wolf down some of the red [*adom*] stuff, this red stuff, because I'm faint' (that's why they named him Edom).

³¹Ya'aqob said, 'Sell me your birthright today.' ³²Esaw said, 'Here, I'm about to die. What use is a birthright to me?' ³³Ya'aqob said, 'Swear to me today.' So he swore to him. He sold his birthright to Ya'aqob, ³⁴and Ya'aqob gave Esaw bread and lentil stew. He ate and drank, and got up and went. So Esaw despised the birthright.

26 There was a famine in the country, apart from the first famine that happened in Abraham's time, and Yitshaq went to Gerar, to Abimelek, king of the Pelishtites. ²Yahweh appeared to him and said, 'Don't go down to Misrayim. Dwell in the country that I'm telling you about. ³Reside in this country. I shall be with you and I shall bless you, because I shall give you and your offspring all these regions. I shall implement the oath that I swore to Abraham your father. ⁴I shall make your offspring as numerous as the stars in the heavens, and I shall give your offspring all these regions, and all the nations on earth will bless themselves by your offspring, ⁵inasmuch as Abraham listened to my voice and kept my charge, my orders, my decrees and my instructions.'

⁶So Yitshaq lived in Gerar. ⁷The people in the place asked about his wife, and he said 'She's my sister', because he was afraid to say 'my wife' in case 'the people in the place kill me because of Ribqah, because she's good-looking'. ⁸But when he'd been there some time, Abimelek king of the Pelishtites looked out through the window and saw: there was Yitshaq playing about with Ribqah his wife.

Do we ever learn? – take two

⁹Abimelek called for Yitshaq and said, 'Here, really she's your wife! How did you come to say "She's my sister"?' Yitshaq said to him, 'Because I said, "So I don't die because of her."' ¹⁰Abimelek said, 'What is this that you've done to us? Almost, someone from the people could have slept with your wife and brought liability upon us.' ¹¹Abimelek ordered the entire people: 'Anyone who touches this man or his wife will absolutely be put to death.'

¹²Yitshaq sowed in that country, and that year reaped a hundredfold. Yahweh blessed him. ¹³The man got big, and went on doing so, until he got very big indeed. ¹⁴He had livestock, flock and herd, and a large body of servants, and the Pelishtites were jealous of him. ¹⁵All the wells that his father's servants had dug in the time of Abraham his father, the Pelishtites stopped up and filled with soil, ¹⁶and Abimelek said to Yitshaq, 'Go away from us, because you're much too numerous for us.'

¹⁷So Yitshaq went from there, camped in Wadi Gerar and lived there. ¹⁸Yitshaq again dug the water wells that they had dug in the time of Abraham his father and that the Pelishtites had stopped up after Abraham's death. He named them by the same names as his father had named them.

¹⁹Yitshaq's servants dug in the wadi and found there a well of spring water, ²⁰but the Gerar shepherds got into an argument with Yitshaq's shepherds, saying 'The water's ours.' He named the well Eseq ['Contention'] because they contended with him. ²¹They dug another well and got into an argument over it, too, and he named it Sitnah ['Opposition']. ²²He went on from there and dug another well, and they didn't argue over it, so he named it Rehobot ['Wide Places'] and said, 'Now Yahweh has made it wide for us and we'll be fruitful in the region.' ²³From there he went up to Be'er Sheba.

We've seen clearly that Yahweh is with you

²⁴Yahweh appeared to him that night and said, 'I am the God of Abraham your father. Don't be afraid, because I shall be with you, and I shall bless you and make your offspring numerous on account of Abraham my servant.' ²⁵He built an altar there, called in Yahweh's name and spread his tents there, and Yitshaq's servants dug out a well there.

²⁶Now Abimelek went to him from Gerar with Ahuzzat his aide and Phikol his army officer. ²⁷Yitshaq said to them, 'Why have you come to me, when you were hostile to me and you sent me off from being with you?' ²⁸They said, 'We've seen clearly that Yahweh is with you, so we said, "There should please be a vow between us", between us and you. We want to solemnize a pact with you. ²⁹If you deal badly with us . . . ! – as we haven't touched you and as we've done only good with you, and sent you off in peace. You're now one blessed by Yahweh.'

³⁰So Yitshaq made a banquet for them, and they ate and drank. ³¹They started early in the morning and swore, each to the other. Yitshaq sent them off and they went from being with him in peace. ³²That day, Yitshaq's servants came and told him about the matter of a well that they'd dug, and said to him, 'We've found water.' ³³So he called it Shib'ah ['Sworn Oath']. That's why the name of the town is Be'er Sheba until this day.

³⁴When Esaw was a man of forty years, he got as wife Yehudit daughter of Be'eri the Hittite, and Ba'semat daughter of Elon the Hittite, ³⁵but they became a source of bitterness in spirit to Yitshaq and Ribqah.

Parents take sides

27 When Yitshaq was old and his eyes had become too dim to see, he called Esaw his older son and said to him, 'Son!' He said to him, 'I'm here.' ²He said, 'Here, please: I'm old. I don't know the day of my death. ³So now, pick up your equipment, please, your quiver and your bow, and go out to the open country, and hunt game for me. ⁴Make me a dish the way I like, and bring it to me so I can eat, and I will give you my personal blessing before I die.' ⁵Ribqah was listening when Yitshaq was speaking to Esaw his son.

So Esaw went into the country to hunt game to bring, ⁶and Ribqah said to Ya'aqob her son: 'Here, I heard your father speaking to Esaw your brother, saying ⁷"Bring me game and make me a dish so I can eat, and I will bless you before Yahweh before I die." ⁸So now, son, listen to my voice, to what I'm ordering you. ⁹Please go to the flock and get me two choice kid goats from there, and I'll make them into a dish for your father, the way he likes, ¹⁰and you can bring it to your father so he can eat, so he may bless you before he dies.'

¹¹Ya'aqob said to Ribqah his mother, 'Here, my brother Esaw is a hairy man and I'm a smooth-skinned man. ¹²Maybe my father will feel me and in his eyes I shall be like someone playing a trick, and I shall bring on myself slight and not blessing.' ¹³His mother said to him, 'Your slight be on me, son. Just listen to what I say. Go and get them for me.' ¹⁴So he went and got them and brought them to his mother, and his mother made a dish the way his father liked.

The trick

¹⁵Ribqah got herself the clothes of Esaw her older son, the best ones, which were with her in the house, and put them on Ya'aqob her younger son. ¹⁶The skin of the kid goats she put on his hands and on the smooth part of his neck, ¹⁷and she put the dish, and the bread that she had made, into the hand of Ya'aqob her son.

¹⁸He came to his father and said, 'Father!' He said, 'I'm here. Who are you, son?' ¹⁹Ya'aqob said to his father, 'I'm Esaw your firstborn. I've done as you spoke to me. Please get up, sit and eat some of my game, so you may give me your personal blessing.' ²⁰Yitshaq said to his son, 'How were you so quick in finding it, son?' He said, 'Because Yahweh your God brought it about for me.' ²¹Yitshaq said to Ya'aqob, 'Please come up so I can feel you, son, whether you're really Esaw my son or not.' ²²Ya'aqob came up to Yitshaq his father, and he felt him and said, 'The voice is Ya'aqob's voice, but the hands are Esaw's hands.' ²³He didn't recognize him because his hands were like the hands of Esaw his brother, hairy.

So he blessed him. ²⁴He said, 'Are you really my son Esaw?' He said, 'I am.' ²⁵He said, 'Bring it up to me so I can eat some of my son's game, in order that I can give you my personal blessing.' He brought it up to him and he ate, and he brought him wine and he drank. ²⁶His father Yitshaq said to him, 'Please come up and kiss me, son.' ²⁷He came up and kissed him, and he smelled his clothes.

So he blessed him: 'See: my son's smell is like the smell of the open country that Yahweh has blessed. ²⁸God give you from the dew of the heavens and from the richness of the earth, a large quantity of grain and new wine. ²⁹Peoples are to serve you, nations to bow low to you. Be lord to your brothers; your mother's sons are to bow low to you. Cursed be the people who curse you, blessed be those who bless you.'

The alternative blessing

³⁰When Yitshaq had finished blessing Ya'aqob and Ya'aqob had scarcely gone right out

from the presence of Yitshaq his father, Esaw his brother came in from his hunting. ³¹He, too, made a dish and brought it to his father and said to his father, 'May my father get up and eat some of his son's game, so you may give me your personal blessing.' ³²Yitshaq his father said to him, 'Who are you?' He said, 'I'm your son, your firstborn, Esaw.' ³³Yitshaq trembled, trembled with force, and said, 'Then who was that who hunted game and brought it to me and I ate of it all before you came, and I blessed him? Yes, he will come to be blessed.'

³⁴When Esaw heard his father's words, he cried out with a very loud and bitter cry. He said to his father, 'Bless me, me as well, father!' ³⁵He said, 'Your brother came with guile and took your blessing.' ³⁶He said, 'He's called "Ya'aqob", isn't he? He's grabbed me [*aqab*] these two times. He took my birthright, and there, he's taken my blessing now.' And he said, 'Haven't you saved a blessing for me?'

³⁷Yitshaq answered Esaw, 'There, I've made him lord in relation to you. I've given him all his brothers as servants and sustained him with grain and new wine. So what can I therefore do for you, son?' ³⁸Esaw said to his father, 'Do you have one blessing, father? Bless me, me as well, father!' Esaw lifted up his voice and cried.

³⁹Yitshaq his father answered him, 'There, your settlement will be from the richness of the earth and from the dew of the heavens above. ⁴⁰By your sword you'll live, and you will serve your brother. But as you wander you'll break his yoke from your neck.'

⁴¹Esaw was antagonistic to Ya'aqob because of the blessing with which his father had blessed him, and Esaw said to himself, 'When the time for grieving over my father arrives, I shall kill Ya'aqob my brother.'

Reasons to get out from here

⁴²Ribqah was told the words of Esaw her older son, and she sent and called for Ya'aqob her younger son, and said to him, 'Here, Esaw your brother is going to console himself by killing you. ⁴³Now, son, listen to my voice. Set off, take flight to Harran to Laban my brother ⁴⁴and stay with him for some time till your brother's wrath turns away, ⁴⁵till your brother's anger with you turns away and he puts out of mind what you've done to him. And I'll send and get you from there. Why should I be bereaved of both of you in one day?'

⁴⁶So Ribqah said to Yitshaq, 'I'm dismayed about my life because of the Hittite women. If Ya'aqob takes a wife from among the Hittite women like these, from the women of this country, what good will life be for me?'

28 So Yitshaq called for Ya'aqob, blessed him and ordered him, 'You're not to take a wife from among the Kena'anite women. ²Set off for yourself to Paddan Aram to the house of Betu'el, your mother's father, and get yourself a wife from there from among the daughters of Laban, your mother's brother. ³May God Shadday bless you and make you fruitful and make you numerous, so you become a congregation of peoples. ⁴May he give you Abraham's blessing, you and your offspring with you, so you take possession of the country where you're residing, which God gave Abraham.'

⁵So Yitshaq sent Ya'aqob off and he went to Paddan Aram to Laban ben Betu'el, the Aramite, the brother of Ribqah, the mother of Ya'aqob and Esaw.

⁶Esaw saw that his father Yitshaq had blessed Ya'aqob and sent him off to Paddan Aram to get himself a wife from there, and in blessing him had ordered him: 'You're not to take a wife from among the Kena'anite women', ⁷and Ya'aqob had listened to his father and mother and gone to Paddan Aram. ⁸Esaw saw that the Kena'anite women were bad in the eyes of Yitshaq his father. ⁹So Esaw went to Yishma'e'l and got himself as wife Mahalat daughter of Yishma'e'l, Abraham's son, sister of Nebayot, as an addition to his wives.

The stairway to heaven

¹⁰Ya'aqob left Be'er Sheba and went to Harran. ¹¹He came upon a site and stayed the night there because the sun had gone. He got one of the stones from the site and put it at his head and lay down in that site.

¹²He had a dream. There – a ramp was put up on the earth with its top reaching to the heavens, and there – God's envoys were going up and down on it. ¹³And there – Yahweh was

standing by him. He said, 'I am Yahweh, the God of Abraham your father and the God of Yitshaq. The ground that you're lying on, I shall give to you and to your offspring. ¹⁴Your offspring will be like the earth's soil. You'll break out to the west, to the east, to the north and to the south. All the kin-groups on the earth will bless themselves by you, and by your offspring. ¹⁵There, I shall be with you. I shall keep you wherever you go and bring you back to this land, because I won't abandon you until I've done what I've spoken to you of.'

¹⁶Ya'aqob woke up from his sleep and said, 'Yahweh is definitely here in this site, and I myself didn't know!' ¹⁷He was in awe, and he said, 'How awe-inspiring is this site! This is none other than a house of God, and that is a gateway into the heavens!'

¹⁸Ya'aqob started early in the morning, took the stone where he had put his head, set it up as a column and poured oil on the top of it. ¹⁹He named the site Bet-el [Bethel; 'House of God'] – Luz was the name of the town at first, however. ²⁰And Ya'aqob made a pledge: 'If God will be with me, and will keep me on this journey that I'm going on, and will give me bread to eat and clothes to wear, ²¹and I come back to my father's house with things being well, then Yahweh will be God for me, ²²and this stone that I've set up as a column will be God's house, and of everything that you give me I will rigorously give a tenth to you.'

Ya'aqob shows his muscle

29 Ya'aqob took up his journey and went to the country of the Easterners. ²He looked, and there – a well in the fields, and three herds of sheep lying there by it, because people used to water the herds from that well. The stone on the well's mouth was big; ³all the herds would gather there, and people would roll the stone off the well's mouth and water the sheep, and put the stone back in its place on the well's mouth.

⁴Ya'aqob said to them, 'Brothers, where are you from?' They said, 'We're from Harran.' ⁵He said to them, 'Do you know Laban ben Nahor?' They said, 'We know him.' ⁶He said to them, 'Are things well with him?' They said, 'They're well. There – Rahel [Rachel] his daughter is coming with the sheep.' ⁷He said, 'Here, it's still the middle of the day. It's not time for the livestock to gather. Water the sheep and go pasture them.' ⁸They said, 'We can't, till all the herds gather and people roll the stone from on the well's mouth and we water the sheep.'

⁹While he was still speaking with them, Rahel came with the sheep that belonged to her father, because she was a shepherd. ¹⁰When Ya'aqob saw Rahel daughter of Laban, his mother's brother, and the flock of Laban, his mother's brother, Ya'aqob came up, rolled the stone from on the well's mouth and watered the flock of Laban his mother's brother; ¹¹and Ya'aqob kissed Rahel and lifted his voice and cried. ¹²Ya'aqob told Rahel that he was her father's brother and that he was Ribqah's son, and she ran and told her father. ¹³When Laban heard the report of Ya'aqob, his sister's son, he ran to meet him, kissed him and hugged him, and brought him into his house. He told Laban all these things, ¹⁴and Laban said to him, 'Certainly you're my own bone and flesh.' He stayed with him for a period of a month.

The deceiver deceived

¹⁵Laban said to Ya'aqob, 'Because you're my brother, are you to serve me for nothing? Tell me: what are your wages to be.' ¹⁶Now Laban had two daughters. The name of the elder was Le'ah and the name of the younger Rahel. ¹⁷Le'ah's eyes were soft, but Rahel was attractive in shape and attractive in appearance. ¹⁸Ya'aqob loved Rahel. So he said, 'I'll serve you seven years for Rahel, your younger daughter.' ¹⁹Laban said, 'For me to give her to you will be better than for me to give her to another man. Stay with me.' ²⁰So Ya'aqob served seven years for Rahel, but in his eyes they were like a few days because of his love for her. ²¹Then Ya'aqob said to Laban, 'Give me my wife, since my time is complete, so I may have sex with her.' ²²Laban gathered all the people of the place and made a banquet, ²³but in the evening he got Le'ah his daughter and brought her to him, and he had sex with her. (²⁴Laban gave her Zilpah his maidservant, to Le'ah his daughter as her maidservant.)

²⁵So in the morning: there, it was Le'ah! He said to Laban, 'What's this that you've done to

me? It was for Rahel that I served with you, wasn't it? Why have you beguiled me?' ²⁶Laban said, 'It's not done like that in our place, giving the younger one before the firstborn. ²⁷Complete the week for the one, and we'll give you the other as well, for the service that you'll give with me for another seven years more.' ²⁸Ya'aqob did so. He completed the week for the one, then he gave him Rahel his daughter as wife. (²⁹Laban gave Rahel his daughter Bilhah his maidservant as her maidservant.)

³⁰So Ya'aqob had sex with Rahel and also loved Rahel more than Le'ah, and he served with him another seven years more.

I want to know what love is

³¹Yahweh saw that Le'ah was disliked and he opened her womb; whereas Rahel was infertile. ³²So Le'ah got pregnant and gave birth to a son, and named him Re'uben, because (she said), 'Yahweh has seen [*ra'ah*] my humbling; now my husband will love me [*ye'ehabeni*].' ³³She got pregnant again and gave birth to a son, and said, 'Yahweh has heard [*shama*] that I'm disliked and has given me this one as well', so she named him Shim'on [Simeon]. ³⁴She got pregnant again and gave birth to a son, and said, 'Now this time my husband will become attached [*lava*] to me, because I've given birth to three sons for him.' That's why he named him Levi. ³⁵She got pregnant again and gave birth to a son and said, 'This time I shall confess [*yadah*] Yahweh.' That's why she named him Yehudah [Judah]. Then she stopped giving birth.

30

Rahel saw that she couldn't give birth for Ya'aqob. Rahel was jealous of her sister and she said to Ya'aqob, 'Give me children! Otherwise, I'm going to die!' ²Ya'aqob's anger raged at Rahel. He said, 'Am I in the place of God, who has held back the fruit of the womb from you?' ³She said, 'Here's my handmaid Bilhah. Have sex with her, so she can give birth on my knees and I can also be built up through her.' ⁴So she gave him Bilhah her maidservant as wife, and Ya'aqob had sex with her. ⁵Bilhah got pregnant and gave birth to a son for Ya'aqob. ⁶Rahel said, 'God has given judgement [*dan*] for me; yes, he's listened to my voice and given me a son.' That's why she named him Dan. ⁷Bilhah, Rahel's maidservant, got pregnant again and gave birth to a second son for Ya'aqob. ⁸Rahel said, 'An almighty wrestling match [*naphtulim*] I've fought with my sister; yes, I've won.' So she named him Naphtali.

Wives, sons and a daughter

⁹Le'ah saw that she had stopped giving birth, and she got Zilpah her maidservant and gave her to Ya'aqob as wife. ¹⁰Zilpah, Le'ah's maidservant, gave birth to a son for Ya'aqob, ¹¹and Le'ah said, 'Luck [*gad*] has come!' So she named him Gad. ¹²Zilpah, Le'ah's maidservant, gave birth to a second son for Ya'aqob, ¹³and Le'ah said 'What good fortune [*oshri*] I have, because daughters will call me fortunate.' So she named him Asher.

¹⁴In the days of the wheat harvest, Re'uben went and found love-plants in the fields and brought them to Le'ah his mother. Rahel said to Le'ah, 'Please give me some of your son's love-plants.' ¹⁵She said to her, 'Was it a small thing, your taking my husband, and you're also going to take my son's love-plants?' Rahel said, 'Therefore he can sleep with you tonight in return for your son's love-plants.'

¹⁶In the evening Ya'aqob came from the fields, and Le'ah went out to meet him and said, 'I'm the one you're to have sex with, because I've paid a hire charge for you, with my son's love-plants.' So he slept with her that night, ¹⁷and God listened to Le'ah. She got pregnant and gave birth to a fifth son for Ya'aqob. ¹⁸Le'ah said, 'God gave me my hire charge [*sakar*], because I gave my maidservant to my husband.' So she named him Yissakar [Issachar].

¹⁹Le'ah got pregnant again, and gave birth to a sixth son for Ya'aqob. ²⁰Le'ah said, 'God has given me a good endowment [*zebed*]; this time my husband will elevate me [*yizbeleni*], because I've given birth to six sons for him.' So she named him Zebulun. ²¹Later, she gave birth to a daughter, and named her Dinah.

²²But God was mindful of Rahel. God listened to her and opened her womb, ²³and she got pregnant and gave birth to a son, and said, 'God has gathered up [*asaph*] my reviling.' ²⁴So she named him Yoseph [Joseph], saying 'May Yahweh add [*yoseph*] another son to me!'

The competition to be the shrewdest sheep farmer

²⁵When Rahel had given birth to Yoseph, Ya'aqob said to Laban, 'Send me off, so I may go to my place, to my country. ²⁶Give me my wives and my children for whom I've served you so I may go, because you yourself know the service that I've given you.' ²⁷Laban said to him, 'Please, if I've found grace in your eyes: I've divined that Yahweh has blessed me because of you.' ²⁸So he said, 'Specify your wages with me and I'll give it to you.' ²⁹He said to him, 'You yourself know how I've served you and how your livestock have been with me, ³⁰because the little that you had before me has broken out so as to become a large number. Yahweh has blessed you wherever I've been. But now, when am I myself also to do something for my household?'

³¹He said, 'What could I give you?' Ya'aqob said, 'You won't give me anything. If you'll do this thing for me, I'll pasture your flock again, I'll keep them. ³²I'll pass through your entire flock today, removing from there every speckled and spotted sheep, and every dark sheep among the lambs, and the spotted and speckled among the goats. It will be my wages. ³³My faithfulness will avow for me on the future day when you come to look at my wages before you. Every one with me that's not speckled or spotted among the goats or dark among the lambs: that one with me will have been stolen.'

³⁴Laban said, 'There, yes, let it be in accordance with your word.' ³⁵But that day he removed the streaked and spotted he-goats and all the speckled and spotted she-goats, every one that had white on it, and every dark one among the lambs. He put them into the care of his sons, ³⁶and put three days' journey between him and Ya'aqob while Ya'aqob was pasturing the rest of Laban's flock.

Trouble follows

³⁷Ya'aqob got for himself fresh canes of poplar, and almond and plane, and peeled white stripes in them, exposing the white that was on the rods. ³⁸The canes that he had peeled he stationed in the troughs, in the water containers that the flock came to drink from, in front of the flock. They were in heat and they came to drink, ³⁹so the flock were in heat by the canes, and the flock gave birth to streaked, speckled and spotted young. ⁴⁰The lambs Ya'aqob divided off, and put the flock's faces towards the streaked and the completely dark animals in Laban's flock. So he put herds for himself each on its own and didn't put them by Laban's flock. ⁴¹Every time the flock was in heat, the well-built females, Ya'aqob would put the canes in the troughs before the eyes of the flock so they would be in heat by the canes. ⁴²But with the feebler in the flock, he didn't put them there. So the feeble ones were Laban's and the well-built ones were Ya'aqob's.

⁴³So the man broke out very greatly. He had a large flock, maidservants, servants, camels and donkeys.

31

But he heard the words of Laban's sons: 'Ya'aqob has taken everything that was our father's. It's from what was our father's that he's made all this substance.' ²And Ya'aqob saw Laban's face: there, it wasn't the same with him as it had been in previous days.

³And Yahweh said to Ya'aqob, 'Go back to your ancestors' country, to your homeland. I will be with you.'

The divisiveness of stuff

⁴Ya'aqob sent and called Rahel and Le'ah to the fields, to his flock, ⁵and said to them, 'I see your father's face, that it's not the same towards me as it was in previous days, but my father's God has been with me.

⁶You yourselves know that I've served your father with all my energy, ⁷but your father – he's played about with me and changed my wages ten times. But God didn't let him deal badly with me. ⁸If he would say, "The speckled will be your wages", the entire flock would give birth to speckled. If he would say, "The streaked will be your wages", the entire flock would give birth to streaked. ⁹God has taken away your father's livestock and given them to me.

¹⁰At the time of the flock's being in heat, in a dream I lifted my eyes and looked: there,

the rams that were mounting the flock were streaked, speckled and mottled. ¹¹In the dream God's envoy said to me, "Ya'aqob!" I said "I'm here!" ¹²He said, "There, please lift up your eyes and look. All the rams that are mounting the flock are streaked, speckled and mottled, because I've seen everything that Laban has been doing to you. ¹³I am the God of Bet-el, where you anointed a column, where you made a pledge to me. Now, set off, get out of this country, go back to the country that is your homeland."'

¹⁴Rahel and Le'ah answered him, 'Do we still have a share, a domain, in our father's household? ¹⁵Aren't we deemed outsiders by him, because he sold us and also totally consumed the silver paid for us? ¹⁶Because all the wealth that God has rescued from our father: it belongs to us and to our children. So now, do everything that God has said to you.'

The secret leaving

¹⁷So Ya'aqob set off. He put his children and his wives on camels ¹⁸and drove all his livestock and all his property that he had gained, the livestock he had acquired, which he had gained in Paddan Aram, to come to Yitshaq his father in the country of Kena'an.

¹⁹Now Laban had gone to shear his flock, and Rahel stole the effigies that belonged to her father. ²⁰Ya'aqob stole away without Laban the Aramite knowing, by not telling him that he was taking flight.

²¹So he took flight, he and all that he had. He set off and crossed the river and set his face towards the highland of Gil'ad. ²²It was told Laban on the third day that Ya'aqob had fled. ²³He took his brothers with him and pursued after him a seven days' journey, and caught up with him in the highland of Gil'ad. ²⁴But God came to Laban the Aramite in a dream by night and said to him, 'Keep watch over yourself so you don't speak anything with Ya'aqob, either good or bad.'

²⁵Laban reached Ya'aqob when Ya'aqob had pitched his tent in the highland, and Laban had pitched, with his brothers, in the highland of Gil'ad. ²⁶Laban said to Ya'aqob, 'What have you done? You stole away without me knowing and you drove my daughters like captives of the sword. ²⁷Why did you secretly take flight and steal away from me and not tell me? I would have sent you off with rejoicing and with singing, with tambourine and with guitar. ²⁸You didn't give me leave to kiss my sons and my daughters. Now you've been idiotic in doing that. ²⁹It's in the almightiness of my hand to deal badly with you. But the God of your father said to me last night: "Keep watch over yourself to avoid speaking anything with Ya'aqob, either good or bad."

³⁰So now: you have indeed gone because you were very keen for your father's household. Why have you stolen my gods?'

The ironic confrontation

³¹Ya'aqob answered Laban, 'Because I was afraid, because I said, "So that you don't seize your daughters from me." ³²The person with whom you find your gods will not live. In front of our brothers, examine for yourself what I have and take it for yourself.' Ya'aqob didn't know that Rahel had stolen them.

³³Laban came into Ya'aqob's tent, into Le'ah's tent and into the two handmaids' tent, but didn't find them. He went out of Le'ah's tent and came into Rahel's tent. ³⁴Now Rahel had taken the effigies, put them in the camel saddle and sat on them. Laban felt through everything in the tent and didn't find them. ³⁵She said to her father, 'May it not cause rage in my lord's eyes that I cannot get up before you, because a woman's period is upon me.' So he searched but didn't find the effigies.

³⁶It enraged Ya'aqob and he got into an argument with Laban. Ya'aqob avowed to Laban, 'What is my affront, what is my wrongdoing, that you chased after me, ³⁷that you felt through all my possessions? What did you find of all your household possessions? Put it here in front of my brothers and your brothers, so they can decide between the two of us.

³⁸These twenty years I've been with you. Your ewes and your goats haven't miscarried. I haven't eaten rams from your flock. ³⁹I haven't brought you animals that had been killed; I myself dealt with the loss. From my hand you would look for what was stolen by day and what was stolen by night. ⁴⁰I became: by day

heat consumed me and by night frost. My sleep fled from my eyes. ⁴¹I've had these twenty years in your household; I served you fourteen years for your two daughters and six years for your flock, and you changed my wages ten times. ⁴²If the God of my father, the God of Abraham and the Reverence of Yitshaq, had not been mine, now you would have sent me off empty-handed. But God saw my humbling and the weariness of the palms of my hands, and he decided last night.'

A family divided by miles

⁴³Laban answered Ya'aqob, 'The daughters are my daughters, the children are my children, the flock is my flock. All that you see is mine. But about my daughters: what can I do today about them or about their children to whom they have given birth? ⁴⁴So now, come, let's solemnize a pact, you and I, and it will be a witness between you and me.'

⁴⁵So Ya'aqob took a stone and set it up as a column, ⁴⁶and Ya'aqob said to his brothers, 'Collect stones.' They got stones and made a heap, and they ate there by the heap. ⁴⁷Laban called it Yegar Sahaduta, while Ya'aqob called it Gal'ed ['Witness Mound' in Aramaic and Hebrew]. ⁴⁸Laban said, 'This heap is a witness between me and you today.' That's why he named it Gal'ed, ⁴⁹and 'The Watchtower' [hammitspah], because (he said), 'May Yahweh watch between me and you when one is hidden from the other. ⁵⁰If you humble my daughters or take wives on top of my daughters: when there's no one with us, see, God will be a witness between me and you.'

⁵¹And Laban said to Ya'aqob, 'Here is this heap and here is the column that I have thrown up between me and you. ⁵²This heap will be a witness and the column will be a witness that I will not go past this heap to you and you will not go past this heap to me, or this column, to act badly. ⁵³The God of Abraham and the God of Nahor (the God of their ancestor) decide between us.'

Ya'aqob swore by the Reverence of his father Yitshaq, ⁵⁴and Ya'aqob offered a sacrifice at the mountain and invited his brothers to eat bread. They ate bread and stayed the night at the mountain. ⁵⁵Laban started early in the morning, kissed his children and his daughters, and blessed them. Then Laban set off and went back to his place.

Ya'aqob scared

32 As Ya'aqob went on his way, God's envoys came upon him. ²When he saw them, Ya'aqob said, 'This is God's camp', and he named that place Mahanayim ['Two Camps']. ³Ya'aqob sent envoys before him to Esaw his brother in the country of Se'ir, in Edom's region. ⁴He ordered them: 'You're to say this to my lord, to Esaw: "Your servant Ya'aqob has said this: 'While I've resided with Laban and remained till now, ⁵oxen, donkeys and flock, and servants and maidservants, have come to belong to me. I've sent to tell my lord so as to find grace in your eyes.'"'

⁶The envoys came back to Ya'aqob, saying, 'We came to your brother, to Esaw, and yes, he's coming to meet you, and 400 men with him.' ⁷Ya'aqob was very fearful. It put pressure on him. He divided the people that were with him, the flock, the herd and the camels into two camps, ⁸and said 'If Esaw comes to the one camp and strikes it down, the remaining camp will escape.'

⁹Ya'aqob said, 'God of my father Abraham, God of my father Yitshaq, Yahweh, you who said to me, "Go back to your country, to your homeland, and I shall do good things with you", ¹⁰I'm too small for all the acts of commitment and all the truthfulness with which you've acted towards your servant. With my cane I crossed this Yarden and now I've become two camps. ¹¹Save me from the hand of my brother, please, from the hand of Esaw, because I'm frightened of him, in case he comes and strikes me down, mother with children. ¹²You yourself said, "I shall definitely do good things with you and make your offspring like the sand of the sea, which cannot be counted because of the large number."'

Buying off a brother

¹³He stayed the night there that night, then got an offering for Esaw his brother from what had come into his care: ¹⁴two hundred she-goats and twenty he-goats, two hundred ewes and

twenty rams, ¹⁵thirty milch camels and their young, forty cows and ten bulls, and twenty she-donkeys and ten he-donkeys. ¹⁶He put them into the care of his servants, herd by herd on its own, and said to his servants, 'Cross over before me, but put a space between herd and herd.'

¹⁷He ordered the first: 'Esaw my brother will meet you and ask you, "To whom do you belong? Where are you going? To whom do these belong, before you?" ¹⁸You're to say, "They're your servant Ya'aqob's. They're an offering sent to my lord, to Esaw. Here, he himself is behind us as well."' ¹⁹He ordered both the second and the third and also all the ones who were going behind the herds: 'You're to speak these very words to Esaw when you reach him. ²⁰You're also to say, "Here, your servant Ya'aqob is behind us"', because (he said), 'I'll mollify his face with an offering that goes ahead of my face, then afterwards I'll face him, and maybe he'll welcome my face.' ²¹Thus the offering crossed ahead of his face, while he stayed that night in the camp.

²²So he set off that night and took his two wives, his two maidservants and his eleven children, and crossed the Yabboq crossing. ²³He took them and got them to cross the wadi and got what belonged to him across.

God struggles

²⁴Ya'aqob was left on his own, and a man wrestled [*aboq*] with him until dawn rose. ²⁵He saw that he had not overcome him, so he touched him at his hip socket, and Ya'aqob's hip socket was put out as he wrestled with him. ²⁶He said, 'Let me go off, because the dawn has risen.' He said, 'I won't let you go off unless you bless me.' ²⁷He said to him, 'What is your name?' He said, 'Ya'aqob.' ²⁸He said, 'You will no longer be named Ya'aqob, but Yisra'el [Israel], because you have striven [*sarah*] with God and with human beings and have prevailed.' ²⁹Ya'aqob asked, 'Tell me your name, please.' He said, 'Why is it that you ask my name?' But he blessed him there.

³⁰Ya'aqob named the place Peni'el ['God's Face'], 'because I saw God face to face, but my life was rescued.' ³¹The sun rose on him as he crossed by Penu'el. He was limping because of his hip. ³²That's why the Israelites don't eat the thigh muscle that's on the hip socket until this day, because he touched Ya'aqob at the hip socket, at the thigh muscle.

33

Ya'aqob lifted his eyes and looked: there, Esaw was coming, and with him 400 men. He divided the children among Le'ah, Rahel and the two maidservants, ²and put the maidservants and their children first, Le'ah and her children after them, and Rahel and Yoseph last. ³He himself passed on before them and bowed to the ground seven times until he came right up to his brother. ⁴Esaw ran to meet him, embraced him, threw his arms round his neck and kissed him, and they cried.

An amicable parting

⁵He lifted his eyes and saw the women and the children, and said 'Who are these of yours?' He said, 'The children with whom God has graced your servant.' ⁶The maidservants came up, they and their children, and bowed low. ⁷Le'ah also came up, she and her children, and bowed low. Last, Yoseph came up, he and Rahel, and they bowed low. ⁸He said, 'What do you mean by this entire camp that I've met?' Ya'aqob said, 'To find grace in my lord's eyes.'

⁹Esaw said, 'I have much, brother. What you have must remain yours.' ¹⁰Ya'aqob said, 'No, please. If I've found grace in your eyes, please, take my offering from my hand, because on account of this I have seen your face, like seeing God's face, and you accepted me. ¹¹Please take my blessing which has been brought to you, because God has graced me, and because I have everything.' So he urged him, and he took it.

¹²Then he said, 'Let's move on and go. I'll go in front of you.' ¹³But he said to him, 'My lord knows that the children are frail and the flock and herd are suckling with me. Should they drive them hard for one day, all the flock will die. ¹⁴My lord should please pass on before his servant. I myself will lead on gently, at the pace of the cattle that are before me and at the pace of the children, until I come to my lord in Se'ir.' ¹⁵Esaw said, 'May I please place with you some of the company that's with me?' He said, 'Why is this? I want to find grace in my lord's eyes.'

¹⁶So Esaw went back that day on his journey to Se'ir, ¹⁷while Ya'aqob moved on to Sukkot, built himself a house there and made bivouacs

[*sukkot*] for his livestock. That's why they named the place Sukkot.

The seduction

¹⁸Ya'aqob came with things being well to the town of Shekem, which was in the country of Kena'an, when he came from Paddan Aram, and he camped facing the town. ¹⁹He acquired the plot in the fields where he spread his tent from the sons of Hamor, Shekem's father, for a hundred qesitas. ²⁰He put up an altar there and called it 'God, the God of Yisra'el'.

34 Dinah daughter of Le'ah, to whom she had given birth for Ya'aqob, went out to see the daughters of the region. ²Shekem ben Hamor, the Hivvite, the leader of the region, saw her, took her and slept with her. He forced her, ³but he himself was attached to Dinah, Ya'aqob's daughter. He loved the girl, and tried to reassure the girl. ⁴Shekem said to Hamor his father: 'Get me this young woman as wife.'

⁵When Ya'aqob heard that he had defiled Dinah his daughter, his sons were with his livestock in the fields, so Ya'aqob remained silent until they came. ⁶Hamor, Shekem's father, went out to Ya'aqob to speak with him. ⁷When Ya'aqob's sons came from the fields, the men were pained when they heard. It deeply enraged them, because he had done something villainous in Yisra'el in sleeping with Ya'aqob's daughter. Such a thing is not done.

⁸Hamor spoke with them: 'Shekem my son, he got attracted to your daughter. Please give her to him as wife. ⁹Make marriages with us: give your daughters to us and take our daughters for yourselves. ¹⁰You can live with us and the region will be before you. Live and move about in it, acquire holdings in it.' ¹¹Shekem said to her father and to her brothers, 'May I find grace in your eyes: what you say to me, I will give. ¹²Set a very large marriage payment and gift upon me, and I will give as you say to me. But give me the girl as wife.'

The sign of a pact becomes a ploy

¹³Ya'aqob's sons answered Shekem and Hamor his father with guile when they spoke, because he'd defiled their sister Dinah. ¹⁴They said to them, 'We can't do this thing, give our sister to a man who has a foreskin, because that would be a reviling to us. ¹⁵Only on this basis could we consent to you: if you become like us by every male of yours being circumcised, ¹⁶and we will give our daughters to you and take your daughters for ourselves and we will live with you, and we'll become one people. ¹⁷But if you won't listen to us by being circumcised, we'll take our daughter and go.'

¹⁸Their words were good in the eyes of Hamor and in the eyes of Hamor's son Shekem, ¹⁹and the boy didn't delay doing the thing, because he wanted Ya'aqob's daughter.

Now he was the most honoured person in his father's household. ²⁰So Hamor and his son Shekem came to the gateway of their town and spoke to the men of their town: ²¹"These people are peaceable with us. They should live in the region and move about in it. This region – here, it's wide enough for them. We'll take their daughters for ourselves and give our daughters to them. ²²Only on this basis will the people consent to us to live with us, to become one people: by every male of ours being circumcised as they are circumcised. ²³Their livestock and their acquisitions and all their animals: will they not become ours? Let's just consent to them so they will live with us.' ²⁴They listened to Hamor and to Shekem his son, all the people who went out to the gateway of his town; and every male, all the people who went out to the gateway of his town, were circumcised.

Should our sister be treated like a whore?

²⁵On the third day, when they were hurting, two of Ya'aqob's sons, Shim'on and Levi, Dinah's brothers, got each his sword, came to the town when it was confident, and killed every male. ²⁶Hamor and Shekem his son they killed with the mouth of the sword. They got Dinah from Shekem's house and left, ²⁷while Ya'aqob's sons came on the men who had been run through and plundered the town because they had defiled their sister. ²⁸Their flock, their herd and their donkeys, what was in the town and what was in the fields, they took. ²⁹All their resources, all their little ones and all their women, they captured and plundered, with everything that was in the houses.

³⁰Ya'aqob said to Shim'on and Levi, 'You've brought disaster on me, making me stink to the people who live in the country, the Kena'anite and the Perizzite. I'm few in number. They'll gather against me and strike me down and I'll be annihilated, I and my household.' ³¹But they said, 'Should he treat our sister like a whore?'

35 God said to Ya'aqob, 'Set off and go up to Bet-el. Live there and make an altar there for the God who appeared to you when you were taking flight from your brother Esaw.' ²Ya'aqob said to his household and to all who were with him, 'Remove the foreign gods that are among you. Purify yourselves. Change your clothes. ³We shall set off to go up to Bet-el and make an altar there for the God who answered me on the day when I was under pressure and has been with me on the way that I've gone.' ⁴They gave Ya'aqob all the foreign gods that were in their hand, and the rings that were in their ears, and Ya'aqob buried them under the oak that was near Shekem.

The passing of Ya'aqob's first love

⁵As they moved on, an almighty terror came over the towns that were round about them, and they didn't pursue after Ya'aqob's sons. ⁶So Ya'aqob came to Luz, which is in the country of Kena'an (i.e. Bet-el), he and all the company that was with him. ⁷He built an altar there and called the place 'God of Bet-el', because God had appeared to him there when he was taking flight from his brother. ⁸Deborah, Ribqah's nanny, died, and was buried below Bet-el, beneath the oak. So they named it Wailing Oak.

⁹God appeared to Ya'aqob again when he had come from Paddan Aram, and he blessed him. ¹⁰God said to him, 'Your name is Ya'aqob. You'll no longer be named Ya'aqob; rather, Yisra'el will be your name.' So he named him Yisra'el. ¹¹God said to him, 'I am God Shadday. Be fruitful and numerous. A nation and a congregation of nations will come into being from you. Kings will come out of your insides. ¹²The country that I gave to Abraham and to Yitshaq I shall give to you, and I shall give the country to your offspring after you.' ¹³God went up from him at the place where he spoke with him, ¹⁴and Ya'aqob put up a column at the place where God had spoken with him, a stone column, and poured out a libation on it and poured oil on it. ¹⁵Ya'aqob named the place where God spoke with him Bet-el.

¹⁶They moved on from Bet El, and there was still a distance in the country so as to come to Ephrat, but Rahel gave birth, and had a tough time in giving birth. ¹⁷When she was having a tough time in giving birth, the midwife said to her, 'Don't be afraid, because this one is a son for you, too.' ¹⁸As her breath was leaving her, because she was dying, she named him Ben-oni ['Son of My Trouble']; but his father called him Binyamin [Benjamin; 'Son of My Right Hand']. ¹⁹So Rahel died and was buried on the road to Ephrat (i.e. Bet Lehem). ²⁰Ya'aqob put up a column over her grave (it's the column at Rahel's grave until today).

Ya'aqob and Yisra'el, Esaw and Edom

²¹Yisra'el moved on and spread his tent beyond Herd Tower. (²²While Yisra'el was dwelling in that region, Re'uben went and slept with Bilhah, his father's secondary wife; and Yisra'el heard.)

Ya'aqob's sons were twelve:
²³the sons of Le'ah: Ya'aqob's firstborn,
  Re'uben; Shim'on; Levi; Yehudah; Yissakar;
  and Zebulun;
²⁴the sons of Rahel: Yoseph and Binyamin;
²⁵the sons of Bilhah, Rahel's maidservant:
  Dan and Naphtali;
²⁶the sons of Zilpah, Le'ah's maidservant:
  Gad and Asher.

These were Ya'aqob's sons who were born to him in Paddan Aram.

²⁷Ya'aqob came to Yitshaq his father at Mamre at Arba Township (i.e. Hebron), where Abraham and Yitshaq resided. ²⁸Yitshaq was a man of 180 years. ²⁹Yitshaq breathed his last and died, and was gathered to his kin, old and full of years. Esaw and Ya'aqob, his sons, buried him.

36 This is the line of Esaw (i.e. Edom). ²Esaw got his wives from the daughters of Kena'an: Adah daughter of Elon the Hittite, Oholibamah daughter of Anah, the daughter of Tsib'on the Hivvite, ³and Ba'semat daughter of Yishma'e'l, the sister of Nebayot. ⁴Adah gave birth to Eliphaz for Esaw, Ba'semat gave birth to Re'u'el, ⁵and Oholibamah gave birth to Ye'ush, Yalam and Qorah.

These are the sons of Esaw who were born to him in the country of Kena'an. ⁶Esaw took his wives, his sons and his daughters, and the people in his household, his livestock, all his animals and all his acquisitions that he had gained in the country of Kena'an, and went to a country away from Ya'aqob his brother, ⁷because their property was too big for them to live together and the country where they were residing couldn't support them because of their livestock. ⁸So Esaw lived in the highland of Se'ir (Esaw is Edom).

Excluded but not forgotten

⁹This is the line of Esaw, the ancestor of Edom, in the highland of Se'ir. ¹⁰These are the names of Esaw's sons:

Eliphaz, son of Esaw's wife Adah;
Re'u'el, son of Esaw's wife Ba'semat.

¹¹The sons of Eliphaz were Teman, Omar, Tsepho, Ga'tam and Qenaz.
¹²Timna was a secondary wife to Esaw's son Eliphaz; she gave birth to Amaleq for Eliphaz.
These were the descendants of Esaw's wife Adah.
¹³These were the sons of Re'u'el: Nahat, Zerah, Shammah and Mizzah.
These were the descendants of Esaw's wife Ba'semat.
¹⁴These were the sons of Esaw's wife Oholibamah daughter of Anah, the daughter of Tsib'on: she gave birth to Ye'ush, Yalam and Qorah for Esaw.
¹⁵These are the clans among Esaw's descendants. The descendants of Eliphaz, Esaw's firstborn:

the Teman clan   ¹⁶the Qorah clan
the Omar clan   the Ga'tam clan
the Tsepho clan   the Amaleq clan
the Qenaz clan

These are the clans of Eliphaz in the country of Edom; these are the descendants of Adah.

¹⁷These are the descendants of Re'u'el, Esaw's son:

the Nahat clan   the Shammah clan
the Zerah clan   the Mizzah clan

These are the clans of Re'u'el in the country of Edom; these are the descendants of Ba'semat, Esaw's wife.

¹⁸These are the descendants of Oholibamah, Esaw's wife:

the Ye'ush clan   the Qorah clan
the Ya'lam clan

These are the clans of Oholibamah daughter of Anah, Esaw's wife.

¹⁹These are the descendants of Esaw and these are their clans (i.e. Edom).

Kings in Edom

²⁰These are the sons of Se'ir the Horite, the people living in the country: Lotan, Shobal, Tsib'on, Anah, ²¹Dishon, Etser and Dishan. These are the Horites' clans, Se'ir's descendants, in the country of Edom.
²²The sons of Lotan were Hori and Hemam; Lotan's sister was Timna.
²³These are the sons of Shobal: Alvan, Mahanat, Ebal, Shepho and Onam.
²⁴These are the sons of Tsib'on: both Ayyah and Anah (he was the Anah who found the hot springs in the wilderness when he was pasturing the donkeys of Tsib'on his father).
²⁵These are the children of Anah: Dishon and Oholibamah, Anah's daughter.
²⁶These are the sons of Dishan: Hemdan, Eshban, Itran and Keran.
²⁷These are the sons of Etser: Bilhan, Za'avan and Aqan.
²⁸These are the sons of Dishan: Uts and Aran.
²⁹These are the Horites' clans: the clans Lotan, Shobal, Tsib'on, Anah, ³⁰Dishon, Etser and Dishan. These are the Horites' clans by their clans in the country of Se'ir.

³¹These are the kings who reigned in the country of Edom before a king reigned among the Yisra'elites:
³²Bela ben Be'or reigned in Edom; his town's name was Dinhabah.
³³Bela died and Yobab ben Zerah from Botsrah reigned in his place.

³⁴Yobab died and Husham from the Temanites' country reigned in his place. ³⁵Husham died and Hadad ben Bedad, who struck down Midyan in Mo'ab's region, reigned in his place; his town's name was Avit. ³⁶Hadad died and Samlah from Masrekah reigned in his place. ³⁷Samlah died and Sha'ul from Broads on the River reigned in his place. ³⁸Sha'ul died and Ba'al ben Akbor reigned in his place. ³⁹Ba'al Hanan ben Akbor died and Hadar reigned in his place; his town's name was Pa'u, and his wife's name was Mehetabel daughter of Matred, the daughter of Gold Water.

⁴⁰These are the names of Esaw's clans by their kin-groups, by their places, with their names:

the Timna clan	the Pinon clan
the Alvah clan	⁴²the Qenaz clan
the Yetet clan	the Teman clan
⁴¹the Oholibamah clan	the Mibtsar clan
	⁴³the Magdi'el clan
the Elah clan	the Iram clan

These are the clans of Edom, by their settlements in the country that is their holding (i.e. Esaw, Edom's ancestor).

The dreamer

37 Ya'aqob lived in the country where his father had resided, the country of Kena'an. ²This is Ya'aqob's line.

Yoseph, when he was seventeen years of age, was pasturing the flock with his brothers; he was a boy with the sons of Bilhah and Zilpah, his father's wives. Yoseph brought bad criticism of them to their father. ³Now Yisra'el loved Yoseph above all his sons, because he was the son of his old age. He made an ornamented coat for him. ⁴His brothers saw that their father loved him above all his brothers, and they became hostile to him and couldn't speak peaceably to him.

⁵Yoseph had a dream and told his brothers, and they were yet more hostile to him. ⁶He said to them, 'Please listen to this dream that I've had. ⁷There – we were binding sheaves in the middle of the fields. There – my sheaf got up, yes, stood. And there – your sheaves were gathering round and bowing low to my sheaf.' ⁸His brothers said to him, 'Are you really to reign over us? Or are you really to rule over us?' They were yet more hostile to him because of his dreams and because of his words.

⁹He had another dream and recounted it to his brothers. 'Here – I had another dream. There – the sun and the moon and eleven stars were bowing down to me.' ¹⁰He recounted it to his father and to his brothers, and his father reprimanded him and said to him, 'What's this dream that you've had? Are we really to come, I and your mother and your brothers, to bow low to the ground to you?' ¹¹So his brothers were jealous of him, while his father kept the thing in mind.

¹²His brothers went to pasture their father's flock at Shekem. ¹³Yisra'el said to Yoseph, 'Your brothers are pasturing at Shekem, aren't they. Come on, I'll send you to them.' He said to him, 'Here I am.'

The dreamer walks into a trap

¹⁴So he said to him, 'Go and see if things are well with your brothers, and if things are well with the flock, please, and bring back word to me.' He sent him from the Hebron Vale and he came to Shekem. ¹⁵A man found him: there, he was wandering about in the fields. The man asked him, 'What are you looking for?' ¹⁶He said, 'I'm looking for my brothers. Do tell me, please, where they're pasturing.' ¹⁷The man said, 'They've moved on from here, because I heard them say, "Let's go to Dotan."'

Yoseph followed his brothers and found them at Dotan. ¹⁸They saw him from a distance, and before he got near them they plotted to put him to death. ¹⁹They said one to another, 'Here, that master of dreams is coming! ²⁰So now, come on, let's kill him and throw him into one of the cisterns. We'll say a bad animal ate him. We'll see what will become of his dreams.'

²¹But Re'uben heard them and rescued him from their hand. He said, 'We won't take his life.' ²²Re'uben said to them, 'Don't shed his blood. Throw him into this cistern that's in the

wilderness. Don't lay a hand on him' (in order that he might rescue him from their hand and give him back to his father). ²³So when Yoseph came to his brothers, they stripped Yoseph of his coat, the ornamented coat that was on him, ²⁴and took him and threw him into the cistern. (The cistern was empty; there was no water in it.)

²⁵They sat down to eat bread, but lifted their eyes and looked: there, a caravan of Yishma'e'lites coming from Gil'ad, their camels carrying spices, balm and myrrh, going to take them down to Misrayim. ²⁶Yehudah said to his brothers, 'What's the gain when we kill our brother and cover up his blood? ²⁷Come on, let's sell him to the Yishma'e'lites. Our hands – they shouldn't be on him, because he's our brother, our flesh.' His brothers listened.

The fate of the famous coat

²⁸So Midyanite men, traders, passed by, and they pulled and got Yoseph up out of the cistern. They sold Yoseph to the Yishma'e'lites for twenty silver pieces, and they brought Yoseph to Misrayim.

²⁹Re'uben went back to the cistern, and there – Yoseph wasn't in the cistern. He tore his clothes ³⁰and went back to his brothers and said, 'The child isn't there! And I – where am I going to go?'

³¹They got Yoseph's coat, slaughtered a goat, dipped the coat in the blood ³²and sent off the ornamented coat so they might bring it to their father, and they said, 'We found this. Please recognize: is it your son's coat, or not?' ³³He recognized it and said, 'My son's coat! A bad animal has devoured him! Yoseph has been torn to pieces!' ³⁴Ya'aqob tore his clothes, put sack round his hips and took up grieving for his son for a long time. ³⁵All his sons and daughters set about consoling him, but he refused to be consoled and said, 'I shall go down to She'ol to my son grieving.' So his father bewailed him.

³⁶Meanwhile the Midyanites sold him into Misrayim, to Potiphar, Par'oh's courtier, the guards officer.

38

At that time Yehudah went down from his brothers and turned aside near an Adullamite man; his name was Hirah. ²Yehudah saw there the daughter of a Kena'anite man, whose name was Shua, and he took her. He had sex with her, ³she got pregnant, and she gave birth to a son and named him Er. ⁴She got pregnant again and gave birth to a son, and named him Onan. ⁵Once more she got pregnant and gave birth to a son, and named him Shelah. He was at Kezib when she gave birth to him.

A daughter-in-law betrayed

⁶Yehudah got a wife for his firstborn, Er. Her name was Tamar. ⁷But Er, Yehudah's firstborn, did what was bad in Yahweh's eyes, and Yahweh let him die. ⁸Yehudah said to Onan, 'Have sex with your brother's wife. Be a brother-in-law to her. Set up offspring for your brother.' ⁹But Onan knew that the offspring would not be his, and when he had sex with his brother's wife he would let it be lost on the ground so he wouldn't give offspring to his brother. ¹⁰But what he did was bad in Yahweh's eyes, and Yahweh also let him die. ¹¹Yehudah said to Tamar his daughter-in-law, 'Live as a widow in your father's household till my son Shelah grows up', because (he said), 'So he doesn't also die, like his brothers.' So Tamar went and lived in her father's household.

¹²Time went on, and Shua's daughter, Yehudah's wife, died. Yehudah was consoled, and went up to the men who were shearing his flock, he and his neighbour Hirah the Adullamite, to Timnah. ¹³It was told Tamar: 'Here, your father-in-law is coming up to Timnah for the shearing of his flock.' ¹⁴Tamar removed her widow's clothes from upon her, covered herself with a veil and wrapped herself up, and sat at the entrance to Two Wells, which is on the road to Timnah, because she saw that Shelah had grown up but she had not been given to him as wife.

¹⁵Yehudah saw her and thought she was a whore, because she had covered her face. ¹⁶He turned aside to her by the road and said 'Come on, can I have sex with you?' because he didn't know that it was his daughter-in-law. She said, 'What will you give me when you have sex with me?' ¹⁷He said, 'I myself will send a kid goat from the flock.' She said, 'If you give

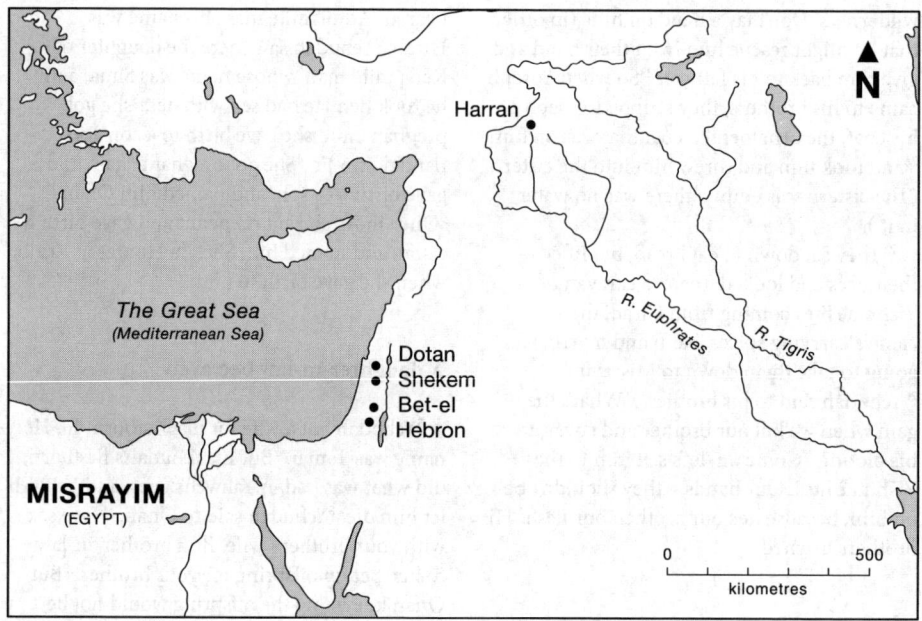

Genesis 38: Ya'aqob (Jacob)

me a pledge till you send it.' ¹⁸He said, 'What's the pledge that I should give you?' She said, 'Your seal and your cord, and the staff that's in your hand.' He gave them to her and he had sex with her, and she got pregnant by him.

Another deceiver deceived

¹⁹She set off and went, and removed her veil from upon her and put on her widow's clothes. ²⁰Yehudah sent the kid goat by the hand of the Adullamite, his neighbour, to get the pledge from the woman's hand, but he couldn't find her. ²¹He asked the people of her place: 'Where's that hierodule, the one at Two Wells, by the road?' They said, 'There's been no hierodule here.' ²²He went back to Yehudah and said, 'I couldn't find her. Furthermore, the people of the place said, "There's been no hierodule here."' ²³Yehudah said, 'She can have it for herself, so that we don't become an object of contempt. Here, I sent her this kid goat, but you couldn't find her.'

²⁴Some three months later, it was told Yehudah: 'Tamar your daughter-in-law has been whoring. Indeed, there, she's pregnant through whoring.' Yehudah said, 'Bring her out. She should be burned.' ²⁵As she was being brought out, she sent to her father-in-law, saying: 'It's by the man to whom these belong that I'm pregnant.' So she said, 'Please recognize: who's the one to whom these seal and cord and staff belong?' ²⁶Yehudah recognized them and said, 'She is more in the right than me, because of the fact that I didn't give her to my son Shelah.' He didn't have sex with her again.

²⁷At the time of her giving birth, there – twins were in her womb. ²⁸When she was giving birth, one put out a hand, and the midwife took a red thread and tied it on his hand, saying 'This one came out first.' ²⁹But when he took back his hand, his brother came out, and she said, 'What a breakout you've made for yourself!' So they named him Perets ['Breakout']. ³⁰Afterwards his brother, on whose hand was the red thread, came out. They named him Zerah ['Shining'].

But Yahweh was with Yoseph

39 So Yoseph had been taken down to Misrayim and a Misrayimite, Potiphar, Par'oh's courtier, the guards officer, had acquired him from the hand of the Yishmae'lites who had taken him down there.

²But Yahweh was with Yoseph and he became a successful man. He was in the household of his Misrayimite lord, ³and his lord saw that Yahweh was with him and that everything that he was doing, Yahweh made succeed in his hand. ⁴So Yoseph found grace in his eyes. He ministered to him, and he appointed him over his household and put into his hand everything that belonged to him.

⁵From the time that he appointed him over his household and over everything that belonged to him, Yahweh blessed the Misrayimite's household because of Yoseph. Yahweh's blessing was on everything that belonged to him, in the house and in the fields. ⁶He abandoned everything that he had into Yoseph's hands, and with him he didn't know about anything except the bread that he was eating.

Yoseph was attractive in shape and attractive in appearance, ⁷and subsequently his lord's wife set her eyes on Yoseph and said, 'Sleep with me.' ⁸He refused, and said to his lord's wife, 'Here, with me, my lord doesn't know about what's in the house. Everything that belongs to him he's put into my hand. ⁹There's no one bigger in this household than me. He hasn't held back anything from me except you, because you're his wife. How could I do this massively bad thing, and do wrong in relation to God?' ¹⁰When she spoke to Yoseph day after day he didn't listen to her about sleeping beside her or being with her.

¹¹On such a day he came into the house to do his work. None of the people of the household was there in the house. ¹²She caught hold of him by his coat, saying 'Sleep with me.' He abandoned his coat in her hand, fled and went outside.

The false allegation

· ¹³When she saw that he had abandoned his coat in her hand and fled outside, ¹⁴she called the people of the household and said to them: 'Look, he brought us a Hebrew man to fool about with us! He came to me in order to sleep with me and I called out in a loud voice, ¹⁵and when he heard that I raised my voice and called out, he abandoned his coat beside me and fled, and went outside.' ¹⁶She set his coat down beside her until his lord came home, ¹⁷and she spoke to him in the same words: 'The Hebrew servant that you brought to us came to me in order to fool about with me, ¹⁸and when I raised my voice and called out he abandoned his coat beside me and fled outside.'

¹⁹When his lord heard his wife's words that she spoke to him, 'These very things your servant did to me', his anger raged. ²⁰Yoseph's lord took him and put him in the jailhouse, the place where the king's prisoners were imprisoned. So he was there in the jailhouse, ²¹but Yahweh was with Yoseph and he extended commitment to him, and gave him grace in the eyes of the jailhouse officer.

²²The jailhouse officer put into Yoseph's care all the prisoners who were in the jailhouse. Everything that they were doing there, he was the one doing it. ²³The jailhouse official didn't look at any matter that was in his care, because Yahweh was with him and whatever he was doing Yahweh made succeed.

40 Subsequently, the king of Misrayim's wine waiter and baker did wrong in relation to their lord the king of Misrayim. ²Par'oh was furious with his two courtiers, with the chief wine waiter and with the chief baker, ³and he put them in the keep at the guards officer's house, in the jailhouse, the place where Yoseph was confined.

Interpretations belong to God

⁴The guards officer appointed Yoseph to them and he ministered to them. They had been some time in the keep, ⁵and the two of them had a dream, each his own dream the same night, each in accordance with the interpretation of his dream – the king of Misrayim's wine waiter and baker, who were confined in the jailhouse. ⁶Yoseph came to them in the morning and saw that they were vexed. ⁷He asked Par'oh's courtiers who were with him in the keep in his lord's house, 'Why are your faces looking bad today?' ⁸They said to him, 'We had a dream, and there's no one to interpret it.' Yoseph said to them, 'Interpretations belong to God, don't they. Please recount them to me.'

⁹The chief wine waiter recounted his dream to Yoseph: 'In my dream: there, a vine before

me. ¹⁰On the vine were three branches. Even as it was budding, its blossom came out and its clusters ripened as grapes. ¹¹Now Par'oh's cup was in my hand, and I got the grapes, pressed them into Par'oh's cup and placed the cup into Par'oh's palm.'

¹²Yoseph said to him, 'This is the interpretation. The three branches are three days. ¹³In yet three days Par'oh will lift up your head and put you back in your position. You'll place Par'oh's cup in his hand in accordance with the former rule when you were his wine waiter.

¹⁴But be mindful of me with you, when things are good for you. Act in commitment with me, please, and make mention of me to Par'oh so you get me out of this house. ¹⁵Because I was actually stolen from the country of the Hebrews, and also I've done nothing here that they should have put me in the cistern.'

The interpreter forgotten

¹⁶The chief baker saw that he had interpreted it as something good, and he said to Yoseph, 'In my dream, also: there, three wicker baskets on my head, ¹⁷and in the top basket, all kinds of food for Par'oh, the work of a baker. But the birds were eating them from the basket, from on my head.' ¹⁸Yoseph answered, 'This is the interpretation. The three baskets are three days. ¹⁹In yet three days, Par'oh will lift up your head from on you and hang you on a tree, and the birds will eat your flesh from on you.'

²⁰On the third day, Par'oh's birthday, he made a banquet for all his servants, and lifted up the head of the chief wine waiter and the head of the chief baker among his servants. ²¹He put the chief wine waiter back into his wine-waiting so that he placed the cup in Par'oh's palm ²²and the chief baker he hanged, as Yoseph had interpreted to them. ²³But the chief wine waiter was not mindful of Yoseph. He put him out of mind.

41

At the end of two years, Par'oh himself was dreaming, and there, he was standing by the Ye'or [Nile]. ²There, from the Ye'or seven cows going up, attractive in appearance and sturdy in body, and they pastured among the reeds. ³And there, seven more cows going up from the Ye'or after them, bad-looking in appearance and thin in body, and they stood beside the cows on the bank of the Ye'or. ⁴The cows that were bad-looking in appearance and thin in body ate the seven cows that were attractive in appearance and sturdy.

Par'oh woke up, ⁵went to sleep and dreamt a second time. There, seven ears of grain growing up on a single stalk, sturdy and good-quality. ⁶And there, seven ears that were thin and scorched by the east wind springing up after them. ⁷The thin ears swallowed the seven sturdy, full ears. Par'oh woke up. There, it was a dream.

⁸In the morning his spirit was agitated, and he sent and called for all Misrayim's diviners and all its experts. Par'oh recounted his dream to them. But no one could interpret them for Par'oh.

The interpreter remembered

⁹The chief wine waiter spoke with Par'oh: 'I'm going to make mention of my wrongdoings today. ¹⁰When Par'oh was furious with his servants and put me in the keep in the guards officer's house, me and the chief baker, ¹¹we had a dream the same night, I and he. We each dreamt in accordance with the interpretation of his dream. ¹²There with us was a Hebrew boy, a servant of the guards officer. We recounted them to him and he interpreted our dreams for us. Each one in accordance with his dream he interpreted. ¹³As he interpreted it for us, so it happened. I was put back into my position and him they hanged.'

¹⁴So Par'oh sent and called for Yoseph. They got him to run from the cistern, he shaved and changed his clothes, and he came to Par'oh. ¹⁵Par'oh said to Yoseph, 'I had a dream and there is no one to interpret it. I've heard it said about you, that you can listen to a dream and interpret it.' ¹⁶Yoseph answered Par'oh: 'Not me. God is the one who will answer with things that will be well for Par'oh.'

¹⁷Par'oh spoke with Yoseph. 'In my dream: there was I, standing by the bank of the Ye'or. ¹⁸There, from the Ye'or seven cows going up, sturdy in body and attractive in appearance, and they pastured among the reeds. ¹⁹And

there, seven more cows going up after them, poor and very bad-looking in appearance, thin in body. I haven't seen the like of them in the entire country of Misrayim for bad quality. ²⁰The thin, bad-looking cows ate the first seven sturdy cows. ²¹So they came inside them, but it wouldn't have been known that they'd come inside them. Their appearance was as bad as it was at the beginning. And I woke up. ²²Then I saw in my dream, there, seven ears of grain growing up on one stalk, full and good-quality; ²³and there, seven ears of grain springing up after them, withered, thin, scorched by the east wind. ²⁴The seven thin ears swallowed the seven good ears.

I said it to the diviners but there was no one to tell me.'

Save first, spend afterwards

²⁵Yoseph said to Par'oh, 'Par'oh's dream is one. God has told Par'oh what he's going to do. ²⁶The seven good cows are seven years and the seven good ears are seven years. It's one dream. ²⁷The seven empty, bad-quality cows that were going up after them are seven years, as are the seven thin ears of grain, scorched by the east wind. There will be seven years of famine. ²⁸That's the word that I've spoken to Par'oh.

God has let Par'oh see what he's going to do. ²⁹There, seven years are coming, great abundance in the entire country of Misrayim, ³⁰but seven years of famine will arise after them, and the entire abundance in the country of Misrayim will be put out of mind. The famine will finish off the country. ³¹The abundance in the country won't be acknowledged in the face of that famine afterwards, because it will be very heavy. ³²And concerning the repeating of the dream to Par'oh, twice: the thing is established by God. God is hurrying to do it.

³³So now, Par'oh should look for a discerning, smart man and set him over the country of Misrayim. ³⁴Par'oh should act and set appointees over the country and take a fifth of the country of Misrayim in the seven years of abundance. ³⁵They should collect all food in these good years that are coming and lay up grain in the towns as food, under Par'oh's care, and keep it. ³⁶The food will be for appointing for the country for the seven years of famine that are going to happen in the country of Misrayim, so the country is not cut off by the famine.'

³⁷The thing was good in the eyes of Par'oh and in the eyes of all his servants, ³⁸and Par'oh said to his servants, 'Shall we find a man like this man, in whom is the spirit of God?'

Yoseph as prime minister

³⁹So Par'oh said to Yoseph, 'Given that God has let you know all this, there's no one smart and discerning like you. ⁴⁰You – you will be in charge of my household, and to your bidding all my people will acquiesce. Only with respect to the throne will I be greater than you.' ⁴¹So Par'oh said to Yoseph, 'See, I'm putting you in charge of the entire country of Misrayim.' ⁴²Par'oh removed his signet ring from on his hand and put it on Yoseph's hand, had him clothed in linen robes and put a gold chain on his neck. ⁴³He had him ride in the chariot of his second-in-command, and they called out before him, 'Bow down!' So he put him in charge of the entire country of Misrayim. ⁴⁴Par'oh said to Yoseph, 'I'm Par'oh, but without you no one will raise his hand or his foot in the entire country of Misrayim.'

⁴⁵Par'oh named Yoseph Tsaphenat Pane'ah and gave him Asenat, the daughter of Potiphera, priest in On [Heliopolis], as wife. So Yoseph went out in charge of the country of Misrayim.

⁴⁶Yoseph was a man of thirty years when he stood before Par'oh, the king of Misrayim. Yoseph went out from before Par'oh and passed through the entire country of Misrayim. ⁴⁷In the seven years of abundance, the country produced by fistfuls, ⁴⁸and he collected all the food of the seven years that passed in the country of Misrayim and put food in the towns; the food of a town's fields that was round it he put in the middle of it. ⁴⁹Yoseph laid up the grain like the sand of the sea in vast quantities until he left off from counting, because counting was impossible.

⁵⁰Two sons were born to Yoseph before the famine year came; Asenat, the daughter of Potiphera, priest in On, gave birth to them for him. ⁵¹Yoseph named the firstborn Menashsheh [Manasseh], because 'God has made me forget [*nasha*] all my oppression and

my father's entire household.' ⁵²The second he named Ephrayim, because 'God has made me fruitful [*pharah*] in the country of my humbling.'

Grain in Misrayim

⁵³The seven years of abundance that passed in the country of Misrayim finished ⁵⁴and the seven years of famine started to come, as Yoseph had said. The famine happened in all the countries, but in the entire country of Misrayim there was bread. ⁵⁵When the entire country of Misrayim was hungry and the people cried out to Par'oh for bread, Par'oh said to all Misrayim, 'Go to Yoseph, do what he says to you.'

⁵⁶When the famine was over the entire face of the earth, Yoseph opened all that was in them and sold grain to the Misrayimites.

So the famine became strong in the country of Misrayim, ⁵⁷while the entire world came to Misrayim to Yoseph to buy grain because the famine was heavy in the entire world,

42 and Ya'aqob saw that there was grain in Misrayim. So Ya'aqob said to his sons, 'Why do you look at one another?' ²He said, 'Here, I've heard that there's grain in Misrayim. Go down there and buy us grain from there, so we may live and not die.' ³So Yoseph's ten brothers went down to buy grain from Misrayim. ⁴Binyamin, Yoseph's brother, Ya'aqob didn't send with his brothers, because (he said) 'in case harm comes to him.'

⁵So Yisra'el's sons came to buy grain among the people who came, because the famine happened to the country of Kena'an. ⁶Now Yoseph was the prime minister over the country, the one who sold grain to all the people of the country. So Yoseph's brothers came and bowed low to him, their faces to the ground. ⁷Yoseph looked at his brothers and recognized them, but he acted like a stranger to them and spoke toughly with them. He said to them, 'Where have you come from?' They said, 'From the country of Kena'an, to buy food.'

Yoseph remembers his dream

⁸So Yoseph recognized his brothers but they didn't recognize him. ⁹Yoseph brought to mind the dreams that he had about them. He said to them, 'You're investigating; you've come to see the country's vulnerability.' ¹⁰They said to him, 'No, my lord! Your servants – they've come to buy grain. ¹¹We're all of us sons of one man. We're honest men. Your servants haven't been investigating.' ¹²He said to them, 'No, you came to see the country's vulnerability.' ¹³They said, 'Your servants, we were twelve brothers, the sons of one man in the country of Kena'an, but there, the youngest is with our father at the moment, and one is no more.'

¹⁴Yoseph said to them, 'It's as I spoke to you: "You're investigating." ¹⁵By this you'll be tested: by the life of Par'oh, you won't leave here unless your youngest brother comes here. ¹⁶Send one of you so he can get your brother. You, be imprisoned, so your words will be tested, whether there is truthfulness in you. And if not, by the life of Par'oh, you're investigating.'

¹⁷He gathered them in the keep for three days. ¹⁸On the third day, Yoseph said to them, 'Do this and you'll live; I am in awe of God. ¹⁹If you're honest, one of your brothers must be imprisoned in the house where you're kept while you go and bring grain for the famine in your households, ²⁰and your youngest brother you're to bring to me so your words may be shown to be trustworthy and you don't die.'

So they did so, ²¹and said to one another, 'Well, we're paying the penalty for our brother. We saw the pressure in his spirit when he pleaded for grace with us and we didn't listen. That's why this pressure has come to us.' ²²And Re'uben answered them: 'I spoke to you, saying: "Don't do wrong in relation to the child", didn't I, and you didn't listen. Yes, his blood – there, it's being required.'

What game is Yoseph playing?

²³Now they didn't know that Yoseph was listening, because there was an interpreter between them. ²⁴He turned away from them and cried, then came back to them and spoke to them, and took Shim'on from among them and imprisoned him before their eyes. ²⁵But Yoseph ordered that they should fill their containers with grain, put back their silver, each man, into his sack and give them provisions for the journey.

So he did this for them, ²⁶they loaded their grain on to their donkeys, and they went from there. ²⁷One of them opened his sack to give feed to his donkey at the lodging and he saw his silver. There it was, in the mouth of his bag. ²⁸He said to his brothers, 'My silver has been put back! Really, here it is, in my bag!' Their heart sank. They turned trembling to one another, saying: 'What is this that God has done to us?'

²⁹They came to Ya'aqob their father in the country of Kena'an and told him all that had happened to them: ³⁰'The man who is lord of the country spoke toughly with us and treated us as people who were investigating the country. ³¹We said to him, "We're honest. We haven't been investigating. ³²We were twelve brothers, the sons of our father; one is no more and the youngest is with our father in the country of Kena'an at the moment." ³³But the man who is lord of the country said to us, "By this I shall know that you're honest. Leave one of your brothers with me, take something for the famine in your households and go, ³⁴and bring your youngest brother to me, so I may know that you're not people investigating but are honest. I'll give your brother to you and you can move about in the country."'

³⁵Then, as they were emptying their sacks, there – each man's silver pouch was in his sack. They looked at their silver pouches, they and their father, and they were afraid.

There's no alternative

³⁶Ya'aqob their father said to them, 'I'm the one you've bereaved of children. Yoseph is no more and Shim'on is no more and you will take Binyamin. It's all happened to me.' ³⁷But Re'uben said to his father: 'You may put my two sons to death if I don't bring him back to you. Put him into my care and I myself will bring him back to you.' ³⁸But he said, 'My son is not to go down with you, because his brother is dead and he alone remains. If harm comes to him on the journey you're going on, you'll send my grey hair down to She'ol with sadness.'

43 But because the famine in the country was heavy, ²when they'd finished eating the grain that they'd brought from Misrayim, their father said to them, 'Go back and buy us a little food.' ³Yehudah said to him: 'The man solemnly testified against us: "You shall not see my face unless your brother is with you." ⁴If you do send our brother with us, we'll go down and buy food for you. ⁵But if you don't send him, we won't go down, because the man said to us, "You will not see my face unless your brother is with you."'

⁶Yisra'el said, 'Why did you deal badly with me by telling the man you had another brother?' ⁷They said, 'The man asked and asked about us and about our homeland, saying "Is your father still alive? Do you have a brother?" and we told him these things at his bidding. Could we possibly know that he would say, "Bring your brother down"?'

When I am bereaved, I am bereaved

⁸Yehudah said to Yisra'el his father, 'Send the boy with me so we can set off and go, and live and not die, both we and you and also our little ones. ⁹I personally guarantee him. From my hand you can look for him. If I don't bring him back to you and set him before you, I shall have done wrong in relation to you for all time. ¹⁰Because if we had not delayed, by now we could have got back here twice.'

¹¹Yisra'el their father said to them, 'If it's to be so, then, do this. Get some of the country's products in your containers and take them down to the man as an offering: a little balm and a little syrup, spices and myrrh, pistachios and almonds. ¹²And take twice the silver in your hand. Take back in your hand the silver that was put back in the mouth of your bags. Maybe it was a mistake. ¹³And your brother: take him and set off and go back to the man. ¹⁴May God Shadday himself give you compassion before the man so he may release your other brother to you, and Binyamin. And me – when I'm bereaved, I'm bereaved.' ¹⁵So the men took this offering and took twice the silver in their hand, and Binyamin, and they set off and went down to Misrayim and stood before Yoseph.

¹⁶Yoseph saw Binyamin with them and said to the person in charge of his household, 'Bring the men into the house and slaughter an animal and prepare it, because the men will eat with me at noon.' ¹⁷The man did as Yoseph said. The man brought the men into Yoseph's house, ¹⁸but

the men were afraid because they were brought into Yoseph's house. They said, 'It's because of the silver that was put back in our bags the first time that we have been brought in, to overwhelm us and fall on us and take us as servants, with our donkeys.'

Yoseph can hardly control himself

[19] So they came up to the man who was in charge of Yoseph's household and spoke to him at the entrance of the house. [20] They said, 'Pardon me, my lord, we only came down the first time to buy food. [21] But when we came to the lodging, we opened our bags and there, each man's silver was in the mouth of his bag, our silver by its weight. We have brought it back in our hand, [22] while we have brought down other silver with us to buy food. We don't know who put our silver in our bags.'

[23] He said, 'Things are well with you. Don't be afraid. Your God, the God of your father, gave you the treasure in your bags, as your silver came to me.' And he brought Shim'on out to them. [24] So the man took the men into Yoseph's house, gave them water and they washed their feet, and gave them feed for their donkeys. [25] They prepared the offering for when Yoseph came at noon, because they had heard that they were to eat a meal there.

[26] Yoseph came home and they brought him the offering that was in their hand in the house, and they bowed low to him to the ground. [27] He asked them whether things were well: 'Are things well with your aged father of whom you spoke? Is he still alive?' [28] They said, 'Things are well with your servant our father. He's still alive', and they bent their head and bowed low. [29] He lifted his eyes and saw Binyamin his brother, his mother's son, and said, 'Is this your youngest brother of whom you spoke to me?' And he said, 'God show grace to you, my son.' [30] Then Yoseph hurried because his insides burned for his brother and looked for somewhere to cry, and came to a room and cried there.

Another pressure

[31] He washed his face and went out and controlled himself and said, 'Serve the meal.' [32] They served him on his own and them on their own and the Misrayimites who were eating with him on their own, because Misrayimites couldn't eat a meal with the Hebrews because this would be an offence to Misrayimites. [33] But they sat before him, the firstborn according to his birthright and the youngest according to his being the youngest, while the men looked in astonishment each at his neighbour. [34] People carried loads to them from before him, and Binyamin's load was five times bigger than all their loads. They drank and were merry with him.

44

He ordered the person in charge of his household: 'Fill the men's bags with food, as much as they can carry, and put each person's silver in the mouth of his bag. [2] And my chalice, the silver chalice, put in the mouth of the bag belonging to the youngest, with the silver for his grain.' He acted in accordance with the word that Yoseph spoke.

[3] When morning dawned and the men had been sent off, they and their donkeys, [4] though they had left the town, they had not gone far when Yoseph said to the person in charge of his household, 'Set off and pursue after the men. Catch up with them and say to them, "Why have you made good with bad for good? [5] Isn't this the one that my lord drinks from and practises divination with? You've acted badly in what you did."'

[6] He caught up with them and spoke these words to them. [7] They said to him, 'Why does my lord speak words such as these? Far be it from your servants to do such a thing as this. [8] Here, the silver that we found in the mouth of our bags we brought back to you from the country of Kena'an. So how would we steal silver or gold from your lord's house? [9] With whichever of your servants it's found, he will die, and also we will become servants to my lord.'

Yehudah pleads

[10] He said, 'Indeed, now, in accordance with your words, so it will be. The one with whom it's found shall be my servant. You will be free of guilt.' [11] So they hurried, each man, and lowered his bag to the ground, and they opened, each man, his bag. [12] He searched, beginning with the eldest and finishing with the youngest,

and the chalice was found in Binyamin's bag. ¹³They tore their clothes, and loaded, each man, his donkey and went back to the town.

¹⁴Yehudah and his brothers came to Yoseph's house. He was still there. They fell on the ground before him. ¹⁵Yoseph said to them, 'What is this deed that you've done? Didn't you know that a man like me practises divination?' ¹⁶Yehudah said, 'What could we say to my lord? What could we speak? How could we show we are in the right? God has found out your servants' waywardness. Here we are, servants to my lord, both we and the one in whose hand the chalice was found.' ¹⁷But he said, 'Far be it from me to do this. The man in whose hand the chalice was found: he will become my servant. You: go up with things being well to your father.'

¹⁸Yehudah came up to him and said, 'Pardon me, my lord, can your servant speak a word in my lord's ear and your anger not rage at your servant, because you are like Par'oh. ¹⁹My lord asked his servants, "Do you have a father or brother?" ²⁰and we said to my lord, "We have an aged father and the child of his old age, the youngest. Since his brother is dead, he alone remains of his mother's, and his father loves him." ²¹You said to your servants, "Bring him down to me so I can set my eye on him." ²²We said to my lord, "The boy cannot abandon his father. If he abandons his father, he will die." ²³But you said to your servants, "If your youngest brother doesn't come down with you, you will not see my face again."

You will send my grey hair down to Sheol with grief

²⁴When we went up to your servant my father, we told him my lord's words. ²⁵Our father said, "Go back, get a little food for us", ²⁶and we said, "We can't go down. If our youngest brother is with us we can go down, because we won't be able to see the man's face with our youngest brother not being with us."
²⁷Your servant my father said to us, "You yourselves know that my wife gave birth to two sons for me. ²⁸The one went away from me, and I said, 'Yes, he's been torn to pieces.' I haven't seen him until now. ²⁹Should you take this one from being with me as well, and harm comes,

you will send my grey hair down to She'ol with the bad fortune."
³⁰When I now come to your servant my father and the boy is not with us, given that his life is bound up with his life, ³¹when he sees the boy is not there, he'll die. Your servants will send your servant our father's grey hair down to She'ol with sadness. ³²Because your servant pledged the boy with my father, saying: "If I don't bring him back to you, I shall have done wrong in relation to my father permanently." ³³So your servant will please now stay as my lord's servant in place of the boy. The boy must go up with his brothers. ³⁴Because how can I go up to my father with the boy not with me, or I will see the bad fortune that will come on my father.'

Not you but God

45 Yoseph couldn't control himself in front of all the people who were stationed by him. He called, 'Get everyone out from being with me!' So no one stood with him when Yoseph made himself known to his brothers. ²But he raised his voice in crying, and the Misrayimites heard and Par'oh's household heard. ³Yoseph said to his brothers, 'I'm Yoseph! Is my father still alive?' His brothers couldn't answer him because they were fearful at his presence.

⁴Yoseph said to his brothers, 'Please come up to me', and they came up. He said, 'I'm Yoseph your brother, whom you sold into Misrayim. ⁵But now: don't be pained, don't let it make you rage at yourselves because you sold me here, because it was to save life that God sent me before you. ⁶Because this has been two years of famine within the country, and there will be five more years in which there will be no ploughing or reaping. ⁷But God sent me before you to put in place for you a group remaining on the earth, to keep it alive for you as a big escape group. ⁸So now it was not you who sent me here but God. He's made me a father for Par'oh and lord of all his household, and ruling over the entire country of Misrayim.

⁹Hurry and go up to my father and say to him, "Your son Yoseph has said this: 'God has made me into lord of all Misrayim. Come down to me, don't stand waiting. ¹⁰You will live in the

Goshen region and be near me, you and your children and your grandchildren, your flock, your herd and all that's yours. ¹¹I shall provide for you there because there will be five more years of famine, so you and your household and all that's yours doesn't become dispossessed.'"

'Yoseph's brothers have come'

¹²Here, your eyes can see and my brother Binyamin's eyes can see that it's my mouth that's speaking to you. ¹³You're to tell my father about all my splendour in Misrayim and all that you've seen, and hurry and bring my father down here.' ¹⁴He fell on his brother Binyamin's neck and cried, and Binyamin cried on his neck, ¹⁵and he kissed all his brothers and cried on them, and after that his brothers spoke with him.

¹⁶When the announcement made itself heard in Par'oh's household, 'Yoseph's brothers have come', it was good in the eyes of Par'oh and in the eyes of his servants. ¹⁷Par'oh said to Yoseph, 'Say to your brothers, "Do this: load your animals and go, come to the country of Kena'an. ¹⁸Get your father and your households and come to me. I shall give you the best of the country of Misrayim and you will eat the fat of the country. ¹⁹You yourself are ordered, do this: get yourselves from the country of Misrayim wagons for your little ones and your wives, and carry your father and come. ²⁰Your eye is not to feel pity about your stuff, because the best of the entire country of Misrayim will be yours."'

²¹Yisra'el's sons did so. Yoseph gave them wagons at Par'oh's bidding and gave them provisions for the journey. ²²To them all he gave changes of clothing for each individual. To Binyamin he gave 300 pieces of silver and five changes of clothing. ²³To his father he sent as follows: ten donkeys carrying some of the good things of Misrayim, and ten she-donkeys carrying grain, bread and provisions for his father for the journey. ²⁴So he sent his brothers off, and as they went, he said to them, 'Don't be agitated on the way.'

'My son Yoseph is still alive!'

²⁵So they went up from Misrayim and came to the country of Kena'an to Ya'aqob their father ²⁶and told him: 'Yoseph is still alive, and actually he's ruling over the entire country of Misrayim.' His heart went numb, because he didn't trust them. ²⁷But they spoke to him all Yoseph's words that he had spoken to them, and he saw the wagons that Yoseph sent to carry him, and the spirit of Ya'aqob their father came alive. ²⁸Yisra'el said, 'Great! My son Yoseph is still alive! I must go and see him before I die!'

46

So Yisra'el moved with all that was his and came to Be'er Sheba. He offered sacrifices to the God of his father Yitshaq, ²and God said to Yisra'el in a great vision at night, 'Ya'aqob, Ya'aqob!' He said, 'I'm here.' ³He said, 'I am God, the God of your father. Don't be afraid of going down to Misrayim, because I shall make you into a big nation there. ⁴I myself will go down with you to Misrayim and I myself will also definitely bring you up from there. Yoseph is the one who will place his hand on your eyes.'

⁵So Ya'aqob set off from Be'er Sheba. Yisra'el's sons carried Ya'aqob their father, their little ones and their wives in the wagons that Par'oh had sent to carry him, ⁶they got their livestock and the property that they had acquired in the country of Kena'an, and Ya'aqob and all his offspring with him came to Misrayim. ⁷His sons and his grandsons with him, his daughters and his granddaughters – all his offspring he brought with him to Misrayim.

The Seventy

⁸These are the names of the descendants of Yisra'el who came to Misrayim, Ya'aqob and his descendants.

Ya'aqob's firstborn, Re'uben; ⁹Re'uben's sons: Hanok, Pallu, Hetsron and Karmi.
¹⁰Shim'on's sons: Yemu'el, Yamin, Ohad, Yakin, Tsohar and Sha'ul, the son of a Kena'anite woman.
¹¹Levi's sons: Gershon, Qehat and Merari.
¹²Yehudah's sons: Er, Onan, Shelah, Perets and Zerah (but Er and Onan had died in the country of Kena'an); Perets's sons were Hetsron and Hamul.
¹³Yissakar's sons: Tolah, Puvvah, Yob and Shimron.
¹⁴Zebulun's sons: Sered, Elon and Yahle'el.

¹⁵These are the sons of Le'ah, to whom she gave birth for Ya'aqob in Paddan Aram, and his daughter Dinah. Every person, his sons and his daughters: thirty-three.

¹⁶Gad's sons: Tsiphyon, Haggi, Shuni, Etsbon, Eri, Arodi and Ar'eli.

¹⁷Asher's sons: Yimnah, Yishvah, Yishvi and Beri'ah, with Serah their sister. Beri'ah's sons: Heber and Malki'el.

¹⁸These are the sons of Zilpah, whom Laban gave to his daughter Le'ah. She gave birth to these for Ya'aqob: sixteen persons.

¹⁹The sons of Ya'aqob's wife Rahel: Yoseph and Binyamin. ²⁰To Yoseph were born in the country of Misrayim Menashsheh and Ephrayim, to whom Asenat, the daughter of Potiphera, priest in On, gave birth for him.

²¹Binyamin's sons: Bela, Beker, Ashbel, Gera, Na'aman, Ehi, Rosh, Muppim, Huppim and Ard.

²²These are the sons of Rahel who were born to Ya'aqob. Every person: fourteen.

²³Dan's sons: Hushim.

²⁴Naphtali's sons: Yahtse'el, Guni, Yetser and Shillem.

²⁵These are the sons of Bilhah, whom Laban gave to his daughter Rahel. She gave birth to these for Ya'aqob. Every person: seven.

²⁶Every person belonging to Ya'aqob who came to Misrayim, the people who went out of his loins, apart from the wives of Ya'aqob's sons, every person: sixty-six. ²⁷Yoseph's sons who were born to him in Misrayim, the persons: two. Every person belonging to Ya'aqob's household who came to Misrayim: seventy.

I can die now

²⁸He had sent Yehudah before him to Yoseph, to give directions before him to Goshen. So they came to the Goshen region, ²⁹and Yoseph harnessed his chariot and went up to meet Yisra'el his father in Goshen. He appeared to him, and he fell on his neck and cried on his neck again and again. ³⁰Yisra'el said to Yoseph, 'I can die now, after I've seen your face, that you're still alive.'

³¹Yoseph said to his brothers and to his father's household, 'I'll go up and tell Par'oh: "My brothers and my father's household, who were in the country of Kena'an – they have come to me. ³²The men are shepherds of a flock, because they've been livestock men, and their flock and their herd and all that's theirs – they've brought them." ³³So when Par'oh calls for you and says, "What's your work?" ³⁴say "Your servants have been livestock men from our youth till now, both we and our ancestors", so that you may live in the Goshen region, because every shepherd of a flock is an offence to Misrayimites.'

47

So Yoseph came and told Par'oh, 'My father and my brothers, their flock and their herd and all that's theirs – they've come from the country of Kena'an. There, they're in the Goshen region.' ²He took some of the total number of his brothers, five of them, and presented them before Par'oh. ³Par'oh said to his brothers, 'What is your work?' They said to Par'oh, 'Your servants are shepherds of a flock, both we and our ancestors.' ⁴They said to Par'oh, 'We have come to reside in the country because there's no pasture for your servants' flock, because the famine is heavy in the country of Kena'an. So now may your servants please live in the Goshen region.' ⁵Par'oh said to Yoseph: 'Given that your father and your brothers have come to you, ⁶the country of Misrayim is before you. Get your father and your brothers to live in the best part of the country. They should live in the Goshen region, and if you know that there are capable men among them, make them livestock officials over all that's mine.'

State provision

⁷Yoseph brought Ya'aqob his father and got him to stand before Par'oh, and Ya'aqob blessed Par'oh. ⁸Par'oh said to Ya'aqob, 'What is the span of the years of your life?' ⁹Ya'aqob said to Par'oh, 'The span of the years of my residing is 130 years. Small and bad has been the span of the years of my life. They haven't reached the span of the years of my ancestors' lives by the span of their residing.'

¹⁰Ya'aqob blessed Par'oh and left Par'oh's presence, ¹¹and Yoseph got his father and his brothers to live and gave them a holding in the

country of Misrayim, in the best part of the country, in the Ra'meses region, as Par'oh had ordered. ¹²Yoseph provided his father, his brothers and his father's entire household with bread by the number of the little ones.

¹³But bread: there was none in the entire country, because the famine was very heavy. The country of Misrayim and the country of Kena'an withered because of the famine. ¹⁴Yoseph collected all the silver that was to be found in the country of Misrayim and in the country of Kena'an in payment for the grain that they were buying. Yoseph brought the silver into Par'oh's house.

¹⁵When the silver from the country of Misrayim and from the country of Kena'an came to an end, all Misrayim came to Yoseph, saying, 'Give us bread: why should we die in front of you, because the silver has gone.' ¹⁶Yoseph said, 'Bring your livestock, and I'll give it to you in exchange for your livestock, if the silver's gone.' ¹⁷So they brought their livestock to Yoseph and Yoseph gave them bread in exchange for the horses, for the livestock in the flock, for the livestock in the herd and for the donkeys. He sustained them with bread in exchange for all their livestock that year.

The nationalization of land

¹⁸When that year came to an end, they came to him the next year and said to him, 'We won't hide from my lord that the silver has come to an end, and the animal stocks belong to my lord: nothing remains before my lord except our bodies and our land. ¹⁹Why should we die before your eyes, both we and our land? Acquire us and our land in exchange for bread. We ourselves and our land will become serfs to Par'oh. Give seed, so we may live and not die, and the land not become a waste.' ²⁰So Yoseph acquired all the land in Misrayim for Par'oh, because the Misrayimites, each of them, sold his fields because the famine was so hard on them, and the country came to belong to Par'oh. ²¹The people: he got them to pass over into the towns from one end of Misrayim's border to its other end. ²²He only didn't acquire the priests' land, because the priests had a statutory allotment from Par'oh and they ate their allotment that Par'oh gave them. Therefore they didn't sell their land.

²³Yoseph said to the people, 'Here, today I've acquired you and your land for Par'oh. Here's seed for you. You are to sow the land, ²⁴and with the yield you are to give a fifth to Par'oh, but four-fifths will be yours, as seed for the fields and as food for you and for those in your households, and for eating by your little ones.' ²⁵They said, 'You've kept us alive. May we find grace in the eyes of my lord. We will become serfs to Par'oh.'

²⁶Yoseph made it a decree, until this day, for the land in Misrayim: a fifth is Par'oh's. Only the land of the priests on their own didn't become Par'oh's.

Still remembering his first love

²⁷So Yisra'el lived in the country of Misrayim in the Goshen region. They acquired holdings in it, they were fruitful and they became very numerous. ²⁸Ya'aqob lived seventeen years in the country of Misrayim. Ya'aqob's span, the years of his life, was 147 years.

²⁹The days drew near for Yisra'el to die, and he called his son Yoseph and said to him, 'Please, if I've found grace in your eyes, put your hand under my thigh, please, and act in commitment and truthfulness with me. Please don't bury me in Misrayim. ³⁰I shall lie down with my ancestors and you're to carry me from Misrayim and bury me in their burial-place.' He said, 'I will act in accordance with your word.' ³¹He said, 'Swear to me.' He swore to him, and Yisra'el bowed low at the head of the bed.

48 Subsequently, they said to Yoseph, 'Here, your father is ill', so he took his two sons with him, Menashsheh and Ephrayim. ²They told Ya'aqob, 'Here, your son Yoseph is coming to you.' Yisra'el summoned up his strength and sat up on the bed. ³Ya'aqob said to Yoseph, 'God Shadday, he appeared to me at Luz in the country of Kena'an and blessed me, ⁴and said to me, "Here, I'm making you fruitful and numerous and making you a congregation of peoples and giving this country to your offspring after you as a permanent holding."

⁵Now, your two sons who were born to you in the country of Misrayim before my coming to you in Misrayim: they're mine. Like Re'uben

and Shim'on, they are to be mine. ⁶Your family that you father after them will be yours. As regards their domain they will be called with the name of their brothers. ⁷I – when I was coming from Paddan, Rahel died, alas, in the country of Kena'an, on the journey, when there was still a distance so as to come to Ephrat, and I buried her there on the road to Ephrat' (i.e. Bet Lehem).

The younger again ahead of the elder

⁸So when Yisra'el saw Yoseph's sons, he said 'Who are these?' ⁹Yoseph said to his father, 'They're my sons, whom God has given me here.' He said, 'Please get them to me, so I may bless them.' ¹⁰Now Yisra'el's eyes were heavy because of age, and he couldn't see.

He brought them up to him, and he kissed them and hugged them. ¹¹Yisra'el said to Yoseph, 'To see your face! I didn't expect it. And here – God has let me see your offspring as well.' ¹²Yoseph got them off his knees and bowed low, with his face to the ground. ¹³Yoseph took the two of them, Ephrayim with his right hand to Yisra'el's left, and Menashsheh with his left hand to Yisra'el's right, and brought them up to him.

¹⁴Yisra'el put out his right hand and put it on Ephrayim's head (though he was the younger one) and his left hand on Menashsheh's head, crossing his hands, because Menashsheh was the firstborn, ¹⁵and he blessed Yoseph: 'May the God before whom my fathers Abraham and Yitshaq walked, the God who has been shepherding me from whenever until this day, ¹⁶the envoy who has restored me from every bad fortune, bless the boys. May I be named through them, I and my ancestors Abraham and Yitshaq. May they abound so as to become a large number in the middle of the country.'

¹⁷Yoseph saw that his father was putting his right hand on Ephrayim's head and it was bad in his eyes. He took hold of his father's hand to remove it from on Ephrayim's head on to Menashsheh's head. ¹⁸Yoseph said to his father, 'Not like that, father, because this one is the firstborn. Place your right hand on his head.' ¹⁹But his father refused and said, 'I know, son, I know. He will become a people as well, he will become big as well, but nevertheless his younger brother will be bigger than him and his offspring will become a full number of nations.'

²⁰So that day he blessed them: 'By you Yisra'el will bless, saying: "God make you like Ephrayim and Menashsheh."' But he put Ephrayim before Menashsheh.

Deathbed promises and predictions (1)

²¹Yisra'el said to Yoseph: 'Here, I'm going to die, but God will be with you and will take you back to the country of your ancestors. ²²I myself am giving you one shoulder [*shekem*] above your brothers, which I took from the hand of the Amorites with my sword and with my bow.'

49

Ya'aqob called his sons and said, 'Gather together and I shall tell you what is to befall you in a later time. ²Collect together and listen, sons of Ya'aqob, listen to Yisra'el your father.'

³Re'uben, you're my firstborn,
 my energy and the firstfruit of my strength.
Though excelling in dignity and excelling in
 vigour,
⁴turbulent as water, you are not to excel.
Because you climbed into your father's bed,
 then profaned it; he climbed on to my
 mattress.

⁵Shim'on and Levi, brothers,
 their pikes are instruments of violence.
⁶May I myself not come into their council,
 may I myself not join in their congregation.
Because when they were angry, they killed
 people;
 when it was acceptable to them, they
 hamstrung oxen.
⁷Cursed be their anger because it was vigorous,
 their outburst because it was tough.
I will divide them in Ya'aqob,
 scatter them in Yisra'el.

Deathbed promises and predictions (2)

⁸You are Yehudah;
 your brothers will confess you.
With your hand on your enemies' neck,
 your father's sons will bow low to you.

⁹Yehudah is a lion cub;
  from the prey, son, you've gone up.
He's bent down, lain like a lion,
  like a cougar – who will make him rise?
¹⁰The staff will not depart from Yehudah,
  the sceptre from between his feet,
Until tribute comes to him
  and the submission of the peoples is his.
¹¹He ties his donkey to a vine,
  the offspring of his she-donkey to a choice vine.
He washes his apparel in wine,
  his garments in grape-blood.
¹²His eyes are darker than wine,
  his teeth whiter than milk.

¹³Zebulun is to dwell by the sea shore
  he's to be by the shore for ships;
  his flank at Tsidon.

¹⁴Yissakar is a sturdy donkey
  lying among the sheepfolds.
¹⁵He saw a place to settle down – how good it was,
  and the country – how lovely.
He bent his shoulder to the labouring,
  became a serf work force.

¹⁶Dan is to give judgement [*yadin*] for his people
  as one of Yisra'el's clans.
¹⁷Dan is to be a snake by the road,
  a viper by the path,
One that bites the horse's heels
  so its rider falls backwards.

¹⁸For your deliverance I have waited, Yahweh.

¹⁹Gad: a raiding gang [*gedud*] will raid him,
  but he himself will raid at its heel.

²⁰From Asher: his bread will be rich,
  and he will give a king's delicacies.

²¹Naphtali is a hind set free,
  who gives lovely fawns.

Deathbed promises and predictions (3)

²²Yoseph is a fruitful branch,
  a fruitful branch by a spring,
  branches that run over a wall.
²³The archers were ferocious
  and shot at him and assaulted him.
²⁴But his bow stayed firm
  and his arms and hands were agile,
Because of the hands of Ya'aqob's Champion,
  because the Shepherd, Yisra'el's Stone, was there,
²⁵Because of your father's God, he helps you,
  and Shadday, he blesses you,
With the blessings of the heavens above,
  the blessings of the deep lying below,
The blessings of the breasts and the womb,
  ²⁶the blessings of your father.
They have been stronger than the blessings of the ancient mountains,
  up to the bounty of the age-old hills.
May they come on Yoseph's head,
  on the crown of the one who was consecrated from his brothers.

²⁷Binyamin is a wolf who tears apart,
  in the morning he eats prey,
  at evening he shares out spoil.

²⁸All these are the twelve Yisra'elite clans and this is what their father spoke to them. So he blessed them. Each of them according to his blessing he blessed them.

²⁹He ordered them and said to them, 'I'm being gathered to my kin. Bury me with my ancestors in the cave that's in the field of Ephron the Hittite, ³⁰in the cave that's in the field at Makpelah which is east of Mamre, in the country of Kena'an, the field that Abraham acquired from Ephron the Hittite as a burial holding ³¹(there they buried Abraham and Sarah his wife, there they buried Yitshaq and Ribqah his wife, there I buried Le'ah), ³²an acquisition (the field and the cave that's in it) from the Hittites.'

³³Ya'aqob finished giving orders to his sons, gathered his feet into the bed, breathed his last and was gathered to his kin.

The great mourning

50 Yoseph fell on his father's face and wailed over him and kissed him. ²Yoseph ordered the physicians who were his servants to embalm his father. When the physicians embalmed Yisra'el, ³they fulfilled forty days for him, because that's how they used to fulfil the days for embalming.

The Misrayimites bewailed him seventy days, ⁴and when the days of bewailing him had passed, Yoseph spoke to Par'oh's household: 'Please, if I have found grace in your eyes, please speak in Par'oh's ears: ⁵"My father himself got me to swear: 'Here, I'm dying; in the grave that I dug for myself in the country of Kena'an, there you're to bury me.' So I shall now go up, please, and bury my father, and come back."'

⁶Par'oh said, 'Go up and bury your father as he got you to swear.' ⁷So Yoseph went up to bury his father. All Par'oh's servants went up with him, and the elders in his household, all the elders in the country of Misrayim, ⁸Yoseph's entire household, his brothers and his father's household. Only the little ones, and their flock and their herd, did they abandon in the Goshen region. ⁹Both chariotry and cavalry went up with him. It was a very substantial camp.

¹⁰They came to the Thorn Threshing Floor, which is across the Yarden, and held a very great and heavy lament there. He made seven days of grieving for his father. ¹¹The Kena'anite people living in the country saw the grieving at Thorn Threshing Floor and said, 'This is a heavy grieving on the part of the Misrayimites.' That's why it was named 'The Misrayimite Grieving', which is across the Yarden.

¹²His sons did thus for him, as he had ordered them, ¹³and his sons carried him to the country of Kena'an and buried him in the cave in the field at Makpelah, the field that Abraham acquired as a burial holding from Ephron the Hittite, east of Mamre.

Am I in the place of God?

¹⁴Then Yoseph went back to Misrayim, he and his brothers and all the people who had gone up with him to bury his father, after he had buried his father. ¹⁵Yoseph's brothers saw that their father was dead, and said, 'What if Yoseph feels hostile to us and really gets back at us for all the bad fate that we dealt to him?' ¹⁶So they gave order to Yoseph: 'Your father gave order before his death: ¹⁷"Say this to Yoseph: 'Oh, please carry your brothers' affront and their wrongdoing, that they dealt a bad fate to you.'" So now please carry the affront of the servants of your father's God.' Yoseph cried when they spoke to him. ¹⁸His brothers also came and fell before him and said, 'Here are we as servants to you.'

¹⁹Yoseph said to them, 'Don't be afraid. Am I in the place of God? ²⁰Whereas you yourselves thought up something bad for me, God thought it up for good, in order to act today to keep alive a numerous people. ²¹So now, don't be afraid. I myself will provide for you and your little ones.' Thus he consoled them and reassured them.

²²So Yoseph lived in Misrayim, he and his father's household. Yoseph lived 110 years ²³and saw the third generation of Ephrayim; the children of Makir ben Menashsheh were also born on Yoseph's knees. ²⁴Then Yoseph said to his brothers, 'I'm going to die, but God will definitely attend to you and take you up from this country to the country that he swore to Abraham, to Yitshaq and to Ya'aqob.' ²⁵Yoseph got Yisra'el's sons to swear, saying: 'God will definitely attend to you, and you're to take up my bones from here.' ²⁶Yoseph died, a man of 110 years. They embalmed him and put him in a coffin in Misrayim.

Exodus

Exodus tells the story of Israel's beginnings as a people. It starts off with the Israelites as state serfs in Egypt, and its first half recounts how Yahweh forces the Egyptian king to release them so they can go and hold a festival for Yahweh. After a further, final showdown between Yahweh and the king at the Reed Sea, they're able to get to the mountain where their leader, Moses, had earlier met with this God.

The second half relates the renewing of the pact or covenant relationship between Yahweh and Israel and Israel's construction of the splendid portable sanctuary whose specifications Yahweh gives Moses. The book first provides all the specifications and then repeats them in its account of how Israel did as Yahweh said. The story ends with Yahweh coming to dwell among Israel in this sanctuary.

The bridge between the two halves of the book is Yahweh's initial meeting with Israel at Mount Sinai. Whereas in Genesis Yahweh didn't explicitly lay down much by way of expectations of his people, his getting Israel out of their serfdom provides a new basis for his laying down expectations of them. These begin with the Ten Commandments, which embody some basic principles for life. The list sums up a number of the concerns that underlie much of the expression of Yahweh's decrees for Israel's life that are expounded in the Old Testament as a whole. It combines some basic obligations that most cultures would accept (no murder, no theft, and so on) with some obligations that would raise eyebrows among other peoples (worship only Yahweh, don't make images, stop working one day a week), and it ends with a final *coup de grâce* that sends anyone away with their tail between their legs (no coveting). The further decrees that follow the Ten Commandments spell out these obligations in sample areas of life. Once again, other Middle Eastern peoples would not be surprised to find directives to avoid the ill-treatment of servants, or procedures for resolving conflicts in the community, but would notice the distinctiveness of instructions about Israel's worship of Yahweh alone.

Exodus is a narrative with a beginning, a middle and an end. Yet it's not self-contained. It continues the story begun in Genesis, and the background for Yahweh's getting Israel out of Egypt lies in things Yahweh had promised in Genesis. At the end, it leads into Leviticus, which relates more of what Yahweh told Moses at Sinai, and it leads on further into the subsequent books that will relate how God continued to pursue his project of settling Israel in Canaan.

As is the case with Genesis, we don't know who wrote Exodus or when it was written, but we can see how its story informed Israel over the centuries about what it was as a people, and what it was supposed to be. The fact that Yahweh rescued Israel from Egypt was a basis for continuing to trust him and for being the kind of community that protects people from harsh servitude rather than ill-treating them as servants. Yahweh's putting Pharaoh in his place provided reason for trusting in and submitting to Yahweh as King and not thinking that the imperial power of the day held the real power. The story of Yahweh's laying out the blueprint for a rather different kind of sanctuary from the temple that Israel later built would give food for thought to a people that liked to devise its own worship and its own worship buildings.

Like Genesis, Exodus is more like a movie based on fact than either a piece of pure fiction or a pure historical narrative. One aspect of its genius is the way it discusses complex theological questions as it tells its story. What is the relationship between God's sovereignty and the sovereignty of a political figure like the Pharaoh? What do we mean by talking about the presence of God? How does God cope with the rebelliousness of his own people in a way that does justice to his faithfulness and mercy and to his sacredness and integrity? In telling its story, Exodus walks round questions such as these, looks at them from various angles and thus resources its readers in thinking about them.

On not rendering to Caesar

1 So these are the names of the sons of Yisra'el [Israel] who came to Misrayim [Egypt] with Ya'aqob [Jacob] (each with his household they came): ²Re'uben, Shim'on [Simeon], Levi and Yehudah [Judah]; ³Yissakar [Issachar], Zebulun and Binyamin [Benjamin]; ⁴Dan and Naphtali; Gad and Asher. ⁵Every person of those who came out of Ya'aqob's loins, they were seventy persons, Yoseph [Joseph] being in Misrayim. ⁶Yoseph died, as did all his brothers, and all that generation, ⁷but the Yisra'elites – they were fruitful and they teemed, they became vast and very, very numerous. The country became full of them.

⁸A new king rose up over Misrayim who didn't acknowledge Yoseph. ⁹He said to his people, 'Here, the people of the Yisra'elites is vaster and more numerous than us. ¹⁰Come on, let's act smart with it so it doesn't become so vast that when battle comes, it even gathers together with our enemies and does battle against us, and goes up from the country.' ¹¹So they set workforce officials over it in order to humble it by means of its labours. It built supply towns for Par'oh [Pharaoh], Pitom and Ra'amses. ¹²But as they would humble it, so it would become vaster and break out. They were dismayed about the Yisra'elites.

¹³So the Misrayimites made the Yisra'elites serve with harshness. ¹⁴They made their lives hard with tough servitude, with mortar, with bricks and with every form of servitude in the fields. Every form of the servitude that they had them undertake was with harshness.

¹⁵The king of Misrayim said to the Hebrew midwives (one of whom was named Shiphrah, the second Pu'ah), ¹⁶'When you're delivering the Hebrew women, look at the

Exodus 1: Mosheh (Moses)

stones. If it's a son, put him to death, but if it's a daughter, she may live.' ¹⁷But the midwives lived in awe of God and didn't do as the king of Misrayim had spoken to them. They let the boys live. ¹⁸The king of Misrayim called for the midwives and said to them, 'Why have you done this thing and let the boys live?' ¹⁹The midwives said to Par'oh, 'Because the Hebrew women are not like the Misrayimite women, because they're lively. Before the midwife comes to them, they give birth.'

How some women continue to defeat Par'oh

²⁰God was good to the midwives, and the people became vast and very numerous. ²¹Because the midwives lived in awe of God, he made households for them. ²²Then Par'oh ordered all his people, 'Every son who's born, you're to throw into the Ye'or [Nile], but every daughter you can let live.'

2 A man from the household of Levi went and got a daughter of Levi. ²The woman got pregnant and gave birth to a son, and she saw he was good-looking. She hid him for three months ³but she couldn't hide him any longer. So she got a papyrus container for him, tarred it with tar and with bitumen, put the child in it and put it in the reeds by the bank of the Ye'or. ⁴His sister took a stand at a distance so she would know what would be done to him.

⁵Par'oh's daughter went down to bathe in the Ye'or, while her girls were walking on the bank of the Ye'or. She saw the container in the middle of the reeds and sent her handmaid, and she got it. ⁶She opened it and saw the child: there, a boy crying. She felt pity for him, and said, 'This is one of the Hebrews' children.' ⁷His sister said to Par'oh's daughter, 'Shall I go and call for a woman from the Hebrew women who is nursing for you, so she can nurse the child for you?' ⁸Par'oh's daughter said to her, 'Go!' The girl went and called for the child's mother. ⁹Par'oh's daughter said to her, 'Take this child and nurse him for me. I myself will give you your wages.' So the woman took the child and nursed him, ¹⁰and the child grew up. Then she brought him to Par'oh's daughter and he became her son. She named him Mosheh [Moses]; she said, 'Because I pulled him out [*mashah*] from the water.'

From guerrilla to fugitive

¹¹During that time, Mosheh grew up, and he went out to his brothers and saw their labours. He saw a Misrayimite man striking down a Hebrew man, one of his brothers. ¹²He turned his face this way and that, saw that there was no one, and struck down the Misrayimite and hid him in the sand.

¹³He went out the next day and there, two Hebrew men were fighting. He said to the one in the wrong, 'Why do you strike down your neighbour?' ¹⁴He said, 'Who made you someone as an official and an authority over us? Are you thinking of killing me as you killed the Misrayimite?' Mosheh was afraid. He said, 'Then the thing has become known!' ¹⁵And Par'oh heard about this thing and sought to kill Mosheh, but Mosheh took flight from before Par'oh and lived in the country of Midyan.

He lived by a well. ¹⁶Now a Midyanite priest had seven daughters. They came and drew and filled the troughs to water their father's flock, ¹⁷but shepherds came and drove them away. Mosheh got up and delivered them, and watered their flock.

¹⁸They came to Re'u'el their father, and he said, 'How have you been so quick in coming today?' ¹⁹They said, 'A Misrayimite man rescued us from the hand of the shepherds. He actually drew water for us as well, and watered the flock.' ²⁰He said to his daughters, 'So where is he? Why did you abandon the man? Call him so he can eat a meal.'

²¹Mosheh resolved to live with the man, and he gave Tsipporah his daughter to Mosheh. ²²She gave birth to a son and he named him Gershom, because (he said) 'I've become a resident [*ger*] in a foreign country.'

It was an ordinary working day

²³During that long time the king of Misrayim died, and the Yisra'elites groaned because of their servitude. They cried out, and their cry for help because of their servitude went up to God. ²⁴God listened to their groan, and God was mindful of his pact with Abraham, with Yitshaq [Isaac] and with Ya'aqob. ²⁵God saw the Yisra'elites. God acknowledged it.

3 Now Mosheh was shepherding the flock of Yitro [Jethro] his father-in-law, the Midyanite priest. He had driven the flock to the far side of the wilderness and come to God's mountain, to Horeb. ²Yahweh's envoy appeared to him in a fiery flame out of the middle of a bush. He saw, and there, the bush was burning up with fire but the bush wasn't consumed. ³Mosheh said, 'I must turn aside and see this great sight. Why doesn't the bush burn up?' ⁴Yahweh saw that he turned aside to see.

God called to him out of the middle of the bush and said, 'Mosheh, Mosheh!' He said, 'I'm here.' ⁵He said, 'Don't draw near here. Take your boots off your feet, because the place you're standing on is sacred ground.' ⁶And he said, 'I'm the God of your father, the God of Abraham, the God of Yitshaq and the God of Ya'aqob.' Mosheh hid his face, because he was afraid to look at God.

⁷Yahweh said, 'I really have seen my people's humbling in Misrayim, and I've listened to their outcry on account of their bosses, because I've acknowledged their sufferings. ⁸I've come down to rescue it from the hand of Misrayim and take it up from that country to a good, wide country, a country flowing with milk and syrup, to the place of the Kena'anite [Canaanite], the Hittite, the Amorite, the Perizzite, the Hivvite and the Yebusite. ⁹So now, here, the Yisra'elites' outcry has come to me, and I've also seen the affliction that the Misrayimites are imposing on them. ¹⁰So now, go, and I'll send you to Par'oh to get my people, the Yisra'elites, out of Misrayim.'

Who God will be

¹¹Mosheh said to God, 'Who am I, that I should go to Par'oh and get the Yisra'elites out of Misrayim?' ¹²He said, 'Because I will be with you. This will be the sign for you that I've sent you. When you get the people out of Misrayim, you'll all serve God on this mountain.'

¹³Mosheh said to God, 'Here, I'm going to come to the Yisra'elites and say to them, "The God of your ancestors – he has sent me to you", and they will say to me, "What is his name?" What shall I say to them?' ¹⁴God said to Mosheh, 'I will be what I will be.' He said, 'Say this to the Yisra'elites, "I will be" sent me to you.' ¹⁵God said further to Mosheh, 'Say this to the Yisra'elites: "Yahweh, the God of your ancestors, the God of Abraham, the God of Yitshaq and the God of Ya'aqob, sent me to you." This is my name permanently; this is my designation to all generations.

¹⁶Go, gather Yisra'el's elders, and say to them, "Yahweh, the God of your ancestors, the God of Abraham, Yitshaq and Ya'aqob, has appeared to me, saying 'I really have attended to you and to what's being done to you in Misrayim. ¹⁷I've said, I will take you up, out from humbling in Misrayim, to the country of the Kena'anite, the Hittite, the Amorite, the Perizzite, the Hivvite and the Yebusite, to a country flowing with milk and syrup.'"

¹⁸They will listen to your voice, and you are to come, you and Yisra'el's elders, to the king of Misrayim and say to him, "Yahweh, the God of the Hebrews – he's met with us. So now, we must please go three days' journey into the wilderness to sacrifice for Yahweh our God."

People will need evidence

¹⁹I myself acknowledge that the king of Misrayim won't allow you to go, not even because of a strong hand. ²⁰But I shall put out my hand and strike Misrayim down with all the extraordinary things that I shall do among them. After this he'll send you off, ²¹and I shall give this people grace in the eyes of Misrayim. When you go, you won't go empty-handed. ²²A woman will ask from her neighbour, and from the woman residing in her house, for objects of silver and objects of gold and clothes, and you will put them on your sons and on your daughters. You will strip Misrayim.'

4 Mosheh answered: 'But there, they won't trust in me, they won't listen to my voice, because they'll say, "Yahweh didn't appear to you."'

²Yahweh said to him, 'What's this in your hand?' He said, 'A staff.' ³He said, 'Throw it on the ground.' He threw it on the ground, and it became a snake. Mosheh fled from before it. ⁴Yahweh said to Mosheh, 'Put out your hand and grasp it by its tail' (so he put out his hand and took strong hold of it, and it became a staff in his fist) ⁵'in order that they

may trust that Yahweh appeared to you – the God of your ancestors, the God of Abraham, the God of Yitshaq and the God of Ya'aqob.'

⁶Yahweh said to him further, 'Put your hand into the fold of your coat, please.' He put his hand into the fold of his coat, and took it out, and there – his hand was scaly, like snow. ⁷He said, 'Put your hand back into the fold of your coat' (so he put his hand back into the fold of his coat, then took it out of the fold of his coat – and there, it had gone back like his flesh) ⁸so if they don't trust you and listen to the voice of the first sign, they may listen to the voice of the later sign.

Some final attempts to say 'No'

⁹If they don't even trust in these two signs and listen to your voice, get some of the water of the Ye'or and pour it on the dry ground, and the water that you get from the Ye'or will become blood on the dry ground.'

¹⁰Mosheh said to Yahweh, 'Pardon me, Lord: I haven't been a man of words in previous days or since you've spoken to your servant, because I'm heavy of mouth, heavy of tongue.' ¹¹Yahweh said to him, 'Who made the mouth for human beings, or who makes someone dumb or deaf, seeing or blind? Isn't it me, Yahweh? ¹²So now go, and I myself will be with your mouth, and I'll instruct you what you're to say.'

¹³He said, 'Pardon me, Lord: please send by the hand [of someone else] you can send.' ¹⁴Yahweh's anger raged against Mosheh, but he said, 'Isn't there Aharon [Aaron] your brother, the Levite? I know that he can really speak. And also – there, he's going to come out to meet you. When he sees you, he'll rejoice in his heart. ¹⁵You're to speak to him and put the words in his mouth. I myself be with your mouth and with his mouth, and I'll instruct you what you're to do. ¹⁶But he's the one who will speak for you to the people. He – he'll be a mouth for you, and you – you'll be God for him. ¹⁷But take in your hand this staff, with which you'll do the signs.'

¹⁸So Mosheh went and returned to Yitro his father-in-law and said to him, 'I must please go and return to my brothers in Misrayim and see whether they're still alive.' Yitro said to Mosheh, 'Go; may things be well.'

The migrant returns

¹⁹So Yahweh said to Mosheh in Midyan, 'Go, go back to Misrayim, because all the people who were seeking your life are dead.' ²⁰Mosheh took his wife and his sons, mounted them on a donkey and went back to the country of Misrayim.

Mosheh took God's staff in his hand. ²¹Yahweh said to Mosheh, 'When you go back to Misrayim, look at all the proofs that I put in your hand and do them before Par'oh. But I myself will make his mind adamant so he doesn't send the people off. ²²You're to say to Par'oh, "Yahweh has said this: 'Yisra'el is my son, my firstborn. ²³I have said to you, "Send my son off so he can serve me", but you've refused to send him off. Here, I'm going to kill your son, your firstborn."'"

²⁴On the way, at a lodging place, Yahweh met up with him and sought to put him to death, ²⁵but Tsipporah got a flint and cut off her son's foreskin, touched his feet with it and said, 'Because you're a bridegroom of shed blood to me!' ²⁶And he slackened his hold on him. (At that time she said 'a bridegroom of shed blood', regarding the circumcision.)

²⁷Yahweh said to Aharon, 'Go and meet Mosheh in the wilderness.' He went and met up with him at God's mountain and kissed him. ²⁸Mosheh told Aharon all Yahweh's words that he had sent him with and all the signs that he had ordered him with, ²⁹and Mosheh and Aharon went and gathered all the elders of the Yisra'elites. ³⁰Aharon spoke all the words that Yahweh had spoken to Mosheh, he did the signs before the people's eyes, ³¹and the people trusted. They heard that Yahweh had attended to the Yisra'elites and had seen their humbling, and they bent their heads and bowed low.

I don't acknowledge Yahweh

5 Afterwards, Mosheh and Aharon went and said to Par'oh, 'Yahweh has said this: "Send my people Yisra'el off so they may hold a festival for me in the wilderness."' ²But Par'oh said, 'Who is Yahweh that I should listen to his voice about sending Yisra'el off? I don't acknowledge Yahweh and I won't send Yisra'el off, either.'

³So they said, 'In that the God of the Hebrews has met with us, we must please go a three days' journey into the wilderness and sacrifice for Yahweh our God so that he doesn't come on us with epidemic or with sword.' ⁴The king of Misrayim said to them, 'Mosheh and Aharon, why should you release the people from their work? Get to your labours.' ⁵And Par'oh said, 'Here, the people of the country are now vast, and you'll make them stop from their labours?'

⁶That day Par'oh ordered the bosses over the people and its overseers: ⁷'You will not continue to give the people straw for making brick, as in previous days. They themselves can go and collect straw for themselves. ⁸But you're to set for them the quantity of bricks that they were making in previous days. You will not cut it down, because they're slacking. That's why they're crying out, "Let's go and offer sacrifice for our God." ⁹Service should weigh heavy on the men so they may do it and not listen to deceptive words.'

¹⁰So the people's bosses and its overseers went out and said to the people, 'Par'oh has said this: "I'm not giving you straw. ¹¹You go, get straw for yourselves from wherever you may find it, but not a thing is to be cut down from your service."'

Divide and rule

¹²The people dispersed through the entire country of Misrayim to gather stubble for straw, ¹³while the bosses hounded them: 'Get your work finished, each day's requirement on its day, just like when there was the straw.' ¹⁴The Yisra'elites' overseers, whom Par'oh's bosses had put over them, were struck down: 'Why have you not finished your decreed amount of brickmaking, as in previous days, either yesterday or today?'

¹⁵The Yisra'elites' overseers came and cried out to Par'oh, 'Why do you act like this towards your servants? ¹⁶No straw is given to your servants but they're saying to us, "Bricks! Make them." Here, your servants are being struck down, but the wrongdoing is your people's.' ¹⁷But he said, 'You're slacking, slacking. That's why you're saying, "We want to go sacrifice for Yahweh." ¹⁸So now go, serve. Straw will not be given you, but you must give the tally of bricks.'

¹⁹The Yisra'elites' overseers saw that things were bad for them in his saying 'You're not to cut down your bricks, each day's requirement on its day.' ²⁰They came upon Mosheh and Aharon taking their stand to meet them when they went out from Par'oh, ²¹and they said to them, 'May Yahweh look at you and exercise authority, because you made our smell stink in the eyes of Par'oh and in the eyes of his servants, putting a sword in their hand to kill us.'

²²Mosheh went back to Yahweh and said, 'Lord, why have you dealt badly with this people? Why is it that you sent me? ²³From the time when I came to Par'oh to speak in your name, he's dealt badly with this people, and you haven't rescued your people at all.'

6 Yahweh said to Mosheh, 'Now you'll see what I shall do to Par'oh, because he will send them off by means of a strong hand. By means of a strong hand he will drive them out of his country.'

My people – your God

²God spoke to Mosheh and said to him, 'I am Yahweh. ³I appeared to Abraham, to Yitshaq and to Ya'aqob as God Shadday, but by my name Yahweh I didn't make myself known to them. ⁴I also implemented my pact with them to give them the country of Kena'an, the country of their residing, in which they were residents. ⁵I have also now personally listened to the groan of the Yisra'elites, whom the Misrayimites are treating as serfs, and I've been mindful of my pact. ⁶Therefore say to the Yisra'elites, "I am Yahweh. I shall get you out from under the labours of Misrayim and rescue you from their servitude. I shall restore you by an outstretched arm and by great acts of authority. ⁷I shall take you for myself as a people and I shall be God for you, and you will acknowledge that I am Yahweh your God, the one who got you out from under the labours of Misrayim. ⁸I shall bring you to the country that I swore to give to Abraham, to Yitshaq and to Ya'aqob. I shall give it to you as a possession. I am Yahweh."'

⁹Mosheh spoke in this way to the Yisra'elites but they didn't listen to Mosheh because of a worn-out spirit and because of tough servitude.

¹⁰Yahweh spoke to Mosheh: ¹¹'Come speak to Par'oh king of Misrayim so he may send off the

Yisraëlites from his country.' ¹²Mosheh spoke before Yahweh: 'Here, the Yisraëlites didn't listen to me, so how will Par'oh listen to me, when I'm foreskinned of lips?' ¹³But Yahweh spoke to Mosheh and Aharon and gave them orders about the Yisraëlites and about Par'oh king of Misrayim, to get the Yisraëlites out of the country of Misrayim.

The family register

¹⁴These are the heads of their ancestral households:
The descendants of Re'uben, Yisra'el's firstborn: Hanok and Pallu, Hetsron and Karmi; these are Re'uben's kin-groups.
¹⁵The descendants of Shim'on: Yemu'el, Yamin, Ohad, Yakin, Tsohar, and Sha'ul, the son of a Kena'anite woman; these are Shim'on's kin-groups.
¹⁶These are the names of Levi's descendants by their lines of descent: Gershon, Qehat and Merari (the span of Levi's life was 137 years).
¹⁷The descendants of Gershon: Libni and Shim'i, by their kin-groups.
¹⁸The descendants of Qehat: Amram, Itshar, Hebron and Uzzi'el (the span of Qehat's life was 133 years).
¹⁹The descendants of Merari: Mahli and Mushi.
These are Levi's kin-groups by their lines of descent:
²⁰Amram got himself as wife Yokebed, his aunt. She gave birth to Aharon and Mosheh for him (the span of Amram's life was 137 years).
²¹The descendants of Itshar: Qorah, Nepheg and Zikri.
²²The descendants of Uzzi'el: Misha'el, Eltsaphan and Sitri.
²³Aharon got for himself as wife Elisheba, the daughter of Amminadab and sister of Nahshon; she gave birth to Nadab and Abihu, El'azar and Itamar, for him.
²⁴The descendants of Qorah: Assir, Elqanah and Abi'asaph; these are the kin-groups of the Qorahites.
²⁵El'azar ben Aharon got for himself as wife one of Puti'el's daughters, and she gave birth to Pinhas for him.

These are the heads of the Levites' ancestral households by their kin-groups.
²⁶That was Aharon and Mosheh to whom Yahweh said, 'Get the Yisraëlites out of the country of Misrayim by their armies.' ²⁷They were the people who spoke to Par'oh king of Misrayim about getting the Yisraëlites out of Misrayim. That was Mosheh and Aharon.

The stiffening of Par'oh's resolve

²⁸On the day Yahweh spoke to Mosheh in the country of Misrayim, ²⁹and Yahweh spoke to Mosheh: 'I am Yahweh: speak to Par'oh king of Misrayim all that I'm going to speak to you', ³⁰Mosheh said before Yahweh, 'Here, I am foreskinned of lips, so how will Pharoah listen to me?'

7 But Yahweh said to Mosheh, 'Look, I am making you God to Par'oh, and Aharon your brother will be your prophet. ²You – you are to speak all that I order you, and Aharon your brother is to speak to Par'oh so he may send off the Yisraëlites from his country. ³But I myself will toughen Par'oh's mind so I may do my many signs and proofs in the country of Misrayim. ⁴Par'oh won't listen to you, and I shall set my hand against Misrayim, and I shall get my armies, my people, the Yisraëlites, out of the country of Misrayim, with great acts of authority. ⁵So the Misrayimites will acknowledge that I am Yahweh when I stretch out my hand over Misrayim and get the Yisraëlites out from among them.'

⁶Mosheh and Aharon did as Yahweh ordered them; so they did. ⁷Mosheh was a man of eighty years and Aharon a man of eighty-three years when they spoke to Par'oh.

⁸Yahweh said to Mosheh and to Aharon: ⁹'When Par'oh speaks to you, "Give us a proof for yourselves", you're to say to Aharon, "Get your staff and throw it before Par'oh; it is to become a serpent."' ¹⁰So Mosheh and Aharon came to Par'oh and did so, as Yahweh ordered. Aharon threw his staff before Par'oh and before his servants, and it became a serpent. ¹¹Par'oh, too, called for the experts and the sorcerers, and the Misrayimite wizards did so, too, with their spells. ¹²They threw, each one, his staff and they became serpents. Then Aharon's staff swallowed their staffs. ¹³But Par'oh's mind

was adamant, and he didn't listen to them, as Yahweh had spoken.

The Ye'or becomes blood

¹⁴Yahweh said to Mosheh, 'Par'oh's mind is heavy. He refuses to send the people off. ¹⁵Go to Par'oh in the morning. There, he'll be going out to the water. Take your stand to meet him at the edge of the Ye'or. The staff that turned into a snake – take it in your hand. ¹⁶Say to him, "Yahweh, the God of the Hebrews, has sent me to you to say, 'Send my people off so they may serve me in the wilderness.' But here, you haven't listened so far.

¹⁷Yahweh has said this: 'Because of this you'll acknowledge that I am Yahweh.' Here, I'm going to strike the water in the Ye'or with the staff that's in my hand, and it will turn into blood. ¹⁸The fish that are in the Ye'or – they'll die. The Ye'or will stink. The Misrayimites will be loath to drink water from the Ye'or.'"

¹⁹Yahweh said to Mosheh, 'Say to Aharon, "Get your staff and stretch out your hand over the water of Misrayim, over its rivers, over its canals, over its ponds, over every body of water, so they become blood. There'll be blood in the entire country of Misrayim, even in wood and stone [containers]."'

²⁰Mosheh and Aharon did so, as Yahweh ordered. He lifted the staff and struck the water in the Ye'or before the eyes of Par'oh and before the eyes of his servants, and all the water that was in the Ye'or turned into blood. ²¹The fish that were in the Ye'or – they died. The Ye'or stank. The Misrayimites couldn't drink water from the Ye'or. There was blood in the entire country of Misrayim.

²²But Misrayimite experts did so with their spells, and Par'oh's mind was adamant and he didn't listen to them, as Yahweh had spoken. ²³Par'oh turned his face and came to his house. He didn't give his mind to this, either. ²⁴All Misrayim dug round the Ye'or for water to drink, because they couldn't drink from the Ye'or water.

Praying for the oppressor

²⁵Seven days were fulfilled after Yahweh struck the Ye'or,

8 then Yahweh said to Mosheh, 'Come to Par'oh and say to him, "Yahweh has said this: 'Send my people off so they may serve me. ²If you're going to refuse to send them off: here, I'm going to hit your entire border with frogs. ³The Ye'or will teem with frogs. They'll climb up and come into your house, into your bedroom and into your bed, and into your servants' house, and in among your people, and into your ovens and into your mixing bowls. ⁴Yes, on to you and on to your people and on to all your servants the frogs will climb up.'"'

⁵Yahweh said to Mosheh, 'Say to Aharon, "Stretch out your hand with your staff over the rivers, over the canals and over the ponds, and get the frogs to climb up on to the country of Misrayim."' ⁶Aharon stretched out his hand over the water in Misrayim, and the frogs came up and covered the country of Misrayim. ⁷But the experts did so with their spells and got the frogs to climb up on to the country of Misrayim.

⁸Par'oh called for Mosheh and Aharon and said, 'Entreat Yahweh to remove the frogs from me and from my people, and I'll send the people off so they may sacrifice for Yahweh.' ⁹Mosheh said to Par'oh, 'You may have the honour over me about when I entreat for you, for your servants and for your people, to cut off the frogs from you and from your houses. Only in the Ye'or will they remain.' ¹⁰He said, 'Tomorrow'. He said, 'According to your word, in order that you may acknowledge that there's no one like Yahweh our God. ¹¹The frogs will depart from you, from your houses, from your servants and from your people. Only in the Ye'or will they remain.'

An epidemic of lice

¹²Mosheh and Aharon went out from Par'oh, Mosheh cried out to Yahweh about the frogs that he had brought on Par'oh, ¹³and Yahweh acted in accordance with Mosheh's word. The frogs died away from the houses, from the courtyards and from the fields. ¹⁴They piled them up, heaps and heaps. The country stank. ¹⁵But when Par'oh saw that there was relief, he firmed up his mind and didn't listen to them, as Yahweh had spoken.

¹⁶Yahweh said to Mosheh, 'Say to Aharon, "Hold out your staff and strike the country's soil so it becomes lice in the entire country of Misrayim."' ¹⁷They did so. Aharon stretched out his hand with his staff and struck the country's soil, and lice were on human beings and on animals. All the country's soil became lice in the entire country of Misrayim. ¹⁸The experts did so with their spells to make lice issue, but they couldn't. So the lice were on human beings and on animals. ¹⁹The experts said to Par'oh, 'This is the finger of God.' But Par'oh's mind was adamant and he didn't listen to them, as Yahweh had spoken.

²⁰Yahweh said to Mosheh, 'Start early in the morning and take your stand before Par'oh. There, he'll be going out to the water. You're to say to him, "Yahweh has said this: 'Send my people off so they may serve me. ²¹Because if you don't send my people off – here, I'm going to send swarms of flies on you, on your servants, on your people and on your houses. The houses of Misrayim will be full of the swarms of flies, and also the ground that they walk on. ²²But on that day I'll make a distinction between the Goshen region on which my people stand, so there's no swarm of flies there, in order that you may acknowledge that I am Yahweh, within the country. ²³I shall put a redemption between my people and your people. Tomorrow this sign will come about."'"

Swarms of flies

²⁴Yahweh did so. Heavy swarms of flies came into Par'oh's house and into his servants' house. In the entire country of Misrayim the country was devastated in the face of the swarms of flies. ²⁵Par'oh called for Mosheh and Aharon and said, 'Go, sacrifice for Yahweh your God within the country.' ²⁶Mosheh said, 'It isn't established to do so, because what we sacrifice for Yahweh our God is an offence to Misrayimites. If we sacrifice what is an offence to Misrayimites before your eyes, won't they stone us? ²⁷We want to go three days' journey into the wilderness to sacrifice for Yahweh our God, as he says to us.'

²⁸Par'oh said, 'I myself will send you off so you may sacrifice for Yahweh your God in the wilderness. Only don't go any great distance. Entreat for me.' ²⁹Mosheh said, 'Here I am, going out from before you, and I'll entreat Yahweh so the swarms of flies depart from Par'oh and from his servants and from his people tomorrow. Only, Par'oh must not again play about by not sending the people off to sacrifice for Yahweh.'

³⁰Mosheh went out from before Par'oh and entreated Yahweh. ³¹Yahweh acted in accordance with Mosheh's word and removed the swarms of flies from Par'oh, from his servants and from his people. Not one remained. ³²But Par'oh firmed up his mind this time, too, and did not send the people off.

The distinction between Misrayim and Yisra'el

9 Yahweh said to Mosheh: 'Come to Par'oh and speak to him: "Yahweh, the God of the Hebrews, has said this: 'Send my people off so they may serve me. ²Because if you refuse to send them off and still keep strong hold on to them, ³here – Yahweh's hand is going to be on your livestock that's in the fields, on the horses, on the donkeys, on the camels, on the herd and on the flock, with a very heavy pestilence. ⁴But Yahweh will make a distinction between Yisra'el's livestock and Misrayim's livestock. Of all that belongs to the Yisra'elites not a thing will die. ⁵Yahweh has fixed a set time: tomorrow Yahweh will do this thing in the country.'"

⁶Yahweh did this thing next day. All Misrayim's livestock died; of the Yisra'elites' livestock, not one died. ⁷Par'oh sent, and there – not even one of Yisra'el's livestock had died. But Par'oh's mind was firm. He didn't send off the people.

⁸Yahweh said to Mosheh and to Aharon, 'Get yourselves fistfuls of kiln ash. Mosheh is to toss it into the heavens before Par'oh's eyes. ⁹It will become dust on the entire country of Misrayim, and on human beings and on animals it will become an inflammation breaking out in blisters in the entire country of Misrayim.'

¹⁰They got the kiln ash and stood before Par'oh. Mosheh tossed it into the heavens and it became an inflammation breaking out in blisters on human beings and on animals. ¹¹The wizards were not able to stand before

Mosheh because of the inflammation, because the inflammation was on the wizards and on all Misrayim. ¹²But Yahweh made Par'oh's mind adamant and he didn't listen to them, as Yahweh has spoken to Mosheh.

The acknowledgement needed

¹³Yahweh said to Mosheh, 'Start early in the morning and take your stand before Par'oh, and say to him, "Yahweh, the God of the Hebrews, has said this: 'Send my people off so they may serve me. ¹⁴Because this time I'm going to send all my blows towards your mind, and on your servants and on your people, in order that you may acknowledge that there's no one like me, in the entire country. ¹⁵Because by now, had I sent my hand and struck down you and your people with an epidemic, you would have been effaced from the country. ¹⁶Yet for this purpose I've let you stand, for the purpose of getting you to see my energy and for the sake of recounting my name in the entire country. ¹⁷You're still exalting yourself over my people so as not to send them off.

¹⁸Here, this very time tomorrow I'm going to make it rain very heavy hail, such as hasn't happened in Misrayim from the day of its founding until now. ¹⁹So now, send to bring into safety your livestock and everything that you have in the fields. Any human beings or animals that are found in the fields and don't gather in the house, the hail will come down on them and they'll die.'"

²⁰Anyone among Par'oh's servants who was in awe of Yahweh's word got his servants and his livestock to flee into their houses, ²¹but whoever didn't give his mind to Yahweh's word abandoned his servants and his livestock in the fields. ²²And Yahweh said to Mosheh, 'Stretch out your hand over the heavens so hail may come through the entire country of Misrayim, on human beings and on animals and on all the plants of the wild in the country of Misrayim.'

Par'oh flip-flop

²³So Mosheh stretched out his staff over the heavens. As Yahweh sent a great noise, and hail and fire fell on the ground, Yahweh rained hail on the country of Misrayim. ²⁴Hail came, with fire flashing about in the middle of the hail, very heavy, such as had not come in the entire country of Misrayim since it became a nation. ²⁵In the entire country of Misrayim, the hail struck down everything that was in the fields, both human beings and animals. All the plants in the fields it struck down, and all the trees in the fields it broke off. ²⁶Only in the Goshen region, where the Yisra'elites were, was there no hail.

²⁷Par'oh sent and called for Mosheh and Aharon and said to them, 'This time I've done wrong. Yahweh is in the right and I and my people are in the wrong. ²⁸Entreat Yahweh so this may be plenty of almighty noise and hail, and I shall send you off. You'll stay no longer.'

²⁹Mosheh said to him, 'As I go out of the town, I shall spread the palms of my hands to Yahweh. The great noise – it will leave off, the hail – it will be no more, in order that you may acknowledge that the country belongs to Yahweh. ³⁰But you and your servants: I know that you are not yet in awe of Yahweh.' ³¹The flax and the barley were struck down, because the barley was ripening and the flax was budding, ³²but the wheat and hulled wheat were not struck down, because they are late-ripening.

³³Mosheh went out of the town from being with Par'oh and spread the palms of his hands to Yahweh, and the great noise and the hail left off and the rain didn't pour on the earth. ³⁴But Par'oh saw that the rain, the hail and the great noise had left off, and he did wrong again and firmed up his mind, he and his servants. ³⁵So Par'oh's mind remained adamant and he didn't send the Yisra'elites off – as Yahweh had spoken through Mosheh.

An epidemic of locusts

10 Yahweh said to Mosheh, 'Come to Par'oh, because I've hardened his mind and his servants' mind in order to set these signs of mine in his midst ²and in order that you may recount in the ears of your son and your grandson how I acted abusively against Misrayim, and my signs that I have set among them, so you may acknowledge that I am Yahweh.'

³So Mosheh and Aharon came to Par'oh and said to him, 'Yahweh the God of the Hebrews has said this: "How long do you refuse to humble yourself before me? Send my people off so they may serve me. ⁴Because if you refuse to send my people off – here, I'm going to bring a locust swarm into your border tomorrow. ⁵It will cover the face of the land; people won't be able to see the land. It will eat the rest of what escaped, which remained to you from the hail. It will eat every tree that grows for you, from the fields. ⁶They will fill your houses, all your servants' houses and all Misrayim's houses, something that your fathers and grandfathers didn't see, from the day they came into existence on the land until this day."' And he turned his face and went out from being with Par'oh.

⁷Par'oh's servants said to him, 'How long will this man be a snare for us? Send the people off so they may serve Yahweh their God. Don't you yet acknowledge that Misrayim is lost?' ⁸So Mosheh and Aharon were brought back to Par'oh, and he said to them, 'Go, serve Yahweh your God. Who exactly are going?' ⁹Mosheh said, 'With our young and with our old we will go, with our sons and with our daughters, with our flock and with our herd we will go, because it's Yahweh's festival for us.'

Repentance and more flip-flop

¹⁰He said to them, 'May Yahweh be with you indeed when I send you and your little ones off! See, you have something bad in view. ¹¹Definitely not. You men do go and serve Yahweh, because this is what you're seeking.' And they were driven out of Par'oh's presence. ¹²Yahweh said to Mosheh, 'Stretch out your hand over the country of Misrayim with the locust swarm, so it may come over the country of Misrayim and eat all the plants in the country, anything that the hail left remaining.' ¹³So Mosheh stretched out his staff over the country of Misrayim and Yahweh drove an east wind through the country all that day and all night. When the morning came, the east wind had carried the locust swarm. ¹⁴The locust swarm came over the entire country of Misrayim and settled down in the entire border of Misrayim, very heavy. There had not been a locust swarm like it before it, and after it there would not be. ¹⁵It covered the face of the entire country. The country was dark. It ate all the plants in the country and all the fruit on the trees that the hail had left. Nothing green was left of the trees or the plants in the fields in the entire country of Misrayim.

¹⁶Par'oh hurried to call for Mosheh and for Aharon and said, 'I've done wrong against Yahweh your God and against you. ¹⁷But now, please carry my wrongdoing only this time. Entreat Yahweh your God that he only remove this death from me.'

¹⁸He went out from being with Par'oh and entreated Yahweh, ¹⁹and Yahweh changed a very strong west wind. It carried the locust swarm and threw it into the Reed Sea. Not one of the locust swarm remained in the entire border of Misrayim. ²⁰But Yahweh made Par'oh's mind adamant and he didn't send the Yisra'elites off.

You won't see my face again

²¹Yahweh said to Mosheh, 'Stretch out your hand over the heavens so there may be darkness over the country of Misrayim and so one can feel darkness.' ²²Mosheh stretched out his hand over the heavens and there was thick darkness through the entire country of Misrayim for three days. ²³No one could see his brother and no one could get up from where he was for three days. But for all the Yisra'elites there was light in their settlements.

²⁴Par'oh called for Mosheh and said, 'Go, serve Yahweh. Only your flock and your herd must be laid down. Even your little ones can go with you.' ²⁵Mosheh said, 'You yourself are to give into our hand sacrifices and burnt offerings so we may make them for Yahweh our God, ²⁶and also our livestock will go with us (not a hoof will remain behind) because we shall take some of it to serve Yahweh our God, and we ourselves won't know with what we shall serve Yahweh until we come there.'

²⁷But Yahweh made Par'oh's mind adamant and he was not willing to send them off. ²⁸Par'oh said to him, 'Get away from me! Keep watch over yourself: don't see my face again, because on the day you see my face, you'll die.' ²⁹Mosheh said, 'You've spoken correctly. I shall not see your face ever again.'

The final threat

11 Yahweh said to Mosheh, 'There's yet one more blow I shall bring on Par'oh and on Misrayim. After that, he will send you off from here. When he sends you off, it will be complete. He will finally drive you out of here. ²Speak in the ears of the people, please, so they ask for objects of silver and gold, each man from his neighbour and each woman from her neighbour.' ³Yahweh gave the people grace in the eyes of Misrayim. Mosheh himself was also very big in the country of Misrayim in the eyes of Par'oh's servants and in the eyes of the people.

⁴Mosheh said, 'Yahweh has said this: "At midnight, I'm going out among the Misrayimites. ⁵Every firstborn in the country of Misrayim will die, from the firstborn of Par'oh who sits on the throne to the firstborn of the maidservant who is behind the millstones, and every firstborn of the animals." ⁶There will be a loud cry in the entire country of Misrayim such as has not been and will not be again. ⁷But at any of the Yisra'elites a dog won't growl, either at a person or at an animal, in order that you may acknowledge that Yahweh makes a distinction between Misrayim and Yisra'el. ⁸All these servants of yours will come down to me and bow low to me saying, "Get out, you and all your people who follow you." After, that I'll go out.' He went out from Par'oh's presence in an angry rage.

⁹Yahweh had said to Mosheh, 'Par'oh won't listen to you, in order that my proofs may become numerous in the country of Misrayim', ¹⁰and Mosheh and Aharon had performed all these proofs before Par'oh, but Yahweh had made Par'oh's mind adamant and he had not sent the Yisra'elites off from his country.

Instructions for a solemn celebration

12 Yahweh said to Mosheh and to Aharon in the country of Misrayim: ²'This month is to be the beginning of the months for you. It's to be the first of the months in the year for you. ³Speak to the entire Yisra'elite assembly: "On the tenth of this month they're to get for themselves, each man, a lamb for the ancestral family, a lamb for the household. ⁴If the household is too small for a lamb, he and his neighbour near his household are to get one, on the basis of a count of the persons. Each person according to what he will eat, you're to calculate for the lamb. ⁵Your lamb is to be whole, male, a year old. You may get it from the sheep or from the goats.

⁶It's to be in your keeping until the fourteenth day of this month, then the entire Yisra'elite assembled congregation are to slaughter it at twilight. ⁷They're to get some of the blood and put it on the two doorposts and on the lintel of the houses where they'll eat it. ⁸They're to eat the meat this night. They're to eat it roasted in fire, with flatbread and bitters. ⁹Don't eat any of it raw or boiled (boiled in water), please, but rather roasted in fire, including its head, with its legs and its innards. ¹⁰You're not to leave any of it until morning. What's left of it until morning, you're to burn in fire.

¹¹This is how you're to eat it: your hips wrapped round, your boots on your feet, your cane in your hand. You're to eat it in haste. It's a Pesah [Passover] for Yahweh. ¹²I shall pass through the country of Misrayim this night and strike down every firstborn in the country of Misrayim, human beings and animals. On all the Misrayimite gods I shall perform acts of authority. I am Yahweh.

¹³But for you the blood will be a sign on the houses where you are. I'll see the blood and pass over you. No blow to devastate will come on you when I strike down the country of Misrayim.

A reminder

¹⁴This day is to be for you a reminder. You're to observe it as a festival for Yahweh. Through your generations you're to observe it, a permanent decree. ¹⁵For seven days you're to eat flatbread. On the first day you're totally to eliminate yeast from your houses (because anyone who eats leavened bread – that person shall be cut off from Yisra'el), from the first day to the seventh day.

¹⁶On the first day it's a sacred occasion and on the seventh day a sacred occasion for you. No work will be done among you. Only what is to be eaten by a person, that alone may be

prepared by you. ¹⁷You're to keep Flatbread, because on this particular day I got your armies out of the country of Misrayim. You're to keep this day through your generations, a permanent decree. ¹⁸In the first month on the fourteenth day in the evening, you're to eat flatbread, until the twenty-first day of the month in the evening. ¹⁹For seven days yeast is not to be found in your houses, because anyone who eats leavened bread – that person shall be cut off from the Yisra'elite assembly, whether being a resident or a native. ²⁰You will eat no leavened bread. In all your settlements you will eat flatbread."'

²¹Mosheh called for all Yisra'el's elders and said to them, 'Go out, get yourselves sheep for your kin-groups and slaughter the Pesah. ²²Get a bunch of hyssop, dip it in the blood that's in the basin, and touch the lintel and the two doorposts with the blood that's in the basin. You – you're not to go outside, anyone, from the entrance of his house until morning. ²³Yahweh will pass through to hit Misrayim, but he will see the blood on the lintel and on the two doorposts. Yahweh will pass by the entrance and not let the devastater come into your households to hit them.

The scream

²⁴You're to keep this word as a permanent decree for yourself and for your descendants. ²⁵When you come into the country that Yahweh will give you, as he spoke, you're to keep this service. ²⁶When your children say to you, "What is this service for you?" ²⁷you're to say, "It's the Pesah sacrifice for Yahweh, because he passed over the Yisra'elites' households in Misrayim, when he hit Misrayim but rescued our households."' The people bent their heads and bowed low.
²⁸The Yisra'elites went and did as Yahweh ordered Mosheh and Aharon; so they did. ²⁹In the middle of the night Yahweh struck down every firstborn in the country of Misrayim, from the firstborn of Par'oh who sat on the throne to the firstborn of the captive who was in the cistern, and every firstborn of an animal. ³⁰Par'oh got up in the night, he and all his servants and all Misrayim, and there was a loud crying out in Misrayim, because

there was no household where there was not someone dead. ³¹He called for Mosheh and Aharon in the night and said, 'Set off, get out from among my people, both you and the Yisra'elites. Go, serve Yahweh in accordance with your word. ³²Both your flock and your herd – take them as you have spoken. Go. But bless me also.'
³³Misrayim was firm with the people, hurrying to send them off from the country, because (they said), 'We're all going to be dead.' ³⁴So the people picked up their dough before it was leavened, their mixing bowls wrapped in their clothes, on their shoulder.
³⁵The Yisra'elites had acted in accordance with Mosheh's word and asked the Misrayimites for objects of silver and gold, and clothes, ³⁶and Yahweh had given the people grace in the eyes of the Misrayimites so they had let them ask. So they stripped the Misrayimites.

A huge company

³⁷The Yisra'elites moved on from Ra'meses to Sukkot, some 600,000 men on foot apart from little ones. ³⁸A mixed crowd also went up with them, and a flock and herd, very substantial livestock. ³⁹They baked the dough they had brought out of Misrayim into flatbread loaves because it was not leavened, because they'd been driven out of Misrayim and hadn't been able to delay, and also they hadn't made provisions for themselves.
⁴⁰The Yisra'elites' settlement that they had had in Misrayim lasted 430 years. ⁴¹At the end of 430 years, on that particular day all Yahweh's armies came out of the country of Misrayim. ⁴²It was a night of keeping watch for Yahweh, in getting them out of the country of Misrayim. For the Yisra'elites through their generations this night is one of keeping watch for Yahweh.
⁴³Yahweh said to Mosheh and Aharon, 'This is the Pesah decree. While no one born of a foreigner may eat of it, ⁴⁴any person who is a servant, acquired for silver, but you've circumcised him – he may then eat of it. ⁴⁵A settler or employee may not eat of it.
⁴⁶It's to be eaten in one house. You may not take any of the meat outside the house. You may not break any bone of it. ⁴⁷The entire

Yisra'elite assembly is to do this. ⁴⁸When someone is a resident with you and makes Pesaḥ for Yahweh, every male belonging to him is to be circumcised, and then he may draw near to perform it; he'll be like a native of the country. But anyone who is foreskinned may not eat of it. ⁴⁹There is to be one instruction for the native and for the person who is a resident among you.'

⁵⁰All the Yisra'elites did as Yahweh ordered Mosheh and Aharon; so they did. ⁵¹This particular day Yahweh got the Yisra'elites out of the country of Misrayim by their armies.

The reminders

13 Yahweh spoke to Mosheh: ²'Make every firstborn sacred for me; the one who opens every womb among the Yisra'elites, human being or animal, is mine.'

³Mosheh said to the people, 'Be mindful of this day when you got out of Misrayim, out of a household of serfs, because Yahweh got you out of it by strength of hand. No leavened bread is to be eaten. ⁴Today you're going out, in the month of Aviv. ⁵When Yahweh brings you into the country of the Kena'anites, the Hittites, the Amorites, the Hivvites and the Yebusites, which he swore to your ancestors to give you, a country flowing with milk and syrup, you're to perform this service in this month.

⁶For seven days you're to eat flatbread, and on the seventh day there's to be a festival for Yahweh. ⁷Flatbread is to be eaten through the seven days. Leavened bread is not to appear among you. Yeast is not to appear among you in your entire border. ⁸You're to tell your child on that day, "It's because of what Yahweh did for me when I got out of Misrayim." ⁹It will be a sign for you on your hand and a reminder between your eyes, in order that Yahweh's instruction may be in your mouth, because Yahweh got you out of Misrayim with a strong hand. ¹⁰You're to keep this decree at its set time from year to year.

¹¹When Yahweh brings you into the country of the Kena'anites as he swore to you and to your ancestors, and gives it to you, ¹²you're to pass on every opener of the womb to Yahweh. Every opener (the drop of an animal that belongs to you), the males are Yahweh's.

¹³Any donkey's opener you're to redeem with a sheep; if you don't redeem it, you're to break its neck. Every human opener among your children, you're to redeem.

The long way round

¹⁴When your child asks in the future "What is this?" you're to say to him, "Yahweh got us out of Misrayim, out of a household of serfs, by strength of hand. ¹⁵When Par'oh was tough about sending us off, Yahweh killed every firstborn in the country of Misrayim, both human firstborn and animal firstborn. That's why I'm sacrificing for Yahweh every opener of the womb, the males, but I redeem the firstborn among my sons." ¹⁶So it will be a sign on your hand and a symbol between your eyes, because Yahweh got us out of Misrayim by strength of hand.'

¹⁷When Par'oh sent the people off, God didn't lead them by the road to the Pelishtites' [Philistines'] country because it was near, because (God said), 'So that the people don't have a change of heart when they see battle, and turn back to Misrayim.' ¹⁸God made the people go round by the wilderness road to the Reed Sea.

The Yisra'elites went up from the country of Misrayim organized into companies. ¹⁹Mosheh took Yoseph's bones with him, because he had made the Yisra'elites solemnly swear, 'God will definitely attend to you, and you're to take up my bones from here with you.' ²⁰They moved on from Sukkot and camped at Etam at the edge of the wilderness, ²¹with Yahweh going before them by day in a cloud pillar to lead them on the way and by night in a fire pillar to give them light, so they could go by day or night. ²²The cloud pillar by day and the fire pillar by night would not move away from before the people.

One kind of fear turns to another

14 Yahweh spoke to Mosheh: ²'Speak to the Yisra'elites: they're to turn back and camp before Pi Hahirot, between Migdol and the sea. You're to camp before Ba'al Tsephon, opposite it, by the sea. ³Par'oh will say of the Yisra'elites, "They're lost in the region. The wilderness has closed in on them." ⁴I shall make Par'oh's mind adamant and he'll pursue after them, so I may show my splendour through Par'oh and all his force, and the Misrayimites may acknowledge that I am Yahweh.' They did so.

⁵It was told the king of Misrayim that the people had taken flight, and the mind of Par'oh and his servants towards the people changed. They said, 'What's this that we've done, that we've sent Yisra'el off from serving us?' ⁶He harnessed his chariot and took his people with him, ⁷and took 600 picked chariotry, and the entire Misrayimite chariotry, with adjutants over all of them.

⁸So Yahweh made the mind of Par'oh king of Misrayim adamant and he pursued after the Yisra'elites as the Yisra'elites were leaving with hand high. ⁹The Misrayimites pursued after them and overtook them camping by the sea, all Par'oh's chariot horses, his riders and his force, near Pi Hahirot, opposite Ba'al Tsephon.

¹⁰As Par'oh got near, the Yisra'elites lifted their eyes, and there, the Misrayimites were moving on after them, and they were very fearful. The Yisra'elites cried out to Yahweh, ¹¹and said to Mosheh, 'Was it for lack of graves in Misrayim that you took us to die in the wilderness? What's this you've done to us in getting us out of Misrayim? ¹²Isn't this the thing we spoke to you in Misrayim, "Leave off from us and we'll serve the Misrayimites, because serving the Misrayimites is better for us than dying in the wilderness"?'

Why should you cry out to me?

¹³Mosheh said to the people, 'Don't be fearful. Take your stand and see Yahweh's deliverance, which he'll effect for you today. Because the Misrayimites you've seen today you won't see any more, ever again, permanently. ¹⁴Yahweh – he will do battle for you. You – you can stay quiet.'

¹⁵Yahweh said to Mosheh, 'Why should you cry out to me? Speak to the Yisra'elites so they may move on. ¹⁶You yourself, lift up your staff and stretch out your hand over the sea and divide it so the Yisra'elites may come into the middle of the sea on the dry ground.

¹⁷And I – here am I, making the Misrayimites' mind adamant so they come after them. I shall show my splendour through Par'oh and through all his force, through his chariotry and through his cavalry. ¹⁸The Misrayimites will acknowledge that I am Yahweh when I show my splendour through Par'oh, through his chariotry and through his cavalry.'

¹⁹God's envoy, who had been going before the Yisra'elite camp, moved on and went behind them, and the cloud pillar moved on from before them and stood behind them, ²⁰so it came between the Misrayimite camp and the Yisra'elite camp. So there was the cloud and the darkness, though it lit the night.

The one didn't draw near the other all night, ²¹but Mosheh stretched out his hand over the sea and Yahweh caused the sea to go by means of a vigorous east wind, all night, and made the sea into parched ground. So the water split ²²and the Yisra'elites came into the middle of the sea on the dry ground, with the water a wall for them on their right and on their left. ²³The Misrayimites pursued, and all Par'oh's horse, his chariotry and his cavalry came into the middle of the sea.

The good kind of fear returns

²⁴At the morning watch Yahweh looked out at the Misrayimite camp through the fire and cloud pillar, and made the Misrayimite camp turmoil. ²⁵He jammed the wheels of its chariotry so they drove them with difficulty. Misrayim said, 'I must flee from before Yisra'el, because Yahweh is battling for them against Misrayim.'

²⁶Yahweh said to Mosheh, 'Stretch out your hand over the sea, so the water comes back over Misrayim, over its chariotry and over its cavalry.' ²⁷Mosheh stretched out his hand over the sea, and as morning turned its face the sea came back to its regular position while the Misrayimites were fleeing to meet it. So Yahweh shook the Misrayimites off into the middle of the sea. ²⁸The water came back and covered the chariotry and the cavalry. As for all Par'oh's force coming behind them into the sea, not one of them remained. ²⁹But the Yisra'elites: they had gone on dry ground in the middle of the sea with the water a wall for them on their right and on their left.

³⁰Yahweh delivered Yisraʼel that day from the hand of Misrayim. Yisraʼel saw Misrayim dead on the shore of the sea. ³¹Yisraʼel saw the great control with which Yahweh had acted against Misrayim, and they were in awe of Yahweh. They trusted in Yahweh and in his servant Mosheh.

Yes, Yahweh reigns

15 Then Mosheh and the Yisraʼelites sang this song for Yahweh. They said:

I'll sing for Yahweh because he acted
    majestically, so majestically:
  horse and its rider he threw into the sea.
²Yah is my vigour and my strength:
  he became my deliverance.
This is my God – I'll glorify him:
  my father's God – I'll exalt him.
³Yahweh is a strong man;
  Yahweh is his name.
⁴Parʼoh's chariotry and his force he threw into
    the sea,
  the pick of his adjutants sank in the Reed Sea.
⁵Deeps covered them,
  they went down into the depths like a stone.
⁶Your right hand, Yahweh, was triumphant in
    energy;
  your right hand, Yahweh, smashed the
    enemy.
⁷In the greatness of your majesty you tore down
    those who rose up against you;
  you sent off your rage, it devoured them like
    straw.
⁸At the blast of your nostrils
  water piled up.
Floods stood up as a heap,
  deeps solidified in the heart of the sea.
⁹The enemy said, 'I'll pursue, overtake;
  I'll share out spoil, my appetite will have its
    fill.
I'll bare my sword,
  my hand will dispossess them.'
¹⁰You blew with your blast, the sea covered
    them;
  they sank like lead in the august water.
¹¹Who is like you among the gods, Yahweh,
  who is like you, triumphant in sacredness,
Awe-inspiring in praises,
  doing extraordinary things?
¹²You stretched out your hand,
  earth swallowed them.
¹³In your commitment you've led the people
    that you restored,
  in your vigour you've guided them to your
    sacred abode.
¹⁴Peoples have heard and shuddered,
  writhing has seized the people living in
    Peleshet [Philistia].
¹⁵Then Edom's chiefs have become fearful,
  Moʼab's leaders.
A shudder has seized them,
  all the people living in Kenaʼan have melted.
¹⁶Alarm and dread have fallen upon them;
  through your arm's greatness they have
    become as still as stone,
Until your people have passed, Yahweh,
  until the people you acquired have passed.
¹⁷You've brought them and planted them on the
    mountain that is your domain,
  the established place for you to live in that
    you've made, Yahweh,
The sanctuary, Lord, your hands have
    established:
¹⁸Yahweh will reign for ever and ever!

Dancing, singing, protesting

¹⁹Because Parʼoh's horse, his chariotry and his riders came into the sea, and Yahweh let the sea's water come back on them, whereas the Yisraʼelites went on dry ground in the middle of the sea. ²⁰Miryam the prophetess, Aharon's sister, took a tambourine in her hand, and all the women went out after her with tambourines and with dancing. ²¹Miryam chanted for them:

Sing for Yahweh, because he has acted
    majestically, so majestically:
  horse and its rider he threw into the sea.

²²Mosheh got Yisraʼel to move on from the Reed Sea and they went out into the Shur Wilderness. They went for three days in the wilderness, and found no water. ²³They came to Marah [Bitter] and couldn't drink water from Marah because it was bitter; that's why they named it Marah. ²⁴The people protested at Mosheh: 'What are we to drink?' ²⁵He cried out to Yahweh, and Yahweh pointed

out some wood. He threw it into the water and the water became sweet.

He made a decree, a ruling for them there; he tested them there. ²⁶He said, 'If you listen attentively to the voice of Yahweh your God, do what is right in his eyes, give ear to his orders and keep all his decrees, I won't bring on you any of the diseases that I brought on Misrayim, because I am Yahweh your healer.'

²⁷They came to Elim. There were twelve springs of water there and seventy palms. They camped there by the water.

Protests in the wilderness

16 The entire assembly of the Yisra'elites moved on from Elim and came to the Syn Wilderness, which is between Elim and Sinay, on the fifteenth day of the second month after their leaving the country of Misrayim.
²The entire assembly of the Yisra'elites protested against Mosheh and Aharon in the wilderness. ³The Yisra'elites said to them, 'If only we had died by Yahweh's hand in the country of Misrayim when we sat by a pot of meat and ate bread till we were full – because you've brought us out into this wilderness to make this entire congregation die of hunger!'
⁴Yahweh said to Mosheh, 'Here, I'm going to rain bread for you from the heavens so the people may go out and glean a day's allocation on its day, in order that I may test it, whether it will walk by my instruction or not. ⁵On the sixth day they will prepare what they bring in and it will be double what they glean each day.'
⁶Mosheh and Aharon said to all the Yisra'elites, 'In the evening, then you will acknowledge that it was Yahweh who got you out of the country of Misrayim, ⁷and in the morning, then you'll see Yahweh's splendour, when he listens to your protests against Yahweh. But we – what are we that you protest against us?' ⁸Mosheh said, 'When Yahweh gives you meat in the evening to eat and bread in the morning till you're full, when Yahweh listens to your protests that you're making against him: what are we? Your protests are not against us but against Yahweh.'
⁹So Mosheh said to Aharon, 'Say to the entire assembly of the Yisra'elites, "Draw near before Yahweh, because he's listened to your protests."'

One day at a time

¹⁰As Aharon spoke to the entire assembly of the Yisra'elites, they turned their face to the wilderness, and there, Yahweh's splendour appeared in a cloud, ¹¹and Yahweh spoke to Mosheh: ¹²'I've listened to the Yisra'elites' protests. Speak to them: "At twilight you shall eat meat and in the morning you shall have your fill of bread, and you will acknowledge that I am Yahweh your God."'
¹³In the evening quail came up and covered the camp, and in the morning there was a layer of dew round the camp. ¹⁴The layer of dew came up, and there, on the face of the wilderness something fine, flaky, fine like frost, on the earth.
¹⁵The Yisra'elites saw it and said each to his brother, 'What [*maan*] is it?' because they didn't know what it was. Mosheh said to them, 'It's the bread that Yahweh has given you as food. ¹⁶This is the thing that Yahweh has ordered. Glean some of it, each of you, as much as he will eat, a gallon per head for the number of persons you are. You're to get it, each individual for the people who are in his tent.'
¹⁷The Yisra'elites did so. They gleaned, one person getting much, one getting little. ¹⁸But when they measured it by the gallon, the one who got much didn't have excess and the one who got little didn't lack. They had gleaned, each individual, as much as he would eat. ¹⁹Mosheh said to them, 'No one is to leave any of it over until morning.' ²⁰But they didn't listen to Mosheh. People left some of it over until morning, and it bred maggots and stank, and Mosheh was furious with them.

Manna

²¹So they gleaned it morning by morning, each person, as much as he would eat. When the sun got hot, it would melt. ²²On Friday they gleaned double bread, two gallons for a single person. All the assembly's leaders came and told Mosheh. ²³He said to them, 'It's what Yahweh spoke. Tomorrow is a stopping, a sacred sabbath [*shabbat*, 'stop'] for Yahweh. Bake what you will bake and boil what you will boil, and lay up for yourselves all that's surplus for keeping until morning.'

²⁴They laid it up until morning as Mosheh ordered. It didn't stink and there was no breeding in it. ²⁵Mosheh said, 'Eat it today, because today is a sabbath for Yahweh. Today you won't find it in the fields. ²⁶For six days you're to glean, but on the seventh day, the sabbath – there'll be none then.'

²⁷On the seventh day some of the people went out to glean, but they didn't find any. ²⁸Yahweh said to Mosheh, 'How long do you people refuse to keep my orders and my instructions? ²⁹See that it's Yahweh who's given you the sabbath. That's why he's giving bread for two days on the sixth day. Stay each person where he is. No one's to go out of his place on the seventh day.' ³⁰So the people stopped on the seventh day.

³¹The household of Yisra'el named it *maan* [manna]. It was like coriander seed, white. Its taste was like wafers with sweetener. ³²Mosheh said, 'This is the thing that Yahweh has ordered: "A full gallon of it is to be for keeping through your generations, in order that people may see the bread that I let you eat in the wilderness when I got you out of the country of Misrayim."' ³³So Mosheh said to Aharon, 'Get a container and put a full gallon of *maan* in it, and lay it up before Yahweh for keeping through your generations.' ³⁴As Yahweh ordered Mosheh, Aharon laid it up before the Affirmation, for keeping.

Hit the rock

³⁵The Yisra'elites ate the *maan* for forty years until they came to the edge of the country of Kena'an. (³⁶A gallon is a tenth of a barrel.)

17 The entire Yisra'elite assembly moved on from the Syn Wilderness by stages at Yahweh's bidding. They camped at Rephidim, but there was no water for the people to drink, ²and the people got into an argument with Mosheh. They said, 'Give us water so we can drink!' Mosheh said to them, 'Why argue with me? Why test Yahweh?' ³But the people were thirsty there for water.

So the people protested against Mosheh: 'Why was it that you brought us up from Misrayim to have me and my children and my livestock die of thirst?' ⁴Mosheh cried out to Yahweh, 'What shall I do about this people? A little while and they'll stone me!'

⁵Yahweh said to Mosheh, 'Pass before the people, take some of Yisra'el's elders with you and your staff with which you struck the Ye'or in your hand, and go. ⁶There, I'll be standing before you there on the crag at Horeb. You're to strike the crag, and water will come out of it, and the people will drink.'

Mosheh did so before the eyes of Yisra'el's elders. ⁷He named the place Massah and Meribah ['Testing' and 'Argument'], because of the Yisra'elites' arguing and because of their testing Yahweh by saying, 'Is Yahweh among us or isn't he?'

The first assailant

⁸Amaleq came and battled with Yisra'el at Rephidim. ⁹Mosheh said to Yehoshua [Joshua], 'Choose some men for us and go out and do battle against Amaleq. Tomorrow I'm going to take my stand on top of the hill with God's staff in my hand.'

¹⁰Yehoshua did as Mosheh told him by battling against Amaleq, while Mosheh, Aharon and Hur went up to the top of the hill. ¹¹As Mosheh would raise his hand, Yisra'el would prevail, but as he would rest his hand, Amaleq would prevail. ¹²So when Mosheh's hands were heavy, they got a stone and put it under him and he sat on it, while Aharon and Hur took hold of his hands, one on this side and one on that. So his hands were trustworthy until sundown ¹³and Yehoshua overwhelmed Amaleq and its people with the mouth of the sword.

¹⁴Yahweh said to Mosheh, 'Write this in a document as a reminder, and put it into Yehoshua's ears, how I shall totally wipe out Amaleq's memory from under the heavens.' ¹⁵Mosheh built an altar and named it 'Yahweh My Banner', ¹⁶and said, 'A hand against Yah's throne! There will be a battle for Yahweh against Amaleq from generation to generation!'

The first convert

18 Yitro the Midyanite priest, Mosheh's father-in-law, heard all that God had done for Mosheh and for his people Yisra'el, how Yahweh had got Yisra'el out of Misrayim. ²So Yitro, Mosheh's father-in-law, got Tsipporah, Mosheh's wife (after her sending away) ³and her two sons (of whom one had the name Gershom because – he said – 'I've been a resident [ger] in a foreign country' ⁴and the other had the name Eli'ezer because 'the God of my father has been my help [ezer] and rescued me from Par'oh's sword'), ⁵and Yitro, Mosheh's father-in-law, came with his sons and his wife to Mosheh in the wilderness where he was camped at God's mountain.

⁶He had said to Mosheh, 'I, your father-in-law Yitro, am coming to you with your wife and her two sons with her.' ⁷Mosheh went out to meet his father-in-law. He bowed low and kissed him. Each of them asked his neighbour about whether things were well, and they came into the tent.

⁸Mosheh recounted to his father-in-law all that Yahweh had done to Par'oh and to Misrayim for Yisra'el's sake, all the hardship that had befallen them on the way and how Yahweh had rescued them. ⁹Yitro rejoiced over all the good that Yahweh had done for Yisra'el when he rescued them from the hand of Misrayim. ¹⁰Yitro said, 'Yahweh be blessed, who rescued you from the hand of Misrayim and from the hand of Par'oh, who rescued the people from under the hand of Misrayim. ¹¹Now I acknowledge that Yahweh is greater than all gods, because in this matter they asserted themselves against them.' ¹²Yitro, Mosheh's father-in-law, got a burnt offering and sacrifices for God, and Aharon and all Yisra'el's elders came to eat a meal before God with Mosheh's father-in-law.

On not doing everything yourself

¹³Next day Mosheh sat to decide things for the people, and the people stood round Mosheh from the morning until the evening. ¹⁴Mosheh's father-in-law saw all that he was doing for the people and said, 'What's this thing that you're doing for the people? Why are you sitting on your own with the entire people taking a stand round you from morning until evening?' ¹⁵Mosheh said to his father-in-law, 'Because the people come to me to enquire of God. ¹⁶When they have something, it comes to me and I decide between one person and his neighbour, and I enable them to know God's decrees and his instructions.'

¹⁷Mosheh's father-in-law said to him, 'The thing that you're doing isn't good. ¹⁸You'll totally wear yourself out, both you and this people that's with you, too, because the thing's too heavy for you. You can't do it on your own. ¹⁹So now listen to my voice. I'll give you some counsel. And God be with you! You yourself be near God for the people and you yourself bring the things to God, ²⁰and make clear to them the decrees and the instructions and enable them to acknowledge the way in which they're to go and the action that they're to take. ²¹But from the entire people, you yourself are to behold capable individuals who live in awe of God, truthful individuals, who are hostile to dishonest gain, and to set them over them as divisional officials, section officials, unit officials and group officials, ²²to decide things for the people at all times. Every big thing they'll bring to you but every small thing they'll decide themselves. Make things lighter for yourself; they will carry things with you. ²³If you do this thing (and so God orders you), you'll be able to stand, and also this entire people will come to its place with things being well.'

²⁴Mosheh listened to the voice of his father-in-law and did everything that he said. ²⁵Mosheh chose capable individuals from all Yisra'el and made them heads over the people, divisional officials, section officials, unit officials and group officials. ²⁶They would decide things for the people at all times. The tough thing they'd bring to Mosheh, but every small thing they'd decide themselves.

²⁷Then Mosheh sent his father-in-law off, and he went his way to his own country.

Two kinds of preparation for meeting God

19 At the beginning of the third month after the Yisra'elites came out of the country of Misrayim, on that day they came to the Sinay Wilderness. ²They moved on from Rephidim, came to the Sinay Wilderness and camped in the wilderness. Yisra'el camped there in front of the mountain ³and Mosheh went up to God.

Yahweh called to him from the mountain: 'You're to say this to the household of Ya'aqob and to tell the Yisra'elites, ⁴"You yourselves saw what I did to Misrayim. I lifted you on eagles' wings and brought you to me. ⁵So now, if you really listen to my voice and keep my pact, you'll be for me personal treasure from among all the peoples. Because the entire earth is mine, ⁶but you in particular will be a priestly kingdom, a sacred nation, for me." These are the words that you're to speak to the Yisra'elites.'

⁷Mosheh came and called for the people's elders and set before them all these words that Yahweh ordered him. ⁸The entire people answered together, 'Everything that Yahweh spoke we will do.' Mosheh took the people's words back to Yahweh, ⁹and Yahweh said to Mosheh, 'Here, I'm coming to you in a thick cloud, so the people may hear when I speak with you and also may trust in you permanently.'

So Mosheh told Yahweh the people's words, ¹⁰and Yahweh said to Mosheh, 'Go to the people and make them sacred today and tomorrow, and get them to wash their clothes. ¹¹They're to be ready for the third day, because on the third day Yahweh will come down before the eyes of the entire people on Mount Sinay. ¹²You're to set bounds for the people round about, saying "Keep watch over yourselves about going up the mountain or touching its border. Anyone who touches the mountain is absolutely to be put to death. ¹³No hand is to touch him, because he's simply to be stoned or simply to be shot with arrows. Whether it's an animal or a person, he's not to live. When the ram's horn sounds out, they may go up the mountain."'

Beware the electric nature of a meeting with God

¹⁴So Mosheh came down from the mountain to the people and made the people sacred, and they washed their clothes. ¹⁵He said to the people, 'Be ready for the third day. Don't approach a woman.'

¹⁶On the third day, when the morning came, there were sounds, lightning-flashes and heavy cloud on the mountain, and the very strong sound of a horn. The entire people that was in the camp trembled. ¹⁷But Mosheh got the people to come out of the camp to meet God, and they took their stand at the bottom of the mountain.

¹⁸Now Mount Sinay smoked, all of it, as a result of the fact that Yahweh had come down on it in fire. His smoke went up like the smoke of a kiln. The entire mountain trembled greatly. ¹⁹The horn's sound was getting stronger and stronger. When Mosheh would speak, God would answer him with the sound.

²⁰So Yahweh came down on Mount Sinay, to the top of the mountain, and Yahweh called Mosheh to the top of the mountain. Mosheh went up, ²¹but Yahweh said to Mosheh, 'Go down, testify against the people so they don't tear through to Yahweh to look, or many of them will fall. ²²The priests also, who come up to Yahweh, must make themselves sacred, so Yahweh doesn't break out against them.' ²³Mosheh said to Yahweh, 'The people cannot come up to Mount Sinay, because you yourself testified against us, "Set bounds for the mountain and make it sacred."' ²⁴But Yahweh said to him, 'Go, get down, then you come up, and Aharon with you, but the priests and the people are not to tear through to come up to Yahweh, so he doesn't break out against them.' ²⁵So Mosheh went down to the people and said it to them.

A rule of life

20 God spoke all these words: ²'I am Yahweh your God who got you out of the country of Misrayim, out of a household of serfs.

³For you there will be no other gods in my presence.

⁴You will not make yourself a sculpture or any shape that's in the heavens above, that's on the earth below or that's in the water under the earth. ⁵You will not bow low to them and you will not serve them. Because I, Yahweh your God, am the passionate God, attending to parents' waywardness in connection with children, with thirds and with fourths, for people who are hostile to me, ⁶but acting in commitment towards thousands for people who are loyal to me and who keep my orders.

⁷You will not lift up the name of Yahweh your God in respect of something empty, because Yahweh will not free of guilt a person who lifts up his name in respect of something empty.

⁸Be mindful of the sabbath day to make it sacred. ⁹For six days you can serve and do all your work, ¹⁰but the seventh day is a sabbath for Yahweh your God. You will not do any work, you, your son or your daughter, your servant or your handmaid, your animal or your resident who is in your communities. ¹¹Because in six days Yahweh made the heavens, the earth, the sea and all that's in them, and settled down on the seventh day. That's why Yahweh blessed the seventh day and made it sacred. ¹²Honour your father and your mother, in order that your time may be long on the land that Yahweh your God is going to give you.
¹³You will not murder.
¹⁴You will not be adulterous.
¹⁵You will not steal.
¹⁶You will not avow false testimony against your neighbour.
¹⁷You will not desire your neighbour's household: you will not desire your neighbour's wife, his servant or his handmaid, his ox or his donkey, or anything your neighbour has.'

No manufactured gods

¹⁸While the entire people were looking at the sounds, the flashes, the sound of the horn, and the smoking mountain – as the people looked, they hesitated and stood at a distance. ¹⁹They said to Mosheh, 'You speak with us and we'll listen. God mustn't speak with us, or we'll die.' ²⁰Mosheh said to the people, 'Don't be afraid, because God has come in order to test you, and in order that awe for him may be upon your faces, so you don't do wrong.' ²¹But the people stood at a distance, whereas Mosheh went up to the denseness where God was.

²²Yahweh said to Mosheh, 'You're to say this to the Yisra'elites: "You yourselves saw how I spoke with you from the heavens. ²³With me you will not make gods of silver and you will not make gods of gold for yourselves. ²⁴An altar of soil you will make for me, and you will sacrifice on it your burnt offerings and your well-being offerings, your flock and your herd. At every site where I cause my name to be commemorated, I'll come to you and bless you. ²⁵If you make an altar out of stones for me, you will not build it of cut stone, because when you've wielded your cutter on them, you'll have made them ordinary. ²⁶You will not go up my altar by steps, so your nakedness will not be exposed on it."

Treating bondservants properly

21 These are the rulings that you're to set before them.
²When you acquire a Hebrew servant, he's to serve for six years. In the seventh he's to leave as a free man, for nothing. ³If he comes by himself, he leaves by himself. If he possesses a wife, his wife leaves with him.
⁴If his lord gives him a wife and she gives birth to sons or daughters for him, the wife and her children belong to her lord. He leaves by himself. ⁵If the servant explicitly says, "I am loyal to my lord, my wife and my children. I won't leave as a free man", ⁶his lord is to bring him up to God and bring him up to the door or the doorpost, and his lord is to pierce his ear with an awl. He's his servant permanently.
⁷When someone sells his daughter as a handmaid, she doesn't leave as servants do. ⁸If she is bad in the eyes of her lord, who had designated her for himself, he's to let her be redeemed. He doesn't have the power to sell her to a foreign people, because of his breaking faith with her. ⁹But if he was designating her for his son, he's to deal with her in accordance with the ruling for daughters. ¹⁰If he takes himself another wife, he will not withhold her food, her clothing or her time. ¹¹If he doesn't do these three things for her, she may leave for nothing, without payment.

An eye for an eye

¹²Someone who strikes a man down, so he dies, is absolutely to be put to death. ¹³Someone who didn't set a trap, but God made him fall into his hand: I shall set a site for you where he may flee. ¹⁴But when someone asserts himself against his neighbour so as to kill him with shrewdness, you're to take him from beside my altar to die.
¹⁵Someone who strikes down his father or his mother is absolutely to be put to death.

¹⁶Someone who kidnaps a person, and he sells him or he's found in his possession, is absolutely to be put to death. ¹⁷Someone who slights his father or his mother is absolutely to be put to death.

¹⁸When people get into an argument and one strikes his neighbour with a stone or with his fist and he doesn't die but he falls into bed, ¹⁹if he gets up and walks about outside on his staff, the one who struck him can be free of guilt, only he's to pay for his sitting around, and definitely to get him healed. ²⁰When someone strikes his servant or his handmaid with a club and he dies under his hand, he's definitely to submit to redress. ²¹Yet if he stands after a day or two, he's not to be subjected to redress, because he's his own silver.

²²When men fight and they hit a pregnant woman and her children come out but there's no harm, he's definitely to make compensation, as the woman's husband may lay on him, or give it by arbitration. ²³If there's harm, you're to give life for life, ²⁴eye for eye, tooth for tooth, hand for hand, foot for foot, ²⁵burn for burn, wound for wound, bruise for bruise. ²⁶When someone strikes his servant's eye or his handmaid's eye and devastates it, he's to send him off as a free person because of his eye. ²⁷If someone makes his servant's tooth or his handmaid's tooth fall out, he's to send him off as a free person because of his tooth.

The goring ox and the missing ox

²⁸When an ox gores a man or a woman and he dies, the ox is absolutely to be stoned and its flesh is not to be eaten, but the ox's owner can be free of guilt. ²⁹But if the ox has been inclined to gore in previous days, and it's been testified with its owner, and he doesn't keep it in and it causes the death of a man or a woman, the ox is to be stoned and its owner is also to be put to death. ³⁰If a ransom is laid on him, he's to give the redemption price for his life in accordance with all that's laid on him. ³¹Should it either gore a son or gore a daughter, it's to be done to him in accordance with this ruling. ³²If the ox gores a servant or a handmaid, he's to give silver, thirty sheqels, to his lord, and the ox is to be stoned.

³³When someone opens a cistern or when someone digs a cistern and doesn't cover it, and an ox or a donkey falls into it, ³⁴the cistern's owner is to make good. He's to give back silver to its owner, but the dead thing will be his. ³⁵When someone's ox injures his neighbour's ox and it dies, they're to sell the live ox and divide the silver, and also divide the dead thing. ³⁶If it was known that the ox was inclined to gore in previous days and its owner doesn't keep it in, he must definitely make good, ox for ox, but the dead thing will be his.

22 When someone steals an ox or sheep and slaughters it or sells it, he's to make good with five from the herd for the ox or four from the fold for the sheep. (²If the thief is found while breaking in and he's struck down and dies, no bloodshed is counted in respect of him. ³If the sun had risen on him, bloodshed is counted in respect of him.) He's definitely to make good; if he doesn't have it, he's to be sold for his theft. ⁴If the thing stolen (either ox or donkey or sheep, alive) is actually found in his possession, he's to make good double.

More problems on the farm

⁵When someone burns up a field or vineyard (or sends off his animals so they burn up someone else's field), he's to make good from the good things of his field or from the good things of his vineyard. ⁶When a fire breaks out and reaches the thorns, so stacked grain or standing grain or the field is consumed, the person who caused the burn is definitely to make good.

⁷When someone gives his neighbour silver or things to keep but it's stolen from the man's house, if the thief is found, he's to make good double. ⁸If the thief isn't found, the owner of the house is to draw near to God [to testify] that he didn't lay hand on his neighbour's work. ⁹Over any breach of trust, over an ox or donkey or sheep or garment or any loss about which someone says, 'This is it', the thing involving the two of them is to come to God. The one whom God says is in the wrong is to make good double to his neighbour.

¹⁰When someone gives his neighbour a donkey or ox or sheep or any animal to keep and it dies or is injured or is taken off, with no one seeing, ¹¹there's to be an oath to Yahweh between the two of them that he hasn't laid his

hand on his neighbour's work. Its owner is to accept it, and he's not to make good. ¹²But if it's actually stolen from him, he's to make good to its owner. ¹³If it gets mauled at all, he's to bring it as evidence. For something mauled, he's not to make good.

On taking advantage of people

¹⁴When someone asks for something from his neighbour and it's injured or it dies, its owner not being with it, he's definitely to make good. ¹⁵If its owner was with it, he's not to make good. If it was a hire, he comes into its hire.

¹⁶If a man seduces a young girl who's not betrothed and sleeps with her, he's to make the actual marriage payment for her as a wife for himself. ¹⁷If her father absolutely refuses to give her to him, he's to weigh out silver in accordance with the marriage payment for young girls.

¹⁸A medium: you will not allow her to live. ¹⁹Anyone who has sex with an animal: is absolutely to be put to death. ²⁰Someone who sacrifices to a god other than Yahweh alone: is to be devoted.

²¹A resident: you will not oppress or afflict him, because you were residents in the country of Misrayim. ²²Any widow or orphan: you will not humble them. ²³If you humble them at all, when they cry aloud to me, I shall listen attentively to their cry. ²⁴My anger will rage and I shall kill you with the sword. Your wives will become widows, your children orphans.

²⁵If you lend silver to my people, to a humble person who is with you, you will not be like a lender to him. You will not make him pay interest. ²⁶If you take your neighbour's coat as a pledge, before sundown you will give it back to him, ²⁷because it alone is his covering, his wrapping for his skin. What is he to sleep in? When he cries out to me, I shall listen, because I am gracious.

You know what it's like to be a resident alien

²⁸You will not slight God or curse a leader among your people. ²⁹Your fullness and the pressing of your grapes: you will not delay them. The firstborn of your sons: you will give him to me. ³⁰You will do this with your oxen and with your sheep. It will be seven days with its mother; on the eighth day you will give it to me. ³¹You will be sacred people to me. You will not eat meat from an animal mauled in the fields; you will throw it to the dogs.

23 You will not carry an empty report. Don't put your hand in with a faithless person to become a felonious witness. ²You will not follow a majority to act badly. You will not avow in an argument so as to bend after a majority, so as to bend it. ³Neither will you defer to a poor person in his argument.

⁴When you come upon an ox belonging to your enemy or his donkey, straying, you will take it straight back to him. ⁵When you see a donkey belonging to someone who is hostile to you lying down under its load and you would refrain from loosening [the load] for it, you will definitely loosen it with him.

⁶You will not bend a poor person's ruling when he is in an argument. ⁷A false statement: stay distant from it. Someone who is free of guilt and is in the right: don't kill him, because I do not treat the person who is in the right as in the wrong. ⁸A bribe: don't accept it, because a bribe blinds people who can see and overturns the statements of people who are in the right. ⁹A resident: you will not afflict him; you yourselves know the feelings of a resident, because you were residents in the country of Misrayim.

The principle of the seventh

¹⁰For six years you're to sow your land and gather its yield. ¹¹The seventh, you're to allow it to lie and leave it alone. The needy among your people may eat, and what they leave the creatures of the wild may eat. So you're to do for your vineyard and for your olive. ¹²For six days you can do your work, but on the seventh day you're to stop, in order that your ox and your donkey may find relief and the offspring of your handmaid and the resident may find refreshment.

¹³You're to keep watch concerning everything I've said to you. You will not commemorate the name of other gods. It will not be heard in your mouth.

¹⁴On three occasions in the year you're to hold a festival for me. ¹⁵You're to keep

the Flatbread Festival: for seven days you're to eat flatbread as I ordered you, at the set time in the month of Aviv [March–April], because in it you left Misrayim; and people are not to appear before me empty-handed; ¹⁶the Harvest Festival: the first products of your work, of what you sow in the fields; the Ingathering Festival at the end of the year, when you gather your work from the fields. ¹⁷Three times in the year, every male among you is to appear before the Lord Yahweh.

¹⁸You will not offer the blood of a sacrifice for me accompanied by leavened bread. The fat from a festival for me will not stay until morning. ¹⁹The very first of the first products of your land you're to bring to the house of Yahweh your God.

You will not cook a kid goat in its own mother's milk.

How to get into the promised land

²⁰Here, I'm going to send an envoy before you to keep you on the way and to bring you to the place that I've prepared. ²¹Keep watch before him. Listen to his voice. Don't defy him, because he won't carry your rebellions, because my name is within him. ²²But if you do really listen to his voice and do everything I speak, I'll be an enemy to your enemies, an adversary to your adversaries, ²³because my envoy will go before you and bring you to the Amorite, the Hittite, the Perizzite, the Kena'anite, the Hivvite and the Yebusite, and I shall efface them. ²⁴You will not bow low to their gods, you will not serve them, you will not do as they do, but completely tear them down and completely break up their columns. ²⁵You are to serve Yahweh your God. He will bless your bread and your water, and I will remove illness from among you. ²⁶There'll be no one miscarrying or infertile in your country. I'll bring to completion the number of your days.

²⁷I shall send off a dread of me before you and it will throw into turmoil all the people among whom you come. I shall make all your enemies turn their back before you. ²⁸I shall send a hornet before you, and it will drive out the Hivvites, the Kena'anites and the Hittites from before you.

²⁹I shall not drive them out from before you in one year, in case the country becomes a desolation and the creatures of the wild multiply against you. ³⁰Little by little I shall drive them out from before you until you're fruitful and you have the country as a domain. ³¹I shall set your border from the Reed Sea to the Pelishtites' Sea and from the wilderness to the River [Euphrates], because I shall give into your hand the people living in the country and you will drive them out from before you. ³²You will not solemnize a pact with them or with their gods. ³³They won't live in your country, in case they cause you to do wrong in relation to me because you serve their gods, because it would be a snare to you.'

Seeing God

24 He said to Mosheh, 'Go up to Yahweh, you and Aharon, Nadab and Abihu, and seventy of the Yisra'elite elders. Bow low from afar. ²Mosheh alone is to come up to Yahweh; they're not to come up and the people are not to go up with him.'

³Mosheh came and recounted all Yahweh's words to the people, all the rulings. The entire people answered with one voice: 'All the things Yahweh spoke of, we will do.' ⁴Mosheh wrote down all Yahweh's words.

Mosheh started early in the morning and built an altar beneath the mountain, and twelve columns for the twelve Yisra'elite clans. ⁵He sent the Yisra'elite boys and they offered up burnt offerings and made well-being sacrifices of bulls. ⁶Mosheh took half the blood and put it in basins, and half the blood he tossed over the altar. ⁷He got the pact document and read it in the people's ears. They said, 'All that Yahweh spoke of, we will do, we will obey.' ⁸Mosheh took the blood, tossed it over the people, and said, 'Here is the blood of the pact that Yahweh has solemnized with you on the basis of all these words.'

⁹Then Mosheh and Aharon, Nadab and Abihu, and seventy of the Yisra'elite elders went up, ¹⁰and saw the God of Yisra'el. Under his feet was something like a sapphire pavement, like the actual heavens for purity. ¹¹Against the Yisra'elites' 'pillars' he didn't put out his hand. They beheld God, and they ate and drank.

¹²Yahweh said to Mosheh, 'Go up to me on the mountain and be there. I shall give you the stone tablets with the instruction and the order that I've written, to instruct them.' ¹³So Mosheh and Yehoshua his minister set off, and Mosheh went up to God's mountain. ¹⁴To the elders he said, 'Stay here for us till we come back to you. Here are Aharon and Hur with you. Anyone who has things to raise can come up to them.'

How to build a sanctuary

¹⁵So Mosheh went up the mountain. The cloud covered the mountain ¹⁶and Yahweh's splendour dwelt on Mount Sinay. The cloud covered it for six days and on the seventh day he called to Mosheh from the middle of the cloud. ¹⁷The appearance of Yahweh's splendour was like devouring fire on the top of the mountain before the eyes of the Yisra'elites. ¹⁸Mosheh came into the middle of the cloud and went up the mountain. Mosheh was on the mountain for forty days and forty nights.

25 Yahweh spoke to Mosheh: ²"Speak to the Yisra'elites so they get a contribution for me. You're to get the contribution for me from every individual whose heart makes him free. ³This is the contribution that you're to get from them: gold, silver, copper; ⁴blue, purple and bright crimson, linen, goats' [hair], ⁵ram skins dyed red, dolphin skins, acacia wood; ⁶oil for lighting, spices for the anointing oil and the aromatic incense; ⁷onyx stones and stones for the mountings for the chasuble and for the pouch. ⁸They're to make me a sanctuary, so that I may dwell among them. ⁹In accordance with everything that I'm going to let you see, the pattern of the dwelling and the pattern of all the articles in it, so you're to make it.

¹⁰They're to make an acacia wood chest, its length two and a half cubits, its width a cubit and a half, and its height a cubit and a half. ¹¹You are to overlay it with pure gold, overlay it inside and outside, and make a gold moulding on it all round. ¹²You're to cast four gold rings for it and put them on its four feet, two rings on one side of it and two on the other. ¹³You're to make acacia wood poles and overlay them with gold, ¹⁴and insert the poles into the rings on the sides of the chest, so as to carry the chest by them. ¹⁵The poles are to be in the rings of the chest; they are not to depart from it. ¹⁶Put into the chest the affirmation that I shall give you.

The expiation cover and the table

¹⁷You're to make an expiation cover of pure gold, its length two and a half cubits and its width a cubit and a half, ¹⁸and to make two gold sphinxes (of hammered work you're to make them) at the two ends of the expiation cover. ¹⁹You're to make one sphinx at one end and the other sphinx at the other end; you're to make the sphinxes issuing from the expiation cover at its two ends. ²⁰The sphinxes are to be spreading their wings upwards, shielding the expiation cover with their wings, and with their faces one towards the other; the sphinxes' faces will be towards the expiation cover.

²¹You're to put the expiation cover on the chest, on top, and put into the chest the affirmation that I shall give you. ²²I shall keep an appointment with you there and speak with you from above the expiation cover, from between the sphinxes that are above the affirmation chest, all that I shall order you for the Yisra'elites.

²³You're to make an acacia wood table, its length two cubits, its width one cubit and its height a cubit and a half. ²⁴You're to overlay it with pure gold and make a gold moulding for it all round. ²⁵You're to make a rim for it, a handbreadth all round, and to make a gold moulding for its rim all round. ²⁶You're to make four gold rings for it and put the rings at the four corners that are at its four legs. ²⁷The rings are to be close by the rim as housing for the poles for carrying the table. ²⁸You're to make the poles of acacia wood and overlay them with gold. The table will be carried by means of them.

²⁹You're to make its dishes, its ladles, its pitchers and its bowls, with which the drink offering will be poured – you're to make them of pure gold. ³⁰You're to put the presence bread on the table before my presence, regularly.

The candelabrum

³¹You're to make a candelabrum of pure gold. The candelabrum is to be made of hammered

Exodus 25: The sanctuary – Yahweh's dwelling

work, its base and its stem. Its cups, its flowers and its petals are to come from it; ³²six stems going out from its flanks, three stems of the candelabrum from its one flank and three stems of the candelabrum from its second flank; ³³three cups made like almond blossom on one stem, flower and petal, three stems made like almond blossom on another stem, flower and petal; so for the six stems going out from the candelabrum.

³⁴On the candelabrum four cups made like almond blossom, its flowers and its petals; ³⁵a flower beneath two stems issuing from it, and a flower beneath two stems issuing from it, and a flower beneath two stems issuing from it, for the six branches going out from the candelabrum; ³⁶their flowers and their stems are to come from it, all of it a single hammered work, pure gold. ³⁷You're to make its seven lamps (they are to put up its lamps so they give light on the area before it) ³⁸and its tongs and its pans of pure gold. ³⁹It will be made of a talent of pure gold, with all these articles.

⁴⁰See that you act by the pattern for them that you're being shown on the mountain.

How to weave a sanctuary

26 You're to make the dwelling from ten pieces of woven linen and from blue, purple and bright crimson, and to make them with sphinxes, designer's work. ²The length of each piece, twenty-eight cubits and the width of each piece, four cubits – one size for all the pieces. ³Five of the pieces are to be joining one to the other, and the other five pieces are to be joining one to the other.

⁴You're to make loops of blue on the lip of the one piece at the edge in its joined set,

and to make them in this way at the lip of the edging piece in the second joined set. ⁵You're to make fifty loops on the one piece and make fifty loops at the edge of the piece that's in the second joined set, with the loops holding one to the other. ⁶You're to make fifty gold clasps and to join the pieces one to the other with the clasps so the dwelling becomes one unit.

⁷You're to make pieces from goats' [hair] for a tent over the dwelling; you're to make eleven pieces. ⁸The length of each piece, thirty by the cubit; the width, four by the cubit each piece; one size for the eleven pieces. ⁹You're to join five of the pieces on their own, and six of the pieces on their own, and double the sixth piece near the front of the tent.

¹⁰You're to make fifty loops on the lip of one outermost piece in a joined set, and fifty loops on the lip of the piece in the other joined set. ¹¹You're to make fifty copper clasps and insert the clasps into the loops and join the tent so it becomes one unit.

¹²The overhang that's surplus in the tent's pieces: the half-piece that's surplus is to overhang the back of the dwelling, ¹³while the cubit at one end and the cubit at the other end in the surplus of the tent's pieces will be hung over the flanks of the dwelling on one side and on the other side, to cover it. ¹⁴And you're to make a covering for the tent of ram skins dyed red, with a covering of dolphin skins above it.

How to build a sanctuary

¹⁵You're to make the planks for the dwelling of acacia wood, standing upright. ¹⁶The length of a plank, ten cubits; the width of a plank, a cubit and a half, each one; ¹⁷two projections for a plank, parallel one to the other. So you're to do for all the dwelling's planks. ¹⁸You're to make the planks for the dwelling: twenty planks for the south (southern) aspect; ¹⁹you're to make forty silver sockets under the twenty planks, two sockets under a plank for its two projections and two sockets under the next plank for its two projections. ²⁰For the dwelling's second side, for the north aspect: twenty planks, ²¹with their forty silver sockets, two sockets under a plank and two sockets under the next plank.

²²For the back of the dwelling, to the west, you're to make six planks, ²³and you're to make two planks for the corners of the dwelling, at the back. ²⁴They're to be double underneath, but together they're to be whole at its top, at the one ring. So it will be for both of them: they'll form two corners. ²⁵Thus there will be eight planks with their silver sockets, sixteen sockets: two sockets under one plank and two sockets under the next plank.

²⁶You're to make bars of acacia wood: five for the planks in one side of the dwelling, ²⁷five bars for the planks in the second side of the dwelling, and five bars for the planks in the side of the dwelling at the back, to the west, ²⁸with the central bar in the middle of the planks running from end to end. ²⁹You're to overlay the planks with gold and to make their rings of gold as housing for the bars, and to overlay the bars with gold.

³⁰You're to set up the dwelling in accordance with the ruling about it that you've been enabled to see on the mountain.

The curtain, the screen and the altar

³¹You're to make a curtain of blue, purple and bright crimson, and of woven linen. It's to be made as designer's work, with sphinxes. ³²You're to put it on four posts of acacia overlaid with gold, with their gold hooks, on four silver sockets. ³³You're to put the curtain under the clasps and bring the affirmation chest there, behind the curtain. The curtain will make a distinction between the sacred place and the especially sacred place for you. ³⁴You're to put the expiation cover on the affirmation chest in the especially sacred place. ³⁵You're to place the table outside the curtain and the candelabrum in front of the table on the south side of the dwelling, and to put the table on the north side. ³⁶You're to make a screen for the tent entrance, of blue, purple and bright crimson, and of woven linen, embroiderer's work, ³⁷and to make for the screen five posts of acacia and overlay them with gold, with their gold hooks, and to cast for them five copper sockets.

27 You're to make the altar of acacia wood, five cubits in length, five cubits in width (the altar will be square), and three cubits in height, ²and to make its horns on its four corners (its horns are to come from it), and overlay it with copper. ³You're to make its buckets for clearing it of waste, its shovels, its basins, its forks and its pans: you're to make all its utensils of copper. ⁴You're to make a grating for it, a mesh made of copper, and make on the mesh four copper rings at its four corners. ⁵You're to put it beneath the altar ledge, underneath; the mesh is to be halfway up the altar. ⁶You're to make poles for the altar, poles of acacia wood, and overlay them with copper. ⁷The poles are to be inserted into the rings and the poles are to be on the two sides of the altar when it's carried. ⁸You're to make it hollow, of boards. As it has been shown you on the mountain, so they are to make it.

The courtyard

⁹You're to make a courtyard for the dwelling:
On the south (southern) aspect: hangings for the courtyard, woven linen, a hundred by the cubit the length on the one aspect;
¹⁰its twenty posts and their twenty sockets, copper; the posts' hooks and their clasps, silver.
¹¹So also on the north aspect along the length: hangings, a hundred cubits the length; its twenty posts and their twenty sockets, copper; the posts' hooks and their clasps, silver.
¹²The width of the courtyard on the west aspect: hangings, fifty cubits; their posts, ten; their sockets, ten.
¹³The width of the courtyard on the front aspect, the east, fifty cubits: ¹⁴hangings, fifteen cubits to the shoulder; their posts, three; their sockets, three; ¹⁵for the second shoulder, hangings, fifteen cubits; their posts, three; their sockets, three.
¹⁶For the courtyard gateway: a screen, twenty cubits, of blue, purple and bright crimson, and of woven linen, embroiderer's work; their posts, four; their sockets, four. ¹⁷All the courtyard's posts around: clasped with silver; their hooks, silver; their sockets, copper. ¹⁸The length of the courtyard, a hundred by the cubit; the width, fifty consistently; the height, five cubits; of woven linen. Their sockets, copper; ¹⁹for all the articles in the dwelling in all its service, and all its pegs and all the courtyard's pegs, copper.

²⁰You yourself are to order the Yisra'elites that they are to get you pure pressed olive oil for lighting, for putting up a lamp regularly. ²¹In the appointment tent, outside the curtain which is over the affirmation, Aharon and his sons are to arrange it from evening till morning before Yahweh, a permanent decree through their generations for the Yisra'elites.

How to dress a priest

28 You yourself are to have Aharon your brother presented to you, and his sons with him, from among the Yisra'elites, to act as priests for me: Aharon, Nadab and Abihu, El'azar and Itamar, Aharon's sons. ²Make sacred garments for Aharon your brother, for splendour and for glory. ³You yourself are to speak to all the people who are smart in their thinking, the people I've filled with a smart spirit, so they may make Aharon's garments, for making him sacred to act as priest for me.

⁴These are the garments that they're to make: pouch, chasuble, coat, woven tunic, turban and sash. They're to make the sacred garments for Aharon your brother and for his sons to act as priests for me ⁵when they get the gold, the blue, purple and bright crimson, and linen.

⁶They're to make the chasuble of gold, of blue, purple and bright crimson, and of woven linen, designer's work. ⁷It will have two shoulder pieces joining to its two corners, so it will be joined. ⁸The chasuble's design-work strap, which is on it, is to be like its work, coming from it: of gold, of blue, purple and bright crimson, and of woven linen.

⁹You're to get two onyx stones and engrave on them the names of Yisra'el's sons, ¹⁰six of their names on the one stone and the remaining six names on the second, by their lines of descent. ¹¹As craftsman's work in stone, with seal engravings, you're to engrave the two stones with the names of Yisra'el's sons. You're to make them surrounded by gold braids. ¹²You're to put the two stones on the chasuble's shoulder pieces as reminder stones for Yisra'el's sons. Aharon is to carry their names before Yahweh on his two shoulder pieces for a reminder.

¹³You're to make braids of gold ¹⁴and two chains of pure gold, as plaitings. You're to make them as woven work and to put the woven chains on the braids.

The decision pouch

¹⁵You're to make a decision pouch, designer's work. You're to make it like the work of the chasuble, of gold, of blue, purple and bright crimson, and of woven linen. ¹⁶It's to be square and folded double, its length a handbreadth and its width a handbreadth. ¹⁷You're to fill it with a filling of stones, four rows of stones:

the first row: a row of carnelian, chrysolyte and emerald;
¹⁸the second row: turquoise, sapphire and amethyst;
¹⁹the third row: jacinth, agate and crystal;
²⁰the fourth row: beryl, onyx and jasper.

They're to be set in gold in their fillings. ²¹The stones will correspond to the names of Yisra'el's sons, twelve corresponding to their names. With seal engravings, each corresponding to its name, they will be for the twelve clans. ²²On the pouch you're to make plaited chains, woven work, pure gold.

²³You're to make two gold rings on the pouch and to put the two rings on the two edges of the pouch. ²⁴You're to put the two gold weavings on the two rings at the edges of the pouch. ²⁵The two ends of the two weavings you're to put on the two braids, and you're to put them on the chasuble's shoulder pieces near its front. ²⁶You're to make two gold rings and put them on the two edges of the pouch at its lip, which is on the side nearer the chasuble. ²⁷You're to make two gold rings and put them on the chasuble's two shoulder pieces underneath, near the front, close by its join, above the chasuble's design-work strap. ²⁸They're to attach the pouch by its rings to the chasuble's rings with a blue cord, so it's on the chasuble's design-work strap and so the pouch doesn't come loose from on the chasuble.

²⁹Aharon is to carry the names of Yisra'el's sons on the decision pouch over his heart when he goes into the sacred place, for a reminder before Yahweh regularly. ³⁰You're to put into the decision pouch the Urim and Tummim, so they're over Aharon's heart when he comes in before Yahweh. Aharon is to carry the decision-making for the Yisra'elites over his heart before Yahweh regularly.

The coat and the medallion

³¹You're to make the chasuble coat, all blue. ³²There's to be an opening for the head in the middle of it. The lip for its opening all round is to be weaver's work (it's to be like the opening of a vest for it) so it doesn't tear. ³³On its hems you're to make pomegranates of blue, purple and bright crimson, on its hems all round, and gold bells among them all round, ³⁴a gold bell and a pomegranate, a gold bell and a pomegranate, on the coat's hems all round. ³⁵It's to be on Aharon for ministering so its sound may be heard when he comes into the sacred place before Yahweh and when he goes out, so he does not die.

³⁶You're to make a medallion of pure gold and engrave on it with seal engravings, "Sacred for Yahweh". ³⁷You're to put it on a blue cord so it's on the turban. It's to be near the front of the turban. ³⁸It's to be on Aharon's forehead so Aharon can carry the waywardness associated with the sacred objects that the Yisra'elites make sacred in connection with any of their sacred gifts. It will be on his forehead regularly, for their acceptance before Yahweh.

³⁹You're to weave the tunic of linen, you're to make a turban of linen and you're to make a sash, embroiderer's work.

⁴⁰For Aharon's sons you're to make tunics, and you're to make them sashes and to make mitres for them, for splendour and for glory. ⁴¹You're to put them on Aharon your brother and on his sons with him, and to anoint them, commission them and make them sacred, so they can act as priests for me.

⁴²You're to make cloth shorts for them to cover their naked flesh. They're to go from the hips to the thighs ⁴³and they're to be on Aharon and on his sons when they come into the appointment tent or when they come up to the altar to minister in the sacred place, so that they don't carry waywardness and die. It's a permanent decree for him and for his offspring after him.

The first ordination offering

29 This is the thing that you're to do for them in making them sacred to act as priests for me. Get one bull from the herd and two rams, whole, ²and flatbread and loaves of flatbread mixed with oil, and flat wafers spread with oil. You're to make them of fine wheat flour. ³You're to put them in a basket and present them in the basket, with the bull and with the two rams.

⁴Aharon and his sons you're to present at the entrance of the appointment tent and wash them with water. ⁵You're to get the garments and clothe Aharon with the tunic, the chasuble coat, the chasuble and the pouch, to wind the chasuble on him with the chasuble's design-work strap, ⁶place the turban on his head, put the sacred diadem on the turban, ⁷get the anointing oil, pour it on his head and anoint him.

⁸And you're to present his sons, clothe them with tunics, ⁹wrap round them with a sash, Aharon and his sons, and bind mitres on them. The priesthood will be theirs by a permanent decree.

You're then to commission Aharon and his sons. ¹⁰Present the bull before the appointment tent. Aharon and his sons are to lean their hands on the bull's head, ¹¹and you're to slaughter the bull before Yahweh at the entrance of the appointment tent. ¹²You're to get some of the bull's blood and put it on the altar's horns with your finger, and all the rest of the blood you're to pour out at the altar's base. ¹³You're to get all the fat that covers the innards, the lobe on the liver, and the two kidneys and the fat that's on them, and turn them into smoke on the altar. ¹⁴The bull's flesh, its skin and its intestines you're to burn in fire outside the camp. It's a decontamination.

The second ordination offering

¹⁵You're to get the one ram, Aharon and his sons are to lean their hands on the ram's head, ¹⁶and you're to slaughter the ram, get its blood and toss it over the altar all round. ¹⁷You're to cut up the ram into its parts, wash its innards and its legs, put them along with its parts and along with its head, ¹⁸and turn the entire ram into smoke on the altar. It's a burnt offering for Yahweh, a nice smell. It's a gift offering for Yahweh.

¹⁹Then you're to get the second ram, Aharon and his sons are to lean their hands on the ram's head, ²⁰and you're to slaughter the ram. You're to get some of its blood and put it on the lobe of Aharon's ear and on the lobe of his sons' right ear, on the thumb of their right hand and on the big toe of their right foot, and toss the rest of the blood over the altar all round. ²¹You're to get some of the blood that's on the altar and some of the anointing oil and spatter it on Aharon, on his garments, on his sons and on his sons' garments with him. So he will become sacred, he, his garments, his sons and his sons' garments with him.

²²You're to get from the ram the fat, the broad tail, the fat covering the innards, the lobe of the liver, the two kidneys, the fat that's on them, and the right thigh, because it's the commissioning ram, ²³and one round of bread, one loaf of bread made with oil and one wafer from the basket of flatbread that's before Yahweh, ²⁴put everything on Aharon's palms and on his sons' palms, and elevate them as an elevation offering before Yahweh. ²⁵Then you're to get them from their hand and turn them into smoke on the altar along with the burnt offering, for a nice smell before Yahweh. It's a gift offering for Yahweh.

The next generation

²⁶You're to get the breast from Aharon's commissioning ram and elevate it as an elevation offering before Yahweh, and it will be your portion. ²⁷You're to make sacred the breast, the elevation offering and the thigh that was the contribution, which was offered up and which was taken up from the commissioning ram, from what belonged to Aharon and from what belonged to his sons, ²⁸and it will belong to Aharon and to his sons, as a permanent decree from the Yisra'elites, because it's a contribution. It will be a contribution from the Yisra'elites from the well-being sacrifices, their gift for Yahweh.

²⁹Aharon's sacred garments will be for his sons after him, for anointing and commissioning them in them. ³⁰For seven days the one of his sons who acts as priest in his place is to put them on, the one who comes into the

appointment tent to minister in the sacred place. ³¹You're to get the commissioning ram and cook its flesh at the sacred site, ³²and Aharon and his sons are to eat the ram's flesh and the bread that's in the basket, at the entrance of the appointment tent. ³³The people for whom expiation was made with them in commissioning them, in making them sacred, they're to eat them; an outsider is not to eat them, because they're sacred. ³⁴If some of the commissioning flesh or some of the bread is left over until morning, you're to burn what is left over in fire. It's not to be eaten, because it's sacred.

How to start and end the day

³⁵You're to act towards Aharon and his sons in accordance with all that I've ordered you. For seven days you're to commission them. ³⁶You're to make a bull as a decontamination each day, for total expiation, and you're to decontaminate the altar through your making expiation on it, and to anoint it, to make it sacred. ³⁷For seven days you're to make expiation on the altar and make it sacred, so the altar becomes especially sacred, and anything that touches the altar becomes sacred.

³⁸This is what you're to make on the altar: two sheep, a year old, regularly each day. ³⁹Make one sheep in the morning and make the second sheep at twilight, ⁴⁰with a tenth of fine flour mixed with pressed oil (a quarter of a gallon) and a libation (a quarter of a gallon of wine for the one sheep). ⁴¹You're to make the second sheep at twilight. You're to make it in the same way as the morning grain offering and its libation, for a nice smell, a gift offering for Yahweh, ⁴²a regular burnt offering through your generations at the entrance of the appointment tent before Yahweh, where I shall keep an appointment with you to speak to you there, ⁴³and keep an appointment with the Yisra'elites there. It will become sacred through my splendour. ⁴⁴I will make the appointment tent and the altar sacred, and I will make Aharon and his sons sacred to act as priests for me. ⁴⁵I shall dwell among the Yisra'elites, I shall be God for them, ⁴⁶and they will acknowledge that I am Yahweh their God who got them out of the country of Misrayim to dwell among them. I am Yahweh their God.

The incense altar

30 You're to make an altar for burning incense. You're to make it of acacia wood, ²its length a cubit, its width a cubit (square) and its height two cubits, with its horns coming from it. ³You're to overlay it with pure gold – its top, its sides all round and its horns. You're to make a gold moulding for it all round. ⁴You're to make two gold rings for it under its moulding, on its two sides, and to make them on its two flanks so they can be housing for poles to carry it with. ⁵You're to make the poles of acacia wood and overlay them with gold.

⁶You're to put it before the curtain that's over the affirmation chest (before the curtain that's over the affirmation) where I will keep an appointment with you. ⁷Aharon is to burn sweet-smelling incense on it. Morning by morning when he looks after the lamps he's to burn it. ⁸And when Aharon sets up the lamps at twilight he's to burn incense regularly before Yahweh through your generations. ⁹You're not to offer up outside incense on it (either a burnt offering or a grain offering), and you're not to pour a libation on it. ¹⁰Aharon is to make expiation on its horns once a year with the blood of a decontamination for complete expiation. Once a year he's to make expiation on it through your generations. It's especially sacred for Yahweh.'

The ransom price

¹¹Yahweh spoke to Mosheh: ¹²'When you take the sum of the Yisra'elites in connection with their register, they're to give for Yahweh, each individual, the ransom price for his life, when you register them, so there isn't an epidemic among them when you register them. ¹³This is what they're to give, each person who passes on to the register: a half-sheqel by the sanctuary sheqel (twenty grains to the sheqel) – a half-sheqel contribution for Yahweh. ¹⁴Each person passing on to the register, from the age of twenty years and upwards, is to give the contribution for Yahweh. ¹⁵The wealthy person is not to do more and the poor person is not to do less than the half-sheqel, in giving Yahweh's contribution to make expiation for your lives. ¹⁶You're to take the silver of complete expiation

from the Yisraʾelites and give it for the service of the appointment tent. It's to be for the Yisraʾelites a reminder before Yahweh, to make expiation for your lives.'

¹⁷Yahweh spoke to Mosheh: ¹⁸'You're to make a copper basin and a copper stand for it, for washing, and to put it between the appointment tent and the altar. Put water there, ¹⁹so Aharon and his sons may wash their hands and their feet from it. ²⁰When they go into the appointment tent they're to wash with water so they don't die. Or when they come up to the altar to minister by turning into smoke a gift offering for Yahweh, ²¹they're to wash their hands and their feet so they don't die. For them it's to be a permanent decree, for him and for his offspring, through their generations.'

How to make incense

²²Yahweh spoke to Mosheh: ²³'You yourself, get yourself the chief spices: liquid myrrh, 500; spiced cinnamon, half that, 250; fragrant cane, 250; ²⁴cassia, 500 – by the sanctuary sheqel; and olive oil, a gallon. ²⁵You're to make it into sacred anointing oil, the best blend, blender's work. It will be the sacred anointing oil. ²⁶With it you're to anoint the appointment tent, the affirmation chest, ²⁷the table and all its articles, the candelabrum and its articles, the incense altar, ²⁸the burnt offering altar and all its articles, and the basin and its stand. ²⁹You're to make them sacred so that they become especially sacred. Anyone who touches them will become sacred. ³⁰You're to anoint Aharon and his sons and make them sacred to act as priests for me.

³¹You're to speak to the Yisraʾelites: "This will be the sacred anointing oil for me through your generations. ³²It's not to be poured on the flesh of anyone, and you're not to make any like it, by its proportions. It's sacred. It's to be sacred for you. ³³Anyone who blends some like it or puts some of it on an outsider shall be cut off from his kin."'

³⁴Yahweh said to Mosheh, 'Get yourself aromatic spices – stacte, onyka and galbanum. Of aromatic spices and pure frankincense there's to be equal weight. ³⁵You're to make them into blended incense, blender's work, salted, pure, sacred. ³⁶You're to beat some of it into powder and put some of it before the affirmation in the appointment tent where I shall keep an appointment with you. It's to be especially sacred for you. ³⁷The incense that you make, you're not to make by its proportions for yourselves. For you it's to be sacred for Yahweh. ³⁸Anyone who makes some like it to smell of it shall be cut off from his kin.'

The first spiritual gifting

31 Yahweh spoke to Mosheh: ²'See, I've called for Betsalʾel ben Uri, son of Hur, of the clan of Yehudah, by name. ³I've filled him with a divine spirit, with smartness, with discernment and with knowledge, in any workmanship, ⁴for making designs so as to make things with gold, with silver and with copper, ⁵in cutting stone for mountings and in carving wood, for working in any craft.

⁶And I: here, I have put with him Oholiʾab ben Ahisamak of the clan of Dan, and into the mind of everyone who is smart in mind I have put smartness, so they can make everything that I've ordered you: ⁷the appointment tent, the chest for the affirmation, the expiation cover that will be on it, all the articles in the tent, ⁸the table and its articles, the pure gold candelabrum and all its articles, the incense altar, ⁹the burnt offering altar and all its articles, the basin and its stand, ¹⁰the liturgical garments, the sacred garments for Aharon the priest, and his sons' garments for acting as priests, ¹¹the anointing oil and the aromatic incense for the sacred place. In accordance with all that I've ordered you they are to act.'

¹²Yahweh said to Mosheh: ¹³'You yourself, speak to the Yisraʾelites: "Nevertheless, my sabbaths you're to keep, because it's a sign between me and you through your generations, for acknowledging that I Yahweh have made you sacred. ¹⁴You're to keep the sabbath because it's sacred for you. The person who treats it as ordinary is absolutely to be put to death. When anyone does work on it, that person shall be cut off from among his kin. ¹⁵For six days work can be done. On the seventh day there is a complete stop [*shabbat shabbaton*], sacred for Yahweh. Anyone who does work on the sabbath day is absolutely to be put to death.

¹⁶The Yisra'elites are to keep the sabbath, making sabbath through their generations, a permanent pact. ¹⁷Between me and the Yisra'elites it will be a permanent sign. Because in six days Yahweh made the heavens and the earth, and on the seventh day he stopped and found refreshment."'

Meanwhile, at the foot of the mountain

¹⁸He gave Mosheh (when he had finished speaking with him on Mount Sinay) the two affirmation tablets, stone tablets written by God's finger.

32 But the people saw that Mosheh was shamefully long about coming down from the mountain. So the people congregated against Aharon and said to him, 'Up, make us gods who will go before us, because this Mosheh, the man who brought us up from the country of Misrayim – we don't know what's happened to him.' ²So Aharon said to them, 'Tear off the gold rings that are in the ears of your wives, your sons and your daughters, and bring them to me.'

³The entire people tore off the gold rings that were in their ears and brought them to Aharon. ⁴He took it from their hand, shaped it with a tool and made it into a bullock figurine. They said, 'Yisra'el, these are your gods who brought you up from the country of Misrayim.'

⁵Aharon saw and built an altar before it. Aharon called out, 'Tomorrow is a festival for Yahweh!' ⁶So they started early next day and offered up burnt offerings and brought up well-being sacrifices. The people sat down to eat and to drink, and set about enjoying themselves.

⁷Yahweh spoke to Mosheh: 'Get yourself down, because your people whom you brought up from the country of Misrayim have acted devastatingly. ⁸They have departed quickly from the way that I ordered them. They've made themselves a bullock figurine, and bowed low to it and sacrificed to it, and said, "Yisra'el, these are your gods who brought you up from the country of Misrayim."'

⁹Yahweh said to Mosheh, 'I've looked at this people. Here, it's a tough-necked people. ¹⁰So now, let me be, so my anger may rage against them and I may finish them off, and make you into a big nation.'

How to pray for rebels and how to lose your temper

¹¹Mosheh sought the goodwill of Yahweh his God: 'Yahweh, why should your anger rage against your people whom you got out of the country of Misrayim by great energy and by a strong hand? ¹²Why should the Misrayimites say, "It was in connection with something bad that he got them out, to kill them in the mountains and finish them off from on the face of the ground"? Turn back from your angry rage. Relent of bringing something bad to your people. ¹³Be mindful of Abraham, Yitshaq and Yisra'el, your servants, to whom you swore by your own self: "I will make your offspring as numerous as the stars in the heavens, and this entire country of which I spoke I will give to your offspring and they will have it as their permanent domain."' ¹⁴And Yahweh relented of the bad thing he spoke of bringing to his people.

¹⁵Then Mosheh turned his face and went down from the mountain with the two affirmation tablets in his hand, tablets written on both their surfaces. They were written this side and that. ¹⁶The tablets were God's work. The writing was God's writing, cut on the tablets.

¹⁷Yehoshua heard the sound of the people with their shouting and said to Mosheh, 'The sound of battle in the camp!' ¹⁸But he said,

It's not the sound of singing in strength,
and it's not the sound of singing in weakness,
the sound of singing that I'm hearing.

¹⁹When he got near the camp, he saw the bullock and dancing. Mosheh's anger raged and he threw the tablets from his hands and broke them up beneath the mountain. ²⁰He got the bullock that they had made and burned it in fire. He ground it until it became fine, scattered it on the face of the water and made the Yisra'elites drink it.

'This bullock came out'

²¹Mosheh said to Aharon, 'What did this people do to you that you brought upon it this great wrong?' ²²Aharon said, 'May my

lord's anger not rage. You know this people, that it's the epitome of what is bad. ²³They said to me, "Make us gods that will go before us, because this Mosheh, the man who brought us up from the country of Misrayim – we don't know what has happened to him." ²⁴So I said to them, "Whoever has gold, tear it off." They gave it to me and I threw it into the fire, and this bullock came out.'

²⁵Mosheh saw the people – it was gone wild, because Aharon had let it go wild, with contempt for those who rose up against them. ²⁶Mosheh stood in the camp gateway and said, 'Who belongs to Yahweh – to me!' All the Levites gathered to him. ²⁷He said to them, 'Yahweh, Yisra'el's God, has said this: "Put, each person, his sword on his thigh. Pass through and come back from gateway to gateway in the camp and kill each person his brother, each person his friend and each person the one near to him."'

²⁸The Levites acted in accordance with Mosheh's word, and of the people that day there fell some 3,000 people. ²⁹Mosheh said, 'They've commissioned you today for Yahweh, because each person was against his son and against his brother, to bestow a blessing on you today.'

³⁰Next day Mosheh said to the people, 'You – you've done a great wrong, but I'll now go up to God. Maybe I can make expiation for your wrongdoing.' ³¹So Mosheh went back to Yahweh and said, 'Oh, it was a great wrong this people did when they made gold gods for themselves. ³²But now, if you could carry their wrongdoing . . . But if not, please wipe me out from the document that you wrote.'

³³Yahweh said to Mosheh, 'Whoever did wrong in relation to me, I'll wipe him out from my document. ³⁴So now, get going, lead the people where I spoke you of. There, my envoy – he'll go before you, but on the day I attend to them, I shall attend to them in respect of their wrongdoing.'

A place where people could check things out with God

³⁵Yahweh hit the people because they made the bullock, which Aharon made,

33

and Yahweh spoke to Mosheh: 'Get going, go up from here, you and the people that you brought up from the country of Misrayim, to the country that I swore to Abraham, to Yitshaq and to Ya'aqob, saying "To your offspring I will give it." ²I shall send an envoy before you and drive out the Kena'anite, the Amorite, the Hittite, the Perizzite, the Hivvite and the Yebusite – ³to a country flowing with milk and syrup. Because I shall not go up among you, because you're a tough-necked people, in case I finish you off on the way.' ⁴When the people heard this bad thing, they took up grieving and no one put on his finery.

⁵Yahweh said to Mosheh, 'Say to the Yisra'elites, "You're a tough-necked people. Were I to go up among you for one moment, I could finish you off. So now, take your jewellery off you, so I may know what I should do with you."' ⁶So the Yisra'elites stripped off their jewellery from Mount Horeb onwards.

⁷Now Mosheh would take a tent and spread it for himself outside the camp, some distance from the camp. He called it the appointment tent. Anyone seeking something from Yahweh would go out to the appointment tent that was outside the camp.

⁸When Mosheh went out to the tent, the entire people would get up and stand, each person at his tent entrance, and look at Mosheh until he came into the tent. ⁹As Mosheh came into the tent, the cloud pillar would come down and stand at the tent entrance, and he would speak with Mosheh. ¹⁰The entire people would see the cloud pillar standing at the tent entrance, and the entire people would get up and bow low, each person at his tent entrance. ¹¹Yahweh would speak to Mosheh face to face, as someone speaks to his neighbour, and he would go back to the camp, though his minister, Yehoshua ben Nun, a boy, would not move away from inside the tent.

Rock of Ages

¹²Mosheh said to Yahweh, 'Look, you're saying to me, "Take this people up", but you yourself haven't made known to me whom you'll send with me. And you yourself said, "I've acknowledged you by name; indeed, you've found grace in my eyes." ¹³So now, please, if I've actually found grace in your

eyes, please let me know your way, so I may acknowledge you, in order that I may find grace in your eyes. Look, because this nation is your people.'

[14]He said, 'My face – it will go, and I'll enable you to settle down.' [15]He said to him, 'If your face doesn't go, don't take us up from here. [16]By what means would it be acknowledged, then, that I've found grace in your eyes, I and your people, unless by your going with us, so we may be distinct, I and your people, from any other people on the face of the ground?' [17]Yahweh said to Mosheh, 'This thing, too, that you've spoken of, I will do, because you've found grace in my eyes and I've acknowledged you by name.'

[18]He said, 'Please let me see your splendour.' [19]He said, 'I myself will pass all my goodness before your face and call out the very name of Yahweh before you: I grace whomever I grace and have compassion on whomever I have compassion.' [20]But he said, 'You can't see my face, because a human being can't see me and stay alive.'

[21]But Yahweh said, 'Here is a place with me. Take your stand on the crag. [22]When my splendour passes, I'll put you in a crack in the crag and lay the palm of my hand over you until I've passed by. [23]Then I'll remove my palm and you'll see my back, whereas my face won't be seen.'

Now I will confirm the pact

34 Yahweh said to Mosheh, 'Carve yourself two stone tablets like the first ones, and I'll write on the tablets the words that were on the first tablets, which you broke up. [2]Be ready by the morning, and come up Mount Sinay in the morning and take your stand before me there on the top of the mountain. [3]No one's to come up with you, nor is anyone to appear on the entire mountain, nor are flock or herd to pasture near the mountain.' [4]So he carved two stone tablets like the first ones.

Mosheh started early in the morning and went up Mount Sinay as Yahweh ordered him. He took the two stone tablets in his hand. [5]Yahweh came down in a cloud, took his stand with him there and called out the very name of Yahweh. [6]Yahweh passed before his face.

Yahweh called out, 'Yahweh, God compassionate and gracious, long-tempered, big in commitment and truthfulness, [7]preserving commitment towards the thousands, carrying waywardness, rebellion and wrongdoing; he certainly doesn't treat people as free of guilt, attending to parents' waywardness in connection with children and with grandchildren, with thirds and with fourths.'

[8]Mosheh hurried and bent his head to the ground and bowed low, [9]and said, 'Please, if I have indeed found grace in your eyes, will the Lord, will the Lord please go among us? Because this is a tough-necked people, pardon our waywardness and our wrongdoing. Have us as your domain.'

[10]He said, 'Here, I am going to solemnize a pact. In front of all your people I will do extraordinary things that haven't been created in the entire earth or among all the nations. The entire people among whom you are will see how awe-inspiring is the deed of Yahweh that I'm going to do with you.

Promises and decrees reaffirmed

[11]See that you keep what I'm ordering you today. Here I am, I'm going to drive out from before you the Amorite, the Kena'anite, the Hittite, the Perizzite, the Hivvite and the Yebusite.
>[12]Keep watch over yourself so that you don't solemnize a pact with the people living in the country into which you're coming, so that it doesn't become a snare among you. [13]Because you're to demolish their altars, break up their columns and cut down their totem poles. [14]Because you will not bow low to any god, because Yahweh, whose name is 'Passionate', is the passionate God. [15]You are not to solemnize a pact with the people living in the country. They will whore after their gods and sacrifice for their gods, and someone will call you and you'll eat of his sacrifice. [16]You'll take some of his daughters for your sons, and his daughters will whore after their gods, and get your sons to whore after their gods.
>[17]You will not make cast-metal gods for yourself.

¹⁸You're to keep the Flatbread Festival. For seven days you're to eat flatbread, which I ordered at the set time in the month of Aviv, because in the month of Aviv you got out of Misrayim. ¹⁹Every opener of the womb is mine, and all your livestock that's born male, the first offspring of ox and sheep. ²⁰A donkey's opener you're to redeem with a sheep, but if you don't redeem it, you're to break its neck. Every firstborn among your children, you're to redeem.

People may not appear before me empty-handed.

²¹For six days you can serve, but on the seventh day you're to stop. In ploughing and in harvest you're to stop.

The magnificent presence

²²You're to perform the Shabu'ot Festival for yourself, the first products of the wheat harvest, and the Ingathering Festival, the turning of the year. ²³Three times in the year all your males are to appear before the Lord Yahweh, Yisra'el's God, ²⁴because I shall dispossess nations from before you and widen your border, and no one will desire your land when you go up to appear before Yahweh your God three times in the year.

²⁵You will not slaughter the blood of a sacrifice for me accompanied by leavened bread.

The sacrifice of the Pesah Festival will not stay until morning.

²⁶The very first of the first products of your land you're to bring to the house of Yahweh your God.

You will not cook a kid goat in its mother's milk.'

²⁷Yahweh said to Mosheh, 'Write these words for yourself, because on the basis of these words I solemnize a pact with you and with Yisra'el.'

²⁸He was there with Yahweh for forty days and forty nights; he didn't eat food and he didn't drink water. He wrote on the tablets the words of the pact, the Ten Words.

²⁹When Mosheh came down from Mount Sinay with the two affirmation tablets in Mosheh's hand as he came down from the mountain, Mosheh didn't know that the skin of his face emanated through his speaking with him. ³⁰Aharon and all the Yisra'elites saw Mosheh: there, the skin of his face emanated. They were afraid to come up to him. ³¹Mosheh called to them, and Aharon and all the assembly's leaders came back to him and Mosheh spoke to them. ³²Afterwards, all the Yisra'elites came up and he gave them orders about all that Yahweh had spoken with him on Mount Sinay.

³³When Mosheh had finished speaking with them he put a veil on his face. ³⁴When Mosheh came before Yahweh to speak with him he would remove the veil until he came out. Then he would come out and speak to the Yisra'elites about what he had been ordered. ³⁵The Yisra'elites would see Mosheh's face, how the skin of Mosheh's face emanated, and Mosheh would put back the veil on his face until he came to speak with him.

The commission

35 Mosheh got the entire assembly of the Yisra'elites to congregate, and he said to them, 'These are the things that Yahweh has ordered you to do. ²For six days work can be done, but on the seventh day it will be sacred for you, a complete stopping, for Yahweh. Anyone who does work on it is to be put to death. ³You're not to burn a fire among all your settlements on the stopping day.'

⁴Mosheh said to the entire assembly of the Yisra'elites: 'This is the thing that Yahweh has ordered. ⁵Get from among yourselves a contribution for Yahweh. Everyone who's free in heart can bring Yahweh's contribution: gold, silver, copper; ⁶ blue, purple and bright crimson, linen, goats' [hair]; ⁷ram skins dyed red, dolphin skins, acacia wood; ⁸oil for lighting, spices for the anointing oil and the aromatic incense, ⁹onyx stones and stones for the mountings for the chasuble and for the pouch.

¹⁰Everyone who is smart of mind among you, they're to come and make everything that Yahweh has ordered: ¹¹the dwelling, the tent and its covering, its clasps and its planks, its bars, its posts and its sockets, ¹²the chest and its poles, the expiation cover and the screen

curtain, ¹³the table, its poles and all its articles, and the presence bread, ¹⁴the candelabrum for lighting, its articles, its lamps and the oil for lighting, ¹⁵the incense altar and its poles, the anointing oil and the aromatic incense, the entrance screen for the dwelling entrance, ¹⁶the altar for the burnt offering, the copper grating that it has, its poles and all its articles, the basin and its stand, ¹⁷the hangings for the courtyard, its posts and its sockets, and the screen for the courtyard gateway, ¹⁸the pegs for the dwelling, the pegs for the courtyard and their ropes, ¹⁹the liturgical garments for ministering in the sacred place, the sacred garments for Aharon the priest, and the garments for his sons to act as priests.'

The enthusiastic giving

²⁰The entire assembly of the Yisra'elites went out of Mosheh's presence, ²¹then came, every individual whose mind lifted him up and everyone whose spirit made him free, and brought a contribution for Yahweh for the work on the appointment tent and for all its service, and for the sacred garments.

²²They came, men along with women, everyone who was free in heart, and brought brooches, earrings, rings and necklaces – all objects of gold, each individual who brought an offering of gold for Yahweh. ²³Everyone with whom there could be found blue, purple and bright crimson, linen, goats' [hair], ram skins dyed red or dolphin skins, brought them. ²⁴Everyone who was taking up a contribution of silver or copper brought the offering for Yahweh. Everyone with whom acacia wood could be found for any of the work for the service brought it. ²⁵Every woman who was smart of mind spun with her hands and brought the spinning, blue, purple and bright crimson, and linen. ²⁶All the women whose mind lifted them up with smartness spun the goats' [hair]. ²⁷The leaders brought onyx stones and stones for the mountings on the chasuble and on the pouch, ²⁸the spice and the oil for lighting, for the anointing oil and for the aromatic incense. ²⁹Every man and woman whose heart made them free to bring for all the work that Yahweh ordered them to do, through Mosheh – the Yisra'elites brought a free offering for Yahweh.

The over-enthusiastic giving

³⁰Mosheh said to the Yisra'elites: 'Look, Yahweh has called by name for Betsal'el ben Uri, son of Hur, of the clan of Yehudah. ³¹He's filled him with a divine spirit, with smartness, with discernment and with knowledge, in any workmanship, ³²for drafting designs to make things with gold, with silver and with copper, ³³in cutting stone for mountings and in carving wood, to make things in any design craft. ³⁴He's put in his mind how to teach, he and Oholi'ab ben Ahisamak of the clan of Dan. ³⁵He's filled them with smartness of mind to do any work: the craftsman, the designer, the embroiderer in blue, purple and bright crimson, and in linen, and the weaver, workers in any craft and makers of designs.

36 So Betsal'el and Oholi'ab and everyone smart of mind, in whom Yahweh has put smartness and discernment so as to know how to do the work for the service in the sacred place, are to do all that Yahweh ordered.'

²So Mosheh called for Betsal'el and Oholi'ab and everyone smart of mind, into whose mind Yahweh had put smartness, everyone whose mind lifted him up, to draw near for the work, to do it. ³They got from before Mosheh every contribution that the Yisra'elites had brought for the work for the service in the sacred place, to do it.

When those people still brought to him a free gift, morning by morning, ⁴all the smart people doing all the work in the sacred place came, one by one from his work, which they were doing, ⁵and said to Mosheh, 'The people are bringing much, more than enough for the service involved in the work that Yahweh ordered us to do.' ⁶So Mosheh made an order and they passed the sound through the camp, 'No man or woman is to do any more work towards the contribution for the sacred place.' So the people finished bringing. ⁷The work was enough for the work, to do it. It left some over.

Hangings for the dwelling

⁸The people who were doing the work, everyone who was smart of mind, made the dwelling of ten pieces of woven linen and blue, purple and bright crimson; with sphinxes,

designer's work, he made them. ⁹The length of each piece, twenty-eight cubits, and the width of each piece, four cubits – one size for all the pieces. ¹⁰He joined five of the pieces one to the other, and joined the other five pieces one to the other. ¹¹He made loops of blue on the lip of the one piece at the edge of its joined set, and in this way made them at the lip of the edging piece in the second joined set. ¹²He made fifty loops on the one piece and made fifty loops at the edge of the piece that's in the second joined set, with the loops holding one to the other. ¹³He made fifty gold clasps, and joined the pieces to one another with the clasps so the dwelling became one unit.

¹⁴He made pieces from goats' [hair] for a tent over the dwelling; eleven pieces he made them. ¹⁵The length of each piece thirty by the cubit; the width four cubits each piece, one size for the eleven pieces. ¹⁶He joined five of the pieces on their own, and six of the pieces on their own. ¹⁷He made fifty loops on the lip of one outermost piece in a joined set, and fifty loops on the lip of the piece in the other joined set. ¹⁸He made fifty copper clasps to join the tent so it became one unit. ¹⁹He made a covering for the tent of ram skins dyed red and a covering of dolphin skins above it.

The frame for the dwelling

²⁰He made the planks for the dwelling of acacia wood, standing upright, ²¹the length of a plank ten cubits, the width of a plank a cubit and a half, each one, ²²two projections for each plank, parallel one to the other. So he did for all the dwelling's planks. ²³He made the planks for the dwelling:
twenty planks for the south (southern) aspect; ²⁴he made forty silver sockets under the twenty planks, two sockets under the one plank for its two projections and two sockets under the next plank for its two projections.
²⁵For the dwelling's second side, on the north aspect: twenty planks, ²⁶with their forty silver sockets, two sockets under the one plank and two sockets under the next plank.
²⁷For the back of the dwelling, to the west, he made six planks, ²⁸and he made two planks for the corners of the dwelling, at the back. ²⁹They were double underneath, but together they were whole at its top, at the one ring. So he made it for both of them, for the two corners. ³⁰Thus there were eight planks with their silver sockets, sixteen sockets: two sockets under one plank and two sockets under the next plank.

³¹He made bars of acacia wood: five for the planks in one side of the dwelling, ³²five bars for planks in the second side of the dwelling, and five bars for the planks in the dwelling at the back, to the west. ³³He made the central bar in the middle of the planks running from end to end. ³⁴The planks he overlaid with gold. The rings he made of gold as housing for the bars, and he overlaid the bars with gold.

The affirmation chest and the expiation cover

³⁵He made the curtain of blue, purple and bright crimson, and woven linen. He made it as designer's work, with sphinxes. ³⁶He made for it four posts of acacia and overlaid them with gold, with their gold hooks, and he cast for them four silver sockets. ³⁷He made a screen for the tent entrance, of blue, purple and bright crimson, and woven linen, embroiderer's work, ³⁸and its five posts with their hooks. He overlaid their tops and their clasps with gold. The five sockets were copper.

37 Betsal'el made the chest of acacia wood, its length two and a half cubits, its width a cubit and a half, and its height a cubit and a half. ²He overlaid it with pure gold, inside and outside, and made a gold moulding for it all round. ³He cast four gold rings for it, on its four feet, two rings on one side of it and two on the other. ⁴He made poles of acacia wood and overlaid them with gold, ⁵and inserted the poles into the rings on the sides of the chest, for carrying the chest.

⁶He made an expiation cover of pure gold, its length two and a half cubits and its width a cubit and a half, ⁷and he made two gold sphinxes (of hammered work he made them) at the two ends of the expiation cover, ⁸one sphinx at one end and the other sphinx at the other end. He made the sphinxes coming from the expiation cover at its two ends. ⁹The sphinxes were spreading their wings upwards, shielding

the expiation cover with their wings, and with their faces one towards the other; the sphinxes' faces were towards the expiation cover.

The candelabrum

¹⁰He made the table of acacia wood, its length two cubits, its width one cubit and its height a cubit and a half. ¹¹He overlaid it with pure gold and made a gold moulding for it all round. ¹²He made a rim of a handbreadth for it all round and made a gold moulding for its rim all round. ¹³He made four gold rings for it and put the rings at the four corners that were at its four feet. ¹⁴The rings were close by the rim as housing for the poles for carrying the table. ¹⁵He made the poles of acacia wood and overlaid them with gold. ¹⁶He made the articles that would be on the table – its dishes, its ladles, its pitchers and its bowls, in which the drink offering would be poured – of pure gold.

¹⁷He made the candelabrum of pure gold. He made the candelabrum of hammered work, its base and its stem. Its cups, its flowers and its petals came from it; ¹⁸six stems going out from its flanks, three stems of the candelabrum from its one flank and three stems of the candelabrum from its second flank; ¹⁹three cups made like almond blossom on one stem, flower and petal, three stems made like almond blossom on another stem, flower and petal; so for the six stems going out from the candelabrum. ²⁰On the candelabrum four cups made like almond blossom, its flowers and its petals; ²¹a flower beneath two stems issuing from it, and a flower beneath two stems issuing from it, and a flower beneath two stems issuing from it, for the six branches going out from it; ²²their flowers and their stems came from it, all of it a single hammered work, pure gold. ²³He made its seven lamps, its tongs and its pans of pure gold. ²⁴He made it and all its articles out of a talent of pure gold.

The altars

²⁵He made the incense altar of acacia wood, its length a cubit, its width a cubit (square) and its height two cubits; its horns came from it. ²⁶He overlaid it with pure gold – its top, its sides all round and its horns. He made a gold moulding for it all round. ²⁷He made two gold rings for it under its moulding, on its two sides, on its two flanks, for housing for the poles to carry it with. ²⁸He made the poles of acacia wood and overlaid them with gold. ²⁹He made the sacred anointing oil and the pure aromatic incense, blender's work.

38 He made the altar for burnt offering of acacia wood, its length five cubits, its width five cubits (square) and its height three cubits. ²He made its horns on its four corners (its horns came from it) and overlaid it with copper. ³He made all the altar's utensils: the buckets, the shovels, the basins, the forks and the pans; he made all its utensils of copper. ⁴He made a grating for the altar, a mesh made of copper, below its ledge, underneath, halfway up it. ⁵He cast four rings at the four corners of the copper mesh as housing for the poles. ⁶He made the poles of acacia wood and overlaid them with copper, ⁷and inserted the poles into the rings on the two sides of the altar for carrying it with. He made it hollow, of boards.

⁸He made the copper basin and its copper stand with the mirrors of the women who served, who did their serving at the entrance of the appointment tent.

The courtyard

⁹He made the courtyard:
on the south (southern) aspect: hangings for the courtyard, woven linen, a hundred by the cubit; ¹⁰their twenty posts and their twenty sockets, copper; the posts' hooks and their clasps, silver;
¹¹on the north aspect: a hundred by the cubit; their twenty posts and their twenty sockets, copper; the posts' hooks and their clasps, silver;
¹²on the west aspect: hangings, fifty by the cubit; their posts, ten; their sockets, ten; the posts' hooks and their clasps, silver;
¹³on the front aspect, the east: fifty by the cubit: ¹⁴hangings, fifteen cubits to the shoulder; their posts, three; their sockets, three; ¹⁵for the second shoulder (on each side of the courtyard gateway), hangings,

fifteen cubits; their posts, three; their sockets, three; ¹⁶all the courtyard hangings, woven linen, all round; ¹⁷the sockets for the posts, copper; the hooks and the clasps of the posts, silver; the overlay of their tops, silver; all the courtyard posts were clasped with silver; ¹⁸the screen for the courtyard gateway, embroiderer's work: blue, purple and bright crimson, and woven linen, twenty cubits in length, its height (by width) five cubits, close by the courtyard hangings; ¹⁹their four posts and their four sockets, copper; their hooks, silver; the overlay of their tops and their clasps, silver; ²⁰all the pegs for the dwelling and for the courtyard all round, copper.

²¹This is the register of the dwelling, the affirmation dwelling, which was made at Mosheh's bidding, the Levites' service at the hand of Itamar ben Aharon the priest. ²²Betsal'el ben Uri, son of Hur of the clan of Yehudah – he made all that Yahweh had ordered Mosheh, ²³and with him Oholi'ab ben Ahisamak of the clan of Dan, the craftsman, the designer, and the embroiderer in blue, purple and bright crimson, and in linen.

How much it was!

²⁴All the gold that was made into the work, in all the work in the sacred place and that was the gold of the elevation offering: 29 talents and 730 sheqels (by the sanctuary sheqel). ²⁵The silver in the assembly register: 100 talents and 1,775 sheqels (by the sanctuary sheqel), ²⁶a fraction per head (a half-sheqel by the sanctuary sheqel) for each person passing through the register, from the age of twenty years and upwards: 603,550 people. ²⁷The 100 talents of silver were for casting the sockets for the sacred place and the curtain sockets, 100 sockets for the 100 talents, a talent for a socket. ²⁸He made the 1,775 sheqels into hooks for the posts, overlaid their tops and clasped them.

²⁹The copper of the elevation offering: 70 talents and 2,400 sheqels. ³⁰With it he made the entrance sockets for the appointment tent, the copper altar and the copper grating that it had, and all the altar's utensils; ³¹the courtyard sockets all round and the courtyard gateway sockets; and all the dwelling's pegs and all the courtyard's pegs all round.

39 From the blue, purple and bright crimson, they made the liturgical garments for ministering in the sacred place, and they made the sacred garments that were for Aharon, as Yahweh had ordered Mosheh.

²He made the chasuble of gold, of blue, purple and bright crimson, and of woven linen. ³They beat out sheets of gold and cut wires for working into the middle of the blue, of the purple, of the bright crimson and of the linen, designer's work. ⁴They made joining shoulder pieces for it; it was joined to two of its corners. ⁵Its chasuble's design-work strap, which was on it, came from it; it was made like its work, gold, blue, purple, bright crimson and woven linen, as Yahweh had ordered Mosheh.

The pouch

⁶They made the onyx stones surrounded by gold braids, engraved with seal engravings corresponding to the names of Yisra'el's sons. ⁷He put them on the chasuble's shoulder pieces as reminder stones for Yisra'el's sons, as Yahweh had ordered Mosheh.

⁸He made the pouch as designer's work like the work of the chasuble, gold, blue, purple and bright crimson, and woven linen. ⁹It was square. They made the pouch folded double, a handbreadth its length and a handbreadth its width, folded double. ¹⁰They filled it with four rows of stones:

the first row: a row of carnelian, chrysolyte and emerald;
¹¹the second row: turquoise, sapphire and amethyst;
¹²the third row: jacinth, agate and crystal;
¹³the fourth row: beryl, onyx and jasper.

They were surrounded by gold braids in their fillings. ¹⁴The stones corresponded to the names of Yisra'el's sons, twelve corresponding to their names, with seal engravings, each corresponding to its name, for the twelve clans.

¹⁵On the pouch they made plaited chains, woven work, pure gold. ¹⁶They made two gold

braids and two gold rings and put the two rings on the two edges of the pouch. ¹⁷They put the two gold weavings on the two rings at the edges of the pouch. ¹⁸The two ends of the two weavings they put on the chasuble's shoulder pieces near its front.

As Yahweh had ordered

¹⁹They made two gold rings and put them on the two edges of the pouch at its lip, which is on the side nearer the chasuble. ²⁰They made two gold rings and put them on the chasuble's two shoulder pieces underneath, near the front, close by its join, above the chasuble's design-work strap. ²¹They attached the pouch by its rings to the chasuble's rings with a blue cord, so it was on the chasuble's design-work strap and the pouch would not come loose from on the chasuble, as Yahweh had ordered Mosheh.
²²They made the chasuble coat, weaver's work, all blue, ²³the opening of the coat in the middle of it like the opening of a vest, with the lip for its opening all round so it would not tear. ²⁴On the coat's hems they made pomegranates of blue, purple and bright crimson, woven, ²⁵and they made bells of pure gold and put the bells in among the pomegranates on the coat's hems all round, ²⁶a bell and a pomegranate, a bell and a pomegranate, on the coat's hems all round, for ministering, as Yahweh had ordered Mosheh. ²⁷They made linen tunics, weaver's work, for Aharon and for his sons, ²⁸the linen turban, ornamental linen mitres, cloth shorts (woven linen), ²⁹and the sash of woven linen, blue, purple and bright crimson, embroiderer's work, as Yahweh had ordered Mosheh.
³⁰They made the medallion, the sacred diadem of pure gold, and wrote on it a seal inscription, 'Sacred for Yahweh'. ³¹They put a blue cord on it so as to put it on the turban above, as Yahweh had ordered Mosheh.

And Mosheh blessed them

³²So the entire service of the dwelling, the appointment tent, finished. The Yisra'elites did everything in accordance with all that Yahweh had ordered Mosheh, so they did. ³³They brought the dwelling to Mosheh with the tent and all its articles – its clasps, its planks, its bars, its posts, its sockets, ³⁴the covering of ram skins dyed red, the covering of dolphin skins, the screen curtain, ³⁵the affirmation chest and its poles and the expiation cover; ³⁶the table and all its articles and the presence bread; ³⁷the pure candelabrum, its lamps (lamps in order) and all its articles, and the oil for lighting; ³⁸the gold altar, the anointing oil, the aromatic incense and the screen for the tent entrance; ³⁹the copper altar, the copper grating that it had, its poles and all its articles, the basin and its stand; ⁴⁰the courtyard hangings, its posts and its sockets, the screen for the courtyard gateway, its cords and its pegs; and all the articles for the service of the dwelling, the appointment tent; ⁴¹the liturgical garments for ministering in the sacred place, the sacred garments for Aharon the priest, and his sons' garments for acting as priests.
⁴²In accordance with all that Yahweh had ordered Mosheh, so the Yisra'elites had done the entire service. ⁴³Mosheh saw all the work: there, they had done it. As Yahweh had ordered, so they had done. And Mosheh blessed them.

Instructions for assembling and sanctifying

40 Yahweh spoke to Mosheh: ²'On the first day of the first month you're to set up the dwelling, the appointment tent. ³You're to place there the affirmation chest and screen over the chest with the curtain. ⁴You're to bring in the table and see to its arrangement, bring in the candelabrum and put up its lamps, ⁵put the gold incense altar before the affirmation chest, and place the screen for the courtyard gateway.
⁶You're to put the altar for burnt offering before the entrance of the dwelling, the appointment tent, ⁷put the basin between the appointment tent and the altar and put water there, ⁸place the courtyard all round, and put in place the screen for the courtyard gateway.
⁹You're to get the anointing oil and anoint the dwelling and everything that's in it, and make it and all its articles sacred, so it may be

sacred. ¹⁰You're to anoint the altar for burnt offering and all its articles and make the altar sacred, so the altar may be especially sacred, ¹¹and you're to anoint the basin and its stand and make it sacred.

¹²You're to present Aharon and his sons at the entrance of the appointment tent and wash them with water, ¹³put the sacred garments on Aharon, and anoint him and make him sacred so he may act as priest for me. ¹⁴You're to present his sons and put tunics on them, ¹⁵and anoint them as you anointed their father so they may act as priests for me. Their anointing will continue to be for them for a permanent priesthood, through their generations.'

¹⁶Mosheh acted in accordance with all that Yahweh had ordered him, so he did.

Yahweh's splendour fills the dwelling

¹⁷In the first month in the second year, on the first of the month, the dwelling was set up. ¹⁸Mosheh set up the dwelling.

He put its sockets and placed its planks and put its bars and set up its posts. ¹⁹He spread the tent over the dwelling and put the tent covering over it, on top, as Yahweh had ordered Mosheh. ²⁰He got the affirmation and put it in the chest, placed the poles on the chest and put the expiation cover on the chest, on top, ²¹brought the chest into the dwelling, placed the screening curtain and screened off the affirmation chest, as Yahweh had ordered Mosheh. ²²He put the table in the appointment tent on the side of the dwelling, northward, outside the curtain, ²³and saw to the arrangement of bread on it before Yahweh, as Yahweh had ordered Mosheh.

²⁴He placed the candelabrum in the appointment tent in front of the table on the side of the dwelling southward, ²⁵and put up the lamps before Yahweh, as Yahweh had ordered Mosheh. ²⁶He placed the gold altar in the appointment tent before the curtain, ²⁷and burned aromatic incense on it, as Yahweh had ordered Mosheh. ²⁸He placed the screen for the dwelling entrance, ²⁹and placed the altar for burnt offering at the entrance of the dwelling, the appointment tent, and offered up the burnt offering and the grain offering on it, as Yahweh had ordered Mosheh. ³⁰He placed the basin between the appointment tent and the altar and put water for washing there, ³¹so that Mosheh and Aharon and his sons could wash their hands and their feet from it, ³²so they could wash when they came into the appointment tent and when they drew near the altar, as Yahweh had ordered Mosheh. ³³He set up the courtyard all round the dwelling and the altar and put in place the screen for the courtyard entrance.

When Mosheh finished the work, ³⁴the cloud covered the appointment tent, and Yahweh's splendour filled the dwelling. ³⁵Mosheh couldn't go into the appointment tent because the cloud dwelt over it and Yahweh's splendour filled the dwelling.

³⁶When the cloud lifted from over the dwelling, the Yisra'elites would move on, during all their movements. ³⁷If the cloud didn't lift, they wouldn't move on until the day it lifted, ³⁸because Yahweh's cloud would be over the dwelling by day and the fire would be in it by night, before the eyes of Yisra'el's entire household during all their movements.

Leviticus

Leviticus takes its name from the Levites, the people who traced their descent back to Jacob's son Levi. Among them were the descendants of Aaron, Levi's great-grandson; they were the priests, people who had responsibility for key aspects of the offering of sacrifices. The other descendants of Levi, the non-priestly Levites, are commonly referred to simply as 'the Levites', for short; they were responsible for the many practical aspects of worship in the sanctuary.

The priests and the (other) Levites also had important responsibility for teaching people about what it means to be a proper Israelite, and much of Leviticus comprises a handbook on matters the Levites need to know about, in order to give such teaching. It also covers matters the priests and Levites themselves need to know about, in order to do their own work.

Chapters 1—7 of the book comprise instructions for them about how to offer the different sacrifices, which can be

- a way of giving something to God as an act of worship;
- a way of sharing in a fellowship meal with God, especially when one had reason to express gratitude to God for some blessing;
- a way of finding purification or decontamination when one was affected by a taboo;
- a way of making reparation for wrongdoing (sacrifice was not directly a means by which one found forgiveness for sins; that came on the basis of God's mercy and grace when one repented).

These opening chapters of the book thus pose challenges to us about worship, about giving to God, about fellowship with God, about purification and about reparation.

Chapters 8—10 recount how Moses ordains Aaron and his sons, how they begin their ministry, but then how things go terribly wrong. Leviticus thus continues the story in Exodus.

Chapters 11—16 revert to detailed instructions. They now concern things that make people taboo and thus forbidden to come into the sanctuary. Many of these are things that clash with Yahweh's own nature, particularly death and sex. The rules in Leviticus can drive readers to face the reality of death and face the way we can make sex into a god. Infringing such taboos would defile the sanctuary and risk making God unwilling to be there. An annual expiation day purifies the sanctuary from the effect of such breaches.

Chapters 17—27 offer miscellaneous instructions about ordinary people's lives, with an underlying concern for Israel to be different, to be sacred as God is sacred. It means maintaining distinctions such as those between God and sex or God and death, and also maintaining distinctions of a moral kind. Behaviour that doesn't match Yahweh's moral character is at least as reprehensible as behaviour that doesn't match other aspects of who God is.

The rules for life cover much of the same ground as Exodus 20—24. Genesis to Deuteronomy as a whole is a compilation of teachings that the Holy Spirit inspired during Israel's history, when different contexts required God to give the people different guidance to match different situations. The teaching in Leviticus suggests a context when Israel had become a nation with a central government, a capital and a 'proper' temple.

Attributing the instructions to Moses then affirms that these instructions are outworkings of principles that Moses would affirm. They're the kind of thing Moses would say if he were living in the time of (say) Hezekiah in the eighth century, 500 years after Moses – though we don't know which particular century Leviticus actually comes from.

Giving to God: something from your herd

1 He called Mosheh [Moses]; Yahweh spoke to him from the appointment tent: ²"Speak to the Yisra'elites [Israelites] and say to them: "When one of you presents an offering of an animal for Yahweh, you may present your offering from the herd or from the flock.

³If his offering is a burnt offering from the herd, he's to present a male that's whole. He's to present it at the entrance of the appointment tent, for his acceptance before Yahweh. ⁴He's to lean his hand on the head of the burnt offering so it may be acceptable for him, to make expiation for him. ⁵He's to slaughter the animal from the herd before Yahweh, and Aharon's [Aaron's] sons, the priests, are to present the blood and toss the blood over the altar that's at the entrance of the appointment tent, all round.

⁶He's to skin the burnt offering and cut it up into its parts. ⁷The sons of Aharon the priest are to put fire on the altar and arrange wood on the fire, ⁸and Aharon's sons, the priests, are to arrange the parts, with the head and with the suet, on the wood that's on the fire that's on the altar. ⁹He's to wash its innards and its legs in water, and the priest is to turn the entire thing into smoke at the altar, a burnt offering, a gift offering, a nice smell for Yahweh.

Giving something smaller

¹⁰If his offering as a burnt offering is from the flock, from the sheep or from the goats, he's to present a male that's whole. ¹¹He's to slaughter it before Yahweh at the side of the altar, to the north, and Aharon's sons, the priests, are to toss its blood over the altar, all round. ¹²He's to cut it up into its parts, and the priest is to arrange them with its head and with its suet on the wood that's on the fire that's on the altar. ¹³He's to wash the innards and the legs with water, and the priest is to present the entire thing and turn it into smoke at the altar. It's a burnt offering, a gift offering, a nice smell for Yahweh.

¹⁴If his offering for Yahweh is a burnt offering from the birds, he's to present his offering from doves or from young pigeons. ¹⁵The priest is to present it at the altar, wring its head and turn it into smoke at the altar. Its blood is to be drained out against the side of the altar. ¹⁶He's to remove its crop with its plumage and throw it beside the altar to the east, to the place for waste. ¹⁷The priest is to tear it open by its wings, not divide it, and turn it to smoke at the altar on the wood that's on the fire. It's a burnt offering, a gift offering, a nice smell for Yahweh.

The grain offering

2 When a person presents as an offering a grain offering for Yahweh, his offering is to be fine flour. He's to pour oil on it and put frankincense on it ²and bring it to Aharon's sons, the priests. He's to scoop from there a fistful from its fine flour and from its oil, along with all its frankincense, and the priest is to turn its commemorative portion into smoke at the altar, a gift offering, a nice smell for Yahweh. ³The rest of the grain offering is for Aharon and his sons, something especially sacred from Yahweh's gift offerings.

⁴When you present as an offering a grain offering baked in an oven: fine flour, loaves of flatbread mixed with oil, or flat wafers spread with oil. ⁵If your offering is a grain offering on a griddle, it's to be fine flour mixed with oil, flatbread; ⁶break it into bits and pour oil on it. It's a grain offering. ⁷If your offering is a grain offering in a pan, it's to be made of fine flour in oil.

⁸You may bring for Yahweh a grain offering that's made from these, and one is to present it to the priest and he will bring it up to the altar. ⁹The priest is to take up from the grain offering its commemorative portion and turn it into smoke at the altar, a gift offering, a nice smell for Yahweh. ¹⁰The rest of the grain offering is for Aharon and his sons, something especially sacred from Yahweh's gift offerings.

Season with salt

¹¹No grain offering that you present for Yahweh is to be made with yeast, because all leavened bread and all syrup – you're not to turn any of it into smoke as a gift offering for Yahweh. ¹²You may present them for Yahweh as an offering of the very first [of the harvest], but they may not go up to the altar as a nice smell.

¹³You're to season with salt your every offering that's a grain offering. You're not to let the salt of your pact with God cease from your grain offering. With every offering of yours you're to present salt.

¹⁴If you present a first-products grain offering for Yahweh, you're to present young ears, roasted in fire, kernels from the plantation, as your first-products grain offering. ¹⁵You're to put oil on it and place frankincense on it; it's a grain offering. ¹⁶The priest is to turn its commemorative portion into smoke, some of its kernels and of its oil, along with all its frankincense, as a gift offering for Yahweh.

The sacrifice shared with Yahweh

3 If his offering is a well-being sacrifice: if he's presenting something from the herd, whether male or female, he's to present it as one that's whole, before Yahweh. ²He's to lean his hand on his offering's head and slaughter it at the entrance of the appointment tent, and Aharon's sons, the priests, are to toss the blood over the altar, all round. ³He's to present from the well-being sacrifice, as a gift offering for Yahweh, the fat covering the innards, all the fat that's on the innards, ⁴the two kidneys and the fat that's on them, which is on the loins, and the lobe on the liver; he's to remove it along with the kidneys. ⁵Aharon's sons are to turn it into smoke at the altar, along with the burnt offering that's on the wood that's on the fire, a gift offering, a nice smell for Yahweh.

⁶If his offering as a well-being sacrifice for Yahweh is from the flock, whether male or female, he's to present it as one that's whole. ⁷If he's presenting a sheep as his offering, he's to present it before Yahweh, ⁸lean his hand on his offering's head and slaughter it before the appointment tent. Aharon's sons are to toss its blood over the altar, all round.

All fat belongs to Yahweh

⁹He's to present from the well-being sacrifice, as a gift offering for Yahweh, its fat, the broad tail, whole (which he's to remove close by the backbone), the fat covering the innards, all the fat that's on the innards, ¹⁰the two kidneys and the fat that's on them, which is on the loins, and the lobe on the liver; he's to remove it along with the kidneys. ¹¹The priest is to turn it into smoke at the altar as a meal, as a gift offering for Yahweh.

¹²If his offering is a goat, he's to present it before Yahweh, ¹³lean his hand on its head and slaughter it before the appointment tent. Aharon's sons are to toss its blood over the altar, all round. ¹⁴He's to present from it as his offering, as a gift offering for Yahweh, the fat covering the innards and all the fat that's on the innards, ¹⁵the two kidneys and the fat that's on them, which is on the loins, and the lobe on the liver; he's to remove it along with the kidneys. ¹⁶The priest is to turn them into smoke at the altar as a meal, as a gift offering, as a nice smell.

All fat belongs to Yahweh. ¹⁷It's a permanent decree through your generations in all your settlements. You will not eat any fat or any blood.'"

When a priest does wrong by mistake

4 Yahweh spoke to Mosheh: ²"Speak to the Yisra'elites: "When a person does wrong by mistake in connection with any of Yahweh's orders about what should not be done, and does one of them . . .

³If the anointed priest does wrong and brings liability on the people, for his wrong that he did he's to present for Yahweh a bull from the herd, one that's whole, as a decontamination. ⁴He's to bring the bull to the entrance of the appointment tent before Yahweh, lean his hand on the bull's head and slaughter the bull before Yahweh. ⁵The anointed priest is to get some of the bull's blood and bring it into the appointment tent. ⁶The priest is to dip his finger in the blood and spatter some of the blood seven times before Yahweh, before the curtain of the sacred place.

⁷The priest is to put some of the blood on the horns of the altar of aromatic incense that's in the appointment tent, before Yahweh, and to pour out all the bull's blood at the base of the altar for burnt offering, at the entrance of the appointment tent.

⁸All the fat of the decontamination bull: he's to take up from it the fat covering the innards, all the fat that's on the innards, ⁹the two kidneys

and the fat that's on them, which is on the loins, and the lobe on the liver; he's to remove it along with the kidneys ¹⁰as it's taken up from an ox that's a well-being sacrifice. The priest is to turn them into smoke at the altar for burnt offering. ¹¹The bull's skin and all its flesh, along with its head, its legs, its innards and its intestines: ¹²he's to take the entire bull out to a pure place outside the camp, to where the waste is poured out, and burn it on wood in fire. It's to burn at the place where the waste is poured out.

When the assembly does wrong by mistake

¹³If the entire Yisra'elite assembly make a mistake and something escapes the eyes of the congregation, and they do something in connection with any of Yahweh's orders about what should not be done, and incur liability, ¹⁴and the wrong that they did in connection with it becomes known, the congregation are to present a bull from the herd as a decontamination. They're to bring it before the appointment tent, ¹⁵the assembly's elders are to lean their hands on the bull's head before Yahweh, and one is to slaughter the bull before Yahweh.

¹⁶The anointed priest is to bring some of the bull's blood into the appointment tent. ¹⁷The priest is to dip his finger in the blood and spatter it seven times before Yahweh, before the curtain. ¹⁸He's to put some of the blood on the horns of the altar that's before Yahweh, which is in the appointment tent, and to pour out all the blood at the base of the altar for burnt offering, at the entrance of the appointment tent.

¹⁹All its fat he's to take up from it and turn it into smoke at the altar. ²⁰He's to do to the bull as he did to the decontamination bull; so he's to do to it, and make expiation for them, and it will be pardoned them. ²¹He's to take the bull out, outside the camp, and burn it as he burned the first bull. It's a decontamination for the congregation.

When a leader does wrong by mistake

²²When a leader does wrong and does something in connection with any of Yahweh's orders about what should not be done, by mistake, and incurs liability, ²³or someone causes him to acknowledge his wrong that he did, he's to bring as his offering a he-goat from the flock, one that's whole. ²⁴He's to lean his hand on the goat's head and slaughter it in the place where one slaughters the burnt offering before Yahweh. It's a decontamination. ²⁵The priest is to get some of the decontamination blood with his finger and put it on the horns of the altar for burnt offering, and to pour out its blood at the base of the altar for burnt offering. ²⁶All its fat he's to turn into smoke at the altar, like the fat of the well-being sacrifice. So he's to make expiation for him because of his wrongdoing, and it will be pardoned him.

When an individual does wrong by mistake

²⁷If an individual person from the country's people does wrong by mistake, in doing something in connection with any of Yahweh's orders about what should not be done, and incurs liability, ²⁸or someone causes him to acknowledge his wrong that he did, he's to bring as his offering a she-goat from the flock, one that's whole, a female, for his wrong that he did. ²⁹He's to lean his hand on the head of the decontamination and slaughter the decontamination in the place of burnt offering. ³⁰The priest is to get some of its blood with his finger and put it on the horns of the altar for burnt offering, and to pour out all its blood at the altar's base. ³¹All its fat he's to remove, as the fat was removed from the well-being sacrifice, and the priest is to turn it into smoke at the altar, as a nice smell for Yahweh. So the priest is to make expiation for him, and it will be pardoned him.

³²If he brings a sheep as his offering as a decontamination, he's to bring a female that's whole. ³³He's to lean his hand on the head of the decontamination and slaughter it as a decontamination in the place where one slaughters the burnt offering. ³⁴The priest is to get some of the blood of the decontamination with his finger and put it on the horns of the altar for burnt offering, and to pour out all its blood at the altar's base. ³⁵All its fat he's to remove, as the fat from the sheep of a well-

being sacrifice is removed, and the priest is to turn them into smoke at the altar over Yahweh's gift offering. So the priest is to make expiation for him for his wrong that he did, and it will be pardoned him.

Making reparation

5 When a person does wrong: he heard the sound of a vow and he was a witness (either he saw or he knew). If he doesn't tell, he carries his waywardness. ²Or a person who touches any taboo thing (either the corpse of a taboo creature, the corpse of a taboo domestic animal or the corpse of a taboo teeming creature) and it escapes him, but he's become taboo and he's liable. ³Or when he touches something human that's taboo (in connection with anything taboo for him, by which one becomes taboo) and it escapes him, but he's come to know it and he's liable. ⁴Or when a person swears, blurting with his lips, to act badly or to do good, in connection with anything that a human being may blurt out in an oath, and it escapes him, but he's come to know it and he's liable.

In connection with one of these matters: ⁵when he's liable in connection with one of these matters, he must make confession of what he's done wrong in connection with it, ⁶and bring his reparation to Yahweh for his wrong that he did: a female from the flock, a ewe-lamb or a she-goat from the flock, as a decontamination; and the priest is to make expiation for him in relation to his wrongdoing. ⁷If his hand doesn't extend to enough for a sheep, he's to bring to Yahweh as his reparation for what he's done wrong two doves or two young pigeons, one as a decontamination and one as a burnt offering. ⁸He's to bring them to the priest and he's to present the one that's a decontamination first, wring its head from near its neck, but not divide it, ⁹and spatter some of the decontamination blood against the side of the altar. The remainder of the blood is to drain at the altar's base. It's a decontamination. ¹⁰The second he's to make as a burnt offering in accordance with the ruling.

So the priest is to make expiation for him because of his wrong that he did, and it will be pardoned him.

More occasions for reparation

¹¹If his hand doesn't stretch to two doves or two young pigeons, he's to bring as his offering for what he did wrong a tenth of a barrel of fine flour as a decontamination. He's not to place oil on it and he's not to put frankincense on it, because it's a decontamination. ¹²He's to bring it to the priest, and the priest is to scoop out of it a fistful as a commemorative portion and turn it into smoke at the altar over Yahweh's gift offering. It's a decontamination. ¹³So the priest is to make expiation for him because of his wrong that he did in connection with one of these matters, and it will be pardoned him. It will be the priest's, like the grain offering.'"

¹⁴Yahweh spoke to Mosheh: ¹⁵"When a person commits a trespass and does wrong by mistake in connection with Yahweh's sacred things, he's to bring his reparation to Yahweh, a ram that's whole from the flock on the basis of the evaluation (in silver by sheqels, by the sanctuary sheqel), as a reparation. ¹⁶For what he did wrong in connection with the sacred thing, he's to make good and add a fifth to it, and give it to the priest. The priest will make expiation for him with the reparation ram, and it will be pardoned him.

¹⁷If a person, when he does wrong and does one of all the things that Yahweh has ordered should not be done, but he didn't know, he'll be liable and he'll carry his waywardness. ¹⁸He's to bring to the priest a ram that's whole from the flock, on the basis of the evaluation as a reparation. The priest will make expiation for him because of his mistake that he made when he didn't know, and it will be pardoned him. ¹⁹It's a reparation. He incurred liability to Yahweh.'

Wrongdoing against Yahweh and wrongdoing against other people

6 Yahweh spoke to Mosheh: ²"When a person does wrong and commits a trespass against Yahweh and is deceptive towards his fellow in connection with something entrusted or something deposited with him or by seizing, or he defrauds his fellow, ³or he finds something lost and is deceptive about it and swears in falsehood, regarding one of all the things that a human being may do so as to do wrong by them: ⁴when he does wrong and is liable, he's to give back the thing that he seized or the thing that he got by fraud or the thing that was entrusted to him or the lost thing that he found, ⁵or anything regarding which he swore in falsehood. He's to make good for it in terms of its total sum and add to it a fifth of it. He's to give it to the person to whom it belongs, on the day of his reparation.

⁶As his reparation he's to bring Yahweh a ram that's whole from the flock, on the basis of the evaluation as a reparation, to the priest. ⁷The priest will make expiation for him before Yahweh and it will be pardoned him in respect of the one thing out of all the things that he might do, to incur liability by it.'

⁸Yahweh spoke to Mosheh: ⁹'Order Aharon and his sons: "This is the instruction about the burnt offering. The burnt offering is on the hearth, on the altar, all night until the morning. The altar fire is to be kept burning on it. ¹⁰Then the priest is to put on his cloth tunic and put on his cloth shorts over his flesh and take up the waste to which the fire devours the burnt offering on the altar and put it beside the altar. ¹¹He's then to take off his garments, put on other garments and take out the waste outside the camp to a pure place.

Priests' instructions about grain offerings

¹²The fire on the altar is to be kept burning on it; it's not to go out. The priest is to burn wood on it morning by morning, arrange the burnt offering on it and turn into smoke the fat parts of the well-being sacrifices on it. ¹³A continual fire is to be kept burning on the altar; it's not to go out.

¹⁴This is the instruction about the grain offering. Aharon's sons are to bring it before Yahweh before the altar. ¹⁵He's to take up from it in his fist some of the fine flour of the grain offering and some of its oil and all the frankincense that's on the grain offering, and burn its commemorative portion into smoke for Yahweh at the altar, a nice smell. ¹⁶The rest of it Aharon and his sons are to eat. It's to be eaten as flatbread in the sacred place; they're to eat it in the appointment tent courtyard.

¹⁷It's not to be baked with yeast. I've given it to them as their share from my gift offerings. It's especially sacred, like the decontamination and the reparation. ¹⁸Any male among Aharon's descendants may eat it (a permanent decree through your generations) from Yahweh's gift offerings. Anything that touches them becomes sacred."'

¹⁹Yahweh spoke to Mosheh: ²⁰'This is Aharon and his sons' offering, which they're to present for Yahweh on the day of his anointing: a tenth of a gallon of fine flour as a regular grain offering, half of it in the morning and half of it in the evening. ²¹It's to be made on a griddle, with oil. You're to bring it blended. You're to present it as baked bits of the grain offering, broken pieces, a nice smell for Yahweh. ²²The priest anointed in his place from among his sons is to make it (a permanent decree) for Yahweh. It's to be turned into smoke, a whole offering. ²³Every grain offering by a priest is to be a whole offering. It will not be eaten.'

Priests' instructions about the decontamination and reparation

²⁴Yahweh spoke to Mosheh: ²⁵'Speak to Aharon and to his sons: "This is the instruction about the decontamination. In the place where the burnt offering is slaughtered, the decontamination is to be slaughtered, before Yahweh. It's especially sacred. ²⁶The priest who offers it as a decontamination is to eat it. It's to be eaten in the sacred place, in the appointment tent courtyard. ²⁷Anything that touches its flesh becomes sacred, and when some of its blood spatters on a garment, you're to wash what it spatters on, in the sacred place. ²⁸A clay container in which it's boiled is to be broken. If it was boiled in a copper container, it's to be scoured and rinsed with water. ²⁹Any male among the priests may eat it. It's especially sacred. ³⁰But no decontamination may be eaten from which some of its blood has been brought into the appointment tent to make expiation in the sacred place. It's to be burned in fire.

7 This is the instruction about the reparation. It's especially sacred. ²In the place where they slaughter the burnt offering

they're to slaughter the reparation. Its blood he's to toss over the altar all round. ³From it he's to present all its fat: the broad tail, the fat covering the innards, ⁴ the two kidneys and the fat that's on them, which is on the loins, and the lobe on the liver; he's to remove it along with the kidneys. ⁵The priest is to turn them into smoke at the altar as a gift offering for Yahweh. It's a reparation. ⁶Any male among the priests may eat it. He's to eat it in the sacred place. It's especially sacred.

The several reasons for a well-being sacrifice

⁷As is the decontamination, so is the reparation; there's one instruction for them. The priest who makes expiation by it, it belongs to him. ⁸The priest who presents an individual's burnt offering – the skin of the burnt offering that he presents belongs to the priest; it's to be his. ⁹Any grain offering that's baked in the oven, and any that's made in the pan or on a griddle, belongs to the priest who presents it; it's to be his. ¹⁰Any grain offering that's mixed with oil or dry is to belong to Aharon's sons, each the same as his brother.

¹¹This is the instruction about the well-being sacrifice that someone presents for Yahweh. ¹²If he presents it as a thanksgiving, along with the thanksgiving he's to present flat loaves mixed with oil, flat wafers spread with oil, and fine flour blended, loaves mixed with oil, ¹³along with the loaves of leavened bread. He's to present his offering along with his thanksgiving well-being sacrifice. ¹⁴From it he's to present one from each offering as a contribution for Yahweh, to the priest who tosses the blood of the well-being sacrifice: it's to be his.

¹⁵The flesh of his thanksgiving well-being sacrifice is to be eaten on the day of its offering. He's not to leave any of it till morning. ¹⁶If the sacrifice he offers is a pledge or free offering, it's to be eaten on the day he presents his sacrifice, though what is left of it may be eaten on the next day, ¹⁷but what is left of the flesh of the sacrifice is to be burned in fire on the third day. ¹⁸If any of the flesh of his well-being sacrifice is eaten at all on the third day, the one who presents it won't find acceptance. It won't be deemed for him. It will be an objectionable thing. The person who eats of it will carry his waywardness.

The priest's allocations

¹⁹Flesh that touches anything taboo will not be eaten. It will be burned in fire. [Other] flesh: anyone who is pure may eat flesh. ²⁰But the person who eats the flesh from a well-being sacrifice, which is Yahweh's, when his taboo is on him – that person shall be cut off from his kin. ²¹A person who touches anything taboo (a human taboo or a taboo animal or any taboo atrocity) and eats from the flesh of Yahweh's well-being sacrifice – that person shall be cut off from his kin.'"

²²Yahweh spoke to Mosheh: ²³'Speak to the Yisra'elites: "You will not eat any of the fat of ox or sheep or goat. ²⁴The fat from a corpse and the fat from something mauled may be used for any work, but you will not eat it at all. ²⁵When anyone eats the fat from an animal from which one may present a gift offering for Yahweh, the person who eats shall be cut off from his kin.

²⁶You will not eat any blood in any of your settlements, of bird or of animal. ²⁷Any person who eats any blood, that person shall be cut off from his kin."'

²⁸Yahweh spoke to Mosheh: ²⁹'Speak to the Yisra'elites: "One who presents his well-being sacrifice for Yahweh, he's to bring his offering for Yahweh from his well-being sacrifice. ³⁰His hands are to bring Yahweh's gift offerings. He's to bring the fat along with the breast – the breast for elevating as an elevation offering before Yahweh.

³¹The priest is to turn the fat into smoke at the altar, and the breast is to be for Aharon and his sons. ³²The right thigh you're to give as a contribution to the priest from your well-being sacrifices. ³³The one of Aharon's sons who presents the blood of the well-being sacrifices, and the fat: the right thigh is to be his portion, ³⁴because I've taken the breast of the elevation offering and the thigh of the contribution from the Yisra'elites from their well-being sacrifices and given them to Aharon the priest and to his sons (as a permanent decree) from the Yisra'elites."'

The ordination begins

35This is Aharon's anointing share and his sons' anointing share from Yahweh's gift offerings on the day he presents them to act as priests for Yahweh, 36which Yahweh ordered to give them on the day of his anointing them (a permanent decree from the Yisra'elites through their generations).
37This is the instruction for the burnt offering, for the grain offering, for the decontamination, for the reparation, for the commissioning and for the well-being sacrifice, 38with which Yahweh ordered Mosheh at Mount Sinay on the day he ordered the Yisra'elites to present their offerings for Yahweh, in the Sinay Wilderness.

8 Yahweh spoke to Mosheh: 2'Get Aharon and his sons with him, and the garments, the anointing oil, the decontamination bull, the two rams and the basket of flatbread, 3and congregate the entire assembly at the entrance of the appointment tent.'
4Mosheh did as Yahweh ordered him, and the assembly congregated at the entrance of the appointment tent. 5Mosheh said to the assembly, 'This is the thing that Yahweh has ordered to do.'
6Mosheh presented Aharon and his sons and washed them with water. 7He put the tunic on him, wrapped him with the sash, clothed him with the coat, put the chasuble on him, wrapped him with the chasuble's design-work strap and wound it to him with it. 8He placed the pouch on him and put into the pouch the Urim and Tummim. 9He placed the turban on his head and placed on the turban near the front of it the gold medallion, the sacred diadem, as Yahweh ordered Mosheh.

The vestments

10Mosheh got the anointing oil and anointed the dwelling and everything that was in it, and made them sacred. 11He sprinkled some of it on the altar seven times and anointed the altar and all its articles, and the basin and its stand, to make them sacred. 12He poured some of the anointing oil on Aharon's head and anointed him, to make him sacred.
13Mosheh presented Aharon's sons, clothed them in tunics, wrapped them with a sash and bound mitres on them, as Yahweh ordered Mosheh. 14He brought up the decontamination bull. Aharon and his sons leaned their hands on the head of the decontamination bull, 15and he slaughtered it. Mosheh got the blood and put it on the altar's horns all round with his finger and decontaminated the altar, and poured out the blood at the altar's base. So he made it sacred for making expiation on it. 16He got all the fat that was on the innards, the lobe of the liver, the two kidneys and their fat, and Mosheh turned them into smoke at the altar. 17The bull, its skin, its flesh and its intestines he burned in fire outside the camp, as Yahweh ordered Mosheh.
18He presented the ram for the burnt offering, Aharon and his sons leaned their hands on the ram's head, 19and he slaughtered it. Mosheh tossed the blood over the altar all round 20and cut up the ram into its parts. Mosheh turned the head, the parts and the suet into smoke, 21and the innards and the legs he washed with water.

So Mosheh turned the entire ram into smoke at the altar. It was a burnt offering, as a nice smell. It was a gift offering for Yahweh, as Yahweh ordered Mosheh.

The commissioning offering

22Then he presented the second ram, the commissioning ram. Aharon and his sons leaned their hands on the ram's head, 23and he slaughtered it. Mosheh got some of its blood and put it on the lobe of Aharon's right ear, on the thumb of his right hand and on the big toe of his right foot. 24He presented Aharon's sons, and Mosheh put some of the blood on the lobe of their right ear, on the thumb of their right hand and on the big toe of their right foot.

Mosheh tossed the blood over the altar all round. 25He got the fat – the broad tail, all the fat that was on the innards, the lobe of the liver, the two kidneys and their fat, and the right thigh – 26and from the basket of flatbread that was before Yahweh he got one loaf of flatbread, one loaf of bread made with oil, and one wafer, and placed them on the fat parts and on the right thigh.
27He put everything on Aharon's palms and on his sons' palms and elevated them as an

elevation offering before Yahweh. ²⁸Mosheh took them from on their palms and turned them into smoke at the altar along with the burnt offering. They were a commissioning offering, as a sweet smell. It was a gift offering for Yahweh. ²⁹Mosheh got the breast and elevated it as an elevation offering before Yahweh. From the commissioning ram it was Mosheh's portion, as Yahweh ordered Mosheh.

³⁰Mosheh got some of the anointing oil and some of the blood that was on the altar and spattered it on Aharon and on his garments, and on his sons and on his sons' garments with him, and made them sacred, Aharon and his garments and his sons and his sons' garments with him.

Seven days in the appointment tent

³¹Mosheh said to Aharon and to his sons: 'Boil the flesh at the entrance of the appointment tent. You're to eat it there, with the bread that's in the commissioning basket, as I ordered: "Aharon and his sons are to eat it." ³²The rest of the flesh and of the bread you're to burn in fire. ³³You will not go out of the entrance of the appointment tent for seven days until the day when the days of your commissioning are complete, because for seven days he will commission you. ³⁴As he has done this day, Yahweh has ordered to do, to make expiation for you. ³⁵You're to stay at the entrance of the appointment tent, day and night, for seven days, and keep Yahweh's charge, so you don't die, because so I've been ordered.'

³⁶Aharon and his sons did all the things that Yahweh ordered through Mosheh.

9 On the eighth day Mosheh called for Aharon and his sons, and Yisraʾel's elders, ²and said to Aharon, 'Get yourself a bullock from the herd as a decontamination and a ram as a burnt offering, ones that are whole, and present them before Yahweh. ³And speak to the Yisraʾelites: "Get a he-goat from the flock as a decontamination, a bullock and a lamb (ones that are a year old, that are whole) as a burnt offering, ⁴an ox and a ram as a well-being offering to sacrifice before Yahweh, and a grain offering mixed with oil, because today Yahweh will appear to you."'

Aharon's offerings

⁵So they took what Mosheh ordered to the front of the appointment tent, and the entire assembly drew near and stood before Yahweh. ⁶Mosheh said, 'This is the thing that Yahweh ordered that you do, so Yahweh's splendour may appear to you.'

⁷Mosheh said to Aharon, 'Draw near the altar and make your decontamination and your burnt offering and make expiation for yourself and for the people, and make the people's offering and make expiation for them, as Yahweh has ordered.'

⁸So Aharon drew near the altar and slaughtered the decontamination bullock that was his. ⁹Aharon's sons presented the blood to him and he dipped his finger in the blood and put it on the altar's horns, and poured out the blood at the altar's base. ¹⁰The fat, the kidneys and the lobe from the liver from the decontamination he turned into smoke at the altar, as Yahweh ordered Mosheh. ¹¹The flesh and the skin he burned in fire outside the camp.

¹²He slaughtered the burnt offering, and Aharon's sons passed the blood to him and he tossed it over the altar all round. ¹³They passed the burnt offering to him in its parts, with the head, and he turned it into smoke on the altar. ¹⁴He washed the innards and the legs and turned them into smoke along with the burnt offering on the altar.

Yahweh's splendour appears

¹⁵Then he presented the people's offering. He got the decontamination goat which was the people's, slaughtered it and made it a decontamination, like the first. ¹⁶He presented the burnt offering and made it in accordance with the ruling. ¹⁷He presented the grain offering, filled his palm from it and turned it into smoke on the altar, apart from the morning burnt offering. ¹⁸He slaughtered the ox and the ram, the well-being sacrifice that was the people's, and Aharon's sons passed the blood to him (and he tossed it over the altar, all round), ¹⁹and the fat parts from the ox and the ram, the broad tail, the covering, the kidneys and the lobe of the liver. ²⁰They placed the fat parts on the breasts and turned the fat parts into smoke at the altar. ²¹The breasts and the

right thigh Aharon elevated as an elevation offering before Yahweh, as Mosheh ordered. ²²Aharon lifted up his hands to the people and blessed them, then came down from making the decontamination, the burnt offering and the well-being sacrifice. ²³Mosheh and Aharon went into the appointment tent, and came out and blessed the people. Then Yahweh's splendour appeared to the entire people, ²⁴and fire came out from before Yahweh and devoured the burnt offering and the fat parts on the altar. The entire people saw, and resounded, and fell on their faces.

Disaster strikes

10 But Aharon's sons, Nadab and Abihu, each took his pan, put fire in it, placed incense on it and presented before Yahweh outside fire, which he had not ordered them. ²Fire came out from before Yahweh and devoured them. They died before Yahweh.

³Mosheh said to Aharon, 'It's what Yahweh spoke of:

> In the people who draw near me I will show
> myself sacred
> and before the face of the entire people I will
> show splendour.'

Aharon was silent, ⁴but Mosheh called for Misha'el and Eltsaphan, sons of Uzzi'el, Aharon's uncle, and said to them, 'Draw near, carry your brothers from before the sacred place, outside the camp.' ⁵They drew near and carried them by their tunics outside the camp, as Mosheh said.

⁶Mosheh said to Aharon and to El'azar and Itamar his sons, 'Don't bare your heads, and you will not tear your clothes, so you don't die and he becomes furious with the entire assembly. Your brothers, Yisra'el's entire household, may bewail the burning that Yahweh has brought about. ⁷You will not go out of the entrance of the appointment tent, so you will not die, because Yahweh's anointing oil is on you.' They did as Mosheh said.

⁸Yahweh spoke to Aharon, ⁹'Don't drink wine or liquor, you or your sons with you, when you go into the appointment tent, so you will not die (a permanent decree, through your generations), ¹⁰so you can make a distinction between the sacred and the ordinary and between the taboo and the pure, ¹¹and instruct the Yisra'elites in all the decrees that Yahweh has spoken to them through Mosheh.'

On being careful with the decrees

¹²Mosheh spoke to Aharon and to El'azar and to Itamar, his remaining sons: 'Get the grain offering that's left from Yahweh's gift offerings and eat it as flatbread beside the altar, because it's especially sacred. ¹³You're to eat it in the sacred place, because it's a decree for you and a decree for your sons from Yahweh's gift offerings, because I've been ordered so. ¹⁴The breast of the elevation offering and the thigh of the contribution you may eat in a pure place, you and your sons and your daughters with you, because they have been given (a decree for you and a decree for your children) from the Yisra'elites' well-being sacrifices. ¹⁵They're to bring the thigh of the contribution and the breast of the elevation offering, along with the gift offerings of fat things, to elevate as an elevation offering before Yahweh, and it will be yours and your children's with you (as a permanent decree) as Yahweh has ordered.'

¹⁶Then Mosheh enquired urgently about the decontamination goat. There, it had been burned. He was furious with El'azar and Itamar, Aharon's remaining sons, and said, ¹⁷'Why didn't you eat the decontamination, in the sacred place, because it's especially sacred, and he's given it to you to carry the assembly's waywardness, to make expiation for them before Yahweh? ¹⁸Here, its blood was not brought into the sacred place, inside. You should certainly eat it in the sacred place, as I ordered.'

¹⁹ But Aharon spoke to Mosheh: 'Here, today they have presented their decontamination and their burnt offering before Yahweh, and things like these have happened to me. Had I eaten the decontamination today, would it have been good in Yahweh's eyes?' ²⁰Mosheh listened, and it was good in his eyes.

You are what you eat

11 Yahweh spoke to Mosheh and to Aharon: ²'Speak to the Yisra'elites: "These are the creatures that you may eat, of all the animals that are on the earth: ³anything that has a divided hoof (that has a cleft in its hoofs) that brings up the cud – among the animals, you may eat it. ⁴This, however, you will not eat, of those that bring up the cud or of those that have a divided hoof:

> the camel, because it brings up its cud but it doesn't have a divided hoof – it's taboo for you;
> ⁵the rock badger, because it brings up the cud but it doesn't have a divided hoof – it's taboo for you;
> ⁶the hare, because it brings up the cud but it doesn't have a divided hoof – it's taboo for you;
> ⁷the pig, because it has a divided hoof (it has a cleft in its hoof) but it doesn't chew the cud – it's taboo for you.

⁸You will not eat of their meat and you will not touch their corpse – they're taboo for you.

⁹This you may eat of everything that's in the water: anything that has fins and scales, in the water, in the seas and in the wadis – you may eat them. ¹⁰But anything that doesn't have fins and scales, in the water and in the wadis, of any teeming things of the water and of any living thing that's in the water – they're an atrocity for you. ¹¹Given that they will be an atrocity for you, from their flesh you will not eat and you're to treat their corpse as an atrocity. ¹²Anything in the water that does not have fins and scales is an atrocity for you.

How touch produces taboo

¹³These you're to treat as an atrocity from the birds – they're not to be eaten, they're an atrocity:

> the eagle, the vulture, the osprey, ¹⁴the kite, the falcon (any of its species), ¹⁵the raven (any of its species), ¹⁶the ostrich, the nighthawk, the seagull, the hawk (any of its species), ¹⁷the tawny owl, the cormorant, the screech owl, ¹⁸the barn owl, the pelican, the swan, ¹⁹the stork, the heron (any of its species), the hoopoe and the bat.

²⁰Any teeming, flying thing walking on all fours is an atrocity for you. ²¹However, you may eat this: of any teeming, flying thing walking on all fours that has bending legs above its feet to leap with on the earth, ²²of them you may eat these:

> the locust (any of its species), the winged locust (any of its species), the cricket (any of its species), the grasshopper (any of its species).

²³But any other teeming, flying thing that has four legs is an atrocity for you.

²⁴By these you make yourself taboo; anyone who touches their corpse becomes taboo until the evening, ²⁵and anyone who carries their corpse is to wash his clothes and becomes taboo until the evening:

> ²⁶By any animal that does have hoofs but they have no cleft, or that doesn't bring up the cud. They're taboo for you; anyone who touches them becomes taboo.
> ²⁷Any that walks on its hands, among all the creatures that walk on all fours, are taboo for you. Anyone who touches their corpse becomes taboo until the evening.
> ²⁸Someone who carries their corpse is to wash his clothes and become taboo until the evening. They're taboo for you.

How other contact produces taboo

²⁹This is taboo for you among the things that teem on the earth:

> the mole, the mouse, the lizard (any of its species), ³⁰the ferret, the gecko, the crocodile, the skink and the chameleon.

³¹These are the taboo things for you among everything that teems.

> Anyone who touches them when they're dead becomes taboo until the evening.
> ³²Anything on which one of them falls when they're dead becomes taboo, of any article of wood, clothing, skin or sacking.
> Any article that can be used for work is to be put in water; it becomes taboo until the evening, then it becomes pure.
> ³³Any clay container inside which one of them falls – anything that's inside it becomes taboo, and you're to break it.
> ³⁴Of anything that would be eaten on to which water comes, it becomes taboo. Anything that would be drunk in any container becomes taboo.
> ³⁵Anything on which one of their corpses falls becomes taboo.

An oven or a stove is to be smashed; they're taboo, and they're to be taboo for you. ³⁶However, a spring or a cistern (a container for water) continues to be pure, but a person who touches their corpse [in it] becomes taboo. ³⁷When one of their corpses falls on any seed for sowing, which is to be sown, it's pure. ³⁸But when water is put on seed and one of their corpses falls on it, it becomes taboo for you.

The importance of making distinctions

³⁹When one of the animals that's for eating by you dies, someone who touches its corpse becomes taboo until the evening. ⁴⁰One who eats of its corpse is to wash his clothes; he becomes taboo until the evening. One who carries its corpse is to wash his clothes; he becomes taboo until the evening. ⁴¹Everything that teems on the earth is an atrocity. It's not to be eaten. ⁴²Anything that goes on its belly and anything that goes on all fours, and further anything that has many feet: regarding anything that teems on the earth, you will not eat them, because they're an atrocity. ⁴³You're not to make yourselves into an atrocity through anything that teems. You will not make yourselves taboo through them and become taboo through them, ⁴⁴because I am Yahweh your God. You're to make yourselves sacred and be sacred, because I am sacred. You will not make yourselves taboo through any teeming thing that moves on the earth, ⁴⁵because I am Yahweh who brought you up from the country of Misrayim [Egypt] to be your God. You're to be sacred, because I am sacred.

⁴⁶This is the instruction about animals, birds, and all living creatures that move in the water, and concerning all creatures that teem on the earth, ⁴⁷for making a distinction between the taboo and the pure and between the living things that are eaten and the living things that may not be eaten.'"

The childbirth taboo

12 Yahweh spoke to Mosheh: ²"Speak to the Yisra'elites: "When a woman brings forth offspring and gives birth to a male, she becomes taboo for seven days; she becomes taboo as in the days of flowing when she's unwell. (³On the eighth day the flesh of his foreskin is to be circumcised.)

⁴For thirty-three days she's to live in a state of blood purifying. She will not touch anything sacred or go into the sanctuary until the completion of her days of purifying. ⁵If she gives birth to a female, she becomes taboo for two weeks as in her flowing and she's to live for sixty-six days in a state of blood purifying.

⁶At the completion of her days of purifying, for a son or a daughter, she's to bring a year-old lamb as a burnt offering, and a young pigeon or dove as a decontamination, to the priest at the entrance of the appointment tent. ⁷He's to present it before Yahweh and make expiation for her, and she'll become pure from her flow of blood. This is the instruction about someone giving birth to a male or to a female.

⁸If her hand can't find enough for a sheep, she's to get two doves or two young pigeons, one for a burnt offering and one for decontamination, and the priest is to make expiation for her, and she'll become pure.'"

Scaliness (aka leprosy)

13 Yahweh spoke to Mosheh and to Aharon: ²"When there is in the skin of a person's body a swelling or rash or spot and it becomes an outbreak of scaliness in the skin of his body, he's to be brought to Aharon the priest or to one of his sons, the priests, ³and the priest is to look at the outbreak in the skin of the body. If the hair in the outbreak has turned white and the outbreak's appearance is deeper than the skin of his body, the outbreak is scaliness. When the priest sees it, he's to pronounce him taboo.

⁴If it's a white spot in the skin of his body, its appearance is not deeper than the skin, and the hair hasn't turned white, the priest is to confine [the person with] the outbreak for seven days. ⁵On the seventh day the priest is to look: there, if the outbreak has stood still, in his eyes, and the outbreak hasn't spread in the skin, the priest is to confine him for a second seven days.

⁶The priest is to look at him on the second seventh day: there, if the outbreak has faded

and the outbreak hasn't spread in the skin, the priest is to pronounce him pure. It's a rash. He's to wash his clothes, and he'll become pure. ⁷But if the rash actually spreads in the skin after his appearing to the priest for his purity pronouncement, he's to appear a second time to the priest, ⁸and the priest will look, and there, the rash has spread in the skin, the priest is to pronounce him taboo. It's scaliness.

Dealing with uncertainty

⁹When there's an outbreak of scaliness in a person and he's brought to the priest, ¹⁰if the priest looks, and there, a white swelling in the skin, and it's turned the hair white, with a living growth of live flesh in the swelling: ¹¹it's dormant scaliness in the skin of his body, and the priest will pronounce him taboo. He won't confine him, because he's taboo.

¹²If the scaliness does break out in the skin and the scaliness covers the entire skin of [the person with] the outbreak, from his head to his feet, everything visible to the priest's eyes, ¹³so the priest looks and there, the scaliness has covered his entire body, he'll pronounce [the person with] the outbreak pure. All of him has turned white. He's pure.

¹⁴But on the day live flesh appears in him, he becomes taboo. ¹⁵When the priest sees the live flesh, he's to pronounce him taboo. The live flesh is taboo. It's scaliness. ¹⁶Or when the live flesh again turns white, he's to come to the priest ¹⁷and the priest is to look, and there, the outbreak has turned white, then the priest is to pronounce [the person with] the outbreak pure. He's pure.

¹⁸When there's an eruption in the skin of someone's body and it heals, ¹⁹but in the place of the eruption there's a white swelling or a white-reddish spot, he's to appear to the priest ²⁰and the priest is to look and there, it's lower than the skin and its hair has turned white, then the priest is to pronounce him taboo. It's an outbreak of scaliness that has broken out in the eruption. ²¹But if the priest looks at it and there, no white hair is in it, it's not lower than the skin and it's pale, then the priest is to confine him for seven days. ²²If it does spread in his skin, the priest is to pronounce him taboo. It's an outbreak. ²³But if the spot halts in its place (it hasn't spread), it's the scab from the eruption. The priest is to pronounce him pure.

Burns and scabies

²⁴Or when there's a burn from fire in the skin of a body and the living growth from the burn becomes a white-reddish or white spot, ²⁵if the priest looks at it, and there, the hair has turned white in the spot and its appearance is deeper than the skin: it's scaliness that's broken out in the burn. The priest is to pronounce him taboo. It's an outbreak of scaliness. ²⁶But if the priest looks at it and there, in the spot is no white hair, and it's not lower than the skin and it's pale, the priest is to confine him for seven days. ²⁷The priest is to look at him on the seventh day. If it's actually spread in the skin, the priest is to pronounce him taboo. It's an outbreak of scaliness. ²⁸But if the spot halts in its place (it hasn't spread in the skin) and it's pale, it's the swelling from the burn. The priest is to pronounce him pure, because it's the scab from the burn.

²⁹When there's an outbreak in a man or a woman in the head or in the beard, ³⁰and the priest looks at the outbreak, and there, its appearance is deeper than the skin and there's thin yellow hair in it, the priest is to pronounce him taboo. It's scabies; it's scaliness in the head or the beard. ³¹But when the priest looks at the scabies outbreak and there, its appearance is not deeper than the skin, but there's no black hair in it, the priest is to confine [the person with] the scabies outbreak for seven days. ³²The priest is to look at the outbreak on the seventh day: there, the scabies hasn't spread and no yellow hair has come in it, and the scabies' appearance is not deeper than the skin, ³³the person is to shave, but not shave the scabies, and the priest is to confine [the person with] the scabies for a second seven days.

Spots and hair loss

³⁴The priest is to look at the scabies on the seventh day: there, the scabies hasn't spread in the skin and its appearance is not deeper than the skin, so the priest is to pronounce him pure. He's to wash his clothes, and he'll become

pure. ³⁵But if the scabies actually spreads after his purity pronouncement, ³⁶the priest is to look at him. There, the scabies has spread in his skin. The priest will not seek for yellow hair. The person is taboo. ³⁷But if in his eyes the scabies has halted and black hair has grown in it, the scabies has healed. The person is pure. The priest is to pronounce him pure.

³⁸When there are spots in the skin of a man or a woman's body, white spots, ³⁹and the priest looks, and there, the spots in the skin of their body are pale, white, it's a sore that's broken out in the skin. The person is pure.

⁴⁰When a man's head becomes hairless: he's bald, he's pure. ⁴¹If his head becomes hairless from the side of his face: his hair is receding, he's pure. ⁴²But when there's a white-reddish outbreak in the bald part or in the receding part, it's scaliness breaking out in his bald part or in his receding part, ⁴³and the priest is to look at him. There, the swelling from the outbreak is white-reddish in his bald part or in his receding part, like the appearance of scaliness in the skin of the body, ⁴⁴the man has been made scaly. He's taboo. The priest is to pronounce him taboo. His outbreak is in his head.

⁴⁵Somone who's been made scaly, who has the outbreak in him: his clothes are to be torn, his head is to be bared, he's to cover his lip and he's to call, "Taboo, taboo". ⁴⁶For all the time that the outbreak is in him, he becomes taboo. While he's taboo, he's to live apart. His dwelling will be outside the camp.

Scaliness in clothing

⁴⁷When there's an outbreak of scaliness in clothing, in wool clothing or in fabric clothing, ⁴⁸whether in the warp or in the woof of the fabric or of the wool, or in a skin or in anything worked from skin, ⁴⁹and the outbreak is greenish or reddish in the clothing or in the skin, whether in the warp or in the woof, or in any skin article: it's an outbreak of scaliness. It's to be shown to the priest. ⁵⁰The priest is to look at the outbreak and confine [the thing with] the outbreak for seven days. ⁵¹He's to look at the outbreak on the seventh day. When the outbreak has spread in the clothing, whether in the warp or in the woof or in the skin, for any work for which the skin may be used, the outbreak is a malignant scaliness. It's taboo. ⁵²He's to burn the cloth, whether warp or woof, in wool or in fabric or any skin article in which there is the outbreak, because it's a malignant scaliness. It's to be burned in fire.

⁵³But if the priest looks, and there, the outbreak in the clothing, whether in the warp or in the woof or in any skin article, hasn't spread, ⁵⁴the priest is to order that they wash the thing with the outbreak in it, and 'confine' it for a second seven days. ⁵⁵The priest is to look at the outbreak after it has been washed, and there, the outbreak hasn't changed its appearance, though the outbreak hasn't spread, it's taboo. You're to burn it in fire. It's a fungus, in its bald side or in its receding side.

⁵⁶But if the priest looks, and there, the outbreak is pale after it's been washed, he's to tear it out from the clothing or from the skin, either from the warp or from the woof. ⁵⁷If it appears again in the clothing, either in the warp or in the woof, or in any skin article, it's breaking out. You're to burn in fire the thing in which is the outbreak. ⁵⁸But the clothing, either the warp or the woof or any skin article that you wash so that the outbreak departs from them, it's to be washed a second time, and it will become pure.

⁵⁹This is the instruction for an outbreak of scaliness in clothing, wool or fabric, either the warp or the woof, or for any skin article, for pronouncing it pure or pronouncing it taboo.'

Being restored to the assembly

14 Yahweh spoke to Mosheh: ²'This is to be the instruction for the person with scaliness, on the day of his purifying. He's to be brought to the priest; ³the priest is to go outside the camp. The priest is to look, and there, the outbreak of scaliness has healed from the person with scaliness, ⁴so the priest is to order that someone get for the person purifying himself two pure live birds, cedar wood, scarlet yarn and hyssop.

⁵The priest is to order that he slaughter one bird in a clay container over fresh water. ⁶The live bird he's to take, with the cedar wood, the scarlet yarn and the hyssop, and dip them with the live bird in the blood of the bird that

was slaughtered over the fresh water. ⁷He's to spatter it over the person purifying himself from the scaliness, seven times, and purify him, and to send off the live bird over the face of the fields.

⁸The person purifying himself is to wash his clothes, shave all his hair and bathe in water, and he'll become pure. Afterwards, he may go into the camp, but he's to live outside his tent for seven days. ⁹On the seventh day he's to shave all his hair – his head, his beard and his eyebrows. He's to shave all his hair, wash his clothes and bathe his body in water, and he'll become pure.

¹⁰On the eighth day he's to get two sheep that are whole, and one ewe a year old that's whole, three tenths of grain-offering fine flour, mixed with oil, and one pint of oil. ¹¹The priest who is purifying is to stand the person who's purifying himself with them, before Yahweh, at the entrance of the appointment tent.

The decontamination rite

¹²The priest is to get one sheep and present it as a reparation, with the pint of oil, and to elevate them as an elevation offering before Yahweh. ¹³He's to slaughter the sheep in the place where one slaughters the decontamination and the burnt offering, in the sacred place, because the reparation is like the decontamination; it belongs to the priest. It's especially sacred.

¹⁴The priest is to get some of the blood of the reparation. The priest is to put it on the lobe of the ear of the person purifying himself (the right), on the thumb of his right hand and on the big toe of his right foot. ¹⁵The priest is to get some of the pint of oil and pour it on to the priest's palm, the left. ¹⁶And the priest is to dip his right finger in the oil that's on his left palm and sprinkle some of the oil with his finger seven times before Yahweh. ¹⁷Some of the rest of the oil that's on his palm the priest is to put on the lobe of the ear of the person purifying himself (the right), on the thumb of his right hand and on the big toe of his right foot, over the blood of the reparation. ¹⁸The rest of the oil that's on the priest's palm he's to put on the head of the person purifying himself. So the priest is to make expiation for him before Yahweh. ¹⁹The priest is to make the decontamination and make expiation for the person purifying himself from his taboo.

Afterwards, he's to slaughter the burnt offering. ²⁰The priest is to offer up the burnt offering and the grain offering at the altar. So the priest will make expiation for him, and he'll become pure.

For someone of limited means

²¹If he's poor and his hand doesn't stretch to it, he's to get one sheep as a reparation, to be an elevation offering to make expiation for him, one tenth of fine flour mixed with oil as a grain offering, a pint of oil, ²²and two doves or two young pigeons, as his hand stretches to it. One will be a decontamination and one a burnt offering.

²³He's to bring them to the priest on the eighth day for his purifying, to the entrance of the appointment tent, before Yahweh. ²⁴The priest is to get the reparation sheep and the pint of oil, and the priest is to elevate them as an elevation offering before Yahweh. ²⁵He's to slaughter the reparation sheep, and the priest is to get some of the blood of the reparation and put it on the lobe of the ear of the person purifying himself (the right), on the thumb of his right hand and on the big toe of his right foot.

²⁶The priest is to pour some of the oil on to the priest's palm, the left, ²⁷and the priest is to spatter some of the oil that's on his left palm with the finger of his right hand seven times before Yahweh. ²⁸Some of the oil that's on his palm the priest is to put on the lobe of the ear of the person purifying himself (the right), on the thumb of his right hand and on the big toe of his right foot, on the place with the reparation blood. ²⁹The rest of the oil that's on the priest's palm he's to put on the head of the person purifying himself, to make expiation for him before Yahweh.

³⁰He's to make an offering of one of the doves or young pigeons, from whichever his hand stretches to ³¹(whichever his hand stretches to), one the decontamination and one the burnt offering, along with the grain offering. So the priest is to make expiation before Yahweh for the person purifying himself.

³²This is the instruction for the person on whom there's an outbreak of scaliness, whose hand doesn't stretch, in his purifying.'

Scaliness in a house

³³Yahweh spoke to Mosheh and to Aharon: ³⁴'When you come into the country of Kena'an [Canaan], which I'm giving you as a holding, and I put an outbreak of scaliness in a house in the country that's your holding, ³⁵the house's owner is to come and tell the priest, "Something like an outbreak has appeared to me in the house." ³⁶The priest is to order that they clear the house before the priest comes to look at the outbreak, so nothing that's in the house becomes taboo. After this, the priest will come to look at the house. ³⁷He will look at the outbreak, and there, if the outbreak in the house's walls is greenish or reddish depressions and their appearance is lower than the wall, ³⁸the priest is to come out from the house to the entrance of the house and confine it for seven days.

³⁹The priest is to come back on the seventh day and look, and there, the outbreak has spread in the house's walls. ⁴⁰The priest is to order that they take out the stones in which is the outbreak and throw them outside the town into a taboo place. ⁴¹He's to get the house scraped, from the house all round, and they're to pour out the earth that they've scraped off, outside the town into a taboo place. ⁴²They're to get other stones and bring them in the place of the stones, and get other earth and coat the house.

⁴³If the outbreak comes back and breaks out in the house after he's pulled out the stones and after the scraping of the house and after the coating, ⁴⁴the priest is to come and look, and there, the outbreak has spread in the house. It's a malignant scaliness. ⁴⁵He's to demolish the house, its stones, its wood and all the soil from the house, and take it out to a taboo place outside the town.

Purifying a house

⁴⁶Someone who goes into the house through all the time he's confined it becomes taboo until the evening. ⁴⁷Someone who sleeps in the house is to wash his clothes. Someone who eats in the house is to wash his clothes.

⁴⁸If the priest actually comes and looks, and there, the outbreak hasn't spread in the house after the coating of the house, the priest is to pronounce the house pure, because the outbreak has healed. ⁴⁹To decontaminate the house, he's to get two birds, cedar wood, bright crimson and hyssop. ⁵⁰He's to slaughter one bird in a clay container over fresh water. ⁵¹He's to get the cedar wood and the hyssop and the bright crimson and the live bird and dip them in the blood of the slaughtered bird and in the fresh water, and spatter the house seven times. ⁵²He's to decontaminate the house with the bird's blood, with the fresh water, with the live bird, with the cedar wood, with the hyssop and with the bright crimson, ⁵³then send off the live bird outside the town to the fields. So he will make expiation for the house, and it will become pure.

⁵⁴'This is the instruction for every outbreak of scaliness, for scabies, ⁵⁵for scaliness in cloth or for a house, ⁵⁶for a swelling, for a rash or for a spot, ⁵⁷to give instruction on the day of becoming taboo and on the day of becoming pure. This is the instruction about scaliness.'

A man's genital discharge

15 Yahweh spoke to Mosheh and to Aharon: ²'Speak to the Yisra'elites: "When any man is discharging from his flesh, his discharge is taboo. ³This will be his taboo through his discharge, whether his flesh runs with his discharge or his flesh seizes up because of his discharge – it's his taboo: ⁴any bedding that the man who is discharging lies on becomes taboo. Any object that he sits on becomes taboo. ⁵A person who touches his bedding is to wash his clothes and bathe in water, and he becomes taboo until the evening.

⁶Someone who sits on the object that the man who is discharging sits on is to wash his clothes and bathe in water, and he becomes taboo until the evening. ⁷Someone who touches the flesh of the man who is discharging is to wash his clothes and bathe in water, and he becomes taboo until the evening. ⁸When the man who is discharging spits on someone who

is pure, he's to wash his clothes and bathe in water, and he becomes taboo until the evening. ⁹Any saddle that the man who is discharging rides on becomes taboo. ¹⁰Anyone who touches anything that was under him becomes taboo until the evening, and someone who carries them is to wash his clothes and bathe in water, and he becomes taboo until the evening. ¹¹Anyone whom the man who is discharging touches when he hasn't rinsed his hands in water is to wash his clothes and bathe in water, and he becomes taboo until the evening. ¹²A clay object that the man who is discharging touches is to be broken, and any wood object is to be rinsed in water.

More on genital discharges and emission of semen

¹³When the man who is discharging is pure from his discharge, he's to count for himself seven days for his purifying, wash his clothes and bathe his body in fresh water, and he'll become pure. ¹⁴On the eighth day he's to get himself two doves or two young pigeons and come before Yahweh at the entrance of the appointment tent, and give them to the priest. ¹⁵The priest is to make them as offerings, one as a decontamination, one as a burnt offering. So the priest is to make expiation for him before Yahweh because of his discharge.

¹⁶When an emission of semen goes out from a man, he's to bathe his entire body in water, and he becomes taboo until the evening. ¹⁷Any clothing or any skin on which the emission of semen comes is to be washed in water, and it becomes taboo until the evening. ¹⁸A woman that the man sleeps with involving an emission of semen, they're to bathe in water and they become taboo until the evening.

¹⁹When a woman is discharging, if her discharge in her flesh is blood, she's to be in her flowing for seven days. Anyone who touches her becomes taboo until the evening. ²⁰Anything that she lies on in her flowing becomes taboo, and anything that she sits on becomes taboo. ²¹Anyone who touches her bedding is to wash his clothes and bathe in water, and he becomes taboo until the evening. ²²Anyone who touches any article on which she sits is to wash his clothes and bathe in water, and he becomes taboo until the evening. ²³Whether it's on the bedding or on the article on which she sits, through touching it he becomes taboo until the evening. ²⁴If a man actually sleeps with her, her flowing comes on him. He becomes taboo for seven days, and any bedding on which he lies becomes taboo.

On keeping away from taboo

²⁵When a woman's discharge of blood flows for many days not during her flowing, or when she discharges beyond her flowing, for all the days of her discharge her taboo will be like the days of her flowing. She's taboo. ²⁶Any bedding on which she lies all the days of her discharge will be for her like the bedding during her flowing. Any article that she sits on becomes taboo, like the taboo during her flowing. ²⁷Anyone who touches them becomes taboo. He's to wash his clothes and bathe in water, and he becomes taboo until the evening.

²⁸If she's pure from her discharge, she's to count for herself seven days, and afterwards she'll become pure. ²⁹On the eighth day she's to get herself two doves or two young pigeons and bring them to the priest at the entrance of the appointment tent. ³⁰The priest is to make one as a decontamination and one as a burnt offering. So the priest is to make expiation for her before Yahweh, from her taboo discharge.

³¹You're to consecrate the Yisra'elites from their taboo, so they won't die through their taboo, through bringing taboo on my dwelling among them.

³²This is the instruction about someone from whom an emission of semen goes out and who becomes taboo through it, ³³about a woman when she's unwell, about someone who has their discharge, male or female, and about the man who sleeps with a woman who is taboo.'

The expiation day

16 Yahweh spoke to Mosheh and Aharon after the death of Aharon's two sons when they drew near before Yahweh and died. ²Yahweh said to Mosheh: 'Speak to your brother Aharon: he's not to come at any time into the sacred place, inside the curtain, before the expiation cover that's on the chest, so he doesn't die, because I appear in a cloud, over the expiation cover. ³In this way Aharon is to come into the sacred place: with a bull from the herd as a decontamination, and a ram as a burnt offering. ⁴He's to put on a sacred linen tunic, and cloth shorts are to be on his body. He's to wrap on a cloth sash and wind on a cloth turban. They're sacred garments; he's to wash his body in water and then put them on. ⁵From the assembly of the Yisra'elites he's to get two goats from the flock as a decontamination and a ram as a burnt offering. ⁶Aharon is to present the decontamination bull that is his and make expiation for himself and for his household, ⁷and to get the two goats and set them before Yahweh at the entrance of the appointment tent. ⁸Aharon is to put lots on the two goats, one lot for Yahweh and one lot for Azazel. ⁹Aharon is to present the goat on to which the lot came for Yahweh and to make it as a decontamination. ¹⁰The goat on to which the lot came for Azazel is to stand alive before Yahweh, to make expiation on it and to send it off to Azazel to the wilderness.

Expiation for the sanctuary

¹¹Aharon is then to present the decontamination bull which is his, and make expiation for himself and for his household. He's to slaughter the decontamination bull that is his, ¹²and get a panful of burning coals from on the altar from before Yahweh, and his fistfuls of fine aromatic incense, and bring it inside the curtain. ¹³He's to put the incense on the fire before Yahweh so the incense cloud covers the expiation cover that's on the affirmation, so he won't die. ¹⁴He's to get some of the bull's blood and spatter it with his finger on the surface of the expiation cover to the east, and before the expiation cover he's to spatter some of the blood seven times with his finger. ¹⁵Then he's to slaughter the decontamination goat that's the people's, bring its blood inside the curtain and do with the blood as he did with the bull's blood. He's to spatter it on the expiation cover and before the expiation cover. ¹⁶So he will make expiation for the sacred place from the Yisra'elites' taboos and from their rebellions, in relation to all their wrongdoings.

So he's to do for the appointment tent, which dwells with them in the middle of their taboos. ¹⁷No human being is to be in the appointment tent when he goes in to make expiation in the sacred place, until his coming out. So he will make expiation for himself, for his household and for the entire Yisra'elite congregation.

The goat for Azazel

¹⁸Then he's to go out to the altar that's before Yahweh and make expiation on it. He's to get some of the bull's blood and some of the goat's blood and put it on the altar's horns all round. ¹⁹He's to spatter some of the blood on it seven times with his finger. So he will purify it and make it sacred from the Yisra'elites' taboos. ²⁰When he's finished making expiation for the sacred place, the appointment tent and the altar, he's to present the live goat. ²¹Aharon is to lean both his hands on the live goat's head and confess over it all the wayward acts of the Yisra'elites and all their rebellions in relation to all their wrongdoings, put them on the goat's head and send it off by means of an appointed person into the wilderness. ²²The goat is to carry on it all their wayward acts to a region that's cut off. He's to send off the goat into the wilderness.

²³Then Aharon is to go into the appointment tent and take off the cloth garments that he put on when he went into the sacred place, and set them down there. ²⁴He's to bathe his body in water in the sacred place, put on his garments, go out and make his burnt offering and the people's burnt offering, and make expiation for himself and for the people. ²⁵The fat of the decontamination he's to turn into smoke at the altar. ²⁶The person who sent off the goat to Azazel is to wash his clothes and bathe his body in water, and after that come into the camp.

The discipline of the seventh month

²⁷He's to take out the decontamination bull and the decontamination goat (whose blood was brought in to make expiation in the sacred place) outside the camp, and burn in fire their

skins, their flesh and their intestines. ²⁸The one who burns them is to wash his clothes and bathe his body in water, and after that come into the camp.

²⁹This is to be a permanent decree for you: in the seventh month on the tenth of the month you're to humble yourselves and not do any work, the native and the person who is a resident among you, ³⁰because on this day he makes expiation for you to purify you from all your wrongdoings; you will become pure before Yahweh. ³¹It will be a total stop for you. You're to humble yourselves (a permanent decree).

³²The priest whom he anoints and commissions to act as priest in his father's place is to make expiation. He's to put on the cloth garments, the sacred garments. ³³He's to make expiation for the sacred sanctuary, to make expiation for the appointment tent and the altar, and to make expiation for the priests and for the entire people of the congregation. ³⁴This is to be a permanent decree for you, to make expiation for the Yisra'elites from all their wrongdoings once in the year.'

He did as Yahweh ordered Mosheh.

Slaughtering animals at the sanctuary

17 Yahweh spoke to Mosheh: ²'Speak to Aharon, to his sons and to all the Yisra'elites: "This is the thing that Yahweh has ordered. ³An individual person from Yisra'el's household who slaughters an ox or sheep or goat in the camp or slaughters it outside the camp ⁴and doesn't bring it to the entrance of the appointment tent to present as an offering for Yahweh before Yahweh's dwelling: blood will be deemed for that person. He's shed blood. That person shall be cut off from among his people."

⁵It is in order that the Yisra'elites may bring their sacrifices that they're making on the face of the fields – may bring them to Yahweh at the entrance of the appointment tent, to the priest, and make them into well-being sacrifices for Yahweh, ⁶and the priest may toss their blood over Yahweh's altar at the entrance of the appointment tent and turn the fat into smoke as a nice smell for Yahweh, ⁷and they may no more make their sacrifices to goat-demons

after whom they're whoring. This is to be a permanent decree for them, through their generations.

⁸You're to say to them: "Anyone, anyone from Yisra'el's household or from the people who reside among you who offers up a burnt offering or a sacrifice ⁹and doesn't bring it to the entrance of the appointment tent to make it as an offering for Yahweh, that individual shall be cut off from his kin. ¹⁰And an individual person from Yisra'el's household or from the people who reside among you who eats any blood: I will set my face against the life of the person who eats the blood and cut it off from among its people, ¹¹ᵃbecause the life of the body is in the blood."

It's the blood that makes expiation

¹¹ᵇI myself have given it to you on the altar to make expiation for your lives, because it's the blood that makes expiation, by means of the life. ¹²That's why I've said to the Yisra'elites, "No person from among you will eat blood, nor will the people who reside among you eat blood."

¹³An individual person from the Yisra'elites or from the people who reside among you who catches a game animal or a bird that may be eaten is to pour out its blood and cover it with soil. ¹⁴Because its blood is the life of all flesh. It simply is its life. So I've said to the Yisra'elites, "You will not eat the blood of any flesh, because its blood is the life of all flesh. Anyone who eats it shall be cut off."

¹⁵Any person who eats a corpse or something mauled, either a native or a resident, is to wash his clothes and bathe in water, and he becomes taboo until the evening, then he becomes pure. ¹⁶If he doesn't wash them and doesn't bathe his body, he carries his waywardness.'

18 Yahweh spoke to Mosheh: ²'Speak to the Yisra'elites: "I am Yahweh your God. ³You will not act in accordance with the practice of the country of Misrayim in which you lived, and you will not act in accordance with the practice of the country of Kena'an where I'm bringing you. You will not walk by their decrees. ⁴You're to act on my rulings and keep my decrees, walking by them. I am Yahweh your God. ⁵You're to keep my decrees and my rulings, by which the person who acts on them may live. I am Yahweh.

Forbidden sexual relationships

⁶No individual person will approach any close relative so as to expose their nakedness. I am Yahweh.
⁷You will not expose your father's nakedness or your mother's nakedness. It's your mother; you will not expose her nakedness.
⁸You will not expose the nakedness of your father's wife; it's your father's nakedness.
⁹You will not expose the nakedness of your sister – your father's daughter or your mother's daughter, born in the household or born outside.
¹⁰You will not expose the nakedness of your son's daughter or your daughter's daughter, their nakedness, because they are your nakedness.
¹¹You will not expose the nakedness of your father's wife's daughter, your father's offspring; she's your sister. You will not expose her nakedness.
¹²You will not expose the nakedness of your father's sister; she's your father's relative.
¹³You will not expose the nakedness of your mother's sister, because she's your mother's relative.
¹⁴You will not expose the nakedness of your father's brother. You will not approach his wife; she's your aunt.
¹⁵You will not expose the nakedness of your daughter-in-law. She's your son's wife; you will not expose her nakedness.
¹⁶You will not expose the nakedness of your brother's wife. It's your brother's nakedness.
¹⁷You will not expose the nakedness of a woman and her daughter. You will not take her son's daughter or her daughter's daughter and expose her nakedness. They're relatives. It's a deliberate wickedness.

How Kena'an vomited out its inhabitants

¹⁸You will not take a wife alongside her sister so as to cause pressure, so as to expose her nakedness beside her during her lifetime.
¹⁹You will not approach a woman during her taboo flowing, so as to expose her nakedness.
²⁰You will not have sex with the wife of your fellow, so as to become taboo through her.
²¹You will not give any of your offspring for passing across to the Shameful King; you will not treat the name of your God as ordinary. I am Yahweh.
²²You will not sleep with a male as one sleeps with a woman. It's an offensive act.
²³You will not have sex with any animal so as to become taboo by it, and no woman is to present herself before an animal so as to lie down with it. It's a perversion.
²⁴Don't make yourself taboo through any of these things, because by all these the nations that I'm going to send off from before you made themselves taboo. ²⁵The country became taboo and I've attended to it for its waywardness, and the country has vomited out the people living in it. ²⁶You yourselves are to keep my decrees and my rulings; you will not perform any of these offensive acts, the native or the person who is a resident among you, ²⁷because the people who were in the country before you performed all these offensive acts, and the country became taboo. ²⁸The country is not to vomit you out because you make it taboo, as it has vomited out the nations that were before you. ²⁹Because anyone who performs any of these offensive acts – the persons who perform them shall be cut off from among their people.
³⁰ You're to keep my charge so you don't perform any of the offensive decrees that were performed before you. You're not to make yourselves taboo through them. I am Yahweh your God.'"

Be sacred as I am sacred

19 Yahweh spoke to Mosheh: ²"Speak to the entire Yisra'elite assembly: "You're to be sacred, because I, Yahweh your God, am sacred.
³An individual is to live in awe of his mother and his father and keep my sabbaths. I am Yahweh your God.

⁴Don't turn your face to non-entities and don't make figurine gods for yourselves. I am Yahweh your God.

⁵When you make a well-being sacrifice for Yahweh, make it so it may be for your acceptance. ⁶It's to be eaten on the day you sacrifice it, or the next day. What is left until the third day is to be burned in fire. ⁷If it's actually eaten on the third day, it will be an objectionable thing. It won't find acceptance. ⁸The one who eats it – he will carry his waywardness, because he's treated as ordinary something sacred that belongs to Yahweh. That person shall be cut off from his kin.

⁹When you reap the harvest of your land, each of you will not finish off harvesting the side of your field, and you will not gather the gleanings of your harvest ¹⁰or scour your vineyard or glean your vineyard's windfall. You're to leave them for the humble and for the resident. I am Yahweh your God.

¹¹You will not steal, you will not deceive, and you will not cheat, one individual his fellow.

¹²You will not swear falsely by my name and treat the name of your God as ordinary. I am Yahweh.

¹³You will not defraud your neighbour and you will not seize things.

The wages of an employee will not stay with you until morning.

¹⁴You will not slight the deaf and you will not put an obstacle before the blind but live in awe of your God. I am Yahweh.

Let creation be

¹⁵You will not do evil in making a decision: you will not honour the person of someone who is poor and you will not respect the person of someone who is big; you will make a decision for your fellow with faithfulness.

¹⁶You will not live as a slanderer among your kin.

You will not take the stand against your neighbour's life. I am Yahweh.

¹⁷You will not be hostile to your brother in your mind; you will firmly reprove your fellow, so you do not carry liability because of him.

¹⁸You will not take redress and you will not hold on to things in relation to members of your people, but be loyal to your neighbour as to yourself. I am Yahweh.

¹⁹You're to keep my decrees.

You will not mate two kinds of animals; you will not sow your field with two kinds; you will not put cloth woven of two kinds on to yourself.

²⁰When a man sleeps with a woman (has sex) and she's a maidservant designated to someone but she hasn't actually been redeemed or given her freedom, there's to be an inquiry. They will not be put to death, because she had not been freed, ²¹but he's to bring his reparation to Yahweh to the entrance of the appointment tent, a ram as a reparation, ²²and the priest is to make expiation for him with the reparation ram before Yahweh for the wrong that he did. So it will be pardoned for him in respect of the wrong that he did.

²³When you come into the country and you plant any edible tree, you're to treat its fruit as its foreskin. For three years it's to be foreskinned to you. It's not to be eaten. ²⁴In the fourth year all its fruit will be sacred, an expression of great praise to Yahweh. ²⁵In the fifth year you may eat its fruit – so as to increase its yield for you. I am Yahweh your God.

Yisra'el's distinctiveness

²⁶You will not eat anything with the blood. You will not cast spells and you will not practise augury.

²⁷You will not trim the side of your head, you will not do violence to the side of your beard, ²⁸you will not make a gash on your flesh for someone and you will not make the mark of a cut on yourselves. I am Yahweh.

²⁹Don't treat your daughter as ordinary by making her act the whore, so the country doesn't whore and become full of deliberate wickedness.

³⁰You're to keep my sabbaths and live in awe of my sanctuary. I am Yahweh.

[31] Don't turn your face to ghosts and don't seek spirits, so as to become taboo through them. I am Yahweh your God. [32] You're to get up in the presence of the grey-haired, respect the person of the elderly and live in awe of your God. I am Yahweh. [33] When a person is a resident with you in your country, you will not wrong him. [34] The person who is a resident with you is to be for you like a native from among you. You're to be loyal to him as someone like you, because you were residents in the country of Misrayim. I am Yahweh your God. [35] You will not do evil over a ruling – over length, over weight or over volume. [36] You're to have true balances, true weights, a true barrel and a true gallon. I am Yahweh your God who got you out of the country of Misrayim, [37] and you're to keep all my decrees and all my rulings, and act on them. I am Yahweh.'"

Yisra'el's sacredness

20 Yahweh spoke to Mosheh: [2] "Say to the Yisra'elites: "An individual person from the Yisra'elites or from the people residing in Yisra'el who gives one of his offspring to the Shameful King is absolutely to be put to death. The people of the country are to pelt him with stones. [3] I myself will set my face against that man and cut him off from among his people, because he's given one of his offspring to the Shameful King, in order to make my sanctuary taboo and treat my sacred name as ordinary. [4] If the people of the country actually hide their eyes from that man when he gives one of his offspring to the Shameful King, so they don't put him to death, [5] I myself will set my face against that man and against his kin-group, and cut off him and all those who whore after him, and thus whore after the Shameful King, from among their people.

[6] The person who turns his face to ghosts and to spirits to whore after them: I shall set my face against that person and cut him off from among his people. [7] You're to make yourselves sacred and to be sacred, because I am Yahweh your God. [8] You're to keep my decrees and act on them. I am Yahweh who makes you sacred.

[9] When an individual person who slights his father and his mother – he's absolutely to be put to death. He's slighted his father and his mother. His shed blood is against him.

Rules about sex

[10] When someone is adulterous with someone's wife (is adulterous with his neighbour's wife), the adulterer and the adulteress are absolutely to be put to death. [11] Someone who sleeps with his father's wife has exposed his father's nakedness. The two of them are absolutely to be put to death. Their shed blood is against them. [12] Someone who sleeps with his daughter-in-law is absolutely to die. The two of them have committed a perversion. Their shed blood is against them. [13] Someone who sleeps with a male as one sleeps with a woman – the two of them have performed an offensive act. They are absolutely to be put to death. Their shed blood is against them. [14] Someone who takes a woman and her mother: it's a deliberate wickedness. They are to burn him and them in fire. There will not be a deliberate wickedness among you. [15] Someone who has sex with an animal is absolutely to be put to death, and you're to kill the animal. [16] A woman who approaches any animal to lie down with it: you're to kill the woman and the animal. They are absolutely to be put to death. Their shed blood is against them. [17] Someone who takes his sister, his father's daughter or his mother's daughter, and he sees her nakedness and she sees his nakedness: it's a shameful thing. They shall be cut off before their people's eyes. He's exposed his sister's nakedness. He will carry his waywardness. [18] When a man sleeps with a woman who's unwell and exposes her nakedness, he has bared her flow and she herself has exposed her blood flow. Both of them shall be cut off from among their people. [19] You will not expose the nakedness of your mother's sister or your father's sister, because he's bared his flesh. They will carry their waywardness.

²⁰Someone who sleeps with his aunt has exposed his uncle's nakedness. They will carry their waywardness. They will die childless. ²¹Someone who takes his brother's wife – it's a defilement. He's exposed his brother's nakedness. They will be childless.

Yisra'el's distinctiveness

²²You're to keep all my decrees and all my rulings, and act on them, so the country where I'm bringing you to live won't vomit you out. ²³You will not walk by the decrees of the nations that I'm sending off from before you because they did all these things. I was dismayed about them ²⁴and I said to you, 'You're the ones who will take possession of their land.' I myself shall give it to you to possess, a country flowing with milk and syrup. I am Yahweh your God, who has made you distinct from the peoples. ²⁵So you're to make a distinction between the pure animal and the taboo, between the taboo bird and the pure. You will not make yourselves into an atrocity through an animal or a bird or anything that moves on the ground, which I've made distinct, for you to treat as taboo. ²⁶You're to be sacred for me, because I Yahweh am sacred, and I've made you distinct from the peoples to be mine.

²⁷When there's a ghost or spirit in a man or a woman, they are absolutely to be put to death. People are to pelt them with stones. Their shed blood will be on their own heads.'"

The priests' discipline

21 Yahweh said to Mosheh: 'Speak to the priests, Aharon's sons: "No one is to make himself taboo for a [dead] person among his kin, ²except for his relative who's near to him – for his mother, for his father, for his son, for his daughter, for his brother, ³or for his sister who's a young girl and is near to him, who hasn't yet come to belong to a man; for her he may make himself taboo. ⁴He will not make himself taboo as a husband among his kin, so as to become ordinary.

⁵They will not make a bald patch on their head, they will not shave the side of their beard and they will not make a gash on their flesh. ⁶They are to be sacred for their God and they will not treat the name of their God as ordinary, because they present Yahweh's gift offerings, their God's meal, so they're to be sacred. ⁷They will not take a woman who's a whore and who's ordinary, and they will not take a woman divorced by her husband, because he's sacred for his God. ⁸You're to treat him as sacred, because he presents your God's meal. He's to be sacred for you, because I am sacred, Yahweh who makes you sacred. ⁹When the daughter of an individual priest becomes ordinary by whoring, she makes her father ordinary. She's to be burned in fire.

¹⁰The priest who is greater than his brothers, on whose head the anointing oil has been poured and whom they have commissioned to put on the garments, will not bare his head or tear his clothes. ¹¹He will not go in near any dead people; he will not become taboo for his father or for his mother. ¹²He will not go out of the sanctuary and treat his God's sanctuary as ordinary, because the consecration of his God's anointing oil is on him. I am Yahweh.

¹³That man is to take a woman in her virginity. ¹⁴A widow or divorcee or someone made ordinary by whoring – these he will not take. Rather, he's to take a young girl from his kin, ¹⁵so he doesn't make his offspring among his kin ordinary, because I am Yahweh who makes him sacred."'

Priestly distinctives

¹⁶Yahweh spoke to Mosheh: ¹⁷"Speak to Aharon: "Through their generations, no individual from your offspring in whom there's a defect is to draw near to present his God's meal. ¹⁸Because no individual in whom there's a defect is to draw near: one blind or lame or disfigured or deformed, ¹⁹or one who has an injury to his leg or an injury to his hand, ²⁰or one who is a hunchback or dwarf or defective in his eye or [has] scab or sore or crushed testicle. ²¹No individual from Aharon's offspring in whom there's a defect will come up to present Yahweh's gift offerings. There being a defect in him, he will not come up to present Yahweh's meal. ²²He may eat his God's meal, from the especially sacred and from the sacred.

²³Nevertheless he will not go to the curtain and he will not come up to the altar, because there's a defect in him. He will not treat my great sanctuary as ordinary, because I am Yahweh who makes it sacred.'"

²⁴Mosheh spoke to Aharon and to his sons and to all the Yisra'elites.

22 Yahweh spoke to Mosheh: ²'Speak to Aharon and to his sons so they stay consecrated from the Yisra'elites' sacred things (and don't treat my sacred name as ordinary), which they are making sacred for me. I am Yahweh. ³Say to them: "Through your generations, any one of all your offspring who comes near the sacred things that the Yisra'elites make sacred for Yahweh and his taboo is on him, that person shall be cut off from before me. I am Yahweh."

Dealing with sacred food

⁴No individual person from Aharon's offspring who has been made scaly or is discharging will eat of the sacred things until he becomes pure. Someone who touches anything taboo through a [dead] person, or an individual from whom there's an emission of semen, ⁵or an individual who touches anything that teems for which he becomes taboo or a human being for whom he becomes taboo: for any taboo of his, ⁶the person who touches it becomes taboo until the evening and will not eat of the sacred things unless he's bathed his body in water ⁷and the sun has gone down, and he's become pure. Afterwards, he may eat of the sacred things, because it's his meal. ⁸He will not eat a corpse or something mauled so as to become taboo through it. I am Yahweh.

⁹They're to keep my charge, and not carry wrongdoing because of it and die through it because they treat it as ordinary. I am Yahweh who makes them sacred. ¹⁰No outsider will eat something sacred. A settler with a priest, or an employee, will not eat something sacred. ¹¹When a priest acquires someone as his own for silver, he may eat of it, and someone born in his household – they may eat of his meal. ¹²When a priest's daughter comes to belong to an individual who is an outsider, she will not eat of the contribution among the sacred things. ¹³But when a priest's daughter becomes a widow or divorcee and she has no offspring, and comes back to her father's household as in her youth, she may eat of her father's meal. But no outsider may eat of it.

¹⁴When an individual eats something sacred by mistake, he's to add to it a fifth of it and give the priest the sacred thing. ¹⁵They will not treat the Yisra'elites' sacred things as ordinary, which they take up for Yahweh, ¹⁶and make them carry waywardness requiring reparation through their eating their sacred things, because I am Yahweh who makes them sacred.'

Acceptable sacrifices

¹⁷Yahweh spoke to Mosheh: ¹⁸'Speak to Aharon and to his sons and to all the Yisra'elites: "An individual person from Yisra'el's household or from the residents in Yisra'el who presents his offering in connection with any of their pledges or with any of their free offerings that they present for Yahweh as a burnt offering: ¹⁹for your acceptance, a male – among the herd, among the flock or among the goats – that's whole. ²⁰Any in which there's a defect you will not present because it won't be for acceptance for you.

²¹When someone presents a well-being sacrifice for Yahweh, to fulfil a pledge or as a free offering, among the herd or among the flock, it's to be whole, for acceptance; there will be no defect in it. ²²Blind or injured or disfigured or suppurating or with scabs or sores: you will not present these for Yahweh and you will not put any of them on the altar as a gift offering for Yahweh. ²³You may make into a free offering an ox or sheep that's deformed or stunted, but for a pledge it will not find acceptance.

²⁴You will not present for Yahweh something bruised, crushed, torn or cut. In your country you will not make an offering ²⁵or present as your God's meal any of these from the hand of a foreigner, because their deformity in them is a defect in them. They won't find acceptance for you."'

²⁶Yahweh spoke to Mosheh: ²⁷'When an ox or sheep or goat is born, it's to be under its mother for seven days. From the eighth day onwards, it will find acceptance as an offering, a gift offering for Yahweh. ²⁸You will not

slaughter a cow or sheep with its offspring on the same day. ²⁹When you make a thanksgiving sacrifice for Yahweh, offer it so it may be for your acceptance. ³⁰It's to be eaten on that day. You will not leave any of it until morning. I am Yahweh.

³¹You're to keep my orders and act on them. I am Yahweh. ³²You will not treat my sacred name as ordinary, so I may show myself sacred among the Yisra'elites. I am Yahweh, who made you sacred, ³³the one who got you out of the country of Misrayim to be your God. I am Yahweh.'

The set times

23 Yahweh spoke to Mosheh: ²'Speak to the Yisra'elites: "These are Yahweh's set times, which you're to call for as sacred occasions. They're my set times. ³For six days, work may be done. On the seventh a complete stop [*shabbat shabbaton*], a sacred occasion. You will not do any work. It's a sabbath for Yahweh in all your settlements.

⁴These are Yahweh's set times, the sacred occasions, which you're to call for at their set time. ⁵In the first month on the fourteenth of the month at twilight, Yahweh's Pesah [Passover], ⁶and on the fifteenth day of this month, the Flatbread Festival for Yahweh. For seven days you're to eat flatbread. ⁷On the first day it's to be a sacred occasion for you; you will not do any servile work. ⁸You're to present a gift offering for Yahweh for seven days. On the seventh day, a sacred occasion, you will not do any servile work."'

⁹Yahweh spoke to Mosheh: ¹⁰'Speak to the Yisra'elites: "When you come into the country that I'm giving you and you reap its harvest, you're to bring the first sheaf of your harvest to the priest. ¹¹He's to elevate the sheaf before Yahweh for your acceptance. On the day after the sabbath the priest is to elevate it. ¹²On the day of your elevating the sheaf, you're to make a lamb that's whole, a year old, into a burnt offering for Yahweh, ¹³with its grain offering of two tenths of fine flour mixed with oil, a gift offering for Yahweh, a nice smell, and its libation, wine, a quarter of a gallon. ¹⁴You will not eat bread or roasted grain or plantation-growth until this particular day, until you bring the offering to your God (a permanent decree through your generations in all your settlements).

The first harvests

¹⁵You're to count seven sabbaths for yourselves from the day after the sabbath, from the day you bring the elevation sheaf. They're to be whole weeks. ¹⁶You're to count until the day after the seventh sabbath, fifty days, and present an offering of new grain for Yahweh.

¹⁷From your settlements you're to bring two loaves of elevation bread. They're to be two tenths of fine flour. They're to be baked with yeast, as first products for Yahweh. ¹⁸You're to present with the bread seven lambs that are whole, a year old, one bull from the herd and two rams. They're to be a burnt offering for Yahweh, with their grain offering and their libations, a gift offering, a nice smell for Yahweh. ¹⁹And you're to make one he-goat from the flock into a decontamination, and two sheep, a year old, into a well-being sacrifice. ²⁰The priest is to elevate them with the first-products bread as an elevation offering before Yahweh, along with the two sheep. They're to be sacred for Yahweh, for the priest.

²¹You're to call for this particular day. It's to be a sacred occasion for you; you're to do no servile work (a permanent decree in all your settlements through your generations).

²²When you reap the harvest of your land, each of you will not finish off harvesting the edge of your field and you will not gather the gleanings of your harvest. You will leave them for the humble and for the resident. I am Yahweh your God."'

²³Yahweh spoke to Mosheh: ²⁴'Speak to the Yisra'elites: "In the seventh month on the first of the month there's to be a stop for you, a reminder with a horn blast, a sacred occasion. ²⁵You will do no servile work. You're to present a gift offering for Yahweh."'

The Day of Complete Expiation

²⁶Yahweh spoke to Mosheh: ²⁷'But then: on the tenth of this seventh month is the Day of Complete Expiation. It's to be a sacred occasion

for you. You're to humble yourselves and present a gift offering for Yahweh. ²⁸You will do no work on this particular day, because it's the Day of Complete Expiation, to make expiation for you before Yahweh your God. ²⁹Because any person who is not humbled on this particular day is to be cut off from his kin, ³⁰and any person who does any work on this particular day – I'll cause that person to perish from among his people. ³¹You will not do any work (a permanent decree through your generations in all your settlements). ³²It's to be a complete stop [shabbat shabbaton] for you, and you're to humble yourselves. On the ninth of the month in the evening, from evening to evening, you're to make your sabbath stop.'

³³Yahweh spoke to Mosheh: ³⁴"Speak to the Yisra'elites: "On the fifteenth day of this seventh month is the Sukkot Festival for Yahweh, for seven days. ³⁵On the first day, a sacred occasion; you will do no servile work. ³⁶For seven days you are to present a gift offering for Yahweh. On the eighth day it's to be a sacred occasion for you. You're to present a gift offering for Yahweh. It's an assembly; you will not do any servile work.

³⁷These are Yahweh's set times that you're to call for as sacred occasions for presenting a gift offering for Yahweh: burnt offering and grain offering, sacrifice and libations, a day's allocation on its day, ³⁸apart from Yahweh's sabbaths, from your gift offerings, from all your pledges and from all your free offerings that you give for Yahweh.

The Sukkot (Tabernacles) Festival and the candelabrum

³⁹But then, on the fifteenth day of the seventh month, when you've gathered in the yield of the country, you're to observe Yahweh's festival, for seven days: on the first day a stop and on the eighth day a stop. ⁴⁰On the first day you're to get yourselves the fruit of magnificent trees, branches of palm, boughs of green trees, and poplars from the wadi, and rejoice before Yahweh your God for seven days. ⁴¹You're to observe it as a festival for Yahweh for seven days in the year (a permanent decree through your generations). In the seventh month you're to observe it. ⁴²You're to live in bivouacs [sukkot] for seven days – every native in Yisra'el, they're to live in bivouacs – ⁴³in order that your generations may acknowledge that I made the Yisra'elites live in bivouacs when I got them out of the country of Misrayim. I am Yahweh your God.'"

⁴⁴Mosheh called for Yahweh's set times to all the Yisra'elites.

24 Yahweh spoke to Mosheh: ²'Order the Yisra'elites that they're to get for you clear pressed olive oil for lighting, for putting up a lamp regularly. ³Outside the affirmation curtain in the appointment tent, Aharon is to order it from evening to morning before Yahweh regularly (a permanent decree through your generations). ⁴On the pure candelabrum he's to order the lamps before Yahweh regularly.

⁵You're to get fine flour and bake it into twelve loaves. One loaf is to be two tenths. ⁶You're to place them in two rows, six in a row, on the pure table before Yahweh. ⁷You're to put pure frankincense with the row. It will be a commemorative portion for the bread, a gift offering for Yahweh. ⁸Sabbath day by sabbath day he's to order it before Yahweh, regularly, a permanent pact on the part of the Yisra'elites. ⁹It's to belong to Aharon and to his sons and they're to eat it in a sacred place, because it's especially sacred for him from Yahweh's gift offerings (a permanent decree).'

An eye for an eye

¹⁰A Yisra'elite woman's son, who was a Misrayimite man's son, went out among the Yisra'elites, and the Yisra'elite woman's son and a Yisra'elite got into a fight in the camp. ¹¹The Yisra'elite woman's son cursed the name and slighted it. So they brought him to Mosheh (his mother's name was Shelomit bat Dibri, of the clan of Dan) ¹²and they placed him under keep for things to be made clear to them at Yahweh's bidding.

¹³Yahweh spoke to Mosheh: ¹⁴"Take the slighter outside the camp. All the people who heard are to lean their hands on his head, and the entire assembly is to stone him.

¹⁵You're to speak to the Yisra'elites: "An individual person who slights his God will carry his wrongdoing. ¹⁶A person who curses Yahweh's name is absolutely to be put to death. The entire assembly is indeed to stone him. As

with the resident, so with the native, for his cursing the name he's to be put to death.

¹⁷An individual who strikes down any human being is absolutely to be put to death. ¹⁸One who strikes down an animal is to make good for it, life for life. ¹⁹An individual who causes an injury to his fellow: as he did, so it's to be done to him, ²⁰fracture for fracture, eye for eye, tooth for tooth. As he causes an injury to the person, so it's to be caused to him. ²¹One who strikes down an animal is to make good for it, but one who strikes down a human being is to be put to death. ²²There's to be one ruling for you; it's to be as with the resident, so with the native, because I am Yahweh your God."

²³Mosheh spoke to the Yisra'elites, and they took the slighter outside the camp and pelted him with stones. The Yisra'elites did as Yahweh ordered Mosheh.

Sabbaths for the land

25 Yahweh spoke to Mosheh at Mount Sinay: ²"Speak to the Yisra'elites: "When you come into the country I'm giving you, the country is to make a sabbath stop for Yahweh. ³For six years you may sow your field and for six years you may prune your vineyard and gather its yield, ⁴but in the seventh year there's to be a complete stop [*shabbat shabbaton*] for the country, a sabbath for Yahweh. You will not sow your field, you will not prune your vineyard, ⁵ you will not reap your harvest's aftergrowth, you will not cut the grapes of your free vines. It's to be a year of stopping for the country. ⁶The country's sabbath will be food for you, for you yourself, for your servant and for your handmaid, for your employee and for your resident living with you, ⁷for your animals and for the creatures that are in your country: all its yield will be for eating.

⁸You're to count seven sabbaths of years for yourselves, seven times seven years, so that the time period of your seven sabbaths of years will be forty-nine years. ⁹You're to make a blasting horn pass through in the seventh month, on the tenth of the month; on the Day of Complete Expiation you're to make the horn pass through your entire country. ¹⁰You're to make the fiftieth year sacred and call for a release in the country for all the people living in it. It's to be a ram's horn year for you. You're to go back, each individual, to his holding, and to go back, each individual, to his kin-group. ¹¹The year, that fiftieth year, is to be a ram's horn year for you: you will not sow, you will not reap its aftergrowth and you will not cut its free vines, ¹²because it's a ram's horn year. It's to be sacred for you. You will eat the yield from the field.

The 'Jubilee', the ram's horn year

¹³In this ram's horn year you're to go back, each individual, to his holding. ¹⁴When you sell something to your fellow, or buy from your fellow's hand, you're not to wrong one another. ¹⁵It's by the count of the years since the ram's horn year that you're to buy from your fellow; it's by the count of the years of yield that he's to sell to you. ¹⁶On the basis of the large number of the years you'll pay a high price to him; on the basis of the low number of the years you'll pay a low price to him, because it's the count of the yields that he's selling to you. ¹⁷You will not wrong one another but live in awe of your God, because I am Yahweh your God.

¹⁸You're to act on my decrees and keep my rulings and act on them, so you may live on the land in confidence. ¹⁹The land will give its fruit and you'll eat your fill and live in confidence on it. ²⁰When you say, 'What are we to eat in the seventh year if we don't sow or gather our yield?', ²¹I shall order my blessing for you in the sixth year and it will generate the yield for three years. ²²You'll sow the eighth year and eat from the yield of the old; until the ninth year, until its yield comes in, you'll eat the old. ²³The land will not be sold permanently because the land belongs to me, because you're residents, settlers, living with me. ²⁴In the entire land that's your holding, you're to grant restoration for the land.

When your brother does badly

²⁵When your brother does poorly and sells part of his holding, his restorer who is near to him is to come to him and restore what his brother has sold. ²⁶When an individual

doesn't have a restorer, but his means stretch and provide enough for its restoration, ²⁷he's to think over the years since his sale and give the surplus back to the individual to whom he sold it, and go back to his holding. ²⁸If his means don't provide enough for giving it back to him, what he sold will be in the possession of the person who bought it until the ram's horn year. It will go out in the ram's horn year and he will go back to his holding.
²⁹If an individual sells a dwelling house in a walled town, its restoration may happen up to the completion of a year from its sale. Through the time, its restoration may happen. ³⁰If it's not restored up to the fulfilling of a whole year for it, the house (which is in a town that has a wall) will transfer permanently to the person who bought it, through his generations. It will not go out in the ram's horn year.
³¹Given that houses in villages that have no wall all round are to be thought of as fields in the country, restoration may happen for it, and it will go out in the ram's horn year. ³²The Levites' towns, the houses in the towns in their holding: there may be permanent restoration for the Levites. ³³Something that one of the Levites may restore (a house sale when the town is in his holding) will go out in the ram's horn year, because the houses in the Levites' towns are their holding among the Yisra'elites. ³⁴The pastureland fields belonging to their towns will not be sold, because it's a permanent holding for them.

Not like slaves

³⁵When your brother does poorly and his means fall to you, you're to take strong hold of him as a resident, a settler, so he can stay alive with you. ³⁶You're not to take interest or profit from him; you're to live in awe of your God, so your brother can stay alive with you. ³⁷You will not give your money to him at interest and you will not give him your food for profit. ³⁸I am Yahweh your God who got you out of the country of Misrayim to give you the country of Kena'an, to be God for you.
³⁹When your brother does badly with you, and he sells himself to you, you will not make him serve with servile service. ⁴⁰He's to be with you as an employee, as a settler. Until the ram's horn year he's to serve with you, ⁴¹then he's to go out from you, he and his children with him, and go back to his kin-group, to his ancestors' holding. ⁴²Because they're my servants, whom I got out of the country of Misrayim, they will not sell themselves as a servant is sold. ⁴³You're not to hold sway over him with harshness. You're to live in awe of your God.
⁴⁴Your servant and your handmaid who belong to you from the nations that are round you – from them you may buy a servant or a handmaid, ⁴⁵and also from the children of the settlers who are resident with you. You may buy from them and from their kin-groups that are with you, that give birth in your country, and they will be your holding. ⁴⁶You may have them as a domain for your children after you, to possess as a permanent holding. By means of them you may get service. But over your brothers, the Yisra'elites, over one another you will not hold sway with harshness.

Servitude to a foreigner

⁴⁷When the means of a resident (a settler with you) stretch, but your brother with him does badly, and he sells himself to the resident (the settler with you) or to an offshoot of a resident's kin-group, ⁴⁸after he's sold himself, restoration may happen for him; one of his brothers may restore him, ⁴⁹or his uncle or his uncle's son may restore him, or any close relative from his kin-group may restore him. Or when his means stretch, he may restore himself.
⁵⁰He's to think with the person who bought him, from the year when he sold himself to him until the ram's horn year, and the silver for his sale will be in accordance with the number of years. As it would be for the time of an employee he'll be with him. ⁵¹If there are still many years, on the basis of them he's to give back for his restoration some of the silver that was his price, ⁵²and if few years remain until the ram's horn year, he's to think about himself, and on the basis of his years he's to give back for his restoration. ⁵³He's to be with him like an employee by the year. He's not to hold sway over him with harshness in your eyes. ⁵⁴If he doesn't restore himself in these ways, he's to go out in the ram's horn year, he and his children with him, ⁵⁵because the

Yisraelites are my servants. They're my servants whom I got out of the country of Misrayim. I am Yahweh your God.

26 You will not make non-entities for yourselves, you will not set up a sculpture or a column for yourselves and you will not put a carved stone in your country to bow low to it, because I am Yahweh your God. ²You're to keep my sabbaths and to live in awe of my sanctuary. I am Yahweh.

Promises

³If you walk by my decrees, and keep my orders and act on them, ⁴I shall give your rains in their time, so the country will give its produce and the trees of the fields will give their fruit. ⁵For you, threshing will overtake reaping and reaping will overtake sowing. You'll eat your bread to the full and live in confidence in your country. ⁶I shall put peace in the country and you will lie down with no one making you tremble. I shall eliminate the bad animal from the country and a sword won't pass through your country. ⁷You will pursue your enemies and they will fall to the sword before you. ⁸Five of you will pursue a hundred and a hundred of you will pursue 10,000. Your enemies will fall to the sword before you.

⁹I shall turn my face to you and make you fruitful and make you numerous. I shall implement my pact with you. ¹⁰You'll eat old stuff stored but then take out the old in favour of the new. ¹¹I shall put my dwelling among you and my soul won't spurn you. ¹²I shall walk about among you. I shall be God for you and you will be a people for me. ¹³I am Yahweh your God who got you out of the country of Misrayim, from being servants to them. I broke the bars of your yoke and let you walk tall.

Warnings

¹⁴But if you don't listen to me and don't act on all these orders, ¹⁵if you reject my decrees and your soul spurns my rulings so as not to act on all my orders and so as to contravene my pact, ¹⁶I shall also do this to you. I shall appoint terror over you, wasting away and fever, finishing off the eyes and consuming the life. You will sow your seed with empty results; your enemies will eat it. ¹⁷I shall set my face against you and you will take a beating before your enemies. Your foes will hold sway over you and you will flee when there's no one pursuing you.

¹⁸And if for all these things you don't listen to me, I shall continue disciplining you sevenfold for your wrongdoings. ¹⁹I shall break the majesty of your vigour. I shall make your heavens like iron and your land like copper. ²⁰Your energy will be used up with empty results. Your land won't give its produce. The trees in the land won't give their fruit.

²¹If you walk contrary with me and are not willing to listen to me, I shall add a sevenfold calamity against you in accordance with your wrongdoings. ²²I shall send off creatures of the wild against you and they will make you childless and cut off your animals. They will reduce you so your roads become desolate.

²³And if through these things you don't accept discipline in relation to me, and you walk contrary with me, ²⁴I myself too will walk contrary with you. I myself will also strike you down sevenfold for your wrongdoings. ²⁵I shall bring a sword against you, taking the redress in the pact. You'll gather into your towns, and I'll send off an epidemic among you and you'll be given into an enemy's hand. ²⁶When I break your staff of bread, ten women will bake your bread in one oven, and give back your bread by weight. You'll eat but you won't be full.

More warnings

²⁷And if because of this you don't listen to me and you walk contrary with me, ²⁸I'll walk with you in contrary wrath. I myself will again discipline you sevenfold for your wrongdoings. ²⁹You will eat the flesh of your sons and you will eat the flesh of your daughters. ³⁰I shall annihilate your shrines and cut down your incense stands and put your carcases on your idols' carcases.

I myself will renounce you ³¹and make your towns a waste. I'll make your sanctuaries desolate. I won't smell your nice smells. ³²I myself will make your country desolate; your enemies who live in it will be desolate at it. ³³I shall scatter you among the nations and draw a sword after you. Your country will become a desolation. Your towns will become a waste. ³⁴Then the country will make amends for its sabbaths, through all the time of desolation while you're in your enemies' country. Then the country will stop [*shabat*], and make up for its sabbaths. ³⁵All the time of desolation it will stop what it didn't stop during your sabbaths when you were living on it.

³⁶Those who remain among you: I'll bring faintness into their heart in their enemies' countries. The sound of a leaf being blown away will chase them. They'll flee as people do from the sword, and they'll fall when there's no one chasing. ³⁷They'll collapse over one another as if before the sword when there's no one chasing. You won't have the ability to stand before your enemies.

More promises

³⁸So you will perish among the nations. Your enemies' country will devour you. ³⁹Those who remain among you will rot through their waywardness in your enemies' countries. Yes, through their ancestors' waywardness they will rot with them.

⁴⁰But they will confess their waywardness and their ancestors' waywardness in their trespass that they committed against me; and also they walked contrary with me. ⁴¹When I also walk contrary with them and bring them into their enemies' country, if by chance their foreskinned mind bows down and then they make amends for their waywardness, ⁴²I shall be mindful of my pact with Ya'aqob [Jacob], and also my pact with Yitshaq [Isaac] and also my pact with Abraham. I shall be mindful, and I shall be mindful of the country.

⁴³The country will be left by them so it may make amends for its sabbaths by being desolate without them, and they themselves will make amends for their waywardness because – yes, because they rejected my rulings and their soul renounced my decrees. ⁴⁴But even for this, when they are in their enemies' country I won't reject them and I won't renounce them so as to finish them off, contravening my pact with them, because I am Yahweh their God. ⁴⁵I shall be mindful for them of the pact with the original people whom I got out of the country of Misrayim before the eyes of the nations, to be God for them. I am Yahweh.'"

⁴⁶These are the decrees, the rulings and the instructions that Yahweh gave between him and the Yisra'elites at Mount Sinay through Mosheh.

Promises to God

27 Yahweh spoke to Mosheh: ²"Speak to the Yisra'elites: "When an individual fulfils a pledge to Yahweh on the basis of the evaluation of persons, ³the evaluation is to be:

A male from the age of twenty years until the age of sixty years, the evaluation is to be fifty silver sheqels (by the sanctuary sheqel).

⁴If it's a female, the evaluation is to be thirty sheqels.

⁵If it's someone from the age of five years until the age of thirty years, the evaluation is to be: a male twenty sheqels, for a female ten sheqels.

⁶If it's someone from the age of one month until the age of five years, the evaluation is to be: a male five silver sheqels; for a female the evaluation is to be three silver sheqels.

⁷If it's someone the age of sixty years and upwards: if it's a male, the evaluation is to be fifteen sheqels, and for a female ten sheqels.

⁸If someone has done too badly for the evaluation, they're to get him to stand before the priest and the priest will evaluate him; the priest is to evaluate him on the basis of what the means of the pledge-maker stretch to.

⁹If it's an animal, one of the ones that people may present as an offering for Yahweh, all of what someone gives for Yahweh is to be sacred; ¹⁰he will not exchange it and he will not substitute for it, good for bad or bad for good, and if he does actually substitute one animal for another, it and its substitute will be sacred.

¹¹If it's any taboo animal, one of the ones that people don't present as an offering for Yahweh, he's to get the animal to stand before the priest ¹²and the priest will

evaluate it; whether good or bad, it's to be in accordance with the priest's evaluation, ¹³and if he actually restores it, he's to add a fifth to the evaluation.

On making things sacred

¹⁴If an individual makes his house sacred, as a thing sacred for Yahweh, the priest is to evaluate it. Whether good or bad, as the priest evaluates it, so it will stand. ¹⁵If the person who makes it sacred restores his house, he's to add to it a fifth of the silver of the evaluation, and it will be his.

¹⁶If an individual makes sacred for Yahweh some of the field that's his holding, the evaluation is to be on the basis of its seed: ten barrels of barley seed to fifty silver sheqels. ¹⁷If he makes his field sacred from the ram's horn year, it will stand in accordance with the evaluation. ¹⁸But if he makes his field sacred after the ram's horn year, the priest is to count the silver on the basis of the years that remain until the ram's horn year, and the evaluation will decrease.

¹⁹If the person who made it sacred actually restores the field, he's to add to it a fifth of the silver of the evaluation, and it will stand for him. ²⁰If he doesn't restore the field, or if he's sold the field to another man, it can't be restored any more. ²¹When the field goes out in the ram's horn year, it will be sacred for Yahweh, like a field that's been devoted. It will belong to the priest as his holding.

²²If he makes sacred for Yahweh a field he bought that's not a field belonging to his holding, ²³the priest is to count for him the proportion of the evaluation until the ram's horn year and he's to give the evaluation on that day as something sacred for Yahweh. ²⁴In the ram's horn year the field is to go back to the one from whom he bought it, to the one whose holding in the country it is.

²⁵Every evaluation is to be by the sanctuary sheqel; the sheqel is to be twenty grams.

Things that belong to God

²⁶However, a firstborn (which is born first for Yahweh) among animals: an individual will not make it sacred, whether ox or sheep. It belongs to Yahweh. ²⁷But if it's among taboo animals he may redeem it at the evaluation and add to it a fifth of it. If it's not restored, it's to be sold at the evaluation. ²⁸However, anything that an individual devotes to Yahweh from all that belongs to him, from human beings or animals or fields in his holding, will not be sold and will not be restored. Anything that's devoted is especially sacred for Yahweh. ²⁹No one who is devoted from among human beings will be redeemed. He's absolutely to be put to death.

³⁰Every tenth of the land, from the land's seed, from the trees' fruit, belongs to Yahweh. It's sacred for Yahweh. ³¹If an individual actually restores some of his tenth, he's to add to it a fifth of it. ³²Every tenth of herd and flock, every one that passes under the club, the tenth is to be sacred for Yahweh. ³³A person will not seek out between good and bad and he will not exchange it. If he actually exchanges it, both it and the exchanged one will be sacred. It will not be restored."

³⁴These are the orders that Yahweh gave Mosheh for the Yisra'elites at Mount Sinay.

Numbers

The book of Numbers takes its name from the two counts of the assembly's members that almost bookend the work as a whole – they come in chapter 1 and chapter 26. These two chapters give virtually the same report of the assembly's total numbers (603,550 men the first time, 601,730 the second time). Considerable significance attaches to that similarity in light of what happens in-between the two counts.

The story of the first count introduces ten chapters that relate ways in which Yahweh gets the Israelites ready to resume their journey to Canaan. The chapters are Israel's marching orders. They thus both close the account of Israel's stay at Sinai and open the account of that journey. So the whole of the second half of Exodus, the entire book of Leviticus and the first third of Numbers all deal with the time at Sinai, which occupies less than a year in the nation's life. The space given to this year reflects how important the time at Sinai is in the Old Testament, and how important are the instructions God gives Israel in connection with its stay at Sinai.

The middle third of Numbers (chapters 11—21) tells of the Israelites' actual journey from Sinai to the edge of Canaan. In contrast to the account of the year at Sinai, this fairly short sequence of chapters covers enough time for a whole generation to pass on. The distance from Mount Sinai to Canaan is only 150 miles, so it should have taken only a couple of weeks, but the Israelites actually took years over it. The reason emerges from the stories that Numbers tells. The journey was characterized by a series of rebellions on Israel's part that led Yahweh to resolve that the generation of Israelites who came out of Egypt should be allowed to die out and not get to Canaan. It would be the next generation that got into the land.

The Old and New Testaments see these stories as full of warnings for Israel and for the Church. Psalm 95 reminds enthusiastic worshippers in the temple about their ancestors' rebellions against Yahweh and that whole generation's consequent failure to reach the settled life in Canaan that was their destiny, with the implication that later generations could lose the land if they follow their ancestors' example. Hebrews 3—4 puts the same warning before people who believe in Jesus. In 1 Corinthians 10 Paul refers back to these stories to make the same point. Believers in Jesus, too, need to be wary about worshipping other gods, engaging in sexual immorality, testing Christ, or grumbling, in the way the exodus-wilderness generation did.

The last third of Numbers (chapters 22—36) sees Israel poised finally to enter Canaan, camped just the other side of the River Jordan. These chapters begin with the blessing of Israel by Bil'am [Baalam], which suggests one way in which we are coming near the end of the story that began with Yahweh's promise of blessing and land to Abraham. Balaam restates Yahweh's promise as Abraham's descendants are about to take possession of this land. The significance of Moses' second count of the people then lies in the fact that the people still number approximately the same as they did when they were at Sinai. Yahweh has preserved them despite their rebellion.

The number of 600,000 or so men, which implies two or three million people when one includes their wives and children, is hardly the actual number of people that were there at the time. Deuteronomy will later comment that Israel is rather a small people, and the figure of two or three million is out of proportion to the population of Egypt or Canaan at this time – or to the population of Israel itself over succeeding centuries. It looks as if something odd has happened to the numbers. One plausible explanation is that the word for 'thousand' is also a word for a family or an army division; the word comes with this sense in Numbers 1.16. Behind these figures, then, might be the idea that Israel numbers 600 families – which makes good sense.

A head count

1 Yahweh spoke to Mosheh [Moses] in the Sinay Wilderness in the appointment tent, on the first of the second month in the second year after they got out of the country of Misrayim [Egypt]: ²"Take a head count of the entire assembly of the Yisra'elites [Israelites] by their kin-groups, by their ancestral households, according to the number of the names of every male by their heads, ³from the age of twenty years and upwards, everyone in Yisra'el who goes out in the army. You're to register them by their troops, you and Aharon [Aaron]. ⁴An individual person for each clan is to be with you. The individual will be head of his ancestral household.

⁵These are the names of the men who are to stand with you:

for Re'uben, Elitsur ben Shede'ur;
⁶for Shim'on [Simeon], Shelumi'el ben Tsurishadday;
⁷for Yehudah [Judah], Nahshon ben Amminadab;
⁸for Yissakar [Issachar], Netan'el ben Zu'ar;
⁹for Zebulun, Eli'ab ben Helon;
¹⁰for the sons of Yoseph [Joseph] –
for Ephrayim, Elishama ben Ammihud,
for Menashsheh, Gamli'el ben Pedahtsur;
¹¹for Binyamin [Benjamin], Abidan ben Gid'oni;
¹²for Dan, Ahi'ezer ben Ammishadday;
¹³for Asher, Pag'i'el ben Okran;
¹⁴for Gad, Elyasaph ben De'u'el;
¹⁵for Naphtali, Ahira ben Enan.'

¹⁶These were the people named from the assembly as leaders of their ancestral clans. They were the heads of the Yisra'elite divisions.
¹⁷Mosheh and Aharon got these men who had been designated by their names, ¹⁸and congregated the entire assembly on the first of the second month. They made their descent known on the basis of their kin-groups by their ancestral household according to the number of the names, from the age of twenty years and upwards, head by head. ¹⁹As Yahweh ordered Mosheh, he registered them in the Sinay Wilderness.

From Re'uben to Yissakar

²⁰They were:

The descendants of Re'uben, Yisra'el's firstborn
their lines of descent by their kin-groups by their ancestral household
according to the number of the names head by head
every male from the age of twenty years and upwards, everyone who goes out in the army
²¹their register for the clan of Re'uben: 46,500.

²²For Shim'on's descendants
their lines of descent by their kin-groups by their ancestral household
its register according to the number of the names head by head
every male from the age of twenty years and upwards, everyone who goes out in the army
²³their register for the clan of Shim'on: 59,300.

²⁴For Gad's descendants
their lines of descent by their kin-groups by their ancestral household
according to the number of the names
from the age of twenty years and upwards, everyone who goes out in the army
²⁵their register for the clan of Gad: 45,650.

²⁶For Yehudah's descendants
their lines of descent by their kin-groups by their ancestral household
according to the number of the names
from the age of twenty years and upwards, everyone who goes out in the army
²⁷their register for the clan of Yehudah: 74,600.

²⁸For Yissakar's descendants
their lines of descent by their kin-groups by their ancestral household
according to the number of the names
from the age of twenty years and upwards, everyone who goes out in the army
²⁹their register for the clan of Yissakar: 54,400.

From Zebulun to Naphtali

³⁰For Zebulun's descendants
their lines of descent by their kin-groups by
   their ancestral household
according to the number of the names
from the age of twenty years and upwards,
   everyone who goes out in the army
³¹their register for the clan of Zebulun:
   57,400.

³²For Yoseph's descendants:
For Ephrayim's descendants
their lines of descent by their kin-groups by
   their ancestral household
according to the number of the names
from the age of twenty years and upwards,
   everyone who goes out in the army
³³their register for the clan of Ephrayim:
   40,500.

³⁴For Menashsheh's descendants
their lines of descent by their kin-groups, by
   their ancestral household
according to the number of the names
from the age of twenty years and upwards,
   everyone who goes out in the army
³⁵their register for the clan of Menashsheh:
   32,200.

³⁶For Binyamin's descendants
their lines of descent by their kin-groups by
   their ancestral household
according to the number of the names
from the age of twenty years and upwards,
   everyone who goes out in the army
³⁷their register for the clan of Binyamin:
   35,400.

³⁸For Dan's descendants
their lines of descent by their kin-groups by
   their ancestral household
according to the number of the names
from the age of twenty years and upwards,
   everyone who goes out in the army
³⁹their register for the clan of Dan: 62,700.

⁴⁰For Asher's descendants
their lines of descent by their kin-groups by
   their ancestral household
according to the number of the names
from the age of twenty years and upwards,
   everyone who goes out in the army
⁴¹their register for the clan of Asher: 41,500.

⁴²For Naphtali's descendants
their lines of descent by their kin-groups by
   their ancestral household
according to the number of the names
from the age of twenty years and upwards,
   everyone who goes out in the army
⁴³their register for the clan of Naphtali:
   53,400.

Levi

⁴⁴This is the register that Mosheh, Aharon and Yisra'el's leaders made (there were twelve, one individual each for his ancestral household). ⁴⁵The entire register of the Yisra'elites by their ancestral household from the age of twenty years and upwards, everyone who goes out in the army in Yisra'el: ⁴⁶the entire register was 603,550.

⁴⁷The Levites were not registered among them by their ancestral clan. ⁴⁸Yahweh had spoken to Mosheh: ⁴⁹'Only, you will not register the clan of Levi or take their head count among the Yisra'elites. ⁵⁰You yourself appoint the Levites over the affirmation dwelling, over all its articles and over everything that belongs to it. They're to carry the dwelling and all its articles and they're to minister to it. They're to camp round the dwelling. ⁵¹When the dwelling sets out, the Levites are to take it down, and when the dwelling camps, the Levites are to set it up. An outsider who comes near is to be put to death.

⁵²The Yisra'elites are to camp each with his camp, each with his standard, by their companies. ⁵³But the Levites are to camp round the affirmation tent, so fury doesn't come on the Yisra'elite assembly. The Levites are to keep the charge of the affirmation dwelling.'

⁵⁴The Yisra'elites acted in accordance with all that Yahweh ordered Mosheh; so they acted.

The order for the journey: Levi at the centre

2 Yahweh spoke to Mosheh and to Aharon: ²"The Yisra'elites are to camp each by his standard with the ensigns of their ancestral households. They're to camp at a distance round the appointment tent.'

³The people camping to the front, to the east: the standard of Yehudah's camp, by their companies.
    The Yehudahites' leader: Nahshon ben Amminadab.
⁴His company, their register: 74,600.
⁵Camping by it, the clan of Yissakar.
    The Yissakarites' leader: Netan'el ben Tsu'ar.
⁶His company, their register: 54,400.
⁷The clan of Zebulun.
    The Zebulunites' leader: Eli'ab ben Helon.
⁸His company, their register: 57,400.
⁹The entire register of Yehudah's camp: 186,400 by their companies.
They're to move on first.

¹⁰The standard of Re'uben's camp, to the south, by their companies.
    The Re'ubenites' leader: Elitsur ben Shede'ur.
¹¹His company, their register: 46,500.
¹²Camping by it, the clan of Shim'on.
    The Shim'onites' leader: Shelumi'el ben Tsuri-shadday.
¹³His company, their register: 59,300.
¹⁴And the clan of Gad.
    The Gadites' leader: Elyasaph ben Re'u'el.
¹⁵His company, their register: 45,650.
¹⁶The entire register of Re'uben's camp: 151,450 by their companies.
They're to move on second.

¹⁷The appointment tent, the Levites' camp, is to set out in the middle of the camps. As they camp, so they're to move on, each in its own place, by their standards.

The order for the journey: the arrangement completed

¹⁸The standard of Ephrayim's camp by their companies, to the west.
    The Ephrayimites' leader: Elishama ben Ammihud.
¹⁹His company, their register: 40,500.
²⁰By it, the clan of Menashsheh.
    The Menashshites' leader: Gamli'el ben Pedahtsur.
²¹His company, their register: 32,200.
²²And the clan of Binyamin.
    The Binyaminites' leader: Abidan ben Gid'oni.
²³His company, their register: 35,400.
²⁴The entire register of Ephrayim's camp: 108,100 by their companies.
They're to move on third.

²⁵The standard of Dan's camp, to the north, by their companies.
    The Danites' leader: Ahi'ezer ben Ammishadday.
²⁶His company, their register: 62,700.
²⁷Camping by it, the clan of Asher.
    The Asherites' leader: Pag'i'el ben Okran.
²⁸His company, their register: 41,500.
²⁹And the clan of Naphtali.
    The Naphtalites' leader: Ahira ben Enan.
³⁰His company, their register: 53,400.
³¹The entire register of Dan's camp: 157,600.
They're to move on last, by their standards.

³²This was the register of the Yisra'elites by their ancestral households. The entire register of the camps by their companies: 603,550.
³³The Levites were not registered among the Yisra'elites, as Yahweh ordered Mosheh.
³⁴So the Yisra'elites acted in accordance with all that Yahweh ordered Mosheh. In this way they camped by their standards and in this way they moved on, each by his kin-group according to his ancestral household.

Yahweh's claim on Levi

3 These are Aharon's and Mosheh's lines of descent on the day Yahweh spoke with Mosheh at Mount Sinay. ²These are the names of Aharon's sons: the firstborn Nadab, and Abihu, El'azar and Itamar. ³These are the names of Aharon's sons, the anointed priests whom he commissioned to act as priests. ⁴Nadab and Abihu died before Yahweh when they presented outside fire before Yahweh in the Sinay Wilderness. They didn't have sons, so El'azar and Itamar acted as priests in the presence of Aharon their father.

⁵Yahweh spoke to Mosheh: ⁶'Present the clan of Levi and have them stand before Aharon the priest to minister to him. ⁷They're to keep his charge and the charge of the entire assembly before the appointment tent by performing the service of the dwelling. ⁸They're to keep all the articles in the appointment tent, the Yisra'elites' charge, by performing the service of the dwelling. ⁹You're to give the Levites to Aharon and to his sons; they're wholly given to him from among the Yisra'elites. ¹⁰Aharon and his sons you're to appoint to keep watch over their priestly work; the outsider who comes near is to be put to death.'

¹¹Yahweh spoke to Mosheh: ¹²'Here, I myself have taken the Levites from among the Yisra'elites in place of every firstborn, the one who opens the womb, from the Yisra'elites. The Levites are to be mine, ¹³because every firstborn is mine. On the day I struck down every firstborn in the country of Misrayim I made sacred for me every firstborn in Yisra'el, human and animal. They're mine. I am Yahweh.'

¹⁴Yahweh spoke to Mosheh in the Sinay Wilderness: ¹⁵'Register the Levites by their ancestral households, by their kin-groups. Every male from the age of one month and upwards, you're to register them.' ¹⁶So Mosheh registered them at Yahweh's bidding, as he was ordered. ¹⁷These were Levi's sons by their names: Gershon, Qehat and Merari. ¹⁸These were the names of Gershon's sons by their kin-groups: Libni and Shim'i; ¹⁹Qehat's sons by their kin-groups: Amram and Yitshar, Hebron and Uzzi'el; ²⁰ᵃMerari's sons by their kin-groups: Mahli and Mushi.

Levi's kin-groups

²⁰ᵇThese were Levi's kin-groups by their ancestral households.

²¹Gershon's:
the Libnite kin-group and the Shim'ite kin-group: they were the Gershonite kin-groups. ²²Their register by number, every male from the age of one month and upwards – their register: 7,500.
²³The Gershonite kin-groups were to camp behind the dwelling, to the west.
²⁴The leader of the Gershonite ancestral household was El'asaph ben La'el.
²⁵The Gershonites' charge in the appointment tent: the dwelling and the tent, its covering, the curtain for the entrance of the appointment tent, ²⁶the courtyard hangings, the curtain for the entrance of the courtyard which is next to the dwelling and next to the altar all round, and its ropes, in respect of its entire service.

²⁷Qehat's:
the Amramite kin-group, the Yitsharite kin-group, the Hebronite kin-group and the Uzzi'elite kin-group: they were the Qehatite kin-groups.
²⁸By the number of every male from the age of one month and upwards: 8,600, keeping the charge of the sacred things.
²⁹The kin-groups of the Qehatites were to camp on the side of the dwelling to the south.
³⁰The leader of the ancestral household of the Qehatite kin goups was Elitsaphan ben Uzzi'el.
³¹Their charge: the chest, the table, the candelabrum, the altars, the sacred articles with which people would minister, the curtain and its entire service.
³²The senior Levite leader, El'azar ben Aharon the priest: appointment over the people who keep the charge of the sacred things.

³³Merari's:
the Mahlite kin-group and the Mushite kin-group: they were the Merarite kin-groups.
³⁴Their register by number, every male from the age of one month and upwards: 6,200.
³⁵The leader of the ancestral household of the Mararite kin-groups: Tsuri'el ben Abihayil. They were to camp on the side of the dwelling to the north.
³⁶The appointment regarding the charge of the Merarites: the dwelling's planks, its bars, its posts, its sockets, all its articles and all its service; ³⁷and the courtyard posts all round, their sockets, their pegs and their ropes.

The count of the firstborn

³⁸The people camping before the dwelling, in front, before the appointment tent, to the

east: Mosheh and Aharon and his sons, having charge of the sanctuary in connection with the Yisra'elites' charge (an outsider who drew near was to be put to death). ³⁹The entire register of the Levites, which Mosheh and Aharon made at Yahweh's bidding, by their kin-groups, every male from the age of one month and upwards: 22,000.

⁴⁰Yahweh said to Mosheh, 'Register every firstborn male belonging to the Yisra'elites from the age of one month and upwards and get the number of their names; ⁴¹and take the Levites for me (I am Yahweh) in place of every firstborn among the Yisra'elites, and the Levites' animals in place of every firstborn among the Yisra'elites' animals.' ⁴²So Mosheh registered, as Yahweh ordered him, every firstborn among the Yisra'elites. ⁴³Every firstborn male by the number of the names from the age of one month and upwards, by their register: 22,273.

⁴⁴Yahweh spoke to Mosheh: ⁴⁵"Take the Levites in place of every firstborn among the Yisra'elites, and the Levites' animals in place of their animals. The Levites are to be mine. I am Yahweh. ⁴⁶As the redemption price for the 273 from the firstborn of the Yisra'elites who are surplus, above and beyond the Levites: ⁴⁷you're to take five sheqels each per head. You're to take it by the sanctuary sheqel (a sheqel is twenty grams). ⁴⁸You're to give the silver to Aharon and to his sons as the redemption price for those who are surplus among them.'

⁴⁹So Mosheh took the redemption silver from those who were surplus, above and beyond those redeemed by the Levites. ⁵⁰From the firstborn of the Yisra'elites he took the 1,365 by the sanctuary sheqel, ⁵¹and Mosheh gave the redemption silver to Aharon and to his sons at Yahweh's bidding, as Yahweh ordered Mosheh.

Dismantling the camp

4 Yahweh spoke to Mosheh and Aharon: ²"Take a head count of the Qehatites from among the Levites, by their kin-groups, by their ancestral household, ³from the age of thirty years and upwards until the age of fifty years, everyone coming in for duty to do work in the appointment tent. ⁴This is the service of the Qehatites in the appointment tent: the especially sacred things.

⁵Aharon and his sons are to come in when the camp is setting off, take down the screen curtain and cover the affirmation chest with it. ⁶They're to put a dolphin-skin covering on it, spread an all-blue cloth on top and place its poles. ⁷Over the presence table they're to spread a blue cloth and put on it the dishes, the ladles, the pitchers and the libation bowls; and the regular bread is to be on it. ⁸They're to spread over them a bright crimson cloth, cover it with a dolphin-skin covering and place its poles.

⁹They're to get a blue cloth and cover the candelabrum for lighting, its lamps, its tongs, its pans and all its oil containers with which they minister to it. ¹⁰They're to put it and all its articles into a dolphin skin covering and put them on a frame. ¹¹Over the gold altar they're to spread a blue cloth, cover it with a dolphin-skin covering and place its poles.

The need to be wary

¹²They're to get all the articles for the ministry in which they minister in the sacred place, put them into a blue cloth, cover them with a dolphin-skin covering and put them on a frame. ¹³They're to clear the altar of waste and spread on it a purple cloth. ¹⁴They're to put on it all the utensils with which they minister on it, the pans, the forks, the shovels and the basins, all the altar's utensils, spread over it a dolphin-skin covering and place its poles.

¹⁵Aharon and his sons are to finish covering the sacred things and all the sacred articles when the camp is moving on, and after that the Qehatites are to come in to carry them. They will not touch the sacred things, and die. These things are for carrying by the Qehatites, in the appointment tent.

¹⁶The appointment of El'azar ben Aharon the priest: the lighting oil, the aromatic incense, the regular grain offering and the anointing oil; appointment over the entire dwelling and everything that's in it – the sacred place and its articles.'

¹⁷Yahweh spoke to Mosheh and to Aharon: ¹⁸'Don't let the clan of Qehatite kin-groups be cut off from among the Levites. ¹⁹Do this for them, and they will live and not die when they come up to the things that are especially

sacred. Aharon and his sons are to go in and place each individual over his service, for his carrying. ²⁰But they're not to come in to look as people are demolishing the sacred place, and die.'

The Gershonites and the Merarites

²¹Yahweh spoke to Mosheh: ²²'Take a head count of the Gershonites, them too, by their ancestral household, by their kin-groups. ²³From the age of thirty years and upwards to the age of fifty years you're to register them, everyone coming in to do duty by performing service in the appointment tent. ²⁴This is the service of the Gershonite kin-groups in serving and in carrying: ²⁵they're to carry the pieces of the dwelling, the appointment tent and its covering, the dolphin-skin covering that's on it, on top, the curtain for the appointment tent entrance, ²⁶the courtyard hangings, the curtain for the entrance of the courtyard gateway which is next to the dwelling and next to the altar all round, its ropes, all the articles in their service and everything that's done in connection with them; so they will serve.

²⁷It's at the bidding of Aharon and his sons that all the Gershonites' service is to happen, as regards all their carrying and as regards all their service. You're to appoint them over them in having charge of all their carrying. ²⁸This is the service of the Gershonites' kin-groups in the appointment tent and their charge at the direction of Itamar ben Aharon the priest.

²⁹The Merarites: you're to register them by their kin-groups, by their ancestral household. ³⁰From the age of thirty years and upwards until the age of fifty years you're to register them, everyone coming in for duty, to perform the service of the appointment tent. ³¹This is their charge in their carrying, in connection with all their service in the appointment tent: the dwelling's planks, its bars, its posts, its sockets, ³²the courtyard's posts all round, their sockets, their pegs and their ropes. For all their articles and for all their service and by their names you're to register the articles in their charge, their carrying. ³³These are the service of the Merarite kin-groups as regards all their service in the appointment tent at the direction of Itamar ben Aharon the priest.'

The register of the Levite kin-groups

³⁴So Mosheh, Aharon and the assembly's leaders registered the Qehatites by their kin-groups and by their ancestral household, ³⁵from the age of thirty years and upwards until the age of fifty years, everyone coming in for duty for service in the appointment tent. ³⁶Their register by their kin-groups was 2,750. ³⁷This was the register of the Qehatite kin-groups, everyone serving in the appointment tent, which Mosheh and Aharon made at Yahweh's bidding through Mosheh.

³⁸The register of the Gershonites by their kin-groups and by their ancestral household, ³⁹from the age of thirty years and upwards until the age of fifty years, everyone coming in for duty for service in the appointment tent: ⁴⁰their register by their kin-groups, by their ancestral household, was 2,630. ⁴¹This was the register of the kin-groups of the Gershonites, everyone serving in the appointment tent, which Mosheh and Aharon made at Yahweh's bidding.

⁴²The register of the kin-groups of the Merarites by their kin-groups, by their ancestral household, ⁴³from the age of thirty years and upwards until the age of fifty years, everyone coming for duty for service in the appointment tent: ⁴⁴their register by their kin-groups was 3,200. ⁴⁵This was the register of the kin-groups of the Merarites, which Mosheh and Aharon made at Yahweh's bidding through Mosheh.

⁴⁶The entire register that Mosheh and Aharon and the Yisra'elite leaders made, the Levites by their kin-groups and by their ancestral household, ⁴⁷from the age of thirty years and upwards until the age of fifty years, everyone coming in to serve (the service of serving and the service of carrying) in the appointment tent: ⁴⁸their register was 5,580. ⁴⁹At Yahweh's bidding they registered them through Mosheh, each individual according to his service and to his carrying, his register that Yahweh ordered Mosheh.

Breaking faith

5 Yahweh spoke to Mosheh: ²'Order the Yisra'elites that they send off from the camp anyone who's been made scaly, anyone who's discharging and anyone who's taboo through a [dead] person. ³Male and female, you're to send them off. You're to send them off outside the camp so they won't make taboo the camp of the people among whom I'm dwelling.' ⁴The Yisra'elites did so; they sent them off outside the camp. As Yahweh spoke to Mosheh, so the Yisra'elites did.

⁵Yahweh spoke to Mosheh: ⁶"Speak to the Yisra'elites: if a man or a woman does one of all the things that are wrong to a human being, thus breaking faith with Yahweh, the person is liable. ⁷They're to confess their wrong that they did. He's to make reparation for its sum total, add to it a fifth of it and give it to the person to whom he's liable. ⁸If the person doesn't have a restorer to make reparation to, the reparation that's made belongs to Yahweh, to the priest, in addition to the ram of complete expiation with which he makes expiation for him.

⁹Every contribution in connection with all the sacred things belonging to the Yisra'elites that they present to the priest is to be his. ¹⁰Each one, his sacred things are to be his; what the person gives the priest is to be his.'

Breaking faith in the context of marriage

¹¹Yahweh spoke to Mosheh: ¹²"Speak to the Yisra'elites: "When an individual's wife goes off and breaks faith with him, ¹³and someone has slept with her and they had sex but it was concealed from the eyes of her husband and she's kept it secret, but she has made herself taboo but there's no witness against her and she was not caught, ¹⁴but a jealous spirit has come over him and he's become jealous in respect of his wife when she has made herself taboo; or a jealous spirit has come over him and he's become jealous in respect of his wife when she hasn't made herself taboo: ¹⁵the man is to bring his wife to the priest, and to bring as an offering for her a tenth of a barrel of barley flour; he will not pour oil on it and he will not put frankincense on it, because it's a grain offering of jealousy, a grain offering of mindfulness, which makes someone mindful of waywardness.

¹⁶The priest is to present her and get her to stand before Yahweh. ¹⁷The priest is to get sacred water in a clay container. The priest is to get some of the earth that's on the dwelling floor and the priest is to put it in the water. ¹⁸The priest is to get the woman to stand before Yahweh and to bare the woman's head and put on her palms the grain offering of mindfulness, the grain offering of jealousy. In the priest's hand is to be the bitter water that brings a curse. ¹⁹The priest is to get her to swear: he's to say to the woman, 'If no one has slept with you, and if you haven't gone off in taboo while married to your husband, you can be free of guilt from this bitter water that brings a curse.

A spirit of jealousy

²⁰But you: when you've gone off while married to your husband and you've made yourself taboo, and a man other than your husband has had sex with you ²¹(the priest is to get the woman to swear the avowed oath, and the priest is to say to the woman), may Yahweh make you a vow and an oath among your people, when Yahweh makes your thigh fall and your womb swell. ²²May this water that brings a curse come into your insides so as to make your womb swell and your thigh fall.' And the woman is to say, 'Yes, yes'. ²³The priest is to write these vows on a document and wipe them off into the bitter water, ²⁴and get the woman to drink the bitter water that brings a curse, so the water that brings a curse may come into her, becoming bitter.

²⁵The priest is to get from the woman's hand the grain offering of jealousy, lift up the grain offering before Yahweh and present it at the altar. ²⁶The priest is to scoop the commemorative portion from the grain offering and turn it into smoke at the altar. Afterwards, he's to get the woman to drink the water.

²⁷When he's got her to drink the water, if she's made herself taboo and broken faith with her husband, the water that brings a curse, becoming bitter, will come into her, her womb will swell and her thigh fall, and the woman will become the exemplar for a vow among her people. ²⁸But if she hasn't made herself taboo and she's pure, she'll be free of guilt and she'll be fruitful.

²⁹This is the instruction regarding incidences of jealousy, when a woman goes off while

married to her husband and becomes taboo, ³⁰or a jealous spirit comes over a man and he becomes jealous in respect of his wife and gets the woman to stand before Yahweh and the priest acts on this entire instruction toward her. ³¹The man will be free of guilt for waywardness when that woman carries her waywardness.'"

The Nazirite pledge

6 Yahweh spoke to Mosheh: ²'Speak to the Yisra'elites: "When a man or woman makes himself distinct to make a pledge as a consecrated person, to be consecrated for Yahweh, ³he's to stay consecrated from wine and liquor. He will not drink wine vinegar or liquor vinegar, he will not drink grape juice and he will not eat grapes, fresh or dried. ⁴All the time of his consecration he will not eat anything that's made from the grapevine, either seeds or skin.

⁵All the time of his consecration pledge, no razor will pass over his head; until the fulfilling of the time that he is consecrated for Yahweh, he's to be sacred, growing the locks of the hair of his head. ⁶All the time of his being consecrated for Yahweh he will not come in to a dead person. ⁷For his father and for his mother, for his brother and for his sister: he will not make himself taboo for them when they die, because his consecration for his God is on his head. ⁸All the time of his consecration, he's sacred for Yahweh.

⁹When someone does die near him suddenly, unexpectedly, and makes the head of his consecration taboo, he's to shave his head on the day he becomes pure. He's to shave it on the seventh day, ¹⁰and on the eighth day he's to bring two doves or two young pigeons to the priest at the entrance of the appointment tent. ¹¹The priest is to make one into a decontamination and one into a burnt offering, and he's to make expiation for him for the wrongdoing in connection with the [dead] person. On that day he's to make his head sacred ¹²and put into effect his time of consecration for Yahweh. He's to bring a year-old lamb as a reparation. The previous time will fall away, because his consecration became taboo.

Yahweh bless you and keep you

¹³This is the instruction for the consecrated person. On the day of the fulfilling of his consecration time, they're to bring him to the entrance of the appointment tent. ¹⁴He's to bring as his offering for Yahweh a year-old lamb, one that's whole, as a burnt offering; a year-old ewe, one that's whole, as a decontamination; a ram, one that's whole, as a well-being sacrifice; ¹⁵a basket of flatbread made from fine flour, loaves mixed with oil; flat wafers spread with oil; their grain offering; and their libations.

¹⁶The priest is to present them before Yahweh, make the decontamination and its burnt offering, ¹⁷and make the ram a well-being sacrifice for Yahweh, along with the basket of flatbread. The priest is to make its grain offering and its libation. ¹⁸The consecrated person is to shave the head of his consecration at the entrance of the appointment tent. He's to get the hair from the head of his consecration and put it on the fire that's under the well-being sacrifice.

¹⁹The priest is to get the ram's shoulder, boiled, a loaf of flatbread from the basket and a flat wafer, and put them on the palms of the consecrated person, after his shaving of his consecration. ²⁰The priest is to elevate them as an elevation offering before Yahweh. It's sacred for the priest, along with the breast of the elevation offering and along with the thigh of the contribution. Afterwards, the consecrated person may drink wine.

²¹This is the instruction concerning the consecrated person. Someone who pledges his offering to Yahweh along with his consecration, apart from what his means stretch to: on the basis of his pledge, that which he pledges, so he's to do, along with the instruction for his consecration.'"

²²Yahweh spoke to Mosheh: ²³'Speak to Aharon and to his sons: "In this way you're to bless the Yisra'elites, saying to them:

²⁴Yahweh bless you and keep you!
²⁵Yahweh shine his face towards you and be gracious to you!
²⁶Yahweh lift his face towards you and make things be well for you!

²⁷They're to put my name on the Yisra'elites so I myself bless them."'

Provision for the sanctuary

7 On the day Mosheh finished setting up the dwelling, he anointed it and made it sacred with all its articles, and the altar with all its articles – he anointed them and made them sacred. ²The Yisra'elite leaders, the heads of their ancestral household (they were the leaders of the clans, who stood over their register) presented ³and brought their offering before Yahweh: six covered wagons and twelve cattle, a wagon for two leaders and an ox for each. They presented them before the dwelling, ⁴and Yahweh said to Mosheh, ⁵'Receive them from them so they can perform service for the appointment tent, and give them to the Levites, each on the basis of his service.'

⁶So Mosheh received the wagons and the cattle, and gave them to the Levites. ⁷Two wagons and four cattle he gave to the Gershonites on the basis of their service. ⁸Four wagons and eight cattle he gave to the Merarites on the basis of their service, at the direction of Itamar ben Aharon the priest. ⁹To the Qehatites he didn't give any, because the service of the sanctuary was upon them; they would carry it on their shoulder. ¹⁰The leaders presented the altar's dedication gift on the day it was anointed. When the leaders presented their offering before the altar, ¹¹Yahweh said to Mosheh: 'One leader each day, they're to present their offering for the altar dedication.'

Offerings by Yehudah, Yissakar, Zebulun

¹²The one who presented his offering on the first day was Nahshon ben Amminadab, of the clan of Yehudah. ¹³His offering: a silver dish, its weight 130 sheqels; a silver basin, seventy sheqels by the sanctuary sheqel; the two of them full of fine flour mixed with oil, for a grain offering; ¹⁴a gold ladle of ten sheqels, full of incense; ¹⁵a bull from the herd; a ram; a year-old lamb as a burnt offering; ¹⁶a he-goat from the flock as a decontamination; ¹⁷and as a well-being sacrifice, two cattle, five rams, five he-goats, five year-old lambs. This was the offering of Nahshon ben Amminadab. ¹⁸On the second day, Netan'el ben Tsu'ar, leader of Yissakar, presented. ¹⁹He presented as his offering a silver dish, its weight 130 sheqels; a silver basin, seventy sheqels by the sanctuary sheqel; the two of them full of fine flour mixed with oil, for a grain offering; ²⁰a gold ladle of ten sheqels, full of incense; ²¹a bull from the herd; a ram; a year-old lamb as a burnt offering; ²²a he-goat from the flock as a decontamination; ²³and as a well-being sacrifice, two cattle, five rams, five he-goats, five year-old lambs. This was the offering of Netan'el ben Tsu'ar.

²⁴On the third day, the leader of the Zebulunites, Eli'ab ben Helon. ²⁵His offering: a silver dish, its weight 130 sheqels; a silver basin, seventy sheqels by the sanctuary sheqel; the two of them full of fine flour mixed with oil, for a grain offering; ²⁶a gold ladle of ten sheqels, full of incense; ²⁷a bull from the herd; a ram; a year-old lamb as a burnt offering; ²⁸a he-goat from the flock as a decontamination; ²⁹and as a well-being sacrifice, two cattle, five rams, five he-goats, five year-old lambs. This was the offering of Eli'ab ben Helon.

Offerings by Re'uben, Shim'on, Gad

³⁰On the fourth day, the leader of the Re'ubenites, Elitsur ben Shede'ur. ³¹His offering: a silver dish, its weight 130 sheqels; a silver basin, seventy sheqels by the sanctuary sheqel; the two of them full of fine flour mixed with oil, for a grain offering; ³²a gold ladle of ten sheqels, full of incense; ³³a bull from the herd; a ram; a year-old lamb as a burnt offering; ³⁴a he-goat from the flock as a decontamination; ³⁵and as a well-being sacrifice, two cattle, five rams, five he-goats, five year-old lambs. This was the offering of Elitsur ben Shede'ur.

³⁶On the fifth day, the leader of the Shim'onites, Shelumi'el ben Tsurishadday. ³⁷His offering: a silver dish, its weight 130 sheqels; a silver basin, seventy sheqels by the sanctuary sheqel; the two of them full of fine flour mixed with oil, for a grain offering; ³⁸a gold ladle of ten sheqels, full of incense; ³⁹a bull from the herd; a ram; a

year-old lamb as a burnt offering; ⁴⁰a he-goat from the flock as a decontamination; ⁴¹and as a well-being sacrifice, two cattle, five rams, five he-goats, five year-old lambs. This was the offering of Shelumi'el ben Tsurishadday.
⁴²On the sixth day, the leader of the Gadites, Elyasaph ben De'u'el. ⁴³His offering: a silver dish, its weight 130 sheqels; a silver basin, seventy sheqels by the sanctuary sheqel; the two of them full of fine flour mixed with oil, for a grain offering; ⁴⁴a gold ladle of ten sheqels, full of incense; ⁴⁵a bull from the herd; a ram; a year-old lamb as a burnt offering; ⁴⁶a he-goat from the flock as a decontamination; ⁴⁷and as a well-being sacrifice, two cattle, five rams, five he-goats, five year-old lambs. This was the offering of Elyasaph ben De'u'el.

Offerings by Ephrayim, Menashsheh, Binyamin

⁴⁸On the seventh day, the leader of the Ephrayimites, Elishama ben Ammihud. ⁴⁹His offering: a silver dish, its weight 130 sheqels; a silver basin, seventy sheqels by the sanctuary sheqel; the two of them full of fine flour mixed with oil, for a grain offering; ⁵⁰a gold ladle of ten sheqels, full of incense; ⁵¹a bull from the herd; a ram; a year-old lamb as a burnt offering; ⁵²a he-goat from the flock as a decontamination; ⁵³and as a well-being sacrifice, two cattle, five rams, five he-goats, five year-old lambs. This was the offering of Elishama ben Ammihud.
⁵⁴On the eighth day, the leader of the Menashshites, Gamli'el ben Pedah-tsur. ⁵⁵His offering: a silver dish, its weight 130 sheqels; a silver basin, seventy sheqels by the sanctuary sheqel; the two of them full of fine flour mixed with oil, for a grain offering; ⁵⁶a gold ladle of ten sheqels, full of incense; ⁵⁷a bull from the herd; a ram; a year-old lamb as a burnt offering; ⁵⁸a he-goat from the flock as a decontamination; ⁵⁹and as a well-being sacrifice, two cattle, five rams, five he-goats, five year-old lambs. This was the offering of Gamli'el ben Pedah-tsur.
⁶⁰On the ninth day, the leader of the Binyaminites, Abidan ben Gid'oni. ⁶¹His offering: a silver dish, its weight 130 sheqels; a silver basin, seventy sheqels by the sacred sheqel; the two of them full of fine flour mixed with oil, for a grain offering; ⁶²a gold ladle of ten sheqels, full of incense; ⁶³a bull from the herd; a ram; a year-old lamb as a burnt offering; ⁶⁴a he-goat from the flock as a decontamination; ⁶⁵and as a well-being sacrifice, two cattle, five rams, five he-goats, five year-old lambs. This was the offering of Abidan ben Gid'oni.

Offerings by Dan, Asher, Naphtali

⁶⁶On the tenth day, the leader of the Danites, Ahi'ezer ben Ammishadday. ⁶⁷His offering: a silver dish, its weight 130 sheqels; a silver basin, seventy sheqels by the sanctuary sheqel; the two of them full of fine flour mixed with oil, for a grain offering; ⁶⁸a gold ladle of ten sheqels, full of incense; ⁶⁹a bull from the herd; a ram; a year-old lamb as a burnt offering; ⁷⁰a he-goat from the flock as a decontamination; ⁷¹and as a well-being sacrifice, two cattle, five rams, five he-goats, five year-old lambs. This was the offering of Ahi'ezer ben Ammishadday.
⁷²On the eleventh day, the leader of the Asherites, Pag'i'el ben Okran. ⁷³His offering: a silver dish, its weight 130 sheqels; a silver basin, seventy sheqels by the sanctuary sheqel; the two of them full of fine flour mixed with oil, for a grain offering; ⁷⁴a gold ladle of ten sheqels, full of incense; ⁷⁵a bull from the herd; a ram; a year-old lamb as a burnt offering; ⁷⁶a he-goat from the flock as a decontamination; ⁷⁷and as a well-being sacrifice, two cattle, five rams, five he-goats, five year-old lambs. This was the offering of Pag'i'el ben Okran.
⁷⁸On the twelfth day, the leader of the Naphtalites, Ahira ben Enan. ⁷⁹His offering: a silver dish, its weight 130 sheqels; a silver basin, seventy sheqels by the sanctuary sheqel; the two of them full of fine flour mixed with oil, for a grain offering; ⁸⁰a gold ladle of ten sheqels, full of incense; ⁸¹a bull from the herd; a ram;

a year-old lamb as a burnt offering; ⁸²a he-goat from the flock as a decontamination; ⁸³and as a well-being sacrifice, two cattle, five rams, five he-goats, five year-old lambs. This was the offering of Ahira ben Enan.

Mosheh heard God speak

⁸⁴This was the altar's dedication gift on the day of its anointing, from Yisra'el's leaders: silver dishes, twelve; silver basins, twelve; gold ladles, twelve; ⁸⁵130 sheqels of silver for each dish; seventy sheqels for each basin; all the silver of the containers, 2,400 sanctuary sheqels; ⁸⁶twelve gold ladles full of incense (ten sheqels each ladle by the sanctuary sheqel); all the gold of the ladles, 120 sheqels. ⁸⁷All the herd for the burnt offering, twelve bulls; rams, twelve; year-old lambs, twelve (and their grain offering); he-goats from the flock, twelve, as a decontamination. ⁸⁸All the herd for the well-being sacrifice: twenty-four bulls; rams: sixty; he-goats: sixty; year-old lambs: sixty. This was the altar's dedication gift after its anointing.

⁸⁹When Mosheh came into the appointment tent to speak with him, he heard the voice speaking to him from above the expiation cover that was on the affirmation chest, from between the two sphinxes. He spoke to him.

8 Yahweh spoke to Mosheh: ²'Speak to Aharon: "When you put up the lamps, the seven lamps are to give light near the front of the candelabrum."' ³Aharon did so. He put up its lamps near the front of the candelabrum, as Yahweh ordered Mosheh. ⁴This was the workmanship of the candelabrum: it was hammered work of gold, hammered work from its base to its petal. In accordance with the picture that Yahweh had let Mosheh see, so he made the candelabrum.

The dedication of the Levites

⁵Yahweh spoke to Mosheh: ⁶'Get the Levites from among the Yisra'elites and purify them. ⁷You're to do this to them to purify them. Spatter decontamination water on them, and they are to pass a razor over their entire flesh and wash their clothes, and they'll become pure. ⁸They're to get a bull from the herd and its grain offering, fine flour mixed with oil, and you're to get a second bull from the herd as a decontamination.

⁹You're to present the Levites before the appointment tent and congregate the entire assembly of the Yisra'elites, ¹⁰and present the Levites before Yahweh. The Yisra'elites are to lean their hands on the Levites, ¹¹and Aharon is to elevate the Levites as an elevation offering before Yahweh from the Yisra'elites, so they may be there to perform service for Yahweh. ¹²The Levites are to lean their hands on the bulls' head. Make one as a decontamination and one as a burnt offering for Yahweh, to make expiation for the Levites.

¹³You're to get the Levites to stand before Aharon and before his sons and elevate them as an elevation offering for Yahweh. ¹⁴You're to make the Levites distinct from among the Yisra'elites. The Levites are to be mine. ¹⁵Afterwards, the Levites are to come to serve the appointment tent. You're to purify them and elevate them as an elevation offering, ¹⁶because they're irrevocably given to me from among the Yisra'elites in place of the first issue of every womb, the firstborn of every one of the Yisra'elites. I've taken them for myself. ¹⁷Because every firstborn among the Yisra'elites is mine, of human beings and of animals.

On the day I struck down every firstborn in the country of Misrayim, I made them sacred for myself. ¹⁸I've taken the Levites in place of every firstborn of the Yisra'elites, ¹⁹and given the Levites irrevocably to Aharon and to his sons from among the Yisra'elites to perform the Yisra'elites' service in the appointment tent and to make expiation for the Yisra'elites, so no epidemic will come on the Yisra'elites through the Yisra'elites' coming up to the sanctuary.'

The Levites' service and semi-retirement

²⁰Mosheh, Aharon and the entire Yisra'elite assembly acted towards the Levites in accordance with all that Yahweh ordered Mosheh for the Levites. The Yisra'elites did so for them. ²¹The Levites decontaminated themselves and washed their clothes, and Aharon elevated them as an elevation

offering before Yahweh, and made expiation for them to purify them. ²²Afterwards the Levites came to perform their services in the appointment tent before Aharon and before his sons. As Yahweh ordered Mosheh concerning the Levites, so they did for them.

²³Yahweh spoke to Mosheh: ²⁴"This is how it is to be for the Levites. From the age of twenty-five years and upwards they're to come to do duty in the service of the appointment tent. ²⁵From the age of fifty years they're to go back from the duty of service. They will not serve any more. ²⁶One may minister to his brothers in the appointment tent by keeping watch, but they will not perform service. Thus you will do for the Levites regarding their charge.

9 Yahweh spoke to Mosheh in the Sinay Wilderness in the second year of their getting out of the country of Misrayim, in the first month: ²"The Yisra'elites are to make the Pesah [Passover] at its set time. ³You're to make it on the fourteenth day of this month at twilight, at its set time in accordance with all its decrees and in accordance with all it rulings.' ⁴So Mosheh spoke to the Yisra'elites about making the Pesah ⁵and they made the Pesah in the first [month], on the fourteenth day of the month, at twilight, in the Sinay Wilderness. In accordance with all that Yahweh ordered Mosheh, so the Yisra'elites did.

God's flexibility

⁶There were some men who were taboo through a [dead] person and couldn't make the Pesah on that day, so they drew near before Mosheh and before Aharon on that day. ⁷Those men said to him, 'Though we're taboo through a [dead] person, why should we hold back from presenting Yahweh's offering at its set time among the Yisra'elites?' ⁸Mosheh said to them 'Wait so I can listen to what Yahweh orders for you.'

⁹Yahweh spoke to Mosheh: ¹⁰"Speak to the Yisra'elites: "When an individual person becomes taboo through a [dead] person or is on a long journey (one of you or of your future generations) and he makes Pesah for Yahweh, ¹¹they're to make it in the second month on the fourteenth day at twilight. With flatbread and bitters they're to eat it. ¹²They will not let any of it remain until morning and they will not break a bone of it: in accordance with every decree for the Pesah they will make it. ¹³But the individual who is pure or hasn't been on a journey and leaves off from making the Pesah: that person shall be cut off from his kin, because he didn't present Yahweh's offering at its set time. That individual will carry his wrongdoing.

¹⁴When someone is a resident with you and makes the Pesah for Yahweh: in accordance with the decree for the Pesah and in accordance with the ruling concerning it, so he is to make it. There's to be one decree for you, both for the resident and for the native of the country.'"

The prompting of the cloud

¹⁵On the day they set up the dwelling, the cloud covered the dwelling belonging to the affirmation tent. In the evening it would be over the dwelling, like the appearance of fire, until morning. ¹⁶So it would be regularly: the cloud would cover it, with the appearance of fire at night. ¹⁷At the bidding of the cloud lifting from over the tent, after this the Yisra'elites would move on, while at the place where the cloud would dwell, there the Yisra'elites would camp. ¹⁸At Yahweh's bidding the Yisra'elites would move on, and at Yahweh's bidding they would camp; through the entire time the cloud would dwell over the dwelling, they would camp.

¹⁹When the cloud stayed over the dwelling for a long time, the Yisra'elites would keep Yahweh's charge and not move on. ²⁰When it was the case that the cloud would be over the dwelling for a period of time, at Yahweh's bidding they would camp and at Yahweh's bidding they would move on. ²¹When it was the case that the cloud was there from evening to morning, as the cloud lifted in the morning they would move on. Day or night, when the cloud would lift, they would move on.

²²Whether two days or a month or some time, while the cloud stayed over the dwelling so as to dwell over it, the Yisra'elites would camp and would not move on, and when it went up they would move on. ²³At Yahweh's bidding they would camp and at Yahweh's bidding they would move on. They kept Yahweh's charge at Yahweh's bidding through Mosheh.

The signal for the journey

10 Yahweh spoke to Mosheh: ²'Make for yourself two silver trumpets. You're to make them of hammered work and they will be for you for the calling of the assembly and for the camps' moving on. ³They will sound out on them, and the entire assembly is to keep an appointment with you at the entrance of the appointment tent ⁴(if they sound out on one, the leaders – the heads of the Yisra'elite divisions – are to keep an appointment with you). ⁵You will sound a blast, and the camps that are to the east are to move on. ⁶You will sound a second blast, and the camps that are to the south are to move on. They will sound a blast for their setting out. ⁷When you call for them as a congregation, you will sound out but you won't give a blast. ⁸It will be Aharon's sons, the priests, who blow on the trumpets. They will be for you a permanent decree through your generations.

⁹When you come in battle in your country against someone who attacks you, you're to give a blast on the trumpets so you may be remembered before Yahweh your God and be delivered from your enemies. ¹⁰On your day of celebration, at your set times and at the beginning of your months, you're to sound out on the trumpets over your burnt offerings and over your well-being sacrifices. They will be for you a reminder before your God. I am Yahweh your God.'

¹¹In the second year, in the second month, on the twentieth of the month, the cloud went up from above the affirmation dwelling ¹²and the Yisra'elites moved on into their journeys from the Sinay Wilderness. Then the cloud dwelt in the Pa'ran Wilderness.

The order of the march

¹³They moved on at the beginning at Yahweh's bidding through Mosheh. ¹⁴At the beginning the Yehudahites' standard moved on by their companies. Over its company was Nahshon ben Amminadab. ¹⁵Over the company of the Yissakarites' clan was Netan'el ben Tsu'ar. ¹⁶Over the company of the Zebulunites' clan was Eli'ab ben Helon. ¹⁷The dwelling would be taken down and the Gershonites and the Merarites (who carried the dwelling) would move on.

¹⁸The standard of Re'uben's camp would move on by their companies. Over its company was Elitsur ben Shede'ur. ¹⁹Over the company of the Shim'onites' clan was Shelumi'el ben Tsuri Shadday. ²⁰Over the company of the Gadites' clan was Elyasaph ben De'u'el. ²¹The Qehatites (who carried the sanctuary) would move on; people would set up the dwelling for when they came.

²²The standard of the Ephrayimites' camp would move on by their companies. Over its company was Elishama ben Ammihud. ²³Over the company of the Menashshites' clan was Gamli'el ben Pedah-tsur. ²⁴Over the company of the Binyaminites' clan was Abidan ben Gid'oni.

²⁵The standard of the Danites' camp would move on, bringing up the rear for all the camps by their companies. Over its company was Ahi'ezer ben Ammi Shadday. ²⁶Over the company of the Asherites' clan was Pag'i'el ben Okran. ²⁷Over the company of the Naphtalites' clan was Ahira ben Enan.

²⁸These were the Yisra'elites' ways of moving on by their companies. So they moved on.

²⁹Mosheh said to Hobab ben Re'u'el the Midyanite, Mosheh's father-in-law, 'We're moving on to the place of which Yahweh said, "I shall give it to you." Go with us and we'll bring good to you, because Yahweh has spoken of good things for Yisra'el.' ³⁰He said to him, 'I won't go. Instead I'll go to my country, to my homeland.'

³¹He said, 'Please don't abandon us, because of this: you know where we can camp in the wilderness. You will be our eyes. ³²Because you go with us, that good that Yahweh brings with us we'll bring to you.'

On missing garlic

³³They moved on from Yahweh's mountain three days' journey, with Yahweh's pact chest moving on before them on the three days' journey to investigate a place to settle down for them, ³⁴and with Yahweh's cloud over them by day as they moved on from the camp. ³⁵When the chest moved on, Mosheh said:

Numbers 10: The wilderness

Up, Yahweh, so your enemies disperse,
so the people who are hostile to you flee from
before you!

³⁶When it halted, he would say:

Go back, Yahweh,
to the countless thousands of Yisra'el!

11 But the people became veritable complainers in Yahweh's ears about their bad fortune. Yahweh heard, and his anger raged. Yahweh's fire burned up among them and devoured the edge of the camp. ²The people cried out to Mosheh and Mosheh pleaded with Yahweh, and the fire died down. ³They named that place Tab'erah ['Burning'] because Yahweh's fire had burned up among them.

⁴Now the other people that they had collected, who were among them, were full of longing, and the Yisra'elites also again wailed and said, 'If only someone would give us meat to eat! ⁵We remember the fish that we could eat in Misrayim for nothing, the cucumbers, the melons, the leeks, the onions and the garlic, ⁶but now our throats are dry. There isn't anything before our eyes except this *maan*.' ⁷The *maan* was like coriander seed; its appearance was like the appearance of resin. ⁸The people went about and gathered it, ground it with millstones or pounded it in a mortar, and cooked it in a pot and made it into loaves. Its taste was like the taste of rich cream. ⁹When the dew came down on the camp at night, the *maan* would come down on it.

Like a nurse carrying a baby

¹⁰Mosheh heard the people wailing in their kin-groups, each person at the entrance of his tent. Yahweh's anger raged right up, and it was bad in Mosheh's eyes.

¹¹Mosheh said to Yahweh, 'Why have you dealt badly with your servant? Why have I not found grace in your eyes, that you've put the burden of this entire people on me? ¹²Am I the one who conceived this entire people or am I the one who gave birth to it, that you should say to me, "Carry it in your arms, as a nurse carries a baby", to the land that you swore to its ancestors? ¹³From where could there be meat for me to give to this entire people when they wail at me, saying "Give us meat so we can eat"? ¹⁴I myself can't carry this entire people alone, because it's too heavy for me. ¹⁵If this is how you're dealing with me, if I've found grace in your eyes, please just kill me, so I may not look at my bad fortune.'

¹⁶Yahweh said to Mosheh, 'Collect for me seventy individuals from Yisra'el's elders, people of whom you know that they are elders of the people and overseers of it. Get them to the appointment tent so they take their stand there with you. ¹⁷I shall come down and speak with you there, and draw off some of the spirit that's on you and put it on them, so they can carry the burden of the people with you and you won't carry it alone.

Is Yahweh short-handed?

¹⁸To the people you're to say, "Make yourselves sacred for tomorrow and you will eat meat, because you've been wailing in Yahweh's ears, 'If only someone would give us meat to eat, because it was good for us in Misrayim.' Yahweh will give you meat, and you'll eat. ¹⁹You'll eat not one day and not two days and not five days and not ten days and not twenty days: ²⁰for a full month, till it comes out of your nose and it's loathsome to you, because you've rejected Yahweh who is among you, and you've wailed before him, saying 'Why oh why did we come out of Misrayim?'"

²¹Mosheh said, 'The people that I'm in the middle of are 600,000 men on foot. You said, "I'll give them meat to eat for a full month." ²²Can a flock and a herd be slaughtered for them so that one could find it for them? Or can all the fish in the sea be collected for them so that one could find it for them?' ²³Yahweh said to Mosheh, 'Is Yahweh's hand short? Now you will see whether my affirmation comes about for you or not.'

²⁴Mosheh went out and spoke Yahweh's words to the people. He collected seventy individuals from the elders of the people and got them to stand round the tent. ²⁵Yahweh came down in a cloud and spoke to him, and drew some of the spirit that was on him and put it on the seventy individual elders. When the spirit alighted on them, they prophesied, but they didn't do it again.

If only all Yahweh's people were prophets

²⁶Two men remained in the camp. The name of the first was Eldad and the name of the second was Medad. The spirit alighted on them and they were among those written down, but they had not gone out to the tent. They prophesied in the camp. ²⁷A boy ran and told Mosheh, 'Eldad and Medad are prophesying in the camp.' ²⁸Yehoshua [Joshua] ben Nun, Mosheh's minister from his youth, answered: 'My lord Mosheh, restrain them!' ²⁹Mosheh said to him, 'Are you jealous for me? If only all Yahweh's people were prophets, that Yahweh would put his spirit on them!' ³⁰And Mosheh joined the camp, he and Yisra'el's elders.

³¹Then a wind moved on from Yahweh, brought quail across from the sea and dropped them over the camp, quite a day's journey on one side and quite a day's journey on the other side, all round the camp, and quite a metre deep on the face of the earth. ³²The people set to, all that day and all night and all the next day, and collected the quail. The person who got little collected a hundred barrels. They spread and spread them for themselves all round the camp. ³³But while the meat was still between their teeth, before it was chewed, Yahweh's anger raged against the people, and Yahweh struck the people down in a very great calamity.

³⁴They named that place Qibrot Hatta'avah ['Longing Graves'] because they buried there the people who had been longing. ³⁵From Qibrot Hatta'avah the people moved on to Hatserot ['Settlements'].

12 They were at Hatserot and Miryam spoke against Mosheh, with Aharon, about the matter of the Kushite [Sudanese] wife he had taken, because he'd taken a Kushite wife. ²They said, 'Has Yahweh really spoken only through Mosheh? He's also spoken through us, hasn't he.' And Yahweh heard. ³Now Mosheh as a man was very ordinary, more so than any human being who has been on the face of the earth.

Mosheh's supreme authority

⁴Yahweh suddenly said to Mosheh, to Aharon and to Miryam, 'Go out, the three of you, to the appointment tent.' The three of them went out, ⁵and Yahweh came down in the cloud pillar, stood at the tent entrance, and called for Aharon and Miryam. The two of them went out ⁶and he said, 'Listen to my words, please. If there's a prophet of yours, I, Yahweh, make myself known to him in a vision, I speak to him in a dream. ⁷Not so my servant Mosheh. In my entire household he's trustworthy. ⁸I speak to him mouth to mouth, in a vision and not in conundrums. He beholds Yahweh's form. So why were you not afraid to speak against my servant, against Mosheh?'

⁹So Yahweh's anger raged against them and he went, ¹⁰and as the cloud departed from above the tent, there – Miryam was made scaly, like snow. Aharon turned his face to Miryam – there, she was made scaly. ¹¹Aharon said to Mosheh, 'My lord, please, don't hold against us the wrong with which we acted stupidly, the wrong which we did. ¹²Please, she mustn't be like someone dead, whose flesh is half eaten away when he comes out of his mother's womb.' ¹³So Mosheh cried out to Yahweh, 'God, please, heal her, please!' ¹⁴Yahweh said to Mosheh, 'Were her father simply to spit in her face, would she not be in disgrace for seven days? She's to shut herself outside the camp for seven days, and afterwards join.' ¹⁵So Miryam shut herself outside the camp for seven days, but the people didn't move on until Miryam joined. ¹⁶Afterwards the people moved on from Hatserot and camped in the Pa'ran Wilderness.

A spy story

13 Yahweh spoke to Mosheh: ²'Send yourself people so they can investigate the country of Kena'an [Canaan], which I'm giving to the Yisra'elites. You're to send one person each per ancestral clan, each one a leader among them.' ³So Mosheh sent them from the Pa'ran Wilderness, at Yahweh's bidding. All of them were people who were leaders of the Yisra'elites. ⁴These are their names:

for the clan of Re'uben, Shammua ben Zakkur;
⁵for the clan of Shim'on, Shaphat ben Hori;
⁶for the clan of Yehudah, Kaleb (Caleb) ben Yephunneh;
⁷for the clan of Yissakar, Yig'al ben Yoseph;
⁸for the clan of Ephrayim, Hoshea ben Nun;
⁹for the clan of Binyamin, Palti ben Raphu;
¹⁰for the clan of Zebulun, Gaddi'el ben Sodi;
¹¹for the clan of Yoseph (for the clan of Menashsheh), Gaddi ben Susi;
¹²for the clan of Dan, Ammi'el ben Gemalli;
¹³for the clan of Asher, Setur ben Mika'el;
¹⁴for the clan of Naphtali, Nahbi ben Vophsi;
¹⁵for the clan of Gad, Ge'u'el ben Maki.

¹⁶These are the names of the people that Mosheh sent to investigate the country. (Mosheh called Hoshea ben Nun 'Yehoshua'.)

¹⁷Mosheh sent them to investigate the country of Kena'an and said to them, 'Go up here into the Negeb, then go up into the highland. ¹⁸You're to look at the country: what's it like? The people that lives in it: is it strong? Is it weak? Is it few or many? ¹⁹What's the country like that it's living in? Is it good or bad? What are the towns that it lives in – in encampments or in fortifications? ²⁰What's the country like? Is it rich or poor? Are there trees in it or are there not? You're to assert your strength, and get some of the country's fruit.' The time was the time of the first of the grapes.

The good news and the bad news

²¹So they went up and investigated the country from the Tsin Wilderness as far as Rehob (Lebo Hamat). ²²They went up into the Negeb and came as far as Hebron. (Ahiman, Sheshay and Talmay, the descendants of Anaq, were there; Hebron was built seven years before Tso'an in Misrayim.) ²³They came as far as Cluster Wadi, and cut from there a branch

and a cluster of grapes (they carried it on a frame by means of two of them), and some pomegranates and some figs. ²⁴They called that place Cluster Wadi on account of the cluster that the Yisra'elites cut from there. ²⁵They came back from investigating the country at the end of forty days.

²⁶So they went, and then came to Mosheh and to Aharon and to the entire assembly of the Yisra'elites at Qadesh in the Pa'ran Wilderness, brought back word to them and to the entire assembly, and let them see the country's fruit. ²⁷They recounted to him, 'We came to the country that you sent us to. Yes, it flows with milk and syrup, and this is its fruit. ²⁸Only, the people living in the country is substantial, and the towns are fortified, very large. Also, we saw the descendants of Anaq there. ²⁹Amaleq is living in the Negeb region, the Hittites, Yebusites and Amorites are living in the highland, and the Kena'anites are living by the sea and by the side of the Yarden [Jordan].'

³⁰Kaleb hushed the people before Mosheh. He said, 'Let's simply go up and take possession of it, because we can definitely prevail against it.'

Listen to the bad news

³¹But the people who went up with him said, 'We can't go up against the people, because it's stronger than us', ³²and they put out criticism of the country that they had investigated to the Yisra'elites: 'The country that we passed through to investigate is a country that devours the people living in it, and the entire people that we saw within it are people of stature. ³³We saw the Nephilim ['Fallen'] there (the Anaqites were from the Nephilim). In our eyes we were like grasshoppers, and so we were in their eyes.'

14 The entire assembly lifted up their voice and gave it out, and the people wailed that night. ²All the Yisra'elites protested against Mosheh and against Aharon. The entire assembly said to them, 'If only we had died in the country of Misrayim or if only we had died in this wilderness! ³Why is Yahweh bringing us into this country to fall by the sword? Our wives and our little ones will become plunder. Wouldn't it be good for us to go back to Misrayim?' ⁴They said one to another, 'Let's appoint a head, and go back to Misrayim.'

⁵Mosheh and Aharon fell on their faces before the entire assembled congregation of the Yisra'elites. ⁶Yehoshua ben Nun and Kaleb ben Yephunneh from the people who had investigated the country tore their clothes ⁷and said to the entire assembly of the Yisra'elites: 'The country that we passed through to investigate it is a very, very good country. ⁸If Yahweh delights in us, he will bring us to this country and give it to us, a country that flows with milk and syrup. ⁹Only you're not to rebel against Yahweh. You're not to be afraid of the people of the country, because they're our bread, their shade has departed from over them, but Yahweh is with us. Don't be afraid of them.'

Mosheh uses his usual argument

¹⁰But the entire assembly said to pelt them with stones, while Yahweh's splendour appeared in the appointment tent to all the Yisra'elites, ¹¹and Yahweh said to Mosheh, 'How long will this people disdain me? How long will they not put their trust in me, for all the signs I've done among them? ¹²I'll strike it down with an epidemic and dispossess it, and make you into a bigger and more numerous nation than it.'

¹³Mosheh said to Yahweh, 'But the Misrayimites will hear, because you brought this people up by your energy from among them, ¹⁴and they'll tell the people living in this country. They've heard that you, Yahweh, are among this people, you Yahweh who've appeared in plain sight with your cloud standing over them, you who go before them in a cloud pillar by day and in a fire pillar by night. ¹⁵You can put this people to death like one man, but the nations that have heard report of you will say, ¹⁶ "Because Yahweh couldn't bring this people into the country that he swore to them, he's slaughtered them in the wilderness."

¹⁷So now, may my Lord's energy be great as you spoke: ¹⁸"Yahweh, long-tempered and big in commitment, carrying waywardness and rebellion, but he certainly doesn't treat people as free of guilt, attending to parents' waywardness in connection with children, with thirds and with fourths." ¹⁹Please pardon this people's waywardness in accordance with the greatness of your commitment from Misrayim even as far as here.'

Pardon but punishment

²⁰Yahweh said, 'I pardon, in accordance with your words. ²¹Yet as I live and as Yahweh's splendour fills the entire world, ²²because all the people who have seen my splendour and my signs that I did in Misrayim and in the wilderness have tested me these ten times and not listened to my voice, ²³if they see the country that I swore to their ancestors . . .

None who disdained me will see it. ²⁴But my servant Kaleb, as a consequence of the fact that there was another spirit with him – he fully followed after me. I shall bring him into the country that he came to, and his offspring will take possession of it. ²⁵Since the Amaleqites and the Kena'anites live in the valley, tomorrow turn your face and move on for yourselves into the wilderness by the Reed Sea road.'

²⁶So Yahweh spoke to Mosheh and to Aharon: ²⁷'How long for this bad assembly that protest against me? I've listened to the Yisra'elites' protests that they utter against me. ²⁸Say to them: "As I live (Yahweh's declaration), if I don't . . .

As you spoke in my ears, so I shall do to you. ²⁹In this wilderness your carcases will fall, the entire register of you by your entire number, from the age of twenty years and upwards, who have protested against me. ³⁰If you come into the country that I lifted up my hand [in an oath] to let you dwell in it, except Kaleb ben Yephunneh and Yehoshua ben Nun . . .

³¹Your little ones whom you said would become plunder – I shall bring them in. They will know the country that you've rejected. ³²But your carcases – you will fall in this wilderness.

A useless change of mind

³³While your children are shepherding in the wilderness for forty years, they will carry your whoring, until your carcases come to an end in the wilderness. ³⁴In the wilderness, for the days that you investigated the country, forty, one day each per year you will carry your wayward acts, forty years. You will know my antagonism. ³⁵I, Yahweh, have spoken. If I don't do this to this entire bad assembly that are making an appointment against me . . . In this wilderness they will come to an end. There they will die."'

³⁶The people whom Mosheh had sent to investigate the country and who had come back and made the entire assembly protest against him by putting out criticism about the country: ³⁷the people who put out the bad criticism of the country died in an epidemic before Yahweh. ³⁸But Yehoshua ben Nun and Kaleb ben Yephunneh lived on, of those people who went to investigate the country.

³⁹Mosheh spoke these words to all the Yisra'elites, and the people took up great grieving. ⁴⁰They started early in the morning and went up to the mountain ridge, saying 'Here we are, we'll go up to the place that Yahweh said, because we did wrong.' ⁴¹Mosheh said, 'Why are you contravening Yahweh's bidding when that won't succeed? ⁴²Don't go up, because Yahweh is not among you. Then you won't take a beating before your enemies. ⁴³Because the Amaleqites and the Kena'anites will be there before you and you'll fall by the sword. Because of the fact that you've turned back from following Yahweh, Yahweh won't be with you.' ⁴⁴They insisted on going up to the mountain ridge, but Yahweh's pact chest and Mosheh didn't move away from within the camp, ⁴⁵and the Amaleqites and the Kena'anites who were living in that highland came down, and struck them down and crushed them as far as Hormah.

Offerings in the country where they will settle

15 Yahweh spoke to Mosheh: ²'Speak to the Yisra'elites: "When you come into the country where you will have your settlements, which I'm giving you, ³and you make a gift offering to Yahweh, a burnt offering or a sacrifice, in fulfilling a pledge or as a free offering or at your set times, to make a nice smell for Yahweh, from the herd or from the flock: ⁴the person presenting his offering to Yahweh is to present a grain offering of fine flour, a tenth, mixed with a quarter of a gallon of oil. ⁵You're also to make wine into a libation, a quarter of a gallon, with the burnt offering or sacrifice, for each sheep. ⁶Or for a ram you're to make a grain offering of fine flour, two tenths, mixed with oil, a third of a gallon, ⁷and you're to present wine for a libation, a third of a gallon, a nice smell for Yahweh.

⁸When you make an animal from the herd into a burnt offering or a sacrifice to fulfil a pledge or a well-being sacrifice for Yahweh, ⁹they're to present with the animal from the herd a grain offering of fine flour, three tenths, mixed with oil, half a gallon. ¹⁰And you're to present wine as a libation, half a gallon, as a gift offering, a nice smell for Yahweh.

¹¹It's to be done in this way with each ox or with each ram or with a young one among the sheep or among the goats, ¹²in accordance with the number that you make. In this way you're to make it for each in accordance with their number. ¹³Every native is to make these in this way in presenting a gift offering, a nice smell for Yahweh.

The first of the baking

¹⁴When someone who resides with you as a resident, or who is among you through your generations, makes a gift offering, a nice smell for Yahweh: as you make it, so the congregation is to make it. ¹⁵One decree for you and for someone who is a resident, a permanent decree through your generations: it will be the same for you and for the resident, before Yahweh. ¹⁶There will be one instruction and one ruling for you and for the person who is a resident with you.'"

¹⁷Yahweh spoke to Mosheh: ¹⁸"Speak to the Yisra'elites: "When you come into the country where I'm bringing you, ¹⁹when you eat of the bread of the country, you're to take up a contribution for Yahweh. ²⁰The first of your baked goods (a loaf) you're to take up as a contribution for Yahweh. Like the contribution from the threshing floor, so you're to take it up. ²¹From the first of your baked goods you're to give a contribution for Yahweh, through your generations.

²²When you make a mistake and don't act on any of these orders that Yahweh has spoken to Mosheh, ²³anything that Yahweh ordered you by means of Mosheh, from the day that Yahweh ordered it and onwards through your generations: ²⁴if it was done by mistake, away from the assembly's eyes, the entire assembly is to make a bull from the herd into a burnt offering, as a nice smell for Yahweh, with its grain offering and its libation, in accordance with the ruling, and a he-goat from the flock as a decontamination. ²⁵The priest is to make expiation for the entire assembly of the Yisra'elites and it will be pardoned them, because it was a mistake and they've brought their offering as a gift offering for Yahweh and as their decontamination before Yahweh, for their mistake. ²⁶It will be pardoned for the entire assembly of the Yisra'elites and for the person who is a resident among them, because for the entire people it was by mistake.

The intentional and the unintentional

²⁷If an individual does wrong by mistake, he's to present a year-old she-goat as a decontamination. ²⁸The priest is to make expiation for the person who made the mistake by his wrongdoing (by mistake), before Yahweh, to make expiation for him, so it may be pardoned for him. ²⁹The native among the Yisra'elites, and for the person who is a resident among you: there's to be one instruction for you for one who acts by mistake.

³⁰But the person who acts with hand upraised, from natives or residents: Yahweh is the one he's insulting. That person shall be cut off from among his people, ³¹because it's Yahweh's word he's scorned and Yahweh's order he's contravened. That person shall absolutely be cut off. There's waywardness on him.'"

³²The Yisra'elites were in the wilderness and they found someone collecting wood on the sabbath day. ³³The people who found him collecting wood presented him to Mosheh, to Aharon and to the entire assembly, ³⁴and they placed him under keep because it had not been specified what should be done to him. ³⁵Yahweh said to Mosheh, 'The person must absolutely be put to death by the entire assembly pelting him with stones outside the camp.' ³⁶So the entire assembly took him outside the camp and pelted him with stones so he died, as Yahweh ordered Mosheh.

³⁷Yahweh said to Mosheh: ³⁸"Speak to the Yisra'elites and say to them: they're to make themselves a fringe on the corners of their clothes, through their generations. They're to put on the hem's fringe a purple cord. ³⁹You

will have the fringe and look at it, and be mindful of all Yahweh's orders and do them, and not investigate the things you whore after, following your mind and your eyes, ⁴⁰in order that you may be mindful and may act on all my orders, and be sacred for your God. ⁴¹I am Yahweh your God who got you out of the country of Misrayim to be God for you. I am Yahweh your God.'

Ambition

16 Qorah ben Yitshar, son of Qehat son of Levi, got both Datan and Abiram, sons of Eli'ab, and On ben Pelet, son of Re'uben, ²and they rose up before Mosheh with 250 men from the Yisra'elites, leaders of the assembly, people called for by the assembly, men with a name. ³They congregated against Mosheh and against Aharon and said to them, 'You have too much, when the entire assembly, all of them, are sacred, and Yahweh is among them! Why do you raise yourselves above Yahweh's congregation?' ⁴Mosheh heard, and fell on his face. ⁵He spoke to Qorah and to his entire group: 'In the morning Yahweh can let it be acknowledged who is his and who is sacred, and he can have them draw near to him. The one he chooses is the one he will have draw near to him. ⁶Do this. Get yourself pans (Qorah and his entire group) ⁷and put fire in them and place incense on them before Yahweh, tomorrow. The person whom Yahweh chooses, he's the sacred one. You have too much, sons of Levi.'

⁸Mosheh said to Qorah: 'Please listen, you Levites. ⁹Is it too little for you that Yisra'el's God has made you distinct from the Yisra'elite assembly by having you draw near to him to perform the service of Yahweh's dwelling and to stand before the assembly to minister to them? ¹⁰He's had you draw near, you and all your brothers the Levites with you, and you seek the priesthood also. ¹¹Therefore you and your entire group are making an appointment against Yahweh. And what is Aharon that you protest against him?'

¹²Mosheh sent to call for Datan and Abiram the sons of Eli'ab but they said, 'We won't go up. ¹³Is it too little that you brought us up from a country flowing with milk and syrup to let us die in the wilderness, that you also continue to play the ruler over us? ¹⁴Certainly you haven't brought us into a country flowing with milk and syrup, and given us a domain of fields and vineyards. Will you gouge out these people's eyes? We won't go up.'

Yahweh must judge

¹⁵It was very infuriating to Mosheh. He said to Yahweh, 'Don't turn your face to their offering. I haven't taken one donkey from them. I haven't dealt badly with one of them.' ¹⁶Mosheh said to Qorah, 'You and your entire company, be before Yahweh, you and they and Aharon, tomorrow. ¹⁷Get, each person, his pan, put incense on it and present it before Yahweh, each person his pan, 250 pans, and you and Aharon each his pan.'

¹⁸They got, each person, his pan, put fire on them and placed incense on them, and stood at the entrance of the appointment tent, as did Mosheh and Aharon. ¹⁹Qorah congregated the entire assembly against them at the entrance of the appointment tent.

Yahweh's splendour appeared to the entire assembly, ²⁰and Yahweh spoke to Mosheh and to Aharon: ²¹'Make yourselves distinct from among this assembly so I may finish them off in a moment!' ²²They fell on their faces and said, 'God, the God of the spirits of all flesh! One person does wrong. Are you furious with the entire assembly?'

²³So Yahweh spoke to Mosheh: ²⁴'Speak to the assembly: "Go up from round the dwelling of Qorah, Datan and Abiram."' ²⁵Mosheh got up and went to Datan and Abiram, and the Yisra'elite elders followed him. ²⁶He spoke to the assembly: 'Please move away from near the tents of these faithless people and don't touch anything that belongs to them, so you don't get swept away because of all their wrongdoings.' ²⁷ᵃSo they went up from near the dwelling of Qorah, Datan and Abiram, all round.

A frightening act of creation

²⁷ᵇNow Datan and Abiram had come out, standing at the entrance of their tents, with their wives, their children and their little ones.

²⁸Mosheh said, 'By this you will acknowledge that it was Yahweh who sent me to do all these things, that they're not from my mind. ²⁹If these people die as all human beings die, and what is appointed for all human beings comes to them, then it was not Yahweh who sent me. ³⁰But if Yahweh performs an act of creation, and the ground opens its mouth and swallows them and all who belong to them so that they go down to She'ol alive, then you will know that these men have disdained Yahweh.'

³¹As he finished speaking all these words, the ground that was underneath them split, ³²and the earth opened its mouth and swallowed them and their households, all who belonged to Qorah and all the property. ³³Those people and all that belonged to them went down alive to She'ol. The earth covered over them. They perished from among the congregation. ³⁴All Yisra'el that was round them fled at the sound they made, because they said, 'So that the earth doesn't swallow us!' ³⁵And fire came out from Yahweh and devoured the 250 people presenting the incense.

³⁶Yahweh spoke to Mosheh: ³⁷'Say to El'azar ben Aharon the priest that he's to take up the pans from within what is burned and scatter the fire some way away, because they've become sacred. ³⁸The pans of these who did wrong at the cost of their lives: they're to make them into beaten sheets as plating for the altar, because people have presented them before Yahweh and they've become sacred. They're to be a sign for the Yisra'elites.'

Fury goes out from Yahweh

³⁹So El'azar the priest got the copper pans that the people who had been burned up had presented, and beat them into plating for the altar ⁴⁰as a reminder for the Yisra'elites that no one who is an outsider who is not from Aharon's offspring is to draw near to offer incense before Yahweh, so he won't become like Qorah and his company, as Yahweh spoke through Mosheh. ⁴¹The entire assembly of the Yisra'elites protested against Mosheh and against Aharon next day: 'You put Yahweh's people to death!' ⁴²When the assembly congregated against Mosheh and against Aharon, they turned their face to the appointment tent and there – the cloud covered it and Yahweh's splendour appeared. ⁴³Mosheh and Aharon came to the front of the appointment tent, ⁴⁴and Yahweh spoke to Mosheh: ⁴⁵'Get up from among this assembly, so I may finish them off in a moment!' They fell on their faces, ⁴⁶and Mosheh said to Aharon, 'Get the pan and put fire on it from on the altar and place incense and take it quickly to the assembly and make expiation for them, because fury has gone out from before Yahweh; the epidemic has started.'

⁴⁷Aharon got it, as Mosheh spoke, and ran into the middle of the congregation. There, the epidemic had started among the people. He put on the incense and made expiation for the people. ⁴⁸He stood between the dead and the living, and the epidemic held back. ⁴⁹The people who were dead through the epidemic were 14,700, apart from the people who were dead on account of Qorah. ⁵⁰Aharon went back to Mosheh at the entrance of the appointment tent when the epidemic had held back.

The staff that budded

17 Yahweh spoke to Mosheh: ²'Speak to the Yisra'elites and get from them a staff each per ancestral household from all their leaders, for the ancestral households, twelve staffs. You're to write each individual's name on his staff, ³and write Aharon's name on Levi's staff, because there's one staff for the head of their ancestral household. ⁴Set them down in the appointment tent before the affirmation, where I make an appointment to meet with you. ⁵The individual whom I choose, his staff will bud, and I shall rid myself of the protests of the Yisra'elites which they're uttering against you.'

⁶Mosheh spoke to the Yisra'elites, and all their leaders gave him one staff each per leader, twelve staffs for their ancestral households, with Aharon's staff among their staffs. ⁷Mosheh set the staffs down before Yahweh in the appointment tent. ⁸Next day Mosheh went into the appointment tent and there, Aharon's staff belonging to Levi's household had budded. It had put out buds and issued blossoms and dealt almonds. ⁹Mosheh took out all the staffs from before Yahweh to all the Yisra'elites, and they looked and got each person his staff.

¹⁰Yahweh said to Mosheh, 'Put Aharon's staff back before the affirmation for keeping as a sign for the rebels, so their protests at me may finish, so they don't die.' ¹¹Mosheh did as Yahweh ordered him; so he did. ¹²But the Yisra'elites said to Mosheh, 'Here, we breathe our last, we're lost, all of us are lost! ¹³Anyone who comes near Yahweh's dwelling at all will die. Have we come to an end, breathing our last?'

Provision for the priests

18 Yahweh said to Aharon, 'You, your sons and your ancestral household with you carry the sanctuary's waywardness, and you and your sons with you carry your priesthood's waywardness. ²Also, present with you your brothers, the clan of Levi, your ancestral clan, so they may join [*lavah*] with you and minister to you, as you and your sons with you are before the affirmation tent. ³They're to keep your charge and the charge of the entire tent, yet they're not to draw near to the articles of the sanctuary or to the altar, so both they and you don't die. ⁴They're to join with you and keep charge of the appointment tent, in relation to all the service of the tent. No outsider is to draw near to you.

⁵You're to keep charge of the sanctuary and charge of the altar, so there won't be fury on Yisra'el again. ⁶I myself, I here take your brothers the Levites from among the Yisra'elites for you as a gift given to Yahweh to perform the service of the appointment tent ⁷while you and your sons with you keep your priesthood in relation to every matter involving the altar and what is inside the curtain. So you will serve. I make your priesthood a service that is a gift. But the outsider who comes near is to be put to death.'

⁸Yahweh spoke to Aharon: 'I myself: I here give you charge of my contributions, in relation to all the sacred things belonging to the Yisra'elites. To you I give them in connection with your anointing, and to your sons, as a permanent decree. ⁹This will be yours from the things that are especially sacred, from the fire: every offering of theirs, with every grain offering of theirs, with every decontamination of theirs and with every reparation of theirs, which they render to me as especially sacred things. It belongs to you and to your sons.

¹⁰You may eat of the especially sacred things. Any male may eat it. It's to be sacred for you.

The sacred gifts

¹¹And this will be yours: the contribution that they give, including every elevation offering by the Yisra'elites, I give them to you and to your sons and to your daughters with you, as a permanent decree. Anyone who is pure in your household may eat it. ¹²All the "fat" of fresh oil and all the "fat" of new wine, and grain: the first of them, which they give to Yahweh, I give them to you. ¹³The first products of everything that will be in their country which they bring to Yahweh will be yours. Anyone who is pure in your household may eat them.

¹⁴Everything devoted in Yisra'el will be yours. ¹⁵Every opener of the womb of any being that people present to Yahweh, among human beings and among animals, will be yours; however, you will definitely redeem the firstborn of a human being, and you will redeem the firstborn of a pure animal. ¹⁶His redemption: at one month old you're to redeem at the evaluation of five silver sheqels by the sanctuary sheqel (it is twenty grams). ¹⁷However, the firstborn of an ox or the firstborn of a sheep or the firstborn of a goat you will not redeem. They're sacred. You're to toss their blood on the altar and burn their fat into smoke as a gift offering, as a nice smell for Yahweh. ¹⁸But their flesh will be yours; like the breast of the elevation offering and the right thigh, it will be yours.

¹⁹Every contribution of things that are sacred that the Yisra'elites take up for Yahweh I give to you, and to your sons and to your daughters with you, as a permanent decree. It's a permanent salt pact before Yahweh for you and for your offspring with you.'

The tithes

²⁰Yahweh said to Aharon, 'In their country you will not have a domain. There will be no share for you among them. I am your share, your domain, among the Yisra'elites. ²¹And to the Levites I here give every tenth

in Yisra'el as a domain in return for their service that they're performing, the service of the appointment tent. ²²The Yisra'elites will no more draw near the appointment tent, carrying wrongdoing that would mean they die. ²³The Levite – he will perform the service of the appointment tent, but they – they will carry their waywardness (a permanent decree through your generations). But among the Yisra'elites they will not receive a domain, ²⁴because the Yisra'elites' tenth, which they take up for Yahweh as a contribution, I give to the Levites as a domain. That's why I've said regarding them, among the Yisra'elites they will not receive a domain."

²⁵Yahweh spoke to Mosheh: ²⁶"And to the Levites you're to speak and to say to them: "When you get from the Yisra'elites the tenth which I've given you from them as your domain, you're to take up from it a tenth of the tenth as a contribution for Yahweh. ²⁷It will be deemed for you as your contribution, like the grain from the threshing floor and like the fullness from the vat. ²⁸So you yourselves are also to take up Yahweh's contribution from all your tenths which you get from the Yisra'elites, and you're to give Yahweh's contribution from them to Aharon the priest. ²⁹From all your gifts you're to take up the entire contribution for Yahweh from it, the sacred part of it from all its 'fat.'"

³⁰You're to say to them, "When you take up its 'fat' from it, it will be deemed for the Levites like the yield of the threshing floor and the yield of the vat. ³¹You may eat it in any place, you and your household, because it's wages for you in return for your service in the appointment tent. ³²You won't carry any wrongdoing on account of it when you've taken up its 'fat' from it. But you will not treat the sacred things of the Yisra'elites as ordinary, so you don't die."

Death defiles

19 Yahweh spoke to Mosheh and to Aharon: ²"This is a decree of instruction that Yahweh has ordered: "Speak to the Yisra'elites, so that they get you a red cow that's whole, one in which there's no defect and on which no yoke has come. ³You're to give it to El'azar the priest and they're to take it outside the camp and slaughter it before him. ⁴El'azar the priest is to get some of its blood with his finger and spatter some of its blood seven times in front, before the appointment tent. ⁵They're to burn the cow before his eyes; they're to burn its skin, its flesh and its blood, along with its intestines. ⁶The priest is to get cedar wood, hyssop and scarlet yarn, and throw them into the middle of the fire burning the cow. ⁷The priest is to wash his clothes and bathe his flesh in water, and afterwards to go into the camp. The priest will be taboo until the evening ⁸and the person who burned it – he's to wash his clothes in water and bathe his flesh in water and he'll be taboo until the evening.

⁹A person who's pure is to gather the cow's ashes and set them down outside the camp in a pure place. The assembly of the Yisra'elites is to have them for keeping as water for flowing. It will be a decontamination. ¹⁰The one who gathers the cow's ashes is to wash his clothes and he will be taboo until the evening. It will be a permanent decree for the Yisra'elites and for the person who is a resident among you.

¹¹Someone who touches the dead body of any human person will be taboo for seven days. ¹²If he decontaminates himself with it on the third day and on the seventh day, he will become pure. If he doesn't decontaminate himself on the third day and on the seventh day, he will not become pure. ¹³Anyone who touches the dead body of a human person who dies and doesn't decontaminate himself makes Yahweh's dwelling taboo. That person shall be cut off from Yisra'el. Because the water for flowing hasn't been tossed over him, he will be taboo. His taboo will still be on him.

Purification from defilement

¹⁴This is the instruction. When a human being dies in a tent, anyone going into the tent and anyone who's in the tent will be taboo for seven days. ¹⁵Every open container with no lid fastened on it is taboo. ¹⁶Anyone who touches on the face of the fields someone run through by the sword or someone who has died or a human bone or a grave will be taboo for seven days.

¹⁷They're to get for the taboo person some of the ashes from the decontamination burning and put fresh water on it in a container.

¹⁸A pure person is to get hyssop and dip it in the water and spatter it on the tent and on all the containers and on the individuals who were there and on the one who touched the bone or the person run through or the person who died or the grave. ¹⁹The pure person is to spatter it on the taboo person on the third day and on the seventh day so he will decontaminate him on the seventh day. He's to wash his clothes and bathe in water, and he will become pure in the evening. ²⁰An individual who becomes taboo and doesn't decontaminate himself: that person shall be cut off from among the congregation, because he has made Yahweh's sanctuary taboo. The water for flowing hasn't been tossed over him. He's taboo. ²¹It's to be a permanent decree for them.

The one who spatters the water for flowing is to wash his clothes. One who touches the water for flowing will be taboo until the evening. ²²Everything that the taboo person touches will become taboo and the person who touches him will become taboo until the evening.'"

Mosheh's one mistake

20 The Yisra'elites, the entire assembly, came to the Tsin Wilderness in the first month, and the people lived at Qadesh. Miryam died there and was buried there.

²But there was no water for the assembly, and they congregated against Mosheh and against Aharon. ³The people got into an argument with Mosheh: 'If only we had breathed our last when our brothers breathed their last before Yahweh! ⁴Why have you brought Yahweh's congregation into this wilderness to die there, us and our animals? ⁵Why did you get us to go up from Misrayim to bring us to this bad place, not a place of seed or fig or vine or pomegranate? And there's no water to drink.'

⁶Mosheh and Aharon came from before the congregation to the entrance of the appointment tent and fell on their faces. Yahweh's splendour appeared to them ⁷and Yahweh spoke to Mosheh: ⁸'Get the staff and congregate the assembly, you and Aharon your brother, and speak to the cliff before their eyes and it will give its water; you will make water come out of the cliff for them and provide drink for the assembly and their animals.' ⁹So Mosheh got the staff from before Yahweh as he ordered him, ¹⁰and Mosheh and Aharon gathered the congregation before the cliff, and he said to them, 'Please listen, you rebels! Are we to make water come out of this cliff for you?' ¹¹Mosheh lifted up his hand and struck the cliff with his staff, twice. Much water came out, and the assembly and their animals drank. ¹²But Yahweh said to Mosheh and to Aharon, 'Because you didn't trust in me so as to make me sacred before the Yisra'elites' eyes, therefore you won't bring this congregation into the country that I'm giving them.' ¹³That's Meribah ['Argument'] Water, where the Yisra'elites got into an argument with Yahweh, and he showed his sacredness among them.

Seeking to live peacefully

¹⁴Mosheh sent envoys from Qadesh to the king of Edom: 'Your brother Yisra'el has said this: you yourself know all the hardship that has befallen us. ¹⁵Our ancestors went down into Misrayim and we lived in Misrayim for a long time, but the Misrayimites dealt badly with us and our ancestors. ¹⁶We cried out to Yahweh and he listened to our voice. He sent an envoy and got us out of Misrayim. So here we are, in Qadesh, a town on the edge of your border. ¹⁷May we please pass through your country. We won't pass through field or through vineyard, and we won't drink water from wells. We'll go along the King's Road. We won't turn off right or left till we pass through your border.'

¹⁸But Edom said to him, 'You're not to pass through me or I'll come out with the sword to meet you.' ¹⁹The Yisra'elites said to him, 'We'll go up by the causeway. If we drink your water, I and my livestock, I'll give you its price. It'll be nothing as we'll pass through only on foot.' ²⁰But he said, 'You will not pass through.' Edom went out to meet him with a substantial company, with a strong hand. ²¹So Edom refused to let Yisra'el pass through its border, and Yisra'el turned from it.

²²So they moved on from Qadesh and the Yisra'elites came, the entire assembly, to Mount Hor. ²³Yahweh said to Mosheh and to Aharon at Mount Hor, on the border of the country of Edom, ²⁴'Aharon is to join his kin, because he will not come into the country that I'm

giving to the Yisra'elites, on account of the fact that you [two] rebelled against my bidding about Meribah Water. **²⁵**Get Aharon and El'azar his son and take them up Mount Hor. **²⁶**Get Aharon to take off his garments, and get El'azar his son to put them on. Aharon will be gathered and die there.'

Aharon joins his ancestors

²⁷Mosheh did as Yahweh ordered. They went up Mount Hor before the eyes of the entire assembly **²⁸**and Mosheh got Aharon to take off his garments and got El'azar his son to put them on. Aharon died there on the top of the mountain, and Mosheh and El'azar came down from the mountain. **²⁹**The assembly saw that Aharon had breathed his last, and they bewailed Aharon for thirty days, the entire Yisra'elite household.

21 The Kena'anite, the king of Arad, who lived in the Negeb, heard that Yisra'el was coming by the Atarim road, and he battled against Yisra'el and took some of them captive. **²**Yisra'el made a pledge to Yahweh: 'If you actually give this people into my hand, I will devote their towns.' **³**Yahweh listened to Yisra'el's voice and gave the Kena'anites over, and they devoted [*haram*] them and their towns. So they named the place Hormah.

⁴They moved on from Mount Hor by the Reed Sea road to go round the country of Edom. The people's spirit became short on the way **⁵**and the people spoke against God and against Mosheh: 'Why did you bring us up from Misrayim to die in the wilderness, because there's no bread and there's no water and our appetite is dismayed about the pathetic bread?' **⁶**Yahweh sent off against the people venomous snakes that bit the people, and a large company from Yisra'el died. **⁷**The people came to Mosheh and said, 'We did wrong in that we spoke against Yahweh and against you. Plead with Yahweh to remove the snakes from us.' Mosheh pleaded on behalf of the people **⁸**and Yahweh said to Mosheh, 'Make yourself a venomous thing and put it on a standard. Anyone who's bitten but looks at it will live.' **⁹**So Mosheh made a copper snake and placed it on a standard, and if a snake bit an individual, he would look to the copper snake and live.

Sihon king of the Amorites

¹⁰The Yisra'elites moved on and camped at Obot, **¹¹**then moved on from Obot and camped at Iyyim in the Regions Across, in the wilderness over against Mo'ab on the east. **¹²**From there they moved on and camped by Wadi Zered. **¹³**From there they moved on and camped across the Arnon, which is in the wilderness that extends from the Amorite border . . .

(because the Arnon is the border of Mo'ab, between Mo'ab and the Amorites; **¹⁴**that's why it's said in the Document about Yahweh's Battles, 'Waheb in Suphah and the wadis; the Arnon **¹⁵**and the slope of the wadis that stretches to the Ar settlement and lies at Mo'ab's border')

¹⁶. . . and from there to Be'er ['Well'] . . .

(that's the well of which Yahweh said to Mosheh, 'Gather the people and I'll give them water', **¹⁷**then Yisra'el sang this song:

> Go up, well – sing for it,
> **¹⁸**well that the officials dug,
> That the important ones among the
> people sank,
> with a sceptre, with their staffs)

and from the wilderness to Mattanah, **¹⁹**and from Mattanah to Nahali'el, and from Nahali'el to Bamot, **²⁰**and from Bamot to the ravine that's in Mo'ab's region, to the top of Pisgah, which overlooks The Wasteland.

²¹Yisra'el sent envoys to Sihon, king of the Amorites: **²²**'I want to pass through your country. We won't turn off into your field or into your vineyard. We won't drink water from your well. We'll go by the King's Road till we pass through your border.' **²³**But Sihon didn't let Yisra'el pass though his border. Sihon gathered his entire company and went out to meet Yisra'el, into the wilderness. He came to Yahats and battled against Yisra'el. **²⁴**But Yisra'el struck him down with the mouth of the sword and took possession of his country from the Arnon as far as the Yabboq, as far as the Ammonites, because the Ammonites' border was strong. **²⁵**Yisra'el took all these towns.

Og king of Bashan

So Yisra'el lived in all the Amorites' towns, in Heshbon and in all its daughter-towns, ²⁶because Heshbon was the town of Sihon, king of the Amorites, and he had battled against the former king of Mo'ab and taken his entire country from his hand as far as the Arnon. ²⁷That's why the poets say:

> Come to Heshbon, which is built up,
>   and which is founded, Sihon's town.
> ²⁸Because fire went out from Heshbon,
>   flame from Sihon's township,
> Devouring Ar in Mo'ab,
>   the masters of the Arnon Heights.
> ²⁹Ah, you, Mo'ab,
>   you were lost, people of Kemosh!
> He gave over his sons, the survivors,
>   his daughters into captivity,
> to the king of the Amorites, Sihon.
> ³⁰But their dominion is lost,
>   Heshbon as far as Dibon.
> We wrought desolation as far as Nophah,
>   which is as far as Medeba.

³¹So Yisra'el lived in the country of the Amorites. ³²Mosheh sent people to investigate Ya'zer, and they captured its daughter-villages and dispossessed the Amorites who were there. ³³Then they turned the face and went up the Bashan road, and Og king of Bashan came out to meet them, he and his entire company, for a battle at Edre'i. ³⁴Yahweh said to Mosheh, 'Don't be afraid of him, because I give him, his entire company and his country into your hand. You're to do to him as you did to Sihon king of the Amorites who was living in Heshbon.' ³⁵They struck down him, his sons and his entire company until they let no survivor remain to him, and they took possession of his country.

22 Then the Yisra'elites moved on and camped in the Mo'ab steppes across the Yarden from Yeriho [Jericho].

Balaq panics

²Balaq ben Tsippor saw all that Yisra'el had done to the Amorites, ³and Mo'ab was in great dread before the people because it was numerous. So Mo'ab was dismayed about the Yisra'elites, ⁴and Mo'ab said to the elders of Midyan, 'The congregation will now lick up everything around us like an ox licks up the grass in the fields.'

Balaq ben Tsippor was king of Mo'ab at that time ⁵and he sent envoys to Bil'am [Balaam] ben Be'or in Petor, which is by the river, the country of his kinsfolk, to call for him: 'Here, a people has come out of Misrayim – here, it has covered the face of the earth, and it's living near me. ⁶So now please curse this people for me, because it's more numerous than me. Maybe I'll be able to strike it down and drive it out of the country, because I know that the one whom you bless is blessed and the one whom you curse is cursed.'

⁷So Mo'ab's elders and Midyan's elders went with divination material in their hand, came to Bil'am and spoke Balaq's words to him. ⁸He said to them, 'Stay the night here tonight and I'll bring back word to you as Yahweh speaks to me.' So the officials from Mo'ab stayed with Bil'am.

⁹God came to Bil'am and said, 'Who are these people with you?' ¹⁰Bil'am said to God, 'Balaq ben Tsippor, king of Mo'ab, has sent to me: ¹¹"Here is the people that came out of Misrayim, and it has covered the face of the earth. Come now and damn it for me. Maybe I'll be able to do battle against it and drive it out."' ¹²God said to Bil'am, 'You will not go with them. You will not curse the people, because it's blessed.'

Bil'am says no then yes

¹³Bil'am got up in the morning and said to Balaq's officials, 'Go to your country, because Yahweh has refused to let me go with you.' ¹⁴So the officials of Mo'ab set off and came to Balaq and said, 'Bil'am refused to go with us.'

¹⁵Balaq once again sent officials, more and more honoured than these. ¹⁶They came to Bil'am and said to him, 'Balaq ben Tsippor has said this: please don't hold back from going to me, ¹⁷because I shall definitely honour you much, and everything that you say I will do. Please go and damn this people for me.' ¹⁸Bil'am answered Balaq's servants, 'If Balaq were to give me his house full of silver and

gold, I couldn't contravene the bidding of Yahweh my God, in doing something small or big. [19]But now, please stay here, you too, tonight, so I may know what Yahweh may further speak with me.'

[20]God came to Bil'am in the night and said to him, 'If the people have come to call for you, set off, go with them, but only the word that I speak to you – it is what you are to do.' [21]So Bil'am got up in the morning, saddled his donkey and went with the officials of Mo'ab.

[22]But Yahweh's anger raged because he was going, and Yahweh's envoy took his stand on the road as an adversary to him. He was riding on his donkey and his two boys were with him. [23]The donkey saw Yahweh's envoy standing in the road with his drawn sword in his hand, so the donkey turned away from the road and went into the fields. Bil'am struck the donkey to turn it away on to the road. [24]Then Yahweh's envoy stood in a vineyards lane, with a barrier this side and a barrier that side. [25]The donkey saw Yahweh's envoy and squeezed itself against the wall, and squeezed Bil'am's foot against the wall. He again struck her.

The donkey speaks

[26]Again Yahweh's envoy passed on and stood in a narrow place where there was no room to turn away right or left, [27]and the donkey saw Yahweh's envoy and lay down under Bil'am. Bil'am's anger raged and he struck the donkey with his stick. [28]Yahweh opened the donkey's mouth and she said to Bil'am, 'What have I done to you, that you've struck me these three times?' [29]Bil'am said to the donkey, 'Because you've acted abusively to me! If only there were a sword in my hand, because I would now kill you.' [30]The donkey said to Bil'am, 'Am I not the donkey that you've ridden on ever since you had me until this day? Have I at all shown myself in the habit of doing this to you?' He said, 'No.'

[31]Yahweh opened Bil'am's eyes and he saw Yahweh's envoy standing in the road with his drawn sword in his hand, and he bent his head and bowed low on his face. [32]Yahweh's envoy said to him, 'Why have you struck your donkey these three times? Here, I'm the one who came out as an adversary, because the journey before me was urgent. [33]The donkey saw me and turned away before me these three times. If she hadn't turned away from before me, then I would rather also have killed you now but kept her alive.' [34]Bil'am said to Yahweh's envoy, 'I did wrong, because I didn't know that you were standing to meet me in the road. So now, if it's bad in your eyes, I'll go back.' [35]Yahweh's envoy said to Bil'am, 'Go with the people. But you're to speak nothing but the word that I speak to you.' So Bil'am went with Balaq's officials.

Balaq instructs Bil'am

[36]Balaq heard that Bil'am was coming and went out to meet him at Mo'ab Town, which is on the Arnon border, which is at the farthest point of the border. [37]Balaq said to Bil'am, 'I sent urgently to you to call for you, didn't I. Why didn't you go to me? Am I truly unable to honour you?' [38]Bil'am said to Balaq, 'Here, I've come to you now. Am I really able to speak anything? The word that God puts in my mouth: I shall speak it.'

[39]Bil'am went with Balaq, and they came to Hutstsot Township. [40]Balaq sacrificed cattle and sheep and sent them off to Bil'am and to the officials who were with him. [41]In the morning Balaq got Bil'am and took him up Master's Heights. From there he looked at the edge of the people.

23 Bil'am said to Balaq, 'Build me seven altars here and make an offering for me here of seven bulls and seven rams.' [2]Balaq did as Bil'am spoke, and Balaq and Bil'am offered up a bull and a ram on each altar. [3]Bil'am said to Balaq, 'Take your stand by your burnt offering and I shall go. Maybe Yahweh will come to meet me, and whatever is the word that he lets me see, I shall tell you.'

He went to a bare place. [4]And God met with Bil'am. He said to him, 'I've laid out seven altars and offered up a bull and a ram on each altar.' [5]And Yahweh put a thing in Bil'am's mouth and said, 'Go back to Balaq and speak in this way.' [6]He went back to him. There he was, standing by his burnt offering, he and all the officials of Mo'ab.

Bil'am's message

⁷He took up his poem:

From Aram Balaq led me,
   Mo'ab's king from the eastern mountains:
'Go, curse Jacob for me;
   go, condemn Yisra'el.'
⁸How can I slight what God has not slighted,
   how can I condemn what God has not condemned?
⁹For from the top of the crags I see him,
   from the hills I behold him.
There, a people that dwells apart,
   that does not think of itself as one of the nations.
¹⁰Who can count the earth of Ya'aqob [Jacob],
   or the number of Yisra'el's dust cloud?
May I myself die the death of the upright;
   may my future be like his!

¹¹Balaq said to Bil'am, 'What have you done to me? It was to slight my enemies that I got you. Here, you've greatly blessed them!' ¹²He answered, 'It's what Yahweh puts in my mouth that I keep watch to speak, isn't it.' ¹³So Balaq said to him, 'Please get yourself with me to another place where you can see him. From there you will see only the edge of them. You won't see all of them. You can slight them for me from there.' ¹⁴He took him to Lookouts Field, to the top of Pisgah, built seven altars, and offered up a bull and a ram on each altar. ¹⁵He said to Balaq, 'Take your stand in this way by your offering. I myself will seek a meeting here.'
¹⁶Yahweh met with Bil'am and put a word in his mouth, and said, 'Go back to Balaq and speak in this way.' ¹⁷He came to him and there he was, standing by his offering, the officials of Mo'ab with him. Balaq said to him, 'What did Yahweh say?'

Balaq tries again

¹⁸Bil'am took up his poem:

Get up, Balaq, listen;
   give ear to me, ben Tsippor.
¹⁹God is not a human person so he lies,
   a human being so he relents.
Would he say and not do,
   speak and not implement it?
²⁰Here, 'Bless' I received;
   when he blesses, I can't turn it back.
²¹He has not envisaged trouble in Ya'aqob,
   he has not visualized oppression in Yisra'el.
Yahweh its God is with it,
   the acclamation of a king is in it,
²²God who got them out of Misrayim
   is like an oryx's horns for it.
²³Because there's no spell against Ya'aqob,
   no magic against Yisra'el.
It is said just once about Ya'aqob,
   and about Yisra'el, what God is doing.
²⁴Here – a people that gets up like a cougar,
   raises itself like a lion.
It doesn't lie down until it eats prey
   and drinks the blood of people who have been run through.

²⁵Balaq said to Bil'am, 'Neither properly slight them nor properly bless them.' ²⁶Bil'am answered Balaq, 'I've spoken to you, haven't I: "Everything that Yahweh speaks with me, I must do."' ²⁷Balaq said to Bil'am, 'Please do go, I'll take you to another place. Maybe it will be all right in God's eyes to slight them for me from there.' ²⁸So Balaq took Bil'am to the top of Pe'or, which overlooks the face of The Wasteland. ²⁹Bil'am said to Balaq, 'Build me seven altars here and make an offering of seven bulls and seven rams for me.' ³⁰Balaq did as Bil'am said, and offered up a bull and a ram on each altar.

Ya'aqob's good tents

24 Bil'am had seen that it was good in Yahweh's eyes to bless Yisra'el, and he didn't go as on other times to find spells but set his face towards the wilderness. ²Bil'am lifted his eyes and saw Yisra'el dwelling by its clans, and God's spirit came on him.
³He took up his poem:

A declaration of Bil'am ben Be'or,
   a declaration of a man who is opened of eye,
⁴A declaration of one who hears God's words,
   one who beholds Shadday's vision,
   falling, with eyes uncovered:
⁵How good are your tents, Ya'aqob,
   your dwellings, Yisra'el,

⁶Like wadis that spread out,
    like gardens by a river,
Like aloes that Yahweh has planted,
    like cedars by water.
⁷Water will flow from its branches,
    its seed will be in much water.
Its king will rise above Agag,
    its kingdom will go up high.
⁸God who brought it out of Misrayim
    is like an oryx's horns to it.
It will devour nations, its attackers,
    crush their bones, hit with its arrows.
⁹It bent down, lay like a lion,
    like a cougar: who would rouse it?
The people who bless you – such a person is
        blessed,
    the people who curse you – such a person is
        cursed!

¹⁰Balaq's anger raged against Bil'am and he struck the palms of his hands. Balaq said to Bil'am, 'I called for you to damn my enemies, but here, you've actually blessed, these three times!' ¹¹So take flight for your life now to your own place. I said I would really honour you, but here, Yahweh has held you back from honour.' ¹²Bil'am said to Balaq, 'I also spoke to your envoys whom you sent to me, didn't I: ¹³"If Balaq were to give me his house full of gold and silver, I couldn't contravene Yahweh's bidding by doing good or bad out of my own mind. What Yahweh speaks, I shall speak." ¹⁴So now: here I am, going to my people. Come, I shall counsel you about what this people will do to your people in a later time.'

Bil'am's last words

¹⁵He took up his poem:

A declaration of Bil'am ben Be'or,
    a declaration of a man who is opened of eye,
¹⁶A declaration of one who hears God's words,
    who has knowledge from the One on High,
One who beholds Shadday's vision,
    falling, with eyes uncovered:
¹⁷I see it, but not now;
    I behold it, but not near.
A star has made a way from Ya'aqob,
    a staff has risen from Yisra'el.
It has hit Mo'ab's crown,
    the skull of all the Setites.
¹⁸Edom has become a possession,
    Se'ir has become a possession, of its enemies,
While Yisra'el is acting forcefully;
    ¹⁹from Ya'aqob one will hold sway
    and obliterate what survives of the town.

²⁰He saw Amaleq and took up his poem:

If Amaleq is first among the nations,
    but its future: it will perish permanently.

²¹He saw the Qenites and took up his poem:

Your settlement is powerful,
    your nest placed in the cliff.
²²Yet Qayin will be for burning up,
    for how long will Ashshur take you captive?

²³He took up his poem:

Ah, who will live
    apart from God's determining it?
²⁴Ships from Kittim's shore
    will humble Ashshur.
They will humble Eber,
    but it, too, will perish permanently.

²⁵Bil'am set off and went and turned back to his place, and Balaq, too, went on his way.

25

But while Yisra'el lived at Acacias, the people started whoring with the Mo'abite women. ²They called the people to their gods' sacrifices, and the people ate and bowed low to their gods. ³So Yisra'el bound itself to Master-of-Pe'or, and Yahweh's anger raged against Yisra'el. ⁴Yahweh said to Mosheh, 'Get all the heads of the people and execute them for Yahweh in the light of the sun, so Yahweh's angry rage may turn back from Yisra'el.' ⁵So Mosheh said to Yisra'el's leaders, 'Each of you kill his men who bound themselves to Master-of-Pe'or.'

The passion of Pinhas and of Yahweh

⁶And there, a man from among the Yisra'elites came and presented a Midyanite woman to his brothers before the eyes of Mosheh and before the eyes of the entire

assembly of the Yisra'elites; they were wailing at the entrance of the appointment tent. ⁷Pinhas ben El'azar, the son of Aharon the priest, saw it, got up from among the assembly, took a spear in his hand, ⁸came after the Yisra'elite man into the pavilion and thrust the two of them through, the Yisra'elite man and the woman, through to her insides.

The epidemic held back from the Yisra'elites, ⁹but the people who died through the epidemic were 24,000.

¹⁰Yahweh spoke to Mosheh: ¹¹'Pinhas ben El'azar, the son of Aharon the priest – he's turned back my wrath from the Yisra'elites by his showing my passion among them, so I didn't finish off the Yisra'elites in my passion. ¹²Therefore say: here, I am giving him my pact that things will be well. ¹³It will be for him and for his offspring after him as a permanent priestly pact, on account of the fact that he was passionate for his God and made expiation for the Yisra'elites.'

¹⁴The name of the Yisra'elite man struck down (the one who was struck down with the Midyanite woman) was Zimri ben Salu, leader of an ancestral household belonging to the Shim'onites. ¹⁵The name of the Midyanite woman who was struck down was Kozbi bat Tsur; he was head of the clans in an ancestral household in Midyan.

¹⁶Yahweh spoke to Mosheh: ¹⁷'Attack the Midyanites, strike them down, ¹⁸because they were attacking you with their wiles which they practised towards you, on account of Pe'or and on account of Kozbi, the daughter of a Midyanite leader, their sister, who was struck down on the day of the epidemic on account of Pe'or.'

Another head count: Re'uben, Shim'on, Gad

26 After the epidemic, Yahweh said to Mosheh and to El'azar ben Aharon the priest, ²'Take a head count of the entire assembly of the Yisra'elites from the age of twenty years and upwards by their ancestral household, everyone in Yisra'el who goes out in the army.' ³Mosheh and El'azar the priest spoke with them in the Mo'ab steppes by the Yarden at Yeriho: ⁴'From the age of twenty years and upwards . . .', as Yahweh ordered Mosheh.

The Yisra'elites who came out of the country of Misrayim:

⁵Re'uben, Yisra'el's firstborn – Re'uben's descendants:
of Hanok, the Hanokite kin-group; of Pallu, the Pallu'ite kin-group; ⁶of Hetsron, the Hetsronite kin-group; of Karmi, the Karmite kin-group.
⁷These were the kin-groups of the Re'ubenites. Their register was 43,730.
⁸Sons of Pallu: Eli'ab.
⁹Sons of Eli'ab: Nemu'el, Datan and Abiram. Datan and Abiram were the people called for by the assembly who campaigned against Mosheh and against Aharon within Qorah's group when they campaigned against Yahweh, ¹⁰and the earth opened its mouth and swallowed them with Qorah, when the company died, when fire devoured the 250 people and they became a banner. ¹¹(Qorah's sons didn't die.)

¹²Shim'on's descendants by their kin-groups: of Nemu'el, the Nemu'elite kin-group; of Yamin, the Yaminite kin-group; of Yakin, the Yakinite kin-group; ¹³of Zerah, the Zarhite kin-group; of Sha'ul, the Sha'ulite kin-group. ¹⁴These were the kin-groups of the Shim'onites. 22,200.

¹⁵Gad's descendants by their kin-groups: of Tsephon, the Tsephonite kin-group; of Haggi, the Haggite kin-group; of Shuni, the Shunite kin-group; ¹⁶of Ozni, the Oznite kin-group; of Eri, the Erite kin-group; ¹⁷of Arod, the Arodite kin-group; of Ar'eli, the Ar'elite kin-group.
¹⁸These were the kin-groups of the Gadites. By their register: 40,500.

Yehudah, Yissakar, Zebulun, Menashsheh, Ephraim

¹⁹Yehudah's sons: Er and Onan. Er and Onan died in the country of Kena'an.
²⁰Yehudah's descendants by their kin-groups were:
of Shelah, the Shelahite kin-group; of Perets, the Partsite kin-group; of Zerah, the Zarhite kin-group.

²¹Perets's descendants were: of Hetsron, the Hetsronite kin-group; of Hamul, the Hamulite kin-group.
²²These were the kin-groups of Yehudah. By their register: 76,500.

²³Yissakar's descendants by their kin-groups: of Tola, the Tola'ite kin-group; of Puvah, the Punite kin-group; ²⁴of Yashub, the Yashubite kin-group; of Shimron, the Shimronite kin-group.
²⁵These were the kin-groups of Yissakar. By their register: 64,300.

²⁶Zebulun's descendants by their kin-groups: of Sered, the Sardite kin-group; of Elon, the Elonite kin-group; of Yahle'el, the Yahle'elite kin-group.
²⁷These were the kin-groups of the Zebulunites. By their register: 60,500.

²⁸Yoseph's descendants by their kin-groups, Menashsheh and Ephrayim.

²⁹Menashsheh's descendants: of Makir, the Makirite kin-group.
Makir fathered Gil'ad; of Gil'ad: the kin-group of the Gil'adites.
³⁰These were Gil'ad's descendants: I'ezer, the I'ezrite kin-group; of Heleq, the Helqite kin-group; ³¹Asri'el, the Asri'elite kin-group; Shekem, the Shekemite kin-group; ³²Shemida, the Shemida'ite kin-group; Hepher, the Hephrite kin-group.
³³Tselophhad ben Hepher – he had no sons, only daughters; the names of Tselophhad's daughters were Mahlah, No'ah, Hoglah, Milkah and Tirtsah.
³⁴These were the kin-groups of Menashsheh. And their register: 52,700.

³⁵These were Ephrayim's descendants by their kin-groups:
of Shutelah, the Shutalhite kin-group; of Beker, the Bakrite kin-group; of Tahan, the Tahanite kin-group.
³⁶These were Shutelah's descendants: of Eran, the Eranite kin-group.
³⁷These were the kin-groups of Ephrayim's descendants. By their register: 32,500.
These were Yoseph's descendants by their kin-groups.

³⁸Binyamin's descendants by their kin-groups: of Bela, the Bal'ite kin-group; of Ashbel, the Ashbelite kin-group; of Ahiram, the Ahiramite kin-group; ³⁹of Shephupham, the Shephuphamite kin-group; of Hupham, the Huphamite kin-group.
⁴⁰Bela's sons were Ard and Na'aman. The Ardite kin-group; of Na'aman, the Na'amanite kin-group.
⁴¹These were Binyamin's descendants by their kin-groups. And by their register: 45,600.

Dan, Asher, Naphtali, Levi

⁴²These were Dan's descendants by their kin-groups:
of Shuham, the Shuhamite kin-group. These were the kin-groups of Dan by their kin-groups.
⁴³All the kin-groups of the Shuhamites, by their register: 64,400.

⁴⁴Asher's descendants by their kin-groups: of Imnah, the Imnahite kin-group; of Yishvi, the Yishvite kin-group; of Beri'ah, the Beri'hite kin-group.
⁴⁵Of Beri'ah's descendants: of Heber, the Hebrite kin-group; of Malki'el, the Malki'elite kin-group.
⁴⁶The name of Asher's daughter was Serah.
⁴⁷These were the kin-groups of Asher's descendants. By their register: 53,400.

⁴⁸Naphtali's descendants by their kin-groups:
of Yahtse'el, the Yahtse'elite kin-group; of Guni, the Gunite kin-group; ⁴⁹of Yetser, the Yitsrite kin-group; of Shillem, the Shillemite kin-group.
⁵⁰These were the kin-groups of Napthali by their kin-groups. And by their register: 45,400.

⁵¹This was the register of the Yisra'elites: 601,730.
⁵²Yahweh spoke to Mosheh: ⁵³"To these people the country is to be shared out as a domain by the number of the names. ⁵⁴For a big group, you're to make its domain big, and for a small group, you're to make its domain small. Each is to be given its domain in

accordance with its register. ⁵⁵Only, the country is to be shared out by lot. By the names of the ancestral clans they're to have a domain. ⁵⁶In accordance with the lot its domain is to be shared out, between big and small.'

⁵⁷This was the register of the Levites by their kin-groups:
of Gershon, the Gershonite kin-group; of Qehat, the Qehatite kin-group; of Merari, the Merarite kin-group.
⁵⁸These were the kin-groups of Levi:
the Libnite kin-group, the Hebronite kin-group, the Mahlite kin-group, the Mushite kin-group, the Qorahite kin-group
 Qehat fathered Amram, ⁵⁹and the name of Amram's wife was Yokebed bat Levi, to whom [her mother] gave birth for Levi in Misrayim. She gave birth to Aharon, Mosheh and Miryam their sister for Amram. ⁶⁰To Aharon were born Nadab and Abihu, El'azar and Itamar, ⁶¹but Nadab and Abihu died when they presented outside fire before Yahweh.
⁶²Their register was 23,000, every male from one month and upwards, because they were not registered among the Yisra'elites, because no domain was given to them among the Yisra'elites.

Five pushy women

⁶³This was the register by Mosheh and El'azar the priest that they made of the Yisra'elites in the Mo'ab steppes by the Yarden at Yeriho. ⁶⁴Among these there was not one person from the register by Mosheh and Aharon the priest that they made of the Yisra'elites in the Sinay Wilderness, ⁶⁵because Yahweh had said to them, 'They will definitely die in the wilderness.' Not one of them remained except Kaleb ben Yephunneh and Yehoshua ben Nun.

27 The daughters of Tselophhad ben Hepher, son of Gil'ad son of Makir son of Menashsheh, of the kin-group of Menashsheh ben Yoseph, presented themselves. These are the names of his daughters: Mahlah, No'ah, Hoglah, Milkah and Tirtsah. ²They stood before Mosheh, before El'azar the priest, and before the leaders and the entire assembly, at the entrance of the appointment tent, and said, ³'Our father died in the wilderness. He was not among the group who kept an appointment against Yahweh, in Qorah's group, because he died for his own wrongdoing. He had no sons. ⁴Why should our father's name disappear from among his kin-group because he had no son? Give us a holding among our father's brothers.'

⁵Mosheh presented their case before Yahweh, ⁶and Yahweh said to Mosheh, ⁷'The daughters of Tselophhad are speaking correctly. Do give them a holding, a domain among their father's brothers. Pass their father's domain over to them.

⁸You're to speak to the Yisra'elites: "When an individual dies and he had no son, you're to pass his domain over to his daughter. ⁹If he had no daughter, you're to give his domain to his brothers. ¹⁰If he had no brothers, you're to give his domain to his father's brothers. ¹¹If his father had no brothers, you're to give his domain to the nearest relative he had from his kin-group, and he will take possession of it. It's to be a ruling decree for the Yisra'elites, as Yahweh ordered Mosheh."'

Appointing a new leader

¹²Yahweh said to Mosheh, 'Go up this mountain in the Regions Across and look at the country that I'm giving the Yisra'elites. ¹³When you've looked at it, you too will be gathered to your kin as Aharon your brother was gathered to them, ¹⁴as you rebelled against my bidding when the assembly argued in the Tsin Wilderness, in connection with making me sacred in their eyes by means of the water' (i.e. Meribah Water at Qadesh in the Tsin Wilderness).

¹⁵Mosheh spoke to Yahweh: ¹⁶'Yahweh, the God of the spirits of all flesh, must appoint an individual over the assembly ¹⁷who will go out before them and come in before them, who will take them out and bring them in, so Yahweh's assembly won't be like a flock that has no shepherd.' ¹⁸Yahweh said to Mosheh, 'Get yourself Yehoshua ben Nun, an individual who has spirit in him. Lean your hand on him. ¹⁹Stand him before El'azar the priest

and before the entire assembly and give him orders before their eyes, ²⁰and put on him some of your dignity in order that the entire assembly of the Yisra'elites may listen. ²¹He will stand before El'azar the priest and he will ask for the decision of the Urim before Yahweh for him. At his bidding they will go out and at his bidding they will come in, he and all the Yisra'elites with him, the entire assembly.' ²²Mosheh did as Yahweh ordered him. He got Yehoshua, stood him before El'azar the priest and before the entire assembly, ²³leaned his hands on him and gave him orders, as Yahweh spoke through Mosheh.

Daily and weekly offerings

28 Yahweh spoke to Mosheh: ²'Order the Yisra'elites: "You're to keep watch about presenting to me my offering, my bread, as my gift offerings, a nice smell for me, at its set time." ³You're to say to them, "This is the gift offering that you're to present to Yahweh:
lambs a year old that are whole, two per day as a regular burnt offering ⁴(you're to make one lamb in the morning and to make the second lamb at twilight);
⁵a tenth of a barrel of fine flour as a grain offering, mixed with a quarter of a gallon of pressed oil ⁶(the regular burnt offering made at Mount Sinay, as a nice smell, a gift offering for Yahweh);
⁷its libation a quarter of a gallon for the one lamb (pour it in the sanctuary as a liquor libation for Yahweh);
⁸you're to make the second lamb at twilight; like the morning grain offering and like its libation you're to make it, a gift offering, a nice smell for Yahweh.
⁹On the sabbath day:
two lambs a year old that are whole;
two tenths of fine flour as a grain offering, mixed with oil, with its libation;
¹⁰a burnt offering for each sabbath along with the regular burnt offering and its libation.

New Year and Pesah

¹¹At the beginning of your months you're to present
a burnt offering for Yahweh: two bulls from the herd, one ram and seven lambs a year old that are whole;
¹²three tenths of fine flour as a grain offering, mixed with oil, for each bull;
two tenths of fine flour as a grain offering, mixed with oil, for each ram;
¹³a tenth each of fine flour as a grain offering, mixed with oil, for each lamb:
a burnt offering, a nice smell, a gift offering for Yahweh;
¹⁴and their libations will be half a gallon of wine for a bull, a third of a gallon for a ram and a quarter of a gallon for a lamb. This is the month-by-month burnt offering for the months of the year. ¹⁵And one he-goat from the flock as a decontamination for Yahweh is to be made, along with the regular burnt offering, with its libation.
¹⁶In the first month, on the fourteenth day of the month, is Pesah for Yahweh, ¹⁷and on the fifteenth day of this month there is a festival. For seven days flatbread is to be eaten. ¹⁸On the first day, a sacred occasion. You will not do any servile work. ¹⁹You're to present
a gift offering, a burnt offering, for Yahweh: two bulls from the herd, one ram, and seven lambs a year old; they're to be ones of yours that are whole;
²⁰their grain offering: you're to make fine flour mixed with oil, three tenths for a bull and two tenths for a ram; ²¹you're to make a tenth for each lamb, for the seven lambs;
²²one he-goat from the flock as a decontamination, to make expiation for you.
²³You're to make these apart from the morning burnt offering, which is for the regular burnt offering. ²⁴You're to make ones like these each day for seven days as a meal, a gift offering, a nice smell for Yahweh. It's to be made along with the regular burnt offering, with its libation.
²⁵On the seventh day it's to be a sacred occasion for you. You will not do any servile work.

The Shabu'ot Festival and the seventh month

²⁶On the day of the first products, when you present a new grain offering for Yahweh,

during your Shabu'ot Festival, it's to be a sacred occasion for you. You will not do any servile work. ²⁷You're to present
- a burnt offering as a nice smell for Yahweh, two bulls from the herd, one ram, seven lambs a year old;
- ²⁸their grain offering, fine flour mixed with oil, three tenths for each bull, two tenths for each ram, ²⁹a tenth each for each lamb, for the seven lambs;
- ³⁰one he-goat from the flock to make expiation for you.

³¹You're to make them apart from the regular burnt offering and its grain offering (they are to be ones of yours that are whole), and their libations.

29 In the seventh month on the first of the month it's to be a sacred occasion for you. You will not do any servile work. It's to be for you the day of a horn blast. ²You're to make
- a burnt offering as a nice smell for Yahweh: a bull from the herd, a ram, seven lambs a year old that are whole;
- ³their grain offering: fine flour mixed with oil, three tenths for the bull, two tenths for the ram ⁴and one tenth for each lamb, for the seven lambs;
- ⁵one he-goat from the flock as a decontamination to make expiation for you;
- ⁶apart from the month's burnt offering and its grain offering, and the regular burnt offering and its grain offering and their libations in accordance with the rulings for them, as a nice smell, a gift offering for Yahweh.

The Pilgrimage Festival celebrations

⁷On the tenth of this seventh month it's to be a sacred occasion for you and you're to humble yourselves. You will not do any work. ⁸You're to present for Yahweh
- a burnt offering, a nice smell, a bull from the herd, a ram, seven lambs a year old (they're to be ones of yours that are whole);
- ⁹their grain offering: fine flour mixed with oil, three tenths for the bull, two tenths for each ram ¹⁰and one tenth for each lamb, for the seven lambs;
- ¹¹one he-goat from the flock as a decontamination;

apart from the decontamination for complete expiation and the regular burnt offering and its grain offering, and their libations.

¹²On the fifteenth day of the seventh month it's to be a sacred occasion for you. You will not do any servile work. You're to hold a festival for Yahweh for seven days. ¹³You're to present
- a burnt offering, a gift offering, a nice smell for Yahweh: thirteen bulls from the herd, two rams, fourteen lambs a year old (they're to be whole);
- ¹⁴their grain offering: fine flour mixed with oil, three tenths for each bull for the thirteen bulls, two tenths for each ram for the two rams ¹⁵and one tenth for each lamb for the fourteen lambs;
- ¹⁶one he-goat from the flock as a decontamination;

apart from the regular burnt offering, its grain offering, and its libation.

¹⁷On the second day:
- twelve bulls from the herd, two rams, fourteen lambs a year old (ones that are whole);
- ¹⁸their grain offering and their libations for the bulls, for the rams and for the lambs, by their number in accordance with the ruling;
- ¹⁹one he-goat from the flock as a decontamination;

apart from the regular burnt offering, its grain offering and their libations.

²⁰On the third day:
- eleven bulls, two rams, fourteen lambs a year old (ones that are whole);
- ²¹their grain offering and their libations for the bulls, for the rams and for the lambs, by their number in accordance with the ruling;
- ²²one he-goat as a decontamination;

apart from the regular burnt offering, its grain offering and its libation.

Days four to eight

²³On the fourth day:
- ten bulls, two rams, fourteen lambs a year old (ones that are whole);

²⁴their grain offering and their libations for the bulls, for the rams and for the lambs, by their number in accordance with the ruling; ²⁵one he-goat from the flock as a decontamination;

apart from the regular burnt offering, its grain offering and its libation. ²⁶On the fifth day:

nine bulls, two rams, fourteen lambs a year old (ones that are whole); ²⁷their grain offering and their libations for the bulls, for the rams and for the lambs, by their number in accordance with the ruling; ²⁸one he-goat as a decontamination;

apart from the regular burnt offering, its grain offering and its libation. ²⁹On the sixth day:

eight bulls, two rams, fourteen lambs a year old (ones that are whole); ³⁰their grain offering and their libations for the bulls, for the rams and for the lambs, by their number in accordance with the ruling; ³¹one he-goat as a decontamination;

apart from the regular burnt offering, its grain offering and its libation. ³²On the seventh day:

seven bulls, two rams, fourteen lambs a year old (ones that are whole); ³³their grain offering and their libations for the bulls, for the rams and for the lambs, by their number in accordance with the ruling; ³⁴one he-goat as a decontamination;

apart from the regular burnt offering, its grain offering and its libation. ³⁵On the eighth day it's to be an assembly for you. You will not do any servile work. ³⁶You're to present

a burnt offering, a gift offering, a nice smell for Yahweh: a bull, a ram, seven lambs a year old (ones that are whole); ³⁷their grain offering and their libations for the bull, for the ram and for the lambs, by their number in accordance with the ruling; ³⁸one he-goat as a decontamination;

apart from the regular burnt offering, its grain offering and its libation. ³⁹These you're to make for Yahweh at your set times (apart from your pledges and your free offerings) as your burnt offerings, your grain offerings, your libations and your well-being sacrifices."

⁴⁰Mosheh said it to the Yisra'elites in accordance with everything that Yahweh ordered Mosheh.

Promises that affect other people

30 Mosheh spoke to the heads of the Yisra'elites' clans: 'This is the thing Yahweh has ordered: ²when a man makes a pledge to Yahweh or swears an oath to take on an obligation for himself, he will not treat his word as ordinary. He's to act in accordance with everything that comes out of his mouth.

³When a woman makes a pledge to Yahweh or takes on an obligation, in her father's household in her youth, ⁴and her father hears of her pledge or her obligation that she takes on for herself, and her father is silent towards her, all her pledges stand and every obligation of hers that she's taken on herself stands. ⁵But if her father restrains her on the day he hears it, none of her pledges or her obligations that she's taken on for herself stand. Yahweh will pardon her because her father has restrained her.

⁶If actually she comes to belong to a husband when there are pledges binding her or an extravagance that came from her lips that she's taken on for herself, ⁷and her husband hears and is silent towards her on the day he hears, then her pledges stand and her obligation that she's taken on for herself stands. ⁸But if her husband restrains her on the day he hears and contravenes her pledge that was binding her or the extravagance that came from her lips that she had taken on for herself, Yahweh will pardon her. (⁹But the pledge of a widow or a divorcee, everything that she's taken on for herself, stands in respect of her.)

Speak now or for ever hold your peace

¹⁰If in her husband's household she's made a pledge or taken on an obligation for herself by an oath ¹¹and her husband has heard and has been silent towards her (he hasn't restrained her), all her pledges stand and every obligation that she's taken on for herself stands. ¹²But if

her husband does contravene them on the day he hears it, nothing coming from her lips in relation to her pledges or to an obligation that she's taken on for herself stands. Her husband has contravened them and Yahweh will pardon her. ¹³Every pledge and every sworn obligation to humble herself, her husband may let stand or her husband may contravene. ¹⁴If her husband remains quite silent towards her from one day to the next, he lets stand all her pledges and all the obligations that are upon her. He lets them stand because he was silent towards her on the day he heard. ¹⁵If he does contravene them after hearing it, he carries her waywardness.'

¹⁶These are the decrees that Yahweh ordered Mosheh between a husband and his wife, between a father and his daughter in her youth, in her father's household.

Unfinished business

31 Yahweh spoke to Mosheh: ²'Take redress for the Yisra'elites from the Midyanites; afterwards, you will be gathered to your kin.' ³Mosheh spoke to the people: 'Some men from among you are to equip themselves for war and go against Midyan to carry out Yahweh's redress on Midyan. ⁴You're to send off to war a division for each clan, for all the Yisra'elite clans.'

⁵So from the Yisra'elite divisions, a division offered themselves for each clan, twelve divisions equipped for war. ⁶Mosheh sent them off to the war, a division for each clan, with Pinhas ben El'azar as the priest for the war, the sacred articles and the trumpets for sounding in his hand. ⁷They made war against Midyan as Yahweh ordered Mosheh, slaughtered every male ⁸and killed the Midyanite kings: along with the others run through by them, Evi, Reqem, Tsur, Hur and Reba, the five Midyanite kings. And they killed Bil'am ben Be'or with the sword.

⁹The Yisra'elites captured the Midyanite women and their little ones and took as plunder all their animals, all their livestock and all their resources. ¹⁰All their towns among their settlements and all their enclosures they burned in fire. ¹¹They took all the spoil and all the gains, human beings and animals, ¹²and brought the captives, the gains and the spoil to Mosheh and to El'azar the priest, and to the Yisra'elite assembly at the camp in the Mo'ab steppes by the Yarden at Yeriho.

The danger of contamination

¹³Mosheh, El'azar the priest and all the leaders of the assembly came to meet them outside the camp. ¹⁴Mosheh was furious with the people appointed over the force, the divisional officers and the section officers, who had come from battling in the war. ¹⁵Mosheh said to them, 'You've let every female live! ¹⁶Here, at Bil'am's word they were the ones who for the Yisra'elites came to be a means of instigating a trespass against Yahweh in the matter of Pe'or, so that the epidemic came on Yahweh's assembly. ¹⁷So now, kill every male among the little ones and kill every woman who has had sex with someone, who has slept with a man. ¹⁸But all the little ones among the women, who haven't had sex, who haven't slept with a man – let them live for yourselves.

¹⁹You yourselves, camp outside the camp for seven days. Everyone who killed someone and everyone who touched someone who had been run through – you're to decontaminate yourselves on the third day and on the seventh day, you and your captives. ²⁰All clothing, every skin article, everything made of goats' hair and every wood article – you're to decontaminate yourelves.'

²¹El'azar the priest said to the strong men who had come to the battle, 'This is the decree of instruction that Yahweh has ordered Mosheh. ²²However, the gold and the silver, the copper and the iron, the tin and the lead, ²³every object that goes through fire, you're to pass through fire and it will become pure. However, it's to decontaminate itself with the water for flowing. Everything that doesn't go through fire is to pass through water. ²⁴You're to wash your clothes on the seventh day, so you become pure. Afterwards, you may come into the camp.'

Counting the plunder

²⁵Yahweh said to Mosheh: ²⁶'Take the sum total of the gains that were captured, human

beings and animals – you and El'azar the priest and the ancestral heads of the assembly. ²⁷You're to halve the gains between the people who took part in the battle, who went out to the war, and the entire assembly. ²⁸But you're to take up a levy for Yahweh from the people who were in the battle, the people who went out to the war, one living thing in 500, from human beings, from the herd, from donkeys and from the flock. ²⁹You're to take it from their half and give it to El'azar the priest as Yahweh's gift. ³⁰And from the Yisra'elites' half you're to take one that's withheld from fifty, from human beings, from the herd, from donkeys, from the flock and from all the animals, and give them to the Levites, who keep charge of Yahweh's dwelling.'

³¹Mosheh and El'azar the priest did as Yahweh ordered Mosheh. ³²The gains, above and beyond the plunder that the war company took: flock, 675,000; ³³herd, 72,000; ³⁴donkeys, 61,000; ³⁵human beings (from the women who had not had sex, who had not slept with a man), all the people 32,000.

³⁶So the half share of the people who went out in the war was: the number of sheep 337,500, ³⁷so Yahweh's levy from the flock was 675; ³⁸the herd 36,000, so Yahweh's levy 72; ³⁹donkeys 30,500, so Yahweh's levy 61; ⁴⁰human beings 16,000, so Yahweh's levy 32 people. ⁴¹Mosheh gave the levy, Yahweh's gift, to El'azar the priest, as Yahweh had ordered Mosheh.

The levy

⁴²From the Yisra'elites' half which Mosheh divided off from the men who went to war, ⁴³the community's half: from the flock, 337,500; ⁴⁴the herd, 36,000; ⁴⁵donkeys, 30,500; ⁴⁶human beings, 16,000. ⁴⁷Mosheh took from the Yisra'elites' half the one withheld from 50 of the human beings and of the animals and gave them to the Levites who keep charge of Yahweh's dwelling, as Yahweh had ordered Mosheh.

⁴⁸The people who had been appointed for the army divisions (the divisional officers and the section officers) drew near to Mosheh. ⁴⁹They said to Mosheh, 'Your servants have taken the sum total of the men who were in the battle who were in our control, and no one has absented himself from us. ⁵⁰We are presenting Yahweh's offering, each individual who found a gold article: a bangle or a bracelet, a ring, an earring or a necklace, for making expiation for ourselves before Yahweh.' ⁵¹Mosheh and El'azar the priest took the gold from them, all the articles of workmanship. ⁵²All the gold, the gift that they took up for Yahweh, came to 16,750 sheqels, from the divisional officers and from the section officers; ⁵³the people in the army had taken plunder each individual for himself.

⁵⁴So Mosheh and El'azar the priest took the gold from the divisional officers and from the section officers and brought it into the appointment tent as a reminder for the Yisra'elites before Yahweh.

Cattle country

32 Now the Re'ubenites and the Gadites had much livestock, very numerous, and they looked at the country of Ya'zer and Gil'ad: there, the place was a place for livestock. ²So the Gadites and Re'ubenites came and said to Mosheh, to El'azar the priest and to the assembly's leaders, ³'Atarot, Dibon, Ya'zer, Nimrah, Heshbon, El'alah, Sebam, Nebo and Be'on, ⁴the region that Yahweh has struck down before the Yisra'elite assembly, is livestock country, and your servants have livestock.'

⁵So they said, 'If we have found grace in your eyes, may this region be given to your servants as a holding. Don't make us cross the Yarden.' ⁶Mosheh said to the Gadites and to the Re'ubenites, 'Are your brothers to come into battle while you people live here? ⁷Why would you restrain the Yisra'elites' mind from crossing into the country that Yahweh has given them? ⁸Your fathers did so when I sent them from Qadesh Barnea to look at the country. ⁹They went up as far as Cluster Wadi and looked at the country but restrained the Yisra'elites' mind so they wouldn't come into the country that Yahweh had given them. ¹⁰And Yahweh's anger raged that day and he swore: ¹¹"If the people who went up from Misrayim, from the age of twenty years and upwards, see the land that I swore to Abraham, Yitshaq and Ya'aqob . . . Because they didn't fully follow after me", ¹²except Kaleb ben

Yephunneh the Qenizzite and Yehoshua ben Nun, because they fully followed after Yahweh. ¹³Yahweh's anger raged against Yisra'el and he made them wander in the wilderness for forty years until the entire generation that acted badly in Yahweh's eyes was finished.

¹⁴So here, you've risen in place of your fathers as a multitude of wrongdoers to add further to Yahweh's angry rage towards Yisra'el. ¹⁵When you turn back from following him, he will once again settle it down in the wilderness, and you'll destroy this entire people.'

Mutual support

¹⁶They came up to him and said, 'We'll build sheepfolds here for our livestock and towns for our little ones, ¹⁷but we ourselves will equip ourselves as shock troops before the Yisra'elites till we've enabled them to come to their place, while our little ones live in the fortified towns, because of the people who live in the country. ¹⁸We won't come back to our houses till the Yisra'elites, each one, has entered into his domain. ¹⁹Because we won't have a domain with them across the Yarden yonder, because our domain has come to us across the Yarden on the east.'

²⁰Mosheh said to them. 'If you do this thing, if you equip yourselves before Yahweh for battle, ²¹and every one of you who is equipped crosses over the Yarden before Yahweh till he's dispossessed his enemies from before him ²²and the country is in subjection before Yahweh, you can come back afterwards and be free in relation to Yahweh and to Yisra'el, and this region will be your holding before Yahweh. ²³But if you don't do so: there, you will have done wrong in relation to Yahweh. Acknowledge the wrongdoing you would do, which will find you. ²⁴Build yourselves towns for your little ones and folds for your sheep. But what has gone out of your mouth, you're to do.'

²⁵The Gadites and Re'ubenites said to Mosheh, 'Your servants will do as my lord is ordering. ²⁶Our little ones, our wives, our livestock and all our animals will be there in the towns of Gil'ad, ²⁷while your servants will cross over for battle, everyone equipped for war before Yahweh for battle, as my lord is saying.'

The region across the Yarden

²⁸So Mosheh gave an order about them to El'azar the priest, to Yehoshua ben Nun and to the ancestral heads of the clans of the Yisra'elites. ²⁹Mosheh said to them, 'If the Gadites and Re'ubenites cross over the Yarden with you, each one equipped for battle before Yahweh, and the country is in subjection before you, you may give them the region of Gil'ad as a holding, ³⁰but if they don't cross over equipped with you, they will receive holdings among you in the country of Kena'an.'

³¹The Gadites and Re'ubenites avowed, 'What Yahweh has spoken to your servants, so we will do. ³²We ourselves will cross over equipped before Yahweh to the country of Kena'an, but the domain which is our holding will be with us across the Yarden.'

³³So Mosheh gave to them (to the Gadites, to the Re'ubenites and to the half-clan of Menashsheh ben Yoseph) the kingdom of Sihon king of the Amorites and the kingdom of Og king of Bashan, the country with its towns in the territories of the country's towns, all round. ³⁴The Gadites built up Dibon, Atarot, Aro'er, ³⁵Atrot Shophan, Ya'zer, Yogbehah, ³⁶Bet Nimrah and Bet Haran, as fortified towns and sheepfolds. ³⁷The Re'ubenites built up Heshbon, El'ale, Qiryatayim, ³⁸Nebo, Ba'al Me'on (these were changed in name) and Sibmah. They gave names to the towns that they built up.

³⁹The descendants of Makir ben Menashsheh went to Gil'ad, captured it and dispossessed the Amorites who were there. ⁴⁰Mosheh gave Gil'ad to Makir ben Menashsheh and he lived there. ⁴¹When Ya'ir ben Menashsheh went and captured their villages, he named them Ya'ir's Villages. ⁴²When Nobah went and captured Qenat and its daughter-towns, he named it Nobah, after his own name.

The stages of the journey

33 These were the movements of the Yisra'elites who came out of the country of Misrayim by their troops at the direction of Mosheh and Aharon. ²Mosheh wrote down their departure points for their movements at Yahweh's bidding. These were the movements by their starting points.

³They moved on from Ra'meses in the first month, on the fifteenth day of the first month. On the day after the Pesah the Yisra'elites went out with hands high before the eyes of all Misrayim ⁴as the Misrayimites were burying the people Yahweh had struck down among them, every firstborn; on their gods Yahweh had performed acts of authority.

⁵The Yisra'elites moved on from Ra'meses and camped at Sukkot.

⁶They moved on from Sukkot and camped at Etam, which is on the edge of the wilderness.

⁷They moved on from Etam and turned back towards Pi Hahirot, which is on the east of Ba'al Tsephon, and camped near Migdol.

⁸They moved on from Pene Hahirot, passed through the middle of the sea into the wilderness, went three days' journey in the Etam Wilderness and camped at Marah.

⁹They moved on from Marah, came to Elim, and at Elim there were twelve springs of water and seventy palms, and they camped there.

¹⁰They moved on from Elim and camped by the Reed Sea.

¹¹They moved on from the Reed Sea and camped in the Syn Wilderness.

¹²They moved on from the Syn Wilderness and camped at Dophqah.

¹³They moved on from Dophqah and camped at Alush.

¹⁴They moved on from Alush and camped at Rephidim, and there was no water for the people to drink there.

Up to the death of Aharon

¹⁵They moved on from Rephidim and camped in the Sinay Wilderness.

¹⁶They moved on from the Sinay Wilderness and camped at Qibrot Hatta'avah.

¹⁷They moved on from Qibrot Hatta'avah and camped at Hatserot.

¹⁸They moved on from Hatserot and camped at Ritmah.

¹⁹They moved on from Ritmah and camped at Rimmon Perets.

²⁰They moved on from Rimmon Perets and camped at Libnah.

²¹They moved on from Libnah and camped at Rissah.

²²They moved on from Rissah and camped at Qehelat.

²³They moved on from Qehelat and camped at Mount Shepher.

²⁴They moved on from Mount Shepher and camped at Haradah.

²⁵They moved on from Haradah and camped at Maqhelot.

²⁶They moved on from Maqhelot and camped at Tahat.

²⁷They moved on from Tahat and camped at Terah.

²⁸They moved on from Terah and camped at Mitqah.

²⁹They moved on from Mitqah and camped at Hashmonah.

³⁰They moved on from Hashmonah and camped at Moserot.

³¹They moved on from Moserot and camped at Bene Ya'aqan.

³²They moved on from Bene Ya'aqan and camped at Hor Haggidgad.

³³They moved on from Hor Haggidgad and camped at Yotbatah.

³⁴They moved on from Yotbatah and camped at Abronah.

³⁵They moved on from Abronah and camped at Etsyon Geber.

³⁶They moved on from Etsyon Geber and camped in the Tsin Wilderness – i.e. Qadesh.

³⁷They moved on from Qadesh and camped at Mount Hor on the edge of the country of Edom.

³⁸Aharon the priest went up Mount Hor at Yahweh's bidding and died there in the fortieth year after the Yisra'elites left the country of Misrayim, in the fifth month, on the first of the month. ³⁹Aharon was a man of 123 years when he died on Mount Hor.

⁴⁰The Kena'anite, the king of Arad (he was living in the Negeb, in the country of Kena'an), heard about the coming of the Yisra'elites.

Almost the end

⁴¹They moved on from Mount Hor and camped at Tsalmonah.

⁴²They moved on from Tsalmonah and camped at Punon.
⁴³They moved on from Punon and camped at Obot.
⁴⁴They moved on from Obot and camped at Iyyim in the Regions Across, within the border of Mo'ab.
⁴⁵They moved on from Iyyim and camped at Dibon Gad.
⁴⁶They moved on from Dibon Gad and camped at Almon Diblatayim.
⁴⁷They moved on from Almon Diblatayim and camped in the mountains of the Regions Across, near Nebo.
⁴⁸They moved on from the mountains of the Regions Across and camped in the Mo'ab steppes by the Yarden at Yeriho.
⁴⁹They camped by the Yarden from Bet Hayeshimot as far as Acacias Meadow in the Mo'ab steppes.
⁵⁰Yahweh spoke to Mosheh in the Mo'ab steppes by the Yarden at Yeriho: ⁵¹"Speak to the Yisra'elites and say to them: "When you're crossing the Yarden into the country of Kena'an, ⁵²you're to dispossess all the people living in the country from before you, obliterate all their carvings, obliterate all their cast images and annihilate all their shrines, ⁵³and to take possession of the country and live in it, because I am giving the country to you to take possession of. ⁵⁴You're to have the country as a domain by lot by your kin-groups. For a large one you're to make its domain large and for a small one to make its domain small. Wherever the lot comes out for it, that's where it will be for it, as you enter into your domain by your ancestral clans.
⁵⁵If you don't dispossess the people living in the country from before you, the ones among them whom you allow to remain will be barbs in your eyes and thorns in your sides. They will attack you in the country where you're living, ⁵⁶and what I imagined doing to them I'll do to you.'"

The dimensions of the country

34 Yahweh spoke to Mosheh: ²'Order the Yisra'elites: "When you come into the country of Kena'an, this is the country that will fall to you as a domain, the country of Kena'an by its borders.

³Your southern aspect will go from the Tsin Wilderness along the sides of Edom. Your southern border will go from the end of the Salt Sea on the east. ⁴Your border will be south of Scorpions Ascent and pass on to Tsin and its furthest extent will be south of Qadesh Barnea. It will extend to Hatsar-addar and pass on to Atsmon. ⁵The border will go round from Atsmon to the Misrayimite Wadi and its furthest extent will be at the Sea.
⁶The western border: it will be the Great Sea for you. This will be your western border, the Great Sea.
⁷This will be your northern border: from the Great Sea you're to mark out Mount Hor for yourselves. ⁸From Mount Hor you're to mark out Lebo Hamat. The border's furthest extent will be Tsedad ⁹and the border will extend to Ziphron; its furthest extent will be Hatsar Enan. This will be your northern border.
¹⁰You're to mark out for yourselves as your eastern border from Hatsar Enan to Shepham. ¹¹The border will go down from Shepham to Hariblah on the east of Ayin. The border will go down and hit the flank of the Kinneret Sea on the east.
¹²The border will go down to the Yarden and its furthest extents will be the Salt Sea. This will be your country in respect of your borders all round."'
¹³Mosheh ordered the Yisra'elites: 'This is the country that you're to enter into as a domain by lot, which Yahweh ordered to give to the nine-and-a-half clans, ¹⁴because the clan of the Re'ubenites by their ancestral household, the clan of the Gadites by their ancestral household and the half-clan of Menashsheh have received their domain, ¹⁵in that the two-and-a-half clans have received their domain across the Yarden at Yeriho on the east, towards the sunrise.'

Twelve trusted men

¹⁶Yahweh spoke to Mosheh: ¹⁷"These are the names of the people who will make the country into domains for you: El'azar the priest and Yehoshua ben Nun. ¹⁸You're to get one leader from each clan to make the country into domains. ¹⁹These are the people's names:

for the clan of Yehudah, Kaleb ben Yephunneh; ²⁰for the clan of the Shim'onites, Shemu'el ben Ammihud; ²¹for the clan of Binyamin, Elidad ben Kislon; ²²for the clan of the Danites as leader, Buqqi ben Yogli; ²³for the Yosephites:

> for the clan of the Menashshites as leader, Hanni'el ben Ephod; ²⁴and for the clan of the Ephrayimites as leader, Qemu'el ben Shiphtan;

²⁵for the clan of the Zebulunites as leader, Elitsaphan ben Parnak; ²⁶for the clan of the Yissakarites as leader, Palti'el ben Azzan; ²⁷for the clan of the Asherites as leader, Ahihud ben Shelomi; ²⁸and for the clan of the Naphtalites as leader, Pedahel ben Ammihud.'

²⁹These are the people whom Yahweh ordered to make the country into domains for the Yisra'elites in the country of Kena'an.

35 Yahweh spoke to Mosheh in the Mo'ab steppes by the Yarden at Yeriho: ²'Order the Yisra'elites that they're to give the Levites towns to live in, out of the domain they hold, and they're to give the Levites the towns' pastureland round them. ³The towns will be theirs to live in and their pasturelands will be for their animals, for their property and for all their creatures. ⁴The pasturelands of the towns that you're to give the Levites will be from the town wall outwards, 500 metres round. ⁵Outside the town, you're to measure on the east side 1,000 metres, on the south side 1,000 metres, on the west side 1,000 metres and on the north side 1,000 metres, with the town in the middle. This will be the towns' pasturelands for them.

The asylum towns

⁶The towns that you give to the Levites will be the six asylum towns that you give a killer to flee to, but you're to give forty-two towns along with them. ⁷All the towns that you give to the Levites will be forty-eight towns, them and their pasturelands. ⁸The towns that you give from the Yisra'elites' holding: from a large one make it large and from a small one make it small. Each in proportion to the domain it receives is to give some of its towns to the Levites.'

⁹Yahweh spoke to Mosheh: ¹⁰'Speak to the Yisra'elites: "When you're crossing the Yarden into the country of Kena'an, ¹¹you're to appoint for yourselves towns that will be asylum towns for you, so a killer who strikes down a person by accident may flee there. ¹²The towns will be an asylum for you from the restorer. The killer will not die until he's stood before the assembly for a ruling.

¹³The towns that you're to set: you're to have six asylum towns. ¹⁴You're to set three towns across the Yarden and set three towns in the country of Kena'an. They will be asylum towns. ¹⁵For the Yisra'elites, for the resident and for the settler among them, these six towns are to be for asylum for anyone who strikes down a person by accident to flee there.

¹⁶But if he struck him down with an iron object and he died, he's a killer; the killer is absolutely to be put to death. ¹⁷If he struck him down with a stone in his hand by which someone might die and he dies, he's a killer; the killer is absolutely to be put to death. ¹⁸Or if he struck him down with a wooden object in his hand by which someone might die and he dies, he's a killer; the killer is absolutely to be put to death. ¹⁹The blood restorer himself is to put the killer to death. On coming upon him, he's to put him to death.

Deciding on responsibility

²⁰If he knocks him down in hostility or he threw something at him with deliberation and he died, ²¹or he struck him down with his hand in enmity and he died, the one who struck down is absolutely to be put to death. He's a killer. The blood restorer is to put the killer to death on coming upon him.

²²But if he knocked him down on meeting him without enmity, or threw any object at him without deliberation ²³or with any stone by which he might die, without seeing, but he made it fall on him and he died, but he was not his enemy and was not seeking something bad for him, ²⁴the assembly is to decide between the one who strikes down and the blood restorer. ²⁵The assembly is to rescue the killer from the hand of the blood restorer.

The assembly is to take him back to his asylum town, to which he had fled, and he's to live in it until the death of the great priest whom they anointed with the sacred oil. ²⁶But if the killer actually goes out of the boundary of his asylum town to which he's fled, ²⁷and the blood restorer finds him outside the boundary of his asylum town, and the blood restorer kills the killer, there's no blood attaching to him, ²⁸because he was to live in his asylum town until the great priest's death. After the great priest's death the killer may go back to the region of his holding.

²⁹These are to be the ruling decree for you through your generations in all your settlements.

³⁰Anyone who strikes a person down, it's at the mouth of witnesses that people may kill the killer, and one witness will not avow against a person so he dies. ³¹You will not accept a ransom for the life of a killer who is in the wrong and should die, because he is absolutely to be put to death. ³²And you will not accept a ransom in respect of fleeing to his asylum town, so that he may go back to live in the region before the priest's death. ³³You will not pollute the country where you are, because blood pollutes the country and the country cannot be expiated for blood that has been shed in it except by the blood of the one who shed it. ³⁴You will not make taboo the country in which you're living, within which I'm dwelling, because I am Yahweh dwelling among the Yisra'elites.'"

The five pushy women pushed back a bit

36 The ancestral heads of the kin-group of the descendants of Gil'ad ben Makir, son of Menashsheh, from the kin-groups of the Yosephites, drew near and spoke before Mosheh and before the leaders, the ancestral heads of the Yisra'elites. ²They said, 'Yahweh ordered my lord to give the country to the Yisra'elites as a domain by lot, and my lord was ordered by Yahweh to give our brother Tselophhad's domain to his daughters. ³But they may become wives of someone from the members of the other Yisra'elite clans, and their domain will disappear from our ancestral domain and add to the domain of the clan to which they come to belong; it will disappear from our domain by lot. ⁴And if the Yisra'elites have a ram's horn [year], their domain will add to the domain of the clan to which they belong; from the domain of our ancestral clan their domain will disappear.'

⁵So Mosheh ordered the Yisra'elites at Yahweh's bidding: 'The Yosephite clan are speaking correctly. ⁶This is the thing that Yahweh has ordered concerning Tselophhad's daughters: "They may become the wives of whoever is good in their eyes, yet they're to become wives of a kin-group in their father's clan. ⁷The domain of the Yisra'elites will not go round from clan to clan, because the Yisra'elites are to attach themselves, each individual, to his clan's ancestral domain. ⁸Any daughter who possesses a domain from the Yisra'elites' clans is to become the wife of someone from a kin-group in her ancestral clan, in order that the Yisra'elites may possess, each person, his ancestral domain. ⁹No domain will go round from a clan to another clan because the clans of the Yisra'elites are to attach themselves, each individual, to his domain."'

¹⁰As Yahweh ordered Mosheh, so Tselophhad's daughters did. ¹¹Mahlah, Tirtsah, Hoglah, Milkah and No'ah, Tselophhad's daughters, became wives of their uncles' sons. ¹²They became wives in the kin-groups of the descendants of Menashsheh ben Yoseph, and their domain was in the clan of their ancestral kin-group.

¹³These are the orders and the rulings that Yahweh gave to the Yisra'elites through Mosheh in the Mo'ab steppes by the Yarden at Yeriho.

Deuteronomy

The name 'Deutero-nomy' gives the impression that this document gives us a 'second law', and that's not a bad description of it. The first law is then the teaching Yahweh gave Moses at Sinay, which dominates the second half of Exodus and the whole of Leviticus. Deuteronomy is another version of that teaching, retreading much of the same ground as the first. We noted in the Introduction to Leviticus that the Torah brings together several versions of the way God laid the law down to Israel over the centuries. God guided his people in changing social contexts by means of people such as priests, prophets and writers, who in effect presented their teaching as what Moses would say if he were here now, and people accepted it as such. They recognized that it was Moses' God who had been speaking to them in their new context.

In Deuteronomy as in Leviticus, the social context is more developed and urban than it is in the older teaching in Exodus. But Deuteronomy no longer looks at matters that priests especially need to know about, as Leviticus does. It talks about issues such as the sort of person the king ought to be and the need to tell the difference between a real prophet and a pretend prophet. That last question was a lively one in Jeremiah's day, and it wouldn't be surprising if that period (the seventh century) forms the background to Deuteronomy. One of the kings of that time, Josiah, attempted a brave reform of Judah's life and religion, seeking to remove features that reflected more the way the Canaanites and the Assyrians thought of God than the way the Israelites ought to think of God (you can read his story in 2 Kings 22—23), and there are overlaps between Josiah's reformation and the teaching of Deuteronomy.

Another feature of Deuteronomy that makes sense against this background is its emphasis on the pact between Yahweh and Israel, which it portrays along the lines of the treaty relationship that obtained between the imperial power of Assyria and a little people like Judah. In effect Deuteronomy says, 'You know how the Assyrians expect you to relate to them, with them as the big power and you expected to do what they say? Well, I'll tell you who is really the big power and what *he* expects you to do.'

As a treaty/pact/covenant document, Deuteronomy outlines as follows:

1—3   The relationship between the two parties in the past
4—11 The big power's basic expectations, especially of loyalty
12—26 The big power's detailed expectations
27   Regulations for the formalizing of the relationship
28—30 The blessings of cooperation, and the opposite
31—34 Moses' final words

The long section of detailed expectations compares with another kind of document we know from the Middle East, one in which a king would expound some of his social and legal policies.

Jesus suggests several guidelines for discerning how we learn from Deuteronomy. He takes some key principles for relating to God from Deuteronomy 4—11 (see Matthew 4.1–11). He declares that the Torah as a whole is an exposition of Deuteronomy 6.5 and Leviticus 19.18 (see Matthew 22.37), so that in reading Deuteronomy it's always worth asking how its requirements are an exposition of love for God or love for one's neighbour. Jesus also takes up Deuteronomy's own affirmation that it is written the way it is because it makes allowance for people's stubbornness (Matthew 19.1–8), so that in reading Deuteronomy, it's also worth asking, how is God making allowance for our stubbornness here?

Mosheh (Moses) begins his last sermon

1 These are the words that Mosheh spoke to all Yisra'el [Israel] across the Yarden [Jordan] in the wilderness, in the steppe near Suph, between Pa'ran and Tophel, Laban, Hatserot and Di Zahab. (²It's eleven days from Horeb by way of Mount Se'ir to Qadesh Barnea.) ³In the fortieth year in the eleventh month on the first of the month, Mosheh spoke to the Yisra'elites in accordance with everything Yahweh had ordered him for them, ⁴after he had struck down Sihon king of the Amorites who was living in Heshbon and Og king of Bashan who was living in Ashtarot (in Edre'i). ⁵Across the Yarden, in the country of Mo'ab, Mosheh resolved to expound this instruction.

⁶Yahweh our God himself spoke to us at Horeb: 'Your stay at this mountain has been long. ⁷Turn your face, move yourselves on, come to the highland of the Amorites and to all their neighbours in the steppe, in the highland, in the foothills, in the Negeb, on the sea coast (the country of the Kena'anites [Canaanites]) and the Lebanon, as far as the big river (the River Euphrates). ⁸See, I've put the country before you. Come and take possession of the country that Yahweh swore to your ancestors, to Abraham, to Yitshaq [Isaac] and to Ya'aqob [Jacob], to give to them and to their offspring after them.'

⁹I said to you at that time, 'I can't carry you alone; ¹⁰Yahweh your God has made you numerous. Here you are today, like the stars in the heavens in the large number. ¹¹May Yahweh the God of our ancestors add to you as you are, a thousand times, and bless you as he spoke to you. ¹²Alone, how can I carry the weight of you, the burden of you and your arguing? ¹³Provide for yourselves people who are smart, discerning and knowledgeable for your clans, and I will make them into your heads.'

Recalling the time in the wilderness

¹⁴You answered me, 'The thing that you spoke of is good to do.' ¹⁵So I got your clan heads, people who were smart and knowledgeable, and made them heads over you, divisional officials, section officials, unit officials, group officials and overseers for your clans. ¹⁶I ordered the people in authority over you at that time: 'Listen between your brothers and exercise authority faithfully between an individual and his brother and a resident. ¹⁷You will not recognize a person in making a decision. Listen to the small as you listen to the big. You will be in dread of no one's person, because decision-making belongs to God. The thing that's too tough for you, present to me, and I'll listen to it.'

¹⁸I gave you orders at that time about all the things that you should do. ¹⁹We moved on from Horeb and went through that entire great, awe-inspiring wilderness that you saw on the way to the Amorite highland, as Yahweh our God ordered us, and we came as far as Qadesh Barnea. ²⁰I said to you, 'You've come as far as the Amorite highland, which Yahweh our God is giving to us. ²¹See, Yahweh your God has put the country before you. Go up, take possession, as Yahweh the God of your ancestors spoke to you. Don't be afraid. Don't be scared.'

²²You all drew near to me and said, 'Let's send people before us so they can check out the country for us and bring us back word about the way by which we should go up, and the towns that we shall come to.' ²³The thing was good in my eyes, and I got from you twelve people, one individual for each clan. ²⁴They turned their face and went up into the highland and came as far as Cluster Wadi. They investigated it ²⁵and got some of the country's fruit in their hand and carried it down to us. They brought us back word, and said, 'The country that Yahweh our God is giving us is good.'

Recalling the failure of nerve

²⁶But you were not willing to go up. You rebelled against the bidding of Yahweh your God. ²⁷You muttered in your tents and said, 'It was because of Yahweh's hostility towards us that he got us out of the country of Misrayim [Egypt] to give us into the hand of the Amorites, to annihilate us. ²⁸Where are we going up to? Our brothers have made our minds melt, saying "It was a people bigger and taller than us, and towns big and fortified to the heavens, and also Anaqites, that we saw there."'

²⁹I said to you, 'You will not be frightened; you will not be afraid of them. ³⁰Yahweh your God is going before you. He will do battle for you, in accordance with all that he did with you in Misrayim before your eyes, ³¹and in the wilderness where you saw how Yahweh your God carried you as a man carries his son, on the entire way that you went until you came to this place. ³²Despite this fact, you don't trust in Yahweh your God ³³who goes before you on the way to investigate a place for you to camp, in fire by night (to enable you to see the way by which you should go) and in a cloud by day.'

³⁴Yahweh heard the sound of your words and he was furious. He swore, ³⁵'If an individual among these people, this bad generation, sees the good country that I swore to give to your ancestors . . . ³⁶Except Kaleb [Caleb] ben Yephunneh, he will see it. To him I'll give the country on which he set foot, and to his descendants, because of the fact that he fully followed after Yahweh.'

How Mosheh paid a price

³⁷With me, too, Yahweh showed himself angry, on your account, saying 'You too will not come there. ³⁸Yehoshua [Joshua] ben Nun, who stands before you, he will come there. Strengthen him, because he's the one who will enable Yisra'el to take it as a domain.

³⁹Your little ones, who you said would become plunder, and your children who haven't got to know good from bad today, they'll come there. To them I'll give it. They'll take possession of it. ⁴⁰But you, turn your face for yourselves, move on into the wilderness by the Reed Sea road.'

⁴¹You answered, 'We've done wrong in relation to Yahweh. We ourselves will go up and do battle in accordance with all that Yahweh our God ordered us.' And you wrapped on your battle gear, each person, and got ready to go up into the highland. ⁴²But Yahweh said to me, 'Say to them, "You will not go up and you will not do battle, because I will not be among you so that you don't take a beating before your enemies."'

⁴³I spoke to you, but you didn't listen. You rebelled against Yahweh's bidding and asserted yourselves and went up into the highland. ⁴⁴And the Amorites who live in that highland came out to meet you and pursued you as bees do. They crushed you in Se'ir as far as Hormah. ⁴⁵You again wailed before Yahweh, but Yahweh didn't listen to your voice. He didn't give ear to you. ⁴⁶So you stayed at Qadesh for a long time, the very time that you stayed there.

2 Then we turned our face and moved on into the wilderness by the Reed Sea road, as Yahweh spoke to me. We went round the highland of Se'ir for a long time.

The beginning of the end

²Then Yahweh said to me: ³'Your going round this highland has been long. Turn your face for yourselves north. ⁴Order the people: "You're going to pass through the border of your brothers, Esaw's descendants, who live in Se'ir. They'll be afraid of you. You're to keep close watch on yourselves: ⁵don't engage them, because I shall not give you any of their country, as much as the sole of a foot treads on, because I gave Esaw Mount Se'ir as a possession. ⁶You may buy food from them for silver so you may eat, and you may also purchase water from them for silver so you may drink. ⁷Because Yahweh your God has blessed you in all the action of your hand. He's known your going through this great wilderness. Yahweh your God being with you these forty years, you haven't lacked anything."'

⁸We passed on, away from our brothers, Esaw's descendants, who live in Se'ir, away from the steppe road, away from Elat and from Etsyon Geber. We turned our face and passed by the Mo'ab Wilderness road. ⁹Yahweh said to me, 'Don't attack Mo'ab. Don't engage them in battle, because I shall not give you any of its country as a possession, because I gave Ar to Lot's descendants as a possession.

(¹⁰The Terrors lived in it before, a big and numerous people, and as tall as the Anaqites. ¹¹They are also thought of as Repha'ites, like the Anaqites, but the Mo'abites call them Terrors. ¹²The Horites lived in Se'ir before, but Esaw's descendants dispossessed them, annihilated them from before them and lived in their place, as Yisra'el did in connection with the country it came to possess, which Yahweh gave them.)

¹³Now, set off, get yourselves across Wadi Zered.' So we crossed Wadi Zered.

When the old generation is gone

¹⁴The time that we were going from Qadesh Barnea until we crossed Wadi Zered was thirty-eight years, until the entire generation of men of battle came to an end from within the camp, as Yahweh swore about them. ¹⁵Indeed, Yahweh's hand was against them to root them out from within the camp, until they came to an end. ¹⁶When all the men of battle came to an end, dying from within the camp, ¹⁷Yahweh spoke to me: ¹⁸'Today you're passing through Mo'ab's border, through Ar, ¹⁹and you will draw near to the Ammonites. Don't attack them. Don't engage with them, because I shall not give you any of the Ammonites' country as a possession, because I've given it to Lot's descendants as a possession.

(²⁰It is also thought of as the country of the Repha'ites; they lived in it before. The Ammonites call them Zamzummites, ²¹a people big and numerous, and as tall as the Anaqites. Yahweh annihilated them from before them, and they dispossessed them and lived in their place, ²²as he did for Esaw's descendants who live in Se'ir, in that he annihilated the Horites from before them. They dispossessed them and lived in their place, until this day. ²³The Avvites who lived in villages as far as Azzah [Gaza] – the Kaphtorites who came from Kaphtor annihilated them and lived in their place.)

²⁴Set off, move on, cross Wadi Arnon, see, I've given Sihon king of Heshbon, the Amorite, into your hand, he and his country. Start taking possession. Engage them in battle. ²⁵This day I shall start putting dread of you and fear of you on the face of the peoples under the entire heavens, peoples who will hear report of you and tremble and shake before you.'

An attempt to be peaceful

²⁶I sent envoys from the Easterlies Wilderness to Sihon king of Heshbon with words of peace: ²⁷'I want to pass through your country by the road. I shall go by the road. I shall not turn aside right or left. ²⁸You can sell me food for silver so I may eat, and you can give me water for silver so I can drink. I only want to pass through on foot ²⁹(as Esaw's descendants who live in Se'ir did for me, and the Mo'abites who live in Ar) until I cross the Yarden into the country that Yahweh our God is giving us.'

³⁰But Sihon king of Heshbon was not willing to let us pass through, because Yahweh had toughened his spirit and made his mind firm in order to give him into your hand this very day. ³¹Yahweh said to me, 'See, I've started giving over before you Sihon and his country. Start taking possession of his country.'

³²Sihon came out to meet us in battle, he and his entire people, at Yahats, ³³but Yahweh our God gave him over before us and we struck him down, he and his sons and his entire people. ³⁴We captured all his towns at that time and devoted every town, men, women and little ones. We let no survivor remain. ³⁵Only the animals did we take as plunder for ourselves, and the spoil in the towns that we captured. ³⁶From Aro'er, which is on the edge of Wadi Arnon, and the town that's in the wadi, as far as Gil'ad, there was no township that was too high for us. Yahweh our God gave over everything before us. ³⁷Only, you didn't draw near to the country of the Ammonites, the entire bank of Wadi Yabboq and the towns in the highland – everything that Yahweh our God ordered.

3 We turned our face and went up the Bashan road. Og king of Bashan came out to meet us in battle, he and his entire company, at Edre'i. ²Yahweh said to me, 'Don't be afraid of him, because I've given him into your hand, him and his entire people and his country. You're to do to him as you did to Sihon king of the Amorites, who was living in Heshbon.'

The man with the huge iron bed

³So Yahweh our God also gave Og king of Bashan into our hand, he and his entire company. We struck him down until no survivor remained to him. ⁴We captured all his towns at that time. There was no township

that we didn't take from them: sixty towns (the entire Argob area, Og's kingdom in Bashan), ⁵all these towns fortified with a lofty wall, doors and a bar, apart from the country towns, very many. ⁶We devoted them as we did Sihon king of Heshbon, devoting every town: men, the women and the little ones. ⁷But all the animals and the spoil in the towns we took as plunder for ourselves.

⁸So at that time we took from the hand of the two Amorite kings the country that was across the Yarden, from Wadi Arnon as far as Mount Hermon (⁹the Tsidonites call Hermon Siryon and the Amorites call it Senir), ¹⁰all the towns in the flatland, all Gil'ad and all Bashan as far as Salkah and Edre'i, the towns of Og's kingdom in Bashan . . .

(¹¹Because only Og king of Bashan remained of what was left of the Repha'ites. There, his bed, a bed made of iron – it's in Rabbah of the Ammonites, isn't it – was five metres in its length and two metres in its width by the human measure. ¹²So we took possession of this region at that time. From Aro'er, which is near Wadi Arnon, and half the highland of Gil'ad and its towns, I gave to the Re'ubenites and to the Gadites. ¹³The rest of Gil'ad and all Bashan, Og's kingdom, I gave to the half-clan of Menashsheh. The entire Argob area (all that part of Bashan used to be called the region of the Repha'ites): ¹⁴Ya'ir ben Menashsheh received the entire Argob area as far as the border of the Geshurites and the Ma'akatites. He named them after his own name (Bashan), Ya'ir's Villages, until this day. ¹⁵To Makir I gave Gil'ad. ¹⁶To the Re'ubenites and to the Gadites I gave the part of Gil'ad as far as Wadi Arnon, the middle of the wadi, the border and as far as Wadi Yabboq, the Ammonites' border.)

¹⁷. . . the steppe, and the Yarden as the border from Kinneret as far as the Steppe Sea (the Salt Sea) beneath the Pisgah slopes on the east.

The plea Yahweh will not answer

¹⁸I ordered you at that time: 'Yahweh your God has given you this country, to take possession of it. You're to cross equipped before your brothers, the Yisra'elites, all the forceful men. ¹⁹Only your wives, your little ones and your livestock (I know that you have much livestock) are to stay in your towns which I've given you, ²⁰till Yahweh enables your brothers to settle down like you and they too take possession of the country that Yahweh your God is giving them across the Yarden. Then you may go back each individual to his possession, which I have given you.'

²¹I ordered Yehoshua at that time, 'Your eyes see all that Yahweh your God did to these two kings. So will Yahweh do to all the kingdoms into which you're crossing. ²²You will not be afraid of them, because Yahweh your God – he will do battle for you.'

²³I pleaded with Yahweh for grace at that time: ²⁴'My Lord Yahweh, you yourself started to let your servant see your greatness and your strong hand. Who is the God in the heavens or on the earth who does things like your deeds and your acts of strength? ²⁵I want to cross, please, and see the good country that's across the Yarden, this good highland and the Lebanon.'

²⁶But Yahweh was incensed with me on your account, and wouldn't listen to me. Yahweh said, 'That's plenty for you. Don't ever speak to me again about this matter. ²⁷Go up to the top of Pisgah, lift up your eyes west, north, south and east. Look with your eyes, because you will not cross this Yarden. ²⁸Give Yehoshua orders, get him to be strong and to stand firm, because he's the one who will cross before this people, and he will enable them to take possession of the country you will see.'

²⁹So we stayed in the ravine near Bet Pe'or.

What nation has a story like Yisra'el's?

4 Now, Yisra'el, listen to the decrees and to the rulings that I am teaching you to act on, in order that you may live, and go in and take possession of the country that Yahweh the God of your ancestors is giving you. ²You will not add to the word that I'm ordering you and you will not take away from it, in keeping the orders of Yahweh your God that I'm giving you. ³Your eyes are the ones that saw what Yahweh did in connection with Master-of-Pe'or, that Yahweh your God eliminated from among you every individual who followed Master-of-Pe'or, ⁴but you who attached yourselves to Yahweh your God are all of you alive today.

⁵See, I am teaching you decrees and rulings, as Yahweh my God has ordered me, so you may act in this way within the country where you're coming to take possession of it. ⁶Keep them and act on them, because it will be your smartness and your discernment before the eyes of the peoples, who will listen to all these decrees and say, 'Really, this great nation is a smart and discerning people.'

⁷Because who is a great nation that has gods near to it like Yahweh our God whenever we call to him? ⁸Who is a great nation that has decrees and rulings as faithful as this entire instruction that I'm putting before you today? ⁹Only keep watch on yourself, keep your own person carefully, so you don't put out of mind the things that your eyes have seen, and so they don't depart from your mind all the days of your life. And get your children and your grandchildren to acknowledge them.

The attraction of images

¹⁰The day that you stood before Yahweh your God at Horeb, when Yahweh said to me, 'Congregate the people for me so I may get them to listen to my words, that they may learn to live in awe of me all the time that they live on the land, and may teach their children': ¹¹you drew near and stood beneath the mountain. The mountain was burning up with fire to the heart of the heavens, dark with cloud and denseness. ¹²Yahweh spoke to you from the middle of the fire; you could hear the sound of the words, but you couldn't see a shape, only a sound. ¹³He told you about his pact which he ordered you to act on, the ten words, and he wrote them on two stone tablets. ¹⁴And at that time Yahweh ordered me to teach you decrees and rulings for you to act on in the country where you're crossing over to take possession of it.

¹⁵Keep close watch on yourselves, because you didn't see any shape on the day Yahweh spoke to you at Horeb from the middle of the fire, ¹⁶so that you don't act devastatingly and make yourselves a shaped sculpture (any figure, the form of a male or female, ¹⁷the form of any animal that's on the earth, the form of any winged bird that flies in the heavens, ¹⁸the form of anything moving on the ground, the form of any fish that's in the water below the earth), ¹⁹and so you don't raise your eyes to the heavens and look at the sun, the moon and the stars, the entire army in the heavens, and stray and bow low to them and serve them, when Yahweh your God allocated them to all the peoples under all the heavens. ²⁰Yahweh took you and got you out of the iron furnace, out of Misrayim, to be a people for him, his domain, this very day.

Annihilation and restoration

²¹Yahweh showed himself angry with me because of your words, and he swore that I would not cross the Yarden and not come into the good country that Yahweh your God is giving you as a domain. ²²Because I'm going to die in this country. I'm not crossing the Yarden. You're going to cross and take possession of this good country.

²³Keep watch on yourselves so you don't put out of mind the pact of Yahweh your God, which he solemnized with you, and make yourselves a shaped sculpture of anything, about which Yahweh your God has given you orders. ²⁴Because Yahweh your God is a devouring fire, a passionate God.

²⁵When you father children and grandchildren and you become sleepy in the country, and you act devastatingly and make a shaped sculpture of anything, and do what is bad in the eyes of Yahweh your God so as to provoke him, ²⁶I call the heavens and the earth to testify against you today that you will quickly quite perish from on the country where you're crossing the Yarden to take possession of it. You won't stay a long time on it, because you will be totally annihilated. ²⁷Yahweh will disperse you among the peoples. Few in number of you will remain among the nations where Yahweh drives you, ²⁸and there you will serve gods made by human hands of wood and stone, which cannot see, cannot listen, cannot eat and cannot smell.

²⁹But you will seek Yahweh your God from there, and you will find, when you enquire of him with your entire heart and with your entire being ³⁰when you're under pressure. All these things will befall you in a later time, but

you will turn back to Yahweh your God and listen to his voice. ³¹Because Yahweh your God is a compassionate God. He won't let go of you. He won't devastate you. He won't put out of mind the pact with your ancestors, which he swore to them.

Has the like of it ever been heard?

³²Because do ask about an earlier time, which was before you, from the day when God created humanity on the earth, and from one end of the heavens to the other end of the heavens, whether anything like this great thing has happened or anything like this has made itself heard. ³³Has a people heard a god's voice speaking from the middle of the fire, as you yourself heard, and stayed alive? ³⁴Or has a god tried to come to take a nation for himself from within a nation, by trials, by signs, by proofs, by battle, by a strong hand, by an extended arm and by great awe-inspiring deeds, in accordance with all that Yahweh your God did for you in Misrayim before your eyes? ³⁵You yourselves have been allowed to see, so as to acknowledge that Yahweh is God. There's no other apart from him. ³⁶From the heavens he let you hear his voice to discipline you, and on the earth he let you see his great fire. You heard his words from the middle of the fire.

³⁷On account of the fact that he loved your ancestors, he chose their offspring after them, and got you out of Misrayim by his presence, by his great energy, ³⁸to dispossess bigger and more numerous nations than you from before you, to bring you in to give you their country as a domain this very day, ³⁹so you may acknowledge today and make it come back to your mind that Yahweh is God in the heavens above and on the earth below (there's no other) ⁴⁰and may keep his decrees and his orders which I'm giving you today, so things may be good for you and for your children after you, in order that your time may be long on the land that Yahweh your God is giving you for all time.

What Yahweh said face to face

⁴¹Then Mosheh made three towns distinct, across the Yarden towards the rising of the sun, ⁴²for a killer to flee there who kills his neighbour without knowing and when he was not hostile to him in previous days, so he could flee to one of the towns and live: ⁴³Betser in the wilderness in the flatland, for the Re'ubenites; Heights-in-Gil'ad, for the Gadites; and Golan, in Bashan, for the Menashshites.

⁴⁴This is the instruction that Mosheh put before the Yisra'elites; ⁴⁵these are the affirmations, the decrees and the rulings that Mosheh spoke to the Yisra'elites when they had got out of Misrayim, ⁴⁶across the Yarden, in the ravine near Bet Pe'or, in the country of Sihon king of the Amorites who had been living in Heshbon, whom Mosheh and the Yisra'elites struck down when they had got out of Misrayim. ⁴⁷They took possession of his country and the country of Og king of Bashan, the two kings of the Amorites, which were across the Yarden towards the rising of the sun, ⁴⁸from Aro'er which is on the bank of Wadi Arnon and as far as Mount Si'on (i.e. Hermon), ⁴⁹and all the steppe across the Yarden to the east and as far as the Steppe Sea, beneath the Pisgah slopes.

5 Mosheh called all Yisra'el and said to them: Listen, Yisra'el, to the decrees and the rulings that I'm speaking in your ears today. You're to learn them and keep them by acting on them.

²Yahweh our God solemnized a pact with us at Horeb. ³It was not with our parents that Yahweh solemnized this pact but with us ourselves, these people here today, all of us who are alive. ⁴Face to face Yahweh spoke with you on the mountain from the middle of the fire ⁵(I was standing between Yahweh and you at that time to tell you Yahweh's word, because you were afraid of the fire and you didn't go up on the mountain):

Ten words

⁶'I am Yahweh your God who got you out of the country of Misrayim, out of a household of serfs.

⁷For you there will be no other gods in my presence.

⁸You will not make yourself a sculpture of any shape that's in the heavens above, that's on the earth below or that's in the water under the earth. ⁹You will not bow low to

them and you will not serve them. Because I, Yahweh your God, am the passionate God, attending to parents' waywardness in connection with children and with thirds and with fourths for people who are hostile to me, ¹⁰but acting in commitment towards thousands for people who are loyal to me and to people who keep my orders.

¹¹You will not lift up the name of Yahweh your God in respect of something empty, because Yahweh will not free of guilt a person who lifts up his name in respect of something empty.

¹²Keep the sabbath day so as to make it sacred, as Yahweh your God has ordered you. ¹³For six days you can serve and do all your work, ¹⁴but the seventh day is a sabbath for Yahweh your God. You will not do any work, you, your son or your daughter, your servant or your handmaid, your ox or your donkey or any of your animals, or the resident who is in your communities, in order that your servant and your handmaid may rest like you. ¹⁵You're to be mindful that you were a servant in the country of Misrayim but Yahweh your God got you out of there with a strong hand and an extended arm. That's why Yahweh your God has ordered you to make the sabbath day.

¹⁶Honour your father and your mother as Yahweh your God has ordered you, in order that your time may be long, and in order that things may be good for you, on the land that Yahweh your God is giving you.

¹⁷You will not murder.

¹⁸You will not be adulterous.

¹⁹You will not steal.

²⁰You will not avow empty testimony against your neighbour.

²¹You will not desire your neighbour's wife. You will not long for your neighbour's house or his field, his servant or his handmaid, his ox or his donkey, or anything that your neighbour has.'

If only . . .

²²These words Yahweh spoke to your entire congregation at the mountain from the middle of the fire (the cloud and the denseness) in a loud voice. He didn't add anything. He wrote them on two stone tablets and gave them to me.

²³When you heard the voice from the middle of the darkness, and the mountain was burning up with fire, you drew near to me, all your clan heads and your elders, ²⁴and said, 'Here, Yahweh our God has let us see his splendour and his greatness, and we've heard his voice from the middle of the fire. This day we've seen that God can speak with a human being and he can live.

²⁵But now, why should we die? Because this great fire will devour us. If we continue to hear the voice of Yahweh our God any more, we will die. ²⁶Because who is there of all flesh that has listened to the living God's voice speaking from the middle of the fire like us and lived? ²⁷You draw near and listen to everything that Yahweh our God says, and you can speak to us everything that Yahweh our God speaks to you, and we will listen and do it.'

²⁸Yahweh listened to the sound of your words as you spoke to me. Yahweh said to me, 'I've listened to the sound of this people's words that they have spoken to you. They've done what is good in everything that they spoke. ²⁹If only this will be their mind, to live in awe of me and to keep all my orders at all times, in order that things may be good for them and for their children permanently. ³⁰Go, say to them: "Get yourselves back to your tents." ³¹But you, stand here with me and I shall speak to you the entire order (the decrees and the rulings) that you're to teach them so they will do them in the country that I'm giving them, to take possession of it.'

Listen, Yisra'el

³²You're to keep them by acting as Yahweh your God has ordered you. You will not turn aside right or left. ³³You're to walk in every way that Yahweh your God has ordered you, in order that you may live and things may be good for you and you may stay a long time in the country that you're to take possession of.

6 This is the order (the decrees and rulings) that Yahweh your God has ordered to teach you, to act on in the country where you're crossing over to take possession of it, ²in order that you may live in awe of Yahweh your God by keeping all his decrees and his orders that I'm giving you – you, your children and your grandchildren – all the days of your life, and in order that your time may be long. ³You're to listen, Yisra'el, and keep them by acting on them so things will be good for you and so you may become very numerous, as Yahweh the God of your ancestors spoke to you (a country flowing with milk and syrup).

⁴Listen, Yisra'el: Yahweh our God Yahweh one. ⁵You're to be loyal to Yahweh your God with your entire mind, with your entire being, with your entire might.

⁶These words that I'm ordering you today are to be on your mind. ⁷You're to drive them home to your children and speak of them when you're staying at home and when you're going on a journey, when you lie down and when you get up. ⁸You're to tie them as a sign on your hand. They're to be bands between your eyes, ⁹and you're to write them on the doorposts of your house and on your gateways.

When your children ask questions

¹⁰When Yahweh your God brings you into the country that he swore to your ancestors, to Abraham, to Yitshaq and to Ya'aqob, to give you, great and good towns that you haven't built, ¹¹houses full of everything good that you haven't filled, cisterns dug that you haven't dug, vineyards and olive groves that you haven't planted, and you eat and are full, ¹²keep watch on yourself so you don't put Yahweh out of mind, the one who got you out of the country of Misrayim, out of a household of serfs.

¹³You're to live in awe of Yahweh your God, to serve him and to swear in his name. ¹⁴You will not follow other gods from among the gods of the peoples that are round you, ¹⁵because Yahweh your God among you is a passionate God, so that the anger of Yahweh your God doesn't rage against you and he annihilate you from on the face of the land.

¹⁶You will not test Yahweh your God as you tested him at Massah ['Testing']. ¹⁷Keep carefully the orders of Yahweh your God, his affirmations and his decrees which he has given you. ¹⁸You're to do what is right and good in Yahweh's eyes in order that things may be good for you and you may come in and take possession of the good country that Yahweh swore to your ancestors, ¹⁹by driving out all your enemies from before you, as Yahweh has spoken.

²⁰ When your child asks you in the future, 'What were the affirmations, the decrees and the rulings that Yahweh our God ordered you?', ²¹you're to say to your child, 'We were Par'oh's serfs in Misrayim, and Yahweh got us out of Misrayim with a strong hand. ²²Yahweh put great, bad signs and proofs against Misrayim, against Par'oh and against his entire household, before our eyes, ²³and he got us out of there in order that he might bring us in to give us the country that he swore to our ancestors. ²⁴Yahweh ordered us to act on all these decrees, to live in awe of Yahweh our God for our good at all times, to keep us alive, this very day. ²⁵It will be our right standing, when we keep this entire order before Yahweh our God by acting on it, as he ordered us.'

Yahweh's attraction

7 When Yahweh your God brings you into the country where you're coming to take possession of it, and clears away many nations from before you (the Hittite, the Girgashite, the Amorite, the Kena'anite, the Perizzite, the Hivvite and the Yebusite, seven nations bigger and more numerous than you), ²and Yahweh your God gives them up before you and you strike them down, you're to devote them totally. You will not solemnize a pact with them. You will not grace them. ³You will not make marriages with them. You will not give your daughter to his son or take his daughter for your son, ⁴because he'll turn your son aside from following me and they'll serve other gods, and the anger of Yahweh will rage against you and he'll quickly annihilate you. ⁵Rather, you're to do this to them. You're to demolish their altars. You're to break up their columns. You're to cut down their totem poles. You're to burn their statues in fire.

⁶Because you're a people sacred for Yahweh your God. It was you that Yahweh your God chose to become a people that is personal treasure for him from all the peoples on the

face of the ground. ⁷It wasn't because of your larger number than all the peoples that Yahweh got attracted to you and chose you, because you were smaller than all the peoples. ⁸Rather, it was because of Yahweh's loyalty to you, and because of his keeping the oath that he swore to your ancestors, that Yahweh got you out with a strong hand, redeemed you out of a household of serfs, out of the hand of Par'oh king of Misrayim.

⁹You're to acknowledge that Yahweh your God is God, the trustworthy God, keeping the pact and commitment to people who are loyal to him and keep his orders, to a thousand generations, ¹⁰but one who makes good to people who are hostile to him, to the person's face, by obliterating him. He isn't slow with someone who's hostile to him; to his face he makes good to him. ¹¹So you're to keep the order (the decrees and the rulings) that I'm giving you today, by acting on it.

The hornet

¹²On the basis that you listen to these rulings and keep and act on them, Yahweh your God will keep for you the pact and commitment that he swore to your ancestors. ¹³He will be loyal to you, bless you and make you numerous. He will bless the fruit of your womb and the fruit of your land, your grain, your new wine and your fresh oil, the drop of your domestic animals and the young of your flock, on the land that he swore to your ancestors to give you. ¹⁴You will be blessed above all the peoples. There will not be among you male or female who is infertile, or among your animals. ¹⁵Yahweh will remove from you every illness, and none of the bad illnesses of Misrayim, which you know, will he place on you. He'll put them on the people who are hostile to you.

¹⁶You're to devour all the peoples that Yahweh your God is giving over to you. Your eye will not pity them. You will not serve their gods, because it will be a snare to you. ¹⁷When you say inside, 'These nations are more numerous than me – how will I be able to dispossess them?', ¹⁸you will not be afraid of them. You're to be resolutely mindful of what Yahweh your God did to Par'oh and to all Misrayim, ¹⁹the great tests that your eyes saw, the signs and the proofs, the strong hand and the extended arm by which Yahweh your God got you out. Yahweh your God will act in that way to all the peoples before whom you're afraid.

²⁰Yahweh your God will also send off a hornet against them until those who remain, and who are hiding from before you, perish. ²¹You will not be frightened before them, because Yahweh your God is among you, a great and awe-inspiring God.

Little by little

²²Yahweh your God will clear away those nations from before you little by little. You won't be able to finish them off quickly, so the creatures of the wild don't become too numerous for you. ²³But Yahweh your God will give them over before you and throw them into a great turmoil until their annihilation. ²⁴He will give their kings into your hand and you will eliminate their name from under the heavens. No one will take a stand before you until you've annihilated them.

²⁵The statues of their gods you're to burn in fire. You will not desire the silver and gold on them and take it for yourself, so you don't trap yourself by it, because it would be an offensive act to Yahweh your God. ²⁶You will not bring an offensive thing into your house, and become an object for devoting, like it. You're to treat it as totally abominable, totally offensive, because it's an object for devoting.

8

The entire order that I'm giving you today you're to keep by acting on it, in order that you may live and become numerous, and come and take possession of the country that Yahweh swore to your ancestors. ²You're to be mindful of the entire way that Yahweh your God had you go these forty years in the wilderness, in order that he might humble you by testing you so as to know what was in your mind, whether you would keep his orders or not. ³He humbled you and let you be hungry and fed you the *maan* which you hadn't known and your ancestors had not known, in order that he might get you to acknowledge that human beings don't live on the basis of bread alone but on the basis of everything that comes out of Yahweh's mouth. ⁴Your clothing hasn't worn out from upon you and your foot hasn't swollen these forty years.

The danger of forgetting

⁵You're to acknowledge in your mind that as someone disciplines his son, Yahweh your God disciplines you, ⁶and you're to keep the orders of Yahweh your God by walking in his ways and by living in awe of him. ⁷Because Yahweh your God is bringing you into a good country, a country of wadis with water, springs and depths issuing, in valley and in mountain, ⁸a country of wheat, barley, vine, fig and pomegranate, a country of olive oil and syrup, ⁹a country where you can eat bread without being short, where you won't lack anything, a country whose stones are iron and from whose mountains you can dig copper. ¹⁰You will eat and be full and bless Yahweh your God for the good country that he's given you.

¹¹Keep watch on yourself so you don't put Yahweh your God out of mind by not keeping his orders, his rulings and his decrees which I'm giving you today, ¹²so you don't eat and get full, and build good houses and live in them, ¹³and your herd and your flock increase, and your silver and gold increase, and everything that you have increases, ¹⁴and your mind exalts itself and you put out of mind Yahweh your God who got you out of the country of Misrayim, out of a household of serfs, ¹⁵the one who had you go through the great, awe-inspiring wilderness with venomous snake and scorpion, and desert where there was no water, who got water out of a flint crag for you, ¹⁶who enabled you to eat *maan* in the wilderness, which your ancestors had not known, in order that he might humble you and in order that he might test you, so as to do good to you in your later life, ¹⁷and you say inside, 'My energy and the might of my hand generated these resources for me.'

The importance of remembering

¹⁸You're to be mindful of Yahweh your God, that he's the one who is giving you the energy to generate resources, in order to implement the pact that he swore to your ancestors, this very day. ¹⁹If you do put Yahweh your God out of mind and follow other gods and serve them and bow low to them, I testify against you today that you will totally perish. ²⁰Like the nations whom Yahweh is making perish from before you, so you will perish, since you don't listen to the voice of Yahweh your God.

9 Listen, Yisra'el. Today you're crossing the Yarden to go in to dispossess nations bigger and more numerous than you: big towns fortified to the heavens, ²a big and tall people, the Anaqites whom you yourselves know and of whom you've heard it said, 'Who can take a stand before the descendants of Anaq?' ³You're to acknowledge today that Yahweh your God – he's crossing before you, a devouring fire. He's the one who will destroy them. He's the one who will put them down before you so you'll dispossess them and make them perish quickly, as Yahweh has spoken to you.

⁴Don't say inside, when Yahweh your God has driven them out from before you, 'It's because of my faithfulness that Yahweh brought me in to take possession of this country.' It's because of the faithlessness of these nations that Yahweh is dispossessing them from before you. ⁵It's not because of your faithfulness or because of the uprightness of your mind that you're going in to take possession of their country. It's because of the faithlessness of these nations that Yahweh your God is dispossessing them from before you, and in order to implement the word that Yahweh swore to your ancestors, to Abraham, to Yitshaq and to Ya'aqob.

Not because of your faithfulness

⁶You're to acknowledge that it's not because of your faithfulness that Yahweh your God is giving you this good country, to take possession of it, because you're a tough-necked people. ⁷Be mindful, don't put out of mind, how you infuriated Yahweh your God in the wilderness. From the day that you left the country of Misrayim till you came to this place, you've been rebellious towards Yahweh.

⁸At Horeb you infuriated Yahweh and he showed himself angry enough with you to annihilate you, ⁹when I went up the mountain to get the stone tablets, the tablets of the

pact that Yahweh had solemnized with you. I stayed on the mountain forty days and forty nights. I ate no bread and I drank no water. ¹⁰Yahweh gave me the two stone tablets written on by God's finger, with all the very things on them that God had spoken with you on the mountain from the middle of the fire on the day of the congregation. ¹¹At the end of forty days and forty nights Yahweh gave me the two stone tablets, the pact tablets.

¹²But Yahweh said to me, 'Get up, go down from here quickly, because your people whom you got out of Misrayim have acted devastatingly. They've departed quickly from the way that I ordered them. They've made a figurine for themselves.' ¹³And Yahweh said to me, 'I've looked at this people, and here, it's a tough-necked people. ¹⁴Let me go, so I can annihilate them and wipe out their name from under the heavens, and make you into a more numerous and vast nation than them.'

¹⁵I turned my face and came down from the mountain (the mountain was burning up with fire) with the two tablets of the pact in my two hands. ¹⁶I looked, and there, you'd done wrong in relation to Yahweh your God. You'd made a bullock figurine for yourselves. You'd departed quickly from the way that Yahweh had ordered you. ¹⁷I took hold of the two tablets and threw them out of my two hands and broke them up before your eyes.

Effective intercession

¹⁸I made myself fall before Yahweh. Like the first time, for forty days and forty nights I ate no bread and drank no water on account of all the wrong that you'd committed in doing what was bad in Yahweh's eyes so as to provoke him, ¹⁹because I was in dread before the anger and wrath with which Yahweh was furious towards you so as to annihilate you. Yahweh listened to me that time, too. ²⁰With Aharon [Aaron], Yahweh showed himself very angry, enough to annihilate him, but I also interceded on Aharon's behalf at that time. ²¹The wrongful thing that you'd made, the bullock, I got it and burned it in fire and crushed it and ground it well until it became fine as powder, and I threw its powder into the wadi coming down from the mountain.

²²At Tab'erah and at Massah and at Qibrot Hatta'avah you were people who infuriated Yahweh. ²³When Yahweh sent you from Qadesh Barnea, saying 'Go up and take possession of the country that I've given you', you rebelled against the bidding of Yahweh your God. You didn't trust in him and you didn't listen to his voice. ²⁴You've been rebellious in relation to Yahweh from the day I knew you.

²⁵I made myself fall before Yahweh for the forty days and forty nights that I made myself fall, because Yahweh said he would annihilate you. ²⁶I interceded with Yahweh and said, 'My Lord Yahweh, don't devastate your people, your domain, which you redeemed by your greatness, which you got out of Misrayim with a strong hand. ²⁷Be mindful of your servants, of Abraham, of Yitshaq and of Ya'aqob. Don't turn your face to the obstinacy of this people, to its faithlessness, to its wrongdoing, ²⁸so the country from which you got us out doesn't say, "It was because Yahweh couldn't bring them into the country of which he spoke to them and because he was hostile to them that he got them out, to let them die in the wilderness." ²⁹They are your people, your domain, which you got out by your great energy and your extended arm.'

The ten words re-inscribed

10 At that time Yahweh said to me, 'Carve yourself two stone tablets like the first ones, and go up to me on the mountain, and make yourself a wooden chest. ²I'll write on the tablets the words that were on the first tablets, which you broke up, and you're to put them in the chest.' ³So I made an acacia wood chest and carved two stone tablets like the first. I went up the mountain with the two tablets in my hand, ⁴and he wrote on the tablets the same text as the first, the ten words that Yahweh spoke to you on the mountain from the middle of the fire on the day of the congregation. Yahweh gave them to me ⁵and I turned my face and came down from the mountain, and put the tablets in the chest that I had made. So they've been there, as Yahweh ordered me.

⁶The Yisra'elites moved on from Bene-ya'aqan Wells to Moserah. There Aharon died

and he was buried there, and El'azar his son acted as priest in his place. ⁷From there they moved on to Gudgod, and from Gudgod to Yotbat, a region of wadis with water. ⁸At that time Yahweh made the clan of Levi distinct, to carry Yahweh's pact chest, to stand before Yahweh to minister to him, and to bless in his name, until this day. ⁹Therefore Levi hasn't had a share, a domain, with his brothers. Yahweh is his domain, as Yahweh your God spoke to him.

¹⁰So I – I stood on the mountain as at the first time for forty days and forty nights, and Yahweh listened to me once again. Yahweh was not willing to devastate you. ¹¹Yahweh said to me, 'Set off, go, move on before the people, so they may come in and take possession of the country that I swore to their ancestors to give them.'

Attraction and attachment

¹²Now, Yisra'el, what is Yahweh your God asking of you except to live in awe of Yahweh your God so as to walk in all his ways, to be loyal to him and to serve Yahweh your God with your entire mind and with your entire being, ¹³so as to keep Yahweh's orders and his decrees that I'm giving you today for your good?

¹⁴Here, to Yahweh your God belong the heavens, the highest heavens, the earth and everything that's in it. ¹⁵Only Yahweh got attracted to your ancestors so as to be loyal to them, and chose their offspring after them, you, from all the peoples, this very day. ¹⁶So circumcise the foreskin of your mind. You will not toughen your neck any more. ¹⁷Because Yahweh your God – he's the God over the gods, the Lord over the lords, the God great, mighty and awe-inspiring, who doesn't honour a person and doesn't accept a bribe. ¹⁸He makes a ruling for the orphan and the widow and he is loyal to the resident by giving him bread and clothing. ¹⁹So you're to be loyal to the resident, because you were residents in the country of Misrayim.

²⁰Yahweh your God: you're to live in awe of him, serve and attach yourselves to him, and swear by his name. ²¹He's to be your praise and he's to be your God who did for you these great, awe-inspiring things that your eyes saw. ²²As seventy persons your ancestors went down to Misrayim, but now Yahweh your God has made you like the stars in the heavens in the large number.

It was you

11 So you're to be loyal to Yahweh your God and keep his charge, his decrees, his rulings and his orders at all times. ²You're to acknowledge today that it was not with your children, who didn't know and who didn't see the discipline of Yahweh your God, his greatness, his strong hand and his extended arm, ³his signs and his deeds that he did in the middle of Misrayim to Par'oh king of Misrayim and to all his country, ⁴and what he did to Misrayim's force, to its horses and to its chariotry, over whose heads Yahweh made the water of the Reed Sea flow when they pursued after you, and in this way destroyed them until this day, ⁵and what he did for you in the wilderness until you came as far as this place, ⁶and what he did to Datan and to Abiram, the sons of Eli'ab the Re'ubenite, whom the earth opened its mouth and swallowed, them, their households, their tents and everything that existed that was in their company, in the middle of all Yisra'el . . .

⁷Rather it was your eyes that saw every great deed that Yahweh did. ⁸So you're to keep the entire order that I'm giving you today, in order that you may be strong and may go in and take possession of the country where you're crossing over to take possession of it, ⁹and in order that you may stay a long time on the land that Yahweh swore to your ancestors to give to them and to their offspring, a country flowing with milk and syrup.

A country that drinks water from the heavens

¹⁰Because the country where you're coming to take possession of it is not like the country of Misrayim, from where you got out, where you sow your seed and water it by foot, like a vegetable garden. ¹¹The country where you're crossing over to take possession of it is a country of mountains and valleys, one

that drinks water from the heavens' rain, ¹²a country that Yahweh your God enquires after. The eyes of Yahweh your God are on it regularly from the year's beginning until the year's end.

¹³If you really do listen to my orders that I'm giving you today by being loyal to Yahweh your God and by serving him with your entire mind and with your entire being, ¹⁴I will give rain on your country in its time, early rain and late rain, and you'll gather in your grain, your new wine and your fresh oil. ¹⁵I'll give grass in your fields for your animals and you'll eat and be full. ¹⁶Keep watch on yourselves so your mind is not naive and you depart, and serve other gods and bow low to them, ¹⁷and Yahweh's anger rages against you, and he holds back the heavens and there's no rain, and the ground doesn't give its produce, and you quickly perish from on the good country that Yahweh is giving you.

¹⁸You're to put these words on to your mind and on to your person. Tie them as a sign on your hand. They're to be bands between your eyes. ¹⁹You're to teach them to your children by speaking of them when you're staying at home and when you're going on a journey, when you're lying down and when you're getting up, ²⁰and you're to write them on the doorposts of your house and on your gateways, ²¹in order that your days and your children's days may be many on the land that Yahweh swore to your ancestors to give them, as many as the days of the heavens over the earth.

Blessing or slighting

²²Because if you carefully keep this entire order that I'm giving you by acting on it, being loyal to Yahweh your God by walking in all his ways and by attaching yourselves to him, ²³Yahweh will dispossess all these nations from before you and you will take possession of nations bigger and more numerous than you. ²⁴Every place on which the sole of your foot treads will be yours. From the wilderness and the Lebanon, from the river (the River Euphrates) as far as the Western Sea will be your border. ²⁵No one will take a stand against you. Yahweh your God will put dread of you and fear of you on the face of the entire country on which you tread, as he's spoken to you.

²⁶Look, I'm putting before you today blessing and slight: ²⁷the blessing because you listen to the orders of Yahweh your God that I'm giving you today, ²⁸and the slight if you don't listen to the orders of Yahweh your God but depart from the way that I'm ordering you today by following other gods that you haven't acknowledged. ²⁹When Yahweh your God brings you into the country where you're coming to take possession of it, you're to put the blessing on Mount Gerizim and the slight on Mount Ebal. ³⁰They're across the Yarden, beyond the sunset road in the country of the Kena'anites who live in the steppe near Gilgal, beside the Moreh Oaks, aren't they. ³¹Because you're crossing the Yarden to go in to take possession of the country that Yahweh your God is giving you so you may take possession of it and live in it. ³²You're to keep all the decrees and the rulings that I'm putting before you today, by acting on them.

On not following your instincts

12 These are the decrees and the rulings that you're to keep by acting on them, in the country that Yahweh the God of your ancestors has given you to take possession of it, all the time that you're living on the land. ²You're to obliterate, totally, all the sites where the nations that you're dispossessing have served their gods, on high mountains and on hills and under any verdant tree. ³You're to tear down their altars, break up their columns, burn their totem poles in fire, cut down the statues of their gods and obliterate their name from that site. ⁴You will not act for Yahweh your God in that way.

⁵Rather you're to enquire at the site that Yahweh your God chooses from all your clans, to put his name there for him to dwell. You're to come there ⁶and bring there your whole offerings and your sacrifices, your tenths and the contribution from your hand, your pledges and your free offerings, and the firstlings of your herd and of your flock. ⁷You're to eat there before Yahweh your God and rejoice in every undertaking of your hand (you and your households) in which Yahweh your God has blessed you.

⁸You will not act in accordance with anything that we are doing here today, an individual doing anything that's all right in his eyes, ⁹because until now you haven't come to the place to settle down, to the domain that Yahweh your God is giving you. ¹⁰You're to cross the Yarden and live in the country that Yahweh your God is giving you as a domain. He will enable you to settle down free of all your enemies all round, and you will live in confidence. ¹¹And the site where Yahweh your God chooses to have his name dwell, you're to bring there everything that I'm ordering you: your burnt offerings and your sacrifices, your tenths, the contribution from your hand and every choice thing among the pledges that you make to Yahweh.

Freedom to 'sacrifice' nearer home

¹²So you're to rejoice before Yahweh your God, you, your sons and your daughters, your servants and your handmaids, and the Levite who is in your communities (because he has no share, no domain with you). ¹³Keep watch on yourself so you don't offer up your burnt offerings at every site that you see. ¹⁴Rather, at the site that Yahweh chooses in one of your clans, there you're to offer up your burnt offerings, and there you're to act on everything that I'm ordering you. ¹⁵Only, at any longing of your appetite you may 'sacrifice' and eat meat in accordance with the blessing of Yahweh your God that he's given you, in all your communities. Taboo and pure people may eat it, like the gazelle and like the deer. ¹⁶Only, the blood you will not eat. You're to pour it on the earth like water. ¹⁷In your communities you will not be able to eat the tenth of your grain, new wine and fresh oil, or the firstlings of your herd and flock, or any pledges that you make, or your free offerings or the contribution from your hand. ¹⁸Rather, you're to eat them before Yahweh your God at the site that Yahweh your God chooses, you, your son and your daughter, your servant and your handmaid, and the Levite who is in your communities, and you're to rejoice before Yahweh your God in every undertaking of your hand. ¹⁹Keep watch on yourself so you don't abandon the Levite all your days on your land.

²⁰When Yahweh your God widens your border, as he spoke to you, and you say, 'I want to eat meat', because your appetite longs to eat meat, at any longing of your appetite you may eat meat. ²¹When the site that Yahweh your God chooses to put his name there is far from you, you may 'sacrifice' from your herd or from your flock that Yahweh has given you as I've ordered you, and you may eat in your communities, at the longing of your appetite.

Not eating the blood

²²However, as the gazelle and the deer are eaten – in this way you're to eat it. Taboo and pure people may eat it together. ²³Only, be firm about not eating the blood, because the blood is the life. You will not eat the life with the meat. ²⁴Given that you will not eat it, you're to pour it on the earth like water. ²⁵You will not eat it, in order that things may be good for you and for your descendants after you, because you do what's right in Yahweh's eyes. ²⁶Only, your sacred things that you have, and your pledges, you're to take up, and come to the site that Yahweh chooses. ²⁷You're to make your burnt offerings, the meat and the blood, on the altar of Yahweh your God. The blood of your sacrifices is to be poured on the altar of Yahweh your God, but the meat you may eat. ²⁸Keep and listen to all these words that I'm ordering you, in order that things may be good for you and for your descendants after you permanently, because you do what is good and right in the eyes of Yahweh your God. ²⁹When Yahweh your God cuts down the nations where you're coming to dispossess them from before you, and you dispossess them and live in their country, ³⁰keep watch on yourself so you're not trapped into following them after they've been annihilated from before you, and so you don't enquire of their gods, saying 'How do these nations serve their gods, so I may also act in the same way?' ³¹You will not act in this way towards Yahweh your God, because they do for their gods everything that's an offence to Yahweh, that to which he's hostile, because they even burn their sons and their daughters in fire for their gods.

³²Every thing that I'm ordering you, you're to keep by acting on it. You will not add to it and you will not take away from it.

False prophets

13 When a prophet or someone who has a dream rises among you, and gives you a sign or a proof ²(and the sign or the proof of which he spoke to you comes about), saying 'Let's follow other gods (which you haven't acknowledged) and serve them': ³you will not listen to the words of that prophet or that one who has the dream, because Yahweh your God is testing you so as to know whether you're people who are loyal to Yahweh your God with your entire mind and with your entire being. ⁴You're to follow Yahweh your God. You're to live in awe of him. His orders you're to keep and to his voice you're to listen. He's the one you're to serve, and you're to attach yourselves to him.

⁵That prophet or that one who has the dream: he's to be put to death, because he spoke defiance against Yahweh your God (who got you out of the country of Misrayim and redeemed you from a household of serfs) to drive you from the way that Yahweh your God ordered you to walk in. So you will burn away the bad thing from among you.

⁶When your brother, your mother's son, or your son or your daughter, or the wife in your arms, or your neighbour who is as close to you as your own self, incites you in secret, saying 'Let's go and serve other gods' (which you yourself and your ancestors haven't acknowledged), ⁷from the gods of the peoples that are round you, the ones near to you or the ones far away from you, from one end of the country to the other end of the country, ⁸you will not agree with him, you will not listen to him.

Your eye will not pity him. You will not spare him or conceal him, ⁹but simply kill him. Your own hand will be the first against him, to put him to death, and the hand of the entire people afterwards. ¹⁰Pelt him with stones so he dies, because he sought to drive you away from Yahweh your God who got you out of the country of Misrayim, out of a household of serfs.

¹¹All Yisra'el will hear and live in awe and will not again do the likes of this bad thing among you.

When someone leads the town astray

¹²When you hear in one of your towns that Yahweh your God is giving you to live in, ¹³'People who are scoundrels have gone out from among you and have driven away the people living in their town, saying "Let's go and serve other gods"' (which you haven't acknowledged), ¹⁴you're to enquire well and search out and ask. And there, the thing is established truthful, this offensive act was done among you. ¹⁵Strike down hard the people living in that town with the mouth of the sword. Devote it, everything that's in it and its animals, with the mouth of the sword. ¹⁶All its spoil you're to collect in the middle of the square, and burn the town and all its spoil with fire as a whole offering for Yahweh your God. It's to become a permanent ruin. It will not be built up again.

¹⁷Not a thing from what was to be devoted will attach itself to your hand, in order that Yahweh may turn back from his angry rage and show you compassion. He will be compassionate to you and make you numerous, as he swore to your ancestors, ¹⁸because you listen to the voice of Yahweh your God by keeping all his orders that I'm giving you today, by doing what is right in the eyes of Yahweh your God.

14 You are the children of Yahweh your God. You will not cut yourselves or make a bald space between your eyes for a dead person, ²because you're a people sacred for Yahweh your God. Yahweh chose you to be his, a people that is personal treasure, from all the peoples that are on the face of the ground.

You are what you eat

³You may not eat anything offensive.
⁴These are the animals that you may eat: ox, young one from the sheep, young one from the goats, ⁵deer, gazelle, roebuck, wild goat, ibex, antelope, mountain sheep, ⁶any animal that has a divided hoof (that

has a cleft in its hoofs) that brings up its cud; you may eat it. ⁷This, however, you may not eat: ones that bring up their cud or have a divided hoof (have a cleft in their hoof) – the camel, the hare and the rock badger, because they bring up their cud but don't have a divided hoof; they're taboo for you; ⁸the pig, because it has a divided hoof but doesn't bring up its cud; it's taboo for you.

You will not eat of their meat and you will not touch their corpse.

⁹This you may eat of everything that's in the water: anything that has fins and scales you may eat. ¹⁰But anything that has no fins and scales you may not eat; it's taboo for you. ¹¹Any pure bird you may eat. ¹²This is what you may not eat of them: the eagle, the vulture, the osprey, ¹³the kite, the falcon, the buzzard (any of its species), ¹⁴every raven (any of its species), ¹⁵the ostrich, the nighthawk, the seagull, the hawk (any of its species), ¹⁶the tawny owl, the screech owl, the barn owl, ¹⁷the pelican, the swan, the cormorant, ¹⁸the stork, the heron (any of its species), the hoopoe and the bat. ¹⁹Any teeming, flying thing is taboo for you. It may not be eaten. ²⁰Any pure flying thing you may eat. ²¹You may not eat any corpse (though you may give it to the resident who is in your communities so he may eat it, or sell it to a foreigner), because you're a people sacred for Yahweh your God.

You will not cook a kid goat in its own mother's milk.

Tithes

²²You're carefully to take a tenth of the entire yield from your seed that your fields produce, year by year. ²³Before Yahweh your God at the site where Yahweh chooses to have his name dwell, you're to eat the tenth of your grain, your new wine and your fresh oil, and the firstlings of your herd and your flock, in order that you may learn to live in awe of Yahweh your God at all times. ²⁴When the journey's too big for you, because you can't carry it (because the site that Yahweh your God chooses to put his name there is too far for you) because Yahweh your God blesses you, ²⁵you may turn it into silver, tie up the silver in your possession, go to the site that Yahweh your God chooses ²⁶and give the silver for anything that your appetite longs for: herd, flock, wine, liquor, anything that your appetite asks for. You're to eat there before Yahweh your God and rejoice, you and your household, ²⁷and you will not abandon the Levite who's in your communities, because he has no share, no domain with you.

²⁸At the end of three years you will take out the entire tenth of your yield in that year, but set it down in your communities. ²⁹The Levite (because he has no share, no domain of his own with you) and the resident, the orphan, and the widow who is in your communities, will come and eat and be full, in order that Yahweh your God may bless you in all the action of your hand that you perform.

Helping people get back on their feet

15 At the end of seven years you're to effect a release. ²This is the thing about the release: anyone in a position to make a loan from his hand who makes a loan to his neighbour is not to exact it of his neighbour, his brother, when the release for Yahweh has been called. ³You may exact it of a foreigner, but whatever of yours is with your brother, your hand is to release.

⁴Yet there won't be a needy person among you, because Yahweh will truly bless you in the country that Yahweh your God is giving you as a domain, to take possession of it, ⁵if only you really listen to the voice of Yahweh your God, by keeping this entire order that I'm giving you today, by acting on it. ⁶When Yahweh your God has blessed you as he spoke to you, you'll lend to many nations but you yourself won't borrow. You'll rule over many nations but over you they won't rule.

⁷When there's a needy person among you, one of your brothers, inside one of your communities in the country that Yahweh your God is giving you, you will not firm up your mind and you will not close your hand against your needy brother, ⁸because you're to open your hand wide to him and generously

lend enough for the lack that he has. ⁹Keep watch on yourself so a thing doesn't come into your scoundrelous mind, 'The seventh year, the release year, is drawing near', so your eye works badly towards your needy brother and you don't give anything to him, and he calls to Yahweh about you and it becomes a wrong done by you. ¹⁰Give generously to him. Your mind must not work badly when you give to him, ¹¹because the needy person won't leave off from within the country. That's why I'm ordering you, 'Open your hand wide to your weak and your needy brother in your country.'

When servants decline their freedom

¹²When your brother, a Hebrew man or a Hebrew woman, sells himself to you, he may serve you for six years, and in the seventh year you're to send him off from you as a free person. ¹³When you send him off from you as a free person, you will not send him off empty-handed. ¹⁴You're to supply him liberally from your flock, from your threshing floor and from your winepress. With what Yahweh your God has blessed you, you're to give to him. ¹⁵Be mindful that you were a serf in the country of Misrayim and Yahweh your God redeemed you. That's why I'm ordering this thing today.

¹⁶When he says to you, 'I won't go out from you', because he's loyal to you and your household, because things have been good for him with you, ¹⁷you're to get an awl and put it through his ear and through the door, and he'll be your servant permanently. You're also to do this for your handmaid. ¹⁸When you send him off from you as a free person, it shouldn't be tough in your eyes, because he's served you for six years for the equivalent of the wages of an employee. And Yahweh your God will bless you in all that you do.

¹⁹Every male firstling that's born in your herd and in your flock you're to make sacred for Yahweh your God. You will not serve with the firstling of your ox and you will not shear the firstling of your flock. ²⁰You're to eat it before Yahweh your God year by year at the site that Yahweh chooses, you and your household. ²¹But when there's a defect in it, lameness or blindness, any bad defect, you're not to sacrifice it for Yahweh your God. ²²You may eat it in your communities, taboo and pure together, like the gazelle and the deer. ²³Only, its blood you will not eat. You're to pour it on the earth like water.

Pesah (Passover)

16 Keep the month of Abib and make Pesah for Yahweh your God, because in the month of Abib Yahweh your God got you out of Misrayim, by night. ²You're to sacrifice the Pesah for Yahweh your God from flock or herd at the site where Yahweh chooses to have his name dwell. ³You will not eat any leavened bread along with it. For seven days you're to eat flatbread (humble bread) with it, because it was in haste that you got out of the country of Misrayim, in order that you may be mindful of the day you got out of the country of Misrayim, all the days of your life. ⁴Yeast will not appear among you, within your entire border, for seven days, and none of the meat that you sacrifice on the evening of the first day will stay until morning.

⁵You will not be able to sacrifice the Pesah within one of your communities that Yahweh your God is giving you. ⁶Rather, you're to sacrifice the Pesah at the site where Yahweh your God chooses to have his name dwell, in the evening, at sunset, the set time of your getting out of Misrayim. ⁷You're to cook and eat at the site that Yahweh your God chooses, and turn your face in the morning and go to your tents. ⁸For six days you're to eat flatbread and on the seventh day there's to be an assembly for Yahweh your God; you will not do any work.

Shabu'ot and Sukkot (Weeks or Pentecost, and Tabernacles)

⁹You're to count seven weeks [*shabu'ot*] for yourself; from when you start the sickle in the standing grain you're to start counting seven weeks. ¹⁰You're to make the Shabu'ot Festival for Yahweh your God, by the measure of the free offering from your hand that you give, as Yahweh your God blesses you. ¹¹You're to rejoice before Yahweh your God, you, your son and your daughter, your servant and your handmaid, the Levite who is in your communities and the resident, the orphan and the widow who are

among you, at the site where Yahweh your God chooses to have his name dwell. ¹²You're to be mindful that you were a serf in Misrayim, and to keep and act on these decrees.

¹³You're to make the Sukkot Festival for yourself for seven days when you've gathered things in from your threshing floor and from your winepress. ¹⁴You're to rejoice at your festival, you, your son and your daughter, your servant and your handmaid, the Levite and the resident, the orphan and the widow who are in your communities. ¹⁵For seven days you're to hold a festival for Yahweh your God at the site that Yahweh chooses, because Yahweh your God will bless you in your entire yield and in all the action of your hands. You will be simply rejoicing.

¹⁶Three times in the year every male of yours is to appear before Yahweh your God at the site that he chooses, at the Flatbread Festival, at the Shabu'ot Festival and at the Sukkot Festival. He's not to appear before Yahweh empty-handed: ¹⁷each in accordance with the gift in his possession, in accordance with the blessing of Yahweh your God that he's given you.

Absolute faithfulness

¹⁸You're to make yourself authorities and officials in all the communities that Yahweh your God is giving you for your clans. They're to exercise faithful authority for the people. ¹⁹You will not twist the exercise of authority. You will not honour persons. You will not accept a bribe, because a bribe blinds the eyes of smart people and twist the words of faithful people. ²⁰You're to pursue absolute faithfulness in order that you may live and take possession of the country that Yahweh your God is giving you.

²¹You will not plant for yourself as a totem pole any tree beside the altar of Yahweh your God which you will make for yourself, ²²and you will not set up a column for yourself, to which Yahweh your God is hostile.

17

You will not sacrifice for Yahweh your God an ox or a sheep in which there's a defect, anything bad, because it's an offensive act to Yahweh your God.

²When there is found among you, in one of your communities that Yahweh your God is giving you, a man or a woman who does something bad in the eyes of Yahweh your God by contravening his pact ³and has gone and served other gods and bowed down to them, to the sun or to the moon or to any of the heavenly army, which I haven't ordered, ⁴and it's told to you, you're to listen and enquire well. And there, the thing is established as truthful, this offensive act was done in Yisra'el. ⁵You're to take out that man or that woman who did this bad thing, to your gateways, and pelt them with stones so they die.

Making judgements

⁶At the mouth of two witnesses or three witnesses is a person to be put to death. He will not be put to death at the mouth of one witness. ⁷The hand of the witnesses is to be the first against him to put him to death, and the hand of the entire people afterwards, so you burn away the bad thing from among you.

⁸When a matter is too hard for you to decide, between one instance of bloodshed and another, between one judgement and another, or between one assault and another (matters of argument in your communities), you're to set off and go up to the site that Yahweh your God chooses ⁹and come to the Levitical priests, to the person in authority that's there at that time, and enquire. They'll tell you the word of decision, ¹⁰and you're to act in accordance with the word that they tell you, from that site that Yahweh chooses. You're to keep it by acting in accordance with everything that they instruct you.

¹¹You're to act in accordance with the instruction that they give you and by the ruling that they say to you. You will not turn aside from the word that they tell you, right or left. ¹²The individual who acts with assertiveness rather than listening to the priest who stands to minister to Yahweh your God there, or to the person in authority: that individual is to die, so you may burn away what is bad from Yisra'el, ¹³and so the entire people may listen and live in awe and not assert themselves again.

Kings

¹⁴When you come into the country that Yahweh your God is giving you and you take

possession of it and you're living in it, and you say 'I intend to set a king over me, like all the nations that are round me', ¹⁵you may indeed set over you a king whom Yahweh your God chooses. From among your brothers you may set a king over you. You cannot put over you an individual who's a foreigner, who's not your brother.

¹⁶Only, he will not acquire many horses for himself and he will not get the people to go back to Misrayim in order that he may acquire many horses, when Yahweh has said to you, 'You will never again go back that way.' ¹⁷He will not acquire many wives for himself, so his mind does not turn aside, and he will not make very much silver and gold for himself.

¹⁸When he sits on his royal throne, he's to write for himself a copy of this instruction on a document, from before the Levitical priests. ¹⁹It's to be with him and he's to read out of it all the days of his life in order that he may learn to live in awe of Yahweh his God, by keeping all the words of this instruction and these decrees by acting on them, ²⁰so his mind doesn't rise above his brothers and so he doesn't depart from the order, right or left, in order that he may stay a long time over his kingdom, he and his sons, within Yisra'el.

Priests and Levites

18 The Levitical priests, the entire clan of Levi, are to have no share, no domain, with Yisra'el. They will eat Yahweh's gift offerings, as its domain. ²It will have no domain among its brothers. Yahweh is its domain, as he spoke to it.

³This is to be the priests' due from the people, from those who are offering a sacrifice, whether an ox or a sheep: he will give the priest the shoulder, the jaws and the stomach. ⁴You're to give him the first of your grain, your new wine and your fresh oil, and the first shearing of your flock. ⁵Because Yahweh your God has chosen him out of all your clans to stand to minister in Yahweh's name, he and his descendants for all time.

⁶When a Levite comes from one of your communities, from all Yisra'el where he's been a resident, and comes with any longing of his own to the site that Yahweh chooses, ⁷he may minister in the name of Yahweh his God like all his brother Levites who are standing there before Yahweh. ⁸They're to eat equal shares, apart from his assets through his ancestors.

⁹When you come into the country that Yahweh your God is giving you, you will not learn to act in accordance with the offensive practices of those nations. ¹⁰There will be no one present among you who makes his son or his daughter pass through fire, who engages in divination, who practises augury, who casts spells, who practises sorcery, ¹¹who uses enchantment, who asks things of ghosts and spirits, or who enquires of the dead. ¹²Because anyone who does these things is an offence to Yahweh. It's because of these offensive acts that Yahweh your God is dispossessing them before you.

Prophets

¹³You're to be people of integrity with Yahweh your God. ¹⁴Because these nations that you're dispossessing listen to people who practise augury and to diviners, but you: Yahweh your God hasn't made it so for you.

¹⁵Yahweh your God will make a prophet arise for you from among you, from your brothers, like me. You're to listen to him, ¹⁶in accordance with all that you asked of Yahweh your God at Horeb on the day of the congregation, saying 'I won't any more listen to the voice of Yahweh my God and I won't look any longer at this great fire, so I don't die.' ¹⁷Yahweh said to me, 'They did a good thing in what they spoke. ¹⁸I shall make a prophet arise for them from among their brothers like you. I shall put my words in his mouth and he will speak to them all that I order him. ¹⁹The individual who doesn't listen to my words that he speaks in my name – I myself will enquire of him.

²⁰Moreover, the prophet who presumes to speak a word in my name that I didn't order him to speak or who speaks in the name of other gods: that prophet shall die. ²¹When you say to yourself, "How will we know the word that Yahweh hasn't spoken?": ²²what the prophet speaks in Yahweh's name but the word doesn't come about, come true, that's the word that Yahweh didn't speak. The prophet spoke it presumptuously. You will not be in dread of him.'

Asylum towns

19 When Yahweh your God cuts down the nations whose country Yahweh your God is giving you and you dispossess them and you live in their towns and in their houses, ²you're to distinguish for yourself three towns within your country that Yahweh your God is giving you, to take possession of it. ³You're to measure the journey for yourself and divide into three the border of your country that Yahweh your God gives you as a domain, so any killer may be able to flee there.

⁴This is the thing with the killer who flees there so he may live – one who strikes down his neighbour without knowing, and wasn't hostile to him in previous days, ⁵but who comes into the forest with his neighbour to chop wood, and his hand thrusts with the axe to cut down a tree and the iron slips off the wooden part and finds his neighbour and he dies. He can flee to one of these towns so he may live, ⁶so the blood restorer doesn't pursue after the killer when his feelings are hot and overtake him, because the journey is long, and strike him down a fatal blow, when he was not liable to the death sentence because he hadn't been hostile to him in previous days. ⁷That's why I'm ordering you, 'You're to distinguish three towns for yourself.'

⁸If Yahweh your God widens your border as he swore to your ancestors and gives you the entire country that he spoke of giving to your ancestors, ⁹when you keep this entire order that I'm giving you today by acting on it, by being loyal to Yahweh your God and by walking in his ways at all times, you're to add for yourself three more towns along with these three. ¹⁰Thus the blood of the person who is free of guilt will not be shed within your country that Yahweh your God is giving you as a domain so that the shed blood comes on you.

An eye for an eye

¹¹But when an individual is hostile to his neighbour, lies in wait for him, sets on him and strikes him down with a fatal blow so he dies, and he flees to one of these towns, ¹²the elders of his town are to send and get him from there and give him into the hand of the blood restorer, so he dies. ¹³Your eye will not pity him. You're to burn away from Yisra'el the blood of the person who is free of guilt, so things may be good for you.

¹⁴You will not move aside your neighbour's boundary marker, which previous generations laid down, in your domain which you will have as yours in the country that Yahweh your God is giving you to take possession of it.

¹⁵One witness will not stand up against someone regarding any waywardness or regarding any wrong, in connection with any wrong that he does. At the mouth of two witnesses or at the mouth of three witnesses the thing will stand up.

¹⁶When a felonious witness stands up against someone to avow defiance against him, ¹⁷the two people who have the argument are to take their stand before Yahweh, before the priests or the authorities who are there at that time, ¹⁸and the authorities will enquire well.

There, the witness is a false witness. He has avowed a falsehood against his brother. ¹⁹You're to do to him as he intended to do to his brother, and burn away the bad thing from among you, ²⁰while the remaining people will hear and live in awe, and will never again do the likes of this bad deed among you. ²¹Your eye will not pity: life for life, eye for eye, tooth for tooth, hand for hand, foot for foot.

How to make war

20 When you go out for battle against your enemies and you see horse and chariotry, a company bigger than you, you will not be afraid of them, because Yahweh your God, who got you out of the country of Misrayim, will be with you. ²When you're drawing near for battle, the priest is to come up and speak to the company, ³and say to them: 'Listen, Yisra'el. You're drawing near for battle against your enemies today. Your heart is not to be soft. Don't be afraid, don't be in haste, don't be frightened before them, ⁴because Yahweh your God is going with you to do battle for you with your enemies, to deliver you.'

⁵The officials will speak to the company: 'Who is the individual who's built a new house and not dedicated it? He's to go and turn back to his house, so he doesn't die in battle and

another individual dedicate it. ⁶Who is the individual who's planted a vineyard and not initiated it? He's to go and turn back to his house, so he doesn't die in battle and another individual initiate it. ⁷Who is the individual who's betrothed a woman and not taken her? He's to go and turn back to his house so he doesn't die in battle and another individual take her.'

⁸The officials are to speak further to the people and say, 'Who is the individual who's afraid and whose mind is frail? He's to go and turn back to his house so his brothers' mind doesn't melt like his mind.'

⁹When the officials have finished speaking to the company, they're to appoint army officers at the head of the company.

How to make war impractical

¹⁰When you draw near to a town to do battle against it, you're to call for peace to it. ¹¹If it answers with peace and opens up to you, the entire people that's to be found in it will become yours, as a workforce. They'll serve you. ¹²If it doesn't make peace with you and does battle with you, you're to besiege it, ¹³and Yahweh your God will give it into your hand. You're to strike down all its males with the mouth of the sword. ¹⁴Only, the women, the little ones, the animals and everything that's in the town, all its spoil, you may take as plunder for yourself, and devour your enemy's spoil, which Yahweh your God has given you.

¹⁵So you're to do to all the towns that are very far from you, which are not among the towns belonging to these nations here. ¹⁶Only, from the towns of these peoples that Yahweh your God is giving you as a domain you will not let any person live, ¹⁷because you're to devote them totally (the Hittite, the Amorite, the Kena'anite, the Perizzite, the Hivvite and the Yebusite), as Yahweh your God has ordered you, ¹⁸in order that they may not teach you to act in accordance with all their offensive practices, which they have performed for their gods, and you do wrong towards Yahweh your God.

¹⁹When you besiege a town for a long time in battling against it to capture it, you will not devastate its trees by thrusting an axe against them, because you're to eat from them. You will not cut them down, because are the trees of the open country human beings, to come before you in a siege work? ²⁰Only, trees that you know are not trees for food, them you may devastate and cut down so you may build a siege work against the town that's doing battle with you, until its fall.

Murder desecrates the land

21 When a person who has been run through is found, fallen in the fields, on the land that Yahweh your God is giving you to take possession of, and it's not known who struck him down, ²your elders or your authorities are to go out and take measurements to the towns that are round the person who has been run through. ³The town near the person who has been run through – that town's elders are to get a heifer from the herd that hasn't been made to serve, that hasn't pulled in a yoke. ⁴That town's elders are to take the heifer down to a flowing wadi that has not served, not been sown, and to break the heifer's neck there, in the wadi.

⁵The Levitical priests will come up, because Yahweh your God chose them to minister to him and to bless in Yahweh's name, and every argument and every assault rests on their pronouncement. ⁶All the elders of that town who were near to the person who has been run through will wash their hands over the heifer whose neck has been broken in the wadi. ⁷They will avow: 'Our hands didn't shed this blood; our eyes didn't see. ⁸Make expiation for your people Yisra'el whom you redeemed, Yahweh. Don't put the blood of a person who's free of guilt among your people Yisra'el.' And the blood will be expiated for them. ⁹You yourself will burn away the blood of the person who is free of guilt from among you, because you do what's right in Yahweh's eyes.

The loved and the unloved

¹⁰When you go out for battle against your enemies, and Yahweh your God gives them into your hand and you take them captive, ¹¹and you see among the captives a woman

who's attractive in appearance, you fancy her, you get her for yourself as wife, ¹²you bring her inside your house, she shaves her head, trims her nails, ¹³removes her captive clothes from her, lives in your house, and bewails her father and her mother for a whole month, and after this you have sex with her and you become her husband and she becomes your wife: ¹⁴if you then don't want her, you're to send her off for herself. You will not at all sell her for silver. You will not do what you like with her, since you've humbled her.

¹⁵When a man has two wives and one is loved and one disliked, and they've borne him sons, the loved and the disliked, and the firstborn son belongs to the disliked one, ¹⁶on the day he gives what he has to his sons as their domain, he cannot treat as firstborn the son of the one who is loved in disregard of the son of the one who is disliked who was the firstborn. ¹⁷Rather he's to treat as the firstborn the son of the one who is disliked, by giving him a double share in all that is found to him, because he's the first of his vigour. The due of the firstborn is his.

¹⁸When an individual has a defiant and rebellious son who doesn't listen to his father's voice or to his mother's voice, and they discipline him but he doesn't listen to them, ¹⁹his father and his mother are to get hold of him and take him out to the town's elders, to the gateway of his place. ²⁰They're to say to the town's elders, 'This son of ours is defiant and rebellious. He doesn't listen to our voice. He's a wastrel and a drunkard.' ²¹All the town's people are to pelt him with stones so he dies. So you will burn away the bad thing from among you; all Yisra'el will hear and live in awe.

Responsibilities

²²When there's a wrong that carries a death sentence against a man and he's put to death, and you hang him up on a tree, ²³you will not let his corpse stay the night on the tree. Rather, you're to make sure you bury him that day, because someone hanged up is a slight to God, and you will not make taboo your land that Yahweh your God is giving you as a domain.

22 You will not see your brother's ox or his sheep straying, and hide from them. You're definitely to get them back to your brother. ²If your brother is not near to you or you don't know him, take it home to your house so it may be with you until your brother enquires about it and you can give it back to him. ³You're to act in this way with his donkey and to act in this way with his clothing and to act in this way with anything lost by your brother, which gets lost from him and which you find. You can't hide. ⁴You will not see your brother's donkey or his ox falling on the road and hide from them. You must definitely get it up with him.

⁵A man's things will not be on a woman and a man will not wear a woman's clothing, because anyone who does these things is offensive to Yahweh your God.

⁶When a bird's nest happens to be before you on the road, in any tree or on the earth, with young ones or eggs and the mother sitting on the young or on the eggs, you will not take the mother along with the offspring. ⁷You're absolutely to send off the mother, but you may take the offspring for yourself, in order that things may be good for you and you may stay a long time.

⁸When you build a new house, you're to make a wall for your roof so you don't put shed blood on your household when someone falling down falls from it.

Accusations against a girl

⁹You will not sow your vineyard with two species, so the full harvest doesn't become sacred (the seed that you sow and the vineyard's yield). ¹⁰You will not plough with ox and with donkey together. ¹¹You will not wear a mixture of wool and linen together. ¹²You're to make yourself tassels on the four corners of your garment with which you cover yourself.

¹³When a man takes a wife and has sex with her, but dislikes her ¹⁴and makes accusations about her and causes her to have a bad name, and says 'I took this woman and had sex with her, and I didn't find in her the evidence of virginity', ¹⁵the girl's father and her mother are to get the evidence of the girl's virginity and bring it out to the town's elders at the gateway. ¹⁶The girl's father is to say to the elders, 'I gave my daughter to this man as wife but he came

to dislike her. ¹⁷Here, that man has made accusations, saying "I didn't find the evidence of virginity in your daughter." This is the evidence of my daughter's virginity.' And they will lay out the cloth before the town's elders. ¹⁸Then that town's elders are to get the man, chastise him, ¹⁹charge him a hundred in silver and give it to the girl's father, because he caused a Yisra'elite young girl to have a bad name. And she can be his wife; he will not be able to send her off through his entire life.

²⁰But if this thing was truthful, if the evidence of virginity was not found for the girl, ²¹they're to bring the girl to the entrance of her father's house, and the people of her town are to pelt her with stones so she dies, because she's done something villainous in Yisra'el by whoring in her father's household. So you will burn away the bad thing from among you.

Sex in the city and in the country

²²When a man is found sleeping with a woman who's married to a husband, they are to die, both of them, the man who slept with the woman and the woman. So you will burn away the bad thing from Yisra'el.

²³When there's a girl who's a young girl betrothed to a man, and a man finds her in the town and sleeps with her, ²⁴you're to take the two of them out to the gateway of that town and pelt them with stones so they die (the girl on account of the fact that she didn't cry out in the town, and the man on account of the fact that he humbled his neighbour's wife). So you will burn away the bad thing from among you. ²⁵But if the man finds the betrothed girl in the fields and the man takes strong hold of her and sleeps with her, the man who slept with her is alone to die. ²⁶You're not to do anything to the girl. There's no wrong that deserves death attaching to her, because this thing is like an individual who sets upon his neighbour and kills him, ²⁷because he found her in the fields. Should the betrothed girl have cried out, there was no one to deliver her.

²⁸When a man finds a girl who's a young girl who's not betrothed and takes hold of her and sleeps with her and they're found out, ²⁹the man who slept with her is to give the girl's father fifty in silver and she can be his wife.

Since he humbled her, he can't send her off through his entire life.

³⁰No individual will take his father's wife. He will not uncover his father's garment.

Attitudes to foreigners

23 No one whose testicles are crushed or whose penis is cut off will come into Yahweh's congregation. ²No one misbegotten will come into Yahweh's congregation; even his tenth generation will not come into Yahweh's congregation.

³No Ammonite or Mo'abite will come into Yahweh's congregation; even their tenth generation will not come into Yahweh's congregation ever, ⁴because of the fact that they didn't meet you with bread and with water on the way, when you got out of Misrayim, and because he hired against you Bil'am ben Be'or from Petor in Aram-of-the-Two-Rivers, to slight you ⁵(but Yahweh your God was not willing to listen to Bil'am, and for you Yahweh your God turned the slight into blessing, because Yahweh your God is loyal to you). ⁶You will not enquire after their welfare or what is good for them through your entire life, permanently.

⁷You will not take offence at an Edomite, because he's your brother; you will not take offence at an Misrayimite, because you were a resident in his country. ⁸Children that are born to them, their third generation, may come into Yahweh's congregation.

⁹When you go out as a camp against your enemies, you're to keep yourselves away from any bad thing. ¹⁰When there is among you an individual who is not pure because of a nocturnal emission, he's to go outside the camp. He will not come inside the camp. ¹¹When evening is turning its face, he's to wash in water, and as the sun goes down he may come inside the camp.

¹²There's to be an area for you outside the camp and you're to go out there, outside. ¹³You're to have a stick along with your equipment, and when you've sat outside, you're to dig with it and go back and cover your excrement. ¹⁴Because Yahweh your God walks about inside your camp to rescue you and to give over your enemies before you, your camp

is to be sacred. He's not to see in you something indecent and turn back from following you.

The runaway servant

¹⁵You will not hand over to his lord a servant who escapes to you from his lord. ¹⁶He's to live with you, among you in the place that he chooses in one of your communities, in one that seems good to him. You will not do him wrong.

¹⁷No one from among Yisra'el's women will become a hierodule, and no one from among Yisra'el's men will become a hierodule. ¹⁸A whore's 'gift' and a dog's fee will not come into the house of Yahweh your God for any pledge, because both of them would be an offence to Yahweh your God.

¹⁹You will not charge interest to your brother: interest on silver, interest on food or interest on anything that can be the subject of interest. ²⁰To a foreigner you may charge interest, but to your brother you will not charge interest, in order that Yahweh your God may bless you in every venture of your hand in the country where you're coming to take possession of it.

²¹When you make a pledge to Yahweh your God, you will not put off making good on it, because Yahweh your God will definitely require it from you, and there will be wrongdoing counted against you, ²²but when you leave off from pledging, there will not be wrongdoing counted against you. ²³What comes out from your lips you're to keep and act on, as you freely made a pledge to Yahweh your God, which you spoke with your own mouth.

²⁴When you come into your neighbour's vineyard, you may eat grapes in accordance with your appetite until you're full, but you will not put them into your container. ²⁵When you come into your neighbour's standing grain, you may pluck ears with your hand, but you will not put a sickle to your neighbour's standing grain.

The pain and the joy of marriage

24 When a man takes a wife and becomes her husband, if she doesn't find grace in his eyes because he finds something indecent in her, and he writes her a divorce document, puts it in her hand and sends her off from his household, ²and she leave his household, goes and comes to belong to another man, ³but the other man dislikes her, writes her a divorce document, puts it in her hand and sends her off from his household, or when the other man who took her as his wife dies, ⁴her first husband who sent her off cannot take her again as his wife after she's been made taboo, because it would be an offence before Yahweh. You will not do wrong to the country that Yahweh your God is giving you as a domain.

⁵When a man takes a new wife he will not go out in the army, and he will not pass over to it for anything. For a year he is to be free for his household so he may enable his wife whom he's taken to rejoice.

⁶Someone may not take a hand mill or an upper millstone as security, because he would be taking a life as security.

⁷When an individual is found kidnapping a person from among his brothers, from among the Yisra'elites, so he can turn him into a slave and sell him, that kidnapper is to die. So you will burn away the bad thing from among you.

⁸Keep careful watch on yourself in an outbreak of scaliness by acting in accordance with everything that the Levitical priests instruct you. As I ordered them, you're to keep watch so as to act. ⁹Be mindful of what Yahweh your God did to Miryam on the journey when you'd got out of Misrayim.

On sacred inefficiency

¹⁰When you make a loan of any kind to your neighbour, you're not to go into his house to get his collateral. ¹¹You're to stand outside while the individual to whom you're making the loan brings the collateral to you outside. ¹²If he's someone humble, you will not sleep with his collateral. ¹³You're definitely to give his collateral back to him at sunset so he may sleep in his covering and bless you, and there will be faithfulness counted for you before Yahweh your God.

¹⁴You will not defraud a humble and needy employee from your brothers or from your residents who are in your country, in your

communities. ¹⁵You're to give him his payment on the day. The sun will not go down on it, because he's humble and he's basing his life on it, and he will call out to God against you, and there will be wrongdoing counted against you.

¹⁶Parents will not be put to death for children and children will not be put to death for parents. People are to be put to death, an individual for his own wrongdoing.

¹⁷You will not twist the exercise of authority in respect of a resident or orphan, and you will not take a widow's coat as security. ¹⁸You're to be mindful that you were a serf in Misrayim and Yahweh your God redeemed you from there. That's why I'm ordering you to do this thing.

¹⁹When you reap your harvest in your fields and you overlook a sheaf in the fields, you will not go back to get it. It's to belong to the resident, to the orphan and to the widow, in order that Yahweh your God may bless you in all the action of your hands. ²⁰When you beat your olive tree, you will not go over it after you. It's to belong to the resident, to the orphan and to the widow. ²¹When you cut the grapes from your vineyard, you will not pick it over after you. It's to belong to the resident, to the orphan and to the widow. ²²You're to be mindful that you were a serf in the country of Misrayim. That's why I'm ordering you to do this thing.

Maintaining the family name

25 When there's an argument between people and they come up for a decision, and they decide for them and pronounce one in the right and the other in the wrong, ²if the one in the wrong is to be beaten, the one who makes decision is to have him fall down and beaten before him with a number that's enough for his wrongdoing. ³While he may have him beaten forty times, he will not do more, so he doesn't do more beating on top of these, a huge beating, and your brother is slighted in your eyes.

⁴You will not muzzle an ox when it's threshing.

⁵When brothers live together and one of them dies and has no son, the dead man's wife will not go elsewhere, to a man who's an outsider. Her brother-in-law is to have sex with her; he's to take her as his wife and act as brother-in-law to her. ⁶The first son to whom she gives birth will take his place in the name of his dead brother so his name is not wiped out from Yisra'el.

⁷If the man doesn't want to take his sister-in-law, his sister-in-law is to go up to the gateway, to the elders, and say, 'My brother-in-law won't set up a name in Yisra'el for his brother. He's not willing to act as brother-in-law to me.' ⁸His town's elders will call for him and speak to him. If he stands firm and says 'I don't want to take her', ⁹his sister-in-law will come up to him before the eyes of the elders, pull his boot from on his foot, spit in his face and avow, 'In this way it's done to the man who doesn't build up his brother's household.' ¹⁰It will be named in Yisra'el, 'the household of the man who had his boot pulled off'.

Not to forget Amaleq

¹¹When men fight one another, a man and his brother, and the wife of one comes near to rescue her husband from the hand of the one who is striking him, puts out her hand and takes strong hold of him by his private parts, ¹²you're to cut off her fist. Your eye will not pity.

¹³You will not have in your bag two stones, big and small. ¹⁴You will not have in your house two measures, big and small. ¹⁵You're to have a stone that's perfect and faithful, a measure that's perfect and faithful, in order that your days may be many on the land that Yahweh your God is giving you. ¹⁶Because anyone who does these things, anyone who does evil, is an offence to Yahweh your God.

¹⁷Be mindful of what Amaleq did to you on the journey, when you had got out of Misrayim. ¹⁸He met you on the journey and attacked you from the rear (all the ones who were shattered at the back of you), when you were faint and weary. He was not in awe of God. ¹⁹When Yahweh your God enables you to settle down free of all your enemies all round in the country that Yahweh your God is giving you as your domain, to take possession of it, you're to erase the memory of Amaleq from under the heavens. You will not put it out of mind.

A refugee has become a great nation

26 When you come into the country that Yahweh your God is giving you as a domain, and you take possession of it and live in it, ²you're to get some of the first of all the fruit of the land that you bring in from your country that Yahweh your God is giving you, put it in a basket and go to the site where Yahweh your God chooses to have his name dwell. ³You're to come to the priest who is there at that time and say to him, 'I tell Yahweh your God today that I've come into the country that Yahweh swore to our ancestors to give them.' ⁴The priest will take the basket from your hand and set it down before the altar of Yahweh your God. ⁵You are to avow before Yahweh your God: 'My father was an Aramite refugee and he went down to Misrayim and resided there as a few people, but there he became a big, numerous and substantial nation. ⁶The Misrayimites dealt badly with us, humbled us and put tough servitude on us, ⁷but we cried out to Yahweh the God of our ancestors, and Yahweh listened to our voice. He saw our humbling, our hardship and our affliction. ⁸Yahweh got us out of Misrayim with a strong hand, with an extended arm, with great awe-inspiring action, with signs and with proofs. ⁹He brought us to this place and gave us this country, a country flowing with milk and syrup. ¹⁰So now, here, I've brought the first of the fruit of the land that you, Yahweh, have given me.'

You will set it down before Yahweh your God and bow low before Yahweh your God, ¹¹and rejoice in all the good that Yahweh your God has given you and your household, you, the Levite and the resident who is among you.

A mutual commitment

¹²When you finish setting aside the entire tenth of your yield in the third year, the year of the tenth, and give to the Levite, to the resident, to the orphan and to the widow, so they may eat in your communities and be full, ¹³you're to say before Yahweh your God, 'I've cleared out what was sacred from the house. Further, I've given it to the Levite, to the resident, to the orphan and to the widow, in accordance with your entire order that you gave me. I haven't contravened any of your orders.

I haven't put them out of mind.
¹⁴I haven't eaten of it while in sorrow.
I haven't cleared out any of it while taboo.
I haven't given any of it to a dead person.

I've listened to the voice of Yahweh my God. I've acted in accordance with everything that you ordered me. ¹⁵Look out from your sacred abode, from the heavens, and bless your people Yisraël and the land that you've given us, as you swore to our ancestors, a country flowing with milk and syrup.'

¹⁶This day Yahweh your God is ordering you to act on these decrees and rulings. You're to keep them and act on them with your entire mind and with your entire being. ¹⁷You've got Yahweh to say today that he'll be your God and that you'll walk in his ways, keep his decrees, his orders and his rulings, and listen to his voice. ¹⁸And Yahweh has got you to say today that you'll be a people that is personal treasure, as he spoke to you, that you'll keep all his orders, ¹⁹that he'll put you on high over all the nations that he made, for praise, for fame and for glory, and that you'll be a people sacred to Yahweh your God, as he spoke.

Inscribed stones

27 Mosheh and the Yisraëlite elders ordered the people: 'Keep the entire order that I'm giving you today. ²On the day that you cross the Yarden into the country that Yahweh your God is giving you, you're to set up for yourself big stones. You're to coat them in plaster ³and write on them all the words in this instruction, when you cross in order that you may go into the country that Yahweh your God is giving you, a country flowing with milk and syrup, as Yahweh the God of your ancestors spoke to you.

⁴So when you cross the Yarden you're to set up on Mount Ebal these stones about which I'm ordering you today, and coat them in plaster, ⁵and build an altar there for Yahweh your God, an altar of stones. You will not wield iron on them; ⁶you're to build the altar of Yahweh your God from whole stones. You're to

offer up whole offerings on it for Yahweh your God, ⁷and make well-being sacrifices, eat there and rejoice before Yahweh your God. ⁸And you're to write on the stones all the words in this instruction. Make it good and plain.'

⁹Mosheh and the Levitical priests spoke to all Yisra'el: 'Be quiet and listen, Yisra'el. This day you've become a people belonging to Yahweh your God. ¹⁰You're to listen to the voice of Yahweh your God and act on his orders and on his decrees, which I'm ordering you today.'

¹¹Mosheh ordered the people that day: ¹²'These are to stand to bless the people on Mount Gerizim, when you cross the Yarden: Shim'on [Simeon], Levi, Yehudah [Judah], Yissakar [Issachar], Yoseph [Joseph] and Binyamin [Benjamin]. ¹³These are to stand for the slight on Mount Ebal: Re'uben, Gad, Asher, Zebulun, Dan and Naphtali.

Curses

¹⁴The Levites will avow to every individual in Yisra'el, in a loud voice:

¹⁵Cursed is the individual who makes a sculpture or figurine, an offensive thing to Yahweh, the making of a craftsman's hands, and sets it up in secret.

The entire people are to avow, "Yes!"
¹⁶Cursed is one who slights his father or his mother.

The entire people is to avow, "Yes!"
¹⁷Cursed is one who moves aside his neighbour's boundary marker.

The entire people is to avow, "Yes!"
¹⁸Cursed is one who misdirects a blind person on the road.

The entire people is to avow, "Yes!"
¹⁹Cursed is one who twists the exercise of authority for a resident, an orphan or a widow.

The entire people is to avow, "Yes!"
²⁰Cursed is one who sleeps with his father's wife, because he's uncovered his father's garment.

The entire people is to avow, "Yes!"
²¹Cursed is one who sleeps with any animal.

The entire people is to avow, "Yes!"
²²Cursed is one who sleeps with his sister, his father's daughter or his mother's daughter.

The entire people is to avow, "Yes!"

²³Cursed is one who sleeps with his mother-in-law.

The entire people is to avow, "Yes!"
²⁴Cursed is one who strikes down his neighbour in secret.

The entire people is to avow, "Yes!"
²⁵Cursed is one who accepts a bribe to strike down a person who is free of guilt.

The entire people is to avow, "Yes!"
²⁶Cursed is someone who doesn't implement the words in this instruction and act on them.

The entire people is to avow, "Yes!"

Blessings

28 If you listen attentively to the voice of Yahweh your God so as to keep all his orders which I'm giving you today by acting on them, Yahweh your God will put you on high over all the nations on the earth. ²All these blessings will come on you and overtake you when you listen to the voice of Yahweh your God:

³Blessed are you in the town and blessed are you in the fields.
⁴Blessed is the fruit of your womb, the fruit of your land, the fruit of your animals, the drop of your domestic animals and the young of your flock.
⁵Blessed is your basket and your kneading bowl.
⁶Blessed are you in your coming in and blessed are you in your going out.

⁷Yahweh will make your enemies who set upon you take a beating before you. They will come out against you by one route but flee before you by seven routes.

⁸Yahweh will order blessing on you in your barns and in every venture of your hand. He will bless you in the country that Yahweh your God is giving you. ⁹Yahweh will set you up as his sacred people, as he swore to you, because you keep the orders of Yahweh your God and walk in his ways. ¹⁰All the peoples of the earth will see that Yahweh's name has been called out over you and they will live in awe of you. ¹¹Yahweh will make you more than abound with good things, in the fruit of your womb, in the fruit of your animals and in the fruit of your land, on the land that Yahweh swore

to your ancestors to give them. ¹²Yahweh will open for you his storehouse of goodness, the heavens, to give rain on the earth in its time and to bless every action of your hand. You will lend to many nations but you won't borrow.

¹³Yahweh will make you the head and not the tail, and you will be only on top and not at the bottom, when you listen to the orders of Yahweh your God that I'm giving you today, keeping them by acting on them, ¹⁴and don't turn aside from all the things that I'm ordering you today, right or left, by following other gods to serve them.

Curses once more

¹⁵But if you don't listen to the voice of Yahweh your God, keeping all his orders and his decrees that I'm giving you today by acting on them, all these slights will come on you and overtake you.

- ¹⁶Cursed are you in the town and cursed are you in the fields.
- ¹⁷Cursed is your basket and your kneading bowl.
- ¹⁸Cursed is the fruit of your womb, the fruit of your land, the drop of your domestic animals and the young of your flock.
- ¹⁹Cursed are you in your coming in and cursed are you in your going out.

²⁰Yahweh will send off against you curse, turmoil and rebuke in every venture of your hand that you undertake, until you're annihilated and until you perish quickly in the face of the bad nature of your practices by which you've abandoned me. ²¹Yahweh will make epidemic attach itself to you until he finishes you off from upon the land where you're coming to take possession of it. ²²Yahweh will strike you down with wasting, with fever, with inflammation, with heatwave, with drought, with blight and with mildew, and they'll pursue you until you perish. ²³The heavens that are above your head will be copper and the earth that's under you will be iron. ²⁴Yahweh will make the rain of your country dust, and earth will descend on you from the heavens until you're annihilated. ²⁵Yahweh will make you take a beating before your enemies. You will go out against him by one route but flee before him by seven routes. You will become a thing of horror to all the kingdoms of the earth. ²⁶Your corpse will become food for all the birds of the heavens and for the animals of the earth, with no one to make them tremble.

Troubles

²⁷Yahweh will strike you down with the inflammation of Misrayim, with haemorrhoids, with sores and with rashes, from which you won't be able to find healing. ²⁸Yahweh will strike you down with madness, with blindness and with confusion of mind. ²⁹You'll be groping at noon as the blind person gropes in darkness. You won't make a success of your journeys. You will only be defrauded and robbed all the time, with no one to deliver.

³⁰You'll betroth a wife but another man will sleep with her. You'll build a house but you won't live in it. You'll plant a vineyard but you won't initiate it. ³¹Your ox slaughtered before your eyes: and you won't eat of it. Your donkey stolen before you: and it won't come back to you. Your flock given over to your enemies: and you'll have no one to deliver. ³²Your sons and your daughters given over to another people, with your eyes looking and spending themselves for them all the time: and there'll be no power in your hand. ³³A people you don't acknowledge will eat the fruit of your ground and all your weariness. You'll be only defrauded and crushed all the time. ³⁴You'll be made insane by the sight that your eyes see. ³⁵Yahweh will strike you down with bad inflammation, on your knees and on your thighs, from which you won't be able to find healing, from the sole of your foot to the crown of your head.

³⁶Yahweh will make you, and the king whom you set over you, go to a nation that you haven't acknowledged, you or your ancestors. There you'll serve other gods, wood and stone. ³⁷You'll be something shocking, an object lesson and a subject of taunting among all the peoples where Yahweh drives you.

Defeat

³⁸You'll take much seed out to the field but you'll gather little because the locust will

devour it. ³⁹You'll plant vineyards and serve them but you won't drink wine and you won't gather because the worm will eat them. ⁴⁰You'll have olive trees through your entire border, but you won't apply oil because your olive tree will drop off. ⁴¹You'll father sons and daughters but they won't be yours because they'll go into captivity. ⁴²Insects will take possession of all your trees and the fruit of your ground. ⁴³The resident who's among you will go up higher and higher above you and you'll descend lower and lower. ⁴⁴He'll lend to you and you won't lend to him. He'll be head and you'll be tail.

⁴⁵All these slights will come on you, and they'll pursue you and overtake you until you're annihilated, because you didn't listen to the voice of Yahweh your God, keeping his orders and his decrees which he gave you. ⁴⁶They'll be permanent signs and proofs against you and against your offspring. ⁴⁷Since you didn't serve Yahweh your God with rejoicing and with a good heart because of the large quantity of everything, ⁴⁸you'll serve your enemies whom Yahweh will send off against you, in hunger and in thirst, in nakedness and in lack of everything. He'll put an iron yoke on your neck until he's annihilated you.

⁴⁹Yahweh will bring against you a nation from afar, from the end of the earth, as the eagle swoops, a nation whose tongue you can't listen to, ⁵⁰a nation hard-faced that won't honour the person of the elderly and won't show grace to the young, ⁵¹and will eat the fruit of your animals and the fruit of your ground until you're annihilated, that won't leave you grain, new wine or fresh oil, the drop of your domestic animals or the young of your flock, until it has let you perish.

The horrors of siege

⁵²It will besiege you in all your communities until the fall of your lofty and fortified walls on which you're relying, in the entire country. It will besiege you in all your communities in the entire country that Yahweh your God has given you. ⁵³You'll eat the offspring of your womb, the flesh of your sons and your daughters, whom Yahweh your God has given you, in the siege and in the stress that your enemy puts on you.

⁵⁴The soft individual among you and the one who is very sensitive – his eye will be mean towards his brother and towards the wife in his arms and towards the rest of his children whom he has remaining, ⁵⁵so that he won't give one of them any of the flesh of his children that he eats, because he doesn't have anything remaining for himself, in the siege and in the stress that your enemy puts on you in all your communities.

⁵⁶The woman who is soft among you and sensitive, who hasn't ventured to set the sole of her foot on the ground because of being sensitive and soft – her eye will be mean towards the husband in her arms, towards her son and towards her daughter, ⁵⁷towards her afterbirth that comes out beneath her feet and towards her children to whom she gives birth, because she will eat them in secret, as a result of her lack of everything, in the siege and in the stress that your enemy puts on you in your communities.

⁵⁸If you don't keep all the words in this instruction that are written in this document by acting on them, so as to live in awe of this honoured and awe-inspiring name, Yahweh your God, ⁵⁹Yahweh will bring extraordinary calamities on you and calamities on your offspring, big and lasting calamities, bad and lasting diseases. ⁶⁰He will bring back on you every illness of Misrayim before which you were in dread, so that they attach themselves to you.

No resting place

⁶¹Yahweh will also bring on you every disease and every calamity that's not written in this instruction document, until you're annihilated. ⁶²You'll remain as a few people, although you were like the stars in the heavens in your large number, because you didn't listen to the voice of Yahweh your God. ⁶³As Yahweh delighted over you in doing good to you and in multiplying you, so Yahweh will delight over you in letting you perish and annihilating you. You'll be torn from upon the land where you're coming in to take possession of it.

⁶⁴Yahweh will disperse you among the peoples from one end of the earth to the other end of the earth, and you'll serve other gods

there that you haven't acknowledged, you or your ancestors. ⁶⁵And among those nations you won't rest. There'll be no place to settle for the sole of your foot. Yahweh will give you there an anxious mind, spending of eyes and languishing of the entire being. ⁶⁶Your life will be hanging at a distance from you. You'll be terrified night and day. You won't trust your life. ⁶⁷In the morning you'll say, "If only it were evening", and in the evening you'll say, "If only it were morning", because of dread in your mind that you feel and because of the sight of your eyes that you see. ⁶⁸Yahweh will take you back to Misrayim in ships, by a way that I said you would not again see, and you'll sell yourselves there to your enemies as servants and maidservants, but there will be no buyer.'

29

These are the words of the pact that Yahweh ordered Mosheh to solemnize with the Yisra'elites in the country of Mo'ab, apart from the pact that he solemnized with them at Horeb.

The mystery of obedience and disobedience

²Mosheh called all Yisra'el and said to them: 'You yourselves have seen all that Yahweh did before your eyes in the country of Misrayim, to Par'oh, to all his servants and to his entire country, ³the great tests that your eyes saw, those great signs and proofs. ⁴But Yahweh hasn't given you a mind to acknowledge or eyes to see or ears to listen, until this day. ⁵I enabled you to go through the wilderness for forty years. Your clothes didn't wear out on you and your boot didn't wear out on your foot, ⁶you didn't eat bread and you didn't drink wine or liquor, in order that you might acknowledge that I am Yahweh your God. ⁷You came to this place and Sihon king of Heshbon and Og king of Bashan came out to meet you in battle but we struck them down, ⁸took their country, and gave it to the Re'ubenites, to the Gadites and to the half-clan of Menashsheh, as their domain.

⁹You're to keep the words in this pact and act on them, in order that you may thrive in everything that you do. ¹⁰You're standing today, all of you, before Yahweh your God – your heads, your clans, your elders, your officials, every individual in Yisra'el, ¹¹your little ones, your wives, your resident who is within the camps, from the person who chops your wood to the one who draws your water – ¹²for you to pass over into the pact of Yahweh your God and into its vow, which Yahweh your God is solemnizing with you today, ¹³in order that he may set you up today as a people for him and that he may be God for you, as he spoke to you and as he swore to your ancestors, to Abraham, to Yitshaq and to Ya'aqob. ¹⁴Not with you alone am I solemnizing this pact and this vow; ¹⁵rather with the one who is here with us today standing before Yahweh our God, and with the one who is not here with us today.

Why this angry fury?

¹⁶Because you yourselves acknowledge the fact that we lived in the country of Misrayim and the fact that we passed through the middle of the nations that you did pass through, ¹⁷and you saw their abominations and their idols, wood and stone, silver and gold, which were with them.

¹⁸Beware that there is not among you a man or a woman, a kin-group or a clan, whose mind is turning about today from Yahweh our God to go to serve those nations' gods. Beware that there is not among you a root sprouting a poisonous and bitter plant. ¹⁹When he hears the words of this vow he may bless himself inside, saying "Things will go well for me when I walk by the determination of my mind, in order to augment the well-watered with the dry." ²⁰Yahweh will not be willing to pardon him. Rather, Yahweh's anger will then smoke, with his passion, against that man. The entire vow written in this document will descend on him. Yahweh will wipe out his name from under the heavens. ²¹Yahweh will distinguish him from all the Yisra'elite clans for bad experiences, in accordance with all the vows in the pact written in this instruction document.

²²The next generation will say – your children who come after you, and the foreigner who comes from a distant country and sees the calamities on that country and its diseases that Yahweh will have brought on it (²³its entire country, burning with sulphur and salt, won't be sown and won't bloom, and no grass will grow in it, like the overthrow of Sedom and

Amorah, Admah and Tseboyim, which Yahweh overthrew in his anger and in his wrath): ²⁴all the nations will say, "Why did Yahweh act like this to this country? Why this great angry rage?"

The things hidden and the things revealed

²⁵They will say, "On account of the fact that they abandoned the pact of Yahweh the God of their ancestors which he solemnized with them when he got them out of the country of Misrayim, ²⁶and went and served other gods and bowed low to them, gods that they had not acknowledged and he had not allocated to them. ²⁷Yahweh's anger raged at that country so as to bring on it every curse that's written in this document. ²⁸Yahweh rooted them up from on their land in anger, in wrath and in great rage, and sent them off to another country this very day."

²⁹The things that are hidden belong to Yahweh our God, but the things that are revealed belong to us and to our children permanently, to act on all the words of this instruction.

30 But when all these things come on you (the blessing and the curse that I've put before you) and you bring them back to mind among all the nations where Yahweh your God has driven you away, ²and turn back to Yahweh your God and listen to his voice in accordance with everything that I'm ordering you today, you and your children, with your entire mind and with your entire being, ³Yahweh your God will bring back your good fortune. He will have compassion on you and again gather you from all the peoples where Yahweh your God has dispersed you.

⁴If your people who've been driven away are at the end of the heavens, from there Yahweh your God will gather you, from there he'll get you. ⁵Yahweh your God will bring you to the country that your ancestors took possession of and you'll take possession of it. He'll be good to you and he'll make you more numerous than your ancestors.

In your mouth and in your mind

⁶Yahweh your God will circumcise your mind and the mind of your offspring so that you are loyal to Yahweh your God with your entire mind and with your entire being, in order that you may live. ⁷Yahweh your God will put all these vows on your enemies, on the people who are hostile to you, who have pursued you. ⁸You yourselves will come back and listen to Yahweh's voice and act on all his orders that I'm giving you today.

⁹Yahweh your God will make you abound in all the action of your hand, in the fruit of your womb, in the fruit of your animals and in the fruit of your land, for good, because Yahweh will again rejoice over you for good, as he rejoiced over your ancestors, ¹⁰when you listen to the voice of Yahweh your God so as to keep his orders and his decrees that are written in this instruction document, when you turn back to Yahweh your God with your entire mind and with your entire being.

¹¹Because this order that I'm giving you today is not too extraordinary for you, and it's not far away. ¹²It's not in the heavens, to make you say, "Who will go up to the heavens for us and get it for us, and enable us to listen to it so we may act on it?" ¹³It's not across the sea, to make you say, "Who will go across the sea for us and get it for us, and enable us to listen to it so we may act on it?" ¹⁴Because the thing is very near you, in your mouth and in your mind, so as to act on it. ¹⁵See, today I've put before you life and good things, death and bad things. ¹⁶I'm ordering you today to be loyal to Yahweh your God by walking in his ways and by keeping his orders, his decrees and his rulings, so you may live and be numerous, and so Yahweh your God may bless you in the country where you're coming to take possession of it.

Choose life

¹⁷But if your mind turns about and you don't listen, and you stray and bow low to other gods and serve them, ¹⁸I tell you today that you will quite perish. You won't stay a long time on the land where you're crossing the Yarden to come to take possession of it. ¹⁹I call the heavens and the earth to testify against you today. I've put life and death before you, blessing and curse. You're to choose life, in order that you and your offspring may

live, ²⁰by being loyal to Yahweh your God by listening to his voice and by attaching yourself to him, because that means your life and your long stay living on the land that Yahweh swore to your ancestors, to Abraham, to Yitshaq and to Ya'aqob, to give them.'

31

Mosheh went and spoke these words to all Yisra'el: ²'I am a man of 120 years. Today I can no longer go out and come in, and Yahweh has said to me, "You will not cross this Yarden." ³Yahweh your God – he's crossing before you, and he himself will annihilate these nations from before you so you may dispossess them. Yehoshua is the one who is crossing before you, as Yahweh has spoken.

⁴Yahweh will do to them as he did to Sihon and to Og, the kings of the Amorites, and to their country, whom he annihilated. ⁵Yahweh will give them up before you and you're to act towards them in accordance with the entire order that I gave you. ⁶Be strong and stand firm. Don't be afraid and don't be frightened before them, because Yahweh your God, he's going with you. He won't let go of you. He won't abandon you.'

Teaching to read

⁷Mosheh called Yehoshua and said to him before the eyes of all Yisra'el, 'Be strong and stand firm, because you're the one who will go with this people into the country that Yahweh swore to their ancestors to give them, and you'll enable them to have it as their domain. ⁸Yahweh himself is going before you. He'll be with you. He won't let go of you. He won't abandon you. You won't be afraid. You won't be scared.'

⁹Mosheh wrote this instruction and gave it to the priests, Levi's descendants who carried Yahweh's pact chest, and to all the Yisra'elite elders. ¹⁰Mosheh ordered them, 'At the end of seven years, at the time set for the release year, at the Sukkot Festival, ¹¹when all Yisra'el comes to appear before Yahweh your God at the site that he chooses, you're to read out this instruction before all Yisra'el, in their ears. ¹²Congregate the people – the men and the women, the little ones and the resident who is in your communities – in order that they may listen, and in order that they may learn and live in awe of Yahweh your God, and keep all the things in this instruction by acting on them. ¹³Their children who haven't acknowledged it – they're to listen and learn to live in awe of Yahweh your God all the time that you're living on the land where you're crossing the Yarden to take possession of it.'

¹⁴Yahweh said to Mosheh: 'Here, the time for you to die has drawn near. Call for Yehoshua and take your stand in the appointment tent so I may give him my orders.' So Mosheh and Yehoshua went and took their stand in the appointment tent, ¹⁵and Yahweh appeared in the tent, in a cloud pillar. The cloud pillar stood at the entrance of the tent.

Write down this song

¹⁶Yahweh said to Mosheh: 'Here, you're going to lie down with your ancestors. This people will set off and whore after the foreign gods of the country where it's coming, within it. It will abandon me and contravene my pact, which I solemnized with it, ¹⁷and my anger will rage against it on that day. I shall abandon them and hide my face from them. It will be for devouring. Many bad experiences and pressures will befall it. On that day it will say, "Isn't it on account of the fact that our God was not among us that these bad experiences have befallen us?" ¹⁸But I myself will quite hide my face on that day because of all the bad things that it has done, because it has turned its face to other gods.

¹⁹So now write down this song for yourselves and teach it to the Yisra'elites. Place it in their mouths in order that this song may be for me a witness against the Yisra'elites. ²⁰When I bring it into the land that I swore to its ancestors, flowing with milk and syrup, and it eats and is full and becomes enriched, and turns its face to other gods, and they serve them and disdain me, and it contravenes my pact, ²¹and when many bad experiences and pressures befall it, this song will avow before it as a witness, because it won't be put out of mind from the mouth of its offspring. Because I know its inclination, which it's forming today, before I bring it into the country that I swore.' ²²So Mosheh wrote down this song that day and taught it to the Yisra'elites.

²³He ordered Yehoshua ben Nun, 'Be strong and stand firm, because you're the one who will

enable the Yisra'elites to go into the country that I swore to their ancestors. I will be with you.'

A truthful God

²⁴When Mosheh had finished writing down the words in this instruction on a document, until it was complete, ²⁵Mosheh ordered the Levites, who carried Yahweh's pact chest: ²⁶'Take this instruction document and place it by the side of the pact chest of Yahweh your God. It's to be there as a witness against you. ²⁷Because I myself know your rebelliousness and the toughness of your neck. There, you've been rebellious with Yahweh while I've still been alive with you, today, and you will certainly be after my death. ²⁸Congregate to me all the elders of your clans and your officials so I may speak these words in their ears and call the heavens and the earth to testify against you. ²⁹Because I know that after my death you will behave in a totally devastating way and depart from the path on which I've ordered you, and that bad fortune will meet you in a later time, because you do what is bad in Yahweh's eyes so as to provoke him by the action of your hands.'

³⁰So Mosheh spoke in the ears of the entire Yisra'elite congregation the words of this song, until it was complete.

32

Give ear, heavens, so I may speak;
    the earth is to listen to the words of my mouth.

²May my grasp of things fall like rain,
    my speech drop like dew,
Like showers on grass,
    like a downpour on shoots.
³Because I call out the name of Yahweh:
    ascribe greatness to our God!
⁴The crag: his action is perfect,
    because all his ways are authoritative.
A trustworthy God with whom there's no evil;
    he is faithful and upright.

Is this the way you repay Yahweh?

⁵They have acted devastatingly with him, not as his children,
    with a defect in them, a perverse and crooked generation.
⁶Do you deal this to Yahweh,
    as a people that is villainous and not smart?
He's your Father who brought you into being, isn't he,
    the one who made you and established you.
⁷Be mindful of the time of old,
    consider the years of generation after generation.
Ask your father, and he will tell you,
    your elders, and they will say it to you.
⁸When the One on High gave the nations domains,
    divided up humanity,
He set the boundaries of the peoples,
    according to the number of the divine beings,
⁹Because Yahweh's share is his people,
    Ya'aqob is the allocation that is his domain.
¹⁰He found him in a wilderness region,
    in a howling desert wasteland.
He surrounded him, he looked after him,
    he preserved him like the pupil of his eye.
¹¹Like an eagle that stirs its nest,
    hovers over its young,
He spread his wings, took him,
    carried him on his pinions.
¹²Yahweh alone led him,
    there was no foreign god with him.
¹³He let him ride on the heights of the earth,
    he ate the fruit of the field.
He let him suckle on honey from a cliff,
    on oil from the flint of a crag,
¹⁴Curds from the herd, milk from the flock,
    with the fat of lambs,
Rams of Bashan and he-goats,
    with the kidney fat of wheat,
and the blood of the grape you drank,
    foaming wine.

¹⁵But Yeshurun got fat and kicked;
    you got fat, heavy and gross.
He took leave of the God who made him,
    despised the crag who delivered him.
¹⁶They aroused his passion with outside gods,
    provoked him with offensive things.
¹⁷They sacrificed to demons, no-god,
    gods they had not acknowledged,
New ones that had come from nearby,
    whom your ancestors didn't recognize.

¹⁸You forgot the crag who fathered you,
  put out of mind the God who was in labour with you.

Yahweh saw the provocation

¹⁹Yahweh saw and disdained them,
  because of the provocation of his sons and his daughters.
²⁰He said, 'I shall hide my face from them,
  and I shall see what is their future.
Because they're a contrary generation,
  children in whom there's no trustworthiness.
²¹Those people aroused my passion with a no-god,
  provoked me with their hollow things.
So I – I shall arouse their passion with a non-people,
  provoke them with a villainous nation.
²²Because a fire has blazed in my anger,
  and burned to lowest She'ol.
It has devoured the earth and its produce,
  set on fire the foundations of the mountains.
²³I shall gather bad things upon them,
  finish up my arrows against them.
²⁴Wasted by hunger, eaten by fever,
  bitter devastation,
I shall send off against them animal fangs,
  with the venom of creatures that crawl in the dirt.
²⁵The sword will bereave outside,
  dread from the rooms,
Both young man and young girl,
  the nursing baby with the grey-haired man.
²⁶I said I would cut them in pieces,
  I would eliminate the memory of them from humanity.
²⁷Except that I dreaded the provocation of the enemy,
  so that their attackers don't recognize,
So that they don't say, "Our hand is high,
  Yahweh has not done any of this!"
²⁸Because they're a nation lost for counsel;
  there's no insight in them.
²⁹If they were smart, they would understand this,
  they would have insight into their future.
³⁰How does one pursue a thousand,
  and two make ten thousand flee,
If it's not that their crag has sold them,
  Yahweh has delivered them up?

Their crag is not like our crag

³¹Because their crag is not like our crag –
  our enemies may be the judges.
³²Because their vine is from Sedom's vine,
  from Amorah's fields.
Their grapes are poisonous grapes,
  their clusters are bitter for them.
³³Their wine is the venom of asps,
  vipers' cruel poison.
³⁴It's laid up with me, isn't it,
  sealed up in my storehouses?
³⁵Redress and making good are mine
  at the time when their foot slips.
Because the day of their calamity is near,
  the things that are destined for them are making speed.
³⁶Because Yahweh will act in judgement for his people,
  will relent concerning his servants,
When he sees that their hand has failed,
  and there's no one, bound or released.
³⁷He will say, 'Where are their gods,
  the crag in which they took shelter,
³⁸Those who ate the fat of their sacrifices,
  drank the wine of their libations?
They should set off and help you;
  he should become a place to hide for you.
³⁹See, now, that I,
  I am the one.
There's no God beside me;
  I myself put to death and I make alive.
I hit and I myself will heal;
  there's no one rescues from my hand.
⁴⁰Because I raise my hand to the heavens,
  and I say: "As I live permanently:
⁴¹If I sharpen the flashing of my sword,
  and my hand takes hold of authority,
I shall give back redress to my attackers,
  I shall make good to the people who're hostile to me.
⁴²I shall make my arrows drunk with blood,
  my sword will devour flesh,
From the blood of the person who's been run through and the captive,
  from the long-haired head of the enemy."

The song shared

⁴³Resound over his people, you nations,
  because he takes redress for the blood of his servants.
He gives back redress to his attackers
  and makes expiation for his land, for his people.'

⁴⁴Mosheh came and spoke all the words of this song in the people's ears, he and Hoshea ben Nun. ⁴⁵Mosheh finished speaking all these words to all Yisra'el, ⁴⁶then said to them: 'Give your mind to all these words that I'm testifying against you today, which you're to order your children to keep by acting on them, all the words in this instruction. ⁴⁷Because it's not an empty thing for you. Rather, it's your life. Through this thing you'll stay a long time on the land where you're crossing the Yarden to take possession of it.' ⁴⁸Yahweh spoke to Mosheh that very day: ⁴⁹'Climb this mountain in the Regions Across, Mount Nebo, which is in the country of Mo'ab, which is facing Yeriho [Jericho], and look at the country of Kena'an, which I'm giving to the Yisra'elites as a holding. ⁵⁰You're to die on the mountain where you're climbing, and you're to be gathered to your kin, as Aharon your brother died on Mount Hor and was gathered to his kin, ⁵¹because of the fact that you trespassed against me among the Yisra'elites at Meribat Qadesh Water in the Tsin Wilderness, because of the fact that you didn't make me sacred among the Yisra'elites, ⁵²because you're to look at the country from a distance, but you will not come there, to the country that I'm giving to the Yisra'elites.'

Mosheh's final blessing: Re'uben, Yehudah, Levi

33 This is the blessing that Mosheh, the supernatural man, gave the Yisra'elites before his death:

²Yahweh came from Sinay,
  rose on them from Se'ir,
  shone from Mount Pa'ran.
He arrived from Sacred Myriads,
  from the south to them at the slope.
³As one who indeed holds the people dear,
  all its sacred ones are in your hand.
They themselves bowed at your foot,
  as the one who utters your words.
⁴The instruction with which Mosheh ordered us,
  the possession of Ya'aqob's congregation.
⁵He became king in Yeshurun,
  when the heads of the people gathered,
  Yisra'el's clans together.
⁶Re'uben is to live and not die,
  but it's to become few in number.

⁷This of Yehudah – he said:

Listen to Yehudah's voice, Yahweh,
  bring him to his people.
Make his hands powerful for him;
  may you be a help against his attackers.

⁸Of Levi he said:

Your Urim and Tummim
  be with the one who was loyal to you,
Whom you tested at Massah ['Testing'],
  argued with at Meribah ['Argument'] Water,
⁹The one who said of his father and of his mother,
  'I haven't looked at him',
And did not recognize his brothers,
  did not acknowledge his children,
Because they kept your word,
  preserved your pact.
¹⁰They will instruct Ya'aqob in your rulings,
  Yisra'el in your instruction.
They will place incense before your nose
  and a whole offering on your altar.
¹¹Bless his forcefulness, Yahweh,
  may you grace the action of his hands.
Hit the hips of the people who rise up against him,
  and the people who are hostile to him, so that they cannot rise up.

Binyamin, Yoseph, Zebulun

¹²Of Binyamin he said:

Yahweh's beloved
  is to dwell in confidence with him.

He will be surrounding him at all times;
    he will be dwelling between his shoulders.

¹³Of Yoseph he said:

His region be blessed by Yahweh,
    from the choice things of the heavens, from the dew,
    and from the deep that lies down below,
¹⁴From the choice things of the sun's yield,
    from the choice things of the moon's produce,
¹⁵From the top of the ancient mountains,
    from the choice things of the age-old hills,
¹⁶From the choice things of the earth and its fullness,
    and the acceptance of the one who dwelt at the bush.
It's to come on Yoseph's head,
    on the crown of the prince of his brothers.
¹⁷His magnificence is that of a firstling ox,
    his horns the horns of an oryx.
With them he's to gore the peoples,
    the ends of the earth all at once.
They are Ephrayim's myriads,
    They are Menashsheh's thousands.

¹⁸Of Zebulun he said:

Rejoice, Zebulun, as you go out,
    and Yissakar in your tents.
¹⁹They're to call peoples to the highland,
    there they will offer right sacrifices.
Because they will suck on the abundance of the seas
    and on the hidden treasures of the shore.

Gad, Dan, Naphtali, Asher

²⁰Of Gad he said:

Blessed the one who widens Gad,
    dwelling like a cougar!
He will tear an arm, yes a crown;
²¹he's seen the best for himself.
Because there is the commander's plot, reserved,
    and he's come to the people's heads.
He's put Yahweh's faithfulness into action,
    his acts of authority with Yisra'el.

²²Of Dan he said:

Dan is a lion cub
    that will leap out from Bashan.

²³Of Naphtali he said:

Naphtali, enjoying the acceptance
    and full of the blessing of Yahweh,
    take possession west and south.

²⁴Of Asher he said:

Blessed of sons is Asher,
    may he be accepted by his brothers,
    dipping his foot in oil,
²⁵Your bolts iron and copper,
    your strength as long as your days.

²⁶Yeshurun, there's none like God,
    riding the heavens as your help,
    the skies in his majesty.
²⁷The ancient God is an abode,
    underneath are the age-old arms.
He drove out the enemy from before you,
    and said, 'Annihilate!'
²⁸So Yisra'el dwells in confidence,
    Ya'aqob's spring is left alone,
In a country of grain and new wine;
    yes, its heavens drop down dew.
²⁹Your good fortune, Yisra'el – who is like you,
    a people finding deliverance through Yahweh,
Your shield who is your help,
    the one who is your majestic sword?
Your enemies will cower before you,
    and you yourself will tread on their backs.

Dying outside the promised land

34 So Mosheh went up from the Mo'ab steppes to Mount Nebo, to the top of Pisgah, which is opposite Yeriho, and Yahweh let him see the entire country, Gil'ad as far as Dan, ²all Naphtali, the region of Ephrayim and Menashsheh, the entire region of Yehudah as far as the Western Sea, ³the Negeb and the Plain (the Valley of Jericho, the town of palms) as far as Tso'ar. ⁴Yahweh said to him, 'This is the country that I swore to Abraham, to Yitshaq and to Ya'aqob, "To your offspring

I will give it." I've let you see it with your eyes, but you will not cross there.'

⁵So Mosheh, Yahweh's servant, died there in the country of Mo'ab at Yahweh's bidding, ⁶and he buried him in a ravine in the country of Mo'ab near Bet Pe'or. No one knows his grave until this day. ⁷Mosheh was a man of 120 years when he died. His eye was not weak and his strength had not gone. ⁸The Yisra'elites bewailed Mosheh in the Mo'ab steppes for thirty days, then the days of grieved bewailing for Mosheh came to an end.

⁹Now Yehoshua ben Nun was full of a discerning spirit because Mosheh had leaned his hands on him, and the Yisra'elites listened to him and did as Yahweh ordered Mosheh. ¹⁰There didn't again rise in Yisra'el a prophet like Mosheh, whom Yahweh acknowledged face to face, ¹¹in all the signs and the miracles that Yahweh sent him to do in the country of Misrayim for Par'oh, for all his servants and for all his country, ¹²and in all the strong hand and in all the great awe-inspiring power that Mosheh showed before the eyes of all Yisra'el.

Joshua

The book of Joshua marks a new beginning to the story of Israel in Canaan. Yet the story continues straight on without a break. Deuteronomy had looked forward to the Israelites occupying Canaan; Joshua describes how they did so. Further back, Genesis had told of God's promise that Abraham's descendants would come to possess this land, and the book of Joshua relates how God fulfilled that promise. So Joshua also marks an end.

There are two stages to its account of the fulfilment. The first half of the book relates how the Israelites came to occupy the land. The second half relates how they allocated it among their clans.

But the story also incorporates two complications. The first half also lists areas of the country that Israel didn't conquer. These were the areas where most of the more powerful Canaanites lived. Israel mostly settled in the highland where hardly anyone else lived. Israelites hearing this story would be unable to suppress a smile, because the areas Israel failed to occupy were the best parts of the country. Sometimes Joshua speaks simply of them not occupying these areas, which might imply it was their fault. Sometimes it speaks of them being unable to occupy them, which implies that God didn't enable them to complete their occupation.

The other complication is that there indeed were a number of spectacular moments when the Israelites did not follow God's instructions: see especially the stories about Achan and about the Gib'onites (Joshua 7 and 9). This aspect of the story also points to the implication that, while they are not entirely to blame for their failure to occupy the whole country, they do carry some of the blame.

So the people see all God's promises fulfilled, but they don't; and they live by Yahweh's instructions, but they don't. The book thus epitomizes the dynamic of the portrait of the people of God in both Testaments. It encourages us to rejoice in God's fulfilling his promises but also to face the extent to which he hasn't, yet to live in confident hope that he will do so. It encourages us to be realistic about our own obedience to God and also to commit ourselves anew to keeping our commitment to the pact God has made with us.

Two other aspects of the book often trouble people. The story of how 'Joshua fit the battle of Jericho' is well known. Unfortunately, archaeological investigations suggest that no one lived in Jericho in Joshua's time, nor in Ai, whose conquest follows that of Jericho in the book. So the stories of the Israelites' capture of these towns don't correspond to what happened in these particular places. Why might God have inspired Israelite storytellers to develop imaginative stories about the taking of these towns (whose ruins would be familiar)? What the stories do is give concrete expression to the fact that God did give the country to Israel in an amazing way, and to the fact that the Israelites were always in danger of disobeying God.

The other aspect of the book that often troubles people is the fact that Joshua can look like a story about the Israelites committing genocide. This fact seems not to have troubled the New Testament writers, who didn't see the story of Joshua as incompatible with believing in Jesus. Stephen (in Acts 7) and Hebrews 11 are enthusiastic about Israel's violent occupation of Canaan. They don't assume that the story provides a warrant for subsequent acts of genocide, and neither does the Old Testament – Israel didn't regularly go around annihilating people. The occupation of the country by Joshua was a one-off act of judgement by God. The Canaanites were getting what they deserved for practices such as sacrificing children; they were not just innocent victims. Ironically, though, the book itself makes clear that the Israelites actually didn't commit genocide. The Canaanites continued in the country for centuries.

Just one river to cross

1 After the death of Mosheh [Moses], Yahweh's servant, Yahweh said to Yehoshua [Joshua] ben Nun, Mosheh's minister: ²'Mosheh my servant is dead. Set off now, cross this Yarden [Jordan], you and this entire people, into the country that I'm giving to them, to the Israelites. ³Every place on which the sole of your foot treads I give you, as I spoke to Mosheh. ⁴From the wilderness and this Lebanon, as far as the big river (the River Euphrates), all the country of the Hittites, as far as the Great Sea on the west, will be your border. ⁵No one will take a stand before you all the days of your life. As I was with Mosheh, I'll be with you. I won't let go of you; I won't abandon you. ⁶Be strong, stand firm, because you're the one who'll enable this people to take as their domain this country that I swore to their ancestors to give them. ⁷Only be strong, stand very firm, so as to keep by acting in accordance with the entire instruction that Mosheh my servant ordered you. Don't turn aside from it right or left, in order that you may thrive everywhere you go. ⁸This instruction document will not move away from your mouth. You're to murmur it day and night in order that you may keep by acting in accordance with everything written in it, because then you'll make your journey successful, then you'll thrive. ⁹I've ordered you, "Be strong, stand firm", haven't I? Don't be frightened, don't be scared, because Yahweh your God will be with you everywhere you go.'

¹⁰So Yehoshua ordered the people's overseers: ¹¹'Pass through the middle of the camp and order the people, "Prepare provisions for yourselves, because in three days more you're going to cross this Yarden, to go in to take possession of the country that Yahweh your God is giving you, to take possession of it."'

Another spy mission

¹²To the Re'ubenites, to the Gadites and to the half-clan of Menashsheh, Yehoshua said: ¹³'Be mindful of the thing that Mosheh, Yahweh's servant, ordered you: "Yahweh your God is letting you settle down and is giving you this region. ¹⁴Your wives, your little ones, and your livestock can stay in the region that Mosheh gave you across the Yarden, but you're to cross, organized into companies, before your brothers, all the forceful strong men. You're to help them ¹⁵till Yahweh enables your brothers to settle down like you and they also take possession of the region that Yahweh your God is giving them. Then you can go back to the region that you're to take possession of and you can take possession of it, which Mosheh, Yahweh's servant, gave you across the Yarden, to the east."'

¹⁶They answered Yehoshua: 'All that you've ordered us we'll do. Everywhere that you send us we'll go. ¹⁷Just as we listened to Mosheh, so we'll listen to you. May Yahweh simply be with you as he was with Mosheh. ¹⁸Any individual who rebels against your bidding and doesn't listen to your words regarding everything that you order him is to be put to death. Simply be strong and stand firm.'

2 From Acacias, Yehoshua ben Nun sent two men to investigate quietly: 'Go and look at the country, and at Yeriho [Jericho].' They went, and came to the house of a woman who was a whore named Rahab, and they slept there. ²It was told to the king of Yeriho: 'Here, some men came here tonight, some of the Yisra'elites [Israelites], to check out the country.' ³So the king of Yeriho sent to Rahab: 'Bring out the men who came to you, who've come to your house, because they've come to check out the entire country.' ⁴The woman had taken the two men and hidden them. So she said, 'Yes, the men came to me. I didn't know where they were from. ⁵The gateway was about to be shut at dark and the men went out. I don't know where the men went. Hurry, pursue after them, because you can overtake them.'

Meanwhile, in the whorehouse

⁶Now she had taken them up to the roof and hidden them among the flax stalks that she had on the roof, laid out. ⁷The men pursued after them on the Yarden road, down to the fords. And after their pursuers had gone out, they shut the gateway.

⁸Before those men went to sleep, she went up to them on the roof. ⁹She said to the men, 'I acknowledge that Yahweh has given you the

country, that a dread of you has fallen on us, and that all the people living in the country have melted away before you, ¹⁰because we heard how Yahweh dried up the water of the Reed Sea before you when you got out of Misrayim [Egypt] and what you did to the two Amorite kings who were across the Yarden, to Sihon and to Og, whom you devoted. ¹¹We heard, and our mind melted. There was no spirit rising up in anyone in the face of you, because Yahweh your God is God in the heavens above and on the earth below.

¹²So now, please swear to me by Yahweh, because I've acted in commitment with you, that you'll also act in commitment with my father's household. Give me a truthful sign ¹³that you'll let my father and my mother live, and my brothers and my sisters, and everyone who belongs to them, and that you'll save our lives from death.' ¹⁴The men said to her, 'Our lives in place of you, to the death, if you don't tell about our business here. When Yahweh gives us the country, we'll act in commitment and truthfulness with you.'

The scarlet cord

¹⁵She let them down by a rope through the window, because her house was in the fortification, so she was living in the fortification. ¹⁶She said to them, 'Go to the highland so the pursuers don't come upon you, and hide there for three days till the pursuers come back, and afterwards you can go on your way.' ¹⁷The men said to her, 'We'll be free of this oath to you, which you've got us to take: ¹⁸here, when we're coming into the country, you're to tie this line of scarlet cord in the window through which you've let us down, and you're to gather to yourself your father, your mother, your brothers, your entire ancestral household, in the house. ¹⁹Anyone who goes out of the doors of your house outside – his blood will be on his head and we'll be free of guilt. Anyone who's with you in the house, his blood will be on our head if a hand is laid on him. ²⁰But if you tell people about this thing of ours, we will be free from the oath to you which you've got us to take.' ²¹She said, 'In accordance with your words,

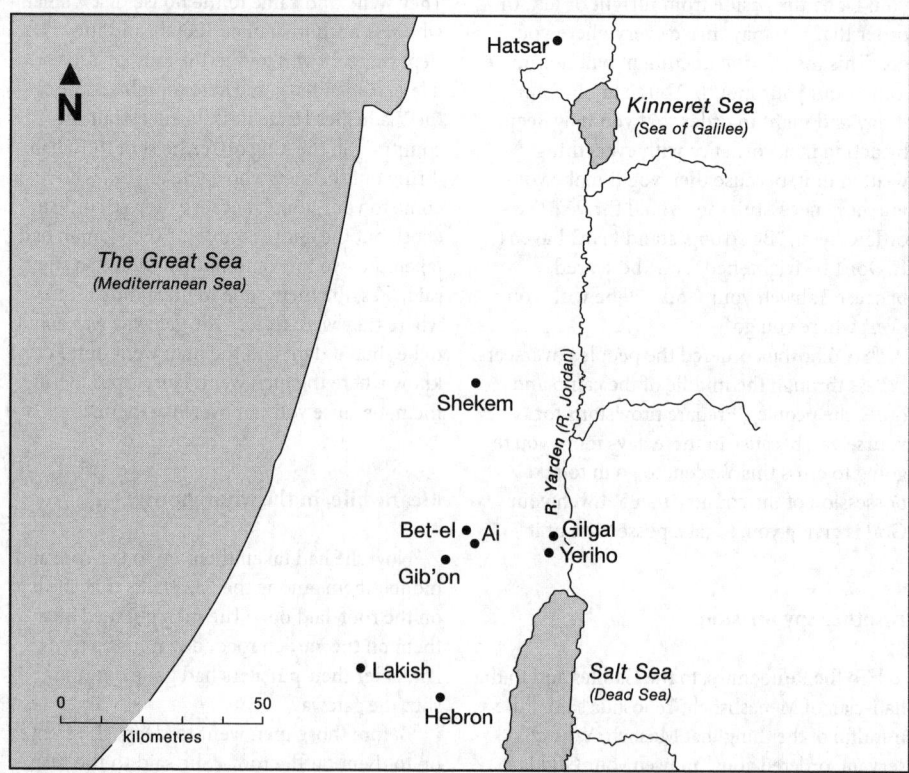

Kena'an (Canaan) at the time of Yeshoshua (Joshua)

so it will be.' She sent them off and they went, and she tied the scarlet line in her window. ²²So they went, and came into the highland and stayed there for three days until the pursuers came back. The pursuers had searched on the entire road but had not found them. ²³The two men came down again from the highland, crossed over, and came to Yehoshua ben Nun. They recounted to him all the things that had befallen them, ²⁴and said to Yehoshua, 'Yahweh has given the entire country into our hand. What's more, all the people living in the country have melted away before us.'

On getting your feet wet

3 Yehoshua started early in the morning and they moved on from Acacias, and came to the Yarden, he and all the Yisra'elites. They stayed the night there before they were to cross over. ²After three days the overseers passed through the middle of the camp ³and ordered the people, 'When you see the pact chest of Yahweh your God, and the Levitical priests carrying it, you yourselves are to move on from your place and follow it ⁴(yet there's to be a distance between you and it, some 1,000 metres by measure – don't go near it), in order that you may know the way whereby you're to go, because you haven't passed this way in previous days.'
⁵Yehoshua said to the people, 'Make yourselves sacred, because tomorrow Yahweh will do extraordinary things among you.' ⁶Yehoshua said to the priests, 'Carry the pact chest and pass through before the people.' So they carried the pact chest and went before the people.
⁷Yahweh said to Yehoshua, 'This day I shall start to make you great in the eyes of all Yisra'el so they may acknowledge that I'm with you as I was with Mosheh. ⁸You yourself are to order the priests carrying the pact chest: "When you come to the edge of the Yarden water, you're to stand in the Yarden."'
⁹Yehoshua said to the Yisra'elites, 'Come up here and listen to the words of Yahweh your God.' ¹⁰Yehoshua said, 'By this you will acknowledge that the living God is among you and that he will totally dispossess from before you the Canaanite, the Hittite, the Hivvite, the Perizzite, the Girgashite, the Amorite and the Yebusite. ¹¹Here is the pact chest of the Lord of all the earth, passing through the Yarden before you. ¹²Now get yourselves twelve men from the Yisra'elite clans, one man per clan. ¹³When the soles of the feet of the priests carrying the chest of Yahweh, Lord of all the earth, set down in the Yarden water, the Yarden water will break off (the water coming down from higher up) and stand as a single heap.'

The Yarden stops

¹⁴So when the people moved on from their tents to cross over the Yarden, the priests carrying the pact chest were before the people. ¹⁵As the people carrying the chest came as far as the Yarden and the feet of the priests carrying the chest dipped into the edge of the water (the Yarden overflows all its banks the entire time of harvest), ¹⁶the Yarden water coming down from higher up stood; it rose as a single heap a great way off at Adam, a town near Tsaretan. Going down to the Steppe Sea (the Salt Sea), it completely broke off. So the people crossed near Yeriho. ¹⁷The priests carrying Yahweh's pact chest stood on dry ground in the middle of the Yarden, steady, while all Yisra'el were crossing on dry ground until the entire nation had come to an end of crossing the Yarden.

4 When the entire nation had come to an end of crossing the Yarden, Yahweh said to Yehoshua: ²'Get yourselves twelve men from the people, one man each from a clan, ³and order them, "Carry yourselves twelve stones from here, from the middle of the Yarden, from the place where the priests' feet stood steady. Take them across with you and set them down at the place where you stay the night tonight." ⁴So Yehoshua called twelve men whom he settled on from the Yisra'elites, one man for each clan. ⁵Yehoshua said to them, 'Cross before the chest of Yahweh your God, into the middle of the Yarden, and lift up for yourselves, each man, a stone on to his shoulder, corresponding to the number of the Yisra'elites' clans, ⁶in order that this may be a sign among you. When your children ask in the future, "What are these stones of yours?", ⁷you're to say to them, 'The Yarden water broke off before Yahweh's

pact chest; when it crossed the Yarden, the Yarden water broke off." These stones will be a permanent reminder for the Yisraelites.'

Looking forwards and backwards

⁸The Yisraelites did so, as Yehoshua ordered. They carried twelve stones from the middle of the Yarden, as Yahweh spoke to Yehoshua, corresponding to the number of the Yisraelites' clans, took them across with them to the place where they were going to stay, and set them down there. ⁹Yehoshua set up twelve stones in the middle of the Yarden at the place where the feet of the priests carrying the pact chest had stood. They have been there until this day. ¹⁰The priests carrying the chest were standing in the middle of the Yarden until everything had come to an end that Yahweh had ordered Yehoshua to speak to the people, in accordance with everything Mosheh had ordered Yehoshua. The people hurried and crossed, ¹¹and when the entire people had come to an end of crossing, Yahweh's chest and the priests crossed before the people.

¹²The Re'ubenites, the Gadites and the half-clan of Menashsheh crossed, organized into companies before the Yisraelites, as Mosheh had spoken to them. ¹³Some 40,000 men equipped for war crossed before Yahweh to the Yeriho steppes for battle. ¹⁴On that day Yahweh made Yehoshua great in the eyes of all Yisrael. They lived in awe of him as they had lived in awe of Mosheh, all the days of his life.

¹⁵Yahweh said to Yehoshua: ¹⁶'Order the priests carrying the affirmation chest to go up out of the Yarden.' ¹⁷So Yehoshua ordered the priests: 'Go up out of the Yarden', ¹⁸and when the priests carrying Yahweh's pact chest went up out of the middle of the Yarden and the soles of the priests' feet stepped on to the dry ground, the Yarden water turned back to its place and went over all its banks as in previous days.

What do these stones mean?

¹⁹When the people went up from the Yarden on the tenth of the first month, they camped at Gilgal, on the eastern border of Yeriho. ²⁰These twelve stones that they had got from the Yarden, Yehoshua set up at Gilgal. ²¹He said to the Yisraelites, 'When your children ask their parents in the future, "What are these stones?", ²²you're to let your children know, "On dry land Yisrael crossed this Yarden", ²³because Yahweh your God dried up the Yarden water before you until you crossed, as Yahweh your God did to the Reed Sea, which he dried up before us until we crossed, ²⁴in order that all the peoples of the earth might acknowledge how strong is Yahweh's hand, in order that you might live in awe of Yahweh your God for all time.'

5 When all the kings of the Amorites who were across the Yarden on its western side and all the kings of the Kena'anites [Canaanites] who were near the Sea heard that Yahweh had dried up the Yarden water before the Yisraelites until they had crossed, their mind melted and there was no longer any spirit left in them because of the Yisraelites.

Foreskin Hill

²At that time Yahweh said to Yehoshua, 'Make yourself flint knives and circumcise the Yisraelites again, a second time.' ³So Yehoshua made himself flint knives and circumcised the Yisraelites at Foreskin Hill.

⁴This is the reason why Yehoshua circumcised the entire people that got out of Egypt, the males. Every one (the men of battle) had died in the wilderness on the way, when they had got out of Egypt. ⁵While the entire people that got out had been circumcised, they had not circumcised the entire people born in the wilderness on the way, when they had got out of Egypt. ⁶Because for forty years the Yisraelites had gone in the wilderness until the entire nation (the men of battle who had got out of Egypt) were gone, the people who had not listened to Yahweh's voice and to whom Yahweh had sworn not to let them see the land that Yahweh had sworn to their ancestors to give us, a land flowing with milk and syrup. ⁷In that he had made their sons arise in their place, they are the people Yehoshua circumcised because they were foreskinned, because they had not circumcised them on the way.

⁸When they had come to an end of circumcising the entire nation, they stayed in their place in the camp until they had

recovered. ⁹Yahweh said to Yehoshua, 'Today I've rolled away the reviling of Egypt from upon you.' So they've named that place Gilgal ['Rolling'] until this day. ¹⁰The Yisra'elites camped at Gilgal and made the Pesah [Passover] on the fourteenth day of the month in the evening, in the Yeriho steppes. ¹¹They ate from the country's produce the day after Pesah, flatbread and roasted grain that actual day. ¹²The *maan* stopped the day after they ate from the country's produce. There was no longer any *maan* for the Yisra'elites. They ate from the yield of the country of Kena'an that year.

Which side are you on?

¹³When Yehoshua was at Yeriho, he lifted his eyes and saw: there, a man standing opposite him, a drawn sword in his hand. Yehoshua went to him and said to him, 'Are you for us or for our attackers?' ¹⁴He said, 'No, because it's as Yahweh's army officer that I've now come.' Yehoshua fell on his face to the ground before him. He bowed low and said to him, 'What is my lord going to speak to his servant?' ¹⁵Yahweh's army officer said to Yehoshua, 'Take your boot off your foot, because the place on which you're standing is sacred.' Yehoshua did so.

6 Now Yeriho was closed, closed tight, before the Yisra'elites. No one was going out and no one was coming in. ²Yahweh said to Yehoshua, 'See, I've given Yeriho and its king, the forceful strong men, into your hand. ³You're to go round the town, all the men of battle circling the town once. You're to do this for six days, ⁴while seven priests carry seven ram's horns before the chest. On the seventh day you're to go round the town seven times, while the priests blow on the horns. ⁵At the drawing out of a blast on the ram's horn, when you hear the noise of the horn, the entire company is to give a great shout, the town's wall will fall flat, and the company are to go up, each individual straight ahead.'

⁶So Yehoshua ben Nun called the priests and said to them, 'Carry the pact chest, while seven priests carry seven ram's horns before Yahweh's chest.' ⁷He said to the company, 'Pass on, go round the town, while the body equipped for a campaign passes on before Yahweh's chest.'

Come blow your horn

⁸When Yehoshua had said it to the company, the seven priests carrying the seven ram's horns passed on before Yahweh and blew on the horns, and Yahweh's pact chest followed them, ⁹while the body equipped for a campaign was going before the priests blowing the horns, and the rearguard was going behind the chest, with a continuing blowing on the horns. ¹⁰Yehoshua ordered the company, 'You will not shout, you will not make your voice heard, no word will come out of your mouth, until the time I say to you, "Shout!", and you'll shout.'

¹¹So he had Yahweh's chest go round the town, circling it once, then they came to the camp and stayed the night in the camp. ¹²Yehoshua started early in the morning and the priests carried Yahweh's chest, ¹³while the seven priests carrying seven ram's horns before Yahweh's chest were continuing to go and blow on the horns, the body equipped for a campaign was going before them, and the rearguard was going behind Yahweh's chest, with a continuing blowing on the horns. ¹⁴They went round the town once on the second day and came back to the camp. So they did for six days.

¹⁵On the seventh day they started early, at sunrise, went round the town in accordance with this rule, seven times; only on that day did they go round the town seven times. ¹⁶The seventh time, the priests blew on the horns and Yehoshua said to the company, 'Shout, because Yahweh has given you the town. ¹⁷The town is to be an object devoted to Yahweh, it and everything that's in it, except that Rahab the whore will live, she and everyone who is with her in the house, because she hid the envoys that we sent. ¹⁸Only, you keep yourselves from what's to be devoted so you don't become a thing that's to be devoted, and you take anything from what's to be devoted and make the Yisra'elite camp into a thing that's to be devoted. You will bring disaster on it. ¹⁹All the silver and gold and the objects of copper and iron are sacred to Yahweh. They're to come into Yahweh's treasury.'

And the walls came tumbling down

²⁰So the company shouted and they blew on the horns, and when the company heard

the sound of the horn, the company gave a great shout, the wall fell flat and the company went up into the town, each individual straight ahead. They captured the town ²¹and devoted everything that was in the town, man and woman, young and old, ox and sheep and donkey, with the mouth of the sword.

²²To the two men who had investigated the country Yehoshua said, 'Come into the house of the woman who's a whore and bring out of there the woman and everyone who belongs to her, as you swore to her.' ²³So the young men who'd done the investigating came in and brought out Rahab, her father and her mother, her brothers and everyone who belonged to her. They brought out her entire kin-group, and set them down outside the Yisra'elite camp.

²⁴The town they burned in fire with everything that was in it, except that the silver and the gold and the objects of copper and iron they put in the treasury of Yahweh's house, ²⁵and Yehoshua let Rahab the whore live, with her ancestral household and everyone who belonged to her. She's lived among Yisra'el until this day, because she hid the envoys whom Yehoshua sent to investigate Yeriho.

²⁶At that time Yehoshua swore, 'Cursed before Yahweh be the man who sets about building this town, Yeriho. At the cost of his firstborn may he found it and at the cost of his little one may he put up its doors.' ²⁷Yahweh was with Yehoshua and report of him went through the entire country.

7 But the Yisra'elites committed a trespass in connection with things to be devoted. Akan ben Karmi, son of Zabdi son of Zerah of the clan of Yehudah [Judah], took some of the things that were to be devoted, and Yahweh's anger raged against the Yisra'elites.

Take it easy

²Yehoshua sent men 'from Yeriho to Ha'ay [Ai, 'The Ruin']', which is by Bet Aven ['Trouble House'], east of Bet-el. He said to them, 'Go up and investigate the region.' The men went up and investigated Ha'ay, ³and came back to Yehoshua and said to him, 'The entire company should not go up. Some two or three thousand men should go up and strike down Ha'ay. You shouldn't make the entire company get weary there, because they are few.' ⁴So some 3,000 of the company went up, but they took flight before the men of Ha'ay. ⁵The men of Ha'ay struck down some thirty-six of them, and pursued them before the gateway as far as the quarries and struck them down on the slope.

The company's mind melted, turned to water. ⁶Yehoshua tore his clothes and fell on his face to the ground before Yahweh's chest until the evening, he and Yisra'el's elders, and they put dirt on their head. ⁷Yehoshua said, 'Oh, Lord Yahweh, why did you bring this people across the Yarden at all, to give us into the hand of the Amorites to obliterate us? If only we had resolved to live across the Yarden. ⁸As for me, Lord, what am I to say after Yisra'el has turned its back before its enemies? ⁹The Kena'anites and all the people living in the country will hear and surround us and cut off our name from the earth, and what will you do about your great name?'

¹⁰Yahweh said to Yehoshua, 'Get yourself up. Why are you falling on your face there? ¹¹Yisra'el has done wrong. Yes, they've contravened my pact about which I gave them orders. They've both taken some of the things that were to be devoted, and they've stolen, and they've acted deceitfully, and they've put things in their bags. ¹²The Yisra'elites won't be able to stand before their enemies, they'll turn their back before their enemies, because they've become something to be devoted. I shall not be with you any more unless you annihilate from among you the thing that's to be devoted.

Coveting can kill

¹³Get up, make the people sacred. You're to say, "Make yourselves sacred for tomorrow, because Yahweh, the God of Yisra'el, has said this: There's something to be devoted among you, Yisra'el. You can't stand before your enemies until you've removed what is to be devoted from among you."

¹⁴In the morning you're to draw near by your clans. The clan that Yahweh takes is to draw near by kin-groups. The kin-group that Yahweh takes is to draw near by households. The household that Yahweh takes is to draw near man by man. ¹⁵The one who is taken in the net is to burn in fire, he and everything

that belongs to him, because he contravened Yahweh's pact and because he did something villainous in Yisra'el.'

¹⁶Yehoshua started early in the morning and presented Yisra'el by its clans, and the clan of Yehudah was taken. ¹⁷He presented the kin-group of Yehudah, and he took the kin-group of Zerah. He presented the kin-group of the Zarhites man by man, and Zabdi was taken. ¹⁸He presented his household man by man, and Akan ben Karmi, son of Zabdi son of Zerah of the clan of Yehudah, was taken. ¹⁹Yehoshua said to Akan, 'Son, please give honour to Yahweh, the God of Yisra'el, and make confession to him. Please tell me what you've done. Don't hide it from me.' ²⁰Akan answered Yehoshua, 'Truly I'm the one who's done wrong against Yahweh, the God of Yisra'el. This actual thing is what I did. ²¹I saw in the spoil a fine coat from Shin'ar, and 200 sheqels of silver, and a bar of gold fifty sheqels in weight. I desired them and took them. There, they're buried in the ground inside my tent, with the silver underneath.'

²²Yehoshua sent envoys and they ran to the tent, and there, it was buried in his tent, with the silver underneath. ²³They took them from inside the tent and brought them to Yehoshua and to all the Yisra'elites, and they laid them out before Yahweh.

Purging away the trespass

²⁴Yehoshua took Akan ben Zerah, the silver, the coat, the gold bar, and his sons, his daughters, his ox, his donkey, his flock, his tent and everything that he had, he and all Yisra'el with him, and brought them up to Disaster Vale. ²⁵Yehoshua said, 'How you've brought disaster on us! Yahweh will bring disaster on you this day.' All Yisra'el pelted him with stones. They burned them in fire and executed them by stoning, ²⁶and raised a great heap of stones over them until this day. And Yahweh turned back from his angry burning.

That's why they've named that place Disaster Vale, until this day.

8 Yahweh said to Yehoshua, 'Don't be afraid. Don't be dismayed. Take the entire battle company with you and set off, go up to Ha'ay. See, I've given into your hand the king of Ha'ay, his town, his people and his region. ²You're to do to Ha'ay and to its king as you did to Yeriho and to its king, only its spoil and its animals you may treat as plunder for yourselves. Set yourself an ambush for the town, behind it.'

³So Yehoshua and all the battle company set off to go up to Ha'ay. Yehoshua chose 30,000 men, forceful strong men, sent them by night ⁴and ordered them, 'See, you're going to be men in an ambush for the town, behind the town. Don't be very far from the town, and all of you be ready. ⁵I and the entire company that's with me – we'll draw near the town, and when they come out to meet us like the first time, we'll flee before them. ⁶They'll come out after us till we've drawn them away from the town, because they'll say "They're fleeing before us like the first time." So we'll flee before them, ⁷and you'll get up out of the ambush and take possession of the town. Yahweh your God will give it into your hand. ⁸When you've taken the town, set the town on fire. You're to act in accordance with Yahweh's word. See, I've given you orders.'

The game plan executed

⁹So Yehoshua sent them, they went to the ambush, and they settled down between Bet-el and Ha'ay, west of Ha'ay. Yehoshua stayed the night among the company. ¹⁰Yehoshua started early in the morning and numbered the company, and he and Yisra'el's elders went up before the company to Ha'ay. ¹¹All the battle company that was with him went up, moved close and came in front of the town, and camped north of Ha'ay. There was a ravine between them and Ha'ay.

¹²So he had taken some 5,000 men and set them as an ambush between Bet-el and Ha'ay, west of the town, ¹³and the company set up the entire camp, which was north of the town, and its rearguard west of the town. Yehoshua had gone that night into the middle of the vale.

¹⁴When the king of Ha'ay saw it, the men of the town hurried and started early and went out to meet Yisra'el in battle, he and all his company, at the set place facing the steppe; he didn't know that there was an ambush for him behind the town. ¹⁵Yehoshua and all Yisra'el let themselves be beaten before them and fled by the wilderness road. ¹⁶The entire company

that was in Ha'ay cried out to one another to pursue after them, and they pursued after Yehoshua and tore out of the town. [17]Not a man remained in Ha'ay or Bet El who didn't go out after Yisra'el. They left the town open and pursued after Yisra'el.

[18]Yahweh said to Yehoshua, 'Hold out the javelin that's in your hand towards Ha'ay, because I shall give it into your hand.' Yehoshua held out the javelin that was in his hand towards the town, [19]while the ambush quickly got up out of its place. They ran when he held out his hand, came into the town and captured it, and hurried and set the town on fire.

Ha'ay becomes a ruin

[20]The men of Ha'ay turned their face behind them and looked: there, smoke from the town went up to the heavens. There was no capacity in them to go this way or that when the company fleeing to the wilderness turned on to the pursuer, [21]and Yehoshua and all Yisra'el saw that the ambush had taken the town and that smoke from the town had gone up, and they turned back and struck down the men of Ha'ay. [22]When these [Yisra'elites] came out of the town to meet them, in relation to Yisra'el they were in the middle, some [Yisra'elites] on one side and some on the other. They struck them down so they didn't let anyone remain to it as escapee or survivor. [23]The king of Ha'ay they took alive and presented him to Yehoshua.

[24]When Yisra'el had finished slaughtering all the people living in Ha'ay in the fields, in the wilderness where they had pursued them, and all of them had fallen to the mouth of the sword until they had come to an end, all Yisra'el went back to Ha'ay and struck it down with the mouth of the sword.

[25]All those who fell that day, both men and women, were 12,000, all the people living in Ha'ay. [26]Yehoshua didn't take back his hand with which he held out his javelin until he had devoted all the people living in Ha'ay. [27]Only the animals and the spoil in that town did Yisra'el take as plunder for themselves, in accordance with Yahweh's word with which he had ordered Yehoshua. [28]Yehoshua burned Ha'ay and made it a permanent ruin, a desolation until this day. [29]The king of Ha'ay he hanged on a tree until the time of evening. At sunset Yehoshua ordered, and they took down his corpse from the tree, threw it at the entrance of the town gateway and set up over it a great heap of stones, until this day.

It's over even when it's not over

[30]Then Yehoshua built an altar for Yahweh the God of Yisra'el on Mount Ebal, [31]as Mosheh Yahweh's servant ordered the Yisra'elites, as it is written in Mosheh's instruction document: an altar of whole stones on which no one had wielded iron. They offered up on it burnt offerings for Yahweh and made well-being sacrifices. [32]He wrote there on the stones a copy of Mosheh's instruction that he had written, before the Yisra'elites. [33]All Yisra'el, its elders, the overseers and its rulers, were standing on each side of the chest, facing the Levitical priests who carried Yahweh's pact chest, resident and native alike, half of them facing Mount Gerizim and half of them facing Mount Ebal, as Mosheh Yahweh's servant had ordered beforehand, to bless the people of Yisra'el.

[34]After this, he read out all the words of the instruction, the blessing and the slight, in accordance with all that's written in the instruction document. [35]There was not a word of all that Mosheh ordered that Yehoshua didn't read out in front of Yisra'el's entire congregation, with the women and little ones and the residents who were going among them.

9 When all the kings who were across the Yarden heard, in the highland, in the foothills and on the entire coast of the Great Sea to near the Lebanon (the Hittite, the Amorite, the Kena'anite, the Perizzite, the Hivvite and the Yebusite), [2]they gathered together to battle with Yehoshua and with Yisra'el, with one accord.

How to take Yisra'el in

[3]The people living in Gib'on heard what Yehoshua had done to Yeriho and to Ha'ay, [4]and they for their part acted with shrewdness. They went and behaved like envoys, but got worn-out sacks for their donkeys and worn-out wineskins, cracked and mended,

⁵with worn-out, patched boots on their feet, and worn-out clothes on themselves, and all the bread they had as their provisions was dry and hard. ⁶They went to Yehoshua in the camp at Gilgal and said to him and to the Yisra'elites, 'We've come from a country far away, so now, solemnize a pact with us.'

⁷The Yisra'elites said to the Hivvites, 'Maybe you're living among us. How can I solemnize a pact with you?' ⁸They said to Yehoshua, 'We are your servants.' Yehoshua said to them, 'Who are you? Where do you come from?'

⁹They said to him, 'Your servants have come from a country very far away by reason of the name of Yahweh your God, because we've heard the report about him, about all that he did in Misrayim, ¹⁰and all that he did to the two Amorite kings who were across the Yarden, to Sihon king of Heshbon and to Og king of Bashan who was in Ashtarot. ¹¹Our elders and all the people living in our country said to us, "Get in your hand provisions for the journey and go to meet them and say to them: 'We are your servants, so now, solemnize a pact with us.'" ¹²This is our bread: we brought it hot as our provision from our houses on the day we left to go to you, but now – here, it's dry and hard. ¹³These wineskins that we filled new – here, they've cracked. These clothes of ours and boots of ours have worn out from the great length of the journey.'

¹⁴The people took some of their provisions and didn't ask for Yahweh's bidding. ¹⁵Yehoshua made peace with them and solemnized a pact with them to let them live, and the assembly's leaders swore an oath to them.

How to swallow your pride

¹⁶At the end of three days after they solemnized the pact with them, they heard that they were near them, living among them.

¹⁷The Yisra'elites moved on and came to their towns on the third day. Their towns were Gib'on, Qephirah, Be'erot and Ye'arim Township. ¹⁸The Yisra'elites didn't strike them down because the assembly's leaders had sworn to them by Yahweh the God of Yisra'el. The entire assembly protested at the leaders, ¹⁹but all the leaders said to the entire assembly, 'We ourselves swore to them by Yahweh the God of Yisra'el. We can't now touch them. ²⁰We'll do this to them: we'll let them live, so that there won't be fury against us because of the oath we swore to them', ²¹so the leaders said to them, 'They're to live', but they became woodchoppers and water carriers for the entire assembly, as the leaders spoke concerning them.

²²So Yehoshua called them and spoke to them: 'Why did you beguile us in saying, "We live very far away from you", and you're living among us? ²³You're now cursed. None of you will stop being a servant, both woodchoppers and water carriers for my God's house.' ²⁴They answered Yehoshua, 'Because it had been clearly told to your servants that Yahweh your God ordered Mosheh his servant to give you the entire country and to annihilate all the people living in the country from before you. We were very fearful for our lives from before you, so we did this thing. ²⁵But now, here we are, in your hand. Act towards us in accordance with what is good and with what is right in your eyes to act towards us.'

²⁶He did so to them: he rescued them from the hand of the Yisra'elites, and they didn't slaughter them. ²⁷That day Yehoshua made them woodchoppers and water carriers for the assembly and for Yahweh's altar, until this day, at the site that he would choose.

Five kings panic

10 ¹When Adonay-tsedeq king of Yerushalaim [Jerusalem] heard that Yehoshua had taken Ha'ay and devoted it (as he had done to Yeriho and its king, so he had done to Ha'ay and its king), and that the inhabitants of Gib'on had made peace with Yisra'el and were among them, ²people were very fearful, because Gib'on was a big town, like one of the royal towns, and because it was bigger than Ha'ay, and all its men were strong men. ³So Adonay-tsedeq king of Yerushalaim sent to Hoham king of Hebron, to Pir'am king of Yarmut, to Yaphia king of Lakish and to Debir king of Eglon, saying ⁴'Go up to me and help me, and we'll strike down Gib'on, because it's made peace with Yehoshua and with the Yisra'elites.'

⁵So the five Amorite kings, the king of Yerushalaim, the king of Hebron, the king of Yarmut, the king of Lakish and the king of

Eglon, they and their entire camp, gathered together, went up, camped against Gib'on and did battle against it. ⁶The people of Gib'on sent to Yehoshua in the camp at Gilgal, saying 'Don't slacken your hands from your servants, go up to us quickly, deliver us, help us, because all the kings of the Amorites, the people living in the highland, have collected together against us.' ⁷So Yehoshua went up from Gilgal, he and the entire battle company with him, all the forceful strong men.

⁸Yahweh said to Yehoshua, 'Don't be afraid of them, because I've given them into your hand. Not one of them will stand before you.' ⁹Yehoshua came on them by surprise; he had gone up all night from Gilgal, ¹⁰and Yahweh put them into a turmoil before Yisra'el. He struck them down in a great rout at Gib'on and pursued them on the road to the Bet-horon ascent, and struck them down as far as Azeqah and as far as Maqqedah.

No compromise

¹¹While they were fleeing from before Yisra'el (they were on the Bet-horon descent), Yahweh threw big stones at them from the heavens, as far as Azeqah. More died who died through the hailstones than the Yisra'elites slaughtered with the sword.

¹²Yehoshua spoke to Yahweh then, on the day Yahweh gave over the Amorites before the Yisra'elites, and said before the eyes of Yisra'el,

> Sun stand still at Gib'on,
> moon at the Ayyalon Vale!
> ¹³The sun stood still,
> the moon halted,
> Until a nation
> took redress from its foes.
> (It's written on the Document of the Upright One, isn't it.)

The sun stood in the middle of the heavens and didn't hasten to set, the like of a whole day. ¹⁴There hasn't been anything like that day before it or after it for Yahweh's listening to someone's voice, because Yahweh was battling for Yisra'el.

¹⁵Yehoshua and all Yisra'el with him went back to the camp at Gilgal, ¹⁶and these five kings fled and hid in a cave at Maqqedah. ¹⁷It was told Yehoshua, 'Five kings have been found hiding in a cave at Maqqedah.' ¹⁸Yehoshua said, 'Roll big stones to the cave's mouth and appoint men over it to keep them. ¹⁹But you, don't halt; pursue after your enemies and hit them from the rear. Don't let them come to their towns, because Yahweh your God has given them into your hand.' ²⁰When Yehoshua and the Yisra'elites had finished striking them down in a great rout until they had come to an end, though some survivors escaped from them and came to their fortified towns, ²¹the entire company went back to the camp to Yehoshua at Maqqedah in safety. No one loosened his tongue about the Yisra'elites.

Open the cave

²²Yehoshua said, 'Open the cave mouth and bring these five kings out of the cave to me.' ²³They did so: they brought these five kings out of the cave to him, the king of Yerushalaim, the king of Hebron, the king of Yarmut, the king of Lakish, the king of Eglon. ²⁴When they brought these kings out to Yehoshua, Yehoshua called all the Yisra'elites and said to the commander over the men of battle who had gone with him, 'Draw near; put your feet on the necks of these kings.' They drew near and put their feet on their necks. ²⁵Yehoshua said to them, 'Don't be afraid. Don't be scared. Be strong, stand firm, because Yahweh will act like this to all your enemies with whom you're battling.'

²⁶After this, Yehoshua struck them down. He put them to death and hanged them on five trees. They were hanged on the trees until the evening. ²⁷At the time when the sun went down, Yehoshua gave an order and they took them down from the trees, threw them into the cave where they had hidden, and put big stones on the cave mouth, until this very day.

²⁸That day Yehoshua captured Maqqedah and struck it down, it and its king, with the mouth of the sword. He devoted them, along with every person who was in it. He didn't let a survivor remain. He did to the king of Maqqedah as he had done to the king of Yeriho. ²⁹Yehoshua and all Yisra'el with him passed on from Maqqedah to Libnah and

battled with Libnah, ³⁰and Yahweh gave it, too, into Yisra'el's hand, it and its king. He struck it down with the mouth of the sword, along with every person who was in it. He didn't let a survivor remain in it. He did to its king as he had done to the king of Yeriho.

Welcome to the wild wild west

³¹Yehoshua and all Yisra'el with him passed on from Libnah to Lakish and camped against it and battled against it, ³²and Yahweh gave Lakish into Yisra'el's hand. He captured it on the second day and struck it down with the mouth of the sword, along with every person who was in it, in accordance with all that he had done to Libnah. ³³Horam king of Gezer had gone up then to help Lakish, but Yehoshua struck down him and his company until he didn't let a survivor remain to him.

³⁴Yehoshua and all Yisra'el with him passed on from Lakish to Eglon and camped against it and battled against it. ³⁵That day they captured it and struck it down with the mouth of the sword. Every person who was in it he devoted that day, in accordance with all that he had done to Lakish. ³⁶Yehoshua and all Yisra'el with him went up from Eglon to Hebron and battled against it. ³⁷They captured it and struck it down with the mouth of the sword, its king and all its towns and every person who was in it. He didn't let a survivor remain, in accordance with all that he had done to Eglon. He devoted it and every person who was in it.

³⁸Yehoshua and all Yisra'el with him went back to Debir and battled against it. ³⁹He captured it and its king and all its towns. They struck them down with the mouth of the sword and devoted every person who was in it. He didn't let a survivor remain. As he had done to Hebron, so he did to Debir and to its king, and as he had done to Libnah and to its king.

Welcome to the wild wild north

⁴⁰Yehoshua struck down the entire country: the highland, the Negeb, the foothills and the slopes, with all their kings. He didn't let a survivor remain. Anything that breathed he devoted, as Yahweh the God of Yisra'el had ordered. ⁴¹Yehoshua struck them down from Qadesh Barnea to Azzah [Gaza], all the Goshen region, and as far as Gib'on. ⁴²All these kings and their country Yehoshua captured at a single stroke, because Yahweh the God of Yisra'el was battling for Yisra'el. ⁴³Then Yehoshua and all Yisra'el with him went back to the camp at Gilgal.

11 When Yabin king of Hatsor heard, he sent to Yobab king of Madon, to the king of Shimron, to the king of Akshaph, ²to the kings who were to the north, in the highland, in the steppe south of Kinneret, in the foothills and in the Dor Heights on the west, ³the Kena'anite on the east and on the west, the Amorite, the Hittite, the Perizzite and the Yebusite in the highland, and the Hivvite beneath Hermon in the region of The Watchtower. ⁴They went out, those and their entire camp with them, a company as numerous as the sand that's on the seashore in its large number, with very numerous horse and chariotry. ⁵All these kings arranged to meet, and came and camped together at Merom Water to do battle with Yisra'el.

⁶Yahweh said to Yehoshua, 'Don't be afraid before them, because tomorrow at this very time I'm going to give all of them up, run through before Yisra'el. You're to hamstring their horses and burn their chariots in fire.' ⁷So Yehoshua and all his battle company with him came on them at Merom Water by surprise. They fell on them, ⁸and Yahweh gave them into Yisra'el's hand. They struck them down and pursued them as far as Great Tsidon, as far as Misrephot Water, and as far as Watchtower Valley on the east, and struck them down until they let no survivor remain. ⁹Yehoshua did to them as Yahweh had said to him: he hamstrung their horses and burned their chariots in fire.

The entire country taken

¹⁰Yehoshua turned back at that time and captured Hatsor, and its king he struck down with the sword, because Hatsor was formerly head of all these kingdoms. ¹¹They struck down every person who was in it with the mouth of the sword, devoting them. Nothing that breathed was left, while he burned Hatsor in fire.

¹²All these royal towns and their kings Yehoshua captured. He struck them down with the mouth of the sword and devoted them, as Mosheh Yahweh's servant had ordered. ¹³Yet all the towns that were standing on their mound Yisra'el didn't burn, except that Yehoshua burned Hatsor alone. ¹⁴All the spoil in these towns and the animals the Yisra'elites took as plunder for themselves. They struck down only all the human beings with the mouth of the sword until they had annihilated them; they didn't let anything that breathed remain. ¹⁵As Yahweh had ordered Mosheh his servant, so Mosheh had ordered Yehoshua, and so Yehoshua did. He didn't take out anything from all that Yahweh had ordered Mosheh.

¹⁶So Yehoshua took this entire country: the highland, the entire Negeb, the entire Goshen region, the foothills, the steppe, the highland of Yisra'el and its foothills, ¹⁷from Bald Mountain which goes up to Se'ir and as far as Ba'al Gad in the Lebanon Valley beneath Mount Hermon. He captured all their kings, struck them down and put them to death.

¹⁸For a long time Yehoshua did battle with all these kings. ¹⁹There was no town that made peace with the Yisra'elites except the Hivvites living in Gib'on. They took everything in battle, ²⁰because it issued from Yahweh to stiffen their heart to meet with Yisra'el in battle, in order that he might devote them without there being any grace for them – in order that rather he might annihilate them, as Yahweh had ordered Mosheh.

The kings east of the Yarden

²¹At that time Yehoshua came and cut down the Anaqites from the highland, from Hebron, from Debir, from Anab, from the entire highland of Yehudah and from the entire highland of Yisra'el, with their towns. Yehoshua devoted them. ²²None of the Anaqites were left in the country of the Yisra'elites. Only in Azzah, in Gat and in Ashdod did they remain.

²³So Yehoshua took the entire country, in accordance with all that Yahweh spoke to Mosheh, and Yehoshua gave it to Yisra'el as its domain, in accordance with their divisions, for the clans. And the country was calm from battle.

12 These are the kings of the country whom the Yisra'elites struck down and whose land they took possession of across the Yarden on the east side, from Wadi Arnon as far as Mount Hermon and the entire steppe, on the east side:

²Sihon king of the Amorites, who lived in Heshbon, ruling from Aro'er, which is on the bank of Wadi Arnon, the middle of the wadi, and half of Gil'ad, as far as Wadi Yabboq, the Ammonites' border; ³and the steppe as far as the Kinneret Sea, on the east side; and as far as the Steppe Sea (the Salt Sea), on the east side, the Bet Hayeshimot road; and on the south side, beneath the Pisgah slopes.

⁴The border of Og king of Bashan, from what was left of the Repha'ites, who lived in Ashtarot and in Edre'i, ⁵ruling over Mount Hermon, over Salkah and over all Bashan, as far as the border of the Geshurites and the Ma'akatites, and half of Gil'ad, the border of Sihon king of Heshbon.

⁶Mosheh Yahweh's servant and the Yisra'elites had struck them down, and Mosheh Yahweh's servant had given it as a possession to the Re'ubenites, to the Gadites and to the half-clan of Menashsheh.

The kings west of the Yarden

⁷These are the kings of the country whom Yehoshua and the Yisra'elites struck down across the Yarden on the west side, from Ba'al Gad in the Lebanon Valley as far as Bald Mountain, which goes up to Mount Se'ir, which Yehoshua gave to the Yisra'elite clans to be a possession, in accordance with their divisions, ⁸in the highland, in the foothills, in the steppe, in the slopes, in the wilderness and in the Negeb (the Hittite, the Amorite, the Kena'anite, the Perizzite, the Hivvite and the Yebusite):

⁹A king of Yeriho	A king of Hebron
A king of Ha'ay, which is near Bet-el	¹¹A king of Yarmut
	A king of Lakish
¹⁰A king of Yerushalaim	¹²A king of Eglon

A king of Gezer
A king of Hatsor
¹³A king of Debir
²⁰A king of Shimron Meron
A king of Geder
¹⁴A king of Hormah
A king of Akshaph
A king of Arad
²¹A king of Ta'nak
¹⁵A king of Libnah
A king of Megiddo
A king of Adullam
²²A king of Qedesh
¹⁶A king of Maqqedah
A king of Yoqne'am in Carmel
A king of Bet-el
¹⁷A king of Tappuah
²³A king of Dor in Dor Height
A king of Hepher
¹⁸A king of Apheq
A king of Goyim in Gilgal
A king of the Sharon
¹⁹A king of Madon
²⁴A king of Tirtsah

All kings: thirty-one.

Yehoshua's time is almost over

13 Now Yehoshua was old, going on in years. Yahweh said to him, 'You yourself have become old, you have gone on in years, while the country is very great that remains, to take possession of it. ²This is the country that remains:

All the areas of the Pelishtites [Philistines] and all the Geshurites, ³from the Shihor, which is east of Misrayim, as far as the border of Eqron to the north, which is thought of as belonging to the Kena'anites (the five Pelishtite lords, the Azzahites, the Ashdodites, the Ashqelonites, the Gittites and the Eqronites); the Avvites ⁴on the south; the entire Kena'anite country, Me'arah belonging to the Tsidonites as far as Apheq (as far as the Amorites' border); ⁵the country of the Giblites and the entire Lebanon on the east from Ba'al Gad beneath Mount Hermon as far as Lebo' Hamat; ⁶all the people living in the highland from the Lebanon as far as Misrephot Water (all the Tsidonites).

I myself will dispossess them from before the Yisra'elites. Only let it fall by lot to Yisra'el as its domain, as I've ordered you. ⁷So now share out this country as a domain to the nine clans and the half-clan of Menashsheh.'

⁸With it, the Re'ubenites and the Gadites had taken their domain which Mosheh gave them across the Yarden to the east, as Mosheh Yahweh's servant gave them:

⁹From Aro'er which is on the bank of Wadi Arnon, and the town which is in the middle of the wadi; the entire Medeba flatland as far as Dibon; ¹⁰all the towns of Sihon king of the Amorites who reigned in Heshbon, as far as the Ammonites' border; ¹¹Gil'ad and the border of the Geshurites and the Ma'akatites; all of Mount Hermon; all of Bashan as far as Salkah, ¹²and the entire kingdom of Og in Bashan, who had reigned in Ashtarot and in Edre'i (he remained from what was left of the Repha'ites). Mosheh had struck them down and dispossessed them, ¹³but the Yisra'elites didn't dispossess the Geshurites and the Ma'akatites; Geshur and Ma'akah have lived among Yisra'el until this day.

¹⁴Only to the clan of Levi did he not give a domain. The gift offerings of Yahweh the God of Yisra'el are its domain, as he spoke to it.

The clans east of the Yarden

¹⁵So Mosheh gave to the clan of the Re'ubenites, by their kin-groups, ¹⁶and it became their border:

From Aro'er, which is on the bank of Wadi Arnon, and the town in the middle of the wadi, and the entire flatland, as far as Medeba; ¹⁷Heshbon and all its towns, which are in the flatland; Dibon, Master's Heights, Bet Ba'al Me'on, ¹⁸Yahats, Qedemot, Mepha'at, ¹⁹Qiryatayim, Sibmah, Tseret Shahar on the vale mountain, ²⁰Bet Pe'or, the Pisgah slopes and Bet Hayeshimot, ²¹all the towns of the flatland, the entire kingdom of Sihon king of the Amorites who reigned in Heshbon, whom Mosheh struck down, he and the Midyanite leaders Evi, Reqem, Tsur, Hur and Reba, Sihon's appointees, living in the country. ²²Bil'am ben Be'or the diviner the Yisra'elites killed with the sword, to add to the people run through by them. ²³The Re'ubenites' border was the Yarden and the edge of it. This was the Re'ubenites'

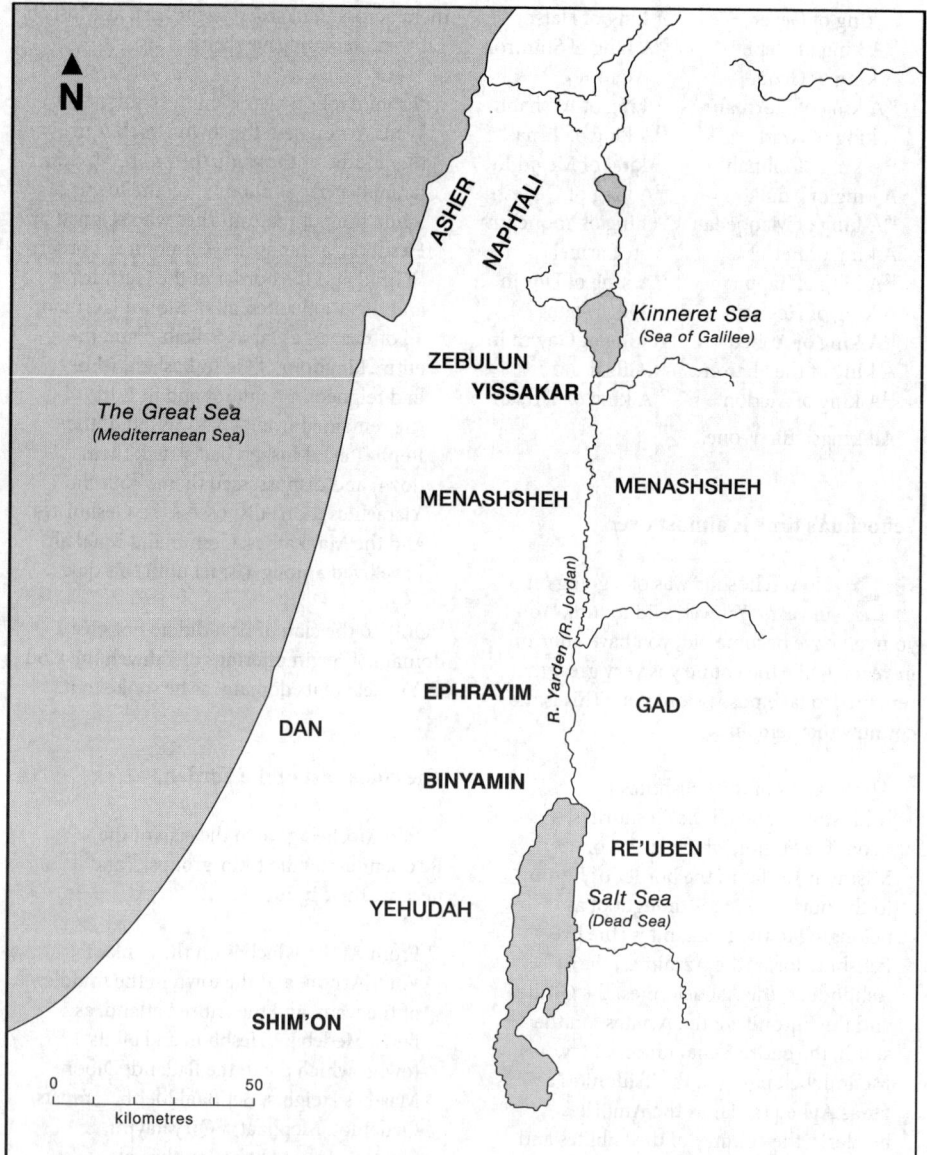

Joshua 13: The twelve clans

domain by their kin-groups, the towns and their villages.

[24]Mosheh gave to the clan of Gad, to the Gadites, by their kin-groups, [25]and it became their border:

Ya'zer; all the towns in Gil'ad; half the Ammonites' country as far as Aro'er which is east of Rabbah; [26]from Heshbon as far as Watchtower Height and Betonim, from Mahanayim as far as the border of Debir; [27]in the vale, Height House, Bet Nimrah, Sukkot and Tsaphon, the rest of the kingdom of Sihon king of Heshbon; and the Yarden and the edge as far as the end of the Kinneret Sea, across the Yarden on the east side. [28]This was the Gadites' domain by their kin-groups, the towns and their villages.

²⁹Mosheh gave to the half-clan of Menashsheh, so it came to belong to the half-clan of the Menashshites by their kin-groups, ³⁰and it became their border:

> From Mahanayim, all of Bashan, the entire kingdom of Og king of Bashan, all Ya'ir's Villages in Bashan, sixty towns, ³¹half of Gil'ad, and Ashtarot and Edre'i, Og's royal towns in Bashan, for the descendants of Makir son of Menashsheh, for half the Makirites, by their kin-groups.

The promise to Kaleb (Caleb)

³²These are what Mosheh made into domains in the Mo'ab steppes across the Yarden east of Yeriho. ³³To the clan of Levi Mosheh didn't give a domain. Yahweh the God of Yisra'el is their domain, as he spoke to them.

14 These are what the Yisra'elites received as their domain in the country of Kena'an, which El'azar the priest, Yehoshua ben Nun and the ancestral heads of the Yisra'elites' clans made into domains, ²their domain by lot, as Yahweh ordered through Mosheh, for the nine clans and the half-clan, ³because Mosheh had given the domain of the two clans and the half-clan across the Yarden, and to the Levites he had given no domain among them, ⁴because the Yosephites [Josephites] were two clans, Menashsheh and Ephrayim, and they didn't give the Levites a share in the country, but rather towns to live in and pasturelands for their livestock and for their cattle. ⁵As Yahweh ordered Mosheh, so the Yisra'elites did, and shared out the country.

⁶The Yehudahites came up to Yehoshua at Gilgal, and Kaleb ben Yephunneh the Qenizzite said to him, 'You yourself know the thing that Yahweh spoke to Mosheh, the supernatural man, concerning me and concerning you, at Qadesh Barnea. ⁷I was a man of forty years when Mosheh Yahweh's servant sent me from Qadesh Barnea to investigate the country, and I brought him back word in accordance with how things were in my mind.

⁸My brothers who went up with me made the people's mind melt, but I myself fully followed after Yahweh my God. ⁹That day, Mosheh swore: "If the country on which your foot trod doesn't become a permanent domain for you and for your descendants, because you fully followed after Yahweh my God . . ."

The country has rest from war

¹⁰So now, here, Yahweh has kept me alive, as he spoke, these forty-five years from when Yahweh spoke this word to Mosheh when Yisra'el went through the wilderness. So now, here, I am today a man of eighty-five years. ¹¹I'm still as strong today as on the day Mosheh sent me. As my energy was then, so is my energy now for battle, both for going out and for coming in. ¹²So now, give me this highland that Yahweh spoke of on that day, because you yourself heard that day that Anaqites are there, and big fortified towns. Maybe Yahweh will be with me and I shall take possession of them as Yahweh spoke.'

¹³Yehoshua blessed him and gave Hebron to Kaleb ben Yephunneh as his domain. ¹⁴Therefore Hebron came to belong to Kaleb ben Yephunneh the Qenizzite as his domain, until this day, because he fully followed Yahweh the God of Yisra'el. (¹⁵Hebron's name formerly was Arba's Township; he was the big man among the Anaqites.)

And the country was calm from battle.

Yehudah's borders

15 The lot fell for the Yehudahites' clan, by their kin-groups, to the Edomite border, the Tsin Wilderness to the south the bottom edge.

> ²Their southern border went from the end of the Salt Sea, from the tongue that turns southward, ³extended to the south of Scorpions Ascent, passed on to Tsin, went up south of Qadesh Barnea, passed on by Hetsron, went up to Addar, turned to Qarqa, ⁴passed on to Atsmon and extended to the Misrayimite Wadi. The border's furthest extents were at the sea. This will be your southern border.
>
> ⁵The border to the east: the Salt Sea as far as the edge of the Yarden.
>
> The border on the northern side, from the tongue of the sea, from the end of

the Yarden: ⁶the border went up by Bet Hoglah and passed north of Bet Ha'arabah. The border went up by Bohan ben-Re'uben Stone. ⁷The border went up to Debir from Disaster Vale, and northward turning its face to Gilgal, which is in front of Red Rocks Ascent, which is south of the wadi. The border passed on to Shemesh Spring Water. Its furthest extents went to Treader Spring. ⁸The border went up by Ben-hinnom Ravine along the Yebusite flank on the south (i.e. Yerushalaim). The border went up to the top of the mountain which is opposite Hinnom Ravine to the west, which is at the edge of Repha'ites Vale to the north. ⁹The border curved from the top of the mountain to Nephtoah Water Spring and extended to the towns of Mount Ephron. The border curved by Ba'alah (i.e. Ye'arim Township). ¹⁰The border turned from Ba'alah westward to Mount Se'ir, passed by the flank of Mount Ye'arim northward (i.e. Kesalon), went down to Bet-shemesh and passed on to Timnah. ¹¹The border extended to the flank of Eqron northward. The border curved to Shikkeron, passed on to Mount Ba'alah and extended by Yabne'el. The border's furthest extents were at the sea.

¹²The western border: the Great Sea and the border.

This was the border of the Yehudahites all round by their kin-groups.

Aksah insists

¹³In accordance with Yahweh's bidding to Yehoshua, he gave to Kaleb ben Yephunneh a share among the Yehudahites, Arba's Township, the ancestor of Anaq (i.e. Hebron). ¹⁴Kaleb dispossessed from there the three Anaqites, Sheshay, Ahiman and Talmay, the descendants of Anaq. ¹⁵He went up from there against the people living in Debir; the name of Debir was formerly Sepher Township. ¹⁶Kaleb said, 'The person who strikes down Sepher Township and captures it: I'll give him Aksah my daughter as wife.' ¹⁷Otni'el ben Qenaz, Kaleb's brother, captured it, and he gave him Aksah his daughter as wife.

¹⁸When she came, she incited him to ask for some fields from her father. She got down from her donkey and Kaleb said to her, 'What is it?' ¹⁹She said, 'Give me a blessing, because you've given me a region in the south. Give me waterholes.' So he gave her the upper waterholes and the lower waterholes.

Yehudah's towns

²⁰This is the domain of the Yehudahites' clan by their kin-groups.

²¹The towns at the edge of the Yehudahites' clan, near the Edomite border, in the Negeb, were:

Qabtse'el, Eder, Yagur, ²²Qinah, Dimonah, Ad'adah, ²³Qedesh, Hatsor, Yitnan, ²⁴Ziph, Telem, Be'alot, ²⁵Hatsor Hadattah, Qeriyyot Hetsron (i.e. Hatsor), ²⁶Amam, Shema, Moladah, ²⁷Gaddah Village, Heshmon, Bet Pelet, ²⁸Shu'al Village, Be'er Sheba, Bizyotyah, ²⁹Ba'alah, Iyyim, Etsem, ³⁰Eltolad, Kesil, Hormah, ³¹Tsiqlag, Madmannah, Sansannah, ³²Leba'ot, Shilhim, Ayin and Rimmon.

All the towns: twenty-nine, and their villages.

³³In the foothills:

Eshta'ol, Tsor'ah, Ashnah, ³⁴Zanoah, Gannim Spring, Tappuah, Enam, ³⁵Yarmut, Adullam, Sokoh, Azeqah, ³⁶Sha'arayim, Aditayim, Gederah and Gederotayim.

Fourteen towns and their villages.

³⁷Tsenan, Hadashah, Gad Tower, ³⁸Dil'an, The Watchtower, Yoqte'el, ³⁹Lakish, Botsqat, Eglon, ⁴⁰Kabbon, Lahmas, Kitlish, ⁴¹Gederot, Bet-dagon, Na'amah and Maqqedah.

Sixteen towns and their villages.

⁴²Libnah, Eter, Ashan, ⁴³Yiphtah, Ashnah, Netsib, ⁴⁴Qe'ilah, Akzib and Mareshah.

Nine towns and their villages.

⁴⁵Eqron, its daughter-towns, and its villages; ⁴⁶from Eqron westward, everything that was in the vicinity of Ashdod and their villages, ⁴⁷Ashdod, its daughter-towns, and its villages; Azzah, its daughter-towns and its villages, as far as the Misrayimite Wadi, and the Great Sea and the edge.

⁴⁸In the highland:

Shamir, Yattir, Sokoh, ⁴⁹Dannah, Sannah Township (i.e. Debir), ⁵⁰Anab, Eshtemoh, Anim, ⁵¹Goshen, Holon and Giloh.
Eleven towns and their villages.
⁵²Arab, Rumah, Esh'an, ⁵³Yanum, Bet-tappuah, Apheqah, ⁵⁴Humtah, Arba's Township (i.e. Hebron) and Tsi'or.
Nine towns and their villages.
⁵⁵Ma'on, Karmel, Ziph, Yuttah, ⁵⁶Yizre'e'l, Yoqde'am, Zanoah, ⁵⁷Qayin, Gib'ah and Timnah.
Ten towns and their villages.
⁵⁸Halhul, Bet-tsur, Gedor, ⁵⁹Ma'arat, Bet-anot and Elteqon.
Six towns and their villages.
⁶⁰Ba'al Township (i.e. Ye'arim Township) and Rabbah.
Two towns and their villages.

⁶¹In the wilderness:

Bet Ha'arabah, Middin, Sekakah, ⁶²Nibshan, Salt Town and Gedi Spring.
Six towns and their villages.

⁶³But the Yehudahites couldn't dispossess the Yebusites, the people living in Yerushalaim, and the Yebusites have lived with the Yehudahites in Yerushalaim until this day.

The Yosephites

16 The lot extended for the Yosephites from the Yarden at Yeriho, at the Yeriho water towards the sunrise, through the wilderness, going up from Yeriho into the highland to Bet-el. ²It extended from Bet-el to Luz and passed on to the Arkites' border at Atarot. ³It went down to the west to the Yaphletites' border, as far as the border of Lower Bet-horon and as far as Gezer. Its furthest extents were at the sea. ⁴So the Yosephites received their domain – Menashsheh and Ephrayim. ⁵The border of the Ephrayimites by their kin-groups, was:

The border of their domain towards the sunrise was Atrot Addar as far as Upper Bet Horon. ⁶The border extended to the sea, to Mikmetat on the north. The border turned towards the sunrise at Ta'anat Shiloh and passed by it east of Yanoah. ⁷It went down from Yanoah to Atarot and to Na'arat, came to Yeriho and extended to the Yarden. ⁸From Tappuah the border extends to the west by Wadi Qanah. Its furthest extents were at the sea. This was the domain of the Ephrayimites' clan by their kin-groups, ⁹and the towns distinguished for the Ephrayimites within the domain of the Menashshites, all the towns and their villages.

¹⁰But they didn't dispossess the Kena'anites who were living in Gezer. The Kena'anites have lived within Ephrayim until this day, but they have been a serf workforce.

17 The lot fell for the clan of Menashsheh, because he was Yoseph's firstborn. For Makir, Menashsheh's firstborn and Gil'ad's father (because he was a man of battle): Gil'ad and Bashan had become his. ²So it fell for the remaining Menashshites by their clans, for the descendants of Abi'ezer, for the descendants of Heleq, for the descendants of Asri'el, for the descendants of Shekem, for the descendants of Hepher and for the descendants of Shemida. These were the male descendants of Menashsheh, Yoseph's son, by their kin-groups.

Menashsheh (and Tselophhad's daughters again)

³Now Tselophhad ben Hepher, son of Gil'ad son of Makir son of Menashsheh, had no sons, but only daughters. These are the names of his daughters: Mahlah, No'ah, Hoglah, Milkah and Tirtsah. ⁴They drew near before El'azar the priest, before Yehoshua ben Nun and before the leaders, saying 'Yahweh himself ordered Mosheh to give us a domain among our brothers.' So he gave them a domain among their father's brothers in accordance with Yahweh's bidding.

⁵Menashsheh's shares fell as ten, apart from the region of Gil'ad and Bashan which are across the Yarden, ⁶because Menashsheh's daughters received a domain among his sons,

while the region of Gil'ad belonged to the remaining descendants of Menashsheh.

⁷Menashsheh's border was: from Asher to Mikmetat, which is east of Shekem. The border goes to the south, to the people living in Tappuah Spring (⁸the Tappuah region belonged to Menashsheh, but Tappuah on the border of Menashsheh belonged to the Ephrayimites). ⁹The border goes down by Wadi Qanah. South of the wadi, these towns belonged to Ephrayim, among Menashsheh's towns, with Menashsheh's border north of the wadi and its furthest extents at the sea. ¹⁰To the south belongs to Ephrayim, to the north to Menashsheh, and the sea was its border. They come to Asher on the north and Yissakar [Issachar] on the east, ¹¹but in Yissakar and in Asher, to Menashsheh belonged Bet-she'an and its daughter-towns, Yible'am and its daughter-towns, the people living in Do'r and its daughter-towns, the people living in Dor Spring and its daughter-towns, the people living in Ta'nak and its daughter-towns, and the people living in Megiddo and its daughter-towns (Three Heights).

¹²But the Menashshites couldn't take possession of these towns; the Kena'anites resolved to stay in this region. ¹³When the Yisra'elites became strong, they made the Kena'anites into a workforce, but they didn't dispossess them at all.

A challenge for Yoseph

¹⁴The Yosephites spoke with Yehoshua: 'Why have you given me as my domain one lot, one allocation, when I'm a numerous people that Yahweh has blessed, up until now?' ¹⁵Yehoshua said to them, 'If you're a numerous people, get yourself up into the forest and clear it for yourself, there in the region of the Perizzite and the Repha'ites, when the highland of Ephrayim is too narrow for you.'

¹⁶The Yosephites said, 'The highland isn't available to us, and there's iron chariotry among all the Kena'anites who live in the vale region, the ones who are in Bet-she'an and in its daughter-towns and the ones who are in the Yizre'el Vale.' ¹⁷Yehoshua said to the household of Yoseph, to Ephrayim and to Menashsheh: 'You're a numerous people. You have great energy. You won't have one lot, ¹⁸because the highland will be yours, because it's forest but you'll clear it, and its furthest extents will be yours because you'll dispossess the Kena'anite when they have iron chariotry, when they're strong.'

18 The entire assembly of the Yisra'elites congregated at Shiloh and placed the appointment tent there, with the country in subjection before them. ²But there remained seven clans among the Yisra'elites to whom they had not shared out their domain.

Surveying the land

³So Yehoshua said to the Yisra'elites, 'How long are you going to be slack about coming to take possession of the country that Yahweh the God of your ancestors has given you? ⁴Provide yourselves three men per clan and I'll send them to set off and go through the country, and write it up on the basis of their domain. Then they're to come to me. ⁵They can allocate it for themselves into seven shares. Yehudah is to stay by its border in the south and the household of Yoseph are to stay by their border in the north.

⁶You, you're to write up the country as seven shares and bring it to me here so I can throw lots for you here before Yahweh our God. ⁷Because there's no share for the Levites among you, because Yahweh's priesthood is their domain, and Gad, Re'uben and the half-clan of Menashsheh have received their domain across the Yarden towards the sunrise, which Mosheh, Yahweh's servant, gave them.'

⁸The men set off and went. Yehoshua ordered the men who were going to write up the country: 'Go, go about the country, and write it up, come back to me, and I'll pitch the lot for you here before Yahweh in Shiloh.' ⁹So the men went and passed through the country, and wrote it up on a document by towns as seven shares. They came to Yehoshua in the camp at Shiloh ¹⁰and Yehoshua pitched the lot for them in Shiloh before Yahweh. So Yehoshua divided up the country before Yisra'el in accordance with their divisions.

Binyamin (Benjamin)

¹¹The lot of the Binyaminites' clan by their kin-groups went up. The border of their lot extended between the Yehudahites and the Yosephites.
¹²Their border on the north side ran from the Yarden. The border went up to Yeriho's northern flank and went up into the highland westward. Its furthest extents were at the Bet Aven Wilderness. ¹³The border passed on from there to Luz, to the flank of Luz southward (i.e. Bet-el). The border went down to Atrot Addar by the mountain which is on the south of Lower Bet-horon.
¹⁴The border curved and turned on the west side southward from the mountain which is opposite Lower Bet-horon southward. Its furthest extents were at Ba'al Township (i.e. Ye'arim Township), a town of the Yehudahites. This was the west side.
¹⁵The south side: from the edge of Ye'arim Township the border extended westward, and extended to Nephtoah Water Spring.
¹⁶The border went down to the edge of the mountain which is opposite Ben-hinnom Ravine, which is in Repha'ites Vale to the north. It went down Hinnom Ravine to the Yebusite flank on the south and went down to Treader Spring. ¹⁷It curved on the north, extended to Shemesh Spring and extended to Gelilot, which is in front of Red Rocks Ascent. It went down to Bohan ben-Re'uben Stone, ¹⁸passed on to the flank near the steppe, northward, and went down to the steppe. ¹⁹The border passed on to the flank of Bet-hoglah, northward. The border's furthest extents were at the tongue of the Salt Sea to the north, at the end of the Yarden to the south. This was the southern border.
²⁰The Yarden constituted its border on the east side.

This is the Binyaminites' domain by its borders all round, by their kin-groups. ²¹The towns of the Binyaminites' clan by their kin-groups were:

Yeriho, Bet-hoglah, Qetsits Vale, ²²Bet Ha'arabah, Tsemarayim, Bet-el, ²³Avvim, Parah, Ophrah, ²⁴Ammonah Hamlet, Ophni and Geba.

Twelve towns and their villages.
²⁵Gib'on, The Height, Be'erot, ²⁶The Watchtower, Kephirah, Motsah, ²⁷Reqem, Yirpe'el, Tar'alah, ²⁸Tsela, Eleph and the Yebusite (i.e. Yerushalaim), Gib'ah, Township.

Fourteen towns and their villages.

This is the Binyaminites' domain by their kin-groups.

Shim'on (Simeon), Zebulun

19 The second lot went out for Shim'on, for the Shim'onites' clan by their kin-groups. Their domain was within the Yehudahites' domain. ²They had as their domain:

Be'er-sheba (or Sheba), Moladah, ³Shu'al Village, Balah, Etsem, ⁴Eltolad, Betul, Hormah, ⁵Tsiqlag, Bet-markabot, Susah Village, ⁶Bet Leba'ot and Sharuhen.

Thirteen towns and their villages.
⁷Ayin, Rimmon, Eter, Ashan.

Four towns and their villages, ⁸and all the villages that are round these towns, as far as Ba'alat Be'er, Ra'mat Negeb.

This is the domain of the Shim'onites' clan by their kin-groups. ⁹The Shim'onites' domain was part of the Yehudahites' share because the Yehudahites' share was too big for them, and the Shim'onites received a domain within their domain.
¹⁰The third lot went up for the Zebulunites by their clans.

The border of their domain ran as far as Sarid. ¹¹Their border went up westward to Mar'alah, came to Dabbeshet and came to the wadi which is opposite Yoqne'am.
¹²It turned back from Sarid towards the sunrise, along the border of Kislot Tabor. It extended to Daberat and went up to Yaphia.
¹³From there it passed on to the east, towards the sunrise, to Gat Hepher, to Et Qatsin. It extended to Rimmon, curving to Ne'ah.
¹⁴It turned (the northern border) to Hannaton. Its furthest extents were Yiphtah-'el Ravine, ¹⁵Qattat, Nahalal, Shimron, Yid'alah and Bet Lehem.

Twelve towns and their villages. ¹⁶This is the Zebulunites' domain by their kin-groups, these towns and their villages.

Yissakar, Asher

¹⁷The fourth lot went out for Yissakar, for the Yissakarites by their kin-groups.
¹⁸Their border was Yizre'e'l, Kesulot, Shunem, ¹⁹Haparayim, Shi'on, Anaharat, ²⁰Rabbit, Qishyon, Ebets, ²¹Remet, Gannim Spring, Haddah Spring and Bet Patstsets.
²²The border came to Tabor, Shahatsim and Bet Shemesh.
The Yarden was the furthest extents of their border.
Sixteen towns and their villages.
²³This is the domain of the Zebulunites' clan by their kin-groups, the towns and their villages.
²⁴The fifth lot went out for the Asherites' clan by their kin-groups.
²⁵Their border was Helqat, Hali, Beten, Akshaph, ²⁶Alammelek, Am'ad and Mish'al.
It came to Karmel on the west and Shihor Libnat.
²⁷It turned back towards the sunrise, to Bet Dagon, and came to Zebulun and Yiphtah-'el Ravine to the north, Bet Ha'emeq and Ne'i'el.
It extended to Kabul on the north, ²⁸Ebron, Rehob, Hammon and Qanah, as far as Great Tsidon. ²⁹The border turned back to The Height and as far as the fortified town of Tsor. The border turned back to Hosah. Its furthest extents were at the sea in the area of Akzib, ³⁰Ummah, Apheq and Rehob.
Twenty-two towns and their villages.
³¹This is the domain of the Asherites' clan by their kin-groups, these towns and their villages.

Naphtali, Dan

³²The sixth lot went out for the Naphtalites, for the Naphtalites by their kin-groups.
³³Their border ran from Heleph, Betsa'anannim Oak, Adami Hanneqeb and Yabne'el as far as Laqqum, and the Yarden was its furthest extents.

³⁴The border turned back westward to Aznot Tabor and went out from there to Huqoq.
It came to Zebulun on the south.
It came to Asher on the west and Yehudah at the Yarden towards the sunrise.
³⁵Its fortified towns: Tsiddim, Tser, Hammat, Raqqat, Kinneret, ³⁶Adamah, The Height, Hatsor, ³⁷Qedesh, Edre'i, Hatsor Spring, ³⁸Yir'on, Migdal-el, Horem, Bet-anat and Bet Shemesh.
Nineteen towns and their villages.
³⁹This is the domain of the Naphtalites' clan by their kin-groups, the towns and their villages.
⁴⁰The seventh lot went out for the Danites by their kin-groups. ⁴¹The border of their domain was Tsor'ah, Eshta'ol, Shemesh Town, ⁴²Sha'alabbin, Ayyalon, Yitlah, ⁴³Elon, Timnah, Eqron, ⁴⁴Elteqeh, Gibbeton, Ba'alat, ⁴⁵Yehud, Bene-beraq, Gat-rimmon, ⁴⁶Yarkon Water, Raqqon, with the border near Yapho.

⁴⁷But the Danites' border got away from them, and the Danites went up and battled with Leshem and captured it. They struck it down with the mouth of the sword, took possession of it and lived in it. They named it Dan in accordance with the name of their ancestor Dan.

⁴⁸This is the domain of the Danites' clan by their kin-groups, these towns and their villages.

⁴⁹So they finished making the country into domains by its borders. The Yisra'elites gave a domain to Yehoshua ben Nun among them. ⁵⁰At Yahweh's bidding they gave him the town that he asked for, Timnat-serah in the highland of Ephrayim. He built up the town and lived in it.
⁵¹These are the domains that El'azar the priest, Yehoshua ben Nun and the heads of the ancestral households made for the Yisra'elites' clans by lot in Shiloh before Yahweh at the entrance of the appointment tent. So they finished sharing out the country.

The asylum towns

20 Yahweh spoke to Yehoshua: ²"Speak to the Yisra'elites: "Give yourselves the asylum towns about which I spoke to you through Mosheh, ³for a killer who strikes a person down by accident (without realizing), to flee there. They will be an asylum for you from the blood restorer.

⁴He will flee to one of these towns, and stand at the entrance of the town gateway and speak in the hearing of that town's elders. They will receive him into the town among them, and give him a place so he can live with them. ⁵When the blood restorer pursues after him, they will not surrender the killer into his hand, because he struck down his neighbour without realizing and he was not hostile to him in previous days.

⁶He is to live in that town until he stands before the assembly for a decision, until the death of the great priest who is there at that time. Then the killer may go back and come to his town and to his home, to the town from which he fled."'

⁷So they made sacred Qedesh in Galilee in the highland of Naphtali; Shekem in the highland of Ephrayim; and Arba's Township (i.e. Hebron) in the highland of Yehudah. ⁸Across the Yarden (Yeriho) towards the sunrise, they made Betser in the wilderness on the flatland, from the clan of Re'uben; Heights-in-Gil'ad from the clan of Gad; and Golan in Bashan from the clan of Menashsheh.

⁹These were the set towns for all the Yisra'elites and for the person who is residing among them to flee there, anyone who struck someone down by accident, so that he would not die by the hand of the blood restorer until he stood before the assembly.

The Levites' needs

21 The heads of the Levites' ancestral households came up to El'azar the priest, to Yehoshua ben Nun and to the heads of the ancestral households of the Yisra'elites' clans. ²They spoke to them at Shiloh in the country of Kena'an: 'Yahweh himself ordered through Mosheh to give us towns to live in, with their pasturelands for our animals.' ³So the Yisra'elites gave the Levites part of their domain in accordance with Yahweh's bidding, these towns and their pasturelands.

⁴The lot went out for the Qehatite kin-groups: for the descendants of Aharon [Aaron] the priest, from the Levites, it was from the clan of Yehudah, from the clan of Shim'on, from the clan of Binyamin, by lot, thirteen towns.

⁵For the remaining Qehatites: from the kin-groups of the clan of Ephrayim, from the clan of Dan and from the half-clan of Menashsheh, by lot, ten towns.

⁶For the Gershonites: from the kin-groups of the clan of Yissakar, from the clan of Asher, from the clan of Naphtali and from the half-clan of Menashsheh in Bashan, by lot, thirteen towns.

⁷For the Merarites by their kin-groups: from the clan of Re'uben, from the clan of Gad and from the clan of Zebulun, twelve towns.

⁸The Yisra'elites gave the Levites these towns and their pasturelands, as Yahweh said through Mosheh, by lot.

The Aharonites and the other Qehatites

⁹From the Yehudahites' clan and from the Shim'onites' clan they gave these towns, which will be named, ¹⁰for the descendants of Aharon from the Qehatite kin-groups of the Levites, because the first lot was for them.

¹¹They gave to them Arba's Township, the ancestor of the Anaqites (i.e. Hebron) in the highland of Yehudah, and its pastureland round it. ¹²The town's fields and its villages they gave to Kaleb ben Yephunneh as his holding, ¹³but to the descendants of Aharon the priest, they gave the killer's asylum town, Hebron, and its pastureland, Libnah and its pastureland, ¹⁴Yattir and its pastureland, Eshtemoa and its pastureland, ¹⁵Holon and its pastureland, Debir and its pastureland, ¹⁶Spring and its pastureland, Yuttah and its pastureland, and Bet Shemesh and its pastureland.

Nine towns from these two clans.

¹⁷And from the clan of Binyamin: Gib'on and its pastureland, Geba and its pastureland, ¹⁸Anatot and its pastureland, and Almon and its pastureland.

Four towns.

¹⁹All the towns of the descendants of Aharon, the priests: thirteen towns and their pasturelands.

²⁰For the kin-groups of the Qehatites, the remaining Levites of the Qehatites, the towns in their lot were:

From the clan of Ephrayim, ²¹they gave them the killer's asylum town, Shekem, and its pastureland in the highland of Ephrayim, Gezer and its pastureland, ²²Qibtsayim and its pastureland, and Bet Horon and its pastureland.
Four towns.
²³From the clan of Dan: Elteqe and its pastureland, Gibbeton and its pastureland, ²⁴Ayyalon and its pastureland, Gat-rimmon and its pastureland.
Four towns.
²⁵From the half-clan of Menashsheh: Ta'nak and its pastureland, and Gat-rimmon and its pastureland.
Two towns.

²⁶All the towns: ten, and their pasturelands, for the remaining kin-groups of the Qehatites.

The Gershonites and the Merarites

²⁷For the Gershonites, of the kin-groups of the Levites:

From the half-clan of Menashsheh, the killer's asylum town, Golan in Bashan and its pastureland, and Be'eshterah and its pastureland.
Two towns.
²⁸From the clan of Yissakar: Qishron and its pastureland, Dobrat and its pastureland, ²⁹Yarmut and its pastureland, and Gannim Spring and its pastureland.
Four towns.
³⁰From the clan of Asher: Mish'al and its pastureland, Abdon and its pastureland, ³¹Helqat and its pastureland, and Rehob and its pastureland.
Four towns.
³²From the clan of Naphtali, the killer's asylum town, Qedesh in Galilee, and its pastureland, Hammot Do'r and its pastureland, and Qartan and its pastureland.
Three towns and their pasturelands.

³³All the towns of the Gershonites by their kin-groups: thirteen towns and their pasturelands.
³⁴For the kin-groups of the Merarites, the remaining Levites:

From the clan of Zebulun: Yoqne'am and its pastureland, Qartah and its pastureland, ³⁵Dimnah and its pastureland, and Nahalal and its pastureland.
Four towns.
³⁶From the clan of Gad, the killer's asylum town, Heights-in-Gil'ad and its pastureland, Mahanayim and its pastureland, ³⁷Heshbon and its pastureland, and Ya'zer and its pastureland.
All the towns, four.

³⁸All the towns of the Merarites by their kin-groups, the remaining kin-groups of the Levites: their lot was twelve towns.

³⁹All the Levites' towns within the Yisra'elites' holding: forty-eight towns and their pasturelands. ⁴⁰These would be the towns, town by town and its pastureland round it – so for all these towns.

Not one word failed

⁴¹So Yahweh gave Yisra'el the entire country that he had sworn to give to their ancestors. They took possession of it and lived in it. ⁴²Yahweh enabled them to settle down all around in accordance with everything that he had sworn to their ancestors. Not one individual of all their enemies stood against them; all their enemies Yahweh gave into their hand. ⁴³No word fell, of every good word that God had spoken to the household of Yisra'el. Everything came about.

22 Then Yehoshua called the Re'ubenites, the Gadites and the half-clan of Menashsheh, ²and said to them: 'You yourselves have kept everything that Mosheh, Yahweh's servant, ordered you, and you've listened to my voice in everything that I ordered you. ³You haven't abandoned your brothers this long time until this day. You've kept the charge from the order of Yahweh your God. ⁴But Yahweh your God has now enabled your brothers to settle down, as he spoke to them. So now, turn your face and get yourselves to your tents, to the region of your holding which Mosheh Yahweh's servant gave you across the Yarden. ⁵Only keep careful watch to act on the order and the instruction that Mosheh Yahweh's servant gave you by being loyal to Yahweh your God, by walking in all his ways, by keeping his orders, by attaching yourselves to him, and by serving him with your entire mind and with your entire being.'

A little local difficulty

⁶Yehoshua blessed them and sent them off, and they went to their tents. ⁷To one half-clan of Menashsheh Mosheh had given [land] in Bashan, and to the other half-clan Yehoshua had given it with their brothers across the Yarden to the west. Further, when Yehoshua sent them off to their tents and blessed them, ⁸he said to them, 'Go back to your tents with great riches, with very much livestock, with silver and with gold, with copper and with iron, and with very much clothing. Share out the spoil of your enemies with your brothers.' ⁹So the Re'ubenites, the Gadites and the half-clan of Menashsheh turned back and went from being with the Yisra'elites at Shiloh, which is in the country of Kena'an, to go the region of Gil'ad, to the land of their holding, which they had acquired at Yahweh's bidding through Mosheh.

¹⁰They came to the area of the Yarden which is in the country of Kena'an, and the Re'ubenites, the Gadites and the half-clan of Menashsheh built an altar there at the Yarden, an altar big in appearance. ¹¹The Yisra'elites heard: 'Here, the Re'ubenites, the Gadites and the half-clan of Menashsheh have built an altar near the land of Kena'an, in the area of the Yarden, across from the Yisra'elites.'

¹²So the Yisra'elites heard, and the entire assembly of the Yisra'elites congregated at Shiloh to go up to war against them. ¹³The Yisra'elites sent Pinhas ben El'azar, the priest, to the Re'ubenites, the Gadites and the half-clan of Menashsheh in the region of Gil'ad, ¹⁴and ten leaders with him, one leader for each ancestral household, for all the clans of Yisra'el. They were, each individual, the head of an ancestral household for the Yisra'elite divisions.

Misunderstanding cleared up

¹⁵They came to the Re'ubenites, the Gadites and the half-clan of Menashsheh in the region of Gil'ad and spoke with them: ¹⁶'The entire assembly of Yisra'el has said this: "What is this trespass that you've committed against Yisra'el's God in turning back today from following Yahweh, in your building yourselves an altar, rebelling today against Yahweh? ¹⁷Was the waywardness at Pe'or a small thing to us, from which we haven't purified ourselves this day (and an epidemic came on Yahweh's assembly), ¹⁸and you yourselves turn back from following Yahweh today? If you rebel against Yahweh, tomorrow he will be furious with the entire assembly of Yisra'el.

¹⁹Yet if the land of your holding is taboo, get yourselves across into the land of Yahweh's holding where Yahweh's dwelling is, and hold land among us. Don't rebel against Yahweh and don't rebel against us by your building yourselves an altar other than the altar of Yahweh our God. ²⁰When Akan ben Zerah trespassed in connection with devoting, fury came on the entire assembly, didn't it. He wasn't the only one who breathed his last for his waywardness."'

²¹The Re'ubenites, the Gadites and the half-clan of Menashsheh answered the heads of the Yisra'elite divisions: ²²'The God over the gods, Yahweh, the God over the gods, Yahweh, he knows, and Yisra'el – it will know: if it was in rebellion or in trespass against Yahweh, don't deliver us today ²³for building ourselves an altar to turn back from following Yahweh. Or if it was for offering up a burnt offering or a grain offering on it, or if for making well-being sacrifices on it, Yahweh – may he look for it from us. ²⁴But if it wasn't out of anxiety about something that we did this, saying "Tomorrow your children may say to our children, 'What do you and Yahweh the God of Yisra'el have in common? ²⁵Yahweh has made the Yarden a border between us and you, Re'ubenites and Gadites. You have no share in Yahweh.'" Your children would make our children stop living in awe of Yahweh.

A happy ending

²⁶So we said, "Let's please act for ourselves by building an altar, not for burnt offering and

not for sacrifice. ²⁷Rather it will be a witness between us and you and coming generations, for performing Yahweh's service before him, with our burnt offerings and with our sacrifices and with our well-being offerings, and your children will not say tomorrow to our children, 'You have no share in Yahweh.'" ²⁸We said, "When they say it to us and to our generations tomorrow, we'll say, 'Look at the pattern of Yahweh's altar which our fathers made, not for burnt offering and not for sacrifice, but it's a witness between us and you.'" ²⁹Far be it from us for us to rebel against Yahweh and turn back today from following Yahweh by building an altar for burnt offering, for grain offering and for sacrifice, apart from the altar of Yahweh our God that's before his dwelling.'

³⁰Pinhas the priest, and the congregation's leaders (the heads of the Yisra'elite divisions) who were with him, listened to the things that the Re'ubenites, the Gadites and the Menashshites spoke of, and it was good in their eyes. ³¹Pinhas ben El'azar the priest said to the Re'ubenites, the Gadites and the Menashshites, 'Today we acknowledge that Yahweh is among us, in that you haven't committed this trespass against Yahweh. Therefore you've saved the Yisra'elites from Yahweh's hand.'

³²Pinhas ben El'azar the priest and the leaders went back from the Re'ubenites and from the Gadites from the region of Gil'ad to the country of Kena'an to the Yisra'elites and took back word to them. ³³The thing was good in the Yisra'elites' eyes and they blessed God. They didn't speak of going up against them to make war, to devastate the land in which the Re'ubenites and the Gadites were living.

³⁴The Re'ubenites and the Gadites named the altar, that it was a 'Witness between us that Yahweh is our God'.

Beware of the other peoples' faiths

23 A long time later, after Yahweh had enabled Yisra'el to settle down from all their enemies around, and when Yehoshua was old, going on in years, ²Yehoshua called all Yisra'el, its elders, its leaders, its rulers and its overseers, and said to them, 'I myself have got old, I've gone on in years. ³You yourselves have seen everything that Yahweh your God did to all these nations from before you, because Yahweh your God – he's the one who was battling for you. ⁴See, I've caused the lot to fall for you on these remaining nations as a domain for your clans, from the Yarden (yes, all the nations I cut off) and the Great Sea in the west.

⁵Yahweh your God – he will push them out from before you and dispossess them from before you so you may take possession of their country as Yahweh your God spoke to you. ⁶You're to be very firm about keeping everything written in Mosheh's instruction document by acting on it, without departing from it right or left, ⁷and without coming among these nations (these that remain with you). You will not commemorate their gods' name, you will not swear, you will not serve them and you will not bow low to them. ⁸Rather, you're to attach yourselves to Yahweh your God, as you've done until this day.

⁹Yahweh has dispossessed great and numerous nations from before you, and you: not one individual stood against you until this day. ¹⁰One individual from among you can pursue a thousand, because Yahweh your God – he has been battling for you, as he spoke to you.

Beware of contravening the pact

¹¹You're to keep careful watch for yourselves so as to be loyal to Yahweh your God, ¹²because if you do turn back and attach yourselves to what is left of these nations (these that remain with you) and intermarry with them and have sex with them and they with you, ¹³you're to acknowledge clearly that Yahweh your God won't continue to dispossess these nations from before you. To you they will become a trap and a snare, a whip on your sides and thorns in your eyes, until you perish from on this good land that Yahweh our God has given you.

¹⁴Here I am, going the way of all the earth now. You're to acknowledge with your entire mind and with your entire being that not one word has fallen down of all the good things of which Yahweh your God spoke to you. Everything has come about for you. Not one word of them has fallen down. ¹⁵But as every good thing of which Yahweh your God spoke to you has come about for you, so Yahweh

will cause every bad experience to come about for you, until he's eliminated you from on this good land that Yahweh your God has given you. ¹⁶When you contravene the pact of Yahweh your God that he ordered you, and go and serve other gods and bow low to them, Yahweh's anger will rage against you and you will perish quickly from on this good country that he's given you.'

24

Yehoshua gathered all Yisra'el's clans at Shekem and called Yisra'el's elders, its leaders, its rulers and its overseers, and they took their stand before God.

Think back over the story

²Yehoshua said to all the people, 'Yahweh, Yisra'el's God, has said this: "Across the river, your ancestors (Terah, Abraham's father and Nahor's father) lived of old and served other gods. ³I got your ancestor Abraham from across the river and enabled him to go through the entire country of Kena'an, and I made his offspring numerous. I gave him Yitshaq [Isaac], ⁴and gave Yitshaq Ya'aqob [Jacob] and Esaw, and I gave Esaw the highland of Se'ir as his domain, while Ya'aqob and his sons went down to Misrayim.

⁵I sent Mosheh and Aharon and I hit Misrayim as I acted in its midst. Afterwards, I got you out. ⁶I got your ancestors out of Misrayim and you came to the sea. The Misrayimites pursued after your ancestors with chariotry and with cavalry, to the Reed Sea. ⁷They cried out to Yahweh and he put darkness between you and the Misrayimites. He made the sea come over them and it covered them. Your eyes saw what I did to the Misrayimites.

You stayed in the wilderness a long time, ⁸but I brought you to the country of the Amorites who were living across the Yarden. They battled with you but I gave them into your hand and you took possession of their country. I eliminated them from before you. ⁹Balaq ben Tsippor king of Mo'ab rose up and battled with Yisra'el. He sent and called for Bil'am ben Be'or to slight you. ¹⁰But I was not willing to listen to Bil'am and he really had to bless you. So I saved you from his hand.

¹¹You crossed the Yarden and came to Yeriho. The Yeriho landowners, the Amorite, the Perizzite, the Kena'anite, the Hittite, the Girgashite, the Hivvite and the Yebusite, battled against you, but I gave them into your hand. ¹²I sent off a hornet before you and it drove them out from before you (two Amorite kings), not by your sword and not by your bow. ¹³I've given you a country for which you didn't get weary, towns that you didn't build but you've lived in, eating from vineyards and olive groves that you didn't plant."

'You can't serve Yahweh.' 'Yes we can!'

¹⁴So now, live in awe of Yahweh and serve him with integrity and with truthfulness. Remove the gods that your ancestors served across the river and in Misrayim, and serve Yahweh. ¹⁵If it's bad in your eyes to serve Yahweh, choose for yourselves today whom you'll serve, whether the gods that your ancestors served who were beyond the river, or the gods of the Amorites whose country you're living in. I and my household, we will serve Yahweh.'

¹⁶The people answered, 'Far be it from us to abandon Yahweh to serve other gods, ¹⁷because Yahweh our God – he's the one who got us and our ancestors up from the country of Misrayim, from a household of serfs, and who did before our eyes these great signs, and kept us the entire way that we went and among all the peoples through whom we passed; ¹⁸and Yahweh drove out all the peoples (the Amorites) living in the country from before us. We'll serve Yahweh as well, because he's our God.'

¹⁹Yehoshua said to the people, 'You can't serve Yahweh, because he's a sacred God. He's a passionate God. He won't carry your rebellions and wrongdoings. ²⁰When you abandon Yahweh and serve foreign gods, he'll turn back and bring bad fortune to you and finish you off, after he's been good to you.'

²¹The people said to Yehoshua, 'No, because Yahweh is the one we'll serve.' ²²Yehoshua said to the people, 'You're witnesses against yourselves that you yourselves have chosen for yourselves Yahweh, to serve him.' They said, 'We're witnesses.' ²³'So now remove the foreign gods that are among you and direct your mind to Yahweh the God of Yisra'el.' ²⁴The people said to Yehoshua, 'Yahweh our God we will serve. To his voice we will listen.'

Confirming the pact anew

²⁵Yehoshua solemnized a pact for the people that day and laid down for them a decree and a ruling, at Shekem. ²⁶Yehoshua wrote these things in God's instruction document. He got a big stone and set it up there under the oak that was in Yahweh's sanctuary. ²⁷Yehoshua said to all the people, 'Here, this stone – it will be a witness against us, because it – it heard all Yahweh's words that he spoke with us. It will be a witness against you, so you don't act deceitfully towards your God.' ²⁸And Yehoshua sent the people off, each to their domain.

²⁹After that, Yehoshua ben Nun, Yahweh's servant, died, a man of 110 years. ³⁰They buried him within the border that was his domain in Timnat-serah in the highland of Ephrayim, north of Mount Ga'ash.

³¹Yisra'el served Yahweh all the time of Yehoshua and all the time of the elders who lived on after Yehoshua and who acknowledged all Yahweh's action that he undertook for Yisra'el. ³²The bones of Yoseph, which the Yisra'elites had brought up from Misrayim, they buried in Shekem on the plot in the fields that Ya'aqob had acquired from the sons of Hamor, Shekem's father, for a hundred qesitas. It had become a domain of the Yosephites.

³³El'azar ben Aharon died and they buried him on the hill of Pinhas his son, which had been given him in the highland of Ephrayim.

Judges

A quick read of Joshua can give one the impression that the story that now follows will relate how everyone lives happily ever after, but the close of Joshua made clear that the Israelites have by no means entered into full possession of the land of Canaan. Moreover, Joshua's challenges to the Israelites at the end of Joshua also raise the question of how faithful Israel will be in fulfilling its own promises.

Judges begins (1.1—2.5) by focusing on the areas of the country over which Israel does not yet have control, and it thus conveys a gloomier impression than the book of Joshua as a whole. Further, the areas that remain under Canaanite control are the most populous areas and the ones most worth possessing. Like Joshua, Judges here moves between 'they didn't gain control' and 'they couldn't gain control' of these areas.

A second introduction to the book (2.6—3.4) then outlines a pattern that runs through much of the book. It introduces a series of stories that relate how Israelites turn away from adherence to Yahweh to serve other deities. Yahweh then himself turns away and leaves them to the mercy of their neighbours. In due course this experience of discipline makes them turn back to Yahweh, and he produces a deliverer who can rescue them from their adversaries.

It is these deliverers who provide the book with its title, 'Judges', though that English word is thus misleading. I use the expression 'exercise authority' to match the rendering elsewhere in this translation. But these leaders are people who don't have an official position like a governor or a king but who by dint of God's spirit coming on them are able to do what needs doing for Israel. Their personalities and gifts are also involved, though they tend to be the kind of people who wouldn't be in positions of official leadership if there were official leaders. God chooses and uses somebody's little brother, somebody who is handicapped, a son of Anat (a name that suggests he is a Canaanite), and then the greatest of the leaders who is – a woman.

Nor are these leaders commonly people of great faith or insight or a high standard of morality. Indeed, there is a troubling arc to the sequence of their stories. As the book unfolds, the leaders become more and more ambiguous figures. They can get the job done, but they lack the moral qualities that one would like to see accompanying their exercise of leadership.

In this respect they mirror the people themselves, and the later chapters in Judges turn it into the most distasteful and disturbing book in the Bible. It becomes a relentless portrayal of human stupidity, failure, and moral and social blindness. Women pay a heavy price in the conflicts and the abuses it reports, though women also exercise remarkable initiatives in different stories in the book.

Its own repeated comment in the closing chapters is that people were doing what was all right in their own eyes, and it adds the further comment that of course there was no king in Israel. The implication is that a king would be able to do something about the situation. The book thus provides some background to the introduction of kings in the next book, 1 Samuel.

If you add up the periods covered by the times of crisis and subsequent quiet in the book, you end up with a history occupying several hundred years. There isn't actually room for that long a period between Joshua (about 1200 BC) and Saul (about 1050 BC). A closer look at the stories, however, reveals that they all concern events and deliverances that are more or less local. They don't involve all the clans. So the periods of years to which the book refers can be overlapping – a time of crisis in one area can be a time of quiet in another. It's then theologically significant that the book portrays all the crises and deliverances as involving 'Israel'. When one suffers, all suffer. Trouble for one part of the body is trouble for the body as a whole.

Real life is more complicated

1 After Yehoshua's [Joshua's] death, the Yisra'elites [Israelites] asked of Yahweh, 'Who is to go up for us against the Kena'anites [Canaanites] first, to do battle with them?' ²Yahweh said, 'Yehudah [Judah] is to go up. Here, I am giving the country into his hand.' ³Yehudah said to Shim'on [Simeon], his brother, 'Go up with me into my lot so we can do battle against the Kena'anites, and I'll go with you into your lot as well.' So Shim'on went with him. ⁴Yehudah went up, and Yahweh gave the Kena'anite and the Perizzite into their hand. They struck them down at Bezeq, 10,000 people.

⁵They found Adoni Bezeq at Bezeq and battled against him, and struck down the Kena'anite and the Perizzite. ⁶Adoni Bezeq fled, but they pursued after him. They caught him and cut off his thumbs and big toes. ⁷Adoni-bezeq said, 'Seventy kings, with thumbs and big toes cut off, used to be gleaning under my table. As I have done, so God has made good to me.' They brought him to Yerushalaim [Jerusalem], and he died there.

⁸The Yehudahites battled against Yerushalaim, captured it and struck it down with the mouth of the sword, and the town they sent up in fire. ⁹Afterwards, the Yehudahites went down to battle against the Kena'anites living in the highland, the Negeb and the foothills.

¹⁰Yehudah went against the Kena'anites who were living in Hebron (Hebron's name was Arba's Township before). They struck down Sheshay, Ahiman and Talmay. ¹¹From there, it went against the people living in Debir (Debir's name was Sepher Township before).

¹²Kaleb [Caleb] said, 'The man who strikes down Sepher Township and captures it: I'll give him Aksah my daughter as wife.' ¹³Otni'el ben Qenaz, Kaleb's brother who was younger than him, captured it, and he gave him Aksah his daughter as wife. ¹⁴When she came, she incited him to ask for some fields from her father. She got down from her donkey and Kaleb said to her, 'What is it?' ¹⁵She said to him, 'Give me a blessing, because you've given me a region in the south. Give me waterholes.' So Kaleb gave her the upper waterholes and the lower waterholes.

Who could and who couldn't

¹⁶The descendants of the Qenite, Mosheh's [Moses'] father-in-law, went up from Palms Town with the Yehudahites into the Yehudah Wilderness that's south of Arad, and he went and lived with the people. ¹⁷Yehudah went with its brother Shim'on and they struck down the Kena'anites living in Tsepat. They devoted it [haram], and named the town Hormah. ¹⁸Yehudah captured Azzah [Gaza] and its border, Ashqelon and its border, and Eqron and its border. ¹⁹Yahweh was with Yehudah, and it took possession of the highland, because it couldn't dispossess the people living in the vale because they had iron chariotry. ²⁰They gave Hebron to Kaleb as Mosheh spoke, and he dispossessed the three Anaqites from there. ²¹But the Yebusites living in Yerushalaim the Binyaminites [Benjaminites] didn't dispossess. The Yebusites have lived with the Binyaminites in Yerushalaim until this day.

²²Yoseph's [Joseph's] household, they too, went up to Bet-el; Yahweh was with them. ²³Yoseph's household investigated Bet-el (the town's name was Luz before), ²⁴and the men keeping watch saw a man coming out of the town and said to him, 'Show us the way into the town, will you, and we will act in commitment with you.' ²⁵He showed them the way into the town and they struck down the town with the mouth of the sword, but the man and his entire kin-group they sent off. ²⁶The man went to the Hittites' region and built a town, and named it Luz. That's its name until this day.

²⁷Menashsheh didn't take possession of Bet-she'an and its daughter-towns, Ta'nak and its daughter-towns, the people living in Dor and its daughter-towns, the people living in Yible'am and its daughter-towns, or the people living in Megiddo and its daughter-towns. The Kena'anites were resolved to live in this region. ²⁸When Yisra'el became strong it made the Kena'anites into a workforce, but it didn't dispossess them at all.

Wailing

²⁹Ephrayim didn't dispossess the Kena'anites who were living in Gezer; the Kena'anites lived among them in Gezer. ³⁰Zebulun didn't

dispossess the people living in Qitron or the people living in Nahalol; the Kena'anites lived among them and became a workforce. ³¹Asher didn't dispossess the people living in Akko or the people living in Tsidon, Ahlab, Akzib, Helbah, Aphiq or Rehob. ³²The Asherites lived among the Kena'anites living in the region, because they didn't dispossess them. ³³Naphtali didn't dispossess the people living in Bet-shemesh or the people living in Bet-anat. They lived among the Kena'anites living in the region and the people living in Bet-shemesh and Bet Anat became a workforce for them.

³⁴The Amorites forced the Danites into the highland because they didn't let them come down into the vale. ³⁵The Amorites resolved to stay in Mount Heres in Ayyalon and in Sha'albim. But the hand of Yoseph's household became heavy and they became a workforce. ³⁶The Amorites' border went from Scorpions Ascent, from Sela, on upwards.

2 Yahweh's envoy went up from Gilgal to Bokim and said, 'I enabled you to go up from Misrayim [Egypt] and I brought you to the country that I swore to your ancestors. I said, "I will not contravene my pact with you, ever. ²You yourselves will not solemnize a pact towards the people living in this country. You're to tear down their altars." But you didn't listen to my voice. What is this you've done? ³So I've also said, "I won't drive them out from before you. They'll be at your sides and their gods will be a snare to you."' ⁴When Yahweh's envoy spoke these words to all the Yisra'elites, the people lifted up their voice and wailed, ⁵and named that place Bokim ['Wailers'], but they sacrificed there to Yahweh.

The power of forgetting

⁶Yehoshua had sent the company off, and the Yisra'elites had gone each person to his domain to take possession of the country. ⁷The people served Yahweh all Yehoshua's time and all the time of the elders who lived on after Yehoshua, who had seen all Yahweh's great work that he did for Yisra'el.

⁸Yehoshua ben Nun, Yahweh's servant, died, a man of 110 years, ⁹and they buried him within the border that was his domain at Timnat-heres in the highland of Ephrayim, north of Mount Ga'ash. ¹⁰That entire generation also joined its ancestors, and another generation arose after them who didn't acknowledge Yahweh, or the work he had done for Yisra'el either. ¹¹The Yisra'elites did what was bad in Yahweh's eyes. They served the Masters ¹²and abandoned Yahweh, their ancestors' God, who had got them out of the country of Misrayim. They followed other gods from among the gods of the peoples who were round them, and bowed low to them, and provoked Yahweh.

¹³So they abandoned Yahweh and served the Master and the Ashtars, ¹⁴and Yahweh's anger raged against Yisra'el and he gave them into the hand of people who plundered them. He surrendered them into the hand of their enemies all round. They could no longer stand before their enemies. ¹⁵Wherever they went out, Yahweh's hand was against them to make things go badly, as Yahweh had spoken and as Yahweh had sworn to them. It put great pressure on them.

¹⁶Yahweh made people to exercise authority arise and they delivered them from the hand of their plunderers, ¹⁷but they also didn't listen to the people who exercised authority for them, because they whored after other gods and bowed low to them. They departed quickly from the way that their ancestors had walked by listening to Yahweh's orders. They didn't do so.

When Yahweh feels sorry for them

¹⁸When Yahweh made people to exercise authority arise for them, Yahweh would be with the one exercising authority and he would deliver them from the hand of their enemies all the time of the one exercising authority, because Yahweh felt sorry on account of their groan in the face of the people afflicting and crushing them. ¹⁹But when the one exercising authority died, they would go back to acting more devastatingly than their ancestors in following other gods to serve them and bow low to them. They didn't drop any of their practices and their tough-minded way.

²⁰So Yahweh's anger raged against Yisra'el. He said, 'Since this nation have contravened the pact with which I ordered their ancestors and haven't listened to my voice, ²¹I for my part will not continue to dispossess anyone from

before them, from the nations that Yehoshua left when he died', ²²in order to test Yisra'el by them, whether they're keeping Yahweh's way by walking in them, as their ancestors kept it, or not. ²³So Yahweh had let these nations settle down without dispossessing them quickly, and had not given them into Yehoshua's hand.

3 These are the nations that Yahweh let settle down, to test Yisra'el by them, all who had not known any of the battles in Kena'an, ²only in order for Yisra'el's generations to know them, by teaching them about battle – only the people who had not known them before: ³the five Pelishtite lords and all the Kena'anites, the Tsidonites and the Hivvites living in the highland of the Lebanon from Ba'al Hermon Mountain as far as Lebo Hamat. ⁴They were for testing Yisra'el by them, to know whether they would listen to Yahweh's order which he had given their ancestors through Mosheh.

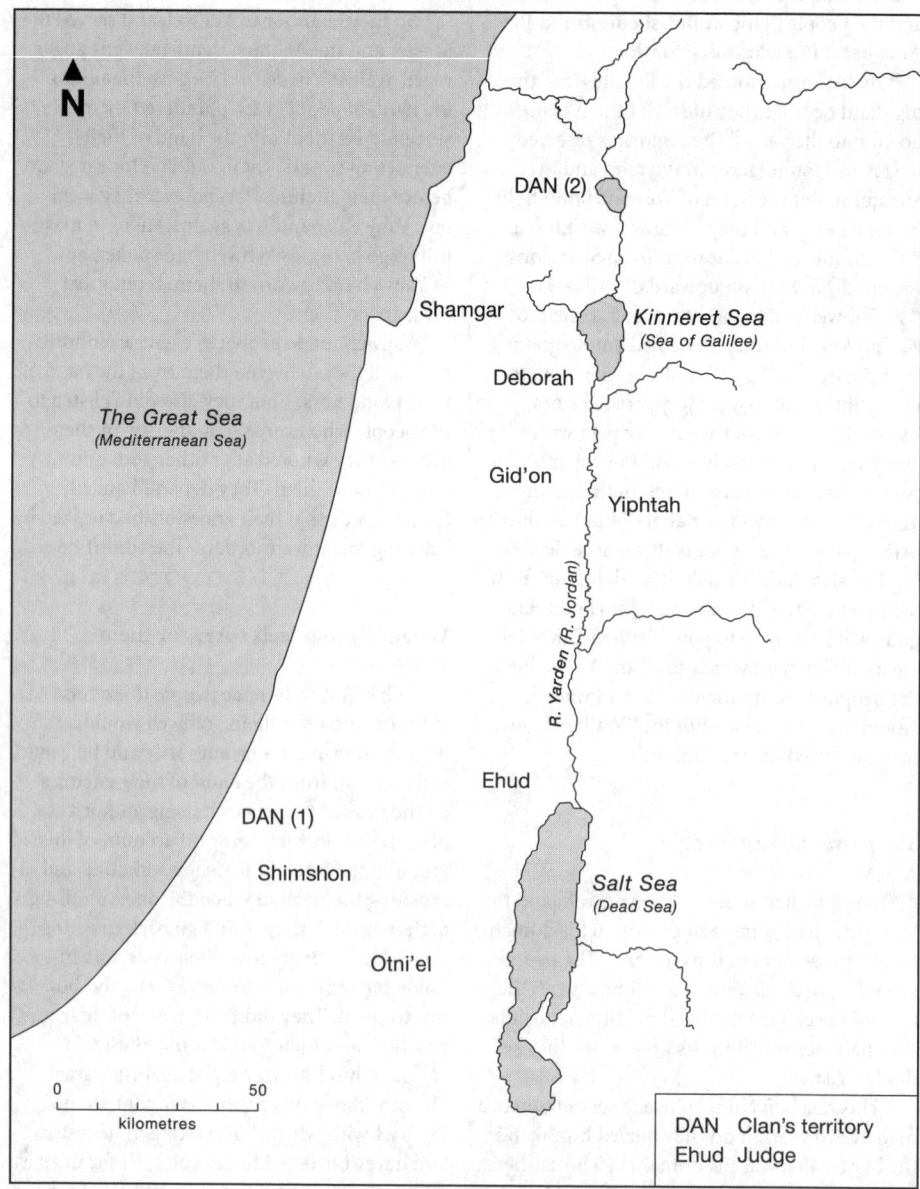

The 'major' judges

Kaleb's little brother again

⁵So the Yisra'elites lived among the Kena'anite, the Hittite, the Amorite, the Perizzite, the Hivvite and the Yebusite, ⁶and got their daughters for themselves as wives and gave their daughters to their sons, and served their gods. ⁷The Yisra'elites did what was bad in Yahweh's eyes. They put Yahweh their God out of mind and served the Masters and the Asherahs. ⁸Yahweh's anger raged against Yisra'el and he surrendered them into the hand of Kushan Rish'atayim, the king of Aram-of-the-Two-Rivers. The Yisra'elites served Kushan Rish'atayim for eight years.

⁹The Yisra'elites cried out to Yahweh and Yahweh made a deliverer arise for the Yisra'elites and he delivered them: Otni'el ben Qenaz, Kaleb's brother who was younger than him. ¹⁰Yahweh's spirit came on him and he exercised authority for Yisra'el. He went out to battle and Yahweh gave Kushan Rish'atayim, the king of Aram, into his hand. His hand was powerful over Kushan Rish'atayim, ¹¹and the region was calm for forty years.

Otni'el ben Qenaz died, ¹²and the Yisra'elites again did what was bad in Yahweh's eyes. Yahweh made Eglon king of Mo'ab strong over Yisra'el because they did what was bad in Yahweh's eyes, ¹³and he got the Ammonites and Amaleq to join him. He went and struck Yisra'el down, and took possession of Palms Town. ¹⁴The Yisra'elites served Eglon king of Mo'ab for eighteen years.

Another unlikely saviour

¹⁵The Yisra'elites cried out to Yahweh and Yahweh made a deliverer arise for them, Ehud ben Gera, a Binyaminite, a man restricted in his right hand. The Yisra'elites sent an offering by his hand to Eglon king of Mo'ab. ¹⁶Ehud made himself a sword with two edges, half a metre in length. He wrapped it on under his uniform on his right side, ¹⁷and presented the offering to Eglon king of Mo'ab. Now Eglon was a very stout man.

¹⁸When he had finished presenting the offering, he sent off the company who had been carrying the gift, ¹⁹but he himself went back from the sculptures that are near Gilgal and said, 'I have a secret message for you, Your Majesty.' He said, 'Silence', and all the people who stood by him went out from his presence. ²⁰When Ehud came to him, he was sitting in the cool upper quarters that he had, alone. Ehud said, 'I have a word from God for you.' He got up from his seat, ²¹and Ehud put out his left hand, took the sword from on his right side and plunged it into his insides. ²²Even the handle went in after the blade, and the fat closed over the blade, because he didn't pull the sword out of his insides. The dirt came out.

²³Ehud went out through the porch, shut the doors of the upper quarters on him and locked them ²⁴as he went out.

His servants came and looked: there, the doors of the upper quarters were locked. They said, 'Yes, he's relieving himself in the cool lounge', ²⁵and waited until they were shamed. But there – he wasn't opening the doors of the upper quarters. So they got the key and opened them, and there – their lord was fallen on the ground, dead.

²⁶Ehud had escaped while they delayed, and had passed the sculptures. He escaped to Se'irah ²⁷and, when he came, blew on the horn in the highland of Ephrayim. The Yisra'elites went down with him from the highland; he was before them. ²⁸He said to them 'Pursue after me, because Yahweh has given your enemies, Mo'ab, into your hand.' They went down after him and captured Mo'ab's Yarden [Jordan] crossings, and didn't let anyone cross. ²⁹They struck down Mo'ab at that time, some 10,000 men, every individual hefty and everyone a forceful man. Not one escaped. ³⁰So Mo'ab bowed down that day under Yisra'el's hand, and the region was calm for eighty years.

Shamgar, Deborah, Lapiddot and Baraq

³¹After him there was Shamgar ben Anat. He struck down 600 Pelishtites [Philistines] with an ox goad. He, too, was one who delivered Yisra'el.

4 The Yisra'elites again did what was bad in Yahweh's eyes when Ehud had died, ²and Yahweh surrendered them into the hand of Yabin king of Kena'an who reigned in Hatsor. His army officer was Sisera; he was living in

Haroshet Haggoyim. ³The Yisra'elites cried out to Yahweh because he had 900 iron chariots, and he had afflicted Yisra'el through his strength for twenty years.

⁴Now Deborah, a woman who was a prophetess, the wife of Lapiddot, was exercising authority for Yisra'el at that time. ⁵She would sit under Deborah's Palm between The Height and Bet-el in the highland of Ephrayim, and the Yisra'elites would go up to her for a decision.

⁶She sent and called for Baraq ben Abino'am, from Qedesh in Naphtali, and said to him, 'Yahweh the God of Yisra'el has ordered you, has he not: "Go, march to Mount Tabor, and take with you 10,000 men from the Naphtalites and from the Zebulunites. ⁷I shall march Sisera, Yabin's army officer, to you, to Wadi Qishon, with his chariotry and his horde, and I shall give them into your hand."'

⁸Baraq said to her, 'If you go with me, I'll go, but if you don't go with me, I won't go.' ⁹She said, 'I'll definitely go with you, only it won't be your glory on the journey that you're going on, because it's into the hand of a woman that Yahweh will surrender Sisera.' So Deborah set off and went with Baraq to Qedesh, ¹⁰and Baraq called out Zebulun and Naphtali to Qedesh. Ten thousand men went up after him, and Deborah went up with him. ¹¹Now Heber the Qenite had split from Qayin, from the descendants of Hobab, Mosheh's father-in-law, and spread his tent by the oak at Tsa'anannim, which was near Qedesh.

¹²They told Sisera that Baraq ben Abinoam had gone up to Mount Tabor, ¹³and Sisera called out all his chariotry (900 iron chariots) and all the company that was with him from Haroshet-goyim to Wadi Qishon.

Ya'el

¹⁴Deborah said to Baraq, 'Set off, because this is the day that Yahweh has given Sisera into your hand. Yahweh has gone out before you, hasn't he.' So Baraq went down from Mount Tabor, with 10,000 men behind him, ¹⁵and Yahweh threw Sisera, all his chariotry and all the camp into confusion at the mouth of the sword before Baraq.

Sisera got down from his chariot and fled on foot, ¹⁶while Baraq pursued after the chariotry and after the camp as far as Haroshet Haggoyim. Sisera's entire camp fell to the mouth of the sword. Not even one was left.

¹⁷Now Sisera had fled on foot to the tent of Ya'el, the wife of Heber the Qenite, because there was peace between Yabin king of Hatsor and the household of Heber the Qenite. ¹⁸Ya'el came out to meet Sisera and said to him, 'Turn aside, sir, turn aside to me. Don't be afraid.' So he turned aside to her into the tent and she covered him with a rug. ¹⁹He said to her, 'Please give me a little water to drink, because I'm thirsty.' She opened a skin of milk and gave him a drink, and covered him. ²⁰He said to her, 'Stand at the tent entrance. If someone comes and asks you, "Is there anyone here?" you're to say, "There's no one."'

²¹But Ya'el, Heber's wife, got a tent peg and picked up a hammer in her hand. She came to him stealthily and drove the peg through his temple so it went down into the ground; he was in a deep sleep, he was weary. So he died.

²²And there was Baraq, pursuing Sisera. Ya'el went out to meet him. She said to him, 'Come, I'll let you see the man that you're looking for.' He came in to her, and there was Sisera, fallen dead, the peg in his temple.

²³That day God made Yabin king of Hatsor bow down before the Yisra'elites. ²⁴The Yisra'elites' hand kept getting tougher on Yabin king of Kena'an until they had cut down Yabin king of Kena'an.

Yahweh's faithful acts

5 Deborah (and Baraq ben Abino'am) sang that day:

²At people exercising authority who were
 letting themselves go in Yisra'el,
 at a company offering itself freely: bless
  Yahweh!
³Listen, kings,
 give ear, sovereigns!
I myself, I shall sing for Yahweh,
 I shall make music for Yahweh the God of
  Yisra'el.

⁴Yahweh, when you came out from Se'ir,
 when you marched from Edomite
  country,

Earth trembled,
   yes, heavens poured,
Yes, clouds poured water,
   ⁵when mountains quaked,
Before Yahweh the one of Sinay,
   before Yahweh the God of Yisra'el.

⁶In the time of Shamgar ben Anat,
   in the time of Ya'el,
Journeys left off,
   people going on paths went by roundabout ways.
⁷Peasantry left off,
   left off in Yisra'el,
Until I, Deborah, arose,
   arose as mother in Yisra'el.
⁸It chose new gods,
   then there was battling in the gateways.
Shield and spear did not appear
   among 40,000 in Yisra'el.
⁹My heart was with Yisra'el's commanders,
   who offered themselves freely in the company.

Bless Yahweh,
   ¹⁰riders on tawny donkeys!
You who sit on saddle blankets,
   you who go on a journey, talk.
¹¹Above the voice of dealers among watering holes,
   there they are to commemorate Yahweh's faithful acts,
Faithful acts for his peasantry in Yisra'el;
   then Yahweh's company went down to the gateways.

Who came and who didn't

¹²Stir, stir, Deborah,
   Stir, stir, sound out a song!
Set off, Baraq,
   take your captives, ben Abino'am!
¹³Then those of the august ones who were left came down,
   Yahweh's company came down for me among the strong men,
¹⁴From Ephrayim people whose root is in Amaleq,
   after you, Binyamin with your kin.
From Makir commanders came down,
   from Zebulun people wielding the marshal's staff.

¹⁵The officers in Yissakar [Issachar] were with Deborah;
   as Yissakar, so was Baraq,
   sent into the vale behind him.
Among Re'uben's divisions,
   great searchings of heart.
¹⁶Why did you sit among the folds
   to listen to the whistlings for the flocks?
Among Re'uben's divisions,
   great searchings of heart.
¹⁷Gil'ad dwelled across the Yarden;
   Dan: why did he stay by the ships?
Asher lived at the sea coast
   and dwelled by its harbours.
¹⁸Zebulun was a people that reviled its life to the death;
   Naphtali was on the heights of the fields.

¹⁹Kings came, battled,
   kings of Kena'an battled then.
At Ta'nak by Megiddo's water
   they got no gain of silver.
²⁰From the heavens the stars battled,
   from their causeways they battled with Sisera.
²¹Wadi Qishon swept them away,
   the rushing wadi, Wadi Qishon:
   go on with vigour, my soul!
²²Then horse hoofs pounded,
   with the galloping, the galloping of his sturdy ones.
²³'Curse Meroz', Yahweh's envoy said,
   'utterly curse the people living in it,
Because they didn't come when Yahweh was helping,
   when Yahweh was helping against the strong men.'

Sisera's mother waits

²⁴Most blessed of women be Ya'el,
   wife of Heber the Qenite,
   most blessed of tent women.
²⁵He asked for water, she gave milk;
   in a bowl fit for august people she presented curds.
²⁶She put out her hand for the peg,
   her right hand for the labourers' hammer.
She hammered Sisera, smashed his head,
   hit and pierced his temple.
²⁷Between her feet he bent down,
   he fell, he lay.

Between her feet he bent down, he fell;
    where he bent down, there he fell, destroyed.

²⁸Through the window Sisera's mother peered,
    she gazed through the lattice.
'Why is his chariot taking time to come,
    why have the rumblings of his chariots delayed?'
²⁹The smartest of her ladies answer her,
    indeed she gives back her word to herself:
³⁰"They've found and shared out the spoil, haven't they,
    a woman, two women, for each man,
Spoil of dyed cloth for Sisera,
    spoil of dyed cloth embroidered,
    two embroidered cloths for the necks as spoil."

³¹So may all your enemies perish, Yahweh,
    but may his friends be like the sun coming out in its strength.

The region was calm for forty years.

The man hiding to beat out wheat

6 The Yisra'elites did what was bad in Yahweh's eyes and he gave them into the hand of Midyan for seven years. ²The hand of Midyan was powerful over Yisra'el. Because of Midyan, the Yisra'elites made themselves hideouts that were in the mountains, caves and strongholds. ³If Yisra'el had sown, Midyan, Amaleq and the Easterners would go up. They would go up against it ⁴and camp against them, and devastate the region's yield until you come to Azzah. They wouldn't let anything remain alive in Yisra'el, either sheep or ox or donkey, ⁵because they and their livestock would go up with their tents. They would come like a locust swarm in their large number. There was no counting them or their camels.

So they came into the region to devastate it, ⁶and Yisra'el became very low before Midyan. The Yisra'elites cried out to Yahweh. ⁷When the Yisra'elites cried out to Yahweh on account of Midyan, ⁸Yahweh sent someone as a prophet to the Yisra'elites. He said to them, 'Yahweh the God of Yisra'el has said this: "I'm the one who got you up from Misrayim, got you out of the household of serfs, ⁹rescued you from the hand of Misrayim and from the hand of all the people who afflicted you. I drove them out from before you and gave you their country. ¹⁰I said to you, 'I am Yahweh your God. You will not live in awe of the gods of the Amorites in whose country you're living.' But you didn't listen to my voice."'

¹¹Yahweh's envoy came and sat under the oak at Ophrah that belonged to Yo'ash the Abi'ezrite. His son Gid'on [Gideon] was beating out wheat in the winepress to keep it safe from before Midyan. ¹²Yahweh's envoy appeared to him and said to him, 'Yahweh is with you, forceful strong man.' ¹³Gid'on said to him, 'Pardon me, my Lord: Yahweh is with us? So why has all this befallen us? Where are all his extraordinary acts that our ancestors recounted to us, saying "Yahweh got us up from Misrayim, didn't he"? Yahweh has now left us alone and given us into Midyan's fist.'

Asking for a sign

¹⁴Yahweh turned his face to him and said, 'Go in this energy of yours and deliver Yisra'el from Midyan's fist. I've sent you, haven't I.' ¹⁵He said to him, 'Pardon me, my Lord: how can I deliver Yisra'el? Here, my family is the poorest in Menashsheh and I'm the youngest in my father's household.' ¹⁶Yahweh said to him, 'But I'll be with you, and you'll strike Midyan down as if they were one man.'

¹⁷He said to him, 'If I've found grace in your eyes, please perform a sign for me that you're the one speaking with me. ¹⁸Don't move away from here, please, until I come to you and bring my offering out and set it down before you.' He said, 'I myself will stay until you come back.'

¹⁹When Gid'on had come in, he prepared a kid goat from the flock and a barrel of flour into flatbread. When he'd put the meat in a basket and put the broth in a pot, he took them out to him under the oak. So he brought them up ²⁰and God's envoy said to him, 'Get the meat and the flatbread and set them down on this rock, and pour out the broth.' He did so. ²¹Yahweh's envoy put out the end of the staff that was in his hand and touched the meat and the flatbread. Fire went up from the crag and devoured the meat and the flatbread, as Yahweh's envoy went from before his eyes.

²²Gid'on saw that it was Yahweh's envoy. Gid'on said, 'Oh, Lord Yahweh, that therefore

I've seen Yahweh's envoy face to face!' ²³Yahweh said to him, 'Things will be well for you. Don't be afraid. You won't die.'

²⁴Gid'on built an altar there for Yahweh and called it 'Yahweh-things-will-be-well'. Until this day it's still in Ophrah of the Abi'ezrites.

The mixed-up father

²⁵That night Yahweh said to him, 'Get the ox bullock that belongs to your father and a second bullock of seven years. Tear down the Master's altar that belongs to your father and cut down the totem pole that's by it, ²⁶and build an altar for Yahweh your God on the top of this stronghold, in proper order. Get the second bullock and offer it up as a burnt offering with the wood of the totem pole that you cut down.' ²⁷So Gid'on got ten men from among his servants and did as Yahweh had spoken to him, but as he was too afraid of his father's household and of the people of the town to do it by day, he did it by night.

²⁸The people of the town started early in the morning and there, the Master's altar was demolished, the totem pole that was by it was cut down and the second bull was sacrificed on the altar that had been built. ²⁹They said, one to his neighbour, 'Who did this thing?' They enquired and sought, and said, 'Gid'on ben Yo'ash did this thing.' ³⁰The people of the town said to Yo'ash, 'Bring your son out: he's to die, because he demolished the Master's altar and because he cut down the totem pole that was by it.' ³¹But Yo'ash said to all who stood round him, 'Do you yourselves argue for the Master? Or do you yourselves deliver him? The person who argues for him should be put to death by morning. If he's a god, he should argue for himself, because someone has demolished his altar.' ³²That day they called him Yerubba'al ('Master-Must-Argue'), saying 'The Master must argue against him, because he demolished his altar.'

The fleece

³³Now all Midyan, Amaleq and the Easterners gathered together, crossed over and camped in the Yizre'e'l Vale, ³⁴and Yahweh's spirit clothed itself in Gid'on. He blew on the horn, and the Abi'ezrites had themselves called out to follow him. ³⁵When he sent envoys through all Menashsheh, they too had themselves called out to follow him, and when he sent envoys through Asher, through Zebulun and through Naphtali, they went up to meet them.

³⁶Gid'on said to God, 'If you're really going to deliver Yisra'el by my hand, as you spoke: ³⁷here, I'm placing a wool fleece on the threshing floor. If there's dew on the fleece alone but on all the ground it's dry, I'll acknowledge that you will deliver Yisra'el by my hand as you spoke.' ³⁸So it happened. He started early next day, squeezed the fleece and wrung out dew from the fleece, a full bowl of water.

³⁹Gid'on said to God, 'May your anger not rage against me and I'll speak just one more time. May I please test with the fleece only one more time. May there please be dry on the fleece alone but on all the ground may there be dew.' ⁴⁰God did so that night. There was dry on the fleece alone but on the ground there was dew.

7 Yerubba'al (i.e. Gid'on) and all the company with him started early and camped above Harod Spring; the Midyanite camp was north of him at Moreh Hill, in the vale. ²Yahweh said to Gid'on, 'The company that's with you is too big for me to give Midyan into their hand, so Yisra'el doesn't take glory for itself over me, saying "My hand delivered me." ³Now call out, please, in the ears of the company, "Whoever is afraid and trembling is to go back and fly from Mount Gil'ad."' Twenty-two thousand of the company went back; 10,000 remained.

How to increase the odds against yourself

⁴Yahweh said to Gid'on, 'The company is still big. Get them to go down to the water and I'll smelt them for you there. The one of whom I say to you, "This one is to go with you", he's to go with you. Everyone that I say to you, "This one's not to go with you", he's not to go.'

⁵So he got the company to go down to the water. Yahweh said to Gid'on, 'Everyone who laps from the water with his tongue as a dog laps, you're to place apart; and everyone who bends down on his knees to drink.' ⁶The

number of people who lapped with their hand into their mouth was 300. All the rest of the company bent down on their knees to drink water. ⁷Yahweh said to Gid'on, 'With the 300 men who were lapping I shall deliver you and give Midyan into your hand, while the entire company are to go each individual to his place.' ⁸So they got the company's provisions in their hand, and their horns, while he sent off every Yisra'elite, each one to his tents, but kept strong hold of the 300 men.

The Midyanite camp was below him in the vale. ⁹That night Yahweh said to him, 'Set off, go down against the camp, because I've given it into your hand. ¹⁰If you're afraid to go down, you yourself go down to the camp with Purah your boy ¹¹and listen to what they speak of, and afterwards your hands will be strong and you'll go down against the camp.' So he himself went down with Purah his boy to the edge of where the men organized into companies were in the camp. ¹²Midyan, Amaleq and all the Easterners were lying in the vale like a locust swarm in their large number, and there was no counting their camels, like the sea on the seashore in their large number.

The man with a dream

¹³Gid'on came, and there, a man was recounting a dream to his neighbour. He said, 'Here, I had a dream. There, a loaf of barley bread was rolling against the Midyanite camp. It came to a tent and struck it down, and it fell. It turned it over, upside down. The tent fell.' ¹⁴His neighbour answered, 'This is nothing but the sword of Gid'on ben Yo'ash, the Yisra'elite. God has given Midyan and the entire camp into his hand.' ¹⁵When Gid'on heard the recounting of the dream and its explaining, he bowed low. He went back to the Yisra'elite camp and said, 'Set off, because Yahweh has given the Midyanite camp into your hand.'

¹⁶He divided the 300 men into three units and put horns into the hand of each of them, with empty pitchers and torches inside the pitchers. ¹⁷He said to them, 'Look at me and do the same. Here am I, coming against the edge of the camp. As I do, so you're to do. ¹⁸I'll blow on my horn, I and everyone who's with me, and you're to blow on your horns, as well, round the entire camp, and you're to say, "Yahweh's and Gid'on's!"'

¹⁹So Gid'on and the 300 men who were with him came against the edge of the camp at the start of the middle watch. They had only then actually set up the watchmen. They blew on the horns, with the pitchers to be smashed that were in their hand, ²⁰and the three units blew on their horns and broke the pitchers and took strong hold of the torches in their left hand while the horns for blowing were in their right hand. They called, 'Yahweh's sword and Gid'on's' ²¹and stood each person where he was round the camp. The entire camp ran and shouted and fled. ²²The 300 horns blew and Yahweh set one person's sword against his neighbour in the entire camp. The camp fled as far as Bet Shittim, towards Tsererah, as far as the edge of Meholah Meadow near Tabbat.

Oreb and Ze'eb

²³Yisra'elites from Naphtali, from Asher and from all Menashsheh had themselves called out, and pursued after Midyan, ²⁴while Gid'on sent envoys through the entire highland of Ephrayim saying, 'Go down to meet Midyan and capture their water as far as Bet Barah and the Yarden.' All the Ephrayimites had themselves called out, and they captured the water as far as Bet Barah and the Yarden. ²⁵They captured two Midyanite officers, Oreb and Ze'eb, and killed Oreb at Oreb's Crag and killed Ze'eb at Ze'eb's Winepress. So they pursued Midyan, and the head of Oreb and Ze'eb they brought to Gid'on from across the Yarden.

8 But the Ephrayimites said to him, 'Why did you do this thing to us, not calling for us when you went to battle against Midyan?' They argued with him strongly. ²He said to them, 'What have I done now compared with you? Aren't Ephrayim's gleanings better than Abi'ezer's reaping? ³Into your hand God gave the Midyanite officers Oreb and Ze'eb. What could I do compared with you?' Then their feelings against him relaxed, when he spoke this word.

⁴Gid'on came to the Yarden. He was crossing, he and the 300 men who were with him, faint as they were pursuing. ⁵He said to the people of Sukkot, 'Please give us loaves of bread for the

company that's after me, because they're faint and I'm pursuing after Zebah and Tsalmunna, the Midyanite kings.' ⁶The officials of Sukkot said to him, 'Is the fist of Zebah and Salmunna in your hand now, that we should give your army bread?' ⁷Gid'on said, 'Therefore, when Yahweh gives Zebah and Salmunna into my hand, I'll thresh your flesh with wilderness thorns and with briars.'

⁸From there he went up to Penu'el and spoke to them in this same way, and the people of Penu'el answered him as the people of Sukkot had answered. ⁹So he also said to the people of Penu'el, 'When I come back with things being well, I'll demolish this tower.'

They were my brothers

¹⁰Now Zebah and Tsalmunna were at Qarqor and their camp with them, some 15,000, all that was left of the entire camp of the Easterners; the fallen were 120,000 men drawing the sword. ¹¹Gid'on went up the tent-dwellers road, east of Nobah and Yogbehah, and struck down the camp when the camp was feeling confident. ¹²Zebah and Tsalmunna fled and he pursued after them. He captured the two Midyanite kings, Zebah and Tsalmunna, and made the entire camp tremble.

¹³Gid'on ben Yo'ash came back from the battle, from Heres Ascent. ¹⁴He captured a boy from among the people of Sukkot and questioned him, and he wrote down for him the officials of Sukkot and its elders, seventy-seven people. ¹⁵He came to the people of Sukkot and said, 'Here are Zebah and Tsalmunna, about whom you reviled me, saying "Is the fist of Zebah and Salmunna in your hand, that we should give bread to your weary men?"' ¹⁶He got the town's elders, and wilderness thorns and briars, and taught the people of Sukkot with them. ¹⁷The tower at Penu'el he demolished, and he killed the town's people.

¹⁸He said to Zebah and to Tsalmunna, 'Where are the men that you killed at Tabor?' They said, 'They were just like you, the very appearance of a king's sons.' ¹⁹He said, 'They were my brothers, my mother's sons. As Yahweh lives, if you had let them live, I would not have killed you.' ²⁰He said to Yeter, his firstborn, 'Get up, kill them.' But the boy didn't draw his sword, because he was afraid, because he was still a boy. ²¹Zebah and Tsalmunna said, 'You yourself get up and attack us, because "As a man is, so is his strength."' So Gid'on got up and killed Zebah and Tsalmunna, and took the crescents that were on their camels' necks.

'I'm not the hero; the hero is God'

²²The Yisra'elites said to Gid'on, 'Rule over us, both you and your son and your grandson, because you've delivered us from the hand of Midyan.' ²³Gid'on said to them, 'I myself won't rule over you and my son won't rule over you. Yahweh is the one who will rule over you.'

²⁴But Gid'on said to them, 'I will ask something of you. Each man, give me the earring that was his spoil' (because they had gold earrings, because they were Yishma'e'lites). ²⁵They said, 'We'll certainly give them.' They spread out a coat and threw there, each man, the earring that was his spoil. ²⁶The weight of the gold earrings that he asked for came to 1,700 in gold, apart from the crescents, pendants and purple robes that were on the Midyanite kings, and apart from the collars that were on their camels' necks. ²⁷Gid'on made it into a chasuble and placed it in his town, in Ophrah. All Yisra'el whored after it there. It became a snare to Gid'on and to his household.

²⁸So Midyan bowed down before the Yisra'elites. They didn't raise their head again. The region was calm for forty years in Gid'on's time.

²⁹Yerubba'al ben Yo'ash went and lived at home. ³⁰Gid'on had seventy sons who issued from his own body, because he had many wives. ³¹His secondary wife who was in Shekem also gave birth to a son for him; he named him Abimelek. ³²Gid'on ben Yo'ash died in a good old age and was buried in his father Yo'ash's tomb in Ophrah of the Abi'ezrites.

The man who would be king

³³When Gid'on died, the Yisra'elites again whored after the Masters, and they made the Pact Master into god for themselves. ³⁴The Yisra'elites didn't keep Yahweh their God in

mind, the one who rescued them from the hand of all their enemies round them. ³⁵They didn't act in commitment with the household of Yerubba'al (Gid'on) in accordance with all the good that he had done in Yisra'el.

9

Abimelek, son of Yerubba'al, went to Shekem to his mother's brothers and spoke to them and to the entire kin-group in his mother's ancestral household: ²'Speak, will you, in the ears of all the Shekem landowners: "Which is better for you, seventy men ruling over you (all the sons of Yerubba'al), or one man ruling over you? Be mindful that I am your own flesh and blood."' ³His mother's brothers spoke all these things about him in the ears of all the Shekem landowners. Their mind turned away to follow Abimelek, because (they said), 'He's our brother', ⁴and they gave him seventy in silver from the house of the Pact Master. With these, Abimelek hired empty-headed and wild men and they followed him. ⁵He came to his father's house in Ophrah and killed his brothers, the sons of Yerubba'al, seventy men on one stone. But Yotam, youngest son of Yerubba'al, was left, because he hid.

⁶All the Shekem landowners and the entire Bet Millo gathered, and went and installed Abimelek as king by the oak at the column which was in Shekem.

A parable about leadership

⁷People told Yotam and he went and stood on top of Mount Gerizim. He lifted his voice and called to them: 'Listen to me, Shekem landowners, so God may listen to you. ⁸The trees went with resolve to anoint a king over themselves. They said to the olive tree, "Do reign over us." ⁹The olive tree said to them, "Should I leave off from my richness, I by whom people honour God and human beings, and go to wave over the trees?" ¹⁰So the trees said to the fig tree, "You go reign over us." ¹¹The fig tree said to them, "Should I leave off from my sweetness, my good fruit, and go to wave over the trees?" ¹²So the trees said to the vine, "You go reign over us." ¹³The vine said to them, "Should I leave off from my new wine, which makes God and human beings rejoice, and go to wave over the trees?"

¹⁴So all the trees said to the thorn bush, "You go reign over us." ¹⁵The thorn bush said to the trees, "If you're going to anoint me as king over you with truthfulness, come take shelter in my shade. But if not, may fire come out of the thorn bush and devour the cedars of the Lebanon."

¹⁶So now, if you've acted in truthfulness and integrity and made Abimelek king, and if you've done something good by Yerubba'al and by his household, and if you've acted towards him in accordance with the dealing of his hands – ¹⁷that my father battled on your account and threw his life a distance away and rescued you from the hand of Midyan . . . ¹⁸But you people have risen up against my father's household today and killed his sons, seventy men on one stone, and made Abimelek, his handmaid's son, king over the Shekem landowners, because he's your brother.

Ambition rebounds

¹⁹If you've acted in truthfulness and integrity with Yerubba'al and with his household this day, rejoice in Abimelek, and may he rejoice in you, too. ²⁰But if not, may fire come out from Abimelek and devour the Shekem landowners and Bet Millo, and may fire come out from the Shekem landowners and from Bet Millo and devour Abimelek!' ²¹Then Yotam took flight. He escaped and went to Be'er, and lived there, away from the presence of Abimelek his brother.

²²Abimelek held office over Yisra'el for three years, ²³but God sent a bad spirit between Abimelek and the Shekem landowners, and the Shekem landowners broke faith with Abimelek, ²⁴so that the violence against the seventy sons of Yerubba'al might come home and so that the bloodshed be put on Abimelek their brother who killed them and on the Shekem landowners who had strengthened his hands in the killing of his brothers. ²⁵The Shekem landowners laid ambushes for him on the tops of the mountains and robbed anyone who passed by them on the road, and it was told Abimelek.

²⁶Ga'al ben Ebed and his brothers came and passed through Shekem, and the Shekem landowners put their trust in him. ²⁷They went out to the fields, cut their vineyards and trod them, and made a great celebration.

They came into their god's house and ate and drank, and slighted Abimelek. ²⁸Ga'al ben Ebed said, 'Who is Abimelek, and who is Shekem, that we should serve him? Isn't he the son of Yerubba'al, and Zebul is his appointee? Serve the men of Hamor, the ancestor of Shekem! Why should we be people who serve him? ²⁹If only this people were in my hand! I would remove Abimelek. Someone would have said to Abimelek, "Amass your army and go out!"'

The ambush

³⁰Zebul, the town official, heard the words of Ga'al ben Ebed, and his anger raged. ³¹He sent envoys to Abimelek at Tormah to say, 'Here, Ga'al ben Ebed and his brothers are coming to Shekem, and here, they're besieging the town against you. ³²So now, set off by night, you and the company that's with you, and make an ambush in the fields. ³³In the morning, at sunrise, you should start early and charge against the town. Here, he and the company that's with him are going to go out against you, and you can do to him whatever your hand finds to do.'

³⁴So Abimelek and the entire company that was with him set off by night and laid an ambush against Shekem in four columns. ³⁵Ga'al ben Ebed went out and stood at the entrance of the town gateway, and Abimelek and the company that was with him arose from the ambush.

³⁶Ga'al saw the company and said to Zebul, 'There, a company is coming down from the tops of the mountains!' Zebul said to him, 'You're seeing the shadow of the mountains as if they were men.' ³⁷Ga'al spoke once again and said, 'There, a company is coming down from the centre of the land, and a company is coming from the Elon Me'onenim road!' ³⁸Zebul said to him, 'Where then is your mouth with which you say, "Who is Abimelek that we should serve him?" This is the company that you rejected, isn't it! Please go out now, and do battle against it!'

³⁹So Ga'al went out before the Shekem landowners and battled against Abimelek, ⁴⁰but Abimelek pursued him and he fled from before him. Many people fell, run through, as far as the entrance of the gateway. ⁴¹Abimelek stayed in Arumah, but Zebul drove out Ga'al and his brothers from living in Shekem.

Undone by a woman

⁴²Next day, the people went out to the fields, and Abimelek was told. ⁴³He got the company, divided it into three columns and set an ambush in the fields. He looked: there was the people coming out from the town. He set upon them and struck them down. ⁴⁴Abimelek and the columns that were with him charged and stood at the entrance of the town gateway. The other two columns charged against everyone who was in the fields and struck them down, ⁴⁵while Abimelek was battling against the town all that day. He captured the town and killed the people that were in it, demolished the town and sowed it with salt.

⁴⁶All the Shekem Tower landowners heard, and came into a tunnel at the house of the Pact God. ⁴⁷It was told Abimelek that all the Shekem Tower landowners had collected together. ⁴⁸Abimelek went up Mount Tsalmon, he and the entire company that was with him. Abimelek got axes in his hand, cut a tree branch, lifted it and put it on his shoulder. He said to the company that was with him, 'What you have seen I did, hurry, do like me.' ⁴⁹The entire company also cut a branch each, followed Abimelek, placed them against the tunnel and set fire to the tunnel over them. All the people in the Shekem Tower also died, some thousand men and women.

⁵⁰Abimelek then went to Tebets, camped against Tebets and captured it. ⁵¹There was a strong tower inside the town and all the men and women, all the town's landowners, fled there, shut themselves in and went up on to the tower roof. ⁵²Abimelek came right up to the tower and battled against it, and drew up close to the tower entrance to burn it in fire. ⁵³But a woman threw an upper millstone on Abimelek's head and broke his skull. ⁵⁴He quickly called to the boy carrying his things and said to him, 'Draw your sword and put me to death, so they don't say of me, "A woman killed him."' So his boy thrust him through, and he died.

⁵⁵The Yisra'elites saw that Abimelek was dead, and went each man to his place.

Peace for a while

⁵⁶So God turned back Abimelek's bad action which he had undertaken towards his father, in killing his seventy brothers, ⁵⁷and God turned back on their head all the bad action of the people of Shekem. The slight by Yotam son of Yerubba'al came true for them.

10 After Abimelek, there arose to deliver Yisra'el Tola ben Pu'ah, son of Dodo, a Yissakarite. He was living in Shamir in the highland of Ephrayim. ²He exercised authority for Yisra'el for twenty-three years. He died, and was buried in Shamir.

³After him, there arose Ya'ir the Gil'adite. He exercised authority for Yisra'el for twenty-two years. ⁴He had thirty sons riding on thirty donkey colts, and he had thirty towns (they call them Ya'ir's Villages until this day) which were in the region of Gil'ad. ⁵Ya'ir died and was buried in Qamon.

⁶But the Yisra'elites again did what was bad in Yahweh's eyes and served the Masters, the Ashtars, the gods of Aram, the gods of Tsidon, the gods of Mo'ab, the gods of the Ammonites and the gods of the Pelishtites. They abandoned Yahweh and did not serve him. ⁷Yahweh's anger raged against Yisra'el and he surrendered them into the hand of the Pelishtites and into the hand of the Ammonites. ⁸They shattered and crushed the Yisra'elites that year – for eighteen years, all the Yisra'elites who were across the Yarden in the Amorites' country, which was in Gil'ad. ⁹The Ammonites also crossed the Yarden to battle against Yehudah, against Binyamin and against the household of Ephrayim. It put great pressure on Yisra'el.

¹⁰So the Yisra'elites cried out to Yahweh: 'We've done wrong against you, because we've abandoned our God and served the Masters.'

God finds it hard to be tough

¹¹Yahweh said to the Yisra'elites, 'Isn't it the case that from the Misrayimites, from the Amorites, from the Ammonites, from the Pelishtites . . . ¹²And the Tsidonites and Amaleq and Ma'on, they afflicted you, and you cried out to me and I delivered you from their hand. ¹³But you – you abandoned me and served other gods. Therefore I won't deliver you again.

¹⁴Go and cry out to the gods that you've chosen. They can deliver you in your time of pressure.'

¹⁵But the Yisra'elites said to Yahweh, 'We've done wrong. You yourself, act towards us in accordance with what's good in your eyes. Only please rescue us this day.' ¹⁶They removed the foreign gods from among them and served Yahweh, and his heart was overwhelmed by Yisra'el's oppression.

¹⁷The Ammonites had themselves called out and camped in Gil'ad, and the Yisra'elites gathered and camped at The Watchtower. ¹⁸The company (Gil'ad's officers) said, one to his neighbour, 'Who is the man who will start battling against the Ammonites? He's to be head over all the people who live in Gil'ad.'

11 Now Yiphtah the Gil'adite was a forceful strong man, but he was the son of a whore. Gil'ad fathered Yiphtah, ²but Gil'ad's wife gave birth to sons for him, and his wife's sons grew up and drove Yiphtah out. They said to him, 'You're to have no domain of your own in our father's household, because you're the son of another woman.' ³So Yiphtah ran away from before his brothers and lived in the region of Good. Empty-headed people collected together to Yiphtah and went out with him.

⁴After a time, the Ammonites battled with Yisra'el, ⁵and when the Ammonites battled with Yisra'el, the Gil'adite elders went to get Yiphtah from the region of Good. ⁶They said to Yiphtah, 'Come, will you, and be our commander, so we can battle against the Ammonites.'

An invitation Yiphtah can't refuse

⁷Yiphtah said to the Gil'adite elders, 'You're the people who were hostile to me and drove me out of my father's household, aren't you. So why have you come to me now when things are pressing for you?' ⁸The Gil'adite elders said to Yiphtah, 'That's why we've come back to you now, so you can go with us and battle against the Ammonites, and you will be head of all the people living in Gil'ad for us.' ⁹Yiphtah said to the Gil'adite elders, 'If you're bringing me back to battle against the Ammonites and Yahweh gives them over before me, I myself will be your head.' ¹⁰The Gil'adite elders said to Yiphtah, 'Yahweh

himself will be listening between us if we don't act in accordance with your word, just so.' ¹¹So Yiphtah went with the Gil'adite elders, and the people made him head and commander over them. Yiphtah spoke all his words before Yahweh at The Watchtower.

¹²Yiphtah sent envoys to the Ammonites' king to say, 'What is between me and you that you've come against me to battle against my land?' ¹³The Ammonites' king said to Yiphtah's envoys, 'Yisra'el took my land when it went up from Misrayim, from the Armon as far as the Yabboq, and as far as the Yarden. So now do give it back peacefully.'

¹⁴Yiphtah once again sent envoys to the Ammonites' king. ¹⁵He said to him, 'Yiphtah has said this: "Yisra'el didn't take Mo'ab's land or the Ammonites' land, ¹⁶because when they went up from Misrayim, Yisra'el went through the wilderness as far as the Reed Sea, then came to Qadesh. ¹⁷Yisra'el sent envoys to the king of Edom to say, 'Please may I pass through your country', but the king of Edom didn't listen. It also sent to the king of Mo'ab and he wasn't willing. Yisra'el lived at Qadesh, ¹⁸then went through the wilderness and went round the country of Edom and the country of Mo'ab, and came east of the country of Mo'ab. They camped across the Arnon and they didn't come inside Mo'ab's border, because Mo'ab's border is the Arnon.

How Yisra'el tried to be peaceable

¹⁹Then Yisra'el sent envoys to Sihon king of the Amorites, king of Heshbon. Yisra'el said to him, 'Please may I pass through your country to get to my place.' ²⁰But Sihon didn't trust Yisra'el to pass through his border. Sihon gathered his entire company and camped at Yahats, and battled with Yisra'el. ²¹But Yahweh the God of Yisra'el gave Sihon and his entire company into Yisra'el's hand, and they struck them down. So Yisra'el took possession of the entire country of the Amorites living in that country. ²²They took possession of the entire border of the Amorites from the Arnon as far as the Yabboq, and from the wilderness to the Yarden.

²³So now, Yahweh the God of Yisra'el – he dispossessed the Amorites from before his people Yisra'el, and are you to dispossess it? ²⁴Won't you possess what Kemosh your god enabled you to possess, and we'll possess all that Yahweh our God dispossessed from before us? ²⁵And are you now so much better than Balaq ben Tsippor, king of Mo'ab? Did he argue at all with Yisra'el or battle at all with them? ²⁶While Yisra'el has been living in Heshbon and in its daughter-towns, in Ar'or and in its daughter-towns, and in all the towns that are on the sides of the Arnon for 300 years, why haven't you rescued them during this time? ²⁷I for my part haven't wronged you, but you for your part are dealing badly with me by battling against me. May Yahweh, who exercises authority, decide authoritatively today between the Yisra'elites and the Ammonites."'

²⁸The Ammmonites' king didn't listen to the words of Yiphtah which he sent to him. ²⁹Then Yahweh's spirit came on Yiphtah and he passed through Gil'ad and Menashsheh, passed Watchtower in Gil'ad and from Watchtower in Gil'ad passed on to the Ammonites.

The man whose promise makes the blood run cold

³⁰Yiphtah made a pledge to Yahweh: 'If you do actually give the Ammonites into my hand, ³¹then the one coming out to meet me, who comes out of the doors of my house when I come back from the Ammonites with things being well, will be Yahweh's. I shall offer this one up as a burnt offering.'

³²So Yiphtah passed on to the Ammonites to do battle against them, and Yahweh gave them into his hand. ³³He struck them down from Aro'er as far as when you come to Minnit, twenty towns, and as far as Keramim Meadow, in a very great rout. So the Ammonites bowed down before the Yisra'elites.

³⁴Yiphtah came home to The Watchtower, and there was his daughter coming out to meet him with a tambourine and with dancing. There was just her, an only child; apart from her he had no son or daughter. ³⁵When he saw her, he tore his clothes and said, 'Oh, my daughter, you've bent me down, bent me down; you yourself have become someone bringing disaster on me. I opened my mouth myself to Yahweh. I can't go back.' ³⁶She said to him,

'Father, you opened your mouth to Yahweh. Do to me as it came from your mouth, after Yahweh has performed full redress for you from your enemies, the Ammonites.'

³⁷She said to her father, 'May this thing be done for me. Let me go for two months so I can walk and go down on the mountains and bewail my girlhood, I and my friends.' ³⁸He said, 'Go', and sent her for two months. She and her friends went and bewailed her girlhood on the mountains. ³⁹At the end of two months she came back to her father and he performed the pledge that he had made in connection with her. She had not had sex with a man.

It became a decree in Yisra'el: ⁴⁰from time to time Yisra'elite girls would go to commemorate the daughter of Yiphtah the Gil'adite, for four days in the year.

Shibboleth

12 Then the Ephrayimites had themselves called out, crossed to Tsaphon and said to Yiphtah, 'Why did you cross over to battle against the Ammonites and not call for us to go with you? We'll burn your house in fire over you.' ²Yiphtah said to them, 'I was involved in an argument, my people and the Ammonites, seriously. I called out to you and you didn't deliver me from their hand. ³I saw that you were not a deliverer and I took my life in the palm of my hand and passed over to the Ammonites, and Yahweh gave them into my hand. So why have you gone up against me this day to do battle against me?'

⁴Yiphtah collected all the Gil'adites and did battle with Ephrayim. The Gil'adites struck Ephrayim down, because they said, 'You're Ephrayimite escapees, Gil'ad within Ephrayim – within Menashsheh.' ⁵Gil'ad captured Ephrayim's Yarden crossings, and when Ephrayimite escapees would say, 'I want to cross', the Gil'adites said to him, 'Are you an Ephrayimite?', and he said, 'No'. ⁶They then said to him, 'Say *shibbolet*, please', and he said *sibbolet*, and couldn't speak in that way. So they took hold of him and killed him by the Yarden crossings. Forty-two thousand Ephrayimites fell at that time.

⁷Yiphtah exercised authority for Yisra'el for six years. Then Yiphtah the Gil'adite died, and was buried in the towns of Gil'ad.

⁸After him, Ibtsan from Bet Lehem exercised authority for Yisra'el. ⁹He had thirty sons and thirty daughters whom he sent off abroad, and he brought in thirty girls for his sons from abroad. He exercised authority for Yisra'el for seven years. ¹⁰Ibtsan died, and was buried in Bet Lehem.

¹¹After him, Elon the Zebulunite exercised authority for Yisra'el. He exercised authority for Yisra'el for ten years. ¹²Elon the Zubulunite died, and was buried in Ayyalon in the region of Zebulun.

¹³After him, Abdon ben Hillel the Pir'atonite exercised authority for Yisra'el. ¹⁴He had forty sons and thirty grandsons, riding on seventy donkeys. He exercised authority for Yisra'el for eight years. ¹⁵Abdon ben Hillel the Pir'atonite died, and was buried in Pir'aton in the region of Ephrayim, in the highland of the Amaleqites.

Entertaining angels unawares

13 The Yisra'elites again did what was bad in Yahweh's eyes and Yahweh gave them into the hand of the Pelishtites for forty years.

²There was a certain man from Tsor'ah, from the kin-group of Dan. His name was Manoah. His wife was infertile; she had not given birth. ³Yahweh's envoy appeared to the woman and said to her, 'Here, please, you're infertile, you haven't given birth, but you're going to get pregnant and give birth to a son. ⁴So now keep watch, please, so you don't drink wine or liquor and don't eat anything taboo, ⁵because here, you're going to get pregnant and give birth to a son, and no razor is to go up on to his head, because the boy is to be a consecrated person for God from the womb. He's the one who will start to deliver Yisra'el from the hand of the Pelishtites.'

⁶The woman came and said to her husband, 'A supernatural man came to me; his appearance was like that of a divine envoy, very awe-inspiring. I didn't ask him where he was from and he didn't tell me his name. ⁷He said to me, "Here, you're going to get pregnant and give birth to a son. So now don't drink wine or liquor and don't eat anything taboo, because the boy's to be a consecrated person for God from the womb until the day of his death."'

⁸Manoah entreated Yahweh: 'Pardon me, Lord, may the supernatural man whom you sent please come to us again and instruct us what we're to do for the boy who's to be born?' ⁹God listened to Manoah's voice, and God's envoy again came to the woman. She was sitting in the fields and Manoah her husband was not with her. ¹⁰The woman hurried and ran and told her husband, and said to him, 'There, the man who came that day has appeared to me.'

A logical woman

¹¹Manoah got up and followed his wife. He came to the man and said to him, 'Are you the man who spoke to the woman?' He said, 'I am.' ¹²Manoah said, 'May your words come true now! What will be the rule for the boy and the work for him?' ¹³Yahweh's envoy said to Manoah, 'The woman is to keep watch in connection with everything that I said. ¹⁴Of anything that comes from the grapevine she's not to eat. Wine and liquor she's not to drink. Anything taboo she's not to eat. Everything that I ordered her, she's to keep watch.'
¹⁵Manoah said to Yahweh's envoy, 'We'll please hold you back and prepare a kid goat from the flock before you.' ¹⁶Yahweh's envoy said to Manoah, 'If you hold me back, I won't eat of your meal, but if you make a burnt offering, you may offer it up for Yahweh' (because Manoah didn't know that it was Yahweh's envoy). ¹⁷Manoah said to Yahweh's envoy, 'What is your name? When your words come true, we will honour you.' ¹⁸Yahweh's envoy said to him, 'Why is it that you ask my name when it's extraordinary?'
¹⁹Manoah got a kid goat from the flock and a grain offering and offered them up on a crag for Yahweh, and he did something extraordinary as Manoah and his wife were looking. ²⁰When the flame went up from on the altar to the heavens, Yahweh's envoy went up in the altar flame as Manoah and his wife were looking. They fell on their faces to the earth. ²¹Yahweh's envoy didn't appear ever again to Manoah and his wife.
Then Manoah knew that it had been Yahweh's envoy. ²²Manoah said to his wife, 'We'll die, we'll die, because we've seen God!' ²³His wife said to him, 'If Yahweh wanted to put us to death, he wouldn't have received the burnt offering and the grain offering from our hand and he wouldn't have let us see all these things, or just now have let us hear something like this.'
²⁴The woman gave birth to a son and named him Shimshon [Samson]. The boy grew, and Yahweh blessed him. ²⁵Yahweh's spirit started to impel him in Dan's Camp between Tsor'ah and Eshta'ol.

The right one for me

14 Shimshon went down to Timnah and saw a woman in Timnah among the Pelishtite girls. ²He went up and told his father and his mother and said, 'I saw a woman in Timnah among the Pelishtite girls, so now, get her for me as wife.' ³His father and his mother said to him, 'Isn't there a wife among your brothers' girls or among all my people, that you're going to take a wife from the foreskinned Pelishtites?' Shimshon said to his father, 'Get that one for me, because she's right in my eyes.' ⁴His father and his mother didn't know that it stemmed from Yahweh, because he was looking for an opportunity from the Pelishtites. At that time the Pelishtites were ruling over Yisra'el.
⁵Shimshon went down to Timnah with his father and his mother and they came as far as the vineyards at Timnah. And there, a lion whelp, roaring as it met him. ⁶Yahweh's spirit thrust itself on to him and he tore it apart as one might tear apart a kid. There was nothing in his hand. He didn't tell his father and his mother what he'd done.
⁷He went down and spoke to the woman. She was right in Shimshon's eyes. ⁸He went back some time later to get her, and he turned aside to see the remains of the lion. There, a swarm of bees was in the lion's corpse, with honey. ⁹He scraped it out into his palms and went on, eating it. He went to his father and to his mother and gave them some, and they ate it. He didn't tell them that he had scraped the honey from the lion's corpse.
¹⁰His father went down to the woman and Shimshon made a banquet there, because that was what the young men used to do. ¹¹When they saw him, they got thirty good friends and they came to be with him.

The conundrum

12Shimshon said to them, 'I shall propound a conundrum to you, please. If you can properly explain it to me in the seven days of the banquet and solve it, I'll give you thirty shirts and thirty changes of clothing. **13**But if you can't explain it, you're to give me thirty shirts and thirty changes of clothing.' They said to him, 'Propound your conundrum and we'll listen.' **14**He said to them:

> From the eater there came out something to eat,
> From the vigorous there came out something sweet.

They couldn't explain the conundrum for three days.

15On the seventh day they said to Shimshon's wife, 'Coax your husband so he explains the conundrum for us, or else we'll burn you and your father's household in fire. Was it to dispossess us that you invited us? Wasn't it?' **16**So Shimshon's wife wailed at him and said, 'Really you dislike me. You don't love me. You propounded a conundrum to my people and you haven't explained it to me.' He said to her, 'There, I didn't explain it to my father and to my mother, and am I to explain it to you?' **17**She wailed at him for the seven days that their banquet lasted. On the seventh day he explained it to her, because she pressed him, and she explained the conundrum to the members of her people. **18**So the men of the town said to him on the seventh day, before the sun went down:

> What's sweeter than honey,
> What's more vigorous than a lion?

He said to them,

> If you had not ploughed with my heifer
> You would not have solved my conundrum!

19Yahweh's spirit thrust itself on to him and he went down to Ashqelon and from them he struck down thirty men. He got their strip and gave the changes of clothing to the men who had explained the conundrum. But his anger raged and he went up to his father's house. **20**Shimshon's wife came to belong to his good friend, one who had been his friend.

Shimshon's redress

15 After some time, during the time of the wheat harvest, Shimshon visited his wife with a kid goat from the flock. He said, 'I want to come in and have sex with my wife in the room', but her father wouldn't let him come in. **2**Her father said, 'I said for sure that you totally disliked her and I gave her to your good friend. Her little sister is better than her. She can be yours in place of her, can't she?' **3**Shimshon said to them, 'This time I'm free of guilt in relation to the Pelishtites when I deal badly with them!' **4**Shimshon went and caught 300 foxes and got torches. He made them face tail to tail and put a torch between two tails, in the middle, **5**set fire to the torches and sent them off into the Pelishtites' standing grain. He burned up the stacked grain, and both the standing grain and the olive vineyard. **6**The Pelishtites said, 'Who did this?' And they said, 'Shimshon, the son-in-law of the Timnite, because he took his wife and gave her to his good friend.' So the Pelishtites went up and burned her and her father in fire.

7Shimshon said to them, 'If you act like this, I shall definitely have redress against you, and only after shall I leave off.' **8**He struck them down, leg upon thigh, in a great rout. He then went down and lived in a cleft in Etam Rock. **9**The Pelishtites went up and camped against Yehudah and ran loose in Lehi, **10**and the Yehudahites said, 'Why have you gone up against us?' They said, 'We've gone up to bind Shimshon, to do to him as he did to us.' **11**So 3,000 men from Yehudah went down to the cleft in Etam Rock and said to Shimshon, 'Don't you acknowledge that the Pelishtites are ruling over us? So why have you done this to us?' He said to them, 'As they did to me, so I did to them.'

Jawbone

12They said to him, 'It's to bind you that we've gone down, to give you over into the Pelishtites' hand.' Shimshon said to them,

'Swear to me that you yourselves won't attack me.' ¹³They said to him, 'No, but we'll simply bind you and give you over into their hand. We definitely won't put you to death.' So they bound him with two new ropes and got him to go up from the Rock. ¹⁴As he came to Lehi and the Pelishtites shouted on meeting him, Yahweh's spirit thrust itself on to him and the ropes that were on his arms became like flax that burns up in fire. His bonds melted from on his hands. ¹⁵He found a fresh donkey jawbone, put out his hand and got it, and struck down a thousand men with it. ¹⁶Shimshon said,

> With a donkey jawbone – a donkey-heap, two donkey-heaps;
> With a donkey jawbone I've struck down a thousand.

¹⁷As he finished speaking, he threw the jawbone from his hand. He called that place Lehi ['Jawbone'] Height.
¹⁸He was very thirsty. He called to Yahweh and said, 'You yourself have given this great deliverance by your servant's hand. Now am I to die of thirst and fall into the hand of the foreskinned?' ¹⁹God split the hollow that was at Lehi, and water came out from it. He drank, and his spirit came back and he revived. That's why it has been named Haqqore ['The Caller'] Spring, which is in Lehi, until this day.
²⁰He exercised authority for Yisra'el in the time of the Pelishtites for twenty years.

Love actually

16 Shimshon went to Azzah and saw there a woman who was a whore, and he had sex with her. ²Someone said to the Gazites, 'Shimshon has come here.' They came round and laid an ambush for him all night at the town gateway. They were still all night, saying 'At morning light, we'll kill him.' ³But Shimshon lay in bed until midnight, then got up at midnight, took hold of the doors of the town gateway and the two gateposts, pulled them out with the bar, put them on his shoulders and took them up to the top of the mountain that's east of Hebron.
⁴After that he loved a woman in Wadi Soreq named Delilah. ⁵The Pelishtites' lords went up to her and said to her, 'Coax him and see whereby is his great energy and whereby we can overcome him and bind him, so as to subdue him. We – we'll each give you 1,100 in silver.'
⁶So Delilah said to Shimshon, 'Please tell me whereby is your great energy and whereby you could be bound so as to subdue you.' ⁷Shimshon said to her, 'If they bind me with seven fresh cords that haven't been dried, I'd become weak. I'd be like any human being.' ⁸So the Pelishtites' lords took up to her seven fresh cords that hadn't been dried and she bound him with them, ⁹while the ambush was sitting waiting for her in a room. She said to him, 'Pelishtites are on you, Shimshon!', and he snapped the tendons as a strand of fibre snaps when it smells fire. So his energy didn't become known.
¹⁰Delilah said to Shimshon, 'Here, you've played about with me. You've spoken lies to me. Now, please tell me whereby you could be bound.' ¹¹He said to her, 'If they actually bind me with new ropes with which no work has been done, I'd become weak, I'd be like any human being.' ¹²So Delilah got new ropes and bound him with them, and said to him, 'Pelishtites are on you, Shimshon!', while the ambush was sitting waiting in a room. He snapped them from on his arms like a thread.

He didn't realize that Yahweh had left him

¹³Delilah said to Shimshon, 'Until now you've played about with me. You've spoken lies to me. Tell me whereby you could be bound.' He said to her, 'If you weave seven braids from my head with the web.' ¹⁴She pinned it with a peg and said to him, 'Pelishtites are on you, Shimshon!' He woke up from his sleep and pulled out the peg (the loom) and the web.
¹⁵She said to him, 'How can you say "I love you" when your mind isn't with me? These three times you've played about with me and not told me whereby is your great energy.' ¹⁶Because she pressed him with her words all the time and begged him, and his spirit was tired to death, ¹⁷he told her everything in his mind. He said to her, 'No razor has gone up on my head, because I've been a consecrated person for God from my mother's womb. If my hair were cut, my energy would depart from me and I'd be weak. I'd be like any human

being.' ¹⁸Delilah saw that he had told her everything in his mind, and she sent and called for the Pelishtites' lords: 'Come up this time, because he's told me everything in his mind.' The Pelishtites' lords went up to her and took up the silver in their hand.

¹⁹She got him to go to sleep on her lap, and called for a man and cut off the seven braids on his head. She started to humble him, and his energy departed from him. ²⁰She said, 'Pelishtites are on you, Shimshon!' He woke up from his sleep and said, 'I'll go out as at other times and shake myself free.' He didn't know that Yahweh had departed from him.

²¹The Pelishtites took hold of him and gouged out his eyes. They took him down to Azzah and bound him in copper shackles, and he became a grinder in the prison.

But Shimshon's hair began to grow again

²²But the hair on his head started to grow, when it had been cut off.

²³Now the Pelishtites' lords gathered to offer a great sacrifice for Dagan their god, and for a celebration. They said, 'Our god has given Shimshon, our enemy, into our hand.' ²⁴The people saw him and praised their god, because (they said) 'Our god has given our enemy into our hand, the one who wasted our country and multiplied the number of us run through.' ²⁵When their heart felt good, they said 'Call for Shimshon. He must make fun for us.' So they called for Shimshon from the prison house and he entertained them.

They stood him between the pillars, ²⁶and Shimshon said to the boy who had a strong hold of him by the hand, 'Let me be and let me feel the pillars that the house depends on, so I can lean on them.' ²⁷The house was full of men and women. All the Pelishtites' lords were there. On the roof were some 3,000 men and women watching Shimshon, making fun.

²⁸Shimshon called to Yahweh and said, 'My Lord Yahweh, please be mindful of me. Please just this once, God, make me strong so I can take redress from the Pelishtites, redress for one of my two eyes.' ²⁹And Shimshon grasped the two middle pillars that the house was established on and leaned on them, one with his right hand and one with his left. ³⁰Shimshon said, 'I myself can die with the Pelishtites', and he pushed energetically. The house fell on the lords and on the entire company that was in it. The people whom he put to death when he died were more than he put to death when he lived.

³¹His brothers and his father's entire household went down, lifted him, took him up, and buried him between Tsor'ah and Eshta'ol in the grave of Manoah his father. He had exercised authority for Yisra'el for twenty years.

Everyone did what was all right in their own eyes

17 There was a man from the highland of Ephrayim; his name was Mikah. ²He said to his mother, 'The 1,100 in silver that were taken from you, and you uttered a curse and also said it in my ears: here, the silver is with me. I'm the one who took it.' His mother said, 'May my son be blessed by Yahweh.' ³He gave back the 1,100 in silver to his mother, and his mother said 'I'm definitively making the silver sacred for Yahweh from my hand for my son to make a statue and a cast image. I now give it back to you.' ⁴So he gave the silver back to his mother and she got 200 in silver and gave it to a smith. He made a statue and a cast image, and it was in Mikah's house.

⁵This man Mikah had a house of God. He made a chasuble and effigies, and commissioned one of his sons and he became priest for him. ⁶At that time there was no king in Yisra'el. An individual would do what was all right in his own eyes. ⁷But there was a boy from Bet Lehem in Yehudah, from the clan of Yehudah. He was a Levite and had been residing there, ⁸but this individual went from the town, from Bet Lehem in Yehudah, to reside wherever he could find somewhere, and he came to the highland of Ephrayim, as far as the house of Mikah, as he made his way. ⁹Mikah said to him, 'Where do you come from?' He said to him, 'I'm a Levite from Bet Lehem in Yehudah but I'm going so as to reside wherever I can find somewhere.' ¹⁰Mikah said to him, 'Stay with me. You'll be a father and a priest for me. I'll give you ten in silver a year, a set of clothes and your living.' So the Levite went. ¹¹The Levite agreed to live with the man, and the boy became to him like one of his sons.

¹²So Mikah commissioned the Levite, and the boy became priest for him. He was in Mikah's household. ¹³Mikah said, 'Now I know that Yahweh will be good to me, because the Levite has become priest for me.'

Desperate Dan

18 At that time there was no king in Yisra'el, and at that time the clan of Dan was looking for a domain for itself to live in, because until that day nothing had fallen to it as a domain among Yisra'el's clans.

²The Danites sent from their kin-group five men from their total number, men of ability, from Tsor'ah and from Eshta'ol, to investigate the country and search it out. So they said to them, 'Go and search out the country', and they came to the highland of Ephrayim, as far as Mikah's house, and stayed the night there.

³When they were near Mikah's house and recognized the young Levite's accent they turned aside there and said to him, 'Who brought you here? What are you doing in this place? What are you here for?' ⁴He said to them, 'Mikah acted like this and like this for me. He hired me and I became priest for him.' ⁵They said to him, 'Please ask of God so we can know if the journey on which we're going will be successful.' ⁶The priest said to them, 'Go, things will be well. The journey on which you're going is in front of Yahweh.'

⁷The five men went and came to Layish. They saw the people that was within it, living in confidence in accordance with the rule of the Tsidonites, calm and confident, with no one in the region possessing them by force, bringing shame regarding anything; though they were far away from the Tsidonites and had nothing to do with anyone.

⁸So they came to their brothers in Tsor'ah and Eshta'ol, and their brothers said to them, 'What did you find?' ⁹They said, 'Set off, let's go up against them, because we've looked at the region: there, it's very good, and you're sitting still! Don't be slow to go, to come and take possession of the region. ¹⁰When you come, you'll come to a people that feels confident, and the region is wide on both sides. Because God has given it into your hand, a place where there's no lack of anything that's in the earth.'

The unfortunate Mikah

¹¹So 600 men of the Danite clan from Tsor'ah and Eshta'ol, wrapped round with battle equipment, moved on from there ¹²and went up and camped in Ye'arim Township in Yehudah (for that reason they call that place 'Dan's Camp' until this day – there, it's west of Ye'arim Township). ¹³They passed on from there to the highland of Ephrayim and came as far as Mikah's house. ¹⁴The five men who had gone to investigate the region of Layish said to their brothers, 'Do you know that in these houses there is a chasuble and effigies and a statue and a cast image? Now acknowledge what you're to do.'

¹⁵They turned aside there and came into the young Levite's house at Mikah's house and asked him whether things were well with him, ¹⁶while 600 men wrapped round with battle equipment were standing at the entrance of the gateway (the men who were from the Danites). ¹⁷The five men who had gone to investigate the country went up, came in there, took the statue, the chasuble, the effigies and the cast image, while the priest was standing at the entrance of the gateway, with the 600 men wrapped round with battle equipment.

¹⁸When these men came into Mikah's house and took the statue with the chasuble, the effigies and the cast image, the priest said to them, 'What are you doing?' ¹⁹They said to him, 'Quiet. Put your hand on your mouth. Go with us and become a father and a priest for us. Is it better for you to be a priest for the household of one man or to be a priest for a clan, a kin-group in Yisra'el?'

²⁰The priest's heart felt good, so he got the chasuble, the effigies and the cast image, and came among the company. ²¹They turned their face and went, and put the little ones, the livestock and the valuables before them.

The unfortunate people of Layish

²²When they had gone a distance from Mikah's house, the men who were in the households that were near Mikah's house had themselves called out, caught up with the Danites ²³and called to the Danites. They turned round and said to Mikah, 'What's the

matter with you, that you've had yourself called out?' ²⁴He said, 'You took my gods that I made, and the priest, and you went. What do I still have? And you say to me, "What's the matter with you?"' ²⁵The Danites said to him, 'Don't make your voice heard among us, or men who are fierce in spirit may come upon you and gather up your life and the life of your household.'

²⁶So the Danites went on their way. Mikah saw that they were stronger than him, turned his face and went back to his house, ²⁷while they took what Mikah had made and the priest that he had. They came to Layish, to a people calm and confident, and struck them down with the mouth of the sword, and burned their town in fire. ²⁸There was no one to rescue because it was far away from Tsidon and they had nothing to do with anyone (it was in the vale that belonged to Bet-rehob).

They built up the town and lived in it, ²⁹and named the town Dan, after the name of Dan, their ancestor, who had been born to Yisra'el (the town's name was Layish originally, however). ³⁰The Danites set up the statue for themselves, and Yehonatan ben Gershom, son of Mosheh, he and his sons, were priests for the clan of Dan until the time of the country's exile. ³¹They put in place for themselves Mikah's statue that he had made, the entire time that the house of God was at Shiloh.

The broken marriage that might recover

19 At that time, when there was no king in Yisra'el, a Levite individual residing in the remote parts of the highland of Ephrayim got himself a woman as a secondary wife from Bet Lehem in Yehudah, ²but his wife whored against him and went from being with him to her father's household in Bet Lehem in Yehudah, and she was there for a full four months. ³Her husband set off and followed her to speak to her heart to get her to come back. His boy and a pair of donkeys were with him. She let him come into her father's house, and the girl's father saw him and rejoiced to meet him. ⁴His father-in-law, the girl's father, took strong hold of him, and he stayed with him for three days. They ate and drank and stayed the night there.

⁵On the fourth day they started early in the morning and got up to go, but the girl's father said to his son-in-law, 'Strengthen your heart with a bit of bread, and go afterwards.' ⁶So the two of them sat down and ate together, and drank. The girl's father said to the man, 'Do resolve to stay the night. Your heart will feel good.' ⁷The man got up to go, but his father-in-law pressed him, and he went back and stayed the night there.

⁸They started early in the morning on the fifth day to go, but the girl's father said, 'Do strengthen your heart and wait till the day declines', and the two of them ate. ⁹The man got up to go, he and his wife and his boy, but his father-in-law, the girl's father, said to him, 'Here, please, the day is slackening towards evening. Please stay the night. Here, it's the time of day for spreading tents. Stay the night here. Your heart will feel good, and you can start early on your way tomorrow and go to your tent.'

A foreign town won't be safe?

¹⁰The man was not willing to stay the night, and he got up and went. He came as far as in front of Yebus (i.e. Yerushalaim). With him were a pair of laden donkeys, and his wife was with him. ¹¹As they were near Yebus and the day had worn far on, the boy said to his lord, 'Come on, please let's turn aside into this town of the Yebusites and stay the night in it.' ¹²His lord said to him, 'We won't turn aside into a foreign town where there aren't any Yisra'elites. We'll pass on as far as Gib'ah.'

¹³So he said to his boy, 'Come on, we'll get near one of the places and stay the night in Gib'ah or in The Height.' ¹⁴So they passed on, and as they went, the sun set on them beside Gib'ah which belongs to Binyamin, ¹⁵and they turned aside there to come in to stay the night in Gib'ah.

They came in and sat in the town square, but there was no one gathering them into his house to stay the night. ¹⁶But there, an old man came in from his work, from the fields, in the evening. The man was from the highland of Ephrayim; he was a resident in Gib'ah, while the men of the place were Binyaminites. ¹⁷He lifted his eyes and saw the man on a journey, in the town square.

The old man said, 'Where are you going and where do you come from?' ¹⁸He said to him, 'We're passing through from Bet-lehem in Yehudah as far as the remote parts of the highland of Ephrayim. I'm from there but I went as far as Bet Lehem in Yehudah and I'm going to Yahweh's house. But there's no one gathering me into his house. ¹⁹Our donkeys have got both straw and fodder and I and your handmaid and the boy with your servants have also got bread and wine. There's no lack of anything.' ²⁰The old man said, 'Welcome to you. All your needs are definitely my responsibility. You're definitely not to stay the night in the square.'

The horrific ending

²¹So he brought him into his house and fed the donkeys, and they bathed their feet and ate and drank. ²²While they were making their heart feel good, there, men from the town, scoundrels, surrounded the house, banging on the door. They said to the man who was the master of the house, the old man, 'Bring out the man who came to your house, so we can have sex with him.'

²³The man who was the master of the house went out to them and said to them, 'No, my brothers, don't do something so bad, will you, after this man has come to my house. Don't perform this villainy. ²⁴Here is my daughter, a young girl, and his wife. I'll bring them out to you, please. Humble them. Do to them what's good in your eyes. But to this man you will not perform this villainy.'

²⁵The men were not willing to listen to him, so the man took strong hold of his wife and made her go out to them, outside. They had sex with her and acted abusively to her all night until morning, and sent her off as dawn came up. ²⁶The woman came as morning turned its face and fell at the entrance of the man's house where her lord was, until daylight.

²⁷Her lord got up in the morning, opened the doors of the house and went out to go on his journey, and there was the woman who was his secondary wife, fallen at the entrance of the house, her hands on the threshold. ²⁸He said to her, 'Get up, let's go.' There was no response, so he got her on to the donkey.

The man set off and went to his own place. ²⁹He came to his house and got a knife, took strong hold of his wife, cut her up limb by limb into twelve parts and sent her off through Yisra'el's entire border. ³⁰Everyone who saw said, 'Such a thing hasn't happened and hasn't been seen from the day the Yisra'elites went up from the country of Misrayim until this day. Apply yourself to this. Take counsel. Speak.'

The outrage

20 All the Yisra'elites went out and the assembly congregated as one person, from Dan as far as Be'er Sheba and the region of Gil'ad, to Yahweh at The Watchtower. ²The cornerstones of the entire people, all Yisra'el's clans, took their stand as the congregation of God's people, 400,000 men on foot, drawing a sword. ³The Binyaminites heard that the Yisra'elites had gone up to The Watchtower.

The Yisra'elites said, 'Speak: how did this bad thing happen?' ⁴The man who was a Levite, the husband of the woman who had been killed, said, 'I came, I and my secondary wife, to Gib'ah which belongs to Binyamin, to stay the night. ⁵The landowners in Gib'ah set upon me and surrounded the house against me at night. They thought about killing me and they humbled my wife, and she died. ⁶So I took hold of my wife and cut her in pieces, and sent her off through every area in Yisra'el's domain, because they had committed a deliberate wickedness that's an act of villainy in Yisra'el. ⁷Here, all you Yisra'elites, come up with your word, your counsel, here and now!'

⁸The entire company got up as one man, saying 'We won't go, not one of us, to his tent; we won't depart, not one of us, to his home. ⁹This is the thing that we will now do to Gib'ah, against it, by lot. ¹⁰We'll get ten men per hundred for all Yisra'el's clans, a hundred per thousand, a thousand per ten thousand, to get provisions for the company, to take action by going to Geba in Binyamin in accordance with the total villainy that it's done in Yisra'el.'

The redress that misfires

¹¹So all the Yisra'elites gathered against the town, united as one man. ¹²The Yisra'elite

clans sent men through all the Binyaminite clans, saying 'What is this bad thing that has happened among you? ¹³So now give us the scoundrels who are in Gib'ah. We'll put them to death and burn away what is bad from Yisra'el.' But the Binyaminites were not willing to listen to the voice of their brothers, the Yisra'elites, ¹⁴and the Binyaminites gathered from the towns to Gib'ah to go out to do battle with the Yisra'elites.

¹⁵That day the Binyaminites registered from the towns 26,000 men drawing a sword, apart from the people living in Gib'ah, with 700 picked men registered ¹⁶from this entire company, 700 picked men restricted in their right hand, each one able to sling a stone at a hair and not go wrong.

¹⁷The Yisra'elites apart from Binyamin registered 400,000 men drawing a sword, each one a man of battle. ¹⁸They set off and went up to Bet-el and asked of God: the Yisra'elites said, 'Who's to go up for us first for the battle with the Binyaminites?' Yahweh said, 'Yehudah first.' ¹⁹The Yisra'elites set off in the morning and camped against Gib'ah.

²⁰So the Yisra'elites went out to do battle with Binyamin. The Yisra'elites lined up for battle with them at Gib'ah, ²¹but the Binyaminites went out from Gib'ah and devastated Yisra'el that day, 22,000 men to the ground. ²²The company (the Yisra'elites) summoned up its strength and again lined up for battle in the place where they had lined up the previous day. ²³The Yisra'elites went up and wailed before Yahweh until the evening and asked of Yahweh, 'Shall we go up again to battle with the descendants of Binyamin my brother?' and Yahweh said, 'Go up against him.' ²⁴So the Yisra'elites drew near to the Binyaminites on the second day, ²⁵but Binyamin came out from Gib'ah to meet them on the second day and devastated the Yisra'elites, 18,000 more to the ground, all these men drawing a sword.

The ambush that succeeds

²⁶All the Yisra'elites and the entire company went up and came to Bet-el. They wailed and sat there before Yahweh and fasted that day until the evening, and offered up burnt offerings and well-being sacrifices before Yahweh. ²⁷The Yisra'elites asked of Yahweh (God's pact chest was there at that time ²⁸and Pinhas son of El'azar son of Aharon was standing before him at that time), 'Shall I go out once more to battle with the descendants of Binyamin my brother, or leave off?' Yahweh said, 'Go up, because I shall give them into your hand tomorrow.'

²⁹Yisra'el put men in ambush against Gib'ah all round. ³⁰On the third day the Yisra'elites went up against the Binyaminites and lined up against Gib'ah as on other times, ³¹and the Binyaminites came out to meet the company. They were drawn away from the town and began to strike down some of the company, run through, as on other times, on the causeways (of which one goes up to Bet-el and one to Gib'ah) in the fields, some thirty men in Yisra'el. ³²The Binyaminites said, 'They've taken a beating before us as before', but the Yisra'elites had said, 'We'll flee and draw them away from the town on to the causeways.'

³³So while all the Yisra'elites got up from their place and lined up at Ba'al Tamar, the Yisra'elite ambush was breaking out from its place, from the Geba wilderness, ³⁴and 10,000 picked men from all Yisra'el came from south of Gib'ah. The battle was heavy and they didn't acknowledge that something bad was closing in on them. ³⁵So Yahweh defeated Binyamin before Yisra'el. That day the Yisra'elites devastated Binyamin, 25,100 men, all these drawing a sword. ³⁶ᵃThe Binyaminites saw that they had taken a beating.

The terrible slaughter of Binyamin

³⁶ᵇThe Yisra'elites had given ground to Binyamin, because they relied on the ambush that they set against Gib'ah. ³⁷While one ambush quickly charged against Gib'ah, the other ambush advanced and struck down the entire town with the mouth of the sword. ³⁸The set time for the Yisra'elites with the ambush was: make a great uprising of smoke go up from the town ³⁹and the Yisra'elites would turn about in the battle. While Binyamin started striking down some thirty men in Yisra'el, run through, because (they said) 'It's taking a terrible beating before us like the first battle', ⁴⁰when the uprising (the smoke column) started to go up from the town, Binyamin

turned his face behind him, and there, the entire town had gone up into the heavens. ⁴¹Yisraʼel circled round and Binyamin became fearful because it saw that something bad had closed in on it. ⁴²They turned their face before Yisraʼel to the wilderness road, but the battle caught up with it, while the men from the towns were devastating it inside it. ⁴³They surrounded Binyamin, pursued him to Menuhah and trod him down as far as in front of Gibʼah on the east. ⁴⁴There fell of Binyamin 18,000 that day, all these forceful men. ⁴⁵They turned their face and fled to the wilderness, to Rimmon Cliff, but on the causeways they gleaned 5,000 men, then caught up with them at Gidʼom, and struck down 2,000 of them. ⁴⁶So all the fallen from Binyamin that day were 25,000 men drawing a sword, all these forceful men. ⁴⁷Six hundred men turned their face and fled to the wilderness, to Rimmon Cliff, and lived at Rimmon Cliff for four months, ⁴⁸while the Yisraʼelites went back to the Binyaminites and struck them down with the mouth of the sword – both the entire town (the people), and the animals and everything that was to be found. They also burned in fire all the towns that were to be found.

How not to save the situation

21 Now the Yisraʼelites had sworn at The Watchtower, 'None of us will give his daughter to Binyamin as a wife.' ²The company came to Bet-el and sat there before God until the evening. They lifted up their voice, and wailed and wailed, loudly. ³They said, 'Why, Yahweh God of Yisraʼel, has this happened in Yisraʼel, so a clan is counted missing today from Yisraʼel?'
⁴Next day the people started early and built an altar there, and offered up whole offerings and well-being sacrifices. ⁵The Yisraʼelites said, 'Who is there from all Yisraʼel's clans that didn't come up in the congregation to Yahweh?' Because there had been a great oath regarding anyone who didn't come up to Yahweh at The Watchtower: 'He will absolutely be put to death.'
⁶So the Yisraʼelites felt sorry towards Binyamin their brother and said, 'Today a clan has been cut off from Yisraʼel. ⁷What can we do for them, for wives for those who are left, when we have sworn by Yahweh not to give them any of our daughters as wives?'
⁸They said, 'Who is there from Yisraʼel's clans who didn't go up to Yahweh at The Watchtower?' There, no one had come from Yabesh-in-Gilʼad to the camp, to the congregation; ⁹the company had registered, and there was no one there from the people living in Yabesh-in-Gilʼad. ¹⁰So the assembly sent 12,000 of the forceful men and ordered them, 'Go and strike down the people living in Yabesh-in-Gilʼad with the mouth of the sword, and the women and little ones. ¹¹This is the thing that you're to do: you're to devote every male and every woman who has slept with a male.'
¹²But they found from the people living in Yabesh-in-Gilʼad 400 young girls who had not had sex by sleeping with a male, and they brought them to the camp at Shiloh, which is in the country of Kenaʼan. ¹³The entire assembly sent and spoke to the Binyaminites who were at Rimmon Cliff and called out peace to them. ¹⁴So Binyamin came back at that time and they gave them the women whom they'd let live from the women of Yabesh-in-Gilʼad.

Everyone was doing what was all right in his own eyes

But they didn't find for them [all] in this way. ¹⁵As the company felt sorry for Binyamin because Yahweh had made a breach in Yisraʼel's clans, ¹⁶the elders of the assembly said, 'What can we do for wives for those who are left, because the women have been annihilated from Binyamin?' ¹⁷They said, 'An escape possession for Binyamin – a clan will not be wiped out from Yisraʼel! ¹⁸But we ourselves can't give them wives from among our daughters' (because the Yisraʼelites had sworn, 'Cursed is the person who gives a wife to Binyamin').
¹⁹So they said, 'Here, from time to time it's Yahweh's festival at Shiloh' (which is north of Bet-el, east of the causeway going up from Bet-el to Shekem and south of Lebonah). ²⁰They ordered the Binyaminites, 'Go and make an ambush in the vineyards ²¹and look. There, if the daughters of Shiloh go out to join in the dances, you go out of the vineyards. Each of you capture a wife for himself from

the daughters of Shiloh, and go to the region of Binyamin. ²²When their fathers or their brothers come to argue with us, we'll say to them, "Be gracious to us over them, because we didn't each get his wife in the battle, because you yourselves didn't give them to them at a time when you would be liable."

²³The Binyaminites did so and carried off wives in accordance with their number from the dancers whom they seized. Then they went and returned to their domain, and built up the towns and lived in them.

²⁴The Yisra'elites went off from there at that time, each to his clan and to his kin-group. They left from there, each to his domain.

²⁵At that time there was no king in Yisra'el. Each person would do what was all right in his own eyes.

Ruth

Ruth is a short story about the aftermath of a series of calamities that befalls an Israelite family. Although Ruth herself may be the book's most prominent character, Na'omi is almost as important, and it is worth also reading the story from the angles of Elimelek, Mahlon, Kilyon, Orpah, Boaz, Obed, and other characters who are even more minor.

In the Hebrew Bible Ruth appears in the company of the Song of Songs, Lamentations, Ecclesiastes and Esther. The Jewish community reads each of these 'Five Scrolls' on one main occasion each year. Ruth is used at the Shabu'ot Festival (Pentecost), in the light of its focus on harvest. The story also provides fine examples of commitment to the Torah, and the giving of the Torah became a theme of the Shabu'ot Festival.

In the order of books in the English Bible, Ruth offers a breath of fresh air after the unpleasantness of the later stories in Judges. It contributes to the transition from Judges to 1 and 2 Samuel in another way, in that we discover at the very end of Ruth that we are reading the story of how David acquired his great-grandmother. That note adds extra significance to the fact that the book's heroine is a Moabite. Elsewhere, the Scriptures emphasize the importance of not intermarrying with people such as Moabites who could lead Israelites to serve other gods. Ruth makes explicit that foreigners who come to serve Yahweh are a different matter. Israel is always open to such foreigners. Its faith is not ethnically based.

The book presupposes a cultural context in which the men have the formal authority in society, and it tells a story about how women may nevertheless be able to take responsibility for their destiny. It makes little reference to God directly acting, and it thus reminds readers how God often works via human planning and initiative and through coincidences. And it shows how a traditional culture can provide safety nets for vulnerable people through the expectations laid on the 'restorer' (English translations often use the word *redeemer*). The restorer is a senior member of the extended family who is expected to be willing to use his resources to help members of the family get back on their feet and to restore equilibrium when things get out of order.

How Na'omi's life falls apart

1 During the time when the people who exercised authority were doing so, there was a famine in the country and a man went from Bet Lehem in Yehudah [Judah] to reside in Mo'abite country, he, his wife and his two sons. ²The man's name was Elimelek, his wife's name was Na'omi, and his two sons' names were Mahlon and Kilyon – Ephratites from Bet Lehem in Yehudah.

So they came to Mo'abite country and they were there, ³but Elimelek, Na'omi's husband, died. She remained, she and her two sons. ⁴They took up for themselves Mo'abite wives; the name of the first was Orpah and the name of the second, Ruth. They lived there some ten years, ⁵but the two of them, Mahlon and Kilyon, also died, and the woman was left without her two sons and without her husband.

⁶She set off, she and her daughters-in-law, and went back from Mo'abite country, because she had heard in Mo'abite country that Yahweh had attended to his people by giving them bread. ⁷So she left the place where she was, her two daughters-in-law with her, and they went on the road to go back to the region of Yehudah.

⁸But Na'omi said to her two daughters-in-law, 'Go, get back, each one to her mother's household. May Yahweh act in commitment with you as you've acted with the dead men and with me. ⁹May Yahweh grant to you that you find a place to settle down, each one in the household of her husband.' She kissed them and they lifted up their voice and cried. ¹⁰They said to her, 'But we should go back with you to your people.'

The choice

¹¹Na'omi said, 'Go back, my daughters, why should you go with me? Do I still have sons inside me so they can become husbands for you? ¹²Go back, my daughters, go, because I'm too old to belong to a man. If I said there's hope for me, even if I both belonged to a man tonight and also gave birth to sons, ¹³would you therefore wait until they grew up, would you therefore hold yourself back from belonging to a man? No, my daughters, because things are much more bitter for me than for you, because Yahweh's hand has gone out against me.'

¹⁴They lifted up their voice and cried again and Orpah kissed her mother-in-law, but Ruth attached herself to her. ¹⁵So she said, 'There, your sister-in-law has gone back to her people and to her gods. Go back after your sister-in-law.' ¹⁶Ruth said, 'Don't press me to abandon you by turning back from following you, because where you go I shall go and where you stay the night I shall stay the night. Your people will be my people and your God will be my God. ¹⁷Where you die I'll die, and there I'll be buried. So may Yahweh do to me, and so may he do more, if death divides between me and you . . .'

¹⁸She saw that she was showing herself firm about going with her, and she left off from speaking to her. ¹⁹So the two of them went on until they came to Bet Lehem. When they came to Bet Lehem, the entire town was astir over them. They said, 'Is this Na'omi?' ²⁰She said to them, 'Don't call me Na'omi ['Lovely'], call me Mara ['Bitter'], because Shadday has made things very bitter for me. ²¹I went full. Yahweh has brought me back empty. Why do you call me Na'omi when Yahweh has humbled me, when Shadday has dealt badly with me?'

She's a Mo'abite, for goodness' sake!

²²So Na'omi went back, she and Ruth the Mo'abite her daughter-in-law with her, coming back from Mo'abite country. They came to Bet Lehem at the beginning of the barley harvest.

2 Now Na'omi had a relative of her husband's, a forceful strong man, from Elimelek's kin-group. His name was Bo'az. ²Ruth the Mo'abite said to Na'omi, 'Please, may I go to the fields and I'll glean among the ears of grain behind someone in whose eyes I may find grace.' She said to her, 'Go, daughter.' ³So she went.

She came and gleaned in the fields behind the reapers and chance took her to the share in the fields belonging to Bo'az, who was from Elimelek's kin-group. ⁴And there was Bo'az, coming from Bet Lehem. He said to the reapers, 'Yahweh be with you', and they said to him, 'Yahweh bless you.' ⁵Bo'az said to his boy who was standing by the reapers, 'Who does that girl belong to?' ⁶The boy who was standing by the reapers said, 'She's a Mo'abite girl who came back with Na'omi from Mo'abite country. ⁷She said, "Please, may I glean and gather among the sheaves behind the reapers." She came and stood from then, in the morning, until now. Her stay in the house has been short.'

⁸Bo'az said to Ruth, 'Listen, daughter, will you. You're not to go to glean in another field. No, you will not pass on from here. Attach yourself to my girls, ⁹your eyes on the field that they reap. Follow them. I've ordered the boys not to touch you, haven't I. When you're thirsty, go to the containers and drink from what the boys draw.'

The God of coincidences

¹⁰She fell on her face and bowed low to the ground and said to him, 'Why have I found grace in your eyes, as you're recognizing me, and I'm a foreigner?' ¹¹Bo'az answered her, 'It's been fully told me everything that you've done for your mother-in-law after the death of your husband. You abandoned your father and your mother and the country that was your homeland and went to a people that you had not acknowledged in previous days. ¹²May Yahweh make good for your deed. May your wages be complete from Yahweh the God of Yisra'el [Israel], under whose skirts you've come to take shelter.' ¹³She said, 'May I find grace in your eyes, sir, because you've comforted me and spoken to your maidservant's heart, and I'm not one of your maidservants.'

¹⁴Bo'az said to her at the mealtime, 'Come up here and eat some of the bread and dip your bit in the vinegar.' So she sat by the side of the reapers, he passed her the roasted grain, and she ate and was full, and she had some left over. ¹⁵She got up to glean, and Bo'az ordered his boys, 'She can also glean among the sheaves, and you will not put her down. ¹⁶You can also pull some out for her from the bundles, and abandon them and she can glean. You will not reprimand her.'

¹⁷She gleaned in the fields until the evening and beat out what she'd gleaned. It came to something like a barrel of barley. ¹⁸She picked it up and came to the town, and her mother-in-law saw what she'd gleaned, and she got out and gave her what was left over from when she'd been full.

¹⁹Her mother-in-law said to her, 'Where did you glean today? Where did you work? Blessed be the man who recognized you.' She told her mother-in-law who she had worked with and said, 'The name of the man that I worked with today was Bo'az.'

How not to leave the initiative to the man

²⁰Na'omi said to her daughter-in-law, 'May he be blessed by Yahweh, who hasn't abandoned his commitment with the living and with the dead.' Na'omi said to her, 'The man is a close relative of ours. He's one of our restorers.' ²¹Ruth the Mo'abite said, 'He also said to me, "You're to attach yourself to my boys until they've finished the entire harvest that belongs to me."' ²²Na'omi said to Ruth, her daughter-in-law, 'Daughter, it will be good that you go out with his girls, and people don't come upon you in another field.' ²³So she attached herself to Bo'az's girls to glean until the finish of the barley harvest and the wheat harvest, and lived with her mother-in-law.

3 Na'omi her mother-in-law said to her, 'My daughter, shouldn't I seek a place for you to settle down that will be good for you? ²So now, Bo'az is our relative, isn't he. You've been with his girls. Here, he's winnowing the barley on the threshing floor tonight. ³Have a bath, put on your make-up, put on your best clothes and go down to the threshing floor. Don't make yourself known to the man until he's finished eating and drinking. ⁴When he lies down and you know the place where he lies down, come in and uncover his feet and lie down. He himself will tell you what you should do.' ⁵She said to her, 'Everything that you say to me, I'll do.'

⁶She went down to the threshing floor and acted in accordance with all that her mother-in-law had ordered her. ⁷Bo'az ate and drank and his heart felt good. He came to lie down at the edge of the heap. She came quietly, uncovered his feet and lay down.

The obstacle to a happy ending

⁸In the middle of the night the man gave a start and twisted round: there, a woman lying at his feet! ⁹He said, 'Who are you?' She said, 'I'm Ruth, your handmaid. You should spread your skirt over your handmaid, because you're a restorer.' ¹⁰He said, 'May you be blessed of Yahweh, daughter. You've made your last act of commitment better than your first in not following the young men, whether a poor one or a wealthy one. ¹¹So now, my daughter, don't be afraid; all that you say I will do for you, because everyone at my people's gateway acknowledges that you're a forceful woman. ¹²But now, because it's true that I'm a restorer, but there's also a restorer nearer than me, ¹³stay the night tonight, and in the morning, if he will act as restorer, good, he may act as restorer. But if he doesn't want to act as your restorer, I myself will act as your restorer, as Yahweh lives. Lie down until the morning.'

¹⁴So she lay at his feet until the morning but got up before one person could recognize his neighbour. He said, 'It shouldn't become known that the woman came to the threshing floor', ¹⁵but he said, 'Bring the shawl that you have on and hold it.' She held it and he weighed out six measures of barley and put it on her.

He went to the town, ¹⁶and she came to her mother-in-law. She said, 'How are you, my daughter?' She told her all that the man had done for her, ¹⁷and said, 'He gave me these six measures of barley, because he said "Don't come to your mother-in-law empty-handed."' ¹⁸She said, 'Stay, my daughter, until you know how the matter falls, because the man won't relax. Rather he'll finish the thing today.'

How not to get overextended in property ownership

4 Now Bo'az had gone up to the gateway and sat down there. And there, the restorer of whom Bo'az had spoken was passing. He said, 'Come over, sit down here, so-and-so.' He turned aside and sat down. ²He got ten men from the town's elders and said, 'Sit down here', and they sat down. ³He said to the restorer, 'The share in the fields that belonged to our brother, to Elimelek: Na'omi, who has come back from Mo'abite country, is disposing of it. ⁴I myself said, "I must open your ear, saying 'Acquire it in the presence of the people who are sitting here, in the presence of the elders of my people. If you're to act as restorer, restore, but (if he's not to restore) do tell me, so I may know, because there's no one to act as restorer apart from you, but I'm after you.'" He said, 'I'll act as restorer.' ⁵But Bo'az said, 'On the day you acquire the fields from Na'omi's hand and from Ruth the Mo'abite, you will have acquired the dead man's wife, to set up the dead man's name over his domain.' ⁶The restorer said, 'I can't act as restorer for myself, or I'll devastate my domain. You act as restorer for yourself regarding my position as restorer, because I cannot act as restorer.'

⁷Now this is how it was formerly in Yisra'el, in connection with acting as restorer and with transfer. To make any matter firm, a man took off his boot and gave it to his neighbour. This was the attestation process in Yisra'el. ⁸So the restorer said to Bo'az, 'Acquire it for yourself', and took off his boot. ⁹Bo'az said to the elders and the entire people, 'You're witnesses today that I've acquired from Na'omi's hand everything that belonged to Elimelek and everything that belonged to Kilyon and Mahlon. ¹⁰I've also acquired Ruth the Mo'abite, Mahlon's wife, for myself as wife, to set up the dead man's name over his domain, so the dead man's name is not cut off from among his brothers and from the gateway of his place. You're witnesses today.'

How David acquired his grandfather

¹¹The entire company that was at the gateway and the elders said, 'Witnesses! May Yahweh make the woman who is coming into your house like Rahel and like Le'ah, both of whom built up Yisra'el's household. Act capably in Ephratah, call out a name in Bet Lehem! ¹²May your household be like the household of Perets, to whom Tamar gave birth for Yehudah, through the offspring that Yahweh will give you through this girl.'

¹³So Bo'az got Ruth and she became his wife. He had sex with her and Yahweh enabled her to get pregnant. She gave birth to a son, ¹⁴and the

women said to Naʽomi, 'Yahweh be blessed, who hasn't held back a restorer for you today. May his name be called out in Yisraʽel! ¹⁵For you he will be one who gives life back and provides for your old age, because your daughter-in-law who loves you has borne him, she who has been better for you than seven sons.'

¹⁶Naʽomi got the child and put him in her arms and became a nurse for him. ¹⁷The neighbours named him, saying 'A son has been born to Naʽomi', and named him Obed. He was father of Yishay [Jesse], father of David.

¹⁸This is the family history of Perets. Perets fathered Hetsron. ¹⁹Hetsron fathered Ram. Ram fathered Amminadab. ²⁰Amminadab fathered Nahshon. Nahshon fathered Salmah. ²¹Salmon fathered Boʽaz. Boʽaz fathered Obed. ²²Obed fathered Yishay. Yishay fathered David.

1 Samuel

In the English Bible, 1 Samuel follows on from Ruth. That story ends by telling us about a line of people descended from Ruth and Boaz, the last of whom is David, and 1 Samuel is another take on David's backstory – on the process that led to David's becoming king. To complement that point, in the Hebrew Bible 1 Samuel directly follows Judges. Judges ends with a rueful comment on how people have been doing what was all right in their own eyes because there was no king in Israel. The implication is that Israel needed someone to exercise ongoing authority and get people to take Yahweh seriously. A king might be able to do so.

It's the first of two books named after Samuel. He did not write them; he dies halfway through 1 Samuel. But he is a huge figure in 1 Samuel, one of the three big men in the book. The account of his birth is a powerful story of a woman's boldness in coming before God with the pain in her life and in challenging God to do something about it, and of this woman's courage in then giving up the son who is the answer to her prayers, so that he can be Yahweh's servant.

Samuel is the last of the 'judges', the leaders of Israel who dominate the book of Judges, people who act effectively and with great authority though without the official position of someone like a king. Samuel is also the first great prophet. It's no coincidence that Yahweh produces him at the same time as kings emerge in Israel. One of the chief responsibilities of a prophet is to be the king's conscience, to challenge him about what he ought to be doing – and more often about what he ought not to be doing. Samuel is responsible for designating and anointing Saul, the second of the three huge figures, and then for pronouncing Yahweh's decommissioning of him. He is then responsible for designating and anointing David. He even reappears at the end of the book, coming back from the dead to meet with Saul on the eve of Saul's last battle.

The background to Samuel's anointing of Saul is the people's desire to have a king like other peoples. This desire fits with that comment at the end of Judges, yet the people are going back on a distinctive aspect of their life, the principle that Yahweh is their king, though humanly speaking it's hard to imagine how they could have gone on as a people without some form of central government to replace the decentralized system whereby no organization holds the clans together. Although asking for a king implies rejecting Yahweh as king, Yahweh accedes to their request and nominates the king. Chapters 8—12 of the book expound all sides of Samuel's and Yahweh's attitude to kingship, which one may infer applies to other forms of leadership. There are advantages and disadvantages to having a leader. It costs people, in varying ways.

Yahweh's mixed feelings about Israel having kings is the background to Saul's having successes but then experiencing Yahweh's rejection for failures that may not seem very culpable. He is a tragic figure, a man enlisted to do a job that Yahweh didn't really want done and that he himself didn't really want, but who becomes attached to the job even as he is making mistakes that lead to his rejection. Eventually Yahweh sends a 'bad spirit' to Saul – not an evil spirit (the Old Testament doesn't talk about those) but a depressed and angry spirit, a bad temper.

The third huge figure is David, who is designated by Yahweh as Saul's successor and who shows himself to be someone who always trusts in Yahweh and is a courageous fighter, a faithful subject, a magnetic personality, an energetic campaigner, a ruthless commander, a shrewd compromiser and a magnanimous victor. Although anointed by Samuel in Yahweh's name, before becoming king he has to wait until Yahweh has finished with Saul; he is also a man who is prepared to wait rather than trying to force things. Eventually Saul and his son Jonathan (David's best friend) meet their death in battle, which opens up the future for David.

The pain of childlessness

1 There was a man from Twin Heights in Tsophim, from the highland of Ephrayim, whose name was Elqanah ben Yeroham, son of Elihu son of Tohu son of Tsuph, an Ephrayimite. ²He had two wives; the name of one was Hannah, the name of the second was Peninnah. Peninnah had children, but Hannah had no children.

³That man used to go up from his town from year to year to bow low and to sacrifice for Yahweh of Armies at Shiloh. The two sons of Eli, Hophni and Pinhas, were priests for Yahweh there.

⁴A day came when Elqanah sacrificed, and he would give portions to his wife Peninnah and to all her sons and her daughters. ⁵To Hannah he would give a portion for two people because he loved Hannah, whereas Yahweh had closed up her womb, ⁶and her rival would provoke her greatly to make her fret because Yahweh had closed up her womb. ⁷So he would do, year after year. As often as she went up to Yahweh's house, she would provoke her in this way, and she would cry and not eat. ⁸Elqanah, her husband, said to her, 'Hannah, why do you cry, why don't you eat, why does your heart feel bad? Aren't I better for you than ten sons?'

⁹Hannah got up after the eating in Shiloh and after the drinking. Eli the priest was sitting on the seat by the doorpost of Yahweh's palace. ¹⁰She was bitter in spirit but she made a plea to Yahweh and cried and cried, ¹¹and she made a pledge. She said, 'Yahweh of Armies, if you actually look at your handmaid's humbling and you're mindful of me, and you don't put your handmaid out of mind but give your handmaid a male offspring, I'll give him to Yahweh all the days of his life. No razor will go up on his head.'

A face transformed

¹²Because she was doing much pleading before Yahweh, and Eli was watching her mouth, ¹³and Hannah was speaking in her heart (only her lips were quivering, but her voice did not make itself heard), Eli thought she was drunk. ¹⁴Eli said to her, 'How long will you behave like a drunk? Put your wine away from you.' ¹⁵Hannah answered, 'No, sir, I'm a tough-spirited woman and I haven't drunk wine or liquor. I've poured myself out before Yahweh. ¹⁶Don't make your handmaid into a scoundrelous woman, because it was out of the dimensions of my tetchiness and my provocation that I've spoken until now.' ¹⁷Eli answered, 'Go, things will be well. The God of Yisra'el: he will give the thing that you've asked of him.' ¹⁸She said, 'May your maidservant find grace in your eyes.'

The woman went on her way and ate, and her face was no longer [the same]. ¹⁹They started early in the morning, bowed low before Yahweh, and went back and came to their home in The Height. Elqanah had sex with his wife Hannah and Yahweh was mindful of her, ²⁰and at the end of the year Hannah had got pregnant. She gave birth to a son and named him Shemu'el [Samuel], because 'I asked [sha'al] for him from Yahweh.'

²¹The man, Elqanah, went up with his entire household to offer Yahweh the yearly sacrifice and his pledge, ²²but Hannah didn't go up, because (she said to her husband) 'When the boy is weaned I'll bring him. We'll see Yahweh's face, and he'll live there permanently.' ²³Elqanah her husband said to her, 'Do what's good in your eyes; stay till you've weaned him. Only, may Yahweh implement his word.' So the woman stayed and nursed her son until she'd weaned him. ²⁴She took him up with her when she had weaned him, with a three-year-old bull, a barrel of flour and a skin of wine, and brought him to Yahweh's house at Shiloh. He was a boy. ²⁵They slaughtered the bull and brought the boy to Eli.

On giving up your son

²⁶She said, 'Pardon me, sir, as surely as you live, sir, I'm the woman who stood with you here to make my plea to Yahweh. ²⁷It was for this boy that I made my plea, and Yahweh gave me what I asked of him. ²⁸I myself am also giving him to Yahweh; for all the days that he lives he's given to Yahweh.' He bowed low there to Yahweh,

2 and Hannah made her plea:

My heart has exulted in Yahweh,
  my horn has lifted high through Yahweh.

My mouth has opened wide at my enemies,
  because I have rejoiced in your deliverance.
²There's no sacred one like Yahweh,
  because there's no one apart from you,
  there's no crag like our God.
³Don't do much speaking of lofty, lofty speech,
  nor should outspoken speech come out of
    your mouth.
Because Yahweh is a God who knows;
  by him actions are weighed.
⁴The bows of strong men are broken,
  but people who were falling have belted on
    forcefulness.
⁵People who were full have hired themselves
    out for bread,
  but the hungry left off from being hungry.
While the infertile woman has given birth to
    seven,
  the woman with many children is withered.
⁶Yahweh is one who puts to death and brings
    to life,
  sends down to She'ol and brings up.
⁷Yahweh is one who makes poor and makes
    wealthy,
  puts down, also lifts up.
⁸He is one who raises the poor from the dirt,
  lifts up the needy from the dump,
To sit with important people;
  he gives them a seat of splendour as their
    domain.
Because earth's pillars belong to Yahweh;
  he set the world upon them.
⁹He keeps the feet of the people who are loyal
    to him,
  but the faithless go silent into the darkness.
Because it's not by energy that a person
    prevails;
¹⁰Yahweh – people who argue with him
    shatter.
The One on High thunders in the heavens;
  Yahweh judges the ends of the earth.
He gives vigour to his king,
  lifts up the horn of his anointed one.

Ministers who indulge themselves

¹¹Elqanah went home to The Height, while the boy was ministering to Yahweh in the presence of Eli the priest. ¹²Now Eli's sons were scoundrels; they didn't acknowledge Yahweh. ¹³The priests' rule with the people was: when each person was offering a sacrifice, the priest's boy would come while the meat was boiling, with a three-pronged fork in his hand. ¹⁴He would thrust it into the pan or the kettle or the cauldron or the pot; all that the fork brought up, the priest would take with it. In this way they would act with all Yisra'el [Israel] who came there to Shiloh. ¹⁵Further, before they turned the fat into smoke, the priest's boy would come and say to the individual making the sacrifice, 'Give over some meat for roasting for the priest; he won't take boiled meat from you, only raw.' ¹⁶Should the individual say to him, 'They should actually turn the fat into smoke now, then take for yourself whatever your appetite longs for', he would say 'No, but you're to give it over now, or I'm taking it by force.'
¹⁷The boys' wrongdoing in Yahweh's presence was very great, because the men disdained Yahweh's offering.
¹⁸So Shemu'el was ministering in the presence of Yahweh, a boy wrapped round in a linen chasuble. ¹⁹His mother would make a little coat for him and bring it up for him from year to year when she went up with her husband to offer the yearly sacrifice. ²⁰Eli would bless Elqanah and his wife and say, 'May Yahweh give you offspring from this woman in place of the one she asked for from Yahweh', and they would go to their place. ²¹Because Yahweh attended to Hannah, she got pregnant and she gave birth to three sons and two daughters, but the boy Shemu'el grew up with Yahweh.

Why do you kick at my sacrifices?

²²When Eli was very old, he heard of all that his sons were doing to all Yisra'el and how they were sleeping with the women who fulfilled duties at the entrance of the appointment tent. ²³He said to them, 'Why do you do such actions as these that I am hearing of, bad actions of yours, from all these people? ²⁴Don't, my sons, because the report is not good that I'm hearing Yahweh's people passing on. ²⁵If an individual does wrong against an individual, God may plead for him, but if an individual does wrong against Yahweh, who will make a plea for him?' But they wouldn't listen to their father's voice because Yahweh wanted to put them to death. ²⁶But the boy Shemu'el was continuing

to grow and seem good both with Yahweh and with people.

²⁷A supernatural man came to Eli and said to him: 'Yahweh has said this: "Did I clearly reveal myself to your father's household when they were in Misrayim [Egypt], belonging to Par'oh's [Pharaoh's] household? ²⁸I chose him out of all Yisra'el's clans as a priest for me, to go up on my altar, to burn incense, to carry a chasuble before me, and I gave your father's household all the Yisra'elites' gift offerings. ²⁹Why do you kick at my sacrifice and at my offering which I ordered, at my abode? You've honoured your sons more than me in fattening yourselves on the first of every offering of Yisra'el as my people.

A trustworthy priest

³⁰Therefore (a declaration of Yahweh the God of Yisra'el), I did say that your household and your father's household would go about before me permanently, but now (Yahweh's declaration), far be it from me, because the people who honour me I honour, but the people who despise me will become slight. ³¹Here, a time is coming when I shall cut off your arm and the arm of your father's household, so that there will be no one as an elder in your household. ³²You will look at the pressure that comes on [my] abode, despite all the good that is done to Yisra'el, and there will be no one as an elder in your household for the entire time. ³³While I shall not cut off every individual of yours from my altar, so as to consume your eyes and make your spirit grieve, the entire abundance of your household: people will die. ³⁴This will be the sign for you that will come on your two sons, on Hophi and Pinhas: the two of them will die on one day.

³⁵I shall set up for myself a trustworthy priest. He will act in accordance with what is in my mind and in my spirit. I shall build a trustworthy household for him and he will go about before my anointed one for all time. ³⁶Anyone who is left of your household will come to bow low to him for a payment in silver and a loaf of bread. He will say, 'Assign me to one of the priestly duties so I can eat a bit of bread.'"

A summons, not a call

3 The boy, Shemu'el, was ministering to Yahweh in the presence of Eli. Yahweh's word was rare at that time; there was no vision spreading about. ²On a day when Eli was lying

Yisra'el at the time of Shemu'el (Samuel)

down in his place (his eyes had started to fail; he couldn't see) ³but God's lamp had not yet gone out, and Shemu'el was lying down in Yahweh's palace where God's chest was, ⁴Yahweh called to Shemu'el.

He said, 'I'm here', ⁵and ran to Eli and said, 'I'm here, because you called to me.' He said, 'I didn't call. Go back, lie down.' He went and lay down. ⁶Yahweh called yet again, 'Shemu'el', and Shemu'el got up and went to Eli and said, 'I'm here, because you called to me.' He said, 'I didn't call, son, go back, lie down.' ⁷Now Shemu'el hadn't yet acknowledged Yahweh; Yahweh's word hadn't yet revealed itself to him.

⁸Yahweh again called Shemu'el, a third time, and he got up, went to Eli and said, 'I'm here, because you called to me.' Eli perceived that Yahweh was calling to the boy. ⁹Eli said to Shemu'el, 'Go, lie down, and if he calls to you, you're to say, "Speak, Yahweh, because your servant is listening."' So Shemu'el went and lay down in his place.

¹⁰Yahweh came and took his stand and called as at the other times, 'Shemu'el, Shemu'el'. Shemu'el said, 'Speak, because your servant is listening.'

The message no one would want to give

¹¹Yahweh said to Shemu'el, 'Here, I'm going to do a thing in Yisra'el such that everyone who hears it – both his ears will tingle. ¹²That day I shall implement regarding Eli everything I spoke concerning his household, beginning and finishing it. ¹³I told him that I'm going to exercise authority over his household permanently for the waywardness that he knew about, that his sons were slighting [me] for themselves and he didn't stop them. ¹⁴Therefore I swear concerning Eli's household: if the waywardness of Eli's household finds expiation by sacrifice or by offering, permanently . . .'

¹⁵Shemu'el lay down until the morning, then opened the doors of Yahweh's house. But Shemu'el was afraid of telling Eli the vision. ¹⁶Eli called Shemu'el: 'Shemu'el, my son'. He said, 'I'm here.' ¹⁷He said, 'What was the thing that he spoke to you? Don't hide any of it from me, please. May God do so to you, and may he do more, if you hide from me anything of all that he said to you.' ¹⁸Shemu'el told him all the things and didn't hide it from him. He said, 'He is Yahweh. He will do what is good in his eyes.'

¹⁹Shemu'el grew up, and as Yahweh was with him, he didn't allow any of his words to fall to the ground. ²⁰All Yisra'el from Dan as far as Be'er Sheba acknowledged that Shemu'el was trustworthy as a prophet belonging to Yahweh. ²¹Yahweh again appeared at Shiloh, in that Yahweh revealed himself to Shemu'el at Shiloh with Yahweh's word,

4 and Shemu'el's word came to all Yisra'el.

Get the chest

¹ᵇYisra'el went out to meet the Pelishtites [Philistines] in battle, and camped at Help Stone [Eben Ha'ezer], while the Pelishtites camped at Apheq. ²The Pelishtites lined up to meet Yisra'el and the battle spread, and Yisra'el took a beating before the Pelishtites. They struck down some 4,000 men in their line in the fields.

³The company came to the camp and Yisra'el's elders said, 'Why did Yahweh defeat us today before the Pelishtites? Let's get Yahweh's pact chest from Shiloh for ourselves, so he will come among us and deliver us from our enemies' fist.' ⁴So the company sent to Shiloh and carried from there the pact chest of Yahweh of Armies, who sits above the sphinxes. Eli's two sons, Hophni and Pinhas, were with God's pact chest there.

⁵When Yahweh's pact chest came into the camp, all Yisra'el gave a great shout, and the earth resounded. ⁶The Pelishtites heard the sound of the shout and said, 'What's this sound of a great shout in the Hebrews' camp?' They came to know that Yahweh's chest had come into the camp.

⁷The Pelishtites were afraid, because they said, 'A god has come into the camp', and they said, 'Alas for us! A thing like this has not happened to us in previous days. ⁸Alas for us! Who will rescue us from the hand of these august gods? These are the gods that struck down the Misrayimites in total defeat in the wilderness. ⁹Summon up your strength, be men, Pelishtites, so you don't serve the Hebrews as they served you. Be men! Do battle!'

¹⁰So the Pelishtites did battle and Yisra'el took a beating. They fled, each one to his tents. The rout was very great, and from Yisra'el 30,000

men on foot fell, ¹¹while God's chest was taken, and Eli's two sons, Hophni and Pinhas, died.

The splendour is gone

¹²A Binyaminite [Benjaminite] man ran from the line and came to Shiloh that day, with his uniform torn and earth on his head. ¹³He came, and there, Eli was sitting on a seat by the road, watching, because his heart was trembling for God's chest. When the man came to tell of it in the town, the entire town cried out. ¹⁴Eli heard the sound of the cry and said, 'What's this sound of an uproar?' The man hurried and came, and told Eli.

¹⁵Eli was a man of ninety-eight years. His eyes were set and he couldn't see. ¹⁶The man said to Eli, 'I'm the one coming from the line. I myself fled from the line today.' He said, 'What was the thing that happened, son?' ¹⁷The man bringing the news replied, 'Yisra'el fled before the Pelishtites. It was both a great disaster to the company, and also your two sons, Hophni and Pinhas, are dead, and God's chest was taken.' ¹⁸When he made mention of God's chest, he fell backwards from on his seat by the side of the gateway. His neck broke and he died, because the man was old and heavy. He had exercised authority for Yisra'el for forty years.

¹⁹His daughter-in-law, Pinhas's wife, was pregnant, soon to give birth. She heard the report about God's chest being taken and her father-in-law and her husband being dead, and she bent down and gave birth, because her labour pains came over her. ²⁰At the time of her dying, the women standing by her spoke: 'Don't be afraid, because you've given birth to a son.' She didn't answer. She didn't give her mind to it.

²¹She called the boy Ikabod ['Where Is the Splendour?'], saying 'The splendour has gone into exile from Yisra'el', in connection with God's chest being taken, and with her father-in-law and with her husband. ²²She said, 'The splendour has gone into exile from Yisra'el, because God's chest has been taken.'

You can't mess with the chest

5 When the Pelishtites took God's chest, they brought it from Help Stone to Ashdod. ²The Pelishtites took God's chest and brought it to Dagon's house and set it beside Dagon. ³The Ashdodites started early next day and there was Dagon, fallen on his face on the ground before Yahweh's chest. So they took Dagon and put him back in his place.

⁴They started early in the morning next day and there was Dagon, fallen on his face on the ground before Yahweh's chest, with Dagon's head and both the palms of his hands cut off, on the threshold. Only [the body of] Dagon remained to him. ⁵That's why Dagon's priests and all the people who come to Dagon's house don't tread on Dagon's threshold in Ashdod, until this day.

⁶Yahweh's hand was heavy on the Ashdodites. He desolated them and struck them down with haemorrhoids, Ashdod and its territories. ⁷The Ashdodites saw that it was so, and said, 'The chest of Yisra'el's God is not to stay with us, because his hand has been tough with us and with Dagon our god.' ⁸They sent and gathered all the Pelishtites' lords to them and said, 'What shall we do with the chest of Yisra'el's God?' They said, 'The chest of Yisra'el's God should get itself round to Gat.' So they took the chest of Yisra'el's God round. ⁹After they had taken it round, Yahweh's hand came against the town with a great turmoil. He struck the town's people from young to old, and haemorrhoids broke out on them.

¹⁰So they sent God's chest off to Eqron. But when God's chest came to Eqron, the Eqronites cried out, 'They've brought the chest of Yisra'el's God round to me to put me and my people to death.' ¹¹So they sent off and gathered all the Pelishtites' lords and said, 'Send the chest of Yisra'el's God off so it goes back to its place. It will not put me and my people to death', because there was a deathly turmoil in the entire town. God's hand was very heavy there. ¹²The men who didn't die were struck down by the haemorrhoids. The town's cry for help went up to the heavens.

The need for reparation

6 Yahweh's chest was in the Pelishtites' country for seven months. ²The Pelishtites called for the priests and for the diviners: 'What shall we do about Yahweh's chest? Let us know what we're to send it off with to its place.' ³They said, 'If you're going to send off the chest of Yisra'el's God, don't send if off empty-handed. Rather, you're definitely to send a reparation back to him. Then you'll find healing. He'll get himself acknowledged by you; why should his hand not depart from you?'

⁴They said, 'What's the reparation that we should send back to him?' They said, 'Five gold haemorrhoids and five gold rats, the number of the Pelishtites' lords, because the same epidemic came to all of them, and to your lords. ⁵You're to make models of your haemorrhoids and models of your rats that have been devastating the country, and give honour to the God of Yisra'el. Maybe he will ease his hand from upon you and from upon your gods and from upon your country. ⁶Why would you harden your mind as Misrayim and Par'oh hardened their mind? When he had acted abusively to them, they sent them off and they went, didn't they.

⁷So now, get and make ready a new cart and two nursing cows on which no yoke has come. Harness the cows to the cart but take their young ones back home, from following them. ⁸Get Yahweh's chest and put it on the cart. The gold articles that you're sending back to him as a reparation you're to put in a receptacle by its side, and send it off so it goes, ⁹and you're to look. If it goes up the road to his border, to Bet Shemesh, he's the one who did this huge bad thing to you. If not, we'll know that it was not his hand touched us. It was a chance that happened to us.'

¹⁰The people did so. They got two nursing cows, harnessed them to a cart, shut up their young ones at home, ¹¹and put Yahweh's chest on the cart, with the receptacle and the gold rats and the models of their haemorrhoids.

Too hot to handle

¹²The cows went straight by the road, on the Bet Shemesh road. By a causeway they went steadily and lowed and didn't depart right or left, with the Pelishtites' lords following them as far as the Bet Shemesh border.

¹³Bet Shemesh people were reaping the wheat harvest in the vale. They lifted up their eyes and saw the chest, and rejoiced to see it. ¹⁴The cart came to the fields of Yehoshua of Bet-shemesh and stood there. There was a big stone there. They split the wood of the cart and offered up the cows as a burnt offering for Yahweh. ¹⁵The Levites took down Yahweh's chest and the receptacle that was with it, in which were the gold articles, and put them on the big stone. The people of Bet-shemesh offered up whole offerings and offered sacrifices that day for Yahweh. ¹⁶The Pelishtites' five lords looked, and went back to Eqron that day.

¹⁷These are the gold haemorrhoids that the Pelishtites gave back as a reparation to Yahweh: one for Ashdod, one for Azzah [Gaza], one for Ashqelon, one for Gat, one for Eqron. ¹⁸The gold rats: the number of all the Pelishtites' towns belonging to the Pelishtites' five lords, both fortified town and country hamlet, as far as the big stone on which they set down Yahweh's chest, until this day in the fields of Yehoshua of Bet-shemesh.

¹⁹But he struck down the people of Bet-shemesh because they looked in Yahweh's chest. He struck down seventy individuals (50,000 individuals) among the people. The people took up grieving because Yahweh had struck the people down with a heavy blow.

²⁰The people of Bet-shemesh said, 'Who can stand before Yahweh, this sacred God? To whom might he go up from us?' ²¹So they sent envoys to the people living in Ye'arim Township to say, 'The Pelishtites have sent Yahweh's chest back. Come down, take it up to you.'

7 The people of Ye'arim Township came and took Yahweh's chest up and brought it into the house of Abinadab, on the hill. They made his son El'azar sacred to keep Yahweh's chest.

Yahweh helped us as far as this

²From the day the chest lived at Ye'arim Township time went on; twenty years passed. The entire household of Yisra'el grieved after Yahweh, ³and Shemu'el said to the entire household of Yisra'el, 'If with your entire heart you're coming back to Yahweh, remove the foreign gods and the Ashtars from among you. Direct your heart firmly towards Yahweh and serve him alone, and he will rescue you from

the hand of the Pelishtites.' ⁴So the Yisra'elites removed the Masters and the Ashtars and served Yahweh alone.

⁵Shemu'el said, 'Gather all Yisra'el at The Watchtower and I'll plead with Yahweh on your behalf.' ⁶They gathered at The Watchtower and drew water and poured it out before Yahweh. They fasted that day and said there, 'We have done wrong against Yahweh.' So Shemu'el exercised authority for the Yisra'elites at The Watchtower.

⁷The Pelishtites heard that the Yisra'elites had gathered at The Watchtower and the Pelishtites' lords went up against Yisra'el. The Yisra'elites heard and were afraid of the Pelishtites. ⁸So the Yisra'elites said to Shemu'el, 'Don't be deaf to us and not cry out to Yahweh our God so he may deliver us from the hand of the Pelishtites.' ⁹So Shemu'el got a suckling lamb and offered it up as a whole burnt offering for Yahweh. Shemu'el cried out to Yahweh on behalf of Yisra'el, and Yahweh answered him. ¹⁰As Shemu'el was offering up the burnt offering, the Pelishtites were coming up for battle against Yisra'el, but Yahweh thundered with a loud voice that day against the Pelishtites and threw them into a turmoil, and they took a beating before Yisra'el. ¹¹The Yisra'elites went out from The Watchtower, pursued the Pelishtites and struck them down as far as below Bet Kar.

¹²Shemu'el got a stone and put it between The Watchtower and The Tooth, and named it 'Help Stone'. He said, 'As far as this Yahweh helped us.' ¹³The Pelishtites bowed down and didn't any more come within Yisra'el's border again. Yahweh's hand was against the Pelishtites all the days of Shemu'el. ¹⁴The towns that the Pelishtites had taken from Yisra'el came back to Yisra'el, from Eqron as far as Gat. Yisra'el rescued their border from the hand of the Pelishtites, and there was peace between Yisra'el and the Amorites.

Appoint us a king

¹⁵Shemu'el exercised authority for Yisra'el all the days of his life. ¹⁶He went year by year and travelled round to Bet-el, Gilgal and The Watchtower and exercised authority for Yisra'el at all these sites; ¹⁷then his return to The Height, because his home was there. He exercised authority for Yisra'el there and built an altar for Yahweh there.

8 When Shemu'el was old, he made his sons into people who exercised authority for Yisra'el. ²The name of his firstborn son was Yo'el and the name of his second Abiyyah; they were authorities in Be'er Sheba. ³But his sons didn't walk in his ways. They turned after profit and accepted bribes, and overturned the exercise of authority.

⁴So all Yisra'el's elders gathered and came to Shemu'el at The Height, ⁵and said to him, 'Here, you've got old and your sons haven't walked in your ways. Now appoint us a king to exercise authority for us like all the nations.' ⁶The thing was bad in Shemu'el's eyes, when they said 'Give us a king to exercise authority for us', and Shemu'el made a plea to Yahweh.

⁷Yahweh said to Shemu'el, 'Listen to the people's voice in everything that they say to you, because it's not you they've rejected, because it's me they've rejected from being king over them. ⁸In accordance with all the deeds they've done from the day I brought them up from Misrayim and until this day, they've abandoned me and served other gods, so they're doing also to you. ⁹So now listen to their voice. Only testify against them solemnly and tell them about the authority of the king who will reign over them.'

What a king will be like

¹⁰Shemu'el spoke all Yahweh's words to the people who were asking for a king from him. ¹¹He said, 'This will be the authority of the king who will reign over you. Your sons he'll take and make into his chariotry and into his cavalry for himself and they'll run before his chariotry, ¹²making them divisional officers and unit officers for himself, and for ploughing his fields and reaping his harvest and making his battle equipment and his chariot equipment. ¹³Your daughters he'll take as perfumers, cooks and bakers. ¹⁴Your fields, your vineyards and your olive groves, the best, he'll take and give to his servants. ¹⁵Of your seed and your vineyards he'll take a tenth and give to his courtiers and to his servants. ¹⁶Your servants and your maidservants, your best young men and your donkeys, he'll take and make into his

workforce. ¹⁷Of your flock he'll take a tenth and you yourselves will become servants to him. ¹⁸You will cry out on that day on account of your king whom you've chosen for yourselves, but Yahweh will not answer you on that day.'

¹⁹The people refused to listen to Shemu'el's voice and said, 'No! Rather, there is to be a king over us, ²⁰so we can become like all the nations. Our king will exercise authority, and go out before us and fight our battles.' ²¹Shemu'el listened to all the people's words and spoke them in Yahweh's ears. ²²Yahweh said to Shemu'el, 'Listen to their voice. Make a king for them.' Shemu'el said to the Yisra'elites, 'Go, each one, to his town.'

How Sha'ul lost some donkeys

9 There was a man from Binyamin; his name was Qish ben Abi'el, son of Tseror son of Bekorat son of Aphiah, a Binyaminite – a forceful man. ²He had a son; his name was Sha'ul [Saul], young and good-looking. There was no one better-looking among the Yisra'elites than him. From his shoulders up, he was loftier than all the people.

³Donkeys belonging to Qish, Sha'ul's father, got lost, and Qish said to Sha'ul his son, 'Please take one of the boys with you, and set off and go look for the donkeys.' ⁴They passed through the highland of Ephraim and passed through the region of Shalishah, but they didn't find them. They passed through the region of Sha'alim, but they were not there. They passed through the region of Binyamin and didn't find them. ⁵When they came to the region of Tsuph, Sha'ul said to his boy who was with him, 'Come on, let's go back, so my father doesn't leave off from the donkeys and get anxious about us.'

⁶He said to him, 'Here, please, there's a supernatural man in this town. The man is honoured. Everything that he speaks does come about. Let's go there now. Maybe he'll tell us about our journey that we've gone on.' ⁷Sha'ul said to his boy, 'But here, we can go, but what are we to bring the man, because the bread is exhausted from our bags and there's no present to bring to the supernatural man. What is there with us?' ⁸The boy again answered Sha'ul, 'Here, there's a quarter-sheqel of silver present in my hand. I'll give it to the supernatural man so he can tell us about our journey.' (⁹Formerly in Yisra'el, an individual said this when he was going to enquire of God: 'Come on, let's go to the seer', because the prophet today was formerly called the seer.)

An extraordinary coincidence

¹⁰So Sha'ul said to his boy, 'Your words are good. Come on, let's go.' So they went to the town where the supernatural man was. ¹¹When they were going up the ascent to the town and they found girls going out to draw water, they said to them, 'Is the seer here?' ¹²They answered them, 'He is, there, before you. Hurry now, because today he's come to the town because the people have a sacrifice at the shrine today. ¹³As you come into the town, there you'll find him before he goes up to the shrine to eat, because the people won't eat until he comes, because he has to say the blessing for the sacrifice. After that, the people who've been invited will eat. So now, go up, because this very day you'll find him.' ¹⁴So they went up to the town. As they were coming into the middle of the town – there was Shemu'el, going out to meet them, going up to the shrine.

¹⁵Now Yahweh had had a word in Shemu'el's ear the day before Sha'ul came: ¹⁶'This very time tomorrow I shall send you a man from the region of Binyamin, and you're to anoint him as ruler over my people Yisra'el. He will deliver my people from the hand of the Pelishtites, because I've seen my people, because their cry has come to me.' ¹⁷When Shemu'el saw Sha'ul, Yahweh himself avowed to him, 'Here is the man of whom I said to you, "This is the man who will put some restraint on my people."' ¹⁸Sha'ul went up to Shemu'el in the middle of the gateway and said, 'Please tell me where the seer's house is.'

An unexpected banquet

¹⁹Shemu'el answered Sha'ul, 'I'm the seer. Go up before me to the shrine and you can eat with me today. I'll send you off in the morning, but everything that's on your mind I'll tell you. ²⁰As for your donkeys that got lost three days ago: don't set your mind on them, because

they've been found. And who is the object of all Yisra'el's desire? You and your entire ancestral household.' ²¹Sha'ul answered, 'I'm a Binyaminite, aren't I, from the smallest of Yisra'el's clans, and my kin-group is the littlest of all the kin-groups in the clans of Binyamin. Why have you spoken to me of such a thing?' ²²Shemu'el took Sha'ul and his boy, brought them into the hall and gave them a place at the head of the people who had been invited; they were some thirty individuals. ²³Shemu'el said to the cook, 'Give me the portion that I gave you, about which I said to you, "Put it by you."' ²⁴The cook lifted up the thigh and what was on it and put it before Sha'ul.

He said, 'There is what has remained, put before you. Eat, because it was kept for you for the set time when I said "I am inviting the people."' So Sha'ul ate with Shemu'el that day, ²⁵then they came down from the shrine to the town, and he spoke with Sha'ul on the roof.

How Sha'ul found more than he bargained for

²⁶They started early, and at break of day Shemu'el called to Sha'ul on the roof: 'Get up, and I'll send you off.' Sha'ul got up, and the two of them, he and Shemu'el, went outside. ²⁷As they were going down to the edge of the town Shemu'el said to Sha'ul, 'Say to the boy that he's to pass on before us' (and he passed on) 'but you stand here this very moment and I shall let you hear God's word.'

10 Shemu'el got a flask of oil and poured it on his head and kissed him, and said, 'Yahweh anoints you as ruler over his domain, does he not. ²When you go from being with me today, you'll find two men by Rahel's grave within the border of Binyamin at Tseltsah. They'll say to you, "The donkeys that you went to look for have been found. Here, your father's given up on the thing about the donkeys and got anxious about you, saying 'What shall I do about my son?'" ³You're to go on from there, and further on you'll come as far as Tabor Oak. Three men will find you there, coming up to God to Bet-el, one carrying three kid goats, one carrying three loaves of bread and one carrying a skin of wine.

⁴They'll ask you if things are well with you, and they'll give you two loaves of bread. You're to accept them from their hand.

⁵After this you're to come to God's Hill, where the Pelishtites' outpost is. When you come into the town there, you'll come upon a group of prophets going down from the shrine, with mandolin, tambourine, pipe and guitar before them. They'll be prophesying. ⁶Yahweh's spirit will thrust itself on to you and you'll prophesy with them. You'll turn into another person. ⁷When these signs come about for you, do for yourself what your hand finds, because God will be with you.

Is Sha'ul a prophet, too?

⁸You're to go down before me to Gilgal. There; I'm going to come down to you to offer up burnt offerings and to make well-being sacrifices. You're to wait seven days until I come to you and make known to you what you're to do.' ⁹As he turned his face to go from being with Shemu'el, God gave him another mind.

All these signs came about that day. ¹⁰They came there, to the hill, and here – a group of prophets coming to meet him. God's spirit thrust itself on to him and he prophesied among them. ¹¹Everyone who knew him in previous days looked – and here, he was prophesying with prophets. The people said, one to his neighbour, 'What's this that's happened to ben Qish? Is Sha'ul among the prophets, too?' ¹²One person from there answered, 'And who is their father?' That's why it became an aphorism, 'Is Sha'ul among the prophets, too?' ¹³He finished prophesying and came to the shrine.

¹⁴Sha'ul's uncle said to him and to his boy, 'Where did you go?' He said, 'To look for the donkeys. We saw that they weren't there, and we came to Shemu'el.' ¹⁵Sha'ul's uncle said, 'Please tell me what Shemu'el said to you.' ¹⁶Sha'ul said to his uncle, 'He did tell us that the donkeys had been found.' As for the matter of the kingship, he didn't tell him what Shemu'el said.

How not to evade being enlisted

¹⁷Shemu'el called out the people to Yahweh at The Watchtower. ¹⁸He said to the Yisra'elites,

'Yahweh the God of Yisra'el has said this: "I am the one who brought Yisra'el up from Misrayim. I rescued you from the hand of Misrayim and from the hand of all the kingdoms that afflicted you", [19]but today you people have rejected your God who was a deliverer for you from all your bad experiences and your pressures. You said to him, "No, rather you're to set a king over us." So now, take your stand before Yahweh by your clans and by your families.'

[20]Shemu'el presented all the Yisra'elite clans, and the clan of Binyamin was taken. [21]He presented the clan of Binyamin by its kin-groups and the kin-group of the Matrites arose, and Sha'ul ben Qish was taken. They looked for him but he couldn't be found, [22]so they asked of Yahweh again, 'Has anyone else come here?' Yahweh said, 'There, he's hiding with the things.' [23]They ran and got him from there and he took his stand among the people. He was loftier than all the people, from his shoulders up. [24]Shemu'el said to all the people, 'Have you seen the one that Yahweh has chosen, that there's no one like him among all the people?' All the people shouted and said, 'Long live the king.'

[25]Shemu'el spoke to the people about the rule for the kingship, wrote it in a document and set it down before Yahweh. Then Shemu'el sent all the people off, each to his house. [26]Sha'ul also went to his house at Gib'ah, and with him went the force whose heart God had touched. [27]When scoundrels said, 'How can this man deliver us?', and despised him and didn't bring him an offering, he was like someone deaf.

Anger as a fruit of the Spirit

11 Nahash the Ammonite went up and camped against Yabesh-in-Gil'ad. All the men of Yabesh said to Nahash, 'Solemnize a pact to us and we'll serve you.' [2]Nahash the Ammonite said to them, 'On this basis I'll solemnize one to you, on the basis of gouging out the right eye of every one of you. I'll make it a reviling to all Yisra'el.' [3]The elders of Yabesh said to him, 'Let us go for seven days and we'll send envoys through all Yisra'el's border. If there's no one who'll be a deliverer for us, we'll come out to you.'

[4]The envoys came to Gib'ah-of-Sha'ul and spoke the words in the people's ears, and the entire people lifted up their voice and wailed. [5]And there, Sha'ul was coming in behind the herd from the fields. Sha'ul said, 'What's happened to the people, that they're wailing?' They told him the words of the men from Yabesh.

[6]God's spirit thrust itself on to Sha'ul when he heard these words, and his anger raged right up. [7]He got a pair from the herd and cut them up and sent them off through the entire border of Yisra'el by the hand of envoys, saying 'Anyone of you who doesn't go out after Sha'ul and after Shemu'el: so it will be done to his herd.' Dread of Yahweh fell on the people and they went out as one person. [8]He numbered them at Bezeq; there were 300,000 Yisra'elites and 30,000 Yehudahites [Judahites]. [9]They said to the envoys who had come, 'Say this to the people of Yabesh-in-Gil'ad: "Tomorrrow there will be deliverance for you, when the sun gets hot."' The envoys came and told the people of Yabesh and they rejoiced. [10]The people of Yabesh said, 'Tomorrow we'll go out to you and you can act towards us in accordance with everything that's good in your eyes.'

No redress

[11]Next day Sha'ul made the company into three units, and they came into the middle of the camp during the morning watch and struck down Ammon until the day got hot. Those who remained dispersed; among them there did not remain two together. [12]The people said to Shemu'el, 'Who was the person who said "Is Sha'ul to reign over us?" Give the people over and we'll put them to death.' [13]But Sha'ul said, 'No one is to be put to death this day, because today Yahweh has brought about deliverance in Yisra'el.'

[14]Shemu'el said to the people, 'Come, let's go to Gilgal and renew the kingship there.' [15]So all the people went to Gilgal and made Sha'ul king there before Yahweh at Gilgal. They made well-being sacrifices there before Yahweh. Sha'ul and all the Yisra'elites rejoiced greatly there.

12 Shemu'el said to all Yisra'el, 'Here, I listened to your voice regarding all that you said to me and I made a king reign over you. [2]So now, there is your king walking about before you. I myself am old and grey, but my sons – here they are, with you. I myself have walked about before you from my youth until this day. ³Here I am. Vow against me in the presence of Yahweh and in the presence of his anointed. Whose ox have I taken? Whose donkey have I taken? Whom have I defrauded? Whom have I crushed? From whose hand have I taken a ransom so I might close my eyes to him? I'll give it back to you.'

⁴They said, 'You haven't defrauded us, you haven't crushed us, you haven't taken anything from anyone's hand.' ⁵He said to them, 'Yahweh is witness against you, and his anointed is witness this day, that you haven't found anything in my hand.' They said, 'He is witness.' ⁶Shemu'el said to the people, 'Yahweh, who made Mosheh and Aharon [Moses and Aaron] and who brought your ancestors up from the country of Misrayim.

Take your stand and face facts

⁷So now take your stand so that I may enter into judgement with you before Yahweh on the basis of all Yahweh's acts of faithfulness which he performed with you and with your ancestors. ⁸When Ya'aqob [Jacob] came to Misrayim and your ancestors cried out to Yahweh, Yahweh sent Mosheh and Aharon and got your ancestors out of Misrayim and enabled them to live in this place. ⁹But they put Yahweh their God out of mind and he sold them into the hand of Sisera the army officer at Hatsor, into the hand of the Pelishtites and into the hand of the king of Mo'ab, and they battled against them. ¹⁰They cried out to Yahweh and said, "We've done wrong, because we've abandoned Yahweh and served the Masters and the Ashtars, but now, deliver us from the hand of our enemies and we will serve you." ¹¹Yahweh sent Yerubba'al, Bedan, Yiphtah and Shemu'el, and rescued you from the hand of your enemies all round, and you lived in confidence. ¹²But you saw that Nahash king of the Ammonites was coming against you and you said to me, "No, rather a king must reign over us", when Yahweh your God was your king.

¹³So now, here is the king that you chose, that you asked for. Here, Yahweh has put a king over you. ¹⁴If you live in awe of Yahweh, serve him, listen to his voice and do not rebel against Yahweh's bidding, and both you and the king who reigns over you follow Yahweh your God . . .

¹⁵But if you don't listen to the voice of Yahweh your God but rebel against Yahweh's bidding, Yahweh's hand will be against you and against your ancestors.

The sin of not praying

¹⁶Further, take your stand now and see this great thing that Yahweh is going to do before your eyes. ¹⁷It's the wheat harvest today, isn't it. I shall call to Yahweh and he will give thunder and rain. You will acknowledge and see that you did a thing that was extremely bad in Yahweh's eyes, in asking for a king for yourselves.'

¹⁸So Shemu'el called to Yahweh and Yahweh gave thunder and rain that day. All the people were in great awe of Yahweh and of Shemu'el. ¹⁹All the people said to Shemu'el, 'Plead on behalf of your servants to Yahweh your God so we don't die, because we've added something bad to all our wrongdoings in asking for a king for ourselves.'

²⁰Shemu'el said to the people, 'Don't be afraid. You yourselves have undertaken all this bad action. Nevertheless don't turn aside from following Yahweh. Serve Yahweh with your entire mind. ²¹You're not to turn aside, because [it would be] after something empty, things that are no use and cannot rescue, because they're empty. ²²Because Yahweh won't take leave of his people, for the sake of his great name, because Yahweh resolved to make you a people for him. ²³Further, as for me, far be it from me to do wrong against Yahweh by leaving off from pleading for you. I shall instruct you in the way that's good and right. ²⁴Nevertheless, live in awe of Yahweh and serve him in truthfulness with your entire mind, because you can see how he has done great things for you. ²⁵But if you actually do what's bad: both you and your king, you'll be swept away.'

The king takes decisive action

13 Sha'ul had been one year reigning and he reigned two years over Yisra'el. ²Then Sha'ul chose for himself 3,000 men from Yisra'el; 2,000 were with Sha'ul at Mikmas and in the highland at Bet-el, and 1,000 were with Yonatan [Jonathan] at Gib'ah-in-Binyamin. The rest of the company he sent off, each one, to his tents.

³Yonatan struck down the Pelishtites' outpost that was at Geba, and the Pelishtites heard. Sha'ul himself blew on the horn throughout the country, saying 'The Hebrews are to hear!' ⁴and all Yisra'el heard: 'Sha'ul has struck down the Pelishtites' outpost, and now Yisra'el has come to stink to the Pelishtites.' The people had themselves called out behind Sha'ul at Gilgal, ⁵while the Pelishtites gathered to battle with Yisra'el: 30,000 chariotry, 6,000 cavalry and a company like the sand that is on the seashore in their large number. They went up and camped at Mikmas, east of Bet Aven. ⁶When the Yisra'elites saw that things were pressing for them, that the company was hard pressed, the company hid in caves, in thickets, in cliffs, in pits and in cisterns, ⁷while Hebrews crossed the Yarden [Jordan] to the region of Gad and Gil'ad.

Sha'ul was still at Gilgal, while the entire company following him trembled. ⁸He waited seven days for the set time that Shemu'el said, but Shemu'el didn't come to Gilgal, and the company was dispersing from him. ⁹So Sha'ul said, 'Bring up to me the burnt offering and the well-being sacrifices', and he offered up the burnt offering. ¹⁰As he finished offering up the burnt offering, there was Shemu'el coming. Sha'ul went out to meet him, to bless him.

You've been stupid

¹¹But Shemu'el said, 'What have you done?' Sha'ul said, 'When I saw that the company was dispersing from me, and you yourself had not come at the set time, and the Pelishtites were gathering at Mikmas, ¹²I said, "The Pelishtites will now come down to me at Gilgal and I haven't sought to gain Yahweh's goodwill." So I forced myself and offered up the burnt offering.'

¹³Shemu'el said to Sha'ul, 'You've been idiotic. You haven't kept the order of Yahweh your God, which he gave you. Because Yahweh would now have made your kingship over Yisra'el stand permanently, ¹⁴but now your kingship won't stand. Yahweh has sought for himself a man in accordance with his own mind. Yahweh has ordered that he is to be ruler over his people, because you haven't kept what Yahweh ordered you.' ¹⁵And Shemu'el set off and went up from Gilgal to Gib'ah-in-Binyamin.

Sha'ul numbered the company of those that could be found with him, some 600 men. ¹⁶Sha'ul and Yonatan his son and the company that could be found with them were staying at Geba in Binyamin and the Pelishtites had camped at Mikmas. ¹⁷A group wreaking devastation went out of the Pelishtites' camp in three columns. One column would turn its face towards the Ophrah road, towards the Shu'al region. ¹⁸One column would turn its face towards the Bet Horon road. One column would turn its face towards the border road overlooking Tsebo'im Ravine, towards the wilderness.

¹⁹Now no smith could be found in all the country of Yisra'el because the Pelishtites had said, 'So that the Hebrews cannot make sword or lance.' (²⁰So all Yisra'el went down to the Pelishtites for anyone to sharpen his ploughshare, his pick, his axe and his sickle. ²¹The charge was two thirds of a sheqel for the ploughshare and for the picks, and a third for a fork, for the axes and for setting the goad.) ²²So on a day of battle no sword or lance could be found in the hand of any of the company that was with Sha'ul and with Yonatan, though it could be found belonging to Sha'ul and to Yonatan his son.

A bright idea on the part of Yonatan (Yehonatan)

²³So the Pelishtites' garrison had gone out to the pass at Mikmas.

14 A day came and Yonatan ben Sha'ul said to the boy who was his equipment-bearer, 'Come on, let's cross over to the Pelishtites' garrison that's across over there.' He didn't tell his father. ²Sha'ul was staying on the edge of Gib'ah, under the pomegranate tree which is at Migron. The company that was with him was some 600 men, ³with Ahiyyah ben Ahitub, who was brother of Ikabod ben Pinhas, son of Eli, Yahweh's priest at Shiloh, carrying a chasuble; the company didn't know that Yonatan had gone.

⁴Between the crossings by which Yonatan sought to cross to the Pelishtites' garrison

there was a craggy outcrop on one side of the crossing and a craggy outcrop on the other side of the crossing. The name of the one was Swamp and the name of the other was Thorn. ⁵The one outcrop was a pillar on the north near Mikmas, the other on the south near Geba.

⁶So Yehonatan said to the boy who was his equipment-bearer, 'Come on, let's cross over to the garrison of these foreskinned men. Maybe Yahweh will act on our behalf, because Yahweh has no difficulty in delivering by many or by few.' ⁷His equipment-bearer said to him, 'Do all that's in your mind. Follow your inclination. Here, I'm with you. Just what's in your mind.'

⁸Yehonatan said, 'Here, we're going to cross over to the men and we'll show ourselves to them. ⁹If they say this to us, "Stay still till we reach you", we'll stand where we are and not go up to them. ¹⁰But if they say this, "Come up to us", we'll go up, because Yahweh will have given them into our hand. This will be the sign for us.'

Yonatan and his boy

¹¹So the two of them showed themselves to the Pelishtites' garrison, and the Pelishtites said, 'There, Hebrews coming out of the holes where they hid themselves.' ¹²The men in the garrison avowed to Yonatan and to his equipment-bearer, 'Come up to us and we'll make you acknowledge something.' Yonatan said to his equipment-bearer, 'Come up after me, because Yahweh has given them into the hand of Yisraʼel.' ¹³Yonatan went up on his hands and his feet with his equipment-bearer behind him. And they fell before Yonatan, with his equipment-bearer putting them to death behind him. ¹⁴The first blow that Yonatan and his equipment-bearer struck was some twenty men, in some half a furlong of an acre of field. ¹⁵There was trembling in the camp, in the field and in the entire company, while the garrison and the group wreaking devastation also trembled, and the earth shook. It became a supernatural trembling.

¹⁶Shaʼul's lookouts at Gibʼah-in-Binyamin saw: there, the turmoil was surging. It went hither and thither. ¹⁷Shaʼul said to the company that was with him, 'Take a count, will you, and see who's gone from us.' They took a count and there, Yonatan and his equipment-bearer were not there. ¹⁸Shaʼul said to Ahiyyah, 'Bring up God's chest' (because God's chest was at that time with the Yisraʼelites).

¹⁹But while Shaʼul spoke to the priest, the turmoil that was in the Pelishtites' camp continued to go on and increase, so Shaʼul said to the priest, 'Take away your hand', ²⁰and Shaʼul and the entire company that was with him had themselves called out and came to the battle. There, one person's sword was against his neighbour, a very great confusion. ²¹Some Hebrews had belonged to the Pelishtites in previous days, people who had gone up with them into the camp all round, and they too came to be with the Yisraʼel that was with Shaʼul and Yonatan, ²²while all the Yisraʼelites hiding in the highland of Ephrayim heard that the Pelishtites had fled, and they too caught up with them in battle. ²³ᵃYahweh delivered Yisraʼel that day.

A taste of honey

²³ᵇWhen the battle passed beyond Bet Aven, ²⁴the Yisraʼelites were hard pressed that day. Shaʼul had got the company to swear, 'Cursed is the man who eats a meal before evening, when I've taken redress from my enemies', and the entire company hadn't tasted a meal.

²⁵Now the whole country came into the forest and there was honey on the face of the field. ²⁶So the company came into the forest, and there, honey flowing. But no one put his hand to his mouth, because the company was in awe of the oath.

²⁷But Yonatan hadn't heard his father get the company to swear, and he stretched out the end of the cane that was in his hand, dipped it into a honeycomb and brought his hand back to his mouth, and his eyes lit up. ²⁸Someone from the company avowed, 'Your father actually got the company to swear, "Cursed is the man who eats food today", and the company has got weary.' ²⁹Yonatan said, 'My father has brought disaster on the country. Please see that my eyes lit up when I tasted this bit of honey. ³⁰Yes, if only the company had actually eaten of its enemies' spoil that it found today, because now wouldn't the calamity for the Pelishtites have been great.'

³¹They struck the Pelishtites down that day from Mikmas to Ayyalon, but the company

got very weary. ³²So the company pounced on the spoil, got flock, herd and calves, and slaughtered them on the ground. The company ate with the blood.

³³People told Sha'ul: 'There, the company are doing wrong in relation to Yahweh by eating with the blood.' He said, 'You've broken faith. Roll a big stone to me now.' ³⁴Sha'ul said, 'Spread out among the company and say to them, "Bring up to me each one his ox and each one his sheep and slaughter it here, and you can eat. You are not to do wrong in relation to Yahweh by eating with the blood."' So the entire company brought up, each one, his ox in his possession that night and slaughtered it there. ³⁵Sha'ul built an altar for Yahweh. It was the first he built as an altar for Yahweh.

The fog of war clarified

³⁶Sha'ul said, 'Let's go down after the Pelishtites tonight and plunder among them till morning light, and not let one person remain among them.' They said, 'Do all that's good in your eyes.' But the priest said, 'Let's draw near to God here.' ³⁷So Sha'ul asked of God, 'Shall I go down after the Pelishtites? Will you give them into Yisra'el's hand?' But he didn't answer him that day. ³⁸Sha'ul said, 'Come up to here, all you cornerstones of the company. Get to know and see how this wrong has happened today. ³⁹Because as Yahweh who delivers Yisra'el lives, even if it is through Yonatan my son, he will absolutely be put to death.' From the entire company there was no one answered him.

⁴⁰He said to all Yisra'el, 'You're to be on one side, and I and Yonatan my son will be on the other side.' The company said to Sha'ul, 'Do what is good in your eyes.' ⁴¹Sha'ul said to Yahweh the God of Yisra'el, 'Grant the truth.' Yonatan and Sha'ul were taken and the company came out. ⁴²Sha'ul said, 'Make it fall between me and Yonatan my son.' Yonatan was taken.

⁴³Sha'ul said to Yonatan, 'Do tell me what you've done.' Yonatan told him: 'I just took a taste, with the end of the cane that was in my hand, of a bit of honey. Here I am. I will die.' ⁴⁴Sha'ul said, 'May God do thus and may he do more [to me], because you absolutely must die, Yonatan.' ⁴⁵But the company said to Sha'ul, 'Is Yonatan to die when he brought about this great deliverance in Yisra'el? Far be it, as Yahweh lives, if a hair of his head is to fall to the ground, because he has acted this day with God.' So the company redeemed Yonatan and he didn't die. ⁴⁶But Sha'ul gave up from following the Pelishtites, and the Pelishtites went to their place.

The successful king

⁴⁷When Sha'ul had taken the kingship over Yisra'el, he did battle all round against all his enemies, against Mo'ab, against the Ammonites, against Edom, against the kings of Tsobah and against the Pelishtites. Anyone who would turn his face, he treated as faithless. ⁴⁸He acted forcefully, struck down Amaleq and rescued Yisra'el from the hand of its despoiler.

⁴⁹Sha'ul's sons were Yonatan, Yishvi and Malki-shua. The name of his two daughters – the name of the firstborn, Merab, the name of the younger, Mikal. ⁵⁰The name of Sha'ul's wife: Ahino'am bat Ahima'ats. The name of his army officer: Abiner ben Ner, Sha'ul's uncle. ⁵¹Both Qish, Sha'ul's father, and Ner, Abner's father, was Abi'el's son.

⁵²There was fierce battling against the Pelishtites all Sha'ul's time, but Sha'ul would see anyone who was a strong man or any forceful individual and get him to join him.

15 Shemu'el said to Sha'ul, 'It was me that Yahweh sent to anoint you as king over his people, over Yisra'el. So listen now to the voice (the words) of Yahweh. ²Yahweh of Armies has said this: "I am attending to what Amaleq did to Yisra'el when he set upon them on the way, when they were going up from Misrayim. ³Now go and strike down Amaleq and devote everything that it has. You will not spare it. Put to death both man and woman, both child and baby, both ox and sheep, both camel and donkey."'

⁴Sha'ul got the company to listen, and numbered them at Tela'im, 200,000 men on foot and 10,000 men from Judah. ⁵Sha'ul came as far as the town of Amaleq and lay in wait in the wadi. ⁶Sha'ul said to the Qenites, 'Go, move away, go down from among the Amaleqites, so I don't gather you up with them, given that you acted in commitment with all the Yisra'elites when they went up from Misrayim.' So the Qenites departed from among Amaleq.

The king who wasn't ruthless enough

⁷Sha'ul struck down Amaleq from Havilah until you come to Shur, which is east of Misrayim. ⁸He captured Agag king of Amaleq alive, while the entire company he devoted with the mouth of the sword. ⁹But Sha'ul and the company spared Agag and the best of the flock, the herd, the second-born and the lambs, everything that was good. They were not willing to devote them. But every object that was despised and emaciated – they devoted it. ¹⁰Yahweh's word came to Shemu'el: ¹¹'I relent of having Sha'ul reign as king, because he's turned from following me and hasn't implemented my words.' It enraged Shemu'el and he cried out to Yahweh all night.

¹²Shemu'el started early in the morning to meet Sha'ul. It was told Shemu'el, 'Sha'ul's come to Carmel. Here, he's been putting up a monument for himself. Then he turned round and passed on, and went down to Gilgal.' ¹³Shemu'el came to Sha'ul, and Sha'ul said to him, 'Blessed are you by Yahweh! I've implemented Yahweh's word.' ¹⁴Shemu'el said, 'So what's this sound of a flock in my ears, and the sound of a herd that I'm hearing?' ¹⁵Sha'ul said, 'They brought them from the Amaleqites, because the company spared the best of the flock and the herd to sacrifice for Yahweh your God. The rest we devoted.'

¹⁶Shemu'el said to Sha'ul, 'Slow down, and I shall tell you what Yahweh spoke to me last night.' He said to him, 'Speak.' ¹⁷Shemu'el said, 'Though you were small in your eyes, you're the head of Yisra'el's clans. Yahweh anointed you as king over Yisra'el ¹⁸and Yahweh sent you on a journey. He said to you, "Go and devote the wrongdoers, Amaleq. Do battle against them until you've finished them off." ¹⁹Why didn't you listen to Yahweh's voice but pounce on the spoil and do what was bad in Yahweh's eyes?'

Listening is better than sacrificing

²⁰Sha'ul said to Shemu'el, 'I listened to Yahweh's voice! I went on the journey that Yahweh sent me on. I brought Agag king of Amaleq, but Amaleq I devoted. ²¹The company took flock and herd from the spoil, the first of what was to be devoted, to sacrifice for Yahweh your God at Gilgal.' ²²Shemu'el said,

> Are burnt offerings and sacrifices as pleasing
>   to Yahweh
>   as listening to Yahweh's voice?
> Here, listening is better than sacrificing,
>   heeding than the fat of rams.
> ²³Because rebellion: the wrongdoing that comes
>   from divination,
> arrogance: the trouble that comes from
>   effigies.
> Since you rejected Yahweh's word,
>   he has rejected you from being king.

²⁴Sha'ul said to Shemu'el, 'I did wrong, because I transgressed Yahweh's bidding and your words, because I was afraid of the company and I listened to their voice. ²⁵But now, please carry my wrongdoing. Come back with me and I will bow low to Yahweh.' ²⁶Shemu'el said to Sha'ul, 'I will not come back with you, because you rejected Yahweh's word and Yahweh has rejected you from being king over Yisra'el.' ²⁷And Shemu'el turned round to go.

He took strong hold of the corner of his coat, and it tore, ²⁸and Shemu'el said to him, 'Yahweh has torn the kingship of Yisra'el from you today and given it to a neighbour of yours who is better than you. ²⁹Further, Yisra'el's Enduring One does not speak falsely and does not relent, because he's not a human being so as to relent.'

³⁰He said, 'I did wrong. Now please honour me in the presence of the elders of my people and in the presence of Yisra'el, and come back with me, and I will bow low to Yahweh your God.' ³¹So Shemu'el went back after Sha'ul and Sha'ul bowed low to Yahweh.

³²Shemu'el said, 'Bring up to me Agag king of Amaleq.' Agag went to him in chains. Agag said, 'Yes! The bitterness of death is departing!' ³³But Shemu'el said, 'As your sword made women childless, so your mother will become childless beyond other women.' And Shemu'el cut Agag down before Yahweh at Gilgal.

Yahweh sees into the heart

³⁴Shemu'el went to The Height while Sha'ul went up to his home at Gib'ah-of-Sha'ul. ³⁵Shemu'el didn't see Sha'ul again until the day

of his death, because Shemu'el took up grieving for Sha'ul when Yahweh had relented that he had made Sha'ul king over Yisra'el.

16 But Yahweh said to Shemu'el, 'How long are you going to take up grieving for Sha'ul, when I myself have rejected him from being king over Yisra'el? Fill your horn with oil and go: I shall send you to Yishay [Jesse] the Bet-lehemite because I've seen a king for myself among his sons.' ²Shemu'el said, 'How can I go? Sha'ul will hear and kill me.' Yahweh said, 'You're to take a heifer in your possession and say "It's to sacrifice for Yahweh that I've come", ³and invite Yishay to the sacrifice. I myself will let you know what you're to do and you're to anoint for me the one that I say to you.'

⁴Shemu'el did what Yahweh spoke. He came to Bet Lehem, and the town's elders trembled to meet him and said, 'Does your coming mean things are well?' ⁵He said, 'Things are well. It's to sacrifice for Yahweh that I've come. Make yourselves sacred and come with me to the sacrifice.' He made Yishay and his sons sacred and invited them to the sacrifice.

⁶When they came, he saw Eli'ab and said, 'Surely his anointed is in front of Yahweh!' ⁷But Yahweh said to Shemu'el, 'Don't look at his appearance or at the loftiness to which he stands, because I've rejected him, because it's not what a human being sees, because a human being sees what appears to the eyes, but Yahweh sees into the mind.' ⁸Yishay called Abinadab and had him pass before Shemu'el,

1 Samuel 16: Sha'ul (Saul) and David

but he said, 'Yahweh has not chosen this one either.' ⁹Yishay had Shammah pass, but he said, 'Yahweh has not chosen this one either.' ¹⁰Yishay had his seven sons pass before Shemu'el, but Shemu'el said to Yishay, 'Yahweh has not chosen these.'

Yahweh's good spirit and Yahweh's bad spirit

¹¹Shemu'el said to Yishay, 'Have the boys come to an end?' He said, 'The little one still remains, but there, he's tending the flock.' Shemu'el said to Yishay, 'Send and get him, because we won't sit down till he comes here.' ¹²So he sent and brought him. He was tanned, with lovely eyes, good-looking. Yahweh said, 'Get up, anoint him, because this is the one.' ¹³Shemu'el got the horn of oil and anointed him among his brothers. Yahweh's spirit thrust itself on to David from that day onwards. And Shemu'el set off and went to The Height.

¹⁴Now Yahweh's spirit had departed from Sha'ul and a bad spirit from Yahweh had terrified him. ¹⁵Sha'ul's servants said to him, 'Please, here, a bad spirit from God is terrifying you. ¹⁶Please, our lord should say that your servants who are before you should look for someone who knows how to play the guitar. When the bad spirit from God is upon you, he would play and it would be good for you.' ¹⁷Sha'ul said to his servants, 'Look for someone who is good at playing for me, please, and bring him to me.' ¹⁸One of the boys answered, 'Here, I've seen a son of Yishay the Bet-lehemite who knows how to play. He's a forceful strong man, a man of battle, but smart with words and good-looking, and Yahweh is with him.'

¹⁹So Sha'ul sent envoys to Yishay and said, 'Send me David your son, who's with the flock.' ²⁰Yishay got a donkey, bread, a skin of wine and a kid-goat from the flock, and sent them by the hand of David his son to Sha'ul. ²¹David came to Sha'ul and stood by him. He liked him a lot and he became an equipment-bearer for him. ²²Sha'ul sent to Yishay to say, 'May David please stand before me, because he's found grace in my eyes.' ²³When the spirit from God would come to Sha'ul, David would get the guitar and play by hand, and there would be relief for Sha'ul. It was good for him. The bad spirit would depart from him.

The frightening champion

17 The Pelishtites gathered their camp for battle. They gathered at Sokoh which belongs to Yehudah and camped between Sokoh and Azeqah, at Dammim End, ²while Sha'ul and the Yisra'elites gathered and camped in Oak Vale and lined up for battle to meet the Pelishtites. ³The Pelishtites were standing on a mountain on one side and Yisra'el was standing on a mountain on the other side, with the ravine between them.

⁴A representative went out from the Pelishtites' camps, Golyat [Goliath] his name, from Gat, his height three metres and a handbreadth, ⁵a copper helmet on his head. He was clothed in a coat of mail (the weight of the coat was 5,000 sheqels of copper), ⁶with copper shin guards on his legs, a copper javelin between his shoulders, ⁷the wood of his lance like a weavers' rod, the point of his lance 600 sheqels of iron, and a shield-bearer walking before him.

⁸He stood and called to the ranks of Yisra'el: 'Why should you go out and line up for battle? I'm the Pelishtite, aren't I, and you're Sha'ul's servants. Choose yourselves someone who will go down against me. ⁹If he succeeds in battling with me and strikes me down, we'll become servants to you. If I'm the one who succeeds over him and strikes him down, you'll become servants to us and serve us.' ¹⁰The Pelishtite said, 'I myself revile Yisra'el's ranks this day. Give me a man and we'll do battle together.'

¹¹Sha'ul and all Yisra'el listened to these words of the Pelishtite, and they were scared, very frightened.

The boy gets the chance to see

¹²Now David was the son of an Ephratite individual from Bet Lehem in Yehudah; his name was Yishay. He had eight sons. In the time of Sha'ul the man was old, going on in age among men. ¹³Yishay's three eldest sons had gone, gone after Sha'ul to the battle. The names

of his three sons who had gone into the battle were Eli'ab the firstborn, his second Abinadab and the third Shammah, ¹⁴while David was the youngest. The three oldest had gone after Sha'ul, ¹⁵while David was going and coming back from being with Sha'ul to shepherd his father's flock in Bet-lehem.

¹⁶The Pelishtite went up, starting early and doing it in the evening, and took his stand for forty days.

¹⁷Yishay said to David his son, 'Get a barrel of this roasted grain and ten loaves of this bread, please, and run them to the camp for your brothers. ¹⁸And these ten wedges of cheese, you're to bring to the divisional officer. You're to attend to your brothers, as to whether things are well with them, and get some reassurance from them, ¹⁹while Sha'ul and they and all the Yisra'elites are in Oak Vale doing battle with the Pelishtites.'

²⁰David started early in the morning, left the flock to a keeper, picked things up, went as Yishay had ordered him, and came to the encampment when the force was going out to the line and shouting for the battle. ²¹Yisra'el and the Pelishtites lined up, line to meet line.

²²David left the things with him in the hand of the equipment-keeper and ran to the line. He came and asked his brothers whether things were well with them. ²³While he was speaking with them, there, the representative was going up (Golyat the Pelishtite was his name, from Gat) from the Pelishtites' lines. He spoke these same words, and David listened.

You're too young and inexperienced

²⁴When all the Yisra'elites saw the man, they fled from before him. They were very frightened. ²⁵A Yisra'elite said, 'Have you seen this man going up? Because he's going up to revile Yisra'el. The man who strikes him down, the king will give him great wealth and give him his daughter and make his father's household tax-free in Yisra'el.'

²⁶So David said to the men standing with him, 'What will be done for the man who strikes down that Pelishtite and removes reviling from Yisra'el? Because who is this foreskinned Pelishtite that he's reviled the lines of the living God?' ²⁷The company said to him this same thing, 'So it will be done for the man who strikes him down.'

²⁸Eli'ab, David's older brother, heard him speaking to the men, and Eli'ab's anger raged at David. He said, 'Why is it that you've come down? And who did you leave that little flock alone in the wilderness with? I myself know your assertiveness and the bad inclination in your mind, that you've come down in order to see the battle.' ²⁹David said, 'What have I done now? Wasn't that just a word?' ³⁰He turned from being near him towards another man and said this same thing. The company gave word back to him that was the same as the first.

³¹The words that David spoke were heard and they told Sha'ul, and he got hold of him. ³²David said to Sha'ul, 'No one's heart should fail him. Your servant himself will go and battle with this Pelishtite.' ³³Sha'ul said to David, 'You can't succeed in going to this Pelishtite to battle with him, because you're a boy and he's been a strong man from his boyhood.'

How to recycle your killer instinct

³⁴David said to Sha'ul, 'Your servant has been shepherding over the flock for his father. A lion or a bear comes and carries off a sheep from the flock, ³⁵and I go out after it and strike it down and rescue it from its mouth. It rises up against me and I get strong hold of it by its beard and strike it down and put it to death. ³⁶Both lion and bear your servant has struck down. This foreskinned Pelishtite will be like one of them, because he's reviled the ranks of the living God.' ³⁷And David said, 'Yahweh who rescued me from the hand of the lion and from the hand of the bear: he will rescue me from the hand of this Pelishtite.' Sha'ul said to David, 'Go, and Yahweh be with you.'

³⁸Sha'ul clothed David in his uniform and put a copper helmet on his head and clothed him in a coat of mail. ³⁹David wrapped his sword over his uniform and resolved to walk, because he hadn't tried it. But David said to Sha'ul, 'I can't walk in these because I haven't tried them.' So David removed them off him, ⁴⁰took his stick in his hand, chose five smooth stones for himself from the wadi, put them in the shepherds' bag which he had, in the pouch,

with his sling in his hand, and went up to the Pelishtite. ⁴¹The Pelishtite kept walking and drawing near to David, with the shield-bearer before him.

⁴²The Pelishtite looked out and saw David, and despised him because he was a boy, tanned and lovely in appearance. ⁴³The Pelishtite said to David, 'Am I a dog that you're coming against me with sticks?' And the Pelishtite slighted David by his gods. ⁴⁴The Pelishtite said to David, 'Come to me, and I'll give your flesh to the birds of the heavens and to the animals of the wild.'

There is a God in Yisra'el

⁴⁵David said to the Pelishtite, 'You're coming against me with sword, with lance and with javelin, but I'm coming against you in the name of Yahweh of Armies the God of Yisra'el's lines, whom you've reviled. ⁴⁶This day Yahweh will deliver you into my hand and I shall strike you down and remove your head from you. I shall give the carcases of the Pelishtites' camp this day to the birds of the heavens and to the creatures of the earth. All the earth will acknowledge that Yisra'el has a God, ⁴⁷and this entire congregation will acknowledge that it is not by sword or by lance that Yahweh delivers, because the battle belongs to Yahweh and he will give you people into our hand.'

⁴⁸When the Pelishtite got up and walked and drew near to meet David, David hurried and ran to the line to meet the Pelishtite. ⁴⁹David put his hand into the bag, got a stone from there, slung it and struck the Pelishtite on his forehead. The stone sank into his forehead. He fell on his face to the ground. ⁵⁰So David was stronger than the Pelishtite with sling and with stone. He struck the Pelishtite down and put him to death. There was no sword in David's hand, ⁵¹so David ran, stood over the Pelishtite, got his sword, pulled it from its sheath and put him to death. He cut off his head with it.

The Pelishtites saw that their strong man was dead, and they fled. ⁵²The Yisra'elites and Yehudahites got up, shouted, and pursued after the Pelishtites until you come to the ravine and to the gateways of Eqron. The Pelishtites who were run through fell on the Sha'arim road as far as Gat and as far as Eqron. ⁵³The Yisra'elites came back from chasing after the Pelishtites and despoiled their camp. ⁵⁴David got the Pelishtite's head and brought it to Yerushalaim [Jerusalem]. His equipment he put in his own tent.

Sha'ul has struck down his thousands, David his ten thousands

⁵⁵When Sha'ul saw David going out to meet the Pelishtite, he said to Abner, the army officer, 'The boy, whose son is he, Abner?' Abner said, 'On your life, Your Majesty, if I know.' ⁵⁶The king said, 'You ask whose son the kid is.' ⁵⁷When David came back from striking down the Pelishtite, Abner got him and brought him before Sha'ul, with the Pelishtite's head in his hand. ⁵⁸Sha'ul said to him, 'Whose son are you, my boy?' David said, 'The son of your servant Yishay the Bet Lehemite.'

18 When he'd finished speaking to Sha'ul, the person of Yehonatan bound itself to David's person. Yehonatan became loyal to him as a person like himself. ²Sha'ul took him that day and didn't let him go back to his father's household. ³Yehonatan and David solemnized a pact because he was loyal to him as a person like himself. ⁴Yehonatan took off the coat that he had on and gave it to David, with his uniform, and along with his sword, with his bow and with his belt.

⁵David went out wherever Sha'ul would send him; as he was successful, Sha'ul set him over the men of battle. It was good in the eyes of the entire company, and also in the eyes of Sha'ul's servants.

⁶But when they had come home, when David got back from striking down the Pelishtite, the women came out from all the towns in Yisra'el for singing and dances to meet King Sha'ul, with tambourines, with celebration and with triangles. ⁷The women who were having fun chanted,

Sha'ul has struck down his thousands,
David his ten thousands.

⁸And it really enraged Sha'ul. This thing was bad in his eyes. He said, 'They've given David ten thousands and given me thousands. Only the kingship will yet be his.' ⁹Sha'ul was eyeing David from that day on.

Daughters are just political pawns

10Next day a bad spirit from God thrust itself on Sha'ul and he prophesied inside the house while David was playing by hand, as he did each day. There was a lance in Sha'ul's hand **11**and Sha'ul threw the lance. He said 'I'll pin David to the wall'; but David turned from before him, twice. **12**Sha'ul was afraid before David because Yahweh was with him and had departed from Sha'ul, **13**and Sha'ul moved him away from being with him and made him a divisional officer, so he went out and came in before the company. **14**David was successful on all his journeys; Yahweh was with him. **15**Sha'ul saw that he was very successful, and he was in dread before him, **16**but all Yisra'el and Yehudah loved David, because he was going out and coming in before them.

17Sha'ul said to David, 'Here's my oldest daughter Merab. I'll give her to you as wife. Only be a forceful man for me and engage in Yahweh's battles' (Sha'ul had said, 'My hand must not be against him. The Pelishtites' hand is to be against him'). **18**David said to Sha'ul, 'Who am I and what is my life, my father's kin-group in Yisra'el, that I should become the king's son-in-law?'

19Then at the time for giving Merab, Sha'ul's daughter, to David, she was given as wife to Adri'el the Meholatite. **20**But Mikal, Sha'ul's daughter, loved David, and they told Sha'ul. The thing was all right in his eyes. **21**Sha'ul said, 'I'll give her to him and she'll become a snare to him, so the Pelishtites' hand may be against him.' So Sha'ul said to David, 'Through number two you're to become my son-in-law, right now.'

Twice as many deaths as Sha'ul asks for

22Sha'ul ordered his servants, 'Speak to David quietly: "Here, the king delights in you and all his servants love you. So now, become the king's son-in-law."' **23**The king's servants spoke these words in David's ears. David said, 'Is it a slight thing in your eyes, becoming the king's son-in-law, when I am a destitute, slight person?' **24**Sha'ul's servants told him, 'These very words David spoke.'

25Sha'ul said, 'Say this to David: "The king will have no delight in a marriage gift except in a hundred Pelishtite foreskins, to have redress on the king's enemies"' (Sha'ul thought to have David fall by the hand of the Pelishtites). **26**His servants told these things to David, and the thing was all right in David's eyes, for becoming the king's son-in-law. The days were not complete **27**but David got up and went, he and his men, and struck down 200 of the Pelishtites. David brought their foreskins and they fulfilled the number for the king so that he might become the king's son-in-law. So Sha'ul gave him Mikal his daughter as wife.

28Sha'ul saw and acknowledged that Yahweh was with David, and Mikal Sha'ul's daughter loved him, **29**and Sha'ul grew more afraid of David. Sha'ul became hostile to David all the time.

30The Pelishtites' officers went out, and as many times as they went out, David was more successful than all Sha'ul's servants. His name was highly esteemed.

19

Sha'ul spoke to Yonatan his son and to all his servants about bringing about David's death, but Yehonatan Sha'ul's son delighted in David very much, **2**and Yehonatan told David: 'Sha'ul my father is seeking to bring about your death, so now, please keep watch in the morning, stay in a secret place and hide. **3**I myself will go out and stand at my father's hand in the fields where you are, and I'll speak to my father about you. I'll see what, and tell you.'

A bad spirit from Yahweh

4Yehonatan spoke good things of David to Sha'ul his father. He said to him, 'The king shouldn't do wrong to his servant, to David, because he hasn't done wrong to you, and because his actions have been very good for you. **5**He put his life in the palm of his hand and struck down the Pelishtite, and Yahweh brought about a great deliverance for all Yisra'el. You saw and you rejoiced. Why should you do wrong, shedding the blood of a person who is free of guilt, by bringing about David's death for nothing?' **6**Sha'ul listened to Yehonatan's voice, and Sha'ul swore, 'As Yahweh lives, if he is put to death . . .'

7So Yehonatan called to David and Yehonatan told him all these things, and

Yehonatan brought David to Sha'ul and he was before him as in previous days. ⁸Again there was a battle and David went out to battle with the Pelishtites and struck them down in a great rout, and they fled from before him.

⁹But a bad spirit from Yahweh came on Sha'ul. He was sitting in his house with his lance in his hand, and David was playing by hand, ¹⁰and Sha'ul sought to pin David to the wall, but he slipped away from before Sha'ul, and he pinned the lance into the wall. David fled and escaped that night. ¹¹Sha'ul sent envoys to David's house to keep watch on him and put him to death in the morning, but Mikal his wife told David, 'If you don't escape with your life tonight, you'll be put to death tomorrow.'

Is Sha'ul among the prophets, too?

¹²So Mikal let David down through the window and he went and escaped and took flight. ¹³Mikal got the effigies and put them in the bed, and put a goat's hair quilt at its head and covered it with clothing. ¹⁴Sha'ul sent envoys to get David, but she said, 'He's ill.' ¹⁵So Sha'ul sent the envoys to see David, saying 'Bring him up to me in the bed, to put him to death.' ¹⁶The envoys came and there, the effigies in the bed and the goat's hair quilt at its head. ¹⁷Sha'ul said to Mikal, 'Why did you beguile me like that and help my enemy get away so he escaped?' Mikal said to Sha'ul, 'He himself said to me, "Help me get away. Why should I put you to death?"'

¹⁸When David took flight and escaped, he came to Shemu'el at The Height and told him all that Sha'ul had done to him. He went, he and Shemu'el, and they stayed in the cabins. ¹⁹It was told Sha'ul, 'There, David's in the cabins at The Height.' ²⁰Sha'ul sent envoys to get David. He saw a group of prophets prophesying, and Shemu'el standing presiding over them. God's spirit came on Sha'ul's envoys and they too prophesied. ²¹People told Sha'ul, so he sent more envoys, but they prophesied, too. Sha'ul again sent, the third envoys, and they prophesied, too.

²²So he also went to The Height. He came as far as the great cistern which is at Seku and asked, 'Where are Shemu'el and David?' Someone said, 'There, in the cabins at The Height.' ²³He went there, to the cabins at The Height, and God's spirit came on him, too. He walked on and prophesied until he came to the cabins at The Height. ²⁴He too stripped off his clothes, and he too prophesied before Shemu'el. He fell down naked all that day and all night. That's why they say, 'Is Sha'ul among the prophets, too?'

A test of Sha'ul's attitude

20 David took flight from the cabins at The Height and came and said before Yehonatan, 'What have I done, what is my waywardness, what is my wrongdoing before your father, that he is seeking my life?' ²He said to him, 'Far be it! You will not die. Here, my father doesn't do anything big or anything small but he has a word in my ear. Why would my father conceal this thing from me? This won't be.' ³But David also swore, 'Your father does know that I've found grace in your eyes, and he's said, "Yehonatan isn't to know this, so he won't be pained." Actually, as Yahweh lives and as you yourself live, there's really just a step between me and death.' ⁴Yehonatan said to David, 'What you yourself say, I will do for you.'

⁵David said to Yehonatan, 'Here, tomorrow is the new month. I'm definitely to sit with the king to eat. You should send me off and I'll hide in the fields until the third evening. ⁶If your father does attend to me, you're to say, "David did ask me about running to Bet-lehem, his town, because there's the annual sacrifice for the entire kin-group there." ⁷If he says this: "Good", things are well for your servant, but if it really enrages him, acknowledge that some bad action is certain from him. ⁸You're to act in commitment with your servant because you've brought your servant into a pact before Yahweh with you. If there's waywardness in me, put me to death yourself. Why is it that you should bring me back to your father?'

⁹Yehonatan said, 'Far be it from you! Because if I do get to know that some bad action by my father is certain to come on you, wouldn't I tell you about it?' ¹⁰David said to Yehonatan, 'Who will tell me if your father gives you a tough answer?'

Loyalty

[11] Yehonatan said to David, 'Come on, let's go out to the fields.' The two of them went out to the fields, [12] and Yehonatan said to David, 'Yahweh the God of Yisra'el! When I search out my father this very time tomorrow or the third day, and there – things are good for David, I shall then send to you and have a word in your ear, won't I. [13] May Yahweh act thus to Yehonatan and act thus again: when some bad action towards you seems good to my father, I will have a word in your ear and send you off, and you can go to where things will be well. And may Yahweh be with you as he was with my father. [14] While I'm still alive, will you not act in Yahweh's commitment with me, and I will not die. [15] And will you not cut off your commitment from my household, ever, not even when Yahweh has cut off David's enemies, each one, from the face of the ground. [16] Yehonatan has solemnized it with David's household. Yahweh will look for it from the hand of (the enemies of) David.' [17] Yehonatan again got David to swear by his loyalty to him, because he was loyal to him with the loyalty of his person.

[18] Yehonatan said to him, 'Tomorrow is the new month and you'll draw attention, because your seat will draw attention. [19] The third day, go right down and come to the place where you hid on the day you did it before, and stay beside the Ezel Stone. [20] When I myself shoot three arrows by the side of it, directing them for myself to a target, [21] there – I shall send the boy, "Go, find the arrows." If I do say to the boy, "There, the arrows are away from you over here, get them", you're to come, because things are well for you, and there's nothing, as Yahweh lives. [22] But if I say this to the kid, "There, the arrows are away from you over there", go, because Yahweh has sent you off. [23] The word that we have spoken, you and I: here, Yahweh is between you and me permanently.'

Rage and shaming

[24] So David hid in the fields. The new month came and the king sat down to eat for the meal. [25] The king sat on his seat as usual, in the seat by the wall. Yehonatan got up and Abner sat at Sha'ul's side, but David's place drew attention. [26] Sha'ul didn't speak a thing that day because (he said), 'There's been some chance thing so that he's not pure. Yes, he's not pure.' [27] Then the day after the new month, the second day, David's place drew attention, and Sha'ul said to Yehonatan his son, 'Why didn't ben Yishay come to the meal either yesterday or today?' [28] Yehonatan answered Sha'ul, 'David did ask me about going to Bet Lehem. [29] He said, "Please send me off, because we have a kin-group sacrifice in the town and my brother has given me an order. So now, if I've found grace in your eyes, please, I'll escape and see my brothers." That's why he hasn't come to the king's table.' [30] But Sha'ul's anger raged at Yehonatan. He said to him, 'Son of a perverse, rebellious woman! I know that you're choosing ben Yishay, aren't you, to your shame and to the shame of your mother's nakedness? [31] Because all the days that ben Yishay is alive on the earth, you and your kingship won't be established. So now, send and get him to me, because he deserves death.' [32] Yehonatan answered Sha'ul his father, 'Why is he to be put to death, what has he done?' [33] And Sha'ul threw the lance at him to strike him down. So Yehonatan acknowledged that it was determined by his father to put David to death. [34] Yehonatan got up from the table in an angry rage and didn't eat a meal on the second day of the new month because he felt pain for David because his father had shamed him.

The play with the arrows

[35] In the morning Yehonatan went out to the fields for the meeting with David, a young boy with him. [36] He said to his boy, 'Run, please find the arrows that I'm shooting.' When the boy ran, and he shot an arrow so that it passed him, [37] the boy came to the location of the arrow that Yehonatan had shot, and Yehonatan called after the boy, 'Isn't the arrow away from you, over there?' [38] Yehonatan called after the boy, 'Hurry, be quick, don't stand there!' So Yehonatan's boy gathered the arrows and came to his lord. [39] The boy didn't know anything. Only Yehonatan and David knew about the thing. [40] Yehonatan gave the equipment to the boy that he had and said to him, 'Go, bring it to the town.'

⁴¹When the boy had come and David had got up from towards the south, he fell on his face to the ground and bowed low three times, and they kissed one another and cried with one another, until David did so greatly. ⁴²Yehonatan said to David, 'Go to where it will be well, because the two of us have sworn in Yahweh's name, "Yahweh be between me and you and between my offspring and your offspring permanently."' So David got up and went, while Yehonatan came to the town.

21

David came to Nob, to Ahimelek the priest. Ahimelek trembled to meet David. He said to him, 'Why are you alone, and there's no one with you?' ²David said to Ahimelek the priest, 'When the king gave me an order about a matter, he said to me, "No one is to know anything about the matter on which I'm sending you and about which I gave you order." I've let the boys know about such and such a place. ³So now, what do you have at hand? Do put five loaves of bread in my hand, or what can be found.'

Re-enter Golyat's sword

⁴The priest answered David, 'There's no ordinary bread at hand. Rather, there's sacred bread, if the boys have only kept themselves from women.' ⁵David answered the priest, 'No, women have been withheld from us, as in previous days. When I've gone out, the boys' bodies have been sacred, when it was an ordinary journey. How much more today, when it's sacred, [they are sacred] in body.' ⁶So the priest gave him what was sacred, because there wasn't any bread there except the presence bread that had been removed from before Yahweh so as to put warm bread, at the time when it's taken away.

⁷Now there that day, held back before Yahweh, was one of Sha'ul's servants; his name was Do'eg the Edomite, chief of Sha'ul's shepherds.

⁸David said to Ahimelek, 'Isn't there a lance or a sword at hand here? Because I didn't take my sword or my equipment in my hand, because the king's business was pressing.' ⁹The priest said, 'The sword of Golyat the Pelishtite whom you struck down in Oaks Vale – here, it's wrapped in a cloth behind the chasuble. If you're to take it for yourself, take it, because there's none other apart from it here.' David said, 'There's none like it. Give it to me.'

¹⁰So David set off and took flight that day from before Sha'ul and came to Akish king of Gat. ¹¹Akish's servants said to him, 'This is David, the king of the country, isn't it. This is the man they chant about during the dances, isn't it:

Sha'ul has struck down his thousands,
David his ten thousands.

¹²David took these words to heart and became much afraid before Akish the king of Gat. ¹³So he disguised his good sense before their eyes and behaved oddly while in their control. He scratched on the gateway doors and let his saliva go down his beard. ¹⁴Akish said to his servants, 'Here, you see a man who's acting crazy. Why do you bring him to me? ¹⁵Am I lacking crazy people, that you bring this one to act crazy for me? Is this man to come into my household?'

The Adullam Cave

22

David went from there and escaped to the Adullam Cave. His brothers and his father's entire household heard, and they went down to him there. ²Everyone under pressure, everyone who had a creditor and everyone who was personally bitter collected themselves together to him, and he became their leader. There were some 400 men with him.

³David went from there to The WatchTower in Mo'ab and said to the king of Mo'ab, 'May my father and my mother please come out to be with you until I know what God will do for me.' ⁴So he led them into the presence of the king of Mo'ab and they stayed with him all the time David was at the stronghold. ⁵But Gad the prophet said to David, 'You're not to stay at the stronghold. Go, take yourself to the region of Yehudah.' So David went, and came to the Heret Forest.

⁶Sha'ul heard that David and the men who were with him had been discovered. Sha'ul was sitting at Gib'ah under the oak on the height, with his lance in his hand and all his servants standing by him. ⁷Sha'ul said to his

servants who were standing by him, 'Listen, please, Binyaminites. Will ben Yishay give fields and vineyards to all of you? Will he make all of you divisional officers or section officers? ⁸Because all of you have conspired against me. There's no one who has a word in my ear when my son solemnizes things with ben Yishay. There's none of you who's feeling sick for me and has a word in my ear when my son has set up my servant to lie in ambush for me this very day.'

⁹Do'eg the Edomite (he was standing with Sha'ul's servants) answered, 'I saw ben Yishay coming to Nob, to Ahimelek ben Ahitub. ¹⁰He asked of Yahweh for him, and gave him provisions, and gave him the sword of Golyat the Pelishtite.' ¹¹The king sent to call for Ahimelek ben Ahitub the priest, and his father's entire household, the priests who were at Nob. All of them came to the king.

The danger of being identified with David

¹²Sha'ul said, 'Listen, will you, ben Ahitub.' He said, 'Here I am, my lord.' ¹³Sha'ul said to him, 'Why have you conspired against me, you and ben Yishay, in giving him bread and a sword, and asking of God for him, so he can rise up against me and lie in ambush this very day?' ¹⁴Ahimelek answered the king, 'But who among all your servants is as trustworthy as David, the king's son-in-law, the officer over your bodyguard and honoured in your household? ¹⁵Was it today I started asking of God for him? Far be it from me. The king should not lay anything against his servant, against my father's entire household, because your servant didn't know anything small or great about all this.'

¹⁶But the king said, 'You are definitely to die, Ahimelek, you and your father's entire household.' ¹⁷The king said to the runners standing by him, 'Turn round and put Yahweh's priests to death, because their hand is also with David, and because they knew that he was taking flight and they didn't have a word in my ear.' The king's servants were not willing to put out their hand to attack Yahweh's priests, ¹⁸so the king said to Do'eg, 'You turn and attack the priests.' Do'eg the Edomite turned and was the one who attacked the priests and put them to death that day, eighty-five men bearing the linen chasuble. ¹⁹He struck down Nob, the priests' town, with the mouth of the sword – both man and woman, child and baby, ox, donkey and sheep, with the mouth of the sword.

²⁰One son of Ahimelek ben Ahitub escaped; his name was Ebyatar [Abiathar]. He took flight after David. ²¹Ebyatar told David that Sha'ul had killed Yahweh's priests, ²²and David said to Ebyatar, 'I knew that day when Do'eg the Edomite was there that he would definitely tell Sha'ul. I was responsible for every life in your father's household. ²³Stay with me. Don't be afraid, because whoever seeks your life will be someone who seeks my life, because you will be in my charge.'

David on the run

23 They told David: 'Here, the Pelishtites are battling aginst Qe'ilah, and they're despoiling the threshing floors.' ²David asked of Yahweh, 'Shall I go and strike down these Pelishtites?' Yahweh said to David, 'Go and strike the Pelishtites down and deliver Qe'ilah.' ³David's men said to him, 'Here, we're afraid here in Yehudah, and how much more when we go to Qe'ilah against the Pelishtites' lines.' ⁴David asked of Yahweh yet again, and Yahweh answered him, 'Set off, go down to Qe'ilah, because I'm going to give the Pelishtites into your hand.' ⁵So David went with his men to Qe'ilah and did battle against the Pelishtites, drove off their livestock and struck them down in a great rout. So David delivered the people living in Qe'ilah.

⁶Now when Ebyatar ben Ahimelek had taken flight to David (at Qe'ilah), a chasuble had come down in his hand. ⁷It was told Sha'ul that David had come to Qe'ilah. Sha'ul said, 'God has transferred him into my hand, because he's shut himself in by coming into a town with doors and a bar.' ⁸Sha'ul got the entire company to listen about a battle, about going down to Qe'ilah to besiege David and his men. ⁹David got to know that Sha'ul was devising something bad against him, and he said to Ebyatar the priest, 'Bring up the chasuble.'

¹⁰David said, 'Yahweh, God of Yisra'el, your servant has heard for certain that Sha'ul is seeking to come to Qe'ilah to devastate the town because of me. ¹¹Will the Qe'ilah landowners deliver me into his hand? Will

Sha'ul come down as your servant heard? Yahweh, God of Yisra'el, please tell your servant.' Yahweh said, 'He will come down.' ¹²David said, 'Will the Qe'ilah landowners deliver me and my men into Sha'ul's hand?' Yahweh said, 'They will deliver.' ¹³So David and his men, some 600 people, set off, got out of Qe'ilah and went about wherever they could go. It was told Sha'ul that David had escaped from Qe'ilah and he left off from setting out.

¹⁴David stayed in the wilderness in the strongholds; he stayed in the highland, in the Ziph Wilderness. Sha'ul looked for him all the time but God didn't give him into his hand.

Slippery cliff

¹⁵But David saw that Sha'ul had set out to seek his life when David was in the Ziph Wilderness at The Forest. ¹⁶Yehonatan, Sha'ul's son, set off and went to David at The Forest and strengthened his hand in God. ¹⁷He said to him, 'Don't be afraid, because the hand of Sha'ul my father will not find you. You yourself will reign over Yisra'el and I will be second to you. Even Sha'ul my father acknowledges it's so.' ¹⁸The two of them solemnized a pact before Yahweh, and David stayed in The Forest, while Yehonatan went home.

¹⁹Ziphites went up to Sha'ul at Gib'ah, saying 'David's hiding with us, isn't he, in the strongholds in The Forest, on Hakilah Hill, which is south of The Wasteland. ²⁰So now, with all the longing to come down that you yourself have, Your Majesty, come down and we'll deliver him into the king's hand.' ²¹Sha'ul said, 'May you be blessed by Yahweh because you've spared me. ²²Go, will you, and establish things further. Get to know and see the place where his foot goes, who has seen him there, because they've said to me, "He acts very shrewdly." ²³Look and get to know of all the hiding places where he hides, and come back to me with things established, and I'll go with you. If he's in the region, I'll search for him among all the divisions of Yehudah.'

²⁴They set off and went to Ziph before Sha'ul. David and his men were in Ma'on Wilderness in the steppe, to the south of The Wasteland. ²⁵Sha'ul and his men went to search, and people told David. He went down to The Cliff and stayed in Ma'on Wilderness. Sha'ul heard and pursued after David to Ma'on Wilderness. ²⁶Sha'ul went on one side of the mountain while David and his men were on the other side of the mountain. David was making haste to get away from before Sha'ul, while Sha'ul and his men were surrounding David and his men so as to seize them, ²⁷when an envoy came to Sha'ul saying 'Hurry, come, because the Pelishtites have made a raid on the country.' ²⁸So Sha'ul went back from pursuing after David and went to meet the Pelishtites. That's why they called that place Slippery Cliff.

Sha'ul pays a visit in a cave

²⁹David went up from there and stayed in the strongholds at Gedi Spring.

24 When Sha'ul came back from following the Pelishtites, they told him, 'There, David's in the Gedi Spring Wilderness.' ²Sha'ul got 3,000 picked men from all Yisra'el and went to look for David and his men in the direction of Ibex Rocks. ³He came to sheepfolds by the road and a cave there, and Sha'ul came in to relieve himself, while David and his men were sitting in the innermost parts of the cave.

⁴David's men said to him, 'Here, it's the day that Yahweh said to you, "Here, I'm giving your enemy into your hand and you can do to him as seems good in your eyes."' David got up and cut off the corner of Sha'ul's coat quietly, ⁵but afterwards, David's heart struck him because he'd cut the corner off that belonged to Sha'ul. ⁶He said to his men. 'Far be it from me by Yahweh, if I should do this thing to my lord, to Yahweh's anointed, in putting out my hand against him, when he's Yahweh's anointed!' ⁷David tore his men apart with the words and didn't let them rise up against Sha'ul.

When Sha'ul set off from the cave and went on his way, ⁸David set off afterwards and went out of the cave. He called after Sha'ul, 'My lord king!' Sha'ul looked behind him and David bent his head, face to the ground, and bowed low. ⁹David said to Sha'ul, 'Why do you listen to people's words, saying "There, David is seeking something bad for you"? ¹⁰Here, this day your eyes have seen the fact that Yahweh gave you into my hand today in the cave, and they said to kill you, but I had pity on you. I said I wouldn't put out my hand against my lord, because he is Yahweh's anointed.

A dead dog? A flea?

[11] My father, look and look some more at the corner of your coat in my hand, because when I cut off the corner of your coat, I didn't kill you. Acknowledge and see that there's nothing bad and no rebellion in my hand. I haven't wronged you, but you're hunting down my life so as to take it. [12] May Yahweh decide between me and you! May Yahweh take redress from you, whereas my hand will not be against you. [13] As the old aphorism says, "It's from faithless people that faithlessness comes." Given that my hand will not be against you, [14] after whom has the king of Yisra'el gone out? After whom are you pursuing? After a dead dog? After a single flea? [15] May Yahweh be judge and may he decide between me and you. May he look and settle my argument and decide for me from your hand.'

[16] When David finished speaking these words to Sha'ul, Sha'ul said, 'Is this your voice, my son David?' Sha'ul lifted up his voice and wailed. [17] He said to David, 'You're more faithful than me, because you've dealt me good things but I've dealt you bad things. [18] Today you yourself have told of the good that you did to me, the fact that Yahweh delivered me into your hand and you didn't kill me. [19] When someone finds his enemy and sends him off on his way with good . . . Yahweh himself will make good to you with good in return this day for what you've done for me. [20] And now, here, I acknowledge that you will definitely reign as king and Yisra'el's kingdom will rise up in your hand. [21] So now, swear to me by Yahweh, if you cut off my offspring after me, if you annihilate my name from my father's household . . .'

[22] David swore to Sha'ul, and Sha'ul went home, while David and his men went up to the stronghold.

The man with the sheep business

25 Shemu'el died, and all Yisra'el collected and lamented for him. They buried him at his home, at The Height.

David set off and went down to the Pa'ran Wilderness. [2] Now a man in Ma'on with his business in Carmel: this man was very big. He had a flock of 3,000, and 1,000 goats, and he was shearing his flock in Carmel. [3] The man's name was Nabal and his wife's name was Abigayil; the woman was good in her insight and attractive in her appearance, but the man was tough and bad in his practices, though he was a Kalebite [Calebite].

[4] David heard in the wilderness that Nabal was shearing his flock [5] and David sent ten boys. David said to the boys, 'Go up to Carmel and come to Nabal and ask of him in my name whether things are well for him. [6] Say this: "Long life! May things be well for you, may things be well for your household and may things be well for all that is yours! [7] So now, I've heard that you have people shearing. Your shepherds have now been with us. We haven't let them be put to shame and nothing of theirs has been counted missing all the time that they were in Carmel. [8] Ask your boys and they'll tell you. So may the boys find grace in your eyes, because we've come on a good day. Give what your hand finds to your servants, please, and to your son, to David."'

[9] David's boys came and spoke all these very words to Nabal in David's name, and let be. [10] Nabal answered David's servants, 'Who is David, who is ben Yishay? There are many servants breaking away today, each from his lord. [11] Should I take my bread and my water and the meat I've slaughtered for my shearers and give them to men who are from I don't know where?'

Abigayil gets to work

[12] David's boys turned round for their journey and went back, and came and told him all these very words. [13] David said to his men, 'Wrap on, each one, his sword.' They wrapped on, each one, his sword, and David also wrapped on his sword. Some 400 men went up after David while 200 stayed by the things.

[14] One of the boys told Abigayil, Nabal's wife, 'Here, David sent envoys from the wilderness to bless our lord, but he screamed at them, [15] though the men had been very good to us. We weren't shamed and we didn't count anything

missing all the time we were going about with them when we were in the fields, ¹⁶while they were a wall round us both by night and by day all the time we were with them shepherding the flock. ¹⁷So now, acknowledge and see what you should do, because something bad is certain for our lord and for his entire household, but he's a scoundrel to speak to.'

¹⁸Abigayil hurried and got two hundred loaves of bread, two skins of wine, five prepared sheep, five measures of roasted grain, a hundred raisin blocks and two hundred fig blocks, put them on donkeys ¹⁹and said to her boys, 'Pass on before me. Here, I'm coming after you.' She didn't tell her husband Nabal. ²⁰While she was riding on the donkey and going down under the cover of the mountain, there, David and his men were going down to meet her. So she ran into them.

²¹Now David had said, 'It really was something false, that I kept watch on everything that belonged to this man in the wilderness and nothing of all that belonged to him has been counted missing, and he has given back something bad to me in return for something good. ²²May God do so to (the enemies of) David and may he do so more if by morning I leave remaining, out of all who belong to him, one person who pisses against a wall.'

Fool by name and fool by nature

²³Abigayil saw David, and hurried and got down from on the donkey. She fell on her face before David, and bowed to the ground. ²⁴So she fell at his feet and said, 'The waywardness is in me myself, my lord. May your handmaid please speak in your ears. Listen to your handmaid's words. ²⁵My lord should please not give his mind to this scoundrel, to Nabal, because he's the same as his name. "Villain" [*nabal*] is his name and villainy goes with him.

Now I, your handmaid, didn't see my lord's boys whom you sent. ²⁶But now, my lord, as Yahweh lives, and as you yourself live, Yahweh who has held you back from coming into bloodshed and finding deliverance for yourself by your own hand! Now may your enemies and the people who seek what is bad for my lord be like Nabal! ²⁷And now may this blessing that your maidservant has brought for my lord be given to the boys who go about after my lord.

²⁸Please bear with your handmaid's rebellion, because Yahweh will definitely make for my lord a trustworthy household, because my lord is engaged in Yahweh's battles, and nothing bad will be found in you through your days. ²⁹When someone sets about pursuing you and seeking your life, my lord's life will be bound up in the bundle of the living with Yahweh your God, but the life of your enemies he will hurl away, in the middle of a sling's hollow. ³⁰And when Yahweh acts towards my lord in accordance with everything good that he has spoken concerning you, and charges you to be ruler over Yisraèl, ³¹this is not to be a cause of collapsing or stumbling of mind for my lord – to have shed blood for nothing and for my lord to have found deliverance for himself. And when Yahweh has been good to my lord, you are to be mindful of your handmaid.'

A marriage of convenience

³²David said to Abigayil, 'Yahweh the God of Yisraèl be blessed, who sent you this day to meet me. ³³Blessed be your good judgement and blessed be you yourself, who restrained me this day from coming into bloodshed and finding deliverance for myself by my hand. ³⁴Yet, as Yahweh the God of Yisraèl lives, who held me back from dealing badly with you: if you had not hurried and come to meet me, by morning light there would definitely not have been left to Nabal one person who pisses against a wall.'

³⁵David took from her hand what she brought for him, and he said to her, 'Go home, things will be well. See, I've listened to your voice and had regard for you.'

³⁶Abigayil came to Nabal, and there, he had a banquet in his house, like a royal banquet. Nabal's heart was good in him and he was very drunk, so she didn't tell him anything small or great until morning light. ³⁷In the morning, when the wine had left Nabal, his wife told him these things, and his heart died inside him. He turned to stone. ³⁸Some ten days later Yahweh struck Nabal and he died.

³⁹David heard that Nabal had died, and said, 'Yahweh be blessed, who has settled the argument over my reviling at the hand

of Nabal, and held back his servant from something bad. Yahweh has made Nabal's bad action come back on his head.' And David sent and spoke with Abigayil in connection with getting her for himself as a wife. ⁴⁰David's servants came to Abigayil at Carmel and spoke to her: 'David has sent us to you to get you for him as a wife.' ⁴¹She got up and bowed low, face to the ground, and said, 'Here is your handmaid, a maidservant to wash my lord's servants' feet.' ⁴²Abigayil hurried and got up, and mounted a donkey with her five girls behind her, and followed David's envoys. So she became his wife.

⁴³As David had got Ahino'am from Yizre'e'l, the two of them also became his wives. ⁴⁴Sha'ul had given Mikal his daughter, David's wife, to Palti ben Layish, who was from Gallim.

Who can lay hands on Yahweh's anointed?

26 The Ziphites came to Sha'ul at Gib'ah, saying 'David's hiding on Hakilah Hill, isn't he, over against The Wasteland.' ²Sha'ul set off and went down to the Ziph Wilderness, 300 picked men of Yisra'el with him, to look for David in the Ziph Wilderness. ³Sha'ul camped on Hakilah Hill, which is over against The Wasteland, by the road. David was staying in the wilderness, and he saw that Sha'ul had come after him into the wilderness. ⁴David sent men to investigate and got to know as established fact that Sha'ul had come.

⁵Then David set off and came to the place where Sha'ul had camped. David saw the place where Sha'ul lay down with Abner ben Ner his army officer, Sha'ul lying down in the encampment and the company camping round him. ⁶David avowed to Ahimelek the Hittite and to Abishay ben Tseruyah, Yo'ab's brother, 'Who'll go down with me to Sha'ul, to the camp?' Abishay said, 'I'll go down with you.'

⁷David and Abishay came to the company by night, and there, Sha'ul was lying asleep in the encampment, with his lance stuck in the earth by his head, and Abner and the company lying round him. ⁸Abishay said to David, 'God has surrendered your enemy into your hand today, so now I'll strike him down with the lance, please, with one thrust into the earth. I won't need to do it twice.'

⁹David said to Abishay, 'You're not to do violence to him, because who has put out his hand against Yahweh's anointed and been free of guilt?' ¹⁰David said, 'As Yahweh lives, no, Yahweh will strike him, or his day will come and he'll die, or he'll go down to battle and be swept away. ¹¹Far be it from me by Yahweh to put out my hand against Yahweh's anointed. But now get the lance that's at his head and the water jug, please, and let's take ourselves off.'

Sha'ul's protectors' failure

¹²So David got the lance and the water jug from by Sha'ul's head and they took themselves off, with no one seeing and no one knowing and no one waking up, because all of them were asleep, because a coma from Yahweh had fallen on them.

¹³David crossed over to the other side and stood on top of the mountain at a distance; the space between them was great. ¹⁴David called to the company and to Abner ben Ner, 'Answer, Abner, won't you!' Abner answered, 'Who are you who've called to the king?' ¹⁵David said to Abner, 'Aren't you a man? Who is like you in Yisra'el? Why haven't you kept watch over your lord the king? Because one from the company came to do violence to the king, your lord. ¹⁶This thing that you've done isn't good. As Yahweh lives, you people deserve death because you haven't kept watch over your lord, over Yahweh's anointed. Look now. Where are the king's lance and the water jar, which were by his head?'

¹⁷Sha'ul recognized David's voice and he said 'Is this your voice, my son David?' David said, 'My voice, my lord king', ¹⁸and he said, 'Why is it that my lord is pursuing after his servant? Because what have I done? What bad action is in my hand? ¹⁹So now my lord the king should please listen to his servant's words. If it's Yahweh who has incited you against me, may he smell an offering, but if it's human beings, may they be cursed before Yahweh, because they've driven me away so I can't attach myself to Yahweh's domain today, saying "Go serve other gods." ²⁰So now may my blood not fall to the ground at a distance from Yahweh's presence, because the king of Yisra'el has gone out to look for a flea, as he might hunt a partridge in the mountains.'

I've been idiotic

²¹Sha'ul said, 'I've done wrong. Come back, my son David, because I won't deal badly with you again, on account of the fact that my life has been esteemed in your eyes this day. Here, I've been idiotic and I've made very great mistakes.' ²²David answered, 'Here's the king's lance. One of the boys may come across and get it. ²³Yahweh himself will return a person's faithfulness and his trustworthiness, in that Yahweh gave you over into my hand today and I was not willing to put out my hand against Yahweh's anointed. ²⁴Here, as your life has been important in my eyes this day, so may my life be important in Yahweh's eyes and may he rescue me from every pressure.' ²⁵Sha'ul said to David, 'Blessed are you, my son David. May you both do much and also succeed much.'

David went on his way, while Sha'ul went back to his place.

27 David said to himself, 'I shall be swept away now one day by Sha'ul's hand. There's nothing good for me but to make a final escape to the Pelishtites' country. Sha'ul will despair of me, of looking for me any more within Yisra'el's entire border, and I'll escape from his hand.' ²So David set off and crossed over, he and 600 men who were with him, to Akish ben Ma'ok, king of Gat. ³David lived with Akish in Gat, he and his men, each with his household, David with his two wives Ahino'am the Yizre'e'lite and Abigayil the wife of Nabal the Carmelite. ⁴It was told Sha'ul, 'David has taken flight to Gat', and he didn't look for him any more.

⁵David said to Akish, 'If I've found grace in your eyes, may they give me a place in one of the country towns so I can live there. Why should your servant live in the royal town with you?' ⁶So that day Akish gave him Tsiqlag. That's why Tsiqlag has belonged to the kings of Yehudah until this day. ⁷The length of time that David lived in the Pelishtites' country was a year and four months.

David's ruthless cunning

⁸David and his men went up and made a raid on the Geshurites, the Gizrites and the Amaleqites, because they were peoples living in the country that extends from Olam as you come to Shur, and as far as the country of Misrayim. ⁹David would strike down the country and not let a man or woman live, but take flock and herd, donkey, camels and clothes, and go back and come to Akish. ¹⁰Akish would say, 'Whom did you raid just now?', and David would say, 'The Negeb of Yehudah' or 'The Negeb of the Yerahme'elites' or 'The Negeb of the Qenites'. ¹¹David wouldn't let man or woman live for bringing to Gat, saying 'So they don't tell about us, "David did this."' Such was his rule all the time that he lived in the Pelishtites' country. ¹²Akish came to trust David, saying 'He's made himself totally stink among his people, among Yisra'el. He'll be a servant for me permanently.'

28 During that time the Pelishtites collected their camp for war so as to battle against Yisra'el. Akish said to David, 'You do know that you're to go out with me in the camp, you and your men.' ²David said to Akish, 'Therefore, you yourself will know what your servant might do.' Akish said to David, 'Therefore I will make you my bodyguard permanently.'

³Now Shemu'el had died, and all Yisra'el had lamented for him and had buried him at The Height, at his town; and Sha'ul had removed the ghosts and the spirits from the country. ⁴The Pelishtites collected and came and camped at Shunem; Sha'ul collected all Yisra'el and camped at Gilboa. ⁵Sha'ul saw the Pelishtites' camp and was afraid; his heart trembled much. ⁶Sha'ul asked of Yahweh but Yahweh didn't answer him, either by dreams or by Urim or by prophets.

What do you do when you're desperate?

⁷So Sha'ul said to his servants, 'Look for a woman who is a ghost-mistress for me so I can go to her and enquire through her.' His servants said to him, 'There, a woman who is a ghost-mistress is in Dor Spring.' ⁸Sha'ul disguised himself and put on other clothes and went, he and two men with him, and came to the woman at night. He said, 'Please divine through a ghost for me. Bring up for me the one that I shall say to you.'

⁹The woman said to him, 'Here, you yourself know what Sha'ul has done, that he's cut off ghosts and spirits from the country. Why are you laying a trap for my life, to bring about my death?' ¹⁰Sha'ul swore to her by Yahweh: 'As Yahweh lives, if waywardness befalls you through this thing . . .'
¹¹So the woman said, 'Who shall I bring up for you?' He said, 'Shemu'el. Bring him up for me.' ¹²The woman saw Shemu'el and cried out in a loud voice. The woman said to Sha'ul, 'Why have you beguiled me? You're Sha'ul.' ¹³The king said to her, 'Don't be afraid. But what have you seen?' The woman said to Sha'ul, 'It's a divine being I've seen coming up from the earth.' ¹⁴He said to her, 'What's he look like?' She said, 'An old man is coming up. He's wearing a coat.' Sha'ul knew that it was Shemu'el. He bent his head, face to the ground, and bowed low.
¹⁵Shemu'el said to Sha'ul, 'Why have you disturbed me by bringing me up?' Sha'ul said, 'Things are very pressing for me. The Pelishtites are battling with me. God has departed from me. He hasn't answered me any more, either by means of prophets or by dreams. I called to you to enable me to know what I should do.'

Shemu'el still speaks straight

¹⁶Shemu'el said, 'So why do you ask me when Yahweh has departed from you and become your adversary? ¹⁷Yahweh has done to you as he spoke by means of me. Yahweh has torn the kingship from your hand and given it to your neighbour, to David, ¹⁸when you didn't listen to Yahweh's voice and didn't perform his angry rage on Amaleq. That's why Yahweh has done this thing to you this day. ¹⁹Yahweh will also give Yisra'el with you into the hand of the Pelishtites. Tomorrow you and your sons will be with me. Yahweh will also give the Yisra'elite camp into the hand of the Pelishtites.'
²⁰Sha'ul hurried and fell full length on the ground. He was very frightened by Shemu'el's words, while also there was no energy in him because he had not eaten bread all day and all night. ²¹The woman came to Sha'ul and saw that he was very fearful. She said to him, 'Here, your maidservant listened to your voice and I put my life in the palm of my hand. I listened to your words which you spoke to me, ²²so now please listen to your maidservant's voice as well. I want to put a bit of bread before you. Eat, and there'll be energy in you when you go on your way.' ²³He refused and said, 'I won't eat', but his servants pressed him, as well as the woman, and he listened to their voice. He got up from the ground and sat on the bed.
²⁴The woman had a stall-fed calf in the house. She hurried and slaughtered it, got flour and kneaded it, and baked it into flatbread. ²⁵She brought it up before Sha'ul and before his servants and they ate. Then they got up, and went that night.

29 The Pelishtites collected their entire camp at Apheq, while Yisra'el was camping at the spring which is in Yizre'e'l ²and the Pelishtites' lords were passing on by sections and by divisions, with David and his men passing on with Akish at the end.

The Pelishtites' lords are wiser than Akish

³The Pelishtites' officers said, 'What are these Hebrews?' Akish said to the Pelishtites' officers, 'This is David, the servant of Sha'ul, king of Yisra'el, isn't it, who's been with me for this time (these years). I haven't found any fault in him from the day he fell away until this day.' ⁴The Pelishtites' officers were furious with him. The Pelishtites' officers said to him, 'Send the man back. He should go back to his place, where you appointed him. He shouldn't go down with us in the battle, so he won't become an adversary to us in the battle. How could this man find acceptance with his lord – it was with those men's heads, wasn't it. ⁵This is the David of whom they used to chant during the dance, isn't it:

Sha'ul has struck down his thousands,
David his ten thousands.

⁶So Akish called for David and said to him, 'As Yahweh lives, you're upright and your going out and coming in with me in the camp is good in my eyes, because I haven't found anything bad in you from the day you came to me until this day. But in the eyes of the lords you're not good. ⁷So now go back, go while things are well, and you won't do anything bad in the eyes of the

Pelishtites' lords.' ⁸David said to Akish, 'But what have I done and what have you found in your servant from the day when I came to be before you until this day, that I shouldn't come and do battle with the enemies of my lord the king?' ⁹Akish answered David, 'I acknowledge that you are good in my eyes, like God's envoy. Nevertheless the Pelishtites' officers have said, "He will not go up with us in the battle." ¹⁰So now, start early in the morning, you and your lord's servants who have come with you. Start early in the morning and when you have light, go.'

¹¹So in the morning David started early, he and his men, to go to return to the Pelishtites' country, while the Pelishtites went up to Yizre'e'l.

The disaster while their back was turned

30 When David and his men came to Tsiqlag, on the third day, the Amaleqites had made a raid on the Negeb and on Tsiqlag. They'd struck down Tsiqlag and burned it in fire ²and taken captive the women who were in it, from the youngest to the oldest. They hadn't put anyone to death but they'd driven them off and gone on their way.

³So David and his men came to the town: there, it was burnt in fire and their wives, their sons and their daughters had been taken captive. ⁴David and the company that was with him lifted up their voice and wailed until there was no energy in them to wail. ⁵David's two wives had been taken captive, Ahino'am the Yizre'elite and Abigayil the wife of Nabal the Carmelite.

⁶It put great pressure on David, because the company said to pelt him with stones, because the entire company's spirit was bitter, each person over his sons and his daughters. But David summoned up his strength through Yahweh his God. ⁷David said to Ebyatar the priest, son of Ahimelek, 'Bring up the chasuble for me, please.' Ebyatar brought up the chasuble to David. ⁸David asked of Yahweh, 'Should I pursue after this raiding gang, will I overtake it?' He said to him, 'Pursue, because you will indeed overtake and you will indeed rescue.'

⁹So David went, he and 600 men who were with him, and came as far as Wadi Besor. While the people who were to be left halted, ¹⁰David pursued, he and 400 men; 200 men who were too faint to cross Wadi Besor halted.

The informant

¹¹They found a Misrayimite man in the fields and took him to David. They gave him bread and he ate, and they let him drink water, ¹²and gave him a piece of a fig block and two raisin blocks. He ate and his spirit came back to him (because he hadn't eaten bread and hadn't drunk water for three days and three nights). ¹³David said to him, 'Who do you belong to and where are you from?' He said, 'I'm a Misrayimite boy, the servant of an Amaleqite. My lord abandoned me because I got ill, three days ago, ¹⁴when we had made an incursion against the Negeb of the Keretites and against what belongs to Yehudah and against the Negeb of Kaleb, and we burned Tsiqlag in fire.'

¹⁵David said to him, 'Will you take me down to this raiding gang?' He said, 'Swear to me by God, if you put me to death or if you deliver me into my lord's hand . . . And I will take you down to this gang.' ¹⁶So he took them down and there they were, left to themselves on the face of the ground, eating and drinking and feasting on all the vast spoil that they had taken from the Pelishtites' country and from the region of Yehudah.

¹⁷David struck them down from dusk until the evening of the next day. Not one of them escaped, except 400 young men who mounted camels and fled. ¹⁸David rescued everything that Amaleq had taken. And David rescued his two wives. ¹⁹Nothing was missing to them, both the young and the old, sons and daughters, and from the spoil and all that they had taken for themselves. David got everything back. ²⁰David took the entire flock, while they drove the herd before that livestock. They said, 'This is David's spoil.'

All should share

²¹David came to the 200 men who were too faint to follow David, so that they had let them stay at Wadi Besor. They went out to meet David and to meet the company that was with him. David went up with the company and he asked them whether things were well. ²²Every bad man and scoundrel of the men who had gone with David answered, 'Since they didn't go with me, we shouldn't give them any of the

spoil that we rescued, except an individual his wife and his children, so they can drive them off and go.'

²³David said, 'You will not do so, my brothers, with what Yahweh has given us. He has kept us and given over the raiding gang that came against us, into our hand. ²⁴Who would listen to you regarding this thing? Because as will be the share of the person who went down into the battle, so will be the share of the person who stayed with the things. They will share it out together.' ²⁵From that day onwards he made it a decree and a rule for Yisra'el, until this day.

²⁶David came to Tsiqlag and sent off some of the spoil to the elders of Yehudah, to his friends, saying 'Here's your blessing from the spoil of Yahweh's enemies', ²⁷to the ones in Betel, to the ones in the Negeb Heights, to the ones in Yattir, ²⁸to the ones in Aro'er, to the ones in Siphmot, to the ones in Eshtemoa, ²⁹to the ones in Rakal, to the ones in the towns of the Yerahme'elites, to the ones in the towns of the Qenites, ³⁰to the ones in Hormah, to the ones in Ashan Cistern, to the ones in Atak ³¹and to the ones in Hebron, to all the places where David had gone about, he and his men.

A last act of loyalty to Sha'ul

31 When the Pelishtites battled against Yisra'el, the Yisra'elites fled from before the Pelishtites and fell, run through, on Mount Gilboa. ²The Pelishtites caught up with Sha'ul and with his sons, and the Pelishtites struck down Yehonatan, Abinadab and Malki-shua, Sha'ul's sons.

³The battle was hard against Sha'ul, and the archers (the bowmen) found him; he was run through by the archers. ⁴Sha'ul said to his equipment-bearer, 'Draw your sword and thrust me through with it, so these foreskinned men don't come and thrust me through and act abusively to me.' But his equipment-bearer wasn't willing because he was very fearful, so Sha'ul took the sword and fell on it. ⁵His equipment-bearer saw that Sha'ul was dead and he too fell on his sword and died with him. ⁶So Sha'ul died, with his three sons, and his equipment-bearer, as well as all his men, all together on that day.

⁷The Yisra'elites who were across the vale and who were across the Yarden saw that the Yisra'elites had fled and that Sha'ul and his sons were dead, and they abandoned their towns and fled (the Pelishtites came and lived in them).

⁸Next day the Pelishtites came to strip the people who were run through. They found Sha'ul and his three sons fallen on Mount Gilboa, ⁹cut off his head and stripped off his equipment. They sent off through the country of the Pelishtites all round to proclaim the news to the house of their idols and to the people. ¹⁰They put his equipment in the house of the Ashtars, and his body they fastened to the wall of Bet Shan. ¹¹But the people living in Yabesh-in-Gil'ad heard about it, about what the Pelishtites had done to Sha'ul, ¹²and they set off, every forceful man. They went all night and got Sha'ul's body and his sons' bodies from the walls of Bet-shan. They came to Yabesh and burned them there, ¹³then got their bones and buried them under the tamarisk at Yabesh, and fasted for seven days.

2 Samuel

The story in 2 Samuel is a tragedy. In a broad sense a tragedy is any terrible event, but we can also use the word to describe a certain kind of story, one that relates how someone important and successful experiences the collapse of everything that made him or her important and successful. While this collapse may come about through bad luck, it may come about through bad decisions whose terrible consequences could hardly have been foreseen, yet which with hindsight seem inevitable. The tragedy in 2 Samuel is the tragedy of David.

Ironically, the background to David's tragedy is another one, that of Saul. Given the circumstances of Saul's becoming king, it might not seem surprising that his reign ends unhappily. David plays a key role in his downfall, without intending to do so – indeed, David seeks to honour Saul as the king anointed by Yahweh. But Saul's story unravels and he dies in battle, along with Jonathan, his son and David's best friend. Their death opens up the way for David to succeed Saul. He has already been designated by God for this position, but the process whereby he gets there is a human one.

Naturally enough, the people of Judah, David's own clan, are ready to recognize him, but the people of the northern clans are aware of other options from within their own number – specifically, someone from Saul's household might seem a natural choice. But the possible candidates and the party supporting them gradually disappear, so that the northern clans drift into giving their own recognition to David.

David then makes an astute move in conquering Jerusalem. Although it sits in the middle of areas assigned to the Israelite clans, the town is still occupied by the Yebusites. David conquers it and makes it his capital. Its position and its history mean that no clan identifies with it, so it has the potential to be viewed as neutral territory, as David's town. Yahweh later declares that he chose it, but in 2 Samuel, it's David who takes the initiative in choosing it.

The dynamics of this process recur in the decision to build a permanent sanctuary for worship of Yahweh in Jerusalem. Again it is David's idea. Yahweh is not enthusiastic about it, because he doesn't want to be stuck in a fixed place, but he yields to it. He goes on to make a commitment to David that removes some of the ambiguity of his earlier attitude to the idea of having kings. He now promises David that his line will permanently occupy the throne over Israel. His immediate successor will be the king who actually builds the sanctuary in Jerusalem.

In the event, he will be the only successor to reign over the whole of Israel, and after a few centuries Davidic rule over Judah will come to an end. God's promise about David's line thus leads in due course to the hope of a Messiah. The word *Messiah* means *Anointed*, and in the Old Testament it applies to actual kings (and priests). But when there are no kings in the present, it comes to refer to the king whom God must surely set up one day.

David wins more spectacular victories but then everything starts to unravel. The second half of 2 Samuel tells of a catastrophic series of events in David's life, for most of which he is directly or indirectly responsible. They centre on his relationships with people inside and outside his family rather than on political or military events. He has shown himself to be a brilliant leader, but he is a disaster as a human being.

It might seem surprising that he is described as a man after God's heart. The description need only mean that he is the man God chose; it doesn't imply that his heart was in tune with God's heart. But in later pages of the Old Testament he is viewed as a model who contrasts positively with many other kings. For all his wrongdoing and foolishness, at least he stayed faithful to Yahweh and stayed trusting in Yahweh.

The fraud that will come unstuck

1 After Sha'ul's [Saul's] death, and when David had come back from striking down the Amaleqites, David stayed in Tsiqlag for two days, ²and on the third day – there, a man coming from the camp, from being with Sha'ul, with his clothes torn and earth on his head. When he came to David he fell to the ground and bowed low. ³David said to him, 'Where do you come from?' He said to him, 'I escaped from Yisra'el's [Israel's] camp.' ⁴David said to him, 'What was it that happened? Please tell me.' He said how the company fled from the battle and also many of the company fell and died and also Sha'ul and Yehonatan [Jonathan] his son died.

⁵David said to the boy who told him, 'How do you know that Sha'ul is dead, and Yehonatan his son?' ⁶The boy who told him said, 'I just happened to be on Mount Gilboa, and there, Sha'ul was leaning on his lance, and there, chariotry and cavalry caught up with him. ⁷He turned his face behind him and saw me and called to me. I said, "Here I am." ⁸He said to me, "Who are you?" I said to him, "I'm an Amaleqite." ⁹He said to me, "Stand over me, please, and put me to death, because doom has taken hold of me, when my life is still entirely in me." ¹⁰So I stood over him and put him to death because I acknowledged that he would not live after he had fallen. I took the diadem that was on his head and a bracelet that was on his arm and brought them to my lord, here.'

¹¹David took strong hold of his clothes and tore them, he and all the men who were with him as well. ¹²They lamented and wailed and fasted until evening for Sha'ul, for Yehonatan his son, for Yahweh's company and for the household of Yisra'el, because they had fallen by the sword.

How are the mighty fallen

¹³David said to the boy who told him, 'Where are you from?' He said, 'I'm the son of a resident, an Amaleqite.' ¹⁴David said to him, 'How were you not afraid to put out your hand to do violence to Yahweh's anointed?' ¹⁵David called for one of the boys and said, 'Come up, attack him!' He struck him down and he died. ¹⁶David said to him, 'Your blood is on your own head, because your own mouth avowed against you, "I put Yahweh's anointed to death."'

¹⁷David chanted this elegy over Sha'ul and over Yehonatan his son, ¹⁸and he said to teach the Yehudahites 'The Bow' (there, it's written on the Document of the Upright One):

¹⁹The gazelle, Yisra'el, is run through on your heights:
  how have the strong men fallen.
²⁰Don't tell it in Gat,
  don't announce the news in Ashqelon's streets,
Lest the Pelishtites' [Philistines'] daughters celebrate,
  lest the daughters of the foreskinned exult.
²¹Mountains of Gilboa, may there be no dew,
  no rain on you or fields of contributions,
Because there the strong men's shield was fouled,
  the shield of Sha'ul, no more rubbed with oil.
²²From the blood of the slain,
  from the fat of strong men,
The bow of Yehonatan did not turn back,
  the sword of Sha'ul did not go back empty.
²³Sha'ul and Yehonatan, loved and delighted in,
  in their life and in their death they were not parted.
They were swifter than eagles,
  they were stronger than lions.
²⁴Daughters of Yisra'el,
  wail over Sha'ul,
Who clothed you in scarlet and finery,
  who put gold ornaments on your apparel.
²⁵How have the strong men fallen
  in the middle of the battle.
Yehonatan, run through on your heights,
  ²⁶it's depressing for me because of you.
My brother Yehonatan,
  you were very lovely to me.
Your loyalty was extraordinary to me,
  more than the loyalty of women.
²⁷How have the strong men fallen
  and the articles of battle perished!

Two kings

2 After this, David asked of Yahweh, 'Should I go up into one of the towns of Judah?' Yahweh said to him, 'Go up.' David said, 'Where should I go up?' He said, 'To Hebron.'

2 Samuel 1: David

²So David went up there, he and also his two wives Ahino'am the Yizre'e'lite and Abigayil the wife of Nabal the Carmelite, ³and David took up his men who were with him, each man and his household, and they lived in the Hebron towns. ⁴The Yehudahites [Judahites] came and anointed David as king there over the household of Yehudah.

They told David, 'The people who buried Sha'ul were the people of Yabesh-in-Gil'ad.' ⁵So David sent envoys to the people of Yabesh-in-Gil'ad and said to them, 'Blessed are you by Yahweh because you acted in this commitment with your lord, with Sha'ul, and buried him. ⁶So now may Yahweh act in commitment and truthfulness with you, and I myself will also do this good thing with you, because you did this thing. ⁷So now, may your hands be strong, be forceful men, because your lord Sha'ul is dead, and further the household of Yehudah have anointed me as king over them.'

⁸Now Abner ben Ner, army officer for Sha'ul, had got Shameful-man son of Sha'ul [Ish-boshet ben Sha'ul], got him to go across to Mahanayim, ⁹and made him king for Gil'ad, for the Ashurites, for Yizre'e'l, for Ephrayim and for Binyamin [Benjamin] – for Yisra'el, all of it. ¹⁰Shameful-man son of Sha'ul was a man of forty years when he became king over Yisra'el and he reigned for two years. However, the household of Yehudah was following David. ¹¹The length of the time that David was king in Hebron over the household of Yehudah was seven years and six months.

The boys fight it out

¹²Abner ben Ner went out, he and the servants of Shameful-man son of Sha'ul, from Mahanayim to Gib'on, ¹³when Yo'ab ben Tseruyah and David's servants went out and met them at the Gib'on pool, together. One group sat at the pool on one side, the other group at the pool on the other side. ¹⁴Abner said to Yo'ab, 'The boys should get up, shouldn't they, and make fun before us!' Yo'ab said, 'They should get up!' ¹⁵They got up and went across by number, twelve for Binyamin and for Shameful-man son of Sha'ul, and twelve of David's servants. ¹⁶Each one took strong hold of his neighbour's head, with his sword into his neighbour's side; thus they fell together. So they called that place Helqat Hatstsurim ['Blades Share'], which is in Gib'on.

¹⁷The battle was very tough that day, and Abner and the Yisra'elites took a beating before David's servants. ¹⁸The three sons of Tseruyah were there, Yo'ab, Abishay and Asah'el. Now Asah'el was quick on his feet, like one of the gazelles that are in the wild. ¹⁹Asah'el pursued after Abner, and didn't turn aside as he went, to the right or to the left, from following Abner.

²⁰Abner turned his face behind him and said, 'Is it you, Asah'el?' He said, 'It's me.' ²¹Abner said to him. 'Turn yourself to your right or to your left and take hold of one of the boys for yourself and get his strip for yourself.' But Asah'el wasn't willing to turn aside from following him. ²²Abner once more said to Asah'el, 'Turn yourself aside from following me! Why should I strike you down to the ground? How could I lift up my face to Yo'ab your brother?' ²³But he refused to turn aside, and Abner struck him down with the end of his lance, in his abdomen. The lance came out from behind and he fell there and died where he was. Everyone who came to the place where Asah'el had fallen and died, halted.

The struggle for power

²⁴Yo'ab and Abishay pursued after Abner as the sun went down and they came to Ammah Hill, which is east of Giah on the Gib'on Wilderness road. ²⁵The Binyaminites collected behind Abner and became one company, and they stood on the top of a hill. ²⁶Abner called to Yo'ab, 'Is the sword to devour permanently? Do you not acknowledge that it will be bitter at the end? For how long will you not say to the company to turn back from following their brothers?' ²⁷Yo'ab said, 'As God lives, if you hadn't spoken, it would rather be in the morning that the company would then give up, each person, from following his brother.' ²⁸So Yo'ab blew on the horn, and the entire company halted. They didn't pursue after Yisra'el any longer and didn't do battle any more. ²⁹When Abner and his men had gone through the steppe all that night, they crossed the Yarden [Jordan], went all through the gorge and came to Mahanayim.

³⁰When Yo'ab had gone back from following Abner, he collected his entire company, and from David's servants nineteen men were counted missing, with Asah'el, ³¹while David's servants had struck down from Binyamin and among Abner's men 360; they had died. ³²They carried Asah'el and buried him in his father's grave, which is in Bet Lehem. Then Yo'ab and his men went all night, and it got light for them in Hebron.

3 The battle between Sha'ul's household and David's household was long-drawn-out, though David was growing stronger and Sha'ul's household was growing weaker. ²Sons were born to David in Hebron. His firstborn was Amnon, by Ahino'am the Yizre'e'lite. ³His second was Kil'ab, by Abigayil, the wife of Nabal the Carmelite. The third was Abshalom, the son of Ma'akah bat Talmay, king of Geshur. ⁴The fourth was Adoniyyah, the son of Haggit. The fifth was Shephatyah, the son of Abital. ⁵The sixth was Yitre'am, by Eglah, David's wife. These were born to David in Hebron.

Abner's power play?

⁶As the battle was going on between Sha'ul's household and David's household, Abner was asserting his strength in Sha'ul's household. ⁷Now Sha'ul had a secondary wife; her name was Ritspah bat Ayyah. [Shameful-man] said to Abner, 'Why have you had sex with my father's wife?' ⁸It really enraged Abner at Shameful-man's words. He said, 'Am I a dog's head that belongs to Yehudah? Today I act in commitment with the household of Sha'ul your father, to his brothers and to his friends, and I haven't let you be found in David's hand, and today you attribute waywardness to me with the woman. ⁹May God do this to Abner and may he do more to him, because as Yahweh swore to David, so I will do for him, ¹⁰to let the kingship pass over from Sha'ul's household and establish David's throne over Yisra'el and over Yehudah, from Dan as far as Be'er Sheba.' ¹¹He couldn't say back anything further to Abner, for fear of him.

¹²Abner sent envoys to David, in place of himself, saying 'Whose is the country? You should solemnize your pact with me, and here, my hand will be with you to get all Yisra'el to come round to you.' ¹³He said, 'Good, I myself will solemnize a pact with you. I'm going to ask only one thing from you: you will not see my face unless beforehand you bring Mikal, Sha'ul's daughter, when you come to see my face.' ¹⁴And David sent envoys to Shameful-man son of Sha'ul, saying 'Give over my wife Mikal whom I betrothed to myself for a hundred Pelishtite foreskins.' ¹⁵Shameful-man sent and got her from being with the husband, from being with Palti'el ben Layish. ¹⁶Her husband went with her, wailing as he followed her as far as Bahurim, but Abner said to him, 'Go, go back', and he went back.

Abner miscalculates

¹⁷Abner had word with Yisra'el's elders: 'Even in previous days, you were seeking David as king over you. ¹⁸So now, act, because Yahweh has said of David, "By the hand of David my servant I will deliver my people Yisra'el from the hand of the Pelishtites and from the hand of all their enemies."' ¹⁹Abner both spoke in Binyamin's ear, and Abner also went to speak in David's ear in Hebron of all that was good in the eyes of Yisra'el and in the eyes of the entire household of Binyamin.

²⁰Abner came to David at Hebron, twenty men with him, and David made a banquet for Abner and for the men who were with him. ²¹Abner said to David, 'I'll set off and go and collect all Yisra'el for my lord the king so they can solemnize a pact with you and you can reign over all that your appetite longs for.' David sent Abner off and he went, with things being well.

²²But there, David's servants and Yo'ab came from a raiding gang, and brought much spoil with them. Abner was not with David in Hebron because David had sent him off and he had gone, with things being well. ²³When Yo'ab and the entire army that was with him came, people told Yo'ab, 'Abner ben Ner came to the king, and he sent him off; he went with things being well.'

²⁴Yo'ab came to the king and said, 'What have you done? Here was Abner coming to you. Why did you send him off? He's totally gone. ²⁵You know Abner ben Ner, that he would have come to deceive you and to know your coming and your going and to know everything that you're doing.'

The elimination of Abner

²⁶Yo'ab went out from being with David and sent envoys after Abner, and they brought him back from the Sirah cistern. David didn't know. ²⁷So Abner came back to Hebron, Yo'ab took him aside inside the gateway to speak with him in private, but struck him down there, in the abdomen. He died for the blood of Asah'el his brother.

²⁸David heard afterwards and said, 'I and my kingdom are free of guilt before Yahweh permanently for the shedding of the blood

of Abner ben Ner. ²⁹May it whirl on the head of Yo'ab and on his father's entire household. May there not be cut off from Yo'ab's household someone with a discharge or someone with scaliness, or a man who takes strong hold of the spindle or falls by the sword or lacks bread.' ³⁰Yo'ab and Abishay his brother had killed Abner because of the fact that he had put Asah'el their brother to death at Gib'on in the battle.

³¹David said to Yo'ab and to the entire company that was with him, 'Tear your clothes and wrap on sack and lament before Abner', while King David was going behind the bier. ³²So they buried Abner at Hebron. The king lifted up his voice and wailed at Abner's grave. The entire company wailed. ³³The king chanted for Abner:

> Should Abner have been dying
>   the death of a villain?
> ³⁴Your hands were not tied up,
>   your feet were not in chains.
> They were brought together like someone
>   falling –
>   before evil men you fell.

So the entire company continued to wail over him.

The disabled son

³⁵The entire company came to get David to eat bread while it was still day, but David swore, 'May God do this to me and may he do more if I taste bread or anything before sunset.' ³⁶When the entire company recognized, it was good in their eyes, as everything that the king did was good in the eyes of the entire company. ³⁷The entire company and all Yisra'el acknowledged that day that putting Abner ben Ner to death did not come from the king.

³⁸The king said to his servants, 'You acknowledge, do you not, that a leader and a great man has fallen this day in Yisra'el. ³⁹And I myself am raw today, though anointed king, whereas these men, the sons of Tseruyah, are tougher than me. May Yahweh make good to the person who does what is bad in accordance with the bad thing that he did.'

4 Ben Sha'ul heard that Abner had died at Hebron, and his hands went slack, while all Yisra'el was fearful. ²Now ben Sha'ul had two men who were officers over raiding gangs. The name of one was Ba'anah and the name of the second was Rekab, sons of Rimmon the Be'erotite, of the Binyaminites because Be'erot was also counted with Binyamin. ³The Be'erotites had taken flight to Gittayim, and they have been residents there until this day.

⁴Now Yehonatan son of Sha'ul had a son who was injured in both feet. He was a boy of five years when the report about Sha'ul and Yehonatan came from Yizre'e'l. His nurse had carried him and fled, and as she was making haste to flee, he fell, so he limped. His name was Mephiboshet ['From-Shame's-Mouth'].

The elimination of Sha'ul's other son

⁵So the sons of Rimmon the Be'erotite, Rekab and Ba'anah, went and at the very heat of the day came to Shameful-man's house. He was taking a midday lie-down. ⁶So there, they came inside the house like people getting wheat and struck him down in the abdomen. Then Rekab and Ba'anah his brother escaped. ⁷They had come to the house when he was lying on his bed in his bedroom, struck him down and put him to death, and they removed his head, took his head, went by the Steppe road all night ⁸and brought Shameful-man's head to David at Hebron. They said to the king, 'Here is the head of Shameful-man son of Sha'ul, your enemy who sought your life. This day Yahweh has given my lord the king full redress from Sha'ul and his offspring.'

⁹David answered Rekab and Ba'anah his brother, the sons of Rimmon the Be'erotite, 'As Yahweh lives, who has redeemed my life from every pressure: ¹⁰when someone told me, "Here, Sha'ul is dead", and in his eyes he was like someone bringing good news, I seized him and killed him in Tsiqlag, one to whom I might have given something for the news. ¹¹How much more when faithless men have killed a faithful man in his house on his bed! I will seek his blood from your hand and burn you away from the country, won't I.' ¹²So David ordered the boys and they killed them, cut off their hands and their feet, and hanged them over the pool at Hebron. The head of Shameful-man they took and buried in Abner's grave at Hebron.

David becomes king and Yerushalaim (Jerusalem) becomes his city

5 Then all the Yisra'elite clans came to David at Hebron and said, 'Here, we are your flesh and blood. ²Further, in previous days, when Sha'ul was king over us, you were the one who took Yisra'el out and brought Yisra'el in. Yahweh said to you, "You're the one who will shepherd my people Yisra'el. You're the one who will be ruler over Yisra'el."'

³So all Yisra'el's elders came to the king at Hebron, King David solemnized a pact to them at Hebron before Yahweh, and they anointed David as king over Yisra'el. ⁴David was a man of thirty years when he began to reign and he reigned for forty years: ⁵in Hebron he reigned over Yehudah for seven years and six months, and in Yerushalaim he reigned for thirty-three years over all Yisra'el and Yehudah.

⁶The king and his men went to Yerushalaim against the Yebusites, the inhabitants of the region. They said to David, 'You won't come in here. Actually, the blind and the lame could have removed you' (saying, 'David won't come in here'). ⁷But David captured the Zion stronghold (i.e. David's Town). ⁸David said on that day, 'Anyone striking down the Yebusites (the blind and the lame, treated with hostility by David himself – that's why they say, "A blind or lame person will not come into the house") should take possession of the conduit.'

⁹David lived in the stronghold and named it 'David's Town'. David built it up all round from the Fill to the house. ¹⁰David went on getting bigger and bigger, as Yahweh the God of Armies was with him. ¹¹Hiram king of Tsor [Tyre] sent envoys to David with cedar wood, craftsmen in wood and craftsmen in stone for walls, and they built a house for David.

For the sake of David's people Yisra'el

¹²David acknowledged that Yahweh had established him as king over Yisra'el and that he had exalted his kingship for the sake of his people Yisra'el. ¹³David took more secondary wives and wives from Yerushalaim after he came from Hebron, and more sons and daughters were born to David. ¹⁴These are the names of the children born to him in Yerushalaim: Shammua, Shobab, Natan, Shelomoh [Solomon], ¹⁵Yibhar, Elishua, Nepheg, Yaphia, ¹⁶Elishama, Elyada and Eliphelet.

¹⁷The Pelishtites heard that they had anointed David as king over Yisra'el, and all the Pelishtites went up to look for David. David heard, and went down to the stronghold. ¹⁸When the Pelishtites came, they ran loose in Repha'ites Vale. ¹⁹David asked of Yahweh, 'Shall I go up against the Pelishtites? Will you give them into my hand?' Yahweh said to David, 'Go up, because I shall definitely give the Pelishtites into your hand', ²⁰and David came to Ba'al-peratsim. David struck them down there and said, 'Yahweh has broken out on my enemies before me like a breakout of water.' That's why they named that place Ba'al Peratsim ['Master of Breakouts']. ²¹They abandoned their idols there, and David and his men carried them off.

²²The Pelishtites yet again went up and ran loose in Repha'ites Vale. ²³David asked of Yahweh, but he said, 'You will not go up. Make a turn round behind them and come to them from the direction of the weeper trees. ²⁴When you hear the sound of marching in the tops of the weeper trees, then take action, because Yahweh will have gone out before you to strike down the Pelishtites' camp.' ²⁵David did so, as Yahweh ordered him, and struck down the Pelishtites from Geba as far as when you come to Gezer.

Little things can have terrible consequences

6 David again gathered every picked man in Yisra'el, 30,000. ²David set off and went, he and the entire company that was with him, from Ba'alim-in-Yehudah to take up from there God's chest over which the name is called out (the name of Yahweh of Armies who sits above the sphinxes). ³They transported God's chest on a new wagon and carried it from Abinadab's house, which was on the hill, with Uzza and Ahyo, Abinadab's sons, driving the new wagon. ⁴So they carried it from Abinadab's house, which was on the hill, with God's chest, with Ahyo going before the chest, ⁵and David and the entire household of Yisra'el made fun before Yahweh with all juniper wood [instruments], with guitars, with mandolins, with tambourines, with rattles and with cymbals.

⁶But they came as far as Nakon's threshing floor, and Uzza reached out to God's chest and grasped it because the cattle had stumbled, ⁷and Yahweh's anger raged at Uzzah. God struck him down there because of the blunder. He died there near God's chest.

⁸It really enraged David that Yahweh had broken out at Uzzah (he called that place Perets Uzzah ['Breakout at Uzzah'], until this day). ⁹David was afraid of Yahweh that day and said, 'How can Yahweh's chest come to me?' ¹⁰So David was not willing to move Yahweh's chest to him, to David's Town. David got it to turn aside to the house of Obed-edom the Gittite.

¹¹Yahweh's chest stayed at the house of Obed Edom the Gittite for three months. Yahweh blessed Obed Edom and his entire household, ¹²and it was told King David, 'Yahweh has blessed the household of Obed Edom and all that belongs to him on account of God's chest', so David went and brought up God's chest from Obed Edom's house to David's Town with rejoicing.

How David honoured himself today!

¹³When the people carrying Yahweh's chest had taken six steps he sacrificed a bull and a fatling, ¹⁴with David whirling before Yahweh with all his vigour, and David wrapped round in a linen chasuble, ¹⁵and David and all the household of Yisra'el bringing up Yahweh's chest with a shout and with the sound of a horn. ¹⁶Yahweh's chest was coming into David's Town as Mikal, Sha'ul's daughter, was looking out through the window. She saw King David jumping and whirling before Yahweh, and she despised him inside.

¹⁷They brought in Yahweh's chest and put it in its place inside the tent that David had spread for it. David offered up burnt offerings and well-being sacrifices before Yahweh. ¹⁸David finished offering up the burnt offering and the well-being sacrifices, blessed the people in the name of Yahweh of Armies, ¹⁹and shared out to the entire people, to the entire Yisra'elite horde, both men and women, to each individual, a round of bread, a date block and a raisin block.

The entire people went each person to his house, ²⁰and David went back to bless his household. Mikal, Sha'ul's daughter, came out to meet David, but she said, 'How the king of Yisra'el honoured himself today when he exposed himself today before the eyes of his servants' handmaids, as one of the empty-headed people totally exposes himself!'

²¹David said to Mikal, 'It was before Yahweh, who chose me rather than your father and his entire household to charge me to be ruler over Yahweh's people, over Yisra'el. I'll make fun before Yahweh ²²and slight myself yet more than this and be low in my own eyes, but with the handmaids that you speak of, with them I'll find honour.'

²³To Mikal, Sha'ul's daughter, no child was born till the day of her death.

Yahweh doesn't like settling down

7 When the king had gone to live in his house, when Yahweh had given him a settled position in relation to all his enemies around, ²the king said to Natan the prophet, 'Please look: I'm living in a cedar house, but God's chest is living inside a tent.' ³Natan said to the king, 'Go do everything that's in your mind, because Yahweh is with you.'

⁴But that night Yahweh's word came to Natan: ⁵'Go and say to my servant, to David, "Yahweh has said this: 'Are you to build me a house to live in? ⁶Because I haven't lived in a house from the day that I took the Yisra'elites up from Misrayim [Egypt] till this day. I've been going about in a tent as a dwelling. ⁷Everywhere I went about among all the Yisra'elites, did I speak a word with one of the Yisra'elite clan leaders whom I ordered to shepherd my people Yisra'el, saying "Why have you not built me a cedar house?"'"

⁸'So now you're to say this to my servant, to David, "Yahweh of Armies has said this: 'I myself took you from the pasture, from following the flock, to be ruler over my people, over Yisra'el, ⁹and I've been with you everywhere you've gone. I've cut off all your enemies from before you and I shall make a big name for you, like the name of the big people

who are on the earth. ¹⁰I shall make a place for my people, for Yisra'el, and plant them. They will dwell in their place and not tremble again. Evil people won't humble them again as they did previously, ¹¹from the day that I ordered leaders over my people Yisra'el. I shall give you a settled position in relation to all your enemies.

A house and a household

Yahweh tells you that Yahweh will make a house(hold) for you. ¹²When your days are full and you lie down with your ancestors, I shall set up your offspring after you, who will come out from inside you, and I shall establish his kingship. ¹³He is the one who will build a house for my name. I shall establish his royal throne permanently. ¹⁴I myself will become a father to him and he will become a son to me. When he goes wrong, I shall reprove him with a club in the hand of human beings, with the blows of human hands, ¹⁵but my commitment will not depart from him as I removed it from Sha'ul, whom I removed from before you. ¹⁶Your household and your kingship will be trustworthy permanently before you. Your throne will be established permanently."'

¹⁷In accordance with all these words and in accordance with this entire vision, so Natan spoke to David.

¹⁸King David came and sat before Yahweh, and said, 'Who am I, Lord Yahweh, and who are my household, that you have brought me as far as this? ¹⁹Moreover, this has been small in your eyes, Lord Yahweh. You've spoken further about your servant's household for the distant future. This is instruction about a human being, Lord Yahweh: ²⁰what more can David speak to you? You yourself have acknowledged your servant, Lord Yahweh. ²¹On account of your word and in accordance with your mind you're doing this entire big thing, making it known to your servant.

No God like Yahweh, no people like Yisra'el

²²Thus you are great, Lord Yahweh, because there is no one like you, no God except you, in all that we have heard with our ears. ²³And who is like your people, like Yisra'el, a nation on the earth that God went to redeem for himself as a people, to make for himself a name, and to do big and awe-inspiring things (for you all) for your country before your people whom you redeemed for yourself from Misrayim (nations and their gods). ²⁴You established your people Yisra'el for yourself as a people permanently, and you Yahweh became God for them.

²⁵Now, Yahweh God, the word that you have spoken about your servant and about his household – establish it permanently and do as you have spoken. ²⁶May your name be great permanently: "Yahweh of Armies is God over Yisra'el". May your servant David's household be established before you. ²⁷Because you, Yahweh of Armies, God of Yisra'el, have opened your servant's ear, saying "I will build a household for you." That's why your servant has found his courage to make this plea to you.

²⁸Now, Lord Yahweh, you are God, and your words are truthful. You have spoken this good thing to your servant. ²⁹Now resolve to bless your servant's household so it will be before you permanently, because you, Lord Yahweh, have spoken. May your servant's household be blessed permanently through your blessing.'

David's victories

8 Subsequently, David struck down the Pelishtites and made them bow down. David took the reins of control from the hand of the Pelishtites. ²He also struck down the Mo'abites. He measured them with a length of cord, making them lie down on the ground. He measured two lengths for putting them to death and one full length for letting them live. The Mo'abites became servants to David, bringing offerings. ³David struck down Hadad'ezer ben Rehob king of Tsobah, when he was going to put back his monument at the River Euphrates. ⁴David captured from him 1,700 cavalry and 20,000 men on foot. David hamstrung all the chariotry but of them left a hundred chariotry.

⁵Aramites from Dammeseq [Damascus] came to help Hadad'ezer king of Tsobah, and David struck down 22,000 men in Aram. ⁶David put outposts in Aram of Dammeseq and the Aramites became servants to David, bringing

offerings. Yahweh delivered David in every place where he went. ⁷David took the gold quivers that Hadad'ezer's servants had and brought them to Yerushalaim, ⁸and from Betah and from Berotay, Hadad'ezer's towns, King David took very much copper.

⁹To'i king of Hamat heard that David had struck down Hadad'ezer's entire force, ¹⁰and To'i sent Yoram his son to King David to ask him about whether things were well and to bless him, because he had battled against Hadad'ezer and had struck him down, on account of the fact that Hadad'ezer had been involved in battles with To'i. In his hand were objects of silver, objects of gold and objects of copper. ¹¹King David also made them sacred for Yahweh, with the silver and the gold that he made sacred from all the nations that he had subjugated: ¹²from Edom, from Mo'ab, from the Ammonites, from the Pelishtites, from Amaleq and from the spoil of Hadad'ezer ben Rebob king of Tsobah.

David's best time

¹³David made a name when he came back from striking down the Aramites in Salt Ravine, 18,000. ¹⁴He put outposts in Edom. When he put outposts in all Edom, all Edom became servants to David. Yahweh delivered David wherever he went. ¹⁵David reigned over all Yisra'el and David exercised authority in faithfulness for all his people.

¹⁶Yo'ab ben Tseruyah was over the army.
Yehoshaphat ben Ahilud was recorder.
¹⁷Tsadoq [Zadok] ben Ahitub and Abimelek ben Ebyatar were priests.
Tserayah was secretary.
¹⁸Benayah ben Yehoyada: both the Keretites and the Peletites.
David's sons were priests.

9 David said, 'Is there anyone still left of Sha'ul's household, so I can act in commitment with him for the sake of Yehonatan?' ²There was a servant belonging to Sha'ul's household; his name was Tsiba. They called for him to David, and the king said to him, 'Are you Tsiba?' He said, 'Your servant'. ³The king said, 'Is there no one at all still left of Sha'ul's household so that I can act in God's commitment with him?' Tsiba said to the king, 'There's still a son of Yehonatan; he's injured in both feet.' ⁴The king said to him, 'Where is he?' Tsiba said to the king, 'There, he's at the house of Makir ben Ammi'el, in Lo Debar.' ⁵King David sent and got him from the house of Makir ben Ammi'el, from Lo Debar. ⁶Mephiboshet ben Yehonatan, son of Sha'ul, came to David, fell on his face and bowed low. David said, 'Mephiboshet!' He said, 'Here is your servant.' ⁷David said to him, 'Don't be afraid, because I'll definitely act in commitment with you for the sake of Yehonatan your father. I'll give back to you all the fields of Sha'ul, your father, and you yourself may eat bread at my table regularly.' ⁸He bowed low and said, 'What is your servant, that you have turned your face to a dead dog like me?'

Mephiboshet ('From-Shame's-Mouth')

⁹The king called for Tsiba, Sha'ul's boy, and said to him, 'Everything that belonged to Sha'ul and to his entire household I am giving to your lord's son. ¹⁰You are to serve the land for him, you, your sons and your servants, and bring it so it may be bread for your lord's son, so he may eat it. But Mephiboshet, your lord's son, himself is to eat bread continually at my table' (Tsiba had fifteen sons and twenty servants). ¹¹Tsiba said to the king, 'In accordance with all that my lord the king orders his servant, so your servant will act, "with Mephiboshet eating at my table like one of the king's sons".'
¹²Mephiboshet had a young son; his name was Mika. Everyone who lived in Tsiba's household – they were servants of Mephiboshet, ¹³though Mephiboshet lived in Yerushalaim, because he was eating at the king's table regularly. He was lame in both feet.

10 Subsequently, the king of the Ammonites died, and Hanun his son began to reign in place of him. ²David said, 'I will act in commitment with Hanun ben Nahash, as his father acted in commitment with me.' So David sent by the hand of his servants to console him over his father. David's servants came to the Ammonites' country, ³but the Ammonites' officials said to Hanun their lord, 'Is David honouring your father, in your eyes, because he sent you people offering consolation? It's for the sake of searching out the town and investigating it so as to overthrow it that David sent his servants to you, isn't it.'

⁴So Hanun got David's servants, clipped off half their beard and cut their clothes in half up to their behinds, and sent them off. ⁵People told David and he sent to meet them, because the men were very ashamed. The king said, 'Stay in Yeriho [Jericho] until your beard grows, then you can come back.'

⁶The Ammonites saw that they stank with David, and the Ammonites sent and hired Aramites from Bet-rehob and Aramites from Tsobah (20,000 men on foot), the king of Ma'akah (1,000 men) and men from Tob (12,000).

Yo'ab's victories

⁷David heard and sent Yo'ab and the entire army, the strong men. ⁸The Ammonites went out and lined up for battle at the entrance of the gateway, with the Aramites from Tsobah and Rehob, the men from Tob, and Ma'akah alone in the fields. ⁹Yo'ab saw that the face of battle was against him in front and behind. He picked some of all the picked men of Yisra'el and lined them up to meet the Aramites, ¹⁰while he gave the rest of the company into the hand of Abshay his brother and lined them up to meet the Ammonites. ¹¹He said, 'If the Aramites are too strong for me, you'll be my deliverance, and if the Ammonites are too strong for you, I'll go to deliver you. ¹²Be strong, and let's summon up our strength on behalf of our people and on behalf of our God's towns, as Yahweh does what is good in his eyes.'

¹³So Yo'ab went up for the battle against the Aramites, he and his company who were with him, and they fled from before him. ¹⁴When the Ammonites saw that the Aramites had fled, they fled from before Abishay and came into the town. So Yo'ab turned back from fighting the Ammonites, and came to Yerushalaim.

¹⁵The Aramites saw that they had taken a beating before Yisra'el, and they gathered together. ¹⁶Hadad'ezer sent and got the Aramites who were from across the river to go out, and they came to Helam, with Shobak,

Hadad'ezer's army officer, at their head. ¹⁷It was told David, and he gathered all Yisra'el, crossed the Yarden and came to Hela'm, and the Aramites lined up to meet David and did battle with him. ¹⁸The Aramites fled from before Yisra'el. David killed 700 of the Aramite chariotry and 40,000 cavalry, and struck down Shobak, his army officer; he died there. ¹⁹All the kings who were servants of Hadad'ezer saw that they had taken a beating before Yisra'el and they made peace with Yisra'el and served them. The Aramites were afraid to deliver the Ammonites any more.

The view from the roof

11 ¹At the turn of the year, at the time when the kings go out, David sent Yo'ab and his servants with him, and all Yisra'el, and they devastated the Ammonites and besieged Rabbah, while David was staying in Yerushalaim.

²During evening time David got up from his bed and walked about on the roof of the king's house, and from on the roof saw a woman bathing. The woman was very good-looking. ³David sent and enquired about the woman. They said, 'She's Bat-sheba bat Eli'am, the wife of Uriyyah the Hittite, isn't she.' ⁴David sent envoys, got her, and she came to him. He slept with her, while she was making herself sacred from her taboo, and she went back to her house.

⁵The woman got pregnant, and she sent and told David, 'I'm pregnant.' ⁶David sent to Yo'ab, 'Send Uriyyah the Hittite to me.' Yo'ab sent Uriyyah to David. ⁷So Uriyyah came to him, and David asked him about how well things were with Yo'ab and how well things were with the company and how well things were with the battle. ⁸Then David said to Uriyyah, 'Go down to your house and bathe your feet.' Uriyyah went out from the king's house, and a present from the king followed him.

⁹But Uriyyah slept at the entrance of the king's house with all his lord's servants. He didn't go down to his house. ¹⁰They told David, 'Uriyyah didn't go down to his house.' David said to Uriyyah, 'Didn't you come from a journey? Why didn't you go down to your house?' ¹¹Uriyyah said to David, 'The chest and Yisra'el

and Yehudah are staying at Sukkot, and my lord Yo'ab and my lord's servants are camped on the face of the fields, and should I myself come to my house to eat and drink and sleep with my wife? By your life, by your very life, if I were to do this thing...'

¹²David said to Uriyyah, 'Stay here today, too, and tomorrow I'll send you off.' So Uriyyah stayed in Yerushalaim that day.

One moral mistake can lead to another

Next day ¹³David called for him, he ate before him and drank, and he got him drunk. But in the evening he went out to lie in his bed with his lord's servants. He didn't go down to his house. ¹⁴So in the morning David wrote a letter to Yo'ab and sent it by the hand of Uriyyah. ¹⁵He wrote in the letter, 'Place Uriyyah near the front of the fiercest battle, and pull back from after him so he may be struck down and die.' ¹⁶So when Yo'ab was keeping watch on the town, he put Uriyyah in the place where he knew that there were forceful men. ¹⁷The men of the town came out and battled against Yo'ab, and of the company some of David's servants fell. Uriyyah the Hittite also died.

¹⁸Yo'ab sent and told David all the things about the battle. ¹⁹He ordered the envoy: 'When you finish speaking all the things about the battle to the king, ²⁰if the king's temper rises and he says to you, "Why did you go up to the town to battle? Didn't you know that they would shoot from on the wall? ²¹Who struck down Abimelek ben Yerubbeshet? Wasn't it a woman who threw down an upper millstone on him from on the wall and he died at Tebets? Why did you go up to the wall?" then you are to say, "Your servant Uriyyah the Hittite also died."'

²²The envoy went, and came and told David all that Yo'ab had sent him with. ²³The envoy said to David, 'The men prevailed against us and came out against us into the fields. Then we were against them as far as the entrance of the gateway. ²⁴But the archers shot at your servants from on the wall and some of the king's servants died; and your servant Uriyyah the Hittie also died.'

²⁵David said to the envoy, 'Say this to Yo'ab: "This thing is not to be bad in your eyes, because the sword devours one way and another way. Make your battle stronger against the town and tear it down." Strengthen him.'

But the thing David had done was bad in Yahweh's eyes

²⁶Uriyyah's wife heard that Uriyyah her husband was dead, and she lamented over her master. ²⁷The grieving passed, and David sent and gathered her to his house. She became a wife for him, and gave birth to a son for him.

But the thing that David did was bad in Yahweh's eyes.

12 So Yahweh sent Natan to David. He came to him and said to him, 'There were two men in a town, one wealthy, one destitute. ²The wealthy man had a very large flock and herd. ³The destitute man didn't have anything except one small ewe that he had acquired. He had let it live and it had grown up with him and with his children, all together. It used to eat from his bit, drink from his cup and sleep in his arms. It was like a daughter to him. ⁴A traveller came to the wealthy man, but he spared taking something from his flock or from his herd to prepare for the man on a journey who had come to him. He took the destitute man's ewe and prepared it for the man who had come to him.'

⁵David's anger raged right up at the man. He said to Natan, 'As Yahweh lives, the man who did this deserves death. ⁶He should make good fourfold for the ewe on account of the fact that he did this thing, and since he didn't spare.'

⁷Natan said to David, 'You're the man. Yahweh the God of Yisra'el has said this: "I myself anointed you as king over Yisra'el. I myself rescued you from Sha'ul's hand. ⁸I gave you your lord's household and your lord's wives into your arms. I gave you the household of Yisra'el and Yehudah. If that's little, I would have added to you as much again as these. ⁹Why did you despise Yahweh's word by doing what is bad in my eyes? Uriyyah the Hittite you struck down with the sword and his wife you took as your wife. Him you killed, with the sword of the Ammonites. ¹⁰So now the sword won't depart from your household, permanently, because of the fact that you despised me and took Uriyyah the Hittite's wife to be a wife for you."

The man who has learned how to be a prophet

[11] Yahweh has said this: "Here, I'm going to make something bad arise for you from your household. I shall take your wives before your eyes and give them to your neighbour. He'll sleep with your wives before the eyes of this sun. [12] Because you yourself acted in secret, but I myself will do this thing before all Yisra'el and before the sun.'"

[13] David said to Natan, 'I've acted wrongly against Yahweh.' Natan said to David, 'Yes. Because Yahweh has made your wrongdoing pass on, you will not die. [14] Nevertheless, because you've totally disdained (the enemies of) Yahweh by this act, yes, the child born to you will definitely die.' [15] And Natan went home.

Yahweh struck the child to whom Uriyyah's wife gave birth for David, and it became ill. [16] David sought God for the boy. David made a fast and came and stayed the night and lay on the ground. [17] The elders in his household got up over him to make him get up from the ground but he wasn't willing, and he didn't eat a meal with them.

[18] On the seventh day the child died. David's servants were afraid to tell him that the child had died, because (they said), 'Here, when the child was alive, we spoke to him and he didn't listen to our voice. How can we say to him, "The child is dead"? He may do something bad.' [19] David saw that his servants were whispering to one another and David perceived that the child was dead. David said to his servants, 'Is the child dead?' They said, 'He's dead.'

Death and new life

[20] David got up from the ground, bathed, put on his oils and changed his clothes. He came to Yahweh's house and bowed low. Then he came to his house and asked and they presented him with a meal and he ate. [21] His servants said to him, 'What's this thing that you've done? When the child was alive, you fasted and wailed. Now that the child is dead, you've got up and eaten a meal.' [22] He said, 'While the child was still alive, I fasted and wailed because I said, "Who knows? Yahweh may be gracious to me. The child may live." [23] But now he's dead, why on earth should I fast? Can I bring him back again? I'm going to him, but he won't come back to me.'

[24] David consoled Bat-sheba his wife and had sex with her. He slept with her and she gave birth to a son, and named him Shelomoh [Solomon]. Because Yahweh loved him, [25] he sent by means of Natan the prophet and named him 'Beloved-by-Yah', on account of Yahweh.

[26] Yo'ab battled against Rabbah of the Ammonites and captured the royal town. [27] Yo'ab sent envoys to David and said, 'I've battled against Rabbah – yes, captured the water town. [28] So now, gather the rest of the company and camp against the town and capture it, so that I myself don't capture the town and my name is called out over it.'

[29] So David gathered the entire company and went to Rabbah, battled against it and captured it. [30] He got their king's crown from on his head (its weight was a talent of gold, with precious stones) and it came on to David's head, while he took out very much spoil from the town. [31] The people that was in it he took out and put them to saws, iron harrows and iron axes, or transferred them to brickworking. So he would do to all the Ammonites' towns. Then David and the entire company went back to Yerushalaim.

Amnon's plot

13 Subsequently: Absalom, David's son, had an attractive sister; her name was Tamar. Amnon, David's son, was in love with her. [2] It was pressing for Amnon, so that he became ill on account of Tamar his sister, because she was a young girl but it was unimaginable in Amnon's eyes to do anything about her.

[3] Now Amnon had a friend; his name was Yonadab ben Shim'ah, David's brother. Yonadab was a very smart man. [4] He said to him, 'Prince, why are you down like this, morning by morning? Won't you tell me?' Amnon said to him, 'Tamar, my brother Absholom's sister – I'm in love with her.' [5] Yonadab said to him, 'Lie on your bed and act ill. Your father will come to see you and you're to say to him, "May Tamar my sister please come and give me

bread to eat. May she prepare the food before my eyes in order that I may see and eat from her hand.'"

⁶So Amnon lay down and acted ill, the king came to see him, and Amnon said to the king, 'May Tamar my sister come and make a couple of pancakes before my eyes, so I may eat from her hand.' ⁷So David sent to Tamar his daughter, saying 'Please go to Amnon your brother's house and make him some food.' ⁸Tamar went to Amnon her brother's house; he was lying down. She got dough and kneaded it and made pancakes before his eyes, and cooked the pancakes.

⁹She got the pan and poured them out before him, but he refused to eat. Amnon said, 'Get everyone to go out from me', and everyone went out from him. ¹⁰Amnon said to Tamar, 'Bring the food into the room so I can eat from your hand.' Tamar got the pancakes that she'd made, brought them to Amnon her brother in the room ¹¹and brought them up to him to eat, but he took strong hold of her and said to her, 'Come to bed with me, sister.'

The rape of a sister

¹²She said to him, 'Don't, brother. Don't humble me, because such a thing is not done in Yisra'el. Don't do this villainous thing. ¹³I, where would I take my reviling? And you, you'll be just one of the villains in Yisra'el. So now, please speak to the king, because he wouldn't withhold me from you.' ¹⁴But he wasn't willing to listen to her voice. He took hold of her and humbled her and bedded her.

¹⁵Amnon then felt a very great hostility for her, in that the hostility that he felt for her was greater than the love he had felt for her. Amnon said to her, 'Get up, go.' ¹⁶She said to him, 'No, because this bad act is greater than the other that you did with me, sending me away.' But he wasn't willing to listen to her. ¹⁷He called the boy who ministered to him and said 'Please send this woman off, away from my presence, outside, and bolt the door after her.'

¹⁸She had a long-sleeved gown on, because the young princesses used to dress in such robes. His minister took her outside and bolted the door after her. ¹⁹Tamar put earth on her head, tore the long-sleeved gown that she had on, put her hand on her head and went her way, crying out as she went.

²⁰Abshalom her brother said to her, 'Sister, was it Aminon your brother who was with you? Now, sister, quieten down. He's your brother. Don't set your mind on this thing.' Tamar stayed, a desolate woman, in Absalom her brother's house. ²¹When King David heard about all these things, it really enraged him. ²²Absalom didn't speak with Amnon anything bad or good, because Absalom was hostile to Amnon because of the fact that he had humbled Tamar his sister.

The strife between brothers

²³Two full years later, Absalom's shearers were at Ba'al Hatsor, which is near Ephrayim, and Absalom invited all the princes. ²⁴Absalom came to the king and said, 'Please, here are your servant's shearers. Will the king and his servants please go with your servant?' ²⁵The king said to Absalom, 'No, son, we won't all of us go, we won't be a burden to you.' He pressed him, but he wasn't willing to go, but he gave them his blessing. ²⁶So Absalom said, 'But won't Amnon my brother please go with us?' The king said to him, 'Why should he go with you?' ²⁷But Absalom pressed him, and he sent with him Amnon and all the princes.

²⁸Absalom ordered his boys, 'Watch when Amnon's heart is good because of the wine, will you, and I'll say to you, "Strike Amnon down": put him to death, don't be afraid. I myself am the one who's given you the order, am I not. Be strong. Be forceful men.' ²⁹Absalom's boys did to Amnon as Absalom ordered, and all the princes got up, each one on his mule, and fled.

³⁰While they were on the way, the report came to David: 'Absalom has struck down all the princes – not one of them was left!' ³¹David got up and tore his clothes and lay on the ground. All his servants stood, their clothes torn. ³²But Yonadab ben Shim'ah, David's brother, avowed, 'My lord should not say that all the young princes are dead, because Amnon alone is dead, because it's been determined at Absalom's bidding since the day Amnon humbled Tamar his sister. ³³So now my lord the

king should not take the thing to heart, saying "All the princes are dead", because Amnon alone is dead.'

The woman from Teqoa

³⁴Abshalom took flight, and the lookout boy lifted up his eyes and looked: there, a large company going from the road behind him, from the side of the mountain. ³⁵Yonadab said to the king, 'There, the princes have come. In accordance with your servant's word, so it has happened.' ³⁶As he finished speaking, there, the princes came; they lifted up their voice and wailed. The king and all his servants also uttered a very great wail. ³⁷When Abshalom took flight and went to Talmay ben Ammihud king of Geshur, he took up grieving over his son all the time.

³⁸When Abshalom had taken flight and gone to Geshur, he was there for three years, ³⁹then going out to Abshalom consumed King David, because he had found consolation over Amnon, that he was dead.

14 Yo'ab ben Tseruyah knew that the king's mind was on Abshalom, ²and Yo'ab sent to Teqoa and got a smart woman from there. He said to her, 'Please act as someone grieving and dress in grieving clothes. Don't put on oils; be like a woman who's been grieving for a long time over someone who has died. ³You're to come to the king and speak to him in this way.' Yo'ab put the words into her mouth, ⁴and the Teqo'ite woman said them to the king. She fell on her face to the ground, bowed low, and said, 'Deliver, Your Majesty!'

⁵The king said to her, 'What do you need?' She said, 'Well, I'm a woman who's a widow; my husband has died. ⁶Your maidservant had two sons. The two of them fought in the fields and there was no one to rescue them from each other. One of them struck the other down and put him to death. ⁷And here, the entire kin-group has risen up against your maidservant and said, "Give us the one who struck his brother down so we may put him to death for the life of his brother whom he killed. We'll annihilate the heir, too." So they'll quench the ember that remains to me, and not give my husband a name or someone remaining on the face of the ground.' ⁸The king said to the woman, 'Go home and I'll give an order concerning you.'

The parable explained

⁹The Teqo'ite woman said to the king, 'On me be the waywardness, my lord king, and on my ancestral household; the king and his throne be free of guilt.' ¹⁰The king said, 'Anyone who speaks to you, bring him to me, and he will never touch you again.' ¹¹She said, 'The king is, please, to be mindful of Yahweh your God so that the restorer of blood does not bring more devastation and they do not annihilate my son.' He said, 'As Yahweh lives, if one hair of your son's falls to the ground . . .'

¹²The woman said, 'May your maidservant please speak a word to my lord the king.' He said, 'Speak.' ¹³The woman said, 'So why have you thought things up in this way against God's people? By the king's speaking this thing, he is like someone liable to condemnation, in that the king does not let his banished son come back. ¹⁴Because we shall all finally die, like water poured out on the ground that cannot be gathered up. But God does not take up the life of one who thinks of ways so that someone who is banished does not stay banished from him.

¹⁵So now, in that I have come to speak this word to my lord the king because the people have frightened me, your maidservant said, "I must speak to the king; perhaps the king will act on your handmaid's word, ¹⁶because the king will listen and rescue his handmaid from the fist of someone annihilating me and my son together from God's domain." ¹⁷Your maidservant said, "May the word of my lord the king please be for my relief, because my lord the king is like God's envoy in listening to what is good and what is bad." May Yahweh your God be with you.'

The king won

¹⁸The king answered the woman, 'Please don't hide a thing from me of what I am asking you.' The woman said, 'My lord the king may please speak.' ¹⁹The king said, 'Is Yo'ab's hand

with you in all this?' The woman answered, 'By your own life, my lord the king, if anyone could go to the right or to the left from all that my lord the king spoke, because your servant Yo'ab – he's the one who gave me orders and who put all these things in your maidservant's mouth. [20]It was for the sake of changing the face of the thing that your servant Yo'ab did this thing. My lord is smart with the same smartness as God's envoy in knowing everything that's in the country.'

[21]The king said to Yo'ab, 'Here, I'm going to do this thing. Go and get the boy, Abshalom, back.' [22]Yo'ab fell on his face on the ground and bowed low and blessed the king. Yo'ab said, 'Today your servant acknowledges that I have found grace in your eyes, my lord king, in that the king has acted on your servant's word.'

[23]Yo'ab set off and went to Geshur and brought Abshalom to Yerushalaim. [24]But the king said, 'He's to go round to his house and not see my face.' So Abshalom went round to his house and didn't see the king's face.

The field set on fire

[25]Compared with Abshalom, there was no one in all Yisra'el as attractive, no one to admire so much. From the sole of his foot to the crown of his head there was no defect in him. [26]When he shaved his head (at the end of each year when he would shave – because it was too heavy for him, so he would shave it), he would weigh the hair on his head: 200 sheqels by the royal weight. [27]There were born to Abshalom three sons and one daughter, and her name was Tamar; she became a woman who was attractive in appearance.

[28]Abshalom lived in Yerushalaim for two years but didn't see the king's face. [29]Then Abshalom sent to Yo'ab so as to send him to the king, but he wouldn't come to him. He sent again, a second time, but he wasn't willing to come. [30]So he said to his servants, 'Look, Yo'ab's share is by the side of me and he has barley there. Go and set it on fire.' Abshalom's servants set the share on fire.

[31]Yo'ab got up and came to Abshalom at home and said to him, 'Why did your servants set my share on fire?' [32]Abshalom said to Yo'ab, 'Here, I sent to you, saying "Come here", so I could send you to the king to say "Why did I come from Geshur? It would be good for me if I were still there." Now, I should see the king's face, and if there is any waywardness in me, he may put me to death.' [33]So Yo'ab came to the king and told him, and he called for Abshalom. He came to the king and bowed low to him, with his face to the ground before the king, and the king kissed Abshalom.

Abshalom prepares for a coup

15 Subsequently, Abshalom made ready for himself a chariot and horses, with fifty men running before him. [2]Abshalom would start early and stand by the side of the road to the gateway. When anyone had an argument that was to come to the king for a decision, Abshalom called to him and said, 'What town are you from?', and the person said, 'Your servant is from one of the Yisra'elite clans', [3]and Abshalom said to him, 'Look, your words are good and straight, but you have no one from the king to listen.'

[4]Abshalom said, 'If only someone would make me an authority in the country so that anyone who had an argument for decision could come to me and I would see he was recognized as in the right.' [5]When someone drew near to bow low to him, he would put out his hand and take strong hold of him and kiss him. [6]Abshalom acted in this manner to all Yisra'el who would come to the king for a decision. So Abshalom stole the heart of the Yisra'elites.

[7]At the end of forty years Abshalom said to the king, 'I want please to go and make good my pledge that I made to Yahweh in Hebron, [8]because your servant made a pledge when I was living in Geshur in Aram, saying "If Yahweh lets me actually go back to Yerushalaim, I will serve Yahweh."' [9]The king said to him, 'Go; things will be well.' So he set off and went to Hebron.

[10]But Abshalom sent followers through all Yisra'el's clans, saying 'When you hear the sound of the horn, you're to say, "Abshalom has become king in Hebron!" [11]Two hundred people from Yerushalaim had gone with Abshalom, invited and going in integrity. They didn't know anything. [12]And Abshalom

sent for Ahitophel the Gilonite, David's counsellor, from his town, from Giloh, when he was offering sacrifices. The conspiracy became powerful, and the company going with Abshalom was growing.

David's flight

¹³Someone came telling David, 'The Yisra'elites' mind has gone after Abshalom.' ¹⁴David said to all his servants who were with him in Yerushalaim, 'Get up, let's take flight, because there'll be no escape group for us from before Abshalom. Hurry, go, so he doesn't hurry and catch up with us and hurl something bad upon us and strike the town down with the mouth of the sword.' ¹⁵The king's servants said to the king, 'In accordance with all that my lord the king chooses, here are your servants.' ¹⁶The king went out with his entire household after him, but the king abandoned ten secondary wives to keep the house.

¹⁷So the king went out with the entire company after him, and halted at the farthest house, ¹⁸with all his servants passing on his side, and all the Keretites and all the Peletites, and all the Gittites (600 men who had come after him from Gat), passing on before the king. ¹⁹The king said to Ittay the Gittite, 'Why should you go with us, too? Go back and stay with the king, because you're a foreigner, and also you're an exile in relation to your place. ²⁰You came yesterday. Why should I get you to wander with us today as we go, when I'm going wherever I'm going? Turn back and take your brothers back with you in commitment and truthfulness.'

²¹Ittay answered the king, 'As Yahweh lives and as my lord the king lives, in the place where my lord the king is, whether for death or for life, there will your servant be.' ²²David said to Ittay, 'Go, pass on.' So Ittay the Gittite passed on, with all his men and all the little ones who were with him.

Turn Ahitophel's advice into stupidity

²³As the entire region was wailing in a loud voice and the entire company was passing on, and the king was passing over Wadi Qidron, and the entire company was passing on before the wilderness road, ²⁴and there also Tsadoq and all the Levites with him were carrying the chest of God's pact, they put God's chest down (and Ebyatar went up) until the company had finished passing on from the town.

²⁵But the king said to Tsadoq, 'Take God's chest back into the town. If I find grace in Yahweh's eyes, he will let me come back and let me see it and its home. ²⁶But if he says this: "I don't want you", here I am: he can do with me as it is good in his eyes.' ²⁷So the king said to Tsadoq the priest, 'Do you see? You go back to the town and things will go well, with Ahima'ats your son and Yehonatan ben Ebyatar (your two sons) with you. ²⁸See, I'm going to wait in the steppes in the wilderness until word comes from you to tell me.'

²⁹So Tsadoq and Ebyatar took God's chest back to Yerushalaim and stayed there, ³⁰while David was going up the Olives Ascent, wailing as he was going up, with his head covered; he was walking barefoot, while the entire company that was with him covered each one his head. They went up wailing as they were going up. ³¹When David was told, 'Ahitophel is among the conspirators with Abshalom', David said, 'Please turn Ahitophel's counsel into idiocy, Yahweh!'

Two loyal friends

³²David was coming as far as the top where people would bow low to God, and there was Hushay the Arkite to meet him, his coat torn and earth on his head. ³³David said to him, 'If you pass on with me, you'll be a burden to me. ³⁴But if you go back to the town and say to Abshalom, "I'm your servant, Your Majesty – I used to be your father's servant in the past, but now I'm your servant", you can contravene Ahitophel's counsel for me. ³⁵Tsadoq and Ebyatar the priests will be with you there, won't they. And every word that you hear from the king's house you can tell Tsadoq and Ebyatar the priests. ³⁶There, their two sons, Tsadoq's Ahima'ats and Ebyatar's Yehonatan, are with them. You can send to me through them everything that you hear.' ³⁷So Hushay, David's friend, came to the town as Abshalom was coming to Yerushalaim.

16 When David had passed a little beyond the top, there, Tsiba, a servant of Mephiboshet, met him with a pair of donkeys, saddled. On them were two hundred loaves of bread, a hundred raisin blocks, a hundred of summer fruit and a skin of wine. ²The king said to Tsiba, 'Why have you got these?' Tsiba said, 'The donkeys are for the king's household to ride, the bread and the summer fruit are for eating by the boys, and the wine is for drinking by people who are weary in the wilderness.' ³The king said, 'And where is your lord's son?' Tsiba said to the king, 'There, he's staying in Yerushalaim, because he's said, "Today the household of Yisra'el will give me back my father's kingship."' ⁴The king said to Tsiba, 'Here, to you belongs everything that belonged to Mephiboshet.' Tsiba said, 'I bow low. May I find grace in your eyes, my lord king.'

Shim'i's slighting

⁵King David came as far as Bahurim and there, someone from the kin-group of Sha'ul's household was going out from there. His name was Shim'i ben Gera. As he went out he was slighting ⁶and pelting David and all King David's servants with stones, with the entire company and all the strong men at his right and at his left. ⁷Shim'i said this as he slighted him: 'Get out, get out, you man of bloodshed, you scoundrel! ⁸Yahweh is giving back to you all the bloodshed in the household of Sha'ul, in whose place you became king. Yahweh has given the kingship into the hand of Abshalom your son, and here you are, in a bad situation, because you're a man of bloodshed.'

⁹Abishay ben Tseruyah said to the king, 'Why should this dead dog slight my lord the king? I shall pass on, please, and remove his head!' ¹⁰But the king said, 'What do you and I have in common, you sons of Tseruyah? He can slight in this way because Yahweh has said to him, "Slight David." Who is to say, "Why have you done that?"?' ¹¹David said to Abishay and to all his servants, 'Here, my son who came out from inside me, is seeking my life. How much more now a Binyaminite? Let him be. He can slight, because Yahweh has said it to him. ¹²Maybe Yahweh will look at the waywardness done to me and Yahweh will give back good to me in place of his slighting this day.'

¹³David and his men went on their way, while Shim'i was going along the side of the mountain alongside him, slighting and pelting him with stones alongside him and throwing earth as he went. ¹⁴The king came with the entire company that was with him, faint, and he refreshed himself there.

Ahitophel's advice

¹⁵Now Abshalom and the entire company, the Yisra'elite men, came to Yerushalaim, and Ahitophel with him. ¹⁶When Hushay the Arkite, David's friend, came to Abshalom, Hushay said to Abshalom, 'Long live the king, long live the king.' ¹⁷Abshalom said to Hushay, 'Is this your commitment to your friend? Why didn't you go with your friend?' ¹⁸Hushay said to Abshalom, 'No, because the one whom Yahweh has chosen, he and this company and all the Yisra'elite men – I shall be for him. I shall stay with him. ¹⁹Second, whom should I serve? Before his son, shouldn't I. As I served before your father, so I shall be before you.'

²⁰Abshalom said to Ahitophel, 'Give your counsel: what shall we do?' ²¹Ahitophel said, 'Have sex with your father's secondary wives whom he left to keep the house. All Yisra'el will hear that you have let yourself stink with your father, and the hands of all the people who are with you will be strong.' ²²They spread a tent for Abshalom on the roof and Abshalom had sex with his father's secondary wives before the eyes of all Yisra'el.

²³At that time the counsel of Ahitophel which he gave was like when one asks of a word from God. So it was with all Ahitophel's counsel both for David and for Abshalom.

17 Ahitophel said to Abshalom, 'I should please pick 12,000 men and set off and pursue after David tonight ²so that I come on him when he's weary and weak-handed. I'll make him tremble, and the entire company that's with him will flee. I'll strike down the king alone ³and bring back the entire company to you. When everyone has come back (it's the man you're seeking), the entire people will be at peace.' ⁴The thing seemed right in the eyes of

Abshalom and in the eyes of all Yisra'el's elders, ⁵but Abshalom said, 'Call for Hushay the Arkite as well, please, so we can hear what's in his mouth as well.' ⁶Hushay came to Abshalom and Abshalom said to him: 'This very word Ahitophel spoke. Shall we act on his word? If not, you speak.'

Good advice treated as folly

⁷Hushay said to Abshalom, 'The counsel Ahitophel has given is not good this time.' ⁸Hushay said, 'You yourself know your father and his men, that they're strong men. They're as fierce-spirited as a bear in the wild that has lost its cubs, and your father is a man of battle. But he won't stay the night with the company. ⁹There, he will now be hiding in one of the pits or in one of the places.

And when some of the men fall at the beginning, a person who hears will hear and say, "Defeat has come on the company that goes after Abshalom!" ¹⁰That man, even if he's a forceful man whose heart's like the heart of a lion, will totally melt, because all Yisra'el knows that your father is a strong man, as are the forceful men who are with him.

¹¹Rather I counsel that all Yisra'el from Dan as far as Be'er-sheba (like the sand on the seashore in numbers) gather together to join you, with you personally going among them. ¹²We'll come against him in one of the places where he may be found and we'll light on him as the dew falls on the ground. None will be left of him and of all the men who are with him, not even one. ¹³If he gathers together into a town, all Yisra'el is to bring ropes to that town and we'll drag it as far as the wadi until not even a pebble is to be found there.'

¹⁴Abshalom and all the Yisra'elite men said, 'The counsel of Hushay the Arkite is better than the counsel of Ahitophel'; Yahweh had ordered the contravening of Ahitophel's good counsel so that Yahweh might bring a bad fate on Abshalom. ¹⁵Hushay said to Tsadoq and to Ebyatar the priests, 'In this and this way Ahitophel counselled Abshalom and the elders of Yisra'el, but in this and this way I myself counselled. ¹⁶Now send off quickly and tell David, "Don't stay the night at the wilderness crossings. Further, cross right over so that he isn't swallowed up, the king and the entire company that's with him."'

Ahitophel's suicide

¹⁷Yehonatan and Ahima'ats were halting at Treader's Spring, a maid would go and tell them, and they would go and tell King David, because they couldn't be seen coming into the town. ¹⁸But a boy saw them and told Abshalom. The two of them went quickly and came to the house of someone in Bahurim. He had a well in his courtyard and they went down there. ¹⁹The wife got a length of cloth and spread it over the face of the well, and scattered groats on it, so that nothing would become known. ²⁰Abshalom's servants came to the woman at the house and said, 'Where are Ahima'ats and Yehonatan?' The woman said to them, 'They crossed over the water brook.' They searched, but didn't find them, and went back to Yerushalaim.

²¹After they had gone, they got up from the well and went and told King David. They said to David, 'Set off and cross the water quickly, because Ahitophel has given counsel about you in such-and-such a way.' ²²So David set off, he and the entire company that was with him, and crossed the Yarden before morning light, until not one was missing who had not crossed the Yarden.

²³When Ahitophel saw that his counsel was not acted on, he saddled his donkey, set off and went home to his town. He gave orders concerning his household, and hanged himself. He died and was buried in his father's grave.

²⁴David was coming to Mahanayim when Abshalom crossed the Yarden, he and all the men of Yisra'el with him. ²⁵Abshalom had put Amasa over the army in place of Yo'ab. Amasa was the son of a man whose name was Yitra the Yisra'elite, who had had sex with Abigayil bat Nahash, the sister of Tseruyah, Yo'ab's mother. ²⁶Yisra'el and Abshalom camped in the region of Gil'ad.

David agrees to stay behind

²⁷When David came to Mahanayim, Shobi ben Nahash from Rabbat of the Ammonites, Makir ben Ammi'el from Lo Debar, and

Barzillay the Gil'adite from Rogelim ²⁸brought up for David and for the company that was with him bedding, basins, potter's containers, wheat, barley, flour, roasted grain, beans, lentils, roasted grain, ²⁹syrup, curds, a flock, and cheese from the herd to eat, because (they said), 'The company's hungry and faint and thirsty in the wilderness.'

18 David numbered the company that was with him and set over them divisional officers and section officers. ²David sent off the company, a third in the hand of Yo'ab, a third in the hand of Abishay ben Tseruyah, Yo'ab's brother, and a third in the hand of Ittay the Gittite. The king said to the company, 'I myself will definitely go out with you as well.' ³But the company said, 'You're not to go out, because if we do flee, they won't put their mind to us. If half of us die, they won't put their mind to us. Because there are now 10,000 like us. So now, it will be good that you're available to us from the town to help.' ⁴So the king said to them, 'Whatever is good in your eyes I'll do.'

The king stood at the side of the gateway as the entire company went out by sections and by divisions. ⁵The king ordered Yo'ab, Abishay and Ittay, 'Gently for me with the boy, with Abshalom.' The entire company heard the the king ordering all the officers concerning Abshalom.

⁶The company went out to the fields to meet Yisra'el. The battle took place in the Ephrayim Forest ⁷and the Yisra'elite company took a beating there before David's servants. It was a great defeat there that day – 20,000 men. ⁸The battle took place there, spread over the face of the entire region. The forest did more devouring of the company than what the sword devoured that day.

Abshalom meets his death

⁹Abshalom met up with David's servants while Abshalom was riding on a mule. The mule came under the tangle of a big oak and his head caught hold of the oak. He was given up between the heavens and the earth as the mule that was under him passed on.

¹⁰Someone saw and told Yo'ab, 'Here, I've seen Abshalom hanging in an oak!' ¹¹Yo'ab said to the man who told him, 'Here, you saw, why didn't you strike him down to the ground there? It would have been on me to give you ten pieces of silver and a belt.' ¹²The man said to Yo'ab, 'If I were weighing on my palms a thousand pieces of silver, I wouldn't put out my hand against the prince, because in our ears the king ordered you and Abishay and Gittay, "Keep watch, whoever you are, over the boy Abshalom." ¹³If I'd acted falsely against his life, when nothing hides from the king, you yourself would have taken your stand at a distance.'

¹⁴Yo'ab said, 'I won't wait for you, therefore.' He took three sticks into his fist and plunged them into Abshalom's heart. While he was still alive in the heart of the oak, ¹⁵ten boys, Yo'ab's equipment-bearers, came round, struck Abshalom down and put him to death. ¹⁶Yo'ab blew on the horn, and the company turned back from pursuing after Yisra'el, because Yo'ab held the company back. ¹⁷They took Abshalom and threw him into a big pit in the forest, and put up a very big heap of stones over it, while all Yisra'el fled, each person to his tents.

(¹⁸While he was alive Abshalom himself had got and put up for himself the column that's in King's Vale, because (he said), 'I have no son in order to commemorate my name.' People have named the column 'Abshalom's Monument', until this day.)

¹⁹When Ahima'ats ben Tsadoq said, 'May I run and bring news to the king that Yahweh has acted with authority for him from his enemies' hand', ²⁰Yo'ab said to him, 'You're not to be a man with news this day. You may bring news another day. This day you're not to bring news, because the king's son is dead.'

The news reaches David

²¹So Yo'ab said to a Kushite [Sudanese], 'Go tell the king what you have seen.' The Sudanese bowed low to Yo'ab and ran. ²²Ahima'ats ben Tsadoq once again said to Yo'ab, 'Whatever happens, may I myself also please run, after the Kushite?' Yo'ab said, 'Why is it that you're going to run, son, when there'll be no reward available for you?' ²³'Whatever happens, I'll run.' So he said to him, 'Run.' Ahima'ats ran by way of the plain, and passed the Kushite.

²⁴David was sitting between the two gateways. The lookout at the gateway roof went to the wall. He lifted up his eyes and looked: there, a man running alone. ²⁵The lookout called and told the king. The king said, 'If he's alone, there's news on his lips.' He continued to draw nearer, ²⁶and the lookout saw another man running. The lookout called to the gateman, 'There, a man running alone', and the king said, 'He's bringing news, as well.' ²⁷The lookout said, 'I see the first runner; it's like the running of Ahima'ats ben Tsadoq.' The king said, 'He's a good man; he comes with good news.'
²⁸Ahima'ats called out to the king, 'Things are well', bowed low to the king, on his face to the ground, and said, 'Yahweh your God be blessed, who delivered up the men who lifted up their hand against my lord the king!' ²⁹The king said, 'Is it well with the boy, with Absalom?' Ahima'ats said, 'I saw a big uproar when the king's servant Yo'ab was sending your servant but I didn't know what it was.'
³⁰The king said, 'Come round; take your stand there.' He came round and halted, ³¹and there, the Kushite was coming. The Kushite said, 'May my lord the king receive the news that Yahweh has acted with authority for you today from the hand of all the people who rose up against you.' ³²The king said to the Kushite, 'Is it well with the boy, with Absalom?' The Kushite said, 'May my lord the king's enemies and all who rise up against you to do something bad be like the boy.'

Inconsiderate grief?

³³The king shook. He went up to the upper story of the gateway and wailed. As he went he said this: 'My son Absalom, my son, my son Absalom, if only I had died, I in place of you, Absalom, my son, my son.'

19 It was told Yo'ab, 'Here, the king is wailing and has taken up grieving over Absalom.' ²The deliverance that day turned to grieving for the entire company when the company heard that day, 'The king is in pain over his son.' ³The company stole in when they came into the town that day, as a company that has battled steals in ashamed when they've fled in the battle, ⁴while the king covered his face. The king cried out in a loud voice, 'My son, Absalom, Absalom, my son, my son.'

⁵Yo'ab came to the king at home and said, 'You've made the faces of all your servants ashamed today, people who saved your life today and the life of your sons and your daughters, the life of your wives and the life of your secondary wives, ⁶by being loyal to the people who are hostile to you and by being hostile to the people who are loyal to you. Because you've told them today that officers and servants are nothing to you. Because I know today that, were Absalom alive and all of us dead today, then it would be all right in your eyes.

⁷So now, get up, go out, encourage your servants! Because I swear by Yahweh, when you do not come out – if anyone stays the night with you tonight . . . It will be bad for you, worse than any bad experience that has come upon you from your youth until now.' ⁸So the king got up and sat in the gateway, and when they told the entire company, 'Here, the king is sitting in the gateway', the entire company came before the king.

Bringing David back

When Yisra'el fled, each person to his tents, ⁹the entire people was arguing. among all the Yisra'elite clans: 'It was the king who rescued us from our enemies' fist, and he was the one who saved us from the hand of the Pelishtites. He has now taken flight from the country because of Absalom, ¹⁰but Absalom, whom we anointed over us, is dead in battle. So now, why are you sitting still with regard to bringing the king back?'

¹¹King David himself sent to Tsadoq and to Ebyatar, the priests, saying 'Speak to the elders of Yehudah, saying "Why are you last to bring the king back to his house?"' (when the words of all Yisra'el came to the king at his house). ¹²'You're my brothers, you're my flesh and blood. Why should you be last to bring the king back? ¹³And to Amasa say, "You're my flesh and blood, aren't you. May God do this to me and may he do more if you do not become officer over the army before me all the time, in place of Yo'ab."'

¹⁴He turned the mind of all the Yehudahites as one individual, and they sent to the king:

'Come back, you and all your servants.' ¹⁵The king went back and came as far as the Yarden, while Yehudah came to Gilgal to go to meet the king, to bring the king across the Yarden. ¹⁶Shim'i ben Gera, the Binyaminite who was from Bahurim, hurried and came down with the Yehudahites to meet King David, ¹⁷and a thousand Binyaminites with him, while Tsiba, a boy from Sha'ul's household, and his fifteen sons and his twenty servants with him, rushed to the Yarden before the king. ¹⁸The crossing took place to get the king's household across and for him to do what was good in his eyes when Shim'i ben Gera fell down before the king as he was crossing the Yarden.

Mercy in victory

¹⁹He said to the king, 'May my lord not think of waywardness in connection with me. Don't be mindful of how your servant was wayward on the day when my lord the king left Yerushalaim, by the king giving his mind to it. ²⁰Because your servant acknowledges that I myself did wrong, but here – today I have come, the first of all Yoseph's [Joseph's] household to go down to meet my lord the king.'

²¹Abishay ben Tseruyah answered, 'On account of this, will Shim'i not be put to death, because he slighted Yahweh's anointed?' ²²David said, 'What do you and I have in common, sons of Tseruyah, that you should be an adversary to me today? Is an individual in Yisra'el to be put to death today? Because I know that today I'm king over Yisra'el, don't I.' ²³So the king said to Shim'i, 'You will not die', and the king swore to him. ²⁴Mephiboshet son of Sha'ul also went down to meet the king. He had not done his feet, he had not done his moustache and he had not washed his clothes from the day the king went until the day when he came with things being well.

²⁵When he came to Yerushalaim to meet the king, the king said to him, 'Why didn't you go with me, Mephiboshet?' ²⁶He said, 'My lord king, my servant beguiled me, because your servant said, "I want to saddle my donkey and ride on it and go with the king, because your servant is lame." ²⁷But he went about [speaking] against your servant to my lord the king, when my lord the king is like God's envoy. Do what is good in your eyes. ²⁸Because there was no one in my father's entire household except people who deserved death before my lord the king, but you put your servant among the people who eat at your table. What right do I have any more to cry out any more to the king?'

²⁹The king said to him, 'Why should you speak any more about these things? I say: you and Tsiba are to share out the fields.' ³⁰But Mephiboshet said to the king, 'He can even take all of it after my lord the king has come home with things being well.'

Barzillay says 'No thank you'

³¹Now Barzillay the Gil'adite had come down from Rogelim and he crossed over the Yarden with the king, to send him off at the Yarden. ³²Barzillay was very old, a man of eighty years; he was the one who had provided for the king during his stay at Mahanayim, because he was a very big man. ³³The king said to Barzillay, 'You cross over with me, and I'll provide for you with me in Yerushalaim.' ³⁴But Barzillay said to the king, 'How many will be the full years of my life, that I should go up to Yerushalaim with the king? ³⁵I'm a man of eighty years today. Do I know the difference between good and bad? Or can your servant taste what he eats and what he drinks or still listen to the sound of men and women singing? So why should your servant still be a burden to my lord the king? ³⁶Hardly could your servant cross the Yarden with the king. Why should the king deal this thing to me? ³⁷May your servant go back, and I shall die in my town near the grave of my father and my mother. But here is your servant Kimham. He should cross with my lord the king. Do for him what is good in your eyes.'

³⁸The king said, 'Kimham may cross with me, and I myself will do for him what is good in your eyes. Anything that you choose from me I will do for you.'

³⁹So the entire company crossed the Yarden. When the king crossed, the king kissed Barzillay and blessed him and he went back to his place, ⁴⁰and the king crossed over to Gilgal; Kimhan crossed with him.

Tension between Yisra'el and Yehudah

When the entire Yehudahite company took the king across, and also half of the Yisra'elite company, ⁴¹there, all the Yisra'elites were coming to the king. They said to the king, 'Why did our brothers, the Yehudahites, steal you away and take the king and his household across the Yarden, and all David's men with him?' ⁴²All the Yehudahites answered the Yisra'elites, 'Because the king is near to us! Why is it that rage came over you at this thing? Have we actually eaten anything of the king's, or has preference been given to us?'

⁴³The Yisra'elites answered the Yehudahites, 'We have ten shares in the king, so in David as well we have more than you. So why have you slighted us, so that our word wasn't first in connection with bringing our king back?' But the Yehudahites' word was tougher than the Yisra'elites' word.

20 But a scoundrel happened to be there; his name was Sheba ben Bikri, a Binyaminite. He blew on the horn and said, 'We have no share in David, we have no domain in ben Yishay – each man to his tents, Yisra'el!' ²All the Yisra'elites rose up from following David to follow Sheba ben Bikri, but the Yehudahites attached themselves to their king, from the Yarden to Yerushalaim. ³David came to his house in Yerushalaim. The king got the ten secondary wives whom he had made stay to keep the house, and put them in a house that was under guard. He provided for them but he didn't have sex with them. They were confined until the day of their death, in living widowhood.

⁴The king said to Amasa, 'Call out the Yehudahites for me in three days, and you yourself, stand here.' ⁵Amasa went to call out Yehudah, but he delayed beyond the time that he had set him. ⁶David said to Abishay, 'Now Sheba ben Bikri will make things worse for us than Abshalom. You take your lord's servants and pursue after him so he doesn't find fortified towns for himself, and tear out our eye.'

Yo'ab deals with Amasa

⁷Yo'ab's men, the Keretites and the Peletites, and all the strong men, went out after him; they went out from Yerushalaim to pursue after Sheba ben Bikri. ⁸When they were near the big stone which is at Gib'on, Amasa himself came before them. Yo'ab was belted in his uniform (his clothing), and over it there was the belt for a sword, fastened on his hips in its sheath. When he went out, it fell down. ⁹Yo'ab said to Amasa, 'Are things well with you, brother?', and Yo'ab's right hand took hold of Amasa's beard, to kiss him, ¹⁰but Amasa didn't keep watch for the sword that was in Yoab's hand, and he struck him down with it in his abdomen and made his insides pour out on to the ground. He didn't do it to him a second time. He died.

While Yo'ab and Abishay his brother pursued after Sheba ben Bikri, ¹¹and one of Yo'ab's boys stood over him and said, 'Whoever delights in Yo'ab and whoever is for David – after Yo'ab!', ¹²and Amasa was rolling in blood in the middle of the causeway, the man saw that the entire company halted. So he took Amasa round from the causeway into the fields and threw a garment over him, because everyone who came on him saw and halted. ¹³When he had been removed from the causeway, everyone passed on after Yo'ab to pursue after Sheba ben Bikri. ¹⁴He had passed through all the Yisra'elite clans to Meadow (Bet Ma'akah). All the Be'erites congregated and came after him also.

¹⁵So they came and besieged him in Bet Ma'akah Meadow. They heaped up a ramp against the town and it stood against the rampart. The entire company that was with Yo'ab were seeking to devastate it to make the wall fall.

An intelligent woman saves her town

¹⁶But a smart woman called from the town, 'Listen, listen! Please say to Yo'ab, "Draw near here so I can speak to you."' ¹⁷He drew near to her. The woman said, 'Are you Yo'ab?' He said, 'I am.' She said to him, 'Listen to your handmaid's words.' He said, 'I'm listening.' ¹⁸She said, 'People did speak previously, saying "They should just ask at Meadow", and thus they finished things. ¹⁹Whereas I'm among the truthful who are committed to peace in Yisra'el, you're seeking to put to death a town that's a mother in Yisra'el. Why would you swallow up Yahweh's domain?'

²⁰Yo'ab answered, 'Far be it from me, far be it from me, if I should swallow up or devastate. ²¹Things aren't like that. Rather, someone from the highland of Ephrayim, Sheba ben Bikri his name, has raised his hand against the king, against David. Give him alone over, and I'll go from the town.' The woman said to Yo'ab, 'There, his head is going to be thrown over the wall to you.'

²²The woman came to the entire people with her smart thinking, and they cut off the head of Sheba ben Bikri and threw it to Yo'ab. He blew on the horn and the men dispersed from the town, each one to his tents, while Yo'ab went back to Yerushalaim, to the king.

²³Yo'ab was over the entire Yisra'elite army. Benayah ben Yehoyada was over the Keretites and over the Peletites. ²⁴Adoram was over the workforce. Yehoshaphat ben Ahilud was the recorder. ²⁵Sheva was secretary. Tsadoq and Ebyatar were priests. ²⁶Ira the Ya'irite was also a priest for David.

Mother love

21 There was a famine in the time of David for three years, year after year. David sought Yahweh's face, and Yahweh said, 'It's in connection with Sha'ul and with the blood-stained household, because he put the Gib'onites to death.' ²So the king called for the Gib'onites and said to them (the Gib'onites were not among the Yisra'elites but rather among what was left of the Amorites, but the Yisra'elites had sworn to them, and Sha'ul had sought to strike them down in his passion for the Yisra'elites and Yehudah) – ³David said to the Gib'onites, 'What shall I do for you? How shall I make expiation, so you can bless Yahweh's domain?'

⁴The Gib'onites said to him, 'We have no [rights to] silver or gold with Sha'ul or with his household and we have no [rights to] put a man to death in Yisra'el.' So he said, 'Whatever you're going to say, I'll do for you.' ⁵They said to the king, 'The man who finished us off and who thought we could be annihilated so we would not take our stand within Yisra'el's entire border; ⁶seven of the men from among his descendants are to be given to us and we will execute them for Yahweh at Gib'ah-of-Sha'ul, Yahweh's chosen one.' The king said, 'I myself will give them.'

⁷The king spared Mephiboshet ben Yehonatan, son of Sha'ul, because of the oath before Yahweh between David and Yehonatan son of Sha'ul. ⁸The king got the two sons of Ritspah bat Ayyah to whom she gave birth for Sha'ul, Armoni and Mephiboshet, and the five sons of Mikal daughter of Sha'ul, to whom she gave birth for Adri'el ben Barzillay the Meholatite, ⁹and gave them into the hand of the Gib'onites. They executed them on the mountain before Yahweh. The seven of them fell together. These men were put to death during the first days of harvest, during the beginning of barley harvest.

¹⁰But Ritspah bat Ayyah got sack and spread it on a crag for herself from the beginning of harvest until water poured on them from the heavens. She didn't let the birds of the heavens settle on them by day or the creatures of the wild by night.

A final resting place

¹¹It was told David what Ritspah bat Ayyah, Sha'ul's secondary wife, had done, ¹²and David went and got the bones of Sha'ul and the bones of Yehonatan his son from the Yabesh-in-Gil'ad landowners, who had stolen them from the square in Bet-shan where the Pelishtites had hung them on the day the Pelishtites struck down Sha'ul at Gilboa. ¹³He took up from there the bones of Sha'ul and the bones of Yehonatan his son, and they gathered the bones of the men who had been executed. ¹⁴They buried the bones of Sha'ul and Yehonatan his son in the region of Binyamin in a side chamber in the grave of Qish his father. They did all that the king ordered, and God let himself be entreated for the country subsequently.

¹⁵There was again a battle by the Pelishtites with Yisra'el. David went down, he and his servants with him, and did battle with the Pelishtites. David got weary ¹⁶and Ishbi Benob (who was among the descendants of the Healer, and the weight of whose lance was 300 sheqels, made of copper, and he was belted in new things) thought to strike David down. ¹⁷But Abishay ben Tseruyah helped him, struck down the Pelishtite and put him to death. Then

David's men swore to him, 'You will not go out with us to battle any more, so that you do not extinguish Yisra'el's lamp.'

[18] Subsequently there was again a battle with the Pelishtites at Gob. Then Sibbekay the Hushatite struck down Saph, who was among the descendants of the Healer.

[19] There was again a battle with the Pelishtites at Gob, and Elhanan ben-Ya'are Oregim, the Bet Lehemite, struck down Golyat the Gittite; the wood of his lance was like a weavers' rod.

[20] There was again a battle at Gat. There was a man of stature with six fingers on his hands and six toes on his feet, twenty-four in number; he also was a descendant of the Healer. [21] He reviled Yisra'el, and Yonatan ben Shim'i, David's brother, struck him down.

[22] These four had descended from the Healer in Gat. They fell by the hand of David and by the hand of his servants.

The God of the storm

22

David spoke the words of this song to Yahweh on the day Yahweh rescued him from the fist of all his enemies and from the fist of Sha'ul.

[2] Yahweh, my crag,
   my stronghold, the one who enables me to survive,
[3] My God, my crag in which I take shelter,
   my shield, the horn that delivers me, my turret,
My retreat, my deliverer,
   you deliver me from violence.
[4] As one to be praised, I call on Yahweh,
   and from my enemies I find deliverance.
[5] Because death's waves overwhelmed me,
   Beliyya'al's wadis terrified me,
[6] She'ol's ropes surrounded me,
   death's snares met me.
[7] In my pressure I called on Yahweh,
   to my God I called.
He listened to my voice from his palace,
   my cry for help was in his ears.

[8] And the earth quaked and rocked,
   the heavens' foundations shook.
They quaked because it enraged him;
[9] smoke went up in his anger,
Fire from his mouth consumed,
   coals burned up from him.
[10] He spread the heavens and came down,
   with thundercloud beneath his feet.
[11] He rode on a sphinx and flew,
   he appeared on the wings of the wind.
[12] He made darkness round him a bivouac –
   a mass of water, clouds of mist.
[13] From the brightness in front of him
   fiery coals burned up.
[14] Yahweh thundered from the heavens,
   the One on High gave out his voice.
[15] He sent off arrows and scattered them,
   lightning, and routed them.
[16] The canyons of the sea appeared,
   the worlds' foundations became visible,
Through Yahweh's reprimand,
   at the breath of his angry wind.

I have kept Yahweh's ways(?)

[17] He sent from on high, he got me,
   he drew me out of much water.
[18] He rescued me from my vigorous enemy,
   from people hostile to me, because they stood too firm for me.
[19] They met me on the day of my disaster,
   but Yahweh became my support.
[20] He brought me out into a roomy place;
   he pulled me out because he delighted in me.
[21] Yahweh dealt to me in accordance with my faithfulness;
   in accordance with the purity of my hands he gave back to me.
[22] Because I have kept Yahweh's ways
   and not been faithless to my God.
[23] For all his rulings have been before me;
   his decrees – I haven't departed from them.
[24] I've been a person of integrity with him,
   and I've kept myself from waywardness I might have done.
[25] So Yahweh has given back to me in accordance with my faithfulness,
   in accordance with my purity before his eyes.
[26] With the committed person you show commitment,
   with the man of integrity you show integrity.
[27] With the pure person you show purity,
   but with the crooked you show yourself refractory.

²⁸A humble people you deliver,
    but you avert your eyes from exalted people.
²⁹For you, Yahweh, are my lamp;
    it's Yahweh who illumines my darkness.
³⁰For with you I can rush at a barricade,
    with my God I can scale a wall.
³¹God: his way has integrity,
    Yahweh's word is proven.
He is a shield
    to all who take shelter with him.
³²Because who is God apart from Yahweh,
    who is a crag apart from our God?

I will confess you among the nations

³³God is my stronghold, my forcefulness;
    he released one who had integrity in his way:
³⁴One who fashions my feet like a deer,
    enables me to stand on the heights,
³⁵Trains my hands for battle
    so that my arms could bend a copper bow.
³⁶You gave me your shield that delivered;
    your avowal made me great.
³⁷You widened my step beneath me;
    my ankles did not slip.
³⁸I pursued my enemies and annihilated them;
    I did not turn back until I had finished them off.
³⁹I devoured them, hit them, they could not get up;
    they fell beneath my feet.
⁴⁰You belted me with forcefulness for battle,
    you bent down beneath me the people who rose up against me.
⁴¹My enemies you made turn tail for me,
    the people who were hostile to me – and I wiped them out.
⁴²They looked, but there was no deliverer –
    to Yahweh, but he did not answer them.
⁴³I ground them fine like the earth in the ground,
    like the mud in the streets I crushed them, beat them out.
⁴⁴You enabled me to survive from arguments with my people,
    you kept me as head of nations,
A people I did not acknowledge serve me;
    ⁴⁵foreigners cowered before me.
On hearing with the ear, they listened to me;
    ⁴⁶foreigners wilted,
    came quaking out of their strongholds.
⁴⁷Yahweh lives, my crag be blessed,
    may God, the crag who delivers me, be exalted,
⁴⁸The God who gives me total redress,
    subjects peoples under me,
⁴⁹Who gets me out from my enemies,
    exalts me above the people who rise up against me,
    rescues me from violent men!
⁵⁰Therefore I will confess you, Yahweh, among the nations,
    and make music for your name,
⁵¹A tower bringing deliverance to his king,
    acting with commitment to his anointed,
    to David and to his offspring permanently.

David's last words

23 These are David's last words.

An utterance of David ben Yishay,
    an utterance of the man set up by the One on High,
The anointed of the God of Jacob,
    the delight of Yisra'el's melodies.
²Yahweh's spirit spoke through me,
    his utterance was on my tongue.
³The God of Yisra'el said,
    the crag of Yisra'el spoke to me:
One who rules over people as a faithful man,
    one who rules in awe of God,
⁴Is like the morning light when the sun rises,
    a morning with no clouds;
Because of brightness, because of rain,
    there's growth from the earth.
⁵My household is established with God, is it not,
    because he has made a permanent pact for me,
    laid out in every respect and secured.
He will bring to accomplishment, will he not,
    all my deliverance and all I delight in.
⁶But scoundrels are like thistles, thrown away, all of them,
    because people do not take them in the hand.
⁷The person who touches them
    equips himself with iron or the wood of a lance,
    and they totally burn up where they lie.

David's strong men

⁸These are the names of the strong men that David had:

The one who sits in the seat, a Tahkemonite, chief of the Three, was Adino the Etsnite, against 800, run through on one occasion. ⁹After him El'azar ben Dodo, son of Ahohi, one of the Three Strong Men with David when they reviled the Pelishtites who had gathered there for battle. The Yisra'elites went up, ¹⁰but he set to and struck down the Pelishtites until his hand got weary. But his hand attached itself to his sword and Yahweh brought about a great deliverance that day. The company came back after him, only to plunder. ¹¹After him Shamma ben Agee the Hararite. The Pelishtites had gathered at Lahi and there was a plot in the fields there full of lentils. Whereas the company had fled from before the Pelishtites, ¹²he took his stand in the middle of the plot and defended it, and struck down the Pelishtites. Yahweh brought about a great deliverance.

¹³Three of the Thirty Heads went down and came at harvest to David at the Adullam Cave. A force of Pelishtites was camped in Repha'ites Vale. ¹⁴David was then in the stronghold and an outpost of Pelishtites was then at Bet Lehem. ¹⁵David had a longing and said, 'If only someone could give me a drink of water from the Bet-lehem cistern that's at the gateway!' ¹⁶The Three Strong Men broke through the Pelishtites' camp, drew water from the Bet-lehem cistern that's at the gateway, carried it and brought it to David. But he was unwilling to drink it. He poured it out for Yahweh ¹⁷and said, 'Far be it from me by Yahweh that I should do this. Should the blood of the men who went at the cost of their lives . . .?' So he was unwilling to drink it. These are things that the Three Strong Men did.

The Three, the Thirty, the Thirty-Seven

¹⁸Abishay, the brother of Yo'ab ben Tseruyah, was head of a Three. He was wielding his lance against 300, run through. He had a name among the Three. ¹⁹Of the Three, he was the most honoured, wasn't he. He became officer for them, but he didn't come to the [other] Three. ²⁰Benayahu ben Yehoyada was a forceful man, prolific in deeds, from Qabtse'el. He struck down the two of Ari'el of Mo'ab. It was he who went down and struck down a lion inside a cistern on a snowy day, ²¹and it was he who struck down a Misrayimite man, an impressive man. In the Misrayimite's hand there was a lance, but he went down to him with a club, seized the lance out of the Misrayimite's hand and killed him with his lance. ²²These things Benayahu ben Yehoyada did, and he had a name among the Three Strong Men. ²³Of the Thirty, he was most honoured, but he did not come to the Three. David put him in charge of his guard.

²⁴Among the Thirty:

Asah-el, Yo'ab's brother
Elhanan ben Dodo (Bet Lehem)
²⁵Shammah the Harodite
Eliqa the Harodite
²⁶Helets the Paltite
Ira ben Iqqesh the Teqo'ite
²⁷Abi'ezer the Anatotite
Mebunnay the Hushatite
²⁸Tsalmon the Ahohite
Mahray the Netophatite
²⁹Heleb ben Ba'anah the Netophatite
Ittay ben Ribay from Gib'ah-of-the-Binyaminites
³⁰Benayahu, a Pir'atonite
Hidday from the Ga'ash Wadis
³¹Abi-albon the Arbatite
Azmavet the Barhumite
³²Elyahba the Sha'albonite
The sons of Yashen, Yehonatan
³³Shammah the Hararite
Ahi'am ben Sharar the Ararite
³⁴Eliphelet ben Ahasbay, son of the Ma'akatite
Eli'am ben Ahitophel the Gilonite
³⁵Hetsray the Carmelite
Pa'aray the Arbite
³⁶Yig'al ben Natan from Tsobah
Bani the Gadite
³⁷Tseleq the Ammonite
Nahray the Be'erotite, equipment-bearer for Yo'ab ben Tseruyah
³⁸Ira the Yitrite
Gareb the Yitrite
³⁹Uriyyah the Hittite

Thirty-seven in all.

When counting was wrong

24 Yahweh's anger raged against Yisra'el again and he incited David against them, saying 'Go count Yisra'el and Yehudah.' [2]So the king said to Yo'ab, the officer over the force that was with him, 'Go round all the Yisra'elite clans from Dan as far as Be'er Sheba, please, and number the company, so I may know the company's count.'

[3]Yo'ab said to the king, 'May Yahweh your God add to the company a hundred times over compared with what they are, while the eyes of my lord the king are watching, but why does my lord the king want this thing?' [4]But the king's word was strong toward Yo'ab and over the force's officers, so Yo'ab and the force's officers went out from the king's presence to number the company, Yisra'el.

[5]They crossed the Yarden and camped in Aro'er, to the south of the town, which is in the middle of Wadi Gad, and on to Ya'zer. [6]They came to Gil'ad and to the region of Tahtim Hodshi and came to Dan Ya'an and round to Tsidon. [7]They came to the fortress of Tsor and all the towns of the Hivvites and the Kena'anites [Canaanites] and went on to the Negeb of Yehudah (Be'er Sheba). [8]They went about the entire country and at the end of nine months and twenty days came to Yerushalaim. [9]Yo'ab gave the king the number for the registration of the company: Yisra'el came to 800,000 forceful men drawing the sword, and the men of Yehudah came to 500,000.

[10]David's mind struck him down after he had counted the company, and David said to Yahweh, 'I have acted very wrongly in what I've done. But now, Yahweh, please make your servant's waywardness pass on, because I've been very idiotic.'

I would rather fall into God's hands than into human hands

[11]David got up in the morning when Yahweh's word came to Gad the prophet, David's seer: [12]'Go and speak to David, "Yahweh has said this: 'I'm holding out three things over you. Choose one of them for yourself and I shall do it to you.'"' [13]Gad came to David and told him. He said to him, 'Are seven years of famine to come to you in the country, or are you to have three months of flight before your attackers as he pursues you, or are there to be three days of epidemic in your country? Now acknowledge it and see what word I'm to take back to the one who sent me.' [14]David said to God, 'It's very pressurizing for me. We will fall into Yahweh's hands, please, because his compassion is great. I will not fall into a human hand.'

[15]So Yahweh put an epidemic on Yisra'el from the morning until the set time, and there died of the company, from Dan as far as Be'er Sheba, 70,000 individuals. [16]The envoy put out his hand to Yerushalaim to devastate it, but Yahweh relented of the bad thing and said to the envoy devastating the company, 'So much! Now slacken your hand!'

Yahweh's envoy was by the threshing floor of Aravnah the Yebusite. [17]David said to Yahweh when he saw the envoy who was striking the company down: 'Here, I'm the one who did wrong. I'm the one who went astray. These people are the flock; what did they do? Your hand should please be against me and against my father's household.'

I won't offer worship that costs me nothing

[18]Gad came to David that day and said to him, 'Go up, set up an altar for Yahweh at the threshing floor of Aravnah the Yebusite.' [19]David went up in accordance with Gad's word, as Yahweh ordered.

[20]Aravnah looked out and saw the king and his servants crossing to him. Aravnah went out and bowed low to the king, his face to the ground. [21]Aravnah said, 'Why has my lord the king come to his servant?' David said, 'To acquire the threshing floor from you, to build an altar for Yahweh, so the epidemic may hold back from the company.' [22]Aravnah said to David, 'My lord the king may take it and offer up what is good in his eyes. See, the cattle as the burnt offering and the threshing boards and the cattle's equipment as wood. [23]Aravnah gives everything to the king, Your Majesty.' Aravnah said to the king, 'May Yahweh your God accept you.'

[24]The king said to Aravnah, 'No, because I will definitely acquire them from you for a

price. I will not offer up for Yahweh my God burnt offerings that cost nothing.' So David acquired the threshing-floor and the cattle for fifty silver sheqels. ²⁵David built an altar there for Yahweh and offered up burnt offerings and well-being sacrifices, and Yahweh let himself be entreated for the country. The epidemic held back from against Yisra'el.

1 Kings

The first book of Kings continues the story from 2 Samuel – indeed, one might have expected the opening chapters to be part of 2 Samuel, because they relate the closing scenes of David's life.

Almost half of 1 Kings then tells the story of the reign of Solomon, the last of the three kings who ruled Israel as a whole. A series of motifs from the stories of Saul and David recur in his story. One is the involvement of God's choice and of human process. In Saul's story, God's choice was the dominant factor, even though it was a choice God never wanted to make (because it wasn't God's idea to have kings). David's story interweaves the fact of God's choosing with a human process whereby much of Israel expects someone from Saul's family to succeed him, an expectation that complicates the process of David's succession. In Solomon's story, the conflictual human process is the dominant factor.

Conflict is more broadly the second motif. Saul's story is dominated by the need to get victory over the Philistines. David is the person who actually achieves this victory, and also deals with peoples such as the Ammonites and Moabites. Solomon thus inherits a kingdom whose international position is stable; it is indeed the dominant force in the region.

The nature of the kings' achievements thus varies. Saul begins with a great deliverance of Jabesh Gilead but achieves little else. David takes Jerusalem and builds on his military victories by making it the nation's capital, and he makes plans for a temple for Yahweh there. Solomon builds this temple and builds up the town in other spectacular ways.

The fourth motif is the trajectory of the kings' reigns. In each case the story unfolds in a way that emphasizes early achievements but then portrays an unravelling. Each king is undone by the pressures and temptations of his position and/or by his personal weaknesses. Whereas for Saul, making his own decisions was his downfall and for David his problem was a wandering eye and a general incompetence in relationships, for Solomon it was the diplomatic marriages that imperilled Israel's faithfulness to Yahweh. Solomon's story thus emphasizes his facilitating of the worship of other deities, which results from the diplomatic move of taking a number of wives from other peoples in order to cement relations with them. But the account of his building achievements also hints at his oppression of the ordinary people who have to pay much of the price for this work, and Solomon fulfils Samuel's warnings about the cost of having kings.

The hints become more explicit statements on the lips of his people after he dies. They want the next king to be less oppressive, but he declines, and this leads to the defection of ten of the Israelite clans and their setting up an alternative state. Because it in fact comprises the bulk of the clans, it retains the name 'Israel'. The state with the Davidic king, centred on Jerusalem, is merely 'Judah'.

The rest of 1 Kings interweaves the stories of Israel and Judah, which often involve conflict between the two states. The first king of Israel sets up an alternative worship structure with sanctuaries at the two ends of the kingdom. It also involves forms of worship that use images of God, flouting the basic principle that Yahweh cannot be imaged. The worship thus follows a regular human instinct to make images of the deity, an instinct that features in the traditional worship of Canaan from which the people of Yahweh were supposed to distance themselves. A dominant theme in the interwoven story of Israel and Judah is then how faithful the two peoples are in their worship of Yahweh: whether they worship Yahweh in inappropriate ways or worship other deities. In general, the worship of Israel is more problematic than that of Judah.

The problematic nature of this worship is important background to the emergence of prophets who confront the nation rather than supporting it (as the prophets did in David's day). These prophets are also involved as Yahweh's agents in initiating coups in Israel.

David in his dotage

1 Now King David was old, advanced in years. They covered him with clothes but he couldn't get warm, ²so his servants said to him, 'They should look for a young girl for my lord the king so she can stand before the king and be his caregiver. She can lie in your arms, and my lord the king will get warm.' ³So they looked for an attractive girl in the entire territory of Yisra'el [Israel], and found Abishag the Shunammite and brought her to the king. ⁴The girl was very attractive. She became the king's caregiver and she ministered to him, but the king didn't have sex with her.

⁵Now Adoniyyah ben Haggit was elevating himself, saying 'I shall be king', and he prepared himself chariotry and cavalry and fifty men running ahead of him. ⁶His father had not pained him in all his years by saying 'Why have you acted like this?' Further, he was very good-looking, and [his mother] had given birth to him after Abshalom. ⁷He had words with Yo'ab ben Tseruyah and with Ebyatar [Abiathar] the priest, and they supported Adoniyyah, ⁸but Tsadoq [Zadok] the priest, Benayahu ben Yehoyada, Natan the prophet, Shim'i, Re'i and David's strong men were not with Adoniyyah.

⁹Adoniyyah sacrificed sheep and cattle and fatlings at Zohelet Stone beside Treader Spring, and called all his brothers, the king's sons, and all the Yehudahites [Judahites], the king's servants, ¹⁰but Natan the prophet, Benayahu, the strong men and Shelomoh [Solomon] his brother he didn't call.

¹¹Natan said to Bat-sheba, Shelomoh's mother, 'You've heard, haven't you, that Adoniyyah ben Haggit has become king, whereas our lord David has not acknowledged it? ¹²So now go (may I please give you counsel) and save your life and the life of your son Shelomoh. ¹³Go, come to King David and say to him, "My lord the king, you yourself swore to your handmaid, didn't you, 'Your son Shelomoh – he will become king after me, it's he who will sit on my throne.' So why has Adoniyyah become king?" ¹⁴There, while you're still speaking there with the king, I myself will come after you and fill out your words.'

How to manipulate the old man in order to get things done

¹⁵So Bat-sheba came to the king in his room. The king was very old and Abishag the Shunammite was ministering to the king. ¹⁶Bat-sheba bent her head and bowed low to the king. The king said, 'What's on your mind?' ¹⁷She said to him, 'My lord, you yourself swore by Yahweh your God to your handmaid, "Shelomoh your son – he will become king after me; it's he who will sit on my throne." ¹⁸But now, here, Adoniyyah has become king, though my lord the king did not now acknowledge it. ¹⁹He has sacrificed oxen and firstlings and sheep in large number and called all the king's sons and Ebyatar the priest and Yo'ab the army officer, but Shelomoh your servant he didn't call. ²⁰So you, my lord king – the eyes of all Yisra'el are on you to tell them who is to sit on my lord king's throne after him. ²¹Or when my lord king lies down with his ancestors, I and my son Shelomoh will be [treated as] wrongdoers.'

²²And there, she was still speaking with the king, and Natan the prophet came. ²³They told the king, 'Here's Natan the prophet.' He came before the king and bowed low on his face to the ground to the king. ²⁴Natan said, 'My lord king, you yourself have said, "Adoniyyah will reign after me, he'll sit on my throne!" ²⁵Because he went down today and sacrificed oxen and fatlings and sheep in large number and called all the king's sons and the army officers and Ebyatar the priest. There they are, eating and drinking before him. They've said, "Long live King Adoniyyah." ²⁶But me, myself your servant, and Tsadoq the priest, and Benayahu ben Yehoyada, and Shelomoh your servant, he didn't call. ²⁷Did this thing come from my lord king and had you not made known to your servant who was to sit on my lord king's throne after him?'

Shelomoh enthroned

²⁸King David answered, 'Call Bat-sheba to me!' She came before the king and stood before the king. ²⁹The king swore, 'As Yahweh lives, who redeemed my life from every pressure, ³⁰indeed as I swore to you by Yahweh the God

of Yisra'el that Shelomoh your son would reign after me, and he would sit on my throne in place of me, so I will do this day.' ³¹Bat-sheba bent her head, face to the ground, and bowed low to the king, and said, 'Long live my lord King David!'

³²King David said, 'Call to me Tsadoq the priest and Natan the prophet and Benayahu ben Yehoyada.' They came before the king ³³and the king said to them, 'Take with you your lord's servants and have Shelomoh my son ride on the mule that belongs to me and have him go down to Gihon. ³⁴Tsadoq the priest is to anoint him there, with Natan the prophet, as king over Yisra'el. You're to blow on a horn and say, "Long live King Shelomoh!" ³⁵And go up after him so he comes and sits on my throne. He will reign in place of me. Him I have ordered to be chief over Yisra'el and over Yehudah.' ³⁶Benayahu ben Yehoyada answered the king, 'Yes, so may Yahweh the God of my lord king say it! ³⁷As Yahweh has been with my lord king, so may he be with Shelomoh. May he make his throne greater than the throne of my lord king David!'

³⁸So Tsadoq the priest went down, with Natan the prophet and Benayahu ben Yehoyada, and the Keretites and the Peletites, and they had Shelomoh ride on King David's mule and had him go to Gihon. ³⁹Tsadoq the priest got the horn of oil from the tent and anointed Shelomoh. They blew on the horn and the entire company said, 'Long live King Shelomoh!' ⁴⁰The entire company went up after him. The company were playing on pipes and rejoicing greatly. The earth split with the sound of them.

The danger when a coup fails

⁴¹Adoniyyah heard, he and all the people who had been called who were with him, as they had finished eating. Yo'ab heard the sound of the horn and said, 'Why the sound of the township in turmoil?' ⁴²While he was still speaking, there, Yonatan ben Ebyatar the priest came. Adoniyyah said, 'Come in, because you're a reliable man, and you announce good news.'

⁴³But Yonatan answered Adoniyyah, 'Well, our lord King David has made Shelomoh king! ⁴⁴The king has sent with him Tsadoq the priest and Natan the prophet and Benayahu ben Yehoyada, and the Keretites and the Peletites, and they've had him ride on the king's mule. ⁴⁵Tsadoq the priest and Natan the prophet have anointed him as king at Gihon, and they went up from there rejoicing and the township was in an uproar. That was the sound that you heard. ⁴⁶Also Shelomoh has sat on the royal throne. ⁴⁷And also, the king's servants came to bless our lord King David, saying "May your God make Shelomoh's name better than your name and make his throne greater than your throne." And the king has bowed low on his bed. ⁴⁸And also the king said this: "Blessed be Yahweh the God of Yisra'el who has today given someone sitting on my throne, and my eyes are seeing it."'

⁴⁹All the people who had been called who were for Adoniyyah trembled, got up and went each one his way, ⁵⁰while Adoniyyah was afraid of Shelomoh and got up and went and took strong hold of the altar horns. ⁵¹It was told Shelomoh, 'There, Adoniyyah is afraid of King Shelomoh. There, he's grasped the altar horns, saying "King Shelomoh must swear to me this very day: if he puts his servant to death with the sword..."'

⁵²Shelomoh said, 'If he becomes a reliable man, not one of his hairs will fall to the ground, but if something bad is found in him, he will die.' ⁵³So King Shelomoh sent and they got him to come down from the altar. He came and bowed low to King Shelomoh, and Shelomoh said to him, 'Go to your house.'

David's last will and testament

2 The days for David to die drew near, and he ordered Shelomoh his son: ²'I am going the way of all the earth. You're to be strong and be a man, ³and to keep the charge of Yahweh your God by walking in his ways, by keeping his decrees, his orders, his rulings and his affirmations as written in Mosheh's [Moses'] instruction, in order that you may thrive in everything you do and everywhere you turn your face, ⁴in order that Yahweh may implement his word which he spoke to me: "If your sons keep watch over their way by walking before me in truthfulness with

their entire mind and with their entire being, there will not be cut off for you someone on Yisra'el's throne."

⁵Further, you yourself know what Yo'ab ben Tseruyah did to me, what he did to the two officers of Yisra'el's armies, to Abner ben Ner and to Amasa ben Yeter. He killed them, and put the bloodshed of battle into peacetime. He put the bloodshed of battle on his belt that's round his hips and on his boot that's on his feet. ⁶Act in accordance with your smartness but don't let his white hair go down to She'ol in peace.

⁷The sons of Barzillay the Gil'adite: act with commitment to them so that they are among the people who eat at your table, because they approached me when I took flight from before Abshalom your brother. ⁸But here, Shim'i ben Gera the Binyaminite [Benjaminite] from Bahurim is with you. He uttered a grievous slight of me on the day I went to Mahanayim, but when he came down to meet me at the Yarden [Jordan] I swore to him by Yahweh, "If I put you to death by the sword . . ."

⁹But now, don't treat him as free of guilt, because you're a smart man and you'll know how you should act towards him and have his white hair go down to She'ol in blood.'

A not-very subtle request

¹⁰So David lay down with his ancestors and was buried in David's Town. ¹¹The time that David reigned over Yisra'el was forty years. In Hebron he reigned seven years; in Yerushalaim he reigned thirty-three years. ¹²Shelomoh sat on David his father's throne and his kingship was well established.

¹³Adoniyyah ben Haggit came to Bat-sheba, Shelomoh's mother. She said, 'Is your coming in peace?' He said, 'In peace', ¹⁴and said, 'I have a word for you.' She said, 'Speak.' ¹⁵He said, 'You yourself know that the kingship was mine. All Yisra'el had set their faces towards me reigning. But the kingship turned round and became my brother's, because it was his from Yahweh. ¹⁶But now I'm making one request from you yourself. Don't turn my face back.' She said to him, 'Speak.' ¹⁷He said, 'Please say to Shelomoh the king (because he won't turn your face back) that he should give me Abishag the Shunammite as wife.' ¹⁸Bat-sheba said, 'Very well, I myself will speak to the king about you.'

¹⁹Bat-sheba came to King Shelomoh to speak to him about Adoniyyah. The king got up to meet her and bowed low to her. He sat on his throne and placed a throne for the king's mother, and she sat at his right. ²⁰She said, 'I'm going to make one small request from you yourself. Don't turn back my face.' The king said to her, 'Ask, mother, because I shall not turn your face back.' ²¹She said, 'Abishag the Shunammite should be given to Adoniyyah your brother as wife.'

²²King Shelomoh answered his mother, 'Why are you asking for Abishag the Shunammite for Adoniyyah? Ask for the kingship for him, because he's my brother who's older than me – for him and for Ebyatar the priest and for Yo'ab ben Tseruyah.' ²³King Shelomoh swore by Yahweh: 'May God act in this way to me, and do more in this way, because Adoniyyah has spoken this word at the cost of his life. ²⁴So now, as Yahweh lives, who has established me and made me sit on the throne of David my father, and made me a household, as he spoke: today Adoniyyah will indeed be put to death.'

The penalty for backing the wrong horse

²⁵So King Shelomoh sent by the hand of Benayahu ben Yehoyada, and he came upon him and he died. ²⁶And to Ebyatar the priest, the king said 'Go to Anatot to your fields, because you deserve death, but on this day I shall not put you to death, because you carried my Lord Yahweh's chest before David my father and because you let yourself be humbled in all that my father let himself be humbled.' ²⁷So Shelomoh drove Ebyatar out from being Yahweh's priest, fulfilling Yahweh's word which he spoke about the household of Eli in Shiloh.

²⁸When the report came to Yo'ab (because Yo'ab had turned away to follow Adoniyyah, though he had not turned away to follow Abshalom), Yo'ab fled to Yahweh's tent and took strong hold of the altar horns. ²⁹It was told King Shelomoh that Yo'ab had fled to Yahweh's tent. There, he was beside the altar. Shelomoh sent Benayahu ben Yehoyada, saying 'Go, come upon him.'

³⁰Benayahu came to Yahweh's tent and said to him, 'The king has said this: "Out!"' He said, 'No! Rather I shall die here.' Benayahu took word back to the king, 'Yo'ab spoke like this; he answered me like this.' ³¹The king said to him, 'Do as he spoke, and come upon him and bury him and remove the blood shed for nothing that Yo'ab poured out, from upon me and from upon my father's household. ³²Yahweh will bring back his blood on his head, because he came upon two men more faithful and better than him and killed them with the sword, when my father David didn't know, Abner ben Ner, Yisra'el's army officer, and Amasa ben Yeter, Yehudah's army officer. ³³Their shed blood is to come back on Yo'ab's head and on the head of his offspring permanently. But for David, for his offspring, for his household and for his throne, may things be well from Yahweh permanently.'

³⁴So Benayahu ben Yehoyada went up and came upon him and put him to death. He was buried in his house in the wilderness. ³⁵The king made Benayahu ben Yehoyada in charge of the army in place of him, while the king made Tsadoq the priest in place of Ebyatar.

The man who might have thought twice

³⁶The king sent and called for Shim'i, and said to him, 'Build yourself a house in Yerushalaim and live there. You will not go out from there anywhere. ³⁷On the day you go out and cross Wadi Qidron, acknowledge clearly that you will definitely die; your blood will be on your own head.' ³⁸Shim'i said to the king, 'The word is good. As my lord king spoke, so your servant will do.' So Shim'i lived in Yerushalaim for a long time.

³⁹But at the end of three years two of Shim'i's servants took flight to Akish ben Ma'akah king of Gat. People told Shim'i, 'There, your servants are in Gat.' ⁴⁰So Shim'i set off, saddled his donkey and went to Gat to Akish to look for his servants.

So Shim'i went, and brought his servants from Gat, ⁴¹but it was told Shelomoh that Shim'i had gone from Yerushalaim to Gat and had come back. ⁴²The king sent and called for Shim'i. He said to him, 'I got you to swear by Yahweh and I testified to you, didn't I, "On the day you go out and go anywhere, you're to acknowledge clearly that you will definitely die", and you said to me, "The word is good. I've listened." ⁴³So why didn't you keep the oath before Yahweh and the order that I gave you?' ⁴⁴The king said to Shim'i, 'You yourself know all the bad dealing (which you acknowledge in your heart) that you undertook towards David my father. Yahweh will bring back your bad dealing on your head, ⁴⁵whereas King Shelomoh will be blessed and David's throne will be established before Yahweh permanently.' ⁴⁶And the king gave orders to Benayahu ben Yehoyada, and he went out and came upon him and put him to death.

So the kingship was established in Shelomoh's hand.

3 Shelomoh made a marriage relationship with Par'oh king of Misrayim [Pharaoh king of Egypt]; he took Par'oh's daughter and brought her to David's Town until he had finished building his house and Yahweh's house and the wall of Yerushalaim all round. ²Only, the people were sacrificing at the shrines because the house for Yahweh's name was not yet built up to that time, ³but Shelomoh was loyal to Yahweh in walking by the decrees of David his father; only, he was sacrificing and burning incense at the shrines.

What do you most want?

⁴The king went to Gib'on to sacrifice there, because it was the biggest shrine; Shelomoh would offer up a thousand burnt offerings on that altar. ⁵At Gib'on Yahweh appeared to Shelomoh in a dream by night. God said, 'Ask for what I should give you.' ⁶Shelomoh said, 'You yourself acted in great commitment with your servant David my father as he walked before you in truthfulness and faithfulness and in uprightness of mind with you. You have kept this great commitment for him and given him a son sitting on his throne this very day.

⁷Now, Yahweh my God, you yourself have made your servant king in place of my father David, when I am a small boy who doesn't know how to go out and come in. ⁸Your servant is among your people that you chose, a numerous people that can't be measured or counted because of the large number. ⁹So you should

give your servant a listening mind to decide cases for your people, to discern between good and bad, because who can exercise authority for this substantial people of yours?'

[10]The thing was good in the Lord's eyes, that Shelomoh had asked for this thing. [11]God said to him, 'Since you've asked for this thing and you haven't asked for a long life for yourself and haven't asked for wealth for yourself and haven't asked for the life of your enemies, but asked for yourself to be discerning in hearing a case: [12]there, I'm acting in accordance with your words. Here, I am giving you a smart and discerning mind such that there has not been anyone like you before you and there will not arise anyone like you after you. [13]What you did not ask I am also giving you, both wealth and splendour for all your days, such that there has not been anyone like you among the kings. [14]If you walk in my ways by keeping my decrees and my orders as your father David walked, I will make your days long.'

[15]Shelomoh woke up. There, a dream. He came to Yerushalaim and stood before the Lord's pact chest, and offered up whole offerings and made well-being sacrifices, and made a banquet for all his servants.

Two mothers, one baby

[16]Then two women who were prostitutes came to the king and stood before him. [17]The one woman said, 'Pardon me, my lord, I and this woman are living in one house. I gave birth with her in the house. [18]On the third day after I gave birth, this woman also gave birth. We were together. There was no outsider in the house with us, only the two of us in the house. [19]This woman's son died in the night because she lay on it, [20]and she got up in the middle of the night and took my son from beside me while your handmaid was asleep, laid him in her arms and laid her dead son in my arms. [21]So I got up in the morning to nurse my son and there – he was dead. But I considered him closely in the morning, and there – it was not my son, whom I had given birth to.' [22]The other woman said, 'No, because the live one is my son and the dead one is your son', while the first woman was saying, 'No, because the dead one is your son and the live one is my son.'

So they spoke before the king, [23]and the king said, 'The one woman is saying "This is my son, the live one, and the dead one is your son", while the other one is saying, "No, because the dead one is your son, and the live one is mine."' [24]The king said, 'Get me a sword.' They brought a sword before the king. [25]The king said, 'Divide the live child in two and give half to one and half to the other.' [26]The woman whose son was the live one said to the king (because her insides burned for her son) – she said, 'Pardon me, my lord, give her the live baby, my lord. Don't actually put it to death', whereas the other was saying, 'It won't be either mine or yours – divide it.' [27]The king answered, 'Give her the live baby. Don't actually put it to death. She's its mother.'

[28]When all Yisra'el heard the decision that the king had made, they were in awe before the king, because they saw that there was divine smartness within him for exercising authority.

Shelomoh's administration

4 So King Shelomoh was king over all Yisra'el. [2]These were the officials that he had:

Azaryahu ben Tsadoq (the priest);
[3]Elihoreph and Ahiyyahu, sons of Shisha (secretaries);
Yehoshaphat ben Ahilud (the recorder);
[4]Benayahu ben Yehoyada (in charge of the army);
Tsadoq and Ebyatar (priests);
[5]Azaryahu ben Natan (in charge of the prefects);
Zabud ben Natan the priest (the king's friend);
[6]Ahishar (in charge of the household);
Adoniram ben Abda (in charge of the workforce).

[7]Shelomoh had twelve prefects over all Yisra'el; they would provide for the king and his household. There would be a month per year for each for provisioning. [8]These were their names:
the son of Hur, in the highland of Ephrayim;
[9]the son of Deqer, in Maqats, in Sha'albim, Bet Shemesh and Bet Hanan Oak;
[10]the son of Hesed, in Arubot: Sokoh and the entire region of Hepher was his;

¹¹the son of Abinadab: all Do'r Height (Taphat, Shelomoh's daughter, was his wife);
¹²Ba'ana ben Ahilud: Ta'anak, Megiddo, and all Bet She'an, which is beside Tsaratan, below Yizre'e'l, from Bet She'an as far as Meholah Meadow, as far as across from Yoqmo'am;
¹³the son of Geber: in Heights-in-Gil'ad, the Villages of Ya'ir ben Menashsheh which are in Gil'ad, were his; the district of Argob, which is in Bashan, sixty big towns with a wall and a copper bar, were his;
¹⁴Ahinadab ben Iddo: Mahanayim;
¹⁵Ahima'ats: in Napthali (also he took Basemat, Shelomoh's daughter, as wife);
¹⁶Ba'ana ben Hushay: in Asher and in Alot;
¹⁷Yehoshaphat ben Paruah: in Yissakar [Issachar];
¹⁸Shim'i ben Ela: in Binyamin;
¹⁹Geber ben Uri: in the region of Gil'ad (the country of Sihon king of the Amorites and Og the king of Bashan), and the one prefect who was in the region.
²⁰Yehudah and Yisra'el were as many as the sand that's by the sea in large number, eating, drinking and rejoicing.

Shelomoh's prosperity and his smartness

²¹Shelomoh was ruling over all the kingdoms from the River to the country of the Pelishtites [Philistines], as far as the border of Misrayim, bringing offerings and serving Shelomoh all the days of his life. ²²Shelomoh's food for one day was thirty ten-gallon measures of fine flour, sixty ten-gallon measures of ordinary flour, ²³ten sturdy cattle, twenty pasture cattle and a hundred sheep, apart from deer, gazelle, roebuck and fattened geese, ²⁴because he was holding sway over all of Beyond the River, from Tiphsah as far as Azzah [Gaza], over all the kings of Beyond the River, and he had peace on all his borders, all round.

²⁵Yehudah and Yisra'el lived in confidence, each person under his vine and under his fig tree, from Dan as far as Be'er-sheba, all Shelomoh's days. ²⁶Shelomoh had 40,000 stalls of horses for his chariotry and 12,000 cavalry. ²⁷These prefects would provide for King Shelomoh and for everyone who approached King Shelomoh's table, each for his month. They did not let anything be lacking. ²⁸As for the barley and the straw for the horses and for the steeds, they would bring it to the place where he would be, each person according to the ruling for him.

²⁹God gave Shelomoh smartness and understanding in very great measure and width of mind like the sand that's on the seashore. ³⁰Shelomoh's smartness was greater than the smartness of all the Qedemites and all the smartness of the Misrayimites. ³¹He was smarter than all humanity, than Etan the Ezrahite, and Heman, Kalkol and Darda, the sons of Mahol. His name was among all the nations around. ³²He spoke 3,000 aphorisms and his songs were 1,005. ³³He spoke about trees from the cedar that's in the Lebanon as far as the hyssop that comes out on the wall. He spoke about animals, about birds, about moving things and about fish. ³⁴They came from all the peoples to listen to Shelomoh's smartness, from all the kings of the earth who had heard of his smartness.

The chance to build a house for Yahweh

5 Hiram king of Tsor [Tyre] sent his servants to Shelomoh because he had heard that they had anointed him as king in place of his father, because Hiram had always been loyal to David. ²Shelomoh sent to Hiram to say, ³'You yourself know of David my father, that he was not able to build a house for the name of Yahweh his God because of the battle that surrounded him until Yahweh put them beneath the soles of his feet. ⁴But now Yahweh my God has made things settle for me all round. There's no adversary and there's nothing bad happening.

⁵So here I'm saying to build a house for the name of Yahweh my God, as Yahweh spoke to David my father: "Your son, whom I will put on your throne in place of you, he will build the house for my name." ⁶So now, order that they cut down cedars for me from the Lebanon. My servants will be with your servants, and your servants' wages – I will give it to you in accordance with anything that you say, because you yourself know that there is no one among us who knows about cutting down trees like the Tsidonites.'

⁷When Hiram heard Shelomoh's words, he rejoiced greatly. He said, 'Yahweh be blessed

today, who has given David a smart son over this numerous people.' ⁸Hiram sent to Shelomoh: 'I've heard what you sent me. I myself will do all you want in cedar trees and in juniper trees. ⁹My servants will get them down from the Lebanon to the sea. It'll be me who makes them into rafts at the sea for the place that you send to me, and I'll split them up there. It'll be you who carries them, and you who'll do what I want in giving bread to my household.'

The labourers for the building

¹⁰So Hiram was giving Shelomoh cedar wood and juniper wood, all that he wanted, ¹¹while Shelomoh gave Hiram 20,000 ten-gallon measures of wheat as provision for his household and 20,[000] ten-gallon measures of pressed oil. Thus Shelomoh would give Hiram year by year. ¹²Because Yahweh gave Shelomoh smartness, as he had spoken to him, there was peace between Hiram and Shelomoh. The two of them solemnized a pact.

¹³King Shelomoh raised a workforce from all Yisra'el; the workforce came to 30,000 men. ¹⁴He sent them to the Lebanon 10,000 per month in shifts. They would be a month in the Lebanon, two months at home. Adoniram was in charge of the workforce.

¹⁵Shelomoh had 70,000 load-carriers and 80,000 stonecutters in the highland, ¹⁶apart from Shelomoh's prefect officers who were in charge of the work, 3,300 holding sway over the company who were doing the work. ¹⁷The king gave them orders and they transported big stones, fine stones, so as to found the house with hewn stones. ¹⁸Shelomoh's builders, Hiram's builders and men from Byblos shaped them, and prepared the wood and the stones for building the house.

6 In the four hundred and eightieth year of the Yisra'elites' getting out of the country of Misrayim, in the fourth year in the month Ziv (i.e. the second month) of Shelomoh's reign over Yisra'el, he built the house for Yahweh. ²The house that King Shelomoh built for Yahweh:

> its length was thirty metres;
> its width ten metres;
> its height fifteen metres.

³The porch on the front of the hall of the house:

> its length was ten metres (along the width of the house);
> its width five metres (along the front of the house).

⁴He made recessed latticed windows for the house, ⁵against the wall of the house he built an extension all round (the walls of the house round the hall and the inner sanctuary), and he made side rooms all round.

> ⁶The lowest extension: its width was two and a half metres;
> the middle: its width was three metres;
> the third: its width was three and a half metres;

because he put supports for the house all round outside so as not to fasten them to the walls of the house.

If you walk

⁷When the house was built, it was built of whole quarry stone. Hammers or chisel, any iron tool, did not make itself heard in the house when it was built. ⁸The entrance to the middle side room was on the right side of the house, and winding stairs went up to the middle one and from the middle one to the third.

⁹So he built the house and finished it, and panelled the house with beams and planks of cedar. ¹⁰He built the extension against the entire house, two and a half metres its height, and secured the house with cedar wood.

¹¹Yahweh's word came to Shelomoh: ¹²'This house that you're building: if you walk by my decrees and act by my rulings and keep all my orders, walking by them, I will implement with you my word that I spoke to David your father. ¹³I will dwell among the Yisra'elites and I will not abandon my people Yisra'el.'

¹⁴So Shelomoh built the house and finished it. ¹⁵He built the walls of the house on the inside with cedar planks from the floor of the house up to the ceiling walls. He overlaid it with wood on the inside and overlaid the floor

1 Kings 6: The temple of Shelomoh (Solomon)

of the house with juniper planks. ¹⁶He built with cedar boards ten metres from the sides of the house, from the floor as far as the walls, and built for it inside an inner room as the very sacred place. ¹⁷The house (i.e. the hall, in front) was twenty metres. ¹⁸The cedar for the house within: carving of melons and open flowers, everything cedar. No stone was visible.

¹⁹He prepared an inner room inside the house, within, to put Yahweh's pact chest there. ²⁰In front of the inner room it was ten metres in length, ten metres in width and ten metres in its height. He overlaid it with beaten gold and overlaid the altar with cedar.

The inner room

²¹Shelomoh overlaid the house inside with beaten gold, and passed gold chains in front of the inner room and overlaid it with gold. ²²So the entire house he overlaid with gold until the entire house was complete, and the entire altar belonging to the inner room he overlaid with gold. ²³In the inner room he made two sphinxes of oil wood; its height was five metres. ²⁴One sphinx's wing was two and a half metres and the second sphinx's wing was two and a half metres. From the ends of its wings to the other ends of its wings was five metres, ²⁵and the second sphinx was five metres: one measure and one profile for the two sphinxes. ²⁶The height of one sphinx was five metres, and so the second sphinx.

²⁷He put the sphinxes in the middle of the inner house. They spread the sphinxes' wings so that the wing of the one touched the wall and the wing of the second sphinx was touching the second wall, with their wings towards the middle of the house, wing touching wing. ²⁸He overlaid the sphinxes with gold, ²⁹and all the walls of the house, all round, he carved with carved engravings of sphinxes, palms and open flowers, inside and outside. ³⁰The floor of the house he overlaid with gold, inside and outside.

³¹As the entrance of the inner room he made doors of oil wood, the upright (the doorposts) fivefold, ³²the two doors of oil wood. He carved on them carvings of sphinxes, palms and open flowers, and overlaid them with gold. He hammered the gold on to the sphinxes and on to the palms. ³³In this way he made for the entrance to the hall doorposts of oil wood, out of a quarter, ³⁴and two doors of juniper wood, one door of two leaves folding and the other door of two leaves folding. ³⁵He carved sphinxes, palms and open flowers and overlaid them with gold, fitted on to the chiselling. ³⁶He built the inner courtyard with three rows of hewn stone and a row of cedar timbers.

The forest-like meeting house

³⁷In the fourth year Yahweh's house was founded, in the month of Ziv, ³⁸and in the

eleventh year in the month of Bul (i.e. the eighth month) the house got finished in keeping with all his words and with all his rulings. He built it over seven years.

7 His own house Shelomoh built over thirteen years. He finished his entire house ²and built the Lebanon Forest house:
its length fifty metres, its width twenty-five metres and its height fifteen metres;
on four rows of cedar pillars, with cedar timbers on the pillars;
³it was panelled with cedar above, on top of the planks that were on the forty-five pillars (fifteen per row);
⁴frames, three rows, face to face, three times;
⁵all the entrances and the doorposts, square in frame, in front, face to face, three times;
⁶the porch of pillars he made, twenty-five metres its length and fifteen metres its width;
a porch in front of them and pillars and a canopy in front.

⁷He made the porch for the throne where he would exercise authority (the authority porch). It was covered in cedar from floor to floor. ⁸His house where he would live (the other courtyard within the porch) was of this same making. He would make a house for Par'oh's daughter, whom Shelomoh took, like this porch. ⁹All these things:
fine stone, hewn according to measure, trimmed with a trimmer, inside and outside, from foundation to coping, from outside as far as the big courtyard;
¹⁰the foundation: fine stones, big stones, five-metre stones and four-metre stones;
¹¹on top: fine stones, hewn according to measure, and cedar;
¹²the big courtyard all round: three rows of hewn stone and a row of cedar timbers, both for the inner courtyard of Yahweh's house and for the house's porch.

The other Hiram

¹³King Shelomoh sent and got Hiram from Tsor. ¹⁴He was the son of a woman who was a widow from the clan of Naphtali, but his father had been a Tsorite, a coppersmith. He was full of smartness, of understanding and of knowledge for doing all work in copper. So he came to King Shelomoh and did all his work.
¹⁵He shaped the two pillars, of copper.
The height of one pillar was nine metres.
A line of six metres would go round the second pillar.
¹⁶Two capitals he made to put on the tops of the pillars, cast in copper; the height of one capital was two and a half metres and the height of the second capital was two and a half metres.
¹⁷Nets of netted work, twists of chainwork, for the capitals that were on the top of the pillars, seven for one capital, seven for the second capital.
¹⁸He made the pillars with two rows all round on each net, to cover the capitals that were on the top of the pomegranates, and in this way he made it for the second capital.
¹⁹The capitals that were on the top of the pillars made of lotuses, in the porch, two metres.
²⁰The capitals on the two pillars also above, next to the bulge that was across from the net.
The 200 pomegranates in rows all round on the second capital.
²¹He set up the pillars for the porch of the hall: he set up the right pillar and named it 'He-Establishes' and set up the left pillar and named it 'In-Him-Is-Strength'.
²²On the top of the pillars: lotus work.
So the work on the pillars was complete.

The 'sea' and its stands

²³He made the sea, cast:
five metres from its lip to its lip, circular all round, two and a half metres its height;
a line of fifteen metres would go round it all round;
²⁴melons under its lip going round it, all round, five metres, encircling the sea all round; two rows of melons cast with its casting;
²⁵standing on twelve cattle, three facing north, three facing west, three facing south, three facing east, with the sea on them, above, and all their rears inwards;
²⁶its thickness a handbreadth;
its lip like the making of the lip of a cup, a lotus petal;

it could contain 2,000 five-gallon measures. ²⁷He made the ten stands, copper:
the length of one stand two metres, two metres its width, and one and a half metres its height;
²⁸this was the making of a stand: they had rims, and rims between the frames;
²⁹on the rims that were between the frames, lions, cattle and sphinxes;
on the frames a stand;
on top and below the lions and the cattle, spirals of hammered making;
³⁰four copper wheels for each stand, and copper axles;
its four legs had shoulder-pieces under the basin;
the shoulder-pieces, cast, with spirals across from each;
³¹its mouth inside the capital and half a metre above;
its mouth circular, the making of a stand, three quarters of a metre;
also on the mouth, carvings;
their rims square, not circular;
³²the four wheels below the rims;
the wheels' supports in the stand;
the height of a wheel three quarters of a metre;
³³the making of the wheels like the making of a chariot wheel;
their supports, their backs, their spokes and their hubs, all cast;
³⁴four shoulder-pieces at the four corners of each stand; from the stand its shoulder-pieces;
³⁵at the top of the stand a circular band all round, the height a quarter of a metre;
on the top of the stand, its handles and its rims coming from it.

The engraved sphinxes

³⁶He engraved on the panels of its handles and on its rims sphinxes, lions and palms, according to the space on each, with spirals all round. ³⁷Like this he made the ten stands, each cast, one measure, one shape for all of them. ³⁸He made ten copper basins. Each basin would contain 45-gallon measures, each basin two metres, each on its stand, for the ten stands. ³⁹He put the stands five at the right shoulder of the house and five at the left shoulder of the house. The sea he put at the right shoulder of the house to the east, towards the south. ⁴⁰Hiram made the basins, the shovels and the bowls.

So Hiram finished doing all the work that he did for King Shelomoh at Yahweh's house:
⁴¹two pillars;
two globes for the capitals that were on the top of the pillars;
two nets to cover the two globes for the capitals that were on the top of the pillars;
⁴²the 400 pomegranates for the two nets, two rows of pomegranates for each net, to cover the two globes for the capitals that were on the face of the pillars;
⁴³the ten stands and the ten basins on the stands;
⁴⁴the one sea and the twelve cattle beneath the sea;
⁴⁵the buckets, the shovels, the basins, all these articles that Hiram made for King Shelomoh for Yahweh's house, polished copper.
⁴⁶The king cast them in the Yarden Plain, in the earthen compactness between Sukkot and Tsaretan. ⁴⁷Shelomoh left all the articles alone [unweighed], because of the very, very large number; the weight of the copper was not searched out.
⁴⁸Shelomoh made all the articles that were for Yahweh's house:
the gold altar;
the table on which was the presence bread, gold;
⁴⁹the lights (five on the right and five on the left) in front of the inner room, beaten gold;
the flowers, the lamps and the tongs, gold;
⁵⁰the basins, the snuffers, the sprinklers, the ladles and the pans, beaten gold;
the hinges for the doors of the inner house, for the very sacred place, for the doors of the house, for the hall, gold.

The work completed

⁵¹So all the work that King Shelomoh had done for Yahweh's house was complete, and Shelomoh brought in the sacred things from David his father; the silver, the gold and the

articles he put in the treasuries of Yahweh's house.

8 Then Shelomoh congregated Yisra'el's elders (all the heads of the clans, the Yisra'elites' ancestral leaders) to King Shelomoh in Yerushalaim, to take up Yahweh's pact chest from David's Town (i.e. Tsiyyon [Zion]). ²All the Yisra'elites congregated to King Shelomoh in the month of Etanim at the festival (i.e. the seventh month). ³All Yisra'el's elders came and the priests carried the chest. ⁴They took up Yahweh's chest, the appointment tent and all the sacred articles that were in the tent. The priests and the Levites took them up ⁵while King Shelomoh and the entire assembly of Yisra'el who had assembled to him were with him before the chest, sacrificing sheep and cattle that could not be numbered and could not be counted because of the large number.

⁶The priests brought Yahweh's pact chest to its place, to the inner room of the house, to the very sacred place, under the sphinxes' wings, ⁷because the sphinxes were spreading their wings to the chest's place; the sphinxes screened the chest and its poles from above. ⁸The poles extended and the heads of the poles could be seen from the sacred place in front of the inner room, but they could not be seen outside. They have been there until this day. ⁹There was nothing in the chest, only the two stone tablets that Mosheh had set down there at Horeb, when Yahweh solemnized things with the Yisra'elites, when they got out from the country of Misrayim.

¹⁰When the priests went out from the sacred place and the cloud was filling Yahweh's house, ¹¹the priests were not able to stand to minister before the cloud, because Yahweh's splendour was filling Yahweh's house.

The God who dwells in the cloud

¹²Then Shelomoh said:

Yahweh has said he would dwell in a thundercloud.
¹³I have indeed built a stately house for you, an established place for you to live in to the ages.

¹⁴The king turned his face round and blessed Yisra'el's entire congregation, as Yisra'el's entire congregation was standing. ¹⁵He said, 'Blessed be Yahweh the God of Yisra'el who spoke by his own mouth with David my father, and by his own hand has fulfilled it: ¹⁶"From the day that I got my people Yisra'el out of Misrayim I didn't choose a town from all Yisra'el's clans to build a house for my name to be there, but I chose David to be in charge of my people Yisra'el."

¹⁷It was in David my father's mind to build a house for the name of Yahweh the God of Yisra'el, ¹⁸but Yahweh said to David my father, "In that it was in your mind to build a house for my name, you did well that it was in your mind. ¹⁹Only you yourself will not build the house. Rather, your son, who is going to come out from your insides, he will build the house for my name."

²⁰Yahweh has implemented his word that he spoke. I have arisen in place of David my father, I have sat on Yisra'el's throne as Yahweh spoke and I have built the house for the name of Yahweh the God of Yisra'el. ²¹I have set a place there for the chest where Yahweh's pact is, which he solemnized with our ancestors when he got them out of the country of Misrayim.'

²²Shelomoh stood before Yahweh's altar in front of the entire congregation of Yisra'el and spread out his palms to the heavens.

Will God really live on earth?

²³He said, 'Yahweh, God of Yisra'el, there is no god like you in the heavens above or on the earth beneath, keeping pact and commitment for your servants who walk before you with their entire mind, ²⁴who has kept for your servant David my father what you spoke to him. You spoke with your own mouth and with your own hand you have fulfilled it, this very day.

²⁵So now, Yahweh, God of Yisra'el, keep for your servant David my father what you spoke to him: "There will not be cut off for you someone before me sitting on Yisra'el's throne, if only your sons keep watch over their way in walking before me as you have walked before me." ²⁶So now, God of Yisra'el, may your word please prove trustworthy that you spoke to your servant David my father.

²⁷Because will God truly live on the earth? There – the heavens, even the highest heavens, could not contain you, certainly not this house that I have built. ²⁸But turn your face towards your servant's plea and towards his prayer for grace, Yahweh my God, so as to listen to the resounding cry and to the plea that your servant is making before you today, ²⁹so that your eyes are opened towards this house night and day, towards the place of which you've said, "My name will be there", so as to listen to the plea that your servant makes towards this place. ³⁰May you listen to the prayer for grace by your servant and your people Yisra'el, which they make towards this place. May you yourself listen towards the place where you live, towards the heavens, listen and pardon.

Some things to pray for

³¹Someone who does wrong, an individual to his neighbour, and he takes up an oath against him to get him to swear, and the oath comes before your altar in this house, ³²may you yourself listen in the heavens, and act, and exercise authority for your servants, so as to show the person in the wrong to be in the wrong, bringing his conduct on his head, and to show the person in the right to be in the right, bringing to him in accordance with his being in the right.

³³When your people Yisra'el take a beating before an enemy because they do wrong in relation to you, but they turn back to you and confess your name and plead and pray for grace towards you in this house, ³⁴may you yourself listen in the heavens and pardon your people Yisra'el's wrongdoing and take them back to the land that you gave to their ancestors.

³⁵When the heavens hold back and there's no rain because they do wrong in relation to you, but they plead towards this place and confess your name, and turn back from their wrongdoing because you humble them, ³⁶may you yourself listen in the heavens and pardon the wrongdoing of your servants, of your people Yisra'el, when you instruct them in the good way that they should walk in, and give rain on your country that you gave your people as a domain.

More things to pray for

³⁷When famine happens in the country, when an epidemic happens, blight, mildew, locust, caterpillar, when it happens; when its enemy besieges it in the region of its settlements; any affliction, any illness; ³⁸any plea, any prayer for grace that any human being belonging to your entire people Yisra'el may have, who acknowledge, each one, the affliction of his heart and spreads out his palms towards this house, ³⁹may you yourself listen in the heavens, the established place where you live, and pardon, and act, and give to the individual in accordance with all his ways, in that you know his mind (because you alone know the mind of all human beings), ⁴⁰in order that they may live in awe of you all the days that they are alive on the face of the ground that you gave to our ancestors.

⁴¹Further, to the foreigner who is not of your people Yisra'el but comes from a distant country for the sake of your name (⁴²because they hear of your big name, your strong hand and your extended arm) and comes and pleads towards this house, ⁴³may you yourself listen in the heavens, in the established place where you live, and act in accordance with everything for which the foreigner calls to you, in order that all earth's peoples may acknowledge your name so as to live in awe of you like your people Yisra'el and to acknowledge that your name is called out over this house that I have built.

⁴⁴When your people goes out to battle against its enemy by the way that you send them and they plead to Yahweh in the direction of the town that you have chosen and the house that I have built for your name, ⁴⁵may you listen in the heavens to their plea and to their prayer for grace, and decide for them.

One more

⁴⁶When they do wrong in relation to you (because there is no human being who doesn't do wrong) and you're angry with them and you give them up before an enemy, and their captors take them off captive to the enemy's country, far or near, ⁴⁷and they turn their mind back in the country where they are captive,

and turn back and pray towards you for grace in their captors' country, saying "We've done wrong, we've been wayward, we've been faithless", ⁴⁸and they turn back to you with their entire mind and with their entire being in the country of their enemies who have taken them off captive, and make their plea to you in the direction of their country that you gave their ancestors, the town that you've chosen and the house that I've built for your name, ⁴⁹may you listen in the heavens, in the established place where you live, to their plea, their prayer for grace, and decide for them, ⁵⁰and pardon your people who've done wrong in relation to you, for all their acts of rebellion that they have committed against you, and give them compassion before their captors so they may have compassion on them, ⁵¹because they are your people, your domain, which you got out of Misrayim, from inside the iron furnace, ⁵²so that your eyes are opened to your servant's prayer for grace and to your people Yisra'el's prayer for grace, so that you listen to them every time they call to you, ⁵³because you yourself made them distinct for yourself as a domain from all the peoples of the earth, as you spoke by means of Mosheh your servant when you got our ancestors out of Misrayim, Lord Yahweh.'

Blessings

⁵⁴When Shelomoh had finished making to Yahweh all this plea and prayer for grace, he got up from before Yahweh's altar, from bending down on his knees with his palms spread out to the heavens, ⁵⁵and stood and blessed the entire congregation of Yisra'el, in a loud voice:

⁵⁶'Blessed be Yahweh, who has given his people Yisra'el a place to settle down in accordance with all that he spoke. Not one word has fallen down of all his good word that he spoke by means of Mosheh his servant. ⁵⁷May Yahweh our God be with us as he was with our ancestors and may he not abandon us, may he not leave us, ⁵⁸by inclining our mind to him so that we walk in all his ways and keep his orders, his decrees and his rulings that he ordered our ancestors. ⁵⁹May these words of mine that I have made as a plea before Yahweh be near to Yahweh our God day and night so that he may decide for his servant and decide for his people Yisra'el, each day's requirement in its day, ⁶⁰in order that all the peoples of the earth may acknowledge that Yahweh is God; there is no other. ⁶¹And may your mind be perfect with Yahweh your God so as to walk in his decrees and keep his orders this very day.'

⁶²The king and all Yisra'el with him were making sacrifice before Yahweh. ⁶³Shelomoh made as well-being sacrifices, which he made for Yahweh, 22,000 cattle and 120,000 sheep. So the king and all the Yisra'elites dedicated Yahweh's house. ⁶⁴That day the king made the middle part of the court sacred, which was in front of Yahweh's house, because he made the burnt offering, the grain offering and the fat parts of the well-being sacrifices there, because the copper altar that was before Yahweh was too small to contain the burnt offering, the grain offering and the fat parts of the well-being sacrifices.

Yahweh appears again, with a warning

⁶⁵Shelomoh made the festival at that time, he and all Yisra'el with him (a big congregation from Lebo Hamat as far as the Misrayimite Wadi) before Yahweh our God for seven days, then seven days, fourteen days. ⁶⁶On the eighth day he sent the people off and they blessed the king. They went to their tents, rejoicing and good-hearted because of all the good things that Yahweh had done for David his servant and for Yisra'el his people.

9 When Shelomoh had finished building Yahweh's house and the king's house and everything that drew Shelomoh's attraction that he wanted to do, ²Yahweh appeared to Shelomoh a second time, as he had appeared to him at Gib'on. ³Yahweh said to him, 'I've listened to your plea and your prayer for grace which you've made before me. I've made this house that you have built sacred, so as to put my name there permanently. My eyes and my mind will be there for all time.

⁴You yourself, if you walk before me as David your father walked, with wholeness of mind and with uprightness, acting in accordance with all that I've ordered you, you will keep my decrees and my rulings, ⁵and I will set up your kingly throne over Yisra'el permanently, as I

spoke to David your father: "There will not be cut off for you someone on Yisra'el's throne." ⁶If you all and your sons actually turn back from following me and don't keep my orders, my decrees that I've put before you, and you go and serve other gods and bow low to them, ⁷I will cut off Yisra'el from on the face of the land that I gave them, and the house that I have made sacred for my name I will send off from before my face. Yisra'el will become an object lesson and a taunt among all the peoples.

⁸Whereas this house is high, anyone who passes by it will be desolate and will whistle. They will say, "Why did Yahweh act in that way to this country and to this house?" ⁹And people will say, "On account of the fact that they abandoned Yahweh their God who got their ancestors out of the country of Misrayim, and took strong hold of other gods and bowed low to them and served them. That's why Yahweh brought upon them all this bad experience.'"

Building projects

¹⁰At the end of the twenty years while Shelomoh built the two houses, Yahweh's house and the king's house, ¹¹when Hiram king of Tsor had supported Shelomoh with cedar wood and with juniper wood and with gold, all he wanted, King Shelomoh then gave Hiram twenty towns in the region of Galilee. ¹²Hiram went out from Tsor to see the towns that Shelomoh had given him, but they were not right in his eyes. ¹³He said, 'What are these towns that you've given me, brother?' He called them the Region of Kabul ['Like-Nothing'], until this day. ¹⁴(Hiram had sent the king 120 talents of gold.)

¹⁵This is the account of the workforce that King Shelomoh raised to build Yahweh's house, his own house, the Fill, the Yerushalaim wall, and Hatsor, Megiddo and Gezer, ¹⁶when Par'oh king of Misrayim had gone up and taken Gezer, burned it with fire, killed the Kena'anites who lived in the town and given it as a dowry to his daughter, Shelomoh's wife. ¹⁷Shelomoh built up Gezer, Lower Bet Horon, ¹⁸Ba'alat and Tadmor in the wilderness, within the country, ¹⁹and all the supply towns that Shelomoh had, the chariot towns, the cavalry towns and the things Shelomoh felt an attraction for building in Yerushalaim, in the Lebanon and in all the country that he ruled.

²⁰The entire people that was left of the Amorite, the Hittite, the Perizzite, the Hivvite and the Yebusite, who were not born of the Yisra'elites (²¹their descendants who were left after them in the country, whom the Yisra'elites were not able to devote), Shelomoh raised as a serf workforce until this day. ²²Of the Yisra'elites Shelomoh did not make anyone a serf; rather they were men of battle, his servants, his officers, his adjutants, his chariot officers and his cavalry; ²³these were the prefect officers who were in charge of the work for Shelomoh, 550, holding sway over the company doing the work. ²⁴Yet Par'oh's daughter went up from David's Town to her house which he built for her. Then he built the Fill.

Enter the queen of Sheba

²⁵Three times a year Shelomoh used to offer up burnt offerings and well-being sacrifices on the altar that he built for Yahweh, and burn incense with it (the one that was before Yahweh). So he completed the house.

²⁶King Shelomoh made a fleet at Etsyon-geber, which is by Elot on the shore of the Reed Sea in the country of Edom. ²⁷In the fleet Hiram sent his servants, shipmen who knew the sea, with Shelomoh's servants. ²⁸They came to Ophir and got gold from there, 420 talents, and brought it to King Shelomoh.

10 Since the queen of Sheba had been hearing report of Shelomoh in connection with Yahweh's name, she came to test him with conundrums. ²She came to Yerushalaim with a very substantial force, camels carrying spices, very much gold and precious stones. She came to Shelomoh and spoke to him of everything that was in her mind, ³and Shelomoh told her about all the things she said. Nothing was concealed from the king that he didn't tell her.

⁴The queen of Sheba saw all Shelomoh's smartness, the house that he had built, ⁵the food on his table, the seating of his servants, the standing of his ministers and their dress, his wine waiters, and his burnt offering that he would offer up at Yahweh's house, and there was no longer any breath left in her.

Far more impressive than I had been told

⁶She said to the king, 'The thing was true that I heard in my country about your words and about your smartness. ⁷I didn't trust in the words until I came and my eyes saw. But here, the half had not been told me. You have more smartness and good things than the report that I heard. ⁸The blessings of your people, the blessings of these servants of yours who are standing continually before you, listening to your smartness! ⁹May Yahweh your God be blessed, who delighted in you so as to put you on Yisra'el's throne in Yahweh's loyalty to Yisra'el, permanently. He made you king to exercise authority with faithfulness.'

¹⁰She gave the king 120 talents of gold, very many spices and precious stones. There never again came spices in the quantity that the queen of Sheba gave King Shelomoh. ¹¹Hiram's fleet, which carried gold from Ophir, also brought very much almug wood and precious stones. ¹²The king made the almug wood into supports for Yahweh's house and for the king's house and into guitars and mandolins for the singers. Such almug wood has not come and has not been seen until this day. ¹³King Shelomoh himself gave the queen of Sheba all that she wanted, that she asked for, beyond what he gave her in accordance with what King Shelomoh possessed. Then she turned her face and went to her country, she and her servants.

¹⁴The weight of the gold that came to Shelomoh in one year was 666 talents of gold, ¹⁵apart from what came from the traders, from the merchants' business, and all the kings of Arabia and the governors of the region. ¹⁶King Shelomoh made 200 body-shields of hammered gold (he would raise 600 gold pieces for each shield) ¹⁷and 300 hand-shields of hammered gold (he would raise three pounds of gold for each shield). The king put them in the Lebanon Forest house.

Throne, fleet, trade

¹⁸The king made a big ivory throne and overlaid it with refined gold, ¹⁹with six steps to the throne, and a circular top for the throne at the back of it, and arms on this side and on that side of the place where one sat, and two lions standing beside the arms, ²⁰and twelve lions standing there on the six steps on this side and on that side. None was made like this for any kingdom.

²¹All King Solomon's drinking vessels were of gold and all the vessels in the Lebanon Forest house were beaten gold, none silver – it was not thought of for anything in Shelomoh's days, ²²because the king had a Tarshish fleet at sea with Hiram's fleet. Once in three years the Tarshish fleet would come carrying gold and silver, tusks, monkeys and peacocks.

²³King Shelomoh was bigger than all the kings of the earth in wealth and in smartness. ²⁴All the earth was seeking audience with Shelomoh to listen to his smartness, which God had put into his mind, ²⁵and they were bringing each his offering: silver objects and gold objects, robes, weaponry and spices, horses and mules, each year's requirement in its year. ²⁶Shelomoh gathered chariotry and cavalry, and had 1,400 chariotry and 12,000 cavalry. He settled them in chariot towns, and with the king in Yerushalaim.

²⁷The king made the silver in Yerushalaim like the stones, and made the cedars like the wild fig trees that are in the foothills in the large number. ²⁸The origin of the horses that Shelomoh had was from Misrayim and from Qewe. The king's dealers would get them from Qewe at a price; ²⁹a chariot went up (it came out from Misrayim) for 600 silver pieces, a horse for 150. In this way they would get them out by their own hand to all the kings of the Hittites and to the kings of Aram.

Diplomatic marriages

11 Now King Shelomoh loved many foreign women (and Par'oh's daughter), Mo'abites, Ammonites, Edomites, Tsidonites and Hittites, ²from the nations of which Yahweh had said to the Yisra'elites, 'You will not have sex with them and they will not have sex with you. They will surely turn away your mind after their gods.' To them Shelomoh attached himself in love. ³He had 700 consorts and 300 secondary wives, and his wives did turn away his mind.

⁴So in Shelomoh's old age, his wives did turn his mind away after other gods. His mind

became not perfect with Yahweh his God like the mind of David his father. ⁵Shelomoh followed Shameful Ashtar the god of the Tsidonites and Milkom the abomination of the Ammonites. ⁶Shelomoh did what was bad in Yahweh's eyes and did not fully follow Yahweh like David his father. ⁷Shelomoh built a shrine for Kemosh the abomination of Mo'ab on the mountain that's facing Yerushalaim, and for the Shameful King, the abomination of the Ammonites. ⁸He did so for all his foreign wives who were burning incense and sacrificing to their gods.

⁹Yahweh showed himself angry with Shelomoh because his mind turned away from Yahweh the God of Yisra'el who had appeared to him twice ¹⁰and had given him orders about this thing, not to follow other gods. He didn't keep what Yahweh ordered. ¹¹Yahweh said to Shelomoh, 'Since this has been with you, and you haven't kept my pact and my decrees which I ordered you, I will tear the kingdom right away from you and give it to your servant. ¹²Yet in your days I won't do it, for the sake of David your father; from the hand of your son I will tear it away. ¹³Only, the entire kingdom I will not tear away; one clan I will give to your son, for the sake of David my servant and for the sake of Yerushalaim, which I chose.'

Adversaries

¹⁴Yahweh made rise as an adversary for Shelomoh Hadad the Edomite. He was from the royal offspring in Edom. ¹⁵When David had been with Edom, Yo'ab went up to bury the people who had been run through, and he had struck down every male in Edom, ¹⁶because for six months Yo'ab and all Yisra'el stayed there until he had cut down every male in Edom. ¹⁷But Adad took flight, he and some Edomite men, some of his father's servants, with him, so as to come to Misrayim; Hadad was a small boy. ¹⁸They set off from Midyan and came to Pa'ran, took some men with them from Pa'ran and came to Misrayim, to Par'oh king of Misrayim. He gave him a house, said there would be bread for him and gave him land.

¹⁹Hadad found grace greatly in Par'oh's eyes and he gave him his wife's sister, the sister of Tahpenes, the queen, as wife. ²⁰Tahpenes' sister gave birth to Genubat, his son, for him. Tahpenes weaned him within Par'oh's household, and Genubat was in Par'oh's household among Par'oh's sons.

²¹When Hadad heard in Misrayim that David had lain down with his ancestors and that Yo'ab the army officer was dead, Hadad said to Par'oh, 'Send me off, so I may go to my country.' ²²Par'oh said to him, 'What do you lack with me, that here, you're seeking to go to your country?' He said, 'No, but do send me off.'

²³And God made rise for him as an adversary Retson ben Elyada, who had taken flight from Hadad'ezer king of Tsobah, his lord. ²⁴He collected men round him and became officer over a raiding gang (when David was killing them); they went to Dammeseq [Damascus] and lived there, and reigned in Dammeseq. ²⁵He was an adversary to Yisra'el all Shelomoh's days, along with the bad thing that Hadad was. He harassed Yisra'el. He reigned over Aram.

Yarob'am (Jeroboam)

²⁶Now Yarob'am ben Nebat, an Ephratite from Tseredah (his mother's name was Tseru'ah, a woman who was a widow), a servant of Shelomoh, raised a hand against the king. ²⁷This was the thing in connection with which he raised a hand against the king. When Shelomoh built the Fill, he secured the breach in David his father's town. ²⁸This individual Yarob'am was a forceful strong man, and Shelomoh saw the boy when he was doing work and appointed him over the entire labour force in the household of Yoseph.

²⁹At that time, when Yarob'am went out of Yerushalaim, Ahiyyah the Shilonite, the prophet, found him on the road. He was covering himself with a new coat and the two of them were alone in the open country. ³⁰Ahiyyah seized the new coat that was on him and tore it into twelve pieces. ³¹He said to Yarob'am, 'Take yourself ten pieces, because Yahweh the God of Yisra'el has said this: "Here am I, tearing the kingdom from Shelomoh's hand and giving you the ten clans. ³²One clan will be his, for the sake of my servant David and for the sake of Yerushalaim, the town that I chose from all Yisra'el's clans. ³³Because they've

abandoned me and bowed low to Shameful Ashtar the god of the Tsidonites, to Kemosh the god of Mo'ab and to Milkom the god of the Ammonites, and have not walked in my ways by doing what is upright in my eyes, my decrees and my rulings, like David his father. ³⁴I shall not take the entire kingdom from his hand and I shall make him leader all the days of his life for the sake of David my servant, whom I chose, who kept my orders and my decrees. ³⁵But I shall take the kingdom from his son's hand and give it to you (the ten clans). ³⁶To his son I will give one clan for the sake of there always being hegemony for David my servant before me in Yerushalaim, the town that I chose for myself to put my name there. ³⁷But you I shall take, and you will reign over all that your appetite longs for. You will be king over Yisra'el. ³⁸If you listen to all that I command you, walk in my ways and do what is upright in my eyes by keeping my decrees and my orders as David my servant did, I will be with you and I will build for you a trustworthy household as I built for David, and I will give Yisra'el to you. ³⁹I will humble David's offspring on account of this (yet not for all time).'"

Rehab'am (Rehoboam)

⁴⁰Shelomoh sought to put Yarob'am to death, but Yarob'am set off and took flight to Misrayim to Shishaq king of Misrayim, and he was in Misrayim until Shelomoh's death. ⁴¹The rest of the things about Shelomoh, all that he did and his smartness, they're written on the document about things regarding Shelomoh, aren't they. ⁴²The time that Shelomoh reigned in Yerushalaim over all Yisra'el was forty years. ⁴³Then Shelomoh lay down with his ancestors and was buried in David his father's town, and Rehab'am his son began to reign in place of him.

12 Rehab'am went to Shekem, because all Yisra'el had come to Shekem to make him king. ²When Yarob'am ben Nebat heard while he was still in Misrayim, where he had taken flight from before King Shelomoh (so Yarob'am lived in Misrayim), ³they sent and called for him. Yarob'am came with the entire congregation of Yisra'el and they spoke to Rehab'am: ⁴'Your father – he made our yoke tough. So you, now, lighten something of your father's tough servitude and of his heavy yoke that he put on us, and we'll serve you.' ⁵He said to them, 'Go for three more days, and come back to me.' The people went, ⁶and King Rehab'am took counsel with the elders who had been standing before Shelomoh his father when he was alive: 'How do you counsel me to give back word to this people?' ⁷They spoke to him, 'If today you'll be a servant to this people, and serve them, and answer them and speak good words to them, they'll be your servants for all time.'

Declining the chance to be a servant leader

⁸But he abandoned the elders' counsel which they gave him and took counsel with the young men who grew up with him, who were standing before him. ⁹He said to them, 'What are you going to counsel, so that we may give back word to this people who spoke to me, "Lighten something of the yoke that your father put on us"?' ¹⁰The young men who grew up with him spoke with him: 'You should say this to this people who spoke to you, "Whereas your father made our yoke heavy, you, lighten it from on us" – you should speak like this to them: "My little finger is thicker than my father's hips. ¹¹So now, whereas my father imposed a heavy yoke on you, I myself will add to your yoke. Whereas my father disciplined you with whips, I myself will discipline you with scorpions."'

¹²Yarob'am and the entire people came to Rehab'am on the third day as the king had spoken, 'Come back to me on the third day', ¹³and the king answered the people toughly. He abandoned the counsel of the elders that they had given him ¹⁴and spoke to them in accordance with the counsel of the young men: 'Whereas my father made your yoke heavy, I myself will add to your yoke. Whereas my father disciplined you with whips, I myself will discipline you with scorpions.' ¹⁵The king didn't listen to the people, because it was a turn of affairs from Yahweh in order to implement his word, which Yahweh had spoken by means of Ahiyyah the Shilonite to Yarob'am ben Nebat.

¹⁶All Yisra'el saw that the king had not listened to them, and the people gave word back to the king:

What share do we have in David?
 – we have no domain in ben Yishay [Jesse].
To your tents, Yisra'el;
 now see to your own household, David.

So Yisra'el went to its tents, [17]though the Yisra'elites who were living in the towns of Yehudah – Rehab'am reigned over them. [18]King Rehab'am sent Adoram, who was in charge of the workforce, but all Yisra'el pelted him with stones and he died, while King Rehab'am got himself together to get up into the chariot to flee to Yerushalaim.

[19]So Yisra'el has rebelled against David's household until this day.

Yahweh confronts Rehab'am

[20]When all Yisra'el heard that Yarob'am had come back, they sent and called him to the

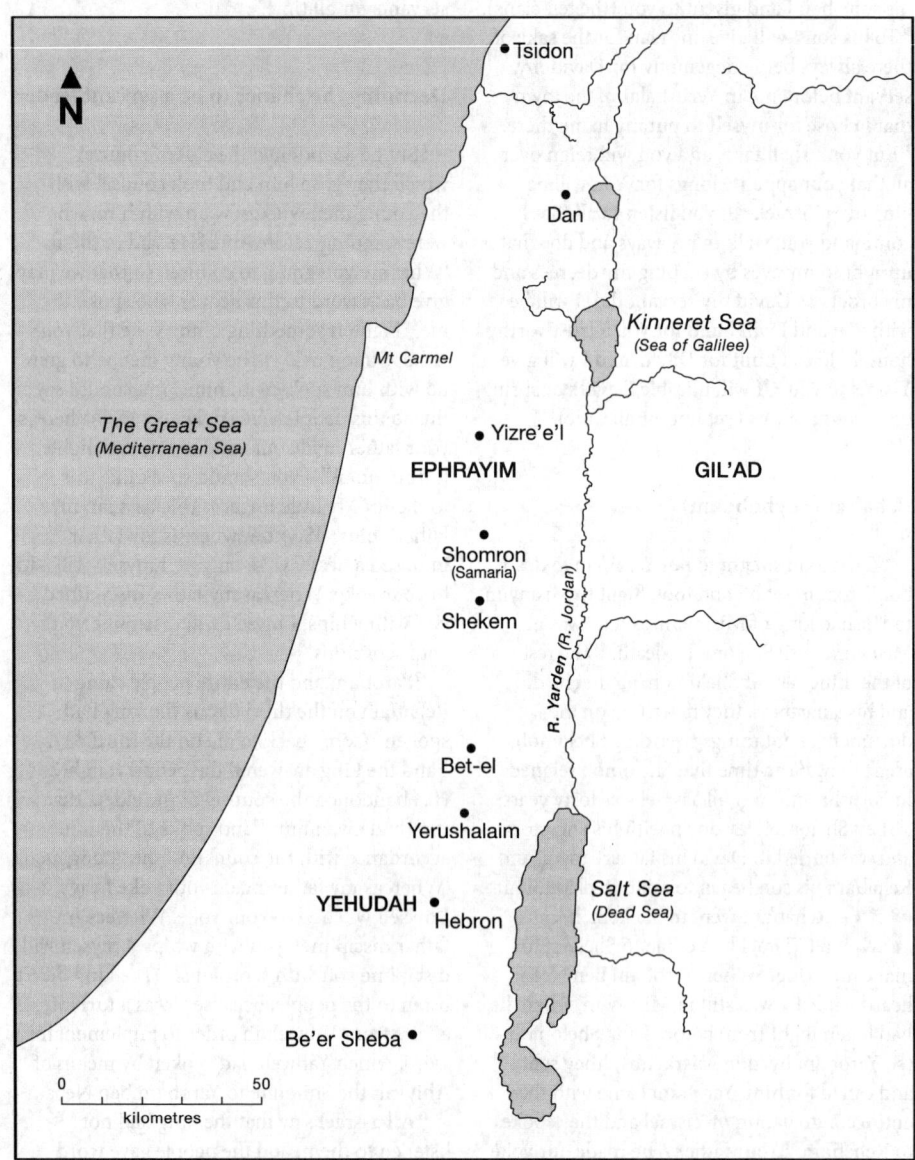

1 Kings 12: The two nations – Ephrayim and Yehudah (Ephraim and Judah)

assembly and made him king over all Yisra'el. No one followed David's household except the clan of Yehudah alone.

²¹Rehab'am came to Yerushalaim and congregated Yehudah's entire household and the clan of Binyamin, 180,000 picked men doing battle, to go to battle with the household of Yisra'el, to get the kingship back for Rehab'am son of Shelomoh. ²²But God's word came to Shema'yah, the supernatural man: ²³'Say to Rehab'am son of Shelomoh king of Yehudah, and to the entire household of Yehudah and Binyamin and the rest of the people: ²⁴"Yahweh has said this: 'You will not go up, you will not go to battle with your Yisra'elite brothers. Go back each one to his house, because this thing has come about from me.'" They listened to Yahweh's word and turned back to go, in accordance with Yahweh's word.

²⁵Yarob'am built up Shekem in the highland of Ephrayim and lived there; then he went out from there and built up Penu'el. ²⁶Yarob'am said to himself, 'The kingship will now go back to the household of David: ²⁷if this people go up to make sacrifices in Yahweh's house in Yerushalaim, this people's mind will turn back to their lord, to Rehab'am king of Yehudah. They'll kill me and turn back to Rehab'am king of Yehudah.' ²⁸So the king took counsel and made two gold bullocks. He said to them, 'It's too much for you to go up to Yerushalaim. Yisra'el, here are your gods who brought you up from the country of Misrayim.' ²⁹He placed the one in Bet-el and the other he put in Dan, ³⁰and this thing became a wrongdoing; the people went before the one as far as Dan. ³¹And he made the house at the shrines and made priests from the sections of the people who were not from the Levites.

The destiny of Yarob'am's altar

³²Yarob'am made a festival in the eighth month, on the fifteenth day of the month, like the festival that was in Yehudah, and went up on to the altar. He acted in this way at Bet-el, sacrificing to the bullocks that he had made.

So he put in place at Bet El the priests of the shrines that he had made ³³and went up on the altar that he had made at Bet-el on the fifteenth day of the eighth month, which he devised out of his own mind, and made a festival for the Yisra'elites. He went up on to the altar to burn an offering,

13 and there, a supernatural man came from Yehudah by Yahweh's word to Bet-el, when Yarob'am was standing on the altar to burn an offering. ²He called out against the altar by Yahweh's word: 'Altar, altar, Yahweh has said this: "Here, a son is going to be born to David's household (Yo'shiyyahu [Josiah] his name). He will sacrifice on you the priests of the shrines who burn offerings on you. People will burn human bones on you."' ³He gave a sign that day: 'This is the sign that Yahweh has spoken: "There, the altar is going to split apart and the waste that's on it will pour out."'

⁴When the king heard the word of the supernatural man which he called out against the altar at Bet-el, Yarob'am put out his hand from above the altar, saying, 'Seize him!' But his hand which he put out against him dried up and he couldn't take it back to himself, ⁵while the altar split apart and the waste from the altar poured out in accordance with the sign that the supernatural man had given by Yahweh's word. ⁶The king avowed to the supernatural man, 'Please seek the goodwill of Yahweh your God and plead for me so that my hand comes back to me.' The supernatural man sought Yahweh's goodwill and the king's hand came back to him, and became as it was previously.

Another prophet in Bet-el

⁷The king spoke to the supernatural man: 'Do come with me to the house and have some sustenance, and I'll give you a gift.' ⁸The supernatural man said to the king, 'If you give me half your household I won't come with you; I won't eat bread or drink water in this place, ⁹because that's how he ordered me, by Yahweh's word: "You will not eat bread and you will not drink water, and you will not go back by the way that you went".' ¹⁰So he went by another way and didn't go back by the way that he came to Bet-el.

¹¹Now an old prophet was living in Bet-el. His son came and recounted to him everything that the supernatural man had done this day

in Bet-el, the words that he had spoken to the king. They recounted them to their father ¹²and their father spoke to them: 'Where exactly is the way he went?' His sons had seen the way that the supernatural man had gone, who had come from Yehudah. ¹³He said to his sons, 'Saddle the donkey for me.' They saddled the donkey for him and he mounted it ¹⁴and went after the supernatural man. He found him sitting under an oak. He said to him, 'Are you the supernatural man who came from Yehudah?' He said, 'I am.' ¹⁵He said to him, 'Go with me to my house and eat some bread.' ¹⁶He said, 'I can't go back with you or come with you. I won't eat bread and I won't drink water with you in this place, ¹⁷because a thing came to me by Yahweh's word, "You will not eat bread and you will not drink water there; you will not go back by going the way that you went."'

Prophets, and when to ignore them

¹⁸He said to him, 'I am also a prophet, like you, and an envoy spoke to me by Yahweh's word: "Get him to go back with you to your house so he can eat bread and drink water."' He was lying to him. ¹⁹But he went back with him and ate bread in his house and drank water.

²⁰As they were sitting at the table, Yahweh's word came to the prophet who had got him to go back, ²¹and he called out to the supernatural man who had come from Yehudah, 'Yahweh has said this: "Since you have rebelled against Yahweh's bidding and not kept the order that Yahweh your God gave you, ²²but have gone back and eaten bread and drunk water in the place of which he spoke to you, 'You're not to eat bread and you're not to drink water', your corpse will not come to your ancestors' grave."'

²³After he had eaten bread and after he had drunk, he saddled for him the donkey belonging to the prophet whom he had got to go back, ²⁴and he went, but a lion met him on the way and put him to death. His corpse was thrown on the way. The donkey was standing beside it and the lion was standing beside the corpse, ²⁵and there, some men were passing and they saw the corpse thrown on the way with the lion standing beside the corpse. They came and spoke of it in the town where the old prophet was living. ²⁶The prophet who had got him to go back from the way heard and said, 'It's the supernatural man who rebelled against Yahweh's bidding. Yahweh has given him over to the lion and it's mauled him and put him to death in accordance with Yahweh's word, which he spoke to him.'

²⁷He spoke to his sons: 'Saddle the donkey for me', and they saddled it. ²⁸He went and found his corpse thrown on the way, with the donkey and the lion standing beside the corpse. The lion had not eaten the corpse and it had not mauled the donkey.

²⁹The prophet took up the supernatural man's corpse, laid it on the donkey and took it back. So it came to the old prophet's town for lamenting and burying it. ³⁰He laid his corpse in his own grave and they lamented over it, 'Oh, my brother!' ³¹After burying him he said to his sons, 'When I die, bury me in the grave where the supernatural man is buried; lay my bones beside his bones, ³²because the word that he called out by Yahweh's word against the altar that's in Bet-el and against all the houses at the shrines that are in the towns of Shomron [Samaria] will definitely come about.'

³³After this thing Yarob'am did not turn back from his bad ways but again made priests for the shrines from all sections of the people. Anyone who wanted commissioned himself and became priests of the shrines. ³⁴This thing was the wrongdoing of Yarob'am's household both to efface and to annihilate it from upon the face of the ground.

When the apostate king's son gets ill

14 At that time Abiyyah ben Yarob'am got ill. ²Yarob'am said to his wife, 'Set off, please, make yourself look different so people won't know that you're Yarob'am's wife, and go to Shiloh. There, the prophet Ahiyyah is there. It was he who spoke of me that I would be king over this people. ³Take ten loaves of bread in your hand, and some crackers and a jar of syrup, and come to him. It's he who will tell you what will happen to the boy.'

⁴Yarob'am's wife did so. She set off and went to Shiloh and came to the house of Ahiyyah. Ahiyyahu couldn't see, because his eyes had set, through his old age, ⁵but Yahweh himself

had said to Ahiyyahu, 'Here, Yarob'am's wife is coming to enquire for a word from you concerning her son, because he's ill. You're to speak such and such things to her. But when she comes she'll be acting like a stranger.'

Tough prophet, tough message

⁶So when Ahiyyahu heard the sound of her feet as she came through the entrance, he said 'Come in, wife of Yarob'am. Why is it you're acting like a stranger?

I'm sent to you with something tough. ⁷Go say to Yarob'am, "Yahweh the God of Yisra'el has said this: 'Since I raised you from among the people and made you chief over my people Yisra'el ⁸and tore the kingship from David's household and gave it to you, but you have not been like my servant David who kept my orders and followed me with all his mind by doing only what was upright in my eyes, ⁹and you've dealt more badly in what you've done than all who were before you, and gone and made yourself other gods and cast images, so as to provoke me, and me you've thrown behind your back, ¹⁰therefore here I am bringing bad fortune to Yarob'am's household. I shall cut off for Yarob'am the one who pisses against a wall (bound or freed) in Yisra'el. I shall burn away after Yarob'am's household, as one burns away dung, until it's finished. ¹¹The person who belongs to Yarob'am who dies in the town the dogs will eat; the person who dies in the open country the birds of the heavens will eat. Because Yahweh has spoken.'"

¹²So you, set off, go to your house. When your foot comes to the town, the child will die. ¹³All Yisra'el will lament for him and bury him, because this person alone who belongs to Yarob'am will come into a grave since in him something good has been found in relation to Yahweh the God of Yisra'el, in the household of Yarob'am. ¹⁴But Yahweh will set up for himself a king over Yisra'el who will cut off the household of Yarob'am. This is the day, and what even now? ¹⁵Yahweh will strike Yisra'el down as a reed sways in the water and he will uproot Yisra'el from upon this good ground that he gave to their ancestors, and scatter them beyond the River, since they've made their totem poles that provoke Yahweh. ¹⁶He will give Yisra'el over on account of Yarob'am's wrongdoings that he committed and that he caused Yisra'el to commit.'

¹⁷Yarob'am's wife set off and went, and came to Tirtsah. She was coming through the threshold of the house as the boy died. ¹⁸They buried him, and all Yisra'el lamented for him in accordance with Yahweh's word which he had spoken by means of his servant Ahiyyahu the prophet.

¹⁹The rest of the things about Yarob'am, how he did battle and how he reigned: there, they're written on the document about things of the time regarding the kings of Yisra'el. ²⁰The time that Yarob'am reigned was twenty-two years; then he lay down with his ancestors, and Nadab his son began to reign in place of him.

In Yehudah: Rehab'am

²¹Rehab'am son of Shelomoh reigned in Yehudah. Rehab'am was a man of forty-one years when he began to reign and he reigned seventeen years in Yerushalaim, the town where Yahweh chose to put his name out of all the clans of Yisra'el. His mother's name was Na'amah the Ammonite. ²²Yehudah did what was bad in Yahweh's eyes and aroused greater passion in him than anything that their ancestors had done by the wrongdoings that they did. ²³They too built for themselves shrines, columns and totem poles on every lofty hill and under every verdant tree. ²⁴There were also hierodules in the country. They acted in accordance with all the offensive practices of the nations that Yahweh dispossessed before the Yisra'elites.

²⁵In the fifth year of King Rehab'am, Shishaq king of Misrayim went up against Yerushalaim ²⁶and took the treasures of Yahweh's house and the treasures of the king's house. He took everything. He took the gold shields that Shelomoh had made; ²⁷King Rehab'am made copper shields in place of them and appointed them to the control of the officers in charge of the runners who kept watch over the entrance to the king's house. ²⁸Whenever the king came to Yahweh's house the runners would carry them, then take them back to the runners' chamber.

²⁹The rest of the things about Rehab'am and all that he did are written on the document about things of the time regarding the kings

of Yehudah, aren't they. ³⁰There was battle between Rehab'am and Yarob'am all the time.

Abiyyam, Asa

³¹Rehab'am lay down with his ancestors and was buried with his ancestors in David's Town. His mother's name was Na'amah the Ammonite. Abiyyam his son began to reign in place of him.

15 It was in the eighteenth year of King Yarob'am ben Nebat that Abiyyam began to reign over Yehudah. ²He reigned three years in Yerushalaim. His mother's name was Ma'akah bat Abishalom. ³He walked in all the wrongdoings of his father, which he did before him. His mind was not perfect with Yahweh his God like the mind of David his father. ⁴Because it was for David's sake that Yahweh his God gave him hegemony in Yerushalaim by setting up his son after him and by having Yerushalaim stand, ⁵because David did what was upright in Yahweh's eyes and did not turn aside from anything that he ordered him all the days of his life, except in the thing about Uriyyah the Hittite. ⁶There was battle between Rehab'am and Yarob'am all the days of his life.

⁷The rest of the things about Abiyyam and all that he did are written on the document about things of the time regarding the kings of Yehudah, aren't they. There was battle between Abiyyam and Yarob'am. ⁸Abiyyam lay down with his ancestors and they buried him in David's Town. Asa his son began to reign in place of him.

⁹It was in the twentieth year of Yarob'am king of Yisra'el that Asa began to reign as king of Yehudah. ¹⁰He reigned forty-one years in Yerushalaim. His mother's name was Ma'akah bat Abishalom. ¹¹Asa did what was upright in Yahweh's eyes, like David his ancestor. ¹²He put away the hierodules from the country and removed all the idols that his ancestors had made. ¹³In addition, Ma'akah his mother he removed from being queen mother, because she had made a monstrosity for Asherah. Asa cut down her monstrosity and burned it in Wadi Qidron, ¹⁴though the shrines did not disappear. Yet Asa's mind was perfect with Yahweh all his days. ¹⁵He brought into Yahweh's house the sacred things belonging to his father and his own sacred things, silver, gold and articles.

Asa and Ben-hadad

¹⁶There was battle between Asa and Ba'sha king of Yisra'el all their days. ¹⁷Ba'sha king of Yisra'el went up against Yehudah and built up The Height, so as not to grant Asa king of Yehudah anyone going out or coming in. ¹⁸Asa got all the silver and gold that was left in the treasuries of Yahweh's house and the treasuries of the king's house and gave them into the hand of his servants, and King Asa sent them to Ben-hadad ben-Tabrimmon son of Hezyon king of Aram, who lived in Dammeseq, saying ¹⁹'A pact between me and you, between my father and your father: here, I have sent you a bribe of silver and gold. Go contravene your pact with Ba'sha king of Yisra'el so he may go up from me.'

²⁰Ben-hadad listened to King Asa and sent the officers of the forces that he had against Yisra'el's towns. He struck down Iyyon, Dan, Bet-ma'akah Meadow and all Kinnerot, on top of all the region of Naphtali. ²¹When Ba'sha heard, he left off building up The Height and stayed in Tirtsah, ²²while King Asa got all Yehudah to listen (there was no one free of obligation) and they carried the stones from The Height and its timber with which Ba'sha had built, and with them King Asa built up Geba in Binyamin and The Watchtower.

²³The rest of all the things about Asa, all his strength, all that he did and the towns that he built up, are written on the document about things of the time regarding the kings of Yehudah. Only, at the time when he was old he had an illness in his feet. ²⁴Asa lay down with his ancestors and was buried with his ancestors in David his father's town. Yehoshaphat his son began to reign in place of him.

In Ephrayim: Nadab, Ba'sha

²⁵Now Nadab ben Yarob'am had become king over Yisra'el in the second year of Asa king of Yehudah. He reigned over Yisra'el two years. ²⁶He did what was bad in Yahweh's eyes; he walked in the way of his father and in his wrongdoing, which he caused Yisra'el to commit. ²⁷Ba'sha ben Ahiyyah, of the household of Yissakar, conspired against him. Ba'sha struck him down at Gibbeton, which

belonged to the Pelishtites, while Nadab and all Yisra'el were besieging Gibbeton. ²⁸Ba'sha put him to death in the third year of Asa king of Yehudah and became king in place of him. ²⁹When he began to reign he struck down Yarob'am's entire household and did not allow anyone breathing to remain to Yarob'am until he had annihilated it, in accordance with Yahweh's word which he spoke by means of his servant Ahiyyah the Shilonite ³⁰because of the wrongs that Yarob'am committed and that he caused Yisra'el to commit, with his provocation that he offered to Yahweh the God of Yisra'el.

³¹The rest of the things about Nadab and all that he did are written on the document about things of the time regarding the kings of Yisra'el, aren't they.

³²There was battle between Asa and Ba'sha king of Yisra'el all their days. ³³It was in the third year of Asa king of Yehudah that Ba'sha ben Ahiyyah began to reign over all Yisra'el in Tirtsah, for twenty-four years. ³⁴He did what was bad in Yahweh's eyes. He walked in the way of Yarob'am and in his wrongdoing that he caused Yisra'el to commit.

16

Yahweh's word came to Yehu ben Hanani, against Ba'sha: ²"Since I raised you from the ground and made you chief over my people Yisra'el, but you have walked in the way of Yarob'am and caused my people Yisra'el to do wrong, so as to provoke me with their wrongdoings, ³here, I'm going to burn away after Ba'sha and after his household. I shall make your household like the household of Yarob'am ben Nebat. ⁴The person belonging to Ba'sha who dies in the town, the dogs will eat; and the person belonging to him who dies in the open country, the birds of the heavens will eat."

The devastating word

⁵The rest of the things about Ba'sha, what he did and his strength, are written on the document about things of the time regarding the kings of Yisra'el, aren't they. ⁶Ba'sha lay down with his ancestors and was buried in Tirtsah, and Elah his son began to reign in place of him. ⁷But by means of Yehu ben Hanani the prophet, Yahweh's word had come regarding Ba'sha and regarding his household also, because of all that was bad that he did in Yahweh's eyes, so as to provoke him by the action of his hands, in being like Yarob'am's household, and because he had struck it down.

⁸It was in the twenty-sixth year of Asa king of Yehudah that Elah ben Ba'sha began to reign over Yisra'el in Tirtsah, for two years. ⁹His servant Zimri, officer in charge of half the chariotry, conspired against him. When he was in Tirtsah getting drunk in the house of Artsa who was in charge of the household at Tirtsah, ¹⁰Zimri came in, struck him down and put him to death, in the twenty-seventh year of Asa king of Yehudah. He began to reign in place of him, ¹¹and when he began to reign, as soon as he sat on his throne, he struck down Ba'sha's entire household. He did not let anyone who pisses against a wall remain to him, either a restorer of his or a friend of his.

¹²So Zimri annihilated Ba'sha's entire household, in accordance with Yahweh's word that he spoke regarding Ba'sha by means of Yehu the prophet ¹³and regarding all Ba'sha's wrongdoings and Elah his son's wrongdoings that they had committed and that they had caused Yisra'el to commit, so as to provoke Yahweh the God of Yisra'el with their hollow things. ¹⁴The rest of the things about Elah and all that he did are written on the document about things of the time regarding the kings of Yisra'el, aren't they.

King for a week

¹⁵It was in the twenty-seventh year of Asa king of Yehudah that Zimri reigned seven days in Tirtsah, when the company was encamped at Gibbeton which belonged to the Pelishtites. ¹⁶The company encamped heard, 'Zimri has conspired, and he has actually struck down the king', and all Yisra'el made Omri the army officer king over Yisra'el that day in the camp. ¹⁷Omri went up, and all Yisra'el with him, from Gibbeton, and they besieged Tirtsah. ¹⁸When Zimri saw that the town was taken, he came into the citadel in the king's house and burned the king's house with fire over himself. So he died ¹⁹because of his wrongdoings that he committed by doing what was bad in Yahweh's eyes by walking in the way of Yarob'am, and through his wrongdoing that he committed

by causing Yisra'el to do wrong. ²⁰The rest of the things about Zimri and his conspiracy which he formed are written on the document about things of the time regarding the kings of Yisra'el, aren't they.

²¹Then the people of Yisra'el split in half. Half the people followed Tibni ben Ginat to make him king, and half followed Omri. ²²The company that followed Omri was stronger than the company of those who followed Tibni ben Ginat, but Tibni died and Omri began to reign.

²³It was in the thirty-first year of Asa king of Yehudah that Omri began to reign over Yisra'el, for twelve years. In Tirtsah he reigned six years, ²⁴then he acquired the Shomron Mountain from Shemer for two talents of silver, built up the mountain, and called the town he built by the name of Shemer, the lord of the Shomron Mountain.

²⁵Omri did what was bad in Yahweh's eyes; he dealt badly more than all who were before him. ²⁶He walked in all the way of Yarob'am ben Nebat and in his wrongdoing that he caused Yisra'el to commit so as to provoke Yahweh the God of Yisra'el with their hollow things. ²⁷The rest of the things about Omri, what he did and his strength that he showed, are written on the document about things regarding the kings of Yisra'el, aren't they.

Ah'ab and Izebel (Jezebel)

²⁸Omri lay down with his ancestors and was buried in Shomron, and Ah'ab his son began to reign in place of him.²⁹Ah'ab ben Omri began to reign over Yisra'el in the thirty-eighth year of Asa king of Yehudah. Ah'ab ben Omri reigned over Yisra'el in Shomron twenty-two years. ³⁰Ah'ab ben Omri did what was bad in Yahweh's eyes, more than all who were before him. ³¹Was it a slight thing, his walking in the wrongdoings of Yarob'am ben Nebat, that he took as wife Izebel bat Etba'al, king of the Tsidonites, and went and served the Master? He bowed low to him ³²and set up an altar for the Master at the Master's house which he built in Shomron, ³³and Ah'ab made a totem pole. Ah'ab continued to act so as to provoke Yahweh the God of Yisra'el more than all the kings of Yisra'el who were before him.

³⁴In his time Hi'el the Bet Elite built up Yeriho [Jericho]. With Abiram his firstborn he founded it and with Segub his youngest he put up its doors, in accordance with Yahweh's word which he spoke by means of Yehoshua ben Nun.

17 Eliyyahu [Elijah] the Tishbite from the inhabitants of Gil'ad said to Ah'ab, 'As Yahweh lives, the God of Yisra'el before whom I have stood, if during these years there will be dew or rain except at the bidding of my word...'

²Yahweh's word came to him: ³'Go from here. Turn your face east and hide in Wadi Kerit, which faces the Yarden. ⁴You will drink from the wadi and I have ordered the ravens to provide for you there.' ⁵He went and acted in accordance with Yahweh's word. He went and stayed in Wadi Kerit, which faces the Yarden, ⁶while the ravens were bringing him bread and meat in the morning and bread and meat in the evening, and he drank from the wadi.

The ravens and the widow

⁷After a time the wadi dried up because there was no rain in the country. ⁸Yahweh's word came to him: ⁹'Set off, go to Tsarephat which belongs to Tsidon and stay there. Here, I have ordered a woman there who is a widow to provide for you.'

¹⁰He set off and went to Tsarephat, and came to the entrance to the town. There, a woman who was a widow was gathering wood there. He called to her, 'Please get me a little water in a container so I can drink', ¹¹and she went to get it. He called to her, 'Please get me a bit of bread in your hand.' ¹²She said, 'As Yahweh your God lives, if I have anything baked, only a fistful of flour in a jar and a little oil in a jug... So here I am, collecting a couple of pieces of wood and I shall come and make it for me and for my son, and we'll eat it and die.'

¹³Eliyyahu said to her, 'Don't be afraid. Come, act in accordance with your word, only make me a small loaf from there first and bring it out to me, and make one for you and for your son afterwards. ¹⁴Because Yahweh the God of Yisra'el has said this: "The jar of flour will not be finished and the jug of oil will not lack until the day Yahweh gives rain on the

face of the ground."' ¹⁵She went and acted in accordance with Eliyyahu's word, and she ate, she and he and her household for some time. ¹⁶The jar of flour was not finished and the jug of oil did not lack, in accordance with Yahweh's word which he spoke by means of Eliyyahu.

Back from the dead

¹⁷After these things, the son of the woman who was mistress of the household got ill. His illness grew very severe, until no breath remained in him. ¹⁸She said to Eliyyahu, 'What is between you and me, supernatural man? You've come to me to bring my waywardness to mind and put my son to death.' ¹⁹He said to her, 'Give me your son.' He took him out of her arms and brought him up to the upper floor where he was staying, laid him on his bed ²⁰and called to Yahweh: 'Yahweh my God, the woman with whom I am residing, are you really going to deal badly with her by putting her son to death?' ²¹He measured himself out over the child three times and called to Yahweh, 'Yahweh my God, please may this child's breath come back inside him!' ²²Yahweh listened to the voice of Eliyyahu. The child's breath came back inside him and he came alive. ²³Eliyyahu got the child and took him down from the upper floor into the house, and gave him to his mother. Eliyyahu said, 'Look, your son is alive.' ²⁴The woman said to Eliyyahu, 'Now I do acknowledge that you are a supernatural man and Yahweh's word in your mouth is truthful.'

18 After much time, Yahweh's word came to Eliyyahu, in the third year: 'Go appear to Ah'ab, and I will give rain on the face of the ground.' ²So Eliyyahu went to appear to Ah'ab. Now the famine was severe in Shomron, ³and Ah'ab had called for Obadyah, who was in charge of the household. Obadyah was someone who lived greatly in awe of Yahweh. ⁴When Izebel cut off Yahweh's prophets, Obadyah had got a hundred prophets and hidden them, fifty individuals to a cave, and provided them with bread and water. ⁵Ah'ab said to Obadyah, 'Go through the country, to all the water springs and to all the wadis. Perhaps we'll find grass so we can keep horse and mule alive so we don't cut off some of the animals.'

The man who served God and king

⁶They split the country for themselves so as to pass through it. While Ah'ab went one way alone and Obadyah went the other way alone, ⁷and Obadyah was on the way, there, Eliyyahu met him. He recognized him and fell on his face, and said, 'Is this you, my lord Eliyyahu?' ⁸He said to him, 'It's me. Go say to your lord, "There's Eliyyahu."'

⁹He said, 'What wrong have I done that you're giving your servant into the hand of Ah'ab, to put me to death? ¹⁰As Yahweh your God lives, if there's a nation or kingdom to which my lord has not sent to seek you out . . . They say, "He's not here", and he makes the kingdom or the nation swear that it can't find you. ¹¹And now you're saying, "Go say to your lord, 'There's Eliyyahu'", ¹²and I myself will go from being with you and Yahweh's spirit will carry you to where I don't know, and I'll come to tell Ah'ab and he won't find you and he'll kill me, when your servant has lived in awe of Yahweh from my youth. ¹³It's been told my lord, hasn't it, what I did when Izebel killed Yahweh's prophets and I hid a hundred of Yahweh's prophets, fifty individuals to a cave, and fed them bread and water. ¹⁴And now you're saying, "Go say to your lord, 'There's Eliyyahu'", and he'll kill me.'

¹⁵Eliyyahu said, 'As Yahweh of Armies lives, before whom I have stood, I will indeed appear to him today.' ¹⁶So Obadyah went to meet Ah'ab and told him, and Ah'ab went to meet Eliyyahu. ¹⁷When Ah'ab saw Eliyyahu, Ah'ab said to him, 'Is this you, troubler of Yisra'el?' ¹⁸He said, 'I haven't troubled Yisra'el. Rather, you and your father's household have, by abandoning Yahweh's orders and following the Masters. ¹⁹So now, send to gather all Yisra'el to me to Mount Carmel, with the 450 prophets of the Master and the 400 prophets of Asherah who eat at Izebel's table.'

There are times when you have to choose

²⁰So Ah'ab sent among all the Yisra'elites and gathered the prophets to Mount Carmel. ²¹Eliyyahu came up to the entire people and said, 'How long are you going to dither between two positions? If Yahweh is God,

follow him. If it's the Master, follow him.' The people didn't answer him a word.

²²Then Eliyyahu said to the people, 'I alone am left as a prophet of Yahweh. The Master's prophets are 450 individuals. ²³They're to give us two bulls, and they're to choose one bull for themselves, divide it up and put it on the wood, but not set fire. I shall prepare the other bull and put it on the wood, but not set fire. ²⁴You will call in your god's name; I'll call in Yahweh's name. The God who answers by fire – he is God.' The entire people answered, 'What you say is good.'

²⁵So Eliyyahu said to the Master's prophets, 'Choose one bull for yourselves and prepare it first, because you're the majority. Call on your god's name but don't set fire.' ²⁶They took the bull that someone gave them, prepared it and called on the Master's name from morning until midday, saying 'Master, answer us', but there was no sound, no one answering. They jumped round the altar that people had made.

²⁷At midday Eliyyahu played about with them: 'Call in a loud voice, because he's a god, but it's because he's talking or he's moving or he's on a journey. Perhaps he's asleep and he'll wake up.' ²⁸So they called in a loud voice and slashed themselves in accordance with their ruling with swords and with spears until blood flowed over them. ²⁹After midday passed they prophesied until the time for presenting the offering, but there was no sound, no one answering, no heeding.

Yahweh, he is God

³⁰Then Eliyyahu said to the entire people, 'Come up to me.' The entire people came up to him and he mended Yahweh's altar that was torn down. ³¹Eliyyahu got twelve stones, in accordance with the number of the twelve clans of the sons of Ya'aqob [Jacob] (to whom Yahweh's word had come, 'Yisra'el will be your name'). ³²He built the stones into an altar in Yahweh's name and made a trench, like a receptacle for a two-measure barrel of seed, round the altar. ³³He laid out the wood and divided the bull and put it on the wood.

³⁴He said, 'Fill four jars with water and pour it over the burnt offering and over the wood.' He said, 'Do it a second time.' They did it a second time. He said, 'Do it a third time.' They did it a third time. ³⁵The water went round the altar and he also filled the trench with water.

³⁶At the time for presenting the offering, Eliyyahu the prophet came up and said, 'Yahweh, God of Abraham, Yitshaq [Isaac] and Yisra'el, today may it be acknowledged that you are God in Yisra'el and that I am your servant, and that by your word I have done all these things. ³⁷Answer me, Yahweh, answer me, so that this people may acknowledge that you Yahweh are God and that you yourself have turned their mind round.'

³⁸Yahweh's fire fell and consumed the burnt offering, the wood, the stones and the earth, and the water that was in the trench it licked up. ³⁹The entire people saw and fell on their faces and said, 'Yahweh, he is God; Yahweh, he is God.' ⁴⁰Eliyyahu said to them, 'Capture the Master's prophets. None of them must escape.' They captured them, and Eliyyahu took them down to Wadi Qishon and slaughtered them there.

The prophet takes flight

⁴¹Eliyyahu said to Ah'ab, 'Go up, eat and drink, because there's a rumbling sound of rain.' ⁴²Ah'ab went up to eat and to drink, while Eliyyahu went up to the top of Carmel, crouched to the ground and put his face between his knees. ⁴³He said to his boy, 'Please go up and look in the direction of the sea.' He went up and looked and said, 'There isn't anything.' He said 'Go back', seven times. ⁴⁴On the seventh he said, 'There, a small cloud, like a person's fist, going up from the west.' He said, 'Go up, say to Ah'ab, "Hitch up, and get down, so that the rain won't hold you back."' ⁴⁵Right then, right then, when the heavens grew black with clouds and wind, there was a great downpour.

Ah'ab got into his chariot and went to Yizre'e'l. ⁴⁶Yahweh's hand came on Eliyyahu, he hitched things round his hips, and he ran before Ah'ab as far as when you come to Yizre'e'l.

19 Ah'ab told Izebel all that Eliyyahu had done and all about how he had killed all the prophets with the sword, ²and Izebel sent an envoy to Eliyyahu saying, 'May the gods do like this and may they do more, because this very time tomorrow I shall make your life like the life of one of them.'

³He was afraid, and he set off and went for his life. He came to Be'er Sheba which belongs to Yehudah, left his boy behind there, ⁴and he himself went a day's journey into the wilderness. He came and sat under a broom bush and asked for his life, that he might die: 'It's too much. Take my life now, Yahweh, because I'm no better than my ancestors.'

The low murmuring sound

⁵He lay down and slept under a broom bush. And there, an envoy touching him. He said to him, 'Get up, eat.' ⁶He looked, and there, by his head a loaf baked on coals and a jar of water. He ate and drank, and lay down again. ⁷Yahweh's envoy came back a second time and touched him and said, 'Get up, eat, because the journey is too much for you.' ⁸He got up and ate and drank, and went in the energy of that food for forty days and forty nights as far as God's mountain, Horeb.

⁹He came to a cave there and stayed the night there. And there, Yahweh's word came to him. He said to him, 'What is there for you here, Eliyyahu?' ¹⁰He said, 'I've been very passionate for Yahweh, the God of Armies, because the Yisra'elites have abandoned your pact. Your altars they've torn down; your prophets they've killed with the sword. I alone am left, and they've been seeking my life, to take it.' ¹¹He said, 'Go out and stand on the mountain before Yahweh.' There was Yahweh passing, and a great, strong wind, splitting mountains and breaking up cliffs before Yahweh (Yahweh was not in the wind), after the wind an earthquake (Yahweh was not in the earthquake), ¹²after the earthquake a fire (Yahweh was not in the fire) and after the fire a low murmuring sound.

¹³When Eliyyahu heard it, he wrapped his face in his coat, went out and stood at the cave's entrance. And there, a voice came to him and said, 'What is there for you here, Eliyyahu?' ¹⁴He said, 'I've been very passionate for Yahweh, the God of Armies, because the Yisra'elites have abandoned your pact. Your altars they've torn down, your prophets they've killed with the sword. I alone am left, and they've been seeking my life, to take it.'

The chilling commission

¹⁵Yahweh said to him, 'Go, turn back on your way, to the Dammeseq wilderness. You're to come and anoint Haza'el as king over Aram. ¹⁶And Yehu ben Nimshi you're to anoint as king over Yisra'el, and Elisha ben Shaphat, from Meholah Meadow, you're to anoint as prophet in place of you. ¹⁷The person who escapes from Haza'el's sword, Yehu will put to death. The person who escapes from Yehu's sword, Elisha will put to death. ¹⁸But I will leave in Yisra'el 7,000, all the knees that have not bent down to the Master and every mouth that has not kissed him.'

¹⁹So he went from there and found Elisha ben Shaphat. He was ploughing with twelve pairs in front of him; he was with the twelfth. Eliyyahu crossed over to him and threw his coat towards him. ²⁰He abandoned the cattle, ran after Eliyyahu and said, 'I shall kiss my father and my mother, please, and follow you.' He said to him, 'Go, turn back, because what have I done to you?' ²¹He went back from following him, took a pair of cattle and sacrificed it. With the cattle's equipment he cooked them (the meat) and gave it to the people, and they ate. Then he set off and followed Eliyyahu, and ministered to him.

20 Now Ben-hadad king of Aram had collected his entire force, thirty-two kings with him, and horse and chariotry. He went up and besieged Shomron. He did battle against it ²and sent envoys to the town to Ah'ab king of Yisra'el, ³and said to him, 'Ben-hadad has said this: "Your silver and your gold are mine; your good wives and children are mine."' ⁴The king of Yisra'el answered, 'In accordance with your word, my lord king, I and all that I have are yours.'

The point to say no

⁵The envoys went back and said, 'Ben-hadad has said this: "When I sent to you saying 'You're to give me your silver and your gold, your wives and your children': ⁶rather at this

very time tomorrow I shall send my servants to you and they will search your house and your servants' houses, and everything that's desirable in your eyes they will put into their own hand and take.'" ⁷The king of Yisra'el called for all the country's elders and said, 'Please acknowledge and see how this man is seeking something bad, because he sent to me for my wives and for my children, for my silver and for my gold, and I didn't hold them back from him.' ⁸All the elders and the entire people said to him, 'Don't listen. You will not agree.' ⁹So he said to Ben-hadad's envoys, 'Say to my lord the king, "Everything about which you sent to your servant at first, I will do, but this thing I cannot do."' The envoys went and took back word. ¹⁰Ben-hadad sent to him: 'May the gods do like this and may they do more if the earth of Shomron suffices for handfuls for the entire company that's behind me.' ¹¹The king of Yisra'el answered, 'Speak: "The one who buckles on should not take pride like the one who loosens."'

¹²When he heard this word (he was drinking, he and the kings, at Sukkot), he said to his servants, 'Get set', and they got set against the town. ¹³But there, a prophet came up to Ah'ab king of Yisra'el and said, 'Yahweh has said this: "You've seen all of this big horde? Here, I'm giving it into your hand today, and you will acknowledge that I am Yahweh."' ¹⁴Ah'ab said, 'Through whom?' He said, 'Yahweh has said this: "Through the provincial officials' boys".' He said, 'Who will hitch up for the battle?' He said, 'You.'

The boys lead the way to victory

¹⁵So he registered the provincial officers' boys (they were 232) and after them registered the entire company, all the Yisra'elites (7,000), ¹⁶and they went out at midday. Ben-hadad was getting drunk at Sukkot, he and the thirty-two kings helping him. ¹⁷The provincial officials' boys went out first. Ben-hadad sent, and they told him, 'Some men have gone out from Shomron.' ¹⁸He said, 'If they've gone out for peace, capture them alive – and if they've gone out for battle, capture them alive.' ¹⁹But these men went out from the town, the provincial officials' boys with the force that was behind them, ²⁰and they struck down each his man. So the Aramites fled, and the Yisra'elites pursued them. Ben-hadad king of Aram escaped on a horse, with cavalry.

²¹The king of Yisra'el went out and struck down the horse and the chariotry. He struck the Aramites down in a great rout. ²²But the prophet came up to the king of Yisra'el and said to him, 'Go, assert your strength, acknowledge and see what you're to do, because at the turn of the year the king of Aram is going to go up against you.'

²³Now the king of Aram's servants said to him, 'Their God is a mountain God. That's why they were stronger than us. However, we should do battle with them in the flatland. If we will not be stronger than them . . . ²⁴This is the thing you should do. Remove the kings, each from his place, and put governors in their places. ²⁵You should count for yourself a force like the force that fell away from being with you, horse for horse, chariot for chariot, so we can battle with them in the flatland, if we will not be stronger than them . . .'

He listened to their voice and did so.

Ben-hadad tries again

²⁶At the turn of the year Ben-hadad registered the Aramites and went up to Apheq for battle with Yisra'el. ²⁷When the Yisra'elites had been registered and provided for, they went to meet them. The Yisra'elites camped opposite them like two bare flocks of goats, while the Aramites filled the region. ²⁸A supernatural man came up and said to the king of Yisra'el, 'Yahweh has said this: "Since the Aramites have said, 'Yahweh is a mountain God, he's not a vale God', I shall give all of this big horde into your hand, and you will acknowledge that I am Yahweh."'

²⁹One side camped opposite the other side for seven days. On the seventh day the battle began, and the Yisra'elites struck down the Aramites, 100,000 men on foot on one day. ³⁰The ones who were left fled to Apheq, into the town, but the wall fell on the 27,000 men who were left.

Now Ben-hadad had fled and come into the town, to an inner room. ³¹His servants said to him, 'Here, please, we've heard that the kings of the household of Yisra'el – that they are kings who show commitment. Please let's put sack on our hips and ropes on our head and go out to the king of Yisra'el. Perhaps he will let you live.' ³²So they wrapped sack on their hips and ropes on their heads, came to the king of Yisra'el and said, 'Your servant Ben-hadad has said, "Please let me live."' He said, 'Is he still alive? He's my brother.' ³³Now the men could divine and they speedily caught it from him, and said, 'Ben-hadad is your brother.' He said, 'Go on, get him.'

A prophet puts on a disguise

Ben-hadad went out to him and he got him up into the chariot. ³⁴He said to him, 'The towns that my father got from your father, I'll give back, and you may put street markets for yourself in Dammeseq as my father put them in Shomron.'

[Ahab said,] 'And I myself in pact will send you off.' He solemnized a pact towards him and sent him off.

³⁵Now a certain man from among the people who prophesied said to his neighbour, 'By Yahweh's word, please strike me down.' But the man refused to strike him down. ³⁶He said to him, 'Since you haven't listened to Yahweh's voice, there, you will be going from being with me and a lion will strike you down.' He went from beside him and a lion found him and struck him down.

³⁷He found another man and said, 'Please strike me down', and the man struck him down and wounded him. ³⁸Then the prophet went and stood for the king by the road and disguised himself with a bandage over his eyes. ³⁹As the king was passing, he cried out to the king, 'Your servant went out in the middle of the battle and there, a man turned aside and brought a man to me and said, "Keep watch over this man! If he's actually counted missing, it will be your life in place of his life, or you'll weigh out a talent of silver." ⁴⁰But your servant was doing things here and there and he – he wasn't there.' The king of Yisra'el said to him, 'Thus you yourself have determined the decision about you.'

⁴¹He speedily removed the bandage from on his eyes and the king of Yisra'el recognized him, that he was one of the prophets. ⁴²He said to him, 'Yahweh has said this: "Since you sent off from your hand the man who was to be devoted to me, it will be your life in place of his life and your people in place of his people."' ⁴³The king of Yisra'el went to his house ill-disposed and vexed, and came to Shomron.

Nabot and the family land

21 After these things, as Nabot the Yizre'e'lite had a vineyard that was in Yizre'e'l beside the palace of Ah'ab king of Shomron, ²Ah'ab spoke to Nabot: 'Give me your vineyard so it can be a vegetable garden for me, because it's right beside my house. In place of it I'll give you a better vineyard than it. If it's good in your eyes, I'll give you silver as the price for this one.' ³But Nabot said to Ah'ab, 'Far be it from me by Yahweh that I give you my ancestors' domain.'

⁴Ah'ab came to his house ill-disposed and vexed because of the word that Nabot the Yizre'e'lite had spoken to him when he said 'I won't give you my ancestors' domain.' He lay on his bed and turned his face round, and didn't eat bread. ⁵Izebel his wife came to him and spoke to him: 'Why is it that your spirit's ill-disposed and you're not eating bread?' ⁶He spoke to her: 'I spoke to Nabot the Yizre'e'lite and said to him, "Give me your vineyard for silver, or if you want I'll give you a vineyard in place of it", but he said, "I won't give you my vineyard."' ⁷Izebel his wife said to him, 'You should now exercise kingship over Yisra'el. Get up, eat bread so you may be in good heart. I myself will give you the vineyard of Nabot the Yizre'e'lite.'

⁸She wrote documents in Ah'ab's name, sealed them with his seal, and sent the documents to the elders and to the important people who were living in the town with Nabot. ⁹She wrote in the documents: 'Call a fast and sit Nabot at the head of the people, ¹⁰and sit two scoundrels in front of him. They are to testify against him: "You have 'blessed' God and the king", and take him out and stone him so that he dies.'

The capital of corruption

¹¹The men of the town, the elders and the important people who were living in his town,

did as Izebel sent to them, as was written in the documents that she sent to them. ¹²They called a fast and sat Nabot at the head of the people. ¹³The two scoundrels came and sat in front of him. The two scoundrels testified against Nabot in front of the people, 'Nabot "blessed" God and the king', and they took him outside the town and pelted him with stones, and he died.

¹⁴They sent to Izebel: 'Nabot has been stoned. He has died.' ¹⁵When Izebel heard that Nabot had been stoned and had died, Izebel said to Ah'ab, 'Set off, take possession of the vineyard of Nabot the Yizre'e'lite, which he refused to give you for silver, because Nabot is not alive. Rather he's dead.' ¹⁶When Ah'ab heard that Nabot was dead, Ah'ab set off to go down to the vineyard of Nabot the Yizre'e'lite to take possession of it.

¹⁷But Yahweh's word came to Eliyyahu the Tishbite: ¹⁸'Set off, go down to meet Ah'ab king of Yisra'el who is in Shomron: there, in Nabot's vineyard, where he's gone down to take possession of it. ¹⁹You're to speak to him: "Yahweh has said this: 'Have you murdered and also taken possession?'" You're to speak to him: "Yahweh has said this: 'In the place where dogs lapped up Nabot's blood, dogs will lap up your blood, yours too.'"'

The dogs will eat Izebel

²⁰Ah'ab said to Eliyyahu, 'Have you found me, my enemy?' He said, 'I've found you, since you sold yourself to do what is bad in Yahweh's eyes. ²¹"Here am I: I'm going to deal badly with you. I'm going to burn away after you and cut off for Ah'ab the one who pisses against a wall (bound or freed) in Yisra'el. ²²I will make your household like the household of Yarob'am ben Nebat and like the household of Ba'sha ben Ahiyyah, for the provocation that you have offered, and you caused Yisra'el to do wrong."

²³Yahweh has also spoken about Izebel: "The dogs will eat Izebel on the rampart of Yizre'e'l. ²⁴The person who belongs to Ah'ab who dies in the town the dogs will eat; the person who dies in the open country the birds of the heavens will eat."' (²⁵Indeed there was no one like Ah'ab who sold himself to do what was bad in Yahweh's eyes, whom Izebel his wife incited. ²⁶He acted most offensively in following idols, in accordance with everything that the Amorites did, whom Yahweh dispossessed from before the Yisra'elites.)

²⁷When Ah'ab heard these words, he tore his clothes and put sack on his body, and fasted. He lay down in sack and went about quietly. ²⁸And Yahweh's word came to Eliyyahu the Tishbite: ²⁹'Have you seen that Ah'ab has bowed down before me? Since he has bowed down before me, I will not bring the bad fortune in his days. In the days of his son I will bring the bad fortune on his household.'

The prophet with ten horns

22 They stayed three years while there was no battle between Aram and Yisra'el. ²In the third year Yehoshaphat king of Yehudah went down to the king of Yisra'el. ³The king of Yisra'el had said to his servants, 'Do you acknowledge that Heights-in-Gil'ad belongs to us but we are sitting still instead of taking it from the hand of the king of Aram?' ⁴So he said to Yehoshaphat, 'Will you go with me for battle at Heights-in-Gil'ad?' Yehoshaphat said to the king of Yisra'el, 'I'll be the same as you, my company the same as your company, my horses the same as your horses.' ⁵But Yehoshaphat said to the king of Yisra'el, 'Please enquire for Yahweh's word today.'

⁶So the king of Yisra'el collected the prophets, some 400 individuals, and said to them, 'Shall I go up against Heights-in-Gil'ad for the battle, or leave off?' They said, 'Go up, and the Lord will give it into the king's hand.' ⁷But Yehoshaphat said, 'Is there no further prophet of Yahweh here, so we can enquire of him?' ⁸The king of Yisra'el said to Yehoshaphat, 'There's one further individual to enquire of Yahweh from, but I myself dislike him because he doesn't prophesy good for me, but bad: Mikayehu ben Yimlah.' Yehoshaphat said, 'The king shouldn't say that.' ⁹So the king of Yisra'el called to a courtier and said, 'Do hurry Mikayehu ben Imlah.'

¹⁰As the king of Yisra'el and Yehoshaphat king of Yehudah were sitting, each on his throne, dressed in robes, at the threshing floor at the entrance to the gateway at Shomron, and all the prophets were prophesying before them,

¹¹Tsidqiyyah ben Kena'anah had made himself iron horns, and he said, 'Yahweh has said this: "With these you will gore the Aramites until you have finished them off."' ¹²All the prophets were prophesying in this way: 'Go up to Heights-in-Gil'ad and succeed. Yahweh will give it into the king's hand.'

¹³Now the envoy who went to call for Mikayehu spoke to him: 'Here, please, the prophets' words are good for the king as one bidding. Your word should please be like the word of one of them. You should speak of something good.' ¹⁴Mikayehu said, 'As Yahweh lives, what Yahweh says to me – I will speak it.'

Who will entice Ah'ab?

¹⁵He came to the king and the king said to him, 'Mikayehu, shall we go up to Heights-in-Gil'ad for battle, or shall we leave off?' He said to him, 'Go up and succeed. Yahweh will give it into the king's hand.' ¹⁶The king said to him, 'How many times am I going to get you to swear that you won't speak to me anything but truth in Yahweh's name?'

¹⁷So he said, 'I saw all Yisra'el scattering towards the mountains like a flock that have no shepherd. Yahweh said, "These people have no lords. They should go back, each to his house, with things being well."' ¹⁸The king of Yisra'el said to Yehoshaphat, 'I said to you, "He won't prophesy good fortune for me, but only bad", didn't I.'

¹⁹He said, 'Therefore listen to Yahweh's word. I saw Yahweh sitting on his throne, with the entire heavenly army standing by him on his right and on his left. ²⁰Yahweh said, "Who will entice Ah'ab so he'll go up but fall at Heights-in-Gil'ad?" One said "In this way" and another said "In this way". ²¹Then a spirit went out and stood before Yahweh and said, "I'm the one who'll entice him." Yahweh said to him, "How?" ²²He said, "I'll go out and become a false spirit in the mouth of all his prophets." He said, "You're to entice. Yes, you'll be able to. Go out and do it." ²³So now, there, Yahweh put a spirit of falsehood in the mouth of all these prophets, in that Yahweh has spoken of something bad for you.'

²⁴Tsidqiyyahu ben Kena'anah went up and struck Mikayehu on the jaw, and said, 'Which way did Yahweh's spirit pass from being with me to speak with you?' ²⁵Mikayehu said, 'There, you're going to see, on that day when you come to an innermost room to hide.'

You can disguise but you can't hide

²⁶The king of Yisra'el said, 'Get Mikayehu and take him back to Amon the town official and to Yo'ash the king's son, ²⁷and say "The king has said this: 'Put this man in the cells and give him slave bread and slave water until I come with things being well.'"' ²⁸Mikayehu said, 'If you really do come back with things being well, Yahweh did not speak through me.' (And he said, 'Listen, you peoples, all of them.')

²⁹So the king of Yisra'el went up with Yehoshaphat king of Yehudah to Heights-in-Gil'ad. ³⁰The king of Yisra'el said to Yehoshaphat, 'I'm putting on disguise and coming into battle, but you, dress in your robes.' So the king of Yisra'el put on disguise and came into battle.

³¹Now the king of Aram had ordered the thirty-two chariot officers that he had, 'You will not battle anyone small or great except the king of Yisra'el alone.' ³²When the chariot officers saw Yehoshaphat and said, 'Yes, he's the king of Yisra'el', they turned aside to him to do battle. But Yehoshaphat cried out, ³³and when the chariot officers saw that he was not the king of Yisra'el, they turned back from following him. ³⁴But a man drew his bow innocently, and struck the king of Yisra'el between the links and the armour. He said to his charioteer, 'Turn your hand, get me out from the camp, because I'm wounded.'

³⁵The battle mounted that day, while the king was kept standing in his chariot opposite the Aramites. But he died in the evening. The blood from the wound poured down into the base of the chariot. ³⁶A shout passed through the camp as the sun set: 'Each man to his town, each man to his land.'

³⁷So the king died and came to Shomron, and they buried the king in Shomron. ³⁸They washed off the chariot by the pool in Shomron, and the dogs licked up his blood as the prostitutes bathed, in accordance with the word of Yahweh that he had spoken.

The fleet that sank

³⁹The rest of the things about Ah'ab, all that he did, the ivory house that he built and all the towns that he built up, are written on the document about things of the time regarding the kings of Yisra'el, aren't they. ⁴⁰Ah'ab lay down with his ancestors, and Ahazyahu, his son, began to reign in place of him.

⁴¹Yehoshaphat ben Asa had become king over Yehudah in the fourth year of Ah'ab king of Yisra'el. ⁴²Yehoshaphat was a man of thirty-five years when he began to reign and he reigned in Yerushalaim twenty-five years. His mother's name was Azubah bat Shilhi. ⁴³He walked in all the way of Asa his father. He did not turn aside from it, in doing what was upright in Yahweh's eyes. Yet the shrines did not disappear; the people were still sacrificing and burning incense at the shrines. ⁴⁴Yehoshaphat made peace with the king of Yisra'el. ⁴⁵The rest of the things about Yehoshaphat, and his strength with which he acted and with which he battled, are written on the document about things of the time regarding the kings of Yehudah, aren't they. ⁴⁶The rest of the hierodules who were left in the time of Asa his father he burned away from the country.

⁴⁷There being no king in Edom, a prefect was king, ⁴⁸and Yehoshaphat made Tarshish ships to go to Ophir for gold, but he didn't go because the ships broke up at Etsyon Geber. ⁴⁹It was then that Ahazyahu ben Ah'ab said to Yehoshaphat, 'My servants should go on the ships with your servants', but Yehoshaphat was not willing.

⁵⁰Yehoshaphat lay down with his ancestors and was buried with his ancestors in David his ancestor's town, and Yehoram his son began to reign in place of him.

⁵¹Now Ahazyahu ben Ah'ab had become king over Yisra'el in Shomron in the seventeenth year of Yehoshaphat king of Yehudah. He reigned over Yisra'el two years. ⁵²He did what was bad in Yahweh's eyes; he walked in the way of his father and in the way of his mother, and in the way of Yarob'am ben Nebat, who had caused Yisra'el to do wrong. ⁵³He served the Master and bowed low to him, and provoked Yahweh the God of Yisra'el in accordance with all that his father did.

2 Kings

The division of the books of Kings into two is arbitrary; the narrative continues seamlessly. The first two thirds of 2 Kings continue the interwoven account of Israel and Judah, with the involvement of prophets such as Elijah and Elisha. While the background of the book's opening chapters is tension between Israel (and Judah) and Syria (Aram), on the horizon is the bigger power of Assyria, the first great Middle Eastern empire to have an impact on Israel and Judah. The middle of the book relates how the Assyrians invade Israel and attempt to require them to function as Assyria's underlings, but Israel resists and in due course the Assyrians invade again, conquer the Israelite capital, Samaria, transport its people and replace them with people from other parts of their empire. Subsequently, the Assyrians did take action to enable these immigrants to know how they should properly worship Yahweh in this land of his, and in some respects they do, but many people continue to worship the gods they had followed in the countries they came from. The aftermath of this forced migration forms background to relations between Judah and Samaria about which we read in Ezra.

The second book of Kings pauses at this point to explain what has happened, not politically but religiously (see 2 Kings 17). The fall of Samaria happened because of its people's false worship of Yahweh and its worship of other deities, its resistance to its prophets, to its covenant and to the rules of that covenant, and its practices such as human sacrifice. The interwovenness of the political and the religious in the story supports the suggestion that one of the key themes in 2 Kings is the interwovennness of divine sovereignty and human sovereignty in politics. Sometimes human leaders do things they wish to do, and it can form part of positive things God wishes to achieve. Sometimes human leaders do things they want to do, and it can form part of negative things God wishes to do. Sometimes human leaders do things they want to do, and it works against God's purpose, and he then frustrates their aims.

The last part of 2 Kings tells more briefly the less complicated story of the last generations of Judah when it has become the rump embodiment of Israel. The story begins with the great King Hezekiah. He also experiences invasion by Assyria, but he is faithful to Yahweh and he has on his side the temple in Jerusalem and the promise to David, not to say the prophet Isaiah. The Assyrians wreak havoc in Judah but fail to take Jerusalem, which constitutes Yahweh's great act of deliverance.

Sadly, Hezekiah's son is the renegade Manasseh, who experiences more Assyrian pressure, adopts much of northern Israel's apostate ways, but reigns much longer than he therefore should. His grandson Josiah is both motivated and politically able to revert to Hezekiah's commitments. In the course of cleaning up the temple, his envoys discover a scroll of Moses' Torah there which causes panic when people read of the consequences that follow practices like the ones Manasseh sponsored. The discovery thereby encourages further reform. Overlaps with what Josiah does suggest that the Torah scroll may have been a version of what we call Deuteronomy.

Alas, it seems that the policies Manassah implemented are too deeply ingrained to be eliminated, and after Josiah's untimely death things revert to the way they were, which results in Jerusalem and Judah going through the same experience that northern Israel and Samaria had had. The account of the fall of Jerusalem and associated events has a pained atmosphere that conveys something of the grief of the people who went through the experience.

The book of 2 Kings comprises the last part the gargantuan work that began in Genesis and it takes the story down to the time of the people who will have heard the story read when it was first compiled. It thus helps them understand who they are and how they need to look at themselves. As is often the case with stories or histories, reading it from the end is illuminating.

One of the factors that has influenced God in keeping the state of Judah in being is the promise he had made that he would never let David's line of kings disappear, and the last event related by 2 Kings is the release of a deposed and exiled king of Judah. It is a hint that God has indeed not abandoned his promises.

The lord of the flies

1 Mo'ab rebelled against Yisra'el [Israel] after Ah'ab's death.
²Ahazyah fell through the lattice in his upper quarters, which were in Shomron [Samaria], and he was ill. He sent envoys and said to them, 'Go enquire of the Fly Master, the god of Eqron, whether I will live on after this illness.' ³But Yahweh's envoy – he spoke to Eliyyahu [Elijah] the Tishbite: 'Set off, go up to meet the king of Shomron's envoys and speak to them: "Is it for lack of a God in Yisra'el that you're going to enquire of the Fly Master, the god of Eqron? ⁴So, therefore, Yahweh has said this: 'The bed that you have climbed into, you won't get down from, because you will actually die.'"' And Eliyyahu went.
⁵The envoys went back to him, and he said to them, 'Why is it that you've come back?' ⁶They said to him, 'There was a man came up to meet us and he said to us, "Go, turn back to the king who sent you, and speak to him: 'Yahweh has said this: "Is it for lack of a God in Yisra'el that you are sending to enquire of the Fly Master, the god of Eqron? Therefore the bed that you have climbed into, you won't get down from, because you will actually die."'"' ⁷He spoke to them, 'What was the manner of the man who came up to meet you and spoke these words to you?' ⁸They said to him, 'A man with lots of hair and a leather wrap belted round his hips.' He said, 'It was Eliyyahu the Tishbite.'
⁹He sent to him an officer over fifty and his fifty men, and he went up to him. There, he was sitting on the top of a mountain. He spoke to him: 'Supernatural man, the king himself has spoken: come down.' ¹⁰Eliyyahu answered the officer over fifty, 'If I'm a supernatural man, may fire come down from the heavens and consume you and your fifty men!' And fire came down from the heavens and consumed him and his fifty men.

Fire from the heavens again

¹¹He again sent to him another officer over 50 and his 50 men. He went up and spoke to him, 'Supernatural man, the king himself has said this: "Come down speedily!"' ¹²Eliyyahu answered them, 'If I'm a supernatural man, may fire come down from the heavens and consume you and your 50 men!' And supernatural fire came down from the heavens and consumed him and his 50 men.
¹³He again sent a third officer over 50 and his 50 men. The third officer over 50 went up, and came and bent down on his knees in front of Eliyyahu and asked him for grace. He spoke to him: 'Supernatural man, please may my life and the life of these 50 servants of yours be valuable in your eyes! ¹⁴Here, fire fell from the heavens and consumed the previous two officers over 50 and their 50 men. But now, may my life be valuable in your eyes.'
¹⁵Yahweh's envoy spoke to Eliyyahu: 'Go down with him. Don't be afraid of him.' So he set off and went down with him to the king, ¹⁶and spoke to him: 'Yahweh has said this: "Since you sent envoys to enquire of the Fly Master, the god of Eqron: is it for lack of a God in Yisra'el to enquire of his word? Therefore the bed that you have climbed into, you will not get down from, because you will actually die."'
¹⁷He died in accordance with Yahweh's word which Eliyyahu spoke. Yehoram began to reign in place of him, in the second year of Yehoram ben Yehoshaphat king of Yehudah [Judah], because he had no son. ¹⁸The rest of the things about Ahazyahu, what he did, are written on the document about things of the time regarding the kings of Yisra'el, aren't they.

Eliyyahu's cloak

2 When Yahweh took Eliyyahu up to the heavens in a hurricane, Eliyyahu had gone with Elisha from Gilgal. ²Eliyyahu said to Elisha, 'Stay here, please, because Yahweh has sent me as far as Bet-el.' Elisha said, 'As Yahweh lives and as you yourself live, if I abandon you . . .' So they went down to Bet-el. ³The people who prophesied who were at Bet-el went out to Elisha and said to him, 'Do you know that today Yahweh is going to take your lord from being your head?' He said, 'Yes, I myself know. Be quiet.'
⁴Eliyyahu said to him, 'Elisha, stay here, please, because Yahweh has sent me to Yeriho [Jericho].' He said, 'As Yahweh lives and as you yourself live, if I abandon you . . .' So they came

to Yeriho. ⁵The people who prophesied who were at Yeriho went up to Elisha and said to him, 'Do you know that today Yahweh is going to take your lord from being your head?' He said, 'Yes, I myself know. Be quiet.'

⁶Eliyyahu said to him, 'Stay here, please, because Yahweh has sent me to the Yarden [Jordan].' He said, 'As Yahweh lives and as you yourself live, if I abandon you . . .' So the two of them went, ⁷while fifty men from among the people who prophesied went and stood at a distance, far off, and the two of them stood at the Yarden.

⁸Eliyyahu got his cape, rolled it up and struck the water. It divided in both directions and the two of them crossed on dry ground.

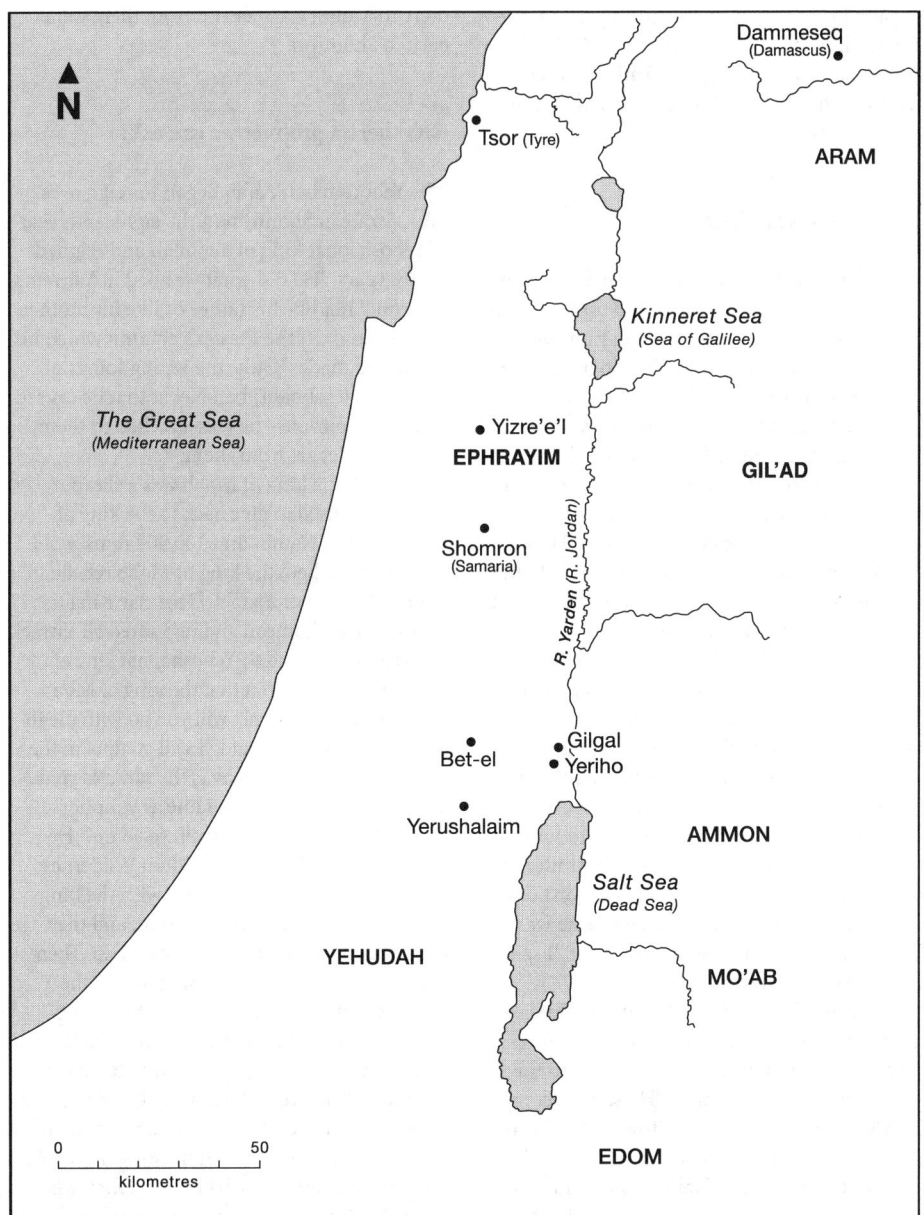

2 Kings 2: Eliyyahu (Elijah) and Elisha

⁹As they crossed, Eliyyahu said to Elisha, 'Ask what I should do for you before I'm taken from being with you.' Elisha said, 'A double share in your spirit should please come to me.' ¹⁰He said, 'You've been tough in asking. If you see me taken from being with you, so it will happen for you. If not, it won't happen.'

¹¹As they were continuing to walk and speak, there – fiery chariotry and fiery horses. They separated the two of them and Eliyyahu went up in a hurricane to the heavens, ¹²while Elisha was looking and crying out, 'Father, father, Yisra'el's chariotry and cavalry!' Then he could no longer see.

No more miscarriage

He took strong hold of his clothes and tore them into two pieces, ¹³and lifted up Eliyyahu's cape which had fallen from upon him. He went back and stood at the Yarden bank. ¹⁴He got Eliyyahu's cape which had fallen from upon him, struck the water and said, 'Where is Yahweh, the God of Eliyyahu? Yes, him?' He struck the water, it divided in both directions and Elisha crossed. ¹⁵The people who prophesied who were at Yeriho, at a distance, saw him and said, 'Eliyyahu's spirit has alighted on Elisha!' They came to meet him and bowed low to the ground before him.

¹⁶They said to him, 'Here, please, with your servants there are fifty men, forceful people. They should please go and look for your lord in case Yahweh's spirit has taken him up and thrown him down on one of the mountains or in one of the ravines.' He said to them, 'You will not send.' ¹⁷But they pressed him until he was shamed, and he said, 'Send.' They sent fifty men and they looked for three days but didn't find him. ¹⁸They came back to him while he was staying in Yeriho, and he said to them, 'I said to you, "Don't go", didn't I.'

¹⁹The town's people said to Elisha, 'Here, please, the settlement in the town is good, as my lord sees, but the water is bad and the region causes miscarriage.' ²⁰He said, 'Get me a new bowl and put salt in it.' They got it for him ²¹and he went out to the water outlet and threw the salt there. He said, 'Yahweh has said this: "I am healing this water. No more will death and miscarriage come from there."' ²²The water became healthy, until this day, in accordance with the word of Elisha which he spoke.

²³He went up from there to Bet-el. He was going up the road and small boys came out of the town and mocked him: 'Go up, baldy, go up, baldy!' ²⁴He turned his face behind him and saw them and slighted them in Yahweh's name, and two bears came out of the forest. Of them they mauled forty-two boys. ²⁵He went from there to Mount Carmel and from there went back to Shomron.

Isn't there a prophet we can ask?

3 Yehoram ben Ah'ab began to reign over Yisra'el in Shomron in the eighteenth year of Yehoshaphat king of Yehudah and reigned twelve years. ²He did what was bad in Yahweh's eyes, only not like his father or like his mother, and he removed the Master's column which his father had made. ³Only, the wrongdoings of Yarob'am [Jeroboam] ben Nebat that he caused Yisra'el to commit – he was attached to them and didn't depart from them.

⁴Now Mesha king of Mo'ab was a sheep breeder. He used to give back to the king of Yisra'el 100,000 lambs and 100,000 rams' wool. ⁵When Ah'ab died, the king of Mo'ab rebelled against the king of Yisra'el. ⁶That day King Yehoram left Shomron and registered all Yisra'el. ⁷He went on to send to Yehoshaphat king of Yehudah to say, 'Given that the king of Mo'ab has rebelled against me, will you go with me to Mo'ab for battle?' He said, 'I will go up; I'm the same as you, my company is the same as your company, my horse is the same as your horse.' ⁸He said, 'By which road shall we go up?' He said, 'The road through the Edom Wilderness.'

⁹So the king of Yisra'el went, with the king of Yehudah and the king of Edom, and they went round on the road for seven days. Then there was no water for the camp or for the animals that were behind them. ¹⁰The king of Yisra'el said, 'Oh no! Yahweh has called for these three kings to give them into the hand of Mo'ab!' ¹¹But Yehoshaphat said, 'Isn't there a prophet of Yahweh here so we can enquire of Yahweh from him?' One of the king of Yisra'el's servants answered, 'Elisha ben Shaphat, who poured water on Eliyyahu's hands, is here.' ¹²Yehoshaphat said, 'Yahweh's word is with

him.' So the king of Yisra'el and Yehoshaphat and the king of Edom went down to him.

The water that looked like blood

¹³Elisha said to the king of Yisra'el, 'What do you and I have in common? Go to your father's prophets and to your mother's prophets.' The king of Yisra'el said to him, 'No, because Yahweh has called for these three kings to give them into the hand of Mo'ab.' ¹⁴Elisha said, 'As Yahweh of Armies lives, before whom I stand, if I did not have regard for Yehoshaphat king of Yehudah, I would not look to you or see you. ¹⁵But now, get me a musician' (when the musician played, Yahweh's hand would come on him).

¹⁶Then he said, 'Yahweh has said this: "This wadi is going to make pools, pools." ¹⁷Because Yahweh has said this: "You will not see wind, you will not see rain, but that wadi – it will fill with water. Both you and your cattle and your livestock will drink." ¹⁸This is a slight thing in Yahweh's eyes: and he will give the Mo'abites into your hand. ¹⁹You will strike down every fortified town and every choice town. Every good tree you will fell, all springs of water you will stop up and every good plot you will make suffer with stones.' ²⁰And in the morning at the time for making the offering – there, water was coming from the direction of Edom. The region filled with water.

²¹Now all the Mo'abites had heard that the kings had gone up to battle against them. They had themselves called out, from everyone who could fasten a belt and upwards, and they stood at the border. ²²In the morning they started early, and when the sun rose over the water, from a distance the Mo'abites saw the water red like blood. ²³They said, 'This is blood! The kings have actually been put to the sword. Each man has struck down his neighbour. Now, to the plunder, Mo'abites!' ²⁴They came to the Yisra'elite camp, but the Yisra'elites set to and struck down the Mo'abites, and they fled from before them.

An ultimate sacrifice

So they came into it and struck down Mo'ab. ²⁵The towns they tore down, on every good plot they threw each man his stone and covered it, every water spring they stopped up and every good tree they would fell, until what was left remaining in Qir Hareset was its stones. The slingers surrounded it and struck it down.

²⁶The king of Mo'ab saw that the battle was too hard for him and he got with him 700 men drawing a sword to break through to the king of Edom, but they couldn't. ²⁷So he got his eldest son who was to reign in place of him, and offered him up as a burnt offering on the wall. A great fury came on Yisra'el, and they moved on from there and went back to the land.

4 Now a woman, one of the wives of the people who prophesied, cried out to Elisha, 'Your servant, my husband, is dead, and you yourself acknowledge that your servant was someone who has lived in awe of Yahweh, and a creditor is coming to take my two children for himself as servants.' ²Elisha said to her, 'What am I to do for you? Tell me what you have in the house.' She said, 'Your maidservant has nothing at all in the house except a jug of oil.' ³He said, 'Go and ask for containers for yourself from outside, from all the people who live near you, empty containers. Don't make it a few. ⁴Come in, shut the door behind you and behind your sons, and pour into all these containers. The full one, remove.'

⁵She went from being with him and shut the door behind her and behind her sons. People were bringing them up to her and she was pouring. ⁶When the containers were full, she said to her son, 'Bring up another container to me', but he said to her, 'There isn't another container'; and the oil halted. ⁷She came and told the supernatural man. He said, 'Go sell the oil and make good your debt, and you and your children can live on what's left.'

The woman who had almost everything

⁸One day Elisha passed through to Shunem. A big woman was there and she took strong hold of him so he would eat bread. Whenever he passed through, he would turn aside there to eat bread. ⁹She said to her husband, 'Here, please, I know that it's a sacred supernatural man who passes by us regularly. ¹⁰Please let's make a little upstairs room with a wall and put a bed for him there and a table and a chair

and a lamp. When he comes to us he can turn aside there.'

¹¹One day he came there and turned aside to the upstairs room and lay down there, ¹²and said to Gehazi, his boy, 'Call this Shunammite woman.' He called her and she stood before him. ¹³He said to him, 'Please say to her, "Here, you've acted towards us with all this concern. What is there to do for you? Is there something to speak to the king for you, or to the army officer?"' She said, 'I'm living among my own people.' ¹⁴He said, 'So what is there to do for her?' Gehazi said, 'Well, she doesn't have a son, and her husband is old.' ¹⁵He said, 'Call her.' He called her and she stood in the entrance. ¹⁶He said, 'At this season, at [nature's] reviving time, you're going to embrace a son.' She said, 'Don't, my lord, supernatural man, don't lie to your maidservant.' ¹⁷But the woman got pregnant and gave birth to a son at this season at reviving time, as Elisha spoke to her.

¹⁸The child grew up, but one day he went out to his father, to the reapers, ¹⁹and he said to his father, 'My head, my head!' He said to a boy, 'Carry him to his mother.' ²⁰He carried him and brought him to his mother, and he sat on her knees until noon, and died. ²¹She took him up, laid him down on the supernatural man's bed, closed up behind him and went out.

Did I ask for a son?

²²She called her husband and said, 'Please send me one of the boys and one of the she-donkeys so I can run to the supernatural man, and come back.' ²³He said, 'Why are you going to him today? It's not new month or sabbath.' She said, 'Things will be well.' ²⁴She saddled the donkey and said to her boy, 'Drive, go, don't hold back from riding unless I say it to you.' ²⁵So she went, and came to the supernatural man at Mount Carmel. When the supernatural man saw her from a distance, he said to Gehazi his boy, 'There's that Shunammite woman. ²⁶Now please run to meet her and say to her, "Are things well with you? Are things well with your husband? Are things well with the child?"' She said, 'Things are well.' ²⁷She came to the supernatural man at the mountain and took strong hold of his feet. Gehazi came up to push her away, but the supernatural man said, 'Let go of her, because her entire being is bitter to her, whereas Yahweh has hidden it from me and not told me.' ²⁸She said, 'Did I ask for a son from my lord? I said, "Don't deceive me", didn't I.' ²⁹He said to Gehazi, 'Wrap things round your hips, take my staff in your hand and go. When you meet someone, you will not bless him, and when someone blesses you, you will not answer him. Place my staff on the boy's face.' ³⁰But the boy's mother said, 'As Yahweh lives and as you yourself live, if I abandon you . . .'

So he set off and followed her. ³¹Now Gehazi passed on before them and placed the staff on the boy's face. But there was no sound and no heeding. He went back to meet him and told him, 'The boy has not woken up.' ³²Elisha came to the house and there – the boy was dead, laid on his bed. ³³He came in and shut the door behind the two of them and pleaded with Yahweh.

Death and life

³⁴He climbed up and lay on the child, put his mouth on his mouth, his eyes on his eyes, his palms on his palms, and crouched over him. And the child's flesh warmed up. ³⁵He went back and went into the house here and there, then climbed up and crouched over him, and the boy sneezed seven times. Then the boy opened his eyes. ³⁶He called Gehazi and said, 'Call this Shunammite woman.' He called her and she came to him. He said, 'Take up your son.' ³⁷She came, and fell at his feet and bowed low to the earth, and took up her son and went out.

³⁸When Elisha went back to Gilgal and there was a famine in the region, and the people who prophesied were sitting before him, he said to his boy, 'Put the big pot on and cook stew for the people who prophesy.' ³⁹One went out into the wild to gather herbs, found a vine of the wild and gathered gourds of the wild from it, enough to fill his garment. He came and sliced them into the pot of stew, because they didn't know them. ⁴⁰They poured it out for the people to eat, but as they ate some of the stew and they cried out, they said, 'There's death in the pot, supernatural man.' They couldn't eat it. ⁴¹He said, 'So get some flour', and he threw it into the pot and said, 'Pour it out for the company

so that they eat.' And there was nothing bad in the pot. ⁴²Now a man came from Ba'al Shalishah and brought the supernatural man some first-products bread, twenty barley loaves and some plantation growth on the stalk. He said, 'Give it to the company so they can eat.' ⁴³His minister said, 'How can I put this before a hundred individuals?' He said, 'Give it to the company so they can eat. Because Yahweh has said this: "Eat and have some left."' ⁴⁴So he put it before them, they ate and they had some left, in accordance with Yahweh's word.

The little girl who knows

5 Now Na'aman, army officer of the king of Aram, was a big man before his lord, and held in high regard, because through him Yahweh had given deliverance to Aram. Now the man was a forceful strong man, with scaliness. ²The Aramites had gone out as raiding gangs and had taken captive a little girl from the country of Yisra'el. She was before Na'aman's wife ³and she said to her mistress, 'If only my lord were before the prophet who's in Shomron. Then he would restore him from his scaliness.' ⁴He came and told his lord, 'The girl who's from the country of Yisra'el has spoken such and such', ⁵and the king of Aram said, 'Come on, go, I'll send a document to the king of Yisra'el.' So he went, took in his hand ten talents of silver, 6,000 gold pieces and ten changes of clothes, ⁶and brought the document to the king of Yisra'el, saying: 'Now, when this document comes to you: here, I've sent Na'aman my servant to you so you may restore him from his scaliness.'

⁷When the king of Yisra'el read the document, he tore his clothes and said, 'Am I God, to put to death and make alive, that this man is sending to me to restore someone from his scaliness? Rather, please acknowledge for sure and see, that he is seeking a confrontation with me.'

⁸When Elisha the supernatural man heard that the king of Yisra'el had torn his clothes, he sent to the king: 'Why have you torn your clothes? He should please come to me, so he may acknowledge that there is a prophet in Yisra'el.'

⁹Na'aman came with his horses and with his chariotry and halted at the entrance of Elisha's house. ¹⁰Elisha sent an envoy to him to say, 'Go and wash seven times in the Yarden so your flesh may come back for you, and be pure.'

A skin disorder removed

¹¹Na'aman was furious and went. He said, 'Here, I said to myself, "He'll definitely come out and stand and call in the name of Yahweh his God and wave his hand at the place and restore the scaliness. ¹²Amanah and Pharpar, the rivers in Dammeseq [Damascus], are better than all the water in Yisra'el, aren't they. I could wash in them and be pure, couldn't I.' So he turned his face and went in wrath. ¹³But his servants came up and spoke to him: 'Father, had the prophet spoken to you of a big thing, wouldn't you do it? How much more when he said to you, "Wash, and be pure"?'

¹⁴So he went down and dipped in the Yarden seven times in accordance with the word of the supernatural man, and his flesh came back like a little boy's. He was pure. ¹⁵He went back to the supernatural man, he and all his camp, and came and stood before him, and said, 'Here, please, I acknowledge that there is no God in all the earth except in Yisra'el. So now please take a blessing from your servant.' ¹⁶He said, 'As Yahweh lives, before whom I stand, if I take anything...'

He pressed him to take it, but he refused. ¹⁷Na'aman said, 'Then please may there not be given to your servant a mule pair's load of earth, because your servant will no longer make a burnt offering or a sacrifice to any other god but Yahweh. ¹⁸With regard to this thing, may Yahweh pardon your servant: when my lord comes into Rimmon's house to bow down there and he leans on my hand and I bow down there in Rimmon's house – when I bow down in Rimmon's house, may Yahweh pardon your servant in this thing.' ¹⁹He said to him, 'Go, and things will be well.'

He went a distance in the region from him, ²⁰and Gehazi, Elisha the supernatural man's boy, said, 'Here, my lord has held back Na'aman this Aramite from taking from his hand what he brought. As Yahweh lives, I shall run after him and take something from him.'

A skin disorder imposed

²¹So Gehazi pursued after Na'aman. Na'aman saw him running after him, fell from his chariot to meet him and said, 'Are things well?' ²²He said, 'Things are well. My lord has sent me to say, "Here, just now two boys have come to me from the highland of Ephrayim, from among the people who prophesy. Please give them a talent of silver and two changes of clothes."' ²³Na'aman said, 'Resolve to take two talents!' He pressed him, and tied up two talents of silver in two bags and two changes of clothes and gave them to two of his boys. They carried them before him. ²⁴He came to the acropolis, took them from their hand, deposited them in the house and sent the men off.

So they went, ²⁵while he came and stood with his lord. Elisha said to him, 'Where have you come from, Gehazi?' He said, 'Your servant hasn't gone here or there.' ²⁶He said to him, 'My mind didn't go along as the man turned from his chariot to meet you? Is it time to take silver or to take clothes or olive trees or vineyards or sheep or cattle or servants or maidservants? ²⁷Na'aman's scaliness will attach itself to you and to your offspring permanently.' He went out from before him, made scaly like snow.

6 The people who prophesied said to Elisha, 'Here, please, the place where we're living before you is too confined for us. ²Please let's go as far as the Yarden and get a beam each from there and make ourselves a place there to live in.' He said, 'Go.' ³One said, 'Please resolve to go with your servants.' He said, 'I'll go.' ⁴He went with them and they came to the Yarden. They cut down trees, ⁵but one was felling a beam and the iron fell into the water. He cried out, 'Oh, my lord, and it was borrowed!' ⁶The supernatural man said, 'Where did it fall?' He let him see the place, and he cut down a stick and threw it there, and it made the iron float. ⁷He said, 'Take it up for yourself', and he put out his hand and got it.

Horses and chariots of fire round Elisha

⁸Now the king of Aram was battling against Yisra'el, and he took counsel with his servants, saying, 'My camp will be at such and such a place', ⁹but the supernatural man sent to the king of Yisra'el saying, 'Keep watch not to pass by this place, because the Aramites are going down there.' ¹⁰So the king of Yisra'el sent to the place that the supernatural man had said to him and warned him, and kept watch there more than once or twice.

¹¹The mind of the king of Aram was agitated about this thing. He called his servants and said to them, 'Won't you tell me who of us is on the king of Yisra'el's side?' ¹²One of his servants said, 'No, my lord king, rather it's Elisha, the prophet who's in Yisra'el, who tells the king of Yisra'el the things that you speak in your bedroom.' ¹³He said, 'Go and see where he is so I can send and get him.'

It was told him, 'There, in Dotan', ¹⁴and he sent horses and chariotry there, with a substantial force. They came by night and encircled the town. ¹⁵The supernatural man's minister started early and got up and went out, and there, a force was surrounding the town, with horses and chariotry. His boy said to him, 'Oh no, my lord, what shall we do?' ¹⁶He said, 'Don't be afraid, because there are more with us than with them.' ¹⁷Elisha pleaded, 'Yahweh, please open his eyes so he sees.' Yahweh opened the boy's eyes and he saw: there, the highland was full of fiery horses and chariotry surrounding Elisha.

The depths to which people can be driven

¹⁸They came down against him, and Elisha pleaded with Yahweh, 'Please strike down this nation with dazzling.' He struck them down with dazzling in accordance with Elisha's word. ¹⁹Elisha said to them, 'This isn't the way, and this isn't the town. Follow me and I'll enable you to go to the man that you're looking for', and he enabled them to go to Shomron.

²⁰When they came to Shomron, Elisha said, 'Yahweh, open these people's eyes so they can see.' Yahweh opened their eyes and they saw: there, they were inside Shomron. ²¹The king of Yisra'el said to Elisha, on seeing them, 'Shall I strike them down, strike them down, father?' ²²He said, 'You will not strike them down. Do you strike down people whom you took captive with your sword and with your bow? Put bread and water before them so they can eat and drink, and go to their lords.' ²³He made a great

banquet for them, and they ate and drank. Then he sent them off and they went to their lords, and the Aramite raiding gangs no longer came into Yisra'el.

²⁴Subsequently, Ben-hadad king of Aram collected his entire camp and went up and besieged Shomron, ²⁵and there was a big famine in Shomron. There, they were besieging it until a donkey's head was eighty silver pieces and a quarter of a litre of pigeon dung was five silver pieces. ²⁶The king of Yisra'el was passing by on the wall when a woman cried out to him: 'Deliver me, my lord king!' ²⁷He said, 'Don't. Yahweh must deliver you. From where am I to deliver you – from the threshing floor or from the winepress?' ²⁸But the king said to her, 'What's the matter?' She said, 'This woman said to me, "Give up your son and we'll eat him today, and we'll eat my son tomorrow", ²⁹and we cooked my son and ate him. The next day I said to her, "Give up your son and we'll eat him", but she hid her son.'

The men who gave up

³⁰When the king heard the woman's words, he tore his clothes, and as he passed by on the wall, the people saw: there, sack on his flesh, inside. ³¹He said, 'May God do this to me and may he do more if the head of Elisha ben Shaphat stays on him today.'

³²While Elisha was sitting in his house and the elders were sitting with him, he sent a man from before him. Before the envoy came to him, he himself said to the elders, 'Do you see that this murderous man has sent to remove my head? See, when the envoy comes, shut the door and press him against the door. The sound of his lord's feet will be behind him, won't it.'

³³While he was still speaking with them, there, the envoy was coming down to him. He said, 'Here, this is the bad fate coming from Yahweh. How can I wait for Yahweh any more?'

7 Elisha said, 'Listen to Yahweh's word. Yahweh has said this: "This very time tomorrow: a measure of fine flour will be for a sheqel, two measures of barley for a sheqel, at the gateway of Shomron."' ²The adjutant on whose hand the king leaned answered the supernatural man, 'There, were Yahweh making apertures in the heavens, would this thing happen?' He said, 'There, you're going to see it with your eyes, but you won't eat of it.'

³Now there were four men with scaliness at the entrance to the gateway. They said, one to his neighbour, 'Why are we sitting here until we die? ⁴If we say, "Let's go into the town", there's famine in the town and we'll die there, and if we sit here, we'll die. So now, come on, let's surrender to the Aramite camp. If they let us live, we'll live. If they put us to death, we'll die.' ⁵ᵃSo they set off at dusk to come to the Aramite camp.

The mysterious panicked flight

⁵ᵇThey came to the edge of the Aramite camp, and there – no one was there. ⁶The Lord had made the Aramite camp hear the sound of chariotry, the sound of horse, the sound of a big force, and they had said to one another, 'Here, the king of Yisra'el has hired against us the kings of the Hittites and the kings of Misrayim [Egypt], to come against us.' ⁷They had set off and fled at dusk. They had abandoned their tents and their horses and their donkeys, the camp as it was, and fled for their life.

⁸So these men with scaliness came to the edge of the camp and came into a tent and ate and drank and carried silver and gold and clothes from there and went and buried it, and went back and came into another tent and carried silver and gold and clothes from there and went and buried it. ⁹But they said each to his neighbour, 'We're not doing right. This day is a day of good news. We're keeping quiet. And should we wait until morning light, waywardness will find us out. Now, come on, let's go and tell the king's household.' ¹⁰So they came and called to the town gateman. They told them, 'We came to the Aramite camp and there, no one and no human sound was there, but horse tied up and donkey tied up and tents as they were.'

¹¹The gatemen called, and they told the king's household, within. ¹²The king got up in the night and said to his servants, 'May I please tell you what the Aramites have done to us? They know that we're starving, and they've gone out of the camp to hide in the fields, saying "When they go out from the town we'll capture them alive and come into the town."'

Was it just a coincidence? (1)

¹³One of his servants answered, 'People should please take five of the remaining horses, the ones that have remained here. There, they are like the entire horde of Yisra'el that have remained here: there they are, like the entire horde of Yisra'el that have come to an end. So let's send them and see.'

¹⁴They got two chariots of horses and the king sent them after the Aramite camp, saying 'Go and see.' ¹⁵They followed them as far as the Yarden and there, the entire road was full of clothes and articles that the Aramites had thrown away in their haste. The envoys came back and told the king. ¹⁶So the people went out and plundered the Aramite camp, and it was a measure of fine flour for a sheqel and two measures of barley for a sheqel, in accordance with Yahweh's word.

¹⁷Now in charge of the gateway the king had appointed the adjutant on whose hand he leaned, and the people trampled on him in the gateway and he died, as the supernatural man had spoken when the king went down to him, ¹⁸when the supernatural man said to the king, 'Two measures of barley for a sheqel and a measure of fine flour for a sheqel, it will be at this very time tomorrow at the gateway of Shomron.' ¹⁹The adjutant had answered the supernatural man, 'There, were Yahweh making apertures in the heavens, would something such as this happen?' And he had said, 'There, you're going to see it with your eyes, but you won't eat of it.' ²⁰It happened to him. The people trampled him in the gateway and he died.

Was it just a coincidence? (2)

8 Now Elisha had spoken to the woman whose son he brought to life: 'Set off and go, you and your household, and reside wherever you can reside, because Yahweh has called for a famine and it is indeed going to come on the country for seven years.' ²The woman set off and acted in accordance with the word of the supernatural man. She went, she and her household, and resided in the Pelishtites' [Philistines'] country seven years.

³At the end of the seven years the woman came back from the Pelishtites' country and went out to cry out to the king about her house and about her fields. ⁴The king was speaking with Gehazi, the supernatural man's boy, saying, 'Please tell me all the big things that Elisha has done.' ⁵He was recounting to the king how he had brought the dead person to life, and there, the woman whose son he had brought to life was crying out to the king about her house and about her fields. Gehazi said, 'My lord king, this is the woman and this is her son whom Elisha brought to life.' ⁶The king asked the woman and she recounted it to him, and the king gave her a courtier, saying, 'Get back all that belongs to her and all the yield from her fields from the day she abandoned the country until now.'

⁷Elisha came to Dammeseq, when Ben-hadad king of Aram was ill. It had been told him, 'The supernatural man is coming here.' ⁸The king said to Haza'el, 'Take an offering in your hand and go to meet the supernatural man and enquire of Yahweh from him, "Will I live on after this illness?"'

The assassination

⁹Haza'el went to meet him and took an offering in his hand, all the good things of Dammeseq, forty camel loads. He came and stood before him and said, 'Your son, Ben-hadad king of Aram, sent me to you, saying "Will I live on after this illness?"' ¹⁰Elisha said to him, 'Go say to him: "You will definitely live on." But Yahweh has let me see that he will definitely die.' ¹¹He made his face stay firm, until he was shamed. But the supernatural man cried, ¹²and Haza'el said, 'Why is my lord crying?' He said, 'Because I know the bad things that you will do to the Yisra'elites. Their fortifications you will set on fire. Their young men you will slay with the sword. Their little ones you will tear to pieces. Their pregnant women you will rip open.' ¹³Haza'el said, 'What is your servant, a dog, that he should do this big thing?' Elisha said, 'Yahweh has let me see you as king over Aram.'

¹⁴He went from Elisha and came to his lord. He said to him 'What did Elisha say to you?' He said, 'He said to me, "You will definitely live on."' ¹⁵But next day he got a cloth, dipped it in water and spread it over his

face, and he died. So Haza'el began to reign in place of him.

¹⁶In the fifth year of Yoram ben Ah'ab king of Yisra'el, whereas Yehoshaphat had been king of Yehudah, Yehoram ben Yehoshaphat began to reign as king of Yehudah. ¹⁷He was a man of thirty-two years when he began to reign and he reigned eight years in Yerushalaim.

¹⁸He walked in the way of the kings of Yisra'el, as Ah'ab's household had done, because he had Ah'ab's daughter as wife. He did what was bad in Yahweh's eyes. ¹⁹But Yahweh was not willing to devastate Yehudah, for the sake of David his servant, as he had said to him that he would give him hegemony for his sons for all time.

Two kings called Yoram/Yehoram

²⁰In his days Edom rebelled from under Yehudah's hand, and they made a king reign over themselves. ²¹Yoram crossed to Tsa'ir, he and all the chariotry with him. He set off by night and struck down the Edomites (who were surrounding him) and the chariotry officers, and the company fled to their tents. ²²But Edom has rebelled from under Yehudah's hand until this day. Then Libnah rebelled at this time.

²³The rest of the things about Yoram and all that he did are written on the document about things of the time regarding the kings of Yehudah, aren't they. ²⁴Yoram lay down with his ancestors and was buried with his ancestors in David's Town, and Ahazyahu his son began to reign in place of him.

²⁵It was in the twelfth year of Yoram ben Ah'ab king of Yisra'el that Ahazyahu ben Yehoram began to reign in Yehudah. ²⁶Ahazyahu was a man of twenty-two years when he began to reign and he reigned one year in Yerushalaim. His mother's name was Atalyahu bat Omri, king of Yisra'el.

²⁷He walked in the way of the household of Ah'ab and did what was bad in Yahweh's eyes like Ah'ab's household, because he was an in-law of Ah'ab's household. ²⁸He went with Yoram ben Ah'ab for battle with Haza'el king of Aram at Heights-in-Gil'ad. The Aramites struck down Yoram, ²⁹and King Yoram went back to heal in Yizre'e'l from the wounds with which the Aramites had struck him down at The Height when he was battling with Haza'el king of Aram, while Ahazyahu ben Yehoram king of Yehudah went down to see Yoram ben Ah'ab because he was ill.

The anointing of another assassin

9 Now Elisha the prophet had called one of the people who prophesied and said to him, 'Wrap things round your hips, take this flask of oil in your hand and go to Heights-in-Gil'ad. ²When you come there, look for Yehu ben Yehoshaphat son of Nimshi, there. You're to come and get him up from among his brothers and bring him to an inner room. ³Take the flask of oil, pour it on his head and say, "Yahweh has said this: 'I anoint you king over Yisra'el'", and open the door and flee; don't wait.'

⁴So the boy (the prophet's boy) went to Heights-in-Gil'ad. ⁵When he came, there, the officers of the force were sitting. He said, 'I have a word for you, officer.' Yehu said, 'For whom out of all of us?' He said, 'For you, officer.'

⁶He got up and came into the house, and he poured the oil on his head and said to him, 'Yahweh, the God of Yisra'el, has said this: "I anoint you king for Yahweh's people, for Yisra'el. ⁷You're to strike down the household of Ah'ab, your lord, and I will take redress from the hand of Izebel [Jezebel] for the shed blood of my servants the prophets and the shed blood of all Yahweh's servants. ⁸The entire household of Ah'ab will perish, and I shall cut off for Ah'ab the one who pisses against a wall (bond or freed) in Yisra'el. ⁹I shall make Ah'ab's household like the household of Yarob'am ben Nebat and like the household of Ba'sha ben Ahiyyah. ¹⁰And Izebel: the dogs will eat her in a Yizre'e'l plot and there will be no one burying her.' And he opened the door and fled.

The man who drives like a madman

¹¹When Yehu went out to his lord's servants, they said to him, 'Are things well? Why did this madman come to you?' He said to them, 'You know the man and his talk.' ¹²They said, 'Lies! Tell us, please.' He said, 'This and that

very thing he said to me: "Yahweh has said this: 'I anoint you king for Yisra'el.'"' ¹³They made speed and got each person his coat and put it under him on the top step, and blew on a horn and said, 'Yehu has become king!' ¹⁴So Yehu ben Yehoshaphat son of Nimshi conspired against Yoram.

Now Yoram had been keeping watch at Heights-in-Gil'ad, he and all Yisra'el, from before Haza'el king of Aram, ¹⁵but King Yehoram had gone back to heal in Yizre'e'l from the wounds with which the Aramites had struck him down when he was battling with Haza'el king of Aram.

So Yehu said, 'If it's your desire, no one is to escape and go out of the town to go to tell of it in Yizre'e'l.' ¹⁶Yehu got into his chariot and went to Yizre'e'l, because Yoram was lying there, and Ahazyah king of Yehudah had come down to see Yehoram. ¹⁷The lookout was standing on the tower in Yizre'e'l and saw Yehu's pack as it was coming. He said, 'I see a pack!' Yehoram said, 'Get a rider and send him to meet them. He's to say, "Are things well?"' ¹⁸The horse rider went to meet him and said, 'The king has said this: "Are things well?"' Yehu said, 'What do you and "Are things well" have in common? Turn round after me.' The lookout told them, 'The envoy came right to them, but he didn't come back.'

¹⁹He sent a second horse rider. He came to them and said, 'The king has said this: "Are things well?"' And Yehu said, 'What do you and "Are things well" have in common? Turn round after me.' ²⁰The lookout told them, 'The envoy came right to them, but he didn't come back. The driving is like the driving of Yehu ben Nimshi, because he drives like a madman.'

The whorings of Izebel

²¹Yehoram said, 'Hitch up!', and they hitched up his chariot. Yehoram king of Yisra'el went out, with Ahazyahu king of Yehudah, each in his chariot. They went out to meet Yehu, and found him on the plot of Nabot the Yizre'e'lite. ²²When Yehoram saw Yehu he said, 'Are things well, Yehu?' He said, 'What can be well while the whorings of Izebel your mother and her sorceries are so many?' ²³Yehoram turned his hands round and fled, and said to Ahazyahu, 'Guile, Ahazyah!', ²⁴as Yehu put his hand to his bow and struck down Yehoram between the shoulders. The arrow went out through his heart and he bowed down on his knees in his chariot.

²⁵He said to Bidqar his adjutant, 'Take him up, throw him into the plot of field belonging to Nabot the Yezre'e'lite, because remember me and you riding as a pair behind Ah'ab his father when Yahweh took up this oracle about him: ²⁶"If I did not see Nabot's shed blood and his sons' shed blood yesterday (Yahweh's proclamation) ... And I will make it good to you on this plot (Yahweh's proclamation)." So now take him up, throw him on the plot in accordance with Yahweh's word.'

²⁷When Ahazyah king of Yehudah saw it, he fled by the Bet Haggan road. Yehu pursued after him and said, 'Him as well, strike him down' – in his chariot at the Gur Ascent, which is by Yible'am. He fled to Megiddo and died there. ²⁸His servants took him in a chariot to Yerushalaim and buried him in his grave with his ancestors in David's Town. ²⁹It had been in the eleventh year of Yoram ben Ah'ab that Ahazyah began to reign over Yehudah.

Izebel puts on her make-up

³⁰Yehu came to Yizre'e'l, and when Izebel heard, she put mascara on her eyes and made her hair look good and watched through the window. ³¹When Yehu came through the gateway, she said 'Are things well, Zimri, slayer of his lord?' ³²He lifted his face to the window and said, 'Who is with me? Who?' Two or three courtiers looked towards him. ³³He said, 'Drop her down!' They dropped her down, and some of her blood spattered on the wall and on the horses, and they trampled her.

³⁴He came in and ate and drank, and said 'Please attend to this accursed woman and bury her, because she's the daughter of a king.' ³⁵They went to bury her, but they couldn't find anything of her, only the skull and the feet and the palms of her hands. ³⁶They came back and told him, and he said, 'It's Yahweh's word that he spoke by means of his servant Eliyyahu the Tishbite: "On a Yizre'e'l plot the dogs will eat Izebel's flesh. ³⁷Izebel's carcase will be like manure on the face of the fields on a Yizre'e'l plot, so that people cannot say, 'This is Izebel.'"'

10 Now Ah'ab had seventy sons in Shomron. Yehu wrote documents and sent them to Shomron, to the officials in Yizre'e'l, the elders, and to Ah'ab's guardians, saying, ²'Now, when this document comes to you, and your lord's sons are with you, and chariotry and horses are with you, and a fortified city, and weaponry, ³see who is the best and most upright of your lord's sons, put him on his father's throne and do battle for your lord's household.' ⁴But they were very, very fearful, and said, 'Here, two kings didn't stand before him; how can we stand?' ⁵So the one in charge of the household, the one in charge of the town, the elders and the guardians sent to Yehu saying, 'We are your servants. Everything that you say to us we will do. We will not make anyone king. Do what is good in your eyes.'

Seventy heads fall

⁶So he wrote them a second document: 'If you're on my side and you're going to listen to my voice, take the heads of the men (your lord's sons) and come to me this very time tomorrow in Yizre'e'l.' The king's sons, seventy of them, were with the big people in the town, who were bringing them up. ⁷When the document came to them, they got the king's sons, slaughtered the seventy, put their heads in baskets and sent them to him in Yizre'e'l. ⁸An envoy came and told him, 'They've brought the heads of the king's sons.' He said, 'Put them in two heaps at the entrance to the town gateway until morning.' ⁹In the morning he went out and stood and said to the entire people, 'You are in the right. There, I myself conspired against my lord and killed him, but who struck down all these? ¹⁰Acknowledge how nothing will fall to the earth of Yahweh's word, which Yahweh spoke concerning the household of Ah'ab, since Yahweh has done what he spoke by means of his servant Eliyyahu.' ¹¹Yehu struck down all that remained of the household of Ah'ab in Yizre'e'l, and all his big people, his friends and his priests, until he let no survivor remain to him.

¹²Then he set off; he came, and went to Shomron; he was at the shepherds' binding house on the way, ¹³and when Yehu found brothers of Ahazyahu king of Yehudah, he said, 'Who are you?' They said, 'We are brothers of Ahazyahu. We've come down regarding whether things are well with the king's sons and the queen's sons.' ¹⁴He said, 'Capture them alive.' They captured them alive but slew them at the binding house cistern, forty-two individuals. He didn't let one of them remain.

The great festival for Ba'al

¹⁵He went from there and found Yehonadab ben Rekab, coming to meet him. He blessed him and said to him, 'Is your mind upright, as my mind is with your mind?' Yehonadab said, 'It is.' 'Since it is, give me your hand.' He gave him his hand and took him up to him into the chariot. ¹⁶He said, 'Go with me and see my passion for Yahweh.' So he got him to ride in his chariot. ¹⁷He came to Shomron and struck down all the people who remained to Ah'ab in Shomron until he had annihilated them, in accordance with Yahweh's word that he spoke to Eliyyahu.

¹⁸Yehu collected all the people and said to them, 'Whereas Ah'ab served the Master a little, Yehu will serve him much. ¹⁹So now, all the Master's prophets, all his servants and all his priests – call them to me. Not one is to be counted missing, because I have a big sacrifice for the Master. No one who is counted missing will live.' Yehu was acting with guile in order that he might obliterate the Master's servants.

²⁰So Yehu said, 'Make a sacred assembly for the Master', and they called it. ²¹Yehu sent through all Yisra'el, and all the Master's servants came. Not one remained who didn't come. They came to the Master's house; the Master's house filled, end to end. ²²He said to the person in charge of the wardrobe, 'Get out apparel for all the Master's servants.' He got the apparel out for them. ²³Yehu came with Yehonadab ben Rekab into the Master's house and said to the Master's servants, 'Search, and see that there are none of Yahweh's servants here with you, but rather the Master's servants alone.' ²⁴They came to make sacrifices and burnt offerings, while Yehu had placed for himself eighty people outside and had said, 'The individual who escapes from the people that I am bringing into your hands: his life in place of his life.'

The sacrifice

²⁵When he'd finished making the burnt offering, Yehu said to the runners and to the adjutants, 'Come, strike them down. No one is to get out.' The runners and the adjutants struck them down with the edge of the sword and threw them down. They went right to the town in the Master's house, ²⁶got out the columns in the Master's house and burned them. ²⁷They demolished the Master's columns and demolished the Master's house and turned it into latrines, until this day.

²⁸So Yehu annihilated the Master from Yisra'el; ²⁹only, the wrongdoings of Yarob'am ben Nebat that he caused Yisra'el to commit – Yehu did not depart from them (the gold bullocks that were at Bet-el and that were at Dan). ³⁰But Yahweh said to Yehu, 'Since you've done what is good, in doing what was upright in my eyes (in accordance with all that was in my mind you have acted towards the household of Ah'ab), sons to the fourth [generation] will sit on Yisra'el's throne for you.' ³¹But Yehu did not keep watch to walk by the instruction of Yahweh the God of Yisra'el with his entire mind. He did not depart from the wrongdoings of Yarob'am that he caused Yisra'el to commit.

³²In those days Yahweh began to reduce Yisra'el, and Haza'el struck them down through Yisra'el's entire territory ³³from the Yarden eastward, the entire region of Gil'ad (the Gadites, the Re'ubenites and the Menashshites), from Aro'er, which is by Wadi Arnon, both Gil'ad and Bashan.

³⁴The rest of the things about Yehu, all that he did and all his strength, are written on the document about things of the time regarding the kings of Yisra'el, aren't they. ³⁵Yehu lay down with his ancestors and they buried him in Shomron, and Yeho'az his son began to reign in place of him. ³⁶The time that Yehu had reigned over Yisra'el was twenty-eight years in Shomron.

The boy king-in-waiting

11 When Atalyah, Ahazyahu's mother, saw that her son was dead, she set to and obliterated all the royal offspring. ²But Yehosheba the daughter of King Yoram, sister of Ahazyahu, got Yo'ash ben Ahazyah and stole him away from among the king's sons who were being put to death, him and his nanny, in a bedroom. They concealed him from Atalyahu and he wasn't put to death. ³He was with her in Yahweh's house hiding six years, while Atalyah was reigning over the country. ⁴In the seventh year, Yehoyada sent and got the centurions of the Karites and of the runners and brought them to him into Yahweh's house. He solemnized a pact with them and made them swear in Yahweh's house, and let them see the king's son.

⁵He ordered them, 'This is the thing that you're to do: a third of you who are coming in on the sabbath and keeping watch over the king's house, ⁶a third at the Sur Gate and a third at the gateway behind the runners: you're to keep watch over the house, as a defence. ⁷The two sections among you, all who are going out on the sabbath, will keep watch over Yahweh's house for the king. ⁸You're to encircle the king all round, each man with his equipment in his hand. Anyone who comes against the ranks is to be put to death. Be with the king when he goes out and when he comes in.'

⁹The centurions acted in accordance with all that Yehoyada the priest ordered. They took each his men who were coming in on the sabbath with those who were going out on the sabbath, and came to Yehoyada the priest. ¹⁰The priest gave the centurions the lance and the bows that belonged to King David, which were in Yahweh's house. ¹¹The runners stood, each with his equipment in his hand, from the shoulder of the house on the right to the shoulder of the house on the left, at the altar and at the house, in charge of the king all round.

An unusual covenant

¹²Then he got the king's son out and put the diadem and the affirmation on him, and they made him king and anointed him. They clapped the palms of their hands and said 'Long live the king.'

¹³Atalyah heard the sound of the runners, the people, and came to the people at Yahweh's

house. ¹⁴She saw, there, the king was standing by the pillar in accordance with the ruling, the officials with the trumpets by the king, and the entire people of the country rejoicing and blowing on trumpets. Atalyah tore her clothes and called, 'Conspiracy, conspiracy!'

¹⁵Yehoyada the priest ordered the centurions appointed over the force, 'Take her out between the rows. The person who follows her, put to death with the sword' (because the priest said she should not be put to death in Yahweh's house). ¹⁶They laid hands on her and she came by way of the Horses' Entrance to the king's house, and she was put to death there.

¹⁷Yehoyada solemnized a pact between Yahweh, the king and the people, that they would be a people for Yahweh, and between the king and the people. ¹⁸The entire people of the country came to the Master's house and tore it down. Its altars and its images they broke up, doing it well, and Mattan, the Master's priest, they killed before the altars.

The priest set appointees over Yahweh's house. ¹⁹He got the centurions, the Karites, the runners and the entire people of the country, and they took the king down from Yahweh's house. They came by way of the Runners' Gate to the king's house, and he sat on the kings' throne.

²⁰The entire people of the country rejoiced, while the town was calm, when they had put Atalyahu to death with the sword at the king's house. ²¹Yeho'ash was seven years of age when he began to reign.

A plan to restore the temple

12 It was in the seventh year of Yehu that Yeho'ash began to reign and he reigned forty years in Yerushalaim. His mother's name was Tsibyah from Be'er-sheba. ²Yeho'ash did what was upright in Yahweh's eyes all his days that Yehoyada the priest taught him. ³Only, the shrines did not disappear; the people were still sacrificing and burning incense at the shrines.

⁴Yeho'ash said to the priests, 'All the silver from the sacred offerings that's brought into Yahweh's house, the silver that's current for an individual (the silver for persons), his evaluation, all the silver that it comes into an individual's mind to bring to Yahweh's house, ⁵the priests are to take for themselves, each from his assessor, and they themselves are to strengthen the defects in the house, everywhere a defect is found.'

⁶But in the twenty-third year of King Yeho'ash the priests had not strengthened the defects in the house. ⁷So King Yeho'ash called Yehoyada the priest, with the priests, and said to them, 'Why are you not strengthening the defects in the house? So now don't take the silver from your assessors but give it for the defects in the house.'

⁸The priests consented not to take silver from the people and not to strengthen the defects in the house. ⁹Yehoyada the priest got a chest, bored a hole in its lid and put it by the altar, on the right when one comes into Yahweh's house. The priests who were keeping watch over the threshold would put there all the silver that was brought to Yahweh's house. ¹⁰When they saw that the amount of silver in the chest was great, the royal scribe went up with the big priest and they tied up and counted the silver that was found in Yahweh's house.

Not the fate he deserved

¹¹So they would put the silver that had been quantified into the hands of the men doing the work, who had been appointed to Yahweh's house. They would have it go out to the carpenters and to the builders who were doing things in Yahweh's house, ¹²and to the masons and to the stonecutters, and for acquiring wood and dressed stones to strengthen the defects in Yahweh's house, and for all that would need to go out in connection with Yahweh's house. ¹³Yet silver basins, snuffers, bowls, trumpets, all gold articles and silver articles, were not made for Yahweh's house from the silver brought into Yahweh's house, ¹⁴because they would give it to the people doing the work so they would strengthen Yahweh's house.

¹⁵They didn't keep a reckoning of the men into whose hand they would give the silver to give to the people doing the work, because they were acting with trustworthiness. ¹⁶Reparation silver and decontamination silver would not be brought into Yahweh's house; it would be the priests'.

[17]Then Haza'el king of Aram went up and battled against Gat, and captured it, and Haza'el set his face to go up to Yerushalaim. [18]Yeho'ash king of Yehudah got all the sacred things that Yehoshaphat, Yehoram and Ahazyahu, his ancestors, kings of Yehudah, had made sacred, and his own sacred things, and all the gold that could be found in the treasuries of Yahweh's house and the king's house, and sent them to Haza'el king of Aram, and he went up from Yerushalaim.

[19]The rest of the things about Yo'ash, and all that he did, are written on the document about things of the time regarding the kings of Yehudah, aren't they. [20]His servants arose and formed a conspiracy, and struck down Yo'ash at Fill House, which goes down to Silla. [21]Yozabad ben Shim'at and Yehozabad ben Shomer, of his servants – they struck him down and he died. They buried him with his ancestors in David's Town, and Amatsyah his son began to reign in place of him.

God sees Yisra'el's affliction

13 In the twenty-third year of Yo'ash ben Ahazyahu king of Yehudah, Yeho'ahaz ben Yehu began to reign over Yisra'el in Shomron, for seventeen years. [2]He did what was bad in Yahweh's eyes and followed the wrongdoings of Yarob'am ben Nebat that he caused Yisra'el to commit. He did not depart from it.

[3]So Yahweh's anger raged against Yisra'el and he gave them into the hand of Haza'el king of Aram and into the hand of Ben-hadad ben Haza'el, all the time. [4]Yeho'ahaz sought to gain Yahweh's goodwill and Yahweh listened to him, because he saw Yisra'el's affliction, how the king of Aram afflicted them. [5]Yahweh gave Yisra'el a deliverer and they got out from under the hand of Aram, and the Yisra'elites lived in their tents as they had in previous days. [6]Yet they didn't depart from the wrongdoings of Yarob'am's household that it caused Yisra'el to commit. They walked in them, and further, the totem pole stood in Shomron. ([7]Because he didn't leave a company to Yeho'ahaz, except 50 cavalry, 10 chariotry and 10,000 men on foot, because the king of Aram had obliterated them and made them like earth for trampling.)

[8]The rest of the things about Yeho'ahaz and all that he did, and his strength, are written on the document about things of the time regarding the kings of Yisra'el, aren't they. [9]Yeho'ahaz lay down with his ancestors and they buried him in Shomron. Yo'ash his son began to reign in place of him. [10]It was in the thirty-seventh year of Yo'ash king of Yehudah that Yeho'ash ben Yeho'ahaz began to reign over Yisra'el in Shomron, for sixteen years. [11]He did what was bad in Yahweh's eyes. He didn't depart from all the wrongdoings of Yarob'am ben Nebat that he caused Yisra'el to commit. He walked in them.

[12]The rest of the things about Yo'ash, all that he did, and his strength in that he battled with Amatsyah king of Yehudah, are written on the document about things of the time regarding the kings of Yisra'el, aren't they. [13]Yo'ash lay down with his ancestors, and Yarob'am sat on his throne. Yo'ash was buried in Shomron with the kings of Yisra'el.

The God who has to be merciful

[14]Now Elisha was ill with the illness of which he died, and Yo'ash king of Yisra'el went down to him. He wept upon his face and said, 'Father, father, the chariotry of Yisra'el and its cavalry!' [15]Elisha said to him, 'Get a bow and arrows.' He got himself a bow and arrows. [16]He said to the king of Yisra'el, 'Mount your hand on the bow.' He mounted his hand. Elisha put his hands on the king's hands [17]and said, 'Open the window to the east.' He opened it. Elisha said, 'Shoot', and he shot. He said, 'Yahweh's deliverance arrow! A deliverance arrow against Aram! You will strike down Aram at Apheq so as to finish it off!'

[18]He said, 'Get the arrows', and he got them. He said to the king of Yisra'el, 'Strike the ground.' He struck three times, and stopped. [19]The supernatural man was furious with him and said, 'Striking five or six times! Then you would have struck Aram so as to finish it off, but now it will be three times that you strike Aram.'

[20]Elisha died and they buried him. Now raiding gangs from Mo'ab would come into the country at the coming of the new year. [21]People were burying someone and there – they saw a raiding band, and they threw the man into

Elisha's grave. He went, and touched Elisha's bones, and came to life and stood on his feet.

²²Now Haza'el king of Aram afflicted Yisra'el all the days of Yeho'ahaz, ²³but Yahweh was gracious to them and had compassion on them. He turned his face to them for the sake of his pact with Abraham, Yitshaq [Isaac] and Ya'aqob [Jacob]. He was not willing to devastate them, and he has not thrown them out from before his face until now.

²⁴Haza'el king of Aram died, and Ben-hadad his son began to reign in place of him. ²⁵Yeho'ash ben Yeho'ahaz took back again from the hand of Ben-hadad ben Haza'el the towns that he had taken from the hand of his father Yeho'ahaz in battle. Three times Yo'ash struck him down and got back the Yisra'elite towns.

Individuals are put to death for their own wrongdoing

14 In the second year of Yo'ash ben Yo'ahaz king of Yisra'el, Amatsyahu ben Yo'ash king of Yehudah began to reign. ²He was a man of twenty-five years when he began to reign and he reigned twenty-nine years in Yerushalaim. His mother's name was Yeho'addan from Yerushalaim. ³He did what was upright in Yahweh's eyes, only not like David his ancestor; in accordance with all that Yo'ash his father did, he did. ⁴Only, the shrines did not disappear; the people were still sacrificing and burning incense at the shrines.

⁵When the kingship was strong in his control, he struck down his servants who had struck down the king, his father. ⁶But the sons of the people who had struck him down, he did not put to death, as it is written in Mosheh's [Moses'] instruction document where Yahweh ordered: 'Parents will not be put to death for children and children will not be put to death for parents. Rather, an individual will be put to death for his own wrongdoing.' ⁷It was he who struck down Edom in Salt Ravine, 10,000, and captured The Cliff in the battle. He named it Yoqte'el, until now.

⁸Then Amatsyah sent envoys to Yeho'ash ben Yeho'ahaz son of Yehu, king of Yisra'el, saying, 'Come on, let's face each other.' ⁹Yeho'ash king of Yisra'el sent to Amatsyahu king of Yehudah, saying, 'A thistle that was in the Lebanon sent to a cedar that was in the Lebanon, saying "Give your daughter to my son as wife." But an animal of the wild that was in the Lebanon passed by and trampled the thistle. ¹⁰You have indeed struck down Edom and your mind has lifted you up. Enjoy your splendour but stay in your house. Why engage with bad fortune and fall, you and Yehudah with you?'

The king who didn't listen

¹¹Amatsyahu didn't listen. So Yeho'ash king of Yisra'el went up and they faced each other, he and Amatsyahu king of Yehudah at Bet-shemesh, which belongs to Yehudah. ¹²Yehudah took a beating before Yisra'el and they fled each man to his tents. ¹³Amatsyahu king of Yehudah, son of Yeho'ash ben Ahazyahu – Yeho'ash king of Yisra'el captured him at Bet-shemesh, came to Yerushalaim and broke down the Yerushalaim wall at the Ephrayim Gate as far as the Corner Gate, 200 metres. ¹⁴He took all the gold and the silver and all the articles that were to be found in Yahweh's house and in the treasuries of the king's house, and pledges, and went back to Shomron.

¹⁵The rest of the things about Yeho'ash, what he did, and his strength and how he battled with Amatsyahu king of Yehudah, are written on the document about things of the time regarding the kings of Yisra'el, aren't they. ¹⁶Yeho'ash lay down with his ancestors and was buried in Shomron with the kings of Yisra'el, and Yarob'am his son began to reign in place of him.

¹⁷Amatsyahu ben Yo'ash king of Yehudah lived after the death of Yeho'ash ben Yeho'ahaz king of Yisra'el fifteen years. ¹⁸The rest of the things about Amatsyahu are written on the document about things of the time regarding the kings of Yehudah, aren't they. ¹⁹People formed a conspiracy against him in Yerushalaim and he fled to Lakish, but they sent after him to Lakish and put him to death there. ²⁰But they carried him on horses and he was buried in Yerushalaim with his ancestors in David's Town. ²¹All the people of Yehudah got Azaryah (he was sixteen years of age) and made him king in place of his father Amatsyahu. ²²It was he who built up Elat. He had got it back for Yehudah after the king lay down with his ancestors.

The king who heard from Yonah [Jonah]

[23]In the fifteenth year of Amatsyahu ben Yo'ash king of Yehudah, Yarob'am ben Yo'ash king of Yisra'el began to reign in Shomron, for forty-one years. [24]He did what was bad in Yahweh's eyes; he didn't depart from all the wrongdoings of Yarob'am ben Nebat that he caused Yisra'el to commit. [25]It was he who got Yisra'el's territory back from Lebo Hamat as far as the Steppe Sea, in accordance with the word of Yahweh the God of Yisra'el which he spoke by means of his servant Yonah ben Amittay the prophet, who was from Gat-hepher. [26]Because Yahweh saw Yisra'el's very bitter humbling (neither bound nor freed) and there was no helper for Yisra'el. [27]Yahweh had not spoken of wiping out Yisra'el's name from under the heavens, and he delivered them by the hand of Yarob'am ben Yo'ash.

[28]The rest of the things about Yarob'am, all that he did, and his strength, how he battled and how he got back Dammeseq and Hamat belonging to Yehudah in Yisra'el, are written on the document about things of the time regarding the kings of Yisra'el, aren't they. [29]Yarob'am lay down with his ancestors, with the kings of Yisra'el, and Zekaryah his son began to reign in place of him.

15 It was in the twenty-seventh year of Yarob'am king of Yisra'el that Azaryah ben Amatsyah king of Yehudah began to reign. [2]He was sixteen years of age when he began to reign and he reigned fifty-two years in Yerushalaim. His mother's name was Yekolyahu from Yerushalaim. [3]He did what was upright in Yahweh's eyes in accordance with all that Amatsyahu his father did. [4]Only, the shrines did not disappear; the people were still sacrificing and burning incense at the shrines. [5]Yahweh touched the king and he was made scaly until the day of his death. He lived in a house apart, while Yotam the king's son was in charge of the household, exercising authority over the people in the country.

A war crime

[6]The rest of the things about Azaryahu and all that he did are written on the document about things of the time regarding the kings of Yehudah, aren't they. [7]Azaryah lay down with his ancestors and they buried him with his ancestors in David's Town, and Yotam his son began to reign in place of him.

[8]It was in the thirty-eighth year of Azaryahu king of Yehudah that Zekaryahu ben Yarob'am began to reign over Yisra'el in Shomron, for six months. [9]He did what was bad in Yahweh's eyes as his ancestors had done. He didn't depart from the wrongdoings of Yarob'am ben Nebat that he caused Yisra'el to commit. [10]Shallum ben Yabesh conspired against him; he struck him down before the people, put him to death and began to reign in place of him. [11]The rest of the things about Zekaryah, there they are, written on the document about things of the time regarding the kings of Yisra'el. [12]That was Yahweh's word which he spoke to Yehu: 'Sons to the fourth [generation] will sit on Yisra'el's throne for you.' So it came about.

[13]Shallum ben Yabesh began to reign in the thirty-ninth year of Uzziyyah king of Yehudah, and reigned for a full month in Shomron. [14]Menahem ben Gadi went up from Tirtsah, came to Shomron, and struck down Shallum ben Yabesh in Shomron and put him to death. He began to reign in place of him. [15]The rest of the things about Shallum and his conspiracy that he formed, there they are, written on the document about things of the time regarding the kings of Yisra'el.

[16]Then Menahem struck down Tiphsah and everyone who was in it and its territories, from Tirtsah, because it didn't open up, so he struck it down. He split open all its pregnant women.

The Assyrians start to cause trouble

[17]It was in the thirty-ninth year of Azaryah king of Yehudah that Menahem ben Gadi began to reign over Yisra'el, for ten years. [18]He did what was bad in Yahweh's eyes; he didn't depart from the wrongdoings of Yarob'am ben Nebat that he caused Yisra'el to commit, all his days. [19]Pul king of Ashshur [Assyria] came against the country, and Menahem gave Pul a thousand talents of silver so that his hands would be with him to strengthen the kingship in his hand. [20]Menahem put the silver out on Yisra'el, on all the forceful strong men, to give to the king of Ashshur, fifty sheqels of silver for

each man, and the king of Ashshur went back and did not stop there in the country.

²¹The rest of the things about Menahem and all that he did are written on the document about things of the time regarding the kings of Yisra'el, aren't they. ²²Menahem lay down with his ancestors, and Peqahyah his son began to reign in place of him.

²³It was in the fiftieth year of Azaryah king of Yehudah that Peqahyah ben Menahem began to reign over Yisra'el in Shomron, for two years. ²⁴He did what was bad in Yahweh's eyes; he didn't depart from the the wrongdoings that Yarob'am ben Nebat caused Yisra'el to commit. ²⁵Peqah ben Remalyahu, his adjutant, conspired against him and struck him down in Shomron in the citadel of the king's house (with Argob and with Aryeh, so along with him were fifty men from the Gil'adites). He put him to death and began to reign in place of him.

²⁶The rest of the things about Peqahyah, all that he did, there they are, written on the document about things of the time regarding the kings of Yisra'el.

Land begins to be lost

²⁷It was in the fifty-second year of Azaryah king of Yehudah that Peqah ben Remalyahu began to reign over Yisra'el in Shomron, for twenty years. ²⁸He did what was bad in Yahweh's eyes; he didn't depart from the wrongdoings that Yarob'am ben Nebat caused Yisra'el to commit. ²⁹In the days of Peqah king of Yisra'el, Tiglat-pil'eser king of Ashshur came and took Iyyon, Bet-ma'akah Meadow, Yanoah, Qedesh, Hatsor, Gil'ad, and the Galilee, the entire region of Naphtali, and exiled them to Ashshur.

³⁰Hoshea ben Elah formed a conspiracy against Peqah ben Remalyahu, and struck him down. He put him to death and began to reign in place of him, in the twentieth year of Yotam ben Uzziyyah. ³¹The rest of the things about Peqah and all that he did, there they are, written on the document about things of the time regarding the kings of Yisra'el.

³²It was in the second year of Peqah ben Remalyahu king of Yisra'el that Yotam ben Uzziyyahu king of Yehudah began to reign. ³³He was a man of twenty-five years when he began to reign and he reigned sixteen years in Yerushalaim. His mother's name was Yerusha bat Tsadoq. ³⁴He did what was upright in Yahweh's eyes; in accordance with all that Uzziyyahu his father had done, he did. ³⁵Only, the shrines did not disappear; the people were still sacrificing and burning incense at the shrines. It was he who built up the Upper Gate of Yahweh's house.

³⁶The rest of the things about Yotam that he did are written on the document about things of the time regarding the kings of Yehudah, aren't they. ³⁷During that time Yahweh began to send Retsin king of Aram and Peqah ben Remalyahu against Yehudah. ³⁸Yotam lay down with his ancestors and was buried with his ancestors in David his ancestor's town, and Ahaz his son began to reign in place of him.

How not to render to Caesar

16 It was in the seventeenth year of Peqah ben Remalyahu that Ahaz ben Yotam king of Yehudah began to reign. ²Ahaz was a man of twenty years when he began to reign and he reigned sixteen years in Yerushalaim. He did not do what was upright in the eyes of Yahweh his God like David his ancestor ³but walked in the way of the kings of Yisra'el. Further, his own son he passed through the fire in accordance with the offensive practices of the nations that Yahweh dispossessed from before the Yisra'elites. ⁴He sacrificed and burned incense at the shrines, on the hills and under every verdant tree.

⁵Then Retsin king of Aram and Peqah ben Remalyahu king of Yisra'el went up to Yerushalaim for battle. They besieged Ahaz but couldn't win the battle. ⁶At that time Retsin king of Aram took back Elat for Aram. He cleared out the Yehudahites from Elot, and Edomites came to Elat and have lived there until this day.

⁷Ahaz sent envoys to Tiglat-pileser king of Ashshur saying, 'I am your servant and your son. Go up and deliver me from the fist of the king of Aram and from the fist of the king of Yisra'el, who are rising up against me.' ⁸Ahaz got the silver and the gold that could be found in Yahweh's house and in the treasuries of the king's house and sent them to the king of Ashshur as a bribe, ⁹and the king of Ashshur

listened to him. The king of Ashshur went up to Dammeseq, captured it, exiled it to Qir and put Retsin to death.

¹⁰King Ahaz went to meet Tiglat-pileser king of Ashshur at Dammeseq, and saw the altar at Dammeseq. King Ahaz sent Uriyyah the priest a picture of the altar and a plan of it, for every aspect of making it, ¹¹and Uriyyah the priest built the altar. In accordance with all that King Ahaz had sent from Dammeseq, so Uriyyah the priest did, before King Ahaz came from Dammeseq.

A new altar

¹²The king came from Dammeseq and the king saw the altar. The king drew near the altar, went up on it, ¹³and turned into smoke his burnt offering and his grain offering, poured his libation, and tossed the blood of the well-being offerings that he had, on the altar.

¹⁴The copper altar that was before Yahweh, he brought near from the front of the house (between his altar and Yahweh's house) and put it by the side of his altar, to the north. ¹⁵King Ahaz ordered Uriyyah the priest, 'On the big altar, turn into smoke the morning burnt offering and the evening grain offering, the king's burnt offering and his grain offering, the burnt offering of the entire people of the country, their grain offering and their libations. All the blood of the burnt offering and all the blood of the sacrifice you're to toss on it. The copper altar will be for me to consult at.' ¹⁶Uriyyah the priest acted in accordance with all that King Ahaz ordered.

¹⁷King Ahaz cut off the stands' rims and removed the basin from on them, took down the sea from on the copper cattle that were beneath it and put it on a pavement of stones, ¹⁸and the sabbath covered-way that they had built in the house and the king's outside entrance he moved round to Yahweh's house, on account of the king of Ashshur.

¹⁹The rest of the things about Ahaz that he did are written on the document about things of the time regarding the kings of Yehudah, aren't they. ²⁰Ahaz lay down with his ancestors and was buried with his ancestors in David's Town, and Hizqiyyahu [Hezekiah] his son began to reign in place of him.

The fall of the northern kingdom

17 It was in the twelfth year of Ahaz king of Yehudah that Hoshea ben Elah began to reign over Yisra'el in Shomron, for nine years. ²He did what was bad in Yahweh's eyes, only not like the kings of Yisra'el who were before him.

³Shalman'eser king of Ashshur went up against him, and Hoshea became his servant and gave back an offering to him. ⁴But the king of Ashshur found a conspiracy in Hoshea, when he sent envoys to So king of Misrayim and did not take up an offering to the king of Ashshur, as he did year by year. So the king of Ashshur detained him, and confined him in the cells.

⁵Then the king of Ashshur went up against the entire country. He went up to Shomron and besieged it for three years. ⁶In the third year of Hoshea, the king of Ashshur took Shomron. He exiled Yisra'el to Ashshur and made them live at Halah and at Habor, the River Gozan and the towns of Maday [Media].

⁷It happened because the Yisra'elites did wrong in relation to Yahweh their God who had got them up from the country of Misrayim, from under the hand of Par'oh king of Misrayim [Pharaoh king of Egypt]. They had lived in awe of other gods ⁸and had walked by the decrees of the nations that Yahweh had dispossessed from before the Yisra'elites, and the kings of Yisra'el that they made.

⁹The Yisra'elites had imputed things that were not so to Yahweh their God and built for themselves shrines in all their towns, from a keepers' tower to a fortified town. ¹⁰They put up columns and totem poles for themselves on every lofty hill and under every verdant tree. ¹¹They burned incense there in all the shrines, like the nations that Yahweh exiled from before them. They undertook bad things so as to provoke Yahweh. ¹²They served idols, of which Yahweh had said to them, 'You will not do this thing.'

By means of every prophet

¹³Yahweh had testified against Yisra'el (and against Yehudah) by means of every prophet of his, every seer, saying, 'Turn back from your

bad ways, keep my orders and my decrees in accordance with the entire instruction that I ordered your ancestors and that I sent to you by means of my servants the prophets.' ¹⁴They didn't listen. They toughened their neck, like the neck of their ancestors who didn't trust in Yahweh their God. ¹⁵They rejected his decrees, his pact which he solemnized with their ancestors, and his affirmations which he testified against them. They followed hollowness and became hollow, followed the nations that were round them, ones that Yahweh had ordered them not to act like them.

¹⁶They abandoned all the orders of Yahweh their God, and made a cast image (two bullocks) for themselves, made a totem pole, bowed low to the entire heavenly army and served the Master. ¹⁷They made their sons and their daughters pass through fire, engaged in divination and practised augury, and sold themselves to do what was bad in Yahweh's eyes so as to provoke him.

¹⁸Yahweh showed himself very angry with Yisra'el and he removed them from before his face; only the clan of Yehudah remained, alone, ¹⁹though Yehudah, too, did not keep the orders of Yahweh their God but walked by the decrees of Yisra'el that they made.

²⁰So Yahweh rejected all Yisra'el's offspring and humbled them. He gave them into the hand of pillagers until he threw them out from his presence. ²¹When he tore Yisra'el from David's household, they made Yarob'am ben Nabat king, and Yarob'am drove Yisra'el away from following Yahweh and caused them to commit great wrong. ²²The Yisra'elites walked in all the wrongdoings of Yarob'am that he committed; they did not depart from them, ²³until Yahweh turned Yisra'el aside from his presence, as he spoke by means of all his servants the prophets. So Yisra'el went into exile from upon its soil to Ashshur, until this day.

The forced immigrants

²⁴The king of Ashshur brought people from Babel, from Kutah, from Avva, and from Hamat and Sepharvayim, and made them live in the towns of Shomron in place of the Yisra'elites. They took possession of Shomron and lived in its towns. ²⁵When they first lived there, they didn't live in awe of Yahweh, and Yahweh sent lions against them; they became killers among them. ²⁶They said to the king of Ashshur, 'The nations that you exiled and made to live in the towns of Shomron don't know the ruling of the country's god, and he's sent lions against them, and there, they are putting them to death, because they don't know the ruling of the country's god.'

²⁷So the king of Ashshur ordered, 'Make one of the priests go there that you exiled from there. They're to go and live there and instruct them in the ruling of the god of the land.' ²⁸So one of the priests that they exiled from

2 Kings 17: The fall of Ephrayim and Yehudah (Ephraim and Judah)

Shomron came and lived in Bet-el and was instructing them in how they were to live in awe of Yahweh. ²⁹But they were making nation by nation its own god, and they set them down in the house at the shrines that the Shomronites had made, nation by nation in their towns where they were living. ³⁰The people from Babel made Sukkot-benot, the people from Kut made Nergal, the people from Hamat made Ashima, ³¹the Avvites made Nibhaz and Tartaq, the Sepharvites were burning their children in fire for Adrammelek and Anammelek, the gods of Sepharvayim. ³²They were living in awe of Yahweh, but they made themselves shrine priests from their sections. They were acting for them in the houses at the shrines.

³³So they were living in awe of Yahweh and they were serving their gods in accordance with the ruling of the nations from which they had exiled them. ³⁴Until this day they are acting in accordance with the previous rulings. They are not living in awe of Yahweh and they are not acting in accordance with their decrees, with their rulings, with the instruction and with the order that Yahweh gave the sons of Ya'aqob, whose name he made into Yisra'el.

The copper snake

³⁵Yahweh had solemnized a pact with them and ordered them, 'You will not live in awe of other gods; you will not bow low to them, you will not serve them and you will not sacrifice to them. ³⁶Rather, Yahweh who got you up from the country of Misrayim by great energy and by an outstretched arm: you are to live in awe of him, bow low to him and sacrifice to him. ³⁷The decrees, the rulings, the instruction and the order that he wrote for you, you're to keep by acting on it, always. You will not live in awe of other gods. ³⁸The pact that I've solemnized with you, you will not put out of mind. You will not live in awe of other gods. ³⁹Rather you will live in awe of Yahweh your God, and it's he who will rescue you from the hand of all your enemies.' ⁴⁰But they hadn't listened. Rather they'd been acting in accordance with their previous ruling.

⁴¹And these nations became people who were in awe of Yahweh but were also serving their sculptures. Their children and grandchildren are also acting as their ancestors acted, until this day.

18 It was in the third year of Hoshea ben Elah king of Yisra'el that Hizqiyyah ben Ahaz began to reign as king of Yehudah. ²He was a man of twenty-five years when he began to reign and he reigned twenty-nine years in Yerushalaim. His mother's name was Abi bat Zekaryah. ³He did what was upright in Yahweh's eyes in accordance with all that David his ancestor did. ⁴It was he who removed the shrines, broke up the columns, cut down the totem pole, and crushed the copper snake that Mosheh had made, because until that time the Yisra'elites had been burning incense to it (it was called 'The Copper').

The faithfulness and the rebellion of Hizqiyyahu

⁵It was on Yahweh the God of Yisra'el that he relied. After him there was no one like him among all the kings of Yehudah, or that were before him. ⁶He stuck to Yahweh. He did not depart from following him but kept his orders, which Yahweh had given Mosheh, ⁷and Yahweh was with him. Wherever he went out, he thrived.

But he rebelled against the king of Ashshur and didn't serve him, ⁸and he himself struck down the Pelishtites as far as Azzah [Gaza] and its borders, from the keepers' tower to the fortified town.

⁹In the fourth year of King Hizqiyyahu (i.e. the seventh year of Hoshea ben Elah king of Yisra'el) Shalman'eser king of Ashshur went up against Shomron and besieged it. ¹⁰They captured it at the end of three years; in the sixth year of Hizqiyyah (i.e. the ninth year of Hoshea king of Yisra'el) Shomron was captured, ¹¹and the king of Ashshur exiled the Yisra'elites to Ashshur and settled them in Halah and in Habor, the River Gozan and the towns of Maday, ¹²because of the fact that they didn't listen to the voice of Yahweh their God but transgressed his pact, all that Mosheh Yahweh's servant had ordered. They didn't listen and they didn't act.

¹³In the fourteenth year of King Hizqiyyahu, Sanherib [Sennacherib] king of Ashshur went up against all the fortified towns of Yehudah and captured them. ¹⁴Hizqiyyah king of

Yehudah sent to the king of Ashshur at Lakish saying, 'I have done wrong. Turn back from me. What you put upon me, I will carry.' The king of Ashshur placed on Hizqiyyah king of Yehudah 300 talents of silver and thirty talents of gold. ¹⁵Hizqiyyah gave him all the silver that could be found in Yahweh's house and in the treasuries of the king's house. ¹⁶At that time Hizqiyyah cut down the doors of Yahweh's palace and the posts that Hizqiyyah king of Yehudah had overlaid, and gave them to the king of Ashshur.

Shut up like a bird in a cage (as Sanherib put it)

¹⁷The king of Ashshur sent the Tartan, the Rab-saris and the Rab-shaqeh from Lakish to King Hizqiyyahu in Yerushalaim with a heavy force. They went up, and came to Yerushalaim and stood at the Upper Pool channel, which is by the Washer's Field causeway. ¹⁸They called to the king, and Elyaqim ben Hilqiyyahu who was in charge of the household, Shebna the secretary and Yo'ah ben Asaph the recorder went out to them.

¹⁹The Rab-shaqeh said to them, 'Say to Hizqiyyahu, please, "The Great King, the king of Ashshur, has said this: 'What is this reliance that you have? ²⁰You've said, "Just the word on some lips are counsel and strength for the battle." Now, on whom have you relied, that you've rebelled against me? ²¹Now, there, you've relied for yourself on the support of this broken reed, on Misrayim, which when someone leans on it, comes into his palm and pierces it. Such is Par'oh king of Misrayim to all the people who rely on him. ²²But when you say to me, "On Yahweh our God – we've relied on him", he's the one whose shrines and whose altars Hizqiyyahu has removed, isn't he, and who's said to Yehudah and to Yerushalaim, "Before this altar you're to bow low in Yerushalaim."

²³But now, please make a wager with my lord the king of Ashshur. I'll give you 2,000 horses if you can put riders on them for yourself. ²⁴So how could you turn back the face of the governor of one of my lord's lesser servants and rely on Misrayim for chariotry and for cavalry for yourself? ²⁵Is it now without Yahweh that I've gone up to this place to devastate it? It was Yahweh who said to me, "Go up to this country and devastate it."'"'

Don't speak in their language

²⁶Elyaqim ben Hilqiyyahu, Shebna and Yo'ah said to the Rab-shaqeh, 'Please speak to your servants in Aramaic, because we're listening. Don't speak to us in Yehudahite in the ears of the people, which is on the wall.' ²⁷The Rab-shaqeh said to them, 'Was it to your lord and to you that my lord sent me to speak these words? Wasn't it to the individuals who are sitting on the wall, to eat their faeces and to drink the water between their legs with you?'

²⁸The Rab-shaqeh stood and called in a loud voice in Yehudahite, and spoke: 'Listen to the word of the Great King, the king of Ashshur. ²⁹The king has said this: "Hizqiyyahu must not deceive you", because he won't be able to rescue you from his hand. ³⁰And Hizqiyyahu must not get you to rely on Yahweh, saying "Yahweh will definitely rescue us; this town won't be given into the hand of the king of Ashshur." ³¹Don't listen to Hizqiyyahu.

Because the king of Ashshur has said this: "Make a blessing [agreement]with me. Go out to me, and eat each one his vine and each one his fig tree, and drink each one the water from his cistern, ³²until I come and take you to a country like your country, a country of grain and new wine, a country of bread and vineyards, a country of fresh olive oil and syrup, and you will live and not die. Don't listen to Hizqiyyahu when he incites you, saying, 'Yahweh will rescue us.' ³³Have the gods of the nations actually rescued, one of them, his country from the hand of the king of Ashshur? ³⁴Where were the gods of Hamat and Arpad? Where were the gods of Sepharvayim, Hena and Ivvah? Indeed did they rescue Shomron from my hand? ³⁵Who was it among all the gods of the countries that rescued their country from my hand, that Yahweh should rescue Yerushalaim from my hand?"'

Perhaps Yahweh will listen

³⁶They were silent. They didn't answer him a word, because it was the king's order, 'Don't

answer him.' ³⁷But Elyaqim ben Hilqiyyah who was in charge of the household, Shebna the secretary and Yo'ah ben Asaph the recorder came to Hizqiyyahu, their clothes torn, and told him the Rab-shaqeh's words.

19 When King Hizqiyyahu heard, he tore his clothes and covered himself in sack. He came into Yahweh's house ²but he sent Elyaqim, who was in charge of the household, Shebna the secretary and the priestly elders, covering themselves in sack, to Yesha'yahu [Isaiah] ben Amots the prophet. ³They said to him, 'Hizqiyyahu has said this: "This is a day of pressure, reproof and disdain, because 'children have come to breaking but there's no energy to give birth'. ⁴Perhaps Yahweh your God will listen to all the words of the Rab-shaqeh, whom the king of Ashshur his lord sent to revile the living God, and will issue a reproof for the words that Yahweh your God heard, and you will lift up a plea on behalf of the remains that are to be found here."'

⁵King Hizqiyyahu's servants came to Yesha'yahu, ⁶and Yesha'yahu said to them, 'You're to say this to your lord: "Yahweh has said this: 'Don't be afraid before the words you've heard with which the king of Ashshur's boys have insulted me. ⁷Here, I'm going to put a spirit in him, and he'll hear a report and go back to his country, and I shall cause him to fall by the sword in his country.'"'

⁸The Rab-shaqeh went back and found the king of Ashshur battling against Libnah, because he heard that he had moved on from Lakish, ⁹ᵃand he heard about Tirhaqah king of Kush [Sudan], 'There, he's gone out to battle with you.'

What to do with tricky mail

⁹ᵇHe again sent envoys to Hizqiyyahu, saying ¹⁰'You're to say this to Hizqiyyahu king of Yehudah: "Your God on whom you're relying mustn't deceive you, saying, 'Yerushalaim won't be given into the hand of the king of Ashshur.' ¹¹Here, you yourself have heard what the kings of Ashshur have done to all the countries, devoting them, and are you the one who'll be rescued? ¹²Did the gods of the nations that my ancestors devastated rescue them – Gozan, Harran, Retseph, and the Edenites who were in Tela'ssar? ¹³Where is the king of Hamat, the king of Arpad, the king of La'ir, Sepharvayim, Hena and Yivvah?"'

¹⁴Hizqiyyahu took the documents from the envoys' hand, read them out and went up to Yahweh's house. Hizqiyyahu spread it before Yahweh, ¹⁵and Hizqiyyahu pleaded before Yahweh: 'Yahweh, Yisra'el's God, sitting above the sphinxes: you are God, you alone, for all the kingdoms of the earth. You are the one who made the heavens and the earth. ¹⁶Yahweh, bend your ear and listen. Yahweh, open your eyes and see. Listen to the words of Sanherib that he has sent to revile the living God.

¹⁷Truly, Yahweh, the kings of Ashshur have put to the sword the nations, and their own country, ¹⁸and put their gods into the fire, because they were not gods but rather the making of human hands, wood and stone, and they obliterated them. ¹⁹But now, Yahweh our God, please deliver us from his hand, so that all the kingdoms of the earth may acknowledge that you alone are Yahweh God.'

²⁰Yesha'yahu ben Amots sent to Hizqiyyahu saying, 'Yahweh, Yisra'el's God, with whom you pleaded concerning Sanherib king of Ashshur, has said this: "I have heard." ²¹ᵃThis is the word that Yahweh has spoken about him.

Yahweh's own ridicule

²¹ᵇMaiden Miss Tsiyyon
    despises you, she ridicules you.
Behind you Miss Yerushalaim
    has shaken her head.
²²Whom have you reviled and insulted,
    against whom have you lifted your voice?
You've raised your eyes on high
    against Yisra'el's sacred one.
²³By the hand of your envoys
    you've reviled the Lord, and said:
'With the large number of my chariotry
    I'm the one who's gone up
to the mountains' height,
    Lebanon's farthest parts.
I've cut down the highest of its cedars,
    the choicest of its junipers.
I've come to its ultimate lodge,
    its forest of farmland.

²⁴'I'm the one who's dug
   and drunk foreign water.
I've dried with the sole of my feet
   all Misrayim's streams.'

²⁵Haven't you heard?
   – long ago I did it.
In days of old I formed it;
   now I've made it come about.
It's happened, crashing fortified towns
   into wasted heaps.
²⁶Their inhabitants, short of ability,
   are scared and shamed.
They were vegetation of the fields,
   green herbage,
Grass on the roofs,
   blasted before it grows up.
²⁷Your staying, your going out, and your
      coming I know,
   and your raging at me.
²⁸Since you raged at me,
   and your din came up into my ears,
I shall put my hook in your nose,
   my bit in your mouth,
I shall make you go back
   by the way that you came.

The promise for Hizqiyyahu

²⁹This will be the sign for you:

This year, eat the natural growth;
   in the second year, the secondary
      growth.
In the third year sow and reap,
   plant vineyards and eat their fruit.
³⁰An escape group from Yehudah's household
      that remains
   will add root downwards and produce fruit
      above.
³¹Because a remainder will go out from
      Yerushalaim,
   and an escape group from Mount Tsiyyon.
The passion of Yahweh of Armies
   will do this.

³²Therefore Yahweh has said this concerning
the king of Ashshur:

He will not come into this town;
   he will not shoot an arrow there.

He will not approach it with a shield;
   he will not heap up a ramp against it.
³³By the way that he comes he will go back;
   into this city he will not come
      (Yahweh's declaration).
³⁴I will shield this town so as to deliver it,
   for my sake and for the sake of David my
      servant.

³⁵That night Yahweh's envoy went out and struck down 185,000 in the Ashshurites' camp. People started early in the morning – there, all of them were dead corpses.

³⁶Sanherib king of Ashshur moved on and went, and returned and lived in Nineveh. ³⁷He was bowing low in the house of Nisrok his god when Adrammelek and Sar'etser his sons struck him down with the sword. While they escaped to the country of Ararat, Esar-haddon his son began to reign in place of him.

How to gain God's sympathy

20 In those days Hizqiyyahu became deathly ill. Yesha'yahu ben Amots the prophet came to him and said to him, 'Yahweh has said this: "Give orders to your household, because you're dying. You won't live on."' ²He turned his face round to the wall and pleaded with Yahweh, ³'Oh, Yahweh, please be mindful of how I've walked about before you in truth and with a perfect mind, and done what is good in your eyes.' Hizqiyyahu cried and cried much.

⁴Yesha'yahu had not gone out of the middle courtyard when Yahweh's word came to him: ⁵'Go back and say to Hizqiyyahu, the chief of my people, "Yahweh, the God of David your ancestor, has said this: 'I have listened to your plea, I've seen your tears. Here, I'm going to heal you. On the third day you'll go up to Yahweh's house. ⁶I shall add fifteen years to your time. From the fist of the king of Ashshur I shall rescue you and this town, and I shall shield this town for my sake and for David my servant's sake.'"' ⁷Yesha'yahu said, 'Get a block of figs.' They got one and put it on the inflammation and he lived on.

⁸Hizqiyyahu had said to Yesha'yahu, 'What will be the sign that Yahweh will heal me and I shall go up to Yahweh's house on the third day?' ⁹Yesha'yahu said, 'This will be the sign for you

from Yahweh that Yahweh will do the thing that he has spoken of. The shadow has gone ten steps. Can it go back ten steps?' [10]Yehizqiyyahu said, 'It's a slight thing for the shadow to extend ten steps, not that the shadow should turn back ten steps.' [11]So Yesha'yahu the prophet called to Yahweh and he made the shadow go back ten steps on the steps where it had gone down, on the steps of Ahaz.

How to lose God's sympathy

[12]At that time Ber'odak Bal'adan ben Bal'adan king of Babel sent documents and an offering to Hizqiyyahu because he had heard that Hizqiyyahu was ill. [13]Hizqiyyahu heard about them and let them see his entire repository house, the silver, the gold, the spices and the fine oil, and his equipment house and everything that was to be found in his storehouses. There was not a thing that Hizqiyyahu didn't let them see in his house and in his entire realm.

[14]Yesha'yahu the prophet came to King Hizqiyyahu and said to him, 'What did these men say? Where did they come from to you?' Hizqiyyahu said, 'From a far country; they came from Babel.' [15]He said, 'What did they see in your house?' Hizqiyyahu said, 'They saw everything that's in my house. There wasn't a thing that I didn't let them see in my storehouses.'

[16]Yesha'yahu said to Hizqiyyahu, 'Listen to Yahweh's word: [17]"There, days are going to come when everything that's in your house, and that your ancestors have stored up until this day, will be carried to Babel. Not a thing will be left", Yahweh has said. [18]"Some of your descendants who will issue from you, whom you will father, will be taken and will become courtiers in the palace of the king of Babel."'

[19]Hizqiyyahu said to Yesha'yahu, 'The word of Yahweh that you have spoken is good.' He said, 'Isn't it so, if there'll be well-being and truthfulness in my days?'

[20]The rest of the things about Hizqiyyahu and all his strength, and how he made the pool and the channel and brought the water into the town, are written on the document about things of the time regarding the kings of Yehudah. [21]Hizqiyyahu lay down with his ancestors and Menashsheh his son began to reign in place of him.

How to be the bad guy

21 Menashsheh was twelve years of age when he began to reign and he reigned fifty-five years in Yerushalaim. His mother's name was Hephtsibah. [2]He did what was bad in Yahweh's eyes in accordance with the offensive practices of the nations that Yahweh dispossessed from before the Yisra'elites. [3]He rebuilt the shrines that Hizqiyyahu his father obliterated, and set up altars for the Master and made a totem pole, as Ah'ab king of Yisra'el had done. He bowed low to all the heavenly army and served them. [4]He built altars in Yahweh's house of which Yahweh had said, 'In Yerushalaim I will put my name.' [5]He built altars for all the heavenly army in the two courtyards of Yahweh's house. [6]He made his son pass through fire and practised augury and divination and dealt with ghosts and spirits. He did much that was bad in Yahweh's eyes, so as to provoke him.

[7]He put a sculpture of Asherah that he made in the house of which Yahweh said to David and to Shelomoh [Solomon] his son, 'In this house and in Yerushalaim, which I chose from all Yisra'el's clans, I will put my name permanently. [8]And I shall not continue to make Yisra'el's foot wander from the land that I gave their ancestors, only if they keep watch to act in accordance with all that I ordered them, and regarding the entire instruction that my servant Mosheh ordered them.' [9]But they didn't listen, and Menashsheh got them to wander so as to deal badly more than the nations that Yahweh annihilated from before the Yisra'elites.

[10]Yahweh spoke by means of his servants the prophets: [11]"Since Menashsheh king of Yehudah has done these offensive things (he has dealt badly more than all that the Amorites did who were before him) and has also caused Yehudah to do wrong with his idols, [12]therefore Yahweh the God of Yisra'el has said this: "Here, I am going to bring bad fortune on Yerushalaim and Yehudah such that everyone who hears it – both his ears will screech.

Wiping the dish clean

[13]Over Yerushalaim I will stretch Shomron's measuring line and the household of Ah'ab's

scale. I will wipe Yerushalaim clean as one wipes a dish clean, wipe it and turn it on its face. ¹⁴I will leave the remains of my domain and give them into the hand of their enemies. They will be plunder and spoil for all their enemies, ¹⁵since they've done what is bad in my eyes and they've been provoking me from the day that I got their ancestors out of Misrayim until this day."'

¹⁶Further, Menashsheh poured out very much blood of people who were free of guilt, until he filled Yerushalaim end to end, beside the wrong that he caused Yehudah to commit in doing what was bad in Yahweh's eyes. ¹⁷The rest of the things about Menashsheh, all that he did and the wrongdoing that he committed, are written on the document about things of the time regarding the kings of Yehudah, aren't they. ¹⁸Menashsheh lay down with his ancestors and was buried in the garden of his house, in Uzza's Garden, and Amon his son began to reign in place of him.

¹⁹Amon was a man of twenty-two years when he began to reign and he reigned two years in Yerushalaim. His mother's name was Meshullemet bat Haruts, from Yotbah. ²⁰He did what was bad in Yahweh's eyes, as Menashsheh his father did. ²¹He walked in all the way that his father walked, and served the idols that his father served and bowed low to them. ²²He abandoned Yahweh, his ancestors' God, and did not walk in Yahweh's way. ²³Amon's servants conspired against him and put the king to death in his house, ²⁴but the people of the country struck down all those who had conspired against King Amon. The people of the country made Yo'shiyyahu [Josiah] king in place of him.

²⁵The rest of the things about Amon that he did are written on the document about things of the time regarding the kings of Yehudah, aren't they. ²⁶They buried him in his grave in Uzza's Garden, and his son Yo'shiyyahu began to reign in place of him.

Last chance to take the Torah and the Prophets seriously

22 Yo'shiyyahu was eight years of age when he began to reign and he reigned thirty-one years in Yerushalaim. His mother's name was Yedidah bat Adayah, from Botsqat. ²He did what was upright in Yahweh's eyes and walked in the entire way of David his ancestor. He did not depart right or left.

³In the eighteenth year of King Yo'shiyyahu, the king sent Shaphan ben Atsalyahu son of Meshullam to Yahweh's house, saying ⁴'Go up to Hilqiyyahu the big priest so he may weigh the silver that's been brought to Yahweh's house, which the people keeping watch over the threshold have gathered from the people. ⁵They're to put it into the hand of the people doing the work who were appointed to Yahweh's house, so they may give it to the people doing the work who are in Yahweh's house, to strengthen the defects in the house, ⁶to the craftsmen, to the builders, to the masons, and for the acquiring of wood and hewn stones to strengthen the house. ⁷Only there will be no reckoning made with them of the silver given into their hand, because they're acting with trustworthiness.'

⁸Hilqiyyahu, the big priest, said to Shaphan, the secretary, 'I've found an instruction document in Yahweh's house.' Hilqiyyahu gave the document to Shaphan and he read it out. ⁹Shaphan the secretary came to the king and took back word to the king: 'Your servants have melted down the silver that was found in the house and they've given it into the hand of the people doing the work who were appointed to Yahweh's house.' ¹⁰And Shaphan the secretary told the king, 'Hilqiyyah the priest gave me a document.' Shaphan read it out before the king.

The tough and gentle prophetess

¹¹When the king heard the words in the instruction document, he tore his clothes. ¹²The king ordered Hilqiyyah the priest, Ahiqam ben Shaphan, Akbor ben Mikayah, Shaphan the secretary and Asayah the king's servant, ¹³'Go enquire of Yahweh on my behalf and on behalf of the people and on behalf of all Yehudah about the words in this document that's been found, because great is Yahweh's wrath that has set on fire against us because our ancestors didn't listen to the words in this document by acting in accordance with everything that's written for us.'

¹⁴Hilqiyyahu the priest went, with Ahiqam, Akbor, Shaphan and Asayah, to Huldah the prophetess, wife of Shallum ben Tikvah son of Harhas, keeper of the robes; she was living in Yerushalaim in the Second Quarter. They spoke to her.

¹⁵She said to them, 'Yahweh the God of Yisra'el has said this: "Say to the man who sent you to me: ¹⁶"Yahweh has said this: "Here, I'm going to bring bad fortune to this place and to its inhabitants, all the things in the document that the king of Yehudah read out, ¹⁷because of the fact that they abandoned me and burned incense to other gods in order to provoke me with all the actions of their hands. My wrath will set on fire against this place and it will not douse."''

¹⁸But to the king of Yehudah who sent you to enquire of Yahweh, you're to say this to him: "Yahweh the God of Yisra'el has said this: 'The words that you have heard: ¹⁹since your mind softened and you bowed down before Yahweh when you heard what I had spoken against this place and against its inhabitants (becoming a desolation and a slighting) and you tore your clothes and cried before me, I for my part have also listened (Yahweh's declaration). ²⁰Therefore, here, I am going to gather you to your ancestors and you will gather yourself to your great grave with things being well. Your eyes will not see all the bad fortune that I am going to bring on this place."'' They took the word back to the king.

The covenant and the clean-up

23 The king sent and gathered to him all the elders of Yehudah and Yerushalaim, ²and the king went up to Yahweh's house, with everyone in Yehudah and all the inhabitants of Yerushalaim with him, and the priests and the prophets, and the entire people, young and old. He read out in their ears all the words in the pact document found in Yahweh's house. ³The king stood by the pillar and solemnized a pact before Yahweh, to follow Yahweh and keep his orders, his affirmations and his decrees with their entire mind and with their entire being, by setting up the words of this pact that were written on this document. The entire people stood by the pact.

⁴The king ordered Hilqiyyahu the big priest, the priests of the second order, and the people keeping watch over the threshold to take out from Yahweh's palace all the articles made for the Master and for Asherah and for the entire heavenly army, and he burned them outside Yerushalaim in the Qidron Fields, and carried their dust to Bet-el. ⁵He did away with the clergy whom the kings of Yehudah had made to burn incense in the shrines in the towns of Yehudah and the areas round Yerushalaim, and the people who burned incense for the Master, for the sun, for the moon, for the constellations and for the entire heavenly army. ⁶He took the totem pole out of Yahweh's house, outside of Yerushalaim, to Wadi Qidron, and burned it in Wadi Qidron, crushed it to dust and threw its dust over the grave of the ordinary people. ⁷He demolished the houses of the hierodules that were in Yahweh's house, where the women were weaving 'houses' for the totem pole.

⁸He brought all the priests from the towns of Yehudah and defiled the shrines where the priests burned incense, from Geba as far as Be'er-sheba. He demolished the shrines at the gateways, which were at the entrance of the gateway of Yehoshua, the official over the town, which were on one's left at the town gateway. ⁹Yet the priests of the shrines did not go up to Yahweh's altar in Yerushalaim; rather, they ate flatbread among their brothers.

Honouring the long-ago prophets

¹⁰He defiled the Hearth which is in the Ben-hinnom Ravine so that no one would make his son or his daughter pass through fire to the Shameful King. ¹¹He did away with the horses that the kings of Yehudah gave for the sun, from the entrance of Yahweh's house, near the hall of Natan-melek the courtier, which was in the precincts. He burned the sun chariots in fire. ¹²The altars that were on the roof of Ahaz's upper quarters, which the kings of Yehudah had made, and the altars that Menashsheh had made in the two courtyards of Yahweh's house, the king demolished. He ran from there and threw their dust into Wadi Qidron.

¹³The shrines that were facing Yerushalaim, which were south of Destroyer Mountain, which

Shelomoh king of Yisra'el had built for Shameful Ashtar the abomination of the Tsidonites, for Kemosh the abomination of Mo'ab and for Milkom the offence of the Ammonites, the king defiled. ¹⁴He broke up the columns and cut up the totem poles and filled their site with human bones.

¹⁵Also the altar which was at Bet-el (the shrine that Yarob'am ben Nebat, who caused Yisra'el to do wrong, made) – also that altar and the shrine, he demolished. He burned the shrine and beat it to dust, and burned the totem pole.

¹⁶Yo'shiyyahu turned his face and saw the graves that were there on the mountain. He sent and got the bones from the graves and burned them on the altar, and defiled it in accordance with Yahweh's word that the supernatural man called out, who called out these things. ¹⁷He said, 'What's that sign that I'm looking at?' The people of the town said to him, 'The grave of the supernatural man who came from Yehudah and called out these things that you have done to the Bet-el altar.' ¹⁸He said, 'Let him be. No one is to disturb his bones.' So they saved his bones, and the bones of the prophet who came from Shomron.

The incomparable reformer

¹⁹All the houses at the shrines that were in the towns of Shomron, which the kings of Yisra'el had made so as to provoke, Yo'shiyyahu also removed. He acted towards them in accordance with the actions that he undertook at Bet'el. ²⁰He sacrificed all the priests of the shrines who were there, on the altars, and burned human bones on them, and went back to Yerushalaim.

²¹The king ordered the entire people: 'Make Pesah [Passover] for Yahweh your God as is written on this pact document.' ²²Because it had not been made like this Pesah since the days of the leaders who had led Yisra'el or all the days of the kings of Yisra'el and the kings of Yehudah. ²³Rather, in the eighteenth year of King Yo'shiyyahu this Pesah was made for Yahweh in Yerushalaim.

²⁴The ghosts, the spirits, the effigies, the idols and all the abominations that were to be seen in the country of Yehudah and in Yerushalaim, Yo'shiyyahu also burned away, in order to implement the things in the instruction that were written on the document that Hilqiyyahu the priest had found in Yahweh's house.

²⁵Before him there was no king like him who turned back to Yahweh with his entire mind, with his entire being and with his entire might in accordance with Mosheh's entire instruction, and after him none rose up like him. ²⁶Yet Yahweh did not turn back from the great angry rage with which his anger raged against Yehudah because of all the provocative acts with which Menashsheh had provoked him. ²⁷Yahweh said, 'Yehudah, too, I shall remove from before my face, as I removed Yisra'el. I shall reject this town that I chose, Yerushalaim, and the house of which I said, "My name will be there."'

The loss of Yo'shiyyahu

²⁸The rest of the things about Yo'shiyyahu and all that he did are written on the document about things of the time regarding the kings of Yehudah, aren't they. ²⁹In his days Par'oh Neko king of Misrayim went up against the king of Ashshur at the River Euphrates. King Yo'shiyyahu went to meet him, but he put him to death at Megiddo when he saw him. ³⁰His servants transported him dead from Megiddo and brought him to Yerushalaim, and buried him in his grave.

The people of the country got Yeho'ahaz ben Yo'shiyyahu, and anointed him and made him king in place of his father. ³¹Yeho'ahaz was a man of twenty-three years when he began to reign and he reigned three months in Yerushalaim. His mother's name was Hamutal bat Yirmeyahu, from Libnah. ³²He did what was bad in Yahweh's eyes in accordance with all that his ancestors had done. ³³Par'oh Neko confined him at Riblah in the region of Hamat to stop him reigning in Yerushalaim, and put a levy on the country of a hundred talents of silver and a talent of gold.

³⁴Par'oh Neko made Elyaqim ben Yo'shiyyahu king in place of his father, but turned his name into Yehoyaqim. He took Yeho'ahaz, and he came to Misrayim and died there. ³⁵The silver and the gold Yehoyaqim gave to Par'oh, only

he assessed the country so as to give the silver in accordance with Par'oh's bidding. Each person according to his assessment, he exacted the silver and the gold from the people of the country so as to give it to Par'oh Neko.

³⁶Yehoyaqim was a man of twenty-five years when he began to reign and he reigned eleven years in Yerushalaim. His mother's name was Zebudah bat Pedayah, from Rumah. ³⁷He did what was bad in Yahweh's eyes, in accordance with all that his ancestors did.

How things start to collapse

24 In his days Nebukadne'tstsar king of Babel went up and Yehoyaqim became his servant for three years, but he turned back and rebelled against him. ²Yahweh sent against him raiding gangs of the Kasdites [Babylonians], raiding gangs from Aram, raiding gangs from Mo'ab and raiding gangs of the Ammonites. He sent them against Yehudah to obliterate it, in accordance with Yahweh's word which he spoke by means of his servants the prophets. ³Indeed, it was at Yahweh's bidding that it happened to Yehudah, to remove them from before his face because of Menashsheh's wrongdoings, in accordance with all that he did, ⁴and also the blood of people who were free of guilt that he had shed. He had filled Yerushalaim with the blood of people free of guilt, and Yahweh was not willing to pardon.

⁵The rest of the things about Yehoyaqim and all that he did are written on the document about things of the time regarding the kings of Yehudah, aren't they. ⁶Yehoyaqim lay down with his ancestors and his son Yehoyakin began to reign in place of him. ⁷The king of Misrayim did not go out of his country again, because the king of Babel had taken all that had belonged to the king of Misrayim from the Misrayimite Wadi as far as the River Euphrates.

⁸Yehoyakin was eighteen years of age when he began to reign and he reigned three months in Yerushalaim. His mother's name was Nehushta bat Elnatan, from Yerushalaim. ⁹He did what was bad in Yahweh's eyes, in accordance with all that his father did. ¹⁰At that time the servants of Nebukadne'tstsar king of Babel went up to Yerushalaim and the town came under siege. ¹¹Nebukadne'tstsar king of Babel came against the town while his servants were besieging it, ¹²and Yehoyakin king of Yehudah went out to the king of Babel, he, his mother, his servants, his officials and his courtiers. The king of Babel took him in the eighth year of his reign.

The first Yehudahite exile and the final siege

¹³He took away from there the treasures of Yahweh's house and the treasures of the king's house, and cut off all the gold objects that Shelomoh had made in Yahweh's palace, as Yahweh had said. ¹⁴He exiled all Yerushalaim, all the officials and all the forceful strong men, 10,000 exiles, and every craftsman and smith. No one remained apart from the poorest element of the people in the country. ¹⁵He exiled Yehoyakin to Babel, and the king's mother, the king's wives, his courtiers and the country's leaders he made go as exiles from Yerushalaim to Babel, ¹⁶with all the forceful men, 7,000 (and craftsman and smith, 1,000), all of them the strong men doing battle. The king of Babel made them come as exiles to Babel.

¹⁷The king of Babel made Mattanyah, his uncle, king in place of him, and turned his name to Tsidqiyyahu [Zedekiah]. ¹⁸Tsidqiyyahu was twenty-one years of age when he began to reign and he reigned eleven years in Yerushalaim. His mother's name was Hamutal bat Yirmeyahu, from Libnah. ¹⁹He did what was bad in Yahweh's eyes in accordance with all that Yehoyaqim had done, ²⁰because of the fact that Yahweh's anger was against Yerushalaim and against Yehudah until he threw them out of his presence.

Tsidqiyyahu rebelled against the king of Babel,

25 and in the ninth year of his reign, in the tenth month, on the tenth of the month, Nebukadne'tstsar king of Babel came against Yerushalaim, he and his entire force. He camped against it and built blockades all round. ²The town came under siege until the eleventh year of King Tsidqiyyahu. ³On the ninth of the month the famine had become overwhelming in the town and there was no bread for the people of the country. ⁴ᵃThe town broke open, and all the men of battle [left] in the night by way of the gateway between the double wall which was by the king's garden, while the Kasdites were all round the town.

The destruction and the second Yehudahite exile

⁴ᵇHe went by the steppe road, ⁵but the Kasdite force pursued after the king. They overtook him in the Yeriho steppes when his entire force had scattered from him. ⁶They captured the king and took him up to the king of Babel at Riblah, and he pronounced a decision about him. ⁷Tsidqiyyahu's sons they slaughtered before his eyes, Tsidqiyyahu's eyes he gouged out, and he bound him with copper chains and brought him to Babel.

⁸In the fifth month, on the seventh of the month (i.e. the nineteenth year of King Nebukadne'tstsar king of Babel), Nebuzar'adan the chief of the guards, servant of the king of Babel, came to Yerushalaim ⁹and burned Yahweh's house, the king's house and all the houses in Yerushalaim. Every house of a big person he burned in fire. ¹⁰The walls round Yerushalaim, the entire Kasdite force that was with the chief of the guards demolished. ¹¹The rest of the people who remained in the town and the people who had submitted (who had submitted to the king of Babel) and the rest of the horde, Nebuzar'adan the chief of the guards took into exile, ¹²but some of the poorest elements in the country the chief of the guards let remain as vinedressers and farm workers.

¹³The copper pillars that were in Yahweh's house, and the stands and the copper sea that were in Yahweh's house, the Kasdites broke up and carried their copper to Babel. ¹⁴The buckets, the shovels, the snuffers, the ladles and all the copper articles with which they ministered, they took. ¹⁵The pans and the sprinklers, whatever was of gold and whatever was of silver, the chief of the guards took. ¹⁶The two pillars, the one sea and the stands that Shelomoh made for Yahweh's house – there was no weighing the copper in all these articles. ¹⁷The height of the one pillar was nine metres, with a copper capital on it; the height of the capital was one and a half metres, with a net with pomegranates on the capital all round, all of it copper, and like these was the second pillar with the net.

Is it the end or is there hope?

¹⁸The chief of the guards took Serayah the head priest, Tsephanyahu the number two priest and the three keepers of the threshold, ¹⁹and from the town he took a courtier who was appointee over the men of battle, and five people from the heads who were before the king, who were found in the town, the secretary of the army officer who mustered the people of the country, and sixty individuals from the people of the country who were found in the town. ²⁰Nebuzar'adan the chief of the guards took them and made them go to the king of Babel at Riblah. ²¹The king of Babel struck them down and put them to death at Riblah, in the region of Hamat.

So Yehudah went into exile from upon its land, ²²while the people that remained in the country of Yehudah whom Nebukadne'tstsar king of Babel allowed to remain – he appointed over them Gedalyahu ben Ahiqam son of Shaphan. ²³All the officers of the forces, they and their men, heard that the king of Babel had appointed Gedalyahu, and they came to Gedalyahu at The Watchtower, with Yishma'e'l ben Netanyah, Yohanan ben Qareah, Serayah ben Tanhumet the Netophatite and Ya'azanyahu son of the Ma'akatite, and their men. ²⁴Gedalyahu swore to them and to their men, and said, 'Don't be afraid of the Kasdites' servants. Stay in the country. Serve the king of Babel. Things will be good for you.'

²⁵But in the seventh month Yishma'e'l ben Netanyah son of Elishama, of royal descent, came with ten men with him, and struck down Gedalyahu and put him to death, him and the Yehudahites and the Kasdites who were with him at The Watchtower. ²⁶And all the people, young and old, and the officers over the forces, set off and came to Misrayim, because they were afraid of the Kasdites.

²⁷But in the thirty-seventh year of the exile of Yehoyakin king of Yehudah, in the twelfth month, on the twenty-seventh of the month,

Ewil-merodak king of Babel, in the year he began to reign, lifted up the head of Yehoyakin king of Yehudah from the cells. ²⁸He spoke of good things with him, gave him a seat above the seat of the kings who were with him in Babel ²⁹and changed his prison clothes. He ate bread before him regularly for his entire life. ³⁰His provision was given him as a regular provision from the king, a day's allocation on its day, for his entire life.

1 Chronicles

The first book of Chronicles retells the entire story from Adam to David which is told in Genesis to Samuel. Why does it do so, and why does the Bible include two versions of the story? One could compare the fact that the New Testament includes four versions of the Jesus story. It would be less confusing to have just one. But a good story can be told from different angles, and the more you tell it, the more illuminating it becomes. You get a different take on it, you get a different author's angle on what it means and you look at it from the perspective of a different audience.

The first thing that strikes you when you start reading Chronicles is that the opening third is just lists of names. In part, that's the way it summarizes the entire story from Adam to David. It's a bit like the opening frames of an episode in a TV serial that provide a lightning reminder of the story so far. This 'series' as a whole is going to focus on David, but the audience needs to see David in his context in the entire story of Israel – indeed, the entire story of the world. This entire story leads up to him. But the chapters also preserve lots of other information that helps the readers know where they came from. The coverage is uneven; perhaps it simply preserves what was available.

The lists of names include references to people living much later than David's day, and Book One of Chronicles as a whole leads into Book Two which takes the story on through another five centuries after David, up to the time when people from Judah are taken off into exile and are then encouraged to return to Jerusalem to rebuild the temple. So Chronicles was not written in David's day, which makes that focus striking. Chronicles is a version of Israel's story told by someone living in Jerusalem in the time of the Second Temple and told for people living in that context. The books of Ezra and Nehemiah and the visions in Daniel give us some insight into events during those times.

Why does Chronicles focus on David? The answer emerges when we consider the book's angle on its hero. Its interest lies not in the great warrior or the smart operator of 1 and 2 Samuel, nor is he the intriguing human being with clay feet that those books also portray. Those books also relate how David set going the process whereby the first temple was built, and it's this aspect of David's achievement that interests Chronicles.

Its angle would be significant for people living in Second Temple times. They were hard times. The community in Judah that centred on Jerusalem was a shadow of its former self. Geographically it was the size of a county, not a country. Politically it was a colony of the Persian Empire. Its faith and its life were often under pressure from neighbouring peoples. When things are like that, how do you hold on?

The Old Testament gives people several complementary answers. The prophets' answer is that you look to the future and tell yourself that things are going to get better. Judah was not just whistling in the wind when it lived by such hopes. God had made a commitment to David that God could not get out of, and people could live in the light of promises that God would one day send them a new David.

A complementary answer is that you look to the past, to what God has done in the past, and it is this answer that attracts Chronicles. Its interest in the past doesn't focus on creation, Abraham, the exodus, or Joshua, but on David. It does so from this angle, David as founder of the temple worship. Telling that story encourages people in Jerusalem to live in the present, because for all the limitations of present experience, one great privilege they do have is the daily round of temple worship. Some of the lists in the first third of the book, and the lists in the last third, relate to the actual arrangements for worship and other aspects of community life in David's day, and in the time of the book's readers.

That daily worship is also significant for people who don't live in Jerusalem. The priest in an English church used to ring the church bell before going into church morning and evening. People who could not respond to the summons could know that the priest was conducting the prayers and could join in at a distance. Elsewhere in Judah, people could know that temple worship was being offered and could associate themselves with it. They could even do so from many miles away, as Daniel did.

In the beginning

1 Adam, Seth, Enosh, ²Kenan, Mahalalel, Yared, ³Hanok [Enoch], Methuselah, Lamek, ⁴Noah, Shem, Ham and Yaphet.
⁵Yaphet's sons: Gomer, Magog, Maday, Yavan [Greece], Tubal, Meshek and Tiras.
⁶Gomer's sons: Ashkenaz, Diphat and Togarmah.
⁷Yavan's sons: Elishah, Tarshish, Kittites and Rodanites.
⁸Ham's sons: Kush [Sudan], Misrayim [Egypt], Put and Kena'an [Canaan].
⁹Kush's sons: Seba, Havilah, Sabta, Ra'ama and Sabteka.
Ra'ama's sons: Sheba and Dedan.
¹⁰Kush fathered Nimrod; he was the first to be a strong man on the earth.
¹¹Misrayim fathered Ludites, Anamites, Lehabites, Naphtuhites, ¹²Patrusites, Kasluhites (Pelishtites [Philistines] came out from there) and Kaphtorites.
¹³Kena'an fathered Tsidon (his firstborn), Het, ¹⁴the Yebusite, the Amorite, the Girgashite, ¹⁵the Hivvite, the Arkite, the Sinite, ¹⁶the Arvadite, the Tsemarite and the Hamatite.
¹⁷Shem's sons: Elam, Ashshur, Arpakshad, Lud, Aram, Uts, Hul, Geter and Meshek.
¹⁸Arpakshad fathered Shelah and Shelah fathered Eber.
¹⁹To Eber two sons were born:
The name of the one was Peleg ['Division'] because in his days the earth divided.
His brother's name was Yoktan.
²⁰Yoktan fathered Almodad, Sheleph, Hatsarmavet, Yerah, ²¹Hadoram, Uzal, Diklah, ²²Ebal, Abima'el, Sheba, ²³Ophir, Havilah and Yobab; all these were Yoktan's sons.
²⁴Shem, Arpakshad, Shelah, ²⁵Eber, Peleg, Re'u, ²⁶Serug, Nahor, Terah, ²⁷Abram (i.e. Abraham).
²⁸Abraham's sons: Yitshaq [Isaac] and Yishma'e'l; ²⁹these are their lines of descent:
Yishma'el's firstborn, Nebayot, Qedar, Adbe'el, Mibsam, ³⁰Mishma, Dumah, Massa, ³¹Hadad, Tema, Yetur, Naphish and Qedemah; these are Yishma'e'l's sons.
³²The sons of Qeturah, Abraham's secondary wife: she gave birth to Zimran, Yoqshan, Medan, Midyan, Yishbaq and Shuah.
Yoqshan's sons: Sheba and Dedan.
³³Midyan's sons: Ephah, Epher, Hanok, Abida and Elda'ah; all these were Qeturah's sons.

Esaw's line

³⁴Abraham fathered Yitshaq.
Yitshaq's sons: Esaw and Yisra'el.
³⁵Esaw's sons: Eliphaz, Re'u'el, Ye'ush, Ya'lam and Qorah.
³⁶Eliphaz's sons: Teman, Omar, Tsephi, Ga'tam, Qenaz, Timna, and Amaleq;
³⁷Re'u'el's sons: Nahat, Zerah, Shammah and Mizzah;
³⁸Se'ir's sons: Lotan, Shobal, Tsib'on, Anah, Dishon, Etser and Dishan;
³⁹Lotan's sons: Hori and Homam; and Timna was Lotan's sister;
⁴⁰Shobal's sons: Alyan, Manahat, Ebal, Shephi and Onam;
Tsib'on's sons: Ayyah and Anah;
⁴¹Anah's sons: Dishon;
Dishon's sons: Hamran, Eshban, Yitran and Keran;
⁴²Etser's sons: Bilhan, Za'avan, Ya'aqan;
Dishan's sons: Uts and Aran.
⁴³These are the kings who reigned in the country of Edom before a king reigned among the Yisra'elites:
Bela ben Be'or; his town's name was Dinhabah.
⁴⁴Bela died, and Yobab ben Zerah from Botsrah began to reign in place of him.
⁴⁵Yobab died, and Husham from the Temanites' country began to reign in place of him.
⁴⁶Husham died, and Hadad ben Bedad, who struck down Midyan in Mo'ab's area, began to reign in place of him; his town's name was Avit.
⁴⁷Hadad died, and Samlah from Masrekah began to reign in place of him.
⁴⁸Samlah died, and Sha'ul from Broads-on-the-River began to reign in place of him.
⁴⁹Sha'ul died, and Ba'al Hanan ben Akbor began to reign in place of him.
⁵⁰Ba'al Hanan died, and Hadad began to reign in place of him; his town's name was

Pa'i, and his wife's name was Mehetabel bat Matred, the daughter of Gold Water. ⁵¹Hadad died.
The Edomite clans were:
the Timna clan;
the Alvah clan;
the Yetet clan;
⁵²the Oholibamah clan;
the Elah clan;
the Pinon clan;
⁵³the Qenaz clan;
the Teman clan;
the Mibtsar clan;
⁵⁴the Magdi'el clan;
the Iram clan.
These were the Edomite clans.

The beginning of Yehudah's line

2 These are Yisra'el's sons:
Re'uben, Shim'on, Levi, Yehudah, Yissakar, Zebulun, ²Dan, Yoseph, Binyamin, Naphtali, Gad, and Asher.
³Yehudah's sons: Er, Onan and Shelah (the three were born to him from Bat-shua the Kena'anite); Er, Yehudah's firstborn, was bad in Yahweh's eyes, and he put him to death; ⁴since Tamar his daughter-in-law gave birth to Perets and Zerah for him, altogether Yehudah's sons were five.
⁵Perets's sons: Hezron and Hamul;
⁶Zerah's sons: Zimri, Etan, Heman, Kalkol and Dara – five altogether;
⁷Karmi's sons: Akar ['Trouble'], the troubler of Yisra'el, who trespassed on something devoted;
⁸Etan's sons: Azaryah;
⁹Hezron's sons, who were born to him: Yerahme'el, Ram and Kelubay;
¹⁰Ram fathered Amminadab, Amminadab fathered Nahshon, a leader of the Yehudahites, ¹¹Nahshon fathered Salma, Salma fathered Bo'az, ¹²Bo'az fathered Obed, and Obed fathered Yishay.
¹³Yishay fathered Eli'ab as his firstborn, Abinadab the second, Shim'a the third, ¹⁴Netan'el the fourth, Radday the fifth, ¹⁵Otsem the sixth, David the seventh.
¹⁶Their sisters were Tseruyah and Abigayil. Tseruyah's sons: Abshay, Yo'ab and Asah'el – three.

¹⁷Abigayil gave birth to Amasa; Amasa's father was Yeter the Yishma'e'lite.
¹⁸Kaleb ben Hezron fathered children with Azubah his wife, and with Yeri'ot; these were her sons: Yesher, Shobab and Ardon.
¹⁹Azubah died and Kaleb took himself Ephrat, who gave birth to Hur for him.
²⁰Hur fathered Uri and Uri fathered Betsal'el.
²¹Afterwards, Hezron had sex with a daughter of Makir, father of Gil'ad; he had taken her when he was a man of sixty years and she gave birth to Segub for him.
²²Segub fathered Ya'ir; he had twenty-three towns in the region of Gil'ad, ²³but Geshur and Aram took from them the Villages of Ya'ir, Qenat and its daughter-towns, sixty towns; all these were sons of Makir, father of Gil'ad.
²⁴After Hezron's death in Kaleb Ephratah, Hezron's wife Abiyyah gave birth to Ashhur, father of Teqoa, for him.

Yehudah's line

²⁵The sons of Yerahme'el, Hezron's firstborn, were: the firstborn Ram, Bunah, Oren, Ozem and Ahiyyah.
²⁶Yerahme'el had another wife and her name was Atarah; she was the mother of Onam.
²⁷The sons of Ram, Yerahme'el's firstborn, were: Ma'ats, Yamin and Eqer.
²⁸Onam's sons were: Shammay and Yada. Shammay's sons: Nadab and Abishur.
²⁹The name of Abishur's wife was Abihayil; she gave birth to Ahban and Molid for him.
³⁰Nadab's sons: Seled and Appayim. Seled died without sons.
³¹Appayim's sons: Yish'i;
Yish'i's sons: Sheshan;
Sheshan's sons: Ahlay.
³²The sons of Yada, Shammay's brother: Yeter and Yonatan.
Yeter died without sons.
³³Yonatan's sons: Pelet and Zaza.
These were Yerahme'el's sons.
³⁴Sheshan did not have sons, but rather daughters, but Sheshan had a Misrayimite servant and his name was Yarha; ³⁵Sheshan

gave his daughter to Yarha his servant as wife, and she gave birth to Attay for him. ³⁶Attay fathered Natan, Natan fathered Zabad, ³⁷Zabad fathered Ephlal, Ephlal fathered Obed, ³⁸Obed fathered Yehu, Yehu fathered Azaryah, ³⁹Azaryah fathered Helets, Helets fathered El'asah, ⁴⁰El'asah fathered Sismay, Sismay fathered Shallum, ⁴¹Shallum fathered Yeqamyah and Yeqamyah fathered Elishama.

Kaleb's line

⁴²The sons of Kaleb, Yerahme'el's brother:
Mesha his firstborn; he was the father of Ziph.
The sons of Mareshah, father of Hebron.
⁴³Hebron's sons: Qorah, Tappuah, Reqem, and Shema.
⁴⁴Shema fathered Raham the father of Yorqo'am.
Reqem fathered Shammay.
⁴⁵Shammay's son was Ma'on; Ma'on was the father of Bet-tsur.
⁴⁶Ephah, Kaleb's secondary wife, gave birth to Haran, Motsa and Gazez.
Haran fathered Gazez.
⁴⁷Yahday's sons: Regem, Yotam, Geshan, Pelet, Ephah and Sha'aph.
⁴⁸Kaleb's secondary wife Ma'akah gave birth to Sheber and Tirhanah, ⁴⁹she gave birth to Sha'aph the father of Madmannah, Sheva the father of Makbenah, and the father of Gib'a, and Kaleb's daughter was Aksah; ⁵⁰these were Kaleb's children.

The son of Hur, Ephratah's firstborn: Shobal father of Ye'arim Township, ⁵¹Salma father of Bet-lehem, Hareph father of Bet-gader. ⁵²Shobal father of Ye'arim Township had sons, Haro'eh, half of the Menuhot, ⁵³and the kin-groups of Ye'arim Township: the Itrites, the Putites, the Shumatites and the Mishra'ites (from these the Tsor'atites and the Eshta'olites came).
⁵⁴Salma's sons: Bet Lehem, Netophatites, Atrot Bet Yo'ab, half the Manahatites (the Tsor'ites), ⁵⁵and the kin-groups of the secretaries living in Ya'bets, Tir'atites, Shim'atites, Sukatites; these are the Qenites who come from Hamat, father of Rekab's household.

David's line

3 These were David's sons who were born to him in Hebron:
the firstborn Amnon, by Ahino'am the Yizre'e'lite;
the second Daniyye'l, by Abigayil the Carmelite;
²the third Abshalom, the son of Ma'akah the daughter of Talmay king of Geshur;
the fourth Adoniyyah, the son of Haggit;
³the fifth Shephatyah, by Abital;
the sixth Yitre'am, by Eglah his wife.
⁴Six were born to him in Hebron; he reigned there seven years and six months, in Yerushalaim he reigned thirty-three years, ⁵and these were born to him in Yerushalaim:
Shim'a, Shobab, Natan and Shelomoh [Solomon] – four by Bat-shua bat Ammi'el; ⁶Yibhar, Elishama, Eliphelet, ⁷Nogah, Nepheg, Yaphia, ⁸Elishama, Elyada and Eliphelet – nine.
⁹All were David's sons, besides the secondary wives' sons; and Tamar was their sister.

¹⁰Shelomoh's son: Rehab'am [Rehoboam]; his son Abiyyah; his son Asa; his son Yehoshaphat; ¹¹his son Yoram; his son Ahazyahu; his son Yo'ash; ¹²his son Amatsyahu; his son Azaryah; his son Yotam; ¹³his son Ahaz; his son Hizqiyyahu; his son Menashsheh; ¹⁴his son Amon; his son Yo'shiyyahu.

¹⁵Yo'shiyyahu's sons: the first-born Yohanan, the second Yehoyaqim, the third Tsidqiyyahu, the fourth Shallum.
¹⁶Yehoyaqim's sons: his son Yekonyah, his son Tsidqiyyahyu.
¹⁷The sons of Yekonyah, the captive: She'alti'el his son, ¹⁸Malkiram, Pedayah, Shen'atstsar, Yeqamyah, Hoshama and Nedabyah.
¹⁹Pedayah's sons: Zerubbabel and Shim'i. Zerubbabel's sons: Meshullam and Hananyah; and Shelomit was their sister.
²⁰Hashubah, Ohel, Berekyah, Hasadyah, Yushab Hesed – five;
²¹Hananyah's son: Pelatyah and Yesha'yah; Rephayah's sons, Arnan's sons, Obadyah's sons, Shekanyah's sons;
²²Shekanyah's sons: Shemayah;

Shemayah's sons: Hattush, Yig'al, Bariah, Ne'aryah and Shaphat – six;
²³Ne'aryah's son: Elyo'enay, Hizqiyyah and Azriqam – three;
²⁴Elyo'enay's sons: Hodavyah, Elyashib, Pelayah, Aqqub, Yohanan, Delayah and Anani – seven.

The prayer of Ya'bets

4 Yehudah's sons: Perets, Hezron, Karmi, Hur and Shobal.
²Re'ayah ben Shobal fathered Yahat; Yahat fathered Ahumay and Lahad; these were the kin-groups of the Tsor'atites.
³The father of Etam, these: Yizre'e'l, Yishma and Yidbash, and their sister's name was Hatslelponi.
⁴Penu'el was the father of Gedor and Ezer was the father of Hushah.
These were the sons of Hur, the firstborn of Ephratah, the father of Bet Lehem.
⁵Asshur the father of Teqoa had two wives, Hel'ah and Na'arah.
⁶Na'arah gave birth to Ahuzzam, Hepher, Temeni and Ha'ahashtari for him; these were Na'arah's sons.
⁷Helah's sons: Tseret, Tsohar and Etnan.
⁸Qots fathered Anub, Hatstsobebah and the kin-groups of Aharhel ben Harum.
⁹Ya'bets was more honourable than his brothers. His mother had named him Ya'bets 'Because I gave birth to him in suffering pain [*otseb*]'. ¹⁰Ya'bets called to the God of Yisra'el, 'If only you will really bless me and enlarge my territory and your hand will be with me and you will act against bad fortune so that I don't suffer pain'. God brought about what he asked.
¹¹Kelub, Shuhah's brother, fathered Mehir; he was father of Eshton.
¹²Eshton fathered Bet Rapha, Paseah, and Tehinnah, father of Ir Nahash; these were the people of Rekah.

More Yehudahites

¹³Qenaz's sons: Otni'el and Seryah; Otni'el's sons: Hatat ¹⁴and Me'onotay; he fathered Ophrah.
Seryah fathered Yo'ab, father of Craftsmen's Ravine (because they were craftsmen).
¹⁵The sons of Kaleb ben Yephunneh: Iru, Elah and Na'am, the sons of Elah, and Qenaz.
¹⁶Yehallel'el's sons: Ziph, Ziphah, Tirya and Asar'el.
¹⁷Ezrah's sons: Yeter, Mered, Epher and Yalon.
She got pregnant with Miryam, Shammay and Yishbah father of Eshtemoa; ¹⁸his Yehudahite wife gave birth to Yered father of Gedor, Heber father of Soko, and Yequti'el father of Zanoah; these were the sons of Bityah, daughter of Par'oh [Pharaoh], whom Mered took.
¹⁹The sons of Hodiyyah's wife, Naham's sister: the father of Qe'ilah the Garmite and Eshtemoa the Ma'akatite.
²⁰Shimon's sons: Amnon, Rinnah, Benhanan and Tilon.
Yishi's sons: Zohat and Ben-zohet.
²¹The sons of Shelah son of Yehudah: Er father of Lekah, La'addah father of Mareshah, the kin-groups of the linen service household at Bet Ashbea, ²²Yoqim, the people of Kozeba, Yo'ash and Saraph who ruled in Mo'ab, and Yashubi Lehem (the words are ancient). ²³They were the potters and the people who lived at Neta'im and Gederah; they lived there with the king, in working for him.

Descendants of Shim'on

²⁴Shim'on's sons: Nemu'el, Yamin, Yarib, Zerah, Sha'ul;
²⁵Shallum his son, Mibsam his son, Mishma his son;
²⁶Mishma's sons: Hammu'el his son, Zakkur his son, Shim'i his son;
²⁷Shim'i had sixteen sons and six daughters, but his brothers didn't have many sons. Their entire kin-group did not produce as many as the Yehudahites. ²⁸They lived

in Be'er-sheba	in Hormah
in Moladah	in Tsiqlag,
in Hatsar Shu'a,	³¹in Bet Markabot
²⁹in Bilhah	in Hatsar Susim
in Etsem	in Bet Bir'i
in Tolad	and in Sha'arayim.
³⁰in Betu'el	

These were their towns until David began to reign; ³²and their villages, Etam, Ayin, Rimmon, Token and Ashan (five towns), ³³and all their villages that were round these towns as far as Ba'al. These were their settlements.

They had their enrolment by genealogy:

³⁴Meshobab	Yeshohayah
Yamlek	Asayah
Yoshah ben Amatsyah	Adi'el Yesimi'el
³⁵Yo'el	Benayah
Yehu ben Yoshibyah son of Serayah son of Asi'el	³⁷Ziza ben Shiph'i son of Allon son of Yedayah son of Shimri son of Shema'yah
³⁶Elyo'enay Ya'aqobah	

³⁸These who come by name were leaders in their kin-groups.

Their ancestral households broke out so as to become a large number ³⁹and went to the approaches to Gedor on the east of the ravine to look for pasture for their flock. ⁴⁰They found rich, good pasture and the region was wide on both sides, calm and peaceful, because the people who lived there before had been from Ham, ⁴¹but these people who are written down by name came in the days of Hizqiyyahu king of Yehudah and struck down their tents, and the Me'unites who were found there devoted them until this day, and settled in place of them, because there was pasture for their flock there. ⁴²Of them, some of the Shim'onites went to Mount Se'ir – 500 people, with Pelatyah, Ne'aryah, Rephayah and Uzzi'el, the sons of Yishi, at their head. ⁴³They struck down the remaining escapees of Amaleq, and they have lived there until this day.

Re'uben

5 The sons of Re'uben, Yisra'el's firstborn (because he was the firstborn, but when he defiled his father's bed, his birthright was given to the sons of Yoseph, the son of Yisra'el, and he was not for enrolment by genealogy on the basis of the birthright, ²because Yehudah was strong among his brothers and a chief came from him, but the birthright belonged to Yoseph) – ³the sons of Re'uben, Yisra'el's firstborn: Hanok, Pallu, Hezron and Karmi.

⁴The sons of Yo'el: Shema'yah his son, Gog his son, Shim'i his son, ⁵Mikah his son, Re'ayah his son, Ba'al his son, ⁶and Be'erah his son, whom Tillegat Pilne'eser king of Ashshur exiled; he was leader of the Re'ubenites.

⁷His brothers by his kin-groups according to the enrolment by genealogy, by their lines of descent: the head, Ye'i'el, Zekaryahu ⁸and Bela ben Azaz son of Shema son of Yo'el. He lived in Aro'er and as far as Nebo and Ba'al Me'on, ⁹and to the east he lived as far as when you come to the wilderness this side of the River Euphrates, because their cattle became many in Gil'ad. ¹⁰In the days of Sha'ul [Saul] they did battle with the Hagri'tes, and they fell by their hand. So they lived in their tents over the entire face of east of Gil'ad.

¹¹Gad's sons lived opposite them in the region of Bashan as far as Salkah: ¹²Yo'el the head, Shapham the second, Ya'nay and Shaphat, in Bashan. ¹³Their brothers by their ancestral households: Mika'el, Meshullam, Sheba, Yoray, Ya'akan, Zia and Eber – seven. ¹⁴These were the sons of Abihayil ben Huri son of Gil'ad son of Mika'el son of Yeshishay son of Yahdo son of Buz. ¹⁵Ahi ben Abdi'el son of Guni was head of their ancestral household. ¹⁶They lived in Gil'ad, in Bashan, in its daughter-towns, and in all the Sharon pasturelands, to their farthest extent. ¹⁷All of them were enrolled by genealogy in the days of Yotam king of Yehudah and in the days of Yarob'am [Jeroboam] king of Yisra'el.

The warriors

¹⁸Re'uben's sons, the Gadites and the half-clan of Menashsheh: of the forceful men carrying shield and sword, drawing the bow and trained in battle, 44,760 able to go out in the army, ¹⁹did battle with the Hagri'tes, Yetur, Naphish and Nodab, ²⁰and sought help against them. The Hagri'tes and all the people who were with them were given into their hand, because they cried out to God in the battle and he let himself be entreated by them because they relied on him. ²¹They captured

1 Chronicles 5: The twelve clans

their livestock, 50,000 camels, 250,000 sheep, 2,000 donkeys and 100,000 people, ²²because many fell, run through, because the battle was God's. They lived in place of them until the exile.

²³The people in the half-clan of Menashsheh lived in the region. They were numerous from Bashan as far as Ba'al Hermon, Senir and Mount Hermon. ²⁴These were the heads of their ancestral households: Epher, Yish'i, Eli'el, Azri'el, Yirmeyah, Hodavyah and Yahdi'el, forceful strong men, men with names, heads of their ancestral households.

²⁵But they trespassed against their ancestors' God and whored after the gods of the peoples of the country, whom God had annihilated

from before them. ²⁶And the God of Yisra'el stirred the spirit of Pul king of Ashshur (the spirit of Tillegat Pilneser king of Ashshur) and he took them into exile – the Re'ubenites, the Gadites and the half-clan of Menashsheh. He brought them to Halah, Habor, and the River Gozan, until this day.

Levi's sons

6 Levi's sons: Gershon, Qehat and Merari.

²Qehat's sons: Amram, Yitshar, Hezron and Uzzi'el;

³Amram's sons: Aharon [Aaron], Mosheh [Moses] and Miryam;

Aharon's sons: Nadab and Abihu, El'azar and It'amar.

⁴El'azar fathered Pinhas
Pinhas fathered Abishua
⁵Abishua fathered Buqqi
Buqqi fathered Uzzi
⁶Uzzi fathered Zerahyah
Zerahyah fathered Merayot
⁷Merayot fathered Amaryah
Amaryah fathered Ahitub
⁸Ahitub fathered Tsadoq
Tsadoq fathered Ahima'ats
⁹Ahima'ats fathered Azaryah
Azaryah fathered Yohanan
¹⁰Yohanan fathered Azaryah (it was he who acted as priest in the house that Shelomoh built in Yerushalaim)
¹¹Azaryah fathered Amaryah
Amaryah fathered Ahitub
¹²Ahitub fathered Tsadoq
Tsadoq fathered Shallum
¹³Shallum fathered Hilqiyyah
Hilqiyyah fathered Azaryah
¹⁴Azaryah fathered Serayah
Serayah fathered Yehotsadaq
¹⁵Yehotsadaq went when Yahweh exiled Yehudah and Yerushalaim by the hand of Nebukadne'tstsar

¹⁶Levi's sons: Gershom, Qehat and Merari.

¹⁷These are the names of Gershom's sons: Libni and Shim'i.

¹⁸Qehat's sons: Amram, Yitshar, Hebron and Uzzi'el.

¹⁹Merari's sons: Mahli and Mushi.

These are the kin-groups of Levi by their ancestors:

²⁰Gershom's: Libni his son, Yahat his son, Zimmah his son, ²¹Yo'ah his son, Iddo his son, Zerah his son, Ye'ateray his son;

²²Qehat's sons: Amminadab his son, Qorah his son, Assir his son, ²³Elqanah his son, Ebyasaph his son, Assir his son, ²⁴Tahat his son, Uri'el his son, Uzziyyah his son and Sha'ul his son;

²⁵Elqanah's sons: Amasay and Ahimot;
²⁶Elqanah;

Elqanah's sons: Tsopay his son, Nahat his son, ²⁷Eli'ab his son, Yeroham his son, Elqanah his son;

²⁸Shemu'el's [Samuel's] sons: the firstborn and the second (Abiyyah);

²⁹Merari's sons: Mahli, Libni his son, Shim'i his son, Uzzah his son, ³⁰Shim'a his son, Haggiah his son, Asayah his son.

The singers

³¹These whom David put in place over the singing in Yahweh's house, from when the chest was set down, ³²were ministering before the dwelling, the appointment tent, with singing, until Shelomoh built Yahweh's house in Yerushalaim. They stood in connection with their service in accordance with the ruling given to them. ³³These were the people who stood, with their sons:

Of the Qehatites:

Heman the singer, son of Yo'el son of Shemu'el ³⁴son of Elqanah son of Yeroham son of Eli'el son of Toah ³⁵son of Tsuph son of Elqanah son of Mahat son of Amasay ³⁶son of Elqanah son of Yo'el son of Azaryah son of Tsephanyah ³⁷son of Tahat son of Assir son of Ebyasaph son of Qorah ³⁸son of Yitshar son of Qehat son of Levi son of Yisra'el.

³⁹His brother Asaph who stood at his right – Asaph ben Berekyahu son of Shim'a ⁴⁰son of Mika'el son of Ba'aseyah son of Malkiyyah ⁴¹son of Etni son of Zerah son of Adayah ⁴²son of Etan son of Zimmah son of Shim'i ⁴³son of Yahat son of

Gershom son of Levi. ⁴⁴The Merarites, their brothers, were on the left: Etan ben Qishi son of Abdi son of Malluk ⁴⁵son of Hashabyah son of Amatsyah son of Hilqiyyah ⁴⁶son of Amtsi son of Bani son of Shemer ⁴⁷son of Mahli son of Mushi son of Merari son of Levi. ⁴⁸Their brother Levites were given to all the service at the dwelling, God's house, ⁴⁹while Aharon and his sons were burning incense on the burnt-offering altar and on the incense altar in connection with all the work in the very sacred place and in connection with making expiation for Yisra'el in accordance with all that Mosheh, God's servant, ordered.

Aharon's family's settlements

⁵⁰These are the sons of Aharon: El'azar his son, Pinhas his son, Abishua his son, ⁵¹Buqqi his son, Uzzi his son, Zerahyah his son, ⁵²Merayot his son, Amaryah his son, Ahitub his son, ⁵³Tsadoq his son, Ahima'ats his son. ⁵⁴These are their settlements, by their enclosures, in their territory:

> To Aharon's sons, the Qehatite kin-group (because theirs was the lot), ⁵⁵they gave them Hebron in the region of Yehudah and its surrounding pasturelands, ⁵⁶but the town's fields and its villages they gave to Kaleb ben Yephunneh. ⁵⁷To Aharon's sons they gave the asylum towns, Hebron, Libnah and its pasturelands, Yattir, Eshtemoa and its pasturelands, ⁵⁸Hilen and its pasturelands, Debir and its pasturelands, ⁵⁹Ashan and its pasturelands, and Bet Shemesh and its pasturelands. ⁶⁰From the clan of Binyamin, Geba and its pasturelands, Alemet and its pasturelands, and Anatot and its pasturelands. All their towns thirteen among their kin-groups.
> ⁶¹To the remaining sons of Qehat from the clan kin-group, from the half-clan, the half of Menashsheh by lot, ten towns.
> ⁶²To the sons of Gershom by their kin-groups, from the clan of Yissakar, from the clan of Asher, from the clan of Naphtali and from the clan of Menashsheh in Bashan, thirteen towns.
> ⁶³To the sons of Merari by their kin-groups, from the clan of Re'uben, from the clan of Gad and from the clan of Zebulun, by lot twelve towns.

⁶⁴So the Yisra'elites gave the Levites the towns and their pasturelands. ⁶⁵They gave them by lot from the clan of the Yehudahites and from the clan of the Shim'onites and from the clan of the Binyaminites these towns that they call by their names.

The Qehatites, the Gershomites and the Merarites

⁶⁶Some of the kin-groups of the Qehatites: there were towns in their territory from the clan of Ephrayim. ⁶⁷They gave them
> the asylum towns;
> Shekem and its pasturelands in the highland of Ephrayim;
> Gezer and its pasturelands;
> ⁶⁸Yoqme'am and its pasturelands;
> Bet Horon and its pasturelands;
> ⁶⁹Ayyalon and its pasturelands;
> Gat-rimmon and its pasturelands;
> ⁷⁰and from the half-clan of Menashsheh
> Aner and its pasturelands;
> Bil'am and its pasturelands for the remaining kin-group of the Qehatites who remained.
> ⁷¹To the Gershomites:
> from the half-clan of Menashsheh, Golan in Bashan and its pasturelands and Ashtarot and its pasturelands;
> ⁷²from the clan of Yissakar, Qedesh and its pasturelands, Dobrat and its pasturelands, ⁷³Heights and its pasturelands, Anem and its pasturelands;
> ⁷⁴from the clan of Asher, Mashal and its pasturelands, Abdon and its pasturelands, ⁷⁵Huqoq and its pasturelands, and Rehob and its pasturelands;
> ⁷⁶ from the clan of Naphtali, Qedesh-in-Galilee and its pasturelands, Hammon and its pasturelands, and Qiryatayim and its pasturelands.
> ⁷⁷To the Merarites, those who remain:
> from the clan of Zebulun, Rimmono and its pasturelands, Tabor and its pasturelands;
> ⁷⁸across the Yarden [Jordan] at Yeriho [Jericho], on the east of the Yarden:
> from the clan of Re'uben, Betser in the wilderness and its pasturelands, Yahtsah

and its pasturelands, ⁷⁹Qedemot and its pasturelands, and Mepha'at and its pasturelands; ⁸⁰and from the clan of Gad, Heights-in-Gil'ad and its pasturelands, Mahanayim and its pasturelands, ⁸¹Heshbon and its pasturelands, and Ya'zer and its pasturelands.

Down to our own day: Yissakar, Binyamin, Naphtali, Menashsheh

7 Yissakar's sons: Tola, Pu'ah, Yashub and Shimron – four. ²Tola's sons: Uzzi, Rephayah, Yeri'el, Yahmay, Yibsam and Shemu'el, heads of their ancestral households belonging to Tola, forceful strong men; by their lines of descent, their number in David's days, 22,600. ³Uzzi's sons: Yizrahyah; Yizrahyah's sons: Mika'el, Obadyah, Yo'el and Yishshiyyah – five, all of them heads; ⁴with them, by their lines of descent, by their kin-groups, army raiding gangs ready for battle, 36,000, because they had many wives and children. ⁵Their brothers in all the kin-groups of Yissakar, forceful strong men, their enrolment by genealogy, 87,000, all of them.
⁶Binyamin: Bela, Beker and Yedi'a'el – three. ⁷Bela's sons: Etsbon, Uzzi, Uzzi'el, Yerimot and Iri – five, heads of ancestral households, forceful strong men, their enrolment by genealogy, 22,034. ⁸Beker's sons: Zemirah, Yo'ash, El'ezer, Eli'onay, Omri, Yeremot, Abiyyah, Anatot, and Alemet, all these sons of Beker, ⁹their enrolment by genealogy by their lines of descent, heads of their ancestral households, forceful strong men, 20,200. ¹⁰Yedi'a'el's sons: Bilhan; Bilhan's sons: Ye'ush, Binyamin, Ehud, Kena'anah, Zetan, Tarshish and Ahishahar, ¹¹all these sons of Yedi'a'el, ancestral heads, forceful strong men, 17,200 able to go out in the army to battle.
(¹²And Shuppim and Huppim, Ir's sons; Hushim; Aher's sons.)
¹³Naphtali's sons: Yahtsi'el, Guni, Yetser and Shallum, sons of Bilhah.

¹⁴Menashsheh's sons: Asri'el, to whom his Aramite secondary wife gave birth; she gave birth to Makir, father of Gil'ad. ¹⁵Makir took a wife for Huppim and for Shuppim; his sister's name was Ma'akah. The name of the second was Tselophhad; Tselophhad had daughters. ¹⁶Ma'akah, Makir's wife, gave birth to a son and named him Peresh; his brother's name: Sheresh; his sons: Ulam and Reqem. ¹⁷Ulam's sons: Bedan.
These were the sons of Gil'ad ben Makir son of Menashsheh; ¹⁸his sister Hammoleket gave birth to Ishhod, Abi'ezer and Mahlah. ¹⁹Shemida's sons were Ahyan, Shekem, Liqhi and Ani'am.

Down to our own day: Ephrayim, Asher

²⁰Ephrayim's sons: Shutelah, Bered his son, Tahat his son, Ele'adah his son, Tahat his son, ²¹Zabad his son, Shutelah his son, and Ezer and Ele'ad. The men of Gat who were born in the region killed them, because they went down to take their cattle. ²²Ephrayim their father grieved for many days, and his brothers came to comfort him. ²³He had sex with his wife and she got pregnant and gave birth to a son. He named him Beri'ah because there had been actual bad fortune [*bera'ah*] in his household. ²⁴His daughter was She'erah. She built up Bet-horon (Lower and Upper) and Uzzen She'erah.
²⁵Rephah his son, Resheph, Telah his son, Tahan his son, ²⁶La'dan his son, Ammihud his son, Elishama his son, ²⁷Non his son, Yehoshua his son: ²⁸their holding and their settlements were Bet-el and its daughter-towns, and on the east Na'aran, and on the west Gezer and its daughter-towns, Shekem and its daughter-towns, as far as Ayyah and its daughter-towns, ²⁹and alongside the Menashshites Bet-she'an and its daughter-towns, Ta'anak and its daughter-towns, Megiddo and its daughter-towns, Do'r and its daughter-towns. The sons of Yoseph the son of Yisra'el lived in these.
³⁰Asher's sons: Yimnah, Yishvah, Yishvi and Beri'ah, and Serah their sister.
³¹Beriah's sons: Heber and Malki'el.

He was Birzayit's father. ³²Heber fathered Yaphlet, Shomer, Hotam and Shua their sister. ³³Yaphlet's sons: Pasak, Bimhal and Ashvat; these were Yaphlet's sons. ³⁴Shemer's sons: Ahi, Rohgah, Hubbah and Aram. ³⁵The son of Helem his brother: Tsophah, Yimna, Shelesh and Amal. ³⁶Tsophah's sons: Suah, Harnepher, Shu'al, Beri, Yimrah, ³⁷Betser, Hod, Shamma, Shilshah, Yitran and Be'era. ³⁸Yeter's sons: Yephunneh, Pispah and Ara. ³⁹Ulla's sons: Arah, Hanni'el and Ritsya.

⁴⁰All these sons of Asher, heads of the ancestral households, proven men, forceful strong men, heads among the leaders. Their enrolment by genealogy in the army in battle: their number, 26,000 men.

Down to our own day: Binyamin

8 Binyamin fathered Bela his firstborn, Ashbel the second, Aharah the third, ²Nohah the fourth and Rapha the fifth. ³Bela had sons: Addar, Gera, Abihud, ⁴Abishua, Na'aman, Ahoah, ⁵Gera, Shephupham and Huram.

⁶These are Ehud's sons, ancestral heads of the inhabitants of Geba, but they exiled them to Manahat: ⁷Na'aman, Ahiyyah and Gera; he exiled them and fathered Uzza and Ahihud.

⁸Shaharayim fathered sons in the open country in Mo'ab after he had sent them away (Husham and Ba'ara were his wives); ⁹by Hodesh his wife he fathered Yobab, Tsibya, Mesha, Malkam, ¹⁰Ye'uts, Sakeyah and Mirmah; these were his sons, ancestral heads; ¹¹by Hushim he fathered Ahitub and Elpa'al.

¹²The sons of Elpa'al: Eber, Misham, Shemed (he built Ono and Lod and its daughter-towns), ¹³Beri'ah and Shema (they were ancestral heads of the inhabitants of Ayyalon – they put to flight the inhabitants of Gat), ¹⁴Ahyo, Shashaq and Yeremot.

¹⁵Zebadyah, Arad, Eder, ¹⁶Mika'el, Yishpah and Yoha were Beri'ah's sons.

¹⁷Zebadyah, Meshullam, Hizqi, Heber, ¹⁸Yishmeray, Yizliah and Yobab were Elpa'al's sons.

¹⁹Yaqim, Zikri, Zabdi, ²⁰Eli'enay, Zilletay, Eli'el, ²¹Adayah, Bera'yah and Shimrat were Shim'i's sons.

²²Yishpan, Eber, Eli'el, ²³Abdon, Zikri, Hanan, ²⁴Hananyah, Elam, Antotiyyah, ²⁵Yiphdeyah and Penu'el were Shashaq's sons.

²⁶Shamsheray, Sheharyah, Atalyah, ²⁷Ya'areshyah, Eliyyah and Zikri were Yeroham's sons.

²⁸These were the ancestral heads by their lines of descent. These heads lived in Yerushalaim.

Sha'ul's family

²⁹Gib'on's father lived in Gib'on. His wife's name was Ma'akah. ³⁰His firstborn son Abdon, Tsur, Qish, Ba'al, Nadab, ³¹Gedor, Ahyo and Zeker. ³²Miklot fathered Shim'ah. They also lived opposite their brothers in Yerushalaim, with their brothers. ³³Ner fathered Qish, Qish fathered Sha'ul, and Sha'ul fathered Yehonatan, Malki-shua, Abinadab and Eshba'al. ³⁴Yehonatan's son was Merib Ba'al. Merib Ba'al fathered Mikah.

³⁵Mikah's sons: Piton, Melek, Ta'area and Ahaz.

³⁶Ahaz fathered Yeho'addah; Yeho'addah fathered Alemet, Azmavet and Zimri. Zimri fathered Motsa.

³⁷Motsa fathered Bin'a, Rapha his son, El'asah his son, Atsel his son.

³⁸Atsel had six sons; these are their names: Azriqam, Bokeru, Yishma'e'l, She'aryah, Obadyah and Hanan; all these were Atsel's sons.

³⁹The sons of Esheq his brother: Ulam his firstborn, Ye'ush the second and Eliphelet the third.

⁴⁰Ulam's sons were forceful strong men, drawing the bow, and they produced a large number of children and grandchildren, 150, all these Binyaminites.

9 All Yisra'el was enrolled by genealogy: there, they are written down on the document about the kings of Yisra'el. But Yehudah was taken into exile to Babel because of their trespass.

The returners

²The first people settling who were on their holding in their towns were Yisra'el, priests, Levites and assistants, ³while some Yehudahites, some Binyaminites, some Ephrayimites and some Menashshehites settled in Yerushalaim: ⁴Utay ben Ammihud son of Omri son of Imri son of Bani, from the sons of Perets son of Yehudah. ⁵Of the Shilonites: Asayah the firstborn and his sons. ⁶Of the sons of Zerah: Ye'u'el and his brothers – 690. ⁷Of the Binyaminites: Sallu ben Meshullam son of Hodavyah son of Hassenu'ah, ⁸Yibneyah ben Yeroham, Elah ben Uzzi son of Mikri, and Meshullam ben Shephatyah son of Re'u'el son of Yibneyah, ⁹and their brothers, by their lines of descent – 956. All these people were ancestral heads of their ancestral households. ¹⁰Of the priests: Yedayah, Yehoyarib, Yakin, ¹¹and Azaryah ben Hilqiyyah son of Meshullam son of Tsadoq son of Merayot son of Ahitub, chief over God's house, ¹²and Adayah ben Yeroham son of Pashhur son of Malkiyyah, and Ma'asay ben Adi'el son of Yahzerah son of Meshullam son of Meshillemit son of Immer, ¹³and their brothers, heads of their ancestral households – 1,760, forceful strong men for the work in the service of God's house. ¹⁴Of the Levites: Shema'yah ben Hashshub son of Azriqam son of Hashabyah, of the Merarites; ¹⁵and Baqbaqqer, Heresh, Galal, and Mattanyah ben Mika son of Zikri son of Asaph; ¹⁶and Obadyah ben Shemayah son of Galal son of Yedutun; and Berekyah ben Asa son of Elqanah who lived in the villages of the Netophatites.

The gatemen

¹⁷The gatemen: Shallum, Aqqub, Talmon, Ahiman, with their brother Shallum the head. ¹⁸Until now they have been at the King's Gate on the east, gatemen for the Levites' camp. ¹⁹Shallum ben Qore son of Ebyasaph son of Qorah and his brothers belonging to his ancestral household, the Qorahites, were in charge of the work involved in the service, keeping watch over the tent thresholds; their ancestors had been in charge of Yahweh's camp as people keeping watch over the entrance. ²⁰Pinhas ben El'azar was chief over them before; Yahweh was with him. ²¹Zekaryah ben Meshelemyah was gateman at the door of the appointment tent. ²²All of them, people proven as gatemen at the thresholds – 212. They were in their villages enrolled by genealogy. David and Shemu'el the seer had established them in their position of trust. ²³They and their sons were in charge of the gateways of Yahweh's house (of the tent house) by watches. ²⁴The gatemen were on the four sides, east, west, north and south. ²⁵Their brothers in the villages were to come every seven days on a schedule, with these men, ²⁶because the four strongest gatemen (they were Levites) were in the position of trust; they were in charge of the halls and of the treasuries in God's house. ²⁷They stayed the night round God's house because the watch was their responsibility and they were in charge of the opening morning by morning.

Sha'ul's family background

²⁸Some of them were in charge of the articles used in the service, because they would bring them in with a count and take them out with a count. ²⁹Some of them were put in charge of the articles, both all the sacred articles and the flour, the wine, the oil, the incense and the spices ³⁰(some of the priests were the people who made the blend of the spices). ³¹Mattityah of the Levites (he was the firstborn of Shallum the Qorahite) was in the position of trust in charge of the making of the griddle cakes. ³²Some of the Qehatites from among their brothers were in charge of the row bread, to prepare it sabbath by sabbath.

³³These are the singers, the ancestral heads of the Levites, in the halls, free, because responsibility was upon them day and night in the work. ³⁴These were the ancestral heads of the Levites by their lines of descent. These heads lived in Yerushalaim.

³⁵Gib'on's father Ye'i'el lived in Gib'on (his wife's name was Ma'akah) ³⁶with his firstborn

son Abdon, Tsur, Qish, Ba'al, Ner, Nadab, ³⁷Gedor, Ahyo, Zekaryah and Miklot.
  ³⁸Miklot fathered Shim'am, and they too lived in Yerushalaim opposite their brothers, with their brothers.
  ³⁹Ner fathered Qish, Qish fathered Sha'ul, Sha'ul fathered Yehonatan, Malki-shua, Abinadab and Eshba'al; ⁴⁰Yehonatan's son was Merib Ba'al; Meri-ba'al fathered Mikah.
  ⁴¹Mikah's sons: Piton, Melek and Ta'area.
  ⁴²Ahaz fathered Yarah; Yarah fathered Alemet, Azmavet and Zimri; Zimri fathered Motsa.
  ⁴³Motsa fathered Bin'a, Raphayah his son, El'asah his son, Atsel his son.
  ⁴⁴Atsel had six sons; these are their names: Azriqam, Bokeru, Yishma'e'l, She'aryah, Obadyah and Hanan; these were Atsel's sons.

The end of Sha'ul

10 Now the Pelishtites battled against Yisra'el. The Yisra'elites fled from before the Pelishtites and fell, run through, on Mount Gilboa, ²and the Pelishtites caught up with Sha'ul and with his sons. The Pelishtites struck down Yonatan, Abinadab and Malki-shua, Sha'ul's sons. ³The battle was hard against Sha'ul, and the archers found him with an arrow; he was run through by the archers.
  ⁴Sha'ul said to his equipment-bearer, 'Draw your sword and thrust me through with it, so these foreskinned men don't come and deal abusively with me.' But his equipment-bearer wasn't willing, because he was very fearful. So Sha'ul took the sword and fell on it. ⁵His equipment-bearer saw that Sha'ul was dead and he too fell on his sword and died. ⁶So Sha'ul died, with his three sons; his entire household died, all together. ⁷All the Yisra'elites who were in the vale saw that people had fled and that Sha'ul and his sons were dead, and they abandoned their towns and fled (the Pelishtites came and lived in them).
  ⁸Next day the Pelishtites came to strip the people who had been run through. They found Sha'ul and his sons fallen on Mount Gilboa, ⁹stripped him, took up his head and his equipment, and sent them off through the Pelishtites' country all round, to announce the news to their idols and their people. ¹⁰They put his equipment in the house of their gods, and his skull they fastened to the house of Dagan.
  ¹¹All Yabesh-in-Gil'ad heard all that the Pelishtites had done to Sha'ul, ¹²and they set off, every forceful man, took up the corpse of Sha'ul and the corpses of his sons, and brought them to Yabesh. They buried their bones under the oak at Yabesh and fasted for seven days.
  ¹³Sha'ul died because of his trespass, which he committed against Yahweh in regard to Yahweh's word which he had not kept, and also in asking something of a spirit, so as to make enquiry; ¹⁴he didn't enquire of Yahweh. So he put him to death and turned the kingship over to David ben Yishay.

David anointed

11 All Yisra'el collected to David at Hebron, saying, 'Here, we are your flesh and blood. ²Further, in previous days, even when Sha'ul was king, you were the one who took Yisra'el out and brought Yisra'el in. Yahweh your God said to you, "You're the one who'll shepherd my people Yisra'el. You're the one who'll be chief over my people Yisra'el."'
  ³So all Yisra'el's elders came to the king at Hebron, David solemnized a pact towards them at Hebron before Yahweh, and they anointed David as king over Yisra'el in accordance with Yahweh's word by means of Shemu'el.
  ⁴David and all Yisra'el went to Yerushalaim (i.e. Yebus); the Yebusites were there as inhabitants of the region. ⁵The inhabitants of Yebus said to David, 'You won't come in here', but David captured the Zion stronghold (i.e. David's Town). ⁶David said, 'Anyone striking down the Yebusites first will be head and officer.' Yo'ab ben Tseruyah went up first and became head.
  ⁷David lived in the stronghold; that's why they named it 'David's Town'. ⁸He built up the town all round, from the Fill all round, while Yo'ab brought to life the remainder of the town. ⁹David went on getting bigger and bigger, as Yahweh of Armies was with him.
  ¹⁰These are the heads of the strong men that David had, the people who asserted their strength with him in his kingship, with all Yisra'el, in making him king in accordance

with Yahweh's word concerning Yisra'el, [11]and these are the number of the strong men that David had.

Yashob'am the Hakmonite was head of the adjutants. He was wielding his lance against 300, run through on one occasion. [12]After him was El'azar ben Dodo, the Ahohite; he was one of the Three Strong Men, [13]and he was with David at Pas Dammim when the Pelishtites gathered there for battle. A plot of field was full of barley. Whereas the company fled from before the Pelishtites [14]they made a stand in the middle of the plot, defended it and struck down the Pelishtites. Yahweh brought about a great deliverance.

Some spectacular exploits

[15]Three of the Thirty Heads went down to the crag to David at the Adullam Cave. The Pelishtite camp was camped in Repha'ites Vale. [16]David was then in the stronghold, and an outpost of Pelishtites was then at Bet Lehem. [17]David had a longing and said, 'If only someone could give me a drink of water from the Bet-lehem cistern that's at the gateway!' [18]The Three broke through the Pelishtites' camp, drew water from the Bet-lehem cistern that's at the gateway, and carried it and brought it to David. But David was unwilling to drink it. He poured it out for Yahweh [19]and said, 'Far be it from me by God that I should do this. Am I to drink the blood of these men, at the cost of their lives?' – because they had brought it at the cost of their lives. So he was unwilling to drink it. These are things that the Three Strong Men did.

[20]Abshay, the brother of Yo'ab, was head of a Three. He was wielding his lance against 300, run through. He had a name among the Three. [21]Of the Three, he was doubly honoured, and he became officer for them, but he didn't come to the [other] Three.

[22]Benayah ben Yehoyada was a forceful man, prolific in deeds, from Qabtse'el. He struck down the two of Ari'el from Mo'ab. It was he who went down and struck down a lion inside a cistern on a snowy day, [23]and it was he who struck down a Misrayimite man, a huge man of two metres. In the Misrayimite's hand there was a lance like a weavers' rod, but he went down to him with a club, seized the lance from the Misrayimite's hand and killed him with his lance. [24]These things Benayah ben Yehoyada did, and he had a name among the Three Strong Men. [25]Of the Thirty, there he is, most honoured, but he didn't come to the Three. David put him in charge of his guard.

The forceful strong men

[26]The forceful strong men:

Asah-el, Yo'ab's brother
Elhanan ben Dodo from Bet Lehem
[27]Shammot the Harorite
Helets the Palonite
[28]Ira ben Iqqesh the Teqo'ite
Abi'ezer the Anatotite
[29]Sibbekay the Hushatite
Ilay the Ahohite
[30]Mahray the Netophatite
Heled ben Ba'anah the Netophatite
[31]Ittay ben Ribay from Gib'ah-of-the-Binyaminites
Benayah the Pir'atonite
[32]Huray from the Ga'ash Wadis
Abi'el the Arbatite
[33]Azmavet the Bahrumite
Elyahba the Sha'albonite
[34]The sons of Hashem the Gizonite
Yonatan ben Shageh the Hararite
[35]Ahi'am ben Sakar the Hararite
Eliphal ben Ur
[36]Hepher the Mekeratite
Ahiyyah the Pelonite
[37]Hetsro the Carmelite
Na'aray ben Ezbay
[38]Yo'el, Natan's brother
Mibhar ben Hagri
[39]Tseleq the Ammonite
Nahray the Berotite, equipment-bearer for Yo'ab ben Tseruyah
[40]Ira the Yitrite
Gareb the Yitrite
[41]Uriyyah the Hittite
Zabad ben Ahlay
[42]Adina ben Shiza, the Re'ubenite, head of the Re'ubenites, and thirty with him
[43]Hanan ben Ma'akah
Yoshaphat the Mitnite
[44]Uzziyya the Ashteratite
Shama and Ye'i'el sons of Hotam the Aro'erite
[45]Yedi'a'el ben Shimri and Yoha his brother the Titsite
[46]Eli'el the Mahavite
Yeribay and Yoshavyah sons of Elna'am
Yitmah the Mo'abite
[47]Eli'el, Obed and Ya'asi'el the Metsobayite

A time of encouragement

12 These are the people who came to David at Tsiqlag when he was still held back because of Sha'ul ben Qish. They were among the strong men helping in battle, ²able to wield the bow, right-handed and left-handed with stones and with arrows from the bow, from among Sha'ul's brothers from Binyamin.

³The head, Ahi'ezer, and Yo'ash, the sons of Shema'ah the Gib'atite
Yezi'el and Pelet, the sons of Azmavet
Berakah
Yehu the Anatotite
⁴Yishma'yah the Gib'onite, a strong man among the Thirty, and in charge of the Thirty
Yirmeyah
Yahazi'el
Yohanan
Yozabad the Gederatite
⁵Eluzay
Yerimot
Be'alyah
Shemaryahu
Shephatyahu the Haruphite
⁶Elqanah, Yishsheyahu, Azar'el, Yo'ezer and Yashob'am, the Qorahites
⁷Yo'e'lah and Zebahyah, sons of Yeroham from Gedor

⁸Forceful strong men from the Gadites made themselves distinct to join David at the stronghold in the wilderness, forceful strong men in the army, ready for battle, able to wield shield and spear, with their face the face of a lion, and making speed like gazelles on the mountains:

⁹Ezer the head
Obadyah the second
Eli'ab the third
¹⁰Mishmannah the fourth
Yirmeyah the fifth
¹¹Attay the sixth
Eli'el the seventh
¹²Yohanan the eighth
Elzabad the ninth
¹³Yirmeyahu the tenth
Makbannay the eleventh

¹⁴These of the Gadites were army heads, the smallest for a hundred, the biggest for a thousand. ¹⁵These were those people who crossed the Yarden in the first month when it was filling up over all its banks, and put to flight all the vale people to the east and to the west.

A time for caution

¹⁶Some Binyaminites and Yehudahites came as far as the stronghold to David, ¹⁷and David went out before them. He avowed to them, 'If you've come to me so that things may go well, to help me, my mind will be one with you, but if it's to beguile me in relation to my attackers when there is no violence in my fists, may our ancestors' God see and reprove.' ¹⁸And a spirit put on Amasay, head of the Thirty:

> For you, David, and with you, ben Yishay, may things be well;
> May things be well for you, and things be well for the person who helps you,
> Because your God has helped you.

So David received them and made them into the heads of his raiding gangs.

¹⁹Some of Menahsheh submitted to David when he came with the Pelishtites for battle against Sha'ul, but they didn't help them because the Pelishtites' lords in council sent him off, saying, 'He'll submit to his lord, Sha'ul, at the cost of our heads.' ²⁰When he went to Tsiqlag, some Menashshites submitted to him, Adnah, Yozabad, Yedi'a'el, Mika'el, Yozabad, Elihu and Tsillethay, chiliarchs belonging to Menashsheh. ²¹It was those people who helped David against the raiding gang, because all of them were forceful strong men. They became officers in the army, ²²because day by day people were coming to David to help him, until the camp was as big as God's camp.

Time for celebration

²³These are the numbers of the heads of the people equipped for the army who came to David at Hebron to turn over Sha'ul's kingship to him in accordance with Yahweh's bidding:
²⁴Yehudahites carrying shield and spear – 6,800 equipped for the army.
²⁵Of the Shim'onites, forceful strong men for the army – 7,100.
²⁶Of the Levites – 4,600; ²⁷Yehoyada, the chief of Aharon, and with him 3,700; ²⁸and Tsadoq, a boy, a forceful strong man, and his ancestral household, 22 officers.
²⁹Of the Binyaminites, Sha'ul's brothers, 3,000 (until now the majority of them were keeping watch for Sha'ul's household).
³⁰Of the Ephrayimites, 20,800 forceful strong men, people with names in their ancestral household.

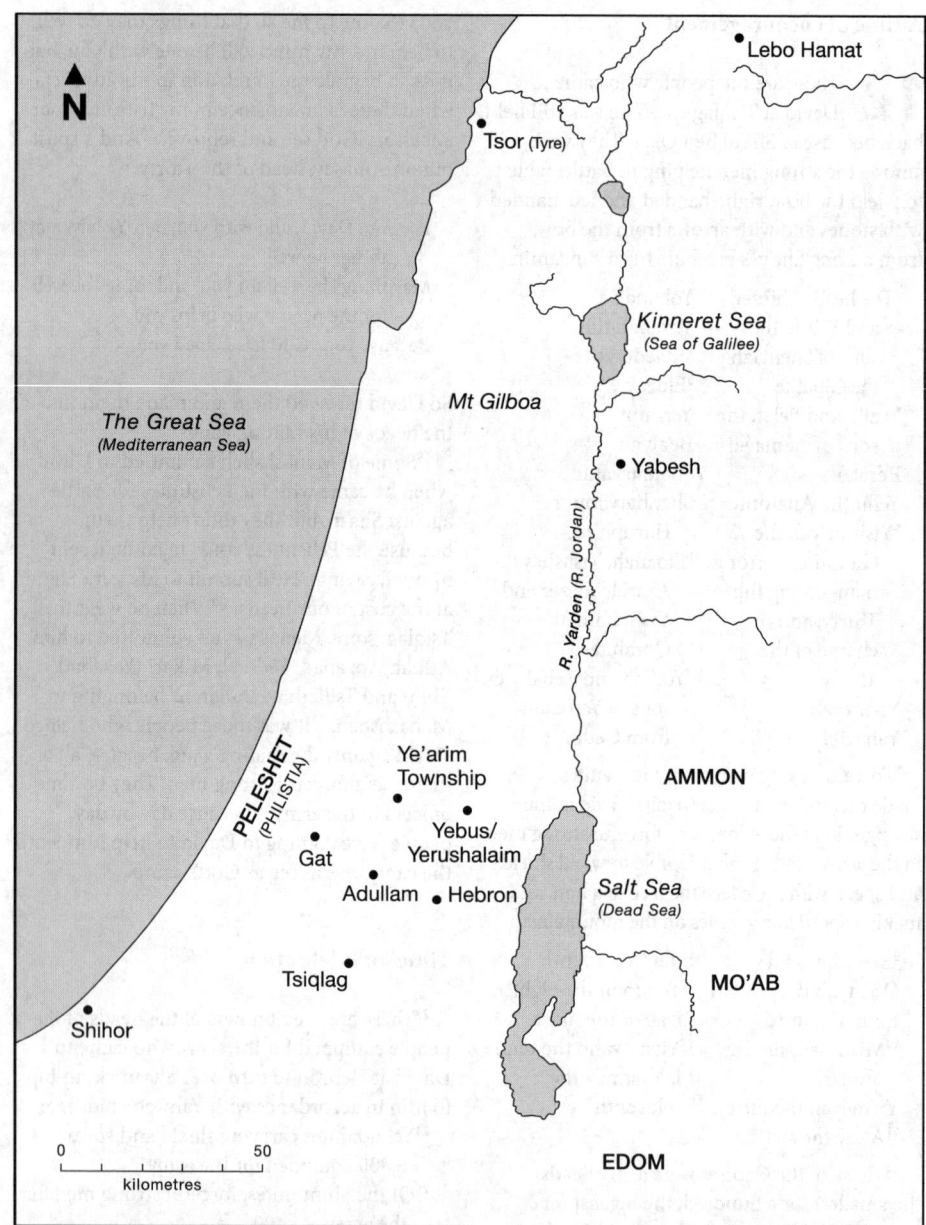

1 Chronicles 12: David

³¹Of the half-clan of Menashsheh, 18,000, who were designated by their names to come to make David king.

³²Of the Yissakarites, people who had understanding of the times so as to know what Yisra'el should do – their heads 200, and all their brothers at their bidding.

³³Of Zebulun, people able to go out in the army, lining up for battle with all battle equipment – 50,000 to help, without a double mind.

³⁴From Naphtali, 1,000 officers, and with them, with shield and lance – 37,000.

³⁵From the Danites, people lining up for battle – 28,600.

³⁶From Asher, people able to go out in the army to line up for battle – 40,000. ³⁷From across the Yarden, from the Re'ubenites, the Gadites and the half-clan of Menashsheh, with all battle army equipment – 120,000. ³⁸All these men of battle, assisting the line-up, with a perfect mind, came to Hebron to make David king over all Yisra'el, while all the remainder of Yisra'el also were of one mind in making David king. ³⁹They were there with David for three days eating and drinking, because their brothers had prepared it for them. ⁴⁰People who were near to them as far as Yissakar, Zebulun and Naphtali were also bringing food on donkeys, on camels, on mules and on cattle, edibles of flour, fig blocks, raisin blocks, wine, oil, cattle and sheep in quantity, because there was rejoicing in Yisra'el.

A frightening outburst

13 David took counsel with the chiliarchs and centurions, every chief, ²and David said to the entire Yisra'elite congregation, 'If it seems good to you and it's from Yahweh our God, let's break out and send to our remaining brothers in all the regions of Yisra'el, and with them the priests and the Levites in their pastureland towns, so they may collect to us ³and we may turn our God's chest over to us, because we didn't enquire of him in Sha'ul's days.' ⁴The entire congregation said to do so, because the thing was upright in the eyes of the entire people.

⁵So David congregated all Yisra'el from Shihor in Misrayim as far as Lebo Hamat, to bring God's chest from Ye'arim Township. ⁶David and all Yisra'el went up to Ba'alah (to Ye'arim Township which belongs to Yehudah) to take up from there the chest of God, Yahweh who sits above the sphinxes, which is called by the name. ⁷They transported God's chest on a new wagon from Abinadab's house, with Uzza and Ahyo driving the wagon ⁸and David and all Yisra'el making fun before God with all their vigour, with songs, with guitars, with mandolins, with tambourines, with cymbals and with trumpets. ⁹But they came as far as Kidon's threshing floor and Uzza put out his hand to grasp the chest, because the cattle had stumbled. ¹⁰Yahweh's anger raged at Uzza and he struck him down on account of the fact that he had put out his hand to the chest. He died there before God. ¹¹It enraged David that Yahweh had broken out at Uzza. He called that place Perets Uzza ['Breakout at Uzza'], until this day.

¹²David was afraid of God that day, saying, 'How can I bring God's chest to me?' ¹³So David did not move the chest to him, to David's Town. He got it to turn aside to the house of Obed-edom the Gittite. ¹⁴God's chest stayed with Obed Edom's household in his house for three months, and Yahweh blessed the household of Obed-edom and everything he had.

When you need to know what to do

14 Hiram king of Tsor [Tyre] sent envoys to David, with cedar wood, craftsmen in walls and craftsmen in wood, to build him a house. ²David acknowledged that Yahweh had established him as king over Yisra'el, because his kingship had been exalted exceptionally high for the sake of his people Yisra'el.

³David took more wives in Yerushalaim and David fathered more sons and daughters. ⁴These are the names of the ones born, who were his in Yerushalaim: Shammua, Shobab, Natan, Shelomoh, ⁵Yibhar, Elishua, Elpelet, ⁶Nogah, Nepheg, Yaphia, ⁷Elishama, Be'elyada and Eliphelet.

⁸The Pelishtites heard that David had been anointed as king over all Yisra'el, and all the Pelishtites went up to look for David. David heard, and went out before them. ⁹When the Pelishtites came, they raided Repha'ites Vale. ¹⁰David asked of God, 'Shall I go up against the Pelishtites? Will you give them into my hand?' Yahweh said to him, 'Go up, and I shall give them into your hand.' ¹¹So they went up to Ba'al Peratsim, and David struck them down there. David said, 'God has broken out on my enemies by my hand like a breakout of water.' That's why they named that place Ba'al Peratsim ['Master of Breakouts']. ¹²They abandoned their gods there. David said it, and they were burned in fire.

¹³The Pelishtites again raided the vale. ¹⁴David again asked of God, but God said to him, 'You will not go up after them. Make a

turn away from them and come to them from the direction of the weeper trees. [15]When you hear the sound of marching in the tops of the weeper trees, then you're to go out in battle, because God will have gone out before you to strike down the Pelishtite camp.' [16]David did as God ordered him, and they struck down the Pelishtite camp from Gib'on as far as Gezer.

[17]David's name went out through all the countries as Yahweh put a dread of him on all the nations.

Preparations for taking the chest

15 He made houses for himself in David's Town, and prepared a place for God's chest and pitched a tent for it. [2]Then David said no one was to carry God's chest but only the Levites, because Yahweh chose them to carry Yahweh's chest and to minister to him permanently. [3]David congregated all Yisra'el to Yerushalaim to take up Yahweh's chest to its place which he had prepared for it. [4]David gathered the Aharonites and the Levites:

[5]of the Qehatites, Uri'el the official and his brothers – 120;

[6]of the Merarites, Asayah the official and his brothers – 220;

[7]of the Gershomites, Yo'el the official and his brothers – 130;

[8]of the Elitsaphanites, Shemayah the official and his brothers – 200;

[9]of the Hebronites, Eli'el the official and his brothers – 80;

[10]of the Uzzi'elites, Amminadab the official and his brothers – 112.

[11]David called for Tsadoq and for Ebyatar the priests, and of the Levites for Uri'el, for Asayah, for Yo'el, for Shemayah, for Eli'el and for Amminadab. [12]He said to them, 'You are the Levites' ancestral heads. Make yourselves sacred, you and your brothers, so that you may take up the chest of Yahweh, the God of Yisra'el, to where I have prepared for it. [13]Because you were not there the first time, Yahweh our God broke out on us, because we did not enquire of him in accordance with the ruling.'

[14]The priests and the Levites made themselves sacred for taking up the chest of Yahweh, the God of Yisra'el. [15]The Levites carried God's chest as Mosheh had ordered in accordance with Yahweh's word, on their shoulder, with poles on them. [16]David said to the Levites' officials to get their brothers, the singers, with musical instruments, guitars, mandolins and cymbals, to stand, making things heard by raising their voice in rejoicing.

The great celebration

[17]So the Levites got to stand:
Heman ben Yo'el;
of his brothers Asaph ben Berekyahu;
of the Merarites, their brothers, Etan ben Qushayahu;
[18]with them their brothers as number two Zekaryahu, son, Ya'azi'el, Shemiramot, Yehi'el, Unni, Eli'ab, Benayahu, Ma'aseyahu, Mattityahu, Eliphalehu, Miqneyahu, Obed Edom and Ye'i'el, the gatemen;
[19]the singers Heman, Asaph and Etan making things heard on copper cymbals;
[20]Zekaryah, Azi'el, Shemiramot, Yehi'el, Unni, Eli'ab, Ma'aseyahu and Benayah with guitars, on 'Eternal Things';
[21]Mattityahu, Eliphelehu, Miqneyahu, Obed Edom, Ye'i'el and Azazyahu with mandolins, on 'The Eighth';
[22]Kenanyahu, the Levites' official, with prophecy, to exercise discipline with prophecy because he was discerning;
[23]Berekyah and Elqanah, the chest's gatemen;
[24]Shebanyahu, Yoshaphat, Netan'el, Amasay, Zekaryahu, Benayah and Eli'ezer the priests, sounding on the trumpets before God's chest;
Obed Edom and Yehiyyah the chest's gatemen.
[25]David, Yisra'el's elders and the chiliarchs went to take up Yahweh's pact chest from Obed-edom's house with rejoicing. [26]As God helped the Levites carrying Yahweh's pact chest, they sacrificed seven bulls and seven rams, [27]with David clad in a robe of Misrayimite linen, and all the Levites who were carrying the chest, and the singers, and Kenanyah the singers' prophetic officer, and on David a linen chasuble, [28]as all Yisra'el were taking up Yahweh's pact chest with a shout, with the sound of a horn, with trumpets and

with cymbals, making things heard with guitars and mandolins. ²⁹Yahweh's pact chest was coming into David's Town as Mikal, Sha'ul's daughter, was looking out through the window. She saw King David jumping and having fun, and she despised him inside.

16 They brought in God's chest and put it inside the tent that David had pitched for it, and presented burnt offerings and well-being sacrifices before God. ²David finished offering up the burnt offering and the well-being sacrifices, blessed the people in Yahweh's name, ³and shared out to each person in Yisra'el, man and woman, to each individual a round of bread, a date block and a raisin block.

Sing to Yahweh, all the earth!

⁴He put some of the Levites before Yahweh's chest as ministers, to make mention, to confess and to praise Yahweh the God of Yisra'el:
⁵Asaph the head;
number two to him, Zekaryah;
Ye'i'el, Shemiramot, Yehi'el, Mattityah,
Eli'ab, Benayahu, Obed Edom and Ye'i'el,
with guitars as instruments and with mandolins;
Asaph making things heard with the cymbals;
⁶Benayahu and Yahazi'el the priests with trumpets regularly before God's pact chest.
⁷Then on that day David first put confession of Yahweh into the hand of Asaph and his brothers:

⁸Confess Yahweh, call out in his name,
    get his deeds acknowledged among the peoples.
⁹Sing for him, make music for him,
    talk of all his extraordinary deeds.
¹⁰Take pride in his sacred name;
    the heart of those who seek Yahweh should rejoice.
¹¹Enquire of Yahweh and his vigour;
    seek his face continually.
¹²Be mindful of his extraordinary deeds, which he has done,
    his signs and the rulings of his mouth,
¹³Offspring of Yisra'el his servant,
    descendants of Ya'aqob [Jacob], his chosen ones.
¹⁴He is Yahweh our God;
    his rulings are in all the earth.
¹⁵Be mindful of his pact permanently,
    the word he ordered for a thousand generations,
¹⁶Which he solemnized with Abraham,
    his oath to Yitshaq,
¹⁷Made to stand for Ya'aqob as a decree,
    for Yisra'el as a lasting pact,
¹⁸Saying, 'To you I will give the country of Kena'an
    as an allocation and as your domain.'
¹⁹When you were few in number,
    a tiny group, and sojourning in it,
²⁰And they went about from nation to nation,
    from a kingdom to another people.
²¹He didn't leave be anyone to oppress them,
    but reproved kings on account of them:
²²'Don't touch my anointed ones,
    don't deal badly towards my prophets.'

All the people said, 'Yes!'

²³Sing for Yahweh all the earth,
    announce the news of his deliverance, from day to day.
²⁴Recount his splendour among the nations,
    among all the peoples his extraordinary deeds.
²⁵Because Yahweh is great and much to be praised;
    he is to be held in awe above all gods.
²⁶Because all the gods of the peoples are non-entities,
    whereas Yahweh made the heavens.
²⁷Grandeur and magnificence are before him,
    vigour and glory at his site.
²⁸Kin-groups of the peoples, give Yahweh,
    give Yahweh splendour and vigour.
²⁹Give Yahweh the splendour due to his name,
    take up an offering and come before him.
Bow low to Yahweh in his sacred glory;
    ³⁰tremble before him, all the earth.
Yes, the world stands firm, it does not slip;
    ³¹the heavens should rejoice, the earth be glad.
They should say among the nations,
    'Yahweh has become king.'
³²The sea should roar and everything that fills it,
    the open country should triumph and all that's in it.

³³Then the trees in the forest should resound
> before Yahweh,
> because he is coming to exercise authority
> over the earth.
³⁴Confess Yahweh, because he is good,
> because his commitment lasts permanently.
³⁵Say, 'Deliver us, our God who delivers,
> collect us and rescue us from the nations,
To confess your sacred name,
> to glory in your praise.'
³⁶Blessed be Yahweh the God of Yisra'el
> from age to age.

All the people said 'Yes' and 'Praise Yahweh.' ³⁷And he abandoned before Yahweh's pact chest there:
> Asaph and his brothers to minister before the chest regularly in connection with each day's requirement in its day; ³⁸Obed Edom and their brothers – sixty-eight; Obed Edom ben Yeditun and Hosah as gatemen; ³⁹Tsadoq the priest and his brothers, the priests, before Yahweh's dwelling at the shrine which was at Gib'on, ⁴⁰to offer up burnt offerings for Yahweh on the burnt-offering altar regularly, morning and evening, in connection with all that is written in Yahweh's instruction with which he ordered Yisra'el; ⁴¹with them Heman, Yedutun and the remainder of the proven men who were designated by their names to confess Yahweh 'because his commitment is permanent'; ⁴²with them (Heman and Yedutun) trumpets and cymbals for the people who make things heard, and instruments for a song to God;
> the sons of Yedutun at the gateway.

⁴³The entire people went each one to his house and David turned to bless his household.

Who builds a house, and what kind?

17 When David had gone to live in his house, David said to Natan the prophet, 'Here am I living in a cedar house and Yahweh's pact chest is under tent cloths.' ²Natan said to David, 'Do everything that's in your mind, because God is with you.'

³But that night God's word came to Natan: ⁴'Go and say to David my servant, "Yahweh has said this: 'It's not you who will build me a house to live in. ⁵Because I haven't lived in a house from the day that I brought Yisra'el up, until this day. I've been from tent to tent, and from a dwelling. ⁶Everywhere I went about in all Yisra'el, did I speak a word to one of the people exercising authority in Yisra'el whom I ordered to shepherd my people, saying "Why have you not built me a cedar house?"'"

⁷So now you're to say this to my servant, to David: "Yahweh of Armies has said this: 'I myself took you from the pasture, from following the flock, to be chief over my people Yisra'el, ⁸and I've been with you everywhere you've gone. I've cut off all your enemies from before you and I shall make for you a name like the name of the big people who are on the earth. ⁹I shall make a place for my people Yisra'el and plant it. It will dwell in its place and not tremble again. Evil people will not wear it down again as they did previously, ¹⁰from the days when I ordered leaders over my people Yisra'el. I shall make all your enemies bow down.

And I tell you: Yahweh will build a house(hold) for you. ¹¹When your days are full for going to be with your ancestors, I shall set up your offspring after you, who will be one of your sons, and I shall establish his kingship. ¹²He is the one who will build me a house. I shall establish his throne permanently. ¹³I myself will become a father to him and he will become a son to me. I shall not remove my commitment from him as I removed it from the one who was before you. ¹⁴I shall let him stand in my house and in my kingship permanently. His throne will become established permanently.'"

There is no one like Yahweh

¹⁵In accordance with all these words and in accordance with this entire vision, so Natan spoke to David.

¹⁶King David came and sat before Yahweh and said, 'Who am I, Yahweh God, and who are my household, that you have brought me as far as this? ¹⁷And this has been small in your eyes, God. You've spoken about your servant's household for the distant future. You've seen

me as one of lofty human form, Yahweh God. ¹⁸What more can David add regarding your servant's honour? You yourself have acknowledged your servant. ¹⁹Yahweh, for your servant's sake and in accordance with your own mind you are doing this entire big thing, making known all the big things.

²⁰Yahweh, there is no one like you, no God except you, in all that we've heard with our ears. ²¹And who is like your people Yisra'el, a nation on the earth that God went to redeem for himself as a people, to make yourself a name for big and awe-inspiring deeds, in driving nations out from before your people that you redeemed from Misrayim. ²²You made your people Yisra'el into a people for yourself permanently, and you Yahweh became God for them.

²³Now, Yahweh, the word that you have spoken about your servant and about his household – may it be trustworthy permanently. Do as you have spoken. ²⁴May it be trustworthy so that your name may be great permanently: "Yahweh of Armies, the God of Yisra'el, is God for Yisra'el". May your servant David's household be established before you. ²⁵Because you, my God, have opened your servant's ear about building him a household. That's why your servant has found it to plead before you.

²⁶Now, Yahweh, you are God. You've spoken this good thing about your servant. ²⁷Now you've resolved to bless your servant's household so it will be before you permanently, because you, Yahweh, have blessed, and it is blessed permanently.'

Wars and rumours of wars

18 Subsequently, David struck down the Pelishtites and made them bow down; David took Gat and its daughter-towns from the hand of the Pelishtites. ²He struck down the Mo'abites, and the Mo'abites became David's servants, bringing offerings. ³David struck down Hadad'ezer king of Tsobah Hamat, when he was going to put up his monument at the River Euphrates. ⁴David captured from him 1,000 chariotry, 7,000 cavalry and 20,000 men on foot. David hamstrung all the chariotry, but of them left 100 chariotry.

⁵Aramites from Dammeseq [Damascus] came to help Hadad'ezer king of Tsobah, and David struck down the Aramites, 22,000 men. ⁶David put men in Aram of Dammeseq, and the Aramites became David's servants, bringing offerings. Yahweh delivered David in every place where he went. ⁷David took the gold quivers that were with Hadad'ezer's servants and brought them to Yerushalaim, ⁸and from Tibhat and from Kun, Hadad'ezer's towns, David took very much copper with which Shelomoh made the copper sea, the columns and the copper articles.

⁹To'u king of Hamat heard that David had struck down the entire force of Hadad'ezer king of Tsobah, ¹⁰and he sent Hadoram his son to King David to ask him about whether things were well and to bless him, on account of the fact that he had battled against Hadad'ezer and had struck him down, on account of the fact that Hadad'ezer had been involved in battles with To'u.

All the gold, silver and copper objects – ¹¹David also made them sacred for Yahweh, with the silver and the gold that he took up from all the nations, from Edom, from Mo'ab, from the Ammonites, from the Pelishtites and from Amaleq. ¹²When Abishay ben Tseruyah struck down Edom in Salt Ravine, 18,000, ¹³ᵃhe put outposts in Edom; all Edom became David's servants.

Suspicion and humiliation

¹³ᵇYahweh delivered David wherever he went. ¹⁴David reigned over all Yisra'el, and he was exercising authority in a faithful way for his entire people.

¹⁵Yo'ab ben Tseruyah was over the army.
Yehoshaphat ben Ahihud was recorder.
¹⁶Tsadoq ben Ahitub and Abimelek ben
   Ebyatar were priests.
Shavsha was secretary.
¹⁷Benayah ben Yehoyada was over the
   Keretites and the Peletites.
David's sons were the first people at the
   king's right hand.

19 Subsequently, Nahash king of the Ammonites died, and his son began to reign in place of him. ²David said, 'I will act in commitment with Hanun ben Nahash, because his father acted in commitment with me.' So David sent envoys to console him about his father. David's servants came to the Ammonites' country to Hanun, to console him, ³but the Ammonites' officials said to Hanun, 'Is David honouring your father, in your eyes, because he sent you people offering consolation? It's for the sake of searching out and overthrowing, investigating the country, that his servants have come to you, isn't it.'

⁴So Hanun got David's servants, clipped them and cut their clothes in half up to their behinds, and sent them off. ⁵People went and told David about the men and he sent to meet them, because the men were very ashamed. The king said, 'Stay in Yeriho until your beard grows and you can come back.' ⁶The Ammonites saw that they stank with David. So Hanun and the Ammonites sent a thousand silver talents to hire themselves chariotry and cavalry from Aram-of-the-Two-Rivers, Aram Ma'akah and Tsobah. ⁷They hired themselves 32,000 chariotry, the king of Ma'akah and his company, and came and camped before Medeba, while the Ammonites gathered from their towns and came for battle. ⁸David heard and sent Yo'ab and the entire army, the strong men.

Be strong and show yourself strong

⁹The Ammonites went out and lined up for battle at the entrance to the town, with the kings who came in the open country on their own. ¹⁰Yo'ab saw that the face of the battle was against him in front and behind. He picked some of all the picked men in Yisra'el and lined them up to meet the Aramites, ¹¹while he gave the rest of the company into the hand of Abshay his brother and they lined up to meet the Ammonites. ¹²He said, 'If the Aramites are too strong for me, you'll be my deliverance, and if the Ammonites are too strong for you, I'll deliver you. ¹³Be strong, and let's assert our strength on behalf of our people and on behalf of our God's towns, as Yahweh does what is good in his eyes.'

¹⁴So Yo'ab went up before the Aramites for the battle, he and his company who were with him, and they fled from before him. ¹⁵When the Ammonites saw that the Aramites had fled, they too fled from before Abishay his brother and came into the town. So Yo'ab came to Yerushalaim.

¹⁶The Aramites saw that they had taken a beating before Yisra'el, and they sent envoys and got the Aramites who were from across the River to go out, with Shophak, Hadad'ezer's army officer, at their head. ¹⁷It was told David, and he gathered all Yisra'el, crossed the Yarden, came to them and lined up against them.

So David lined up to meet the Aramites in battle, and they did battle with him. ¹⁸The Aramites fled from before Yisra'el and David killed 7,000 of the Aramite chariotry and 40,000 men on foot, and put to death Shophak the army officer. ¹⁹The servants of Hadad'ezer saw that they had taken a beating before Yisra'el and they made peace with David and served him. The Aramites were not willing to deliver the Ammonites any more.

Giants of men

20 At the time of the turn of the year, at the time when the kings go out, Yo'ab led out the army force, devastated the Ammonites' country, and came and besieged Rabbah, while David was staying in Yerushalaim. Yo'ab struck down Rabbah and tore it down. ²David got their king's crown from on his head and found its weight a talent of gold, with precious stones in it. It came on to David's head, as he took out very much spoil from the town. ³The people that was in it he took out and submitted to saws, iron harrows and axes. So David would do to all the towns of the Ammonites. Then David and the entire company went back to Yerushalaim.

⁴Subsequently, a battle started at Gezer with the Pelishtites. Then Sibbekay the Hushatite struck down Sippay, one of the descendants of the Repha'ites. So they bowed down. ⁵There was again a battle with the Pelishtites. Elhanan ben Ya'ir struck down Lahmi, brother of Golyat [Goliath] the Gittite; the wood of his lance was like a weavers' rod. ⁶There was again a battle at Gat, and there was a man of stature with twenty-four fingers and toes, six on each. ⁷He

reviled Yisra'el, and Yehonatan ben Shim'a, David's brother, struck him down. ⁸These had descended from the Healer in Gat. They fell by the hand of David and by the hand of his servants.

Temptation and fall

21 ¹An adversary stood up against Yisra'el and incited David to count Yisra'el. ²So David said to Yo'ab and to the company's officers, 'Go number Yisra'el, from Be'er Sheba as far as Dan, and bring it to me so I may know their number.' ³Yo'ab said, 'May Yahweh add to his people a hundred times as many as they are. My lord king, all of them are my lord's servants, aren't they. Why does my lord seek this? Why should it bring liability on Yisra'el?' ⁴But when the king's word was strong over Yo'ab, Yo'ab went out and went about in all Yisra'el, then came to Yerushalaim. ⁵Yo'ab gave David the number for the registration of the people. All Yisra'el was 1,100,000 men drawing the sword; Yehudah was 470,000 men drawing the sword; ⁶Levi and Binyamin he did not register among them because the king's word was offensive to Yo'ab.

⁷This thing was bad in God's eyes, and he struck Yisra'el down. ⁸David said to God, 'I've acted very wrongly in that I have done this thing. But now, please make your servant's waywardness pass away, because I've been very idiotic.' ⁹Yahweh spoke to Gad, David's seer: ¹⁰'Go and speak to David: "Yahweh has said this: 'I'm holding out three things to you. Choose one of these for yourself and I shall do it for you.'"' ¹¹Gad came to David and said to him, 'Yahweh has said this: "Accept for yourself ¹²either three years of famine, or three months of being swept away before your adversaries, with your enemies' sword overtaking, or three days of Yahweh's sword and epidemic in the country and Yahweh's envoy causing devastation in the entire territory of Yisra'el." So now see what word I am to take back to the one who sent me.'

¹³David said to Gad, 'It's very pressurizing for me. I shall fall into Yahweh's hand, please, because his compassion is very great. Into a human hand I will not fall.'

No cost-free offerings

¹⁴So Yahweh put an epidemic on Yisra'el and 70,000 individuals from Yisra'el fell. ¹⁵God sent an envoy to Yerushalaim to devastate it, but as he was devastating it, Yahweh saw and relented over the bad thing and said to the devastating envoy, 'So much! Now slacken your hand.' Yahweh's envoy was standing by the threshing floor of Ornan the Yebusite. ¹⁶David lifted his eyes and saw Yahweh's envoy standing between the earth and the heavens with his drawn sword in his hand extended over Yerushalaim. David and the elders, covered in sack, fell on their faces. ¹⁷David said to God, 'I'm the one who said to number the people, aren't I. I'm the one who did wrong and did what was definitely bad. These people are the flock; what did they do? Yahweh my God, your hand should please be against me and against my ancestral household, not as an epidemic against your people.'

¹⁸Now Yahweh's envoy said to Gad to say to David that David should go up to set up an altar for Yahweh at the threshing floor of Ornan the Yebusite. ¹⁹David went up at Gad's word which he spoke in Yahweh's name. ²⁰Ornan came back and saw the envoy (his four sons with him were hiding; Ornan was threshing wheat). ²¹David came to Ornan and Ornan looked and saw David, went out of the threshing floor and bowed low to David, face to the ground.

²²David said to Ornan, 'Give me the threshing-floor site so I can build an altar for Yahweh on it. Give it to me at the full price so that the epidemic may hold back from the people.' ²³Ornan said to David, 'Take it for yourself. My lord the king may do what is good in his eyes. See, I'm giving the cattle as the burnt offerings and the threshing boards as wood and the wheat as the grain offering. All of it, I'm giving.' ²⁴But King David said to Ornan, 'No, because I will definitely acquire them at the full price, because I won't lift up to Yahweh what belongs to you. I won't offer up a burnt offering that cost nothing.'

Preparations begin

²⁵So David gave Ornan 600 gold sheqels in weight for the site. ²⁶David built an altar there

for Yahweh and offered up burnt offerings and well-being sacrifices. He called to Yahweh, and he answered him with fire from the heavens on the burnt-offering altar. ²⁷Yahweh said it to the envoy and he put his sword back into its sheath.

²⁸At that time, when David saw that Yahweh had answered him at the threshing floor of Ornan the Yebusite, he sacrificed there. ²⁹Yahweh's dwelling which Mosheh made in the wilderness, and the burnt-offering altar, were at the shrine at Gib'on at that time, ³⁰and David could not go before it to enquire of God because he was terrified before the sword of Yahweh's envoy.

22 David said, 'This is the house of Yahweh God. This is the burnt-offering altar for Yisra'el.'

²David said to assemble the resident aliens who were in the country of Yisra'el, and he got them to stand as hewers to hew dressed stones for building God's house. ³David prepared iron in quantity for the nails for the doors of the gateways and for the clasps, copper in quantity, beyond weighing, ⁴and cedar logs beyond numbering (because the Tsidonites and the Tsorites brought cedar logs in quantity to David). ⁵David said, 'Shelomoh my son is a boy and green, and the house to build for Yahweh is to be exceptionally big so as to have a name and glory in all the countries. I should please prepare for him.' So David prepared in quantity before he died.

⁶He called Shelomoh his son, and ordered him to build a house for Yahweh the God of Yisra'el.

The man of peace for a time of peace and a place of peace

⁷David said to Shelomoh his son, 'I myself – it was in my mind to build a house for the name of Yahweh my God, ⁸but Yahweh's word came to me: "You've shed blood in quantity and fought big battles. You will not build a house for my name, because you've shed much blood on the earth before me. ⁹Here, a son has been born to you. He'll be a settled man. I'll enable him to settle down from all his enemies all round, because his name will be Shelomoh and I'll give peace [*shalom*] and calm upon Yisra'el in his days. ¹⁰It's he who will build a house for my name. He'll become a son to me and I'll become a father to him. I'll establish his kingly throne over Yisra'el permanently."

¹¹Now, son, may Yahweh be with you, and may you succeed and build the house of Yahweh your God, as he spoke concerning you. ¹²Yet may Yahweh give you insight and understanding and may he order you over Yisra'el, and so that you keep the instruction of Yahweh your God. ¹³Then you will succeed, if you keep watch over acting on the decrees and the rulings that Yahweh ordered Mosheh for Yisra'el.

Be strong and stand firm. Don't be afraid, don't be scared. ¹⁴Here, by my restraint I've prepared for Yahweh's house 100,000 talents of gold, 1,000,000 talents of silver, and copper and iron beyond weighing (because it was in quantity). I've prepared logs and stones, but you can add to them. ¹⁵With you in large numbers are workmen (hewers, craftsmen in stone and wood, and every kind of smart person in all work), ¹⁶the gold, the silver, the copper and the iron, beyond numbering. Set to and do it. May Yahweh be with you.'

¹⁷David ordered all Yisra'el's officials to help Shelomoh his son: ¹⁸'Yahweh your God is with you, isn't he, and he's enabled you to settle all round, because he's given into my hand the inhabitants of the country, and the country is in subjection before Yahweh and before his people. ¹⁹Now give your mind and your being to enquiring of Yahweh your God, and set to and build Yahweh your God's sanctuary so as to bring Yahweh's pact chest and God's sacred articles to the house that's built for Yahweh's name.'

The Levites' divisions

23 When David was old and full of years, he made Shelomoh his son king over Yisra'el. ²David gathered all the officials of Yisra'el, and the priests and the Levites. ³The Levites were numbered, from age thirty and upwards; their head count for the males was 38,000. ⁴Of these, in charge of the work in Yahweh's house were 24,000; overseers and authorities, 6,000; ⁵4,000 gatemen; and 4,000 praising Yahweh 'with instruments that I made for praising'. ⁶David allocated them to divisions:

The sons of Levi: Gershon, Qehat and Merari. ⁷The Gershonites: La'dan and Shim'i.
⁸La'dan's sons: the head Yehi'el, Zetam and Yo'el – three.
⁹Shim'i's sons: Shelomit, Hazi'el and Haran – three.
These were La'dan's ancestral heads.
¹⁰Shim'i's sons: Yahat, Zina, Ye'ush and Beri'ah; these were Shim'i's sons – four.
¹¹Yahat was the head, Zina the second, and Ye'ush and Beri'ah did not have many sons so they became an ancestral household with one appointment.
¹²Qehat's sons: Amram, Yitshar, Hebron and Uzzi'el – four.
¹³Amram's sons: Aharon and Mosheh. Aharon was distinguished to make sacred the very sacred things, he and his sons permanently, to burn incense before Yahweh, to minister to him and to bless in his name, permanently.
¹⁴Mosheh, the supernatural man: his sons were named after the clan of Levi.
¹⁵Mosheh's sons: Gershom and Eli'ezer.
¹⁶Gershom's sons: Shebu'el the head.
¹⁷Eli'ezer's sons were Rehabyah the head; Eli'ezer didn't have other sons but Rehabyah's sons were exceptionally numerous.
¹⁸Yitshar's sons: Shelomit the head.
¹⁹Hebron's sons: Yeriyyahu the head, Amaryah the second, Yahazi'el the third and Yeqam'am the fourth.
²⁰Uzzi'el's sons: Mikah the head and Yishshiyyah the second.
²¹Merari's sons: Mahli and Mushi. Mahli's sons: El'azar and Qish.
²²El'azar died and didn't have sons, but rather daughters, and the sons of Qish, their brothers, took them.
²³Mushi's sons: Mahli, Eder and Yeremot – three.

The Levites' roles

²⁴These are the Levites by their ancestral households – the ancestral heads as they were registered by a headcount of names, the people doing the work in connection with the service of Yahweh's house, from age twenty and upwards. ²⁵Because David said, 'Yahweh the God of Yisra'el has settled his people down and come to dwell in Yerushalaim permanently, ²⁶so also for the Levites there's no carrying the dwelling and all its articles, for its service.' ²⁷Because by the last words of David, those are the number of the Levites from the age of twenty and upwards. ²⁸Because their standing was at the side of the Aharonites for the service of Yahweh's house:
over the courtyards and over the halls;
over the purity of everything that was sacred, and the work involved in the service of God's house;
²⁹the row bread, the fine flour for a grain offering, the flatbread wafers, the griddle loaves, the mixed loaves, and every weight and measure;
³⁰standing morning by morning to confess and praise Yahweh, and similarly in the evening;
³¹all offering up of burnt offerings for Yahweh for the sabbaths, for the new months and for the appointed festivals by number, in accordance with the ruling for them, regularly, before Yahweh.
³²So they would keep watch over the appointment tent, over what was sacred, and over the Aharonites, their brothers, for the service of Yahweh's house.

24
The divisions of the Aharonites. Aharon's sons: Nadab and Abihu, El'azar and Itamar. ²Nadab and Abihu died before their father and they had no sons, so El'azar and Itamar acted as priests. ³David, Tsadoq of the sons of El'azar, and Ahimelek of the sons of Itamar allocated them to their appointment by their service. ⁴El'azar's sons were found to be more numerous by male heads than Itamar's sons, so they allocated El'azar's sons as sixteen heads of ancestral households and Itamar's sons as eight heads of ancestral households. ⁵They allocated them by lots, both of them, because they were the sacred place's officials and God's officials, from El'azar's sons and from Itamar's sons.

The Aharonites' divisions

⁶Shema'yah ben Netan'el the secretary, of the Levites, wrote them down before the king, the officials, Tsadoq the priest, Ahimelek ben Ebyatar, and the ancestral heads of the priests

and of the Levites – an ancestral household taken for El'azar, then one taken for Itamar.

⁷The first lot came out for Yehoyarib
the second for Yeda'yah
⁸the third for Harim
the fourth for Se'orim
⁹the fifth for Malkiyyah
the sixth for Miyyamin
¹⁰the seventh for Haqqots
the eighth for Abiyyah
¹¹the ninth for Yeshua
the tenth for Shekanyahu
¹²the eleventh for Eliyashib
the twelfth for Yaqim
¹³the thirteenth for Huppah
the fourteenth for Yeshebe'ab
¹⁴the fifteenth for Bilgah
the sixteenth for Immer
¹⁵the seventeenth for Hezir
the eighteenth for Happitstsets
¹⁶the nineteenth for Petahyah
the twentieth for Yehezqe'l
¹⁷the twenty-first for Yakin
the twenty-second for Gamul
¹⁸the twenty-third for Delayahu
the twenty-fourth for Ma'azyahu

¹⁹These were their appointment, in relation to their service, for coming into Yahweh's house in accordance with the ruling for them by means of Aharon their father, as Yahweh the God of Yisra'el had ordered him.
²⁰Of the Levites who were left:

Of Amram's sons: Shuba'el;
Shuba'el's sons: Yehdeyahu;
²¹of Rehabyahu – of Rehabyahu's sons: the head Yishshiyyah.
²²Of the Yitsharites: Shelomot;
of Shelomot's sons: Yahat.
²³Yeriyyahu's sons: Amaryahu the second, Yahazi'el the third, Yeqam'am the fourth.
²⁴Uzzi'el's sons: Mikah;
of Mikah's sons: Shamir;
²⁵Mikah's brother: Yishshiyyah;
of Yishshiyyah's sons: Zekaryahu.
²⁶Merari's sons: Mahli and Mushi;
the sons of Ya'aziyyahu, his son (²⁷Merari's sons by Ya'aziyyahu, his son): Shoham, Zakkur, and Ibri;
²⁸of Mahli: El'azar (he did not have sons);
²⁹of Qish – Qish's sons: Yerahme'el;
³⁰Mushi's sons: Mahli, Eder and Yerimot.

These were the sons of the Levites by the ancestral households.
³¹They also let lots fall, along with their Aharonite brothers, before David the king, Tsadoq, Ahimelek, and the ancestral heads of the priests and the Levites, the ancestral head along with his younger brother.

25
And David and the army officers made distinct for the service the sons of Asaph, Heman and Yedutun, who prophesied with guitars, mandolins and tambourines.

The watches

The number of them (the people fulfilling the work in connection with their service) was:
²Asaph's sons: Zakkur, Yoseph, Netanyah and Asar'elah, Asaph's sons at the side of Asaph, who prophesied at the side of the king;
³Yedutun – Yedutun's sons: Gedalyah, Tseri, Yeshayahu, Hashabyahu, Mattityahu, six, at the side of Yedutun their father with the mandolin, who prophesied in confessing and praising Yahweh;
⁴Heman – Heman's sons: Buqqiyyahu, Mattanyahu, Uzzi'el, Shebu'el, Yerimot, Hananyah, Hanani, Eli'atah, Giddalti, Romamti Ezer, Yoshbeqashah, Malloti, Hotir and Mahazi'ot. ⁵All these sons of Heman the king's seer with God's words, to lift up his horn. God gave Heman fourteen sons and three daughters, ⁶all these by their father's side in singing in Yahweh's house with cymbals, mandolins and guitars, for the service of God's house.

Asaph, Yedutun and Heman were by the king's side. ⁷Their number with their brothers, trained in singing for Yahweh, every one discerning: 288. ⁸They let lots fall for the watch, the big man along with the young man, discerning man with learner.

⁹The first lot (Asaph's) came out for Yoseph;
Gedalyah, the second, he, his brothers and his sons – 12;
¹⁰the third Zakkur, his sons and his brothers – 12;
¹¹the fourth for Yitsri, his sons and his brothers – 12;
¹²the fifth Netanyah, his sons and his brothers – 12;

¹³the sixth Buqqiyyah, his sons and his brothers – 12;
¹⁴the seventh Yesar'elah, his sons and his brothers – 12;
¹⁵the eighth Yesha'yahu, his sons and his brothers – 12;
¹⁶the ninth Mattanyahu, his sons and his brothers – 12;
¹⁷the tenth Shim'i, his sons and his brothers – 12;
¹⁸eleventh Azar'el, his sons and his brothers – 12;
¹⁹the twelfth for Hashabyah, his sons and his brothers – 12;
²⁰for the thirteenth Shuba'el, his sons and his brothers – 12;
²¹for the fourteenth Mattityahu, his sons and his brothers – 12;
²²for the fifteenth for Yeremot, his sons and his brothers – 12;
²³for the sixteenth for Hananyahu, his sons and his brothers – 12;
²⁴for the seventeenth for Yoshbeqashah, his sons and his brothers – 12;
²⁵for the eighteenth for Hanani, his sons and his brothers – 12;
²⁶for the nineteenth for Malloti, his sons and his brothers – 12;
²⁷for the twentieth for Eli'atah, his sons and his brothers – 12;
²⁸for the twenty-first for Hotir, his sons and his brothers – 12;
²⁹for the twenty-second for Giddalti, his sons and his brothers – 12;
³⁰for the twenty-third for Mahazi'ot, his sons and his brothers – 12;
³¹for the twenty-fourth for Romamti Ezer, his sons and his brothers – 12.

The gatemen

26 The divisions of the gatemen:

Qorahites: Meshelemeyahu ben Qore of the sons of Asaph;
²of Meshelemeyahu, sons: Zekaryahu the firstborn, Yedi'a'el the second, Zebadyahu the third, Yatni'el the fourth, ³Elam the fifth, Yehohanan the sixth, Elyeho'enay the seventh.
⁴Of Obed Edom, sons: Shema'yah the firstborn, Yehozabad the second, Yo'ah the third, Sakar the fourth, Netan'el the fifth, ⁵Ammi'el the sixth, Yissakar the seventh, Pe'ulletay the eighth (because God blessed him);
⁶to Shema'yah his son sons were born who ruled for their ancestral households because they were forceful strong men;
⁷Shema'yah's sons: Otni, Repha'el, Obed, Elzabad;
his brothers, forceful men: Elihu and Semakyahu;
⁸all these of the sons of Obed Edom, they, their sons and their brothers, people forceful in their energy for the service – of Obed Edom, sixty-two.
⁹Meshelemeyahu had sons and brothers, forceful men – eighteen.
¹⁰Hosah of the Merarites had sons: Shimri the head (because he was not the firstborn but his father made him head), ¹¹Hilqiyyahu the second, Tebalyahu the third, Zekaryahu the fourth; all sons and brothers of Hoseh – thirteen.

¹²These are the gatemen's divisions by the strong men who were the heads, in watches along with their brothers, to minister in Yahweh's house. ¹³They let lots fall, small and big alike, gateway by gateway:
¹⁴the lots to the east fell to Shelemyahu;
Zekaryahu his son, a counsellor with insight: they let lots fall and his lot came out to the north;
¹⁵for Obed Edom, to the south, and for his sons, the stores;
¹⁶for Suppim and for Hosah, to the west, with the Shalleket Gate on the upper causeway.
Watch along with watch:
¹⁷to the east, six Levites;
to the north, four daily;
to the south, four daily;
for the stores, two by two;
¹⁸at the colonnade to the west, four at the causeway, two at the colonnade.
¹⁹These are the divisions of the gatemen belonging to the Qorahites and the Merarites.

The Levites' responsibilities

²⁰The Levites:
Ahiyyah in charge of the treasuries of God's house and the treasuries of the sacred things.

²¹La'dan's sons, the sons of the Gershonites belonging to La'dan, the ancestral heads of La'dan the Gershonite: Yehi'eli. ²²Yehi'eli's sons: Zetam and Yo'el his brother, in charge of the treasuries of Yahweh's house; ²³of the Amramites, the Yitsharites, the Hebronites and the Uzzi'elites: ²⁴Shebu'el ben Gershom, the son of Mosheh, chief over the treasuries. ²⁵His brothers by Eli'azar: Rehabyahu his son, Yesha'yahu his son, Yoram his son, Zikri his son and Shelomit his son. ²⁶That Shelomit and his brothers were in charge of all the treasuries of the sacred things that David the king made sacred, with the ancestral heads, for the chiliarchs, the centurions and the army officers; ²⁷some of the spoil from battles they made sacred for strengthening Yahweh's house; ²⁸everything that Shemu'el the seer, Sha'ul ben Qish, Abner ben Ner and Yo'ab ben Tseruyah made sacred (anyone who made something sacred) was in the control of Shelomit and his brothers. ²⁹Of the Yitsharites: Kenanyahu and his sons – in connection with work outside, in charge of Yisra'el as overseers and authorities. ³⁰Of the Hebronites: Hashabyahu and his brothers, forceful men, 1,700, with an appointment over Yisra'el across the Yarden westward regarding all Yahweh's work and regarding the king's service. ³¹Of the Hebronites, Yeriyyah the head of the Hebronites by his lines of descent, by his ancestors: in the fortieth year of David's reign they were enquired after, and forceful strong men were found among them in Ya'zir-in-Gil'ad; ³²his brothers, forceful men, 2,700, ancestral heads – David the king appointed them in charge of the Re'ubenites, the Gadites and the half-clan of Menashsheh in connection with everything of God's and everything of the king's.

The army roster

27 The Yisra'elites by their number (the ancestral heads, the chiliarchs, the centurions and their overseers who ministered to the king in everything concerning the divisions that came in and went out month by month, all the months of the year); each division was 24,000:

²in charge of the first division, for the first month: Yashob'am ben Zabdi'el, in charge of his division of 24,000 – ³of the sons of Perets, the head over all the army officers, for the first month; ⁴in charge of the second month's division: Doday the Ahohite in charge of his division with Miqlot the chief, in charge of his division of 24,000; ⁵the third army officer, for the third month: Benayah ben Yehoyada, the head priest, in charge of his division of 24,000; ⁶that was Benayah the strongest man among the Thirty and in charge of the Thirty and his division, Ammizabad his son; ⁷the fourth, for the fourth month: Asah-el, Yo'ab's brother, and Zebadyah his son after him, in charge of his division of 24,000; ⁸the fifth, for the fifth month: the officer Shamhut the Yizrahite, in charge of his division of 24,000; ⁹the sixth, for the sixth month: Ira ben Iqqesh, the Teqo'ite, in charge of his division, 24,000; ¹⁰the seventh, for the seventh month: Helets the Pelonite, from the Ephrayimites, in charge of his division of 24,000; ¹¹the eighth, for the eighth month: Sibbekay, the Hushatite of the Zerahites, in charge of his division of 24,000; ¹²the ninth, for the ninth month: Abi'ezer, the Anatotite of Binyamin, in charge of his division of 24,000; ¹³the tenth, for the tenth month: Mahray, the Netophatite of the Zerahites, in charge of his division of 24,000; ¹⁴the eleventh, for the eleventh month: Benayah, the Peratonite from the Ephrayimites, in charge of his division of 24,000; ¹⁵the twelfth, for the twelfth month: Helday the Netophatite of Otni'el, in charge of his division of 24,000.

The administration

¹⁶In charge of the Yisra'elite clans:

for the Re'ubenites: chief, Eli'ezer ben Zikri; for the Shim'onites: Shephatyahu ben Ma'akah;

¹⁷for the Levites: Hashabyah ben Qemu'el;
for Aharon: Tsadoq;
¹⁸for Yehudah: Elihu, from David's brothers;
for Yissakar: Omri ben Mika'el;
¹⁹for Zebulun: Yishma'yahu ben Obadyahu;
for Naphtali: Yerimot ben Azri'el;
²⁰for the Ephrayimites: Hoshea ben Azizyahu;
for the half-clan of Menashsheh: Yo'el ben Pedayah;
²¹for the half of Menashsheh in Gil'ad: Yiddo ben Zekaryahu;
for Binyamin: Ya'asi'el ben Abner;
²²for Dan: Azar'el ben Yeroham.

These were the officers of the Yisra'elite clans. ²³David did not take their number for the people of twenty years or less, because Yahweh had said he would make Yisra'el as numerous as the stars in the heavens, ²⁴though Yo'ab ben Tseruyyah began to count, but he did not finish; at this, fury came on Yisra'el and the number did not go into the number of the things concerning King David.

²⁵In charge of the king's treasuries: Azmavet ben Adi'el;
in charge of the treasuries in the open country (in the towns, in the hamlets and in the towers): Yehonatan ben Uzziyyahu;
²⁶in charge of the people doing work in the open country, in the service of the ground: Ezri ben Kelub;
²⁷in charge of the vineyards: Shim'i the Ramatite;
in charge of what was in the vineyards for the wine treasuries: Zabdi the Shiphmite;
²⁸in charge of the olive trees and the wild fig trees that were in the foothills: Ba'al Hanan the Gederite;
in charge of the oil treasuries: Yo'ash;
²⁹in charge of the cattle pasturing in Sharon: Shirtay the Sharonite;
in charge of the cattle in the vales: Shaphat ben Adlay;
³⁰in charge of the camels: Obil the Ishma'elite;
in charge of the she-donkeys: Yehdeyahu the Meronotite;
³¹in charge of the flocks: Yaziz the Hagrite.

All these were officials over the property that belonged to King David.

³²Yehonatan, David's uncle, was a counsellor; he was a discerning person and a secretary. Yehi'el ben Hackmoni was with the king's sons. ³³Ahitophel was counsellor to the king. Hushay the Arkite was the king's friend. ³⁴After Ahitophel were Yehoyada ben Benayah and Ebyatar.

Yo'ab was the king's army officer.

David's commission

28 David congregated in Yerushalaim all Yisra'el's officials, the clan officials, the divisional officials who ministered to the king, the chiliarchs, the centurions, and the officials over all the property and cattle belonging to the king and to his sons, with the courtiers and the strong men, every forceful strong man. ²David the king rose to his feet and said, 'Listen to me, my brothers, my people. I – it was in my mind to build a place to settle down for Yahweh's pact chest, for our God's footstool, and I have prepared for building it. ³But God said to me, "You aren't the one to build a house for my name because you're a man of battles; you've shed blood."

⁴Yahweh the God of Yisra'el chose me from my father's entire household to be king over Yisra'el permanently, because he chose Yehudah as chief, and in Yehudah's household, my father's household and from my father's sons he accepted me to make me king over all Yisra'el. ⁵And from all my sons (because Yahweh has given me many sons) he chose Shelomoh my son to sit on Yahweh's kingly throne over Yisra'el. ⁶He said to me, "Shelomoh your son – he will build my house and my courtyards, because I've chosen him as a son to me, and I myself will become a father to him. ⁷I will establish his reign permanently if he is strong in acting on my orders and my rulings this very day."

⁸So now before the eyes of all Yisra'el, Yahweh's congregation, and in the ears of our God: keep and enquire of all the orders of Yahweh our God in order that you may possess the good country and give it to your children as their domain after you permanently.

⁹And you, Shelomoh my son: acknowledge your father's God and serve him with a perfect mind and with a willing being, because Yahweh enquires of all minds and discerns every inclination in people's intentions. If you enquire of him, he will be found by you,

but if you abandon him, he will spurn you permanently. ¹⁰See, now, that Yahweh has chosen you to build a house for the sanctuary. Be strong and act!'

The plan and the charge

¹¹David gave Shelomoh his son the plan for the porch, its houses, its storerooms, its upper quarters, its inside rooms, the house for the expiation cover, ¹²the plan for all that was with him by the spirit for the courtyards of Yahweh's house and for all the halls around, for the treasuries in God's house and for the treasuries for sacred things, ¹³for the divisions of the priests and the Levites and all the work involved in the service of Yahweh's house, for all the articles involved in the service of Yahweh's house, ¹⁴for the gold with the weight (for the gold for all the articles used service by service), for the silver vessels with the weight (for all the articles used service by service), ¹⁵the weight for the gold candelabra and the gold lamps, with the weight candelabrum by candelabrum and its lamps, and for the silver candelabra, with the weight for the candelabrum and its lamps in accordance with the service of candelabrum by candelabrum, ¹⁶the weighed gold for the tables for the row [of bread] table by table, and silver for the silver tables, ¹⁷the forks, the basins and the pitchers, pure gold, for the gold vessels, with the weight vessel by vessel, and the silver vessels, with the weight vessel by vessel, ¹⁸for the incense altar refined gold, with the weight, and for the plan for the chariot, the gold sphinxes spreading and shielding Yahweh's pact chest, ¹⁹'all of it in writing, through Yahweh's hand upon me. He has given me insight into all the plan's workings.'

²⁰David said to Shelomoh his son, 'Be strong and stand firm, and act. Don't be afraid, don't be scared, because Yahweh God, my God, is with you. He won't let go of you, he won't abandon you, until the finishing of all the work in connection with the service of Yahweh's house. ²¹Here are the divisions of the priests and the Levites for the service of God's house, and with you in all the work everyone who is free with smartness for every service, and the officials and all the people in connection with all your words.'

David's provision

29 David the king said to the entire congregation, 'Shelomoh my son, the one God chose, is a boy and green, though the work is big, because the castle is not for a human being but for Yahweh God. ²With all my energy I have prepared for my God's house the gold for the gold things, the silver for the silver, the copper for the copper, the iron for the iron, the logs for the logs, onyx stones and settings, stones of antimony and colour, every precious stone, and alabaster stones, in quantity. ³And further, through my acceptance in my God's house, I have gold and silver as personal treasure that I'm giving for my God's house on top of all I have prepared for the sacred house: ⁴3,000 talents of gold (Ophir gold), 7,000 talents of refined silver to overlay the houses' walls (⁵the gold for the gold, the silver for the silver), and for all the work in the hand of the craftsmen. So who is going to give freely, commissioning himself to Yahweh today?'

⁶The ancestral officials, the Yisra'elite clans' officials, the chiliarchs, the centurions and the officials over the king's work gave freely. ⁷They gave for the service of God's house 5,000 talents of gold, 10,000 darics, 10,000 talents of silver, 18,000 talents of copper and 100,000 talents of iron. ⁸The person who had stones to be found with him – they gave them to the treasury of Yahweh's house, into the hand of Yehi'el the Gershonite. ⁹The people rejoiced over their free giving because it was with a perfect mind that they had given freely for Yahweh. David the king, too, rejoiced greatly.

Who am I and who is my people?

¹⁰David blessed Yahweh before the eyes of the entire congregation. David said, 'You are to be blessed, Yahweh, God of Yisra'el our father, from age to age. ¹¹Yours, Yahweh, is greatness, strength, glory, honour and grandeur, because everything in the heavens and on the earth is yours, Yahweh – the kingship and pre-eminence in relation to everything, as head. ¹²Wealth and splendour come from before you. You rule over everything. In your hand are energy and strength. It's in your hand to make

anyone big or strong. ¹³So now, our God, we confess you and praise your glorious name.

¹⁴But who am I and who is my people that we hold on to the energy to give freely like this, because everything comes from you, and it's from your hand that we've given you. ¹⁵Because we are resident aliens before you, transients like all our ancestors. Our days are like a shadow on the earth, and without hope. ¹⁶Yahweh our God, all this mass that we have prepared to build a house for you, for your sacred name, is from your hand. Everything is yours.

¹⁷My God, I acknowledge that you test the mind and that integrity is what you accept. I myself with my integrity of mind have freely given all these things, and now your people who have presented themselves here – I have seen them giving freely to you with rejoicing. ¹⁸Yahweh, God of Abraham, Yitshaq and Yisra'el, our ancestors, keep this permanently as the inclination of the intentions in your people's mind, and establish their mind in relation to you. ¹⁹To Shelomoh my son give a perfect mind to keep your orders, your affirmations and your decrees, and to do it all, and to build the castle for which I have prepared.'

Full of years

²⁰David said to the entire congregation, 'Bless Yahweh your God, please.' The entire congregation blessed Yahweh, their ancestors' God. They knelt and bent their heads to Yahweh and to the king ²¹and made sacrifices for Yahweh and offered up burnt offerings for Yahweh the next day after that day: 1,000 bulls, 1,000 rams, 1,000 lambs, with their libations, sacrifices in large numbers for all Yisra'el. ²²They ate and drank before Yahweh that day with great rejoicing.

They again made Shelomoh ben David king and anointed him for Yahweh as chief, and Tsadoq as priest. ²³Shelomoh sat on Yahweh's throne as king in place of his father. He was successful and all Yisra'el listened to him. ²⁴All the officials, the strong men, and also all King David's sons, gave their support to Shelomoh the king. ²⁵Yahweh made Shelomoh exceptionally big before the eyes of all Yisra'el and gave him a royal grandeur that had not been on any king over Yisra'el before him.

²⁶When David ben Yishay reigned over all Yisra'el, ²⁷the time that he reigned over Yisra'el was forty years. In Hebron he reigned seven years and in Yerushalaim he reigned thirty-three. ²⁸He died in a good old age full of years, of wealth and of honour, and Shelomoh his son began to reign in place of him. ²⁹The things about David the king, early and late, there they are, written down in the things of Shemu'el the seer, in the things of Natan the prophet and in the things of Gad the seer, ³⁰with his entire reign and his might, and the times that passed for him, for Yisra'el and for the kingdoms of the earth.

2 Chronicles

Like 1 Chronicles, 2 Chronicles is a history of Israel that focuses on the history of the temple and its worship. The first part (chapters 1—9) retells the story of Solomon's reign with a focus on his activity in building the temple, on the basis of the preparation and provision that David completed.

The middle part (chapters 10—28) retells the story of the two centuries when Judah and Ephraim were divided into two nations, but it does so by focusing almost entirely on Judah. By setting up its independent state, Ephraim has cut itself off from Jerusalem and cut itself off from the household of David. In effect it has cut itself off from the real people of God, so its story does not really belong in that story. The book makes clear that it comes from the Second Temple period, when the Persian king has made it possible for Judahites to rebuild the temple but when Judah is merely a Persian colony and an embattled little community whose relationships with surrounding Persian colonies are difficult. The stories of Ezra and Nehemiah open a window into some of that trickiness. One of the most difficult is with the people of Samaria, who are the people now living in the area of what was once Ephraim. The second book of Chronicles encourages Judah to trust in its special relationship with God and not be threatened by or tempted into compromise with Samaria/Ephraim.

One way its stories offer encouragement is the way they relate monumental victories that Judah won over those two centuries when Ephraim and Judah were separate peoples. The battles are told larger than life in a way that enhances their excitement and their encouragement. The numbers are way out of line with the actual size of the peoples of the day, and even more out of line with the size of the peoples for whom Chronicles' version of the stories was written. The stories underline the way that trust in God, not the size of your army, is the key to survival and to success.

The last part of the book (chapters 29—36) returns to giving more focused attention to the temple. It covers the period after the downfall of Ephraim to the Assyrians, though it ignores that event because Ephrayim's story is not really part of the story of Israel. (The use of the word 'Israel' is often confusing in the Old Testament, but especially in 2 Chronicles. On one hand, 'Israel' was the usual political name of the northern kingdom, and it is then set over against 'Judah'. On the other hand, 'Israel' denotes the people that God chose, the people of Abraham and Moses and David. In this sense Chronicles can refer to Judah as 'Israel'. Let the reader beware! I myself refer to the northern kingdom by its other name, Ephraim, to try to reduce the confusion.)

This last part of the book has two heroes, Hezekiah and Josiah, who were both involved in reforming the temple's worship. The odd thing about Josiah is that having acted with great faithfulness to Yahweh, he died quite young. His story contrasts with that of his grandfather, Manasseh, an apostate king who nevertheless reigned for fifty-five years. Chronicles offers implicit explanations of those disparities by describing how Manasseh repented of his wrongdoing while Josiah ignored a word from God in taking on the battle in which he died. Chronicles is thus able to affirm the truth of one of its important themes, that God is faithful and responsive to the people who are faithful and responsive to him but that failing in your faithfulness and responsiveness leads to trouble.

The book almost closes with Judah's own undoing of the reforms of Hezekiah and Josiah and with the temple's destruction by the Babylonians. But finally the Persian emperor declares that he has a commission from Yahweh (!) to rebuild the temple, and he encourages Judahites in exile throughout his empire to go back to Jerusalem to do it. That last little paragraph is also the first paragraph in the story in Ezra and Nehemiah, and the order of the books in the English Bible encourages us to read them in this sequence. But in most Hebrew Bibles these books come at the very end, in the order Ezra–Nehemiah–Chronicles, which points to the possibility that Ezra and Nehemiah are not the sequel to Chronicles; Chronicles is the prequel to Ezra–Nehemiah. That overlap between Chronicles and Ezra is the way Chronicles encourages its readers to see it as such a prequel. It offers further encouragement to see the book as speaking to the needs and pressures and questions of the Second Temple period.

What would you like me to give you?

1 Shelomoh [Solomon] ben David showed himself strong over his kingdom; Yahweh his God was with him and made him exceptionally big. ²Shelomoh spoke to all Yisra'el (to the chiliarchs and the centurions, to the authorities and to every leader in all Yisra'el, the ancestral heads), ³and Shelomoh and the entire congregation with him went to the shrine which was at Gib'on, because God's appointment tent, which Mosheh [Moses], Yahweh's servant, made in the wilderness, was there, ⁴though God's chest David had taken up from Ye'arim Township when David had prepared for it, because he had pitched a tent for it in Yerushalaim. ⁵But the copper altar, which Betsal'el ben Uri the son of Hur had made, was there before Yahweh's dwelling. So Shelomoh and the congregation enquired of it. ⁶There Shelomoh went up on the copper altar before Yahweh, which was at the appointment tent, and offered up a thousand burnt offerings on it.

⁷That night God appeared to Shelomoh and said to him, 'Ask for what I should give you.' ⁸Shelomoh said to God, 'You yourself acted in great commitment with David my father and you have made me king in place of him. ⁹Now, Yahweh God, may your word with David my father prove trustworthy, because you have made me king over a people as numerous as the earth on the ground. ¹⁰Now give me smartness and knowledge so that I may go out and come in before this people. Because who can exercise authority for this great people of yours?'

¹¹God said to Shelomoh, 'Since this was in your mind, and you haven't asked for wealth and possessions and honour, or the life of the people hostile to you, nor was it even long life that you asked for, but you've asked for smartness and knowledge so you can exercise authority for my people over which I've made you king, ¹²smartness and knowledge are going to be given to you, and wealth and possessions and honour I will give to you, which have not belonged in this way to the kings who have been before you, nor will belong in this way to those after you.'

Shelomoh's flourishing

¹³Shelomoh came, apropos the shrine which was at Gib'on, to Yerushalaim from before the appointment tent, and reigned over Yisra'el.

¹⁴Shelomoh gathered chariotry and cavalry; he had 1,400 chariotry and 12,000 cavalry. He settled them in chariot towns and with the king in Yerushalaim. ¹⁵The king made the silver and the gold in Yerushalaim like the stones, and made the cedars like the wild fig trees that are in the foothills, in the large number. ¹⁶The origin of the horses that Shelomoh had was from Misrayim [Egypt] and from Qewe. The king's dealers would get them from Qewe at a price; ¹⁷they took up a chariot (they brought it out from Misrayim) for 600 silver pieces, a horse for 150. In this way they would get them out by their own hand to all the kings of the Hittites and to the kings of Aram.

2 Shelomoh said to build a house for Yahweh's name and a house for himself as king. ²Shelomoh numbered 70,000 carriers, 80,000 hewers in the highland and 3,600 supervisors over them.

³Shelomoh sent to Huram king of Tsor [Tyre], saying, 'As you did with David my father when you sent him cedars to build himself a house to live in: ⁴here, I'm going to build a house for the name of Yahweh my God, to make sacred for him for burning spiced incense before him, and the regular row [of bread], and burnt offerings morning and evening, for the sabbaths, for the new months and for the appointed occasions of Yahweh our God. This is laid upon Yisra'el permanently. ⁵The house that I'm going to build will be big, because our God is bigger than all gods. ⁶But who can hold on to the energy to build him a house, because the heavens, even the highest heavens cannot contain him, so who am I that I should build him a house except for burning incense before him?

What's needed for the house of God

⁷But now send me someone who's smart at working in gold, in silver, in copper, in iron, in purple, scarlet and blue, and who knows how to do engraving, with the smart people

who're with me in Yehudah and in Yerushalaim whom David my father prepared. ⁸And send me cedar, juniper and algum logs from the Lebanon, because I acknowledge that your servants know about cutting Lebanese logs. And there, my servants will be with your servants ⁹to prepare logs in large number for me, because the house that I'm going to build will be big, extraordinary. ¹⁰Here, for the choppers, the people who cut the logs, I'm giving: crushed wheat for your servants, 20,000 ten-gallon measures; barley, 20,000 ten-gallon measures; wine, 20,000 five-gallon measures; and oil, 20,000 five-gallon measures.'

¹¹Huram king of Tsor said in a written message, and sent to Shelomoh, 'In Yahweh's loyalty to his people he has made you king over them.' ¹²Huram said, 'Blessed be Yahweh the God of Yisra'el who made the heavens and the earth, who gave David the king a smart son, who knows about insight and understanding, who will build a house for Yahweh and a house for himself as king. ¹³So now I'm sending someone smart who knows about understanding, Huram Abi, ¹⁴the son of one of the Danite women and his father a Tsorite man, who knows about working in gold, in silver, in copper, in iron, in stones, in wood, in purple, in blue, in fine linen and in scarlet, and how to do all engraving and to do any designing that will be given him, with your smart people and the smart people of my lord David your father. ¹⁵And now the wheat, the barley, the oil and the wine that my lord said, he should send them to his servants. ¹⁶We ourselves will cut down trees from the Lebanon in accordance with all your need and we will bring them to you as rafts by sea to Yafo, and you can take them up to Yerushalaim.'

The work begins

¹⁷Shelomoh numbered all the people who were resident aliens who were in the country of Yisra'el, following on the numbering of them by David his father. They were found to be 153,600. ¹⁸Of them he made 70,000 carriers, 80,000 hewers in the highland and 3,600 supervisors to get the company to serve.

3 And Shelomoh began building Yahweh's house in Yerushalaim on Mount Moriyyah where he had appeared to David his father, at David's site which he had prepared, at the threshing floor of Ornan the Yebusite. ²He began to build in the second month, on the second, in the fourth year of his reign. ³These were Shelomoh's foundation for building God's house:
 the length 30 metres (by the former measure); the width 10 metres;
⁴the porch corresponding to the length, corresponding to the width of the house, 10 metres;
 the height 60 metres.
He overlaid it on the inside with pure gold. ⁵The big house he covered with juniper wood, and he covered it with fine gold. He put on top of it palms and chains. ⁶He decorated the house with precious stones for glory; the gold was Parvayim gold. ⁷He covered the house (the beams, the thresholds, and its walls and its doors) with gold, and engraved sphinxes on the walls.

⁸He made the very sacred house: its length corresponding to the house's width, ten metres, and its width ten metres. He covered it with fine gold, 600 talents, ⁹the weight of the nails fifty sheqels of gold. The upper quarters he covered in gold.

¹⁰In the very sacred house he made two sphinxes, sculptured work, and they overlaid them with gold. ¹¹The sphinxes' wings: their length ten metres – the wing of the first two-and-a-half metres touching the wall of the house and the other wing two-and-a-half metres touching the other sphinx's wing, ¹²the other sphinx's wing two-and-a-half metres touching the wall of the house and the other wing two-and-a-half metres attaching to the first sphinx's wing, ¹³these sphinxes' wings spreading ten metres; they were standing on their feet with their faces to the house.

The features of the house

¹⁴He made the expiation cover of purple, blue, scarlet and fine linen, and made sphinxes on it. ¹⁵Before the house he made two pillars sixteen metres in length; the capital that was on top of it was two and a half metres. ¹⁶He made chains in the inner room and put them on top of the pillars, and he made a hundred

pomegranates and put them into the chains. ¹⁷He set up the pillars in front of the palace, one on the right and one on the left. He named the right 'He-Establishes' and the left 'In-Him-Is-Strength'.

4 He made a copper altar, ten metres its length, ten metres its width, five metres its height. ²He made the sea, cast:

five metres from its lip to its lip, circular all round, two and a half metres its height;
a line of fifteen metres would go round it all round;
³figures of cattle under it round it, all round, ten metres, encircling the sea all round;
two rows of the cattle, cast along with its casting;
⁴standing on twelve cattle, three facing north, three facing west, three facing south, three facing east, with the sea on them, above, and all their rears inwards;
⁵its thickness a handbreadth;
its lip like the making of the lip of a cup, a lotus petal;
taking strong hold of 10,000 gallons, which it would hold.

⁶He made ten basins and put them five on the right and five on the left, for washing in them. In them they would rinse the work for the burnt offering, while the sea was for the priests' washing in. ⁷He made the ten gold candelabra in accordance with the ruling for them and put them in the palace, five on the right and five on the left. ⁸He made ten tables and set them in the palace, five on the right and five on the left. He made a hundred gold sprinklers. ⁹He made the priests' courtyard and the big enclosure and doors for the enclosure, and their doors he overlaid with copper. ¹⁰He put the sea at the right shoulder, to the east, towards the south.

The work completed

¹¹Huram made the basins, the shovels and the bowls. So Huram finished doing all the work that he did for King Shelomoh in God's house:
¹²two pillars;
the two globes and capitals on the top of the pillars;
two nets to cover the two globes for the capitals that were on the top of the pillars;
¹³the 400 pomegranates for the two nets, two rows of pomegranates for each net, to cover the two globes for the capitals that were on the face of the pillars;
¹⁴he made the stands and he made the basins on the stands;
¹⁵the one sea and the twelve cattle under it;
¹⁶the buckets, the shovels, the basins and all their articles that Huram his father made for King Shelomoh for Yahweh's house, polished copper.

¹⁷The king cast them in the Yarden [Jordan] Plain, in the earthen compactness between Sukkot and Tsaretan. ¹⁸Shelomoh made all these articles, a large number, so that the weight of the copper was not searched out. ¹⁹Shelomoh made all the articles that were in God's house:
the gold altar;
the table on which was the presence bread;
²⁰the candelabra and their lamps for burning in accordance with the ruling, before the inner room, beaten gold;
²¹the flowers, the lamps and the tongs, gold (i.e. solid gold);
²²the snuffers, the sprinklers, the ladles and the pans, beaten gold;
the entrance for the house, its doors, the inside parts for the very sacred place, and the doors of the house for the palace, gold.

5 So all the work that Shelomoh did for Yahweh's house was complete, and Shelomoh brought in the sacred things from David his father; the silver, the gold and all the articles he put in the treasuries of God's house.

When you can tell God is present

²Then Shelomoh congregated Yisra'el's elders (all the heads of the clans, the Yisra'elites' ancestral leaders) to Yerushalaim, to take up Yahweh's pact chest from David's Town (i.e. Zion). ³Every individual in Yisra'el congregated to the king at the festival (i.e. the seventh month). ⁴All Yisra'el's elders came and the Levites carried the chest. ⁵They took up the chest, the appointment tent and all the sacred articles that were in the tent. The priests, the Levites, took them up ⁶while King Shelomoh and the entire assembly of Yisra'el who had assembled to him before the chest

were sacrificing sheep and cattle that could not be numbered and could not be counted because of the large number.

⁷The priests brought Yahweh's pact chest to its place, to the inner room of the house, to the very sacred place, under the sphinxes' wings. ⁸The sphinxes were spreading their wings over the chest's place; the sphinxes covered the chest and its poles from above. ⁹The poles extended and the heads of the poles coming from the chest could be seen in front of the inner room, but they could not be seen outside. It has been there until this day. ¹⁰There was nothing in the chest, only the two tablets that Mosheh put in at Horeb, when Yahweh solemnized things with the Yisra'elites when they got out from Misrayim.

¹¹When the priests went out of the sacred place (because all the priests who were to be found had made themselves sacred – there was no keeping to the divisions), ¹²the Levite singers, all of them, Asaph, Heman and Yedutun, and their sons and their brothers, dressed in linen, with tambourines and with guitars and mandolins, were standing east of the altar, and with them were 120 priests blowing trumpets. ¹³When the trumpeters and the singers as one made one sound to be heard to praise and confess Yahweh and raised a sound on trumpets, on tambourines and on musical instruments, and praised Yahweh 'Because he is good, because his commitment is permanent', the house filled with a cloud – Yahweh's house. ¹⁴The priests could not stand ministering before the cloud because Yahweh's splendour filled God's house.

A thick cloud and a stately house

6 Then Shelomoh said:

Yahweh has said he would dwell in a
    thundercloud,
²but I myself have built you a stately house,
    an established place for you to live in to the ages.

³The king turned his face round and blessed Yisra'el's entire congregation, as Yisra'el's entire congregation was standing. ⁴He said, 'Blessed be Yahweh the God of Yisra'el who spoke by his own mouth with David my father, and by his own hand has fulfilled it: ⁵"From the day when I got my people out of the country of Misrayim I didn't choose a town from all Yisra'el's clans to build a house for my name to be there and I didn't choose anyone to be chief over my people Yisra'el. ⁶But I have chosen Yerushalaim for my name to be there, and I have chosen David to be in charge of my people Yisra'el."

⁷It was in David my father's mind to build a house for the name of Yahweh the God of Yisra'el, ⁸but Yahweh said to David my father, "In that it was in your mind to build a house for my name, you did well that it was in your mind. ⁹Only you yourself will not build the house. Rather your son, who is going to come out from your insides, he will build the house for my name."

¹⁰Yahweh has implemented his word that he spoke. I have arisen in place of David my father, I have sat on Yisra'el's throne as Yahweh spoke and I have built the house for the name of Yahweh the God of Yisra'el. ¹¹I have set there the chest where Yahweh's pact is, which he solemnized with the Yisra'elites.'

God dwells with humanity on earth!

¹²He stood before Yahweh's altar in front of the entire congregation of Yisra'el and spread out his palms ¹³(because Shelomoh had made a copper platform and put it in the middle of the enclosure, its length two and a half metres, its width two and a half metres and its height one and a half metres; so he stood on it, and knelt on his knees in front of the entire congregation of Yisra'el, and spread out his palms to the heavens).

¹⁴He said, 'Yahweh, God of Yisra'el, there is no god like you in the heavens or on the earth, keeping pact and commitment to your servants who walk before you with their entire mind, ¹⁵who has kept for your servant David my father what you spoke to him. You spoke with your own mouth and with your own hand you have fulfilled it, this very day.

¹⁶So now, Yahweh, God of Yisra'el, keep for your servant David my father what you spoke to him: "There will not be cut off for you someone before me sitting on Yisra'el's throne, if only your sons keep watch over their way in

walking by my instruction, as you have walked before me." ¹⁷So now, Yahweh, God of Yisra'el, may your word prove trustworthy that you spoke to your servant David.

¹⁸Because will God truly live with humanity on the earth? There, the heavens, even the highest heavens, could not contain you, certainly not this house that I've built. ¹⁹But turn your face towards your servant's plea and towards his prayer for grace, Yahweh my God, so as to listen to the resounding cry and the plea that your servant's uttering before you, ²⁰so that your eyes are opened towards this house day and night, towards the place of which you said you would put your name there, so as to listen to the plea that your servant makes towards this place. ²¹May you listen to the prayers for grace by your servant and your people Yisra'el, which they make towards this place. May you yourself listen from the place where you live, from the heavens, listen and pardon.'

Be one who listens to us

²²If someone does wrong to his neighbour, and he takes up an oath against him to get him to swear, and the oath comes before your altar in this house, ²³may you yourself listen from the heavens and act and exercise authority for your servants, so as to turn it back on the one who is in the wrong, bringing his conduct on his head, and to show the person in the right to be in the right, giving to him in accordance with his being in the right.

²⁴If your people Yisra'el take a beating before an enemy because they do wrong in relation to you, but they turn back and confess your name and plead and pray for grace before you in this house, ²⁵may you yourself listen from the heavens and pardon your people Yisra'el's wrongdoing and take them back to the land that you gave to them and to their ancestors.

²⁶When the heavens hold back and there's no rain because they do wrong in relation to you, but they plead towards this place and confess your name, when they turn back from their wrongdoing because you humble them, ²⁷may you yourself listen in the heavens and pardon the wrongdoing of your servants, your people Yisra'el, when you instruct them in the good way that they should walk in, and give rain on your country that you gave your people as a domain.

²⁸When famine happens in the country, when an epidemic happens, blight, mildew, locust or caterpillar, when it happens; when its enemies besiege it in the region of their settlements; any affliction or any illness; ²⁹any plea, any prayer for grace that any human being may have or your entire people Yisra'el may have, who acknowledge each one his affliction or illness, and he spreads out his palms towards this house, ³⁰may you yourself listen from the heavens, the established place where you live, and pardon, and give to the individual in accordance with all his ways (in that you know his mind because you alone know the mind of human beings), ³¹in order that that they may live in awe of you by walking in your ways all the days that they are alive on the face of the ground that you gave to our ancestors.

No ethnic limits to Yahweh

³²Further, to the foreigner who is not of your people Yisra'el but comes from a distant country for the sake of your big name, your strong hand and your extended arm, and comes and pleads towards this house, ³³may you yourself listen from the heavens, from the established place where you live, and act in accordance with everything for which the foreigner calls to you, in order that all earth's peoples may acknowledge your name, and so as to live in awe of you like your people Yisra'el and to acknowledge that your name is called out over this house that I have built.

³⁴When your people goes out to battle against its enemies by the way that you send them and they plead to you in the direction of this town that you have chosen and the house that I have built for your name, ³⁵may you listen from the heavens to their plea and to their prayer for grace, and decide for them.

³⁶When they do wrong in relation to you (because there is no human being who doesn't do wrong) and you're angry with them and you give them up before an enemy, and their captors take them off captive to a country far or near, ³⁷and they turn their mind back in the country where they are captive, and turn back

and pray towards you for grace in the country of their captivity, saying, "We've done wrong, we've been wayward, we've been faithless", ³⁸and they turn back to you with their entire mind and with their entire being in the country of their captivity where people have taken them off captive, and make their plea in the direction of their country that you gave their ancestors, the town that you've chosen, and to the house that I've built for your name, ³⁹may you listen from the heavens, from the established place where you live, to their plea, their prayers for grace, and decide for them, and pardon your people who have done wrong in relation to you.

⁴⁰Now, my God, may your eyes please be opened and your ears be heeding to a plea from this place.

A committed people can rejoice

⁴¹So now,

Yahweh God, rise to your settled place,
    you and your powerful chest.
May your priests, Yahweh God,
    clothe themselves in deliverance.
May your committed people rejoice in good
    things,
⁴²Yahweh God.
Don't turn back the face of your anointed ones;
    be mindful of your servant David's acts of
    commitment.'

7 When Shelomoh had finished pleading, and the fire had come down from the heavens and consumed the burnt offering and the sacrifices, and Yahweh's splendour had filled the house, ²the priests couldn't come into Yahweh's house because Yahweh's splendour filled Yahweh's house. ³When all the Yisra'elites saw the fire and Yahweh's splendour on the house, they bent down, face to the ground, on the pavement. They bowed low and confessed Yahweh, 'Because he is good, because his commitment lasts permanently'.

⁴When the king and all the people made sacrifice before Yahweh, ⁵King Shelomoh sacrificed 22,000 cattle and 120,000 sheep, and the king and the entire people dedicated God's house, ⁶while the priests were standing at their watches, the Levites with the instruments for singing to Yahweh, which David the king had made for confessing Yahweh, 'Because his commitment lasts permanently', with David's praise in their hand, and the priests blowing trumpets in front of them, and all Yisra'el standing.

⁷Shelomoh made sacred the middle of the courtyard which was before Yahweh's house, because he made the burnt offerings and the fat parts of the well-being sacrifices there, because the copper altar that Shelomoh had made couldn't contain the burnt offering, the grain offering and the fat parts. ⁸Shelomoh made the festival at that time for seven days, and all Yisra'el with him, a very big congregation, from Lebo Hamat as far as the Misrayimite Wadi.

⁹On the eighth day they made an assembly, because they made the dedication of the altar for seven days and the festival for seven days. ¹⁰On the twenty-third day of the seventh month he sent the people off to their tents, rejoicing and good-hearted because of the good things that Yahweh had done for David, for Shelomoh and for Yisra'el his people.

If my people

¹¹Shelomoh had finished Yahweh's house and the king's house. Everything that had come into Shelomoh's mind to do in Yahweh's house and in his own house he succeeded in doing. ¹²And Yahweh appeared to Shelomoh at night and said to him, 'I've listened to your plea and chosen this place for myself as a house for sacrifice. ¹³If I hold back the heavens and there's no rain, or if I order the locust to consume the country, or if I send off an epidemic against my people, ¹⁴and my people over whom my name is called out bow down and plead and seek my face, and turn back from their bad ways, I myself will listen from the heavens and pardon their wrongdoing, and heal their country. ¹⁵My eyes will now be opened and my ears be heeding to this place's plea. ¹⁶So now I've chosen and made sacred this house for my name to be there permanently. My eyes and my mind will be there for all time.

¹⁷You yourself, if you walk before me as David your father walked, acting in accordance

with all that I've ordered you, and you keep my decrees and my rulings, ¹⁸I will set up your kingly throne as I solemnized it to David your father, saying "There will not be cut off for you someone ruling in Yisra'el."

¹⁹But if you people turn back and abandon my decrees and my orders that I've put before you, and you go and serve other gods and bow low to them, ²⁰I will uproot them from upon my land that I gave them, and this house that I've made sacred for my name I will throw out from before my face and make it into an object lesson and a taunt among all the peoples. ²¹This house, which has been high – everyone who passes by it will be desolate and will say, "Why did Yahweh act in that way to this country and to this house?" ²²And people will say, "On account of the fact that they abandoned Yahweh their ancestors' God who got them out of the country of Misrayim, and took strong hold of other gods and bowed low to them and served them. That's why he brought upon them all this bad fate."'

Shelomoh's other projects

8 At the end of the twenty years while Shelomoh built Yahweh's house and his own house ²(and the towns that Huram gave Shelomoh – he built them up and got Yisra'elites to live there), ³Shelomoh went to Hamat Tsobah and overpowered it, ⁴and built Tadmor in the wilderness, and all the supply towns that he built in Hamat. ⁵He built Upper Bet Horon and Lower Bet Horon as fortified towns (walls, gateways and a bar), ⁶Ba'alat and the supply towns that belonged to Shelomoh, all the chariotry towns and the cavalry towns – every attraction that Shelomoh had for building in Yerushalaim, in the Lebanon and in all the country he ruled.

⁷The entire people that were left of the Hittite, the Amorite, the Perizzite, the Hivvite and the Yebusite, who were not of Yisra'elite birth (⁸of their descendants who were left after them in the country, whom the Yisra'elites had not finished off), Shelomoh raised them as a workforce until this day. ⁹Of the Yisra'elites, whom Shelomoh did not make into servants for his work: rather they were men of battle, adjutant officers, and officers over his chariotry and his cavalry, ¹⁰and these were King Shelomoh's prefect officers, 250, holding sway over the people.

¹¹Par'oh's [Pharaoh's] daughter Shelomoh took up from David's Town to the house that he built for her, because (he said), 'My wife will not live in the house of David king of Yisra'el, because those places where Yahweh's chest has come are sacred.'

¹²Shelomoh then offered up burnt offerings for Yahweh on Yahweh's altar which he built before the porch, ¹³offering up each day's requirement in its day in accordance with Mosheh's order for the sabbaths, the new months and the three appointed occasions in the year, on the Flatbread Festival, on the Shabu'ot Festival and on the Sukkot Festival.

¹⁴In accordance with the ruling of David his father, he put in place the priests' divisions for their service, the Levites for their watches to praise and to minister in front of the priests, each day's requirement in its day, and the gatemen by their divisions, gateway by gateway, because this was the order of David, the supernatural man. ¹⁵They did not depart from the king's order regarding the priests or the Levites in connection with anything, or in connection with the treasuries.

There had been nothing like it

¹⁶So all Shelomoh's work was established from the day Yahweh's house was founded and until Yahweh's house was finished, complete. ¹⁷Shelomoh then went to Etsyon-geber and to Elot on the sea coast in the country of Edom. ¹⁸Huram sent ships to him by the hand of his servants; his servants knew the sea. They came with Shelomoh's servants to Ophir and got gold from there, 450 talents, and brought it to King Shelomoh.

9 Since the queen of Sheba heard report of Shelomoh, she came to test Shelomoh in Yerushalaim with conundrums, with a very substantial force, both camels carrying spices, and gold in quantity, and precious stones. She came to Shelomoh and spoke with him of everything that was in her mind, ²and Shelomoh told her about all the things she said. Nothing was concealed from Shelomoh that he didn't tell her.

³The queen of Sheba saw Shelomoh's smartness, the house that he had built, ⁴the food on his table, the seating of his servants, the standing of his ministers and their dress, his wine waiters and their dress, and his stairway by which he would go up to Yahweh's house, and there was no longer any breath in her.

⁵She said to the king, 'The thing is true that I heard in my country about your words and about your smartness. ⁶I didn't believe their words until I came, and my eyes saw, but here, half of the extent of your smartness had not been told me; you exceed the report that I heard. ⁷The blessings of your people, the blessings of these servants of yours who are standing continually before you and listening to your smartness! ⁸May Yahweh your God be blessed, who delighted in you so as to put you on his throne as king for Yahweh your God, in your God's loyalty to Yisra'el in enabling them to stand, permanently, and made you king over them to exercise authority with faithfulness.'

All that she wanted

⁹She gave the king 120 talents of gold, spices in very large quantity and precious stones. There never again came spice like that spice that the queen of Sheba gave King Shelomoh. ¹⁰Huram's servants and Shelomoh's servants, who brought gold from Ophir, also brought algum wood and precious stones. ¹¹The king made the algum logs into causeways for Yahweh's house and for the king's house and into guitars and mandolins for the singers. Ones like these had not been seen before in the country of Yehudah. ¹²King Shelomoh himself gave the queen of Sheba all that she wanted, that she asked for, beyond what she brought to the king. Then she turned round and went to her country, she and her servants.

¹³The weight of the gold that came to Shelomoh in one year was 666 talents of gold, ¹⁴apart from what the traders and the merchants were bringing; and all the kings of Arabia and the governors of the region were bringing gold and silver to Shelomoh. ¹⁵King Shelomoh made 200 body-shields of hammered gold (he would raise 600 gold pieces for each shield) ¹⁶and 300 hand-shields of hammered gold (he would raise 300 pieces of gold for each shield). The king put them in the Lebanon Forest house.

¹⁷The king made a big ivory throne and overlaid it with refined gold, ¹⁸with six steps to the throne, and a gold footstool for the throne attached, and arms on this side and on that side of the place where one sat, and two lions standing beside the arms, ¹⁹and twelve lions standing there on the six steps on this side and on that side; none was made like this for any kingdom.

Tusks, monkeys and peacocks

²⁰All King Shelomoh's drinking vessels were gold and all the vessels in the Lebanon Forest house were beaten gold – silver was not thought of for anything in Shelomoh's days, ²¹because the king had a fleet going to Tarshish with Huram's servants. Once in three years the Tarshish fleet would come carrying gold and silver, tusks, monkeys and peacocks.

²²King Shelomoh was bigger than all the kings of the earth in wealth and in smartness. ²³All the kings of the earth were seeking audience with Shelomoh to listen to his smartness, which God had put into his mind, ²⁴and they were bringing each his offering: silver objects and gold objects, robes, weaponry and spices, horses and mules, each year's requirement in its year. ²⁵Shelomoh had 4,000 stalls for horses and chariots and 12,000 cavalry. He settled them in chariot towns, and with the king in Yerushalaim.

²⁶He was ruling over all the kings from the River as far as the Pelishtites' [Philistines'] country and as far as the Misrayimite border. ²⁷The king made the silver in Yerushalaim like the stones, and made the cedars like the wild fig trees that are in the foothills in the large number. ²⁸They were getting horses out of Misrayim for Shelomoh, and out of all the countries.

²⁹The rest of the things about Shelomoh, early and late, are written in the words of Natan the prophet, in the prophecy of Ahiyyah the Shilonite and in the visions of Ye'do the seer concerning Yarob'am [Jeroboam] ben Nebat, aren't they. ³⁰Shelomoh reigned in Yerushalaim over all Yisra'el forty years. ³¹Shelomoh lay down with his ancestors and they buried him

in the town of David his father. Rehab'am [Rehoboam] his son began to reign in place of him.

How Rehab'am could win people's allegiance

10 Rehab'am went to Shekem, because all Yisra'el had come to Shekem to make him king. ²But when Yarob'am ben Nebat heard while he was in Misrayim, where he had taken flight from before Shelomoh the king, Yarob'am came back from Misrayim, ³and they sent and called for him. Yarob'am and all Yisra'el came and spoke to Rehab'am: ⁴"Your father – he made our yoke tough. So now, lighten something of your father's tough servitude and of his heavy yoke that he put on us, and we'll serve you."

⁵He said to them, 'In three more days, come back to me.' The people went, and ⁶King Rehab'am took counsel with the elders who had been standing before Shelomoh his father when he was alive: 'How do you counsel me to give back word to this people?' ⁷They spoke to him: 'If you're good to this people and accept them and speak good words to them, they'll be servants to you for all time.'

⁸But he abandoned the elders' counsel which they gave him and took counsel with the young men who grew up with him, who were standing before him. ⁹He said to them, 'What are you going to counsel, so that we may give back word to this people who spoke to me: "Lighten something of the yoke that your father put upon us"?' ¹⁰The young men who grew up with him spoke with him: 'You should say this to the people who spoke to you: "Whereas your father made our yoke heavy, you, lighten it from on us" – you should say this to them: "My little finger is thicker than my father's hips. ¹¹So now, whereas my father imposed a heavy yoke on you, I myself will add to your yoke. Whereas my father disciplined you with whips, I myself will with scorpions."'

How to forfeit people's allegiance

¹²Yarob'am and all the people came to Rehab'am on the third day as the king had spoken, "Come back to me on the third day", ¹³and the king answered them toughly. So King Rehab'am abandoned the elders' counsel ¹⁴and spoke to them in accordance with the young men's counsel: 'I shall make your yoke heavy. I myself shall add to it. Whereas my father disciplined you with whips, I myself will with scorpions.' ¹⁵The king didn't listen to the people, because the turn of affairs came from God in order that Yahweh might implement his word, which he had spoken by means of Ahiyyahu the Shilonite to Yarob'am ben Nebat.

¹⁶All Yisra'el [saw] that the king had not listened to them, and the people said back to the king:

What share do we have in David? –
 we have no domain in ben Yishay.
Each one to your tents, Yisra'el;
 now see to your own household, David.

So all Yisra'el went to their tents, ¹⁷though the Yisra'elites who were living in the towns of Yehudah – Rehab'am reigned over them. ¹⁸King Rehab'am sent Hadoram, who was in charge of the workforce, but the Yisra'elites pelted him with stones and he died, though King Rehab'am got himself together to climb up into the chariot to flee to Yerushalaim.

¹⁹So Yisra'el rebelled against David's household, until this day.

11 Rehab'am came to Yerushalaim and congregated the household of Yehudah and Binyamin, 180,000 picked men doing battle, to go to battle with Yisra'el and get the kingship back for Rehab'am. ²But Yahweh's word came to Shema'yahu, the supernatural man: ³'Say to Rehab'am son of Shelomoh king of Yehudah, and to all Yisra'el in Yehudah and in Binyamin: ⁴"Yahweh has said this: 'You will not go up, you will not go to battle with your brothers. Go back each one to his home, because this thing has come about from me.'" They listened to Yahweh's words and turned back from going against Yarob'am.

People from Ephrayim join Rehab'am

⁵Rehab'am lived in Yerushalaim but built up towns as a fortress in Yehudah. ⁶He built up Bet-lehem, Etam, Teqoa, ⁷Bet-tsur, Soko, Adullam, ⁸Gat, Mareshah, Ziph, ⁹Adorayim,

Lakish, Azeqah, ¹⁰Tsorah, Ayyalon and Hebron, which are in Yehudah and in Binyamin, as fortress towns. ¹¹He strengthened the fortresses and put chiefs in them, and treasuries of food, oil and wine, ¹²and in each and every town shields and spears. He strengthened them very greatly.

So Yehudah and Binyamin were his, ¹³while the priests and the Levites who were in all Yisra'el took their stand with him, from all their territory, ¹⁴because the Levites abandoned their pasturelands and their holding and went to Yehudah and to Yerushalaim (because Yarob'am and his sons rejected them from acting as priests for Yahweh ¹⁵and put in place priests for himself for the shrines for the goats and for the calves that he made). ¹⁶Following them from all the Yisra'elite clans, the people who were giving their mind to seek Yahweh the God of Yisra'el came to Yerushalaim to sacrifice for Yahweh, their ancestors' God. ¹⁷They strengthened the kingdom of Yehudah and enabled Rehab'am to be firm for three years, because they walked in the way of David and Shelomoh for three years.

¹⁸Rehab'am took Mahalat bat Yerimot, the son of David, and Abihayil bat Eli'ab, the son of Yishay. ¹⁹She gave birth to sons for him, Ye'ush, Shemaryah and Zaham. ²⁰After her he took Ma'akah bat Abshalom. She gave birth for him to Abiyyah, Attay, Ziza and Shelomit. ²¹Rehab'am loved Ma'akah bat Abshalom more than all his wives and his secondary wives (because he had 18 wives and 60 secondary wives, and fathered 28 sons and 60 daughters).

²²Rehab'am put in place Abiyyah son of Ma'akah as head, as chief among his brothers, because it was to make him king. ²³He was discerning and he got some of all his sons to break out to all the regions of Yehudah and Binyamin, to all the fortified towns, gave them provisions in quantity and asked for a horde of wives.

You abandon me; I abandon you

12 When Rehab'am had established his kingship and he was strong, he abandoned Yahweh's instruction, he and all Yisra'el with him, ²and in the fifth year of King Rehab'am, Shishaq king of Misrayim went up against Yerushalaim because they had trespassed against Yahweh, ³with 1,200 chariotry and 60,000 cavalry; there was no numbering of the company that came with him from Misrayim (Lubites, Sukkiyyites and Kushites). ⁴He captured the fortified towns that belonged to Yehudah and came as far as Yerushalaim.

⁵Shema'yah the prophet came to Rehab'am and the Yehudahite officers who had gathered in Yerushalaim in face of Shishaq, and said to them, 'Yahweh has said this: "You people have abandoned me, so I myself have also abandoned you into the hand of Shishaq."' ⁶The Yisra'elite officers and the king bowed down and said, 'Yahweh is in the right.' ⁷When Yahweh saw that they had bowed down, Yahweh's word came to Shema'yah: 'They have bowed down. I will not devastate them, but in a little while will give them an escape group. My wrath will not pour out on Yerushalaim by means of Shishaq, ⁸but rather they will be servants to him and will acknowledge [the difference between] serving me and serving the kingships of the earth.'

⁹Shishaq king of Misrayim went up against Yerushalaim and took the treasures of Yahweh's house and the treasures of the king's house. He took everything. He took the gold shields that Shelomoh had made; ¹⁰King Rehab'am made copper shields in place of them and appointed them to the control of the officers in charge of the runners who kept watch over the entrance to the king's house. ¹¹Whenever the king came to Yahweh's house the runners came and they would carry them, then take them back to the runners' chamber.

¹²So when he bowed down, Yahweh's anger turned back from him and did not completely devastate him; and in Yehudah there were good things, too.

A salt covenant

¹³King Rehab'am showed himself strong in Yerushalaim and reigned, in that he was a man of forty-one years when he began to reign and he reigned seventeeen years in Yerushalaim, the town that Yahweh chose to put his name there out of all Yisra'el's clans. His mother's name was Na'amah the Ammonite. ¹⁴But he did

what was bad, because he didn't establish his mind to enquire of Yahweh.

¹⁵The things about Rehab'am, early and late, are written in the words of Shema'yah the prophet and Iddo the seer regarding enrolment by genealogy, aren't they. There were battles between Rehab'am and Yarob'am all the time. ¹⁶Rehab'am lay down with his ancestors and was buried in David's Town, and Abiyyah his son began to reign in place of him.

13 In the eighteenth year of King Yarob'am, Abiyyah began to reign over Yehudah. ²Three years he reigned in Yerushalaim. His mother's name was Mikayahu bat Uri'el, from Gib'ah. There was a battle between Abiyyah and Yarob'am, ³and Abiyyah hitched up for the battle with a force of strong men of battle, 400,000 picked men, while Yarob'am lined up with him for battle with 800,000 picked men – strong, forceful.

⁴Abiyyah got up on Mount Tsemarayim, which is in the highland of Ephrayim, and said, 'Listen to me, Yarob'am and all Yisra'el. ⁵It's for you to acknowledge, isn't it, that Yahweh the God of Yisra'el gave kingship over Yisra'el to David permanently, to him and to his sons, by a salt pact. ⁶Yarob'am ben Nebat, a servant of Shelomoh ben David, rose up and rebelled against his lord. ⁷There collected to him empty-headed scoundrels, and they took a firm stand against Rehab'am son of Shelomoh when Rehab'am was a boy and green in mind, and he didn't assert his strength before them. ⁸Now you're saying you'll assert your strength before Yahweh's kingship in the hand of David's sons. Whereas you're a numerous horde and you have with you the gold calves that Yarob'am made for you as gods, ⁹you drove out Yahweh's priests, the Aharonites and the Levites, didn't you, and made priests for yourselves, like the peoples of the countries. Anyone who comes to commission himself, with a bull from the herd and seven rams, becomes a priest, for no-gods.

Don't do battle with Yahweh

¹⁰But for us, Yahweh is our God. We haven't abandoned him. The priests ministering to Yahweh are Aharonites, with the Levites at work, ¹¹burning up whole offerings for Yahweh morning by morning and evening by evening, with spiced incense and the row of bread on the pure table, and the gold candelabrum and its lamps to burn evening by evening, because we are keeping the charge of Yahweh our God, but you people have abandoned it. ¹²So here, God is with us, at the head, and his priests with resounding trumpets to sound against you. Yisra'elites, don't battle with Yahweh, your ancestors' God, because you won't succeed.'

¹³Now Yarob'am had sent an ambush round to come from behind them, so they were before Yehudah, and the ambush was behind them. ¹⁴Yehudah turned their face, and there – the battle was in front and behind for them. They cried out to Yahweh, with the priests blowing on the trumpets, ¹⁵and the men of Yehudah shouted. When the men of Yehudah shouted, God himself hit Yarob'am and all Yisra'el before Abiyyah and Yehudah. ¹⁶The Yisra'elites fled from before Yehudah and God gave them into their hand. ¹⁷Abiyyah and his company struck them down in a great rout. There fell of Yisra'el, run through, 500,000 picked men.

¹⁸So the Yisra'elites bowed down at that time and the Yehudahites stood firm because they relied on Yahweh, their ancestors' God. ¹⁹Abiyyah pursued after Yarob'am and captured some towns from him, Bet-el and its daughter-towns, Yeshanah and its daughter-towns, and Ephrayin and its daughter-towns. ²⁰Yarob'am did not retain energy any more in the days of Abiyyahu, and Yahweh struck him and he died, ²¹but Abiyyahu showed himself strong. He got himself 14 wives and fathered 22 sons and 16 daughters. ²²The rest of the things about Abiyyah, his ways and his words, are written in the commentary of the prophet Iddo.

We rest on thee

14 Abiyyah lay down with his ancestors and they buried him in David's Town, and Asa his son began to reign in place of him. In his days the country was calm ten years. ²Asa did what was good and upright in the eyes of Yahweh his God. ³He removed the alien altars and the shrines, broke up the columns and cut down the totem poles. ⁴He said to Yehudah that they were to look to Yahweh, their ancestors' God, and to act on the instruction and the order. ⁵From all the towns in Yehudah he removed the shrines and the incense stands. The kingdom was calm before him, ⁶and he built up fortified towns in Yehudah because the country was calm and there was no battle made with him in those years, because Yahweh enabled him to settle down. ⁷He said to Yehudah, 'Let's build up these towns and surround them with a wall and towers, gateways and bars, while the country is before us, because we've enquired of Yahweh our God. We've enquired of him and he has enabled us to settle down all round.' So they built and they were successful.

⁸Asa had a force carrying body-shield and spear from Yehudah, 300,000 men, and from Binyamin 280,000 men carrying hand-shield and drawing a bow. All these were forceful strong men. ⁹Zerah the Kushite went out against them with a force of 1,000,000 and 300 chariots, and came as far as Mareshah. ¹⁰Asa went out before him and lined up for battle in the Tsephat Ravine near Mareshah. ¹¹Asa called to Yahweh his God: 'Yahweh, there is no one compared with you to help, between the numerous and the powerless. Help us, Yahweh our God, because we lean on you and in your name we've come against this horde. You are Yahweh our God. A mere human being is not to hold on with you.'

God's spirit comes

¹²Yahweh hit the Kushites before Asa and before Yehudah, and the Kushites fled. ¹³Asa and the company that was with him pursued them as far as Gerar, and some of the Kushites fell. There was no saving of life for them, because they broke up before Yahweh and before his camp.

They took up very much spoil ¹⁴and struck down all the towns round Gerar, because a dread of Yahweh was on them. They plundered all the towns because there was much plunder in them. ¹⁵They also struck down the cattle tents and captured sheep in large number and camels, then went back to Yerushalaim.

15 Azaryahu ben Oded – God's spirit came on him ²and he went out before Asa and said to him, 'Listen to me, Asa and all Yehudah and Binyamin. Yahweh is with you when you are with him. If you enquire of him he will be found by you, but if you abandon him, he will abandon you. ³For a long time Yisra'el had no true God, no priest instructing and no instruction, ⁴but in the pressure upon it, it turned back to Yahweh the God of Yisra'el. They sought him, and he let himself be found by them.

⁵In those times there was no well-being for the person who went out or for the person who came in, because there was much turmoil among all the inhabitants of the countries. ⁶Nation was crushed by nation, town by town, because God put them into a turmoil with every kind of pressure. ⁷But you: be strong. Your hands are not to slacken, because there will be wages for your work.'

⁸When Asa heard these words, the prophecy of Oded the prophet, he showed himself strong and got rid of the abominations from the entire country of Yehudah and Binyamin and from the towns that he had captured from the highland of Ephrayim, and he renovated Yahweh's altar which was before Yahweh's porch.

Taking the initiative in covenant

⁹He collected all Yehudah and Binyamin and the resident aliens with them from Ephrayim and Menashsheh and from Shim'on, because people from Yisra'el in great number had submitted to him when they saw that Yahweh his God was with him. ¹⁰They collected in Yerushalaim in the third month of the fifteenth year of Asa's reign. ¹¹They sacrificed for Yahweh that day some of the spoil; they brought 700 cattle and 7,000 sheep ¹²and came into a pact to enquire of Yahweh their ancestors' God, with their entire mind and with their entire being. ¹³Anyone who would not enquire of Yahweh the God of Yisra'el would be put to death, whether small or great, man or woman. ¹⁴They swore to Yahweh with a loud voice, with a shout, with trumpets and with horns. ¹⁵All Yehudah rejoiced over the oath because they swore with their entire mind and sought him with their entire heart, and he let himself be found by them. Yahweh enabled them to be settled all round.

¹⁶In addition, Ma'akah mother of Asa the king he removed as queen mother, because she had made a monstrosity for Asherah. Asa cut

down her monstrosity, turned it to dust and burned it in Wadi Qidron, ¹⁷though the shrines did not disappear from Yisra'el. Yet Asa's mind was perfect all his days. ¹⁸He brought into God's house the sacred things belonging to his father and to him, silver, gold and articles, ¹⁹while no battle happened until the thirty-fifth year of Asa's reign.

16 In the thirty-sixth year of Asa's reign, Ba'sha king of Yisra'el went up against Yehudah and built up The Height so as not to grant Asa king of Yehudah anyone going out or coming. ²Asa got silver and gold out from the treasuries of Yahweh's house and the king's house and sent to Ben-hadad king of Aram who lived in Dammeseq [Damascus], saying, ³'A pact between me and you and between my father and your father: here, I've sent you silver and gold; go contravene your pact with Ba'sha king of Yisra'el so that he may go up from me.'

God's eyes are ranging through the earth

⁴Ben-hadad listened to King Asa and sent the officers of the forces that he had against Yisra'el's towns. He struck down Iyyon, Dan, Water Meadow and all the supply places, the towns in Naphtali. ⁵When Ba'sha heard, he left off building up The Height and stopped his work, ⁶while Asa the king got all Yehudah and they carried the stones from The Height and its timber with which Ba'sha had built, and with them he built up Geba and The Watchtower.

⁷But at that time Hanani the seer came to Asa king of Yehudah and said to him, 'For your leaning on the king of Aram and not leaning on Yahweh your God, because of this the king of Aram's force has escaped from your hand. ⁸The Kushites and the Lubites were a force in large numbers, of chariotry and cavalry, very many, weren't they, but when you leaned on Yahweh, he gave them into your hand. ⁹Because Yahweh – his eyes are ranging through the entire earth, to show himself strong with people whose mind is perfect towards him. You've been very idiotic in connection with this, because from now on there will be battles with you.' ¹⁰Asa was provoked by the seer, and he put him into the stocks because he was in a rage with him on account of this, and Asa oppressed some of the people at that time.

¹¹There, the things about Asa, early and late – there they are, written on the document about the kings of Yehudah and Yisra'el. ¹²In the thirty-ninth year of his reign Asa had an ailment in his feet, until his ailment was exceptionally serious, and further, in his ailment he did not enquire of Yahweh but with physicians. ¹³Asa lay down with his ancestors and died in the forty-first year of his reign. ¹⁴They buried him in the graveyard that he had cut for himself in David's Town. They laid him in his bed, which they filled with spices and perfumes blended by blending work, and they made for him a very great fire.

A teaching mission

17 Yehoshaphat his son began to reign in place of him and showed himself strong over Yisra'el. ²He put a force in all the fortified towns of Yehudah and put outposts in the country of Yehudah and in the towns of Ephrayim that Asa his father had captured.

³Yahweh was with Yehoshaphat because he walked in the earlier ways of David his ancestor and did not enquire of the Masters. ⁴He enquired of the God of his father and walked by his orders, not in accordance with the practice of Yisra'el. ⁵Yahweh established the kingship in his hand and all Yehudah gave offerings to Yehoshaphat, so that he had wealth and splendour in quantity. ⁶His mind was lofty in Yahweh's ways, and further he removed the shrines and the totem poles from Yehudah.

⁷In the third year of his reign he sent his officials Ben-hayil, Obadyah, Zekaryah, Netan'el and Mikayahu to teach in the towns of Yehudah, ⁸and with them the Levites Shema'yahu, Netanyahu, Zebadyahu, Asah'el, Shemiramot, Yehonatan, Adoniyyah, Tobiyyahu and Tob Adoniyyah, the Levites, and with them Elishama and Yehoram, the priests. ⁹They taught in Yehudah, Yahweh's instruction document being with them. They went round through all the towns of Yehudah and taught among the people.

¹⁰A dread of Yahweh was on all the kingships of the countries that were round Yehudah and they didn't battle with Yehoshaphat. ¹¹Some Pelishtites were bringing Yehoshaphat offerings

and silver as a levy; also the Arabs were bringing him flocks: 7,700 rams and 7,700 goats.

¹²So Yehoshaphat was getting bigger and bigger. He built castles and supply towns in Yehudah; ¹³he had much work in the towns of Yehudah, and men of battle, forceful strong men, in Yerushalaim. ¹⁴These, their registering by their ancestral households was:

> for Yehudah as chiliarchs –
> Adnah the officer, and with him 300,000 forceful strong men;
> ¹⁵next to him Yehohanan the officer, and with him 280,000;
> ¹⁶next to him Amasyah ben Zikri, who gave freely for Yahweh, and with him 200,00 forceful strong men;
> ¹⁷and from Binyamin –
> a forceful strong man, Elyada, and with him 200,000 men able to wield bow and shield;
> ¹⁸next to him Yehozabad, and with him 180,000 men equipped for the army.

¹⁹These were the people ministering to the king, apart from the people that the king put in the fortified towns in all Yehudah.

The prophet whom Ah'ab didn't like

18 Yehoshaphat had wealth and splendour in quantity. He made a marriage alliance with Ah'ab, ²and at the end of some years went down to Ah'ab in Shomron [Samaria]. Ah'ab sacrificed sheep and cattle in quantity for him and for the company that was with him, and incited him into going up to Heights-in-Gil'ad.

³Ah'ab king of Yisra'el said to Yehoshaphat king of Yehudah, 'Will you go with me to Heights-in-Gil'ad?' He said to him, 'I'll be the same as you, my company the same as yours, with you in the battle.' ⁴But Yehoshaphat said to the king of Yisra'el, 'Please enquire for Yahweh's word today.'

⁵So the king of Yisra'el collected the prophets, 400 individuals, and said to them, 'Shall we go to Heights-in-Gil'ad for battle, or shall I leave off?' They said, 'Go up, and God will give it into the king's hand.' ⁶But Yehoshaphat said, 'There isn't any further prophet of Yahweh here, is there, so we may enquire of him?' ⁷The king of Yisra'el said to Yehoshaphat, 'There is one further individual to enquire of Yahweh from, but I myself dislike him because he doesn't prophesy good for me but always bad. He's Mikayehu ben Yimlah.' Yehoshaphat said, 'The king shouldn't say that.' ⁸So the king of Yisra'el called to a courtier and said, 'Hurry Mikayehu ben Yimlah.'

⁹As the king of Yisra'el and Yehoshaphat king of Yehudah were sitting, each on his throne, dressed in robes, sitting at the threshing-floor at the entrance to the gateway of Shomron, and all the prophets were prophesying before them, ¹⁰Tsidqiyyahu ben Kena'anah had made himself iron horns, and he said, 'Yahweh has said this: "With these you will gore the Aramites until you have finished them off."' ¹¹All the prophets were prophesying in this way: 'Go up to Heights-in-Gil'ad and succeed! Yahweh will give it into the king's hand.'

The lying spirit

¹²Now the envoy who went to call for Mikayehu spoke to him: 'Here, the prophets' words are good for the king, as one bidding. Your word should please be like one of them. You should speak of something good.' ¹³Mikayehu said, 'As Yahweh lives, what my God says to me – I will speak it.'

¹⁴He came to the king and the king said to him, 'Mikah, shall we go up to Heights-in-Gil'ad for battle, or should I leave off?' He said, 'Go up, and succeed! They will be given into your hand.' ¹⁵The king said to him, 'How many times am I going to get you to swear that you won't speak to me anything but truth in Yahweh's name?'

¹⁶So he said, 'I saw all Yisra'el scattered on the mountains like a flock that have no shepherd. Yahweh said, "These people have no lords. They should go back, each to his house, with things being well."' ¹⁷The king of Yisra'el said to Yehoshaphat, 'I said to you, "He won't prophesy something good for me, but rather something bad", didn't I.'

¹⁸He said, 'Therefore, listen to Yahweh's word. I saw Yahweh sitting on his throne, with the entire heavenly army standing to his right and his left. ¹⁹Yahweh said, "Who'll entice

Ah'ab king of Yisra'el so he'll go up but fall at Heights-in-Gil'ad?" One spoke, saying "Like this", and another saying "Like this". ²⁰Then a spirit went out and stood before Yahweh and said, "I'm the one who'll entice him." Yahweh said to him, "How?" ²¹He said, "I'll go out and become a false spirit in the mouth of all his prophets." He said, "You are to entice him. Yes, you'll be able to. Go out and do it." ²²So now, there, Yahweh put a false spirit in the mouth of these prophets of yours, in that Yahweh has spoken of something bad for you.'

The power of chance

²³Tsidqiyyahu ben Kena'anah went up and struck Mikayehu on the jaw, and said, 'Which way did Yahweh's spirit pass from being with me to speak with you?' ²⁴Mikayehu said, 'Here, you are going to see, on that day when you come to an innermost room to hide.'

²⁵The king of Yisra'el said, 'Get Mikayehu and take him back to Amon the town official and to Yo'ash the king's son ²⁶and say, "The king has said this: 'Put this man in the cells and give him slave bread and slave water until I come back with things being well.'"' ²⁷Mikayehu said, 'If you really do come back with things being well, Yahweh did not speak through me.' (And he said, 'Listen, you peoples, all of them.')

²⁸So the king of Yisra'el went up with Yehoshaphat king of Yehudah to Heights-in-Gil'ad. ²⁹The king of Yisra'el said to Yehoshaphat, 'I'm putting on disguise and coming into battle, but you, dress in your robes.' So the king of Yisra'el put on disguise and they came into battle.

³⁰Now the king of Aram had ordered his chariot officers, 'You will not battle anyone small or great except the king of Yisra'el alone.' ³¹When the chariot officers saw Yehoshaphat and said 'He's the king of Yisra'el', they turned round to him to do battle. But Yehoshaphat cried out and Yahweh helped him. God incited them away from him, ³²and when the chariot officers saw that it was not the king of Yisra'el, they turned back from following him. ³³But a man drew his bow innocently and struck the king of Yisra'el between the links and the armour. He said to his charioteer, 'Turn your hand, get me out from the camp, because I'm wounded.'

³⁴The battle mounted that day, while the king of Yisra'el was keeping himself standing in the chariot opposite the Aramites until the evening. But he died towards the time of the sun's setting.

Proper exercise of authority

19 Yehoshaphat king of Yehudah went back to Yerushalaim to his house with things being well, ²but Yehu ben Hanani the seer went out before him. He said to King Yehoshaphat, 'Do you help the faithless, are you loyal to the people hostile to Yahweh? For this, there is fury upon you from before Yahweh. ³Yet good things are found with you, because you burned away the totem poles in the country and set your mind on enquiring of God.'

⁴Yehoshaphat lived in Yerushalaim, but he again went out among the people from Be'er Sheba as far as the highland of Ephrayim and got them to come back to Yahweh, their ancestors' God. ⁵He put in place authorities in the country in all the fortified towns in Yehudah, town by town.

⁶He said to the authorities, 'Watch what you're doing, because it's not for a human being that you exercise authority but for Yahweh, who is with you when you speak an authoritative word. ⁷So now, a dread of Yahweh is to be upon you. Keep watch and act, because with Yahweh our God there is no evil or honouring of the face or taking of a bribe.' ⁸(Also in Yerushalaim Yehoshaphat put in place some of the Levites and the priests and some of the ancestral heads of Yisra'el for the exercise of Yahweh's authority and for arguments.)

They came back to Yerushalaim ⁹and he ordered them, 'You're to act like this: with awe for Yahweh, with truthfulness and with a perfect mind. ¹⁰Every argument that comes to you from your brothers who are living in their towns, between blood and blood, between instruction and order, decrees or rulings, you're to warn them so that they don't become liable before Yahweh and fury come on you and on your brothers. So you will do, and you won't become liable. ¹¹Here, Amaryahu the head priest is over you in everything to do with Yahweh, and Zebadyahu ben Yishma'el is the chief of Yehudah's household in everything to do with the king. The Levite overseers are before you. Be strong when you act. Yahweh be with the good.'

How to pray in a political crisis

20 Subsequently the Mo'abites and the Ammonites, and some of the Me'unites, came against Yehoshaphat for battle. ²People came and told Yehoshaphat, 'A great horde is coming against you from across the sea, from Aram. There, they're at Hatsetson Tamar (i.e. Gedi Spring).' ³Yehoshaphat was afraid and gave himself to enquiring of Yahweh, and he called a fast for all Yehudah. ⁴Yehudah collected to seek help from Yahweh; from all the towns in Yehudah, too, people came to seek Yahweh.

⁵Yehoshaphat stood in the congregation of Yehudah and Yerushalaim in Yahweh's house before the new court. ⁶He said, 'Yahweh, our ancestors' God: you are God in the heavens and one who rules all the kingships of the nations, are you not. In your hand are energy and strength. There's no one able to take a stand with you. ⁷It was you, our God, wasn't it, who dispossessed the inhabitants of this country from before your people Yisra'el and gave it to the offspring of Abraham your friend permanently. ⁸They lived in it and built you a sanctuary in it for your name, saying ⁹"If bad fortune comes upon us (the sword exercising authority, or epidemic, or famine), we will stand before this house and before you, because your name is in this house, and we will cry out to you because of the pressure on us, and you will listen and deliver."

¹⁰Now, there, people from Ammon and Mo'ab and Mount Se'ir, into which you did not let Yisra'el come when they came from the country of Misrayim (rather they departed from being against them and did not annihilate them), ¹¹here – they are dealing to us by coming to drive us out from your possession which you let us possess. ¹²Our God, you will exercise authority over them, won't you, because there's no energy in us before this great horde that's coming against us. We don't know what we'll do, but our eyes are on you.' ¹³All Yehudah was standing before Yahweh, also their little ones, their wives and their children.

The two stages whereby we see answers to prayer

¹⁴Then Yahazi'el ben Zekaryahu son of Benayah son of Ye'i'el son of Mattanyah, the Levite, one of the sons of Asaph – Yahweh's spirit came on him in the middle of the congregation, ¹⁵and he said, 'Heed, all Yehudah, inhabitants of Yerushalaim and King Yehoshaphat. Yahweh has said this to you: "Don't be afraid, don't be scared before this great horde, because the battle is not yours but God's. ¹⁶Tomorrow, go down against them. There they'll be, going up by the Tsits Ascent. You'll find them at the end of the wadi, before the Yeru'el Wilderness. ¹⁷It's not for you to battle on this occasion. Take your position, stand and see Yahweh's deliverance of you, Yehudah and Yerushalaim. Don't be afraid, don't be scared. Tomorrow, go out before them. Yahweh will be with you."'

¹⁸Yehoshaphat bowed his head, face to the ground, and all Yehudah and the inhabitants of Yerushalaim fell before Yahweh to bow low to Yahweh. ¹⁹The Levites from the Qehatites and from the Qorahites stood up to praise Yahweh the God of Yisra'el with an exceptionally loud voice.

²⁰They started early in the morning and went out to the Teqoa Wilderness. When they went out, Yehoshaphat stood and said, 'Listen to me, Yehudah and inhabitants of Yerushalaim. Stand firm in faith in Yahweh your God and you will stand firm; stand firm in faith in his prophets and you will succeed.' ²¹He took counsel with the people and put in place people singing for Yahweh and praising his sacred glory as they went out before the armed company, and saying, 'Confess Yahweh, because his commitment is permanent.'

²²At the time when they began resounding and praising, Yahweh set ambushes against the people of Ammon, Mo'ab and Mount Se'ir who were coming to Yehudah, and they took a beating. ²³The people of Ammon and Mo'ab stood against the inhabitants of Mount Se'ir to devote and annihilate them. When they'd

finished off the inhabitants of Se'ir, they helped, each individual, to devastate his neighbour.

Relief and thanksgiving

²⁴When Yehudah came to a watchtower towards the wilderness and they turned their faces towards the horde – there, they were corpses fallen to the ground. There was no escape group. ²⁵Yehoshaphat came with his company to plunder their spoil and they found among them, in quantity, both property and corpses and desirable articles. They rescued things for themselves until they couldn't carry anything. They were plundering the spoil for three days because there was so much. ²⁶On the fourth day they congregated in Blessing Vale (because they blessed Yahweh there, that's why people have called the place Blessing Vale until this day). ²⁷Everyone from Yehudah and Yerushalaim went back with Yehoshaphat at their head, going back to Yerushalaim with rejoicing, because Yahweh had let them rejoice over their enemies. ²⁸They came to Yerushalaim with mandolins, with guitars and with trumpets, to Yahweh's house. ²⁹Dread of God came over all the kingships in the countries when they heard that Yahweh had battled with Yisra'el's enemies. ³⁰So Yehoshaphat's kingship was calm; his God enabled him to settle down all round.

³¹Yehoshaphat began to reign over Yehudah as a man of thirty-five years, when he began to reign, and he reigned twenty-five years in Yerushalaim. His mother's name was Azubah bat Shilhi. ³²He walked in the way of his father Asa and did not turn aside from it in doing what was upright in Yahweh's eyes. ³³Yet the shrines did not disappear and the people did not set their minds on their ancestors' God.

³⁴The rest of the things about Yehoshaphat, early and late – there they are, written in the words of Yehu ben Hanani, which were entered into the document about the kings of Yisra'el. ³⁵But subsequently, Yehoshaphat king of Yehudah joined with Ahazyah king of Yisra'el; he was faithless in so doing. ³⁶He joined with him in making ships to go to Tarshish. They made the ships at Etsyon Geber. ³⁷Eli'ezer ben Dodavahu from Mareshah prophesied against Yehoshaphat: 'As you've joined with Ahazyahu, Yahweh is breaking out on your work.' And the ships broke up and had to hold back from going to Tarshish.

The son who killed his brothers

21 Yehoshaphat lay down with his ancestors and was buried with his ancestors in David's Town, and his son Yehoram began to reign in place of him. ²He had brothers, Yehoshaphat's sons: Azaryah, Yehi'el, Zekaryahu, Azaryahu, Mika'el and Shephatyahu. All these were sons of Yehoshaphat king of Yisra'el. ³Their father gave them many gifts of silver and of gold, and of choice things, with fortified towns in Yehudah, but the kingship he gave to Yehoram, because he was the firstborn.

⁴Yehoram rose up over his father's kingship and showed himself strong, and killed all his brothers with the sword, and also some Yisra'elite ministers. ⁵Yehoram was a man of thirty-two years when he began to reign and he reigned eight years in Yerushalaim. ⁶He walked in the way of the kings of Yisra'el, as Ah'ab's household had done, because he had Ah'ab's daughter as wife. He did what was bad in Yahweh's eyes. ⁷But Yahweh was not willing to devastate David's household, for the sake of the pact that he solemnized towards David, and as he had said he would give him and his sons hegemony for all time.

⁸In his days Edom rebelled from under Yehudah's hand and got a king to reign over them. ⁹Yehoram went across with his officers and all his chariotry with him. He rose by night and struck down the Edomites, who were surrounding him and the chariot officers. ¹⁰But Edom has rebelled from under Yehudah's hand until this day. Then Libnah rebelled from under his hand at that time, because he had abandoned Yahweh, his ancestors' God. ¹¹He also made shrines in the highland of Yehudah, and got the inhabitants of Yerushalaim to whore, and drove Yehudah away.

How to be really unpopular

¹²A document from Eliyyahu [Elijah] the prophet came to him, saying 'Yahweh the

God of David your ancestor has said this: "Since you have not walked in the ways of Yehoshaphat your father and in the ways of Asa king of Yehudah ^{13}but have walked in the way of the kings of Yisra'el, and got Yehudah and the inhabitants of Yerushalaim to whore, as the household of Ah'ab got them to whore, and your brothers, your father's household, who were better men than you, you have also killed – ^{14}here, Yahweh is going to inflict a great beating on your people, on your sons, on your wives and on all your property, ^{15}and you yourself with a great illness, with an illness of the insides, until your insides come out because of the illness, days upon days."

^{16}Yahweh made the spirit of the Pelishtites and the Arabs who were near the Kushites rise against Yehoram. ^{17}They went up against Yehudah, broke into it and took captive all the property that could be found belonging to the king's house, and also his sons and his wives. No son remained to him except Yeho'ahaz, the youngest of his sons.

^{18}After all this, Yahweh hit him in his insides with an illness without healing. ^{19}After days upon days, as the end of two years came, his insides came out with his illness, and he died because of the bad illness. His people did not make a fire for him like the fire for his ancestors. ^{20}He was a man of thirty-two years when he began to reign and he reigned eight years in Yerushalaim but went without people caring. They buried him in David's Town but not in the kings' graves.

22
The inhabitants of Yerushalaim made Ahazyahu, his youngest son, king in place of him, because the raiding gang which came into the camp with Arabs had killed all the older ones. So Ahazyahu ben Yehoram began to reign as king of Yehudah.

Two forceful women

^{2}Ahazyahu was a man of twenty-two years when he began to reign and he reigned one year in Yerushalaim. His mother's name was Atalyahu bat Omri. ^{3}He too walked in the ways of Ah'ab's household, because his mother was his counsellor in acting faithlessly. ^{4}He did what was bad in Yahweh's eyes, like Ah'ab's household, because they became his counsellors after his father's death, to his devastation. ^{5}He also went by their counsel when he went to battle with Yehoram ben Ah'ab king of Yisra'el, against Haza'el king of Aram at Heights-in-Gil'ad. The Aramites struck Yoram down, ^{6}so he went back to heal in Yizr'e'el because they had been striking him down (the people who struck him down at The Height when he was battling with Haza'el king of Aram).

Now Azaryahu ben Yehoram king of Yehudah went down to see Yehoram ben Ah'ab in Yizr'e'el because he was ill. ^{7}But from God came the treading down of Ahazyahu for coming to Yoram. When he came, he went out with Yehoram to Yehu ben Nimshi whom Yahweh had anointed to cut down Ah'ab's household. ^{8}When Yehu entered into judgement with Ah'ab's household, he found the Yehudahite officers and Ahazyahu's nephews, Ahazyahu's ministers, and killed them. ^{9}He looked for Ahazyahu and took him captive; he was hiding in Shomron. They brought him to Yehu and put him to death. They buried him, because (they said), 'He's the son of Yehoshaphat, who enquired of Yahweh with his entire mind.'

Ahazyahu's household could not retain energy for reigning. ^{10}When Atalyahu, Ahazyahu's mother, saw that her son was dead, she set to and obliterated all the royal offspring of Yehudah's household. ^{11}But Yehoshab'at, the king's daughter, got Yo'ash ben Ahazyahu and stole him away from among the king's sons who were being put to death and put him and his nanny in a bedroom. Yehoshab'at bat Yehoram, the wife of Yehoyada the priest, concealed him (because she was Ahazyahu's sister) from Atalyahu, and she didn't put him to death. ^{12}He was with them in God's house hiding for six years, while Atalyah was reigning over the country.

Two covenants among people

23
In the seventh year, Yehoyada showed himself strong and got the centurions, Azaryahu ben Yeroham, Yishma'e'l ben Yehohanan, Azaryahu ben Obed, Ma'aseyahu ben Adayahu and Elishaphat ben Zikri, into a pact with him. ^{2}They went round in Yehudah

and collected the Levites from all the towns in Yehudah, and the ancestral heads of Yisra'el. They came to Yerushalaim ³and the entire congregation solemnized a pact in God's house with the king.

He said to them, 'Here, the king's son will reign, as Yahweh spoke concerning David's sons. ⁴This is the thing that you're to do: a third of you who are coming in on the sabbath as priests and as Levites are to be gatemen on the thresholds, ⁵a third in the king's house, a third at the Foundation Gate, the entire people in the courts of Yahweh's house. ⁶No one is to come into Yahweh's house except the priests and the ministering Levites; they may come in because they are sacred, but the entire people is to keep Yahweh's charge. ⁷The Levites are to encircle the king all round, each with his equipment in his hand. Anyone who comes into the house is to be put to death. They are to be with the king when he comes in and when he goes out.'

⁸The Levites and all Yehudah acted in accordance with all that Yehoyada the priest ordered. They took each his men who were coming in on the sabbath with those who were going out on the sabbath (because Yehoyada the priest did not free the divisions). ⁹Yehoyada the priest gave the centurions the lances, the hand-shields and the body-shields that belonged to King David, which were in God's house. ¹⁰He put in place the entire people, each with his weapon in his hand, from the shoulder of the house on the right as far as the shoulder of the house on the left, at the altar and at the house, in charge of the king all round. ¹¹Then they got the king's son out, put the diadem and the affirmation on him, and made him king. Yehoyada and his sons anointed him and said, 'Long live the king!'

A new covenant with God

¹²Atalyahu heard the sound of the people running and praising the king and came to the people at Yahweh's house. ¹³She saw, there, the king was standing by his pillar at the entrance, and the officials with their trumpets by the king, and the entire people of the country rejoicing and blowing on trumpets, and the singers with musical instruments, who were helping them to know how to give praise.

Atalyahu tore her clothes and said, 'Conspiracy, conspiracy!'

¹⁴Yehoyada the priest sent out the centurions who were appointed over the force and said to them, 'Take her out between the rows. The person who follows her is to be put to death with the sword' (because the priest said, 'You will not put her to death in Yahweh's house'). ¹⁵They laid hands on her and she came to the Horse Gate entrance to the king's house, and they put her to death there.

¹⁶Yehoyada solemnized a pact between himself and the entire people and the king, that they would be a people for Yahweh. ¹⁷The entire people came to the Master's house and tore it down. Its altars and its images they broke down, and Mattan, the Master's priest, they killed before the altars.

¹⁸Yehoyada put the appointments in Yahweh's house in the hand of the Levite priests to whom David had given a share over Yahweh's house in offering up Yahweh's burnt offerings in accordance with what is written in Mosheh's instruction, with rejoicing and with song on the basis of David's directions. ¹⁹He put in place the gatemen at the gateways of Yahweh's house so that anyone who was defiled in any way should not come in. ²⁰He got the centurions, the august people, the people's rulers and all the people of the country, and took the king down from Yahweh's house. They brought him through the Upper Gate to the king's house and seated the king on the royal throne. ²¹The entire people of the country rejoiced, while the town was quiet, when they had put Atalyahu to death by the sword.

Boy king, insistent young man

24 Yo'ash was seven years of age when he began to reign and he reigned forty years in Yerushalaim. His mother's name was Tsibyah, from Be'er Sheba. ²Yo'ash did what was upright in Yahweh's eyes all the days of Yehoyada the priest. ³Yehoyada got him two wives, and sons and daughters were born to him.

⁴Subsequently, it came into Yo'ash's mind to renovate Yahweh's house. ⁵He collected the priests and the Levites and said to them, 'Go out to the towns of Yehudah and collect silver from all Yisra'el to strengthen your God's

house, each year's requirement in its year. You're to make speed about the thing.' But the Levites didn't make speed. ⁶So the king called for Yehoyada the head and said to him, 'Why have you not required of the Levites to bring from Yehudah and from Yerushalaim the levy of Mosheh, Yahweh's servant, and the congregation of Yisra'el, to the affirmation tent?' ⁷Because the faithless Atalyahu – her sons had broken into God's house, and further had made all the sacred things in Yahweh's house for the Masters.

⁸So the king said, and they made a chest and put it at the gateway of Yahweh's house, outside, ⁹and they gave voice in Yehudah and in Yerushalaim to bring to Yahweh the levy of Mosheh, Yahweh's servant, made on Yisra'el in the wilderness. ¹⁰All the officials and the entire people rejoiced and brought it, and threw it into the chest until they'd filled it. ¹¹At the time when they would bring the chest to the king's appointees by the hand of the Levites, when they saw that the silver was much, the king's secretary and the head priest's appointee would come and empty the chest and carry it and take it back to its place. So they did day by day, and they gathered silver in quantity.

¹²The king and Yehoyada gave it to the people doing the work, the service for Yahweh's house, and they were hiring masons and craftsmen to renovate Yahweh's house, and also craftsmen in iron and copper to strengthen Yahweh's house.

But when the mentor's gone . . .

¹³The people doing the work did it, and restoration progressed by the work at their hand. They set up God's house in accordance with its design and made it stand firm. ¹⁴When they'd finished, they brought before the king and Yehoyada the remainder of the silver and they made articles for Yahweh's house, articles for ministry and the burnt offerings, ladles, and gold and silver articles. They were offering up burnt offerings in Yahweh's house regularly all the days of Yehoyada.

¹⁵But Yehoyada grew old and became full of years and died, a man of 130 years when he died. ¹⁶They buried him in David's Town with the kings, because he had done good things in Yisra'el with God and God's house. ¹⁷But after Yehoyada's death the officials of Yehudah came and bowed low to the king. Then the king listened to them ¹⁸and they abandoned the house of Yahweh, their ancestors' God, and served the totem poles and the idols, and fury came on Yehudah and Yerushalaim because of this liability of theirs.

¹⁹Yahweh sent prophets among them to turn them back to Yahweh, and they testified against them, but they didn't give ear. ²⁰God's spirit clothed Zekaryahu ben Yehoyada, the priest, and he stood above the people and said to them: 'God has said this: "Why are you transgressing Yahweh's orders? You will not succeed. Because you have abandoned Yahweh, he has abandoned you."' ²¹But they conspired against him and pelted him with stones, by the king's order, in the court of Yahweh's house. ²²So Yo'ash the king was not mindful of the commitment with which Yehoyada his father had acted with him, and he killed his son. As he died he said, 'May Yahweh see and require.'

²³At the turn of the year, a force from Aram went up against him. They came to Yehudah and Yerushalaim and eliminated all the people's officers from the people. All their plunder they sent off to the king of Dammeseq, ²⁴ᵃbecause the Aramite force had come with a few men but Yahweh gave into their hand a force of a very large number because they had abandoned Yahweh, their ancestors' God.

Boy king, insistent young man, apostate adult

²⁴ᵇSo they executed acts of authority upon Yo'ash, ²⁵and when they went from him (because they abandoned him with many wounds), his servants conspired against him because of the shedding of the blood of the sons of Yehoyada the priest, and they killed him on his bed. So he died and they buried him in David's Town, but they didn't bury him in the kings' graves. ²⁶These were the people who conspired against him: Zabad ben Shim'at (the Ammonite woman) and Yehozabad ben Shimrit (the Mo'abite woman). ²⁷His sons, the quantity of prophecy against him, and the founding of God's house – there, they are written in the exposition in the document about the kings.

His son Amatsyahu began to reign in place of him.

25 Amatsyahu began to reign as a man of twenty-five years and he reigned twenty-nine years in Yerushalaim. His mother's name was Yeho'addan, from Yerushalaim. ²He did what was upright in Yahweh's eyes, only not with a perfect mind. ³When the kingship was strongly in his control, he killed his servants who had struck down the king, his father, ⁴but the children he didn't put to death, because it was in accordance with what is written in the instruction in Mosheh's document where Yahweh ordered, 'Parents will not die because of children and children will not die because of parents. Rather, it is as an individual for his own wrongdoing that people are to die.'

⁵Amatsyahu collected the Yehudahites and set them by ancestral households under chiliarchs and centurions, for all Yehudah and Binyamin. He registered them from the age of twenty upwards and found them to be 300,000 picked men able to go out in the army, able to grasp spear and shield. ⁶He hired from Yisra'el 100,000 forceful strong men for a hundred talents of silver. ⁷But a supernatural man came to him saying, 'Your Majesty, the army of Yisra'el is not to come with you, because Yahweh is not with Yisra'el (all the Ephrayimites). ⁸Rather, come, you act, be strong for battle. God could make you collapse before an enemy, because there's energy in God to help and to make collapse.'

A war crime

⁹Amatsyahu said to the supernatural man, 'But what am I to do about the hundred talents that I gave to the Yisra'elite raiding gang?' The supernatural man said, 'Yahweh has the means to give you much more than this.' ¹⁰So Amatsyahu made them distinct (the raiding gang that had come to him from Ephrayim) for them to go to their own place. Their anger raged greatly against Yehudah, and they went back to their place in angry fury.

¹¹But Amatsyahu showed himself strong and drove his company, and went to Salt Ravine. He struck down the men of Se'ir, 10,000, ¹²and the Yehudahites captured 10,000 alive, brought them to the top of The Cliff, and threw them down from the top of The Cliff; all of them tore apart. ¹³But the men in the raiding gang that Amatsyahu sent back from going with him to the battle made a raid against the Yehudahite towns from Shomron as far as Bet Horon, struck down 3,000 of them and took much plunder.

¹⁴After Amatsyahu came from striking down the Edomites, he brought the gods of the people of Se'ir and set them up for himself as gods, and he would bow low before them and burn incense for them. ¹⁵Yahweh's anger raged at Amatsyahu and he sent a prophet to him. He said to him, 'Why have you enquired of the gods of the people who did not rescue their people from your hand?' ¹⁶When he spoke to him, he said to him, 'Have we made you a counsellor to the king? Leave off for yourself! Why should they strike you down.' The prophet left off, and said, 'I know that God has counselled to devastate you, because you have done this and not listened to my counsel.'

What counts as effective counsel

¹⁷Amatsyahu king of Yehudah took counsel and sent to Yo'ash ben Yeho'ahaz son of Yehu, king of Yisra'el, saying 'Come on, let's face each other.' ¹⁸Yo'ash king of Yisra'el sent to Amatsyahu king of Yehudah, saying, 'A thistle that was in the Lebanon sent to a cedar that was in the Lebanon, saying "Give your daughter to my son as wife." But an animal of the wild that was in the Lebanon passed by and trampled the thistle. ¹⁹You've said, "There, you've struck down Edom", and your mind has lifted you up, so that you behave with splendour. Stay in your house now. Why stir up something bad? You'll fall, you and Yehudah with you.'

²⁰Amatsyahu didn't listen, because it was from God, in order that he might give them into his hand, because he'd enquired of the Edomite gods. ²¹So Yo'ash king of Yisra'el went up, and he and Amatsyahu king of Yehudah faced each other at Bet Shemesh, which belongs to Yehudah. ²²Yehudah took a beating before Yisra'el and they fled each man to his tents. ²³Amatsyahu king of Yehudah, son of Yo'ash son of Yeho'ahaz – Yo'ash king of Yisra'el captured him at Bet Shemesh, brought him to Yerushalaim and broke down the Yerushalaim

wall from the Ephrayim Gate as far as the Corner Gate, 200 metres. ²⁴He took all the gold and the silver and all the articles that were to be found in God's house with Obed Edom, and the treasuries of the king's house, and hostages, and went back to Shomron.

²⁵Amatsyahu ben Yo'ash king of Yehudah lived after the death of Yo'ash ben Yeho'ahaz king of Yisra'el fifteen years. ²⁶The rest of the things about Amatsyahu, early and late, there, they are written on the document about the kings of Yehudah and Yisra'el, aren't they. ²⁷After the time when Amatsyahu departed from following Yahweh, people formed a conspiracy against him in Yerushalaim and he fled to Lakish, but they sent after him to Lakish and put him to death there. ²⁸They carried him on horses and buried him in Yerushalaim with his ancestors in the Town of Yehudah.

A young man's achievements

26 All the people of Yehudah got Uzziyyahu (he was sixteen years of age) and made him king in place of his father Amatsyahu. ²It was he who built up Elot. He had got it back for Yehudah after the king lay down with his ancestors.

³Uzziyyahu was sixteen years of age when he began to reign and he reigned fifty-two years in Yerushalaim. His mother's name was Yekolyah, from Yerushalaim. ⁴He did what was upright in Yahweh's eyes in accordance with all that Amatsyahu his father did. ⁵He came to enquire of God in the days of Zekaryahu, who enabled him to understand awe for God, and in the days when he enquired of Yahweh, God enabled him to be successful.

⁶He went out and battled against the Pelishtites and broke through the wall of Gat, the wall of Yabneh and the wall of Ashdod, and built up towns in Ashdod and among the Pelishtites. ⁷God helped him against the Pelishtites, against the Arabs who lived in Gur-ba'al, and the Me'unites. ⁸The Ammonites gave offerings to Uzziyyahu, and his name went as far as the entry point to Misrayim, because he became exceptionally strong. ⁹Uzziyyahu built towers in Yerushalaim on the Corner Gate, on the Ravine Gate and on the Angle, and made them strong. ¹⁰He built towers in the wilderness and hewed many cisterns, because he had much livestock, and in the foothills and in the flatland – ploughmen and vinedressers in the mountains and in the farmland, because he loved the ground.

On the separation of church and state, Old Testament style

¹¹Uzziyyahu had a battle force, men able to go out in the army as a raiding gang by the number of their registering by the hand of Ye'i'el the secretary and Ma'aseyahu the overseer, in the control of Hananyahu from the king's officials. ¹²The total number of the ancestral heads of the forceful strong men was 2,600, ¹³and in their control an army force of 307,500 able to do battle with forceful energy to help the king against the enemy.

¹⁴Uzziyyahu prepared for them, for the entire army, shields, spears, helmets, coats of armour, bows and slingstones. ¹⁵He made in Yerushalaim contrivances, an inventor's invention, to be on the towers and on the corners, for shooting arrows and big stones. His name went out far, because he did extraordinarily in acquiring help, until he was strong.

¹⁶But when he became strong, his mind became lofty, until he acted devastatingly. He trespassed against Yahweh his God, and came into Yahweh's palace to burn incense on the incense altar. ¹⁷Azaryahu the priest followed him; with him were eighty priests of Yahweh, forceful men. ¹⁸They stood against Uzziyyahu the king and said to him, 'It's not for you, Uzziyyahu, to burn incense for Yahweh, but for the priests, the Aharonites, who have been made sacred, to burn incense. Get out of the sanctuary, because you've trespassed. It will not mean splendour for you from Yahweh God.'

¹⁹Uzziyyahu was furious, the censer for burning incense in his hand. When he got furious with the priests, scaliness broke out on his forehead before the priests in Yahweh's house, by the incense altar. ²⁰Azaryahu the head priest turned his face to him, with all the priests: there, he was scaly on his forehead. They hurried him from there, and he himself hastened to get out, because Yahweh had touched him. ²¹Uzziyyahu the king was made

scaly until the day of his death. He lived in a house apart as a person who was scaly, because he was cut off from Yahweh's house, while Yotam his son was in charge of the king's house, exercising authority over the people in the country.

The son who had learned a lesson

²²The rest of the things about Uzziyyahu, early and late, Yesha'yahu [Isaiah] ben Amots the prophet wrote. ²³Uzziyyahu lay down with his ancestors, but they buried him with his ancestors in the burial field that belonged to the kings because (they said), 'He was made scaly.' Yotam his son began to reign in place of him.

27 Yotam was a man of twenty-five years when he began to reign and he reigned sixteen years in Yerushalaim. His mother's name was Yerushah bat Tsadoq. ²He did what was upright in Yahweh's eyes in accordance with all that his father Uzziyyahu had done, only he did not come into Yahweh's palace. But the people acted devastatingly. ³It was he who built up the Upper Gate of Yahweh's House, and built on a large scale on the Ophel Wall. ⁴He built up towns in the highland of Yehudah, and in the forests he built castles and towers. ⁵When he battled with the king of the Ammonites he was stronger than them; the Ammonites gave him that year 100 talents of silver, 10,000 ten-gallon measures of wheat and 10,000 of barley. This the Ammonites gave back to him – and in the second and third year. ⁶Yotam showed himself strong because he established his ways before Yahweh his God. ⁷The rest of the things about Yotam, and all his battles and his ways – there they are, written on the document about the kings of Yisra'el and Yehudah. ⁸He was a man of twenty-five years when he began to reign and he reigned sixteen years in Yerushalaim. ⁹Yotam lay down with his ancestors and they buried him in David's Town, and Ahaz his son began to reign in place of him.

28 Ahaz was a man of twenty years when he began to reign and he reigned sixteen years in Yerushalaim. He did not do what was upright in Yahweh's eyes like David his ancestor, ²but walked in the ways of the kings of Yisra'el. He even made cast images for the Masters. ³He was the one who burned incense in the Ben-himmon Ravine and burned up his sons in fire in accordance with the offensive practices of the nations that Yahweh dispossessed from before the Yisra'elites. ⁴He sacrificed and burned incense at the shrines, on the hills and under every verdant tree.

The warning to the victors

⁵So Yahweh his God gave him into the hand of the king of Aram, and they struck him down, took captive a large group of his and brought them to Dammeseq. He was also given into the hand of the king of Yisra'el; he struck him down in a great rout. ⁶Peqah ben Remalyahu killed 120,000 in Yehudah on one day, all forceful men, because of their abandoning Yahweh, their ancestors' God. ⁷Zikri, the Ephrayimite strong man, killed Ma'aseyahu the king's son, Azriqam the chief over the house, and Elqanah, number two to the king, ⁸and the Yisra'elites took captive 200,000 of their brothers, wives, sons and daughters, and also plundered much spoil from them and brought the plunder to Shomron. ⁹There was a prophet of Yahweh there, Oded by name. He went out before the army which was coming to Shomron and said to them, 'Here, because of the wrath of Yahweh your ancestors' God with Yehudah, he gave them into your hand and you killed them in a fury that reached as far as the heavens. ¹⁰And now you are saying that you'll subjugate the people of Yehudah and Yerushalaim as your servants and maidservants, while you yourselves – with you there are only liabilities in relation to Yahweh your God, aren't there. ¹¹So now listen to me. Give back the captives that you've taken from your brothers, because the angry rage of Yahweh is on you.'

¹²People from among the heads of the Ephrayimites, Azaryahu ben Yehohanan, Berekyahu ben Meshillemot, Yehizqiyyahu ben Shallum and Amasa ben Hadlay, rose up against the people coming from the army. ¹³They said to them, 'You will not bring the captives here, because it will be a liability upon us in relation to Yahweh; you're saying you'll add to our wrongdoings and to our liabilities, because our liability is great and there's angry

rage against Yisra'el.' ¹⁴So the armed men abandoned the captives and the plunder before the officers and the entire congregation.

The administrators with compassion

¹⁵The people who were designated by their names set to, took strong hold of the captives and clothed all the naked with the spoil. They both clothed them and gave them boots and food and drink, and bathed them and led them (everyone who was collapsing) on donkeys, and brought them to Yeriho (Palms Town) beside their brothers, and went back to Shomron.

¹⁶At that time King Ahaz sent to the kings of Ashshur for help for himself. ¹⁷The Edomites had again come and struck down Yehudah and taken captives, ¹⁸and the Pelishtites had raided the towns in the foothills and in the Negeb belonging to Yehudah. They had taken Bet-shemesh, Ayyalon, Gederot, Soko and its daughter-townships, Timnah and its daughter-townships, and Gimzo and its daughter-townships, and gone to live there, ¹⁹because Yahweh made Yehudah bow down on account of Ahaz king of Yisra'el, because he had been lax in Yehudah and had trespassed against Yahweh.

²⁰Tillegat Pilne'eser king of Ashshur came out against him and put him under pressure; he did not strengthen him, ²¹because Ahaz had divided up Yahweh's house and the house of the king and the officers and given it to the king of Ashshur, but it was no help to him.

²²In his time of pressure he added to his trespassing against Yahweh, that King Ahaz, ²³and sacrificed to the gods of Dammeseq who had struck him down; he had said, 'Because the gods of the king of Aram help them, I will sacrifice to them so that they may help me.' So those became the cause of his collapsing, and that of all Yisra'el. ²⁴Ahaz gathered the articles from God's house and cut up the articles from God's house. He shut the doors of God's house and made himself altars in every corner of Yerushalaim. ²⁵In each and every town in Yehudah, he made shrines to burn incense for other gods, and provoked Yahweh, his ancestors' God.

²⁶The rest of the things about him and all his ways, early and late – there they are, written on the document about the kings of Yehudah and Yisra'el. ²⁷Ahaz lay down with his ancestors and they buried him in the town, in Yerushalaim, because they didn't bring him into the graves of the kings of Yisra'el. His son Yehizqiyyahu [Hezekiah] began to reign in place of him.

The new David

29 Yehizqiyyahu began to reign as a man of twenty-five years and reigned twenty-nine years in Yerushalaim. His mother's name was Abiyyah bat Zekaryahu. ²He did what was upright in Yahweh's eyes in accordance with all that David his ancestor did. ³He, in the first year of his reign, in the first month, opened the doors of Yahweh's house and strengthened them.

⁴He brought the priests and the Levites and gathered them in the eastern square, ⁵and said to them, 'Listen to me, Levites. Make yourselves sacred now and make sacred the house of Yahweh, your ancestors' God. Take out the defilement from the sacred place. ⁶Because our fathers trespassed and did what was bad in the eyes of Yahweh our God, and abandoned him. They turned their faces from Yahweh's dwelling. They turned their back. ⁷They also shut the porch's doors and put out the lamps. They didn't burn incense and they didn't offer up a burnt offering in the sacred place for the God of Yisra'el. ⁸So Yahweh's fury came on Yehudah and Yerushalaim. He made them a thing of horror and desolation and a thing to whistle at, as you see with your own eyes. ⁹There, our fathers have died by the sword and our sons and daughters and wives have been in captivity on account of this.

¹⁰It's now in my mind to solemnize a pact towards Yahweh the God of Yisra'el so that his angry rage may turn back from us. ¹¹My sons, don't be negligent now, because you're the ones Yahweh chose to stand before him to minister for him, to be people who minister and burn incense for him.'

¹²So the Levites set to:

Mahat ben Amasay and Yo'el ben Azaryahu, of the Qehatites;
of the sons of Merari, Qish ben Abdi and Azaryahu ben Yehallel'el;

of the Gershonites, Yo'ah ben Zimmah and Eden ben Yo'ah; ¹³of the sons of Elitsaphan, Shimri and Ye'i'el; of the sons of Asaph, Zekaryahu and Mattanyahu; ¹⁴of the sons of Heman, Yehi'el and Shim'i; and of the sons of Yedutun, Shema'yah and Uzzi'el.

The great purification

¹⁵They gathered their brothers and made themselves sacred, and came in accordance with the king's order, by Yahweh's words, to purify Yahweh's house. ¹⁶The priests came into the inside of Yahweh's house to purify it, and took out all that was defiled that they found in Yahweh's palace into the court of Yahweh's house. The Levites received it to take it outside to Wadi Qidron. ¹⁷They began to make it sacred on the first of the first month, and on the eighth of the month they came to Yahweh's porch. They made Yahweh's house sacred in eight days, and on the sixteenth day of the first month they finished.

¹⁸Then they came inside to Hizqiyyahu the king and said, 'We've purified Yahweh's entire house, the burnt-offering altar and all its implements, and the table for the row [of bread] and all its implements. ¹⁹All the implements that King Ahaz spurned when he was king, when he trespassed, we've prepared and made sacred. There they are, before Yahweh's altar.'

²⁰Yehizqiyyahu the king started early, gathered the town officials and went up to Yahweh's house. ²¹They brought seven bulls, seven rams, seven lambs and seven goats as a purification offering for the kingship, for the sanctuary and for Yehudah. He said to the Aharonites, the priests, to offer them up on Yahweh's altar. ²²They slaughtered the cattle, and the priests received the blood and tossed it against the altar. They slaughtered the rams and tossed the blood against the altar. They slaughtered the lambs and tossed the blood against the altar. ²³They took up the goats for the purification offering before the king and the congregation, and they leaned their hands on them. ²⁴The priests slaughtered them and made the purification with their blood to make expiation for all Yisra'el, because the king had said that the burnt offering and the purification offering were for all Yisra'el. ²⁵He put the Levites in place in Yahweh's house with cymbals, with mandolins and with guitars, by the order of David, Gad the king's seer and Natan the prophet, because the order was through Yahweh through his prophets.

What God has made possible

²⁶So the Levites stood with David's instruments and the priests with the trumpets, ²⁷and Hizqiyyahu said to offer up the burnt offering at the altar. At the time when the burnt offering began, Yahweh's song and the trumpets began, along with the instruments of David king of Yisra'el, ²⁸with the entire congregation bowing low, the singers singing and the trumpeters trumpeting, all of it until they finished the burnt offering. ²⁹When they'd finished offering it up, the king and all who were to be found with him bent down and bowed low. ³⁰Yehizqiyyahu the king with the officers said to the Levites to praise Yahweh in the words of David and of Asaph the seer, and they praised with rejoicing and bent their heads and bowed low.

³¹Yehizqiyyahu avowed, 'You have now commissioned yourselves to Yahweh. Come up and bring sacrifices and thank offerings to Yahweh's house.' The congregation brought sacrifices and thank offerings, and everyone who was free in heart, a burnt offering. ³²The number of burnt offerings that the congregation brought was 70 cattle, 100 rams, 200 lambs as a burnt offering for Yahweh, all these. ³³The sacred things were 600 cattle and 3,000 from the flocks. ³⁴Only the priests were few and they could not skin all the burnt offerings, so their brothers, the Levites, added to their strength until the finishing of the work and until the priests had made themselves sacred (because the Levites were more upright in mind in making themselves sacred than the priests). ³⁵Also there were burnt offerings in quantity with the fat parts of the well-being sacrifices and with the libations for the burnt offering.

So the service of Yahweh's house was established, ³⁶and Yehizqiyyahu rejoiced, with all the people, over what God had established for the people, because the thing had happened so rapidly.

One nation

30 Yehizqiyyahu sent to all Yisra'el and Yehudah and also wrote communiqués to Ephrayim and Menashsheh to come to Yahweh's house in Yerushalaim to make Pesah [Passover] for Yahweh, the God of Yisra'el. [2]The king took counsel, he and his officials and the entire congregation in Yerushalaim, about making the Pesah in the second month, [3]because they couldn't do it at that time because the priests had not made themselves sacred in sufficiency, and the people had not assembled to Yerushalaim.

[4]The thing was upright in the king's eyes and in the congregation's eyes. [5]So they put in place a word to pass an announcement through all Yisra'el from Be'er-sheba as far as Dan about coming to make Pesah for Yahweh, the God of Yisra'el, in Yerushalaim, because they hadn't done it in large numbers as it is written.

[6]The runners went out with the communiqués from the hand of the king and his officials, through all Yisra'el and Yehudah, in accordance with the king's order, saying 'Yisra'elites, turn back to Yahweh the God of Abraham, Yitshaq and Yisra'el, and he will turn back to the escape group that remains to you from the fist of the kings of Ashshur. [7]Don't be like your fathers and like your brothers who trespassed against Yahweh, their ancestors' God, and he made them into a desolation, as you see. [8]Don't toughen your neck now like your ancestors. Give your hand to Yahweh, come to his sanctuary which he made sacred permanently, serve Yahweh your God, so that his angry rage may turn back from you. [9]When you turn back to Yahweh, your brothers and your children will find compassion before their captors and they will come back to this country, because Yahweh your God is gracious and compassionate, and he will not turn aside his face from you if you turn back to him.'

Laughter and response

[10]The runners were passing from town to town in the region of Ephrayim and Menashsheh and as far as Zebulun, but they were making fun of them and ridiculing them. [11]Yet people from Asher, Menashsheh and Zebulun bowed down and came to Yerushalaim. [12]God's hand was on Yehudah, too, to give them one mind to act on the order of the king and the officials by Yahweh's word.

[13]So a numerous people gathered to Yerushalaim to make the Flatbread Festival in the second month, a congregation in very large numbers. [14]They set to and removed the altars that were in Yerushalaim and removed all the incense stands and threw them into Wadi Qidron.

[15]They slaughtered the Pesah on the fourteenth of the second month, while the priests and the Levites were ashamed, and made themselves sacred and brought burnt offerings to Yahweh's house. [16]They stood in their position in accordance with the ruling for them, in accordance with the instruction of Mosheh the supernatural man, the priests tossing the blood from the Levites' hand.

[17]Because much of the congregation had not made themselves sacred, the Levites were in charge of the slaughter of the Pesah animals for everyone who was not pure, to make them sacred for Yahweh, [18]because most of the people (much of the group from Ephrayim and Menashsheh, Yissakar and Zebulun) had not purified themselves, but they ate the Pesah not in accordance with what is written, because Yehizqiyyahu had pleaded for them: 'May the good Yahweh expiate on behalf of [19]everyone who has set his mind on enquiring of God, Yahweh his ancestors' God, though not in accordance with purification in the sacred place.' [20]Yahweh listened to Yehizqiyyahu and healed the people.

The great rejoicing

[21]The Yisra'elites who were to be found in Yerushalaim made the Flatbread Festival for seven days with great rejoicing and the Levites and the priests praising Yahweh daily with powerful instruments for Yahweh. [22]Yehizqiyyahu spoke to encourage all the Levites who showed good insight for Yahweh, and they ate what was appointed for the seven days, making well-being sacrifices and confessing Yahweh, their ancestors' God. [23]The entire congregation took counsel to make another seven days, and made seven

days with rejoicing, ²⁴because Hizqiyyahu king of Yehudah raised for the congregation 1,000 bulls and 7,000 from the flock, while the officials raised for the congregation 1,000 bulls and 10,000 from the flock, and the priests made themselves sacred in large numbers.

²⁵The entire congregation of Yehudah rejoiced, with the priests and the Levites, the entire congregation that came from Yisra'el, and the resident aliens who had come from the country of Yisra'el but who lived in Yehudah. ²⁶So there was great rejoicing in Yerushalaim, because from the days of Shelomoh ben David king of Yisra'el there had not been something like this in Yerushalaim. ²⁷The Levite priests rose and blessed the people. And there was listening to their voice; their plea came to his sacred abode, to the heavens.

31 When they had finished all this, all Yisra'el who were to be found went out to the towns of Yehudah and broke up the columns, cut down the totem poles and demolished the shrines and the altars from all Yehudah and Binyamin, and in Ephrayim and Menashsheh, until they had finished. Then all the Yisra'elites went back each to his holding, to their towns.

Embarras de richesse

²Yehizqiyyahu put in place the divisions of the priests and the Levites, by their divisions, each in accordance with his service (with regard to the priests and the Levites), for the burnt offering and the well-being offerings, to minister and to confess and to praise in the gateways of Yahweh's camps; ³and the king's share, from his property, for the burnt offerings – the morning and the evening burnt offerings and the burnt offerings for sabbaths, for beginning of months and for set times, as it is written in Yahweh's instruction. ⁴He said to the people, the inhabitants of Yerushalaim, to give the priests' and Levites' share, in order that they might hold fast to Yahweh's instruction.

⁵When the word broke out, the Yisra'elites produced much of the very first of grain, new wine, fresh oil, syrup and all the yield of the field. They brought a tenth of everything, in quantity. ⁶The people of Yisra'el and Yehudah who lived in the towns of Yehudah – they too brought a tenth of cattle and flock and a tenth of sacred things that had been made sacred for Yahweh their God, and put them in heaps upon heaps. ⁷In the third month they began to found the heaps and in the seventh month they finished.

⁸Yehizqiyyahu and the officials came and saw the heaps, and blessed Yahweh and his people Yisra'el. ⁹Yehizqiyyahu enquired of the priests and the Levites about the heaps ¹⁰and Azaryahu the head priest, of the household of Tsadoq, said to him, 'From when they began bringing the contribution into Yahweh's house, there's been eating and being full and having a quantity remain, because Yahweh has blessed his people, and this horde remains over.' ¹¹So Yehizqiyyahu said to prepare halls in Yahweh's house, and they prepared them, ¹²ªand brought in the contribution, the tenth and the sacred things, truthfully.

The trustworthy administrators

¹²ᵇThe chief over them was Kananyahu the Levite; Shim'i his brother was number two. ¹³Yehi'el, Azazyahu, Nahat, Asah'el, Yerimot, Yozabad, Eli'el, Yismakyahu, Mahat and Benayah were appointees under the control of Kananyahu and Shim'i his brother, by the appointment of Yehizqiyyahu the king and Azaryahu the chief over God's house. ¹⁴Qore ben Yimnah the Levite, gateman on the east, was in charge of the free offerings to God, to give out the contribution for Yahweh and the very sacred things. ¹⁵In his control were Eden, Minyamin, Yeshua, Shema'yahu, Amaryahu and Shekanyahu, in the priests' towns in their trustworthy position, to give out to their brothers by their divisions, old and young alike:

¹⁶apart from their enrolment by genealogy,
   to males from three years and upwards;
to everyone who came into Yahweh's house,
   each day's requirement in its day, for their
   service in their watches, by their divisions;
¹⁷the priests' enrolment by genealogy, by
   their ancestral households;
the Levites from twenty years and upwards
   in their watches, by their divisions,
¹⁸and (in line with the enrolment by
   genealogy of all their little ones, their

wives, their sons and their daughters) to the entire congregation, because in their trustworthy position they would make themselves very sacred. [19]And to the Aharonites, the priests, in their towns' pastureland fields, everywhere town by town: men who were designated by their names were to give portions to every male among the priests, and to the entire enrolment by genealogy among the Levites. [20]Yehizqiyyahu acted like this in all Yehudah. He did what was good, upright and trustworthy before Yahweh his God. [21]In all the work that he began in the service of God's house and in the instruction and in the order, by enquiring of his God with his entire mind, he acted and succeeded.

The Assyrian crisis

32 After these things with their trustworthiness, Sanherib [Sennacherib] king of Ashshur came. He came against Yehudah, camped against the fortified towns and said he would break into them for himself. [2]Yehizqiyyahu saw that Sanherib had come with his face directed to battle against Yerushalaim [3]and took counsel with his officials and his strong men about blocking the water in the springs that were outside the town. They helped him, [4]and a large company collected and blocked all the springs and the stream flowing through the middle of the country, saying 'Why should the kings of Ashshur come and find much water?' [5]He showed himself strong and built up all the wall that had been broken through, and raised the towers on it, and outside it another wall. He strengthened the Fill in David's Town and made weaponry in quantity, and shields, [6]and put battle officers over the people.

He collected them to him in the square at the town gateway and spoke to encourage them: [7]'Be strong and stand firm. Don't be afraid, don't be scared in face of the king of Ashshur and in face of the entire horde that's with him, because with us is one greater than with him. [8]With him is an arm of flesh, but with us is Yahweh our God to help us and to fight our battles.' The people leaned on the words of Yehizqiyyahu king of Yehudah.

[9]Subsequently, Sanherib king of Ashshur sent his servants to Yerushalaim (he was at Lakish, and his command with him) to Yehizqiyyahu king of Yehudah and to all Yehudah who were in Yerushalaim, saying, [10]'Sanherib king of Ashshur has said this: "On what are you relying, living in a siege in Yerushalaim? [11]Yehizqiyyahu is inciting you to give yourselves over to dying by hunger and by thirst, isn't he, in saying, 'Yahweh our God will rescue us from the fist of the king of Ashshur.' [12]He, Yehizqiyyahu, removed his shrines and his altars, didn't he, and said to Yehudah and to Yerushalaim, 'Before one altar you are to bow low, and on it burn incense.'

The superpower's boast

[13]You acknowledge what I and my ancestors have done to all the peoples of the countries, don't you. Were the gods of the countries' nations at all able to rescue their country from my hand? [14]Which among all the gods of these nations that my ancestors devoted was able to rescue his people from my hand, that your God should be able to rescue you from my hand? [15]Hizqiyyahu should not now deceive you. He should not incite you like this. Don't trust him. Because no god of any nation or kingdom has been able to rescue his people from my hand or from the hand of my ancestors. Certainly your gods will not rescue you from my hand."'

[16]His servants spoke further against Yahweh God and against Yehizqiyyahu his servant, [17]and he wrote documents to revile Yahweh the God of Yisra'el and to say about him, 'Like the gods of the countries' nations that did not rescue their people from my hand, so Yehizqiyyahu's God will not rescue his people from my hand.' [18]They called in a loud voice in Yehudahite to the people of Yerushalaim who were on the wall, to make them afraid and fearful, in order that they might take the town. [19]They spoke of Yerushalaim's God as they spoke about the gods of the peoples of the earth, the making of human hands.

[20]Yehizqiyyahu the king and Yesha'yahu ben Amots the prophet pleaded about this and cried out to the heavens, [21]and Yahweh sent an envoy and he effaced every forceful strong man, chief and officer in the camp of the king of Ashshur. He went back in shame to his

country. He came into his god's house, and there some of the people who had come out from inside him made him fall by the sword.

Even Yehizqiyyahu can stumble

²²Yahweh delivered Yehizqiyyahu and Yerushalaim's inhabitants from the hand of Sanherib king of Ashshur and from the hand of everyone. He led them all round ²³and many were bringing offerings for Yahweh to Yerushalaim and choice things for Yehizqiyyahu king of Yehudah. He rose high in the eyes of all the nations from then on.

²⁴In those days Yehizqiyyahu became deathly ill, but he pleaded to Yahweh, and he spoke to him and gave him a sign, ²⁵but Yehizqiyyahu did not give back in accordance with the dealing done to him, because his mind became lofty. So there was fury on him and on Yehudah and Yerushalaim. ²⁶But Yehizqiyyahu bowed down, when his mind had become lofty, he and the inhabitants of Yerushalaim, and Yahweh's fury didn't come on them in Yehizqiyyahu's days.

²⁷Yehizqiyyahu had wealth and splendour, very great. He made himself treasuries for silver, for gold, for precious stone, for spices, for shields and for all desirable objects, ²⁸supplies of the yield of grain, new wine and fresh oil, and stalls for each and every cattle, and flocks for folds. ²⁹He made himself towns and livestock, flocks and cattle, in large numbers, because God gave him very much property. ³⁰He, Yehizqiyyahu, blocked the Upper Gihon water outlet and directed it down on the west of David's Town. Yehizqiyyahu succeeded in all his action. ³¹And so with the spokesmen of the officials from Babel who sent to him to enquire about the sign that happened in the country, when God abandoned him to test him so as to know everything in his mind.

³²The rest of the things about Yehizqiyyahu and his acts of commitment – there they are, written in the vision of Yesha'yahu ben Amots the prophet, on the document regarding the kings of Yehudah and Yisra'el. ³³Yehizqiyyahu lay down with his ancestors and they buried him in the upper floor of the graves of David's sons, and all Yehudah and the inhabitants of Yerushalaim did him honour when he died. Menashsheh his son began to reign in place of him.

The possibility of repentance

33 Menashsheh was twelve years of age when he began to reign and he reigned fifty-five years in Yerushalaim. ²He did what was bad in Yahweh's eyes in accordance with the offensive practices of the nations that Yahweh dispossessed from before the Yisra'elites. ³He rebuilt the shrines that Yehizqiyyahu his father had demolished, set up altars for the Masters and made totem poles, and bowed low to all the heavenly army and served them. ⁴He built altars in Yahweh's house, of which Yahweh had said, 'In Yerushalaim my name will be permanently.' ⁵He built altars for all the heavenly army in the two courtyards of Yahweh's house. ⁶He himself made his sons pass through fire in Ben-hinnom Ravine. He practised augury, divined, acted as a medium, and dealt with ghosts and spirits. He did much that was bad in Yahweh's eyes, so as to provoke him.

⁷He put the image sculpture that he made in God's house, of which God had said to David and to Shelomoh his son, 'In this house and in Yerushalaim, which I chose from all Yisra'el's clans, I will put my name permanently. ⁸And I will never again remove Yisra'el's foot from upon the land that I put in place for their ancestors, only if they keep watch to act on all that I ordered them – the entire instruction, the decrees and the rulings by means of Mosheh.' ⁹Menashsheh made Yehudah and Yerushalaim and the inhabitants of Yerushalaim wander so as to deal badly, more than the nations that Yahweh annihilated from before the Yisra'elites.

¹⁰Yahweh spoke to Menashsheh and to his people but they didn't heed, ¹¹so Yahweh brought against them the officers of the army belonging to the king of Ashshur. They took Menashsheh captive in hooks, bound him with copper shackles and made him go to Babel. ¹²But when he was under pressure, he sought the goodwill of Yahweh his God. He bowed right down before his ancestors' God ¹³and pleaded to him. He let himself be entreated by him and listened to his prayer for grace, and let him go back to Yerushalaim to his kingship. So Menashsheh acknowledged that Yahweh was God.

Menashsheh and Amon

¹⁴Subsequently he built an outer wall for David's Town, west of Gihon, in the wadi and as you come through the Fish Gate. It went round the Ophel. He made it very lofty. He put forceful officers in all the fortified towns in Yehudah. ¹⁵He removed the foreign gods and the image from Yahweh's house and all the altars that he had built on the mountain of Yahweh's house and in Yerushalaim, and threw them outside the town. ¹⁶He built up Yahweh's altar and made on it well-being sacrifices and thank offerings. He said to Yehudah to serve Yahweh the God of Yisra'el, ¹⁷though the people were still sacrificing at the shrines, only for Yahweh their God.

¹⁸The rest of the things about Menashsheh, his plea to his God, and the words of the seers who spoke to him in the name of Yahweh his God – there they are, on the things of the kings of Yisra'el. ¹⁹His plea and his being entreated by him, and all his wrongdoing and his trespass, and the sites in which he built shrines and put in place totem poles and sculptures, before he bowed down – there, they're written in the words of his seers. ²⁰Menashsheh lay down with his ancestors and they buried him in his house, and Amon his son began to reign in place of him.

²¹Amon was a man of twenty-two years when he began to reign and he reigned two years in Yerushalaim. ²²He did what was bad in Yahweh's eyes, as Menashsheh his father had done. To all the sculptures that Menashsheh his father had made, Amon sacrificed and served them. ²³He did not bow down before Yahweh as Menashsheh his father bowed down, but rather he, Amon, made his liability great. ²⁴His servants conspired against him and put him to death in his house, ²⁵but the people of the country struck down those who had conspired against King Amon. The people of the country made Yo'shiyyahu his son king in place of him.

The great reformer

34 Yo'shiyyahu [Josiah] was eight years of age when he began to reign and he reigned thirty-one years in Yerushalaim. ²He did what was upright in the eyes of Yahweh and walked in the ways of David his ancestor. He did not depart right or left.

³In the eighth year of his reign when he was still a boy he began to enquire of the God of David his ancestor, and in the twelfth year began to purify Yehudah and Yerushalaim of the shrines, the totem poles, the sculptures and the cast images. ⁴They demolished the Masters' altars before him, and the incense stands that were above, over them, he cut down. The totem poles, the sculptures and the cast images he broke up, made dust of them and threw it over the face of the graves of the people who had sacrificed to them. ⁵The priests' bones he burned on their altars. He purified Yehudah and Yerushalaim, ⁶and in the towns of Menashsheh, Ephrayim and Shim'on, and as far as Naphtali, and in their ruins all round, ⁷he demolished the altars and the totem poles, crushed the sculptures to dust and cut down the incense stands in the entire country of Yisra'el, and went back to Yerushalaim.

⁸In the eighteenth year of his reign, when he had purified the country and the house, he sent Shaphan ben Atsalyahu, Ma'aseyahu the town official and Yo'ah ben Yo'ahaz the recorder to strengthen the house of Yahweh his God. ⁹They came to Hilqiyyahu the big priest and gave him the silver that had been brought to God's house, which the Levites who keep watch over the threshold had gathered from the hand of Menashsheh and Ephrayim, from the entire remainder of Yisra'el and from all Yehudah and Binyamin and the inhabitants of Yerushalaim.

¹⁰They gave it into the hand of the one doing the work, the people appointed in Yahweh's house. The ones doing the work who were doing it in Yahweh's house gave it for dealing with the defects and for strengthening the house. ¹¹They gave it to craftsmen and masons for acquiring hewn stones and logs for the clasps and for roofing the houses that the kings of Yehudah had let become devastated.

The worrying discovery

¹²The men were acting with trustworthiness in the work:
    appointed in charge of them: Yahat and
        Obadyahu, Levites from the Mararites,
        and Zekaryah and Meshullam from the
        Qehatites, to supervise;

the Levites, everyone with understanding of musical instruments, ¹³both in charge of the carriers and supervising everyone doing the work, service by service; some of the Levites: secretaries, overseers and gatemen.

¹⁴When they were taking out the silver that had been brought to Yahweh's house, Hilqiyyahu the priest found a document of Yahweh's instruction by means of Mosheh. ¹⁵Hilqiyyahu avowed to Shaphan the secretary, 'I've found an instruction document in Yahweh's house.' Hilqiyyahu gave the document to Shaphan, ¹⁶and Shaphan brought the document to the king. He also took word back to the king: 'All that was given into your servants' hands, they're doing. ¹⁷They've melted down the silver that was found in Yahweh's house and given it into the hand of the appointees and into the hand of the people doing the work.' ¹⁸And Shaphan the secretary told the king, 'Hilqiyyahu the priest gave me a document', and he read it out before the king.

¹⁹When the king heard the words in the instruction, he tore his clothes. ²⁰The king ordered Hilqiyyahu, Ahiqam ben Shaphan, Abdon ben Mikah, Shaphan the secretary and Asayah the king's servant, ²¹'Go enquire of Yahweh on my behalf and on behalf of the remainder in Yisra'el and Yehudah about the words in the document that's been found, because great is Yahweh's wrath that's poured upon us because our ancestors didn't keep Yahweh's word by acting in accordance with everything that's written on this document.'

²²Hilqiyyahu and those whom the king [had said] went to Huldah the prophetess, wife of Shallum ben Toqhat son of Hasrah, keeper of the robes; she was living in Yerushalaim in the Second Quarter. They spoke to her in this way.

The prophetess speaks straight

²³She said to them, 'Yahweh the God of Yisra'el has said this: "Say to the man who sent you to me: ²⁴"Yahweh has said this: "Here, I'm going to bring bad fortune on this place and its inhabitants, all the curses written on the document that they read out before the king of Yehudah, ²⁵because of the fact that they abandoned me and burned incense to other gods, in order to provoke me with all the actions of their hands, so that my wrath will pour out on this place and will not go out."'''

²⁶But to the king of Yehudah who sent you to enquire of Yahweh, you're to say to him, "Yahweh the God of Yisra'el has said this: 'The words that you have heard: ²⁷since your mind softened and you bowed down before God when you heard his words about this place and about its inhabitants, and you bowed down before me and tore your clothes and cried before me, I for my part have also listened (Yahweh's declaration). ²⁸Here, I'm going to gather you to your ancestors, and you'll gather yourself to your great grave with things being well. Your eyes will not see all the bad fortune that I'm going to bring on this place and on its inhabitants.'"'

They took word back to the king ²⁹and the king sent and gathered all the elders of Yehudah and Yerushalaim. ³⁰The king went up to Yahweh's house, with everyone in Yehudah, the inhabitants of Yerushalaim, the priests, the Levites, and all the people, old and young. He read out in their ears all the words of the pact document found in Yahweh's house. ³¹The king stood in his position and solemnized a pact before Yahweh to follow Yahweh and to keep his orders, his affirmations and his decrees with his entire mind and with his entire being, by acting on the words of the pact that were written on this document. ³²He got everyone who was to be found in Yerushalaim and Binyamin to stand, and the inhabitants of Yerushalaim acted in accordance with the pact of God, their ancestors' God.

Preparations for a great celebration

³³Yo'shiyyahu removed all the offensive things from all the regions that belonged to the Yisra'elites and got everyone who was to be found in Yisra'el to give their service to Yahweh their God. All his days they did not depart from following Yahweh, their ancestors' God.

35 Yo'shiyyahu made Pesah for Yahweh in Yerushalaim; they slaughtered the Pesah on the fourteenth of the first month. ²He put in place the priests at their watches and he strengthened them for the service of Yahweh's house. ³He said to the Levites, who helped all Yisra'el understand, who were sacred for Yahweh, 'Put the sacred chest in the house that Shelomoh ben David, king of Yisra'el, built. There's no carrying it on the shoulder for you now; serve Yahweh your God and his people Yisra'el now.

⁴Establish yourselves by your ancestral households according to your divisions, by the writing of David king of Yisra'el and by the writing of Shelomoh his son. ⁵Stand in the sacred place by the ancestral household groupings of your brothers (the members of the people) and the ancestral household divisions of the Levites, ⁶and slaughter the Pesah. Make yourselves sacred and prepare it for your brothers, acting in accordance with Yahweh's word by means of Mosheh.'

⁷Yo'shiyyahu raised for the members of the people flocks, lambs and goats (all of it for the Pesah occasions for everyone who was to be found) to the number of 30,000, and cattle 3,000, these from the king's property. ⁸His officials raised a free offering for the people, for the priests and for the Levites; Hilqiyyah, Zekaryahu and Yehi'el, the chiefs over God's house, gave for the Pesah occasions 2,600, and 300 cattle. ⁹Kananyahu, Shema'yahu and Netan'el his brothers, and Hashabyahu, Ye'i'el and Yozabad, the Levites' officials, raised for the Levites for the Pesah occasions 5,000, and 500 cattle.

No Pesah (Passover) like this for centuries

¹⁰So the service was prepared. The priests stood in their position, with the Levites by their divisions in accordance with the king's order. ¹¹They slaughtered the Pesah and the priests tossed some of the blood they had while the Levites were doing the skinning. ¹²They removed the burnt offering to give them to the groups by ancestral households, to the members of the people, to present to Yahweh in accordance with what is written in Mosheh's document, and so for the cattle. ¹³They cooked the Pesah in fire in accordance with the ruling, and the sacred things they cooked in pots, in cauldrons and in pans, and ran them to all the members of the people.

¹⁴After, they prepared things for themselves and for the priests, because the priests, the Aharonites, were involved in offering up the burnt offering and the fat parts until evening, while the Levites prepared for themselves and for the priests, the Aharonites. ¹⁵The singers, the Asaphites, were in their place in accordance with the order of David, Asaph, Heman and Yedutun the king's seer, and the gatemen were at gateway by gateway: there was no departing from their service for them, because their Levite brothers prepared for them.

¹⁶The entire service of Yahweh was prepared that day, making the Pesah and offering up burnt offerings on Yahweh's altar in accordance with the order of King Yo'shiyyahu. ¹⁷The Yisra'elites who were to be found made the Pesah at that time, and the Flatbread Festival, for seven days. ¹⁸Pesah had not been made like this in Yisra'el since the days of Shemu'el [Samuel] the prophet. No kings of Yisra'el had made one like the Pesah that Yo'shiyyahu made, with the priests, the Levites, all Yehudah and Yisra'el to be found, and the inhabitants of Yerushalaim. ¹⁹This Pesah was made in the eighteenth year of Yo'shiyyahu 's reign.

One fatal mistake

²⁰After all this, when Yo'shiyyahu had established the house, Neko king of Misrayim went up to do battle at Karkemish on the Euphrates, and Yo'shiyyahu went out to meet him.

²¹He sent envoys to him saying, 'What is there between you and me, king of Yehudah? You're not the one I'm against today, but against the household that's doing battle with me. God said I should hurry. Hold yourself back from God, who's with me, so he doesn't devastate you.'

²²But Yo'shiyyahu didn't turn his face round from him but disguised himself to do battle against him. He didn't listen to the words of Neko from the mouth of God but came to battle in the Megiddo Valley, ²³and the archers shot King Yo'shiyyahu. The king said to his servants, 'Get me out, because I'm badly hurt.' ²⁴His servants got him out of the chariot, put him on the second-in-command's chariot and took him to Yerushalaim, but he died. He was buried

in his ancestors' graves, and all Yehudah and Yerushalaim was mourning over Yo'shiyyahu. ²⁵Yirmeyahu [Jeremiah] lamented over Yo'shiyyahu, and all the singers (male and female) have spoken of Yo'shiyyahu in their laments until this day. They made them a decree in Yisra'el. There, they're written in the laments. ²⁶The rest of the things about Yo'shiyyahu and his acts of commitment in accordance with what is written in Yahweh's instruction, ²⁷his words early and late: there, they are written on the document about the kings of Yisra'el and Yehudah.

36 The people of the country got Yeho'ahaz ben Yo'shiyyahu and made him king in place of his father in Yerushalaim.

The rebellious end

²Yeho'ahaz was a man of twenty-three years when he began to reign and he reigned three months in Yerushalaim, ³but the king of Misrayim removed him in Yerushalaim and levied the country for a hundred talents of silver and a talent of gold. ⁴The king of Misrayim made Elyaqim his brother king over Yehudah and Yerushalaim and changed his name to Yehoyaqim. Neko took Yo'ahaz his brother and brought him to Misrayim.

⁵Yehoyaqim was a man of twenty-five years when he began to reign and he reigned eleven years in Yerushalaim. He did what was bad in the eyes of Yahweh his God. ⁶Nebukadne'tstsar king of Babel went up against him and bound him with copper shackles to make him go to Babel. ⁷Nebukadne'tstsar brought some of the articles from Yahweh's house and put them in his palace in Babel. ⁸The rest of the things about Yehoyaqim and the offensive things that he did, and what was found against him – there, they are written on the document about the kings of Yisra'el and Yehudah. His son Yehoyakin began to reign in place of him.

⁹Yehoyakin was eighteen years of age when he began to reign and he reigned three months and ten days in Yerushalaim. He did what was bad in Yahweh's eyes. ¹⁰At the turn of the year King Nebukadne'tstsar sent and brought him to Babel with desirable articles from Yahweh's house. He made Tsidqiyyahu, his brother, king over Yehudah and Yerushalaim.

¹¹Tsidqiyyahu was twenty-one years of age when he began to reign and he reigned eleven years in Yerushalaim. ¹²He did what was bad in the eyes of Yahweh his God and did not bow down before Yirmeyahu the prophet from Yahweh's mouth. ¹³Further, he rebelled against Nebukadne'tstsar, who had made him swear by God. He toughened his neck and firmed up his mind from turning back to Yahweh the God of Yisra'el. ¹⁴Further, all the officials of the priests and the people committed many acts of trespass, in accordance with the offensive practices of the nations, and defiled Yahweh's house which he had made sacred in Yerushalaim.

The land fulfils its sabbaths

¹⁵Yahweh, their ancestors' God, sent to them by means of his envoys, starting early and sending, because he had pity on his people and on his abode. ¹⁶But they were mocking God's envoys, despising his words and scoffing at his prophets, until Yahweh's wrath against his people rose, until there was no healing.

¹⁷So he brought up the king of the Kasdites [Babylonians] against them. They killed their young men by the sword in their sacred house. He did not have pity on young man or young girl, elder or greybeard. He gave everything into his hand. ¹⁸All the articles in God's house, big and small, the treasures of Yahweh's house, and the treasures of the king and his officers – he brought everything to Babel. ¹⁹They burned God's house and demolished the wall of Yerushalaim. They burned all its citadels with fire and devastated all its desirable objects.

²⁰He exiled to Babel the people who remained from the sword and they became his and his sons' servants until Parsite [Persian] kingship reigned, ²¹to fulfil Yahweh's word by the mouth of Yirmeyahu, until the country made amends for its sabbaths. All the days of its desolation it stopped [*shabat*], to fill up seventy years.

²²But in the first year of Koresh king of Paras [Cyrus king of Persia], fulfilling Yahweh's word by the mouth of Yirmeyahu, Yahweh stirred the spirit of Koresh king of Paras, and he made an announcement pass through his entire

kingdom, and also in writing: ²³'Koresh king of Paras has said this:

> Yahweh the God of the heavens has given me all the kingdoms of the earth, and he himself has appointed me to build him a house in Yerushalaim, which is in Yehudah. Whoever among you from all his people: may Yahweh his God be with him, and he is to go up.

Ezra

Ezra and Nehemiah were originally one book; they were divided into two some time after Christ's day. They tell the story of the community in Judah over the first hundred years after the moment when Judahites who had been taken off into exile (or whose parents had been taken off into exile) were allowed to return to Judah to rebuild the temple, in about 539 BC. The books thus continue the story told in Kings and in Chronicles. But whereas those books relate a fairly continuous story, Ezra-Nehemiah is episodic.

- First, Ezra 1—6 tells of the actual return of some of those Judahites, by the commission of the Persian emperor and in fulfilment of the promise of Jeremiah, and of their rebuilding of the temple. In relating this story, Ezra 1—6 emphasizes the problem of opposition from the other little peoples that surrounded Judah, all of them provinces of the Persian Empire. The prophets Haggai and Zechariah were allies of Zerubbabel the governor and Joshua the priest in getting the community to complete the work. But the work does get completed, and the achievement is reason for a great celebration.

- Without warning Ezra 7—10 then jumps forward half a century to the mission of Ezra himself. The opening date indicates that he came from Babylon to Jerusalem in 458 BC. (That fact in itself makes evident that by no means all Judahites had accepted the chance to join in the move to Jerusalem described in Ezra 1—6.) He comes as a theologian who is an expert in the Torah of Moses, and he brings a copy of the Torah with him in order to campaign for people in Jerusalem to implement what it says. It wouldn't be surprising if this mission marks the moment when the 'Books of Moses' (Genesis to Deuteronomy) have reached the form in which we know them. Ezra comes to Jerusalem with the support of the Persian emperor, who will have seen the advantage to him of having a good administrative order in the province, of a kind that the people themselves would accept. A key feature of Ezra's work is his persuading Judahites to terminate their marriages with people from the other communities around, which imperilled the distinctiveness of Israel as God's people.

- Next the story moves to the mission of Nehemiah (Nehemiah 1—7). Nehemiah came from Susa in Persia to Jerusalem in 445 BC. He has heard in Susa of the broken-down state of things in Jerusalem. He first prays, then he too gets the support of the emperor (whose butler he is) for him to go to Jerusalem to do something about it. His signature achievement is the rebuilding of the city's walls, again despite opposition from neighbouring communities. But he also campaigns for the community to be generous rather than self-serving as it lives with the economic pressures of the times.

- Finally the two books give some account of Ezra and Nehemiah working together, and of some further events (Nehemiah 8—13). This last section of the story involves the community reading the Torah and accepting a commitment to aspects of the way of life that marks them out that were apparently neglected, such as proper observance of the sabbath and support for the temple and its worship. The story also speaks of action to get more people to come and live in Jerusalem, which will have been discouraged by the city's broken-down state. The books close with further action by Nehemiah to deal with offensive practices such as trading on the sabbath (again) and intermarrying with people from other communities that could lead them into unfaithfulness (again). It is an important initiative in seeing that the people of God stayed in being and did not cease to exist through assimilation.

So if one was going to subdivide Ezra-Nehemiah, it might have been more illuminating to divide it into four parts, not just two.

Yahweh stirs the emperor and the people

1 In the first year of Koresh king of Paras [Cyrus king of Persia], fulfilling Yahweh's word from the mouth of Yirmeyah [Jeremiah], Yahweh stirred the spirit of Koresh king of Paras, and he made an announcement pass through his entire kingdom, and also in writing: ²Koresh king of Paras has said this:

> Yahweh the God of the heavens has given me all the kingdoms of the earth, and he himself has appointed me to build him a house in Yerushalaim, which is in Yehudah. ³Whoever among you from all his people: may his God be with him, and may he go up to Yerushalaim which is in Yehudah and build the house of Yahweh the God of Yisra'el; he is the God who is in Yerushalaim. ⁴Anyone who remains, from all the places where he is a resident – the people of his place are to support him with silver, with gold, with property and with cattle, along with the free offering for the house of God which is in Yerushalaim.

⁵So the ancestral heads of Yehudah and Binyamin, and the priests and the Levites, everyone whose spirit God stirred, set to so as to go up to build up Yahweh's house which is in Yerushalaim. ⁶All the people who were round about them strengthened their hands with silver articles, with gold, with property, with cattle and with choice things, apart from every free offering. ⁷Koresh the king took out the articles belonging to Yahweh's house that Nebukadne'tstsar had taken out from Yerushalaim and put in his god's house. ⁸Koresh king of Paras took them out by the hand of Mitredat the treasurer, and counted them out to Sheshbatstsar, the Yehudahite leader. ⁹These are their count:

> gold bowls: 30;
> silver bowls: 1,000;
> knives: 29;
> ¹⁰gold dishes: 30;
> double silver bowls: 410;
> other articles: 1,000.
> ¹¹All the articles of gold and of silver: 5,400.

All these Sheshbatstsar took up when the exiles were taken up from Babel to Yerushalaim.

Who we were

2 These are the people of the province, who went up from among the captives in exile whom Nebukadne'tstsar king of Babel had exiled to Babel and who went back to Yerushalaim and Yehudah, each to his town, ²who came with Zerubbabel, Yeshua, Nehemyah, Serayah, Re'elayah, Mordokay, Bilshan, Mispar, Bigvay, Rehum, Ba'anah.

The number of the men belonging to the Yisra'elite people:

Ancient Near East at the time of Ezra

³sons of Par'osh 2,172
⁴sons of Shephatyah 372
⁵sons of Arah 775
⁶sons of Pahat Mo'ab (by the sons of Yeshua, Yo'ab) 2,812
⁷sons of Elam 1,254
⁸sons of Zattu 945
⁹sons of Zakkay 760
¹⁰sons of Bani 642
¹¹sons of Bebay 623
¹²sons of Azgad 1,222
¹³sons of Adoniqam 666
¹⁴sons of Bigvay 2,056
¹⁵sons of Adin 454
¹⁶sons of Ater (by Yehizqiyyah) 98
¹⁷sons of Betsay 323
¹⁸sons of Yorah 112
¹⁹sons of Hashum 223
²⁰sons of Gibbar 95
²¹sons of Bet-lehem 123
²²people of Netophah 56
²³people of Anatot 128
²⁴sons of Azmavet 42
²⁵sons of Arim Township, Kephirah and Be'erot 743
²⁶sons of The Height and Geba 621
²⁷people of Mikmas 122
²⁸people of Bet-el and Ha'ay 223
²⁹sons of Nebo 52
³⁰sons of Magbish 156
³¹sons of the other Elam 1,254
³²sons of Harim 320
³³sons of Lod, Hadid and Ono 725
³⁴sons of Yereho 345
³⁵sons of Sena'ah 3,630
³⁶The priests:
sons of Yeda'yah (by the household of Yeshua) 973
³⁷sons of Immer 1,052
³⁸sons of Pashhur 1,247
³⁹sons of Harim 1,017
⁴⁰The Levites:
sons of Yeshua and Qadmi'el (by the sons of Hodavyah) 74
⁴¹The singers:
sons of Asaph 128

Gatemen, assistants and undocumented people

⁴²The sons of the gatemen:
sons of Shallum
sons of Ater
sons of Talmon
sons of Aqqub
sons of Hatita
sons of Shobay altogether 139
⁴³The assistants:
sons of Tsiha
sons of Hasupha
sons of Tabba'ot
⁴⁴sons of Qeros
sons of Si'aha
sons of Padon
⁴⁵sons of Lebanah
sons of Hagabah
sons of Aqqub
⁴⁶sons of Hagab
sons of Shalmay
sons of Hanan
⁴⁷sons of Giddel
sons of Gahar
sons of Re'ayah
⁴⁸sons of Retsin
sons of Neqodah
sons of Gazzam
⁴⁹sons of Uzza
sons of Paseah
sons of Besay
⁵⁰sons of Asnah
sons of Me'unim
sons of Nephusim
⁵¹sons of Baqbuq
sons of Haqupha
sons of Harhur
⁵²sons of Batslut
sons of Mehida
sons of Harsha
⁵³sons of Barqos
sons of Sisera
sons of Temah
⁵⁴sons of Netsiah
sons of Hatipha

⁵⁵The sons of Shelomoh's [Solomon's] servants:
sons of Sotay
sons of Hassopheret
sons of Peruda
⁵⁶sons of Ya'alah
sons of Darqon
sons of Giddel
⁵⁷sons of Shephatyah
sons of Hattil
sons of Pokeret Hatstsebayim
sons of Ami

⁵⁸All the assistants and the sons of Shelomoh's servants 392.

⁵⁹These are the people who came up from Tel Melah, Tel Harsha, Kerub, Addan, Immer, but who could not tell their ancestral household and their origin, whether they were from Yisra'el:

⁶⁰sons of Delayah
sons of Tobiyyah
sons of Neqoda 652
⁶¹Of the sons of the priests:
sons of Habayah
sons of Haqqots
sons of Barzillay (who had taken a wife from the daughters of Barzillay the Gil'adite and was called by their name):

⁶²these looked for their record in the enrolment by genealogy but they couldn't be found, and they were deconsecrated from the priesthood. ⁶³The administrator said to them that they should not eat of the very sacred things until there was a priest standing with Urim and Tummim.

⁶⁴The entire congregation altogether 42,360;
⁶⁵apart from their servants and handmaids: these were 7,337;
and they had 200 male and female singers;
⁶⁶their horses 736; their mules 245; ⁶⁷their camels 435; their donkeys 6,720.

New beginnings

⁶⁸Some of the ancestral heads, when they came to Yahweh's house in Yerushalaim, gave

a free offering for God's house, to put it in its place on its established site. ⁶⁹In accordance with their energy, to the treasury for the work they gave gold, 61,000 drakmas; silver, 5,000 minas; and priests' robes, 100. ⁷⁰The priests, the Levites, some of the people, the singers, the gatemen and the assistants went to live in their towns, and all Yisra'el in their towns.

3 When the seventh month arrived, with the Yisra'elites in their towns, the people gathered as one person in Yerushalaim. ²Yeshua ben Yotsadaq and his brother priests, and Zerubbabel ben She'alti'el and his brothers, set to and built the altar of the God of Yisra'el, to offer up burnt offerings on it as is written in the instruction of Mosheh [Moses] the supernatural man. ³They established the altar on its established site because they were in dread of the peoples of the countries, and they offered up burnt offerings on it for Yahweh, the burnt offerings for morning and for evening. ⁴They made the Sukkot Festival as it is written, and the burnt offering day by day, by the number in accordance with the ruling, each day's requirement in its day, ⁵and afterwards the regular burnt offering and the ones for the new months and for all the occasions set by Yahweh that were made sacred, and for anyone making a free offering for Yahweh.

⁶From the first day of the seventh month they began to offer up burnt offerings for Yahweh, though Yahweh's palace had not been started. ⁷They gave silver to the hewers and to the craftsmen, and food, drink and oil to the Tsidonites and to the Tsorites, to bring cedar logs from the Lebanon by sea to Yafo, in accordance with the authorization to them by Koresh king of Paras.

Shouts of joy and the sound of crying

⁸In the second year of their coming to the house of God at Yerushalaim, in the second month, Zerubbabel ben She'alti'el and Yeshua ben Yotsadaq, and the rest of their brothers (the priests, the Levites and all the people who had come from the captivity to Yerushalaim) began, and put in place the Levites from people of twenty years and upwards to supervise the work on Yahweh's house. ⁹Yeshua, his sons and his brothers, and Qadmi'el and his sons (descendants of Yehudah) stood up together to oversee the one doing the work on God's house (the sons of Henadad, their sons and their brothers, the Levites).

¹⁰When the builders started Yahweh's palace, they put in place the priests in their vestments with trumpets, and the Levites, the sons of Asaph, with cymbals, to praise Yahweh in accordance with the directions of David king of Yisra'el. ¹¹They sang responsively in praise and confession to Yahweh, 'Because he is good, because his commitment stands permanently for Yisra'el', and the entire people gave a big shout in praise of Yahweh, because Yahweh's house had been started. ¹²While many of the priests and the Levites and the ancestral heads, the old men who had seen the first house, at the start on this house before their eyes were crying with a loud voice, many were raising their voice in a shout of rejoicing. ¹³The people couldn't recognize the sound of the shout of rejoicing from the sound of the people's crying, because the people were giving a big shout. The sound was audible from afar.

4 The adversaries of Yehudah and Binyamin heard that the people from the exile were building a palace for Yahweh the God of Yisra'el, ²and they came up to Zerubbabel and to the ancestral heads and said to them, 'We'll build with you, because we enquire of your God like you, and we've been sacrificing for him since the days of Esar Haddon king of Ashshur, who got us up here.'

Offers of help refused

³Zerubbabel, Yeshua and the remainder of the ancestral heads of Yisra'el said to them, 'It's not for you and for us to build a house for our God, because we as one will build for Yahweh the God of Yisra'el, as Koresh king of Paras ordered us.'

⁴Then the people of the country were making the hands of the people of Yehudah slacken and making them fearful to build. ⁵They were bribing counsellors against them so as to contravene their counsel all the days of Koresh king of Paras and until the reign of Doryavesh [Darius] king of Paras, ⁶and in the reign of Ahashverosh [Xerxes], at the beginning of his

reign, they wrote an accusation against the inhabitants of Yehudah and Yerushalaim.

⁷Then in the days of Artahshasta [Artaxerxes], Bishlam, Mitredat, Tabe'el and the remainder of his associates wrote to Artahshasta king of Paras. The writing of the document was in Aramaic and translated.

(Aramaic.) ⁸Rehum the administrator and Shimshay the secretary wrote a communiqué about Yerushalaim to King Artahshasta as follows.

⁹Rehum the administrator, Shimsay the secretary and the remainder of their associates, the authorities and officials, of Tarpel, Paras, Erek, Babel, Shushan (i.e. the Elamites) ¹⁰and the remainder of the peoples that the great and glorious Osnapper [Ashurbanipal] exiled and made live in the town of Shomrayin [Samaria] and the remainder of Beyond-the-River province (so now ¹¹this is a copy of the communiqué they sent him) to Artahshasta the king.

Your servants, men of Beyond-the-River province:

So now ¹²be it known to the king that the Yehudahites who came up from you to us have come to Yerushalaim. They are building up the rebellious and wicked town. They have completed the walls and strengthened the foundations. ¹³Now be it known to the king that if this town is built up and its walls are completed, they will not give tribute, taxes or tolls, so the kings' interests will suffer harm.

A pattern of tension running through the story

¹⁴Now since we share the salt of the palace and it's not right for us to see the king's dishonour, therefore we have sent and made it known to the king ¹⁵so that they may search in the document with your ancestors' records. You will find in the records document and acknowledge that this town is a rebellious town, harmful to kings and provinces. People have been making mutiny in it from days of old. Because of that this town was destroyed. ¹⁶We make it known to the king that if this town is built up and its walls are completed, as a result of that you will not have a share in Beyond-the-River.

¹⁷The king sent a message:

To Rehum the administrator, Shimshay the secretary, the remainder of their associates who live in Shomrayin, and the remainder of Beyond-the-River, good wishes.

So now ¹⁸the letter that you sent to us was explained, read out before me. ¹⁹A decree was made by me, and they searched and found that this town from days of old has risen against kings. Rebellion and mutiny have been made in it. ²⁰There have been powerful kings over Yerushalaim and they have exercised authority over the whole of Beyond-the-River. Tribute, taxes and tolls were rendered to them. ²¹Now make a decree to stop these men. That town will not be built up until the order is made by me. ²²Be careful about acting negligently in this. Why should damage grow so as to harm kings?

²³When a copy of the letter from Artahshasta the king was read out before Rehum, Shimshay the secretary and their associates, they went with speed to Yerushalaim to the Yehudahites and stopped them with compelling force.

To return to the time of the temple building . . .

²⁴So work stopped on God's house in Yerushalaim. It stopped until the second year of the reign of Doryavesh king of Paras, 5 and Haggay the prophet and Zekaryah ben Iddo prophesied to the Yehudahites who were in Yehudah and in Yerushalaim in the name of the God of Yisra'el, over them. ²Then Zerubbabel ben She'alti'el and Yeshua ben Yotsadaq set to and began to build God's house in Yerushalaim, God's prophets being with them, supporting them.

³At that time Tattenay the governor of Beyond-the-River, Shetar Bozenay and their associates came to them and said this to them: 'Who made you a decree to build this house and finish these supplies?' ⁴Then we said to them, 'What are the names of the men who are constructing this building?' ⁵But God's eye was on the Yehudahite elders, and they didn't stop them while an account could go to Doryavesh, and then they would bring back a letter about this.

⁶A copy of the communiqué that Tattenay governor of Beyond-the-River, Shetar Bozenay and his associates, the officials of Beyond-the-River, sent to Doryavesh the king. ⁷They sent a message to him, and in it was written as follows:

> To Doryavesh the king, all good wishes. ⁸Be it known to the king that we went to Yehudah province to the house of the great God. It's being built up of dressed stone, and wood is being set in the walls. This work is being done punctiliously and it is succeeding in their hand. ⁹Then we asked of these elders as follows: 'Who made you a decree to build this house and finish these supplies?' ¹⁰We also asked for their names to make them known to you, so that we could write down the name of the men who are at their head.

A defence

> ¹¹They sent back a message like this to us: 'We are the servants of the God of the heavens and the earth. We are building up the house that was built many years before this, when a great king of Yisra'el built it and completed it. ¹²Yet because our ancestors angered the God of the heavens, he gave them into the hand of Nebukadne'tstsar king of Babel, the Kasdite. He destroyed this house and exiled the people to Babel. ¹³However, in the first year of Koresh king of Babel, Koresh the king made a decree to build up this house of God. ¹⁴The articles belonging to the house of God, of gold and silver, which Nebukadne'tstsar took out of the palace in Yerushalaim and brought to the palace in Babel, Koresh the king also took out of the palace in Babel and they gave them to someone named Sheshbatstsar whom he made governor. ¹⁵He said to him, "Take up these articles, go off, put them in the palace in Yerushalaim. And the house of God is to be built up on its place." ¹⁶This Sheshbatstsar then came and made a start on the house of God in Yerushalaim. From then until now it's been being built, but it's not complete.'

> ¹⁷Now, if it seems good to the king, there should be a search in the king's treasure-house there in Babel, if it's the case that a decree was made by Koresh the king for building up that house of God in Yerushalaim. And may the king send us his wish concerning this.

6

Then a decree was made by Doryavesh the king and they searched in the documents house where treasures were kept in Babel.

An astounding result

²But a scroll was found in the fortress at Ahmeta in Maday [Media] province. In it was written as follows:

> Memorandum. ³In the first year of Koresh the king, Koresh the king made a decree: 'The house of God in Yerushalaim. The house is to be built up, a place where people make sacrifices, with its foundations buttressed, its height 30 metres, its width 30 metres, ⁴three courses of dressed stone and a course of new wood. The expense will be paid by the king's house. ⁵Also the articles belonging to the house of God, of gold and silver, which Nebukadne'tstsar took out of the palace in Yerushalaim and brought to Babel are to be given back. It is to go to the palace in Yerushalaim to its place. You are to deposit it in God's house.'

> ⁶'Now Tattenay governor of Beyond-the-River, Shetar Bozenay and their associates, officials of Beyond-the-River, stay away from there. ⁷Leave the work on this house of God alone. The governor of the Yehudahites and the elders of the Yehudahites are to build up

this house of God on its place, ⁸and a decree is made by me about what you're to do with these elders of the Yehudahites, to build up this house of God. The expense is to be paid punctiliously to these men out of the assets of the king, out of the tribute from Beyond-the-River, so as not to cause a stop. ⁹Whatever they need, both young bulls, rams and lambs for burnt offerings for the God of the heavens, wheat, salt, wine and oil, in accordance with the word of the priests in Yerushalaim – it's to be given them day by day without fail, ¹⁰so that they may present pleasing sacrifices to the God of the heavens and pray for the life of the king and his sons.

¹¹And a decree is made by me that anyone who defies this message, wood will be removed from his house and he will be lifted up and beaten upon it, and his house will be made forfeit, because of this. ¹²And may the God who had his name dwell there overthrow any king or people who puts out a hand to defy – to damage this house of God in Yerushalaim. I, Doryavesh, have made a decree. It's to be put into effect scrupulously.'

Success and celebration

¹³Then Tattenay governor of Beyond-the-River, Shetar Bozenay and their associates, in keeping with what Doryavesh the king sent, accordingly acted punctiliously. ¹⁴The elders of the Yehudahites built, and succeeded through the prophesying of Haggay the prophet and Zekaryah ben Iddo. They built and finished by the decree of the God of Yisra'el and by the decree of Koresh, Doryavesh and Artahshasta king of Paras. ¹⁵This house was completed on the third day of the month of Adar; it was in the sixth year of the reign of Doryavesh the king.

¹⁶The Yisra'elites, the priests, the Levites and the remainder of the exiles made the dedication of this house of God with celebration. ¹⁷For the dedication of this house of God they presented 100 bulls, 200 rams, 400 lambs and twelve goats as a purification offering for all Yisra'el, according to the number of the clans of Yisra'el. ¹⁸They set up the priests in their divisions and the Levites in their groups for the service of God in Yerushalaim, in accordance with what is written in Mosheh's document.

¹⁹The people from the exile made the Pesah [Passover] on the fourteenth of the first month, ²⁰because the priests had purified themselves, and the Levites altogether were pure, all of them. They slaughtered the Pesah for all the people from the exile, for their brother priests and for themselves. ²¹The Yisra'elites who had come back from the exile ate, with everyone who had made himself distinct from the defilement of the nation in the country, to join them to enquire of Yahweh the God of Yisra'el. ²²They made the Flatbread Festival for seven days with rejoicing, because Yahweh had made them rejoice when he turned round the mind of the king of Ashshur to them so as to strengthen their hands in the work on the house of God, the God of Yisra'el.

Enter the priest-theologian

7 After these things, in the reign of Artahshasta king of Paras, Ezra ben Serayah, son of Azaryah son of Hilqiyyah ²son of Shallum son of Tsadoq son of Ahitub ³son of Amaryah son of Azaryah son of Merayot ⁴son of Zerahyah son of Uzzi son of Buqqi ⁵son of Abishua son of Pinhas son of El'azar son of Aharon the head priest – ⁶that Ezra went up from Babel. He was a smart scholar in the instruction of Mosheh which Yahweh the God of Yisra'el had given. In accordance with the hand of Yahweh his God upon him, the king had given him everything that he sought.

⁷Some Yisra'elites, some priests, Levites, singers, gatemen and assistants went up to Yerushalaim in the seventh year of Artahshasta the king, ⁸and he came to Yerushalaim in the fifth month (it was the king's seventh year), ⁹because on the first of the first month it was the start of the journey up from Babel, and on the first of the fifth month he came to Yerushalaim in accordance with the good hand of his God upon him, ¹⁰because Ezra had set his mind to enquire of Yahweh's instruction so as both to keep and to teach decree and ruling in Yisra'el.

¹¹This is a copy of the letter that King Artahshasta gave Ezra the priest-scholar, scholar in things concerning Yahweh's orders and his decrees for Yisra'el:

¹²Artahshasta, king of kings, to Ezra the priest-scholar in the instruction of the God of the heavens (and so on). Now: ¹³a decree is made by me that anyone in my kingdom from the people of Yisra'el and its priests and Levites who freely offers to go to Yerushalaim with you may go. ¹⁴Because you are sent by the king and his seven counsellors to enquire about Yehudah and Yerushalaim on the basis of the instruction of your God which is in your hand, ¹⁵and to take silver and gold that the king and his counsellors have made as a free offering for the God of Yisra'el whose dwelling is in Yerushalaim, ¹⁶and any silver and gold that you find in all Babel province, with the free offering of the people and the priests that they make for the house of their God in Yerushalaim.

What we owe, and what we give because we want to

¹⁷Therefore with this money acquire punctiliously bulls, rams and lambs, and their grain offerings and their drink offerings, and present them on the altar in the house of your God in Yerushalaim. ¹⁸And what seems good to you and to your brothers to do with the remainder of the silver and the gold, in accordance with the will of your God, you may do. ¹⁹The articles given to you for the service of your God's house, deliver before God in Yerushalaim. ²⁰The remainder of the needs of your God's house that it falls to you to give, you may give from the king's treasure-house.

²¹I, Artahshasta the king – by me a decree is made to all the treasurers in Beyond-the-River, that anything Ezra the priest-scholar in the instruction of the God of the heavens asks of you is punctiliously to be done, ²²up to 100 talents of silver, to 100 ten-gallon measures of wheat, to 100 five-gallon measures of wine, to 100 five-gallon measures of oil, and salt without prescribed limit. ²³Anything that is by the decree of the God of the heavens is to be done scrupulously for the house of the God of the heavens, so that fury does not come on the realm of the king and his sons. ²⁴And to you we make it known that all priests, Levites, musicians, gatemen, assistants and workers in this house of God – it's not permitted to impose tribute, taxes and tolls on them.

²⁵You, Ezra, in accordance with your God's smartness which is in your possession, appoint authorities and judges who will give judgement for all the people in Beyond-the-River, for all who acknowledge your God's instructions, and make them known to anyone who does not acknowledge them. ²⁶Anyone who does not observe the instruction of your God and the instruction of the king, judgement will be done to him punctiliously, whether by death, by banishment, by confiscation of property or by imprisonment.

God working through the king

²⁷Blessed be Yahweh, our ancestors' God, who put into the king's mind in this way to glorify Yahweh's house which is in Yerushalaim ²⁸and extended commitment to me before the king and his counsellors and all the king's officials, the powerful men.

I myself showed myself strong in accordance with the hand of Yahweh my God upon me, and collected heads from Yisra'el to go up with me.

8 These are the ancestral heads and the enrolment by genealogy of the people who went up with me in the reign of Artahshasta the king from Babel:

²of the sons of Pinhas, Gershom;
of the sons of Itamar, Daniyy'el;
of the sons of David, Hattush, ³of the sons of Shekanyah;
of the sons of Parosh, Zekaryah, and with him were enrolled by genealogy 150 males;
⁴of the sons of Pahat Mo'ab, Elyeho'enay ben Zerahyah, and with him 200 males;
⁵of the sons of Shekanyah, ben Yahazi'el, and with him 300 males;
⁶and of the sons of Adin, Ebed ben Yonatan, and with him 50 males;
⁷and of the sons of Elam, Yesha'yah ben

Atalyah, and with him 70 males; ⁸and of the sons of Shephatyah, Zebadyah ben Mika'el, and with him 80 males; ⁹of the sons of Yo'ab, Obadyah ben Yehi'el, and with him 218 males; ¹⁰and of the sons of Shelomit, ben Yosiphyah, and with him 160 males; ¹¹and of the sons of Bebay, Zekaryah ben Bebay, and with him 28 males; ¹²and of the sons of Azgad, Yohanan ben Haqqatan, and with him 110 males; ¹³and of the sons of Adoniqam, the last ones – these are their names: Eliphelet, Ye'i'el and Shemayah, and with them 60 males; ¹⁴and of the sons of Bigvay, Utay and Zakkur, and with him 70 males.

God's good hand

¹⁵I collected them at the river that comes to Ahava and we camped there for three days. I considered the people and the priests, and didn't find any of the Levites there. ¹⁶So I sent for Eli'ezer, for Ari'el, for Shema'yah, for Elnatan, for Yarib, for Elnatan, for Natan, for Zekaryah and for Meshullam as heads, and for Yoyarib and for Elnatan as people of understanding, ¹⁷and ordered them to Iddo, the head at Kasiphaya, the [worship] site, and put words in their mouth to speak to Iddo, his brother, the assistants at Kasiphaya, the site, to bring us ministers for the house of our God. ¹⁸In accordance with the good hand of our God upon us they brought us a man of insight from the sons of Mahli ben Levi, son of Yisra'el, namely Sherebyah, and his sons and his brothers, eighteen people, ¹⁹and Hashabyah and with him Yesha'yah of the sons of Merari, his brothers and their sons, twenty people, ²⁰and of the assistants that David and the officials had given for the service of the Levites, 220 assistants; all of them were recorded by name. ²¹I called a fast there at the River Ahava to humble ourselves before our God so as to seek from him a straightforward journey for us and for our little ones and for all our property, ²²because I was ashamed to ask the king for a force and cavalry to help us against an enemy on the way, because we'd said to the king, 'The hand of our God is upon all who seek him, for good, but his vigour and his anger are on all who abandon him.' ²³So we fasted and sought God about this, and he let himself be entreated by us.

The journey and the arrival

²⁴I distinguished twelve of the priestly officials, Sherebyah and Hashabyah and with them ten of their brothers, ²⁵and weighed out to them the silver, the gold and the articles, the contribution for our God's house that the king, his counsellors, his officials, and all Yisra'el who were to be found, had raised. ²⁶I weighed out into their hand the silver, 650 talents; the silver articles, 100 talents, the gold, 100 talents; ²⁷the gold bowls, twenty, worth 100 darics; and two articles of good, shining copper, as precious as gold. ²⁸I said to them, 'You are sacred for Yahweh, and the articles are sacred, and the silver and the gold are a free offering for Yahweh, your ancestors' God. ²⁹Be watchful and keep them until you weigh them out before the priestly officials, the Levites and the ancestral officials of Yisra'el in Yerushalaim in the halls of Yahweh's house.' ³⁰The priests and the Levites received the weighed-out silver and gold and the articles to bring to Yerushalaim to our God's house. ³¹We moved on from the River Ahava on the twelfth of the first month to go to Yerushalaim. The hand of our God was upon us and he rescued us from an enemy's fist and ambush on the way. ³²We came to Yerushalaim, stayed there three days, ³³and on the fourth day the silver and the gold and the articles were weighed out in our God's house into the hand of Meremot ben Uriyyah the priest and with him El'azar ben Pinhas, and with them Yozabad ben Yeshua and No'adyah ben Binnuy, the Levites, ³⁴everything by number/by weight. The entire weight was written down at that time. ³⁵The people who had come from the captivity, the people from the exile, presented burnt offerings for the God of Yisra'el, 12 bulls for all Yisra'el, 96 rams, 77 lambs and 12 goats as a purification offering. The whole was a burnt offering for Yahweh. ³⁶They gave the king's instructions to the king's satraps and the governors of Beyond-the-River, and they supported the people and the house of God.

The importance of keeping distinct

9 When these things finished, the officials came up to me to say, 'The people of Yisra'el and the priests and the Levites have not made themselves distinct from the peoples of the countries in light of their offensive practices (of the Kena'anite [Canaanite], the Hittite, the Perizzite, the Yebusite, the Ammonite, the Mo'abite, the Misrayimite [Egyptian] and the Amorite), ²because they've got some of their daughters for themselves and for their sons, and the sacred seed has mixed with the peoples of the countries, while the hand of the officials and the overseers has been first in this trespass.' ³When I heard this thing, I tore my garment and my coat, pulled hair from my head and from my beard, and sat desolate. ⁴Anyone who trembled at the words of the God of Yisra'el was gathering to me because of the exiles' trespass. I was sitting desolate until the evening offering. ⁵At the evening offering I got up from my self-affliction but bent down on my knees in my torn garment and coat and spread out my palms to Yahweh my God, ⁶and said, 'My God, I'm disgraced and ashamed to lift up my face to you, my God, because our wayward acts have grown above our head, and our liability is great, as far as the heavens. ⁷From the days of our ancestors until this day we've been in great liability, and through our wayward acts we've been given into the hand of the kings of the countries, we, our kings, our priests, with sword, with captivity, with plunder and with shame of face, this very day.

⁸Now for a little while there's been grace from Yahweh our God, in letting an escape group remain for us and giving us a stake in his sacred place, in our God's brightening our eyes and giving us a little life in our servitude. ⁹Because we're serfs, but in our serfdom our God hasn't abandoned us but has extended commitment to us before the kings of Paras so as to give us life, to raise up our God's house and make its wastes stand, and to give us a fence in Yehudah and in Yerushalaim.

How to make your people's confession

¹⁰But now what can we say, our God, after this? Because we've abandoned your orders ¹¹that you issued by means of your servants the prophets, saying, "The country into which you're going to take possession of it is a country polluted by the pollution of the peoples of the countries, through their offensive practices with which they've filled it from end to end in their defilement. ¹²So now don't give your daughters to their sons or get their daughters for your sons. You will not enquire after their well-being or benefit, ever, so that you may be strong and eat the good of the country and enable your children to possess it permanently."

¹³After all that's come upon us because of our bad ways and our great liabilities, when you, our God, have held back [in punishing] below our waywardness, and given us an escape group like this, ¹⁴shall we go back to contravening your orders and intermarrying with the peoples who are characterized by these offensive practices? You will be angry with us so as to finish us off, so that there's no people remaining, no escape group, won't you. ¹⁵Yahweh, God of Yisra'el, you're in the right, because we remain as an escape group this very day. Here we are before you with our liability, but there's no standing before you on account of this.'

10 While Ezra was pleading and making confession, crying and falling down before God's house, a very great congregation from Yisra'el, men, women and children, collected to him, because the people were crying bitterly. ²Shekanyah ben Yehi'el of the sons of Elam answered Ezra, 'We've trespassed against our God and got foreign women come to live from the peoples of the country. But now there's hope for Yisra'el over this, ³so now let's solemnize a pact towards our God to get all the women and those born from them to go away, by the counsel of my lord and of those who tremble at our God's order. It should be done in accordance with the instruction. ⁴Set to, because the thing rests on you, and we're with you. Be strong and act.'

Where there's commitment there's hope

⁵Ezra set to and swore the priestly officials, the Levites and all Yisra'el to act in accordance with this word, and they swore. ⁶Ezra got up

from his place before God's house and went into the hall of Yehohanan ben Elyashib. When he went there, he didn't eat food and he didn't drink water, because he was grieving over the exiles' trespass.

⁷They passed an announcement through Yehudah and Yerushalaim to all the people from the exile, that they should collect in Yerushalaim. ⁸Anyone who didn't come in three days, in accordance with the counsel of the officials and the elders – all his property would be devoted and he himself would be distinguished from the exile congregation.

⁹So all the men of Yehudah and Binyamin collected in Yerushalaim in three days; it was the ninth month, the twentieth of the month. All the people sat in the square at God's house, trembling about the thing and because of the rains.

¹⁰Ezra the priest got up and said to them, 'You've trespassed. You've got foreign women come to live, adding to Yisra'el's liability. ¹¹But now, make confession to Yahweh, your ancestors' God, and do what is acceptable to him. Make yourselves distinct from the peoples of the country and from the foreign women.'

¹²The entire congregation answered with a loud voice, 'Yes, it's for us to act in accordance with your word. ¹³Nevertheless the company is large and the time is the rains. We don't have the energy to stand outside, and it's not the work of one day or of two, because we've become greatly rebellious in this thing. ¹⁴Our officials should please stand [here] for the entire congregation, and anyone in our towns who's got foreign women come to live should come at set times, and with them the elders town by town, and its authorities, until we turn back the angry rage of our God from us over this thing.' ¹⁵Only Yonatan ben Asah'el and Yahzeyah ben Tiqvah stood against this, but Meshullam and Shabbatay the Levites helped them.

The tough action

¹⁶The people from the exile acted in this way. Ezra the priest, the men who were the ancestral heads, for their ancestral family, and all of them by their names, made themselves distinct and sat on the first day of the tenth month to enquire into the thing. ¹⁷They finished with all the men who'd got foreign women to come to live, by the first day of the first month.

¹⁸There were found among the sons of the priests who'd got foreign women to come to live:

Yeshua ben Yotsadaq and his brothers Ma'aseyah, Eli'ezer, Yarib and Gedalyah; ¹⁹they gave their hand that they would send away their wives and, being liable, a ram from the flock, for their liability;
²⁰of the sons of Immer, Hanani and Zebadyah;
²¹of the sons of Harim, Ma'aseyah, Eliyyah, Shema'yah, Yehi'el and Uzziyyah;
²²of the sons of Pashhur, Elyo'enay, Ma'aseyah, Yishma'e'l, Netan'el, Yozabad, and El'asah;

²³of the Levites:
Yozabad, Shim'i, Qelayah (i.e. Qelita), Petahyah, Yehudah and Eli'ezer;

²⁴of the singers:
Eliyashib;

of the gatemen:
Shallum, Telem and Uri.
²⁵Of the Yisra'elites:
of the sons of Parosh, Ramyah, Yizzeyah, Malkiyyah, Miyyamin, El'azar, Malkiyyah and Benayah;
²⁶of the sons of Elam, Mattanyah, Zekaryah, Yehi'el, Abdi, Yeremot and Eliyyah;
²⁷of the sons of Zattu, Elyo'enay, Elyashib, Mattanyah, Yeremot, Zabad and Aziza;
²⁸of the sons of Bebay, Yehohanan, Hananyah, Zabbay, Atlay;
²⁹of the sons of Bani, Meshullam, Malluk, Adayah, Yashub, She'al and Ramot;
³⁰of the sons of Patah Mo'ab, Adna, Kelal, Benayah, Ma'aseyah, Mattanyah, Betsal'el, Binnuy and Menashsheh;
³¹of the sons of Harim, Eli'ezer, Ishshiyyah, Malkiyyah, Shema'yah, Shim'on, ³²Binyamin, Malluk, Shemaryah;
³³of the sons of Hashum, Mattenay, Mattattah, Zabad, Eliphelet, Yeremay, Menashsheh, Shim'i;
³⁴of the sons of Bani, Ma'aday, Amram and U'el, ³⁵Benayah, Bedeyah, Keluhu, ³⁶Vanyah, Meremot, Elyashib,

³⁷Mattanyah, Mattenay, Ya'asay, ³⁸Bani, Binnuy, Shim'i, ³⁹Shelemyah, Natan, Adayah, ⁴⁰Maknadebay, Shashay, Sharay, ⁴¹Azar'el, Shelemyahu, Shemaryah, ⁴²Shallum, Amaryah, Yoseph;

⁴³of the sons of Nebo, Ye'i'el, Mattityah, Zabad, Zebina, Yadday and Yo'el, Benayah. ⁴⁴All these had got foreign wives, and there were some of them who were women who had had children.

Nehemiah

For an introduction, see the introduction to Ezra.

Survivors troubled and disgraced

1 The words of Nehemyah ben Hakalyah.

In the month of Kislev in the twentieth year, when I was in Shushan, the fortress, ²Hanani, one of my brothers, came, he and some men from Yehudah, and I asked them about the Yehudahites, the escape group that remained from the captivity, and about Yerushalaim. ³They said to me, 'The remaining people, who remain from the captivity there in the province, are in a very bad way and are subject to reviling there in the province, with Yerushalaim's wall broken down and its gateways set on fire.' ⁴When I heard these things I sat and cried and grieved for days. I was fasting and pleading before the God of the heavens.

⁵I said, 'Oh! Yahweh, God of the heavens, great and awe-inspiring God, keeping pact and commitment for people who are loyal to him and keep his orders! ⁶Please may your ear become heeding and your eyes opened to listen to the plea of your servant that I'm making before you today, day and night, for the Yisra'elites [Israelites] your servants, making confession concerning the wrongdoings of the Yisra'elites that we have committed in relation to you. I and my ancestral household have done wrong. ⁷We've acted very ruinously in relation to you. We haven't kept the orders, the decrees and the rulings with which you ordered Mosheh [Moses] your servant.

⁸Be mindful, please, of the word with which you ordered Mosheh your servant: "Should you people trespass, I for my part will scatter you among the peoples, ⁹but should you turn back to me and keep my orders and do them, if the people who've been driven away are at the end of the heavens, from there I will collect them and bring them to the place where I chose to have my name dwell." ¹⁰And they are your servants and your people whom you redeemed by your great energy and your strong hand. ¹¹ᵃOh! Lord, please may your ear become heeding to your servant's plea and to the plea of your servants who want to live in awe of your name. Please enable your servant to succeed today and give him compassion before this man.'

Boldness (and discretion) as a king's servant

2 ¹¹ᵇNow I was the king's butler, and in the month of Nisan in the twentieth year of Artahshasta [Artaxerxes] the king, when wine was before him, I carried the wine and gave it to the king. I hadn't been in a bad way before him, ²so the king said to me, 'Why is your face looking bad when you're not ill? This is nothing but something bad on your mind.' I became very much afraid, ³but I said to the king, 'Long live the king! Why should my face not look bad when the town where my ancestors' graves are lies waste and its gateways have been consumed by fire?'

⁴The king said to me, 'What are you asking for?' I pleaded with the God of the heavens ⁵and said to the king, 'If it seems good to the king and if your servant seems good before you, that you send me to Yehudah to the town of my ancestors' graves so that I may build it up.' ⁶The king said to me, with the consort sitting beside him, 'How long will your journey be? When will you come back?' So it seemed good before the king and he sent me, and I gave him a date.

⁷I said to the king, 'If it seems good to the king, may they give me communiqués for the governors of Beyond-the-River so that they may let me pass until I come to Yehudah, ⁸and a communiqué to Asaph the keeper of the park which belongs to the king so that he may give me logs for roofing the gateways of the fortress that belongs to the house, for the town wall and for the house to which I shall come.' The king gave them to me in accordance with the good hand of my God upon me. ⁹I came to the governors of Beyond-the-River and gave them the king's communiqués. The king sent with me officers of a force and cavalry. ¹⁰But Sanballat the Horonite and Tobiyyah the Ammonite servant heard, and it seemed very bad to them that someone had come to seek something good for the Yisra'elites.

A secret survey

¹¹I came to Yerushalaim and I was there for three days, ¹²then I set to by night, I and

a few men with me. I didn't tell anyone what my God had put into my mind to do for Yerushalaim, and there was no animal with me except the animal that I was riding on. ¹³I went out through the Ravine Gate by night, to the Jackals Spring and to the Rubbish Gate. I was examining the Yerushalaim walls that had been broken down and its gateways that had been consumed by fire. ¹⁴I passed on to the Spring Gate and to the King's Pool, but there was no room for the animal under me to pass. ¹⁵So I was going up through the wadi by night and I was examining the wall, then I went back and came in through the Ravine Gate.

Thus I went back, ¹⁶while the overseers didn't know where I'd gone or what I was doing, and I hadn't until now told the Yehudahites, the priests, the important people, the overseers and the rest of the people who were going to be doing the work. ¹⁷I said to them, 'You see the bad situation that we're in, that Yerushalaim lies waste and its gateways have been set on fire. Come, let's build up the Yerushalaim wall and no longer be subject to reviling.' ¹⁸I told them of my God's hand, that it was good upon me, and also of the king's words that he said to me, and they said, 'Let's set to and build.' So they strengthened their hands for the good work.

¹⁹Sanballat the Horonite, Tobiyyah the Ammonite servant and Geshem the Arab heard, and they ridiculed us and despised us. They said, 'What's this thing that you're doing? Are you rebelling against the king?' ²⁰I sent back word to them: 'The God of the heavens – he'll enable us to succeed. We, his servants – we'll set to and build. You have no share or right or record in Yerushalaim.'

Everyone played their part (1)

3 So Elyashib the big priest and his brother priests set to and built up the Sheep Gate. They made it sacred and put in place its doors, and as far as the Hundred Tower they made it sacred, as far as Hanan'el's Tower;
²next to him the men of Yereho [Jericho] built;
next to him Zakkur ben Imri built;
³the Fish Gate, the sons of Hassena'ah built up; they roofed it and put in place its doors, its bolts and its bars;
⁴next to them Meremot ben Uriyyah son of Haqqots did the strengthening;
next to them Meshullam ben Berekyah son of Meshezab'el did the strengthening;
next to them Tsadoq ben Ba'ana did the strengthening;
⁵next to them the Teqo'ites did the strengthening, but their august people didn't give their neck to the service of their lord;
⁶the Yeshanah Gate, Yoyada ben Paseah and Meshullam ben Besodeyah did the strengthening of; they roofed it and put in place its doors, its bolts and its bars;
⁷next to them Melatyah the Gib'onite and Yadon the Meronotite did the strengthening (people of Gib'on and The Watchtower, the seat of the Beyond-the-River governor);
⁸next to him Uzzi'el ben Harhayah (goldsmiths) did the strengthening;
next to him Hananyah of the perfumers did the strengthening, but they abandoned Yerushalaim as far as the wide wall;
⁹next to them Rephayah ben Hur, official over half the district of Yerushalaim, did the strengthening;
¹⁰next to them Yedayah ben Harumaph did the strengthening, in front of his house;
next to him Hattush ben Hashabneyah did the strengthening;
¹¹a second section Malkiyyah ben Harim and Hashshub ben Paha Mo'ab did the strengthening, and the Ovens Tower.

Everyone played their part (2)

¹²Next to him Shallum ben Hallohesh, official over half the district of Yerushalaim, did the strengthening, he and his daughters;
¹³the Ravine Gate, Hanun and the inhabitants of Zanoah did the strengthening; they built it up and put in place its doors, its bolts and its bars, and 500 metres in the wall as far as the Rubbish Gate;

¹⁴the Rubbish Gate, Malkiyyah ben Rekab, official over the district of Bet-hakkerem, did the strengthening; he built it up and put in place its doors, its bolts and its bars;

¹⁵the Spring Gate, Shallun ben-Kol-hozeh the official over the district of The Watchtower did the strengthening; he built it up, covered it, and put in place its doors, its bolts and its bars, and the wall of the Shelah Pool belonging to the King's Garden, and as far as the steps going down from David's Town;

¹⁶after him Nehemyah ben Azbuq, official over half the district of Bet-tsur, did the strengthening as far as opposite David's graves, as far as the man-made pool and as far as the Strong Men's House;

¹⁷after him the Levites did the strengthening: Rehum ben Bani;

next to him Hashabyah, official over half the district of Qe'ilah, did the strengthening for his district;

¹⁸after him their brothers did the strengthening: Bavvay ben Henadad, official over half the district of Qe'ilah;

¹⁹next to him Ezer ben Yeshua, official over The Watchtower, did the strengthening of a second section, from opposite the ascent to the armoury at the corner;

²⁰after him Baruk ben Zakkay burned [with zeal]; he did the strengthening of a second section, from the corner as far as the entrance of the house of Elyashib the big priest.

Everyone played their part (3)

²¹After him Meremot ben Uriyyah son of Haqqots did the strengthening of a second section, from the entrance of Elyashib's house and as far as the end of Elyashib's house;

²²after him the priests who were the people of the plain did the strengthening;

²³after him Binyamin and Hashshub did the strengthening opposite their house;

after him Azaryah ben Ma'aseyah son of Ananyah did the strengthening beside his house;

²⁴after him Binnuy ben Henadad did the strengthening of a second section, from the house of Azaryah to the corner, to the angle;

²⁵Palal ben Uzzay: from opposite the corner and the tower going out from the king's upper house which belongs to the court of the guard;

after him Pedayah ben Parosh ²⁶(the assistants were living on the Ophel as far as opposite the Water Gate to the east and the projecting tower);

²⁷after him the Teqo'ites did the strengthening of a second section from opposite the big projecting tower as far the Ophel wall;

²⁸above the Horses Gate, the priests did the strengthening, each one opposite his house;

²⁹after him Tsadoq ben Immer did the strengthening opposite his house;

after him Shema'yah ben Shekanyah, keeper of the East Gate, did the strengthening;

³⁰after him Hananyah ben Shelemyah and Hanun ben Tsalaph (the sixth) did the strengthening of a second section;

after him Meshullam ben Berekyah did the strengthening opposite his room;

³¹after him Malkiyyah of the goldsmiths did the strengthening as far as the house of the assistants and the merchants, opposite the Registration Gate and as far as the upper floor at the angle;

³²between the upper floor of the angle to the Sheep Gate the goldsmiths and the merchants did the strengthening.

Reasons for discouragement

4 When Sanballat heard that we were building up the wall, it enraged him. He was greatly provoked. He ridiculed the Yehudahites ²and said before his brothers and the Shomron [Samaria] force, 'What are the feeble Yehudahites doing? Will they abandon it for themselves? Will they sacrifice? Will they finish in the day? Will they bring to life the stones from the heaps of earth, when they're burnt?' ³Tobiyyah the Ammonite, being beside him, said, 'What they're building, if a fox went up, he'd breach their wall of stones.'

⁴'Listen, our God, because we've become an object of contempt. May their reviling turn

Nehemiah 4: Nehemyah's Yerushalaim (Nehemiah's Jerusalem)

back on their own head. Make them into spoil in a land of captivity. ⁵Don't cover over their waywardness. Their wrongdoing should not be blotted out from before you, because they've uttered provocation in front of the builders.'

⁶So we built up the wall, and the entire wall joined up until it was half done. The mind of the people was on doing it. ⁷But when Sanballat, Tobiyyah, the Arabs, the Ammonites and the Ashdodites heard that restoration of the Yerushalaim walls had progressed in that the broken parts had begun to close up, it enraged them very much, ⁸and all of them conspired together to come to battle against Yerushalaim and cause confusion in it. ⁹We pleaded with our God and put in place a watch over them day and night in the face of them.

¹⁰But Yehudah said,

> The carrier's energy has collapsed,
>   and there is much earth.
> We ourselves are not able
>   to build up the wall.

¹¹And our adversaries said, 'They won't know and they won't see when we come in among them and kill them, and stop the work.' ¹²And when the Yehudahites who lived beside them came, they said to us ten times from all the places, 'You should come back to us.'

Sword and trowel, faith and hope

[13] So I put in place at the lowest parts of the space behind the wall at the exposed points – I put the people in place by kin-groups with their swords, their lances and their bows. [14] I looked, and I stood up and said to the important people, to the overseers and to the rest of the people, 'Don't be afraid of them. The Lord, the one who is great and awe-inspiring – be mindful of him and do battle for your brothers, your sons and your daughters, your wives and your homes.'

[15] When our enemies heard that it had become known to us and that God had contravened their counsel, we went back to the wall, all of us, each to his work. [16] But from that day, half of my boys were doing the work and half of them were holding strongly on to lances, shields, bows and armour, with the officials behind the entire house of Yehudah [17] who were building up the wall. The basket-carriers who were transporting: with one hand he was doing the work and with one he was holding strongly on to the weapon. [18] The builders were fixed each with his sword on his hips, but they were building. And the person who sounded the horn was beside me.

[19] I said to the important people, to the overseers and to the rest of the people, 'There's much work, and widely spread, and we're divided on the wall, far away one from another. [20] At the place where you hear the sound of the horn, collect there to us. Our God – he'll battle for us.' [21] So we were doing the work with half of them holding strongly on to lances, from when dawn came up until the stars came out. [22] Further, at that time I said to the people, 'Each man and his boy should stay the night within Yerushalaim; they'll be a watch for us at night and they'll work by day.' [23] I, my brothers, my boys and the men in the watch behind me – we didn't take off our clothes, each one, with his weapon at the water.

The community's moral challenge

5 But there was a great outcry by the people and their wives towards their Yehudahite brothers. [2] There were some saying, 'Our sons and our daughters, we are many. We must get grain so we can eat and live.' [3] There were some saying, 'Our fields, our vineyards, our homes – we're mortgaging them so we can get grain during a famine.' [4] And there were some saying, 'We've borrowed silver for the king's tax – our fields and our vineyards. [5] Now, our flesh is the same as our brothers' flesh, our children are the same as their children, but here – we're binding our sons and our daughters as servants. Some of our daughters are bound. There's no power in our hand; our fields and our vineyards belong to other people.'

[6] It enraged me very much when I heard their outcry and these words. [7] When my mind had counselled me, I argued with the important people and the overseers: 'Are you advancing loans, one with his brother?', and I set a big congregation against them. [8] I said to them, 'We acquired our Yehudahite brothers who'd been sold to the Gentiles, as far as it lay in us. Will you indeed sell your brothers so that they may be sold to us?'

They were silent. They couldn't find a word. [9] I said, 'The thing that you're doing isn't good. Will you not walk in awe of God to avoid reviling before our Gentile enemies? [10] Indeed, I, my brothers and my boys are advancing loans of silver and grain with them. Please let's abandon this advancing loans. [11] Please give them back this very day their fields, their vineyards, their olive trees and their houses, and the percentage on the silver, the grain, the new wine and the fresh oil that you're advancing them.'

Putting your money where your mouth is

[12] They said, 'We'll give them back, and we won't seek anything from them. We'll act in this way, as you're saying.' So I called for the priests and swore them to act in accordance with this word. [13] I also shook out my pocket and said, 'May God shake out like this anyone who does not implement this word, from his house and from his labour. May he become shaken out like this and empty.' The entire congregation said 'Yes', and praised Yahweh, and the people acted in accordance with this word.

[14] Further, from the day I was ordered to become governor in the country of Yehudah, from the twentieth year until the thirty-second

year of Artaḥshasta the king, twelve years, I with my brothers didn't eat the governor's food. ¹⁵The previous governors who were before me made things heavy for the people, and for food and wine for one day took from them forty sheqels of silver (further, their boys had power over the people). I didn't do so, out of awe for God. ¹⁶And further, I strengthened the work on this wall; we didn't acquire fields, and all my boys were collected there for the work. ¹⁷The Yehudahites and the overseers, 150 individuals, and the people who came to us from the nations that were round us, were at my table. ¹⁸What was being prepared for one day, an ox, six choice sheep, and birds, they were prepared for me with all kinds of wine in quantity at an interval of ten days, but with this I didn't seek the governor's food, because the service was heavy on this people.

¹⁹Be mindful for me of all that I've done for this people, my God, for good.

Don't trust anybody

6 When it came to be heard by Sanballat, Tobiyyah, by Geshem the Arab and by the rest of our enemies, that we had built up the wall and that no breach was left in it (though up to that time I hadn't put in place doors in the gateways), ²Sanballat and Geshem sent to me: 'Come, let's meet together at Kephirim in Ono Valley.' But these men were thinking to do something bad to me, ³so I sent envoys to them saying, 'I'm doing some big work and I can't come down. Why should the work stop when I slacken hold of it and come down to you?' ⁴They sent me this same message four times, and I sent this same message back to them. ⁵Sanballat sent me this same message with his boy a fifth time, with an open communiqué in his hand, ⁶written in it: 'Among the nations it's come to be heard (and Gashmu says): you and the Yehudahites are thinking to rebel. That's why you're building up the wall. You're going to be their king, according to these words. ⁷You've also put prophets in place to call out in Yerushalaim about you, "A king in Yehudah". It will now make itself heard to the king, these very words. So now go, and let's take counsel together.'

⁸I sent to him: 'Nothing like these things that you're saying has happened; rather you're devising things out of your own mind', ⁹because they were all of them making us afraid, saying 'Their hands will slacken from the work and it won't be done.'

So now strengthen my hands.

The work completed

¹⁰I myself came to the house of Shema'yah ben Delayah son of Mehetab'el, when he was confined. He had said,

Let's meet in God's house,
  inside the palace.
Let's shut the doors of the palace,
  because they're coming to kill you,
  by night they're coming to kill you.

¹¹I said, 'Will a person like me take flight? And who is there like me who may go into the palace and live? I won't come.' ¹²I realized: there, God had not sent him, because he'd spoken the prophecy about me when Obiyyah and Sanballat had hired him. ¹³It was to this end that he'd been hired, to the end that I'd be afraid and I'd act in this way and do wrong, and they'd have a bad name, in order that they could revile me. ¹⁴Be mindful, my God, of Tobiyyah, and of Sanballat in accordance with these acts of his, and also of Noadyah the prophetess and of the rest of the prophets who were making me afraid.

¹⁵The wall was complete on the twenty-fifth of Elul, after fifty-two days. ¹⁶When all our enemies heard, all the nations that were round us were afraid, and they fell greatly in their own eyes because they acknowledged that this work had been done by our God.

¹⁷Also in those days, the important people among the Yehudahites were having many communiqués go to Tobiyyah, and ones that were Tobiyyah's were coming to them, ¹⁸because many people in Yehudah were under oath to him, because he was a son-in-law of Shekanyah ben Arah, and Yehohanan his son had taken the daughter of Meshullam ben Berekyah. ¹⁹Further, they were saying good things about him before me, and they were letting my words go out to him when Tobiyyah sent communiqués to make me afraid.

The need for a new population

7 When the wall was built and I'd put in place the doors, they appointed the gatemen, the singers and the Levites. ²I ordered in charge of Yerushalaim Hanani my brother and Hananyah the fortress officer, because he was truly a trustworthy man and one who lived in awe of God more than many. ³I said to them, 'The Yerushalaim gateways will not open until the sun is hot; until those men are standing in position they must shut the doors and hold them fast. And put in place the inhabitants of Yerushalaim as watches, one individual at his watch and another individual opposite his own house.'

⁴Now the town was wide on both sides and big, but the people within it was small, and there were no houses built up. ⁵My God put it into my mind and I collected the important people, the overseers and the people, for enrolment by genealogy. I found the document with the roll of the people who went up at the first, and found written in it:

⁶These are the people of the province who went up from among the captives in exile whom Nebukadne'tstsar king of Babel had exiled and who went back to Yerushalaim and to Yehudah, each to his town, ⁷who came with Zerubbabel, Yeshua, Nehemyah, Azaryah, Ra'amyah, Nahamani, Mordecay, Bilshan, Misperet, Bigvay, Nehum, Ba'anah.

The number of the men belonging to the Yisra'elite people:

⁸sons of Par'osh 2,172
⁹sons of Shephatyah 372
¹⁰sons of Arah 652
¹¹sons of Pahat Mo'ab (by the sons of Yeshua and Yo'ab) 2,818
¹²sons of Elam 1,254
¹³sons of Zattu 845
¹⁴sons of Zakkay 760
¹⁵sons of Binnuy 648
¹⁶sons of Bebay 628
¹⁷sons of Azgad 2,322
¹⁸sons of Adoniqam 667
¹⁹sons of Bigvay 2,067
²⁰sons of Adin 655
²¹sons of Ater (by Hizqiyyah) 98
²²sons of Hashum 328
²³sons of Bezay 324
²⁴sons of Hariph 112
²⁵sons of Gib'on 95
²⁶people of Bet-lehem and Netophah 188
²⁷people of Anatot 128
²⁸people of Bet-azmavet 42
²⁹sons of Ye'arim Township, Kephirah and Be'erot 743
³⁰sons of The Height and Geba 621
³¹people of Mikmas 122
³²people of Bet-el and Ha'ay 123
³³people of the other Nebo 52
³⁴people of the other Elam 1,254
³⁵sons of Harim 320
³⁶sons of Yereho 345
³⁷sons of Lod, Hadid and Ono 721
³⁸sons of Sena'ah 3,930

Ministers on the roll

³⁹The priests:
sons of Yeda'yah (by the household of Yeshua) 973
⁴⁰sons of Immer 1,052
⁴¹sons of Pashhur 1,247
⁴²sons of Harim 1,017

⁴³The Levites:
sons of Yeshua (by Qadmi'el, by the sons of Hodavyah) 74

⁴⁴The singers:
sons of Asaph 148

⁴⁵The gatemen:
sons of Shallum
sons of Ater
sons of Talmon
sons of Aqqub
sons of Hatita
sons of Shobay
altogether 138

⁴⁶The assistants:
sons of Tsiha
sons of Hasupha
sons of Tabba'ot
⁴⁷sons of Qeros
sons of Si'ah
sons of Padon
⁴⁸sons of Lebanah
sons of Hagabah
sons of Shalmay
⁴⁹sons of Hanan
sons of Giddel
sons of Gahar
⁵⁰sons of Re'ayah
sons of Retsin
sons of Neqodah
⁵¹sons of Gazzam
sons of Uzza
sons of Paseah
⁵²sons of Besay
sons of Me'unim
sons of Nephishesim
⁵³sons of Baqbuq
sons of Haqupha
sons of Harhur
⁵⁴sons of Batslit
sons of Mehida
sons of Harsha
⁵⁵sons of Barqos
sons of Sisera
sons of Temah
⁵⁶sons of Netsiah
sons of Hatipha

⁵⁷The sons of Shelomoh's [Solomon's] servants:
sons of Sotay
sons of Sopheret
sons of Perida
⁵⁸sons of Ya'ela
sons of Darqon
sons of Giddel
⁵⁹sons of Shephatyah
sons of Hattil
sons of Pokeret Hatstsebayim
sons of Amon

⁶⁰All the assistants and the sons of Shelomoh's servants 392.

⁶¹These are the people who came up from Tel Melah, Tel Harsha, Kerub, Addan and Immer, but who could not tell their ancestral household and their origin, whether they were from Yisra'el:

⁶²sons of Delayah	sons of Haqqots
sons of Tobiyyah	sons of Barzillay (who
sons of Neqoda	had taken a wife
642	from the daughters of
	Barzillay the Gil'adite
⁶³Of the priests:	and was called by
sons of Habayah	their name):

⁶⁴these looked for their record in the enrolment by genealogy but it was not found, and they were deconsecrated from the priesthood. ⁶⁵The administrator said to them that they should not eat of the very sacred things until there was a priest standing with Urim and Tummim.

The need for a new community

⁶⁶The entire congregation altogether 42,360;
⁶⁷apart from their servants and handmaids: these were 7,337;
and they had 245 male and female singers;
⁶⁸their horses 736; their mules 245; ⁶⁹camels 435; donkeys 6,720.

⁷⁰Some of the ancestral heads gave to the work. The administrator gave to the treasury gold (1,000 drakmas), basins (50), priests' robes (530). ⁷¹Some of the ancestral heads gave to the work treasury gold (20,000 drakmas) and silver (2,200 minas). ⁷²What the remainder of the people gave: gold (20,000 drakmas), silver (2,000) and priests' robes (67).

⁷³The priests, the Levites, the gatemen, the singers, some of the people, the assistants and all Yisra'el went to live in their towns. The seventh month arrived, with the Yisra'elites in their towns,

8 and the entire people gathered as one person to the square that's before the Water Gate, and said to Ezra the scholar to bring Mosheh's instruction document with which Yahweh had ordered Yisra'el. ²Ezra the priest brought the instruction before the congregation (men and women and all who could understand when they listened) on the first day of the seventh month. ³He read out in it before the square which is before the Water Gate from dawn until midday, in front of the men and the women and the people who could understand, with the ears of the entire people towards the instruction document.

⁴Ezra the scholar stood on a wooden tower that they made for the thing. There stood beside him Mattityah, Shema, Anayah, Uriyyah, Hilqiyyah and Ma'aseyah on his right, and at his left Pedayah, Misha'el, Malkiyyah, Hashum, Hashbaddanah, Zekaryah, Meshullam. ⁵Ezra opened the document before the eyes of the entire people, because he was above the entire people, and as he opened it, the entire people stood. ⁶Ezra blessed Yahweh, the great God, and the entire people answered, 'Yes, yes', with a raising of their hands, then bent their heads and bowed low to Yahweh, faces on the ground. ⁷Yeshua, Bani, Sherebyah, Yamin, Aqqub, Shabbetay, Hodiyyah, Ma'aseyah, Qelita, Azaryah, Yozabad, Hanan, Pela'yah, and the Levites, helped the people understand the instruction, with the people in their place. ⁸They read out in the document, in God's instruction, explaining and giving insight so they understood the reading.

Mourning or celebration?

⁹Nehemyah (he was the administrator), Ezra the priest-scholar and the Levites who were helping the people understand said to the entire people, 'Today is sacred for Yahweh your God. Don't mourn, don't cry', because the entire people were crying as they heard the words of the instruction. ¹⁰He said to them, 'Go, eat rich food, drink sweet drinks and send off portions to anyone who has nothing prepared, because today is sacred for our Lord. Don't be in pain, because joy in Yahweh is your protection.' ¹¹The Levites were silencing the entire people, saying 'Hush, because today is sacred, don't be in pain.' ¹²So the entire people went to eat and drink and send off portions and make great rejoicing, because

they understood the things that they had made known to them. ¹³On the second day, the ancestral heads of the entire people, the priests and the Levites gathered to Ezra the scholar, to get insight into the words of the instruction. ¹⁴They found written in the instruction that Yahweh had ordered by means of Mosheh that the Yisra'elites should live in bivouacs [*sukkot*] in the festival in the seventh month ¹⁵and that they should make heard and should pass on an announcement in all their towns and in Yerushalaim: 'Go out into the mountains and bring olive branches, pine-tree branches, myrtle branches, palm branches and leafy tree branches to make bivouacs, as it is written.' ¹⁶So the people went out and brought them, and made themselves bivouacs, each person on his roof, or in their courtyards, in the courtyards of God's house, in the square at the Water Gate or in the square at the Ephrayim Gate. ¹⁷The entire congregation of people who had come back from the captivity made bivouacs and lived in the bivouacs, because the Yisra'elites had not done so since the days of Yehoshua [Joshua] ben Nun until that day, and there was very great rejoicing. ¹⁸So he read out in the document of God's instruction day by day, from the first day until the last day. They made festival for seven days and an assembly on the eighth day, in accordance with the ruling.

How to make your confession

9 On the twenty-fourth day of this month the Yisra'elites assembled with fasting and with sack, and earth on themselves. ²The offspring of Yisra'el distinguished themselves from all foreigners and stood and confessed their wrongdoings and their ancestors' wayward acts. ³They got up in their position and read out in Yahweh their God's instruction document for a quarter of the day, and for a quarter they were confessing and bowing low to Yahweh their God.

⁴On the Levites' stairway Yeshua and Bani (Qadmi'el, Shebanyah, Bunni, Sherebyah, Bani, Kenani) got up and cried out in a loud voice to Yahweh their God. ⁵The Levites Yeshua and Qadmi'el (Bani, Hashabneyah, Sherebyah, Hodiyyah, Petahyah) said, 'Get up, bless Yahweh your God from age to age:

May people bless your glorious name,
    though exalted above all blessing and praise.
⁶You are Yahweh, you alone;
    you made the heavens,
The highest heavens and all their army,
    the earth and all that's on it,
    the seas and all that's in them.
You give life to all of them,
    and the army in the heavens bow low to you.

⁷You are Yahweh, the God who chose Abram and got him to go out from Ur of the Kasdites, and made his name Abraham. ⁸You found his mind trustworthy before you and you solemnized the pact with him to give the country of the Kena'anite [Canaanite], the Hittite, the Amorite, the Perizzite, the Yebusite and the Girgashite – to give [it] to his offspring. You implemented your words, because you're faithful.

⁹You saw our ancestors' humbling in Misrayim [Egypt] and you heard their cry at the Reed Sea. ¹⁰You performed signs and proofs against Par'oh [Pharaoh] and against all his servants and against all the people of his country because you acknowledged that they asserted themselves over them, and you made a name for yourself this very day.

Self-assertion and pardon

¹¹You split the sea before them and they passed through the middle of the sea on dry ground, but you threw their pursuers into the depths, like a stone into vigorous water. ¹²With a cloud column you led them by day, and with a fire column by night, to give light for them on the way in which they were to go.

¹³On Mount Sinai you came down and spoke with them from the heavens. You gave them upright rulings and truthful instructions, good decrees and orders. ¹⁴Your sacred sabbath you caused to be acknowledged by them, and you ordained for them orders, decrees and instruction by means of Mosheh your servant. ¹⁵Bread from the heavens you gave them for their hunger, and you made water go out from

a cliff for them, for their thirst. You said to them to go and take possession of the country that you had raised your hand [to swear] to give them.

¹⁶But they, our ancestors, asserted themselves, toughened their neck and didn't listen to your orders. ¹⁷They refused to listen and were not mindful of your extraordinary deeds, which you'd done with them. They toughened their neck and appointed a head so as to go back to their serfdom, in their rebelliousness.

But you are a pardoning God, gracious and compassionate, long-tempered and big in commitment, and you didn't abandon them, ¹⁸even when they made themselves a calf figurine and said, "This is your God who got you up from Misrayim." They committed great acts of disdain. ¹⁹But you in your great compassion – you didn't abandon them in the wilderness. The cloud column didn't depart from them by day to lead them on the way, nor the fire column by night to give light to them and on the way in which they were to go.

Provision and rebellion

²⁰You gave them your good spirit to enable them to succeed. You didn't withhold your *maan* [manna] from their mouth and you gave them water for their thirst. ²¹When for forty years you provided for them in the wilderness, they didn't lack, their clothes didn't wear out and their feet didn't swell. ²²You gave them kingdoms and peoples, and allocated these as a border. They took possession of the country of Sihon, which was the country of the king of Heshbon, and the country of Og king of Bashan.

²³You made their children as many as the stars in the heavens and brought them to the country that you said to their parents to go in to possess. ²⁴The children came and took possession of the country. You made the inhabitants of the country, the Kena'anites, bow down before them, and you gave them into their hand, both their kings and the peoples of the country, to do with them in accordance with what was acceptable to them. ²⁵They took fortified towns and rich land and took possession of houses full of every good thing: hewn cisterns, vineyards, olives and fruit trees, in large number. They ate, were full, grew stocky and revelled in your great goodness.

²⁶But they defied and rebelled against you and threw your instruction behind their back. They killed your prophets who testified against them to get them to come back to you, and they committed great acts of disdain. ²⁷You gave them into the hand of their adversaries and they oppressed them. In their time of pressure they cried out to you and from the heavens you yourself would listen. In accordance with your great compassion you gave them deliverers and they delivered them from the hand of their adversaries.

Servants or serfs

²⁸But when things settled down for them, they again dealt badly before you. You abandoned them into the hand of their enemies and they held sway over them. They again cried out to you, and from the heavens you yourself would listen and rescue them in accordance with your great compassion, time after time. ²⁹You testified against them to get them to come back to your instruction, but they themselves asserted themselves and didn't listen to your orders. They did wrong by your rulings, which a person should act on and live by. They presented a defiant shoulder, they toughened their neck and they didn't listen.

³⁰You prolonged things for them for many years and testified against them by your spirit by means of your prophets, but they didn't give ear, so you gave them into the hand of the peoples of the countries. ³¹But in your great compassion you didn't make an end of them and you didn't abandon them, because you are a God gracious and compassionate.

³²So now, our great God, strong and awe-inspiring, keeping pact and commitment, may all the suffering not seem small before you that has found us, our kings, our officials, our priests, our prophets, our ancestors and all your people, from the days of the kings of Ashshur until this day. ³³You are in the right over everything that has come upon us, because you've acted truthfully, but we've acted faithlessly. ³⁴Our kings, our officials, our priests and our ancestors – they didn't act on your instruction and they didn't heed your orders and your affirmations that you

testified against them. ³⁵Despite their kingship and despite your great goodness that you gave them and despite the wide and rich country that you gave before them, they didn't serve you and they didn't turn back from their bad ways.

³⁶Here we are, serfs today. The country you gave our ancestors to eat its fruit and its goodness, here we are, serfs on it. ³⁷Its great yield belongs to the kings that you've put over us because of our wrongdoings. They're ruling over our bodies and among our animals in accordance with what is acceptable to them. We're under great pressure.

Putting your life where your mouth is

³⁸Because of all this, we are confirming a pledge and putting it in writing, and on the sealed document are our officials, our Levites and our priests.'

10

So on the sealed documents are Nehemyah ben Hakalyah, the administrator and

Tsidqiyyah	Meremot
²Serayah	Obadyah
Azaryah	⁶Daniyye'l
Yirmeyah	Ginneton
³Pashhur	Baruk
Amaryah	⁷Meshullam
Malkiyyah	Abiyyah
⁴Hattush	Miyyamin
Shebanyah	⁸Ma'azyah
Malluk	Bilgay
⁵Harim	Shema'yah

These were the priests. ⁹The Levites:

Yeshua ben Azanyah, Binnuy of the sons of Henadad, Qadmi'el; ¹⁰their brothers Shebanyah, Hodiyyah, Qelita, Pela'yah, Hanan, ¹¹Mika, Rehob, Hashabyah, ¹²Zakkur, Sherebyah, Shebanyah, ¹³Hodiyyah, Bani, Beninu.

¹⁴The heads of the people:

Par'osh	Bani
Pahat Mo'ab	¹⁵Bunni
Elam	Azgad
Zattu	Bebay
¹⁶Adoniyyah	²²Pelatyah
Bigvay	Hanan
Adin	Anayah
¹⁷Ater	²³Hoshea
Hizqiyyah	Hananyah
Azzur	Hashshub
¹⁸Hodiyyah	²⁴Hallohesh
Hashum	Pilha
Betsay	Shobeq
¹⁹Hariph	²⁵Rehum
Anatot	Hashabnah
Nebay	Ma'aseyah
²⁰Magpi'ash	²⁶and Ahiyyah
Meshullam	Hanan
Hezir	Anan
²¹Meshezab'el	²⁷Malluk
Tsadoq	Harim
Yaddua	Ba'anah

²⁸The remainder of the people, the priests, the Levites, the gatemen, the singers, the assistants and everyone who made themselves distinct from the peoples of the countries to God's instruction, their wives, their sons and their daughters, everyone who knows, having understanding, ²⁹were taking strong hold of their brothers, the august ones among them, and coming into a curse and into an oath to walk by God's instruction that was given by means of Mosheh, God's servant, and to keep and act on all the orders of Yahweh our Lord, and his rulings and his decrees.

On being specific

³⁰Namely:

We will not give our daughters to the peoples of the country and we will not take their daughters for our sons.

³¹The peoples of the country who bring items of merchandise or any grain on the sabbath day to sell, we will not get from them on the sabbath, or on a sacred day.

We will leave alone the seventh year and the loan linked to any pledge.

³²We have put in place for ourselves orders to impose on ourselves one third of a sheqel per year for the service of our God's house, ³³for the bread in the row, the regular grain offering and for the regular burnt offering, that of the sabbaths, of the

new months, for the appointed occasions, for sacred things and for purification offerings to make expiation for Yisra'el, and all the work in our God's house. ³⁴We have let lots fall for the wood offering (the priests, the Levites and the people) to bring it to our God's house by ancestral households at designated times year by year to burn up on the altar of Yahweh our God, as it is written in the instruction. ³⁵And to bring the first fruits of our ground and the first fruits of every fruit of every tree year by year for Yahweh's house, ³⁶and the firstborn of our sons and of our animals, as it is written in the instruction, and to bring the firstborn of our cattle and of our flocks to our God's house to the priests who minister in our God's house. ³⁷We will bring the first of our dough, our contributions, and the fruit of every tree, new wine and fresh oil, to the priests to the halls in our God's house, and the tenth of our ground to the Levites; the Levites are the ones who collect the tenths in all the towns where we serve. ³⁸The priest, the son of Aaron, is to be with the Levites during the tenthing by the Levites, and the Levites are to take up a tenth of the tenth to our God's house, to the halls of the treasure-house, ³⁹because the Yisra'elites and the Levites are to bring to the halls the contribution of grain, new wine and fresh oil. The sanctuary articles, the priests who minister, the gatemen and the singers are there. We will not abandon our God's house.

The sacred town (1)

11 The people's officials lived in Yerushalaim, while the remainder of the people let lots fall to get one out of ten to come to live in Yerushalaim, the sacred town, while nine tenths were in the towns. ²The people blessed all the individuals who decided freely to live in Yerushalaim.

³These are the heads of the province who lived in Yerushalaim; while in the towns of Yehudah people lived in their towns, each individual on his holding, Yisra'el, the priests, the Levites, the assistants and the descendants of Shelomoh's servants, ⁴and some of the Yehudahites and some of the Binyaminites [Benjaminites] lived in Yerushalaim.

Of the Yehudahites:
Atayah ben Uzziyyah son of Zekaryah son of Amaryah son of Shephatyah son of Mahalal'el of the descendants of Perets; ⁵and Ma'aseyah ben Baruk son of Kol-hozeh son of Hazayah son of Adayah son of Yoyarib son of Zekaryah son of the Shilonite.
⁶All the descendants of Perets who were living in Yerushalaim: 468 forceful men.
⁷These are the Binyaminites:
Sallu ben Meshullam son of Yo'ed son of Pedayah son of Qolayah son of Ma'aseyah son of Iti'el son of Yesha'yah;
⁸and after him Gabbay, Sallay: 928.
⁹Yo'el ben Zikri was appointee in charge of them;
and Yehudah ben Hassenu'ah was second-in-command over the town.
¹⁰Of the priests:
Yeda'yah ben Yoyarib, Yakin, ¹¹Serayah ben Hilqiyyah son of Meshullam son of Tsadoq son of Merayot son of Ahitub, chief over God's house, ¹²and their brothers doing the work for the house: 822;
Adayah ben Yeroham son of Pelalyah son of Amtsi son of Zekaryah son of Pashhur son of Malkiyyah, ¹³and his brothers, ancestral heads: 242;
and Amashsay ben Azar'el son of Ahzai son of Meshillemot son of Immer, ¹⁴and their brothers, forceful strong men: 128; Zabdi'el ben Haggedolim was appointee in charge of them.

The sacred town (2)

¹⁵Of the Levites:
Shema'yah ben Hashshub, son of Azriqam son of Hashabyah son of Bunni;
¹⁶and Shabbetay and Yozabad in charge of the outside work for God's house, of the heads of the Levites;
¹⁷Mattanyah ben Mikah son of Zabdi son of Asaph, head; at prayer, the one who began the confession;
Baqbuqyah, second-in-command, one of his brothers;

and Abda ben Shammua son of Galal son of Yedutun. ¹⁸All the Levites in the sacred town: 284. ¹⁹The gatemen:

Aqqub, Talmon and their brothers who watched at the gateways: 172.

²⁰The remainder of Yisra'el, the priests, the Levites in all the towns of Yehudah, each on his property.

²¹The assistants were living on the Ophel; Tsipha and Gishpa were in charge of the assistants.

²²The Levites' appointee in Yerushalaim was Uzzi ben Bani son of Hashabyah son of Mattanyah son of Mika, of the Asaphite singers, in charge of the work in God's house, ²³because there was an order from the king concerning them, a pledge about the singers, each day's requirement in its day. ²⁴Petahyah ben Meshezab'el, of the descendants of Zerah son of Yehudah, was at the king's hand in connection with everything regarding the people.

²⁵As for the villages, with their fields: some of the Yehudahites lived in Arba's Township and its daughter-towns, in Dibon and its daughter-towns, and in Yeqabtse'el and its villages, ²⁶in Yeshua, in Moladah, in Bet Pelet, ²⁷in Hatsar Shu'al, in Be'er Sheba and its daughter-towns, ²⁸in Tsiqlag, in Mekonah and its daughter-towns, ²⁹in En Rimmon, in Tsorah, in Yarmut, ³⁰Zanoah, Adullam and their villages, Lakish and its fields, and Azeqah and its daughter-towns. So they camped from Be'er-sheba to the Hinnom Ravine.

³¹The Binyaminites:

from Geba, Mikmash, Ayyah, and Bet-el and its daughter-towns; ³²Anatot, Nob, Ananyah, ³³Hatsor, Ramah, Gittayim, ³⁴Hadid, Tsebo'im, Neballat, ³⁵Lod and Ono, Craftsmen's Ravine. ³⁶Some of the Levites who were Yehudah's allocations belonged to Binyamin.

Priests and Levites in the community

12 These are the priests and the Levites who went up with Zerubbabel ben She'alti'el and Yeshua:

Serayah
Yirmeyah
Ezra
²Amaryah
Malluka
Hattush
³Shekanyah
Rehum
Meramot
⁴Iddo
Ginnetoy

Abiyyah
⁵Miyyamin
Ma'adyah
Bilgah
⁶Shema'yah
Yoyarib
Yeda'yah
⁷Sallu
Amoq
Hilqiyyah
Yeda'yah

These were the heads of the priests and their brothers in the time of Yeshua. ⁸The Levites:

Yeshua, Binnuy, Qadmi'el, Sherebyah, and Yehudah;

Mattanyah, in charge of confession songs, he and his brothers;

⁹Baqbuqyah and Unni, their brothers, were opposite them for the watches.

¹⁰Yeshua fathered Yoyaqim, Yoyaqim fathered Elyashib, Elyashib fathered Yoyada, ¹¹Yoyada fathered Yonatan, Yonatan fathered Yaddua.

¹²In the time of Yoyaqim, priests who were the ancestral heads were:

for Serayah, Merayah
for Yirmeyah, Hananyah
¹³for Ezra, Meshullam
for Amaryah, Yehohanan
¹⁴for Meliku, Yonatan
for Shebanyah, Yoseph
¹⁵for Harim, Adna
for Merayot, Helqay
¹⁶for Iddo, Zekaryah
for Ginneton, Meshullam

¹⁷for Abiyyah, Zikri
for Minyamin
for Mo'adyah, Piltay
¹⁸for Bilgah, Shammua
for Shema'yah, Yehonatan
¹⁹and for Yoyarib, Mattenay
for Yeda'yah, Uzzi
²⁰for Sallay, Qallay
for Amoq, Eber
²¹for Hilqiyyah, Hashabyah
for Yeda'yah, Netan'el

²²The Levites in the time of Elyashib, Yoyada and Yohanan, and Yaddua, written down as ancestral heads (and the priests in the reign of Doryavesh the Parsite); ²³the Levites as ancestral heads written down on the document about things of the time right up to the time of Yohanan ben Elyashib; ²⁴so the Levites' heads: Hashabyah, Sherebyah, Yeshua ben Qadmi'el and their brothers opposite them, for

praising, for confessing, by the order of David the supernatural man, watch responding to watch; ²⁵Mattanyah, Baqbuqyah, Obadyah, Meshullam, Talmon, Aqqub, keeping watch as gatemen at the storerooms by the gateways. ²⁶These were in the time of Yoyaqim ben Yeshua son of Yotsadaq, and in the time of Nehemyah the governor and Ezra the priest-scholar.

Dedication choirs

²⁷At the dedication of the Yerushalaim wall, they looked for the Levites from all their places to get them to come to Yerushalaim to make a dedication with rejoicing, with confessions and with song, cymbals, mandolins and with guitars. ²⁸The singers gathered both from the plain round Yerushalaim and from the villages of the Netophatites, ²⁹from Bet Hagilgal, and from the fields of Geba and Azmavet, because the singers had built themselves villages round Yerushalaim. ³⁰The priests and the Levites purified themselves and purified the people, the gateways and the wall.

³¹I got the officials of Yehudah to go up on to the wall and I put in place two big confessions and processions:

> To the right on the wall to the Rubbish Gate. ³²Hosha'yah and half the officials of Yehudah followed them, ³³with Azaryah, Ezra and Meshullam, ³⁴Yehudah, Binyamin, Shema'yah, Yirmeyah, ³⁵some of the priests' sons with trumpets, Zekaryah ben Yonatan son of Shema'yah son of Mattanyah son of Mikayah son of Zakkur son of Asaph, ³⁶his brothers Shema'yah and Azar'el, Milalay, Gilalay, Ma'ay, Netan'el, Yehudah, Hanani, with the musical instruments of David the supernatural man, and Ezra the scholar before them. ³⁷Above the Spring Gate, straight ahead of them they went up the ascent to David's Town by the ascent to the wall, above David's house, and as far as the Water Gate on the east.
> ³⁸The second confession which went the opposite way with me behind it and half

the people, on the wall above the Ovens Tower as far as the wide wall, ³⁹and above the Ephrayim Gate, by the Yeshanah Gate, by the Fish Gate, Hananel's Tower, the Hundred Tower and as far as the Sheep Gate. They halted at the Guard Gate.

⁴⁰The two confessions halted at God's house, as did I and half the overseers with me, ⁴¹and the priests Elyaqim, Ma'aseyah, Minyamin, Mikayah, Elyo'enay, Zekaryah, Hananyah, with trumpets, ⁴²and Ma'aseyah, Shema'yah, El'azar, Uzzi, Yehohanan, Malkiyyah, Elam and Ezer. The singers made themselves heard, with Yizrahyah the appointee. ⁴³They made big sacrifices that day and rejoiced, because God had enabled them to rejoice greatly. The women and the children also rejoiced. The rejoicing in Yerushalaim was heard from afar.

Intermarriage again

⁴⁴On that day they appointed people over the treasury rooms for the contributions, for first fruits and for the tenths, to collect in them (for the fields belonging to the towns) the portions mentioned by the instruction for the priests and for the Levites, because there was rejoicing in Yehudah over the priests and over the Levites who stood ⁴⁵and kept their God's watch and the purity watch, and the singers and the gatemen, in accordance with the order of David, Shelomoh his son ⁴⁶(because in the days of David and Asaph of old, there were heads of the singers and a song of praise and confession to God). ⁴⁷In the days of Zerubbabel and in the days of Nehemyah all Yisra'el were giving the singers and the gatemen's portions, each day's requirement in its day, and making things sacred for the Levites, while the Levites were making things sacred for the Aaronites.

13 On that day there was a reading out in Mosheh's document in the ears of the people and it was found written in it that an Ammonite or Mo'abite should not come into God's congregation, permanently, ²because they did not meet the Yisra'elites with bread and with water but hired Bil'am [Balaam] to slight them (but our God turned the slighting into blessing). ³When they heard the instruction, they distinguished the entire mixed crowd from Yisra'el.

⁴Before this, Elyashib the priest had been put in a hall in our God's house. Being near to Tobiyyah, ⁵he had made for him a big hall where before they had been putting the grain offering, the incense, the articles, the tenth of grain, new wine and fresh oil, the order for the Levites, the singers and the gatemen, and the contribution for the priests.

More frustrations

⁶During all this time I was not in Yerushalaim because in the thirty-second year of Artahshasta king of Babel I came to the king, but at the end of a period of time I asked of the king ⁷and came to Yerushalaim. I considered the bad thing that Elyashib had done for Tobiyyah in making a room for him in the courtyards of God's house. ⁸It seemed very bad to me. I threw all the articles of Tobiyyah's household outside from the hall ⁹and said they should purify the halls, and I put back there the articles from God's house, the grain offering and the incense.

¹⁰I got to know that the Levites' portions had not been given, so that the Levites and the singers doing the work had taken flight each to his field. ¹¹I argued with the overseers and said, 'Why has God's house been abandoned?' I collected them and put them in place at their position, ¹²and all Yehudah brought the tenth of the grain, the new wine and the fresh oil into the treasuries. ¹³I made as treasurers in charge of the treasuries Shelemyah the priest, Tsadoq the secretary, Pedayah from the Levites, and next to them Hanan ben Zakkur son of Mattanyah, because they were reckoned trustworthy, and it was up to them to make allocations to their brothers.

¹⁴Be mindful of me, my God, because of this. Don't blot out my acts of commitment, which I have performed in God's house and in its duties.

¹⁵In those days I saw people in Yehudah treading winepresses on the sabbath, and bringing grain heaps and stacking them on donkeys, and also wine, grapes, figs and every load, and bringing them into Yerushalaim on the sabbath day. I testified on the day when they sold provisions ¹⁶and when the Tsorites who lived there were bringing fish and all merchandise and selling on the sabbath to Yehudahites and in Yerushalaim, ¹⁷and I argued with the important people in Yehudah: 'What is this bad thing that you're doing, and profaning the sabbath day? ¹⁸Our ancestors acted like this, didn't they, and our God brought on us all this bad fortune, and on this town. You're bringing more rage against Yisra'el by profaning the sabbath.'

Desecration and trespass

¹⁹When the gateways of Yerushalaim grew dark before the sabbath, I said that the doors should shut, and I said that they should not open them until after the sabbath. Given that I put in place some of my boys at the gateways, no load would come in on the sabbath day. ²⁰The merchants and the people selling all merchandise stayed the night outside Yerushalaim once or twice, ²¹but I testified against them: 'Why are you staying the night opposite the wall? If you do it again, I'll lay hands on you'; from that time they didn't come on the sabbath. ²²I said to the Levites that they should purify themselves and come keep watch over the gateways to make the sabbath day sacred.

Be mindful of this for me as well, my God, and have pity on me in accordance with the abundance of your commitment.

²³In those days I also saw the Yehudahites had got Ashdodite, Ammonite and Mo'abite women to come to live. ²⁴Their children were speaking half in Ashdodite, and none of them knew how to speak Yehudahite, but in accordance with the tongue of one people or the other. ²⁵I argued with them and slighted them, and struck some of them down and pulled out their hair, and made them swear by God: 'If you give your daughters to their sons or if you get some of their daughters for your sons or for yourselves . . . ²⁶It was in these things that Shelomoh king of Yisra'el did wrong, wasn't it. Among the many nations there was no king like him. He was loved by God, and God made him king over all Yisra'el; foreign women caused even him to do wrong. ²⁷Are we to listen to you doing this great bad thing, trespassing against our God by getting foreign women come to live?'

⁲⁸One of the sons of Yoyada, the son of Elyashib the big priest, was son-in-law to Sanballat the Horonite. I made him take flight from me. ²⁹Be mindful with regard to them, my God, because they polluted the priesthood, the pact of the priesthood and the Levites.

³⁰I purified them of everything foreign and put the watches in place for the priests and for the Levites, each one in his work, ³¹and for the wood offering at designated times and for the first fruits. My God, be mindful for me for good.

Esther

In the 1930s, the Nazi regime in Germany formulated a 'final solution to the Jewish question' that involved the killing of all the Jews in Germany and in the areas of Europe it controlled. The book of Esther tells the story of the first great attempt at such a 'final solution' formulated by a Persian state official, Haman, in the fifth century BC. It is the same period as Ezra and Nehemiah and another reminder that by no means did all Judahites return to Jerusalem after the exile.

Haman's plan is frustrated as a result of some coincidences and some brave acceptance of responsibility by a young woman called Hadassah whose Persian name was Esther. As it happens, the king has dismissed his queen because she wouldn't be put on display at a party; and as it happens, Esther wins a beauty contest and becomes the next queen. She is therefore in a position to get the king to reverse his decision to have Haman's plan implemented and to give the Judahites permission to kill any Persians who are foolish enough to attack them anyway (which a large number are).

The story is full of irony, humour and exaggeration, such as the twelve-month beauty preparation and Haman's twenty-five-metre-high gallows on which he ends up being hanged himself. It makes no reference to God or prayer or the Torah and it thus puts the emphasis on Judahites taking responsibility for their destiny and on coincidences. It therefore both contrasts with and compares with the exodus story. It testifies to God's involvement in ensuring that his people are preserved, but it keeps that involvement operative behind the scenes – in the way we usually experience it.

The woman who won't play ball

1 In the days of Ahashverosh [Xerxes], that Ahashverosh who reigned from Hoddu [India] as far as Kush [Sudan] over 127 provinces – ²in those days, when King Ahashverosh sat on his royal throne which was in the Shushan fortress, ³in the third year of his reign, he made a banquet for all his officials and his servants. The force of Paras and Maday [Persia and Media], the nobles and the officials of the provinces were before him, ⁴while he let them see the wealth of his royal splendour and the glorious dignity of his greatness for many days – 180 days.

⁵At the fulfilment of these days the king made a banquet for the entire people to be found in the Shushan fortress, great to small, for seven days, in the courtyard of the king's palace garden:

⁶white cloth, cotton and blue cloth, held by bands of fine linen and purple to silver rods and alabaster pillars;
couches of gold and silver on a pavement of porphyry, alabaster, marble and mosaic;
⁷giving of drinks in gold vessels (vessels differing from one another);
much royal wine in accordance with the king's liberality;
⁸drinking in accordance with the rule 'There's no one restraining', because the king had laid it down in this way with every senior person in his household, to act in accordance with what was acceptable, individual by individual.

⁹Queen Vashti also made a women's banquet at the royal house of King Ahashverosh.

¹⁰On the seventh day, when the king was in good heart because of the wine, he said to Mehuman, Bizzeta, Harbona, Bigta, Abagta, Zetar and Karkas, the seven eunuchs who ministered to the presence of King Ahashverosh, ¹¹to get Vashti the queen to come before the king in her royal diadem, to let the peoples and the officials see her beauty, because she was good-looking. ¹²ᵃQueen Vashti refused to come at the king's word by means of the eunuchs.

The men who are afraid

¹²ᵇThe king was quite furious. His wrath burned up in him. ¹³The king said to the experts who knew the times (because this was the thing with the king in relation to all the people who knew law and judgement; ¹⁴near to him were Karshena, Shetar, Admata, Tarshish, Meres, Marsena and Memukan, the seven officials of Paras and Maday who could see the king and sat in first place in the realm), ¹⁵'According to law, what should be done with Queen Vashti because she has not acted on the word of King Ahashverosh by means of the eunuchs?'

¹⁶Memukan said before the king and the officials, 'It's not against the king alone that Vashti the queen has gone astray, but against all the officials and against all the peoples that are in all King Ahashverosh's provinces. ¹⁷Because the thing about the queen will get out to all the women, so as to make them despise their masters in their eyes, when they say, "King Ahashverosh said to get Vashti the queen to come before him, and she didn't come." ¹⁸This day the leading women of Paras and Maday who have heard the thing about the queen will say it to all the king's officials, with quite enough despising and fury.

¹⁹If it seems good to Your Majesty, a royal word should issue from his presence and it should be written in the laws of Paras and Maday, and not pass away, that Vashti will not come before King Ahashverosh. The king should give her royal position to another woman who is better than her. ²⁰The king's proclamation that he makes will make itself heard in all his realm (because it's great), and all the women will give dignity to their masters, great to small.'

²¹The thing seemed good in the eyes of the king and the officials, and the king acted in accordance with Memukan's word. ²²He sent documents to all the king's provinces, to each province in accordance with its script and to each people in accordance with its language, for every man to be ruling in his household and to be speaking in accordance with the language of his own people.

The beauty contest

2 Subsequently, when King Ahashverosh's wrath had subsided, he was mindful of Vashti and what she had done and what had been determined against her. ²The king's boys ministering to him said, 'They should seek for the king young, good-looking girls. ³The king should appoint people in all the provinces of his realm so they can collect every young, good-looking girl to the Shushan fortress, to the women's household, into the control of Hege, the king's eunuch who keeps watch over the women, and their cleansing treatments should be given them. ⁴The girl who seems good in the king's eyes should reign in place of Vashti.' The thing seemed good in the king's eyes, and he did so.

⁵Now there was a Yehudahite [Judahite] man in the Shushan fortress named Mordokay ben Ya'ir son of Shim'i son of Qish, a Binyaminite [Benjaminite], ⁶who had been taken into exile from Yerushalaim with the group of exiles that had been exiled with Yekonyah [Jehoiachin] king of Yehudah, which Nebukadne'tstsar king of Babel took into exile. ⁷He was guardian of Hadassah (i.e. Esther), his uncle's daughter, because she had no father or mother. The girl was lovely of figure and good-looking. When her father and mother died, Mordokay took her as a daughter to him.

⁸When the king's word, his law, made itself heard and many girls collected to the Shushan fortress into the control of Hegay, Esther was taken into the king's household into the control of Hegay, who kept watch over the women. ⁹The girl seemed good in his eyes and she gained commitment before him. He hastened to give to her her cleansing treatments and her portions, and the seven girls who had been looked out to give to her from the king's household. He changed her and her girls to the best part of the women's household. ¹⁰Esther did not tell of her people or her family, because Mordokay had ordered her not to tell of it.

The girl who pays a price

¹¹Each and every day Mordokay used to walk about before the courtyard of the women's household so as to know about Esther's welfare and what was being done with her.

¹²When a turn arrived, girl by girl, for coming to King Ahashverosh, at the end of things happening to her in accordance with the law for the women, for twelve months (because their cleansing days were fulfilled like this, six months with oil of myrrh and six months with perfumes and women's cleansing treatments), ¹³in this way the girl came to the king: everything that she would say would be given her, so as to come with her from the women's household to the king's household. ¹⁴Whereas she came in the evening, in the morning she went back to the second women's household, into the control of Sha'ashgaz, the king's eunuch who kept watch over the secondary wives. She would not come again to the king unless the king wanted her and she was called for by name.

¹⁵When the turn arrived for Esther bat Abihayil (uncle of Mordokay, who had taken her as daughter to him) to come to the king, she did not seek anything except what Hegay the king's eunuch who kept watch over the women said. Esther would gain grace in the eyes of everyone who saw her.

¹⁶Esther was taken to King Ahashverosh in his royal household in the tenth month (i.e. the month of Tebet) in the seventh year of his reign. ¹⁷The king liked Esther more than all the women and she gained grace and commitment before him more than all the young girls, and he put a royal diadem on her head and made her queen in place of Vashti. ¹⁸The king made a great banquet for all his officials and his servants, 'Esther's Banquet'. He made a holiday for the provinces and gave gifts in accordance with the capacity of the king.

Amaleq *redivivus*

¹⁹When the young girls collected a second time, Mordokay was sitting at the king's gateway. ²⁰Esther had not told of her family or her people, as Mordokay had ordered her; Esther did as Mordokay said, as when she was in guardianship with him.

²¹During that time, when Mordokay was sitting at the king's gateway, Bigtan and Teresh, two of the king's eunuchs who kept watch over the threshold, became furious and sought to lay hand on King Ahashverosh. ²²The thing became known to Mordokay, he told Esther the queen, and Esther told the king in Mordokay's name. ²³The thing was enquired into and found to be so, and the two of them were hanged on

a pole. It was written in the document about things of the time, before the king.

3 Subsequently, King Ahashverosh promoted Haman ben Hammedata the Agagite. He elevated him and put his seat above all the officials who were with him. ²All the king's servants who were at the king's gateway would kneel and bow low to Haman, because the king had ordered this regarding him. But Mordokay didn't kneel and didn't bow low. ³The king's servants who were at the king's gateway said to Mordokay, 'Why are you transgressing the king's order?' ⁴But when they said it to him day by day, he didn't listen to them.

They told Haman, to see whether Mordokay's words would stand, because he had told them that he was a Yehudahite. ⁵Haman saw that Mordokay was not kneeling or bowing low to him, and Haman filled with wrath, ⁶but in his eyes he despised laying hand on Mordokay alone, because they had told him Mordokay's people, and Haman sought to annihilate all the Yehudahites who were in Ahashverosh's entire kingdom – Mordokay's people.

The lottery that meant death

⁷In the first month (i.e. the month of Nisan) in King Ahashverosh's twelfth year, they made *pur* (i.e. the lot) fall before Haman, from day to day and from month to month: [it fell on] the twelfth (i.e. the month of Adar). ⁸Haman said to King Ahashverosh, 'There is a people, spread about and divided among the peoples in all the provinces in your kingdom, and their laws are different from every people. They don't act on the king's laws, and it's not advantageous for the king to let them be. ⁹If it seems good to Your Majesty, it should be written down to obliterate them. I will weigh out 10,000 talents of silver into the hands of those who do the work, to bring into the king's treasuries.'

¹⁰The king removed his ring from on his hand and gave it to Haman ben Hammedata the Agagite, the Yehudahites' adversary. ¹¹The king said to Haman, 'The silver is given to you, and the people, to do with it as seems good in your eyes.'

¹²So the king's secretaries were called for in the first month, on the thirteenth day of it, and it was written down in accordance with all that Haman had ordered, to the king's satraps and to the governors who were over each and every province and to the officials people by people, province by province, in accordance with its script, and people by people in accordance with its language, written in the name of King Ahashverosh and sealed with the king's ring. ¹³Documents were sent by means of the runners to all the king's provinces regarding annihilating, killing and eliminating all the Yehudahites, from young to old, little ones and women, on one day, on the thirteenth of the twelfth month (i.e. Adar), and for despoiling them as plunder. ¹⁴A copy of the document was to be given out as a law in each and every province, shown to all the peoples so that they would be ready for this day.

¹⁵The runners went out, driven by the king's word, and the law was given out in the Shushan fortress. While the king and Haman sat down to a banquet, the town of Shushan was perplexed.

The risk that needs taking

4 When Mordokay got to know of all that had been done, Mordokay tore his clothes and put on sack and earth. He went out into the middle of the town and cried out with a loud and bitter cry. ²He came as far as before the king's gateway, because there was no coming into the king's gateway in sack clothing. ³In each and every province, the place where the king's word and his law arrived, there was great mourning on the part of the Yehudahites, fasting, weeping and lamenting; sack and earth were laid down for most people.

⁴Esther's girls and her eunuchs came and told her, and the queen went all-a-tremble. She sent Mordokay clothes to put on so he could remove the sack from on him, but he didn't accept them. ⁵Esther called for Hatak, one of the king's eunuchs whom he had put in place before her, and ordered him to Mordokay to get to know what this was and why this was happening.

⁶Hatak went out to Mordokay in the town square which was before the king's gateway ⁷and Mordokay told him everything that had happened to him and the details about the silver that Haman said he would weigh out to the king's treasuries for the Yehudahites, to

obliterate them. ⁸He gave him a copy of the document containing the law that had been given out in Shushan for their annihilation, to let Esther see and to tell her, and to order her to come to the king and seek grace with him and enquire before him concerning her people.

⁹Hatak came and told Esther Mordokay's words, ¹⁰but Esther said to Hatak and ordered him to Mordokay, ¹¹'All the king's servants and the people of the king's provinces know that any man or woman who comes to the king in the inner courtyard who has not been called for – he has one law, to put them to death, unless the king extends to him the gold sceptre, and he lives. And I haven't been called for to come to the king these thirty days.'

The possibility of a non-miraculous miracle

¹²They told Mordokay Esther's words, ¹³and Mordokay said to take back word to Esther: 'Don't imagine within yourself that you'll escape in the king's household better than all the Yehudahites, ¹⁴because if you stay quite silent at this time, relief and rescue will arise for the Yehudahites from a place, but you and your father's household will perish. Who knows if it was for a time like this that you arrived at the royal position?'

¹⁵Esther said to take back word to Mordokay: ¹⁶'Go assemble all the Yehudahites to be found in Shushan and fast for me. Don't eat or drink for three days, night or day. I, too, will fast with my girls in this way, and in this way I'll come to the king, which is not in accordance with the law. And as I perish, I perish.' ¹⁷Mordokay passed it on and acted in accordance with everything that Esther ordered him.

5 On the third day, Esther put on royal dress and stood in the inner courtyard of the king's house, opposite the king's house, while the king was sitting on his royal throne in the royal house opposite the entrance to the house. ²When the king saw Esther the queen standing in the courtyard, she gained grace in his eyes. The king extended to Esther the gold sceptre that was in his hand and Esther drew near and touched the head of the sceptre.

³The king said to her, 'What do you have, Esther, queen? What's your request? Up to half the kingdom, it will be given you.' ⁴Esther said, 'If it seems good to the king, may the king and Haman come today to the banquet that I have made for him.' ⁵The king said, 'Hurry Haman to act on Esther's word.' So the king and Haman came to the banquet that Esther had made.

The girl who knows how to work her man

⁶The king said to Esther at the wine banquet, 'What's your petition? It will be given you. What's your request? Up to half the kingdom, it will be done.' ⁷Esther answered, 'My petition, my request: ⁸if I have found grace in the king's eyes and if it seems good to the king to grant my petition, to act on my request, may the king and Haman come to the banquet that I will make for them, and tomorrow I will act in accordance with the king's word.'

⁹Haman went out that day rejoicing and good-hearted, but when Haman saw Mordokay at the king's gateway and he didn't get up and didn't tremble because of him, Haman filled with wrath at Mordokay. ¹⁰But Haman controlled himself and came to his house. He sent and got his friends and Zeresh his wife to come. ¹¹Haman recounted to them the splendour of his wealth and the large number of his sons and all the way that the king had promoted him and that he had elevated him above the officials and the king's servants. ¹²And Haman said, 'Indeed, Esther the queen did not get anyone to come to the banquet with the king that she made, except me. Tomorrow, too, I am called to her with the king. ¹³But all this does not seem advantageous to me every time that I see Mordokay the Yehudahite sitting at the king's gateway.'

¹⁴Zeresh his wife with all his friends said to him, 'They should make a pole twenty-five metres high, and in the morning you should say to the king that they should hang Mordokay on it; and go with the king to the banquet rejoicing.' The thing seemed good to Haman and he made the pole.

6 That night the king's sleep took flight and he said to bring the records document (the things about the time). They were being read out before the king ²and it was found written that Mordokay had told of Bigtana and Teresh, two of the king's eunuchs among the guards of the threshold, who had sought to lay a hand on King Ahashverosh. ³The king said, 'What dignity or promotion was done for Mordokay for this?' The king's boys, his ministers, said, 'Nothing was done with him.'

Haman comes unstuck

⁴The king said, 'Who's in the courtyard?' Now Haman had come into the outer courtyard of the king's house to say to the king to hang Mordokay on the pole that he had prepared for him. ⁵The king's boys said to him, 'There's Haman standing in the courtyard.' The king said, 'He's to come in.' ⁶Haman came in, and the king said to him, 'What's to do with a man whose dignity the king wants?' Haman said to himself, 'For whom would the king want dignity more than me?'

⁷So Haman said to the king, 'A man whose dignity the king wants: ⁸they should bring royal apparel that the king has worn and a horse on which the king has ridden and on whose head a royal diadem has been put, ⁹and put the apparel and the horse into the hand of one of the king's noble officials. They should clothe the man whose dignity the king wants, have him ride on the horse through the town square and call out before him, 'This is what is done for the man whose dignity the king wants!'

¹⁰The king said to Haman, 'Hurry, get the apparel and the horse, as you've spoken, and do that for Mordokay the Yehudahite, who sits in the king's gateway. No word of all that you have spoken should fall.' ¹¹Haman got the apparel and the horse, clothed Mordokay, had him ride through the town square and called out before him, 'This is what is done for the man whose dignity the king wants.'

¹²Mordokay went back to the king's gateway while Haman hastened to his house, mourning and head covered. ¹³Haman recounted to Zeresh his wife and to all his friends everything that had happened to him. His smart people and Zeresh his wife said to him, 'If Mordokay, before whom you have begun to fall, is of Yehudahite origin, you will not overcome him, because you will surely fall before him.'

Fates reversed

¹⁴While they were still speaking with him, the king's eunuchs arrived and hastened to bring Haman to the banquet that Esther had made.

7 So the king and Haman came to drink with Esther the queen, ²and the king said to Esther again on the second day at the wine banquet, 'What's your petition, Queen Esther? It will be given you. What's your request, up to half the kingdom? It will be done.' ³Esther answered, 'If I've found grace in your eyes, Your Majesty, and if it seems good to Your Majesty, may my life be given me as my petition, and my people as my request, ⁴because I and my people have been sold for annihilating, killing and obliterating. Had we been sold as servants and as maidservants, I would have kept silent, because the adversity would not be commensurate to the damage to the king.'

⁵King Ahashverosh said – he said to Esther the queen, 'Who's this? Where's this man who is so full of himself to act like this?' ⁶Esther said, 'The man who's an adversary and an enemy is this bad man Haman.' As Haman was terrified before the king and the queen, ⁷in his wrath the king set off from the wine banquet for the palace garden, while Haman stayed to seek for his life with Esther the queen, because he saw that a bad fate was certain for him from the king.

⁸When the king came back from the palace garden into the wine banquet house, Haman was falling on the couch where Esther was. The king said, 'Is he also to violate the queen with me, in the house?' As the word went out from the king's mouth, they covered Haman's face. ⁹Harbonah, one of the eunuchs before the king, said, 'In addition, there's the pole that Haman made for Mordokay, who spoke something good for the king, standing in Haman's house, twenty-five metres high.' The king said, 'Hang him on it.'

The right to self-defence

¹⁰So they hanged Haman on the pole that he had set up for Mordokay, and the king's wrath subsided.

8 That day King Ahashverosh gave over the household of Haman, the Yehudahites' adversary, to Esther the queen, while Mordokay came before the king because Esther had told of what he was to her. ²The king removed his ring, which he had taken away from Haman, and gave it to Mordokay, and Esther put Mordokay in charge of Haman's household.

³Esther again spoke before the king, and fell before his feet and cried. She sought grace from him to take away the bad action of Haman the Agagite, the intention that he had thought up against the Yehudahites. ⁴The king extended to Esther the gold sceptre and Esther got up and stood before the king. ⁵She said, 'If it seems good to the king, if I have found grace before him, if the thing seems proper before the king and I seem good in his eyes, may things be written to turn back the documents, the intention of Haman ben Hammedata the Agagite, which he wrote so as to obliterate the Yehudahites who are in all the king's provinces, ⁶because how can I look upon the bad fate that will befall my people? How can I look upon my family's obliteration?'

⁷King Ahashverosh said to Esther the queen and to Mordokay the Yehudahite, 'Here, I have given Esther the household of Haman and they have hanged him on the pole because he put out his hand against the Yehudahites. ⁸You yourselves – write as it seems good in your eyes concerning the Yehudahites in the king's name and seal it with the king's ring' (because a document that's been written in the king's name and sealed with the king's ring can't be turned back).

Rejoicing with relief

⁹So the king's secretaries were called at that time, in the third month (i.e. the month of Sivan) on the twenty-third of it, and it was written in accordance with all that Mordokay ordered, to the Yehudahites and to the satraps, the governors and the officials of the provinces that are from Hoddu as far as Kush, 127 provinces, province by province in accordance with its script, and people by people in accordance with its language, and to the Yehudahites in accordance with their script and in accordance with their language.

¹⁰He wrote in King Ahashverosh's name, sealed it with the king's seal, and sent documents by the hand of the runners on horses, riding royal relay steeds, the offspring of racehorses, ¹¹that the king permitted the Yehudahites who were in each and every town to congregate and stand up for themselves, so as to annihilate, to kill and to obliterate the entire force of a people or province attacking them, little ones and women, and to plunder their spoil ¹²on one day, in all King Ahashverosh's provinces, on the thirteenth of the twelfth month (i.e. the month of Adar), ¹³a copy of the document to be given out as a law in each and every province, shown to all the peoples, so that the Yehudahites would be ready for this day to take redress from their enemies. ¹⁴The runners went out riding royal relay steeds, hastening and driven by the king's word, and the law was given out in the Shushan fortress.

¹⁵When Mordokay went out from before the king in royal apparel, blue and white, a big gold crown, and a robe of fine linen and purple, the town of Shushan shouted and rejoiced. ¹⁶For the Yehudahites there was light and rejoicing, joy and dignity. ¹⁷In each and every province and in each and every town, in a place where the king's word and his law arrived, there was rejoicing and joy for the Yehudahites, a banquet and a good time. Many of the peoples of the country professed to be Yehudahites, because dread of the Yehudahites had fallen upon them.

The slaughter

9 So in the twelfth month (i.e. the month of Adar), on the thirteenth, the day when the king's word and his law were due to be acted on, on the day when the Yehudahites' enemies expected to be in power over them, that was turned round, so that the Yehudahites – they were in power over the people hostile to them. ²The Yehudahites in their towns in all King Ahashverosh's provinces congregated to lay a hand on people who sought something bad for them, but no one stood up before them, because dread of them had fallen on all the peoples. ³All the king's provincial officials, satraps, governors and people doing work were elevating the Yehudahites, because dread of Mordokay had fallen on them, ⁴because

Mordokay was big in the king's house and report of him was going through all the provinces, because the man Mordokay was getting bigger and bigger.

⁵So the Yehudahites struck down all their adversaries with a stroke of the sword, with killing and obliteration, and acted against the people hostile to them in accordance with what was acceptable to them. ⁶In the Shushan fortress the Yehudahites killed and obliterated 500 people, ⁷and killed Parshandata, Dalphon, Aspata, ⁸Porata, Adalya, Aridata, ⁹Parmashta, Arisay, Ariday and Vayzata, ¹⁰the ten sons of Haman ben Hammedata, the Yehudahites' adversary, but they did not lay their hand on the plunder.

¹¹That day the number of the people killed in the Shushan fortress came before the king, ¹²and the king said to Esther the queen, 'Given that in the Shushan fortress the Yehudahites have slaughtered and obliterated 500 people, and Haman's ten sons, in the remainder of the king's provinces what have they done? But what's your petition? It will be given you. What else is your request? It will be done.' ¹³Esther said, 'If it seems good to the king, may it be given to the Yehudahites who are in Shushan tomorrow also to act in accordance with today's law, and may they hang Haman's ten sons on the pole.' ¹⁴The king said this was to be done, and a law was given out in Shushan and they hanged Haman's ten sons.

The commemoration

¹⁵So the Yehudahites who were in Shushan congregated again on the fourteenth day of the month of Adar and killed 300 people in Shushan, but did not lay their hand on the plunder. ¹⁶The remainder of the Yehudahites, who were in the king's provinces, congregated and stood up for themselves and got relief from their enemies. They killed 75,000 of the people hostile to them, but did not lay their hand on the plunder, ¹⁷on the thirteenth day of the month of Adar. They let be on its fourteenth and made it a day of banquet and rejoicing, ¹⁸while the Yehudahites who were in Shushan congregated on its thirteenth and on its fourteenth, but let be on its fifteenth and made it a day of banquet and rejoicing. ¹⁹That's why the rural Yehudahites, who live in the rural towns, make the fourteenth day of the month of Adar into rejoicing and banquet, a good time and one of sending portions one to his neighbour.

²⁰Mordokay wrote down these things and sent documents to all the Yehudahites who were in all King Ahashverosh's provinces, near and far, ²¹to lay upon them to make the fourteenth day of the month of Adar, and its fifteenth day, each and every year, ²²as the days when the Yehudahites got relief for themselves from their enemies and the month that turned for them from sadness to rejoicing and from grief to a good time – to make them days of banquet and celebration, and sending portions one to his neighbour and gifts to the needy.

²³The Yehudahites accepted what they had begun to do and what Mordokay had written to them, ²⁴because Haman ben Hammedata the Agagite, the adversary of all the Yehudahites, had thought to obliterate the Yehudahites and had caused the *pur* to fall (i.e. the lot) so as to crush them and obliterate them. ²⁵But when it came before the king, he said with the document: his bad intention, which he had thought up against the Yehudahites, should come back on to his own head, and they should hang him and his sons on the pole. ²⁶ᵃOn account of this they called these days Purim, after the word *pur*.

A law that will last

²⁶ᵇOn account of this, on account of all the words in this communiqué and what they had seen – on account of such things and what had come to them, ²⁷the Yehudahites implemented and accepted for themselves and for their offspring and for all who would join them, so that it should not pass away, to make these two days, in accordance with the document about them and in accordance with their time, each and every year, ²⁸these days being commemorated and made in each and every generation, family, province and town. These days of Purim will not pass away from among the Yehudahites, and their commemoration will not cease from their offspring.

²⁹Esther the queen, daughter of Abihayil, and Mordokay the Yehudahite wrote with all

force to implement this second communiqué about Purim. ³⁰He sent documents to all the Yehudahites in the 127 provinces in Ahashverosh's realm, words about well-being and truthfulness, ³¹to implement these days of Purim at their times as Mordokay the Yehudahite and Esther the queen implemented them for themselves, and as they had implemented for themselves and for their offspring words about the fasts and their outcry. ³²Esther's word implemented these statements about Purim and it was written down in the document.

10 King Ahashverosh put a workforce on the country and the shores across the sea. ²All his forceful and strong action, and the detail about the importance of Mordokay which the king conferred on him, are written down on the document with the things of the time regarding the kings of Maday and Paras, aren't they, ³because Mordokay the Yehudahite was second-in-command to King Ahashverosh, important to the Yehudahites and accepted by the large number of his brothers, enquiring after what was good for his people and speaking of well-being for all its offspring.

Job

The book of Job is something like the script for a play – there's no indication that it was performed, but it could have been. The main part of the book is an argument between Job, three of his friends, an angry young man who appears later, and then Yahweh himself, who eventually responds to Job. The framework for the argument is the story of how Job, someone exemplary in his commitment to Yahweh and someone who has done really well in life, loses everything in a series of calamities, and how Yahweh eventually restores him. The argument happens in poetry, which puts us on the track of the fact that this isn't simply the transcript of something that happened, though the basic story line reflects things that happen often enough, and in this sense I imagine it is based on fact.

But the book's point isn't dependent on its being factual. The point about the book is to discuss various approaches to handling the way that people do experience the kind of horrifying tragedy that comes to Job. In this work, discussing the issue doesn't mean trying to explain why people suffer. It's not about the problem of evil, or theodicy, in this sense. It's more about how one lives with an experience like Job's. And it presupposes that the experience of tragedy raises even bigger questions about the very nature of our relationship with God and the basis of that relationship.

Making these questions the basis of an argument between the participants enables the book to look at the questions from different angles. All these angles have some truth to them, though they are not all very relevant to Job.

1. The book's starting point is that there is a relationship of deep mutual commitment between Job and God. But that starting point raises the question whether Job is committed to God because it means God blesses him. The story therefore imagines God agreeing that Job should be tested by taking away his blessings, to see how he reacts; and Job passes the test. So the first insight about the relationship between God and us is that it's based on the free trust and commitment between God and us, not on what we get out of it; and that tragedy can be a means of testing us. (In this introduction to the book, a key role is played by 'The Adversary', who is a member of God's staff whose job it is to make sure that people don't get away with things that they shouldn't get away with. He is a safeguard against God being too soft. In English translations, he is often referred to as Satan, but this is misleading.)
2. The second insight about the relationship is that Job can have an exceptional freedom in expressing his grief, anguish and puzzlement, and in expressing to God his anger, frustration and sense of betrayal (see chapters 3—27).
3. A third insight is expressed time and time again by Job's three friends (interwoven in chapters 3—27), who know that tragedy often issues from our disobedience. The problem is that often it does not. But often it does, so their insight is a real one, though it's irrelevant to Job.
4. The poem about wisdom in Job 28 reminds readers that awe and thus obedience in relation to God is the key to being smart.
5. The insight expressed by the angry young man (chapters 32—37) is that tragedy can be something through which God speaks to you and through which he draws you nearer to himself. It too is a real insight, but not very relevant to Job.
6. When God appears (chapters 38—41) he reminds Job that he is God and Job isn't, and that the world doesn't circulate round Job. If Job thinks he can run the world better than God, he should try. Tragedy drives one to recognize that one must and can trust God and submit to God.
7. The close of the story affirms that in the end God is faithful. The fact that most people's stories don't end as comfortably as Job's makes it all the more important to affirm this truth about God.

The man of integrity

1 There was a man in the country of Uz named Iyyob [Job]. That man was a person of integrity and upright, in awe of God and turning aside from what is bad. ²There had been born to him seven sons and three daughters. ³His acquisitions comprised 7,000 sheep, 3,000 camels, 500 yoke of cattle, 500 she-donkeys and a very large servant body. That man was bigger than all eastern people.

⁴His sons used to make a feast at the house of an individual on his day, and send and call for their three sisters to eat and to drink with them. ⁵When the days of the feast had made their round, Iyyob would send and make them sacred. He would start early in the morning and offer up burnt offerings for the number of them all, because (Iyyob said) 'Perhaps my children have done wrong and "blessed" God inside.' In this way Iyyob would act continually.

⁶There was a day when the divine beings came to take their stand with Yahweh. The adversary, too, came among them. ⁷Yahweh said to the adversary, 'From where do you come?' The adversary answered Yahweh, 'From roaming on the earth and from walking about on it.' ⁸Yahweh said to the adversary, 'Have you applied your mind to my servant Iyyob, because there's no one like him on the earth, a person of integrity and upright, in awe of God and turning aside from what is bad?'

⁹The adversary answered Yahweh, 'Is it for nothing that Iyyob lives in awe of God? ¹⁰Have you yourself not hedged about him and about his household and about everything that he has, all round? You've blessed the action of his hands, and his acquisitions have spread through the earth. ¹¹However, put out your hand, please, and touch everything that he has. If he doesn't "bless" you to your face ...'

¹²Yahweh said to the adversary, 'There, everything that he has is in your hand. Only against him you may not put out your hand.' So the adversary went out from being in Yahweh's presence.

When life falls apart

¹³There was a day when his sons and his daughters were eating and drinking wine in the house of their oldest brother ¹⁴when an envoy came to Iyyob and said, 'The cattle were ploughing and the she-donkeys were pasturing next to them, ¹⁵and Sabeans fell and took them, and struck down the boys with the edge of the sword. I alone am the only one who has escaped to tell you.'

¹⁶While this man was still speaking, another came and said, 'Fire from God fell from the heavens and burned up the flocks and the boys, and consumed them. I alone am the only one who has escaped to tell you.'

¹⁷While this one was still speaking, another came and said, 'Kasdites made three columns and made a dash on the camels and took them, and struck down the boys with the edge of the sword. I alone am the only one who has escaped to tell you.'

¹⁸While this one was still speaking, another came and said, 'Your sons and your daughters were eating and drinking wine in the house of their oldest brother, ¹⁹and there – a big wind came from across the wilderness and touched the four corners of the house. It fell on the young people and they died. I alone am the only one who has escaped to tell you.'

²⁰Iyyob got up, tore his coat and shaved his head, fell to the ground and bowed low, ²¹and said, 'Naked I came out of my mother's womb, and naked I will go back there. Yahweh gave and Yahweh has taken. Yahweh's name be blessed.'

²²In all this Iyyob did not do wrong. He did not ascribe corruptness to God.

The wise silence of friends

2 There was a day when the divine beings came to take their stand with Yahweh. The adversary, too, came among them to take his stand with Yahweh. ²Yahweh said to the adversary, 'From where do you come?' The adversary answered Yahweh, 'From roaming on the earth and from walking about on it.' ³Yahweh said to the adversary, 'Have you applied your mind to my servant Iyyob, because there's no one like him on the earth, a person of integrity and upright, in awe of God and turning aside from what is bad? He's still holding strongly to his integrity whereas you incited me against him to swallow him up for nothing.'

⁴The adversary answered Yahweh, 'Skin for skin! All that a man has he will give for the sake of his life. ⁵However, put out your hand, please, and touch his bones and his flesh. If he doesn't "bless" you to your face...'

⁶Yahweh said to the adversary, 'There he is, in your hand. Only keep his life.' ⁷So the adversary went out from Yahweh's presence and struck Iyyob down with a bad inflammation from the sole of his foot as far as the crown of his head, ⁸and he got himself a piece of pot to scratch himself with as he was sitting among ashes.

⁹His wife said to him, 'Are you still holding strongly to your integrity? "Bless" God and die.' ¹⁰He said to her, 'Like the speaking of one of the villainous women, you too speak. We accept good fortune from Yahweh. Do we not accept bad fortune?' In all this Iyyob didn't do wrong with his lips.

¹¹Three friends of Iyyob heard about all these bad things that had come upon him, and they came each one from his place: Eliphaz the Temanite, Bildad the Shuhite and Tsophar the Na'amatite. They met together by agreement to come to express their sorrow to him and to comfort him, ¹²but they raised their eyes from afar and didn't recognize him. They raised their voice and cried. They ripped, each one, his coat and they threw earth over their heads, to the heavens.

¹³They sat with him on the ground seven days and seven nights with no one speaking a word to him because they saw that his suffering was very great.

Iyyob: Perish the day I was born

3 Subsequently, Iyyob opened his mouth and slighted his day. ²Iyyob avowed:

³Perish the day on which I was born,
    and the night that said 'A male has been conceived!'
⁴That day should be darkness,
    God above should not enquire about it,
    and light should not shine on it.
⁵Darkness and deathly shadow should reclaim it,
    cloud should dwell over it.
Blackness by day should terrify it,
    ⁶that night – shadow should take it.
It should not be one with the days of the year,
    it should not come in the number of months.
⁷There, that night should be barren,
    no resounding should come in it.
⁸The people who curse a day should damn it,
    the people ready to rouse Livyatan [Leviathan].
⁹Its dusk stars should be dark,
    it should hope for light when there is none.
It should not see the eyelids of dawn,
    ¹⁰because it did not shut the doors of my womb,
    and conceal oppression from my eyes.

Iyyob: Life means turmoil, death means rest

¹¹Why did I not die at birth,
    go out from the womb and breathe my last?
¹²Why did knees meet me,
    or why breasts that I would suck?
¹³Because now I would be lying and calm,
    I would have slept then and would rest myself,
¹⁴With kings and the counsellors of the earth,
    who build up ruins for themselves,
¹⁵Or with officials who have gold,
    who fill their houses with silver.
¹⁶Or why was I not like a buried stillborn,
    like babies that have not seen the light?
¹⁷There the faithless leave off causing turmoil;
    there people wearied of energy rest.
¹⁸All at once prisoners relax;
    they don't hear the boss's voice.
¹⁹Small and big are there;
    the servant is free of his master.

²⁰Why does he give light to the oppressed,
    life to the bitter in spirit,
²¹People who wait for death but there is none,
    who search for it more than hidden treasures,
²²Who rejoice with gladness,
    who are joyful, because they find a grave,
²³To the man whose way has concealed itself,
    and whom God has hedged about?
²⁴Because my sighing comes before my food,
    my groans pour out like water.
²⁵Because I dreaded something and it happened to me,
    what I was terrified of comes to me.
²⁶I was not at ease, I was not calm,
    I did not rest, and turmoil came.

Eliphaz: Can a mere human being be in the right in God's eyes?

4 Eliphas the Temanite answered:

²Should one venture a word to you, will you be distraught?
  but holding back utterances: who could?
³Here, you have disciplined many,
  you would strengthen weak hands.
⁴Your utterances would enable one who was collapsing to get up,
  you would firm up bending knees.
⁵Yet now it comes to you, and you are distraught;
  it touches you, and you are fearful.
⁶Is your awe not your assurance,
  and the integrity of your ways your hope?
⁷Be mindful, please: who is that person free of guilt who has perished,
  where did the upright people disappear?
⁸As I have seen, the people who plough trouble,
  and sow oppression, reap them.
⁹By God's breath they perish,
  by his angry blast they come to a finish.
¹⁰The lion's roar, the cub's sound,
  the teeth of the whelps – they crumple;
¹¹The tiger perishes for lack of prey,
  the cougar's children scatter.

¹²A word stole to me,
  my ear got a whisper of it.
¹³In uneases from visions of the night,
  when deep sleep falls on human beings,
¹⁴Dread befell me, and trembling,
  and brought dread to the mass of my bones.
¹⁵A wind was sweeping over my face,
  it was bristling the hair on my flesh.
¹⁶It was halting, but I didn't recognize its appearance,
  the form in front of my eyes.
I heard a murmur, a voice:
¹⁷'Can a mere human being be in the right before God,
  can a man be pure before his maker?'
¹⁸If he does not trust his servants,
  and attributes folly to his envoys,
¹⁹How much more people who dwell in mud houses,
  whose foundation is in the dirt,
  so that people crush them before [they crush] a moth.
²⁰Between morning and evening they are struck down;
  without anyone noticing they perish permanently.
²¹Is it not that, when their tent cord is pulled up from them,
  they die, and without smartness?

Eliphaz: God frustrates the intentions of the shrewd

5 Please call – is anyone going to answer you,
  and to which of the sacred ones will you turn your face?
²Because provocation kills the dense person,
  passion puts the simple-minded to death.
³I myself have seen a dense person who was taking root,
  but I have immediately declared his home cursed.
⁴His children will be far from deliverance;
  they will collapse in the gateway and with no one to rescue.
⁵A hungry person will eat his harvest, will take it into baskets,
  and thirsty people will pant after their resources.
⁶Because trouble does not grow out from dirt,
  oppression does not spring up from the ground.
⁷Because a human being may be born for oppression
  and plagues go flying lofty.

⁸However, I myself enquire of God,
  and before God I set my words,
⁹One who does big things of which there is no searching out,
  extraordinary deeds until there is no numbering,
¹⁰The one who gives rain on the face of the earth,
  sends water on the face of the countryside,
¹¹Setting the lowly on high,
  so that mourners soar to deliverance,
¹²Contravening the intentions of the shrewd,
  so that their hands don't achieve adeptness,
¹³Capturing smart people through their shrewdness,
  so that the counsel of the clever sweeps away.
¹⁴By day they meet with darkness,
  at noon they grope as in the night.

¹⁵But he delivers the needy person from the sword of their mouth,
   from the hand of the strong;
¹⁶So there is hope for the poor person,
   and evil shuts its mouth.

Eliphaz: God wounds but binds up

¹⁷There – the good fortune of the man God reproves;
   so don't reject Shadday's correction.
¹⁸Because he is the one who wounds but binds up,
   he hits but his hands heal.
¹⁹During six attacks he will rescue you;
   during seven, bad things will not affect you.
²⁰In famine he redeems you from dying;
   in battle – from the hands of the sword.
²¹During the scourge of the tongue, you will hide,
   you will not be afraid of destruction when it comes.
²²Of destruction and of blight you will make fun;
   you will not be afraid of the animals of the country.
²³Because your pact is with the stones of the field,
   and the animals of the wild are made at peace with you.
²⁴You will acknowledge that there is well-being in your tent;
   you will attend to your home and not miss anything.
²⁵You will acknowledge that your offspring are many,
   your descendants like the grass of the earth.
²⁶You will come to the grave in fullness,
   as a sheaf comes up at its time.
²⁷There – we have searched this out and it is so;
   listen to it, acknowledge it for yourself.

Iyyob: There's no help for me

6 Iyyob answered:

²If only my provocation could be truly weighed,
   and people could lift on the scales the malice shown to me, altogether.
³Because it would now be heavier than the sand of the seas;
   that is why my words have been wild.
⁴Because Shadday's arrows are in me,
   their poison my spirit drinks up,
   God's terrors line up against me.
⁵Does a wild donkey bray over grass,
   does an ox bellow over its fodder?
⁶Is something insipid eaten without salt,
   is there taste in the juice of a mallow?
⁷My appetite refuses to touch;
   those things are like food for when I am ill.
⁸If only my request would come about,
   and God would grant my hope,
⁹That God would show willing and crush me,
   let loose his hand and cut me off.
¹⁰It would still be my consolation
   (though I would contort with writhing that wouldn't spare),
   because I have not disowned the things said by the Sacred One.

¹¹What energy do I have that I should wait,
   what end do I have that I should prolong my life?
¹²Is my energy the energy of stones,
   or is my flesh copper?
¹³Surely there is no help for me in myself,
   and adeptness has driven itself away from me.

Iyyob: You call this friendship?

¹⁴As for one who refuses commitment to his friend,
   he abandons awe for Shadday.
¹⁵My brothers have broken faith like a wadi,
   like the canyons with wadis that pass away,
¹⁶That are dark with ice,
   when snow piles over them.
¹⁷At the time when they flow, they've expired;
   in the heat, they've disappeared from their place.
¹⁸Caravans divert their path;
   they go up into the wasteland and perish.
¹⁹Caravans from Tema have looked to them,
   travelling groups from Sheba have hoped in them.
²⁰They're confounded, because they had trusted;
   they came right to it and they're shamed.

²¹Because now you've become nothing;
   you see something fearful and you're afraid.
²²Did I say to you, 'Give me –
   out of your energy pay a bribe on my behalf?
²³Save me from the hand of my adversary,
   from the hand of violent people redeem me'?

²⁴Instruct me, and I myself will be quiet;
  enable me to understand how I've erred.
²⁵How painful are upright things that have been said –
  but how does reproof from you reprove?
²⁶Do you think up utterances for reproof,
  and are the sayings of a despairing man for the wind?
²⁷Would you also make the lot fall for an orphan,
  and barter over your friend?
²⁸But now, show willing, turn your face to me;
  if I lie to your face . . .
²⁹Please turn back, there should not be evil;
  turn back, my right standing is still intact.
³⁰Is there evil on my tongue,
  or can my palate not discern malice?

Iyyob to God: A human being has hard service on earth

7 A mere human being has hard service on earth, doesn't he,
  and his days are like the days of an employee,
²Like a servant who longs for shadow,
  and like an employee who hopes for his wages.
³Thus I have been given months of emptiness as my domain,
  nights of oppression have been counted out for me.
⁴If I lie down, I say
  'When shall I get up?'
But evening drags on,
  and I am full of tossings until morning twilight.
⁵My flesh is clothed in maggots,
  and clods of earth,
my skin has become broken and oozing.
⁶My days have been swifter than a weaver's shuttle,
  and they've come to a finish in an absence of thread.
⁷Be mindful that my life is wind;
  my eye will not again see good things.
⁸The eye that sees me will not behold me;
  your eye will be on me, but I will be no more.
⁹A cloud comes to a finish and goes;
  so the person who goes down to She'ol does not come up.
¹⁰He does not go back to his home again;
  his place does not recognize him again.

Iyyob: What are human beings that you pay them so much attention?

¹¹Indeed I will not hold back my mouth;
  I will speak in the pressure of my spirit,
  I will talk in the bitterness of my entire being.
¹²Am I the Sea or the Dragon,
  that you set a watch over me?
¹³When I've said, 'My bed will comfort me,
  my mattress will carry part of my talk',
¹⁴You scare me with dreams,
  and terrify me with visions.
¹⁵My entire being would choose strangling,
  death, away from my bones.
¹⁶I've rejected it, I shall not live permanently;
  leave off from me, because my days are hollow.
¹⁷What is a mere human being that you make him great,
  and that you set your mind on him,
¹⁸That you attend to him each morning
  and test him every moment?
¹⁹How long will you not look away from me,
  not slacken hold of me until I swallow my spit?
²⁰If I've done wrong, what do I do to you,
  you who preserve humanity?
Why have you made me into a target for yourself
  so that I've become a burden to myself?
²¹Why do you not carry my rebellion
  and let my waywardness pass?
Because I shall now lie down in the earth,
  and when you look urgently for me, I will be no more.

Bildad: On learning from the past

8 Bildad the Shuhite answered:

²How long will you utter these things?
  – the sayings of your mouth are a massive wind.
³Does God twist the exercise of authority,
  does Shadday twist what is right?
⁴If your sons did wrong in relation to him,
  he sent them into the hand of their rebellion.
⁵If you yourself look urgently for God,
  and seek for grace with Shadday,
⁶If you're clean and upright,
  surely he will now arise for you
  and he will make good your faithful estate:
⁷your beginning may have been small,
  but your end will grow very great.

⁸Because ask the former generation, please,
   set your mind to what their ancestors searched
      out,
⁹Because we are of yesterday and we don't know,
   because our days on earth are a shadow.
¹⁰They can instruct you, can't they, and say to you,
   and get utterances out from their mind?
¹¹Can papyrus get tall where there's no marsh,
   can reed grow without water?
¹²While still in its shoot form when it's not cut,
   it would wither before any grass does.
¹³So are the paths of all who put God out of
      mind;
   the hope of the impious man perishes.
¹⁴His assurance breaks off,
   his trust is a spider's house.
¹⁵He relies on his house but it doesn't stand;
   he takes strong hold of it but it does not hold.
¹⁶While he may be moist before the sun,
   and his shoot may go out over his garden,
¹⁷His roots may interweave over a heap,
   may behold a house among stones,
¹⁸If they swallow him up from his place,
   it denies him: 'I didn't see you.'
¹⁹There, that's the joy of his way;
   and from the earth another springs.
²⁰On the other hand, God does not reject the man
      of integrity,
   and does not take strong hold of the hand of
      the person who acts badly.
²¹He will fill your mouth with laughter again,
   and your lips will shout.
²²The people hostile to you will clothe themselves
      in disgrace;
   the tent of the faithless will be no more.

Iyyob: God does not answer

9 Iyyob answered:

²Truly I acknowledge that it is so;
   but how can a mere human being be in the
      right with God?
³If he wants to argue with him,
   he doesn't answer him once in a thousand.
⁴Smart in mind and firm in energy –
   who has been tough with him and been at
      peace? –
⁵The one who moves mountains though they don't
      acknowledge him,
   who overturns them in his anger,
⁶Who shakes the earth from its place
   so that its pillars shudder,
⁷Who says to the sun that it should not shine
   and seals over the stars,
⁸Who spread out the heavens by himself
   and trod on the back of the sea,
⁹Who is the maker of the Bear, Orion,
   Pleiades and the rooms of the South,
¹⁰Who does big things, beyond searching out,
   extraordinary deeds, beyond numbering.
¹¹If he were to pass by me, I would not see,
   were he to sweep past, I would not discern
      him.
¹²If he were to snatch away, who could make him
      turn back,
   who could say to him, 'What are you
      doing?'
¹³God – he doesn't turn back his anger;
   under him Rahab's helpers bow low.
¹⁴How much less can I be one to answer him,
   to choose words against him?
¹⁵Though I am in the right, I would not answer
      him;
   I would ask for grace from the one who
      exercises authority for me.
¹⁶If I called and he answered me,
   I would not trust that he would give ear to my
      voice,
¹⁷He who crushes me for a trifle,
   and multiplies my wounds for nothing.
¹⁸He doesn't let me get my breath back,
   but fills me with bitterness.
¹⁹If it's about energy – there, he is firm;
   if it's about exercising authority – who can
      enable me to meet him?
²⁰Though I were in the right, my mouth would
      declare me in the wrong;
   I am a man of integrity, but it could declare me
      crooked.

Iyyob: There is no arbiter between us

²¹Whereas I am a man of integrity, I don't
      acknowledge myself,
   I reject my life.
²²It's all the same, that's why I say
   'He finishes off the person of integrity and the
      faithless.'
²³If a scourge suddenly puts to death,
   he ridicules the plight of people who are free
      of guilt.

²⁴When the earth is given into the hand of the faithless,
   he covers the face of the people who exercise authority in it –
   if not he, then who is it?

²⁵My days have been swifter than a runner;
   as they've taken flight, they haven't seen good things.
²⁶They've swept by like boats of reed,
   as an eagle that swoops on prey.
²⁷If my saying is, 'I'll put my talk out of mind,
   I'll abandon my look and be cheerful',
²⁸I'm terrified of all my pains,
   I know that you won't hold me free of guilt.
²⁹I am the one who'll be declared in the wrong;
   why then should I get weary in vain?
³⁰If I wash with soap,
   and cleanse the palms of my hands with caustic,
³¹You would then dip me in a pit,
   so that my clothes would take offence at me.
³²Because he isn't a man like me so I could answer him,
   should we come to make a ruling together.
³³No, there's no arbiter between us
   who might lay his hand on the two of us.
³⁴Were he to remove his club from upon me,
   so that dread of him might not terrify me,
³⁵I would speak and not be afraid of him,
   because I am not like this in myself.

10

With my entire being I loathe my life;
   I shall let loose my talk for myself,
   I shall speak in the bitterness of my being.
²I will say to God, 'Don't declare me in the wrong;
   let me know what it is you argue with me about.
³Does it seem good to you that you oppress,
   that you reject the labour of your fists
   and smile on the counsel of faithless people?

Iyyob: Do you have eyes of flesh?

⁴Do you have eyes of flesh,
   do you see as a mere human being sees?
⁵Are your days like the days of a mere human being,
   are your years like the years of a man,
⁶That you seek for my waywardness,
   enquire after my wrongdoings?

⁷Although you know that I'm not in the wrong,
   and there's no one who rescues from your hand.
⁸Whereas your hands shaped me and made me,
   altogether, all round, you've swallowed me up.
⁹Be mindful, please, that you made me like mud:
   but you turn me back to earth.
¹⁰Did you not pour me out like milk,
   set me like cheese?
¹¹You clothed me with skin and flesh,
   wove me with bones and sinews.
¹²You showed me life and commitment,
   your attention watched over my spirit.
¹³But these things you hid in your mind,
   I know that this was in your thinking:
¹⁴If I did wrong, you would watch me,
   and not hold me free of the guilt of my waywardness.
¹⁵If I'm in the wrong, alas for me:
   but if I am in the right, I can't lift my head,
Full of being slighted,
   drenched with my humbling.
¹⁶Should [my head] stand high, you'd hunt me like a cub,
   and again show extraordinary power against me.
¹⁷You bring new witnesses in front of me,
   increase your vexation towards me,
   changes of hard service with me.

¹⁸So why did you get me out of the womb?
   – I could have breathed my last, and eye not seen me.
¹⁹I could have been as if I never was,
   I could have been carried from the womb to the grave.
²⁰My days are few, aren't they, so leave off,
   get away from me so I may look cheerful for a moment,
²¹Before I go (and I will not come back)
   to a country of darkness and deathly shadow,
²²A land of gloom like darkness,
   deathly shadow without order,
   so that it shines like dark.

Tsophar: Can you plumb God's depth?

11

Tsophar the Na'amatite answered:

²Should an abundance of words not be answered,
   or should a man with lip be treated as in the right?

³Your prattle may silence human beings,
  you may ridicule and there may be no one to
    rebuke,
⁴You may say 'My grasp of things is clean,
  and I have been pure in your eyes',
⁵However, would that God might speak
  and open his lips with you,
⁶And tell you the secrets of being smart,
  because there are two sides to adeptness and
    you should acknowledge
  that God lets some of your waywardness be
    forgotten for you.

⁷Could you find God's reaches,
  or find Shadday's completeness?
⁸The loftiness of the heavens – what can you do,
  deeper than She'ol – what can you know?
⁹Its measure is longer than the earth,
  wider than the sea.
¹⁰If he sweeps by and takes captive and
    congregates,
  who can turn him back?
¹¹Because he knows empty men;
  when he sees trouble, does he not discern?
¹²A hollow man will get a mind
  when a wild donkey is born a human being.
¹³If you direct your mind
  and spread your palms towards him,
¹⁴If there is trouble in your hand, put it far
    away,
  and don't let evil dwell in your tents,
¹⁵Because then you will lift your face, free of
    blemish,
  and you will be constrained, but you won't be
    afraid.
¹⁶Because you yourself will put trouble out of
    mind,
  you'll remember it as water that has passed
    by.
¹⁷Your life span will rise brighter than
    noonday;
  though it be gloomy, it will become like
    morning.
¹⁸You'll be confident, because there'll be hope;
  when you search, you'll take your rest in
    confidence.
¹⁹You'll lie down and there'll be no one to
    disturb,
  and many will seek your goodwill.
²⁰But the eyes of the faithless will fail,
  retreat vanishes from them,
  their hope is a dying breath.

Iyyob: You're so smart

12 Iyyob answered:

²Truly you are the people
  and smartness will die with you.
³I too have a mind like you, I don't fall lower than
    you,
  and in whose thinking are there not things like
    these?
⁴I shall become one who is a laughing stock to his
    friend,
  who calls to God and he answers;
  one in the right, a man of integrity, is a
    laughing stock.
⁵While there is contempt for calamity in the
    thought of the person who is secure,
  it is prepared for people whose foot slips.
⁶Tents stay at ease for robbers
  and people who provoke God have
    confidence,
  as people whom God has brought into his
    hand.

⁷However, please ask the animals so they can
    instruct you,
  and the birds of the heavens so they can tell
    you,
⁸Or talk to the earth so it may instruct you,
  and so the fish of the sea can recount it to
    you.
⁹Who does not acknowledge, among all these,
  that Yahweh's hand has done this,
¹⁰The one in whose hand is the life of every living
    thing,
  and the spirit of all human flesh?
¹¹The ear tests utterances, doesn't it,
  as the palate tastes food for itself.
¹²Among the aged lies smartness,
  in length of days lies discernment.

¹³With him are smartness and strength,
  to him belong counsel and discernment.
¹⁴On one hand, he tears down and it is not built
    up,
  he locks up a man and he is not released.
¹⁵On the other, he holds back the water and it
    dries up,
  he sends it off and it overwhelms the country.
¹⁶With him are vigour and adeptness,
  to him belong the person who goes astray and
    the one who leads astray.

Iyyob: Just listen, will you?

¹⁷He makes counsellors go stripped,
  makes people who exercise authority go crazy.
¹⁸He loosens the bond put on by kings,
  ties a belt round their hips.
¹⁹He makes priests go stripped,
  overthrows the enduring.
²⁰He removes speech from trustworthy men,
  takes the discretion of elders.
²¹He pours contempt on leaders,
  slackens the belt of the strong.
²²He reveals mysteries from the darkness,
  gets deathly shadow out into the light.
²³He lifts up nations and obliterates them,
  expands nations and leads them.
²⁴He removes the mind from the heads of a
    country's people,
  and makes them wander in a wasteland where
    there's no way.
²⁵They grope in the darkness where there is no
    light,
  and he makes them wander like a drunk.

13 There, my eye has seen all this,
  my ear has heard and understood it.
²Corresponding to your knowledge, I too know;
  I don't fall lower than you.
³However, I myself will speak to Shadday,
  I want to reprove God.
⁴However, you are smearers of falsehood,
  non-entity physicians, all of you.
⁵If only you would simply be quiet;
  it would be smartness for you.
⁶Please listen to my reproof,
  heed the arguments from my lips.
⁷Is it for God that you speak evil,
  or for him that you speak deceitfully?
⁸Is it for him that you show regard,
  or for God that you argue?
⁹Would it be good if he searched you out,
  would you play about with him as one plays
    about with a mere human being?
¹⁰He would reprove you strongly,
  even if you covertly show regard.
¹¹His dignity would terrify you, wouldn't it,
  and dread of him would fall on you.
¹²Your reminders are aphorisms made of ash,
  your responses are responses made of mud.
¹³Be quiet for me and I myself will speak;
  there will befall me whatever may.

¹⁴Why do I lift my flesh between my teeth,
  put my life into the palms of my hands?
¹⁵There, though he may slay me, I will not wait,
  yet I will defend my ways to his face.
¹⁶That, too, will be deliverance for me,
  that an impious person does not come before
    him.
¹⁷Listen attentively to my utterances,
  to my declaration in your ears.

Iyyob: God, why do you conceal your face?

¹⁸Here, please, I have lined up a case;
  I know that I am the one who will prove to be
    in the right.
¹⁹Who is the one who will argue with me?
  – because now I would be quiet and breathe
    my last.
²⁰Yet don't do two things with me,
  then I need not conceal myself from
    your face:
²¹Take the palm of your hand far from me;
  may dread of you not scare me.
²²Call and I will be the one who answers,
  or I will speak and you speak back to me.
²³How many are my acts of waywardness and my
    wrongdoings?
  – make known to me my rebellion and my
    wrongdoing.

²⁴Why do you conceal your face,
  and think of me as an enemy to you?
²⁵Do you frighten a leaf that's being blown away,
  do you pursue dried-up chaff,
²⁶That you should write down bitter things
    for me
  and make me own the wayward acts of my
    youth,
²⁷Put my feet in the stocks,
  keep watch on all my paths,
  put a mark on the roots of my feet?
²⁸And that is one who wears out like something
    rotten,
  like a garment moth has eaten.

14 A human being, born of a woman,
  is short in days and full of turmoil.
²Like a flower, he comes up but withers,
  takes flight like a shadow and does not stand.
³Yes, at this person you open your eye,
  and bring me into making a ruling with you.

⁴Who can bring clean from defiled?
  – not one person.
⁵If his days are determined, the number of his months is with you,
  you have set his limits and he cannot pass them,
⁶Turn away from him so that he may leave off,
  until he's happy with his day, like an employee.

Iyyob: If only you would hide me in She'ol

⁷Because there is hope for a tree;
  if it is cut down, it can renew itself again,
  and its sucker will not leave off.
⁸If its root grows old in the earth,
  and its stump dies in the earth,
⁹At the scent of water it will bud
  and make a shoot like a plant.
¹⁰But a man – he dies and is prostrate;
  a human being breathes his last, and where is he?
¹¹The water goes from a sea,
  a river becomes parched and dry,
¹²And a man lies down and does not get up,
  until the heavens are no longer.
They don't wake up,
  they don't rise from their sleep.

¹³If only you would hide me in She'ol,
  conceal me until your anger turns back,
Set a limit for me and be mindful of me:
¹⁴if a man were to die, could he come to life?
All the days of my hard service
  I would wait until my renewal came.
¹⁵You would call and I myself would answer you;
  for the making of your hands you would long.
¹⁶Because now when you counted my steps,
  you would not keep watch for my wrongdoings.
¹⁷My rebellion would be sealed up in a pouch;
  you would coat over my waywardness.

¹⁸However, a falling mountain crumbles,
  and a crag dislodges from its place,
¹⁹Water wears away stones,
  its torrents wash away the earth from the ground:
And you obliterate a mere human being's hope;
  ²⁰you overpower him permanently and he goes;
  you alter his face and send him off.
²¹His sons find honour but he doesn't know,
  or they are insignificant and he doesn't discern it.
²²Only, his flesh hurts him
  and his own self grieves for him.

Eliphaz: Are you really so smart?

15 Eliphaz the Temanite answered:

²Would a smart man answer with windy knowledge,
  fill his belly with the east wind,
³Argue with talk that's no use,
  and utterances by which he cannot profit?
⁴Indeed you – you contravene awe,
  you restrain talk before God.
⁵Because your waywardness teaches your mouth,
  you choose the tongue of shrewd people.
⁶Your mouth declares you in the wrong, not I;
  your lips testify against you.

⁷Are you the first human being who was born,
  or were you birthed before the hills?
⁸Do you listen in God's cabinet,
  or do you restrain smartness to yourself?
⁹What do you know and we don't know it,
  or understand and it is not in our possession?
¹⁰Among us are a grey-haired man, an old man,
  mightier in days than your father.
¹¹Are God's comforts too small for you,
  a word in gentleness with you?
¹²Why does your mind capture you,
  why do your eyes flash,
¹³That you turn back your spirit on God
  and let out your utterances from your mouth?
¹⁴What is a human being that he should be clean,
  one born of woman that he should be in the right?
¹⁵There, in his sacred ones he does not trust,
  and the heavens are not clean in his eyes.
¹⁶How much less one offensive and foul,
  a man drinking evil like water.
¹⁷I will explain, listen to me,
  and what I have beheld I will recount,
¹⁸Things that smart people tell,
  and have not concealed, from their ancestors.
¹⁹To them alone the land was given,
  when no stranger passed among them.

Eliphaz: What happens to the faithless

²⁰All the days of the faithless man, he writhes,
  the number of years that are hidden for the violent man.
²¹Dreadful sounds are in his ears;
  when he is doing well, a robber comes upon him.

²²He is not sure of coming back from darkness;
 he is spied over for the sword.
²³He wanders about for bread, where is it?
 – he knows that the day of darkness is
  prepared, at his hand.
²⁴Pressure terrifies him, anguish overwhelms him,
 like a king ready to attack.
²⁵Because he stretched out his hand against God,
 acted the strong man against Shadday.
²⁶He runs against him head down
 with the thickness of his shields' backs,
²⁷Because he has covered his face with fat
 and put brawn on his thighs.
²⁸But he will dwell in ruined towns,
 houses that people don't live in,
 that have prepared to be heaps.
²⁹He will not be wealthy, his resources will not
  rise up;
 their gains will not extend over the land.
³⁰He will not depart from darkness,
 flame will wither his shoot;
 he will depart by the wind from his mouth.
³¹He should not trust in emptiness, leading
   himself astray,
 because emptiness will be his recompense.
³²Before his time he will wither;
 his branches will not be verdant.
³³He will do violence to his unripe grapes like a
   vine,
 he will throw off his blossom like an olive tree.
³⁴Because the impious man's assembly is barren,
 and fire consumes the tents of one who gives
   bribes.
³⁵He conceives oppression and gives birth to
   trouble;
 their womb prepares guile.

Iyyob: Comforters? More like troublemakers

16   Iyyob answered:

²I have heard many things like these;
 all of you are oppressive comforters.
³Is there a limit to windy words –
 what ails you that you answer?
⁴I too could speak like you
 if you yourselves were in my own place.
I could sound out against you in utterances
 and shake my head over you.

⁵I could firm you up with my speech;
 the moving of my lips could hold things back.
⁶If I speak, my hurt does not hold back;
 but if I leave off, what goes from me?
⁷Indeed he has now worn me out;
 you have desolated my whole assembly.
⁸You have shrivelled me, it's become a witness;
 my gauntness rises up against me, it testifies
   against me.
⁹His anger has torn and been hostile to me,
 he's gnashed his teeth at me.
My adversary sharpens his eyes towards me;
 ¹⁰people have gaped at me with their mouth.
With reviling they've struck me on the cheek,
 they mass together against me.
¹¹God has delivered me up to an evildoer,
 thrown me into the hands of the faithless.
¹²I was at ease, but he's shattered me,
 he's grasped me by the neck and smashed me,
He's set me up for himself as a target,
 ¹³his archers surround me.
He pierces my kidneys and doesn't spare;
 he pours my bile on the earth.
¹⁴He assaults me, with assault on top of assault;
 he runs at me like a strong man.
¹⁵I've sewn sack over my skin
 and buried my horn in the earth.
¹⁶My face is red from crying
 and over my eyelids is deathly shadow,
¹⁷Although there was no violence in my fists
 and my plea was clean.

Iyyob: A witness in the heavens?

¹⁸Earth, don't cover my blood;
 there must not be a place for my cry.
¹⁹Even now, there – my witness is in the heavens,
 my advocate is on high.
²⁰Though my friends are people who scorn me,
 my eye pours out to God.
²¹He will issue reproof for a man with God
 [as] a human being does for his friend.
²²Because numbered years will come
 and I will go the path on which I shall not
   come back.

17   My spirit is broken, my days are
       extinguished,
 the graves are for me.

²If it's not the case that mockeries are with me,
   and on their recalcitrance my eye lodges . . .
³Please put my pledge by you –
   who is the one who will clap my hand?
⁴Because you've hidden their mind from insight;
   therefore you will not be exalted.
⁵'For a meal he tells on friends,
   and his children's eyes fail':
⁶He has made me a proverb for peoples,
   I shall become something at which to spit in the face.
⁷My eye has grown dim from provocation,
   my limbs are like a shadow, all of them.

⁸The upright are desolate at this,
   the one who is free of guilt arises against the impious.
⁹The faithful person grasps his way;
   the man who is pure of hands grows firmer.
¹⁰However, all of you, please come back again –
   but I will not find a smart man among you.
¹¹My days have passed, my strategies have snapped,
   the desires of my heart.
¹²They make night into day;
   light is nearer than darkness.
¹³If I hope for She'ol as my home,
   lay out my bed in the darkness,
¹⁴I call out to the Pit, 'You are my father',
   to the worm, 'My mother', 'My sister'.
¹⁵Where then is my hope,
   who can behold my hope?
¹⁶Will they go down to the poles of She'ol,
   will we descend together to the earth?

Bildad: Reaffirming the moral foundation of the world

18 Bildad the Shuhite answered:

²How long until you put an end to utterances?
   – consider, and afterwards we will speak.
³Why are we thought of as cattle,
   stupid in your eyes?
⁴One who tears himself apart with his anger –
   for your sake will the earth be abandoned,
   will a crag dislodge from its place?

⁵Yes, the light of the faithless goes out,
   the flame of his fire doesn't shine.
⁶Light darkens in his tent,
   his lamp above him goes out.

⁷His vigorous steps become short,
   his own counsel throws him down,
⁸Because he's thrust into a net by his own feet;
   he walks about on to the mesh.
⁹A trap grasps him by the heel,
   clamps get strong hold of him.
¹⁰A rope for him is hidden in the earth,
   a trap for him on the trail.
¹¹All around, terrors terrify him,
   shatter him at his feet.
¹²Trouble is hungry for him,
   disaster has prepared for his stumbling.
¹³It consumes his skin-covered limbs;
   death's firstborn consumes his limbs.
¹⁴His confidence tears away from his tent,
   and it marches him to the king of terrors.
¹⁵Fire dwells in his tent,
   sulphur scatters over his home.
¹⁶Below, his roots dry up;
   above, his foliage withers.
¹⁷Commemoration of him perishes from the country,
   and he has no name in the outside world.
¹⁸They thrust him out from light to darkness,
   drive him out of the world.
¹⁹He has no posterity, no offspring, among his people,
   and he has no survivor in his place where he resided.
²⁰At his day people in the west are desolate,
   people in the east grasp horror.
²¹Indeed, these are the dwellings of the evildoer,
   this is the place of the one who did not acknowledge God.

Iyyob: Ten times you've shamed me

19 Iyyob answered:

²How long will you torment my entire being,
   crush me with utterances?
³These ten times you have shamed me;
   you feel no disgrace when you abuse me.
⁴Yet truly, should I have erred,
   my error lodges with me.
⁵If you truly magnify yourselves above me,
   and argue with me on the basis of my reviling,
⁶Acknowledge here that God has put me in the wrong,
   has put siege works round me.

⁷If I cry out 'Violence', I don't get an answer;
    if I call for help, there's no exercise of authority.
⁸He's barred my path and I can't pass,
    and he sets darkness over my trails.
⁹He's stripped my splendour from me,
    removed the crown on my head.
¹⁰He tears me down all round, and I am gone;
    he uproots my hope like a tree.
¹¹He makes his anger rage against me;
    he thinks of me as like his adversaries for him.
¹²His raiding gangs come on all together,
    they've built up their way against me,
    they've camped at my tent all round.

Iyyob: I know that my restorer lives, but . . .

¹³He's put my brothers far from me;
    my acquaintances have indeed become strangers to me.
¹⁴The people near to me and the people I knew have left off,
    the people residing in my house have put me out of mind.
¹⁵My servant girls think of me as a stranger;
    I've become a foreigner in their eyes.
¹⁶I've called to my servant but he doesn't answer,
    when with my own mouth I ask him for grace.
¹⁷My breath is strange to my wife,
    I'm loathsome to my siblings.
¹⁸Even little children have rejected me;
    when I get up, they speak against me.
¹⁹All my confidential friends have taken offence at me,
    and those I've been loyal to have turned against me.
²⁰My bone sticks to my skin and my flesh,
    and I've escaped by the skin of my teeth.
²¹Be gracious to me, be gracious to me, you're my friends,
    because God's hand has touched me.
²²Why do you pursue me like God,
    and why aren't you full of my flesh?
²³If only here my utterances were written down,
    if only they were inscribed in a document,
²⁴With an iron pen and lead,
    engraved on a crag permanently.
²⁵But I myself know that my restorer is alive,
    and as the last will get up on the earth.
²⁶After my skin has thus been stripped,
    away from my flesh I will behold God,
²⁷Whom I will behold for myself;
    my eyes will have seen him, and not a stranger.
My inner being within my chest fails,
²⁸when you say, 'How have we pursued him?'
The root of the thing is found in me;
²⁹be terrified of the sword for yourselves.
Because your wrath is wayward acts that deserve the sword,
    in order that you may acknowledge that there is judgement.

Tsophar: My uneases

20 Tsophar the Na'amatite answered:
²This is why my uneases make me speak back,
    because of my feelings within me.
³When I hear correction that shames me,
    a spirit from my understanding makes me answer.
⁴Do you acknowledge this: from of old,
    from the placing of humanity on the earth,
⁵That the resounding of faithless people is of the briefest,
    the rejoicing of the impious is for a moment?
⁶If his exaltation climbs to the heavens
    and his head touches the clouds,
⁷Like his dung he perishes permanently;
    people who saw him say, 'Where is he?'
⁸Like a dream he flies away and people cannot find him;
    he is driven away like a night vision.
⁹Though an eye looked on him, it does not do so again;
    his place beholds him no more.
¹⁰His children seek the grace of poor people,
    his hands give back his vigour.
¹¹His bones were full of his youthfulness,
    but with him it lies down in the earth.
¹²If something bad is sweet in his mouth
    as he hides it under his tongue,
¹³As he spares it and does not abandon it,
    but holds it back inside his palate,
¹⁴His food in his stomach turns
    into the venom of asps within him.
¹⁵The resources he has swallowed he vomits,
    as God discharges it from his insides.

Tsophar: How wickedness gets its reward

¹⁶He sucks the poison of asps,
  the viper's tongue kills him.
¹⁷He is not to see the streams,
  the rivers, the wadis of syrup and cream.
¹⁸He gives back the gains and doesn't swallow,
  he doesn't exult in the very resources from his trading.
¹⁹Because he crushed, abandoned poor people,
  seized a house when he was not building it,
²⁰Because he doesn't know ease inside him,
  he doesn't let any of what he desired escape.
²¹There'll be no survivor to eat it;
  therefore his good things will not endure.
²²When his abundance is full, pressure will overtake him;
  every hand of the oppressor will come upon him.
²³May he be for the filling of his belly,
  may he send off on him his angry rage,
  and rain it upon him as his food.

²⁴When he takes flight from an iron weapon,
  a copper arrow will pass through him.
²⁵When he pulls it out and it comes out of his body,
  the shining thing out of his gall bladder,
Dreads come upon him,
  ²⁶all darkness is hidden up for his treasures.
Fire will consume him, unfanned;
  may it pasture on the survivor in his tent.
²⁷The heavens will reveal his waywardness,
  the earth is going to rise up for him.
²⁸May a flood exile his household,
  torrents on the day of his anger.
²⁹This is the faithless person's share from God,
  the domain spoken of by God.

Iyyob: If only wickedness did get its reward!

21   Iyyob answered:

²Listen properly to my utterance;
  may this be the comfort you offer.
³Bear with me while I myself speak,
  and after I have spoken, you may ridicule.
⁴Am I: is my talk towards a human being,
  so why should my spirit not be short?
⁵Turn your face to me and be desolated,
  put your hand on your mouth.
⁶If I am mindful, I am terrified;
  trembling grasps my flesh.
⁷Why do faithless people live on,
  as they grow older, also get stronger in resources?
⁸Their offspring are established before them, with them,
  their descendants are before their eyes.
⁹Their households are doing well, without fear;
  with no club of God on them.
¹⁰His bull breeds and does not fail;
  his cow delivers and does not miscarry.
¹¹They send off their little ones like sheep,
  their children skip about.
¹²They lift their voice to tambourine and guitar,
  rejoice to the sound of the pipe.
¹³They finish their days with good things,
  and in peace go down to She'ol.
¹⁴They say to God, 'Depart from us,
  we don't want to acknowledge your ways.
¹⁵What is Shadday that we should serve him,
  and how do we profit when we pray to him?'
¹⁶There, are their good things not in their own hand,
  though the counsel of faithless people is far away from me.

Iyyob: Your words of comfort are hollow

¹⁷How often does the lamp of faithless people go out,
  and the disaster due to them come upon them,
  the destiny he shares out in his anger.
¹⁸They should be like straw before wind,
  like chaff that a tempest seizes.
¹⁹Whereas God may hide up his trouble for his children,
  he should make it good to him, so that he acknowledges it.
²⁰His eyes should see his destruction;
  he should drink Shadday's wrath.
²¹Because what will he want for his household after him,
  when the number of his months has been curtailed?

²²Can one teach God knowledge,
  when he is the one who exercises authority over people on high?
²³One person dies in his full strength,
  all peaceable and at ease.

²⁴His pails are full of milk
   and the marrow in his bones is juicy.
²⁵Another person dies bitter in himself;
   he has not tasted good things.
²⁶All together they lie down in the earth
   and worms cover over them.

²⁷There, I know your intentions,
   the strategies with which you will do violence
      against me,
²⁸That you will say, 'Where is the leader's house,
   where is the tent that was the dwelling of the
      faithless people?'
²⁹Have you not asked people who pass by on the
      way,
   not recognized their evidences,
³⁰That on the day of disaster a bad person is held
      back,
   on the day when outbursts are carried along.
³¹Who tells of his conduct to his face;
   when he has acted, who makes good to him?
³²When he is carried along to the graves,
   and someone watches over his tomb,
³³The clods in the wadi are sweet to him;
   behind him everyone follows,
   and there is no numbering those before him.
³⁴So how can you comfort me with hollowness?
   – the things that you say back: trespass
      remains.

Eliphaz rewrites Iyyob's life

22 Eliphaz answered:

²Is a man useful to God,
   that a person of insight should be of benefit
      to him?
³Is it a delight to Shadday when you are in the right,
   or is there profit when you show integrity in
      your ways?
⁴Is it because of your awe that he reproves you,
   comes to make a ruling with you?
⁵Are your bad ways not great,
   and is there no end to your acts of waywardness?
⁶Because you take pledges from your brothers for
      nothing,
   you strip the clothes of the naked.
⁷You don't give water to the weary person,
   you hold back bread from the hungry,
⁸As a strong man to whom the land belongs,
   a man held in high regard who lives on it.
⁹Widows you've sent off empty,
   the strength of orphans is crushed.
¹⁰That's why traps are all round you,
   and sudden dread frightens you,
¹¹Or darkness when you cannot see,
   and a flood of water that covers you.
¹²God is lofty in the heavens, isn't he;
   see the peak of the stars, how high!
¹³You've said, 'What does God know,
   can he exercise authority through the
      thundercloud?
¹⁴The clouds are a screen for him and he doesn't see,
   as he goes about the circuit of the heavens.'

Eliphaz: Come back!

¹⁵Do you keep watch on the age-old path
   that men of trouble have trod,
¹⁶Who were shrivelled up when it was not time,
   whose foundation was washed away in a river,
¹⁷People who said to God, 'Depart from us',
   and 'What will Shadday do for them?'
¹⁸But he was the one who filled their houses with
      good things;
   the counsel of faithless people is far away
      from me.
¹⁹Faithful people see and celebrate,
   the one who is free of guilt ridicules them:
²⁰'Is it not the case that those who rose against us
      have disappeared,
   and what was left of them the fire has
      consumed?'

²¹Please be of benefit to him and be at peace;
   by these things good will come to you.
²²Please take instruction from his mouth
   and lay up in your mind the things he said.
²³If you come back to Shadday you'll be built up,
   when you move evil far from your tent.
²⁴You'll regard precious metal as earth,
   Ophir gold as a crag in the wadis.
²⁵Shadday will be your precious metal,
   choice silver for you,
²⁶When you then revel in Shadday,
   and lift your face to God.
²⁷You'll pray to him and he will listen to you,
   and you'll make good your pledges.
²⁸You'll determine something and it will arise
      for you,
   and on your ways light will shine.

²⁹When people make others fall, you'll say 'Lift
  them up',
  and he'll deliver the downcast of eyes.
³⁰He'll rescue one who is not free of guilt –
  he'll find rescue through the cleanness of your
  palms.

Iyyob: Who moved?

23 Iyyob answered:

²My talk is indeed rebellious today,
  though my hand is heavy with my groaning.
³If only I knew how I could find him,
  could come as far as his established place.
⁴I'd lay out my case before him,
  fill my mouth with reproofs.
⁵I'd get to know the utterances he would answer
  me,
  I'd understand what he'd say to me.
⁶Would he argue with me with abundance of
  energy?
  – no, surely he'd set his mind on me.
⁷There it would be an upright man who would
  enter into reproof with him,
  and I would survive permanently from the one
  who exercises authority over me.
⁸If I go east, he is not there,
  and west, I don't discern him,
⁹North where he acts, I don't behold him;
  he may turn south, but I don't see him.
¹⁰But he knows the way that is mine;
  if he tests me, I'll come out as gold.
¹¹My foot has grasped his track,
  I've kept his way and not turned aside.
¹²From the order of his lips I haven't moved away,
  I've hidden up the sayings of his mouth more
  than my portion of food.
¹³He is one; who can turn him back?
  – what he himself desires, he does,
¹⁴Because he'll bring to completion what was
  decreed regarding me,
  and there are many things like these in his
  mind.
¹⁵Therefore I'm fearful of his presence;
  when I consider, I'm in dread of him.
¹⁶God has made my mind soft;
  Shadday has made me fearful,
¹⁷But I haven't expired before the darkness;
  from before me he has covered the gloom.

Iyyob: Why are times not kept by Shadday?

24 Why are times not hidden up by
  Shadday?
  – those who acknowledge him do not behold
  his days.
²People remove boundary stones,
  seize a flock and pasture it,
³Drive away the orphans' donkey,
  take the widow's bull as a pledge,
⁴Turn aside the needy from the road:
  the humble in the land have been made to hide
  together.
⁵There, they're wild donkeys in the wilderness,
  who go out in the course of their work.
Looking urgently for prey, the steppe belongs
  to it,
  food for the boys.
⁶In the open country they harvest its fodder,
  and glean the vineyard of the faithless.
⁷They stay the night naked, without clothing;
  there's no covering against the cold.
⁸They get wet from the mountain rain,
  and without a shelter they embrace a crag.
⁹People seize the orphan from the breast,
  take the baby of a humble person as a
  pledge.
¹⁰They go about naked, without clothing,
  and hungry, though they carry sheaves.
¹¹Between their terraces they press oil,
  and they tread the winepresses, but they are
  thirsty.
¹²From the town men groan,
  the entire being of people run through cries
  for help,
  but God does not lay a charge of corruptness.

Iyyob: Who can prove me a liar?

¹³Those people – they are among those who are
  rebels against the light,
  they don't recognize its ways,
  they don't live in its trails.
¹⁴At first light the murderer gets up
  so he may slay the humble and needy,
And in the evening become like a thief,
  ¹⁵while the eye of the adulterer watches for
  dusk,
Saying 'No eye will behold me',
  and he puts a cover on his face.

¹⁶He breaks into houses in the dark,
by day they shut themselves in; they don't acknowledge light.
¹⁷Because for them, all together, morning is deathly shadow,
because he recognizes deathly shadow's terrors.

¹⁸He should be a slight thing on the face of the water,
their domain in the land should be slighted;
no one should turn his face by way of their vineyards.
¹⁹Both drought and heat seize snow water,
and She'ol, people who have done wrong.
²⁰The womb should put him out of mind,
the worm should find him sweet.
No longer should he be kept in mind;
evil should break like a tree.
²¹He deals badly with the infertile woman, who does not give birth,
he does no good to the widow.
²²He drags off the sturdy by means of his energy;
he rises up, and he should not trust in his life.
²³He gives himself confidence and leans on it,
and his eyes are on their ways.

²⁴They are on high for a while, then there is nothing of them;
they are brought low, like a mallow they shrivel,
like a head of grain they wither.
²⁵If it is not so, who can prove me a liar,
make my utterance into nothing?

Bildad: Even the stars are not clean

25 Bildad the Shuhite answered:

²Rule and dread are with him;
he brings about well-being in his heights.
³Is there any numbering of his raiding gangs,
or on whom does his light not rise?
⁴And how can a mere human being be right with God,
how can someone born of a woman be clean?
⁵There, even the moon is not bright
and the stars are not clean in his eyes.
⁶How much less a mere human being, a worm,
or a man, a maggot.

Iyyob: The edges of his ways

26 Iyyob answered:

²How you have helped someone without energy,
delivered an arm without vigour!
³How you have counselled someone without smartness,
and made known adeptness in abundance!
⁴With whom have you told utterances,
and whose breath came out from you?

⁵The ghosts are made to writhe
beneath the water, with those who dwell in it.
⁶She'ol is naked in front of him,
there is no cover for Abaddon.
⁷The one who stretched out the north over the waste,
suspended earth over nothingness,
⁸Wrapped the water in his clouds
(and the thundercloud did not break beneath them),
⁹Enclosed the view of his throne,
spread his thundercloud over it.
¹⁰He drew a borderline on the face of the water
at light's boundary with darkness.
¹¹The heavens' pillars quake,
they are aghast at his reprimand.
¹²By his energy he stirred up the sea,
by his understanding he hit Rahab.
¹³By his wind the heavens became clear;
his hand ran through the twisting snake.
¹⁴There, these are the edges of his ways,
and what a whisper is the word that we hear of him,
so who understands the thunder of his strength?

Iyyob: I do identify with the people of integrity

27 Iyyob again took up his poem:

²By the life of God who has dismissed the exercise of authority for me,
Shadday who has made my life bitter,
³All the while there is breath in me,
and God's spirit is in my nostrils,
⁴If my lips speak evil,
or my tongue – if it murmurs deceit . . .

⁵Far be it from me that I should say you are right;
   until I breathe my last I will not dismiss my
      integrity from me.
⁶I hold strongly to my being in the right and I will
      not slacken hold of it;
   my conscience does not revile me for any of
      my days.

⁷May my enemy be like the faithless,
   may the one who rises against me be like the
      evildoer.
⁸Because what is the hope of the impious man
      when he is cut down,
   when God requires his life?
⁹Will God listen to his cry,
   when pressure comes upon him,
¹⁰Or will he revel in Shadday,
   call God at any time?
¹¹I will instruct you in God's hand,
   what is with Shadday I will not hide.
¹²There, you have beheld, all of you,
   so why this total hollowness you manifest?

Iyyob: And I do affirm that wicked people get their deserts

¹³This is the share of the person who is faithless
      with God,
   the domain that violent people get from
      Shadday.
¹⁴If his children are many – it is for the sword,
   and his descendants will not be full of bread.
¹⁵The people who survive him will be buried by
      death,
   and their widows will not cry.
¹⁶If he heaps up silver like earth,
   and prepares clothing like mud,
¹⁷He may prepare, but a faithful person will wear,
   and a person free of guilt will share out the
      silver.
¹⁸He has built a house like a nest,
   like the bivouac a watchman makes,
¹⁹He may lie down a wealthy man but he will not
      do so again;
   when he opens his eyes, there is none of it.
²⁰Terrors overtake him like water;
   by night a tempest has seized him.
²¹The east wind lifts him and he has gone;
   it sweeps him from his place.
²²It throws itself at him and does not spare,
   though he takes flight urgently from its hand.

²³It claps the palms of its hands at him
   and whistles at him from its place.

Interlude: There is a mine for silver . . .

28 Indeed there is a source for silver,
   a place for gold that people will refine.
²Iron is taken from the earth,
   stone that someone pours as copper.
³He has put an end to darkness,
   and to every limit, he was searching out.
Stone in darkness and deathly shadow
   ⁴has been broken open by a wadi, away from
      any resident.
Forgotten people, away from anyone's foot, have
      dangled,
   away from a human being they've swayed.
⁵Earth from which food comes forth
   has been changed like fire below it.
⁶Its stones were the place of sapphire,
   and it had gold dust.
⁷The bird of prey did not know the trail,
   the falcon's eye has not gazed on it.
⁸Majestic beasts have not made a way to it,
   the cub has not advanced on it.
⁹Someone has put out his hand against the flint,
   overturned the mountains by the root,
¹⁰He has split channels through the crags
   and his eye has seen every precious thing.
¹¹He has dammed up the sources of the rivers
   so that he might bring hidden things out into
      the light.

. . . but where can wisdom be found?

¹²But smartness: from where can it be found,
   where is understanding's place?
¹³No human being can know its comparative
      value,
   and it's not found in the country of the living.
¹⁴The deep says, 'It's not in me';
   the sea says, 'It's not with me.'
¹⁵Fine gold can't be given in its place;
   silver can't be weighed out as its price.
¹⁶It can't be balanced against Ophir gold,
   against precious onyx or sapphire.
¹⁷Gold or crystal can't compare with it,
   or containers of fine gold be its exchange.
¹⁸Coral and jasper can't be brought to mind;
   a pouch of smartness is more than rubies.

¹⁹Topaz from Kush cannot compare with
   it;
  it can't be balanced against pure gold.

²⁰So smartness: from where does it come,
  where is understanding's place?
²¹It hides from the eyes of every living thing;
  from the birds in the heavens it conceals itself.
²²Abaddon and death say,
  'With our ears we've heard report of it.'
²³God understands the way to it;
  he's the one who knows its place.
²⁴Because he's the one who looks to the ends of
   the earth,
  sees beneath all the heavens.
²⁵In setting a weight for the wind,
  and establishing the water by measure,
²⁶When setting a decree for the rain
  and a way for the bolt of thunder,
²⁷Then he saw it and took account of it,
  established it and also searched it out.
²⁸And he said to humanity:
  'There, smartness is awe for the Lord,
  understanding is departing from evil.'

Iyyob: The way things were (1)

29 Iyyob again took up his poem:

²If only it was like the months of the past,
  like the days when God was keeping watch over
   me,
³When his lamp was shining over my head,
  when I was walking through the darkness with
   his light,
⁴As I was in my days early in the year,
  when God's confidences were at my tent,
⁵When Shadday was still with me,
  my boys were round me,
⁶When my steps bathed in cream,
  and the crag poured streams of oil for me.
⁷When I went out of the township gateway,
  set my seat in the square,
⁸Boys saw me and withdrew,
  old men got up, stood.
⁹Officials held back utterances,
  put the palm of their hand to their mouth.
¹⁰The voices of rulers were quiet,
  their tongue stuck to their palate.
¹¹When the ear heard, it wished me good fortune;
  when the eye saw, it testified to me.

Iyyob: The way things were (2)

¹²Because I rescued the humble person crying for
   deliverance,
  the orphan and the one who had no one to
   help.
¹³The blessing of the person who was perishing
   would come upon me;
  I made the heart of the widow resound.
¹⁴I clothed myself in faithfulness so that it clothed
   itself in me;
  the [proper] exercise of authority by me was
   coat and turban.
¹⁵I was eyes to the blind person,
  I was feet to the lame.
¹⁶I was father to the needy;
  I sought out the argument of the person I did
   not know.
¹⁷I broke the jaws of the evildoer
  and threw the prey from his teeth.
¹⁸I said, 'I shall breathe my last with my nest,
  I shall make my days as many as the phoenix,
¹⁹My root opened to the water,
  dew lodging in my branches,
²⁰My splendour fresh with me,
  my bow renewing itself in my hand.'
²¹People listened to me and waited,
  they kept themselves quiet for my counsel.
²²After my utterance they would not speak again;
  upon them my word would drop.
²³They would wait for me as for rain,
  they would open their mouth as for the late rain.
²⁴When I would make fun with them, they would
   not believe it;
  the light of my face they would not discount.
²⁵I would choose the way for them and sit as head,
  I would dwell like a king among his troops,
  like one who comforts mourners.

Iyyob: The way things are (1)

30 But now people make fun of me,
   people younger than me in days,
People whose fathers I would have rejected
  from putting with my sheep dogs.

²Indeed, what use would the energy of their hands be to me,
    when their vigour has perished from them,
³People who in want and desolate hunger flee,
    to the arid ground, the edge of devastating devastation,
⁴Who pick the saltwort on bushes;
    the root of broom is their food.
⁵They are driven out from society,
    people shout at them like a thief,
⁶So they dwell in the gully of wadis,
    holes in the earth and rocks.
⁷They bray among the bushes,
    huddle under the thistles,
⁸Villains, yes, nameless people,
    they are struck down from the country.
⁹And now I've become their song,
    I've become something to talk about for them.

¹⁰People take offence at me, they stay far from me,
    but they don't hold back spit from my face.
¹¹Because someone has loosened my bow and humbled me,
    before me they've let loose restraint.
¹²When a brood arises at my right,
    they let my feet loose,
    and build up their paths to disaster against me.
¹³They break down my trail to express malice to me;
    they profit though they have no helper.
¹⁴They come as through a wide breach,
    beneath the devastation they roll in.
¹⁵Terrors are turned upon me;
    like the wind it pursues my honour.
My deliverance passes on like a cloud,
    ¹⁶so now my life pours out for me.
Days of humbling grasp me,
    ¹⁷night pierces my bones for me,
    and the things that gnaw at me don't rest.

Iyyob: The way things are (2)

¹⁸With abundance of energy he grasps my clothing,
    belts me like the neck of my garment.
¹⁹He has thrown me into the mud,
    and I've come to resemble earth and ashes.

²⁰I cry for help to you but you don't answer me,
    though I stood, and you considered me.
²¹You turn into someone cruel to me;
    with the might of your hand you're hostile to me.
²²You lift me to the wind, make me ride on it,
    and dissolve me with a crash.
²³Indeed I know you'll take me back to death,
    to the appointed home for every living person.
²⁴Surely no one puts out his hand against a ruin,
    if in his calamity there is a cry for help regarding these things.
²⁵If I did not cry for one whose day was tough –
    my entire being grieved for the needy.
²⁶Indeed I hoped for good things, but bad things came;
    I waited for light, but darkness came.
²⁷My insides churn and don't stop,
    my days of humbling meet me.
²⁸I walk about dark, without warmth;
    when I get up in the congregation I cry for help.
²⁹I've become a brother to jackals,
    a friend to ostriches.
³⁰My skin turns black on me,
    my bones burn with heat.
³¹My guitar has become for mourning,
    my pipe for the sound of people crying.

Iyyob: The way I have walked (1)

31 ¹I sealed a pact for my eyes,
    so how could I consider a girl?
²What is the share that God gives from above,
    the domain that Shadday gives from the heights?
³It's disaster for the evildoer, isn't it,
    ruin for the people who devise trouble.
⁴He himself sees my ways, doesn't he,
    takes account of all my steps.
⁵Have I walked with emptiness,
    has my foot hastened after guile?
⁶He should weigh me on faithful scales,
    so that God may acknowledge my integrity.

⁷If my step turns aside from the way,
    or my mind has gone after my eyes,
    or a blemish has stuck to my palms,
⁸May I sow but another eat,
    may my descendants be uprooted.

⁹If my mind has been enticed by a woman
    or I have lain in wait at my neighbour's door,
¹⁰May my wife grind for another,
    and over her may other men kneel,

¹¹Because this would have been a deliberate wickedness;
it would be waywardness for the mediators to deal with,
¹²Because it is a fire that consumes to Abaddon,
and it would uproot my entire yield.

Iyyob: The way I have walked (2)

¹³If I've rejected the case of my servant or my maidservant
when they argued with me,
¹⁴What will I do when God arises;
when he pays attention, what will I say back?
¹⁵Didn't my maker make him inside his mother,
didn't one person prepare us in the womb?

¹⁶If I hold back from the want of poor people,
or let a widow's eyes fail,
¹⁷And eat my bit of food alone,
so that the orphan has not eaten of it,
¹⁸Because from my youth he has grown up with me like a father,
and I have guided her from my mother's womb;
¹⁹If I see someone perishing for lack of clothing,
and a needy person has no covering,
²⁰If his insides have not blessed me
when he would get warm from the shearing of my sheep,
²¹If I have shaken my hand against the orphan
because I could see that I had help at the gateway;
²²My shoulder blade should fall from the shoulder,
my forearm break from the joint,
²³Because disaster from God would be dread to me
and I could not endure his dignity.

Iyyob: The way I have walked (3)

²⁴If I've made gold my assurance
or said to fine gold, 'My confidence',
²⁵If I rejoice because my resources are great,
because my hand has found a massive amount,
²⁶If I see light when it shines,
or the bright moon going,
²⁷And my mind was enticed in secret
and my hand kissed my mouth,
²⁸That, too, would be waywardness calling for mediation,
because I would have been deceiving God above.
²⁹If I rejoice in the calamity of someone hostile to me
or thrill when bad fortune found him –
³⁰But I haven't given my mouth to wrongdoing,
to asking for his life by a curse.
³¹If the men in my tent have not said,
'If only there was someone who had not been full of his meat!'
³²No stranger lodges in the street;
I open my doors to the path.
³³If I covered my rebellion like Adam,
hiding my waywardness in my heart,
³⁴Because I fear the great horde,
and the contempt of kin-groups would terrify me,
so that I would keep quiet and not go out of my entrance . . .

³⁵If only I had someone listening to me:
here is my mark – Shadday should answer me,
the one who argues with me should write a document.
³⁶If I did not carry it on my shoulder,
bind it on me as my crown.
³⁷I would tell him the number of my steps,
present it as to a ruler.

³⁸If my land cries out against me
and its furrows weep together,
³⁹If I have consumed its energy without silver
and made its owners sigh,
⁴⁰In place of wheat may thistle come up,
in place of barley, stinkweed.

The words of Iyyob have come to an end.

Elihu: The angry young man

32 These three men stopped answering Iyyob, because he was in the right in his eyes. ²But anger raged in Elihu ben Barak'el the Buzite, of the family of Ram. His anger raged at Iyyob because he thought himself more in the right than God, ³and his anger raged at his three friends because they didn't find an answer although they declared him in the wrong. ⁴While Elihu had waited for Iyyob with his words because they were older than him in years, ⁵Elihu saw that there was no answer in the mouth of the three men, and his anger raged. ⁶So Elihu ben Barak'el the Buzite answered:

I am young in years
    and you are old.
For this reason I hesitated and was afraid
    of explaining what I know to you.
⁷I said, 'Age should speak,
    abundance of years should make smartness known.'
⁸Nevertheless it is the spirit in a human being,
    the breath of Shadday, that gives understanding.
⁹It's not the advanced people who are smart
    or the elders who understand the exercise of authority.
¹⁰Therefore I say, 'Listen to me,
    I myself will explain what I know, I as well.'
¹¹There, I've waited for your words,
    I've given ear to your understanding.
While you searched out utterances,
    ¹²I was giving consideration to you.
But there, there is no one who has reproved Iyyob,
    none of you has answered the things he said.
¹³Beware that you say, 'We've found smartness;
    God must blow him away, not a human being.'
¹⁴He did not line up utterances for me,
    and I shall not give back reply to him with the things you said.

¹⁵Because they are fearful, they haven't answered any more;
    utterances have moved on from them.
¹⁶I waited when they didn't speak,
    when they halted, they didn't answer any more.
¹⁷I myself will answer, I too, with my share,
    I will declare what I know, I too.
¹⁸Because I am full of utterances;
    the spirit in my insides constrains me.
¹⁹There, my insides are like wine that isn't open,
    like skins of new wine that burst.
²⁰I must speak so it will relieve me,
    I shall open my lips and answer.
²¹Please, I will not show regard for anyone
    or give titles to any person.
²²Because I don't know how to give titles;
    my maker would soon carry me off.

Elihu: Don't argue with God

33 However, please listen to my utterances, Iyyob,
    give ear to all I have to say.
²Here, please, I'm opening my lips,
    my tongue is speaking in my palate.
³The things I say are the uprightness of my mind;
    my lips utter knowledge, purified.
⁴God's spirit made me;
    Shadday's breath keeps me alive.
⁵If you can, speak back to me;
    lay it out before me, take your stand.
⁶Here am I, the same as you to God;
    I was nipped from clay, I too.
⁷There, dread of me should not terrify you;
    pressure from me should not be heavy on you.

⁸You indeed have said in my ears,
    I could hear the sound of the utterances:
⁹'I am clean, without rebellion;
    I am pure and there's no waywardness in me.
¹⁰There, he finds occasions for opposition to me,
    he thinks of me as his enemy.
¹¹He puts my feet in the stocks,
    he watches all my paths.'
¹²There, in this you're not in the right;
    I shall answer to you, that God is greater than a mere human being.
¹³Why do you argue with him,
    because he doesn't answer any of someone's words?
¹⁴Because God speaks once,
    and twice, though he does not behold it.

Elihu: How God tries to win us back

¹⁵In a dream, a vision in the night,
    when deep sleep falls on people,
    during slumbers in bed,
¹⁶Then he opens the ear of people,
    and in disciplining them perturbs them,
¹⁷To turn a person away from an action
    and cover a man's majesty from him.
¹⁸He holds his life back from the Pit,
    his existence from crossing the River.
¹⁹He is reproved by pains on his bed,
    constant argument in his bones.
²⁰His existence makes him loathe bread,
    his life desirable food.

²¹His flesh fails so that it cannot be seen,
   his bones that could not be seen are laid bare.
²²His life draws near to the Pit,
   his existence to the bringers of death.
²³If there is an envoy by him,
   one spokesperson from the thousand,
To tell of the person's uprightness,
   ²⁴and be gracious to him and say,
'Redeem him from going down to the Pit,
   I have found a ransom':
²⁵His flesh healthier than his youth,
   he will go back to his young days.
²⁶He will pray to God and he will accept him;
   he will see his face with a shout.
So he will give back his right standing to the person;
   ²⁷he will sing to people and say,
'I did wrong and twisted what was upright,
   and it was not advantageous for me.
²⁸He redeemed my life from passing into the Pit;
   my existence will see light.'
²⁹There, God does all these things,
   twice, three times with a man,
³⁰To bring him back from the Pit
   so that he may be alight with the light of life.

³¹Heed, Iyyob, listen to me;
   be quiet, and I will speak.
³²If there are things to say, speak back;
   speak, because I want you to be in the right.
³³If there are not, you listen to me;
   be quiet, and I will teach you smartness.

Elihu: Drinking ridicule like water

34 Elihu answered:

²Listen to my utterances, you smart people;
   give ear to me, you who have knowledge.
³Because the ear tests utterances,
   as the palate tastes something to eat.
⁴Let's choose a ruling for ourselves,
   let's acknowledge between ourselves what is good.
⁵Because Iyyob has said, 'I'm in the right;
   God has turned aside the case about me.
⁶Regarding the case about me, I declare it a lie,
   my arrow-wound grave, without having rebelled.'
⁷What man is like Iyyob,
   who drinks ridicule like water?
⁸He travels in company with people who devise trouble,
   and he walks with faithless people,
⁹Because he's said, 'There's no benefit to a man,
   in his being accepted with God.'

¹⁰Therefore, you sensible people,
   listen to me.
Far be it for God to act in faithlessness,
   for Shadday to do evil.
¹¹Because he makes good for a person's action to him,
   and in accordance with an individual's path he makes him meet with things.
¹²Indeed, in truth God does not act faithlessly;
   Shadday does not twist the exercise of authority.
¹³Who appointed the earth to him,
   who set the world [to him], all of it?
¹⁴If he sets his mind to it,
   he can gather his spirit and his breath to him.
¹⁵All flesh would breathe their last together
   and humanity go back to earth.
¹⁶So if there is to be understanding, listen to this,
   give ear to the sound of my utterances.
¹⁷Is someone indeed in control who is hostile to the [proper] exercise of authority
   – do you declare the faithful, strong one to be in the wrong?
¹⁸He is the one who says to a king, 'Scoundrel',
   to rulers, 'Faithless',
¹⁹ªWho does not show regard to officials
   and does not recognize the important person before the poor.

Elihu: Tested to the limit

¹⁹ᵇBecause all of them are the making of his hands;
   ²⁰suddenly they die, in the middle of the night.
A people is in turmoil and they pass away;
   a sturdy person is removed, not by human hand.
²¹Because his eyes are on an individual's ways;
   he sees all his steps.
²²There is no darkness, there is no deathly shadow,
   for people who devise trouble to hide there.
²³Because he doesn't lay down a set time for an individual
   to go to God for a ruling.

²⁴He shatters strong people without searching out,
   and puts others in place instead of them.
²⁵Thus he recognizes their deeds;
   he overturns them in the night and they
      collapse.
²⁶He pummels them among the faithless
   in a place where people see.
²⁷Because of the fact that they have departed from
      following him;
   they have not had insight into any of his ways,
²⁸So as to cause the cry of the poor to come to
      him,
   so that he listens to the cry of the humble.
²⁹Should he be calm, who can call him faithless,
   should he hide his face, who can behold him?
He is over nation and over individual together,
   ³⁰to stop the impious person reigning,
   to stop a people's traps.
³¹Because has someone said to God,
   'I will carry it, I will not act ruinously.
³²What I cannot behold, instruct me in yourself;
   if I have done evil, I will not do so again'?
³³Is he to make good in the way you think, when
      you've rejected him?
   – because you should choose, not I;
   speak what you know.
³⁴People with sense say to me,
   a smart man listening to me:
³⁵'Iyyob doesn't speak with knowledge,
   his words are not with insight.
³⁶Would that Iyyob were tested to the limit,
   about replies befitting people who devise
      trouble.
³⁷Because he adds to his wrongdoing:
   he abounds in rebellion among us,
   and multiplies the things he says to God.'

Elihu: What difference do you make to God?

35 Elihu answered:

²Do you think this is a good ruling,
   when you say, 'I am more in the right than
      God'?
³When you say, how does it benefit you –
   'How do I profit more than from wrongdoing?'
⁴I myself will make utterances back to you,
   and your friends with you.
⁵Look to the heavens and see,
   behold the skies that are lofty above you.

⁶If you have done wrong, what do you do to him,
   and if your rebellions have been many, what do
      you do to him?
⁷If you are in the right, what do you give him,
   or what does he get from your hand?
⁸Your faithlessness affects a person like yourself,
   your being in the right affects a human being.

⁹Because of the multitude of the oppressed, people
      cry out;
   they cry for help because of the power
      exercised against so many,
¹⁰But no one says, 'Where is God my maker,
   who gives melodies in the night,
¹¹Who teaches us more than the animals of the
      earth,
   makes us smarter than the birds in the
      heavens?'
¹²They cry out there but he does not answer
   before the majesty of bad people.
¹³Indeed God does not listen to emptiness,
   Shadday does not behold it.
¹⁴How much less when you say you don't behold
      him,
   your case is before him, and you wait for him,
¹⁵And now that his anger has given no attention,
   and he has not given much acknowledgement
      to rebellion.
¹⁶Iyyob opens his mouth with hollowness,
   multiplies words that are without knowledge.

Elihu: The God who opens our ear

36 Elihu again spoke:

²Wait for me a little and I will explain to you,
   because there are yet utterances to be said for
      God.
³I will carry my knowledge from far away,
   and I will ascribe faithfulness to my maker.
⁴Because truly my utterances are not false;
   one with integrity in knowledge is with you.

⁵There, God is strong but he doesn't reject –
   strong in energy of mind.
⁶He doesn't let the faithless person live,
   and he gives a ruling for the humble people.
⁷He doesn't hold back his eyes from faithful
      people,
   but seats them with kings on a throne,
   permanently, and they are lofty.

⁸If people are bound in chains,
　　caught in humbling bonds,
⁹He tells them what they've done,
　　and their acts of rebellion, that they acted big.
¹⁰He opens their ear to correction
　　and says how they should turn back from trouble.
¹¹If they listen and serve,
　　they'll finish their days with good things,
　　their years in happiness.
¹²But if they don't listen, they'll cross the River,
　　they'll breathe their last without knowledge.
¹³But the impious of mind lay up anger,
　　they don't cry for help when he binds them.
¹⁴They die in youth,
　　their existence among the hierodules.
¹⁵He pulls the humble person out through his humbling,
　　and opens their ear through affliction.

Elihu: God is great, and we cannot know

¹⁶Indeed, he has drawn you away from the brink of pressure,
　　to a broad place where there is no constraint, instead of it,
　　and what is laid on your table is full of richness.
¹⁷But you're full of the judgement due to the faithless person;
　　judgement and the exercise of authority take hold.
¹⁸Because wrath mustn't draw you away through wealth;
　　a large amount of ransom money must not turn you aside.
¹⁹Would your wealth line up, without pressure,
　　and all your energetic efforts?
²⁰Don't long for the night,
　　to take up peoples where they are.
²¹Keep watch, don't turn your face to trouble,
　　because you've chosen this rather than humbling.
²²There, God towers in his energy;
　　who is an instructor like him?
²³Who has appointed his way for him,
　　who has said, 'You've done evil'?
²⁴Be mindful that you should exalt what he does,
　　which people have sung about.
²⁵All humanity has beheld it;
　　a human being looks at it from afar.
²⁶There, God is great, and we cannot know –
　　of the number of his years there is no searching out.
²⁷Because he draws up the drops of water
　　that distil as rain in his mist,
²⁸Which the skies pour down,
　　dispense upon humanity as a shower.
²⁹Indeed, can one understand the spreading of cloud,
　　the thunders from his bivouac?
³⁰There, he spreads his lightning over it,
　　he uncovers the roots of the sea.
³¹Because by these things he governs peoples,
　　gives food in abundance.
³²He covers over the palms of his hands with lightning,
　　and orders it against its mark.
³³His thunder tells of him,
　　his angry passion against evil.

Elihu: The awe-inspiring Creator

37 Indeed at this my heart trembles
　　and leaps from its place.
²Listen, listen to the raging of his voice,
　　the murmur that comes out from his mouth.
³Beneath the entire heavens he lets it loose,
　　and his lightning over the corners of the earth.
⁴After it, a voice roars;
　　he thunders with his majestic voice.
He doesn't hold them back
　　when his voice makes itself heard;
⁵God thunders with his voice in extraordinary ways,
　　does great things that we cannot know,
⁶When he says to the snow,
　　'Fall on the earth',
And the downpour of rain,
　　his vigorous downpour of the rains.
⁷On every human being's hand he imposes a seal,
　　so that everyone may acknowledge what he does.
⁸Living things come into the lair,
　　lie down in their den.
⁹The tempest comes out of its room,
　　the cold from the driving winds.
¹⁰By God's breath he makes ice,
　　and the expanse of water into something frozen.
¹¹He also loads the cloud with moisture,
　　scatters his lightning thundercloud,

¹²And it turns round and round at his directions,
so that they do all that he commands them.
Over the face of the earthly world,
¹³either for the exercise of his club, or for the sake of his earth,
or for the sake of his commitment – he makes them happen.

¹⁴Give ear to this, Iyyob;
stand and consider God's extraordinary deeds.
¹⁵Do you know how God lays things upon them,
how the lightning from his thundercloud shines out?
¹⁶Do you know about the balancing of the clouds,
the extraordinary deeds of the one who is perfect in knowledge,
¹⁷You whose clothes become hot,
when the earth is calm because of the south wind?
¹⁸Could you spread the skies with him,
hard like a mirror of cast metal?
¹⁹Help us know what we're to say to him;
we can't lay it out, from before darkness.
²⁰Will it be announced to him that I shall speak,
has someone said that he is confused?
²¹But now, people cannot look at the light,
when it is bright in the skies.
And the wind has passed and cleared them,
²²when gold comes from the north.
God On High, awe-inspiring in grandeur,
²³Shadday: we couldn't find him.
Great in energy and in the exercise of authority,
but with abundance of faithfulness, he doesn't humble.
²⁴Therefore people live in awe of him,
though he doesn't look at any of the smart-minded.

Yahweh: You need to accept your limits

38 Yahweh answered Iyyob from a hurricane:

²Who is this who darkens counsel
by utterances without knowledge?
³Belt up your thighs like a man, please,
so I can ask you and you can let me know.

⁴Where were you when I founded the earth?
– tell, if you know and understand.
⁵Who set its dimensions, since you will know,
or who stretched a line over it?
⁶On what were its bases sunk,
or who threw its cornerstone,
⁷When the morning stars resounded together
and all the divine beings shouted?

⁸And who shut the sea in with doors,
when it gushed from the womb it came out of,
⁹When I made cloud its clothing,
thundercloud its blanket,
¹⁰Decreed my limit for it,
set a bar and doors,
¹¹And said, 'You may come as far as this,
but not go further;
here it's set, at the majesty of your waves'?

¹²Since your days began, have you ordered morning,
let the dawn know its place,
¹³For it to grasp the earth by the corners,
so that faithless people shake out of it?
¹⁴It turns like clay under a seal,
so that they stand out like a garment.
¹⁵From faithless people their light holds back,
and their high arm breaks.

¹⁶Have you come to the springs of the sea,
or walked about through the reaches of the deep?
¹⁷Have the gateways of death opened to you,
or can you see the gateways of deathly shadow?
¹⁸Have you considered the expanses of the earth?
– tell, if you know it all.

Yahweh: What do you really know?

¹⁹Where is the way to where light dwells,
and darkness – where is its place,
²⁰That you may take it to its territory,
and understand the trails to its home?
²¹You know, because you were coming to birth then,
and the number of your years is many.

²²Have you come to the storehouses of snow,
or can you see the storehouses of hail,
²³Which I have held back for the time of pressure,
for the day of drawing near and of battle?
²⁴Where then is the way to where lightning is shared out,
where the east wind is scattered over the earth?

²⁵Who cut a channel for the torrent,
 and a way for the bolt of thunder,
²⁶To rain on land with no people,
 wilderness with no one in it,
²⁷To satisfy the devastated devastation,
 and make a crop of grass flourish?
²⁸Does the rain have a father,
 or who fathered the drops of dew?
²⁹From whose womb did the ice come out,
 the frost from the heavens, who fathered it,
³⁰When water hardens like stone,
 and the surface of the deep freezes?

³¹Can you tie Pleiades' bonds,
 or loose Orion's belt?
³²Can you lead out Mazzarot at its time,
 or lead out the Bear with its children?
³³Do you know the decrees of the heavens,
 or can you implement its authority on earth?

³⁴Can you lift up your voice to the cloud,
 so that a flood of water may cover you?
³⁵Can you send off shafts of lightning so that they go,
 and say to you, 'Here we are!'
³⁶Who put smartness in the ibis,
 or who gave understanding to the cockerel?
³⁷Who can give an account of the skies with smartness,
 and tilt the water skins in the heavens,
³⁸When earth pours into a mass,
 and clods are made to stick together?

Yahweh: Could you care for nature?

³⁹Can you hunt prey for a lion,
 and fill the appetite of whelps,
⁴⁰When they crouch in dens,
 lie in wait in a bivouac?
⁴¹Who prepares its provision for the raven
 when its young cry for help to God
 and wander without food?

39 Do you know the time for the mountain goats to give birth,
 keep watch as the deer goes into labour?
²Do you count the months they complete,
 or know the time for their giving birth?
³They crouch so that they may deliver their young,
 as they send off their pains.
⁴Their offspring become strong, they grow up in the open,
 they go out and don't come back to them.

⁵Who sends off the wild donkey, free,
 and who looses the ropes of the wild mule,
⁶Whose home I made the steppe,
 its dwellings the salty land?
⁷It makes fun of the uproar of the township;
 it doesn't listen to the shouts of a driver.
⁸It ranges mountains as its pasture,
 and searches after any green thing.

⁹Is an oryx willing to serve you,
 will it lodge by your feeding trough?
¹⁰Can you hold an oryx with a harness to the furrow,
 will it till the vales behind you?
¹¹Can you rely on it because its energy is great,
 and abandon your toil to it?
¹²Can you trust it that it will bring back your seed,
 and gather it to your threshing floor?

¹³The wing of the screechers exults:
 is it a stork's wing and plumage?
¹⁴Because she abandons her eggs on the earth,
 lets them get warm on the earth,
¹⁵And puts out of mind that a foot may crush it,
 or a creature of the wild trample it.
¹⁶She's tough with her offspring so that they are not hers,
 her toil is in vain, without dread.
¹⁷Because God made her forget smartness,
 didn't give a share of understanding to her.
¹⁸At the time when she flaps on high,
 she makes fun of the horse and its rider.

Yahweh: So many extraordinary creatures!

¹⁹Do you give the horse its strength,
 do you clothe its neck with a mane?
²⁰Do you make it quiver like a locust?
 – the grandeur of its snort is a dread.
²¹They paw with force; it rejoices in its energy,
 as it goes out to meet the weapons.
²²It makes fun of dread, doesn't frighten,
 doesn't turn back from the face of the sword.
²³By it a quiver resounds,
 a flash of lance and javelin.
²⁴With shaking and raging it swallows the earth,
 and it can't stand firm when there's the sound of the horn.

²⁵At the blast of the horn it says, 'Ah',
and from far away it smells battle,
the thunder of the officers, and the shout.

²⁶Is it by your understanding that the hawk takes flight,
spreads its wings to the south?
²⁷Is it at your bidding that the eagle is lofty,
and that it puts its nest high?
²⁸It dwells on the cliff,
and lodges on an outcrop of the cliff, a stronghold.
²⁹From there it searches for food,
from far away its eyes look out,
³⁰So its young drink blood;
where there are people who have been run through, there it is.

40 Yahweh answered Iyyob:

²Does the person who argues with Shadday correct him?
– the one who reproves God must answer it.

³Iyyob answered Yahweh:

⁴There, I am slight, what could I say back?
– I put my hand to my mouth.
⁵I have spoken once, and I will not answer –
twice, and I will not do so again.

Yahweh: Think about the Great Creature

⁶But Yahweh answered Iyyob from a hurricane:

⁷Belt up your thighs like a man, please,
so I can ask you and you can let me know.
⁸Would you indeed contravene my exercise of authority,
declare me in the wrong in order that you may be in the right?
⁹Do you have an arm like God,
or can you thunder with a voice like his?
¹⁰Adorn yourself with majesty and loftiness, please,
clothe yourself in splendour and grandeur.
¹¹Scatter your angry outbursts about,
see every majestic person and bring him low.
¹²See every majestic person and make him bow down,
throw down the faithless where they stand.
¹³Bury them in the earth all together,
conceal their faces in the hidden place.
¹⁴And I too will confess you,
that your right hand can bring deliverance to you.

¹⁵There, please, is the Great Creature, which I made along with you,
which eats grass like cattle.
¹⁶There, please, its energy is in its insides,
its vigour in the muscles of its stomach.
¹⁷It hangs its tail like a cedar,
the sinews of its thighs are intertwined.
¹⁸Its bones are tubes of copper,
its limbs like a bar of iron.
¹⁹It is the first of God's ways;
its maker can draw near with his sword.
²⁰Because the mountains carry produce for it,
and all the animals of the wild have fun there,
²¹It lies down underneath the lotuses,
in the cover of the reeds and in the marsh.
²²The lotuses screen it as its shade,
the willows of the wadi surround it.
²³There – when the river gushes, it doesn't make haste;
it's confident that Yarden [Jordan] bursts forth at its bidding.
²⁴Can someone take it by its eyes
or pierce its nose, in traps?

Yahweh: Think about Livyatan

41 Can you pull in Livyatan with a fishhook
or tie down its tongue with a rope?
²Can you put a reed in its nose
or pierce its jaw with a hook?
³Will it make many prayers for grace to you,
will it speak smooth words to you?
⁴Will it seal a pact with you
that it will be taken as a lifelong servant?
⁵Will you have fun with it like a bird
or put it on a leash for your girls?
⁶Will partners barter over it,
will they divide it up among the dealers?
⁷Can you fill its skin with harpoons
or its head with fish spears?
⁸Lay your fist on it,
be mindful of the battle, don't do it again.
⁹There, hope for [capturing] it tells a lie
– isn't one even overwhelmed at the sight of it?

¹⁰No one is so cruel that he gets it to rise;
   so who is the one who takes a stand before me?
¹¹Who confronts me so that I make good?
   – under the entire heavens, things are mine.

¹²I will not be silent about its limbs or its strong word,
   or the grace of its frame.
¹³Who has stripped off the surface of its garment,
   who can come with a double bridle for it?
¹⁴Who has opened the doors of its face?
   – its teeth all round are a dread.
¹⁵Its back is rows of shields,
   shut up with a tight seal.
¹⁶One comes up to the other;
   a breath could not come between them.
¹⁷They stick each one to its brother;
   they clasp each other and cannot separate.
¹⁸Its sneezes flash lightning,
   its eyes are like the eyelids of dawn.
¹⁹From its mouth go torches,
   sparks of fire escape.
²⁰From its nostrils smoke goes out,
   like a pot heated, with rushes.
²¹Its breath sets coals on fire;
   flame goes out from its mouth.

Iyyob relents

²²In its neck vigour lodges;
   dismay leaps before it.
²³The folds of its flesh stick;
   it is cast on it, it doesn't slip.
²⁴Its heart is cast like stone,
   cast like a bottom millstone.
²⁵At its rising up, divine beings are in dread;
   at its crashes, they fail.
²⁶The sword that reaches it does not prevail –
   spear, dart or lance.
²⁷It thinks of iron as straw,
   of copper as rotten wood.
²⁸Arrow doesn't make it take flight;
   sling stones turn into chaff for it.
²⁹A club is thought of as chaff;
   it makes fun of the shaking of a javelin.
³⁰Its underparts are sharp bits of pot;
   it spreads a threshing sledge on mud.
³¹It makes the deep boil like a pot,
   it makes the sea like a pot of ointment.
³²Behind it, it lightens a trail;
   one would think the deep to be white hair.
³³There is no one on the earth to rule it,
   made without fright.
³⁴It sees everything lofty;
   it is king over all noble creatures.

42 Iyyob answered Yahweh:

²I acknowledge that you can do anything;
   no strategy is impracticable for you.
³'Who is this who darkens counsel without knowledge?'
   – thus I told of things that I did not understand,
   things too extraordinary for me, that I did not know.
⁴'Listen, please, and I myself will speak;
   I will ask and you can let me know.'
⁵I have listened to you with the listening of an ear,
   and now my eye has seen you.
⁶Therefore I reject and find consolation
   about earth and ashes.

So they all lived happily ever after

⁷After Yahweh had spoken these words to Iyyob, Yahweh said to Eliphaz the Temanite, 'My anger rages against you and against your two friends, because you haven't spoken to me what is established truth, like my servant Iyyob. ⁸So now get yourselves seven bulls and seven rams, go to my servant Iyyob and offer up a burnt offering on your behalf. Iyyob my servant can plead for you, because I will show regard to him so as not to act with you in the light of your villainy, because you haven't spoken to me what is established truth, like my servant Iyyob.' ⁹Eliphaz the Temanite, Bildad the Shuhite and Tsophar the Na'amatite went and did as Yahweh spoke to them.

Yahweh showed regard to Iyyob. ¹⁰When Yahweh restored Iyyob's fortunes after he pleaded on behalf of his friends, Yahweh increased all that Iyyob had to double. ¹¹All his brothers and all his sisters and all his former acquaintances came and ate a meal with him at his house. They consoled and comforted him for all the bad things that Yahweh had brought on him, and they gave him a piece of silver each and a gold ring each.

¹²When Yahweh blessed the latter part of Iyyob's life more than the former, he had 14,000 sheep, 6,000 camels, 1,000 yoke of cattle and

1,000 donkeys. ¹³He had seven sons and three daughters. ¹⁴He named the first Yemimah, the second Ketsiyah and the third Qeren Happuk. ¹⁵There could not be found women as beautiful as Iyyob's daughters in the entire country. And their father gave them a domain among their brothers.

¹⁶Afterwards, Iyyob lived 140 years, and saw his sons and his grandsons, four generations. ¹⁷Iyyob died old and full of years.

Psalms

The book of Psalms is a collection of 150 things that we can say to God. In putting it that way, I oversimplify slightly, as a few psalms have God speaking to us, but the vast majority are prayers and praises addressed to God. You could say that they are Israel's hymn book and prayer book.

They are divided into five books – English translations make that point explicit with the headings 'Book One' (at the beginning), 'Book Two' (at Psalm 42), and so on. The five books of Psalms thus parallel the five books of the Torah. The Torah comprises teaching on what God has done for Israel and on the life God expects of Israel. The Psalms comprise teaching on the nature of praise and prayer. But they teach not by giving instructions but by giving examples. The examples divide into a few main types.

1. There are hymns of praise for who God is and for the great things God has done in creation and for his people. They refer to the exodus and to God's involvement in Israel's subsequent story. But they also emphasize how all the nations should therefore come to acknowledge this God.
2. There are prayers of protest about the way things are now working out, which contrasts with the affirmations appearing in the praise hymns. There are protests that belong on the lips of the people as a whole, of their leader and of individuals. They describe how Israel itself has been defeated, how its leader is under attack, and how an individual is overwhelmed by people's attacks or accusations. One noteworthy feature is the amount of space they give to description of the plight and suffering of the people who are praying; they are much less specific about what they expect God to do beyond acting to rescue. While formulating this description no doubt offers release for them, its more direct point is to get God to notice and take action. And sometimes before these psalms end, they already express the conviction that God has heard the pleas, so that the person praying can look forward to the act of God that will follow.
3. There are some prayers that presuppose the reality of that kind of experience but are more dominated by a note of trust and hope.
4. There are songs of praise that testify to the way God has responded to a prayer of this kind and has delivered the people or the leader or the individual. A noteworthy feature of them is the way they mingle addressing God in thanksgiving and addressing other people in testimony. They are designed both to glorify God and to build up the faith and trust of people who have not had this experience of deliverance.

A few psalms don't fit into these categories. Some speak from God or from a human teacher to the community rather than from human beings to God. The first two psalms are examples, Psalm 1 being a challenge to faithful living, Psalm 2 a declaration about God's faithfulness to the Davidic king. Such psalms remind worshippers that they can't be involved in praise or prayer unless they are people living faithful lives. And they remind them that the God of whom the psalms speak is one involved in the political affairs of the nation and committed to fulfilling his purpose in the world. The fact that there was no Davidic king after the fall of Jerusalem meant that the psalms' references to the king became promises and declarations of hope about the Davidic king that God would surely enthrone again one day, and this development is part of the background to references to them in the New Testament.

The Davidic king is an important figure in the Psalms, though the references to David in the introductions to the psalms don't imply that he wrote them. The introductions relate to ways in which the Psalms were used in worship (e.g. tunes), and we don't understand many of the terms they use. However many psalms David may have written, his position as the patron of the Temple means that they all appear under his sponsorship. The key to using the Psalms is the realization that they are designed for ongoing use by the people of God and by individuals, so that who wrote them is not very important.

Psalm 1 You have a choice

¹ The blessings of someone who has not walked
  by the counsel of the faithless,
Or stood on the way of wrongdoers,
  or lived in the settlement of the arrogant!
²Rather, his delight is in Yahweh's instruction,
  and he murmurs about his instruction day and
    night.
³He's like a tree planted by channels of water,
  which gives its fruit in its time,
And its foliage doesn't fade;
  all that he does succeeds.
⁴Not so the faithless people;
  rather, they're like the chaff that the wind blows
    away.
⁵Therefore the faithless don't rise up when a ruling
    is given,
  nor wrongdoers in the assembly of the faithful.
⁶Because Yahweh acknowledges the way of the
    faithful,
  but the way of the faithless perishes.

Psalm 2 God laughs on his people's behalf

¹Why have nations crowded together,
  and peoples murmur about something empty,
²Earth's kings take a stand,
  leaders made plans together,
  against Yahweh and against his anointed –
³'We'll break off their means of discipline,
  throw off their ropes from us'?
⁴The one who sits in the heavens makes fun;
  the Lord ridicules them.
⁵Then he speaks to them in his anger,
  terrifies them with his rage.
⁶'But I myself installed my king on Tsiyyon [Zion],
  my sacred mountain!'
⁷I shall recount Yahweh's decree:
  he said to me,
'You're my son;
  today I myself have fathered you.
⁸Ask of me and I'll make nations your domain,
  earth's ends your holding.
⁹You'll smash them with an iron club,
  shatter them like an object made by a potter.'
¹⁰So now, show some insight, you kings,
  accept discipline, you people who exercise
    authority in the earth.
¹¹Serve Yahweh with awe,
  rejoice with trembling, surrender sincerely,
¹²So that he doesn't get angry
  and you perish as regards the way,
Because his anger will soon burn up;
  the blessings of all who take shelter with him!

Psalm 3 You're not alone

A composition. For David when he took flight from Abshalom his son.

¹Yahweh, how many are my adversaries;
  many people are rising up against me.
²Many people are saying of me,
  'There's no deliverance in God for him!' *(Rise)*
³But you are Yahweh, a shield about me,
  my splendour, the one who lifts my head
    high.
⁴With my voice I would call to Yahweh,
  and he's answered me from his sacred
    mountain. *(Rise)*
⁵I myself have lain down and slept;
  I've woken up, because Yahweh sustains me.
⁶I'm not afraid of a company of myriads
  that has set itself against me all round.

⁷Rise up, Yahweh,
  deliver me, my God,
Because you've struck all my enemies on the jaw;
  you've smashed the teeth of the faithless.
⁸Deliverance belongs to Yahweh,
  your blessing is on your people. *(Rise)*

Psalm 4 Who can I turn to?

The leader's. With strings. A composition. David's.

¹When I call, answer me,
  my faithful God!
Under pressure you widened me;
  be gracious to me and listen to my plea!

²You people, how long will the one I honour be
    for shaming,
  will you be loyal to something empty, will you
    seek a lie? *(Rise)*
³So acknowledge that Yahweh has distinguished
    the committed person for himself;
  Yahweh is the one who listens when I call to
    him.

⁴Tremble and don't do wrong;
   say it in your heart on your bed and be quiet.
   (Rise)
⁵Offer faithful sacrifices,
   and put your confidence in Yahweh.
⁶Increased numbers of people are saying,
   'Who will enable us to see good fortune?
   – the light of your face has fled from upon us, Yahweh.'
⁷You've put rejoicing in my heart
   from the time when their grain and their new wine has increased.
⁸In well-being I will lie down and sleep, all at once,
   because you alone are Yahweh;
   you enable me to live in confidence.

Psalm 5 Pleading with the King

The leader's. To flutes. A composition. David's.

¹Give ear to the things I say, Yahweh,
   consider my murmur.
²Heed the sound of my cry for help,
   my King and my God, because it's with you I plead.
³Yahweh, at morning may you listen to my voice,
   at morning I lay it out to you and wait.
⁴Because you're not a God who delights in faithlessness;
   that which is bad can't reside with you.
⁵Wild people can't take their stand in front of your eyes;
   you're hostile to all who devise trouble.
⁶You obliterate people who speak a lie;
   at someone of blood and guile, Yahweh takes offence.
⁷But I myself will come to your house through the abundance of your commitment;
   I will bow low to your sacred palace in awe of you.
⁸Yahweh, lead me in your faithfulness
   for the sake of the people who are watching for me;
   make your way direct before me.
⁹Because there's no established truth in their mouth;
   their inner being is malice.

Their throat is an opened grave,
   they're slippery with their tongue.
¹⁰Have them make restitution, God;
   they should fall by means of their own counsels.
Because of the abundance of their rebellions drive them out,
   because they've defied you.
¹¹But may all the people who take shelter with you rejoice,
   may they resound permanently.
As you protect them,
   may the people who are loyal to your name triumph in you.
¹²Because you yourself bless the faithful person, Yahweh;
   you surround him with acceptance like a body-shield.

Psalm 6 The way prayer makes a difference

The leader's. With strings. On the eighth [tone]. A composition. David's.

¹Yahweh, don't reprove me in your anger,
   don't discipline me with your wrath.
²Be gracious to me, Yahweh, because I'm faint;
   heal me, Yahweh, because my bones shake in fearfulness.
³My entire being shakes in great fearfulness,
   and you, Yahweh – how long?
⁴Turn back, Yahweh, pull me out,
   deliver me for the sake of your commitment!
⁵Because there's no commemoration of you in death;
   in Sheol who confesses you?
⁶I'm weary of my groaning, I make my bed swim every night,
   I melt my mattress with my tears.
⁷My eye has wasted away through provocation,
   grown old because of all my adversaries.
⁸Depart from me, all you who devise trouble,
   because Yahweh has heard the sound of my crying.
⁹Yahweh has heard my prayer for grace;
   Yahweh receives my plea.
¹⁰All my enemies will be shamed and be very fearful;
   they will turn back and be shamed instantly.

Psalm 7 The Judge is on your side

Lament. David's, which he sang for Yahweh concerning the Kushite [Sudanese] words. The Binyaminite.

¹Yahweh my God, in you I take shelter
 – deliver me from all the people who are pursuing me, rescue me,
²So that one doesn't tear me apart like a lion, ripping me to pieces when there's no one to rescue.
³Yahweh my God, if I did this, if there's evil in the palms of my hands,
⁴If I have dealt something bad to my friend, but pulled out my adversary without reason,
⁵May the enemy pursue me and overtake me, may he trample my life to the ground, may he lay down my splendour in the dirt.
 (Rise)

⁶Rise up, Yahweh, in your anger;
 lift yourself up at the great outburst of my adversaries.
Awake, my God, you must order the exercise of authority;
⁷the assembly of the nations should come round you.
Take your seat over it on high;
⁸Yahweh must rule the peoples.
Exercise authority for me, Yahweh,
 in accordance with my faithfulness and with my integrity, over me.
⁹The bad ways of faithless people must please come to an end,
 and you must establish the faithful person.

The faithful God
 is one who tests minds and inner being.
¹⁰God is my shield on high,
 one who delivers people who are upright in mind.
¹¹God exercises authority for the faithful person;
 God condemns each day.
¹²If someone doesn't turn back, he whets his sword;
 he's directed his bow and fixed it.
¹³He's fixed deadly weapons for himself,
 he makes his arrows into flames.
¹⁴There, someone twists with trouble,
 he's pregnant with oppression, he gives birth to falsehood.
¹⁵He's dug a cistern and made it deep,
 but he's fallen into the hole he makes.
¹⁶His act of oppression comes back on to his own head,
 his violence comes down on his own skull.

¹⁷I will confess Yahweh in accordance with his faithfulness
 and make music to the name of Yahweh, the One on High.

Psalm 8 Thus far and no further

The leader's. On the Gittite. A composition. David's.

¹Yahweh our God,
 how august is your name in all the earth,
You who put your grandeur above the heavens
 ²by the mouth of babies and sucklings.
You founded something vigorous to deal with your adversaries,
 to stop the enemy and the person taking redress.
³When I see the heavens, the things that your fingers made,
 moon and stars that you established,
⁴What are people that you are mindful of them,
 human beings that you attend to them?
⁵But you made them fall short of God by a little,
 and you crown them with honour and magnificence.
⁶You let them rule over the things that your hands made;
 you put everything under their feet –
⁷Sheep and cattle, all of them,
 and the animals of the wild, too,
⁸The birds of the heavens, the fish of the sea,
 what passes over the paths in the seas.
⁹Yahweh our God,
 how mighty is your name in all the earth!

Psalm 9 Praise and thanksgiving as a key to prayer

The leader's. Secrets. The son's. A composition. David's.

¹I will confess you, Yahweh, with my whole mind,
 I will recount all your extraordinary deeds.

²I will rejoice and exult in you,
  I will commemorate your name, the One on
    High.
³When my enemies turn back,
  they collapse and perish before you,
⁴Because you exercised authority for me and
    made a judgement for me;
  you sat on your throne as one who exercises
    authority in faithfulness.
⁵You reprimanded nations, you obliterated the
    faithless person,
  you wiped out their name for ever and ever.
⁶The enemy is finished, ruins permanently;
  you uprooted towns, their commemoration
    perished.
Them! ⁷But Yahweh sits for ever;
  he established his throne for exercising
    authority.
⁸He's the one who exercises authority for the
    world with faithfulness,
  he gives judgement for the peoples with
    uprightness.
⁹Yahweh became a turret for the downtrodden
    person,
  a turret for times of pressure,
¹⁰So that people who acknowledge your name will
    rely on you,
  because you didn't abandon people who
    enquired of you, Yahweh.

¹¹Make music for Yahweh who sits in Tsiyyon,
  tell among the peoples of his deeds,
¹²Because the one who enquires about bloodshed
    was mindful of them,
  he didn't put out of mind the cry of the
    humble.
¹³Be gracious to me, Yahweh,
  see my humbling at the hand of the people
    hostile to me,
  you who lift me up from death's gateways,
¹⁴In order that I may recount all your
    praiseworthy acts;
  in the gateways of Miss Tsiyyon I will rejoice in
    your deliverance.
¹⁵Nations plunged into the pit they made;
  in the net that they hid, their foot caught.
¹⁶Yahweh caused himself to be acknowledged, he
    made an authoritative decision;
  by the act of his own fists the faithless person
    trapped himself. *(Recitation. Rise)*
¹⁷Faithless people should turn back to She'ol,
  all the nations that put Yahweh out of mind,
¹⁸Because the needy person will not be out of
    mind without end,
  or the hope of the humble perish permanently.
¹⁹Rise up, Yahweh, a human being should not
    exercise power,
  nations should enter into judgement in your
    presence.
²⁰Appoint something fearful for them, Yahweh;
  nations should acknowledge that they are
    human beings. *(Rise)*

Psalm 10 The wretched of the earth

¹Why do you stand far off, Yahweh,
  hide in times of pressure?
²When the faithless person in his position of
    majesty hounds the humble,
  they should catch themselves by the strategies
    that they have thought up.
³Because the faithless person has praised the
    longing of his appetite
  and blessed the greedy person.
The faithless person has disdained Yahweh,
  ⁴in accordance with the loftiness of his look.
'God won't enquire, he's not here';
  in all his strategies ⁵his ways are profane.
All the time your acts of authority are high up, at
    a distance from him;
  all his adversaries – he snorts at them.
⁶He's said to himself, 'I shall not slip, generation
    after generation';
  'I shall not be in bad circumstances,' ⁷he's
    sworn.
His mouth is full of acts of guile and repression;
  under his tongue are oppression and trouble.
⁸He lives in a hiding place in the villages,
  so that in complete secret he can kill someone
    free of guilt.
His eyes watch for the wretched person;
  ⁹he waits in secret like a lion in its lair.
He waits to catch the humble;
  he catches the humble by dragging him in his
    net.
¹⁰The wretched, collapsing, sinks down,
  and falls because he is so numerous.
¹¹He's said to himself, 'God has put it out of
    mind,
  he's hidden his face, he's never looked.'
¹²Rise up, Yahweh;
  God, lift your hand,
  don't put the humble out of mind.

¹³Why has the faithless person disdained God,
    said to himself, 'He does not enquire'?
¹⁴You've seen, because you yourself
    look out at oppression and vexation.
Giving it into your hand, the wretched abandons
        it to you;
    the orphan – you're the one who has been a
        helper.
¹⁵Break the arm of the faithless and the bad
        person,
    so that when you enquire after his faithlessness,
        you will not find it.

¹⁶Yahweh will be king for ever and ever;
    the nations will have perished from his
        country.
¹⁷When you've heard the longing of the humble,
        Yahweh,
    you establish their mind, you bend your ear,
¹⁸To exercise authority for orphan and
        downtrodden;
    no one from the earth will frighten ever again.

Psalm 11 Flee or stay?

The leader's. David's.

¹With Yahweh I take shelter;
    how can you say to me,
'Flit to your mountain, bird,
    ²because there – the faithless direct a bow.
They've set their arrow on a string,
    to shoot in the shadow at the people who're
        upright in mind.
³When the foundations are torn down,
    the faithful person – what can he do?'

⁴Yahweh is in his sacred palace,
    Yahweh whose throne is in the heavens.
His eyes behold,
    his eyelids examine human beings.
⁵Yahweh examines the faithful person,
    and the faithless, and the ones who love
        violence –
    his entire being is hostile to them.
⁶He rains coals of fire and sulphur on the faithless
        people;
    a scorching wind is the portion in their cup.
⁷Because Yahweh is faithful, he loves faithful
        deeds;
    the upright person – his face beholds him.

Psalm 12 Sometimes God speaks

The leader's. On the eighth [tone]. A
composition. David's.

¹Deliver, Yahweh, because the committed person
        has come to an end,
    because the people who are true have vanished
        from among humankind.
²An individual speaks emptiness to his
        neighbours;
    with smooth lip through a double mind they
        speak.
³Yahweh should cut off all the smooth lips,
    the tongue that speaks big things,
⁴The people who've said, 'With our tongues we
        will be strong:
    our lips will be with us – who will be lord over
        us?'

⁵'Because of the destruction of the humble,
        because of the cry of the needy,
    now I will rise up,' Yahweh says.
'I will set myself up as deliverance,'
    he testifies to him.

⁶Yahweh's words are pure words,
    silver purified in a furnace on the ground,
        refined seven times.
⁷Yahweh, you will keep them;
    you will preserve us from the generation that
        lasts permanently.
⁸All round, the faithless walk about,
    as flimsiness stands high for humankind.

Psalm 13 How long, how long, how long, how long?

The leader's. A composition. David's.

¹How long, Yahweh: will you put me out of mind
        permanently,
    how long will you hide your face from me?
²How long must I lay up [people's] plans in my
        entire being,
    sadness in my heart day by day,
    – how long will my enemy stand high over
        me?
³Look out, answer me, Yahweh my God;
    give light to my eyes, so that I don't sleep in
        death,

⁴So that my enemy doesn't say, 'I've finished him off',
   my adversaries celebrate because I slip.
⁵But I myself trust in your commitment;
   my heart will celebrate your deliverance.
I will sing to Yahweh,
   because he has dealt to me.

Psalm 14 What a rogue says to himself

The leader's. David's.

¹A villain has said to himself,
   'There's no God here.
People have become devastating, offensive, in their action;
   there's no one doing good here.'
²From the heavens Yahweh has looked out at humankind,
To see if there is someone insightful,
   enquiring of God.
³Everyone has departed, altogether they're foul;
   there's no one doing good here, there isn't even one.
⁴They don't acknowledge him, do they, all the people devising trouble,
   who eat my people.
They've eaten food;
   they haven't called Yahweh.

⁵They're experiencing dreadful terror there,
   because God is among the faithful circle.
⁶You people may shame the humble person's counsel,
   but Yahweh is his shelter.

⁷If only there were deliverance for Yisra'el from Tsiyyon,
   when Yahweh turns back his people's fortunes.
Ya'aqob [Jacob] will celebrate,
   Yisra'el will rejoice!

Psalm 15 How to dwell with God

A composition. David's.

¹Yahweh, who may reside in your tent,
   who may dwell on your sacred mountain?
²One who walks with integrity, acts with faithfulness,
   and speaks truth inside.
³He has not gone about talking,
   has not done wrong to his neighbour,
   has not taken up reviling against someone near him.
⁴In his eyes a contemptible person is to be rejected,
   but he honours people who live in awe of Yahweh;
   he has sworn to bring about something bad and not changed it.
⁵He has not given his silver on interest,
   and not taken a bribe against someone free of guilt;
   one who does these things, who does not slip ever.

Psalm 16 I've set Yahweh in front of me

An inscription. David's.

¹Keep me, God,
   because I take shelter with you.
²I've said of Yahweh,
   'My Lord, you are my good, none above you',
³To the sacred ones who are in the country,
   and the august ones in whom is all my delight.
⁴Their pains will be many,
   the people who attend to another [god].
I will not pour their blood libations;
   I will not take up their names on my lips.
⁵Yahweh, my allocated share, my cup,
   you're the one who takes hold of my lot.
⁶Apportionments have fallen to me in lovely places;
   yes, a perfect domain for me.
⁷I will bless Yahweh who has counselled me;
   yes, by night my inner being disciplines me.
⁸I have set Yahweh in front of me continually;
   because he's at my right hand, I shall not slip.
⁹Therefore my entire being rejoices,
   my spirit celebrates,
   yes, my flesh will dwell in confidence.
¹⁰Because you won't abandon my life to She'ol,
   you won't give over someone committed to you to see the Abyss.
¹¹You will let me know the path to life,
   joyful fulfilment with your face,
   lovely things at your right hand permanently.

Psalm 17 Go on, look into my heart

A plea. David's.

^{1}Listen in faithfulness, Yahweh,
  heed my resounding cry.
Give ear to my plea,
  on lips that are without guile.
^{2}May an authoritative ruling for me go out from
    your presence;
  may your eyes behold what is upright.
^{3}Were you to test my mind, visit me by night,
  try me, you wouldn't have found [anything]
  – I had determined that my mouth would not
    transgress.
^{4}As for human actions, in accord with the word of
    your lips,
  I myself have kept watch on the paths of the
    robber.
^{5}My steps have taken hold of your tracks,
  my feet have not slipped.
^{6}I myself call you, because you will answer me,
    God;
  bend your ear to me, listen to my word.
^{7}Act in an extraordinary way with deeds of
    commitment,
  you who deliver those who take shelter with
    you
  from the people who rise up against them, by
    your right hand.
^{8}Keep me like the apple of your eye,
  in the shadow of your wings hide me,
^{9}From the faithless who've destroyed me,
  the enemies of my life who surround me.
^{10}They've closed their minds,
  with their mouth they have spoken with
    majesty.
^{11}Our steps – they've now surrounded us;
  their eyes – they set them to extend through
    the country.
^{12}His appearance is like a lion that's eager to tear,
  like a whelp that sits in ambush.
^{13}Rise up, Yahweh,
  meet him face to face, bring him down!
Enable me to survive from the faithless with your
    sword,
  ^{14}from human beings with your hand,
    Yahweh.
From human beings – in their lifetime will you fill
    their belly,
  with their share in life and with what you have
    stored up.
Their children are to be full,
  and they are to leave what they have over to
    their own young.
^{15}When I behold your face in faithfulness,
  I will be full with your form when I awake.

Psalm 18.1–24 Rescued from death

The leader's. Yahweh's servant's. David's, who spoke to Yahweh the words of this song on the day Yahweh rescued him from the fist of all his enemies and from the hand of Sha'ul [Saul]. He said:

^{1}I dedicate myself to you, Yahweh, my strength,
  ^{2}Yahweh my cliff, my fortress, the one who
    enables me to survive,
My God, my crag in which I take shelter,
  my shield, the horn that delivers me, my turret.
^{3}As one to be praised, I called Yahweh,
  and from my enemies I found deliverance.
^{4}Death's ropes have overwhelmed me,
  Beliyya'al's wadis terrified me,
^{5}She'ol's ropes have surrounded me,
  death's snares have confronted me.
^{6}In my pressure I called on Yahweh,
  I cried for help to my God.

^{7}And the earth has quaked and rocked,
  the mountains' foundations shook.
They've quaked because it enraged him;
  ^{8}smoke has gone up in his anger.
Fire from his mouth consumed,
  coals have burned up from him.
^{9}He's spread the heavens and come down,
  with thundercloud beneath his feet.
^{10}He's ridden on a sphinx and flown,
  swooped on the wings of the wind.
^{11}He's made darkness his hiding place round
    him,
  his bivouac water cloud, masses of mist.
^{12}From the brightness in front of him, through his
    masses there have passed
  hail and fiery coals.
^{13}Yahweh has thundered in the heavens,
  the One on High gave out his voice.
Hail and fiery coals:
  ^{14}he's sent off his arrows and scattered them,
  shot lightning and routed them.
^{15}Canyons of water have appeared,
  the world's foundations have come into sight,

At your reprimand, Yahweh,
  at the breath of your angry wind.
¹⁶He sent from on high, he got me,
  he drew me out of much water.
¹⁷He rescued me from my vigorous enemy,
  from people hostile to me, because they stood
    too firm for me.
¹⁸They met me on the day of my disaster,
  but Yahweh has become a support for me.
¹⁹He's brought me out into a roomy place;
  he's pulled me out because he delighted in me.
²⁰Yahweh has dealt to me in accordance with my
    faithfulness;
  in accordance with the purity of my hands he
    gave back to me,
²¹Because I have kept Yahweh's ways
  and not been faithless to my God.
²²Because all his rulings have been in front of
    me;
  his decrees I didn't let depart from me.
²³I've been a person of integrity with him;
  I've kept myself from waywardness I might
    have done.
²⁴So Yahweh has given back to me in accordance
    with my faithfulness,
  in accordance with the purity of my hands
    before his eyes.

Psalm 18.25–50 The one who keeps my lamp alight

²⁵With the committed person you show
    commitment;
  with the man of integrity you show integrity.
²⁶With the pure you show yourself pure;
  with the crooked you show yourself
    refractory.
²⁷Because you're one who delivers a humble
    people
  but puts down exalted eyes.
²⁸Because you're the one who keeps my lamp
    alight;
  it's Yahweh my God who illumines my
    darkness.
²⁹Because with you I can rush at a barricade;
  with my God I can scale a wall.
³⁰God: his way has integrity;
  Yahweh's word is proven.
He is a shield
  to all who take shelter with him.

³¹Because who is God apart from Yahweh,
  who is a crag except our God?
³²God is the one who belts me with forcefulness,
  and makes my way one that has integrity,
³³Who fashions my feet like a deer,
  enables me to stand on the heights,
³⁴Who trains my hands for battle,
  so that my arms could bend a copper bow.
³⁵You've given me your shield that delivered;
  your right hand sustained me, your avowal
    made me great.
³⁶You widened my step beneath me;
  my ankles have not slipped.
³⁷I pursued my enemies so that I could overtake
    them;
  I didn't turn back until I finished them off.
³⁸I hit them and they couldn't get up;
  they fell beneath my feet.
³⁹You've belted me with forcefulness for battle;
  you bent down beneath me the people who
    rose up against me.
⁴⁰My enemies you've made turn tail for me;
  the people who were hostile to me – I wiped
    them out.
⁴¹They cried for deliverance, but there was no
    deliverer –
  [cried] to Yahweh, but he has not answered
    them.
⁴²I ground them fine like earth before the wind,
  flattened them like mud in the streets.
⁴³You enabled me to survive from arguments with
    the people,
  you set me as head of nations.
A people I did not acknowledge serve me;
⁴⁴on hearing with the ear, they listened to me.
Foreigners wither before me,
⁴⁵foreigners wilt and come quaking out of their
    strongholds.

⁴⁶Yahweh lives, my crag be blessed,
  may my God who delivers be exalted,
⁴⁷The God who gives me total redress,
  and subjects peoples under me,
⁴⁸Who enabled me to escape from my enemies,
  yes, exalts me above the people who rise up
    against me,
  rescues me from the violent man!

⁴⁹Therefore I will confess you, Yahweh, among the
    nations,
  and make music for your name,

⁵⁰The one who gives great acts of deliverance to
    his king,
  acting with commitment to his anointed,
    to David and to his offspring permanently!

Psalm 19 The mystery of sin

The leader's. A composition. David's.

¹The heavens are recounting God's splendour,
    the sky is telling of what his hands made.
²Day by day it pours out speech,
    night by night it proclaims knowledge.
³There's no speech, there are no words,
    whose voice does not make itself heard.
⁴In all the earth their noise has gone out,
    at the end of the world their utterances.
For the sun he put a tent in them;
  ⁵it's like a groom going out of his dressing
      room.
It rejoices to run the path, like a strong man,
  ⁶as its going out is from the end of the
      heavens.
Its completed circuit is at their [other] end,
  and there's nothing hidden from its heat.

⁷Yahweh's instruction has integrity,
    bringing life back.
Yahweh's affirmation is trustworthy,
    making the naïve smart.
⁸The things Yahweh has determined are upright,
    rejoicing the mind.
Yahweh's order is clean,
    enlightening the eyes.
⁹Awe for Yahweh is pure,
    standing permanently.
Yahweh's rulings are true;
    they're faithful altogether.
¹⁰They're more desirable than gold,
    than much pure gold,
Sweeter than syrup,
    than the juice of honeycombs.
¹¹Yes, your servant takes warning through them,
    and in keeping them there are great results.

¹²Who can understand mistakes?
    – free me from things that are hidden;
  ¹³yes, hold your servant back from assertive
      deeds.
May they not rule over me, then I'll be whole,
  and free of great rebellion.

¹⁴May the sayings of my mouth be acceptable to
    you,
  and the murmur of my mind before you,
    Yahweh, my crag and my restorer.

Psalm 20 Chariotry, horses, Yahweh

The leader's. A composition. David's.

¹May Yahweh answer you on the day of pressure,
    the name of Ya'aqob's God set you on high.
²May he send your help from the sacred place,
    support you from Tsiyyon.
³May he be mindful of all your offerings,
    enrich your burnt sacrifice. *(Rise)*
⁴May he give to you what is in accordance with
    your mind,
  fulfil every counsel of yours.
⁵May we resound at your deliverance,
    in the name of our God we'll lift our banners:
  may Yahweh fulfil all your requests.

⁶Now I acknowledge
    that Yahweh has delivered his anointed.
He answers him from his sacred heavens,
    with the mighty acts of deliverance of his right
      hand.
⁷These people [make mention] of chariotry, those
      people of horses,
  but as for us – we make mention of the name of
      Yahweh our God.
⁸Those people have bent down and fallen,
    but as for us – we've risen up and taken our
      stand.
⁹'Yahweh, deliver the king!'
    – may he answer us on the day we call.

Psalm 21 An embodiment of blessing

The leader's. A composition. David's.

¹Yahweh, the king rejoices in your vigour,
    how greatly he takes joy in your deliverance!
²You gave him the longing of his heart;
    the request of his lips you didn't deny.
³Because you meet him with blessings of good,
    set on his head a crown of pure gold.
⁴When he asked for life from you, you gave
      him,
  length of days for ever and ever.

⁵Great is his splendour through your deliverance,
  grandeur and magnificence you bestow on
    him.
⁶Because you make him [an embodiment of]
    blessing permanently,
  you gladden him with rejoicing at your
    presence.
⁷Because the king trusts in Yahweh
  and by the commitment of the One on High he
    doesn't slip.

⁸Your hand finds all your enemies,
  your right hand finds the people hostile to you.
⁹You make them like a blazing furnace
  at the time of your appearing.
Yahweh in anger swallows them up;
  fire consumes them.
¹⁰Their posterity you destroy from the earth,
  their offspring from among humanity.
¹¹When they've directed something bad against
    you,
  thought up a strategy, they don't succeed.
¹²Because you set them back
  when you aim at their faces with your bows.
¹³Be on high, Yahweh, in your vigour
  – we will sing and make music about your
    strength.

Psalm 22.1–18 My God, my God, why?

The leader's. On Dawn Help. A composition.
David's.

¹My God, my God, why have you abandoned me,
  far away from delivering me, from the word I
    yell?
²My God, I call by day but you don't answer,
  and by night – there's no quietness for me.

³But you sit as the sacred one,
  the great praise of Yisra'el.
⁴In you our ancestors trusted;
  they trusted and you enabled them to
    survive.
⁵To you they cried out and they escaped;
  in you they trusted and they were not
    shamed.

⁶But I'm a worm, not a person,
  an object of reviling for human beings, an
    object of contempt for the people.
⁷All who see me ridicule me,
  open their mouth, shake their head.
⁸'He should commit it to Yahweh, he must enable
    him to survive,
  he must rescue him, because he delights in
    him.'

⁹Because you're the one who enabled me to break
    out of the womb,
  enabled me to trust at my mother's breast.
¹⁰On you I was thrown from birth;
  from my mother's womb you were my God.
¹¹Don't be far away from me,
  because pressure is near, and there's no one to
    help.

¹²Many bulls have surrounded me,
  sturdy Bashan steers have encircled me.
¹³Tearing and roaring lions
  have opened their mouth at me.
¹⁴I've spilled out like water,
  all my bones have become loose.
My mind's become like wax;
  it's melted inside me.
¹⁵My energy's withered like a piece of pot,
  my tongue sticks to my palate.
You've put me into death's earth,
  ¹⁶because dogs have surrounded me.
An assembly of bad people has hemmed me in;
  my hands and feet have shrivelled.
¹⁷I can count all my bones,
  while those people look out and see me.
¹⁸They divide my clothes for themselves;
  for my garments they let lots fall.

Psalm 22.19–31 When you know that God has heard

¹⁹But you, Yahweh, don't be far away
  – my strength, come quickly as my help.
²⁰Rescue my life from the sword,
  my very self from the dog's power.
²¹Deliver me from the lion's mouth;
  may you have answered me from the oryxes'
    horns.

²²I will recount your name to my brothers;
  in the middle of the congregation I will praise
    you.
²³You who live in awe of Yahweh, praise him,
  all Ya'aqob's offspring, honour him!

Revere him,
  all Yisra'el's offspring!
²⁴Because he hasn't despised, he hasn't treated as abominable,
  the lament of the humble.
He hasn't hidden his face from him
  but listened to his cry for help to him.
²⁵From you will be my praise in the great congregation;
  my pledges I will make good in front of the people who live in awe of him.
²⁶Humble people will eat and be full;
  people who enquire of Yahweh will praise him
  – may your heart live permanently.
²⁷All the ends of the earth will be mindful and turn back to Yahweh;
  all the kin-groups of the nations will bow low before you.
²⁸Because kingship belongs to Yahweh;
  he rules over the nations.
²⁹All the enriched of the earth have eaten, and bowed low;
  before him all the people who are going down into the earth will kneel,
  and the person who hasn't been able to keep himself alive.
³⁰Offspring will serve him;
  a generation to come will be told of my Lord.
³¹They will recount his faithfulness to a people to be born,
  because he has acted.

Psalm 23 In the dark of the canyon

A composition. David's.

¹My shepherd being Yahweh, I don't lack;
  ²he enables me to lie down in grassy pastures.
He leads me to settled water;
  ³he turns my life back.
He guides me in faithful tracks
  for the sake of his name.
⁴Even when I walk in a deathly dark ravine,
  I'm not afraid of bad fortune,
Because you're with me;
  your club and your cane – they comfort me.

⁵You spread a table before me
  in front of my adversaries.
You've enriched my head with oil;
  my cup fills me up.
⁶Yes, goodness and commitment pursue me
  all the days of my life.
I shall go back to Yahweh's house
  for long days.

Psalm 24 Will God let you in? Will you let God in?

David's. A composition.

¹The earth and what fills it are Yahweh's,
  the world and the people who live in it.
²Because he founded it on the seas,
  set it on the rivers.

³Who goes up on to Yahweh's mountain,
  who gets up in his sacred place?
⁴One clean as to the palms of his hands and pure in mind,
  who has not lifted up himself to emptiness
  and not sworn so as to beguile.
⁵He lifts a blessing from Yahweh
  and faithfulness from his God who delivers.
⁶This is the circle of people who enquire of him,
  Ya'aqob who seek your face. *(Rise)*

⁷Lift your heads, gateways;
  lift yourself up, age-old doors,
  so that the glorious King may come in.
⁸'Who is he, then, the glorious King?'
  – Yahweh the vigorous one and the strong man,
  Yahweh the strong man in battle.
⁹Lift up your heads, gateways;
  lift up, age-old doors,
  so that the glorious King may come in.
¹⁰'Who is that, then, the glorious King?'
  – the glorious King is Yahweh of Armies.
  (Rise)

Psalm 25 I can't wait

David's.

¹To you, Yahweh,
  I lift my entire being, ²my God.
I've trusted in you – I must not be shamed;
  my enemies must not exult about me.

³Yes, all the people who hope in you will not be shamed;
   the people who break faith without reason will be shamed.
⁴Enable me to acknowledge your ways, Yahweh,
   teach me your paths.
⁵Direct me in your truthfulness and teach me,
   because you're my God who delivers;
   in you I have hoped all day.
⁶Be mindful of your compassion, Yahweh, and your commitment,
   because they are age-old.
⁷Don't be mindful of the wrongs of my youth
   and my acts of rebellion.
In accordance with your commitment be mindful of me yourself,
   for the sake of your goodness, Yahweh.
⁸Yahweh is good and upright;
   therefore he instructs wrongdoers in the way.
⁹He directs the humble by his authority,
   teaches the humble his way.
¹⁰All Yahweh's paths are commitment and truthfulness
   to people who keep his pact, his affirmations.
¹¹For the sake of your name, Yahweh,
   pardon my waywardness, because it's great.
¹²Who, then, is the individual who lives in awe of Yahweh?
   – he instructs him in the way he should choose.
¹³His life lodges in goodness,
   and his offspring possess the country.
¹⁴Yahweh's confidences are with people who live in awe of him,
   and his pact, in enabling them to acknowledge him.
¹⁵My eyes are continually towards Yahweh,
   because he's the one who gets my feet out of the net.
¹⁶Turn your face to me and be gracious to me,
   because I'm alone and humble.
¹⁷The pressures in my mind have widened;
   get me out from my straits.
¹⁸Look at my humbling and oppression;
   carry all my wrongdoings.
¹⁹Look at my enemies, how they are many,
   and at the violent hostility they show to me.
²⁰Keep my life, rescue me;
   I must not be shamed, because I've taken shelter with you.
²¹Integrity and uprightness must preserve me,
   because I've hoped in you.
²²God, redeem Yisra'el
   from all its pressures.

Psalm 26 I wash my hands in innocence

David's.

¹Exercise authority for me, Yahweh,
   because I – I have walked in integrity.
In Yahweh I've trusted;
   I don't slip.
²Probe me, Yahweh, try me,
   test my inner being and my mind.
³Because your commitment is in front of my eyes;
   I walk about by your truthfulness.
⁴I haven't sat with empty men;
   I don't come with deceitful people.
⁵I'm hostile to the congregation of people who deal badly;
   I don't sit with the faithless.
⁶I wash the palms of my hands with freedom from guilt
   so that I may go about your altar, Yahweh,
⁷To let people hear the sound of confession,
   to recount all your extraordinary deeds.
⁸Yahweh, I'm loyal to the abode that is your house,
   the dwelling place of your splendour.
⁹Don't gather me up with wrongdoers,
   my life with men of bloodshed,
¹⁰In whose hand is deliberate wickedness,
   and whose right hand is full of bribes.
¹¹But I'm one who walks in my integrity;
   redeem me, be gracious to me!
¹²My foot has stood on level ground;
   in the great congregation I will bless Yahweh.

Psalm 27 One thing

David's.

¹Yahweh is my light, my deliverance:
   of whom should I be afraid?
Yahweh is the stronghold of my life:
   of whom should I be in dread?
²When people who deal badly drew near me,
   to devour my flesh,
My adversaries and my enemies:
   those people collapsed, fell.
³If an army camps against me,
   my heart will not be afraid.

If battle arises against me,
   during this I trust.

⁴One thing I've asked from Yahweh,
   it's what I seek,
For me to live in Yahweh's house,
   all the days of my life,
To behold Yahweh's loveliness,
   and to consult each morning in his palace.
⁵Because he keeps me safe in his shelter
   on the day of bad fortune.
He hides me in his tent as a hiding place;
   he lifts me high on a crag.
⁶So now my head is high,
   above my enemies round me.
In his tent I will offer noisy sacrifices;
   I will sing and make music for Yahweh.

⁷Listen, Yahweh, to my voice when I call;
   be gracious to me, answer me.
⁸For you my mind said,
   'Seek my face!'
Your face I seek, Yahweh:
   ⁹don't hide your face from me.
Don't turn aside your servant in anger;
   you've been my help.
Don't leave me, don't abandon me,
   my God who delivers.
¹⁰When my father and my mother have abandoned me,
   then Yahweh will take me in.
¹¹Instruct me in your way, Yahweh,
   lead me on a level path.
In view of the people watching for me,
   ¹²don't give me over to the will of my adversaries.
Because there have arisen against me false witnesses,
   a person who testifies violence.
¹³Unless I trusted to see good things from Yahweh
   in the country of the living . . .
¹⁴Hope in Yahweh, be strong,
   may your mind stand firm, hope in Yahweh!

Psalm 28 Our vigour and God's

David's.

¹To you, Yahweh, I call;
   my crag, don't be deaf towards me,
So that you aren't silent in relation to me,
   and I become like the people who go down into the Cistern.
²Listen to the sound of my prayers for grace,
   when I cry for help to you,
When I lift up my hands
   to your sacred inner room.
³Don't drag me off with faithless people,
   with people who devise trouble,
People who speak of well-being with their neighbours,
   when there is bad dealing in their mind.
⁴Give to them in accordance with their doings,
   in accordance with the badness of their deeds.
In accordance with the action of their hands give to them,
   give back their dealing to them.
⁵Because they don't consider Yahweh's acts,
   the work of his hands;
   may he tear them down and not build them up.

⁶Yahweh be blessed,
   because he's heard the sound of my prayers for grace.
⁷Yahweh is my vigour and my shield;
   in him my mind has trusted, and I will find help.
My mind has exulted,
   and I will glorify him with my song.
⁸Yahweh is vigour for him and stronghold;
   he is the great deliverance of his anointed.
⁹Deliver your people, bless your domain,
   shepherd them and carry them permanently.

Psalm 29 Yahweh's voice produces convulsions

A composition. David's.

¹Give Yahweh, you divine beings,
   give Yahweh splendour and vigour.
²Give Yahweh the glory of his name,
   bow low to Yahweh in sacred array.
³Yahweh's voice was over the water,
   the glorious God thundered,
   Yahweh over mighty water.
⁴Yahweh's voice was with energy;
   Yahweh's voice was with magnificence.
⁵Yahweh's voice breaks cedars;
   Yahweh breaks off cedars of Lebanon.
⁶He makes them jump like a calf,
   Lebanon and Siryon like a young oryx.

⁷Yahweh's voice splits flames of fire,
⁸Yahweh's voice convulses the wilderness,
Yahweh convulses the Qadesh Wilderness.
⁹Yahweh's voice convulses oaks,
strips forests.
In his palace everyone in it says,
'In splendour ¹⁰Yahweh sat on high;
Yahweh sat as king permanently.'
¹¹Yahweh gives vigour to his people;
Yahweh blesses his people with well-being.

Psalm 30 I prayed, Yahweh answered, Yahweh acted

A composition. A song at the dedication of the house. David's.

¹I will exalt you, Yahweh, because you put me down,
but did not let my enemies rejoice about me.
²Yahweh my God,
I cried for help to you, and you healed me.
³Yahweh, you got my life up from She'ol,
you kept me alive from going down into the Cistern.
⁴Make music for Yahweh, you who are committed to him,
confess his sacred commemoration,
⁵Because there's a moment in his anger,
a life in his acceptance.
In the evening crying lodges,
but at morning there's resounding.

⁶I – I had said when I was at ease,
'I shall not slip ever.'
⁷Yahweh, in your acceptance
you'd put in place vigour for my mountain.
You hid your face;
I became fearful.
⁸To you, Yahweh, I would call,
to my Lord I would pray for grace.
⁹'What would be the gain in my blood being shed,
in my going down to She'ol?
Can the earth confess you,
can it tell of your truthfulness?
¹⁰Listen, Yahweh, be gracious to me;
Yahweh, be a helper for me.'

¹¹You turned my lament into dancing for me,
you undid my sack and belted me with rejoicing,
¹²so that my heart might make music and not stop;
Yahweh my God, I will confess you permanently.

Psalm 31 My times are in your hand

The leader's. A composition. David's.

¹Since I've taken shelter with you, Yahweh,
may I never be shamed;
enable me to survive by your faithfulness.
²Bend your ear to me,
hurry and rescue me.
Be for me a crag, a stronghold,
a fortress to deliver me.
³Because you're my cliff, my stronghold;
for your name's sake lead me and guide me.
⁴Do get me out of the net that they concealed for me,
because you're my stronghold.
⁵Into your hand I assign my spirit;
you've redeemed me, Yahweh, truthful God.
⁶I'm hostile to people who keep things that are empty and hollow;
I myself trust in Yahweh.
⁷I shall celebrate and rejoice in your commitment,
you who've seen my humbling;
you've acknowledged the pressures on me.
⁸You haven't delivered me into the hand of the enemy;
you've stood my feet in a wide place.

⁹Be gracious to me, Yahweh,
because there's pressure on me.
My eye wastes away because of vexation;
my entire being and my body.
¹⁰Because my life comes to a finish in sadness,
my years in groaning.
My energy has collapsed because of my waywardness,
my bones waste away.
¹¹Before all my adversaries I've become an object of reviling,
and very much so for my neighbours,
A dread to my acquaintances;
people who see me in the street flee away from me.
¹²I'm put out of mind like someone who's died;
I've become like a container perishing.
¹³Because I've heard the smears of many people,
alarm all round,

As they scheme together against me;
 they've conspired to take my life.
¹⁴But I – I've trusted in you, Yahweh;
 I've said, 'You are my God.'
¹⁵My times are in your hand;
 rescue me from the hand of my enemies, from my pursuers.
¹⁶May your face shine upon your servant;
 deliver me, in your commitment.
¹⁷Yahweh, may I not be shamed, because I have called you;
 may the faithless people be shamed.
As they go silent to She'ol,
 ¹⁸may false lips be quiet,
Which speak arrogantly against the faithful,
 with majesty and contempt.
¹⁹How much good you have,
 which you've stored up for those who live in awe of you,
With which you've acted towards those who take shelter with you,
 in front of people.
²⁰You hide them in a hiding place in your presence from human plots.
You conceal them in a bivouac
 from arguing tongues.

²¹Yahweh be blessed,
 because he has been extraordinary in his commitment to me,
 as a town besieged.
²²I myself had said in my haste,
 'I'm cut off at a distance from your eyes.'
On the contrary, you heard my voice praying for grace,
 when I cried out for help to you.
²³Be loyal to Yahweh, all you who are committed to him;
 Yahweh preserves the people who are true,
 but makes good plentifully to the person who acts with majesty.
²⁴Be strong; your mind should stand firm,
 all you who wait for Yahweh.

Psalm 32 Love covers a multitude of sins

David's. An instruction.

¹The blessings of the one whose rebellion is carried,
 whose wrongdoing is covered!
²The blessings of the person
 whose waywardness Yahweh does not think about,
 in whose spirit there is no deceit!
³When I was silent,
 my bones wasted away with my anguish all day.
⁴Because day and night your hand was heavy on me;
 my strength was sapped [as] in summer drought. *(Rise)*
⁵I acknowledged my wrongdoing to you;
 I didn't cover my waywardness.
I said, 'I shall confess my rebellions to Yahweh',
 and you yourself carried the waywardness of my wrongdoing. *(Rise)*
⁶Because of this everyone who is committed should plead with you,
 at the time when he is found out.
Yes, when much water overwhelms,
 it will not reach him.
⁷You're a hiding place for me, you preserve me from trouble,
 you surround me with survival shouts.

⁸'I shall give you insight, instruct you in the way you should go;
 I shall offer counsel, my eye on you.
⁹Don't be like a horse,
 like a mule that has no understanding,
Whose advance requires curbing with bit and bridle,
 or there is no coming near you.'

¹⁰Many are the pains of the faithless,
 but the person who trusts in Yahweh – commitment surrounds him.
¹¹Rejoice in Yahweh, celebrate, you faithful;
 shout, all you upright of mind.

Psalm 33 God's commitment fills the earth

¹Resound, faithful people, in Yahweh;
 praise is fitting for the upright.
²Confess Yahweh with the mandolin;
 make music for him with the ten-stringed guitar.
³Sing him a new song;
 do well in playing, with a shout.
⁴Because Yahweh's word is upright,
 and every act of his is done in truthfulness.
⁵He's loyal to faithfulness in exercising authority;
 Yahweh's commitment fills the earth.

⁶By Yahweh's word the heavens were made,
  by the breath of his mouth all their army,
⁷Gathering the sea's water as in a dam,
  putting the deeps in treasuries.

⁸All the earth is to live in awe of Yahweh;
  all the world's inhabitants are to revere him.
⁹Because he's the one who spoke, and it happened;
  he's the one who ordered, and it stood up.
¹⁰Yahweh has contravened the nations' counsel,
  frustrated the peoples' intentions.
¹¹Yahweh's counsel stands permanently,
  the intentions of his mind for generation after generation.
¹²The blessings of the nation for which Yahweh is its God,
  the people he chose as a domain for himself!
¹³From the heavens Yahweh has looked,
  seen all humanity.
¹⁴From the established place where he lives he's gazed
  at all the people who live on the earth,
¹⁵The one who shapes their mind, all together,
  who considers all their actions.

¹⁶There is no king who delivers himself by the abundance of his resources;
  a strong man doesn't rescue himself by the abundance of his energy.
¹⁷The horse is a falsehood for deliverance,
  and by the abundance of its forcefulness it doesn't provide escape.
¹⁸There, it's Yahweh's eye that's on people who live in awe of him,
  people who wait for his commitment,
¹⁹To rescue their life from death,
  and keep them alive in famine.
²⁰Our entire being hopes for Yahweh;
  he is our help and our shield.
²¹Because in him our heart rejoices;
  because in his sacred name we've trusted.
²²May your commitment be over us, Yahweh,
  as we've waited for you.

Psalm 34 Look to him and become bright

David's. When he concealed his sanity before Abimelek so that he drove him out, and he went.

¹I will bless Yahweh all the time;
  his praise will be in my mouth continually.
²In Yahweh my entire being takes pride;
  the humble should listen and rejoice.
³Magnify Yahweh with me;
  we'll exalt his name together.
⁴I enquired of Yahweh and he answered me,
  and rescued me from all my terrors.
⁵People look to him and become bright;
  their faces need not be confounded.
⁶This humble man called and Yahweh himself listened,
  and delivered him from all his pressures.
⁷Yahweh's envoy camps round the people who live in awe of him
  and pulls them out.
⁸Taste and see that Yahweh is good;
  the blessings of the man who takes shelter with him!
⁹Live in awe of Yahweh, you who are his sacred ones,
  because there's no lack for people who live in awe of him.
¹⁰Lions are destitute and starve,
  but people who enquire of Yahweh don't lack any good thing.
¹¹Come, children, listen to me;
  I'll teach you about awe for Yahweh.
¹²Who's the individual who delights in life,
  who loves days for seeing good fortune?
¹³Preserve your tongue from what is bad,
  your lips from speaking a lie.
¹⁴Depart from what's bad and do what's good;
  seek well-being, pursue it.
¹⁵Yahweh's eyes are on the faithful,
  his ears are to their cry for help.
¹⁶Yahweh's face is against people who do what's bad,
  to cut off their commemoration from the country.
¹⁷People cry out, and Yahweh listens,
  and rescues them from all their pressures.
¹⁸Yahweh is near to the people who are breaking inside,
  and delivers the people who are crushed in spirit.
¹⁹When the bad things that come to the faithful person are many,
  Yahweh rescues him from them all.
²⁰He keeps all his bones;
  not one of them breaks.
²¹Bad fortune brings the death of the faithless person,
  and the people who are hostile to the faithful incur liability.

²²Yahweh redeems the life of his servants,
and none who take shelter with him incur liability.

Psalm 35.1–16 Argue for me

David's.

¹Argue with the people who argue with me, Yahweh,
battle with the people who battle me.
²Take strong hold of hand-shield and body-shield,
and arise as my help.
³Draw lance and pike
to meet my pursuers.
Say to me,
'I am your deliverance.'
⁴They must be shamed and disgraced,
the people seeking my life.
They must turn backwards and be confounded,
the people thinking up something bad for me.
⁵They must be like chaff before the wind,
with Yahweh's envoy chasing.
⁶Their way must be darkness and slipperiness,
with Yahweh's envoy pursuing them.
⁷Because for nothing they've hidden their net's pit for me,
for nothing they dug it for my life.
⁸Devastation must come that he doesn't know,
his own net that he hid must catch him,
as devastation may he fall into it.
⁹But my entire being will rejoice in Yahweh,
it shall be glad at his deliverance.
¹⁰All my bones will say,
'Yahweh, who is like you,
One who rescues the humble person from the one stronger than him,
the humble and needy person from the robber?'

¹¹Violent witnesses arise,
people who ask me about what I don't acknowledge.
¹²They make good to me with bad for good,
mourning for my entire being.
¹³But I – when they were ill,
my clothing was sack.
I humbled myself with fasting,
and my plea would turn back to my heart.
¹⁴I walked about as if it was my friend, as if it was a brother;
as if I were a mother grieving, mourning, gloomy.
¹⁵But at my stumbling they've rejoiced and gathered,
gathered against me as assailants.
People I didn't know
have torn at me and not stopped.
¹⁶As the most profane twisted people who ridicule,
they have ground their teeth against me.

Psalm 35.17–28 'We've swallowed him up!'

¹⁷Lord, how long until you see?
– bring back my life from their devastation,
my dear life from the lions.
¹⁸I shall confess you in the great congregation,
among a numerous people I shall praise you.
¹⁹My lying enemies must not rejoice at me,
the people hostile to me for nothing, who glint their eyes.
²⁰Because they don't speak of peace;
they're against the quiet people in the country.
They think up false statements,
²¹and they've widened their mouth against me.
They have said,
'Ah, ah, our eye has seen it!'
²²You've seen, Yahweh, don't be silent;
Lord, don't be far away from me!
²³Stir yourself, wake up, to exercise authority for me,
to argue for me, my God and Lord!
²⁴Exercise authority for me in accordance with your faithfulness,
Yahweh my God; they mustn't rejoice over me.
²⁵They must not say inside, 'Ah, our desire!'
– they must not say, 'We've swallowed him up!'
²⁶They must be shamed and confounded altogether,
the people who rejoice at bad fortune coming to me.
They must be clothed in disgrace and shame,
the people who act big over me.
²⁷They must resound and rejoice,
the people who delight in the faithfulness shown me,
So that they will say continually, 'Yahweh is great,
the one who delights in the well-being of his servant.'
²⁸And my tongue will tell of your faithfulness,
of your praise all day.

Psalm 36 Your truthfulness reaches to the skies

The leader's. Yahweh's servant's. David's.

¹A rebellious utterance by a faithless person
   is in my mind.
There is no reverence for God
   in front of his eyes.
²Because he flatters himself in his own eyes,
   about being found out for his waywardness,
      about meeting hostility.
³The words of his mouth are trouble and deceit;
   he's left off having insight, doing good.
⁴He thinks up trouble on his bed,
   he takes his stand on a no-good way, he doesn't
      reject what is bad.

⁵Yahweh, your commitment is in the heavens,
   your truthfulness reaches as far as the skies.
⁶Your faithfulness is like supernatural mountains,
   your authority is like the great deep.
Human being and animal you deliver, Yahweh;
   ⁷how valuable is your commitment.
Divine beings and human beings
   take shelter in the shadow of your wings.
⁸They feast on the richness of your house,
   you let them drink from your lovely wadi.
⁹Because with you there is a living spring;
   in your light we see light.

¹⁰Draw out your commitment to the people who
      acknowledge you,
   your faithfulness to the upright in mind.
¹¹The majestic foot must not come on me,
   the hand of faithless people must not make me
      flee.
¹²The people who devise trouble have fallen there,
   they have been thrown down, they can't get up.

Psalm 37.1–20 The humble will enter into possession of the land

David's.

¹Don't get into a rage because of people who deal
      badly,
   don't get passionate because of people who do
      evil.
²Because like grass they fade quickly,
   like green plants they wither.
³Trust in Yahweh and do good,
   dwell in the country and pasture on
      truthfulness.
⁴Revel in Yahweh,
   and he'll give you the requests of your heart.
⁵Commit your way to Yahweh;
   trust in him and he'll act,
⁶He'll bring out faithfulness for you like light,
   exercise of authority for you like midday.
⁷Be still before Yahweh,
   and wait patiently for him.
Don't get into a rage with the person who makes
      his way successful,
   with the individual who acts on his strategies.
⁸Let go of anger, abandon wrath;
   don't get into a rage, only to do something
      bad.
⁹Because people who deal badly will be cut off,
   but those who hope in Yahweh – they'll enter
      into possession of the country.
¹⁰Yet a little while and there'll be no faithless
      person;
   you'll consider his place, and there'll be no one.
¹¹The humble – they'll enter into possession of the
      country
   and revel in abundance of well-being.
¹²The faithless person schemes against the faithful
   and grinds his teeth against him.
¹³The Lord makes fun of him,
   because he's seen that his day will come.
¹⁴Faithless people have drawn the sword,
   and directed their bow,
To make the humble and needy fall,
   to slaughter people who are upright in their
      way.
¹⁵Their sword will come into their own heart,
   their bows will break.
¹⁶Better is the little of the faithful
   than the great mass of the faithless.
¹⁷Because the arms of the faithless will break,
   but Yahweh upholds the faithful.
¹⁸Yahweh will acknowledge the days of people of
      integrity,
   and their domain will last permanently.
¹⁹They won't be shamed at a time when things are
      bad,
   and in days of famine they'll be full.
²⁰Because faithless people will perish,
   Yahweh's enemies.
They'll come to a finish like the most valuable of
      pastures,
   come to a finish in smoke.

Psalm 37.21–40 What I've seen and not seen

²¹The faithless person borrows and cannot make good,
  but the faithful person is gracious and gives.
²²Because the people blessed by him will enter into possession of the country,
  but the people slighted by him will be cut off.
²³A man's steps are established by Yahweh,
  when he delights in his way.
²⁴When he falls he's not thrown headlong,
  because Yahweh supports with his hand.
²⁵I was young and yes, I'm old,
  but I haven't seen a faithful person abandoned,
  or his offspring seeking bread.
²⁶All day he's gracious and lends,
  and his offspring are a blessing.
²⁷Depart from what's bad and do good,
  and dwell permanently.
²⁸Because Yahweh is loyal to the exercise of authority,
  and doesn't abandon people committed to him.
They are kept watch over permanently,
  but the offspring of the faithless are cut off.
²⁹Faithful people will enter into possession of the country,
  and dwell for ever and ever.
³⁰The mouth of the faithful person murmurs smartness,
  and his tongue speaks with authority.
³¹His God's instruction is in his mind;
  his steps don't slip.
³²The faithless person watches for the faithful,
  and seeks to put him to death.
³³Yahweh doesn't abandon him into his hand,
  and doesn't declare him in the wrong when entering into judgement about him.
³⁴Hope in Yahweh,
  and keep his way.
He'll raise you up so that you enter into possession of the country;
  when the faithless are cut off, you'll see.
³⁵I've seen a faithless man, violent,
  arousing himself like a verdant native tree,
³⁶But he passed on – there, he was gone;
  I sought him and he couldn't be found.
³⁷Keep watch on the person of integrity, see the upright person,
  because there is a future for the man of peace.
³⁸But rebels are annihilated all at once;
  the future of the faithless is cut off.
³⁹The deliverance of the faithful comes from Yahweh,
  their stronghold in time of pressure.
⁴⁰Yahweh helps them and enables them to survive,
  he enables them to survive from the faithless and delivers them,
  because they take shelter with him.

Psalm 38 Suffering can sometimes link to sin

A composition. David's. For commemoration.

¹Yahweh, don't reprove me in your fury,
  or discipline me in your wrath.
²Because your arrows have descended on me,
  your hand has descended upon me.
³There's no integrity in my body by reason of your condemnation;
  there's no well-being in my bones by reason of my wrongdoings.
⁴Because my wayward acts have passed over my head;
  like a heavy burden, they're too heavy for me.
⁵My wounds have smelled and festered
  by reason of my denseness.
⁶Because I went astray, I'm utterly bowed down;
  all day I've gone about gloomy.
⁷Because my thighs are full of burning,
  and there is no integrity in my body.
⁸I've become numb, utterly crushed;
  I howl because of the rumbling in my heart.
⁹Lord, all my longing is in front of you;
  my groaning has not hidden from you.
¹⁰My heart has taken flight, my energy has abandoned me;
  the light in my eyes – they, too, are not with me.
¹¹My friends and my neighbours
  stand back at a distance from my affliction.
The people near me have stood far off,
  ¹²and people who seek my life have laid traps.
People who enquire about something bad for me have spoken malice;
  all day they murmur lies.
¹³But I myself am like a deaf person, I cannot hear,
  like a dumb person who cannot open his mouth.
¹⁴I've become like someone who doesn't hear;
  there's no reproof in my mouth.

¹⁵Because I've waited for you, Yahweh;
   you – you will answer, Lord my God.
¹⁶Because I said, 'They must not rejoice about me;
   when my foot slipped, they acted big over me.'
¹⁷Because I am set for stumbling;
   my pain is in front of me continually.
¹⁸Because I tell of my waywardness,
   I'm anxious because of my wrongdoings.
¹⁹My mortal enemies are numerous,
   the people hostile to me with falsehood are many.
²⁰The people who make good with something bad for something good
   attack me on account of my pursuing what is good.
²¹Don't abandon me, Yahweh;
   my God, don't be far from me.
²²Hurry to my help,
   Lord my deliverance.

Psalm 39 Just a breath

The leader's. Yedutun's. A composition. David's.

¹I said, 'I shall keep watch on my ways,
   so that I don't do wrong with my tongue.
I shall keep a muzzle on my mouth,
   as long as a faithless person is in front of me.'
²I was dumb, in silence;
   I was quiet, more than it was good.
And as my pain stirred,
   ³my mind became heated inside me.
As I murmured, fire burned up;
   I spoke out with my tongue.

⁴Get me to acknowledge my end, Yahweh,
   the number of my days, what it is.
⁵There, you made my days handbreadths;
   my span is as nothing in front of you.
Yes, every human being, standing firm, is simply a breath; *(Rise)*
⁶yes, it's as a shadow that a person walks about.
Yes, it's for a breath that people are in turmoil;
   someone may heap up, but not know who's going to gather them in.

⁷So now, what have I hoped for, Lord?
   – my waiting is for you.
⁸Rescue me from all my acts of rebellion,
   don't make me an object of reviling to the villain.

⁹I was dumb, I didn't open my mouth,
   because you were the one who acted.
¹⁰Turn away your affliction from me;
   because of the blow of your hand I – I am finished.
¹¹With reproofs for waywardness you've disciplined someone,
   and consumed like a moth what he desires;
   yes, every human being is a breath. *(Rise)*

¹²Listen to my plea, Yahweh, give ear to my cry for help,
   don't be silent at my crying.
Because I'm a sojourner with you,
   a transient like all my ancestors.
¹³Look away from me so that I may smile,
   before I go and there is nothing of me.

Psalm 40 I didn't hide your faithfulness within my heart

The leader's. David's. A composition.

¹I hoped and hoped in Yahweh,
   and he bent to me and listened to my cry for help.
²He got me up from a roaring cistern,
   from the overflowing mud.
He set up my feet on a cliff,
   he established my steps.
³He put a new song in my mouth,
   an act of praise to our God.
Many could see it and live in awe,
   and trust in Yahweh.

⁴The blessings of the man
   who makes Yahweh his trust
And has not turned his face to the arrogant
   or to people who follow a lie!
⁵You, Yahweh, my God,
   have done many things.
Your extraordinary deeds and your intentions for us
   – there is no one to set alongside you.
Were I to tell and speak,
   they are too numerous to recount.
⁶Sacrifice and offering you didn't want
   – you dug ears for me;
   burnt offering and purification offering you didn't ask for.
⁷Then I said, 'Here, I've come;
   in a written scroll it is inscribed for me.'

⁸I wanted to do what's acceptable to you, my God;
   your instruction was within my inmost self.
⁹I announced the news of your faithfulness in the great congregation;
   there – I wouldn't close my lips,
   as, Yahweh, you yourself know.
¹⁰I didn't hide your faithfulness within my heart;
   I told of your truthfulness and your deliverance.
I didn't conceal your true commitment
   before the great congregation.

¹¹You, Yahweh,
   may you not close up your compassion from me;
   may your true commitment preserve me continually.
¹²Because bad experiences have surrounded me, beyond numbering.
My wayward acts have caught up with me;
   I haven't been able to see.
They're more numerous than the hairs on my head;
   my mind has abandoned me.
¹³Show acceptance, Yahweh, by rescuing me;
   Yahweh, hurry to my help.
¹⁴May they be shamed and reviled altogether,
   the people who seek my life, to destroy it.
May they turn backwards and be confounded,
   the people who want what is bad for me.
¹⁵May they be desolate on account of their shame,
   the people who say to me 'Ah, ah!'
¹⁶May they celebrate and rejoice in you, all the people who seek you;
   may they say continually 'Yahweh is great',
   the people loyal to your deliverance.

¹⁷But I'm humble and needy;
   may my Lord take thought for me.
You're my help and the one who enables me to survive;
   my God, don't delay!

Psalm 41.1–12 Learning from the poor

The leader's. A composition. David's.

¹The blessings of the one who has insight into the poor person,
   whom Yahweh saves on the day when bad things happen!
²Yahweh keeps watch over him and keeps him alive,
   and blesses him in the country,
   and you won't give him to the appetite of his enemies.
³Yahweh sustains him on his sickbed;
   his entire bed you've transformed, in his illness.
⁴I myself said, 'Yahweh, be gracious to me;
   heal me, because I have done wrong in relation to you.'
⁵My enemies speak of bad fortune for me:
   'When will he die, and his name perish?
⁶If he comes to see [someone],
   he speaks emptiness.
His mind collects trouble for himself,
   which he speaks when he goes outside.'
⁷All the people hostile to me whisper together against me;
   they think up bad things for me.
⁸'A lethal pestilence besets him;
   in that he has lain down, he won't get up again.'
⁹Even my friend whom I trusted,
   one who eats bread with me,
   has acted big against me as a cheat.
¹⁰But you, Yahweh, be gracious to me,
   raise me up, and I'll make good to them.

¹¹Through this I have acknowledged that you delighted in me,
   because my enemy does not shout over me,
¹²And I – in my integrity you've taken hold of me,
   and stood me up before you permanently.

Psalm 41.13 An interim closing act of praise

¹³Yahweh the God of Yisra'el be blessed,
   from age to age,
Amen, amen.

Psalm 42 Where is your God?

The leader's. An instruction. The Qorahites'.

¹Like a deer that strains towards water canyons,
   so my entire being strains towards you, God.
²My entire being is thirsty for God,
   for the living God;

When will I come
  and appear before God?
³My crying has become my food,
  day and night,
While people say to me all day,
  'Where is your God?'
⁴These things I shall bring to mind,
  as I pour out my entire being within me:
That I shall pass along in the shelter,
  lead people right to God's house,
With a voice of resounding and confession,
  the festive crowd.
⁵Why do you bow low, my entire being,
  [why] are you in turmoil within me?
Wait for God, because I shall yet confess him
  for the deliverance that comes from his face.

⁶My God, my entire being bows low within me;
  therefore I bring you to mind,
From the Yarden [Jordan] region and the Hermons,
  from Little Mountain.
⁷Deep is calling to deep,
  in the sound of your waterfalls.
All your breakers and your waves
  have passed over me.
⁸By day may Yahweh order his commitment,
  and by night may his song be with me.
A plea to my living God:
⁹I will say to God, my cliff,
'Why have you put me out of mind,
  why do I go about gloomy,
With affliction from an enemy,
  ¹⁰with murder in my bones?
My adversaries have reviled me,
  while they say to me all day,
'Where is your God?'
¹¹Why do you bow low, my entire being,
  and why are you in turmoil within me?
Wait for God, because I shall yet confess him,
  as the deliverance of my face and my God.

Psalm 43 God's light and truthfulness to lead me

¹Exercise authority for me, God,
  argue for my cause.
From a nation that is not committed,
  from a deceitful and evil individual, enable me
    to survive.
²Because you are God my stronghold;
  why have you rejected me?
Why do I go about gloomy,
  through an enemy's affliction?
³Send your light and your truthfulness, they will
    lead me;
  they will bring me to your sacred mountain, to
    your great dwelling,
⁴So that I can come to God's altar,
  to the God in whom I rejoice joyfully,
And confess you with the guitar,
  God my God.
⁵Why do you bow low, my entire being,
  and why are you in turmoil within me?
Wait for God, because I shall yet confess him
  as the deliverance of my face and my God.

Psalm 44.1–16 It's not in my bow that I trust

The leader's. The Qorahites.' An instruction.

¹God, we've heard with our ears,
  our ancestors have recounted to us,
The deed you did in their days, in past days,
  ²you yourself with your own hand.
You dispossessed nations and planted them;
  you brought bad fortune on peoples and sent
    them off.
³Because it was not by their sword that they
    entered into possession of the country,
  it was not their arm that delivered them,
But your hand and your arm, and the light of your
    face,
  because you accepted them.
⁴You are my king, God;
  order Ya'aqob's deliverance!
⁵Through you we charge at our adversaries,
  by your name we tread down our attackers.
⁶Because it's not in my bow that I trust;
  my sword doesn't deliver me.
⁷Because you've delivered us from our adversaries,
  and shamed the people hostile to us.
⁸God is the one whom we praise all day;
  your name we shall confess permanently. *(Rise)*

⁹Yet you've rejected and disgraced us,
  and you don't go out with our armies.
¹⁰You turn us back from the adversary,
  and the people hostile to us have plundered us
    at will.
¹¹You make us like sheep for food,
  and you've scattered us among the nations.

¹²You sell your people without profit;
 you didn't go high in their price.
¹³You make us an object of reviling to our
 neighbours,
 an object of ridicule and derision to the people
 round us.
¹⁴You make us an object lesson among the
 nations,
 something to shake the head at among the
 peoples.
¹⁵All day my disgrace is in front of me;
 the shame of my face has covered me,
¹⁶At the voice of the person reviling and insulting,
 at the presence of the enemy exacting redress.

Psalm 44.17–26 Wake up, God!

¹⁷All this has come upon us and we haven't put
 you out of mind;
 we haven't been false to your pact.
¹⁸Our mind has not turned backwards;
 our steps have not deviated from your path,
¹⁹That you should have crushed us into the place
 of jackals,
 covered us over with deathly darkness.
²⁰If we'd put our God's name out of mind,
 and spread our palms to a foreign god,
²¹God would search this out, wouldn't he,
 because he knows the mind's secrets.
²²Rather, it's because of you that we've been run
 through all day;
 we have been thought of as sheep for slaughter.

²³Rise up, why do you sleep, Lord?
 – wake up, don't reject permanently!
²⁴Why do you hide your face,
 put our humbling and affliction out of mind?
²⁵Because our being bows down in the earth,
 our heart clings to the ground.
²⁶Get up as our help,
 redeem us for the sake of your commitment!

Psalm 45 The marriage challenge

The leader's. On Lotuses. The Qorahites'. An
instruction. A love song.

¹My mind stirs with a fine message;
 I'm speaking my work to a king,
 my tongue is the pen of a speedy secretary.

²You're the most handsome of human beings;
 grace is poured on to your lips
 – therefore God has blessed you permanently.
³Wrap your sword on to your side,
 strong man, with your grandeur and
 magnificence,
⁴and in your magnificence win.
Ride in the cause of truthfulness and faithful
 lowliness,
 so that your right hand directs you to awe-
 inspiring deeds.
⁵Your arrows are sharpened;
 peoples are beneath you.
They fall in the heart of the king's enemies;
 ⁶your throne, God's, is lasting and permanent.
Your royal club is an upright club;
 ⁷you're loyal to faithfulness and you're hostile to
 faithlessness.
Therefore God, your God,
 has anointed you with celebratory oil beyond
 your companions.
⁸All your clothes are myrrh, aloes and cassia;
 from your great ivory palace strings entertain
 you.
⁹The great princess stands in your jewels,
 the queen at your right hand in gold of Ophir.

¹⁰Listen, young lady, look, bend your ear;
 put out of mind your people, your father's
 household.
¹¹The king will desire your beauty;
 because he's your lord, bow low to him.
¹²The daughter-town of Tsor [Tyre] will seek your
 goodwill with a gift,
 the wealthiest of the people ¹³with all splendour.

To the inside, the princess, with her gold
 embroidery,
 her dress ¹⁴of coloured cloth, will be taken to
 the king,
The girls behind her, her friends,
 will be brought to you.
¹⁵They'll be taken with joyful celebration;
 they'll come into the king's palace.
¹⁶In place of your ancestors will be your sons;
 you will appoint them as officials throughout
 the country.

¹⁷I shall make mention of your name in every
 generation after generation;
 therefore peoples will confess you lastingly,
 permanently.

Psalm 46 Be still and know that I am God

The leader's. The Qorahites'. On Secrets. A song.

[1] God is for us shelter and vigour,
   a help in pressures, readily to be found.
[2] Therefore we're not afraid when the earth moves,
   when mountains slip into the middle of the seas.
[3] Its water may be in turmoil and foam,
   the mountains may quake when it lifts up high.
   (Rise)

[4] A river with its streams rejoices God's town,
   the sacred place where the great dwelling of the One on High is.
[5] God being in the middle of it, it will not slip;
   God helps it as morning turns its face.
[6] Nations are in turmoil, kingdoms slip;
   when he gives his voice, earth dissolves.
[7] Yahweh of Armies is with us;
   Ya'aqob's God is a turret for us. *(Rise)*

[8] Go behold the deeds of Yahweh,
   who is causing great destruction in the earth,
[9] Stopping battles
   as far as the end of the earth,
When he breaks up the bow and snaps the lance,
   burns chariots in the fire.
[10] 'Relax, and acknowledge that I am God;
   I will be high among the nations, I will be high in the earth.'
[11] Yahweh of Armies is with us;
   Ya'aqob's God is a turret for us. *(Rise)*

Psalm 47 The outrageous confession

The leader's. The Qorahites'. A composition.

[1] All you peoples, clap the palms of your hands,
   shout to God with a resounding voice.
[2] Because Yahweh, the One on High, is awe-inspiring,
   the great king over all the earth.
[3] He subdues peoples under us,
   nations under our feet.
[4] He chooses our domain for us,
   the majesty of Ya'aqob to whom he is loyal. *(Rise)*
[5] God has gone up with a shout,
   Yahweh with the sound of a horn.
[6] Make music for God, make music;
   make music for our king, make music.
[7] Because God is king of all the earth;
   make music with insight.
[8] God has become king over the nations;
   God has sat on his sacred throne.
[9] The leaders of the peoples have gathered,
   the people of Abraham's God.
Because the shields of the earth belong to God;
   he has gone up very high.

Psalm 48 Our town

A song. A composition. The Qorahites'.

[1] Yahweh is great, and much to be praised,
   in our God's town.
His sacred mountain [2] is a beauty of a height,
   the greatest joy in all the earth.
The heights of Tsaphon are Mount Tsiyyon,
   the great king's town.
[3] In its citadels God
   has caused himself to be acknowledged as a turret.
[4] Because there – the kings assembled,
   passed along together.
[5] When those men saw, they were stunned,
   they were frightened, they made haste.
[6] Trembling grasped them there,
   writhing like a woman in labour.
[7] With an east wind
   you break up Tarshish ships.
[8] As we've heard, so we've seen,
   in Yahweh of Armies' town,
In our God's town,
   which God will establish permanently. *(Rise)*
[9] God, we have reflected on your commitment,
   within your palace.
[10] God, like your name,
   so your praise reaches to the ends of the earth.
Your right hand is full of faithfulness;
   [11] Mount Tsiyyon will rejoice.
Yehudah's towns will celebrate
   on account of your rulings.
[12] Go round Tsiyyon, circle it,
   count its towers.
[13] Set your mind on its rampart,
   tour its citadels,
So that you can recount to a future age
   [14] that this is God,

Our God lastingly and permanently
— he will direct us against death.

Psalm 49 You can't take it with you

The leader's. The Qorahites'. A composition.

[1]Listen to this, all you peoples;
give ear, all you inhabitants of the world,
[2]Both ordinary people and important people,
wealthy and needy together.
[3]My mouth will speak smartness,
the murmur from my mind will be understanding.
[4]I shall bend my ear to a poem,
resolve my conundrum with the guitar.

[5]Why should I be afraid in bad days,
when the waywardness of people cheating me surrounds me,
[6]People who trust in their resources,
and take pride in the abundance of their wealth?
[7]Huh; it definitely can't redeem someone;
it can't give God his ransom.
[8]The redemption of his life would be expensive;
it would be insufficient permanently,
[9]So that he should live on permanently,
not see the Pit.
[10]Because one can see that smart people die,
the dimwit and stupid person perish together.
They abandon their resources to others,
[11]whereas their inward thought is that their home will be permanent,
Their dwelling to generation after generation
— they had called lands by their names.
[12]A human being does not lodge in honour;
he is like cattle that are terminated.
[13]This is the way things are for them, the people characterized by dim-wittedness,
and after them the people who accept their talk. *(Rise)*
[14]Like sheep they've headed for She'ol;
death shepherds them.
The upright hold sway over them at morning,
and their form is for wasting in She'ol,
away from its lofty home.

[15]Yet God will redeem my life from the hand of She'ol,
because he will take me. *(Rise)*

[16]Don't be afraid when someone becomes wealthy,
when the splendour of his house becomes great,
[17]Because when he dies he doesn't take it all;
his splendour doesn't go down after him.
[18]If he blesses himself in his lifetime,
and people confess you, that you do well for yourself,
[19]He comes to the circle of his ancestors;
never does he see the light.
[20]A human being in honour but who does not have understanding
is like cattle that are terminated.

Psalm 50 Keep it simple

A composition. Asaph's.

[1]God, Yahweh God, has spoken,
and called the earth from the rising of the sun
as far as its going down.
[2]From Tsiyyon, the fullness of beauty,
God has shone out; [3]our God comes and cannot be silent.
Fire devours before him,
and round him it has stormed greatly.
[4]He calls to the heavens above,
and to the earth for a judgement about his people.
[5]'Gather to me the people committed to me,
the people who sealed a pact with me over a sacrifice.'
[6]The heavens have told of his faithfulness,
because he is a God who exercises authority. *(Rise)*

[7]Listen, my people, and I will speak;
Yisra'el, and I will testify against you —
I am God, your God.

[8]About your sacrifices I don't reprove you,
and your burnt offerings are continually in front of me.
[9]I would not take a bull from your house,
goats from your pens.
[10]Because every animal in the forest is mine,
the cattle on a thousand mountains.
[11]I know every bird in the mountains,
and every creature of the wild is with me.
[12]If I were hungry, I would not say so to you,
because the world and what fills it is mine.

¹³Do I eat the flesh of the sturdy
   or drink the blood of goats?
¹⁴Sacrifice a thank-offering to God,
   and make good your pledges to the One on High.
¹⁵Call me on the day of pressure;
   I'll pull you out, then you'll honour me.

¹⁶But to the faithless person, God has said:
   What's your business, recounting my decrees,
   and taking my pact on to your mouth,
¹⁷When you're one hostile to discipline,
   and you throw my words behind you?
¹⁸If you've seen a thief, you've accepted him,
   and your lot has been with adulterers.
¹⁹You've given your mouth to bad dealing;
   you harness your tongue to deceit.
²⁰As you sit you speak against your brother,
   with your mother's son you find fault.
²¹These things you've done and I have been silent;
   you've thought I really was like you.
I reprove you and lay it out before your eyes;
   ²²please consider this, you who put God out of mind,
   so that I don't tear you apart and there's no one to rescue.

²³The person who sacrifices a thank-offering honours me,
   and the person who directs his way
   – I let him see God's deliverance.

Psalm 51 Teach me to repent

The leader's. A composition. David's. When Natan the prophet came to him as he had come to Bat-sheba.

¹Be gracious to me, God, in accordance with your commitment.
   in accordance with the abundance of your compassion wipe away my rebellions.
²Wash me thoroughly from my waywardness,
   cleanse me from my wrongdoing.
³Because I myself acknowledge my rebellions;
   my wrongdoing is in front of me continually.
⁴In relation to you alone have I acted wrongly,
   and done what is bad in your eyes,
In order that you are faithful in your speaking,
   clean in your exercise of authority.
⁵On one hand, in waywardness I was birthed,
   in wrongdoing my mother conceived me.
⁶On the other, you delight in truthfulness in hidden places;
   in the secret place you make me acknowledge smartness.
⁷Remove my wrongdoing with hyssop so I'm pure,
   wash me so I'm whiter than snow.
⁸Let me listen to joy and rejoicing;
   may the bones you've crushed celebrate.
⁹Hide your face from my wrongdoings,
   wipe away all my wayward acts.
¹⁰Create for me a pure mind, God;
   renew an established spirit within me.
¹¹Don't throw me out of your presence;
   don't take your sacred spirit from me.
¹²Give back to me the joy of being delivered by you;
   may your generous spirit sustain me.

¹³I will teach rebels your ways,
   and wrongdoers will turn back to you.
¹⁴Rescue me from shed blood, God,
   the God who delivers me;
   my tongue will resound concerning your faithfulness.
¹⁵Lord, open my lips,
   and my mouth will tell of your praise.
¹⁶Because you wouldn't delight in a sacrifice, were I to give it;
   you wouldn't accept a burnt offering.
¹⁷Godly sacrifices are a broken spirit;
   a broken, crushed mind, God, you would not despise.

¹⁸Do good to Tsiyyon through your acceptance;
   build up Yerushalaim's walls.
¹⁹Then you will delight in faithful sacrifices,
   burnt offering and whole offering;
   then people will take bulls up on to your altar.

Psalm 52 How to stand tall

The leader's. An instruction. David's. When Do'eg the Edomite came and told Sha'ul, 'David came to Ahimelek's house.'

¹Why do you take pride in what is bad, strong man,
   when God's commitment holds all day?
²Your tongue thinks up malice,
   like a sharpened razor, you who're acting with deceit.

³You're loyal to what is bad rather than what is good,
  to falsehood rather than faithful words. *(Rise)*
⁴You're loyal to all devouring words,
  you deceitful tongue.
⁵God will indeed tear you down permanently,
  break you and pull you from your tent,
  uproot you from the land of the living. *(Rise)*

⁶Faithful people will see and be in awe,
  and make fun of him:
⁷"There's the man
  who didn't make God his stronghold,
But trusted in the abundance of his wealth,
  found vigour in his malice."
⁸But I'm like a verdant olive tree
  in God's house.
I have trusted in God's commitment lastingly and permanently;
  ⁹I will confess you permanently, because you've acted.
And I will hope in your name, because it's good,
  in front of the people committed to you.

Psalm 53 There's no God here

The leader's. On Pipe. An instruction. David's.

¹A villain has said to himself,
  'There's no God here.'
People have been devastating and offensive in evil;
  there's no one doing good here.
²From the heavens God has looked out
  at human beings,
To see if there is someone insightful,
  enquiring of God.
³The whole of it has turned backwards, altogether they're foul;
  there's no one doing good, there isn't even one.
⁴They don't acknowledge, do they, the people devising trouble,
  who eat my people?
They've eaten food;
  they haven't called God.

⁵They're experiencing dreadful terror there,
  when there had been no terror.
Because God is scattering the bones of the one camping against you;
  you've shamed them, because God has rejected them.

⁶If only there were deliverance for Yisra'el from Tsiyyon,
  when God turns back his people's fortunes.
Ya'aqob will celebrate,
  Yisra'el will rejoice!

Psalm 54 With a free offering I will sacrifice to you

The leader's. With strings. An instruction. David's. When the Ziphites came and told Sha'ul, 'David's hiding with us, isn't he.'

¹God, deliver me by your name,
  by your strength give judgement for me.
²God, listen to my plea,
  heed the sayings of my mouth.
³Because aliens have risen up against me,
  frightening people have sought my life,
  people who haven't put God in front of them.
⁴Here – God is my helper,
  my Lord is the very sustainer of my life.
⁵May he make the bad experience come back to the people who are watching for me;
  in your truthfulness wipe them out.
⁶With a free offering I will sacrifice to you,
  I will confess your name, Yahweh, because it's good.
⁷Because it has rescued me from every pressure,
  and my eye has looked at my enemies.

Psalm 55 Throwing things on to God

The leader's. With strings. An instruction. David's.

¹God, give ear to my plea,
  don't hide from my prayer for grace.
²Heed me and answer me;
  I'm frantic in my talking and I reel,
³At the voice of the enemy,
  in the face of the oppression of the faithless.
Because they make trouble fall down on me,
  and in anger they harass me.
⁴My mind whirls within me,
  deathly dreads have fallen upon me.
⁵Fear and trembling come into me,
  horror has covered me.
⁶I said, 'If only I had wings;
  like a pigeon I could fly and dwell somewhere.'

⁷There, I would go far away in flight,
   I would lodge in the wilderness. *(Rise)*
⁸I would hurry to a place where I could survive,
   from the sweeping wind, from the
      hurricane.

⁹Lord, swallow up, divide their speech,
   because I've seen violence and argument in the
      town.
¹⁰Day and night they go round it on its walls,
   while trouble and oppression are inside it.
¹¹Malice is within it;
   repression and deceit don't move away from its
      square.
¹²Because it's not an enemy that reviles me, which
      I could bear,
   or someone hostile to me that has acted big
      over me,
   from whom I could hide,
¹³But you, a person of my kind,
   my companion, someone I knew,
¹⁴Together we would enjoy confidences
   as we walked about in the throng into God's
      house.

¹⁵Great desolation on them,
   they should go down to She'ol alive,
   because there are bad dealings in their
      residence, among them.
¹⁶I am one who calls to God;
   Yahweh will deliver me.
¹⁷Evening and morning and noon I talk,
   and I am in turmoil, but he has listened to my
      voice.
¹⁸He has redeemed my life in well-being from my
      encounter,
   because many indeed were with me.
¹⁹God listens and puts them down,
   the one who sits of old, *(Rise)*
The one in whom there are no changes;
   but they had no awe of God.
²⁰He put out his hand against his friends,
   he violated his pact.
²¹The butter in his mouth was smooth,
   but encounter was in his mind.
His words were softer than oil,
   but they – they were unsheathed swords.

²²Throw on to Yahweh what is given you,
   and he himself will sustain you.
He will never let
   the faithful person fall down.

²³God, you yourself will bring them down,
   to the deepest pit,
The people of bloodshed and deceit
   will not have half their days,
   but I – I will trust in you.

Psalm 56 I am afraid, I'm not afraid

The leader's. On the Silent Pigeon of Far-off Places. David's. An inscription. When the Pelishtites [Philistines] seized him in Gat.

¹Be gracious to me, God, because a man has
      hounded me;
   all day a man of battle afflicts me.
²The people watching for me have hounded me
      all day,
   because those battling me from a lofty position
      are many.
³On the day I am afraid,
   I do trust in you.
⁴In God whose word I praise,
   in God I've trusted.
I'm not afraid:
   what can flesh do to me?
⁵All day they pervert my words;
   all their intentions to deal badly are against me.
⁶They stir up strife, they lie in ambush, those people,
   they keep watch on my steps,
   as if they're hoping for my life.
⁷For the trouble they devise, reduce them to
      survivors,
   in anger put the peoples down, God.

⁸You've recorded my lamenting,
   you yourself have put my tears into your flask;
   they're in your record, aren't they.
⁹Then my enemies will turn back
      on the day I call;
   I know this, because God is mine.
¹⁰In God whose word I praise,
   in Yahweh whose word I praise,
¹¹In God I've trusted, I'm not afraid:
   what can a human being do to me?
¹²Given that pledges to you are binding upon me,
      God,
   I shall make good my thank-offerings to you,
¹³Because you've rescued my life from death,
   my foot from tripping up, haven't you,
So that I might walk about before God,
   in the light of life.

Psalm 57 My mind is set

The leader's. Do Not Destroy. David's. An inscription. When he fled from before Sha'ul into the cave.

¹Be gracious to me, God, be gracious to me,
  because my life has taken shelter with you,
And in the shadow of your wings I shall take
    shelter
  until malice passes.
²I will call to God, the One on High,
  to God who is going to bring it to an end for me.
³May he send from the heavens and deliver me,
  as he reviles the one who hounds me. *(Rise)*
May God send his commitment
  and his truthfulness ⁴to my life.
I shall lie down among lions,
  devouring human beings,
Their teeth a pike and arrows,
  their tongue a sharp sword.
⁵Rise above the heavens, God,
  your splendour above all the earth.

⁶People set a net for my feet;
  my life was bowing down.
They dug a pit before me;
  they fell right into it. *(Rise)*
⁷My mind is set, God,
  my mind is set.
I shall sing and make music;
  ⁸wake up, my heart.
Wake up, mandolin and guitar;
  I shall wake up the dawn.
⁹I will confess you among the peoples, Lord,
  I will make music for you among the nations.
¹⁰Because your commitment is big, as far as the
    heavens,
  your truthfulness as far as the skies.
¹¹Rise above the heavens, God,
  your splendour above all the earth.

Psalm 58 A challenge to the principalities and powers

The leader's. Do Not Destroy. David's. An instruction.

¹You gods, do you truly speak with faithfulness,
  exercise authority for human beings with
    uprightness?
²Actually, with your mind you devise acts of evil
    in the country;
  with your hands you deal out violence.
³Faithless people go astray from the womb;
  people who speak lies are wayward from birth.
⁴Their poison is like snake poison,
  like a deaf viper that blocks its ear,
⁵That does not listen to the voice of the charmers,
  the expert weaver of spells.
⁶God, smash their teeth in their mouth;
  break the fangs of the lions, Yahweh.
⁷They should vanish like water when it goes away;
  when one aims his arrows, so should they dry
    up.
⁸Like a snail that vanishes as it goes,
  like a woman's stillbirth, they should not
    behold the sun.
⁹Before your pots sense the thorn,
  as a living person, so should rage whirl them off.
¹⁰The faithful person will rejoice when he beholds
    redress,
  when he bathes his feet in the blood of the
    faithless.
¹¹Someone will say, 'Yes, there is fruit for the
    faithful,
  yes, there are gods exercising authority in the
    country.'

Psalm 59 My turret

The leader's. Do Not Destroy. David's. An instruction. When Sha'ul sent and watched his house so as to put him to death.

¹Rescue me from my enemies, my God;
  do set me on high above the people who rise up
    against me.
²Rescue me from those who devise trouble,
  deliver me from people of bloodshed.
³Because there, they lie in wait for my life;
  vigorous people stir up strife against me.
Not for my rebellion, not for my wrongdoing,
    Yahweh,
  ⁴nor for my waywardness, do they run and set
    themselves up.
Stir yourself to meet me, and look,
  ⁵yes, you, Yahweh God Armies,
  God of Yisra'el.
Wake up to attend to all the nations;
  don't show grace to any of the people who
    break faith, who devise trouble. *(Rise)*

⁶They come back at evening,
 they howl like a dog and go round the town.
⁷There, they bellow with their mouth,
 swords on their lips, because who is listening?
⁸But you, Yahweh, make fun of them,
 you ridicule all the nations.
⁹My vigour, I keep watch for you,
 because God is my turret.
¹⁰The God committed to me will meet me,
 God will enable me to look at the people who are watching for me.
¹¹Don't kill them, in case my people are unmindful;
 by your resources, make them wander.
Put them down, Lord our shield,
 ¹²for the wrongdoing of their mouth, the word of their lips.
So that they are caught by their majesty
 and by the oath and by the lie they recount.
¹³Finish them off in wrath,
 finish them off so they are no more,
So that people may acknowledge that God rules in Ya'aqob,
 to the ends of the earth. *(Rise)*
¹⁴They come back at evening,
 they howl like a dog and go round the town.
¹⁵Those people – they wander about for food;
 if they are not full they stay the night.
¹⁶But I – I will sing about your vigour,
 I will resound at morning about your commitment.
Because you've become my turret,
 a retreat on the day when I was under pressure.
¹⁷My vigour, to you I will make music,
 because God is my turret,
 the God committed to me.

Psalm 60 How to deal with unfulfilled promises

The leader's. On The Lotus of Testimony. An inscription. David's. For teaching. When he fought Aram-of-the-Two-Rivers and Aram Tsobah, and Yo'ab went back and struck down Edom in Salt Ravine, 12,000 men.

¹God, you've rejected us, broken us,
 been angry – turn back to us!
²You've shaken the country, torn it open
 – mend its splits, because it's slipped.
³You've made your people see tough things,
 you've made us drink wine that caused us to stagger.
⁴You have given people who live in awe of you a banner to flee to
 because of the bow. *(Rise)*
⁵In order that your beloved people may pull out,
 deliver with your right hand, answer me.

⁶God had spoken by his sacredness:

'I will exult as I allocate Shekem
 and measure out Sukkot Vale.
⁷Gil'ad will be mine,
 Menashsheh will be mine,
Ephrayim will be a stronghold for my head,
 Yehudah my sceptre,
⁸Mo'ab will be my washbasin,
 against Edom I will throw my boot;
 raise a shout against me, Peleshet [Philistia]!
⁹Who will conduct me to the fortified town,
 who would lead me to Edom?'

¹⁰You yourself have rejected us, God, haven't you,
 you don't go out with our armies, God.
¹¹Grant us help against the adversary,
 given that human deliverance is empty.
¹²Through God we will act with forcefulness;
 he's the one who will trample on our adversaries.

Psalm 61 How to pray with your leader

The leader's. On a stringed instrument. David's.

¹Listen to my resounding noise, God,
 heed my plea.
²From the end of the earth I call to you,
 while my heart flags.
To a crag that rises high above me may you lead me,
 ³because you've been a shelter for me,
 a vigorous tower before the enemy.

⁴I shall reside in your tent permanently,
 I shall shelter in the hiding place of your wings. *(Rise)*
⁵Because you, God, have listened to my pledges;
 you gave their possession to the people who hold your name in awe.

⁶You will add days to the king's days;
  his years will be like generation after generation.
⁷He will live permanently before God;
  appoint commitment and truthfulness so they
    may preserve him.
⁸Thus I shall make music to your name
    permanently,
  in making good my pledges day by day.

Psalm 62 Silence towards God

The leader's. On Yedutun. A composition. David's.

¹Indeed, towards God my entire being is silent;
  from him my deliverance comes.
²Indeed, he is my crag and my deliverance,
  my turret – I shall not slip far.
³How long will you attack someone,
  commit murder, all of you?
Like a bent wall, a fence that's been pulled down
  – ⁴indeed, they have taken counsel so as to pull
    him down from his dignity.
They accept lying;
  they bless with their mouth, but inside they
    slight. *(Rise)*

⁵Indeed, be silent towards God, my entire being,
  because from him my hope comes.
⁶Indeed, he's my crag, my deliverance,
  my turret – I shall not slip.
⁷On God rests my deliverance and my splendour;
  my strong rock, my shelter, is God in person.
⁸Trust in him at all times, you people,
  pour out your heart before him;
  God is our shelter. *(Rise)*

⁹Indeed, human beings are hollow,
  people are a lie.
Going up on scales,
  they're less than hollow, altogether.
¹⁰Don't trust in fraud, don't put hollow hopes in
    robbery;
  resources – when they bear fruit, don't set your
    mind on them.
¹¹God spoke of one thing,
  two things that I heard:
That God has vigour ¹²and you, Lord, have
    commitment,
  that you yourself make good for someone in
    accordance with his action.

Psalm 63 I am mindful of you on my bed

A composition. David's. When he was in the Wilderness of Yehudah.

¹God, you are my God, I look urgently for you,
  my whole person thirsts for you.
My body aches for you,
  in a dry, faint country without water.
²Yes, in the sacred place I've beheld you,
  seeing your vigour and your splendour.
³Because your commitment is better than life;
  my lips will extol you.
⁴Yes, I shall bless you throughout my life;
  in your name I shall lift up the palms of my
    hands.
⁵As with juiciness and richness my appetite will
    be full,
  and with resounding lips my mouth will give
    praise,
⁶If I am mindful of you on my bed,
  murmur about you during the watches.
⁷Because you've been my help,
  and in the shade of your wings I shall resound.
⁸My whole person has clung after you;
  your right hand has taken hold of me.

⁹But those people, who seek devastation for my
    life,
  will come into the depths of the earth.
¹⁰The people who hurl someone on to the edges of
    the sword
  will be the prey of jackals.
¹¹But the king – he will rejoice in God;
  everyone who swears by him will take pride,
  because the mouth of people who speak
    falsehood is stopped up.

Psalm 64 The failure of the well-plotted plot

The leader's. A composition. David's.

¹Listen to my voice, God, as I talk,
  may you preserve my life from the enemy's
    terror.
²May you hide me from the council of people
    dealing badly,
  from the crowd of people devising trouble,
³Who have whetted their tongue like a sword,
  who have directed their bitter word like arrows,

⁴To shoot from hiding at the person of integrity
– they shoot at him suddenly and they're not afraid.
⁵They take strong hold for themselves of a word about bad dealing,
they recount it, in hiding traps.
They've said 'Who will see them?'
⁶as they plot evil.
'We have completed a plot that's well plotted;
the inner thinking of a person and his mind are deep.'
⁷But God has shot them with an arrow;
suddenly the blows that strike them down have come.
⁸They've made it collapse on themselves with their tongue;
all who look at them shake their head.
⁹Everyone was in awe; they've told of God's act,
they've gained insight into his deed.
¹⁰The faithful person rejoices in Yahweh
and takes shelter with him;
all the upright in mind take pride.

Psalm 65 The God of atonement and the God of the harvest

The leader's. A composition. David's. A song.

¹To you silence is praise,
God in Tsiyyon.
To you a pledge is made good,
²the one who listens to a plea.
All flesh come right to you
³with wayward words.
Whereas our rebellions would have been too strong for me,
you yourself expiate them.
⁴The blessings of the person you choose and bring near,
so that he dwells in your courtyards!
May we be full with the good things of your house,
your sacred palace.
⁵Answer us with awe-inspiring deeds in faithfulness,
God who delivers us!

Object of trust for all the ends of the earth
and the far-off sea,
⁶Who established the mountains by his energy,
who is belted with strength,
⁷Who stills the din of the seas,
the din of their waves, yes, the tumult of the peoples.
⁸The people who live at the ends are in awe at your signs;
you make the entry points of morning and evening resound.

⁹You've attended to the earth and watered it;
you greatly enrich it.
God's channel is full of water;
you prepare their grain.
Because in this way you prepare it:
¹⁰saturating its furrows, smoothing its ridges,
You soften it with rains,
you bless its growth.
¹¹You've crowned the year with your good things;
your cart tracks flow with richness.
¹²The pastures of the wilderness flow,
the hills wrap on celebration.
¹³The meadows put on flocks,
the vales envelop themselves in wheat,
they shout, and sing too.

Psalm 66 I shall make good my pledges

The leader's. A song. A composition.

¹Shout for God, all the earth,
²make music for the splendour of his name!
Make his praise splendour,
³say to God, 'How awe-inspiring are your acts!
At the abundance of your vigour
your enemies wither before you.
⁴All the earth bow low to you,
they make music to you, make music to your name!' *(Rise)*

⁵Come and see the deeds of God,
the one who is awe-inspiring for his activity in relation to human beings.
⁶He turned sea into dry land,
so they could cross the river on foot.
There let us rejoice in him,
⁷the one who rules permanently by his strength!
His eyes watch the nations;
the defiant – they should not rise up against him. *(Rise)*

⁸Peoples, bless our God,
let the sound of his praise be heard,

⁹The one who places us in life,
    and doesn't give our foot to slipping.
¹⁰Because you've tried us, God;
    you've refined us like someone refining silver.
¹¹You let us come into a net,
    put a constraint on our hips.
¹²You let someone ride at our head,
    we've come into fire and into water,
    but you've got us out into flourishing.

¹³I shall come into your house with burnt offerings,
    I shall make good my pledges to you,
¹⁴The ones that my lips uttered,
    that my mouth spoke when I was under pressure.
¹⁵As burnt offerings I will offer up fatlings to you,
    with the aroma of rams;
    I'll make ready bulls with goats. *(Rise)*
¹⁶Come listen and I'll recount,
    all you who live in awe of God,
    what he's done for me.
¹⁷To him with my mouth I called;
    he was exalted by my tongue.
¹⁸If I could have seen trouble in my heart,
    my Lord would not listen.
¹⁹In fact God listened,
    heeded the sound of my plea.
²⁰God be blessed,
    the one who didn't turn aside my plea
    or his commitment from me!

Psalm 67 Bless us, and let other peoples acknowledge it

The leader's. With strings. A composition. A song.

¹May God be gracious to us and bless us,
    may he shine his face with us, *(Rise)*
²For the acknowledging of your way in the earth,
    your deliverance in all the nations.
³May peoples confess you, God,
    may peoples confess you, all of them.
⁴May countries rejoice and resound,
    because you exercise authority over peoples with uprightness,
    you guide nations in the earth. *(Rise)*
⁵May peoples confess you, God,
    may peoples confess you, all of them.
⁶As earth has given its produce,
    may God, our God, bless us.
⁷May God bless us,
    may all the ends of earth live in awe of him.

Psalm 68.1–18 Father of the orphan, protector of the widow

The leader's. David's. A composition. A song.

¹When God arises, his enemies scatter,
    the people hostile to him flee before him.
²You blow them away like smoke blowing away,
    like wax melting before fire.
The faithless perish before God,
    ³but the faithful rejoice.
They exult before God,
    they celebrate with rejoicing.

⁴Sing to God,
    make music to his name.
Lift up the one who rides on the clouds,
    whose name is Yah, and exult before him.
⁵Father for orphans, judge for widows,
    is God in his sacred abode.
⁶God enables people who are alone to live at home,
    brings out prisoners in chains,
    yet the defiant dwell in parched land.

⁷God, when you went out before your people,
    when you marched through the wilderness, *(Rise)*
⁸Earth shook, yes, heavens poured,
    before God, the one of Sinay,
    before God, the God of Yisra'el.
⁹You shed generous rain, God;
    your own domain, when it was languishing –
    you yourself provided for it.
¹⁰Your dwelling – they've lived in it;
    you provide for the humble with your goodness, God.
¹¹The Lord gives a word;
    the women announcing the news are a great army.
¹²Kings of armies flee, flee;
    the young girls of the house share the spoil,
¹³though they stay among the sheepfolds,
The wings of a dove covered in silver,
    its pinions in pale gold.
¹⁴When Shadday scatters kings there,
    it snows on Tsalmon.

¹⁵Mount Bashan is a supernatural mountain,
  Mount Bashan is a many-peaked mountain.
¹⁶Why do you keep watch, mountains, peaks,
  on the mountain that God desired as his place to live?
  – yes, Yahweh will dwell there permanently.
¹⁷God's chariotry were myriads, thousands doubled;
  the Lord was among them at Sinay in sacredness.
¹⁸You went up on high, you took captives,
  to get gifts among people,
Yes, defiant ones,
  to dwell as Yah God.

Psalm 68.19–35 Kingdoms of the earth, sing to God

¹⁹The Lord be blessed day by day;
  the God who is our deliverance supports us.
  (Rise)
²⁰God is for us a God of deliverance;
  to Yahweh God belong departures to death.
²¹Yes, God hits his enemies' head,
  the hairy crown of the one who walks about in his great liability.
²²The Lord said, 'I'll bring them back from Bashan,
  I'll bring them back from the depths of the sea,
²³In order that your foot may hit in blood;
  your dogs' tongue – its share may be from your enemies.'
²⁴People saw your journeyings, God,
  the journeyings of my God, my king, into the sacred place.
²⁵Singers came first, then string-players,
  amid girls playing tambourines.
²⁶In the great congregation that bless God,
  Yahweh, you [who issued] from Yisra'el's fountain.
²⁷There was little Binyamin, holding sway over them,
  Yehudah's officials, their noisy crowd,
Zebulun's officials, Naphtali's officials:
²⁸your God ordered vigour for you.
Be vigorous, God,
  you who acted for us ²⁹from your palace;
Right up to Yerushalaim to you
  kings will bring tribute.

³⁰Reprimand the creature in the reeds,
  the assembly of sturdy among the bullocks, the peoples.
Trampling on those who accept silver,
  you scattered peoples who delight in confrontations.
³¹Envoys will come from Misrayim [Egypt],
  Kush will run with its hands to God.

³²Kingdoms of the earth, sing to God,
  make music to the Lord, *(Rise)*
³³To the one who rides on the highest heavens of old
  – there, he gives out his voice, a vigorous voice.
³⁴Give vigour to God, whose majesty is over Yisra'el,
  his vigour in the skies.
³⁵God, you are to be held in awe in your most sacred place,
  the one who is God of Yisra'el.
He gives vigour and great might to his people;
  God be blessed.

Psalm 69.1–18 Passion means persecution

The leader's. On Lotuses. David's.

¹Deliver me, God,
  because the water has come up to my neck.
²I've sunk in a deep flood;
  there's no foothold.
I've come into torrents of water;
  a deluge has overwhelmed me.
³I've become weary with calling,
  my throat has become dry.
My eyes fail,
  waiting for my God.
⁴They are more numerous than the hairs on my head,
  the people hostile to me for nothing.
Numerous are the people who are trying to put an end to me,
  my enemies, with falsehood.
What I haven't stolen,
  then I must give back.
⁵God, you yourself know my denseness;
  the things for which I'm liable are not hidden from you.

⁶The people who hope in you must not be shamed through me,
  Lord Yahweh of Armies.

The people who seek you must not be disgraced
through me,
God of Yisra'el.
⁷Because it's on account of you that I've carried reviling,
that disgrace has covered my face.
⁸I've become a stranger to my brothers,
an alien to my mother's children.
⁹Because passion for your house has consumed me;
the words of reviling with which people have reviled you have fallen on me.
¹⁰I cried with fasting, with my entire being,
and it became words of reviling for me.
¹¹I made sack my clothing,
and I became an object lesson for them.
¹²The people who sit at the gateway talk about me;
– the drinkers' song.
¹³But I: my plea to you, Yahweh,
is a time of acceptance.
God, in the abundance of your commitment answer me,
in the truthfulness of your deliverance.
¹⁴Rescue me from the mud; I must not sink;
may I be rescued from the people hostile to me,
from the torrents of water.
¹⁵The deluge of water must not overwhelm me,
the flood must not swallow me,
the pit must not close its mouth over me.
¹⁶Answer me, Yahweh, because your commitment is good;
in accordance with the abundance of your compassion turn your face to me.
¹⁷Don't hide your face from your servant,
because I'm under pressure, hurry, answer me.
¹⁸Draw near to me, restore me;
because of my enemies, redeem me.

²²May their table become a trap before them,
a snare for their allies.
²³May their eyes go dark so they can't see,
may their hips shudder continually.
²⁴Pour out your condemnation on them;
may your angry rage overtake them.
²⁵May their encampment become desolate,
may there be no one living in their tents.
²⁶Because you – the person you struck down,
they've pursued,
and the suffering of the people run through by you, they've heralded.
²⁷Put waywardness on top of their waywardness;
may they not come to your faithfulness.
²⁸May they be erased from the document of living people;
may they not be written down with the faithful.
²⁹When I'm humble and suffering,
may your deliverance set me on high, God.
³⁰I shall praise God's name with a song,
I shall magnify it with confession.
³¹It will seem good to Yahweh more than an ox,
a bull with horns and divided hoofs.
³²Humble people have seen and rejoiced;
you who enquire of God – may your spirit revive.
³³Because Yahweh is going to listen to the needy,
and not despise his captives.
³⁴May heavens and earth praise him,
seas and everything that moves in them.
³⁵Because God will deliver Tsiyyon
and build Yehudah's towns.
People will live there and possess it,
³⁶the offspring of his servants will hold it as their domain,
people who are loyal to his name will dwell in it.

Psalm 69.19–36 Trusting God with your anger

¹⁹You yourself know my reviling,
my shame, my disgrace.
All the people watching for me are in front of you;
²⁰reviling has broken my spirit, and I'm ailing.
I've hoped for someone to sympathize but there's no one,
for comforters but I haven't found any.
²¹People have put poison in my food,
for my thirst they've given me vinegar to drink.

Psalm 70 Telling God what to do

The leader's. David's. For commemoration.

¹God, to rescue me,
Yahweh, to my help, hurry!
²They should be shamed and reviled,
the people who seek my life.
They should turn backwards and be confounded,
the people who want what is bad for me.
³They should turn back on account of their disgrace,
the people who say, 'Ah, ah!'

⁴They should celebrate and rejoice in you, all the
   people who seek you;
  they should say continually, 'God is great',
   the people loyal to your deliverance.
⁵But I am humble and needy –
   God, hurry to me.
You're my help and the one who enables me to
   survive;
  Yahweh, don't delay!

Psalm 71.1–16 From birth through to old age

¹I have taken shelter with you, Yahweh;
   I must not be shamed ever.
²In your faithfulness rescue me, enable me to
   survive,
  bend your ear to me, deliver me.
³Be for me a crag,
   an abode for coming to continually,
  Which you've ordered to deliver me,
   because you're my cliff, my fastness.
⁴My God, enable me to survive from the fist of the
   faithless,
  from the grip of the evildoer and robber.
⁵Because you have been my hope, Lord Yahweh,
   the one whom I've trusted from my youth.
⁶On you I have leaned from birth,
   from my mother's womb.
You've been my support;
   my praise has continually been of you.
⁷I've been a true sign for many people,
   as you have been my strong shelter.
⁸My mouth is full of your praise,
   of your glory all day.

⁹Don't cast me off for my old age,
   when my energy is finished, don't abandon me.
¹⁰Because my enemies have said of me,
   and people who keep watch for my life have
    taken counsel together:
¹¹'Since God has abandoned him, pursue him,
   seize him, because there's no one to rescue
    him.'
¹²God, don't be far from me;
   my God, hurry to my help.
¹³They should be shamed and finished,
   the people who attack my life.
They should dress themselves in reviling and
   disgrace,
  the people who seek something bad for me.

¹⁴But I – I will wait continually,
   and add to all your praise.
¹⁵My mouth – it will recount your faithfulness,
   your deliverance all day.
Because I don't know how to write,
   ¹⁶I'll come with the mighty acts of my Lord
    Yahweh,
   I'll make mention of your faithfulness, yours
    alone.

Psalm 71.17–24 You've taught me and I will tell of it

¹⁷God, you have taught me from my youth,
   and until now I tell of your extraordinary
    deeds.
¹⁸So even until my old age and grey hair,
   God, don't abandon me,
Until I tell of your strength to a generation,
   [tell] to everyone who is to come your strength,
   ¹⁹and your faithfulness, God, on high.
You who have done big things, God
   – who is like you?
²⁰You who have let me see pressures,
   many and bad,
Will give me life again,
   and from the depths of the earth bring me up
    again.
²¹You will grant me much greatness
   and turn round to comfort me.
²²And I myself will confess you with a mandolin
   for your truthfulness, God.
I will make music for you with the guitar,
   sacred one of Yisra'el.
²³My lips will resound when I make music for
   you,
  and my entire being, which you've redeemed.
²⁴Yes, my tongue will talk of your faithfulness all
   day,
  because they have been shamed, because they
   have been confounded,
  the people who sought something bad for me.

Psalm 72.1–17 How to pray for the government

Shelomoh's [Solomon's].

¹God, give the king your rulings,
   the royal son your faithfulness.

²May he give judgement for your people with faithfulness,
  your humble ones with authority.
³May the mountains bear well-being for the people,
  and the hills, in faithfulness.
⁴May he exercise authority for the humble among the people,
  deliver the needy, crush the fraud.
⁵May they live in awe of you while the sun shines,
  and before the moon, generation after generation.
⁶May he come down like rain on mown grass,
  like downpours, an overflowing on the earth.
⁷May the faithful person flourish in his days,
  and abundance of well-being, until the moon is no more.
⁸May he hold sway from sea to sea,
  from the river to the ends of the earth.
⁹May wildcats kneel before him,
  may his enemies lick the dust.
¹⁰May the kings of Tarshish and foreign shores bring back an offering.
May the kings of Sheba and Seba
  present a gift.
¹¹May all kings bow low to him,
  all nations serve him.
¹²Because he rescues the needy person crying for deliverance
  and the humble person who has no helper.
¹³May he have pity on poor and needy,
  so that he delivers the lives of needy people.
¹⁴From repression and from violence may he restore their life,
  and may their blood be valuable in his eyes.
¹⁵May he live and be given
  gold from Sheba.
May pleas be said on his behalf continually;
  all day may people pray for blessing for him.
¹⁶May there be an abundance of grain in the country,
  on the top of the mountains.
May his fruit shake like Lebanon,
  may people thrive from the town like the grass in the country.
¹⁷May his name be permanent,
  before the sun may his name have offspring,
So that people may pray to be blessed through him;
  may all nations count him fortunate.

Psalm 72.18–20 Another interim closing act of praise

¹⁸Yahweh God,
  the God of Yisra'el be blessed,
  the one who alone does extraordinary things.
¹⁹His splendid name be blessed permanently;
  may the entire earth fill with his splendour.
Amen, amen.

²⁰The pleas of David ben Yishay [Jesse] end.

Psalm 73.1–14 I had nearly tripped

Composition. Asaph's.

¹Indeed, God is good to Yisra'el,
  to the pure in heart.
²But I – my feet all but turned away,
  my steps were nearly tipped out.
³Because I was passionate about the wild people,
  the well-being of the faithless that I can see.
⁴Because there are no stresses threatening their death,
  and their chest is portly.
⁵In oppression from people they have no part;
  they are not afflicted like other people.
⁶Therefore majesty is round their neck;
  a coat of violence wraps round them.
⁷Their eye bulges because of hardness;
  the schemes in their mind have overflowed.
⁸They scoff and speak of dealing badly,
  from their position on high they speak of fraud.
⁹They've set their mouth in the heavens,
  and their tongue walks about on the earth.
¹⁰Thus hammering comes back to his people,
  and full waters are drained by them.
¹¹And they say, 'How does God know,
  is there knowledge with the One on High?'
¹²There – these are the faithless people, at ease permanently,
  as they have amassed resources.
¹³Indeed, it was with empty results that I had kept my heart clean
  and washed the palms of my hands in freedom from guilt,
¹⁴I've come to be afflicted all day,
  and my reproof happens each morning.

Psalm 73.15–28 God redeems now

¹⁵If I had said I would recount it thus,
 there, I would have broken faith with the circle of your children.
¹⁶But when I thought about how to know about this,
 it was oppressive in my eyes,
¹⁷Until I came to God's great sanctuary,
 so that I might consider their end.
¹⁸Indeed, you will set them among deceptions;
 you're making them fall to lies.
¹⁹How they're coming to desolation suddenly;
 they're come to an end, they're finished, through terrors.
²⁰Like a dream on waking, Lord,
 on stirring, you will despise their shadow.

²¹When my mind is embittered,
 and in my inner being I'm cut through,
²²Then I'm stupid and I don't know things;
 I became an animal with you.
²³But I've been with you continually;
 you've grasped my right hand.
²⁴By your counsel you lead me,
 and afterwards you will take me to splendour.
²⁵Whom do I have in the heavens?
 – and with you, I haven't wanted anyone on the earth.
²⁶Though my flesh and my mind are finished,
 God is my mind's crag and my share permanently.
²⁷Because there – the people who are far from you perish;
 you're terminating everyone who whores in relation to you.
²⁸But I – nearness to God is good for me;
 I've made my Lord Yahweh my shelter,
 so as to recount all your deeds.

Psalm 74 Destruction, blasphemy, villainy

An instruction. Asaph's.

¹God, why have you rejected us permanently,
 [why] does your anger smoke at the flock you pasture?
²Be mindful of your assembly,
 which you acquired long ago,
Which you restored as the clan that was your domain,
 Mount Tsiyyon, where you dwelt.
³Lift up your steps to the perpetual desolations,
 every bad action that the enemy undertook in the sacred place.
⁴Your adversaries roared inside your appointed places,
 they made their own signs into signs.
⁵It could be recognized as like someone bringing up axes against a thicket of trees.
⁶And now its engravings altogether
 they were smashing with hatchet and cleavers.
⁷They sent off your sanctuary in fire, down to the ground;
 they defiled the dwelling of your name.
⁸They said to themselves, 'We'll put them down altogether';
 they burned all God's appointed places in the country.
⁹We couldn't see our signs, there was no longer a prophet,
 there was no one with us who knew how long.
¹⁰Until when, God, will the adversary blaspheme,
 will the enemy revile your name permanently?
¹¹Why do you turn back your hand,
 withhold your right hand in the fold of your coat?

¹²But God, my king of old,
 the one who effects acts of deliverance in the middle of the earth:
¹³You're the one who parted the sea by your vigour,
 you smashed the dragons' heads on the water.
¹⁴You're the one who crushed Livyatan's heads,
 so you could make it food for a company of wildcats.
¹⁵You're the one who split spring and wadi,
 you're the one who dried up perennial rivers.
¹⁶Day is yours, night is also yours;
 you're the one who established the light, the sun.
¹⁷You're the one who set all earth's boundaries;
 summer and winter – you're the one who shaped them.

¹⁸Be mindful of this: an enemy has blasphemed, Yahweh,
 a villainous people has reviled your name.
¹⁹Don't give the life of your dove to an animal,
 don't put out of mind permanently the life of your humble ones.
²⁰Look at the pact,
 because the dark places in the country are full of pastures of violence.

²¹The broken must not turn back shamed;
   the humble and needy should praise your name.
²²Rise, God, argue for your judgement,
   be mindful of your reviling by villains all day.
²³Don't put out of mind the voice of your adversaries,
   the din of the people who rise against you,
      going up continually.

Psalm 75 The promise of an intoxicating chalice

The leader's. Do Not Destroy. A composition. Asaph's. A song.

¹We have confessed you, God, we have confessed,
   and when your name drew near, people have recounted your extraordinary deeds.
²'Indeed I will take the set time,
   when I myself will exercise authority with uprightness.
³Whereas earth and all its inhabitants are trembling,
   I am the one who ordered its pillars. *(Rise)*
⁴I have said to the wild people, 'Don't be wild',
   and to the faithless, 'Don't lift your horn.
⁵Don't lift your horn high,
   [or] speak with forward neck.'

⁶Because it's not from the east or from the west,
   not from the mountains' pasturage,
⁷But God exercises authority;
   this person he puts down, that person he lifts up.
⁸Because there is a chalice in Yahweh's hand,
   with fermented wine, full of spices.
He's pouring from it, they will indeed drain its dregs;
   all the faithless on the earth will drink.
⁹But I – I will tell of it permanently,
   I will make music for Ya'aqob's God.
¹⁰'Whereas I will cut all the horns of the faithless,
   the horns of the faithful person I will lift up.'

Psalm 76 To be held in awe by earth's kings

The leader's. With strings. A composition. Asaph's. A song.

¹God made himself be acknowledged in Yehudah,
   in Yisra'el his name is great.
²His shelter came to be in Shalem,
   his abode in Tsiyyon.
³There he shattered the bow's flames,
   shield, sword and battle. *(Rise)*
⁴You were resplendent,
   august on the mountains of prey.
⁵The sturdy-hearted let themselves be plundered,
   they fell into a deep sleep,
None of the forceful men could lift their hands
   ⁶at your reprimand, God of Ya'aqob.
Both chariot and horse lay stunned;
   ⁷you – you were to be held in awe.
Who can stand before you
   in the time of your anger?
⁸From the heavens you let your judgement be heard;
   the earth was in awe and was still,
⁹When God rose to exercise authority,
   to deliver all the humble in the land. *(Rise)*
¹⁰Because human wrath confesses you;
   you wrap on the remainder of your wrath.

¹¹Give pledges and make them good, to Yahweh your God;
   all those round him bring tribute to the one who is to be held in awe.
¹²He curbs the spirit of leaders;
   he is to be held in awe by earth's kings.

Psalm 77 Has God changed?

The leader's. On Yedutun. Asaph's. A composition.

¹With my voice to God, yes, I will cry out;
   with my voice to God, yes, so that he may give ear to me.
²On the day when I was under pressure,
   I have enquired of my Lord.
My hand has reached out by night and does not grow numb;
   my entire being refuses to find comfort.
³I shall be mindful of God and be in turmoil,
   I shall talk as my spirit faints. *(Rise)*
⁴You've grasped the guards on my eyes;
   I've been constrained and I can't speak.
⁵I've thought of days of old,
   years of ages past.
⁶I shall be mindful of my song by night,
   as I murmur in my heart, and my spirit has sought hard.

⁷Will it be permanently that my Lord rejects,
  and never again shows acceptance?
⁸Has his commitment ceased to exist permanently,
  his word come to an end for generation after generation?
⁹Has God put out of mind the showing of grace,
  or shut off his compassion in anger? *(Rise)*

¹⁰I said, 'That has distressed me:
  the change in the right hand of the One on High.'
¹¹I shall be mindful of Yah's deeds;
  yes, I shall be mindful of your extraordinary deeds of old.
¹²I shall murmur about your every act,
  I shall talk of your deeds.
¹³God, your way is characterized by sacredness;
  who is a god as great as God?
¹⁴You are the God who performs extraordinary deeds;
  you caused your vigour to be acknowledged among the peoples.
¹⁵You restored your people with your arm,
  the descendants of Ya'aqob and Yoseph. *(Rise)*
¹⁶Water saw you, God;
  when water saw you, it would convulse.
Yes, deeps would tremble;
  ¹⁷clouds poured down water.
Skies gave voice;
  yes, your arrows would go about.
¹⁸The sound of your thunder was in the whirlwind,
  lightning lit up the world.
The earth trembled and shook;
  ¹⁹your way was in the sea.
Your paths were in mighty water,
  though your steps were not acknowledged.
²⁰You led your people like a flock
  by the hand of Mosheh [Moses] and Aharon [Aaron].

Psalm 78.1–11 Pass on the story

An instruction. Asaph's.

¹Give ear to my instruction, my people;
  bend your ear to the sayings of my mouth.
²I shall open my mouth with a poem,
  pour out conundrums from of old.
³Things that we have heard and acknowledged,
  that our ancestors have recounted to us,
⁴We will not hide from their descendants,
  recounting to the next generation,
The praises of Yahweh and his vigour,
  the extraordinary things that he did.

⁵He implemented an affirmation in Ya'aqob,
  put instruction in Yisra'el,
Which he ordered our ancestors
  to get their descendants to acknowledge,
⁶In order that the next generation might acknowledge them,
  descendants who would be born,
So they might rise up and recount them to their descendants,
  ⁷so they might put their assurance in God,
And not put out of mind God's acts,
  but observe his orders,
⁸And not become like their ancestors,
  a defiant and rebellious generation,
A generation that did not set its mind,
  and whose spirit was not true to God.

⁹The Ephrayimites, equipped as archers,
  turned back on the day of meeting [in battle].
¹⁰They didn't keep God's pact
  but refused to walk by his instruction.
¹¹They put out of mind his deeds,
  the extraordinary things that he had let them see.

Psalm 78.12–31 God's generosity and people's response

¹²In the sight of their ancestors he had done something extraordinary,
  in the country of Misrayim, in the region of Tso'an.
¹³He divided the sea and enabled them to pass through it,
  he made the water stand like a mound.
¹⁴He led them by means of a cloud by day,
  and all night by means of a fiery light.
¹⁵He divided crags in the wilderness,
  and enabled them to drink like the deeps, abundantly.
¹⁶He got streams out from a cliff,
  and made water flow down like rivers.
¹⁷But they went on repeatedly doing wrong in relation to him,
  and defying the One on High in the desert.

¹⁸They tested God with [deliberation of] their mind,
  in asking food for themselves.
¹⁹They spoke against God:
  'Can God lay a table in the wilderness?
²⁰Yes, he struck a crag and water flowed,
  wadis gushed.
Can he also give bread,
  or provide meat for his people?'
²¹Therefore Yahweh listened and raged;
  fire broke out against Ya'aqob,
  and also anger arose against Yisra'el,
²²Because they didn't trust in God,
  they didn't rely on his deliverance.
²³So he ordered the skies above,
  opened the doors of the heavens.
²⁴He rained *maan* [manna] on them to eat,
  gave them grain from the heavens.
²⁵Each one ate food fit for the sturdy;
  he sent them provisions to fill them.
²⁶He would make the east wind move in the heavens,
  he drove the south wind by his vigour.
²⁷He rained meat on them like earth,
  winged birds like the sand at the seas.
²⁸He made them fall inside his camp,
  round his great dwelling.
²⁹They ate, and they were very full;
  he would bring them their longing.
³⁰They hadn't turned aside from their longing,
  their food was still in their mouth,
³¹When God's anger rose against them,
  and he killed some of their beefiest,
  put down Yisra'el's youth.

Psalm 78.32–55 Responsiveness is short-lived, but so is wrath

³²For all this they did wrong again,
  and didn't trust in all his extraordinary deeds.
³³He made their days end in hollowness,
  their years in terror.
³⁴If he killed them, they would enquire of him,
  turn back and look urgently for God.
³⁵They were mindful that God was their crag,
  God on High their restorer.
³⁶But they deceived him with their mouth,
  with their tongue they would lie to him.
³⁷Their mind was not set with him;
  they didn't stay true to his pact.
³⁸But because he was compassionate,
  he would expiate waywardness and not devastate.
He repeatedly turned his anger back;
  he didn't stir all his wrath.
³⁹He was mindful that they were flesh,
  a passing wind that doesn't come back.
⁴⁰How much they would defy him in the wilderness,
  pain him in the wasteland.
⁴¹Repeatedly they tested God,
  upset Yisra'el's Sacred One.
⁴²They weren't mindful of his hand,
  the day when he redeemed them from the adversary,
⁴³When he put his signs in Misrayim,
  his portents in the region of Tso'an.
⁴⁴He turned their great river into blood;
  people couldn't drink from their streams.
⁴⁵He would send off a swarm against them and it ate them,
  frogs and they devastated them.
⁴⁶He gave their produce to the caterpillar,
  their crop to the locust.
⁴⁷He killed their vine with hail,
  their wild figs with flood.
⁴⁸He surrendered their animals to hail,
  their livestock to lightning flashes.
⁴⁹He would send off among them his angry rage,
  outburst, condemnation and pressure,
A delegation of bad envoys,
⁵⁰that would clear a trail for his anger.
He didn't hold back their life from death
  but surrendered their existence to epidemic.
⁵¹He struck down every firstborn in Misrayim,
  the first issue of vigour in the tents of Ham.
⁵²He got his people on the move like sheep,
  drove them like a flock in the wilderness.
⁵³He led them in confidence and they were not fearful,
  but their enemies – the sea covered them.
⁵⁴He brought them to his sacred territory,
  the mountain that his right hand acquired.
⁵⁵He dispossessed nations before them,
  allotted them a share as their domain;
  he enabled Yisra'el's clans to dwell in their tents.

Psalm 78.56–72 When God woke up

⁵⁶But they tested and defied God On High;
  they didn't keep his affirmations.

⁵⁷They turned backwards and broke faith like their
    ancestors;
  they turned like a deceitful bow.
⁵⁸They vexed him with their shrines,
  aroused his passion with their images.
⁵⁹God listened and raged,
  and quite rejected Yisraèl.
⁶⁰He left the dwelling at Shiloh,
  the tent where he had dwelt among humanity.
⁶¹He gave his vigour to captivity,
  his glory to the hand of the adversary.
⁶²He surrendered his people to the sword;
  he raged at his own domain.
⁶³Fire consumed its young men,
  and its girls were not lamented.
⁶⁴Its priests fell by the sword;
  its widows could not cry.

⁶⁵But my Lord woke up like someone asleep,
  like a strong man shouting because of wine.
⁶⁶He beat back his adversaries,
  gave them permanent reviling.
⁶⁷He rejected Yoseph's tent,
  didn't choose the clan of Ephrayim.
⁶⁸He chose the clan of Yehudah,
  Mount Tsiyyon, to which he was loyal.
⁶⁹He built his sanctuary like the heights,
  like the earth that he founded permanently.
⁷⁰He chose David as his servant
  and took him from the sheep pens.
⁷¹He brought him from following the ewes
  to shepherd Ya'aqob his people,
  Yisraèl his domain.
⁷²He shepherded them in accordance with the
    integrity of his mind;
  he would lead them by the skilful acts of his fists.

Psalm 79 How long will your passion burn?

A composition. Asaph's.

¹God, nations came into your domain,
  defiled your sacred palace,
  made Yerushalaim into ruins.
²They gave your servants' corpses
  as food to the birds of the heavens,
  the flesh of the people committed to you to the
    creatures of the earth.
³They poured out their blood like water
  round Yerushalaim with no one to bury them.
⁴We became an object of reviling to our
    neighbours,
  of ridicule and derision to the people round us.
⁵How long, Yahweh – will you be angry
    permanently,
  will your passion burn up like fire?
⁶Pour out your wrath on the nations
  which have not acknowledged you,
On the kingdoms
  which have not called on your name.
⁷Because they have consumed Ya'aqob,
  and desolated his home.
⁸Don't keep in mind the wayward acts of the past
    for us;
  may your compassion meet us quickly,
  because we've got very low.
⁹Help us, our God who delivers,
  for the sake of the splendour of your name.
Rescue us, make expiation for our wrongdoings,
  for the sake of your name.
¹⁰Why should the nations say,
  'Where is their God?'
May redress for your servants' blood that was
    poured out
  be acknowledged among the nations before
    our eyes.
¹¹May the captive's groan come before you;
  in accordance with the greatness of your
    might
  preserve the people about to die.
¹²Give back to our neighbours sevenfold, into
    their heart,
  their reviling with which they've reviled you,
    Lord.
¹³But we are your people,
  the flock you shepherd.
We will confess you permanently;
  to generation after generation we will recount
    your praise.

Psalm 80 Bring back! Come back!

The leader's. For Lotuses. An affirmation.
Asaph's. A composition.

¹You who shepherd Yisraèl, give ear,
  you who drive Yoseph like a flock.
You who sit above the sphinxes, shine out
  ²before Ephrayim, Binyamin and Menashsheh.
Stir your might,
  come as deliverance for us.

³God, bring us back,
   shine your face so we may find deliverance.

⁴Yahweh, God Armies,
   how long have you fumed at your people's plea?
⁵You've fed them weeping as food,
   made them drink tears by measure.
⁶You've set us at contention with our neighbours;
   our enemies ridicule us at will.

⁷God Armies, bring us back,
   shine your face so we may find deliverance.
⁸You moved a vine from Misrayim,
   dispossessed nations and planted it.
⁹You cleared a way before it,
   it put its roots down and filled the country.
¹⁰Mountains were covered by its shade,
   supernatural cedars by its branches.
¹¹It put out its boughs as far as the sea,
   its shoots to the river.
¹²Why have you broken open its walls,
   so that all the people who pass by the way pluck it?
¹³The boar from the forest tears at it,
   the creature of the wild feeds on it.

¹⁴God Armies, please come back,
   look from the heavens and see,
Attend to this vine,
   ¹⁵the stock that your right hand planted,
And over the offspring you took firm hold of for yourself.
¹⁶Burned in fire, cut;
   at the reprimand from your face they perish.
¹⁷May your hand be upon the one at your right hand,
   upon the man you took firm hold of for yourself.
¹⁸We will not turn backwards from you;
   give us life, and we will call on your name.
¹⁹Yahweh, God Armies, bring us back,
   shine your face so that we may find deliverance.

Psalm 81 Praising and listening

The leader's. On the Gittite. Asaph's.

¹Resound for God our vigour,
   shout for Ya'aqob's God.
²Raise the music, strike the tambourine,
   the melodious guitar with the mandolin.
³Blow the horn at the new month,
   at the full moon for our festival day.
⁴Because it's a decree of Yisra'el,
   a ruling of Ya'aqob's God,
⁵An affirmation he laid on Yoseph,
   when he went out over the country of Misrayim.

I listen to a lip I had not acknowledged:
   ⁶'I removed his shoulder from the burden;
   his fists passed on from the basket.
⁷Under pressure you called and I pulled you out,
   I answered you in the secret place of thunder.
I tested you at Argument Water:
   ⁸"Listen, my people, and I will testify to you;
   Yisra'el, if you listen to me . . .
⁹There will not be for you a foreign god,
   you will not bow low to an alien god.
¹⁰I Yahweh am your God,
   the one who brought you up from the country of Misrayim;
   widen your mouth and I will fill it."
¹¹But my people didn't listen to my voice;
   Yisra'el was unwilling in relation to me.
¹²So I sent them off in the determination of their mind,
   so that they might walk by their own counsels.
¹³If only my people were listening to me,
   [if only] Yisra'el would walk about in my ways.
¹⁴In a little while I would put down their enemies,
   turn my hand against their adversaries.'
¹⁵The people hostile to Yahweh would wither at him,
   and their fate would be permanent.
¹⁶He let them eat of the best of wheat;
   'From the crag I filled you with syrup.'

Psalm 82 Challenging the gods and God

A composition. Asaph's.

¹God is standing in the divine assembly;
   among the gods he exercises authority.
²How long will you [gods] exercise authority for evil,
   show regard to faithless people? *(Rise)*
³Exercise authority for the poor and the orphan,
   show faithfulness to the humble and the destitute.
⁴Enable the poor and the needy to survive,
   rescue them from the hand of the faithless.
⁵They don't acknowledge,
   they don't consider.
As they walk about in darkness,
   all earth's foundations slip.

⁶I myself said, 'You're gods,
   offspring of the One on High, all of you.
⁷Therefore you will die like a human being,
   fall like one of the officials.'
⁸Arise, God, exercise authority for the earth,
   because you possess all the nations as your
      domain.

Psalm 83 Don't be calm, God

A song. A composition. Asaph's.

¹God, don't keep your silence, don't be mute,
   don't be calm, God.
²Because there – your enemies are in turmoil,
   the people who are hostile to you have reared
      their head.
³They formulate shrewd confidences against your
      people,
   they take counsel with one another against the
      people you cherish.
⁴They've said, 'Come on, let's wipe them out from
      being a nation,
   so that Yisra'el's name will be brought to mind
      no more.'
⁵Because they've taken counsel together with one
      mind;
   against you they seal a pact –
⁶The tents of Edom and the Yishma'e'lites
      [Ishmaelites],
   Mo'ab and the Hagrites,
⁷Gebal, Ammon and Amaleq,
   Peleshet with the inhabitants of Tsor.
⁸Ashshur, too, has joined with them;
   they've become a source of strength for Lot's
      descendants. *(Rise)*

⁹Act towards them like Midyan,
   like Sisera, like Yabin, at the Qishon Wadi.
¹⁰They were destroyed at Dor Spring;
   they became manure for the ground.
¹¹Treat them – their leaders like Oreb and like Ze'eb,
   all their chiefs like Zebah and Tsalmunna,
¹²People who said, 'Let's take possession
   of God's pastures for ourselves.'
¹³My God, make them like a whirl,
   like stubble before the wind.
¹⁴Like fire that burns up a forest,
   like a flame that sets mountains on fire,
¹⁵So may you chase them with your hurricane,
   terrify them with your tempest.

¹⁶Fill their faces with slighting,
   so that they seek your name, Yahweh.
¹⁷May they be shamed and terrified permanently,
   may they be confounded and may they perish.
¹⁸May they acknowledge that you, whose name is
      Yahweh,
   you alone are the One on High over all the earth.

Psalm 84 The one day and the thousand days

The leader's. On the Gittite. The Qorahites'. A composition.

¹How much loved is your fine dwelling,
   Yahweh of Armies.
²My entire being yearned, yes it failed,
   for Yahweh's courtyards,
So that my mind and my body
   might resound for the living God.
³Yes, a bird – it found a home,
   a pigeon a nest for itself,
Where it put its young – your great altar,
   Yahweh of Armies, my King and my God.
⁴The blessings of the people who live in your house,
   who can still praise you! *(Rise)*
⁵The blessings of the person whose vigour comes
      through you,
   the causeways in their mind!
⁶The people who pass through Balsam Vale
   make it a spring.
Yes, the first rain will cover it with blessings;
   ⁷they will go from rampart to rampart.
The God of gods will appear in Tsiyyon,
   ⁸Yahweh God Armies.

Listen to my plea, give ear,
   God of Ya'aqob. *(Rise)*
⁹See our shield, God,
   look to the face of your anointed.
¹⁰Because a day in your courtyards is better than
      a thousand,
   I would choose being at the threshold of my
      God's house,
Rather than dwelling in the tents of the faithless
      person,
   ¹¹because Yahweh God is sun and shield.
Yahweh gives grace and splendour;
   he does not withhold good for people who walk
      with integrity.
¹²Yahweh of Armies,
   the blessings of the person who trusts in you!

Psalm 85 Faithfulness and well-being have embraced

The leader's. The Qorahites'. A composition.

[1] Yahweh, you accepted your country,
 you turned back Ya'aqob's fortunes.
[2] You carried your people's waywardness,
 you covered all their wrongdoings.
[3] You withdrew all your outburst,
 you turned from your angry burning.
[4] Turn us back, God who delivers us,
 contravene your vexation with us.
[5] Will you be angry at us permanently,
 prolong your anger to generation after generation?
[6] Will you yourself not again bring us to life,
 so that your people may rejoice in you?
[7] Yahweh, let us see your commitment,
 give us your deliverance.

[8] I will listen to what the God Yahweh will speak,
 because he will speak of well-being,
To his people and to those committed to him,
 those who do not turn back to dim-wittedness.
[9] Indeed his deliverance is near for people who live in awe of him,
 so that his splendour may settle in our country.
[10] Commitment and truthfulness – they've met;
 faithfulness and well-being – they've embraced.
[11] Truthfulness – it springs up from the earth;
 faithfulness – it has looked down from the heavens.
[12] Yes, Yahweh – he will give good things;
 our land – it will give its produce.
[13] Faithfulness – it will walk about before him
 as he sets his feet on the way.

Psalm 86 A servant leans on his master

A plea. David's.

[1] Bend your ear, Yahweh, answer,
 because I'm humble and needy.
[2] Keep watch over my life, because I'm committed;
 deliver your servant – you are my God.
As one who trusts in you, [3] be gracious to me, my Lord,
 because to you I call all day.
[4] Make your servant's entire being rejoice,
 because to you, my Lord, I lift up my being.
[5] Because you, my Lord, are good and pardoning,
 big in commitment to everyone who calls you.
[6] Give ear to my plea, Yahweh,
 heed the sound of my prayers for grace.
[7] On the day when I'm under pressure I call you,
 because you answer me.
[8] There is no one like you among the gods, my Lord,
 and there are no acts like yours.
[9] All the nations that you've made will come
 and bow low before you, my Lord.
They will honour your name,
[10] because you're great, one who does extraordinary things.
You are God, you alone;
[11] instruct me in your way, Yahweh.
I will walk about by your truthfulness;
 may my mind be one, in awe at your name.
[12] I will confess you, my Lord, my God, with all my mind;
 I will honour your name permanently.
[13] Because your commitment is great over me;
 you will rescue my life from deepest She'ol.
[14] God, assertive people have arisen against me,
 an assembly of terrifying people has sought my life.
Whereas they haven't put you in front of them,
[15] you are my Lord,
The compassionate and gracious God,
 long-tempered and big in commitment and truthfulness.
[16] Turn your face to me and be gracious to me,
 give your vigour to your servant.
Deliver the son of your handmaid,
[17] show me a sign for good,
So that the people who are hostile to me may see and be shamed,
 because you, Yahweh, have helped me and comforted me.

Psalm 87 Glorious things of thee are spoken, Tsiyyon

The Qorahites'. A composition. A song.

[1] Founded by him among the sacred mountains,
[2] Yahweh is loyal to Tsiyyon's gates
 more than all Ya'aqob's dwellings.

³Honourable things are spoken in you,
  God's town. *(Rise)*
⁴I will make mention of Rahab and Babel
  to the people who acknowledge me.
There are Peleshet, Tsor, with Kush
  – each was born there.
⁵To Tsiyyon it will be said,
  'Each and every one was born in it.'
He is the one who will establish it, the One on
  High;
⁶Yahweh will record, in writing down the
  peoples,
  'Each was born there.' *(Rise)*
⁷They sing as they dance,
  'All my fountains are in you.'

Psalm 88 A cry from the grave

A song. A composition. The Qorahites'. The leader's. On Pipe. For affliction. An instruction. Heman the Ezrahite's.

¹Yahweh, my God who delivers,
  by day I have cried out, by night in front of
    you.
²May my plea come before you;
  bend your ear to my resounding noise.
³Because my whole person is full of bad
    experiences;
  my life has arrived at She'ol.
⁴I am thought of with the people who go down
    into the Cistern,
  I've become like a man without strength,
⁵An outcast among the dead, like people run
    through,
  lying in the grave,
Of whom you've been mindful no more,
  when they are cut off from your hand.
⁶You've put me in the deepest Cistern,
  in dark places, in the depths.
⁷Upon me your wrath has pressed down;
  with all your breakers you've humbled me.
    (Rise)
⁸You've taken my acquaintances far from me,
  made me a great offence to them.
I'm confined so that I cannot go out,
  ⁹my eye has become dim through humbling.
I've called you, Yahweh, each day,
  I've stretched out my palms to you.
¹⁰Do you do extraordinary things for the dead,
  do ghosts rise to confess you? *(Rise)*
¹¹Is your commitment recounted in the grave,
  your truthfulness in Abaddon?
¹²Are your extraordinary deeds made known in
    the darkness,
  your faithfulness in the land of forgetting?
¹³But I, Yahweh, I've cried to you for help,
  in the morning my plea meets you.
¹⁴Yahweh, why do you reject me,
  hide your face from me?
¹⁵I'm afflicted, breathing my last since youth;
  I've borne your dreads, I despair.
¹⁶Your acts of rage have passed over me,
  your acts of terror have destroyed me.
¹⁷They are round me like water all day,
  they've encircled me altogether.
¹⁸You've taken friend and neighbour far from me,
  my acquaintances – darkness.

Psalm 89.1–18 The stable world

An instruction. Ethan the Ezrahite's.

¹Of Yahweh's acts of commitment I will sing
    permanently,
  for generation after generation I will cause his
    truthfulness to be acknowledged with my
    mouth.
²Because I've said, 'Your commitment is built up
    permanently;
  the heavens – you establish your truthfulness
    in them.'

³'I sealed a pact for my chosen,
  I swore to David my servant:
⁴"I will establish your offspring permanently,
  I will build your throne for generation after
    generation."'

⁵In the heavens they confess your extraordinary
    deeds, Yahweh,
  yes, your truthfulness in the congregation of
    the sacred ones.
⁶Because who in the sky can equal Yahweh,
  can compare with Yahweh among the divine
    beings,
⁷The God inspiring great reverence in the council
    of the sacred ones,
  inspiring awe above all those round him?
⁸Yahweh, God of Armies, who is like you,
  mighty Yah, with your truthfulness
    surrounding you?

⁹You rule over the majesty of the sea;
    when it lifts its waves, you're the one who can still them.
¹⁰You're the one who crushed Rahab, like someone run through;
    with your vigorous arm you scattered your enemies.
¹¹The heavens are yours, yes, the earth is yours,
    the world and what fills it: you're the one who founded them.
¹²North and south – you're the one who created them;
    Tabor and Hermon – they resound at your name.
¹³To you belongs an arm with strength;
    your hand is vigorous, your right hand stands high.
¹⁴Faithfulness in the exercise of authority is the establishment of your throne;
    commitment and truthfulness come to meet your face.
¹⁵The blessings of the people that acknowledges the shout,
    that walks about in the light of your face, Yahweh!
¹⁶In your name they celebrate all day,
    in your faithfulness they stand high.
¹⁷Because you're their vigorous glory;
    through your acceptance our horn stands high.
¹⁸Because our shield belongs to Yahweh,
    our king to Yisra'el's Sacred One.

Psalm 89.19–37 The stable promise

¹⁹Then you spoke in a vision to the people committed to you:
    'I put help on a strong man,
    I raised high one chosen from the people.
²⁰I found David, my servant,
    with my sacred oil I anointed him,
²¹The one with whom my hand will be established;
    yes, my arm will enable him to stand firm.
²²No enemy will extort from him,
    or evil person humble him.
²³I will crush his adversaries before him,
    beat down the people hostile to him.
²⁴My truthfulness and commitment will be with him,
    and in my name his horn will stand high.
²⁵I will set his hand on the sea,
    his right hand on the great river.
²⁶That man will call me, "You're my father,
    my God, the crag that delivers me."
²⁷Yes, I myself will make him my firstborn,
    on high in relation to earth's kings.
²⁸Permanently will I keep my commitment to him;
    my pact will be true for him.
²⁹I will set his offspring evermore,
    his throne like the days of the heavens.
³⁰If his sons abandon my instruction,
    don't walk by my rulings,
³¹If they profane my decrees
    don't keep my orders,
³²I will attend to their rebellion with a club,
    their waywardness with blows,
³³But my commitment I will not contravene from him;
    I will not be false to my truthfulness.
³⁴I will not profane my pact;
    what's come out of my lips I will not change.
³⁵Once and for all I've sworn by my sacredness:
    'If I lie to David . . .'
³⁶His offspring will be there permanently,
    his throne like the sun in front of me,
³⁷Like the moon, which is established permanently,
    a witness in the sky that's truthful.' *(Rise)*

Psalm 89.38–51 But is the promise stable?

³⁸But you yourself have rejected, spurned,
    burst out with your anointed.
³⁹You've renounced your servant's pact,
    profaned his diadem to the earth.
⁴⁰You've broken through all his walls,
    made his fortifications a ruin.
⁴¹All the people who pass his way have plundered him;
    he's become an object of reviling to his neighbours.
⁴²You've lifted high his adversaries' right hand,
    you've made all his enemies rejoice.
⁴³Yes, you've turned back his sword's blade,
    not enabled him to rise up in the battle.
⁴⁴You've made his purity cease;
    his throne you've hurled to the earth.
⁴⁵You've cut short the days of his youth,
    clothed him in shame. *(Rise)*

⁴⁶How long, Yahweh – will you hide permanently,
    will your wrath burn up like fire?

⁴⁷Be mindful – I, what a short span,
   for what emptiness you created all human beings.
⁴⁸Who is the man who can live on and not see death,
   can enable himself to escape from She'ol's hand?
   (Rise)
⁴⁹Where are your former acts of commitment, my Lord,
   which you swore to David in your truthfulness?
⁵⁰Be mindful, my Lord, of your servant's reviling,
   which I've carried in my heart,
Of all the many peoples
   ⁵¹who have reviled,
Of your enemies, Yahweh,
   those who have reviled the steps of your anointed.

Psalm 89.52 Amen anyway

⁵²Yahweh be blessed permanently.
   Amen, amen.

Psalm 90 God's time and our time

A plea. Mosheh's, supernatural man.

¹Lord, you were an abode for us,
   generation after generation.
²Before mountains were birthed
   and you laboured with the earth and the world,
From age to age,
   you were God.
³You would turn back mere human beings, right to being crushed;
   you said, 'Turn back, people!'
⁴Because a thousand years
   in your eyes were like a day,
Yesterday when it passes,
   or a watch in the night.
⁵You swept them away in sleep,
   though in the morning they would be like grass that grows fresh.
⁶In the morning it can flourish and grow fresh;
   by evening it dries up and withers.
⁷Because we are finished through your anger,
   through your wrath we have been fearful.
⁸You've set our wayward acts in front of you,
   our youthful deeds in the light of your face.
⁹Because all our days have turned their face through your outburst;
   we've finished up our years as murmuring.
¹⁰The days of our years in themselves are seventy years, or with strength eighty years.
But their drive has been oppression and trouble,
   because it's passed by speedily and we've flown away.
¹¹Who acknowledges the vigour of your anger,
   and your outburst, in accordance with awe for you?
¹²In counting our days, so make us acknowledge it,
   in order that we may bring home a smart mind.
¹³Turn back, Yahweh, how long?
   – relent about your servants.
¹⁴Fill us in the morning with your commitment,
   and we will resound and rejoice all our days.
¹⁵Enable us to rejoice in accordance with the days of your humbling us,
   the years we've seen bad fortune.
¹⁶May your deed appear to your servants,
   your magnificence for their descendants.
¹⁷May the Lord's loveliness come about,
   our God for us.
Establish the deed of our hands for us;
   yes, the deed of our hands – establish it.

Psalm 91 Shadow of the Almighty

¹As someone who lives in the hiding place of the One on High,
   who lodges in the shade of Shadday,
²I say of Yahweh, 'My shelter,
   my stronghold, my God in whom I trust.'
³Because he's the one who will rescue you from the hunter's trap,
   from the malicious epidemic.
⁴With his pinion he'll cover you,
   and under his wings you'll find shelter;
   his truthfulness will be a body-shield, a rampart.
⁵You needn't be afraid of something dreadful by night,
   of an arrow that flies by day,
⁶Of an epidemic that walks in the dark,
   of a scourge that destroys at noon.
⁷A thousand may fall at your side,
   ten thousand at your right hand
   – it will not reach to you.

⁸You'll only look with your eyes
   and see a making good to the faithless.
⁹Because you're one who has made Yahweh
      'My abode',
   the One on High your shelter.
¹⁰Nothing bad will be given access to you,
   no harm will approach your tent.
¹¹Because he'll order his envoys to you,
   to keep you in all your ways.
¹²They'll carry you on the palms of their hands
   so you don't hit your foot on a stone.
¹³You'll tread on cub and viper,
   you'll trample on lion and serpent.
¹⁴'Because he's attracted to me, I shall enable him
      to survive;
   I shall set him on high, because he's
      acknowledged my name.
¹⁵He will call me and I'll answer, I'll be with him
      when he is under pressure,
   I'll pull him out and honour him.
¹⁶I'll fill him with long days,
   and show him my deliverance.'

Psalm 92 A psalm used on the sabbath

A composition. A song. For the sabbath day.

¹It's good to confess Yahweh,
   to make music for your name, you who are the
      One on High,
²To tell of your commitment in the morning,
   and of your truthfulness at night,
³With ten-string and with mandolin,
   with recitation, on the guitar.
⁴Because you've made me rejoice, Yahweh, by
      your act;
   at the deeds of your hands I resound.
⁵How great your deeds have been, Yahweh;
   your intentions were very deep.
⁶The stupid person – he doesn't acknowledge,
   the dimwit – he doesn't understand this:
⁷When the faithless flourish like grass,
   and all the people who devise trouble thrive,
It's to be annihilated for all time,
   ⁸whereas you are up on high permanently,
      Yahweh.
⁹Because there – your enemies, Yahweh,
   because there – your enemies perish;
   all the people who devise trouble scatter.
¹⁰But you've raised up my horn like an oryx,
   my exhaustion with refreshing oil.
¹¹My eye has looked at the people who're watching
      for me;
   the people who rise against me, dealing badly
      – my ears can hear them.
¹²The faithful person is like a date palm that
      flourishes,
   like a Lebanese cedar that grows great,
¹³Planted in Yahweh's house,
   which flourish in our God's courtyards.
¹⁴They still fruit in old age,
   they become verdant and fresh,
¹⁵Telling that Yahweh is upright,
   my crag in whom there is no evil.

Psalm 93 Is the earth vulnerable?

¹Yahweh began to reign,
   he put on majesty;
   Yahweh put on, belted on vigour.
Yes, the world is established, it doesn't slip;
   ²your throne is established since long ago,
   you are from of old.
³Rivers lifted up, Yahweh,
   rivers lifted up their voice,
   rivers lift up their crushing.
⁴Above the voices of much water,
   august, the sea's breakers,
   Yahweh was august on high.
⁵Your affirmations have been very truthful,
   your sacredness has adorned your house,
   Yahweh, for long days.

Psalm 94 The God of redress

¹God of total redress, Yahweh,
   God of total redress, shine out.
²Rise up as the one who exercises authority over
      the earth,
   give back their dealing to the majestic people.
³How long will the faithless, Yahweh,
   how long will the faithless exult,
⁴Will they pour out, speak assertively,
   will all the people who devise trouble hold
      forth?
⁵They crush your people, Yahweh,
   they humble your domain.
⁶They kill the widow and alien,
   they murder the orphan.
⁷And they say, 'Yah does not see,
   Ya'aqob's God does not consider it.'

⁸Consider, you stupid among the people,
  you dimwits, when will you show some insight?
⁹The one who plants the ear – he listens, doesn't he;
  the one who shapes the eye – he looks, doesn't he.
¹⁰The one who disciplines nations – he reproves, doesn't he,
  the one who teaches humanity about knowledge.
¹¹Yahweh knows about humanity's intentions,
  that they are hollow.
¹²The blessings of the man whom you discipline, Yah,
  and teach from your instruction,
¹³To give him calm from bad times,
  until a pit is dug for the faithless person!
¹⁴Because Yahweh does not leave his people,
  does not abandon his domain.
¹⁵Because authority will come right back to faithfulness,
  and all those who are upright in mind will follow it.

¹⁶Who rises up for me with the people dealing badly,
  who takes a stand for me with the people devising trouble?
¹⁷Were Yahweh not a help for me,
  soon I myself would have dwelt in silence.
¹⁸If I said, 'My foot is slipping',
  your commitment, Yahweh, sustains me.
¹⁹When anxieties multiply inside me,
  your comforts give me pleasure.
²⁰Can a malicious throne ally with you,
  someone who shapes oppression by means of a decree?
²¹They gang up against the life of the faithful person,
  they condemn to death the person who's free of guilt.
²²But Yahweh has been a turret for me,
  my God a crag that's a shelter.
²³He has turned back their troublemaking on them,
  he will put an end to them through their bad ways;
  Yahweh our God will put an end to them.

Psalm 95 Will you just shut up and listen?

¹Come, let's resound for Yahweh,
  let's shout for our crag who delivers us.
²Let's draw near to his face with confession;
  we'll shout for him with melodies.
³Because Yahweh is the great God,
  the great king over all gods,
⁴The one in whose hand are the far reaches of the earth,
  and to whom the mountain peaks belong,
⁵The one to whom the sea belongs (he made it)
  and the dry land (his hands shaped it).

⁶Come, let's bow low, let's bend down,
  let's bow the knee before Yahweh our maker.
⁷Because he's our God
  and we're the people he pastures,
  the sheep in his hand.

Today, if you listen to his voice,
  ⁸don't toughen your mind as you did at Meribah ['Argument'],
As on the day at Massah ['Testing'] in the wilderness,
  ⁹when your ancestors tested me.
They tried me, though they'd seen my action;
  ¹⁰for forty years I loathed the generation.
I said, 'They're a people who go astray in mind,
  and they – they have not acknowledged my ways,
¹¹Of whom I swore in my anger,
  "If they come to my place to settle down . . ."'

Psalm 96 Yes, Yahweh has begun to reign

¹Sing for Yahweh a new song,
  sing for Yahweh all the earth!
²Sing for Yahweh, bless his name,
  announce the news day after day of his deliverance!
³Recount his splendour among the nations,
  his extraordinary deeds among all the peoples!
⁴Because Yahweh is great and much to be praised;
  he's to be held in awe above all gods.
⁵Because all the nations' gods are non-entities,
  whereas Yahweh made the heavens.
⁶Grandeur and magnificence are before him,
  vigour and glory in his sanctuary.

⁷Bestow on Yahweh, you kin-groups of the peoples,
  bestow on Yahweh splendour and vigour.
⁸Bestow on Yahweh the splendour due to his name,
  carry an offering and come into his courtyards.

⁹Bow low to Yahweh in his sacred splendour;
 tremble before him, all the earth.
¹⁰Say among the nations, 'Yahweh has begun to reign!'
 – yes, the world will stand firm, it will not slip.
He will give judgement for the peoples with uprightness;
 ¹¹the heavens may rejoice and the earth celebrate.
The sea and what fills it may thunder,
 ¹²the field and all that is in it exult.
Then all the trees in the forest may resound
 ¹³before Yahweh, because he is coming.
Because he is coming to exercise authority over the earth;
 he will exercise authority over the world with faithfulness,
 over the peoples with truthfulness.

Psalm 97 The real King of kings

¹Yahweh has begun to reign, earth should celebrate,
 many foreign shores should rejoice!
²Cloud and darkness are round him,
 faithfulness in exercising authority is the establishment of his throne.
³Fire goes before him
 and has set on fire his adversaries all round.
⁴His lightning flashes have lit up the world;
 the earth has seen and convulsed.
⁵Mountains like wax have melted before Yahweh,
 before the Lord of all the earth.
⁶The heavens have told of his faithfulness,
 and all the peoples will see his splendour.
⁷They will be shamed, all those who serve an image,
 those who take pride in non-entities;
 all the gods have bowed low to him.

⁸Tsiyyon has listened and rejoiced,
 the daughter-towns of Yehudah have celebrated,
 on account of your authoritative rulings, Yahweh.
⁹Because you, Yahweh, are the One on High over all the earth,
 you have ascended very high over all the gods.
¹⁰You who are loyal to Yahweh, be hostile to what is bad;
 he keeps watch on the lives of people committed to him,
 he rescues them from the hand of the faithless.

¹¹Light has been sown for the faithful person,
 rejoicing for those who are upright in mind.
¹²Rejoice in Yahweh, you faithful,
 confess the commemoration of his sacredness!

Psalm 98 Revealed to the eyes of the nations

A composition.

¹Sing for Yahweh a new song,
 because he has performed extraordinary deeds!
His right hand has wrought deliverance for him,
 yes, his sacred arm.
²Yahweh has caused his deliverance to be acknowledged;
 to the eyes of the nations he has revealed his faithfulness.
³He has been mindful of his commitment and his truthfulness
 to the household of Yisra'el.
All the ends of the earth have seen
 the deliverance of our God.

⁴Shout for Yahweh, all the earth,
 break out and resound and make music!
⁵Make music for Yahweh with the guitar,
 with the guitar and the sound of music!
⁶With trumpets and the sound of the horn,
 shout before the King, Yahweh!
⁷The sea and what fills it should thunder,
 the world and the people who live in it.
⁸Rivers should clap the palms of their hands,
 mountains should resound together,
⁹Before Yahweh, because he has come
 to exercise authority over the earth.
He exercises authority over the world with faithfulness,
 over the peoples with uprightness.

Psalm 99 The one who carries things

¹Yahweh has begun to reign – peoples should tremble;
 the one who sits above the sphinxes – the earth should shake.
²In Tsiyyon Yahweh is great,
 and he is on high over all the peoples.
³They should confess your name, great and awe-inspiring
 – he is sacred.

⁴With the vigour of a king, loyal to the exercise of
        authority,
    you are the one who established uprightness.
Authority and faithfulness in Ya'aqob:
    you are the one who implemented them.
⁵Lift Yahweh our God high
    and bow low to his footstool
    – he's sacred.

⁶Mosheh, and Aharon among his priests,
    and Shemu'el [Samuel] among the people who
        call his name,
They were people calling to Yahweh, and he
        himself would answer them,
⁷in the pillar of cloud he would speak to them.
They kept his affirmations, the decree he gave
        them;
⁸Yahweh our God, you answered them.
You became a God who carried things for them,
    but one who exacted redress for their actions.
⁹Lift Yahweh our God high and bow low to his
        sacred mountain
    – because Yahweh our God is sacred.

Psalm 100 Shout for Yahweh, all the earth

A composition. For the thank-offering.

¹Shout for Yahweh, all the earth,
    ²serve Yahweh with rejoicing,
    come before him with resounding.
³Acknowledge that Yahweh is God,
    he is the one who made us and we are his,
    his people and the sheep he pastures.
⁴Come into his gateways with confession,
    his courtyards with praise,
    confess him, bless his name.
⁵Because Yahweh is good,
    his commitment is permanent,
    his truthfulness to generation after generation.

Psalm 101 The leadership challenge

David's. A composition.

¹I will sing of commitment and the exercise of
        authority,
    for you Yahweh I will make music.
²I will show insight in the way that has integrity;
    when will you come to me?
I will go about with integrity in my mind
    within my household.
³I will not set in front of my eyes anything of
        Beliyya'al;
    I'm hostile to the action of deviant people
    – it will not stick to me.
⁴A crooked mind will depart from me;
    I will not acknowledge bad ways.
⁵The person who speaks against his neighbour in
        secret
    – I will put an end to him.
The person lofty in his own eyes and wide of
        mind
    – I will not tolerate him.
⁶My eyes will be on the person who is trustworthy
        in the country,
    to live with me.
The person who walks on the way of integrity
    – he will minister to me.
⁷The person who practises deceit
    will not live within my household.
The person who speaks lies
    will not be established in front of my eyes.
⁸Each morning I will put an end to all the people
        who are faithless in the country,
    so as to cut off from Yahweh's town all who
        devise trouble.

Psalm 102.1–11 My heart's withered

A plea. For a humble person when he is faint
and pours out his talk before Yahweh.

¹Yahweh, listen to my plea;
    may my cry for help come to you.
²Don't hide your face from me
    on a day when there is pressure for me.
Bend your ear to me;
    on the day when I call, be quick, answer me.
³Because my days are finished in smoke,
    my bones have burned as in a fireplace.
⁴My heart's been stricken like grass and it's
        withered,
    because I've put out of mind eating my food.
⁵Because of the sound of my groaning,
    my bone sticks to my flesh.
⁶I've come to resemble a tawny owl of the
        wilderness,
    I've become like a screech owl of the ruins.
⁷I've been awake and I've become like a bird,
    alone on a roof.

⁸All day my enemies have reviled me;
  people whom I call crazy have sworn oaths by me.
⁹Because I've eaten ashes like bread
  and mixed my drink with tears,
¹⁰In the face of your condemnation and your fury,
  because you picked me up and threw me out.
¹¹My days are like an extended shadow,
  and I – I wither like grass.

Psalm 102.12–28 I have hope for Tsiyyon, but is there hope for me?

¹²But you, Yahweh – you will sit permanently,
  your commemoration will continue for generation after generation.
¹³You – you will arise, you will have compassion on Tsiyyon,
  because it's time to be gracious to it, because the set time has come.
¹⁴Because your servants have accepted its stones,
  and been gracious to its earth.
¹⁵Nations will live in awe of Yahweh's name,
  all earth's kings of your splendour.
¹⁶Because Yahweh has built up Tsiyyon,
  has appeared in his splendour.
¹⁷He has turned his face to the plea of the naked person
  and not despised their plea.
¹⁸May this be written down for the next generation,
  so that a people to be created may praise Yah,
¹⁹Because he has looked down from his sacred height,
  from the heavens Yahweh has looked at the earth,
²⁰To listen to the prisoner's cry,
  to release people doomed to death,
²¹For the recounting of Yahweh's name in Tsiyyon,
  his praise in Yerushalaim,
²²When peoples collect together,
  yes, kingdoms, to serve Yahweh.

²³He has humbled my energy on my way,
  he has cut my days.
²⁴I will say, 'My God, don't take me up
  in the middle of my days.
Your years continue generation after generation;
  ²⁵before, you founded the earth,
  and the heavens are the making of your hands.
²⁶Whereas they may perish,
  you will stand.
All of them could wear out like a coat;
  like clothing you could pass them on.
They would pass on, ²⁷but you are the one,
  and your years will not come to an end.
²⁸May your servants' children dwell,
  and their offspring endure, before you.'

Psalm 103 He has distanced our rebellions from us

David's.

¹Bless Yahweh, my entire being;
  all my being, [bless] his sacred name.
²Bless Yahweh, my entire being;
  don't put out of mind all his dealings.
³He's the one who pardons all your waywardness,
  who heals all your illnesses,
⁴Who restores your life from the Pit,
  who garlands you with commitment and compassion,
⁵Who fills you in your finery with goodness,
  so that your youth renews like an eagle.
⁶Yahweh performs faithful deeds,
  acts of authority for all the oppressed.
⁷He would make his ways known to Mosheh,
  his deeds to the Yisra'elites.
⁸Yahweh is compassionate and gracious,
  long-tempered and big in commitment.
⁹He doesn't argue permanently,
  he doesn't hold on to it for a long time.
¹⁰He hasn't acted towards us in accordance with our wrongdoings;
  he hasn't dealt to us in accordance with our wayward acts.
¹¹Because in accordance with the loftiness of the heavens over the earth,
  his commitment has been strong over people who hold him in awe.
¹²In accordance with the distance of east from west,
  he has distanced our rebellions from us.
¹³In accordance with a father's compassion for his children,
  Yahweh has had compassion for people who hold him in awe.
¹⁴Because he himself knows our frame;
  he is mindful that we are earth.

¹⁵A mere human being: his days are like grass;
  like a flower in the fields – that's how he
    blooms.
¹⁶When the wind passes by it, it is no more;
  its place doesn't recognize it any more.
¹⁷But Yahweh's commitment lasts from age to age
  for people who hold him in awe, and his
    faithfulness to their grandchildren,
¹⁸For people who keep his pact
  and are mindful of the things he has
    determined, so that they perform them.
¹⁹Yahweh established his throne in the heavens;
  his reign rules over everything.
²⁰Bless Yahweh, his envoys,
  energetic strong men performing his word,
    listening to the sound of his word.
²¹Bless Yahweh, all his armies,
  his ministers doing what is acceptable to him.
²²Bless Yahweh, all his works,
  in all the places where he rules.
Bless Yahweh, my entire being.

Psalm 104.1–23 Provision for human beings and donkeys

¹Bless Yahweh, my entire being!
  – Yahweh my God, you became very great.
You put on grandeur and magnificence,
  ²wrapping on light like a coat,
Stretching the heavens like a tent,
  ³one fixing his lofts in the water,
One making clouds his transport,
  one going about on the wings of the wind,
⁴Making his envoys of winds,
  his ministers of flaming fire.
⁵He founded the earth on its establishments,
  so that it would never slip, ever.
⁶You covered it with the deep like a garment,
  so that the water would stand above the
    mountains.
⁷At your reprimand they would flee;
  at the sound of your thunder they would make
    haste.
⁸They would go up mountains, they would go
    down valleys,
  to the place that you founded for them.
⁹You set a boundary they were not to pass;
  they would not again cover the earth.
¹⁰You're the one who sends out springs in wadis,
  so that they go about between the mountains.
¹¹They water every animal of the field;
  donkeys break their thirst.
¹²By them the birds of the heavens dwell;
  from among the branches they give voice.
¹³You're one who waters mountains from his lofts
  – from the fruit of your deeds the earth has its
    fill.
¹⁴You are one who grows grass for the cattle,
  and plants for the service of human beings,
To make bread go out from the earth,
  ¹⁵and wine that rejoices a person's heart,
To make the face shine with oil,
  and bread that sustains a person's heart.
¹⁶Yahweh's trees get their fill,
  the cedars of Lebanon that he planted,
¹⁷Where birds nest,
  the stork – the junipers are its home.
¹⁸The lofty mountains belong to the ibex,
  the cliffs are a shelter for the rock badgers.
¹⁹He made the moon for set times;
  the sun knows its setting.
²⁰You bring darkness so that it becomes night:
  in it every creature of the forest moves about.
²¹The lions roar for prey,
  yes, in seeking their food from God.
²²When the sun rises, they gather,
  and crouch in their abodes.
²³Human beings go out to their work,
  and to their service until evening.

Psalm 104.24–35 Withdrawing breath, giving breath

²⁴How the things you made multiplied, Yahweh;
  you made them all with smartness;
  the earth is full of your possessions.
²⁵That's the sea, great,
  and wide in reach.
There are moving things without number,
  living things small and great.
²⁶There ships go about,
  Livyatan that you shaped to have fun in it.
²⁷All of them look to you,
  to give their food at its time.
²⁸You give them, they gather;
  you open your hand, they have their fill of good
    things.
²⁹You hide your face, they're fearful;
  you gather up their breath, they breathe their
    last,
  and go back to their earth.

³⁰You send out your breath, they are created,
and you renew the face of the ground.

³¹May Yahweh's splendour be permanent;
may Yahweh rejoice in his deeds,
³²The one who looks on the earth and it trembles;
he touches the mountains and they smoke.
³³I will sing for Yahweh while I live,
I will make music for my God while I'm still here.
³⁴May my talk be pleasant to him;
I myself will rejoice in Yahweh.
³⁵May wrongdoers come to an end from the earth;
faithless people – may there be none of them any more.
Bless Yahweh, my entire being;
praise Yah.

Psalm 105.1–22 Tell your story

¹Confess Yahweh, call in his name,
make known his deeds among the peoples.
²Sing for him, make music for him,
talk about all his extraordinary deeds.
³Take pride in his sacred name;
the heart of all who seek Yahweh should rejoice.
⁴Enquire of Yahweh and his vigour;
seek his face continually.
⁵Be mindful of his extraordinary deeds, those which he has done,
his portents and the rulings of his mouth,
⁶You offspring of Abraham his servant,
descendants of Ya'aqob, his chosen ones.

⁷He is Yahweh our God;
his rulings are in all the earth.
⁸He has been mindful permanently of his pact,
the word he ordered to a thousand generations,
⁹That which he sealed to Abraham,
and swore to Yitshaq [Isaac].
¹⁰He established it as a decree to Ya'aqob,
to Yisra'el as a lasting pact,
¹¹saying, 'I will give the country of Kena'an [Canaan] to you,
as a share, your domain.'
¹²When they were few in number,
little and resident aliens in it,
¹³And they went about from nation to nation,
from one kingdom to another people,
¹⁴He did not allow anyone to oppress them,
but reproved kings on account of them:

¹⁵'Don't touch my anointed ones,
don't do wrong to my prophets.'

¹⁶He called for hunger on the country;
every staff of bread he broke.
¹⁷He sent before them an individual
who was sold as a servant, Yoseph.
¹⁸They subjected his foot to the fetter;
iron came on to his person.
¹⁹Until the time his word came about,
Yahweh's saying refined him.
²⁰A king sent and freed him,
a ruler of peoples, and released him.
²¹He made him lord of his household,
ruler over all his possessions,
²²To constrain his officials according to his will,
and to make his elders smart.

Psalm 105.23–45 In order that they might keep his decrees

²³Yisra'el came to Misrayim;
Ya'aqob resided in the country of Ham.
²⁴He made his people very fruitful,
made them more numerous than their adversaries.
²⁵He turned their mind against his people,
to scheme against his servants.
²⁶He sent Mosheh his servant,
Aharon whom he had chosen.
²⁷They placed among them words about his signs,
his portents in the country of Ham.
²⁸He sent darkness, and it became dark;
they did not defy his word.
²⁹He turned their water into blood,
and put their fish to death.
³⁰Their country teemed with frogs,
in their kings' rooms.
³¹He spoke, and a swarm came,
mosquitoes in all their territory.
³²He made their rain hail,
flaming fire in their country.
³³He struck down their vine and their fig tree,
broke down the trees in their territory.
³⁴He spoke, and the locust came,
the grasshopper without number.
³⁵It ate all the vegetation in their country,
ate the fruit of their land.
³⁶He struck down every firstborn in their country,
the first of all their vigour.

³⁷He got them out, with silver and gold;
   none among their clans collapsed.
³⁸Misrayim rejoiced when they got out,
   because dread of them had fallen on them.
³⁹He spread a cloud for covering,
   and a fire to light the night.
⁴⁰They asked and he brought quail,
   and he would fill them with bread from the heavens.
⁴¹He opened a crag and water flowed,
   went in dry places as a river.
⁴²Because he was mindful of his sacred word
   with Abraham his servant,
⁴³He got his people out with joy,
   his chosen ones with resounding.
⁴⁴He gave them the nations' countries,
   and they took possession of the labour of the peoples,
⁴⁵In order that they might keep his decrees
   and observe his instructions.
Praise Yah!

Psalm 106.1–22 He gave them what they asked

¹Praise Yah! –
   confess Yahweh, because he is good,
   because his commitment is permanent.
²Who can utter Yahweh's mighty acts,
   get people to listen to all his praises?
³The blessings of people who keep watch over the exercise of authority,
   of the person who does what is faithful at all times!
⁴Be mindful of me, Yahweh, when you act with acceptance towards your people,
   attend to me when you deliver them,
⁵So that I may see the good things that come to your chosen,
   rejoice in the rejoicing of your nation,
   take pride with your domain.
⁶We've done wrong with our ancestors,
   we've been wayward, we've been faithless.
⁷Our ancestors in Misrayim did not have insight into your extraordinary deeds,
   they were not mindful of the magnitude of your acts of commitment.
⁸But he delivered them for the sake of his name,
   so that his might would be acknowledged.
⁹He reprimanded the Reed Sea and it dried up,
   and he enabled them to go through the deeps like a wilderness.
¹⁰He delivered them from the hand of the one who was hostile to them,
   restored them from the hand of the enemy.
¹¹Water covered their adversaries;
   not one of them was left.
¹²They trusted in his words,
   and sang his praise.
¹³They quickly put his deeds out of mind;
   they did not wait for his counsel.
¹⁴They felt a deep longing in the wilderness,
   they tested God in the wasteland.
¹⁵He gave them what they asked,
   but sent a wasting in their entire being.
¹⁶They were jealous of Mosheh in the camp,
   of Aharon, Yahweh's sacred one.
¹⁷The earth opened and swallowed Datan,
   closed over Abiram's assembly.
¹⁸Fire burned up among their assembly,
   a flame that set on fire the faithless.
¹⁹They made a bullock at Horeb,
   bowed low to an image.
²⁰They exchanged their splendour
   for the representation of an ox eating grass.
²¹They put out of mind their deliverer,
   the one who had done great things in Misrayim,
²²Extraordinary deeds in the country of Ham,
   awe-inspiring deeds at the Reed Sea.

Psalm 106.23–47 Deliver us in the same way!

²³He said he would annihilate them,
   except that Mosheh, his chosen,
Stood in the breach before him,
   to turn back his wrath from devastating.
²⁴They rejected the beautiful country,
   and didn't trust in his word.
²⁵They muttered in their tents,
   and didn't listen to Yahweh's voice.
²⁶So he raised his hand [to swear] to them,
   that he would make them fall in the wilderness,
²⁷Make their offspring fall among the nations,
   and scatter them among the countries.
²⁸They joined the Master-of-Pe'or,
   and ate sacrifices offered for the dead.
²⁹They provoked by their deeds,
   and an epidemic broke out among them.

³⁰But Pinhas stood and intervened,
and the epidemic held back.
³¹It was thought of for him as a faithful deed,
generation after generation permanently.
³²They angered at Meribah Water;
it was bad for Mosheh because of them.
³³Because they rebelled against his spirit,
he was rash with his tongue.

³⁴They didn't devastate the peoples,
as Yahweh had said to them.
³⁵They mixed with the nations,
and learned what they did.
³⁶They served their images;
they became a snare for them.
³⁷They sacrificed their sons
and their daughters to demons.
³⁸They shed the blood of someone free of guilt,
the blood of their sons and their daughters,
Whom they sacrificed to the images of Kena'an,
so that the land became ungodly through the bloodshed.
³⁹They became defiled through their deeds;
they whored in their actions.
⁴⁰Yahweh's anger burned against his people,
he loathed his domain.
⁴¹He gave them into the hand of the nations;
people hostile to them ruled over them.
⁴²Their enemies afflicted them,
and they bowed down under their hand.
⁴³Many times he would rescue them,
but those people – they were rebellious in their counsel.
They sank low because of their waywardness,
⁴⁴and he saw the pressure that came to them.
When he heard their resounding shout,
⁴⁵he was mindful of his pact to them.
He relented in accordance with the magnitude of his acts of commitment,
⁴⁶and made them objects of compassion
before all their captors.

⁴⁷Deliver us, Yahweh our God,
collect us from the nations,
To confess your sacred name,
to glory in your praise.

Psalm 106.48 Another amen

Yahweh, the God of Yisra'el, be blessed,
from age to lasting age!
All the people is to say,
'Amen'; praise Yah!

Psalm 107.1–22 Let the redeemed of the Lord say so

¹Confess Yahweh, because he is good,
because his commitment is permanent.
²The people restored by Yahweh are to say it,
those whom he restored from the hand of the adversary,
³And collected from the countries,
from the north and from the west.

⁴They wandered in the wilderness, in the wasteland;
they didn't find the way to a settled town.
⁵Hungry, thirsty too,
their entire being within them fainted.
⁶But they cried out to Yahweh in the pressure that came to them,
and he rescued them from their straits.
⁷He directed them by a straight way,
so as to go to a settled town.
⁸They are to confess to Yahweh his commitment,
his extraordinary deeds for human beings,
⁹Because he has sated the person who is scurrying about,
and filled the hungry person with good things.

¹⁰People living in darkness and deathly gloom,
prisoners of humbling and iron,
¹¹Because they had defied the things God said,
despised the counsel of the One on High:
¹²He humbled their heart with oppression;
they collapsed without a helper.
¹³But they cried out to Yahweh in the pressure that came to them,
and he delivered them from their straits.
¹⁴He got them out of darkness and deathly gloom,
and would break their bonds.
¹⁵They are to confess to Yahweh his commitment,
his extraordinary deeds for human beings.
¹⁶Because he has broken up copper doors,
shattered iron bars.

¹⁷Dense people, because of their rebellious way,
and through their acts of waywardness,
experienced humbling.
¹⁸Their appetite loathed all food;
they reached death's gateways.

¹⁹But they cried out to Yahweh in the pressure
    that came to them,
  and he delivered them from their straits.
²⁰He sent his word and healed them;
  he released them from their deep pit.
²¹They are to confess to Yahweh his commitment,
  his extraordinary deeds for human beings.
²²They are to offer thanksgiving sacrifices,
  and tell of his deeds with resounding noise.

Psalm 107.23–43 Consider Yahweh's acts of commitment

²³People who go down to the sea in ships,
  doing work in extensive waters,
²⁴These people – they saw Yahweh's deeds,
  and his extraordinary deeds in the deep.
²⁵He spoke and set a hurricane in place,
  and it lifted its waves.
²⁶They went up to the heavens, they went down to the depths;
  their entire being melted away in their trouble.
²⁷They reeled and staggered like a drunk,
  and all their smartness swallowed itself up.
²⁸But they cried out to Yahweh in the pressure
    that came to them,
  and he delivered them from their straits.
²⁹He turned the hurricane into stillness;
  their waves went quiet.
³⁰They rejoiced when they became silent,
  and he led them to the haven they wanted.
³¹They are to confess to Yahweh his commitment,
  his extraordinary deeds for human beings.
³²They are to exalt him in the congregation of the people,
  and praise him in the session of the elders.

³³He turns rivers into wilderness,
  water outlets into thirsty land,
³⁴Fruitful land into salt marsh,
  because of the bad ways of the people who live in it.
³⁵He turns wilderness into a pool of water,
  dry land into water outlets.
³⁶He has let hungry people live there;
  they have established a settled town.
³⁷They've sown fields and planted vineyards,
  and they have produced fruit, a yield.
³⁸He's blessed them and they've increased greatly,
  and he doesn't let their cattle decrease.
³⁹But they have decreased and become low
  through oppression, bad fortune and sadness.
⁴⁰He pours contempt on leaders,
  and makes them wander in a waste where there is no way.
⁴¹But he sets the needy person on high out of humbling,
  and makes their kin-groups like a flock.

⁴²The upright will see and rejoice;
  all evil has stopped its mouth.
⁴³Who is the smart person who will keep watch on these things?
  – they will consider Yahweh's acts of commitment.

Psalm 108 Urging God to act in the light of his promises

A song. A composition. David's.

¹My mind is established, God,
  I will sing and make music, yes, my entire being.
²Wake up, mandolin and guitar;
  I will wake the dawn.
³I will confess you among the peoples, Yahweh,
  I will make music for you among the nations.
⁴Because your commitment is great, over the heavens,
  your truthfulness up to the skies.
⁵Be high over the heavens, God,
  over all the earth your splendour.
⁶In order that the people you love may be pulled out,
  deliver me by your right hand and answer me.

⁷God had spoken by his sacredness:
  'I will exult as I allocate Shekem
  and measure out Sukkot Vale.
⁸Gil'ad will be mine,
  Menashsheh will be mine.
Ephrayim will be a stronghold for my head,
  Yehudah my sceptre.
⁹Mo'ab will be my washbasin,
  over Edom I will throw my boot,
  over Peleshet I will shout out.
¹⁰Who will conduct me to the fortified town,
  who would lead me to Edom?

¹¹You've rejected us, haven't you, God;
  you don't go out with our armies, God.

¹²Grant us help against the adversary,
    given that human deliverance is empty.
¹³Through God we will act with forcefulness;
    he is the one who will trample on our adversaries.

Psalm 109.1–19 How to deal with being swindled

The leader's. David's. A composition.

¹God, my praise, don't be silent,
    ²because it's a faithless mouth,
And a deceitful mouth, that people have opened against me;
    they have spoken with me by means of a lying tongue.
³With hostile words they've surrounded me,
    and battled against me for nothing.
⁴In return for my friendliness they accuse me;
    so I [am making] a plea.
⁵They've brought on me bad in return for good,
    hostility in return for my friendliness.

⁶'Appoint a faithless person over him,
    an accuser who will stand at his right hand.
⁷When he enters into judgement, may he come out as faithless;
    may his plea lead to condemnation.
⁸May his days be few;
    may another person take his appointment.
⁹May his children become orphans,
    his wife a widow.
¹⁰May his children wander about,
    ask and enquire from their ruins.
¹¹May the creditor strike at all that he has,
    may strangers plunder his earnings.
¹²May he have no one showing commitment,
    may there be no one being gracious to his orphans.
¹³May his succession be for cutting off,
    in the next generation may their name be blotted out.
¹⁴May the waywardness of his ancestors stay in mind for Yahweh,
    may his mother's wrongdoings not be blotted out.
¹⁵May they be in front of Yahweh continually;
    may he cut off their commemoration from the earth.
¹⁶Because of the fact that he was not mindful to keep commitment,
But pursued the person who was humble and needy,
    and the one crushed in spirit, to put him to death.
¹⁷He liked slighting, and it came about for him;
    he didn't want blessing, and it was far from him.
¹⁸He put on slighting like a coat,
    it came into his insides like water,
    into his bones like oil.
¹⁹May it be for him like clothing in which he covers himself,
    and as a belt that he wraps round continually.'

Psalm 109.20–31 Wages for accusers

²⁰May this be the wages of my accusers from Yahweh,
    the people who speak what is bad against me.
²¹So you, Yahweh, Lord,
    deal with me for the sake of your name;
    because your commitment is good, rescue me.
²²Because I am humble and needy,
    and my heart is run through within me.
²³Like a shadow as it lengthens, I am gone;
    I am shaken off like a locust.
²⁴My knees have collapsed from hunger;
    my body has wasted, away from fatness.
²⁵I – I have become an object of reviling to them;
    when they see me, they shake their head.
²⁶Help me, Yahweh my God,
    deliver me in accordance with your commitment,
²⁷So that people may acknowledge that this is your hand,
    that you, Yahweh, you have done it.
²⁸Those people may slight me, but you – may you bless;
    they will have arisen and been disgraced, but your servant will rejoice.
²⁹May my accusers put on shame,
    may they wrap round their disgrace like a coat.

³⁰I will confess Yahweh greatly with my mouth,
    in the middle of many people I will praise him,
³¹Because he stands at the right hand of the needy person,
    to deliver him from the people who exercise authority over him.

Psalm 110 Enemies become footstool

David's. A psalm.

¹Yahweh's proclamation to my lord:
  'Sit at my right
    until I make your enemies your footstool.'
²Yahweh will send your vigorous sceptre out from Tsiyyon;
  hold sway among your enemies.
³Your people are willing offerings
  on the day you deploy your forces.
In sacred magnificence from the womb of dawn
  the dew of your youths is yours.
⁴Yahweh has sworn,
  and will not relent:
'You are a priest permanently
  after the manner of Melkitsedeq.'
⁵The Lord is at your right;
  he has hit kings on the day of his anger.
⁶He judges among the nations, filling them with bodies;
  he has hit heads over the earth, far and wide.
⁷From the wadi by the way he drinks;
  therefore he can raise his head.

Psalm 111 The lasting pact

¹Praise Yah! –
  I will confess Yahweh with my whole mind
  in the council of the upright, the assembly.
²Yahweh's doings are great,
  enquired about for all their delights.
³His action is grandeur and magnificence,
  his faithfulness stands permanently.
⁴He achieved commemoration for his extraordinary deeds;
  Yahweh is gracious and compassionate.
⁵He has given meat to people who live in awe of him;
  he is mindful of his pact permanently.
⁶He told his people of the energy of his doings
  in giving them the domain of the nations.
⁷The doings of his hands are true and authoritative;
  all the things he has determined are truthful,
⁸Established lastingly and permanently,
  done in truth and uprightness.
⁹He sent redemption to his people,
  he ordered his pact permanently.
His name is sacred and to be held in awe;
  ¹⁰awe for Yahweh is the essence of smartness.
Good insight belongs to all who do them;
  his praise stands permanently.

Psalm 112 Blessed so as to bless

¹Praise Yah! –
  the blessings of the person who lives in awe of Yahweh,
  who delights much in his orders!
²His offspring will become a strong man in the country;
  the generation of the upright will be blessed.
³Riches and wealth are in his house,
  and his faithfulness stands permanently.
⁴He rises in the darkness as light for the upright,
  gracious, compassionate and faithful.
⁵Good is the person who is gracious and lends,
  as he fulfils his words with the [proper] exercise of authority.
⁶Because he will not slip, ever;
  the faithful person will become an object of commemoration permanently.
⁷He is not afraid of bad news;
  his mind is established, reliant on Yahweh.
⁸His mind is held firm so that he is not afraid,
  until he looks on his adversaries.
⁹He spreads abroad as he gives to the needy;
  his faithfulness stands permanently.
His horn will stand high in splendour;
  ¹⁰the faithless person will see and be vexed.
He will grind his teeth and waste away;
  the longing of faithless people will perish.

Psalm 113 The one who gets down low to look

¹Praise Yah! –
  praise, Yahweh's servants,
  praise Yahweh's name!
²May Yahweh's name be blessed,
  now and permanently!
³From the rising of the sun to its setting,
  Yahweh's name be praised!
⁴Yahweh is on high over all nations,
  his splendour is over the heavens!
⁵Who is like Yahweh our God,
  the one who goes on high to sit,
⁶Who gets down low to look,
  in the heavens and the earth,

⁷Who lifts up the poor person from the earth,
 raises the needy person from the rubbish heap,
⁸To enable them to sit with leaders,
 with the leaders of the people,
⁹Who enables the childless woman to sit in the household,
 the mother of children, rejoicing?
Praise Yah!

Psalm 114 The sacred place

¹When Yisra'el got out from Misrayim,
 Ya'aqob's household from a jabbering people,
²Yehudah became its sacred place,
 Yisra'el its realm.
³When the sea saw, it fled;
 the Yarden – it was turning back.
⁴The mountains – they jumped like rams,
 the hills like the children of the flock.
⁵What was it with you, sea, that you were fleeing,
 Yarden, that you were turning back,
⁶Mountains that you were jumping like rams,
 hills like the children of the flock?
⁷Tremble, before the Lord, earth,
 before Ya'aqob's God,
⁸Who turned the crag into a pool of water,
 basalt into a spring of water.

Psalm 115 The gods with bodies that don't work

¹Not to us, Yahweh,
 not to us,
But to your name give splendour,
 for your commitment, for your truthfulness.
²Why should the nations say,
 'Where is their God, please?'
³Whereas our God is in the heavens;
 everything that he wants he has done.
⁴Their images are silver and gold,
 the making of human hands.
⁵They have a mouth but they don't speak,
 they have eyes but they don't see,
⁶They have ears but they don't hear,
 they have a nose but they don't smell,
⁷Their hands but they don't feel, their feet but they don't walk about;
 they don't murmur with their throat.
⁸Their makers become like them,
 everyone who relies on them.

⁹Yisra'el, rely on Yahweh!
 – he is their help and their shield.
¹⁰Household of Aharon, rely on Yahweh!
 – he is their help and their shield.
¹¹People who live in awe of Yahweh, rely on Yahweh!
 – he is their help and their shield.
¹²In that Yahweh has been mindful of us, he will bless us;
 he will bless Yisra'el's household,
 he will bless Aharon's household.
¹³He will bless the people who live in awe of Yahweh,
 the small along with the great.
¹⁴May Yahweh add to you,
 to you and to your children.
¹⁵May you be blessed by Yahweh,
 maker of heavens and earth.
¹⁶The heavens are heavens belonging to Yahweh,
 but the earth he gave to human beings.
¹⁷Whereas the dead do not praise Yah,
 nor any who go down to silence,
¹⁸We – we will bless Yah,
 now and permanently.
Praise Yah!

Psalm 116 I will make good my pledges

¹I am loyal, because Yahweh listens
 to my voice, my prayers for grace.
²Because he has bent his ear to me,
 and through my days I will call.

³Death's ropes encompassed me,
 She'ol's restraints found me.
When I find pressure and sadness,
⁴I call out in Yahweh's name:
'Oh now, Yahweh,
 save my life!'
⁵Yahweh is gracious and faithful;
 our God is compassionate.
⁶Yahweh keeps watch over simple people;
 I sank low, and he delivered me.
⁷Turn back, my entire being, to your rest,
 because Yahweh – he has dealt to you.
⁸Because you pulled out my life from death,
 my eye from tears, my foot from being pushed down,
⁹I can walk about before Yahweh
 in the land of the living.

¹⁰I trust, because I could say,
  'I – I have become very low.'
¹¹I – I said in my haste,
  'Every human being lies.'
¹²What shall I give back to Yahweh,
  for all his dealings with me?
¹³I will lift the deliverance cup,
  and call out in Yahweh's name.
¹⁴I will make good my pledges to Yahweh,
  right in front of all his people, please.
¹⁵Valuable in Yahweh's eyes
  is the death of people who are committed to him.
¹⁶Oh, Yahweh,
  because I am your servant,
I am your servant, the son of your handmaid;
  you loosed my bonds.
¹⁷I will make a thanksgiving sacrifice to you,
  I will call in Yahweh's name.
¹⁸I will make good my pledges to Yahweh,
  right in front of all his people, please,
¹⁹in the courtyards of Yahweh's house,
  in the middle of Yerushalaim.
Praise Yah!

Psalm 117 A lot in a few words

¹Praise Yahweh, all you nations,
  extol him all you peoples.
²Because his commitment to us has been strong;
  Yahweh's truthfulness is permanent.
Praise Yah.

Psalm 118 This is the day that the Lord has made

¹Confess Yahweh, because he is good,
  because his commitment is permanent.
²Yisraʾel is please to say,
  'His commitment is permanent.'
³Aharon's household is please to say,
  'His commitment is permanent.'
⁴The people who live in awe of Yahweh are please to say,
  'His commitment is permanent.'
⁵Out of constraint I called Yah;
  Yah answered me with roominess.
⁶Because Yahweh is mine, I will not be afraid;
  what can a human being do to me?
⁷Yahweh is mine as my helper,
  and I shall look on the people who are hostile to me.
⁸It's better to take shelter with Yahweh
  than to rely on human beings.
⁹It's better to take shelter with Yahweh
  than to rely on leaders.
¹⁰All nations surrounded me;
  in Yahweh's name I can indeed wither them.
¹¹They surrounded me, yes, surrounded me;
  in Yahweh's name I can indeed wither them.
¹²They surrounded me like bees;
  they've been extinguished like a fire of thorns
  – in Yahweh's name I can indeed wither them.
¹³You pushed me hard, so as to fall,
  but Yahweh – he helped me.
¹⁴Yah was my vigour and protection,
  and he became my deliverance.
¹⁵The noise of resounding and deliverance
  was in the tents of the faithful.
Yahweh's right hand acts with forcefulness,
  ¹⁶Yahweh's right hand lifts up high,
  Yahweh's right hand acts with forcefulness.
¹⁷I shall not die, but live,
  and recount Yah's deeds.
¹⁸Yahweh severely disciplined me,
  but didn't give me over to death.
¹⁹Open the faithful gateways to me;
  when I come through them, I shall confess Yahweh.
²⁰This is Yahweh's gateway;
  faithful people come through it.
²¹I will confess you, because you answered me
  and became deliverance for me.
²²'The stone that the builders spurned
  became the head cornerstone.'
²³This came about from Yahweh;
  it's been extraordinary in our eyes.
²⁴This was the day that Yahweh made;
  so that we would celebrate and rejoice in it.
²⁵Oh, Yahweh, will you deliver us, please?
  – oh, Yahweh, enable us to succeed, please.
²⁶Blessed be the one who comes in Yahweh's name;
  we are blessing you from Yahweh's house.
²⁷Yahweh is God; he has shone light to us
  – tie the festal offering with cords to the horns of the altar.
²⁸You are my God and I will confess you;
  my God, I will exalt you.

²⁹Confess Yahweh, because he is good,
  because his commitment is permanent.

Psalm 119.1–24 God's laws as the way to blessing

¹The blessings of people who have integrity in their way,
  who walk by Yahweh's instruction!
²The blessings of people who observe his affirmations,
  who enquire of him with their entire mind!
³Indeed, they have not done evil;
  they have walked in his ways.
⁴You yourself have given the order that the things you have determined
  are to be well kept.
⁵Oh that my ways may be firm
  in keeping your decrees!
⁶Then I shall not be shamed
  when I look to all your orders.
⁷I will confess you with uprightness of mind
  as I learn of your faithful rulings.
⁸I will keep your decrees;
  don't totally abandon me.

⁹How can a youth keep his path clean?
  – by keeping watch in accordance with your word.
¹⁰I've enquired of you with my whole mind;
  don't let me stray from your orders.
¹¹I've treasured your words in my mind
  in order that I may not do wrong in relation to you.
¹²Blessed are you, Yahweh;
  teach me your decrees.
¹³With my lips I've recounted
  all the rulings of your mouth.
¹⁴In the way of your affirmations
  I've rejoiced as over all riches.
¹⁵I shall talk about the things you have determined
  and look to your paths.
¹⁶In your decrees I will take pleasure;
  I will not put out of mind your words.

¹⁷Deal to your servant
  so that I may live, and keep your word.
¹⁸Open my eyes so that I may look
  to extraordinary things from your instruction.
¹⁹I'm a sojourner on the earth;
  don't hide your orders from me.
²⁰My entire being has failed with longing
  for your rulings all the time.
²¹You've reprimanded the assertive;
  cursed are the people who stray from your orders.
²²Roll away from me reviling and shame,
  because I've observed your affirmations.
²³Although officials have sat, have spoken against me,
  your servant talks about your decrees.
²⁴Yes, your affirmations are my pleasure,
  my counsellors.

Psalm 119.25–48 Standing on the promises

²⁵My entire being is stuck in the earth:
  bring me to life in accordance with your word.
²⁶I recounted my ways and you answered me;
  teach me your decrees.
²⁷Help me understand the way of the things you have determined,
  so that I may talk about your extraordinary deeds.
²⁸My entire being has wept itself away through sorrow;
  set me up in accordance with your word.
²⁹Remove the way of falsehood from me;
  grace me with your instruction.
³⁰I've chosen the way of truthfulness;
  I've set out your rulings.
³¹I've stuck to your affirmations;
  Yahweh, don't shame me.
³²I run the way of your orders,
  because you widen my mind.

³³Teach me the way of your decrees, Yahweh,
  so that I may preserve it to the utmost.
³⁴Help me understand, so that I may observe your instruction,
  and keep it with all my mind.
³⁵Direct me on the trail of your orders,
  because I delight in it.
³⁶Bend my mind to your affirmations
  and not to profit.
³⁷Help my eyes pass from seeing emptiness;
  bring me to life by your way.
³⁸Implement for your servant what you've said,
  that which was for people who live in awe of you.
³⁹Make my reviling, which I dread, pass,
  because your rulings are good.
⁴⁰There, I long for the things you've determined;
  in your faithfulness bring me to life.

⁴¹So may your commitment come to me, Yahweh,
  your deliverance in accordance with what
     you've said.
⁴²And I shall answer the person who reviles me
     with a word,
  because I've relied on your word.
⁴³So don't snatch right away from my mouth your
     truthful word,
  because I've waited for your rulings.
⁴⁴And I will keep your instruction continually,
  lastingly and permanently.
⁴⁵So I will walk about in wideness,
  because I've enquired of the things you've
     determined.
⁴⁶And I will speak of your affirmations in front of
     kings,
  and not be shamed.
⁴⁷So I will take pleasure in your orders,
  to which I am loyal.
⁴⁸And I will lift the palms of my hands to your
     orders, to which I am loyal,
  and I will talk about your decrees.

Psalm 119.49–72 Teach me

⁴⁹Be mindful of your word to your servant,
  upon which you've caused me to wait.
⁵⁰This is my comfort in my humbling,
  that what you've said has brought me to life.
⁵¹Though the assertive have mocked me greatly,
  I haven't turned away from your instruction.
⁵²I've been mindful of your rulings from of old,
  Yahweh, and found comfort.
⁵³Rage has grasped me because of the faithless
     people,
  who abandon your instruction.
⁵⁴Your decrees have been my protection
  in the house where I reside.
⁵⁵I've been mindful by night of your name,
     Yahweh,
  and I've kept your instruction.
⁵⁶This is how it's been for me,
  because I've observed the things you've
     determined.
⁵⁷Yahweh being my share,
  I've said I would keep your words.
⁵⁸I've sought your goodwill with all my heart;
  be gracious to me in accordance with what
     you've said.
⁵⁹I've thought about my ways
  and turned back my feet to your affirmations.
⁶⁰I've hurried and not delayed
  to keep your orders.
⁶¹Though the ropes of the faithless were round
     me,
  I haven't put out of mind your instruction.
⁶²In the middle of the night I get up
  to confess you for your faithful rulings.
⁶³I'm a friend to all who live in awe of you
  and to the people who keep the things you've
     determined.
⁶⁴The earth is full of your commitment, Yahweh;
  teach me your decrees.

⁶⁵You've done good things with your servant,
  Yahweh, in accordance with your word.
⁶⁶Teach me goodness of discretion and
     acknowledgement,
  because I've trusted in your orders.
⁶⁷Before I became low I was going astray,
  but now I've kept what you said.
⁶⁸You're good and you do good;
  teach me your decrees.
⁶⁹The assertive have smeared falsehood over me,
  whereas I observe the things you've determined
     with my whole mind.
⁷⁰Their mind is thick like fat,
  whereas I've taken pleasure in your instruction.
⁷¹It was good for me that I was humbled,
  in order that I might learn your decrees.
⁷²The instruction that comes from your mouth is
     better for me
  than thousands of gold and silver pieces.

Psalm 119.73–96 Waiting

⁷³Given that your hands made me, established me,
  help me understand so that I may learn your
     orders.
⁷⁴People who live in awe of you will see and
     rejoice,
  because I've waited for your word.
⁷⁵I've acknowledged, Yahweh, that your rulings
     are faithful,
  and in truthfulness you've humbled me.
⁷⁶May your commitment become my comfort,
     please,
  in accordance with what you've said to your
     servant.
⁷⁷May your compassion come to me so that I may
     live,
  because your instruction is my pleasure.

⁷⁸May the assertive be shamed, because they have
    put me in the wrong by means of falsehood,
  whereas I talk about the things you've
    determined.
⁷⁹May the people who live in awe of you turn back
    to me,
  the people who acknowledge your
    affirmations.
⁸⁰May my mind be of integrity in your decrees
  in order that I may not be shamed.

⁸¹My entire being fails [in looking] for your
    deliverance;
  for your word I've waited.
⁸²My eyes fail regarding what you've said,
  in saying 'When will you comfort me?'
⁸³When I've become like a water-skin in smoke,
  I haven't put out of mind your decrees.
⁸⁴How many are your servant's days:
  when will you act with authority against my
    pursuers?
⁸⁵The assertive have dug pits for me,
  which is not in accordance with your
    instruction.
⁸⁶All your orders are truthful;
  when people pursue me with falsehood, help
    me.
⁸⁷They've almost finished me off in the country,
  but I haven't abandoned the things you've
    determined.
⁸⁸In accordance with your commitment bring me
    to life,
  so that I may keep the affirmations of your
    mouth.

⁸⁹Your word is permanent, Yahweh,
  standing in the heavens.
⁹⁰Your truthfulness lasts generation after
    generation;
  you established the earth and it has stood firm.
⁹¹As for your rulings, they've stood firm today,
  because all are your servants.
⁹²Were not your instruction my pleasure,
  I would then have perished through my
    humbling.
⁹³Never will I put out of mind the things you've
    determined,
  because by means of them you've brought me
    to life.
⁹⁴I am yours, deliver me,
  because I've enquired of the things you've
    determined.

⁹⁵Whereas faithless people have hoped to make
    me perish,
  I show understanding of your affirmations.
⁹⁶As for every finish, I've seen an end,
  but your order is very wide.

Psalm 119.97–120 I can be smarter than my professor

⁹⁷How loyal I am to your instruction!
  – all day it is my talk.
⁹⁸Your orders make me smarter than my enemies,
  because they are mine permanently.
⁹⁹I've gained more insight than all my teachers,
  because your affirmations are my talk.
¹⁰⁰I show more understanding than the elders,
  because I've observed the things you've
    determined.
¹⁰¹I've kept back my foot from every bad path,
  in order that I might keep your word.
¹⁰²I haven't departed from your rulings,
  because you've instructed me.
¹⁰³How smooth the things you say have been to
    my palate,
  more than syrup to my mouth.
¹⁰⁴Through the things you've determined I show
    understanding;
  therefore I oppose every false path.

¹⁰⁵Your word is a lamp to my foot,
  a light to my trail.
¹⁰⁶I swore and set it up,
  that I would keep your faithful rulings.
¹⁰⁷I am low, very low, Yahweh;
  bring me to life in accordance with your word.
¹⁰⁸Please accept the free offerings of my mouth,
    Yahweh,
  and teach me your rulings.
¹⁰⁹My life is in the palm of my hand continually,
  but I haven't put out of mind your instruction.
¹¹⁰Faithless people have placed a trap for me,
  but I haven't strayed from the things you've
    determined.
¹¹¹I've made your affirmations my own
    permanently,
  because they are the joy of my heart.
¹¹²I've bent my mind to act on your decrees,
  permanently, to the utmost.

¹¹³I'm hostile to divided people,
  and I'm loyal to your instruction.

^{114}Since you've been my shelter and shield,
  I've waited for your word.
^{115}Depart from me, you who deal badly,
  so that I may observe my God's orders.
^{116}Hold me up in accordance with what you said,
    so that I may live;
  don't let me be ashamed of my expectation.
^{117}Sustain me so that I may find deliverance,
  and have regard to your decrees continually.
^{118}You've thrown out everyone who wanders from
    your decrees,
  because their deceptiveness is false.
^{119}As dross, you've made all the faithless people in
    the country cease;
  therefore I'm loyal to your affirmations.
^{120}My flesh shivers in reverence for you;
  I live in awe of your rulings.

Psalm 119.121–144 The opening up of your words gives light

^{121}I've made faithful rulings;
  don't leave me to oppressors.
^{122}Make a pledge to your servant for good things;
  the assertive must not oppress me.
^{123}My eyes fail [in looking] for your deliverance,
  for what you said about your faithfulness.
^{124}Act with your servant in accordance with your
    commitment,
  and teach me your decrees.
^{125}As I am your servant, help me understand,
  so that I may acknowledge your affirmations.
^{126}It's a time for Yahweh to act;
  people have violated your instruction.
^{127}Therefore I'm loyal to your orders,
  more than to gold and silver.
^{128}Therefore I've treated as upright everything that
    you've determined about everything;
  I've been hostile to every false path.
^{129}Your affirmations are extraordinary things;
  therefore my entire being has observed them.
^{130}The opening up of your words gives light,
  helping the simple to understand.
^{131}I opened wide my mouth and panted,
  because I longed for your orders.
^{132}Turn your face to me and be gracious to me,
  in accordance with your ruling for people who
    are loyal to your name.
^{133}Establish my feet by what you say,
  so that no evil may have power over me.
^{134}Redeem me from human oppression,
  so that I may keep the things you've
    determined.
^{135}Shine your face on your servant,
  and teach me your decrees.
^{136}My eyes have run down streams of water,
  because people have not kept your instruction.

^{137}You're faithful, Yahweh,
  and upright in your rulings.
^{138}You've ordered the faithfulness of your
    affirmations,
  and the truthfulness, exceedingly.
^{139}My passion has devoured me,
  because my adversaries have put your words
    out of mind.
^{140}What you say has been much proven,
  and your servant is loyal to it.
^{141}Although I am small and despised,
  I haven't put out of mind the things you've
    determined.
^{142}Your faithfulness is a faithfulness that is
    permanent,
  and your instruction is truth.
^{143}Although pressure and straits have found me,
  your orders are my pleasure.
^{144}The faithfulness of your affirmations is
    permanent;
  help me understand so that I may live.

Psalm 119.145–160 My eyes have anticipated the watches

^{145}I've called with all my heart; answer me,
    Yahweh,
  so that I may observe your decrees.
^{146}I've called you – deliver me,
  so that I may keep your affirmations.
^{147}I've anticipated the twilight and cried for help,
  as I waited for your word.
^{148}My eyes have anticipated the watches,
  to talk about what you've said.
^{149}Listen to my voice in accordance with your
    commitment;
  Yahweh, bring me to life in accordance with
    your ruling.
^{150}People who pursue deliberate wickedness are
    near;
  they are far from your instruction.
^{151}You are near, Yahweh,
  and all your orders are true.

¹⁵²Of old I've acknowledged from your affirmations
   that you founded them permanently.

¹⁵³See my humbling, pull me out,
   because I haven't put out of mind your instruction.
¹⁵⁴Argue my cause and restore me;
   in the light of what you've said, bring me to life.
¹⁵⁵Deliverance is far from the faithless,
   because they haven't enquired of your decrees.
¹⁵⁶Your compassion is great, Yahweh;
   bring me to life in accordance with your rulings.
¹⁵⁷Although my pursuers and adversaries are many,
   I haven't turned away from your affirmations.
¹⁵⁸I've seen people who break faith and loathed them,
   people who didn't keep what you said.
¹⁵⁹See that I've been loyal to the things you've determined;
   Yahweh, bring me to life in accordance with your commitment.
¹⁶⁰Truthfulness is the first principle of your word,
   and every faithful ruling of yours is permanent.

Psalm 119.161–176 The appeal of the lost sheep

¹⁶¹Officials have pursued me for nothing,
   but my heart has revered your word.
¹⁶²I rejoice over what you've said,
   like someone who finds much plunder.
¹⁶³Whereas I'm hostile to and take offence at falsehood,
   I'm loyal to your instruction.
¹⁶⁴I've praised you seven times a day
   for your faithful rulings.
¹⁶⁵There is much well-being for people who are loyal to your instruction,
   and there isn't anything that can make them collapse.
¹⁶⁶I've looked for your deliverance, Yahweh,
   and acted on your orders.
¹⁶⁷I've kept your affirmations with my entire being;
   I am totally loyal to them.
¹⁶⁸I've kept the things you've determined and your affirmations,
   because all my ways are in front of you.

¹⁶⁹May my resounding come near your presence, Yahweh;
   in accordance with your word, help me understand.
¹⁷⁰May my prayer for grace come before you;
   in accordance with what you've said, rescue me.
¹⁷¹May my lips pour forth praise,
   because you teach me your decrees.
¹⁷²May my tongue chant of what you've said,
   because all your orders are faithful.
¹⁷³May your hand come to my help,
   because I've chosen the things you've determined.
¹⁷⁴I've longed for your deliverance, Yahweh,
   and your instruction is my pleasure.
¹⁷⁵May my entire being live and praise you,
   and may your rulings help me.
¹⁷⁶I've wandered like a lost sheep:
   look for your servant,
   because I haven't put your orders out of mind.

Psalm 120 Peaceableness

A song of the ascents.

¹To Yahweh, when I was under pressure,
   I called and he answered me.
²Yahweh, rescue my life from false lips,
   from a deceitful tongue.
³What will it give you, what will it add to you, deceitful tongue?
⁴The arrows of a strong man, sharpened,
   with coals of broom shrubs.
⁵Oh for me, that I've resided with Meshek,
   dwelt with Qedar's tents.
⁶A long time I've been dwelling
   with someone hostile to peace.
⁷I am for peace, but when I speak,
   they are for battle.

Psalm 121 Peacefulness

A song for the ascents.

¹I raise my eyes to the mountains:
   from where does my help come?

²My help comes from Yahweh,
  maker of heavens and earth.
³He doesn't give your foot to slipping;
  your keeper doesn't doze.
⁴There, he doesn't doze and he doesn't sleep,
  Yisra'el's keeper.
⁵Yahweh is your keeper, Yahweh is your shade,
  at your right hand.
⁶By day the sun will not strike you down,
  or the moon by night.
⁷Yahweh will keep you from everything bad;
  he will keep your life.
⁸Yahweh will keep your going out and your
    coming in,
  from now and permanently.

Psalm 122 Praying for Yerushalaim

A song of the ascents. David's.

¹I rejoiced when people said to me,
  'We'll go to Yahweh's house.'
²Our feet have been standing
  in your gates, Yerushalaim,
³Yerushalaim, which is built
  as a town that is joined together to itself,
⁴Where the clans went up, Yah's clans,
  (an affirmation for Yisra'el),
  to confess Yahweh's name.
⁵Because thrones for exercising authority sat there,
  thrones for David's household.
⁶Ask for the well-being of Yerushalaim;
  may people who are loyal to it be secure.
⁷May there be well-being in your rampart,
  ease in your citadels.
⁸For the sake of my brothers and my friends
  I shall please speak of well-being for you.
⁹For the sake of the house of Yahweh our God
  I will seek good things for you.

Psalm 123 Praying for grace

A song of the ascents.

¹To you I raise my eyes,
  you who sit in the heavens.
²There, like the eyes of servants
  towards the hand of their masters,
Like the eyes of a maidservant
  towards the hand of her mistress,

So are our eyes towards Yahweh our God,
  until he is gracious to us.
³Be gracious to us, Yahweh, be gracious,
  because we've become very full of contempt.
⁴Our entire being has become very full for itself
  of the ridicule of complacent people,
  of the contempt of majestic people.

Psalm 124 Our help is the name of the Lord

A song of the ascents. David's.

¹Were it not Yahweh who was ours,
  Yisra'el is please to say,
²Were it not Yahweh who was ours
  when people arose against us,
³Then they would have swallowed us alive
  in their angry burning against us.
⁴Then the water – it would have carried us off;
  the torrent – it would have passed right over us.
⁵Then it would have passed right over us,
  the seething water.
⁶Yahweh be blessed,
  who did not give us as prey to their teeth.
⁷Our life is like a bird
  that has escaped from the hunters' trap.
The trap – it broke;
  and we – we escaped.
⁸Our help is the very name of Yahweh,
  maker of heavens and earth.

Psalm 125 Mountains round Yerushalaim, Yahweh round his people

A song of the ascents.

¹The people who rely on Yahweh are like Mount
    Tsiyyon,
  which will not slip – it will sit permanently.
²Yerushalaim – mountains are round it;
  Yahweh – he is round his people,
  now and permanently.
³Because the faithless club will not rest
  over the allocation of the faithful,
In order that the faithful do not put
  their hands to evil.

⁴Do good, Yahweh, to the people who are good,
  yes, to the people who are upright in their mind.

⁵But the people who bend their crooked ways,
   may Yahweh make them go, the people who
      devise trouble;
   well-being [be] on Yisraʼel!

Psalm 126 Dreaming, crying, resounding

A song of the ascents.

¹When Yahweh turned back Tsiyyon's fortunes,
   we became like people dreaming.
²Then our mouth would fill with laughter,
   our tongue with resounding.
Then they would say among the nations,
   'Yahweh has shown greatness in acting with
      them.'
³Yahweh has shown greatness in acting with us;
   we became people celebrating.

⁴Turn back our fortunes, Yahweh,
   like canyons in the Negev.
⁵May people who sow with crying
   reap with resounding.
⁶The person who goes, but goes crying,
   carrying the seed bag –
As he comes, may he come with resounding,
   carrying his sheaves.

Psalm 127 Insomnia

A song of the ascents. Shelomoh's.

¹If Yahweh doesn't build a house,
   in vain the builders have laboured on it.
If Yahweh doesn't keep a town,
   in vain the one who keeps watch has been
      wakeful.
²It is in vain for you, being people early to get up,
   people late to sit down,
People who eat bread of toil
   – yes, he gives sleep to his beloved.

³There, sons are your domain from Yahweh;
   the fruit of the womb is a reward.
⁴Like arrows in a strong man's hand
   – so are the sons of youth.
⁵The blessings of the man
   who has filled his quiver!
Of them he will not be shamed
   when they speak with enemies in the gateway.

Psalm 128 Blessings and good things

A song of the ascents.

¹The blessings of anyone who lives in awe of Yahweh,
   who walks in his ways!
²Because you will eat the fruit of the palms of
      your hands,
   your blessings and good things of yours.
³Your wife like a fruitful vine
   in the inner rooms of your house,
Your children like the slips of olive trees
   round your table.
⁴There, surely thus will he be blessed,
   a man who lives in awe of Yahweh.
⁵May Yahweh bless you from Tsiyyon;
   you can look at the good things of Yerushalaim,
All the days of your life,
   ⁶and look at your grandchildren;
   well-being [be] on Yisraʼel!

Psalm 129 Atrocities

A song of the ascents.

¹People have attacked me much since my youth,
   Yisraʼel is please to say,
²People have attacked me much,
   though not prevailed over me.
³Over my back ploughmen have ploughed;
   they made long furrows.
⁴Yahweh is faithful;
   he cut through the ropes of the faithless people.
⁵May they be shamed and may they turn
      backwards,
   all the people who are hostile to Tsiyyon.
⁶May they become like the grass on roofs
   that withers before someone has plucked it,
⁷With which a reaper has not filled his fist,
   or a gatherer his arm,
⁸And passers-by have not said,
   'Yahweh's blessing on you;
   we bless you in Yahweh's name.'

Psalm 130 From the depths

A song of the ascents.

¹From the depths I have called you, Yahweh:
   ²Lord, listen to my voice.

May your ears become attentive
    to the sound of my prayers for grace.
³If you keep watch on wayward acts, Yah:
    Lord, who can stand?
⁴Because with you there is pardon,
    in order that you may be held in awe.
⁵I have hoped for Yahweh,
    my entire being has hoped.
For his word I have waited,
    ⁶my entire being for the Lord,
More than people keeping watch for the morning,
    people keeping watch for the morning.
⁷Yisra'el, wait for Yahweh,
    because with Yahweh there is commitment.
With him the redemption will be great,
    ⁸when he himself redeems Yisra'el from all its
        wayward acts.

Psalm 131 No big ideas

A song of the ascents. David's.

¹Yahweh, my mind has not been lofty,
    my eyes have not looked high.
I haven't gone about with big ideas
    or extraordinary deeds beyond me.
²If I haven't conformed
    and quietened my entire being . . .
Like someone nursed with its mother,
    so my entire being is nursed with me.
³Yisra'el, wait for Yahweh,
    now and for evermore.

Psalm 132 If you build it, he will come

A song of the ascents.

¹Yahweh, be mindful for David
    of all his being humbled,
²In that he swore to Yahweh,
    pledged to Ya'aqob's Champion,
³'If I come into my tent, my house,
    if I climb into my bed, my couch,
⁴If I give sleep to my eyes,
    slumber to my eyelids,
⁵Until I find the place belonging to Yahweh,
    the dwelling belonging to Ya'aqob's Champion . . .'

⁶There, we heard of it at Ephrata,
    we found it in the Ya'ar fields.

⁷Let's come to his dwelling,
    let's bow low to his footstool.
⁸Rise, Yahweh, to your place, to settle down,
    you and your powerful chest.
⁹Your priests put on faithfulness,
    the people who are committed to you resound.
¹⁰For the sake of David your servant,
    don't turn back the face of your anointed one.

¹¹Yahweh swore to David in truthfulness,
    he will not turn back from it:
'One from the fruit of your body
    I will put on your throne.
¹²If your sons keep my pact,
    my affirmations that I will teach them,
For all time their sons
    also will sit on your throne.
¹³Because Yahweh chose Tsiyyon,
    which he wanted as a seat for himself.
¹⁴For all time this is my place to settle down,
    where I will sit, because I wanted it.
¹⁵Its supplies I will greatly bless;
    its needy people I will fill with bread.
¹⁶Its priests I will clothe with deliverance,
    its committed people will resound loudly.
¹⁷There I will make David's horn flourish;
    I am setting up a lamp for my anointed one.
¹⁸Its enemies I will clothe in shame,
    but on him his crown will sparkle.'

Psalm 133 Brothers living as one

A song of the ascents. David's.

¹There, how good and how lovely
    is brothers living as one,
²Like good oil on the head,
    going down on to the beard,
Aharon's beard,
    which goes down on the collar of his clothes,
³Like the dew of Hermon,
    which goes down on the mountains of Tsiyyon.
Because there Yahweh ordered blessing,
    life for evermore.

Psalm 134 How to end the day

A song of the ascents.

¹There, bless Yahweh, all you servants of Yahweh,
    you who stand in Yahweh's house at night.

²Raise your hands to the sacred place
  and bless Yahweh.
³May Yahweh bless you from Tsiyyon
  – the one who is maker of heavens and earth.

Psalm 135 Anything that Yahweh has wished, he has done

¹Praise Yah! –
  praise Yahweh's name;
  praise, servants of Yahweh,
²You who stand in Yahweh's house,
  in the courtyards of the house of our God.
³Praise Yah, because Yahweh is good;
  make music for his name, because it's lovely.
⁴Because Yah chose Ya'aqob for himself,
  Yisra'el as his personal treasure.

⁵Because I myself acknowledge that Yahweh is
    great;
  our Lord above all gods.
⁶Anything that Yahweh has wished,
  he has done in the heavens and on the earth,
In the seas and all the depths,
  ⁷making clouds rise from the end of the earth.
He has made flashes of lightning for the rain,
  getting wind out from his storehouses,
⁸The one who struck down the firstborn of
    Misrayim,
  both human beings and cattle.
⁹He sent signs and portents
  in the middle of Misrayim
  against Par'oh [Pharaoh] and against all his
    servants,
¹⁰The one who struck down many nations
  and killed numerous kings,
¹¹Sihon king of the Amorites,
  Og king of Bashan,
And all the kingdoms of Kena'an,
  ¹²and gave their country as a domain,
  a domain for Yisra'el his people.

¹³Yahweh, your name is permanent;
  Yahweh, your commemoration is through
    generation after generation.
¹⁴Because Yahweh acts in judgement for his
    people
  and gets relief in connection with his servants.

¹⁵The nations' images are silver and gold,
  the making of human hands.

¹⁶They have a mouth but they don't speak,
  they have eyes but they don't see.
¹⁷They have ears but they don't hear;
  no, there's no breath in their mouths.
¹⁸Their makers will become like them,
  anyone who relies on them.

¹⁹Household of Yisra'el, bless Yahweh;
  household of Aharon, bless Yahweh.
²⁰Household of Levi, bless Yahweh;
  you who live in awe of Yahweh, bless Yahweh.
²¹Yahweh be blessed from Tsiyyon,
  the one who dwells in Yerushalaim.
Praise Yah!

Psalm 136 His commitment is permanent

¹Confess Yahweh, because he is good
  (because his commitment is permanent).
²Confess the God of gods
  (because his commitment is permanent).
³Confess the Lord of lords
  (because his commitment is permanent).
⁴The one who did big, extraordinary things alone
  (because his commitment is permanent),
⁵Who made the heavens with understanding
  (because his commitment is permanent),
⁶Who spread the earth over the water
  (because his commitment is permanent),
⁷Who made the big lights
  (because his commitment is permanent),
⁸The sun to rule the day
  (because his commitment is permanent),
⁹The moon and the stars to rule the night
  (because his commitment is permanent),
¹⁰Who struck down Misrayim through their
    firstborn
  (because his commitment is permanent),
¹¹And got Yisra'el out from the middle of them
  (because his commitment is permanent),
¹²With a strong hand and an extended arm
  (because his commitment is permanent),
¹³The divider of the Reed Sea into two divisions
  (because his commitment is permanent),
¹⁴Who let Yisra'el pass through the middle of it
  (because his commitment is permanent),
¹⁵But shook Par'oh and his force into the Reed Sea
  (because his commitment is permanent),
¹⁶The one who enabled his people to go through
    the wilderness
  (because his commitment is permanent),

¹⁷The one who struck down great kings
   (because his commitment is permanent),
¹⁸Who killed august kings
   (because his commitment is permanent),
¹⁹Sihon king of the Amorites
   (because his commitment is permanent),
²⁰Og king of Bashan
   (because his commitment is permanent),
²¹And gave their country as a domain
   (because his commitment is permanent),
²²A domain for Yisra'el his servant
   (because his commitment is permanent),
²³Who was mindful of us in our lowliness
   (because his commitment is permanent),
²⁴And tore us away from our adversaries
   (because his commitment is permanent),
²⁵Giver of food to all flesh
   (because his commitment is permanent).
²⁶Confess the God of the heavens
   (because his commitment is permanent).

Psalm 137 Mindfulness, God's and ours

¹By the rivers of Babel,
   there we sat, yes, we cried
   as we were mindful of Tsiyyon.
²On the poplars in the middle of it
   we hung our guitars.
³Because there they asked,
   our captors, for the words of a song,
The people who play about with us, for rejoicing:
   'Sing us one of the Tsiyyon songs!'
⁴How can we sing Yahweh's song
   on foreign soil?
⁵If I put you out of mind, Yerushalaim,
   may my right hand put out of mind.
⁶May my tongue stick to my palate
   if I am not mindful of you,
If I do not exalt Yerushalaim
   above the pinnacle of my rejoicing.

⁷Yahweh, be mindful for the Edomites
   of Yerushalaim's day,
The people who were saying, 'Strip it,
   strip it, to its foundation.'
⁸Ms Babel, you who are to be destroyed:
   the blessings of the person who makes good
      to you
   for the thing that you dealt to us.
⁹The blessings of the person who grasps your babies
   and dashes them on the cliff.

Psalm 138 How to be defiant in spirit

David's.

¹I will confess you with all my heart,
   in front of the gods I will make music for you.
²I will bow low to your sacred palace,
   and confess your name for your commitment
      and for your truthfulness,
Because you have made great above everything
   your name, your word.
³On the day I called, you answered me;
   you make me defiant in my being, with vigour.
⁴All earth's kings will confess you, Yahweh,
   because they will have heard the sayings of
      your mouth.
⁵They will sing of Yahweh's ways,
   because Yahweh's splendour will be great.v
⁶Because Yahweh is on high, but he sees the lowly;
   lofty, he acknowledges from afar.
⁷If I walk in the middle of pressure you will give
      me life;
   on account of my enemies' anger you will put
      out your hand.
Your right hand will deliver me;
⁸Yahweh will bring it to an end for me.
Yahweh, your commitment is permanent;
   don't slacken your hold of the things your
      hands made.

Psalm 139 Openness

The leader's. David's. A composition.

¹Yahweh, you've searched me out and got to know
      me:
²you yourself have got to know my sitting and
      my rising,
   you've understood my intention, from far
      away.
³My walking and my reclining you've measured;
   with all my ways you've become familiar.
⁴Because there's not an utterance on my tongue
   – there, Yahweh, you've got to know it all.
⁵Behind and in front you've bound me,
   and put the palm of your hand on me.
⁶Your knowledge is too extraordinary for me;
   it's towered high, I can't prevail over it.

⁷Where could I go from your spirit,
   where could I take flight from your face?

⁸If I were to go up to the heavens, you would be there;
　if I were to make She'ol my bed – there you would be.
⁹Were I to take dawn's wings,
　dwell on the far side of the sea,
¹⁰There, too, your hand could lead me away,
　your right hand could grasp me.
¹¹Were I to say, 'The darkness can certainly seize me,
　light can be night round me',
¹²Darkness, too, would not be too dark for you,
　and night would be light like day;
　darkness and light are the same.

¹³Because you are the one who created my inner being,
　when you wove me in my mother's womb.
¹⁴I will confess you, on account of the fact that I was made distinct in an awe-inspiring way;
　the things you made were extraordinary.
I myself acknowledge you fully;
　¹⁵my frame was not concealed from you,
When I was made in secret,
　when I was embroidered in earth's depths.
¹⁶Your eyes saw me as an embryo,
　and on your document were written, all of them,
The days that were shaped,
　when there was not one of them.
¹⁷So for me, how valuable were your intentions, God,
　how numerous was the sum of them!
¹⁸If I could count them, they would be more than the sand;
　when I've come to an end, I will still be with you.

¹⁹If you would only slay the faithless person, God,
　and people of bloodshed would depart from me,
²⁰People who speak of you in connection with a strategy,
　your adversaries who have lifted you up for emptiness.
²¹I'm hostile to people who are hostile to you, Yahweh, am I not,
　and I loathe people who rise up against you.
²²With complete hostility I'm hostile to them;
　they've become enemies for me.

²³Search me out, God, and acknowledge my mind;
　test me and acknowledge my concerns.

²⁴See if there is an idolatrous way in me
　and lead me in the ancient way.

Psalm 140 The shield

The leader's. A composition. David's.

¹Pull me out, Yahweh, from the bad person,
　preserve me from the individual of great violence,
²People who've thought up bad things in their mind,
　who stir up battles every day.
³They've sharpened their tongue like a snake;
　a spider's poison is under their lips. *(Rise)*
⁴Keep me from the hand of the faithless person, Yahweh,
　preserve me from the individual of great violence,
People who've thought up how to trip my steps;
　⁵majestic people have hidden a trap for me, and ropes.
They've spread a net by the side of the track,
　they've set snares for me. *(Rise)*

⁶I've said to Yahweh, 'You are my God';
　give ear, Yahweh, to the sound of my prayer for grace.
⁷Yahweh, my Lord, the [one with the] vigour that delivers me,
　you've shielded my head on the day of weaponry.
⁸Yahweh, don't grant the wishes of the faithless person;
　don't let his plan succeed so that they are exalted. *(Rise)*
⁹The head of the people who surround me
　– may the oppression caused by their lips cover them.
¹⁰May burning coals tumble on them with fire;
　may it make them fall into pits so that they don't get up.
¹¹May the person with a [violent] tongue not be established in the country;
　the violent person – may bad fortune hunt him into pens.
¹²I've come to acknowledge that Yahweh makes a judgement for the humble,
　a ruling for the needy.
¹³Yes, the faithful will confess your name;
　the upright will live in your presence.

Psalm 141 On keeping one's mouth shut

A composition. David's.

¹Yahweh, when I call you, hurry to me,
  give ear to my voice when I call to you.
²May my plea be established as incense before you,
  the lifting of the palms of my hands as the evening offering.
³Set a watch at my mouth, Yahweh,
  keep guard at the door of my lips.
⁴Don't let my mind turn away to something bad,
  to have dealings in faithlessness
  with people who devise trouble.
So I shall not feed on their delights;
  ⁵the faithful person may hit me with commitment and reprove me.
May choice oil not adorn my head,
  because my plea is still against their bad ways.
⁶When their authorities have fallen at the sides of the cliff,
  they will listen to the things I say, because they are lovely.

⁷Like someone cleaving and splitting the earth,
  our bones have been scattered at the mouth of She'ol.
⁸Because my eyes are towards you, Yahweh my Lord,
  with you I have taken shelter, don't expose my life.
⁹Keep me from the sides of the trap that they have laid for me,
  and from the snares of people who devise trouble.
¹⁰May the faithless fall into their own nets all at once,
  while I myself pass through.

Psalm 142 A prisoner's plea

An instruction. David's. When he was in the cave. A plea.

¹With my voice I will cry out to Yahweh,
  with my voice I will pray for grace to Yahweh.
²I will pour out my talk before him;
  the pressure on me I will declare before him.
³When my spirit faints away within me,
  you're the one who knows my trail.
On the way that I walk about,
  they've hidden a trap for me.
⁴Look at my right hand and see
  – there's no one who recognizes me.
Retreat has failed for me;
  there's no one who enquires about my life.
⁵I've cried out to you, Yahweh;
  I've said, 'You're my shelter,
  my share in the land of the living.'
⁶Heed my resounding shout,
  because I've been brought very low.
Rescue me from my pursuers,
  because they stand too firm for me.
⁷Get me out of my prison,
  to confess your name.
Round me faithful people will gather,
  because you've dealt to me.

Psalm 143 God's faithfulness, not mine

A composition. David's.

¹Yahweh, listen to my plea,
  give ear to my prayer for grace, in your truthfulness,
  answer me in your faithfulness.
²Don't come into the exercise of authority with your servant,
  because no living person counts as faithful before you.
³Because my enemy has pursued my life,
  crushed my existence to the earth,
Made me live in darkness,
  like people long dead.
⁴My spirit has fainted away within me;
  my mind is desolate inside me.
⁵I have been mindful of the days of old,
  I've murmured about all you had done,
  I would talk about the action of your hands.
⁶I've spread out my hands to you,
  my entire being has been like dry earth in relation to you. *(Rise)*

⁷Be quick, answer me, Yahweh;
  my spirit is finished.
Don't hide your face from me,
  so that I shall be like the people who go down into the Cistern.
⁸Let me hear of your commitment in the morning,
  because it's on you that I've relied.

Let me know the way that I should walk,
    because it is to you that I've lifted up my soul.
⁹Rescue me from my enemies, Yahweh;
    with you I've found cover.
¹⁰Teach me to do what's acceptable to you,
    because you are my God.
May your good spirit lead me
    on level ground.
¹¹For the sake of your name, Yahweh, give me life;
    in your faithfulness will you get me out of the pressure on me.
¹²In your commitment will you put an end to my enemies,
    obliterate all the people who are attacking me,
    because I'm your servant.

Psalm 144 The God who snatches away

David's.

¹Yahweh, my crag, be blessed,
    the one who trains my hands for encounter,
    my fingers for battle,
²The one committed to me, my fastness,
    my turret, the one who enables me to survive,
My shield, the one with whom I take shelter,
    who subdues my people under me.

³Yahweh, what is a human person that you should acknowledge him,
    a mere human being that you should think about him?
⁴A human person is like a breath,
    his days like a passing shadow.
⁵Yahweh, spread your heavens and come down,
    touch the mountains so that they smoke.
⁶Make lightning flash and scatter them,
    send your arrows and rout them.
⁷Send your hands from on high,
    snatch me away, rescue me,
From the great water,
    from the hand of foreigners,
⁸Whose mouth has spoken emptiness,
    and whose right hand is a right hand of falsehood.

⁹God, I will sing
    a new song for you,
    on a ten-stringed mandolin I will make music for you.
¹⁰As the one who gives deliverance to kings,
    who snatches away David his servant,
From the deadly sword ¹¹snatch me away,
    rescue me from the hand of foreigners,
Whose mouth has spoken emptiness,
    and whose right hand is a right hand of falsehood.

¹²In that our sons are like saplings,
    nourished in their youth,
Our daughters are like a corner pillar,
    carved in the pattern of a palace,
¹³Our storehouses are full
    of provisions of this kind and that kind,
Our flocks number thousands, myriads in our fields,
    ¹⁴our cattle are laden,
There is no breach and no going out
    and no cry in our squares:
¹⁵The blessings of the people that has it like this,
    the blessings of the people whose God is Yahweh!

Psalm 145 Thine is the kingdom, the power and the glory

An act of praise. David's.

¹I will exalt you, my God, King;
    I will bless your name lastingly and permanently.
²Every day I will bless you;
    I will praise your name lastingly and permanently.
³Yahweh is great and much to be praised;
    of his greatness there is no searching out.
⁴One generation will extol your works to another generation,
    and tell of your mighty acts.
⁵Of the glorious magnificence of your grandeur,
    and your extraordinary deeds, I will talk.
⁶People will speak of the might of your awe-inspiring acts;
    your greatness – I will recount it.
⁷They will pour forth commemoration of your great goodness,
    and resound at your faithfulness.
⁸Yahweh is gracious and compassionate,
    long-tempered and big in commitment.
⁹Yahweh is good to all;
    his compassion is over all the things he made.

¹⁰All the things you made will confess you,
   Yahweh;
  the people committed to you will bless you.
¹¹They will talk of the splendour of your reign,
  they will speak of your might,
¹²To get his mighty acts acknowledged by human
   beings,
  the splendour and magnificence of his reign.
¹³Your reign is a reign over all ages,
  your rule over generation after generation.

¹⁴Yahweh supports all who are falling,
  and lifts upright all who are bent down.
¹⁵The eyes of all look to you,
  and you give them their food at its time.
¹⁶You open your hand,
  and fill every living thing with your
   acceptance.
¹⁷Yahweh is faithful in all his ways,
  committed in all his actions.
¹⁸Yahweh is near to all who call him,
  to all who call him in truth.
¹⁹He acts with acceptance to the people who live
   in awe of him;
  he listens to their cry for help and delivers
   them.
²⁰Yahweh keeps watch over all who are loyal to
   him,
  but he devastates all the faithless.
²¹My mouth will speak Yahweh's praise;
  all flesh will bless his sacred name,
   lastingly and permanently.

Psalm 146 Don't rely on leaders

¹Praise Yah! –
  praise Yahweh, my entire being.
²I will praise Yahweh through my life,
  I will make music for my God while I exist.
³Don't rely on leaders,
  on a human being with whom there is no
   deliverance.
⁴His breath leaves, he goes back to his ground;
  on that day, his deliberations have perished.
⁵The blessings of the one who has Ya'aqob's God
   as his help,
  whose expectation is of Yahweh his God,
⁶Maker of heavens and earth,
  the sea and all that is in them!
The one who keeps faith permanently,
  ⁷exercising authority for the oppressed,

Giving food to the hungry
  – Yahweh frees captives.
⁸Yahweh opens the blind;
  Yahweh lifts upright the people who are bent
   down.
Yahweh is loyal to the faithful;
  ⁹Yahweh keeps watch over the resident aliens.
He relieves orphan and widow,
  but subverts the way of the faithless.
¹⁰Yahweh will reign permanently
  – your God, Tsiyyon, for generation after
   generation.
Praise Yah!

Psalm 147 Reasons for hope

¹Praise Yah! –
  because making music for our God is good,
  because glorifying the one who is our praise is
   beautiful.
²Yahweh is the builder of Yerushalaim,
  he gathers those of Yisra'el who were driven
   out.
³He's the one who heals the broken in heart,
  and bandages their wounds.
⁴He calculates the number of the stars
  and pronounces the names of them all.
⁵Our Lord is great and mighty in energy;
  of his understanding there is no reckoning.
⁶Yahweh restores the humble,
  brings down the faithless to the earth.

⁷Chant for Yahweh with confession,
  make music for our God with the guitar.
⁸He's the one who covers the heavens with
   clouds,
  provides rain for the earth,
  makes the mountains grow grass.
⁹He gives their food to cattle,
  to the offspring of the raven when they call.
¹⁰He doesn't delight in the strength of a horse;
  he doesn't value the thighs of a person.
¹¹Yahweh values people who live in awe of him,
  people who put their expectation in his
   commitment.

¹²Yerushalaim, extol Yahweh,
  praise your God, Tsiyyon,
¹³Because he's made strong the bars of your
   gateways,
  blessed your children within you.

¹⁴He gives your territory well-being,
   fills you with the finest of wheat.
¹⁵He sends his utterance to the earth;
   his word runs quickly.
¹⁶He gives snow like wool;
   he scatters frost like ash.
¹⁷He throws his hail like bits of bread;
   who can stand before his ice?
¹⁸He sends his word and melts them;
   when he blows his breath, water flows.
¹⁹He tells his words to Ya'aqob,
   his decrees and his rulings to Yisra'el.
²⁰He has not done so for any nation;
   his rulings – they don't know them.
   Praise Yah!

Psalm 148 Reasons for praise

¹Praise Yah! –
   praise Yahweh from the heavens,
   praise him in the heights.
²Praise him, all his envoys,
   praise him all his armies.
³Praise him, sun and moon,
   praise him, all bright stars.
⁴Praise him, highest heavens,
   and you water that is above the heavens.
⁵They should praise Yahweh's name,
   because it was he who gave the order so they
      were created.
⁶He set them in place lastingly and
      permanently,
   he gave a decree and it will not pass.

⁷Praise Yahweh from the earth,
   sea monsters and all depths,
⁸Fire and hail, snow and fog,
   hurricane doing his word,
⁹Mountains and all hills,
   fruit trees and all cedars,
¹⁰Creatures and all cattle,
   things that move and winged birds,
¹¹Kings of the earth and all peoples,
   officials and all authorities in the earth,
¹²Young men and young women too,
   old and young too.
¹³They should praise Yahweh's name,
   because his name alone is on high.
His grandeur is over the earth and the heavens,
   ¹⁴but he has lifted up a horn for his people,
A reason for praise for all who are committed to
      him,
   for the Yisra'elites, the people who come near
      him.
   Praise Yah!

Psalm 149 Dance and slaughter

¹Praise Yah! –
   sing for Yahweh a new song,
   his praise in the congregation of the committed
      people.
²Yisra'el is to rejoice in its maker,
   the children of Tsiyyon are to celebrate their King.
³They are to praise his name in dancing;
   tambourine and guitar are to make music for him.
⁴Because Yahweh accepts his people;
   he adorns the humble with deliverance.
⁵The committed people are to exult in their
      splendour,
   they are to resound on their beds,
⁶Acclamations of God in their throat
   and a two-edged sword in their hand,
⁷To execute redress on the nations,
   reproofs on the peoples,
⁸To bind their kings with shackles,
   their nobles with iron chains,
⁹To execute on them the ruling that is written
   – it will be magnificence for all the people
      committed to him.
   Praise Yah!

Psalm 150 The praise of God, the eternal Creator, is finished and completed

¹Praise Yah! –
   praise God in his sacred place,
   praise him in his strong firmament.
²Praise him in his acts of strength,
   praise him in accordance with his immense
      greatness.
³Praise him with the blast of the horn,
   praise him with mandolin and guitar.
⁴Praise him with tambourine and dancing;
   praise him with strings and pipe.
⁵Praise him with cymbals that can be heard,
   praise him with noisy cymbals.
⁶Every breath should praise Yah:
   praise Yah!

Proverbs

The book called 'Proverbs' is indeed dominated by one-liners that express a truth, often vividly and concretely, but it is the middle third of the book (chapters 10—22) that is most characterized by these sayings. The first third (chapters 1—9) is a collection of something more like sermonettes that may occupy half a chapter. The last third is a mixture of the two.

They all have in common that they are teaching about life that bases itself on how life itself works out in practice – or at least on how it's supposed to work out. Proverbs doesn't appeal to the exodus or the covenant and it doesn't refer to the Torah or to the Prophets. It does presuppose that the God of Israel is the real God (it uses the name Yahweh) and it presupposes that life must always be lived within the framework of faithfulness and uprightness. But while it takes that framework for granted, it then works empirically. It fits with this feature of Proverbs that it is a part of the Old Testament that has close parallels with works we know from other Middle Eastern cultures (the 'Thirty Sayings' in chapters 22—24 parallel an Egyptian set of Thirty Sayings). Proverbs thus recognizes that God has not left the world as a whole without any awareness of his ways, of right and wrong, and of how life works. Such awarenesses are hardwired into humanity.

The proverbs are 'Solomon's', though the implication is not that he wrote them. Indeed, you could almost say that nobody 'writes' proverbs – at least the one-liners. They just happen. Solomon is the patron of the worldly wisdom that appears in Proverbs (and in Ecclesiastes and the Song of Songs) as David is the patron of psalmody. If we wonder about the background of the material in Proverbs, then three contexts are worth bearing in mind.

First, much of the material presents itself as the teaching that parents offer their children. While this image may have become a figure of speech, the family is indeed the natural first context in which people are encouraged to grow up from naïvety to smartness. Such teaching in Proverbs would ultimately go back to way before Solomon's day. One can imagine its teaching in the context of the life of the clan in Genesis. And the story of Joseph illustrates a number of the themes of Proverbs.

Second, scattered through the book are a number of observations about kings and how to relate to them, and that material suggests another context in which the material could naturally be used: the training of young men and women for the administration. Beyond the explicit references to the king there are many other references to wise speech, the dynamics of decision-making, and self-control that would be important for people involved in the administration.

Third, the opening part of the book also includes some reflection on the nature of creation, of God's involvement in creation and of the way creation reflects something of God. That reflection makes one think in terms of the syllabus for theological education in Israel. By New Testament times the 'scribes' were certainly people who had been involved in theological education. We don't know how it developed in Israel, but it wouldn't be surprising if Proverbs was a set text in theological schools when they came into being.

The opening chapters speak of Smartness as a woman who is its embodiment, and the last verses of the book comprise a description of the resourceful woman. It occupies 22 lines, one line for each letter of the Hebrew alphabet, so that it describes the resourceful woman from A to Z. The poem shows how extensive were the opportunities for a woman in Israel – in this case, a woman who is the mistress of a household, but she is active outside the house and not just inside. Alongside the metaphor of Ms Smartness and the picture of the resourceful woman is the metaphor of Ms Stupidity and the picture of the woman who can lead a man astray. In the Torah, the point would be that sexual dallying and adultery are wrong. In Proverbs, the point is that they are also really stupid.

Knowledge, ethics and spirituality

1 ¹Aphorisms of Shelomoh [Solomon] ben David king of Yisra'el:

²So as to know smartness and discipline,
  to understand words that express understanding,
³To get discipline so as to act with insight,
  faithfulness, the exercise of authority, and uprightness,
⁴To give shrewdness to the naïve,
  knowledge and strategy to the youth,
⁵So that the smart person may listen and increase in his grasp,
  the understanding may acquire skill,
⁶So as to understand an aphorism and a parable,
  the words of the smart and their conundrums:
⁷The first principle of knowledge is awe for Yahweh;
  dense people despise smartness and discipline.

⁸Listen to your father's discipline, son,
  don't leave your mother's instruction,
⁹Because they're a graceful garland for your head,
  a chain for your neck.
¹⁰Son, if wrongdoers entice you, don't be willing,
  ¹¹if they say 'Go with us.
Let's lie in wait for blood,
  let's ambush someone free of guilt, for nothing.
¹²Let's swallow them alive, like She'ol –
  whole, like people going down to the Cistern.
¹³We'll find every sort of valuable riches,
  we'll fill our houses with spoil.
¹⁴Let your lot fall among us;
  there'll be one purse for us all.'
¹⁵Son, don't go on the way with them;
  keep your foot from their trail.
¹⁶Because their feet run to bad dealing,
  they hurry to shed blood.
¹⁷Because it's for nothing that a net is spread
  before the eyes of any owner of wings.
¹⁸But those people lie in wait for their own blood,
  they ambush their own lives.
¹⁹Such are the paths of everyone who gets wrongful gain;
  it takes the life of its owners.

The naïve, the arrogant, the dimwit

²⁰Smartness resounds in the open streets,
  in the squares she gives her voice.
²¹At the head of the noisy places,
  at the entrances of the gateways,
  in the town she says her words.

²²'How long will you naïve people be loyal to naïvety?
  – arrogant people desire arrogance for themselves.
Dimwits are hostile to knowledge;
  ²³do turn back at my rebuke.
Here, I will pour out my spirit to you,
  I will let you know my words.
²⁴Since I called but you refused me,
  I stretched out my hand but there was no one heeding,
²⁵You've spurned all my counsel,
  and you weren't willing for my rebuke,
²⁶I myself too will make fun of your disaster;
  I shall ridicule when what you dread comes,
²⁷When what you dread comes like devastation,
  and your calamity arrives like a tempest,
  when trouble and disaster come upon you.
²⁸Then they'll call me but I won't answer,
  they'll look urgently for me but they won't find me,
²⁹Because of the fact that they were hostile to acknowledgement,
  didn't choose awe for Yahweh.
³⁰They weren't willing for my counsel,
  they spurned every rebuke of mine.
³¹They'll eat the fruit of their way,
  they'll have their fill of their own counsels.
³²Because the turning back of the naïve will kill them,
  and the ease of dimwits will obliterate them.
³³But the person who listens to me will dwell in confidence,
  safe from the dread of bad fortune.'

The household that goes down to death

2 ¹Son, if you take the things I say,
  hide up my orders with you,
²Getting your ear to heed smartness,
  inclining your mind to understanding,
³If you indeed call to understanding,
  give your voice to understanding,
⁴If you seek it like silver,
  search for it like treasure,
⁵Then you'll understand awe for Yahweh,
  you'll find acknowledgement of God.

⁶Because Yahweh gives smartness;
  from his mouth come acknowledgement and understanding.
⁷He hides up adeptness for the upright,
  being a shield for people who walk with integrity,
⁸Preserving the paths of authority,
  he keeps watch on the way of people committed to him.
⁹Then you'll understand faithfulness and authority,
  and uprightness, every good track.
¹⁰Because smartness will come into your mind,
  acknowledgement be lovely to your entire being.
¹¹Strategy will keep watch over you,
  understanding will preserve you,
¹²Rescuing you from the way of the bad person,
  from the one speaking things that are crooked,
¹³People who abandon upright paths,
  going in the ways of darkness,
¹⁴Who rejoice to deal badly,
  celebrate the crooked actions of the bad person,
¹⁵People whose paths are crooked,
  who are deviant in their tracks;
¹⁶Rescuing you from the other woman,
  from the alien woman who is slippery in the things she says,
¹⁷Who abandons the partner of her youth,
  puts out of mind her pact with God.
¹⁸Because her household goes down to death,
  her tracks to the ghosts.
¹⁹Anyone who comes to her doesn't come back;
  he doesn't reach the paths of life;
²⁰In order that you may walk in the way of good people,
  keep the paths of the faithful.
²¹Because the upright will dwell in the country,
  the people of integrity will be left in it.
²²But the faithless will be cut off from the country,
  the people who break faith will be ripped up from it.

Commitment, truthfulness, trust

3 Son, don't put my instruction out of mind;
  your mind is to observe my orders,
²Because length of days and years of life
  and well-being is what they will add to you.
³Commitment and truthfulness must not abandon you;
  bind them on your neck, write them on the tablet of your mind.
⁴Thus find grace and good insight,
  in the eyes of God and of human beings.
⁵Rely on Yahweh with all your mind,
  don't lean on your own understanding.
⁶In all your ways acknowledge him,
  and he himself will keep your paths straight.
⁷Don't become smart in your own eyes;
  live in awe of Yahweh and depart from what's bad.
⁸It will be health for your body,
  a tonic for your bones.
⁹Honour Yahweh with your riches,
  with the first of all your yield.
¹⁰Your barns will fill with plenty,
  your vats will overflow with new wine.
¹¹Don't reject Yahweh's discipline, son,
  don't be dismayed at his reproof.
¹²Because the one Yahweh is loyal to, he reproves,
  just like a father the son he accepts.

The tree of life

¹³The blessings of the person who finds smartness,
  the person who obtains understanding!
¹⁴Because her profit is better than the profit of silver,
  her yield than pale gold.
¹⁵She's more valuable than rubies;
  nothing you delight in equals her.
¹⁶Length of days is in her right hand;
  in her left hand wealth and splendour.
¹⁷Her ways are lovely ones;
  all her trails are well-being.
¹⁸She's a tree of life to people who take strong hold of her;
  one who gets hold of her is blessed.
¹⁹It was by smartness that Yahweh founded the earth;
  he established the heavens by understanding.
²⁰By his knowledge the deeps split,
  and the skies would drop dew.

²¹Son, they must not deviate from your eyes;
  preserve adeptness and strategy.
²²They will be life for your whole person,
  and grace for your neck.

²³Then you'll go your way with confidence,
    and you won't hit your foot.
²⁴If you lie down, you won't be fearful;
    you'll lie down and your sleep will be pleasant.
²⁵You won't be afraid of a sudden terror
    or of the devastation of the faithless when it comes,
²⁶Because Yahweh will be your assurance,
    and will keep your foot from being caught.

²⁷Don't withhold good from the one to whom it's due
    when it's in your hand to act.
²⁸Don't say to your neighbour, 'Go, and come back,
    I'll give it tomorrow', when it's with you.
²⁹Don't devise something bad against your neighbour,
    when he's living with a feeling of security with you.
³⁰Don't argue with someone for nothing,
    if he hasn't dealt you something bad.
³¹Don't be jealous of a violent individual,
    and don't choose any of his ways.
³²Because a deviant person is offensive to Yahweh;
    his confidences are with upright people.
³³Yahweh's curse is on the household of the faithless person,
    but he blesses the home of faithful people.
³⁴If he himself behaves arrogantly to the arrogant,
    to the humble he gives grace.
³⁵Smart people will have splendour as their domain,
    but dimwits take up slighting.

On discipline

4 Listen to a father's discipline, sons,
    heed, so as to acknowledge understanding.
²Because I give you a good grasp;
    don't abandon my instruction.
³Because I was a son to my father,
    tender and the only one before my mother.
⁴He instructed me and said to me,
    'Your mind is to take hold of my words;
    keep my orders and you'll live.'

⁵Acquire smartness, acquire understanding;
    don't put it out of mind and don't turn away
    from the sayings of my mouth.
⁶Don't abandon her and she'll keep you;
    be loyal to her and she'll protect you.

⁷The first principle of smartness is, acquire smartness,
    and among all the things you acquire, acquire understanding.
⁸Exalt her and she'll elevate you;
    she'll honour you when you embrace her.
⁹She'll give your head a graceful garland,
    she'll present you with a glorious diadem.
¹⁰Listen, son, and take my sayings,
    and the years of your life will be many.
¹¹I instruct you in the way of smartness,
    I direct you in upright tracks.
¹²As you go, your step will not be in straits;
    if you run, you won't collapse.
¹³Take a strong hold of discipline, don't slacken hold,
    preserve it, because it's your life.
¹⁴Don't come on to the path of faithless people,
    don't walk in the way of people who deal badly.
¹⁵Avoid it, don't pass through it;
    turn from it and pass by.
¹⁶Because they won't sleep if they don't act badly;
    they're robbed of their sleep if they don't make someone collapse.
¹⁷Because they eat bread that comes from faithlessness
    and drink wine that comes from violent acts.
¹⁸But the path of the faithful is like dawn light,
    getting more light until the establishing of the day.
¹⁹The way of faithless people is very darkness;
    they don't acknowledge how they will collapse.

On resisting temptation

²⁰Son, heed my words,
    bend your ear to the things I say.
²¹They must not deviate from your eyes;
    keep them within your mind.
²²Because they are life to the people who find them,
    health for one's whole body.
²³Above everything that you keep watch over,
    preserve your mind,
    because from it things go out into life.
²⁴Keep away from you crookedness of mouth;
    put deviousness of lips far away.
²⁵Your eyes must turn forward,
    your eyelids be straight ahead of you.

⁲⁶Weigh the track for your foot;
 all your ways must be firm.
²⁷Don't turn right or left;
 keep your foot away from evil.

5 Heed my smartness, son,
 bend your ear to my understanding,
²So as to keep strategy,
 and so that your lips may protect knowledge.
³Because the lips of an alien woman drip honey,
 her mouth is smoother than oil.
⁴But her end is as bitter as gall,
 sharp as a two-edged sword.
⁵Her feet go down to death,
 her steps take hold of She'ol.
⁶So that she doesn't weigh the path to life,
 her tracks wander, though she doesn't acknowledge it.
⁷So now, sons, listen to me,
 and don't depart from the sayings of my mouth.
⁸Keep your way far from her,
 don't go near the entrance to her house,
⁹So that you don't give your wealth to other people,
 your years to someone cruel,
¹⁰So that strangers don't eat their fill of your energy,
 and [the fruit of] your pains are in the house of a foreigner.
¹¹You'll groan at your end,
 when your flesh and body are finished.
¹²You'll say, 'How I was hostile to discipline,
 and my mind spurned rebuke.
¹³I didn't listen to my instructors' voice,
 I did not bend my ear to my teachers.
¹⁴I was soon in every kind of bad situation
 in the middle of the assembled congregation.'

Crazy for love

¹⁵Drink water from your cistern,
 running water from within your well.
¹⁶Should your fountains gush outside,
 your streams of water in the squares?
¹⁷They should be for you alone,
 so that there's none for strangers with you.
¹⁸May your spring be blessed,
 may you rejoice in the wife of your youth,
¹⁹She's a doe to love,
 a graceful deer.
Her breasts should drench you all the time;
 be crazy on her love continually.
²⁰Why be crazy on a stranger, son,
 and embrace the arms of a foreigner?
²¹Because an individual's ways are in front of Yahweh's eyes;
 he weighs all his tracks.
²²His wayward acts capture the faithless person;
 he gets taken hold of by the ropes of his wrongdoing.
²³That person dies for lack of discipline;
 he's crazy on the abundance of his denseness.

6 Son, if you've given a guarantee for your neighbour,
 clapped the palms of your hands for a stranger,
²Trapped yourself by the sayings of your mouth,
 caught yourself by the sayings of your mouth:
³Do this then,
 son, and rescue yourself.
When you've come into the palm of your neighbour's hand,
 go, lower yourself, press your neighbour.
⁴Don't give sleep to your eyes
 or slumber to your eyelids.
⁵Rescue yourself like a gazelle from the hand,
 like a bird from the hand, of a hunter.

⁶Go to the ant, you sloth,
 look at its ways and get smart.
⁷One that has no commander,
 overseer, or ruler,
⁸Prepares its bread in summer,
 gathers its food at harvest.
⁹How long will you lie down, you sloth,
 when will you get up from your sleep?
¹⁰A little sleep, a little slumber,
 a little folding of the hands to lie down,
¹¹And your destitution will come like someone walking about,
 your want like someone with a shield.

¹²Someone who is a scoundrel, an evil individual,
 going with a crooked mouth,
¹³Winking his eyes, speaking with his feet,
 pointing with his fingers,
¹⁴Crooked actions in his mind, devising something bad;
 all the time he lets loose disputes.
¹⁵Therefore suddenly his disaster will come on him,
 in an instant he'll break, with no healing.

Jealousy and wrath

¹⁶These are six things Yahweh is hostile to,
 seven offensive to his entire being:
¹⁷Haughty eyes, a false tongue,
 and hands shedding the blood of someone free of guilt,
¹⁸A mind devising troublesome intentions,
 feet hurrying to run to something bad,
¹⁹Someone who breathes out lies as a false witness,
 and someone who lets loose disputes between brothers.

²⁰Son, observe your father's order,
 don't leave your mother's instruction.
²¹Fasten them into your mind continually,
 bind them on to your neck.
²²When you're going about, it will lead you,
 when you lie down it will keep watch over you,
 when you wake up, it will talk to you.
²³Because an order is a lamp and instruction is a light,
 and the rebuke that disciplines is a way to life,
²⁴To keep you from the woman who is bad,
 from the smoothness of the tongue of an alien woman.
²⁵Don't desire her beauty in your heart;
 she must not take you with her eyelids.
²⁶Because for a woman who's a whore,
 [the cost is] as much as a loaf of bread.
 But a man's wife,
 she'll capture your dear life.
²⁷Can someone scoop up fire into the fold of his coat,
 and his clothes will not burn?
²⁸If someone walks about on coals,
 will his feet not burn?
²⁹So it is with one who has sex with his neighbour's wife;
 no one who touches her will go free.
³⁰People don't despise a thief when he steals
 to fill his appetite, when he's hungry.
³¹But if he's found out, he'll make good sevenfold;
 he'll give all the riches of his household.
³²One who commits adultery with a woman is lacking in sense;
 one who does it is devastating himself.
³³He'll find injury and slighting;
 his reviling will not wipe away.
³⁴Because jealousy means a man's wrath;
 he won't spare on the day of redress.
³⁵He won't show regard for any compensation;
 he won't agree, even when you offer a big bribe.

Let me tell you a story

7 Son, keep my words,
 store up my orders with you.
²Keep my orders and live,
 and my instruction as the apple of your eye.
³Fasten them on your fingers,
 write them on the tablet of your mind.
⁴Say to smartness, 'You're my sister',
 and call understanding 'Friend',
⁵To keep you from the alien woman,
 the foreign woman who is smooth in the things she says.

⁶Because through the window of my house,
 by way of my lattice, I looked out,
⁷And I saw among the naïve, I considered among the young men,
 a youth lacking in sense.
⁸He was passing along the street by her corner,
 he was walking the way to her house,
⁹At dusk, in the evening of the day,
 at the approach of night and darkness.
¹⁰There, a woman to meet him,
 dressed as a whore, restrained in heart.
¹¹She's noisy and defiant;
 her feet don't stay in her house.
¹²Now in the street, now in the squares,
 and by every corner, she lies in wait.
¹³She takes strong hold of him and kisses him,
 makes her face forceful and says to him,
¹⁴'Though well-being sacrifices were incumbent on me,
 today I've made good my pledges.
¹⁵Therefore I've come out to meet you,
 to look urgently for your face, and I've found you.
¹⁶I've spread my couch with coverlets,
 coloured Egyptian linens.
¹⁷I've perfumed my bed,
 with myrrh, aloes and cinnamon.
¹⁸Come on, let's drench ourselves in love until morning,
 let's exult in lovemaking.
¹⁹Because the man isn't here in his house,
 he's gone on a journey a long way.
²⁰He's taken a bag of silver in his hand;
 he'll come home at the middle of the month.'

The story has a solemn end

²¹She's turned him away with the abundance of
her grasp of things,
with the smoothness of her lips she drives him.
²²All at once he's going after her,
like an ox that comes to the slaughter,
Like a dense person bounding into constraint,
²³until an arrow pierces his liver,
Like a bird rushing into a trap,
when it doesn't know it will be at the cost of
its life.

²⁴So now listen to me, sons,
heed the sayings of my mouth.
²⁵Your mind isn't to turn into her ways;
don't wander into her trails.
²⁶Because she's made many fall, run through;
numerous are all the ones killed by her.
²⁷Her house is a major road to She'ol,
going down to death's rooms.

8 Smartness calls, doesn't she;
understanding gives her voice.
²At the highest point along the trail,
at the crossroads, she takes her stand.
³At the side of the gateways at the township entrance,
at the way in to the entrances, she resounds.
⁴'People, I call to you,
my voice is to humankind.
⁵Understand shrewdness, you naïve;
understand sense, you dimwits.
⁶Listen, because I speak honourable things;
the opening of my lips, upright things.
⁷Because my palate murmurs truth;
faithlessness is offensive to my lips.
⁸All the sayings of my mouth are characterized by
faithfulness;
there's nothing crooked or twisted in them.
⁹All of them are straight to someone of
understanding,
upright to people who have found knowledge.
¹⁰Take my discipline and not silver,
knowledge more than choice pale gold.
¹¹Because smartness is better than rubies,
and no delights can compare with her.

Let me tell you my story

¹²I, smartness, dwell with shrewdness;
I find knowledge of strategies.
¹³Awe for God
is hostility to what is bad.
Majesty and majesticness and the bad way,
and a crooked mouth, I am hostile to.
¹⁴Mine are counsel and adeptness;
I am understanding, I have strength.
¹⁵By me kings reign
and rulers decree what is faithful;
¹⁶By me officials govern,
leaders, all who exercise authority faithfully.
¹⁷I am loyal to people who are loyal to me;
people who look urgently for me find me.
¹⁸Wealth and splendour are with me,
enduring riches and faithfulness.
¹⁹My fruit is better than pale gold, even than fine
gold,
my yield than choice silver.
²⁰I walk about in the way of faithfulness,
among the trails of authority,
²¹Giving a domain to people who are loyal with
substance,
and I fill their treasuries.

²²Yahweh acquired me at the beginning of his
way,
before his actions of old.
²³Long ago I was formed,
at the beginning, at earth's origins.
²⁴When there were no deeps I was birthed,
when there were no springs heavy with water.
²⁵Before the mountains were settled,
before the hills I was birthed,
²⁶While he had not yet made the earth and
fields,
and the first of the world's lumps of earth.
²⁷When he established the heavens, I was there,
when he marked out the horizon on the face of
the deep,
²⁸When he made the skies above firm,
when the deep's fountains were vigorous,
²⁹When he set its limit for the sea,
so that its water might not transgress his
bidding.
When he marked out earth's foundations,
³⁰I was a child by his side.
I was full of pleasure day by day,
having fun before him all the time,
³¹Having fun in his world, in his earth,
and full of pleasure in humanity.

³²So now, sons, listen to me:
the blessings of people who keep my ways!

³³Listen to discipline and become smart, don't put it out of mind;
³⁴the blessings of the person who listens to me,
Seeking my gateways keenly day by day,
  keeping watch at the posts of my entrances!
³⁵Because one who finds me finds life,
  and obtains acceptance from Yahweh.
³⁶But one who wrongs me does violence to his life;
  all who are hostile to me are loyal to death.'

The two voices

9 Smartness has built her house;
  she's hewn her seven pillars.
²She's slaughtered her animals, mixed her wine,
  indeed set her table.
³She's sent her girls so she can call,
  on the township's high elevations,
⁴'Whoever is naïve should turn aside here';
  one who is lacking in sense, she says to him,
⁵'Come, eat my bread,
  drink of the wine I've mixed.
⁶Abandon naïvety and live,
  walk in the way of understanding.'

⁷One who disciplines an arrogant person gets slighting for himself;
  one who reproves someone faithless, a hurt for himself.
⁸Don't reprove an arrogant person or he'll be hostile to you;
  reprove someone smart and he'll be loyal to you.
⁹Give something to someone smart and he'll get yet smarter;
  make something known to a faithful person and he'll increase in his grasp.
¹⁰Awe for Yahweh is the beginning of smartness;
  understanding lies in acknowledgement of the Sacred One.
¹¹Because through me your days will be many
  and the years of your life will increase.
¹²If you're smart, you're smart for your benefit;
  if you're arrogant, you'll carry it alone.

¹³The Dimwit Woman is noisy;
  naïvety, and she doesn't acknowledge anything.
¹⁴She sits at the entrance of her house,
  on a seat at the township's heights,
¹⁵Calling to passers-by, people making their paths straight:
¹⁶'Whoever is naïve should turn aside here.'
The person who is lacking in sense, she says to him,
¹⁷'Stolen water is sweet, a secret meal is lovely.'
¹⁸He doesn't acknowledge that the ghosts are there;
  the people she calls are in the depths of She'ol.

The mouth of the faithful is fruitful

10 Shelomoh's aphorisms.

A smart son rejoices a father,
  but a dimwit son is a mother's sorrow.
²Treasures that come from faithlessness don't profit,
  but faithfulness rescues from death.
³Yahweh doesn't let the faithful person go hungry,
  but he thwarts the malice of faithless people.
⁴A lazy fist makes destitute,
  but the hand of determined people makes wealthy.
⁵One who gathers in summer is an insightful son;
  one who sleeps in harvest is a disgraceful son.
⁶There are blessings on the head of the faithful person,
  but the mouth of faithless people conceals violence.
⁷The commemoration of the faithful person becomes a blessing,
  but the name of faithless people rots.
⁸One who is smart of mind accepts orders,
  but one dense of lips comes to ruin.
⁹One who walks in integrity walks in confidence,
  but one who makes his ways crooked gets known.
¹⁰One who winks an eye gives hurt,
  and one dense of lips comes to ruin.
¹¹The mouth of a faithful person is a fountain of life,
  but the mouth of faithless people conceals violence.
¹²Hostility stirs up disputes,
  but loyalty covers over all acts of rebellion.
¹³Smartness is found on the lips of the person of understanding,
  but there's a club on the back of one who is lacking in sense.

¹⁴Smart people store up knowledge,
  but the mouth of a dense person is ruin drawing near.
¹⁵The riches of the wealthy person are his strong township;
  their destitution is the ruin of the poor.
¹⁶The earnings of the faithful person make for life;
  the yield of the faithless person makes for wrongdoing.

The dimwit's real fun

¹⁷One who keeps correction is on the path to life,
  one who abandons reproof goes astray.
¹⁸Someone who conceals hostility with false lips,
  and the one who issues charges, he's a dimwit.
¹⁹Where there's an abundance of words, rebellion doesn't leave off,
  but one who holds back his lips is insightful.
²⁰The tongue of a faithful person is choice silver;
  the mind of faithless people is worth little.
²¹The lips of a faithful person pasture many,
  but dense people die for lack of sense.
²²Yahweh's blessing – it makes wealthy,
  and painful toil doesn't add to it.
²³Real fun for a dimwit is implementing a deliberate wickedness,
  but for someone of understanding, it's smartness.
²⁴The dread of a faithless person – it comes to him,
  but the longing of faithful people is granted.
²⁵When a tempest passes, the faithless person isn't there,
  but the faithful person is a lasting foundation.
²⁶Like vinegar to the teeth, like smoke to the eyes,
  so is the lazy person to the people who sent him.
²⁷Awe for Yahweh prolongs days,
  but the years of the faithless shorten.
²⁸The waiting of faithful people will be rejoicing,
  but the hope of faithless people will perish.
²⁹Yahweh is a stronghold for someone of integrity in his way,
  but the ruin of people who devise trouble.
³⁰The faithful person will never slip,
  but the faithless will not dwell in the country.
³¹The mouth of the faithful person is fruitful with smartness,
  but the crooked tongue will be cut off.
³²The lips of the faithful person know what finds acceptance,
  but the mouth of the faithless, things that are crooked.

On lying scales

11 Lying scales are an offence to Yahweh,
  and a perfect weight is what he accepts.
²Assertiveness comes, and slighting comes,
  but with modest people there is smartness.
³The integrity of the upright guides them,
  but the deviousness of people who break faith destroys them.
⁴Riches don't avail on the day of an outburst [of wrath],
  but faithfulness rescues from death.
⁵The faithfulness of a man of integrity makes his way straight,
  but the faithless person falls by his faithlessness.
⁶The faithfulness of the upright rescues them,
  but people who break faith are captured through malice.
⁷At the death of a faithless person hope perishes,
  and waiting for riches perishes.
⁸The faithful person pulls out from pressure,
  and the faithless person comes in in place of him.
⁹With the mouth the impious person devastates his neighbour,
  but through the knowledge of the faithful, people pull out [from trouble].
¹⁰When things are good for the faithful, the township exults;
  when the faithless perish, there is resounding.
¹¹By the blessing of the upright a township rises up,
  but by the mouth of the faithless it's torn down.
¹²One who despises his neighbour lacks sense,
  and a person of understanding keeps quiet.
¹³Someone who goes about as a slanderer reveals a confidence,
  but someone trustworthy of spirit conceals a thing.
¹⁴When there's no steering, a people falls,
  but deliverance comes with an abundance of counsellors.

¹⁵A bad person will do badly when he stands surety for a stranger,
but someone hostile to people clapping hands will be secure.

The gold ring in a pig's nose

¹⁶A woman of grace takes hold of splendour,
and violent men take hold of wealth.
¹⁷A person of commitment deals to himself;
someone cruel troubles his own self.
¹⁸One who is faithless makes a false profit,
but someone who sows faithfulness,
a trustworthy wage.
¹⁹One established in faithfulness goes to life,
but one who pursues what is bad, to his death.
²⁰The crooked in mind are an offence to Yahweh,
but people of integrity in their way are the ones he accepts.
²¹Hand to hand, the bad person will not go free of guilt,
but the offspring of the faithful will escape.
²²A gold ring in a pig's nose
is a beautiful woman turning aside from discretion.
²³The longing of the faithful is only good;
the hope of the faithless is for an outburst [of wrath].
²⁴There is one who scatters and gets still more,
and one who holds back beyond what is upright, only to be in want.
²⁵A person of blessing will be enriched,
and someone who drenches – he'll also be drenched.
²⁶One who withholds grain – the people will curse him,
but blessing will be on the head of one who sells.
²⁷Someone who urgently looks for what is good seeks acceptance,
but the one who looks for what is bad, it comes on him.
²⁸One who relies on his wealth – he falls,
but the faithful flourish like foliage.
²⁹Someone who troubles his household gets wind as his domain,
and someone dense is a servant to one who is smart of mind.
³⁰The fruit of a faithful person is a tree of life,
but a smart person takes lives.
³¹If someone who is faithful on earth is made good,
how much more the faithless person and the wrongdoer.

The one who knows his animal's appetite

12 One who befriends correction befriends knowledge,
but one who is hostile to reproof is stupid.
²One who is good obtains acceptance from Yahweh,
but he regards a man of strategies as faithless.
³A person cannot be established through faithlessness,
but the root of the faithful will not slip.
⁴A resourceful woman is her husband's crown,
but a shameful one is like decay in his bones.
⁵The intentions of the faithful are the [proper] exercise of authority;
the steering of the faithless is deceit.
⁶The words of the faithless are a deadly ambush,
but the mouth of the upright rescues them.
⁷Overturn the faithless and they're not there,
but the household of the faithful stands.
⁸On the basis of his insight an individual is praised,
but one who's crooked in mind comes to contempt.
⁹Better one who is slighted but is his own servant
than one who looks honourable but lacks bread.
¹⁰A faithful person knows his animal's appetite,
but the compassion of the faithless is cruel.
¹¹One who serves his land will have his fill of bread,
but one who pursues empty things lacks sense.
¹²The faithless person desires what is a trap for bad people,
but the root of the faithful gives.
¹³In the rebellion of lips is a snare for a bad person,
but a faithful person gets out of pressure.
¹⁴From the fruit of an individual's mouth he has his fill of good things,
and the dealing of someone's hands comes back to him.

Silence, words and smartness

¹⁵The way of a dense person is upright in his eyes,
but the smart person listens to counsel.

¹⁶A dense person – his vexation makes itself known at the time,
  but a shrewd person conceals a slighting.
¹⁷Someone who testifies truthfully tells things with faithfulness,
  but a false witness with deceit.
¹⁸There is one who rants like sword-thrusts,
  but the tongue of smart people is a healing.
¹⁹A truthful lip is established permanently,
  but a false tongue lasts for the blink of an eye.
²⁰Deceit is in the mind of people who devise something bad,
  but for people who counsel well-being, there is rejoicing.
²¹No trouble befalls the faithful person,
  but the faithless are full of bad fortune.
²²False lips are an offence to Yahweh;
  people who act truthfully are the ones he accepts.
²³A shrewd person conceals knowledge,
  but the mind of dimwits calls out denseness.
²⁴The hand of determined people rules,
  but [someone characterized by] laziness will belong to a workforce.
²⁵Anxiety in someone's mind weighs it down,
  but a good word makes it rejoice.
²⁶A faithful person shows his neighbour the path,
  but the way of the faithless leads them astray.
²⁷Laziness will not roast game,
  but the riches of a person are valuable – determined.
²⁸On the path of faithfulness there is life,
  and on the way of its trail, no death.

Hope deferred sickens the heart

13 A smart son [listens] to a father's discipline,
  but someone arrogant doesn't listen to a reprimand.
²From the fruit of his mouth a person eats what is good,
  but the appetite of the people who break faith is for violence.
³One who preserves his mouth preserves his life,
  but one who opens his lips wide – ruin is his.
⁴The lazy person – his appetite desires, but there is nothing;
  the appetite of the determined is enriched.
⁵A faithful person is hostile to a lying word,
  but a faithless person stinks and comes to confounding.
⁶Faithfulness preserves [the person of] integrity in the way,
  but faithlessness overturns a wrong[doer].
⁷There is one who acts wealthy but there's nothing,
  one who acts destitute but there's much riches.
⁸The ransom for someone's life is his wealth,
  but one who is destitute doesn't listen to a reprimand.
⁹The light of the faithful rejoices,
  but the lamp of the faithless goes out.
¹⁰Only by means of assertiveness does someone produce strife;
  smartness is with people who take counsel.
¹¹Riches gained from emptiness diminish,
  but someone who gathers by hand makes it grow.
¹²Hope deferred sickens the heart,
  but longing that comes about is a tree of life.

The company you keep

¹³One who despises a word, it will be ruinous for him,
  but one who lives in awe of an order, he'll be made good.
¹⁴The instruction of a smart person is a fountain of life,
  for departing from deadly snares.
¹⁵Good insight gives grace,
  but the way of people who break faith is strong.
¹⁶Every shrewd person acts with knowledge,
  but a dimwit spreads denseness.
¹⁷A faithless envoy falls into bad fortune,
  but a trustworthy emissary – healing.
¹⁸Destitution and slighting – one who rejects discipline,
  but one who keeps watch on correction is honoured.
¹⁹Longing that comes about is pleasant to the appetite,
  but departing from bad ways is an offence to the dimwit.
²⁰One who walks with smart people gets smart,
  but the friend of dimwits does badly.
²¹Bad fortune pursues wrongdoers,
  but good fortune makes good to the faithful.
²²A good man gives a domain to grandchildren,
  but the resources of the wrongdoer are stored up for the faithful person.

²³The fallow ground of the destitute – abundance of food,
 but it's swept away for want of the exercise of authority.
²⁴Someone who holds back his club is hostile to his son,
 but one who loves him gets him up early with discipline.
²⁵The faithful person eats to fill his appetite,
 but the stomach of the faithless lacks.

Even in laughter a heart may hurt

14 The smartest of women builds her house,
 but denseness tears it down with her own hands.
²One who lives in awe of Yahweh walks in uprightness,
 but one who despises him is deviant in his ways.
³In the mouth of the dense person there is a shoot of majesty,
 but the lips of smart people keep watch over them.
⁴When there are no oxen the stall is clean,
 but there's abundance of yield through the energy of a bull.
⁵A trustworthy witness doesn't lie,
 but a false witness testifies lies.
⁶Someone arrogant seeks smartness and there is none,
 but knowledge is easy for the person of understanding.
⁷Go at a distance from the dimwit;
 you won't have known knowledgeable lips.
⁸The smartness of someone shrewd means understanding his way,
 but the denseness of dimwits is deception.
⁹Dense people are arrogant about reparation,
 but between upright people there is acceptance.
¹⁰The heart knows its own bitterness,
 and in its rejoicing a stranger doesn't share.
¹¹The house of the faithless will be devastated,
 but the tent of the upright will flourish.
¹²There is a way that is upright before someone,
 but its end is the ways of death.
¹³Even in laughter a heart may hurt,
 and rejoicing – its end may be grief.
¹⁴Someone who turns backwards in heart will be full from his ways,
 and a good person from his deeds.
¹⁵A naïve person trusts in anything,
 but someone shrewd understands his step.
¹⁶A smart person is afraid and turns aside from what is bad,
 but a dimwit rages and is confident.

Oppressing the poor reviles their maker

¹⁷One who is short-tempered will do dense things,
 and a person of strategies will meet with hostility.
¹⁸The naïve get denseness as their domain,
 but the shrewd wear a crown of knowledge.
¹⁹Bad people bow down before good people,
 and the faithless at the gateways of someone faithful.
²⁰Even with his neighbour someone destitute meets with hostility,
 but the friends of a wealthy person are many.
²¹One who despises his neighbour is a wrongdoer,
 but one who is gracious to the humble: his blessings!
²²People who devise bad things go astray, don't they,
 but people who devise good things: commitment and truthfulness.
²³In all painful toil there will be profit,
 but the word of lips: only being in want.
²⁴Their wealth is the crown of the smart,
 but the denseness of dimwits is denseness.
²⁵A truthful witness saves lives,
 but one who testifies lies, deceit.
²⁶In awe for Yahweh, vigorous security,
 and for one's children it will be a shelter.
²⁷Awe for Yahweh is a fountain of life,
 to depart from deadly snares.
²⁸The glory of a king lies in the abundance of a people,
 and in the absence of a nation lies the ruin of a ruler.
²⁹Long-temperedness is abundant in understanding,
 but shortness of spirit exalts denseness.
³⁰A healthy mind is life for the flesh,
 but passion is rot for the bones.
³¹One who oppresses a poor person reviles his maker,
 but one who is gracious to a needy person honours him.

³²In his bad fortune a faithless person is thrown down,
  but a faithful person finds shelter when he's dying.
³³In the mind of a person of understanding smartness settles,
  and in the middle of dimwits it makes itself known.
³⁴Faithfulness exalts a nation,
  but wrongdoing is a reproach to peoples.
³⁵The acceptance of a king [will be] towards an insightful servant,
  but his outburst will be [towards] a shameful one.

A gentle response turns back wrath

15 A gentle answer turns back wrath,
  but a painful word arouses anger.
²The tongue of the smart makes knowledge good,
  but the mouth of dimwits pours out denseness.
³Yahweh's eyes are in every place,
  observing the bad and the good people.
⁴A healing tongue is a tree of life,
  but deviation in it is brokenness in spirit.
⁵A dense person spurns his father's discipline,
  but one who keeps watch on reproof shows shrewdness.
⁶The house of the faithful person: much riches,
  but in the yield of the faithless, trouble.
⁷The lips of the smart spread knowledge,
  but the mind of dimwits – not so.
⁸The sacrifice of the faithless is an offence to Yahweh,
  but the plea of the upright is acceptable to him.
⁹The way of the faithless person is an offence to Yahweh,
  but he is loyal to one who pursues faithfulness.
¹⁰Discipline is bad to one who abandons the path,
  but one who is hostile to reproof dies.
¹¹She'ol and Abaddon are in front of Yahweh;
  how much more the minds of human beings.
¹²Someone arrogant doesn't befriend one who reproves him;
  he doesn't go to the smart.
¹³A rejoicing heart makes the face good,
  but by hurt in the heart the spirit is crushed.
¹⁴The mind of a person of understanding seeks knowledge,
  but the mouth of dimwits feeds on denseness.
¹⁵All the days of a humble person are bad,
  but a good heart is a continual feast.
¹⁶Better a little with awe for Yahweh,
  than much treasure and turmoil with it.

Better a helping of greens when love is there

¹⁷Better a helping of greens when love is there,
  than a fattened bull when hostility is with it.
¹⁸A wrathful man stirs up a dispute,
  but one who is long-tempered calms an argument.
¹⁹The way of a lazy person is like a hedge of thorn,
  but the path of the upright is cleared.
²⁰A smart son rejoices his father,
  but a dim-witted man despises his mother.
²¹Denseness is a joy to one who lacks sense,
  but a person of understanding makes his going upright.
²²Intentions get contravened when there is no counsel,
  but with an abundance of counsellors they get implemented.
²³In the answer of his mouth there is rejoicing for a person,
  and a word at its time – how good!
²⁴The path of life is upwards for someone insightful,
  in order to depart from She'ol below.
²⁵Yahweh tears down the house of the majestic,
  but establishes the boundary of the widow.
²⁶Bad intentions are an offence to Yahweh,
  but lovely sayings are pure.
²⁷One who gets dishonest gain troubles his household,
  but one who is hostile to a gift will live.
²⁸The mind of a faithful person murmurs so as to answer,
  but the mouth of faithless people pours out bad things.
²⁹Yahweh is far away from the faithless,
  but listens to the plea of the faithful.
³⁰The lamp of the eyes rejoices the heart;
  good news enriches the bones.
³¹The ear that listens to life-giving reproof lodges among the smart.
³²One who leaves go of discipline despises himself,
  but one who listens to reproof acquires sense.
³³Awe for Yahweh is smartness's discipline;
  lowliness is before splendour.

Yahweh weighs spirits

16 ¹The ordering of the mind belongs to a human being,
but the answer of the tongue comes from Yahweh.
²All an individual's ways are clean in his eyes,
but Yahweh weighs spirits.
³Roll your actions on to Yahweh,
and your intentions will be established.
⁴Every deed of Yahweh is for what it answers,
even the faithless person for a bad day.
⁵Anyone lofty of mind is an offence to Yahweh;
hand to hand he won't go free of guilt.
⁶By commitment and truthfulness waywardness is expiated,
and with awe for Yahweh there's a departing from anything bad.
⁷When Yahweh accepts an individual's ways,
he causes even his enemies to be at peace with him.
⁸Better is a little with faithfulness
than abundance of yield without judgement.
⁹The mind of a person thinks out his course,
but Yahweh establishes his step.
¹⁰There is divination on a king's lips;
in giving judgement, one doesn't trespass against his bidding.
¹¹Balance and scales for judgement belong to Yahweh;
all the stones in the bag are his making.
¹²Acting with faithlessness is an offence to kings,
because the throne stands on faithfulness.
¹³Faithful lips are what kings accept;
he's loyal to one who speaks upright things.
¹⁴The king's wrath is death's envoy,
but someone smart will expiate it.
¹⁵There is life in the light of the king's face,
and his acceptance is like a cloud with spring rain.
¹⁶Acquiring smartness – how much better than pale gold,
and acquiring understanding is to be chosen rather than silver.

Majesty, loftiness; brokenness, collapsing

¹⁷The causeway of the upright: departing from anything bad;
one who preserves his way keeps his life.
¹⁸Majesty goes before brokenness,
loftiness of spirit before collapsing.
¹⁹Lowliness of spirit with the humble
is better than sharing plunder with the majestic.
²⁰One who is insightful about a thing will find good fortune,
and one who relies on Yahweh, his blessings.
²¹One who is smart of mind is called understanding,
and sweetness of lips increases people's grasp.
²²The insight of people who possess it is a fountain of life,
but denseness is the discipline of dense people.
²³The mind of someone smart makes his speech insightful,
and on his lips it increases people's grasp.
²⁴Lovely sayings are a honeycomb,
sweet to the entire being and healing for the body.
²⁵There is a road that is right before someone,
but its end is roads that lead to death.
²⁶The appetite of a labourer labours for him,
because his mouth is pressing on him.
²⁷A scoundrel digs for bad things,
and on his lip is a veritable scorching fire.
²⁸A crooked person lets loose a dispute,
and a gossip separates a friend.
²⁹A violent person misleads his neighbour,
and makes him go in a way that isn't good.
³⁰A person winks his eyes in thinking up crooked things;
he purses his lips when he's finished something bad.
³¹Grey hair is a glorious crown;
it's found by way of faithfulness.
³²Better to be long-tempered than a strong man,
and one ruling over his spirit than one taking a town.
³³The lot is cast in the fold of the coat,
but every ruling it makes is from Yahweh.

Yahweh tests minds

17 ¹Better a dry bit of bread and ease with it,
than a house full of sacrifices with arguments.
²An insightful servant will rule over a disgraceful son,
and share in the domain among the brothers.
³The crucible for silver, the furnace for gold,
and Yahweh tests minds.

⁴Someone who deals badly heeds a lip that brings trouble;
  falsehood gives ear to a malicious tongue.
⁵One who ridicules a destitute person reviles his maker;
  one who rejoices at disaster will not go free of guilt.
⁶Grandchildren are the crown of elders,
  and their parents are the glory of children.
⁷A plentiful tongue isn't fitting for a villain,
  much less a false tongue for a leader.
⁸A bribe is a gracious stone in its owner's eyes;
  wherever he turns his face, he'll thrive.
⁹One who seeks loyalty covers over rebellion,
  but one who repeats a thing separates a friend.
¹⁰A reprimand gets down into a person of understanding,
  more than lashes into a dimwit – a hundred.
¹¹A bad person seeks only rebellion,
  but a cruel envoy will be sent off against him.
¹²Let a bereaved bear meet with someone,
  but not a dimwit in his denseness.
¹³Someone who gives back something bad for something good –
  bad fortune will not move away from his household.
¹⁴The beginning of a dispute releases water,
  so before contention breaks out, abandon it.

A rejoicing heart enhances healing

¹⁵One who declares a faithless person faithful or declares a faithful person faithless,
  both of them are an offence to Yahweh.
¹⁶Why is the price in a dimwit's hand
  for acquiring smartness, when he has no sense?
¹⁷A neighbour is a friend at any time;
  a brother is born for pressure.
¹⁸Someone lacking in sense claps the palm of his hand,
  standing surety before his neighbour.
¹⁹One who likes rebellion likes strife;
  one who makes his entrance lofty seeks breaking down.
²⁰Someone crooked of mind doesn't find good fortune,
  and someone who twists with his tongue falls into bad fortune.
²¹One begets a dimwit to one's grief,
  and the father of a villain doesn't rejoice.
²²A rejoicing heart enhances healing,
  but a crushed spirit dries up bones.
²³A faithless person takes a bribe from the fold of his coat,
  to bend the paths of the exercise of authority.
²⁴Smartness is before someone of understanding,
  but the eyes of the dimwit are at the end of the earth.
²⁵A dimwit son is a vexation to his father,
  and bitterness to the one who gave birth to him.
²⁶Surely penalizing a faithful person is not good –
  striking down leaders for uprightness.
²⁷One who has knowledge holds back his words;
  a person of understanding is cool of spirit.
²⁸Even a dense person, keeping silence, is thought smart;
  one who keeps his lips closed, understanding.

Yahweh's name is a refuge

18 One who isolates himself seeks what he longs for;
  he breaks out against all adeptness.
²The dimwit doesn't delight in understanding,
  but rather in disclosing his thinking.
³When a faithless person comes, contempt also comes,
  and with slighting comes reviling.
⁴The words from someone's mouth are deep water;
  a fountain of smartness is a flowing wadi.
⁵Showing regard to the faithless person is not good,
  by turning away the faithful person when exercising authority.
⁶The lips of a dimwit come into an argument,
  and his mouth calls to blows.
⁷The mouth of a dimwit is his ruin,
  and his lips are a snare for his life.
⁸The words of a gossip are like bites of food,
  and they go down into the inner rooms of the stomach.
⁹Really, one who slackens in his work –
  he is brother to a master of devastation.
¹⁰Yahweh's name is a strong tower,
  into which the faithful person runs and is high up.
¹¹A wealthy person's riches are his strong township,
  and like a high wall, in his thinking.

¹²Before being broken, someone's mind is lofty,
  but before splendour comes lowliness.

A crushed spirit – who can bear it?

¹³One who gives word back before he listens –
  it's his denseness and shame.
¹⁴A person's spirit sustains his illness,
  but a crushed spirit – who can bear it?
¹⁵An understanding mind acquires knowledge,
  and the ear of smart people seeks knowledge.
¹⁶A person's gift widens the way for him,
  and conducts him before big people.
¹⁷The first person in a dispute seems in the right,
  then his neighbour comes and examines him.
¹⁸The lot stops disputes,
  and separates numerous people.
¹⁹A brother acting rebelliously is stronger than a strong township,
  and disputes are like the barrier of a citadel.
²⁰From the fruit of someone's mouth his stomach gets full;
  from the yield of his lips he gets full.
²¹Death and life are in the hand of the tongue;
  those who love it eat its fruit.
²²When someone finds a wife, he finds something good,
  and obtains acceptance from Yahweh.
²³The destitute person speaks prayers for grace,
  but the wealthy person answers fierce things.
²⁴There are neighbours to act like neighbours,
  and there's one who's loyal, sticking firmer than a brother.

Riches make many friends

19 Better one who's destitute who walks with integrity
  than one who's crooked with his lips and he's a dimwit.
²Surely without knowledge appetite isn't good,
  and one who's hasty on his feet goes wrong.
³A person's denseness overturns his way,
  but his mind rages against Yahweh.
⁴Riches make many friends,
  and a poor person becomes separate from his friend.
⁵A false witness will not go free of guilt,
  one who testifies lies will not escape.
⁶Many seek the goodwill of a leader,
  and everyone befriends the person with a gift.
⁷All the brothers of a destitute person are hostile to him –
  how much more do his neighbours keep their distance from him;
  someone who pursues things to say – he doesn't have them.
⁸One who acquires sense befriends himself;
  one who keeps understanding finds good fortune.
⁹A false witness will not go free of guilt,
  and one who testifies lies will perish.
¹⁰Luxury isn't fitting for a dimwit,
  certainly not for a servant to rule over officials.
¹¹A person's insight lengthens his anger,
  and his glory is to pass over an act of rebellion.
¹²The king's rage is a growl like a lion's,
  and his acceptance is like dew on grass.
¹³A dimwit son is malicious to his father,
  but a woman's disputes are a continuing drip.
¹⁴House and riches are a domain from parents,
  but a woman of insight comes from Yahweh.

The peril of laziness

¹⁵Laziness makes deep sleep fall,
  and a slack person gets hungry.
¹⁶One who keeps an order keeps his life;
  one who despises his ways will die.
¹⁷One who's gracious to a poor person lends to Yahweh,
  and he'll make good to him for his dealing.
¹⁸Discipline your son when there's hope,
  and don't apply yourself to putting him to death.
¹⁹One who's big in wrath carries a penalty;
  if you rescue him, you'll do it again.
²⁰Listen to counsel and accept discipline,
  in order that you may be smart when you come to the end.
²¹Many intentions may be in a person's mind,
  but Yahweh's counsel is the one that gets implemented.
²²A person's longing is his reproach,
  but a destitute person is better than a liar.
²³Awe for Yahweh leads to life;
  one eats one's fill, spends the night, doesn't fear bad fortune.
²⁴The lazy person buries his hand in the bowl;
  he can't even bring it back to his mouth.

²⁵Strike down someone arrogant and the naïve person will become shrewd;
reprove someone of understanding – he'll understand knowledge.
²⁶One who destroys a father, puts a mother to flight,
is a son who brings shame and confounding.
²⁷Son, leave off listening to discipline,
and you'll stray from words of knowledge.
²⁸A witness who's a scoundrel is arrogant towards the exercise of authority,
and the mouth of faithless people swallows trouble.
²⁹Acts of authority are prepared for the arrogant,
and blows for the back of dimwits.

Drink is noisy

20 ¹Wine is arrogant, drink is noisy,
and anyone who goes astray through them isn't smart.
²The king's dreadfulness is a growl like a lion's;
one who infuriates him wrongs himself.
³Ceasing from an argument is splendour for a person,
but every dense person breaks out.
⁴After autumn the lazy person doesn't plough,
and he asks at harvest, and there's nothing.
⁵The counsel in someone's mind is deep water,
but someone understanding can draw it up.
⁶An abundance of people may call out, 'a person of commitment',
but a person of truthfulness who can find?
⁷A faithful person walks about with integrity –
the blessings of his children after him!
⁸A king sitting on a throne of judgement
winnows all that's bad with his eyes.
⁹Who can say, 'I've kept my mind clean,
I'm pure from my offence'?
¹⁰Different stones, different measures,
both of them are an offence to Yahweh.
¹¹It is indeed by his deeds that a youth lets himself be recognized,
whether his action is clean and whether it's upright.
¹²The ear listens, the eye sees;
Yahweh made both of them.
¹³Don't love sleep, so that you don't become poor;
open your eyes, be full of bread.
¹⁴'Bad, bad', says the buyer,
and goes off, then takes pride.
¹⁵There is gold and abundance of jewels,
but lips with knowledge are a valuable object.

Don't say, 'I'll recompense a bad deed'

¹⁶Take his garment, because he made a pledge to a stranger;
bind him, on account of a foreign woman.
¹⁷Dishonest bread is pleasant to someone,
but afterwards his mouth will fill with gravel.
¹⁸Intentions are established through counsel;
do battle with steering.
¹⁹One who reveals a confidence goes about as a slanderer;
don't share with someone who has his lips open.
²⁰One who slights his father and his mother,
his lamp will go out at the approach of darkness.
²¹A domain hastened at the beginning,
at the end of it will not be blessed.
²²Don't say, 'I'll make good for a bad deed';
hope in Yahweh and he'll deliver you.
²³Different stones are an offence to Yahweh;
deceptive scales are not good.
²⁴A man's steps come from Yahweh;
how can someone understand his way?
²⁵It's a snare when someone is wild regarding making something sacred,
and consults after vows.
²⁶A smart king winnows faithless people,
and turns back the wheel over them.
²⁷The breath of a person is Yahweh's lamp,
revealing all the rooms in your insides.
²⁸Commitment and truthfulness protect a king;
he maintains his throne by commitment.
²⁹The glory of youths is their energy;
the magnificence of elders is their grey hair.
³⁰Blows that wound scour things that are bad,
and beatings, the rooms of one's insides.

The way of a man can be strange

21 ¹The king's mind is a water channel in Yahweh's hand,
which he bends wherever he wants.
²Someone's entire way is upright in his own eyes,
but Yahweh weighs minds.
³Exercising authority in a faithful way
is to be chosen for Yahweh over a sacrifice.

⁴Exaltedness of eyes and wideness of mind:
   the fallow ground of the faithless is
      wrongdoing.
⁵The intentions of the determined person do end
      up in gain,
   but anyone who's hasty does end up in want.
⁶Working for treasures by means of a false
      tongue
   is a breath driven away, people seeking death.
⁷The destructiveness of the faithless sweeps them
      off,
   because they refuse to exercise [proper]
      authority.
⁸The way of a man: twisting, and strange,
   but his action: clean and upright.
⁹Living on a corner of the roof is better
   than a disputatious woman and a shared house.
¹⁰The appetite of the faithless person desires what
      is bad;
   his neighbour isn't graced in his eyes.
¹¹Through the punishing of someone arrogant a
      naïve person gets smart,
   and through gaining insight into someone
      smart he gets knowledge.
¹²One who is faithful gains insight into the
      household of the faithless person,
   turning over the faithless to their bad fortune.
¹³One who shuts his ear to the cry of the poor
      person –
   he too will call and not be answered.
¹⁴A gift in secret calms anger,
   a bribe in the fold of the coat, vigorous wrath.
¹⁵Exercising authority means rejoicing for the
      faithful
   but ruin to one who brings trouble.
¹⁶Someone who wanders from the way of insight
   will settle down in the congregation of ghosts.

The sacrifice of the faithless is an offence

¹⁷One who loves rejoicing: a person in want;
   one who loves wine and oil will not get wealthy.
¹⁸The faithless person is a ransom for someone
      faithful,
   and one who breaks faith, in place of upright
      people.
¹⁹Living in a wilderness region is better
   than a disputatious and vexatious woman.
²⁰Desirable treasure and oil are in the home of
      someone smart,
   but a dimwit of a person will swallow them up.
²¹One who pursues faithfulness and commitment
   finds life, faithfulness and splendour.
²²Someone smart went up to a town of strong
      men
   and brought down the stronghold in which it
      was confident.
²³One who keeps his mouth and his tongue
   keeps his life from pressures.
²⁴The assertive, presumptuous person – arrogant
      his name –
   acts in an outburst of assertiveness.
²⁵The longing of the lazy person puts him to
      death,
   because his hands have refused to act.
²⁶All day someone may feel longing,
   but the faithful gives and doesn't hold back.
²⁷The sacrifice of the faithless is an offence,
   yes, because he brings it with a deliberate
      wickedness.
²⁸A lying witness will perish,
   but someone who listens to the end will speak.
²⁹A faithless person looks forceful in his face,
   but one who is upright – he understands his
      way.
³⁰There's no smartness, there's no understanding,
   there's no counsel in front of Yahweh.
³¹The horse is prepared for the day of battle
   but the deliverance belongs to Yahweh.

Rich and poor meet

22 A name is to be chosen rather than
      much wealth;
   grace is better than silver and than gold.
²Wealthy and destitute meet;
   Yahweh makes all of them.
³Someone shrewd sees something bad and hides;
   naïve people pass on and pay the penalty.
⁴The effect of lowliness is awe for Yahweh,
   wealth, splendour and life.
⁵Thorns (traps) are in the way of the crook;
   one who keeps watch on his life stays far from
      them.
⁶Initiate a youth with regard to his way;
   even when he gets old, he won't depart from it.
⁷The wealthy person rules over the destitute,
   and the borrower is a servant to the one who
      lends.
⁸One who sows evil will reap trouble;
   the club with which he expresses his outburst
      will be finished off.

⁹One who is good of eye will be blessed,
　because he gives of his bread to the poor person.
¹⁰Drive out the arrogant person and dispute will depart;
　judgement and slighting will cease.
¹¹One who is loyal to being pure in mind,
　grace on his lips, the king is his friend.
¹²Yahweh's eyes preserve knowledge,
　but he overturns the words of one who breaks faith.
¹³Someone lazy says, 'A lion in the street,
　in the middle of the square I shall be murdered!'
¹⁴The mouth of alien women is a deep pit;
　one condemned by Yahweh falls there.
¹⁵Denseness is bound up in a youth's mind;
　the club of discipline will take it far away from him.
¹⁶One who oppresses the poor person: it's to make much for himself;
　one who gives to the wealthy person: it's only to come to want.

Thirty sayings: from 1 to 5

¹⁷Bend your ear, listen to smart people's words,
　and apply your mind to my knowledge.
¹⁸Because it will be lovely when you keep them inside you;
　they will be prepared all at once on your lips.
¹⁹So that your reliance may be on Yahweh,
　I enable you to know them today – yes, you.
²⁰I've written for you thirty, haven't I,
　with counsels and knowledge,
²¹To enable you to know the truest of truthful sayings,
　so as to take back sayings in truthfulness to the people who send you.

²²[1] Don't rob the poor person because he's poor,
　and don't crush the humble person at the gateway.
²³Because Yahweh will argue their cause,
　and despoil the people who despoil them of life.
²⁴[2] Don't befriend someone characterized by anger,
　and you will not come with someone of frequent wrath,
²⁵So that you don't learn his paths,
　and get a snare for your life.
²⁶[3] Don't be among the people who clap the palm of the hand,
　among the people who stand surety for debts.
²⁷If you have nothing to make good with,
　why should someone take your bed from under you?
²⁸[4] Don't remove an age-old boundary mark,
　one that your ancestors made.
²⁹[5] You've beheld someone quick at his work?
　– he'll stand before kings,
　he won't stand before people who are in the dark.

Thirty sayings: from 6 to 14

23 [6] When you sit to dine with a ruler,
　understand well who is before you.
²Put a knife to your throat
　if you're someone with an appetite.
³Don't long for his titbits,
　given that it's a lying meal.

⁴[7] Don't get weary in order to become wealthy;
　out of your understanding, leave off.
⁵Should your eyes flit upon it, it's gone,
　because it definitely makes itself wings;
　like an eagle, it flies to the heavens.

⁶[8] Don't eat the meal of someone who is bad of eye,
　and don't be desirous of his titbits.
⁷Because like a hair in the throat, so is he;
　he says to you, 'Eat and drink',
　but his heart isn't with you.
⁸The bit you've eaten you'll throw up,
　and ruin your lovely words.

⁹[9] In the ears of a dimwit don't speak,
　because he'll despise the insight of your utterances.

¹⁰[10] Don't remove an age-old boundary mark,
　and don't come into the fields of orphans.
¹¹Because their restorer is strong;
　he'll argue their cause with you.

¹²[11] Bring your mind to discipline,
　and your ear to knowledgeable sayings.

¹³[12] Don't withhold discipline from a youth;
    if you strike him down with a club, he won't die.
¹⁴You may strike him down with a club,
    and rescue his life from She'ol.

¹⁵[13] Son, if your mind is smart,
    my mind will rejoice, mine too.
¹⁶My inner being will exult,
    when your lips speak with uprightness.

¹⁷[14] Your mind must not be jealous of wrongdoers,
    but rather of [people who live in] awe for
        Yahweh all day.
¹⁸Rather there will be a future,
    and your hope will not cut off.

Thirty sayings: from 15 to 18

¹⁹[15] You, my son, listen, and be smart,
    and direct your mind on the way.
²⁰Don't become among the people who toss down wine,
    among those who gorge themselves on meat.
²¹Because one who tosses down and gorges will
        lose his possession,
    and slumbering will clothe him in rags.

²²[16] Listen to your father who begot you,
    and don't despise your mother when she's old.
²³Acquire truth, don't sell it –
    smartness, discipline and understanding.
²⁴The father of someone faithful will truly celebrate,
    the one who begets someone smart will rejoice
        in him.
²⁵May your father and your mother rejoice,
    the one who gave birth to you celebrate.

²⁶[17] Give your mind to me, son,
    may your eyes preserve my ways.
²⁷Because a whore is a deep pit,
    a foreign woman is a narrow well.
²⁸Indeed, she lies in wait as if for prey,
    and multiplies the people who break faith
        among humanity.

²⁹[18] Who has 'Oh', who has 'Aagh',
    who has disputes, who has talk,
Who has wounds for nothing,
    who has bleary eyes?
³⁰People who linger over wine,
    who come to investigate mixed wine.

³¹Don't look at wine because it's red,
    because it gives its eye in the chalice,
    goes about smoothly.
³²At its finish it bites like a snake,
    poisons like a viper.
³³Your eyes will see strange things,
    your mind will speak twisted things.
³⁴You'll become like someone lying down in the
        middle of the sea,
    like someone lying down on the top of the rigging.
³⁵'Though they struck me down, I didn't hurt,
    though they beat me, I didn't know.
When will I wake up? –
    I'll seek it once again!'

Thirty sayings: from 19 to 30

24 [19] Don't be jealous of bad people,
    don't desire to be with them.
²Because their mind mutters destruction,
    and their lips speak of oppression.

³[20] By smartness a house gets built,
    and by understanding it gets established.
⁴By knowledge its rooms get filled
    with all valuable and lovely riches.

⁵[21] A smart man is vigour itself,
    someone knowledgeable firms his energy.
⁶Because by steering you do battle to your advantage,
    and deliverance comes through an abundance
        of counsellors.

⁷[22] Smartness is too high for a dense person;
    at the gateway he doesn't open his mouth.

⁸[23] While they may call one who intends to deal
        badly
    'a master of strategies',
⁹Dense deliberate wickedness, an expression of
        denseness, is wrongdoing,
    and an arrogant person is an offence to people.

¹⁰[24] Should you slacken on a day of constraint,
    your energy will be constrained.

¹¹[25] Rescue people who are being taken off to
        death,
    who are slipping towards slaughter; if you hold
        back . . .

¹²When you say, 'There, we didn't know this',
   the one who weighs minds will discern, won't he.
The one who preserves your life, he will know,
   and will give back to a person in accordance with his deed.
¹³[26] Eat syrup, son, because it's good,
   liquid honey, sweet to your palate.
¹⁴In this way acknowledge smartness for your appetite;
   if you find it, there's a future,
   and your hope will not be cut off.
¹⁵[27] Don't lie in wait, faithless one, at the home of a faithful person,
   don't destroy his dwelling.
¹⁶Because seven times a faithful person may fall, and rise,
   but the faithless will collapse through one bad fortune.
¹⁷[28] When your enemy falls, don't rejoice,
   and when he collapses, your heart should not celebrate,
¹⁸So that Yahweh doesn't see and it's bad in his eyes,
   and he turns back his anger from him.
¹⁹[29] Don't get heated at people who do bad things,
   don't get jealous of the faithless,
²⁰Because there's no future for the bad person;
   the lamp of the faithless goes out.
²¹[30] Live in awe of Yahweh, son, and of the king,
   and don't share with people who are changing,
²²Because suddenly disaster may arise for them,
   and ruin from both of them: who can know?

Another set of sayings

²³These also belong to the sages.

Recognizing the person in exercising authority isn't good:
²⁴someone saying to the faithless person 'You're in the right.'
Peoples curse him,
   nations condemn him.
²⁵But for people who issue reproof, things will be lovely,
   and upon them will come the blessing of good things.
²⁶He kisses with the lips,
   the one who speaks back with straight words.
²⁷Prepare your work outside,
   get it ready in the fields for yourself;
   afterwards build your house.
²⁸Don't become a witness against your neighbour for nothing;
   will you mislead with your lips?
²⁹Don't say, 'As he did to me, so I'll do to him,
   I'll give back to the man in accordance with his deed.'
³⁰I passed by the field of someone lazy,
   and by the vineyard of one lacking sense.
³¹There, it had all come up in weeds,
   chickpeas covered its surface,
   its stone wall was torn down.
³²When I myself beheld, I applied my mind;
   when I saw, I grasped some discipline.
³³A little sleep, a little slumber,
   a little folding of the hands to lie down,
³⁴And your destitution comes walking about,
   your want like someone with a shield.

Golden apricots in silver settings

25 These, too, are aphorisms of Shelomoh, which the men of Hizqiyyahu [Hezekiah] king of Yehudah compiled.

²It's God's splendour to conceal a thing,
   but kings' splendour to explore a thing.
³The heavens regarding height, the earth regarding depth,
   and the mind of kings – there's no exploring.
⁴Remove dross from silver,
   and an article comes out for the smith;
⁵Remove the faithless person before a king,
   and his throne is established in faithfulness.
⁶Don't magnify yourself before a king,
   and don't stand in the place of big people,
⁷Because it's better for someone to say to you 'Go up there',
   than move you down before a leader.

What your eyes have seen
  ⁸should not go out into an argument quickly,
In case – what will you do at the end of it,
  when your neighbour puts you to shame?
⁹Argue for your cause with your neighbour,
  but don't reveal someone else's confidence,
¹⁰In case someone who hears it reproaches you
  and the charge against you doesn't turn back.
¹¹Golden apricots in silver settings
  is a word appropriately spoken.
¹²A gold earring or an ornament of fine gold
  is someone smart reproving into a listening ear.
¹³Like the cold of snow at harvest time
  is a trustworthy envoy to the people who sent him;
  he brings back his lord's soul.
¹⁴Clouds and wind but no rain
  is someone who takes pride in a false gift.

A gentle tongue can break a bone

¹⁵Through being long-tempered a commander can be enticed;
  a gentle tongue can break a bone.
¹⁶When you find syrup, eat enough for yourself,
  so that you don't get your fill of it and throw up.
¹⁷Make your foot rare at your neighbour's house,
  so that he doesn't get his fill of you and become hostile to you.
¹⁸A hammer, a sword, a sharpened arrow,
  is someone who testifies against his neighbour as a false witness.
¹⁹A bad tooth and a wobbly foot,
  is confidence in someone who breaks faith on a day of pressure.
²⁰One who takes off a coat on a cold day,
  vinegar on a wound,
  and a singer of songs to a bad heart.
²¹If someone hostile to you is hungry, give him bread to eat;
  if he's thirsty, give him water to drink,
²²Because you're heaping coals on his head,
  and Yahweh will make good to you.
²³A north wind may give birth to rain,
  and a secretive tongue a condemning face.
²⁴Living on a corner of the roof is better
  than a disputatious woman and a shared house.
²⁵Cold water to a dry throat
  is good news from a far-off land.
²⁶A muddied spring, a ruined fountain,
  is a faithful person slipping before a faithless person.
²⁷Eating much syrup isn't good,
  nor is it splendid to investigate people's splendour.
²⁸A town that's been opened up, where there's no wall,
  is someone for whose spirit there's no restraint.

The dimwit

26 Like snow during summer and like rain during harvest,
  so splendour is not fitting for a dimwit.
²Like a sparrow flitting and like a swallow flying,
  so being slighted for nothing will not come about.
³A whip for a horse, a bridle for a donkey,
  and a club for the back of dimwits.
⁴Don't answer a dimwit in accordance to his denseness,
  so that you don't become like him, you too.
⁵Answer a dimwit in accordance with his denseness,
  so he doesn't become smart in his own eyes.
⁶Someone cutting off his feet, drinking violence,
  sending words by means of a dimwit.
⁷Legs hang down from someone disabled,
  and an aphorism in the mouth of dimwits.
⁸Like binding a stone in a sling,
  so is one who gives splendour to a dimwit.
⁹A thorn grows up into the hand of a drunk
  and an aphorism in the mouth of dimwits.
¹⁰An archer running through everyone
  and one who hires a dimwit or hires people passing through.
¹¹As a dog goes back to its vomit,
  a dimwit repeats his denseness.
¹²I've seen someone smart in his own eyes;
  there's hope for a dimwit more than for him.
¹³A lazy person says, 'There's a lion cub on the road,
  a lion among the squares.'
¹⁴The door turns on its hinge,
  the lazy person on his bed.
¹⁵The lazy person buries his hand in the bowl;
  he's too weary to bring it back to his mouth.
¹⁶The lazy person is smarter in his own eyes
  than seven people speaking back with discretion.

When there's no gossip, disputes go quiet

¹⁷One who takes strong hold of the ears of a passing dog
   is one who bursts out in an argument that isn't his.
¹⁸Like a madman who is shooting
   fiery arrows of death,
¹⁹So is someone who beguiles his neighbour
   and says, 'I was having fun, wasn't I.'
²⁰In the absence of wood a fire goes out,
   and when there's no gossip, disputes go quiet.
²¹Charcoal for embers and wood for a fire,
   and a disputatious person for heating up an argument.
²²The words of a gossip are like bites of food,
   and they go down into the rooms of the stomach.
²³Silver dross laid over a pot,
   burning lips but a bad mind.
²⁴With his lips a hostile person disguises himself;
   inside him, he puts deceit.
²⁵When he makes his voice gracious, don't trust him;
   because seven offences are in his mind.
²⁶His hostility will be concealed by deception;
   his bad action will reveal itself in a congregation.
²⁷One who digs a pit will fall into it;
   one who rolls a stone, it will come back on to him.
²⁸A false tongue is hostile to the people crushed by it;
   a smooth mouth works a pushing down.

Trustworthy are the wounds of a friend

27 Don't take pride in tomorrow,
   because you don't know what a day will give birth to.
²A stranger should praise you and not your mouth,
   a foreigner and not your lips.
³A stone is weighty and sand is heavy,
   but a dense person's vexation is heavier than both of them.
⁴The cruelty of wrath and the flooding of anger:
   but who can stand before jealousy?
⁵Reproof openly expressed is better
   than friendship concealed.
⁶The wounds of a friend are trustworthy;
   the kisses of someone hostile are importunate.
⁷Someone full despises honey,
   but someone hungry: anything bitter is sweet.
⁸Like a sparrow flitting from its nest,
   so is someone flitting from his place.
⁹Oil and incense rejoice the heart,
   and the sweetness of one's friend, more than one's own counsel.
¹⁰Don't abandon your friend or your father's friend,
   and don't come to your brother's house on your day of disaster.
Better one who dwells near
   than a brother far away.
¹¹Be smart, son, and rejoice my heart,
   so I may speak back to one who reviles me with a word.
¹²When someone shrewd sees something bad, he hides;
   naïve people pass on and pay the penalty.
¹³Take his garment, because he made a pledge to a stranger;
   bind him, on account of a foreign woman.

The crucible of praise

¹⁴One who blesses his neighbour in a loud voice
   in the morning, early:
   it will be thought of for him as a slighting.
¹⁵A continuing drip on a rainy day,
   and a disputatious woman, are similar.
¹⁶People who hide her could hide the wind,
   or he could grasp oil in his right hand.
¹⁷Iron sharpens iron,
   and a person sharpens the face of his friend.
¹⁸One who guards a fig tree will eat its fruit,
   and one who keeps watch on his lord will be honoured.
¹⁹Like water, face to face,
   so the heart of a person to a person.
²⁰She'ol and Abaddon don't get full,
   and the eyes of a human being don't get full.
²¹A crucible for silver, a furnace for gold,
   and an individual for a mouth praising him.
²²If you grind the dense person in a mortar,
   in the middle of the grain in a pestle,
   his denseness will not depart from him.
²³You should really know the faces of your flock,
   apply your mind to your herds,
²⁴Because riches aren't permanent
   or a crown for generation after generation.

²⁵Hay goes away and new grass appears
    and the growth of the mountains is gathered.
²⁶Lambs are for your clothing,
    goats for the price of a field,
²⁷Enough goats' milk for your meal,
    for a meal for your household and life for your young girls.

¹³One who covers his rebellions will not succeed,
    but one who confesses and abandons will be shown compassion.
¹⁴The blessings of the person who continually reveres,
    whereas one who toughens his mind falls to bad fortune.

Interest and profiteering

28 The faithless flee when there's no one pursuing,
    but faithful people are as confident as a lion.
²When there's rebellion in the country,
    its rulers are many.
But when there's someone who understands,
    someone who knows, established order will last long.
³A man who is destitute and who oppresses the poor:
    rain beating down and there's no bread.
⁴People who abandon instruction praise the faithless person;
    people who keep instruction fight against them.
⁵Bad people don't understand the exercise of authority,
    but people who seek Yahweh understand everything.
⁶Better someone destitute walking in integrity,
    than someone crooked in his ways, but he's wealthy.
⁷An understanding son observes instruction,
    but one who befriends gluttons disgraces his father.
⁸Someone who increases his riches through interest and profiteering
    amasses it for someone who will be gracious to the poor.
⁹One who turns his ear aside from listening to instruction:
    even his plea is an offence.
¹⁰One who misleads the upright into a bad way,
    he'll fall into his own pit, but people of integrity get good things as their domain.
¹¹A wealthy person is smart in his own eyes,
    but a poor person of understanding can search him out.
¹²At the exulting of the faithful there's much glorying,
    but at the rise of the faithless, people have to be searched for.

The peril of shutting the eyes

¹⁵A roaring lion or an advancing bear:
    a faithless ruler over a poor people.
¹⁶A leader lacking understanding and abundant in acts of oppression;
    one hostile to dishonest gain will extend his days.
¹⁷When one oppressed by shedding someone's blood
    flees to a cistern, people should not take hold of him.
¹⁸A person who walks in integrity will find deliverance,
    but one who's crooked in his ways will fall at once.
¹⁹One who serves his land will be full of bread,
    but one who pursues empty things will be full of destitution.
²⁰A person of trustworthy deeds will be abundant in blessings,
    but one hasty to get wealthy will not go free of guilt.
²¹Recognizing a person isn't good,
    but a man may rebel for a bit of bread.
²²One who is bad in eye hurries for riches,
    and doesn't acknowledge that lack will come to him.
²³One who reproves a person in the end
    will find more grace than one who makes his tongue smooth.
²⁴One who robs his father and his mother
    and says 'It's not an act of rebellion' –
    he is a companion of one who devastates.
²⁵One wide of appetite provokes dispute,
    but one who relies on Yahweh will be enriched.
²⁶One who relies on his own mind – he's a dimwit,
    but one who walks in smartness – he'll escape.
²⁷One who gives to a destitute person – there's no lack,
    but one who shuts his eyes – many are the curses.
²⁸When the faithless rise up, people hide,
    and when they perish, the faithful become many.

You could suddenly break and there could be no healing

29 ¹A person of many reproofs who toughens his neck
will suddenly break, and there will be no healing.
²When the faithful increase, the people rejoice,
but when a faithless person rules, the people groan.
³Someone who loves smartness rejoices his father,
but one who befriends whores obliterates riches.
⁴A king enables a country to stand by the exercise of authority,
but a man of great deceit tears it down.
⁵A man who flatters his neighbour
spreads a net for his steps.
⁶In the rebellion of someone bad there's a snare,
but a faithful person resounds and rejoices.
⁷A faithful person acknowledges the cause of the poor;
a faithless person doesn't understand acknowledgement.
⁸Arrogant people stir up a township,
but the smart turn back anger.
⁹Someone smart may enter into judgement with a dense person,
but he'll rage and have fun and there'll be no settlement.
¹⁰People inclined to bloodshed may be hostile to someone of integrity,
but the upright will seek the person out.
¹¹A dimwit lets all his spirit out;
someone smart holds it back.
¹²A ruler who gives heed to a false word:
all his ministers will be faithless.
¹³A destitute man and a man given to deceit meet:
Yahweh enlightens the eyes of them both.

How the throne will stand firm

¹⁴A king who exercises authority for the poor in truth:
his throne will be established permanently.
¹⁵Club and reproof give smartness,
but a youth sent off shames his mother.
¹⁶When the faithless increase, rebellion increases,
but the faithful will see their downfall.
¹⁷Discipline your son and he'll enable you to settle down,
and give much delight to your entire being.
¹⁸When there's no vision, the people throw off restraint,
but someone who keeps instruction – his blessings!
¹⁹By words a servant will not be disciplined,
when he understands but there's no answer.
²⁰If you behold someone hasty with his words,
there's hope for a dimwit more than for him.
²¹Someone who indulges his servant from youth:
at the end he'll become his offspring.
²²Someone angry provokes a dispute,
and someone given to wrath rebels much.
²³A person's majesty will make him fall,
but one lowly of spirit will take hold of splendour.
²⁴Someone who shares with a thief is hostile to himself;
he hears the oath and doesn't tell.
²⁵A person's trembling sets a snare,
but one who relies on Yahweh will be set on high.
²⁶Many seek the regard of a ruler,
but the ruling about a person comes from Yahweh.
²⁷An evildoer is an offence to the faithful,
and someone upright in his way is an offence to the faithless person.

I'm just a weary sojourner but I have some words from God

30 ¹Words of Agur ben Yaqeh. The oracle. The man's pronouncement to Iti'el, to Iti'el and Ukal.

²Truly I'm a brute more than a person,
and I don't have human understanding.
³I haven't learned smartness
and I don't possess the knowledge of the sacred ones.
⁴Who has gone up to the heavens and come down,
who has gathered the wind in his open hands?
Who has confined the water in a cloak,
who has set all earth's ends?
What is his name and what is his son's name,
if you know?
⁵Everything God says is tested;
he's a shield to those who take shelter with him.
⁶Don't add to his words,
so that he doesn't reprove you and you prove a liar.

⁷Two things I ask of you;
    don't hold back from me before I die.
⁸Emptiness and a lying word keep far from me,
    destitution and wealth don't give me,
    let me grab the bread that is my due,
⁹So that I don't get full and renounce
    and say, 'Who is Yahweh?'
Or so that I don't get poor and rob,
    and take the name of my God.

¹⁰Don't mention a servant to his lord,
    in case he slight you, and you're liable.

¹¹A generation that slights its father,
    and doesn't bless its mother!
¹²A generation that's pure in its own eyes,
    but its filth isn't washed off!
¹³A generation – how its eyes are high,
    and its eyelids rise!
¹⁴A generation whose teeth are swords,
    and their jaws knives,
To consume the humble from the earth,
    the needy from humanity!

Creation and numbers

¹⁵The leech has two daughters,
    'Give, give!'
These are three things that don't get full,
    four that don't say 'Plenty!' –
¹⁶She'ol, a barren womb,
    a country that isn't full of water,
    and fire that doesn't say 'Plenty!'

¹⁷The eye that ridicules a father
    and despises obedience to a mother:
The ravens in the wadi will gouge it out,
    and young eagles will eat it.

¹⁸Those are three things too extraordinary for me,
    four that I don't know:
¹⁹An eagle's way in the heavens,
    a snake's way on a crag,
A ship's way in the heart of the sea,
    and a man's way with a girl.

²⁰Such is the way of an adulterous woman:
    she eats and wipes her mouth,
    and says, 'I haven't brought trouble.'

²¹Under three things the earth shudders,
    and under four that it cannot bear:
²²Under a servant when he becomes king,
    and villain when he's full of bread,
²³Under a woman who has met with hostility
    when she marries,
    and a maidservant when she dispossesses her mistress.

²⁴Those are four smallest things on earth,
    but they are the smartest of the smart:
²⁵Ants are a people not strong,
    but they prepare their bread in summer;
²⁶Hyraxes are a people not numerous,
    but they make their home in a cliff;
²⁷Locusts have no king,
    but they go out organized, all of them;
²⁸You can take hold of a lizard in your hands,
    but it's in a king's palaces.

²⁹Those are three things good in their stride,
    four that are good in moving:
³⁰The lion is the strong man among animals,
    it doesn't turn back from before anyone;
³¹One belted round the hips; or a goat;
    and a king – no rising against him.

³²If you've been villainous in exalting yourself,
    and if you've schemed – hand on your mouth!
³³Because pressing milk issues in butter,
    pressing the nose issues in blood,
    and pressing anger issues in an argument.

The demon drink

31 The words of King Lemu'el. A pronouncement with which his mother disciplined him.

²What, my son, what, son of my womb,
    what, son of my pledges?
³Don't give your resources to women,
    your ways to women who wipe out kings.
⁴It's not for kings, Lemuel,
    not for kings to drink wine,
    and for rulers, or liquor.
⁵In case they drink and put out of mind what has been decreed,
    and are hostile to the cause of all humble people.
⁶Give liquor to someone who is perishing,
    wine to one who is bitter inside.

⁷He can drink and put out of mind his destitution,
   and his oppression he won't keep in mind any
      more.
⁸Open your mouth for the dumb,
   for the cause of all the people who are passing
      away.
⁹Open your mouth, exercise authority faithfully,
   give judgement for the humble and needy
      person.

The resourceful woman

¹⁰Who can find a resourceful woman?
   – her value is far above rubies.
¹¹Her husband's mind relies on her,
   and he lacks no spoil.
¹²She deals him good, not bad,
   all the days of her life.
¹³She looks for wool and flax,
   and works with delight with the palms of her
      hands.
¹⁴She becomes like a trader's ships,
   when she brings her bread from far away.
¹⁵She rises while it's still night,
   and gives a bite to her household,
   and an allocation to her girls.
¹⁶She schemes about a field and gets it;
   from the fruit of the palms of her hands she
      plants a vineyard.
¹⁷She wraps her hips in vigour,
   and firms up her arms.
¹⁸She checks that her trading is good;
   her lamp doesn't go out at night.
¹⁹She puts out her hands to the spindle,
   and her palms take hold of the wheel.
²⁰She opens her palm to the humble person,
   puts out her hands to the needy person.
²¹She isn't afraid for her household because of
      snow,
   because her entire household is dressed in
      crimson.
²²She makes coverlets for herself;
   her clothing is linen and purple.
²³Her husband is acknowledged at the gateways,
   as he sits with the country's elders.
²⁴She makes fabric and sells it,
   and gives a sash to the merchant.
²⁵Vigour and magnificence are her clothing;
   she can make fun of a future day.
²⁶She opens her mouth with smartness;
   committed instruction is on her tongue.
²⁷She watches over the goings of her household;
   she doesn't eat the bread of laziness.
²⁸Her children rise up and declare her blessed;
   her husband praises her:
²⁹'Many women produce resources,
   but you surpass all of them.'
³⁰Grace is false, beauty is hollow,
   but a woman who lives in awe of Yahweh –
      she is to take pride.
³¹Give to her from the fruit of her hand;
   her deeds should praise her at the
      gateways.

Ecclesiastes

Ecclesiastes is one of the most reassuring books in the Bible in the way it encourages us to face facts about how life is. Whereas Proverbs majors on positive aspects to the way life works out, Ecclesiastes acknowledges that things are more complicated than a first, surface reading of Proverbs might seem to imply. Often Ecclesiastes proceeds by quoting the kind of observation that appears in Proverbs and saying 'Yes, but . . .'

A substantial chunk of the beginning of the book takes Solomon as a test case for looking at life, though the book never mentions Solomon by name. It refers to the author as Qohelet, which is related to the Hebrew word for 'congregation'. I translate it as 'congregant'. An implication of using this name is that this book is proper 'congregational teaching', proper teaching for the people of God. It refers to its 'hero' as 'David's son', which probably suggests Solomon, though there are many other people to whom the phrase applies. But Solomon was the man who had everything – women, wisdom, achievement, power, pleasure. So he provides a test case for whether these things can make life worthwhile. And his answer is, they don't.

It's not that these things are totally useless. They are all worthwhile. But they are not ultimately significant. They don't provide the ultimate answers. In the absence of such ultimate answers, really everything is 'hollow'. This declaration forms a bracket round the book as a whole. When one looks empirically at life in the world, one can see ways in which things make sense and ways in which life is worthwhile, but also ways in which they don't make sense and in which the things that people tell themselves make life worthwhile are not really of ultimate significance. Qohelet encourages us to remember that they are nevertheless things that 'God gives' – that phrase recurs in the book. There's some value in seeking to live a faithful life and in enjoying life with one's family, work, and food and drink. It's not enough, but it's not nothing.

Everything is hollow

1 ¹The words of Congregant, son of David,
king in Yerushalaim.

²Utter hollowness, said Congregant,
  utter hollowness, everything is hollow.
³What value is there for a person
  in all the labour that he undertakes under
    the sun?

⁴A generation goes, a generation comes;
  the earth stands permanently.
⁵The sun rises and the sun sets
  and rushes to its place where it rises.
⁶The wind goes to the south and turns round to
    the north,
  it turns, turns as it goes,
  and on its turnings the wind goes back.
⁷All the wadis go to the sea, but the sea isn't full;
  to the place where the wadis go,
  there they go again.
⁸All the things are laborious;
  no one could speak of it.
The eye isn't replete as regards looking,
  the ear isn't full as regards listening.
⁹What has happened is what will happen;
  what has occurred is what will occur;
  there's nothing new under the sun.
¹⁰Where there is a thing that someone says,
  'See this, it's new',
Already it has happened
  for ages that were before us.
¹¹There is no commemoration for the earlier
    people,
  and also for future people who are to come.
For them there will be no commemoration,
  with the people who will be in the future.

A king's achievement

¹²I, Congregant, began to reign over Yisra'el in Yerushalaim. ¹³I gave my mind to looking into and exploring with smartness everything that occurs under the heavens. It's a bad business God gave human beings to be busy with. ¹⁴I saw all the actions that occur under the sun. There, everything is hollow, a shepherding of wind.

¹⁵Something crooked cannot become straight,
  and something lacking cannot be counted.

¹⁶I myself spoke inside myself: 'Here, I've got big and increased in smartness above everyone who has been over Yerushalaim before me. My mind has seen much of smartness and knowledge. ¹⁷I've given my mind to a knowledge of smartness and a knowledge of madness and apparent insight. I've come to acknowledge that this, too, was a shepherding of wind.

¹⁸Because with abundance of smartness there's
    much vexation,
  and one who increases knowledge increases
    pain.

2 ¹I myself said inside myself, 'Come on, please, I'll test you with rejoicing. Look into what's good.' There, that is also hollow.

²Of having fun, I said, 'It's mad',
  and of rejoicing, 'What does this do?'

³I explored inside myself, stretching my flesh with wine while directing my mind with smartness and taking hold of idiocy, until I could see which one was good for human beings, which they should practise under the heavens for the number of the days of their life. ⁴I made my achievements big. I built houses for myself, I planted vineyards for myself, ⁵I made gardens and parks for myself and planted in them trees with every fruit. ⁶I made pools of water for myself, to water from them a forest flourishing with trees. ⁷I acquired servants and maidservants and ones born in my household. I also had livestock, herd and flock; I had more than all who were before me in Yerushalaim.

Wealth and learning

⁸I also amassed for myself silver and gold and the personal treasure of kings and provinces. I made for myself male and female singers, and the pleasures of human beings, many women. ⁹I got big and increased more than anyone who was before me in Yerushalaim; also my smartness stood with me. ¹⁰Nothing that my eyes asked for did I keep from them. I didn't hold my mind back from any rejoicing; rather, my mind rejoiced in

all my labour. This was my share from all my labour.

¹¹But I myself turned my face to all the things that my hands had done and to the labour that I had put into doing it. There, everything was hollow, a shepherding of wind. There was no value under the sun.

¹²I turned my face to see smartness, madness and idiocy. Because what will the person do who comes after the king? That which people have already done. ¹³I myself saw that

There is value to smartness over idiocy,
  like the value of light over darkness.
¹⁴The smart person – his eyes are in his head,
  but the dimwit walks in darkness.

But I myself also acknowledged that one experience happens to each of them. ¹⁵So I myself said inside myself: like the experience of the dimwit, so it will happen to me, too. So why have I myself then been exceedingly smart? I spoke inside myself: 'This is hollow, too.' ¹⁶Because there's no commemoration permanently of the smart person, just like the dimwit, in that already in the coming days each will have gone out of mind. But how can the smart man die just like the dimwit? ¹⁷So I was hostile to life, because the action that occurs under the sun is bad with me, because everything is hollow, a shepherding of wind.

¹⁸So I myself was hostile to all the labour that I myself have expended under the sun, which I shall leave to the person who will be after me. ¹⁹Who knows whether he'll be a smart person or an idiot? But he'll hold power over all the labour that I've expended and the smartness that I've exercised under the sun. This too is hollow.

Everything has its time

²⁰So I myself turned round to letting myself despair about all the labour that I've expended under the sun. ²¹Because there's a person whose labour was with smartness, with knowledge and with skill, and he gives his share from it to a person who didn't labour for it. This is also hollow, something very bad. ²²Because what does the person have for all his labour and for his mind's shepherding, with which he's laboured under the sun? ²³Because all his days, his busyness is pain and vexation. By night, too, his mind doesn't lie down. This is also hollow.

²⁴There's nothing better with a person than that he eats and drinks and lets himself see good things through his labour. I myself have also seen that this is from God's hand. ²⁵Because who eats and who hastens apart from me? ²⁶Because to the person who is good before him he gives smartness, knowledge and rejoicing, and to the wrongdoer he gives the busyness of gathering and collecting – to give to someone who is good before God.

This too is hollow, a shepherding of wind.

3 Everything has a moment,
  every purpose under the sun has a time:
²A time of birthing, a time of dying,
  a time of planting, a time of uprooting what is planted,
³A time of killing, a time of healing,
  a time of demolishing, a time of building,
⁴A time of crying, a time of having fun,
  a time of wailing, a time of dancing,
⁵A time of throwing stones, a time of collecting stones,
  a time of embracing, a time of staying far from embracing,
⁶A time of searching, a time of obliterating,
  a time of keeping, a time of throwing out,
⁷A time of tearing, a time of mending,
  a time of being silent, a time of speaking,
⁸A time of being loyal, a time of being hostile,
  a time of battle and a time of peace.

⁹What's the value for the person who acts, in what he labours over? ¹⁰I've seen the busyness that God has given human beings to be busy with. ¹¹He's made everything beautiful in its time; he's also put permanence into their mind, but not so that humanity can find out what God has done from the beginning until the end.

There's no justice

¹²I acknowledged that there is nothing good with them except to rejoice and do what's good in their lifetime. ¹³Also, everyone who eats and drinks and sees good things through all his labour – it's God's gift. ¹⁴I acknowledged that

Everything that God does,
   it will be permanent.
To it there is nothing to add,
   and from it, there's nothing to take away.

God has acted so that people live in awe before him.

¹⁵What has happened already is,
   and that which is to happen has already happened.

And God seeks out what has been driven away. ¹⁶Further, I've seen under the sun:

In the place for the [proper] exercise of
   authority, faithlessness was there,
in the place for faithfulness, faithlessness was
   there.

¹⁷I myself said inside myself,

Over the faithful person and the faithless
   God will exercise authority.
Because there will be a time for every purpose
   and for every activity there.

¹⁸I myself said inside myself with regard to human beings, it's for God to purify them and for them to see that they are animals. ¹⁹Because the experience of human beings and the experience of animals is a single experience for them. Like the dying of the one, so is the dying of the other. Each has the same spirit. The advantage of humanity over animals – there is none, because each is hollow. ²⁰Each goes to the same place. Each came into being from earth and each goes back to earth. ²¹Who knows if the spirit of human beings goes up and the spirit of animals goes down beneath the ground?

²²So I saw that there is nothing better than that a person enjoys his activities, because this is his share, because who can give him discernment to see what will happen after him?

4 I again saw all the oppressed people that are appearing under the sun. There, the tears of the oppressed, and there is no comforter for them; yes, from the hand of their oppressors is the energy, and there is no comforter for them. ²I myself extolled the dead people, who had already died, more than the living people, who were still alive. ³Better than both of them is the one who hasn't yet come into being, who hasn't seen the bad activity that occurs under the sun.

Two people who lie together can be warm

⁴I myself saw all labour and all skill in activity: it's the jealousy of a person by his neighbour. This too is hollow, a shepherding of wind.

⁵The dimwit folds his hands,
   and eats his own flesh.

⁶Better a palmful with settlement than two fistfuls with labour, and a shepherding of wind. ⁷I again saw hollowness under the sun. ⁸There's one person, and he has no second person, either son or brother. And there's no end to all his labour; nor is his eye full of wealth. 'But for whom am I labouring and depriving myself of good things?' This too is hollow, a bad business. ⁹Two are better than one, in that they have better reward for their labour. ¹⁰Because if they fall, one can lift up his companion; but alas for the single person who falls and has no second person to lift him up. ¹¹Further, if two people lie down together, they are warm, but for one – how can he be warm? ¹²And if someone overpowers him (the one person), the two can stand up in front of him. And a triple cord doesn't break quickly. ¹³Better a young man who's poor but smart than a king who's old but a dimwit, who doesn't know how to heed a warning any more, ¹⁴because from the prison house he can get out to become king, even when he was born destitute in the kingdom. ¹⁵I saw all the living who walk about under the sun with the youth, the second [king], who stands in place of him. ¹⁶There was no end to all the people, to all before whom he stood; also those who are after him will not rejoice in him. Because this too is hollow, a shepherding of wind.

Sell your tongue and buy a thousand ears

5 Keep watch on your feet as you go to God's house. Drawing near to listen is better than the giving of a sacrifice by dimwits, because they don't acknowledge that they are doing something bad. ²Don't be hasty with your mouth; your mind shouldn't be quick to let out a word before God, because God is in the heavens and you're on the earth. Thus your words should be few. ³Because

A dream comes with an abundance of busyness,
    and the voice of a dimwit with an abundance of words.

⁴When you make a pledge to God, don't delay making it good, because there's no delight in dimwits. What you pledge, make it good. ⁵It's better that you don't make a pledge than that you make a pledge and don't make it good. ⁶Don't give your mouth to causing your flesh to do wrong. Don't say before the envoy, 'It was a mistake.' Why should God be furious at your voice and destroy what your hands have made? ⁷Because in an abundance of dreams is much hollowness, and many words. Rather, live in awe of God.

⁸If you see oppression of the destitute person and violation of the faithful exercise of authority in the province, don't marvel at the matter, because one who is lofty keeps watch over one who is lofty, and ones who are lofty over them. ⁹The value for the land in every way is this: a king for the field that's worked.

It's not enough but it's not nothing

¹⁰Someone who loves silver doesn't have his fill of silver, nor whoever loves riches of his yield. This too is hollow. ¹¹With the increase of his goods, the people who consume them increase, so what's the profit of their owners except his eyes seeing them? ¹²The sleep of someone who serves is sweet whether he eats little or much, but the richness of the wealthy person doesn't leave him to sleep. ¹³There is a sick bad fortune I saw under the sun: wealth kept by its owner to his bad fortune, ¹⁴or that wealth perishes through a bad business; and he fathers a son but there's nothing in his hand. ¹⁵As he got out from his mother's womb, naked he again goes, as he came; he carries nothing of his labour in his hand when he goes. ¹⁶This too is a sick bad fortune. Corresponding to the way he comes, so he goes, and what's the value to him that he labours for the wind? ¹⁷Further, all his days he eats in darkness with much vexation, illness and fury.

¹⁸Here's what I myself saw as good, that it's beautiful to eat and to drink and to see what's good in all his labour that he expends under the sun for the number of the days of his life that God gives him, because this is his share. ¹⁹Further, each person to whom God gives wealth and possessions and whom he empowers to consume some of them, to take up his share and to rejoice in his labour – this is God's gift. ²⁰Because he won't be very mindful of the days of his life, because God busies him with his mind's rejoicing.

Everyone is going to the same place

6 There's something bad that I saw under the sun, and there's much of it with human beings: ²a person to whom God gives wealth, possessions and splendour, and who has no lack regarding his appetite for anything that he desires, but God doesn't empower him to consume any of it, and a stranger consumes it. This is hollow and a bad sickness. ³If a man fathers a hundred children and lives many years, and however many are the days of his years, his appetite can't be full from the good things: then even if it was not buried, I say the stillbirth is better off than him. ⁴Because it comes in hollowness and it goes in darkness, and its name is covered in darkness; ⁵though it doesn't see or know the sun, that one is more settled than the other one.

⁶Even if he lives a thousand years twice over but doesn't see the good things, each is going to one place, isn't he. ⁷All a person's labour is for his mouth, but his appetite doesn't get full. ⁸Because what's the value for the smart person over the dimwit? What does the humble person have, who knows how to walk in front of the living? ⁹The eyes seeing is better than the appetite journeying. This too is hollow, a shepherding of wind.

¹⁰What happens has already been named, and what a person is has become known. He cannot contend with one who is stronger than him, ¹¹because the more words are, the more is the hollowness. What's the value for a person? ¹²Because who knows what is good for

a person in life for the number of the days of his hollow life? He spends them like a shadow, so who can tell the person what will happen under the sun after him?

Better the house of mourning than the house of feasting

7 A good name is better than good oil,
  and the day of death than the day of birth.
² Going to a house of mourning
  is better than going to a house of feasting,
Inasmuch as that is the end of everyone
  and the living person should put it into his mind.
³ Vexation is better than fun,
  because despite a bad look in the face,
  the mind will be good.
⁴ The mind of smart people is in a house of mourning,
  the mind of dimwits in a house of rejoicing.
⁵ It's better to listen to the reprimand of a smart person
  than be listening to the song of dimwits,
⁶ Because the fun of a dimwit
  is like the sound of thistles under a pot.
But this too is hollow,
  ⁷ because fraud can make a fool out of a smart person,
  and a gift can obliterate the mind.
⁸ The end of something is better than its beginning,
  endurance of spirit is better than loftiness of spirit.
⁹ Don't be quick to feel vexed in your spirit,
  because vexation settles in the heart of dimwits.
¹⁰ Don't say, 'How did it happen
  that the former days were better than these?',
  because it's not out of smartness that you ask about this.
¹¹ Smartness is good, like a domain,
  and something valuable to people who see the sun.
¹² Because as smartness is a veritable shelter,
  silver is a veritable shelter.
But the value of knowledge
  is that smartness keeps its masters alive.

¹³ Look at God's activity,
  because who can straighten
  what he has twisted?
¹⁴ In the day when things are good, be with what is good,
  and in the day when things are bad, see:
God made both this one as well as that one,
  with the result that a person cannot find out anything after him.

I haven't found a woman

¹⁵ I've seen everything in my hollow days.

There's a faithful person who perishes in his faithfulness
  and there's a faithless person who endures in his faithlessness.
¹⁶ Don't be exceedingly faithful
  and don't act excessively smart: why should you be devastated?
¹⁷ Don't be exceedingly faithless and don't be idiotic:
  why should you die when it's not your time?
¹⁸ It's good that you take hold of the one
  but also not let go of your grasp of the other,
  because someone in awe of God will go out with all of them.
¹⁹ Smartness strengthens a smart person
  more than ten people holding power who were there in a town.

²⁰ Because there's no faithful human being on earth who does good and doesn't do wrong. ²¹ Further, don't give your mind to all the things that people speak, so that you don't hear your servant slighting you, ²² because many times your mind also knows that you too have slighted other people.

²³ When I tested all this with smartness, I said 'I shall be smart', but it's far away from me. ²⁴ What happens is far away and deep, deep; who can find it out? ²⁵ I myself turned round with my mind to know and to explore, and to seek smartness and thought, and to know faithlessness as dim-wittedness and idiocy as madness.

²⁶ I myself find more bitter than death the woman who is a great trap, whose mind is a great snare, whose hands are a great chain. One who is good before God escapes from her, but a wrongdoer is caught by her. ²⁷ Look, this is what I've found, Congregant said, adding one thing to another to find some thinking, ²⁸ which I myself sought further but didn't find.

I found one human being among a thousand, but a woman among these I didn't find. ²⁹Only, look at this, I found that God made humanity upright, but they have sought many thoughts.

For every purpose there's a time to make a decision

8 Who is like the smart person,
and who knows the meaning of a saying:
'A person's smartness lightens up his face,
and the strength of his face is changed.'
²I [say]: keep the king's bidding,
and on account of the oath to God ³don't be fearful.
You should go out from before him;
don't stand against something bad.
Because he can do anything that he purposes,
⁴in that the king's word has power,
And who can say to him, 'What are you doing?';
⁵one who keeps an order will not know something bad.
And the time to exercise authority
the mind of a smart person will know.
⁶Because for every purpose there's a time to exercise authority,
when what is bad for a person is great for him.
⁷Because he doesn't know what will happen,
because who can tell him when it will happen?
⁸There's no one who has power over the spirit,
to restrain the spirit,
And there's no one who has power
over the day of death.
There's no discharge during a battle,
and faithlessness cannot rescue the people who are masters of it.

⁹All this I saw as I gave my mind to every action that occurs under the sun, the time when a human being held power over a human being, with bad results for him. ¹⁰And then I saw faithless people buried, when they came from the sacred place. They went about and they were put out of mind in the town where they had so acted. This too is hollow.

To eat and to drink and to rejoice

¹¹When the edict regarding something bad isn't enacted quickly, consequently the mind of people inside them is full of dealing badly, ¹²when a wrongdoer does something bad a hundred times, and it is extended for him. Because I do know that

It will be good for people who live in awe of God,
because they live in awe of him,
¹³And it will not be good for the faithless person
and he won't extend his days, like a shadow,
because he doesn't live in awe of God.

¹⁴There's a hollowness that occurs on the earth, that there are faithful people to whom things befall in accordance with the action of the faithless, and there are faithless people to whom things befall in accordance with the action of the faithful. I said, 'This too is hollow.' ¹⁵So I myself extolled rejoicing, because there's no good for a person under the sun except to eat and to drink and to rejoice. That can accompany him in his labour for the days of his life that God has given him under the sun.

¹⁶When I gave my mind to knowing smartness and looking at the busyness that is fulfilled on the earth (because even day and night one does not see sleep with one's eyes), ¹⁷and I looked at all the action of God: a human being cannot find out about the action that is undertaken under the sun. When a human being persists in seeking, he doesn't find. Even if a smart person says he'll know, he cannot find out.

Remember you're going to die . . .

9 Because all this I put into my mind, and I sifted all this, that faithful and smart people and their acts of service are in God's hands. Both love and hostility: a person doesn't know anything beforehand. ²Everything is as it is for everyone. One experience comes to the faithful person and to the faithless, to the good and to the pure and to the polluted, to the person who sacrifices and to the person who doesn't sacrifice. As the good person so is the wrongdoer. The person who swears is like the person who is afraid of an oath. ³This is something bad about everything that occurs under the sun, that there is one experience for everyone.

Further, the mind of human beings is full of bad things and there is madness in their mind during their life, and afterwards – to the dead. ⁴Because whoever is joined to all the living – there is confidence, because a living dog is better than a dead lion. ⁵Because the living know that they will die, but the dead don't know anything. There is no more reward for them, because their commemoration has gone out of mind. ⁶Both their love and their hostility and their passion has already perished. They have no more share permanently in all that occurs under the sun.

⁷Go, eat your bread with rejoicing, drink your wine with a good mind, because God has already approved your actions. ⁸At all times your clothes should be white and oil should not be lacking on your head. ⁹See life with the woman that you love all the days of your hollow life that you've been given under the sun, all your hollow days, because that is your share in life and in your labour that you expend under the sun. ¹⁰Everything that your hand finds to do, do with all your energy, because there is no action, thought, knowledge or smartness in She'ol, where you're going.

. . . and it may be sooner than you think

¹¹I again saw under the sun that

The race doesn't belong to the swift people,
   the battle doesn't belong to the strong people,
Nor bread to the smart people,
   nor wealth to the discerning people,
Nor grace to the knowledgeable people,
   because time and chance happen to all of them.

¹²Rather, a person cannot know his time.

Like fish that are taken in a bad net
   and like birds that are taken by a trap,

like them, human beings are snared by a bad time when it falls on them suddenly. ¹³This too I've seen as smartness under the sun, and it seemed big to me. ¹⁴There was a small town and the people in it were few. A big king came to it, surrounded it and built big strongholds against it. ¹⁵There was found in it a poor man who was smart, and he saved the town by his smartness, but no one was mindful of that poor man. ¹⁶I myself said,

Smartness is better than strength,
   but the poor man's smartness is despised
   and his words are not listened to.
¹⁷The words of smart people with calmness
   are listened to more than the crying out of a ruler among dimwits.
¹⁸Smartness is better than implements of engagement,
   but one wrongdoer can obliterate much good.

10 When dead flies make a stink,
   they ferment the perfumer's oil.
Outweighing smartness, splendour,
   is a little idiocy.
²The mind of a smart person goes to his right,
   the mind of a dimwit goes to his left.
³Further, on a journey, as an idiot goes, his sense is lacking,
   and he tells everyone that he's an idiot.
⁴If the spirit of the ruler arises against you,
   don't let go of your place,
because calmness can let go of great wrongdoings.

The distressing dynamics of smartness and power

⁵There's something bad I've seen under the sun,
   the very error that comes from someone holding power:
⁶Idiocy has been put in many high positions,
   and wealthy people sit in a lowly place.
⁷I've seen servants on horses,
   and officials walking on the ground like servants.
⁸The person who digs a pit falls into it;
   the person who breaks down a wall – a snake bites him.
⁹The person who quarries stones is hurt by them;
   the person who splits logs is endangered by them.
¹⁰If the iron has become dull,
   and he hasn't sharpened it before,
He must exert more force,
   so smartness is a value for giving success.
¹¹If the snake bites when there's no spell,
   there's no value in a master of the tongue.
¹²The words from the smart person's mouth mean grace,
   but the lips of a dimwit swallow him.
¹³The beginning of the words from his mouth is idiocy

and the end of his mouth is bad madness,
¹⁴But the idiot multiplies words,
> though a person doesn't know what will happen.

And what will happen after him,
> who can tell him?

¹⁵The labour of dimwits wearies him,
> because he doesn't know how to go to a town.

¹⁶Alas for you, country whose king is a youth
> and whose ministers eat in the morning.

¹⁷Your blessings, country whose king is one born of important people
> and whose officials eat at the proper time, for strength and not drinking.

¹⁸Through laziness the roof sags,
> through drooping hands the house drips.

¹⁹For fun people make a meal,
> wine rejoices life;
> silver answers everything.

²⁰Even in your thinking don't slight the king,
> and in your bedroom don't slight a wealthy person,

Because a bird of the heavens may make the sound travel,
> an owner of wings may tell of the thing.

Enjoy your life . . .

11 Send off your bread on the surface of the water,
> because in an abundance of days you will find it.

²Give a share to seven or even to eight,
> because you don't know what bad thing may happen on the earth.

³If the clouds fill,
> they will pour down rain on the earth;

If a tree falls
> on the south or on the north,

In the place where the tree falls,
> there it will be.

⁴Someone who keeps watch on the wind will not sow,
> and someone who sees the clouds will not reap.

⁵As you don't know the way of the wind,
> like the limbs in the womb of a pregnant woman,

So you don't know the action of God
> who does everything.

⁶In the morning sow your seed
> and at evening don't let your hand relax,

Because you don't know
> which one will succeed,

This one or the other,
> or if both of them will be equally good.

⁷The light is sweet
> and it's good for the eyes to see the sun.

⁸Because if a person lives many years,
> he should rejoice in all of them.

But be mindful of the days of darkness,
> because they will be many; everything that will come is hollow.

⁹Rejoice, young man, during your youth;
> your mind should make you feel good in the days of your youth.

Walk about in the ways of your mind
> and in the sights of your eyes.

But acknowledge that for all these things
> God will bring you to account.

Mindful of your creator

¹⁰So remove vexation from your mind
> and make what is bad pass from your body

Because youth and vigour are hollow.

12 So be mindful of your creator in the days of your youth,

Before the bad days come,
> and the years arrive of which you'll say, 'There's no purpose for me in them',

²before it goes dark,

The sun, the light, the moon and the stars,
> and the clouds come back after the rain,

³On the day when the keepers of the house tremble,
> and the strong men stoop.

The women who grind stop because they are few,
> and the women who look through the windows get dark.

⁴The gateways to the street are shut,
> as the sound of the mill becomes low.

One gets up at the sound of a bird,
> but all the songs get weak.

⁵Further, people are afraid of a height
> and there are terrors on the road.

The almond blossoms, the grasshopper carries itself along,
> and the caperberry bears fruit.

But the human being is going to his eternal home
> and the mourners are coming round in the street –

⁶Before the silver cord snaps,
  and the gold bowl breaks,
The jar shatters at the spring,
  and the wheel breaks at the cistern,
⁷The earth goes back to the ground as it was,
  and the spirit goes back to the God who gave it.
⁸Utter hollowness, said Congregant,
  utter hollowness, everything is hollow.

⁹But further: because Congregant was smart, he still taught the people knowledge. He weighed and examined, set in order many aphorisms. ¹⁰Congregant sought to find purposeful words, and what is written was upright. Truthful words, ¹¹smart words, are like goads; the masters of collections are like fixed nails. They were given by one shepherd.

¹²But further, beyond these, son, beware. Of the making of many books there is no end, and much study is a wearying of the body. ¹³The end of the thing; everything has been heard. Live in awe of God and keep his orders, because this is for everyone. ¹⁴Because God brings every action to account, including everything hidden, whether good or bad.

The Song of Songs

The expression 'song of songs' means it's 'the best song'. It's a series of poems about the relationship between two people who are in love. They are poems that describe in an imaginative way moments in a relationship. They may all refer to the same relationship or they may be separate imaginative compositions; there are no indications that they are poems that tell one couple's story. The relationship between the two people is evidently exclusive and it implies a commitment that will surely be lifelong, but the two are not living together, so they are apparently not married. Further, they speak of tensions and conflicts in the community over their relationship, so their relationship is apparently not yet 'official' in the community. They are not betrothed, though in their own minds and hearts they are evidently committed.

The opening description of the songs as Solomonic marks them as expressions of wisdom or smartness in the same way as Proverbs and Ecclesiastes. They are the kind of smart teaching of which Solomon was the patron. The description need not imply that he composed the poems, and what we know of him from his story in Kings and Chronicles doesn't suggest he would have had the kind of experience or would think the kind of way that the poems do. Indeed, he would have a lot to learn from them. (In the imaginative picture in chapter 3, the emphasis lies on his opulence and might rather than on his love.)

There are expressions in the poems that can also describe something about relationships between God and his people: 'I belong to my love and he belongs to me.' But there are no indications that the poems were written to illustrate that relationship or that they were included in the Scriptures on that basis. Indeed, while the Scriptures do use marriage as an image for the relationship between God and his people, the kind of marriage they have in mind in that connection is one where the husband is master and the wife is submissive. The relationship portrayed in the Song of Songs is egalitarian rather than hierarchical, so that most of it does not correspond to the way relationships between God and his people work.

Like Proverbs and Ecclesiastes, the poems issue from reflection on how life actually works out, and what they do is invite people to live in the light of the reality that they describe. They would thus have things to say to young couples and also to the wider community. They have things to say about the wonder of the relationship between two people, and also about its frustrations, fears and pressures.

The way Hebrew works often indicates whether a male or a female is the speaker, and in these poems it is therefore generally possible to know when the man is speaking and when the woman is speaking.

Alone together

1 ¹The Song of Songs, which is Shelomoh's [Solomon's].

Woman ²May he kiss me with some of the
        kisses of his mouth! –
    because your love is better than wine.
³The fragrance – your oils are good,
    your name is oil poured out.
Therefore girls love you;
    ⁴pull me after you, let's run.
The king has brought me into his
        rooms;
    let's celebrate and rejoice in you.
Let's make mention of your love more
        than wine;
    rightly they love you.

⁵I am dark but lovely,
    Yerushalaim daughters,
Like the tents of Qedar,
    like Shelomoh's curtains.
⁶Don't look at me because I'm dark-
        skinned,
    because the sun has stared at me.
My mother's sons were enraged with
        me,
    they made me someone who guards
        the vineyards.
My vineyard, the one I had,
    I didn't guard.
⁷Tell me, you whom my entire being
        loves,
    where do you pasture,
    where do you rest them at midday?
Why should I be like someone
        covering herself
    by the flocks of your companions?

Man ⁸If you don't know for yourself,
        loveliest of women,
    Get yourself out in the tracks of the
        flock,
    pasture your goats
        by the shepherds' dwellings.
⁹To a mare among Par'oh's [Pharaoh's]
        chariots
    I have compared you, my dear.
¹⁰Lovely are your cheeks with earrings,
    your neck with necklaces;
¹¹We will make gold earrings for you,
    with studs of silver.

Woman ¹²While the king was on his couch,
        my nard gave its fragrance.
¹³My love to me is a bag of myrrh
    that lodges between my breasts.
¹⁴My love to me is a cluster of henna
    in the vineyards of Gedi Spring.

Man ¹⁵There you are, so lovely, my dear;
    there you are, so lovely, your eyes
        doves.

The crocus and the apricot

Woman ¹⁶There you are so lovely, my love,
    yes beautiful, yes our couch is
        verdant.
¹⁷Cedars are the beams of our house,
    junipers our rafters.
2 I am a crocus of Sharon,
    a lotus of the vales.

Man ²Like a lotus among thorns,
    so is my dear among the daughters.

Woman ³Like an apricot among the trees of the
        forest,
    so is my love among the sons.
In its shade I desired to sit,
    and its fruit was sweet to my palate.
⁴He brought me into the house of wine,
    and love was his standard over me.
⁵Refresh me with raisins, revive me
        with apricots,
    because I'm ill with love.
⁶His left arm under my head,
    his right arm would embrace me.
⁷I want you to swear, Yerushalaim
        daughters,
    by the gazelles or by the deer in the
        fields:
If you awaken, if you arouse love,
    before it wishes . . .

⁸The sound of my love! – there, he's
        coming,
    leaping over the mountains,
    bounding over the hills.
⁹My love is like a gazelle,
    or a young stag.
There, he's standing, behind our wall,
    gazing from the window, peering
        from the lattice.

¹⁰My love affirmed and said to me:
  'Get yourself up, my dear,
  my lovely one, and get yourself going!
¹¹Because there – the winter has passed,
  the rain has stopped and taken itself off.
¹²The blossoms have appeared in the country,
  the time of music has arrived,
The voice of the dove
  has made itself heard in our country.
¹³The fig tree has ripened its green fruit,
  the blossoming vines have given their fragrance.
Get yourself up, my dear,
  my lovely one, and get yourself going!
¹⁴My dove, in the clefts of the crag,
  in the hiddenness of the cliff,
Let me see your appearance,
  let me hear your voice.
Because your voice is pleasing,
  your appearance is alluring.'

¹⁵Catch the foxes for us, the little foxes,
  ruining the vineyards, when our vineyards are in blossom.

My love is mine and I am his

Woman ¹⁶My love belongs to me and I belong to him,
  the one who pastures among the lotuses.
¹⁷While the day breathes and the shadows flee,
  turn round, be like a gazelle, my love,
  or a young stag on the Beter Mountains.

3 On my bed by night, I searched for the one my entire being loves;
  I searched for him but didn't find him.
²'I'll get up, please, and go round the town,
  through the streets and through the squares.
I'll search for the one my entire being loves;
  I've searched for him but not found him.'
³The watchmen found me as they went round the town:
  'Have you seen the one my entire being loves?'
⁴Scarcely had I passed them,
  when I found the one my entire being loves.
I took hold of him and wouldn't slacken hold of him,
  until I'd brought him to my mother's house,
  to the room of the one who conceived me.
⁵I want you to swear, Yerushalaim daughters,
  by the gazelles or by the deer in the fields:
If you awaken, if you arouse love,
  before it wishes . . .

Man ⁶Who is this coming up from the wilderness,
  like columns of smoke,
Perfumed with myrrh and incense,
  from every powder of a merchant?
⁷There, Shelomoh's bed,
  sixty strong men round it,
  of the strong men of Israel.
⁸All of them are girded with a sword,
  trained in battle,
Each with his sword on his side,
  because of the terror of the night.
⁹King Shelomoh had made himself a sedan,
  of wood from the Lebanon.
¹⁰He had made its posts of silver,
  its base of gold, its seat of purple.
Its inside was inlaid with love
  by the Yerushalaim daughters.
¹¹Go out and look, Tsiyyon [Zion] daughters,
  at King Shelomoh in the crown
With which his mother has crowned him on his wedding day,
  on the day of his heartfelt rejoicing.

Crazy for love

Man **4** There you are, so lovely, my dear,
  there you are, so lovely.
Your eyes are doves
  behind your veil.

Your hair is like a flock of goats
   that stream from Mount Gil'ad.
²Your teeth are like a flock of shorn ewes
   that climb up from the washing,
Which are all of them twinning,
   and there's none bereaved among
      them.
³Like a crimson ribbon are your lips;
   your mouth is lovely.
Like the splitting of a pomegranate
   is your brow behind your veil.
⁴Like David's Tower is your neck,
   built in courses,
Hung with a thousand shields on it,
   all the bows of strong men.
⁵Your two breasts are like two fawns,
   the twins of a gazelle pasturing
      among the lotuses.
⁶While the day breathes,
   and the shadows flee,
I'll get myself to the mountain of myrrh,
   to the hill of incense.
⁷Every part of you is lovely, my dear;
   there's no flaw in you.
⁸With me from Lebanon, my bride,
   with me from Lebanon, you should
      come!
You should gaze from the top of
      Amana,
   from the top of Senir and Hermon,
From the abodes of lions,
   from the mountains of leopards.

⁹You've captured my heart, my sister, my
      bride, you've captured my heart,
   with one of your eyes,
   with one strand of your necklace.
¹⁰How beautiful is your love,
   my sister, my bride!
How much better is your love than
      wine,
   the fragrance of your oils than all
      perfumes!
¹¹Your lips drop honey, my bride;
   syrup and milk are under your
      tongue.
The fragrance of your robes
   is like the fragrance of Lebanon.
¹²A locked garden, my sister, my bride,
   a locked fountain, a sealed fountain:
¹³Your shoots are an orchard of
      pomegranates,
   with choice fruit,
Henna with much spikenard,
   ¹⁴spikenard and saffron,
Cane and cinnamon,
   with all the incense woods,
Myrrh and aloes,
   with all the top perfumes:
¹⁵A garden spring,
   a well of living water,
   flowing from Lebanon.

Nightmares and dreams

Woman ¹⁶Awake, north wind, and come, south
         wind,
      breathe on my garden so its
         perfumes may spread.
      May my love come to his garden,
         and eat its choice fruit!

Man **5** I've come to my garden, my sister,
         my bride.
      I've plucked my myrrh with its
         perfume.

Girls Eat, friends, drink,
      get drunk on love.

Woman ²I was sleeping, but my mind was
         awake;
      the sound of my love, knocking!
      'Open for me, my sister, my dear,
         my dove, my perfect one.
      My head is full of dew,
         my hair with the moisture of night.'
      ³'I've taken off my robe; how can I get
         dressed?
      I've washed my feet, how can I get
         them dirty?'
      ⁴My love put out his hand through the
         hole;
      my heart was in turmoil for him.
      ⁵I myself got up to open to my love;
         my hands dripped with myrrh.
      So my fingers were flowing myrrh
         on the hollows of the bolt.
      ⁶I myself opened the door for my love,
         but my love had turned, passed on.
      My entire being had gone out at his
         speaking;
      I looked for him but I didn't find
         him,
      I called him, but he didn't answer me.

⁷The watchmen found me as they went
  round the town;
 they struck me down, injured me.
 They took my shawl from upon me,
  the watchmen on the walls.
⁸I want you to swear, Yerushalaim
  daughters,
 if you find my love:
 What are you to tell him?
  – that I am ill with love.

How is your love more than another love?

Girls ⁹How is your love more than another
  love,
 most beautiful among women?
 How is your love more than another
  love,
 that you want us to swear in that
  way?

Woman ¹⁰My love is radiant and ruddy,
  outstanding among ten thousand.
¹¹His head is gold, fine gold;
  his hair curly, black as a raven.
¹²His eyes are like doves by water
  canyons,
 bathing in milk, sitting by a full pool.
¹³His cheeks like a bed of spice,
  towers of perfumes.
 His lips are lotuses,
  dripping flowing myrrh.
¹⁴His hands are gold rods,
  covered in Tarshish-stone.
 His stomach is an ivory plate,
  overlaid with sapphires.
¹⁵His legs are alabaster pillars,
  founded on sockets of fine gold.
 His appearance is like the Lebanon,
  choice as the cedars.
¹⁶His palate is total sweetness;
  all of him is desirable.
 This is my love, this is my dear,
  Yerushalaim daughters!

Girls **6** Where has your love gone,
  loveliest among women?
 Where has your love turned his face,
  so we may search for him with you?

Woman ²My love has gone down to his garden,
  to the beds of spice,
 To pasture in the gardens,
  and to pick lotuses.
³I belong to my love and my love
  belongs to me,
 the one who pastures among the
  lotuses.

Man ⁴You're beautiful, my dear, as Tirtsah,
  lovely as Yerushalaim, awe-inspiring
  as bannered armies.
⁵Turn your eyes round from in front
  of me;
 they – they overwhelm me.
 Your hair is like a flock of goats
  that stream from Mount Gil'ad.
⁶Your teeth are like a flock of shorn
  ewes
 that climb up from the washing,
 Which are all of them twinning,
  and there's none bereaved among
  them.
⁷Like the splitting of a pomegranate
  is your brow behind your veil.
⁸There are sixty queens,
  eighty secondary wives,
 Girls without number;
⁹my dove, my perfect one, is
  unique.
 She's unique to her mother,
  she's special to the one who gave
  birth to her.
 Daughters have seen her and called her
  blessed;
  queens and secondary wives have
  praised her.

His desire is towards me

Girls ¹⁰Who is this who looks out like the
  dawn,
 beautiful as the moon,
 Special like the sun,
  awe-inspiring as bannered armies?

Woman ¹¹I went down to the garden of nut-
  trees
  to see the blossoms in the wadi,
 To see the budding of the vine,
  whether the pomegranates had
  bloomed.
¹²Though I didn't know,
  my entire being set me with the
  chariots of my generous people.

Girls	¹³Turn back, turn back, Shulammite; Turn back, turn back, so we may behold you!
Man	Why will you behold the Shulammite, like the Mahanayim dance?

7 How beautiful are your feet
 in sandals, noble daughter!
The curves of your hips are like rings,
 the work of a craftsman's hands.
²Your navel is a round bowl;
 mixed wine will not be lacking.
Your waist is a heap of wheat,
 encircled by lotuses.
³Your two breasts are like two fawns,
 the twins of a gazelle.
⁴Your neck is like an ivory tower,
 your eyes are pools at Heshbon,
By the gate of Bat-rabbim,
 your nose like the Lebanon tower,
Watching towards Damascus,
 ⁵your head upon you like Carmel,
The locks on your head like purple;
 a king is captivated by your tresses.
⁶How beautiful you are, how lovely
 you are,
 love with delights;
⁷This, your stature, is like a palm,
 your breasts are clusters.
⁸I've said, I shall climb the palm,
 I'll take hold of its stems.
May your breasts please be like the
 clusters of the vine,
 the fragrance of your breath like
 apricots,
 ⁹your palate like good wine.

Woman	It goes straight to my love,
	    gliding over the lips of sleepers.
	¹⁰I belong to my love
	    and his desire is towards me.
	¹¹Come, my love, let's go out to the
	    fields,
	    let's lodge in the hamlets.
	¹²Let's start early for the vineyards,
	    let's see if the vine has budded,
	The blossom has opened, the
	    pomegranates have bloomed;
	    there I'll give my love to you.
	¹³The mandrakes have given fragrance,
	    and at our doors are all choice
	    things,

Fresh and also old things, my love,
 I've stored for you.

Love is as fierce as death

Woman	**8** If only you could be made like a
	brother to me,
	    one who was nursing at my mother's
	    breasts.
	When I found you in the street I could
	    kiss you;
	    people would not despise me,
	    either.
	²I would lead you, I would bring you,
	    to the house of my mother, the one
	    who taught me.
	I would get you to drink some spiced
	    wine,
	    some of my pomegranate juice.
	³His left hand would be under my
	    head,
	    his right hand would hold me.
	⁴I want you to swear, Yerushalaim
	    daughters, don't awaken,
	    don't arouse love, before it wishes.

Girls	⁵Who is this coming up from the
	    wilderness,
	    leaning on her love?

Woman	Under the apricot tree I aroused you;
	    there your mother conceived you,
	    there the one who gave birth to
	    you conceived you.
	⁶Make me like a seal on your heart,
	    like a seal on your arm.
	Because love is as fierce as death,
	    passion as tough as She'ol.
	Its darts are darts of fire,
	    a supernatural flame.
	⁷Much water could not quench love,
	    nor rivers overflow it.
	If someone gave all his household's
	    resources for love,
	    people would totally despise him.

Boys	⁸We have a little sister;
	    she doesn't have breasts.
	What shall we do for our sister
	    on the day when she's spoken for?
	⁹If she's a wall,
	    we'll build on it a silver battlement.

	If she's a door, 　　we'll enclose it with cedar 　　　　panelling.		¹²My vineyard is before me; 　　the thousand are yours, Shelomoh, 　　and 200 for the people who guard 　　　　the fruit.

Woman　¹⁰I am a wall
　　　　and my breasts are like towers;
　　Then I've become in his eyes
　　　　like one who finds well-being.
　　¹¹Shelomoh had a vineyard
　　　　in Ba'al Hamon;
　　He gave the vineyard to guards;
　　　　someone would give for its fruit
　　　　a thousand silver pieces.

Man　¹³You who live in the gardens, with
　　　　friends listening:
　　let me hear your voice.

Woman　¹⁴Take flight, my love,
　　　　be like a gazelle,
　　Or like a young stag,
　　　　on the mountains of spices.

Isaiah

The book of Isaiah [Yesha'yahu] is a collection of prophecies addressed to the people of Judah. Isaiah lived in the eighth century BC, a time of crisis for Judah associated with the expansion of the Assyrian Empire into the region. A major focus of Isaiah's prophecies concerns how Judah needs to deal with different aspects of the challenge this crisis brings.

- Chapters 1—12 give dates in the time of King Ahaz, the 730s, when Ephraim and Syria are leaning on Judah to resist Assyria, and Isaiah urges Judah to trust God for its future.
- Chapters 13—23 speak of what God intends to do in relation to the other peoples around Judah, so as to urge Judah not to be afraid of them but not to trust them either.
- Chapters 24—27 widen the horizon to speak of God's purpose for the world as a whole.
- Chapters 28—39 return to focus directly on Judah, but now in the time of King Hezekiah, the 700s, when Ephraim and Syria have fallen and Judah is seeking help from Egypt in order to resist Assyria.

Isaiah's prophecies are thus quite coherently organized on a large scale, though readers are often bemused about the train of thought within these major collections of chapters. The chapters collect short prophecies delivered on different occasions. So any given chapter probably brings together several separate prophecies that did not originally belong together.

Isaiah wants Judah and its king to live by trust in the commitment Yahweh made to David and his successors and to Jerusalem as the place where he himself deigned to dwell. The promises that work out God's commitment to David are ones that help us understand Jesus. But in origin they brought God's word to his people in Isaiah's day. So Christians need to read them as indications of the way God was speaking to his people in that context and as promises that can help us understand Jesus, and understand what God still intends to do.

The first 39 chapters of Isaiah close with a declaration that members of Hezekiah's family are going to end up in exile in Babylon. It happened a century or so later. When we then turn over the page into Isaiah 40 we read a message of comfort to those exiles: the time of their restoration from exile has arrived. Babylon is about to fall to the Persians, which happened in 539 BC.

These prophecies are not couched as promises that one day Yahweh will restore his people. They are declarations that Yahweh is taking that action now. The implication is that they were given in the sixth century, not the eighth century. In the chapters that follow Isaiah 40 we can see links with earlier prophecies in the book. They continue to use Isaiah's favourite title for Yahweh, that he is 'Israel's Holy One' or 'Sacred One'. So in these chapters a prophet or a series of prophets is taking up Isaiah's message and proclaiming what he would say if he were here now. He had spoken of how Yahweh's being Israel's Holy One had been bad news – it meant Yahweh was going to discipline Judah for its rebellion against him. These chapters declare that Yahweh's being Israel's Holy One is now good news for Judah – it is this Holy One who is their restorer. Once again there are prophecies that helped the New Testament understand the significance of Jesus, particularly Isaiah 52.13—53.12. It describes a servant of God who has been persecuted but will be restored. This description will have applied to someone in the prophet's day, but it helped Jesus and people who believed in Jesus to understand him.

When we turn over the page again after Isaiah 40—55, we discover that the situation has again moved on. Isaiah 56—66 relates to the situation of Judah when people have been free to return there after their exile but where things are not as wonderful as they might have expected, and they bring together messages designed to enable the community to live in that context and keep being hopeful and committed. In Isaiah 61 there is a testimony by a prophet called to bring that message, and it is another chapter that Jesus took up and applied to himself.

Haven't you had enough?

1 The vision of Yesha'yahu ben Amots which he beheld concerning Yehudah and Yerushalaim in the days of Uzziyyahu, Yotam, Ahaz and Yehizqiyyahu [Uzziah, Jotham, Ahaz and Hezekiah], kings of Yehudah.

²Listen, heavens, give ear, earth,
  because Yahweh has spoken.
I reared children, I raised them,
  but they – they rebelled against me.
³An ox acknowledges its owner,
  a donkey its master's manger.
Yisra'el doesn't acknowledge,
  my people doesn't show any discernment.
⁴Hey, wrongdoing nation,
  a people heavy with waywardness!
Offspring of people who deal badly, devastating children,
  they've abandoned Yahweh.
They've disdained Yisra'el's sacred one,
  they've become estranged, backwards.

⁵Why will you be struck down more,
  continue being defiant?
The whole head has come to sickness,
  the whole mind is faint.
⁶From the sole of the foot to the head,
  there's no integrity in it.
Bruise, blotch, fresh wound –
  they haven't been pressed out.
They haven't been bandaged,
  it hasn't been softened with oil.
⁷Your country's a desolation,
  your towns burned with fire.
Your land – in front of you,
  foreigners are consuming it,
A desolation, quite overthrown by foreigners,
  ⁸and Miss Tsiyyon [Zion] is left like a shelter in a vineyard,
Like a place to stay the night in a melon field,
  like a town besieged.
⁹Had Yahweh of Armies
  not left us survivors, a few,
We'd have been like Sedom [Sodom],
  we'd have resembled Amorah [Gomorrah].

I'm fed up to the teeth with your worship

¹⁰Listen to Yahweh's word,
  rulers of Sedom!
Give ear to our God's instruction,
  people of Amorah!
¹¹What use to me is the large number of your sacrifices?
  (Yahweh says).
I'm full of burnt offerings of rams
  and the fat of fatlings.
In the blood of bulls and lambs and goats
  I do not delight.
¹²When you come to appear to my face,
  who sought this from your hand?
Trampling my courtyards – ¹³you will do it no more,
  bringing an empty offering.
Incense is an offence to me,
  new month and sabbath, the calling of a convocation.
I cannot bear trouble and assembly;
  ¹⁴your new moons and your appointed times
  my entire being dislikes.
They've become a burden to me
  that I'm weary of carrying.
¹⁵And when you spread the palms of your hands,
  I shall lift up my eyes from you.
Even when you offer many a plea,
  there will be no listening on my part.
Your hands are full of bloodshed –
  ¹⁶wash, get clean.
Remove the badness of your practices
  from in front of my eyes.
Stop dealing badly,
  ¹⁷learn doing good.
Require the exercise of authority, put the oppressor right,
  exercise authority for the orphan, argue for the widow.

¹⁸Come on, please, let's argue it out
  (Yahweh says).
If your wrongdoings are like scarlet,
  they're to be white like snow.
If they're red like crimson,
  they're to be like wool.
¹⁹If you're willing and you listen,
  you will consume the good things of the country.
²⁰But if you refuse and rebel,
  you'll be consumed by the sword;
  because Yahweh's mouth has spoken.

Second-degree manslaughter

²¹Aagh, she's become a whore,
  the trustworthy township, full of the exercise of authority.

Faithfulness was lodging in it,
   but now murderers.
²²Your silver has become slag,
   your drink is diluted with water.
²³Your officers are defiant, the associates of thieves;
   every one of them loves a bribe, chases gifts.
They don't exercise authority for the orphan;
   the widow's cause doesn't come to them.

²⁴Therefore the declaration of the Lord,
   Yahweh of Armies, Yisra'el's champion, is:
'Hey, I shall get relief from my adversaries,
   take redress from my enemies,
      ²⁵turn back my hand against you.

But I shall smelt your slag as with lye,
   remove all your contamination.
²⁶I shall restore your leaders as of old,
   your counsellors as at the beginning.
Afterwards you will be called faithful town,
   trustworthy township.'

²⁷Tsiyyon will find redemption through the
      exercise of authority,
   and the people in it who turn back, through
      faithfulness.
²⁸But there will be a breaking of rebels and
      wrongdoers, all together,
   and the people who abandon Yahweh will be
      finished.
²⁹Because they'll be shamed on account of the
      oaks that you desired;
   you will be confounded on account of the
      gardens that you chose.
³⁰Because you'll be like an oak wilting of foliage,
   like a garden for which there's no water.
³¹The strong person will become tinder,
   his work a spark.
The two of them will burn all together,
   and there will be no one quenching.

2 The word that Yesha'yahu ben Amots beheld concerning Yehudah and Yerushalaim.

Study war no more

²It will come about at the end of the time:

The mountain of Yahweh's house will have
      become established
at the head of the mountains, and it will lift up
      higher than the hills.
All the nations will stream to it;
   ³many peoples will come and say,
'Come on, let's go up to Yahweh's mountain,
   to the house of Ya'aqob's [Jacob's] God,
So he may instruct us in his ways,
   and we may walk in his paths.'
Because instruction will go out from Tsiyyon,
   Yahweh's word from Yerushalaim.
⁴He will exercise authority among the nations,
   and issue reproof to many peoples.
They'll beat their swords into hoes,
   their spears into pruning hooks.
Nation will not carry sword against nation;
   they will no more learn about battle.
⁵Ya'aqob's household, come on,
   let's walk by Yahweh's light.

⁶Because you have left your people alone,
   Ya'aqob's household.
Because they are full from the east,
   yes, of diviners like the Pelishtites [Philistines],
   and they abound in children of foreigners.
⁷Its country's full of silver and gold;
   there's no end to its treasures.
Its country's full of horses;
   there's no end to its chariots.
⁸Its country's full of non-entities;
   they bow low to the making of their hands,
   to what their fingers made.
⁹So humanity bows down, the individual falls
      down
   (may you not carry them).

¹⁰Come into the crag,
   bury yourself in the earth,
Before the fearfulness of Yahweh,
   from the dreadfulness of his majesty.
¹¹Lofty human eyes have fallen down,
   the exaltedness of individuals has bowed down.
Yahweh alone will be on high
   on that day.

The destiny of all that is humanly impressive

¹²Because Yahweh of Armies has a day
   against all majesty and exaltedness,
Against all that is high –
   and it will fall down,

¹³Against all the cedars of the Lebanon, exalted and high,
    against all the oaks of the Bashan,
¹⁴Against all the exalted mountains,
    against all the high hills,
¹⁵Against every lofty tower,
    against every fortified wall,
¹⁶Against every Tarshish ship,
    against all the impressive vessels.
¹⁷Human loftiness will bow down,
    people's exaltedness will fall down.
Yahweh alone will be on high on that day;
    ¹⁸non-entities – they will completely vanish.
¹⁹People will go into caves in the crags,
    into holes in the earth,
From before the fearfulness of Yahweh,
    from the dreadfulness of his majesty,
    when he arises to terrify the country.
²⁰On that day humanity will throw away
    its silver non-entities and its gold non-entities,
Which they made for it to bow down to,
    to the moles and to the bats,
²¹To come into the clefts in the crags,
    into the crevices in the cliffs,
Before the fearfulness of Yahweh,
    from the dreadfulness of his majesty,
    when he arises to terrify the earth.
²²Get yourselves away from humanity,
    that has breath in its nostrils,
    because what is it to count for?

You have a coat, you can be a leader

3 Because there,
    the Lord Yahweh of Armies
Is removing from Yerushalaim and from Yehudah
    supply and support:
All supply of bread
    and all supply of water,
²Strong man and man of battle,
    leader and prophet, diviner and elder,
³Officer over fifty, person held in high regard, counsellor,
    person smart with charms and understanding chants.
⁴I will make youths their officials;
    infants will rule over them.
⁵The people will oppress one another,
    each his neighbour.
The youth will be arrogant towards the elder,
    one who is slighted towards someone honourable.
⁶Because a man will seize one of his brothers,
    his father's household:
'You have a coat, you will be a leader for us,
    this ruin will be under your hand.'
⁷On that day he will shout,
    'I won't be one to bind up.
In my house there's no bread and no coat –
    you won't make me leader of the people.'

⁸Because Yerushalaim has collapsed,
    Yehudah has fallen.
Because their tongue and their practices have been towards Yahweh
    to be rebellious against his glorious eyes.
⁹The look on their face testifies against them;
    they declare their wrongdoing like Sedom and don't hide it.
Aagh, for their lives,
    because they have dealt themselves bad fortune.
¹⁰Say of the faithful person, 'It will be good',
    because they will eat the fruit of their practices.
¹¹Aagh, for the faithless person, 'It will be bad',
    because the dealing of his hands will be done to him.
¹²My people – infants are their bosses,
    women rule over them.
My people – your guides make you wander;
    they've swallowed up the course of your paths.

¹³Yahweh is taking his stand to argue,
    he's rising to give judgement for peoples.
¹⁴Yahweh will come in the exercise of authority
    with his people's elders and its officials.
'You – you've burned up the vineyard,
    the humble person's plunder is in your houses.
¹⁵What do you mean that you crush my people,
    grind the faces of humble ones?
    (a declaration of the Lord Yahweh of Armies).'

Dresses, shawls and purses

¹⁶Yahweh has said:

Since Tsiyyon's daughters are lofty,
    and walk outstretched with their neck,
Flirting with their eyes,
    walking and mincing as they walk,
    and they jingle with their feet,

¹⁷The Lord will bare the crown of Tsiyyon's
daughters,
Yahweh will expose their forehead.

¹⁸On that day the Lord will remove the splendour of the anklets, the bands and the necklaces, ¹⁹the earrings, the bracelets and the veils, ²⁰the hats, the armlets, the scarves, the amulets and the charms, ²¹the rings and the nose rings, ²²the dresses, the capes, the shawls, the purses, ²³the gowns, the blouses, the tiaras, the veils and the sashes.

²⁴Instead of perfume there will be a stench;
instead of a wrap, a rope;
Instead of a hairdo, a shorn head;
instead of a robe, a wrapping of sack;
branding instead of beauty.
²⁵Your men [Tsiyyon] will fall by the sword,
your strength by battle.
²⁶Her gateways will lament and mourn;
she'll be empty, she'll sit on the ground.

4 Seven women will take strong hold of one
man
on that day,
Saying, 'We'll eat our bread,
we'll wear our clothes,
Only may your name be called out over us –
gather up our reviling.'

²On that day, Yahweh's shoot will be
for beauty and for splendour,
And the country's fruit
for majesty and for glory for Yisra'el's escape
group.
³What remains in Tsiyyon,
what is left in Yerushalaim –
'Sacred' will be said of it,
everyone who's been written down for life in
Yerushalaim.

⁴If the Lord has washed away
the filth of Tsiyyon's daughters,
And cleanses from within it
the shed blood of Yerushalaim,
By a spirit of the exercise of authority
and by a spirit of burning away,
⁵Yahweh will create
over the entire establishment of Mount Tsiyyon,
and over its meeting place,
A cloud by day, and smoke,
and a brightness of flaming fire by night.

Because over all the splendour will be a canopy,
⁶and it will be a bivouac,
For shade by day from the heat,
and for shelter and for a hiding place from
storm and from rain.

A singer-songwriter's strange song

5 I want to sing a song for my friend,
my love song about his vineyard.
My friend had a vineyard
on a fertile ridge.
²He dug it and de-stoned it,
and planted it with choice vine.
He built a tower in the middle of it,
and also hewed a press in it.
He hoped it would make grapes,
but it made rotten grapes.
³So now, population of Yerushalaim,
people of Yehudah,
decide, please, between me and my vineyard.
⁴What more was there to do for my vineyard,
and I didn't do in it?
Why, when I hoped for it to make grapes,
did it make rotten grapes?
⁵So now I want to let you know, please,
what I'm doing about my vineyard:
Remove its hedge, so it will be for burning up,
break down its wall so it will be for
trampling,
⁶so that I make an end of it.
It won't be pruned and it won't be hoed;
briar and thorn will grow.
I shall order the clouds
not to send rain on it.
⁷Because the vineyard of Yahweh of Armies
is the household of Yisra'el.
The people of Yehudah
are the planting in which he took pleasure.
He hoped for the exercise of authority, but there –
blood pouring out;
for faithfulness, but there – a cry.

She'ol has broadened its appetite

⁸Hey, people adding house to house,
who join field to field,
Until there's no room,
and you're made to live alone in the middle of
the country.

⁹In my ears Yahweh of Armies [has said]:

If many houses do not become desolation,
    big and good ones without inhabitant . . .
¹⁰Because ten acres of vineyard
    will make five gallons.
Ten barrels of seed
    will make a barrel.

¹¹Hey, people who start early in the morning
    so they can chase liquor,
Stay late in the dusk
    so wine can inflame them.
¹²There'll be guitar and mandolin,
    tambourine and pipe and wine at their banquets.
But Yahweh's deed they don't look to,
    the action of his hands they haven't watched.
¹³Therefore my people are going into exile
    because of not acknowledging.
Its splendour – hungry people,
    its horde – parched with thirst.
¹⁴Therefore She'ol has broadened its appetite,
    opened its mouth without limit.
Its magnificence will go down,
    its horde and its din and the one who exults in it.
¹⁵Human beings bow down, individuals fall down,
    the eyes of the lofty fall down.
¹⁶And Yahweh of Armies is lofty in exercising authority;
    the sacred God shows himself sacred in faithfulness.
¹⁷Lambs will pasture as in their meadow,
    aliens will eat the fatlings' wastes.

¹⁸Hey, people who haul waywardness
    with cords of emptiness,
    and wrongdoing as with cart ropes,
¹⁹Who say, 'He should hurry,
    he should speed up his action, in order that we may see.
It should draw near and come about,
    the counsel of Yisra'el's sacred one, so we may acknowledge.'

²⁰Hey, people who say about what is bad, 'Good',
    and about what is good, 'Bad',
Who make darkness into light,
    and light into darkness,
Who make bitter into sweet,
    and sweet into bitter.

Yahweh will whistle

²¹Hey, people who are smart in their eyes,
    who in their view are understanding.
²²Hey, strong men at drinking wine,
    forceful people at mixing a drink,
²³Who declare a faithless person to be in the right
    in return for a bribe,
And the faithfulness of the faithful people
    they remove from them.
²⁴Therefore: like the consuming of straw in a tongue of fire,
    when hay sinks down in the flame,
Their root will become veritable rot,
    and their blossom will go up like dust,
Because they've rejected the instruction of Yahweh of Armies,
    spurned the word of Yisra'el's sacred one.

²⁵On account of this Yahweh's anger flared against his people;
    he stretched out his hand against it and struck it down.
Mountains shook, and their corpses became
    like refuse in the middle of the streets.
For all this his anger did not turn back;
    his hand was still stretched out.

²⁶He will lift a signal to the nations from afar,
    he will whistle to one from the end of the earth,
    and there – with speed, quick, it will come.
²⁷There's none weary, there's none collapsing, in it;
    it doesn't slumber, it doesn't sleep.
The belt on its waist doesn't come loose,
    the thong on its boots doesn't break.
²⁸Its arrows are sharpened,
    all its bows are directed.
Its horses' hoofs are thought of like flint,
    its wheels like a whirlwind.
²⁹Its roar is like a cougar's;
    it roars like lions.
It growls and seizes prey,
    and carries it off and there's no one rescuing.
³⁰It will growl over it on that day, like the growling of the sea;
    and he will look to the land,
And there, darkness, pressure,
    and the light will have gone dark with its thunderclouds.

A commission to frighten people into repentance

6 In the year King Uzziyyahu died, I saw the Lord sitting on a throne, high and lofty, with his train filling the palace. ²Seraphs were standing above him; each had six wings. With two it would cover its face, with two it would cover its feet, with two it would fly. ³One would call to another, 'Sacred, sacred, sacred, Yahweh of Armies, his splendour is the filling of the entire earth.' ⁴The doorposts on the sills shook at the sound of the one who called, while the house was filling with smoke.

⁵I said, 'Aagh me, because I'm ruined, because I'm a man polluted of lips, and I live among a people polluted of lips, because my eyes have seen the King, Yahweh of Armies.' ⁶But one of the seraphs flew to me, in his hand a coal that he had taken with tongs from on the altar. ⁷He made it touch my mouth, and he said, 'There, this has touched your lips, and your waywardness will depart, your wrongdoing will be expiated.'

⁸I heard the Lord's voice saying, 'Whom shall I send, who will go for us?' I said, 'Here I am, send me.' ⁹He said,

Go, and say to this people:
'Keep listening, but don't understand,
keep looking, but don't acknowledge.'
¹⁰Fatten this people's mind,
make its ears heavy, smear its eyes,
So it doesn't see with its eyes and listen with its
    ears,
and its mind understands and it turns and
    there is healing for it.

¹¹I said, 'For how long, Lord?' He said,

'Until towns have crashed into ruins,
    so that there is no inhabitant,
And houses so that there are no people,
    and the land crashes into ruins, a desolation.'
¹²Yahweh will send the people away;
    vast will be the abandonment in the middle of
        the country.
¹³When there is still a tenth in it,
    it will again be for burning up.
But like a terebinth or like an oak
    of which there's a stump after their felling,
    the sacred seed will be its stump.

Stand firm in faith, or you won't stand at all

7 In the days of Ahaz ben Yotam son of Uzziyyahu king of Yehudah, Retsin king of Aram and Peqah ben Remalyahu king of Yisra'el went up to Yerushalaim for a battle against it, but they couldn't do battle against it.

²It had been told David's household, 'Aram has set down on Ephrayim', and his mind and his people's mind shook like the trees in a forest shaking before wind. ³Yahweh said to Yesha'yahu, 'Go out, please, to meet Ahaz, you and "A Remainder Will Go Back" your son, at the end of the Upper Pool channel at the Washer's Field causeway. ⁴You're to say to him, "Keep watch over yourself, be calm. Don't be afraid; your mind is not to go soft on account of these two stumps of smoking firewood, because of the angry burning of Retsin and Aram and ben Remalyahu. ⁵Since Aram has counselled something bad against you (Ephrayim and ben Remalyahu), saying ⁶'We'll go up against Yehudah and dismay it and break it open for ourselves and enthrone as king within it ben Tabe'el', ⁷the Lord Yahweh has said this:

It won't arise,
    it won't happen.
⁸Because the head of Aram is Dammeseq
        [Damascus],
    and the head of Aram is Retsin.
Within yet sixty-five years
    Ephrayim will shatter from being a people.
⁹The head of Ephrayim is Shomron [Samaria],
    and the head of Shomron is ben Remalyahu.
If you don't stand firm in trust,
    indeed you won't stand firm at all."'

¹⁰Yahweh again spoke to Ahaz: ¹¹'Ask for yourself a sign from Yahweh your God. Make it deep, to She'ol, or make it lofty, to the heights.' ¹²Ahaz said, 'I won't ask, I won't test Yahweh.' ¹³He said, 'Listen, please, household of David. Is it too small for you, wearying human beings, that you weary my God as well? ¹⁴Therefore the Lord – he will give you a sign. There – a girl is pregnant and she's going to give birth to a son, and she'll name him Immanu El ['God Is with Us']. ¹⁵He will

eat yoghurt and syrup in knowing how to reject the bad and choose the good. ¹⁶Because before the boy knows how to reject the bad and choose the good, the land whose two kings you're dismayed at will be abandoned.'

Plunder Hurries Loot Rushes

¹⁷Yahweh will bring on you and on your people and on your father's household days that have not come since the day Ephrayim departed from Yehudah (the king of Ashshur). ¹⁸On that day Yahweh will whistle to the fly that's at the end of the streams of Misrayim [Egypt] and to the bee that's in the country of Ashshur. ¹⁹They'll come and settle down, all of them, in the steep wadis, in the craggy cliffs, in all the thorn bushes and in all the watering holes. ²⁰On that day the Lord will shave with a razor hired beyond the River (with the king of Ashshur) the head and the hair on the feet, and it will also sweep away the beard. ²¹On that day someone will keep alive a heifer from the cattle and two from the flock, ²²but from the quantity of the milk they make he will eat yoghurt, because everyone who's left within the country will eat yoghurt and syrup. ²³On that day every place where there used to be a thousand vines worth a thousand sheqels of silver will be for briar and for thorn. ²⁴With arrows and a bow someone will come there, because the entire country will be briar and thorn. ²⁵But all the hills that are hoed with a hoe – the fear of briar and thorn won't come there; it will be for the roaming of oxen and for the trampling of sheep.

8 Yahweh said to me, 'Get yourself a big panel and write on it with an ordinary stylus, "For Plunder Hurries Loot Rushes".' ²I invoked as trustworthy witnesses for me Uriyyahu the priest and Zekaryahu ben Yeberekyahu. ³I had sex with the prophetess and she got pregnant and gave birth to a son. Yahweh said to me, 'Call him Plunder Hurries Loot Rushes, ⁴because before the boy knows how to call "father" and "mother", someone will carry off Dammeseq's wealth and Shomron's plunder before the king of Ashshur.'

Where to look for guidance

⁵Yahweh spoke to me yet further:

⁶Since this people has rejected
  the water of Shiloah, which goes gently
  (and been glad about Retsin and ben
    Remalyahu),
⁷Therefore: there, the Lord is bringing up against
    them
  the water of the River, substantial, vast
  (the king of Ashshur and all his splendour).
It will rise up over all its canyons
  and go up over its banks.
⁸It will sweep through Yehudah, flood as it passes
    over,
  reach as far as its neck.
Its wings spread out will be
  the filling of the breadth of your country.

God is with us:
  ⁹do what is bad, peoples, and shatter.
Give ear, all you distant parts of the earth;
  belt yourselves and shatter,
Belt yourselves and shatter;
  ¹⁰take counsel, but it will be contravened.
Speak a word, but it won't arise,
  because God is with us.

¹¹Because Yahweh said this to me as he took strong hold of my hand so that he might discipline me out of walking in the way of this people:

¹²You shall not say 'conspiracy'
  about everything that this people says
    'conspiracy' about.
What they're in awe of, you shall not be in awe of,
  and not dread.
¹³Yahweh of Armies – regard him as sacred;
  he's to be the object of your awe, he your dread.
¹⁴He's to be a sacred place, but a stone to trip on,
  a crag to collapse on,
For the two households of Yisra'el –
  a trap and a snare for Yerushalaim's inhabitants.
¹⁵Many people will collapse on them,
  they'll fall and break, be snared and caught.

¹⁶Bind up the testimony, seal the instruction among my disciples. ¹⁷I shall wait for Yahweh, who's hiding his face from Ya'aqob's household, and I shall hope for him. ¹⁸Here am I and the

children Yahweh has given me as signs and portents in Yisra'el from Yahweh of Armies who dwells on Mount Tsiyyon. ¹⁹So when they say to you, 'Enquire of the ghosts and the spirits who chirp and whisper. A people is to enquire of its gods, isn't it, of the dead on behalf of the living, ²⁰for instruction and testimony': if they do not speak in accordance with this word, for which there will be no dawn . . .

Darkness and dawning

²¹It will pass through it wretched and hungry. When it is hungry it will rage and slight its king and its gods. It will turn its face upwards ²²and look to the earth, but there, pressure and darkness, oppressive gloom, driven murkiness,

9

because there will be no dawn for the one that experiences oppression.

As the earlier time has slighted
   the region of Zebulun and the region of Naphtali,
The later one is bringing splendour to the Sea Way,
   the other side of the Yarden [Jordan], Galilee of the nations.
²The people walking in darkness
   has seen big light.
Those living in deathly gloom –
   light has shone on them.
³You've made the nation many,
   you've given it great rejoicing.
They've rejoiced before you like the rejoicing at harvest,
   like people who celebrate at the dividing of spoil.
⁴Because the yoke that burdened it,
   the rod on its shoulder,
The boss's club over it,
   you've shattered as on the day at Midyan.
⁵Because every shoe of someone trampling, with shaking,
   and the coat rolled in shed blood,
Have been for burning,
   consumed by fire.
⁶Because a child has been born to us,
   a son has been given to us,
   and government has come on to his shoulder.

People have called him
   'An Extraordinary Counsellor Is the Strong Man God,
   the Everlasting Father Is an Official for Well-being'.
⁷Of the growing of government and of well-being
   there will be no end, on David's throne and on his kingship,
To establish it and support it,
   with authority and faithfulness,
From now and permanently;
   the passion of Yahweh of Armies will do this.

For all this, his anger did not turn back

⁸The Lord has sent out a word against Ya'aqob,
   and it has fallen on Yisra'el.
⁹But the people, all of it, acknowledge it
   (Ephrayim and the inhabitants of Shomron)
   with loftiness and big-headedness:
¹⁰'Bricks have fallen, but we'll build with dressed stone;
   sycamore-figs have been cut down, but we'll substitute cedars.'
¹¹But Yahweh has lifted high the adversaries of Retsin over it,
   and spurred on its enemies,
¹²Aram from the east, the Pelishtites from the west,
   and they've devoured Yisra'el with their entire mouth.
For all this, his anger did not turn back;
   his hand was still stretched out.

¹³The people didn't turn back to the one who hit it;
   they haven't enquired of Yahweh of Armies.
¹⁴So Yahweh cut off from Yisra'el head and tail,
   palm branch and reed, in one day.
¹⁵The elder and the person held in high regard, he is the head,
   and the prophet who instructs in falsehood, he is the tail.
¹⁶The guides of this people became ones who make them wander;
   the ones who were guided were people who were swallowed up.
¹⁷Therefore the Lord does not rejoice over its young men,
   and does not show compassion for its widows and orphans,
Because all of it is impious and deals badly,
   and every mouth speaks villainy.

For all this, his anger did not turn back;
  his hand was still stretched out.

¹⁸Because faithlessness has burned up like fire,
  which consumes briar and thorn.
It set light to the forest thickets,
  and they swirled as a column of smoke.
¹⁹By the fury of Yahweh of Armies
  the country was scorched.
The people became like a fire consuming;
  one person would not spare his brother.
²⁰He carved to the right but was hungry,
  and ate to the left but was not full;
An individual eats the flesh of his offspring,
  ²¹Menashsheh, Ephrayim, Ephrayim, Menashsheh,
  all together they were against Yehudah.
For all this, his anger did not turn back;
  his hand was still stretched out.

My officers are kings, aren't they

10 Hey, you who make decrees that bring trouble,
  who write documents that bring oppression,
²To subvert the case of poor people,
  and steal the rights of the humble among my people,
So that widows become their spoil,
  and orphans their plunder.
³What will you do on the day when attention is given,
  when devastation comes from afar?
To whom will you flee for help,
  and where will you abandon your splendour?
⁴Except bend beneath a prisoner,
  fall beneath the slain?
For all this, his anger did not turn back;
  his hand was still stretched out.

⁵Hey, Ashshur, my angry club –
  and the mace in their hand is my condemnation.
⁶Against an impious nation I send it;
  I order it against a people towards which I am wrathful,
To seize spoil and to take plunder,
  and to make it into something trampled, like mud in the streets.
⁷But it doesn't picture it this way;
  its mind doesn't think this way.

Because in its mind is to annihilate,
  to cut off nations not a few.
⁸Because it says,
  'My officers are kings, altogether, aren't they.
⁹Kalno's like Karkemish, isn't it, or Hamat like Arpad –
  or Shomron like Dammeseq.
¹⁰As my hand found the non-entity kingdoms
  (and their images were more than Shomron and Yerushalaim) –
¹¹As I did to Shomron and to its non-entities,
  so I will do to Yerushalaim and to its idols, won't I.'

¹²But when the Lord finishes all his action
  against Mount Tsiyyon and against Yerushalaim:
'I will attend to the fruit of the king of Ashshur's big-headedness
  and to the lofty splendour of his eyes.
¹³Because he said, "By the energy of my hand I've acted,
  by my smartness, because I have understanding.
I've removed peoples' borders,
  I've plundered their treasures,
  as a champion I've subdued inhabitants.
¹⁴My hand found, as in a nest,
  the resources of peoples.
Like one gathering abandoned eggs,
  I myself gathered the entire earth.
There was not one flapping a wing,
  or opening its mouth and chirping."'

The remainder of Yisra'el

¹⁵Does the axe glorify itself over the one who chops with it,
  or the saw magnify itself over the one who wields it,
As if the club wields the one who lifts it up,
  as if the mace lifted up the one who is not made of wood?
¹⁶Therefore the Lord Yahweh of Armies will send off
  a wasting disease against his beefy ones.
Beneath its splendour it will burn,
  with a burning like the burning of fire.
¹⁷Yisra'el's light will become fire,
  its sacred one a flame.
It will burn up and consume its thorn and its thistle,
  in one day.

¹⁸The splendour of its forest and its farmland
   it will finish off, soul and body.
It will be like the fading away of a sick person;
   ¹⁹the remainder of the trees in its forest will be
       so few,
   a boy could write them down.

²⁰But on that day,
   no more will the remainder of Yisra'el,
The escape group from Ya'aqob's household,
   lean on the one that struck them down.
They will lean on Yahweh,
   Yisra'el's sacred one, in truth.
²¹The remainder will turn back, the remainder of
       Ya'aqob,
   to God, the God who is a strong man.
²²Though your people, Yisra'el,
   were like the sand of the sea,
It will be a remainder of it that will turn back;
   a finishing is determined, overwhelming
       faithfulness.
²³Because a finish, a thing determined –
   the Lord Yahweh of Armies is going to do it,
   within the entire country.

²⁴Therefore the Lord Yahweh of Armies has said this:

Don't be afraid, my people,
   who dwell on Tsiyyon, of Ashshur,
Which strikes you down with a club
   and raises its mace against you in the manner
       of the Misrayimites.
²⁵Because in a very little while more,
   my condemnation will finish,
   and my anger will be towards their destruction.
²⁶Yahweh of Armies is lifting up a whip against it
   like the striking down of Midyan at the Oreb
       Crag,
Like his mace over the sea,
   and he will raise it in the manner of Misrayim.
²⁷And on that day
   its burden will depart from your shoulder,
Its yoke from upon your neck;
   the yoke will be destroyed in the face of your
       beefiness.

Visions of threat and promise

²⁸He has gone against Ayat, he has passed by Migron,
   at Mikmas he put his equipment in place.

²⁹They crossed at the pass;
   'Geba will be lodging for us.'
The Height trembles,
   Gib'ah of Sha'ul [Saul] has fled.
³⁰Bellow loudly, Bat-gallim, heed, Layshah,
   answer, Anatot!
³¹Madmenah has run away,
   the inhabitants of Gebim have taken refuge.
³²More, today at Nob,
   standing, he will wave his hand
At the mount of Miss Tsiyyon,
   the hill of Yerushalaim.

³³There is the Lord Yahweh of Armies,
   lopping off boughs with a crash.
The loftiest in height are being felled,
   the tall ones fall down.
³⁴The forest thickets will be cut down with iron,
   the Lebanon will fall by the august one.

11 But a shoot will go out from Yishay's
       [Jesse's] stump,
   a branch will fruit from his roots.
²Yahweh's breath will alight on him,
   a breath with smartness and understanding,
A breath with counsel and strength,
   a breath with acknowledgement and awe for
       Yahweh;
³his scent will be awe for Yahweh.
He will not exercise authority by the seeing of his
       eyes,
   he will not reprove by the hearing of his ears.
⁴He will exercise authority with faithfulness for
       the poor,
   and reprove with uprightness for the humble
       people in the country.
He will strike the country down with the club in
       his mouth,
   with the breath from his lips he will put the
       faithless person to death.
⁵Faithfulness will be the belt round his hips,
   truthfulness the belt round his thighs.
⁶Wolf will reside with lamb,
   leopard will lie down with goat,
Calf, lion and fatling together,
   with a little boy driving them.
⁷Cow and bear will pasture,
   their young will lie down together.
Cougar, like cattle,
   will eat straw.
⁸A baby will play over the cobra's burrow;
   an infant will hold its hand over the viper's
       hole.

⁹People will not deal badly, they will not devastate,
  in all my sacred mountain.
Because the country will be full of the
    acknowledgement of Yahweh
  like the water covering the sea.
¹⁰On that day,
  Yishay's root which will be standing
    as a signal for peoples,
  Nations will enquire of him,
    and where he settles down will be [a place of]
      splendour.

A day when there will be a song to sing

¹¹On that day,
    the Lord will again act, a second time,
    with his hand to acquire the remainder of his
      people,
  That remain from Ashshur, from Misrayim, from
      Patros,
    from Kush [Sudan], from Elam, from Shin'ar,
    from Hamat and from the shores across the
      Sea.
¹²He will lift up a signal to the nations,
    and gather the men of Yisra'el who were driven
      out,
  And the women of Yehudah who were scattered
      he will collect
    from the four corners of the earth.
¹³Ephrayim's jealousy will go away,
    and the people putting pressure on Yehudah
      will be cut off.
  Ephrayim won't be jealous of Yehudah,
    and Yehudah won't put pressure on Ephrayim.
¹⁴They will fly against the back of the Pelishtites
      to the west;
    together they will plunder the easterners,
  The putting out of their hand: Edom and Mo'ab;
    the people obeying them: the Ammonites.
¹⁵Yahweh will dry up the tongue of the
    Misrayimite sea,
  and wave his hand over the River
    with the heat of his breath.
  He will strike it down into seven wadis,
    and let people make their way in boots.
¹⁶There will be a causeway for the remainder of
      his people
    that remain from Ashshur,
  As there was for Yisra'el
    on the day it went up from the country of
      Misrayim.

12 You will say on that day,

I will confess you Yahweh, because whereas you
      were angry with me,
  your anger turned back and you comforted me.
²There is God, my deliverance,
  I will be confident and not be fearful,
Because Yah, Yahweh, is my vigour and might,
  and he has been my deliverance.

³You will draw water with joy
  from the deliverance fountains.

⁴And you will say on that day,

Confess Yahweh,
  call out in his name.
Make his deeds known among the peoples,
  make mention that his name is on high.
⁵Make music for Yahweh, because he has acted in
      majesty;
  this is to be acknowledged in the entire earth.
⁶Bellow and resound, inhabitants of Tsiyyon,
  because great among you is Yisra'el's sacred one.

The downfall of the superpower

13 A pronouncement about Babel, which
Yesha'yahu ben Amots beheld.

²On a bare mountain lift up a banner,
  raise your voice to them.
Wave your hand,
  so they'll come through the leaders' entrances.
³I myself have ordered the people I made sacred,
  yes, I've called my strong men in connection
      with my anger,
  the people who exult in my majesty.
⁴The sound of a horde on the mountains,
  the semblance of a great company,
The sound of the din of kingdoms,
  nations gathering:
Yahweh of Armies is numbering
  an army for war.
⁵They're coming from a distant country,
  from the end of the heavens,
Yahweh and the instruments of his
    condemnation,
  to destroy the entire earth.
⁶Howl, because Yahweh's day is near;
  like destruction from the Destroyer it comes.

⁷Therefore all hands go limp,
  every human mind melts.
⁸They're terrified, spasms and throes grasp them,
  they writhe like a birthing woman.
An individual looks aghast at his neighbour;
  their faces are faces aflame.

⁹There, Yahweh's day is coming, ruthless,
  with fury and angry blazing,
To turn the earth into a desolation,
  so it can annihilate its wrongdoers from it.
¹⁰Because the stars in the heavens and their
    constellations
  will not flash their light.
The sun will have gone dark when it comes out,
  the moon will not shine its light.
¹¹I will attend to the world for its bad dealing,
  to the faithless for their waywardness.
I will put a stop to the majesty of the arrogant,
  and make the dignity of the violent fall down.
¹²I will make people scarcer than pure gold,
  human beings than Ophir gold.
¹³Therefore I will make the heavens quake,
  and the earth will shake out of its place,
At the fury of Yahweh of Armies,
  on the day of his angry blazing.
¹⁴Like a hunted gazelle,
  like sheep with no one collecting them,
Each person will turn his face to his people,
  each will flee to his country.
¹⁵Everyone who is found will be thrust through,
  everyone who is swept up will fall by the sword.
¹⁶Their little ones will be smashed before their eyes,
  their homes will be despoiled, their wives bedded.

Deliverance and compassion

¹⁷Here am I, stirring up Maday [the Medes]
    against them,
  who don't think about silver,
Gold – they don't want it,
  ¹⁸but their bows will smash the young,
They won't have compassion on the fruit of the
    womb,
  their eye won't spare children.
¹⁹So Babel, the most splendid of kingdoms,
  the majestic glory of the Kasdites
    [Babylonians],
will become like God's overturning of Sedom
    and Amorah.
²⁰It will not be inhabited ever,
  it will not be dwelt in for generation after
    generation.
Arab will not camp there,
  shepherds will not make flocks lie down there.
²¹Wild creatures will lie down there;
  their houses will be full of owls.
Ostriches will dwell there,
  wild goats will leap about there.
²²Hyenas will live in its citadels,
  dragons in its luxurious palaces.
Its time is near coming,
  its days will not draw on.

14 Because Yahweh will have compassion
    on Ya'aqob
  and will again choose Yisra'el.
He will settle them down on their land and the
    alien will join them,
  and attach themselves to Ya'aqob's household.
²Peoples will get them
  and bring them to their place.
The household of Yisra'el will have them as their
    domain on Yahweh's land
  as servants and maidservants.
They will be captors to their captors
  and will rule over their bosses.

A greeting from the ghosts

³On the day Yahweh settles you down after your suffering, after your turmoil and after the tough service that was imposed on you, ⁴you will take up this poem about the king of Babel:

Ah, the boss has stopped,
  the storm has stopped.
⁵Yahweh has broken the mace of the faithless,
  the club of the rulers,
⁶That strikes down peoples with fury,
  a striking down without turning aside,
Subdues nations in anger,
  a persecution without holding back.
⁷The entire earth has settled down, it's calm;
  people have broken out in resounding.
⁸The juniper trees have also rejoiced over you,
  the cedars of Lebanon:
'Now you've lain down,
  no one will go up who will cut us down.'
⁹She'ol below has been astir for you,
  to meet your coming,

Isaiah 14: Ancient Near East at the time of Yesha'yahu (Isaiah)

Rousing the ghosts for you,
  all earth's big guys,
Raising from their thrones
  all the nations' kings.
¹⁰All of them answer
  and say to you,
'You too have been made weak as we are,
  you have become like us!'
¹¹Your majesty has been taken down to She'ol,
  the sound of your mandolins.
Beneath you worm is spread out,
  maggot is your covering.

Thus you have fallen from the heavens

¹²Ah, you've fallen from the heavens,
  bright one, son of dawn!
You've been felled to the earth,
  enfeebler of nations!
¹³But you yourself said within yourself,
  'I shall go up to the heavens.
Above the supernatural stars
  I shall raise my throne.
I shall sit on the mountain for the appointed
    meeting,
  on the extremities of Tsaphon.

¹⁴I shall go up on cloud tops,
  I will be like the One on High.'
¹⁵Yet you're taken down to She'ol,
  to the extremities of the Pit.
¹⁶The people who see you stare,
  they consider you.
'Is this the man who shook the earth,
  who made kingdoms tremble,
¹⁷Who made the world a veritable wilderness
  and tore down its towns?
Its prisoners he did not release for home,
¹⁸all the nations' kings.'
All of them lay down in splendour,
  each in his 'house'.
¹⁹But you've been thrown away from your tomb,
  like offensive carrion,
Clothed in the slain,
  pierced by the sword,
People who go down to the stones of the Pit
  like a trampled corpse.
²⁰You won't be one with them in burial,
  because you devastated your country, you
    killed your people.
The offspring of people who deal badly
  will not be named permanently.
²¹Prepare a place of slaughter for his children
  because of the waywardness of their ancestors.

They are not to arise and possess the earth,
  so that towns cover the face of the world.
²²I shall arise against them
  (a declaration of Yahweh of Armies),
And cut off for Babel name and remainder,
  offspring and descendants (Yahweh's declaration).
²³I shall make it into the possession of the owl,
  and pools of water;
I shall sweep it with a sweeper bringing annihilation
  (a declaration of Yahweh of Armies).

No one can frustrate Yahweh's plans

²⁴Yahweh of Armies has sworn:

Yes, as I envisaged, so it is happening;
  as I counselled, it arises,
²⁵To break Ashshur in my country –
  I will crush it upon my mountains.
Its yoke will depart from upon them,
  its burden will depart from upon his shoulder.
²⁶This is the counsel that has been formulated for the entire earth,
  this is the hand that is stretched out over all the nations.
²⁷Because Yahweh of Armies has taken counsel,
  and who can contravene it?
His hand is stretched out,
  and who can turn it back?

²⁸In the year King Ahaz died, this pronouncement came:

²⁹Don't rejoice, all you Pelishtites,
  because the club of the one who struck you down has broken.
Because from the snake's root a viper will come out,
  its fruit a flying seraph.
³⁰The firstborn of poor people will pasture,
  the needy will lie down in confidence.
But I will put your root to death with hunger,
  I will slay the remainder of you.
³¹Howl, gateway; cry out, town;
  melt, all you Pelishtites.
Because a cloud is coming from the north,
  and there's no one straggling in its appointed ranks.

³²So what should one answer the nation's envoys? –
  that Yahweh has established Tsiyyon,
  and in it the humble of his people will take shelter.

Compassion for Mo'ab

15 A pronouncement about Mo'ab.

Yes, by night Ar has been destroyed,
  Mo'ab has been terminated.
Yes, by night Qir has been destroyed,
  Mo'ab has been terminated.
²Dibon has gone up to the house,
  to the shrines, to cry.
Over Nebo and over Medeba
  Mo'ab howls.
On every head in it there is shornness, every beard is cut off,
  ³in its streets they wrap on sack.
On its roofs, in its squares,
  everyone in it howls, falling down with crying.
⁴Heshbon and Ele'aleh cry out,
  their voice makes itself heard in Yahats.
Therefore the equipped men of Mo'ab shout,
  its entire being trembles for it.
⁵My heart cries out for Mo'ab –
  its fugitives as far as So'ar, Eglat Shelishiyyah.
Because the ascent of Luhit – with crying they climb it;
  because the road to Horonayim – they raise a broken cry.
⁶Because the water of Nimrim
  becomes a great desolation.
Because the grass is dry, the vegetation is finished,
  there is no greenery.
⁷Therefore the gains they've made and what they have in their charge –
  they carry them across the Willows Wadi.
⁸Because the cry has surrounded Mo'ab's border,
  as far as Eglayim its howl, and in Be'er Elim its howl.
⁹Because Dimon's water is full of blood,
  because I put more on Dimon –
A lion for Mo'ab's escape group,
  for the remainder of the land.

16 Send a ram belonging to the country's ruler,
  from Sela in the wilderness to the mountain of Miss Tsiyyon.

²Like a bird flitting, a nest thrown out,
  are the Mo'abite women at the fords of the Arnon.
³'Bring counsel,
  make a decision.
Make your shadow like night
  in the middle of the day.
Hide the banished, don't betray the fugitive;
  ⁴the people banished from Mo'ab should reside with you.
Be a hiding place for them
  from the face of the destroyer.'

When the oppressor is no more, when destruction finishes,
  when the devastator has come to an end from the country,
⁵A throne will be established with commitment,
  there will sit on it in truthfulness
In David's tent one who exercises authority,
  enquiring after judgement, and quick with faithfulness.

Mo'ab open to learning

⁶We have heard of Mo'ab's majesty,
  very majestic,
Its majesty, its loftiness and its arrogance –
  its empty talk is not like that.
⁷Therefore Mo'ab should howl,
  everyone in it should howl for Mo'ab,
For the raisin blocks from Qir-hareset you should moan,
  utterly stricken.
⁸Because the terraces of Heshbon languish,
  the vines of Sibmah.
The nations' lords have struck down their clusters
  that had reached as far as Ya'zer,
That wandered into the wilderness;
  when its shoots spread, they crossed to the sea.
⁹Therefore I cry with Ya'zer's crying for Ya'zer,
  for Sibmah's vines.
I drench you with my tears,
  Heshbon and Ele'aleh.
Because over your summer fruit and over your harvest
  the cheering has fallen still.
¹⁰Rejoicing and gladness have gathered up from the farmland,
  in the vineyards no one resounds, no one shouts.
Wine in the presses – the treader doesn't tread;
  I have made the cheering stop.
¹¹Therefore my heart murmurs for Mo'ab like a guitar,
  my inner being for Qir Heres.
¹²When Mo'ab appears, when it wearies itself, at the shrine,
Comes to its sanctuary to plead,
  it won't prevail.

¹³This is the word that Yahweh spoke for Mo'ab then. ¹⁴But now Yahweh has spoken: 'In three years in accordance with the years of an employee, Mo'ab's splendour with all its great horde will be slighted. The remainder will be a small thing, tiny, not much.'

Don't worry about the Aramites

17 A pronouncement about Dammeseq.

There is Dammeseq, removed from being a town;
  it will become a fallen ruin.
²The towns of Aro'er will be abandoned,
  they will be for flocks,
  and they will lie down with no one disturbing.
³Fortress will cease from Ephrayim,
  kingship from Dammeseq.
The remainder of Aram
  will become like the Yisra'elites' splendour
  (a declaration of Yahweh of Armies).

⁴On that day
  Ya'aqob's splendour will become poor,
  the beefiness of his body will become thin.
⁵It will be like the gathering of the standing harvest,
  when someone harvests the ears in his arm.
It will be like someone gleaning ears
  in Repha'ites Vale.
⁶There will remain garnerings in it,
  like the beating of an olive tree:
Two, three berries on the top (the height);
  four, five on a fruitful bough
  (a declaration of Yahweh, the God of Yisra'el).
⁷On that day a person will pay regard to his maker,
  and his eyes will look to Yisra'el's sacred one.
⁸He won't pay regard to the altars that are the making of his hands,
  he won't look to what his fingers made,
  both the totem poles and the incense stands.

⁹On that day,
  his strong towns will be
  like an abandoned piece of woodland and height
That people abandoned from before the
    Yisra'elites,
  and it will be a desolation.
¹⁰Yes, you have put out of mind the God who
    delivers you;
  your strong crag you have not kept in mind.
Therefore you may plant the plants of the Lovely
    One
  and sow the cutting of an alien god.
¹¹On the day you plant, you may get them to grow,
  and in the morning you sow, get it to blossom,
Though the harvest disappears
  on the day of sickness and grave pain.

Who would want to be a superpower?

¹²Hey, the horde of many peoples
  that roar like the seas' roar,
The din of nations
  that make a din like the din of mighty water!
¹³Nations make a din like the din of much water,
  but he reprimands it and it flees far away,
Driven like the chaff on the mountains before the
    wind,
  like tumbleweed before a storm.
¹⁴Towards evening time there – terror;
  before morning, it is no more.
This is the share of the people who despoil us,
  the lot of the people who plunder us.

18 Hey, country of the buzzing of wings,
  which is beyond the rivers of Kush,
²Which sends envoys by sea
  in papyrus boats on the face of the water.
Go, swift envoys,
  to a nation towering and smooth,
To a people feared far and near,
  a nation of gibberish and aggressiveness,
  whose country rivers divide.
³All you inhabitants of the world,
  people who dwell in the earth:
At the raising of a signal on the mountains, you
    should look,
  and at the sounding of the horn, you should
    listen.
⁴Because Yahweh has said this to me:
  'I shall be calm and I shall look to my
    established place,

Like glowing heat in daylight,
  like a dew cloud in the heat of harvest.'
⁵Because before harvest, when the blossom is
    complete,
  and the flower becomes a ripening grape,
He will cut the shoots with pruning knives,
  and the tendrils he has removed he will have
    taken away.
⁶They will be abandoned, altogether, to the birds
    of prey of the mountains,
  and to the animals of the earth.
The birds of prey will summer on them
  and all the animals of the earth will winter on
    them.
⁷At that time
  tribute will be brought to Yahweh of Armies,
(A people towering and smooth,
  a people feared far and near,
A nation of gibberish and aggressiveness,
  whose country rivers divide)
To the place of the name of Yahweh of Armies,
  Mount Tsiyyon.

Misrayim at a loss

19 A pronouncement about Misrayim.

There is Yahweh, riding on a swift cloud,
  coming to Misrayim.
Misrayim's non-entities will tremble from before
    him,
  and Misrayim's mind will melt within it.
²I will stir up Misrayimites against Misrayimites,
  and one will do battle against his brother,
One against his neighbour, town against town,
  kingdom against kingdom.
³Misrayim's spirit will drain away within it,
  and I will swallow up its counsel.
They will enquire of the non-entities and of the
    ghosts,
  of the mediums and of the spirits.
⁴But I will put Misrayim
  into the hand of a tough master.
A vigorous king will rule over them
  (a declaration of the Lord Yahweh of
    Armies).

⁵Water will dry up from the sea,
  the river will wither and parch.
⁶Rivers will stink as they get low,
  the channels of Misrayim will dry up.

Reed and rush will wither,
    ⁷the plants by the Ye'or [Nile], by the mouth of the Ye'or.
Everything sown at the Ye'or will wither,
    blow away, and there will be none of it.
⁸The fishermen will lament and mourn,
    all the people who throw a hook into the Ye'or.
The people who spread a net
    on the face of the water will have languished.
⁹The workers with combed flax will be shamed,
    and the weavers of linen.
¹⁰Its textile workers will become crushed,
    all the wage-earners troubled in their entire being.
¹¹The officials at Tso'an are simply dense,
    Par'oh's [Pharaoh's] smart counsellors – stupid counsel.
How can you say to Par'oh,
    'I'm a son of experts, a son of the kings of Qedem?' –
¹²Where on earth are your experts,
    so they may please tell you, may acknowledge
    what Yahweh of Armies has planned against Misrayim.

¹³The officials at Tso'an have become fools,
    the officials at Noph have deceived themselves.
They've made Misrayim wander –
    they, the cornerstone of its clans.
¹⁴Yahweh has mixed within it
    a spirit of distortion.
They'll make Misrayim wander in all it does,
    like the wandering of a drunk in his vomit.
¹⁵There'll be no action by Misrayim
    that head or tail can take,
    palm branch or reed.

Misrayim my people

¹⁶On that day, Misrayim will be like women, and will be trembling and in dread before the shaking of the hand of Yahweh of Armies, which he is shaking against it. ¹⁷The land of Yehudah will be a terror to the Misrayimites. Everyone to whom someone makes mention of it will be fearful in the face of the counsel of Yahweh of Armies, which he is formulating against it. ¹⁸On that day, there will be five towns in the country of Misrayim speaking the tongue of Kena'an [Canaan] and taking oaths to Yahweh of Armies. 'Sun Town', one will be called.

¹⁹On that day there will be an altar for Yahweh in the middle of the country of Misrayim and a column for Yahweh at its border. ²⁰It will be a sign and a testimony for Yahweh of Armies in the country of Misrayim; when they cry out to Yahweh before oppressors, he will send them someone to deliver and argue, and he will rescue them.

²¹Yahweh will cause himself to be acknowledged by the Misrayimites, and the Misrayimites will acknowledge Yahweh on that day. They will serve with sacrifice and offering, and make pledges to Yahweh and make good on them. ²²Yahweh will strike Misrayim, striking but healing, and they will turn back to Yahweh and he will let himself be entreated by them and will heal them.

²³On that day there will be a causeway from Misrayim to Ashshur. Ashshur will come to Misrayim and Misrayim to Ashshur. Misrayim will serve with Ashshur.

²⁴On that day Yisra'el will be the third for Misrayim and for Ashshur, a blessing in the middle of the earth, ²⁵because Yahweh of Armies has blessed it, saying 'Blessed be my people Misrayim, my handiwork Ashshur and my domain Yisra'el.'

Prophet as crazy man

20 In the year the commander-in-chief came to Ashdod when Sargon king of Ashshur sent him, and battled against Ashdod and took it, ²at that time Yahweh spoke by means of Yesha'yahu ben Amots: 'Go, loose the sack from on your hips and unfasten the boot from on your feet.' He did so, going stripped and barefoot. ³Yahweh said, 'As my servant Yesha'yahu has gone stripped and barefoot three years as a sign and portent for Misrayim and Kush, ⁴so the king of Ashshur will drive off the captives of Misrayim and the exiles of Kush, young and old, stripped and barefoot, bare of behind, Misrayim's nakedness. ⁵People will be shattered and shamed because of Kush their confidence and Misrayim their glory.

⁶The one who lives on this foreign shore will say on that day, "There, such is the state of the one on whom we had confidence, where we fled for help, to find rescue from before the king of Ashshur. How can we ourselves escape?"

What is there of the night?

21 A pronouncement about the Sea Wilderness.

Like storms in the Negeb passing through,
  from the wilderness it comes, from a fearful country.
²A tough vision has been told me:
  'The betrayer is betraying, the destroyer is destroying.
Go up, Elam, lay siege, Maday [Media] –
  I have stopped all its groaning.'
³Therefore my hips are full of convulsing,
  pains have grasped me, like the pains of someone giving birth.
I'm too struck down to listen, I'm too terrified to look;
  ⁴my mind wanders, shuddering has overwhelmed me.
The dusk to which I was attracted
  he has turned to horror for me.
⁵Setting the table, spreading the rug,
  eating, drinking . . .
'Get up, officers,
  oil the shield.'

⁶Because the Lord said this to me:

Go, set a watch,
  so he may tell what he sees.
⁷He will see a rider, a cavalry pair,
  a donkey chariot, a camel chariot.
He is to heed, with heeding,
  great heeding.

⁸The lookout called:

On the watchtower, my lord, I've been standing,
  continually by day,
And on my watch I have been taking my position,
  every night.

⁹And there, a chariot with men is coming,
  a cavalry pair.

He avowed:

Babel has fallen, fallen,
  all its gods' images.
He has smashed to the ground ¹⁰my crushed one,
  my son on the threshing-floor.
What I heard from Yahweh of Armies,
  Yisra'el's God, I have told you.

¹¹A pronouncement about Dumah.

Someone is calling to me from Se'ir:
  'Watchman, what is there of the night,
  Watchman, what is there of the night?'
¹²The watchman said,
  'Morning came, and night, too;
  if you enquire, enquire; come back again.'

¹³A pronouncement in the steppe.

In the forest, in the steppe, you lodge,
  caravans of Dedanites.
¹⁴Meet the thirsty one, bring water,
  you who inhabit the country of Tema,
  present the fugitive with his bread.
¹⁵Because they've fled from before swords,
  from before the drawn sword,
From before the directed bow,
  from before the weight of battle.

¹⁶Because the Lord has said this to me:

Yet a year according to the years of an employee,
  all the splendour of Qedar will be finished.
¹⁷The remainder of the number of the bows,
  the strong men of the Qedarites, will be few,
  because Yahweh, Yisra'el's God, has spoken.

Yerushalaim (aka Vision Ravine)

22 A pronouncement about Vision Ravine.

What are you doing here, then,
  that you have gone up, all of you, on to the roofs,
²You, full of din, tumultuous town,
  exultant township?

Those of you who were run through were not run
  through by the sword,
  they were not dead in battle.
³All your leaders fled together,
  without the bow they were captured.
All those of you who were found were captured
  together,
  they took flight far away.
⁴Therefore I have said, 'Look away from me,
  I will express bitterness in crying.
Don't try to comfort me
  over the destruction of the daughter of my
  people.'
⁵Because the Lord Yahweh of Armies
  had a day of tumult, trampling and confusion,
In Vision Ravine someone tearing down the
  wall,
  and a cry for help to the mountain.
⁶Elam carried the quiver,
  in chariotry with men, cavalry;
  Qir bared the shield.
⁷Your choicest vales became full
  of chariotry and cavalry.
They took their stand at the gateway
⁸and it exposed Yehudah's covering.

You'd looked that day
  to the armoury in the Forest House.
⁹The breaches in David's Town –
  you'd seen them, that there were many.
You'd collected the water of the Lower Pool
  ¹⁰and counted the houses in Yerushalaim.
You'd torn down the houses to strengthen the
  wall
  ¹¹and made a basin between the two walls
  for the water from the old pool.
But you didn't look to the one who made it,
  you didn't consider the one who formed it long
  before.

¹²The Lord Yahweh of Armies called
  on that day
To crying and to lamenting,
  to shaving the head and to wrapping on sack.
¹³But here – celebration and rejoicing,
  killing cattle and slaughtering sheep,
Eating meat and drinking wine:
  'Eat and drink, because tomorrow we die!'
¹⁴Yahweh of Armies revealed himself in my ears:
  'If this waywardness of yours is to be expiated
    before you die . . .'
  (the Lord Yahweh of Armies has said).

The administrator who fancied himself

¹⁵The Lord Yahweh of Armies said this:
'Come, go to this administrator, to Shebna,
who is in charge of the house.

¹⁶What are you doing here,
  and whom do you have here,
  that you have hewn a tomb for yourself here,
You who have hewn his tomb on high,
  who has carved a dwelling for himself in the
  cliff?
¹⁷There: Yahweh is going to hurl you far;
  strong man, he's going to grasp you firmly.
¹⁸He's going to roll you up tight, rolling you up
  like a ball,
  to a country broad on both sides.
There you'll die;
  there will be your splendid chariots,
  a slight for your master's house.
¹⁹I shall thrust you out from your position;
  you'll be torn down from your office.

²⁰On that day I shall call my servant Elyaqim ben Hilqiyyahu. ²¹I shall clothe him in your coat and fasten him with your belt, and put your ruling power in his hand. He will become a father to the inhabitants of Yerushalaim and to the household of Yehudah. ²²I shall put the key of David's household on his shoulder; he will open and no one will shut, he will shut and no one will open. ²³I shall fix him as a peg in a trustworthy place; he will be a throne of splendour for his father's household. ²⁴All the splendour of his father's household will hang on him, offspring and shoots, all the little articles, from the bowls to all the jars.'

²⁵On that day (a declaration of Yahweh of Armies) the peg fixed in a trustworthy place will move away. It will be hacked off and it will fall, and the load that's on it will be cut down. Yahweh has indeed spoken.

The great sea power broken

23 A pronouncement about Tsor [Tyre].

Howl, Tarshish ships,
  because it has been destroyed so that there is
  not a house.

After they came from the country of Kittim [Cyprus],
    it was revealed to them.
²Be still, inhabitants of the foreign shore,
    merchants of Tsidon.
Seafarers filled you;
    ³by mighty waters came the seed of Shihor.
The harvest of the Ye'or was its yield,
    and it became the marketplace of the nations.
⁴Be shamed, Tsidon, because the sea has said,
    the stronghold of the sea,
'I haven't laboured, I haven't given birth,
    I haven't brought up young men or raised girls.'
⁵When the report came to Misrayim, they were in anguish,
    when the report came about Tsor.

⁶Cross over to Tarshish;
    howl, inhabitants of the foreign shore.
⁷Is this your exultant one,
    whose antiquity is from ancient days,
Whose feet carried it
    to reside far away?
⁸Who counselled this for Tsor,
    the giver of crowns,
Whose merchants were officials,
    its traders the most honoured in the earth?
⁹Yahweh of Armies counselled it,
    to defile all its splendid majesty,
    to slight all the most honoured in the earth.
¹⁰Pass through your country like the Ye'or, Miss Tarshish;
    there's a harbour no more.
¹¹He stretched out his hand over the sea,
    shook kingdoms.
It was Yahweh gave an order regarding Kena'an,
    to annihilate its strongholds.
¹²He said, 'You will no more exult,
    afflicted maiden, Miss Tsidon.
Get up, cross over to Kittim;
    there will be no settling for you, even there.'
¹³There, the country of the Kasdites –
    this is the people that is no longer.
Ashshur founded it for ships;
    they set up its citadels.
They've stripped its strongholds,
    they've made it into a ruin.

What to do with a whore's fee

¹⁴Howl, ships of Tarshish,
    because your stronghold has been destroyed.

¹⁵On that day,
    Tsor will be put out of mind for seventy years,
    like the days of a king.
At the end of seventy years
    it will be for Tsor like the song about the whore:
¹⁶'Get a guitar, go about the town,
    whore who is put out of mind.
Be good, play, sing many a song,
    in order that you may be brought to mind.'
¹⁷At the end of seventy years
    Yahweh will attend to Tsor.
It will go back to its 'gift' and its whoring
    with all the world's kingdoms on the face of the earth.
¹⁸But its profits and its 'gifts' will be sacred to Yahweh;
    it won't be treasured, it won't be stored,
Because its profit will be for the people who live before Yahweh,
    for eating till they are full, and for fine clothes.

The broken world covenant

24

There:

Yahweh is laying waste to the earth and making it desolate,
    twisting its surface and scattering its inhabitants.
²It will be: as people, so priest;
    as servant, so his lord;
As maidservant, so her mistress;
    as buyer, so seller;
As creditor, so borrower;
    as lender, so the one to whom he lends.
³The earth will be totally wasted,
    it will be totally plundered,
    (because it is Yahweh who has spoken this word).

⁴The earth dries up, withers;
    the world languishes, withers;
    the height languishes with the earth.
⁵The earth was impious under its inhabitants,
    because they transgressed instructions.
They violated statute,
    contravened an age-old pact.
⁶That's why a vow has consumed the earth;
    the people who live in it incurred liability.
That's why earth's inhabitants have been ablaze,
    and few people remain.

⁷The new wine dries up, the vine has languished,
   all the people who were rejoicing in heart groan.
⁸The joy of tambourines has stopped,
   the din of the exultant has left off,
   the joy of the mandolin has stopped.
⁹They do not drink wine with a song,
   liquor is bitter to the one who drinks it.
¹⁰The empty township is broken up,
   every house is closed against entering.
¹¹There's a cry over the wine in the streets,
   all rejoicing has reached evening,
   earth's joy has gone into exile.
¹²Desolation is what remains in the town;
   the gateway is struck down, a ruin.
¹³Because so it will be within the earth,
   among the peoples,
Like the beating of an olive tree,
   like gleanings if the harvest finishes.

¹⁴Those people lift their voice, resound,
   because of Yahweh's majesty they've bellowed from the west.
¹⁵Therefore honour Yahweh in the east,
   in shores across the sea,
   the name of Yahweh, Yisra'el's God.

¹⁶From a corner of the earth we've heard melodies,
   'Splendour belongs to the Faithful One.'
But I said, I waste away,
   I waste away! Oh, me!
People have broken faith,
   in broken faith people have broken faith.

Heavenly powers shamed

¹⁷Dread and pit and trap
   for you who inhabit the earth!
¹⁸The one who flees at the dreadful sound
   will fall into the pit.
The one who climbs up from the pit
   will be caught in the trap.
Because sluices have opened on high,
   and earth's foundations have shaken.
¹⁹The earth has quite broken up;
   earth has quite split up;
   earth has quite slipped.
²⁰The earth quite reels like a drunk,
   it sways about like an overnight shelter.
Its rebellion weighs heavy upon it;
   it will fall, and not get up again.

²¹On that day Yahweh will attend
   to the army of the height, in the height,
   and to the kings of the earth, on the earth.
²²They will be gathered as a gathering,
   as captives in a pit.
They will be imprisoned in a prison,
   but after many days will get attention.
²³The moon will be confounded,
   the sun will be disgraced.
Because Yahweh of Armies will have begun to reign
   in Mount Tsiyyon and in Yerushalaim,
   with his splendour in front of his elders.

25

Yahweh, you are my God, I will exalt you,
   I will confess your name,
Because you have done something extraordinary,
   plans from a distant time, truthfulness, truth.
²Because you've made out of a town a heap,
   a fortified township into a ruin.
The citadel of foreigners is no longer a town;
   it won't be built up ever.
³Therefore a vigorous people will honour you,
   a township of violent nations will revere you.
⁴Because you've been a stronghold for the poor person,
   a stronghold for the needy person in his pressures,
A shelter from rain,
   a shade from heat,
When the spirit of the violent was like winter rain,
   ⁵the din of aliens like heat in the desert.
You subdue the heat with a cloud shade;
   the music of the violent succumbs.

Grief brought to an end

⁶And Yahweh of Armies will make
   for all peoples on this mountain
A banquet with rich foods, a banquet with aged wines,
   juicy rich foods, refined aged wines.
⁷He will swallow up on this mountain the layer of wrapping,
   the wrapping over all the peoples,
The covering that is spread out over all the nations;
   ⁸he will have swallowed up death permanently.
The Lord Yahweh will wipe the tears
   from on all faces.

The reviling of his people
   he will take away from on all the earth;
   because Yahweh is the one who has spoken.

⁹On that day one will say:

There, this is our God,
   we hoped for him and he delivered us.
This is Yahweh, we hoped for him;
   let's celebrate and rejoice in his deliverance.
¹⁰Because Yahweh's hand will alight
   on this mountain.
Mo'ab will be trodden down in its place
   like the treading of straw at Madmenah.
¹¹It will spread out its hands within it,
   as a swimmer spreads his hands to swim.
He will bring down its majesty
   with the spoils of its hands.
¹²The towering fortification of its walls
   he will have laid low, taken down,
   knocked down to the ground, right to the earth.

26 On that day this song will be sung in the country of Yehudah:

We have a strong town;
   he makes walls and rampart into deliverance.
²Open the gateways so that the faithful nation
   may come in,
   one that keeps truthfulness.
³A mind that is sustained, you preserve in well-being,
   in well-being because it's filled with reliance
      on you.
⁴Rely on Yahweh permanently, because in Yah –
   Yahweh is crag for the ages.
⁵Because he has laid low the people who live in
      the height;
   the towering township he brings down.
He brings it down right to the ground,
   knocks it down right to the earth.
⁶The foot treads it down, the feet of the humble
      person,
   the soles of the poor people.

Your dead will live

⁷The path is clear for the faithful person,
   when you level the faithful person's track clear.
⁸Yes, on the path determined by your rulings,
   Yahweh, we have hoped for you.

The longing of our entire being
   has been for your name and your renown.
⁹With my entire being I've longed for you by
      night;
   yes, my spirit within me seeks urgently for you.
Because when your rulings are in the earth,
   the inhabitants of the world learn faithfulness.
¹⁰Were the faithless person shown grace,
   he wouldn't learn faithfulness.
In a country characterized by straightness he does
      what's evil,
   and doesn't live in awe of Yahweh's majesty.
¹¹Yahweh, they don't behold your hand raised;
   they should behold and be shamed.
Your passion for the people,
   yes, your fire for your adversaries, should
      consume them.
¹²Yahweh, may you institute well-being for us,
   because all the things we've done, you did for
      us.
¹³Yahweh our God,
   lords apart from you have been masters over us,
   but of you alone we will make mention, of your
      name.
¹⁴Dead people don't live,
   ghosts don't rise.
That's why you attended to them and annihilated
      them,
   and obliterated any mention of them.
¹⁵You added to the nation, Yahweh;
   when you added to the nation you were
      honoured,
   you furthered all the country's boundaries.
¹⁶Yahweh, under pressure they attended to you,
   a whispered prayer during your correction of
      them.

¹⁷Like a pregnant woman who draws near to
      giving birth,
   who writhes, cries out in her pain,
So have we become,
   because of you, Yahweh.
¹⁸We were pregnant, we writhed,
   it is as if we gave birth to wind.
We don't achieve deliverance in the earth;
   the inhabitants of the world don't fall.

¹⁹Your dead will live, my corpse will rise;
   wake up and resound, you who dwell in the
      earth!
Because your dew is the dew of the lights,
   and you make the country of ghosts fall.

²⁰Go, my people, come into your rooms,
   and shut your door after you.
Hide for a little moment,
   until condemnation passes.
²¹Because there, Yahweh is going to come out from his place,
   to attend to the waywardness of the earth's inhabitants upon them.
The earth will uncover its shed blood,
   and will no more cover over its slain.

Livyatan (Leviathan) meets its end

27 On that day Yahweh will attend with his sword,
tough and big and strong,
To Livyatan the fleeing serpent,
   to Livyatan the twisting serpent;
he will slay the dragon that's in the sea.

²On that day,
   a delightful vineyard, chant of it!
³I Yahweh am going to preserve it;
   moment by moment I will water it.
In case someone attends to it,
   night and day I will preserve it.
⁴I have no wrath;
   if only someone gives me briar and thorn!
In battle I will march against it,
   and set fire to them altogether.
⁵Or he can take hold of my stronghold,
   he can make peace with me,
   peace he can make with me.

⁶Coming days: Ya'aqob will root,
   Yisra'el will bud and blossom,
   and the face of the world will be full of produce.

⁷Did he strike it down like the striking of the one who struck it down,
   was it slain like the slaying of the ones slain by him?
⁸By driving away, by sending off, you argue with it;
   he removed it by a tough blast on a day of east wind.
⁹Therefore by this Ya'aqob's waywardness will be expiated;
   this is the entire fruit of the removing of its wrongdoing.

Through his making all the altar stones
   like shattered blocks of limestone,
   totem poles and incense altars won't stand.
¹⁰Because the fortified town is desolate,
   the abode sent off and abandoned like the wilderness.
There a calf pastures,
   there it lies down and consumes its boughs.
¹¹When its branches wither, they break;
   women come, set light to them.
Because it is not a people of understanding;
   therefore its maker will not have compassion on it,
   its former will not be gracious to it.

¹²On that day
Yahweh will thresh from the channel of the River [Euphrates]
   to the Misrayimite Wadi,
And you will be gleaned
   one by one, Yisra'elites.
¹³On that day
   there will be a sound on a great horn.
The people will come who are perishing in the country of Ashshur,
   and who are scattered in the country of Misrayim.
They will bow low to Yahweh
   on the sacred mountain, in Yerushalaim.

The drunks of Ephrayim and Yehudah

28 Hey, majestic crown of Ephrayim's drunks,
   and its splendid beauty, a fading flower,
One that's on the majestic head of beefy people,
   struck down by wine!
²Here, the Lord has someone strong and powerful,
   like a storm of hail, a destructive tempest.
Like a storm of water, forceful, rushing,
   he has set it down on the earth by his power.
³It will be trampled underfoot,
   the majestic crown of Ephrayim's drunks.
⁴The fading flower, its splendid beauty,
   that's on the majestic head of beefy people,
Will be like a fig before harvest
   that someone sees.
The one who sees it –
   while it's still in his palm, he swallows it.

⁵On that day,
   Yahweh of Armies will become
A splendid crown and a glorious diadem
   for the remainder of his people,
⁶An authoritative spirit
   for the one who sits over the exercise of
      authority,
   and the strength of the people who turn back
      the battle at the gateway.

⁷But these also wander because of wine,
   stagger because of liquor:
Priest and prophet wander because of liquor,
   they're swallowed up by wine, they stagger
      because of liquor.
They wander when they are seeing,
   they go astray in giving judgement.
⁸Because all the tables are full of vomit, filth –
   there's no place.

⁹"Whom does he instruct in knowledge,
   whom does he help to understand a report?
People weaned from milk,
   moving on from the breast?
¹⁰Because order upon order,
   order upon order,
Rule upon rule, rule upon rule,
   a little there, a little there.
¹¹Because with mockings of lip and in another
      tongue
   he speaks to this people,
¹²The one who has said to them,
   "This is the place to settle down,
Settle the weary person down,
   yes, this is the place of repose.'"

But they have not been willing to listen,
¹³so to them Yahweh's word will be
Order upon order,
   order upon order,
Rule upon rule, rule upon rule,
   a little there, a little there,
In order that they may go, but fall back,
   and be broken and snared and captured.

God's strange work

¹⁴Therefore listen to Yahweh's word,
   you arrogant,
Who rule this people,
   which is in Yerushalaim.

¹⁵Because you've said:

'We have solemnized a pact with death,
   with She'ol we've made an agreement.
The sweeping flood, when it passes,
   won't come to us,
Because we've made a lie our shelter,
   we have hidden in falsehood.'

¹⁶Therefore the Lord Yahweh has said this:

Here am I founding in Tsiyyon a stone,
   a testing stone, a valuable cornerstone,
A well-founded foundation;
   the one who stands firm in faith will not be
      hasty.
¹⁷I will make authority the rule,
   faithfulness the weight.
Hail will sweep away the lying shelter;
   water will flood the hiding place.
¹⁸Your pact with death will be covered over,
   your agreement with She'ol won't stand up.
The sweeping flood, when it passes –
   you will be for trampling by it.
¹⁹The times when it passes, it will get you,
   because it will pass morning after morning,
By day and by night,
   and understanding the report will be simply a
      horror.
²⁰Because the bed will be too short for stretching
      out,
   the blanket too narrow for gathering round
      oneself.
²¹Because Yahweh will arise as on Mount Peritsim,
   he will be astir as in Gib'on Vale,
To do his deed – strange is his deed,
   to perform his service – foreign is his service.
²²So now, don't be arrogant,
   or your chains will get strong.
Because I've heard of a finish, a thing determined,
   by the Lord Yahweh of Armies,
   against the entire country.

²³Give ear, listen to my voice,
   heed, listen to what I say.
²⁴Is it all the time that the ploughman ploughs to
      sow,
   opens up and harrows his ground?
²⁵When he's levelled its surface,
   he scatters caraway and sprinkles cumin,
Sets wheat (millet) and barley in its place,
   and spelt in its border, doesn't he.

²⁶One disciplines him for acting with judgement:
  his God instructs him.
²⁷Because caraway isn't threshed with a sled,
  and the wheel of a cart isn't rolled over cumin.
Because caraway is beaten with a rod,
  and cumin with a club.
²⁸Cereal is crushed,
  because the thresher doesn't thresh permanently.
The wheel of his cart may rumble,
  but he doesn't crush it with his horse riders.
²⁹This too comes from Yahweh of Armies;
  he formulates extraordinary plans,
  he shows great skill.

Like a ghost from the earth

29 Hey, God's Hearth, God's Hearth,
  township where David camped!
Add year to year;
  the festivals may come round.
²But I will oppress God's Hearth,
  and there'll be sorrow and sighing.
It will be to me God's very hearth;
  ³I shall camp against you with a very encircling.
I shall lay siege against you with a rampart,
  set up siege works against you.
⁴You'll be lower than the ground when you speak,
  your words will be lower than the earth.
Your voice will be like a ghost from the ground,
  your words will chirp from the earth.
⁵But like fine dust will be the horde of your adversaries,
  like passing chaff the horde of the violent.
In an instant, suddenly,
  ⁶by Yahweh of Armies you will be attended,
With thunder and with shaking, and a loud voice,
  storm and hurricane and a flame of consuming fire.
⁷It will be like a dream, a vision in the night:
  the horde of all the nations,
Which are making war against God's Hearth,
  and all its besiegers and its stronghold and its oppressors.
⁸It will be like when someone hungry dreams,
  and there, he's eating, but he wakes up,
  and his throat is empty,
Or like when someone thirsty dreams,
  and there, he's drinking, but he wakes up,
  and there, he's faint, and his throat is craving.
So will the horde of all the nations be
  that are making war against Mount Tsiyyon.

⁹Wait about and be stupefied,
  blind yourselves and be blind.
They are drunk but not from wine,
  they totter but not from liquor.
¹⁰Because Yahweh has poured over you
  a spirit of coma.
He has closed your eyes, the prophets,
  and covered your heads, the seers.
¹¹The vision of anything has become for you
  like the words of a sealed scroll,
Which they give to someone who knows writing,
  saying 'Read this out, please',
And he says, 'I can't,
  because it's sealed.'
¹²So the scroll is given to someone who doesn't know writing,
  saying 'Read this out, please',
  but he says, 'I don't know writing.'

Who sees us?

¹³The Lord has said,

'Since this people has come near with its mouth,
  and with its lips has honoured me,
But has kept its mind far from me,
  and their awe for me has been a learned human order:
¹⁴Therefore here I am,
  once more doing something extraordinary with this people,
  acting in an extraordinary way, something extraordinary.
The smartness of its smart people will perish,
  the understanding of its people of understanding will hide.'
¹⁵Hey, you who go deeper than Yahweh
  to hide your counsel,
Whose action is in the dark and who say,
  'Who sees us, who knows about us?'
¹⁶Your overturning of things! – if the potter is thought of as like the clay,
  or the thing that's made says of its maker, 'He didn't make me',

Or the pot says of its potter,
'He didn't understand.'

¹⁷In yet a little while,
Lebanon will turn back into farmland, won't it,
and the farmland be thought of as forest.
¹⁸Deaf people will listen on that day to the words of a document,
and out of murk and darkness the eyes of blind people will see.
¹⁹The humble will regain rejoicing in Yahweh,
and the neediest of people will celebrate Yisra'el's Sacred One.
²⁰Because the violent person will not exist, the arrogant person will be finished,
and all the people who are wakeful over trouble will be cut off,
²¹The people who make someone into a wrongdoer with a statement they make,
who trap the judge at the gateway,
and who turn aside the one in the right with empty words.

²²Therefore, Yahweh has said this to Ya'aqob's household, the one who redeemed Abraham:

Ya'aqob won't now be shamed;
his face won't now be pale.
²³Because when he (his descendants) sees
the action of my hands within him,
he'll make my name sacred.
People will make Ya'aqob's Sacred One sacred,
and be in dread of Yisra'el's God.
²⁴The people who wander in spirit will acknowledge understanding,
and the people who complain will learn a grasp of things.

God is our refuge and strength, really?

30 Hey, defiant sons (Yahweh's declaration),
in forming counsel but not from me,
In pouring a drink offering but not from my spirit,
in order to heap wrong on wrong,
²You who go to descend to Misrayim,
but have not asked my bidding,
In protecting yourselves by Par'oh's protection
and in taking shelter in Misrayim's shade.
³But Par'oh's protection will become shame for you,
and shelter in Misrayim's shade, disgrace.
⁴Because his officials have been at Tso'an,
his envoys reach Hanes:
⁵Everyone will have come to shame
because of a people that's no use to them,
No help and no use,
but rather shame and yes, reviling.

⁶A pronouncement about The Animals of the Negeb.

In a country of pressure and distress,
lion and cougar among them,
viper and flying serpent,
They carry their resources on the back of donkeys,
their treasures on the hump of camels,
To a people that's no use,
⁷Misrayim which helps with a breath, emptiness.
Therefore I call this
'They are Rahab sitting.'

⁸Now, come,
write it on a tablet with them,
inscribe it on a scroll,
So that it may be for a future day
a witness permanently.
⁹Because it's a rebellious people,
deceitful children,
Children who didn't wish to listen
to Yahweh's instruction,
¹⁰People who've said to seers,
'Don't see',
And to visionaries,
'Don't give us visions of straightness.
Speak nice things to us,
give us visions that are deceptions.
¹¹Depart from the way, turn away from the path,
make Yisra'el's Sacred One cease from before us.'

¹²Therefore Yisra'el's Sacred One has said this:

Since you've rejected this word,
and relied on fraud and crookedness,
and leaned on it,
¹³Therefore this waywardness will be for you
like a breach falling,
Swelling out in a high wall,
whose breaking comes suddenly, in an instant.
¹⁴Its breaking is like the breaking of a potters' jug,
smashed so he doesn't spare:

Through its smashing there won't be found a fragment
    for picking up fire from a hearth
    or for skimming water from a pool.

Yahweh waits

¹⁵Because the Lord Yahweh, Yisra'el's Sacred One, has said this:

By turning back and settling down you'll find deliverance;
    in calm and reliance will be your strength.
But you were unwilling,
    ¹⁶and you said 'No,
Rather we'll flee on a horse' –
    therefore you'll flee.
'We'll ride on a swift one' –
    therefore your pursuers will be swift.
¹⁷A thousand from before the reprimand of one,
    from before the reprimand of five, you'll flee,
Until you're left like a beacon on the top of a mountain,
    like a banner on a hill.

¹⁸Therefore Yahweh waits to be gracious to you;
    but therefore he will arise to show compassion to you.
Because Yahweh is a God with authority –
    the blessings of all who wait for him!
¹⁹Because, people in Tsiyyon, which dwells in Yerushalaim,
    you really will not weep.
He really will be gracious to you at the sound of your cry;
    as he hears it, he'll have answered you.
²⁰The Lord will give you pressure bread
    and affliction water.
But your instructors will no longer be marginalized;
    your eyes will be seeing your instructors.
²¹Your ears will listen to a word from behind you, saying, 'This is the way, walk in it',
    when you go right and when you go left.
²²You'll defile the plating of your silver images,
    and the sheath of your gold idol.
You'll scatter them like something sick;
    'Get out', you'll say to it.
²³And he'll give the rain for your seed
    with which you sow your ground,
And the bread that's the yield of your ground,
    and it will be rich and fat.
Your livestock will pasture on that day
    in a broad pasture.
²⁴The oxen and the donkeys that serve the ground will eat seasoned fodder
    that's been winnowed with shovel and fork.

The Hearth prepared for the King

²⁵There will be, on every high mountain
    and on every lofty hill,
    streams running with water,
On the day of great slaughter,
    when towers fall.
²⁶But the moon's light will be like the sun's light,
    and the sun's light will be sevenfold,
    like the light of seven days,
On the day when Yahweh bandages his people's wound,
    and heals the wound from his striking down.

²⁷There, Yahweh's name is coming from afar,
    his anger burning, his load a weight.
His lips are full of condemnation,
    his tongue is like a consuming fire.
²⁸His breath is like a rushing wadi
    that comes halfway to the neck,
To shake the nations in an empty shaker,
    with a halter that makes them wander on the peoples' jaws.
²⁹The song will be for you
    like the night when a festival gets made sacred,
The rejoicing of heart like someone going with a pipe,
    to come on Yahweh's mountain, to Yisra'el's crag.
³⁰Yahweh will make the majesty of his voice heard,
    and show the alighting of his arm,
In angry wrath and consuming fiery flame,
    cloudburst, storm and hailstone.
³¹Because at Yahweh's voice
    Ashshur that strikes down with a club will be shattered.
³²Every passing of the appointed mace,
    which Yahweh causes to alight on him,
Will be with tambourines and guitars,
    and with battles involving its shaking he will battle against them.
³³Because the Hearth is laid out already;
    yes, it's prepared for the King.
He's made its firepit deep and wide,
    fire and wood a-plenty,

Yahweh's breath
   like a sulphur wadi burning up in it.

The hawks hovering over the town

31 ⁱHey, you who are going down to Misrayim for help,
   who lean on horses,
Who've relied on chariotry because it's vast,
   and on cavalry because they're very numerous,
And not turned to Yisra'el's Sacred One,
   and not enquired of Yahweh.
²But he too is smart, and he has brought bad fortune,
   and not made his words turn away.
He will arise against the household of people who deal badly,
   and against the help of people who bring trouble.
³The Misrayimites are human, not God,
   their horses are flesh and not spirit.
When Yahweh stretches out his hand,
   helper will collapse and the one who is helped will fall;
   all of them will be finished together.

⁴Because Yahweh has said this to me:

As a lion murmurs,
   or a cougar over its prey
(When a whole group of shepherds
   is called against it,
At their voice it isn't shattered,
   at the horde of them it doesn't succumb),
So Yahweh of Armies will go down
   to fight on Mount Tsiyyon and on its hill.
⁵Like birds flying,
   so Yahweh of Armies will shield Yerushalaim,
Shielding and rescuing,
   passing over and saving.
⁶Turn back to the one whom you have deeply defied,
   Yisra'elites.
⁷Because on that day they will reject, each one,
   his silver non-entities and his gold non-entities,
   which your hands made for you, a wrongdoing.
⁸Ashshur will fall by a sword not human;
   a sword that doesn't belong to a human being will consume it.
It will flee for its life from before the sword;
   its young men will become a workforce.
⁹Its cliff will pass away because of the terror,
   its officers will be shattered because of the ensign
(a declaration of Yahweh, whose fire is in Tsiyyon,
   his furnace in Yerushalaim).

32 ¹There, a king will reign to promote faithfulness;
   as for officials, they'll govern to promote the exercise of authority.
²Each will be a veritable hiding place from wind,
   a place of concealment from rain,
Like channels of water in the desert,
   like the shade of a heavy cliff in a weary country.
³The eyes of people who see won't be blind,
   the ears of people who listen will heed.
⁴The mind of the quick will understand knowledge,
   the tongue of the hesitant will be quick to speak dazzling words.
⁵No more will a villain be called a leader,
   or a rogue called a deliverer.
⁶Because a villain speaks villainy,
   and his mind brings trouble,
Acting impiously,
   and speaking of wandering in regard to Yahweh,
Leaving the hungry person empty,
   and letting the drink of the thirsty fail.
⁷The rogue: his tools are bad,
   he's one who counsels schemes,
To destroy the humble by false words,
   and when the needy person speaks his case.
⁸But a leader will counsel acts of leadership,
   and that man will rise up with acts of leadership.

When the spirit empties itself

⁹Carefree women, get up, listen to my voice;
   confident daughters, give ear to what I say.
¹⁰Some days over a year
   you confident ones will shake,
Because the harvest will be finished,
   the ingathering won't come.
¹¹Tremble, you carefree; shake, you confident,
   strip, be bare, a skirt round your waist,
¹²Lamenting upon your breasts for the lovely fields,
   for the fruitful vine,

¹³For my people's soil,
  which will produce thorn and briar,
Indeed, for all the joyful households,
  the exultant township.
¹⁴Because the fortress will have been deserted,
  the uproar of the town will have been
    abandoned.
Citadel and tower will have become
  empty spaces permanently,
Enjoyment for donkeys,
  pasture for flocks:
¹⁵Until spirit empties on us from on high,
  and wilderness becomes farmland,
  and farmland is thought of as forest.
¹⁶Authority will dwell in the wilderness,
  faithfulness will live in the farmland.
¹⁷The effect of faithfulness will be well-being,
  the service of faithfulness will be calm and
    confidence permanently.
¹⁸My people will live in an abode characterized by
    well-being,
  in secure dwellings, in carefree places to settle
    down.

¹⁹Though it hails when the forest flattens,
  and the town falls utterly down,
²⁰The blessings you will have as you sow by all
    water,
  as you let loose the foot of ox and donkey!

The offensive hope of the city of God

33 Hey, destroyer, and you're not
    destroyed,
  one who breaks faith, and people have not
    broken faith with you!
When you finish destroying you will be destroyed,
  when you stop breaking faith, they'll break
    faith with you.
²Yahweh, be gracious to us,
  we have hoped in you.
Be people's arm every morning,
  yes, our deliverance in time of pressure.
³Before the sound of uproar peoples fled,
  before your rising nations scattered.
⁴Your spoil was gathered like the gathering of
    locusts;
  like the rushing of grasshoppers someone
    rushes on it.
⁵Yahweh is lofty, because he dwells on high;
  he filled Tsiyyon with authority and faithfulness.

⁶He will become the truthfulness of your times;
  smartness and knowledge are the wealth that
    brings deliverance,
  awe for Yahweh – that is its treasure.

⁷There – the people in God's Hearth have cried
    out aloud in the streets,
  the envoys of Shalom cry bitterly.
⁸Causeways have become desolate,
  people passing on the road have ceased.
He has contravened the pact, rejected the towns,
  not taken account of anyone.
⁹The country has withered, wasted away;
  Lebanon is confounded, it has shrivelled.
The Sharon has become like the steppe,
  Bashan and Carmel are shaking things off.
¹⁰'Now I will arise,' Yahweh says,
  'now I will exalt myself, now I will lift myself.
¹¹You will conceive hay, give birth to straw;
  your breath a fire that consumes you.
¹²Peoples will be burnings of lime,
  thorns cut off that are set on fire.
¹³Listen, you far off, to what I have done;
  acknowledge, you that are near, my strength.'

Your eyes will behold the King in his beauty

¹⁴Wrongdoers in Tsiyyon are frightened,
  trembling grasps the impious.
Who of us can reside with consuming fire,
  who of us can reside with the permanent blaze?
¹⁵One who walks in faithfulness,
  speaks uprightly,
Rejects profit from fraud,
  waves the palms of his hands rather than
    grasping a bribe,
Stops his ear rather than listening to talk of
    bloodshed,
  closes his eyes rather than look at what is bad –
¹⁶That person can dwell on the heights,
  with fortresses in the cliffs as his high tower.
His food will be given,
  his water reliable.

¹⁷Your eyes will behold the King in his beauty,
  they'll see the country stretching far.
¹⁸Your mind will murmur about what you dreaded –
  where's the person counting, where's the person
    weighing?
Where's the person counting the towers? –
  ¹⁹when you don't see the barbarous people,

The people too way-out of speech to listen,
> so stammering of tongue that there's no understanding.
²⁰Behold Tsiyyon, the township of our appointed festivals;
> your eyes will see Yerushalaim,
A carefree abode,
> a tent that will not move about,
Whose pegs one will never pull up,
> none of whose ropes will break.
²¹Rather, there the august one, Yahweh, will be for us
> a place of rivers, streams, broad on both sides.
No rowing vessel can go in it,
> no august ship can pass through it.
²²Because Yahweh is the one exercising authority for us,
> Yahweh is the one who makes decrees for us.
Yahweh is our King, he is the one who will deliver us,
²³when your ropes are loose.
They cannot take strong hold on the base of their mast,
> they cannot spread a sail.
Then much spoil is divided,
> lame people take plunder.
²⁴No dweller will say, 'I'm ill';
> the people that lives in it – its waywardness is carried.

Putting down Edom

34 Come near to listen, nations,
> heed, peoples.
The earth and what fills it should listen,
> the world and all who come out from it.
²Because Yahweh has fury for all the nations,
> wrath for all their army.
He's devoting them, giving them to slaughter,
> ³and those of them who are run through will be thrown out.
Their corpses – their stench will go up,
> and the mountains will dissolve with their blood.
⁴All the army of the heavens will rot,
> and the heavens will roll up like a document.
All their army will droop
> like the droop of foliage from a vine,
And the droop from a fig tree,
⁵because my sword will have drunk its fill in the heavens.

There, on Edom it goes down,
> and on a people I am devoting, so as to exercise authority.
⁶Yahweh's sword is full of blood,
> soaked in fat,
In the blood of lambs and goats,
> in fat from the kidneys of rams.
Because Yahweh has a sacrifice in Botsrah,
> a big slaughter in the country of Edom.
⁷Oryxes will go down with them,
> bullocks with sturdy steers.
Their country will be full of blood,
> their earth will be soaked in fat.
⁸Because it's a day of redress for Yahweh,
> a year of making good for Tsiyyon's argument.
⁹Its wadis will turn to pitch,
> its earth to sulphur.
Its country will become pitch burning up;
> ¹⁰day and night it won't go out.
Its smoke will go up permanently;
> from generation to generation it will lie waste.
Lastingly and permanently
> there will be no one passing through it.
¹¹Hawk and hedgehog will possess it,
> owl and raven will dwell in it.
He'll stretch out over it the measuring line of emptiness,
> and the weights of the void ¹²over its nobles.
People will call it 'There's No Kingship There';
> all its officials will be nothing.
¹³Thorns will grow up in its citadels,
> briar and thistle in its fortresses.
It will become an abode of jackals,
> a dwelling for ostriches.
¹⁴Wildcats will meet hyenas,
> a wild goat will call to its neighbour.
Indeed, the night creature is resting there,
> finding herself a place of repose.
¹⁵There the snake is nesting and laying eggs,
> sitting and hatching in its shade.
Yes, there buzzards are gathering,
> each with her mate.

Giving the mute their voice

¹⁶Enquire from in Yahweh's document, and read out:

Not one of these is lacking,
> they do not miss, any of them, her mate,

Because by my mouth he ordered,
    and with his spirit he collected them.
¹⁷He's the one who made the lot fall for them,
    his hand shared it out for them with the line.
They will possess it for all time,
    to generation after generation they will dwell there.

35

The wilderness and the dry land will be glad,
    the steppe will celebrate and bloom like a crocus.
²It will bloom abundantly and celebrate,
    indeed with celebration and resounding.
The Lebanon's splendour will be given it,
    the Carmel and the Sharon's glory.
Those people will see Yahweh's splendour,
    our God's glory.

³Strengthen slackening hands,
    firm up collapsing knees.
⁴Say to the hesitant of mind,
    'Be strong, don't be afraid, there is your God.
Redress will come, God's dealing,
    he will come and deliver you.'

⁵Then the eyes of the blind will open,
    the ears of the deaf will unfasten.
⁶Then the handicapped person will jump like a deer,
    the mute's tongue will resound.
Because water will burst out in the wilderness,
    wadis in the steppe.
⁷The burning sand will become a pool,
    the thirsty ground fountains of water.
In the abode of jackals, its resting place,
    the dwelling will be reed and rush.

⁸There will be a highway there, a way,
    the sacred way it will be called;
    an unclean person won't pass along it.
It will be for them, the one who walks the way;
    stupid people won't wander there.
⁹There'll be no lion there;
    violent beast won't go up on it,
It won't be found there;
    the restored people will go.
¹⁰The people redeemed by Yahweh will go back,
    they will come to Tsiyyon with resounding,
With eternal rejoicing on their head,
    as joy and rejoicing overtake them
    and sorrow and sighing flee.

What are you relying on?

36

In the fourteenth year of King Hizqiyyahu, Sanherib [Sennacherib] king of Ashshur went up against all the fortified towns of Yehudah and captured them. ²The king of Ashshur sent the Rab-shaqeh from Lakish to Yerushalaim to King Hizqiyyahu with a heavy force, and he stood at the Upper Pool channel at the Washer's Field causeway. ³Elyaqim ben Hilqiyyahu who was in charge of the household, Shebna the secretary and Yo'ah ben Asaph the recorder went out to him.

⁴The Rab-shaqeh said to them, 'Say to Hizqiyyahu, please, "The Great King, the king of Ashshur, has said this: 'What is this reliance that you have: ⁵"I've said, 'Just the word on some lips are counsel and strength for battle'"? Now, on whom have you relied, that you've rebelled against me? ⁶There, you've relied on the support of this broken reed, on Misrayim, which when someone leans on it, comes into his palm and pierces it. Such is Par'oh king of Misrayim to all the people who rely on him. ⁷But when you say to me, "On Yahweh our God – we've relied on him", he's the one whose shrines and whose altars Hizqiyyahu removed, isn't he, and who's said to Yehudah and to Yerushalaim, "Before this altar you're to bow low."

⁸But now, please make a wager with my lord the king of Ashshur. I'll give you 2,000 horses if you can put riders on them for yourself. ⁹So how could you turn back the face of the governor of one of my lord's lesser servants and rely on Misrayim for chariotry and for cavalry for yourself? ¹⁰And now, is it without Yahweh that I've gone up to this country to devastate it? It was Yahweh who said to me, "Go up to this country and devastate it."'"

Don't rely on Yahweh

¹¹Elyaqim, Shebna and Yo'ah said to the Rab-shaqeh, 'Please speak to your servants in Aramaic, because we're listening. Don't speak to us in Yehudahite in the ears of the people, which is on the wall.' ¹²The Rab-shaqeh said, 'Was it to your lord and to you that my lord sent me to speak these words? Wasn't it to the individuals

who are sitting on the wall, to eat their faeces and drink the water between their legs with you?'

¹³The Rab-shaqeh stood and said and called in a loud voice in Yehudahite: 'Listen to the words of the Great King, the king of Ashshur. ¹⁴The king has said this: "Hizqiyyahu must not deceive you", because he won't be able to rescue you. ¹⁵And Hizqiyyahu must not get you to rely on Yahweh, saying, "Yahweh will definitely rescue us, this town won't be given into the hand of the king of Ashshur." ¹⁶Don't listen to Hizqiyyahu.

Because the king of Ashshur has said this: "Make a blessing [agreement] with me. Go out to me, and eat each one his vine and each one his fig tree, and drink each one the water from his cistern, ¹⁷until I come and take you to a country like your country, a country of grain and new wine, a country of bread and vineyards. ¹⁸Don't let Hizqiyyahu incite you, saying 'Yahweh will rescue us.' Have the gods of the nations, any of them, rescued his country from the hand of the king of Ashshur? ¹⁹Where were the gods of Hamat and Arpad? Where were the gods of Sepharvayim? And indeed did they rescue Shomron from my hand? ²⁰Who was it among all the gods of these countries that rescued their country from my hand?"'

²¹They were silent. They didn't answer him a word, because it was the king's order, 'Don't answer him.' ²²But Elyaqim ben Hilqiyyahu who was in charge of the household, Shebna the secretary and Yo'ah ben Asaph the recorder came to Hizqiyyahu, their clothes torn, and told him the Rab-shaqeh's words.

A politician's one fatal mistake

37 When King Hizqiyyahu heard, he tore his clothes and covered himself in sack. He came into Yahweh's house, ²but he sent Elyaqim, who was in charge of the household, Shebna the secretary and the priestly elders, covered in sack, to Yesha'yahu ben Amots. ³They said to him, 'Hizqiyyahu has said this: "This day is a day of pressure, reproof and disdain, when 'children have come to breaking but there's no energy to give birth'. ⁴Perhaps Yahweh your God will listen to the words of the Rab-shaqeh, whom the king of Ashshur his lord sent to revile the living God, and will issue a reproof for the words that Yahweh your God has heard, and you will lift up a plea on behalf of the remainder that are to be found here."'

⁵King Hizqiyyahu's servants came to Yesha'yahu, ⁶and Yesha'yahu said to them, 'You're to say this to your lord: "Yahweh has said this: 'Don't be afraid before the words you've heard with which the king of Ashshur's boys have insulted me. ⁷Here – I'm going to put a spirit in him, and he'll hear a report and go back to his country, and I shall cause him to fall by the sword in his country.'"'

⁸The Rab-shaqeh went back and found the king of Ashshur battling against Libnah, because he heard that he had moved on from Lakish, ⁹and he heard about Tirhaqah king of Kush, 'He's gone out to do battle with you.' So he heard and sent envoys to Hizqiyyahu, saying, ¹⁰'You're to say this to Hizqiyyahu king of Yehudah: "Your God on whom you're relying mustn't deceive you, saying 'Yerushalaim won't be given into the hand of the king of Ashshur.' ¹¹Here, you yourself have heard what the kings of Ashshur have done to all the countries, devoting them, and are you the one who'll be rescued? ¹²Did the gods of the nations that my ancestors devastated rescue them – Gozan, Harran, Reseph, and the Edenites who were in Tela'ssar? ¹³Where is the king of Hamat, the king of Arpad, the king of La'ir, Sepharvayim, Hena and Yivvah?"'

Dealing with tricky mail

¹⁴Hizqiyyahu took the documents from the envoys' hand, read it out and went up to Yahweh's house. Hizqiyyahu spread it before Yahweh, ¹⁵and Hizqiyyahu pleaded with Yahweh: ¹⁶'Yahweh of Armies, Yisra'el's God, sitting above the sphinxes: you are God, you alone, for all the kingdoms of the earth. You are the one who made the heavens and the earth. ¹⁷Yahweh, bend your ear and listen. Yahweh, open your eye and see. Listen to all the words of Sanherib that he has sent to revile the living God.

¹⁸Truly, Yahweh, the kings of Ashshur have put to the sword all the countries, and their own country, ¹⁹and put their gods into the fire, because they were not gods but rather

the making of human hands, wood and stone, and they obliterated them. ²⁰But now, Yahweh our God, deliver us from his hand, so that all the kingdoms of the earth may acknowledge that you alone are Yahweh.'

²¹Yesha'yahu ben Amots sent to Hizqiyyahu saying, 'Yahweh, Yisra'el's God, with whom you pleaded concerning Sanherib king of Ashshur, has said this. ²²This is the word that Yahweh has spoken about him:

Maiden Miss Tsiyyon
   despises you, she ridicules you.
Behind you Miss Yerushalaim
   has shaken her head.
²³Whom have you reviled and insulted,
   against whom have you lifted your voice?
You've raised your eyes on high
   towards Yisra'el's sacred one.
²⁴By the hand of your servants
   you've reviled the Lord, and said,
"With the large number of my chariotry I'm the
   one who has gone up
to the mountains' height, Lebanon's farthest
   parts.
I've cut down the highest of its cedars,
   the choicest of its junipers.
I've come to its ultimate height,
   its forest of farmland.
²⁵I'm the one who has dug
   and drunk water,
I've dried with the sole of my feet
   all Misrayim's streams."

Reminder to Sanherib, promise to Hizqiyyahu

²⁶Haven't you heard?
   – long ago I did it.
From days of old I formed it;
   now I've made it come about.
It's happened, crashing fortified towns
   into wasted heaps.
²⁷Their inhabitants, short of ability,
   are scared and shamed.
They were vegetation of the fields,
   green herbage,
Grass on the roofs,
   blasted before it grows up.
²⁸Your sitting, your going out and your coming I
   know,
and your raging at me.
²⁹Since you raged at me,
   and your din came up into my ears,
I shall put my hook in your nose,
   my bit in your mouth,
I shall make you go back
   by the way that you came.'

³⁰This will be the sign for you:

This year, eat the natural growth;
   in the second year, the secondary growth.
In the third year, sow and reap,
   plant vineyards and eat their fruit.
³¹An escape group from Yehudah's household that
   remains
will add root downwards and produce fruit
   above.
³²Because a remainder will go out from
   Yerushalaim,
and an escape group from Mount Tsiyyon.
The passion of Yahweh of Armies
   will do this.

³³Therefore Yahweh has said this concerning the king of Ashshur:

'He will not come into this town;
   he will not shoot an arrow there.
He will not meet it with a shield;
   he will not heap up a ramp against it.
³⁴By the way that he came he will go back;
   into this town he will not come
(Yahweh's declaration).
³⁵I will shield this town so as to deliver it,
   for my sake and for the sake of David my
   servant.'

The praying Hizqiyyahu

³⁶Yahweh's envoy went out and struck down 185,000 in the Ashshurites' camp. People started early in the morning – there, all of them were dead corpses.

³⁷Sanherib the king of Ashshur moved on and went, and returned and lived in Nineveh. ³⁸He was bowing low in the house of Nisrok his god when Adrammelek and Sar'etser his sons struck him with the sword. While they escaped to the country of Ararat, Esar-haddon his son began to reign in place of him.

38 In those days Hizqiyyahu became deathly ill. Yesha'yahu ben Amots the prophet came to him and said to him, 'Yahweh has said this: "Give orders to your household, because you're dying. You won't live on."' ²Hizqiyyahu turned his face round to the wall and pleaded with Yahweh, ³'Oh, Yahweh, please be mindful of how I've walked before you in truth and with a perfect mind, and done what is good in your eyes.' Hizqiyyahu cried and cried much.

⁴Yahweh's word came to Yesha'yahu: ⁵'Go and say to Hizqiyyahu: "Yahweh, the God of David your ancestor, has said this: 'I have listened to your plea, I've seen your tears. Here, I am going to add to your time fifteen years. ⁶From the fist of the king of Ashshur I shall rescue you and this town, and I shall shield this town.'" ⁷This will be the sign for you from Yahweh that Yahweh will do this thing that he has spoken of. ⁸"Here, I'm going to make the shadow go back on the steps, which has gone down on the steps of Ahaz with the sun, back ten steps."' And the sun went back ten steps by the steps that it had gone down.

The prayer

⁹Something written for Hizqiyyahu king of Yehudah, when he was ill and came back to life from his sickness.

¹⁰I myself said,
  'In the middle of my days I shall go.
I've been appointed to She'ol's gateways
  for the rest of my years.'
¹¹I said, 'I shall not see Yah;
  Yah is in the land of the living.
I shall not look to humanity again,
  with the inhabitants of the world.
¹²My dwelling has moved on and gone into exile from me,
  like a shepherd's tent.
I've rolled up my life like a weaver,
  as he cuts me from the loom.
While from day until night you make an end of me,
  ¹³I have composed myself until morning.
Like a lion that thus breaks up all my bones,
  from day until night you make an end of me.
¹⁴Like a swift, a swallow, so I chirp;
  I murmur like a dove.'
My eyes have looked to the height:
'Lord, it's oppression to me, make a pledge to me.
¹⁵What shall I speak of when he has said it to me,
  and he himself has acted?
I shall walk all my years
  in the bitterness of my heart.
¹⁶Lord, in such things people live,
  and in all of them is the life of my spirit;
  may you restore me and let me live.'

¹⁷There – as regards well-being,
  it was bitter for me, bitter.
But you yourself delighted in me,
  out of the pit of nothingness,
Because you threw all my wrongdoings
  behind your back.
¹⁸Because She'ol does not confess you,
  death praise you.
People who go down to the Pit
  don't expect your truthfulness.
¹⁹The living person, the living person, that one confesses you,
  this very day.
A father makes known to his children
  your truthfulness.
²⁰Yahweh will deliver me,
  and we will make music,
All the days of our lives
  at Yahweh's house.

(²¹Yesha'yahu had said, 'They are to get a block of figs and apply it to the infection, and he will live on', and Hizqiyyahu had said, 'What will be the sign that I shall go up to Yahweh's house?')

How to lose God's sympathy

39 At that time Merodak Bal'adan ben Bal'adan king of Babel sent documents and an offering to Hizqiyyahu; he had heard that he had been ill and had regained strength. ²Hizqiyyahu rejoiced about them and let them see his repository house, the silver, the gold, the spices and the fine oil, and his entire equipment house, and everything that was to be found in his storehouses. There was not a thing that Hizqiyyahu didn't let them see in his house and his entire kingdom.

³Yesha'yahu the prophet came to King Hizqiyyahu and said to him, 'What did these men say? Where did they come from to you?' Hizqiyyahu said, 'From a far country, they came to me from Babel.' ⁴He said, 'What did they see in your house?' Hizqiyyahu said, 'They saw everything that's in my house. There wasn't a thing that I didn't let them see in my storehouses.'

⁵Yesha'yahu said to Hizqiyyahu, 'Listen to the word of Yahweh of Armies. ⁶"There, days are going to come when everything that's in your house, and that your ancestors have stored up until this day, will be carried to Babel. Not a thing will be left," Yahweh has said. ⁷"Some of your descendants who will issue from you, whom you will father, will be taken and will become courtiers in the palace of the king of Babel."' ⁸Hizqiyyahu said to Yesha'yahu, 'The word from Yahweh that you have spoken is good.' He said, 'Because there'll be well-being and truthfulness in my days.'

Comfort my people

40 'Comfort, comfort my people',
says your God.
²'Speak to Yerushalaim's heart,
  call to it
That its tour of duty is fulfilled,
  that its waywardness is paid for,
That it has taken from Yahweh's hand
  double for all its wrongdoings.'

³A voice is calling:

'In the wilderness clear Yahweh's way,
  make straight in the steppe a causeway for our
    God.
⁴Every ravine is to rise up,
  every mountain and hill is to fall down.
The ridge is to become level,
  the cliffs a valley.
⁵Yahweh's splendour will appear,
  and all flesh will see it together,
  because Yahweh's mouth has spoken.'

⁶A voice is saying, 'Call',
  but someone says, 'Call what?'
All flesh is grass,
  and all its commitment is like a wild flower's.
⁷Grass withers, a flower fades,
  when Yahweh's wind blows on it.'
'Yes, the people is grass;
  ⁸grass withers, a flower fades –
  but our God's word rises up permanently.'

⁹Get yourself up on to a high mountain
  as a bringer of news to Tsiyyon.
Raise your voice with energy
  as a bringer of news to Yerushalaim.
Raise it, don't be afraid,
  say to Yehudah's towns,
'Here is your God,
  ¹⁰here is the Lord Yahweh.'
He comes as the strong one,
  his arm is going to rule for him.
Here, his reward is with him,
  his earnings before him.
¹¹Like a shepherd who pastures his flock,
  he collects lambs in his arm.
He carries them in his embrace,
  guides the nursing ones.

¹²Who gauged the water in his palm,
  surveyed the heavens with his span,
Measured the world's earth by the gallon,
  weighed the mountains with a balance,
  the hills with scales?
¹³Who directed Yahweh's spirit,
  or as the person to give him counsel made it
    known to him?
¹⁴With whom did he take counsel, so that he
    helped him understand,
  taught him the way to exercise authority,
Taught him knowledge,
  made known to him the way of understanding?
¹⁵There, nations count like a drop from a pan,
  like a cloud on scales;
  there, foreign shores are like a fine cloud that
    rises.
¹⁶Lebanon – there's not enough to burn up,
  its animals – there aren't enough as a burnt
    offering.
¹⁷All the nations are like nothing over against him;
  they count as less than naught, emptiness, to
    him.

Hope means energy

¹⁸So to whom would you compare God,
  or what comparison would you line up for him?

¹⁹The image, which a craftworker casts? –
  a smith beats it out with gold,
  and a smith with silver chains.
²⁰Is it sissoo fit for tribute,
  wood that doesn't rot, that someone chooses?
He seeks for himself a smart craftworker
  to set up an image so it doesn't slip.

²¹You acknowledge, don't you,
  you listen, don't you?
It's been told you from the beginning, hasn't it,
  you've understood earth's foundations, haven't you?
²²There's one who sits above earth's horizon,
  with its inhabitants like grasshoppers,
One who stretched out the heavens like net,
  spread them like a tent for sitting in,
²³One who turns sovereigns into nothing,
  makes earth's authorities pure emptiness.
²⁴They're really not planted, really not sown,
  their stem is really not rooting in the earth,
Then he blows on them and they shrivel,
  and a hurricane carries them off like straw.

²⁵So to whom would you compare me,
  so I could be similar (says the Sacred One)?
²⁶Lift your eyes on high and see –
  who created these?
The one who takes out their army by number
  calls to all of them by name.
Because of the greatness of his power,
  and as one firm in energy, not one lags behind.

²⁷Why do you say, Ya'aqob,
  and speak, Yisra'el,
'My way has hidden from Yahweh,
  a ruling for me passes away from my God'?
²⁸Haven't you acknowledged,
  or haven't you listened?
Yahweh is God of the ages,
  creator of earth's ends.
He doesn't get faint or weary;
  there's no searching out of his understanding.
²⁹He gives energy to the faint,
  and to the one who has no resources he gives much strength.
³⁰Youths may get faint and weary,
  young men may totally collapse.
³¹But people who hope in Yahweh get new energy,
  they grow pinions like eagles.
They run and don't get weary,
  they walk and don't faint.

Don't be afraid

41 Be silent for me, foreign shores;
  peoples must renew their energy.
They must come up, then speak;
  together let us draw near for making a ruling.
²Who aroused someone from the east
  whom faithfulness calls to its heel?
He gives up nations before him,
  enables him to put down kings.
He makes them like earth with his sword,
  like driven straw with his bow.
³As he pursues them, he passes on with things being well
  by a path on which he doesn't come straight.
⁴Who acted and did it,
  calling the generations from the beginning?
I am Yahweh, the first,
  and I myself am with the last.
⁵Foreign shores have seen and become afraid,
  earth's ends tremble,
  they've drawn near and come.
⁶An individual helps his neighbour,
  and says to his brother, 'Be strong!'
⁷Craftworker bids smith be strong,
  one who flattens with a hammer [bids] one who strikes with a mallet.
One who says of the joint, 'It's good',
  strengthens it with fastenings so it doesn't slip.

⁸But you as Yisra'el are my servant,
  as Ya'aqob you're the one that I chose.
As the offspring of Abraham you're my friend,
  ⁹the one of whom I took strong hold from earth's ends,
Called from its corners, and said to you,
  'You're my servant, I chose you, and didn't spurn you.'
¹⁰Don't be afraid, because I'm with you;
  don't be frightened, because I'm your God.
I'm making you firm, yes, helping you,
  yes, supporting you with my faithful right hand.
¹¹There, they'll be shamed and disgraced,
  all who rage at you.
They'll become absolutely nothing, they'll perish,
  the people who argue with you.
¹²You will seek them and not find them,
  the people who attack you.
They'll become absolutely nothing, zero,
  the people who do battle against you.
¹³Because I am Yahweh your God,
  who takes strong hold of your right hand,

Who says to you, 'Don't be afraid,
   I myself am helping you.'

¹⁴Don't be afraid, worm Ya'aqob,
   relics Yisra'el.
I'm helping you (Yahweh's declaration),
   Yisra'el's sacred one is your restorer.
¹⁵There, I'm making you into a harrow,
   a new thresher fitted with points.
You'll trample mountains and crush them,
   and make hills like chaff.
¹⁶You'll winnow them and the wind will carry them,
   the hurricane will scatter them.
And you yourselves will rejoice in Yahweh;
   in Yisra'el's sacred one you'll exult.

Do anything!

¹⁷When the humble and the needy are seeking water,
   but there is none, their tongue is parched with thirst.
I Yahweh will answer them;
   the God of Yisra'el will not abandon them.
¹⁸I will open up rivers on the bare places,
   springs in the middle of the valleys.
I will make the wilderness into a pool of water,
   dry land into water courses.
¹⁹In the wilderness I will put cedar,
   acacia, myrtle and oil tree.
In the steppe I will set juniper,
   maple and cypress, together,
²⁰In order that people may see and acknowledge,
   consider and discern together,
That Yahweh's hand did this,
   Yisra'el's sacred one created it.

²¹'Present your argument,'
   Yahweh says.
'Bring up your strong points,'
   says Ya'aqob's King.
²²They should bring them up
   and tell us what will happen.
The previous events – tell us what they were,
   so we may apply our mind and acknowledge their outcome.
Or let us hear about the coming events,
   ²³tell us things that will arrive after,
   so we may acknowledge that you are gods.
Yes, do something good or do something bad,
   so we may bow low and see together.

²⁴Here, you're less than nothing,
   your action is less than a sigh;
   it's an offence that someone chooses in you.

²⁵I aroused one from the north and he arrived,
   from the rising of the sun one who would call on my name.
He came on viceroys as if they were mire,
   as if he was a potter who treads clay.
²⁶Who told of it from the beginning so we might acknowledge him,
   beforehand so we might say 'He was right'?
No, there was no one telling of it;
   no, there was no one letting us hear about it;
   no, there was no one hearing your words.
²⁷The first for Tsiyyon ('Here, here they are'),
   for Yerushalaim, I give a bringer of news.
²⁸Were I to look, there was no one;
   of them, there was no counsellor,
   who could speak a word back if I asked them.
²⁹There, they are all a bane, their acts are zero,
   their images are a breath, emptiness.

There is my servant

42 There is my servant whom I support,
   my chosen whom I myself accept.
I'm putting my breath on him;
   he will see that my exercise of authority gets out to the nations.
²He won't cry out and he won't raise
   or make his voice heard, in the streets.
³A broken cane he won't snap,
   a flickering lamp he won't snuff.
For the sake of truthfulness he'll see the exercise of authority gets out,
⁴he won't flicker or break,
Until he sets the exercise of authority in the earth,
   as foreign shores wait for his instruction.

⁵The God Yahweh has said this,
   the one who created the heavens and stretched them,
   beating out the earth and its produce,
Giving air to the people on it,
   breath to those who walk on it:
⁶'I am Yahweh, I called you in faithfulness,
   took strong hold of your hand.
I formed you and gave you as a pact for the people,
   a light for the nations,

⁷In opening blind eyes,
   in getting the captive out from the dungeon,
   from the prison people who are living in the dark.
⁸I am Yahweh, that is my name;
   my splendour I do not give to another,
   or my praise to images.
⁹The previous events – here, they came about;
   and I'm telling of new events –
   before they grow, I let you hear.'

¹⁰Sing Yahweh a new song,
   his praise from the end of the earth,
You who go down to the sea, and what fills it,
   foreign shores and those who live in them.
¹¹The wilderness and its towns are to raise their voice,
   the villages where Qedar lives.
The people who live in Sela are to resound,
   they are to yell from the top of the mountains.
¹²They are to ascribe splendour to Yahweh,
   to tell of his praise on foreign shores.

What will we do when God's servant is deaf and blind?

¹³Yahweh goes out like a strong man,
   like a man of battle he arouses his passion.
He shouts, yes roars,
   acts as a strong man against his enemies.
¹⁴'I've been quiet from of old;
   I've been being still and restraining myself.
Like a woman giving birth I shall shriek,
   I shall devastate and crush together.
¹⁵I shall waste mountains and hills,
   wither all their growth.
I shall turn rivers into shores,
   wither wetland.
¹⁶I shall enable blind people to go by a way they haven't known,
   lead them on paths they haven't known.
I shall make the darkness in front of them into light,
   rough places into level ground.
These are the words I am acting on,
   and I will not abandon them.'
¹⁷They're turning back, they're utterly shamed,
   the people who trust in an image,
Who say to an idol,
   'You're our god.'

¹⁸Listen, you deaf people;
   you blind people, look and see!
¹⁹Who is blind except my servant,
   as deaf as my envoy I send?
Who is as blind as the one made good to,
   as blind as Yahweh's servant?
²⁰While seeing many things, you don't heed;
   while opening ears, he doesn't listen.
²¹Yahweh wants, for the sake of his faithfulness,
   that he should magnify the instruction, glorify it.
²²But that is a people plundered and spoiled,
   trapped in holes, all of them,
   and they're confined in jails.
They've become plunder with no rescuer,
   spoil with no one saying, 'Give it back!'
²³Who among you will give ear to this,
   will heed and listen for the future?
²⁴Who gave Ya'aqob as spoil, Yisra'el to plunderers? –
   it was Yahweh, against whom we had done wrong, wasn't it.
They were not willing to walk in his ways,
   they didn't listen to his instruction.
²⁵So he poured wrath upon it,
   his anger and battling vigour.
It blazed upon it all round, but it didn't acknowledge;
   it burned it up, but it doesn't take it into its mind.

You'll still be my witnesses

43 But now Yahweh has said this,
   your creator, Ya'aqob, your former, Yisra'el:
'Don't be afraid, because I'm restoring you;
   I call you by name, you're mine.
²When you pass through water, I'll be with you,
   and through rivers, they won't overwhelm you.
When you go in the middle of fire you won't burn,
   and into flames, they won't consume you.
³Because I am Yahweh your God,
   Yisra'el's Sacred One, your deliverer.
I gave Misrayim as your ransom,
   Kush and Seba in place of you.
⁴Because you were valuable in my eyes;
   you were honoured and I myself was loyal to you,
So that I would give people in place of you,
   nations in place of your life.

⁵Don't be afraid,
    because I'll be with you.
From the east I shall bring your offspring,
    from the west I shall gather you.
⁶I shall say to the north, "Give",
    and to the south, "Don't restrain.
Bring my sons from far away,
    my daughters from the end of the earth,
⁷Everyone called in my name and for my
        splendour,
    whom I created, formed, yes made."'

⁸Take out the people that is blind though it has
        eyes,
    those who are deaf though they have ears.
⁹All the nations must collect together,
    the peoples must gather.
Who among them could tell of this,
    could let us hear of the earlier events?
They must give their witnesses so they may prove
        right,
    so people may listen and say, 'It's true.'
¹⁰You're my witnesses (Yahweh's declaration),
    and my servant whom I chose,
In order that you may acknowledge and trust in
        me,
    and understand that I am the one.
Before me no god was formed,
    and after me there will be none.
¹¹I myself, I am Yahweh,
    and apart from me there's no deliverer.
¹²I'm the one who told of it and delivered;
    I let you hear, and there was no stranger among
        you.
And you're my witnesses (Yahweh's declaration);
    I am God.
¹³Yes, from this day I'm the one,
    and there is no one rescues from my hand;
    I act, and who can make it go back?

I'm sending to Babel

¹⁴Yahweh has said this,
    your restorer, Yisra'el's sacred one:
'For your sake I am sending to Babel,
    and I shall take down all of them as fugitives,
    the Kasdites into their boats with a shout.
¹⁵I am Yahweh, your Sacred One,
    Yisra'el's creator, your King.'
¹⁶Yahweh has said this,
    the one who made a way in the sea,
A path in vigorous water,
    ¹⁷who took out chariot and horse,
    force and vigorous one, altogether.
(They lie down, they don't get up;
    they were extinguished, they went out like a wick):
¹⁸Don't be mindful of the earlier events,
    don't consider previous events.
¹⁹Here am I, doing something new;
    now it is to grow – you will acknowledge it,
        won't you.
Yes, I shall make a way in the wilderness,
    rivers in the desert.
²⁰The animals of the wild will honour me,
    jackals and ostriches,
Because I'm giving water in the wilderness,
    rivers in the desert,
To give drink to my people, my chosen,
    ²¹the people that I formed for myself;
    they will recount my praise.

²²But it's not me you've called on, Ya'aqob,
    because you've been weary of me, Yisra'el.
²³You haven't brought me sheep as your whole
        offerings,
    nor honoured me with your sacrifices.
I haven't made you serve me with an offering,
    nor made you weary with incense.
²⁴You haven't gained me cane with silver,
    nor soaked me with the fat of your sacrifices.
Actually you have made me serve with your
        wrongdoings,
    wearied me with your wayward acts.
²⁵I, I'm the one,
    who wipes away your rebellions for my sake,
    and your wrongdoings I will not keep in mind.
²⁶Remind me; let's enter into judgement together –
    you give an account, so you may prove to be in
        the right.
²⁷Your first ancestor – he did wrong,
    and your interpreters – they rebelled against me.
²⁸So I treated the sacred officials as ordinary,
    give Ya'aqob to being devoted, Yisra'el to taunts.

People will say, 'I am Yahweh's'

44 But now listen, Ya'aqob my servant,
    Yisra'el whom I chose.
²Yahweh your maker has said this,
    your former from the womb, who will help you:
Don't be afraid, my servant Ya'aqob,
    Yeshurun whom I chose.

³Because I shall pour water on the thirsty,
   streams on the dry ground.
I shall pour my spirit on your offspring,
   my blessing on those who go out from you.
⁴They'll grow like a grassy tamarisk,
   like willows by water channels.
⁵One will say, 'I am Yahweh's',
   one will call out in Yahweh's name.
One will write on his hand 'Yahweh's',
   take as his name 'Yisra'el'.

⁶Yahweh, Yisra'el's King, has said this,
   your restorer, Yahweh of Armies:
'I am first and I am last;
   apart from me there is no God.
⁷Who is like me? – he must call out,
   tell and lay it out for me.
Who let people hear of coming events from of old? –
   they must tell us what will happen.
⁸Don't fear or take fright,
I let you hear of it in time past, and told of it, didn't I.
And you're my witnesses:
   is there a God apart from me? –
   but there is no crag, I don't acknowledge one.'

The stupidity of images

⁹People who form an image – all of them are emptiness,
   and the objects of their delight are no use.
They are their witnesses – they don't see and they don't acknowledge,
   in order that they may be shamed.
¹⁰Who forms a god or casts an image
   so that it may be of no use?
¹¹There, all his associates will be shamed;
   craftworkers are but human.
If all of them collect together and stand up,
   they'll be afraid, shamed, together.
¹²A craftworker in metal with a cutter
   works in the fire.
He forms it with hammers,
   works it with his energetic arm.
Should he get hungry, he'd have no energy;
   should he not drink water, he'd be faint.
¹³A craftworker in wood stretches a line,
   outlines it with a chalk.
He makes it with squares,
   outlines it with a compass.
He makes it in the image of a person,
   with the majesty of a human being, to live at home.
¹⁴In cutting himself cedars,
   getting ilex or oak,
He secures it for himself among the trees of the forest,
   plants a pine so the rain may make it grow,
¹⁵So it may be fuel for someone,
   and he takes some of them and gets warm.
He both lights it and bakes bread,
   and also makes a god and bows down to it.
He makes an image and prostrates himself to it,
   ¹⁶while half of it he burns in the middle of the fire.
Over the half of it he eats meat,
   he makes a roast and is full.
He also gets warm and says,
   'Ah, I'm warm, I see a flame.'
¹⁷The remainder of it he makes into a god, into his image,
   to which he will kneel down and bow low.
He will plead with it and say,
   'Rescue me, because you're my god.'
¹⁸They don't acknowledge,
   they don't understand,
Because their eyes are smeared so they don't see,
   their minds so they don't discern.
¹⁹He doesn't bring back to his mind,
   there's no knowledge nor understanding to say,
'Half of it I burned in the middle of the fire,
   also I baked bread on the coals.
I roasted meat and ate,
   and the rest of it I'll make into an offence.
I'll kneel down to a lump of wood' –
   ²⁰feeder on earth!
A deluded mind has directed him,
   and he can't rescue himself.
He can't say,
   'Isn't it a falsehood in my hand?'

No forgetting

²¹Be mindful of these things, Ya'aqob,
   Yisra'el, because you're my servant.
I formed you as a servant, you're mine;
   Yisra'el, there is to be no forgetting.
²²I'm wiping away your rebellions like a cloud,
   your wrongdoings like a thundercloud.
Turn back to me,
   because I'm restoring you.

²³Resound, heavens, because Yahweh has
    acted;
  shout, depths of the earth.
Break out in sound, mountains,
    forest and every tree in it.
Because Yahweh is restoring Ya'aqob,
    and will show his majesty in Yisra'el.

²⁴Yahweh, your restorer, has said this –
    your former from the womb:
'I am Yahweh,
    maker of everything,
Who stretched out the heavens on my own,
    spread out the earth of myself,
²⁵Who contravenes the signs of soothsayers,
    makes fools of diviners,
Turns the smart back,
    makes idiocy of their knowledge,
²⁶Implements his servant's word,
    fulfils his envoys' plan –
Who says of Yerushalaim, "It will be
    inhabited",
    and of Yehudah's towns, "They'll be built up",
    and "I will raise its wastes",
²⁷Who says to the deep,
    "Be wasted – I shall dry up your rivers",
²⁸Who says to Koresh [Cyrus], "My shepherd,
    he'll fulfil my every want",
By saying of Yerushalaim, "It will be built up",
    and to the palace, "Be founded."'

Creator of good and bad things

45 Yahweh has said this to his anointed, to Koresh,
'The one whom I took by the right hand,
Putting down nations before him,
    undoing the hips of kings,
Opening doors before him,
    so that gateways might not shut:
²I will go before you and level walls;
    I will break up copper doors,
    cut up iron bars.
³I will give you dark treasuries
    and hidden hoards,
In order that you may acknowledge that I am
    Yahweh;
        Yisra'el's God is the one who calls you by
        your name.
⁴For the sake of my servant Ya'aqob,
    Yisra'el my chosen,
I called you by your name,
    I designate you though you haven't
        acknowledged me.
⁵I am Yahweh and there is no other;
    apart from me there is no God.
I put the belt on you, though you have not
        acknowledged me,
⁶in order that people may acknowledge,
    from the rise of the sun and from the setting,
That there is none apart from me,
    I am Yahweh and there is no other,
⁷Forming light and creating dark,
    making well-being and creating bad fortune.
I am Yahweh,
    doing all these things.'

⁸Rain, heavens above;
    skies are to pour down faithfulness.
Earth is to open so that deliverance may fruit,
    faithfulness is to burst out all at once;
    I Yahweh have created it.

⁹Hey, you who argue with the one who forms him,
    a pot with earthen pots.
Can clay say to the one who forms it, 'What do
        you do',
    or can the thing you make say, 'It has no handles'?
¹⁰Hey, you who say to a father, 'What do you beget?'
    or to a woman, 'What do you give birth to?'
¹¹Yahweh has said this –
    Yisra'el's Sacred One and the one who forms it:
'Ask me about things to come for my children –
    you can give me orders about the work of my
        hands.
¹²I'm the one who made the earth
    and created humanity upon it.
I – my hands stretched out the heavens,
    I ordered their entire army.
¹³I'm the one who aroused him in faithfulness
    and level all his ways.
He's the one who will build up my town
    and send off my exiles,
Not for payment, not for a bribe,'
    Yahweh of Armies has said.

Every knee will bend

¹⁴Yahweh has said this:

'Misrayim's toil, Kush's profit,
    the Seba'ites, people of stature,

Will pass over to you and be yours;
   they'll follow behind you.
They'll pass over in fetters and bow low to you,
   to you they'll make their plea:
"God is in you only,
   and there's no other, no God.
¹⁵Certainly you're the God who hides,
   God of Yisra'el who delivers."
¹⁶They are shamed, yes, they are disgraced, all of
      them at once,
   they have gone in disgrace, the people who
      craft forms.
¹⁷Yisra'el has found deliverance in Yahweh,
   everlasting deliverance.
You will not be shamed, you will not be disgraced,
   to everlasting ages.'

¹⁸Because Yahweh has said this,
   the creator of the heavens, he is God,
the former of the earth and its maker –
   he established it, he did not create it an
      emptiness,
   he formed it for inhabiting:

'I am Yahweh
   and there is no other.
¹⁹It was not in hiddenness that I spoke,
   in a place in a dark country.
I didn't say to Ya'aqob's offspring,
   "Enquire of me in emptiness."
I am Yahweh, speaking of faithfulness,
   telling of what is right.
²⁰Gather, come, draw near together,
   escapees of the nations.
The people who carry their wooden images have
      not acknowledged,
   the people who plead with a god who does not
      deliver.
²¹Tell out, bring near,
   yes, consult together.
Who let people hear of this beforehand,
   told about it of old?
Was it not I, Yahweh? –
   and there was no other God apart from me,
The faithful God and deliverer;
   there's none except me.
²²Turn your faces to me and find deliverance, all
      the ends of the earth,
   because I am God and there's no other.
²³By myself I've sworn,
   faithfulness has gone out from my mouth,
   a word that will not turn back:
To me every knee will bend,
   every tongue swear.
²⁴"Only in Yahweh (of me it is said)
   are faithful acts and vigour.'"
To him they will come and be shamed,
   all who rage at him.
²⁵In Yahweh all Yisra'el's offspring
   will be faithful and will exult.

Gods you have to carry and the God who carries you

46 Bel has bent down, Nebo is stooping;
   their images have come to belong to
      creatures, to animals.
The things carried by you are loaded as a burden
      for weary ones;
²they've stooped, they've bent down together.
They couldn't save the burden;
   they themselves have gone into captivity.
³Listen to me, Ya'aqob's household,
   all the remainder of Yisra'el's household,
Who've been loaded from birth,
   who've been carried from the womb.
⁴Even until old age I will be the one;
   even until grey-headedness I will be the one
      who will bear.
I'm the one who made, I'm the one who carries;
   I'm the one who bears, and I will save.
⁵To whom can you compare me so I should be
      similar,
   or liken me so we are comparable?
⁶People who lavish gold from a purse,
   or weigh out silver by the rod,
Hire a smith so he may make it into a god
   to which they may fall down, bow low.
⁷They carry it on their shoulder, bear it,
   so they can set it down in its position and it can
      stand;
   from its place it won't move away.
Yes, someone can cry out to it, but it doesn't answer;
   it doesn't deliver him from the pressure on him.
⁸Keep this in mind, be strong,
   bring it back to mind, you rebels,
⁹Keep in mind earlier events of old,
   because I am God and there is no other.
I am God and there is none like me,
¹⁰telling of the outcome from the beginning,
And from beforehand things that haven't been done,
   saying 'My counsel will arise, all I want I shall do,'

¹¹Calling from the east a shriek,
  from a far country the person in my counsel.
I both spoke and will also bring it about;
  I formed and will also do it.
¹²Listen to me, you sturdy of mind,
  you who are far away from faithfulness.
¹³I have brought faithfulness near; it's not far away,
  and my deliverance won't delay.
I shall put deliverance in Tsiyyon,
  my magnificence for Yisra'el.

The unexpected fall of the superpower

47 Get down, sit in the earth, young Miss Babel,
  sit on the ground without a throne, Miss Kasdim.
Because you will not again have people call you
  sensitive and delightful.
²Get the millstones and grind meal,
  expose your hair.
Uncover your tresses, expose your leg,
  cross rivers.
³Your nakedness will be exposed,
  yes, your reviling will be visible.
I shall take redress,
  no one will intervene.
⁴(Our restorer: Yahweh of Armies is his name,
  Yisra'el's Sacred One.)

⁵Sit in silence, enter into darkness,
  Miss Kasdim.
Because you will not again have them call you
  mistress of kingdoms.
⁶I was angry with my people, I treated my domain
  as ordinary,
  I gave them into your hand.
You didn't show compassion to them;
  upon the aged you made your yoke very heavy.
⁷You said, 'I shall be here permanently,
  mistress always.'
You didn't receive these things into your mind;
  you were not mindful of its outcome.

⁸So now listen to this, charming one,
  who sits in confidence,
Who says to herself,
  'I and none else am still here,
I shall not sit as a widow,
  I shall not know the loss of children.'
⁹The two of these will come to you,
  in a moment, on one day.
The loss of children and widowhood
  in full measure will have come upon you.
In the multiplying of your chants
  and in the great abounding of your charms,
¹⁰You've been confident in your bad dealing;
  you said, 'There's no one looking at me.'
Your smartness, your knowledge,
  it turned you back.
You said to yourself,
  'I and none else am still here.'
¹¹But bad fortune is going to come upon you
  whose countercharm you won't know.
Disaster will fall upon you
  that you won't be able to expiate.
There will come upon you suddenly
  devastation that you won't know about.
¹²Stand, please, in your charms and in the
    multiplying of your chants,
  in which you've laboured from your youth.
Perhaps you'll be able to succeed,
  perhaps you will terrify.

I knew you were tough-minded

¹³You're collapsing in the multiplying of your plans;
  they should indeed stand up and deliver you,
The people who observe the heavens,
  who look at the stars,
Who make known for the months
  some of what will come upon you.
¹⁴There, they've become like straw
  that fire burns up.
They can't rescue themselves
  from the power of the blaze.
It's not a coal for warming,
  a flame for sitting before.
¹⁵Such have they been for you,
  those with whom you have laboured,
  your charmers from your youth.
They've wandered, each of them his own way;
  there's no one delivering you.

48 Listen to this, Ya'aqob's household,
  you who call yourselves by Yisra'el's name,
You who came out of Yehudah's water,
  who swear by Yahweh's name,
Who make mention of Yisra'el's God –
  not in truthfulness, not in faithfulness –
²Because they call themselves by the sacred town,
  lean on Yisra'el's God,
  whose name is Yahweh of Armies.

³The earlier events I told about of old,
   from my mouth they came out so I could make
      them heard.
Suddenly I acted and they came about,
   ⁴because of my knowing that you're tough.
Your neck is an iron sinew,
   your forehead copper.
⁵I told you about them of old,
   before they came about I let you hear,
So you couldn't say, 'My icon did them;
   my image, my idol ordered them.'

⁶You've heard – look at all of it;
   will you yourselves not tell of it?
I'm letting you hear of new events right now,
   secrets that you didn't know.
⁷Now they're created, not of old,
   or before today, and you haven't heard of
      them,
   so you could say, 'There, I knew about them.'
⁸No, you haven't heard; no, you haven't known;
   no, of old your ear didn't open up.
Because I knew you would utterly break faith;
   rebel from birth, you were called.

⁹For the sake of my name I delay my anger,
   for the sake of my praise I muzzle it for you
      so that I don't cut you off.
¹⁰There, I smelted you, and not in the silver
      [furnace];
   I chose you in the affliction furnace.
¹¹For my sake, for my sake, I act,
   because how can my splendour be treated as
      ordinary? –
   I will not give it to someone else.

If only . . .

¹²Listen to me, Ya'aqob,
   Yisra'el whom I called.
I'm the one, I'm the first,
   yes, I'm the last.
¹³Yes, it was my hand formed earth;
   my right hand spanned the heavens.
I'm going to call them
   so they stand together.
¹⁴Collect together, all of you, and listen –
   who among them told of these things?
One to whom Yahweh is loyal will do what he
      wants to Babel,
   and his arm to the Kasdites.

¹⁵I, I'm the one who spoke,
   yes, I called him,
   I brought him and he will succeed in his
      journey.
¹⁶Draw near to me,
   listen to this.
Not from the first did I speak in hiddenness;
   from the time it came to be, I was there.

Now the Lord Yahweh
   has sent me, with his spirit.
¹⁷Yahweh has said this – your restorer,
   Yisra'el's Sacred One.
'I am Yahweh your God,
   the one who teaches you to succeed,
Who directs you in the way you should go –
   ¹⁸if only you had heeded my orders.
Your well-being would have been like a river,
   your faithfulness like the waves of the sea.
¹⁹Your offspring would have been like the sand,
   the people who went out from you like its grains.
Your name would not be cut off,
   not be annihilated, from before me.'

²⁰Go out from Babel,
   flee from the Kasdites!
Tell it with resounding voice,
   make it heard.
Send it out to the end of the earth,
   say, 'Yahweh is restoring his servant Yisra'el.'
²¹They were not thirsty
   as he made them go through wastes.
He made water flow from the crag for them,
   he split the crag and water gushed out.

²²There's no well-being
   (Yahweh has said) for faithless people.

The servant's servant

49 Listen, foreign shores, to me;
   heed, peoples far away.
Yahweh called me from the womb,
   from my mother's insides he made mention of
      my name.
²He made my mouth like a sharp sword,
   in the shadow of his hand he hid me.
He made me into a burnished arrow,
   in his quiver he concealed me.
³He said to me, 'You're my servant, Yisra'el;
   in you I will show my majesty.'

⁴But I myself said, 'It was to empty results that I toiled,
   for futility and hollowness that I used up my energy.'
Yet a ruling for me is with Yahweh,
   my earnings are with my God.
⁵Now Yahweh has said –
   the one who formed me from the womb as a servant for him,
By bringing Ya'aqob back to him,
   so that Yisra'el might not withdraw;
And I have found honour in Yahweh's eyes,
   and my God has become my vigour –
⁶He has said, 'It's slight, your being a servant for me
   to raise Ya'aqob's clans and bring back Yisra'el's shoots.
I shall make you into a light of nations,
   to be my deliverance to the end of the earth.'

⁷Yahweh has said this –
   Yisra'el's restorer, its Sacred One –
To one despised in spirit, offensive to nations,
   to a servant of rulers:

Kings will see and rise,
   leaders, and they will fall low,
For the sake of Yahweh, who is trustworthy,
   Yisra'el's Sacred One – he chose you.

⁸Yahweh has said this:

In a time of acceptance I'm answering you,
   on a day of deliverance I'm helping you.
I'll guard you and make you
   into a pact for people,
By raising up the country,
   by giving out the desolate domains,
⁹By saying to captives, 'Go out',
   to people in darkness, 'Appear.'
Along the roads they will pasture,
   on all the bare places will be their pasture.
¹⁰They will not hunger and not thirst;
   khamsin and sun won't strike them down.
Because the one who has compassion on them will lead them,
   and guide them by springs of water.
¹¹I'll make all my mountains into a road;
   my causeways will rise up.
¹²There – these will come from afar;
   there – these from the north and the west,
   and these from the country of Sinim.

Can a mother forget?

¹³Resound, heavens, celebrate, earth,
   break into sound, mountains.
Because Yahweh is comforting his people;
   he will have compassion on his humble ones.

¹⁴But Tsiyyon says, 'Yahweh has abandoned me,
   the Lord has put me out of mind.'
¹⁵Can a woman put her baby out of mind,
   so as not to have compassion on the child of her womb?
Yes, these may put out of mind,
   but I – I cannot put you out of mind.
¹⁶There, on my palms I engraved you;
   your walls are in front of me continually.
¹⁷Your children are hurrying the people who tore you down,
   your devastators will go out from you.
¹⁸Lift your eyes round and look,
   they're all collecting, they're coming to you.
As I am alive (Yahweh's declaration),
   you will indeed put on all of them like jewellery,
   bind them on like a bride.
¹⁹Because your wastes, your devastations,
   your country that was torn down –
Because now you'll be too confined for your population,
   while the people who swallowed you up go away.
²⁰The children of your bereavement
   will yet say in your ears,
'The place is too narrow for me,
   move over for me so I can settle down.'
²¹You'll say to yourself,
   'Who fathered these for me,
When I was bereaved and barren,
   gone into exile and passing away?
These, who reared them,
   there, when I remained alone,
   these – where were they?'

Can prey be taken from a strong man?

²²The Lord Yahweh said this:

Here, I shall raise my hand to the nations,
   to the peoples I will lift up my signal.
They will bring your sons in their embrace,
   carry your daughters on their shoulder.

²³Kings will be your foster fathers,
  their queens your nursing mothers.
Face to the ground they'll bow low to you,
  they'll lick up the earth under your feet.
And you will acknowledge that I am Yahweh;
  those who hope in me will not be shamed.

²⁴Can prey be taken from a strong man
  or the captives of a faithful one escape?

²⁵Because Yahweh has said this:

Yes, the strong man's captives may be taken,
  the prey of the violent may escape.
I myself will argue with the one arguing with
    you,
  and your children I will deliver.
²⁶I'll feed your oppressors with their own flesh;
  they'll be drunk on their own blood as on
    grape juice.
And all flesh will acknowledge
  that I am Yahweh your deliverer,
  Ya'aqob's strong one, your restorer.

50 Yahweh has said this:

Where now is the divorce document
  belonging to your mother whom I sent off?
Or who among my creditors was it
  to whom I sold you?
There – you were sold for your wayward acts,
  and for your rebellions your mother was sent
    off.
²Why did I come and there was no one there,
  did I call and there was no one answering?
Has my hand become far too short for
    redeeming,
  or is there no energy in me to rescue?
There, with my reprimand I can dry up the sea,
  I can make rivers into wilderness.
Their fish will smell because there's no water;
  they'll die of thirst.
³I can clothe the heavens in black,
  make sack their covering.

Will you follow?

⁴The Lord Yahweh gave me a disciples' tongue,
  so as to know how to aid someone faint.
With a word he wakens, morning by morning,
  wakens my ear so as to hear like the disciples.

⁵The Lord Yahweh opened my ear,
  and I didn't rebel, I didn't turn away.
⁶I gave my back to people striking me,
  my cheeks to people pulling out my beard.
I didn't hide my face
  from deep disgrace and spit.
⁷The Lord Yahweh helps me;
  therefore I haven't been disgraced.
Therefore I set my face like flint,
  and I knew I wouldn't be shamed.
⁸The one who shows that I'm in the right is
    near;
  who will argue with me? – let us stand up
    together.
Who's the person with a case against me? –
  he should come forward to me.
⁹There, the Lord Yahweh will help me –
  who's the one who will show that I'm in the
    wrong?
There, all of them will wear out like clothing;
  moth will consume them.

¹⁰Who among you lives in awe of Yahweh,
  listens to his servant's voice?
One who has walked in darkness
  and has no illumination
Must rely on Yahweh's name
  and lean on his God.
¹¹There, all of you who kindle fire,
  who belted on firebrands:
Walk into your fiery flame,
  into the firebrands you've lit.
This is coming about from my hand for you;
  you'll lie down in pain.

Wake up, Yahweh

51 Listen to me, you who pursue faithfulness,
who seek help from Yahweh.
Look to the crag from which you were hewn,
  to the cavity, the hole, from which you were
    dug.
²Look to Abraham your ancestor,
  and Sarah who was labouring with you.
Because he was one when I called him,
  so I might bless him and make him many.
³Because Yahweh is comforting Tsiyyon,
  he's comforting all its wastes.
He's making its wilderness like Eden,
  its steppe like Yahweh's garden.

Gladness and rejoicing will be found there,
  thanksgiving and the sound of music.
⁴Heed me, my people;
  give ear to me, my nation.
Because instruction goes out from me,
  my exercise of authority for the light of
      peoples.
In a flash ⁵my faithfulness is near,
  my deliverance is going out,
  my arm will exercise authority for peoples.
Foreign shores will hope in me,
  they will wait for my arm.
⁶Lift up your eyes to the heavens,
  look to the earth below.
Because the heavens are shredding like smoke,
  the earth will wear out like clothing,
  its inhabitants will die in like manner.
But my deliverance will be permanent,
  my faithfulness will not shatter.

⁷Listen to me, you who acknowledge my
      faithfulness,
  a people with my instruction in its mind.
Don't be afraid of human reviling,
  don't shatter at their taunting.
⁸Because moth will consume them like clothing,
  grub will consume them like wool.
But my faithfulness will be permanent,
  my deliverance to all generations.

⁹Wake up, wake up, put on vigour,
  Yahweh's arm.
Wake up as in days of old,
  generations long ago.
You're the one who split Rahab,
  pierced the dragon, aren't you.
¹⁰You're the one who dried up the sea,
  the water of the great deep,
Who made the depths of the sea
  a way for the restored people to pass, aren't
      you.
¹¹The people redeemed by Yahweh will go back,
  they will come to Tsiyyon with resounding.
With eternal rejoicing on their head,
  as joy and rejoicing overtake them,
  and sorrow and sighing flee.

Wake up, Yerushalaim

¹²I, I am the one who's comforting you –
  who are you to be afraid
Of a mortal who dies,
  of a human being who is treated like grass?
¹³You've put Yahweh your maker out of mind,
  the one who stretched out the heavens and
      founded the earth.
You're fearful constantly, all day,
  of the fury of the oppressor,
  as he is preparing to devastate.
But where is the fury of the oppressor? –
  ¹⁴the one stooping is hastening to be released.
He won't die in the pit,
  he won't lack his bread.
¹⁵I am Yahweh your God,
  one who stills the sea when its waves roar –
  Yahweh of Armies is his name.
¹⁶I've put my words in your mouth,
  and covered you with the shade of my hand,
In planting the heavens and founding the earth,
  in saying to Tsiyyon 'You're my people.'

¹⁷Wake yourself up, wake yourself up,
  get up, Yerushalaim,
You who drank from Yahweh's hand
  his fury cup.
The chalice, the shaking cup,
  you drank, you drained.
¹⁸There was no one guiding her,
  of all the children to whom she gave birth.
There was no one taking her by the hand,
  of all the children she brought up.
¹⁹There were two things befalling you
  (who was to mourn for you?),
Destruction and breaking, famine and sword
  (who was I to comfort you?).
²⁰Your children were overcome,
  they lay down at the entrance to all the streets
  like a snared oryx,
The people full of Yahweh's fury,
  of your God's reprimand.
²¹Therefore please listen to this, humble one,
  drunk but not with wine.
²²Your Lord Yahweh has said this,
  your God who argues for his people:
'There, I'm taking from your hand
  the shaking cup,
My chalice, the fury cup,
  which you will never drink again.
²³I'll put it into the hand of your tormentors,
  the people who said to your neck,
  "Bow down so we may pass over."
And you made your back like the earth,
  like the street for them to pass over.'

Beautiful feet

52 Wake up, wake up,
 put on your vigour, Tsiyyon!
Put on your majestic clothes,
 Yerushalaim, sacred town!
Because the foreskinned or taboo person
 will never again come into you.
²Shake yourself from the earth,
 get up, sit down, Yerushalaim!
They are loosening the bonds from on your neck,
 captive Miss Tsiyyon.

³Because Yahweh has said this:

For nothing you were sold,
 without silver you will be restored.

⁴Because the Lord Yahweh has said this:

My people went down to Misrayim at the beginning
 to reside there.
But Ashshur oppressed them to no purpose,
 ⁵so now what was there for me here (Yahweh's declaration)?
Because my people was taken to no end,
 while its rulers boast (Yahweh's declaration).
And constantly, all day,
 my name stands reviled.
⁶Therefore my people will acknowledge my name,
 therefore on that day [it will acknowledge]
 that I'm the one who speaks – here I am.

⁷How lovely on the mountains are the feet of one who brings news,
 one who lets people hear 'All is well',
One who brings good news, lets people hear of deliverance,
 who says to Tsiyyon, 'Your God has begun to reign.'
⁸A voice! – lookouts are lifting voice,
 together they resound.
Because with both eyes
 they see Yahweh going back to Tsiyyon.
⁹Break out, resound together,
 wastes of Yerushalaim.
Because Yahweh is comforting his people;
 he's restoring Yerushalaim.
¹⁰Yahweh is baring his sacred arm
 before the nations' eyes.
All the ends of the earth
 will see our God's deliverance.

¹¹Depart, depart, get out from there,
 don't touch what is taboo.
Get out from within it, purify yourselves,
 you who carry Yahweh's things.
¹²Because you won't get out in haste,
 you won't go in flight.
Because Yahweh is going before you,
 and Yisra'el's God is bringing up your rear.

Who could have believed it?

¹³There, my servant will thrive,
 he'll rise and lift up and be very high.
¹⁴As many people were appalled at you,
 so his appearance is anointed beyond anyone,
 his look beyond that of human beings.
¹⁵So he'll spatter many nations;
 at him kings will shut their mouths.
Because what hadn't been told them they will have seen,
 and what they hadn't heard they will have understood.

53 Who believed what we heard,
 and upon whom did Yahweh's arm appear?
²He grew before him like a sucker
 or a root out of dry ground.
He had no look and no majesty so we should look at him,
 no appearance so we should want him.
³He was despised and the most frail of human beings,
 a man of great suffering and acquainted with weakness.
As when people hide their face from someone,
 he was despised and we didn't count him.
⁴Yet it was our weaknesses that he carried,
 our great suffering that he bore.
But we ourselves had counted him touched,
 struck down, by God, and afflicted.
⁵But he was the one who was wounded through our rebellions,
 crushed through our wayward acts.
Chastisement to bring us well-being was on him,
 and by means of his being hurt there was healing for us.
⁶All of us like sheep had wandered,
 each had turned his face to his own way.

Yahweh – he let fall on him
   the waywardness of all of us.

The man who kept his mouth shut

⁷He was put down, but he was one who let himself
      be afflicted,
   and he wouldn't open his mouth.
Like a sheep that's led to slaughter
   or like a ewe that's silent before its shearers,
      he wouldn't open his mouth.
⁸By the restraint of authority he was taken;
   who would complain at his generation?
Because he was cut off from the land of the living;
   because of my people's rebellion the touch
      came to him.
⁹He was given his tomb with the faithless,
   his burial mound with the rich person,
Because he'd done no violence,
   and no deceit with his mouth.
¹⁰While Yahweh desired the crushing of the one
      he weakened,
   if with his whole person he lays down a
      reparation offering,
He'll see offspring, he'll prolong his life,
   and Yahweh's desire will succeed in his hand.
¹¹Out of his personal trouble, when he sees he will
      be sated;
   by his acknowledgement my servant will show
      many that he is indeed in the right,
         when he bears their wayward acts.

¹²Therefore I'll give him a share with the many;
   he'll share out the numerous as spoil,
In return for the fact that he exposed his person
      to death,
   when he let himself be numbered with the rebels,
When he was the one who carried the
      wrongdoing of many people,
   and was appealing for the rebels.

A time to cry and a time to whoop

54 Resound, infertile one, you who haven't
      given birth;
   break out into sound and bellow, you who
      haven't laboured.
Because the children of the desolate are many,
   more than the married woman's children
      (Yahweh has said).

²Enlarge your tent space;
   people must stretch your dwelling curtains,
      don't hold back.
Lengthen your ropes, strengthen your pegs,
   ³because you'll spread out right and left.
Your offspring will dispossess the nations,
   they'll inhabit the desolate towns.
⁴Don't be afraid, because you will not be shamed;
   don't be disgraced, because you will not be
      confounded.
Because you will put out of mind the shame of
      your youth,
   you will no more be mindful of the reviling of
      your widowhood.
⁵Because your maker will be the one who marries
      you;
   Yahweh of Armies is his name.
Yisra'el's Sacred One is your restorer;
   he calls himself 'God of all the earth'.
⁶Because it's as a wife abandoned
   and distressed in spirit that Yahweh is calling
      you,
The wife of his youth when she's been spurned,
   your God has said.
⁷For a short moment I abandoned you,
   but with great compassion I'll gather you.
⁸In a burst of anger
   I hid my face from you for a moment,
But with permanent commitment I'm having
      compassion for you
   (your restorer, Yahweh, has said),
⁹because this is Noah's water to me.
In that I swore that Noah's water
   would not pass over the earth again,
So I'm swearing
   not to be angry with you or to reprimand you.
¹⁰Because mountains may move away, hills slip,
   but my commitment will not move away from
      you.
My pact of well-being will not slip,
   the one who has compassion for you, Yahweh,
      has said.

David's covenant will become yours

¹¹Humble, tossing, not comforted –
   here I am, resting your stones in antimony.
I'll found you with sapphires,
   ¹²make chalcedony your pinnacles,
Your gateways into sparkling stones,
   your entire border into delightful stones.

¹³All your children will be Yahweh's disciples;
   great will be your children's well-being.
¹⁴In faithfulness you'll establish yourself;
   you can be far from oppression,
Because you will not be afraid,
   and from shattering, because it will not come
      near you.
¹⁵There, someone need be in dread
   of nothing from me.
Who quarrels with you? –
   he'll fall to you.
¹⁶There, I'm the one who created the smith
   who blows into the fire of coals,
And who brings out a tool for his work,
   and I'm the one who created the destroyer to
      ravage.
¹⁷Any tool formed against you will not succeed;
   you will show to be in the wrong every tongue
      that arises with you for a judgement.

This is the domain of Yahweh's servants,
   their faithfulness from me (Yahweh's declaration).

55 Hey, anyone who's thirsty,
   come for water.
Whoever has no silver, come,
   buy and eat.
Come, buy without silver,
   wine and milk without cost.
²Why weigh out silver for what isn't bread,
   and your labour for what isn't filling?
Listen hard to me and eat what's good;
   you can delight your appetite with rich food.
³Bend your ear, come to me;
   listen, so you may come to life.
I will solemnize for you a permanent pact,
   the trustworthy commitments to David.
⁴Here, I made him a witness for peoples,
   a leader and commander for peoples.
⁵Here, you'll call a nation that you don't
      acknowledge,
   and a nation that doesn't acknowledge you will
      run to you,
For the sake of Yahweh your God,
   and for Yisra'el's Sacred One, because he's
      glorifying you.

Our ideas and plans, and God's

⁶Enquire of Yahweh while he is letting himself be
      found,
   call him while he's near.
⁷The faithless person must abandon his way,
   the person who brings trouble [must abandon]
      his intentions.
He must turn back to Yahweh so he may have
      compassion on him,
   to our God because he does much pardoning.
⁸Because my intentions are not your intentions,
   your ways are not my ways (Yahweh's
      declaration).
⁹Because the heavens are higher than the earth;
   so are my ways higher than your ways,
   my intentions than your intentions.

¹⁰Because as the rain or snow
   falls from the heavens,
And doesn't go back there
   but rather soaks the earth,
And makes it bear and produce,
   and give seed to the sower and bread to the
      eater,
¹¹So will my word be
   that goes out from my mouth.
It will not come back to me empty,
   but rather do that which I wanted,
   achieve that for which I sent it.

¹²Because you'll go out with joy,
   and be brought in with well-being.
The mountains and the hills
   will break out before you in resounding.
All the trees in the open country
   will clap the palms of their hands.
¹³Instead of the thorn a juniper will come up,
   instead of the briar a myrtle will come up.
It will be a memorial for Yahweh,
   a permanent sign that will not be cut down.

An ambiguous 'Because'

56 Yahweh has said this:
Keep the exercise of authority,
   act in faithfulness,
Because my deliverance is near to coming,
   my faithfulness to appearing.
²The blessings of the person who does this,
   the individual who holds on to it,
Keeping the sabbath rather than treating it as
      ordinary,
   and keeping his hand from doing anything
      bad.

³So the foreigner who attaches himself to Yahweh
   is not to say,
'Yahweh will quite separate me
   from among his people.'
The eunuch is not to say,
   'Here am I, a dry tree.'

⁴Because Yahweh has said this:

'To the eunuchs who keep my sabbaths,
   and choose what I want, and hold on to my
      pact –
⁵I will give to them,
   within my house and within my walls,
A memorial and name
   better than sons and daughters.
I will give him a permanent name,
   one that will not be cut off.
⁶And the foreign people
   who attach themselves to Yahweh, to minister
      to him
And to give themselves to Yahweh's name,
   to be servants to him,
Anyone who keeps the sabbath rather than
      treating it as ordinary,
   and holds strongly to my pact,
⁷I will bring them to my sacred mountain,
   and let them rejoice in my prayer house.
Their burnt offerings and their sacrifices
   will be for acceptance on my altar.
Because my house will be called
   a prayer house for all the peoples.'
⁸A declaration of the Lord Yahweh,
   the one gathering the scattered people of Yisra'el:
   'I will gather yet more towards it, to its gathered
      ones.'

Slaughter in the wadis

⁹All you animals of the wild, come and eat –
   all you animals in the forest.
¹⁰Its lookouts are blind,
   all of them; they don't know.
All of them are dumb dogs, they can't bark;
   they're lying snoozing, loving to doze.
¹¹But the dogs are vigorous of appetite;
   they don't know about being full.
And these people – they are shepherds
   that don't know how to discern.
All of them have turned their face to their own way,
   each to his loot, every last bit of it.

¹²'Come on, I'll get wine,
   we'll swill liquor.
Tomorrow will be like this,
   exceedingly, very great!'

57
The faithful person has perished,
   and there was no one taking it into their
      mind.
Committed people are gathered up
   without anyone discerning
That it is from before a bad situation
   that the faithful person has been gathered up.
²He goes while things are well (while they rest on
      their beds),
   the one who walks straight.

³But you people, draw near here,
   children of a diviner.
Offspring of an adulterer and a woman who acts
      the whore,
⁴in whom do you revel?
At whom do you open your mouth wide,
   put out your tongue?
Are you not rebellious children,
   the offspring of falsehood,
⁵You who inflame yourselves among the oaks,
   under any verdant tree,
Who slaughter children in the wadis,
   under the clefts in the cliffs?
⁶Among the deceptions in the wadi is your share;
   they are your allocation.
Yes, to them you've poured a libation,
   you've lifted up an offering:
   in view of these things, should I relent?
⁷On a high and lofty mountain
   you've put your bed.
Yes, you've gone up there
   to offer a sacrifice.
⁸Behind the door and the doorpost
   you've set your memorial.
Because from me you've gone away, you've gone
      up,
   you've opened wide your bed.
You've solemnized things for yourself from them,
   you've been loyal to their bed, you've beheld
      their love.

High and holy, but present with the crushed

⁹You've appeared to the King in your oils,
   you've multiplied your perfumes.

You've sent off your envoys afar,
  you've got them to go down to She'ol.
¹⁰When you grew weary with the length of your way,
  you didn't say, 'It's futile.'
You found life for your capacity;
  therefore you haven't weakened.
¹¹For whom have you felt reverence and awe,
  that you lie?
You haven't been mindful of me;
  you haven't received me into your mind.
I've been still, yes from of old, haven't I,
  but you're not in awe of me.
¹²I myself will tell of your 'faithfulness',
  and your acts – they won't avail you.
¹³When you cry out, your abominable gatherings can rescue you;
  but a wind will carry them all off, a breath will take them.
But the person who takes shelter with me will receive the country as his domain,
  will possess my sacred mountain.

¹⁴Someone has said, 'Build up, build up, clear a way,
  lift high the obstacles from my people's way.'
¹⁵Because the one who is high and lofty has said this,
The one who dwells permanently,
  whose name is 'Sacred One':
'I dwell on high and sacred,
  but with the crushed and low in spirit,
Bringing life to the spirit of people who are low,
  bringing life to the heart of the crushed.
¹⁶Because I will not argue permanently,
  I will not be perpetually irate.
Because before me the spirit would faint,
  the breathing beings I made.
¹⁷At the waywardness of its looting I was irate;
  I hit it, hiding – I was irate.
It lived turning back to the way of its own mind;
  ¹⁸I've seen its ways, but I will heal it.
I'll lead it and make good all comfort to it;
  for its mourners ¹⁹creating as the fruit of lips well-being,
Well-being for one far away and one near
  (Yahweh has said), and I'll heal it.
²⁰But the faithless – they are like the sea tossing,
  because it cannot be calm.
Its waters toss muck and mud;
  ²¹there's no well-being (my God has said) for faithless people.'

(Un)spiritual practices

58 Call with full throat, don't hold back,
  lift your voice like the horn.
Tell my people about their rebellion,
  Ya'aqob's household about their wrongdoings.
²They enquire of me day by day
  and want to acknowledge my ways,
Like a nation that has acted in faithfulness,
  and not abandoned its God's ruling.
They ask me for faithful rulings,
  they want to draw near to God.
³'Why have we fasted and you haven't seen,
  we've humbled ourselves and you haven't acknowledged?'
There – on your fast day you find what you want,
  but you oppress the people who toil for you.
⁴There – you fast for argument and strife,
  and for hitting with faithless fist.
You don't fast this very day
  in such a way as to make your voice heard on high.
⁵Will the fast that I choose be of this very kind,
  a day for a person to humble himself?
Will it be for bowing one's head like a bulrush,
  and spreading sack and ash?
Is it this that you call a fast,
  a day accepted by Yahweh?
⁶This will be the fast I choose, won't it:
  loosing faithless chains,
Untying the cords of the yoke,
  letting the oppressed go free,
  and tearing apart every yoke.
⁷It will be dividing your food with the hungry person, won't it,
  and bringing home the humble, downtrodden.
When you see the naked, you'll cover him,
  and not hide from your fellow flesh and blood.
⁸Then your light will break out like dawn,
  and your restoration will flourish speedily.
Your faithfulness will go before you;
  Yahweh's splendour will gather you.
⁹Then you'll call and Yahweh will answer;
  you'll cry for help and he'll say, 'I'm here.'
If you do away with the yoke from within you,
  the pointing of the finger and the troublesome word,
¹⁰And offer yourself to the hungry person,
  and fill the need of the humble person,
Your light will shine in the darkness,
  your gloom will be like midday.

¹¹Yahweh will guide you continually,
  and fill your appetite in scorched places.
He'll renew your frame
  and you will be like a watered garden,
Like a spring of water
  whose water does not deceive.
¹²People of yours will build up the ruins of old;
  you'll raise the foundations from past generations.
You'll be called 'Repairer of a Breach,
  Restorer of Paths for Living On'.

Honouring the sabbath

¹³If you take back your foot from the sabbath,
  doing the things you want on my sacred day,
Call the sabbath 'Revelling',
  and Yahweh's sacred thing 'Honourable',
And honour it rather than acting in your ways,
  or finding what you want, and speaking your word,
¹⁴Then you'll revel in Yahweh
  and I'll let you ride over the heights of the earth.
I'll let you eat the domain of Ya'aqob your father;
  because Yahweh's mouth has spoken.

59 Here – Yahweh's hand hasn't become too short to deliver,
  his ear hasn't become too heavy to listen.
²Rather, your wayward acts have become separators
  between you and your God.
Your wrongdoings have hidden his face
  so as not to listen to you.
³Because your fists – they've become polluted with blood,
  your fingers – with waywardness.
Your lips – they've spoken falsehood,
  your tongue – it talks of evil.
⁴There's no one calling in faithfulness,
  there's no one entering into judgement with trustworthiness.
Relying on nothingness and speaking emptiness,
  conceiving trouble and giving birth to wickedness.
⁵They've broken open a serpent's eggs,
  they spin a spider's webs.
Someone who eats of their eggs – he will die,
  and one that is smashed – an adder breaks out.
⁶Their webs won't become a garment,
  they won't cover themselves in the things they make.
The things they make are things that bring trouble;
  the doing of violence is in their fists.
⁷Their feet run to what is bad,
  they hurry to shed the blood of one free of guilt.
Their intentions are troublesome intentions,
  destruction and breaking is on their causeways.
⁸The way of well-being they haven't acknowledged,
  and there's no exercise of authority on their tracks.
They've made their paths crooked for themselves;
  no one who walks on it acknowledges well-being.

That's why there's no restoration

⁹That's why the exercise of authority is far from us,
  faithfulness doesn't reach us.
We look for light but there, darkness;
  for brightness, whereas we walk in gloom.
¹⁰We grope like blind people along a wall;
  like people without eyes we grope.
We've fallen over at midday as if it was dusk,
  among sturdy people as if we were dead.
¹¹We rumble like bears, all of us,
  and murmur on like doves.
We look for the exercise of authority but there is none,
  for deliverance that's far from us.

¹²Because our rebellions are many in your sight,
  and our wrongdoings have testified against us.
Because our rebellions are with us,
  and our wayward acts – we acknowledge them.
¹³Rebelling, breaking faith with Yahweh,
  and turning back from following our God,
Speaking of fraud, conceiving defiance,
  and talking words of falsehood inside us.
¹⁴So the exercise of authority has turned away,
  faithfulness stands far off.
Because truthfulness has fallen over in the square,
  and straightness can't come in.
¹⁵Truthfulness has gone missing;
  the one who turns from dealing badly is despoiled.

Yahweh saw and it was bad in his eyes
  that there was no exercise of authority.

¹⁶He saw that there was no one,
  he was devastated that there was no one
    intervening.
But his arm brought deliverance for him;
  his faithfulness – it sustained him.
¹⁷He put on faithfulness like a coat of mail,
  and a deliverance helmet on his head.
He put on redress clothes as clothing,
  he wrapped on passion as a coat.
¹⁸In accordance with their dealings,
  as the One on High he will make good with
    fury to his adversaries,
With dealings to his enemies,
  dealings to foreign shores, he will make good.
¹⁹They will be in awe of Yahweh's name from the
    west,
  and of his splendour from the sunrise.
When an adversary comes like the river,
  Yahweh's wind raises a banner against him.
²⁰He will come to Tsiyyon as restorer,
  to the people who turn from rebellion in Ya'aqob
    (Yahweh's declaration).

²¹'And me – this is my pact with them (Yahweh has said). My breath that is on you, and my words that I've put in your mouth, will not move away from your mouth, from the mouth of your offspring and from the mouth of your offspring's offspring (Yahweh has said) from now and permanently.'

An invitation to imagination

60 Get up, be alight, because your light is coming,
  Yahweh's splendour has shone on you.
²Because there – darkness covers the earth,
  gloom the peoples.
But on you Yahweh will shine;
  his splendour will appear over you.
³Nations will come to your light,
  kings to your shining brightness.
⁴Lift your eyes round and look,
  all of them are collecting, they're coming to you.
Your sons will come from afar,
  your daughters will support themselves on the
    hip.
⁵Then you'll see and glow,
  your mind will be in awe and will swell.
Because the sea's horde will turn to you,
  the resources of nations will come to you.

⁶A mass of camels will cover you,
  dromedaries from Midyan and Ephah;
  all of them will come from Sheba.
They will carry gold and frankincense,
  and bring news of Yahweh's great praise.
⁷All the sheep of Qedar will collect to you,
  rams of Nebayot will minister to you.
They will go up with acceptance on my altar,
  and I will add majesty to my majestic house.
⁸Who are these that fly like a cloud,
  and like doves to their hatches?
⁹Because foreign shores will look for me,
  Tarshish ships at the first,
To bring your sons from afar,
  their silver and their gold with them,
For the name of Yahweh your God, for Yisra'el's
    Sacred One,
  because he has made you majestic.
¹⁰Foreigners will build your walls,
  kings will minister to you.
Because in wrath I struck you,
  but with acceptance I'm having compassion
    on you.
¹¹Your gateways will open continuously,
  day and night they will not shut,
To bring you the nations' resources,
  with their kings being led along.
¹²Because the nation or kingdom that doesn't
    serve you –
  they will perish, and the nations will become a
    total waste.

An invitation to hope

¹³The Lebanon's splendour will come to you,
  juniper, fir and cypress together,
To add majesty to my sacred place,
  so I may honour the place for my feet.
¹⁴They'll walk to you bending down,
  the children of the people who humbled you.
They'll bow low at the soles of your feet,
  all the people who despised you.
They'll call you 'Yahweh's Town,
  the Tsiyyon of Yisra'el's Sacred One'.
¹⁵Instead of being abandoned,
  treated hostilely with no one passing
    through,
I'll make you an object of permanent pride,
  a joy generation after generation.
¹⁶You'll suck the nations' milk,
  suck the kings' breast.

And you will acknowledge that I am Yahweh;
    Ya'aqob's champion is your deliverer and your
        restorer.
¹⁷Instead of copper I'll bring gold,
    instead of iron I'll bring silver,
Instead of wood, copper;
    instead of stone, iron.
I'll make well-being your oversight,
    faithfulness your bosses.
¹⁸Violence will not make itself heard any more in
        your country,
    destruction and breaking in your borders.
You will call deliverance your walls,
    praise your gateways.
¹⁹The sun will no longer be light for you by day,
    and as brightness the moon will not be light
        for you.
Because Yahweh will be light for you
        permanently;
    your God will be your majesty.
²⁰Your sun will not set any more,
    your moon will not withdraw.
Because Yahweh will be light for you
        permanently;
    your mourning days will be complete.
²¹Your people, all of them, will be faithful ones,
    who will possess the country permanently.
They will be the shoot that I plant,
    the work of my hands, to demonstrate majesty.
²²The smallest will become a clan,
    the least a numerous nation.
I am Yahweh;
    I will speed it in its time.

Blown over and anointed

61 The Lord Yahweh's breath is on me,
    because Yahweh has anointed me.
He's sent me to bring news to the humble,
    to bind up the people broken in mind,
To call for release for captives,
    the opening of eyes for prisoners,
²To call for a year of Yahweh's acceptance,
    our God's day of redress,
To comfort all the mourners,
    ³to provide for the people who mourn
        Tsiyyon –
To give them majesty instead of ash,
    festive oil instead of mourning,
A praise garment
    instead of a flickering spirit.

They'll be called faithful oaks,
    Yahweh's planting, to demonstrate majesty.
⁴People will build up permanent ruins,
    raise up the ancestors' desolations.
They'll renew ruined towns,
    desolations from generation after generation.
⁵Strangers will stand and pasture your sheep,
    foreigners will be your farmworkers and
        vinedressers.
⁶You yourselves will be called 'Yahweh's priests',
    you'll be termed 'our God's ministers'.
You'll eat the nations' resources
    and thrive on their splendour.
⁷Instead of your shame, double;
    [instead of] disgrace, people will resound at the
        share you have.

Therefore in their country they'll possess double;
    permanent joy will be theirs.
⁸Because I am Yahweh, one loyal to exercising
        authority,
    hostile to robbery in evil.
I'll give them their earnings in truthfulness;
    a permanent pact I'll solemnize for them.
⁹Their offspring will gain acknowledgement with
        the nations,
    their descendants among the peoples.
All who see them will recognize them,
    that they are offspring Yahweh has blessed.

People who won't let Yahweh rest

¹⁰I shall be ardently glad in Yahweh,
    my entire being will joy in my God.
Because he's clothing me in deliverance clothes,
    wrapping me in a faithfulness coat,
Like a groom who behaves priestly in majesty,
    or like a bride who adorns herself in her things.
¹¹Because as the earth brings out its growth
    and as a garden makes its seed grow,
So the Lord Yahweh will make faithfulness and
        praise grow
    before all the nations.

62 For the sake of Tsiyyon I will not be
    silent,
    for Yerushalaim's sake I will not be calm,
Until its faithfulness goes out like brightness,
    its deliverance like a torch that blazes.
²The nations will see your faithfulness,
    all the kings your splendour.

You'll be called by a new name,
   which Yahweh's mouth will determine.
³You'll be a majestic crown in Yahweh's hand,
   a royal diadem in your God's palm.
⁴You'll no longer be termed 'Abandoned',
   your country will no longer be termed
      'Desolate'.
Rather, you'll be called 'My Delight Is in Her',
   and your country 'Married'.
Because Yahweh delights in you,
   and your country will be married.
⁵Because a young man marries a girl;
   your sons will marry you.
With a groom's gladness over a bride,
   your God will be glad over you.

⁶Upon your walls, Yerushalaim,
   I'm appointing guards.
All day and all night
   they will never be silent.
You who remind Yahweh,
   there's no stopping for you.
⁷Don't give him stopping, until he establishes,
   until he makes Yerushalaim an object of praise
      in the earth.

I had to do it myself

⁸Yahweh has sworn by his right hand,
   by his vigorous arm:

If I give your grain again
   as food for your enemies,
If foreigners drink your new wine,
   for which you've laboured . . .
⁹Because the people who harvest it will eat it,
   and praise Yahweh.
The people who collect it will drink it
   in my sacred courtyards.

¹⁰Pass through, pass through the gateways,
   clear the people's way!
Build up, build up the causeway,
   clear it of stones!
Raise a banner over the peoples –
   ¹¹there, Yahweh has let it be heard to the end of
      the earth.
Say to Miss Tsiyyon,
   'There, your deliverance is coming.
There, his reward is with him,
   his earnings before him.'

¹²People will call them
   'The Sacred People, Ones Restored by Yahweh'.
You'll be called
   'Sought Out, a Town Not Abandoned'.

63

Who's this coming from Edom,
   marked in clothes from Botsrah,
This person majestic in attire,
   stooping in his mighty energy?
'I'm the one speaking in faithfulness,
   mighty to deliver.'
²Why is your attire red,
   your clothes like someone treading in a wine
      trough?
³'I trod a press alone;
   from the peoples there was no one with me.
I tread them in my anger,
   trample them in my fury.
Their spray spatters on my clothes;
   I've stained all my attire.
⁴Because a day of redress has been in my mind,
   my year of restoration has arrived.
⁵But I look, and there's no helper;
   I stare, and there's no support.
So my arm has effected deliverance for me;
   my fury – it's supported me.
⁶I trample peoples in my anger,
   make them drunk in my fury,
   bring down their eminence to the earth.'

On hurting God's sacred spirit

⁷I shall recount Yahweh's acts of commitment,
   Yahweh's praises,
In accordance with all that Yahweh dealt to us,
   the great goodness to Yisra'el's household,
That which he dealt to them in accordance with
      his compassion
   and the greatness of his acts of commitment.
⁸He said, 'Yes, they're my people,
   children who won't be false.'
He became their deliverer;
   ⁹in all their trouble it became troublesome to him.
His personal envoy –
   he delivered them, in his love and pity.
He was the one who restored them, lifted them up,
   carried them all the days of old.
¹⁰But they – they rebelled
   and hurt his sacred spirit.
So he turned into their enemy;
   he himself battled against them.

¹¹But he was mindful of the days of long ago,
  of Mosheh [Moses], of his people.

Where is the one who brought them up from the
    sea,
  the shepherds of his flock?
Where is the one who put within it
  his sacred spirit,
¹²The one who made his majestic arm go
  at Mosheh's right hand,
Dividing the water in front of them
  to make himself a name permanently,
¹³Enabling them to go through the depths like a
    horse in the wilderness,
  so they wouldn't collapse,
¹⁴Like a beast in the valley that goes down,
  so that Yahweh's spirit would enable them to
    settle down?
In that way you drove your people,
  to make a majestic name for yourself.

¹⁵Look out from the heavens,
  see from your sacred and majestic height!
Where are your passion and your acts of strength,
  the roar from inside you and your compassion?
In relation to me they have withheld themselves,
  ¹⁶when you are our Father.
When Abraham wouldn't acknowledge us,
  Yisra'el wouldn't recognize us,
You Yahweh are our Father;
  'Our Restorer from Forever' is your name.
¹⁷Why do you let us wander from your ways,
    Yahweh,
  let our mind be tough so as not to be in awe of
    you?
Turn for the sake of your servants,
  the clans that are your domain.
¹⁸As something small they dispossessed your
    sacred people;
  our adversaries trampled your sanctuary.
¹⁹Permanently we have become people over
    whom you haven't ruled,
  who haven't been called by your name.

But you're our Father

64 Oh that you'd torn apart the heavens
    and gone down,
  that mountains had quaked before you,
²Like fire lighting brushwood,
  so that the fire boils water,
To cause your name to be acknowledged by your
    adversaries,
  so that the nations might tremble before you.
³When you did wonders that we didn't hope for,
  you went down and mountains quaked before
    you.
⁴Never had people heard or given ear,
  eye had not seen,
A God apart from you,
  who acts for one who waits for him.
⁵You met with the one who was joyful and doing
    what was faithful,
  the people who were mindful of you in your
    ways.
There, you yourself got furious,
  and of old we did wrong in relation to them,
  but we were delivered.
⁶We became like something taboo, all of us,
  and all our faithful deeds like menstrual
    clothing.
We withered like leaves, all of us,
  and our wayward acts carry us off like the wind.
⁷There's no one calling on your name,
  stirring himself to take hold of you.
Because you've hidden your face from us,
  and made us fade away at the hand of our
    wayward acts.

⁸But now, Yahweh, you're our Father;
  we're the clay, you're our potter –
  the work of your hand, all of us.
⁹Don't be so very furious, Yahweh,
  don't be mindful of waywardness.
There, please do look at your people, all of us:
  ¹⁰your sacred towns became a wilderness,
Tsiyyon became a wilderness,
  Yerushalaim a devastation.
¹¹Our sacred and majestic house,
  where our ancestors praised you,
Became something consumed by fire,
  and all that we valued became a ruin.
¹²At these things do you restrain yourself, Yahweh,
  do you remain still and let us be humbled so
    much?

Straight-talking meets straight-talking

65 I could be enquired of people who didn't
    ask,
  I could be found by people who didn't seek help
    from me.

I said, 'I'm here, I'm here',
    to a nation that wasn't calling on my name.
²I spread my hands all day
    to a defiant people,
Who walk in a way that is not good,
    following their own intentions.
³The people are ones who provoke me,
    to my face, continually,
Sacrificing in the gardens,
    burning incense on the bricks,
⁴Ones who sit in tombs,
    who spend the night in secret places,
Who eat swine's flesh,
    with a broth of desecrating things in their bowls,
⁵Who say, 'Keep to yourself, don't come near me,
    because I'm too sacred for you.'
These people are smoke in my nostrils,
    a fire burning all day.
⁶There, it's written before me,
    I will not be still, rather I am making good,
I'll make good into their lap ⁷your waywardness
    and your ancestors' waywardness together
    (Yahweh has said).
The people who burned incense on the mountains,
    who reviled me on the hills:
I'm counting out their earnings
    first of all into their lap.

⁸Yahweh has said this:

As the new wine can be found in the cluster,
    and someone will say 'Don't destroy it,
    because there's a blessing in it',
So I will act for my servants' sake,
    so as not to destroy everything.
⁹I shall bring out offspring from Ya'aqob,
    and from Yehudah one who's going to possess my mountains.
My chosen ones will possess it,
    my servants will dwell there.
¹⁰The Sharon will become an abode for sheep,
    Disaster Vale a resting-place for cattle,
    for my people who've enquired of me.
¹¹But you who abandon Yahweh,
    who put out of mind my sacred mountain,
Who set a table for Luck,
    who fill a mixing chalice for Destiny:
¹²I shall destine you to the sword,
    all of you will bend down for slaughter.
Because I called but you didn't answer,
    I spoke but you didn't listen.

You did what was bad in my eyes,
    and what I didn't want, you chose.

The renewed Yerushalaim

¹³Therefore the Lord Yahweh has said this:

There, my servants will eat,
    but you'll be hungry.
There, my servants will drink,
    but you'll be thirsty.
There, my servants will rejoice,
    but you'll be shamed.
¹⁴There, my servants will resound
    from happiness of heart,
But you'll cry out from pain of heart,
    from brokenness of spirit you'll howl.
¹⁵You'll leave your name
    as an oath for my chosen ones,
'So may the Lord Yahweh kill you',
    but for his servants he will call out another name,
¹⁶So that the person who prays for blessing in the country
    will pray for blessing by the God who says 'Amen'.
Because the earlier pressures will have been put out of mind,
    and because they'll have been hidden from my eyes.

¹⁷Because here I am, creating
    new heavens and a new earth.
The earlier ones won't be recollected;
    they won't come into mind.
¹⁸Rather, be glad and celebrate permanently
    what I am creating.
Because here I am, creating Yerushalaim as reason for celebration
    and its people as reason for gladness.
¹⁹I will celebrate Yerushalaim
    and be glad in my people.
There will not make itself heard in it any more
    the sound of weeping or the sound of a cry.
²⁰There will no longer be from there any more
    a baby of [few] days
    or an old person who doesn't fulfil his days.
Because the youth will die as a person of a hundred years,
    and the wrongdoer will be slighted as a person of a hundred years.

²¹They'll build houses and dwell [in them],
    they'll plant vineyards and eat their fruit.
²²They won't build and another dwell;
    they won't plant and another eat.
The days of my people will be like a tree's days;
    my chosen ones will use up the work of their hands.
²³They won't toil with empty result;
    they won't give birth with fearful outcome.
Because they'll be offspring blessed by Yahweh,
    they and their descendants with them.
²⁴Before they call, I myself will answer;
    while they're still speaking, I myself will listen.
²⁵The wolf and the lamb will pasture together,
    the cougar, like cattle, will eat straw,
but the snake – earth will be its food.
People won't deal badly, they won't devastate,
    in all my sacred mountain (Yahweh has said).

Trembling at Yahweh's word

66 Yahweh has said this:

The heavens are my throne,
    the earth is my footstool.
Wherever would be the house that you would build for me,
    wherever would be the place that would be for me to settle down?
²All these things my hand made (Yahweh's declaration),
    and to this person I look:
To the humble, to the broken in spirit,
    one who trembles at my word.

³One who slaughters an ox is one who strikes a person down;
    one who sacrifices a lamb is one who strangles a dog.
One who lifts up an offering – it's pig's blood;
    one who makes a memorial of incense – he worships a bane.
They for their part have chosen their ways,
    their soul delights in their abominations.
⁴I for my part will choose caprices for them,
    and bring upon them what they dread.
Because I called and there was no one answering,
    I spoke and they didn't listen.
They did what was bad in my eyes,
    and what I didn't delight in, they chose.

⁵Listen to Yahweh's word,
    you who tremble at his word.
'Your brothers have said, people who are hostile to you,
    who exclude you for the sake of my name,
"May Yahweh be severe, so that we may see your celebration" –
    they will be shamed.'
⁶The sound of a din from the town,
    a sound from the palace,
The sound of Yahweh
    making good with his dealings to his enemies.

⁷Before she labours she's given birth,
    before pain comes to her she delivers a boy.
⁸Who has heard something like this,
    who has seen things like these?
Can a country be brought through labour in one day,
    or a nation be born in one moment?
Because Tsiyyon is labouring
    and also giving birth to her children.
⁹"Will I myself make a breach
    and not bring to birth? (Yahweh says).
Or will I myself bring to birth
    and close [the womb]? (your God says).'

¹⁰Rejoice with Yerushalaim,
    be glad in her, all you who love her.
Be glad with her in joy,
    all you who mourned over her,
¹¹In order that you may nurse and be full
    from her comforting breast,
In order that you may drink deeply and delight yourself
    from her splendid bosom.

Choose your ending

¹²Because Yahweh has said this:

Here I am, stretching out to her
    well-being like a river,
Like a flooding wadi
    the splendour of the nations,
So you may drink of it as you're carried on her side
    and dandled on her knees.
¹³Like someone whom his mother comforts,
    so I myself will comfort you.

You'll be comforted in Yerushalaim,
¹⁴you'll see, and your heart will be glad,
   and your limbs will flourish like grass.

Yahweh's hand will cause itself to be
   acknowledged among his servants,
   and he will condemn his enemies.
¹⁵Because there – Yahweh will come in fire,
   his chariots like a whirlwind,
To give back his anger in wrath,
   his reprimand in fiery flame.
¹⁶ Because Yahweh is going to enter into
   judgement with fire,
   with his sword, among all flesh;
   the people run through by Yahweh will be many.
¹⁷'The people who make themselves sacred and
   purify themselves for the gardens,
   following after one in the middle,
People who eat the flesh of pig, reptile and mouse
   will come to an end together (Yahweh's
   declaration).'

¹⁸But as for me, on the basis of their deeds and their intentions, the gathering of all the nations and tongues is coming. They'll come and see my splendour. ¹⁹I shall set a sign among them and send off from them survivors to the nations – Tarshish, Pul and Lud, the people who draw the bow, Tubal, Yavan [Greece], the distant shores, which haven't heard report of me and haven't seen my splendour. They will tell of my splendour among the nations.

²⁰They will bring all your kin-group members from all the nations as an offering to Yahweh, by means of horses, chariotry, coaches, mules and dromedaries, to my sacred mountain, Yerushalaim (Yahweh has said), as the Yisra'elites bring the offering in a pure vessel to Yahweh's house. ²¹Also from them I will take people as priests and Levites (Yahweh has said).

²²Because as the new heavens and the new earth that I'm going to make are going to stand before me (Yahweh's declaration), so will your offspring and your name stand. ²³New moon by new moon, sabbath by sabbath, all flesh will come to bow low before me (Yahweh has said).

²⁴But they will go out and look at the corpses of the people who rebel against me. Because their worm will not die and their fire will not go out. They will be a horror to all flesh.

Jeremiah

Jeremiah [Yirmeyahu] lived a century later than Isaiah. He was summoned to be a prophet in 626 BC and he continued prophesying until after the fall of Jerusalem to the Babylonians forty years later. He thus lived through tumultuous years and changing fortunes in Judah. His summons came as King Josiah was involved in a reformation of religious life in Judah and a cleaning up of forms of worship that accepted other Middle Eastern peoples' practices (including sacrificing children) instead of Israel's own. After Josiah's death the nation reverted to those habits, which led to Yahweh's abandoning Jerusalem to the Babylonians. Jeremiah speaks positively of Josiah but spent most of his life confronting kings and people about their faithlessness to Yahweh and to one another.

That confrontation involves him in issuing repeated warnings that this continuing faithlessness will issue in disaster, which makes him a deeply unpopular figure, especially with Judah's leadership. From their perspective he is simply a troublemaker. Slightly illogically, they do not become more tolerant of Jeremiah as a result of the fact that Yahweh keeps not fulfilling his threats. One might have inferred that Jeremiah looked like a prophet who could safely be ignored. Instead they persecute him, imprison him and threaten to kill him. Naturally this has an effect on Jeremiah himself, who doesn't appreciate the fact that he has to keep issuing warnings that don't come true. He expresses his resentment frankly to Yahweh. His book includes many stories about him, presumably written by people such as Baruk who do support him. More surprisingly, his book also incorporates a number of the prayers he prayed, which have a place there not because of an assumption that his readers will be interested in the nature of his relationship with God but because (like the stories) they give readers another angle on his persecution. It is an expression of the attitude the community takes to the God whom he serves.

The book of Jeremiah is not clearly organized like Isaiah and Ezekiel, but we can say that the first half is dominated by his prophecies and by those prayers, while the second half is dominated by stories about him and then by prophecies about other nations.

Some stand-out chapters in his book are:

1. his account of his summons to be a prophet (Jer. 1), which later inspired the prophet who speaks in Isaiah 49 and still later inspired Paul (Gal. 1.15) in their accounts of their summons;
2. his grief over Judah's failure of memory (Jer. 2);
3. his reminder about the fate of Shiloh (Jer. 7);
4. his ridicule of the making of images (Jer. 10);
5. his accepting a command not to marry (Jer. 16);
6. his emphasis on the way God can have a change of mind over his threats and over his promises in the light of the response they receive (Jer. 18);
7. his wrestling with the question of how to tell a false prophet from a true one (Jer. 23);
8. his declaration that the Babylonian king is Yahweh's servant (Jer. 25);
9. his declaration that the exile will last seventy years – both a warning and a promise (also Jer. 25);
10. his confrontation with the prophet Hananiah (Jer. 28);
11. his exhortation to people already exiled in 597 to settle down and not think they are coming back soon (Jer. 29);
12. his promise that after the exile God will make a new covenant with Judah (Jer. 31);
13. his willingness to invest in land at an inauspicious moment (Jer. 32);
14. the account of how he puts his prophecies into writing and enlarges the collection when the king burns his scroll (Jer. 36);
15. the account of his continuing struggle with people resisting Yahweh's expectations after the fall of Jerusalem and their forcing him to flee with them to Egypt (Jer. 39—44);
16. the closing narrative that shows how he was proved right after all (Jer. 52).

Yahweh's summons

1 The words of Yirmeyahu ben Hilqiyyahu, one of the priests of Anatot in the Binyamin [Benjamin] region, ²to whom Yahweh's word came in the days of Yoshiyyahu [Josiah] ben Amon king of Yehudah in the thirteenth year of his reign, ³and came in the days of Yehoyaqim ben Yoshiyyahu king of Yehudah, until the end of the eleventh year of Tsidqiyyahu [Zedekiah] ben Yoshiyyahu king of Yehudah, until Yerushalaim's exile in the fifth month.

⁴Yahweh's word came to me:

⁵Before I formed you in the womb I acknowledged you,
before you went out from the womb I made you sacred.
I made you a prophet concerning the nations.

⁶I said:

Oh, Lord Yahweh –
here, I don't know how to speak,
because I'm a boy.

⁷But Yahweh said to me:

Don't say, 'I'm a boy',
because you're to go out to anyone to whom I send you,
and speak anything that I order you.
⁸Don't be afraid of their faces,
because I'll be with you to rescue you (Yahweh's declaration).

⁹Yahweh put out his hand and touched my mouth, and Yahweh said to me:

Here, I'm putting my words into your mouth:
¹⁰see, I'm appointing you this day
over the nations, over the kingdoms,
To uproot and to pull down, to obliterate and to tear down,
to build and to plant.

¹¹Yahweh's word came to me:

What are you looking at, Yirmeyahu?

I said:

I'm looking at the branch of a watcher tree.

¹²Yahweh said to me:

You've done good in looking,
because I'm watching, over my word, to put it into effect.

The iron pillar

¹³Yahweh's word came to me a second time:

What are you looking at?

I said:

I'm looking at a boiling pot,
with its face facing from the north.

¹⁴Yahweh said to me:

From the north bad things will open out
on all the inhabitants of the country.
¹⁵Because here am I calling
all the kin-groups of the northern kingdoms
(Yahweh's declaration).
They'll come and put each one his throne
at the opening of Yerushalaim's gateways,
Against all its walls round,
and against all Yehudah's towns.
¹⁶I shall speak my rulings to them,
for all their bad dealing, in that they've abandoned me.
They've burned incense to other gods,
bowed low to things their hands made.
¹⁷You, you're to put your belt round your hips,
and get up and speak to them
anything that I myself order you.
Don't shatter before them,
in case I shatter you before them.
¹⁸I – here I am, making you
into a fortified town today,
Into an iron pillar
and copper walls against the entire country,
For Yehudah's kings and its officers,
for its priests and the people of the country.
¹⁹They'll battle against you but they won't prevail over you,
because I'm with you (Yahweh's declaration) to rescue you.

Digging cisterns that leak

2 Yahweh's word came to me: ²Go, call out in Yerushalaim's ears,
Yahweh has said this:

I have kept in mind for you the commitment of your youth,
    your loyalty as a bride,
Your following me through the wilderness,
    through a country not sown.
³Yisra'el was sacred to Yahweh,
    the first fruits of his yield.
All the people who ate of it would incur liability;
    bad fortune would come upon them (Yahweh's declaration).

⁴Listen to Yahweh's word, Ya'aqob's [Jacob's] household,
    all the kin-groups of Yisra'el's household.

⁵Yahweh has said this:

What did your ancestors find that was evil in me,
    that they went far away from me,
Followed something hollow and became hollow,
⁶and didn't say 'Where is Yahweh,
The one who got us up from the country of Misrayim [Egypt]
    and enabled us to go through the wilderness,
Through a country of steppe and pit,
    through a country of drought and deep darkness,
Through a country through which no one passed
    and where no human being lived?'
⁷I enabled you to come into a country of farmland,
    to eat its fruit and its good things.
But you came and defiled my country;
    you made my domain something offensive.
⁸The priests didn't say 'Where is Yahweh?',
    the people controlling the instruction didn't acknowledge me.
The shepherds rebelled against me,
    the prophets prophesied by the Master,
    and followed beings that couldn't prevail in anything.

⁹Therefore I'll argue with you more (Yahweh's declaration)
    and I'll argue with your grandchildren.

¹⁰Because cross over to the shores of Kittim [Cyprus] and see,
    send off to Qedar and consider well,
    see if something like this has happened.
¹¹Has a nation changed its gods,
    when those are not gods?
But my people have changed my splendour
    for what doesn't prevail in anything.
¹²Be devastated at this, heavens,
    shudder, be utterly desolate (Yahweh's declaration).
¹³Because my people have done two bad things:
    they've abandoned me, the fountain of living water,
To dig themselves cisterns, breakable cisterns,
    that don't prevail over water.

'I haven't become defiled'

¹⁴Was Yisra'el a servant, or someone born in a household –
    why has he become plunder?
¹⁵Lions roar over him,
    they've given their voice.
They've made his country a devastation;
    his towns are burned, without inhabitant.
¹⁶The people of Memphis and Tahpanhes
    will also break your skull [Yerushalaim].
¹⁷It's this that does it to you, isn't it –
    your abandoning of Yahweh your God
    at the time when he was enabling you to go on your journey?
¹⁸So now what is there for you in a journey to Misrayim
    to drink the Ye'or's [the Nile's] water?
What is there for you in a journey to Ashshur
    to drink the River's water?
¹⁹Your bad dealing should discipline you,
    your turning back should reprove you.
Acknowledge and see how bad and bitter it is,
    your abandoning Yahweh your God,
And you have no dread towards me
    (a declaration of the Lord Yahweh of Armies).

²⁰Because of old you broke your yoke,
    you tore off your straps, and said, 'I won't serve.'
Because on every high hill and under every verdant tree
    you're lying down as a whore.
²¹I – I planted you as a top-class vine,
    all of it trustworthy seed.

So how have you changed for me
  into the turnings of a foreign vine?
²²Because if you wash with soap
  and use much detergent for yourself,
Your waywardness is inscribed before me
  (a declaration of the Lord Yahweh).

²³How can you say, 'I haven't become defiled,
  I haven't followed the Masters'?
Look at your journey into the Ravine,
  acknowledge what you've done,
A swift camel twisting her journeys,
  ²⁴a wild donkey taught about the wilderness,
Sniffing the wind in the desire of her appetite –
  who can turn back her craving?
None who seek her get tired;
  in her season they find her.

Why do you gad about?

²⁵Hold your foot back from being shoeless
  and your throat from being dry.
But you say, 'It's desperate,
  because I'm loyal to strangers, I shall follow
    them.'
²⁶Like a thief's shame when he's found out,
  so Yisra'el's household was shamed.
They, their kings, their officials,
  their priests, their prophets,
²⁷Were saying to a piece of wood, 'You're our
    father',
  to some stone, 'You gave me birth.'
Because they turned their back to me,
  not their face.
At the time when something bad happened to
    them
  they'd say, 'Arise, deliver us.'
²⁸But where are your gods
  that you made for yourself?
They should arise if they can deliver you,
  at the time when something bad happens to you.
Because your gods have become
  more than the number of your towns, Yehudah.
²⁹Why do you argue with me
  when all of you have rebelled against me?
    (Yahweh's declaration).

³⁰With empty results I struck down your children;
  they didn't accept discipline.
Your sword consumed your prophets
  like a destroying lion.

³¹This generation,
  look at Yahweh's word.
Did I become a wilderness to Yisra'el,
  or a country of deep darkness?
Why did my people say, 'We've wandered off,
  we won't come to you any more'?
³²Can a girl put her jewellery out of mind,
  a bride her adornments?
But my people have put me out of mind,
  days without number.

³³How good you've made your journey in seeking
    love [Yerushalaim];
  therefore you've even taught bad women your
    journeys.
³⁴Further, on your garments is found
  the blood of the lives of needy people who are
    free of guilt
  (you didn't find them breaking in).
Because despite all these things,
  ³⁵you've said, 'I'm free of guilt,
  his anger has surely turned back from me.'
Here I am, entering into judgement with you,
  because of your saying 'I haven't done wrong.'

³⁶Why do you go about so much,
  changing your journey?
Through Misrayim you'll be shamed again,
  as you were shamed through Ashshur.
³⁷Through this you'll again come out
  with your hands on your head.
Because Yahweh has rejected the ones you rely
    on,
  and you won't succeed through them.

Is it possible to come back?

3 Saying: 'If someone sends off his wife, she goes from him, and she comes to belong to another man, can he come back to her again?' That country will be totally profaned, won't it. And you [Yerushalaim] have been whoring with many lovers. Would you come back to me? (Yahweh's declaration).

²Raise your eyes to the bare places and look –
  where have you not been laid?
By the roads you sat for them,
  like a Bedouin in the wilderness.
You profaned the country
  with your whoring and your bad dealing.

³Showers held back,
  there was no rain,
But you had the brazenness of a whore;
  you refused to be shamed.
⁴Now you've called to me, haven't you,
  'Father, you're the partner of my youth.'
⁵'Does he hold on to things permanently
  or keep watch for all time?'
There – you've spoken;
  you've done what was bad, and prevailed.

⁶Yahweh said to me in the days of King Yoshiyyahu, 'Have you seen what Yisra'el did, she who turned back? She was going on to every high mountain and under every verdant tree and whoring there. ⁷I said, "After she's done all these things, she'll come back to me." But she didn't come back. And her faith-breaking sister Yehudah saw. ⁸I saw that because of the acts of adultery that Yisra'el committed, she who turned back, I sent her off and gave her divorce document to her. But her sister Yehudah, she who broke faith, wasn't afraid. She went and acted as a whore, too. ⁹It came about that because of the frivolity of her whoring she profaned the country; she committed adultery with stone and wood. ¹⁰But even in all this, her sister, faith-breaking Yehudah, didn't come back to me with her whole mind but rather with falsehood (Yahweh's declaration).'

Breaking faith

¹¹Yahweh said to me, 'Yisra'el who turned back has shown herself more faithful than Yehudah who broke faith. ¹²Go and call out these words to the north. Say, "Come back, Yisra'el who turned back (Yahweh's declaration); I shall not make my face fall against you, because I am committed (Yahweh's declaration), I don't hold on to things permanently. ¹³Only acknowledge your waywardness, that you've rebelled against Yahweh your God and scattered your journeys to strangers under every verdant tree, and not listened to my voice (Yahweh's declaration).

¹⁴Come back, children who are turning back (Yahweh's declaration), because I'm your master. I'll take you, one from a town, two from a kin-group, and bring you to Tsiyyon [Zion]. ¹⁵I'll give you shepherds in accordance with my will and they'll shepherd you with knowledge and insight.

¹⁶When you increase and are fruitful in the country in those days (Yahweh's declaration), people will no longer say 'Yahweh's pact chest'. It won't come to mind, they won't be mindful of it or give attention; it won't be made again. ¹⁷At that time they'll call Yerushalaim 'Yahweh's Throne', and all the nations will gather to it, to Yahweh's name, to Yerushalaim. People will no more follow the bad determination of their mind.

¹⁸In those days Yehudah's household will go to Yisra'el's household, and they'll come together from the northern country to the country that I gave your ancestors as a domain.

¹⁹I myself had said, 'How gladly I'll put you among my children and give you a desirable country, the most splendid domain of the nations.' I said you'd call me 'Father', and not turn back from following me. ²⁰Actually, as a woman breaks faith with her lover, so you broke faith with me, Yisra'el's household (Yahweh's declaration).'"

I'll heal their turnings

²¹A sound makes itself heard on the bare places,
  the Yisra'elites' crying that pleads for grace.
Because they've misdirected their way,
  they've put Yahweh their God out of mind.
²²Come back, children who are turning back;
  I'll heal your turnings.
'Here we are, we're coming to you,
  because you are Yahweh our God.
²³Yes, what comes from the hills belongs to
    falsehood,
  the uproar from the mountains.
Yes, in Yahweh our God
  is the deliverance of Yisra'el.
²⁴But the Shame has consumed
  our ancestors' labour from our youth,
Their flock and their cattle,
  their sons and their daughters.
²⁵We must lie down in our shame,
  our disgrace should cover us.
Because we've done wrong to Yahweh our God,
  we and our ancestors from our youth until this
    day.

We haven't listened
    to the voice of Yahweh our God.'

4 'If you come back, Yisra'el (Yahweh's declaration),
    come back to me.
If you remove your abominations from before me
    and don't flit,
²But swear "As Yahweh lives",
    in truth and in the faithful exercise of authority,
Nations will pray to be blessed by him,
    and will exult in him.'

³Because Yahweh has said this to Yehudah's people and to Yerushalaim:

Till the tillable land for yourselves,
    and don't sow among thorns.
⁴Circumcise yourselves for Yahweh,
    remove the foreskin from your mind,
People of Yehudah and inhabitants of Yerushalaim,
    so that my wrath doesn't come out like fire,
And burn up with no one putting it out,
    because of the bad nature of your practices.

⁵Tell out in Yehudah,
    make it heard in Yerushalaim,
Say, 'Sound the horn in the country',
    call out, fulfil it, say:
'Gather together, let's go into the fortified towns,
    ⁶raise a banner towards Tsiyyon, take refuge,
    don't stand still.'
Because I'm going to bring something bad from the north,
    a great breaking.

The searing wind

⁷A lion has gone up from its thicket,
    a destroyer of nations has moved on.
He's gone out from his place
    to make your country a devastation.
Your towns will be wasted,
    without inhabitant.
⁸On account of this, wrap on sack,
    lament and howl:
'Yahweh's angry blazing
    isn't turning back from us.'
⁹On that day (Yahweh's declaration)
    the king's mind and the officials' mind will expire.
The priests will be devastated,
    the prophets will be dumbfounded.

¹⁰I said, 'Oh, Lord Yahweh,
    really you've totally deceived this people and Yerushalaim,
In saying "Things will be well for you",
    whereas the sword has reached as far as their throat.'

¹¹At that time it will be said
    concerning this people and concerning Yerushalaim:
On the way to the daughter of my people
    a searing wind comes,
From the bare places in the wilderness,
    not to winnow, not to fan.
¹²A wind too full for these things comes on my behalf;
    now I myself announce rulings against them.
¹³There, one will go up like clouds,
    his chariots like a whirlwind.
His horses are swifter than eagles –
    oh, alas for us, because we are destroyed.

¹⁴Wash your mind of what is bad, Yerushalaim,
    in order that you may find deliverance.
How long will you let your intentions to bring trouble
    lodge within you?
¹⁵Because a voice tells it from Dan,
    it lets trouble be heard from Mount Ephrayim.
¹⁶Make mention to the nations;
    there – make it heard against Yerushalaim.
Watchers are coming from a far-off country,
    they'll give voice against Yehudah's towns.
¹⁷Like people keeping watch on the fields
    they've come against it all round,
    because it has rebelled against me (Yahweh's declaration).

¹⁸Your way and your practices
    have done these things to you.
This is the bad fortune that's come to you, because it's bitter,
    because it's reached your heart.

The empty void

¹⁹My pain, my pain, I writhe, the walls of my heart,
    my heart howls within me, I can't be still.

Because you've heard, my soul,
    the sound of the horn, the battle shout.
²⁰Breaking meets with breaking,
    because the entire country is destroyed.
Suddenly my tents have been destroyed,
    in an instant my tent cloths.
²¹How long shall I see a banner,
    listen to the sound of the horn?

²²Because my people are dense,
    they haven't acknowledged me.
They're idiotic children,
    they're not people who understand.
They're smart at doing what's bad,
    but they don't know how to do good.

²³I looked at the earth and there – it was empty, void;
    and at the heavens – there was no light in them.
²⁴I looked at the mountains and there – they were quaking,
    and all the hills were moving to and fro.
²⁵I looked and there – no human being,
    and every bird in the heavens had fled.
²⁶I looked and there – the farmland was wilderness,
    and all its towns were burned,
In the face of Yahweh,
    in the face of his angry blazing.

²⁷Because Yahweh has said this:

'The entire country will become desolation
    (but I won't make an end).
²⁸On account of this the earth mourns,
    the heavens are dark above.
Since I have spoken, I have made a scheme;
    I haven't relented, I won't turn back from it.'

²⁹At the sound of cavalry and bowman
    the entire town is fleeing.
They've gone into the woods,
    climbed on to the rocks.
The entire town is abandoned,
    there's no inhabitant in it, not one.
³⁰So you who are going to be destroyed,
    what do you do when you dress in scarlet,
When you adorn yourself in gold adornment,
    when you broaden your eyes with mascara?
It's with empty results that you look beautiful;
    your lovers have rejected you, they seek your life.
³¹Because I've heard a voice like someone in pain,
    distress like someone having her first baby,
The voice of Miss Tsiyyon –
    as she gasps, she stretches out the palms of her hands:
'Oh, me, please,
    because my life faints before my killers.'

Can you find anyone?

5 Explore Yerushalaim's streets, please look, and get to know,
    seek in its squares, if you can find anyone,
If there's someone exercising authority
    seeking truthfulness, and I'll pardon it.
²But even when they say, 'As Yahweh lives' –
    therefore they swear in falsehood.

³Yahweh, your eyes look for truthfulness, don't they;
    you struck them down but they didn't feel sick.
When you finished them off,
    they refused to accept discipline.
They made their faces stronger than a cliff;
    they refused to turn back.
⁴I myself said,
    'They're only the poor who act foolishly,
Because they don't acknowledge the way of Yahweh,
    the authority of their God.
⁵I'll go to the big people
    and speak with them,
Because those people acknowledge the way of Yahweh,
    the authority of their God.'
Yet those people had altogether broken the yoke,
    torn off the straps.
⁶That's why the lion from the forest has struck them down,
    the wolf from the steppes destroys them.
The leopard is lying by their townships;
    anyone who goes out from them will be torn to pieces.
Because their rebellions are many,
    their turnings away are numerous.

⁷For what reason should I pardon you? –
    your children have abandoned me and sworn by no-gods.
I filled them and they committed adultery;
    they troop off to the whorehouse.
⁸They were horses in heat, lusty;
    they were bellowing, each for his neighbour's wife.

⁹Shall I not attend to these things (Yahweh's declaration),
 or myself not take redress
 against a nation that's like this one?

¹⁰Go up among its vine-rows and destroy them,
 but don't make an end.
Remove its branches,
 because those people don't belong to Yahweh.
¹¹Because Yisra'el's household and Yehudah's household
 have totally broken faith with me (Yahweh's declaration).
¹²They've acted deceptively towards Yahweh,
 and said 'He isn't the one.
Bad fortune won't come upon us,
 we won't see sword or famine.
¹³The prophets – they'll be but wind,
 the word isn't in them; so it will be done to them.'

Senseless people

¹⁴Therefore Yahweh, God of Armies, has said this, since you people have spoken this thing:

Here I am, putting my words in your mouth as fire:
 this people is the wood, and it will consume them.
¹⁵Here I am, bringing a nation from afar against you,
 Yisra'el's household (Yahweh's declaration).
It's an enduring nation,
 it's an age-old nation,
A nation whose tongue you don't know;
 you can't listen to what it speaks.
¹⁶Its quiver is like an open grave;
 all of them are strong men.
¹⁷It will consume your harvest and your bread;
 it will consume your sons and your daughters.
It will consume your flock and your cattle;
 it will consume your vine and your fig.
It will destroy your fortified towns,
 on which you rely, with the sword.

¹⁸But even in those days (Yahweh's declaration) I won't make an end of you. ¹⁹And when they say, 'On what account did Yahweh our God do all these things to us?', you're to say to them, 'As you abandoned me and served alien gods in your country, so you'll serve foreigners in a country that isn't yours.'

²⁰Tell of this in Ya'aqob's household,
 make it heard in Yehudah:
²¹Listen to this, please, idiotic people,
 without sense,
Who have eyes but don't look,
 have ears but don't listen.
²²It's me that you should be in awe of, isn't it (Yahweh's declaration),
 and before me that you should tremble,
The one who set the sand as a boundary for the sea,
 a permanent limit that it shouldn't pass over.
Its waves toss but don't overcome,
 they roar but don't pass over.
²³But this people has a defiant and rebellious mind;
 they've defied and gone.
²⁴They haven't said to themselves,
 'We must be in awe of Yahweh our God,
Who gives the rain, the early and later rain at its time,
 who keeps watch for us the weeks set for harvest.'
²⁵It's your wayward acts that have turned these things aside,
 your wrongdoings that have withheld good things from you.

How to become sleek

²⁶Because faithless people were found among my people,
 like someone who watches in a bird-catchers' hide.
They've set up a means of destruction so they may capture people,
 ²⁷like a basket full of birds.
So their houses are full of deceit;
 that's how they've got big and rich.
²⁸They've become fat, become sleek;
 further, they've passed over words about bad dealing in giving judgement.
They haven't given judgement for the orphan, so that they might be successful;
 they haven't exercised authority for the needy.
²⁹Shall I not attend to these things (Yahweh's declaration),
 or myself not take redress against a nation that's like this one?

³⁰A devastating thing, a horrifying thing
  has happened in the country.
³¹The prophets prophesy falsely,
  the priests rule on the basis of their own capacity,
And my people like it so –
  but what will you do at the end of it?

6

Take refuge, Binyaminites,
  from inside Yerushalaim!
Sound the horn in Teqoa,
  raise the signal at Bet Hakkerem!
Because something bad is looking out from the north,
  a big breaking.
²I'm terminating Miss Tsiyyon, lovely and refined:
  ³shepherds and their flocks will come to it.
They pitch their tents against it all round,
  they pasture each one his own responsibility.
⁴'Make battle sacred against it,
  set to, we'll go up at noon!'
'Oh, alas for us, because the day is declining,
  because the evening shadows get long.
⁵Set to, we'll go up at night
  and devastate its citadels.'

⁶Because Yahweh of Armies has said this:

Cut down the trees,
  heap up a ramp against Yerushalaim.
The town is appointed;
  within it, all of it is fraud.
⁷Like a well flowing with its water,
  so it flows with its bad dealing.
In it violence and destruction makes itself heard,
  sickness and wound are before me continually.
⁸Accept discipline, Yerushalaim,
  so that I myself don't withdraw from you,
So that I don't make you a devastation,
  a country not inhabited.

Weary of holding in Yahweh's wrath

⁹Yahweh of Armies has said this:

Like a vine they are to glean and glean
  the remainder of Yisra'el.
'Put your hand again
  like a grape-picker over the branches.'
¹⁰To whom shall I speak,
  and testify so they listen?
There, their ear is foreskinned,
  they can't heed.
There, Yahweh's word has become for them
  a reviling; they don't delight in it.
¹¹So Yahweh's wrath – I'm full of it,
  I'm weary of holding it in.
'Pour it on the child in the street
  and on the group of young men, together.
Because both man and woman will be captured,
  the elder with the one full of years.
¹²Their houses will pass to other people,
  fields and wives together.
Because I shall stretch out my hand
  against the inhabitants of the country (Yahweh's declaration).
¹³Because from their smallest to their biggest,
  every one of them is greedy for loot.
Prophet and priest alike,
  every one of them is acting falsely.
¹⁴They've healed my people's break too lightly,
  saying, "Things are well, they're well",
  when they're not well.
¹⁵They've been shameful, because they've done something offensive;
  they neither manifest any shame
  nor do they know how to be disgraced.
Therefore they will fall among the people who fall;
  at the time when I attend to them, they will collapse
  (Yahweh has said).'

The analyst

¹⁶Yahweh has said this:

Stand by the roads, and look,
  ask about the old paths.
Which is the road to good things? –
  walk on it, and find peacefulness for yourselves.
But they said, 'We won't walk',
  ¹⁷so I raised up lookouts for you.
'Heed the sound of the horn',
  but they said, 'We won't heed.'
¹⁸Therefore listen, you nations,
  and acknowledge, you assembly, what will be against them.
¹⁹Listen, earth:
  here am I.
I'm going to bring something bad on this people,
  the fruit of their intentions.

Because they haven't heeded my words,
   and my instruction – they've rejected it.
²⁰What use to me is incense that comes from Sheba,
   or fine cane from a far-off country?
Your burnt offerings don't find acceptance,
   your sacrifices aren't pleasing to me.

²¹Therefore Yahweh has said this:

Here am I; I'm going to set for this people
   things to make them collapse, and they'll
      collapse because of them.
Parents and children together,
   neighbour and friend – they'll perish.

²²Yahweh has said this:

There, a people is going to come from a northern
      country,
   a big nation will arise from earth's remotest
      parts.
²³They take strong hold of bow and javelin;
   it's violent – they don't have compassion.
Their sound is like the sea that roars,
   they ride on horses.
It's lined up like a man for battle,
   against you, Miss Tsiyyon.
²⁴'We've heard report of them, our hands go slack,
   pressure has taken strong hold of us, anguish
      like a woman giving birth.
²⁵Don't go out into the fields, don't walk by the
      road,
   because the enemy has a sword, terror is all
      round.
²⁶My dear people, wrap on sack, roll in the dust,
   make for yourself the mourning for an only
      child,
Bitter lament,
   because suddenly the destroyer will come upon
      us.'

²⁷I made you an analyst among my people,
   a refiner, so you might know and analyse their
      way.
²⁸All of them are the most defiant people,
   people who live by slander,
Copper and iron,
   all of them are people who devastate.
²⁹The bellows are scorched by fire,
   the lead has come to an end.
With empty results the smelter smelted,
   and bad people were not separated out.

³⁰Reject silver, people have called them,
   because Yahweh has rejected them.

Remember Shiloh

7 The word that came to Yirmeyahu from Yahweh: ²'Stand at the gateway of Yahweh's house and call out this word there. You're to say, "Listen to Yahweh's word, all of Yehudah who are coming through these gateways to bow low to Yahweh. ³Yahweh of Armies, Yisra'el's God, has said this: 'Make your ways and your practices good, and I'll let you dwell in this place. ⁴Don't rely for yourselves on words of falsehood: "These buildings are Yahweh's palace, Yahweh's palace, Yahweh's palace." ⁵Rather, make your ways and your practices truly good. If you really exercise authority between an individual and his neighbour, ⁶don't exploit alien, orphan and widow, don't shed the blood of someone who is free of guilt in this place, and don't follow other gods with bad results for yourselves, ⁷I'll let you dwell in this place, in the country that I gave to your ancestors from of old, permanently.

⁸There, you're relying for yourselves on words of falsehood that won't prevail. ⁹Is there stealing, murder, adultery, swearing falsely and burning sacrifices to the Master, and following other gods that you didn't acknowledge, ¹⁰and you come and stand before me in this house over which my name has been called out and say "We are rescued" – in order to do all these offensive things? ¹¹Has it become a cave for thugs in your eyes, this house over which my name has been called out? Yes, I myself, I've been looking (Yahweh's declaration).

¹²Because you can go to my site that was at Shiloh where I let my name dwell before, and look at what I did to it in the face of my people Yisra'el's bad dealing. ¹³So now because of your doing all these things (Yahweh's declaration), and I've spoken to you, starting early, but you haven't listened, and I've called you but you haven't answered, ¹⁴I shall do to the house over which my name has been called out, on which you're relying, the site that I gave to you and your ancestors, as I did to Shiloh. ¹⁵I'll throw you out from my presence as I threw your brothers out, Ephrayim's entire offspring."'

Jeremiah 7: Yehudah (Judah) at the time of Yirmeyahu (Jeremiah)

The prophet forbidden to pray

[16]'You, don't plead for this people, don't lift up a cry or plea for them, don't intercede with me, because I'm not listening to you. [17]You see what they're doing in Yehudah's towns and in Yerushalaim's streets, don't you. [18]The sons are collecting wood, the fathers are lighting the fire and the women are kneading the dough, to make loaves for the Queen of Heaven and to pour libations to other gods, to provoke me. [19]Is it me they're provoking (Yahweh's declaration)? Is it not themselves, in order to bring shame on their faces?'

[20]Therefore the Lord Yahweh has said this: 'Here, my anger, my fury, is going to pour out on this place, on human beings, on animals, on the trees in the open country and on the fruit of the earth. It will burn up and not go out.'

[21]Yahweh of Armies, Yisra'el's God, has said this: 'Add your burnt offerings to your sacrifices, eat meat. [22]Because I didn't speak with your ancestors or order them on the day I got them out of the country of Misrayim regarding matters concerning burnt offering and sacrifice. [23]Rather I ordered them this thing: "Listen to my voice, and I'll be God for you and you'll be a people for me; walk

in every way that I order you so that it may go well for you." ²⁴But they didn't listen, they didn't bend their ear, they walked by their own counsels, by the bad determination of their mind. They went back, not forwards, ²⁵from the day that I got your ancestors out from the country of Misrayim until this day. I sent them all my servants the prophets, starting early and sending daily, ²⁶but they didn't listen to me, they didn't bend their ear, they toughened their neck; they acted badly more than their ancestors.

²⁷You're to speak to them all these things, but they won't listen to you. You're to call them but they won't answer you. ²⁸You're to say to them: "This is the nation that hasn't listened to the voice of Yahweh its God. They haven't accepted discipline. Truthfulness has perished, cut itself off from their mouth."'

Slaughter Ravine

²⁹Shave your hair and throw it away,
   take up a lament on the bare places.
Because Yahweh has rejected and deserted
   the generation with which he's furious.

³⁰Because the Yehudahites have done what is bad in my eyes (Yahweh's declaration). They've set up their abominations in the house over which my name has been called out, so as to defile it. ³¹They've built shrines at Tophet, in the Ben-hinnom Ravine, to burn their sons and daughters in fire, which I didn't order; it didn't come into my mind. ³²Therefore, now, days are coming (Yahweh's declaration) when it will no longer be said 'Tophet and the Ben-hinnom Ravine' but rather 'Slaughter Ravine'. They'll bury in Tophet because there's no other place. ³³This people's carcases will be food for the birds of the heavens and the animals of the land, with no one making them tremble. ³⁴I shall silence from Yehudah's towns and from Yerushalaim's streets the joyful voice, the rejoicing voice, the voice of groom and the voice of bride. Because the country will become a waste.

8 At that time (Yahweh's declaration) people will take out the bones of Yehudah's kings, its officials, the priests, the prophets and Yerushalaim's inhabitants from their graves, ²and expose them to the sun, the moon and all the army of the heavens that they were loyal to and that they served and that they followed and that they enquired of and that they bowed low to. They won't be gathered up and buried; they'll become manure on the face of the ground. ³Death will be preferable to life for all the remainder that remain of this bad kin-group in all the remaining places where I'll drive them (a declaration of Yahweh of Armies).

The misleading scholars

⁴You're to say to them, Yahweh has said this:

When people fall, don't they get up –
   if they turn back, don't they turn back?
⁵Why is this people turning back,
   Yerushalaim, with a permanent turning
      back?
They've taken strong hold on deceit,
   they've refused to turn back.
⁶I've heeded and listened;
   they don't speak dependably.
There's no one relenting of his bad dealing,
   saying 'What did I do?'
All of it has turned back, at a run,
   like a horse flooding into battle.
⁷Even the stork in the heavens –
   it acknowledges its set times.
The dove, the swift and the crane –
   they keep the time for their coming.
But my people – it doesn't acknowledge
   Yahweh's ruling.

⁸How can you say, 'We are smart,
   Yahweh's instruction is with us'?
Actually, there, the false pen of the scholars
   has made it into falsehood.
⁹The smart people have been shamed,
   they've shattered and been captured.
There, they've rejected Yahweh's word;
   what smartness do they have?

¹⁰Therefore I shall give their wives to other men,
   their fields to dispossessors.
Because from small to big,
   every one of them is greedy for loot.
Prophet and priest alike,
   every one of them is acting falsely.

¹¹They've healed my dear people's break too lightly,
   saying, 'Things are well, they're well',
   when they're not well.
¹²They've been shameful, because they've done something offensive;
   they neither manifest any shame
   nor do they know how to be disgraced.
Therefore they will fall among the people who fall;
   at the time when I attend to them, they'll collapse (Yahweh has said).
¹³I shall totally gather them up (Yahweh's declaration):
   there'll be no grapes on the vine,
   no figs on the fig tree.
The leaves will wither,
   and what I have given them will pass away from them.

No balm in Gil'ad?

¹⁴Why are we sitting? – gather up,
   we'll come into the fortified towns and be still there.
Because Yahweh our God is letting us perish
   and drink poisoned water,
Because we've done wrong to Yahweh,
   ¹⁵hoping for things to go well but there's nothing good,
   for a time of healing but here – terror.
¹⁶From Dan its horses' snort has made itself heard:
   at the sound of the neighing of its sturdy ones
   the entire country has shaken.
They came and consumed the country and what fills it,
   the town and the people who live in it.
¹⁷'Because here I am,
   sending off snakes against you,
Vipers for which there's no charming;
   they'll bite you' (Yahweh's declaration).

¹⁸You who cheer me in sorrow,
   my mind is sick.
¹⁹Here is the sound of my dear people's cry for help from the country far away:
'Isn't Yahweh in Tsiyyon,
   or isn't its King in it?'
'Why did they provoke me with their images,
   with hollow foreign beings?'
²⁰Harvest has passed, summer is finished,
   but we ourselves haven't found deliverance.

²¹Because of my dear people's breaking I'm broken,
   I mourn, devastation has taken strong hold of me.
²²Isn't there ointment in Gil'ad,
   or is there no healer there?
Because why has my dear people's restoration not developed?

9 If only my head were water,
   my eye a fountain of tears.
I'd cry day and night
   for those who are run through among my dear people.

²If only I could have a travellers' lodge in the wilderness,
   and abandon my people, go from them,
Because all of them are adulterers,
   a pack of people breaking faith.
³They've directed their tongue, their bow has been falsehood;
   it's not on behalf of truthfulness that they've been strong in the country.
Because they've gone out from something bad, to something bad,
   and not acknowledged me (Yahweh's declaration).
⁴They should keep watch, each person, on his neighbour;
   don't rely on any brother.
Because every brother is totally crooked,
   and every neighbour goes about as a slanderer.
⁵Each one trifles with his neighbour;
   they don't speak the truth.
They've taught their tongue false speech;
   they've got tired being wayward.
⁶You [Yirmeyahu] have lived in the middle of deceit;
   in deceit they've refused to acknowledge me (Yahweh's declaration).

Who is the smart person who understands all this?

⁷Therefore Yahweh of Armies has said this:

Here am I; I'm going to smelt them, test them,
   because how [else] can I act in the face of my dear people?
⁸Their tongue is a sharpened arrow,
   it's spoken deceit.

With his mouth someone speaks with his
   neighbour of how things will be well,
but inside he lays an ambush for him.
⁹For these things shall I not attend to them
      (Yahweh's declaration),
   or on a nation that's like this shall I myself not
      take redress?
¹⁰For the mountains I shall take up crying and
      wailing,
   and for the wilderness pastures a lament.
Because they're laid waste, with no one passing
      through,
   and people don't hear the sound of livestock.
Both the birds of the heavens and the animals,
   they've fled; they've gone.
¹¹I shall make Yerushalaim into heaps of rubble,
   the dwelling of jackals.
Yehudah's towns I shall make into a devastation,
   with no inhabitant.

¹²Who is the smart individual who understands this,
   to whom has Yahweh's mouth spoken so that he
      can tell of it?
On what account has the country perished,
   become wasted like a wilderness, with no one
      passing through?

¹³Yahweh said, 'Because they abandoned my instruction which I put before them. They didn't listen to my voice and they didn't walk by it. ¹⁴They followed the determination of their mind and followed the Masters, as their ancestors taught them.' ¹⁵Therefore Yahweh of Armies, Yisra'el's God, said this: 'Here am I; I'm going to make this people eat bitter plants and make them drink poisoned water. ¹⁶I shall scatter them among the nations that they and their ancestors haven't known. I shall send off the sword after them until I've finished them off.'

The real circumcision

¹⁷Yahweh of Armies has said this:

Show some discernment, and call the lamenting
   women so they may come,
   send for the smart women so they may come.
¹⁸They must hurry and raise a wailing over us,
   so our eyes may run with tears,
   our pupils flow with water.

¹⁹Because the sound of wailing –
   it has made itself heard from Tsiyyon:
'How we are destroyed,
   we are very shamed.
Because we are abandoning our country,
   because they've overthrown our dwellings.'
²⁰Because listen, women, to Yahweh's word;
   your ear must receive the word from his
      mouth.
Teach wailing to your daughters,
   lamentation one woman to her neighbour.
²¹Because death is climbing through our
      windows,
   coming into our citadels,
To cut off children from the streets,
   young men from the squares.

²²Speak like this (Yahweh's declaration):

Human corpses will fall
   like manure on the face of the fields,
Like a sheaf behind the reaper
   with no one gathering it up.

²³Yahweh has said this:

The smart person isn't to exult in his smartness,
   the strong person isn't to exult in his strength,
   the wealthy person isn't to exult in his wealth.
²⁴Rather the person who exults is to exult in this:
   showing insight and acknowledging me,
That I am Yahweh,
   acting with commitment,
With authority and faithfulness in the country,
   because I delight in these things (Yahweh's
      declaration).

²⁵There, days are coming (Yahweh's declaration) when I shall attend to everyone circumcised in the foreskin, ²⁶with Misrayim, Yehudah, Edom, the Ammonites, Mo'ab, and all the people shaved at the forehead who live in the wilderness, because all the nations are foreskinned, and Yisra'el's entire household – foreskinned in mind.

Facing the facts about images

10 Listen to the word that Yahweh spoke to you, Yisra'el's household. ²Yahweh has said this:

Don't learn the nations' way;
   don't shatter at signs in the heavens.
Because the nations may shatter at those,
   ³because the nations' laws are hollow.

Because someone cuts a tree from the forest,
   the work of a craftsman's hands, with an axe.
⁴With silver and gold he beautifies it,
   with nails and hammers he strengthens it, so it doesn't wobble.
⁵They're like a scarecrow in a melon patch;
   they don't speak.
They're carried, carried, because they don't walk;
   don't be in awe of them.
Because they don't do anything bad,
   nor is doing good with them.
⁶There is none like you, Yahweh;
   you are great and your name is great, with strength.
⁷Who would not be in awe of you, king of the nations,
   because it's fitting to you.
Because among all the nations' smart people
   and in all their dominion there's none like you.
⁸As one, they're stupid, dim-witted;
   the correction that comes from hollow beings is wood.
⁹Beaten silver is brought from Tarshish,
   gold from Uphaz,
A craftsman's work, a goldsmith's hands,
   their clothing blue and purple,
   the work of smart people, all of them.
¹⁰But Yahweh is the true God,
   he's the living God, the everlasting King.
At his fury, earth shakes;
   nations can't cope with his condemnation.

¹¹You're to speak in this way to them:

The gods that didn't make the heavens and the earth
   will perish from the earth and from under the heavens.

¹²One who made the earth by his energy,
   established the world by his expertise,
   by his understanding stretched out the heavens –
¹³At his giving voice there was a roar of water in the heavens,
   and he made clouds go up from the end of the earth.
He made lightning for the rain,
   made wind come out from his storehouses.

Discipline with judgement

¹⁴Every human being proves stupid, without knowledge;
   every goldsmith is put to shame by the image,
Because his figure is a falsehood,
   and there's no breath in them.
¹⁵They're hollow, a work for mockery;
   at the time they're attended to, they'll perish.
¹⁶Not like these is Ya'aqob's share,
   because he's the former of everything.
Yisra'el is the clan that is his domain;
   Yahweh of Armies is his name.

¹⁷Gather up your baggage from the country [Yerushalaim],
   you who dwell under siege.

¹⁸Because Yahweh has said this:

Here am I, I'm going to fling away the people who dwell in the country,
   at this moment.
I shall pressure them
   in order that they experience it.

¹⁹Oh, alas for me, on account of my break,
   my wound is sickening,
Whereas myself I had said,
   'This is only a sickness, and I shall bear it.'
²⁰My tent is destroyed, all my tent cords have broken.
   my children have gone out from me, there are none of them,
No one spreading my tent again,
   hanging out my tent cloths.
²¹Because the shepherds are stupid,
   they haven't enquired of Yahweh.
That's why they haven't thrived,
   and all their flock has scattered.
²²A sound, a report – there, it's coming,
   a great shaking from a northern country,
To make Yehudah's towns a devastation,
   the abode of jackals.
²³I acknowledge, Yahweh,
   that an individual's road doesn't belong to him.

It doesn't belong to a person walking
    to set his step.
²⁴Discipline me, Yahweh, only with judgement,
    not in your anger, so you don't make me small.
²⁵Pour your wrath on the nations that haven't
    acknowledged you,
    on the kin-groups that haven't called out in
        your name.
Because they've consumed Ya'aqob,
    consumed him and finished him off, and
        devastated his abode.

No shrugging of God's shoulders

11 The word that came to Yirmeyahu from Yahweh: ²'You people, listen to the words in this pact.'

'So you're to speak them to Yehudah's people and against Yerushalaim's inhabitants, ³and say to them, "Yahweh, Yisra'el's God, has said this: 'The person is cursed who doesn't listen to the words in this pact ⁴that I ordered your ancestors on the day I got them out from the country of Misrayim, from the iron smelter, saying "Listen to my voice and act on them in accordance with all that I order you, and you will be a people for me and I will be God for you", ⁵in order to implement the oath that he swore to your ancestors to give them a country flowing with milk and syrup this very day."'

I said, 'Yes, Yahweh.'

⁶Yahweh said to me, 'Call out all these words in Yehudah's towns and in Yerushalaim's streets: "Listen to the words in this pact and act on them. ⁷Because I testified solemnly to your ancestors on the day I got them out from the country of Misrayim and until this day, starting early to testify, saying 'Listen to my voice.' ⁸But they didn't listen or bend their ear but walked each person by the bad determination of their mind. So I brought on them all the words in this pact that I ordered them to act on but they didn't act on."'

⁹Yahweh said to me, 'A conspiracy can be found among Yehudah's people and among Yerushalaim's inhabitants. ¹⁰They've turned back to the wayward acts of their ancestors of old, who refused to listen to my words. As those people followed other gods, Yisra'el's household and Yehudah's household have contravened my pact that I solemnized with their ancestors.'

Don't pray

¹¹Therefore Yahweh has said this: 'Here am I; I'm going to bring upon them bad fortune from which they won't be able to get away. They'll cry out to me but I won't listen to them. ¹²Yehudah's towns and Yerushalaim's inhabitants will go and cry out to the gods to whom they've been burning incense. But they won't deliver them at all at the time when the bad fortune comes to them. ¹³Because according to the number of your towns, Yehudah, have been your gods, and according to the number of your streets, Yerushalaim, have you set up altars to Shame, altars to burn incense to the Master.'

¹⁴And you, don't plead on this town's account,
    don't raise on its account a resounding shout
        or plea.
Because I won't be listening at the time when they
        call to me
    on account of the bad fortune that comes to
        them.
¹⁵What business does my beloved have in my
        house,
    as she acts on her strategy?
Many will make the sacred flesh pass from you,
    because you deal badly, then you exult.
¹⁶'Verdant olive, beautiful with shapely fruit',
    Yahweh named you.
To a big roaring sound he's set fire to it,
    and its branches have broken.
¹⁷Yahweh of Armies who planted you –
    he's spoken of bad fortune for you,
On account of the bad dealing of Yisra'el's
        household
    and Yehudah's household,
Which they did for themselves
    to provoke me by burning incense to the
        Master.

¹⁸When Yahweh made it known to me so that I
        might know –
    then you let me see their practices.
¹⁹And I myself had been like a docile lamb
    that's led to slaughter.
I didn't know that against me
    they'd thought up their intentions:
'Let's destroy the tree with its sap,
    let's cut him off from the land of the living,
    so that his name isn't mentioned any more.'

²⁰So, Yahweh of Armies, who exercises authority
with faithfulness,
who tests the inner being and the mind:
May I see your redress on them,
because I've laid out my argument to you.

Why do the faithless get away with it?

²¹Therefore Yahweh has said this:

'About the people of Anatot who are seeking
your life, saying "You will not prophesy in
Yahweh's name, then you won't die by our hand."'
²²Therefore Yahweh of Armies has said this:

Here am I; I'm going to attend to them;
the young men will die by the sword.
Their sons and their daughters will die by famine;
²³there will be no remainder of them.
Because I shall bring bad fortune on the people
of Anatot,
the year when they're attended to.

12 You'll be in the right, Yahweh, when I
argue with you,
yet I shall speak of your rulings with you.
Why does the way of the faithless succeed,
why are all the people who break faith at ease?
²You plant them, yes they root;
they go on, yes they produce fruit.
You're near in their mouth,
but far from their inner being.
³But you, Yahweh, have acknowledged me and
seen me,
you've tested my mind in relation to you.
Drive them off like sheep to the slaughter,
make them sacred for the killing day.

⁴How long will the country mourn,
the grass in all the fields wither?
Through the bad action of the people who live in it,
animals and birds come to an end,
Because people say,
'He won't look at our future.'

⁵When you [Yirmeyahu] have run with people on
foot and they've exhausted you,
then how can you compete with horses?
If you're secure in a country where things are well,
then how will you do in the Yarden [Jordan]
jungle?

⁶Because yes, your brothers and your father's
household –
yes, those people have broken faith with you;
yes, those people have called after you in full
voice.
Don't trust them,
when they speak good things to you.

I have abandoned my household

⁷I have abandoned my household,
I have deserted my domain.
I have given my dearly beloved
into her enemies' fist.
⁸My domain has become to me
like a lion in the forest.
She's given her voice against me;
therefore I've been hostile to her.
⁹My domain is a coloured bird of prey;
birds of prey are against her, all round.
Go, gather all the creatures of the wild,
bring them to eat.
¹⁰Many shepherds have devastated my vineyard,
trampled my share.
They've made my desirable share
into a devastated wilderness.
¹¹Someone has made it into a devastation;
it mourns before me, devastated.

The entire country is devastated,
because there's no one taking it into their mind.
¹²Into all the bare places in the wilderness
destroyers have come
because Yahweh's sword consumes.
From one end of the country to the other end of
the country
there's no well-being for all flesh.
¹³They've sown wheat but reaped thorns,
they've pained themselves but they don't
prevail.
So be shamed by your yield
because of Yahweh's angry blazing.

¹⁴Yahweh has said this: 'About all my neighbours who deal badly, who touch the domain that I gave to my people Yisra'el: here am I, I'm going to uproot them from on their land, and Yehudah's household I shall uproot from among them. ¹⁵But after I've uprooted them I shall again show compassion to them and bring them back, each to his domain, each

to his country. ¹⁶If they really learn the ways of my people, swearing by my name "As Yahweh lives" as they taught my people to swear by the Master, they'll be built up among my people. ¹⁷But if they don't listen, I'll uproot that nation, uproot and destroy it (Yahweh's declaration).'

A shorts story

13 Yahweh said this to me: 'Go and get yourself a linen garment and put it round your hips, but don't let it come into water.' ²So I got the garment in accordance with Yahweh's word and put it round my hips. ³Yahweh's word came to me a second time: ⁴"Take the garment that you got, which is round your hips, and set off for Perat. Hide it there in a crevice in the cliff.' ⁵So I went and hid it at Perat as Yahweh ordered me. ⁶After many days Yahweh said to me, 'Set off for Perat and get the garment from there that I ordered you to hide there.' ⁷I went to Perat and dug, and got the garment from the place where I'd hidden it, and there, the garment was destroyed; it wouldn't be useful for anything.

⁸Yahweh's word came to me. ⁹Yahweh said this: 'In this way I shall devastate Yehudah's majesty and Yerushalaim's majesty, which are great. ¹⁰This people that deals badly, who refuse to listen to my words, who walk by the determination of their mind, and who follow other gods to serve them and bow low to them, will become like this garment that isn't useful for anything. ¹¹Because as a garment sticks to someone's hips, so I made Yisra'el's entire household and Yehudah's entire household stick to me (Yahweh's declaration) to be for me a people, a name, praise and splendour. But they didn't listen.

¹²So you're to speak this word to them. Yahweh the God of Yisra'el says this: "Every bottle should be full of wine." They'll say to you, "We know very well that every bottle should be full of wine, don't we." ¹³You're to say to them, "Yahweh has said this: 'Here am I; I'm going to fill all the inhabitants of this country, the kings who sit on David's behalf on his throne, the priests, the prophets and all Yerushalaim's inhabitants – with drunkenness. ¹⁴I shall smash them, one person against his brother, parents and children together

(Yahweh's declaration). I shall not pity and I shall not spare and I shall not have compassion so that I don't devastate them.'"

Can the people change?

¹⁵Listen, give ear, don't be superior,
    because Yahweh has spoken.
¹⁶Give honour to Yahweh your God
    before he brings darkness,
Before your feet stumble
    on the mountains at dusk,
And you hope for light but he turns it into deep
    darkness,
    makes it into dark gloom.
¹⁷If you don't listen to this, my soul will cry in
    hidden places
    before your majesty.
My eye will cry and cry, and run with crying,
    because Yahweh's flock has gone into captivity.

¹⁸Say to the king and to the queen mother,
    'Fall down, sit.
Because your headwear is coming down,
    your glorious crown.'
¹⁹The Negeb towns are closed,
    there's no one opening them.
Yehudah is taken into exile, all of it,
    taken into exile, completely.
²⁰Lift up your eyes
    and look at the people coming from the north.
Where are the sheep that were given you
    [Yerushalaim],
    your glorious flock?
²¹What will you say when he appoints over you
    ones whom you trained for yourself,
    as allies, as your head?
Contractions will take hold of you, won't they,
    like a woman giving birth.
²²And when you say to yourself,
    'Why have these things happened to me?' –
Because of the magnitude of your waywardness
    your skirts have been stripped off and your
    body has been violated.

²³Does the Kushite [Sudanese] change his skin,
    the leopard his spots?
You people too can do good,
    you who have been taught to do bad.
²⁴So I shall scatter them like chaff
    passing away before the wilderness wind.

²⁵This will be your fate,
   your lot measured out from me (Yahweh's declaration),
In that you put me out of mind
   and relied on falsehood.
²⁶Yes, I myself will lift up your skirts over your face,
   and your slighting will become visible,
²⁷Your adulteries and your bellowings,
   your whorish scheming.
On the hills, in the open country,
   I've seen your abominable deeds.
Oh, alas for you, Yerushalaim, you're not clean –
   how much longer will it be?

The God who doesn't answer prayer

14 What came as a word from Yahweh to Yirmeyahu concerning the matter of the drought.

²Yehudah mourns,
   its settlements languish.
People look down to the ground,
   Yerushalaim's crying goes up.
³Their important people send their underlings for water;
   they come to the cisterns, they don't find water.
They return, their vessels empty;
   they're shamed, disgraced, they cover their head.
⁴On account of the fact that the ground has broken up,
   because there hasn't been rain in the country,
The farmers are shamed,
   they cover their head.
⁵When the hind in the open country, too, gives birth,
   it abandons, because there's been no grass.
⁶As the donkeys stand on the bare places,
   they gasp for air like jackals.
Their eyes fail,
   because there's no vegetation.

⁷If our wayward acts avow against us, Yahweh,
   act for the sake of your name.
Because our turnings away are many;
   we've done wrong to you.
⁸Yisra'el's hope,
   its deliverer in time of pressure,
Why should you become like an alien in the country,
   like a traveller who turns aside to lodge?
⁹Why should you become like someone bewildered,
   like a strong man who can't deliver?
But you're among us, Yahweh,
   your name has been called out over us, don't let go of us.

¹⁰Yahweh has said this to this people:

Yes, they've loved straying,
   they haven't restrained their feet.
Given that Yahweh doesn't accept them,
   he'll now be mindful of their waywardness
   and he'll attend to their wrongdoings.

The encouraging prophets

¹¹Yahweh said to me, 'Don't plead for good things on behalf of this people. ¹²When they fast I won't be listening, when they make a burnt sacrifice or offering, I won't be accepting them, because by sword, by famine and by epidemic I'm going to finish them off.' ¹³I said, 'Oh! Lord Yahweh! There, the prophets are saying to them, "You won't see a sword, famine won't happen to you, because I shall give you true well-being in this place."' ¹⁴Yahweh said to me, 'It's falsehood that the prophets have prophesied in my name; I didn't send them, I didn't order them, I didn't speak to them. A false vision, divination and nothingness, their mind's deceit, is what those people are prophesying to you. ¹⁵Therefore Yahweh has said this to the prophets who prophesy in my name when I didn't send them and they're saying, "Sword and famine won't happen in this country": by sword and famine those prophets will come to an end. ¹⁶And the people to whom they're prophesying will be thrown out into Yerushalaim's streets because of famine and sword. There'll be no one burying them – them, their wives, their sons and their daughters. I'll pour out on them their bad fortune.

¹⁷And you're to speak this word to them.

My eyes run down with crying,
   night and day they won't stop.
Because with a great breaking
   the dear daughter of my people has broken,
   a very sickening wound.

¹⁸If I go out into the open country –
   there, people run through by the sword.
If I come into the town –
   there, sicknesses that come from famine.
Because both prophet and priest go round the
      country
   but don't acknowledge it.'

No matter who prayed

¹⁹Have you totally rejected Yehudah,
   have you renounced Tsiyyon with your entire
      being?
Why have you struck us down
   and we have no one healing us? –
Hoping for things to go well, but there's nothing
      good,
   for a time of healing, but there – terror.
²⁰We acknowledge our faithlessness, Yahweh,
   our ancestors' waywardness.
Because we've done wrong to you,
   ²¹don't spurn us, for the sake of your
      name.
Don't disgrace your honoured throne;
   be mindful, don't contravene your pact with
      us.
²²Are there any among the nations' hollow beings
   who make it rain,
or do the heavens give showers?
You're the one, Yahweh our God, aren't you,
   so we hope in you, because you made all these
      things.

15 Yahweh said to me, 'If Mosheh [Moses] and Shemu'el [Samuel] were to stand before me, my soul wouldn't go out to this people. Send them away from my presence. They're to go away. ²When they say to you, "Where shall we go?", say to them, "Yahweh has said this:

Those who are for death, to death;
   those who are for the sword, to the sword;
Those who are for famine, to famine;
   those who are for captivity, to captivity.

³I shall appoint over them four species (Yahweh's declaration):

The sword to slay
   and the dogs to drag off,
The birds of the heavens and the animals of the
      earth
   to eat and to devastate.

⁴I shall make them a horror to all earth's kingdoms on account of Menashsheh ben Yehizqiyyahu king of Yehudah, because of what he did in Yerushalaim."'

I'm tired of relenting

⁵Because who will pity you, Yerushalaim,
   who will grieve for you,
Who will turn aside
   to ask about your well-being?
⁶You are one who has deserted me (Yahweh's
      declaration);
   you go backwards.
So I'm stretching out my hand against you and
      devastating you;
   I'm tired of relenting.
⁷I'm winnowing them with a pitchfork
   in the country's settlements.
I'm bereaving, I'm obliterating my people,
   because of their ways from which they wouldn't
      turn back.
⁸Their widows will be more numerous
   than the sand of the seas.
I shall bring to them (against mother, young man)
   a destroyer at noon.
I shall let shock and terror
   fall on them suddenly.
⁹One who has borne seven languishes,
   she's breathed out her life.
Her sun has set while it's still day;
   she's shamed and confounded.
Their remainder I'll give to the sword
   before their enemies (Yahweh's declaration).

¹⁰Oh, alas for me,
   my mother, that you gave birth to me,
An argumentative man and a disputatious man
   for the entire country.
Although I haven't lent and they haven't lent to me,
   everyone slights me.

¹¹Yahweh said:

If I do not free you for good things,
   if I do not get the enemy to intervene for you
      in a bad time and in a time of distress . . .

¹²Can one break iron,
  iron from the north or copper?
¹³Your wealth [Yerushalaim] and your treasures I
  shall give as plunder,
  not for payment but for all your wrongdoings,
    yes through all your territory.

¹⁴I shall make your enemies [Yirmeyahu] pass on
  through a country they haven't known.
Because fire is blazing in my anger;
  it will blaze against you all.

You've been a deceiver

¹⁵You yourself acknowledge, Yahweh;
  be mindful of me, attend to me.
Grant me redress from my persecutors;
  don't let me be taken, because of your long-
    temperedness.
Acknowledge my bearing of reviling because of
    you;
  ¹⁶your words presented themselves and I
    consumed them.
Your word became joy to me,
  the rejoicing of my mind.
Because your name was called out over me,
  Yahweh God of Armies.
¹⁷I haven't sat in the company of people having
    fun, and exulted;
  because of your hand I've sat alone,
  because you'd filled me with condemnation.
¹⁸Why has my pain become endless,
  my wound grave, refusing to heal?
You really have been to me a veritable
    deceiver,
  water that's not trustworthy.

¹⁹Therefore Yahweh has said this:

If you turn back, I'll let you come back;
  you can stand before me.
If you let out what is valuable rather than what is
    empty,
  you can be my very mouth.
Those people will turn back to you,
  but you yourself won't turn back to them.
²⁰To this people I shall make you
  a copper wall, fortified;
They'll battle against you
  but not prevail over you.
Because I shall be with you

to deliver you and to rescue you (Yahweh's
    declaration).
²¹I will rescue you from the hand of people who
    deal badly,
  redeem you from the fist of the violent.

Your marriage isn't your own

16 Yahweh's word came to me: ²'You will not get yourself a wife and you will not have sons or daughters in this place.' ³Because Yahweh has said this about the sons and the daughters that are born in this place, and about the mothers who give birth to them and about the fathers who father them in this country: ⁴'Sickening deaths they will die. They won't be lamented or buried. As manure on the face of the ground they'll be. By sword and famine they'll come to an end. Their corpse will be food for the birds of the heavens and for the animals of the earth.'

⁵Because Yahweh has said this:

Don't come to a house where there's a wake,
  don't go to lament and grieve for them.
Because I have gathered up my well-being from
    this people
  (Yahweh's declaration), my commitment and
    compassion.
⁶Big people and little people in this country will die;
  they won't be buried.
People won't lament for them,
  they won't gash themselves and they won't
    shave their heads for them.
⁷They won't break bread for them in mourning
  to comfort someone over a death.
They won't give them a cup of comfort to drink,
  for his father or for his mother.
⁸And you're not to come to a house where there's
    a banquet,
  to sit with them to eat and drink.

⁹Because Yahweh of Armies, Yisra'el's God, has
said this:

Here am I – I'm going to make cease from this
    place,
  in front of your eyes and in your days,
The joyful voice and the rejoicing voice,
  the voice of groom and the voice of bride.

Fishers and hunters

10"When you tell this people all these things, and they say to you, "Why has Yahweh spoken against us all this great bad fortune, and what is our waywardness and our wrongdoing that we've committed against Yahweh our God?" **11**you're to say to them, "Because your ancestors abandoned me (Yahweh's declaration) and followed other gods, served them and bowed low to them. They abandoned me and didn't keep my instruction. **12**And you've dealt badly more than your ancestors. There you are, following each of you the bad determination of his mind, so as not to listen to me. **13**So I shall hurl you from upon this country to a country that you haven't known, you or your ancestors, and there you will serve other gods, day and night, in that I won't show you grace."

14Therefore, here, days are coming (Yahweh's declaration) when it will no more be said, "As Yahweh lives, who got the Yisra'elites up from the country of Misrayim," **15**but rather, "As Yahweh lives, who got the Yisra'elites up from the northern country and from all the countries where he'd driven them". I shall bring them back to their country, which I gave their ancestors.'

16Here am I; I'm going to send for many fishers
   (Yahweh's declaration), and they'll fish for
      them.
Afterwards I shall send
   for many hunters and they'll hunt for them,
From on every mountain and from on every hill
   and from the clefts in the cliffs.
17Because my eyes have been upon all their ways;
   they haven't hidden from my presence.
Their waywardness hasn't stayed concealed
   from in front of my eyes.
18So I shall make good to them first,
   double for their waywardness and their
      wrongdoing,
Because of their profaning my country
   with their abominable corpses;
   they filled my domain with their offensive
      practices.

19Yahweh, my vigour and my stronghold,
   my escape in the day of pressure,
To you nations will come
   from earth's ends and say,
'Our ancestors indeed had falsehood as their
      domain,
   hollowness, and there was nothing in them that
      would prevail.
20Can a human being make himself gods? –
   but they're not gods.'

21Therefore here am I, I'm going to make them
      acknowledge it
   at this moment.
I shall make them acknowledge my hand and my
      strength,
   and they will acknowledge that my name is
      Yahweh.

Yahweh tests the inner being

17 Yehudah's wrongdoing is written
   with an iron pen,
Engraved with a diamond point
   on their mind's tablet
And at the horns of their altars
   2in accordance with their children's being
      mindful of their altars and their totem poles,
By a verdant tree and by high hills,
   3the mountains in the open country.
Your resources, all your treasures, I shall give as
      plunder,
   the shrines for your wrongdoing, in all your
      territory.
4You'll forfeit hold (and by your own act)
   of your domain that I gave you.
I shall make you serve your enemies
   in a country that you haven't known.
Because you've lit a fire in my anger
   that will burn permanently.

   5Yahweh has said this:

Cursed is the man
   who relies on human beings,
Makes flesh his strength,
   and his mind turns aside from Yahweh.
6He'll be like a shrub in the steppe;
   it can't see that good will come.
It dwells in parched places in the wilderness,
   salty land where no one lives.
7Blessed is the man who relies on Yahweh,
   and Yahweh is his reliance.
8He'll be like a tree planted by water;
   it sends out its roots by a channel.

It isn't afraid that heat will come;
   its foliage will be verdant.
In a year of drought it isn't anxious;
   it doesn't move away from producing fruit.
⁹The mind is more crooked than anything;
   it's grave – who can know it?
¹⁰I am Yahweh, searching the mind,
   testing the inner being,
To give to an individual in accordance with his ways,
   in accordance with the fruit proper to his practices.

¹¹A partridge hatching when it didn't give birth –
   someone who makes wealth but not by [proper] exercise of authority.
At the midpoint of his days it will abandon him,
   and at his end he'll be a villain.

¹²Splendid throne, on high from of old,
   our sacred place!
¹³Yisra'el's hope, Yahweh,
   all who abandon you will be shamed.
People who turn aside in the country will be written down,
   because they've abandoned
   the fountain of living water, Yahweh.

Making the sabbath sacred

¹⁴Heal me, Yahweh, so I may find healing;
   deliver me, so I may find deliverance,
   because you're my praise.
¹⁵There, those people are saying to me,
   'Where is Yahweh's word? – yes, it should come.'
¹⁶I myself haven't hurried away from being a shepherd after you;
   I haven't longed for the grave day.
You yourself know what has come out from my lips;
   it's been in front of your face.
¹⁷Don't become a terror to me;
   you're my shelter on the day of bad fortune.
¹⁸My persecutors must be shamed;
   I myself must not be shamed.
They're the ones who must shatter;
   I myself must not shatter.
Bring upon them the day of bad fortune,
   break them with a double breaking.

¹⁹Yahweh said this to me: 'Go and stand in the ordinary people's gateway by which Yehudah's kings come in and by which they go out, and in all Yerushalaim's gateways. ²⁰Say to them, "Listen to Yahweh's word, Yehudah's kings and all Yehudah and all Yerushalaim's inhabitants, who come in by these gateways. ²¹Yahweh has said this: 'Keep watch on yourselves, and don't carry a load on the sabbath day or bring them through Yerushalaim's gateways. ²²Don't take out a load from your houses on the sabbath day or do any work. Make the sabbath day sacred, as I ordered your ancestors – ²³but they didn't listen, they didn't bend their ear, but toughened their neck so as not to listen and so as not to accept discipline.

²⁴But if you really listen to me (Yahweh's declaration) so as not to bring a load through the gateways of this town on the sabbath day but make the sabbath day sacred so as not to do any work on it, ²⁵then there will come through this town's gateways kings and officials sitting on David's throne, riding on chariots and horses, they and their officials, Yehudah's people and Yerushalaim's inhabitants. This town will stay permanently. ²⁶People will come from Yehudah's towns, from Yerushalaim's environs, from Binyamin's region, from the foothills, from the mountains and from the Negeb, bringing burnt offering, sacrifice, grain offering and incense, and bringing a thank-offering to Yahweh's house.

²⁷But if you don't listen to me by making the sabbath day sacred and not carrying a load, and you come through Yerushalaim's gateways on the sabbath day, I shall set fire to its gateways, and it will consume Yerushalaim's citadels and not go out.""

Clay in the potter's hand

18 The word that came to Yirmeyahu from Yahweh: ²'Set off and go down to a potter's house, and there I'll let you hear my words.' ³So I went down to a potter's house, and there, he was doing work at the stones. ⁴If the object were to spoil that he was making with clay, in the potter's hand, he'd make it again into another object, as it was right in the potter's eyes to do.

⁵Yahweh's word came to me: ⁶'Like this potter I can do to you, Yisra'el's household (Yahweh's declaration), can't I. There, like clay in the potter's hand, so are you in my hand, Yisra'el's household. ⁷Momentarily I may speak concerning a nation or kingdom about uprooting, demolishing and destroying, ⁸but that nation concerning which I've spoken may turn back from its bad dealing. I may then relent about the exile that I intended to do to it. ⁹But momentarily I may speak concerning a nation or kingdom about building and planting, ¹⁰and it may do what is bad in my eyes so as not to listen to my voice. I may then relent about the good that I said I'd do to it.

¹¹So now, say to Yehudah's people and Yerushalaim's inhabitants, please: "Yahweh has said this: 'Here, I'm shaping bad fortune for you. I'm thinking up intentions concerning you. Turn back, please, each person from his bad way, and make your ways and your practices good.'" ¹²But they'll say, "It's desperate, because we shall follow our intentions, and we shall act, each person by the bad determination of his mind."'

Don't expiate their waywardness

¹³Therefore Yahweh has said this:

Ask among the nations, please:
   who has heard anything like this?
She's done something very horrible,
   Miss Yisra'el.
¹⁴Does Lebanon snow abandon
   the crags in the open country?
Or does foreign water,
   cool streams, uproot?
¹⁵Because my people have put me out of mind,
   so they may burn incense to something empty.
They've made them collapse on their ways,
   the age-old paths,
By walking on [other] tracks,
   a way not built up,
¹⁶To make their country a devastation,
   something to whistle at permanently.
Anyone who passes by it will be devastated
   and will shake his head.
¹⁷Like the east wind
   I shall scatter them in front of the enemy.
At their back, not their face,
   I shall look at them, on their day of disaster.

¹⁸People said, 'Come on, we'll think up some intentions against Yirmeyahu, because instruction won't perish from the priest, counsel from the smart person or word from the prophet. Come on, let's strike him down with the tongue, so we may not heed any of his words.'

¹⁹Heed me, Yahweh,
   listen to the voice of the people who argue with me.
²⁰Is someone to make good with bad, for good? –
   because they've dug a pit for me.
Be mindful of how I stood before you
   to speak good things concerning them,
   to turn away your wrath from them.
²¹Therefore give their children to famine,
   tip them out to the edges of the sword.
Their women should be bereaved of children and widowed,
   their men should be slain by death,
   their young men struck down by the sword in battle.
²²May an outcry make itself heard from their houses,
   when suddenly you bring a raiding gang on them.
Because they've dug a pit to capture me
   and laid snares for my feet.
²³Yahweh, you yourself know
   their entire counsel against me, for my death.
Don't expiate their waywardness,
   don't blot out their wrongdoing from before you.
They should become people caused to collapse before you;
   in the time of your anger, act against them.

The pitcher that's to be pitched

19 Yahweh said this: 'Go and get a potter's earthenware pitcher, and some of the elders of the people and some of the elders of the priests, ²and go out into the Ben-hinnom Ravine, which is at the entrance of the Potsherd Gate, and call out there the words that I shall speak to you. ³Say, "Listen to Yahweh's word, Yehudah's kings and Yerushalaim's inhabitants. Yahweh of Armies, Yisra'el's God, has said this: 'Here am I; I'm going to bring bad fortune on this place such that everyone who hears of it – his ears will ring, ⁴since they've abandoned me, made this place alien, burned sacrifices in it to other gods that they hadn't acknowledged, they, their ancestors and Yehudah's kings. They've filled this place with the blood of people free of guilt. ⁵They've built shrines for the Master for burning their children in fire as burnt offerings to the Master, which I didn't order or speak of; it didn't come up into my mind.

⁶Therefore days are coming (Yahweh's declaration) when this place will no longer be called Tophet or Ben-hinnom Ravine but rather Slaughter Ravine. ⁷I shall pitch out the counsel of Yehudah and Yerushalaim in this place. I shall make them fall by the sword before their enemies, by the hand of people who seek their lives, and give their corpse as food to the birds of the heavens and to the animals of the earth. ⁸I shall make this town into a devastation and something to whistle at; anyone who passes by it will be devastated and will whistle at all its wounds. ⁹I shall cause them to eat the flesh of their sons and the flesh of their daughters, and they'll each eat the flesh of his neighbour in the siege and in the straits that their enemies, the people who seek their lives, impose on them."'

Terror-Is-All-Around

¹⁰And you're to break the pitcher before the eyes of the men who go with you, ¹¹and say to them, "Yahweh of Armies has said this: 'In this way I shall break this people and this town, as one breaks a potter's article, which cannot be mended again. In Tophet they'll bury, because there'll be no place for burying. ¹²Thus I shall do to this place (Yahweh's declaration) and to its inhabitants, to make this town like Tophet. ¹³Yerushalaim's houses and the kings of Yehudah's houses will become like the place Tophet, defiled – that is, all the houses on whose roofs people have burned sacrifices to the entire heavenly army and poured libations to other gods.'"

¹⁴Yirmeyahu came from Tophet where Yahweh had sent him to prophesy, stood in the courtyard of Yahweh's house and said to the entire people: ¹⁵'Yahweh of Armies, Yisra'el's God, has said this: "Here am I; I'm going to bring on this town and on all its towns all the bad fortune of which I've spoken concerning it, because they've toughened their neck so as not to listen to my words."'

20

Pashhur son of Immer, the priest (he was the leading appointee in Yahweh's house), heard Yirmeyahu prophesying these things. ²Pashhur struck the prophet Yirmeyahu down and put him in the stocks at the Upper Binyamin Gate, which is in Yahweh's house.

³Next day Pashhur let Yirmeyahu out from the stocks. Yirmeyahu said to him, 'Yahweh has named you not Pashhur but rather Terror-Is-All-Around. ⁴Because Yahweh has said this: "Here am I; I'm going to give you to terror, you and all your friends. They'll fall by the sword of their enemies, with your eyes seeing it. I shall give all Yehudah into the hand of the king of Babel and he'll exile them to Babel and strike them down with the sword. ⁵I shall give this town's entire wealth – all its profit, all its valuables and all the treasures of Yehudah's kings, I shall give into their enemies' hand. They'll plunder them, take them and carry them off to Babel. ⁶You, Pashhur, and all the people who live in your house – you'll go into captivity. You'll come to Babel, and there you'll die and there you'll be buried, you and all your friends to whom you've prophesied falsely."'

Cursed be the day I was born

⁷You enticed me, Yahweh, I was enticed;
   you've taken strong hold of me and prevailed.
I've become an object of fun all the time,
   everyone ridicules me.
⁸Because every time I speak, I cry out,
   I call out violence and destruction.
Because Yahweh's word has become for me
   reviling and derision all the time.
⁹When I said, 'I won't make mention of him,
   not speak in his name any more',
It became in my mind like a raging fire,
   shut up in my bones.
I was weary of holding it in –
   I couldn't.
¹⁰Because I heard the murmuring of many:
   'Terror is on every side – tell of it, let's tell of it.'
Every person who was my friend –
   they're watching my step:

'Perhaps he can be trapped and we can prevail
  over him,
  and take our redress from him.'

¹¹But Yahweh – he's with me as a violent strong man;
  therefore my persecutors will collapse and not
    win.
They're being utterly shamed, because they aren't
    thriving,
  with a disgrace for all time that won't be put
    out of mind.
¹²Yahweh of Armies, you who test the faithful
    person,
  who see inner being and mind,
May I see your redress on them,
  because to you I've rolled my argument.

¹³Sing for Yahweh,
  praise Yahweh.
Because he's rescued the life of a needy person
  from the hand of people who deal badly.

¹⁴Cursed be the day
  on which I was born.
The day when my mother gave birth to me –
  may it not be blessed.
¹⁵Cursed be the man
  who brought the news to my father,
'A male child has been born to you';
  he made him rejoice so much.
¹⁶That man will become like the towns
  that Yahweh overthrew and didn't relent.
He'll hear an outcry in the morning
  and a shout at noon time,
¹⁷The one who didn't kill me before birth,
  so that my mother became my grave,
  her womb pregnant permanently.
¹⁸Why then did I go out from the womb
  to see oppression and sorrow
  and so my days might consume themselves in
    shame?

The way to life and the way to death

21 The word that came to Yirmeyahu
  from Yahweh when King Tsidqiyyahu
sent to him Pashhur ben Malkiyyah and
Tsephanyah ben Ma'aseyah the priest to say,
²'Enquire on our behalf of Yahweh, please,
because Nebukadre'tstsar king of Babel is doing
battle against us. Perhaps Yahweh will act with
us in accordance with his wonders, so that he
goes up from us.'

³Yirmeyahu said to them, 'You're to say this to
Tsidqiyyahu: ⁴"Yahweh, Yisra'el's God, has said
this: 'Here am I; I'm going to turn back the battle
implements that are in your hand, with which
you're doing battle with the king of Babel and the
Kasdites who are besieging you from outside
the wall, and I shall gather them up into the
middle of this town. ⁵I myself will do battle
against you with hand bent and strong arm, with
anger, with wrath and with great fury. ⁶I shall
strike down this town's inhabitants, human beings
and animals; they'll die in a great epidemic.
⁷After this (Yahweh's declaration) I shall give
Tsidqiyyahu king of Yehudah and his servants
and the people, those who remain in this town
from epidemic, sword and famine, into the
hand of Nebukadre'tstsar king of Babel and
into the hand of their enemies, into the hand of
the people seeking their life. He'll strike them
down with the mouth of the sword. He won't
have pity for them. He won't have mercy. He
won't have compassion.'"

⁸And to this people you are to say, "Yahweh
has said this: 'Here am I, putting before you the
way to life and the way to death. ⁹The one who
lives in this town will die by sword, by famine
or by epidemic. But the one who goes out and
goes over to the Kasdites who are besieging you
will live. His life will be his as a trophy. ¹⁰Because
I have set my face against this town for bad
fortune and not for good fortune (Yahweh's
declaration). Into the hand of the king of Babel
it will be given, and he will burn it in fire.'"

About false confidence

¹¹And to the household of the king of
Yehudah, listen to Yahweh's word. ¹²Household
of David, Yahweh has said this:

Judge with authority morning by morning,
  rescue the person who's been robbed from the
    hand of the oppressor,
So that my wrath doesn't go out like fire,
  and burn up with no one quenching it,
  because of the bad nature of your practices.
¹³Here am I towards you [Yerushalaim], you who
    dwell in the vale,
  a crag in the flatland (Yahweh's declaration).

People who say, "Who can come down against us,
who can come into our abodes?",
¹⁴I shall attend to you
in accordance with the fruit of your practices (Yahweh's declaration).
I shall set fire to its forest
and consume all that's round it.'

22

Yahweh said this: 'Go down to the house of the king of Yehudah and speak there this word. ²Say, "Listen to Yahweh's word, king of Yehudah, you who sit on David's throne and your servants and your people who come through these gateways. ³Yahweh has said this: 'Exercise authority with faithfulness, rescue the person who's been robbed from the hand of the oppressor, don't wrong alien, orphan and widow, don't be violent, don't shed the blood of someone free of guilt in this place. ⁴Because if you really do act on this word, then through this house's gateways will come David's kings sitting on his throne, riding chariot and horses, he and his servants and his people. ⁵But if you don't listen to these words, I swear by myself (Yahweh's declaration) that this house will become a waste.'"

⁶Because Yahweh has said this concerning the house of the king of Yehudah:

You are Gil'ad to me,
the top of Lebanon.
If I don't make you a wilderness,
towns that aren't inhabited . . .
⁷I shall make devastators sacred to go against you,
each with his implements.
They'll cut the choicest of your cedars
and make them fall into the fire.

How to evaluate a king

⁸Many nations will pass by this town and will say, an individual to his neighbour, 'Why did Yahweh act in this way to this great town?' ⁹And they'll say, 'On account of the fact that they abandoned the pact of Yahweh their God and bowed low to other gods and served them.'

¹⁰Don't cry for the one who is dead,
don't lament for him.
Cry and cry for the one who is going,
because he won't come back again
and see the country of his birth.

¹¹Because Yahweh has said this regarding Shallum ben Yoshiyyahu king of Yehudah, who was reigning in place of Yoshiyyahu his father, who has gone out from this place: 'He won't come back here again, ¹²because in the place where they have exiled him, there he'll die. This country he won't see again.'

¹³Hey, one who builds his house without faithfulness,
his lofts without the [proper] exercise of authority!
He makes his neighbour serve for nothing;
he doesn't give him his earnings.
¹⁴The one who says, 'I'll build myself a vast house, spacious lofts.'
He cuts windows for it, panelled with cedar, painted with vermilion.
¹⁵Are you a king
because you're competing in cedar?
Your father – he ate and drank, didn't he,
and acted in faithful exercise of authority.
Then things were good for him,
¹⁶when he gave judgement for the weak and needy.
Then things were good;
this is to acknowledge me, isn't it (Yahweh's declaration).
¹⁷Because you have no eye or mind
except for loot,
For shedding the blood of the one free of guilt,
and for fraud and for extortion.

¹⁸Therefore Yahweh has said this concerning Yehoyaqim ben Yoshiyyahu king of Yehudah:

They won't mourn for him,
'Oh my brother, oh my sister'.
They won't mourn for him,
'Oh my lord, oh His Majesty'.
¹⁹He'll be buried with a donkey's burial,
dragged and dumped outside Yerushalaim's gateways.

The despised potsherd

²⁰Climb the Lebanon and cry out [Yerushalaim],
in the Bashan lift your voice.

Cry out from Abarim,
   because all your friends are broken.
²¹I spoke to you during your peaceful times;
   you said, 'I won't listen.'
This was your way from your youth,
   because you didn't listen to my voice.
²²All your shepherds – the wind will shepherd them;
   your friends will go into captivity.
Because then you'll be shamed and disgraced
   because of all your bad dealing.
²³You who live in the Lebanon, nesting among the cedars,
   how needy of grace you'll be,
When contractions come to you,
   labour like someone giving birth.

²⁴'As I live (Yahweh's declaration), if Konyah ben Yehoyaqim king of Yehudah were the ring on my right hand . . . Because from there I'd tear you off. ²⁵I shall give you into the hand of the people who seek your life, into the hand of the people whom you yourself dread, into the hand of Nebukadre'tstsar king of Babel, into the hand of the Kasdites. ²⁶I'll hurl you and your mother who gave birth to you into another country where you were not born, and there you'll die. ²⁷The country where people will be lifting up their longing to come back: they won't come back there.'

²⁸Is he a despised broken piece of pottery,
   this man Konyahu,
or an implement in which there's no delight?
Why are they being hurled, he and his offspring,
   thrown to a country that they don't know?
²⁹Country, country, country,
   listen to Yahweh's word.
³⁰Yahweh has said this:
'Write down this person as childless,
A man who won't succeed in his time,
   because not one of his offspring will succeed,
Sitting on David's throne
   and ruling again in Yehudah.'

A wicked play on words in a king's name

23

'Hey, shepherds who led astray and scattered my flock (Yahweh's declaration)'. ²Therefore Yahweh, Yisra'el's God, has said this about the shepherds who shepherd my people: 'You – you've let my flock scatter. You've driven them away and not attended to them. Here am I; I'm going to attend to you, to the bad nature of your practices (Yahweh's declaration). ³And I myself will draw together the remainder of my flock from all the countries where I've driven them. I'll take them back to their abode, and they'll be fruitful and become many. ⁴I'll set up shepherds over them and they'll shepherd them, and they won't be afraid any more or shatter or be missing (Yahweh's declaration).

⁵There, days are coming (Yahweh's declaration) when I shall set up for David a faithful branch. He will reign as king and show insight and exercise authority and faithfulness in the country. ⁶In his days Yehudah will find deliverance and Yisra'el will dwell with confidence. This is the name by which he'll be called: "Yahweh Is Our Faithfulness" [Yahweh Tsidqenu]. ⁷Therefore, here, days are coming (Yahweh's declaration) when they will no longer say "As Yahweh lives, who got the Yisra'elites up from the country of Misrayim". ⁸Rather, "As Yahweh lives, who got up and brought the offspring of Yisra'el's household from the northern country" and from all the countries where I will have driven them. And they will live on their land.'

False prophets

⁹Concerning the prophets.

My mind has broken within me,
   all my bones have become weak.
I've become like someone drunk,
   like a man wine has overcome,
Before Yahweh and before his sacred words,
   ¹⁰because the country is full of adulterers.
Because the country mourns before a vow;
   the wilderness pastures have dried up.
People's running has become something bad,
   their strength not right.
¹¹Because both prophet and priest are impious;
   'Even in my house I've found their bad dealing' (Yahweh's declaration).
¹²Therefore their way will become for them like slippery slopes,
   they'll be driven into darkness and they'll fall there.

Because I shall bring bad fortune upon them,
  the year when they're attended to (Yahweh's declaration).
¹³In Shomron's [Samaria's] prophets I saw corruptness:
  they prophesied by the Master and led my people astray.
¹⁴In Yerushalaim's prophets I saw a horror:
  adultery, walking by falsehood,
And they strengthen the hands of people dealing badly,
  so that no one may turn back from his bad dealing.
They've become like Sedom [Sodom] to me, all of them,
  its inhabitants like Amorah [Gomorrah].

¹⁵Therefore Yahweh of Armies has said this concerning the prophets:

Here am I; I'm going to feed this people bitter plants
  and make them drink poisoned water.
Because from Yerushalaim's prophets
  impiety has gone out to the whole country.

¹⁶Yahweh of Armies has said this:

Don't listen to the words of the prophets
  who prophesy to you.
They're giving you something hollow;
  they speak a vision from their mind,
  not from Yahweh's mouth.
¹⁷They're saying to people who disdain Yahweh's word,
  'Things will go well for you.'
To everyone who's walking by the determination of his mind,
  they've said, 'Bad fortune won't come upon you.'

Who has stood in Yahweh's council?

¹⁸Because who has stood in Yahweh's council,
  and seen and listened to his word –
  who has heeded his word and listened?
¹⁹There – Yahweh's hurricane,
  wrath has gone out.
The storm is whirling,
  on the head of the faithless it will whirl.
²⁰Yahweh's anger won't turn back until he's acted,
  until he's implemented the strategies in his mind.
At the end of the time
  you'll understand it fully.
²¹I didn't send the prophets, but those people ran;
  I didn't speak to them, but those people prophesied.
²²If they'd stood in my council,
  they'd have got my people to listen to my word.
They'd have turned them back from their bad way,
  from the bad nature of their practices.

²³Am I a God nearby (Yahweh's declaration),
  and not a God far away?
²⁴If a man hides in a hiding place,
  will I not see him (Yahweh's declaration)?
I fill the heavens and the earth, don't I (Yahweh's declaration).

²⁵'I've listened to what the prophets who prophesy falsehood in my name say: "I've dreamed, I've dreamed." ²⁶How long? Is there in the mind of the prophets who prophesy falsehood, the prophets with deceit in their mind – ²⁷are they intending to get my people to put my name out of mind with their dreams that they recount, each to his neighbour, as their ancestors put my name out of mind because of the Master? ²⁸The prophet who has a dream with him should recount a dream, and the one who has my word with him should speak my word truthfully. What does straw have compared with grain (Yahweh's declaration)? ²⁹My word is like fire (Yahweh's declaration) and like a hammer that shatters a cliff, isn't it.

Another wicked play on words

³⁰Therefore here am I, against the prophets (Yahweh's declaration), who steal my words each from his neighbour. ³¹Here am I, against the prophets (Yahweh's declaration), who take up their tongue and make a "declaration". ³²Here am I, against the prophets of false dreams (Yahweh's declaration) who recount them and lead my people astray with their falsehoods and their recklessness, when I didn't send them, didn't order them. In no way will they prevail for this people (Yahweh's declaration).

³³When this people or the prophet or the priest asks you, "What is Yahweh's burden?" you're to say to them, "You're the burden and

I shall desert you" (Yahweh's declaration). ³⁴As for the prophet and the priest and the people that says, "Yahweh's burden", I shall attend to that person and his household. ³⁵You're to say this, each to his neighbour, each to his brother: "What has Yahweh avowed?" or "What has Yahweh spoken?" ³⁶But don't make mention of Yahweh's burden any more, because the burden will belong to the person with his word, and you will overturn the words of the living God, Yahweh of Armies, our God.

³⁷You're to say this to the prophet: "What did Yahweh avow to you?" or "What did Yahweh speak?" ³⁸If you say "Yahweh's burden" – therefore Yahweh has said this: "Since you said this thing, 'Yahweh's burden', and I had sent to you saying, 'Don't say, "Yahweh's burden"', ³⁹therefore here am I: I shall simply forget you and desert you, you and the town that I gave you and your ancestors, from in front of my face. ⁴⁰I shall put upon you permanent reviling, permanent shame, which won't be put out of mind."'

Lucky figs and unlucky figs

24 Yahweh showed me: there, two baskets of figs placed before Yahweh's palace (after Nebukadre'tstsar king of Babel exiled Yekonyahu ben Yehoyaqim king of Yehudah, Yehudah's officials, the craftworkers and the smiths, from Yerushalaim and brought them to Babel). ²One basket was very good figs, like early figs; one basket was very bad figs that couldn't be eaten because of being bad. ³Yahweh said to me, 'What are you looking at, Yirmeyahu?' I said, 'Figs – the good figs very good, the bad very bad, that couldn't be eaten because of being bad.'

⁴Yahweh's word came to me. ⁵Yahweh, Yisra'el's God, has said this: 'Like these good figs, so I shall mark down for good Yehudah's exile community that I've sent off from this place to the country of the Kasdites. ⁶I shall set my eye on them for good and bring them back to this country. I shall build them and not overthrow. I shall plant them and not uproot. ⁷I shall give them a mind to acknowledge me, that I am Yahweh. They will be a people for me and I shall be God for them, because they will turn back to me with their entire mind.

⁸But like bad figs that can't be eaten because of being bad (because Yahweh has said this), so shall I make Tsidqiyyahu king of Yehudah, his officials and the remainder of Yerushalaim who remain in this country and who are living in the country of Misrayim – ⁹I shall make them a horror, something bad, to all earth's kingdoms, an insult and an example, a taunt and a slighting, in all the places where I drive them. ¹⁰I shall send against them sword, famine and epidemic until they come to an end from on the land that I gave to them and to their ancestors.'

Twenty-three years

25 The word that came to Yirmeyahu concerning the entire people of Yehudah in the fourth year of Yehoyaqim ben Yoshiyyahu king of Yehudah (it was the first year of Nebukadre'tstsar king of Babel), ²which Yirmeyahu the prophet spoke to all Yehudah's people and all Yerushalaim's inhabitants: ³'From the thirteenth year of Yoshiyyahu ben Amon king of Yehudah, to this day, twenty-three years, Yahweh's word has come to me, and I've spoken to you, starting early and speaking, but you haven't listened. ⁴Yahweh has been sending to you all his servants, sending urgently, but you haven't listened. You haven't bent your ear to listen: ⁵"Please turn back each one from his bad way, from the bad nature of your acts, so you may live on the land that Yahweh gave you and your ancestors, from earliest ages to farthest ages. ⁶Don't follow other gods so as to serve them and bow down to them. Don't provoke me with the things your hands have made, and I won't bring bad fortune to you. ⁷But you didn't listen to me (Yahweh's declaration), so as to provoke me with the things your hands have made, to bring bad fortune to you."

⁸Therefore Yahweh of Armies has said this: "Since you haven't listened to my words, ⁹here am I; I'm going to send and get all the northern kin-groups (Yahweh's declaration) and Nebukadre'tstsar king of Babel my servant, and bring them against this country and against its inhabitants, and against all these nations round about. I shall devote them and make them a devastation, something to whistle at, a complete waste permanently. ¹⁰I shall

eliminate from them the sound of celebration and the sound of rejoicing, the sound of bride and the sound of groom, the sound of mill and the light of lamp. [11a]This entire country will become a waste, a desolation.

Seventy years

[11b]These nations will serve the king of Babel for seventy years, [12]but when seventy years are fulfilled, I shall attend to the king of Babel and to that nation (Yahweh's declaration) for their waywardness, to the country of the Kasdites, and make it a desolation permanently. [13]I shall bring on that country all my words that I've spoken against it, all that's written in this book that Yirmeyahu prophesied against all the nations. [14]Because they, too, will serve many nations and great kings. I shall make good to them in accordance with their action and with the work of their hands."

[15]Because Yahweh, Yisra'el's God, has said this to me: "Take this chalice of wine (wrath) from my hand and get all the nations to which I'm sending you to drink it. [16]They will drink and throw up and go mad because of the sword that I'm sending among them."

[17]So I took the chalice from Yahweh's hand and got all the nations to which Yahweh sent me to drink: [18]Yerushalaim and all Yehudah's towns, its kings and its officials, to make them a waste, a desolation, something to whistle at, a slighting, this very day; [19]Par'oh [Pharaoh] king of Misrayim, his servants, his officials, all his people [20]and all the foreign group; all the kings of the country of Uts; all the kings of the country of the Pelishtites [Philistines], Ashqelon, Azzah [Gaza], Eqron and the remainder of Ashdod; [21]Edom, Mo'ab and Ammon; [22]all the kings of Tsor [Tyre], all the kings of Tsidon and the kings of the shore that's across the sea; [23]Dedan, Tema and Buz, and all the people shaved at the forehead; [24]all the kings of Arabia and all the kings of the foreign group who dwell in the wilderness; [25]all the kings of Zimri, all the kings of Elam and all the kings of Maday [Media]; [26]all the northern kings, near or far each to his brother; all the kingdoms of the earth that are on the face of the land; and the king of Sheshak will drink, as the last of them.

The demon drink

[27]'You're to say to them: "Yahweh of Armies, Yisra'el's God, has said this: 'Drink, get drunk, throw up, fall down and don't get up again, because of the sword that I'm sending among you.'" [28]When they refuse to take the chalice from your hand to drink, you're to say to them, "Yahweh of Armies has said this: 'Drink, drink, [29]because here, in the town over which my name has been called out, I'm beginning to make bad things happen, and you, will you really be treated as free of guilt? You will not be treated as free of guilt, because I'm calling a sword against all earth's inhabitants (a declaration of Yahweh of Armies).'"

[30]You're to prophesy all these things to them, and say to them:

Yahweh roars from on high,
    from his sacred dwelling he gives voice,
    he roars and roars against his abode.
He chants a cry like grape-treaders
    to all earth's inhabitants.
[31]The din has come to the end of the earth,
    because Yahweh has an argument for the nations.
He's entering into judgement with all flesh;
    the faithless – he's giving them to the sword
    (Yahweh's declaration).'

[32]Yahweh of Armies has said this:

There something bad going out, from nation to nation;
    a great storm arises from earth's remotest parts.
[33]There will be people run through by Yahweh on that day
From the end of the earth
    as far as the end of the earth.
They won't be lamented
    and they won't be gathered up and they won't be buried;
    they'll become manure on the face of the ground.
[34]Howl, you shepherds, cry out,
    throw yourselves about, you who are eminences over the flock.
Because the days of your slaughter are fulfilled;
    I shall scatter you, and you will fall like a desirable bowl.

³⁵Flight will perish from the shepherds,
  escape from the people who are eminences
    over the flock.
³⁶The sound of the shepherds' cry,
  the howls of the people who are eminences
    over the flock!
Because Yahweh is destroying their pastures;
  ³⁷the meadows with their well-being will be still
  in the face of Yahweh's angry burning.
³⁸He's abandoned his thicket like a lion
  because his country has become a desolation,
In the face of the oppressor's blazing,
  and in the face of his angry blazing.

The threat of martyrdom

26 At the beginning of the reign of Yehoyaqim ben Yoshiyyahu king of Yehudah, this word came from Yahweh: ²'Yahweh has said this: "Stand in the courtyard of Yahweh's house and speak to all Yehudah's towns, the people coming to bow low in Yahweh's house, all the words that I'm ordering you to speak to them. Don't omit a thing. ³Perhaps they'll listen and turn back, each from his bad way, and I shall relent regarding the bad things that I'm intending to do to them because of the bad nature of their practices. ⁴You're to say to them, 'Yahweh has said this: "If you don't listen to me by walking according to the instruction that I've put before you, ⁵listening to the words of my servants the prophets whom I've been sending to you, starting early and sending them (but you haven't listened), ⁶I shall make this house like Shiloh, and make this town a slighting to all the nations of the earth."'"

⁷The priests, the prophets and the entire people listened to Yirmeyahu speaking these words in Yahweh's house, ⁸and when Yirmeyahu finished speaking all that Yahweh had ordered him to speak to the entire people, the priests, the prophets and the entire people seized him, saying: 'You are definitely to die. ⁹Why have you been prophesying in Yahweh's name, "This house will become like Shiloh, and this town will be waste, without inhabitant"?'

So the entire people congregated against Yirmeyahu in Yahweh's house. ¹⁰Yehudah's officials heard these things and went up from the king's house to Yahweh's house and sat in the entrance of Yahweh's New Gate. ¹¹The priests and the prophets said to the officials and to the entire people, 'A sentence of death for this man, because he's prophesied against this town, as you've heard with your own ears.'

Remember Mikah

¹²Yirmeyahu said to all the officials and to the entire people, 'It was Yahweh sent me to prophesy to this house and to this town all the words that you heard. ¹³So now make your ways and your practices good and listen to the voice of Yahweh your God, so Yahweh may relent of the bad thing that he's spoken of against you. ¹⁴And me – here am I in your hand. Do to me in accordance with what is good and right in your eyes. ¹⁵Yet you must fully acknowledge that if you put me to death – that you're putting on yourselves the blood of someone who's free of guilt. Because in truth Yahweh sent me to you to speak all these things in your ears.'

¹⁶The officials and the entire people said to the priests and to the prophets, 'There's no sentence of death, because it was in the name of Yahweh our God that he spoke to us.' ¹⁷Some people from the country's elders got up and said to all the congregation of the people, ¹⁸'Mikah the Morashtite was prophesying in the days of Hizqiyyahu king of Yehudah. He said to Yehudah's entire people:

"Yahweh of Armies has said this:

'Tsiyyon will be ploughed as open countryside.
Yerushalaim will become heaps of rubble,
  the mountain of the house shrines in the
    forest.'"

¹⁹Did Hizqiyyahu king of Yehudah and all Yehudah put him to death at all? Was he not in awe of Yahweh and did he not seek Yahweh's goodwill, so that Yahweh relented of the bad thing that he spoke against them? We're going to do a great bad thing to ourselves.'

Not always the Hollywood ending

²⁰There was also a man prophesying in Yahweh's name, Uriyyahu ben Shema'yahu

from Ye'arim Township. He prophesied against this town and against this people in accordance with all Yirmeyahu's words. ²¹King Yehoyaqim, all his strong men and all the officials heard his words, and the king sent to put him to death. Uriyyahu heard and was afraid and fled, and came to Misrayim. ²²But King Yehoyaqim sent men to Misrayim, Elnatan ben Akbor and men with him, to Misrayim. ²³They got Uriyyahu out of Misrayim and brought him to King Yehoyaqim, and he struck him down with the sword and threw his corpse into the common graves. ²⁴However, the hand of Ahiqam ben Shaphan was with Yirmeyahu so as not to give him into the people's hand to put him to death.

27 At the beginning of the reign of Yehoyaqim ben Yoshiyyahu king of Yehudah, this word came to Yirmeyahu from Yahweh: ²Yahweh said this to me: 'Make yourself straps and bars and put them on your neck, ³and send them to the king of Edom, the king of Mo'ab, the king of the Ammonites, the king of Tsor and the king of Tsidon, by the hand of the envoys who have come to Yerushalaim to Tsidqiyyahu king of Yehudah. ⁴Order them regarding their lords: "Yahweh of Armies, Yisra'el's God, has said this: 'You're to say this to your lords: ⁵"I'm the one who made the earth, the human beings and the animals that are on the face of the earth, by my great energy and by my bent arm, and I give it to whoever is right in my eyes. ⁶So now, I'm giving all these countries into the hand of Nebukadne'tstsar king of Babel my servant. Even the creatures of the wild I'm giving him to serve him. ⁷All the nations will serve him, his son and his grandson, until the time comes for his country, him too. Many nations and great kings will serve him. ⁸The nation or kingdom that won't serve him (Nebukadne'tstsar king of Babel), that won't give its neck to the yoke of the king of Babel: I'll attend to that nation by sword, by famine and by epidemic (Yahweh's declaration) until I have brought them to an end by his hand.

Don't listen to your prophets

⁹So you, don't listen to your prophets, to your augurs, to your dreams, to your mediums or to your diviners, who are saying to you, 'Don't serve the king of Babel.' ¹⁰Because they're speaking falsehood to you, so he may take you far from your country, and I drive you out and you perish. ¹¹But the nation that brings its neck to the yoke of the king of Babel and serves him, I'll allow to stay on its land (Yahweh's declaration) and serve it and live on it."'"

¹²To Tsidqiyyah king of Yehudah I spoke in accordance with these words: 'Bring your necks to the king of Babel's yoke, serve him and his people, and live. ¹³Why should you die, you and your people, by sword, by famine and by epidemic, as Yahweh has said regarding the nation that doesn't serve the king of Babel? ¹⁴Don't listen to the words of the prophets who are saying to you, "Don't serve the king of Babel", because they're prophesying falsehood to you. ¹⁵Because I didn't send them (Yahweh's declaration) and they're prophesying falsely in my name, so that I'll drive you out and you'll perish, you and the prophets who are prophesying to you.'

¹⁶And to the priests and to this entire people I spoke: 'Yahweh has said this: "Don't listen to the words of the prophets who are prophesying to you, 'There, the things from Yahweh's house are going to be brought back from Babel now, very soon', because they're prophesying falsehood to you. ¹⁷Don't listen to them; serve the king of Babel and live – why should this town become a waste? ¹⁸If they are prophets and Yahweh's word is with them, they should please intercede with Yahweh of Armies so that the rest of the things in Yahweh's house, in the house of the king of Yehudah and in Yerushalaim, don't come to Babel."

Things have to get worse

¹⁹Because Yahweh of Armies has said this about the pillars, the Sea, the stands and the rest of the things that remain in this town, ²⁰which Nebukadne'tstsar king of Babel didn't take when he exiled Yekonyah ben Yehoyaqim king of Yehudah from Yerushalaim to Babel, with all the important people from Yehudah and Yerushalaim – ²¹because Yahweh of Armies, Yisra'el's God, has said about the things that remain in Yahweh's house, in the house of the king of Yehudah and in Yerushalaim: ²²"To

Babel they will be brought, and there they will be, until the day when I attend to them (Yahweh's declaration) and take them up and bring them back to this place.'"

28 That year, at the beginning of the reign of Tsidqiyyah king of Yehudah, in the fifth month of the fourth year, Hananyah ben Azzur the prophet, who was from Gib'on, said to me in Yahweh's house in the eyes of the priests and the entire people: ²'Yahweh of Armies, Yisra'el's God, has said this: "I am breaking the king of Babel's yoke. ³In yet two years' time I'm going to bring back to this place all the things from Yahweh's house that Nebukadne'tstsar king of Babel took from this place and brought to Babel. ⁴And I am going to return to this place Yekonyah ben Yehoyaqim king of Yehudah and all Yehudah's exile community who came to Babel (Yahweh's declaration), because I'm breaking the king of Babel's yoke."'

Prophet confronts prophet

⁵Yirmeyahu the prophet said to Hananyah the prophet in the eyes of the priests and the entire people standing in Yahweh's house – ⁶Yirmeyahu the prophet said, 'Amen, so may Yahweh do. May Yahweh act on your words, which you've prophesied, bringing back the things from Yahweh's house and the entire exile community from Babel to this place. ⁷Nevertheless please listen to this word that I'm speaking in your ears and the ears of the entire people. ⁸The prophets who were before me and before you, from of old, prophesied against many countries and about great kingdoms, regarding battle, famine and epidemic. ⁹The prophet who prophesies of things going well – when the prophet's word comes about, he can be acknowledged as one whom Yahweh sent in truth.'

¹⁰Hananyah the prophet took the bar from on Yirmeyahu the prophet's neck and broke it. ¹¹Hananyah said in front of the entire people: 'Yahweh has said this: "In this way I shall break the yoke of Nebukadne'tstsar king of Babel, in yet two years, from on the neck of all the nations."'

Yirmeyahu the prophet went his way. ¹²But Yahweh's word came to Yirmeyahu after Hananyah the prophet broke the bar from on Yirmeyahu the prophet's neck: ¹³'Go and say to Hananyah, "Yahweh has said this: 'You broke bars of wood, but you're to make bars of iron.' ¹⁴Because Yahweh of Armies, Yisra'el's God, has said this: 'I'm putting an iron yoke on the neck of all these nations so that they serve Nebukadne'tstsar king of Babel. They will serve him; even the creatures of the wild I am giving him.'"' ¹⁵And Yirmeyahu the prophet said to Hananyah the prophet, 'Please listen, Hananyah. Yahweh hasn't sent you, and you're one who has made this people trust in falsehood. ¹⁶Therefore Yahweh has said this: "Here am I; I'm going to send you off from on the face of the land. This year you're going to die, because you've spoken of defiance towards Yahweh."'

¹⁷Hananyah the prophet died that year in the seventh month.

Settle down

29 These are the words in a document that Yirmeyahu the prophet sent from Yerushalaim to the rest of the elders of the exile community, the priests, the prophets and the entire people that Nebukadne'tstsar had exiled from Yerushalaim to Babel ²(after King Yekonyah, the queen mother, the courtiers, the officials of Yehudah and Yerushalaim, the craftworkers and the smiths left Yerushalaim), ³by the hand of El'asah ben Shaphan and Gemaryah ben Hilqiyyah, whom Tsidqiyyah king of Yehudah sent to Babel to Nebukadne'tstsar king of Babel.

⁴'Yahweh of Armies, Yisra'el's God, has said this to the entire exile community that I exiled from Yerushalaim to Babel: ⁵"Build houses and live, plant gardens and eat their fruit. ⁶Take wives and have sons and daughters, take wives for your sons and give your daughters to husbands, so they may have sons and daughters. Become many there; don't become few. ⁷Seek the well-being of the town where I've exiled you; plead on its behalf with Yahweh, because in its well-being there will be well-being for you."

⁸Because Yahweh of Armies, Yisra'el's God, has said this: "Your prophets who are among you and your diviners must not deceive you.

You must not listen to your dreams that you're dreaming. ⁹Because they're prophesying to you falsely in my name; I didn't send them (Yahweh's declaration)."

¹⁰Because Yahweh has said this: "At the bidding of the fulfilment for Babel of seventy years I shall attend to you, and act for you on my word about good things, bringing you back to this place. ¹¹Because I myself acknowledge the intentions that I'm formulating for you (Yahweh's declaration), intentions for your well-being and not for bad things, to give you a future, a hope. ¹²You will call me and come and plead with me and I shall listen to you. ¹³You will seek me and find me if you enquire of me with your entire mind, ¹⁴and I'll be able to be found by you (Yahweh's declaration). I shall restore your fortunes, collect you from all the nations and from all the places where I've driven you (Yahweh's declaration), and bring you back to the place from where I've exiled you."

The fate of false prophets

¹⁵Because you have said, "Yahweh has set up prophets for us in Babel." ¹⁶Rather, Yahweh has said this regarding the king who sits on David's throne and the entire people that lives in this town, your brothers who haven't gone out with you into exile – ¹⁷Yahweh of Armies has said this: "Here am I; I'm going to send off against them sword, famine and epidemic. I shall make them like horrible figs that may not be eaten because of being bad. ¹⁸I shall pursue them with sword, famine and epidemic and make them a horror to all the kingdoms of the earth, a vow, a devastation, something to whistle at and a reviling among all the nations where I drive them out, ¹⁹on account of the fact that they haven't listened to my words (Yahweh's declaration), in that I sent them my servants the prophets, starting early and sending. But you haven't listened (Yahweh's declaration). ²⁰So you people, the entire exile community that I sent off from Yerushalaim to Babel, listen to Yahweh's word."

²¹Yahweh of Armies, Yisra'el's God, has said this regarding Ah'ab ben Qolayah and regarding Tsidqiyyahu ben Ma'aseyah who are prophesying to you in my name: "Here am I; I'm going to give them into the hand of Nebukadre'tstsar king of Babel. He will strike them down in front of your eyes. ²²A formula of slighting will be taken from them for the entire exile community of Yehudah in Babel: 'May Yahweh make you like Tsidqiyyahu and like Ah'ab, whom the king of Babel roasted in fire, ²³since they acted with villainy in Yisra'el and both committed adultery with the wives of their neighbours and spoke a word in my name that was false, which I hadn't ordered them.' I am the one who knows and who testifies (Yahweh's declaration)."

Get a grip on that madman

²⁴And regarding Shemayahu the Nehelemite you're to say: ²⁵"Yahweh of Armies, Yisra'el's God, has said this: 'Since you're the one who has sent documents in your name to the entire people in Yerushalaim, to Tsephanyah ben Ma'aseyah the priest and to all the priests, saying, ²⁶"Yahweh has made you priest instead of Yehoyada the priest, so that there might be appointees in Yahweh's house regarding anyone who's mad and is prophesying, and you're to put him into the stocks and into the neck iron: ²⁷so now, why have you not reprimanded Yirmeyahu from Anatot who's prophesying to you? ²⁸Because on account of this he's sent to us in Babel, saying, 'It will be a long time. Build houses and live [there], plant gardens and eat their fruit.'"'"

²⁹Tsephanyah the priest read this document out in the hearing of Yirmeyahu the prophet, ³⁰and Yahweh's word came to Yirmeyahu: ³¹"Send to the entire exile community, saying "Yahweh has said this regarding Shema'yah the Nehelemite: 'Since Shema'yah has prophesied to you and I myself hadn't sent him, and he's got you to trust in falsehood, ³²therefore Yahweh has said this: "Here am I; I'm going to attend to Shema'yah the Nehelemite and to his offspring. He won't have anyone living among this people and he won't see the good things that I'm going to do for this people (Yahweh's declaration), because he's spoken of defiance against Yahweh."'""

30 The word that came to Yirmeyahu from Yahweh: ²"Yahweh, Yisra'el's God, has said this: "Write down for yourself all the words that I've spoken to you in a document. ³Because there, days are coming (Yahweh's declaration) when I shall restore the fortunes of my people Yisra'el and Yehudah", Yahweh has said.'

Is a man giving birth?

⁴So these are the words that Yahweh spoke concerning Yisra'el and Yehudah. ⁵Because Yahweh had said this:

We've heard the sound of trembling,
    dread, and lack of well-being.
⁶Please ask and see if a male is giving birth –
    why have I seen every man
With his hands on his stomach like someone
    giving birth
and why have all faces turned to paleness?
⁷Hey, because that day is big,
    so that there has been none like it.
It will be a time of pressure for Ya'aqob,
    but from it he will find deliverance.

⁸On that day (a declaration of Yahweh of Armies):

I shall break his yoke from on your neck
    and tear off your straps.
They won't serve foreigners any more with it,
    ⁹but they will serve Yahweh their God,
And David their king,
    whom I shall set up over them.
¹⁰So you, don't be afraid, my servant Ya'aqob
    (Yahweh's declaration),
don't shatter, Yisra'el.
Because here am I; I'm going to deliver you from
    far away,
    and your offspring from the country of their
        captivity.
Ya'aqob will again be calm,
    at peace with no one making him tremble.
¹¹Because I am with you (Yahweh's declaration) to
    deliver you,
because I shall make an end among all the
    nations
    where I've scattered you,
Yet of you I won't make an end,
    though I discipline you in exercising
        authority
and don't treat you as free of guilt.

¹²Because Yahweh has said this:

Your break is grave [Yerushalaim],
    your wound sickening.
¹³There's no one giving a judgement about
    treatment;
    there's no healing, growing back, for you.
¹⁴All your allies have put you out of mind,
    they don't enquire of you.
Because I struck you down with an enemy's blow,
    the discipline of someone violent,
On account of the magnitude of your
    waywardness;
    your wrongdoings were numerous.
¹⁵Why do you cry out because of your break,
    that your injury is grave?
It was on account of the magnitude of your
    waywardness,
your wrongdoings were numerous,
    that I did these things to you.

Compassion has the last word

¹⁶Therefore all the people who are consuming you
    will be consumed,
    and all your adversaries (all of them) will go
        into captivity.
Your despoilers will become spoil,
    and all who plundered you I'll give as plunder.
¹⁷Because I shall make restoration grow up for you
    and I shall heal you of your wounds (Yahweh's
        declaration).
Because they've called you 'Outcast',
    'It's Tsiyyon; there's no one enquiring about it.'

¹⁸Yahweh has said this:

Here am I, I'm going to restore the fortunes of
    Ya'aqob's tents,
    and on his dwellings I shall have compassion.
A town will be built on its tell;
    a citadel will sit on its authorized place.
¹⁹Thanksgiving will go out from them,
    and the sound of people having fun.
I shall make them many and they won't become
    few;
    I shall make them honourable and they won't
        become small.
²⁰Its children will be as of old,
    its assembly will stand established before me,
    and I shall attend to all its oppressors.

²¹Its august one will come from within it
  and its ruler will go out from within it.
I shall draw it near and it will come up to me,
  because who is the one
  who would have pledged his own mind to
    come up to me (Yahweh's declaration)?
²²So you will be a people for me
  and I shall be God for you.

²³There is Yahweh's hurricane,
  wrath has gone out.
A storm is raging,
  on the head of the faithless it whirls.
²⁴Yahweh's angry blazing won't turn back until he's acted,
  until he's implemented the strategies in his mind;
  at the end of the time you'll understand it.

31

At that time (Yahweh's declaration):

I shall be God for all Yisra'el's kin-groups
  and they'll be a people for me.

Mourning becomes celebration

²Yahweh said this:

The people found grace in the wilderness,
  those who survived the sword.
As Yisra'el went to find its rest,
³'From afar Yahweh appeared to me.'
With permanent love I loved you;
  therefore I've drawn you out with commitment.
⁴I shall build you up again so that you are built up, Miss Yisra'el.
You will again deck yourself with your tambourine
  and go out in the dance of people having fun.
⁵You will again plant vineyards
  on Shomron's mountains;
  planters will have planted and will begin to have the use of them.
⁶Because there will be a day
  when lookouts call out on Ephrayim's highland,
'Set off so we may go up to Tsiyyon,
  to Yahweh our God.'

⁷Because Yahweh has said this:

Resound with rejoicing for Ya'aqob,
  bellow at the nations' crossroads.
Let them hear, exult and say,
  'Yahweh, deliver your people,
  the remainder of Yisra'el!'
⁸Here am I; I'm going to bring them
  from the northern country.
I shall collect them from the farthest reaches of the earth,
  among them blind and lame,
Pregnant and giving birth, together;
  a great congregation will come back here.
⁹With crying they'll come,
  and with prayers for grace I'll bring them along.
I shall lead them to streams of water
  by a straight way on which they won't collapse.
Because I've been a father to Yisra'el,
  and Ephrayim is my firstborn.

¹⁰Listen to Yahweh's word, you nations,
  tell of it on shores far away:
The one who scattered Yisra'el will collect it,
  and keep it like a shepherd his flock.
¹¹Because Yahweh is redeeming Ya'aqob,
  restoring it from a hand that's too strong for it.
¹²They will come and resound on Tsiyyon's height
  and shine because of Yahweh's good things,
Over grain and over new wine and over fresh oil,
  over newborn of flock and cattle.
Their entire being will become like a watered garden;
  they won't sorrow ever again.
¹³Then a girl will rejoice with dancing,
  young men and old together.
I shall turn their mourning into celebration,
  comfort them and let them rejoice after their grief.
¹⁴I shall saturate the priests' appetite with fat,
  and my people will be full of my good things (Yahweh's declaration).

Rahel (Rachel) comforted

¹⁵Yahweh has said this:

A voice makes itself heard in Ramah,
  lamentation, bitter crying.
Rahel is crying over her children;
  she's refused to find comfort over her children,
  because they're not there.

¹⁶Yahweh has said this:

Restrain your voice from crying
   and your eyes from tears.
Because there will be a reward for your work
   (Yahweh's declaration);
   they will come back from the enemy's country.
¹⁷There is hope for your future (Yahweh's
   declaration);
   your children will come back to their territory.

¹⁸I've heard, I've heard Ephrayim lamenting:
   'You've disciplined me and I've undergone
      discipline
   like a calf that hadn't been trained.
Have me back and I'll turn back,
   because you are Yahweh my God.
¹⁹Because after I turned back I repented;
   after I came to acknowledge it I struck my
      thigh.
I was shamed, yes disgraced,
   because I bore the insult of my youth.'
²⁰Ephrayim is a dear son to me,
   or a child in whom I took pleasure, isn't he.
Because every time I speak against him,
   I'm so mindful of him again.
That's why my insides moan for him,
   I have deep compassion for him (Yahweh's
      declaration).

Sour grapes

²¹Set up markers for yourself,
   put up signposts for yourself.
Give your mind to the causeway,
   the way you went.
Come back, Miss Yisra'el,
   come back to these towns of yours.
²²How long will you waver,
   daughter who's turned back?
Because Yahweh has created something new in
      the country:
   a woman surrounds a man.

²³Yahweh of Armies, Yisra'el's God, has said this:

They will again say this thing
   in the country of Yehudah and in its towns,
      when I restore their fortunes:
'May Yahweh bless you,
   faithful abode, sacred mountain.'
²⁴Yehudah and all its towns together will dwell in
      it as farmers,
   and people will go about with the flock.
²⁵Because I'm saturating the weary person
   and filling everyone who languishes.

²⁶Upon this I woke up and looked,
   and my sleep had been nice for me.

²⁷'There, days are coming (Yahweh's declaration) when I shall sow Yisra'el's house and Yehudah's household with human seed and animal seed. ²⁸As I was watchful over them to uproot, to demolish, to tear down, to obliterate and to deal badly, so I'll be watchful over them to build and to plant (Yahweh's declaration).'

²⁹In those days they will no longer say, 'The parents ate sour grapes but the children's teeth feel rough.' ³⁰Rather, each person will die for his waywardness. Everyone who eats sour grapes, his teeth will feel rough.

The power of being forgiven

³¹'There, days are coming (Yahweh's declaration) when I shall solemnize with Yisra'el's household and with Yehudah's household a new pact, ³²not like the pact that I solemnized with your ancestors on the day I took strong hold of them by the hand to get them out of the country of Misrayim, my pact which they contravened, though I was master over them (Yahweh's declaration). ³³Because this is the pact that I shall solemnize with Yisra'el's household after those days (Yahweh's declaration). I'm putting my instruction inside them and I shall write it on their mind; and I'll be God for them and they'll be a people for me. ³⁴They will no longer teach each person his neighbour and each his brother, saying "Acknowledge Yahweh", because all of them will acknowledge me from the least of them to the biggest of them (Yahweh's declaration), because I shall pardon their waywardness, and their wrongdoing I shall not keep in mind any more.'

³⁵Yahweh has said this
   (the one who gives the sun as light by day,
   the laws of the moon and stars as light by night,

Who stirs up the sea so that its waves roar –
  Yahweh of Armies is his name):

³⁶If these laws move away from before me
  (Yahweh's declaration),
Yisra'el's offspring may also cease
  from being a nation for all time.

³⁷Yahweh has said this:

If the heavens above may be measured
  and earth's foundations below be explored,
Also I may reject the entire offspring of Yisra'el
  for what they've done (Yahweh's declaration).

³⁸There, days are coming (Yahweh's declaration) when the town will be built up for Yahweh from the Hanan'el Tower to the Corner Gate, ³⁹and the measuring line will go out again straight to Gareb Hill and turn to Go'ah. ⁴⁰The entire vale (corpses and ashes) and all the open country as far as Wadi Qidron and as far as the Horses Gate on the east will be sacred for Yahweh. It won't be uprooted or torn down again ever.

On putting your money where your mouth is

32 The word that came to Yirmeyahu from Yahweh in the tenth year of Tsidqiyyahu king of Yehudah (it was the eighteenth year of Nebukadre'tstsar). ²The king of Babel's force were then besieging Yerushalaim, while Yirmeyahu the prophet was confined in the prison courtyard at the king of Yehudah's house, ³where Tsidqiyyahu king of Yehudah had confined him, saying 'Why are you prophesying, "Yahweh has said this: 'Here am I; I'm going to give this town into the hand of the king of Babel, and he'll capture it. ⁴Tsidqiyyahu king of Yehudah won't escape from the hand of the Kasdites because he'll definitely be given into the hand of the king of Babel (his mouth will speak to his mouth, his eyes will see his eyes). ⁵He'll make Tsidqiyyahu go to Babel, and he'll be there until I attend to him (Yahweh's declaration). When you do battle with the Kasdites, you won't succeed."'"

⁶Yirmeyahu said, 'Yahweh's word came to me: ⁷"Here, Hanam'el ben Shallum your uncle is going to come to you, saying, 'Acquire for yourself my field which is in Anatot, because the ruling about restoration belongs to you, so as to acquire it.'"

⁸So Hanam'el my uncle's son came to me in accordance with Yahweh's word, to the prison courtyard, and said to me, "Please acquire my field which is in Anatot in the region of Binyamin, because the ruling about possession belongs to you and the restoration belongs to you; acquire it for yourself." So I knew that it was Yahweh's word. ⁹I acquired the field from Hanam'el my uncle's son, which is in Anatot, and I weighed out the silver to him, seventeen sheqels of silver. ¹⁰I wrote in a document, sealed it, got witnesses and weighed the silver on scales. ¹¹I took the acquisition document, the sealed one (the order and the laws) and the open one, ¹²and gave the acquisition document to Baruk ben Nerayyah son of Mahseyah before the eyes of Hanam'el my cousin and of the witnesses inscribed in the acquisition document and of all the Yehudahites sitting in the prison courtyard.

Are you asking something crazy of me?

¹³I ordered Baruk before their eyes, ¹⁴"Yahweh of Armies, Yisra'el's God, has said this: 'Take these documents, this acquisition document (both the sealed one and this open document) and put them in an earthen container so that they may stand for a long time.'" ¹⁵Because Yahweh of Armies, Yisra'el's God, has said this: "Houses, fields and vineyards will again be acquired in this country."

¹⁶I pleaded with Yahweh after giving the acquisition document to Baruk ben Nerayyah: ¹⁷"Oh, Lord Yahweh! There – you made the heavens and the earth by your great energy and your bent arm. Nothing is too extraordinary for you, ¹⁸one who acts with commitment to thousands but makes good for the waywardness of parents into the lap of their children after them: big strong man God (Yahweh is his name), ¹⁹big in counsel and mighty in deed, you whose eyes are open to all the ways of human beings to give to each person in accordance with his ways and in accordance with the fruit of his practices,

²⁰who put down signs and portents in the country of Misrayim to this day, and in Yisra'el and among humanity, and made a name for yourself this very day. ²¹You got your people Yisra'el out of the country of Misrayim with signs and portents and with a strong hand and a bent arm and with great fearfulness. ²²You gave them this country that you swore to their ancestors to give them, a country flowing with milk and syrup. ²³They came and possessed it, but they didn't listen to your voice or walk by your instruction.

All that you ordered them to do, they didn't do. So you've made all this bad fortune happen to them. ²⁴There – ramps have come to the town to capture it, and the town is being given into the hand of the Kasdites who are doing battle against it, in the face of sword, famine and epidemic. What you said has happened. There you are, looking.

²⁵And now you've said to me, Lord Yahweh, 'Acquire the field for yourself with silver and get witnesses', when this town is given into the hand of the Kasdites.'"

Is anything too extraordinary for Yahweh?

²⁶Yahweh's word came to Yirmeyahu: ²⁷'Here am I, Yahweh, the God of all flesh. Is anything too extraordinary for me?' ²⁸Therefore Yahweh has said this: 'Here am I; I'm going to give this town into the hand of the Kasdites and into the hand of Nebukadre'tstsar king of Babel, and he will capture it. ²⁹The Kasdites who are doing battle against this town will come and set this town on fire and burn it, with the houses where people burned incense on the roofs to the Master and poured drink offerings to other gods, so as to provoke me.

³⁰Because the Yisra'elites and the Yehudahites have been doing only what is bad in my eyes from their youth, because the Yisra'elites have only been provoking me by the things that their hands made (Yahweh's declaration). ³¹Because this town became a cause of my anger and a cause of my wrath to me from the day that they built it until this day, so that I must remove it from before me, ³²on account of all the bad dealing of the Yisra'elites and the Yehudahites which they dealt so as to provoke me, they, their kings, their officials, their priests, their prophets, Yehudah's people and Yerushalaim's inhabitants. ³³They turned their back and not their face to me; when I taught them, starting early and teaching, there were none of them listening so as to accept discipline.

³⁴They put their abominations in the house over which my name has been called out, to defile it, ³⁵and they built up the shrines of the Master in the Ben-hinnom Ravine to make their sons and their daughters pass through the fire to the Shameful King, which I didn't order them (it didn't come into my mind) to do this offensive thing, so as to cause Yehudah to do wrong.'

Land will be acquired again

³⁶But now therefore Yahweh, Yisra'el's God, says this concerning this town of which you're saying, 'It's given into the hand of the king of Babel by sword, by famine and by epidemic': ³⁷'Here am I; I'm going to collect them from all the countries where I've driven them in my anger and wrath and great fury, and bring them back to this place and let them live with confidence. ³⁸They'll be a people for me and I'll be God for them. ³⁹I'll give them a single mind and a single way, to live in awe of me all the days, so that things will be good for them and for their children after them.

⁴⁰I shall solemnize for them a permanent pact that I won't turn back from them, and I shall do good to them. I shall put awe for me in their mind so that they don't turn away from me. ⁴¹I shall have delight towards them, in doing good to them. I shall plant them in this country in truth, with all my mind and soul.'

⁴²Because Yahweh has said this: 'As I have brought to this people all this great bad fortune, so I'm going to bring on them all the good things that I'm speaking about. ⁴³A field will be acquired in this country of which you're saying, "It's a desolation, without human being or animal; it's given into the hand of the Kasdites." ⁴⁴People will acquire fields for silver and write it in a document and seal it and get witnesses, in Binyamin's region, in Yerushalaim's environs, in Yehudah's towns, in the towns in the highland, in the towns in the foothills and in the towns in the Negeb.

Because I shall restore their fortunes (Yahweh's declaration).'

Call me and I shall answer

33 Yahweh's word came to Yirmeyahu a second time, while he was still detained in the prison courtyard: ²'Yahweh has said this (Yahweh is going to do it, he's going to form it, he is going to make sure of it – Yahweh is his name): ³"Call to me and I shall answer, and tell you great things, secret things that you haven't known."

⁴Because Yahweh, Yisra'el's God, has said this about the houses in this town and about the houses of Yehudah's kings that were torn down in connection with the ramps and the sword: ⁵"People are coming to do battle with the Kasdites – and to fill them with the corpses of the people that I will have struck down in my anger and my wrath, in that I've hidden my face from this town because of all their bad dealing.

⁶Here am I, I'm going to make recovery and healing grow up for it. I shall heal and reveal to them abundance of well-being and truth. ⁷I shall restore Yehudah's fortunes and Yisra'el's fortunes and build them up as before. ⁸I shall purify them from all their waywardness with which they did wrong to me, and I shall pardon all their wayward acts with which they did wrong to me and rebelled against me. ⁹For me it will mean a name to celebrate, and praise and splendour, for all the nations of the earth that hear of all the good things that I'm going to do with them, and they will be in awe and will shiver because of all the good things and all the well-being that I'm going to do for it."'

¹⁰Yahweh has said this: 'A voice will make itself heard in this place of which you're saying, "It's desolate, without human being, without animal, in Yehudah's towns and in Yerushalaim's devastated courtyards, without human being, without animal", ¹¹the voice of joy and of celebration, the voice of groom and of bride, the voice of people saying, "Confess Yahweh of Armies, because Yahweh is good, because his commitment lasts permanently", bringing a thank-offering to Yahweh's house, because I shall restore the country's fortunes as before (Yahweh has said).'

Expect great things

¹²Yahweh of Armies has said this: 'In this place, desolate, without human being or animal, and in all its towns, there will again be an abode for shepherds resting a flock. ¹³In the mountain towns, in the lowland towns, in the Negeb towns, in Binyamin's country, in Yerushalaim's environs and in Yehudah's towns, sheep will again pass under the hands of the one counting (Yahweh has said). ¹⁴There, days are coming (Yahweh's declaration) when I shall act on the good word that I spoke concerning Yisra'el's household and Yehudah's household.

¹⁵In those days and at that time I shall grow for David a faithful branch, and he will implement authority and faithfulness in the country. ¹⁶In those days Yehudah will find deliverance, and Yerushalaim will dwell with confidence, and this is what it will be called: "Yahweh Is Our Faithfulness". ¹⁷Because Yahweh has said this: 'There will not be cut off from David someone sitting on the throne of Yisra'el's household. ¹⁸And from the priests, the Levites, there will not be cut off someone before me offering up the whole offering and burning the grain offering and performing the sacrifice, for all time.'

¹⁹Yahweh's word came to Yirmeyahu: ²⁰'Yahweh has said this: "If you people can contravene my pact about the day and my pact about the night so that there's no day and night at their time, ²¹also my pact with David my servant may be contravened so that there's no son for him reigning on his throne, and with the Levites, the priests, ministering to me. ²²As the heavens' army cannot be counted and the sea's sand cannot be measured, so I shall multiply the offspring of David my servant and the Levites who minister to me."'

²³Yahweh's word came to Yirmeyahu: ²⁴'You've seen what this people have spoken, haven't you: "The two kin-groups that Yahweh chose – he's rejected them." They've despised my people so that they are no longer a nation before them.' ²⁵Yahweh has said this: 'If I haven't laid down my pact about day and night, the laws about the heavens and the earth, ²⁶also the offspring of Ya'aqob and the offspring of David my servant may be rejected so as not to take from its offspring rulers for

the offspring of Abraham, Yitshaq [Isaac] and Ya'aqob. Because I shall restore their fortunes and have compassion on them.'

A covenant for freedom

34 The word that came to Yirmeyahu from Yahweh, when Nebukadre'tstsar king of Babel, and his entire force, and all the kingdoms of the earth ruled by his hand and all the peoples, were battling against Yerushalaim and against all its towns: ²'Yahweh, Yisra'el's God, has said this: "Go and say to Tsidqiyyahu king of Yehudah: 'Yahweh has said this: "Here am I, I'm going to give this town into the hand of the king of Babel, and he will burn it in fire. ³You yourself won't escape from his hand, because you'll definitely be seized and be given into his hand. Your eyes will see the eyes of the king of Babel. His mouth will speak to your mouth. You will come to Babel." ⁴Yet listen to Yahweh's word, Tsidqiyyahu king of Yehudah. Yahweh has said this about you: "You will not die by the sword. ⁵You will die with things being well. In accordance with the burning [of incense] for your ancestors, the earlier kings who were before you, so people will burn it for you. 'Oh, lord', they will lament for you, because I myself have spoken the word (Yahweh's declaration).""'" ⁶Yirmeyahu the prophet spoke all these words in Yerushalaim to Tsidqiyyahu king of Yehudah ⁷while the king of Babel's force were battling against Yerushalaim and against all Yehudah's towns that were left, with Lakish and Azeqah, because these remained among Yehudah's towns as fortified towns.

⁸The word that came to Yirmeyahu from Yahweh after King Tsidqiyyahu solemnized a pact with the entire people that was in Yerushalaim to call to them for a release, ⁹for each one to send off his servant and each one his maidservant, the Hebrew man and the Hebrew woman, as free persons, so that they wouldn't serve them, an individual Yehudahite his brother. ¹⁰ᵃAll the officials and the entire people that came into the pact obeyed, by each one sending off his servant and each one his maidservant as free persons, so that they wouldn't serve them any more.

The people who had prayed a dangerous prayer

¹⁰ᵇSo they obeyed and sent them off, ¹¹but afterwards they turned back and got back the servants and the maidservants whom they had sent off as free persons, and subjugated them as servants and maidservants. ¹²Yahweh's word came to Yirmeyahu from Yahweh: ¹³'Yahweh, Yisra'el's God, has said this: "I myself solemnized a pact with your ancestors on the day I got them out of the country of Misrayim, out of a household of servants, saying, ¹⁴'At the end of seven years you're to send off, each one, his Hebrew brother who has sold himself to you and served you for six years; you're to send him off as a free man from being with you.' Your ancestors didn't listen to me; they didn't bend their ear. ¹⁵Just now you yourselves turned back and did what was right in my eyes by calling for a release, each one to his neighbour, and you solemnized a pact before me in the house over which my name has been called out. ¹⁶But you've turned back and profaned my name; you've got back each one his servant and each one his maidservant whom you sent off as free persons to live their life, and you've subjugated them as servants and as maidservants to you."

¹⁷Therefore Yahweh has said this: "You haven't listened to me by calling for a release, each one to his brother, each to his neighbour. Here am I, I'm going to call for a release to you (Yahweh's declaration) – to sword, to epidemic and to famine. I'm going to make you a horror to all earth's kingdoms. ¹⁸I'm going to make the people who are transgressing my pact, who haven't acted on the words in the pact that they solemnized before me, into the calf that they cut into two and passed between its parts: ¹⁹Yehudah's officials and Yerushalaim's officials, the courtiers, the priests and the entire people of the country who passed between the parts of the calf.

The tempting

²⁰So I shall give them into the hand of their enemies, into the hand of those who seek their life. Their corpse will be food for the birds

of the heavens and for the animals of the earth. ²¹Tsidqiyyahu king of Yehudah and his officials I shall give into the hand of their enemies, into the hand of those who seek their life, into the hand of the king of Babel's force who are pulling up from you. ²²Here am I, I'm going to give an order (Yahweh's declaration) and I shall bring them back to this town. They will do battle against it and capture it and burn it with fire, and Yehudah's towns I shall make a desolation without inhabitant."'

35

The word that came to Yirmeyahu from Yahweh in the days of Yehoyaqim ben Yoshiyyahu king of Yehudah: ²'Go to the Rekabites' house and speak with them, and bring them to Yahweh's house to one of the halls and get them to drink wine.'

³So I got Ya'azanyah ben Yirmeyahu son of Habatstsinyah, his brothers, all his sons and the entire household of the Rekabites ⁴and brought them to Yahweh's house to the hall of the sons of Hanan ben Yigdalyahu, the supernatural man, which was near the officials' hall, which was above the hall of Ma'aseyahu ben Shallum, the guard of the threshold. ⁵I put in front of the members of the Rekabites' household bowls full of wine and cups, and said to them, 'Drink wine.' ⁶They said, 'We won't drink wine, because Yonadab ben Rekab our ancestor ordered us, "You're not to drink wine, you or your descendants permanently. ⁷You're not to build a house, you're not to sow seed, you're not to plant a vineyard. They won't be for you. Rather, you're to live in tents all your days, so you may live for many days on the face of the land where you're residing."

Witnessing by your obedience to your special vocation

⁸We've obeyed the voice of Yehonadab ben Rekab our ancestor regarding all he ordered us, not to drink wine all our days, we, our wives, our sons and our daughters, ⁹and not to build houses for us to live in; and we don't have vineyard or field or seed. ¹⁰We've lived in tents and obeyed, and acted in accordance with all that Yonadab our ancestor ordered us. ¹¹But when Nebukadre'tstsar king of Babel went up against the country we said, "Come on, we'll come into Yerushalaim in the face of the Kasdite force and in the face of the Aramite force." So we've lived in Yerushalaim.'

¹²Yahweh's word came to Yirmeyahu: ¹³'Yahweh of Armies, Yisra'el's God, has said this: "Go and say to Yehudah's people and to Yerushalaim's inhabitants: 'Won't you accept discipline by listening to my words (Yahweh's declaration)? ¹⁴It has been implemented, the words of Yehonadab ben Rekab which he ordered his descendants, not to drink wine. They haven't drunk up until this day because they've obeyed their ancestor's order. But I myself have spoken to you, starting early and speaking, but you haven't obeyed me. ¹⁵I've sent to you all my servants the prophets, starting early and sending them, saying "Will you turn back, each one, from his bad way and make your deeds good, and not follow other gods so as to serve them, and you will live on the land that I gave to you and to your ancestors", but you haven't bent your ear, you haven't obeyed me. ¹⁶Because the descendants of Yehonadab ben Rekab have implemented the order of their ancestor which he gave them, but this people – they haven't obeyed me."'

¹⁷Therefore Yahweh, God of Armies, Yisra'el's God, has said this: 'Here am I, I'm going to bring to Yehudah and to all Yerushalaim's inhabitants all the bad fortune of which I spoke against them, since I spoke to them and they haven't listened, I called to them and they haven't answered.' ¹⁸But to the household of the Rekabites Yirmeyahu said, 'Yahweh of Armies, Yisra'el's God, has said this: "Since you obeyed the order of Yehonadab your ancestor and kept all his orders and acted in accordance with all that he ordered you, ¹⁹therefore Yahweh of Armies, Yisra'el's God, has said this: 'There shall not be cut off for Yonadab ben Rekab someone standing before me for all time.'"'

The scroll

36

In the fourth year of Yehoyaqim ben Yoshiyyahu king of Yehudah, this word came to Yirmeyahu from Yahweh: ²'Get yourself a document scroll and write in it all the words that I've spoken to you about Yisra'el, about Yehudah and about all the nations from the day I spoke to you (from the days of Yoshiyyahu) until this day. ³Perhaps Yehudah's household will listen to all the bad things that I'm intending to do to them, so they may turn back each one from his bad way and I may pardon their waywardness and their wrongdoing.'

⁴So Yirmeyahu called Baruk ben Neriyyah, and Baruk wrote from Yirmeyahu's mouth all Yahweh's words that he'd spoken to him, on a document scroll. ⁵Yirmeyahu ordered Baruk, 'I'm under constraint; I can't come to Yahweh's house. ⁶You're to come and read out, in the scroll that you've written from my mouth, the words from Yahweh, in the ears of the people at Yahweh's house on a fast day, and you're also to read them in the ears of all Yehudah who come from their towns. ⁷Perhaps their prayer for grace will fall before Yahweh and they'll turn back each one from his bad way, because Yahweh's anger and wrath are great, of which he's spoken concerning this people.'

⁸Baruk ben Neriyyah acted in accordance with all that Yirmeyahu the prophet ordered him, by reading out in the scroll Yahweh's words at Yahweh's house. ⁹In the fifth year of Yehoyaqim ben Yoshiyyahu king of Yehudah, in the ninth month, they called for a fast before Yahweh, the entire people in Yerushalaim and the entire people coming from Yehudah's towns into Yerushalaim. ¹⁰Baruk read in the scroll Yirmeyahu's words at Yahweh's house in the hall of Gemaryahu ben Shaphan the secretary, in the upper courtyard at the entrance of the new gateway of Yahweh's house, in the ears of the entire people.

The bold miscalculation

¹¹Mikayehu ben Gemaryahu son of Shaphan listened to all Yahweh's words from the scroll, ¹²and went down to the king's house to the secretary's hall. There, all the officials were sitting there: Elishama the secretary, Delayahu ben Shema'yahu, Elnatan ben Akbor, Gemaryahu ben Shaphan, Tsidqiyyahu ben Hananyahu and all the officials. ¹³Mikayehu told them all the words that he'd heard when Baruk read out in the document in the people's ears.

¹⁴All the officials sent Yehudi ben Netanyahu son of Shelemyahu son of Kushi to Baruk, saying, 'The scroll in which you read out in the people's ears – will you get it in your hand and get going.' So Baruk ben Nirayyahu got the scroll in his hand and came to them. ¹⁵They said to him, 'Sit down, please, and read it out in our ears.' Baruk read it out in their ears. ¹⁶When they heard all the words, they were fearful, each towards his neighbour. They said to Baruk, 'We must definitely tell the king all these words.' ¹⁷They asked Baruk, 'Please tell us how you wrote all these words from his mouth.' ¹⁸Baruk said to them, 'From his mouth he called out to me all these words and I was writing them in the document in ink.' ¹⁹The officials said to Baruk, 'Go hide, you and Yirmeyahu. No one is to know where you are.' ²⁰They came to the king in the courtyard; the scroll they deposited in Elishama the secretary's hall, but they told in the king's ears all the words.

²¹The king sent Yehudi to get the scroll, and he got it from Elishama the secretary's hall. Yehudi read it out in the king's ears and in the ears of all the officials standing in attendance on the king. ²²The king was sitting in the winter house (in the ninth month) with the firepot before him, burning. ²³As Yehudi read out three or four columns, he would cut it with a secretary's knife and throw it into the fire that was in the firepot until the entire scroll was finished in the fire that was in the firepot.

Yet more words

²⁴So they weren't fearful and they didn't tear their clothes, the king and all his servants who heard all these words, ²⁵even though Elnatan, Delayyahu and Gemaryahu entreated the king not to burn the scroll; he didn't listen to them. ²⁶The king ordered Yerahme'el the king's son, Serayahu ben Azri'el and Shelemyahu ben Abde'el to get Baruk the secretary and Yirmeyahu the prophet, but Yahweh hid them.

²⁷Yahweh's word came to Yirmeyahu after the king burned the scroll with the words that Baruk wrote from Yirmeyahu's mouth: ²⁸'Get yourself yet another scroll, and write on it all the earlier words that were on the earlier scroll that Yehoyaqim king of Yehudah burned. ²⁹About Yehoyaqim king of Yehudah you're to say, "Yahweh has said this: 'You – you burned this scroll, saying, "Why have you written on it, 'The king of Babel will definitely come and devastate this country and eliminate from it human beings and animals'?" ³⁰Therefore

Yahweh has said this about Yehoyaqim king of Yehudah: 'He will not have someone sitting on David's throne, and his corpse will be thrown out to the heat by day and to the cold by night. ³¹I shall attend to their waywardness for him, for his offspring and for his servants, and bring on them, on Yerushalaim's inhabitants and on Yehudah's people all the bad fortune of which I spoke in connection with them, but they didn't listen.""

³²So Yirmeyahu got another scroll and gave it to Baruk ben Neriyyahu the secretary, and he wrote on it from the mouth of Yirmeyahu all the words on the document that Yehoyaqim king of Yehudah burned in the fire. There were also added to them many words like them.

The king who vacillates

37 King Tsidqiyyahu ben Yoshiyyahu became king in place of Konyahu ben Yehoyaqim; Nebukadre'tstsar king of Babel made him king in the country of Yehudah. ²He didn't listen, he or his servants or the people of the country, to Yahweh's words which he spoke by means of Yirmeyahu the prophet.

³But King Tsidqiyyahu sent Yehukal ben Shelemyah and Tsephanyahu ben Ma'aseyah the priest to Yirmeyahu the prophet to say, 'Will you plead on our behalf with Yahweh our God?' (⁴when Yirmeyahu was coming in and going out among the people and they hadn't put him into a place of confinement, ⁵and when Par'oh's force had come out from Misrayim, and the Kasdites who were besieging Yerushalaim had heard the report about them and had pulled up from Yerushalaim).

⁶Yahweh's word came to Yirmeyahu the prophet: ⁷'Yahweh, Yisra'el's God, has said this: "This is what you people should say to the king of Yehudah who's sending you to me to enquire of me: 'There, Par'oh's force that are coming out to you to help you will go back to their country, to Misrayim. ⁸The Kasdites will come back and will do battle against this town, capture it and burn it in fire.'"

⁹Yahweh has said this: "Don't deceive yourselves by saying, 'The Kasdites will certainly go from against us', because they won't go. ¹⁰If you struck down the entire force of the Kasdites who are doing battle with you, and people who were thrust through remained among them, each in his tent, they'd get up and burn this town in fire."

Until the bread runs out

¹¹When the Kasdite force pulled up from Yerushalaim in the face of Par'oh's force, ¹²Yirmeyahu went out from Yerushalaim to go to the region of Binyamin to divide a share there among the people. ¹³When he was at the Binyamin Gate, a master over the appointment was there; his name was Yir'iyyah ben Shelemyah son of Hananyah. He seized Yirmeyahu the prophet, saying, 'You're going over to the Kasdites.' ¹⁴Yirmeyahu said, 'It's a falsehood. I'm not going over to the Kasdites', but he didn't listen to him. Yir'iyyah seized Yirmeyahu and brought him to the officials. ¹⁵The officials were furious at Yirmeyahu, struck him down and put him in the prison house, the house of Yehonatan the secretary, because they had made it into the jail.

¹⁶When Yirmeyahu had come to the cistern house and to the cells, and Yirmeyahu had lived there for many days, ¹⁷King Tsidqiyyahu sent and got him, and the king asked him in his house in secret, 'Is there a word from Yahweh?' Yirmeyahu said, 'There is', and said, 'You'll be given into the hand of the king of Babel.'

¹⁸And Yirmeyahu said to King Tsidqiyyahu, 'What have I done wrong to you, to your servants and to this people, that you've put me into the jail? ¹⁹And where are your prophets who prophesied to you, "The king of Babel won't come against you or against this country"? ²⁰So now listen please, my lord king; may my plea for grace please fall to you. Don't send me back to the house of Yehonatan the secretary, so I don't die there.' ²¹King Tsidqiyyahu gave an order and they placed Yirmeyahu in the prison courtyard, and gave him a loaf of bread per day from the bakers' street until all the bread came to an end from the town. So Yirmeyahu lived in the prison courtyard.

The king can't prevail

38 Shephatyah ben Mattan, Gedalyahu ben Pashhur, Yukal ben Shelemyah and Pashhur ben Malkiyyah heard the words that Yirmeyahu was speaking to the entire people: ²'Yahweh has said this: "The person who lives in this town will die by sword, by famine or by epidemic, but the one who goes out to the Kasdites will live. His life will be his as a trophy. He'll live." ³Yahweh has said this: "This town will certainly be given into the hand of the king of Babel's force and he'll capture it."'

⁴The officials said to the king, 'This man should please be put to death, because by this means he's slackening the hands of the men of battle who remain in this town, and the hands of the entire people, by speaking to them in accordance with these words, because this man isn't seeking the well-being of this people, but something bad.' ⁵King Tsidqiyyahu said, 'There, he's in your hand, because the king can't prevail against you in a thing.' ⁶So they got Yirmeyahu and threw him into the cistern of Malkiyyahu the king's son, which was in the prison courtyard. They put Yirmeyahu in with ropes. There was no water in the cistern, but only mud. So Yirmeyahu sank into the mud.

⁷Ebed-melek the Kushite, a courtier who was in the king's household, heard that they'd put Yirmeyahu in the cistern. The king was sitting at the Binyamin Gate, ⁸so Ebed-melek went out from the king's house and spoke to the king: ⁹'My lord king, these men have dealt badly in all they've done to Yirmeyahu the prophet, whom they've thrown into the pit. He's dead in this place from hunger, because there's no more bread in the town.' ¹⁰So the king ordered Ebed-melek the Kushite, 'Get thirty people from here with you and pull Yirmeyahu the prophet up from the cistern before he dies.'

The rescue

¹¹Ebed-melek got the men with him and came to the king's house to below the treasury. He got from there old rags and old clothes and sent them to Yirmeyahu in the pit by the ropes. ¹²Ebed-melek the Kushite said to Yirmeyahu, 'Put the old rags and clothes under your armpits, please, under the ropes.' Yirmeyahu did so. ¹³They drew Yirmeyahu up by the ropes and got him up from the cistern. So Yirmeyahu lived in the prison courtyard.

¹⁴King Tsidqiyyahu sent and got Yirmeyahu the prophet to him at the third entrance in Yahweh's house. The king said to Yirmeyahu, 'I'm going to ask you something; don't hide anything from me.' ¹⁵Yirmeyahu said to Tsidqiyyahu, 'When I tell you, won't you definitely put me to death? And when I counsel you, you won't listen to me.' ¹⁶King Tsidqiyyahu swore to Yirmeyahu in secret, 'As Yahweh lives, who made this life for us, if I put you to death or if I give you into the hand of these people who are seeking your life . . .'

¹⁷So Yirmeyahu said to Tsidqiyyahu, 'Yahweh, God of Armies, Yisra'el's God, has said this: "If you do go out to the king of Babel's officers, you yourself will live, and this town won't be burned with fire. You and your household will live. ¹⁸But if you don't go out to the king of Babel's officers, this town will be given into the hand of the Kasdites. They will burn it with fire and you won't escape from their hand."' ¹⁹King Tsidqiyyahu said to Yirmeyahu, 'I'm afraid of the Yehudahites who've submitted to the Kasdites, in case they give me over into their hand and they deal abusively with me.'

Don't tell anyone

²⁰Yirmeyahu said, 'They won't give you over. Please listen to Yahweh's voice, to what I'm speaking to you, so he may do good things for you and you yourself may live. ²¹But if you refuse to go out, this is the word that Yahweh has shown me. ²²There – all the women who remain in the king of Yehudah's household are going to be taken out to the officers of the king of Babel, and there, they're going to say,

The people who were your friends
   have incited you and prevailed over you.
Your feet are stuck in the mire;
   they've turned away back.

²³They're going to take out all your women and children to the Kasdites, and you won't escape from their hand, because you'll be seized by the king of Babel's hand, and you will burn this town in fire.'

²⁴Tsidqiyyahu said to Yirmeyahu, 'No one is to know of these words, and you won't die.

²⁵But when the officials hear that I've spoken with you and they come to you and say to you, "Tell us, please, what you spoke to the king. Don't hide it from us and we won't put you to death. And what did the king speak to you?", ²⁶you're to say to them, "I was letting my plea for grace fall before the king, not to send me back to the house of Yehonatan to die there."

²⁷All the officials came to Yirmeyahu and asked him, and he told them in accordance with all these words that the king had ordered him. So they left off from speaking with him, because the thing hadn't been audible.

²⁸ªYirmeyahu lived in the prison courtyard until the day when Yerushalaim was captured.

The grimmest scene in the Old Testament?

²⁸ᵇWhen Yerushalaim was captured.

39 In the ninth year of Tsidqiyyahu king of Yehudah, in the tenth month, Nebukadre'tstsar king of Babel and his entire force came to Yerushalaim and besieged it. ²In the eleventh year of Tsidqiyyahu, in the fourth month, on the ninth of the month, the town was broken open. ³All the officers of the king of Babel came and sat in the Middle Gate – Nergal Sar-etser, Samgar-nebu, Sar-sekim the head courtier, Nergal Sar-etser the head official and all the remainder of the king of Babel's officers.

⁴When Tsidqiyyahu king of Yehudah and all the men of battle saw them, they fled. They went out by night from the town by the king's garden road, through the gateway between the double wall. He went out on the steppe road. ⁵The Kasdite force pursued after them and overtook Tsidqiyyahu in the Yeriho [Jericho] steppes. They captured him and took him up to Nebukadre'tstsar king of Babel at Riblah in the country of Hamat, and he announced rulings with him. ⁶The king of Babel slaughtered Tsidqiyyahu's sons at Riblah before his eyes, and the king of Babel slaughtered all the important people in Yehudah. ⁷He blinded Tsidqiyyahu's eyes and shackled him in copper chains to bring him to Babel.

⁸The king's house and the people's housing the Kasdites burned in fire, and Yerushalaim's walls they demolished. ⁹The rest of the people who remained in the town and the people who had submitted to him and the rest of the people who remained, Nebuzar'adan the head of the guards took into exile to Babel. ¹⁰Some of the people who were poor, who had nothing, Nebuzar'adan the head of the guards left remaining in the country of Yehudah, and gave them vineyards and fields on that day.

What will happen to Ebed-melek?

¹¹Nebukadre'tstsar king of Babel gave order regarding Yirmeyahu by means of Nebuzar'adan the head of the guards: ¹²'Get him and keep your eyes on him and don't do anything bad to him. Rather, as he speaks to you, so do with him.' ¹³Then sent Nebuzar'adan the head of the guards, Nebushazban the head courtier, Nergal Sar-etser the head officer and all the heads of the king of Babel – ¹⁴they sent and got Yirmeyahu from the prison courtyard and gave him over to Gedalyahu ben Ahiqam son of Shaphan to let him go out to a house. So he lived among the people.

¹⁵A word from Yahweh had come to Yirmeyahu while he was confined in the prison courtyard: ¹⁶'Go and say to Ebed-melek the Kushite: "Yahweh of Armies, Yisra'el's God, has said this: 'Here am I, I'm going to bring about my words regarding this town for bad fortune and not for good. They will come about before you on that day. ¹⁷But I shall rescue you on that day (Yahweh's declaration) and you will not be given into the hand of the people that you're afraid of. ¹⁸Because I shall definitely save you. You will not fall by the sword. Your life will be yours as a trophy, because you've relied on me (Yahweh's declaration).""

40 The word that came to Yirmeyahu from Yahweh after Nebuzar'adan the head of the guards sent him off from The Height, where he'd taken him (he was shackled in chains) among the exile community from Yerushalaim and Yehudah, who were being exiled to Babel. ²The head of the guards took Yirmeyahu and said to him, 'It was Yahweh your God who spoke of this bad fortune for this place, ³and he's brought it about. Yahweh has done as he spoke, because you people did wrong to Yahweh and didn't listen to his voice. So this thing has happened to you.

What will happen to Yirmeyahu?

⁴But now, here: I'm releasing you yourself today from the chains that are on your hand. If it's good in your eyes to come with me to Babel, come, and I'll have my eye on you. But if it's bad in your eyes to come with me to Babel, leave off. Look, all the country is before you. Regarding what is good and what is right in your eyes to go, go there.' ⁵Still he wouldn't go back. 'Or go back to Gedalyah ben Ahiqam son of Shaphan whom the king of Babel has appointed over Yehudah's towns and live with him among the people. Or go anywhere that's right in your eyes to go.' The head of the guards gave him provisions and goods and sent him off. ⁶So Yirmeyahu came to Gedalyah ben Ahiqam at The Watchtower and lived with him among the people who remained in the country.

⁷All the officers in the forces that were in the open country, they and their men, heard that the king of Babel had appointed Gedalyahu ben Ahiqam over the country and that he'd appointed with him the men, the women, the children and those of the poor people of the country who hadn't been exiled to Babel. ⁸They came to Gedalyah at The Watchtower – Yishma'e'l ben Netanyahu, Yohanan and Yonatan the sons of Qareah, Serayah ben Tanhumet, the sons of Ephay the Netophatite, and Yezanyahu the son of the Ma'akatite, they and their men. ⁹Gedalyahu ben Ahiqam son of Shaphan let it be heard by them and by their men, 'Don't be afraid of serving the Kasdites. Go back into the country and serve the king of Babel and things will be good for you. ¹⁰I, here am I, I'm going to live in The Watchtower to serve before the Kasdites who come to us. You, gather up wine, summer fruit and oil, put them in your containers and live in the towns that you'll have seized.'

The fugitives return

¹¹All the Yehudahites who were in Mo'ab, among the Ammonites, in Edom, and those who were in all the countries also heard that the king of Babel had granted a remainder group to Yehudah and that he'd appointed over them Gedalyahu ben Ahiqam son of Shaphan, ¹²and all the Yehudahites came back from all the places where they had been driven. They came to the country of Yehudah to Gedalyahu at The Watchtower and gathered up wine and summer fruit, very much.

¹³Yohanan ben Qareah and all the officers in the forces that were in the open country came to Gedalyahu at The Watchtower ¹⁴and said to him, 'Do you actually know that Ba'alis king of the Ammonites has sent Yishma'e'l ben Netanyah to strike down your life?' But Gedalyahu ben Ahiqam didn't believe them. ¹⁵Yohanan ben Qareah said to Gedalyahu in secret at The Watchtower, 'I shall go, please, and strike down Yishma'e'l ben Netanyah, and no one will know. Why should he strike down your life and scatter all Yehudah who've collected to you, and the remainder of Yehudah perish?' ¹⁶But Gedalyahu ben Ahiqam said to Yohanan ben Qareah, 'Don't do this thing, because you're speaking falsehood about Yishma'e'l.'

41 But in the seventh month Yishma'e'l ben Netanyah son of Elishama, of the royal line, and the king's commanders and ten men with him, came to Gedalyahu ben Ahiqam at The Watchtower. They ate bread there together at The Watchtower, ²and Yishma'e'l ben Netanyah and the ten men who were with him got up and struck down Gedalyahu ben Ahiqam son of Shaphan with the sword and put him to death, the man whom the king of Babel had appointed over the country. ³And all the Yehudahites who were with him (with Gedalyahu at The Watchtower) and the Kasdites who were present there, the men of battle, Yishma'e'l struck down.

The luckless penitents

⁴On the second day after they put Gedalyahu to death, when no one knew, ⁵some people came from Shekem, Shiloh and Shomron, eighty people, shaved bare, clothes torn, bodies gashed, grain offering and incense in their hand to bring to Yahweh's house. ⁶Yishma'e'l ben Netanyah went out from The Watchtower to meet them, crying as he went. When he reached them, he said to them, 'Come to Gedalyahu ben Ahiqam.'

⁷When they came inside the town Yishma'e'l ben Netanyah slaughtered them, into a cistern,

he and the men who were with him. ⁸But ten people were present among them who said to Yishma'e'l, 'Don't put us to death, because we have stores in the open country, grain, barley, oil and syrup.' So he held back and didn't put them to death among their brothers.

⁹The cistern where Yishma'e'l threw all the corpses of the people whom he struck down by the side of Gedalyahu, it was the one that King Asa had made on account of Ba'asha king of Yisra'el; Yishma'e'l ben Netanyah filled it with people who had been run through.

¹⁰Yishma'e'l took captive all the remainder of the company that was at The Watchtower, the king's daughters and all the people who had remained at The Watchtower over whom Nebuzar'adan the head of the guards had appointed Gedalyahu ben Ahiqam. Yishma'e'l ben Netanyah took them captive and went to cross over to the Ammonites. ¹¹But Yohanan ben Qareah and all the officers in the forces that were with him heard all the bad things that Yishma'e'l ben Netanyah had done, ¹²and they got all the people and went to do battle with Yishma'e'l ben Netanyah. They found him by the great pool that's at Gib'on.

¹³When all the company that was with Yishma'e'l saw Yohanan ben Qareah and all the officers in the forces that were with him, they rejoiced. ¹⁴All the company that Yishma'e'l had taken captive from The Watchtower turned round and went back and went to Yohanan ben Qareah.

Turning to God?

¹⁵But Yishma'e'l ben Netanyah, with eight men, escaped from Yohanan and went to the Ammonites. ¹⁶Yohanan ben Qareah and all the officers in the forces that were with him took all the remainder of the company that he brought back from being with Yishma'e'l ben Netanyah from The Watchtower, after he struck down Gedalyah ben Ahiqam (men, men of battle, women, children and courtiers, whom he had brought back from Gib'on). ¹⁷They went and lived at Kimham Khan which is near Bet Lehem, going so as to come to Misrayim ¹⁸on account of the Kasdites, because they were afraid of them because Yishma'e'l ben Netanyah had struck down Gedalyahu ben Ahiqam

whom the king of Babel had appointed over the country.

42 All the officers in the forces, Yohanan ben Qareah, Yezanyah ben Hosha'yah and the entire company, big and small, came up ²and said to Yirmeyahu the prophet, 'May our prayer for grace please fall before you; plead on our behalf with Yahweh your God on behalf of all this remainder, because we remain a few out of many, as your eyes see us. ³May Yahweh your God tell us the way by which we should go and what we should do.'

⁴Yirmeyahu the prophet said to them, 'I've listened. Here am I, I'm going to plead with Yahweh your God in accordance with your words. Everything that Yahweh will answer you, I shall tell you. I won't withhold anything from you.' ⁵They themselves said to Yirmeyahu, 'May Yahweh be a true and truthful witness against us, if we don't act in accordance with everything that Yahweh your God sends you for us. ⁶Whether good or bad, we'll listen to the voice of Yahweh our God to whom we're sending you, for the sake of what will be good for us when we listen to the voice of Yahweh our God.'

Stay, don't go

⁷At the end of ten days Yahweh's word came to Yirmeyahu. ⁸He called to Yohanan ben Qareah, to all the officers in the forces that were with him and to the entire company, to big and small, ⁹and said to them: 'Yahweh, Yisra'el's God, to whom you sent me to let your prayer for grace fall before him, has said this: ¹⁰"If you again live in this country, I will build you up and not tear you down, I will plant you and not uproot, because I regret the bad things that I did to you. ¹¹Don't be afraid of the king of Babel, of whom you are afraid; don't be afraid of him (Yahweh's declaration) because I am with you to deliver you and to rescue you from his hand. ¹²I shall give you compassion, and he will have compassion towards you and take you back to your land."

¹³But if you're going to say, "We won't live in this country" (so as not to listen to Yahweh your God's voice), ¹⁴saying, "No, rather we'll come to the country of Misrayim, where we won't see battle or hear the sound of the

horn or be hungry for bread, and live there": ¹⁵now therefore listen to Yahweh's word, you remainder of Yehudah. Yahweh of Armies, Yisra'el's God, has said this: "If you do set your faces to come to Misrayim, and you come to reside there, ¹⁶the sword that you're afraid of will overtake you there in the country of Misrayim and the famine that you fear will stick close to you there in Misrayim, and you'll die there. ¹⁷All the people who set their faces to come to Misrayim to reside there will die by sword, by famine or by epidemic. There won't be anyone surviving or escaping in the face of the bad fate that I'm going to bring upon you."

An ambassador in chains

¹⁸Because Yahweh of Armies, Yisra'el's God, has said this: "As my anger and my wrath poured out on Yerushalaim's inhabitants, so my wrath will pour out on you when you come to Misrayim. You'll become a vow, a devastation, a slight and a reviling, and you won't again see this place." ¹⁹Yahweh has spoken against you, remainder of Yehudah. Don't come to Misrayim. Acknowledge clearly that I've testified against you this day. ²⁰Because you were deceitful in your entire beings when you yourselves sent me to Yahweh your God, saying "Plead on our behalf to Yahweh our God, and in accordance with all that Yahweh our God says, so tell us and we will act." ²¹I've told you this day, but you haven't listened to the voice of Yahweh your God, even regarding anything with which he sent me to you. ²²So now you must really acknowledge that you'll die by sword, by famine or by epidemic in the place where you want to come to reside.'

43 When Yirmeyahu finished speaking to the entire people all the words of Yahweh their God with which Yahweh their God had sent him to them, all these words, ²Azaryah ben Hosha'yah, Yohanan ben Qareah and all the assertive people were saying to Yirmeyahu, 'You're speaking falsehood. Yahweh our God hasn't sent you to say, "You're not to come to Misrayim to reside there." ³Because Baruk ben Neriyyah is inciting you against us in order to give us into the hand of the Kasdites to put us to death or take us into exile in Babel.'

⁴So Yohanan ben Qareah, all the officers in the forces and the entire people didn't listen to Yahweh's voice so as to stay in the country of Yehudah. ⁵Yohanan ben Qareah and all the officers in the forces took the entire remainder of Yehudah that had come back to reside in the country of Yehudah from all the nations where they had been driven – ⁶men, women, children, the king's daughters and every person whom Nebuzar'adan the head of the guards had set down with Gedalyahu ben Ahiqam son of Shaphan, and Yirmeyahu the prophet and Baruk ben Neriyyahu. ⁷ᵃThey came to Misrayim because they didn't listen to Yahweh's voice.

No escape from Nebukadre'tstsar

⁷ᵇThey came as far as Tahpanhes, ⁸and Yahweh's word came to Yirmeyahu at Tahpanhes: ⁹'Take some big stones in your hand and bury them in clay on the pavement that's at the entrance to Par'oh's house at Tahpanhes, before the eyes of the Yehudahites. ¹⁰You're to say to them, "Yahweh of Armies, Yisra'el's God, has said this: 'Here am I, I'm going to send and get Nebukadre'tstsar king of Babel my servant, and I shall set his throne above these stones (that I've buried) and he will spread his canopy over them. ¹¹He will come and strike down the country of Misrayim: the people destined for death, to death, the people destined for captivity, to captivity, the people destined for the sword, to the sword. ¹²I shall set fire to the houses of the gods of Misrayim and he will burn them and take them captive. He'll delouse the country of Misrayim as a shepherd delouses his coat, and he'll go out from there with things being well. ¹³He'll break up the columns in Sun House which is in the country of Misrayim, and he'll burn the houses of Misrayim's gods with fire.'"

44 The word that came to Yirmeyahu regarding all the Yehudahites who were living in the country of Misrayim, living in Migdol, in Tahpanhes, in Memphis and in the country of Patros. ²'Yahweh of Armies, Yisra'el's God, has said this: "You've seen all the bad fortune that I've brought on Yerushalaim and on all Yehudah's towns. There they are, a waste this day, with no one living in them, ³in the face of the bad dealing that they did, so as to provoke me by going to burn incense to serve other gods that they hadn't acknowledged – they or you or your ancestors. ⁴I sent to you all my servants the prophets, starting early and sending them, to say, 'Please don't do this offensive thing, to which I am hostile.' ⁵But they didn't listen, they didn't bend their ear, so as to turn back from their bad dealing, so as not to burn incense to other gods. ⁶So my wrath and my anger poured out and burned against Yehudah's towns and against Yerushalaim's streets, and they've become a waste, a desolation, this very day."

Things can't get worse, can they?

⁷So now, Yahweh, God of Armies, Yisra'el's God, has said this: "Why are you going to do something that's so bad for yourselves, by cutting off for you man and woman, child and infant, from within Yehudah, so as not to leave a remainder for you, ⁸by provoking me by the practices of your hands, by burning incense to other gods in the country of Misrayim to which you're coming to reside there, in order to cut them off for you and in order to become a slighting and a reviling among all the nations on earth? ⁹Have you put out of mind the bad dealings of your ancestors, the bad dealings of Yehudah's kings, the bad dealings of its wives, your own bad dealings and the bad dealings of your wives, which they did in the country of Yehudah and in Yerushalaim's streets? ¹⁰They were not crushed until this day, they didn't live in awe, they didn't walk by my instruction and by my laws that I put before you and before your ancestors."

¹¹Therefore Yahweh of Armies, Yisra'el's God, has said this. "Here am I, I'm going to set my face against you for bad fortune and to cut off all Yehudah. ¹²I shall take the remainder of Yehudah who have set their face to come to the country of Misrayim to reside there, and they will all come to an end in the country of Misrayim. They will fall by the sword and come to an end by famine. Big and small, by sword and by famine they will die. They will become a vow, a devastation, a slighting and a reviling. ¹³I shall attend to the people living in the country of Misrayim as I attended to Yerushalaim, by sword, by famine and by epidemic. ¹⁴There will be no escapee or survivor of the remainder of Yehudah who are coming to reside there in the country of Misrayim, or to go back to the country of Yehudah when they are lifting up their longing to go back to live there, because they won't go back (except escapees).'"

No, no turning to God

¹⁵All the men who knew that their wives burned incense to other gods, and all the wives standing by, a big congregation, and the entire company who were living in the country of Misrayim at Patros, answered Yirmeyahu, ¹⁶"The word that you've spoken to us in Yahweh's name – we aren't listening to you. ¹⁷Rather, we'll definitely act on every word that's gone out of our mouth, burning incense to the Queen of Heaven and pouring libations to her, as we and our ancestors, our kings and our officials, did in Yehudah's towns and in Yerushalaim's streets, and had our fill of bread and were finding things good, and saw no bad fortune. ¹⁸But from when we left off burning incense to the Queen of Heaven and pouring libations to her, we've lacked everything and we've come to an end by sword and by famine. ¹⁹And when we were burning incense to the Queen of Heaven and pouring libations to her, was it without our husbands that we made cakes to image her and poured libations to her?'

²⁰Yirmeyahu said to the entire company, to the men, to the women and to the entire company who were giving him an answer: ²¹"The incense you burned in Yehudah's towns and in Yerushalaim's streets, you and your ancestors, your kings, your officials and the people of the country – hasn't Yahweh been mindful of them and brought them to mind? ²²Yahweh could no longer bear it, in the face of the bad nature of your practices, in the face of the offensive acts that you committed, so that the country became a waste and a devastation and a slighting, so that there's no inhabitant, this very day. ²³In the face of the way you burned incense and in that you did wrong to Yahweh and didn't listen to Yahweh's voice and didn't walk by his instruction, his laws and his affirmations, that's why this bad fate has happened to you this very day.'

²⁴Yirmeyahu said to the entire company and to all the women, 'Listen to Yahweh's word, all of Yehudah in the country of Misrayim. ²⁵ᵃYahweh of Armies, Yisra'el's God, has said this: "You and your wives – you've spoken by your mouth and with your hands you've fulfilled it, saying 'We'll definitely act on our vows that we made, to burn incense to the Queen of Heaven and pour libations to her.'

A promise for Baruk

²⁵ᵇYou may indeed implement your pledges. You may indeed act upon your pledges." ²⁶Therefore listen to Yahweh's word, all Yehudah who live in the country of Misrayim. "Here am I: I am swearing by my great name (Yahweh has said), if my name will any more be called out in the mouth of anyone from Yehudah, saying 'As the Lord Yahweh lives', in all the country of Misrayim.

²⁷Here am I: I'm going to watch over them for bad things, not for good things. They will come to an end, every individual from Yehudah who's in the country of Misrayim, by sword and by famine, until they're finished off. ²⁸The people who escape the sword will go back from the country of Misrayim to the country of Yehudah few in number, and all the remainder of Yehudah who are coming to the country of Misrayim to reside there will acknowledge whose word will be implemented, mine or theirs.

²⁹This will be the sign for you (Yahweh's declaration) that I'm going to attend to you in this place, so that you may acknowledge that my words against you for bad fortune will indeed be implemented. ³⁰Yahweh has said this: 'Here am I; I'm going to give Par'oh Hophra king of Misrayim into the hand of his enemies and into the hand of the people who are seeking his life, as I gave Tsidqiyyahu king of Yehudah into the hand of Nebukadre'tstsar king of Babel his enemy and one seeking his life.'"

45 The word that Yirmeyahu the prophet spoke to Baruk ben Neriyyah when he wrote these words in a document from Yirmeyahu's mouth in the fourth year of Yehoyaqim ben Yoshiyyahu king of Yehudah: ²'Yahweh, Yisra'el's God, has said this to you, Baruk: ³"You said, 'Oh, me, please, because Yahweh has added sorrow to my pain. I'm weary with my groaning. I haven't found a settled place.'" ⁴You're to say to him, "Yahweh has said this: 'Here, what I built, I'm tearing down; what I planted, I'm uprooting (i.e. the entire country). ⁵You, do you seek big things for yourself? Don't seek them, because here am I, I'm going to bring bad fortune on all flesh (Yahweh's declaration), but I shall give you your life as a trophy in all the places where you go.'"

Par'oh full of talk

46 Things that came as Yahweh's word to Yirmeyahu the prophet about the nations.

²Regarding Misrayim.

About the force of Par'oh Neko king of Misrayim, which was at the River Euphrates at Karkemish, which Nebukadre'tstsar king of Babel struck down in the fourth year of Yehoyaqim ben Yoshiyyahu king of Yehudah:

³Get ready hand-shield and body-shield;
    go up to battle!
⁴Harness the horses;
    get up, cavalry!
Take your position with your helmets,
    polish lances, put on armour!
⁵Why have I seen – they're shattered,
    they're turning back!
Their strong men are struck down, they've fled, fled,
    they haven't turned round, terror is all round (Yahweh's declaration).
⁶The swift is not to flee,
    the strong man is not to escape.
To the north, by the side of the River Euphrates,
    they've collapsed and fallen.
⁷Who is this rises like the Ye'or,
    like streams whose water surges?
⁸It's Misrayim that rises like the Ye'or
    and like streams whose water surges.
It said, 'I'll rise, I'll cover the earth,
    I'll obliterate a town and the people who live in it.'
⁹Rise, horses, rage, chariotry,
    strong men are to go out,

Seba and Put seizing shields,
  Ludites seizing and directing bows.

¹⁰That day belongs to the Lord Yahweh of Armies,
  a day of redress, for taking redress from his adversaries.
The sword will consume, be full,
  will soak in their bloodshed.
Because the Lord Yahweh of Armies has a sacrifice
  in the northern country by the River Euphrates.
¹¹Go up to Gil'ad and get balm,
  young Miss Misrayim.
To empty results you're multiplying healings –
  there's no growing back for you.
¹²Nations have heard your slighting;
  the earth is full of your scream.
Because strong man has collapsed on strong man;
  the two of them have fallen down together.

Par'oh helpless

¹³The word that Yahweh spoke to Yirmeyahu the prophet regarding the coming of Nebukadre'tstsar king of Babel to strike down the country of Misrayim:

¹⁴Tell it in Misrayim, make it heard in Migdal,
  make it heard in Memphis and in Tahpanhes.
Say, 'Take your position, prepare yourself,
  because the sword is consuming all round you.'
¹⁵Why has your champion been swept away?
  – he didn't stand, because Yahweh thrust him down.
¹⁶He's made many people collapse,
  yes, each one has fallen into his neighbour.
They said, 'Set to,
  let's turn back to our people,
To the country of our birth,
  from before the oppressor's sword.'
¹⁷There they called Par'oh king of Misrayim,
  'A din who has let the appointed time pass'.
¹⁸As I live (a declaration of the King,
  Yahweh of Armies is his name):
Like Tabor among the mountains,
  and like Carmel at the sea, one will come.
¹⁹Make for yourself things for exile,
  you who sit as Miss Misrayim.
Because Memphis will become a desolation,
  burned, without inhabitant.
²⁰Misrayim is a beautiful, beautiful heifer;
  a wasp from the north is coming, coming.
²¹Her mercenaries within her, too,
  are like well-fed bullocks.
Yet they're turning round, too,
  they're fleeing together, they're not taking a stand.
Because their day of disaster has come upon them,
  the time when they're attended to.
²²Her sound will be like a snake when it goes,
  with a force they will go.
With axes they're coming to her,
  like fellers of trees.
²³They're cutting down her forest (Yahweh's declaration)
  when it cannot be explored,
Because they're more than locusts;
  there's no numbering of them.
²⁴Miss Misrayim is being shamed,
  given into the hand of the northern people.

But of you I won't make an end

²⁵Yahweh of Armies, Yisra'el's God, has said:

Here am I, attending to Amon of Thebes and to Par'oh, to Misrayim, to its gods, to its kings – to Par'oh and to the people who rely on him. ²⁶I shall give them into the hand of the people who seek their life, into the hand of Nebukadre'tstsar king of Babel and into the hand of his servants. But afterwards it will dwell as in former days (Yahweh's declaration).

²⁷But you, don't be afraid, my servant Ya'aqob;
  don't shatter, Yisra'el.
Because here am I, I'm going to deliver you from far away,
  and your offspring from the country of their captivity.
Ya'aqob will again be calm,
  at peace with no one making him tremble.
²⁸So you, don't be afraid, my servant Ya'aqob (Yahweh's declaration),
  because I'm with you.
Because I shall make an end among all the nations where I've driven you,
But of you I won't make an end,
  though I discipline you in exercising authority,
  and don't treat you as free of guilt.

47

Something that came as Yahweh's word to Yirmeyahu the prophet regarding the Pelishtites, before Par'oh struck down Azzah.

²Yahweh has said this:

There, water is rising from the north,
  and it will become an overwhelming wadi.
They'll overwhelm the country and what fills it,
  the town and the people who live in it.
People will cry out,
  all the country's inhabitants will howl,
³At the sound of the pounding of his sturdy steeds' hooves,
  at the noise of his chariotry, the clatter of its wheels.
Fathers are not turning their faces to children
  because of the slackening of their hands,
⁴Because of the day that's coming
  for the destroying of all the Pelishtites,
For cutting off every helper who survives
  for Tsor and Tsidon.
Because Yahweh is going to destroy the Pelishtites,
  the remainder of Kaphtor's shore.
⁵The shaved head is coming to Azzah,
  Ashqelon is being terminated.
You remainder of their vale,
  how long will you gash yourself?
⁶Hey, sword of Yahweh,
  for how long will you not be calm? –
Gather up into your sheath,
  rest, be still.
⁷How can you be calm
  when Yahweh is ordering it?
For Ashqelon and for the seacoast
  he has set its appointment.

Mo'ab broken

48

Regarding Mo'ab.

Yahweh of Armies, Yisra'el's God, has said this:

Hey for Nebo, that it's destroyed,
  Qiryatayim is shamed, captured.
The stronghold is shamed and it has shattered.
  ²Mo'ab's praise is no more.
In Heshbon they intended something bad against her:
  'Come, let's cut her down from being a nation.'
Madmenah, you'll be still, too;
  the sword will follow you.
³The sound of an outcry from Horonayim,
  destruction and great breaking.
⁴Mo'ab is broken,
  its little ones have let the outcry be heard.
⁵Because the ascent to Luhit –
  with crying one ascends, with crying.
Because on the Horonayim descent
  people have heard the crying distresses about the breaking.
⁶Flee, save your life,
  be like Aro'er in the wilderness!
⁷Because on account of your reliance on what you've made,
  and on your treasures, you too will be captured.
Kemosh will go out into exile,
  his priests and his officials together.
⁸The destroyer will come to every town,
  no town will escape.
The vale will perish,
  the flatland will be desolate, because Yahweh has said.
⁹Give wings to Mo'ab,
  because it's to fly, go out.
Its towns will be for desolation,
  with no inhabitant in them.
¹⁰Cursed is the one who does Yahweh's work deceitfully;
  cursed is the one who holds back his sword from blood.
¹¹Mo'ab has been at peace from its youth;
  it's been still on its lees.
It hasn't been poured from bowl to bowl;
  it hasn't gone into exile.
Therefore its taste has stayed in it,
  its bouquet hasn't changed.
¹²Therefore there – days are coming (Yahweh's declaration)
  when I'll send off decanters to it.
They'll decant it and empty its bowls
  and smash its jugs.
¹³Mo'ab will be shamed because of Kemosh
  as Yisra'el's household was shamed
  because of Bet El, the object of their reliance.
¹⁴How can you say, 'We are strong men,
  forceful men for the battle'?

¹⁵Mo'ab is destroyed, people have gone up to its towns,
  the choicest of its young men have gone down to the slaughter
(The declaration of the King,
  Yahweh of Armies is his name).

A long quiet disturbed

¹⁶Mo'ab's disaster is near to coming,
  its bad fate is hurrying quickly.
¹⁷Condole with it, all you who are round it,
  all you who acknowledge its name.
Say, 'How has the vigorous club broken,
  the splendid mace.'
¹⁸Come down from honour, sit on the thirsty ground,
  you who sit as Miss Dibon.
Because Mo'ab's destroyer has come up against you;
  he's devastated your fortifications.
¹⁹Stand by the road and look out,
  you who live in Aro'er.
Ask the man who flees and the woman who escapes,
  say 'What's happened?'
²⁰Mo'ab is shamed, because it has shattered –
  howl and cry out;
Tell at the Arnon
  that Mo'ab is destroyed.

²¹A ruling has come for the flatland region,
  for Holon, for Yahtsah,
On Mepha'at, ²²on Dibon, on Nebo,
  on Bet Diblatayim, ²³on Qiryatayim,
On Bet Gamul, on Bet Me'on,
  ²⁴on Qeriyyot, on Botsrah,
On all the towns in the country of Mo'ab,
  far and near.

²⁵Mo'ab's horn is cut off,
  its arm broken (Yahweh's declaration).
²⁶Get it drunk, because it's made itself big against Yahweh;
  Mo'ab will wallow in its vomit.
It will be an object of fun, too:
  ²⁷wasn't Yisra'el an object of fun to you?
Was it found among robbers,
  that when you speak of it you shake your head?

²⁸Abandon the towns, dwell in the cliff,
  inhabitants of Mo'ab,
Be like a pigeon that nests
  in the sides of the mouth of a chasm.
²⁹We've heard of Mo'ab's majesty
  (it's very majestic),
Its height and its majesty and its exaltation,
  and the loftiness of its mind.
³⁰I myself know (Yahweh's declaration) its fury;
  its empty talk is not upright, they haven't acted uprightly.

³¹Therefore I will howl for Mo'ab,
  I will cry out regarding Mo'ab, all of it,
  concerning the people of Qir-heres I will murmur.
³²With more crying than for Ya'zer I'll cry for you,
  vine of Sibmah.
Your tendrils crossed the sea,
  to the sea of Ya'zer they reached.
On your summer fruit and on your grapes
  a destroyer has fallen.
³³Rejoicing and celebration gather up from the farmland
  and from the country of Mo'ab.
I've made wine cease from the presses;
  no one treads with a shout;
  the shout is no shout.

My heart moans for Mo'ab

³⁴From the outcry of Heshbon as far as Ele'aleh,
  as far as Yahats, they're giving their voice,
From Tso'ar as far as Horonayim, Eglat Shelishiyyah,
  because the water of Nimrim, too, will become a great desolation.
³⁵I shall stop for Mo'ab (Yahweh's declaration)
  anyone ascending to the shrine,
  anyone burning incense to its gods.
³⁶Therefore my heart for Mo'ab
  moans like a flute.
My heart for the people of Qir-heres
  moans like a flute.
Therefore the profit it made –
  they've perished, ³⁷because every head is shaved,
  every beard cut off.
On all hands there are gashes,
  on hips there's sack.
³⁸On Mo'ab's roofs and in its squares,
  all of it, is lamentation,
Because I've broken Mo'ab
  like a jar no one wants (Yahweh's declaration).
³⁹How it has shattered – wail;
  how Mo'ab has turned its back in shame.

Mo'ab will be an object of fun,
    something to shatter all the people round it.

⁴⁰Because Yahweh has said this:

There, one swoops like an eagle
    and spreads his wings towards Mo'ab.
⁴¹Qeriyyot has been captured,
    the strongholds have been seized.
The mind of Mo'ab's strong men will be
    like the mind of a woman in labour on that day.
⁴²Mo'ab has been destroyed from being a people
    because it made itself big against Yahweh.
⁴³A terror and a pit and a trap
    are against you who live in Mo'ab (Yahweh's
        declaration).
⁴⁴The one who flees from the face of the terror
    will fall into the pit.
The one who climbs out of the pit
    will be captured by the trap.
Because I'll bring to it, to Mo'ab,
    the year of my attending to it (Yahweh's
        declaration).
⁴⁵In Heshbon's shade
    people who are fleeing stop, being out of energy.
Because fire has gone out from Heshbon,
    a flame from within Sihon,
Consumed Mo'ab's forehead,
    the skull of Sha'on's people.
⁴⁶Oh, alas for you, Mo'ab,
    the people of Kemosh have perished.
Because your sons have been taken into captivity,
    your daughters into captivity.

⁴⁷But I shall restore Mo'ab's fortunes
    at the end of the time (Yahweh's declaration).

As far as here is the ruling about Mo'ab.

The wisdom that fails

49
Regarding the Ammonites.

Yahweh has said this:

Does Yisra'el have no sons,
    or no one entering into possession?
Why has Malkam dispossessed Gad
    and its people lived in its towns?
²Therefore – there, days are coming (Yahweh's
        declaration)
    when I shall make the battle alarm heard
    for Rabbah of the Ammonites.
It will become a desolate tell;
    its daughter-townships will be set on fire.
Yisra'el will dispossess
    the people who dispossessed it (Yahweh has said).

³Howl, Heshbon,
    because Ai is destroyed!
Cry out, daughter-townships of Rabbah,
    wrap on sack, lament.
Run to and fro in the enclosures,
    because Malkam is to go into exile,
    his priests and his officials together with him.
⁴Why do you boast of your vales? –
    your vale is flowing away,
Miss-who-turns-back, you who rely on your
        treasures,
    'Who will come against me?'
⁵Here am I, I'm going to bring a terror against you
    (a declaration of the Lord Yahweh of Armies)
        from all those round you.
You'll be driven off, each one straight ahead;
    there'll be no one collecting the fugitive.

⁶But afterwards I shall restore
    the fortunes of the Ammonites (Yahweh's
        declaration).

⁷Regarding Edom.

Yahweh of Armies has said this:

Is there no longer smartness in Teman,
    has counsel perished from the discerning,
    has their smartness gone stale?
⁸Flee, turn round, lie low,
    inhabitants of Dedan.
Because I'm going to bring Esaw's disaster upon
        him,
    the time when I attend to him.
⁹If grape-pickers came to you,
    would they not let gleanings remain?
If robbers [came] by night
    they'd devastate what they needed.
¹⁰But it's I who've stripped Esaw,
    bared his hiding place.
He can't conceal himself; his offspring is destroyed,
    his brothers and his neighbours, and there is
        no one.
¹¹Abandon your orphans, I'll keep them alive;
    your widows may rely on me.

Strong men emasculated

¹²Because Yahweh has said this: 'The people for whom there has been no ruling that they should drink the glass: if they'll certainly drink it, are you one to go totally free of guilt? You won't go free of guilt, because you will certainly drink it. ¹³Because by myself I have sworn (Yahweh's declaration) that Botsrah will be for desolation, for reviling, for wasting, for slighting, and all its towns will be for total waste permanently.'

¹⁴I have heard a report from Yahweh,
    and an envoy is sent among the nations.
Collect together and come to it,
    set to for battle!
¹⁵Because there – I'm going to make you small
    among the nations,
    despised among people.
¹⁶Your dreadfulness has deceived you,
    the assertiveness of your mind.
You who dwell in the clefts of the cliff,
    you who seize the height of the hill,
If you make your nest high like an eagle,
    I will get you down from there (Yahweh's
        declaration).

¹⁷Edom will become a desolation,
    everyone who passes by it will be desolate
And will whistle at all its wounds,
    ¹⁸as at the overthrow of Sedom and Amorah
        and their neighbours (Yahweh has said).
No one will live there,
    no human being will reside there.

¹⁹There, it will be as when a lion comes up
    from the Yarden jungle into an enduring abode,
Because in a moment I shall run him out of it,
    and whoever is chosen for it I shall appoint.
Because who is like me, who can make me testify,
    who is the shepherd who can stand before me?
²⁰Therefore listen to Yahweh's counsel
    which he's devised for Edom,
His intentions which he's formulated
    for the inhabitants of Teman.
If the flock's boys don't drag them away,
    if the abode isn't desolate at them . . .

²¹At the sound of their fall the earth shakes,
    the outcry makes its sound heard at the Sea of
        Reeds.
²²There, like an eagle he goes up and swoops,
    spreads his wings against Botsrah.
The mind of Edom's strong men will be
    like the mind of a woman in labour on that day.

The promise of a future

²³Regarding Dammeseq [Damascus].

Hamat and Arpah are shamed,
    because they've heard a report of something
        bad.
They toss like the sea with anxiety;
    it cannot be calm.
²⁴Dammeseq is weak,
    she's turned her face to flee.
Panic has taken strong hold of her,
    pressure and contractions have grasped her like
        a woman giving birth.
²⁵How has the praiseworthy town not been
        abandoned,
    the town I celebrated?
²⁶Therefore its young men will fall in its squares
    and all its men of battle will become still on
        that day (a declaration of Yahweh of Armies).
²⁷I shall set fire to the wall of Dammeseq;
    it will consume the citadels of Ben-hadad.

²⁸Regarding Qedar and the kingdoms of Hatsor, which Nebukadre'tstsar king of Babel struck down.

Yahweh has said this:

Set to, go up to Qedar,
    destroy the Qedemites!
²⁹They will take their tents and their flocks,
    their tent cloths and all their things.
They'll carry off their camels for themselves;
    they'll call out against them, 'Terror is all
        round.'
³⁰Flit, go way away, lie low,
    inhabitants of Hatsor (Yahweh's declaration).
Because Nebukadre'tstsar king of Babel
    has devised counsel against you,
    has formulated an intention against you.

³¹Set to, go up, to a nation at peace,
    living in confidence (Yahweh's declaration).
It has no gateways and no bars;
    they dwell alone.

³²Their camels will become plunder,
 their horde of livestock, spoil.
I shall scatter to every wind the people shaved at
   the forehead,
 from all sides I shall bring about their disaster
   (Yahweh's declaration).
³³Hatsor will become an abode for jackals,
 a desolation permanently.
No one will live there;
 no human being will reside there.

An unexpected vulnerability

³⁴What came as Yahweh's word to Yirmeyahu the prophet regarding Elam at the beginning of the reign of Tsidqiyyah king of Yehudah.

³⁵Yahweh of Armies has said this:

Here am I, I'm about to break Elam's bow,
 the first principle of their strength.
³⁶I shall bring to Elam four winds
 from the four corners of the heavens.
I shall scatter them to these four winds;
 the nation won't exist
 where Elam's fugitives don't come.
³⁷I shall shatter Elam before its enemies,
 and before the people who seek their life.
I shall bring bad fortune on them,
 my angry blazing (Yahweh's declaration).
I shall send the sword off after them
 until I've finished them off.
³⁸I shall put my throne in Elam
 and obliterate king and officials from there
   (Yahweh's declaration).

³⁹But at the end of the time
 I shall restore Elam's fortunes (Yahweh's
   declaration).

50 The word that Yahweh spoke regarding Babel, regarding the country of the Kasdites, by means of Yirmeyahu the prophet:

²Tell among the nations, make it heard;
 lift a banner, make it heard.
Don't hide it, say, 'Babel is captured,
 Bel is shamed, Merodak has shattered.'
Its idols are shamed,
 its fetishes have shattered.

³Because a northern nation has gone up against it,
 it will make its country a desolation.
There will be no one living in it;
 both human being and animal – they have
   flitted, gone.
⁴In those days and at that time (Yahweh's
   declaration):

The Yisra'elites will come,
 they and the Yehudahites together.
They'll go, and cry as they go,
 and seek Yahweh their God.
⁵They'll ask the way to Tsiyyon,
 and their faces will be towards there.
'Come, join yourselves to Yahweh
 by a permanent pact that won't be put out of
   mind.'
⁶My people were a flock that were lost;
 their shepherds had led them astray.
On the mountains they turned them back,
 from mountain to hill they went.
They put their resting-place out of mind;
 ⁷all the people who found them consumed them.
Their adversaries said, 'We won't incur liability,
 on account of the fact that they did wrong to
   Yahweh,
 the faithful abode, their ancestors' hope, Yahweh.'

Flit from within Babel

⁸Flit from within Babel,
 get out of the country of the Kasdites,
 be like the he-goats before the flock.
⁹Because here, I'm going to arouse,
 and get to go up, against Babel
A congregation of great nations
 from a northern country.
When they line up against it,
 from there it will be captured.
Its arrows like those of an insightful strong man
 won't turn back empty.
¹⁰The Kasdites will become spoil;
 all its despoilers will be full (Yahweh's
   declaration),
¹¹Because you rejoice, because you exult,
 plunderers of my domain,
Because you jump like a heifer with grain;
 you bellow like sturdy ones.
¹²Your mother is very shamed,
 the one who gave birth to you is confounded.

There is the end of the nations:
   wilderness, dry land and steppe.
¹³Because of Yahweh's fury it won't be inhabited,
   it will become a desolation, all of it.
Everyone who passes by Babel will be desolate
   and will whistle at all its wounds.

¹⁴Line up against Babel round about,
   all you who direct a bow.
Shoot at it, don't hold back with an arrow,
   because it's done wrong to Yahweh.
¹⁵Shout against it round about, it's giving its hand,
   its towers are falling,
Its walls are being torn down,
   because that is Yahweh's redress.
Take redress upon it;
   as it has done, do to it.
¹⁶Cut off sower from Babel,
   and seizer of sickle at harvest time.
Before the oppressor's sword
   they'll turn, each one to his people,
   they'll flee, each one to his country.

The superpower that thought it was safe

¹⁷Yisra'el is scattered sheep
   that lions have driven away.
As first the king of Ashshur consumed him,
   then as last Nebukadre'tstsar king of Babel
   crushed his bones.

¹⁸Therefore Yahweh of Armies, Yisra'el's God, has said this:

Here am I, I'm going to attend
   to the king of Babel and to his country
   as I attended to the king of Ashshur.
¹⁹And I shall take Yisra'el back to its abode,
   and it will pasture in the Carmel and the Bashan.
In the highland of Ephrayim and Gil'ad
   its appetite will eat its fill.

²⁰In those days and at that time (Yahweh's declaration):

Yisra'el's waywardness will be looked for, and
      there'll be none;
   Yehudah's wrongdoings – and they won't be
      found,
   because I shall pardon the people I let remain.

²¹Against the country of Double Rebellion,
   go up against her, and to the inhabitants of
      Attention.
Put to the sword and devote the last of them
      (Yahweh's declaration),
   do in accordance with all that I've ordered
      you.
²²The sound of battle in the country,
   a great breaking.
²³How the hammer of the entire earth
   has severed and broken!
How Babel has become
   a desolation among the nations!
²⁴I trapped you and yes, you were captured,
      Babel,
   and you didn't know it.
You were found and also caught,
   because you challenged Yahweh.
²⁵Yahweh opened his storehouse
   and got out the instruments of his
      condemnation,
Because that's the work
   of the Lord Yahweh of Armies
   in the country of the Kasdites.

²⁶Come to it from afar, open its granaries,
   pile it up like heaps,
   devote it, there must be no remainder of it.
²⁷Put to the sword all its bullocks,
   they must go down for slaughter.
Oh, alas for them, because their day is coming,
   the time when they're attended to.
²⁸The sound of fugitives and escapees
   from the country of Babel,
To tell in Tsiyyon
   of the redress of Yahweh our God,
   redress for his palace.

Death and life interweave

²⁹Make it heard to the archers against Babel,
   all those who direct a bow!
Camp against it round about,
   there must not be people who escape.
Make good to it for its action,
   do to it in accordance with all that it did,
Because it asserted itself against Yahweh,
   Yisra'el's sacred one.
³⁰Therefore its young men will fall in the squares,
   and all its men of battle will become still
   on that day (Yahweh's declaration).

³¹Here am I regarding you, assertive one (a
    declaration of the Lord, Yahweh of Armies).
because your day is coming,
    the time when I attend to you.
³²The assertive one will collapse and fall,
    and there will be no one raising him up.
I shall set fire to his towns
    and it will consume all round him.

³³Yahweh of Armies has said this:

The Yisra'elites and the Yehudahites
    are oppressed together.
All their captors have taken strong hold of them
    and refused to send them off.
³⁴Their restorer is strong,
    Yahweh of Armies is his name.
He will argue their case strongly
    in order that he may quieten the country
    and shake up Babel's inhabitants.

³⁵A sword against the Kasdites (Yahweh's
    declaration),
    for Babel's inhabitants, its officials and its experts!
³⁶A sword for the diviners so they become fools,
    a sword for its strong men so they shatter!
³⁷A sword to its horses and for its chariotry,
    and for all the foreign group that's within it,
    so they become women!
A sword to its storehouses, so they're plundered,
³⁸a drought to its water, so it dries up!
Because it's a country of images,
    and through their dreadful objects they'll go
    mad.
³⁹Therefore wildcats will live with jackals,
    and ostriches will live in it.
It won't be lived in again permanently,
    it won't dwell for generation after generation.
⁴⁰Like God's overthrow
    of Sedom, Amorah and their neighbours
    (Yahweh's declaration),
No one will live there,
    no human being will reside in it.

Hands go limp

⁴¹There, a people is coming from the north;
    a big nation and many kings
    are aroused from earth's farthest reaches.
⁴²They take strong hold of bow and spear;
    they're violent and they don't show compassion.

Their sound is like the sea that rumbles;
    they ride on horses,
As someone lined up for battle,
    against you, Miss Babel.
⁴³The king of Babel has heard the report of them,
    his hands have become slack.
Pressure has taken strong hold of him,
    labour like a woman giving birth.
⁴⁴There, it will be as when a lion goes up
    from the Yarden jungle into an enduring
    abode,
Because in a moment I shall run him out of it,
    and whoever is chosen for it I shall appoint.
Because who is like me, who can make me testify,
    who is the shepherd who can stand before me?
⁴⁵Therefore listen to Yahweh's plan
    which he's devised for Babel,
His intentions which he's formulated
    for the country of the Kasdites.
If the flock's boys don't drag them away,
    if the abode isn't desolate at them . . .
⁴⁶At the sound of the seizing of Babel
    the earth shakes,
    the outcry makes itself heard among the
    nations.

51 Yahweh has said this:

Here am I, I'm rousing against Babel
    and for the inhabitants of The-Mind-of-One-
    Who-Rises-Against-Me a devastating wind.
²I shall send strangers off to Babel
    so they'll winnow it and strip its country,
Because they're against it all round,
    on the day of bad fortune.
³The one who directs his bow isn't to direct it
    and isn't to stand in his armour.
Don't spare its young men;
    devote its entire army.
⁴People are to fall run through in the country of
    the Kasdites,
    thrust through in its streets.

Don't get caught

⁵Because Yisra'el and Yehudah were not widowed
    by its God, Yahweh of Armies.
Rather their country was full of liability
    because of Yisra'el's sacred one.
⁶Flee from inside Babel;
    each of you, save his life.

Don't be still because of its waywardness,
  because this is the time of redress for Yahweh;
  he's making good with his dealings to it.
⁷Babel was a gold chalice in Yahweh's hand,
  making the entire earth drunk.
From its wine nations drank;
  therefore nations go mad.
⁸Suddenly Babel has fallen and broken;
  howl over it.
Get balm for its injuries,
  perhaps it may heal.
⁹'We're healing Babel but it hasn't healed;
  abandon it, let's go each to his country.'
Because the ruling for it has reached to the
    heavens,
  lifted to the skies.
¹⁰Yahweh has brought out faithfulness for us;
  come, let's recount in Tsiyyon
  the action of Yahweh our God.

¹¹Polish the arrows, fill the quivers,
  Yahweh has aroused the spirit of Maday's
    [Media's] kings.
Because his strategy against Babel
  is to devastate it.
Because it's Yahweh's redress,
  redress for his palace.
¹²To Babel's walls lift up a banner,
  make a strong watch,
  set up watchmen, prepare ambushes.
Because Yahweh is both scheming and acting on
  what he spoke regarding Babel's inhabitants.
¹³You who dwell by much water, abundant in
    storehouses,
  your end has come, the time for your cutting off.

¹⁴Yahweh of Armies has sworn by his life:

I'm filling you with people like a locust swarm;
  they'll chant a shout over you.
¹⁵One who made the earth by his energy,
  established the world by his smartness,
  by his understanding stretched out the heavens:
¹⁶At his giving voice
  there was a rumble of the water in the heavens.
He brought up clouds from the end of the earth;
  made lightning for the rain,
  brought out wind from his storehouses.

¹⁷Every human being proves dense, without
    knowledge;
  every goldsmith is put to shame by the image,

Because his figure is a falsehood,
  and there's no breath in them.
¹⁸They're hollow, a work for mockery;
  at the time when they're attended to, they'll
    perish.
¹⁹Not like these is Ya'aqob's share,
  because he's the one who formed everything.
And it is the clan that is his domain;
  Yahweh of Armies is his name.

You were my club

²⁰You were my club,
  my battle instruments.
I clubbed nations with you,
  I devastated kingdoms with you.
²¹I clubbed horse and its rider with you,
  I clubbed chariot and its rider with you.
²²I clubbed man and woman with you,
  I clubbed elder and youth with you.
I clubbed young man and girl with you,
  ²³I clubbed shepherd and his flock with you.
I clubbed ploughman and his pair with you,
  I clubbed governors and overseers with you.
²⁴But I shall make good to Babel
  and to all Kasdim's inhabitants
For all their bad dealing,
  which they did in Tsiyyon before your eyes
    (Yahweh's declaration).

²⁵Here am I in relation to you,
  mountain of the devastator (Yahweh's
    declaration),
Destroyer of the entire earth;
  I'm stretching out my hand against you.
I shall roll you from the cliffs
  and make you a burnt mountain.
²⁶They won't get from you
  a cornerstone or foundation stone,
  because you'll be a total desolation
  permanently (Yahweh's declaration).

²⁷Lift up a banner in the earth,
  sound a horn among the nations.
Make nations sacred against it,
  make it heard to kingdoms against it,
  Ararat, Minni, Ashkenaz.
Appoint a marshal against it,
  bring up horses like swarming locust.
²⁸Make nations sacred against it,
  the kings of Maday,

Its governors, all its overseers,
  every country it rules.
²⁹The earth is shaking and writhing
  because Yahweh's intentions are implemented against Babel
To make the country of Babel
  a desolation without inhabitant.
³⁰Babel's strong men are holding back from doing battle;
  they're sitting in the fortresses.
Their strength has failed,
  they've turned into women.
People have set fire to its dwellings,
  its gateway bars have broken.
³¹Runner runs to meet runner,
  messenger to meet messenger,
To tell the king of Babel
  that his town has been captured at one end.
³²The fords have been seized,
  people have set the marshes on fire,
  the men of battle are fearful.

Yahweh takes on Bel

³³Because Yahweh of Armies, Yisra'el's God, has said this:

Miss Babel is like a threshing-floor
  at the time of its treading:
Yet a little while
  and the time of its harvest will come.
³⁴'He consumed me, crushed me,
  did Nebukadre'tstsar king of Babel,
  put me down an empty dish.
He swallowed me like a dragon,
  filled his belly with my tasty things, threw me up.
³⁵The violence done to me and my body be on Babel'
  says the inhabitant of Tsiyyon.
'My blood be on Kasdim's inhabitants'
  says Yerushalaim.

³⁶Therefore Yahweh says this:

Here am I, arguing your case.
  I'll exact redress for you.
I'll wither its sea and dry up its spring.
³⁷Babel will become heaps of rubble,
The abode of jackals, a desolation,
  something to whistle at, with no inhabitant.

³⁸Together, like cougars they roar,
  they've growled like the whelps of lions.
³⁹When they've been made hot I'll set out their drink banquet,
  and get them drunk in order that they may exult,
And sleep an everlasting sleep
  and not wake up (Yahweh's declaration).
⁴⁰I'll take them down like lambs to slaughter,
  like rams along with goats.
⁴¹How Sheshak has been captured,
  the praise of the entire earth has been seized.
How Babel has become
  a desolation among the nations.
⁴²The sea has gone up over Babel;
  it's covered by the rumble of its waves.
⁴³Its towns have become a desolation,
  its country desert and steppe,
A country where no one lives in them,
  where a human being doesn't pass through them.
⁴⁴I shall attend to Bel in Babel
  and make what he's swallowed come out of his mouth.
Nations will no more flood to him;
  even Babel's wall is falling.

An everlasting sleep

⁴⁵Get out from inside it, my people;
  each of you save his life
  from Yahweh's angry blaze.
⁴⁶Beware that your mind doesn't become soft or you become afraid
  at the report that makes itself heard in the country.
A report will come during the year
  and afterwards a report may come during the next year,
Violence in the country,
  ruler against ruler.
⁴⁷Therefore, now, days are coming
  when I shall attend to Babel's images.
Its entire country will be shamed;
  all its people who are run through will fall within it.
⁴⁸The heavens and the earth and all that's in them
  will resound over Babel,
  because from the north the destroyers will come to it (Yahweh's declaration).

⁴⁹Yes, Babel, for the falling of those of Yisra'el who
 have been run through;
 yes, for Babel all in the earth who have been
 run through have fallen.
⁵⁰Survivors of the sword, go,
 don't stand there.
Be mindful of Yahweh from afar;
 Yerushalaim is to come up into your mind.
⁵¹'We were shamed, because we heard
 reviling,
 disgrace covered our faces.
Because strangers came
 into the sacred places in Yahweh's house.'
⁵²Therefore, there, days are coming (Yahweh's
 declaration)
 when I shall attend to its images
 and in the entire country the person who has
 been run through will groan.
⁵³When Babel goes up to the heavens,
 when it fortifies its strong height,
 destroyers will come to it from me (Yahweh's
 declaration).

⁵⁴The sound of a cry from Babel,
 a great breaking from the country of the
 Kasdites.
⁵⁵Because Yahweh is destroying Babel,
 eliminating the loud voice from it.
Their waves are rumbling like much water;
 the din of their voice gives out.
⁵⁶Because there is coming against it
 a destroyer, against Babel.
Its strong men will be captured;
 their bows will shatter.
Because Yahweh is a God of dealings;
 he really makes good.
⁵⁷I shall make its officials and its experts drunk,
 its governors and overseers and strong men.
They will sleep an everlasting sleep
 and not wake up (a declaration of the King,
 whose name is Yahweh of Armies).

In the interests of the living

⁵⁸Yahweh of Armies has said this:

Babel's wall, broad, will be totally levelled,
 its high gateways burned with fire.
Peoples will have toiled for emptiness,
 nations will have got weary for fire.

⁵⁹The word that Yirmeyahu the prophet ordered to Serayah ben Neriyyah son of Mahseyah when he went with Tsidqiyyahu king of Yehudah to Babel in the fourth year of his reign; Serayah was accommodation officer. ⁶⁰Yirmeyahu wrote down all the bad fortune that would come to Babel on a document, all these words that are written concerning Babel. ⁶¹Yirmeyahu said to Serayah, 'When you come to Babel, you're to see that you read out all these words. ⁶²And you're to say, "Yahweh, you yourself have spoken concerning this place that you'll cut it off, so that there won't be anyone living in it, human being or animal, because it's to be a great desolation permanently."

⁶³When you've finished reading out this document, you're to tie a stone to it and throw it into the middle of the Euphrates. ⁶⁴You're to say, "In this way Babel will sink and not rise up because of the bad fortune that I'm going to bring on it. They'll have got weary."'

As far as here it is the words of Yirmeyahu.

The horrifying coda

52 Tsidqiyyahu was twenty-one years of age when he began to reign and he reigned eleven years in Yerushalaim. His mother's name was Hamutal bat Yirmeyahu, from Libnah. ²He did what was bad in Yahweh's eyes in accordance with all that Yehoyaqim had done, ³because of the fact that Yahweh's anger was against Yerushalaim and against Yehudah until he threw them out of his presence.

Tsidqiyyahu rebelled against the king of Babel, ⁴and in the ninth year of his reign, in the tenth month, on the tenth of the month, Nebukadne'tstsar king of Babel came against Yerushalaim, he and his entire force. They camped against it and built blockades all round. ⁵The town came under siege until the eleventh year of King Tsidqiyyahu. ⁶In the fourth month, on the ninth of the month, the famine had become overwhelming in the town and there was no bread for the people of the country. ⁷The town broke open, and all the men of battle fled; they got out of the town in the night by way of the gateway between the double wall which was by the king's garden, while the Kasdites were all round the town.

They went by the steppe road, ⁸but the Kasdite force pursued after the king. They overtook Tsidqiyyahu in the Yeriho steppes when his entire force had scattered from him. ⁹They captured the king and took him up to the king of Babel at Riblah in the region of Hamat, and he announced rulings with him. ¹⁰The king of Babel slaughtered Tsidqiyyahu's sons before his eyes, and also slaughtered all the Yehudahite officials at Riblah. ¹¹Tsidqiyyahu's eyes he gouged out, and he bound him with copper chains. The king of Babel brought him to Babel and put him in the guard house until the day of his death.

Yirmeyahu horribly vindicated

¹²In the fifth month, on the tenth of the month (i.e. the nineteenth year of King Nebukadne'tstsar king of Babel), Nebuzar'adan the chief of the guards stood before the king of Babel in Yerushalaim ¹³and burned Yahweh's house, the king's house and all the houses in Yerushalaim. Every house of a big person he burned in fire. ¹⁴All the walls round Yerushalaim, the entire Kasdite force that was with the chief of the guards demolished. ¹⁵Some of the poorest elements of the people, and the rest of the people who remained in the town, and the people who had submitted (who had submitted to the king of Babel), and the rest of the horde, Nebuzar'adan the chief of the guards took into exile, ¹⁶but some of the poorest elements in the country the chief of the guards let remain as vinedressers and farmworkers.

¹⁷The copper pillars that belonged to Yahweh's house, and the stands and the copper sea that was in Yahweh's house, the Kasdites broke up. They carried all their copper to Babel. ¹⁸The buckets, the shovels, the snuffers, the ladles, the sprinklers and all the copper articles with which they ministered, they took. ¹⁹The basins, the pans, the sprinklers, the pots, the candelabra, the ladles, the bowls, whatever was of gold and whatever was of silver, the chief of the guards took. ²⁰The two pillars, the one sea and the twelve copper cattle that were under the stands, which Shelomoh [Solomon] made for Yahweh's house – there was no weighing the copper in all these articles. ²¹The pillars: the height of one pillar was nine metres; a line of six metres would go round it, and its thickness was four fingers, hollow, ²²with a copper capital on it; the height of the capital was one and a half metres, with a net with pomegranates on the capital all round, all of it copper; like these was the second pillar with pomegranates. ²³There were ninety-six pomegranates towards the wind: all the pomegranates were a hundred above the net all round.

Is it the end or is there hope?

²⁴The chief of the guards took Serayah the head priest, Tsephanyah the number two priest and the three keepers of the threshold, ²⁵and from the town he took a courtier who was appointee over the men of battle, and seven people from the heads who were before the king, who were found in the town, the secretary of the army officer who mustered the people of the country, and sixty individuals from the people of the country who were found inside the town. ²⁶Nebuzar'adan the chief of the guards took them and made them go to the king of Babel at Riblah. ²⁷The king of Babel struck them down and put them to death at Riblah, in the region of Hamat.

So Yehudah went into exile from upon its land.
²⁸This is the company that Nebukadre'tstsar exiled in the seventh year: 3,023 Yehudahites;
²⁹in Nebukadre'tstsar's eighteenth year: 832 people from Yerushalaim;
³⁰in Nebukadre'tstsar's twenty-third year, Nebuzar'adan the head of the guards exiled 745 Yehudahites.
All the people were 4,600.

³¹But in the thirty-seventh year of the exile of Yehoyakin king of Yehudah, in the twelfth month, on the twenty-fifth of the month, Ewil Merodak king of Babel, in the year he began to reign, lifted up the head of Yehoyakin king of Yehudah and got him out of the prison. ³²He spoke of good things with him, gave him his seat above the seat of the kings who were with him in Babel ³³and changed his prison clothes. He ate a meal before him regularly for all the days of his life, ³⁴and his provision was given him as a regular provision from the king of Babel, a day's allocation on its day, until the day of his death, for all the days of his life.

Lamentations

These five prayer-poems grieve over a great disaster that has happened to Yerushalaim. The poems presumably relate to the destruction of Jerusalem by Nebuchadnezzar in 587 BC, though the book doesn't make any concrete references that make that link explicit. But if that disaster is the one Lamentations refers to, it is appropriate that the book thus follows the account of this event in Jeremiah. Tradition identifies Jeremiah as the author, though the poems themselves are anonymous.

Each poem comprises twenty-two verses (except the middle one, with sixty-six), which is the number of letters in the Hebrew alphabet, and the first four poems are alphabetical – that is, the verses begin with the successive letters of the alphabet. They express grief, protest and prayer from A to Z.

The Hebrew Bible has the books of the Bible in a different order from that in the English Bible (which follows the order in the Greek translation of the Bible). The Hebrew Bible groups Lamentations with some other shorter books (Song of Songs, Ruth, Ecclesiastes and Esther) that are used once a year in Jewish communities. Lamentations is used on the sixth day of the month Ab, which overlaps with July–August, to mark the anniversary of the fall of Jerusalem in 587 and in AD 70.

The town bereft

1 Oh! – the town sits alone
     that abounded with a people.
She became like a widow,
   she who was great among the nations.
She who was a queen among the provinces
   became a slave.
²She cries and cries in the night;
   there are tears on her cheeks.
She has no comforter
   from all her allies.
All her friends broke faith with her;
   they became enemies to her.
³Yehudah went into exile after humbling
   and a great amount of servitude.
When she went to live among the nations
   she didn't find a settled place.
All her pursuers caught up with her
   amid her pressures.
⁴The roads to Tsiyyon [Zion] are mourning,
   because of the lack of people coming for the set times.
All her gateways are desolate,
   her priests are groaning.
Her girls are suffering,
   and her – it's hard for her.
⁵Her adversaries became her head,
   her enemies are at peace.
Because Yahweh made her suffer
   on account of the great number of her rebellions.
Her infants went into captivity
   before the adversary.
⁶From Miss Tsiyyon
   all her glory went away.
Her officials became like deer
   that had found no pasture.
They walked without energy
   before the pursuer.
⁷Yerushalaim has been mindful,
   in her days of humbling and wandering,
Of all the desirable things she had,
   which there were from days before.
When her people fell into the hand of the adversary
   and there was no one helping her,
The adversaries saw her,
   made fun of her coming to an end.
⁸Yerushalaim did wrong and did wrong;
   therefore she became taboo.
All the people who had honoured her treated her
     as wretched
   because they saw her exposure.
Yes, she groaned
   and turned backwards.
⁹Though her uncleanness was in her skirts,
   she hadn't been mindful of her future.
She went down in extraordinary ways;
   she had no comforter.
'Yahweh, look at my humbling,
   because the enemy has got big.'
¹⁰The adversary laid his hand
   on all her desirable things.
Because she saw nations
   that came into her sanctuary,
Who you ordered should not come
   into your congregation.
¹¹All her people are groaning,
   looking for bread.
They have given their desirable things
   for food to bring life back.
'Look, Yahweh, heed,
   because I've become wretched.'

It's nothing to you who pass by, is it?

¹²Though it's nothing to you, all you who pass
     along the road,
   heed and look.
Is there any pain like my pain,
   which was dealt out to me,
When Yahweh made me suffer
   on the day of his angry blazing?
¹³From on high he sent fire,
   into my bones, and it held sway over them.
He spread a net for my feet;
   he turned me backwards.
He made me a desolation,
   faint all day long.
¹⁴The yoke of my rebellions was bound on,
   they interweave by his hand.
They came up on to my neck;
   he made my energy collapse.
The Lord gave me
   into the hands of people before whom I cannot stand.
¹⁵The Lord within me threw aside
   all my sturdy men.
He called for a set time against me
   to break my young men.
The Lord trod in a press
   young Miss Yehudah.
¹⁶'On account of these things I'm crying;
   both my eyes are going down with water.

Because a comforter is far from me,
   someone bringing my life back.
My children have become desolate,
   because an enemy was strong.'
[17]Tsiyyon spread out her hands;
   she has no comforter.
Yahweh ordered to Ya'aqob [Jacob]
   the people round him as his adversaries.
Yerushalaim became
   something taboo among them.
[18]'Yahweh is in the right,
   because I rebelled against his bidding.
Listen, please, all you peoples,
   see my pain.
My girls and my young men
   went into captivity.
[19]I called to my friends;
   those people beguiled me.
My priests and my elders
   perished in the town,
When they looked for food for themselves
   so they might bring their life back.
[20]See, Yahweh, how there was pressure on me;
   my insides churned.
My heart turned over within me,
   because I had rebelled and rebelled.
Outside, the sword bereaved;
   at home, very death.
[21]People heard that I was groaning;
   I had no comforter.
When all my enemies heard of my bad fortune,
      they were glad
   that you yourself had acted.
You brought about the day you called for –
   they should be like me.
[22]All their bad action should come before you –
   deal with them,
As you dealt with me
   on account of all my rebellions.
Because my groans are many,
   and my heart is faint.'

Anger

2 Oh! – with his anger the Lord clouds over
   Miss Tsiyyon.
He threw down Yisra'el's glory
   from the heavens to the earth.
He was not mindful of his footstool
   on his day of anger.
[2]The Lord swallowed up all Ya'aqob's pastures
   and didn't spare.
In his fury he tore down
   Miss Yehudah's fortifications.
He brought right to the earth, made ordinary,
   the kingdom and its officials.
[3]He cut off every horn of Yisra'el
   in his angry blazing.
He turned backwards his right hand
   from before the enemy.
He burned up against Ya'aqob like a flaming fire
   consuming all round.
[4]He directed his bow as an enemy,
   took his stand with his right hand as an
      adversary.
He killed everyone
   who was desirable to the eye.
In Miss Tsiyyon's tent
   he poured out his wrath like fire.
[5]The Lord became like an enemy;
   he swallowed up Yisra'el.
He swallowed up all her citadels,
   devastated her fortifications.
He made great in Miss Yehudah
   mourning and moaning.
[6]He violated his shelter like a garden,
   destroyed his set place.
Yahweh caused set time and sabbath
   to be put out of mind in Tsiyyon.
In his angry condemnation he spurned
   king and priest.
[7]The Lord rejected his altar,
   abandoned his sanctuary.
He gave over the walls of her citadels
   into the enemy's hand.
They gave voice in Yahweh's house
   as on the day when it was a set occasion.
[8]Yahweh intended to devastate
   Miss Tsiyyon's wall.
He stretched out a line,
   he didn't turn back his hand from swallowing
      up.
He made rampart and wall mourn;
   together they languished.
[9]Her gateways sank into the earth;
   he obliterated and broke up her bars.
Her king and her officials are among the nations;
   there is no instruction.
Her prophets, too, found
   no vision from Yahweh.
[10]Miss Tsiyyon's elders
   sit on the earth, they're silent.

They've taken up earth on their head,
  they've wrapped on sack.
Yerushalaim's girls
  have lowered their head to the ground.
¹¹My eyes are spent with tears,
  my insides churn.
My heart has poured out to the earth
  on account of the breaking of my dear people,
While infant and suckling faint
  in the township's squares.
¹²To their mothers they say,
  'Where are grain and wine?',
As they faint like someone run through
  in the town's squares,
As their life pours out
  in their mothers' arms.

Is this the town called 'The Joy of All the Earth'?

¹³What can I avow, what can I liken to you,
  Miss Yerushalaim?
What can I compare with you so I may comfort you,
  fair Miss Tsiyyon?
Because your breaking is as big as the sea;
  who can heal you?
¹⁴Your prophets beheld for you
  things that were empty and arid.
They didn't reveal your waywardness
  so as to restore your fortunes.
They beheld for you
  empty prophecies and seductions.
¹⁵All the people who pass your way
  have clapped the palms of their hands at you.
They've whistled and shaken their head
  at Miss Yerushalaim:
'Is this the town of which they used to say,
  "Complete in beauty, a joy to the entire earth"?'
¹⁶Against you all your enemies
  have opened their mouth wide.
They've whistled and ground their teeth,
  they've said, 'We've swallowed her up.
Indeed this is the day that we hoped for;
  we've found it, we've seen it.'
¹⁷Yahweh did what he schemed,
  he accomplished his word,
Which he ordered long ago;
  he tore down and didn't spare.
He let an enemy rejoice over you,
  exalted the horn of your adversaries.

¹⁸Their heart cried out to the Lord;
  Miss Tsiyyon's wall,
Make your tears go down like a wadi,
  day and night.
Don't give yourself respite;
  your dear eye must not stop.
¹⁹Get up, resound at night,
  at the beginning of the watches.
Pour out your heart like water
  in front of the presence of the Lord.
Lift up the palms of your hands to him
  for the life of your infants,
Who faint with hunger
  at the top of all the streets.
²⁰Look, Yahweh, heed
  the one with whom you've dealt like this.
Do women eat their fruit,
  the babies they dandle?
Are priest and prophet killed
  in the Lord's sanctuary?
²¹Young person and old
  lay on the ground in the streets.
My girls and my young men
  fell by the sword.
You killed them on your day of anger,
  you slaughtered them, you didn't spare.
²²You call (as on the day of a set occasion) –
  for terrors for me from all round.
On Yahweh's day of anger
  there was no one escaping or surviving.
Those whom I dandled and raised –
  my enemy finished them off.

The man who saw humbling

3 I am the man who saw humbling,
  by his furious club.
²He drove me and made me go
  in darkness and not light.
³Yes, against me
  repeatedly he'd turn his hand all day long.
⁴He wore away my flesh and my skin,
  he broke my bones.
⁵He built up against me and surrounded me
  with poison and weariness.
⁶He made me live in darkness,
  like those long dead.
⁷He walled me in and I couldn't get out,
  he made my chains heavy.
⁸Even when I'd cry out and call for help,
  he shut out my plea.

⁹He walled in my ways with stonework,
   twisted my paths.
¹⁰He was a lurking bear to me,
   a lion in hiding.
¹¹He diverted my ways and mangled me,
   made me desolate.
¹²He directed his bow and set me up
   as the target for his arrow.
¹³He made the shafts from his quiver
   come into my inner being.
¹⁴I became an object of fun to all my people,
   their song all day long.
¹⁵He filled me with bitter herbs,
   saturated me with vinegar.
¹⁶He broke my teeth on the gravel,
   bent me down in the ashes.
¹⁷My soul gave up on well-being,
   I forgot good things.
¹⁸I said, 'My distinction has perished,
   and my waiting for something from Yahweh.'
¹⁹To be mindful of my humbling and my wandering
   was vinegar and poison.
²⁰My spirit is mindful, so mindful,
   and it bows down within me.

They are new every morning

²¹This I bring back to my mind,
   therefore I shall wait:
²²Yahweh's acts of commitment, that we're not finished,
   that his compassion isn't ended.
²³They're new each morning;
   his truthfulness is great.
²⁴'Yahweh is my share', my entire being said;
   therefore I shall wait for him.
²⁵Yahweh is good to people who hope in him,
   to the person who enquires of him.
²⁶It's good that one waits and keeps still
   for Yahweh's deliverance.
²⁷It's good for a man
   that he carries a yoke in his youth.
²⁸He should sit alone and be still
   when he's put it on him.
²⁹He should put his mouth in the dirt;
   perhaps there's hope.
³⁰He should give his jaw to the one who strikes him down,
   become full of reviling.
³¹Because the Lord
   doesn't reject permanently.
³²Rather he brings suffering, but has compassion,
   in the greatness of his acts of commitment.
³³Because it's not from his heart that he humbles
   and brings suffering to human beings,
³⁴Crushing under his feet
   all earth's prisoners,
³⁵Turning aside the exercise of authority for a man
   in front of the presence of the One on High,
³⁶Putting someone in the wrong in his argument
   when the Lord didn't look.
³⁷Who is it who said and it happened,
   when the Lord didn't order?
³⁸From the mouth of the One on High
   do not the bad things and the good things issue?
³⁹Of what should a living person complain,
   a man in connection with his wrongdoings?
⁴⁰Let's search out and examine our ways
   and turn back to Yahweh.
⁴¹Let's lift up our mind with the palms of our hands
   to God in the heavens.
⁴²When we ourselves rebelled and defied,
   you yourself didn't pardon.
⁴³You wrapped yourself in anger and pursued us,
   you killed and didn't spare.
⁴⁴You wrapped yourself in your cloud
   so that a plea didn't pass through.

Yahweh's shadow side

⁴⁵You make us trash and refuse
   among the peoples.
⁴⁶Against us all our enemies
   have opened their mouth wide.
⁴⁷Terror and trap have become ours,
   ruin and breaking.
⁴⁸My eye flows with streams of water
   because of the breaking of my fair people.
⁴⁹My eye has poured and won't stop,
   without respite,
⁵⁰Until Yahweh looks down
   and sees from the heavens.
⁵¹My eye has dealt hard to my entire being
   because of all the girls in my town.
⁵²My enemies hunted me relentlessly
   like a bird for no reason.
⁵³They put an end to my life in a pit
   and threw stones at me.
⁵⁴Water flowed over my head;
   I said, 'I'm lost.'

⁵⁵I called on your name, Yahweh,
　　from the deepest pit.
⁵⁶You listened to my voice, 'Don't close your ear
　　concerning my relief, to my cry for help.'
⁵⁷You came near on the day when I would call on
　　　you;
　　you said, 'Don't be afraid.'
⁵⁸You pressed the arguments for me, Lord,
　　you restored my life.
⁵⁹You've seen the wrong done to me, Yahweh:
　　exercise authority with a ruling for me.
⁶⁰You've seen all their redress,
　　all their intentions for me,
⁶¹You've listened to their reviling, Yahweh,
　　all their intentions against me,
⁶²The lips of the people who rise up against me
　　and their murmuring against me all day long.
⁶³Look at them sitting and rising;
　　I'm their song.
⁶⁴Give back their dealings to them, Yahweh,
　　in accordance with the action of their hands.
⁶⁵May you give them a covering over their mind,
　　your vow for them.
⁶⁶May you pursue them in anger and annihilate them
　　from under Yahweh's heavens.

What happened to loving mothers

4 Oh! – gold tarnishes,
　　fine gold changes.
Sacred stones pour out
　　at the top of every street.
²Tsiyyon's precious children,
　　worth their weight in pure gold –
Oh, they're thought of like clay vessels,
　　a potter's handiwork.
³Even jackals offer the breast,
　　nurse their young.
My dear people has become cruel,
　　like ostriches in the wilderness.
⁴The suckling's tongue sticks
　　to the roof of its mouth, for thirst.
Infants ask for bread;
　　there's no one offering it to them.
⁵People who ate gourmet food
　　are desolate in the streets.
People brought up in purple
　　cling to rubbish heaps.
⁶The waywardness of my dear people had become
　　　bigger
　　than the wrongdoing of Sedom [Sodom],

Which was overturned in a moment,
　　though hands didn't whirl at it.
⁷Her consecrated people were purer than snow,
　　whiter than milk.
Their frame was redder than coral,
　　their body was sapphire.
⁸Their appearance became blacker than soot;
　　they weren't recognized in the streets.
Their skin shrivelled on their frame;
　　it became dry like wood.
⁹The people run through by the sword were better
　　　off
　　than the people run through by famine,
Those who slip away, thrust through,
　　for lack of the produce of the field.
¹⁰The hands of compassionate women
　　cooked their children.
They became food for them
　　through the breaking of my dear people.
¹¹Yahweh finished up his wrath,
　　poured out his angry blazing.
He kindled a fire in Tsiyyon;
　　it consumed its foundations.

Yahweh's anointed captured

¹²The kings of the earth didn't believe,
　　or all the world's inhabitants,
That adversary or enemy would come
　　through Yerushalaim's gates.
¹³Because of her prophets' wrongdoings,
　　her priests' wayward acts,
People who shed within her
　　the blood of the faithful,
¹⁴They wandered blind through the streets,
　　they were defiled with blood,
Without people being able
　　to touch their clothes.
¹⁵'Go away, polluted', they called to them,
　　'Go away, go away, don't touch.'
When they fled and wandered, people said among
　　　the nations,
　　'They must be resident no longer.'
¹⁶Yahweh's presence divided them up,
　　he no longer looks to them.
They didn't honour the face of priests,
　　they didn't show favour to elders.
¹⁷Our eyes still spend themselves
　　looking for help for ourselves, in vain.
On our watchtowers we watched
　　for a nation that wouldn't deliver.

¹⁸People hounded our steps
   so that we didn't walk in our squares.
Our end was near, our days were full,
   because our end had come.
¹⁹Our pursuers became swifter
   than the eagles in the heavens.
They chased us on the mountains,
   they lay in wait for us in the wilderness.
²⁰The breath of our lungs, Yahweh's anointed,
   was captured in their traps,
The one of whom we had said, 'In his shade
   we will live among the nations.'
²¹Celebrate and rejoice, Miss Edom,
   you who live in the country of Uts.
To you, too, the chalice will pass;
   you'll get drunk and you'll strip naked.
²²Your waywardness is complete, Miss Tsiyyon;
   he will no longer exile you.
He's attending to your waywardness, Miss Edom;
   he's exposing your wrongdoings.

Have you totally rejected us?

5 Be mindful, Yahweh, of what happened to us;
   look, and see our reviling.
²Our domain was turned over to strangers,
   our homes to foreigners.
³We became orphans with no father,
   our mothers actual widows.
⁴We drank our water for money;
   our wood comes for payment.
⁵We were pursued, at our neck;
   we were weary, but there was no settling down for us.
⁶We've put out our hand to Misrayim [Egypt],
   to Ashshur to get a fill of bread.
⁷Our parents did wrong and are no more,
   and we were the ones who carried their wayward acts.
⁸Servants have ruled over us;
   there's no one freeing us from their hand.
⁹It's at the risk of our lives that we bring our bread,
   because of the sword in the wilderness.
¹⁰Our skin was as hot as an oven,
   because of the fever of famine.
¹¹They humbled women in Tsiyyon,
   girls in Yehudah's towns.
¹²Officials were hung up by their hand;
   elders weren't respected.
¹³Young men carried a millstone,
   boys collapsed with wood.
¹⁴Elders turned back from the gate,
   young men from their music.
¹⁵The joy of our heart ceased;
   our dancing was turned to mourning.
¹⁶The crown on our head fell;
   oh, alas for us, because we did wrong.
¹⁷Because of this, our heart has become sick,
   because of these things, our eyes become dark,
¹⁸Because of Mount Tsiyyon, which is desolate;
   jackals have walked about on it.
¹⁹You, Yahweh, sit permanently,
   your throne endures through the generations.
²⁰Why do you put us out of mind permanently,
   abandon us for length of days?
²¹Bring us back to yourself, Yahweh, so we may come back;
   make our days new, as before.
²²But you have totally rejected us,
   you have been utterly furious with us.

Ezekiel

Ezekiel [Yehezqe'l] was a member of the priestly clan in Israel, but before he was old enough to be a priest he was taken off into exile in Babylon with other priestly families in 597 BC. In Babylon he was given a vision of Yahweh and was summoned to be a prophet there to the exiles. The beginning of his prophetic work thus coincided with the last years of Jeremiah's prophetic work. Like Jeremiah, his messages brought much critique of the Jerusalem community and many warnings about disaster coming to it, but also brought promises of a more positive future the other side of the trouble. But whereas Jeremiah delivered the warnings and the promises in Jerusalem itself, Ezekiel delivered his warnings and promises in Babylon. The reason was that the future of Jerusalem was of decisive importance to people who had been taken off from there into exile. They were inclined to think that they would soon be going back home. Yahweh needs to get them to see that they will not soon be going home, because the conduct of priests, prophets, other leaders and ordinary people back home is such (perhaps worse than that of the people in exile) that Yahweh has to bring more chastisement upon them. On the other hand, when the axe has fallen, it will be possible for restoration to happen.

The book of Ezekiel divides neatly in accordance with this profile.

- In chapters 1—3 Ezekiel gives us an account of the vision Yahweh gave him that commissioned him as a lookout-prophet. It is a great vision of Yahweh himself, whose appearing in Babylon indicated that he had not abandoned the people who had been taken off into exile.
- In chapters 4—24 Ezekiel relates a series of visions of what is going on in Jerusalem. He portrays the goings on in Jerusalem as vividly as if he were actually there. No doubt his envisioning was facilitated by the knowledge of things in Jerusalem that he would have gained before he was taken into exile. He portrays the pagan practices that characterized the worship in the Jerusalem temple and the oppressive practices that characterized the life of the city, and he acts out the fall of the city and the exile of its inhabitants. His rhetoric and his acting out are exotic, picturesque, horrifying and not for the squeamish. Everything is subordinate to breaking through the consciousness of his audience.
- In chapters 25—32 Ezekiel begins the transition to the hopeful half of the book. Chapter 24 has referred to the beginning of the city's final siege, whose success (from the Babylonians' perspective) will open up the way to a more hopeful message. The transition lies in prophecies about Judah's neighbours who were often its adversaries (Ammon, Moab, Edom and Philistia), about the great regional trading nation Tyre, and about the nation that Judah often relied on as an ally, Egypt.
- Chapters 33—48 constitute Yahweh's direct promises about Judah's future. They begin with a renewed summons to Ezekiel to act as a watchman-prophet and with the arrival in Babylon of the news that Jerusalem has fallen. Yahweh now commissions Ezekiel to promise Israel's renewal. The promises constitute a series of declarations that Yahweh will take up and be faithful to his long-standing commitments. The people will be properly shepherded, by Yahweh and by a new David. Incursions from a people such as Edom will be stopped and the land that such peoples occupied will be Israel's again. The exiles will be brought back, cleansed and given a new spirit. The nation that feels reduced to dry bones will be brought back to life. The divided people will become one. Renewed threats from strange northern peoples will lead to their elimination. A remarkable new temple will be built and Yahweh will once again dwell there. The country itself will be physically transformed and reallocated. A river will flow from the temple to bring fruitfulness to hostile parts of the country. The city will be renamed 'Yahweh-Is-There'. This last section of the book makes clear that we should not be literalistic in interpreting Ezekiel, and this consideration undermines any suggestion that Ezekiel is referring to Middle Eastern events in our own time or that he is indicating that we should expect or plan for the rebuilding of the Jerusalem temple. But neither should we underestimate the wonder of what Yahweh promises.

God appears in Babel

1 In the thirtieth year, in the fourth, on the fifth of the month, when I was among the exile community by the River Kebar, the heavens opened and I saw a great appearance of God. ²On the fifth of the month (it was the fifth year of King Yoyakin's exile), ³Yahweh's word came to Yehezqe'l ben Buzi, the priest, in the country of the Kasdites by the River Kebar. Yahweh's hand came on him there.

⁴I saw: there, a hurricane wind came from the north, a great cloud, with fire consuming itself, with its brightness all round, with a very gleam of electrum from inside it, from inside the fire, ⁵and from inside it the form of four creatures. This was their appearance. They had human form, ⁶but they had four faces each and four wings each. ⁷Their feet: a straight foot, but the sole of their feet was like the sole of a calf's foot, and they were sparkling like the gleam of burnished copper. ⁸Human hands were under their wings on their four quarters.

Their faces and their wings belonging to the four of them: ⁹their wings touched each other. They wouldn't turn as they went; they'd go, each in the direction of its face. ¹⁰The form of their faces: a human face, but the four of them had a lion's face on the right, and the four of them had an ox's face on the left, and the four of them had an eagle's face. ¹¹So their faces. Their wings were stretching upwards, two belonging to each touching each, and two covering its body. ¹²They'd go each in the direction of its face; to wherever the wind was to go, they'd go. They wouldn't turn as they went.

¹³So the form of the creatures. Their appearance was very coals of fire burning, the very appearance of torches. It was going about between the creatures. The fire had a brightness, and from the fire lightning was coming out. ¹⁴The creatures were running and coming back, the very appearance of lightning-flashes.

The creatures powering the chariot

¹⁵I looked at the creatures. There, one wheel on the earth beside the creatures with its four faces. ¹⁶The wheels' appearance and their construction: the very gleam of topaz. The form of each of the four of them: their appearance and their construction were like a wheel inside a wheel. ¹⁷When they went, they'd go in the direction of their four quarters; they wouldn't turn as they went. ¹⁸Their rims were high and awe-inspiring. Their rims were full of eyes all round, belonging to the four of them. ¹⁹When the creatures went, the wheels would go, beside them. When the creatures lifted above the earth, the wheels lifted. ²⁰Wherever the wind was to go, they'd go there, with the wind going. The wheels would lift alongside them, because the creature's spirit was in the wheels. ²¹When they went, they'd go; when they stopped, they'd stop; when they lifted from on the earth, the wheels would lift alongside them, because the creature's spirit was in the wheels.

²²A form was above the creature's heads, a platform, the very gleam of crystal, awe-inspiring, spread out over their heads, above. ²³Under the platform their wings were straight towards each other. Each had two covering their bodies on one side, and each had two covering on the other side. ²⁴I heard the sound of their wings, the very sound of much water, the very sound of Shadday, when they went, the sound of a tumult, the very sound of an army. When they stopped, they'd relax their wings.

²⁵There was a sound above the platform that was over their head (when they stopped, they'd relax their wings). ²⁶Above the platform that was over their head was the very appearance of sapphire, the form of a throne, and above the form of the throne a form that was a very human appearance on it, above.

A rebellious household

²⁷I saw the very gleam of electrum, the very appearance of fire within it all round, from the appearance of his hips upwards and from the appearance of his hips downwards I saw the very appearance of fire. His brightness was all round. ²⁸The very appearance of the bow that comes in the cloud on a rainy day, such was the appearance of the brightness all round. That was the appearance of the form of Yahweh's splendour.

I saw it and fell on my face, and I heard a voice speaking.

2 He said to me, 'Young man, stand on your feet, so I may speak with you.' ²A wind came into me as he spoke to me. It stood me on my feet and I listened to him speaking to me.

³He said to me, 'Young man, I'm sending you to the Yisra'elites, nations that rebel, who've rebelled against me. They and their ancestors have defied me right up to this day. ⁴The descendants are tough-faced and strong-minded. I'm sending you to them, and you're to say to them, "The Lord Yahweh has said this." ⁵Whether they listen or refuse (because they're a rebellious household), they will acknowledge that a prophet's been among them. ⁶So you, young man, don't be afraid of them and don't be afraid of their words, when thistles and thorns are with you and you're living with scorpions. Don't be afraid of their words, don't shatter because of them, because they're a rebellious household. ⁷You're to speak my words to them whether they listen, or whether they refuse because they're rebellious. ⁸You, young man, listen to what I'm speaking to you. Don't become rebellious like the rebellious household. Open your mouth and eat what I'm going to give you.'

⁹I saw: there, a hand put out to me, and there, in it a document scroll. ¹⁰He spread it out before me. It was written on front and back. Laments, muttering and groaning were written on it.

Strong-headed and tough-minded

3 He said to me, 'Young man, eat what you find. Eat this scroll, and go speak to Yisra'el's household.' ²I opened my mouth and he got me to eat this scroll. ³He said to me, 'Young man, get your stomach to eat, fill your insides with this scroll that I'm giving you.' I ate, and in my mouth it became like syrup for sweetness.

⁴He said to me, 'Young man, go, come to Yisra'el's household and speak with my words to them. ⁵Because not to a people unfathomable of speech and difficult of language – you're sent to Yisra'el's household, ⁶not to many peoples unfathomable of speech and difficult of language whose words you can't listen to. If I didn't send you to them . . .

Those people would listen to you. ⁷But Yisra'el's household won't be willing to listen to you, because they're not willing to listen to me, because Yisra'el's entire household are strong-headed and tough-minded. ⁸There, I'm making your face strong over against their face and your head tough over against their head. ⁹Like a mineral harder than flint I'm making your head. You will not be afraid of them, you will not shatter before them, because they're a rebellious household.'

¹⁰Then he said to me, 'Young man, receive into your mind all my words that I speak to you. Listen with your ears ¹¹and go, come to the exile community, to the members of your people, and speak to them. Say to them, "The Lord Yahweh has said this", whether they listen or refuse.'

¹²Then a wind lifted me, and I heard behind me a great quaking sound: 'Yahweh's splendour be blessed from his place', ¹³and the sound of the creatures' wings beating against each other and the sound of the wheels alongside them: a great quaking sound. ¹⁴When a wind lifted me and took me, I went, bitter and in wrath of my spirit, with Yahweh's hand strong on me.

I shall look for his blood from your hand

¹⁵I came to the exile community at Tel Abib living by the River Kebar. I lived where they were living, lived there desolate for seven days, ¹⁶and at the end of the seven days Yahweh's word came to me: ¹⁷'Young man, I'm making you a lookout for Yisra'el's household. You're to listen to the word from my mouth and warn them from me.

¹⁸When I say about the faithless person, "You will definitely die", and you don't warn him and don't speak to warn the faithless person from his faithless way, to keep him alive: he, the faithless person, will die for his waywardness, but I shall look for his blood from your hand. ¹⁹But you – when you warn the faithless person and he doesn't turn back from his faithlessness, from his faithless way: he will die for his waywardness, but you will have saved your life.

²⁰And when a faithful person turns back from his faithfulness and does what is evil and I put an obstacle before him, he will die, because you didn't warn him. For his

wrongdoing he will die, and his faithful acts that he has done won't be borne in mind, but I shall look for his blood from your hand. ²¹But you, when you warn him (the faithful person) that the faithful person shouldn't do wrong, and he doesn't do wrong, he will definitely live because he let himself be warned, and you yourself will have saved your life.'

²²Yahweh's hand came on me there and he said to me, 'Set off, go out to the valley, and I shall speak with you there.' ²³So I set off and went out to the valley, and there – Yahweh's splendour was standing there, like the splendour that I saw at the River Kebar. I fell on my face, ²⁴ᵃbut a wind came into me and stood me up on my feet.

Acting out a siege

²⁴ᵇHe spoke with me and said to me, 'Come, shut yourself inside your house. ²⁵You, young man, there – they're putting ropes on you and tying you up with them. You're not to go out among them. ²⁶I shall make your tongue stick to your palate and you'll be dumb. To them, you won't be someone who reproves, because they're a rebellious household. ²⁷But when I speak with you, I shall open your mouth and you will say to them, "The Lord Yahweh has said this." The one who listens may listen and the one who refuses may refuse, because they're a rebellious household.

4 You, young man, get yourself a brick, put it before you, and engrave a town on it: Yerushalaim. ²Prepare a siege against it. Build a tower against it. Heap up a ramp against it. Make a camp against it. Set up battering rams against it all round. ³And you, get yourself an iron plate and place it as an iron wall between you and the town, and set your face towards it. It will be under siege; you're to lay siege against it. It will be a sign for Yisra'el's household.

⁴You yourself, lie on your left side and on it put the waywardness of Yisra'el's household. The number of the days that you lie on it, you will carry their waywardness. ⁵I myself am giving you the years of their waywardness, in number 390 days; you will carry the waywardness of Yisra'el's household. ⁶You will finish these, then lie on your right side, a second time, and carry the waywardness of Yehudah's household. Forty days, a day for each year, I'm giving you.

Defiled bread

⁷And towards Yerushalaim's siege you're to set your face and your bared arm, and prophesy against it. ⁸There, I'm putting ropes on you, and you aren't to turn from side to side until you've finished your days of siege. ⁹You're to get yourself wheat, barley, beans, lentils, millet and spelt, put them into a jar and make them into bread for yourself. For the number of days that you're lying on your side, 390 days, you're to eat it.

¹⁰The food that you eat, by weight, twenty sheqels a day, you're to eat at the regular times, ¹¹and water by measure you're to drink, a sixth of a gallon you're to drink at the regular times. ¹²You're to eat it as a barley cake. Cook it on human excrement in their sight.' ¹³Yahweh said, 'In this way the Yisra'elites will eat their bread, defiled, among the nations where I'm driving them.'

¹⁴I said, 'Oh, Lord Yahweh, here, my person hasn't been defiled. I haven't eaten anything found dead or torn by an animal, from my youth until now. Impure meat hasn't come into my mouth.' ¹⁵So he said to me, 'See, I'm going to give you cattle dung instead of human excrement. You can make your bread on that.' ¹⁶But he said to me, 'Young man, here am I, I'm going to break the bread supply in Yerushalaim. They will eat bread by weight in anxiety, and drink water by measure in desolation, ¹⁷so that they run out of bread and water and are desolate in relation to one another, and waste away because of their waywardness.'

Among the nations

5 'You, young man, get yourself a sharp sword. You're to get it for yourself as a barber's razor and pass it over your head and over your beard. Get yourself weighing scales and divide them [the hairs]. ²You're to burn a third in fire inside the town when the days of the siege are fulfilled. Take a third and strike down all round it with the sword. And scatter a third to the wind; I shall draw a sword after them. ³But you're to get from there a few and bind them into the folds of your clothes. ⁴Get some of them again and throw them into the middle of the fire. Burn them in the fire. From this a fire will go out against the entire household of Yisra'el.'

⁵The Lord Yahweh said this: 'This Yerushalaim I put among the nations, with countries round it. ⁶But it rebelled against my rulings with more faithlessness than the nations, and against my laws more than the countries round it. Because people rejected my rulings, and my laws – they didn't walk by them.'

⁷Therefore the Lord Yahweh said this: 'Since you've been more turbulent than the nations that are round you – you haven't walked by my laws, you haven't acted on my rulings and you haven't acted in accordance with the rulings of the nations that are round you'; ⁸therefore the Lord Yahweh said this: 'Here am I over against you, yes, I myself. I shall act on rulings among you before the eyes of the nations. ⁹I shall do in you what I haven't done and the like of which I won't do again, on account of all your offensive practices.

¹⁰Therefore within you parents will eat children and children will eat their parents. I shall execute acts of authority against you and scatter your remainder to every wind. ¹¹Therefore as I live (the Lord Yahweh's declaration) if I don't, because you defiled my sanctuary with all your abominations and all your offensive practices – yes, I myself will shave you, my eye won't spare you, and I myself won't pity you. ¹²A third of you will die in an epidemic or be finished off through famine within you. A third will fall by the sword all round you. And a third I shall scatter to every wind, and draw a sword after them.

About intolerance

¹³So my anger will finish itself up and I shall set down my wrath on them. I shall find relief, and they will acknowledge that I, Yahweh, have spoken in my passion, when I've finished up my wrath against them. ¹⁴I shall make you a waste and an object of reviling among the nations that are round you, in the sight of everyone passing by. ¹⁵It will be a basis for reviling and ridicule, for discipline and desolation, to the nations that are round you, when I execute acts of authority against you in anger, in wrath and in wrathful reproofs. I, Yahweh, have spoken.

¹⁶When I send off the bad arrows of famine on the people who were due for devastating, which I shall send off to devastate you, I shall add to the famine upon you and break the bread supply for you. ¹⁷I shall send off against you famine and bad creatures, and they will bereave you; epidemic and bloodshed will pass through you, and I shall bring the sword against you. I, Yahweh, have spoken.'

6 Yahweh's word came to me: ²'Young man, set your face towards Yisra'el's mountains and prophesy towards them. ³You're to say, "Yisra'el's mountains, listen to the Lord Yahweh's word. The Lord Yahweh said this to the mountains and to the hills, to the canyons and to the ravines: 'Here am I, I'm going to bring a sword against you, and I shall obliterate your shrines. ⁴Your altars will become desolate, your incense stands broken. I shall make those of you who are run through fall before their lumps. ⁵I shall put the Yisra'elites' corpses before their lumps and scatter your bones round your altars ⁶in all your settlements. The towns will be laid waste and the shrines desolate, in order that your altars may be laid waste and may make restitution, your lumps break and cease, your incense stands be cut down and what you've made be wiped out, ⁷and the person who is run through may fall among you. And you will acknowledge that I am Yahweh.

I shall let some be left

⁸But I shall let some be left. When you have people who have escaped the sword among the nations, when you're scattered among the countries, ⁹those of you who escape will be mindful of me among the nations where they've been taken captive, that I've been broken with their whorish mind that turned away from me and with their eyes whoring after their lumps. They'll feel a loathing towards their own selves concerning the bad things that they've done, regarding all their offensive practices. ¹⁰And they will acknowledge that I am Yahweh. Not for

nothing did I speak about bringing all this bad fortune to them.'

¹¹The Lord Yahweh said this: 'Clap with the palm of your hand, stamp with your foot. Say, "Aagh" about all the offensive bad practices of Yisra'el's household, who will fall by sword, by famine and by epidemic. ¹²The person who's far away will die by the epidemic, the one who's near will fall by the sword, and the one who remains and is preserved will die by the famine. I shall finish up my wrath on them. ¹³And you will acknowledge that I am Yahweh when those of them who are run through are among their lumps round their altars towards every high hill, on all the tops of the mountains, under every verdant tree and under every leafy oak, the site where they presented a pleasing fragrance to all their lumps. ¹⁴I shall stretch out my hand against them and make the country desolation and devastation, from the wilderness to Diblah, in all their settlements. And they will acknowledge that I am Yahweh."'

The club has blossomed

7 Yahweh's word came to me: ²'You, young man – the Lord Yahweh has said this to Yisra'el's land: "An end! The end is coming upon the four corners of the country. ³The end is now upon you. I shall send off my anger against you, and I shall exercise authority over you in accordance with your ways. I shall put all your offensive practices upon you. ⁴My eye won't spare you, I shall not have pity, because I shall put upon you your ways and your offensive practices that are within you. And you will acknowledge that I am Yahweh."'

⁵The Lord Yahweh said this: 'A singular bad event, a bad event – there, it's coming. ⁶An end is coming, it's coming. The end is rousing itself against you, there, it's coming. ⁷The doom is coming upon you, you who inhabit the country. The time is coming. The day is near, tumult not cheering on the mountains. ⁸Now it's near.

I shall pour out my wrath on you and finish up my anger against you. I shall exercise authority over you in accordance with your ways, and put all your offensive practices upon you. ⁹My eye will not spare, I shall not have pity. When in accordance with your ways I put them upon you, your offensive practices that are within you, you will acknowledge that I am Yahweh, the one who strikes down.

¹⁰There, the day, there, it's coming. The doom is coming out. The club has blossomed, assertiveness has flourished, ¹¹violence has arisen with a faithless club. Nothing comes from them, not from their horde, not from anything of theirs; there's no distinction in them. ¹²The time is coming, the day is coming close. The buyer shouldn't rejoice, the seller shouldn't mourn, because wrath is upon its entire horde. ¹³Because the seller won't turn back to what he sold, even though their life is still among the living, because the vision about the entire horde won't turn back. Each in his waywardness – they won't keep strong hold on their life.

They'll throw their silver into the streets

¹⁴'They've sounded the horn and made everything ready, but there's no one going to the battle, because my wrath is against its entire horde. ¹⁵The sword is in the street, the epidemic and the famine in the house. The person who's in the field will die by the sword, and the person who's in the town – famine and epidemic will consume him. ¹⁶Those of them that escape – they'll escape but be in the mountains like the pigeons in the ravines, all of them moaning, each in his waywardness. ¹⁷All the hands will go slack, water will go down all the knees. ¹⁸They'll wrap on sack, and shuddering will cover them, with shame on all faces and shornness on all their heads.

¹⁹'They'll throw their silver into the streets; their gold will become taboo. Their silver and their gold won't be able to rescue them on the day of Yahweh's outburst, they won't satisfy people's desire or fill their stomachs, because their waywardness has become the cause of their collapse.

²⁰Its jewelled splendour that he set in majesty, with it they made their offensive images, their abominations with it. Therefore I'm making it taboo for them. ²¹I shall give it into the hand of strangers as plunder, as spoil for the faithless of the earth, and they'll treat it as ordinary. ²²I shall turn away my face from them, and people will treat my treasured place

as ordinary – intruders will come into it and treat it as ordinary.

Inflammatory images

²³Make a chain, because the country is full of bloody exercise of authority, the town is full of violence. ²⁴I shall bring the nations that deal most badly and they will take possession of their houses. I shall put a stop to the majesty of the vigorous. Their sanctuaries will be made ordinary.

²⁵Calamity is coming. People will seek well-being but there will be none. ²⁶Disaster will come upon disaster, report will follow upon report. They will seek a vision from a prophet, but instruction will perish from priest and counsel from elders. ²⁷The king will mourn, the ruler will put on desolation as clothing, the hands of the country's people will tremble. According to their way I shall act with them, and on the basis of their acts of authority I shall exercise authority over them. And they will acknowledge that I am Yahweh.'

8 In the sixth year, in the sixth, on the fifth of the month, I was sitting in my house and the Yehudahite elders were sitting before me, and the hand of the Lord Yahweh fell on me there. ²I looked, and there, a form with a fiery appearance. From the appearance of his hips and downwards there was fire, and from his hips and upwards, a gold appearance, the very gleam of electrum. ³He put out the form of a hand and took me by the hair of my head, and a wind lifted me between the earth and the heavens and brought me to Yerushalaim with a great appearance of God, to the entrance of the gateway to the inner courtyard that faces north, where was the seat of the inflammatory image, which inflames. ⁴There, the splendour of Yisra'el's God was there, like the appearance that I saw in the valley.

⁵He said to me, 'Young man, raise your eyes northward, please.' I raised my eyes in the northward direction, and there, north of the altar gateway, was this inflammatory image, at the entrance. ⁶He said to me, 'Young man, do you see what they're doing, great offensive things that Yisra'el's household are doing here, so that I shall go far from my sanctuary? You will see further great offensive things.'

Religion and violence

⁷He brought me to the entrance of the courtyard. I looked, and there, a hole in the wall. ⁸He said to me, 'Young man, break through the wall, please.' I broke through the wall, and there, a door. ⁹He said to me, 'Come in, look at the offensive bad things that they're doing here.' ¹⁰I came and looked, and there, every form of abominable reptile and animal and all the lumps of Yisra'el's household, carved on the wall all the way round. ¹¹Seventy individuals of the elders of Yisra'el's household, with Ya'azanyahu ben Shaphan standing among them, were standing before them, each with his censer in his hand. The richness of the incense cloud was going up. ¹²He said to me, 'Young man, have you seen what the elders of Yisra'el's household are doing in the dark, each in his image-covered rooms? Because they're saying, "Yahweh isn't looking at us. Yahweh's abandoned the country."'

¹³He said to me, 'You will again see further great offensive things that they're doing.' ¹⁴He brought me to the entrance of the gateway of Yahweh's house that's to the north. There, the women were sitting there, bewailing Tammuz. ¹⁵He said to me, 'Young man, have you seen? You will again see further greater offensive things than these.' ¹⁶He brought me to the inner courtyard of Yahweh's house. There, at the gateway of Yahweh's palace, between the portico and the altar, some twenty-five men, their backs to Yahweh's palace and their faces to the east, and they were bowing low to the east, to the sun.

¹⁷He said to me, 'Young man, have you seen? Is it too slight for Yehudah's household to do the offensive things that they've done here? Because they've filled the country with violence and again provoked me. There they are, putting the branch to their nose. ¹⁸Yes, I myself will act in wrath. My eye won't spare and I shall not pity. They will call in my ears in a loud voice but I shall not listen to them.'

Who are the people who groan and moan?

9 He called in my ears in a loud voice, 'Come near, you who have appointment over the town, each of you with his implement of devastation in his hand.' ²And there – six individuals coming by way of the upper gateway that faces north, each with his implement of demolition in his hand, and an individual among them dressed in linen, with a writing case at his hips. They came and stood beside the copper altar. ³Now the splendour of Yisra'el's God had gone up from on the sphinx on which it had been, to the house's terrace. He called to the one dressed in linen, at whose hips was the writing case. ⁴Yahweh said to him, 'Pass through the middle of the town, through the middle of Yerushalaim, and put an X on the foreheads of the people who are groaning and who are moaning over the offensive things that are done in the middle of it.'

⁵To the others he said in my ears, 'Pass through the town after him and strike down. Your eye must not spare. You must not pity. ⁶Elder, young man, girl, little one, women, you're to kill outright. But any individual on whom is the X – don't go up to them. Start from my sanctuary.' So they started with the men who were the elders who were before the house. ⁷He said to them, 'Defile the house. Fill the courtyards with the people run through. Go out.' They went out and struck the town down.

⁸While they were striking down, I myself remained alone. I fell on my face and cried out and said, 'Aagh, Lord Yahweh, are you going to devastate all that remains of Yisra'el by pouring out your wrath on Yerushalaim?' ⁹He said to me, 'The waywardness of the household of Yisra'el and Yehudah is very, very great. The country is full of bloodshed. The town is full of injustice. Because they've said, "Yahweh has abandoned the country. Yahweh isn't looking." ¹⁰I, too – my eye won't spare and I won't pity. I'm putting their own way on their head.' ¹¹And there – the one clothed in linen, at whose hips was the writing case, was bringing back word: 'I've acted in accordance with all that you ordered me.'

Take fire

10 I looked, and there – on the platform that was over the head of the sphinxes was an actual sapphire stone; the appearance of the form of a throne appeared on it. ²He said to the man clothed in linen, 'Come in between the whirling, underneath the sphinx, fill the hollow of your hands with burning coals from between the sphinxes, and scatter them over the town.' He came in before my eyes. ³The sphinxes were standing at the right of the house when the man came in, and the cloud was filling the inner courtyard.

⁴Yahweh's splendour lifted from above the sphinx above the house's terrace, the house filled with the cloud, and the courtyard was full of the brightness of Yahweh's splendour. ⁵The sound of the sphinxes' wings made itself heard as far as the outer courtyard, like the voice of God Shadday when he speaks. ⁶When he ordered the one dressed in linen, 'Take fire from between the whirling, from between the sphinxes', he came in and stood beside the wheel. ⁷The sphinx put out its hand from between the sphinxes to the fire that was between the sphinxes, took some up and put it into the hollow of the hands of the one dressed in linen. He took it and went out. ⁸(The form of a human hand belonging to the sphinxes appeared under their wings.)

⁹I looked, and there – four wheels beside the sphinxes, one wheel beside one sphinx, another wheel beside another sphinx. The appearance of the wheels: the very gleam of beryl stone. ¹⁰Their appearance: the four of them had one form, as if one wheel were inside another wheel. ¹¹When they went, they'd go in the direction of their four quarters. They wouldn't turn as they went, because the place that the head faced, they'd follow it. They wouldn't turn as they went.

Yahweh leaves

¹²Their entire body – their backs, their hands and their wings – and the wheels were full of eyes all round (the wheels belonging to the four of them; ¹³these wheels had been called 'the whirling' in my ears). ¹⁴Each had four faces. Face one was the sphinx's face. Face two was a human face. The third was a lion's face. The fourth was an eagle's face.

¹⁵The sphinxes lifted; it was the creature that I'd seen by the River Kebar. ¹⁶When the sphinxes went, the wheels would go beside them. When the sphinxes raised their wings to

lift from on the earth, the wheels wouldn't turn from beside them, too. ¹⁷When they stopped, they'd stop, and when they lifted, they'd lift with them, because the creature's spirit was in them.

¹⁸Yahweh's splendour went out from above the house's terrace and stood above the sphinxes. ¹⁹The sphinxes raised their wings and lifted from the earth before my eyes as they went out, with the wheels alongside them. It stood at the entrance of the east gateway of Yahweh's house, with the splendour of Yisra'el's God over them, above. ²⁰It was the creature that I saw below Yisra'el's God at the River Kebar. So I recognized that they were sphinxes. ²¹Each had four faces and each had four wings, with the form of human hands under their wings. ²²The form of their faces – they were the faces that I saw by the River Kebar, their appearance and themselves. They'd each go in the direction of its face.

The pot and the meat

11 A wind lifted me and brought me to the east gateway of Yahweh's house, which faces east. There, at the entrance of the gateway, were twenty-five men. I saw among them Ya'azanyah ben Azzur and Pelatyahu ben Benayahu, officials of the people. ²He said to me, 'Young man, these are the men who think up trouble and formulate bad counsel in this town, ³who say, "The building of houses isn't near. That's the pot, and we're the meat." ⁴Therefore prophesy against them. Prophesy, young man.'

⁵Yahweh's spirit fell on me, and he said to me, 'Say, "Yahweh has said this: 'This is what you've said, Yisra'el's household; I myself know what's come up into your spirit. ⁶You've multiplied the people run through by you in this town. You've filled its streets with people run through.'

⁷Therefore the Lord Yahweh has said this: 'The people run through by you whom you've put in the middle of it: they're the meat. That's the pot, but he's making you go out from the middle of it. ⁸You're afraid of a sword, but I shall bring a sword upon you (the Lord Yahweh's declaration). ⁹I shall make you go out from the middle of it and give you into the hand of strangers. I shall execute acts of authority against you. ¹⁰By the sword you will fall. At Yisra'el's border I shall exercise authority over you, and you will acknowledge that I am Yahweh. ¹¹It won't be a pot for you nor will you be the meat in the middle of it. At Yisra'el's border I shall exercise authority over you, ¹²and you will acknowledge that I am Yahweh, whose laws you didn't follow and whose rulings you didn't act on, but acted in accordance with the rulings of the nations that are round you."'

¹³As I prophesied, Pelatyahu ben Benayahu died. I fell on my face and cried out in a loud voice, 'Aagh, Lord Yahweh, you're finishing off the remainder of Yisra'el.'

A small sanctuary

¹⁴Yahweh's word came to me: ¹⁵'Young man, your brothers, your brothers who are the people in your extended family, Yisra'el's entire household, all of it, are the people of whom Yerushalaim's inhabitants have said, "Get far away from Yahweh. It's being given to us, the country, as a possession." ¹⁶Therefore say, "The Lord Yahweh has said this: 'Because I've made them go far away among the nations and because I've scattered them among the countries but become a small sanctuary for them in the countries where they've come'", ¹⁷therefore say, "The Lord Yahweh has said this: 'I shall collect you from the peoples, gather you from the countries in which I scattered them, and I shall give you Yisra'el's land.' ¹⁸They will come there and remove all their abominations and their offensive practices from them, ¹⁹and I shall give them one mind. I shall put a new spirit within you. I shall remove the mind of stone from their flesh and give them a mind of flesh, ²⁰so that they will follow my laws, and keep my rulings and act on them. They will be a people for me and I shall be God for them. ²¹But the people whose mind is walking after the mind of their abominations and their offensive practices, I'm going to put their way on their own head (a declaration of the Lord Yahweh)."'

²²The sphinxes lifted up their wings, with the wheels alongside them and the splendour of Yisra'el's God over them, above. ²³Yahweh's

splendour went up from over the middle of the town and stood over the mountain that's on the east of the town, ²⁴while a wind lifted me up and brought me to Kasdim to the exile community, by the appearance from God's spirit, and the appearance that I'd seen went up from over me. ²⁵I spoke to the exile community all Yahweh's words that he'd shown me.

Dramatizing exile

12 Yahweh's word came to me: ²'Young man, you're living in the middle of a rebellious household, who have eyes for seeing but don't see, ears for hearing but don't hear, because they're a rebellious household. ³You, young man, prepare things for exile for yourself and go into exile by day before their eyes. Go into exile from your place to another place before their eyes. Perhaps they will see that they're a rebellious household.

⁴You're to take your things out like things for exile by day, before their eyes, and you yourself are to go out in the evening, before their eyes, like people going out into exile. ⁵Before their eyes, break through the wall for yourself and take them out through it. ⁶Before their eyes, you're to lift them on to your shoulder. You're to take it out in the dark. You're to cover your face and not look at the land, because I'm making you a sign for Yisra'el's household.'

⁷I did just as I was ordered. I took my things out by day, like things for exile, and in the evening I broke through the wall for myself with my hand. In the dark I took them out. I lifted them on my shoulder before their eyes.

⁸Yahweh's word came to me in the morning: ⁹'Young man, Yisra'el's household (a rebellious household) said to you, "What are you doing?", didn't they. ¹⁰Say to them, "The Lord Yahweh has said this: 'This pronouncement: the ruler in Yerushalaim and all Yisra'el's household that are among them.'" ¹¹Say, "I'm a sign for you. As I've done, so it will be done to them. They will go into exile, into captivity. ¹²The ruler who's among them will lift them on to his shoulder in the dark. He'll go out through the wall. They'll break through in order to take them out through it. He'll cover his face, because he won't look at the land with his eye. ¹³But I shall spread my net over him, and he'll be caught in my trap. I shall bring him to Babel, to the country of the Kasdites, but he won't see it, and he'll die there. ¹⁴Everyone who's round him, his support staff and all his legions, I shall scatter to every wind, and draw a sword after them.

God won't let things drag on

¹⁵They will acknowledge that I am Yahweh when I scatter them among the nations and disperse them among the countries. ¹⁶But I shall let a few of the people be left from sword, from famine and from epidemic, in order that they may recount all their offensive practices among the nations where they come. And they will acknowledge that I am Yahweh."

¹⁷Yahweh's word came to me: ¹⁸'Young man, you're to eat your food with trembling and drink your water with shuddering and with anxiety, ¹⁹and say to the country's people, "The Lord Yahweh has said this concerning Yerushalaim's inhabitants in the land of Yisra'el: 'They will eat their bread with anxiety and drink their water in desolation, in order that their country may be desolate of what fills it because of the violence of all the people who live in it. ²⁰The inhabited towns will be wasted and the country will become a desolation. And you will acknowledge that I am Yahweh.'"

²¹Yahweh's word came to me: ²²'Young man, what's this saying that you have in the land of Yisra'el, "Days grow long and every vision perishes"? ²³Therefore say to them, "The Lord Yahweh has said this: 'I shall make this saying stop. They won't say it any more in Yisra'el.'" Rather, speak to them: "The days are drawing near, and the thing in every vision." ²⁴Because there won't any more be empty vision or deceptive divination within Yisra'el's household. ²⁵Because I Yahweh shall speak the word that I speak and it will be done. It won't drag on any more. Because in your days, rebellious household, I shall speak a word and do it (a declaration of the Lord Yahweh).'

²⁶Yahweh's word came to me: ²⁷'Young man, there, Yisra'el's household are saying, "The vision that he sees is for many days and he prophesies for far-off times." ²⁸Therefore say to them: "The Lord Yahweh has said this: 'None of the words that I speak will drag on any

more. The word that I speak will be acted on (a declaration of the Lord Yahweh)."'"

About building a wall

13 Yahweh's word came to me: ²"Young man, prophesy against Yisra'el's prophets, who are prophesying. Say to the prophets of their own mind, "Listen to Yahweh's word. ³The Lord Yahweh has said this: 'Hey, against the villainous prophets who follow their own spirit and have seen nothing. ⁴Your prophets have been like jackals among wastes, Yisra'el. ⁵You didn't go up into the breaks and build up the barrier round Yisra'el's household so it would stand in the battle on Yahweh's day. ⁶They saw emptiness and lying divination, those who say "Yahweh's declaration" when Yahweh hadn't sent them, and people expected the implementing of the word. ⁷It was an empty vision that you saw and lying divination that you uttered, wasn't it, saying "Yahweh's declaration" when I myself hadn't spoken.'"

⁸Therefore the Lord Yahweh has said this: "Because you spoke emptiness and saw lies, here am I towards you (a declaration of the Lord Yahweh): ⁹my hand will be against the prophets who see emptiness and who divine lies. They won't be in my people's council. They won't be recorded in the record of Yisra'el's household. They won't come into Yisra'el's land. And you will acknowledge that I am the Lord Yahweh.

¹⁰Because, yes because they've misled my people, saying 'Things will be well', when things won't be well, and 'He's building a divider', and there – they're coating it with paint: ¹¹say to the people coating it with paint, 'It will fall. Pouring rain is coming and I shall send hailstones that will fall, and a hurricane wind will break it up. ¹²There, the wall is falling. It will be said to you, won't it, "Where's the coating that you put on?"'"

¹³Therefore the Lord Yahweh has said this: "I shall make a hurricane wind break out in my wrath, and pouring rain will come in my anger and hailstones in my wrath, to a finish. ¹⁴I shall tear down the wall that you've coated with paint, bring it close to the earth, and its foundation will become visible. When it falls, you will come to a finish within it. And you will acknowledge that I am Yahweh.

Trapping people's lives like birds

¹⁵I shall finish up my wrath on the wall and on the people who coat it with paint, and I shall say to you, 'There's no wall and there are no painters of it, ¹⁶Yisra'el's prophets who prophesy about Yerushalaim and see a vision of things being well for it when things aren't going to be well (a declaration of the Lord Yahweh).'"

¹⁷And you, young man, set your face against your people's daughters, who prophesy out of their own mind. Prophesy against them. ¹⁸You shall say, "The Lord Yahweh has said this: 'Hey, to the women who sew straps on any wrists and make veils for the head of someone of any height, to trap their lives. Should you trap my people's lives but keep yourselves alive for yourselves? ¹⁹You've treated me as ordinary to my people, for handfuls of barley and for crumbs of bread, so as to put to death people who shouldn't die and to keep alive people who shouldn't live, with your lying to my people who listen to lying.'"

²⁰Therefore the Lord Yahweh has said this: "Here am I, against your straps, where you're [like people] hunting the lives of flying creatures. I shall tear them off from your arms and send off [free] the lives that you're hunting, [like] the lives of flying creatures. ²¹I shall tear off your veils and rescue my people from your hand. They will no longer be an object for hunting in your hand. And you will acknowledge that I am Yahweh.

²²Because of your saddening the heart of the faithful person with falsehood when I myself hadn't hurt him, and for your strengthening the hands of the faithless person so that he wouldn't turn back from his bad way so as to stay alive, ²³therefore you won't see emptiness and you won't practise divination any more. I shall rescue my people from your hand. And you will acknowledge that I am Yahweh.'"

Shall I really let myself be enquired of by them?

14 People from among Yisra'el's elders came to me and sat before me, ²and Yahweh's word came to me: ³"Young man, these people have taken up their lumps into their mind and set their waywardness as an obstacle in front of their faces. Shall I really let myself be enquired of by them? ⁴Therefore speak to them: "The Lord Yahweh has said this: 'Any individual from Yisra'el's household who takes up his lumps into his mind and places his waywardness as an obstacle in front of his face, and comes to the prophet, I make an answer to him through it (through the great number of his lumps), ⁵in order to lay hold of Yisra'el's household through its mind, because they've become estranged from me through their lumps, all of them.'"

⁶Therefore say to Yisra'el's household, "The Lord Yahweh has said this: 'Turn back, turn yourselves back from your lumps, turn back your faces from your offensive practices. ⁷Because any individual from Yisra'el's household or from the aliens residing in Yisra'el who becomes estranged from following me and takes up his lumps into his mind and sets his waywardness as an obstacle in front of his face, and comes to the prophet to enquire of him with me – I Yahweh will make an answer to him by myself. ⁸I shall set my face against that individual and make him a sign and a saying. I shall cut him off from among my people. And you will acknowledge that I am Yahweh.'"

⁹When a prophet is enticed and speaks a word, I Yahweh will have enticed that prophet, and I shall stretch out my hand against him and annihilate him from among my people Yisra'el. ¹⁰They will carry their waywardness. The enquirer's waywardness and the prophet's waywardness will be the same, ¹¹in order that Yisra'el's household may not wander again from following me and may not defile itself again with all its rebellions. They will be a people for me and I shall be God for them (a declaration of the Lord Yahweh)."

Noah, Dan'el and Iyyob (Job)

¹²Yahweh's word came to me: ¹³"Young man, when a country does wrong to me by committing a trespass, and I stretch out my hand against it, and I break its bread supply and send famine against it and cut off from it human beings and animals, ¹⁴were these three people within it, Noah, Dan'el and Iyyob, by their faithfulness they would save their own lives (a declaration of the Lord Yahweh). ¹⁵If I let bad creatures pass through the country, and they leave it childless and it becomes a desolation without anyone passing through in face of the creatures, ¹⁶were these three people within it, as I live (a declaration of the Lord Yahweh), neither sons nor daughters would they save. They'd save themselves alone. The country would become a desolation.

¹⁷Or I might bring a sword against that country and say, "A sword is to pass through the country, and I shall cut off from it human beings and animals"; ¹⁸were these three people within it, as I live (a declaration of the Lord Yahweh) they wouldn't save sons or daughters, but would save themselves alone.

¹⁹Or I might send off an epidemic to that country and pour out my wrath on it in bloodshed, cutting off from it human beings and animals; ²⁰were Noah, Dan'el and Iyyob within it, as I live (a declaration of the Lord Yahweh) they wouldn't save a son or a daughter. These people would save themselves alone by their faithfulness.'

²¹Because the Lord Yahweh has said this: 'How much more when I've sent off my four bad judgements – sword, famine, bad creature and epidemic – to Yerushalaim, to cut off from it human beings and animals.

²²But there – an escape group is being left in it, people who are being taken out, sons and daughters. There they are, coming out to you. You will see their way and their deeds, and be comforted about the bad fate that I shall have brought upon Yerushalaim, all that I've brought upon it. ²³They will comfort you because you will see their way and their deeds and you will acknowledge that it was not without reason that I did all that I did against it (a declaration of the Lord Yahweh).'

The useless vine wood

15 Yahweh's word came to me: ²"Young man, how will the vine's wood be better than the wood of any branch that's among the trees of the forest? ³Will wood be taken from it to make anything? Will they take a peg from it to hang an object on? ⁴There, it's put in the fire to be consumed. If the fire consumes the two ends of it and the middle of it is burned, is it useful for anything? ⁵There, when it was whole, it couldn't be made into anything. How much less when the fire consumes it, and it burns, can it be made into anything.

⁶Therefore the Lord Yahweh says this: "As the wood of the vine among the trees of the forest that I gave to the fire for consuming, so I'm giving Yerushalaim's inhabitants. ⁷I'm setting my face against them. They got out from the fire, but the fire will consume them. And you will acknowledge that I am Yahweh when I set my face against them. ⁸I shall make the country a desolation because they committed trespass (a declaration of the Lord Yahweh)."

16 Yahweh's word came to me: ²'Young man, get Yerushalaim to acknowledge its offensive practices. ³You're to say, "The Lord Yahweh has said this to Yerushalaim: 'Your origin and your birth were from the Kena'anites' [Canaanites'] country – your father an Amorite and your mother a Hittite. ⁴Your birth: on the day you were born, no one cut your cord and you weren't washed in water for cleansing. You weren't rubbed with salt at all and you weren't wrapped up at all. ⁵No eye cared about you so as to do one of these things for you to express compassion for you. You were thrown on to the face of the open country in loathing for you on the day you were born. ⁶But I passed by you and looked at you kicking about in your bloodiness and I said to you in your bloodiness, "Live." Yes, I said to you in your bloodiness, "Live."

You're just a whore

⁷I made you big like a plant in the open country, and you grew big. You grew up and came to full loveliness; your breasts formed, your hair flourished, but you were naked, bare. ⁸I passed by you and saw you – there, your time was time for love. I spread my robe over you and covered your nakedness. I took an oath to you and came into a pact with you (a declaration of the Lord Yahweh) and you became mine.

⁹I washed you in water and sluiced off the blood from on you and poured oil over you. ¹⁰I clothed you with embroidery and gave you leather footwear. I wrapped you round in fine linen and covered you in silk. ¹¹I adorned you with jewellery and put bracelets on your hands and a necklace on your neck. ¹²I put a ring on your nose, earrings on your ears and a splendid crown on your head. ¹³So you adorned yourself with gold and silver, and your clothing was of fine linen, silk and embroidery, your food was choice flour, syrup and oil, and you became more and more beautiful, and attained a royal position. ¹⁴Your fame went out among the nations for your beauty, because it was complete through the splendour that I put on you (a declaration of the Lord Yahweh).

¹⁵But you relied on your beauty and whored on the basis of your fame. You poured your whorings on every passer-by. It could become his. ¹⁶You took some of your clothes and made yourself colourful shrines, and whored at them (not things to come, and they will not be). ¹⁷You took your splendid things of gold and of silver that I gave you and made yourself male images and whored with them. ¹⁸You took your embroidered clothes and covered them and offered my oil and incense before them.

Yes, just a whore

¹⁹My food that I gave you, fine flour, oil and syrup that I let you eat, you gave before them as a pleasing fragrance, and so it became (a declaration of the Lord Yahweh). ²⁰You took your sons and your daughters to whom you gave birth for me and sacrificed them to them to eat: were your whorings trivial? ²¹You slaughtered my children and gave them to them by making them pass through [fire].

²²With all your offensive practices and your whorings, you weren't mindful of your young days when you were naked and bare, kicking about in your bloodiness. ²³After all your bad dealing (hey, hey, to you: a declaration of the Lord Yahweh) ²⁴you built yourself an enclosure and made yourself a platform in every square. ²⁵At the top of every street you built your platform and made your beauty something offensive. You spread your legs to every passer-by and multiplied your whorings. ²⁶You whored with the Misrayimites [Egyptians], your neighbours with their big members. You multiplied your whoring to provoke me. ²⁷So there, I'm stretching out my hand to you and

cutting your maintenance. I'm giving you over to the will of people who are hostile to you, the Pelishtite [Philistine] women, who are ashamed of your deliberately wicked way.

²⁸You whored with the Ashshurites because you weren't full. You whored with them, but you were still not full. ²⁹You multiplied your whoring with the trader country, Kasdim, but you were still not full with this. ³⁰How feeble was your mind (a declaration of the Lord Yahweh) when you did all these things, the action of a whorish, powerful woman.

But a strange kind of whore

³¹When you built your enclosure at the top of every street and made your platform in every square, you were not like a whore in scorning a "gift", ³²you adulterous wife who accepts strangers instead of her husband. ³³To all whores men give a fee, but you – you've given fees to all your lovers, and paid them to come to you from all round for your whorings. ³⁴With you it was the opposite from other women, in your whorings. Whoring wasn't done by going after you but through your giving a "gift". A "gift" was not given to you. You were the opposite.

³⁵Therefore listen to Yahweh's word, whore. ³⁶The Lord Yahweh has said this: "Since your copper poured out and your nakedness exposed itself in your whorings with your lovers and with all your offensive lumps, and in accordance with the bloodshed of your children whom you gave to them, ³⁷therefore here am I, I'm going to collect all your lovers to whom you were sweet, each one whom you loved, as well as each one to whom you were hostile. I shall collect them against you from all round and expose your nakedness to them. They will see all your nakedness ³⁸and I shall make for you the judgements appropriate for women who commit adultery or pour out blood.

I shall make you an object of the blood of wrath and passion. ³⁹I shall give you into their hand and they will tear down your enclosure and break down your platforms. They will strip you of your clothes, take your splendid things, and leave you naked and bare. ⁴⁰They will bring up a congregation against you, pelt you with stones and cut you down with their swords. ⁴¹They will burn your houses with fire and execute acts of authority against you before the eyes of many women. I shall make your whoring stop. You will no more give 'gifts', either. ⁴²I shall set down my wrath with you and turn away my passion from you, and be calm and not vexed any more.

Yerushalaim, her mother and her sisters

⁴³Since you weren't mindful of your young days and you infuriated me with all these things, I myself shall also – yes, I shall put your way on your own head (a declaration of the Lord Yahweh). You acted on your deliberate wickedness with your offensive practices, didn't you.

⁴⁴There, everyone who quotes sayings will quote this saying with regard to you: 'Like mother, like daughter'. ⁴⁵You're your mother's daughter, renouncing her husband and her children. You're the sister of your sisters, who renounced their husbands and their children. Your mother was a Hittite, your father an Amorite. ⁴⁶Your big sister was Shomron [Samaria], she and her daughters who were living to the north of you. Your little sister who was living to the south of you was Sedom [Sodom] and her daughters. ⁴⁷You walked in their ways and acted by their offensive practices, didn't you. In a very short while you became more devastating than them in all your ways. ⁴⁸As I live (a declaration of the Lord Yahweh), if Sedom your sister, she and her daughters, had acted as you and your daughters acted . . .

⁴⁹There, this was the waywardness of Sedom your sister: she and her daughters had majesty, plenty of bread, and calm peacefulness, but they didn't take the hand of the humble and needy. ⁵⁰They were lofty and they did something offensive before me. So I removed them, as you have seen.

⁵¹Shomron – she didn't commit half your wrongdoings; you've multiplied your wrongdoings more than her. You made your sisters seem faithful with all your offensive deeds that you did. ⁵²You, too, carry your shame, you who've pleaded for your sisters with your wrongdoings with which you've acted more offensively than them.

They're more faithful than you. Yes, you – be shamed. Carry your disgrace in your making your sisters seem faithful.

But whoring will not be the end of the story

⁵³I shall restore their fortunes, the fortunes of Sedom and her daughters and the fortunes of Shomron and her daughters, and the fortunes of your captivity among them, ⁵⁴in order that you may carry your disgrace and feel disgraced for all that you've done in enabling them to take comfort. ⁵⁵Your sister Sedom and her daughters will go back to what they were before, Shomron and her daughters will go back to what they were before, and you and your daughters will go back to what you were before. ⁵⁶Your sister Sedom was a topic of talk in your mouth in the day of your majesty, wasn't she, ⁵⁷before your bad dealing became open, at the very time of the reviling of the daughters of Aram and all the peoples round her, the daughters of the Pelishtites, who jeer at you from all round. ⁵⁸Your scheming and your offensive deeds – you are going to carry them (Yahweh's declaration).'"

⁵⁹Because the Lord Yahweh has said this: 'Yes, I shall act with you as you've acted, in that you've despised the vow, in contravening the pact. ⁶⁰But I – I shall be mindful of my pact with you in your young days. I shall implement for you a permanent pact. ⁶¹You will be mindful of your ways and feel disgrace when you receive your sisters, the ones who are bigger than you and the ones who are younger than you. I shall give them to you as daughters, though not on the basis of your pact. ⁶²I – I shall implement my pact with you. And you will acknowledge that I am Yahweh, ⁶³in order that you may be mindful and feel shame. It won't be for you to open your mouth again in the face of your disgrace, when I make expiation for you for all that you've done (a declaration of the Lord Yahweh).'"

A tale of two eagles

17 Yahweh's word came to me: ²'Young man, unveil a conundrum, tell Yisra'el's household a parable. ³Say, "The Lord Yahweh has said this: 'A big eagle, big-winged, long-feathered, full-plumaged, with colouring, came to the Lebanon and took the top of a cedar. ⁴He broke off the highest of its shoots, brought it to a merchant country and put it in a traders' town. ⁵He took some of the country's seed and put it in a seed field; he placed it by plentiful water, a willow. ⁶It grew and became a spreading vine, low in height, its branches to turn to him, its roots being beneath it. So it became a vine, produced limbs and sent out shoots. ⁷But there was another big eagle, big-winged, much-plumaged. There – this vine turned its roots towards it and sent out its branches to it for it to water it, away from the beds where it was sown, ⁸though it had been planted in a good field by plentiful water so as to produce boughs, bear fruit, and become an impressive vine.'"

⁹Say, "The Lord Yahweh has said this: 'It may flourish, but he will tear up its roots and strip off its fruit so that it withers, won't he. All the leaves of its growth will wither (not by means of a big arm or by means of a large company) to carry it off by its roots. ¹⁰There, though planted, will it flourish? It will totally wither when the east wind touches it, won't it. It will wither on the beds where it grew.'"

¹¹Yahweh's word came to me: ¹²"Say to the rebellious household, please: "You acknowledge what these things are, don't you." Say: "There, the king of Babel came to Yerushalaim, took its king and its officials, and brought them to him, to Babel. ¹³He took someone from the royal offspring and solemnized a pact with him and put him under a vow, but he took the leaders of the country ¹⁴so that it might be a lowly kingdom and not exalt itself, keeping his pact so as to stand.

A tale of two trees

¹⁵But he rebelled against him by sending his envoys to Misrayim so it would give him horses and a large company. Will he flourish? Will the one who does these things escape? Will he contravene a pact and escape? ¹⁶As I live (a declaration of the Lord Yahweh), if he doesn't die in the place belonging to the king who

made him king, whose vow he despised and whose pact he contravened, inside Babel . . .

¹⁷Par'oh [Pharaoh] won't act towards him with a big force, with a numerous congregation – with battle, with the heaping up of a ramp and with the building of a tower, to cut down many lives. ¹⁸He despised a vow by contravening a pact. There – he gave his hand, but he did all these things. He won't escape. ¹⁹Therefore the Lord Yahweh has said this: 'As I live, if I don't put on his own head my vow that he despised and my pact that he contravened . . .

²⁰I shall spread my net over him, and he'll be caught in my trap. I shall bring him to Babel and enter into judgement with him there for the trespass that he committed against me. ²¹All the fugitives in all his legions will fall by the sword and the remainder will scatter to every wind. And you will acknowledge that I Yahweh have spoken."'

²²Yahweh has said this: 'And I myself shall take from the top of a tall cedar, and put from the highest of its shoots a tender one that I shall break off and myself plant on a lofty, tall mountain. ²³On Yisra'el's high mountains I shall plant it. It will bear boughs and produce fruit, and become an august cedar. Every bird of every wing will dwell beneath it; in the shade of its branches they will dwell. ²⁴All the trees of the field will acknowledge that I am Yahweh. I shall have brought low the exalted tree, exalted the lowly tree, withered the green tree and made the withered tree flourish. I am Yahweh. I have spoken and I shall act.'

Father and son

18 Yahweh's word came to me: ²'What is it to you people using this saying on Yisra'el's land, "Parents eat sour grapes, but children's teeth feel rough"? ³As I live (a declaration of the Lord Yahweh), if you have any more using of this saying in Yisra'el . . .

⁴Here, all lives are mine. As the parent's life, so the child's life, they're mine. The person who sins, he will die. ⁵When an individual is faithful and exercises authority with faithfulness:

⁶he hasn't eaten on the mountains;
nor raised his eyes to the lumps of Yisra'el's household;
nor defiled his neighbour's wife;
nor does he draw near a woman who's taboo;
⁷nor does he oppress an individual;
he gives back the pledge given him for a debt;
nor does he commit robbery;
he gives his bread to the hungry person;
he covers the naked with clothes;
⁸he doesn't give on the basis of earning interest nor take a profit;
he turns his hand back from what is evil;
he makes a truthful judgement between one individual and another:

⁹he walks by my laws and has kept my rulings by exercising truthfulness. He's faithful. He will definitely live (a declaration of the Lord Yahweh).

¹⁰But he fathers a violent son, a shedder of blood, who does one or another of these things, ¹¹when he himself did none of these things. Rather he

has eaten on the mountains;
has defiled his neighbour's wife;
¹²has oppressed the humble and needy;
has committed robbery;
doesn't return a pledge;
has raised his eyes to the lumps;
has done an offensive thing;
¹³has given on the basis of earning interest and taken a profit:

is he to live? He won't live. One who has done any of these offensive things will definitely die. His bloodshed will be against him.

Do I really want the death of a faithless person?

¹⁴But there, he fathers a son, and he sees all his father's wrongdoings that he committed. He sees, and he doesn't act in accordance with them:

¹⁵he hasn't eaten on the mountains;
he hasn't raised his eyes to the lumps of Yisra'el's household;
he hasn't defiled his neighbour's wife;
¹⁶he hasn't oppressed anyone;
he hasn't exacted a pledge;
he hasn't committed robbery;
he has given his bread to a hungry person;
he has covered a naked person with clothes;
¹⁷he has turned his hand back from the humble;
he hasn't taken interest or profit:

he has acted on my rulings; he has walked by my laws. He won't die because of his father's waywardness. He will definitely live. ¹⁸His father, because he practised fraud, committed robbery against his brother and did what was not good among his people: there, he will definitely die for his waywardness.

¹⁹You say, "Why has the son not carried any of the father's waywardness?" But the son has exercised authority with faithfulness, kept all my laws and done them. He will live. ²⁰The person who does wrong, he will die. A son doesn't carry any of the father's waywardness and a father doesn't carry any of the son's waywardness. The faithfulness of the faithful person belongs to him and the faithlessness of the faithless person belongs to him. ²¹But the faithless person when he turns back from all his wrongdoings that he's committed and keeps all my laws and exercises authority with faithfulness, he will definitely live. He won't die. ²²None of the rebellions that he's committed will be kept in mind for him; through the faithfulness with which he's acted, he will live. ²³Do I really want the death of the faithless person (a declaration of the Lord Yahweh) and not his turning back from his ways so that he lives?

Produce yourselves a new mind and a new spirit

²⁴But when the faithful person turns back from his faithfulness and does what is evil in accordance with all the offensive things that the faithless person did, and does them, is he to live? None of his faithful acts that he's done will be kept in mind because of the trespass that he's committed and the wrongdoings that he's done. Through them he will die.

²⁵You say, "The Lord's way isn't just." Listen please, Yisra'el's household. Is it my way that isn't just? It's your ways that aren't just, isn't it. ²⁶When a faithful person turns back from his faithfulness and does what is evil and dies for them, he dies for the wrong that he's done. ²⁷And when a faithless person turns back from his faithlessness that he's done and exercises authority with faithfulness, he keeps himself alive. ²⁸He's seen and turned back from all his rebellions that he's done. He will definitely live. He won't die.

²⁹Yisra'el's household say, "The Lord's way isn't just." Is it my ways that are not just, Yisra'el's household? It's your ways that aren't just, isn't it. ³⁰Therefore I shall exercise authority over you, Yisra'el's household, over each person in accordance with his ways (a declaration of the Lord Yahweh). So turn back, turn yourselves back from all your rebellions, and they won't become a wayward obstacle to you. ³¹Throw away from you all your rebellions that you've committed. Produce yourselves a new mind and a new spirit. Why should you die, Yisra'el's household? ³²Because I don't want the death of the person who dies (a declaration of the Lord Yahweh). So turn back and live!'

A dirge for a nation's rulers

19 'And you, take up a dirge for Yisra'el's rulers. ²Say:

What was your mother? –
  a lioness among lions.
She bedded down among the great cougars,
  reared her cubs.
³She brought up one of her cubs,
  he became a cougar.
He learned to hunt prey,
  he ate human beings.
⁴Nations heard about him,
  he was caught in their pit.
They brought him with hooks
  to the country of Misrayim.

⁵She saw that she'd expected,
  whereas her hope had perished.
She got another of her cubs,
  made him a cougar.
⁶He went about among the lions;
  he became a cougar.
He learned to hunt prey,
  he ate human beings.
⁷He had sex with their widows,
  wasted their towns.
The country and what filled it were desolate
  at the sound of his roaring.
⁸But nations set against him
  from provinces all round.
They spread their net over him;
  he was caught in their pit.
⁹They put him in a cage with hooks,

brought him to the king of Babel.
They brought him into a great stronghold,
    in order that his voice wouldn't make itself heard
        any more on Yisra'el's mountains.

¹⁰Your mother was a real vine (with your blood),
    planted by water.
It became fruitful and green
    because of the abundant water.
¹¹It had vigorous boughs
    fit for the clubs of rulers.
The stature of one grew high, among the clouds,
    and it was visible by its height, by the number of its branches.
¹²But it was uprooted in wrath, thrown to the earth,
    and the east wind withered its fruit.
They broke and withered;
    its vigorous bough – fire consumed it.
¹³So now it's planted in the wilderness,
    in a dry, thirsty country.
¹⁴Fire came out from its bough,
    consumed its branches with its fruit.
It didn't have a vigorous bough,
    a club for ruling.'

It's a dirge. It became a dirge.

When you can't enquire of God

20 In the seventh year, in the fifth, on the tenth of the month, some Yisra'elite elders came to enquire of Yahweh, and sat before me. ²Yahweh's word came to me: ³'Young man, speak to Yisra'el's elders: "The Lord Yahweh has said this: 'Is it to enquire of me that you're coming? As I live, if I shall let myself be enquired of by you (a declaration of the Lord Yahweh) . . .'"

⁴Will you exercise authority over them, will you exercise authority over them, young man? Get them to acknowledge their ancestors' offensive practices. ⁵Say to them, "The Lord Yahweh has said this: 'On the day when I chose Yisra'el, I raised my hand [to swear] to the offspring of Ya'aqob's [Jacob's] household, and when I made myself known to them in the country of Misrayim, I raised my hand to them, saying "I am Yahweh your God." ⁶On that day I raised my hand to them to get them out of the country of Misrayim to a country that I'd sought out for them, flowing with milk and syrup; it was the most splendid of all countries. ⁷I said to them, "Each person, throw away the abominations before your eyes. Don't defile yourselves with Misrayim's lumps. I am Yahweh your God." ⁸But they rebelled against me. They wouldn't listen to me. Each person, they didn't throw away the abominations before their eyes and abandon Misrayim's lumps.

I said I'd pour out my wrath on them, to finish up my anger against them within the country of Misrayim. ⁹But I acted for the sake of my name, so that it might not be treated as ordinary in the eyes of the nations among whom they were, before whose eyes I'd caused myself to be acknowledged by them in getting them out of the country of Misrayim.

They treated the sabbath as ordinary

¹⁰So I got them out of the country of Misrayim and brought them into the wilderness. ¹¹I gave them my laws and made known to them my rulings, which a person may act on and live by. ¹²I also gave them my sabbaths, to become a sign between me and them, so that they might acknowledge that I am Yahweh, who makes them sacred. ¹³But Yisra'el's household rebelled against me in the wilderness. They didn't walk by my laws. They rejected my rulings, which a person may act on and live by, and they quite treated my sabbaths as ordinary.

I said I'd pour my wrath on them in the wilderness, so as to finish them off. ¹⁴But I acted for the sake of my name so that it might not be treated as ordinary in the eyes of the nations before whose eyes I got them out. ¹⁵But I did also raise my hand to them in the wilderness not to bring them into the country that I'd given them, flowing with milk and syrup, the most splendid of all countries, ¹⁶because they'd rejected my rulings and not walked by my laws, and treated my sabbaths as ordinary, because their mind was following their lumps.

¹⁷But my eye had pity on them so as not to devastate them. I didn't bring them to a finish in the wilderness. ¹⁸I said to their children in

the wilderness, "Don't follow your parents' laws and don't keep their rulings, and don't defile yourselves with their lumps. [19]I am Yahweh your God. Walk by my laws and keep my rulings and do them, [20]and make my sabbaths sacred so that they're a sign between me and you, so that you acknowledge that I am Yahweh your God." [21]But the children rebelled against me. They didn't walk by my laws and they didn't keep my rulings by acting on them, which an individual may act on and live by. They treated my sabbaths as ordinary.

I said I'd pour my wrath on them to finish up my anger against them in the wilderness. [22]But I held back my hand and acted for the sake of my name so that it might not be treated as ordinary in the eyes of the nations before whose eyes I'd got them out.

The shrine (*bamah*): come to what (*ba' mah*)?

[23]I did also raise my hand to them in the wilderness to scatter them through the nations and disperse them through the countries, [24]because they didn't act on my rulings but rejected my laws and treated my sabbaths as ordinary, and their parents' lumps were before their eyes. [25]I myself also gave them laws that weren't good and rulings they couldn't live by. [26]I defiled them by their gifts when they made every firstborn of the womb pass through [fire], so that I might desolate them, in order that they might acknowledge that I am Yahweh.'"

[27]Therefore speak to Yisra'el's household, young man, and say to them, "The Lord Yahweh has said this: 'Your ancestors further insulted me with this, by committing trespass against me. [28]I brought them into the country that I'd raised my hand to give them. But they looked at every high hill and every leafy tree and slaughtered their sacrifices there, made the provocation of their offering there, produced their pleasing fragrance there and poured their libations there. [29]I said to them, "What [*mah*] is the shrine [*bamah*] that you're coming to [*ba*]?" (and they've named it *bamah* until this day).'"

[30]Therefore say to Yisra'el's household: "The Lord Yahweh has said this: 'Are you defiling yourselves in the manner of your ancestors and whoring after their abominations, [31]and in presenting your gifts by making your children pass though fire defiling yourselves in connection with all your lumps, until this day? And shall I let myself be enquired of by you, Yisra'el's household? As I live (a declaration of the Lord Yahweh), if I let myself be enquired of by you . . .

[32]What comes up into your spirit will simply not happen, that you're saying, "We'll be like the nations, like the countries' kin-groups, in ministering to wood and stone." [33]As I live (a declaration of the Lord Yahweh), if I don't reign over you with a strong hand and with an arm stretched out and with wrath poured out . . .

Then I will accept you

[34]So I shall get you out from the peoples and collect you from the countries among whom you're scattered, with a strong hand and with an arm stretched out and with wrath poured out. [35]I shall bring you into the wilderness of the peoples and enter into judgement with you there face to face. [36]As I entered into judgement with your ancestors in the wilderness of the country of Misrayim, so I shall enter into judgement with you (a declaration of the Lord Yahweh). [37]I shall get you to pass under a club and bring you into a pact bond. [38]I shall purge out from you the people who rebel and revolt against me; while I shall get them out from the country where they're residing, they will not come into the land of Yisra'el. And you will acknowledge that I am Yahweh.

[39]You, Yisra'el's household: the Lord Yahweh has said this: "Each person, go, serve his lumps, and afterwards, if you don't listen to me. But you won't treat my sacred name as ordinary any more with your gifts and your lumps. [40]Because on my sacred mountain, on Yisra'el's high mountain (a declaration of the Lord Yahweh), there Yisra'el's entire household, all of it, will serve me in the country. There I shall accept them and there I shall ask after your donations and the finest of your offerings with all your sacred things. [41]With your pleasing fragrance I shall accept you when I get you out from the peoples and collect you from the countries in which you're scattered. I shall make myself sacred through you in the eyes of the peoples.

⁴²You will acknowledge that I am Yahweh when I bring you into Yisra'el's land, into the country that I raised my hand to give your ancestors. ⁴³You will be mindful there of your ways and all your deeds by which you defiled yourselves. You will be loathsome in your own sight for all your bad dealings that you've done. ⁴⁴You will acknowledge that I am Yahweh when I deal with you for the sake of my name, not in accordance with your bad ways and your devastating deeds, Yisra'el's household (a declaration of the Lord Yahweh).'"

Slaughter from south to north

⁴⁵Yahweh's word came to me: ⁴⁶'Young man, set your face towards Teman, preach against Darom, prophesy against the open forest of the Southland. ⁴⁷You're to say to the Southland forest, "Listen to Yahweh's word. The Lord Yahweh has said this: 'Here am I, I'm going to light a fire in you. It will consume every green tree and every dry tree in you. The burning flame won't go out. Every face from south to north will be scorched by it. ⁴⁸All flesh will see that I, Yahweh, lit it; it won't go out.'"' ⁴⁹But I said, 'Oh, Lord Yahweh, they're saying of me, "Isn't he a teller of parables?"'

21 Yahweh's word came to me: ²'Young man, set your face against Yerushalaim. Preach against the sanctuaries, prophesy against Yisra'el's land. ³You're to say to Yisra'el's land, "Yahweh has said this: 'Here am I towards you. I shall get my sword out of its sheath and cut off from you faithful and faithless person. ⁴Since I'm going to cut off from you faithful and faithless person, therefore my sword will come out from its sheath against all flesh from south to north, ⁵and all flesh will acknowledge that I, Yahweh, got my sword out of its sheath; it won't go back again.'"

⁶So you, young man, sigh. With a breaking in your hips and with anguish you're to groan before their eyes. ⁷When they say to you, "Why are you groaning?", you're to say, "On account of the report, because it's coming. Every heart will melt. All hands will go limp. Every spirit will faint. Water will go down all knees. There, it's coming, it will happen (a declaration of the Lord Yahweh)."'

⁸Yahweh's word came to me: ⁹'Young man, prophesy: "The Lord Yahweh has said this: 'Say, "A sword, a sword sharpened, yes, and polished, ¹⁰sharpened in order that it can bring slaughter, polished in order that it can be a lightning-flash. Otherwise, could we celebrate the club of my son, which rejects every tree? ¹¹Someone gave it for polishing and for grasping in the fist. The sword is sharpened and polished, for putting into the hand of a killer."'"

The fork in the road

¹²Cry and howl, young man, because it will happen among my people, among all Yisra'el's rulers. They're going to be tossed to the sword, with my people. Therefore strike your thigh. ¹³Because there's going to be a testing, and what if it scorns the club? Will it not happen? (a declaration of the Lord Yahweh).

¹⁴So you, young man, prophesy, clap palm against palm. The sword will come twice, a third time it will be the sword for people run through, a sword of someone run through, the great one who surrounds them, ¹⁵in order that the heart may melt and the fallings be many. At all their gateways I have set the sword's slaughter. Aagh, it's made to be a flash of lightning, sharpened for slaughter. ¹⁶Slash to the right, set yourself to the left, wherever your edges are appointed. ¹⁷I too will clap palm against palm and set down my wrath. I Yahweh have spoken.'

¹⁸Yahweh's word came to me: ¹⁹'You, young man, set for yourself two roads for the king of Babel's sword to come. They'll go out from one country. Choose a place; choose it at the beginning of the road to the town. ²⁰You're to set a road for the sword to come to Rabbah of the Ammonites, and [one] to Yehudah against fortified Yerushalaim. ²¹Because the king of Babel is standing at the split on the road, at the top of the two roads, to perform divination. He's shaking arrows, he's asking effigies, he's looking at a liver.

²²In his right hand was the divination for Yerushalaim, for setting battering rams, for giving the word for murder, for lifting up the voice in the battle shout, for setting battering rams against the gateways, for heaping up a

ramp, for building a tower. ²³To them it will be like empty divination, in the eyes of the people who've been sworn with oaths. But he is one who causes waywardness to be kept in mind, so that they will be taken.'

The sword unsheathed and sheathed

²⁴Therefore the Lord Yahweh has said this: 'Since you've caused your waywardness to be kept in mind, as your rebellions reveal themselves, as your wrongdoings become visible, in all your doings – since you've caused it to be kept in mind, you will be taken in [his] fist.

²⁵And you, Yisra'el's slain, faithless ruler, whose day has come at the time of final waywardness, ²⁶the Lord Yahweh has said this: "Remove the mitre, lift off the crown. It won't stay like this. Exalt the lowly, lower the exalted. ²⁷Ruin, ruin, ruin, I shall make it (indeed, this hasn't happened) until the one comes to whom authority belongs, and I shall give it to him."

²⁸And you, young man, prophesy: "The Lord Yahweh has said this about the Ammonites and about their reviling." You're to say, "Sword, sword, unsheathed for slaughter, polished for finishing off, so as to be a flash of lightning. ²⁹Because of beholding something empty for you, because of divining lies for you, they will give you to the necks of the people run through, faithless people whose day has come at the time of final waywardness.

³⁰Put it back into its sheath. In the place where you were created, in the country of your origin, I shall exercise authority over you. ³¹I shall pour out my condemnation upon you. With my furious fire I shall blow on you. I shall give you into the hand of brutal people, craftsmen in devastation. ³²You will be for fire to consume. Your blood will be in the middle of the country. You won't be remembered. Because I, Yahweh, have spoken."'

Unfaithfulness to people and unfaithfulness to God

22 Yahweh's word came to me: ²'You, young man, will you exercise authority, will you exercise authority, over the bloodshed town, and get it to acknowledge all its offensive practices? ³You're to say, "The Lord Yahweh has said this: 'Town that sheds blood within it, so that its time is coming, and makes lumps for itself, so that it becomes defiled! ⁴Through your blood that you've shed, you've incurred liability, and through the lumps that you've made, you're defiled. You've brought your days near; you've come to your years. Therefore I'm making you an object of reviling for the nations, an object of scorn for all the countries. ⁵The ones near and the ones far away from you will scorn you, defiled of name, abounding in tumult.

⁶There, Yisra'el's rulers were in you, each one with his powerful arm, in order to shed blood:

⁷people have slighted father and mother in you;
towards the alien they've acted with fraud within you;
orphan and widow they've oppressed in you;
⁸you've despised my sacred things and treated my sabbaths as ordinary;
⁹people who spread lies have been in you in order to shed blood;
in you they've eaten on the mountains;
they've acted on their scheming within you;
¹⁰in you a man has exposed his father's nakedness;
they've raped a woman defiled by taboo;
¹¹an individual has done something offensive with his neighbour's wife;
another individual has defiled his daughter-in-law by scheming;
in you an individual has raped his sister, his father's daughter;
¹²in you they've taken a bribe so as to shed blood;
you've taken interest and profit;
you've looted your neighbours by fraud.

You've put me out of mind (a declaration of the Lord Yahweh). ¹³So here, I am clapping my palm about your loot that you've made and over your bloodshed that there's been within you. ¹⁴Will your mind stand firm or your hands be strong for the days when I'm dealing with you? I Yahweh have spoken and I shall act. ¹⁵I shall scatter you among the nations and disperse you among the countries. I shall consume your defilement out of you. ¹⁶You will be treated as ordinary in yourself before the eyes of the nations. And you will acknowledge that I am Yahweh."'

Smelting and slag

[17]Yahweh's word came to me: [18]'Young man, Yisra'el's household has become slag to me. All of them are copper, tin, iron and lead inside a furnace. Silver has become slag. [19]Therefore the Lord Yahweh has said this: "Because all of you have become slag, therefore here am I, I'm going to collect you into the middle of Yerushalaim. [20]The collecting of silver, copper, iron, lead and tin inside the furnace, for blowing fire on it to smelt it: so I shall collect in my anger and wrath, and lay you down, and smelt you. [21]I shall collect you and blow on you with my furious fire and you will be smelted inside it. [22]Like the smelting of silver inside a furnace, so you will be smelted inside it, and you will acknowledge that I, Yahweh, have poured out my wrath upon you."'

[23]Yahweh's word came to me: [24]'Young man, say to it: "You're a country that's not been cleansed, and it's not to be rained on in the day of condemnation:
- [25]its conspiracy of prophets within it is like a roaring lion tearing prey, they've consumed human beings, taken riches and wealth, made many widows within it;
- [26]its priests have violated my instruction and treated my sacred things as ordinary, they haven't distinguished between sacred and ordinary, they haven't enabled people to know the difference between clean and defiled, they've closed their eyes to my sabbaths, and I'm treated as ordinary among them;
- [27]its officials within it are like wolves tearing prey, shedding blood to destroy lives for the sake of gaining loot;
- [28]its prophets have coated them with paint, seeing emptiness and divining lies for them, saying, 'The Lord Yahweh has said this' when Yahweh hasn't spoken;
- [29]the country's people have practised fraud and committed robbery, they've oppressed the humble and needy, and they've defrauded the alien without the proper exercise of authority.

[30]I sought from them someone constructing the wall or standing in the breach before me on behalf of the country, so I might not devastate it, but I didn't find anyone. [31]So I'm pouring out my condemnation on them. In furious fire I'm finishing them off. I'm putting their way on their head (a declaration of the Lord Yahweh)."'

A pornographic story begins

23 Yahweh's word came to me: [2]'Young man, there were two women, the daughters of one mother. [3]They whored in Misrayim. They whored in their youth. Their breasts were pressed there. There men squeezed their girls' nipples. [4]Their names: the older one was Oholah, and her sister was Oholibah. They became mine, and they gave birth to sons and daughters. Their names: Oholah was Shomron and Oholibah was Yerushalaim.

[5]Oholah whored when under me. She doted on her lovers, towards Ashshur, guardsmen [6]clothed in blue, governors and overseers, all of them desirable young men, cavalry riding horses. [7]She gave her whorings to them, all of them the choicest of the Ashshurites, and with each one on whom she doted, with all their lumps, she defiled herself. [8]She didn't abandon her whorings from Misrayim, because men had slept with her in her youth, when they'd squeezed her girl's nipples and poured out their whoring on her. [9]Therefore I gave her into the hand of her lovers, into the hand of the Ashshurites on whom she'd doted. [10]When they had exposed her nakedness, they took her sons and daughters and killed her with the sword. When they implemented rulings against her, she became well known to women.

[11]Her sister Oholibah saw, but her doting was more devastating than hers, and her whorings than her sister's whorings. [12]She doted on Ashshurites, governors and overseers, guardsmen clothed in fullness, cavalry riding horses, all of them desirable young men.

[13]I saw that she defiled herself. The two of them had one way, [14]but she increased her whorings. She saw men engraved on the wall, images of Kasdites engraved in vermilion, [15]girded with a belt round their hips, flowing turbans on their heads, all of them with the appearance of officers, the form of Babelites, Kasdim the country of their birth.

The two sisters

¹⁶So she doted on them on their appearing before her eyes. She sent envoys to them to Kasdim, ¹⁷and the Babelites came to her to her love bed. They defiled her with their whoring. She defiled herself with them, then tore herself away from them. ¹⁸So she exposed her whorings and revealed her nakedness, and I tore myself away from her, as I'd torn myself away from her sister. ¹⁹She multiplied her whorings, being mindful of her young days when she whored in the country of Misrayim. ²⁰She doted on their concubinage, whose flesh was the flesh of donkeys, and their emission the emission of horses. ²¹You attended to the scheming of your youth, when men from Misrayim squeezed your nipples for the sake of your young breasts.'

²²Therefore, Oholibah, the Lord Yahweh has said this: 'Here am I, I'm going to arouse your lovers against you, the ones from whom you tore yourself away. I shall bring them against you from all round: ²³the Babelites, all the Kasdites, Peqod, Shoa, Qoa, all the Ashshurites with them, desirable young men, governors and overseers all of them, officers and men of renown, riding horses all of them. ²⁴They will come against you, armoury, chariot and wheel, and with a congregation of peoples. They will set body-shield, hand-shield and helmet against you all round. I shall put the exercise of authority before them and they will exercise authority over you with their acts of authority. ²⁵So I shall set my passion against you, and they will deal with you in fury. They will remove your nose and your ears, and the last of you will fall by the sword. Those people will take your sons and your daughters, and the last of you will be consumed by fire. ²⁶They will strip you of your clothes and take your majestic things. ²⁷I shall make your scheming cease from you, and your whoring from the country of Misrayim. You won't lift up your eyes to them. You won't be mindful of Misrayim any more.'

Drunkenness and sorrow

²⁸Because the Lord Yahweh has said this: 'Here am I, I'm going to give you into the hand of the people to whom you are hostile, into the hand of the people from whom you tore yourself away. ²⁹They will act towards you with hostility and take all you've toiled for and abandon you naked and bare. The nakedness of your whorings will be visible, your scheming and your whorings. ³⁰They will do these things to you because of your whoring after the nations, on account of the way you defiled yourself with your lumps. ³¹You've walked in the way of your sister, so I shall put her chalice into your hand.'

³²The Lord Yahweh has said this:

'You're to drink your sister's chalice,
  deep and wide;
  it will bring laughter and scorn.
It contains much;
³³you will be full of drunkenness and sorrow,
A chalice of desolating and desolation,
  your sister Shomron's chalice.
³⁴You will drink it and drain it,
  and break it into shards
And tear your breasts,
  because I have spoken (a declaration of the Lord Yahweh).'

³⁵Therefore the Lord Yahweh has said this: 'Since you've put me out of mind and thrown me behind your back, you yourself indeed – carry your scheming and your whoring.'

³⁶Yahweh said to me, 'Young man, will you exercise authority over Oholah and Oholibah. Tell them of their offensive practices. ³⁷Because they've committed adultery and there's blood on their hands. They've committed adultery with their lumps and also made their children, to whom they gave birth for me, pass through [the fire] as food for them. ³⁸Further, they've done this to me: defiled my sanctuary and treated my sabbaths as ordinary. ³⁹When they'd slaughtered their children for their lumps, they came into my sanctuary that day, to treat it as ordinary. There, that's what they did within my house.

Worn out by adultery

⁴⁰Furthermore you would send for men coming from afar, to whom an envoy was sent. There, they came, men for whom you bathed, painted your eyes and donned jewellery. ⁴¹You

sat on an elegant couch with a table spread before it, and you put my incense and my oil on it. ⁴²The sound of a horde feeling at peace was in it, with men from the human mass brought in, drunkards from the wilderness. They put bracelets on the women's hands and a majestic crown on their heads.

⁴³I said of one worn out by adulteries, "Even now they can engage in whorings with her, and she herself", ⁴⁴and they've had sex with her. As men have sex with a whore, so they've had sex with Oholah and Oholibah, scheming women. ⁴⁵But faithful men – they will exercise authority over them, a ruling for women who commit adultery and a ruling for women who've shed blood, because they're women who commit adultery and with blood on their hands.'

⁴⁶Because the Lord Yahweh has said this: 'Take up a congregation against them, give them over to terror and to plunder. ⁴⁷The congregation is to pelt them with stones and cut them down with their swords. They're to kill their sons and their daughters and burn their houses in fire. ⁴⁸I shall put a stop to scheming from the country, and all the women will accept discipline and won't act in accordance with your scheming. ⁴⁹They'll put your scheming upon you. You will carry the wrongdoings involved in your lumps. And you will acknowledge that I am the Lord Yahweh.'

The cooking pot

24 Yahweh's word came to me in the ninth year, in the tenth month, on the tenth of the month: ²'Young man, write for yourself the date today, this very day. The king of Babel is leaning on Yerushalaim on this very day. ³And tell a parable to the rebellious household: "The Lord Yahweh has said this:

'Put the pot on, put it on,
    and pour water into it, too.
⁴Gather its pieces into it,
    every good piece.
Leg and shoulder,
    the choicest of the bones, fill it.
⁵Get the choicest of the flock,
    pile the bones under it, too.
Get it to boil;
    its bones are to cook inside it, too.'

⁶Therefore the Lord Yahweh has said this:

'Oh, town of bloodshed,
    pot in which there's rust,
    whose rust hasn't gone out from it!
Piece by piece get it out
    no lot has fallen on it.
⁷Because the blood she shed was inside her;
    she put it on the face of a cliff.
She didn't pour it on the ground
    to cover over it with earth.
⁸To arouse wrath
    to take redress,
I put the blood she shed on the face of a cliff
    so that it wouldn't be covered.'

⁹Therefore the Lord Yahweh has said this:

'Oh, town of bloodshed,
    I shall make the pile big, too.
¹⁰Get much wood, light the fire,
    cook the meat through.
Mix the spices;
    the bones must burn.
¹¹Stand it on the coals empty,
    in order that it may get hot and its copper burn,
So its defilement may smelt inside it,
    its rust be consumed.
¹²It has wearied the trouble;
    the abundance of its rust doesn't come out from it,
    the rust in the fire.'

¹³Your scheming is your defilement, since I would have cleansed you, but you wouldn't be clean from your defilement. You won't be clean again until I've set down my wrath on you. ¹⁴I Yahweh have spoken. It's coming about and I shall do it. I won't hold back. I won't spare. I won't relent. In accordance with your ways and in accordance with your deeds they are exercising authority over you (a declaration of the Lord Yahweh)."'

The bereavement

¹⁵Yahweh's word came to me: ¹⁶'Young man, here am I, I'm going to take from you the desire of your eyes through an epidemic. But you're not to mourn, you're not to cry, your

tears aren't to come. ¹⁷Groan quietly. Don't make mourning for the dead. Put on your hat. Put your boots on your feet. Don't cover your lips. Don't eat people's food.'

¹⁸I spoke to the people in the morning, and my wife died in the evening. I did in the morning as I'd been ordered, ¹⁹and the people said to me, 'Won't you tell us what these things mean for us, that you're acting so?'

²⁰I said to them, 'Yahweh's word came to me: ²¹"Say to Yisra'el's household: 'The Lord Yahweh has said this: "Here am I, I'm going to treat my sanctuary as ordinary, the pride of your vigour, the desire of your eyes, the object of your heart's pity. Your sons and your daughters whom you abandoned will fall by the sword. ²²You will do as I've done. You won't cover your lips. You won't eat people's food. ²³Your hat on your heads, your boots on your feet, you won't mourn and you won't cry. You will waste away because of your wayward acts and you will groan one to another. ²⁴So Yehezqe'l is to be a sign for you. In accordance with all that he's done, you will do, when it comes about. And you will acknowledge that I am the Lord Yahweh."'

²⁵You, young man, on the day I take from them their stronghold, their splendid object of celebration, the desire of their eyes, the longing of their heart, their sons and their daughters – ²⁶on that day someone who has escaped will come to let you hear it with your ears, won't he. ²⁷On that day your mouth will open to the one who has escaped, and you will speak and no longer be dumb. You will be a sign to them. And they will acknowledge that I am Yahweh."'

Redress is mine: Ammon and Mo'ab

25 Yahweh's word came to me: ²'Young man, set your face against the Ammonites and prophesy against them. ³Say to the Ammonites, "Listen to the word of the Lord Yahweh. The Lord Yahweh has said this: 'Because you said "Ah" about my sanctuary when it was treated as ordinary, and about Yisra'el's land when it became desolate, and about Yehudah's household when they went into exile, ⁴therefore, here am I, I'm going to give you to the Qedemites as a possession. They will set up their encampments in you and put their dwellings in you. Those people will eat your fruit. Those people will drink your milk. ⁵I shall make Rabbah an abode for camels and the Ammonites a fold for sheep. And you will acknowledge that I am Yahweh.'"

⁶Because the Lord Yahweh has said this: "Since you clapped your hand and stamped your foot and rejoiced with all your contempt in your soul about Yisra'el's land, ⁷therefore here am I, I'm going to stretch out my hand against you, and I shall give you as plunder to the nations. I shall cut you off from the peoples, obliterate you from the countries, annihilate you. And you will acknowledge that I am Yahweh."'

⁸The Lord Yahweh has said this: 'Because Mo'ab and Se'ir said, "There – Yehudah's household is like all the nations", ⁹therefore here am I, I'm going to open up Mo'ab's flank from the towns, from its towns on its extremity, the country's splendour – Bet Yeshimot, Ba'al Me'on and Qiryatayim – ¹⁰to the Qedemites, along with the Ammonites. I shall give it as a possession, so that the Ammonites may not be remembered among the nations ¹¹and I shall execute acts of authority against Mo'ab. And they will acknowledge that I am Yahweh.'

Redress meets redress: Edom and Peleshet (Philistia)

¹²The Lord Yahweh said this: 'Because of Edom's action in exacting redress on Yehudah's household and incurring liability when they took redress against them', ¹³therefore the Lord Yahweh has said this: 'I shall stretch out my hand against Edom and cut off from it human being and animal. I shall make it a waste from Teman to Dedan. They will fall by the sword. ¹⁴I shall inflict my redress on Edom by the hand of my people Yisra'el. They will act against Edom in accordance with my anger and with my fury, and they will acknowledge my redress (a declaration of the Lord Yahweh).'

¹⁵The Lord Yahweh has said this: 'Because of the Pelishtites' action in taking redress and because they've exacted redress with personal contempt in devastating with ancient enmity', ¹⁶therefore the Lord Yahweh has said this:

'Here am I, I'm going to stretch out my hand against the Pelishtites and cut off the Keretites, and obliterate what remains of the seacoast. ¹⁷I shall execute great acts of redress against them with acts of wrathful reproof, and they will acknowledge that I am Yahweh when I impose my redress on them.'

Tsor (Tyre): just a place for spreading nets

26 In the eleventh year on the first of the month, Yahweh's word came to me: ²'Young man, since Tsor has said about Yerushalaim, "Ah, the people's gateway has broken, it has turned round to me, I shall be full now it's been laid waste", ³therefore the Lord Yahweh has said this: "Here am I against you, Tsor; I shall make many nations go up against you, like the sea making its waves go up. ⁴They will devastate Tsor's walls and tear down its towers. I shall scrape off its soil and make it into the face of a cliff. ⁵It will become a place for spreading nets in the middle of the sea: because I have spoken (a declaration of the Lord Yahweh). It will become plunder for the nations. ⁶Its daughter-townships that are in the open country will be killed by the sword. And they will acknowledge that I am Yahweh."

⁷Because the Lord Yahweh has said this: "Here am I, I'm going to bring against Tsor from the north Nebukadne'tstsar king of Babel, king of kings, with horse, chariotry, cavalry, a congregation, a great company. ⁸Your daughter-townships in the open country he will kill with the sword. He will build a tower against you, heap up a ramp against you and set a body-shield against you. ⁹He will set his opposing force against your walls and demolish your towers with his axes. ¹⁰From the profusion of his horses their dust will cover you. From the sound of the cavalry, wheel and chariot, your wheels will shake, when he comes through your gateways like people coming into a breached town. ¹¹With the hoofs of his horses he will trample all your streets. He will kill your people with the sword. Your strong columns will descend to earth. ¹²They will plunder your wealth and loot your merchandise. They will tear down your walls and demolish your desirable houses. Your stones, your wood and your soil they will put in the middle of the water.

The sound of music stops

¹³I shall put a stop to the uproar of your songs, and the sound of your guitars will make itself heard no more. ¹⁴I shall make you into the face of a cliff. You will become a place for spreading nets. You won't be built up any more. Because I, Yahweh, have spoken (a declaration of the Lord Yahweh)."

¹⁵The Lord Yahweh has said to Tsor: "At the sound of your downfall, at the groan of the people run through, at the instigation of killing within you, will foreign shores not shake? ¹⁶All the sea's rulers will descend from their thrones. They will remove their robes, strip off their embroidered clothes and put on great trembling. They will sit on the ground and tremble at every moment and be desolate because of you.

¹⁷They will take up a dirge over you and say to you:

Oh, you've perished,
   you who were peopled from the seas,
The renowned town,
   one that was strong on the sea,
It and its inhabitants,
   people that put their terror on all its inhabitants.
¹⁸Now the foreign shores tremble,
   on the day of your downfall.
The foreign shores panic,
   they that are by the sea, at your passing."

¹⁹Because the Lord Yahweh has said this: "When I make you a wasted town, like towns that are not inhabited, when I take up the deep over you and the mighty water covers you, ²⁰I shall make you descend with the people who descend to the Pit, to the people of old, and I shall make you live in the world deep below, like the wastes from of old, with those who descend to the Pit, in order that you won't be inhabited. I shall make 'Splendour in the Country of the Living' – ²¹I shall make you a great horror. There will be nothing of you. You will be sought out, but you won't be found again, ever (a declaration of the Lord Yahweh).'"

Tsor, perfect in beauty?

27 Yahweh's word came to me: ²"You, young man, take up a dirge over Tsor. ³You're to say to Tsor, which lives at the entrance to the sea, trading with the peoples at many foreign shores: "The Lord Yahweh has said this:

Tsor, you said,
 'I am perfect in beauty.'
⁴Your borders were in the heart of the seas;
 your builders perfected your beauty.
⁵With juniper from Senir
 they built all your planks.
They got a cedar from Lebanon
 to make a mast for you.
⁶With oaks from Bashan
 they made your oars.
Your boarding they made of ivory inlaid in cypress
 from the shores of Kittim [Cyprus].
⁷Linen with embroidery from Misrayim became
  your spread,
 to be an ensign for you.
Blue and purple from the shores of Elishah
 became your covering.
⁸The inhabitants of Tsidon and Arvad
 were your rowers.
Your experts, Tsor, were within you;
 they were your sailors.
⁹The elders of Gebel and its experts were within you,
 strengthening your cracks.

All the ships of the sea and their mariners
 were in you to deal in your merchandise.
¹⁰Paras [Persia], Lydia and Put were in your force,
 your men of battle.
They hung shield and helmet in you;
 those men gave you your splendour.
¹¹People from Arvad and Helek
 were on your walls all round.
Gammadites were in your towers,
 they hung their quivers on your walls all round;
 those men perfected your beauty.

The dealer

¹²Tarshish was your dealer because of the quantity of all your wealth; they gave your wares in exchange for silver, iron, tin and lead. ¹³Yavan [Greece], Tubal and Meshek were your traders; they gave your merchandise in exchange for human life and things of copper. ¹⁴From Bet Togarmah they gave horses, cavalry and mules in exchange for your wares. ¹⁵The Dedanites were your traders. Many foreign shores were dealers under your control. They brought back to you ivory tusks and ebony as your payment. ¹⁶Aram was your dealer because of the quantity of your products; they gave your wares in exchange for turquoise, purple, embroidery, fine linen, coral and ruby. ¹⁷Yehudah and the country of Yisra'el were your merchants; they gave your merchandise in exchange for wheat from Minnit and Pannag, syrup, oil and balm. ¹⁸Dammeseq [Damascus] was your dealer because of the quantity of your products, because of the quantity of all your wealth, in wine of Helbon and white wool. ¹⁹Vedan and Yavan gave yarn in exchange for your wares; there was wrought iron, cassia and cane among your merchandise. ²⁰Dedan was your trader in saddlecloths for riding. ²¹Arabia and all Qedar's rulers were dealers under your control in lambs, rams and goats, as your dealers in these.
²²The traders of Sheba and Ra'amah were your traders; they gave your wares in exchange for the finest of all spice and for all precious stone and gold. ²³Haran, Kanneh and Eden, the traders of Sheba, Ashshur and Kilmad, were your traders. ²⁴Those were your traders in fine things, in blue embroidered cloths, and in coloured rugs bound with cords and preserved with cedar, in your market. ²⁵Tarshish ships were your ministers for your merchandise.

The wreck of the *Titanic*

You were full and very heavy
 in the heart of the seas.
²⁶Into the mighty water
 the rowers brought you.
The east wind broke you
 in the heart of the seas.
²⁷Your wealth and your wares, your merchandise,
 your mariners and your sailors,
The men who strengthened your cracks,
 and the people who handled your merchandise,
All your men of battle who were in you,
 and in all your congregation that was within
  you,

Will fall in the heart of the seas
  on the day of your downfall.
²⁸At the sound of your sailors' cry,
  the shorelands will shake.
²⁹All the oarsmen
  will come down from their ships.
The mariners, all the sailors of the sea,
  will stand on the earth.
³⁰They will let their voice be heard concerning you,
  and cry in distress.
They will take up earth on to their head,
  and cover themselves in ash.
³¹For you, they will shave their head,
  and wrap on sack.
They will cry for you with bitterness of soul,
  with bitter lament.
³²For you they will take up a dirge as they groan,
  and lament for you:
'Who was like Tsor,
  like the one silenced in the middle of the sea?'
³³When your wares went out from the seas,
  you filled many peoples.
With the quantity of your wealth and your merchandise
  you enriched earth's kings.
³⁴The time when you broke because of the seas,
  in the depths of the water,
Your merchandise and all your congregation
  fell in the middle of it.
³⁵All the inhabitants of foreign shores
  are desolate over you.
Their kings bristled with horror,
  their faces went dark.
³⁶The dealers among the peoples whistled at you;
  you became a horror, and you're no more, permanently."'

Another king who thinks he's a god

28 Yahweh's word came to me: ²'Young man, say to Tsor's ruler: "The Lord Yahweh has said this: 'Because your mind has been lofty and you've said, "I am a god, I am sitting as a deity – I've taken my seat in the heart of the seas"', when you're a human being and not God, but you made your mind like a deity's mind:

³There, you're smarter than Dan'el;
  nothing hidden baffles you.
⁴Through your smartness and your discernment
  you've made wealth for yourself.
You've made gold and silver in your treasuries
  ⁵through the magnitude of your smartness and
    through your trading.
You've made your wealth great,
  but you've let your mind get lofty because of
    your wealth.

⁶Therefore the Lord Yahweh has said this:

Because of your making your mind
  like the mind of a deity,
⁷Therefore here am I, I'm going to bring against you
  strangers, the most violent of nations.
They will draw their swords against your smart beauty
  and run you through in your splendour.
⁸Down to the Pit they will make you descend;
  you will die the death of someone run through
    in the heart of the seas.
⁹Will you actually say 'I'm a deity'
  before your killers –
Given that you're a human being and not God –
  at the hand of the people who run you through?
¹⁰The death of the foreskinned
  you will die, at the hand of strangers,
  because I have spoken (a declaration of the
    Lord Yahweh).'"

A dirge for a living king

¹¹Yahweh's word came to me: ¹²'Young man, take up a dirge over the king of Tsor. You're to say to him: "The Lord Yahweh has said this:

You were an exact seal,
  full of smartness, perfect in beauty.
¹³You were in Eden, God's garden,
  every precious stone your covering:
Carnelian, topaz and diamond,
  beryl, onyx and jasper,
Sapphire, turquoise and emerald,
  and gold, the work of your tambourines,
And your sockets in you,
  that were prepared on the day of your creation.

¹⁴You were a sphinx, anointed as the protector,
  and I placed you –
  you were on God's sacred mountain.
When you walked about among the fiery stones,
  ¹⁵you were a person of integrity in all your ways,

From the day of your creation,
    until evil appeared in you.
¹⁶Through the quantity of your trading,
    people filled the middle of you with violence.
You did wrong, and I am treating you as ordinary,
    away from God's mountain, and destroying you,
Sphinx the protector,
    from among the fiery stones.
¹⁷Your mind became lofty because of your beauty;
    you devastated your smartness, through your splendour.
I'm throwing you out on to the earth;
    before kings I'm making you something to stare at.
¹⁸Because of the quantity of your wayward acts,
    through the evil of your trading,
You've treated your great sanctuary as ordinary.
    I'm making fire go out from within you and it's devouring you.
I'm making you into ash on the earth
    before the eyes of all who look at you.
¹⁹All who acknowledge you among the peoples
    are becoming desolate at you.
You're becoming a horror,
    and you will be no more, permanently.'"

No more prickling briar

²⁰Yahweh's word came to me: ²¹"Young man, set your face towards Tsidon and prophesy against it. ²²You're to say, "The Lord Yahweh has said this:

Here am I against you, Tsidon;
    I shall get honour within you.
They will acknowledge that I am Yahweh,
    when I execute acts of authority against it.
I shall show myself sacred in it
    ²³and let loose epidemic in it and blood in its streets.
The run through will fall within it
    by the sword that's against it from all round,
    and they will acknowledge that I am Yahweh.

²⁴No more will there be for Yisra'el's household prickling briar and piercing thorn from all the people round them who treat them with contempt. And they will acknowledge that I am the Lord Yahweh.'"

²⁵The Lord Yahweh has said this: 'When I have collected Yisra'el's household from the peoples among whom they're dispersed and I've shown myself sacred among them before the eyes of the nations, they will live on their land that I gave my servant Ya'aqob, ²⁶and live on it with confidence. They will build houses and plant vineyards and live with confidence, when I have executed acts of authority on all the people who treat them with contempt, who are round them. And they will acknowledge that I Yahweh am their God.'

The Ye'or (Nile) is mine: I made it

29 In the tenth year, in the tenth, on the twelfth of the month, Yahweh's word came to me: ²'Young man, set your face against Par'oh king of Misrayim, and prophesy against him and against Misrayim, all of it. ³Speak: "The Lord Yahweh has said this:

Here am I against you,
    Par'oh king of Misrayim,
Big monster stretching out
    in the middle of its channels,
That said, 'My Ye'or is mine;
    I'm the one who made it.'
⁴I shall put hooks in your jaws
    and make the fish in your channels stick to your scales.
I shall get you up from the middle of your channels,
    with all the fish in your channels that stick to your scales.
⁵I shall leave you to the wilderness,
    you and all the fish in your channels.
You will fall on the face of the open country;
    you won't be gathered and you won't be collected.
I'm giving you as food to the creatures of the earth
    and to the birds of the heavens.
⁶And all the inhabitants of Misrayim
    will acknowledge that I am Yahweh.
Since they were something to lean on that was made of reed
    for Yisra'el's household,
⁷When they grasped you in their fist, you would fracture,
    and tear their entire shoulder.
When they leaned on you, you'd break,
    and make their entire hips collapse."

⁸Therefore the Lord Yahweh has said this: "Here am I, I'm going to bring a sword against you. I shall cut off from you human being and animal. ⁹The country of Misrayim will become desolation and waste. And they will acknowledge that I am Yahweh.

Because he said, 'The Ye'or is mine; I'm the one who made it', ¹⁰therefore here am I towards you and towards your channels: I shall make the country of Misrayim an utter waste and desolation, from Migdol to Seweneh, as far as the border with Kush [Sudan]. ¹¹Human foot won't pass through it and animal foot won't pass through it. It won't be inhabited for forty years.

Misrayim as compensation

¹²I shall make the country of Misrayim a desolation in the middle of desolate countries, and its towns in the middle of ruined towns will be a desolation for forty years. I shall scatter the Misrayimites among the nations and disperse them among the countries.'"

¹³Indeed the Lord Yahweh has said this: 'At the end of forty years I shall collect the Misrayimites from the peoples where they've scattered. ¹⁴I shall restore the fortunes of the Misrayimites and bring them back to the country of Patros, on to the country of their origin. They will be a lowly kingdom there. ¹⁵It will be the lowliest of the kingdoms; it won't arise again over the nations. I shall make them small so they don't have dominion over the nations. ¹⁶It won't again be an object of reliance for Yisra'el's household, making it mindful of its waywardness in turning its face after them. And they will acknowledge that I am the Lord Yahweh.'

¹⁷In the twenty-seventh year, on the first of the first month, Yahweh's word came to me: ¹⁸'Young man, Nebukadne'tstsar king of Babel has made his forces serve with great servitude against Tsor. Every head is rubbed bare. Every shoulder is scraped. But he and his forces have no wages from Tsor for the servitude with which they have served on it.'

¹⁹Therefore the Lord Yahweh has said this: 'Here am I, I'm going to give the country of Misrayim to Nebukadne'tstsar king of Babel. He will carry off its wealth, take spoil from it and seize plunder from it, and it will be the wages for his force. ²⁰As his compensation for which he served, I'm giving him the country of Misrayim, because they acted for me (a declaration of the Lord Yahweh).

²¹On that day I shall make a horn grow for Yisra'el's household, and to you I shall give an opening of your mouth among them. And they will acknowledge that I am Yahweh.'

The day of the Lord for Misrayim

30 Yahweh's word came to me: ²'Young man, prophesy: "Yahweh has said this:

Howl, aagh for the day,
    ³because Yahweh's day is near.
A day of cloud,
    a time for nations, it will be.
⁴A sword will come upon Misrayim,
    anguish will fall upon Kush,
When people fall, run through, in Misrayim,
    and people take its wealth, and its foundations
    are torn down.
⁵Kush, Put, Lydia, the entire foreign group,
    Cyrenaica, and members of the country in the
        pact
    will fall by the sword with them.

⁶Yahweh has said this:

The people who support Misrayim will fall;
    its vigorous majesty will go down.
From Migdol to Seweneh
    they will fall there by the sword (a declaration
        of the Lord Yahweh).

⁷They will be desolate among desolate countries, and its towns will be among wasted towns. ⁸And they will acknowledge that I am Yahweh when I put fire in Misrayim, and all its helpers break. ⁹On that day envoys will go out from before me in ships to make confident Kush tremble. Anguish will be upon them on Misrayim's day, because there, it's coming."

¹⁰The Lord Yahweh has said this: "And I shall put a stop to Misrayim's horde by the hand of Nebukadne'tstsar king of Babel. ¹¹He and his company with him, the most violent of nations, are going to be brought to devastate the country. They will draw their swords against

Misrayim and fill the country with the people run through. ¹²I shall make the channels dry ground and sell the country into the hand of bad people. I shall desolate the country and everything in it by the hand of strangers. I, Yahweh, have spoken."

Acts of authority on Misrayim

¹³The Lord Yahweh has said this: "I shall obliterate the lumps and make the non-entities cease from Memphis. There will no longer be a ruler from the country of Misrayim. I shall put fear in the country of Misrayim. ¹⁴I shall desolate Patros. I shall put fire in Tso'an. I shall execute acts of authority in Thebes. ¹⁵I shall pour out my fury on Pelusium, Misrayim's stronghold. I shall cut off the horde of Thebes. ¹⁶I shall put fire in Misrayim. Pelusium will writhe and writhe. Thebes will be torn apart. Memphis: adversaries daily. ¹⁷The young men of Heliopolis and Pi-beset will fall by the sword. Those – they will go into exile. ¹⁸In Tehaphnehes the day will be dark when I break Misrayim's yokes there, and its vigorous majesty comes to a stop in it. Cloud will cover it and its daughter-townships will go into captivity. ¹⁹I shall execute acts of authority in Misrayim, and they will acknowledge that I am Yahweh.'"

²⁰In the eleventh year, in the first, on the seventh of the month, Yahweh's word came to me: ²¹"Young man, I'm breaking the arm of Par'oh king of Misrayim. There, it's not bound up so as to give healing, by putting a bandage to bind it up to strengthen it for grasping a sword.'

²²Therefore the Lord Yahweh has said this: 'Here am I towards Par'oh king of Misrayim. I shall break his arms, the strong one and the broken one. I shall make the sword fall from his hand. ²³I shall scatter the Misrayimites among the nations and disperse them among the countries. ²⁴I shall strengthen the arms of the king of Babel and put my sword in his hand. I shall break the arms of Par'oh. He will groan before him with the groans of someone run through. ²⁵I shall strengthen the arms of the king of Babel, but Par'oh's arms – they will fall. And they will acknowledge that I am Yahweh, when I put my sword into the hand of the king of Babel and he stretches it out against the country of Misrayim. ²⁶I shall scatter the Misrayimites among the nations and disperse them among the countries, and they will acknowledge that I am Yahweh.'

An empire on which the sun never sets?

31 In the eleventh year, in the third, on the first of the month, Yahweh's word came to me: ²'Young man, say to Par'oh king of Misrayim and to his horde: "To whom are you like in your greatness?

³There, Ashshur was a cedar in Lebanon,
 beautiful in boughs, and a shady thicket,
Lofty in height,
 and its top was among the clouds.
⁴Water made it big, the deep made it high,
 going with its rivers round its plantation.
It sent its channels
 to all the trees of the open country.
⁵As a result its height was loftier
 than all the trees of the open country.
Its branches abounded, its boughs extended,
 because of the abundant water in its channel.
⁶All the birds of the heavens
 nested in its branches.
All the animals of the open country
 gave birth under its boughs.
All the great nations
 were living in its shade.
⁷It was beautiful in its great size, in the length of its branches,
 because its root was by abundant water.
⁸Cedars in God's garden didn't overshadow it,
 junipers didn't equal its branches,
 plane trees didn't compare with its boughs.
No tree in God's garden
 equalled it in its beauty.
⁹I made it beautiful
 in the number of its branches.
All the trees of Eden were jealous of it,
 the ones that were in God's garden."

Learn from its fall

¹⁰Therefore the Lord Yahweh has said this: "Since you were lofty in height – and it put its top into the middle of the clouds, and its mind became exalted in its loftiness, ¹¹I gave it into the hand of the leader of the nations so he'd deal effectively with it. In accordance with its

faithlessness I dispossessed it. ¹²Strangers, the most violent of nations, cut it down and left it. Its branches fell on the mountains and in all the ravines, and its boughs broke into all the canyons in the earth. All the peoples of the earth went down from its shade and left it.

¹³Upon it, fallen, all the birds of the heavens dwell, and to its boughs came all the animals of the open country – ¹⁴in order that no trees by water should become lofty in their height or put their top among the clouds, nor should any of their mighty ones, drinkers of water, stand up in their loftiness, because all of them were given over to death, to the country below, among all human beings, with the people who go down to the Pit."

¹⁵The Lord Yahweh has said this: "On the day it went down to She'ol, I caused mourning, I closed the deep over it. I held back its rivers; the abundant water held back. I made Lebanon grieve over it. All the trees of the open country languished over it. ¹⁶At the sound of its fall I made the nations shake, when I made it go down to She'ol with the people who go down to the Pit. In the country below, all the trees of Eden, the choicest and best of Lebanon, all the drinkers of water, found consolation. ¹⁷They also went down with it to She'ol, to the people run through by the sword, and its [supporting] arm, the people who had lived in its shadow among the nations.

¹⁸To whom are you thus like, in honour and in greatness among the trees of Eden? You will be brought down with the trees of Eden to the country below. Among the foreskinned you will lie, with the people run through by the sword. That is Par'oh and his entire horde (a declaration of the Lord Yahweh).'"

The dragon caught

32 In the twelfth year in the twelfth month on the first of the month, Yahweh's word came to me: ²'Young man, take up a dirge over Par'oh king of Misrayim:

Lion of the nations, you are being terminated,
    though you are like the dragon in the water.
You've thrust forth with your rivers,
    you've stirred up the water with your feet,
    you've muddied their rivers.

³The Lord Yahweh has said this:

And I shall spread my mesh over you
    in a congregation of many peoples.
I shall lift you up in my net ⁴and leave you on the earth;
I shall throw you on the face of the open country.
I shall get all the birds of the heavens to dwell on you;
    I shall get the animals of the entire earth to be full from you.
⁵I shall put your flesh on the mountains
    and fill the ravines with your height.
⁶I shall drench the earth
    with the flow of your blood on the mountains,
    and canyons will fill from you.
⁷I shall cover the heavens when I put you out,
    and make their stars dark.
I shall cover the sun with cloud,
    and the moon won't give its light.
⁸All the bright lights in the heavens
    I shall make dark above you.
I shall put darkness on your country
    (a declaration of the Lord Yahweh)
⁹and vex the mind of many peoples,
When I bring you broken among the nations,
    to countries that you haven't known.
¹⁰I shall make many peoples desolate because of you;
    their kings will bristle with horror because of you.
When I whirl my sword in their faces,
    they will tremble at every moment,
Each for his own life,
    on the day of your fall.

The great leveller

¹¹Because the Lord Yahweh has said this:

The king of Babel's sword will come to you;
    ¹²by strong men's swords I shall make your horde fall,
    the most violent among the nations, all of them.
They will destroy Misrayim's majesty;
    its entire horde will be annihilated.
¹³I shall obliterate all its cattle
    from beside abundant water.
Human feet will no more muddy them,
    and animal hoofs won't muddy them.
¹⁴Then I shall settle their water,
    make their rivers go like oil (a declaration of the Lord Yahweh).

¹⁵When I make the country of Misrayim a desolation
 and the country is desolate of what filled it,
When I strike down all the people who live in it,
 they will acknowledge that I am Yahweh.

¹⁶That is a dirge, and people will lament with it;
 the nations' daughters will lament with it.
Over Misrayim and over its entire horde
 they will lament with it (a declaration of the Lord Yahweh).'

¹⁷In the twelfth year, on the fifteenth of the month, Yahweh's word came to me: ¹⁸'Young man, wail for Misrayim's horde. You're to send them down, it and the daughter-townships of mighty nations, to the country deep below, with the people who go down to the Pit. ¹⁹"Than whom are you more beautiful? Go down and be laid down with the foreskinned." ²⁰They will fall among people run through by the sword. The sword has been given over. They're dragging it off with all its hordes. ²¹The mightiest of strong men speak to him from within She'ol, with his helpers. The foreskinned, people run through by the sword, have gone down and lain down. ²²Ashshur is there, and all its congregation, round him his graves, all of them run through, fallen by the sword, ²³whose graves were put in the Pit's far parts, and its congregation was round its grave, all of them run through, fallen by the sword, people who'd spread terror in the country of the living.

The strange consolation

²⁴Elam is there, and all its horde, round its grave, all of them run through, fallen by the sword, people who went down foreskinned to the country deep below, people who had put their terror in the country of the living but carried their shame with the people who go down to the Pit. ²⁵Among the run through they've given it a bed, with all its graves round it, all of them foreskinned, run through by the sword. Because their terror was put in the country of the living, they carried their shame with the people who go down to the Pit; among the run through, he is put.

²⁶Meshek and Tubal and its entire horde are there. Its graves are round it, all of them foreskinned, run through by the sword, because they put their terror in the country of the living. ²⁷They don't lie with the fallen strong men of the foreskinned, who went down to She'ol with their battle equipment and put their swords under their heads. Their wayward acts were upon their frames, because the strong men's terror had been in the country of the living. ²⁸And you yourselves will break among the foreskinned and will lie down with people run through by the sword.

²⁹Edom is there, its kings and all its rulers, who despite their strength are put with the people run through by the sword. Those people lie with the foreskinned and with the people who go down to the Pit. ³⁰The leaders of the north, all of them, are there, and all the Tsidonites, who went down with the people run through despite their terror that issued from their strength, disgraced. They lie foreskinned with the people run through by the sword. They carried their shame with the people who go down to the Pit.

³¹These Par'oh will see, and he will be consoled over his entire horde, Par'oh's people who were run through by the sword, all his force (a declaration of the Lord Yahweh). ³²Because I'm putting my terror in the country of the living. He will be laid down among the foreskinned with the people run through by the sword, Par'oh and his entire horde (a declaration of the Lord Yahweh).'

The lookout

33 Yahweh's word came to me: ²'Young man, speak to the members of your people: "Regarding a country: when I bring the sword against it, and the country's people take someone from their number and make him into their lookout, ³and he sees the sword coming against the country and blows the horn and warns the people, ⁴and someone hears the sound of the horn but doesn't take warning and the sword comes and takes him – his blood will be on his own head. ⁵He heard the sound of the horn but didn't take warning; his blood will be on him. Had that person taken warning, he'd have saved his life. ⁶But should the lookout, when he sees the sword coming, not blow the horn, and the people don't take warning, and the sword comes and takes one of them, that person gets taken because of his own waywardness, but I shall require his blood from the lookout."

⁷So you, young man, I've made you a lookout for Yisra'el's household. You will hear a word from my mouth, and you're to warn them from me. ⁸When I say to the faithless person, "Faithless one, you shall definitely die", and you haven't spoken to warn the faithless person from his way, that faithless person will die because of his waywardness, but I shall require his blood from your hand. ⁹But you – when you've warned the faithless person from his way, to turn back from it, and he hasn't turned from his way, he will die because of his waywardness, but you will rescue your life.

¹⁰But you, young man, say to Yisra'el's household: "You've said this: 'Our rebellions and our wrongdoings rest upon us. Because of them we're wasting away, and how can we live?'" ¹¹Say to them, "As I live (a declaration of the Lord Yahweh), if I want the death of the faithless person . . . rather that the faithless person should turn back from his way and live. Turn back, turn back, from your bad ways. Why should you die, Yisra'el's household?"

The news arrives

¹²So you, young man, say to the members of your people: "The faithfulness of the faithful person won't rescue him on the day of his rebellion, and the faithlessness of the faithless person – he won't fall because of it on the day he turns back from his faithlessness. So the faithful person won't be able to live because of it on the day he commits wrongdoing. ¹³When I say of the faithful person, 'He will indeed live', but he trusts in his faithfulness and does evil, none of his faithful deeds will be kept in mind. Because of the evil that he's done – he will die because of it. ¹⁴And when I say to the faithless person, 'You will definitely die', and he turns back from his wrongdoing and exercises authority faithfully ¹⁵(the faithless person gives back a pledge, makes good for what was stolen, walks by the laws of life, so as not to do evil), he will definitely live, he won't die. ¹⁶None of his wrongdoings that he's committed will be kept in mind for him. He's exercised authority faithfully. He will definitely live."

¹⁷The members of your people say, "The Lord's way isn't right." But they – their way isn't right. ¹⁸When a faithful person turns from his faithfulness and does evil, he will die because of them. ¹⁹When a faithless person turns from his faithlessness and exercises authority faithfully, on account of them that person will live. ²⁰And you say, "The Lord's way isn't right." I exercise authority over each person in accordance with his ways, Yisra'el's household.'

²¹In the twelfth year of our exile, in the tenth, on the fifth of the month, somebody who'd escaped from Yerushalaim came to me, saying, 'The town's been struck down.' ²²Yahweh's hand had come upon me in the evening before the person who'd escaped came, and he'd opened my mouth, before he came to me in the morning. So my mouth had opened. I was no longer dumb.

On how not to listen to a preacher

²³Yahweh's word came to me: ²⁴'Young man, the people living in these wastes on Yisra'el's land are saying, "Abraham was one man, but he came to possess the country, whereas we're many. The country is given to us as a possession." ²⁵Therefore say to them, "The Lord Yahweh has said this: 'You eat with the blood, you raise your eyes to your lumps and you shed blood – and you will enter into possession of the country? ²⁶You've stood by your sword, you've done an offensive thing and you've each defiled his neighbour's wife – and you will enter into possession of the country?'"

²⁷You're to say this to them: "The Lord Yahweh has said this: 'As I live, if the people in the wastes don't fall by the sword and I don't give the people in the open country to the animals for them to eat, and the people in the strongholds and in the caves don't die in an epidemic . . .

²⁸I shall make the country desolating and desolation. Its vigorous majesty will cease, Yisra'el's mountains will be desolate, with no one passing through, ²⁹and they will acknowledge that I am Yahweh, when I make the country desolating and desolation because of all their offensive deeds that they've done.'"

³⁰But you, young man: the members of your people are speaking about you by the walls and in the entrances of the houses. One speaks to

another, a man to his brother: "Come, please, listen to what word is coming out from Yahweh." ³¹They will come to you like a people coming, and sit before you, my people, and listen to your words. But they won't do them, because while they're making amorous sounds with their mouths, their mind is going after their loot. ³²And there are you, like a singer of amorous sounds to them, beautiful in voice and doing well in playing, and they listen to your words but none of them are doing them. ³³But when it comes about (there, it's coming), they will acknowledge that a prophet's been among them.'

The self-indulgent shepherds

34 Yahweh's word came to me: ²'Young man, prophesy against Yisra'el's shepherds. Prophesy and say to them, "About the shepherds, the Lord Yahweh has said this: 'Hey, Yisra'el's shepherds, who've been shepherding themselves: isn't it the flock that shepherds shepherd? ³You eat the fat and clothe yourselves in the wool, you sacrifice the fatlings; you don't shepherd the flock. ⁴You haven't strengthened the weak, nor healed the sick, nor bandaged the broken, nor brought back the scattered, nor sought the missing, but ruled them with harshness and cruelty. ⁵They scattered for lack of a shepherd, and they became food for any animal of the open country when they scattered. ⁶My flock wanders through all the mountains and on every high hill. My flock scattered over the face of the country. There's been no one seeking and no one looking.'"

⁷Therefore, shepherds, listen to Yahweh's word. ⁸'As I live (a declaration of the Lord Yahweh), since my flock's become plunder and my flock's become food for any animal of the open country through the lack of anyone shepherding, and my shepherds haven't sought my flock, but the shepherds have shepherded themselves and not shepherded my flock, if I don't . . .'

⁹Therefore listen, you shepherds, to Yahweh's word. ¹⁰The Lord Yahweh has said this: 'Here am I towards the shepherds. I shall require my flock from their hand. I shall make them stop shepherding the flock, and the shepherds won't shepherd themselves any more. I shall rescue my flock from their mouth. They won't be food for them.'

The good shepherd

¹¹Because the Lord Yahweh has said this: 'Here am I, myself, and I shall enquire after my flock and search for them. ¹²Like a shepherd searching after his herd when he's among his dispersed flock, so I shall search for my flock and rescue them from all the places where they've scattered on the day of cloud and gloom. ¹³I shall get them out from the peoples, collect them from the countries and bring them to their land. I shall shepherd them on Yisra'el's mountains by the canyons and by all the country's settlements. ¹⁴I shall shepherd them on good pasturage; their abode will be on Yisra'el's high mountains. There they will lie down in a good abode, and they will pasture on rich pasturage on Yisra'el's mountains. ¹⁵I myself shall shepherd my flock and I myself shall get them to lie down (a declaration of the Lord Yahweh). ¹⁶I shall seek the missing, bring back the scattered, bandage the broken and strengthen the weak. But the fat and the strong I shall destroy. I shall shepherd with authority.

¹⁷And you, my flock (the Lord Yahweh has said this): here am I, I'm going to decide between one animal and another. About rams and he-goats: ¹⁸is it too little for you that you pasture on good pasturage, but you trample with your feet what's left of your pasturage, and that you drink the clearest of the water, but muddy what's left with your feet, ¹⁹so that my flock pastures on what your feet have trampled and your feet have muddied?'

²⁰Therefore the Lord Yahweh has said this to them: 'Here am I, and I shall decide between fat animal and thin animal. ²¹Since you were pushing with flank and shoulder, and butting with your horns against all the sick, until you scattered them abroad, ²²I shall deliver my flock, and it will no longer be plunder. I shall decide between one animal and another.

The Davidic shepherd

²³And I shall set up over them one shepherd and he will shepherd them, my servant David. He's the one who will shepherd them. He'll be their shepherd. ²⁴I, Yahweh, will be their God, with my servant David ruler among them. I Yahweh have spoken. ²⁵I shall solemnize a

pact of well-being for them. I shall stop bad creatures from the country, and they will live in the wilderness with confidence and sleep in the forests.

²⁶I shall make them and the environs of my hill a blessing. I shall make the rain come down in its season; they will be showers that bring blessing. ²⁷The trees of the open country will give their fruit; the earth will give its produce. People will be on their land with confidence, and they will acknowledge that I am Yahweh, when I break the bars of their yoke and rescue them from the people who make them serve them. ²⁸They will no longer be plunder for the nations. The country's creatures won't eat them and they will live in confidence with no one disturbing them.

²⁹I shall set up for them a plantation of renown, and they will no longer be carried off by famine in the country. They will no longer bear the nations' shame. ³⁰And they will acknowledge that I am Yahweh their God with them and they, Yisra'el's household, are my people (a declaration of the Lord Yahweh). ³¹You, my flock, the flock I shepherd, you're human, and I am your God (a declaration of the Lord Yahweh).'

The two peoples

35 Yahweh's word came to me: ²'Young man, set your face against Mount Se'ir and prophesy against it. ³You're to say to it: "The Lord Yahweh has said this: 'Here am I towards you, Mount Se'ir. I shall stretch out my hand against you and make you desolating and desolation. ⁴Your towns I shall make into a waste and you will be a desolation, and you will acknowledge that I am Yahweh.

⁵Since you had an ancient enmity and you hurled the Yisra'elites into the power of the sword at the time of their calamity, at the time of their final waywardness, ⁶therefore, as I live (a declaration of the Lord Yahweh), I shall make you into blood; blood will pursue you. Given that you were not hostile to blood, blood will pursue you. ⁷I shall make Mount Se'ir desolation and desolating, and I shall cut off from it anyone passing by and anyone coming back. ⁸I shall fill its mountains with its people run through. Your hills, your valleys and all your canyons – people run through by the sword will fall in them. ⁹I shall make you a permanent desolation, your towns won't be inhabited and you will acknowledge that I am Yahweh.

¹⁰Since you said, "The two nations and the two countries will be mine, and we shall possess them" (but Yahweh was there), ¹¹therefore as I live (a declaration of the Lord Yahweh), I shall act in accordance with your anger and with your passion with which you acted out of your hostility to them. I shall cause myself to be acknowledged among them as I exercise authority over you. ¹²You will acknowledge that I Yahweh have heard all your insults, which you've uttered about Yisra'el's mountains: "They're desolate, they've been given to us as food." ¹³You acted big against me with your mouth and you made your words proliferate against me. I myself heard.'"

¹⁴The Lord Yahweh has said this: 'In accordance with the rejoicing over the entire country, I shall make you a desolation. ¹⁵In accordance with your rejoicing over the domain that belonged to Yisra'el's household, because it became desolate, so I shall act towards you. You will become a desolation, Mount Se'ir and all Edom, all of it. And they will acknowledge that I am Yahweh.'

The mountains renewed

36 'And you, young man, prophesy towards Yisra'el's mountains: "Mountains of Yisra'el, listen to Yahweh's word. ²The Lord Yahweh has said this: 'Since the enemy said over you, "Ah", and "The ancient shrines have become ours as a domain", ³therefore prophesy: "The Lord Yahweh has said this: 'Since, yes since they made you desolate and trampled you all round, so that you became the possession of the remaining nations, and you were taken up on to the lip of the tongue and the slur of the people, ⁴therefore, Yisra'el's mountains, listen to the Lord Yahweh's word.

The Lord Yahweh has said this to the mountains, to the hills, to the canyons, to the ravines, to the desolate wastes, and to the abandoned towns that have become plunder and derision to the remaining nations that are all round – ⁵therefore the Lord Yahweh has said: "If I haven't spoken in my passionate anger against the remaining nations and against Edom, all of it, which made my country a possession for itself with wholehearted rejoicing, with contempt of soul, for the sake of pastureland, as plunder...""

⁶Therefore prophesy about Yisra'el's land. You're to say to the mountains, to the hills, to the canyons and to the ravines, "The Lord Yahweh has said this: 'Here am I, I'm going to speak in my passion and in my fury, since you've carried the nations' shame.' ⁷Therefore the Lord Yahweh has said this: 'I myself have raised my hand [to swear]: if the nations that are from all round you don't carry their shame...

⁸But you, Yisra'el's mountains, will produce your boughs and bear your fruit for my people Yisra'el, because they're near coming. ⁹Because here am I towards you, and I shall turn my face to you, and you will be served and sown. ¹⁰I shall make the people on you abundant, Yisra'el's entire household, all of it. The towns will be inhabited, the wastes built up. ¹¹I shall multiply on you human beings and animals; they'll be many and they'll be fruitful. I shall cause you to be inhabited as you were before and I shall make things good for you, better than before for you, and you will acknowledge that I am Yahweh. ¹²I shall get people, my people Yisra'el, to walk upon you. They will come to possess you and you will be their domain. You won't bereave them ever again.""

Yahweh takes pity on his name

¹³The Lord Yahweh has said this: 'Since they're saying to you, "You've been one who devours human beings, who bereaves your nations", ¹⁴therefore you will no more devour human beings, you will not bereave your nations again any more (a declaration of the Lord Yahweh). ¹⁵I shall not let you hear the nations' shaming any more. You will no more carry the peoples' reviling. You will no more make your nations collapse (a declaration of the Lord Yahweh).'

¹⁶Yahweh's word came to me: ¹⁷'Young man, when Yisra'el's household were living on their land, they defiled it with their way and with their deeds. In my eyes their way was like the defilement of a woman who's taboo. ¹⁸So I poured out my fury on them because of the blood they had poured out on the earth, and they had defiled it with their lumps. ¹⁹I scattered them among the nations and they were dispersed among the countries. In accordance with their way and with their deeds I exercised authority over them.

²⁰They came to the nations, wherever they came, and treated my sacred name as ordinary, in that people said of them, "These are Yahweh's people, but they went out of his country." ²¹But I have taken pity on my sacred name, which Yisra'el's household caused to be treated as ordinary among the nations where they came.

²²Therefore say to Yisra'el's household: "The Lord Yahweh has said this: 'It's not for your sake that I'm going to act, Yisra'el's household, but for my sacred name, which you've caused to be treated as ordinary among the nations where you came. ²³I shall make my great name sacred, which has been treated as ordinary among the nations among whom you have caused it to be treated as ordinary, and the nations will acknowledge that I am Yahweh (a declaration of the Lord Yahweh) when I show myself sacred through you before their eyes.

²⁴I shall take you from the nations, collect you from all the countries and bring you to your land. ²⁵I shall toss clean water over you and you'll be clean. From all your defilements and from all your lumps I shall cleanse you.

The gift of a new mind and a new spirit

²⁶I shall give you a new mind and I shall put a new spirit inside you. I shall remove the stony mind from your flesh and give you a fleshy mind, ²⁷and I shall put my spirit inside you. I shall make it so that you walk by my laws and keep my rulings and do them. ²⁸You will live in the country that I gave your ancestors, and you will be my people and I shall be your God. ²⁹I shall deliver you from all your defilements. I shall call for the grain and make it abundant, and not put famine upon you. ³⁰I shall make the fruit of the trees and the produce of the fields abundant, so that you no more receive reviling because of famine among the nations. ³¹You will be mindful of your bad ways and

your practices that were not good, and you will be loathsome in your own sight because of your wayward acts and because of your offensive practices. ³²It's not for your sake that I'm going to act (a declaration of the Lord Yahweh), be it known to you. Be disgraced and ashamed because of your ways, Yisra'el's household."'

³³The Lord Yahweh has said this: 'On the day I cleanse you from all your wayward acts, I shall cause your towns to be inhabited, the wastes will be built up, ³⁴and the desolate country will be served instead of being a desolation in the sight of every passer-by. ³⁵People will say, "That country which was desolate has become like Eden Garden, and the towns that were wasted and desolate and torn down, people live in, fortified." ³⁶The nations that remain all round you will acknowledge that I Yahweh have built up the wastes; I have planted the desolations. I Yahweh have spoken and I shall act.'

³⁷The Lord Yahweh has said this: 'Further, in this I shall let myself be enquired of by Yisra'el's household, to act for them. I shall make people as abundant as a flock. ³⁸Like the flock of sacred ones, like the Yerushalaim flock at its set occasions, so the wasted towns will be full of a human flock, and they will acknowledge that I am Yahweh.'

Dem bones, dem bones, dem dry bones

37 Yahweh's hand came on me and took me out by Yahweh's wind, and set me down in the middle of a valley. It was full of bones. ²He got me to pass through them, all the way round. There, they were very many on the face of the valley. And there, they were very dry. ³He said to me, 'Young man, could these bones come to life?' I said, 'Lord Yahweh, you know.' ⁴He said to me, 'Prophesy to these bones: "You dry bones, listen to Yahweh's word. ⁵The Lord Yahweh has said this to these bones: 'Here, I'm going to make breath come into you, and you will come to life. ⁶I shall put muscles on you, make flesh go up on you, spread skin on you and put breath into you, and you'll come to life, and you will acknowledge that I am Yahweh.'"'

⁷I prophesied as I was ordered, and a sound came as I prophesied, and there – a shaking, and the bones drew near bone to its bone. ⁸I looked, and there, muscles were on them, and flesh went up, and skin spread on them above. But there was no breath in them. ⁹He said to me, 'Prophesy to the breath, prophesy, young man. You're to say to the breath, "The Lord Yahweh has said this: 'Come from the four winds, breath, and breathe into these people who are run through, so that they come to life.'"'

¹⁰So I prophesied as he ordered me, and the breath came into them. They came to life and stood on their feet, a very, very great force.

¹¹He said to me, 'Young man, these bones are Yisra'el's entire household. There, they're saying, "Our bones are dry, our hope has perished, we're totally finished." ¹²Therefore prophesy and say to them, "The Lord Yahweh has said this: 'Here, I'm going to open your graves and get you to go up from your graves, my people, and bring you to Yisra'el's land. ¹³You will acknowledge that I am Yahweh when I open your graves and get you to go up from your graves, my people. ¹⁴I shall put my spirit in you and you will come to life and I shall settle you down on your land, and you will acknowledge that I Yahweh have spoken and acted (Yahweh's declaration).'"'

The two become one

¹⁵Yahweh's word came to me: ¹⁶'And you, young man, get yourself a piece of wood and write on it, "Belonging to Yehudah and to the Yisra'elites who are its associates", and get a piece of wood and write on it, "Belonging to Yoseph (Ephrayim's piece of wood) and all Yisra'el's household that are its associates". ¹⁷Bring them close one to the other so they become one piece of wood. They're to become one in your hand.

¹⁸When members of your people say to you, "Tell us what these things of yours are, won't you", ¹⁹speak to them: "The Lord Yahweh has said this: 'Here am I, I'm going to take Yoseph's piece of wood that's in Ephrayim's hand, and the Yisra'elite clans that are his associates, and I shall put them on it (Yehudah's piece of wood), and make them one piece of wood. They will be one in my hand.'"

²⁰The pieces of wood on which you've written are to be in your hand before their

eyes, ²¹and you're to speak to them, "The Lord Yahweh has said this: 'Here am I, I'm going to get the Yisra'elites from among the nations where they've gone, collect them from all round and bring them to their land. ²²I shall make them into one nation in the country, on Yisra'el's mountains. One king will be king for all of them. There won't be two nations again. They won't divide into two kingdoms ever again. ²³And they won't defile themselves again with their lumps and their abominations and all their rebellions. I shall deliver them from all their settlements in which they did wrong and cleanse them, and they will be my people and I shall be their God.

²⁴My servant David will be king over them and they will all have one shepherd. They will walk by my rulings and keep my laws and do them. ²⁵They'll live in the country that I gave to my servant, to Ya'aqob, in which your ancestors lived. They'll live in it, they and their children and their grandchildren, permanently, with David my servant as their ruler permanently.

²⁶I shall solemnize a pact of well-being for them. It will be a permanent pact with them. I shall give it to them and multiply them, and I shall put my sanctuary among them permanently. ²⁷My dwelling will be with them. I shall be their God and they will be my people. ²⁸And the nations will acknowledge that I am Yahweh, the one who makes Yisra'el sacred, when my sanctuary is among them permanently.'"

Gog and Magog

38 Yahweh's word came to me: ²"Young man, set your face towards Gog, in the country of Magog, the highest ruler in Meshek and Tubal. You're to prophesy against him: ³"The Lord Yahweh has said this: 'Here am I towards you, Gog, highest ruler in Meshek and Tubal. ⁴I shall turn you back and put hooks in your jaws and make you go out, with your entire force, horses and cavalry, clothed in fullness all of them, a great congregation, with body-shield and hand-shield, grasping swords, all of them. ⁵Paras, Kush and Put are with them, all of them with shield and helmet, ⁶Gomer and all its legions, Bet Togarmah in the far parts of the north

and all its legions – many peoples with you. ⁷Be ready, get yourselves ready, you and your entire congregation who are forming round you. You're to be a watch for them. ⁸After many days you will be appointed; at the end of the years you will come to a country restored from the sword, collected from many peoples – against Yisra'el's mountains, which have been a waste continually. But it will have been taken out from the peoples, and they will be living with confidence, all of them. ⁹When you go up, you will come as devastation; you will be like a cloud to cover the country, you and all your legions and many peoples with you.'"

¹⁰The Lord Yahweh has said: 'On that day, things will come up into your mind. You will think up a bad plan. ¹¹You will say, "I shall go up against a country of open villages. I shall come to quiet people living in confidence, all of them, living without walls and without bars or gateways, ¹²to take plunder and seize spoil", to turn your hand against wastes that have become inhabited, and upon a people gathered from the nations, making livestock and possessions, living at the centre of the earth. ¹³Sheba and Dedan, the traders of Tarshish and all its lions will say to you, "Is it to take plunder that you're coming? Is it to seize spoil that you've formed your congregation, to carry off silver and gold, to get livestock and possessions, to take much plunder?"'

The last great battle

¹⁴Therefore prophesy, young man, and say to Gog: 'The Lord Yahweh has said this: "On that day, when my people Yisra'el are living with confidence, you will acknowledge it, won't you, ¹⁵and come from your place, from the far parts of the north, you and many peoples with you, riding horses all of them, a great congregation, a huge force. ¹⁶You'll go up against my people Yisra'el like a cloud to cover the country. At the end of the time it will come about. I shall bring you against my country in order that the nations may acknowledge me when I show myself sacred through you before their eyes, Gog."'

¹⁷The Lord Yahweh said this: 'Are you the one of whom I spoke in earlier days by means of my servants Yisra'el's prophets,

who prophesied in those days for years that I would bring you against them? ¹⁸On that day, on the day Gog comes against Yisraʾel's land (a declaration of the Lord Yahweh), my wrath will go up into my nostrils. ¹⁹In my passion, in my furious fire, I have spoken. If on that day a great earthquake doesn't happen in Yisraʾel's land . . .

²⁰Before me things will quake: the fish in the sea, the birds in the heavens, the animals of the open country, everything that moves on the ground and all the human beings that are on the face of the ground. The mountains will be toppled, the cliffs will fall, every wall will fall to the earth.

²¹I shall call for a sword against him through all my mountains (a declaration of the Lord Yahweh). One person's sword will be against his brother. ²²I shall enter into judgement with him by epidemic and by bloodshed, and I shall pour torrential rain, hailstones, fire and sulphur, on him, on his legions and on the many peoples that are with him. ²³I shall show I am great and show I am sacred and cause myself to be acknowledged before the eyes of many nations. And they will acknowledge that I am Yahweh.'

The peace dividend

39 And you, young man, prophesy against Gog: 'The Lord Yahweh has said this: "Here am I towards you, Gog, the highest ruler of Meshek and Tubal. ²I shall turn you back. I shall lead you along and get you to go up from the far parts of the north and bring you against Yisraʾel's mountains. ³But I shall strike down your bow from your left hand and make your arrows fall from your right hand. ⁴You will fall on Yisraʾel's mountains, you and all your legions and the peoples that are with you. I shall give you as food to birds of prey of every kind and to the animals of the open country ⁵when you fall on the face of the open country, because I have spoken (a declaration of the Lord Yahweh).

⁶I shall send off fire on Magog and on the people who live with confidence on foreign shores, and they will acknowledge that I am Yahweh. ⁷I shall cause my sacred name to be acknowledged among my people Yisraʾel and not let my sacred name be treated as ordinary any more, and the nations will acknowledge that I Yahweh am sacred in Yisraʾel.

⁸There, it's coming, it's happening (a declaration of the Lord Yahweh). It's the day of which I have spoken. ⁹The inhabitants of Yisraʾel's towns will go out and make a fire and burn the weaponry, hand-shield and body-shield, bow and arrows, hand pike and spear. They'll make a fire with them for seven years. ¹⁰They won't carry wood from the open country and they won't cut it from the forests, because they'll make a fire with the weaponry. They'll plunder their plunderers and despoil their despoilers (a declaration of the Lord Yahweh).

Proper burial

¹¹On that day I shall give Gog a place where there will be a grave in Yisraʾel, Travellers' Ravine, east of the sea. It will obstruct travellers; they'll bury Gog and his entire multitude there. They'll call it Gog's Multitude's Ravine. ¹²Yisraʾel's household will bury them to cleanse the country, for seven months; ¹³the entire people of the country will bury them. It will mean renown for them, the day I show my splendour (a declaration of the Lord Yahweh). ¹⁴They will set apart permanent people as travellers in the country, burying (the travellers) ones that remain on the face of the country, to cleanse it. At the end of seven months they'll search. ¹⁵As travellers travel in the country and see human bones, one is to build a marker by it, until the buriers have buried it in Gog's Multitude's Ravine ¹⁶(the name of the town will also be Multitude) and cleansed the country."

¹⁷And you, young man (the Lord Yahweh has said this), say to birds of every kind and to every animal of the open country, "Collect yourselves and come, gather from all round to my sacrifice that I'm going to make for you, a great sacrifice on Yisraʾel's mountains. You'll eat flesh and drink blood. ¹⁸You'll eat strong men's flesh and drink the blood of earth's rulers: rams, lambs, goats, bulls, Bashan fatlings, all of them. ¹⁹You'll eat fat until you're full and drink blood until you're drunk from my sacrifice that I shall have made for you. ²⁰At my table you'll

become full of horses, chariotry, strong men, every man of battle (a declaration of the Lord Yahweh).

I shall not hide my face any more

²¹I shall put my splendour among the nations, and all the nations will see my authoritative decision that I've made and my hand that I've set against them. ²²Yisra'el's household will acknowledge that I Yahweh am their God, from that day onwards. ²³And the nations will acknowledge that Yisra'el's household went into exile for their waywardness, because they trespassed against me. I hid my face from them and gave them into the hand of their adversaries, and all of them fell by the sword. ²⁴It was in accordance with their defilement and with their rebellions that I dealt with them and hid my face from them."

²⁵Therefore the Lord Yahweh has said this: 'Now I shall restore Ya'aqob's fortunes and have compassion on Yisra'el's entire household, and be passionate about my sacred name. ²⁶They will carry their shame and all their trespass that they committed against me when they live on their land with confidence, with no one disturbing them, ²⁷when I bring them back from the peoples and collect them from their enemies' countries and show myself sacred among them before the eyes of many nations. ²⁸They will acknowledge that I Yahweh am their God, when I've exiled them to the nations but gathered them on their land. I shall leave none of them there any more. ²⁹I shall not hide my face from them any more when I've poured out my spirit on Yisra'el's household (a declaration of the Lord Yahweh).'

A town on a mountain

40 In the twenty-fifth year of our exile, at the beginning of the year, on the tenth of the month, in the fourteenth year after the town was struck down, on this very day Yahweh's hand came upon me, and he brought me there. ²In a great appearance of God he brought me to the country of Yisra'el and set me down on a very high mountain. On it was the very structure of a town to the south. ³He brought me to it, and there – a man, his appearance the very appearance of copper, a linen cord in his hand, and a measuring rod. He was standing in the gateway. ⁴The man spoke to me: 'Young man, look with your eyes, listen with your ears and set your mind on everything that I'm going to show you, because you've been brought here in order to show you. Tell Yisra'el's household everything you see.'

⁵There – a wall outside the house, all the way round. In the man's hand was a six-cubit measuring rod, by the cubit-plus-a-handbreadth [three metres]. He measured the structure's width – one rod, and the height – one rod. ⁶He came to the gateway whose face was towards the east, and went up its steps. He measured the gateway's threshold – one rod in depth (the one threshold – one rod in depth). ⁷Each alcove – one rod in length and one rod in width. Between the alcoves – five cubits.

The gateway's threshold next to the gateway's porch, facing the house – one rod. ⁸He measured the gateway's porch facing the house – one rod. ⁹He measured the gateway's porch – eight cubits, and its columns – two cubits; the gateway's porch was facing the house. ¹⁰The gateway alcoves towards the east were three on one side and three on the other side, one measurement for the three of them and one measurement for the columns on each side.

Gateways (1)

¹¹He measured:
  the width of the gateway opening – ten cubits;
  the gateway's length – thirteen cubits;
  ¹²the barrier in front of the alcoves – one
    cubit, so the barrier was one cubit on each
    side;
  the alcove – six cubits on one side and six
    cubits on the other side.
¹³He measured the gateway from the back of an alcove to the back of the other; the width – twenty-five cubits, opening to opening. ¹⁴He made columns – sixty cubits, and next to the column was the gateway courtyard all the way round. ¹⁵Starting at the front of the outer gateway to the front of the inner gateway's porch – fifty cubits. ¹⁶There were narrow windows to the alcoves and to their columns inside the

gateway all the way round, and similarly to the porches there were windows all the way round on the inside, with palms on a column.

[17]He brought me to the outer courtyard, and there – halls, and a pavement made for the courtyard all the way round, 30 halls to the pavement. [18]The pavement was by the side of the gateways, alongside the length of the gateways (the lower pavement). [19]He measured the width from in front of the lower gateway to the front of the outer courtyard – a hundred cubits, east and north.

[20]The gateway whose face was towards the north, belonging to the outer courtyard – he measured its length and its width, [21]its three alcoves on one side and three on the other side, its columns and its porches. Like the measurement of the first gate, its length – fifty cubits, and the width – twenty-five cubits. [22]Its windows, its porches and its palms were like the measurement of the gateway that faced towards the east. By seven steps people would go up on to it, and its porch would be in front of them. [23]There was a gateway to the inner courtyard facing the northern gate as well as the east; he measured from one gateway to the other gateway – a hundred cubits.

Gateways (2)

[24]He took me towards the south. There – a gate towards the south. He measured its columns and its porches, in accordance with these measurements. [25]It and its porches had windows all the way round like these windows; the length – fifty cubits, and the width – twenty-five cubits. [26]There were seven steps up to it. Its porch was in front of them. It had palms, one on one side and one on the other side, on its columns. [27]The inner courtyard had a gateway towards the south. He measured from the gateway to the gateway on the south – a hundred cubits.

[28]He brought me to the inner courtyard through the southern gateway and measured the southern gateway in accordance with these measurements. [29]Its alcoves, its columns and its porches were in accordance with these measurements. It and its porches had windows all the way round. The length – fifty cubits, and the width – twenty-five cubits [30](the porches all the way round, the length – twenty-five cubits, the width – five cubits). [31]Its porch was towards the outer courtyard. There were palms on its columns and eight steps in its staircase.

[32]He brought me to the inner courtyard towards the east and measured the gateway in accordance with these measurements. [33]Its alcoves, its columns and its porches were in accordance with these measurements. It and its porches had windows all the way round. The length – fifty cubits, and the width – twenty-five cubits. [34]Its porch was towards the outer courtyard. There were palms on its columns, on one side and on the other side, and eight steps in its staircase.

[35]He brought me to the northern gateway and measured it in accordance with these measurements – [36]its alcoves, its columns and its porches, and its windows all the way round. The length – fifty cubits, and the width – twenty-five cubits. [37]Its columns were towards the outer courtyard. There were palms on its columns, on one side and on the other side, and eight steps in its staircase.

Provision for the priests and the singers

[38]There was a hall and its entrance in the porch at the gateways, where they would wash the burnt offering. [39]In the gateway porch were two tables on one side and two tables on the other side for slaughtering the burnt offering, the purification offering and the restitution offering on them. [40]On the outer side wall for someone going up to the entrance of the northern gateway were two tables and on the other side wall in relation to the gateway's porch were two tables, [41]four tables on one side and four tables on the other side at the side wall of the gateway, eight tables on which they would slaughter things. [42]The four tables for the burnt offering were of hewn stone. The length – a cubit and a half, the width – a cubit and a half, and the height – a cubit. On them they'd set down the things with which they would slaughter the burnt offering and the sacrifice. [43]There were ledges – one handbreadth, fixed inside all the way round. The flesh of the offering was on the tables.

[44]Outside the inner gateway were the singers' halls in the inner courtyard, one that was on

Start: Eastern gateway

The list approximately follows Ezekiel's walk through the temple
1 Outer gateways
2 Outer courtyard
3 Lower pavement
4 Inner gateways
5 Inner courtyard
6 Altar
7 Sanctuary
8 Most sacred place
9 Rooms for ministers
10 Separate place
11 Building (storage?)
12 Kitchens

Ezekiel 40: The temple in Yehezqe'l's (Ezekiel's) vision

the side wall of the northern gateway with their face towards the south, one on the side wall of the eastern gateway facing towards the north. ⁴⁵He spoke to me: 'This, the hall that faces towards the south, is for the priests having charge of the house. ⁴⁶The hall that faces towards the north is for the priests having charge of the altar. They are the Tsadoqites, who of the Levites draw near Yahweh to minister to him.'

⁴⁷He measured the courtyard. The length – a hundred cubits, the width – a hundred cubits, foursquare. The altar was before the house. ⁴⁸He brought me to the house's porch and measured a porch column – five cubits on one side and five cubits on the other side. The width of the gateway – three cubits on one side and three cubits on the other side. ⁴⁹The length of the porch – twenty cubits, and the width – eleven cubits. It was by steps that people would go up to it. There were pillars by the columns, one on one side, one on the other side.

Yahweh's palace (1)

41 He brought me into the palace and measured the columns – six cubits the width on one side, six cubits the width on the other side (the width of the tent). ²The width of the entrance – ten cubits, and the side walls of the entrance – five cubits on one side and five cubits on the other side. He measured its length – forty cubits, and the width – twenty cubits. ³He came inside and measured an entrance column – two cubits, the entrance – six cubits, and the entrance's width – seven cubits. ⁴He measured its length – twenty cubits, and the width – twenty cubits, before the palace. He said to me, 'This is the especially sacred place.'

⁵He measured the wall of the house – six cubits, and the width of a side room – four cubits, round the house, all the way round. ⁶The side rooms – side room above side room, thirty-three-fold. There were insets in the wall that belonged to the house for the side rooms all the way round, to be supports but so that they wouldn't be supports in the wall of the house. ⁷It widened as it went round higher and higher to the side rooms. Because the house's surrounding went higher and higher all the way round the house, consequently the width of the house went higher, and one would go up from the lowest to the highest via the middle.

⁸I saw belonging to the house a raised area all the way round, the foundations of the side rooms. Its height – the full length of a rod, six cubits, to the joint. ⁹The width of the wall of a side room on the outside – five cubits. What was left clear between the side rooms of the house ¹⁰and between the halls, the width – twenty cubits round the house, all the way round. ¹¹The entrance of a side room towards what was left clear, one entrance towards the north, one entrance to the south, and the width of the place that was left clear – five cubits all the way round. ¹²The building that was towards the front of the separate place at the corner towards the west: the width – seventy cubits. The wall of the building: the width – five cubits all the way round, and its length – ninety cubits.

Yahweh's palace (2)

¹³He measured the house:
 the length – a hundred cubits;
 the separate place, the building and its walls:
  the length – a hundred cubits;
 ¹⁴the width of the front of the house and the separate place on the east – a hundred cubits.

¹⁵He measured the length of the building facing the separate place that was at the back of it, and its galleries on one side and on the other side – a hundred cubits. The palace inside, the courtyard porches ¹⁶(the thresholds), the narrow windows, and the galleries round the three of them by the threshold, they were panelled with wood all the way round. The ground up to the windows, and the windows, they were covered, ¹⁷above the entrance and as far as the house, inside and outside.

On the entire wall, all the way round, inside and outside, was a measured area. ¹⁸Sphinxes and palms were made, a palm between sphinx and sphinx. A sphinx had two faces, ¹⁹a human face towards the palm on one side and a lion face towards the palm on the other side. It was made for the entire house all the way round. ²⁰From the ground to above the entrance the sphinxes and the palms were made, and the palace wall.

²¹The palace: there was a square door frame, and facing the sacred place something with an appearance like the appearance of ²²a wood altar. The height – three cubits, its length – two cubits. It had corners, and its length and its walls were wood. He spoke to me: 'This is the table that's before Yahweh.' ²³The palace had double doors, and the sacred place ²⁴had double doors. The double doors had double doors that could be turned, two doors for one and two doors for the other. ²⁵Sphinxes and palms were made for them (for the palace doors) as they were made for the walls. There was a wood canopy in front of the porch, on the outside. ²⁶There were narrow windows and palms on one side and on the other, on the porch's side walls and the side rooms of the house and the canopies.

The halls

42 He took me out into the outer courtyard by the way towards the north and brought me into the hall that was opposite the separate place and that was opposite the northern building. ²Facing the length – a hundred cubits – was the northern entrance. The width – fifty cubits. ³Opposite the twenty of the inner courtyard, and opposite the pavement of the outer courtyard, one gallery was facing another gallery in threes.

⁴Facing the halls was a walkway (the width – ten cubits, on the inside; a path – one cubit), with its entrances to the north. ⁵The upper halls were cut back, because galleries had an effect on them, more than the lowest and the middle ones in the building, ⁶because they were divided into three, and they had no pillars like the pillars in the courtyards. Therefore it got narrower from the lowest and from the middle, from the ground.

⁷There was a wall outside, alongside the halls, towards the outer courtyard facing the halls. Its length – fifty cubits, ⁸because the length of the halls belonging to the outer court was fifty cubits. So there, in front of the palace, it was a hundred cubits. ⁹From below these halls was the passageway from the east when someone comes here from the outer courtyard.

¹⁰In the width of the wall towards the east, facing the separate place and facing the building, there were halls. ¹¹Towards the front of them was a similar appearance of halls that were towards the north. Corresponding to their length, so was their width. All their exits were in accordance with the prescriptions for them and in accordance with their entrances. ¹²Like the halls' entrances that were towards the south was the entrance at the head of the path, the path in front of the wall going towards the east, as one comes into them.

Separating between the sacred and the ordinary

¹³He said to me, 'The northern halls, the southern halls, that are facing the separate place, are the sacred halls where the priests who come near Yahweh will eat the most sacred things. They will set down the most sacred things there (the grain offering, the purification offering and the restitution offering), because the place is sacred. ¹⁴When the priests come in, they won't go out from the sacred place to the outer courtyard. They'll set down their garments in which they minister there because it's sacred, and put on other garments and go near the people's area.'

¹⁵He finished measuring the inner house and took me out towards the gateway that faces towards the east, and measured all the way round.

¹⁶He measured the eastern side with the measuring rod – 500 (in rods) with the measuring rod, all round.
¹⁷He measured the northern side – 500 (in rods) with the measuring rod, all round.
¹⁸He measured the southern side – 500 (in rods) with the measuring rod.
¹⁹He turned to the southern side and measured – 500 (in rods) with the measuring rod.

²⁰Four sides he measured it. It had a wall all the way round (the length – 500; the width – 500) to separate between the sacred and the ordinary.

Yahweh's splendour is returning

43 He took me to a gateway, the gateway that faces towards the east. ²There – the splendour of Yisra'el's God was coming from the eastern direction, its sound like the sound of much water. The earth was lit up by his splendour. ³The appearance was like the appearance that I saw, like the appearance that I saw when I came to devastate the town, and the great appearance was like the appearance that I saw at the River Kebar. I fell on my face.

⁴Yahweh's splendour came into the house by way of the gateway whose face is towards the east. ⁵A spirit lifted me up and brought me to the inner courtyard. There, Yahweh's splendour was filling the house. ⁶I heard someone speaking to me from the house, while the man was standing next to me. ⁷He said to me, 'Young man: the place for my throne and the place for the soles of my feet, where I shall dwell among the Yisra'elites permanently – Yisra'el's household shall not defile my sacred name any more, they and their kings by their whoring and by their kings' corpses, their mounds. ⁸When they put their threshold with my threshold and their door frame next to my door frame with a wall between me and them, they would defile my sacred name with their offensive deeds that they did, and I consumed them in my anger. ⁹Now they are to put their whoring and their kings' corpses far away from me, and I shall dwell among them permanently.

¹⁰You, young man, tell Yisra'el's household about the house. They're to be ashamed of their wayward acts, but they're to measure out the plan. ¹¹When they're ashamed of all that they did, make known the house's form, its plan, its exits, its entrances, all its forms, all its laws, all its forms and all its instructions. Write it down before their eyes so they may keep its entire form and all its laws, and act on them. ¹²This is the instruction for the house on the mountain top. Its entire boundary all the way round is most sacred. Here, this is the instruction for the house.'

The altar

¹³These are the measurements of the altar in cubits (a 'cubit' is a cubit plus a handbreadth):
the base – a cubit, and the width – a cubit;
its rim at its lip all round – one hand span; this is the altar's mound;
¹⁴from the base in the ground to the lower ledge – two cubits, and the width – one cubit;
from the small ledge to the big ledge – four cubits, and the width – a cubit;
¹⁵the hearth – four cubits, and from the hearth upwards, four horns;
¹⁶the hearth: the length – twelve, the width – twelve, made square on its four sides;
¹⁷the ledge: the length – fourteen, with the width – fourteen, on its four sides;
the rim round it – half a cubit;
the base to it – a cubit round it, with its steps facing east.
¹⁸He said to me, 'Young man, the Lord Yahweh has said this: "These are the laws for the altar on the day it's built, for offering the burnt offering on it and tossing blood on it. ¹⁹You're to give to the Levitical priests who are of the offspring of Tsadoq, who come near to me (a declaration of the Lord Yahweh) to minister to me, a bullock from the herd as a purification offering. ²⁰You're to get some of its blood and put it on its four horns and towards the four corners of the ledge and towards the rim round, and purge it and expiate it. ²¹And you're to get the purification offering bullock and burn it in the appointed place in the house, outside the sanctuary. ²²On the second day you're to present a male goat, whole, as a purification offering.

They're to purge the altar as they purged it with the bull. ²³When you've completed the purging, you're to present a bullock from the herd, whole, and a ram from the flock, whole. ²⁴You're to present them before Yahweh, and the priests are to throw salt on them and offer them as a burnt offering to Yahweh.

Preparations for the splendour's return

²⁵For seven days you're to prepare a goat as a purification offering, daily, and they're to prepare a bullock from the herd and a ram from the flock, whole. ²⁶For seven days they are to expiate the altar, purify it and commission it. ²⁷They're to complete these days, and on the eighth day and onwards the priests are to make your burnt offerings and your fellowship sacrifices on the altar. And I shall accept you (a declaration of the Lord Yahweh)."'

44 He took me back towards the sanctuary's outer gateway that faces east. It was shut. ²Yahweh said to me, 'This gateway is to be shut. It's not to be opened. No one is to come through it, because Yahweh, Yisra'el's God, came through it. It's to be shut. ³As for the ruler, the ruler himself will sit in it to eat bread before Yahweh. By way of the gateway's threshold he may come in and by way of it he may go out.'

⁴He brought me by way of the northern gateway to the front of the house. I looked, and there – Yahweh's splendour was filling Yahweh's house. I fell on my face. ⁵Yahweh said to me, 'Young man, apply your mind, look with your eyes, listen with your ears to all that I'm going to speak with you regarding all the laws for Yahweh's house and all the instructions for it. Set your mind on the entrance into the house with all the exits from the sanctuary. ⁶You're to say to the rebellious, to Yisra'el's household: "The Lord Yahweh has said this: 'You have plenty of all your offensive deeds, Yisra'el's household, ⁷in that you brought foreigners, foreskinned in spirit and foreskinned in flesh, to be in my sanctuary, to make my house ordinary when you present my meal, the fat and blood. You contravened my pact with all your offensive deeds. ⁸You didn't kept the charge of my sacred things; you appointed them as people to keep my charge in my sanctuary for you.'"'

Who can properly minister?

⁹The Lord Yahweh has said this: 'No foreigner, foreskinned in spirit and foreskinned in flesh, is to come into my sanctuary, of any foreigner who's among the Yisra'elites. ¹⁰Rather, the Levites who went far from me when Yisra'el went astray (when they went astray from me, following their lumps) will carry their waywardness, ¹¹but in my sanctuary they will be ministering with oversight at the gateways of the house and ministering to the house. They will slaughter the burnt offering and the sacrifice for the people and they will stand before them to minister to them.

¹²Because they used to minister to them before their lumps, and to Yisra'el's household they were obstacles that tripped them into waywardness, therefore I've raised my hand [to swear] concerning them (a declaration of the Lord Almighty) that they will carry their waywardness. ¹³They're not to come near me to act as priests to me or to come near to any of my sacred things, to the most sacred things. They're to carry their shame, the offensive deeds that they did. ¹⁴But I shall make them guards in charge of the house, for all its service and for all that's done in it.

¹⁵But the Levitical priests who are descendants of Tsadoq, who kept the charge of my sanctuary when Yisra'el's household went astray from me, they may draw near to me to minister to me. They may stand before me to present fat and blood to me (a declaration of the Lord Yahweh). ¹⁶They're the ones to come into my sanctuary. They're the ones to draw near to my table to minister to me, and they will keep my charge.

¹⁷When they come to the gateways of the inner courtyard they're to wear linen garments. They're not to put wool on themselves when they minister in the gateways of the inner courtyard and inside. ¹⁸Linen attire is to be on their head and linen pants round their hips; they're not to wrap on anything sweaty. ¹⁹When they go out to the outer courtyard (to the outer courtyard to the people) they're to take off their garments in which they were ministering, set them down in the sacred halls, and put on other garments, and not make the people sacred by their garments.

Priests

²⁰They're not to shave their head or grow long hair, but definitely to trim their heads. ²¹They're not to drink wine, any priest, when they go into the inner courtyard. ²²They're not to take a widow or a divorcee for themselves as wives, but rather to take a girl from the offspring of Yisra'el's household or a widow who's a priest's widow.

²³They're to teach my people between sacred and ordinary and to enable them to know between clean and defiled. ²⁴In connection with an argument, they're the ones to stand to give a ruling; they're to give a rule by my rulings. They're to keep my instructions and my laws regarding all set occasions, and to keep my sabbaths sacred.

²⁵An individual isn't to go in to someone dead, except that he may defile himself for father or for mother, for a son or for a daughter, for a brother or for a sister who hasn't come to belong to a man. ²⁶After his cleansing they're to count seven days for him, ²⁷and on the day he comes into the sacred place, into the inner courtyard, to minister in the sacred place, he's to present his purification offering (a declaration of the Lord Yahweh).

²⁸They're to have as a domain: I am their domain. You're to give them no holding in Yisra'el; I am their holding. ²⁹The grain offering, the purification offering and the restitution offering – they're the ones to eat them. Everything devoted in Yisra'el will be theirs. ³⁰The first of all the first fruits of everything and every donation of anything, of all your donations, will be the priests'. The first of your dough you're to give to the priest, to make a blessing set down on your house. ³¹The priests aren't to eat anything that's died naturally or any prey, bird or animal.

Constraining the ruler

45 When you allot the country as a domain:

You're to raise a donation for Yahweh, a sacred area of the country: the length – 25,000 in length; the width – 10,000. It's to be a sacred area in its entire border, all round.

²Of this, there's to be 500 by 500 squared all round for the sacred place, and fifty cubits as an open space all round.
³From this measurement you're to measure 25,000 in length and 10,000 in width; in it is to be the sanctuary, the most sacred place. ⁴It will be the sacred area of the country, for the priests, the sanctuary ministers, who draw near to minister to Yahweh. It will be a place for homes for them, and a sanctuary for the sanctuary. ⁵25,000 in length and 10,000 in width will be for the Levites, the ministers of the house, for them as a holding, twenty halls.
⁶The town's holding: you're to give 5,000 in width, and in length 25,000, alongside the sacred donation. It will belong to Yisra'el's entire household.
⁷To the ruler there will belong on one side and on the other side of the sacred donation and of the town's holding, in front of the sacred donation and in front of the town's holding, on the west westwards and on the east eastwards, a length alongside one of the shares, from the western border to the eastern border ⁸of the country. It will be a holding for him in Yisra'el. My rulers are no more to oppress my people. They will give the country to Yisra'el's household, to their clans.'
⁹The Lord Yahweh has said this: 'There's plenty for you, Yisra'el's rulers. Remove violence and destruction. Exercise authority with faithfulness. Lift your expulsions of my people (a declaration of the Lord Yahweh). ¹⁰You're to have faithful balances, a faithful *ephah*, a faithful *bat*. ¹¹The ephah and the bat are to be one size. The bat is to contain a tenth of a *homer*, and the ephah a tenth of a homer. The size will be based on the homer. ¹²The sheqel is twenty *gerahs*. Twenty sheqels plus twenty-five sheqels plus fifteen sheqels are a *mina* for you.

Responsibilities of people and ruler

¹³This is the donation that you're to raise: a sixth of an ephah from a homer of wheat; a sixth of an ephah from a homer of barley; ¹⁴the law for oil – oil by the bat: a tenth of a bat from a kor (ten bats or a homer, because ten bats make a homer);

¹⁵one sheep from the flock, out of 200, from Yisra'el's pastureland for a grain offering, for a burnt offering and for fellowship sacrifices, to make expiation for them (a declaration of the Lord Yahweh).
¹⁶The entire people of the country are to be involved in this donation to the ruler in Yisra'el, ¹⁷but the burnt offerings, the grain offering, the libation – at festivals, at new months and on sabbaths, on all set occasions for Yisra'el's household – are incumbent on the ruler. He is to make the purification offering, the grain offering, the burnt offering and the fellowship sacrifices to make expiation for Yisra'el's household.'
¹⁸The Lord Yahweh has said this: 'On the first of the first month, you're to get a bullock from the herd, whole, and purify the sanctuary. ¹⁹The priest is to get some of the blood of the purification offering and put it on the door frame of the house, on the four corners of the altar's ledge, and on the door frame of the gateway to the inner courtyard. ²⁰So you're to do on the seventh of the month, because of someone making a mistake or being ignorant; you're to expiate the house.
²¹In the first, on the fourteenth day of the month, it's to be Pesah [Passover] for you. For the seven-day festival, flatbread is to be eaten. ²²On that day the ruler is to make on his behalf and on behalf of the entire people a bull as a purification offering. ²³For the seven days of the festival he's to make a burnt offering for Yahweh, seven bullocks and seven rams, whole, daily for the seven days, and as a purification offering a male goat, daily. ²⁴He's to make as a grain offering an ephah for the bullock, an ephah for the ram, and oil: a hin for the ephah. ²⁵In the seventh, on the fifteenth day of the month, during the festival, he's to make it in accordance with these for seven days, in accordance with the purification offering, with the burnt offering, with the grain offering and with the oil.'

Daily, weekly, monthly, annually and spontaneously

46 The Lord Yahweh said this: 'The gateway of the inner court facing east is to be shut for the six days of work, but on the sabbath day it's to be open, and on the new month day it's to be open. ²The ruler is to come in by way of the outer gateway's threshold and to stand at the door frame, and the priests are to make his burnt offering and his fellowship sacrifices. He's to bow low at the gateway's terrace and go out, but the gateway isn't to be shut until evening.

³The country's people are to bow low at that gateway door on sabbaths and on new months, before Yahweh. ⁴The burnt offering that the ruler presents for Yahweh on the sabbath day: six lambs, whole, a ram, whole, ⁵and a grain offering: an ephah for the ram, and for the lambs as a grain offering a gift from his hand, and oil: a hin for the ephah. ⁶On the day of the new month: a bullock from the herd, whole, six lambs and a ram; they're to be whole. ⁷He's to make an ephah for the bullock, an ephah for the ram as a grain offering, and for the lambs as his hand attains to, and oil: a hin for the ephah.

⁸When the ruler comes in, he's to come in by way of the gateway's threshold, and go out the same way. ⁹But when the country's people come in before Yahweh on the set occasions, someone who comes in by way of the northern gateway to bow low is to go out by way of the southern gateway, and someone who comes in by way of the southern gateway is to go out by way of the northern gateway. He isn't to go back by way of the gateway by which he came in but go out by the one opposite him.

¹⁰The ruler will come in among them when they come in, and go out when they go out. ¹¹On festivals and on set occasions the grain offering is to be an ephah for the bullock, an ephah for the ram, for the lambs a gift from his hand, and oil: a hin for the ephah.

Preparations for sacrifices

¹²When the ruler makes a burnt offering as a voluntary offering or fellowship sacrifices as a voluntary offering to Yahweh, someone is to open the gateway facing east for him and he's to make his burnt offering and his fellowship sacrifices as he does on the sabbath day, and he's to go out. Someone is to shut the gateway after he goes out.

¹³With a lamb of the first year, whole, you're to make an offering for the day for Yahweh; morning by morning you're to make it. ¹⁴You're to make a grain offering with it morning by morning: a sixth of an ephah and a third of a hin of oil to moisten the fine flour as a grain offering for Yahweh – permanent laws, regularly. ¹⁵They're to make the lamb, the grain offering and the oil morning by morning, a regular burnt offering.'

¹⁶The Lord Yahweh said this: 'When the ruler gives a gift to one of his sons, it will be his domain; it will belong to his sons. It will be their holding as a domain. ¹⁷But when he gives a gift out of his domain to one of his servants, it will belong to him until the year of release, and go back to the ruler. After all, his sons – his domain is to belong to them. ¹⁸But the ruler isn't to take from the people's domain, oppressing them out of their holding. From his own holding he may give a domain to his sons, so that my people may not be scattered, each person from his holding.'

¹⁹He brought me by the entrance that was by the side of the gateway to the sacred halls belonging to the priests, facing north. There, in the far parts to the west, a place was there. ²⁰He said to me, 'This is the place where the priests are to cook the restitution offering and the purification offering, where they're to bake the grain offering, so as not to have them go out into the outer courtyard and make the people sacred.' ²¹He took me out into the outer courtyard and got me to pass the courtyard's four corners. There, a courtyard in each courtyard corner: ²²in the four corners of the courtyard were enclosed courtyards: length – forty; width – thirty, one measurement for the four of them set in corners, ²³with a ledge all round them (all round the four of them), and cooking places made underneath the ledges all round. ²⁴He said to me, 'These are the kitchens where the ministers in the house will cook the people's fellowship sacrifice.'

Life-giving water

47 He took me back to the entrance of the house. There, water was going out from under the house's terrace, eastward, because the front of the house was to the east. The water was going down from under the right side of the house, south of the altar. ²He took me out by way of the northern gateway and took me round by way of the outside to the outer gateway, the way facing east. There, water was flowing from the right side. ³As the man went out eastward with a line in his hand, he measured 500 metres and got me to pass through the water, ankle-deep water. ⁴He measured 500 and got me to pass through the water, the water being knee-deep. He measured 500 and got me to pass through the hips-deep water. ⁵He measured 500, a wadi that I couldn't pass through because the water had risen, swimming water, a wadi that couldn't be passed through.

⁶He said to me, 'Have you seen, young man?', and got me to go and return to the wadi's bank. ⁷As I returned, there – on the wadi's bank, very many trees, this side and that. ⁸He said to me, 'This water is going out towards the eastern region, going down to the Steppe, and coming to the sea, to the sea of polluted water. The water will become healthy. ⁹Any living being that moves will live wherever the great wadi goes, and the fish will be very abundant because this water comes there. It will be healthy, and anything will live where the wadi comes. ¹⁰Fishermen will stand by it from Gedi Spring to Eglayim Spring, a place for spreading nets. In kind their fish will be like the fish of the Sea, very abundantly great. ¹¹But its swamps and marshes won't become healthy; they're given over to salt.

¹²By the wadi there will grow, on its bank this side and that, every tree for food. Their foliage won't wither, their fruit won't come to an end. By their months they will produce, because their water is going out from the sanctuary. Their fruit will be for food and their foliage for medicine.'

The extent of the country

¹³The Lord Yahweh said this: 'This is the border by which you're to have the country as a domain for Yisra'el's twelve clans (Yoseph – holdings). ¹⁴You're to have it as a domain (each the same as his brother), that which I raised my hand [to swear] to give your ancestors. This country will fall to you as your domain. ¹⁵This is the border of the country:

On the northern side: from the Great Sea by way of Hetlon, Lebo, to Tsedad, ¹⁶Hamat, Berotah, Sibrayim (which is between the border of Dammeseq and the border of Hamat), Hatser Hattikon (which is on the border of Havran). ¹⁷The border will be from the Sea to Hatser Enon, the border of Dammeseq and north, northward, and the border of Hamat: the north side.

¹⁸The eastern side: from between Havran and Dammeseq, and Gil'ad and Yisra'el's country, the Yarden [Jordan], you're to measure from the border to the Eastern Sea: the east side.

¹⁹The southern side: to the south from Tamar as far as the water at Meribot Qadesh, the Wadi, to the Great Sea: the southern side, to the south.

²⁰The western side: the Great Sea from the border as far as opposite Lebo Hamat: this is the western side.

²¹You're to share out this country for yourselves among Yisra'el's clans. ²²You're to allot it as a domain for yourselves and for the aliens residing among you who've had children among you. They're to be like natives among the Yisra'elites. With you they'll receive a domain in the property among Yisra'el's clans. ²³In the clan with which the alien resides, there you're to give him his domain (a declaration of the Lord Yahweh).'

The clans

48 'These are the names of the clans. At the northern end, by the side of the Hetlon road to Lebo-hamat, Hatsar Enan, the border of Dammeseq to the north by the side of Hamat, from the eastern side to the Sea will belong to it: one, Dan.

²At Dan's border, from the eastern side as far as the western side: one, Asher.

³At Asher's border, from the eastern side as far as the western side: one, Naphtali.

⁴At Naphtali's border, from the eastern side as far as the western side: one, Menashsheh.

⁵At Menashsheh's border, from the eastern side as far as the western side: one, Ephrayim.

⁶At Ephrayim's border, from the eastern side as far as the western side: one, Re'uben.

⁷At Re'uben's border, from the eastern side as far as the western side: one, Yehudah.

⁸At Yehudah's border, from the eastern side as far as the western side, will be the donation that you raise, width and length – 25,000, like one of the holdings from the eastern side as far as the western side. The sanctuary will be in the middle of it. ⁹The donation that you raise for Yahweh: length – 25,000; width – 10,000. ¹⁰It will belong to these: the sacred donation to the priests, on the north – 25,000; on the west the width – 10,000; on the east the width – 10,000, and on the south the length – 25,000. Yahweh's sanctuary will be in the middle of it. ¹¹What is made sacred will belong to the priests, the Tsadoqites, who kept my charge, who didn't go astray when the Yisra'elites went astray, as the Levites went astray. ¹²It will belong to them as a donation out of the donation from the country, most sacred, at the Levites' border. ¹³The Levites, alongside the priests' border: length – 25,000, and width – 10,000 (the entire length – 25,000, and the width – 10,000). ¹⁴They're not to sell any of it. A person isn't to exchange or transfer the first fruits of the country, because it's sacred to Yahweh.

¹⁵The 5,000 in width by 25,000 in length that remain: it's ordinary land for the town, for dwelling and for pasture. The town will be in the middle of it. ¹⁶These are its measurements: the northern side – 4,500; the southern side – 4,500; the eastern side – 4,500; and the western side – 4,500. ¹⁷The pasture will belong to the town, northward – 250; southward – 250; eastward – 250; and westward – 250.

Yahweh-Is-There

¹⁸What is left in the country alongside the sacred donation will be 10,000 eastward and 10,000 westward. It will be alongside the sacred donation, and its produce will be for food for the town's servants. ¹⁹One who serves the town – from all Yisra'el's clans they will serve it. ²⁰The entire donation, 25,000 by 25,000 square, you're to raise, the sacred donation with the town's holding. ²¹What is left will belong to the ruler, on this side and on the other of the sacred donation and the town's holding. In front of the 25,000 of the donation as far as the eastern border, and on the west in front of the 25,000 to the western border, alongside the shares, will belong to the ruler. The sacred donation and the sanctuary belonging to the house in the middle of it, ²²and apart from the Levites' holding and the town's holding within what belongs to the ruler, between Yehudah's border and Binyamin's border will belong to the ruler.

²³The rest of the clans:
from the eastern side as far as the western side: one, Binyamin;
²⁴at Binyamin's border, from the eastern side as far as the western side: one, Shim'on;
²⁵at Shim'on's border, from the eastern side as far as the western side: one, Yissakar;
²⁶at Yissakar's border, from the eastern side as far as the western side: one, Zebulun;
²⁷at Zebulun's border, from the eastern side as far as the western side: one, Gad;
²⁸at Gad's border, to the southern side, southward: the border will be from Tamar to the water at Meribat Qadesh, the Wadi, as far as the Great Sea.

²⁹This is the country that you're to allot as a domain to Yisra'el's clans. These will be the shares (a declaration of the Lord Yahweh).
³⁰These are the town's exits:
on the northern side, the measurement is 4,500 ³¹(the town's gateways will be by the names of Yisra'el's clans), three northern gateways: one the Re'uben gateway, one the Yehudah gateway, one the Levi gateway;
³²on the eastern side, 4,500, and three gateways: one the Yoseph gateway, one the Binyamin gateway, one the Dan gateway;
³³on the southern side, the measure is 4,500, and three gateways: one the Shim'on gateway, one the Yissakar gateway, one the Zebulun gateway;
³⁴on the western side, 4,500, their three gateways: one the Gad gateway, one the Asher gateway, one the Naphtali gateway.
³⁵All round – 18,000. The town's name from now on will be "Yahweh-Is-There".

Daniel

The book of Daniel [Daniyye'l] divides into two halves. The first half is a series of stories, amazing but easy to understand. They tell about a series of pressures that come on four Judahite boys taken off into exile in Babylon at the beginning of the sixth century, who are well-born and clever enough to get drafted into the Babylonian administration. The question is, can they survive the pressures as well as succeed there? Will God enable them to do so? God does, and the imperial authorities recognize it.

The second half is a series of dreams and visions (expanding on a first dream vision in chapter 2), amazing and hard to understand. Each of the dreams and visions tells the story from Daniel's own day up to a great crisis four centuries later. In the 160s BC Jerusalem was ruled from Syria as part of the Seleucid Empire, one of the entities into which Alexander the Great's empire split. Its current ruler, Antiochus IV, banned worship in accordance with the Torah and imposed alien forms of worship in Jerusalem. The dreams and visions in Daniel envisage the sequence of empires from Daniel's day up to Antiochus (Babylon, Medo-Persia, Greece, the Seleucids) and promise that at the end of this story God will put the empires down and bring in his own rule.

To judge from parallels with other dream visions from the cultural context, these stories expressed as depictions of the future are actually accounts formulated near the end of the story they tell. The actual future promise in them promises deliverance from Antiochus. And against all the odds the people of Jerusalem did get their freedom from Antiochus, and became masters of their own fate for the first time for many centuries. Of course it wasn't the final end, but it was a kind of anticipation of the final end, like the fall of Jerusalem in AD 70. The visions were thus vindicated and shown to be God-given. The pressures of the time, the persecution and the outrageous action on the part of the emperor recurred a century or two later when the Romans annexed Judea, and the portrait of events helped people in Jesus' day to understand what was going on and to live in hope.

On drawing the line

1 In the third year of the reign of Yehoyaqim king of Yehudah, Nebukadne'tstsar king of Babel came to Yerushalaim and besieged it. ²The Lord gave into his hand Yehoyaqim king of Yehudah and some of the articles from God's house, and he brought them to the country of Shin'ar, to his god's house. He brought the articles to his god's treasure house.

³The king said to Ashpenaz, the chief over his courtiers, to bring some of the Yisra'elites, both some of royal descent and some of the important people ⁴(young men in whom there was no defect, good in appearance, insightful in terms of all smartness, knowledgeable, discerning in knowledge and in whom there was capacity to stand in attendance in the king's palace), and to teach them the learning and the language of the Kasdites. ⁵The king assigned to them a daily allocation from the king's supplies and from the wine he drank, and to bring them up for three years and some of them would stand in attendance before the king.

⁶Among them were some Yehudahites, Daniyye'l, Hananyah, Misha'el and Azaryah, ⁷but the officer over the courtiers determined on names for them. For Daniyye'l he determined on 'Beltesha'tstsar', for Hananyah 'Shadrak', for Misha'el 'Meshack' and for Azaryah 'Abed Nego'.

⁸Daniyye'l determined in his mind that he would not defile himself with the king's supplies and with the wine he drank, and he asked the officer over the courtiers that he might not defile himself. ⁹God gave Daniyye'l commitment and compassion before the officer over the courtiers, ¹⁰but the officer over the courtiers said to Daniyye'l, 'I'm afraid of my lord the king, who assigned your food and your drink. What if he sees your faces thinner than the other young men of your generation and you risk my head with the king?'

The test

¹¹So Daniyye'l said to the guard whom the officer over the courtiers had assigned over Daniyye'l, Hananyah, Misha'el and Azaryah, ¹²'Please test your servants for ten days. They could give us some legumes to eat and water to drink, ¹³and our appearance and the appearance of the young men who eat the king's supplies will be visible before you. Deal with your servants in accordance with what you see.' ¹⁴He listened to them regarding this thing, and tested them for ten days. ¹⁵At the end of ten days their appearance looked better and they were heftier in body than all the young men who were eating the king's supplies. ¹⁶So the guard would carry away their supplies and the wine they were to drink, and give them legumes.

¹⁷These young men, the four of them: God gave them knowledge and insight in all writing and smartness, while Daniyye'l had discernment in all vision and dreams. ¹⁸At the end of the time that the king had said to bring them, the head of the courtiers brought them before Nebukadne'tstsar. ¹⁹The king spoke with them, and from all of them there was not found anyone like Daniyye'l, Hananyah, Misha'el and Azaryah. So they stood in attendance before the king. ²⁰Every matter of discerning smartness that he asked of them, the king found them ten times superior to all the diviners and chanters that were in his entire kingdom.

²¹Daniyye'l was there until the first year of Koresh [Cyrus] the king.

Except the gods, whose home is not with humanity

2 In the second year of Nebukadne'tstsar's reign, Nebukadne'tstsar had dreams. His spirit was agitated, but his sleep came over him. ²The king said to call the diviners, chanters, charmers and Kasdites to tell the king his dreams, and they came and stood in attendance before the king. ³The king said to them, 'I had a dream, and my spirit is agitated to know the dream.' ⁴The Kasdites spoke to the king (in Aramaic): 'Long live the king! Relate the dream to your servants and we'll explain its meaning.' ⁵The king answered the Kasdites: 'A firm decision has issued from me: if you don't make known to me the dream and its meaning, you'll be torn limb from limb and your houses turned into rubble. ⁶But if you explain the dream and its meaning, you'll receive a reward and gift and great honour from me. Now: explain to me the dream and its meaning.'

⁷They answered a second time, 'May Your Majesty relate the dream to his servants, and we'll explain its meaning.' ⁸The king answered, 'I know for sure that you're buying time, because you see that a firm decision has issued from me ⁹that if you don't make the dream known to me, there's a specific decree for you. You've arranged with each other to tell me something false and base, until the situation changes. Now: relate the dream to me, and I'll know that you can explain its meaning.' ¹⁰The Kasdites answered the king, 'There's no one on earth who can explain the thing for the king. Thus no great king or ruler has asked a thing like this of any diviner or chanter or Kasdite. ¹¹The thing that the king is asking is so daunting that there's no one else who can explain it to the king except the gods, whose home is not with humanity.' ¹²At this, the king became furious, very angry, and he said to put to death all Babel's experts.

The God who changes times and eras

¹³So the decree went out and the experts were to be killed, and they looked for Daniyye'l and his companions, to kill them. ¹⁴Daniyye'l responded with shrewdness and judgement to Aryok, the king's chief of police, who had gone out to kill the experts in Babel. ¹⁵He answered Aryok, 'Royal marshal, why is there the severe decree from the king?' Aryok made the thing known to Daniyye'l, ¹⁶and Daniyye'l went and asked the king that he might give him a time, and he would explain the meaning to the king.

¹⁷Then Daniyye'l went to his house and made the thing known to his companions, Hananyah, Misha'el and Azaryah, ¹⁸for them to ask for compassion from the God of the heavens about this mystery, so that Daniyye'l and his companions might not be put to death, with the rest of the experts in Babel.

¹⁹Then the mystery was revealed to Daniyye'l in a vision by night. So Daniyye'l blessed the God of the heavens. ²⁰Daniyye'l avowed:

The name of God be blessed from age to age,
  because smartness and strength are his.
²¹He changes times and eras,
  removes kings and establishes kings.
He gives smartness to the smart,
  knowledge to the people who know discernment.
²²He reveals things that are deep and hidden;
  he knows what's in the dark, and light dwells with him.
²³God of my ancestors, I confess and praise you,
  because you've given me smartness and strength.
You've now made known to me what we asked of you;
  you've made known to us the thing that the king asked.

²⁴Thus Daniyye'l went to Aryok, whom the king had appointed to kill Babel's experts. He came and said this to him: 'Don't kill the experts in Babel. Take me to the king and I'll explain the meaning to the king.'

The dream statue

²⁵With haste Aryok took Daniyye'l before the king and said this to him: 'I've found a man from the Yehudahite exiles who can make known the meaning to the king.' ²⁶The king answered Daniyye'l (whose name was Beltesha'tstsar), 'Can you make known to me the dream that I saw, and its meaning?' ²⁷Daniyye'l answered before the king, 'The mystery about which the king asked – experts, chanters, diviners and exorcists can't explain it to the king. ²⁸But there is a God in the heavens revealing mysteries, and he has made known to King Nebukadne'tstsar what will happen at the end of the time.

Your dream, the visions in your head in bed, was this. ²⁹Your Majesty, in bed your thoughts came concerning what will happen after this, and the one who reveals mysteries made known to you what will happen. ³⁰And I – not because of smartness that there is in me above any other human being has this mystery been revealed to me, but in order that the meaning should be made known to the king, and you may know the thoughts in your mind.

³¹Your Majesty, you were looking, and there – a large statue. This statue was big and its brightness extraordinary, standing in front

of you, an awe-inspiring sight. ³²That statue: its head was of fine gold, its chest and its arms of silver, its stomach and its sides of copper, ³³its legs of iron, its feet partly of iron and partly of pottery. ³⁴You watched as a stone broke off, not by hands, and hit the statue on its feet of iron and pottery, and shattered them. ³⁵All at once the iron, the pottery, the copper, the silver and the gold shattered. They became like chaff from a summer threshing-floor. The wind carried them. No place was found for them. But the stone that hit the statue became a big crag and filled the entire earth.

³⁶That was the dream. We will relate its meaning before the king.

After Nebukadne'tstsar, what?

³⁷You, Your Majesty, king of kings, to whom the God of the heavens gave kingship, sovereignty, power and honour, ³⁸and gave into your hand, wherever they live, human beings, animals of the wild and birds of the heavens, and made you rule over all of them – you're the head of gold. ³⁹In your place another kingship will arise, inferior to you, and another, third kingship, of copper, which will rule over the entire earth. ⁴⁰The fourth kingship will be strong as iron, because iron shatters and smashes anything. Like iron that crushes, it will shatter and crush all these. ⁴¹In that you saw the feet and toes partly of clay pottery and partly of iron, it will be a split kingship, but some of the toughness of iron will be in it. Insofar as you saw iron mixed with earthen pottery, ⁴²and the toes of the feet were partly iron and partly clay, to some extent the kingship will be strong but in part it will be fragile. ⁴³In that you saw the iron mixed with earthen pottery, human beings will unite, but they won't stick with each other, as iron doesn't stick with pottery.

⁴⁴In the time of those kings, the God of the heavens will set up a kingship that won't be destroyed through the ages; the kingship won't pass to another people. It will shatter and terminate all these kingships, and it will stand through the ages, ⁴⁵insofar as you saw that a stone broke off from the crag, not by hands, and shattered the iron, the copper, the pottery, the silver and the gold.

The great God has made known to the king what will happen after this. The dream is true. Its meaning is reliable.'

⁴⁶King Nebukadne'tstsar fell on his face and bowed down before Daniyye'l. He said to present an offering and fragrant oblations to him. ⁴⁷The king answered Daniyye'l, 'Indeed your God is God of gods, Lord of kings, and revealer of mysteries, that you can reveal this mystery.' ⁴⁸The king elevated Daniyye'l and gave him many great gifts. He would have made him ruler over the entire province of Babel and chief officer over all the experts in Babel, ⁴⁹but Daniyye'l asked the king to appoint Shadrak, Meshak and Abed Nego over the administration of the province of Babel, with Daniyye'l at the king's court.

On facing the music

3 Nebukadne'tstsar the king made a gold statue thirty metres in height, three metres in width. He set it up in the Dura Valley in the province of Babel. ²Nebukadne'tstsar the king sent to assemble the satraps, the governors and the commissioners, the counsellors, the treasurers, the judges, the officers, and all the provincial officials, to come for the dedication of the statue that Nebukadne'tstsar the king had set up. ³They assembled, the satraps, the governors and the commissioners, the counsellors, the treasurers, the judges, the officers and all the provincial officials, for the dedication of the statue that Nebukadne'tstsar the king had set up, and they stood in front of the statue that Nebukadne'tstsar had set up.

⁴The herald called out forcefully, 'To you it is being declared, peoples, nations and languages, ⁵at the time when you hear the sound of the horn, pipe, cithara, trigon, psaltery, ensemble and all types of music, you're to fall and bow down to the gold statue that Nebukadne'tstsar the king has set up. ⁶Anyone who doesn't fall and bow down will at that moment be thrown inside a red-hot blazing furnace.' ⁷So at that time when all the peoples heard the sound of the horn, pipe, cithara, trigon, psaltery and all types of music, all the peoples, the nations and the languages would bow down to the gold statue that Nebukadne'tstsar the king had set up.

⁸So at that time some Kasdites came and denounced the Yehudahites. ⁹They avowed to King Nebukadne'tstsar: 'Long live the king! ¹⁰Your Majesty, you gave notice that anyone who hears the sound of the horn, pipe, cithara, trigon, psaltery, ensemble and all types of music is to fall and bow down to the gold image, ¹¹and anyone who doesn't fall and bow down will be thrown inside a red-hot blazing furnace. ¹²There are some Yehudahites whom you appointed over the business of the province of Babel, Shadrak, Meshak and Abed Nego. These men have not taken any notice of you, Your Majesty. They haven't revered your gods or bowed down to the gold image that you've set up.'

But even if our God doesn't rescue us . . .

¹³Nebukadne'tstsar in rage and fury said to bring Shadrak, Meshak and Abed Nego, and these men were brought before the king. ¹Nebukadne'tstsar avowed to them: 'Shadrak, Meshak and Abed Nego, do you really not revere my gods and bow down to the gold statue that I've set up? ¹⁵If you're indeed now ready, at the time when you hear the sound of the horn, pipe, cithara, trigon, psaltery, ensemble and all types of music, to fall and bow down to the statue that I've made . . .

But if you won't bow down, at that moment you'll be thrown inside a red-hot blazing furnace. And who is the god who could rescue you from my hand?' ¹⁶Shadrak, Meshak and Abed Nego answered, 'King Nebukadne'tstsar, we don't need to make any response to this. ¹⁷If our God, whom we revere, exists, he's able to rescue us from the red-hot blazing furnace, and he will rescue us from your hand, Your Majesty. ¹⁸But if he doesn't, be it known to you, Your Majesty, that we won't revere your gods or bow down to the gold statue that you've set up.'

¹⁹Nebukadne'tstsar filled with wrath, and the expression on his face towards Shadrak, Meshak and Abed Nego changed. He avowed that they should heat the furnace seven times higher than it was customary to heat it. ²⁰He said to the strongest men in his forces to tie up Shadrak, Meshak and Abed Nego, to throw them into the red-hot blazing furnace. ²¹These men were tied up in their trousers, shirts, headwear and other clothes, and thrown inside the red-hot blazing furnace. ²²So because of the king's strict word, when the furnace was heated excessively, the flame from the fire killed those men who took up Shadrak, Meshak and Abed Nego.

Four men walking free in the furnace

²³So these three men, Shadrak, Meshak and Abed Nego, fell inside the red-hot blazing furnace, tied up. ²⁴Then Nebukadne'tstsar the king was startled and stood up in haste. He avowed to his advisers, 'Wasn't it three men, bound, that we threw inside the furnace?' They answered the king, 'Certainly, Your Majesty.' ²⁵He avowed, 'There, I see four men, free, walking about inside the fire. There's no effect on them. The appearance of the fourth is like a divine being.'

²⁶Nebukadne'tstsar went near the door of the red-hot blazing furnace. He avowed, 'Shadrak, Meshak and Abed Nego, servants of God on High, come out, come here.' Shadrak, Meshak and Abed Nego came out from inside the fire. ²⁷The satraps, the governors and the commissioners, and the king's advisers, assembled. They looked at these men, on whose bodies the fire had not had power and the hair on whose head was not singed. Their trousers were unaffected. The smell of the fire had not come on them.

²⁸Nebukadne'tstsar avowed, 'The God of Shadrak, Meshak and Abed Nego be blessed, who's sent his envoy and rescued his servants who entrusted themselves to him. They defied the king's word and gave up their body so they might not revere or bow down to any god but their God. ²⁹Notice is given by me that any people, nation or tongue that says something remiss about the God of Shadrak, Meshak and Abed Nego will be torn limb from limb and his house turned into rubble, because there's no other god who can rescue like this.' ³⁰The king promoted Shadrak, Meshak and Abed Nego in the province of Babel.

Nebukadne'tstsar gives his testimony

4 'Nebukadne'tstsar the king to all the peoples, the nations and the languages that live in all the earth. May your well-being abound! ²It has seemed good to me to relate the signs and wonders that God on High has done with me. ³His signs – how great. His wonders – how mighty. His kingship is a kingship that lasts permanently, his rule continues generation after generation.

⁴I, Nebukadne'tstsar, was at peace in my house, flourishing in my palace. ⁵I had a dream and it disturbed me, and images while I was in bed, visions that came into my head, alarmed me. ⁶Notice was given by me to bring all Babel's experts so they could make known the dream's meaning. ⁷The diviners, the chanters, the Kasdites and the exorcists came, and I related the dream before them, but they couldn't make its meaning known to me.

⁸Finally there came before me Daniyye'l, whose name is Beltesha'tstsar in accordance with my God's name, and in whom is the spirit of the sacred gods. I related the dream before him: ⁹"Beltesha'tstsar, chief of the diviners, I know that the spirit of the sacred gods is in you and that no mystery defeats you. Tell me the visions in the dream that I had, and its meaning.

¹⁰The visions that came into my head: I looked, and there, a tree in the middle of the earth. Its height was big. ¹¹The tree grew and became mighty. Its height reached the heavens. It was visible to the end of the entire earth. ¹²Its foliage was lovely, its fruit abundant, and there was food for everyone in it. Beneath it the animals of the wild sheltered. In its branches the birds of the heavens dwelt. From it all humanity fed.

The dream should be for your enemy

¹³I looked in the visions that came into my head in bed, and there, a lookout, a sacred being, coming down from the heavens. ¹⁴He called forcefully, 'Fell the tree, cut off its branches, strip off its foliage, scatter its fruit. The animals must flee from beneath it, the birds from its branches. ¹⁵Yet leave its rooted stump in the earth. With a ring of iron and copper, with the grass of the wild, with the dew of the heavens he is to be watered, and with the animals his share will be in the plants of the earth. ¹⁶His mind is to be changed from that of a human being; the mind of an animal is to be given him. Seven periods are to pass over him. ¹⁷The decision is by the decree of the lookouts, the intent is by the word of the sacred ones, with the object that human beings may acknowledge that the One on High rules over human kingship. He can give it to whomever he wishes and set up over it the lowest of people.'"

¹⁸I, King Nebukadne'tstsar, had this dream. You, Beltesha'tstsar, tell me its meaning, since all my kingdom's experts can't make its meaning known to me. But you can, because the spirit of the sacred gods is in you.'

¹⁹Daniyye'l, whose name was Beltesha'tstsar, was overcome at that very moment. His thoughts alarmed him. The king avowed, 'Beltesha'tstsar, the dream and its meaning shouldn't alarm you.' Daniyye'l avowed, 'My lord, the dream should be for your enemy, its meaning for your foe. ²⁰The tree that you saw that grew and became mighty, its height reached the heavens and it was visible to the end of the entire earth, ²¹its foliage was lovely, its fruit abundant, and there was food for everyone in it, beneath it animals of the wild sheltered, in its branches the birds of the heavens dwelt: ²²you, Your Majesty, are the one who's grown and become mighty. Your stature has grown and reached the heavens, your rule to the end of the earth.

Break with your wrongdoings by faithfulness

²³In that Your Majesty saw a lookout, a sacred one, come down from the heavens and say, "Fell the tree, destroy it, yet leave its rooted stump in the earth; with a ring of iron and copper, with the grass of the wild, with the dew of the heavens he's to be watered, and with the animals his share will be, until seven periods pass over him": ²⁴this is the meaning, Your Majesty.

It is the decision of the One on High that has befallen my lord the king. ²⁵They're going to lead you away from human beings, and your home will be with the animals of the wild. They'll feed you plants, like oxen, and water you with dew from the heavens. Seven periods will pass over you, until you acknowledge that the One on High rules over human kingship. He can give it to whomever he wishes. ²⁶But in that they said to leave the rooted stump of the tree: your kingship is going to arise for you from when you acknowledge that the heavens rule.

²⁷But, Your Majesty, may my counsel be pleasing to you. Break with your wrongdoings by faithfulness, your waywardness by grace to the humble, in case there may be an extending of your being at peace.'

²⁸It all befell King Nebukadne'tstsar. ²⁹At the end of twelve months, he was walking on the royal palace in Babel. ³⁰The king avowed, 'This is great Babel, which I myself built as a royal home by my sovereign might and for my majestic honour.'

A warning implemented

³¹'The thing still on the king's lips, a voice fell from the heavens: 'To you they're saying, King Nebukadne'tstsar: your kingship has passed from you. ³²They're going to lead you away from human beings and your home will be with the animals of the wild. They'll feed you plants, like oxen. Seven periods will pass over you, until you acknowledge that the One on High rules over human kingship and can give it to whomever he wishes.'

³³At that moment the thing was fulfilled upon Nebukadne'tstsar. He was led away from human beings, he ate plants, like oxen, and his body was watered with the dew of the heavens, until his hair had grown long like eagles and his nails like birds.

³⁴'At the end of the time, I, Nebukadne'tstsar, raised my eyes to the heavens. My sanity came back to me and I blessed the One on High, praised and honoured the One Who Lives Permanently, whose rule is a rule that lasts permanently, whose kingship continues generation after generation. ³⁵All earth's inhabitants are counted as nothing. He acts in accordance with his wishes with the force in the heavens and the inhabitants of the earth. There's no one who can restrain his hand or say to him, "What have you done?"

³⁶At that time, my sanity came back to me, and as for the honour of my kingship, my glory and my splendour came back to me.

My advisers and my important people sought audience with me. I was established over my kingdom, and exceeding power was added to me. ³⁷Now I, Nebukadne'tstsar, praise, exalt and honour the King of the Heavens, all of whose deeds are true and his ways just, and who can put down people who walk in pride.'

A party interrupted

5 Belsha'tstsar the king served a big dinner for his thousand important people, and in the presence of the thousand he was drinking wine. ²Belsha'tstsar said, when he tasted the wine, to bring the gold and silver vessels that Nebukadne'tstsar his father had taken from the palace in Yerushalaim so they could drink from them – the king, his important people, his queens and his consorts. ³The gold and silver vessels that had been taken from the palace in God's house in Yerushalaim were brought in, and they drank from them – the king, his important people, his queens and his consorts. ⁴They drank wine and praised gods of gold and silver, copper, iron, wood and stone.

⁵At that moment the fingers of a human hand appeared and wrote, over against the lamp-stand, on the plaster of the wall of the king's palace. The king saw the palm of the hand that wrote. ⁶The king – his face changed colour. His thoughts alarmed him. His hip joints went loose and his knees knocked one against the other. ⁷The king called forcefully to bring the chanters, Kasdites and exorcists. The king avowed to the smart people of Babel, 'Anyone who can read this writing and tell me its meaning will wear the purple, and the gold chain on his neck, and will rule as Third in the kingdom.'

⁸All the king's smart people came, but they couldn't read the writing or make known its meaning to the king. ⁹King Belsha'tstsar became very alarmed, his face changed colour further and his important people were put in turmoil.

You can keep your rewards

¹⁰The queen – because of the words of the king and his important people, she came into

the banquet hall. The queen avowed, 'Long live the king! Your thoughts shouldn't alarm you or your face change colour. [11]There's a man in your kingdom in whom is the spirit of the sacred gods. In your father's days, illumination, insight and smartness like the gods' smartness was found in him. King Nebukadne'tstsar your father appointed him as chief of the diviners, chanters, Kasdites and exorcists – your father as king. [12]Since a remarkable spirit, knowledge and insight – interpreting dreams, explaining puzzles and resolving enigmas – was found in him, in Daniyye'l whom the king named Beltesha'tstsar, Daniyye'l should now be called. He'll relate the meaning.'

[13]Daniyye'l was brought before the king. The king avowed to Daniyye'l, 'You are Daniyye'l, one of the exiles from Yehudah that my father as king brought from Yehudah. [14]I've heard about you, that the spirit of the gods is in you, and illumination, insight and remarkable smartness are found in you. [15]The smart people (the chanters) have now been brought before me so they could read this writing and make its meaning known to me, but they couldn't relate the words' meaning. [16]I myself have heard about you, that you can explain meanings and resolve enigmas. If you can now read the writing and make known its meaning to me, you will wear the purple and the gold chain on your neck, and rule as Third in the kingdom.'

[17]Daniyye'l answered before the king, 'Your gifts can be for you; give your gifts to someone else. Nevertheless I'll read the writing for Your Majesty and make known the meaning to him.

Weighed and found wanting

[18]You, Your Majesty – God on High gave kingship, greatness, majesty and honour to Nebukadne'tstsar, your father. [19]Because of the greatness given him, all peoples, nations and languages trembled and feared before him. Whomever he wished, he killed, and whomever he wished, he kept alive. Whomever he wished, he elevated, and whomever he wished, he put down. [20]When his mind became elevated and his spirit arrogant, so that he became presumptuous, he was taken from his royal throne, and his honour was removed from him. [21]He was led away from human beings, and his mind was made like an animal, his dwelling with wild donkeys. They fed him grass like oxen and his body was watered with the dew of the heavens, until he acknowledged that God on High rules over human kingship and can set up over it whomever he wishes.

[22]But you, his son, Belsha'tstsar, have not humbled your mind because you knew all this, [23]but have elevated yourself above the Lord of the Heavens. They brought the vessels from his house before you, and you, your important people, your queens and your consorts have drunk wine in them, and praised gods of silver and gold, copper, iron, wood and stone, that don't see, don't hear and don't know. But the God who has your breath in his hand, with all your ways, you haven't glorified.

[24]From before him the palm of the hand was sent, and this writing inscribed. [25]This is the writing that was inscribed: "Counted at a mina, a teqel and two halves". [26]This is the meaning of the words: "A mina": God counted out [*mena*] the days of your kingship and handed it over. [27]"A teqel": you've been weighed [*teqal*] on the scales and found deficient. [28]"A half": your kingship has been broken in half [*peras*] and given to Maday and Paras [Media and Persia].'

[29]Belsha'tstsar gave orders and they clothed Daniyye'l with the purple and with the gold chain on his neck and called out concerning him that he would rule as Third in the kingdom.

[30]That night Belsha'tstsar the Kasdite king was killed, [31]and Dareyavesh [Darius] the Maday acquired the kingship, as a man of sixty-two years.

Standing firm in faith

6 It seemed good to Dareyavesh to appoint over his kingdom 120 satraps who would be spread through the entire kingdom, [2]and over them three supervisors, of whom Daniyye'l was one, to whom these satraps would give account, and the king would not be troubled. [3]This man Daniyye'l distinguished himself above the other supervisors and satraps because of the remarkable spirit in him, and the king was inclined to appoint him over the entire kingdom.

[4]The supervisors and satraps were seeking to find some fault on Daniyye'l's part in the

kingdom's affairs, but they couldn't find any fault or corruption because he was trustworthy; no negligence or corruption could be found against him. ⁵Those men said, 'We shall not find any fault in this Daniyye'l unless we find it regarding his God's law.'

⁶So these supervisors and satraps mustered to see the king and said this to him: 'Long live Dareyavesh the king! ⁷All the supervisors of the kingdom, the governors, the satraps, the advisers and the commissioners have taken counsel about the setting up of a royal decree and the enforcing of an injunction that anyone who makes a petition of any god or human being for thirty days, except of you, Your Majesty, will be thrown into a lion pit. ⁸Your Majesty, issue the injunction now and sign the document, so that it may not be changed, as a law of Maday and Paras, which won't pass away.' ⁹So King Dareyavesh signed the document and the injunction.

¹⁰When Daniyye'l got to know that the document had been signed, he went to his house with its windows open at its top, facing Yerushalaim, and three times a day he'd get down on his knees and pray and give thanks before his God, because he'd been doing so before this.

The frustrated king

¹¹Those men mustered and found Daniyye'l petitioning and praying for grace before his God. ¹²They came near and spoke before the king about the royal injunction: 'You signed an injunction, didn't you, that anyone who petitions any god or human being for thirty days except you, Your Majesty, will be thrown into the lion pit.' The king answered, 'The thing stands firm, as a law of Maday and Paras, which won't pass away.' ¹³They answered before the king, 'Daniyye'l, one of the exiles from Yehudah, has not taken notice of you, Your Majesty, or of the injunction that you signed. Three times a day he makes his petition.'

¹⁴When he heard the thing, he was very displeased in himself, and regarding Daniyye'l he set his mind to delivering him. Until sunset he was working on rescuing him. ¹⁵Then those men mustered and said to the king, 'Your Majesty, acknowledge that it is a law of Maday and Paras that any injunction or decree that the king sets up cannot be changed.' ¹⁶Then the king said, and they brought Daniyye'l and threw him into the lion pit.

The king avowed to Daniyye'l, 'Your God whom you revere continually must deliver you.' ¹⁷A stone was brought and put on the mouth of the pit, and the king sealed it with his signet and with the signets of his important people, so that the intention regarding Daniyye'l might not be changed. ¹⁸The king went off to his palace. He spent the night without food; nothing was brought before him. Sleep eluded him.

Shutting the lions' mouths

¹⁹In the morning, the king got up at first light and went off in haste to the lion pit. ²⁰As he drew near to the pit, he cried in an anguished voice to Daniyye'l. The king avowed, 'Daniyye'l, servant of the living God, your God whom you revere continually – could he deliver you from the lions?' ²¹Daniyye'l spoke with the king: 'Long live the king! ²²God sent his envoy and shut the lions' mouth. They haven't injured me, because before him innocence was found in me – and also before you, Your Majesty, I've done no injury.'

²³The king was very glad about him, and said to get Daniyye'l up out of the pit. So Daniyye'l was got up out of the pit. No injury was found in him, because he had trusted in his God. ²⁴The king said, and they brought those men who had attacked Daniyye'l and threw them into the lion pit, them, their children and their wives. They hadn't reached the ground in the pit before the lions overpowered them and crushed all their bones.

²⁵Then Dareyavesh the king wrote to all peoples, nations and languages that live in the entire earth: 'May your well-being abound! ²⁶From me notice is given that in every domain of my kingdom, people must tremble and fear before Daniyye'l's God, because he is the living God and he stands permanently. His kingship is one that will experience no injury, his rule will continue to the end. ²⁷He delivers and rescues and does signs and wonders in the heavens and in the earth. He rescued Daniyye'l from the hand of the lions.'

²⁸So this Daniyye'l flourished during the reign of Dareyavesh and during the reign of Koresh the Parsite [Cyrus the Persian].

The four weird animals

7 In the first year of Belsha'tstsar king of Babel, Daniyye'l had a dream, visions that came into his head in bed. He wrote the dream down.

The beginning of the account: ²Daniyye'l avowed, 'I looked in my vision during the night, and there, the four winds of the heavens stirring up the Great Sea, ³and four huge animals coming up out of the sea, each different from the others.

⁴The first was like a lion but it had an eagle's wings. I looked as its wings were plucked off and it was lifted up from the ground and set on its feet like a human being, and a human mind was given to it.

⁵And there – another, second animal. It was like a bear, but it was lifted up on one side, with three ribs in its mouth, between its teeth. They said this to it: "Get up, eat lots of meat."

⁶After that, I looked, and there – another, like a leopard, but it had four bird's wings on its back. The animal had four heads, and authority was given it.

⁷After that, I looked in the night visions and there – a fourth animal, fearsome, terrifying and extremely powerful. It had huge iron teeth, devouring, crushing and trampling what was left with its feet. It was different from all the animals that were before it. It had ten horns. ⁸I looked at the horns, and there – another small horn came up among them, and three of the first horns were uprooted before it. And there – something like human eyes in this horn, and a mouth speaking great things.

A throne scene

⁹I looked as

Thrones were set in place
   and someone advanced in years sat down.
His clothing was like white snow,
   the hair of his head like lamb's wool.
His throne was flashes of flame,
   its rings a blazing flame.
¹⁰A river of flame was flowing,
   coming out from before him.
A thousand thousands ministered to him,
   a myriad myriads stood in attendance before him.
The court sat,
   and books were opened.

¹¹I looked because of the sound of the great things that the horn was speaking. I looked as the animal was killed. Its body was destroyed and given to the burning fire. ¹²The rest of the animals: their authority was taken away, but an extension of their lives was given to them for a set time.

¹³I looked in my night visions, and there,

With the clouds in the heavens
   someone like a human being came.
He reached the one advanced in years
   and they presented him before him.
¹⁴To him was given authority, honour and kingship;
   all peoples, nations and languages were to revere him.
His authority is an authority that lasts permanently,
   that won't pass away,
   his kingship one that won't be destroyed.

¹⁵I (Daniyye'l) was disturbed in my spirit within me at this. The visions that came into my head alarmed me. ¹⁶I came near one of those standing in attendance and asked him the truth about all this. He told me and made known the meaning of the thing: ¹⁷"These huge animals, of which there were four: four kings will arise from the earth, ¹⁸but the sacred ones on high will acquire the kingship. They will take hold of the kingship permanently, lastingly and permanently."

One who talks big is silenced

¹⁹I wanted to understand about the fourth animal which was different from all of them (extremely fearsome, its iron teeth, its copper

claws), devouring, crushing and trampling what was left with its feet, ²⁰and about the ten horns that were on its head, and the one that came up and three fell before it – and that horn had eyes and a mouth speaking great things, and its appearance was bigger than its companions. ²¹I looked, and that horn made war with the sacred ones and prevailed over them, ²²until the one advanced in years came and judgement was given for the sacred ones on high, and the time arrived and the sacred ones took hold of the kingship.

²³He said this:
"The fourth animal – there will be a fourth kingship in the earth that will be different from all the kingships. It will devour the entire earth, tread it down and crush it. ²⁴The ten horns – from that kingship ten kings will arise.

After them another will arise. He will be different from those before him. He will bring low three kings. ²⁵He will say things against the One on High and oppress the sacred ones on high. He will try to change times and a law. They will be given into his hand for a period, periods and half a period. ²⁶But the court will sit and take away his authority, to annihilate it and obliterate it permanently. ²⁷The kingship, the authority and the greatness of the kingships under the entire heavens will be given to the people of the sacred ones on high. Its kingship will be a kingship lasting permanently. All authorities will revere and bow down to it."

²⁸That's the end of the account.

I Daniyye'l – my thoughts were very alarming to me. My face changed colour. I kept the thing in my mind.'

A ram, a goat and the terminating of offerings

8 In the third year of the reign of Belsha'tstsar the king, a vision appeared to me (me, Daniyye'l), after the one that appeared to me earlier. ²I looked in the vision (when I saw it, I was in Shushan, the fortress town in Elam Province) – I looked in the vision and I was at the Ulay Gate. ³I raised my eyes and looked, and there – a ram standing before the gate. It had two horns. The horns were high, but the one was higher than the other. The high one came up later. ⁴I looked at the ram charging west and north and south. No animals could stand before it. There was no one could rescue from its hand. It acted according to its wishes and got big.

⁵As I was considering it, there, a male goat coming from the west across the face of the entire earth, without touching the ground. The goat, a conspicuous horn between its eyes, ⁶came to the ram that possessed the two horns, which I had seen standing before the gate, and ran at it in energetic wrath. ⁷I looked at it reaching the ram. It raged at it, struck the ram down and broke its two horns. The ram didn't have the energy to stand before it. It threw it to the earth and trampled it. There was no one could rescue the ram from its hand.

⁸The male goat grew very big, but just when it had become so substantial, the big horn broke. Four conspicuous ones came up in its place, towards the four winds in the heavens. ⁹From one of them came up a small horn. It grew abundantly towards the south and towards the east and towards the splendour. ¹⁰It grew as far as the army of the heavens, and made some of the army, some of the stars, fall to earth, and it trampled them. ¹¹It grew as far as the officer over the army. By it the regular offering was removed and his sacred place and an army were overthrown. ¹²It will be set over the regular offering in rebellion; it will throw truthfulness to the ground. It will act and succeed.

The Greek king who goes too far

¹³I heard a sacred one speaking, and another sacred being said to the one who was speaking, 'How long will the vision be – the regular offering and the desolating rebellion, the giving of both the sacred place and the army to trampling?' ¹⁴He said to me, 'For 2,300 evenings and mornings. But the sacred place will emerge in the right.'

¹⁵While I (Daniyye'l) was looking at the vision and seeking understanding, there – standing in front of me was a human-like person, ¹⁶and I heard a human voice within Ulay. It called, 'Gabri'el, help this man

understand the vision.' ¹⁷He came near where I was standing. When he came, I was overwhelmed and I fell on my face. He said to me, 'Understand, young man, that the vision relates to the time of the end.' ¹⁸When he spoke with me, I fell into a trance, on the face of the ground, but he touched me and stood me up where I had been standing. ¹⁹He said, 'Here am I; I'm going to make known to you what will happen at the conclusion of the condemnation, because it's for the time set for the end.

²⁰The ram that you saw, having two horns, is the kings of Maday and Paras.

²¹The buck (the he-goat) is the king of Yavan [Greece].

The big horn between its eyes – that's the first king.

²²The one that broke and four stood up in its place: four kingships will stand up from a nation, but not with its energy.

²³At the conclusion of their kingship, when the rebels reach full measure, a king will arise fierce of face and understanding conundrums. ²⁴His energy will be substantial, but not by his own energy. He will perform extraordinary acts of devastation and he will succeed when he acts. He will devastate the substantial, and a people of sacred ones, ²⁵with his insight. He will succeed in deceit through his power, and through his mind he will get big. With ease he will devastate many, and he will stand against the officer-in-chief. But without a human hand he will break.

²⁶The vision of evening and morning: what has been said is the truth. You, seal the vision, because it relates to many days.'

²⁷I (Daniyye'l) fell ill for some days, but got up and performed the king's business. But I was overcome by the vision and there was no one could help me understand it.

What happened to the seventy years of Jeremiah 29?

9 In the first year of Dareyavesh son of Ahashverosh, of Maday birth, who was made king over the kingdom of the Kasdites – ²in the first year of his reign, I (Daniyye'l) was considering in the Scriptures the number of years that were (Yahweh's word to Yirmeyah the prophet) to be fulfilled for Yerushalaim's wastes, seventy years.

³I set my face towards the Lord God, to make a plea and prayers for grace with fasting, sack and ash. ⁴I pleaded with Yahweh my God and made confession: 'Oh, Lord, great and awe-inspiring God, who keeps pact and commitment to people who are loyal to him and keep his orders: ⁵we did wrong, we were wayward, we were faithless, we rebelled, we turned aside from your orders and your rulings. ⁶We didn't listen to your servants the prophets who spoke in your name to our kings, our officials and our ancestors, and to all the country's people.

⁷To you, Lord, belongs the right; to us, shame of face this very day, to Yehudah's people, to Yerushalaim's inhabitants and to all Yisra'el, near and far, in all the countries where you drove them because of their trespass that they committed against you. ⁸Yahweh, to us belongs shame of face, to our kings, to our officials and to our ancestors, who did wrong to you. ⁹To the Lord our God belong compassion and acts of pardon, because we rebelled against him ¹⁰and didn't listen to the voice of Yahweh our God by walking according to his instructions that he set before us by means of his servants the prophets. ¹¹ᵃAll Yisra'el transgressed your instruction and turned aside so as not to listen to your voice.

Lord, listen, Lord, pardon!

¹¹ᵇThe vow and the oath that was written in the instruction of Mosheh [Moses], God's servant, overwhelmed us. Because we did wrong to him, ¹²he confirmed his word that he spoke against us and against the people who exercised authority over us, by bringing great bad fortune upon us that hasn't been done under the entire heavens as it has been done in Yerushalaim.

¹³As it is written in Mosheh's instruction, all this bad fortune came upon us, but we didn't seek the goodwill of Yahweh our God by turning away from our waywardness and gaining insight through your truthfulness, ¹⁴so Yahweh watched over this bad fortune and brought it on us, because Yahweh our God was in the right in all his actions that he undertook, and we didn't listen to his voice.

¹⁵But now, Lord our God, who got your people out of the country of Misrayim [Egypt] with a strong hand and made yourself a name this very day, we did wrong, we were faithless. ¹⁶Lord, in accordance with all your faithfulness, please may your anger and your wrath turn back from your town, Yerushalaim, your sacred mountain, because through our wrongdoings and our ancestors' wayward acts, Yerushalaim and your people became an object of reviling to all the people round us.

¹⁷So now, listen, our God, to your servant's plea and to his prayers for grace, and shine your face on your desolate sanctuary, for the Lord's sake. ¹⁸Bend your ear, my God, and listen, open your eyes and look at our desolations and at the town over which your name is called, because it's not on the basis of our faithful acts that we're letting our prayers for grace fall before you, but on the basis of your abundant compassion. ¹⁹Lord, listen, Lord, pardon, Lord, heed and act, and don't delay, for your sake, my God, because your name is called over your town and over your people.'

Seventy sevens until that king who goes too far

²⁰I was still speaking, pleading, confessing my wrongdoing and the wrongdoing of my people Yisra'el, and letting my prayers for grace fall before Yahweh my God for my God's sacred mountain – ²¹I was still speaking in my plea when Gabri'el, the person whom I saw in the vision I had before, tired and weary, reached me at the time of the evening offering ²²and enabled me to understand. He spoke with me: 'Daniyye'l, I have now come out to give you insight in understanding. ²³At the beginning of your prayers for grace a word went out, and I myself have come to relate it, because you're held in high regard. So understand the word and gain understanding into the vision.

²⁴Seventy sevens have been assigned for your people and for your sacred town to bring the rebellion to an end, to do away with wrongdoings, to wipe away waywardness, to bring permanent faithfulness, to seal vision and prophet, and to anoint a most sacred place.

²⁵You're to acknowledge and perceive:
from the issuing of a word for restoring and building up Yerushalaim to an anointed, a leader, there are seven sevens;
for sixty-two sevens it will again be built up, square and moat;
but in the pressure of the times, ²⁶after the sixty-two sevens, an anointed will be cut off, and will have neither the town nor the sacred place; a leader to come will devastate a people and its end will come by a flood, but until the end of battle, devastations are determined;
²⁷a pact will prevail for many people for one seven, for half the seven he will suspend sacrifice and offering, and upon a wing will be a great abomination, desolating, until a conclusion and something decreed overwhelms the desolator.'

The last great vision

10 In the third year of Koresh king of Paras, a word revealed itself to Daniyye'l who was called Beltesha'tstsar. The word was true: a great war. He understood the word; he had understanding through the vision.

²In those days I (Daniyye'l) was mourning for a period of three weeks. ³I ate no food held in high regard; meat and wine didn't come into my mouth. I didn't put on make-up at all until the completion of the period of three weeks.

⁴On the twenty-fourth day of the first month I was on the bank of the big river (i.e. Hiddeqel [the Tigris]). ⁵I raised my eyes and looked, and there, a man clothed in linen, his hips belted with pure gold, ⁶his body like topaz, his face like the brightness of lightning, his eyes like fiery torches, his arms and his feet like the gleam of polished copper, and the sound of his words like the sound of thunder. ⁷I (Daniyye'l) alone saw this vision. The people who were with me didn't see the vision, yet a great terror fell on them and they fled into hiding. ⁸So I remained alone. I looked at this great vision. No energy remained in me. My vigour turned to devastation in me. I didn't retain any energy.

⁹I heard the sound of his words, but when I heard the sound of his words, I went into a trance on to my face, with my face to the

ground. ¹⁰But there, a hand touched me and shook me on to my knees and the palms of my hands. ¹¹He said to me, 'Daniyye'l, man held in high regard, understand the words that I'm going to speak to you. Stand up in your place, because I've now been sent to you.' When he spoke this word with me, I stood up, trembling.

A battle in the heavens

¹²He said to me, 'Don't be afraid, Daniyye'l, because from the first day that you set your mind to understand and humble yourself before your God, your words were heard. I've come because of your words. ¹³The officer over the kingdom of Paras was standing over against me for twenty-one days, but there, Mika'el, one of the senior officers, came to help me. So I had remained there with the kings of Paras, ¹⁴but I've come to enable you to understand what will happen to your people at the end of the time, because there's yet a vision for that time.'

¹⁵While he spoke with me in accordance with these words, I put my face to the ground and kept silence. ¹⁶But there, someone with the likeness of human beings touched my lips, and I opened my mouth and spoke to the one standing over against me: 'My lord, because of the vision my convulsions have overthrown me. No energy has remained in me. ¹⁷How can this servant of my lord speak with this my lord when I – no energy now stays in me, no breath remains in me.'

¹⁸The one with a human appearance touched me again and strengthened me. ¹⁹He said, 'Don't be afraid, man held in high regard, things will be well for you. Be strong, be strong.' When he had spoken with me I asserted my strength and said, 'My lord may speak, because you've strengthened me.'

²⁰He said, 'You know why I've come to you, don't you. Now I shall go back to do battle with the officer over Paras. When I go off, there, the officer over Yavan is going to come. ²¹Nevertheless, I shall tell you what is inscribed in the truthful document. No one is asserting his strength with me against these except Mika'el, your [people's] officer.

11 But I – in the first year of Dareyavesh the Maday, my place was to strengthen and fortify him.

On earth as it is in the heavens

²Now I shall tell you some truth. There, three kings more are going to stand for Paras, and a fourth will possess great wealth, more than anyone. In accordance with the strength he gets through his wealth, he will stir up everyone against the kingdom of Yavan. ³A strong man king will arise, rule a great dominion and act in accordance with his will. ⁴But as soon as he arises, his kingdom will break and scatter to the four winds of the heavens, and not to his posterity nor in accordance with the dominion that he ruled, because his kingdom will uproot and belong to other people apart from these.

⁵The southern king will be strong, but one of his officers will be stronger than him, and he will rule a greater dominion than his dominion. ⁶At the end of some years people will make an alliance, and the southern king's daughter will come to the northern king to effect an agreement. But she won't retain the energy of her strength, nor will his strength stand. She will be given up, she and her escorts and the one who fathered her and the one who gave her strength.

In time ⁷one of the shoots from her roots will stand in his place. He will come against the force and come into the stronghold of the northern king. He will act against them and be strong. ⁸Also their gods with their images, with their articles held in high regard, gold and silver, he will take captive to Misrayim. For some years he will stand back from the northern king. ⁹He will come against the kingdom of the southern king but will go back to his own country. ¹⁰His sons will wage war and gather a horde of many forces. It will come repeatedly, and sweep and pass through, and again wage war as far as his stronghold.

The meaningless to and fro

¹¹The southern king will rage and go out and do battle with him (with the northern king). He will raise a large horde, but the horde will be given into his hand. ¹²The horde will be carried off, but his mind will become superior. He will make myriads fall, but he won't prevail. ¹³The northern king will again raise a horde, greater than the first. At the end of a period of

years he will come repeatedly with a great force and with much equipment.

¹⁴In those times many will stand against the southern king. Wild men among your people will raise themselves, to confirm a vision, but they will collapse. ¹⁵The northern king will come, heap up a ramp and capture a fortified town. The southern forces won't stand, even his company of picked soldiers. There will be no energy to stand. ¹⁶The one who comes against him will act as he pleases, and there will be no one standing before him. He will stand in the splendid country, destruction in his hand. ¹⁷He will set his face to come into control of his entire kingdom, but will make an agreement with him and give him a wife, in order to devastate it. But it won't stand, it won't come about for him. ¹⁸He will set his face towards foreign shores and capture many, but a commander will stop his reviling for him so that he won't be able to turn back his reviling for him. ¹⁹He will turn his face back to the strongholds in his own country. But he will collapse and fall and not be found.

²⁰There will stand in his place one who sends round an oppressor of royal splendour. But in a few days he will break, not by anger or battle.

People who break faith with the covenant

²¹There will stand in his place someone despised, to whom they've not given royal honour. He will come with ease and gain power over the kingdom by empty words. ²²Overwhelming forces will be overwhelmed before him and will break; so too a ruler of the pact. ²³Through the making of alliances with him, he will exercise deceit. He will arise and become substantial with a small group, ²⁴with ease. He will come against the richest of provinces and do what his father and forefathers didn't do. Plunder, spoil and wealth he will scatter among people. He will devise plans against fortresses, until a certain time. ²⁵He will assert his strength and his mind against the southern king with a large force. The southern king will do battle with a large and very substantial force, but he won't stand, because people will devise plans against him. ²⁶People who eat his provisions will break him. His force will be overwhelmed. Many will fall, run through. ²⁷The two of them, the kings, their mind set on bad dealing, will speak lies at one table, but it won't succeed, because an end will yet wait for the set time.

²⁸He will go back to his country with great wealth and with his mind against a sacred pact. So he will act and go back to his country. ²⁹At the set time he will come against the south again, but it won't be like the first and the second time. ³⁰Ships from Kittim will come against him, and he will cower and turn back. He will be condemning a sacred pact and he will act. He will go back and heed the people who abandon a sacred pact. ³¹Forces of his will stand and treat the sanctuary, the fortress, as ordinary. They will remove the regular offering and set up the desolating abomination.

³²People who act faithlessly towards a pact he will make into apostates by empty words, but a people that acknowledge their God will be strong and will act. ³³The insightful among the people will help the multitude to understand, but they will fall by sword, by fire, by captivity and by becoming prey, for a time.

The end approaches

³⁴When they fall, they will receive a little help, but many will join them with empty words. ³⁵Some of the insightful people will fall, to refine them, to purify and to cleanse, until the time of the end, because it will yet wait for the set time.

³⁶So the king will do as he pleases. He will exalt himself and magnify himself above every god, and against the God of gods he will speak extraordinary things. He will succeed until condemnation is complete, because what has been decreed has been done. ³⁷To his ancestors' gods he won't heed, nor to the one women hold in high regard. He won't heed any god, because over everything he will magnify himself. ³⁸A stronghold god he will honour in his place. A god whom his ancestors didn't acknowledge he will honour with gold and with silver, with precious stones and with things held in high regard. ³⁹He will attend to the securest of fortresses with the help of an alien god. To those whom he recognizes he will give great honour. He will let them rule over the multitude and divide up land as payment.

⁴⁰At the time of the end the southern king will wrestle with him, but the northern king will storm against him with chariotry, with cavalry and with many ships. He will come against countries, sweep and pass through, ⁴¹and come against the splendid country. Many will fall, but these will escape from his hand: Edom, Mo'ab and the chief part of the Ammonites. ⁴²He will put out his hand on other countries, and the country of Misrayim will not find escape. ⁴³He will rule the treasuries of gold and silver and all the things held in high regard in Misrayim, with the Putites and Kushites [Sudanese] at his heel. ⁴⁴But reports will alarm him from the east and from the north and he will go out in great wrath to destroy and annihilate many. ⁴⁵He will pitch his royal tents between the seas and the splendid sacred mountain. But he will come to his end. There will be no helper for him.

The people who will shine like stars

12 At that time Mika'el will stand, the high officer who stands by the members of your people. There will be a time of pressure such as hasn't happened since it became a nation until that time. But at that time your people will escape, everyone who is found written in the book, ²and many sleeping in the earth country will wake up, some to permanent life, some to great reviling, to permanent abhorrence. ³The insightful people will be bright, like the sky's brightness, and the people who helped many to be faithful like stars, for ever and ever.

⁴You, Daniyye'l, close up the words, seal the book, until the time of the end. Many will run to and fro so that knowledge may increase.'

⁵I (Daniyye'l) looked, and there – two others standing, one on the riverbank this side, one on the riverbank the other side. ⁶Someone said to the man dressed in linen, who was above the water of the river, 'How long until the end of the extraordinary events?' ⁷I listened to the man dressed in linen who was above the water of the river. He raised his right hand and his left hand to the heavens and swore by the Ever-Living One, 'For a set time, set times and a half. When the shattering of the power of the sacred people ends, all these things will come to an end.'

⁸Though I listened, I didn't understand. I asked, 'My lord, what will be the final stage in these events?' ⁹He said, 'Go, Daniyye'l, because the words are closed up and sealed until the time of the end. ¹⁰Many will purify themselves, cleanse themselves and refine themselves, but the faithless will act faithlessly. None of the faithless will understand, but the people of insight will understand.

¹¹From the time when the regular offering is removed and a desolating abomination put in place will be 1,290 days. ¹²The blessings of the one who waits and reaches 1,335 days! ¹³You, go to the end and settle down, so you may stand for your destiny at the end of the time.'

Hosea

Hosea [Hoshea] is the first of the twelve shorter prophetic books that close the Old Testament. Chronologically, Hosea, Amos and Micah belong together, and they reflect a similar set of religious, social and political circumstances. They were all contemporaries of Isaiah ben Amoz. Hosea, however, worked in northern Israel, to which he often refers as Ephraim with its capital in Samaria, rather than in Judah with its capital in Jerusalem. His task was thus to seek to win Ephraim back to Yahweh in order to forestall Yahweh's taking action against it. Occasional references to Judah indicate that Judah needs to learn from Ephraim's bad example and its consequent fate.

Hosea's key image for portraying Ephraim's wrongdoing is that Ephraim is a whore in the sense of someone who is immoral and faithless to her husband, Yahweh. She expresses her whoring both in having recourse to other deities to get their help in making the land and its people fruitful, and also in having recourse to other political allies to get their help in standing up to Assyria as the threatening superpower. In the opening chapters Hosea's own marriage to someone who was unfaithful provides an acted parable of the nation's life.

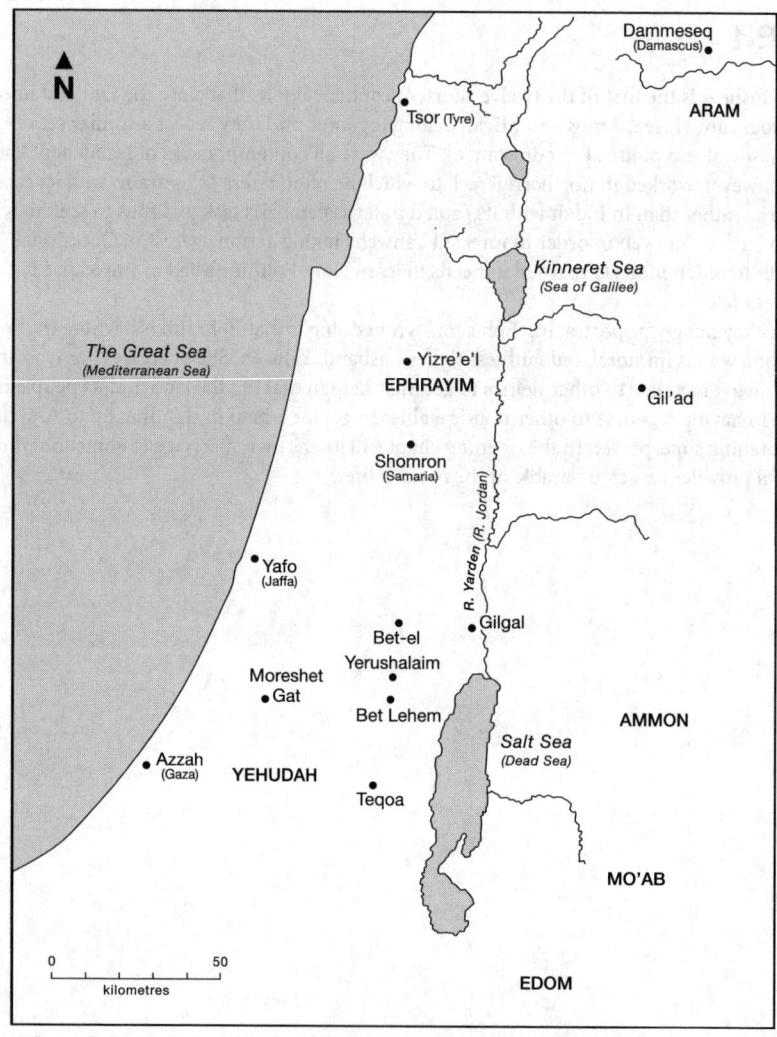

Ephrayim (Ephraim) and Yehudah (Judah) at the time of Hoshea (Hosea)

The whore

1 Yahweh's word which came to Hoshea ben Be'eri in the days of Uzziyah, Yotam, Ahaz and Yehizqiyyah, kings of Yehudah, and in the days of Yarob'am ben Yo'ash king of Yisra'el.

²As the beginning of Yahweh's word through Hoshea, Yahweh said to Hoshea, 'Go get yourself a whorish woman and whorish children, because the country is really whoring away from Yahweh.' ³So he went and got Gomer bat Diblayim.

She got pregnant and gave birth to a son for him. ⁴Yahweh said to him, 'Name him "Yizre'e'l", because in yet a little while I shall attend to the bloodshed in Yizre'e'l upon Yehu's household. I shall stop the kingship of Yisra'el's household. ⁵On that day I shall break Yisra'el's bow in Yizre'e'l Vale'.

⁶She got pregnant again and gave birth to a daughter. He said to him, 'Name her "Not-Compassioned", because I shall no more have compassion again on Yisra'el's household, that I should carry them. ⁷(But on Yehudah's household I will have compassion, and I will deliver them through Yahweh their God – I shall not deliver them through bow, through sword and through battle, through horses and through cavalry.)

⁸She weaned Not-Compassioned, got pregnant and gave birth to a son. ⁹He said, 'Name him "Not-My-People", because you're not my people and I – I shall not be God to you.'

¹⁰But the number of the Yisra'elites will be like the sand at the sea that cannot be measured or counted. In the place where it is said to them 'You are not my people' it will be said to them, 'Children of the living God'. ¹¹The Yehudahites and the Yisra'elites will collect together and make one head for themselves. They will go up from the country, because Yizre'e'l's day will be great.

2 Say to your brothers, 'My people', and to your sisters, 'Compassioned'.

Like mother, like sons and daughters

²Argue with your mother, argue,
  because she isn't my woman and I'm not her man.
She must put away her whoring from her face,
  her adultery from between her breasts.
³Otherwise I shall strip her naked,
  and turn her into like the day she was born.
I shall make her like the wilderness,
  change her into dry land, let her die of thirst.
⁴On her children I shall have no compassion,
  because they're whorish children.
⁵Because their mother has been whorish;
  the one who conceived them has acted shamefully.
Because she's said,
  'I'll go after my lovers,
The ones who give me my bread and my water,
  my wool and my linen, my oil and my drink.'

⁶Therefore, here am I,
  I'm going to hedge up your way with thorn-bushes,
And I shall build a wall for her,
  so she can't find her paths.
⁷She'll pursue her lovers but she won't catch them,
  she'll look for them but she won't find them,
And she'll say,
  'I'll go and return to my first man,
  because it was better for me then than now.'
⁸She – she hasn't acknowledged
  that I myself am the one who gave her
  the grain, the new wine and the fresh oil.

I produced an abundance of silver for her,
  and gold, which they used for the Master.
⁹Therefore, I shall take back
  my grain in its season and
  my new wine at its set time.
I shall rescue my wool and my linen
  for covering her nakedness.
¹⁰Now I shall uncover her villainy
  before her lovers' eyes.
No one will rescue her from my hand,
  ¹¹and I shall make all her celebrating stop,
Her festival, her new month, her sabbath,
  every set event of hers.
¹²I shall devastate her vine and her fig tree,
  of which she's said, 'It's my "gift",
  which my lovers gave me.'
I shall turn them into a forest;
  animals of the wild will consume them.
¹³I shall attend to her for the Masters' days
  when she burns incense for them.
She's decked herself with her ring and her jewellery,
  gone after her lovers,
  and put me out of mind (Yahweh's declaration).

Trouble Vale can become Hope's Door

¹⁴Therefore, here,
  I'm going to charm her,
  and get her to go into the wilderness, and speak to her heart.
¹⁵I shall give her vineyards from there,
  Trouble Vale as Hope's Door.
She'll answer there as in her young days,
  as in the day she went up from the country of Misrayim [Egypt].
¹⁶On that day (Yahweh's declaration) she'll call,
  'My Man';
  she'll no more call me 'My Master'.
¹⁷I shall remove the Masters' names from her mouth;
  they'll be mentioned by their name no more.

¹⁸I shall solemnize a pact for them on that day
  with the creature of the wild,
With the bird in the heavens,
  and with what moves on the ground.
Bow and sword and battle
  I shall break from the country, and enable them to lie down in confidence.

¹⁹I shall marry you to me permanently,
  marry you to me with faithfulness and with the exercise of authority,
With commitment and with compassion,
  ²⁰marry you to me with truth.
You will acknowledge Yahweh,
  ²¹and on that day I shall answer (Yahweh's declaration).
I shall answer the heavens,
  and they will answer the earth.
²²The earth will answer
  with grain, new wine and fresh oil,
Those will answer with Yizre'e'l,
  ²³and shall sow it for myself in the country.
I shall have compassion on Not-Compassioned,
  and I shall say to Not-My-People 'My people'
  and it will say 'My God'.

3 Yahweh said to me further, 'Go, love a woman who is loved by a neighbour and who commits adultery – like Yahweh's love for the Yisra'elites, though they're turning their face towards other gods and loving raisin slabs.' ²So I bought her for myself for fifte silver pieces, a barrel of barley and half a barrel of barley. ³I said to her, 'For a long time you're to live for me. You will not go whoring; you will not belong to a man. So also will I be for you.' ⁴Because for a long time the Yisra'elites are to live with no king, no official, no sacrifice, no pillar, no ephod or effigies. ⁵Afterwards the Yisra'elites will turn back and have recourse to Yahweh their God and David their king. They will be in dread of Yahweh and of his goodness at the end of the time.

No acknowledgement

4 Listen to Yahweh's word,
      Yisra'elites:
Because Yahweh has an argument
  with the country's inhabitants.
Because there's no truthfulness and no commitment,
  no acknowledging of God in the country.
²Vowing, deceit, murder,
  robbery and adultery have spread out;
  bloodshed follows on bloodshed.
³Therefore the country grieves,
  everyone who lives in it languishes,
With the animal in the wild and with the bird in the heavens –
  even the fish in the sea are gathered up.
⁴Yet no one is to argue
  no one is to reprove.
Your people are like people arguing with a priest,
  ⁵and you will collapse by day.
A prophet will also collapse with you by night,
  and I shall terminate your mother.
⁶My people are terminated
  for lack of acknowledgement.
Because you've rejected acknowledgement
  I shall reject you from being a priest for me.
You've put out of mind your God's instruction;
  I shall put out of mind your children, I too.
⁷As they became many, so they did wrong to me;
  I shall exchange their honour for slighting.
⁸They feed on my people's wrongdoing;
  they direct its appetite to their waywardness.
⁹So it will be: as the people, so the priest;
  I shall attend to its ways for it.
I shall bring back its practices for it;
  ¹⁰they will eat but not be full.
They've whored but they won't spread out,
  because they've abandoned Yahweh,
To keep watch ¹¹on whoring,
  as wine and new wine takes away sense.
¹²My people asks things of its piece of wood;
  its stick tells it.
Because a whorish spirit has led it astray;
  they've whored from under their God.
¹³On the tops of the mountains they sacrifice,
  on the hills they burn incense,
Under oak, poplar and terebinth,
  because its shade is good.
That's why your daughters whore,
  your brides commit adultery.
¹⁴I shall not attend to your daughters because they whore,
  or to your brides because they commit adultery.
Because the men themselves consort with whores
  and sacrifice with hierodules,
  and a people that doesn't understand comes to ruin.
¹⁵(If you're whorish, Yisra'el,
  Yehudah must not become liable.)
Don't come to Gilgal, don't go up to Bet Aven ['Trouble House'],
  don't swear 'As Yahweh lives!'

Malcontents have made deep slaughter

¹⁶Because like a defiant cow
   Yisra'el has been stubborn.
Now Yahweh will pasture them
   like sheep on the range.
¹⁷Ephrayim is attached to images;
   leave him to himself.
¹⁸Their drink has gone as they've whored and whored;
   as they've loved and loved, slighting is its 'gift'.
¹⁹The wind has bound it up in its wings,
   so that they'll be shamed because of their sacrifices.

5 Listen to this, priests;
   heed, Yisra'elites.
Give ear, royal household,
   because authority belongs to you.
Because you've been a snare to The Watchtower,
   you've spread a net over Tabor.
²When malcontents have made deep slaughter,
   I was the correction for them all.
³I myself acknowledge Ephrayim;
   Yisra'el has not eluded me.
Because you've now been whoring, Ephrayim;
   Yisra'el has become defiled.
⁴Their practices don't allow them
   to turn back to their God.
Because there's a whorish spirit within them,
   and they don't acknowledge Yahweh.
⁵Yisra'el's majesty will avow against it;
   so Yisra'el and Ephrayim will collapse through their waywardness
   (Yehudah has fallen with them, too).
⁶They may go out with their flock and with their cattle,
   to seek Yahweh.
But they won't find him – he's withdrawn from them;
⁷they've broken faith with Yahweh.
Because they've given birth to alien children,
   the new moon will now consume their shares.

⁸Sound a horn in Gib'ah,
   a trumpet in Ramah.
Raise a shout in Bet Aven,
   after you, Binyamin.
⁹Ephrayim will become a desolation
   on the day of reproof.
Against Yisra'el's clans
   I've made known something truthful.

(¹⁰Yehudah's officials have become like people who move a boundary;
   on them I shall pour out my outburst like water.)

What shall I do with you, Ephrayim?

¹¹Ephrayim is oppressed, crushed by the exercise of authority;
   because he resolved to go after filth:
¹²I myself am like a moth to Ephrayim,
   like rot to Yehudah's household.
¹³Ephrayim saw its sickness,
   Yehudah its sore.
Ephrayim went to Ashshur,
   it sent to the king who would argue.
But that man won't be able to heal you;
   he won't cure you of a sore.
¹⁴Because I shall be like a lion to Ephrayim,
   like a cougar to Yehudah's household.
I, I myself, will tear,
   and as I go I shall carry, and there'll be no one to rescue.

¹⁵I shall go, I shall return to my place,
   until they make restitution,
And seek my face;
   in their pressure they'll seek me urgently:
6 'Come on, let's return to Yahweh,
   because he's the one who tore, but he can heal us.
He strikes down but he can bandage us;
²he can bring us to life after two days.
On the third day he can raise us up,
   so we can live before him.
³When we acknowledge, pursue the acknowledging of Yahweh,
   like dawn his coming out is sure.
He'll come to us like rain,
   like spring rain that waters earth.'
⁴What shall I do with you, Ephrayim,
   what shall I do with you, Yehudah,
When your commitment is like morning cloud,
   like dew going early?

⁵That's why I hewed them down with my prophets,
   killed them with the words of my mouth;
   with rulings against you, light goes out.
⁶Because I wanted commitment not sacrifice,
   acknowledgement of God more than burnt offerings.

⁷But they – as at Adam they transgressed the pact;
   there they broke faith with me.
⁸Gil'ad is a township of people who bring trouble,
   trailed in blood.
⁹The company of priests
   is like gangs waiting for someone.
On the road to Shekem they commit murder,
   when they have committed deliberate wickedness.
¹⁰In Yisra'el's household I have seen something horrible:
   Ephrayim's whoring is there.
Yisra'el has become defiled ¹¹ᵃ(Yehudah, too);
   he's appointed a harvest for you.

A loaf not turned over

7 ¹¹ᵇWhen I restore my people's fortunes,
   as I heal Yisra'el,
Ephrayim's waywardness reveals itself,
   Shomron's [Samaria's] bad dealings.
Because people have practised falsehood, a thief enters,
   a gang has made a dash in the street.
²Their mind doesn't say,
   'I've kept in mind all their bad dealing.'
Now their practices have surrounded them;
   they've been in front of my face.
³They make a king rejoice, with their bad dealing,
   and officials, with their lies.
⁴All of them are committing adultery,
   like an oven burning without a baker.
He stops stirring
   from the kneading of the dough to its yeasting.
⁵On our king's day,
   officials got sick with the heat of wine.
He extended his hand to the arrogant ⁶when they came near,
   their mind like an oven with intrigue.
All night their baker slept,
   in the morning he's burning, like a flaming fire.
⁷All of them burn as hot as an oven,
   they consume their authorities.
All their kings have fallen;
   there's no one among them calling to me.

⁸Ephrayim among the peoples, he wastes away.
   Ephrayim has become a loaf not turned over.
⁹Strangers have consumed his energy,
   and he has not acknowledged it.
Yes, grey hair has spread over him,
   and he has not acknowledged it.
¹⁰Yisra'el's majesty avows against it,
   but they haven't turned back to Yahweh their God.
they haven't sought him despite all this.
¹¹Ephrayim has become like a simple pigeon,
   without sense.
They've called on Misrayim,
   they've gone to Ashshur.
¹²When they go,
   I shall spread my net over them.
Like a bird in the heavens, I shall bring them down;
   I shall correct them in accordance with the report of their assembly.
¹³Oh, these people, because they've strayed from me;
   destruction for them, because they've rebelled against me.
Whereas I'm the one who could redeem them,
   but they themselves have spoken lies about me.
¹⁴They haven't cried out to me in their heart,
   when they wail on their beds.
Over grain and new wine they quarrel;
   they turn against me.
¹⁵I myself corrected them, strengthened their arms,
   but they think up bad things against me.
¹⁶They turn back, not to the One on High;
   they've become like a false bow.
Their officials will fall by the sword
   because of the condemnation of their tongue
   (i.e. their jabbering in the country of Misrayim).

They have made kings, but not through me

8 Horn to your mouth,
   like an eagle over Yahweh's house!
Since they've transgressed my pact,
   rebelled against my instruction.
²To me they cry out,
   'My God, as Yisra'el we've acknowledged you.'
³Yisra'el has rejected what's good;
   an enemy pursues them.
⁴They've made kings, but not through me;
   they've made officials, but I haven't acknowledged them.
With their silver and gold they've made images for themselves,
   in order that [Yisra'el] may be cut off.
⁵He's rejected your bullock, Shomron;
   my anger burns against them.

How long will they be incapable of being free of
    guilt? –
⁶because it was from Yisra'el.
That thing – a metal worker made it;
    it's not a god.
Because Shomron's bullock
    will be broken bits.

⁷Because they sow wind,
    they'll reap a hurricane.
A stalk that has no growth
    doesn't produce flour.
If perhaps it produces,
    strangers will swallow it;
⁸Yisra'el has been swallowed up
    and they have now become among the nations,
Like an object that no one wants,
    ⁹because they've gone up to Ashshur.
A wild donkey on its own,
    Ephrayim has hired lovers.
¹⁰Even when they hire among the nations,
    now I shall collect them.
They've writhed for a while
    because of the burden (king, officers).
¹¹Because Ephrayim has built many altars for
    wrongdoing;
for it, they've become altars for wrongdoing.
¹²Though I write for it many things in my
    instruction,
they've been thought of as alien.
¹³Though they offer sacrifices to me as gifts,
    and eat flesh,
Yahweh doesn't accept them;
    now he'll be mindful of their waywardness.
He'll attend to their wrongdoings;
    those people – they'll go back to Misrayim.
¹⁴Yisra'el has put out of mind its maker
    and built palaces,
    (and Yehudah has built many fortified towns).
I shall send off fire to its towns
    and it will consume its citadels.

I found Yisra'el as like grapes in the wilderness

9 Don't rejoice, Yisra'el, with joy like the
    peoples,
because you've gone whoring away from your
    God.
You have loved the 'gift'
    on every grain threshing-floor.

²Threshing-floor and winepress won't pasture
    them,
new wine will deceive her.
³They won't live in Yahweh's country;
    Ephrayim will go back to Misrayim,
    in Ashshur they'll eat defiled food.
⁴They won't pour wine for Yahweh;
    their sacrifices won't please him.
Like mourners' bread to them,
    all who eat it will be defiled.
Because their bread will be for their own appetite;
    it will not come into Yahweh's house.
⁵What will you do for the set day,
    for the day of Yahweh's festival?
⁶Because there – when they have gone from
    destruction,
Misrayim will collect them, Memphis will bury
    them.
Whereas high regard will attach to their silver,
    briar will dispossess them, bramble will be in
    their tents.
⁷The days of giving attention have come,
    the days of making good have come,
Yisra'el must acknowledge it, though the prophet
    is stupid,
    the person of the spirit is crazy,
On account of the abundance of your waywardness,
    your abundant animosity.
⁸A prophet, with my God,
    is a lookout over Ephrayim.
There's a hunter's snare over all his ways,
    animosity in its God's house.
⁹They've gone deep in devastation, as in the days
    at Gib'ah;
he'll be mindful of their waywardness, he'll
    attend to their wrongdoings.

¹⁰I found Yisra'el
    as like grapes in the wilderness.
I saw your fathers
    as like the first fruit on a fig tree in its beginning.
When those people came to the Master of Pe'or,
    they dedicated themselves to Shame,
    and became abominations like the thing they
    loved.

The King: what would he do for us?

¹¹Ephrayim – their splendour will fly off like a bird,
    away from birth, from the womb, from
    conception.

¹²Even if they rear their children,
  I shall bereave them of people.
Because – oh they, indeed,
  when I turn away from them.
¹³Ephrayim – as I've seen with Tsor [Tyre],
  planted in a meadow,
  so Ephrayim is to take out its children to the
    killer.

¹⁴Give them: Yahweh, what are you to give? –
  give them a miscarrying womb, dry breasts.
¹⁵All their bad dealing was at Gilgal,
  because there I was hostile to them.
Because of the bad nature of their practices,
  I shall drive them from my house.
I shall not add to my love for them;
  all their officials are defiant.

¹⁶Ephrayim is struck down, their root withers,
  they won't produce fruit.
Even when they have children,
  I shall put to death the desired offspring of
    their womb.
¹⁷My God will reject them
  because they haven't listened to him;
  they'll become wanderers among the nations.

10 Yisra'el is a wasting vine;
  its fruit resembles it.
In accordance with the quantity of its fruit, it
  multiplied its altars;
  in accordance with the goodness of its country,
  they made good pillars.
²Because their mind was deceitful,
  now they are to make restitution;
He himself will break down their altars,
  destroy their pillars.
³Because they now say,
  'We have no king;
Because we do not live in awe of Yahweh,
  the King: what would he do for us?'
⁴They've spoken things with empty oaths
  in solemnizing a pact.
The exercise of authority has flourished like
  poisonous growth
  in the furrows of the field.

Sow for yourselves for faithfulness

⁵The population of Shomron fear
  for the bullock of Bet Aven,
Because its people and its priestlings are
  mourning over it
  whereas they celebrate over its splendour.
Because it's going into exile from it;
  ⁶it, too, will be brought to Ashshur,
  a gift to the king so he will argue.
Ephrayim will receive shame,
  Yisra'el will be shamed by its counsel.
⁷Shomron – its king is being terminated,
  like a twig on the face of water.
⁸The shrines of Aven will be annihilated,
  Yisra'el's wrongdoing.
Thorn and thistle
  will grow on their altars.
They will say to the mountains, 'Cover us',
  to the hills, 'Fall on us.'

⁹Since the days of Gib'ah you have done wrong,
  Yisra'el;
  there they stood.
Will battle not overtake them in Gib'ah
  because of evildoers?
¹⁰When it's my desire and I correct them
  peoples will be gathered against them.
When they're disciplined for their double
    waywardness,
  ¹¹though Ephrayim was a trained bullock.
It loved threshing,
  and I – I passed over its good neck.
I shall drive Ephrayim, Yehudah will
    plough,
  Ya'aqob [Jacob] will harrow for itself.

¹²Sow for yourselves for faithfulness,
  reap in proportion to commitment,
  till the tillable ground for yourselves.
It's time for enquiring of Yahweh, until he
    comes,
  and showers faithfulness for you.
¹³You've ploughed faithlessness, you have reaped
    evil,
  you've eaten deceptive fruit.
Because you've relied on your way,
  on the number of your strong men.
¹⁴A din will arise against your people,
  and all your fortifications will be
    destroyed.
Like Shalman's destruction of Bet Arbe'l on a day
  of battle,
  when mother smashed on children.
¹⁵Like this he is doing to you, Bet-el,
  in the face of your bad, bad dealing.

At dawn he's being terminated, being
    terminated,
  Yisra'el's king.

The unfailing nature of a mother's love

11 When Yisra'el was a boy I loved him;
  from Misrayim I called my son.
²I called them;
  thus they went from me.
They sacrifice to the Masters,
  burn incense to images.
³I myself taught Ephrayim to walk,
  lifted them into my arms.
But they didn't acknowledge
  that I healed them.
⁴With human cords I would lead them,
  with loving ties.
For them I was
  someone lifting a baby to the cheek,
  and I bent to him so that I might feed him.

⁵No, they'll go back to the country of
    Misrayim,
  or Ashshur will be their king.
  because they refused to come back.
⁶A sword will whirl against its towns,
  finish off its gate-bars, consume them because
    of their counsels.
⁷My people are bent on turning back from me;
  when they call to the One on High,
  he won't lift them up at all.

⁸How can I give you up, Ephrayim,
  hand you over, Yisra'el?
How can I make you like Admah,
  treat you like Tsebo'im?
My spirit turns round within me,
  my comfort warms all at once.
⁹I shall not act on my angry burning;
  I shall not again devastate Ephrayim.
Because I am God and not a human being,
  the sacred one among you,
  and I shall not come against the town.
¹⁰They will follow Yahweh;
  he will roar like a lion.
When he roars,
  children will come trembling from the west.
¹¹They will come trembling like a bird from
    Misrayim,
  like a pigeon from the country of Ashshur,

I shall let them live in their homes (Yahweh's
    declaration).

Fraud from the womb

¹²Ephrayim has surrounded me with lying,
  Yisra'el's household with deceit.
(Yehudah still wanders with God,
  keeps faith with the sacred ones.)

12 Ephrayim pastures the wind,
  pursues the easterly;
Continually it increases deception and destruction;
  they solemnize a pact with Ashshur,
  and oil is carried to Misrayim.
²Yahweh will argue with Yehudah,
  and attend to Ya'aqob in accordance with his
    ways;
  in accordance with his practices he will give
    back to him.
³In the womb he grabbed his brother,
  and in his strength he struggled with God.
⁴He struggled with the envoy and prevailed;
  he cried and sought grace from him.
He would find him at Bet-el,
  speak with him there,
⁵Yahweh, God of Armies –
  Yahweh is his name.
⁶So you yourself are to turn back to your God;
  keep watch on commitment in the exercise of
    authority,
  and wait for your God always.

⁷A trader in whose hand are deceptive scales
  loves to defraud.
⁸Ephrayim has said, 'Yes, I've become rich,
  I've acquired strength for myself.
In all that I've toiled for they won't find in me
  waywardness that amounts to wrongdoing.'

⁹I am Yahweh your God
  from the country of Misrayim.
I shall make you live in your tents again,
  as in the days of your set occasion.
¹⁰I spoke to the prophets
  and I – I gave many a vision;
  by means of the prophets I shall terminate.
¹¹Is Gil'ad trouble: yes, emptiness;
  in Gilgal did they sacrifice bulls?
Their altars, too,
  are like stone heaps [*gallim*] on the furrows of
    the field.

¹²Ya'aqob fled to the open country of Aram;
Yisra'el served for a wife –
for a wife he kept [sheep].
¹³Through a prophet Yahweh got Yisra'el up from Misrayim,
and through a prophet he was kept.
¹⁴Ephrayim provoked with great bitterness;
his Lord will leave his bloodshed on him,
give back his reviling to him.

Like the morning cloud

13 When Ephrayim spoke, there was trembling,
when he lifted [his voice] in Yisra'el,
but through the Master he became liable and died.
²Now they commit more and more wrongdoing,
and they've made themselves an idol,
Images from their silver in accordance with their insight,
the work of craftsmen, all of it.
With regard to them people are saying,
'Human sacrifices, they kiss bullocks.'
³Therefore they will be like the morning cloud,
like the dew that goes early,
Like chaff that whirls from a threshing-floor,
like smoke from a window.
⁴I am Yahweh your God
from the country of Misrayim.
You will not acknowledge a god apart from me;
there's no deliverer except me.
⁵I acknowledged you in the wilderness,
in a country of droughts.
⁶When they pastured, they were full,
when they were full, their attitude became superior;
therefore they put me out of mind.
⁷So I've become like a cougar to them,
like a leopard I shall lurk by the road.
⁸I shall attack them like a bereaved bear,
rip open the cover of their heart.
I shall consume them like a lion;
the animals of the wild will tear them apart.
⁹Your devastation, Yisra'el,
because in me is your help.
¹⁰Where is your king, then,
so he may deliver you in all your towns,
And your authorities, of whom you said,
'Give me a king and officials'?
¹¹I'd give you a king in my anger
and take him in my outburst.

Birth and death

¹²Ephrayim's waywardness is preserved,
his wrongdoings stored up.
¹³When the pains of giving birth come to him,
he'll be a child who isn't smart.
Because at the time he won't stand
at the breach for children.
¹⁴From She'ol's hand I could redeem them,
from death I could restore them.
Where would be your scourges, death,
where your destruction, She'ol?

Comfort will hide from my eyes,
¹⁵because he's fruitful among brothers.
An easterly will come, Yahweh's wind,
coming up from the wilderness.
His fountain will dry up,
his spring wither.
That will plunder the treasury,
all the objects held in high regard.
¹⁶Shomron is liable,
because it's rebelled against its God.
People will fall by the sword,
their babies will be smashed,
their pregnant women torn open.

14 Turn back, Yisra'el,
to Yahweh your God,
because you've fallen through your waywardness.
²Take words with you,
and turn back to Yahweh;
Say to him, 'Will you carry it all, the waywardness? –
receive something good: for bulls we'll make up with our lips.
³Ashshur isn't to deliver us,
we won't ride on horses.
We will no more say "our God"
to something made by our hands,
because in you the orphan will find compassion.'

⁴I shall heal their turning away, I shall love them freely,
because my anger has turned back from me.

⁵I shall become like dew to Yisraël;
　it will flourish like the lily,
It will strike roots like the Lebanon;
　⁶its shoots will grow
Its splendour will be like an olive
　　tree,
　its fragrance like the Lebanon.
⁷People who sit in its shade will again
　　bring grain to life,
　and flourish like the vine,
　its fame like Lebanon wine.

⁸Ephrayim:
'What shall I have to do with idols any more? –
　I myself have answered and looked to him.
I myself am like a verdant juniper' –
　from me your fruit appears.

⁹Who is smart and discerning about these things,
　is discerning and acknowledges them?
Because Yahweh's ways are straight,
　and the faithful walk in them,
　but rebels collapse by them.

Joel

The first half of Joel [Yo'el] comprises a double description of disaster: a locust epidemic that is portrayed as past and a military invasion that is portrayed as coming. Possibly one is a figure for the other. The book does not give any concrete indication of the century when the disaster(s) happened. Joel's task is to urge Judah to turn to Yahweh in this situation and to promise that Yahweh will then deliver and restore the country. Beyond this restoration, the second half of the book speaks of an unprecedented pouring out of Yahweh's spirit, which will also be associated with a day of world judgement and a final battle between forces of good and forces of wickedness. The natural and/or military catastrophe is an embodiment of 'Yahweh's day', which will come in its final form in those events.

The disaster

1 Yahweh's word that came to Yo'el ben Petu'el.

²Listen to this, you elders;
  give ear, all you inhabitants of the country.
Has this happened in your days,
  or in your ancestors' days?
³Recount it to your children,
  your children to their children,
  and their children to the next generation.

⁴What was left from the cutter, the locust has eaten;
  what was left from the locust, the grub has eaten;
  what was left from the grub, the hopper has eaten.
⁵Wake up, you drunks, and cry;
  howl, all you wine drinkers,
  about the new wine, because it's been cut off from your mouth.
⁶Because a nation has come up against my country,
  numerous, and beyond counting.
Its teeth are a lion's teeth,
  it has a lioness's fangs.
⁷It's made my vine into desolation,
  my fig tree into a stump.
It's stripped its bark and thrown it away;
  its branches have turned white.

⁸Wail like a girl wrapped in sack
  because of the husband of her youth.
⁹Offering and libation has been cut off
  from Yahweh's house;
The priests have mourned,
  Yahweh's ministers.
¹⁰The open country has been destroyed,
  the ground has mourned.
Because the grain has been destroyed,
  the new wine has withered,
  the fresh oil languishes.
¹¹Farmers, be ashamed,
  vinedressers, howl,
Over wheat, over barley,
  because the harvest of the field has perished.
¹²The vine has withered, the fig tree languishes,
  pomegranate, even palm, and apricot.
All the trees of the open country wither,
  because joy has withered from humankind.

All you can do is pray

¹³Wrap on and lament, priests;
  howl, ministers of the altar.
Come, spend the night in sack,
  ministers of my God.
Because offering and libation
  have been held back from Yahweh's house.
¹⁴Declare a sacred fast, call an assembly,
  gather the elders,
  all the inhabitants of the country,
To the house of Yahweh your God,
  and cry out to Yahweh.

¹⁵Ah for the day,
  because Yahweh's day is near;
  it comes like destruction from Shadday ['Destroyer'].
¹⁶Food is cut off, isn't it,
  in front of our eyes,
Rejoicing and celebration
  from Yahweh's house.
¹⁷Seeds have shrivelled under their clods,
  storehouses are desolate.
Granaries are torn down,
  because grain has withered.
¹⁸How the animals have groaned,
  the herds of cattle have been befuddled.
Because they have no pasture,
  even the flocks of sheep suffer punishment.
¹⁹To you, Yahweh, I call,
  because fire has consumed
  the pastures in the wilderness.
Flame has burned
  all the trees in the open country.
²⁰Even the animals of the wild pant for you,
  because the canyons of water dry up.
Fire has consumed
  the pastures in the wilderness.

2 Blow a horn in Tsiyyon [Zion],
  sound out on my sacred mountain.
All the country's inhabitants are to tremble,
  because Yahweh's day has come, because it's near,
²A day of darkness and gloom,
  a day of cloud and murk.

Like dawn spread over the mountains,
  a vast and numerous company.
Nothing like it has happened from of old,
  and it won't happen again after it,
  through the years of generation after generation.

³Before it fire has consumed,
   after it flame blazes.
Before it the country was like Eden Garden,
   but after it, desolate wilderness –
   indeed, no survivors have been left to it.

Who knows, he may turn back

⁴Their appearance is like the appearance of horses;
   like steeds, so they run.
⁵Like the sound of chariots,
   on the tops of the mountains they leap.
Like the sound of a blazing fire
   consuming straw,
Like a numerous company
   lined up for battle.
⁶Before them, peoples shudder;
   all faces have collected a flush.
⁷Like strong men they run,
   like men of battle they climb a wall.
They go each of them on his ways,
   they don't deviate their paths.
⁸They don't jostle one another;
   they go each man on his causeway.
When they fall through the weaponry,
   they don't break off.
⁹They rush at the town,
   they run at the wall.
They climb on the houses,
   through the windows they come in like a robber.

¹⁰Before it earth has quaked,
   heavens have shaken.
Sun and moon have gone dark,
   stars have gathered up their brightness.
¹¹Yahweh – he has given his voice
   before his force.
Because his camp is very vast,
   because numerous is the one performing his
      word.
Because Yahweh's day is great,
   very extraordinary – who can endure it?

¹²But even now (Yahweh's declaration),
   turn back to me with your whole heart,
   with fasting, with crying and with lamenting.
¹³Tear your mind, not your clothes,
   and turn back to Yahweh your God,
Because he is gracious and compassionate,
   long-tempered and vast in commitment,
   and he relents of dealing badly.

¹⁴Who knows, he may turn back and relent,
   and let a blessing remain behind him,
   an offering and a libation for Yahweh your
      God?

¹⁵Blow the horn in Tsiyyon,
   declare a sacred fast, call an assembly.
¹⁶Gather the people, make the congregation
      sacred,
   collect the elders.
Gather the babies
   and those nursing at the breast.
The groom is to go out of his room,
   the bride out of her tent.
¹⁷Between the porch and the altar
   the priests, Yahweh's ministers, are to cry.
They're to say, 'Spare your people, Yahweh,
   don't give your domain to reviling.
   as a byword against them for the nations.
Why should they say among the peoples,
   "Where is their God?"'

The years the locust has eaten

¹⁸So Yahweh became passionate about his country,
   and took pity on his people.
¹⁹Yahweh answered,
   and said to his people,
'Here I am, I'm going to send grain to you,
   new wine and fresh oil – you'll be full of it.
I shall not ever again give you over
   as an object of reviling among the nations.
²⁰I shall put the northerner far from you,
   thrust him into a dry and desolate country,
His face to the eastern sea,
   his rear to the western sea.
His smell will go up, his stench go up,
   because he has acted big.

²¹Don't be afraid, earth, celebrate and rejoice,
   because Yahweh has acted big.
²²Don't be afraid, animals of the wild,
   because the wilderness pastures are green.
Because the tree has borne its fruit,
   fig tree and vine have given their resources.
²³Members of Tsiyyon, celebrate,
   rejoice in Yahweh your God.
Because he's given you
   the autumn rain in faithfulness.
He's made rain come down for you,
   autumn rain and spring rain as before.

²⁴Threshing-floors will be full of grain,
 presses will abound in new wine and fresh oil.
²⁵I shall make good to you for the years
 that the locust and the grub have consumed,
The hopper and the cutter, my big force,
 which I sent off against you.
²⁶You will eat and eat and be full,
 and praise the name of Yahweh your God,
The one who acted in an extraordinary way with you;
 my people won't be ashamed permanently, and you will acknowledge it.
²⁷Because I will be within Yisra'el,
 and I am Yahweh your God.
And there is no other,
 and my people will not be ashamed,
 permanently.

You can't control who receives God's spirit

²⁸After that, I shall pour my breath on all flesh,
 and your sons and your daughters will prophesy.
Your elderly will have dreams,
 your young men will see visions.
²⁹I shall also pour my breath
 on servants and maidservants in those days.

³⁰I shall put portents in the heavens and in the earth,
 blood, fire and columns of smoke.
³¹The sun will turn to darkness,
 the moon to blood,
Before Yahweh's day comes,
 great, extraordinary.
³²But anyone who calls
 in Yahweh's name will escape.
Because on Mount Tsiyyon and in Yerushalaim
 there will be an escape group,
As Yahweh has said,
 among the survivors whom Yahweh is going to call.

3 Because there, in those days
 and at that time,
When I restore the fortunes
 of Yehudah and Yerushalaim,
²I shall collect all the nations
 and get them down to Yehoshaphat ['Yahweh has exercised authority'] Vale.
I shall enter into the exercise of authority with them there
 over my people, my domain, Yisra'el,
 whom they scattered among the nations.
They shared out my country.
 ³and for my people they cast the lot.
They gave a boy for a whore,
 sold a girl for wine and drank it.

⁴Now, what are you in relation to me, Tsor [Tyre] and Tsidon,
 and all you regions of Peleshet [Philistia]?
Are you making good to me with your dealings? –
 if you're dealing out me,
Swiftly, speedily,
 I shall give back your dealings on to your head.
⁵Because it was my silver and my gold you took,
 the good things that I held in high regard you brought into your palaces.
⁶Yehudahites and Yerushalaimites you sold to the Yavanites [Greeks],
 in order to send them far away from their territory.
⁷Here am I, stirring them up from the place to where you sold them,
 and I shall give back your dealings on to your head.
⁸I shall sell your sons and your daughters
 into the hand of the Yehudahites,
And they will sell them into captivity
 to a far-off nation (because Yahweh has spoken).

Beat your hoes into swords

⁹Call out this among the nations,
 declare a sacred battle.
Stir up strong men so they draw near;
 all the men of battle are to go up.
¹⁰Beat your hoes into swords,
 your pruning hooks into spears;
The weakling is to say, 'I'm a strong man' –
 ¹¹hurry, come.
All you nations around, collect yourselves,
 make your strong men go down there, Yahweh.
¹²The nations are to stir themselves and go up
 to Yehoshaphat Vale,
Because there I shall sit to exercise authority
 over all the nations around.

¹³Put out the sickle,
   because the harvest has ripened.
Come, tread,
   because the vat is full.
The presses abound,
   because their bad dealing is great.
¹⁴Hordes, hordes, in Verdict Vale,
   because Yahweh's day is near in Verdict Vale.
¹⁵Sun and moon have gone dark,
   stars have gathered up their brightness;
¹⁶Yahweh roars from Tsiyyon,
   gives voice from Yerushalaim.
Heavens and earth tremble,
   but Yahweh is a shelter for his people,
   a stronghold for the Yisra'elites.
¹⁷You will acknowledge that I am Yahweh,
   your God who dwells on Tsiyyon, my sacred mountain.
Yerushalaim will be sacred;
   strangers will no more pass through it.
¹⁸On that day
   the mountains will drop sweet wine,
The hills will run with milk,
   all Yehudah's canyons will run with water.
A fountain will go out of Yahweh's house
   and water Acacias Wadi.
¹⁹Misrayim [Egypt] will become a desolation,
   Edom will become a wilderness, a desolation,
Because of violence done to the Yehudahites,
   in whose country they shed the blood of one free of guilt.
²⁰But Yehudah will live permanently,
   Yerushalaim for generation after generation.
²¹I shall treat their bloodshed as free of guilt,
   which I have not treated as free of guilt,
   as Yahweh is dwelling on Tsiyyon.

Amos

Yahweh sent Amos from Judah to bring his message to northern Israel (Ephraim) at Bethel, at the southern end of the country. He was a contemporary of Hosea in Ephraim, though they may not have come into contact if Hosea was in the Ephraimite capital, Samaria. Compared with Hosea, Amos pays proportionately more attention to social ills than to religious ills, and he is a gifted communicator. The opening chapters win his audience's attention by lambasting other nations for their war crimes before turning to declare that Ephraim is worse because it had fuller revelation from God. He invites people to come to worship, but then tells them it's an act of rebellion that Yahweh hates. He sings a funeral lament that turns out to be a dirge for the coming demise of the nation itself. He declares that the day of Yahweh will be bad news, not good news. He tells people how he prayed successfully for Yahweh not to act in judgement but then indicates that he had to stop doing so. He warns people that they cannot escape Yahweh even by trying to hide in She'ol. But he also says that judgement will not be the end.

Nations held responsible

1 The words of Amos, who was among the sheep-breeders from Teqoa, which he saw concerning Yisra'el in the days of Uzziyyah king of Yehudah and in the days of Yarob'am ben Yo'ash king of Yisra'el, two years before the earthquake.

²When Yahweh roars from Tsiyyon [Zion],
 gives voice from Yerushalaim,
The shepherds' pastures will mourn,
 Carmel's head will wither.

³Yahweh has said this:

For three rebellions by Dammeseq [Damascus],
 for four I shall not turn it back,
 because of their threshing Gil'ad with iron sledges.
⁴I shall send off fire against Haza'el's house,
 and it will consume Ben-hadad's citadels.
⁵I shall break Dammeseq's bar,
 and I shall cut off inhabitants from Trouble Valley,
A sceptre-holder from Bet-eden,
 and the people of Aram will go into exile to Qir (Yahweh has said).

⁶Yahweh has said this:

For three rebellions by Azzah [Gaza],
 for four I shall not turn it back,
Because of their exiling a complete exile community,
 handing them over to Edom.
⁷I shall send off fire against Azzah's wall,
 and it will consume its citadels.
⁸I shall cut off inhabitants from Ashdod,
 a sceptre-holder from Ashqelon.
I shall turn back my hand against Eqron;
 the remainder of the Pelishtites [Philistines]
  will perish (the Lord Yahweh has said).

⁹Yahweh has said this:

For three rebellions by Tsor [Tyre],
 for four I shall not turn it back,
because of their handing over a complete exile community to Edom;
 they were not mindful of the brotherhood pact.
¹⁰I shall send off fire against Tsor's wall,
 and it will consume its fortresses.

Yehudah too

¹¹Yahweh has said this:

For three rebellions by Edom,
 for four I shall not turn it back,
Because he pursued his brother with a sword,
 devastated his compassion.
His anger tore ceaselessly,
 his outburst kept watch continually.
¹²I shall send off fire against Teman,
 and it will consume Botsrah's citadels.

¹³Yahweh has said this:

For three rebellions by the Ammonites,
 for four I shall not turn it back,
Because of their ripping open pregnant women in Gil'ad,
 in order to enlarge their territory.
¹⁴I shall set fire to Rabbah's wall
 and it will consume its citadels,
With shouting on a day of battle,
 with a hurricane on a stormy day.
¹⁵Their king will go into exile,
 he and his officials together (Yahweh has said).

2 Yahweh has said this:

For three rebellions by Mo'ab,
 for four I shall not turn it back,
 because of his burning the bones of the king of Edom to lime.
²I shall send off fire against Mo'ab,
 and it will consume Qeriyyot's citadels.
Mo'ab will die amid a din,
 amid shouting and the sound of a horn.
³I shall cut off the authority from within it,
 and kill all its officials with him (Yahweh has said).

⁴Yahweh has said this:

For three rebellions by Yehudah,
 for four I shall not turn it back,
Because of their rejecting Yahweh's instruction
 and not keeping his laws.
Their lies led them astray,
 which their ancestors followed.
⁵I shall send off fire against Yehudah,
 and it will consume Yerushalaim's citadels.

And also Ephrayim

⁶Yahweh has said this:

For three rebellions by Yisraʾel,
  for four I shall not turn it back,
Because of their selling a faithful person for silver,
  a needy person for a pair of boots.
⁷You who trample the head of poor people
    into the earth of the ground,
  and twist the way of humble people!
An individual and his father go to a girl,
  in order to treat my sacred name as ordinary.
⁸On garments given in pledge
  they lie down by every altar.
In their God's house they drink
  the wine of people who have been defrauded.

⁹And I'm the one who annihilated the Amorite before them,
  whose height was like the height of cedars,
  and who was as sturdy as oaks.
I annihilated his fruit above
  and his roots below.
¹⁰And I'm the one who took you up
  from the country of Misrayim [Egypt].
I enabled you to go through the wilderness for forty years,
  to take possession of the Amorite's country.
¹¹I raised up prophets from your children,
  consecrated people from your young men.
It is indeed so, isn't it, Yisraʾelites (Yahweh's declaration),
  ¹²but you made the consecrated people drink wine
  and you ordered the prophets, 'You will not prophesy.'

¹³There, I'm going to make a split beneath you
  as a cart makes a split
  when full of its grain.
¹⁴Flight will perish from the swift,
  the strong won't firm up his energy.
The strong man won't save his life,
  ¹⁵the one who wields the bow won't stand.
One swift on his feet won't save himself,
  one riding a horse won't save his life.
¹⁶The firmest of mind among the strong men
  will flee naked on that day (Yahweh's declaration).

Do accidents happen?

3 Listen to this word which Yahweh has spoken about you, Yisraʾelites, about the entire kin-group that I took up from Misrayim:

²Only you did I acknowledge
  from all earth's kin-groups.
Therefore I shall attend to you
  for all your wayward acts.
³Do two walk together
  unless they've taken counsel?
⁴Does a lion roar in the forest
  and it has no prey?
Does a cougar give voice from its abode
  unless it has caught something?
⁵Does a bird fall in a trap on the earth
  and there's no snare there?
Does a trap come up from the ground
  and it hasn't actually caught something?
⁶If a horn sounds in a town,
  doesn't the people tremble?
And if something happens to a town,
  isn't it Yahweh who's acted?
⁷Because the Lord Yahweh does nothing
  except he has revealed his plan
  to his servants the prophets.

⁸A lion has roared,
  who would not be afraid?
The Lord Yahweh has spoken,
  who wouldn't prophesy?

⁹Make it heard in Ashdod's citadels,
  and in the citadels in the country of Misrayim.
Say, 'Gather on Shomron's [Samaria's] mountains,
  look at the great chaos within it,
  the oppressed within it.'
¹⁰They haven't acknowledged acting straight (Yahweh's declaration),
  the people who store up violence and destruction in their citadels.

¹¹Therefore, the Lord Yahweh has said this:

An adversary, round the country:
  he'll pull down your vigour from you,
  and your citadels will be plundered.

¹²Yahweh has said this:

As a shepherd rescues
   from a lion's mouth
Two shank bones
   or the tip of an ear,
So the Yisra'elites will escape,
   the people who live in Shomron,
   with the leg of a bed or the damask of a couch.

¹³Listen, and testify against Ya'aqob's [Jacob's] household
   (a declaration of the Lord Yahweh, God of Armies):
¹⁴On the day I attend to Yisra'el's rebellions for it,
   I shall attend to Bet-el's altars.
The altar's horns will be cut off,
   and will fall to the ground.
¹⁵I shall strike down the winter house
   as well as the summer house.
The ivory houses will perish,
   the great houses will come to an end (Yahweh's declaration).

But you haven't turned back to me

4 Listen to this word,
   you Bashan cows,
You who are on Shomron's mountain,
   you who defraud the poor, who crush the needy,
Who say to their husbands,
   'Bring something so we can drink.'

²The Lord Yahweh has sworn by his sacredness:

There, days are coming upon you
   when someone will carry you off with hooks –
   yes, the last of you with fish hooks.
³Through the breaches you'll go out, each woman straight ahead,
   and you'll be thrown out to Harmon (Yahweh's declaration).

⁴Come to Bet-el and rebel –
   to Gilgal, multiply the rebelling.
Bring your sacrifices every morning,
   your tenths every three days.
⁵Burn your thank-offering of leavened bread,
   call out voluntary offerings, make them heard,
   because so you love it, Yisra'elites (the Lord Yahweh's declaration).
⁶Even though I – I have given you
   emptiness of teeth in all your towns,
Lack of food in all your places,
   but you haven't turned back to me (Yahweh's declaration).
⁷Even though I – I have withheld the rain from you
   when it was still three months to the harvest.
I'd let it rain on one town
   but not let it rain on another town.
One plot would be rained on,
   but a plot on which it would not rain would wither.
⁸Two or three towns would wander
   to another town to drink water.
But they wouldn't be full,
   but you haven't turned back to me (Yahweh's declaration).
⁹I have struck you down with blight and with mildew,
   multiplying it on your gardens and your orchards.
The locust would eat your fig trees and olives,
   but you haven't turned back to me (Yahweh's declaration).
¹⁰I sent off an epidemic among you
   in the manner of Misrayim,
I killed your young men with the sword,
   with your captured horses,
Made the smell of your camps rise, even into your nostrils,
   but you haven't turned back to me (Yahweh's declaration).
¹¹I overthrew some of you
   like the supernatural overthrow of Sedom [Sodom] and Amorah [Gomorrah],
You became like a burning stick pulled out of the fire,
   but you haven't turned back to me (Yahweh's declaration).

When authority becomes poisonous

¹²Therefore this is what I shall do to you, Yisra'el;
   because I shall do this to you,
   get ready to meet your God, Yisra'el.
¹³Because there, one who shapes mountains,
   creates wind,

Tells human beings what his thinking is,
  makes dawn into darkness,
Treads on earth's high places –
  Yahweh, God of Armies, is his name.

5 Listen to this word, which I'm taking up,
  a lament over you, Yisra'el's household.

²She's fallen, she won't get up again,
  Miss Yisra'el;
She's left on her land,
  there's no one to help her up.

³Because the Lord Yahweh has said this:

The town that goes out as a thousand
  will have a hundred remaining.
The one that goes out as a hundred
  will have ten remaining to Yisra'el's household.

⁴Because Yahweh has said this to Yisra'el's household:

Enquire of me, and live,
  ⁵don't enquire of Bet-el,
Don't go to Gilgal,
  don't cross over to Be'er-sheba.
Because Gilgal is definitely to go into exile,
  and Bet-el is to become nothing.
⁶Enquire of Yahweh and live,
  so he doesn't break out like fire
On Yoseph's household, and consume,
  and there's no one to quench it for Bet-el.

⁷You who turn the exercise of authority to
    poison
  and set down faithfulness on the earth!
⁸He's the one who makes Pleiades and Orion,
  turns deep darkness to dawn.
He darkens day into night,
  the one who calls the water of the sea,
Pours it out on the face of the earth –
  Yahweh is his name –
⁹The one who flashes destruction on the vigorous,
  so that destruction comes on the fortification.

¹⁰They are hostile to the one who reproves in the
    gateway,
  they take offence at the one who speaks with
    integrity.
¹¹Therefore, because you tax the poor person,
  take a levy of grain from him:

You've built houses of square stone,
  but you won't live in them.
¹²Because I have got to know your many acts of
    rebellion,
  your numerous wrongdoings.
You adversaries of the faithful, takers of a bribe,
  who have turned aside the needy in the
    gateway.

The day of the Lord as bad news

¹³Therefore the person of insight keeps silent at
    such a time,
  because it's a bad time.
¹⁴Enquire after what is good, not what is bad, in
    order that you may live;
  thus Yahweh, God of Armies, will be with
    you,
  as you've said.
¹⁵Be hostile to what is bad, be loyal to what is
    good,
  establish the exercise of authority in the
    gateway.
Perhaps Yahweh, God of Armies, will be gracious
  to what remains of Yoseph.

¹⁶Therefore Yahweh, God of Armies, the Lord, has said this:

In all the squares lamenting,
  in all the streets they'll say, 'Oh, oh'.
They'll call the farmhand to mourning,
  and for lamenting to the people who know how
    to keen.
¹⁷In all the orchards lamenting,
  when I pass through the middle of you
  (Yahweh has said).

¹⁸Hey, you who wish
  for Yahweh's day.
What good really is Yahweh's day to you? –
  it will be darkness, not light.
¹⁹As when someone flees from before a lion
  and a bear meets him,
Or he comes home,
  leans his hand on a wall,
  and a snake bites him.
²⁰Yahweh's day will be darkness not light, won't it,
  gloom, with no brightness to it.
²¹I've been hostile, I've rejected your festivals;
  I don't savour your assemblies.

²²Even when you offer me burnt offerings,
  and your grain offerings, I shall not accept them.
To a fellowship offering of well-fed animals
  I shall not look.
²³Remove from me the noise of your songs;
  I shall not listen to the music of your mandolins.
²⁴The exercise of authority is to roll like water,
  faithfulness like a perennial wadi.
²⁵Was it sacrifices and an offering that you presented to me
  in the wilderness for forty years,
  household of Yisra'el?

²⁶You will carry Sikkut your king,
  and Kiyyun, your images, the star of your god,
That which you made for yourselves,
  ²⁷and I shall exile you beyond Dammeseq,
  (Yahweh whose name is God of Armies has said).

A warning to people at peace

6 Hey, you people who are at peace on Tsiyyon,
  who are confident on Shomron's mountain,
You notables of the first of the nations,
  to whom Yisra'el's household come.
²Pass over to Kalneh and look,
  go from there to Great Hamat,
  go down to Gat in Peleshet [Philistia].
Are these better than your kingdoms,
  or their territory than your territory,
³You who push away the bad day,
  but bring near the rule of violence,
⁴You who lie on ivory beds,
  lounging on their couches,
Eating lambs from the flock,
  bullocks from within the stall,
⁵Making music to the sound of the mandolin like David,
  people who have composed for themselves on musical instruments,
⁶Drink with bowls of wine,
  anoint themselves with the finest oils,
  but haven't got sick at the breaking of Yoseph?
⁷Therefore now:
  they will go into exile at the head of the exiles,
  and the revelry of the loungers will turn aside.

⁸The Lord Yahweh has sworn by himself
(a declaration of Yahweh, God of Armies):

I detest Ya'aqob's majesty,
  I'm hostile to its citadels,
  I shall deliver up the town and what fills it.
⁹If ten people are left
  in one house, they'll die.
¹⁰If someone's relative lifts him up (the person who burns spices for him)
  to take his bones out of the house,
And says to whoever is in the inner parts of the house,
  'Is anyone still with you?'
He'll say, 'Hush,
  because we're not to mention Yahweh's name.'
¹¹Because there, Yahweh is going to order,
  and he'll strike down the great house to pieces,
  the small house to bits.

¹²Do horses run on a cliff,
  or does one plough it with cattle?
Because you've turned the exercise of authority to venom,
  faithful fruit to poison,
¹³You who rejoice at No-thing,
  who say 'It was by our strength, wasn't it,
  that we took Qarnayim for ourselves?'
¹⁴Because here am I, about to raise up against you,
  Yisra'el's household (a declaration of Yahweh, God of Armies) –
A nation, and they'll afflict you
  from Lebo Hamat to Wadi Arabah.

I wasn't a prophet

7 The Lord Yahweh showed me this: there, he was forming a locust swarm at the beginning of the growth of the spring crop. There – the spring crop after the king's reaping. ²When it had finished consuming the grass in the country, I said, 'Lord Yahweh, please pardon, how can Ya'aqob stand, because it's small.' ³Yahweh relented about this. 'It won't happen', Yahweh said.

⁴The Lord Yahweh showed me this: there, he was calling for an argument by fire. It consumed the Great Deep and it was consuming the plots. ⁵I said, 'Lord Yahweh, please spare, how can Ya'aqob stand, because

it's small.' ⁶Yahweh relented about this. 'It won't happen either', the Lord Yahweh said.

⁷He showed me this: there, the Lord was standing by a lead-weight wall, and in his hand was a lead weight. ⁸Yahweh said to me, 'What are you looking at, Amos?' I said, 'A lead weight'. The Lord said, 'Here am I, I'm going to put a lead weight in the middle of my people Yisra'el. I shall not again pass over it any more. ⁹Yitshaq's [Isaac's] shrines will be desolate, Yisra'el's sanctuaries will be laid waste. I shall rise against Yarob'am's household with the sword.'

¹⁰Amatsyah the priest at Bet-el sent to Yarob'am king of Yisra'el to say, 'Amos has conspired against you within Yisra'el's household. The country can't endure all his words. ¹¹Because Amos has said this: "Yarob'am will die by the sword, Yisra'el will go into exile, exile away from its soil."' ¹²But Amatsyah said to Amos, 'Seer, go, flee for your life to the country of Yehudah, eat bread there, prophesy there. ¹³Don't prophesy again in Bet-el any more, because it's the king's sanctuary. It's the kingdom's house.'

¹⁴Amos answered Amatsyah, 'I wasn't a prophet and I wasn't a prophet's son; rather I was a cattleman and a dresser of sycamore figs. ¹⁵But Yahweh took me from following the flock, and Yahweh said to me, "Go, prophesy to my people Yisra'el."

¹⁶Now, listen to Yahweh's word. You're saying, "You shouldn't prophesy against Yisra'el. You shouldn't preach against Yitshaq's household." ¹⁷Therefore Yahweh has said this: "Your wife will whore in the town. Your sons and your daughters will fall by the sword. Your land will be shared out by measuring line. You yourself will die on unclean land. Yisra'el will go into exile, exile away from its land."'

Amos isn't praying now

8 The Lord Yahweh showed me this: there, a basket of ripe fruit. ²He said, 'What are you looking at, Amos?' I said, 'A basket of ripe fruit'. Yahweh said to me, 'The ripe time has come for my people Yisra'el. I shall not again pass over it any more. ³The palace singers will wail on that day (a declaration of the Lord Yahweh): "He has thrown out many a corpse in every place – hush!"'

⁴Listen to this, you who trample the needy person,
   who make the humble people in the country cease,
⁵Saying, 'When will the new month be over,
   so we can sell wheat,
   and the sabbath, so we can lay out grain –
Making the barrel measure small but the sheqel big,
   falsifying the scales by deceit,
⁶Acquiring the poor people for silver,
   the needy person for a pair of boots,
   and selling sweepings as grain?'
⁷Yahweh has sworn by the Majesty of Ya'aqob,
   'If I ever put out of mind any of their doings ...'

⁸For this, the earth will shake, won't it,
   and everyone who lives in it mourn.
It will all rise like the Ye'or [Nile],
   surge and sink like Misrayim's Ye'or.

⁹On that day (a declaration of the Lord Yahweh),
   I shall make the sun set at noon,
   make the earth dark during daylight.
¹⁰I shall turn your festivals into mourning,
   all your songs into lamenting.
I shall put sack on all hips,
   shortness on every head,
I shall make it like the mourning for an only child,
   its end a truly bitter day.

You can't get away from God

¹¹There, days are coming (a declaration of the Lord Yahweh)
   when I shall send famine through the country –
Not famine of bread, not thirst for water,
   but rather of hearing Yahweh's words.
¹²People will wander from sea to sea
   and roam from north to east,
To seek Yahweh's word,
   but they won't find it.
¹³On that day beautiful girls and young men
   will faint with thirst.
¹⁴People who swear by the liability of Shomron
   and say, 'As your god lives, Dan',
And 'As the way to Be'er-sheba lives',
   will fall and not rise again.

9 I saw the Lord standing by the altar. He said:

Strike down the capitals so the thresholds shake;
  break them off on to the head of all of them.
The last of them I shall kill with the sword;
  not one of them will flee as a fugitive,
  no escapee will survive.
²If they dig into She'ol,
  from there my hand will get them.
If they go up into the heavens,
  I shall get them down.
³If they hide on top of Carmel,
  from there I shall search them out and get them.
If they conceal themselves from in front of my eyes
  at the bottom of the sea,
From there I shall order
  the serpent and it will bite them.
⁴If they go into captivity before their enemies,
  from there I shall order the sword and it will kill them.
I shall set my eye on them for something bad,
  not for something good.

⁵The Lord Yahweh of Armies –
  he touches the earth and it melts,
  and all the people who live in it mourn.
All of it rises like the Ye'or,
  and sinks like Misrayim's Ye'or.
⁶He built his lofts in the heavens
  and founded his structure on the earth,
The one who calls the sea's water
  and pours it over the face of the earth –
  Yahweh is his name.

The day of the Lord as good news again

⁷You're like the Kushites [Sudanese]
  to me, Yisra'elites, aren't you (Yahweh's declaration).
I got Yisra'el up from the country of Misrayim, didn't I –
  and the Pelishtites from Kaphtor, and the Aramites from Qir?

⁸There, the Lord Yahweh's eyes
  are on the kingdom that does wrong;
I annihilate it
  from on the face of the earth.
Except that I shall not totally annihilate
  Ya'aqob's household (Yahweh's declaration).
⁹Because here I am, I'm going to give an order,
  and shake Yisra'el's household among all the nations,
As someone shakes in a sieve,
  and no pebble falls to the earth.
¹⁰All the wrongdoers in my people
  will die by the sword,
The people who say, 'It won't reach,
  it won't come near us.'

¹¹On that day:
  I shall raise David's fallen bivouac
  and repair its breaches,
I shall raise its ruins
  and build it up as in days of old,
¹²In order that they may enter into possession of
  what remains of Edom,
  and all the nations that were called by my name.
  (a declaration of Yahweh who is going to do this).

¹³There, days are coming (Yahweh's declaration):
  when the ploughman will reach the reaper,
  the treader of grapes the one trailing the seed.
The mountains will drop sweet wine,
  all the hills will flow.
¹⁴I shall restore the fortunes of my people Yisra'el;
  they'll build up desolate towns and live there.
They'll plant vineyards and drink their wine,
  they will make gardens and eat their fruits.
¹⁵I shall plant them on their land
  and they won't uproot again
From on their land
  which I have given them (Yahweh your God has said).

Obadiah

Presumably Yahweh gave Obadiah [Obadyah] many other prophecies, but the Judahite community recognized this one as having long-lasting significance. It refers to Edom's involvement in the destruction of Jerusalem, particularly grievous because behind the relationship of Israel and Edom is the relationship between Jacob and Esau as brothers. One might guess that further background is the fact that Edom took over much of the territory Yahweh gave Judah in the centuries that followed.

Who could bring me down to earth?

¹Obadyah's vision.

The Lord Yahweh has said this about Edom; we have heard a report from Yahweh:

An envoy has been sent out among the nations:
  'Rise up – let's rise up against it for battle!'
²Here, I'm making you small among the nations;
  you're going to be very despised.
³The arrogance of your mind has deceived you,
  you who dwell in the clefts of the crag, the height of its abode,
Saying within yourself,
  'Who could take me down to earth?'
⁴If you go up high like an eagle,
  if you put your nest among the stars,
  from there I could bring you down (Yahweh's declaration).

⁵If thieves came to you, if robbers came by night
  (how you are terminated!)
  they would steal what they needed, wouldn't they.
If grape-pickers came to you,
  they'd let gleanings remain, wouldn't they.
⁶How Esaw is being ransacked,
  its hidden treasures sought out!
⁷All the people you were in pact with
  are sending you off to the border.
The people you were in alliance with
  are deceiving you, prevailing over you.
The people who eat your bread set a trap beneath you
  (it has no understanding).

⁸On that day (Yahweh's declaration):

I shall eliminate the experts from Edom, shan't I,
  and understanding from Mount Esaw.
⁹Your strong men will shatter, Teman,
  in order that people will be cut off from Mount Esaw through slaughter.
¹⁰Because of the violence to your brother Ya'aqob [Jacob]
  shame will cover you, and you'll be cut off permanently.
¹¹On the day you stood aside,
  on the day foreigners captured his resources,
When aliens came into his gateways,
  and cast lots for Yerushalaim,
  you, too, were like one of them.

On gloating and taking advantage

¹²You shouldn't have looked at your brother's day,
  the day this alien thing happened to him.
You shouldn't have rejoiced at the Yehudahites
  on the day of their perishing.
You shouldn't have talked big
  on the day of pressure.
¹³You shouldn't have come into my people's gateway
  on the day of their disaster.
You shouldn't have looked, you too, at his bad fortune
  on the day of his disaster.
You shouldn't have reached out at his resources
  on the day of his disaster.
¹⁴You shouldn't have stood at the crossroad
  to cut down his escapees.
You shouldn't have handed over his survivors
  on the day of pressure.
¹⁵Because Yahweh's day is near against all the nations;
  as you did, it will be done to you,
  when your dealings come back on your head.

¹⁶Because as you [Yehudahites] drank
  on my sacred mountain,
All the nations will drink continually,
  drink and swallow,
  and be as if they'd never been.
¹⁷But on Mount Tsiyyon [Zion] there'll be an escape group,
  and it will be sacred.
Ya'aqob's household will dispossess
  the people who dispossessed them.
¹⁸Ya'aqob's household will become a fire,
  Yoseph's household a flame,
Esaw's household straw,
  and they will burn among them, consume them.
Esaw's household
  will have no survivor (because Yahweh has spoken).

¹⁹The Negeb will possess Mount Esaw,
  the Lowland [will possess] the Pelishtites [Philistines].

They will possess the fields of Ephrayim,
  the fields of Shomron [Samaria],
  and Binyamin [will possess] Gil'ad.
²⁰This exile community force belonging to the Yisra'elites
  [will possess] what [belongs to] the Kena'anites [Canaanites] as far as Tsarepat.
The exile community from Yerushalaim which is in Sepharad
  will possess the towns of the Negeb.
²¹Deliverers will go up on Mount Tsiyyon
  to exercise authority over Mount Esaw,
  and the kingship will belong to Yahweh.

Jonah

Yahweh used Jonah [Yonah] to promise Ephraim the recovery of territory from the Arameans (2 Kings 14.25). Thus it would not be surprising if he were unenthusiastic about preaching to the Assyrians because he knows that Yahweh will refrain from destroying them if they repent. The story about him thus warns prophets and other people about underestimating Yahweh's concern for other nations, even domineering superpowers. It thus complements Obadiah in illustrating the other side to Yahweh's attitude to oppressive nations. The story is full of humour and irony, which supports the idea that it is a parable rather than a historical story.

The prophet who runs away

1 Yahweh's word came to Yonah ben Amittay: ²'Set off, go to the great town of Nineveh and call out against it, because their bad dealing has come up before me.' ³But Yonah set off to flee to Tarshish from before Yahweh. He went down to Yafo [Jaffa], found a ship going to Tarshish, paid its fare and went down into it to go with them to Tarshish from before Yahweh. ⁴But Yahweh flung a great wind into the sea, there was a great storm in the sea, and the ship threatened to break up. ⁵The sailors were afraid and cried out each of them to his god. They flung the things that were in the ship into the sea to lighten it of them.

Yonah had gone down into the inmost parts of the vessel, lain down and gone to sleep. ⁶The captain went to see him and said to him, 'What are you doing, sleeping? Get up, call on your god. Perhaps the god will give a thought to us and we won't perish.'

⁷The men said to each other, 'Come on, let's make lots fall so we can know on whose account this bad fate has come to us.' They made lots fall, and the lot fell on Yonah. ⁸They said to him, 'Tell us, please, on whose account this bad fate has come to us. What's your work? Where do you come from? What's your country? What people are you from?' ⁹He said to them, 'I'm a Hebrew. I live in awe of Yahweh the God of the heavens, who made the sea and the dry land.'

¹⁰The men were greatly afraid, and said to him, 'What is this you've done?', when the men knew that he was fleeing from before Yahweh, when he had told them. ¹¹They said to him, 'What shall we do to you so that the sea quietens down from upon us?' (when the sea was growing stormier). ¹²He said to them, 'Lift me up and hurl me into the sea, and the sea will quieten down from upon you, because I acknowledge that it was on my account that this great storm has come upon you.'

How to pray from inside a fish

¹³The men rowed to get back to dry land, but they couldn't, because the sea was growing stormier against them. ¹⁴They called to Yahweh, 'Oh, Yahweh, may we please not perish for this man's life. Don't put upon us the blood of someone free of guilt. Because you, Yahweh – as you wished, you have acted.' ¹⁵They lifted Yonah up and hurled him into the sea; and the sea stopped its raging. ¹⁶The men were in great awe of Yahweh. They offered a sacrifice to Yahweh and made pledges.

¹⁷Yahweh provided a big fish to swallow Yonah, and Yonah was in the fish's insides three days and three nights.

2 Yonah prayed to Yahweh his God from the fish's insides:

²Out of my pressure I called
    to Yahweh and he answered me.
When I called for help from She'ol's belly,
    you listened to my voice.
³You threw me into the deep,
    into the heart of the seas.
The river surrounded me;
    all your breakers and your waves passed over me.
⁴I myself said, 'I've been driven away
    from in front of your eyes.'
Yet I shall again look
    towards your sacred palace.
⁵The water overwhelmed me, up to my neck,
    the deep surrounded me.
Reed was wrapped round my head
⁶at the roots of the mountains.
I went down into the earth,
    its bars were about me permanently.
But you got my life up from the Pit,
    Yahweh my God.
⁷When my life was ebbing away from me,
    I was mindful of Yahweh.
My plea came to you,
    to your sacred palace.
⁸People who keep watch for things that are empty and hollow
    forsake their commitment.
⁹But I – with a voice of thanksgiving I will sacrifice to you;
    for what I have pledged I shall make good –
    deliverance belongs to Yahweh.

¹⁰Yahweh spoke to the fish, and it vomited Yonah on to the dry land.

The reluctant prophet does as he is told

3 Yahweh's word came to Yonah a second time: ²"Set off, go to the great town of

Nineveh and call out to it the thing that I'm going to speak to you.' ³Yonah set off and went to Nineveh in accordance with Yahweh's word. Now Nineveh was an extraordinarily great town, three days walk through. ⁴Yonah started to go through the town, one day's walk. He called out, 'Forty days more, and Nineveh will be overthrown.' ⁵The Ninevites believed God, and called for a fast and put on sack, from the biggest of them to the least of them.

⁶The word reached the king of Nineveh, and he got up from his throne, took off his robe from upon him, covered himself with sack and sat on ash. ⁷He got people to cry out in Nineveh, by the decree of the king and his big people: 'Human being and animal (cattle and flock) are not to taste anything. They're not to pasture; they're not to drink water. ⁸They're to cover themselves in sack, human being and animal, and call on God strongly. They're to turn, each one from his bad way and from the violence that's in their fists. ⁹Who knows, God may turn back and relent, turn back from his anger, and we may not perish.'

¹⁰God saw their actions, that they turned back from their bad way, and God relented of the bad thing that he had spoken about doing to them. He didn't do it.

4 But it seemed bad to Yonah, a very bad thing. He was enraged.

I knew you'd do that

²He prayed to Yahweh: 'Oh, Yahweh, isn't this what I said when I was in my country? That's why I acted previously by fleeing to Tarshish, because I knew that you're a God gracious, compassionate, long-tempered, vast in commitment and relenting about something bad. ³So now, Yahweh, please take my life from me, because my dying will be good, better than my living.' ⁴Yahweh said, 'Was your rage good?'

⁵Yonah went out from the town and sat east of the town. He made a bivouac for himself there and sat under it in the shade until he could see what would happen in the town. ⁶Yahweh God provided a qiqayon vine and it grew up over Yonah so as to be a shade over his head to rescue him from what was bad for him. Yonah rejoiced greatly about the qiqayon. ⁷But God provided a worm when dawn came up next day and it struck down the qiqayon, and it withered; ⁸and when the sun rose, God provided a scorching east wind, and the sun struck down on Yonah's head. He grew faint and asked for his life, that he might die. He said, 'My dying will be good, better than my living.'

⁹God said to Yonah, 'Was your rage good about the qiqayon?' He said, 'It was good, my rage, to the point of death.' ¹⁰Yahweh said, 'You pitied the qiqayon, for which you didn't labour and which you didn't grow, which came into existence overnight and perished overnight. ¹¹Shouldn't I pity the great town of Nineveh, in which there are more than 120,000 human beings who don't know their right hand from their left, and many animals?'

Micah

Micah [Mikah] was a contemporary of Isaiah who worked in Jerusalem at about the same time and brought a similar message, though he originally came from the country rather than from the capital. Like Isaiah, he declares that Yahweh intends to take action against Jerusalem because of the way people with power and resources, and spiritual leaders, take advantage of their position. Like Isaiah, he has to deal with people who don't want prophets to say the kind of thing that as a prophet he says. But like Isaiah, he also looks beyond the coming disaster to Yahweh's restoring the city. It is he who asks what God requires, and answers the question in a powerful formulation (6.8).

Disaster reaches the very gateways

1 Yahweh's word that came to Mikah the Morashtite in the days of Yotam, Ahaz and Yehizqiyyah, kings of Yehudah, which he beheld concerning Shomron [Samaria] and Yerushalaim.

²Listen, peoples, all of you,
 heed, earth and what fills it,
So that the Lord Yahweh may be a witness against you,
 the Lord from his sacred palace.
³Because there – Yahweh is going to come out from his place,
 come down and tread on earth's heights.
⁴The mountains will melt beneath him,
 the vales split,
Like wax before the fire,
 like water propelled down a slope.

⁵All this is for Ya'aqob's [Jacob's] rebellion,
 for the household of Yisra'el's wrongdoings.
What is Ya'aqob's rebellion – it's Shomron, isn't it;
 and what is Yehudah's great shrine – it's Yerushalaim, isn't it.
⁶I shall make Shomron into a ruin in open country,
 plantations for a vineyard.
I shall propel its stones into the ravine,
 expose its foundations.
⁷All its images will be smashed,
 all its 'gifts' burned in fire.
All its idols I shall make into desolation.
 because it collected them from a whore's 'gift',
 and they will go back as a whore's 'gift'.

⁸Because of this I shall lament and howl,
 I shall go barefoot and stripped.
I shall make lament like the jackals,
 mourning like the ostriches.
⁹Because its wound is grave,
 because it's come right to Yehudah.
It's reached right to my people's gateway,
 right to Yerushalaim.
¹⁰Don't tell it in Gat, don't cry at all;
 in Bet Le'aprah roll in earth [*apar*].
¹¹Pass on,
 you inhabitants of Shapir, naked in shame;
The inhabitants of Tsa'anan
 have not gone out.
Bet Etsel is in lamentation;
 it will take its support from you.

¹²Because the inhabitants of Marot
 are sick for something good.
Because bad fortune has come down from Yahweh
 to Yerushalaim's gateway.
¹³Hitch the chariot to the steed,
 inhabitants of Lakish.
It was the beginning of wrongdoing for Miss Tsiyyon [Zion],
 because Yisra'el's rebellions were found in you.
¹⁴Therefore you will give parting gifts
 to Moreshet Gat.
The houses of Akzib will be a deception [*akzab*]
 to Yisra'el's kings.
¹⁵'I shall yet bring a dispossessor to you,
 inhabitants of Mareshah.
Yisra'el's splendour
 will come as far as Adullam.
¹⁶Shave your head, cut off your hair,
 for the children in whom you delighted.
Extend the shaving of your head like an eagle,
 because they've gone into exile from you.'

Don't preach?

2 Hey, you people thinking up trouble,
 doing something bad on their beds.
At morning light they do it,
 because it's in the power of their hand.
²They desire fields and steal them –
 houses, and take them.
They defraud a man and his household,
 an individual and his domain.

³Therefore Yahweh has said this:

Here am I, thinking up a bad fate for this kin-group
 that you won't move your neck away from.
You won't walk tall,
 because it will be a bad time.

⁴On that day,
 someone will lift up a poem against you,
 he'll wail with a wail, a wailing.
He's saying, 'We are destroyed, destroyed,
 he exchanges my people's share.
Aagh, he removes it from me,
 he shares out our fields to someone who turns away.'

⁵Therefore there will be no one for you
    casting the cord by lot
        in Yahweh's congregation.

⁶'Don't preach,' they preach,
    'people are not to preach about these things.
Disgrace won't turn away
    ⁷(should it be said, Ya'aqob's household?).
Has Yahweh's temper become short,
    are these things his acts?'
My words are good, aren't they,
    with someone who walks upright.
⁸But just now my people rises up as an enemy;
    you strip the mantle off the front of the coat
From people passing by with confidence,
    turning back from battle.
⁹The women among my people –
    you drive her out from the household in which
        she delights.
From her infants
    you take my glory permanently.
¹⁰Set off, go,
    because this won't be a place to settle,
On account of defilement that will destroy
    with a grave destruction.
¹¹If someone were going about
    with wind and deceptive falsehood,
'I shall preach to you about wine and about liquor',
    he'd be this people's preacher.

Prophets who lead astray

¹²I shall definitely gather Ya'aqob, all of you,
    I shall definitely collect what remains of Yisra'el.
I shall put them together like a sheep in a fold;
    like a flock in the middle of its pasture,
It will be noisy with people;
    ¹³one who breaks out in front of them is going
        up.
They're breaking out, passing through the
        gateway,
    going out through it.
Their king passes through before them,
    Yahweh at their head.

3 I said, 'Listen, please, heads of Ya'aqob,
    rulers of Yisra'el's household:
It's for you to know how to exercise authority,
    isn't it,
    ²people who are hostile to what is good and
        loyal to what is bad,
Who tear the skin from on my people,
    their flesh from on their bones,
³Who eat my people's flesh
    and strip off their skin from on them,
Break up their bones,
    cut them up as in a pan,
        like meat inside a pot.'
⁴Then they will cry out to Yahweh,
    but he will not answer them.
He will hide his face from them at that time,
    as they've acted badly in their practices.

⁵Yahweh has said this:

About the prophets who lead my people astray,
    who chew with their teeth and call out that
        things will be well,
But someone who puts nothing in their mouths –
    they declare a sacred battle against him.
⁶Therefore there will be night for you, without
        vision,
    darkness for you, without divination.
The sun will set for the prophets,
    the day will be dark for them.
⁷The seers will be ashamed,
    the diviners confounded.
All of them will cover over their lip,
    because there's no answer from God.
⁸But as for me, I'm full of energy, with Yahweh's
        wind,
    and strong authority,
To tell Ya'aqob about its rebellion,
    Yisra'el about its wrongdoing.

The new Jerusalem

⁹Listen to this, please,
    heads of Ya'aqob's household,
    rulers of Yisra'el's household,
You who take offence at the exercise of authority,
    and make what is straight crooked,
¹⁰One who builds Tsiyyon with bloodshed,
    Yerushalaim with evil.
¹¹Its heads exercise authority for a bribe,
    its priests teach for a fee.
Its prophets divine for money,
    but lean on Yahweh:
'Yahweh is among us, isn't he,
    bad fortune won't come upon us.'
¹²Therefore, on account of you,
    Tsiyyon will be a field that is ploughed.

Yerushalaim will become ruins,
  the house's mount a great shrine in a forest.

4

But at the end of the time
  the mountain of Yahweh's house will be
Established at the head of the mountains,
  elevated above the hills.
Peoples will stream to it;
  ²many nations will go and say,
'Come, let's go up to Yahweh's mountain,
  to the house of Ya'aqob's God,
So he may teach us in his ways
  and we may walk in his paths.'
Because instruction will go out from Tsiyyon,
  Yahweh's word from Yerushalaim.
³He will decide between many peoples
  and issue reproof for numerous nations, even
    far away.
They'll beat their swords into hoes,
  their spears into pruning hooks.
Nation won't take up sword against nation;
  they will no more learn about battle.
⁴They will sit, each person
  under his vine and under his fig tree,
With no one disturbing –
  because the mouth of Yahweh of Armies has
    spoken.
⁵Because all the peoples walk,
  each in the name of its god,
But we ourselves will walk
  in the name of Yahweh our God lastingly and
    permanently.

⁶On that day (Yahweh's declaration):

I shall gather the lame, collect the ones driven out,
  and those to whom I've done something bad.
⁷I shall turn the lame into a remainder,
  the outcast into a numerous nation.
Yahweh will reign over them on Mount Tsiyyon
  from now and permanently.
⁸And you, watchtower of the flock,
  citadel, Miss Tsiyyon,
To you will arrive and come
  the former rule, the kingship of Miss
    Yerushalaim.

Is there no king in you?

⁹Now, why do you issue a shout,
  is there not a king in you?
Has your counsellor perished,
  that writhing has taken strong hold of you like
    a woman giving birth?
¹⁰Writhe and scream,
  Miss Tsiyyon, like a woman giving birth.
Because you will now go out from the township
  and dwell in the open country.
You will come as far as Babel,
  but there you will be rescued.
There Yahweh will restore you
  from the fist of your enemies.

¹¹But now many nations
  have gathered against you.
They're saying, 'It shall be profaned,
  our eye shall behold Tsiyyon.'
¹²But those people don't know
  Yahweh's intentions.
They don't understand his plan,
  that he's gathered them like sheaves on the
    threshing-floor.
¹³Rise up, thresh, Miss Tsiyyon,
  because I shall make your horn iron.
I shall make your hoofs copper,
  and you will crush many peoples.
They will devote their dishonest gain to Yahweh,
  their resources to the Lord of the entire earth.

5

Now, you may form a gang, Miss Gang –
  someone has laid siege to us.
They strike down Yisra'el's authority
  on the cheek with a club.
²But you, Bet-lehem in Ephratah,
  small to be among Yehudah's clans,
From you will emerge for me
  someone to be a ruler in Yisra'el
  whose emerging is of old, of ancient days.
³Therefore he will give them up until the time
  when the one who is going to give birth has
    given birth,
And those who are left of his brothers
  come back to the Yisra'elites.
⁴He will stand and shepherd with Yahweh's
    vigour,
  in the majesty of the name of Yahweh his God.
They will live, because now he'll be great, as far as
    the ends of the earth,
  ⁵and this will mean things are well.
Ashshur, when it comes into our country,
  when it treads through our citadels:
We will set up over it seven shepherds,
  eight people as leaders.

⁶They will shepherd the country of Ashshur with
    the sword,
  the country of Nimrod with its entrances.
He will rescue us from Ashshur when it comes
    into our country,
  when it treads through our territory.

What God looks for

⁷Ya'aqob's remainder will become,
  among many peoples,
Like dew from Yahweh,
  like showers on grass,
Which don't wait for people,
  don't look to human beings.
⁸Ya'aqob's remainder will become, among the
    nations,
  among many peoples,
Like a lion among the animals in the forest,
  like a cougar among the flocks of sheep,
Which, if it passes by, tramples and mauls,
  with no one to rescue.
⁹Your hand will rise over your adversaries,
  and all your enemies will be cut off.

¹⁰On that day (Yahweh's declaration):

I shall cut down your horses from among you
  and obliterate your chariots.
¹¹I shall cut down the towns in your country,
  and tear down all your fortresses.
¹²I shall cut down the charms from your hand,
  and you will have no chanters.
¹³I shall cut down your images
  and your pillars from among you.
You will not bow low any more
  to something made by your hands.
¹⁴I shall uproot your totem poles from among you
  and annihilate your towns.
¹⁵But I shall effect redress in anger and wrath
  on the nations that have not listened.

6 Listen, please, to what Yahweh has said:

Get up, argue with the mountains;
  the hills must listen to your voice.
²Listen to Yahweh's argument, mountains,
  enduring ones, earth's foundations.
Because Yahweh has an argument with his people,
  with Yisra'el he issues a reproof.
³'My people, what have I done to you,
  how have I wearied you? – avow against me.
⁴Because I got you up out of the country of
    Misrayim [Egypt],
  redeemed you from a household of servants.
I sent before you
  Mosheh [Moses], Aharon [Aaron] and
    Miryam.
⁵My people, please be mindful
  of what Balaq king of Mo'ab counselled,
  and what Bil'am [Balaam] ben Be'or avowed
    with him,
From Acacias as far as Gilgal,
  for the sake of acknowledging Yahweh's faithful
    acts.'

⁶By what means shall I meet Yahweh,
  bow down to God on High?
Shall I meet him by means of burnt offerings,
  bullocks a year old?
⁷Would Yahweh accept thousands of rams,
  in myriads of streams of oil?
Should I give my firstborn for my rebellion,
  the fruit of my body for my own wrongdoing?
⁸He has told you, people, what is good,
  what Yahweh requires from you:
Rather, exercising authority and being loyal to
    commitment,
  and being diffident in how you walk with your
    God.

Like the gleanings

⁹The voice of Yahweh calls to the town;
  awe for your name is good sense.
Listen to the club
  and the one who set it ¹⁰still.
'Shall I forget the faithless household,
  the faithless storehouses,
  the condemned short measure?
¹¹Would I be clean with faithless scales,
  with a bag of false weights? –
¹²Whose rich people are full of violence,
  whose inhabitants speak falsehood,
  and their tongue is deceit in their mouths?

¹³So I myself am indeed making you sick in
    striking you down,
  desolating you for your wrongdoings.
¹⁴You – you will eat but not be full,
  with your emptiness inside you.
You'll displace, but not save,

and what you save I shall give to the sword.
¹⁵You – you'll sow but not harvest;
   you – you'll tread olives, but not rub with oil,
   and grapes, but not drink wine.
¹⁶You've kept Omri's laws,
   every practice of Ah'ab's household.
You've walked by their policies,
   for the sake of my making you a desolation,
Your inhabitants a hissing,
   and you will bear the reviling of my people.'

7 Aagh, me, because I've become
   like the gatherings of summer fruit,
   like the gleanings of the vintage.
There's no cluster to eat,
   or early fig that my appetite could fancy.
²The committed person has perished from the country,
   there's no one upright among the people.
All of them lie in wait for blood;
   one person hunts his brother with a net.
³Both fists are on what is bad, to do it well:
   the official asking, and the authority, with pay,
The big man speaking
   his appetite's desire, and they weave it together.
⁴The good one among them is like a briar,
   the most upright worse than a thorn hedge.
The day your lookouts described,
   the day when you're attended to, is going to come;
   now the disarray they described will happen.
⁵Don't believe a neighbour,
   don't rely on a friend.
From the one who sleeps in your embrace
   guard the opening of your mouth.
⁶Because son acts villainously to father,
   daughter rises up against her mother,
Daughter-in-law against her mother-in-law;
   a person's enemies are the people in his household.
⁷But I myself will look to Yahweh,
   I shall wait for my God who delivers me;
   my God will listen to me.

Lament, prayer, expectation and worship for the city

⁸Don't rejoice over me, my enemy;
   when I've fallen, I'm getting up.
When I sit in darkness,
   Yahweh will be my light.

⁹I shall carry Yahweh's wrath
   when I've done wrong to him,
Until he gives judgement for me
   and exercises authority for me.
He will get me out into the light,
   I shall see his faithfulness,
¹⁰My enemy will see,
   and shame will cover it,
The one who says to me,
   'Where is he, Yahweh, your God?'
My eyes will look on it;
   now it'll be for trampling
   like mud in the streets.
¹¹A day for building up your walls –
   that will be a day when your boundary will be far away.
¹²That day one will come to you
   from Ashshur and the towns of Misrayim,
From Misrayim as far as the River,
   to sea from sea, to mountain from mountain.
¹³But the earth will become a desolation because of its inhabitants,
   as the fruit of their practices.

¹⁴Pasture your people with your club,
   the flock that's your domain,
Dwelling by itself in a forest
   in the middle of farmland.
May they pasture in Bashan and Gil'ad
   as in days of old,
¹⁵as in the days when you got out of the country of Misrayim.

'When I show it my wonders, ¹⁶nations will see
   and be ashamed of all their strength.
They'll put their hand to their mouth,
   their ears will go deaf.
¹⁷They'll lick earth like a snake,
   like things that crawl on the ground.'

May they come trembling out of their strongholds
   to Yahweh our God,
   may they be in dread and awe of you.
¹⁸Who is a God like you, one who carries waywardness,
   and passes over rebellion for the remainder of his domain.
He doesn't keep strong hold of his anger permanently,
   because he delights in commitment;

¹⁹When he has compassion on us again, he'll
  trample on our wayward acts;
  he'll throw all our wrongdoings into the depths
    of the sea.

²⁰You will show truthfulness to Ya'aqob,
  commitment to Abraham,
  as you swore to our ancestors from days of
    old.

Nahum

One can set Nahum, Habakkuk and Zephaniah alongside Jeremiah, in that they lived a century later than Amos, Hosea and Micah, in the time when Assyria was succeeded by Babylon as the world power. Nahum's vocation was to encourage Jerusalem when it was still under the domination of Assyria with its capital in Nineveh, by promising that Nineveh would be put down. Yahweh's promise through Nahum was fulfilled when Nineveh fell to the Babylonians in 612 BC. But there are few concrete references to Nineveh, so the promises (or warnings) can apply to other great imperial cities such as Babylon – or to Jerusalem itself.

Yahweh the passionate God

1 The pronouncement about Nineveh, the document with the vision of Nahum the Elqoshite.

²Yahweh is a God who is passionate and takes redress;
 Yahweh takes redress and is a possessor of wrath.
Yahweh takes redress on his adversaries,
 maintains it towards his enemies.
³Yahweh is long-tempered but big in energy,
 and certainly doesn't treat people as free of guilt.
Yahweh – his way is in whirlwind and in storm,
 the cloud is the dust from his feet.
⁴He reprimands the sea and withers it,
 dries up all the rivers.
Bashan and Carmel languish,
 Lebanon's blossom languishes.
⁵Mountains quake because of him,
 the hills melt.
The earth lifts from before him,
 the world and all the people who live in it.
⁶Before his condemnation, who can stand,
 and who can rise against his angry burning? –
His wrath pours out like fire,
 and crags shatter because of him.
⁷Yahweh is good, a stronghold on the day of pressure,
 and he acknowledges people who take shelter with him.
⁸With a flood passing
 he makes an end of [the city's] place,
He pursues his enemies into darkness;
 ⁹what do you think up for Yahweh?
He makes an end;
 pressure doesn't rise twice.
¹⁰Because they're tangled among thorns,
 and drunk as with their drink,
they're consumed like straw that is fully dry.

¹¹From you [as a city] has gone out
 one who thinks up something bad against Yahweh,
 one who counsels wickedness.

¹²Yahweh has said this:

If they are allied and thus are many,
 even thus they're cut down and he passes away;
Whereas I afflicted you, I shall afflict you no more.
 ¹³but now I shall break its yoke from on you,
tear off your shackles.

¹⁴Yahweh has given an order against you:
 nothing more from your name will be sown.
From your gods' house I shall cut off
 carved image and cast image.
I shall make your grave,
 because you are slight.
¹⁵There, on the mountains are the feet of a herald,
 letting people hear of well-being.
Observe your festival, Yehudah,
 make good your pledges.
Because he will no more pass through you:
 the scoundrel, all of him, is being cut off.

The empire writes back

2 A shatterer has gone up against you –
 guard the ramparts.
Watch the road, strengthen your hips,
 firm up your energy all you can.
²Because Yahweh is restoring
 Ya'aqob's [Jacob's] majesty like Yisra'el's majesty.
Because wasters have wasted them,
 devastated their branches.

³His strong men's shield is painted red,
 the men in the force clad in scarlet.
The chariotry is with flashing fire on the day it's made ready,
 the junipers are brandished.
⁴In the streets the chariotry race,
 they rush about in the squares,
Their appearance like torches,
 they speed like lightning streaks.
⁵Though he calls to mind his august men, they collapse as they go;
 they hurry to its wall, the shelter is made ready.
⁶The river gates open, the palace melts;
 ⁷it's decreed: it's exiled, it's taken up.
Its handmaids lament like the voice of doves,
 beating on their chests.
⁸Nineveh was like a pool of water of old,
 but they're fleeing.
'Stop, stop',
 but no one can turn them.

⁹Plunder silver, plunder gold,
  there's no limit to the things prepared,
  the splendour from all the things that people
    hold in high regard.

¹⁰Emptiness, just emptiness, waste;
  the mind melts, the knees knock.
All hips tremble,
  the faces of all of them have collected a
    flush.
¹¹Where is the lions' abode,
  the pasture for the cougars,
Where the lion walked,
  the lioness there,
The lion's cub, with no one disturbing,
¹²the lion tearing enough for its cubs,
And strangling for its lionesses –
  it filled its lairs with prey, its abodes with
    prey?
¹³Here am I towards you (a declaration of Yahweh
    of Armies):
  I shall burn up its chariotry in smoke.
The sword will consume your cougars;
  I shall cut off your prey from the earth.
Your envoys' voice
  will no more be listened to.

3 Hey, town of bloodshed,
  all of it deception,
Full of plunder,
  where prey doesn't depart.
²The sound of a whip,
  the sound of the rumble of a wheel,
A horse galloping,
  a chariot jumping,
³Cavalry going up, sword flashing,
  spear glittering, a multitude run through,
A heap of carcases, no end of the corpses,
  people collapse over their corpses.

The invincible falls

⁴Because of the dimensions of the whore's
    whorings,
  the well-favoured expert in charms,
Who sells nations with her whorings,
  kin-groups with her charms,
⁵Here am I towards you (a declaration of Yahweh
    of Armies):
  I shall expose your skirts over your face.
I shall show the nations your nakedness,
  kingdoms your slighting.

⁶I shall throw abominations over you,
  demean you and make a spectacle of you;
⁷All who see you will flee from you
  and say, 'Nineveh is destroyed!
Who will mourn for her,
  where shall I seek for people to comfort
    her?'

⁸Are you better than Thebes of Amon,
  which was sitting on the Ye'or [Nile],
Water surrounding it,
  whose rampart was the sea, its wall made from
    the sea?
⁹Numerous Kush [Sudan]
  and Misrayim [Egypt] without end,
Put and the Lubites
  were your help.
¹⁰Even it was for exile, it went into captivity;
  even its babies were smashed at the head of
    every street.
For its honourable men people threw lots,
  and all its big people were bound in chains.
¹¹Even you will become drunk, you will be in
    hiding;
  even you will seek a refuge from the enemy.
¹²All your fortresses are fig trees, with the first
    fruits;
  if people shake them, they fall into the mouth
    of an eater.
¹³There, your company is women within you,
  to your enemies they are wide open,
The gateways of your country;
  fire is consuming your gate-bars.

¹⁴Draw siege water for yourself,
  strengthen your fortresses,
Tread the clay, trample the mud,
  take strong hold of the brick mould.
¹⁵Fire will consume you there,
  the sword will cut you off, consume you like the
    grasshopper.
Multiply like the grasshopper,
  multiply like the locust.
¹⁶You made your merchants more than the stars
    in the heavens;
  the grasshopper strips and flies.
¹⁷Your guards are like locusts,
  your officials like a pile of grubs,
That settle on walls
  on a cold day.
When the sun comes out, they flee;
  their place, where they are, isn't known.

¹⁸Your shepherds have gone to sleep, king of
    Ashshur;
  your august people settle down.
Your people have scattered over the
    mountains,
  and there's no one collecting them.

¹⁹There's no healing for your break;
  your wound is severe.
All who hear the report of you
  clap the palm of a hand at you,
Because to whom has bad fortune from you
  not passed, continually?

Habakkuk

The bulk of Habakkuk [Habaqquq] takes the form of questions and answers between the prophet and Yahweh. Like other prophets, Habakkuk is horrified at what he sees in Judah and he wants to know what Yahweh intends to do about it. Yahweh declares that he intends to bring the Babylonians to act against Judah. This idea horrifies Habakkuk; Yahweh adds that the Babylonians will get their own comeuppance in due course. The final chapter is a vision of Yahweh's coming to take action in this connection.

Habaqquq protests, Yahweh answers, Habaqquq protests again

1 The pronouncement that Habaqquq the prophet beheld.

²How long have I called for help, Yahweh,
  and you don't listen?
I cry out to you, 'Violence',
  but you don't deliver.
³Why do you make me see trouble,
  why do you look at oppression?
Destruction and violence are in front of me;
  there's been argument, and strife arises.
⁴Therefore instruction ceases,
  the exercise of authority never issues.
Because the faithless person encircles the faithful;
  therefore the exercise of authority issues deformed.

⁵Watch the nations,
  look, and be utterly astounded.
Because I'm going to do something in your days
  that you wouldn't believe when it was told.
⁶Because here am I, I'm going to raise up the Kasdites,
  the bitter, quick-moving nation,
That goes to the far reaches of the earth,
  to possess dwellings that don't belong to it.
⁷It's terrible and fearful;
  from itself its authority and its dignity issues.
⁸Its horses are swifter than leopards,
  keener than wolves at evening;
Its steeds gallop;
  its steeds come from afar.
They fly like an eagle hastening to devour;
  ⁹all of it comes for violence.
The thrust of their faces is forwards;
  it gathers captives like sand.
¹⁰It derides kings,
  rulers are fun to it.
It makes fun of every fortress,
  it fortifies earth and captures it.
¹¹Then the wind sweeps on and passes through,
  and it becomes guilty, because its energy is its god.

¹²You are from of old, Yahweh, are you not;
  my God, my sacredness, you don't die.
Yahweh, you've made it an authority;
  my crag, you have founded it to reprove.
¹³Your eyes are too pure to watch bad dealing,
  you cannot look at oppression.
Why do you look at people who break faith –
  stay still,
  when the faithless person swallows one who is more faithful than him?
¹⁴You made humanity like the fish in the sea,
  like moving things that have no ruler.
¹⁵He's got all of it up with a hook,
  he drags it away in his net,
Gathers it in his trawl;
  that's why he rejoices and celebrates.
¹⁶That's why he sacrifices to his net,
  burns incense to his trawl.
Because through them his share is rich,
  his food luxuriant.
¹⁷Is he therefore to empty his net
  and continually to kill nations,
  not pity?

Yahweh answers again

2 On my watch I shall take my stand,
  station myself at my post.
I shall look to see what he'll speak through me,
  what I shall say back to the reproof that comes to me.

²Yahweh answered me:

Write the vision, make it plain on tablets,
  in order that someone who reads it out can run with it.
³Because there's yet a vision about a set time,
  it testifies about the end, and it won't deceive.
If it's slow, wait for it,
  because it will definitely come, it won't lag.
⁴There, his appetite within him
  is swollen, not upright,
whereas the faithful person will live by his truthfulness.
⁵How much more does wine betray
  the arrogant man.
He won't abide,
  one who's let his appetite be as wide as She'ol.
The one who is like death,
  but he isn't full,
The one who gathers to himself all the nations,
  collects to himself all the peoples.
⁶These people, all of them,
  will raise a poem about him, won't they,
  mocking, conundrums, about him.

Hey, one who accumulates what's not his – how
    long,
  one who makes debts heavy for himself?
⁷Your creditors will suddenly arise, won't they,
  the people who make you tremble will wake up,
  and you will turn into plunder for them.
⁸Because you're one who despoiled many nations,
  all that's left of the peoples will despoil you,
On account of the human bloodshed and the
    violence against the country,
  the township and all the people who live in it.

⁹Hey, one who makes dishonest gain,
  a bad thing for his household,
To set his nest on high,
  to escape from the fist of bad fortune.
¹⁰You've counselled shame for your household,
  cutting off many peoples and doing wrong to
    yourself.
¹¹Because a stone will cry out from a wall,
  and the beam from the wood will answer it.

¹²Hey, one who builds a town through bloodshed
  who establishes a township through evil
    ¹³(there, it's from Yahweh of Armies, isn't it?),
And peoples laboured for the fire,
  nations toiled for emptiness.
¹⁴Because the earth will be full
  so as to acknowledge Yahweh's splendour,
  as the water covers over the sea.

The confrontation

¹⁵Hey, one who makes his neighbour drink,
  pouring out your wrath and your drunken anger,
  in order to look at their naked bodies.
¹⁶You're getting full of slighting rather than of
    splendour;
  drink, and show your foreskin, you too.
The chalice in Yahweh's right hand
  will come round to you,
  with slighting in place of your splendour.

¹⁷Because your violence to Lebanon will cover you,
  your destruction of animals, which terrifies them,
On account of human bloodshed and violence to
    the earth,
  the township and all who live in it.
¹⁸What use is a carved image when its carver has
    shaped it,
  an image, which teaches falsehood,
When the one who shaped it relies on it,
  in making dumb non-entities?
¹⁹Hey, one who says to wood, 'Wake up',
  'Get up', to dumb stone,
  so it may teach.
There, it's cased in gold and silver,
  but there isn't any breath within it.
²⁰But Yahweh is in his sacred palace –
  be silent before him, all the earth.

3 A plea by Habaqquq the prophet; on 'Laments'.

²Yahweh, I've heard a report of you,
  I am in awe, Yahweh, of your action.
Within the years, bring it to life;
  within the years, cause it to be acknowledged;
  in the turmoil, be mindful of compassion.

³God comes from Teman,
  the sacred one from Mount Pa'ran. *(Rise)*
His majesty has covered the heavens,
  his praise has filled the earth.
⁴His brightness comes like dawn,
  its rays from his hand,
  and there is the hiding place of his vigour.
⁵Before him epidemic comes,
  plague comes out at his feet.
⁶He has stood and shaken the earth;
  he has looked, and agitated nations.
Ancient mountains have shattered,
  age-old hills sunk down.
The age-old ways are his,
  ⁷in place of the trouble that I have seen.
Kushan's tents shake,
  the dwellings of Midyan's country.

A vision that God must and will turn to reality

⁸Are you wrathful at the Rivers, Yahweh,
  is your anger at the Rivers,
  is your wrath at the Sea,
When you mount on your horses,
  your chariots that bring deliverance?
⁹You totally bare your bow;
  your clubs are sworn, by your word. *(Rise)*
With the Rivers you split the earth;
  ¹⁰when they've seen you, mountains
    writhe.

A torrent of water has passed by,
   the Deep has given its voice.
The sun has raised its hands in the height,
   ¹¹the moon has stood on high.
Your arrows go to give light,
   the flash of your spear to give brightness.
¹²In condemnation you stride the earth,
   in anger you trample nations.
¹³You have gone out for the deliverance of your people,
   for the deliverance of your anointed.
You have shattered the head of the faithless household,
   laying it bare, foundation to neck. *(Rise)*
¹⁴You have pierced his head with his clubs
   when his strong men were storming out,
To scatter me in their exultation,
   like consuming a humble man in hiding.
¹⁵You have made your way through the sea with your horses,
   with a stirring of much water.

¹⁶I heard and my insides quaked,
   at the sound my lips quivered.
Rot comes into my bones;
   in my place I tremble,
While I settle for the day of pressure,
   for the people who invade us to go up.

¹⁷Because the fig tree may not bud,
   and there may be no produce on the vines,
The product of the olive may deceive,
   and the fields may not produce food,
Someone may cut off the flock from the fold
   and there may be no cattle in the stalls:
¹⁸Yet I shall exult in Yahweh,
   rejoice in the God who delivers me.
¹⁹The Lord Yahweh is my resource,
   he makes my feet like the deer's,
   enables me to tread on the high places.

   The leader's; with strings.

Zephaniah

The introduction to Zephaniah [Tsephanyah] makes him contemporary with the early years of Jeremiah's activity, when King Josiah engaged in a reform of Judah's religious life that for a while undid the apostasy of his grandfather Manasseh. The nature of the charges that Zephaniah issues indicates that any reform process is only partly under way. The threat of Yahweh's day thus hangs over Jerusalem, but it also hangs over the world. And the possibility of restoration holds for Jerusalem, and for the rest of the world. His distinctive declaration to Jerusalem in this connection is that Yahweh is 'within you'.

A people that needs to change

1 Yahweh's word that came to Tsephanyah ben Kushi, son of Gedalyah son of Amaryah son of Hizqiyyah, in the days of Yoshiyyahu ben Amon, king of Yehudah.

²I shall totally gather up everything
    from on the face of the ground (Yahweh's declaration).
³I shall gather up human beings and animals;
    I shall gather up the birds of the heavens and the fish of the sea,
    and the things that make the faithless collapse.
I shall cut off humanity
    from on the face of the ground (Yahweh's declaration).

⁴I shall stretch out my hand against Yehudah,
    and against all the inhabitants of Yerushalaim.
I shall cut off from this place
    the remainder of the Master,
    the names of the priestlings with the priests,
⁵The people who bow low on the roofs
    to the army in the heavens,
Who bow low, who swear, to Yahweh
    and swear by Malkam,
⁶Who turn away from following Yahweh
    and don't seek Yahweh nor enquire of him.

⁷Silence before the Lord Yahweh,
    because Yahweh's day is coming near.
Because Yahweh has prepared a sacrifice,
    made sacred the people he called.
⁸On the day of Yahweh's sacrifice
    I shall attend to the officials,
To the king's sons,
    and to all the people wearing foreign clothing.
⁹I shall attend to all the people who leap on the threshold
    on that day,
Who fill their lord's house
    with violence and deceit.

¹⁰On that day there will be (Yahweh's declaration)
    the sound of an outcry from the Fish Gate
A howl from the Mishneh,
    a big breaking from the hills.
¹¹Howl, you who live in the Maktesh,
    because the entire trading people has perished,
    all those who weigh out silver have been cut off.

¹²At that time
    I shall search Yerushalaim with lamps.
I shall attend to the people
    who are relaxing on their lees,
Who are saying to themselves,
    'Yahweh won't do something good and he won't do something bad.'
¹³Their resources will be for plundering,
    their houses will be for desolation.
They will build houses but not live [there],
    plant vineyards but not drink their wine.

Yahweh's day

¹⁴Yahweh's great day is coming near,
    coming near very quickly.
The sound of Yahweh's day is bitter;
    the strong man is going to shriek there.
¹⁵That day will be a day of outburst,
    a day of pressure and distress,
A day of desolation and devastation,
    a day of darkness and gloom,
A day of cloud and shadow,
¹⁶a day of horn blast and shout,
Against the fortified towns,
    and against the lofty corner towers.
¹⁷I shall bring pressure to the people, they will walk like the blind,
    because they've done wrong to Yahweh.
Their blood will be poured out like earth,
    their marrow like faeces.
¹⁸Neither their silver nor their gold
    will be able to rescue them.
On the day of Yahweh's outburst,
    in his passionate fire,
The entire country will be consumed,
    because he will make an end, yes, how terrible,
    of all the people who live in the country.

2 Pile together, pile it,
    nation that isn't wanted,
²Before the decree's birth,
    the day that passes like chaff,
Before Yahweh's angry blazing
    doesn't come upon you,
Before Yahweh's angry day
    doesn't come upon you.
³Seek Yahweh, all you humble people in the country,
    who have implemented his ruling.

Seek faithfulness, seek lowliness;
  perhaps you can hide on Yahweh's angry day.

Where to look

⁴Because Azzah [Gaza] will become abandoned,
  Ashqelon a desolation.
Ashdod will be dispossessed at midday,
  Eqron uprooted.
⁵Hey, you people who live in the region by the sea,
  the nation of Keretites!
Yahweh's word is against you,
  Kena'an [Canaan], country of the Pelishtites [Philistines]!
I shall obliterate you, without inhabitant.
⁶The region by the sea will become abodes,
  shepherds' cisterns, pens for flocks.
⁷It will be a region
  for the remainder of Yehudah's household.
On these they will pasture;
  in Ashqelon's houses they'll lie down in the evening.
Because Yahweh their God will attend to them,
  and restore their fortunes.
⁸I have heard Mo'ab's reviling,
  the insults of Ammon,
Who have reviled my people,
  talked big over their territory.
⁹Therefore, as I live
  (a declaration of Yahweh of Armies, Yisra'el's God),
Mo'ab will become like Sedom [Sodom],
  the Ammonites like Amorah [Gomorrah]:
The domain of chickweed and a salt-pit,
  desolation permanently.
The remainder of my people will plunder them
  and what is left of my nation will have them as a domain.
¹⁰This is what they'll have instead of their majesty,
  because they reviled and talked big
at the people belonging to Yahweh of Armies.
¹¹Yahweh will be fearsome against them,
  because he's reducing all earth's gods.
All the nations' shores will bow down to him,
  each from its place.
¹²You Kushites [Sudanese], too:
  run through by my sword.
¹³And he'll stretch out his hand against the north,
  and obliterate Ashshur.
He'll make Nineveh a desolation,
  dry like the wilderness.
¹⁴Flocks will lie down in the middle of it,
  every creature in the nation.
Both jackdaw and owl will lodge in its pillars,
  the sound will sing in the windows.
Waste will be on the threshold,
  because the cedar is stripped.
¹⁵This is the exultant town,
  one that sits in confidence,
Saying to itself,
  'I'm the one, there is no other.'
Aagh, it's become a desolation,
  a lair for creatures.
Everyone who passes by it hisses
  and shakes his hand.

Wait for me

3 Hey, rebellious and defiled one,
  oppressive town!
²It hasn't listened to a voice,
  it hasn't accepted correction.
It hasn't relied on Yahweh,
  it hasn't come near to its God.
³Its officials within it
  are roaring lions.
Its authorities are wolves at evening;
  they don't gnaw until morning.
⁴Its prophets are arrogant, people who break faith;
  its priests treat what's sacred as ordinary, they violate instruction.
⁵Yahweh is faithful within it;
  he doesn't do evil.
Morning by morning he gives his ruling,
  at daybreak he doesn't fail,
but the evildoer doesn't acknowledge shame.

⁶I am cutting off nations, their corner towers are becoming desolate;
  I am wasting their streets, so that no one passes through.
Their towns are standing without people,
  with no inhabitant.
⁷I said, 'You'll surely be in awe of me,
  you'll accept correction.'
Then its abode wouldn't be cut off,
  all that I attended to for it.
On the contrary, they've been up early
  and made all their deeds devastating.

⁸Therefore wait for me (Yahweh's declaration),
  for the day when I rise as a witness.

Because it's my ruling to gather nations,
    for me to collect kingdoms,
To pour out on them my condemnation,
    all my angry blazing.
Because in my passionate fire
    the entire earth will be consumed.
⁹Because then I shall transform for the peoples
    purified speech,
So that all of them call on Yahweh's name,
    so that they serve him shoulder to shoulder.
¹⁰From beyond Kush's rivers my suppliants,
    my scattered community, will bring my offering.

God among us

¹¹On that day,
    you [Yerushalaim] won't be ashamed of all your deeds,
    with which you've rebelled against me.
Because then I shall remove from within you
    the people exulting in your majesty.
You'll no more be very superior
    on my sacred mountain.

¹²I shall leave remaining within you
    a humble, poor people,
    and they will find shelter in Yahweh's name.
¹³The remainder of Yisra'el won't do wrong,
    and won't speak lies.
There won't be found in their mouth
    a deceitful tongue.
Because they are the ones who will pasture and lie down,
    with no one disturbing.

¹⁴Resound, Miss Tsiyyon [Zion],
    shout, Yisra'el.
Rejoice and exult with all your heart,
    Miss Yerushalaim.
¹⁵Yahweh is turning aside the rulings about you,
    he's turning back your enemy.
Yahweh, Yisra'el's King, is within you;
    you needn't be afraid of bad things any more.

¹⁶On that day it will be said to Yerushalaim:

Don't be afraid, Tsiyyon;
    your hands shouldn't droop.
¹⁷Yahweh your God is within you,
    a strong man who delivers.
He'll celebrate over you with rejoicing,
    he'll hold his peace in his love,
    he'll be glad over you with resounding.
¹⁸The people who grieve on account of the set occasions –
    I'm gathering them from you;
    upon you they've been a burden, a reviling.
¹⁹Here am I, I'm going to deal with all your oppressors
    at that time.
I shall deliver the lame,
    collect the ones driven out.
I shall make them an object of praise and renown
    whose shame was in the entire earth.

²⁰At that time I shall bring you –
    yes, at the time I shall collect you.
Because I shall make you an object of renown and praise
    among all the peoples of the earth,
    when I restore your fortunes before your eyes
    (Yahweh has said).

Haggai

On conquering Babylon, Cyrus the king of Persia permitted and encouraged Judahites who had been taken into exile there to return to Jerusalem to rebuild the temple. In the short term the work miscarried, and Haggai [Haggay], with whom Zechariah was contemporary, was involved in encouraging the people to take up the work again and complete it, in 520–516. It was apparently his vital role in connection with this crucial event that led to the preserving of his prophecies concerning it. The story, with an account of the role of Haggai and Zechariah, appears in Ezra 1—6.

Concerning remodelling priorities

1 In the second year of Dareyavesh [Darius] the king, in the sixth month, on the first day of the month, Yahweh's word came by means of Haggay the prophet to Zerubbabel ben She'alti'el governor of Yehudah and to Yehoshua ben Yehotsadaq the big priest: ²"Yahweh of Armies has said this: "This people has said, 'The time hasn't come, the time for building Yahweh's house.'""

³Yahweh's word came by means of Haggay the prophet: ⁴"Is it the time for you yourselves to live in your panelled houses, and this house lies waste? ⁵So now Yahweh of Armies has said this: "Apply your mind to your ways. ⁶You've sown much but brought in little. You eat but without having enough. You drink but without getting drunk. You dress but without a person getting warm. And the people who earn wages earn them for a purse with holes."

⁷Yahweh of Armies has said this: "Apply your mind to your ways. ⁸Go up to the highland, bring wood and build the house, and I shall accept it and find honour", Yahweh has said. ⁹"You looked for much, but there – little. You brought it home, and I'd blow on it. On account of what (a declaration of Yahweh of Armies)? On account of my house that lies waste, and you're running each person to his own house. ¹⁰That's why above you the heavens have withheld dew, and the earth has withheld its produce, ¹¹and I've called for drought on the earth, on the mountains, on the grain, on the new wine, on the fresh oil, on all that the ground produces, on human beings, on animals and on all the labour of your fists.'"

¹²Zerubbabel ben She'alti'el, Yehoshua ben Yehotsadaq the big priest and all the remainder of the people listened to the voice of Yahweh their God, and because of Haggay the prophet, as Yahweh their God sent him. So the people were in awe of Yahweh, ¹³and Haggay, Yahweh's envoy in Yahweh's work, said to the people, 'I am with you (Yahweh's declaration).'

A new splendour

¹⁴So Yahweh aroused the spirit of Zerubbabel ben She'alti'el governor of Yehudah, the spirit of Yehoshua ben Yehotsadaq the big priest, and the spirit of all the remainder of the people, and they came and did work on the house of Yahweh of Armies, their God, ¹⁵ᵃon the twenty-fourth day of the sixth.

2 ¹⁵ᵇIn the second year of Dareyavesh the king, in the seventh, on the twenty-first of the month, Yahweh's word came by means of Haggay the prophet: ²"Say, please, to Zerubbabel ben She'alti'el governor of Yehudah, and to Yehoshua ben Yehotsadaq the big priest, and to the remainder of the people: ³"Who among you remains who saw this house in its former splendour? How do you see it now? In comparison with it, it's just nothing in your eyes, isn't it.

⁴But now, be strong, Zerubbabel (Yahweh's declaration), be strong, Yehoshua ben Yehotsadaq, big priest, be strong, all you people of the country (Yahweh's declaration). Act, because I am with you (a declaration of Yahweh of Armies), ⁵the thing that I solemnized with you when you got out of Misrayim [Egypt]. My spirit stays among you. Don't be afraid." ⁶Because Yahweh of Armies has said this: "Once more, shortly, I'm going to shake the heavens and the earth, the sea and the dry land. ⁷I shall shake all the nations, and the things held in high regard belonging to all the nations will come. I shall fill this house with splendour (Yahweh of Armies has said). ⁸Mine is the silver and mine is the gold (a declaration of Yahweh of Armies). ⁹The splendour of this later house will be greater than the earlier one (Yahweh of Armies has said). In this place I shall give you well-being (a declaration of Yahweh of Armies)."

A renewed promise

¹⁰On the twenty-fourth of the ninth in the second year of Dareyavesh, Yahweh's word came to Haggay the prophet. ¹¹Yahweh of Armies said this: 'Ask the priests for instruction, please: ¹²"If someone carries sacred meat in the fold of his garment and touches bread or stew or wine or oil or any other food with the fold, does it become sacred?"' The priests answered, 'No'. ¹³Haggay said, 'If someone taboo because of a body touches any of these, does it become taboo?' The priests answered, 'It becomes taboo.' ¹⁴Haggay responded, 'So is this

people, so is this nation before me (Yahweh's declaration) and so is the action of their hands. What they present there is taboo.

[15]But now, apply your mind, please, from this day and onwards. Before the setting of stone on stone in Yahweh's palace, [16]from when these things happened, someone came to a twenty-measure heap, and there'd be ten; someone came to the wine vat to skim off fifty measures, there'd be twenty. [17]I struck you down with blight, with mildew and with hail, in all the action of your hands, but you were not with me (Yahweh's declaration). [18]Apply your mind, please, from this day and onwards, from the twenty-fourth day of the ninth, from the day when Yahweh's palace was founded. Apply your mind: [19]is there still seed in the barn? Whereas until now the vine, the fig tree, the pomegranate and the olive tree have not borne, from this day I shall bless.'

[20]Yahweh's word came a second time to Haggay on the twenty-fourth of the month. [21]'Say to Zerubbabel governor of Yehudah: "I'm going to shake the heavens and the earth, [22]overturn the throne of the kingdoms, destroy the strength of the nations' kingdoms, and overturn chariotry and its drivers. Horses and their riders will come down, each by his brother's sword.

[23]On that day (a declaration of Yahweh of Armies), I shall take you, Zerubbabel ben She'alti'el my servant (Yahweh's declaration), and make you like a signet, because I've chosen you (a declaration of Yahweh of Armies)."'

Zechariah

Zechariah [Zekaryah] was a contemporary of Haggai, associated with him in the story of the rebuilding of the temple in Ezra 1—6. While Haggai was the bad cop who confronted the people about their failure, Zechariah was the good cop who encouraged them with Yahweh's promises in chapters 1—8, a series of visions and exhortations. Zechariah 9—14 comprises a series of prophecies without concrete indications of a context.

A world at peace

1 In the eighth month in the second year of Dareyavesh [Darius], Yahweh's word came to Zekaryah ben Berekyah, son of Iddo, the prophet. ²'Yahweh felt a great fury with your ancestors. ³You're to say to them, "Yahweh of Armies has said this: 'Turn back to me (a declaration of Yahweh of Armies) and I shall turn back to you (Yahweh of Armies has said). ⁴Don't become like your ancestors, to whom the earlier prophets called out, "Yahweh of Armies has said this: 'Turn back, please, from your bad ways and from your bad practices'", but they didn't listen or heed me (Yahweh's declaration). ⁵Your ancestors: where are they? The prophets: do they live permanently? ⁶Yet my words and my laws that I ordered my servants the prophets: they overtook your ancestors, didn't they, and they turned back and said, "As Yahweh of Armies schemed to do to us in accordance with our ways and with our practices, so he has done with us."'"'

⁷On the twenty-fourth day of the eleventh month (i.e. the month of Shebat) in the second year of Dareyavesh, Yahweh's word came to Zekaryah ben Berekyah, son of Iddo:

⁸I saw by night: there, a man riding on a red horse. He was standing among myrtle trees that were in the deep. Behind him were red, brown and white horses. ⁹I said, 'What are these, my lord?' The envoy who was speaking with me said, 'I'll show you what those are.' ¹⁰The man who was standing among the myrtle trees answered, 'These are ones that Yahweh sent to go round in the earth.' ¹¹They answered Yahweh's envoy who was standing among the myrtle trees, 'We've been going round in the earth. There, the entire earth is living quiet.'

Too peaceful

¹²Yahweh's envoy answered, 'Yahweh of Armies, how long will you not have compassion on Yerushalaim and on Yehudah's towns, which you've been condemning these seventy years?' ¹³Yahweh answered the envoy who was speaking with me with good words, comforting words. ¹⁴The envoy who was speaking with me said to me, 'Call out: "Yahweh of Armies has said this: 'I have felt a great passion for Yerushalaim and for Tsiyyon [Zion], ¹⁵and I – I have been feeling a great fury with the nations that are peaceful, because I was a bit furious, but they helped it become bad fortune.' ¹⁶Therefore Yahweh has said this: 'I'm turning back to Yerushalaim in compassion. My house will be built up in it (a declaration of Yahweh of Armies), and a cord will be stretched over Yerushalaim.'" ¹⁷Call out further: "Yahweh of Armies has said this: 'My towns will again flow with good things. Yahweh will again comfort Tsiyyon and again choose Yerushalaim.'"'

¹⁸I lifted my eyes and looked: there, four horns. ¹⁹I said to the envoy who was speaking with me, 'What are these?' He said to me, 'These are the horns that scattered Yehudah, Yisra'el and Yerushalaim.' ²⁰And Yahweh showed me four smiths. ²¹I said, 'What are these coming to do?' He said, 'These are the horns that scattered Yehudah to such an extent that no one lifted his head. But these have come to disturb them by throwing down the horns of the nations that lifted a horn against the country of Yehudah, to scatter it.'

You can't measure Yerushalaim (Jerusalem)

2 I lifted my eyes and looked: there, a man with a measuring line in his hand. ²I said, 'Where are you going?' He said to me, 'To measure Yerushalaim, to see exactly what is its breadth and its length.' ³But there, the envoy who was speaking with me was going out, and another envoy was going out to meet him. ⁴He said to him, 'Run, speak to that young man: "Yerushalaim will be inhabited as unwalled villages because of the number of people and animals within it. ⁵And I myself shall be for it (Yahweh's declaration) a wall of fire round, and I shall be splendour within it."'

⁶'Hey, hey, flee from the northern country (Yahweh's declaration), because I'm scattering you like the four winds of the heavens (Yahweh's declaration).' ⁷Hey, Tsiyyon, escape, you who live in Miss Babel. ⁸Because Yahweh of Armies has said this (after splendour sent me) regarding the nations who plundered you: the one touching you was touching the apple of his eye. ⁹Because here am I, I'm going to shake my

hand against them. They will become spoil for their servants.' And you will acknowledge that Yahweh of Armies sent me. ¹⁰'Resound, rejoice, Miss Tsiyyon, because here am I – I'm coming to dwell within you (Yahweh's declaration). ¹¹Many nations will attach themselves to Yahweh on that day and will become my people, and I shall dwell within you.'

And you will acknowledge that Yahweh sent me to you. ¹²And Yahweh will have Yehudah as his domain on the sacred ground, and will again choose Yerushalaim.

¹³Hush, all flesh, before Yahweh, because he has roused himself from his sacred abode.

Guilt is not the end

3 He showed me Yehoshua the big priest standing before Yahweh's envoy, and the adversary standing at his right to act as his adversary. ²Yahweh said to the adversary, 'Yahweh reprimand you, adversary, Yahweh who chose Yerushalaim reprimand you. Isn't this a burning stick snatched from the fire?' ³Yehoshua was wearing filthy clothes as he was standing before the envoy.

⁴He avowed to the beings who were standing before him, 'Take the filthy clothes off him', and he said to him, 'Look: I've made your waywardness pass on from you, and you may wear fine robes. ⁵And I've said, "They should put a pure turban on his head."' They put the pure turban on his head and dressed him in clothes as Yahweh's envoy was standing by.

⁶Yahweh's envoy testified against Yehoshua: ⁷'Yahweh of Armies has said this: "If you walk in my ways and keep my charge, you yourself will both judge my house and also keep watch on my courtyards, and I shall give you movement among these who are standing in attendance. ⁸Listen, please, Yehoshua, senior priest, you and your fellows who are sitting before you, because they are people who constitute a sign. Because here am I, I'm going to bring my servant, Branch. ⁹Because here's the stone that I've put before Yehoshua. On one stone are seven eyes. Here am I, I'm going to make its engraving (a declaration of Yahweh of Armies), and I shall remove this country's waywardness in one day.

¹⁰On that day (a declaration of Yahweh of Armies) you will call, each person his neighbour, under his vine and under his fig tree."'

A candelabrum and a promise

4 The envoy who was speaking with me came back and woke me up like someone who wakes up from his sleep. ²He said to me, 'What are you looking at?' I said, 'I looked, and there – a candelabrum of gold, all of it, with its bowl on top of it, and its seven lamps on it, seven spouts each for the lamps that were on top of it, ³and two olive trees by it, one to the right of the bowl and one to its left.' ⁴I avowed to the envoy who was speaking with me, 'What are these, my lord?' ⁵The envoy who was speaking with me answered me, 'Don't you know what these are?' I said, 'No, my lord.' ⁶He answered me . . .

'This is Yahweh's word to Zerubbabel: "Not by resources, not by energy, but by my spirit", Yahweh of Armies has said. ⁷Who are you, big mountain, before Zerubbabel? Into flatland. He will take out the top stone, with shouts of "Grace, grace to it!"'

⁸Yahweh's word came to me: ⁹'Zerubbabel's hands have founded this house and his hands will finish it off.' And you will acknowledge that Yahweh of Armies sent me to you. ¹⁰Because who despises the day of little things? They will rejoice when they see the metal stone in Zerubbabel's hand.

. . . 'These seven are Yahweh's eyes ranging through the entire earth.' ¹¹I avowed to him, 'What are these two olive trees on the right of the candelabrum and on its left?' ¹²And I avowed to him a second time, 'What are the two ears [of grain] of the olive trees that pour out gold from themselves by means of the two gold pipes?' ¹³He said to me, 'Don't you know what these are?' I said, 'No, my lord.' ¹⁴He said, 'These are the two sons of fresh oil who stand by the Lord of the entire earth.'

A flying scroll and a flying container

5 I again lifted my eyes and looked – there, a flying scroll. ²He said to me, 'What are you looking at?' I said, 'I'm looking at a flying scroll. Its length is ten metres and its width five metres.' ³He said to me, 'This is the vow that's going out over the face of the entire country. Because everyone who steals (from this side, according to it) has gone free of guilt, and everyone who swears (from the other side, according to it) has gone free of guilt. ⁴I'm causing it to go out (a declaration of Yahweh of Armies) and it will come into the thief's house and the house of the person who swears by my name for falsehood. It will lodge inside his house and consume it, both its timbers and its stones.'

⁵The envoy who spoke with me went out and said to me, 'Lift up your eyes, please, and look. What's this going out?' ⁶I said, 'What is it?' He said, 'This is the barrel that's going out.' And he said, 'This is their appearance in the entire country.' ⁷And there, a lead disc lifted, and it was a woman sitting inside the barrel. ⁸He said, 'This is Faithlessness.' He thrust her inside the container and thrust the lead disc to its mouth.

⁹I lifted my eyes and looked, and there – two women going out with wind in their wings (they had wings like a stork's wings). They carried the barrel between the earth and the heavens. ¹⁰I said to the envoy who was speaking with me, 'Where are they making the container go?' ¹¹He said to me, 'To build it a house in the country of Shin'ar, which will be established, and it will be settled down there on its established place.'

Settling Yahweh's spirit and making crowns

6 I lifted my eyes again and looked, and there – four chariots going out from between two mountains; the mountains were mountains of copper. ²In the first chariot the horses were red, in the second chariot the horses were black, ³in the third chariot the horses were white, in the fourth chariot the horses were dappled, strong.

⁴I avowed to the envoy who was speaking with me, 'What are these, my lord?' ⁵The envoy answered me, 'These are the four winds of the heavens, going out after standing by the Lord of the entire earth.' ⁶The one where the black horses are – they were going out to the northern country. The white left after them.

The dappled went out to the southern country. ⁷So the strong went out. When they sought to go, so as to go about through the earth, he said, 'Go, go about through the earth.' So they went about through the earth. ⁸He cried out to me and spoke to me: 'Look, the ones going out to the northern country have settled my spirit in the northern country.'

⁹Yahweh's word came to me: ¹⁰'Receive from the exile community, from Helday, from Tobiyyah and from Yeda'yah, and you yourself are to come on that day, to come to the house of Yo'shiyyah ben Tsephanyah, when they've come from Babel: ¹¹you're to receive gold and silver and make crowns and put them on the head of Yehoshua ben Yehotsadaq the big priest, ¹²and say to him, "Yahweh of Armies has said this: 'There is the man whose name is Branch. From his place he will branch out and build Yahweh's palace. ¹³He's the one who'll build Yahweh's palace. He's the one who'll put on majesty, and sit and rule on his throne. A priest will be by his throne, and there'll be peaceful counsel between the two of them.' ¹⁴For Helem, for Tobiyyah, for Yeda'yah and for Hen ben Tsephanyah, the crowns will be a memorial in Yahweh's palace. ¹⁵Distant people will come and build in Yahweh's palace, and you will acknowledge that Yahweh of Armies sent me to you. It will happen if you really do listen to the voice of Yahweh your God."'

Who are you fasting for?

7 In the fourth year of Dareyavesh the king, Yahweh's word came to Zekaryah, on the fourth of the ninth month, in Kislev. ²Bet-el Sar-ezer and Regem Melek and his men sent to seek Yahweh's goodwill ³by saying to the priests who were at the house of Yahweh of Armies and to the prophets, 'Should I cry in the fifth month, consecrating myself, as I have done these how many years?'

⁴A word from Yahweh of Armies came to me: ⁵'Say to all the people of the country and to the priests, "When you fasted and lamented in the fifth and in the seventh even these seventy years, did you really fast for me? ⁶When you eat and when you drink, it's you who eat and you who drink, isn't it. ⁷They're the words that Yahweh called out by means of the

earlier prophets, aren't they, when Yerushalaim was peopled and peaceful, and its towns round it, and the Negeb and the Lowland were peopled?'"
⁸Yahweh's word came to Zekaryah: ⁹'Yahweh of Armies has said this: "Exercise truthful authority, exercise commitment and compassion each person with his brother. ¹⁰Don't oppress widow and orphan, alien and humble. Don't think up bad dealings each person against his brother in his mind." ¹¹But they refused to heed and presented a defiant shoulder. They stopped their ears from listening. ¹²They made their mind concrete so as not to listen to the instruction and the words that Yahweh of Armies sent by his spirit by means of the earlier prophets, and great wrath came from Yahweh of Armies. ¹³As he called but they didn't listen, "so they'll call and I shall not listen", Yahweh of Armies said. ¹⁴"And I blasted them away to all the nations that they hadn't known. The country was desolate behind them from anyone passing through or coming back. They made a country that was held in high regard into a desolation."'

I will make you a blessing

8 A word from Yahweh of Armies came. ²'Yahweh of Armies has said this: "I feel a great passion for Tsiyyon. I feel a fierce passion for it." ³Yahweh has said this: "I'm coming back to Tsiyyon and I shall dwell within Yerushalaim. Yerushalaim will be called 'Truthful Town', and the mountain of Yahweh of Armies 'Sacred Mountain.'"
⁴Yahweh of Armies has said this: "Old men and old women will again sit in Yerushalaim's squares, each with his cane in his hand because of the great number of his days. ⁵The town's squares will be full of boys and girls having fun in its squares."
⁶Yahweh of Armies has said this: "Because it will be fantastic in the eyes of the remainder of this people in those days, will it also be fantastic in my eyes (a declaration of Yahweh of Armies)?"
⁷Yahweh of Armies has said this: "Here am I, I'm going to deliver my people from the eastern country and from the western country, ⁸and bring them, and they will dwell within Yerushalaim. They will be a people for me and I shall be God for them, in truth and faithfulness."
⁹Yahweh of Armies has said this: "Your hands are to be strong, you who are listening to these words in these days from the mouth of the prophets who [were there] on the day when the house of Yahweh of Armies was founded, for building the palace. ¹⁰Because before those days there were no wages for a human being and there were no wages for an animal. For anyone going out or coming in, there was no peace from the adversary. I set all human beings one against his neighbour. ¹¹But now I'm not acting towards the remainder of this people as in earlier days (a declaration of Yahweh of Armies), ¹²because the sowing will be in peace, the vine will give its fruit, the earth will give its produce, the heavens will give their dew, and I shall let the remainder of this people have all these things as a domain. ¹³As you became a slighting among the nations, Yehudah's household and Yisra'el's household, so I shall deliver you and you will become a blessing. Don't be afraid. Your hands are to be strong."

Make me a blessing

¹⁴Because Yahweh of Armies has said this: "As I schemed to do something bad to you when your ancestors infuriated me (Yahweh of Armies said) and didn't relent, ¹⁵so I have again schemed in these days to do good to Yerushalaim and to Yehudah's household. Don't be afraid. ¹⁶These are the things that you're to do. Speak the truth each to his neighbour. Exercise authority with truthful authority that makes for peace in your gateways. ¹⁷Don't think up something bad in your mind each person against his neighbour. Don't love a false oath. Because all these are things to which I'm hostile (Yahweh's declaration).'"
¹⁸The word of Yahweh of Armies came to me. ¹⁹'Yahweh of Armies has said this: "The fast of the fourth, the fast of the fifth, the fast of the seventh and the fast of the tenth will become for Yehudah's household celebration and rejoicing, good set occasions. So love truthfulness and peace."
²⁰Yahweh of Armies has said this: "Peoples and inhabitants of many towns will yet

come, ²¹and the inhabitants of one will go to one another saying, 'Let's go, let's go to seek Yahweh's goodwill and seek Yahweh of Armies. I myself intend to go, yes.' ²²Many peoples will come, numerous nations, to seek Yahweh of Armies in Yerushalaim and to seek Yahweh's goodwill."

²³Yahweh of Armies has said this: "In those days, when ten people from all the nations' tongues will take hold, they'll take hold of the hem of a Yehudahite individual's coat, saying 'We want to go with you, because we've heard that God is with you.'"

The king on a donkey

9 A pronouncement.

Yahweh's word against the country of Hadrak,
    and Dammeseq [Damascus] its place of settling.
Because people's eye will be towards Yahweh,
    all Yisra'el's clans.
²Hamat, too, which borders on it;
    Tsor [Tyre], and Tsidon because it's very smart.
³Tsor has built itself a stronghold,
    it has heaped up silver like earth,
Gold like the mud in the streets;
    ⁴there, the Lord Yahweh will dispossess it.
He'll strike down its resources at sea;
    it will be consumed by fire, itself.
⁵Ashqelon will see and be afraid,
    Azzah [Gaza] will writhe much,
    and Eqron, because its reliance will have withered.
King will perish from Azzah,
    Ashqelon won't be inhabited.
⁶A mongrel will live in Ashdod;
    I shall cut off the majesty of the Pelishtites [Philistines].
⁷But I shall remove the blood it has shed from its mouth,
    and its abominations from between its teeth.
What remains of it, too, will belong to our God,
    and become like a clan in Yehudah,
    while Eqron will be like the Yebusites.
⁸I shall camp for my house as a garrison
    against anyone passing through or coming back.
No oppressor will pass through against them again,
    because now I shall have looked with my eyes.

⁹Celebrate greatly, Miss Tsiyyon;
    shout, Miss Yerushalaim.
There, your king will come to you;
    he'll be faithful and one who finds deliverance,
Humble and riding on a donkey,
    on an ass, the child of a she-ass.
¹⁰I shall cut off chariotry from Ephrayim
    and horse from Yerushalaim.
The bow of battle will be cut off;
    he will speak of peace to the nations.
His rule will be from sea to sea,
    from the River to the ends of the earth.

Crown jewels glittering on his land

¹¹Yes, you [Yerushalaim], by the blood of your pact:
    I'm sending off your captives.
From the pit where there's no water,
    ¹²get back to the fortress, hopeful prisoners.
Yes, today I'm going to announce:
    I shall give back double to you.
¹³Because I'm directing Yehudah for myself as a bow,
    I'm loading Ephrayim.
I shall arouse your sons, Tsiyyon,
    against your sons, Yavan [Greece],
    and make you like a strong man's sword.

¹⁴Yahweh – he'll appear over them,
    his arrow will go out like lightning.
The Lord God will sound on the horn
    and go in southern hurricanes.
¹⁵Yahweh of Armies will shield over them;
    sling stones will consume and tread down.
They will drink, make a noise as with wine,
    be full like a bowl, like the altar's corners.
¹⁶Yahweh our God will deliver them
    on that day, like a flock, his people.
Because they are crown jewels glittering on his land,
    ¹⁷because how good they are and how beautiful they are.
Grain will make the young men flourish,
    new wine the young women.

10 Ask for rain from Yahweh
    at the time of the spring rain;
Yahweh is the one who sends lightning flashes,
    gives them a downpour of rain,
    growth in the fields for each one.

²Because the effigies have spoken trouble,
  the diviners have beheld falsehood.
They speak lying dreams,
  they comfort with hollowness.
Therefore people have strayed like a flock,
  they suffer because there's no shepherd.
³Against the shepherds my anger has blazed,
  I shall attend to the big guys.

Because Yahweh of Armies is attending to his flock,
  Yehudah's household.
He will make them
  like his majestic horse in battle.
⁴From it cornerstone, from it tent peg,
  from it battle bow,
From it will go out
  every overseer, together.
⁵They'll be like strong men,
  trampling the mud of the streets, in battle.
They'll do battle, because Yahweh will be with them;
  they'll shame the people riding horses.

Yehudah's household become strong men

⁶So I shall make Yehudah's household strong men,
  and I shall deliver Yoseph's household.
I shall restore them, because I've had compassion on them;
  they'll be as if I had not rejected them.
Because I am Yahweh,
  their God, and I shall answer them.
⁷Ephrayim will be a veritable strong man;
  their heart will rejoice as with wine.
Their children will see and rejoice;
  their heart will be joyful in Yahweh.
⁸I shall whistle to them and gather them,
  because I have redeemed them.
They will become many, as they were many,
  ⁹though I sowed them among the nations.
In far-off places they will be mindful of me;
  they will live with their children, and come back.
¹⁰I shall bring them back from the country of Misrayim [Egypt],
  collect them from Ashshur.
Though I bring them to the country of Gil'ad and Lebanon,
  room won't be found for them.

¹¹He will pass through the confining sea,
  he will strike down the sea of waves.
All the Ye'or's [Nile's] deeps will dry up,
  and the majesty of Ashshur will be put down.
Misrayim's club will pass away,
  ¹²and I shall make them strong men through Yahweh,
  and in his name they'll go about (Yahweh's declaration).

11 Open your doors, Lebanon,
  so fire can consume your cedars.
²Howl, junipers, because the cedar is falling,
  when the august are being destroyed.
Howl, Bashan oaks,
  because the fortified forest is going down.
³The sound of the shepherds' howling,
  because their eminence is destroyed.
The sound of the lions' roar,
  because Yarden's [Jordan's] majesty is destroyed.

Lying, neglectful, loathsome and stupid shepherds

⁴Yahweh my God said this: 'Tend the flock to be killed, ⁵whose acquirers will kill them and won't be liable, whose sellers will say, "Yahweh be blessed! I shall be rich", and whose shepherds won't have pity on them. ⁶Because I shall no more have pity on the country's inhabitants (Yahweh's declaration). There, I'm going to make people vulnerable, each to his neighbour's hand and to his king's hand. They will crush the country, and I shall not rescue it from their hand.'

⁷So I pastured the sheep to be killed, therefore the lowliest of the flock. I got myself two staffs, I called one 'Beauty', and the other I called 'Binders', and I pastured the sheep. ⁸I disposed of the three shepherds in one month. With my whole being I lost patience with them, and with their whole being they loathed me, too. ⁹So I said, 'I shall not pasture you. The one who dies may die and the one who gets disposed of may get disposed of, and the ones who remain, each may eat the flesh of her neighbour.'

¹⁰I got my staff 'Beauty' and broke it, contravening my pact that I had solemnized with all the peoples. ¹¹So it was contravened

on that day, and the lowliest of the sheep, who were keeping watch towards me, thus acknowledged that it was Yahweh's word. ¹²I said to them, 'If it's good in your eyes, give me my pay; if not, withhold it.' They weighed out my pay, thirty silver pieces. ¹³Yahweh said to me, 'Throw it to the potter' (the worthy magnificence that I was worth to them). So I took the thirty silver pieces and threw them to the potter in Yahweh's house. ¹⁴And I broke my second staff, 'Binders', to contravene the brotherhood between Yehudah and Yisra'el.

¹⁵Yahweh said to me again, 'Get yourself the implements of a stupid shepherd. ¹⁶Because here I am, I'm going to raise up a shepherd in the country who won't attend to the ones who are disposed of or seek the young one or heal the injured or sustain the one who stands firm, but will eat the flesh of the fat one and tear off their hoofs.

¹⁷Hey, non-entity shepherds,
    abandoning the flock:
A sword on your arm
    and on your right eye!
May his arm quite wither,
    his right eye go quite blind!'

A chalice that causes reeling

12 A pronouncement. Yahweh's word concerning Yisra'el.

A declaration of Yahweh,
    the one who stretched out the heavens,
Who founded the earth,
    who shaped the spirit of humanity within it.

²'There, I'm going to make Yerushalaim a chalice that causes reeling to all the peoples around. It will also be against Yehudah during the siege against Yerushalaim.
³On that day, I shall make Yerushalaim a stone hard to lift for all the peoples. All who lift it will seriously injure themselves when all the nations of the earth gather against it.
⁴On that day (Yahweh's declaration), I shall strike down every horse with panic and its rider with madness. Over Yehudah's household I shall open my eyes, but every horse belonging to the peoples I shall strike with blindness.

⁵Yehudah's clans will say to themselves, "Yerushalaim's inhabitants are my strength, through Yahweh of Armies, their God."
⁶On that day, I shall make Yehudah's clans like a firepot among trees, like a fiery torch among sheaves. They will consume all the peoples around, to the right and the left. And Yerushalaim will again live in its place, in Yerushalaim. ⁷Yahweh will deliver Yehudah's tents first, so that the glory of David's household and the glory of Yerushalaim's population will not be greater than Yehudah.'
⁸On that day Yahweh will shield over Yerushalaim's population. Someone among them who is liable to collapse will be like David on that day, and David's household will be like gods, like Yahweh's envoy going before them.
⁹'On that day I shall seek to annihilate all the nations that come against Yerushalaim, ¹⁰but I shall pour out on David's household and on Yerushalaim's population a spirit of grace and of prayers for grace. They will look to me concerning someone they've thrust through, and they will lament over him with the lamentation for an only son, and express distress for him like the distress over a firstborn.

The sword against the shepherd

¹¹On that day the lamentation in Yerushalaim will be great, like the lamentation for Hadad-rimmon in Megiddo Valley. ¹²The country will lament, kin-group by kin-group by itself, the kin-group of David's household by itself and their women by themselves, the kin-group of Natan's household by itself and their women by themselves, ¹³the kin-group of Levi's household by itself and their women by themselves, the kin-group of the Shim'ites by itself and their women by themselves, ¹⁴all the remaining kin-groups kin-group by kin-group by itself and their women by themselves.

13 On that day there will be a fountain opened for David's household and Yerushalaim's inhabitants, for purification and for cleansing.
²And on that day (a declaration of Yahweh of Armies) I shall cut off the names of the images from the country. They won't be mentioned

again. Also the prophets and the defiled spirit I shall cause to pass away from the country. ³When someone prophesies again, his father and his mother, who brought him to birth, will say, "You will not live, because you've spoken falsehood in Yahweh's name." His father and his mother, who brought him to birth, will thrust him through when he prophesies.

⁴On that day the prophets will be ashamed, each one, of his vision when he prophesies. They won't wear a garment of hair so as to deceive. ⁵He will say, "I'm not a prophet, I'm a man who works the ground, because a man acquired me from my youth." ⁶If someone says to him, "What are these wounds between your hands?" he will say, "I was wounded in my friends' house."

⁷Sword, rouse yourself against my shepherd,
    against a man who is my envoy (a declaration
        of Yahweh of Armies).
Strike down my shepherd, the flock is to scatter;
    I shall turn back my hand against the little
        ones.
⁸In all the country (Yahweh's declaration)
    two parts in it will be cut off, will perish.
A third will be left in it.
⁹but I shall bring the third into the fire.
I shall smelt them as one smelts silver,
    test them as one tests gold.
It will call in my name
    and I myself shall answer it,
I shall have said, "It is my people",
    and it will say, "Yahweh is my God."

Yahweh stands on the Mount of Olives

14 There, a day of Yahweh is coming, and your spoil [Yerushalaim] will be shared out within you. ²I shall gather all the nations to Yerushalaim for battle. The town will be captured, the houses will be plundered, the women will be ravished and half the town will go out into exile. But the rest of the people will not be cut off from the town, ³and Yahweh will go out and do battle against those nations, as he does battle on a day of engagement.

⁴On that day his feet will stand on the Mount of Olives which faces Yerushalaim to the east. The Mount of Olives will split in half from east to west, a very big ravine; half of the mountain will move away northward, half of it southward. ⁵You people will flee by the ravine between my mountains, because the ravine between the mountains will reach to Atsal. You will flee as you fled from before the earthquake in the days of Uzziyah king of Yehudah. But Yahweh my God will come – all the sacred ones will be with you.

⁶On that day there won't be light from the glorious ones; they will dwindle. ⁷There'll be one day (it is known to Yahweh), not day and not night; at evening time it will be light. ⁸On that day living water will go out from Yerushalaim, half of it to the eastern sea, half of it to the western sea. It will happen in summer and in winter. ⁹Yahweh will be king over all the earth.

No more trader in Yahweh's house

On that day Yahweh will be one and his name one. ¹⁰The entire country will turn round [and be] like the steppe, from Geba to Rimmon south of Yerushalaim, but it [Yerushalaim] will rise up and stay in its place, from the Binyamin Gate to the place of the First Gate, to the Corner Gate, and from Hananel's Tower to the king's winepresses. ¹¹People will live in it, and devoting will not happen any more. Yerushalaim will live in confidence.

¹²But this will be the epidemic that Yahweh will impose on all the peoples that made war against Yerushalaim: making someone's flesh waste away while he stands on his feet, his eyes waste away in their sockets, and his tongue waste away in their mouth.

¹³On that day a great panic from Yahweh will come upon them. They'll take hold, each person, of his neighbour's hand, and his hand will rise against his neighbour's hand. ¹⁴Yehudah, too, will do battle at Yerushalaim. The resources of all the nations around will be gathered – gold and silver and clothing, a great quantity.

¹⁵Like this epidemic, so will be the epidemic affecting horse, mule, camel, donkey and every animal that will be in those camps. ¹⁶But everyone who is left from all the nations that come against Yerushalaim will go up year by year to bow low to the King, Yahweh of

Armies, and to observe the Sukkot Festival. ¹⁷Whichever does not go up from the kingroups of the earth to Yerushalaim to bow low to the King, Yahweh of Armies, there'll be no rain on them. ¹⁸If Misrayim's kin-group doesn't go up and doesn't come, there'll be none on them; there'll be the epidemic that Yahweh imposes on the nations that don't go up to observe the Sukkot Festival. ¹⁹This will be [the penalty for] the wrongdoing of Misrayim and the wrongdoing of all the nations that don't go up to observe the Sukkot Festival.

²⁰On that day, upon a horse's bells will be 'Sacred to Yahweh'. The pots in Yahweh's house will be like the basins before the altar. ²¹Every pot in Yerushalaim and Yehudah will be sacred to Yahweh of Armies. All the people who offer sacrifice will come and take some of them and cook in them. There'll be no more trader in the house of Yahweh of Armies on that day.

Malachi

The location of Malachi [Mal'aki] in the Old Testament invites us to infer that it belongs, with Haggai and Zechariah, in the period after exiled Judahites were free to return to Jerusalem. The temple is functioning, so it presupposes the completion of their work, while the variety of problems it seeks to handle then fit with the pressures of the subsequent time of Ezra and Nehemiah. It proceeds mostly by means of a to-and-fro argument in which Yahweh or the prophet confronts the community over a series of issues. Its ending with the prospect of Yahweh sending a new Elijah or the old Elijah recommissioned, to herald Yahweh's day, makes it an appropriate close to the Prophets. Also, its ending the Old Testament as a whole (in the Christian ordering of the Old Testament) makes for a deft transition to the New Testament.

Easy-going priests

1 A pronouncement. Yahweh's word to Yisra'el by means of Mal'aki.

²'I've been loyal to you', Yahweh said. But you say, 'How have you been loyal to us?' 'Esaw was Ya'aqob's [Jacob's] brother, wasn't he (Yahweh's declaration). But I was loyal to Ya'aqob ³and I was hostile to Esaw. I'm making his mountains a desolation, his domain to belong to wilderness jackals.' ⁴Because Edom says, 'We've been crushed, but we'll build the wastes again', Yahweh of Armies has said this: 'Those people may build, but I myself will tear down.' They will be called 'Faithless Territory' and 'the people Yahweh has condemned permanently'. ⁵Your own eyes will see it. You yourselves will say, 'Yahweh is great, beyond Yisra'el's territory.'

⁶"'A son honours his father, a servant his lord. If I'm a father, where's the honour for me? If I'm a Lord, where's the awe for me?" Yahweh of Armies said to you, priests who disdain my name. You say, "How have we disdained your name?" ⁷You're presenting defiled food on my altar. You say, "How have we defiled you?" By your saying, "Yahweh's table can be disdained." ⁸When you bring up something blind for sacrifice, there's nothing bad. When you bring up something lame or sick, there's nothing bad. Present it to your governor, please. Will he accept you? Will he have regard to you? (Yahweh of Armies has said). ⁹Now, please seek Yahweh's goodwill so that he shows favour to us. This has come from your hand. Will he have regard to any of you? (Yahweh of Armies has said).

¹⁰'Who indeed is there among you who'll shut the doors, and not light a fire on my altar to no end! I find no delight in you (Yahweh of Armies has said) and I shall not accept an offering from your hand.

A priest's lips keep watch on knowledge

¹¹Because from the sun's rising to its setting my name is great among the nations and in every place incense is offered to my name, and a pure offering, because my name is great among the nations (Yahweh of Armies has said). ¹²But you're treating it as ordinary when you say, "The Lord's table is defiled, and its fruit, its food, can be disdained", ¹³or say, "This is a weariness", and blow it off (Yahweh of Armies has said), or bring something stolen or lame or sick, and bring it as the offering. Should I accept it from your hand (Yahweh has said)? ¹⁴Cursed is the cheat when there's a male in his flock but he pledges and sacrifices to the Lord something devastated. Because I am a great king (Yahweh of Armies has said) and my name is held in awe among the nations.

2 So now to you priests, this order. ²If you don't listen and don't receive it into your mind to give honour to my name (Yahweh of Armies has said), I shall send off a curse among you. I shall curse your blessings. Indeed, I have cursed it, because you don't receive it into your mind. ³Here am I, I'm going to reprimand your seed. I'm going to spread faeces on your faces, the faeces from your festival sacrifice. Someone will carry you out to it. ⁴And you will acknowledge that I have sent off this order to you so that my pact with Levi might exist (Yahweh of Armies has said). ⁵My pact with him was life and well-being, and I gave them to him, with awe. He was in awe of me. He was in dread of my name.

⁶True instruction was in his mouth;
　evil wasn't found on his lips.
In well-being and in uprightness he walked with
　me,
　and he turned many back from waywardness.
⁷Because a priest's lips keep watch on knowledge;
　people seek instruction from his mouth,
　because he's an envoy of Yahweh of Armies.

⁸But you've turned aside from the way. You've made many people collapse through your instruction. You've devastated Levi's pact (Yahweh of Armies has said). ⁹I myself in turn am making you shameful and low to the entire people, on account of the fact that you don't keep watch on my ways but you show regard in the instruction.'

A broader neglected covenant

¹⁰We all of us have one father, don't we. One God created us, didn't he. Why do we break faith, each with his brother, in treating our

ancestors' pact as ordinary? ¹¹Yehudah has broken faith. An offence has been committed in Yisra'el and in Yerushalaim, because Yehudah has treated as ordinary what is sacred to Yahweh, to which he is loyal, and has married the daughter of a strange god. ¹²May Yahweh cut off the person who does this (anyone who arises and anyone who responds) from Ya'aqob's tents, even one who presents an offering to Yahweh of Armies.

¹³And you do this second thing, covering Yahweh's altar with tears, crying and wailing because he's no longer regarding the offering or receiving it with acceptance from your hand, ¹⁴and you've said, 'On account of what?' On account of the fact that Yahweh is a witness between you and the wife of your youth, with whom you've broken faith, when she was your partner and your covenanted woman. ¹⁵Didn't One make us, and isn't the remainder of the spirit his? And what is the One seeking? Godly offspring. So you will guard yourself in your spirit. Someone is not to break faith with the wife of your youth. ¹⁶When he's hostile so as to divorce (Yahweh the God of Yisra'el has said), he makes violence a cover over his clothing (Yahweh of Armies has said). So you're to keep watch for yourself in your spirit and not break faith.

¹⁷You've wearied Yahweh with your words. You've said, 'How have we wearied him?' When you say, 'Everyone who does something bad is good in Yahweh's eyes. In them he takes delight.' Or 'Where is the God who exercises authority?'

3 'Here am I, I'm going to send my envoy, and he'll clear the way before me.' Suddenly there will come to his palace the Lord for whom you are looking.

A full and frank exchange of views

¹ᵇSo the envoy of the pact whom you want – there, he's coming (Yahweh of Armies has said). ²But who's going to endure the day of his coming? Who's going to stand when he appears? Because he'll be like a smelter's fire or like launderer's soap. ³He'll sit smelting and purifying silver. He'll purify the Levites and refine them like gold and silver, and they'll be Yahweh's, people who take up an offering in faithfulness. ⁴The offering of Yehudah and Yerushalaim will please Yahweh as in the days gone by, in former years.

⁵'So I shall come near to you to exercise authority and be an eager witness against the diviners, the adulterers, the people who swear falsely, the people who defraud the employee of his wages, the widow and orphan, and those who turn aside the resident and who are not in awe of me (Yahweh of Armies has said). ⁶Because I am Yahweh, I haven't changed, and you're Ya'aqob's descendants, you haven't come to an end. ⁷Given that from your ancestors' days you've turned aside from my laws and not kept them: come back to me and I'll come back to you (Yahweh of Armies has said).

You'll say, "How shall we come back?" ⁸Does a person cheat God? Because you're cheating me. You'll say, "How have we cheated you?" In tithe and contribution. ⁹You're subjected to a curse, and you're cheating me – the nation, all of it. ¹⁰Bring the entire tithe into the storehouse, so that there may be food in my house, and test me by this, please (Yahweh of Armies has said), if I don't open the heavens' floodgates and empty out blessing on you until there's no need. ¹¹I'll reprimand the devourer for you, and it won't destroy the fruit of the ground for you, and the vine in the open country won't miscarry for you (Yahweh of Armies has said). ¹²All the nations will count you fortunate, because you'll be a delightful land (Yahweh of Armies has said).

A faithful sun with healing in its rays

¹³You've made your words strong against me (Yahweh has said). You'll say, "What have we spoken to ourselves against you?" ¹⁴You've said, "Serving God is empty in results. What was the gain when we kept his charge and walked in gloom before Yahweh of Armies? ¹⁵So now we count the arrogant fortunate. The people who act in faithlessness have both been built up and have also tested God and escaped."'

¹⁶Then the people who were in awe of Yahweh talked, each with his neighbour, and Yahweh heeded and listened, and a remembrance scroll was written before him regarding the people who were in awe of Yahweh and who esteemed his name. ¹⁷'For me

they will be a special possession (Yahweh of Armies has said) for the day that I'm preparing. I shall have pity on them as someone has pity on his son who serves him. ¹⁸You'll again see the difference between the faithful and the faithless, between the one who serves God over against the one who has not served him.

4 Because there – the day is coming, burning like an oven, when all the arrogant and all the people who act in faithlessness will be stubble, and the day that's coming will burn them up (Yahweh of Armies has said) so that it doesn't leave them root or branch. ²But there will rise for you who are in awe of my name a faithful sun with healing in its rays. You'll go out and jump like well-fed bullocks. ³You'll trample the faithless, because they'll be ashes under the soles of your feet, on that day that I'm making (Yahweh of Armies has said).

⁴Be mindful of Mosheh [Moses] my servant's instruction, which I ordered him for all Yisra'el at Horeb, laws and rulings. ⁵There, I'm sending you Eliyyah [Elijah] the prophet before the coming of the great and awe-inspiring day of Yahweh. ⁶He will turn back the mind of parents to children and the mind of children to parents, so that I don't come and strike down the country with "devoting".

An Old Testament glossary

Abaddon
One of the Old Testament's words for the place where dead people are, like **She'ol**. The ordinary word is similar to a Hebrew word meaning 'perish', which may well not be a coincidence. Indeed, the verb can suggest 'destroy', and people might make a link with the fact that death does mean that our bodies decay. But the texts do not make anything of this. The word is simply a name.

affirmation
In the context of expressions such as '**affirmation chest**' or 'affirmation dwelling', affirmation refers to the things **Yahweh** has affirmed as his expectations of **Yisra'el (Israel)** – namely, the Ten Commandments.

affirmation chest
The '**affirmation** chest' is a box a bit more than a metre long, a bit more than half a metre wide and high. The King James Bible (KJV) refers to it as an 'ark', but the word means a box, though it is only occasionally used to refer to chests used for other purposes. It is the *affirmation* chest because it contains the stone tablets inscribed with the Ten Commandments, key expectations God affirmed in connection with establishing the Sinai covenant. It is regularly kept in the sanctuary, but there is a sense in which it symbolizes God's presence (given that **Yisra'el (Israel)** has no images to do so), and in that capacity the Israelites sometimes carry it with them. It is sometimes referred to as the pact chest, with the same meaning.

altar
A structure for offering a sacrifice (the Hebrew word for altar comes from the word for sacrifice), made of earth or stone. An altar might be relatively small, like a table, and the person making the offering would stand in front of it. Or it might be higher and larger, like a platform, and the person making the offering would climb on to it.

Amorites
A term for one of the original ethnic groups in **Kena'an (Canaan)**, though also used to refer to the people of that country as a whole. Genesis 15.16 and 21 illustrates the two uses of the word in close proximity. Indeed, outside the Old Testament 'Amorites' refers to a people living over a much wider area of Mesopotamia. 'Amorites' is thus a little like the word 'America', which commonly refers to the USA but can denote a much broader area of the continent of which the USA is part.

ancestral heads
The heads of the (very) extended families within the twelve clans of **Yisra'el (Israel)**, a family unit rather larger than the household.

Aram, Aramaic, Arameans, Aramites
In the period to which Genesis refers, the Arameans (or Aramites) were a people living in Syria and northern Mesopotamia. Aram later became the name for a more defined political entity in Syria, **Ephrayim**'s (**Ephraim**'s) big north-eastern neighbour; English translations then often refer to it as Syria. The Aramaic language, a sister language of **Hebrew** somewhat in the way Spanish is a sister language of Portuguese or Italian, became the international language of the Middle East. Parts of Ezra, Jeremiah and Daniel are in Aramaic, and it was the everyday language of Palestine in Jesus' day.

Asherah, Ashtar
The word is used both to signify the name of a deity and the name of an aid to worship (the two meanings come close together in 1 Kings 14—15). In **Kena'anite (Canaanite)** religion and elsewhere, strictly Asherah was a particular goddess, but the name came to be used in the plural as a general term for a goddess. As a word for an aid to worship, it denotes something that can be 'erected', 'planted' and 'burned', which suggests a tree-like column or pillar that represented and suggested the presence of the deity.

Ashshur (Assyria)
The first great Middle Eastern superpower, the Assyrians spread their empire westward into Syria-Palestine in the eighth century BC, the time of Amos and Isaiah. They first made **Ephrayim (Ephraim)** part of their empire; then when Ephraim kept trying to assert independence, they invaded Ephraim, destroyed its capital at **Shomron (Samaria)**, transported its people and settled people from other parts of their empire in their place. They also invaded **Yehudah (Judah)** and devastated much of the country, but did not take Jerusalem. Prophets such as Amos and Isaiah describe how **Yahweh** was thus using Assyria as a means of disciplining **Yisra'el (Israel)**.

assistant
These are the *netinim*, people who played a support role in the temple. Etymologically their name implies they are people who were 'given', dedicated to the service of God, or given to the priests and **Levites** as their assistants in fulfilling menial tasks. The people of Gibeon (Josh. 9.27) are not called *netinim*, but the role ascribed to them as water carriers and woodchoppers for the sanctuary conveys an idea of these assistants' work. The assistants came to be treated as among the Levites.

authority
People such as Eli, Samuel, Samuel's sons and the kings 'exercise authority' over **Yisra'el (Israel)** and for Israel. The Hebrew word for someone who exercises such authority, *shopet*, is traditionally translated 'judge', but such leadership is wider than this. In the book called Judges, these **leader**s are people who have no official position like the later kings, but who arise and exercise initiative in a way that brings the people **deliverance** from the trouble they get into. It is a king's job to exercise authority in accordance with **faithfulness** to God and people.

awe
Hebrew uses the same words for being afraid of someone fearful and for respecting someone whom it's appropriate to revere. Occasionally it's hard to be sure which sort of attitude is designated by the word. I have used 'awe' where the context implies the second sort of attitude, which also implies submission and obedience. In the wisdom books, awe is seen as a key aspect of a relationship with God, of crucial importance to understanding God and life. Awe for God has been described as the Old Testament expression for spirituality.

Azazel
The word comes only in the expression 'for Azazel' in Leviticus 16; it might be a deserted and/or rocky place or it might be a demonic power.

Babel (Babylon)
A minor power in the context of **Yisra'el's (Israel's)** early history, in the time of Jeremiah they took over the position of superpower from **Ashshur (Assyria)** and kept that for nearly a century until conquered by **Paras (Persia)**. Prophets such as Jeremiah describe how **Yahweh** was using them as a means of disciplining **Yehudah (Judah)**. Their creation stories, law codes and more philosophical writings help us understand aspects of the Old Testament's equivalent writings, while their astrological religion also forms background to aspects of polemic in the Prophets.

bad
The Old Testament uses this word in a similar fashion to the way English uses the word 'bad' – it can refer both to the bad things that people do and the bad things that happen to us, both to morally bad actions and to bad experiences. Sometimes prophets use the word with both connotations in the same context, pointing towards the fact that bad things often happen because people do bad things – though they know that this is not invariably so. They can thus speak of God doing bad things in the sense of bringing calamity to people.

Beliyya'al
A personification of death, which swallows (*bala*); the word became a term for Satan.

brother
The Hebrew word can refer to blood relatives in a broader sense than the English word – both male and female.

Cistern
A term that can denote the grave as the place where dead people are (see **She'ol**).

commitment
The word corresponds to the Hebrew word *hesed*, which translations render by means of expressions such as 'steadfast love' or 'loving kindness' or 'goodness'. It is the Old Testament equivalent of the special word for love in the New Testament, the word *agapē*. The Old Testament uses this word to refer to an extraordinary act whereby someone pledges himself or herself to someone else in some act of generosity, allegiance or grace when there is no prior relationship between them and therefore no reason why they should do so. Thus in Joshua 2, Rahab appropriately speaks of her protection of the Israelite spies as an act of commitment. It can also refer to a similar extraordinary act that takes place when there is a relationship between people, but one party has let the other party down and therefore has no right to expect any **faithfulness** from the other party. If the party that has been let down continues being faithful, they are showing this kind of commitment. In their response to Rahab, the Israelite spies declare that they will relate to her in this way.

cry, cry out
In describing the Israelites' response when they are oppressed by enemies, Judges uses the word that the Old Testament uses to describe Abel's blood crying out to God, the outcry of the people of Sodom under their oppression, the Israelites' crying out in **Misrayim (Egypt)** and the outcry of people who are unfairly treated within **Yisra'el (Israel)** in later centuries. It denotes an urgent cry that presses God for **deliverance**, a cry that God can be relied on to hear even when people deserve to be having the experience that is assailing them.

cubit
Half a yard or just under half a metre (I usually translate cubit measurements into metres).

day of the Lord
The oldest occurrence of the expression 'the day of the Lord', 'Yahweh's day', comes in Amos 5, which indicates that people saw it as a time when **Yahweh** would bring great blessing on them. Amos declares that the opposite is the case. Henceforth the expression always has sinister connotations. Yahweh's day is a day when Yahweh acts in decisive fashion. It doesn't happen just once; there are various occasions that the Old Testament describes as Yahweh's day, such as Jerusalem's fall in 587 BC and **Babel's (Babylon's)** fall in 539. In Isaiah, Sennacherib's devastation of **Yehudah (Judah)** was such an embodiment of Yahweh's day (22.5).

decontamination
A sacrifice that removes the **taboo** that comes from contravening **Yahweh**'s rulings for life.

deliver, deliverance, deliverer
In the Old Testament, modern translations often use the words 'save', 'saviour' and 'salvation', but this gives a misleading impression. In Christian usage, these words commonly refer to our personal relationship with God and to the enjoyment of heaven. The Old Testament does speak of our personal relationship with God, but it does not use this group of words in that connection. They refer rather to God's practical intervention to get **Yisra'el (Israel)** or the individual out of a mess of some kind, such as false accusations by individuals within the community or invasion by enemies.

devote, devotion
Devoting something to God means giving it over to God irrevocably. Translations use words such as 'annihilated' or 'destroyed', and that is often the implication, but it does not convey the word's distinctive point. You could devote land, or an animal such as a donkey, and in effect Hannah will devote Samuel; the donkey or the human being then belongs to God and is committed to God's service. In effect the Israelites devoted many **Kena'anites (Canaanites)** to God's service in this way; they became people who chopped wood and drew water for the **altar**, its offerings and the rites of the sanctuary. Devoting people to God by killing them as a kind of sacrifice was a practice known from other peoples, which **Yisra'el (Israel)** takes over on its own initiative, but which God validates. Israel knows this is how war works in its world and it assumes it is to operate the same way, and God goes along with that.

disciples of the prophets
Literally, these are the 'sons of the prophets'. The books of 1 and 2 Kings mention communities of such prophets in various places in **Ephrayim (Ephraim)** in the time of Elijah and Elisha. They lived together and apparently made their services available to people who needed guidance from God on some matter. They would be dependent on donations from people who sought their help in this way; the stories indicate that this made them vulnerable to poverty.

Edom, Edomites
Edom is **Yehudah**'s (**Judah**'s) south-eastern neighbour, occupying an area to the south-east of the Dead Sea. As **Yisra'el (Israel)** traces its ancestry back to Jacob, it traces Edom's ancestry back to Jacob's brother Esau. The Old Testament critiques Edom in particular for its inclination to take advantage of Judah's vulnerability and its support of the Babylonians when they captured Jerusalem. Subsequently the Edomites occupied considerable parts of southern Judah.

effigies
The Hebrew word for these is *teraphim*. In 1 Samuel 15.33 the text presupposes a link between the *teraphim* and divination, which involves techniques (like those of astrology) for trying to discover things about the future so that we can make sensible decisions or safeguard against trouble that might come. One form of divination involves consulting the dead. The effigies would be images of family members who had passed (a little like family photographs), whom people would seek to consult on the assumption that they might now know things that their relatives who were still alive could not know. **Yisra'el (Israel)** was not supposed to be involved in such procedures because it was expected to rely more directly on God for guidance.

envoy
A supernatural agent through whom God may appear and work in the world. Standard English translations refer to them as 'angels', but this is inclined to suggest ethereal figures with wings, wearing diaphanous white dresses. Envoys are human-like figures; hence it is possible to give them hospitality without realizing this is who they are (Heb. 13). And they have no wings; hence

their need of a stairway or ramp between heaven and earth (Gen. 28). They appear in order to act or speak on God's behalf, and so fully represent God that they can speak as if they *are* God (Gen. 22). They thus bring the reality of God's presence, action and voice, without bringing such a real presence that it would electrocute mere mortals or shatter their hearing.

ephod
In some passages the Old Testament implies that an ephod is a kind of vestment worn by a priest, but in some passages it at least incorporated something that contained the **Urim and Tummim**.

Ephrayim (Ephraim)
After the reign of David and Solomon, the nation of **Yisra'el (Israel)** split into two. Most of the twelve Israelite clans set up an independent state in the north, separate from **Yehudah (Judah)** and Jerusalem and from the line of David. Because this was the bigger of the two states, politically it kept the name Israel, which is confusing because Israel is still the name of the people as a whole as the people of God. In the Prophets, it is sometimes difficult to tell whether 'Israel' refers to the people of God as a whole or just to the northern state. But sometimes the state is referred to by the name of Ephraim as one of its dominant clans, so I use this term to refer to that northern state, to try to reduce the confusion.

exile
At the end of the seventh century **Babel (Babylon)** became the major power in **Yehudah's (Judah's)** world but Judah was inclined to rebel against its authority. As part of a successful campaign to get Judah to submit properly to its authority, in 597 and in 587 BC the Babylonians transported many people from Jerusalem to Babylon. They made a special point of transporting people in leadership positions, such as members of the royal family and the court, priests and prophets (Ezekiel was one of them). These people were thus compelled to live in Babylonia for the next fifty years or so. Through the same period, people back in Judah were also under Babylonian authority. So they were not physically in exile but they were also living *in* the exile as a period of time. A number of books in the Old Testament indicate that one of the issues they are handling is the pressure this experience brings to people.

expiation
A key concern in Exodus and Leviticus is keeping the sanctuary pure. While God may be able to tolerate a small amount of impurity there (as we can tolerate a small amount of dirt), if the place people have made as a home for God becomes too much affected by things that are alien, then God can hardly carry on living there. So it is important to deal with impurity that comes on the sanctuary through the infringement of **taboo**s. One way of conceiving this is to speak in terms of atonement (at-one-ment), which suggests the healing of a relationship. Another is to speak of propitiation, which suggests the mollifying of someone who was angry. In contrast, expiation relates to the thing that has caused the problem rather than to the person. It suggests the removal or wiping away of a stain. Of course the removal of the stain does mean that the threat to the relationship is gone and it is now possible for God to be in easy relationship with the people; in this sense expiation and at-one-ment are closely related. On the other hand, 'propitiation' is a more questionable idea in connection with Leviticus; while it does imply that God is offended by people and unwilling to associate with them, it does not speak of God being angry with them because of their offences.

faithfulness
In English Bibles this Hebrew word (*tsedaqah*) is usually translated 'righteousness', but it denotes a particular slant on what we might mean by righteousness. It means doing the right thing by the people with whom one is in a relationship, the members of one's community. Thus it is really closer to 'faithfulness' than 'righteousness'.

faithlessness
A word for sin that suggests the opposite of **faithfulness**, an attitude to God and to other people that expresses a contempt for what right relationships deserve.

flatbread
Bread made without being yeasted and allowed to rise.

Greece
In 336 BC, Greek forces under Alexander the Great took control of the **Parsite (Persian)** Empire, but after Alexander's death in 333 his empire split up. The largest part, to the north and east of Palestine, was ruled by one of his generals, Seleucus, and his successors. **Yehudah (Judah)** was under its control for much of the next two centuries, though it was at the extreme southwestern border of this empire and sometimes came under the control of the Ptolemaic Empire in **Misrayim (Egypt)** (ruled by successors of another of Alexander's officers).

Hebrew
Oddly, whereas this word became the term for the language of the Jewish people, it seems not to be an ethnic term in the Old Testament. 'Hebrew' is not the same as 'Israelite'. While Abraham can be designated a Hebrew (Gen. 14.13) and the Israelites might be termed Hebrews, they were not the only Hebrews. Other languages have related words, and all seem to be more sociological terms than ethnic ones, a little like the word 'gypsy'. They suggest people who do not belong to a regular recognized political community. In the New Testament, the Hebrews are Hebrew-speaking **Jews** as opposed to Greek-speaking Jews. So it's confusing to refer to Old Testament Israelites as 'Hebrews'.

hierodule
A type of temple servant, possibly involved in sexual rites.

Jew
The word is a shortened version of the word *yehudi*, which thus denotes a member of the clan or province of **Yehudah (Judah)**. As Judah became the heart of **Yisra'el (Israel)** in the Second Temple period, *yehudim* or 'Jews' became a term for all members of the people of Israel and became a regular term for members of a religious community rather than members of an ethnic group. But this usage mostly belongs to post-Old Testament times, and in the Old Testament the word *yehudim* or 'Jews' would exclude most Israelites. So it's confusing to refer to Old Testament Israelites as 'Jews'.

Kasdites
People from an area within Babylonia who came to rule Babylonia, so that it became a term for Babylonians in general (also sometimes for their expert advisers); an alternative form of the word is Kaldites (hence the traditional English term Chaldeans).

Kena'an, Kena'anites (Canaan, Canaanites)
As the biblical terms for the land of **Yisra'el (Israel)** as a whole and for its indigenous peoples, 'Canaan' and 'Canaanites' are not so much names that refer to a particular ethnic group as shorthand terms for all the peoples native to the land. See also **Amorites**.

leader
The book of Judges is named after the leaders whose stories appear in the book. The traditional term is 'judge', so that they are people who also give their name to the period of time between Joshua and Saul, the 'Judges Period'. But these 'judges' do not usually operate in connection with sorting out legal cases, and 'leaders' gives more the right idea concerning their role. They are people who have no official position like the later kings, but who arise and exercise initiative in a way that brings the clans **deliverance** from the trouble the clans get into.

Levites
Within the clan of Levi, the descendants of Aaron are the priests, the people who have specific responsibilities in connection with offering the community's sacrifices and helping individuals to offer their sacrifices by performing some aspects of the offering such as the sprinkling of the animal's blood. The other Levites fulfil a support and administrative role in the temple and are also involved in teaching the people and in other aspects of leading worship.

Livyatan (Leviathan)
A sea monster who is an embodiment or symbol of tumultuous power asserted against God and the world.

Maday and Paras, Parsites (Media and Persia, Medo-Persia, Persians)
Media lies between Mesopotamia and Persia. In the 550s Cyrus the Great gained control of Media and also of Persia, and turned Medo-Persia into the third Middle Eastern superpower. Cyrus took control of the Babylonian Empire in 539 BC, which opened up the possibility of Judahites returning from **Babel (Babylon)** after the **exile**. **Yehudah (Judah)** and surrounding peoples such as **Shomron (Samaria)**, Ammon and Ashdod were then Persian provinces or colonies. The Persians stayed in power for two centuries until defeated by **Greece**.

Master, Masters
The word *ba'al* is an ordinary Hebrew word for a master or lord or owner, but the word is also used to describe a **Kena'anite (Canaanite)** god. It is thus parallel to the word 'Lord' as used to describe **Yahweh**. Further, in effect 'Master' can be a proper name, like 'Lord'. To make the difference clear, the Old Testament generally uses 'Master' for a foreign god and 'Lord' for the real God, Yahweh. Like other ancient peoples, the Canaanites acknowledged a number of gods, and strictly the Master was simply one of them, though he was one of the most prominent. In addition, a title such as 'The Master of Pe'or' suggests that the Master was believed to be manifest and known in different ways and different places. The Old Testament also uses the plural 'Masters' to refer to Canaanite gods in general.

Misrayim, Misrayimites (Egypt, Egyptians)
The major regional power to the south of **Kena'an (Canaan)** and the country where Jacob's family had found refuge, where they ended up as serfs, and from which the Israelites then needed to escape. In Moses' time Egypt controlled Canaan; in subsequent centuries it was sometimes a threat to **Yisra'el (Israel)**, sometimes a potential ally.

name
The name of someone stands for the person. The Old Testament talks of the temple as a place where God's name dwells. It's one of the ways it handles the paradox involved in speaking of the temple as a place where God lives. It knows this is a nonsense: how could a building contain the God who could not be contained by the entire heavens, no matter how far you could travel across them? Yet **Yisra'el (Israel)** knows that God does in some sense dwell in the temple. They know they can talk with God when they go there; they are aware that they can talk with God anywhere, but there is a special guarantee of this in the temple. They know they can make offerings there and that God will receive them (supposing they are made in good faith). One way they try to square the circle in speaking of the presence of God in the temple is therefore to speak of God's name being present there, because the name sums up the person. Uttering the name of someone you know brings home his or her reality to you; it's almost as if the person is there. When you say someone's name, there is a sense in which you conjure up the person. When people murmur 'Jesus, Jesus' in their prayer, it brings home the reality of Jesus' presence. Likewise, when Israel proclaimed the name **Yahweh** in worship, it brought home the reality of Yahweh's presence.

non-entity
A pejorative term, especially for gods other than **Yahweh**; it resembles the word for God but also a word for 'useless'.

Paras, Parsites (Persia, Persians)
See **Maday and Paras**.

peace
The Hebrew word *shalom* can suggest peace after there has been conflict, but it often points to a richer notion, of fullness of life. The KJV sometimes translates it 'welfare', and modern translations use words such as 'well-being' or 'prosperity'. It suggests that everything is going well for you.

Pelishtites (Philistines)
The Philistines were people who came from across the Mediterranean to settle in **Kena'an (Canaan)** at the same time as the Israelites were establishing themselves in Canaan, so that the two peoples formed an accidental pincer-movement on the existing inhabitants of the country and became each other's rivals for control of the area.

Pesah
A festival in spring commemorating the exodus (commonly rendered in English as Passover).

purification, purification offering, purify
A major concern of the Torah is dealing with the **taboo** that can come on people and places through the effect of something that is alien to who God is, such as contact with death. There is nothing wrong with being involved in burying someone, but you have to give the taint of death time to dissipate or have it removed before coming into God's presence. A purification rite can bring that about.

Rahab (not the woman Rahab in Joshua)
Another name for the creature also called **Livyatan (Leviathan)**.

Reed Sea
Literally 'sea of rushes'; the word is the one that came in Exodus 2 where Miriam left Moses in the reeds by the Nile. It might be one of the northern arms of what we call the Red Sea, either side of Sinai, or it might be an area of marshy lakes within Sinai.

remainder
The Prophets warn that **Yahweh**'s chastisement will mean **Yisra'el (Israel)** (and other peoples) being cut down so that the 'remainder' of them, what 'remains', the 'remnant', will be small. But at least some remainder of Israel will survive – so the idea of a 'remainder' can become a sign of hope. It can also become a challenge – the few that remain are challenged to become a faithful remainder, a faithful remnant.

reside, resident
Verb and noun refer to someone living in a country other than their own, who therefore cannot own land.

restore, restorer
A restorer is a person who is in a position to take action on behalf of someone within his extended family who is in need in order to restore the situation to what it should be. The word overlaps with expressions such as next-of-kin, guardian and redeemer. 'Next-of-kin' indicates the family context that 'restorer' presupposes. 'Guardian' indicates that the restorer is in a position to

be concerned for the person's protection and defence. 'Redeemer' indicates having resources that the restorer is prepared to expend on the person's behalf. The Old Testament uses the term to refer to God's relationship with **Yisra'el (Israel)** as well as to the action of a human person in relation to another, so it implies that Israel belongs to God's family and that God acts on its behalf in the way a restorer does.

rise
This term (*selah*) comes at the end of a number of lines in the Psalms (and in Habakkuk). We do not know what it refers to.

scaliness
A skin condition traditionally translated 'leprosy' and carrying a **taboo**.

secondary wife
Translations use the word 'concubine' to describe people such as Abimelek's mother, but the term used of them does not suggest that they were not properly married. Being a secondary wife rather means that a woman has a different status from that of other wives. It perhaps implies that her son had fewer or no inheritance rights. It may be that a wealthy or powerful man could have several wives with full rights and several secondary wives, or just one of each, or just the former, or even just a secondary wife.

Shabu'ot
'Weeks', a harvest festival in May or June (commonly transliterated as Shavu'ot, and rendered in English as Pentecost).

Shadday
El Shadday (or simply Shadday) is a name for God that the Old Testament especially associates with the time when the name **Yahweh** would not have been known and with people who would not have known that name. Thus it comes in Genesis and it is used in connection with non-Israelites such as Balaam and Job. We do not know the meaning of the name. There are similar-looking words that mean destruction and breast and – in a sister language of **Hebrew** – mountain, so it could originally have meant destructive God or nourishing God or mountain-like God, but we have little evidence that people made any of those connections in the Old Testament. The Greek translation of the Old Testament often rendered it 'Almighty', and this also became the convention in English translations. But the significance of the word is rather that it indicates that we are talking about the true God but talking about this God in a way that people who do not know the name Yahweh could use.

The Shameful King
The **Kena'anite (Canaanite)** god whose name means 'the king'. The name is altered in **Hebrew** by combining it with the word for 'shameful'.

She'ol
The most frequent of the Hebrew names for the place where we go when we die (see also **Abaddon**). In the New Testament it is called Hades. It is not a place of punishment or suffering but simply a resting place for everyone, a kind of non-physical analogue to the tomb as the resting place for our bodies.

sheqel
About half an ounce or ten grams.

Shomron (Samaria)
The city of Samaria was the capital of **Ephrayim (Ephraim)**; it fell to the Assyrians in 722 BC. Many people were then transported there by the Assyrians. Samaria later became the name of the Babylonian and **Parsite (Persian)** province in the area, and for a while its governor had authority over **Yehudah (Judah)**. In the Second Temple period the Judahites were thus ethnically, politically and religiously suspicious of the Samarians. But many of the Samarians were actually more conservative than the Judahites; as their Scriptures they accepted only the Torah.

soul
'Soul' in the English Bible usually represents Hebrew *nephesh* or Greek *psuche*. It can denote the inner person distinguishable and separable from the body but not independent of it; or the inner being of the whole person, their heart or deeply felt emotions; or the whole person comprising physical body plus divine breath; or the life of the person ('her soul was departing'). It does not mean the real person for which the body is a dispensable outward shell.

spirit
The Hebrew word for spirit is also the word for breath and for wind, and the Old Testament sometimes implies a link between these. Spirit suggests dynamic power; God's spirit suggests God's dynamic power. The wind in its forcefulness with its capacity to fell mighty trees is an embodiment of the powerful spirit of God. Breath is essential to life; where there is no breath, there is no life. And life comes from God. So human breath and even animal breath is an offshoot of God's breath.

Sukkot
The word means 'shelters' and refers to the festival in September/October that marks the end of the harvest and also commemorates the way the Israelites had to live in makeshift shelters on the way from **Misrayim (Egypt)** to **Kena'an (Canaan)** (the term is commonly rendered in English as tabernacles or booths).

taboo
I use the word 'taboo' to render the Hebrew word often translated 'impure' or 'unclean', because the Hebrew word suggests a positive quality rather than the absence of purity. There are certain things that are mysterious, extraordinary, perplexing and a bit worrying. Among these are menstruation and childbirth, because they suggest both death and life. These are opposites, and God is the God of life and not of death, yet menstruation (with its association of blood and life) and giving birth (which is both life-giving and very dangerous) bring them into close connection. So contact with them makes people taboo; they cannot go into God's presence until they are purified (see **purification**).

talent
About 40 kilograms or 90 pounds.

trespass
A term to describe sin or wrongdoing. It suggests the idea that in varying ways people owe it to one another to respect the rights that the other person has. So married people owe each other **faithfulness**, and unfaithfulness involves failure to respect that right. Unfaithfulness to **Yahweh** by serving other gods has similar implications; it fails to respect Yahweh's right to allegiance and trust. Devoting to God the plunder from a war means that someone who appropriates some of the plunder fails to respect God's right to it (1 Chron. 2.7). For a king to act as if he was a priest involves similar failure (2 Chron. 26.16).

Tsiyyon (Zion)
The word is an alternative name for the city of Jerusalem. Jerusalem is more a political name; other peoples would refer to the city as 'Jerusalem'. Zion is more a religious name, a designation of the city that focuses on its being the place where **Yahweh** dwells and is worshipped.

Urim and Tummim
The Old Testament never describes the nature of these, but they were somehow means of God's guiding **Yisra'el (Israel)**. It seems they were something like two rocks that had marks on them signifying yes and no. You could ask God a question and if you got two yeses or two nos, God's answer was clear; if you got a mixed message, that meant God was not answering.

Yah
Either an earlier version of the name of God, of which **Yahweh** is then an elaboration (cf. the story in Exod. 3), or an abbreviation of the longer name.

Yahweh
In most English Bibles, the word 'Lord' often comes in all capitals like that, as does also sometimes the word 'God' in similar format. These actually represent the name of God, Yahweh. In later Old Testament times, Israelites stopped using the name Yahweh and started to refer to Yahweh as 'the Lord'. There may be two reasons. They wanted other people to recognize that Yahweh was the one true God, but this strange foreign-sounding name could give the impression that Yahweh was just **Yisra'el's (Israel's)** tribal god. A term such as 'the Lord' was one anyone could recognize. In addition, they did not want to fall foul of the warning in the Ten Commandments about misusing Yahweh's **name**. Translations into other languages then followed suit and substituted an expression such as 'the Lord' for the name Yahweh. The downsides are that this obscures the fact that God wanted to be known by name, that often the text refers to Yahweh and not some other (so-called) god or lord, and that the practice gives the impression that God is much more 'lordly' and patriarchal than actually God is. (The form 'Jehovah' is not a real word but a mixture of the consonants of 'Yahweh' and the vowels of that word for 'Lord', to remind people in reading Scripture that they should say 'the Lord', not the actual name.)

Yahweh of Armies
This title for God usually appears in English Bibles as 'the Lord of Hosts', but it is a more puzzling expression than that implies. The word for Lord is actually the **name** of God, **Yahweh**, and the word for Hosts is the regular Hebrew word for armies; it is the word that appears on the back of an Israeli military vehicle. So more literally the expression means 'Yahweh [of] Armies', which is just as odd in **Hebrew** as 'Goldingay of Armies' would be. Yet in general terms its likely implication is clear; it suggests that Yahweh is the embodiment of or controller of all war-making power, in heaven or on earth.

Yahweh's day
See **day of the Lord**.

Yehudah (Judah)
One of the twelve sons of Jacob, then the clan that traces its ancestry to him, then the dominant clan in the southern of the two states after the time of Solomon. Later, as a **Parsite (Persian)** province or colony, it was known in **Aramaic** as Yehud. Later still, the Roman province known as Judea also included much of the area of **Ephrayim (Ephraim)/Shomron (Samaria)**. In the context of the Old Testament, it's thus less confusing to refer to Judah and to Judahites, not Judeans.

Yisra'el (Israel)
Originally, 'Israel' was the new name God gave Abraham's grandson, Jacob. His twelve sons were then forefathers of the 12 clans that comprise the people Israel. In the time of Saul and David these twelve clans became more of a political entity. So Israel was both the people of God and a nation or state like other nations or states. After Solomon's day, this state split into two separate states, **Ephrayim (Ephraim)** and **Yehudah (Judah)**. Because Ephraim was far the bigger, it often continued to be referred to as Israel. So if one is thinking of the people of God, Judah is part of Israel. If one is thinking politically, Judah is not part of Israel. Once Ephraim has gone out of existence, then for practical purposes Judah *is* Israel, as the people of God.

THE NEW TESTAMENT FOR EVERYONE

TOM WRIGHT

Preface to the New Testament for Everyone

The first thing that happened in the life of the church was *translation*. On the Day of Pentecost, God's powerful wind swept through Jesus' followers, filling them, like the sails of a great ocean-going sailing ship, so that they could take God's good news to the ends of the earth. And they found themselves speaking other languages, so that everyone in the crowd could understand.

Part of the point of Jesus' message, after all, is that it's about God coming to people where they are, not sitting back sternly and waiting for them to come to him. Not for nothing does John call Jesus 'the *word* of God'. There's no point speaking a word that nobody can understand.

So, right from the start, they translated. Sometimes it happened, as at Pentecost, by the direct action of the holy spirit. Mostly, though, it was through people eagerly turning the message into other languages. Much of the time, Jesus himself spoke Aramaic, an updated dialect of Hebrew, but the gospels are written in Greek. Greek was everybody's second language at the time, a bit like English in many parts of our world today. So, since the message was designed to be good news for everyone, not just native speakers of one language, it was important to translate it. Once begun, the process continued.

It took fifteen hundred years for the whole Bible to appear in English, but once that had happened – particularly through the work of one of my lifelong heroes, William Tyndale (d. 1536) – the idea caught on quickly. Several translations appeared during the sixteenth century, culminating in the King James ('Authorized') Version at the start of the seventeenth. And in the twentieth century, too, there have been several new English versions. Some have been quite strict translations, almost word for word; others have been paraphrases, trying to convey the message in a looser, less formal way.

Two questions, then: is this new version really a translation, or a paraphrase? And why do we need yet another one?

It's a translation, not a paraphrase. I have tried to stick closely to the original. But, as with all translations, even within closely related modern European languages, there are always going to be places where you simply can't do it word by word. To do so would be 'correct' at one level and deeply incorrect at another. There is no 'safe' option: all translation is risky, but it's a risk we have to take.

This is particularly so when the language in question is, in the technical sense, 'dead'. Nobody today speaks first-century Greek, so we can't simply phone a native speaker and ask what they mean by a particular phrase. Even if we could do so, there's no guarantee that the person we called would necessarily understand all that a New Testament writer has put into a word, phrase or sentence. The New Testament, after all, is telling a story which is deeply rooted in the ancient scriptures of Israel. Often its key technical terms mean something more like their equivalents in Hebrew than their regular usage in secular, non-Christian Greek.

Greek often goes quite easily into English, but not always. A couple of examples may help, one about little words and one about big ones.

Greek often uses little words to join sentences together; English often makes do with punctuation. (That last sentence is a good example: I could have written '*but* English often makes do with punctuation', but the semicolon does the job more elegantly.) St Paul, in particular, uses the little word *gar* a great deal to connect his sentences, and English versions often translate it as 'for' in the sense of 'because'. But people today don't often use the word 'for' in that way. It sounds formal and stilted, especially if you repeat it over and over as Paul does. People don't say it much in conversation, and a lot of the New Testament is more like conversation than like a great literary work. So, on various occasions, I have done it differently. 'If by the Spirit you put to death the deeds of the body, you will live,' writes Paul in Romans 8.13–14 in the NRSV translation, '*for* all who are led by the Spirit of God are children of God.' I decided, instead of that 'for', to put in the colloquial English 'you see': 'all who are led by the spirit of God, *you see*, are God's children.' Or, sometimes, I have linked the two points by asking a question, and answering it: 'there is no condemnation for those who are in the Messiah, Jesus! *Why not? Because* the law of the spirit of life in the Messiah, Jesus, released you from the law of sin and death' (Romans 8.1–2). That 'Why not? Because . . . ' is how I'd say it, if I were Paul giving a lecture.

Or take the bigger words. Some of the great New Testament words are like ships loaded with several different kinds of cargo, and we simply haven't got words that can carry all that freight today. Thus, for instance, the English word 'righteousness' has been a technical term in theology for many years, and has often been used to translate the Greek *dikaiosynē*. But for many English speakers today it means *self*-righteousness: it's become a proud, 'churchy' sort of word. So what are the alternatives? We simply haven't got them. We want a word that can pack 'justice', 'covenant faithfulness', and 'right standing or relationship' all into the same hold, and can set off, with this cargo safely on board, to sail around the world. There isn't such a word. So I have done my best to bring out the different flavour which *dikaiosynē* seems to carry in this or that passage. I have done the same with *Christos*: most translations simply say 'Christ', but most modern English speakers assume that that word is simply a proper name (as though 'Jesus' were Jesus' 'Christian' name and 'Christ' were his 'surname'). For all sorts of reasons, I disagree; so I have experimented not only with 'Messiah' (which is what the word literally means) but sometimes, too, with 'King'. These experiments are risky. But they also present a glorious opportunity.

It's an opportunity (here is the answer to the second question, why yet another translation?) because translating the New Testament is something that, in fact, each generation ought to be doing. This is a special, peculiar and exciting point about the very nature of Christian faith. Just as Jesus taught us to pray for our *daily* bread, our bread for each day, we can never simply live on yesterday's bread, on the interpretations and translations of previous generations. To be sure, we can and must learn from those who have gone before us in the faith. But they themselves would tell us that living faith requires that we do business with God for ourselves. Inherited spiritual capital may help to get you started, but you need to do fresh work for yourself, to think things through, to struggle and pray and ponder and try things out. And a new translation, as carefully faithful as it ought to be but also as open to new possibilities as it needs to be, is a key tool for that larger task.

There are two ways to use a tool like this. First, it's good to read right through chapters, sections and entire books at a single sitting. The 'books' which make up the New Testament weren't written to be read in ten-verse sections at a time; imagine what would happen if you tried to listen to a symphony that way, or to read a novel at the rate of a single page once a week. I hope this present translation will make it easier for people to do this, to feel the flow and pull, the energy and power, of large chunks at a time.

But, second, it's always worth sitting down with a short passage and studying it intensely, trying to work out precisely what is meant by each sentence, each phrase, each word. And for that (even if you know Greek itself, but especially if you don't) you should always have at least two English translations open in front of you. No one translation – certainly not this one – will be able to give you everything which was there in the Greek. But I hope this one will take its place as one of the two or three that will help the next generation to do its own homework, to acquire its own first-hand, rather than second-hand, understanding of what the New Testament said in its own world, and what it urgently wants to say in ours.

That sense of urgency, indeed, has pushed me into a less formal and academic, and a more deliberately energetic, style. Most of the New Testament isn't 'great literature' in terms of the high standards of the day. Mark's gospel is more like a revolutionary tract; Paul's letters, though capable of poetic brilliance, often seem to reflect the kind of animated discussion you might have after a lecture in a crowded room. Again, it has seemed to me more important to convey that sense of excitement than to imitate the more formal, somewhat stately English prose we know from the traditions of the King James or Revised Standard Versions, good in their way though they have been.

This has affected all kinds of decisions: for instance, how to reproduce Jesus' discussions and debates. We simply don't say, in today's English, 'Jesus answered and said to them, "Go and tell

John what you have seen and heard"'. As with a novel, we'd be much more likely to say, '"Go and tell John", replied Jesus, "what you've seen and heard."' So that's what I've done. I think it makes quite a difference as to how we hear, and feel, the whole story.

In particular, this translation was made originally in order to accompany a series of 'guides' or popular commentaries on the New Testament. This series (*Matthew for Everyone* and the rest) was itself designed for people who would never normally read a 'biblical commentary', but who just wanted some help to get into the text for themselves. People like that might well have been confused if I'd always been saying 'Well, the RSV says this, the NIV says that, but I'm telling you something different.' I wanted to comment on a text without having to make that kind of remark all the time. Equally, as with all translations ever made, I have taken a particular view on point after point of interpretation, and my understanding of the many controversial passages in the New Testament shows up, naturally enough, in the translation as well.

A couple of final comments. First, all translations of the New Testament depend on other people's work in producing editions of the Greek New Testament from the literally thousands of manuscripts that have survived from the first few centuries. From time to time, I have had to make tricky decisions about which text to follow, but in a work of this sort I haven't wanted to distract the reader by inserting notes saying, 'other ancient authorities say . . .'. For that you will have to look elsewhere. In the same way, sometimes whole verses were added to biblical manuscripts, often by scribes who remembered (say) the equivalent passage in Mark to the one they were transcribing from Matthew, or vice versa. Thus, for instance, Matthew 6.15 has crept into some manuscripts of Mark 11, creating an extra verse (26). Modern editions leave these 'extra' verses out, because they aren't there in the best and earliest manuscripts. But occasionally this means that the verse-numbering has to skip, since the numbering was done several centuries ago before these much better manuscripts turned up. Again, translations which include footnotes will make this clear. There are two extra 'endings' for Mark's gospel. They are not found in the best manuscripts. Most likely the original version was damaged; this often happened to scrolls. (Some think Mark intended to stop with 16.8, but I consider this less likely.) Then, some time later, two copyists decided to add 'endings' to round the story off, and these found their way into the manuscript tradition. The shorter of the two endings (printed in double square brackets) doesn't have a verse number. The second is known as Mark 16.9–20.

Finally, I have tried to use gender-neutral language throughout when referring to human beings. Sometimes this has been, to put it mildly, quite difficult. I have often had to use what some people regard as an ugly and ungrammatical form, saying 'they' rather than 'he or she'. This is a classic example of what happens when a language is going through a time of change. That can't be helped. Indeed, it is because languages are constantly changing that we regularly need fresh translations.

My hope and prayer for this book is that many people will discover through it just how exciting and relevant the New Testament really is. If it helps the church as a whole, and individuals within it, to be refreshed in their faith and reinvigorated to take forward God's mission in tomorrow's world, I will be delighted. I have had the amazing privilege of spending the best years of my life studying and teaching the New Testament in both church circles and academic settings, and I hope that this translation will enable that work to reach a wider audience.

I am extremely grateful to my friends and publishers at SPCK in London, especially Simon Kingston and Joanna Moriarty, who commissioned the For Everyone series in the first place and have provided constant encouragement all the way through. And I am very grateful to HarperOne in San Francisco, especially Mickey Maudlin and Mark Tauber, for their publishing this translation in the USA. If only all working relationships could be as happy. I owe a special, enormous debt of gratitude to Dr Michael Lakey of Ripon College Cuddesdon who, in the last stages before publication, has worked through the whole text with a meticulous eye, a theologian's heart, and a grammarian's delight in the precise nuance of language. He has not only rescued me from a few howlers but gently suggested numerous excellent emendations. The mistakes that remain are my own, some of them the result of my not taking his advice.

Finally, in connection with my constant attempt to write clear, brisk English, I should also mention my beloved wife and children. They have regularly stopped me from using long, fuzzy words where short, sharp ones would do instead. This version of the New Testament is dedicated to them in gratitude and love.

Introduction to the New Testament for Everyone

We call them 'books', but the twenty-seven writings that make up the 'New Testament' are much shorter than most 'books' in our world. The longest are about the same length as a short modern paperback; the shortest would struggle to fill a single page in a magazine. But in the first-century world a 'book' usually meant a scroll, a roll of parchment with a stick attached at either end, usually written on one side only. Such 'books' had to be fairly short to avoid getting too bulky; the longest of the New Testament books included about as much as a long scroll could hold.

The early followers of Jesus saw the books that were written about him, and the writings of the first generation or so of his followers, as the indispensable framework for understanding who Jesus really was, what he had achieved in launching God's kingdom 'on earth as in heaven', and what they were called to be and to do as a result. These early writings mattered, in other words, because Jesus matters. He had claimed to be renewing God's covenant ('testament') with Israel, and through Israel with the whole creation; the early Christians believed he had indeed done so. Hence 'new covenant' or 'new testament'. These books are central to all Christian understanding and living because of the centrality of the Jesus to whom they bear witness.

These books offer, in particular, a framework for understanding what the word 'God' itself actually means. At the heart of the New Testament, glimpsed in story, poetry and vision, is the sense that with Jesus, and with his powerful spirit, the one God who had created the world had made himself known in a new way by rescuing that world. This one God was known in worship, but was to be known too in understanding, in thinking things through with the 'renewed mind', as Paul puts it (see Romans 12.2). The writers of these books wanted their hearers (the books were written to be read out loud) not only to think new thoughts about these key topics but *to think in a whole new way*, a way which combined rigorous intellectual engagement with the disciplined imagination of the artist and the praying heart of the believer.

We may suspect that this combination was as challenging to the early Christians as it is for many today. But, they might have said, come into the house by whichever door is the most natural for you, and these books will draw you into the other rooms as well. And the 'house' with these doors, and these rooms, is the home of the one true God, where we all are invited as honoured guests; guests who then discover they are part of the family. The New Testament is designed to issue that invitation, to offer that welcome, and to explain what it all means.

The gospels

For many people, the most natural starting point will be one or other of the four gospels, the books which stand at the head of the New Testament. These offer 'the story of Jesus'; but like all good stories they are much more than just a string of events. For a start, they tell the story of Jesus *as the fulfilment of the ancient story of Israel*. Matthew begins with the genealogy that runs from Abraham to David, from David to the exile in Babylon, and then from David to the Messiah who would save his people and, thereby, the whole world. Mark opens with the prophecies of Isaiah and Malachi that look ahead to the one God renewing the covenant at last; Luke, with a personal story that echoes the books of Samuel, introducing John the Baptist as the one who summed up the Old Covenant dispensation and ushered in the New. John opens with a clear echo of Genesis 1.1 ('in the beginning'): this is the start of the new creation itself.

But there's more. The four gospels also tell the story of Jesus as the story of how the dark forces of evil, active in the wider world, seemed to converge onto a point when Jesus was announcing God's kingdom. Herod the Great, and his son Herod Antipas, loom up threateningly; the populist pressure group called the 'Pharisees' are constantly trying to catch Jesus out and accuse him; tormented souls shriek at him, sneering aristocrats mock him, his own followers misunderstand him and one of them ends up betraying him to the authorities. The Roman governor sums it all up, sending Jesus to his undeserved death. The gospel writers see all this as part of the point: evil gathers itself together and does its worst to Jesus, so that, when he dies under its weight, evil itself loses its ultimate power. That is why, then, the story of Jesus' resurrection from the dead, coming at the conclusion of all four gospels, is not simply a strange 'happy ending' after the crucifixion. It is the launching of God's new creation. This is, indeed, the underlying message of the whole 'New Testament': Israel's God has acted in and through Jesus to renew the covenant with Israel and so to open the way for new creation to be born.

That is why, ultimately, the four gospels demand to be read as the story of *how God became King*. ('What?' people ask. 'Is God not already King?' 'Yes,' answer the gospels, 'but his role has been usurped by the power of evil, and this is the story of how he overcame evil and won back his rightful rule.') They tell the story of Jesus announcing that 'the time is fulfilled' for God's kingdom to appear on earth as in heaven, a reference to scriptural prophecies, especially in the book of Daniel. They also portray Jesus as constantly redefining what that 'kingdom' would look like, through stories and acted symbols, especially healings and celebrations with the 'wrong' kind of people: a very different 'kingdom', then, from the national and military revolution many of his contemporaries were expecting. Throughout, Jesus was talking about 'God's kingdom' *to explain what he himself was doing*, and the four gospel writers put the picture together, particularly through their allusions to Israel's scriptures: this, they are saying, is what it looked like when *Israel's God came back in person to rescue his people and the world*.

The four gospels are thus many-layered stories, which can be read simply to find out 'what happened' but also, in more depth, to discover 'what it meant'. There is no agreement about their date. Many think Mark was the first to be written; it is certainly the shortest, and has a clipped, punchy style, getting straight to the point. Matthew's more leisurely presentation, taking the time to lay out Jesus' public career and teaching in a way which evokes more explicitly the great traditions of Israel, particularly the law of Moses, shows Jesus as the Emmanuel, the God-with-us person, fulfilling every aspect of the scriptural promises up to and including his elevation, as Israel's Messiah, to sovereignty over the whole world. Luke sets Jesus within the wider world of the non-Jewish nations: the story of Israel now fulfilled for the sake of the world. John's breathtaking vision of new creation focuses on Jesus as the true 'Temple', the place where heaven and earth come together, through which his followers are themselves commissioned to be heaven-and-earth people, animated by the new breath of the spirit.

All four gospels, finally, are written in such a way as to show how the movement of Jesus' followers began, and why it must take a certain shape. The mission, the unity, the prayerfulness and the obedience of the church all begin with Jesus' call to the first disciples. They, like the ancient Israelites through the events of the exodus, will discover who they really are through Jesus' own Passover, his final meal which interprets in advance his death and resurrection. The gospels thus invite their readers not just to look back at far-off events – though it matters that those events were unique and unrepeatable – but also to live within the story as it moves forward, or, perhaps better, to allow this story to live in fresh ways in and through them.

The letters

Letters, an obvious substitute for personal presence, mattered more in the ancient world than in today's world of telephones and email. A letter written in, say, Ephesus might take a week to arrive in Corinth by sea, or a month if sent overland, so a writer like Paul would plan thoughtfully what to say. Some of his letters may have been written in a hurry, but in many cases, above all in Romans, it looks as though he has mapped it out carefully and taken pains with the structure and balance.

The letters written by Paul and others were not, however, designed to be systematic presentations of all that the early Christians believed. Not even Romans, Paul's most 'systematic' letter, is like that. The letters cover many topics, but they aim to meet particular needs and challenges and to warn of specific problems and difficulties. In particular, they are regularly attempting, not to close off further thought but to teach the hearers *how to think for themselves* as spirit-led, Jesus-focused communities. No letter could possibly cover everything the writer might have wanted to say; Paul and the others wanted people to take what had been written and to work things out from there. Paul urged his hearers to 'grow up in their thinking'; to be 'transformed by the renewing of the mind'. The letters were an aid to that, not a substitute for it.

There are thirteen letters ascribed to Paul. There is no agreement as to whether he wrote them all, but most would say that the disputed ones come at least from sources close to him. It is actually quite easy to fit the letters (except the 'Pastorals', that is, the two letters to Timothy and the one to Titus) into the narrative of Acts. Thus, if the Pastorals were written by Paul they must reflect a further journey or journeys after the conclusion of Acts, and we must also suppose that Paul had changed his style and tone somewhat.

Paul's letters are, in fact, the only parts of the New Testament which we may date reasonably securely. In my judgment, Galatians is the earliest, written most likely in AD 48; 1 and 2 Thessalonians are written around 50, with 1 Corinthians following in 52–53 and then the 'prison letters' being written from Ephesus in 53–54 (Philippians, Colossians and Philemon, with Ephesians being a circular written to many churches in the region of western Turkey). Then, after Paul's release, he writes 2 Corinthians – the most painful of his letters – while on his way to Corinth for the last time; then, as he is leaving Greece for his journey to Jerusalem and then Rome, he writes Romans. Other schemes are possible but this one has the merit of simplicity and coherence.

The main themes of Paul's letters, and indeed all the other letters in the New Testament, focus on Jesus himself: Jesus as the embodiment of Israel's God, returning to rescue his people and the world; Jesus as Israel's Messiah, summing up in himself the covenantal obedience of Israel from Abraham onwards; Jesus whose death and resurrection form the fulcrum of all history, opening up a new world in which the evil powers have been defeated so that idolatrous and sinful humans can be rescued from their grip; Jesus whose spirit animates the believer and the whole church in the present and will breathe new life into dead bodies at the final resurrection. Jesus, in other words, as the inaugurator of the 'new covenant' (2 Corinthians 3).

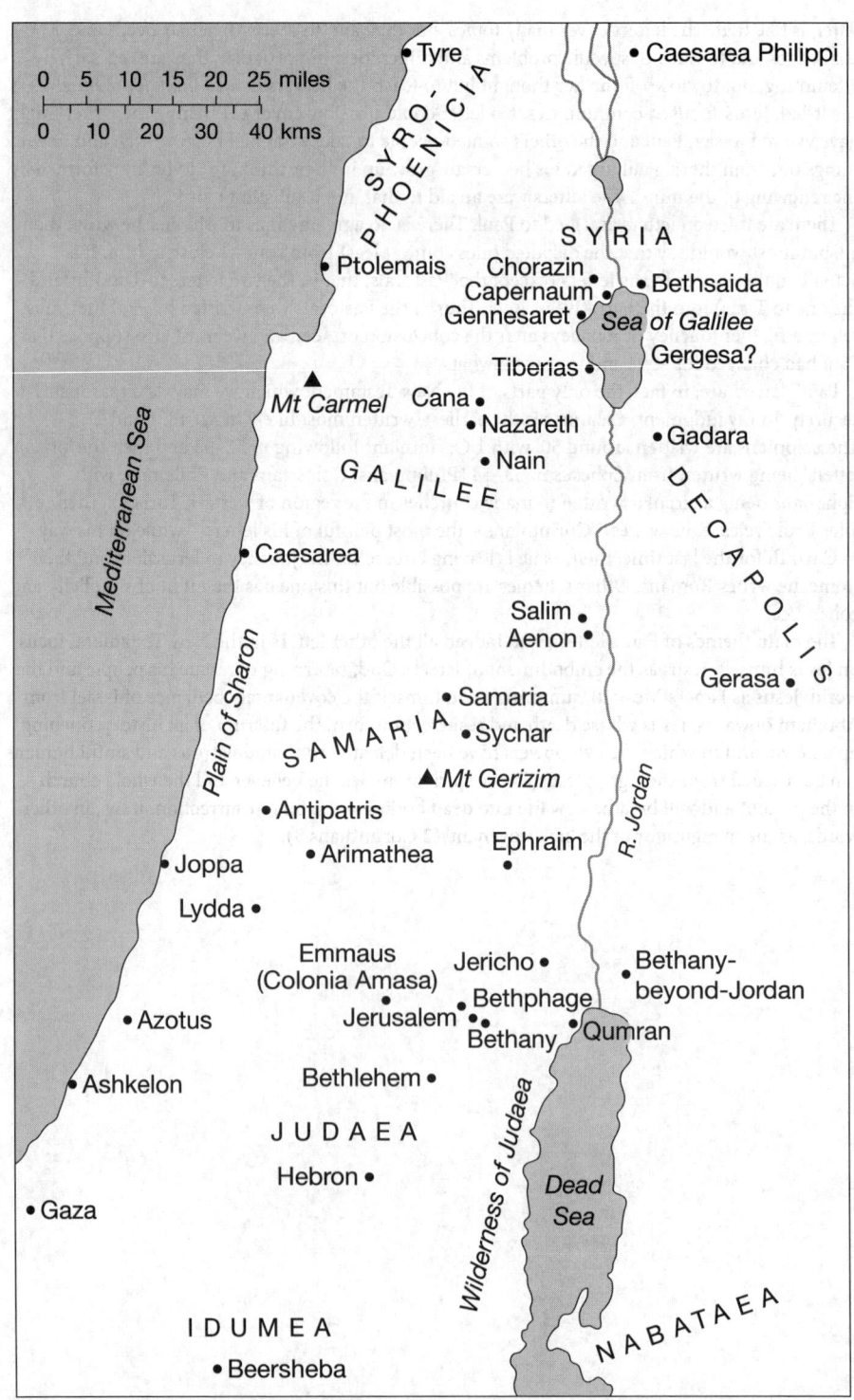

Galilee, Samaria and Judaea in the first century AD

Matthew

All four gospels are emphatically Jewish in tone and content, but Matthew's is the most obviously so. The book is structured around five blocks of Jesus' teaching, corresponding to the five books of Moses. The early chapters have Jesus re-enacting the exodus from Egypt; the closing chapters highlight Jesus' death at Passover. The book opens with a genealogy from Abraham to the Messiah, and closes with a scene echoing Daniel's picture of the enthroned son of man. Matthew repeatedly draws attention to the way in which events concerning Jesus fulfil biblical promises. At every turn he insists that Jesus is what Israel had been waiting for – even though this fulfilment turned out to be shocking.

The genealogy itself tells the whole story, for those with eyes to see. Matthew organizes it into three sequences of fourteen generations, from Abraham to David, David to the Babylonian exile, and the exile to Jesus. Abraham is the founder of the family through whom the one God would rescue the world; David is the king who is promised an heir to rule the world; the Babylonian exile is the point at which, in line with the covenantal warnings in Deuteronomy, the world seems to have won and the promise to be lost for ever. But God's faithfulness continues, and the Messiah is the one who will save his people from their sins. He inaugurates the seventh 'seven', the Jubilee of forgiveness. But the Messiah is not simply the long fulfilment of Israel's promises. He is also 'Emmanuel', 'God with us'.

The story unfolds as Jesus embodies Israel's history, going into Egypt as a baby and then returning, and then, in his baptism, re-enacting the crossing of the Red Sea and the Jordan. In his wilderness temptations, he succeeds where ancient Israel had failed. All this prepares us for Jesus' opening announcement of God's kingdom arriving on earth as in heaven, and his enactment of this, throughout the story, in powerful deeds of healing, in his feasting with tax-collectors and sinners, and in his refashioning of the kingdom-hope in sermon and parable. The five great blocks of teaching open with the Sermon on the Mount (chapters 5—7) and continue with the instructions to the disciples (chapter 10), the parables of seeds and sowing (chapter 13) and the further instructions for his followers' communal life (chapter 18), before the last block mirrors the first in its length (chapters 23—25), looking ahead with warnings and promises to the forthcoming destruction of Jerusalem and the Temple and the rescue and vindication of Jesus' followers.

Throughout the story the question of who Jesus really is, and how exactly he will bring God's kingdom, is never far away. It reaches a central climax with Peter's confession that Jesus is 'the Messiah, the son of the living God', and with the transfiguration. But Matthew leads the eye relentlessly towards the final events of Jesus' dramatic entry into Jerusalem, his action in the Temple, the Last Supper, and the arrest, trial and crucifixion. Matthew makes it clear that these events all interpret one another, and together point to the long-awaited act of divine and messianic rescue: the forces of evil do their worst and are defeated. Texts from the Psalms, Isaiah, Daniel and elsewhere are drawn together to say that this is the ultimate saving act promised all along. The resurrection of Jesus is then the beginning of an entirely new phase of history for the people of God, as Jesus commissions his followers to announce the good news to the whole world.

Jesus' genealogy

1 The book of the family tree of Jesus the Messiah, the son of David, the son of Abraham.

²Abraham became the father of Isaac, Isaac of Jacob, Jacob of Judah and his brothers, ³Judah of Peres and Zara (by Tamar), Peres of Esrom, Esrom of Aram, ⁴Aram of Aminadab, Aminadab of Naason, Naason of Salmon, ⁵Salmon of Boaz (by Rahab), Boaz of Obed (by Ruth), Obed of Jesse, ⁶and Jesse of David the king.

David was the father of Solomon (by the wife of Uriah), ⁷Solomon of Rehoboam, Rehoboam of Abijah, Abijah of Asaph, ⁸Asaph of Jehosaphat, Jehosaphat of Joram, Joram of Uzziah, ⁹Uzziah of Joatham, Joatham of Ahaz, Ahaz of Hezekiah, ¹⁰Hezekiah of Manasseh, Manasseh of Amoz, Amoz of Josiah, ¹¹Josiah of Jeconiah and his brothers, at the time of the exile in Babylon.

¹²After the Babylonian exile, Jeconiah became the father of Salathiel, Salathiel of Zerubbabel, ¹³Zerubbabel of Abioud, Abioud of Eliakim, Eliakim of Azor, ¹⁴Azor of Sadok, Sadok of Achim, Achim of Elioud, ¹⁵Elioud of Eleazar, Eleazar of Matthan, Matthan of Jacob, ¹⁶and Jacob of Joseph the husband of Mary, from whom was born Jesus, who is called 'Messiah'.

¹⁷So all the generations from Abraham to David add up to fourteen; from David to the Babylonian exile, fourteen generations; and from the Babylonian exile to the Messiah, fourteen generations.

The birth of Jesus

¹⁸This was how the birth of Jesus the Messiah took place. His mother, Mary, was engaged to Joseph; but before they came together she turned out to be pregnant – by the holy spirit. ¹⁹Joseph, her husband-to-be, was an upright man. He didn't want to make a public example of her. So he decided to set the marriage aside privately. ²⁰But, while he was considering this, an angel of the Lord suddenly appeared to him in a dream.

'Joseph, son of David,' the angel said, 'don't be afraid to get married to Mary. The child she is carrying is from the holy spirit. ²¹She is going to have a son. You are to give him the name Jesus; he is the one who will save his people from their sins.'

²²All this happened so that what the Lord said through the prophet might be fulfilled: ²³'Look: the virgin is pregnant, and will have a son, and they shall give him the name Emmanuel,' – which means, in translation, 'God with us'.

²⁴When Joseph woke up from his sleep he did what the Lord's angel had told him to. He married his wife, ²⁵but he didn't have sexual relations with her until after the birth of her son. And he gave him the name Jesus.

The Magi visit Jesus

2 When Jesus was born, in Bethlehem of Judaea, at the time when Herod was king, some wise and learned men came to Jerusalem from the East.

²'Where is the one', they asked, 'who has been born to be king of the Jews? We have seen his star rising in the East, and we have come to worship him.'

³When King Herod heard this, he was very disturbed, and the whole of Jerusalem was as well. ⁴He called together all the chief priests and scribes of the people, and enquired from them where the Messiah was to be born.

⁵'In Bethlehem of Judaea,' they replied. 'That's what it says in the prophet:

⁶You, Bethlehem, in Judah's land
are not the least of Judah's princes;
from out of you will come the ruler
who will shepherd Israel my people.'

⁷Then Herod called the wise men to him in secret. He found out from them precisely when the star had appeared. ⁸Then he sent them to Bethlehem.

'Off you go,' he said, 'and make a thorough search for the child. When you find him, report back to me, so that I can come and worship him too.'

⁹When they heard what the king said, they set off. There was the star, the one they had seen rising in the East, going ahead of them! It went and stood still over the place where the child was. ¹⁰When they saw the star, they were

beside themselves with joy and excitement. ¹¹They went into the house and saw the child, with Mary his mother, and they fell down and worshipped him. They opened their treasure-chests, and gave him presents: gold, frankincense and myrrh.

¹²They were warned in a dream not to go back to Herod. So they returned to their own country by a different route.

Travels to Egypt

¹³After the Magi had gone, suddenly an angel of the Lord appeared to Joseph in a dream.

'Get up,' he said, 'and take the child, and his mother, and hurry off to Egypt. Stay there until I tell you. Herod is going to hunt for the child, to kill him.'

¹⁴So he got up and took the child and his mother by night, and went off to Egypt. ¹⁵He stayed there until the death of Herod. This happened to fulfil what the Lord said through the prophet:

Out of Egypt I called my son.

¹⁶When Herod saw that he had been tricked by the Magi, he flew into a towering rage. He dispatched people to kill all the boys in Bethlehem, and in all its surrounding districts, from two years old and under, according to the time the Magi had told him. ¹⁷That was when the word that came through Jeremiah the prophet was fulfilled:

¹⁸There was heard a voice in Rama,
crying and loud lamentation.
Rachel is weeping for her children,
and will not let anyone comfort her,
because they are no more.

¹⁹After the death of Herod, suddenly an angel of the Lord appeared in a dream to Joseph in Egypt.

²⁰'Get up,' he said, 'and take the child and his mother and go to the land of Israel. Those who wanted to kill the child are dead.'

²¹So he got up, took the child and his mother, and went to the land of Israel. ²²But when he heard that Archelaus was ruling Judaea instead of his father Herod, he was afraid to go back there. After being advised in a dream, he went off to the region of Galilee. ²³When he got there, he settled in a town called Nazareth. This was to fulfil what the prophet had spoken:

He shall be called a Nazorean.

The preaching of John the Baptist

3 In those days John the Baptist appeared. He was preaching in the Judaean wilderness.

²'Repent!' he was saying. 'The kingdom of heaven is coming!'

³John, you see, is the person spoken of by Isaiah the prophet, when he said,

The voice of someone shouting in the desert:
'Prepare the route that the Lord will take,
straighten out his paths!'

⁴John himself had clothing made from camel's hair, and a leather belt around his waist. His food was locusts and wild honey. ⁵Jerusalem, and all Judaea, and the whole area around the Jordan, were going off to him. ⁶They were being baptized by him in the river Jordan, confessing their sins.

⁷He saw several Pharisees and Sadducees coming to be baptized by him.

'You brood of vipers!' he said to them. 'Who warned you to escape from the coming wrath? ⁸You'd better prove your repentance by bearing the right sort of fruit! ⁹And you needn't start thinking to yourselves, "We have Abraham as our father." Let me tell you, God is quite capable of raising up children for Abraham from these stones! ¹⁰The axe is already taking aim at the root of the tree. Every tree that doesn't produce good fruit is to be cut down and thrown into the fire.'

Jesus' baptism

¹¹'I am baptizing you with water, for repentance,' John continued. 'But the one who is coming behind me is more powerful than me! I'm not even worthy to carry his sandals. He will baptize you with the holy spirit and

fire! ¹²He's got his shovel in his hand, ready to clear out his barn, and gather all his corn into the granary. But he'll burn up the chaff with a fire that will never go out.'

¹³Then Jesus arrived at the Jordan from Galilee, and came to John to be baptized by him.

¹⁴John tried to stop him.

'I ought to be baptized by you,' he said, 'and are you going to come to me?'

¹⁵'This is how it's got to be right now,' said Jesus. 'This is the right way for us to complete God's whole saving plan.'

So John consented, ¹⁶and Jesus was baptized. All at once, as he came up out of the water, suddenly the heavens were opened, and he saw God's spirit coming down like a dove and landing on him.

¹⁷Then there came a voice out of the heavens.

'This is my son, my beloved one,' said the voice. 'I am delighted with him.'

Temptation in the wilderness

4 Then Jesus was led out into the wilderness by the spirit to be tested by the devil. ²He fasted for forty days and forty nights, and at the end of it was famished. ³Then the tempter approached him.

'If you really are God's son,' he said, 'tell these stones to become bread!'

⁴'The Bible says', replied Jesus, 'that it takes more than bread to keep you alive. You actually live on every word that comes out of God's mouth.'

⁵Then the devil took him off to the holy city, and stood him on a pinnacle of the Temple.

⁶'If you really are God's son,' he said, 'throw yourself down. The Bible does say, after all, that "God will give his angels a command about you"; and "they will carry you in their hands, so that you won't hurt your foot against a stone."'

⁷'But the Bible also says', replied Jesus, 'that you mustn't put the Lord your God to the test!'

⁸Then the devil took him off again, this time to a very high mountain. There he showed him all the magnificent kingdoms of the world.

⁹'I'll give the whole lot to you,' he said, 'if you will fall down and worship me.'

¹⁰'Get out of it, satan!' replied Jesus. 'The Bible says, "Worship the Lord your God, and serve him alone!"'

¹¹Then the devil left him, and angels came and looked after him.

Announcing the kingdom

¹²When Jesus heard that John had been arrested, he went off to Galilee. ¹³He left Nazareth, and went to live at Capernaum, a small town by the sea in the region of Zebulon and Naphtali. ¹⁴This happened so that the word spoken through Isaiah the prophet might come true:

¹⁵The land of Zebulon and the land of Naphtali,
the road by the sea, beyond the Jordan,
Galilee, land of the nations:
¹⁶the people who sat in the dark saw a great light;
light dawned on those who sat in the shadowy
    land of death.

¹⁷From that time on Jesus began to make his proclamation.

'Repent!' he would say. 'The kingdom of heaven is arriving!'

Jesus calls the disciples

¹⁸As Jesus was walking beside the sea of Galilee he saw two brothers, Simon (also called Peter) and Andrew his brother. They were fishermen, and were casting nets into the sea.

¹⁹'Follow me!' said Jesus. 'I'll make you fish for people!'

²⁰Straight away they abandoned their nets and followed him.

²¹He went on further, and saw two other brothers, James the son of Zebedee and John his brother. They were in the boat, mending their nets, with Zebedee their father. He called them. ²²At once they left the boat, and their father, and followed him.

²³He went on through the whole of Galilee, teaching in their synagogues and proclaiming the good news of the kingdom, healing every disease and every illness among the people. ²⁴Word about him went out around the whole of Syria. They brought to him all the people tormented with various kinds of diseases and ailments, demon-possessed people, epileptics, and paralytics, and he healed them. ²⁵Large crowds followed him

from Galilee, the Ten Towns, Jerusalem, Judaea and beyond the Jordan.

The Beatitudes

5 When Jesus saw the crowds, he went up the hillside, and sat down. His disciples came to him. ²He took a deep breath, and began his teaching:

³'Blessings on the poor in spirit! The kingdom of heaven is yours.

⁴'Blessings on the mourners! You're going to be comforted.

⁵'Blessings on the meek! You're going to inherit the earth.

⁶'Blessings on people who hunger and thirst for God's justice! You're going to be satisfied.

⁷'Blessings on the merciful! You'll receive mercy yourselves.

⁸'Blessings on the pure in heart! You will see God.

⁹'Blessings on the peacemakers! You'll be called God's children.

¹⁰'Blessings on people who are persecuted because of God's way! The kingdom of heaven belongs to you.

¹¹'Blessings on you, when people slander you and persecute you, and say all kinds of wicked things about you falsely because of me! ¹²Celebrate and rejoice: there's a great reward for you in heaven. That's how they persecuted the prophets who went before you.'

Fulfilling the law

¹³'You're the salt of the earth! But if the salt becomes tasteless, how is it going to get salty again? It's no good for anything. You might as well throw it out and walk all over it.

¹⁴'You're the light of the world! A city can't be hidden if it's on top of a hill. ¹⁵People don't light a lamp and put it under a bucket; they put it on a lampstand. Then it gives light to everybody in the house. ¹⁶That's how you must shine your light in front of people! Then they will see what wonderful things you do, and they'll give glory to your father in heaven.

¹⁷'Don't suppose that I came to destroy the law or the prophets. I didn't come to destroy them; I came to fulfil them! ¹⁸I'm telling you the truth: until heaven and earth disappear, not one stroke, not one dot, is going to disappear from the law, until it's all come true. ¹⁹So anyone who relaxes a single one of these commandments, even the little ones, and teaches that to people, will be called least in the kingdom of heaven. But anyone who does them and teaches them will be called great in the kingdom of heaven.

²⁰'Yes, let me tell you: unless your covenant behaviour is far superior to that of the scribes and Pharisees, you will never get in to the kingdom of heaven.'

On murder and reconciliation

²¹'You heard that it was said to the ancient people, "You shall not murder"; and anyone who commits murder shall be liable to judgment. ²²But I say to you that everyone who is angry with his brother shall be liable to judgment; anyone who uses foul and abusive language will be liable to the lawcourt; and anyone who says, "You fool", will be liable to the fires of Gehenna.

²³'So, if you are coming to the altar with your gift, and there you remember that your brother has a grievance against you, ²⁴leave your gift right there in front of the altar, and go first and be reconciled to your brother. Then come back and offer your gift. ²⁵Make friends with your opponent quickly, while you are with him in the street, in case your opponent hands you over to the judge, and the judge to the officer, and you find yourself being thrown into jail. ²⁶I'm telling you the truth: you won't get out until you've paid every last copper coin.'

On adultery and oaths

²⁷'You heard', Jesus continued, 'that it was said, "You shall not commit adultery." ²⁸But I say to you: everyone who gazes at a woman in order to lust after her has already committed adultery with her in his heart. ²⁹If your right eye trips you up, tear it out and throw it away. Yes: it's better for you to have one part of your body destroyed than for the whole body to be thrown into Gehenna. ³⁰And if your right hand trips you up, cut it off and throw it away.

Yes: it's better for you to have one part of your body destroyed than for your whole body to go into Gehenna.

³¹'It was also said, "If someone divorces his wife, he should give her a legal document to prove it." ³²But I say to you: everyone who divorces his wife, unless it's in connection with immorality, makes her commit adultery; and anyone who marries a divorced woman commits adultery.

³³'Again, you heard that it was said to the people long ago: "You shall not swear falsely, but you shall give to the Lord what you promised under oath." ³⁴But I say to you: don't swear at all! Don't swear by heaven (it's God's throne!); ³⁵don't swear by the earth (it's God's footstool!); don't swear by Jerusalem (it's the city of the great king!); ³⁶don't swear by your head (you can't make one hair of it turn white or black!). ³⁷When you're talking, say "Yes" when you mean Yes, and "No" when you mean No. Anything more than that comes from the evil one.'

Loving your enemies

³⁸'You heard that it was said, "An eye for an eye, and a tooth for a tooth." ³⁹But I say to you: don't use violence to resist evil! Instead, when someone hits you on the right cheek, turn the other one towards him. ⁴⁰When someone wants to sue you and take your shirt, let him have your cloak, too. ⁴¹And when someone forces you to go one mile, go a second one with him. ⁴²Give to anyone who asks you, and don't refuse someone who wants to borrow from you.

⁴³'You heard that it was said, "Love your neighbour and hate your enemy." ⁴⁴But I tell you: love your enemies! Pray for people who persecute you! ⁴⁵That way, you'll be children of your father in heaven! After all, he makes his sun rise on bad and good alike, and sends rain both on the upright and on the unjust. ⁴⁶Look at it like this: if you love those who love you, do you expect a special reward? Even tax-collectors do that, don't they? ⁴⁷And if you only greet your own family, what's so special about that? Even Gentiles do that, don't they? ⁴⁸Well then: you must be perfect, just as your heavenly father is perfect.'

Piety in secret

6 'When you are practising your piety, mind you don't do it with an eye on the audience! Otherwise, you won't have any reward from your father in heaven.

²'So when you give money to the poor, don't sound a trumpet in front of you. That's what people do when they're just play-acting, in the synagogues and the streets. They do it so that people will be impressed at them. I'm telling you the truth: they've received their reward in full. ³No: when you give money, don't let your left hand have any idea what your right hand is up to. ⁴That way, your giving will be in secret. And your father, who sees in secret, will repay you.

⁵'When you pray, you mustn't be like the play-actors. They love to pray standing in the synagogues and on street corners, so that people will notice them. I'm telling you the truth: they have received their reward in full. ⁶No: when you pray, go into your own room, shut the door, and pray to your father who is there in secret. And your father, who sees in secret, will repay you.'

The Lord's Prayer

⁷'When you pray, don't pile up a jumbled heap of words! That's what the Gentiles do. They reckon that the more they say, the more likely they are to be heard. ⁸So don't be like them. You see, your father knows what you need before you ask him.

⁹'So this is how you should pray:

Our father in heaven,
may your name be honoured.
¹⁰May your kingdom come.
May your will be done,
as in heaven, so on earth.
¹¹Give us today the bread we need now;
¹²and forgive us the things we owe,
as we too have forgiven what was owed to us.
¹³Don't bring us into the great trial,
but rescue us from evil.

¹⁴'Yes: if you forgive people the wrong they have done, your heavenly father will forgive you as well. ¹⁵But if you don't forgive people,

neither will your heavenly father forgive you what you have done wrong.'

On fasting and lasting treasure

¹⁶'When you fast, don't be gloomy like the play-actors. They make their faces quite unrecognizable, so that everyone can see they're fasting. I'm telling you the truth: they have received their reward in full. ¹⁷No: when you fast, tidy your hair and beard the way you normally do, and wash your face, ¹⁸so that others won't notice you're fasting – except your father, privately. Then your father, who sees in private, will repay you.

¹⁹'Don't store up treasure on earth. Moths and rust will eat it away, and robbers will break in and steal it. ²⁰No: store up for yourselves treasure in heaven! Moths and rust don't eat it away there, and no robbers break in and steal it. ²¹Show me your treasure, and I'll show you where your heart is.

²²'The eye is the lamp of the body. So if your eye is honest and clear, your whole body will be full of light. ²³But if your eye is evil, your whole body is in the dark. So, if the light within you turns out to be darkness, darkness doesn't come any darker than that.

²⁴'Nobody can serve two masters. Otherwise, they will either hate the first and love the second, or be devoted to the first and despise the second. You can't serve both God and wealth.'

Do not worry

²⁵'So let me tell you: don't worry about your life – what to eat, what to drink; don't worry about your body – what to wear. There's more to life than food! There's more to the body than a suit of clothes! ²⁶Have a good look at the birds in the sky. They don't plant seeds, they don't bring in the harvest, they don't store things in barns – and your father in heaven feeds them! Think how different you are from them! ²⁷Can any of you add fifteen inches to your height just by worrying about it?

²⁸'And why worry about what to wear? Take a tip from the lilies in the countryside. They don't work; they don't weave; ²⁹but, let me tell you, not even Solomon in all his finery was dressed as well as one of these. ³⁰So if God gives that sort of clothing even to the grass in the field, which is here today and on the bonfire tomorrow, isn't he far more likely to clothe you too, you little-faith lot?

³¹'So don't worry away with your "What'll we eat?" and "What'll we drink?" and "What'll we wear?" ³²Those are all the kinds of things the Gentiles fuss about, and your heavenly father knows you need them all. ³³Instead, make your top priority God's kingdom and his way of life, and all these things will be given to you as well.

³⁴'So don't worry about tomorrow. Tomorrow can worry about itself. One day's trouble at a time is quite enough.'

On judging others

7 'Don't judge people, and you won't be judged yourself. ²You'll be judged, you see, by the judgment you use to judge others! You'll be measured by the measuring-rod you use to measure others! ³Why do you stare at the splinter in your neighbour's eye, but ignore the plank in your own? ⁴How can you say to your neighbour, "Here – let me get that splinter out of your eye," when you've got the plank in your own? ⁵You're just play-acting! First take the plank out of your own eye, and then you'll see clearly enough to take the splinter out of your neighbour's eye.

⁶'Don't give holy things to dogs. Don't throw your pearls to pigs. If you do, they will trample them under their feet – and then turn round and attack you!'

On prayer

⁷'Ask and it will be given to you! Search and you will find! Knock and the door will be opened for you! ⁸Everyone who asks receives; everyone who searches finds; everyone who knocks will have the door opened. ⁹Don't you see? Supposing your son asks you for bread – which of you is going to give him a stone? ¹⁰Or if he asks for a fish – which of you is going to give him a serpent? ¹¹Well then: if you know how to give good gifts to your children,

evil as you are, how much more will your father in heaven give good things to those who ask him!

¹²'So whatever you want people to do to you, do just that to them. Yes; this is what the law and the prophets are all about.'

The two ways

¹³'Go in by the narrow gate. The gate that leads to destruction, you see, is nice and wide, and the road going there has plenty of room. Lots of people go that way. ¹⁴But the gate leading to life is narrow, and the road going there is a tight squeeze. Not many people find their way through.

¹⁵'Watch out for false prophets. They will come to you dressed like sheep, but inside they are hungry wolves. ¹⁶You'll be able to tell them by the fruit they bear: you don't find grapes growing on thorn-bushes, do you, or figs on thistles? ¹⁷Well, in the same way, good trees produce good fruit, and bad trees produce bad fruit. ¹⁸Actually, good trees *can't* produce bad fruit, nor can bad ones produce good fruit! ¹⁹Every tree that doesn't produce good fruit is cut down and thrown on the fire. ²⁰So: you must recognize them by their fruits.

²¹'Not everyone who says to me, "Master, Master" will enter the kingdom of heaven; only people who do the will of my father in heaven. ²²On that day lots of people will say to me, "Master, Master – we prophesied in your name, didn't we? We cast out demons in your name! We performed lots of powerful deeds in your name!"

²³'Then I will have to say to them, "'I never knew you! You're a bunch of evildoers – go away from me!"'

True obedience

²⁴'So, then, everyone who hears these words of mine and does them will be like a wise man who built his house on the rock. ²⁵Heavy rain fell; floods rose up; the winds blew and beat on that house. It didn't fall, because it was founded on the rock. ²⁶And everyone who hears these words of mine and doesn't do them – they will be like a foolish man who built his house on sand. ²⁷Heavy rain fell; floods rose up; the winds blew and battered the house – and down it fell! It fell with a great crash.'

²⁸And so it was, when Jesus finished these words, that the crowds were astonished at his teaching. ²⁹He was teaching them, you see, on his own authority, not like their scribes used to do.

Two healings

8 When Jesus came down from the hillside, large crowds followed him. ²Suddenly someone with a virulent skin disease approached, and knelt down in front of him.

'Master,' he said, 'if you want, you can make me clean!'

³Jesus stretched out his hand and touched him.

'I do want to,' he said. 'Be clean!'

At once his disease was cured.

⁴'Take care', Jesus said to him, 'that you don't say anything to anyone. Instead, go and show yourself to the priest, and make the offering which Moses commanded. That will be a proof to them.'

⁵Jesus went into Capernaum. A centurion came up and pleaded with him.

⁶'Master,' he said, 'my servant is lying at home, paralysed. He's in a very bad state.'

⁷'I'll come and make him better,' said Jesus.

⁸'Master,' replied the centurion, 'I don't deserve to have you come under my roof! Just say the word, and my servant will be healed. ⁹I know what authority's all about, you know – I've got soldiers answering to me, and I can say to one of them, "Go!" and he goes, and to another one, "Come here!" and he comes, and I can say, "Do this," to my slave, and he does it!'

¹⁰Jesus was fair amazed when he heard this.

'I'm telling you the truth,' he said to the people who were following. 'I haven't found faith like this – not even in Israel! ¹¹Let me tell you this: lots of people will come from East and West and join the great party of celebration with Abraham, Isaac and Jacob in the kingdom of heaven. ¹²But the children of the kingdom will be thrown into outer darkness, where people will weep and gnash their teeth.'

¹³Then he turned to the centurion.

'Go home,' he said. 'Let it be for you as you believed.'

And his servant was healed at that very moment.

On following Jesus

¹⁴Jesus went into Peter's house. There he saw Peter's mother-in-law laid low with a fever. ¹⁵He touched her hand. The fever left her, and she got up and waited on him.

¹⁶When evening came, they brought to him many people who were possessed by demons. He cast out the spirits with a word of command, and healed everyone who was sick. ¹⁷This happened so that the word spoken by Isaiah the prophet might come true:

> He himself took our weaknesses
> and bore our diseases.

¹⁸When Jesus saw the crowd all around him, he told them to go across to the other side of the lake. ¹⁹A scribe came up and spoke to him.

'Teacher,' he said, 'I will follow you wherever you go!'

²⁰'Foxes have their dens,' replied Jesus, 'and the birds in the sky have their nests. But the son of man has nowhere he can lay his head.'

²¹'Master,' said another of his disciples, 'let me first go and see to my father's funeral.'

²²'Follow me!' replied Jesus. 'And leave the dead to bury their own dead.'

The calming of the storm

²³So Jesus got into the boat, and his disciples followed him. ²⁴All of a sudden a great storm blew up on the sea, so that the boat was being swamped by the waves. Jesus, however, was asleep. ²⁵They came and woke him up.

'Help! Master! Rescue us!' they shouted. 'We're done for!'

²⁶'Why are you so scared, you little-faith lot?' he replied.

Then he got up and told the wind and the sea to behave themselves, and there was a great calm. ²⁷They were all astonished.

'What sort of man is this,' they said, 'that the winds and the sea do what he says?'

The healing of the demoniacs

²⁸So he went across to the other side, to the region of the Gadarenes. Two demon-possessed men met him, coming out of the tombs. They were very violent and made it impossible for anyone to go along that road. ²⁹'What is it with us and you, son of God?' they yelled. 'Have you come here to torture us ahead of the time?'

³⁰Some way off from where they were there was a large herd of pigs feeding.

³¹'If you cast us out,' the demons begged Jesus, 'send us into the herd of pigs!'

³²'Off you go, then!' said Jesus.

So the demons went out of the men and into the pigs. Then and there the entire herd rushed down the steep slope into the lake, and were drowned in the water.

³³The herdsmen took to their heels. They went off to the town and told the whole tale, including the bit about the demon-possessed men. ³⁴So the whole town came out to see Jesus for themselves. When they saw him, they begged him to leave their district.

The healing of the paralytic

9 Jesus got into the boat, and crossed back over to his own town.

²Some people brought to him a paralysed man lying on a bed. When Jesus saw their faith, he said to the paralysed man, 'Cheer up, my son! Your sins are forgiven!'

³'This fellow's blaspheming!' said some of the scribes to themselves.

⁴Jesus read their thoughts. 'Why let all this wickedness fester in your hearts?' he said. ⁵'Which is easier: to say, "Your sins are forgiven", or to say, "Get up and walk"? ⁶But, to let you know that the son of man has authority on earth to forgive sins' – he spoke to the paralysed man – 'Get up, pick up your bed, and go home!'

⁷And he got up, and went away to his home. ⁸When the crowds saw it they were frightened, and praised God for giving authority like this to humans.

The call of Matthew

⁹As Jesus was walking along, he saw a man called Matthew sitting at the tax-office.

'Follow me!' he said to him. And he rose up and followed him.

¹⁰When he was at home, sitting down to a meal, there were lots of tax-collectors and sinners there who had come to have dinner with Jesus and his disciples. ¹¹When the Pharisees saw it, they said to his disciples, 'Why does your teacher eat with tax-collectors and sinners?'

¹²Jesus heard them.

'It isn't the healthy who need a doctor,' he said, 'it's the sick. ¹³Go and learn what this saying means: "It's mercy I want, not sacrifice." My job isn't to call upright people, but sinners.'

¹⁴Then John's disciples came to him with a question.

'How come,' they asked, 'we and the Pharisees fast a good deal, but your disciples don't fast at all?'

¹⁵'Wedding guests can't fast, can they,' replied Jesus, 'as long as the bridegroom is with them? But sooner or later the bridegroom will be taken away from them. They'll fast then all right.

¹⁶'No one,' he went on, 'sews a patch of unshrunk cloth onto an old coat. The patch will simply pull away from the coat, and you'll have a worse hole than you started with. ¹⁷People don't put new wine into old wineskins, otherwise the skins will split; then the wine will be lost, and the skins will be ruined. They put new wine into new skins, and then both are fine.'

The raising of the little girl

¹⁸As Jesus was saying this, suddenly an official came up and knelt down in front of him.

'It's my daughter!' he said. 'She's just died! But – if you'll come and lay your hand on her, she'll come back to life!'

¹⁹Jesus got up and followed him. So did his disciples.

²⁰Just then a woman appeared. She had suffered from internal bleeding for twelve years. She came up behind Jesus and touched the hem of his coat.

²¹'If I can only touch his coat,' she said to herself, 'I'll be rescued.'

²²Jesus turned round and saw her.

'Cheer up, my daughter!' he said. 'Your faith has rescued you.'

And the woman was healed from that moment.

²³Jesus went into the official's house. There he saw the flute-players, and everybody in a great state of agitation.

²⁴'Go away!' he said. 'The little girl isn't dead. She's asleep!' And they laughed at him.

²⁵So when the crowd had been put out, he went in and took hold of her hand, and she got up. ²⁶The report of this went out around the whole of that region.

Jesus' fame increases

²⁷As Jesus was leaving the area, two blind men followed him, shouting 'Have pity on us, son of David!' at the tops of their voices.

²⁸Jesus went into the house, and the blind men came to him.

'Do you believe that I can do this?' asked Jesus.

'Yes, Master,' they replied.

²⁹Then Jesus touched their eyes. 'As you have believed, so let it happen,' he said. ³⁰And their eyes were opened.

Then Jesus gave them a stern warning. 'Take good care,' he said, 'that nobody gets to know about this.' ³¹But they went out and spread the news in the whole of that region.

³²After they had left, people brought to Jesus a demon-possessed man who couldn't speak. ³³Jesus cast out the demon, and the man spoke. The crowds were amazed. 'Nothing like this ever happened in Israel,' they said. ³⁴But the Pharisees said, 'He casts out demons by the prince of demons.'

³⁵Jesus went around all the towns and villages, teaching in their synagogues, announcing the good news of the kingdom, and healing every disease and every sickness. ³⁶When he saw the crowds, he felt deeply sorry for them, because they were distressed and dejected, like sheep without a shepherd. ³⁷Then he said to his disciples, 'There's plenty of harvest to be had, but not many workers! ³⁸So pray the master of the harvest to send more workers to harvest his fields!'

The Twelve are sent out

10 Jesus called his twelve disciples to him, and gave them authority over unclean spirits, to cast them out and to heal every disease and every sickness.

[2] These are the names of the twelve apostles. First, Simon, who is called Peter ('the rock'), and Andrew his brother; James the son of Zebedee, and John his brother; [3] Philip and Bartholomew, Thomas and Matthew the tax-collector, James son of Alphaeus, and Thaddaeus; [4] Simon the Cananaean; and Judas Iscariot (who betrayed him).

[5] Jesus sent these Twelve off with these instructions.

'Don't go into Gentile territory,' he said, 'and don't go into a Samaritan town. [6] Go instead to the lost sheep of the house of Israel. [7] As you go, declare publicly that the kingdom of heaven has arrived. [8] Heal the sick, raise the dead, cleanse people with skin diseases, cast out demons.

'It was all free when you got it; make sure it's free when you give it. [9] Don't take any gold or silver or copper in your belts; [10] no bag for the road, no second cloak, no sandals, no stick. Workers deserve their pay.

[11] 'When you go into a town or village, make careful enquiry for someone who is good and trustworthy, and stay there until you leave. [12] When you go into the house give a solemn greeting. [13] If the house is trustworthy, let your blessing of peace rest upon it, but if not, let it return to you. [14] If anyone won't welcome you or listen to your message, go out of the house or the town and shake the dust off your feet. [15] I'm telling you the truth: it will be more bearable for Sodom and Gomorrah on the day of judgment than for that town.'

Sheep among wolves

[16] 'See here,' Jesus continued, 'I'm sending you out like sheep surrounded by wolves. So be as shrewd as snakes, and as innocent as doves.

[17] 'Watch out for danger from people around you. They will hand you over to councils, and flog you in their synagogues. [18] You will be dragged before governors and kings because of me, as evidence to them and to the nations. [19] But when they hand you over, don't worry how to speak or what to say. What you have to say will be given to you at that moment. [20] It won't be you speaking, you see; it will be the spirit of your father speaking in you.

[21] 'One brother will betray another to death; fathers will betray children, and children will rebel against their parents and have them put to death. [22] You will be hated by everyone because of my name. But the one who holds out to the end will be delivered.

[23] 'When they persecute you in one town, run off to the next one. I'm telling you the truth: you won't have gone through all the towns of Israel before the son of man comes.'

Warnings and encouragements

[24] 'The disciple isn't greater than the teacher; the slave isn't greater than the master. [25] It's quite enough for the disciple to be like the teacher, and the slave to be like the master. If they called the master of the house 'Beelzebul', think what they're going to call his family!

[26] 'Don't be afraid of them. Nothing is hidden, you see, that won't come to light; nothing is secret that won't be made known. [27] What I tell you in the dark, speak in the light, and what you hear whispered in your ears, announce from the roofs of the houses.

[28] 'Don't be afraid of people who can kill the body, but can't kill the soul. The one you should be afraid of is the one who can destroy both body and soul in Gehenna. [29] How much would you get for a couple of sparrows? A single copper coin if you're lucky? And not one of them falls to the ground without your father knowing about it. [30] When it comes to you – why, every hair on your head is counted. [31] So don't be afraid! You're worth much more than a great many sparrows.'

Jesus causes division

[32] 'So: everyone who owns up in front of others to being on my side, I will own them before my father in heaven. [33] But anyone who disowns me in front of others, I will disown that person before my father in heaven.

[34] 'Don't think it's my job to bring peace on the earth. I didn't come to bring peace – I came

to bring a sword! ³⁵I came to divide a man from his father, a daughter from her mother, and a daughter-in-law from her mother-in-law. ³⁶Yes, you'll find your enemies inside your own front door.

³⁷'If you love your father or mother more than me, you don't deserve me. If you love your son or daughter more than me, you don't deserve me. ³⁸Anyone who doesn't pick up their cross and follow after me doesn't deserve me. ³⁹If you find your life you'll lose it, and if you lose your life because of me you'll find it.

⁴⁰'Anyone who welcomes you, welcomes me; and anyone who welcomes me, welcomes the one who sent me. ⁴¹Anyone who welcomes a prophet in the name of a prophet will receive a prophet's reward; and anyone who receives an upright person in the name of an upright person will receive an upright person's reward. ⁴²Anyone who gives even a cup of cold water to one of these little ones, in the name of a disciple – I'm telling you the truth, they won't go short of their reward!'

Jesus and John the Baptist

11 So when Jesus had finished giving instructions to the twelve disciples, he moved on from there to teach and preach in their towns.

²Meanwhile, John, who was in prison, heard about these messianic goings-on. He sent word through his followers.

³'Are you the one who is coming?' he asked. 'Or should we be looking for someone else?'

⁴'Go and tell John,' replied Jesus, 'what you've seen and heard. ⁵Blind people are seeing! Lame people are walking! People with virulent skin diseases are being cleansed! Deaf people can hear again! The dead are being raised to life! And – the poor are hearing the good news! ⁶And God bless you if you're not upset by what I'm doing.'

The identity of John the Baptist

⁷As the messengers were going away, Jesus began to speak to the crowds about John.

'What were you expecting to see,' he asked, 'when you went out into the desert? A reed wobbling in the wind? ⁸No? Well, then, what were you expecting to see? Someone dressed in silks and satins? If you want to see people like that you'd have to go to somebody's royal palace. ⁹All right, so what *were* you expecting to see? A prophet? Ah, now we're getting there: yes indeed, and much more than a prophet! ¹⁰This is the one the Bible was talking about when it says,

> See, I'm sending my messenger ahead of you
> and he will clear your path before you.

¹¹'I'm telling you the truth: John the Baptist is the greatest mother's son there ever was. But even the least significant person in heaven's kingdom is greater than he is. ¹²From the time of John the Baptist until now the kingdom of heaven has been forcing its way in – and the men of force are trying to grab it! ¹³All the prophets and the law, you see, made their prophecies up to the time of John. ¹⁴In fact, if you'll believe it, he is Elijah, the one who was to come. ¹⁵If you've got ears, then listen!'

Jesus condemns the cities

¹⁶'What picture shall I give you for this generation?' asked Jesus. 'It's like a bunch of children sitting in the town square, and singing songs to each other. ¹⁷This is how it goes:

> You didn't dance when we played the flute,
> you didn't cry when we sang the dirge!

¹⁸'What do I mean? When John appeared, he didn't have any normal food or drink – and people said "What's got into him, then? Some demon?" ¹⁹Then along comes the son of man, eating and drinking normally, and people say, "Ooh, look at him – guzzling and boozing, hanging around with tax-collectors and other riff-raff." But, you know, wisdom is as wisdom does – and wisdom will be vindicated!'

²⁰Then he began to berate the towns where he'd done most of his powerful deeds, because they hadn't repented.

²¹'A curse on you, Chorazin!' he said. 'A curse on you, Bethsaida! If Tyre and Sidon had seen the kind of powerful things you saw, they would have repented long ago with hairshirts and ashes. ²²But I can tell you this: on the day

of judgment Tyre and Sidon will have a better time of it than you will. ²³And what about you, Capernaum? You think you're going to be exalted to heaven, do you? No – you'll be sent down to Hades! If the powerful works that happened in you had happened in Sodom, it would still be standing today. ²⁴But I can tell you this: on the day of judgment the land of Sodom will have a better time of it than you will!'

Jesus' invitation

²⁵At that time Jesus turned to God with this prayer: 'I give you my praise, father, Lord of heaven and earth! You hid these things from the wise and intelligent and revealed them to children! ²⁶Yes, father, that's the way you decided to do it! ²⁷My father gave me everything: nobody knows the son except the father, and nobody knows the father except the son – and anyone the son wants to reveal him to.

²⁸'Are you having a real struggle? Come to me! Are you carrying a big load on your back? Come to me – I'll give you a rest! ²⁹Pick up my yoke and put it on; take lessons from me! My heart is gentle, not arrogant. You'll find the rest you deeply need. ³⁰My yoke is easy to wear, my load is easy to bear.'

Lord of the sabbath

12 At that time Jesus went through the cornfields on the sabbath. His disciples were hungry, and they began to pluck ears of corn and eat them. ²When the Pharisees observed this they said to him, 'Look here! Your disciples are doing something that's not permitted on the sabbath!'

³'Did you never read what David did?' replied Jesus. 'When he and his men were hungry, ⁴they went into God's house and ate the holy bread which neither he nor his men were allowed to eat – only the priests had that right. ⁵Or didn't you read in the law that the priests in the Temple do things on the sabbath which are against sabbath law – and they aren't guilty? ⁶Let me tell you this: something greater than the Temple is here. ⁷If you'd known what this saying means:

Mercy, not sacrifice, is what I really want –

you wouldn't have passed judgment on blameless people. ⁸Yes, you see: the son of man is master of the sabbath, too.'

⁹He left the place and went into their synagogue, ¹⁰where there was a man with a withered hand.

They put the question to him: 'Is it lawful to heal on the sabbath?'

(They asked this so that they could frame a charge against him.)

¹¹'Supposing one of you has just one sheep,' replied Jesus, 'and it falls into a ditch on the sabbath. You'll grab it and haul it out, won't you? ¹²Well then, think how much more important a human being is than a sheep! So, you see, it is permitted to do good on the sabbath.'

¹³Then he said to the man, 'Stretch your hand out.' He stretched it out, and it was restored to health, just like the other one. ¹⁴But the Pharisees went off and plotted against him, with the intention of doing away with him.

The Servant

¹⁵Jesus discovered the plots against him, and left the district. Large crowds followed him, and he healed them all, ¹⁶giving them strict instructions not to tell people about him. ¹⁷This was so that what was spoken through Isaiah the prophet might come true:

¹⁸Look! Here's my servant, whom I chose;
my beloved one, my heart's delight.
My spirit I will place on him,
and he'll announce true judgment
to the whole wide world.
¹⁹He will not argue, nor will he
lift up his voice and shout aloud;
nobody in the streets will hear
his voice. ²⁰He will not break the damaged
reed, or snuff the guttering lamp,
until his judgment wins the day.
²¹The world will hope upon his name.

Jesus and Beelzebul

²²They brought to Jesus a man who was possessed by a demon that made him unable to

see or speak. Jesus healed him, so that the sick man was able to talk and see. ²³All the crowds were astonished.

'He can't be David's Son, can he?' they said.

²⁴The Pharisees heard this.

'The fellow can only cast out demons,' they said, 'because he's in league with Beelzebul, the prince of demons!'

²⁵Jesus knew their thoughts.

'Suppose a kingdom is split down the middle,' he said to them. 'It'll go to rack and ruin! If a city or a household is split down the middle, it's doomed! ²⁶And if the satan drives out the satan, he's split down the middle – so how can his kingdom stay standing?

²⁷'What's more, if I cast out demons by Beelzebul, whose power are your people in league with when they cast them out? Yes, they'll tell you what's what! ²⁸But if I'm casting out demons because I'm in league with God's spirit – well, then, God's kingdom has arrived on your doorstep!

²⁹'Look at it like this. Suppose you want to break into a strong man's house and steal his belongings. How are you going to do that unless you first tie up the strong man? Then you can plunder his house to your heart's content. ³⁰If you're not with me, you're against me. Unless you're gathering the flock with me, you're scattering it.

³¹'So let me tell you this: people will be forgiven for every sin and blasphemy; but blasphemy against the spirit will not be forgiven. ³²If anyone speaks a word against the son of man, it will be forgiven. But if anyone speaks a word against the holy spirit, it won't be forgiven, either in the present age or in the age to come.'

The sign of Jonah

³³'You must make up your mind between two possibilities,' Jesus went on. 'Either the tree is good, in which case its fruit is good; or the tree is bad, in which case its fruit is bad. You can tell the tree by its fruits, after all.

³⁴'You're a family of snakes! How can you say good things when you're bad inside? What the mouth speaks is what fills the heart. ³⁵A good person produces good things from a good storeroom; an evil person produces evil things from an evil storeroom. ³⁶Let me tell you this: on judgment day people will have to own up to every trivial word they say. ³⁷Yes: you will be vindicated by your own words – and you will be condemned by your own words.'

³⁸'Teacher,' responded some of the scribes and Pharisees. 'We would like to see a sign from you.'

³⁹'This wicked and immoral generation is looking for a sign,' replied Jesus. 'But no sign will be given to it – except the sign of Jonah. ⁴⁰Jonah, you see, was in the stomach of the sea-monster for three days and three nights – and in the same way the son of man will be in the heart of the earth for three days and three nights. ⁴¹The men of Nineveh will rise up at the judgment along with this generation and will condemn it. They, after all, repented when they heard Jonah's warnings! And, in case you hadn't noticed, something greater than Jonah is here. ⁴²The Queen of the South will be raised at the judgment with this generation and will condemn it. She, after all, came from the ends of the earth to hear the wisdom of Solomon! And, in case you hadn't noticed, something greater than Solomon is here.'

Jesus' true family

⁴³'When the unclean spirit goes out of a person,' Jesus continued, 'it goes wandering through waterless places looking for somewhere to rest, and doesn't find anywhere. ⁴⁴Then it says, "I'll go back to my house, the one I left." When it gets there it finds it standing empty, clean and tidy. ⁴⁵Then it goes out and collects seven other spirits to join it, spirits worse than itself. They go in and take up residence there. The poor person ends up worse off than they were to start with! And that's what will happen with this wicked generation.'

⁴⁶Suddenly, while he was speaking to the crowds, his mother and his brothers came and stood outside, hoping for a chance to speak to him.

⁴⁷'Look,' someone said to him, 'your mother and your brothers are standing outside wanting to speak to you.'

⁴⁸'Who is my mother?' said Jesus to the person who had spoken to him. 'Who are my brothers?'

⁴⁹Then he stretched out his hand towards his disciples.

'Look!' he said. 'Here are my mother and my brothers. ⁵⁰Yes; anyone who does what my heavenly father wants is my brother, and my sister, and my mother.'

The parable of the sower

13 That very day Jesus went out of the house and sat down beside the sea. ²Large crowds gathered around him, so he got into a boat and sat down. The whole crowd was standing on the shore.

³He had much to say to them, and he said it all in parables.

'Listen!' he said. 'Once there was a sower who went out to sow. ⁴As he sowed, some seed fell beside the path, and the birds came and ate it up. ⁵Some seed fell on rocky soil, where it didn't have much earth. It sprang up at once because it didn't have depth of soil. ⁶But when the sun was high it got scorched, and it withered because it didn't have any root. ⁷Other seed fell in among thorns, and the thorns grew up and choked it. ⁸And other seed fell into good soil, and produced a crop, some a hundred times over, some sixty, and some thirty times over. ⁹If you've got ears, then listen!'

The reason for parables

¹⁰His disciples came to him.

'Why are you speaking to them in parables?' they asked.

¹¹'You've been given the gift of knowing the secrets of the kingdom of heaven,' he replied, 'but they haven't been given it. ¹²Anyone who already has something will be given more, and they will have plenty. But anyone who has nothing – even what they have will be taken away! ¹³That's why I speak to them in parables, so that they may look but not see, and hear but not understand or take it in. ¹⁴Isaiah's prophecy is coming true in them:

> You will listen and listen but won't understand,
> you will look and look but not see.
> ¹⁵This people's heart has gone flabby and fat,
> their ears are muffled and dull,
> their eyes are darkened and shut;
> in order that they won't see with their eyes
> or hear with their ears, or know in their heart,
> or turn back again for me to restore them.

¹⁶But there's great news for *your* eyes: they can see! And for your ears: they can hear! ¹⁷I'm telling you the truth: many prophets and holy people longed to see what you see and didn't see it, and to hear what you hear and didn't hear it.'

The parable of the sower explained

¹⁸'All right, then,' Jesus continued, 'this is what the sower story is all about. ¹⁹When someone hears the word of the kingdom and doesn't understand it, the evil one comes and snatches away what was sown in their heart. This corresponds to what was sown beside the path. ²⁰What was sown on rocky ground is the person who hears the word and immediately receives it with delight, ²¹but doesn't have any root of their own. Someone like that only lasts a short time; as soon as there's any trouble or persecution because of the word, they trip up at once. ²²The one sown among thorns is the one who hears the word, but the world's worries and the seduction of wealth choke the word and it doesn't bear fruit. ²³But the one sown on good soil is the one who hears the word and understands it. Someone like that will bear fruit: one will produce a hundred times over, another sixty, and another thirty times over.'

The parable of the weeds

²⁴He put another parable to them.

'The kingdom of heaven,' he said, 'is like this! Once upon a time a man sowed good seed in his field. ²⁵While the workers were asleep, his enemy came and sowed weeds in among the wheat, and went away. ²⁶When the crop came up and produced corn, then the weeds appeared as well.

²⁷'So the farmer's servants came to him.

'"Master," they said, "didn't you sow good seed in your field? Where have the weeds come from?"

28 "'This is the work of an enemy,'" he replied.

"'So,' the servants said to him, 'do you want us to go and pull them up?'

29 "'No,' he replied. 'If you do that you'll probably pull up the wheat as well, while you're collecting the weeds. 30 Let them both grow together until the harvest. Then, when it's time for harvest, I will give the reapers this instruction: "First gather the weeds and tie them up in bundles to burn them, but gather the wheat into my barn."'

31 He put another parable to them.

'The kingdom of heaven,' he said, 'is like a grain of mustard seed, which someone took and sowed in his field. 32 It's the smallest of all the seeds, but when it grows it turns into the biggest of the shrubs. It becomes a tree, and the birds in the sky can then come and nest in its branches.'

33 He told them another parable.

'The kingdom of heaven is like leaven,' he said, 'which a woman took and hid inside three measures of flour, until the whole thing was leavened.'

34 Jesus said all these things to the crowds in parables. He didn't speak to them without a parable. 35 This was to fulfil what was spoken by the prophet:

I will open my mouth in parables,
I will tell the things that were hidden
since the very foundation of the world.

The parable of the weeds explained

36 Then Jesus left the crowds and went into the house. His disciples came and joined him.

'Explain to us,' they said, 'the parable of the weeds in the field.'

37 'The one who sows the good seed,' said Jesus, 'is the son of man. 38 The field is the world; the good seed are the children of the kingdom. The weeds are the children of the evil one; 39 the enemy who sowed them is the devil. The harvest is the close of the age, and the reapers are angels.

40 'So: when the weeds are gathered and burned in the fire, that's what it will be like at the close of the age. 41 The son of man will send out his angels, and they will collect together out of his kingdom everything that causes offence, and everyone who acts wickedly. 42 They will throw them into the fiery furnace, where there will be weeping and gnashing of teeth. 43 Then the righteous will shine like the sun in the kingdom of their father. If you have ears, then hear!'

Other parables

44 'The kingdom of heaven,' Jesus continued, 'is like treasure hidden in a field. Someone found it and hid it, and in great delight went off and sold everything he possessed, and bought that field.

45 'Again, the kingdom of heaven is like a trader who was looking for fine pearls, 46 and who found one that was spectacularly valuable. He went off and sold everything he possessed, and bought it.

47 'Again, the kingdom of heaven is like a net that was thrown into the sea, and collected every type of fish. 48 When it was full, the fishermen brought it to shore. They sat down and selected the good ones, which they put into a bucket; but they threw out the bad ones. 49 That's what it will be like at the close of the age. The angels will go off and separate the wicked from the righteous, 50 and they will throw them into the fiery furnace, where there will be weeping and gnashing of teeth.

51 'Have you understood all this?' asked Jesus.

'Yes,' they answered.

52 'Well, then,' he said to them, 'every scribe who has been trained for the kingdom of heaven is like a householder who brings out of his storeroom some new things and some old things.'

53 When Jesus had finished these parables, he went away from there.

Opposition in Nazareth

54 Jesus came to the town where he had been brought up. He taught them in their synagogue, and they were astonished.

'Where did this fellow get this wisdom, and these powers?' they said.

55 'Isn't he the carpenter's son? Isn't his mother called Mary, and his brothers James, Joseph, Simon and Judah? 56 And aren't all his

sisters here with us? So where does he get it all from?' ⁵⁷They were offended by him.

So Jesus said to them, 'No prophet lacks respect – except in his own town and his own house!'

⁵⁸And he didn't perform many mighty works there, because they didn't believe.

The death of John the Baptist

14 At that time Herod the Tetrarch heard reports about Jesus.

²'This fellow must be John the Baptist,' he said to his servants. 'He's been raised from the dead! That's why these powers are at work in him.'

³This is what had happened. Herod had seized John, tied him up and put him in prison because of Herodias, the wife of his brother Philip. ⁴John had been telling him that it wasn't right for him to have her. ⁵Herod wanted to kill him, but he was afraid of the crowd, because they reckoned that John was a prophet.

⁶When Herod's birthday came round, the daughter of Herodias danced for the assembled company, and delighted Herod. ⁷So he swore a great oath that he would give her whatever she requested. ⁸Prompted by her mother, she said, 'Give me – here, on a platter – the head of John the Baptizer!' ⁹The king was sorry; but because of his oaths, and his guests, he gave orders for it to be given to her. ¹⁰He sent to the prison and had John beheaded. ¹¹His head was brought on a platter and given to the girl, and she passed it on to her mother. ¹²His disciples came and took away the body and buried it. Then they went and told Jesus.

The feeding of the five thousand

¹³When Jesus heard it, he went away from there in a boat to a deserted spot by himself. The crowds heard it, and followed him on foot from the towns. ¹⁴When he came out and saw the large crowd, he was sorry for them. He healed their sick.

¹⁵When it was evening, the disciples came to him.

'This is a deserted spot,' they said, 'and it's already getting late. Send the crowds away so that they can go into the villages and buy food for themselves.'

¹⁶'They don't need to go away,' said Jesus. 'You give them something to eat.'

¹⁷'All we have here,' they said, 'is five loaves of bread and two fish.'

¹⁸'Bring them here to me,' he said.

¹⁹He told the crowds to sit down on the grass. Then he took the five loaves and the two fish and looked up to heaven. He blessed the loaves, broke them, and gave them to the disciples, and the disciples gave them to the crowds. ²⁰Everybody ate and was satisfied, and they picked up twelve baskets full of broken pieces. ²¹There were about five thousand men who had eaten, besides women and children.

²²Jesus at once made the disciples get into the boat and go on ahead of him to the opposite shore, while he dismissed the crowds.

Jesus walks on water

²³After he had sent the crowds away, Jesus went up the mountain by himself to pray. When evening came he was there by himself. ²⁴The boat had already gone some distance from the shore and was being smashed around by the waves, since the wind was against it.

²⁵At the very dead of night he came towards them, walking on the water. ²⁶The disciples saw him walking on the sea and panicked. 'It's a ghost!' they said, and they screamed in terror. ²⁷But Jesus at once spoke to them.

'Cheer up,' he said, 'it's me! Don't be frightened!'

²⁸'If it's really you, Master,' said Peter in reply, 'give me the word to come to you on the water.'

²⁹'Come along, then,' said Jesus.

Peter got out of the boat and walked on the water and came towards Jesus. ³⁰But when he saw the strong wind he was afraid, and began to sink.

'Master,' he yelled, 'rescue me!'

³¹Jesus at once reached out his hand and caught him.

'A fine lot of faith you've got!' he said. 'Why did you doubt?'

³²They got into the boat, and the wind died down. ³³The people in the boat worshipped him.

'You really are God's son!' they said.

³⁴So they crossed over to the land called Gennesaret. ³⁵The men of that region recognized him and sent word to all the surrounding district. They brought all their sick people to him, ³⁶and begged him to be allowed simply to touch the hem of his clothes. And everyone who touched it was cured.

Discussions of clean and unclean

15 At that time some Pharisees and scribes came from Jerusalem to Jesus. They had a question for him.

²'Why', they said, 'do your disciples go against the tradition of the elders? They don't wash their hands when they eat their food!'

³'Why', Jesus replied, 'do *you* go against the command of God because of your tradition? ⁴What God said was "Honour your father and mother" and "If anyone speaks evil of father or mother, they must certainly die." ⁵But you say, "If anyone says to father or mother, 'What you might have gained from me is given to God', ⁶they don't need to honour their father any more." As a result, you make God's word null and void because of your tradition.

⁷'You play-actors! Isaiah had the right words for you in his prophecy:

⁸This people gives me honour with their lips,
their heart, however, holds me at arm's length.
⁹The worship which they offer me is vain,
because they teach, as law, mere human
    precepts.'

The parable of clean and unclean

¹⁰Then Jesus called the crowd, and said to them, 'Listen and understand. ¹¹What makes someone unclean isn't what goes into the mouth. It's what comes out of the mouth that makes someone unclean.'

¹²Then the disciples came to Jesus.

'Do you know', they said, 'that the Pharisees were horrified when they heard what you said?'

¹³'Every plant that my heavenly father hasn't planted', replied Jesus, 'will be plucked up by the roots. ¹⁴Let them be. They are blind guides. But if one blind person guides another, both of them will fall into a pit.'

¹⁵Peter spoke up. 'Explain the riddle to us,' he said.

¹⁶'Are you still slow on the uptake as well?' replied Jesus. ¹⁷'Don't you understand that whatever goes into the mouth travels on into the stomach and goes out into the toilet? ¹⁸But what comes out of the mouth begins in the heart, and that's what makes someone unclean. ¹⁹Out of the heart, you see, come evil plots, murder, adultery, fornication, theft, false witness, and blasphemy. ²⁰These are the things that make someone unclean. But eating with unwashed hands doesn't make a person unclean.'

The Canaanite woman

²¹Jesus left that place and went off to the district of Tyre and Sidon. ²²A Canaanite woman from those parts came out and shouted, 'Have pity on me, Lord, son of David! My daughter is demon-possessed! She's in a bad way!' ²³Jesus, however, said nothing at all to her.

His disciples came up.

'Please send her away!' they asked. 'She's shouting after us.'

²⁴'I was only sent', replied Jesus, 'to the lost sheep of the house of Israel.'

²⁵The woman, however, came and threw herself down at his feet.

'Master,' she said, 'please help me!'

²⁶'It isn't right', replied Jesus, 'to take the children's bread and throw it to the dogs.'

²⁷'I know, Master. But even the dogs eat the scraps that fall from their master's table.'

²⁸'You've got great faith, haven't you, my friend!' replied Jesus. 'All right; let it be as you wish.'

And her daughter was healed from that moment.

The feeding of the four thousand

²⁹Jesus went away from there, and arrived beside the sea of Galilee. He went up the mountain and sat down. ³⁰Large crowds came to him, with their lame, blind, crippled, mute and many others. They laid them at his feet, and he healed them. ³¹When the crowd saw the mute speaking, the crippled made

whole, the lame walking, and the blind seeing, they were astonished, and they gave praise to the God of Israel.

³²Jesus called his disciples, and said, 'I am really sorry for the crowd. They've been around me now for three days and they haven't got anything to eat. I don't want to send them away hungry; they might faint on the way home.'

³³The disciples said to him, 'Where could we get enough bread to feed a crowd this size, out in the country like this?'

³⁴'How many loaves have you got?' asked Jesus.

'Seven,' they replied, 'and a few fish.'

³⁵Jesus told the crowd to sit down on the ground. ³⁶Then he took the seven loaves and the fish, gave thanks, broke them, and gave them to the disciples, and the disciples gave them to the crowds. ³⁷They all ate and were satisfied. And they picked up seven baskets full of what was left of the broken pieces. ³⁸There were four thousand men who had eaten, besides the women and children.

³⁹Jesus sent the crowds away. Then he got into the boat and went over to the Magadan coast.

The leaven of the Pharisees

16 The Pharisees and Sadducees came to Jesus and tried to catch him out by asking him to show them a sign from heaven.

²This was his reply to them: 'When it's evening you say, "Sky looks like wine, it's going to be fine." ³And in the morning you say, "Red in the sky, rain by and by." Well then: you know how to work out the look of the sky, so why can't you work out the signs of the times? ⁴The generation that wants a sign is wicked and corrupt! No sign will be given to it, except the sign of Jonah.'

With that, he left them and went away.

⁵When the disciples crossed over the lake, they forgot to bring any bread. ⁶'Watch out,' said Jesus to them, 'and beware of the leaven of the Pharisees and Sadducees.'

⁷They discussed it with each other. 'It's because we didn't bring any bread,' they said.

⁸But Jesus knew what they were thinking.

'You really are a little-faith lot!' he said. 'Why are you discussing with each other that you haven't got any bread? ⁹Don't you understand, even now? Don't you remember the five loaves and the five thousand, and how many basketfuls you picked up afterwards? ¹⁰Or the seven loaves and the four thousand, and how many baskets you picked up? ¹¹Why can't you see that I wasn't talking about bread? Watch out for the leaven of the Pharisees and Sadducees!'

¹²Then they understood that he wasn't telling them to beware of the leaven you get in bread, but of the teaching of the Pharisees and Sadducees.

Peter's declaration of Jesus' messiahship

¹³Jesus came to Caesarea Philippi. There he put this question to his disciples: 'Who do people say that the son of man is?'

¹⁴'John the Baptist,' they replied. 'Others say Elijah. Others say Jeremiah, or one of the prophets.'

¹⁵'What about you?' he asked them. 'Who do you say I am?'

¹⁶Simon Peter answered.

'You're the Messiah,' he said. 'You're the son of the living God!'

¹⁷'God's blessing on you, Simon, son of John!' answered Jesus. 'Flesh and blood didn't reveal that to you; it was my father in heaven. ¹⁸And I've got something to tell you, too: you are Peter, the rock, and on this rock I will build my church, and the gates of hell won't overpower it. ¹⁹I will give you the keys of the kingdom of heaven. Whatever you tie up on earth will have been tied up in heaven, and whatever you untie on earth will have been untied in heaven.'

²⁰Then he sternly ordered the disciples not to tell anyone that he was the Messiah.

Jesus predicts his death

²¹From then on Jesus began to explain to his disciples that he would have to go to Jerusalem, and suffer many things from the elders, chief priests and scribes, and be killed, and be raised on the third day.

²²Peter took him and began to tell him off. 'That's the last thing God would want, Master!' he said. 'That's never, ever going to happen to you!'

[23]Jesus turned on Peter. 'Get behind me, satan!' he said. 'You're trying to trip me up! You're not looking at things like God does! You're looking at things like a mere mortal!'

[24]Then Jesus said to his disciples, 'If anyone wants to come after me, they must give themselves up, and pick up their cross, and follow me. [25]Yes: if someone wants to save their life, they must lose it; and if anyone loses their life for my sake they will find it. [26]What use will it be, otherwise, if you win the whole world but forfeit your true life? What will you give to get your life back? [27]You see, the son of man is going to "come in the glory of his father with his angels", and then "he will reward everyone for the work they have done". [28]I'm telling you the truth: some of those standing here will not taste death until they see "the son of man coming in his kingdom".'

The transfiguration

17 After six days Jesus took Peter, James, and James's brother John, and led them off up a high mountain by themselves. [2]There he was transformed in front of them. His face shone like the sun, and his clothes became as white as light. [3]Then, astonishingly, Moses and Elijah appeared to them. They were talking with Jesus.

[4]Peter just had to say something. 'Master,' he said to Jesus, 'it's wonderful for us to be here! If you want, I'll make three shelters here – one for you, one for Moses, and one for Elijah!'

[5]While he was still speaking, a bright cloud overshadowed them. Then there came a voice out of the cloud. 'This is my dear son,' said the voice, 'and I'm delighted with him. Pay attention to him.'

[6]When the disciples heard this, they fell on their faces and were scared out of their wits. [7]Jesus came up and touched them.

'Get up,' he said, 'and don't be afraid.' [8]When they raised their eyes, they saw nobody except Jesus, all by himself.

The question about Elijah

[9]As they were coming down the mountain, Jesus gave them strict instructions. 'Don't tell anyone about the vision,' he said, 'until the son of man has been raised from the dead.'

[10]'So why', asked the disciples, 'do the scribes say that "Elijah must come first"?'

[11]'Elijah does indeed come,' replied Jesus, 'and "he will restore everything". [12]But let me tell you this: Elijah has already come, and they didn't recognize him! They did to him whatever they wanted. That's how the son of man, too, will suffer at their hands.'

[13]Then the disciples realized that he was talking to them about John the Baptist.

Faith that moves mountains

[14]When they came near the crowd, a man approached and knelt in front of him.

[15]'Master,' he said, 'take pity on my son! He suffers from awful fits which are frightful for him. He often falls into the fire, and often into the water. [16]I brought him to your disciples, but they couldn't cure him.'

[17]'You unbelieving and twisted generation!' responded Jesus. 'How much longer must I be with you? How much longer must I put up with you? Bring him here to me.'

[18]Then Jesus rebuked the demon and it came out of him. The boy was cured from that moment.

[19]The disciples came to Jesus in private. 'Why couldn't we cast it out?' they asked.

[20]'Because of your lack of faith,' Jesus replied. 'I'm telling you the truth: if you have faith like a grain of mustard seed, you will say to this mountain, "Move from here to there", and it will move. Nothing will be impossible for you.'

The Temple tax

[22]As they regathered in Galilee, Jesus said to them, 'The son of man is going to be given over into human hands. [23]They will kill him, and on the third day he will be raised.' And they were very sad.

[24]They came to Capernaum, where the officials who collected the Temple tax approached Peter.

'Your teacher pays the Temple tax, doesn't he?' they asked.

[25]'Yes,' he replied.

When he came into the house, Jesus spoke first, 'What d'you think, Simon? When the kings of the world collect taxes or duties, who do they collect them from? From their own families, or from outsiders?'

²⁶'From outsiders,' he replied.

'Well then,' said Jesus, 'that means the families are free. ²⁷But we don't want to give them offence, do we? So why don't you go down to the sea and cast out a hook? The first fish you catch, open its mouth and you'll find a coin. Take that and give it to them for the two of us.'

Humility and danger

18 At that time the disciples came to Jesus.

'So, then,' they said, 'who is the greatest in the kingdom of heaven?'

²Jesus called a child and stood her in the middle of them.

³'I'm telling you the truth,' he said. 'Unless you turn inside out and become like children, you will never, ever, get into the kingdom of heaven. ⁴So if any of you make yourselves humble like this child, you will be great in the kingdom of heaven. ⁵And if anyone welcomes one such child in my name, they welcome me.

⁶'Whoever causes one of these little ones who believe in me to trip up,' he went on, 'it would be better for them to have a huge millstone hung around their neck and be drowned far out in the deep sea. ⁷It's a terrible thing for the world that people will be made to stumble. Obstacles are bound to appear and trip people up, but it will be terrible for the person who makes them come.'

More about the 'little ones'

⁸'But if your hand or your foot causes you to trip up,' Jesus continued, 'cut it off and throw it away. It's better to enter into life crippled or lame than to go into eternal fire with both hands and both feet! ⁹And if your eye causes you to trip up, pull it out and throw it away. Going into life with one eye is better than going into hell with two!

¹⁰'Take care not to despise one of these little ones. I tell you this: in heaven, their angels are always gazing on the face of my father who lives there.

¹²'How does it seem to you? If someone has a hundred sheep and one of them wanders off and goes missing, what will he do? He'll leave the ninety-nine on the hillside and go off after the one that's missing, won't he? ¹³And when, eventually, he finds it, I'll tell you the truth: he will celebrate over that one more than over the ninety-nine who didn't go missing! ¹⁴It's the same with your father in heaven. The last thing he wants is for a single one of these little ones to be lost.'

Reconciliation and prayer in the community

¹⁵'If another disciple sins against you,' Jesus continued, 'go and have it out, just between the two of you alone. If they listen to you, you've won back a brother or sister. ¹⁶But if they won't listen, you should take with you one or two others, so that "everything may be established from the mouth of two or three witnesses". ¹⁷If they won't listen to them, tell it to the assembly. And if they won't listen to the assembly, you should treat such a person like you would a Gentile or a tax-collector. ¹⁸I'm telling you the truth: whatever you tie up on earth will have been tied up in heaven; and whatever you untie on earth will have been untied in heaven.

¹⁹'Again, let me tell you the truth: if two of you come to an agreement on earth about any matter that you want to ask, it will be done for you by my father in heaven. ²⁰Yes: where two or three come together in my name, I'll be there in the midst of them.'

The challenge of forgiveness

²¹Then Peter came to Jesus.

'Master,' he said, 'how many times must I forgive my brother when he sins against me? As many as seven times?'

²²'I wouldn't say seven times,' replied Jesus. 'Why not – seventy times seven?

²³'So, you see,' he went on, 'the kingdom of heaven is like a king who wanted to settle up accounts with his servants. ²⁴As he was beginning to sort it all out, one man was

brought before him who owed ten thousand talents. ²⁵He had no means of paying it back, so the master ordered him to be sold, with his wife and children and everything he possessed, and payment to be made.

²⁶'So the servant fell down and prostrated himself before the master.

'"Be patient with me," he said, "and I'll pay you everything!"

²⁷'The master was very sorry for the servant, and let him off. He forgave him the loan.

²⁸'But that servant went out and found one of his fellow-servants, who owed him a hundred dinars. He seized him and began to throttle him. "Pay me back what you owe me!" he said.

²⁹'The colleague fell down and begged him, "Be patient with me, and I'll pay you!"

³⁰'But he refused, and went and threw him into prison until he could pay the debt.

³¹'So when his fellow-servants saw what had happened, they were very upset. They went and informed their master about the whole affair. ³²Then his master summoned him.

'"You're a scoundrel of a servant!" he said to him. "I let you off the whole debt, because you begged me to. ³³Shouldn't you have taken pity on your colleague, like I took pity on you?"

³⁴'His master was angry, and handed him over to the torturers, until he had paid the whole debt. ³⁵And that's what my heavenly father will do to you, unless each of you forgives your brother or sister from your heart.'

The question about divorce

19 So this is what happened next. When Jesus had finished saying all this, he went away from Galilee and came to the region of Judaea across the Jordan. ²Large crowds followed him, and he healed them there.

³Some Pharisees approached him with a trick question.

'Is it lawful', they asked, 'for a man to divorce his wife for any reason at all?'

⁴'Haven't you read', he replied, 'that the creator from the beginning "made them male and female"? ⁵And this is what he said: "For this reason a man shall leave his father and mother and be joined to his wife, and the two shall become one flesh." ⁶As a result, they are no longer two, but one flesh. So humans shouldn't split up what God has joined together.'

⁷'So then,' they asked, 'why did Moses give the regulation that one should give the woman a certificate of divorce and make the separation legal?'

⁸'Moses gave you this instruction about how to divorce your wives,' replied Jesus, 'because your hearts were hard. But that's not how it was at the beginning. ⁹Let me tell you this: anyone who divorces his wife, except for immorality, and marries another woman, commits adultery.'

Marriage, celibacy and children

¹⁰The disciples said to Jesus, 'If that's the situation of a man with his wife, it would be better not to marry!'

¹¹'Not everyone can accept this word,' replied Jesus; 'only the people it's given to. ¹²You see, there are some eunuchs who are that way from birth. There are some who have been made eunuchs by others. And there are some who have made themselves eunuchs for the sake of the kingdom of heaven. If anyone can receive this, let them do so.'

¹³Then children were brought to Jesus for him to lay his hands on them and pray. The disciples spoke sternly to them. ¹⁴But Jesus said, 'Let the children come to me! Don't stop them! They are the sort the kingdom of heaven belongs to!' ¹⁵And he laid his hands on them.

Then he moved on elsewhere.

The rich young man

¹⁶Suddenly a man came up to Jesus. 'Teacher,' he asked, 'what good thing must I do if I'm to possess the life of the age to come?'

¹⁷'Why come to me with questions about what's good?' retorted Jesus. 'There is One who is good! If you want to enter into life, keep the commandments.'

¹⁸'Which ones?' he asked.

'These ones,' Jesus answered: '"don't murder, don't commit adultery, don't steal, don't tell lies under oath, ¹⁹respect your father and mother", and "love your neighbour as yourself".'

²⁰'I've kept the lot,' said the young man. 'What am I still short of?'

²¹'If you want to complete the set,' Jesus replied, 'go and sell everything you own and give it to the poor. That way you'll have treasure in heaven! Then come and follow me.'

²²When the young man heard him say that, he went away very sad. He had many possessions.

The first and the last

²³Jesus said to his disciples, 'I'm telling you the truth: it's very hard for a rich person to get into the kingdom of heaven. ²⁴Let me say it again: it's easier for a camel to go through the eye of a needle than for a rich person to enter God's kingdom.'

²⁵The disciples were completely flabbergasted when they heard that. 'So who then can be saved?' they asked.

²⁶Jesus looked round at them. 'Humanly speaking,' he replied, 'it's impossible. But everything's possible with God.'

²⁷Then Peter spoke up. 'Look here,' he said, 'we've left everything behind and followed you. What can we expect?'

²⁸'I'm telling you the truth,' Jesus replied. 'In God's great new world, when the son of man sits on his glorious throne, those of you who have followed me will sit on twelve thrones – yes, you! – and rule over the twelve tribes of Israel. ²⁹And anyone who's left houses or brothers or sisters or father or mother or children or estates because of my name will get back a hundred times over, and will inherit the life of that new age. ³⁰But many at the front will find themselves at the back, and the back ones at the front.'

The workers in the vineyard

20 'So you see,' Jesus continued, 'the kingdom of heaven is like a landowner who went out early in the morning to hire workers for his vineyard. ²He agreed with the workers to give them a dinar a day, and sent them off to his vineyard.

³'He went out again in the middle of the morning, and saw some others standing in the market-place with nothing to do.

⁴"You too can go to the vineyard," he said, "and I'll give you what's right." ⁵So off they went.

'He went out again about midday, and then in the middle of the afternoon, and did the same. ⁶Then, with only an hour of the day left, he went out and found other people standing there.

'"Why are you standing here all day with nothing to do?" he asked them.

⁷'"Because no one has hired us," they replied.

'"Well," he said, "you too can go into the vineyard."

⁸'When evening came, the vineyard-owner said to his servant, "Call the workers and give them their pay. Start with the last, and go on to the first."

⁹'So the ones who had worked for one hour came, and each of them received a dinar. ¹⁰When the first ones came, they thought they would get something more; but they, too, each received a dinar.

¹¹'When they had been given it, they grumbled against the landowner. ¹²"This lot who came in last", they said, "have only worked for one hour – and they've been put on a level with us! And we did all the hard work, all day, and in the heat as well!"

¹³'"My friend," he said to one of them, "I'm not doing you any wrong. You agreed with me on one dinar, didn't you? ¹⁴Take it! It's yours! And be on your way. I want to give this fellow who came at the end the same as you. ¹⁵Or are you suggesting that I'm not allowed to do what I like with my own money? Or are you giving me the evil eye because I'm good?"

¹⁶'So those at the back will be at the front, and the front ones at the back.'

The cup he had to drink

¹⁷Jesus was on his way up to Jerusalem. He took the twelve disciples aside in private, while they were on the road, and said to them, ¹⁸'Look here. We're going up to Jerusalem. The son of man will be handed over to the chief priests and the scribes, and they're going to condemn him to death. ¹⁹They will hand him over to the pagans, and they're going to mock him, flog him and crucify him. And on the third day he will be raised.'

²⁰Then the mother of Zebedee's sons came up, with her sons, to Jesus. She bowed low in front of him and indicated that she had a special request to make.

²¹'What d'you want?' he asked her.

'It's about these two sons of mine,' she said to him. 'Please say that, when you're king, they may sit, one at your right hand and one at your left.'

²²'You don't know what you're asking for,' said Jesus. 'Can you two drink the cup I'm going to drink?'

'Yes, we can,' they replied.

²³'Well,' said Jesus, 'so you will drink my cup, then! But sitting at my right and left is not something I can grant. That's up to my father to give to whoever he has in mind.'

²⁴When the other ten heard this they were annoyed with the two brothers. ²⁵But Jesus called them together.

'You know how it is with pagan rulers,' he said. 'They lord it over their subjects. They get all high and mighty and let everybody know it. ²⁶But that's not how it's to be with you. If any of you wants to be great, he must be your servant. ²⁷If any of you wants to be first, he must be the slave of all. ²⁸That's how it is with the son of man: he didn't come to have servants obey him, but to *be* a servant – and to give his life as "a ransom for many".'

The healing of two blind men

²⁹As they were going out of Jericho, a large crowd was following Jesus. ³⁰Just then two blind men were sitting by the wayside, and heard that Jesus was going by. 'Have pity on us, Master, son of David!' they shouted.

³¹The crowd scolded them and told them to be silent. But they shouted out all the more, 'Have pity on us, Master, son of David!'

³²Jesus came to a stop. He called them.

'What d'you want me to do for you?' he asked.

³³'Master,' they replied, 'we want you to open our eyes.'

³⁴Jesus was very moved. He touched their eyes. At once they could see again, and they followed him.

Jesus rides into Jerusalem

21 When they came near to Jerusalem, and arrived at Bethphage on the Mount of Olives, Jesus sent two of the disciples on ahead.

²'Go into the village over there,' he said, 'and at once you'll find a donkey tied up, and a foal beside it. Untie them and bring them to me. ³And if anyone says anything to you, say, "The master needs them, and he'll send them back straight away."'

He sent them off at once.

⁴This happened so that the prophet's words might be fulfilled:

⁵Tell this to Zion's daughter:
look now! Here comes your king;
he's humble, mounted on an ass,
yes, on a foal, its young.

⁶So the disciples went off and did as Jesus had told them. ⁷They brought the donkey and its foal, and put their cloaks on them, and Jesus sat on them.

⁸The huge crowd spread their cloaks on the road. Others cut branches from the trees and scattered them on the road. ⁹The crowds who went on ahead of him, and those who were following behind, shouted out,

Hosanna now to David's Son!
God's blessing on the coming one –
the one who comes in the Lord's own name!
Hosanna in the highest!

¹⁰When they came into Jerusalem, the whole city was gripped with excitement.

'Who is this?' they were saying.

¹¹'This is the prophet, Jesus,' replied the crowds, 'from Nazareth in Galilee!'

The Temple and the fig tree

¹²Jesus went into the Temple and threw out all the people who were buying and selling in the Temple. He upturned the tables of the money-changers and the seats of the dove-sellers.

¹³'This is what the Bible says,' he said to them,

My house will be called a house of prayer –
but you have made it a brigands' lair!'

¹⁴The blind and the lame came to him in the Temple, and he healed them. ¹⁵But

when the chief priests and the scribes saw the remarkable things he was doing, and the children shouting out 'Hosanna to David's son!' in the Temple, they were very cross.

¹⁶'Do you hear what they're saying?' they asked Jesus.

'Yes,' said Jesus. 'Did you never read what it says,

> You called forth praise to rise to you
> from newborn babes and infants too!'

¹⁷Then he left them, and went out of the city to Bethany, where he stayed the night.

¹⁸Early the next morning Jesus went back to the city. He was hungry. ¹⁹He saw a single fig tree beside the road, but when he came up to it he found nothing on it except leaves.

'May you never bear fruit, ever again!' he said to it. Instantly the fig tree withered up.

²⁰The disciples saw it, and were astonished.

'Look how quickly the fig tree has withered up!' they said.

²¹'I'm telling you the truth,' replied Jesus. 'If you have faith, and don't doubt, you will not only be able to do this to a fig tree, but if you say to this mountain, "Be lifted up and thrown into the sea", it will happen. ²²Whatever you ask in prayer, you'll get it, if you believe.'

The question about John

²³Jesus went into the Temple. As he was teaching, the chief priests and the elders of the people came up to him.

'By what right are you doing these things?' they asked him. 'Who gave you this right?'

²⁴'I'm going to ask you one question, too,' replied Jesus, 'and if you tell me the answer then I'll tell you by what right I'm doing these things. ²⁵Where did John's baptism come from? Was it from heaven, or from this world?'

They debated this among themselves. 'If we say "from heaven"; they said, 'he's going to say to us, "So why didn't you believe him?" ²⁶But if we say "from this world", we'll have to watch out for the crowd, because they all reckon that John was a prophet.'

²⁷So they answered Jesus, 'We don't know.'

'Well, then,' said Jesus, 'nor will I tell you by what right I'm doing these things.

²⁸'What d'you think?' he went on. 'Once upon a time there was a man who had two sons.

'He went to the first one and said, "Now then, my boy, off you go and do a day's work in the vineyard."

²⁹'"Don't want to," replied the son; but afterwards he thought better of it and went.

³⁰'He went to the other son and said the same thing.

'"Certainly, Master," he said; but he didn't go.

³¹'So which of the two did what his father wanted?'

'The first,' they answered.

'I'm telling you the truth,' Jesus said to them. 'The tax-collectors and prostitutes are going into God's kingdom ahead of you! ³²Yes: John came to you, in accordance with God's righteous covenant plan, and you didn't believe him – but the tax-collectors and prostitutes believed him. But when you saw it, you didn't think better of it afterwards and believe him.'

The parable of the tenants

³³'Listen to another parable,' Jesus went on. 'Once upon a time there was a householder who planted a vineyard, built a wall for it, dug out a wine-press in it, and built a tower. Then he let it out to tenant farmers and went away on a journey.

³⁴'When harvest time arrived, he sent his slaves to the farmers to collect his produce. ³⁵The farmers seized his slaves; they beat one, killed another, and stoned another. ³⁶Again he sent other slaves, more than before, and they treated them in the same way. ³⁷Finally he sent his son to them.

'"They'll respect my son," he said.

³⁸'But the farmers saw the son.

'"This fellow's the heir!" they said among themselves. "Come on, let's kill him, and then we can take over the property!"

³⁹'So they seized him, threw him out of the vineyard, and killed him.

⁴⁰'Now then: when the vineyard-owner returns, what will he do to those farmers?'

⁴¹'He'll kill them brutally, the wretches!' they said. 'And he'll lease the vineyard to other farmers who'll give him the produce at the right time.'

⁴²'Did you never read what the Bible says?' said Jesus to them:

The stone the builders threw away
is now atop the corner;
it's from the Lord, all this, they say
and we looked on in wonder.

⁴³'So then let me tell you this: God's kingdom is going to be taken away from you and given to a nation that will produce the goods. ⁴⁴Anyone who falls on this stone will be smashed to pieces, and anyone it falls on will be crushed.'

⁴⁵When the chief priests and the Pharisees heard his parables, they knew he was talking about them. ⁴⁶They tried to arrest him, but they were afraid of the crowds, who regarded him as a prophet.

The parable of the wedding feast

22 Jesus spoke to them once again in parables.

²'The kingdom of heaven,' he said, 'is like a king who made a wedding feast for his son. ³He sent his slaves to call the invited guests to the wedding, and they didn't want to come.

⁴'Again he sent other slaves, with these instructions: "Say to the guests, Look! I've got my dinner ready; my bulls and fatted calves have been killed; everything is prepared. Come to the wedding!"

⁵'But they didn't take any notice. They went off, one to his own farm, another to see to his business. ⁶The others laid hands on his slaves, abused them and killed them. ⁷(The king was angry, and sent his soldiers to destroy those murderers and burn down their city.) ⁸Then he said to his slaves, "The wedding is ready, but the guests didn't deserve it. ⁹So go to the roads leading out of town, and invite everyone you find to the wedding." ¹⁰The slaves went off into the streets and rounded up everyone they found, bad and good alike. And the wedding was filled with partygoers.

¹¹'But when the king came in to look at the guests, he saw there a man who wasn't wearing a wedding suit.

¹²'"My friend," he said to him, "how did you get in here without a wedding suit?" And he was speechless. ¹³Then the king said to the servants, "Tie him up, hands and feet, and throw him into the darkness outside, where people weep and grind their teeth."

¹⁴'Many are called, you see, but few are chosen.'

Paying taxes to Caesar

¹⁵Then the Pharisees went and plotted how they might trap him into saying the wrong thing. ¹⁶They sent their followers to him, with the Herodians.

'Teacher,' they said, 'we know that you are truthful, and that you teach God's way truthfully. You don't care what anyone thinks about you, because you don't try to flatter people or favour them. ¹⁷So tell us what you think. Is it lawful to pay tribute to Caesar, or not?'

¹⁸Jesus knew their evil intentions.

'Why are you trying to trick me, you hypocrites?' he said. ¹⁹'Show me the tribute coin.' They brought him a dinar.

²⁰'This . . . image,' said Jesus, 'and this . . . inscription. Who do they belong to?'

²¹'Caesar,' they said.

'Well then,' said Jesus, 'you'd better give Caesar back what belongs to Caesar! And – give God what belongs to God!'

²²When they heard that they were astonished. They left him and went away.

The question of the resurrection

²³The same day some Sadducees came to him. (The Sadducees deny the resurrection.) Their question was this.

²⁴'Teacher,' they began, 'Moses said, "If a man dies without children, his brother should marry his widow and raise up seed for his brother." ²⁵Well now, there were seven brothers living among us. The first got married, and then died, and since he didn't have children he left his wife to his brother. ²⁶The same thing happened with the second and the third, and so on with all seven. ²⁷Last of all the woman died. ²⁸So: in the resurrection, whose wife will she be, of all the seven? All of them had married her, after all.'

²⁹This was Jesus' answer to them: 'You are quite mistaken,' he said, 'because you don't

know your Bibles or God's power. ³⁰In the resurrection, you see, people don't marry or get married off; they are like angels in heaven. ³¹But as for the resurrection of the dead, did you never read what was said to you by God, in these words: ³²"I am the God of Abraham, and the God of Isaac, and the God of Jacob?" He isn't God of the dead, but of the living.'

³³The crowds heard this, and they were astonished at his teaching.

The Great Commandment, and David's Master

³⁴When the Pharisees heard that Jesus had silenced the Sadducees, they got together in a group. ³⁵One of them, a lawyer, put him on the spot with this question.

³⁶'Teacher,' he said, 'which is the most important commandment in the law?'

³⁷'You must love the Lord your God', replied Jesus, 'with all your heart, with all your life, and with all your mind. ³⁸This is the first commandment, and it's the one that really matters. ³⁹The second is similar, and it's this: You must love your neighbour as yourself. ⁴⁰The entire law hangs on these two commandments – and that goes for the prophets, too.'

⁴¹While the Pharisees were gathered there, Jesus asked them, ⁴²'What's your view of the Messiah? Whose son is he?'

'David's,' they said to him.

⁴³'Why then', said Jesus, 'does David (speaking by the spirit) call him "Master", when he says,

⁴⁴The Master says to my master,
sit here at my right hand,
until I place your enemies
down beneath your feet.

⁴⁵'If David calls him "Master", how can he be his son?'

⁴⁶Nobody was able to answer him a single word. From that day on nobody dared ask him anything any more.

Warnings against scribes and Pharisees

23 Then Jesus spoke to the crowds and to his disciples: ²'The scribes and Pharisees', he said, 'sit on the seat of Moses. ³So you must do whatever they tell you, and keep it, but don't do the things they do. You see, they *talk* but they don't *do*. ⁴They tie up heavy bundles which are difficult to carry, and they dump them on people's shoulders – but they themselves aren't prepared to lift a little finger to move them!

⁵'Everything they do is for show, to be seen by people. Yes, they make their prayer-boxes large and their prayer-tassels long, ⁶and they love the chief places at dinners, the main seats in the synagogues, ⁷the greetings in the market-places, and having people call them "Rabbi".

⁸'You mustn't be called "Rabbi". You have one teacher, and you are all one family. ⁹And you shouldn't call anyone "father" on earth, because you have one father, in heaven. ¹⁰Nor should you be called "teacher", because you have one teacher, the Messiah.

¹¹'The greatest among you should be your servant. ¹²People who make themselves great will be humbled; and people who humble themselves will become great.'

Condemnation of scribes and Pharisees (1)

¹³'Woe betide you, scribes and Pharisees, you hypocrites!' Jesus continued. 'You lock up the kingdom of heaven in front of people's faces. You don't go in yourselves, and when other people try to enter, you stop them.

¹⁵'Woe betide you, scribes and Pharisees, you hypocrites! You cross sea and land to make one single Gentile take up Judaism, and when that happens you make the convert twice as much a child of Gehenna as you are yourselves.

¹⁶'Woe betide you, you blind guides! This is what you say: "If anyone swears by the Temple, it's nothing; but if anyone swears by the gold in the Temple, the oath is valid." ¹⁷How crazy and blind can you get! Which is greater, the gold, or the Temple that makes the gold sacred? ¹⁸And you say, "If anyone swears by the altar, it's nothing; but if anyone swears by the gift on it, the oath is valid." ¹⁹How blind you are! Which is greater, the gift, or the altar that makes the gift sacred? ²⁰So whoever swears by the altar swears by it and by everything on it. ²¹And whoever swears by the Temple swears by

it and by the one who lives in it. ²²And whoever swears by heaven swears by the throne of God and by the one who sits on it.'

Condemnation of scribes and Pharisees (2)

²³'Woe betide you, scribes and Pharisees, you hypocrites!' Jesus went on. 'You tithe mint and dill and cumin, and you omit the serious matters of the law like justice, mercy and loyalty. You should have done these, without neglecting the others. ²⁴You're blind guides! You filter out a gnat, but you gulp down a camel!

²⁵'Woe betide you, scribes and Pharisees, you hypocrites! You scrub the outside of the cup and the dish, but the inside is full of extortion and moral flabbiness. ²⁶You blind Pharisee, first make the inside of the cup clean, and then the outside will be clean as well.

²⁷'Woe betide you, scribes and Pharisees, you hypocrites! You're like whitewashed graves, which look very fine on the outside, but inside they are full of the bones of the dead and uncleanness of every kind. ²⁸That's like you: on the outside you appear to be virtuous and law-abiding, but inside you are full of hypocrisy and lawlessness.

²⁹'Woe betide you, scribes and Pharisees, you hypocrites! You build the tombs of the prophets, and you decorate the memorials of the righteous, ³⁰and you say, "If we'd lived in the days of our ancestors, we wouldn't have gone along with them in killing the prophets." ³¹So you testify against yourselves that you are the children of the people who murdered the prophets! ³²Well then, go ahead: complete the work your ancestors began! ³³You snakes, you nest of vipers, how can you escape the judgment of Gehenna?'

Judgment on Jerusalem and its leaders

³⁴'Because of all this,' Jesus concluded, 'I'm sending you prophets, wise men and scribes. Some of them you will kill and crucify. Some of them you will whip in your synagogues. You'll chase them from town to town. ³⁵That's how all the righteous blood that's been shed on earth, from the blood of righteous Abel to the blood of Zechariah son of Barachiah – you murdered him between sanctuary and altar – all that blood will come upon you. ³⁶I'm telling you the solemn truth: it will all come on this generation.

³⁷'Jerusalem, Jerusalem, killing the prophets and stoning those who are sent to you! How often have I longed to gather up your children, the way a hen gathers up her brood under her wings, and you didn't want me to! ³⁸Now, see here: your house has been abandoned by God; it's a ruin. ³⁹Yes, I tell you: you won't see me again from now on until you say, "God's blessing on the coming one, the one who comes in the Lord's own name!"'

The beginning of the birth pangs

24 Jesus left the Temple and went away. As he did so, his disciples came and pointed out the Temple buildings to him. ²'Yes,' he said, 'and you see all these things? I'm telling you the truth: not one stone will be left standing upon another. All of them will be thrown down.'

³As he was sitting on the Mount of Olives, his disciples came to him privately.

'Tell us,' they said, 'when will these things happen? And what will be the sign that you are going to appear as king, and that the end of the age is upon us?'

⁴'Watch out,' replied Jesus. 'Don't let anyone deceive you. ⁵You see, there will be several who will come along, using my name, telling you "I'm the Messiah!" They will fool lots of people. ⁶You're going to hear about wars, actual wars and rumoured ones; make sure you don't get alarmed. This has got to happen, but it doesn't mean the end is coming yet. ⁷Nations will rise against one another, and kingdoms against each other. There will be famines and earthquakes here and there. ⁸All this is just the start of the birthpangs.

⁹'Then they will hand you over to be tortured, and they will kill you. You will be hated by all nations because of my name. ¹⁰Then several will find the going too hard, and they will betray each other and hate each other. ¹¹Many false prophets will arise, and they will deceive plenty of people. ¹²And because lawlessness will be on the increase, many will find their love growing cold. ¹³But the one who

lasts out to the end will be delivered. ¹⁴And this gospel of the kingdom must be announced to the whole world, as a witness to all the nations. Then the end will come.'

The desolating sacrilege

¹⁵'So when you see "the sacrilege that desolates", as Daniel the prophet put it, "standing in the holy place" (the reader should understand), ¹⁶then those who are in Judaea should take to their heels and run to the mountains. ¹⁷If you're up on your roof, don't go down into the house to get things out. ¹⁸If you're in the fields, don't go back to pick up your cloak. ¹⁹It's going to be terrible for pregnant and nursing women during those days. ²⁰Pray that it won't be winter when you have to run away, or for that matter a sabbath. ²¹Yes: there's going to be such great suffering then as has never been since the start of the world until now – no, and won't ever be again. ²²And if those days had not been shortened, nobody at all would have been rescued. But for the sake of God's chosen ones those days will be shortened.

²³'Then if anyone says to you, "Look! Here is the Messiah!" or "Look! There he is!", don't believe them. ²⁴False messiahs will arise, you see, and false prophets too. They will provide great signs and portents, so as to deceive even God's chosen ones, if that were possible. ²⁵Remember, I'm telling you this beforehand! ²⁶'So if someone says to you, "Look! He's out in the wilderness", don't go out. If they say, "Look, he's in the inner room", don't believe them. ²⁷You see, the royal appearing of the son of man will be like the lightning that comes from the East and flashes across to the West. ²⁸Where the carcass is, there the vultures will gather.'

The coming of the son of man

²⁹'Straight away,' Jesus continued, 'after the suffering that those days will bring,

> The sun will turn to darkness,
> and the moon won't give its light;
> the stars will fall from heaven,
> and the powers of heaven will shake.

³⁰'And then the sign of the son of man will appear in heaven; then all the tribes of the earth will mourn. They will see "the son of man coming on the clouds of heaven" with power and great glory. ³¹He will send off his messengers with a great trumpet-blast, and they will collect his chosen ones from the four winds, from one end of heaven to the other.

³²'Learn the hidden meaning from the fig tree. When its branch begins to sprout, and to push out its leaves, then you know that summer is nearly there. ³³So with you: when you see all these things, you will know that it is near, at the very gates. ³⁴I'm telling you the truth: this generation won't be gone before all these things happen. ³⁵Heaven and earth will disappear, but my words will never, ever disappear.'

The unexpected coming

³⁶'Nobody knows what day or time this will happen,' Jesus went on. 'The angels in heaven don't know it, and nor does the son; only the father knows. ³⁷You see, the royal appearing of the son of man will be like the days of Noah.

³⁸'What does that mean? Well, in those days, before the flood, they were eating and drinking, they were getting married and giving children in marriage, right up to the day when Noah went into the ark. ³⁹They didn't know about it until the flood came and swept them all away. That's what it'll be like at the royal appearing of the son of man.

⁴⁰'On that day there will be two people working in the field. One will be taken, the other will be left. ⁴¹There will be two women grinding corn in the mill. One will be taken, the other will be left.

⁴²'So keep alert! You don't know what day your master will come. ⁴³But bear this in mind: if the householder had known what time of night the burglar was going to come, he would have stayed awake and wouldn't have let his house get broken into. ⁴⁴So you too must be ready! The son of man is coming at a time you don't expect.'

The wise and wicked slaves

⁴⁵'So,' Jesus went on, 'who then is the trustworthy and sensible slave, the one

the master will set over his household, so that he will give them their meals at the right time? ⁴⁶Blessings on the servant whom the master, when he comes, finds doing just that. ⁴⁷I'm telling you the truth: he'll promote him to be over all his belongings. ⁴⁸But if the wicked slave says in his heart, "My master's taking his time", ⁴⁹and starts to beat the other slaves, and to feast and drink with the drunkards, ⁵⁰the master of that slave will come on a day he doesn't expect, and at a time he doesn't know. ⁵¹He will cut him in two, and put him along with the hypocrites, where people will weep and grind their teeth.'

The wise and foolish girls

25 'Then,' continued Jesus, 'the kingdom of heaven will be like ten girls who each took their own torches and went out to meet the bridegroom. ²Five of them were silly, and five were sensible. ³The silly ones took their torches, but didn't take oil with them. ⁴The sensible ones took oil, in flasks, along with their torches.

⁵'The bridegroom took his time coming, and they all nodded off and went to sleep. ⁶In the middle of the night a shout went up: "Here's the bridegroom! Come on and meet him!" ⁷Then all the girls got up and trimmed the wicks of their torches.

⁸'The silly ones said to the sensible ones, "Give us some of your oil! Our torches are going out!"

⁹'But the sensible ones answered, "No! If we do that, there won't be enough for all of us together! You'd better go to the dealers and buy some for yourselves."

¹⁰'So off they went to buy oil. But, while they were gone, the bridegroom arrived. The ones who were ready went in with him to the wedding party, and the door was shut.

¹¹'Later on the other girls came back. "Master, Master!" they said. "Open the door for us!"

¹²'"I'm telling you the truth," he said, "I don't know you."

¹³'So keep awake! You don't know the day or the hour.'

The parable of the talents

¹⁴'This is what it will be like,' Jesus went on. 'It will be like a man who was going off on a journey. He summoned his slaves, and handed over control of his property to them. ¹⁵He gave five talents to the first, two to the next, and one to the last – each according to his ability. Then he left.

'Straight away ¹⁶the man who had been given the five talents went out and traded with them, and made five more. ¹⁷Similarly, the one who had received two talents went and made another two. ¹⁸But the one who received a single talent went and dug a hole in the ground, and hid his master's money.

¹⁹'After a long time, the master of those slaves came back and settled accounts with them. ²⁰The man who had received five talents came forward and gave him the other five talents. "Master," he said, "you gave me five talents. Look: I've made another five!" ²¹"Well done indeed," said his master. "You're an excellent slave, and loyal too! You've been trustworthy with small things, and now I'm going to put you in charge of bigger ones. Come and join your master's celebration!"

²²'Then the man who had had the two talents came forward. "Master," he said, "you gave me two talents. Look: I've made another two!" ²³"Well done indeed," said his master. "You're an excellent slave, and loyal too! You've been trustworthy with small things, and now I'm going to put you in charge of bigger ones. Come and join your master's celebration!"

²⁴'Then the man who had had the one talent came forward. "Master," he said, "I knew that you were a hard man. You reap where you didn't sow, and you profit from things you never invested in. ²⁵So I was scared! I went and hid your talent in the ground. Here it is: it's yours, you can have it back."

²⁶'"You're a wicked and lazy slave!" answered his master. "So! You knew that I reap where I didn't sow, and profit from investments I never made? ²⁷Then you should have put my money with the bankers, and when I returned I would have received back what I had with interest!

²⁸'"So take the talent from him," he went on, "and give it to the man who has ten talents." ²⁹(If someone already has something, you see, they will be given more, and they'll have plenty. But if someone has nothing, even what they have will be taken away from them.) ³⁰"But as for this useless slave, throw him outside in

the dark, where people weep and grind their teeth.'"

The sheep and the goats

³¹'When the son of man comes in his glory,' Jesus went on, 'and all the angels with him, then he will sit on his glorious throne. ³²All the nations will be assembled in front of him, and he will separate them from one another, like a shepherd separates the sheep from the goats. ³³He will stand the sheep at his right hand, and the goats at his left.

³⁴'Then the king will say to those on his right, "Come here, you people who my father has blessed. Inherit the kingdom prepared for you from the foundation of the world! ³⁵Why? Because I was hungry and you gave me something to eat. I was thirsty and you gave me something to drink. I was a stranger and you made me welcome. ³⁶I was naked and you clothed me; I was sick and you looked after me; I was in prison and you came to me."

³⁷'Then the righteous will answer him, "Master, when did we see you hungry and feed you, or thirsty and give you a drink? ³⁸When did we see you a stranger and welcome you, or naked and clothe you? ³⁹When did we see you sick or in prison and come to see you?"

⁴⁰'Then the king will answer them, "I'm telling you the truth: when you did it to one of the least significant of my brothers and sisters here, you did it to me."

⁴¹'Then he will say to those on his left hand, "Get away from me! You're accursed! Go to the everlasting fire prepared for the devil and his angels! ⁴²Why? Because I was hungry and you gave me nothing to eat! I was thirsty and you gave me nothing to drink! ⁴³I was a stranger and you didn't welcome me; I was naked and you didn't clothe me; I was sick and in prison and you didn't look after me!"

⁴⁴'Then they too will answer, "Master, when did we see you hungry or thirsty, or a stranger, or naked, or sick, or in prison, and didn't do anything for you?"

⁴⁵'Then he will answer them, "I'm telling you the truth: when you didn't do it for one of the least significant of my brothers and sisters here, you didn't do it for me."

⁴⁶'And they will go away into everlasting punishment, but the righteous will go into everlasting life.'

Preparations for Jesus' death

26 So this is how it finally happened. When Jesus had finished all these sayings, he said to his disciples, ²'In two days' time, as you know, it'll be Passover! That's when the son of man will be handed over to be crucified.'

³Then the chief priests got together with the elders of the people, in the official residence of the high priest, who was called Caiaphas. ⁴They plotted how to capture Jesus by some trick, and kill him.

⁵'We'd better not try anything at the feast,' they said. 'We don't want the people to riot.'

⁶While Jesus was at Bethany, in the house of Simon (known as 'the Leper'), ⁷a woman came to him who had an alabaster vase of extremely valuable ointment. She poured it on his head as he was reclining at the table.

⁸When the disciples saw it, they were furious.

'What's the point of all this waste?' they said. ⁹'This could have been sold for a fortune, and the money could have been given to the poor!'

¹⁰Jesus knew what they were thinking.

'Why make life difficult for the woman?' he said. 'It's a lovely thing, what she's done for me. ¹¹You always have the poor with you, don't you? But you won't always have me. ¹²When she poured this ointment on my body, you see, she did it to prepare me for my burial. ¹³I'm telling you the truth: wherever this gospel is announced in all the world, what she has just done will be told, and people will remember her.'

Passover and betrayal

¹⁴Then one of the Twelve, called Judas Iscariot, went to the chief priests.

¹⁵'What will you give me', he said, 'to hand him over to you?'

They settled the deal with him at thirty pieces of silver. ¹⁶From that moment on, he was watching for an opportunity to hand him over.

¹⁷On the first day of the Feast of Unleavened Bread, the disciples said to Jesus, 'Where do you want us to get the Passover ready for you to eat it?'

¹⁸'Go into the city', he said, 'to a certain man, and say to him, "The Teacher says, 'My time is very close. I'm going to keep the Passover at your house with my disciples.'"'

¹⁹So the disciples did as Jesus had told them, and got the Passover ready.

²⁰When evening came, he settled down with the Twelve. ²¹As they were eating, he said, 'I'm telling you the truth: one of you will betray me.'

²²They were extremely upset, and began to say one by one, 'It's not me, is it, Master?'

²³'It's one who's dipped his hand with me in the dish,' Jesus replied. 'That's the one who will betray me. ²⁴The son of man is on his way, as the Bible said it would happen, but it's misery for the man who hands him over. It would be better for that man if he'd never been born.'

²⁵At this, Judas, who was planning to betray him, said, 'It isn't me, is it, Teacher?'

'You've just said so,' he replied.

The Last Supper

²⁶As they were eating, Jesus took some bread, blessed it, broke it and gave it to the disciples.

'Take it and eat it,' he said, 'this is my body.'

²⁷Then he took a cup; and, after giving thanks, he gave it to them.

'Drink this, all of you,' he said. ²⁸'This is my blood of the covenant, which is poured out for many for the forgiveness of sins. ²⁹But let me tell you this: I will not drink any more from this fruit of the vine, until that day when I drink it new with you in the kingdom of my father.'

³⁰They sang a hymn, and went out to the Mount of Olives.

³¹Then Jesus said to them, 'You are all going to stumble and fall tonight because of me. This is what the Bible says, you see:

I shall strike the shepherd,
and the sheep of the flock will be scattered.

³²'But after I am raised up, I shall go on ahead of you to Galilee.'

³³'Even if everyone else trips and falls,' said Peter in reply to him, 'I'm never going to do that!'

³⁴'I'm telling you the truth,' said Jesus to him, 'this very night, before the cock has crowed, you will deny me three times.'

³⁵'Even if I have to die with you,' said Peter to him, 'I won't ever deny you!'

And all the disciples said the same.

Gethsemane

³⁶So Jesus went with them to the place called Gethsemane.

'You sit here,' he said to the disciples, 'while I go over there and pray.'

³⁷He took Peter and the two sons of Zebedee with him, and began to be very upset and distressed.

³⁸'My soul is overwhelmed with grief,' he said, 'even to death. Stay here and keep watch with me.'

³⁹Then, going a little further on, he fell on his face and prayed.

'My father,' he said, 'if it's possible – please, please let this cup go away from me! But . . . not what I want, but what you want.'

⁴⁰He came back to the disciples and found them asleep.

'So,' he said to Peter, 'couldn't you keep watch with me for a single hour? ⁴¹Watch and pray so that you don't get pulled down into the time of testing. The spirit is eager, but the body is weak.'

⁴²Again, for the second time, he went off and said, 'My father, if it's not possible for this to pass unless I drink it, let your will be done.'

⁴³Again he came and found them asleep; their eyes were heavy. ⁴⁴Once more he left them and went away. He prayed for the third time, using the same words once again. ⁴⁵Then he came back to the disciples.

'You can sleep now,' he said, 'and have a good rest! Look – the time has come, and the son of man is given over into the hands of wicked people! ⁴⁶Get up and let's be going. Look! Here comes the one who's going to betray me!'

Jesus is arrested

⁴⁷While Jesus was still speaking, there was Judas, one of the Twelve. He had come with a

large crowd, with swords and clubs, from the chief priests and the elders of the people. ⁴⁸The one who was intending to betray him gave them a sign: 'The one I kiss – that's him! Grab hold of him!'

⁴⁹So he went up at once to Jesus and said 'Greetings, Teacher!', and kissed him.

⁵⁰'My friend,' said Jesus, 'what have you come to do?'

Then they came and laid hands on Jesus, and arrested him.

⁵¹At that, one of the men with Jesus reached out his hand, drew his sword and hit the high priest's slave, cutting off his ear.

⁵²'Put your sword back where it belongs!' said Jesus to him. 'People who use the sword die by the sword! ⁵³Don't you realize that I could call on my father and have him send me more than twelve legions of angels, just like that? ⁵⁴But how then can the Bible come true when it says this has to happen?'

⁵⁵At that time Jesus said to the crowds, 'Have you really come out with swords and sticks to arrest me, as if I were some kind of brigand? I sat there teaching in the Temple every day, and you didn't arrest me! ⁵⁶But all this has happened so that the writings of the prophets would be fulfilled.'

Then all the disciples abandoned him and ran away.

Jesus before Caiaphas

⁵⁷The people who had arrested Jesus took him off to Caiaphas the high priest. The scribes and elders had already gathered at his house. ⁵⁸Peter, however, followed him at some distance, all the way to the high priest's residence. He went in and sat with the servants, to see how things would work out.

⁵⁹The high priest and the whole council tried to produce false evidence against Jesus, to frame a capital charge and have him killed. ⁶⁰But even though they brought in plenty of lying witnesses, they couldn't find the evidence they wanted. Finally two people came forward ⁶¹and declared: 'This fellow said, "I can destroy God's Temple and build it again in three days!"'

⁶²Then the high priest stood up.

'Aren't you going to answer?' he said to him. 'What are these people accusing you of?'

⁶³But Jesus remained silent.

Then the high priest said to him, 'I put you on oath before the living God: tell us if you are the Messiah, God's son!'

⁶⁴'You said the words,' replied Jesus. 'But let me tell you this: from now on you will see "the son of man sitting at the right hand of the Power, and coming on the clouds of heaven".'

⁶⁵Then the high priest tore his robes.

'He's blasphemed!' he said. 'Why do we need any more witnesses? Look – you've heard his blasphemy, here and now! ⁶⁶What's your verdict?'

'He deserves to die,' they answered.

⁶⁷Then they spat in his face and hit him. Some of them slapped him, ⁶⁸and said, 'Prophesy for us, Mr Messiah! Who was it who hit you?'

Peter's denial

⁶⁹Meanwhile, Peter sat outside in the courtyard.

One of the servant-girls came up to him. 'You were with Jesus the Galilean too, weren't you?' she said.

⁷⁰He denied it in front of everyone.

'I don't know what you're talking about,' he said.

⁷¹He went out to the gateway. Another girl saw him, and said to the people who were there, 'This fellow was with Jesus the Nazarene!'

⁷²Once more he denied it, this time swearing, 'I don't know the man!'

⁷³After a little while the people standing around came up and said to Peter, 'You really are one of them! Look – the way you talk makes it obvious!'

⁷⁴Then he began to curse and swear, 'I don't know the man!' And then, all at once, the cock crowed.

⁷⁵And Peter remembered.

He remembered the words Jesus had spoken to him: 'Before the cock crows, you will deny me three times.'

And he went outside and cried like a baby.

The death of Judas

27 When dawn broke, all the chief priests and elders of the people held a council meeting about Jesus, in order to have him put to death. ²They tied him up, took him off, and handed him over to Pilate, the governor.

³Meanwhile Judas, who had betrayed him, saw that he had been condemned, and was filled with remorse. He took the thirty pieces of silver back to the high priests and elders.

⁴'I've sinned!' he said. 'I betrayed an innocent man, and now I've got his blood on my hands!'

'See if we care!' they replied. 'Deal with it yourself.'

⁵And he threw down the money in the Temple, and left, and went and hanged himself.

⁶'Well now,' said the chief priests, picking up the money. 'According to the law, we can't put it into the Temple treasury. It's the price of someone's blood.'

⁷So they had a discussion, and used it to buy the Potter's Field, as a burial place for foreigners. ⁸(That's why that field is called Blood Field, to this day.) ⁹Then the word that was spoken by Jeremiah the prophet came true:

> They took the thirty pieces of silver,
> the price of the one who was valued,
> valued by the children of Israel;
> ¹⁰and they gave them for the potter's field,
> as the Lord instructed me.

Jesus and Barabbas before Pilate

¹¹So Jesus stood in front of the governor.

'Are you the King of the Jews?' the governor asked him.

'If you say so,' replied Jesus.

¹²The chief priests and elders poured out their accusations against him, but he made no answer.

¹³Then Pilate said to him, 'Don't you hear all this evidence they're bringing against you?'

¹⁴He gave him no answer, not even a word, which quite astonished the governor.

¹⁵Now the governor had a custom. At festival time he used to release one prisoner for the crowd, whoever they chose. ¹⁶Just then they had a famous prisoner, called Jesus Barabbas. ¹⁷So when the people were all gathered there, Pilate said to them, 'Who do you want me to release for you? Jesus Barabbas, or Jesus the so-called Messiah?' ¹⁸(He knew that they'd handed him over out of sheer envy.)

¹⁹While he was presiding in the court, his wife sent a message to him.

'Don't have anything to do with that man,' she said. 'He's innocent! I've had a really bad time today in a dream, all because of him.'

²⁰The high priests and the elders persuaded the crowds to ask for Barabbas, and to have Jesus killed. ²¹So when the governor came back to them again, and asked, 'Which of the two do you want me to release for you?' they said, 'Barabbas!'

²²'So what shall I do with Jesus the so-called Messiah?' asked Pilate.

'Let him be crucified!' they all said.

²³'Why?' asked Pilate. 'What's he done wrong?'

But they shouted all the louder, 'Let him be crucified!'

²⁴Pilate saw that it was no good. In fact, there was a riot brewing. So he took some water and washed his hands in front of the crowd.

'I'm not guilty of this man's blood,' he said. 'It's your problem.'

²⁵'Let his blood be on us!' answered all the people. 'And on our children!'

²⁶Then Pilate released Barabbas for them. He had Jesus flogged, and handed him over to be crucified.

Jesus mocked and crucified

²⁷Then the soldiers of the governor took Jesus into the barracks, and gathered the whole regiment together. ²⁸They took off his clothes and dressed him up in a scarlet military cloak. ²⁹They wove a crown out of thorns and stuck it on his head, and put a reed in his right hand. Then they knelt down in front of him.

'Greetings, King of the Jews!' they said, making fun of him.

³⁰They spat on him. Then they took the reed and beat him about the head. ³¹When they had finished mocking him, they took off the cloak, dressed him in his own clothes again, and led him off to crucify him.

³²As they were going out they found a man from Cyrene, called Simon. They forced him to carry his cross.

³³When they came to the place called Golgotha, which means Skull-Place, ³⁴they gave him a drink of wine mixed with bitter herbs. When he tasted it, he refused to drink it.

35So then they crucified him. They divided up his clothes by casting lots, 36and they sat down and kept watch over him there. 37And they placed the written charge above his head: 'This is Jesus, the King of the Jews.'

38Then they crucified two brigands alongside him, one on his right and one on his left.

Jesus mocked on the cross

39The people who were going by shouted blasphemies at Jesus. They shook their heads at him.

40'So!' they said. 'You were going to destroy the Temple and build it in three days, were you? Save yourself, if you're God's son! Come down from the cross!'

41The chief priests, too, and the scribes and the elders, mocked him.

42'He rescued others,' they said, 'but he can't rescue himself! All right, so he's the King of Israel! – well, let him come down from the cross right now, and then we'll really believe that he is! 43He trusted in God; let God deliver him now, if he's that keen on him – after all, he did say he was God's son!'

44The brigands who were crucified alongside him heaped insults on him as well.

The death of God's son

45From noon until mid-afternoon there was darkness over the whole land. 46About the middle of the afternoon Jesus shouted out in a loud voice, '*Eli, Eli, lema sabachthani!*'

– which means, 'My God, my God, why did you abandon me?'

47Some of the people who were standing there heard it and said, 'This fellow's calling Elijah!'

48One of them ran at once and got a sponge. He filled it with vinegar, put it on a reed, and gave him a drink.

49The others said, 'Wait a bit. Let's see if Elijah is going to come and rescue him!'

50But Jesus shouted out loudly one more time, and then breathed his last breath.

51At that instant the Temple curtain was torn in two, from top to bottom. The earth shook, the rocks were split, 52and the tombs burst open. Many bodies of the sleeping holy ones were raised. 53They came out of the tombs after Jesus' resurrection, and went into the holy city, where they appeared to many people.

54When the centurion and the others with him, keeping watch over Jesus, saw the earthquake and the things that happened, they were scared out of their wits.

'He really was God's son!' they said.

55There were several women there, watching from a distance. They had followed Jesus from Galilee, helping to look after his needs. 56They included Mary Magdalene, Mary the mother of James and Joseph, and the mother of Zebedee's sons.

The burial of Jesus

57When evening came, a rich man from Arimathea arrived. He was called Joseph, and he, too, was a disciple of Jesus. 58He went to Pilate and requested the body of Jesus. Pilate gave the order that it should be given to him.

59So Joseph took the body and wrapped it in a clean linen cloth. 60He laid it in his own new tomb, which he had carved out of the rock. Then he rolled a large stone across the doorway of the tomb, and went away.

61Mary Magdalene was there, and so was the other Mary. They were sitting opposite the tomb.

62On the next day (that is, the day after Preparation Day), the chief priests and the Pharisees went as a group to Pilate.

63'Sir,' they said, 'when that deceiver was still alive, we recall that he said, "After three days, I'll rise again." 64So please give the order for the tomb to be made secure until the third day. Otherwise his disciples might come and steal him away, and then tell the people, "He's been raised from the dead!", and so the last deception would be worse than the first.'

65'You may have a guard,' said Pilate; 'go and make it as secure as you know how.' 66So they went and made the tomb secure, sealing the stone and putting a guard on watch.

The resurrection of Jesus

28 Dawn was breaking on the first day of the week; the sabbath was over. Mary Magdalene, and the other Mary, had come to look at the tomb, ²when suddenly there was a great earthquake. An angel of the Lord came down from heaven. He came to the stone, rolled it away, and sat down on top of it. ³Looking at him was like looking at lightning, and his clothes were white, like snow. ⁴The guards trembled with terror at him, and became like corpses themselves.

⁵'Don't be afraid,' said the angel to the women. 'I know you're looking for Jesus, who was crucified. ⁶He isn't here! He's been raised, as he said he would be! Come and see the place where he was lying –⁷and then go at once, and tell his disciples that he's been raised from the dead, and that he's going on ahead of you to Galilee. That's where you'll see him. There: I've told you.'

⁸The women scurried off quickly away from the tomb, in a mixture of terror and great delight, and went to tell his disciples. ⁹Suddenly, there was Jesus himself. He met them and said, 'Greetings!' They came up to him and took hold of his feet, prostrating themselves in front of him.

¹⁰'Don't be afraid,' said Jesus to them. 'Go and tell my brothers that they should go to Galilee. Tell them they'll see me there.'

The priests and the guards

¹¹While the women were on their way, some of the soldiers who had been on guard went into the city and told the chief priests everything that had happened. ¹²They called an emergency meeting with the elders, allotted a substantial sum of money, and gave it to the soldiers.

¹³'This,' they told them, 'is what you are to say: "His disciples came in the night, while we were asleep, and stole him away." ¹⁴And if this gets reported to the governor, we'll explain it to him and make sure you stay out of trouble.'

¹⁵They took the money and did as they had been instructed. And this story still goes the rounds among the Jews to this day.

The Great Commission

¹⁶So the eleven disciples went off to Galilee, to the mountain where Jesus had instructed them to go. ¹⁷There they saw him, and worshipped him, though some hesitated.

¹⁸Jesus came towards them and addressed them.

'All authority in heaven and on earth,' he said, 'has been given to me! ¹⁹So you must go and make all the nations into disciples. Baptize them in the name of the father, and of the son, and of the holy spirit. ²⁰Teach them to observe everything I have commanded you. And look: I am with you, every single day, to the very end of the age.'

Mark

Mark's is the shortest gospel, and when you read it straight through you can *feel* why: it has a breathless, eager sense, with things happening 'at once', and one dramatic incident following another. Unlike its longer cousins, Matthew and Luke, Mark gets straight to the point and pretty much stays there: who is Jesus, and what was the meaning of his death?

The central scene in which these questions are posed, and answered, comes towards the end of chapter 8, halfway through the story, when Peter blurts out, 'You're the Messiah!' – and Jesus at once tells his followers that they are going to Jerusalem where he will be crucified. But the abrupt opening of the book sets this double truth within a larger and still more startling frame. Quoting Malachi and Isaiah, Mark indicates that John the Baptist is to be understood as the 'messenger' who will prepare the way, as the 'voice in the wilderness' who will be the herald . . . for *Israel's God in person*. Malachi 3 and Isaiah 40 are not about a coming Messiah. They are about Israel's God himself, coming back at last to judge and to save after the long years of extended exile. Mark intends that we should read his fast-paced, dramatic narrative as the story of what it looked like when the one God finally came back.

Mark has comparatively little 'teaching'. What he does have is Jesus acting with authority, healing all sorts and conditions, casting out demons, feasting with tax-collectors, stilling storms, multiplying loaves and fishes – and teasingly chiding his disciples because they kept on misunderstanding what was going on. They knew he was doing things which meant that the one God was taking charge in a whole new way, but though 'the kingdom of God' was a well-known slogan at the time they had never thought it would look like this.

The drama intensifies as they reach the city. On the way, the disciples squabble about who would be the greatest, and Jesus reminds them that in the true 'kingdom' all human power-systems will be stood on their heads – because, he says, 'the son of man didn't come to be waited on. He came to be the servant, to give his life "as a ransom for many"' (10.45). The meaning of the cross is found *inside* the power-reversing meaning of the kingdom. Mark explains the meaning of Jesus' strange action in the Temple, symbolizing its destruction, in a sequence of events and dialogues which highlight Jesus' own role as the last prophet, issuing the last warning to God's rebel subjects. We are not surprised when he is arrested, or that the question of the Temple and its destruction is central at his trial. Jesus responds to the ultimate question of his identity with a devastating combination of Daniel 7 and Psalm 110: he is claiming not only to be Israel's Messiah but to share the throne of the one God. Mark shows us all this in such a way as to make his alert reader conclude, like the Roman centurion at the foot of the cross, that 'this fellow really was God's son' (15.39).

Mark, then, has given us the message, straight from the shoulder: Jesus is the Messiah, the embodiment of Israel's God, dying to rescue his people from their fate. But his book is also full of mysteries: beneath the plain-spoken story we sense huge earthquakes rumbling until, with the women at the tomb on Easter morning, all we can sense is 'trembling and panic' (16.8). They were right to be afraid. The world had been turned upside down. *Their vision of God had been turned inside out.* St Mark's gospel, twenty pages or so of text in a modern translation, still has the capacity to do that for today's readers.

The preaching of John the Baptist

1 This is where the good news starts – the good news of Jesus the Messiah, God's son. ²Isaiah the prophet put it like this ('Look! I am sending my messenger ahead of me; he will clear the way for you!'):

³'A shout goes up in the desert: Make way for the Lord! Clear a straight path for him!'

⁴John the Baptizer appeared in the desert. He was announcing a baptism of repentance, to forgive sins. ⁵The whole of Judaea, and everyone who lived in Jerusalem, went out to him; they confessed their sins and were baptized by him in the river Jordan. ⁶John wore camel-hair clothes, with a leather belt round his waist. He used to eat locusts and wild honey.

⁷'Someone a lot stronger than me is coming close behind,' John used to tell them. 'I don't deserve to squat down and undo his sandals. ⁸I've plunged you in the water; he's going to plunge you in the holy spirit.'

Jesus' baptism

⁹This is how it happened. Around that time, Jesus came from Nazareth in Galilee, and was baptized by John in the river Jordan. ¹⁰That very moment, as he was getting out of the water, he saw the heavens open, and the spirit coming down like a dove onto him. ¹¹Then there came a voice, out of the heavens: 'You are my son! You are the one I love! You make me very glad.'

¹²All at once the spirit pushed him out into the desert. ¹³He was in the desert forty days, and the satan tested him there. He was with the wild beasts, and angels waited on him.

The calling of the disciples

¹⁴After John's arrest, Jesus came into Galilee, announcing God's good news.

¹⁵'The time is fulfilled!' he said; 'God's kingdom is arriving! Turn back, and believe the good news!'

¹⁶As he went along beside the sea of Galilee he saw Simon and his brother Andrew. They were fishermen, and were casting nets into the sea.

¹⁷'Follow me!' said Jesus to them. 'I'll have you fishing for people!'

¹⁸Straight away they left their nets and followed him. ¹⁹He went on a bit, and saw James, Zebedee's son, and John his brother. They were in the boat mending their nets, ²⁰and he called them then and there. They left their father Zebedee in the boat with the hired servants, and went off after him.

Exorcism and healings

²¹They went to Capernaum. At once, on the sabbath, Jesus went into the synagogue and taught. ²²They were astonished at his teaching. He wasn't like the legal teachers; he said things on his own authority.

²³All at once, in their synagogue, there was a man with an unclean spirit.

²⁴'What business have you got with us, Jesus of Nazareth?' he yelled. 'Have you come to destroy us? I know who you are: you're God's Holy One!'

²⁵'Be quiet!' ordered Jesus. 'And come out of him!'

²⁶The unclean spirit convulsed the man, gave a great shout, and came out of him. ²⁷Everyone was astonished.

'What's this?' they started to say to each other. 'New teaching – with real authority! He even tells the unclean spirits what to do, and they do it!'

²⁸Word about Jesus spread at once, all over the surrounding district of Galilee.

²⁹They came out of the synagogue, and went at once (with James and John) into Simon and Andrew's house. ³⁰Simon's mother-in-law was in bed with a fever, and they told Jesus about her right away. ³¹He went in, took her by the hand, and raised her up. The fever left her, and she waited on them.

³²When the sun went down and evening came, they brought to Jesus everyone who was ill, all who were demon-possessed. ³³The whole town was gathered around the door. ³⁴Jesus healed many people suffering from all kinds of diseases, and cast out many demons. He didn't allow the demons to speak, because they knew him.

The healing of a man with a skin disease

³⁵Very early – in the middle of the night, actually – Jesus got up and went out, off to a

lonely place, and prayed. ³⁶Simon, and those with him, followed. ³⁷When they found him, they said, 'Everyone is looking for you!'

³⁸'Let's go off to the other towns around here,' Jesus replied, 'so that I can tell the news to people there too. That's why I came out.'

³⁹So he went into their synagogues, throughout the whole of Galilee, telling the news and casting out demons.

⁴⁰A man with a virulent skin disease came up to him. He knelt down and begged him, 'If you want to, you can make me clean!'

⁴¹Jesus was deeply moved. He reached out his hand and touched him, and said to him, 'I do want to: be clean!' ⁴²The disease left him at once, and he was clean.

⁴³Jesus sent him away at once, with this stern warning: ⁴⁴'Mind you don't say anything to anyone! Just go and show yourself to the priest, and make the offering Moses commanded, to purify yourself and to give them a sign.'

⁴⁵But the man went out and began to tell the news widely. He spread the tale so effectively that Jesus couldn't any longer go publicly into a town. He stayed out in the open country, and people came to him from all around.

The healing of the paralytic

2 Jesus went back again to Capernaum, where, after a few days, word got round that he was at home. ²A crowd gathered, so that people couldn't even get near the door as he was telling them the message.

³A party arrived: four people carrying a paralysed man, bringing him to Jesus. ⁴They couldn't get through to him because of the crowd, so they opened up the roof above where he was. When they had dug through it, they used ropes to let down the stretcher the paralysed man was lying on.

⁵Jesus saw their faith, and said to the paralysed man, 'Child, your sins are forgiven!'

⁶'How dare the fellow speak like this?' grumbled some of the legal experts among themselves. ⁷'It's blasphemy! Who can forgive sins except God?'

⁸Jesus knew at once, in his spirit, that thoughts like this were in the air. 'Why do your hearts tell you to think that?' he asked. ⁹'Answer me this,' he went on. 'Is it easier to say to this cripple, "Your sins are forgiven", or to say, "Get up, pick up your stretcher, and walk"?

¹⁰'You want to know that the son of man has authority on earth to forgive sins?' He turned to the paralytic. ¹¹'I tell you,' he said, 'Get up, take your stretcher, and go home.' ¹²He got up, picked up the stretcher in a flash, and went out before them all.

Everyone was astonished, and they praised God. 'We've never seen anything like this!' they said.

The calling of Levi

¹³Once more Jesus went out beside the sea. All the crowd came to him, and he taught them.

¹⁴As he went along he saw Levi, son of Alphaeus, sitting at the toll booth. 'Follow me!' he said. And he got up and followed him.

¹⁵That's how Jesus came to be sitting at home with lots of tax-collectors and sinners. There they were, plenty of them, sitting with Jesus and his disciples; they had become his followers.

¹⁶When the legal experts from the Pharisees saw him eating with tax-collectors and sinners, they said to his disciples, 'Why does he eat with tax-collectors and sinners?'

¹⁷When Jesus heard it, he said to them, 'It's sick people who need the doctor, not healthy ones. I came to call the bad people, not the good ones.'

Questions about fasting

¹⁸John's disciples, and the Pharisees' disciples, were fasting. People came and said to Jesus, 'Look here: John's disciples are fasting, and so are the Pharisees' disciples; why aren't yours?'

¹⁹'How can the wedding guests fast', Jesus replied, 'if the bridegroom is there with them? As long as they've got the bridegroom with them, they can't fast.

²⁰'Mind you, the time is coming when the bridegroom will be taken away from them. They'll fast then all right.

²¹'No one sews unshrunk cloth onto an old cloak. If they do, the new patch will tear the old cloth, and they'll end up with a worse hole. ²²Nor does anyone put new wine into old

wineskins. If they do, the wine will burst the skins, and they'll lose the wine and the skins together. New wine needs new skins.'

Teachings on the sabbath

[23]One sabbath, Jesus was walking through the cornfields. His disciples made their way along, plucking corn as they went.

[24]'Look here,' said the Pharisees to him, 'why are they doing something illegal on the sabbath?'

[25]'Haven't you ever read what David did,' replied Jesus, 'when he was in difficulties, and he and his men got hungry? [26]He went into God's house (this was when Abiathar was high priest), and ate the "bread of the presence", which only the priests were allowed to eat – and he gave it to the people with him.'

[27]'The sabbath was made for humans,' he said, 'not humans for the sabbath; [28]so the son of man is master even of the sabbath.'

Healing of the man with the withered hand

3 Once more Jesus went to the synagogue. There was a man there with a withered hand. [2]People were watching to see if Jesus would heal him on the sabbath, so that they could frame a charge against him.

[3]'Stand up', said Jesus to the man with the withered hand, 'and come out here.' And he said to them, [4]'Is it lawful to do good on the sabbath, or to do evil? To save life or to kill?' They stayed quiet.

[5]He was deeply upset at their hard-heartedness, and looked round at them angrily. Then he said to the man, 'Stretch out your hand.' He stretched it out – and his hand was restored. [6]The Pharisees went out right away and began to plot with the Herodians against Jesus, trying to find a way to destroy him.

The Twelve are appointed

[7]Jesus went off towards the sea with his disciples, and a large crowd from Galilee followed him. A great company, too, from Judaea, [8]Jerusalem, Idumaea, Transjordan, and the region of Tyre and Sidon, heard what he was doing and came to him.

[9]There was a real danger that he might be crushed by the crowd, so he told his disciples to get a boat ready for him. [10]He healed large numbers, and sick people were pushing towards him to touch him. [11]Whenever unclean spirits saw him, they fell down in front of him and yelled out, 'You are the son of God!' [12]He gave them strict orders not to reveal his identity.

[13]Jesus went up the mountain, and summoned the people he wanted, and they came to him. [14]He appointed twelve (naming them 'apostles') to be with him and to be sent out as heralds, [15]and to have authority to cast out demons. [16]In appointing the Twelve, he named Simon 'Peter'; [17]James, son of Zebedee, and his brother John, he named 'Boanerges', which means 'sons of thunder'. The others were [18]Andrew, Philip, Bartholomew, Matthew, Thomas, James son of Alphaeus, Thaddaeus, Simon the Cananaean, [19]and Judas Iscariot (the one who handed him over).

Jesus and Beelzebul

[20]He went into the house. A crowd gathered again, so that they couldn't even have a meal. [21]When his family heard it, they came to restrain him. 'He's out of his mind,' they said.

[22]Experts who had come from Jerusalem were saying, 'He is possessed by Beelzebul! He casts out demons by the prince of demons!'

[23]Jesus summoned them and spoke to them in pictures. 'How can the Accuser cast out the Accuser? [24]If a kingdom splits into two factions, it can't last; [25]if a household splits into two factions, it can't last. [26]So if the Accuser revolts against himself and splits into two, he can't last – his time is up! [27]But remember: no one can get into a strong man's house and steal his property unless first they tie up the strong man; then they can plunder his house.

[28]'I'm telling you the truth: people will be forgiven all sins, and all blasphemies of whatever sort. [29]But people who blaspheme the holy spirit will never find forgiveness. They will be guilty of an eternal sin.' [30]That was his response to their claim that he had an unclean spirit.

Jesus' family

³¹Jesus' mother and brothers appeared. They waited outside the house, and sent in a message, asking for him.

³²'Look!' said the crowd sitting around Jesus. 'Your mother, your brothers, and your sisters are outside! They're searching for you!'

³³'Who is my mother?' replied Jesus. 'Who are my brothers?'

³⁴He looked around him at the people sitting there in a ring. 'Here is my mother!' he said. 'Here are my brothers! ³⁵Anybody who does God's will is my brother! And my sister! And my mother!'

The parable of the sower

4 Once again Jesus began to teach beside the sea. A huge crowd gathered; so he got into a boat and stationed himself on the sea, with all the crowd on the shore looking out to sea. ²He taught them lots of things in parables. This is how his teaching went.

³'Listen!' he said. 'Once upon a time there was a sower who went out sowing. ⁴As he was sowing, some seed fell beside the path, and the birds came and ate it up. ⁵Other seed fell on the rock, where it didn't have much soil. There was no depth to the ground, so it shot up at once; ⁶but when the sun came up it was scorched, and withered away, because it hadn't got any root. ⁷Other seed fell in among thorns; the thorns grew up and choked it, and it didn't give any crop. ⁸And other seeds fell into good soil, and gave a harvest, which grew up and increased, and bore a yield, in some cases thirtyfold, in some sixtyfold, and in some a hundredfold.'

⁹And he added, 'If you've got ears, then listen!'

¹⁰When they were alone, the people who were around Jesus, with the Twelve, asked him about the parables.

¹¹'The mystery of God's kingdom is given to you,' he replied, 'but for the people outside it's all in parables, ¹²so that "they may look and look but never see, and hear and hear but never understand; otherwise they would turn and be forgiven".

¹³'Don't you understand the parable?' he said to them. 'How are you going to understand all the parables?

¹⁴'The sower sows the word. ¹⁵The ones by the path are people who hear the word, but immediately the Accuser comes and takes away the word that has been sown in them. ¹⁶The ones sown on the rock are those who hear the word and accept it with excitement, ¹⁷but don't have any root in themselves. They are short-term enthusiasts. When the word brings them trouble or hostility they quickly become disillusioned. ¹⁸The others – the ones sown among thorns – are those who hear the word, ¹⁹and the worries of the present age, and the deceit of riches, and desires for other kinds of things, come in and choke the word, so that it produces no fruit. ²⁰But the ones sown on good soil are the people who hear the word and receive it, and produce fruit, some thirtyfold, some sixtyfold, some a hundredfold.'

A lamp on its stand

²¹Jesus said to them, 'When you bring a lamp into a room, do you put it under a bucket, or under a bed? Of course not! It goes on a lampstand. ²²No: nothing is secret except what's meant to be revealed, and nothing is covered up except what's meant to be uncovered. ²³If you have ears, then listen!

²⁴'Be careful with what you hear,' he went on. 'The scales you use will be used for you, and more so. ²⁵If you have something, you'll be given more; but if you have nothing, even what you have will be taken away.'

More seed parables

²⁶'This is what God's kingdom is like,' said Jesus. 'Once upon a time a man sowed seed on the ground. ²⁷Every night he went to bed; every day he got up; and the seed sprouted and grew without him knowing how it did it. ²⁸The ground produces crops by itself: first the stalk, then the ear, then the complete corn in the ear. ²⁹But when the crop is ready, in goes the sickle at once, because harvest has arrived.'

³⁰'What shall we say God's kingdom is like?' he said. 'What picture shall we give of it? ³¹It's like a grain of mustard seed. When it's sown on the ground, it's the smallest of all the seeds of the earth. ³²But when it's sown, it springs up

and becomes the biggest of all shrubs. It grows large branches, so that "the birds of the air make their nests" within its shade.'

³³He used to tell them a lot of parables like this, speaking the word as much as they were able to hear. ³⁴He never spoke except using parables. But he explained everything to his own disciples in private.

Jesus calms the storm

³⁵That day, when it was evening, Jesus said to them, 'Let's go over to the other side.'

³⁶They left the crowd, and took him with them in the boat he'd been in. There were other boats with him too.

³⁷A big windstorm blew up. The waves beat on the boat, and it quickly began to fill. ³⁸Jesus, however, was asleep on a cushion in the stern. They woke him up.

'Teacher!' they said to him, 'We're going down! Don't you care?'

³⁹He got up, scolded the wind, and said to the sea, 'Silence! Shut up!'

The wind died, and there was a flat calm.

⁴⁰Then he said to them, 'Why are you scared? Don't you believe yet?'

⁴¹Great fear stole over them. 'Who *is* this?' they said to each other. 'Even the wind and the sea do what he says!'

The healing of the demoniac

5 So they came over the sea to the land of the Gerasenes. ²When they got out of the boat, they were suddenly confronted by a man with an unclean spirit. ³He was emerging from a graveyard, which was where he lived. Nobody had been able to tie him up, not even with a chain; ⁴he had often been bound with shackles and chains, but he used to tear up the chains and snap the shackles. No one had the strength to tame him. ⁵On and on, night and day, he used to shout out in the graveyard and on the hillside, and slash himself with stones.

⁶When he saw Jesus a long way away, he ran and threw himself down in front of him.

⁷'Why you and me, Jesus?' he shouted at the top of his voice. 'Why you and me, son of the High God? By God, stop torturing me!' –

⁸this last, because Jesus was saying to him, 'Unclean spirit, come out of him!'

⁹'What's your name?' Jesus asked him.

'Legion,' he replied. 'That's my name – there are lots of us!' ¹⁰And he implored Jesus not to send them out of the country.

¹¹It so happened that right there, near the hillside, was a sizeable herd of pigs. They were grazing.

¹²'Send us to the pigs,' begged the spirits, 'so that we can enter them.'

¹³So Jesus gave them permission. The unclean spirits came out and went into the pigs. The herd rushed down the steep slope into the sea – about two thousand of them! – and were drowned.

¹⁴The herdsmen fled. They told it in the town, they told it in the countryside, and people came to see what had happened. ¹⁵They came to Jesus; and there they saw the man who had been demon-possessed, who had had the 'legion', seated, clothed and stone-cold sober. They were afraid. ¹⁶The people who had seen it all told them what had happened to the man – and to the pigs. ¹⁷And they began to beg Jesus to leave their district.

¹⁸Jesus was getting back into the boat, when the man asked if he could go with him. ¹⁹Jesus wouldn't let him.

'Go back home,' he said. 'Go to your people and tell them what the Lord has done for you. Tell them how he had pity on you.'

²⁰He went off, and began to announce in the Ten Towns what Jesus had done for him. Everyone was astonished.

Jairus's daughter and the woman with chronic bleeding

²¹Jesus crossed over once more in the boat to the other side. There a large crowd gathered around him, and he was by the seashore.

²²One of the synagogue presidents, a man named Jairus, arrived. When he saw Jesus he fell down at his feet.

²³'My daughter's going to die! My daughter's going to die!' he pleaded. 'Please come – lay your hands on her – rescue her and let her live!'

²⁴Jesus went off with him. A large crowd followed, and pressed in on him.

²⁵A woman who had had internal bleeding for twelve years heard about Jesus. ²⁶(She'd had a rough time at the hands of one doctor after another; she'd spent all she had on treatment, and had got worse rather than better.) ²⁷She came up in the crowd behind him and touched his clothes. ²⁸'If I can just touch his clothes,' she said to herself, 'I'll be rescued.' ²⁹At once her flow of blood dried up. She knew, in her body, that her illness was cured.

³⁰Jesus knew at once, inside himself, that power had gone out of him. He turned around in the crowd and said, 'Who touched my clothes?'

³¹'You see this crowd crushing you,' said the disciples, 'and you say "Who touched me?"'

³²He looked round to see who had done it. ³³The woman came up; she was afraid and trembling, but she knew what had happened to her. She fell down in front of him and told him the whole truth.

³⁴'My daughter,' Jesus said to her, 'your faith has rescued you. Go in peace. Be healed from your illness.'

The raising of Jairus's daughter

³⁵As he said this, some people arrived from the synagogue president's house.

'Your daughter's dead,' they said. 'Why bother the teacher any more?'

³⁶Jesus overheard the message. 'Don't be afraid!' he said to the synagogue president. 'Just believe!'

³⁷He didn't let anyone go with him except Peter, James and James's brother John. ³⁸They arrived at the synagogue president's house, and saw a commotion, with a lot of weeping and wailing. ³⁹Jesus went inside.

'Why are you making such a fuss?' he said. 'Why all this weeping? The child isn't dead; she's asleep.' ⁴⁰And they laughed at him.

He put them all out. Then he took the child's father and mother, and his companions, and they went in to where the child was. ⁴¹He took hold of her hand, and said to her, '*Talitha koum*', which means 'Time to get up, little girl!' ⁴²At once the girl got up and walked about. (She was twelve years old.) They were astonished out of their wits. ⁴³Then he commanded them over and over not to let anyone know about it, and told them to give her something to eat.

A prophet in his own town

6 Jesus went away from there, and came to his home region. His disciples followed him. ²On the sabbath, he began to teach in the synagogue. When they heard him, lots of people were astonished.

'Where does he get it all from?' they said. 'What's this wisdom he's been given? How does he get this kind of power in his hands? ³Isn't he the handyman, Mary's son? Isn't he the brother of James, Joses, Judah and Simon? And aren't his sisters here with us?' They took offence at him.

⁴'Prophets have honour everywhere', said Jesus, 'except in their own country, their own family, and their own home.'

⁵He couldn't do anything remarkable there, except that he laid hands on a few sick people and cured them. ⁶Their unbelief dumbfounded him.

He went round the villages, teaching.

The Twelve sent out

⁷Jesus called the Twelve, and began to send them out in pairs, giving them authority over unclean spirits. ⁸These were his instructions: they were not to take anything for the road, just one staff; no bread, no bag, no cash in the belt; ⁹to wear sandals, and not to wear a second tunic.

¹⁰'Whenever you go into a house,' he told them, 'stay there until you leave the district. ¹¹If any place doesn't welcome you, or won't listen to you, go away and wipe the dust from your feet as evidence against them.'

¹²They went off and announced that people should repent. ¹³They cast out several demons; and they anointed many sick people with oil, and cured them.

The speculations of Herod

¹⁴Jesus' name became well known, and reached the ears of King Herod.

'It's John the Baptist,' he said, 'risen from the dead! That's why these powers are at work in him.'

¹⁵Other people said, 'It's Elijah!'

Others said, 'He's a prophet, like one of the old prophets.'

¹⁶'No,' said Herod when he heard this. 'It's John. I cut off his head, and he's been raised.'

Herod and John the Baptist

¹⁷What had happened was this. Herod had married Herodias, his brother Philip's wife. ¹⁸John regularly told Herod it wasn't right for him to take his brother's wife; so Herod gave the word, arrested him and tied him up in prison. ¹⁹Herodias kept up a grudge against him and wanted to kill him, but couldn't; ²⁰Herod was afraid of John, knowing that he was a just and holy man. So he protected him, and used to listen to him regularly. What he heard disturbed him greatly, and yet he enjoyed listening to him.

²¹And then, one day, the moment came. There was a great party. It was Herod's birthday, and he gave a feast for his leading retainers, militia officers, and the great and good of Galilee. ²²Herodias's daughter came in and danced, and Herod and his guests were delighted.

'Tell me what you'd like', said the king to the girl, 'and I'll give it you!'

²³He swore to her, over and over again, 'Whatever you ask me, I'll give it you – right up to half my kingdom!'

²⁴She went out, and said to her mother, 'What shall I ask for?'

'The head of John the Baptist,' she replied.

²⁵So she went back at once to the king, all eager, and made her request: 'I want you to give me, right now, on a dish – the head of John the Baptist!'

²⁶The king was distraught. But his oaths on the one hand, and his guests on the other, meant he hadn't the guts to refuse her. ²⁷So he sent a jailer straight away with orders to bring John's head. He went and beheaded him in the prison, ²⁸brought the head on a dish, and gave it to the girl. The girl gave it to her mother.

²⁹When John's followers heard about it, they came and took his body, and buried it in a tomb.

The feeding of the five thousand

³⁰The apostles came back to Jesus and told him all they had done and taught. ³¹'All right,' he said, 'it's time for a break. Come away, just you, and we'll go somewhere lonely and private.' (Crowds of people were coming and going and they didn't even have time to eat.)

³²So they went off privately in the boat to a deserted spot. ³³And . . . crowds saw them going, realized what was happening, hurried on foot from all the towns, and arrived there first. ³⁴When Jesus got out of the boat he saw the huge crowd, and was deeply sorry for them, because they were like a flock without a shepherd. So he started to teach them many things.

³⁵It was already getting late when his disciples came to him and said, 'Look: there's nothing here. It's getting late. ³⁶Send them away. They need to go off into the countryside and the villages and buy themselves some food.'

³⁷'Why don't you give them something?' Jesus replied.

'Are you suggesting', they asked, 'that we should go and spend two hundred dinars and get food for this lot?'

³⁸'Well,' said Jesus, 'how many loaves have you got? Go and see.'

They found out, and said, 'Five, and a couple of fish.'

³⁹Jesus told them to sit everyone down, group by group, on the green grass. ⁴⁰So they sat down in companies, by hundreds and by fifties. ⁴¹Then he took the five loaves and the two fishes, looked up to heaven, blessed the bread, broke it, and gave it to his disciples to give to the crowd. Then he divided the two fish for them all. ⁴²Everyone ate, and had plenty. ⁴³They picked up the leftovers, and there were twelve baskets of broken pieces, and of the fish. ⁴⁴The number of men who had eaten was five thousand.

Jesus walks on water

⁴⁵At once Jesus made his disciples get into the boat and set sail across towards Bethsaida, while he dismissed the crowd. ⁴⁶He took his leave of them and went off up the mountain to pray.

⁴⁷When evening came, the boat was in the middle of the sea, and he was alone on the

shore. ⁴⁸He saw they were having to work hard at rowing, because the wind was against them; and he came to them, about the fourth watch of the night, walking on the sea. He intended to go past them, ⁴⁹but they saw him walking on the sea and thought it was an apparition. They yelled out; ⁵⁰all of them saw him, and they were scared stiff.

At once he spoke to them.

'Cheer up,' he said, 'it's me. Don't be afraid.'

⁵¹He came up to them and got into the boat, and the wind stopped. They were overwhelmed with astonishment; ⁵²they hadn't understood about the loaves, because their hearts were hardened.

⁵³They made landfall at Gennesaret, and tied the boat up. ⁵⁴People recognized Jesus as soon as they got out of the boat, ⁵⁵and scurried about the whole region to bring sick people on stretchers to wherever they heard that he was. ⁵⁶And wherever he went, in villages, towns or in the open country, they placed the sick in the market-places and begged him to let them touch even the hem of his garment. And all who touched it were healed.

God's law and human tradition

7 The Pharisees gathered round Jesus, together with some legal experts from Jerusalem. ²They saw that some of his disciples were eating their food with unclean (that is, unwashed) hands.

³(The Pharisees, you see – and indeed all the Jews – don't eat unless they first carefully wash their hands. This is to maintain the tradition of the elders. ⁴When they come in from the market, they never eat without washing. There are many other traditions which they keep: washings of cups, pots and bronze dishes.)

⁵Anyway, the Pharisees and legal experts asked Jesus, 'Why don't your disciples follow the tradition of the elders? Why do they eat their food with unwashed hands?'

⁶'Isaiah summed you up just right,' Jesus replied. 'Hypocrites, the lot of you! What he said was this:

With their lips this people honour me,
but with their hearts they turn away from me;
⁷all in vain they think to worship me,
all they teach is human commands.

⁸'You abandon God's commands, and keep human tradition!

⁹'So,' he went on, 'you have a fine way of setting aside God's command so as to maintain your tradition. ¹⁰Here's an example: Moses said, "Honour your father and your mother," and, "Anyone who slanders father or mother should die." ¹¹But you say, "If someone says to their father or mother, 'What you might get from me – it's Korban!'" (which means, 'given-to-God'), ¹²you don't let them do anything else for their father or mother! ¹³The net result is that you invalidate God's word through this tradition which you hand on. And there are lots more things like that which you do.'

Clean and unclean

¹⁴Jesus summoned the crowd again.

'Listen to me, all of you,' he said, 'and get this straight. ¹⁵What goes into you from outside can't make you unclean. What makes you unclean is what comes out from inside.'

¹⁷When they got back into the house, away from the crowd, his disciples asked him about the parable.

¹⁸'You didn't get it either?' he asked. 'Don't you see that whatever goes into someone from outside can't make them unclean? ¹⁹It doesn't go into the heart; it only goes into the stomach, and then carries on, out down the drain.' (Result: all foods are clean.)

²⁰'What makes someone unclean', he went on, 'is what comes out of them. ²¹Evil intentions come from inside, out of people's hearts – sexual immorality, theft, murder, ²²adultery, greed, wickedness, treachery, debauchery, envy, slander, pride, stupidity. ²³These evil things all come from inside. They are what make someone unclean.'

The Syrophoenician woman

²⁴Jesus got up, left that place, and went to the region of Tyre. When he took up residence in a house, he didn't want anyone to know, but it wasn't possible for him to remain hidden. ²⁵On the contrary: news of him at once reached a woman who had a young daughter with an unclean spirit. She came and threw

herself down at his feet. ²⁶She was Greek, a Syrophoenician by race; and she asked him to cast the demon out of her daughter.

²⁷'Let the children eat what they want first,' Jesus replied. 'It's not right to take the children's bread and throw it to the dogs.'

²⁸'Well, Master,' she said, 'even the dogs under the table eat the crumbs that the children drop.'

²⁹'Well said!' replied Jesus. 'Off you go; the demon has left your daughter.'

³⁰So she went home, and found the child lying on the bed, and the demon gone.

A deaf and mute man is healed

³¹Jesus went away from the region of Tyre, through Sidon, round towards the sea of Galilee, and into the region of the Ten Towns. ³²They brought to him a man who was deaf and had a speech impediment, and asked that he would lay his hand on him.

³³Jesus took the man off in private, away from the crowd. He put his fingers into his ears, spat, and touched his tongue. ³⁴Then he looked up to heaven, groaned, and said to him, '*Ephphatha*' (that is, 'Be opened'). ³⁵Immediately the man's ears were opened, and his tongue was untied, and he spoke clearly.

³⁶Jesus gave them orders not to tell anyone. But the more he ordered them, the more they spread the news. ³⁷They were totally astonished.

'Everything he does is marvellous!' they said. 'He even makes the deaf hear and the mute speak!'

The feeding of the four thousand

8 Once again, about that time, a large crowd gathered with nothing to eat.

Jesus called the disciples.

²'I'm really sorry for the people,' he said. 'They've been with me three days now, and they haven't got anything to eat. ³If I send them home hungry, they'll collapse on the way. Some of them have come from miles off.'

⁴'Where could you get food for all this lot, out here in the wilderness?' answered his disciples.

⁵'How many loaves have you got?' he asked.
'Seven,' they replied.

⁶He told the crowd to sit down on the ground. Then he took the seven loaves, gave thanks, broke them and gave them to his disciples to share around, and they gave them to the crowd. ⁷They had a few small fish, which he also blessed and told them to distribute. ⁸They ate; they were satisfied; and they took up seven baskets of leftover bits. ⁹There were about four thousand people. And he sent them away.

¹⁰At once Jesus got into the boat with his disciples and went to the region of Dalmanoutha.

The yeast of the Pharisees and Herod

¹¹The Pharisees came out and began to dispute with Jesus. They were asking him for a sign from heaven, to test him out.

¹²Jesus groaned deeply in his spirit. 'Why is this generation looking for a sign?' he said. 'I'm telling you the truth: no sign will be given to this generation.' ¹³He left them again, got into the boat, and crossed over to the other side.

¹⁴They had forgotten to get any bread, and had only one loaf with them in the boat.

¹⁵'Beware!' said Jesus sternly to them. 'Watch out for leaven – the Pharisees' leaven, and Herod's leaven too!'

¹⁶'It must be something to do with us not having any bread,' they said to each other.

¹⁷'Why are you mumbling about not bringing bread?' said Jesus, who knew what they were thinking. 'Don't you get it? Don't you understand? Have your hearts gone hard?

¹⁸Can't you see with your two good eyes?
Can't you hear with your two good ears?

'And don't you remember? ¹⁹When I broke the five loaves for the five thousand, how many baskets full of broken bits were left over?'

'Twelve,' they said.

²⁰'And the seven loaves for the four thousand – how many baskets full of bits were left over?'

'Seven.'

²¹'You still don't get it?'

Peter's declaration of Jesus' messiahship

²²They arrived at Bethsaida. A blind man was brought to Jesus, and they begged him to touch

him. ²³He took his hand, led him off outside the village, and put spittle on his eyes. Then he laid his hands on him, and asked, 'Can you see anything?'

²⁴'I can see people,' said the man, peering around, 'but they look like trees walking about.'

²⁵Then Jesus laid his hands on him once more. This time he looked hard, and his sight came back: he could see everything clearly. ²⁶Jesus sent him back home.

'Don't even go into the village,' he said.

²⁷Jesus and his disciples came to the villages of Caesarea Philippi. On the way he asked his disciples, 'Who are people saying that I am?'

²⁸'John the Baptist,' they said, 'or, some say, Elijah; or, others say, one of the prophets.'

²⁹'What about you?' asked Jesus. 'Who do you say I am?'

Peter spoke up. 'You're the Messiah,' he said.

³⁰He gave them strict orders not to tell anyone about him.

Jesus predicts his death

³¹Jesus now began to teach them something new.

'There's big trouble in store for the son of man,' he said. 'The elders, the chief priests and the scribes are going to reject him. He will be killed – and after three days he'll be raised.' ³²He said all this quite explicitly.

At this, Peter took him aside and started to scold him. ³³But he turned round, saw the disciples, and scolded Peter.

'Get behind me, Accuser!' he said. 'You're thinking human thoughts, not God's thoughts.'

³⁴He called the crowd to him, with his disciples. 'If any of you want to come the way I'm going,' he said, 'you must say "no" to your own selves, pick up your cross, and follow me. ³⁵Yes: if you want to save your life, you'll lose it; but if you lose your life because of me and the message you'll save it. ³⁶After all, what use is it to win the world and lose your life? ³⁷What can you give in exchange for your life? ³⁸If you're ashamed of me and my words in this cheating and sinning generation, the son of man will be ashamed of you when he "comes in the glory of his father with the holy angels".

9 'I'm telling you the truth,' he said; 'some people standing here won't experience death before they see God's kingdom come in power.'

The transfiguration

²A week later, Jesus took Peter, James and John away by themselves, and went up a high mountain. There he was transformed before their eyes. ³His clothes shone with a whiteness that no laundry on earth could match. ⁴Elijah appeared to them, and Moses too, and they were talking with Jesus.

⁵'Teacher,' said Peter as he saw this, 'it's great to be here! I tell you what – we'll make three shelters, one for you, one for Moses and one for Elijah!' ⁶(He didn't know what to say; they were terrified.)

⁷Then a cloud overshadowed them, and a voice came out of the cloud: 'This is my son, the one I love. Listen to him!'

⁸Then, quite suddenly, they looked round and saw nobody there any more, only Jesus with them.

⁹As they came down the mountain, Jesus instructed them not to talk to anyone about what they had seen, 'until', he said, 'the son of man has been raised from the dead'. ¹⁰They held on to this saying among themselves, puzzling about what this 'rising from the dead' might mean.

¹¹'Why then', they asked him, 'do the legal experts say "Elijah must come first"?'

¹²'Elijah does come first,' he replied, 'and his job is to put everything straight. But what do you think it means that "the son of man must suffer many things and be treated with contempt"? ¹³Actually, listen to this: Elijah has already come, and they did to him whatever they wanted. That's what scripture said about him.'

The demon-possessed boy

¹⁴The four of them made their way back to the other disciples. There they saw a large crowd surrounding them, and legal experts arguing with them. ¹⁵As soon as the crowd saw Jesus they were astounded, and they all ran up to greet him.

¹⁶'What's all the fuss about?' he asked.

¹⁷'Teacher,' said someone from the crowd, 'I brought my son to you. He's got a spirit that stops him speaking. ¹⁸Whenever it takes hold of him it throws him on the ground; he foams

at the mouth, and grinds his teeth, and goes rigid. I spoke to your disciples about casting it out, but they couldn't.'

[19] 'You unbelieving generation!' replied Jesus. 'How much longer must I be with you? How much longer must I put up with you? Bring the boy to me.'

[20] They brought him to him. When the spirit saw Jesus, it immediately threw the boy into a convulsion, and he fell on the ground and rolled about, foaming at the mouth.

[21] 'How long has it been like this with him?' asked Jesus.

'Since childhood,' replied the man. [22] 'Often it even throws him into fire or water to kill him. But if you can do anything . . . please, please help us! Have pity on us!'

[23] 'What d'you mean, "If you can"?' said Jesus. 'Everything is possible to someone who believes.'

[24] At this the father gave a great shout. 'I do believe!' he roared. 'Help me in my unbelief!'

[25] Jesus saw that the crowd was getting bigger by the minute. He scolded the unclean spirit: 'Speechless and deaf spirit,' he said, 'I command you – come out of him, and never go back again!'

[26] The spirit yelled, gave the boy a huge convulsion, and came out. The boy seemed to be dead; in fact, several people did say 'He's dead!' [27] But Jesus took him by the hand and helped him to his feet, and he stood up.

[28] 'Why couldn't we cast it out?' asked his disciples, once they were back in the house by themselves.

[29] 'This sort', replied Jesus, 'can only be cast out by prayer.'

True greatness

[30] They went away from there and were travelling through Galilee. Jesus didn't want anyone to know, [31] because he was teaching his disciples.

'The "son of man"', he was saying, 'is to be given over into human hands. They will kill him; and, when he's been killed, after three days he will rise again.'

[32] They didn't understand the saying, and were afraid to ask him.

[33] They came to Capernaum. When they got into the house he asked them, 'What were you arguing about on the road?'

[34] They said nothing, because on the road they had been arguing about which of them was the greatest.

[35] Jesus sat down and called the Twelve.

'If you want to be first,' he said, 'you must be last of all, and servant of all.' [36] He took a small child, and stood it in the middle of them. Then he hugged the child, and said to them, [37] 'If anyone welcomes one child like this in my name, they welcome me. And if anyone welcomes me, it isn't me they welcome, but the one who sent me.'

Warnings about sin

[38] 'Teacher,' said John, 'we saw someone casting out demons in your name. We stopped him, because he wasn't following us.'

[39] 'Don't stop him,' said Jesus. 'No one who does powerful things by my name will be able to say bad things about me soon afterwards. [40] Anyone who's not against us is on our side. [41] Anyone who even gives you a cup of water in my name, because you belong to the Messiah – I'm telling you the truth, that person won't go unrewarded.

[42] 'Think about these little ones who believe in me,' he went on. 'If anyone causes one of them to slip up, it would be much better for that person to have a huge millstone put around their neck, and be thrown into the sea.

[43] 'And if your hand causes you to slip up, cut it off. It's better for you to go into life maimed than to have two hands and go into Gehenna, into the fire that never goes out.

[45] 'And if your foot causes you to slip up, cut it off. It's better for you to go into life lame than to have two feet and be thrown into Gehenna.

[47] 'And if your eye causes you to slip up, throw it away. It's better for you to go into the kingdom of God with one eye than to have two eyes and to be thrown into Gehenna, [48] where

their worm lives on for ever
and the fire can never be quenched.

[49] 'You see, everyone will be salted with fire. [50] Salt is great stuff; but if salt becomes unsalty, how can you make it salty again? You need salt among yourselves. Live at peace with each other.'

Teachings on divorce

10 Jesus left the region, and went to the districts of Judaea across the Jordan. A large crowd gathered around him, and once more, as his custom was, he taught them.

²Some Pharisees approached him with a question. 'Is it permitted', they asked, 'for a man to divorce his wife?' They said this to trap him.

³'Well,' answered Jesus, 'what did Moses command you?'

⁴'Moses permitted us', they replied, 'to write a notice of separation and so to complete the divorce.'

⁵'He gave you that command', said Jesus, 'because you are hardhearted. ⁶But from the beginning of creation

> male and female he made them; ⁷and that's why the man must leave his father and his mother and cleave unto his wife; ⁸so that the two become one flesh.

'There you are, then: they are no longer two, but one flesh. ⁹What God has joined, humans must not split up.'

¹⁰When they were back indoors, the disciples asked him about this.

¹¹'Anyone who divorces his wife', said Jesus, 'and marries someone else commits adultery against her. ¹²And if she divorces her husband and marries someone else she commits adultery.'

¹³People brought children to Jesus for him to touch them. The disciples reprimanded them. ¹⁴But Jesus was angry when he saw it, and said to them, 'Let the children come to me! Don't stop them! The kingdom of God belongs to people like that. ¹⁵I'm telling you the truth: anyone who doesn't receive the kingdom of God like a child will never get into it.'

¹⁶And he hugged them, laid his hands on them, and blessed them.

The rich young ruler

¹⁷As he was setting out on the road, a man ran up and knelt down in front of him.

'Good teacher,' he asked, 'what should I do to inherit the life of the Age to Come?'

¹⁸'Why call me "good"?' replied Jesus. 'No one is good except God alone. ¹⁹You know the commandments:

> Don't kill.
> Don't commit adultery.
> Don't steal.
> Don't swear falsely.
> Don't defraud.
> Honour your father and your mother.'

²⁰'Teacher,' he said, 'I've kept all of them since I was little.'

²¹Jesus looked hard at him, and loved him.

'One more thing,' he said. 'Go away, and whatever you possess – sell it, and give it to the poor. You will have treasure in heaven! Then: come and follow me.'

²²At that, his face fell, and he went off sadly. He was very wealthy.

²³Jesus looked slowly around. Then he said to his disciples, 'How difficult it is for the wealthy to enter the kingdom of God!'

²⁴The disciples were astonished at what he was saying. So Jesus repeated once more, 'Children, it's very hard to enter the kingdom of God! ²⁵It would be easier for a camel to go through the eye of a needle than for a rich man to enter God's kingdom.'

²⁶They were totally amazed, and said to each other, 'So who then can be saved?'

²⁷'It's impossible for mortals,' Jesus said, looking hard at them, 'but it's not impossible for God. All things are possible for God.'

²⁸'Look here,' Peter started up, 'we've left everything and followed you.'

²⁹'I'll tell you the truth,' replied Jesus. 'No one who has left a house, or brothers or sisters, or mother or father, or children, or lands, because of me and the gospel, ³⁰will fail to receive back a hundred times more in the Present Age: houses, brothers, sisters, mothers, children, and lands – with persecutions! – and finally the life of the Age to Come. ³¹But plenty of people at the front will end up at the back, and the back at the front.'

The request of James and John

³²They were on the road, going up to Jerusalem. Jesus was walking ahead of them; they were amazed, and the people following were afraid.

Again he took the Twelve aside and began to tell them what was going to happen to him. ³³'Look,' he said, 'we're going up to Jerusalem. The son of man will be handed over to the chief priests and the legal experts, and they will condemn him to death, and hand him over to the pagans. ³⁴They will taunt him and spit at him and flog him and kill him – and after three days he will rise again.'

³⁵James and John, Zebedee's sons, came up to him.

'Teacher,' they said, 'we want you to grant us whatever we ask.'

³⁶'What do you want me to do for you?' asked Jesus.

³⁷'Grant us,' they said, 'that when you're there in all your glory, one of us will sit at your right, and the other at your left.'

³⁸'You don't know what you're asking for!' Jesus replied. 'Can you drink the cup I'm going to drink? Can you receive the baptism I'm going to receive?'

³⁹'Yes,' they said, 'we can.'

'Well,' said Jesus, 'you will drink the cup I drink; you will receive the baptism I receive. ⁴⁰But sitting at my right hand or my left – that's not up to me. It's been assigned already.'

⁴¹When the other ten disciples heard, they were angry with James and John. ⁴²Jesus called them to him.

'You know how it is in the pagan nations,' he said. 'Think how their so-called rulers act. They lord it over their subjects. The high and mighty ones boss the rest around. ⁴³But that's not how it's going to be with you. Anyone who wants to be great among you must become your servant. ⁴⁴Anyone who wants to be first must be everyone's slave. ⁴⁵Don't you see? The son of man didn't come to be waited on. He came to be the servant, to give his life "as a ransom for many".'

Jesus heals a blind beggar

⁴⁶They came to Jericho. As Jesus, his disciples and a substantial crowd were leaving the town, a blind beggar named Bartimaeus, the son of Timaeus, was sitting by the road. ⁴⁷When he heard it was Jesus of Nazareth, he began to shout out: 'Son of David! Jesus! Take pity on me!'

⁴⁸Lots of people told him crossly to be quiet. But he shouted out all the louder, 'Son of David – take pity on me!'

⁴⁹Jesus came to a stop. 'Call him,' he said. So they called the blind man.

'Cheer up,' they said, 'and get up. He's calling you.'

⁵⁰He flung his cloak aside, jumped up, and came to Jesus.

Jesus saw him coming. ⁵¹'What do you want me to do for you?' he asked.

'Teacher,' the blind man said, 'let me see again.'

⁵²'Off you go,' said Jesus. 'Your faith has saved you.' And immediately he saw again, and he followed him on the way.

The triumphal entry

11 So they approached Jerusalem. They got as far as Bethphage and Bethany, on the Mount of Olives, when Jesus sent two of his disciples on ahead with a specific task.

²'Go to the village over there,' he said to them, 'and as soon as you enter it you will find a colt tied up – one that nobody has ever ridden before. Untie it and bring it here. ³And if anyone says to you, "Why are you doing that?" then say, "The master needs it, and he will return it at once."'

⁴They went off and found the colt tied up beside a door, out in the street; and they untied it.

⁵Some of the bystanders said to them, 'Why are you untying the colt?' ⁶They gave the answer Jesus had told them, and they let them carry on. ⁷So they brought the colt to Jesus and laid their cloaks on it, and he mounted it. ⁸Several people spread their cloaks out in the road. Others did the same with foliage that they had cut in the fields. ⁹Those in front, and those coming behind, shouted out, 'Hosanna! Welcome in the Lord's Name! ¹⁰Welcome to the kingdom of our father David, the kingdom coming right now! Hosanna in the highest!'

¹¹Jesus entered Jerusalem, went into the Temple, and looked all round. It was already getting late, and he returned to Bethany with the Twelve.

Jesus cleanses the Temple

¹²The next day, as they were leaving Bethany, Jesus was hungry. ¹³From some distance away he saw a fig tree covered with leaves, and

hoped to find some fruit on it; but when he came up to it he found nothing but leaves. (It wasn't yet the season for figs.)

¹⁴He addressed the tree directly. 'May no one ever eat fruit from you again,' he said. And his disciples heard.

¹⁵They came into Jerusalem. Jesus went into the Temple and began to drive out the traders, those who bought and sold in the Temple, and overturned the tables of the money-changers and the seats of the dove-sellers. ¹⁶He permitted no one to carry any vessel through the Temple. ¹⁷He began to teach: 'Isn't this what's written,' he said,

> 'My house shall be called
> a house of prayer
> for all the world to share?

But you've made it a brigands' den!'

¹⁸The chief priests and the legal experts heard, and looked for a way to get rid of him. But they were afraid of him, because the whole crowd was astonished at his teaching.

¹⁹When evening came, they went back out of the city.

²⁰As they were returning, early in the morning, they saw the fig tree withered from its roots.

²¹'Look, Teacher!' said Peter to Jesus, remembering what had happened before. 'The fig tree you cursed has withered.'

²²'Have faith in God,' replied Jesus. ²³'I'm telling you the truth: if anyone says to this mountain, "Be off with you – get yourself thrown into the sea", if they have no doubt in their heart, but believe that what they say will happen, it will be done for them. ²⁴That's why I'm telling you, everything that you request in prayer, everything you ask God for, believe that you receive it, and it will happen for you.

²⁵'And when you are standing there praying, if you have something against someone else, forgive them – so that your father in heaven may forgive you your trespasses.'

The authority of Jesus is questioned

²⁷Once more they went into Jerusalem. As Jesus was walking in the Temple he was approached by the chief priests, the legal experts and the elders.

²⁸'By what right do you do these things?' they asked. 'Who gave you the right to do them?'

²⁹'I have one question for you, too,' replied Jesus, 'and if you tell me the answer I shall tell you by what right I do these things. ³⁰Was the baptism of John from heaven, or was it a human invention? What's your answer?'

³¹'Well now,' they muttered to each other, 'if we say it was from heaven, he will say, "Then why didn't you believe him?" ³²But if we say it was a human invention . . .' They were afraid of the crowd, because everyone regarded John as a prophet.

³³'We don't know,' they said to Jesus.

'Nor will I tell you,' replied Jesus, 'by what right I do these things.'

The parable of the tenants

12 Jesus began to speak to them with parables.

'Once upon a time,' he began, 'there was a man who planted a vineyard. He built a fence around it, dug out a wine-press, built a watchtower, and then let it out to tenant farmers. He himself went abroad. ²When the time came he sent a slave to the farmers to collect from them his portion of the vineyard's produce. ³They seized him, beat him and sent him away empty-handed.

⁴'So again he sent another slave to them. This one they beat about the head, and treated shamefully. ⁵He sent another, and they killed him. He sent several more; they beat some and killed others.

⁶'He had one more to send: his beloved son. He sent him to them last of all, thinking "They will respect my son".

⁷'But the tenant farmers said to themselves, "This is the heir! Come on – let's kill him, and we'll get the inheritance!" ⁸So they seized him and killed him, and threw him out of the vineyard.

⁹'So what will the vineyard owner do? He will come and destroy those tenants, and give the vineyard to others. ¹⁰Or haven't you read the scripture which says,

> There is the stone the builders refused;
> now it's in place at the top of the corner.
> ¹¹This happened the way the Lord planned it;
> we were astonished to see it.'

¹²They tried to find a way of arresting him, because they realized he had directed the parable against them. But they were afraid of the crowd. They left him and went away.

On paying taxes to Caesar

¹³They sent some Pharisees to Jesus, and some Herodians, to try to trick him into saying the wrong thing.

¹⁴'Teacher,' they said, 'we know you are a man of integrity; you don't regard anybody as special. You don't bother about the outward show people put up; you teach God's way truly.

'Well then: is it lawful to give tribute to Caesar or not? Should we pay it, or shouldn't we?'

¹⁵He knew the game they were playing. 'Why are you trying to trap me?' he said. 'Bring me a tribute-coin; let me look at it.'

¹⁶They brought one to him.

'This image,' he asked, 'whose is it? And whose is this superscription?'

'Caesar's,' they replied.

¹⁷'Well then,' said Jesus, 'give Caesar back what belongs to Caesar – and give God back what belongs to God!'

They were astonished at him.

Marriage and the resurrection

¹⁸Some Sadducees approached Jesus (Sadducees, by the way, deny the resurrection).

¹⁹'Teacher,' they said, 'Moses wrote for us that "If a man's brother dies, and leaves a wife but no child, the brother should take the wife and raise up descendants for his brother." ²⁰Well now: there were once seven brothers. The first married a wife, and died without children. ²¹The second married the widow, and died without children. The third did so as well, ²²and so did all seven, still without leaving children. Finally the woman died too. ²³So: when they rise again in the resurrection, whose wife will she be? All seven had her, after all.'

²⁴'Where you're going wrong,' replied Jesus, 'is that you don't know the scriptures, or God's power. ²⁵When people rise from the dead, they don't marry, nor do people give them in marriage. They are like angels in heaven.

²⁶'However, to show that the dead are indeed to be raised, surely you've read in the book of Moses, in the passage about the bush, what God says to Moses? "I am Abraham's God, Isaac's God and Jacob's God"? ²⁷He isn't the God of the dead, but of the living. You are completely mistaken.'

The most important commandment

²⁸One of the legal experts came up, and overheard the discussion. Realizing that Jesus had given a splendid answer, he put a question of his own.

'Which commandment,' he asked, 'is the first one of all?'

²⁹'The first one,' replied Jesus, 'is this: "Listen, Israel: the Lord your God, the Lord is one; ³⁰and you shall love the Lord your God with all your heart, and with all your soul, and with all your understanding, and with all your strength." ³¹And this is the second one: "You shall love your neighbour as yourself." No other commandment is greater than these ones.'

³²'Well said, Teacher,' answered the lawyer. 'You are right in saying that "he is one and there is no other beside him", ³³and that "to love him with all the heart, and with all the intelligence, and with all the strength" and "to love one's neighbour as oneself" is worth far more than all burnt offerings and sacrifices.'

³⁴Jesus saw that his answer came out of deep understanding.

'You are not far from God's kingdom,' he said to him.

After that, nobody dared put any more questions to him.

David's son and the widow's mite

³⁵By way of response to it all, Jesus began to teach in the Temple.

'Why do the experts say', he asked, 'that the Messiah is the son of David? ³⁶David himself, inspired by the holy spirit, said:

The Lord said to my Lord:
sit at my right hand,
until I place your enemies
right underneath your feet.

³⁷'David himself calls him "Lord"; how then can he be his son?'

The whole crowd listened to him with delight.

³⁸During his teaching, he said, 'Beware of the lawyers! They like to walk about in long robes, and to be greeted in the market-places. ³⁹They take the chief seats in the synagogue, and the best places at dinner parties. ⁴⁰They devour the property of widows, and make long prayers without meaning them. They will receive all the more condemnation.'

⁴¹As he sat opposite the Temple treasury, he watched the crowd putting money into the almsboxes. Lots of rich people put in substantial amounts. ⁴²Then there came a single poor widow, who put in two tiny coins, together worth a single penny.

⁴³Jesus called his disciples.

'I'm telling you the truth,' he said. 'This poor widow just put more into the treasury than everybody else. ⁴⁴You see, all the others were contributing out of their wealth; but she put in everything she had, out of her poverty. It was her whole livelihood.'

Signs of the end

13 As they were going out of the Temple, one of Jesus' disciples said to him, 'Teacher! Look at these huge stones, and these huge buildings!'

²'You see these enormous buildings?' said Jesus. 'There will not be one single stone left on top of another. They will all be torn down.'

³Peter, James, John and Andrew approached him privately as he was sitting on the Mount of Olives opposite the Temple.

⁴'Tell us,' they asked. 'When will these things happen? What will be the sign that these things are about to be completed?'

⁵'Take care that nobody deceives you,' Jesus began to say to them. ⁶'Plenty of people will come in my name, saying "I'm the one!", and they will lead plenty astray. ⁷But whenever you hear about wars, and rumours about wars, don't be disturbed. These things have to happen, but it doesn't mean the end is here. ⁸One nation will rise up against another; one kingdom will rise up against another. There will be earthquakes from place to place, and famines too. These are the first pains of childbirth.

⁹'But watch out for yourselves. They will hand you over to courts, they will beat you in synagogues; you will stand before rulers and kings because of me, as a witness against them. ¹⁰And the message of the kingdom must first be announced to all the nations. ¹¹And when they put you on trial and hand you over, don't work out beforehand what you are going to say, but say whatever is given you at that moment. It won't be you speaking, you see, but the holy spirit.

¹²'One brother will hand over another to death. Fathers will hand over children. Children will rebel against parents and have them put to death. ¹³And you will be hated by everyone because of my name. But the one who is patient through to the end – that one will be saved.'

Further signs of the end

¹⁴'However,' Jesus continued, 'when you see "the desolating abomination" set up where it ought not to be' (let the reader understand) 'then those who are in Judaea should run away to the mountains. ¹⁵If you're on the housetop, don't go down, and don't go in to get anything from the house. ¹⁶If you're out in the countryside, don't turn back again to pick up your cloak.

¹⁷'It will be a terrible time for pregnant and nursing mothers. ¹⁸Pray that it won't happen in winter. ¹⁹Yes, those days will bring trouble like nothing that's ever happened from the beginning of creation, which God created, until now, or ever will again. ²⁰In fact, if the Lord had not shortened the days, no one would be rescued. But for the sake of his chosen ones, those whom he appointed, he shortened the days.

²¹'So at that time, if someone says to you, "Look – here is the Messiah!" or, "Look – there he is!", don't believe them; ²²because false messiahs and false prophets will arise, and will perform signs and portents to lead astray even God's chosen ones, if that were possible. ²³But you must be on your guard. I've told you everything ahead of time.

²⁴'But in those days, after that suffering,

The sun will be dark as night
and the moon will not give its light;

²⁵the stars will fall from heaven
and the powers in heaven will shake.

²⁶'Then they will see "the son of man coming on clouds with great power and glory". ²⁷And then he will dispatch his messengers, and will gather in his chosen ones from the four winds, from the ends of earth to the ends of heaven.'

Watching for the son of man

²⁸'Learn this lesson from the fig tree. When its branch becomes soft and sprouts leaves, you know that summer is near. ²⁹In the same way, when you see these things happen, you should know that it is near, right at the gates. ³⁰I'm telling you the truth: this generation won't disappear until all of this has happened. ³¹Heaven and earth will disappear, but my words won't disappear.

³²'No one knows, though, the day or the hour. The angels in heaven don't know it; nor does the son; only the father.

³³'Keep watch, stay awake. You don't know when the moment will arrive. ³⁴It's like a man who goes away from home: he leaves his house, giving each of his slaves authority for their own tasks; and he commands the doorkeeper to keep watch. ³⁵Keep watch, then, because you don't know when the master of the house is going to come. It might be at evening, or at midnight, or at cockcrow, or in the morning! ³⁶You don't want him to come suddenly and find you asleep. ³⁷What I am telling you, I am telling everyone: keep watch!'

Jesus is anointed at Bethany

14 Passover – the feast of unleavened bread – was due in two days. The chief priests and the lawyers were plotting how to seize Jesus by a trick, and kill him.

²'We can't do it at the feast,' they said. 'The people might riot.'

³Jesus was in Bethany, at the house of Simon (known as 'the Leper'). While he was at table, a woman came up with an alabaster pot containing extremely valuable ointment made of pure spikenard. She broke the pot and poured the ointment on Jesus' head.

⁴Some of the people there grumbled to one another.

'What's the point of wasting the ointment?' they asked. ⁵'That ointment could have been sold for three hundred dinars, and given to the poor.'

And they were angry with her.

⁶'Leave her alone,' said Jesus. 'Why make trouble for her? She has done a wonderful thing for me. ⁷You have the poor with you always; you can help them whenever you want to. But you won't always have me.

⁸'She has played her part. She has anointed my body for its burial, ahead of time. ⁹I'm telling you the truth: wherever the message is announced in all the world, the story of what she has just done will be told. That will be her memorial.'

¹⁰Judas Iscariot, one of the Twelve, went to the chief priests, to arrange to hand Jesus over to them. ¹¹They were delighted with his proposal, and made an agreement to pay him. And he began to look for a good moment to hand him over.

The Last Supper

¹²On the first day of unleavened bread, when the Passover lambs were sacrificed, Jesus' disciples said to him, 'Where would you like us to go and get things ready for you to eat the Passover?'

¹³He sent off two of his disciples, with these instructions.

'Go into the city, and you will be met by a man carrying a water-pot. Follow him. ¹⁴When he goes indoors, say to the master of the house, "The teacher says, where is the guest room for me, where I can eat the Passover with my disciples?" ¹⁵He will show you a large upstairs room, set out and ready. Make preparations for us there.'

¹⁶The disciples went out, entered the city, and found it exactly as he had said. They prepared the Passover.

¹⁷When it was evening, Jesus came with the Twelve. ¹⁸As they were reclining at table and eating, Jesus said, 'I'm telling you the truth: one of you is going to betray me – one of you that's eating with me.'

¹⁹They began to be very upset, and they said to him, one after another, 'It isn't me, is it?'

20'It's one of the Twelve,' said Jesus, 'one who has dipped his bread in the dish with me. 21Yes: the son of man is completing his journey, as scripture said he would; but it's bad news for the man who betrays him! It would have been better for that man never to have been born.'

22While they were eating, he took bread, blessed it, broke it, and gave it to them.

'Take it,' he said. 'This is my body.'

23Then he took the cup, gave thanks, and gave it to them, and they all drank from it. 24"This is my blood of the covenant," he said, 'which is poured out for many. 25I'm telling you the truth: I won't ever drink from the fruit of the vine again, until that day – the day when I drink it new in the kingdom of God.'

Jesus is arrested

26They sang a hymn, and went out to the Mount of Olives.

27'You're all going to desert me,' said Jesus, 'because it's written,

I shall attack the shepherd
and then the sheep will scatter.

28'But after I am raised up, I will go ahead of you to Galilee.'

29Peter spoke up.

'Everyone else may desert you,' he said, 'but I won't.'

30'I'm telling you the truth,' Jesus replied. 'Today – this very night, before the cock has crowed twice – you will renounce me three times.'

31This made Peter all the more vehement.

'Even if I have to die with you,' he said, 'I will never renounce you.'

And all the rest said the same.

32They came to a place called Gethsemane.

'Stay here', said Jesus to the disciples, 'while I pray.'

33He took Peter, James and John with him, and became quite overcome and deeply distressed. 34'"My soul is disturbed within me", he said, 'right to the point of death. Stay here and keep watch.'

35He went a little further, and fell on the ground and prayed that, if possible, the moment might pass from him.

36'Abba, father,' he said, 'all things are possible for you! Take this cup away from me! But – not what I want, but what you want.'

37He returned and found them sleeping.

'Are you asleep, Simon?' he said to Peter. 'Couldn't you keep watch for a single hour? 38Watch and pray, so that you won't come into the time of trouble. The spirit is eager, but the body is weak.'

39Once more he went off and prayed, saying the same words. 40And again, when he returned, he found them asleep, because their eyes were very heavy. They had no words to answer him. 41But the third time he came, he said to them, 'All right – sleep as much as you like now. Have a good rest. The job is done, the time has come – and look! The son of man is betrayed into the clutches of sinners. 42Get up, let's be on our way. Here comes the man who's going to betray me.'

43At once, while he was still speaking, Judas, one of the Twelve, arrived, accompanied by a crowd, with swords and clubs, from the chief priests, the legal experts, and the elders. 44The betrayer had given them a coded sign: 'The one I kiss – that's him! Seize him and take him away safely.'

45He came up to Jesus at once. 'Rabbi!' he said, and kissed him.

46The crowd laid hands on him and seized him. 47One of the bystanders drew a sword and struck the high priest's servant, cutting off his ear. 48Then Jesus spoke to them.

'Anyone would think', he said, 'you'd come after a brigand! Fancy needing swords and clubs to arrest me! 49Day after day I've been teaching in the Temple, under your noses, and you never laid a finger on me. But the scriptures must be fulfilled.'

50Then they all abandoned him and ran away. 51A young man had followed him, wearing only a linen tunic over his otherwise naked body. 52They seized him, and he left the tunic and ran away naked.

In the high priest's house

53They took Jesus away to the high priest. All the chief priests and the elders and legal experts were assembled. 54Peter followed him at a distance, and came to the courtyard of the high priest's house, where he sat with the servants and warmed himself at the fire.

⁵⁵The chief priests, and all the Sanhedrin, looked for evidence for a capital charge against Jesus, but they didn't find any. ⁵⁶Several people invented fictitious charges against him, but their evidence didn't agree. ⁵⁷Then some stood up with this fabricated charge: ⁵⁸'We heard him say, "I will destroy this Temple, which human hands have made, and in three days I'll build another, made without human hands."'

⁵⁹But even so their evidence didn't agree.

⁶⁰Then the high priest got up in front of them all and interrogated Jesus.

'Haven't you got any answer about whatever it is these people are testifying against you?'

⁶¹Jesus remained silent, and didn't answer a word.

Once more the high priest questioned him. 'Are you the Messiah, the Son of the Blessed One?'

⁶²'I am,' replied Jesus, 'and you will see "the son of man sitting at the right hand of Power, and coming with the clouds of heaven".'

⁶³'Why do we need any more evidence?' shouted the high priest, tearing his clothes. ⁶⁴'You heard the blasphemy! What's your verdict?'

They all agreed on their judgment: he deserved to die.

⁶⁵Some of them began to spit at him. They blindfolded him and hit him, and said, 'Prophesy!' And the servants took charge of him and beat him.

⁶⁶Peter, meanwhile, was below in the courtyard. One of the high priest's servant-girls came up ⁶⁷and saw him warming himself. She looked closely at him, and said, 'You were with Jesus the Nazarene too, weren't you?'

⁶⁸'I don't know what on earth you're talking about,' replied Peter.

He went outside into the forecourt, and the cock crowed.

⁶⁹The servant-girl saw him, and once more began to say to the bystanders, 'This man is one of them.' ⁷⁰But Peter again denied it.

A little while later the bystanders said again to Peter, 'You really are one of them, aren't you? You're a Galilean!'

⁷¹At that he began to curse and swear, 'I don't know this man you're talking about.' ⁷²And immediately the cock crowed for the second time. Then Peter remembered the words that Jesus had said to him: 'Before the cock crows twice, you will renounce me three times.' And he burst into tears.

Jesus before Pilate

15 As soon as morning came, the chief priests held a council meeting with the elders, the legal experts, and the whole Sanhedrin. They bound Jesus, took him off to Pilate, and handed him over.

²'Are you the king of the Jews?' asked Pilate.

'You have said it,' replied Jesus.

³The chief priests laid many accusations against him.

⁴Pilate again interrogated him: 'Aren't you going to make any reply? Look how many things they're accusing you of!'

⁵But Jesus gave no reply at all, which astonished Pilate.

⁶The custom was that at festival time he used to release for them a single prisoner, whoever they would ask for. ⁷There was a man in prison named Barabbas, one of the revolutionaries who had committed murder during the uprising. ⁸So the crowd came up and began to ask Pilate to do what he normally did.

⁹'Do you want me', answered Pilate, 'to release for you "the king of the Jews"?'

¹⁰He said this because he knew that the chief priests had handed him over out of envy. ¹¹The chief priests stirred up the crowd to ask for Barabbas instead to be released to them. So Pilate once again asked them, ¹²'What then do you want me to do with the one you call "the king of the Jews"?'

¹³'Crucify him!' they shouted again.

¹⁴'Why?' asked Pilate. 'What has he done wrong?'

'Crucify him!' they shouted all the louder.

¹⁵Pilate wanted to satisfy the crowd; so he released Barabbas for them. He had Jesus flogged, and handed him over to be crucified.

The crucifixion

¹⁶The soldiers took Jesus into the courtyard, that is, the Praetorium, and called together the whole squad. ¹⁷They dressed Jesus up in purple;

then, weaving together a crown of thorns, they stuck it on him. ¹⁸They began to salute him: 'Greetings, King of the Jews!' ¹⁹And they hit him over the head with a staff, and spat at him, and knelt down to do him homage. ²⁰Then, when they had mocked him, they took the purple robe off him, and put his own clothes back on.

Then they led him off to crucify him. ²¹They compelled a man called Simon to carry Jesus' cross. He was from Cyrene, and was coming in from out of town. He was the father of Alexander and Rufus.

²²They took Jesus to the place called Golgotha, which in translation means 'Skull's Place'. ²³They gave him a mixture of wine and myrrh, but he didn't drink it.

²⁴So they crucified him; they 'parted his clothing between them, casting lots' to see who would get what. ²⁵It was about nine o'clock in the morning when they crucified him. ²⁶The inscription, giving the charge, read: 'The King of the Jews'. ²⁷They also crucified two bandits alongside him, one on his right and one on his left.

²⁹People who were passing by abused him. They shook their heads at him.

'Hah!' they said. 'You were going to destroy the Temple, were you? And build it again in three days? ³⁰Why don't you rescue yourself, and come down from the cross?'

³¹The chief priests and the lawyers were mocking him in the same way among themselves.

'He rescued others,' they said, 'but he can't rescue himself. ³²Messiah, is he? King of Israel, did he say? Well, let's see him come down from the cross! We'll believe him when we see that!'

The two who were crucified alongside him taunted him as well.

The death of Jesus

³³At midday there was darkness over all the land until three in the afternoon. ³⁴At three o'clock Jesus shouted out in a powerful voice, '*Eloi, Eloi, lema sabachthani?*' which means, 'My God, my God, why did you abandon me?'

³⁵When the bystanders heard it, some of them said, 'He's calling for Elijah!'

³⁶One of them ran and filled a sponge with sour wine, put it on a pole, and gave it him to drink.

'Well then,' he declared, 'let's see if Elijah will come and take him down.'

³⁷But Jesus, with another loud shout, breathed his last.

³⁸The Temple veil was torn in two, from top to bottom. ³⁹When the centurion who was standing facing him saw that he died in this way, he said, 'This fellow really was God's son.'

The burial of Jesus

⁴⁰Some women were watching from a distance. They included Mary Magdalene, Mary the mother of the younger James and of Joses, and Salome. ⁴¹They had followed Jesus in Galilee, and had attended to his needs. There were several other women, too, who had come up with him to Jerusalem.

⁴²It was already getting towards evening, and it was the day of Preparation, that is, the day before the sabbath. ⁴³Joseph of Arimathea, a reputable member of the council who was himself eagerly awaiting God's kingdom, took his courage in both hands, went to Pilate, and requested the body of Jesus.

⁴⁴Pilate was surprised that he was already dead. He summoned the centurion, and asked whether he had been dead for some time. ⁴⁵When he learned the facts from the centurion, he conceded the body to Joseph.

⁴⁶So Joseph bought a linen cloth, took the body down, wrapped it in the cloth, and laid it in a tomb cut out of the rock. He rolled a stone against the door of the tomb. ⁴⁷Mary Magdalene and Mary the mother of Joses saw where he was buried.

The resurrection

16 When the sabbath was over, Mary Magdalene, Mary the mother of James, and Salome bought spices so that they could come and anoint Jesus. ²Then, very early on the first day of the week, they came to the tomb, just at sunrise. ³They were saying to one another, 'There's that stone at the door of the tomb – who's going to roll it away for us?'

⁴Then, when they looked up, they saw that it had been rolled away. (It was extremely large.) ⁵So they went into the tomb, and there they saw a young man sitting on the right-hand side. He was wearing white. They were totally astonished.

⁶'Don't be astonished,' he said to them. 'You're looking for Jesus the Nazarene, who was crucified. He has been raised! He isn't here! Look – this is the place where they laid him. ⁷But go and tell his disciples – including Peter – that he is going ahead of you to Galilee. You'll see him there, just like he told you.'

⁸They went out, and fled from the tomb. Trembling and panic had seized them. They said nothing to anyone, because they were afraid.

Two extra endings

[[They gave a brief account to the people around Peter of what they had been told. After this, Jesus himself sent out from East to West, through their work, the sacred and imperishable proclamation of eternal salvation. Amen.]]

⁹[When Jesus was raised, early on the first day of the week, he appeared first of all to Mary Magdalene, from whom he had cast out seven demons. ¹⁰She went and told the people who had been with him, who were mourning and weeping. ¹¹When they heard that he was alive, and that he had been seen by her, they didn't believe it.

¹²After this he appeared in a different guise to two of them as they were walking into the countryside. ¹³They came back and told the others, but they didn't believe them.

¹⁴Later Jesus appeared to the eleven themselves, as they were at table. He told them off for their unbelief and hardheartedness, for not believing those who had seen him after he had been raised.

¹⁵'Go into all the world,' he said to them, 'and announce the message to all creation. ¹⁶Anyone who believes and is baptized will be rescued, but people who don't believe will be condemned. ¹⁷And these signs will happen around those who believe: they will drive out demons in my name, they will speak with new tongues, ¹⁸they will pick up serpents in their hands; and if they drink anything poisonous it won't harm them. They will lay their hands on the sick, and they will get better.'

¹⁹When the Lord Jesus had spoken with them, he was taken up into heaven, and sat down at God's right hand. ²⁰They went out and announced the message everywhere. The Lord worked with them, validating their message by the signs that accompanied them.]

Luke

Some ancient traditions, following a hint in Paul (Colossians 4.14), suppose that Luke was a doctor. Other traditions, not so ancient but still important, claim that he was an artist. For all we know, he may have been both, in which case we have two clues as to the kind of book his gospel might be.

For a start, Luke's gospel shows signs of a scholarly approach, such as we might expect from someone with a degree of academic training. He speaks of having checked his sources, both oral and written, and of his determination to set out 'an orderly account' (1.1) of what had happened. When we put alongside Luke the other similar writings we have, it seems overwhelmingly probable that he used Mark's gospel as a basis for his own, adding plenty of other material, shaping his Markan material and polishing the style as he went along. Mark's is a gospel for someone in a hurry; Luke's is a book to be studied by the wider world.

This wider aim and audience has prompted some to ask whether Luke was a Gentile. We don't know the answer to that, but he was clearly soaked in the scriptures, probably knowing them best in a Greek version. He highlights the way in which the risen Jesus insists that the events of his crucifixion and resurrection were to be understood in the light of the entire scriptural narrative, and how, balancing that, the scriptures themselves were now to be understood in a fresh way in the light of Jesus and by the leading of the spirit. His book is scriptural through and through, but in a quite different way from Matthew's, allowing Israel's scriptures to resonate in the background as he tells the opening stories of the conception and birth of John the Baptist and then of Jesus himself.

What does this mean? This is where Luke-as-an-artist comes into his own. He knows how to tell a story so well that we can see it happening in front of us as if painted by a master. He tells, early on, the story of Mary and Joseph losing the twelve-year-old Jesus in the Passover crowd and spending three days frantically hunting for him before finding him calmly sitting in the Temple, discussing things with the teachers. Luke balances this at the end with the two disciples on the road to Emmaus, distraught for a third day after the crucifixion of the one they thought was to redeem Israel, only to discover that their unexpected companion on the road was Jesus himself, making their hearts burn as he opens the scriptures. Luke expects his readers to find themselves in this story as well. That is what artists aim at.

In particular, Luke has structured his book so as to move fairly quickly through the material corresponding to Mark's first eight chapters, in order then to present most of the gospel in terms of Jesus' journey to Jerusalem. This journey begins, in quite a formal way, in 9.51, and though the next ten chapters contain much besides, Luke steadily leads the eye up to chapter 19, where he paints a scene worthy of a Rembrandt or Titian. From the start the scriptural echoes tell us what is going on: Jesus 'sent messengers ahead of him' (9.52), echoing the promise in Exodus 23.20 and, more darkly, the warning in Malachi 3.1. Jesus' journey to Jerusalem is to be seen in terms of the long-delayed promise that one day YHWH would return to his people in person, to judge and to save. This becomes explicit in 19.11–48, when Jesus tells a story about the king who comes back at last, and then rides into Jerusalem in floods of tears at the fate the city now faces 'because you didn't know the moment when God was visiting you' (verse 44).

Thus, through the human story of Jesus the storyteller and healer, Luke offers us both a work of art for our contemplation and the medicine for the deepest human disease.

Prologue

1 Many people have undertaken to draw up an orderly account of the events that have been fulfilled in our midst. ²It has been handed down to us by the original eyewitnesses and stewards of the word. ³So, most excellent Theophilus, since I had traced the course of all of it scrupulously from the start, I thought it a good idea to write an orderly account for you, ⁴so that you may have secure knowledge about the matters in which you have been instructed.

Gabriel visits Zechariah

⁵In the time when Herod was king of Judaea, there was a priest called Zechariah, of the priestly division of Abijah. His wife, who came from the Aaron family, was called Elisabeth. ⁶Both of them were righteous in God's sight; they followed all the Lord's commandments and ordinances without fault. ⁷They had no children. Elisabeth was barren, and both of them were of an advanced age.

⁸It so happened, when Zechariah was performing his priestly service before God, according to the order of his division, ⁹that the lot fell to him, according to the priestly custom, to go in to the Lord's sanctuary to offer incense. ¹⁰The people were praying outside in a large crowd, at the time of the incense-offering. ¹¹An angel of the Lord appeared to him, standing on the right hand side of the incense-altar. ¹²Zechariah was troubled and terror-struck when he saw the angel.

¹³But the angel said to him: 'Don't be afraid, Zechariah: your prayer has been heard. Your wife Elisabeth will bear you a son, and you shall call his name John. ¹⁴This will bring you joy and celebration, and many will rejoice at his birth. ¹⁵He will be a great man in God's sight; he will drink no wine or strong drink. He will be filled with the holy spirit from his mother's womb, ¹⁶and will turn many of the children of Israel to the Lord their God. ¹⁷He will go before him in the spirit and power of Elijah, and he will turn the hearts of fathers to children, and of unbelievers to the wisdom of the righteous. He will get ready for the Lord a prepared people.'

¹⁸'How can I be sure of this?' said Zechariah to the angel. 'I'm an old man! My wife's not as young as she used to be, either!'

¹⁹'Look here,' replied the angel, 'I'm Gabriel. I stand in God's presence. I was sent to speak to you and give you this splendid news. ²⁰Now, listen: you will be silent – you won't be able to speak – until the day when it all happens, because you didn't believe my words. But they will come true at the proper time.'

²¹Meanwhile, the people were waiting for Zechariah, and were surprised that he was taking such a long time in the sanctuary. ²²But when he came out he couldn't speak to them, and they understood that he had seen a vision in the sanctuary. He made gestures to them, but remained speechless.

²³So, when the days of his priestly service were complete, he went back home. ²⁴After that time, Elisabeth his wife conceived. She stayed in hiding for five months.

²⁵'This is the Lord's doing,' she said; 'at last he has looked on me, and taken away my public shame.'

The annunciation of the birth of Jesus

²⁶In the sixth month, Gabriel the angel was sent from God to a town in Galilee called Nazareth, ²⁷to a virgin engaged to a man called Joseph, from the family of David. The virgin was called Mary.

²⁸'Greetings, favoured one!' said the angel when he arrived. 'May the Lord be with you!'

²⁹She was disturbed at this, and wondered what such a greeting might mean.

³⁰'Don't be afraid, Mary,' said the angel to her. 'You're in favour with God. ³¹Listen: you will conceive in your womb and will have a son; and you shall call his name Jesus. ³²He will be a great man, and he'll be called the son of the Most High. The Lord God will give him the throne of David his father, ³³and he shall reign over the house of Jacob for ever. His kingdom will never come to an end.'

³⁴'How will this happen?' said Mary to the angel. 'I'm still a virgin!'

³⁵'The holy spirit will come upon you,' replied the angel, 'and the power of the Most High will overshadow you. For that reason the holy one who is born from you will be called God's Son.

³⁶'Let me tell you this, too: your cousin Elisabeth, in her old age, has also conceived a son. This is the sixth month for her, a woman who people used to say was barren. ³⁷With God, you see, nothing is impossible.'

³⁸'Here I am,' said Mary; 'I'm the Lord's servant-girl. Let it happen to me as you've said.'

Then the angel left her.

The Magnificat: Mary's song of praise

³⁹Mary got up then and there, and went in excitement to the hill country of Judaea. ⁴⁰She went into Zechariah's house, and greeted Elisabeth. ⁴¹When Elisabeth heard Mary's greeting, the baby gave a leap in her womb. Elisabeth was filled with the holy spirit, ⁴²and shouted at the top of her voice: 'Of all women, you're the blessed one! And the fruit of your womb – he's blessed, too! ⁴³Why should this happen to me, that the mother of my Lord should come to me? ⁴⁴Look – when the sound of your greeting came to my ears, the child in my womb gave a great leap for joy! ⁴⁵A blessing on you, for believing that what the Lord said to you would come true!'

⁴⁶Mary said,

'My soul declares that the Lord is great,
⁴⁷my spirit exults in my saviour, my God.
⁴⁸He saw his servant-girl in her humility;
from now, I'll be blessed by all peoples to come.
⁴⁹The Powerful One, whose name is Holy,
has done great things for me, for me.
⁵⁰His mercy extends from father to son,
from mother to daughter for those who fear him.
⁵¹Powerful things he has done with his arm:
he routed the arrogant through their own cunning.
⁵²Down from their thrones he hurled the rulers,
up from the earth he raised the humble.
⁵³The hungry he filled with the fat of the land,
but the rich he sent off with nothing to eat.
⁵⁴He has rescued his servant, Israel his child,
because he remembered his mercy of old,
⁵⁵just as he said to our long-ago ancestors –
Abraham and his descendants for ever.'

⁵⁶Mary stayed with Elisabeth for three months, and then returned home.

Zechariah's song of praise

⁵⁷The time arrived for Elisabeth's child to be born, and she gave birth to a son. ⁵⁸Her neighbours and relatives heard that the Lord had increased his mercy to her, and they came to celebrate with her.

⁵⁹Now on the eighth day, when they came to circumcise the child, they were calling him by his father's name, Zechariah. ⁶⁰But his mother spoke up.

'No,' she said, 'he is to be called John.'

⁶¹'None of your relatives', they objected, 'is called by that name.'

⁶²They made signs to his father, to ask what he wanted him to be called. ⁶³He asked for a writing tablet, and wrote on it, 'His name is John.'

Everyone was astonished. ⁶⁴Immediately his mouth and his tongue were unfastened, and he spoke, praising God. ⁶⁵Fear came over all those who lived in the neighbourhood, and all these things were spoken of throughout all the hill country of Judaea. ⁶⁶Everyone who heard about it turned the matter over in their hearts.

'What then will this child become?' they said. And the Lord's hand was with him.

⁶⁷John's father Zechariah was filled with the holy spirit, and spoke this prophecy:

⁶⁸'Blessed be the Lord, Israel's God!
He's come to his people and bought them their freedom.
⁶⁹He's raised up a horn of salvation for us
in David's house, the house of his servant,
⁷⁰just as he promised, through the mouths of his prophets,
the holy ones, speaking from ages of old:
⁷¹salvation from our enemies, rescue from hatred,
⁷²mercy to our ancestors, keeping his holy covenant.
⁷³He swore an oath to Abraham our father,
⁷⁴to give us deliverance from fear and from foes,
so we might worship him, ⁷⁵holy and righteous
before his face to the end of our days.
⁷⁶You, child, will be called the prophet of the Highest One,
go ahead of the Lord, preparing his way,
⁷⁷letting his people know of salvation,
through the forgiveness of all their sins.
⁷⁸The heart of our God is full of mercy,
that's why his daylight has dawned from on high,

[79]bringing light to the dark, as we sat in death's shadow,
guiding our feet in the path of peace.'

[80]The child grew, and became powerful in the spirit. He lived in the wilderness until the day when he was revealed to Israel.

The birth of Jesus

2 At that time a decree was issued by Augustus Caesar: a census was to be taken of the whole world. [2](This was the first census, before the one when Quirinius was governor of Syria.) [3]So everyone set off to be registered, each to their own town. [4]Joseph too, who belonged to the house and family of David, went from the city of Nazareth in Galilee to Bethlehem in Judaea, David's city, [5]to be registered with his fiancée Mary, who was pregnant.

[6]So that's where they were when the time came for her to give birth; [7]and she gave birth to her firstborn, a son. She wrapped him up and put him to rest in a feeding-trough, because there was no room for them in the normal living quarters.

[8]There were shepherds in that region, out in the open, keeping a night watch around their flock. [9]An angel of the Lord stood in front of them. The glory of the Lord shone around them, and they were terrified.

[10]'Don't be afraid,' the angel said to them. 'Look: I've got good news for you, news which will make everybody very happy. [11]Today a saviour has been born for you – the Messiah, the Lord! – in David's town. [12]This will be the sign for you: you'll find the baby wrapped up, and lying in a feeding-trough.'

[13]Suddenly, with the angel, there was a crowd of the heavenly armies. They were praising God, saying,

[14]'Glory to God in the highest,
and peace upon earth among those in his favour.'

[15]So when the angels had gone away again into heaven, the shepherds said to each other, 'Well then; let's go to Bethlehem and see what it's all about, all this that the Lord has told us.' [16]So they hurried off, and found Mary and Joseph, and the child lying in the feeding-trough. [17]When they saw it, they told them what had been said to them about this child. [18]And all the people who heard it were amazed at the things the shepherds said to them. [19]But Mary treasured all these things and mused over them in her heart.

[20]The shepherds returned, glorifying and praising God for all they had heard and seen, as it had been told to them.

Simeon and Anna

[21]After eight days, the time came to circumcise the baby. He was called by the name Jesus, which the angel had given him before he had been conceived in the womb.

[22]When the time came for them to be purified according to the law of Moses, they took him up to Jerusalem to present him before the Lord. [23]That's what the law of the Lord says: 'Every firstborn male shall be called holy to the Lord.' [24]They also came to offer sacrifice, according to what it says in the law of the Lord: 'A pair of turtledoves or two young pigeons.'

[25]Now there was a man in Jerusalem named Simeon. He was righteous and devout, waiting for God to comfort Israel, and the holy spirit was upon him. [26]He had been told by the holy spirit that he would not die until he had seen the Lord's Messiah. [27]Led by the spirit, he came into the Temple. As Jesus' parents brought him in, to do for him what the law's regulations required, [28]he took the baby in his arms and blessed God with these words:

[29]'Now, master, you are dismissing your servant in peace,
just as you said.
[30]These eyes of mine have seen your salvation,
[31]which you made ready in the presence of all peoples:
[32]a light for revelation to the nations,
and glory for your people Israel.'

[33]His father and mother were astonished at the things that were said about him. [34]Simeon blessed them.

'Listen,' he said to Mary his mother, 'this child has been placed here to make many in

Israel fall and rise again, and as a sign that will be spoken against ³⁵(yes, a sword will go through your own soul as well), so that the thoughts of many hearts may be disclosed.'

³⁶There was also a prophetess called Anna, the daughter of Phanuel, of the tribe of Asher. She was of a great age, having been widowed after a seven-year marriage, ³⁷and was now eighty-four. She never left the Temple, but worshipped with fasting and prayer night and day. ³⁸She came up at that moment and gave thanks to God, and spoke about Jesus to everyone who was waiting for the redemption of Jerusalem.

³⁹So when they had finished everything according to the law of the Lord, they returned to Galilee, to their town of Nazareth. ⁴⁰The child grew and became strong, and was full of wisdom, and God's grace was upon him.

The boy Jesus

⁴¹Jesus' parents used to go to Jerusalem every year for the Passover festival. ⁴²When he was twelve years old, they went up as usual for the festival. ⁴³When the feast days were over, they began the journey back, but the boy Jesus remained in Jerusalem. His parents didn't know; ⁴⁴they thought he was in the travelling party, and went a day's journey before looking for him among their relatives and friends.

⁴⁵When they didn't find him, they went back to Jerusalem to look for him. ⁴⁶And so it happened that after three days they found him in the Temple, sitting among the teachers, listening to them and asking them questions. ⁴⁷Everyone who heard him was astonished at his understanding and his answers.

⁴⁸When they saw him they were quite overwhelmed.

'Child,' said his mother, 'why did you do this to us? Look – your father and I have been in a terrible state looking for you!'

⁴⁹'Why were you looking for me?' he replied. 'Didn't you know that I would have to be getting involved with my father's work?'

⁵⁰They didn't understand what he had said to them. ⁵¹He went down with them and came to Nazareth, and lived in obedience to them. And his mother kept all these things in her heart.

⁵²So Jesus became wiser and taller, gaining favour both with God and with the people.

The preaching of John the Baptist

3 It was the fifteenth year of the reign of Tiberius Caesar. Pontius Pilate was governor of Judaea; Herod was tetrarch of Galilee; his brother Philip was tetrarch of Ituraea and Trachonitis; Lysanias was tetrarch of Abilene. ²Annas and Caiaphas were the high priests.

At that time, the word of God came to John, the son of Zechariah, in the wilderness. ³He went through all the region of the Jordan, announcing a baptism of repentance for the forgiveness of sins. ⁴This is what is written in the book of the words of Isaiah the prophet:

A voice shouting in the wilderness:
get ready a path for the Lord,
make the roads straight for him!
⁵Every valley shall be filled in,
and every mountain and hill shall be flattened,
the twisted paths will be straightened out,
and the rough roads smoothed off,
⁶and all that lives shall see God's rescue.

⁷'You brood of vipers,' John used to say to the crowds who came out to be baptized by him. 'Who told you to escape from the coming anger? ⁸You'd better prove your repentance by bearing the proper fruit! Don't start saying to yourselves, "We have Abraham as our father"; let me tell you, God can raise up children for Abraham from these stones! ⁹The axe is already standing by the roots of the tree – so every tree that doesn't produce good fruit will be cut down and thrown into the fire.'

John the Baptist confronts the crowds

¹⁰'What shall we do?' asked the crowds.

¹¹'Anyone who has two cloaks,' replied John, 'should give one to someone who hasn't got one. The same applies to anyone who has plenty of food.'

¹²Some toll-collectors came to be baptized. 'Teacher,' they said, 'what should we do?'

¹³'Don't collect more than what is laid down,' he replied.

¹⁴Some soldiers, too, asked John, 'What about us? What should we do?'

'No extortion,' replied John, 'and no blackmail. Be content with your wages.'

¹⁵The people were very excited, and everyone was questioning in their hearts whether John might not be the Messiah. ¹⁶To all of them John responded: 'I am baptizing you with water. But someone is coming who is stronger than I am. I don't deserve to untie his sandal-strap. He will baptize you with the holy spirit and with fire. ¹⁷He will have his winnowing-fork to hand, ready to sort out the mess on his threshing floor and gather the corn into his barn. Any rubbish he will burn with a fire that will never go out.'

¹⁸John urged his news on the people with many other words. ¹⁹But Herod the Tetrarch – whom John had accused in the matter of his brother's wife Herodias, and for all the evil things which Herod had done – ²⁰added this to his list of crimes, that he shut John up in prison.

Jesus' baptism and genealogy

²¹So it happened that, as all the people were being baptized, Jesus too was baptized, and was praying. The heaven was opened, ²²and the holy spirit descended in a bodily form, like a dove, upon him. There came a voice from heaven: 'You are my son, my dear son! I'm delighted with you.'

²³Jesus was about thirty years old at the start of his work. He was, as people thought, the son of Joseph, from whom his ancestry proceeds back in the following line: Heli, ²⁴Matthat, Levi, Melchi, Jannai, Joseph, ²⁵Mattathias, Amos, Nahum, Esli, Naggai, ²⁶Maath, Mattathias, Semein, Josech, Joda, ²⁷Johanan, Rhesa, Zerubbabel, Shealtiel, Neri, ²⁸Melchi, Addi, Kosam, Elmadam, Er, ²⁹Joshua, Eliezer, Jorim, Matthat, Levi, ³⁰Simeon, Judah, Joseph, Jonam, Eliakim, ³¹Melea, Menna, Mattatha, Nathan, David, ³²Jesse, Obed, Boaz, Sala, Nahshon, ³³Amminadab, Admin, Arni, Hezron, Perez, Judah, ³⁴Jacob, Isaac, Abraham, Terah, Nahor, ³⁵Serug, Reu, Peleg, Eber, Shela, ³⁶Kainan, Arphachsad, Shem, Noah, Lamech, ³⁷Methuselah, Enoch, Jared, Mahalaleel, Kainan, ³⁸Enosh, Seth, Adam, and God.

Temptation in the wilderness

4 Jesus returned from the Jordan, filled with the spirit. The spirit took him off into the wilderness ²for forty days, to be tested by the devil. He ate nothing during that time, and at the end of it he was hungry.

³'If you are God's son,' said the devil, 'tell this stone to become a loaf of bread.'

⁴'It is written,' replied Jesus, '"It takes more than bread to keep you alive."'

⁵The devil then took him up and showed him, in an instant, all the kingdoms of the world.

⁶'I will give you authority over all of this,' said the devil, 'and all the prestige that goes with it. It's been given to me, you see, and I give it to anyone I like. ⁷So it can all be yours . . . if you will just worship me.'

⁸'It is written,' replied Jesus, '"The Lord your God is the one you must worship; he is the only one you must serve."'

⁹Then the devil took him to Jerusalem, and stood him on a pinnacle of the Temple.

'If you are God's son,' he said, 'throw yourself down from here; ¹⁰it's written that "He will give his angels a command about you, to look after you"; ¹¹and "They will carry you in their hands, so that you won't hit your foot against a stone."'

¹²'It has been said,' replied Jesus, '"You mustn't put the Lord your God to the test."'

¹³When the devil had finished each temptation, he left him until another opportunity.

Opposition to Jesus in Nazareth

¹⁴Jesus returned to Galilee in the power of the spirit. Word about him went out throughout the whole district. ¹⁵He taught in their synagogues, and gained a great reputation all around.

¹⁶He came to Nazareth, where he had been brought up. On the sabbath, as was his regular practice, he went into the synagogue and stood up to read. ¹⁷They gave him the scroll of the prophet Isaiah. He unrolled the scroll and found the place where it was written:

¹⁸The spirit of the Lord is upon me
because he has anointed me
to tell the poor the good news.

He has sent me to announce release to the
   prisoners
and sight to the blind,
to set the wounded victims free,
¹⁹to announce the year of God's special favour.

²⁰He rolled up the scroll, gave it to the attendant, and sat down. All eyes in the synagogue were fixed on him.

²¹'Today,' he began, 'this scripture is fulfilled in your own hearing.'

²²Everyone remarked at him; they were astonished at the words coming out of his mouth – words of sheer grace.

'Isn't this Joseph's son?' they said.

²³'I know what you're going to say,' Jesus said. 'You're going to tell me the old riddle: "Heal yourself, doctor!" "We heard of great happenings in Capernaum; do things like that here, in your own country!"

²⁴'Let me tell you the truth,' he went on. 'Prophets never get accepted in their own country. ²⁵This is the solemn truth: there were plenty of widows in Israel in the time of Elijah, when heaven was shut up for three years and six months, and there was a great famine over all the land. ²⁶Elijah was sent to none of them, only to a widow in the Sidonian town of Zarephath. ²⁷And there were plenty of people with virulent skin diseases in Israel in the time of Elisha the prophet, and none of them was healed – only Naaman, the Syrian.'

²⁸When they heard this, everyone in the synagogue flew into a rage. ²⁹They got up and threw him out of town. They took him to the top of the mountain on which their town was built, meaning to fling him off. ³⁰But he slipped through the middle of them and went away.

Jesus' authoritative healings

³¹Jesus went down to Capernaum, a town of Galilee. He used to teach them every sabbath. ³²They were astonished at his teaching, because his message was powerful and authoritative.

³³There was a man in the synagogue who had the spirit of an unclean demon. ³⁴'Hey, you!' he yelled out at the top of his voice. 'What's going on with you and me, Jesus of Nazareth? Have you come to destroy us? I know who you are – you're God's Holy One!'

³⁵'Shut up!' Jesus rebuked him. 'Come out of him!'

The demon threw the man down right there in front of them, and came out without harming him. ³⁶Fear came over them all. 'What's all this?' they started to say to one another. 'He's got power! He's got authority! He tells the unclean spirits what to do, and they come out!' ³⁷Word about him went out to the whole surrounding region.

³⁸He left the synagogue and went into Simon's house. Simon's mother-in-law was sick with a high fever, and they asked him about her. ³⁹He stood in front of her, rebuked the fever, and it left her. And straight away she got up and waited on them.

⁴⁰When the sun went down, everyone who had sick people – all kinds of sicknesses – brought them to him. He laid his hands on each one in turn, and healed them. ⁴¹Demons came out of many people, shouting out, 'You are the son of God!' He sternly forbade them to speak, because they knew he was the Messiah.

⁴²When day dawned he left the town and went off to a deserted place. The crowds hunted for him, and when they caught up with him they begged him not to leave them.

⁴³'I must tell the good news of God's kingdom to the other towns,' he said. 'That's what I was sent for.' ⁴⁴And he was announcing the message to the synagogues of Judaea.

The miraculous catch of fish

5 One day, as the crowds were pressing close to him to hear the word of God, Jesus was standing by the lake of Gennesaret. ²He saw two boats moored by the land; the fishermen had gone ashore and were washing their nets. ³He got into one of the boats – it was Simon's – and asked him to put out a little way from the land. Then he sat down in the boat and began to teach the crowd.

⁴When he had finished speaking, he said to Simon, 'Put out into the deeper part, and let down your nets for a catch.'

⁵'Master,' replied Simon, 'we were working hard all night and caught nothing at all. But if you say so, I'll let down the nets.'

⁶When they did so, they caught such a huge number of fish that their nets began to break.

⁷They signalled to their partners in the other boat to come and help them. So they came, and filled both the boats, and they began to sink.

⁸When Simon Peter saw it, he fell down at Jesus' knees.

'Go away,' he said. 'Leave me, Lord! I'm a sinner!' ⁹He and all his companions were gripped with amazement at the catch of fish they had taken; ¹⁰this included James and John, the sons of Zebedee, who were partners with Simon.

'Don't be afraid,' said Jesus to Simon. 'From now on you'll be catching people.'

¹¹They brought the boats in to land. Then they abandoned everything and followed him.

The healing of the man with a virulent skin disease

¹²It so happened that, as Jesus was in one particular town, there was a man whose body was riddled with a virulent skin disease. When he saw Jesus, he fell on his face.

'Lord,' he begged, 'if you want, you can make me clean.'

¹³Jesus stretched out his hand and touched him.

'I do want to,' he said. 'Be clean.'

And the skin disease disappeared immediately.

¹⁴Jesus instructed the man not to tell anyone. 'Go and show yourself to the priest,' he said, 'and make the offering commanded by Moses in connection with your healing, as evidence for them.'

¹⁵The news about Jesus, though, spread all round, and large crowds came to hear and to be healed from their diseases. ¹⁶He used to slip away to remote places and pray.

The healing of the paralytic lowered through the roof

¹⁷One day, as Jesus was teaching, there were Pharisees and legal experts sitting there who had come from every village of Galilee, and from Judaea and Jerusalem. The power of the Lord was with Jesus, enabling him to heal. ¹⁸Just then some men appeared, carrying a paralysed man on a mattress; they were trying to bring him in and lay him before Jesus. ¹⁹The crowd made it impossible for them to get through, so they went up on the roof and let him down through the tiles, mattress and all, so that he landed right in the middle, in front of Jesus.

²⁰Jesus saw what trust they had.

'My friend,' he said, 'your sins are forgiven.'

²¹The legal experts and Pharisees began to argue. 'Who does he think he is?' they said. 'He's blaspheming! Nobody can forgive sins – only God can do that!'

²²Jesus knew their line of thought.

'Why are you complaining in your hearts?' he replied. ²³'Which is easier, to say, "Your sins are forgiven", or to say, "Get up and walk"? ²⁴But if you want to be convinced that the son of man has authority on earth to forgive sins –' (here he turned to the paralysed man) '– I say to you, get up, pick up your mattress, and go home.'

²⁵At once he got up in front of them all, picked up what he'd been lying on, and went off home, praising God.

²⁶A sense of awe came over everyone. They praised God, and were filled with fear. 'We've seen extraordinary things today,' they said.

Questions about table-company and fasting

²⁷After this Jesus went out and saw a tax-collector called Levi, sitting at the tax-office. 'Follow me,' he said. ²⁸And he left everything, got up, and followed him.

²⁹Levi made a great feast for him in his house, and a large crowd of tax-collectors and others were there reclining at table. ³⁰The Pharisees and the legal experts began to grumble to Jesus' disciples.

'Why do you lot eat and drink,' they asked, 'with tax-collectors and sinners?'

³¹'Healthy people don't need a doctor,' replied Jesus. 'It's sick people who do! ³²I haven't come to call the righteous; I'm calling sinners to repentance.'

³³'John's disciples often fast, and say prayers,' they said to him, 'and so do the Pharisees' followers – but your disciples eat and drink.'

³⁴'Can you make the wedding guests fast,' replied Jesus, 'while the bridegroom is with them? ³⁵But the time will come when the bridegroom is taken away from them. That's when they will fast.'

³⁶He added this parable. 'Nobody tears a piece of cloth from a new coat to make a patch on an old one. If they do, they tear the new, and the patch from it won't fit the old one anyway. ³⁷And nobody puts new wine into old wineskins. If they do, the new wine will burst the skins: it will go to waste, and the skins will be ruined too. ³⁸You have to put new wine in new skins. ³⁹And nobody who drinks old wine wants new. "I prefer the old," they say.'

Teachings on the sabbath

6 One sabbath, Jesus was walking through some cornfields. His disciples were plucking and eating ears of grain, rubbing them with their hands.

²'Why', asked some Pharisees, 'are you doing something that isn't permitted on the sabbath?'

³'Haven't you read what David did?' replied Jesus. 'When he and his men were hungry, ⁴he went into God's house and took the "bread of the Presence", which no one but the priests was allowed to eat. He ate some, and gave it to his companions.

⁵'The son of man', he declared, 'is Lord of the sabbath.'

⁶On another sabbath he went into the synagogue and was teaching. A man was there whose right hand was withered. ⁷The scribes and Pharisees were watching him, to see if he would heal him on the sabbath, so that they could find an accusation against him.

⁸He knew what they were thinking.

'Get up,' he said to the man with the withered hand, 'and come out here in the middle.' He got up and came out.

⁹'Let me ask you something,' Jesus said to them. 'Is it lawful to do good on the sabbath or to do evil? To save life or to destroy it?'

¹⁰He looked round at all of them.

'Stretch out your hand,' he said to the man. He did so; and his hand was restored. ¹¹But they were filled with rage, and discussed with each other what they might do to Jesus.

The Beatitudes

¹²It happened around that time that Jesus went up into the mountain to pray, and he spent all night in prayer to God. ¹³When day came, he called his disciples, and chose twelve of them, calling them 'apostles': ¹⁴Simon, whom he called Peter, and Andrew his brother, and James and John, and Philip, Bartholomew, ¹⁵Matthew, Thomas, James son of Alphaeus, Simon who was called 'the hothead', ¹⁶Judas son of James, and Judas Iscariot, who turned traitor.

¹⁷He went down with them, and took up a position on a level plain where there was a large crowd of his followers, with a huge company of people from all Judaea, from Jerusalem, and from the coastal region of Tyre and Sidon. ¹⁸They came to hear him, and to be cured from their diseases. Those who were troubled by unclean spirits were healed, ¹⁹and the whole crowd tried to touch him, because power was going out from him and healing everybody.

²⁰He lifted up his eyes and looked at his disciples, and said:

'Blessings on the poor: God's kingdom belongs to you!
²¹'Blessings on those who are hungry today: you'll have a feast!
'Blessings on those who weep today: you'll be laughing!
²²'Blessings on you, when people hate you, and shut you out, when they slander you and reject your name as if it was evil, because of the son of man. ²³Celebrate on that day! Jump for joy! Don't you see: in heaven there is a great reward for you! That's what their ancestors did to the prophets.
²⁴'But woe betide you rich: you've had your comfort!
²⁵'Woe betide you if you're full today: you'll go hungry!
'Woe betide you if you're laughing today: you'll be mourning and weeping!
²⁶'Woe betide you when everyone speaks well of you: that's what their ancestors did to the false prophets.'

Loving your enemies

²⁷'But this is my word', Jesus continued, 'for those of you who are listening: love your enemies! Do good to people who hate you!

[28]Bless people who curse you! Pray for people who treat you badly!

[29]'If someone hits you on the cheek – offer him the other one! If someone takes away your coat – don't stop him taking your shirt! [30]Give to everyone who asks you, and don't ask for things back when people have taken them.

[31]'Whatever you want people to do to you, do that to them. [32]If you love those who love you, what credit is that to you? Think about it: even sinners love people who love them. [33]Or again, if you do good only to people who do good to you, what credit is that to you? Sinners do that too. [34]If you lend only to people you expect to get things back from, what credit is that to you? Even sinners lend to sinners to get paid back. [35]No: love your enemies, do good and lend without expecting any return. Your reward will be great! You will be children of the Highest! He is generous, you see, to the stingy and wicked. [36]You must be merciful, just as your father is merciful.

[37]'Don't judge, and you won't be judged. Don't condemn, and you won't be condemned. Forgive, and you'll be forgiven. [38]Give, and it will be given to you: a good helping, squashed down, shaken in, and overflowing – that's what will land in your lap. Yes: the ration you give to others is the ration you'll get back for yourself.'

Judging others and true obedience

[39]Jesus told them this riddle. 'What do you get when one blind man guides another? Both of them falling in a ditch! [40]Students can't do better than the teacher; when the course is done, they'll all be just like the teacher.

[41]'Why look at the speck of dust in your brother's eye, when you haven't noticed the plank in your own eye? [42]How can you say to your brother, "Dear brother, let me take the speck out of your eye," when you can't see the plank in your own? You're a fraud! First take the plank out of your own eye, and then you'll see clearly to take the speck out of your brother's eye.

[43]'You see, no good tree bears bad fruit; nor can a bad tree produce good fruit. [44]Every tree is known by its fruit. You don't pick figs from thorns; nor do you get grapes from a briar-bush. [45]The good person brings good things out of the good treasure of the heart; the evil person brings evil things out of evil. What comes out of the mouth is what's overflowing in the heart.

[46]'Why do you call me, "Lord, Lord," and don't do what I say? [47]I'll show you what people are like when they come to me, and hear my words, and do them. [48]They are like a wise man building a house: he dug, he went down deep, and he laid a foundation on rock. When a flood came, the river burst its banks all over the house, but it couldn't shake it because it was well built. [49]But when people hear but don't obey – that's like a man who built a house on the ground, without a foundation. When the river burst over it, it fell down at once. The ruin of that house was devastating.'

The healing of the centurion's servant

7 When Jesus had finished saying all these words in the hearing of the people, he went into Capernaum.

[2]There was a centurion who had a slave who was particularly precious to him. This slave was ill, at the point of death. [3]The centurion heard about Jesus, and sent some Jewish elders to him, to ask him to come and rescue his slave. [4]They approached Jesus and begged him eagerly.

'He deserves a favour like this from you,' they said. [5]'He loves our people, and he himself built us our synagogue.'

[6]Jesus went with them.

When he was not far off from the house, the centurion sent friends to him with a further message.

'Master,' he said, 'don't trouble yourself. I don't deserve to have you come under my roof. [7]That's why I didn't think myself worthy to come to you in person. But – just say the word, and my slave will be healed. [8]You see, I'm used to living under authority, and I have soldiers reporting to me. I say to this one, "Go," and he goes; to another one, "Come," and he comes; and to my slave, "Do this," and he does it.'

[9]When Jesus heard this he was astonished.

'Let me tell you,' he said, turning to the crowd that was following him, 'I haven't found faith of this kind, even in Israel.'

[10]The people who had been sent to him went back to the house. There they found the slave in good health.

The raising of the widow's son

¹¹Not long afterwards, Jesus went to a town called Nain. His disciples went with him, and so did a large crowd. ¹²As he got near to the gate of the city, a young man was being carried out dead. He was the only son of his mother, and she was a widow. There was a substantial crowd of the townspeople with her.

¹³When the master saw her, he was very sorry for her. 'Don't cry,' he said to her. ¹⁴Then he went up and touched the bier, and the people carrying it stood still.

'Young fellow,' he said, 'I'm telling you – get up!' ¹⁵The dead man sat up and began to speak, and he gave him to his mother.

¹⁶Terror came over all of them. They praised God.

'A great prophet has risen among us!' they said. 'God has visited his people!'

¹⁷This report went out about him in the whole of Judaea and the surrounding countryside.

Jesus and John the Baptist

¹⁸The disciples of John the Baptist told him about all these things. John called two of these followers ¹⁹and sent them to the master with this message: 'Are you the Coming One, or should we expect someone else?'

²⁰The men arrived where Jesus was. 'John the Baptist', they said, 'has sent us to you to say, "Are you the Coming One, or should we expect someone else?"'

²¹Then and there Jesus healed several people of diseases, plagues and possession by unclean spirits; and he gave several blind people back their sight. ²²Then he answered them: 'Go and tell John what you have seen and heard: the blind see, the lame walk, people with virulent skin diseases are cleansed, the deaf hear, the dead are raised, the poor hear the gospel. ²³And a blessing on the person who isn't shocked by me!'

²⁴So off went John's messengers.

Jesus then began to talk to the crowds about John. 'Why did you go out into the desert?' he asked. 'What were you looking for? A reed swaying in the breeze? ²⁵Well then, what did you go out to see? Someone dressed in silks and satins? See here, if you want to find people who wear fine clothes and live in luxury, you'd better look in royal palaces. ²⁶So what did you go out to see? A prophet? Yes indeed, and more than a prophet. ²⁷This is the one of whom the Bible says, "Look: I send my messenger before my face; he will get my path ready ahead of me."

²⁸'Let me tell you this,' he went on. 'Nobody greater than John has ever been born of women. But the one who is least in God's kingdom is greater than he is.'

²⁹When all the people, and the tax-collectors, heard that, they praised God for his faithfulness; they had been baptized with John's baptism. ³⁰But the Pharisees and the lawyers, who had not been baptized by John, rejected God's plan for them.

³¹'What picture can I use', Jesus continued, 'for the people of this generation? What are they like? ³²They're like children sitting in the square and calling this old riddle to each other:

> We piped for you and you didn't dance;
> we wailed for you and you didn't cry!

³³'When John the Baptist came, he didn't eat bread or drink wine, and you say, "He's got a demon!" ³⁴When the son of man came, eating and drinking, you say, "Look! A glutton and a drunkard, a friend of tax-collectors and sinners!" ³⁵And wisdom is justified by all her children.'

Jesus anointed by a sinful woman

³⁶A Pharisee asked Jesus to dine with him, and he went into the Pharisee's house and reclined at table. ³⁷A woman from the town, a known bad character, discovered that he was there at table in the Pharisee's house. She brought an alabaster jar of ointment. ³⁸Then she stood behind Jesus' feet, crying, and began to wet his feet with her tears. She wiped them with her hair, kissed his feet, and anointed them with the ointment.

³⁹The Pharisee who had invited Jesus saw what was going on.

'If this fellow really was a prophet,' he said to himself, 'he'd know what sort of a woman this is who is touching him! She's a sinner!'

⁴⁰'Simon,' replied Jesus, 'I have something to say to you.'

'Go ahead, Teacher,' he replied.

⁴¹'Once upon a time there was a moneylender who had two debtors. The first owed him five hundred dinars; the second a tenth of that. ⁴²Neither of them could pay him, and he let them both off. So which of them will love him more?'

⁴³'The one he let off the more, I suppose,' replied Simon.

'Quite right,' said Jesus.

⁴⁴Then, turning towards the woman, he said to Simon, 'You see this woman? When I came into your house, you didn't give me water to wash my feet – but she has washed my feet with her tears, and wiped them with her hair. ⁴⁵You didn't give me a kiss, but she hasn't stopped kissing my feet from the moment I came in. ⁴⁶You didn't anoint my head with oil, but she has anointed my feet with ointment. ⁴⁷So the conclusion I draw is this: she must have been forgiven many sins! Her great love proves it! But if someone has been forgiven only a little, they will love only a little.'

⁴⁸Then he said to the woman, 'Your sins are forgiven.'

⁴⁹'Who is this', the other guests began to say among themselves, 'who even forgives sins?'

⁵⁰'Your faith has saved you,' said Jesus to the woman. 'Go in peace.'

The parable of the sower

8 Soon afterwards, Jesus went about in person, with the Twelve, through the towns and villages, announcing and telling the good news of God's kingdom. ²They were accompanied by various women who had been healed from evil spirits and diseases: Mary who was called 'Magdalene', from whom seven demons had gone out, ³Joanna the wife of Chouza (Herod's steward), and Susanna, and many others. They looked after the needs of Jesus and his companions out of their own pockets.

⁴A large crowd came together, and people came to him from town after town. He spoke to them in parables: ⁵'A sower went out to sow his seed. As he was sowing, some fell by the road, and was trodden on, and the birds of the air ate it up. ⁶Other seed fell on stony ground, and when it came up it withered, because it didn't have any moisture. ⁷Other seed fell in among thorns, and when the thorns grew up they choked it. ⁸Other seed again fell into good soil, and came up, and gave a hundredfold yield.'

As he said this, he called out: 'If you've got ears to hear, then hear!'

⁹His disciples asked him what this parable was about.

¹⁰'You are being let in on the secrets of God's kingdom,' he said, 'but to the rest it happens in parables, so that "they may see but not perceive, and hear but not understand."

¹¹'This is the parable: the seed is the word of God. ¹²Those by the roadside are people who hear, but then the devil comes and takes away the word from their hearts, so that they won't believe it and be saved. ¹³Those on the stony ground are those who hear the word and receive it with delight – but they don't have any root, and so they believe only for a time, and then, when a time of testing comes, they draw back. ¹⁴The seed that falls in among thorns represents people who hear, but as they go on their way they are choked by the cares and riches and pleasures of life, and they don't bear proper, ripening fruit. ¹⁵But those in the good soil are the ones who hear the word and hold on to it with an upright and good heart, and who patiently produce fruit.'

Jesus calms the storm

¹⁶'Nobody lights a lamp', continued Jesus, 'and then hides it under a pot or a bed. They put it on a lampstand, so that people who come in can see the light. ¹⁷You see, nothing is hidden which won't become visible; nothing is concealed that won't come to light.

¹⁸'So be careful how you listen. If you've got something, more will be given to you; if you haven't, even what you imagine you have will be taken away from you.'

¹⁹His mother and brothers came to him, and couldn't get near him because of the crowd. ²⁰So they sent a message to him: 'Your mother and your brothers are standing outside, wanting to see you.'

²¹'Mother and brothers, indeed?' replied Jesus. 'Here are my mother and brothers – people who hear God's word and do it!'

²²One day he got into a boat with his disciples, and suggested that they cross to the other shore. So they set off. ²³As they were sailing, he fell asleep. A violent wind swept down on the lake, and the boat began to fill dangerously with water.

²⁴'Master, Master!' shouted the disciples, coming and waking him up. 'Master, we're lost!'

He got up and scolded the wind and the waves. They stopped, and there was a flat calm.

²⁵'Where's your faith?' he asked them.

They were afraid and astonished. 'Who is this, then,' they asked one another, 'if he can give orders to wind and water, and they obey him?'

The healing of the demoniac

²⁶They sailed to the land of the Gerasenes, which is on the other side from Galilee. ²⁷As he got out on land, a demon-possessed man from the town met him. For a long time he had worn no clothes, and he didn't live in a house but among the tombs. ²⁸When he saw Jesus he screamed and fell down in front of him.

'You and me, Jesus – you and me!' he yelled at the top of his voice. 'What is it with you and me, you son of the Most High God? Don't torture me – please, please don't torment me!' ²⁹Jesus was commanding the unclean spirit to come out of the man. Many times over it had seized him, and he was kept under guard with chains and manacles; but he used to break the shackles, and the demon would drive him into the desert.

³⁰'What's your name?' Jesus asked him.

'Regiment!' replied the man – for many demons had entered him. ³¹And they begged him not to order them to be sent into the pit.

³²A sizeable herd of pigs was feeding on the hillside, and the demons begged him to allow them to go into them. He gave them permission. ³³The demons went out of the man and entered the pigs, and the herd rushed down the steep slope into the lake and was drowned.

³⁴The herdsmen saw what had happened. They took to their heels and spread the news in town and country, ³⁵and people came out to see what had happened. They came to Jesus, and found the man from whom the demons had gone out sitting there at Jesus' feet, clothed and in his right mind. They were afraid. ³⁶People who had seen how the demoniac had been healed explained it to them. ³⁷The whole crowd, from the surrounding country of the Gerasenes, asked him to go away from them, because great terror had seized them. So he got into the boat and returned.

³⁸The man who had been demon-possessed begged Jesus to let him stay with him. But he sent him away. ³⁹'Go back to your home,' he said, 'and tell them what God has done for you.' And he went off round every town, declaring what Jesus had done for him.

Jairus's daughter and the woman with chronic bleeding

⁴⁰Jesus returned. A large crowd was waiting for him, and welcomed him back. ⁴¹A man named Jairus, a ruler of the synagogue, came and fell down in front of his feet. He pleaded with him to come to his house, ⁴²because he had an only daughter, twelve years old, who was dying. So they set off, and the crowd pressed close in around him.

⁴³There was a woman who had had an internal haemorrhage for twelve years. She had spent all she had on doctors, but had not been able to find a cure from anyone. ⁴⁴She came up behind Jesus and touched the hem of his robe. Immediately her flow of blood dried up.

⁴⁵'Who touched me?' asked Jesus.

Everybody denied it. 'Master,' said Peter, 'the crowds are crushing you and pressing you!'

⁴⁶'Somebody touched me,' said Jesus. 'Power went out from me, and I knew it.'

⁴⁷When the woman saw that she couldn't remain hidden, she came up, trembling, and fell down in front of him. She told him, in front of everyone, why she had touched him, and how she had been healed instantly.

⁴⁸'Daughter,' said Jesus, 'your faith has saved you. Go in peace.'

⁴⁹While he was still speaking, someone arrived from the synagogue-ruler's house. 'Your daughter's dead,' he said. 'Don't bother the teacher any longer.'

⁵⁰'Don't be afraid,' said Jesus when he heard it. 'Just believe, and she will be rescued.'

⁵¹When they got to the house, he didn't let anyone come in with them except Peter, John

and James, and the child's father and mother. ⁵²Everyone was weeping and wailing for her.

'Don't cry,' said Jesus. 'She isn't dead; she's asleep.' ⁵³They laughed at him, knowing that she was dead.

⁵⁴But he took her by the hand. 'Get up, child,' he called. ⁵⁵Her spirit returned, and she got up at once. He told them to give her something to eat. ⁵⁶Her parents were astounded, but he told them to tell nobody what had happened.

The Twelve sent out and the feeding of the five thousand

9 Jesus called together the Twelve, and gave them power and authority over all demons, and to cure diseases. ²He sent them out to announce God's kingdom and cure the sick.

³'Don't take anything for the journey,' he said to them, 'no stick, no bag, no bread, no money, no second cloak. ⁴Whenever you go into a house, stay there and leave from there. ⁵If anyone won't receive you, go out of that town and wipe the dust off your feet as evidence against them.'

⁶So off they went, and travelled through the villages, announcing the good news and healing people everywhere.

⁷Herod the Tetrarch heard what was going on, and was very puzzled. Some people were saying that John had been raised from the dead. ⁸Others were saying that Elijah had appeared; still others, that one of the old prophets had arisen.

⁹'I beheaded John,' said Herod, 'but I keep hearing all these things about this other fellow. Who is he?' And he tried to get to see him.

¹⁰The apostles returned and told Jesus what they had done. He took them off and went away privately to a town called Bethsaida. ¹¹When the crowds discovered, they followed him. He welcomed them and spoke to them about the kingdom of God, and he healed those who needed it.

¹²As the day wore on, the Twelve came to Jesus.

'Send the crowd away,' they said, 'so that they can go into the villages and countryside nearby, find somewhere to stay, and get something to eat. We're in quite a lonely spot here.'

¹³'You give them something to eat,' he replied.

'All we've got here', they said, 'is five loaves and a couple of fishes – unless you mean we should go ourselves and buy food for all these people?' ¹⁴(There were about five thousand men.)

'Get them to sit down', Jesus said to them, 'in groups of around fifty each.'

¹⁵They did so, and everyone sat down. ¹⁶Then Jesus took the five loaves and the two fish. He looked up to heaven, blessed the food, divided it, and gave it to the disciples to pass around the crowd. ¹⁷Everyone ate, and was satisfied. They took up twelve baskets of broken bits left over.

Peter's declaration of Jesus' messiahship

¹⁸When Jesus was praying alone, his disciples gathered around him.

'Who do the crowds say I am?' he asked them.

¹⁹'John the Baptist,' they responded. 'And others say Elijah. Others say that one of the ancient prophets has arisen.'

²⁰'What about you?' said Jesus. 'Who do you say I am?'

'God's Messiah,' answered Peter.

²¹He gave them strict and careful instructions not to tell this to anyone.

²²'The son of man,' he said, 'must suffer many things, and be rejected by the elders, and the chief priests, and the legal experts. He must be killed, and raised up on the third day.'

²³He then spoke to them all. 'If any of you want to come after me,' he said, 'you must say No to yourselves, and pick up your cross every day, and follow me. ²⁴If you want to save your life, you'll lose it; but if you lose your life because of me, you'll save it. ²⁵What good will it do you if you win the entire world, but lose or forfeit your own self? ²⁶If you're ashamed of me and my words, the son of man will be ashamed of you, when he comes in the glory which belongs to him, and to the father, and to the holy angels.

²⁷'Let me tell you,' he concluded, 'there are some standing here who won't experience death until they see God's kingdom.'

The transfiguration

²⁸About eight days after this conversation, Jesus took Peter, John and James and went up a

mountain to pray. ²⁹And, as he was praying, the appearance of his face changed, and his clothes became shining white. ³⁰Two men appeared, talking with him: it was Moses and Elijah, ³¹who appeared in glory and were speaking of his departure, which he was going to fulfil in Jerusalem.

³²Peter and those who were with him were heavy with sleep, but they managed to stay awake. They saw his glory, and the two men who were standing there with him.

³³As they were going away from him, Peter said to Jesus, 'Master, it's wonderful for us to be here! Let's make three tents, one for you, one for Moses, and one for Elijah!' He didn't know what he was saying; ³⁴but as the words were coming out of his mouth a cloud appeared and overshadowed them. They were afraid as they entered the cloud. ³⁵And a voice came from the cloud: 'This is my son, my chosen one: listen to him.' ³⁶As the voice spoke, there was Jesus by himself. They kept silent, and told nobody at that time anything of what they had seen.

³⁷The next day, as they were going down from the mountain, a large crowd met them. ³⁸A man from the crowd shouted out, 'Teacher! Please, please have a look at my son! He's my only child, ³⁹and look what's happening to him! A spirit seizes him, and suddenly it shrieks and convulses him, so that he foams at the mouth. It goes on savaging him, and it's almost impossible to get it to leave him. ⁴⁰I begged your disciples to cast it out, but they couldn't.'

⁴¹'You faithless and depraved generation!' said Jesus in reply. 'How long shall I be with you and have to put up with you? Bring your son here.'

⁴²While he was on the way, the demon tore at him and threw him into convulsions. Jesus rebuked the unclean spirit, healed the child, and gave him back to his father. ⁴³Everyone was astonished at the greatness of God.

While they were all still expressing amazement at everything he had done, Jesus said to his disciples, ⁴⁴'Let these words go right down into your ears: the son of man is to be given over into human hands.' ⁴⁵They had no idea what he was talking about. It was hidden from them, so that they wouldn't perceive it, and they were afraid to ask him about what he had said.

The nature of discipleship

⁴⁶A dispute arose among them about which of them was the greatest. ⁴⁷Jesus knew this quarrel was going on in their hearts, so he took a child and stood it beside him.

⁴⁸'If you receive this child in my name,' he said, 'you receive me. And anyone who receives me, receives the one who sent me. Whoever is the least among you – that's the one who is great.'

⁴⁹'Master,' commented John, 'we saw someone casting out demons in your name. We told him to stop, because he wasn't part of our company.'

⁵⁰'Don't stop him,' replied Jesus. 'Anyone who isn't against you is on your side.'

⁵¹As the time came nearer for Jesus to be taken up, he settled it in his mind to go to Jerusalem. ⁵²He sent messengers ahead of him. They came into a Samaritan village to get them ready, ⁵³and they refused to receive him, because his mind was set on going to Jerusalem. ⁵⁴When the disciples James and John saw it, they said, 'Master, do you want us to call down fire from heaven and burn them up?' ⁵⁵He turned and rebuked them, ⁵⁶and they went on to another village.

⁵⁷As they were going along the road a man addressed Jesus.

'Wherever you're going,' he said, 'I'll follow you!'

⁵⁸'Foxes have lairs,' Jesus replied, 'and the birds in the sky have nests; but the son of man doesn't have anywhere to lay his head.'

⁵⁹To another person he said, 'Follow me.'

'Master,' he replied, 'let me first go and bury my father.'

⁶⁰'Let the dead bury their dead,' said Jesus. 'You must go and announce God's kingdom.'

⁶¹'I will follow you, Master,' said another, 'but first let me say goodbye to the people at home.'

⁶²'Nobody', replied Jesus, 'who begins to plough and then looks over his shoulder is fit for God's kingdom.'

Jesus sends out the seventy

10 After this the master commissioned seventy others, and sent them ahead of him in pairs to every town and place where he was intending to come.

²'There's a great harvest out there,' he said to them, 'but there aren't many workers. So plead with the harvest-master to send out workers for the harvest.

³'Off you go now. Remember, I'm sending you out like lambs among wolves. ⁴Take no money-bag, no pack, no sandals – and don't stop to pass the time with anyone on the road. ⁵Whenever you go into a house, first say, "Peace on this house." ⁶If a child of peace lives there, your peace will rest on them; but if not, it will return to you.

⁷'Stay in the same house, and eat and drink what they provide. The worker deserves to be paid, you see. Don't go from house to house. ⁸If you go into a town and they welcome you, eat what is provided, ⁹heal the sick who are there, and say to them, "God's kingdom has come close to you." ¹⁰But if you go into a town and they don't welcome you, go out into the streets of the town and say, ¹¹"Here is the very dust of your town clinging to our feet – and we're wiping it off in front of your eyes! ¹²But you should know this: God's kingdom has come close to you!" Let me tell you, on that day it will be more tolerable for Sodom than for that town.

¹³'Woe betide you, Chorazin! Woe betide you, Bethsaida! If the powerful deeds done in you had been done in Tyre and Sidon, they would have repented long ago, sitting in sackcloth and ashes. ¹⁴But it will be more tolerable for Tyre and Sidon in the judgment than for you. ¹⁵And you, Capernaum – you want to be lifted up to heaven, do you? No: you'll be sent down to Hades!

¹⁶'Anyone who hears you, hears me; anyone who rejects you, rejects me; and anyone who rejects me, rejects the one who sent me.'

The celebration of Jesus

¹⁷The seventy came back exhilarated.

'Master,' they said, 'even the demons obey us in your name!'

¹⁸'I saw the satan fall like lightning from heaven,' he replied. ¹⁹'Look: I've given you authority to tread on snakes and scorpions, and over every power of the enemy. Nothing will ever be able to harm you. ²⁰But – don't celebrate having spirits under your authority. Celebrate this, that your names are written in heaven.'

²¹Then and there Jesus celebrated in the holy spirit.

'I thank you, father,' he said, 'Lord of heaven and earth! You hid these things from the wise and intelligent, and revealed them to babies. Yes, father, that was what you graciously decided. ²²Everything has been given me by my father. Nobody knows who the son is except the father, and nobody knows who the father is except the son, and anyone to whom the son wishes to reveal him.'

²³Jesus then turned to the disciples privately.

'A blessing on the eyes,' he said, 'which see what you see! ²⁴Let me tell you, many prophets and kings wanted to see what you see, and they didn't see it; and to hear what you hear, and they didn't hear it!'

The parable of the good Samaritan

²⁵A lawyer got up and put Jesus on the spot.

'Teacher,' he said, 'what should I do to inherit the life of the coming age?'

²⁶'Well,' replied Jesus, 'what is written in the law? What's your interpretation of it?'

²⁷'You shall love the Lord your God', he replied, 'with all your heart, all your soul, all your strength, and all your understanding; and your neighbour as yourself.'

²⁸'Well said!' replied Jesus. 'Do that and you will live.'

²⁹'Ah,' said the lawyer, wanting to win the point, 'but who is my neighbour?'

³⁰Jesus rose to the challenge. 'Once upon a time,' he said, 'a man was going down from Jerusalem to Jericho, and was set upon by brigands. They stripped him and beat him and ran off leaving him half dead. ³¹A priest happened to be going down that road, and when he saw him he went past on the opposite side. ³²So too a Levite came by the place; he saw him too, and went past on the opposite side.

³³'But a travelling Samaritan came to where he was. When he saw him he was filled with pity. ³⁴He came over to him and bound up his wounds, pouring in oil and wine. Then he put him on his own beast, took him to an inn, and looked after him. ³⁵The next morning, as he was going on his way, he gave the innkeeper

two dinars. "Take care of him," he said, "and on my way back I'll pay you whatever else you need to spend on him."

36"Which of these three do you think turned out to be the neighbour of the man who was set upon by the brigands?'

37"The one who showed mercy on him,' came the reply.

'Well,' Jesus said to him, 'you go and do the same.'

Martha and Mary

38On their journey, Jesus came into a village. There was a woman there named Martha, who welcomed him. 39She had a sister named Mary, who sat at the master's feet and listened to his teaching.

40Martha was frantic with all the work in the kitchen.

'Master,' she said, coming in to where they were, 'don't you care that my sister has left me to do the work all by myself? Tell her to give me a hand!'

41'Martha, Martha,' he replied, 'you are fretting and fussing about so many things. 42Only one thing matters. Mary has chosen the best part, and it's not going to be taken away from her.'

The Lord's Prayer

11 Once Jesus was praying in a particular place. When he had finished, one of his disciples approached.

'Teach us to pray, Master,' he said, 'just like John taught his disciples.'

2'When you pray,' replied Jesus, 'this is what to say:

'Father, may your name be honoured; may your kingdom come; 3give us each day our daily bread; 4and forgive us our sins, since we too forgive all our debtors; and don't put us to the test.'

5'Suppose one of you has a friend,' he said, 'and you go to him in the middle of the night and say, "My dear friend, lend me three loaves of bread; 6A friend of mine is on a journey and has arrived at my house, and I have nothing to put in front of him!" 7He will answer from inside his house, "Don't make life difficult for me! The door is already shut, and my children and I are all in bed! I can't get up and give you anything." 8Let me tell you, even if he won't get up and give you anything just because you're his friend, because of your shameless persistence he will get up and give you whatever you need.

9'So this is my word to you: ask and it will be given you; search and you will find; knock and it will be opened to you. 10You see, everyone who asks receives! Everyone who searches finds! Everyone who knocks has the door opened for them! 11If your son asks you for a fish, is there a father among you who will give him a snake? 12Or if he asks for an egg, will you give him a scorpion? 13Face it: you are evil. And yet you know how to give good presents to your children. How much more will your heavenly father give the holy spirit to those who ask him!'

Jesus and Beelzebul

14Jesus was casting out a demon that prevented speech. When the demon had gone out, the man who had been silent spoke, and the crowd were amazed. 15But some of them said, 'He casts out demons by Beelzebul, the prince of demons!' 16Others, trying to test him out, asked him to produce a sign from heaven.

17Jesus knew what they were thinking.

'Every kingdom split down the middle goes to ruin,' he said. 'If a house turns in on itself, it falls. 18Well then: if even the satan is split down the middle, how can his kingdom last? This', he added, 'is because you say that I cast out demons by Beelzebul!

19'Now look: supposing I do cast out demons by Beelzebul, whose power are your own people using when they cast them out? Think about it: they will be your judges. 20But if it's by God's finger that I cast out demons, then God's kingdom has come upon you.

21'Imagine a strong man, armed to the teeth, guarding his palace. Everything he owns is safe and sound. 22But supposing someone stronger comes and overpowers him, and takes away the armour he was trusting in – then he can help himself and start giving the booty away! 23If you're not with me, you're against me. If you're not gathering with me, you're scattering.

²⁴'When the unclean spirit goes out of a person, it roams through desert landscapes looking for a place to rest. When it doesn't find anywhere, it says to itself, "I shall go back to the house I left behind." ²⁵And it finds the place neat and tidy. ²⁶So it sets off and brings along seven other spirits more evil than itself, and goes back to live there. That person will end up worse off than he began.'

²⁷While he was saying these things, a woman from the crowd raised her voice. 'A blessing on the womb that bore you,' she shouted, 'and the breasts that you sucked!'

²⁸'On the contrary,' replied Jesus. 'A blessing on those who hear God's word and keep it!'

The sign of Jonah

²⁹The crowds kept increasing. Jesus began to say to them, 'This generation is an evil generation! It looks for a sign, and no sign will be given to it except the sign of Jonah. ³⁰Jonah was a sign to the people of Nineveh; just so, the son of man will be a sign to this generation. ³¹The Queen of the South will rise up in the judgment with the men of this generation and will condemn them: she came from the ends of the earth to listen to Solomon's wisdom, and look – something greater than Solomon is here. ³²The men of Nineveh will rise up in the judgment with this generation and will condemn it: they repented at Jonah's preaching, and look – something greater than Jonah is here.

³³'Nobody lights a lamp in order to hide it or put it under a jug. They put it on a lampstand, so that people who come in can see the light. ³⁴Your eye is the lamp of your body. If your eye is focused, your whole body is full of light. But if it's evil, your body is in darkness. ³⁵Watch out, then, in case the light inside you turns to darkness. ³⁶If your whole body is illuminated, with no part in darkness, everything will be illuminated, just as you are by a flash of lightning.'

³⁷While he was speaking, a Pharisee invited him to have dinner at his house. So he went in and sat down. ³⁸The Pharisee, watching him, was surprised that he didn't first wash before dinner.

³⁹'Now, you Pharisees,' said the master to him, 'you clean the outside of the plate and cup, but your insides are full of violent robbery and wickedness. ⁴⁰That's stupid! Didn't the one who made the outside make the inside as well? ⁴¹You should give for alms what's inside the bowl, and then everything will be clean for you.'

Woes against the Pharisees

⁴²'But woe betide you Pharisees!' Jesus continued. 'You tithe mint and rue and herbs of all kinds; and you have sidestepped justice, mercy and the love of God. You should have done these, without missing out the others.

⁴³'Woe betide you Pharisees! You love the chief seats in the synagogues and greetings in the market-places.

⁴⁴'Woe betide you! You are like hidden tombs, and people walk over them without knowing it.'

⁴⁵At this, one of the legal experts spoke up. 'Teacher,' he said, 'when you say this you're insulting us too!'

⁴⁶'Woe betide you lawyers, too!' replied Jesus. 'You give people heavy loads to carry which they can hardly bear, and you yourselves don't lift a finger to help!

⁴⁷'Woe betide you! You build the tombs of the prophets, and your ancestors killed them. ⁴⁸So you bear witness that you approve of what your ancestors did: they killed them, and you build their tombs.

⁴⁹'For all this, God's Wisdom says, "I'm sending you prophets and ambassadors; some of them you will kill and persecute", ⁵⁰so that the blood of all the prophets shed ever since the beginning of the world may be required from this generation – ⁵¹from the blood of Abel to the blood of Zacharias, who died between the altar and the sanctuary. Yes, let me tell you, it will all be required from this generation.

⁵²'Woe betide you lawyers! You have taken away the key of knowledge. You didn't go in yourselves, and you stopped the people who were trying to go in.'

⁵³He went outside, and the scribes and Pharisees began to be very threatening towards him. They interrogated him about several things, ⁵⁴lying in wait for him to catch him in something he might say.

Further warnings

12 Crowds were gathering in their thousands, so much so that they were trampling on each other. Jesus began to say to his disciples, 'Watch out for the leaven of the Pharisees – I mean, their hypocrisy. This is a matter of first importance.

²'Nothing is concealed that won't be uncovered; nothing is hidden that won't be made known. ³So whatever you say in the darkness will be heard in the light, and whatever you speak indoors into someone's ear will be proclaimed from the housetops.

⁴"So, my friends, I have this to say to you: don't be afraid of those who kill the body, and after that have nothing more they can do. ⁵I will show you who to fear: fear the one who starts by killing and then has the right to throw people into Gehenna. Yes, let me tell you, that's the one to fear!

⁶'How much do five sparrows cost? Two copper coins? And not one of them is forgotten in God's presence. ⁷But the hairs of your head have all been counted. Don't be afraid! You are worth more than lots of sparrows.

⁸'Let me tell you: if anyone acknowledges me before others, the son of man will acknowledge that person before God's angels. ⁹But if anyone denies me before others, that person will be denied before God's angels.

¹⁰'Everyone who speaks a word against the son of man will have it forgiven; but the one who blasphemes against the holy spirit will not be forgiven.

¹¹'When they bring you before synagogues, rulers and authorities, don't worry about how to give an answer or what to say. ¹²The holy spirit will teach you what to say at that very moment.'

The parable of the rich fool

¹³Someone from the crowd said to Jesus, 'Teacher, tell my brother to divide the inheritance with me!'

¹⁴'Tell me, my good man,' replied Jesus, 'who appointed me as a judge or arbitrator over you?'

¹⁵'Watch out,' he said to them, 'and beware of all greed! Your life doesn't consist of the sum total of your possessions.'

¹⁶He told them a parable. 'There was a rich man whose land produced a fine harvest. ¹⁷"What shall I do?" he said to himself. "I don't have enough room to store my crops!

¹⁸"'I know!" he said. "I'll pull down my barns – and I'll build bigger ones! Then I'll be able to store all the corn and all my belongings there. ¹⁹And I shall say to my soul, Soul, you've got many good things stored up for many years. Take it easy! Eat, drink, have a good time!"

²⁰'But God said to him, "Fool! This very night your soul will be demanded of you! Now who's going to have all the things you've got ready?" ²¹That's how it is with someone who stores up things for himself and isn't rich before God.

²²'So let me tell you this,' he said to the disciples. 'Don't be anxious about your life – what you should eat; or about your body – what you should wear. ²³Life is more than food! The body is more than clothing! ²⁴Think about the ravens: they don't sow seed, they don't gather harvests, they don't have storehouses or barns; and God feeds them. How much more will he feed you! Think of the difference between yourselves and the birds!

²⁵'Which of you by being anxious can add a day to your lifetime? ²⁶So if you can't even do a little thing like that, why worry about anything else? ²⁷Think about the lilies and the way they grow. They don't work hard, they don't weave cloth; but, let me tell you, not even Solomon in all his glory was dressed up like one of them. ²⁸So if that's how God clothes the grass in the field – here today, into the fire tomorrow – how much more will he clothe you, you little-faith lot!

²⁹'So don't you go hunting about for what to eat or what to drink, and don't be anxious. ³⁰The nations of the world go searching for all that stuff, and your father knows you need it. ³¹This is what you should search for: God's kingdom! Then all the rest will be given you as well. ³²Don't be afraid, little flock. Your father is delighted to give you the kingdom.

³³'Sell your possessions and give alms. Make yourselves purses that don't wear out, a treasure in heaven that lasts for ever, where the thief doesn't come near and the moth doesn't destroy. ³⁴Yes: where your treasure is, there your heart will be too.'

Jesus' call to watchfulness

35'Make sure you're dressed and ready with your lamps alight,' said Jesus. 36'You need to be like people waiting for their master when he comes back from the wedding feast, so that when he comes and knocks they will be able to open the door for him at once. 37A blessing on the servants whom the master finds awake when he comes! I'm telling you the truth: he will put on an apron and sit them down and come and wait on them. 38A blessing on them if he comes in the second watch of the night, or even the third, and finds them like that!

39'But you should know this: if the householder had known what time the thief was coming, he wouldn't have let his house be broken into. 40You too should be ready, because the son of man is coming at a time you don't expect.'

41'Master,' said Peter, 'are you telling this parable for us, or for everyone?'

42'Who then is the faithful and wise servant,' said Jesus, 'whom the master will set over all his household, to give them their allowance of food at the proper time? 43A blessing on the servant that his master, when he comes, finds doing just that! 44I'm telling you truly, he will install him as manager over all his possessions. 45But if that servant says in his heart, "My master is taking his time over coming back," and begins to beat the slaves and slave-girls, to eat and drink and get drunk – 46then the master of that servant will come on a day he doesn't expect him to, and at a moment he didn't imagine, and he will cut him in two. He will give him the same place as the unbelievers.

47'If a servant knew what the master wanted, and didn't get ready, or do what was wanted, the punishment will be a severe beating. 48If the servant didn't know, and did what deserved a beating, it will be a light beating. Much will be required from one who is given much; if someone is entrusted with much, even more will be expected in return.'

Reading the signs of the times

49'I came to throw fire upon the earth,' Jesus continued, 'and I wish it were already alight! 50I have a baptism to be baptized with, and I am under huge pressure until it's happened! 51'Do you suppose I've come to give peace to the earth? No, let me tell you, but rather division. 52From now on, you see, families will be split down the middle: three against two in a family of five, and two against three, 53father against son and son against father, mother against daughter and daughter against mother, mother-in-law against daughter-in-law and daughter-in-law against mother-in-law.

54'When you see a cloud rising in the west,' he said to the crowds, 'you say at once, "It's going to rain," and rain it does. 55When you see the south wind getting up, you say, "It's going to be very hot," and that's what happens. 56You impostors! You know how to work out what the earth and the sky are telling you; why can't you work out what's going on at this very moment?

57'Why don't you judge for yourselves what you ought to do? 58When you go with your accuser before a magistrate, do your best to reach a settlement with him. Otherwise he may drag you in front of the judge, and the judge will hand you over to the officer, and the officer will throw you into jail. 59Let me tell you, you won't get out from there until you have paid the last coin.'

The parable of the fig tree

13 At that moment some people came up and told them the news. Some Galileans had been in the Temple, and Pilate had mixed their blood with that of the sacrifices.

2'Do you suppose,' said Jesus, 'that those Galileans suffered such things because they were greater sinners than all other Galileans? 3No, let me tell you! Unless you repent, you will all be destroyed in the same way.

4'And what about those eighteen who were killed when the tower in Siloam collapsed on top of them? Do you imagine they were more blameworthy than everyone else who lives in Jerusalem? 5No, let me tell you! Unless you repent, you will all be destroyed in the same way.'

6He told them this parable. 'Once upon a time there was a man who had a fig tree in his vineyard. He came to it looking for fruit, and didn't find any. 7So he said to the gardener, "Look here! I've been coming to this fig tree for three years hoping to find some fruit, and I haven't found any! Cut it down! Why should it use up the soil?"

8"'I tell you what, Master,' replied the gardener; "let it alone for just this one year more. I'll dig all round it and put on some manure. 9Then, if it fruits next year, well and good; and if not, you can cut it down.'"

Jesus heals a crippled woman on the sabbath

10One sabbath, Jesus was teaching in one of the synagogues. 11There was a woman there who had had a spirit of weakness for eighteen years. She was bent double, and couldn't stand fully upright. 12Jesus saw her and called to her.

13'Woman,' he said, laying his hands on her, 'you are freed from your affliction.' And at once she stood upright, and praised God.

14The synagogue president was angry that Jesus had healed on the sabbath.

'Look here,' he said to the crowd, 'there are six days for people to work! Come on one of those days and be healed, not on the sabbath day!'

15'You bunch of hypocrites!' replied Jesus. 'You would all be quite happy to untie an ox or a donkey from its stall on the sabbath day and lead it out for a drink! 16And isn't it right that this daughter of Abraham, tied up by the satan for these eighteen years, should be untied from her chains on the sabbath day?'

17At that, all the people who had been opposing him were ashamed. The whole crowd was overjoyed at all the splendid things he was doing.

18So Jesus said, 'What is God's kingdom like? What shall we compare it with? 19It's like a mustard seed that someone took and placed in his garden. It grew, and became a tree, and the birds of the sky made nests in its branches.'

20And again he said, 'What shall we say God's kingdom is like? 21It's like leaven that a woman took and hid in three measures of flour, until the whole thing was leavened.'

Entering through the narrow door

22Jesus went through the towns and villages, teaching as he went, making his way towards Jerusalem.

23'Master,' somebody said to him, 'will there be only a few that are saved?'

24'Struggle hard', Jesus replied, 'to get in by the narrow gate. Let me tell you: many will try to get in and won't be able to. 25When the householder gets up and shuts the door – at that moment you will begin to stand outside and knock at the door and say, "Master, open the door for us." Then he will say in response, "I don't know where you've come from." 26Then you will begin to say, "We ate with you and drank with you, and you taught in our streets!" 27And he will say to you, "I don't know where you people are from. Be off with you, you wicked lot."

28'That's where you'll find weeping and gnashing of teeth: when you see Abraham and Isaac and Jacob and all the prophets in God's kingdom, and you yourselves thrown out. 29People will come from East and West, from North and South, and sit down to feast in God's kingdom. 30And, listen to this: some who are last will be first, and some of the first will be last.'

Jesus grieves over Jerusalem

31Just then some Pharisees came up and spoke to Jesus.

'Get away from here,' they said, 'because Herod wants to kill you.'

32'Go and tell that fox,' replied Jesus, "'Look here: I'm casting out demons today and tomorrow, and completing my healings. I'll be finished by the third day. 33But I have to continue my travels today, tomorrow and the day after that! It couldn't happen that a prophet would perish except in Jerusalem."

34'Jerusalem, Jerusalem! You kill the prophets, and stone the people sent to you! How many times did I want to collect your children, like a hen gathers her brood under her wings, and you would have none of it! 35Look, your house has been abandoned. Let me tell you this: you will never see me until you are prepared to say, "A blessing upon you! Welcome in the name of the Lord!"'

Jesus and the Pharisee

14 One sabbath, Jesus went to a meal in the house of a leading Pharisee. They were keeping a close eye on him.

²There was a man there in front of Jesus who suffered from dropsy. ³So Jesus asked the lawyers and Pharisees, 'Is it lawful to heal on the sabbath or not?' ⁴They remained silent. He took the man, healed him, and dismissed him.

⁵Then he said to them, 'Suppose one of you has a son – or an ox! – that falls into a well. Are you going to tell me you won't pull him out straight away on the sabbath day?' ⁶They had no answer for that.

⁷He noticed how the guests chose the best seats, and told them this parable.

⁸'When someone invites you to a wedding feast,' he said, 'don't go and sit in the best seat, in case some other guest more important is invited, ⁹and the person who invited you both comes and says to you, "Please move down for this man," and you will go to the end of the line covered with embarrassment. ¹⁰Instead, when someone invites you, go and sit down at the lowest place. Then, when your host arrives, he will say to you, "My dear fellow! Come on higher up!" Then all your fellow guests will show you respect. ¹¹All who push themselves forward, you see, will be humbled, and all who humble themselves will be honoured.'

The parable of the great banquet

¹²He then turned to his host. 'When you give a lunch or a supper,' he said, 'don't invite your friends or your family or relatives, or your rich neighbours. They might ask you back again, and you'd be repaid. ¹³When you give a feast, invite the poor, the crippled, the lame and the blind. ¹⁴God will bless you, because they have no way to repay you! You will be repaid at the resurrection of the righteous.'

¹⁵One of the guests heard this, and commented, 'A blessing on those who eat food in God's kingdom!'

¹⁶Jesus said, 'Once a man made a great dinner, and invited lots of guests. ¹⁷When the time for the meal arrived, he sent his servant to say to the guests, "Come now – everything's ready!" ¹⁸But the whole pack of them began to make excuses. The first said, "I've just bought a field, and I really have to go and see it. Please accept my apologies." ¹⁹Another one said, "I've just bought five yoke of oxen, and I've got to go and test them out – please accept my apologies." ²⁰And another one said, "I've just got married, so naturally I can't come." ²¹So the servant went back and told his master all this. The householder was cross, and said to his servant, "Go out quickly into the streets and lanes of the town and bring in here the poor, the crippled, the lame and the blind." ²²"All right, Master," said the servant, "I've done that – but there's still room." ²³"Well then," said the master to the servant, "go out into the roads and hedgerows and make them come in, so that my house may be full! ²⁴Let me tell you this: none of those people who were invited will get to taste my dinner."'

The cost of discipleship

²⁵A large crowd was gathering around him. Jesus turned to face them.

²⁶'If any of you come to me,' he said to them, 'and don't hate your father and your mother, your wife and your children, your brothers and your sisters – yes, and even your own life! – you can't be my disciple. ²⁷If you don't pick up your own cross and come after me, you can't be my disciple.

²⁸'Don't you see? Supposing one of you wants to build a tower; what will you do? You will first of all sit down and work out how much it will cost, to see whether you have enough to finish it. ²⁹Otherwise, when you've laid the foundation and then can't finish it, everyone who sees it will begin to make fun of you. ³⁰"Here's a fellow", they'll say, "who began to build but couldn't finish!"

³¹'Or think of a king, on the way to fight a war against another king. What will he do? He will first sit down and discuss with his advisers whether, with ten thousand troops, he is going to be a match for the other side who are coming with twenty thousand! ³²If they decide he isn't, he will send a delegation, while the other one is still a long way away, and sue for peace.

³³'In the same way, none of you can be my disciple unless you give up all your possessions.

³⁴'Salt is good; but if even the salt loses its savour, how can it be made salty again? ³⁵It's no good for soil and no good for manure. People throw it away. If you have ears, then listen!'

The parables of the lost sheep and the lost coin

15 ¹All the tax-collectors and sinners were coming close to listen to Jesus. ²The Pharisees and the legal experts were grumbling. 'This fellow welcomes sinners!' they said. 'He even eats with them!'

³So Jesus told them this parable. ⁴'Supposing one of you has a hundred sheep,' he said, 'and you lose one of them. What will you do? Why, you'll leave the ninety-nine out in the countryside, and you'll go off looking for the lost one until you find it! ⁵And when you find it, you'll be so happy – you'll put it on your shoulders ⁶and come home, and you'll call your friends and neighbours in. "Come and have a party!" you'll say. "Celebrate with me! I've found my lost sheep!"

⁷'Well, let me tell you: that's how glad they will be in heaven over one sinner who repents – more than over ninety-nine righteous people who don't need repentance.

⁸'Or supposing a woman has ten drachmas and loses one of them. What will she do? Why, she'll light a lamp, and sweep the house, and hunt carefully until she finds it! ⁹And when she finds it she'll call her friends and neighbours in. "Come and have a party!" she'll say. "Celebrate with me! I've found my lost coin!"

¹⁰'Well, let me tell you: that's how glad God's angels feel when a single sinner repents.'

The parable of the Prodigal: the father and the younger son

¹¹Jesus went on: 'Once there was a man who had two sons. ¹²The younger son said to the father, "Father, give me my share in the property." So he divided up his livelihood between them. ¹³Not many days later the younger son turned his share into cash, and set off for a country far away, where he spent his share in having a riotous good time.

¹⁴'When he had spent it all, a severe famine came on that country, and he found himself destitute. ¹⁵So he went and attached himself to one of the citizens of that country, who sent him into the fields to feed his pigs. ¹⁶He longed to satisfy his hunger with the pods that the pigs were eating, and nobody gave him anything.

¹⁷'He came to his senses. "Just think!" he said to himself. "There are all my father's hired hands with plenty to eat – and here am I, starving to death! ¹⁸I shall get up and go to my father, and I'll say to him: 'Father; I have sinned against heaven and before you; ¹⁹I don't deserve to be called your son any longer. Make me like one of your hired hands.'" ²⁰And he got up and went to his father.

'While he was still a long way off, his father saw him and his heart was stirred with love and pity. He ran to him, hugged him tight, and kissed him. ²¹"Father," the son began, "I have sinned against heaven and before you; I don't deserve to be called your son any longer."

²²But the father said to his servants, "Hurry! Bring the best clothes and put them on him! Put a ring on his hand, and shoes on his feet! ²³And bring the calf that we've fattened up, kill it, and let's eat and have a party! ²⁴This son of mine was dead, and is alive again! He was lost, and now he's found!" And they began to celebrate.'

The parable of the Prodigal: the father and the older son

²⁵'The older son was out in the fields. When he came home, and got near to the house, he heard music and dancing. ²⁶He called one of the servants and asked what was going on.

²⁷'"Your brother's come home!" he said. "And your father has thrown a great party – he's killed the fattened calf! – because he's got him back safe and well!"

²⁸'He flew into a rage, and wouldn't go in.

'Then his father came out and pleaded with him. ²⁹"Look here!" he said to his father, "I've been slaving for you all these years! I've never disobeyed a single commandment of yours. And you never even gave me a young goat so I could have a party with my friends. ³⁰But when this son of yours comes home, once he's finished gobbling up your livelihood with his whores, you kill the fattened calf for him!"

³¹'"My son," he replied, "you're always with me. Everything I have belongs to you. ³²But we had to celebrate and be happy! This brother of yours was dead and is alive again! He was lost, and now he's found!"'

The parable of the shrewd manager

16 Jesus said to his disciples, 'Once there was a rich man who had a steward, and charges were laid against him that he was squandering his property. ²So he called him and said to him, "What's all this I hear about you? Present an account of your stewardship; I'm not going to have you as my steward any more!"

³'At this, the steward said to himself, "What shall I do? My master is taking away my stewardship from me! I can't do manual work, and I'd be ashamed to beg . . .

⁴"'I have an idea what to do! – so that people will welcome me into their households when I am fired from being steward."

⁵'So he called his master's debtors to him, one by one. "How much", he asked the first, "do you owe my master?"

⁶"'A hundred measures of olive oil," he replied.

'"Take your bill," he said to him, "sit down quickly, and make it fifty."

⁷"'To another he said, "And how much do you owe?"

'"A hundred measures of wheat," he replied.

'"Take your bill," he said, "and make it eighty."

⁸'And the master praised the dishonest steward because he had acted wisely. The children of this world, you see, are wiser than the children of light when it comes to dealing with their own generation.

⁹'So let me tell you this: use that dishonest stuff called money to make yourselves friends! Then, when it gives out, they will welcome you into homes that will last.'

Teachings on stewardship

¹⁰'Someone who is faithful in a small matter', Jesus continued, 'will also be faithful in a large one. Someone who is dishonest in a small matter will also be dishonest in a large one. ¹¹If you haven't been faithful with that wicked thing called money, who is going to entrust you with true wealth? ¹²And if you haven't been faithful in looking after what belongs to someone else, who is going to give you what is your own?

¹³'Nobody can serve two masters. You will end up hating one and loving the other, or going along with the first and despising the other. You can't serve God and money.'

¹⁴The Pharisees, who loved money, heard all this, and mocked Jesus. ¹⁵So he said to them, 'You people let everyone else know that you're in the right – but God knows your hearts. What people call honourable, God calls abominable!

¹⁶'The law and the prophets lasted until John. From now on, God's kingdom is announced, and everyone is trying to attack it. ¹⁷But it's easier for heaven and earth to pass away than for one dot of an "i" to drop out of the law.

¹⁸'Anyone who divorces his wife and marries another commits adultery, and a person who marries a divorced woman commits adultery.'

The parable of the rich man and Lazarus

¹⁹'There was once a rich man,' said Jesus, 'who was dressed in purple and fine linen, and feasted in splendour every day. ²⁰A poor man named Lazarus, who was covered with sores, lay outside his gate. ²¹He longed to feed himself with the scraps that fell from the rich man's table. Even the dogs came and licked his sores.

²²'In due course the poor man died, and was carried by the angels into Abraham's bosom. The rich man also died, and was buried. ²³As he was being tormented in Hades, he looked up and saw Abraham far away, and Lazarus in his bosom.

²⁴'"Father Abraham!" he called out. "Have pity on me! Send Lazarus to dip the tip of his finger in water and cool my tongue! I'm in agony in this fire!"

²⁵'"My child," replied Abraham, "remember that in your life you received good things, and in the same way Lazarus received evil. Now he is comforted here, and you are tormented. ²⁶Besides that, there is a great chasm standing between us. People who want to cross over from here to you can't do so, nor can anyone get across from the far side to us."

²⁷'"Please, then, father," he said, "send him to my father's house. ²⁸I've got five brothers. Let him tell them about it, so that they don't come into this torture-chamber."

²⁹"'They've got Moses and the prophets,' replied Abraham. 'Let them listen to them.'
³⁰"'No, father Abraham,' he replied, 'but if someone went to them from the dead, they would repent!'
³¹"'If they don't listen to Moses and the prophets,' came the reply, 'neither would they be convinced, even if someone rose from the dead.'"

Forgiveness, faith and obedience

17 Jesus said to his disciples, 'There are bound to be things that trip people up; but woe betide the person who brings them about! ²It would be better to have a millstone hung around your neck, and be thrown into the sea, than to trip up one of these little ones. ³So watch out for yourselves.

'If your brother sins against you, rebuke him; and if he apologizes, forgive him. ⁴Even if he sins against you seven times, and turns round seven times and says "sorry" to you, you must forgive him.'

⁵The apostles said to the master, 'Give us greater faith!'

⁶'If you had faith', replied the master, 'as a grain of mustard seed, you would say to this mulberry tree, "Be uprooted and be planted in the sea", and it would obey you.

⁷'Supposing one of you has a slave ploughing or keeping sheep out in the field. When he comes in, what will you say? "Come here at once, and sit down for a meal?" ⁸No; you will be far more likely to say, "Get something ready for me to eat! Get properly dressed, and wait on me while I eat and drink! After that you can have something to eat and drink yourself." ⁹Will you thank the slave because he did what you told him?

¹⁰'That's how it is with you. When you've done everything you're told, say this: "We're just ordinary slaves. All we've done is what we were supposed to do."'

Ten men healed

¹¹As Jesus was on his way to Jerusalem, he passed along the borderlands between Samaria and Galilee. ¹²As he was going into one particular village he was met by ten men with virulent skin diseases who stayed at some distance from him.

¹³'Jesus, Master!' they called out loudly. 'Have pity on us!'

¹⁴When Jesus saw them he said to them, 'Go and show yourselves to the priests.' And as they went, they were healed.

¹⁵One of them, seeing that he had been healed, turned back and gave glory to God at the top of his voice. ¹⁶He fell on his face in front of Jesus' feet and thanked him. He was a Samaritan.

¹⁷'There were ten of you healed, weren't there?' responded Jesus. 'Where are the nine? ¹⁸Is it really the case that the only one who had the decency to give God the glory was this foreigner?'

¹⁹'Get up, and be on your way,' he said to him. 'Your faith has saved you.'

The coming of the kingdom

²⁰The Pharisees asked Jesus when the kingdom of God was coming.

'God's kingdom', replied Jesus, 'isn't the sort of thing you can watch for and see coming. ²¹People won't say "Look, here it is", or "Look, over there!" No: God's kingdom is within your grasp.'

²²Then Jesus said to the disciples, 'The days are coming when you will long to see one of the days of the son of man, and you won't see it. ²³They will say to you, "Look, there!" or "Look, here!" Don't go off or follow them. ²⁴The son of man in his day will be like lightning that shines from one end of the sky to the other. ²⁵But first he must suffer many things and be rejected by this generation.

²⁶'What will it be like in the days of the son of man? It will be like the days of Noah. ²⁷People were eating and drinking, they were getting married and giving wedding parties, until the day when Noah went into the ark – and that day the flood came and swept them all away. ²⁸And it will be like the days of Lot. They were eating and drinking, they were buying and selling, they were planting and building. ²⁹But on the day when Lot left Sodom, it rained fire and sulphur from the sky and they were all destroyed. ³⁰That's what it will be like on the day when the son of man is revealed.

³¹'On that day anyone up on the roof, with all their possessions in the house, shouldn't go down to get them. Anyone out in the field shouldn't go back to get anything. ³²Remember Lot's wife. ³³If you try to save your life you'll lose it, but anyone who loses it will keep it.

³⁴'Let me tell you, in that night there will be two people sleeping side by side: one will be taken, and the other left behind. ³⁵There will be two women working side by side grinding corn: one will be taken, and the other left behind.'

³⁷'Where will this be, master?' they asked him.

'Where the body is,' replied Jesus, 'there the vultures will gather.'

The parables of the persistent widow and the tax-collector

18 Jesus told them a parable, about how they should always pray and not give up.

²"There was once a judge in a certain town,' he said, 'who didn't fear God, and didn't have any respect for people. ³There was a widow in that town, and she came to him and said, "Judge my case! Vindicate me against my enemy!"

⁴'For a long time he refused. But, in the end, he said to himself, "It's true that I don't fear God, and don't have any respect for people. ⁵But because this widow is causing me a lot of trouble, I will put her case right and vindicate her, so that she doesn't end up coming and giving me a black eye."

⁶'Well,' said the master, 'did you hear what this unjust judge says? ⁷And don't you think that God will see justice done for his chosen ones, who shout out to him day and night? Do you suppose he is deliberately delaying? ⁸Let me tell you, he will vindicate them very quickly. But – when the son of man comes, will he find faith on the earth?'

⁹He told this next parable against those who trusted in their own righteous standing and despised others.

¹⁰'Two men,' he said, 'went up to the Temple to pray. One was a Pharisee, the other was a tax-collector. ¹¹The Pharisee stood and prayed in this way to himself: "God, I thank you that I am not like the other people – greedy, unjust, immoral, or even like this tax-collector. ¹²I fast twice in the week; I give tithes of all that I get."

¹³'But the tax-collector stood a long way off, and didn't even want to raise his eyes to heaven. He beat his breast and said, "God, be merciful to me, sinner that I am." ¹⁴Let me tell you, he was the one who went back to his house vindicated by God, not the other. Don't you see? People who exalt themselves will be humbled, and people who humble themselves will be exalted.'

The rich young ruler

¹⁵People were bringing even tiny babies to Jesus for him to touch them. When the disciples saw it, they forbade them sternly. ¹⁶But Jesus called them. 'Let the children come to me,' he said, 'and don't stop them! God's kingdom belongs to the likes of these. ¹⁷I'm telling you the truth: anyone who doesn't receive God's kingdom like a child will never get into it.'

¹⁸There was a ruler who asked him, 'Good teacher, what must I do to inherit the life of the age to come?'

¹⁹'Why call me good?' said Jesus to him. 'No one is good except God alone. ²⁰You know the commandments: Don't commit adultery, don't kill, don't steal, don't swear falsely, honour your father and mother.'

²¹'I've kept them all', he said, 'since I was a boy.'

²²When Jesus heard that, he said to him, 'There's just one thing you're short of. Sell everything you own, and distribute it to the poor, and you will have treasure in heaven. Then come and follow me.'

²³When he heard that he turned very sad; he was extremely wealthy.

²⁴Jesus saw that he had become sad, and said, 'How hard it is for those with possessions to enter God's kingdom! ²⁵Yes: it's easier for a camel to go through the eye of a needle than for a rich man to enter God's kingdom.'

²⁶The people who heard it said, 'So who can be saved?'

²⁷'What's impossible for humans', said Jesus, 'is possible for God.'

²⁸'Look here,' said Peter, 'we've left everything and followed you.'

²⁹'I'm telling you the truth,' said Jesus, 'everyone who has left house or wife or brothers or parents or children, because of God's kingdom, ³⁰will receive far more in return in the present time – and in the age to come they will receive the life that belongs to that age.'

Jesus heals a blind beggar

³¹Jesus took the Twelve aside.

'Look,' he said, 'we're going up to Jerusalem. Everything that's written in the prophets about the son of man will be fulfilled. ³²Yes: he will be handed over to the pagans; he'll be mocked, abused and spat upon. ³³They will beat him and kill him; and on the third day he'll be raised.'

³⁴They didn't understand any of this. The word was hidden from them, and they didn't know what he meant.

³⁵As they were getting near Jericho there was a blind man sitting by the road, begging. ³⁶When he heard a crowd passing through the town he asked what was going on.

³⁷'Jesus of Nazareth is coming by,' people said to him.

³⁸So he shouted out, 'Jesus – David's son! Have pity on me!'

³⁹The people who were at the front of the group firmly told him to be silent. But he yelled out all the more, 'David's son! Have pity on me!'

⁴⁰Jesus stopped, and told them to bring the man to him. When he came up, he asked him, ⁴¹'What d'you want me to do for you?'

'Master,' he said, 'I want to see again.'

⁴²'Then see again,' said Jesus. 'Your faith has saved you.'

⁴³At once he received his sight again, and followed him, glorifying God. And when all the people saw it, they gave praise to God.

The calling of Zacchaeus

19 They went into Jericho and passed through. ²There was a man named Zacchaeus, a chief tax-collector, who was very rich. ³He was trying to see who Jesus was, but, being a small man, he couldn't, because of the crowd. ⁴So he ran on ahead, along the route Jesus was going to take, and climbed up into a sycamore tree to see him.

⁵When Jesus came to the place, he looked up.

'Zacchaeus,' he said to him, 'hurry up and come down. I have to stay at your house today.'

⁶So he hurried up, came down, and welcomed him with joy.

⁷Everybody began to murmur when they saw it. 'He's gone in to spend time with a proper old sinner!' they were saying.

⁸But Zacchaeus stood there and addressed the master.

'Look, Master,' he said, 'I'm giving half my property to the poor. And if I have defrauded anyone of anything, I'm giving it back to them four times over.'

⁹'Today,' said Jesus, 'salvation has come to this house, because he too is a son of Abraham. ¹⁰You see, the son of man came to seek and to save the lost.'

The king, the servants and the money

¹¹While people were listening to this, Jesus went on to tell a parable. They were, after all, getting close to Jerusalem, and they thought that the kingdom of God was going to appear at once.

¹²'There was once a nobleman,' he said, 'who went into a country far away to be given royal authority and then return. ¹³He summoned ten of his slaves and gave them ten silver coins. "Do business with these", he said, "until I come back." ¹⁴His subjects, though, hated him, and sent a delegation after him to say, "We don't want this man to be our king."

¹⁵'So it happened that when he received the kingship and came back again, he gave orders to summon these slaves who had received the money, so that he could find out how they had got on with their business efforts. ¹⁶The first came forward and said, "Master, your money has made ten times its value!"

¹⁷'"Well done, you splendid servant!" he said. "You've been trustworthy with something small; now you can take command of ten cities."

¹⁸'The second came and said, "Master, your money has made five times its value!"

¹⁹'"You too – you can take charge of five cities."

²⁰'The other came and said, "Master, here is your money. I kept it wrapped in this handkerchief. ²¹You see, I was afraid of you, because you are a hard man: you profit where you made no investment, and you harvest what you didn't sow."

²²'"I'll condemn you out of your own mouth, you wicked scoundrel of a servant!" he replied. "So: you knew that I was a hard man, profiting where I didn't invest and harvesting where I didn't sow? ²³So why didn't you put my money with the bankers? Then I'd have had the interest when I got back!"

²⁴'"Take the money from him," he said to the bystanders, "and give it to the man who's got it ten times over!" ²⁵("Master," they said to him, "he's got ten times that already!")

²⁶'Let me tell you: everyone who has will be given more; but if someone has nothing, even what he has will be taken away from him. ²⁷But as for these enemies of mine, who didn't want me to be king over them – bring them here and slaughter them in front of me.'

The triumphal entry

²⁸With these words, Jesus went on ahead, going up to Jerusalem.

²⁹As they came close, as near as Bethany and Bethphage, at the place called the Mount of Olives, he sent two of the disciples on ahead. ³⁰'Go into the village over there,' he said, 'and as you arrive you'll find a colt tied up, one that nobody has ever ridden. Untie it and bring it here. ³¹If anyone says to you, "Why are you untying it?" you should say, "Because the master needs it."'

³²The two who were sent went off and found it just as Jesus had said to them. ³³They untied the colt, and its owners said to them, "Why are you untying the colt?"

³⁴'"Because the master needs it," they replied.

³⁵They brought it to Jesus, threw their cloaks on the colt, and mounted Jesus on it. ³⁶As he was going along, people kept spreading their cloaks on the road.

³⁷When he came to the descent of the Mount of Olives, the whole crowd of disciples began to celebrate and praise God at the tops of their voices for all the powerful deeds they had seen.

³⁸'Welcome, welcome, welcome with a blessing,' they sang.
'Welcome to the king in the name of the Lord!
'Peace in heaven, and glory on high!'

³⁹Some of the Pharisees from the crowd said to Jesus, 'Teacher, tell your disciples to stop that.'

⁴⁰'Let me tell you,' replied Jesus, 'if they stayed silent, the stones would be shouting out!'

Jesus cleanses the Temple

⁴¹When he came near and saw the city, he wept over it.

⁴²'If only you'd known,' he said, 'on this day – even you! – what peace meant. But now it's hidden, and you can't see it. ⁴³Yes, the days are coming upon you when your enemies will build up earthworks all round you, and encircle you, and squeeze you in from every direction. ⁴⁴They will bring you crashing to the ground, you and your children within you. They won't leave one single stone on another, because you didn't know the moment when God was visiting you.'

⁴⁵He went into the Temple and began to throw out the traders.

⁴⁶'It's written,' he said, 'my house shall be a house of prayer; but you've made it a brigands' cave.'

⁴⁷He was teaching every day in the Temple. But the chief priests, the scribes and the leading men of the people were trying to destroy him. ⁴⁸They couldn't find any way to do it, because all the people were hanging on his every word.

The question about Jesus' authority

20 On one of those days, while Jesus was teaching the people in the Temple, and announcing the good news, the chief priests and the scribes came up with the elders, and said to him, ²'Tell us: by what authority are you doing these things? Or who gave you this authority?'

³'I've got a question for you, too,' said Jesus, 'so tell me this: ⁴was John's baptism from God, or was it merely human?'

⁵'If we say it was from God,' they said among themselves, 'he'll say, So why didn't you believe

him? ⁶But if we say "merely human", all the people will stone us, since they're convinced that John was a prophet.'

⁷So they replied that they didn't know where John and his baptism came from.

⁸'Very well, then,' said Jesus. 'Nor will I tell you by what authority I do these things.'

The parable of the tenants

⁹Jesus began to tell the people this parable. 'There was a man who planted a vineyard, let it out to tenant farmers, and went abroad for a long while. ¹⁰When the time came, he sent a slave to the farmers to collect from them some of the produce of the vineyard. But the farmers beat him and sent him away empty-handed. ¹¹He then sent a further slave, and they beat him, abused him, and sent him back empty-handed. ¹²Then he sent yet a third, and they beat him up and threw him out.

¹³'So the master of the vineyard said, "What shall I do? I'll send my beloved son. They will certainly respect him!" ¹⁴But when the farmers saw him they said to each other, "This is the heir! Let's kill him, and then the inheritance will belong to us!" ¹⁵And they threw him out of the vineyard and killed him.

'So what will the master of the vineyard do? ¹⁶He will come and wipe out those farmers, and give the vineyard to others.'

When they heard this, they said, 'God forbid!' ¹⁷But Jesus looked round at them and said, 'What then does it mean in the Bible when it says,

The very stone the builders refused
now for the corner's top is used?

¹⁸'Everyone who falls on that stone will be smashed to smithereens; but if it falls on anyone, it will crush them.'

¹⁹The scribes and the chief priests tried to lay hands on him then and there. But they were afraid of the people, because they knew that Jesus had told this parable against them.

On paying taxes to Caesar

²⁰So the authorities watched Jesus, and sent people to lie in wait for him. They pretended to be upright folk, but were trying to trap him in something he said, so that they could hand him over to the rule and authority of the governor. ²¹So they asked him this question.

'Teacher,' they said, 'we know that you speak and teach with integrity. You are completely impartial, and you teach God's way and God's truth. ²²So: is it right for us to give tribute to Caesar, or not?'

²³Jesus knew they were playing a trick.

²⁴'Show me a tribute-coin,' he said. 'This image . . . and this inscription . . . who do they belong to?'

'Caesar,' they said.

²⁵'Well, then,' replied Jesus, 'you'd better give Caesar back what belongs to him! And give *God* back what belongs to *him*.'

²⁶They couldn't catch him in anything he said in front of the people. They were amazed at his answer, and had nothing more to say.

Marriage and the resurrection

²⁷Some of the Sadducees came to Jesus to put their question. (The Sadducees deny that there is any resurrection.)

²⁸'Teacher,' they said, 'Moses wrote for us that "If a man's brother dies, leaving a widow but no children, the man should marry the widow and raise up a family for his brother." ²⁹Well, now: there were seven brothers; the eldest married a wife, and died without children. ³⁰The second ³¹and the third married her, and then each of the seven, and they died without children. ³²Finally the woman died as well. ³³So, in the resurrection, whose wife will the woman be? The seven all had her as their wife.'

³⁴'The children of this age,' replied Jesus, 'marry and are given in marriage. ³⁵But those who are counted worthy of a place in the age to come, and of the resurrection of the dead, don't marry, and they are not given in marriage. ³⁶This is because they can no longer die; they are the equivalent of angels. They are children of God, since they are children of the resurrection.

³⁷'But when it comes to the dead being raised, Moses too declares it, in the passage about the burning bush, where scripture describes the Lord as "the God of Abraham, the God of Isaac, and the God of Jacob". ³⁸God

is God, not of the dead, but of the living. They are all alive to him.'

³⁹'That was well said, teacher,' commented some of the scribes, ⁴⁰since they no longer dared ask him anything else.

David's son and the widow's mite

⁴¹Jesus said to them, 'How can people say that the Messiah is the son of David? ⁴²David himself says, in the book of Psalms,

The Lord says to the Lord of mine
sit here at my right hand;
⁴³until I place those foes of thine
right underneath thy feet.

⁴⁴'David, you see, calls him "Lord"; so how can he be his son?'

⁴⁵As all the people listened to him, he said to the disciples, ⁴⁶'Watch out for the scribes who like to go about in long robes, and enjoy being greeted in the market-place, sitting in the best seats in the synagogues, and taking the top table at dinners. ⁴⁷They devour widows' houses, and make long prayers without meaning them. Their judgment will be all the more severe.'

21 He looked up and saw rich people putting their contributions into the Temple treasury. ²He also saw an impoverished widow putting in two tiny copper coins.

³'I'm telling you the truth,' he said. 'This poor widow has put in more than all of them. ⁴They all contributed into the collection out of their plenty, but she contributed out of her poverty, and gave her whole livelihood.'

Signs of the end

⁵Some people were talking about the Temple, saying how wonderfully it was decorated, with its beautiful stones and dedicated gifts.

'Yes,' said Jesus; ⁶'but the days will come when everything you see will be torn down. Not one stone will be left standing on another.'

⁷'Teacher,' they asked him, 'when will these things happen? What will be the sign that it's all about to take place?'

⁸'Watch out that nobody deceives you,' said Jesus. 'Yes: lots of people will come using my name, saying "I'm the one!" and "The time has come!" Don't go following them. ⁹When you hear about wars and rebellions, don't be alarmed. These things have to happen first, but the end won't come at once.

¹⁰'One nation will rise against another,' he went on, 'and one kingdom against another. ¹¹There will be huge earthquakes, famines and plagues in various places, terrifying omens, and great signs from heaven.

¹²'Before all this happens they will lay hands on you and persecute you. They will hand you over to the synagogues and prisons. They will drag you before kings and governors because of my name. ¹³That will become an opportunity for you to tell your story. ¹⁴So settle it in your hearts not to work out beforehand what tale to tell; ¹⁵I'll give you a mouth and wisdom, which none of your opponents will be able to resist or contradict.

¹⁶'You will be betrayed by parents, brothers and sisters, relatives and friends, and they will kill some of you. ¹⁷You will be hated by everyone because of my name. ¹⁸But no hair of your head will be lost. ¹⁹The way to keep your lives is to be patient.'

The distress of Jerusalem predicted

²⁰'But,' continued Jesus, 'when you see Jerusalem surrounded by armies, then you will know that her time of desolation has arrived. ²¹Then people in Judaea should run off to the hills, people in Jerusalem itself should get out as fast as they can, and people in the countryside shouldn't go back into the city. ²²Those will be the days of severe judgment, which will fulfil all the biblical warnings. ²³Woe betide pregnant women, and nursing mothers, in those days! There is going to be huge distress on the earth, and divine anger against this people. ²⁴The hungry sword will eat them up; they will be taken off as prisoners to every nation; and Jerusalem will be trampled by the pagans, until the times of the pagans are done.

²⁵'There will be signs in the sun, the moon and the stars. On earth the nations will be in distress and confusion because of the roaring and swelling of the sea and its waves. ²⁶People will faint from fear, and from imagining all

that's going to happen to the world. The powers of the heavens will be shaken. ²⁷Then they will see "the son of man coming on a cloud" with power and great majesty. ²⁸When all these things start to happen, stand up and lift up your heads, because the time has come for you to be redeemed.'

²⁹He told them this parable. 'Look at the fig tree and all the trees. ³⁰When they are well into leaf, you can see for yourselves and know that summer is upon you. ³¹In the same way, when you see all these things happening, you will know that God's kingdom is upon you. ³²I'm telling you the truth; this generation won't be gone before all of this happens. ³³Heaven and earth may disappear, but these words of mine won't disappear.'

Watching for the son of man

³⁴'So watch out for yourselves,' said Jesus, 'that your hearts may not grow heavy with dissipation and drunkenness and the cares of this life, so that that day comes upon you suddenly, ³⁵like a trap. It will come, you see, on everyone who lives on the face of the earth. ³⁶Keep awake at all times, praying that you may have strength to escape all these things that will happen, and to stand before the son of man.'

³⁷Jesus was teaching in the Temple by day, but at night he went out and stayed in the place called the Mount of Olives. ³⁸And from early morning all the people flocked to him in the Temple, to hear him.

The Last Supper

22 The time came for the festival of unleavened bread, known as Passover. ²The chief priests and the scribes looked for a way to assassinate Jesus, a difficult task because of the crowds.

³The satan entered into Judas, whose surname was Iscariot, who was one of the company of the Twelve. ⁴He went and held a meeting with the chief priests and officers, to discuss how he might hand Jesus over. ⁵They were delighted, and promised to pay him. ⁶He agreed, and started to look for an opportunity to hand him over to them when the crowds weren't around.

⁷The day of unleavened bread arrived, the day when people had to kill the Passover lamb. ⁸Jesus dispatched Peter and John.

'Off you go,' he said, 'and get the Passover ready for us to eat.'

⁹'Where d'you want us to prepare it?' they asked him.

¹⁰'Listen carefully,' said Jesus. 'As you go into the city a man will meet you carrying a jar of water. Follow him, and when he goes into a house, go after him. ¹¹Then say to the householder there, "The teacher says, 'Where is the living-room where I can eat the Passover with my disciples?'" ¹²And he will show you a large upstairs room, laid out and ready. Make the preparations there.'

¹³So they went and found it as he had said to them, and they prepared the Passover.

¹⁴When the time came, Jesus sat down at table, and the apostles with him.

¹⁵'I have been so much looking forward to eating this Passover with you before I have to suffer,' he said to them. ¹⁶'For – let me tell you – I won't eat it again until it's fulfilled in the kingdom of God.'

¹⁷Then he took a cup, and gave thanks, and said, 'Take this and share it among yourselves. ¹⁸Let me tell you, from now on I won't drink from the fruit of the vine until the kingdom of God comes.'

¹⁹Then he took some bread. He gave thanks, broke it and gave it to them.

'This is my body,' he said, 'which is given for you. Do this in memory of me.'

²⁰So too, after supper, with the cup: 'This cup,' he said, 'is the new covenant, in my blood which is shed for you.

²¹'But look here! The hand of the one who will betray me is with me at this table. ²²The son of man is indeed going, as it is marked out for him; but woe betide that man by whom he is betrayed!'

²³They began to ask each other which of them was going to do this.

Prediction of Peter's denial

²⁴A quarrel began among them: which of them was to be seen as the most important?

²⁵'Pagan kings lord it over their subjects,' said Jesus to them, 'and people in power get themselves called "Benefactors". ²⁶That's not how it's to be with you. The most important among you ought to be like the youngest. The leader should be like the servant. ²⁷After all, who is the more important, the one who sits at table or the one who waits on him? The one at table, obviously! But I am with you here like a servant.

²⁸'You are the ones who have stuck it out with me through the trials I've had to endure. ²⁹This is my bequest to you: the kingdom my father bequeathed to me! ³⁰What does this mean? You will eat and drink at my table, in my kingdom, and you will sit on thrones, judging the twelve tribes of Israel.

³¹'Simon, Simon, listen to this. The satan demanded to have you. He wanted to shake you into bits like wheat. ³²But I prayed for you; I prayed that you wouldn't run out of faith. And, when you turn back again, you must give strength to your brothers.'

³³'Master,' replied Simon, 'I'm ready to go with you to prison – or to death!'

³⁴'Let me tell you, Peter,' replied Jesus, 'the cock won't crow today before you have three times denied that you know me.

³⁵'When I sent you out,' Jesus said to them, 'without purse or bag or sandals, were you short of anything?'

'Nothing,' they replied.

³⁶'But now,' he said, 'anyone who has a purse should take it, and the same with a bag. And anyone who doesn't have a sword should sell his cloak and buy one. ³⁷Let me tell you this: when the Bible says, "He was reckoned with the lawless", it must find its fulfilment in me. Yes; everything about me must reach its goal.'

³⁸'Look, Master,' they said, 'we've got a couple of swords here.'

'That's enough!' he said to them.

Jesus is arrested

³⁹So off they went. Jesus headed, as usual, for the Mount of Olives, and his disciples followed him.

⁴⁰When he came to the place, he said to them, 'Pray that you won't come into the trial.' ⁴¹He then withdrew from them about a stone's throw, and knelt down to pray.

⁴²'Father,' he said, 'if you wish it – please take this cup away from me! But it must be your will, not mine.' ⁴³An angel appeared to him from heaven, strengthening him. ⁴⁴By now he was in agony, and he prayed very fervently. And his sweat became like clots of blood, falling on the ground. ⁴⁵Then he got up from praying, and came to the disciples and found them asleep because of sorrow.

⁴⁶'Why are you sleeping?' he said to them. 'Get up and pray, so that you won't come into the trial.'

⁴⁷While he was still speaking, a crowd appeared. The man named Judas, one of the Twelve, was leading them. He came towards Jesus to kiss him, ⁴⁸but Jesus said to him, 'Judas! Are you going to betray the son of man with a kiss?'

⁴⁹Jesus' followers saw what was about to happen.

'Master!' they said. 'Shall we go in with the swords?' ⁵⁰And one of them struck the high priest's servant, and cut off his right ear.

⁵¹'Enough of that!' said Jesus, and healed the ear with a touch.

⁵²Then Jesus spoke to the chief priests, the Temple guardsmen, and the elders who had come after him.

'Anyone would think I was a brigand,' he said, 'for you to come out with swords and clubs! ⁵³Every day I've been in the Temple with you and you never laid hands on me. But your moment has come at last, and so has the power of darkness.'

Peter denies Jesus

⁵⁴So they arrested Jesus, took him off, and brought him into the high priest's house. Peter followed at a distance. ⁵⁵They lit a fire in the middle of the courtyard and sat around it, and Peter sat in among them.

⁵⁶A servant-girl saw him sitting by the fire. She stared hard at him. 'This fellow was with him!' she said.

⁵⁷Peter denied it. 'I don't know him, woman,' he said.

⁵⁸After a little while another man saw him and said, 'You're one of them!'

'No, my friend, I'm not,' replied Peter.

⁵⁹After the space of about an hour, another man insisted, 'It's true! This man was with him; he's a Galilean too!'

⁶⁰'My good fellow,' said Peter, 'I don't know what you're talking about.' And at once, while he was still speaking, the cock crowed. ⁶¹The master turned and looked at Peter, and Peter called to mind the words the master had spoken to him: 'Before the cock crows, this very day, you will deny me three times.' ⁶²And he went outside and wept bitterly.

⁶³The men who were holding Jesus began to make fun of him and knock him about. ⁶⁴They blindfolded him.

'Prophesy!' they told him. 'Who is it that's hitting you?'

⁶⁵And they said many other scandalous things to him.

⁶⁶When the day broke, the official assembly of the people, the chief priests and the scribes came together, and they took him off to their council.

⁶⁷'If you are the Messiah,' they said, 'tell us!'

'If I tell you,' he said to them, 'you won't believe me. ⁶⁸And if I ask you a question, you won't answer me. ⁶⁹But from now on the son of man will be seated at the right hand of God's power.'

⁷⁰'So you're the son of God, are you?' they said.

'You say that I am,' he said to them.

⁷¹'Why do we need any more witnesses?' they said. 'We've heard it ourselves, from his own mouth!'

Jesus before Pilate and Herod

23 The whole crowd of them got up and took Jesus to Pilate.

²They began to accuse him. 'We found this fellow,' they said, 'deceiving our nation! He was forbidding people to give tribute to Caesar, and saying that he is the Messiah – a king!'

³So Pilate asked Jesus, 'You are the king of the Jews?'

'You said it,' replied Jesus.

⁴'I find no fault in this man,' said Pilate to the chief priests and the crowds. ⁵But they became insistent.

'He's stirring up the people,' they said, 'teaching them throughout the whole of Judaea. He began in Galilee, and now he's come here.'

⁶When Pilate heard that, he asked if the man was indeed a Galilean. ⁷When he learned that he was from Herod's jurisdiction he sent him to Herod, who happened also to be in Jerusalem at that time.

⁸When Herod saw Jesus he was delighted. He had been wanting to see him for quite some time now, since he'd heard about him, and hoped to see him perform some sign or other. ⁹He questioned him this way and that, but Jesus gave no answer at all. ¹⁰The chief priests and the scribes stood by, accusing him vehemently. ¹¹Herod and his soldiers treated Jesus with contempt; they ridiculed him by dressing him up in a splendid robe, and sent him back to Pilate. ¹²And so it happened, that very day, that Herod and Pilate became friends with each other. Up until then, they had been enemies.

Pilate pressured by the crowds

¹³So Pilate called the chief priests, the rulers and the people.

¹⁴'You brought this man before me,' he said to them, 'on the grounds that he was leading the people astray. Look here, then: I examined him in your presence and I found no evidence in him of the charges you're bringing against him. ¹⁵Nor did Herod; he sent him back to me. Look: there is no sign that he's done anything to deserve death. ¹⁶So I'm going to flog him and let him go.'

¹⁸'Take him away!' they shouted out all together. 'Release Barabbas for us!' ¹⁹(Barabbas had been thrown into prison because of an uprising that had taken place in the city, and for murder.) ²⁰Pilate spoke to them again, with the intention of letting Jesus go, ²¹but they shouted back, 'Crucify him! Crucify him!'

²²'Why?' he said for the third time. 'What's he done wrong? I can't find anything he's done that deserves death, so I'm going to beat him and let him go.'

²³But they went on shouting out at the tops of their voices, demanding that he be crucified; and eventually their shouts won the day. ²⁴Pilate gave his verdict that their request should be granted. ²⁵He released the man they asked for, the one who'd been thrown into prison because of rebellion and murder, and gave Jesus over to their demands.

²⁶As they led him away, they grabbed a man from Cyrene called Simon, who was coming in to the city from outside, and they forced him to carry the crossbeam behind Jesus.

The crucifixion

²⁷A great crowd of the people followed Jesus, including women who were mourning and wailing for him. ²⁸Jesus turned and spoke to them.

'Daughters of Jerusalem,' he said, 'don't cry for me. Cry for yourselves instead! Cry for your children! ²⁹Listen: the time is coming when you will say, "A blessing on the barren! A blessing on wombs that never bore children, and breasts that never nursed them!" ³⁰At that time people will start to say to the mountains, "Fall on us", and to the hills, "Cover us"! ³¹Yes: if this is what they do with the green tree, what will happen to the dry one?'

³²Two other criminals were taken away with him to be executed. ³³When they came to the place called The Skull, they crucified him there, with the criminals, one on his right and one on his left.

³⁴'Father,' said Jesus, 'forgive them! They don't know what they're doing!'

They divided his clothes, casting lots for them.

³⁵The people stood around watching. The rulers hurled abuse at him.

'He rescued others,' they said, 'let him try rescuing himself, if he really is the Messiah, God's chosen one!'

³⁶The soldiers added their taunts, coming up and offering him cheap wine.

³⁷'If you're the king of the Jews,' they said, 'rescue yourself!'

³⁸The charge was written above him: 'This is the King of the Jews.'

³⁹One of the bad characters who was hanging there began to insult him. 'Aren't you the Messiah?' he said. 'Rescue yourself – and us, too!'

⁴⁰But the other one told him off. 'Don't you fear God?' he said. 'You're sharing the same fate that he is! ⁴¹In our case it's fair enough; we're getting exactly what we asked for. But this fellow hasn't done anything out of order.

⁴²'Jesus,' he went on, 'remember me when you finally become king.'

⁴³'I'm telling you the truth,' replied Jesus, 'you'll be with me in paradise, this very day.'

The death and burial of Jesus

⁴⁴By the time of the sixth hour, darkness came over all the land. ⁴⁵The sunlight vanished until the ninth hour. The veil of the Temple was ripped down the middle. ⁴⁶Then Jesus shouted out at the top of his voice, 'Here's my spirit, father! You can take care of it now!' And with that he died.

⁴⁷The centurion saw what happened, and praised God.

'This fellow', he said, 'really was in the right.'

⁴⁸All the crowds who had come together for the spectacle saw what happened, and they went away beating their breasts. ⁴⁹Those who knew Jesus, including the women who had followed him from Galilee, remained at a distance and watched the scene.

⁵⁰Now there was a man named Joseph, a member of the council. He was a good and righteous man, ⁵¹and had not given his consent to the court's verdict or actions. He was from Arimathea, a town in Judaea, and he was longing for God's kingdom. ⁵²He approached Pilate and asked for Jesus' body. ⁵³He took it down, wrapped it in a shroud, and put it in a tomb hollowed out of the rock, where no one had ever been laid. ⁵⁴It was the day of Preparation, and the sabbath was beginning.

⁵⁵The women who had followed Jesus, the ones who had come with him from Galilee, saw the tomb and how the body was laid. ⁵⁶Then they went back to prepare spices and ointments. On the sabbath they rested, as the commandment specified.

The resurrection

24 The women went to the tomb in the very early morning of the first day of the week, carrying the spices they had prepared. ²They found the stone rolled away from the tomb, ³and when they went in they didn't find the body of the Lord Jesus.

⁴As they were at a loss what to make of it all, suddenly two men in shining clothes stood beside them. ⁵The women were terrified, and bowed their faces towards the ground.

But the men said to them, 'Why look for the living with the dead? ⁶He isn't here – he's been raised! Don't you remember? While you were still in Galilee he told you that ⁷the son of man must be handed over into the hands of sinners, and be crucified, and rise again on the third day.'

⁸And they remembered his words.

⁹They went back, away from the tomb, and told all this to the eleven and all the others. ¹⁰It was Mary Magdalene, Joanna, and Mary the mother of James, and the others with them. They said this to the apostles; ¹¹and this message seemed to them just stupid, useless talk, and they didn't believe them.

¹²Peter, though, got up and ran to the tomb. He stooped down and saw only the graveclothes. He went back home, perplexed at what had happened.

On the road to Emmaus

¹³That very day, two of them were going to a village called Emmaus, which lay about seven miles from Jerusalem. ¹⁴They were discussing with each other all the various things that had taken place. ¹⁵As they were discussing, and arguing with each other, Jesus himself approached and walked with them. ¹⁶Their eyes, though, were prevented from recognizing him.

¹⁷'You're obviously having a very important discussion on your walk,' he said; 'what's it all about?'

They stood still, a picture of gloom. ¹⁸Then one of them, Cleopas by name, answered him.

'You must be the only person around Jerusalem,' he said, 'who doesn't know what's been going on there these last few days.'

¹⁹'What things?' he asked.

'To do with Jesus of Nazareth,' they said to him. 'He was a prophet. He acted with power and he spoke with power, before God and all the people. ²⁰Our chief priests and rulers handed him over to be condemned to death, and they crucified him. ²¹But we were hoping that he was going to redeem Israel!

'And now, what with all this, it's the third day since it happened. ²²But some women from our group have astonished us. They went to his tomb very early this morning, ²³and didn't find his body. They came back saying they'd seen a vision of angels, who said he was alive. ²⁴Some of the folk with us went off to the tomb and found it just as the women had said, but they didn't see *him*.'

²⁵'You are so senseless!' he said to them. 'So slow in your hearts to believe all the things the prophets said to you! Don't you see? ²⁶This is what *had* to happen: the Messiah had to suffer, and then come into his glory!'

²⁷So he began with Moses, and with all the prophets, and explained to them the things about himself throughout the whole Bible.

Jesus revealed at Emmaus

²⁸They drew near to the village where they were heading. Jesus gave the impression that he was going further, ²⁹but they urged him strongly not to.

'Stay with us,' they said. 'It's nearly evening; the day is almost gone.' And he went in to stay with them.

³⁰As he was sitting at table with them he took the bread and gave thanks. He broke it and gave it to them. ³¹Then the eyes of both of them were opened, and they recognized him; and he vanished from their sight.

³²Then they said to each other, 'Do you remember how our hearts were burning inside us, as he talked to us on the road, as he opened up the Bible for us?'

³³And they got up then and there and went back to Jerusalem. There they found the eleven, and the people with them, gathered together. ³⁴They were saying, 'The Lord really has been raised! He's appeared to Simon!' ³⁵Then they told what had happened on the road, and how he was known to them in the breaking of the bread.

Jesus' promise and ascension

³⁶As they were saying this, Jesus himself stood in the midst of them, and said, 'Peace be with you.' ³⁷They were terrified and alarmed, and thought they were seeing a ghost.

³⁸'Why are you so disturbed?' he said. 'Why do these questionings come up in your hearts? ³⁹Look at my hands and feet; it really is me, myself. Touch me and see! Ghosts don't have flesh and bones like you can see I have.'

⁴⁰With these words, he showed them his hands and feet.

⁴¹While they were still in disbelief and amazement from sheer joy, he said to them, 'Have you got something here to eat?' ⁴²They gave him a piece of baked fish, ⁴³which he took and ate in front of them.

⁴⁴Then he said to them, 'This is what I was talking to you about when I was still with you. Everything written about me in the law of Moses, and in the prophets and the Psalms, had to be fulfilled.' ⁴⁵Then he opened their minds to understand the Bible.

⁴⁶'This is what is written,' he said. 'The Messiah must suffer and rise from the dead on the third day, ⁴⁷and in his name repentance, for the forgiveness of sins, must be announced to all the nations, beginning from Jerusalem. ⁴⁸You are the witnesses for all this. ⁴⁹Now, look: I'm sending upon you what my father has promised. But stay in the city until you are clothed with power from on high.'

⁵⁰Then he took them out as far as Bethany, and lifted up his hands and blessed them. ⁵¹As he was blessing them, he was separated from them and carried into heaven.

⁵²They worshipped him, and went back to Jerusalem in great joy. ⁵³They spent all their time in the Temple, praising God.

John

People used to say that John gave us the 'divine' Jesus while the other gospels gave us the 'human' Jesus. But this is clearly wrong, since the others also see Jesus as embodying the one God, and John sees Jesus weeping, troubled in spirit, thirsting and dying, and, still more importantly, playing the role in the divine purposes that was marked out for *humans* from the start. Perhaps a better way to express the difference might be to say that John has put into the first paragraph of his book what the others want their readers to work out step by step.

Certainly John's first paragraph (1.1–18) is one of the most visionary short pieces in the whole history of Christian writing. 'In the beginning was the Word . . . and the Word became flesh.' What does John think he is doing?

He is writing a new Genesis. His whole book is about how the world's creator has come at last to remake that world: chapter 20 is about Jesus' resurrection, but every sentence breathes the life of 'the first day of the week', the start of new creation. But if John's Prologue is a new Genesis 1, then the equivalent of the climax of that great chapter, the creation of humans in the divine image, is precisely the Word becoming flesh. John 1.14 corresponds to Genesis 1.26–28: the one through whom the world was made now becoming the one through whom the world is rescued and remade. This theme runs throughout the gospel, reaching its own climax in 19.5 when Pilate declares 'Here's the man!'

But John is also writing a new Exodus – and this provides the other major clue to his book. Moses led the people out of Egypt and gave them the Torah, to prepare them for God coming in person to dwell with them, in the Tabernacle, and lead them to their inheritance. Now 'the Word became flesh and [literally] "tabernacled in our midst"' (1.14). Jesus is the place where the one God has come to dwell among us and to reveal his true glory. The whole gospel resonates with this Temple-theme, reaching a climax in the 'Farewell Discourses' (chapters 13—17) when Jesus' followers, too, become Temple-people by the promise of the indwelling spirit.

John's gospel divides neatly into two. The first twelve chapters offer a mixture of 'signs' and discourses; the two go together, leading the eye up to the raising of Lazarus in chapter 11 and then the dramatic statement of purpose in chapter 12: Jesus, going to the cross, is going to pass judgment on the 'ruler of the world' and rescue the captives from all the nations (12.23–33). This then leads to the second half, which opens with a statement as important as the Prologue itself: Jesus 'had always loved his own people in the world; now he loved them right through to the end' (13.1). The divine glory and the divine love turn out to be two ways of saying the same thing. Jesus explains to his disciples what it all means, how they in turn must be people of love and unity; then he goes to face 'the ruler of the world' and bear witness to the reality of God's kingdom, the real truth, and the ultimate power (18.33—19.16). Jesus' last words, 'It's all done' (19.30), echo the 'finished' of Genesis 2.1–2. Creation has been rescued. New creation can now begin.

Nobody knows when John's gospel was written. Scholars have suggested dates as late as AD 120 and as early as the middle 30s. It doesn't matter. The revelation of divine love and glory in the true Man, Jesus, continues to evoke faith and life, as John intended that it should (20.31).

The Word made flesh

1 In the beginning was the Word. The Word was close beside God, and the Word was God. ²In the beginning, he was close beside God.

³All things came into existence through him; not one thing that exists came into existence without him. ⁴Life was in him, and this life was the light of the human race. ⁵The light shines in the darkness, and the darkness did not overcome it.

⁶There was a man called John, who was sent from God. ⁷He came as evidence, to give evidence about the light, so that everyone might believe through him. ⁸He was not himself the light, but he came to give evidence about the light.

⁹The true light, which gives light to every human being, was coming into the world. ¹⁰He was in the world, and the world was made through him, and the world did not know him. ¹¹He came to what was his own, and his own people did not accept him. ¹²But to anyone who did accept him, he gave the right to become God's children; yes, to anyone who believed in his name. ¹³They were not born from blood, or from fleshly desire, or from the intention of a man, but from God.

¹⁴And the Word became flesh, and lived among us. We gazed upon his glory, glory like that of the father's only son, full of grace and truth.

¹⁵John gave evidence about him, loud and clear.

'This is the one', he said, 'that I was speaking about when I told you, "The one who comes after me ranks ahead of me, because he was before me."'

¹⁶Yes; it's out of his fullness that we have all received, grace indeed on top of grace. ¹⁷The law, you see, was given through Moses; grace and truth came through Jesus the Messiah. ¹⁸Nobody has ever seen God. The only-begotten God, who is intimately close to the father – he has brought him to light.

The evidence of John

¹⁹This is the evidence John gave, when the Judaeans sent priests and Levites from Jerusalem to ask him, 'Who are you?'

²⁰He was quite open about it; he didn't try to deny it. He said, quite openly, 'I am not the Messiah.'

²¹'What then?' they asked. 'Are you Elijah?'

'No, I'm not,' he replied.

'Are you the Prophet?'

'No.'

²²'Well, then, who *are* you?' they said. 'We've got to take some kind of answer back to the people who sent us. Who do you claim to be?'

²³'I'm a voice calling in the desert,' he said, '"Straighten out the road for the master!"' – just as the prophet Isaiah said.

²⁴The people who had been sent were from the Pharisees. ²⁵They continued to question him.

'So why are you baptizing', they asked, 'if you aren't the Messiah, or Elijah, or the Prophet?'

²⁶'I'm baptizing with water,' John replied. 'But there is someone standing among you that you don't know, ²⁷someone who is to come after me. I'm not good enough to undo his sandal-strap.'

²⁸This took place in Bethany beyond the Jordan, where John was baptizing.

The lamb and the spirit

²⁹The next day, John saw Jesus coming towards him.

'Look!' he said. 'There's God's lamb! He's the one who takes away the world's sin! ³⁰He's the one I was speaking about when I said, "There's a man coming after me who ranks ahead of me, because he was before me!" ³¹I didn't know who it would be, but this was the reason I came to baptize with water – so that he could be revealed to Israel.'

³²So John gave this evidence: 'I saw the spirit coming down like a dove out of heaven and remaining on him. ³³I didn't know who it would be; but the one who sent me to baptize with water said to me, "When you see the spirit coming down and resting on someone, that's the person who will baptize with the holy spirit." ³⁴Well, that's what I saw, and I've given you my evidence: he is the son of God.'

The first disciples

³⁵The following day John was again standing there, with two of his disciples. ³⁶He saw

Jesus walking by, and said, 'Look! There goes God's lamb!'

37 The two disciples heard him say this, and they followed Jesus.

38 Jesus turned and saw them following him.

'What do you want?' he asked.

'Rabbi,' they said (the word means 'teacher'), 'where are you staying?'

39 'Come and see,' he replied.

So they came, and saw where he was staying, and stayed with him that day. It was late in the afternoon.

40 One of the two who heard what John said and followed Jesus was Andrew, Simon Peter's brother. 41 The first person he found was his own brother Simon.

'We've found the Messiah!' he said (that means 'the anointed one', like our word 'Christ'). 42 He brought him to Jesus.

Jesus looked at him.

'So,' he said, 'you're Simon, John's son, are you? We'd better call you Cephas!' (That means 'the Rock', like our word 'Peter'.)

Philip and Nathanael

43 The next day Jesus decided to go to Galilee, where he found Philip.

'Follow me,' he said to him.

44 Philip came from Bethsaida, the town where Andrew and Peter hailed from. 45 Philip found Nathanael.

'We've found him!' he said. 'The one Moses wrote about in the law! And the prophets, too! We've found him! It's Jesus, Joseph's son, from Nazareth!'

46 'Really?' replied Nathanael. 'Are you telling me that something good can come out of Nazareth?'

'Come and see,' replied Philip.

47 Jesus saw Nathanael coming towards him.

'Here he comes,' he said. 'Look at him! He's a real Israelite. Genuine through and through.'

48 'How did you get to know me?' asked Nathanael.

'Oh,' replied Jesus, 'I saw you under the fig tree, before Philip spoke to you.'

49 'Rabbi,' replied Nathanael, 'you're the son of God! You're the king of Israel!'

50 'Wait a minute,' said Jesus. 'Are you telling me that you believe just because I told you I saw you under the fig tree? You'll see a lot more than that!

51 'In fact,' he went on, 'I'm telling you the solemn truth. You'll see heaven opened, and God's angels going up and down upon the son of man.'

Water into wine

2 On the third day there was a wedding at Cana in Galilee. Jesus' mother was there, 2 and Jesus and his disciples were also invited to the wedding.

3 The wine ran out.

Jesus' mother came over to him.

'They haven't got any wine!' she said.

4 'Oh, Mother!' replied Jesus. 'What's that got to do with you and me? My time hasn't come yet.'

5 His mother spoke to the servants.

'Do whatever he tells you,' she said.

6 Six stone water-jars were standing there, ready for use in the Jewish purification rites. Each held about twenty or thirty gallons.

7 'Fill the jars with water,' said Jesus to the servants. And they filled them, right up to the brim.

8 'Now draw some out', he said, 'and take it to the chief steward.' They did so.

9 When the chief steward tasted the water that had turned into wine (he didn't know where it had come from, but the servants who had drawn the water knew), he called the bridegroom.

10 'What everybody normally does', he said, 'is to serve the good wine first, and then the worse stuff when people have had plenty to drink. But you've kept the good wine till now!'

11 This event, in Cana of Galilee, was the first of Jesus' signs. He displayed his glory, and his disciples believed in him.

12 After this, he went down to Capernaum, with his mother, his brothers and his disciples. He remained there for a few days.

Jesus in the Temple

13 It was nearly time for the Judaean Passover, and Jesus went up to Jerusalem.

14 In the Temple he found people selling cows, sheep and doves, and the money-changers

sitting there. ¹⁵He made a whip out of cords and drove them all out of the Temple, sheep, cows and all. He spilt the money-changers' coins onto the ground, and knocked over their tables.

¹⁶'Take these things away!' he said to the people selling doves. 'You mustn't turn my father's house into a market!'

¹⁷His disciples remembered that it was written, 'The zeal of your house has eaten me up.'

¹⁸The Judaeans had this response for him. 'What sign are you going to show us', they said, 'to explain why you're doing this?'

¹⁹'Destroy this Temple,' replied Jesus, 'and I'll raise it up in three days.'

²⁰'It's taken forty-six years to build this Temple,' responded the Judaeans, 'and are you going to raise it up in three days?' ²¹But he was speaking about the 'temple' of his body. ²²So when he was raised from the dead, his disciples remembered that he had said this, and they believed the Bible and the word which Jesus had spoken.

²³While he was in Jerusalem during the Passover festival, several people came to trust in his name, because they had seen the signs he did. ²⁴But Jesus didn't entrust himself to them. He knew everything, ²⁵and had no need for anyone to give him information about people. He himself knew what was inside people.

Jesus and Nicodemus

3 There was a man of the Pharisees called Nicodemus, a ruler of the Judaeans. ²He came to Jesus by night.

'Rabbi,' he said to him. 'We know that you're a teacher who's come from God. Nobody can do these signs that you're doing, unless God is with him.'

³'Let me tell you the solemn truth,' replied Jesus. 'Unless someone has been born from above, they won't be able to see God's kingdom.'

⁴'How can someone possibly be born', asked Nicodemus, 'when they're old? You're not telling me they can go back a second time into the mother's womb and be born, are you?'

⁵'I'm telling you the solemn truth,' replied Jesus. 'Unless someone is born from water and spirit, they can't enter God's kingdom. ⁶Flesh is born from flesh, but spirit is born from spirit. ⁷Don't be surprised that I said to you, You must be born from above. ⁸The wind blows where it wants to, and you hear the sound it makes; but you don't know where it's coming from or where it's going to. That's what it's like with someone who is born from the spirit.'

⁹'How can this be so?' asked Nicodemus.

¹⁰'Well, well!' replied Jesus. 'You're a teacher of Israel, and yet you don't know about all this? ¹¹I'm telling you the solemn truth: we're talking about things we know about. We're giving evidence about things we've seen. But you won't admit our evidence. ¹²If I told you earthly things and you don't believe, how will it be if I tell you heavenly things? Are you going to believe then? ¹³And nobody has gone up into heaven except the one who came down from heaven, the son of man.'

The snake and the love of God

¹⁴'So, just as Moses lifted up the snake in the desert, in the same way the son of man must be lifted up, ¹⁵so that everyone who believes in him may share in the life of God's new age. ¹⁶This, you see, is how much God loved the world: enough to give his only, special son, so that everyone who believes in him should not be lost but should share in the life of God's new age. ¹⁷After all, God didn't send the son into the world to condemn the world, but so that the world could be saved by him.

¹⁸'Anyone who believes in him is not condemned. But anyone who doesn't believe is condemned already, because they didn't believe in the name of God's only, special son. ¹⁹And this is the condemnation: that light has come into the world, and people loved darkness rather than light, because what they were doing was evil. ²⁰For everyone who does evil hates the light; people like that don't come to the light, in case their deeds get shown up and reproved. ²¹But people who do the truth come to the light, so that it can become clear that what they have done has been done in God.'

The bridegroom and his friend

²²After this, Jesus and his disciples went into the countryside of Judaea, and he stayed there with them and baptized. ²³John, too, was baptizing at Aenon, close to Salim. There was

plenty of water there, and people came to him and were baptized. ²⁴This, of course, was before John had been put into prison.

²⁵There was, perhaps inevitably, a dispute between the disciples of John and a Judaean, on the subject of purification. ²⁶They came to John.

'Rabbi,' they said. 'Remember the man who was with you beyond the Jordan, the one you gave evidence about? Well, look! He's baptizing, and everyone's going to him!'

²⁷'Nobody can receive anything unless heaven first gives it,' replied John. ²⁸'You yourselves can bear me out that I said I wasn't the Messiah, but that I was sent ahead of him. ²⁹It's the bridegroom who gets the bride. The bridegroom's friend, who stands nearby and hears him, is very, very happy when he hears the bridegroom's voice. So, you see, my joy is now complete. ³⁰He must increase, but I must decrease.'

³¹The one who comes from above is over everything. The one who is from the earth has an earthly character, and what he says has 'earth' written all over it. The one who comes from heaven is above all. ³²He gives evidence about what he has heard and seen, and nobody accepts his evidence. ³³The one who does accept his evidence has put his signature to the fact that God is true. ³⁴The one God sent, you see, speaks God's words, because he gives the spirit lavishly. ³⁵The father loves the son and has given everything into his hand. ³⁶Anyone who believes in the son shares in the life of God's new age. Anyone who doesn't believe in the son won't see life, but God's wrath rests on him.

The woman of Samaria

4 So when Jesus knew that the Pharisees had heard that he was making more disciples than John, and was baptizing them ²(Jesus himself didn't baptize people; it was his disciples who were doing it), ³he left Judaea and went back to Galilee.

⁴He had to go through Samaria, ⁵and he came to a town in Samaria named Sychar. It was near the place which Jacob gave to his son Joseph. ⁶Jacob's well was there. So Jesus, tired from the journey, sat down there by the well. It was about midday.

⁷A Samaritan woman came to draw water, and Jesus spoke to her.

'Give me a drink,' he said. ⁸(The disciples had gone off into the town to buy food.)

⁹'What!' said the Samaritan woman. 'You, a Jew, asking for a drink from me, a woman, and a Samaritan at that?' (Jews, you see, don't have any dealings with Samaritans.)

¹⁰'If only you'd known God's gift,' replied Jesus, 'and who it is that's saying to you, "Give me a drink", you'd have asked him, and he would have given you living water.'

¹¹'But sir,' replied the woman, 'you haven't got a bucket! And the well's deep! So how were you thinking of getting living water? ¹²Are you greater than our father Jacob, who gave us the well, and drank of it himself, with his sons and his animals?'

¹³'Everyone who drinks this water', Jesus replied, 'will get thirsty again. ¹⁴But anyone who drinks the water I'll give them won't ever be thirsty again. No: the water I'll give them will become a spring of water welling up to the life of God's new age.'

¹⁵'Sir,' the woman said, 'give me this water! Then I won't be thirsty any more, and I won't have to come here to draw from the well.'

Jesus and the woman

¹⁶'Well then,' said Jesus to the woman, 'go and call your husband and come here.'

¹⁷'I haven't got a husband,' replied the woman.

'You're telling me you haven't got a husband!' replied Jesus. ¹⁸'The fact is, you've had five husbands, and the one you've got now isn't your husband. You were speaking the truth!'

¹⁹'Well, sir,' replied the woman, 'I can see you're a prophet . . . ²⁰Our ancestors worshipped on this mountain. And you say that in Jerusalem is the place where people ought to worship.'

²¹'Believe me, woman,' replied Jesus, 'the time is coming when you won't worship the father on this mountain or in Jerusalem. ²²You worship what you don't know. We worship what we do know; salvation, you see, is indeed from the Jews. ²³But the time is coming – indeed, it's here already! – when true worshippers will worship the father in spirit and in truth. Yes; that's the kind of worshippers

the father is looking for. ²⁴God is spirit, and those who worship him must worship in spirit and in truth.'

²⁵'I know that Messiah is coming,' said the woman, 'the one they call "the anointed". When he comes, he'll tell us everything.'

²⁶'I'm the one – the one speaking to you right now,' said Jesus.

Sower and reaper rejoice together

²⁷Just then Jesus' disciples came up. They were astonished that he was talking with a woman; but nobody said 'What did you want?' or 'Why were you talking with her?' ²⁸So the woman left her water-jar, went into the town and spoke to the people.

²⁹'Come on!' she said. 'Come and see a man who told me everything I ever did! You don't think he can be the Messiah, do you?'

³⁰So they left the town and were coming out to him.

³¹Meanwhile the disciples were nagging him.

'Come on, rabbi!' they were saying. 'You must have something to eat!'

³²'I've got food to eat that you know nothing about,' he said.

³³'Nobody's brought him anything to eat, have they?' said the disciples to one another.

³⁴'My food', replied Jesus, 'is to do the will of the one who sent me, and to finish his work! ³⁵Don't you have a saying, "Another four months, then comes harvest"? Well, let me tell you, raise your eyes and see! The fields are white! It's harvest time already! ³⁶The reaper earns his pay, and gathers crops for the life of God's coming age, so that sower and reaper can celebrate together. ³⁷This is where that saying comes true, "One sows, another reaps". ³⁸I sent you to reap what you didn't work for. Others did the hard work, and you've come into the results.'

³⁹Several Samaritans from that town believed in Jesus because of what the woman said in evidence about him, 'He told me everything I did.' ⁴⁰So when the Samaritans came to him, they asked him to stay with them. And he stayed there two days.

⁴¹Many more believed because of what he said.

⁴²'We believe, too,' they said to the woman, 'but it's no longer because of what you told us.

We've heard him ourselves! We know that he really is the one! He's the saviour of the world!'

The official's son

⁴³After the two days in Samaria, Jesus went off from there to Galilee. ⁴⁴Jesus himself gave evidence, after all, that a prophet isn't honoured in his own country. ⁴⁵So when he came to Galilee, the Galileans welcomed him. They had seen all the things he had done in Jerusalem at the festival, since they had been at the festival too.

⁴⁶So he went once more to Cana in Galilee, where he had turned the water into wine.

There was a royal official in Capernaum whose son was ill. ⁴⁷He heard that Jesus had come from Judaea into Galilee, and he went to him and asked him to come down and heal his son, since he was at the point of death.

⁴⁸'Unless you see signs and miracles,' replied Jesus, 'you won't ever believe.'

⁴⁹'Sir,' replied the official, 'come down before my child dies!'

⁵⁰'Off you go!' said Jesus. 'Your son will live!'

The man believed the word which Jesus had spoken to him, and he set off. ⁵¹But while he was still on his way down to Capernaum, his servants met him with the news that his son was alive and well.

⁵²So he asked them what time he had begun to get better.

'Yesterday afternoon, about one o'clock,' they said. 'That's when the fever left him.'

⁵³So the father knew that it had happened at the very moment when Jesus had said to him, 'Your son will live!' He himself believed, and so did all his household.

⁵⁴This was now the second sign Jesus did, when he came out of Judaea into Galilee.

The healing of the disabled man

5 After this there was a Jewish festival, and Jesus went up to Jerusalem.

²In Jerusalem, near the Sheep Gate, there is a pool which is called, in Hebrew, Bethesda. It has five porticoes, ³where there were several sick people lying. They were blind, lame and paralysed.

⁵There was a man who had been there, in the same sick state, for thirty-eight years. ⁶Jesus saw him lying there, and knew that he had been there a long time already.

'Do you want to get well?' he asked him.

⁷'Well, sir,' the sick man replied, 'I don't have anyone to put me into the pool when the water gets stirred up. While I'm on my way there, someone else gets down before me.'

⁸'Get up,' said Jesus, 'pick up your mattress and walk!'

⁹At once the man was healed. He picked up his mattress and walked.

God's son breaks the sabbath!

The day all this happened was a sabbath. ¹⁰So the Judaeans confronted the man who had been healed.

'It's the sabbath!' they said. 'You shouldn't be carrying your mattress!'

¹¹'Well,' he replied, 'the man who cured me told me to pick up my mattress and walk!'

¹²'Oh, really?' they said. 'And who is this man, who told you to pick it up and walk?'

¹³But the man who'd been healed didn't know who it was. Jesus had gone away, and the place was crowded.

¹⁴After this Jesus found the man in the Temple.

'Look!' he said. 'You're better again! Don't sin any more, or something worse might happen to you!'

¹⁵The man went off and told the Judaeans that it was Jesus who had healed him. ¹⁶This was why the Judaeans began to persecute Jesus, because he did these things on the sabbath.

¹⁷This was Jesus' response to them.

'My father', he said, 'is going on working, and so am I!'

¹⁸So for this reason the Judaeans were all the more eager to kill him, because he not only broke the sabbath, but spoke of God as his own father, making himself equal to God.

The coming judgment

¹⁹So Jesus made this response to them.

'I'm telling you the solemn truth,' he said. 'The son can do nothing by himself. He can only do what he sees the father doing. Whatever the father does, the son does too, and in the same way. ²⁰The father loves the son, you see, and shows him all the things that he's doing. Yes: he will show him even greater things than these, and that'll amaze you! ²¹For, just as the father raises the dead and gives them life, in the same way the son gives life to anyone he chooses.

²²'The father doesn't judge anyone, you see; he has handed over all judgment to the son, ²³so that everyone should honour the son just as they honour the father. Anyone who doesn't honour the son doesn't honour the father who sent him.

²⁴'I'm telling you the solemn truth: anyone who hears my word, and believes in the one who sent me, has the life of God's coming age. Such a person won't come into judgment; they will have passed out of death into life. ²⁵I'm telling you the solemn truth: the time is coming – in fact, it's here already! – when the dead will hear the voice of God's son, and those who hear it will live. ²⁶You see, just as the father has life in himself, in the same way he has given the son the privilege of having life in himself. ²⁷He has even given him authority to pass judgment, because he is the son of man.

²⁸'Don't be surprised at this. The time is coming, you see, when everyone in the tombs will hear his voice. ²⁹They will come out – those who have done good, to the resurrection of life, and those who have done evil, to the resurrection of judgment.'

The evidence in support of Jesus

³⁰'I can't do anything on my own authority,' Jesus went on. 'I judge on the basis of what I hear. And my judgment is just, because I'm not trying to carry out my own wishes, but the wishes of the one who sent me.

³¹'If I give evidence about myself, my evidence isn't true. ³²There is someone else who gives evidence about me, and I know that the evidence which he brings about me is true. ³³You sent messengers to John, and he gave evidence about the truth. ³⁴Not that I need evidence from human beings; but I'm saying this so that you may be saved.

35'John was a burning, bright lamp, and you were happy to celebrate in his light for a while. 36But I have greater evidence on my side than that of John. The works which the father has given me to complete – these works, which I'm doing, will provide evidence about me, evidence that the father has sent me. 37And the father who sent me has given evidence about me. You've never heard his voice; you've never seen his form. 38What's more, you haven't got his word abiding in you, because you don't believe in the one he sent.'

Jesus and Moses

39'You study the Bible', Jesus continued, 'because you suppose that you'll discover the life of God's coming age in it. In fact, it's the Bible which gives evidence about me! 40But you won't come to me so that you can have life.

41'I'm not accepting glory from human beings; 42but I know that you haven't got the love of God within you. 43I have come in the name of my father, and you won't receive me. If someone else comes in his own name, you will receive him! 44How can you believe, when you receive glory from one another, and you're not looking for the glory which comes from the one and only God?

45'Don't think that I'm going to accuse you to the father. There is someone who accuses you: it's Moses, the one you've put your hope in! 46You see, if you'd believed Moses, you would have believed me – because it was me he was writing about. 47But if you don't believe his writings, how are you going to believe my words?'

Feeding the five thousand

6 After this Jesus went away to beside the sea of Galilee, that is, the sea of Tiberias. 2A large crowd followed him, because they saw the signs he was doing in healing the sick. 3Jesus went up into the mountain and sat down there with his disciples. 4It was nearly time for the Passover, a Jewish festival.

5Jesus looked up and saw a great crowd coming to him.

'Where are we going to buy bread,' he said to Philip, 'so that they can have something to eat?' 6(He said this to test him. He himself knew what he intended to do.)

7'Even with six months' pay', replied Philip, 'you wouldn't be able to buy enough bread for each of them to have just a little!'

8One of his disciples, Andrew, Simon Peter's brother, joined in.

9'There's a lad here', he said, 'who's got five barley loaves and two fish. But what use are they with this many people?'

10'Make the men sit down,' said Jesus.

There was a lot of grass where they were, so the men sat down, about five thousand in all. 11So Jesus took the loaves, gave thanks and gave them to the people sitting down, and then did the same with the fish, as much as they wanted.

12When they were satisfied, he called the disciples.

'Collect up the bits and pieces left over,' he said, 'so that we don't lose anything.'

13So they collected it up, and filled twelve baskets with broken pieces of the five barley loaves left behind by the people who had eaten.

14When the people saw the sign that Jesus had done, they said, 'This really is the Prophet, the one who is to come into the world.' 15So when Jesus realized that they were intending to come and seize him to make him king, he withdrew again, by himself, up the mountain.

Jesus walking on the water

16When it was evening, Jesus' disciples went down to the seashore. 17They got into a boat, and went across the sea towards Capernaum. It was already getting dark, and Jesus had not yet come to them. 18A strong wind blew up, and the sea began to get rough. 19They had been rowing for about three or four miles when they saw Jesus walking on the sea, coming towards the boat. They were terrified.

20But he spoke to them.

'It's me!' he said. 'Don't be afraid!'

21Then they were eager to take him into the boat; and at once the boat arrived at the land they had been making for.

22The next day the crowd that had remained on the far side of the lake saw that there had only been the one boat there. They knew that Jesus hadn't gone with his disciples, but that the disciples had set off by themselves.

²³But other boats came from Tiberias, near the place where they had eaten the bread after the Lord had given thanks. ²⁴When the crowd saw that neither Jesus nor his disciples were there, they themselves got into the boats and came to Capernaum looking for Jesus.

²⁵When they found him beside the sea, they said to him, 'Rabbi, when did you come here?'

Bread from heaven

²⁶This was Jesus' reply.

'I'm telling you the solemn truth,' he said. 'You aren't looking for me because you saw signs, but because you ate as much bread as you could. ²⁷You shouldn't be working for perishable food, but for food that will last to the life of God's coming age – the food which the son of man will give you, the person whom God the father has stamped with the seal of his approval.'

²⁸'What should we be doing,' they asked him, 'so that we can be doing the work God wants?'

²⁹'This is the work God wants of you,' replied Jesus, 'that you believe in the one he sent.'

³⁰'Well, then,' they said to him, 'what sign are you going to do, so that we can see it and believe you? What work are *you* doing? ³¹Our ancestors ate the manna in the wilderness; it says in the Bible that "he gave them bread from heaven to eat."'

³²'I'm telling you the solemn truth,' Jesus replied. 'It wasn't Moses who gave you the bread from heaven. It was my father who gave you the true bread from heaven. ³³God's bread, you see, is the one who comes down from heaven and gives life to the world.'

³⁴'Master,' they said, 'give us this bread – give it to us always!'

³⁵'I am the bread of life,' replied Jesus. 'Anyone who comes to me will never be hungry! Anyone who believes in me will never be thirsty!'

The father's will

³⁶'But I told you', Jesus continued, 'that you have indeed seen me – and still you don't believe! ³⁷All that the father gives me will come to me; and I won't reject anyone who comes to me, ³⁸because I came down from heaven not to do my own will but the will of the one who sent me. ³⁹And this is the will of the one who sent me, that I should lose nothing out of everything that he has given me, but that I should raise it up on the last day. ⁴⁰This is the will of my father, you see: that all who see the son and believe in him should have the life of God's coming age; and I will raise them up on the last day.'

⁴¹The Judaeans then grumbled about him because he had said, 'I am the bread which came down from heaven.'

⁴²'Isn't this Jesus, Joseph's son?' they said. 'We know his father and mother, don't we? So how can he say "I came down from heaven"?'

⁴³'Don't grumble among yourselves,' answered Jesus. ⁴⁴'No one can come to me unless the father who sent me draws them – and I will raise them up on the last day. ⁴⁵It is written in the prophets, "They shall all be taught by God." Everyone who listens to what comes from the father, and learns from it, comes to me. ⁴⁶Not that anyone has seen the father except the one who is from God; he has seen the father.'

Eating and drinking the son of man

⁴⁷'I'm telling you the solemn truth,' Jesus went on. 'Anyone who believes in me has the life of God's coming age. ⁴⁸I am the bread of life. ⁴⁹Your ancestors in the wilderness ate the manna, and they died. ⁵⁰This is the bread which comes down from heaven, so that people can eat it and not die. ⁵¹I am the living bread which came down from heaven. If anyone eats from this bread, they will live for ever. And the bread which I shall give is my flesh, given for the life of the world.'

⁵²This caused a squabble among the Judaeans.

'How can this fellow give us his flesh to eat?' they asked.

⁵³'I'm telling you the solemn truth,' Jesus replied. 'If you don't eat the flesh of the son of man, and drink his blood, you have no life in yourselves. ⁵⁴Anyone who feasts upon my flesh and drinks my blood has the life of God's coming age, and I will raise them up on the last day. ⁵⁵My flesh is true food, you see, and my blood is true drink. ⁵⁶Anyone who eats my flesh and drinks my blood remains in me, and

I remain in them. ⁵⁷Just as the living father sent me, and I live because of the father, so the one who eats me will live because of me. ⁵⁸This is the bread which came down from heaven; it isn't like the bread which the ancestors ate, and died. The one who eats this bread will share the life of God's new age.'

⁵⁹He said this in the synagogue, while he was teaching in Capernaum.

Division among Jesus' followers

⁶⁰When they heard this, many of Jesus' disciples said, 'This is difficult stuff! Who can bear to listen to it?'

⁶¹Jesus knew in himself that his disciples were grumbling about what he'd said.

'Does this put you off?' he said. ⁶²'What if you were to see the son of man ascending to where he was before? ⁶³It's the spirit that gives life; the flesh is no help. The words that I have spoken to you – they are spirit, they are life. ⁶⁴But there are some of you who don't believe.'

Jesus knew from the beginning, you see, those who didn't believe, and the one who was going to betray him.

⁶⁵'That's why I said', he went on, 'that no one can come to me unless it is given to them by the father.'

⁶⁶From that time on, several of his disciples drew back, and no longer went about with him.

⁶⁷Jesus turned to the Twelve.

'You don't want to go away too, do you?' he asked.

⁶⁸Simon Peter spoke up.

'Master,' he said, 'who can we go to? You're the one who's got the words of the life of the coming age! ⁶⁹We've come to believe it – we've come to know it! – that you are God's holy one.'

⁷⁰'Well,' replied Jesus, 'I chose you twelve, didn't I? And one of you is an accuser!'

⁷¹He was referring to Judas, son of Simon Iscariot. He was one of the Twelve, and he was going to betray him.

Jesus and his brothers

7 After this, Jesus went about in Galilee. He didn't want to go about in Judaea, because the Judaeans were after his blood. ²The time came for the Jewish festival of Tabernacles. ³So Jesus' brothers approached him.

'Leave this place', they said, 'and go to Judaea! Then your disciples will see the works you're doing. ⁴Nobody who wants to become well known does things in secret. If you're doing these things, show yourself to the world!'

⁵Even his brothers, you see, didn't believe in him.

⁶'My time isn't here yet,' replied Jesus, 'but your time is always here. ⁷The world can't hate you, but it hates me, because I am giving evidence against it, showing that its works are evil. ⁸I tell you what: you go up to the feast. I'm not going up to this feast; my time is not yet complete.'

⁹With these words, he stayed behind in Galilee.

Disputes about Jesus

¹⁰But when Jesus' brothers had gone up to the festival, then he himself went up, not openly, but, so to speak, in secret. ¹¹The Judaeans were looking for him at the feast.

'Where is he?' they were saying.

¹²There was considerable dispute about him among the crowds.

'He's a good man!' some were saying.

'No, he isn't,' others would reply. 'He's deceiving the people!'

¹³But nobody dared speak about him openly, for fear of the Judaeans.

¹⁴About the middle of the feast, Jesus went up into the Temple and began to teach. ¹⁵The Judaeans were astonished.

'Where does this fellow get all his learning from?' they asked. 'He's never been trained!'

¹⁶'My teaching isn't my own,' replied Jesus. 'It comes from the one who sent me! ¹⁷If anyone wants to do what God wants, they will know whether this teaching is from God, or whether I'm just speaking on my own account. ¹⁸Anyone who speaks on his own behalf is trying to establish his own reputation. But if what he's interested in is the reputation of the one who sent him, then he is true, and there is no injustice in him.'

Moses and the Messiah

19"Moses gave you the law, didn't he?' Jesus continued. 'But none of you obeys the law. Why are you wanting to kill me?'

20The crowd responded to this.

'You must have a demon inside you!' they said. 'Who is trying to kill you?'

21'Look here,' replied Jesus. 'I did one single thing, and you are all amazed. 22Moses commanded you to practise circumcision (not that it starts with Moses, of course; it comes from the patriarchs), and you circumcise a man on the sabbath. 23Well, then, if a man receives circumcision on the sabbath, so that the law of Moses may not be broken, how can you be angry with me if I make an entire man healthy on the sabbath? 24Don't judge by appearances! Judge with proper and right judgment!'

25Some Jerusalem residents commented, 'Isn't this the man they're trying to kill? 26Look – he's speaking quite openly, and nobody is saying anything to him. You don't suppose our rulers really know he's the Messiah, do you? 27The thing is, we know where he comes from – but when the Messiah appears, nobody will know where he comes from.'

28As Jesus was teaching in the Temple, he shouted out, 'You know me! You know where I come from! I haven't come on my own behalf – but the one who sent me is true, and you don't know him! 29I know him, because I come from him, and he sent me!'

30So they tried to arrest him. But nobody laid hands on him, because his time had not yet come.

Rivers of living water

31Many people from the crowd believed in Jesus.

'When the Messiah comes,' they were saying, 'will he do more signs than this man has done?'

32The Pharisees heard that the crowd was full of this rumour about him, and the chief priests and Pharisees sent servants to arrest him.

33So Jesus said, 'I'm just with you for a little while, and then I'm going to the one who sent me. 34You will look for me and you won't find me, and you can't come where I am.'

35'Where does he think he's going,' said the Judaeans to one another, 'if we won't be able to find him? He's not going to go off abroad, among the Greeks, is he, and teach the Greeks? 36What does he mean when he says, "You'll look for me and you won't find me", and "Where I am, you can't come"?'

37On the last day of the festival, the great final celebration, Jesus stood up and shouted out, 'If anybody's thirsty, they should come to me and have a drink! 38Anyone who believes in me will have rivers of living water flowing out of their heart, just like the Bible says!'

39He said this about the spirit, which people who believed in him were to receive. The spirit wasn't available yet, because Jesus was not yet glorified.

Where does the Messiah come from?

40When they heard these words, some people in the crowd said, 'This man really is "the Prophet"!'

41'He's the Messiah!' said some others.

But some of them replied, 'The Messiah doesn't come from Galilee, does he? 42Doesn't the Bible say that the Messiah is descended from David, and comes from Bethlehem, the city where David was?'

43So there was a division in the crowd because of him. 44Some of them wanted to arrest him, but nobody laid hands on him.

45So the servants went back to the chief priests and the Pharisees.

'Why didn't you get him?' they asked.

46'No man ever spoke like this!' the servants replied.

47'You don't mean to say you've been taken in too?' answered the Pharisees. 48'None of the rulers or the Pharisees have believed in him, have they? 49But this rabble that doesn't know the law – a curse on them!'

50Nicodemus, who went to Jesus earlier, and who was one of their own number, spoke up.

51'Our law doesn't condemn a man, does it, unless first you hear his side of the story and find out what he's doing?'

52'Oh, so you're from Galilee too, are you?' they answered him. 'Check it out and see! No prophet ever rises up from Galilee!'

Adultery and hypocrisy

⁵³They all went off home, **8** and Jesus went to the Mount of Olives. ²In the morning he went back to the Temple. All the people came to him, and he sat down and taught them.

³The scribes and Pharisees brought a woman who had been caught out in adultery. They stood her out in the middle.

⁴'Teacher,' they said to him. 'This woman was caught in the very act of adultery. ⁵In the law, Moses commanded us to stone people like this. What do you say?'

⁶They said this to test him, so that they could frame a charge against him.

Jesus squatted down and wrote with his finger on the ground. ⁷When they went on pressing the question, he got up and said to them, 'Whichever of you is without sin should throw the first stone at her.'

⁸And once again he squatted down and wrote on the ground.

⁹When they heard that, they went off one by one, beginning with the oldest. Jesus was left alone, with the woman still standing there.

¹⁰Jesus looked up.

'Where are they, woman?' he asked. 'Hasn't anybody condemned you?'

¹¹'Nobody, sir,' she replied.

'Well, then,' said Jesus, 'I don't condemn you either! Off you go – and from now on don't sin again!'

The light of the world

¹²Jesus spoke to them again.

'I am the light of the world,' he said. 'People who follow me won't go around in the dark; they'll have the light of life!'

¹³'You're giving evidence in your own case!' said the Pharisees. 'Your evidence is false!'

¹⁴'Even if I do give evidence about myself,' replied Jesus to them, 'my evidence is true, because I know where I came from and where I'm going to. But you don't know where I come from or where I'm going to. ¹⁵You are judging in merely human terms; I don't judge anyone. ¹⁶But even if I do judge, my judgment is true, because I'm not a lone voice; I have on my side the father who sent me. ¹⁷It is written in your law that the evidence of two people is true. ¹⁸I'm giving evidence about myself, and the father who sent me is giving evidence about me.'

¹⁹'Where is your father?' they said to him.

'You don't know me,' replied Jesus, 'and you don't know my father! If you had known me, you would have known my father as well.'

²⁰He said all this in the treasury, while he was teaching in the Temple. Nobody arrested him, though, because his time hadn't yet come.

From below or from above

²¹So Jesus spoke to them once more.

'I am going away,' he said. 'You will look for me, and you will die in your sin. You can't come where I'm going.'

²²'Is he going to kill himself?' asked the Judaeans. 'Is that what he means when he says we can't come where he's going?'

²³'You come from below,' Jesus said to them, 'but I come from above. You are from this world, I am not from this world. ²⁴I told you that you would die in your sins; you see, that's what will happen to you if you don't believe that I am the one.'

²⁵'Who are you?' they asked.

'What I've been telling you from the beginning,' replied Jesus. ²⁶'There are plenty of things I could say about you, yes, and against you too! But the one who sent me is true, and I tell the world what I heard from him.'

²⁷They didn't understand that he was talking about the father.

²⁸So Jesus said to them, 'When you've lifted up the son of man, then you will know that I'm the one, and that I never act on my own initiative; I say exactly what the father taught me. ²⁹And the one who sent me is with me. He hasn't left me alone, because I always do what pleases him.'

The truth will make you free

³⁰As Jesus said all this, several people believed in him.

³¹So Jesus spoke to the Judaeans who had believed in him.

'If you remain in my word,' he said, 'you will truly be my disciples, ³²and you will know the truth, and the truth will make you free.'

33'We are Abraham's descendants!' they replied. 'We've never been anyone's slaves! How can you say that "You'll become free"?'

34'I'm telling you the solemn truth,' Jesus replied. 'Everyone who commits sin is a slave of sin. 35The slave doesn't live in the house for ever; the son lives there for ever. 36So, you see, if the son makes you free, you will be truly free.'

Children of Abraham – or of the devil

37'I know you're Abraham's descendants,' Jesus went on. 'But you're trying to kill me, because my word doesn't find a place among you. 38I am speaking of what I have seen with the father; and you, too, are doing what you heard from your father.'

39'Abraham is our father!' they replied.

'If you really were Abraham's children,' replied Jesus, 'you would do what Abraham did! 40But now you're trying to kill me – me, a man who has told you the truth which I heard from God! That's not what Abraham did. 41You're doing the works of *your* father.'

"There wasn't anything immoral about the way *we* were born!' they replied. 'We've got one father, and that's God!'

42'If God really was your father,' replied Jesus, 'you would love me, because I came from God, and here I am. I didn't come on my own initiative, you see, but he sent me. 43Why don't you understand what I'm saying? It can only be because you can't hear my word. 44You are from your father – the devil! And you're eager to get on with what he wants. He was a murderer from the beginning, and he's never remained in the truth, because there is no truth in him. When he tells lies, he speaks what comes naturally to him, because he is a liar – in fact, he's the father of lies! 45But because I speak the truth, you don't believe me. 46Which of you can bring a charge of sin against me? If I speak the truth, why don't you believe me? 47The one who is from God speaks God's words. That's why you don't listen, because you're not from God.'

Before Abraham, 'I Am'

48This was the Judaeans' response to Jesus.

'Haven't we been right all along,' they said, 'in saying you're a Samaritan, and that you've got a demon inside you?'

49'I haven't got a demon!' replied Jesus. 'I am honouring my father, and you are dishonouring me. 50I'm not looking for my own glory; there is one who is looking after that, and he will be the judge. 51I'm telling you the solemn truth: anyone who keeps my word will never, ever see death.'

52'Now we know that you really *have* got a demon!' replied the Judaeans. 'Look here: Abraham died! So did the prophets! And here are you, saying, "Anyone who keeps my word will never, ever taste death." 53You're not suggesting, are you, that you're greater than our father Abraham? He died, and so did the prophets! Who are you making yourself out to be?'

54'If I do give myself glory,' replied Jesus, 'my glory is nothing. My father is the one who brings me glory – the one you say is "our God"; 55and you don't know him! I know him, though. If I were to say I didn't know him, I would be a liar like you. But I do know him, and I keep his word. 56Your father Abraham celebrated the fact that he would see my day. He saw it and was delighted.'

57'You're not yet fifty years old!' responded the Judaeans. 'Have you seen Abraham?'

58'I'm telling you the solemn truth,' replied Jesus. 'Before Abraham existed, I Am.'

59So they picked up stones to throw at him. But Jesus hid, and left the Temple.

The man born blind

9 As Jesus was going along, he saw a man who had been blind from birth.

2'Teacher,' his disciples asked him, 'whose sin was it that caused this man to be born blind? Did he sin, or did his parents?'

3'He didn't sin,' replied Jesus, 'nor did his parents. It happened so that God's works could be seen in him. 4We must work the works of the one who sent me as long as it's still daytime. The night is coming, and nobody can work then! 5As long as I'm in the world, I'm the light of the world.'

6With these words, he spat on the ground, and made some mud out of his spittle. He spread the mud on the man's eyes.

⁷"Off you go', he said to him, 'and wash in the pool of Siloam' (which means 'sent'). So he went off and washed. When he came back, he could see.

⁸His neighbours, and the people who used to see him begging, remarked on this.

'Isn't this the man', they said, 'who used to sit here and beg?'

⁹'Yes, it's him!' said some of them.

'No, it isn't!' said some others. 'It's somebody like him.'

But the man himself spoke.

'Yes, it's me,' he said.

¹⁰'Well, then,' they said to him, 'how did your eyes get opened?'

¹¹'It was the man called Jesus!' he replied. 'He made some mud, then he spread it on my eyes, and told me to go to Siloam and wash. So I went, and washed, and I could see!'

¹²'Where is he?' they asked.

'I don't know,' he replied.

The blind man's parents

¹³They took the man who had been blind and brought him to the Pharisees. (¹⁴The day Jesus had made the mud, and opened his eyes, was a sabbath.) ¹⁵So the Pharisees began to ask him again how he had come to see.

'He put some mud on my eyes,' he said, 'and I washed, and now I can see!'

¹⁶'The man can't be from God,' some of the Pharisees began to say. 'He doesn't keep the sabbath!'

'Well, but,' replied some of the others, 'how can a man who is a sinner do signs like these?'

And they were divided.

¹⁷So they spoke to the blind man again.

'What have you got to say about him?' they asked. 'He opened your eyes, after all.'

'He's a prophet,' he replied.

¹⁸The Judaeans didn't believe that he really had been blind and now could see. So they called the parents of the newly sighted man, ¹⁹and put the question to them.

'Is this man really your son,' they asked, 'the one you say was born blind? How is it that he can now see?'

²⁰'Well,' replied his parents, 'we know that he is indeed our son, and that he was born blind. ²¹But we don't know how it is that he can now see, and we don't know who it was that opened his eyes. Ask him! He's grown up. He can speak for himself.'

²²His parents said this because they were afraid of the Judaeans. The Judaeans, you see, had already decided that if anyone declared that Jesus was the Messiah, they should be put out of the synagogue. ²³That's why his parents said, 'He's grown up, so you should ask him.'

Is Jesus from God?

²⁴So for the second time they called the man who had been blind.

'Give God the glory!' they said. 'We know that this man is a sinner.'

²⁵'I don't know whether he's a sinner or not,' replied the man. 'All I know is this: I used to be blind, and now I can see.'

²⁶'What did he do to you?' they asked. 'How did he open your eyes?'

²⁷'I told you already,' replied the man, 'and you didn't listen. Why d'you want to hear it again? You don't want to become his disciples too, do you?'

²⁸'You're his disciple,' they scoffed, 'but we are Moses's disciples. ²⁹We know that God spoke to Moses, but we don't know where this man comes from.'

³⁰'Well, here's a fine thing!' replied the man. 'You don't know where he's from, and he opened my eyes! ³¹We know that God doesn't listen to sinners; but if anyone is devout, and does his will, he listens to them. ³²It's never, ever been heard of before that someone should open the eyes of a person born blind. ³³If this man wasn't from God, he couldn't do anything.'

³⁴'You were born in sin from top to toe,' they replied, 'and are *you* going to start teaching *us*?' And they threw him out.

Seeing and not seeing

³⁵Jesus heard that they had thrown the man out. He found him and spoke to him.

'Do you believe in the son of man?' he asked.

³⁶'Who is he, sir,' asked the man, 'so that I can believe in him?'

³⁷'You have seen him,' replied Jesus. 'In fact, it's the person who's talking to you.'

38'Yes, sir,' said the man; 'I do believe.' And he worshipped him.

39'I came into the world for judgment,' said Jesus, 'so that those who can't see would see, and so that those who can see would become blind.'

40Some of the Pharisees were nearby, and they heard this.

'So!' they said. 'We're blind too, are we?'

41'If you were blind,' replied Jesus, 'you wouldn't be guilty of sin. But now, because you say, "We can see", your sin remains.'

The good shepherd

10 'I'm telling you the solemn truth,' said Jesus. 'Anyone who doesn't come into the sheepfold by the gate, but gets in by some other way, is a thief and a brigand. 2But the one who comes in through the gate is the sheep's own shepherd. 3The doorkeeper will open up for him, and the sheep hear his voice. He calls his own sheep by name, and leads them out. 4When he has brought out all that belong to him, he goes on ahead of them. The sheep follow him, because they know his voice. 5They won't follow a stranger; instead, they will run away from him, because they don't know the stranger's voice.'

6Jesus spoke this parable to them, but they didn't understand what it was he was saying to them.

7So he spoke to them again.

'I'm telling you the solemn truth,' he said. 'I am the gate of the sheep. 8All the people who came before me were thieves and brigands, but the sheep didn't listen to them. 9I am the gate. If anyone comes in by me, they will be safe, and will go in and out and find pasture. 10The thief only comes to steal, and kill, and destroy. I came so that they could have life – yes, and have it full to overflowing.'

The shepherd and the sheep

11'I am the good shepherd,' Jesus continued. 'The good shepherd lays down his life for the sheep. 12But supposing there's a hired servant, who isn't himself the shepherd, and who doesn't himself own the sheep. He will see the wolf coming, and leave the sheep, and run away. Then the wolf will snatch the sheep and scatter them. 13He'll run away because he's only a hired servant, and doesn't care about the sheep.

14'I am the good shepherd. I know my own sheep, and my own know me – 15just as the father knows me and I know the father. And I lay down my life for the sheep. 16And I have other sheep, too, which don't belong to this sheepfold. I must bring them, too, and they will hear my voice. Then there will be one flock, and one shepherd.

17'That's why the father loves me, because I lay down my life, so that I can take it again. 18Nobody takes it from me; I lay it down of my own accord. I have the right to lay it down, and I have the right to receive it back again. This is the command I received from my father.'

The Messiah and the father

19So there was again a division among the Judaeans because of what Jesus had said.

20'He's demon-possessed!' some were saying. 'He's raving mad! Why listen to him?'

21'No,' said some others, 'that's not how demon-possessed people talk. Anyway, how could a demon open a blind man's eyes?'

22It was the Feast of the Dedication in Jerusalem. It was winter, 23and Jesus was walking in the Temple, in Solomon's Porch. 24The Judaeans surrounded him.

'How much longer are you going to keep us in suspense?' they asked. 'If you are the Messiah, say so out loud!'

25'I told you,' replied Jesus, 'and you didn't believe. The works which I'm doing in my father's name give evidence about me. 26But you don't believe, because you don't belong to my sheep. 27'My sheep hear my voice. I know them, and they follow me. 28I give them the life of the coming age. They will never, ever perish, and nobody can snatch them out of my hand. 29My father, who has given them to me, is greater than all, and nobody can snatch them out of my father's hand. 30I and the father are one.'

Blasphemy!

31So the Judaeans once more picked up stones to stone him.

³²'I've shown you many fine deeds from the father,' Jesus replied to them. 'Which of these deeds are you stoning me for?'

³³'We're not stoning you for good deeds,' replied the Judaeans, 'but because of blasphemy! Here you are, a mere man, and you're making yourself into God!'

³⁴'It's written in your law, isn't it,' replied Jesus to them, '"I said, you are gods?" ³⁵Well, if the law calls people "gods", people to whom God's word came (and you can't set the Bible aside), ³⁶how can you accuse someone of blasphemy when the father has placed him apart and sent him into the world, and he says, "I am the son of God"?

³⁷'If I'm not doing the works of my father, don't believe me. ³⁸But if I am doing them, well – even if you don't believe me, believe the works! That way you will know and grasp that the father is in me, and I am in the father.'

³⁹So again they tried to arrest him. But Jesus managed to get away from them.

⁴⁰He went off once more across the Jordan, to the place where John had been baptizing at the beginning, and he stayed there. ⁴¹Several people came to him.

'John never did any signs,' they said, 'but everything that John said about this man was true.'

⁴²And many believed in him there.

The death of Lazarus

11 There was a man in Bethany named Lazarus, and he became ill. Bethany was the village of Mary and her sister Martha. (²This was the Mary who anointed the Lord with myrrh, and wiped his feet with her hair; Lazarus, who was ill, was her brother.)

³So the sisters sent messengers to Jesus.

'Master,' they said, 'the man you love is ill.'

⁴When Jesus got the message, he said, 'This illness won't lead to death. It's all about the glory of God! The son of God will be glorified through it.'

⁵Now Jesus loved Martha, and her sister, and Lazarus. ⁶So when he heard that he was ill, he stayed where he was, to begin with, for two days.

⁷Then, after that, he said to the disciples, 'Let's go back to Judaea.'

⁸'Teacher,' replied the disciples, 'the Judaeans were trying to stone you just now! Surely you don't want to go back *there*!'

⁹'There are twelve hours in the day, aren't there?' replied Jesus. 'If you walk in the day, you won't trip up, because you'll see the light of this world. ¹⁰But if anyone walks in the night, they will trip up, because there is no light in them.'

¹¹When he had said this, Jesus added: 'Our friend Lazarus has fallen asleep. But I'm going to wake him up.'

¹²'Master,' replied the disciples, 'if he's asleep, he'll be all right.'

(¹³They thought he was referring to ordinary sleep; but Jesus had in fact been speaking of his death.)

¹⁴Then Jesus spoke to them plainly.

'Lazarus,' he said, 'is dead. ¹⁵Actually, I'm glad I wasn't there, for your sakes; it will help your faith. But let's go to him.'

¹⁶Thomas, whose name was the Twin, addressed the other disciples.

'Let's go too,' he said. 'We may as well die with him.'

The resurrection and the life

¹⁷So when Jesus arrived, he found that Lazarus had already been in the tomb for four days. ¹⁸Bethany was near Jerusalem, about two miles away. ¹⁹Many of the Judaeans had come to Martha and Mary to console them about their brother.

²⁰When Martha heard that Jesus had arrived, she went to meet him. Mary, meanwhile, stayed sitting at home.

²¹'Master!' said Martha to Jesus. 'If only you'd been here! Then my brother wouldn't have died! ²²But even now I know that God will give you whatever you ask him for.'

²³'Your brother will rise again,' replied Jesus.

²⁴'I know he'll rise again,' said Martha, 'in the resurrection on the last day.'

²⁵'I am the resurrection and the life,' replied Jesus. 'Anyone who believes in me will live, even if they die. ²⁶And anyone who lives and believes in me will never, ever die. Do you believe this?'

²⁷'Yes, Master,' she said. 'This is what I've come to believe: that you are the Messiah, the

son of God, the one who was to come into the world.'

Jesus goes to the tomb

²⁸With these words, Martha went back and called her sister Mary.

'The teacher has come,' she said to her privately, 'and he's asking for you.'

²⁹When she heard that, she got up quickly and went to him. ³⁰Jesus hadn't yet got into the village. He was still in the place where Martha had met him.

³¹The Judaeans who were in the house with Mary, consoling her, saw her get up quickly and go out. They guessed that she was going to the tomb to weep there, and they followed her.

³²When Mary came to where Jesus was, she saw him and fell down at his feet.

'Master!' she said. 'If only you'd been here, my brother wouldn't have died!'

³³When Jesus saw her crying, and the Judaeans who had come with her crying, he was deeply stirred in his spirit, and very troubled.

³⁴'Where have you laid him?' he asked.

'Master,' they said, 'come and see.'

³⁵Jesus burst into tears.

³⁶'Look,' said the Judaeans, 'see how much he loved him!'

³⁷'Well, yes,' some of them said, 'but he opened the eyes of a blind man, didn't he? Couldn't he have done something to stop this fellow from dying?'

The raising of Lazarus

³⁸Jesus was once again deeply troubled within himself. He came to the tomb. It was a cave, and a stone was placed in front of it.

³⁹'Take away the stone,' said Jesus.

'But, Master,' said Martha, the dead man's sister, 'there'll be a smell! It's the fourth day already!'

⁴⁰'Didn't I tell you,' said Jesus, 'that if you believed you would see God's glory?'

⁴¹So they took the stone away.

Jesus lifted up his eyes.

'Thank you, father,' he said, 'for hearing me! ⁴²I know you always hear me, but I've said this because of the crowd standing around, so that they may believe that you sent me.'

⁴³With these words, he gave a loud shout: 'Lazarus – come out!'

⁴⁴And the dead man came out. He was tied up, hand and foot, with strips of linen, and his face was wrapped in a cloth.

'Untie him,' said Jesus, 'and let him go.'

⁴⁵The result of all this was that several of the Judaeans who had come to Mary, and who had seen what he had done, believed in him. ⁴⁶But some of them went off to the Pharisees and told them what Jesus had done.

The plan of Caiaphas

⁴⁷So the chief priests and the Pharisees called an assembly.

'What are we going to do?' they asked. 'This man is performing lots of signs. ⁴⁸If we let him go on like this, everyone is going to believe in him! Then the Romans will come and take away our holy place, and our nation!'

⁴⁹But one of them, Caiaphas, the high priest that year, addressed them.

'You know nothing at all!' he said. ⁵⁰'You haven't worked it out! This is what's best for you: let one man die for the people, rather than the whole nation being wiped out.'

⁵¹He didn't say this of his own accord. Since he was high priest that year, it was a prophecy. It meant that Jesus would die for the nation; ⁵²and not only for the nation, but to gather into one the scattered children of God. ⁵³So from that day on they plotted how to kill him.

⁵⁴So Jesus didn't go around openly any longer among the Judaeans. He went away from there to the region by the desert, to a town called Ephraim. He stayed there with the disciples.

⁵⁵The time came for the Judaeans' Passover. Lots of people went up to Jerusalem from the countryside, before the Passover, to purify themselves. ⁵⁶They were looking for Jesus. As they stood there in the Temple, they were discussing him with one another.

'What d'you think?' they were saying. 'Do you suppose he won't come to the festival?'

⁵⁷The chief priests and the Pharisees had given the order that if anyone knew where he was, they should tell them, so that they could arrest him.

Mary and her ointment

12 Six days before the Passover, Jesus came to Bethany. Lazarus was there, the man he had raised from the dead. ²So they made a dinner for him there. Martha served, and Lazarus was among the company at table with him.

³Then Mary took a pound of very expensive perfume, made of pure nard. She anointed Jesus' feet with it, and wiped his feet with her hair. The house was filled with the smell of the perfume.

⁴At this, Judas Iscariot, one of his disciples (the one who was going to betray him), spoke up.

⁵'Why wasn't this ointment sold?' he asked. 'It would have fetched a year's wages! You could have given it to the poor!'

(⁶He didn't say this because he cared for the poor, but because he was a thief. He kept the common purse, and used to help himself to what was in it.)

⁷'Let her alone,' replied Jesus. 'She's been keeping it for the day of my burial! ⁸You always have the poor with you, but you won't always have me.'

Jesus enters Jerusalem

⁹When the great crowd of Judaeans discovered that Jesus was there, they came to Bethany not just because of Jesus, but to see Lazarus, the one he had raised from the dead. ¹⁰So the chief priests planned to kill Lazarus as well, ¹¹because many of the Judaeans were leaving their side on account of him, and were believing in Jesus.

¹²On the next day, the large crowd that had come up for the festival heard that Jesus had come to Jerusalem. ¹³They took palm branches and went out to meet him.

'Hosanna!' they shouted. 'Welcome in the name of the Lord! Welcome to Israel's king!'

¹⁴Jesus found a little donkey and sat on it. As the Bible says,

¹⁵Do not fear, daughter of Zion!
 Look! Your king is coming now;
 sitting on a donkey's colt.

¹⁶His disciples didn't understand this to begin with. But when Jesus was glorified, they remembered that these things had been written about him, and that these things had been done to him. ¹⁷The crowd that was with him when he called Lazarus out of the tomb, and raised him from the dead, told their story. ¹⁸That's why the crowd went out to meet him, because they heard that he had done this sign.

¹⁹The Pharisees conferred.

'You see?' they said to each other. 'It's impossible. There's nothing you can do. Look – the world has gone off after him!'

The seed must die

²⁰Some Greeks had come up with all the others to worship at the festival. ²¹They went to Philip, who was from Bethsaida in Galilee.

'Sir,' they said, 'we would like to see Jesus.'

²²Philip went and told Andrew, and Andrew and Philip went together to tell Jesus.

²³'The time has come,' said Jesus in reply. 'This is the moment for the son of man to be glorified. ²⁴I'm telling you the solemn truth: unless a grain of wheat falls into the earth and dies, it remains all by itself. If it dies, though, it will produce lots of fruit. ²⁵If you love your life, you'll lose it. If you hate your life in this world, you'll keep it for the life of the coming age.

²⁶'If anyone serves me, they must follow me. Where I am, my servant will be too. If anyone serves me, the father will honour them.'

The hour has come

²⁷'Now my heart is troubled,' Jesus went on. 'What am I going to say? "Father, save me from this moment?" No! It was because of this that I came to this moment. ²⁸Father, glorify your name!'

'I have glorified it,' came a voice from heaven, 'and I will glorify it again.'

²⁹'That was thunder!' said the crowd, standing there listening.

'No,' said others. 'It was an angel, talking to him.'

³⁰'That voice came for your sake, not mine,' replied Jesus. ³¹'Now comes the judgment of this world! Now this world's ruler is going to be thrown out! ³²And when I've been lifted up from the earth, I will draw all people to myself.'

³³He said this in order to point to the kind of death he was going to die.

³⁴So the crowd spoke to him again.

'We heard in the law,' they said, 'that the Messiah will last for ever. How can you say that the son of man must be lifted up? Who is this "son of man"?'

³⁵'The light is among you a little while longer,' replied Jesus. 'Keep walking while you have the light, in case the darkness overcomes you. People who walk in the dark don't know where they're going. ³⁶While you have the light, believe in the light, so that you may be children of light.'

With these words, Jesus went away and was hidden from them.

Glory and blindness

³⁷They didn't believe in him, even though he had done so many signs in front of their eyes. ³⁸This was so that the word of Isaiah the prophet might be fulfilled:

> Lord, who believed the story we told?
> Your powerful arm – who saw it unveiled?

³⁹That's why they couldn't believe. As Isaiah again put it,

> ⁴⁰He has caused their eyes to be blind,
> and caused their hearts to be hard;
> so they wouldn't see with their eyes,
> or understand with their hearts,
> or turn, so that I could heal them.

⁴¹Isaiah said this because he saw his glory, and spoke about him.

⁴²Even so, however, quite a few of the rulers did believe in him. But, because of the Pharisees, they didn't declare their faith, for fear of being put out of the synagogue. ⁴³This was because they loved the praise of other people more than the praise of God.

The final challenge

⁴⁴'Anyone who believes in me,' shouted Jesus in a loud voice, 'doesn't believe in me, but in the one who sent me! ⁴⁵Anyone who sees me sees the one who sent me! ⁴⁶I've come into the world as light, so that everyone who believes in me won't need to stay in the dark.

⁴⁷'If anyone hears my words and doesn't keep them, I'm not going to judge them. That wasn't why I came. I came to save the world, not to judge it. ⁴⁸Anyone who rejects me and doesn't hold on to my words has a judge. The word which I have spoken will judge them on the last day.

⁴⁹'I haven't spoken on my own authority. The father who sent me gave me his own command about what I should say and speak. ⁵⁰And I know that his command is the life of the coming age. What I speak, then, is what the father has told me to speak.'

Washing the disciples' feet

13 It was before the festival of Passover. Jesus knew that his time had come, the time for him to leave this world and go to the father. He had always loved his own people in the world; now he loved them right through to the end.

²It was supper-time. The devil had already put the idea of betraying him into the heart of Judas, son of Simon Iscariot. ³Jesus knew that the father had given everything into his hands, and that he had come from God and was going to God. ⁴So he got up from the supper-table, took off his clothes, and wrapped a towel around himself. ⁵Then he poured water into a bowl, and began to wash the disciples' feet, and to wipe them with the towel he was wrapped in.

⁶He came to Simon Peter.

'Master,' said Peter, 'what's this? You, washing my feet?'

⁷'You don't understand yet what I'm doing,' replied Jesus, 'but you'll know afterwards.'

⁸'I'm not going to have you washing my feet!' said Peter. 'Never!'

'If I don't wash you,' replied Jesus, 'you don't belong to me.'

⁹'All right then, Master,' said Simon Peter, 'but not only my feet – wash my hands and my head as well!'

¹⁰'Someone who has washed,' said Jesus to him, 'doesn't need to wash again, except for their feet. They are clean all over. And you are clean – but not all of you.'

[11]Jesus knew, you see, who was going to betray him. That's why he said, 'You are not all clean.'

Like master, like servant

[12]So when he had washed their feet, he put on his clothes and sat down again.

'Do you know what I've done to you?' he asked. [13]'You call me "teacher", and "master", and you're right. That's what I am. [14]Well, then: if I, as your master and teacher, washed your feet just now, you should wash each other's feet. [15]I've given you a pattern, so that you can do things in the same way that I did to you.

[16]'I'm telling you the solemn truth,' he continued. 'The slave isn't greater than the master. People who are sent are not greater than the person who sends them. [17]If you know these things, God's blessing on you if you do them.

[18]'I'm not talking about all of you,' he went on. 'I know the ones I have chosen. What the Bible says has to come true: "The person who ate my bread lifted up his heel against me." [19]I'm telling you this now, before it happens, so that when it does happen you may believe that I am who I am. [20]I'm telling you the solemn truth: anyone who welcomes someone I send, welcomes me, and anyone who welcomes me, welcomes the one who sent me.'

Judas goes out

[21]After saying this, Jesus was troubled in spirit. He told them why.

'I'm telling you the solemn truth,' he said. 'One of you will betray me.'

[22]The disciples looked at each other in shock, wondering who he could be talking about. [23]One of the disciples, the one Jesus specially loved, was reclining at table close beside him. [24]Simon Peter motioned to him to ask who it was he was talking about. [25]So, leaning back against Jesus' chest, he asked him, 'Who is it, Master?'

[26]'It's the one I'm going to give this piece of bread to,' said Jesus, 'when I've dipped it in the dish.'

So he dipped the piece of bread, and gave it to Judas, son of Simon Iscariot. [27]After the bread, the satan entered into him.

'Do it quickly, won't you?' said Jesus to him.

[28]None of the others at the table knew what he meant. [29]Because Judas kept the common purse, some were thinking that he meant, 'Buy what we need for the festival', or that he was to give something to the poor.

[30]So when Judas had taken the bread, he went out at once. It was night.

Love one another

[31]When Judas had gone out, Jesus began to speak.

'Now the son of man is glorified!' he said. 'Now God is glorified in him! [32]And if God is glorified in him, God will glorify him in himself, and glorify him at once. [33]Children, I'm only with you a little longer. You will look for me, and, as I said to the Judaeans that where I was going they couldn't come, so I'm saying the same to you now.

[34]'I'm giving you a new commandment, and it's this: love one another! Just as I have loved you, so you must love one another. [35]This is how everybody will know that you are my disciples, if you have love for each other.'

[36]Simon Peter spoke up.

'Master,' he said, 'where are you going?'

'Where I'm going', replied Jesus, 'you can't follow me just now. You will follow later, though.'

[37]'Master,' Peter replied, 'why can't I follow you now? I will lay down my life for you!'

[38]'Will you really lay down your life for me?' smiled Jesus. 'I'm telling you the solemn truth: by the time the cock crows you will have disowned me three times.'

The way, the truth, the life

14 'Don't let your hearts be troubled,' Jesus continued. 'Trust God – and trust me, too! [2]There is plenty of room to live in my father's house. If that wasn't the case, I'd have told you, wouldn't I? I'm going to get a place ready for you! [3]And if I do go and get a place ready for you, I will come back and take you to be with me, so that you can be there, where I am. [4]And as to where I'm going – you know the way!'

⁵'Actually, Master,' said Thomas to him, 'we don't know where you're going, so how can we know the way?'

⁶'I am the way,' replied Jesus, 'and the truth and the life! Nobody comes to the father except through me. ⁷If you had known me, you would have known my father. From now on you do know him! You have seen him.'

⁸'Just show us the father, then, Master,' said Philip to Jesus, 'and that'll be good enough for us!'

⁹'Have I been with you for such a long time, Philip,' replied Jesus, 'and still you don't know me? Anyone who has seen me has seen the father! How can you say, "Show us the father"? ¹⁰Don't you believe that I am in the father, and the father is in me? The words I'm speaking to you, I'm not speaking on my own initiative. It's the father, who lives within me, who is doing his own works. ¹¹You must trust me that I am in the father and the father is in me. If not, then trust because of all the things you've seen done.'

Another helper

¹²'I'm telling you the solemn truth,' Jesus continued. 'Anyone who trusts in me will also do the works that I'm doing. In fact, they will do greater works than these, because I'm going to the father! ¹³And whatever you ask in my name, I will do it, so that the father may be glorified in the son. ¹⁴If you ask anything in my name, I will do it.

¹⁵'If you love me,' he went on, 'you will keep my commands. ¹⁶And I will ask the father, and he will give you another helper, to be with you for ever. ¹⁷This other helper is the spirit of truth. The world can't receive him, because it doesn't see him or know him. But you know him, because he lives with you, and will be in you.

¹⁸'I'm not going to leave you bereft. I am coming to you. ¹⁹Not long from now, the world won't see me any more; but you will see me. Because I live, you will live too. ²⁰On that day you will know that I am in my father, and you in me, and I in you.

²¹'Anyone who has my commandments and keeps them – that's the person who loves me. Anyone who loves me will be loved by my father, and I will love them and show myself to them.'

My peace I give to you

²²Judas spoke up. (This was the other Judas, not Iscariot.)

'Master,' he said, 'how will it be that you will show yourself to us and not to the world?'

²³'If anyone loves me,' Jesus replied, 'they will keep my word. My father will love them, and we will come to them and make our home with them. ²⁴Anyone who doesn't love me won't keep my word. And the word which you hear isn't mine. It comes from the father, who sent me.

²⁵'I've said all this to you while I'm here with you. ²⁶But the helper, the holy spirit, the one the father will send in my name, he will teach you everything. He will bring back to your mind everything I've said to you.

²⁷'I'm leaving you peace. I'm giving you my own peace. I don't give gifts in the way the world does. Don't let your hearts be troubled; don't be fearful. ²⁸You heard that I said to you, "I'm going away, and I'm coming back to you." If you loved me, you would be happy that I'm going to the father – because the father is greater than me. ²⁹And now I've told you before it happens, so that when it does happen, you may believe.

³⁰'I haven't got much more to say to you. The ruler of the world is coming. He has nothing to do with me. ³¹But all this is happening so that the world may know that I love the father, and that I'm doing what the father has told me to do.

'Get up. Let's be going.'

The true vine

15 'I am the true vine,' said Jesus, 'and my father is the gardener. ²He cuts off every branch of mine that doesn't bear fruit; and he prunes every branch that does bear fruit, so that it can bear more fruit. ³You are already clean. That's because of the word that I've spoken to you.

⁴'Remain in me, and I will remain in you! The branch can't bear fruit by itself, but only if it remains in the vine. In the same way, you

can't bear fruit unless you remain in me. ⁵I am the vine, you are the branches. People who remain in me, and I in them, are the ones who bear plenty of fruit. Without me, you see, you can't do anything.

⁶'If people don't remain in me, they are thrown out, like a branch, and they wither. People collect the branches and put them on the fire, and they are burned. ⁷If you remain in me, and my words remain in you, ask for whatever you want, and it will happen for you. ⁸My father is glorified in this: that you bear plenty of fruit, and so become my disciples.'

Obeying and loving

⁹'As the father loved me,' Jesus continued, 'so I loved you. Remain in my love. ¹⁰If you keep my commands, you will remain in my love, just as I have kept my father's commands, and remain in his love. ¹¹I've said these things to you so that my joy may be in you, and so that your joy may be full.

¹²'This is my command: love one another, in the same way that I loved you. ¹³No one has a love greater than this, to lay down your life for your friends. ¹⁴You are my friends, if you do what I tell you. ¹⁵I'm not calling you "servants" any longer; servants don't know what their master is doing. But I've called you "friends", because I've let you know everything I heard from my father.

¹⁶'You didn't choose me. I chose you, and I appointed you to go and bear fruit, fruit that will last. Then the father will give you whatever you ask in my name. ¹⁷This is my command to you: love one another.'

If the world hates you

¹⁸'If the world hates you,' Jesus went on, 'know that it hated me before it hated you. ¹⁹If you were from the world, the world would be fond of its own. But the world hates you for this reason: that you're not from the world. No: I chose you out of the world.

²⁰'Remember the word that I said to you: servants are not greater than their masters. If they persecuted me, they will persecute you too. If they kept my word, they will keep yours too. ²¹But they will do all these things to you because of my name, because they don't know the one who sent me.

²²'If I hadn't come and spoken to them, they wouldn't be guilty of sin. But now they have no excuse for their sin. ²³(Anyone who hates me, hates my father as well!) ²⁴If I hadn't done, there in the middle of them, the works which nobody else did, they wouldn't be guilty of sin. But now they have seen me, and my father – and they've hated us both! ²⁵All this has happened, however, so that the word written in their law might be fulfilled: "They hated me for no reason."

²⁶'When the helper comes – the one I shall send you from the father, the spirit of truth who comes from the father – he will give evidence about me. ²⁷And you will give evidence as well, because you have been with me from the start.'

The spirit and the world

16 'I've said these things to you', Jesus went on, 'to stop you from being tripped up. ²They will put you out of the synagogues. In fact, the time is coming when anyone who kills you will suppose that they are in that way offering worship to God. ³They will do these things because they haven't known the father, or me. ⁴But I have been talking to you about these things so that, when their time comes, you will remember that I told you about them.

'I didn't say these things to you from the start, because I was with you. ⁵But now I'm going to the one who sent me. None of you asks me, "Where are you going?" ⁶But because I've said these things to you, sorrow has filled your heart. ⁷However, it's the truth that I'm telling you: it's better for you that I should go away. If I don't go away, you see, the helper won't come to you. But if I go away, I will send him to you.

⁸'When he comes, he will prove the world to be in the wrong on three counts: sin, justice and judgment. ⁹In relation to sin – because they don't believe in me. ¹⁰In relation to justice – because I'm going to the father, and you won't see me any more. ¹¹In relation to judgment – because the ruler of this world is judged.'

Your hearts will rejoice

¹²'There are many things I still have to say to you,' Jesus continued, 'but you're not yet strong enough to take them. ¹³When the spirit of truth comes, though, he will guide you in all the truth. He won't speak on his own account, you see, but he will speak whatever he hears. He will announce to you what's to come. ¹⁴He will glorify me, because he will take what belongs to me and will announce it to you. ¹⁵Everything that the father has is mine. That's why I said that he would take what is mine and announce it to you.

¹⁶'Not long from now, you won't see me any more. Then again, not long after that, you will see me!'

¹⁷'What's he talking about?' some of his disciples asked each other. 'What's this business about "not long from now, you won't see me, and again not long after that you will see me"? And what's this about "going to the father"?'

¹⁸They kept on saying it.

'What is this "not long"?'

'What's it all about?'

'We don't know what he means!'

¹⁹Jesus knew that they wanted to ask him. 'You're discussing with each other what I meant, aren't you?' he said. 'You want to know what I meant by saying, "Not long from now, you won't see me; and then again, not long after that, you will see me." That's it, isn't it? ²⁰Well, I'm going to tell you the solemn truth.

'You will weep and wail, but the world will celebrate. You will be overcome with sorrow, but your sorrow will turn into joy. ²¹When a woman is giving birth she is in anguish, because her moment has come. But when the child is born, she no longer remembers the suffering, because of the joy that a human being has been born into the world. ²²In the same way, you have sorrow now. But I shall see you again, and your hearts will celebrate, and nobody will take your joy away from you.'

Ask, and you will receive

²³'On that day,' Jesus went on, 'you won't ask me for anything. I'm telling you the solemn truth: whatever you ask the father in my name, he will give you. ²⁴Up to now, you haven't asked for anything in my name. Ask, and you will receive, so that your joy may be full!

²⁵'I've been saying all this to you in picture-language. The time is coming when I won't speak in pictures any more. Instead, I'll tell you about the father quite plainly. ²⁶On that day you will ask in my name. I won't say I will ask the father on your behalf, ²⁷because the father himself loves you! That's because you have loved me, and have believed that I came from God. ²⁸I came from the father, and I've come into the world. Now I'm leaving the world, and going back to the father.'

²⁹'Ah!' said his disciples. 'Now you're speaking plainly! You're not talking in pictures. ³⁰Now we know that you know all things, and you don't need to have anybody ask you anything. This makes us trust that you came from God.'

³¹'So you do now believe, do you?' replied Jesus. ³²'Look here: the time is coming (in fact, it's now arrived!) when you will be scattered, each of you to his own place. You will leave me alone – though I'm not alone, because the father is with me. ³³I've said these things to you so that you can have peace in me. You'll have trouble in the world. But cheer up! I have defeated the world!'

Glorify the son

17 After Jesus had said this, he lifted up his eyes to heaven.

'Father,' he said, 'the moment has come. Glorify your son, so that your son may glorify you. ²Do this in the same way as you did when you gave him authority over all flesh, so that he could give the life of God's coming age to everyone you gave him. ³And by "the life of God's coming age" I mean this: that they should know you, the only true God, and Jesus the Messiah, the one you sent.

⁴'I glorified you on earth, by completing the work you gave me to do. ⁵So now, father, glorify me, alongside yourself, with the glory which I had with you before the world existed.

⁶'I revealed your name to the people you gave me out of the world. They belonged to you; you gave them to me; and they have kept your word. ⁷Now they know that everything which you gave me comes from you. ⁸I have

given them the words you gave me, and they have received them. They have come to know, in truth, that I came from you. They have believed that you sent me.'

Jesus prays for his people

⁹'I'm praying for them. I'm not praying for the world, but for the people you've given me. They belong to you. ¹⁰All mine are yours; all yours are mine; and I'm glorified in them.

¹¹'I'm not in the world any longer, but they're still in the world; I'm coming to you. Holy father, keep them in your name, the name you've given to me, so that they may be one, just as we are one.

¹²'When I was with them, I kept them in your name, the name you've given me. I guarded them, and none of them has been destroyed (except the son of destruction; that's what the Bible said would happen). ¹³But now I'm coming to you. I'm speaking these things in the world, so that they can have my joy fulfilled in them.

¹⁴'I have given them your word. The world hated them, because they are not from the world, just as I am not from the world. ¹⁵I'm not asking that you should take them out of the world, but that you should keep them from the evil one. ¹⁶They didn't come from the world, just as I didn't come from the world. ¹⁷Set them apart for yourself in the truth; your word is truth. ¹⁸Just as you sent me into the world, so I sent them into the world. ¹⁹And on their account I set myself apart for you, so that they, too, may be set apart for you in the truth.'

That they may be one

²⁰'I'm not praying simply for them. I'm praying, too, for the people who will come to believe in me because of their word. ²¹I am praying that they may all be one – just as you, father, are in me, and I in you, that they too may be in us, so that the world may believe that you sent me.

²²'I have given them the glory which you have given to me, so that they may be one, just as we are one. ²³I in them, and you in me; yes, they must be completely one, so that the world may know that you sent me, and that you loved them just as you loved me.

²⁴'Father, I want the ones you've given me to be with me where I am. I want them to see my glory, the glory which you've given me, because you loved me before the foundation of the world.

²⁵'Righteous father, even the world didn't know you. But I have known you, and these ones have known that you sent me. ²⁶I made your name known to them – yes, and I will make it known; so that the love with which you loved me may be in them, and I in them.'

The arrest of Jesus

18 With these words, Jesus went out with his disciples across the Kidron valley to a place where there was a garden. He and his disciples went in.

²Judas, his betrayer, knew the place, because Jesus often used it as a meeting-place with his disciples. ³So Judas took a band of soldiers, with some servants of the chief priests and the Pharisees, and came there with torches, lights and weapons.

⁴Jesus knew everything that was going to happen to him. He went out to meet them.

'Who are you looking for?' he asked.

⁵'Jesus of Nazareth,' they answered.

'I'm the one,' he said to them.

Judas, his betrayer, was standing there with them. ⁶So when he said, 'I'm the one,' they went back a few paces, and fell down on the ground.

⁷Jesus repeated his question.

'Who are you looking for?' he asked.

'Jesus of Nazareth,' they said.

⁸'I told you, I'm the one!' said Jesus. 'So, if you're looking for me, let these people go.' (⁹He said this so as to fulfil the word he had spoken, when he said, 'I haven't lost any of the people you gave me.')

¹⁰Simon Peter had a sword. He drew it and hit the high priest's servant, cutting off his right ear. The servant's name was Malchus.

¹¹'Put your sword back in its sheath!' said Jesus to Peter. 'Do you imagine I'm not going to drink the cup my father has given me?'

¹²So the band of soldiers, with the officer and the Judaean attendants, arrested Jesus and tied him up. ¹³They led him off first to Annas; he was the father-in-law of Caiaphas, who was high priest that year. ¹⁴It was Caiaphas who had

given advice to the Judaeans that the best thing would be for one man to die for the people.

Peter denies Jesus

¹⁵Simon Peter and another disciple followed Jesus. That other disciple was known to the high priest; he went in to the high priest's courtyard along with Jesus, ¹⁶while Peter stood outside by the gate. So the other disciple, being known to the high priest, went out and spoke to the woman on the gate. Then he brought Peter inside.

¹⁷The woman on the gate spoke to Peter.

'You're not one of that man's disciples too, are you?' she asked.

'No, I'm not,' he replied.

¹⁸It was cold. The slaves and the attendants had made a charcoal fire, and they were standing round it, warming themselves. Peter was standing there with them and warming himself.

¹⁹The high priest asked Jesus about his disciples, and about his teaching.

²⁰'I've spoken to the world quite openly,' replied Jesus. 'I always taught in the synagogue and in the Temple, where all the Judaeans gather. I didn't say anything in secret. ²¹Why are you asking me? There were people who listened to me. Ask them what I said to them. Don't you see? They know what I said.'

²²When Jesus said that, one of the attendants standing there gave him a slap on the face.

'Is that how you answer the high priest?' he said.

²³'If I've said something wrong,' replied Jesus, 'give evidence about what was wrong with it. But if what I said was true, why are you hitting me?'

²⁴So Annas sent him off, still tied up, to Caiaphas the high priest.

²⁵Simon Peter, meanwhile, was standing there and warming himself.

'You're not one of his disciples, are you?' they asked him.

He denied it. 'No, I'm not,' he said.

²⁶Then one of the high priest's slaves, a relative of the man whose ear Peter had cut off, spoke up.

'Didn't I see you in the garden with him?' he said.

²⁷Peter denied it once more. Instantly, the cock crowed.

Pilate and the Judaeans

²⁸So they took Jesus from Caiaphas to the Praetorium, the governor's residence. It was early in the morning. They didn't themselves go inside the Praetorium. They were anxious not to pollute themselves, so that they would still be able to eat the Passover.

²⁹So Pilate went outside and spoke to them.

'What's the charge, then?' he asked. 'What have you got against this fellow?'

³⁰'If he wasn't doing wicked things,' they replied, 'we wouldn't have handed him over to you.'

³¹'Take him yourselves,' said Pilate to them, 'and judge him by your own law.'

'We're not allowed to put anyone to death,' replied the Judaeans. ³²(This was so that the word of Jesus might come true, when he had indicated what sort of death he was going to die.)

My kingdom is not from this world

³³So Pilate went back in to the Praetorium and spoke to Jesus.

'Are you the King of the Jews?' he asked.

³⁴'Was it *your* idea to ask that?' asked Jesus. 'Or did other people tell you about me?'

³⁵'I'm not a Jew, am I?' retorted Pilate. 'Your own people, and the chief priests, have handed you over to me! What have you done?'

³⁶'My kingdom isn't the sort that grows in this world,' replied Jesus. 'If my kingdom were from this world, my supporters would have fought, to stop me being handed over to the Judaeans. So then, my kingdom is not the sort that comes from here.'

³⁷'So!' said Pilate. 'You *are* a king, are you?'

'You're the one who's calling me a king,' replied Jesus. 'I was born for this; I've come into the world for this: to give evidence about the truth. Everyone who belongs to the truth listens to my voice.'

³⁸'Truth!' said Pilate. 'What's that?'

With those words, he went back out to the Judaeans.

'I find this man not guilty!' he said to them. ³⁹'But look here: you've got this custom that I should let someone free at Passover-time. So what about it? Would you like me to release "The King of the Jews"?'

⁴⁰'No!' they shouted. 'We don't want him! Give us Barabbas!'

Now Barabbas was a brigand.

Here's the man!

19 So Pilate then took Jesus and had him flogged. ²The soldiers wove a crown of thorns, put it on his head, and dressed him up in a purple robe. ³Then they came up to him and said, 'Hail, King of the Jews!' And they slapped him.

⁴Pilate went out again.

'Look,' he said to them, 'I'm bringing him out to you, so that you'll know I find no guilt in him.'

⁵So Jesus came out, wearing the crown of thorns and the purple cloak.

'Look!' said Pilate. 'Here's the man!'

⁶So when the chief priests and their attendants saw him, they gave a great shout.

'Crucify him!' they yelled. 'Crucify him!'

'Take him yourselves and crucify him!' said Pilate. 'I find him not guilty!'

⁷'We've got a law,' replied the Judaeans, 'and according to that law he deserves to die! He made himself the son of God!'

No king but Caesar

⁸When Pilate heard that, he was all the more afraid. ⁹He went back into the Praetorium and spoke to Jesus.

'Where do you come from?' he asked.

But Jesus gave him no answer.

¹⁰So Pilate addressed him again.

'Aren't you going to speak to me?' he said. 'Don't you know that I have the authority to let you go, and the authority to crucify you?'

¹¹'You couldn't have any authority at all over me,' replied Jesus, 'unless it was given to you from above. That's why the person who handed me over to you is guilty of a greater sin.'

¹²From that moment on, Pilate tried to let him go.

But the Judaeans shouted at him.

'If you let this fellow go,' they said, 'you are no friend of Caesar! Everyone who sets himself up as a king is speaking against Caesar!'

¹³So when Pilate heard them saying that, he brought Jesus out and sat down at the official judgment seat, called The Pavement (in Hebrew, 'Gabbatha'). ¹⁴It was the Preparation Day of the Passover, and it was about midday.

'Look,' said Pilate, 'here is your king!'

¹⁵'Take him away!' they shouted. 'Take him away! Crucify him!'

'Do you want me to crucify your king?' asked Pilate.

'We have no king', the chief priests replied, 'except Caesar!'

¹⁶Then he handed him over to them to be crucified.

The King of the Jews

So they took Jesus away. ¹⁷He carried his own cross, and went to the spot called 'Skull Place' (in Hebrew, 'Golgotha'). ¹⁸That was where they crucified him. They also crucified two others, one on either side of him, with Jesus in the middle.

¹⁹Pilate wrote a notice and had it placed on the cross:

JESUS OF NAZARETH, THE KING OF THE JEWS

²⁰Lots of the Judaeans read this notice, because the place where Jesus was crucified was close to the city. It was written in Hebrew, Latin and Greek.

²¹So the chief priests said to Pilate, 'Don't write "The King of the Jews"! Write that he *said*, "I am the King of the Jews"!'

²²'What I've written,' replied Pilate, 'I've written.'

²³When the soldiers had crucified Jesus, they took his clothes and divided them into four parts, giving each soldier one part. When they came to his tunic, they found that it was a single piece of cloth, woven from top to bottom.

²⁴'Let's not tear it,' they said to each other. 'Let's throw lots for it, to see who's going to have it.'

This was so that the Bible would be fulfilled, when it says,

They took my clothes and divided them up,
they threw the dice to decide on my garments.

And that's what the soldiers did.

The death of Jesus

²⁵Jesus' mother was standing beside his cross. So was her sister, Mary the wife of Clopas, with Mary Magdalene too. ²⁶Jesus saw his mother, and the disciple he specially loved, standing there.

'Mother,' he said. 'Look! there's your son.'
²⁷Then he spoke to the disciple.
'Look!' he said. 'There's your mother.'
From that time, the disciple welcomed her into his own home.
²⁸After this, Jesus knew that everything had at last been completed.
'I'm thirsty,' he said (fulfilling what the Bible had said).
²⁹There was a jar there full of sour wine. So they put a sponge filled with the sour wine on a hyssop rod and lifted it to his mouth. ³⁰Jesus drank it.
'It's all done!' he said.
Then he let his head drop, and gave up his spirit.

Blood and water

³¹It was the day of Preparation. The coming sabbath was a very special one, and the Judaeans were anxious that the bodies should not remain on the cross during the sabbath. So they asked Pilate to have the legs of the crucified men broken, and their bodies taken away. ³²So the soldiers came and broke the legs of the men who were crucified with Jesus, first the one, then the other. ³³But when they came to Jesus, they saw that he was already dead, so they didn't break his legs. ³⁴Instead, one of the soldiers thrust a spear into his side, and blood and water came out. ³⁵(The one who saw it is giving evidence, and his evidence is true. He knows he's speaking the truth, so that you too may believe.) ³⁶These things, you see, came about so that the Bible might come true: 'No bone of his will be broken.' ³⁷And, again, another passage in the Bible says, 'They shall look on the one whom they pierced.'

The burial of Jesus

³⁸After this, Joseph of Arimathea asked Pilate if he could take Jesus' body away. He was a disciple of Jesus, but he kept it secret because he was afraid of the Judaeans. Pilate gave him permission. So he came and took his body. ³⁹Nicodemus came too (the man who, at first, had visited Jesus by night). He brought a concoction of myrrh and aloes, about a hundred pounds in weight. ⁴⁰They took Jesus' body, and wrapped it up in cloths with the spices, according to the normal Judaean burial custom.

⁴¹There was a garden in the place where he was crucified. In the garden, there was a new tomb in which nobody had ever been buried. ⁴²So, because the tomb was nearby, and because of the Judaean day of Preparation, they buried Jesus there.

The empty tomb

20 On the first day of the week, very early, Mary Magdalene came to the tomb while it was still dark.

She saw that the stone had been rolled away from the tomb. ²So she ran off, and went to Simon Peter, and to the other disciple, the one Jesus loved.

'They've taken the master out of the tomb!' she said. 'We don't know where they've put him!'

³So Peter and the other disciple set off and went to the tomb. ⁴Both of them ran together. The other disciple ran faster than Peter, and got to the tomb first. ⁵He stooped down and saw the linen cloths lying there, but he didn't go in. ⁶Then Simon Peter came up, following him, and went into the tomb. He saw the linen cloths lying there, ⁷and the napkin that had been around his head, not lying with the other cloths, but folded up in a place by itself.

⁸Then the other disciple, who had arrived first at the tomb, went into the tomb as well. He saw, and he believed. ⁹They did not yet know, you see, that the Bible had said he must rise again from the dead.

¹⁰Then the disciples returned to their homes.

Mary Magdalene and the risen Jesus

¹¹But Mary stood outside the tomb, crying. As she wept, she stooped down to look into the tomb. ¹²There she saw two angels, clothed in white, one at the head and one at the feet of where Jesus' body had been lying.

¹³'Woman,' they said to her, 'why are you crying?'

'They've taken away my master,' she said, 'and I don't know where they've put him!'

¹⁴As she said this she turned round, and saw Jesus standing there. She didn't know it was Jesus.

¹⁵'Woman,' Jesus said to her, 'why are you crying? Who are you looking for?'

She guessed he must be the gardener.

'Sir,' she said, 'if you've carried him off somewhere, tell me where you've put him, and I will take him away.'

¹⁶'Mary!' said Jesus.

She turned and spoke in Aramaic.

'Rabbouni!' she said (which means 'Teacher').

¹⁷'Don't cling to me,' said Jesus. 'I haven't yet gone up to the father. But go to my brothers and say to them, "I'm going up to my father and your father – to my God and your God."'

¹⁸Mary Magdalene went and told the disciples, 'I've seen the master!' and that he had said these things to her.

Jesus and the disciples

¹⁹On the evening of that day, the first day of the week, the doors were shut where the disciples were, for fear of the Judaeans. Jesus came and stood in the middle of them.

'Peace be with you,' he said.

²⁰With these words, he showed them his hands and his side. Then the disciples were overjoyed when they saw the master.

²¹'Peace be with you,' Jesus said to them again. 'As the father has sent me, so I'm sending you.'

²²With that, he breathed on them.

'Receive the holy spirit,' he said. ²³'If you forgive anyone's sins, they are forgiven. If you retain anyone's sins, they are retained.'

Jesus and Thomas

²⁴One of the Twelve, Thomas (also known as Didymus), wasn't with them when Jesus came. ²⁵So the other disciples spoke to him.

'We've seen the master!' they said.

'Unless I see the mark of the nails in his hands,' replied Thomas, 'and put my finger into the nail-marks, and put my hand into his side – I'm not going to believe!'

²⁶A week later the disciples were again in the house, and Thomas was with them. The doors were shut. Jesus came and stood in the middle of them.

'Peace be with you!' he said.

²⁷Then he addressed Thomas.

'Bring your finger here,' he said, 'and inspect my hands. Bring your hand here and put it into my side. Don't be faithless! Just believe!'

²⁸'My Lord,' replied Thomas, 'and my God!'

²⁹'Is it because you've seen me that you believe?' replied Jesus. 'God's blessing on people who don't see, and yet believe!'

³⁰Jesus did many other signs in the presence of his disciples, which aren't written in this book. ³¹But these ones are written so that you may believe that the Messiah, the son of God, is none other than Jesus; and that, with this faith, you may have life in his name.

Jesus on the beach

21 After this, Jesus showed himself again to the disciples by the sea of Tiberias. This was how he showed himself.

²Simon Peter, Thomas (known as Didymus), Nathanael from Cana in Galilee, the sons of Zebedee, and two other disciples, were all together.

³Simon Peter spoke up.

'I'm going fishing,' he said.

'We'll go with you,' they replied.

So they went off and got into the boat; but that night they caught nothing.

⁴As dawn was breaking, Jesus stood beside the seashore, but the disciples didn't know that it was Jesus.

⁵'Children,' said Jesus to them, 'haven't you got anything to eat?'

'No!' they replied.

⁶'Cast the net on the right side of the boat,' he said, 'and you'll find something.'

So they cast the net; and now they couldn't draw it in because of the weight of the fish.

⁷So the disciple that Jesus loved spoke to Peter.

'It's the master!' he said.

When Simon Peter heard that it was the master, he wrapped his cloak around him (he had been naked for work), and threw himself into the sea. ⁸The other disciples brought the boat in to land, dragging the net full of fish. They weren't far from shore, about a hundred yards away.

Breakfast by the shore

⁹When they came to land, they saw a charcoal fire laid there, with fish and bread on it.

¹⁰Jesus spoke to them.

'Bring some of the fish you've just caught,' he said.

¹¹So Simon Peter went and pulled the net onto the shore. It was full of large fish, a hundred and fifty-three in all. The net wasn't torn, even though there were so many.

¹²'Come and have breakfast,' said Jesus to them.

None of the disciples dared ask him, 'Who are you?' They knew it was the master.

¹³Jesus came and took the bread and gave it to them, and so also with the fish. ¹⁴This was now the third time that Jesus had appeared to the disciples after he had been raised from the dead.

Jesus and Peter

¹⁵So when they had eaten breakfast, Jesus spoke to Simon Peter.

'Simon, son of John,' he said, 'do you love me more than these?'

'Yes, Master,' he said. 'You know I'm your friend.'

'Well, then,' he said, 'feed my lambs.'

¹⁶'Simon, son of John,' said Jesus again, for a second time, 'do you love me?'

'Yes, Master,' he said. 'You know I'm your friend.'

'Well, then,' he said, 'look after my sheep.'

¹⁷'Simon, son of John,' said Jesus a third time, 'are you my friend?'

Peter was upset that on this third time Jesus asked, 'Are you my friend?'

'Master,' he said, 'you know everything! You know I'm your friend!'

'Well, then,' said Jesus, 'feed my sheep.

¹⁸'I'm telling you the solemn truth,' he went on. 'When you were young, you put on your own clothes and went about wherever you wanted. But when you are old, you'll stretch out your hands, and someone else will dress you up and take you where you don't want to go.'

¹⁹He said this to indicate the sort of death by which Peter would bring God glory. And when he had said this, he added, 'Follow me!'

The beloved disciple

²⁰Peter turned and saw, following them, the disciple that Jesus loved. This was the disciple who had leaned back against Jesus' chest at the supper, and had asked, 'Master, who is it that's going to betray you?'

²¹'Master,' said Peter to Jesus, seeing him there, 'what about him?'

²²'If it's my intention,' replied Jesus, 'that he should remain here until I come, what's that got to do with you? You must follow me!'

²³So the rumour went around the Christian family that this disciple wouldn't die. But Jesus didn't say he wouldn't die. What he said, rather, was this: 'If it's my intention that he should remain here until I come, what's that got to do with you?'

²⁴(This is the disciple who is giving evidence about these things, and who wrote them down. We know that his evidence is true.)

²⁵There are many other things which Jesus did. If they were written down one by one, I don't think the world itself would be able to contain the books that would be written.

The eastern Mediterranean in the first century AD

The Acts of the Apostles

The story of the four gospels is continued in the Acts of the Apostles, written by Luke as 'part two' of his earlier work. He refers back to his gospel as the story of 'everything Jesus began to do and teach' (1.1); the story he now tells is of what Jesus *continued* to do and to teach, through the presence and power of the holy spirit. The story moves outwards: beginning in Jerusalem, the news about Jesus spreads to Judaea, then into the contested territory of Samaria, and then onwards into the wider world, ending up with Paul in Rome announcing God as King and Jesus as Lord openly and unhindered under the nose of Caesar himself. It is easy to be disappointed when reading Acts because the second half tells the story of Paul's missionary journeys, and when he gets to Rome under armed guard to have his appeal heard by Caesar the reader naturally wants to know, 'What happened next?' But the hero of Luke's story is not Paul, but the Jesus-gospel itself. All roads in Luke's world led not only *to* Rome but *from* Rome. Once the gospel has taken root there, it will spread to the rest of the world.

The spirit turns the family of Jesus-followers into a strange kind of new Temple. The Jerusalem Temple was the place where heaven and earth met; many Jews longed for a new event in which the divine glory would fill the 'house' once more, as (for instance) in Exodus 40 or 1 Kings 8. The wind and fire of Pentecost (Acts 2) answer to this expectation, indicating that now the Temple is a community, not a building – which is why, in much of the rest of the book, the moments when the early church clashes with the authorities in Jerusalem and the wider world are often focused on temples. The implicit early Christian claim was that the one God had opened up a new heaven-and-earth reality, which was bound to be a threat to existing structures and authorities.

This leads to suffering and martyrdom. The church which was founded through the kingdom-bringing death and resurrection of the Messiah must itself make its way in the world through the same shadowed valley. There will be opposition, too, from within the movement itself: Acts is not shy about describing sharp disagreements among the early leaders. But, as in the biblical books upon which Luke is drawing, the reader is tacitly invited to see the work of divine providence throughout the strange events. And, as with the four gospels, those who hear and read this story are drawn into it, to face the question of vocation: what will it look like *today* to follow Jesus and make his kingdom known?

Here comes the sequel!

1 Dear Theophilus,
The previous book which I wrote had to do with everything Jesus began to do and teach. ²I took the story as far as the day when he was taken up, once he had given instructions through the holy spirit to his chosen apostles.

³He showed himself to them alive, after his suffering, by many proofs. He was seen by them for forty days, during which he spoke about God's kingdom. ⁴As they were having a meal together, he told them not to go away from Jerusalem, but to wait, as he put it, 'for the father's promise, which I was telling you about earlier. ⁵John baptized with water, you see; but in a few days from now you will be baptized with the holy spirit.'

When, what and how?

⁶So when the apostles came together, they put this question to Jesus. 'Master,' they said, 'is this the time when you are going to restore the kingdom to Israel?'

⁷'It's not your business to know about times and dates,' he replied. 'The father has placed all that under his own direct authority. ⁸What will happen, though, is that you will receive power when the holy spirit comes upon you. Then you will be my witnesses in Jerusalem, in all Judaea and Samaria, and to the very ends of the earth.'

Ascension!

⁹As Jesus said this, he was lifted up while they were watching, and a cloud took him out of their sight. ¹⁰They were gazing into heaven as he disappeared. Then, lo and behold, two men appeared, dressed in white, standing beside them.

¹¹'Galileans,' they said, 'why are you standing here staring into heaven? This Jesus, who has been taken from you into heaven, will come back in the same way you saw him go into heaven.'

Acts 1.6–8

¹²Then they went back to Jerusalem from the hill called the Mount of Olives, which is close to Jerusalem, about the distance you could travel on a sabbath. ¹³They then entered the city ('they' here means Peter, John, James, Andrew, Philip, Thomas, Bartholomew, Matthew, James the son of Alphaeus, Simon the zealot, and Judas the son of James) and went to the upstairs room where they were staying. ¹⁴They all gave themselves single-heartedly to prayer, with the women, including Mary, Jesus' mother, and his brothers.

Restoring the Twelve

¹⁵Around that time Peter stood up in the middle of the gathering, which by this stage numbered about a hundred and twenty.

¹⁶'My dear family,' he said, 'the holy spirit spoke long ago, through the mouth of David, about Judas, who became a guide to the people who arrested Jesus. There it is in the Bible, and it had to come true. ¹⁷He was counted along with us, and he had his own share in the work we've been given.'

(¹⁸Judas, you see, had bought a field with the money his wickedness had brought him, where he fell headlong and burst open, with all his innards gushing out. ¹⁹This became known to everyone who lived in Jerusalem, so that the field was called, in their local language, 'Akeldamach', which means 'Blood-place'.)

²⁰'For this is what it says in the book of the Psalms:

Let his home become desolate
and let nobody live in it;

and again,

Let someone else receive his overseeing task.

²¹'So this is what has to be done. There are plenty of people who have gone about with us all the time that our master Jesus was coming and going among us, ²²starting from John's baptism until the day he was taken from us. Let one of them be chosen to be alongside us as a special witness of his resurrection.'

²³So they chose two: Joseph who was called Barsabbas, with the surname Justus, and Matthias.

²⁴'Lord,' they prayed, 'you know the hearts of all people. Show us which one of these two you have chosen ²⁵to receive this particular place of service and apostleship, from which Judas went away to go to his own place.'

²⁶So they cast lots for them. The lot fell on Matthias, and he was enrolled along with the eleven apostles.

Here comes the power

2 When the day of Pentecost had finally arrived, they were all together in the same place. ²Suddenly there came from heaven a noise like the sound of a strong, blowing wind, and it filled the whole house where they were sitting. ³Then tongues, seemingly made of fire, appeared to them, moving apart and coming to rest on each one of them. ⁴They were all filled with the holy spirit, and began to speak in other languages, as the spirit gave them the words to say.

New words for new news

⁵There were devout Jews from every nation under heaven staying in Jerusalem at that time. ⁶When they heard this noise they came together in a crowd. They were deeply puzzled, because every single one of them could hear them speaking in his or her own native language. ⁷They were astonished and amazed.

'These men who are doing the speaking are all Galileans, aren't they?' they said. ⁸'So how is it that each of us can hear them in our own mother tongues? ⁹There are Parthians here, and Medians, Elamites, people from Mesopotamia, Judaea, Cappadocia, Pontus, Asia, ¹⁰Phrygia and Pamphylia, Egypt and the parts of Libya that belong to Cyrene; there are people from Rome, ¹¹proselytes as well as Jews; there are Cretans and Arabs. We can hear them telling us about the powerful things God has done – *in our own languages!*'

¹²Everyone was astonished and perplexed. 'What does it all mean?' they were asking each other.

¹³But some sneered.

'They're full of new wine!' they said.

Acts 2.5–13

It's all coming true at last!

¹⁴Then Peter got up, with the eleven. He spoke to them in a loud voice.

'People of Judaea!' he began. 'All of you staying here in Jerusalem! There's something you have to know! Listen to what I'm saying! ¹⁵These people aren't drunk, as you imagine. It's only nine o'clock in the morning! ¹⁶No, this is what the prophet Joel was talking about, when he said,

> ¹⁷In the last days, declares God, I will pour out my spirit on all people.
> Your sons and your daughters will prophesy;
> your young men will see visions, your old men will dream dreams;
> ¹⁸yes, even on slaves, men and women alike, will I pour out my spirit in those days, and they shall prophesy.
> ¹⁹And I will give signs in the heavens above, and portents on earth beneath,
> blood and fire and clouds of smoke.
> ²⁰The sun will be turned into darkness, and the moon into blood,
> before the day of the Lord comes, the great and glorious day.
> ²¹And then everyone who calls on the name of the Lord will be saved.

David speaks of Jesus' resurrection

²²'You people of Israel,' Peter continued, 'listen to this. Jesus of Nazareth was a man marked out for you by God through the mighty works, signs and portents which God performed through him right here among you, as you all know. ²³He was handed over in accordance with God's determined purpose and foreknowledge – and you used people outside the law to nail him up and kill him. ²⁴'But God raised him from the dead! Death had its painful grip on him; but God released him from it, because it wasn't possible for him to be mastered by it. ²⁵This, you see, is how David speaks of him:

> I set the Lord before me always;
> because he is at my right hand, I won't be shaken.
> ²⁶So my heart was happy, and my tongue rejoiced, and my flesh, too, will rest in hope.
> ²⁷For you will not leave my soul in Hades, nor will you allow your Holy One to see corruption.
> ²⁸You showed me the path of life, you filled me with gladness in your presence.

²⁹'My dear family, I can surely speak freely to you about the patriarch David. He died and was buried, and his tomb is here with us to this day. ³⁰He was of course a prophet, and he knew that God had sworn an oath to him to set one of his own physical offspring on his throne. ³¹He foresaw the Messiah's resurrection, and spoke about him 'not being left in Hades', and about his flesh 'not seeing corruption'. ³²This is the Jesus we're talking about! God raised him from the dead, and all of us here are witnesses to the fact! ³³Now he's been exalted to God's right hand; and what you see and hear is the result of the fact that he is pouring out the holy spirit, which had been promised, and which he has received from the father.

³⁴'David, after all, did not ascend into the heavens. This is what he says:

> The Lord said to my Lord,
> sit at my right hand,
> ³⁵until I place your enemies underneath your feet.

³⁶'So the whole house of Israel must know this for a fact: God has made him Lord and Messiah – this Jesus, the one you crucified.'

God's rescue plan

³⁷When they heard this, the people in the crowd were cut to the heart.

'Brothers,' they said to Peter and the other apostles, 'what shall we do?'

³⁸'Turn back!' replied Peter. 'Be baptized – every single one of you – in the name of Jesus the Messiah, so that your sins can be forgiven, and you will receive the gift of the holy spirit. ³⁹The promise is for you and for your children, and for everyone who is far away, as many as the Lord our God will call.'

⁴⁰He carried on explaining things to them with many other words.

'Let God rescue you', he was urging them, 'from this wicked generation!'

⁴¹Those who welcomed his word were baptized. About three thousand people were added to the community that day.

The new family

⁴²They all gave full attention to the teaching of the apostles and to the common life, to the breaking of bread and the prayers. ⁴³Great awe fell on everyone, and many remarkable deeds and signs were performed by the apostles.

⁴⁴All of those who believed came together, and held everything in common. ⁴⁵They sold their possessions and belongings and divided them up to everyone in proportion to their various needs. ⁴⁶Day by day they were all together attending the Temple. They broke bread in their various houses, and ate their food with glad and sincere hearts, ⁴⁷praising God and standing in favour with all the people. And every day the Lord added to their number those who were being rescued.

More than he bargained for

3 One day, Peter and John were going up to the Temple at three o'clock in the afternoon, the time for prayer. ²There was a man being carried in who had been lame since birth. People used to bring him every day to the Temple gate called 'Beautiful', so that he could ask for alms from folk on their way in to the Temple. ³When he saw Peter and John going in to the Temple, he asked them to give him some money. ⁴Peter, with John, looked hard at him.

'Look at us,' he said.

⁵The man stared at them, expecting to get something from them.

⁶'I haven't got any silver or gold', Peter said, 'but I'll give you what I have got. In the name of the Messiah, Jesus of Nazareth, get up and walk!'

⁷He grabbed the man by his right hand and lifted him up. At once his feet and ankles became strong, ⁸and he leaped to his feet and began to walk. He went in with them into the Temple, walking and jumping up and down and praising God. ⁹All the people saw him walking

Acts 3.1–10, 11–16

and praising God, ¹⁰and they recognized him as the man who had been sitting begging for alms by the Beautiful Gate of the Temple. They were filled with amazement and astonishment at what had happened to him.

An explanation is called for

¹¹All the people ran together in astonishment towards Peter and John, and the man who was clinging onto them. They were in the part of the Temple known as 'Solomon's Porch'. ¹²Peter saw them all and began to speak.

'Fellow Israelites,' he said, 'why are you amazed at this? Why are you staring at us as though it was our own power or piety that made this man walk? ¹³"The God of Abraham, the God of Isaac, the God of Jacob – the God of our ancestors" – he has glorified his child Jesus, the one you handed over and denied in the presence of Pilate, although he had decided to let him go. ¹⁴But you denied the Holy One, the Just One, and requested instead to have a murderer given to you; ¹⁵and so you killed the Prince of Life. But God raised him from the dead, and we are witnesses to the fact. ¹⁶And it is his name, working through faith in his name, that has given strength to this man, whom you see and know. It is faith which comes through him that has given him this new complete wholeness in front of all of you.'

Restoration and refreshment

¹⁷'Now, my dear family,' Peter continued, 'I know that you acted in ignorance, just as your rulers did. ¹⁸But this is how God has fulfilled what he promised through the mouth of all the prophets, that his Messiah would suffer. ¹⁹So now repent, and turn back, so that your sins may be blotted out, ²⁰so that times of refreshment may come from the presence of the Lord, and so that he will send you Jesus, the one he chose and appointed to be his Messiah. ²¹He must be received in heaven, you see, until the time which God spoke about through the mouth of his holy prophets from ancient days, the time when God will restore all things. ²²Moses said, "The Lord your God will raise up for you a prophet like me, one from among your own brothers; whatever he says to you, you must pay attention to him. ²³And everyone who does not listen to that prophet will be cut off from the people." ²⁴All the prophets who have spoken, from Samuel and his successors, spoke about these days too. ²⁵You are the children of the prophets, the children of the covenant which God established with your ancestors when he said to Abraham, "In your seed shall all the families of the earth be blessed." ²⁶When God raised up his servant he sent him to you first, to bless you by turning each of you away from your wicked deeds.'

Resurrection plus the name of Jesus equals trouble

4 As they were speaking to the people, along came the priests, the chief of the Temple police, and the Sadducees. ²They were thoroughly annoyed that they were teaching the people and proclaiming that 'the resurrection of the dead' had begun to happen in Jesus. ³They seized them and put them under guard until the next day, since it was already evening. ⁴But a large number of the people who had heard the message believed it, and the number of men grew to five thousand.

⁵On the next day their rulers, the elders and the scribes gathered in Jerusalem, ⁶along with Annas the high priest, Caiaphas, John, Alexander and all the members of the high-priestly family. ⁷They stood them in the midst.

'How did you do this?' they asked them. 'What power did you use? What name did you invoke?'

⁸Peter was filled with the holy spirit. 'Rulers of the people and elders,' he said, ⁹'if the question we're being asked today is about a good deed done for a sick man, and whose power it was that rescued him, ¹⁰let it be known to all of you, and to all the people of Israel, that this man stands before you fit and well because of the name of the Messiah, Jesus of Nazareth, whom you crucified, but whom God raised from the dead. ¹¹He is the stone which you builders rejected, but which has become the head cornerstone. ¹²Rescue won't come from anybody else! There is no other name given under heaven and among humans by which we must be rescued.'

The clash of loyalties

¹³When they saw how boldly Peter and John were speaking, and realized that they were untrained, ordinary men, they were astonished, and they recognized them as people who had been with Jesus. ¹⁴And when they saw the man who had been healed standing with them, they had nothing to say in reply. ¹⁵They ordered them to be put out of the assembly while they conferred among themselves.

¹⁶'What can we do to these men?' they said. 'This is a spectacular sign that has happened through them. All Jerusalem knows it, and we can't deny it! ¹⁷But we certainly don't want it to spread any further among the people. So let's threaten them with awful consequences if they speak any more in this name to anybody.'

¹⁸So they called them in and gave them orders not to speak at all, or to teach, in the name of Jesus.

¹⁹But Peter and John gave them this reply.

'You judge', they said, 'whether it's right before God to listen to you rather than to God! ²⁰As far as we're concerned, we can't stop speaking about what we have seen and heard.'

²¹Then they threatened them some more, and let them go. They couldn't find any way to punish them because of the people, since everyone was glorifying God for what had happened. ²²After all, the man to whom this sign of healing had happened was over forty years old.

Look upon their threats

²³When they had been released, they went back to their own people, and told them everything that the chief priests and the elders had said. ²⁴When they heard it, they all together lifted up their voices to God.

'Sovereign Master,' they said, 'you made heaven and earth, and the sea, and everything in them. ²⁵And you said through the holy spirit, by the mouth of our ancestor David, your servant,

> Why did the nations fly into a rage,
> and why did the peoples think empty
>   thoughts?
> ²⁶The kings of the earth arose
> and the rulers gathered themselves together
> against the Lord and against his anointed
>   Messiah.

²⁷'It's true: Herod and Pontius Pilate, together with the nations and the peoples of Israel, gathered themselves together in this very city against your holy child Jesus, the one you anointed, ²⁸to do whatever your hand and your plan had foreordained to take place. ²⁹So now, Master, look on their threats; and grant that we, your servants, may speak your word with all boldness, ³⁰while you stretch out your hand for healing, so that signs and wonders may come about through the name of your holy child Jesus.'

³¹When they had prayed, the place where they were gathered was shaken. They were all filled with the holy spirit, and they boldly spoke the word of God.

Signs of the new covenant

³²The company of those who believed had one heart and soul. Nobody said that they owned their property; instead, they had everything in common. ³³The apostles gave their testimony to the resurrection of the Lord Jesus with great power, and great grace was upon all of them. ³⁴For there was no needy person among them, since any who possessed lands or houses sold them, brought the money from the sale, ³⁵and placed it at the feet of the apostles, who then gave to each according to their need.

³⁶Joseph, a Levite from Cyprus, to whom the apostles gave the surname 'Barnabas' (which means 'son of encouragement'), ³⁷sold some land which belonged to him, brought the money, and laid it at the apostles' feet.

Disaster

5 There was, however, a man named Ananias, married to a woman called Sapphira. He sold some property, ²and, with his wife's knowledge, kept back part of the price. He brought the rest and laid it at the apostles' feet.

³'Ananias!' said Peter. 'Why did the satan fill your heart, to make you tell a lie to the holy

spirit and to keep back part of the price of the land? ⁴While it was still yours, it belonged to you, didn't it? And, when you sold it, it was still in your power! Why did you get such an idea in your heart? It isn't humans that you've lied to: it's God!'

⁵When Ananias heard these words, he fell down and died. Everyone who heard about it was scared out of their wits. ⁶The young men got up, took him away, wrapped up his body and buried him.

⁷After an interval of about three hours, his wife came in, not knowing what had happened.

⁸Peter spoke to her.

'Tell me,' he said, 'did you sell the land for this much?'

'Yes,' she replied, 'that was the price.'

⁹'So why', Peter answered, 'did you agree together to put the holy spirit to the test? Look: the feet of those who have buried your husband are at the door – and they will carry you out too!'

¹⁰At once she fell down at his feet and died. The young men were just coming in, and they found her dead, so they took her out and buried her beside her husband. ¹¹Great fear came upon the whole gathering, and on all who heard about these things.

Healed by Peter's shadow

¹²Many signs and wonders were performed by the apostles among the people. They were all together in Solomon's Porch, ¹³while none of the others dared to join them, though the people spoke highly of them. ¹⁴But more people, a crowd both of men and women, believed in the Lord, and were added to their number. ¹⁵They used to bring the sick into the streets, and place them on beds and mats so that at least Peter's shadow might fall on them as he went by. ¹⁶Crowds gathered from the towns around Jerusalem, bringing people who were sick, or infested with unclean spirits. All of them were cured.

The words of this life

¹⁷Then the high priest got up, and all who were with him, namely the group called the 'Sadducees'. They were filled with righteous indignation, ¹⁸and seized the apostles and put them in the public jail. ¹⁹But an angel of the Lord came in the night, opened the prison doors, and brought them out.

²⁰'Go and take your stand in the Temple,' he said, 'and speak all the words of this Life to the people.'

²¹When they heard this, they went in at early morning and began to teach.

When the high priest arrived with his entourage, they called the official Assembly and all the elders of the children of Israel, and they sent to the prison to have the apostles brought in. ²²But when the attendants went, they didn't find them in the prison. So they came and reported back.

²³'We found the jail shut up with maximum security', they said, 'and the guards were standing in front of the doors. But when we opened up we found nobody inside.'

²⁴When they heard these words, the commander of the Temple police and the chief priests were at a loss about them, with no idea what had happened. ²⁵But then someone came with a message for them.

'Look!' he said. 'The men you put in prison are standing in the Temple and teaching the people!'

²⁶Then the commander went with his attendants and brought them. They didn't use force, though, because they were afraid that the people might stone them.

Human inventions and divine instructions

²⁷So they brought them and stood them in the Assembly. The high priest questioned them.

²⁸'We gave you strict orders, didn't we?' he demanded. 'We told you not to teach in this Name, and look what you're doing! You have filled Jerusalem with your teaching, and you're trying to bring this man's blood on us!'

²⁹'We must obey God, not human beings!' responded Peter and the apostles. ³⁰'The God of our ancestors raised Jesus, after you had laid violent hands on him and hanged him on a tree. ³¹God exalted him to his right hand as Leader and Saviour, to give repentance to Israel and forgiveness of sins. ³²We are witnesses of

these things, and so is the holy spirit, which God gave to those who obey him.'

³³When they heard this, they were infuriated, and wanted to kill them. ³⁴But then a Pharisee by the name of Gamaliel stood up in the Assembly. He was a law-teacher, highly respected by all the people. He ordered the men to be put outside for a short while.

³⁵'Men of Israel,' he said to the gathering, 'be careful what you do to these men. ³⁶Before these times Theudas rose up, claiming to be someone special, and about four hundred men went off to join him. But he was killed, and all the people who had trusted him were dispersed. The movement came to nothing. ³⁷After that, Judas the Galilean arose, in the days of the Census, and drew a crowd after himself. But he was killed, and all those who trusted him were scattered. ³⁸So my advice to you now is this. Leave off from these men; let them be. You see, if this plan or this work is of merely human origin, it will come to ruin. ³⁹But if it's from God – well, you won't be able to stop them. You might even be found to be fighting against God!'

They were persuaded by him, ⁴⁰and they called the apostles back in. They beat them and told them not to speak in the name of Jesus. Then they let them go. ⁴¹They, however, went out from the presence of the Assembly celebrating, because they had been reckoned worthy to suffer disgrace for the Name. ⁴²And all day, in the Temple and from house to house, they did not stop teaching and proclaiming Jesus as the Messiah.

Problems of family living

6 Around that time, as the number of disciples increased, the 'Hellenists' raised a dispute with the 'Hebrews' because their widows were being overlooked in the daily distribution of food. ²So the Twelve called the whole crowd of disciples together.

'Listen,' they said. 'It wouldn't be right for us to leave the word of God to wait on tables. ³So, brothers and sisters, choose seven men from among yourselves who are well spoken of and filled with the spirit and wisdom. We will put them in charge of what needs to be done in this matter. ⁴We will continue to pay attention to prayer and to the ministry of the word.'

Acts 6.9

⁵The whole gathering was pleased with what they said. They chose Stephen, a man full of faith and the holy spirit, and Philip, Prochorus, Nicanor, Timon, Parmenas and Nicolaus (a proselyte from Antioch). ⁶They presented them before the apostles, who prayed and laid their hands on them.

⁷The word of God increased, and the number of disciples in Jerusalem grew by leaps and bounds. This included a large crowd of priests who became obedient to the faith.

Stephen becomes a target

⁸Stephen was filled with grace and power, and performed great signs and wonders among the people. ⁹But some from the 'Freemen's Synagogue', as it was named, and from Cyrene, Alexandria, Cilicia and Asia, stood up and disputed with Stephen. ¹⁰They could not, however, resist the wisdom and the spirit with which he spoke.

¹¹Then they put up men to say, 'We heard this man speaking blasphemous words against Moses and against God!' ¹²They aroused the people, the elders and the scribes. They set upon him, seized him, and took him in front of the Assembly. ¹³They set up false witnesses to say, 'This man never stops speaking words against this holy place and the law! ¹⁴We heard him say that this Jesus the Nazorean will destroy this place, and change the customs which Moses handed down to us!'

¹⁵Everyone who was sitting in the Assembly looked hard at Stephen. They all saw that his face was like the face of an angel.

Stephen tells the story

7 The high priest addressed Stephen. 'Are these things true?' he said.

²'My brothers and fathers,' replied Stephen, 'please give me a hearing.

'The God of glory appeared to our father Abraham when he was in Mesopotamia, before he moved to live in Haran. ³"Leave your land and your family," he said to him, "and go to the land which I will show you." ⁴So he left the land of the Chaldeans and went to live in Haran. Then, from there, after his father's death, God moved him on to this land in which you now live. ⁵God didn't give him an inheritance here, not even a place to stand up in. Instead, he promised (when Abraham still had no child) that he would give it as a possession to his seed after him. ⁶This is what God said to him: that his seed would be strangers in a foreign land, that they would serve there as slaves, and that they would be afflicted for four hundred years. ⁷But God said that he would judge the nation that had enslaved them, and that they would then come out and worship him "on this mountain". ⁸And he gave them the covenant of circumcision. So Abraham became the father of Isaac, and he circumcised him on the eighth day. Isaac became the father of Jacob, and Jacob the father of the twelve patriarchs.

⁹'Now the patriarchs became angry with Joseph, and were jealous of him. They sold him into Egypt. But God was with him, ¹⁰and rescued him from all his troubles and gave him grace and wisdom before Pharaoh, king of Egypt, making him ruler over Egypt and over all his household. ¹¹But then there was a famine over the whole of Egypt and Canaan, which resulted in great hardship. Our ancestors couldn't find food to eat. ¹²Jacob, however, heard that there was grain in Egypt, and sent our ancestors there on an initial visit. ¹³On their second trip, Joseph made himself known to his brothers, and revealed to Pharaoh what family he was from. ¹⁴So Joseph sent and summoned Jacob his father and all the family, seventy-five people in all. ¹⁵Jacob came to Egypt, and he and our ancestors died there. ¹⁶They were brought back to Shechem, and buried in the tomb which Abraham had bought with silver, at a named price, from the sons of Hamor in Shechem.'

Stephen and Moses

¹⁷'God had sworn an oath to Abraham,' Stephen continued. 'When the time drew near for this promise to be fulfilled, the people had increased and multiplied in Egypt, ¹⁸until another king arose over Egypt, one who had not known Joseph. ¹⁹He got the better of our people, and ill-treated our ancestors, forcing them to abandon their newborn children so that they would die.

20'It was at that time that Moses was born, and he was a noble-looking child. He was nursed for three months in his father's house. 21But, when they abandoned him, Pharaoh's daughter claimed him and brought him up as her own son. 22So Moses was educated in the full teaching of Egyptian wisdom, and he was powerful in what he said and did.

23'When he had grown to about forty years old, it came into his heart to see how his family, the children of Israel, were doing. 24He saw someone being wronged, and came to the man's defence; he took revenge on behalf of the man who was being oppressed, by striking down the Egyptian. 25He thought his kinsfolk would grasp the fact that God was sending him to their rescue, but they didn't.

26'The next day he showed up as two Hebrews were fighting, and he tried to bring them back together again. "Now then, you two," he said, "you are brothers! Why are you wronging each other?" 27But the man who was wronging the other wasn't having it. "Who d'you think you are?" he retorted, pushing him away. "Who made you a ruler or judge over us? 28Do you want to kill me in the same way you killed the Egyptian yesterday?" 29At that word, Moses ran away, and lived as a guest in the land of Midian, where he had two sons.

30'After another forty years, an angel appeared to him in the desert at Mount Sinai, in the flame of a burning bush. 31When Moses saw it, he was amazed at the vision. But, as he came closer to see, there came the voice of the Lord: 32"I am the God of your ancestors, the God of Abraham, of Isaac, and of Jacob." Moses was very frightened, and didn't dare to look. 33But the Lord said to him, "Take your sandals off your feet, for the place where you are standing is holy ground. 34I have looked long and hard at the trouble my people are having in Egypt. I have heard their groaning, and I have come down to rescue them. So, come on now: I'm going to send you to Egypt."'

Handmade shrines

35'So', Stephen continued, 'this same Moses – the one they rejected, saying "Who made you a ruler or judge?" – this is the man God sent as ruler and redeemer, by the hand of the angel who had appeared to him in the bush. 36He did signs and wonders in the land of Egypt, and led them out, through the Red Sea and for forty years in the wilderness. 37This is the Moses who said to the children of Israel, "God will raise up a prophet like me from among your brothers." 38And this is the one who was in the Assembly in the desert with the angel who had spoken to him on Mount Sinai, and with our ancestors; and he received living words to give to us.

39'This is the one whom our ancestors had not wanted to obey, but instead rejected him and turned back in their hearts to Egypt, 40by saying to Aaron, "Make us gods who will go before us; for this Moses, who brought us out of the land of Egypt – we don't know what has become of him!" 41They made a calf in those days, and offered sacrifice to an idol. They celebrated things their own hands had made.

42'Then God turned and handed them over to worship the host of heaven, as it stands written in the book of the prophets: "Did you bring sacrifices and offerings to me in those forty years in the wilderness, O house of Israel? 43You took up the tent of Moloch, and the star of your god Rhephan, the carved images you made to worship! I will remove you beyond Babylon!"

44'Our ancestors had the "tent of meeting" in the desert. God had commanded Moses to make it according to the pattern which he had seen. 45Our ancestors in their turn brought it in when, with Joshua, they dispossessed the nations whom God drove out before our ancestors, and it was there until the time of David. 46David found favour with God, and requested permission to establish a Tabernacle for the house of Jacob. 47But it was Solomon who built him a house.

48'The Most High, however, does not live in shrines made by human hands. The prophet put it like this:

49Heaven is my throne, and earth my footstool!
What sort of house will you build me, says the Lord,
or what place will you give me to rest in?
50My own hand made all these, did it not?

51'You stiff-necked people! Your hearts and ears are uncircumcised! You always resist the holy spirit, just as your ancestors did before you! ⁵²Which of the prophets did your ancestors not persecute? And you killed those who announced in advance the coming of the Righteous One – and now you have betrayed him and murdered him. ⁵³You received the law at the command of angels, but you didn't keep it!'

The stoning of Stephen

⁵⁴What Stephen said was a blow right to the heart. When they heard it, they gnashed their teeth against him. ⁵⁵He, however, was filled with the holy spirit, and looked steadily up into heaven. There he saw the glory of God, and Jesus standing at God's right hand.

⁵⁶'Look!' he said. 'I can see heaven opened, and the son of man standing at God's right hand!'

⁵⁷But they yelled at him at the tops of their voices, blocked their ears and made a concerted dash at him. ⁵⁸They bundled him out of the city and stoned him. The witnesses laid down their cloaks at the feet of a young man named Saul.

⁵⁹So they stoned Stephen.

'Lord Jesus,' he cried out, 'receive my spirit.' ⁶⁰Then he knelt down and shouted at the top of his voice, 'Lord, don't let this sin stand against them.'

Once he had said this, he fell asleep.

8 Now Saul was giving his consent to Stephen's death.

That very day a great persecution was started against the church in Jerusalem. Everyone except the apostles was scattered through the lands of Judaea and Samaria. ²Devout men buried Stephen, and made a great lamentation over him. ³But Saul was doing great damage to the church by going from one house to another, dragging off men and women and throwing them into prison.

Samaria, the spirit and Simon Magus

⁴Those who were scattered went all over the place announcing the word. ⁵Philip went off to a town in Samaria and announced the Messiah to them. ⁶The crowds, acting as one, clung to what Philip was saying, as they heard him

Acts 8.4–25

and saw the signs he performed. ⁷For unclean spirits came out of many of them, and several who were paralysed or lame were cured. ⁸So there was great joy in that town.

⁹But there was a man named Simon, who had lived in the town for some while and who practised magic. He used to astonish the Samaritan people, giving out that he was some great personage. ¹⁰Everyone, small and great alike, paid attention to him, and said, 'This man is the one called "God's Great Power"!' ¹¹They had been under his spell for some time, since they were amazed at the magic he could perform. ¹²But when they believed Philip as he was announcing to them the message about God's kingdom and the Name of Jesus the Messiah, they were baptized, men and women alike. ¹³Simon too believed and was baptized, paying close attention to Philip. When he saw signs, and great and powerful deeds, it was his turn to be astonished.

¹⁴When the apostles in Jerusalem heard that Samaria had received God's word, they sent Peter and John to them. ¹⁵When they arrived, they prayed for them, asking that they would receive the holy spirit, ¹⁶since up to that point the spirit had come upon none of them; they had simply been baptized into the name of the Lord Jesus. ¹⁷Then they laid their hands on them, and they received the holy spirit.

¹⁸When Simon saw that the spirit was given through the laying on of the apostles' hands, he offered them money.

¹⁹'Give me this power too,' he said, 'so that anyone I lay my hands on will receive the holy spirit.'

²⁰'You and your silver belong in hell!' retorted Peter. 'Did you really think that God's gift could be bought with money? ²¹You have no part or share in this word! Your heart is not straight before God. ²²So repent from this wickedness, and pray to the Lord. Perhaps he will forgive the scheme you had in your heart. ²³I can see that you are still stuck in the bitter poison and chains of unrighteousness.'

²⁴'Pray to the Lord for me', said Simon in reply, 'that none of what you've said will happen to me.'

²⁵After Peter and John had finished bearing witness and speaking the word of the Lord,

Acts 8.26–40

they returned to Jerusalem, announcing the good news to many Samaritan villages.

Philip and the Ethiopian

[26] An angel of the Lord spoke to Philip.

'Get up and go south,' he said. 'Go to the desert road that runs down from Jerusalem to Gaza.'

[27] So he got up and went. Lo and behold, there was an Ethiopian eunuch, a court official of the Candace (the queen of Ethiopia), who was in charge of her whole treasury. He had come to Jerusalem to worship, [28] and was on his way back home. He was sitting in his chariot and reading the prophet Isaiah.

[29] 'Go up and join his chariot,' said the spirit to Philip. [30] So Philip ran up, and heard him reading the prophet Isaiah.

'Do you understand what you're reading?' he asked.

[31] 'How can I,' he replied, 'unless someone gives me some help?'

So he invited Philip to get up and sit beside him. [32] The biblical passage he was reading was this one:

He was led like a sheep to the slaughter
and as a lamb is silent before its shearers,
so he does not open his mouth.
[33] In his humiliation, judgment was taken away
   from him.
Who can explain his generation?
For his life was taken away from the earth.

[34] 'Tell me,' said the eunuch to Philip, 'who is the prophet talking about? Himself or someone else?'

[35] Then Philip took a deep breath and, starting from this biblical passage, told him the good news about Jesus.

[36] As they were going along the road, they came to some water.

'Look!' said the eunuch. 'Here is some water! What's to stop me being baptized?'

[38] So he gave orders for the chariot to stop, and both of them went down into the water, Philip and the eunuch together, and he baptized him. [39] When they came up out of the water, the spirit of the Lord snatched Philip away, and the eunuch didn't see him any more, but went on his way rejoicing. [40] Philip, however, turned up at Azotus. He went

Acts 9.1–9

through all the towns, announcing the good news, until he came to Caesarea.

The conversion of Saul

9 Meanwhile, Saul was still breathing out threats and murder on the Lord's disciples. He went to the high priest ²and requested from him official letters to the synagogues in Damascus, so that he could find people who belonged to the Way, men and women alike, tie them up and bring them back to Jerusalem.

³While he was on the journey, and was getting near to Damascus, suddenly a light from heaven shone around him. ⁴He fell on the ground and heard a voice speaking to him.

'Saul, Saul!' said the voice. 'Why are you persecuting me?'

⁵'Who are you, Lord?' he asked.

'I am Jesus,' he said, 'and you are persecuting me. ⁶But get up and go into the city, and it will be told you what you have to do.'

⁷The men who were travelling with Saul stood speechless. They heard the voice but couldn't see anybody. ⁸Saul got up from the ground, but when he opened his eyes he couldn't see anything. So they led him by the hand and brought him to Damascus. ⁹He went for three days, being unable to see, and he neither ate nor drank.

Ananias and Saul

¹⁰In Damascus there was a disciple named Ananias. The Lord spoke to him in a vision.

'Ananias!' he said.

'Here I am, Lord,' he replied.

¹¹'Get up', said the Lord to him, 'and go to the street called Straight. Enquire at the house of Judas for a man from Tarsus named Saul. Look – he's praying! ¹²And he has seen, in a vision, a man named Ananias coming and laying his hands on him so that he can see again.'

¹³'Well, Lord,' replied Ananias, 'I've heard about this man from several people . . . all about how he's done wicked things to your holy people in Jerusalem . . . ¹⁴and now he's come

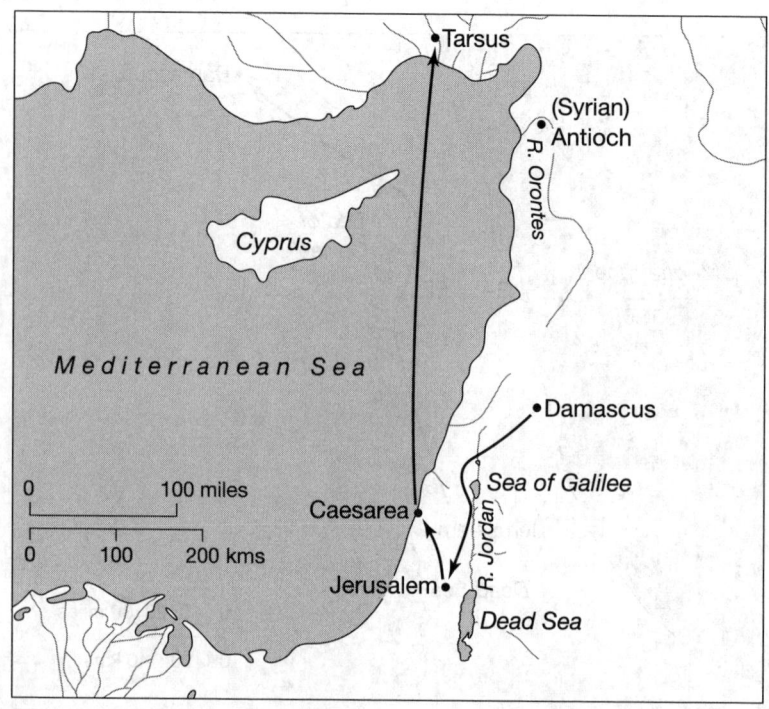

Acts 9.19–26, 30

here with authority from the chief priests to tie up everybody who calls on your Name!'

¹⁵'Just go,' replied the Lord. 'He is a chosen vessel for me, to carry my Name before nations and kings – and the children of Israel, too. ¹⁶I am going to show him how many things he is going to have to suffer for the sake of my Name.'

¹⁷So Ananias set off, went into the house, and laid his hands on him.

'Brother Saul,' he said, 'the Lord has sent me – yes, Jesus, who appeared to you on the road as you were coming here – so that you may be able to see again, and receive the holy spirit.'

¹⁸At once something like scales fell off his eyes, and he was able to see. He got up and was baptized. ¹⁹He had something to eat, and regained his strength.

'He is God's son'

Saul stayed with the disciples in Damascus for a few days. ²⁰At once he proclaimed Jesus in the synagogues, saying, 'This really is the son of God!' ²¹Everyone was astonished, and said, 'Isn't this the man who caused havoc to those in Jerusalem who call on this Name? And here he is, coming to tie them up and take them off to the high priests!' ²²But Saul grew all the stronger, and threw the Jews in Damascus into confusion by demonstrating that Jesus is indeed the Messiah.

²³After some days, the Jews made a plot to kill him, ²⁴but Saul got wind of their plan. They were watching the city gates day and night so that they could do away with him. ²⁵But the disciples took him by night and let him down through the wall, lowering him in a basket.

²⁶When he got back to Jerusalem he tried to join the disciples, but they were all afraid of him, not believing that he really was a disciple. ²⁷But Barnabas took him, brought him to the apostles, and explained to them how he had seen the Lord on the road, and that he had spoken to him, and how in Damascus he had spoken boldly in the name of Jesus.

²⁸He was with them in Jerusalem, coming and going and speaking boldly in the name of the Lord. ²⁹He spoke, as well, to the Hellenists, who tried to kill him. ³⁰But the family heard of it and took him down to Caesarea. There they sent him off to Tarsus.

³¹So the church in all Judaea, Galilee and Samaria found itself at peace. It was built up

Acts 9.32, 35, 36

and gained in numbers, living in the fear of the Lord and the comfort of the holy spirit.

Back to Peter

³²As Peter was going through various places among all the believers, he went down to God's people who lived in Lydda. ³³There he found a paralysed man named Aeneas who had been confined to bed for eight years.

³⁴'Aeneas,' Peter said to him, 'Jesus the Messiah heals you! Stand up and fold up your bed!'

And at once he stood up. ³⁵Everyone who lived at Lydda and Sharon saw it, and they turned to the Lord.

³⁶In Joppa there was a disciple named Tabitha, whose name translates as 'Dorcas'. She was full of good works and generous deeds. ³⁷Around that time she fell ill and died. They washed her and laid her in an upper room. ³⁸Lydda is near Joppa, and the disciples, hearing that Peter was there, sent two men to him with the urgent request that he shouldn't delay, but come to them at once. ³⁹So Peter got up and went with them. When he arrived, they took him to the upper room, where all the widows were weeping. They showed him the tunics and the other clothes that Dorcas had made while she was with them.

⁴⁰Peter requested them all to leave. Then he knelt down and prayed, and turned to the body.

'Tabitha,' he said, 'get up!'

She opened her eyes, and when she saw Peter she sat up. ⁴¹He gave her his hand and lifted her up. Then he called God's people, including the widows, and presented her alive.

⁴²This became known throughout the whole of Joppa, and many believed in the Lord.
⁴³Peter stayed on in Joppa for some days, at the house of Simon the tanner.

Peter's vision

10 In Caesarea there was a man named Cornelius, a centurion with the cohort called 'the Italian'. ²He was devout, and he and all his household revered God. He gave alms generously to the people, and constantly prayed to God.

³He had a vision. Around three o'clock in the afternoon he saw, quite clearly, one of God's angels coming to him.

'Cornelius!' said the angel.

⁴He looked hard at him, terrified.

'What is it, Sir?' he said.

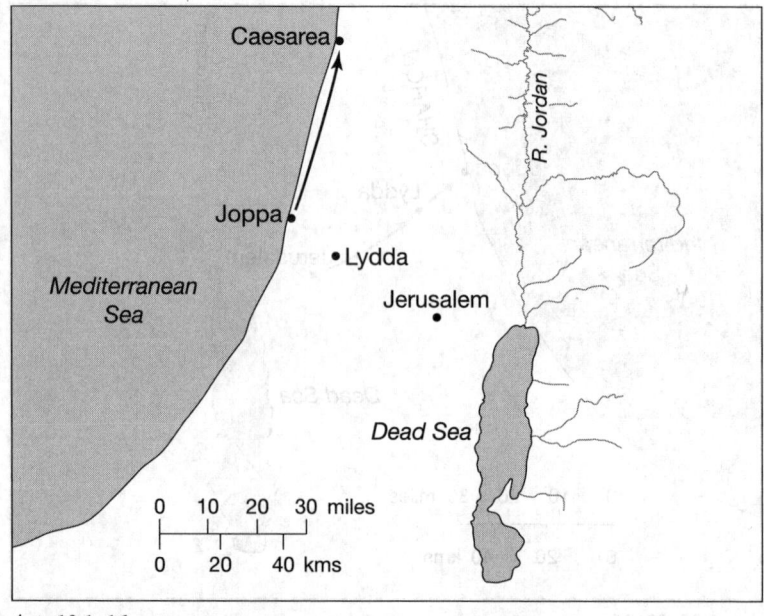

Acts 10.1–16

'Your prayers and your alms have come to God's notice,' said the angel. ⁵'What you must do is this. Send men to Joppa, and ask for someone called Simon, surnamed Peter. ⁶He is staying with a man called Simon, a tanner, whose house is beside the sea.'

⁷When the angel who had spoken with him went away, he called two of his household and a devout soldier from among his retinue. ⁸He explained everything to them, and sent them off to Joppa.

⁹The next day, as they were on their journey and getting near the town, Peter went up onto the roof of the house to pray. It was around midday; ¹⁰he was hungry, and asked for something to eat. While they were preparing it, he fell into a trance. ¹¹He saw heaven opened, and a vessel like a great sail coming down towards the earth, suspended by its four corners. ¹²In the sail there was every kind of four-footed creature, reptiles of the earth and birds of the air. ¹³Then he heard a voice: 'Get up, Peter!' said the voice. 'Kill and eat!'

¹⁴'Certainly not, Master!' said Peter. 'I've never eaten anything common or unclean!'

¹⁵'What God has made clean,' said the voice, coming now for a second time, 'you must not regard as common.'

¹⁶This all happened three times, and then suddenly the sail was whisked back up to heaven.

Peter goes to Cornelius

¹⁷When Peter came to himself, he was puzzled as to what the vision he had seen was all about. Then, suddenly, the men sent by Cornelius appeared, standing by the gate. They had been asking for Simon's house, ¹⁸enquiring if someone by the name of Simon called Peter was staying there. ¹⁹Peter was still pondering the vision, when the spirit spoke to him.

'Look,' said the spirit. 'There are three men searching for you. ²⁰It's all right; get up, go down and go with them. Don't be prejudiced; I have sent them.'

²¹So Peter went down to the men.

'Here I am,' he said. 'I'm the one you're looking for. Why have you come?'

²²'There is a man called Cornelius,' they replied. 'He is a centurion, and he's a righteous and God-fearing man. The whole people of the Jews will testify to him. A holy angel told him in a vision to send for you to come to his house, so that he can hear any words you may have to say.'

²³So he invited them in and put them up for the night.

In the morning he got up and went with them. Some of the believers from Joppa went with him. ²⁴They reached Caesarea the following day. Cornelius had summoned his relatives and close friends and was waiting for him.

²⁵When Peter came in, Cornelius went to meet him. He fell down at his feet and worshipped him.

²⁶'Get up!' said Peter, lifting him up. 'I'm just a man, too.'

²⁷So they talked together, and Peter came in and found lots of people assembled.

²⁸'You must know,' he said to them, 'that it is forbidden for a Jewish man to mix with or visit a Gentile. But God showed me that I should call nobody "common" or "unclean". ²⁹So I came when I was asked, and raised no objections. Do tell me, then, the reason why you sent for me.'

³⁰Cornelius gave him the answer.

'Four days ago,' he said, 'I was praying in my house at around this time, about three o'clock, and suddenly a man stood beside me in shining clothes. ³¹"Cornelius," he said, "your prayer has been heard, and your almsgiving has been remembered by God. ³²So send someone to Joppa and call Simon, who is named Peter; he is staying in the house of Simon the tanner, beside the sea." ³³So I sent for you at once, and you have been kind enough to come. So now we are all here, in God's presence, to listen to everything which the Lord has told you to say.'

Telling the Gentiles about Jesus

³⁴Peter took a deep breath and began.

'It's become clear to me,' he said, 'that God really does show no favouritism. ³⁵No: in every race, people who fear him and do what is right are acceptable to him. ³⁶He sent his word to the children of Israel, announcing peace through Jesus Christ – he is Lord of all! ³⁷You know all about this, and how the word spread through all Judaea, beginning from Galilee after the baptism which John proclaimed.

³⁸'God anointed this man, Jesus of Nazareth, with the holy spirit and with power. He went about doing good and healing all who were overpowered by the devil, since God was with him. ³⁹We are witnesses of everything he did in the land of Judaea and in Jerusalem. They killed him by hanging him on a tree; ⁴⁰but God raised him on the third day, and allowed him to be seen, ⁴¹not indeed by all the people, but by those of us whom God had appointed beforehand. We ate and drank with him after he had been raised from the dead. ⁴²And he commanded us to announce to the people, and to bear testimony, that he is the one appointed by God to be judge of the living and the dead. ⁴³All the prophets give their witness: he is the one! Everyone who believes in him receives forgiveness of sins through his Name.'

⁴⁴While Peter was still speaking these words, the holy spirit fell on everyone who was listening to the word. ⁴⁵The circumcised believers who had accompanied Peter were astonished, because the gift of the holy spirit had been poured out on the Gentiles too. ⁴⁶They heard them speaking with tongues and praising God.

Then Peter spoke up.

⁴⁷'Nobody can deny these people water to be baptized, can they?' he said. 'They have received the holy spirit, just like we did!' ⁴⁸So he ordered them to be baptized in the name of Jesus the Messiah.

Then they asked him to stay for a few days.

Controversy and vindication

11 The apostles, and the brothers and sisters with them in Judaea, heard that the Gentiles had received the word of God. ²So when Peter went up to Jerusalem, those who wanted to emphasize circumcision took issue with him.

³'Why did you do it?' they asked. 'Why did you go in to visit uncircumcised men and eat with them?'

⁴So Peter began to explain it all, step by step.

⁵'I was in the town of Joppa,' he said, 'and I was praying. I was in a trance, and I saw a vision: something like a great sail suspended by its four corners was let down from heaven, and came towards me. ⁶I stared at it, then I began to look in, and I saw four-footed land animals, wild beasts, reptiles and birds of the air. ⁷I heard a voice, saying to me, "Get up, Peter! Kill and eat!" ⁸"Certainly not, Lord," I replied. "Nothing common or unclean has ever entered my mouth!" ⁹Then the voice came from heaven a second time: "What God made clean, you must not regard as common." ¹⁰All this happened three times, and then the whole lot was drawn back up into heaven.

¹¹'Just then, suddenly, three men appeared at the house where I was, sent to me from Caesarea. ¹²The spirit told me to go with them, without raising scrupulous objections. These six brothers also came with me, and we went into the man's house. ¹³He told us that he had seen an angel standing in his house and saying, "Send to Joppa and fetch Simon called Peter, ¹⁴who will speak to you words by which you and all your house will be saved." ¹⁵As I began to speak, the holy spirit fell on them, just as the spirit did on us at the beginning. ¹⁶And I remembered the word which the Lord had spoken: "John baptized with water, but you will be baptized with the holy spirit."

¹⁷'So, then,' Peter concluded, 'if God gave them the same gift as he gave to us when we believed in the Lord Jesus the Messiah, who was I to stand in the way of God?'

¹⁸When they heard this, they had nothing more to say. They praised God.

'Well, then,' they declared, 'God has given the Gentiles, too, the repentance that leads to life!'

Taking root – and a name! – in Antioch

¹⁹The people who had been scattered because of the persecution that came about over Stephen went as far afield as Phoenicia, Cyprus and Antioch, speaking the word only to Jewish people. ²⁰But some from among them, who were from Cyprus and Cyrene in the first place, arrived in Antioch and spoke to the Hellenists as well, announcing the good news of the Lord Jesus. ²¹The Lord's hand was with them, and a large number of people believed and turned to the Lord.

Acts 11.19–30

[22]News of all this reached the ears of the church in Jerusalem, and they sent Barnabas to Antioch. [23]When he arrived and saw the grace of God he was glad, and he urged them all to stay firmly loyal to the Lord from the bottom of their hearts. [24]He was a good man, full of the holy spirit and faith. And a substantial crowd was added to the Lord.

[25]Then Barnabas went to Tarsus to look for Saul [26]and, when he had found him, he brought him to Antioch. They were there a whole year, and were received hospitably in the church, and taught a substantial crowd. And it was in Antioch that the disciples were first called 'Christians'.

[27]Around that time, prophets came from Jerusalem to Antioch. [28]One of them, Agabus by name, stood up and gave an indication through the spirit that there would be a great famine over the whole world. (This took place in the reign of Claudius.) [29]Each of the disciples determined, according to their ability, to send what they could to help the brothers and sisters living in Judaea. [30]They carried out this plan, sending their gift to the elders by the hand of Barnabas and Saul.

Herod kills James

12 Around that time, King Herod began to use violence towards some people in the church. [2]He killed James the brother of John with the sword. [3]When he saw that it pleased the Judaeans, he proceeded to arrest Peter, too. (This was around the time of the Festival of Unleavened Bread.) [4]So, when he had seized him, he put him in prison, and gave four squads of soldiers the job of guarding him, with the intention of bringing him out to the people after Passover. [5]So Peter was kept in prison. But the church prayed earnestly to God on his behalf.

Peter's rescue and Rhoda's mistake

[6]On the night when Herod was intending to bring Peter out, Peter was sleeping between two soldiers, bound with two chains. There were guards on the doors, watching the prison. [7]Suddenly an angel of the Lord stood there, and a light shone in the cell.

The angel hit Peter on the side and woke him up.

'Get up quickly!' he said.

The chains fell off his hands. ⁸Then the angel spoke again.

'Get dressed and put on your sandals,' he said. So Peter did.

'Put on your cloak and follow me,' said the angel.

⁹So he went out, following the angel. He didn't think all this business with the angel was really happening. He thought he was seeing a vision. ¹⁰They went through the first set of guards; then the second; and then they came to the iron gate that led into the city. It opened all by itself. They went out and walked along a street. Suddenly the angel left him.

¹¹Then Peter came to his senses.

'Now I know it's true!' he said. 'The Lord sent his angel and snatched me out of Herod's hands. He rescued me from all the things the Judaeans were intending to do.'

¹²Once he had realized this, he went to the house of Mary, John Mark's mother. Lots of people were gathered there, praying. ¹³Peter knocked at the door in the outer gate, and a maid called Rhoda came to answer it. ¹⁴When she heard Peter's voice, she was so excited she didn't open the gate. Instead, she ran back in and told them that Peter was standing outside the gate.

¹⁵'You're mad!' they said to her. But she insisted that it really was true.

'It must be his angel!' they said.

¹⁶Meanwhile Peter carried on knocking. They opened the door and saw him, and were astonished. ¹⁷He made a sign with his hand for them to be quiet. Then he told them how the Lord had led him out of the prison.

'Tell this to James, and to the other brothers and sisters,' he said.

Then he left, and went somewhere else.

¹⁸When morning came, there was quite a commotion among the guards as to what had become of Peter. ¹⁹Herod looked for him but couldn't find him. He interrogated the guards and ordered them to be put to death. Then he left Judaea and went down to Caesarea, and stayed there.

Herod's vanity and death

²⁰Now Herod was angry with the people of Tyre and Sidon. They all came together to meet

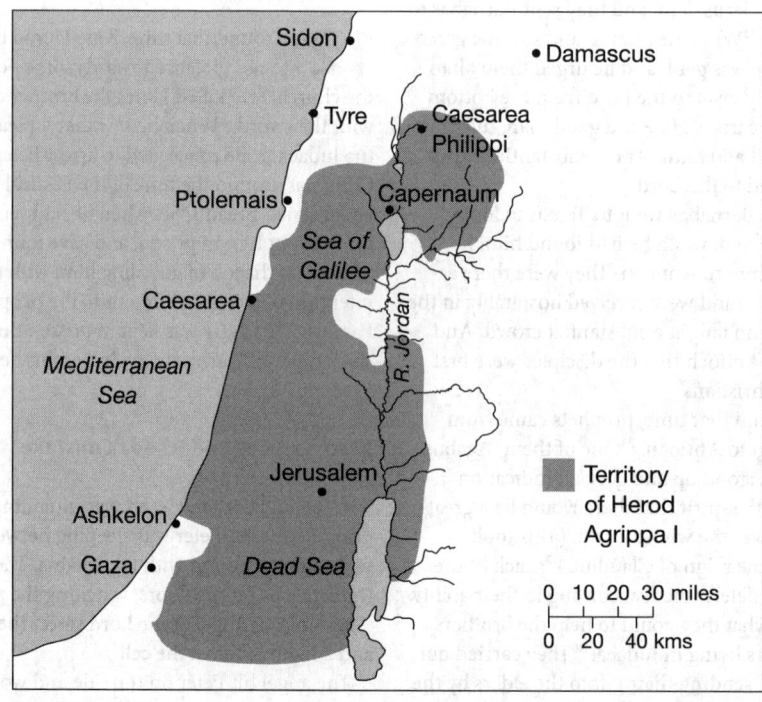

Acts 12.20–25

him, and they persuaded Blastus, who was in charge of the king's bedchamber, to seek a reconciliation. (They were, you see, dependent on the king's country for their food.) ²¹So a day was set, and Herod dressed himself in his royal robes and took his seat on the official platform to make a public address to them.

²²The people began to shout,

'The voice of a god, not of a mortal!'

²³Immediately an angel of the Lord struck him, because he didn't give God the glory. He was eaten by worms and expired.

²⁴But God's word grew and multiplied. ²⁵Barnabas and Saul had by now accomplished their ministry in Jerusalem, and they came back to Antioch, bringing John Mark with them.

Mission and magic

13 In the church at Antioch there were prophets and teachers: Barnabas, Symeon called Niger, Lucius of Cyrene, Manaen from the court of Herod the Tetrarch, and Saul. ²As they were worshipping the Lord and fasting, the holy spirit said, 'Set apart Barnabas and Saul for the work to which I have called them.' ³So they fasted and prayed; and then they laid their hands on them and sent them off.

⁴So off they went, sent out by the holy spirit, and arrived at Seleucia. From there they set sail to Cyprus, ⁵and when they arrived in Salamis they announced God's word in the Jewish synagogues. John was with them as their assistant. ⁶They went through the whole of the island, all the way to Paphos. There they found a magician, a Jewish false prophet named Bar-Jesus. ⁷He was with the governor, Sergius Paulus, who was an intelligent man. He called Barnabas and Saul and asked to hear the word of God. ⁸The magician Elymas (that is the translation of his name) was opposing them, and doing his best to turn the governor away from the faith. ⁹But Saul, also named Paul, looked intently at him, filled with the holy spirit.

¹⁰'You're full of trickery and every kind of villainy!' he said. 'You're a son of the devil! You're an enemy of everything that's right! When are you going to stop twisting the paths that God has made straight? ¹¹Now see here:

Acts 13.1–6

the Lord's hand will be upon you, and you will be blind for a while; you won't even be able to see the sun!'

At once mist and darkness fell on him, and he went about looking for someone to lead him by the hand. ¹²When the governor saw what had happened, he believed, since he was astonished at the teaching of the Lord.

Address in Antioch

¹³Paul and his companions set off from Paphos and came to Perga in Pamphylia. John, however, left them and went back to Jerusalem. ¹⁴But they came through from Perga and arrived in Antioch of Pisidia, where they went into the synagogue on the sabbath day and sat down. ¹⁵After the reading of the law and the prophets, the ruler of the synagogue sent word to them.

'My brothers,' he said, 'if you have any word of exhortation for the people, let us hear it.'

¹⁶So Paul stood up and motioned with his hand for attention.

'Fellow Israelites,' he said, 'and the godfearers among you: listen. ¹⁷The God of this people Israel chose our ancestors, and he raised the people up to greatness during their stay in the land of Egypt. Then he led them out from there with his hand lifted high, ¹⁸and for about forty years he put up with them in the desert. ¹⁹He drove out seven nations from the land of Canaan, and gave them the land as their inheritance ²⁰for about four hundred and fifty years. After that, he gave them judges, up until Samuel the prophet. ²¹After that, they asked for a king, and God gave them Saul the son of Kish, a man from the tribe of Benjamin. He ruled for forty years, ²²and after God had removed him he raised up for them David as king. He is the one to whom God bore witness when he said, "I have found David, son of Jesse, a man after my own heart; he will accomplish all my purpose."

²³'From this man's offspring, in accordance with his promise, God has produced a saviour for Israel: Jesus! ²⁴Before he appeared, John had announced a baptism of repentance for the whole people of Israel. ²⁵As John was finishing

Acts 13.13–25

his course, he said, "What do you suppose I am? I am not the one. But look: someone is coming after me, and I am not worthy to untie the sandals on his feet."

The messianic challenge

[26] 'My brothers and sisters,' Paul continued, 'children of Abraham's family, and the godfearers among you: it is to us that the word of this salvation has been sent! [27] The people who live in Jerusalem, and their rulers, didn't recognize him, and they fulfilled the words of the prophets which are read to them every sabbath by condemning him. [28] Even though they found no reason to condemn him to death, they asked Pilate to have him killed. [29] When they had completed everything that had been written about him in prophecy, they took him down from the cross and put him in a tomb. [30] But God raised him from the dead, [31] and he was seen for several days by those who had come with him from Galilee to Jerusalem. They are now his witnesses to the people.

[32] 'We are here now to bring you the good news which was promised to our ancestors, [33] that God has fulfilled this promise to us, their children, by raising Jesus. This corresponds, indeed, to what is written in the second Psalm:

You are my son; this day I have begotten you.

[34] 'That he raised him from the dead, never more to return to corruption, conforms to what was written:

I will give you the holy and faithful mercies of David.

[35] 'Because, as it says in another place,

You will not hand over your holy one to see corruption.

[36] 'Now David served his own generation, and in the purposes of God he fell asleep and was gathered to his fathers. He did experience corruption. [37] But the one God raised up did not experience corruption. [38] So let it be known to you, my brothers and sisters, that forgiveness of sins is announced through him, and that everything from which you were unable to be set right by the law of Moses, [39] by him every one who believes is set right.

[40] 'Beware, then, lest what the prophets foretold comes true of you:

[41] Look out, you scoffers – be amazed, and disappear!
I am doing something in your days, a work which you wouldn't believe
even if someone were to explain it to you.'

[42] As Paul and Barnabas were leaving, they begged them to come back the next sabbath and tell them more about these things. [43] Many of the Jews and devout proselytes followed them once the synagogue was dismissed. They spoke to them some more, and urged them to remain in God's grace.

A light to the Gentiles

[44] On the next sabbath, almost the whole city came together to hear the word of the Lord. [45] But when the Jews saw the crowds, they were filled with righteous indignation, and spoke blasphemous words against what Paul was saying.

[46] Paul and Barnabas grew very bold.

'God's word had to be spoken to you first,' they declared. 'But since you are rejecting it, and judging yourselves unworthy of the life of God's new age, look! We are turning to the Gentiles! [47] This is what the Lord has commanded, you see:

I have set you for a light to the nations,
so that you can be salvation-bringers to the end of the earth.'

[48] When the Gentiles heard this, they were thrilled, and they praised the word of the Lord. All those who were marked out for the life of God's new age became believers. [49] And the word of the Lord spread through the whole land.

[50] But the Jews incited the devout aristocratic women and the leading men of the city. They stirred up persecution against Paul and Barnabas, and drove them out of their district. [51] They, however, shook the dust off their feet

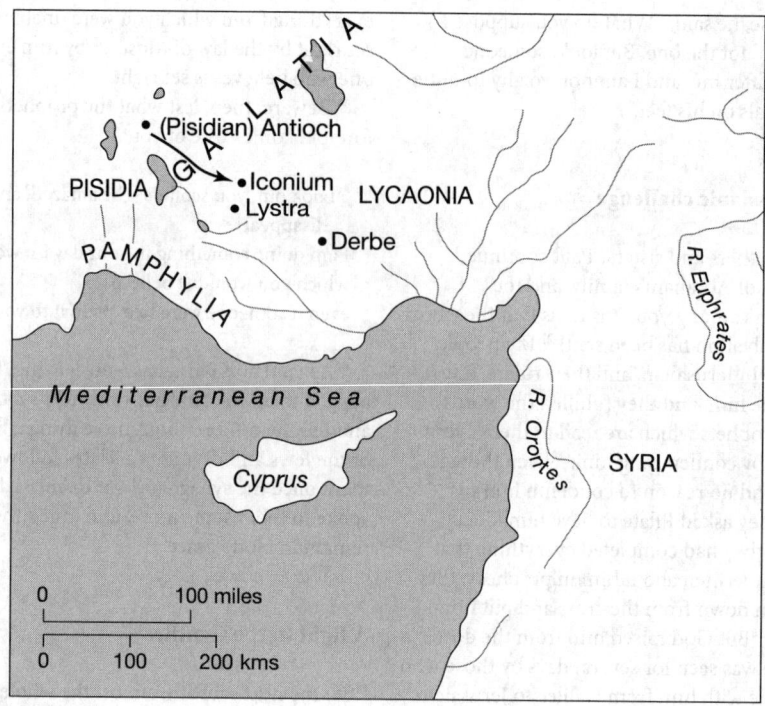

Acts 13.51

and went on to Iconium. ⁵²The disciples were filled with joy and with the holy spirit.

Iconium

14 What happened in Iconium was much the same. They went into the Jewish synagogue and spoke, with the result that a large crowd, both of Jews and of Greeks, came to faith. ²But the unbelieving Jews stirred up and poisoned the minds of the Gentiles against the brothers. ³They stayed there a long time, speaking boldly on behalf of the Lord, who bore them witness to the word of his grace by giving signs and wonders which were done at their hands.

⁴But the inhabitants of the city were divided. Some were with the Jews, and some with the apostles. ⁵But then the Gentiles and Jews, with their rulers, made an attempt to ill-treat them and stone them. ⁶They got wind of it, however, and fled to Lystra and Derbe, cities of Lycaonia, and to the surrounding countryside. ⁷There they went on announcing the good news.

Confusion in Lystra

⁸There was a man sitting in Lystra who was unable to use his feet. He had been lame from his mother's womb, and had never walked. ⁹He heard Paul speaking. When Paul looked hard at him, and saw that he had faith to be made well, ¹⁰he said with a loud voice, 'Stand up straight on your feet!'

Up he jumped, and walked about.

¹¹When the crowds saw what Paul had done, they shouted loudly in the Lycaonian language, 'The gods have come down to us in human form!' ¹²They called Barnabas 'Zeus', and Paul, because he was the main speaker, 'Hermes'. ¹³The priest of Zeus, whose temple was just outside the city, brought oxen and garlands to the city gates. There was a crowd with him, and he was all ready to offer sacrifice.

¹⁴But when the apostles, Paul and Barnabas, heard of it, they tore their clothes and rushed into the crowd.

¹⁵'Men, men,' they shouted, 'what on earth are you doing? We are just ordinary humans, with the same nature as you, and we are bringing you the wonderful message that you

Acts 14.1–7

should turn away from these foolish things to the living God, the one who made heaven and earth and the sea and everything in them. ¹⁶In earlier generations he allowed all the nations to go their own ways, ¹⁷but even then he didn't leave himself without witness. He has done you good, giving you rain from heaven and times of fruitfulness, filling your bodies with food and your hearts with gladness.'

¹⁸Even by saying this, they only just restrained the crowds from offering them sacrifice. ¹⁹But some Jews arrived from Antioch and Iconium, and persuaded the crowds to stone Paul. They dragged him outside the city, thinking he was dead. ²⁰The disciples gathered round him, however, and he got up and went into the city. The next day he and Barnabas went off to Derbe.

Opening the door of faith

²¹They preached in Derbe, and made many disciples. Then they returned to Lystra, Iconium and Antioch, ²²strengthening the hearts of the disciples, and urging them to remain in the faith. They warned them that getting into God's kingdom would mean going through considerable suffering. ²³In every church they appointed elders by laying hands on them. They fasted, prayed, and commended them to the Lord in whom they had believed.

²⁴They went through Pisidia and came to Pamphylia; ²⁵and when they had spoken the word in Perga they went down to Attalia. ²⁶From there they sailed to Antioch, which was where they had been commended to God's grace for the work which they had accomplished. ²⁷Once there, they called the church together, and told them all the things which God had done with them, and how he had opened a door of faith for the Gentiles. ²⁸They stayed there a long time with the disciples.

Is circumcision necessary?

15 Some people came from Judaea to Antioch and, on arrival, began to teach the Christians that they could not be saved unless they were circumcised according to the custom of Moses. ²This caused

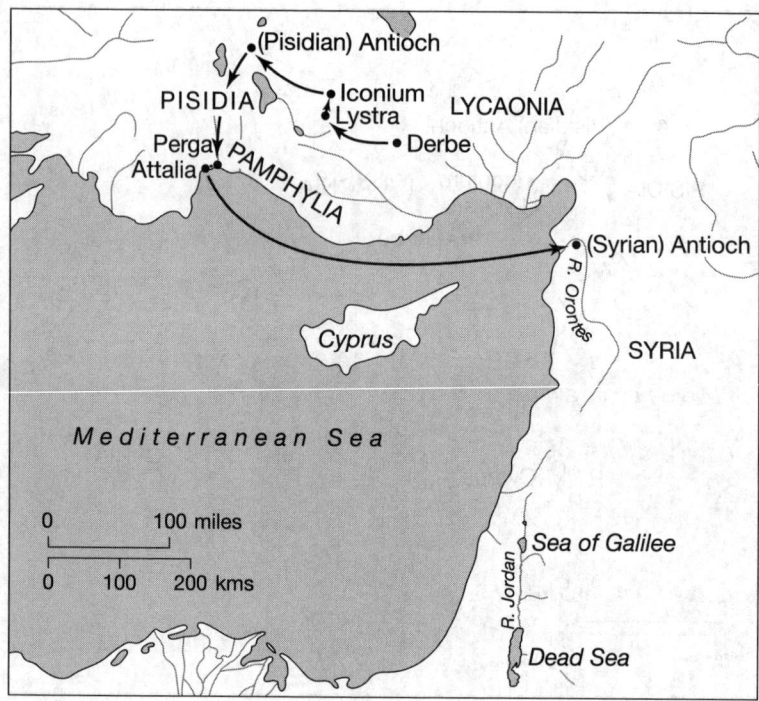

Acts 14.21-28

considerable uproar and dispute between them and Paul and Barnabas, and the church decided to send Paul and Barnabas, and some others from their fellowship, to the apostles and elders in Jerusalem, to try to sort out the problem. ³So they were sent off by the church. They travelled through Phoenicia and Samaria, telling people as they went about the conversion of the Gentiles. They brought great joy to the Christian communities.

⁴When they arrived in Jerusalem they were welcomed by the church, the apostles and the elders, and they told them all the things that God had done with them. ⁵But some believers from the party of the Pharisees stood up.

'They must be circumcised,' they said, 'and you must tell them to keep the law of Moses.'

⁶The apostles and elders gathered together to see what to do about this matter. ⁷After considerable argument, Peter got up.

'My brothers,' he said, 'you know that from our early days together God chose that it should be from my mouth that the Gentiles should hear the word of the gospel and believe. ⁸And God, who knows the heart, bore them witness, by giving them the holy spirit just as he did to us. ⁹He made no distinction between us and them, but he purified their hearts through faith. ¹⁰So now, why are you putting God to the test, by placing a yoke on the disciples' neck which neither we nor our ancestors have been able to bear? ¹¹Rather, we believe that it is by the grace of the Lord Jesus that we shall be saved, just like them.'

The judgment of James

¹²The whole company was silent, and listened to Barnabas and Paul describing the signs and wonders which God had done through them among the Gentiles. ¹³After they had finished, James replied.

'My dear brothers,' he said, 'listen to me. ¹⁴Symeon has explained how, at the beginning, God graciously favoured the Gentiles, to take from them a people for his own name. ¹⁵This, indeed, is in accordance with the words of the prophets, which say,

> ¹⁶After this I will return, and will rebuild the tabernacle of David which had collapsed,

Acts 15.1–11

and I will build the ruins again, and set them straight,
[17]so that the rest of the human race may seek the Lord,
and all the nations upon whom my name has been called.
Thus says the Lord, who has made these things [18]known from of old.

[19]'Therefore this is my judgment: we should not cause extra difficulties for those of the Gentiles who have turned to God. [20]Rather, we should send them a message, warning them to keep away from things that have been polluted by idols, from fornication, from what has been strangled, and from blood. [21]Moses, after all, has from ancient times had people proclaiming him from city to city, since he is read in the synagogues sabbath after sabbath.'

The letter to the churches

[22]Then the apostles and elders, with the whole assembly, decided to send people from their number, Judas Barsabbas and Silas (men well thought of by the Christian community) to Antioch with Paul and Barnabas. [23]They sent a letter with them, which read as follows.

'The apostles and elders send greetings to our Gentile brothers and sisters in Antioch, Syria and Cilicia. [24]Since we have heard that some of our number (not, however, sent by us) have been saying things which have troubled you, causing you distress of heart, [25]we resolved unanimously that it would be best to send to you men whom we have chosen, together with our beloved Barnabas and Paul, [26]who have risked their lives for the name of the Messiah, the Lord Jesus. [27]So we have sent Judas and Silas, and they will tell you the same things face to face. [28]For it seemed good to the holy spirit and to us not to lay any burden on you beyond the following necessary things: [29]that you should abstain from what has been sacrificed to idols, from blood, from what has been strangled, and from fornication. If you keep yourselves from these, you will do well. Farewell.'

[30]So they went off and came down to Antioch, where they gathered the people

together and presented the letter. ³¹When they read it, they were delighted with the message it contained. ³²Judas and Silas, who were themselves prophets, said a good deal to encourage the brothers and sisters, and they gave them strength. ³³When they had spent some time there, they left the family in peace and returned to those who had sent them. ³⁵But Paul and Barnabas stayed on in Antioch, teaching and preaching the word of the Lord, with many others as well.

A huge row

³⁶After some days, Paul said to Barnabas, 'Let's go back and visit the brothers and sisters in all the various cities where we preached the word of the Lord, and see how they are doing.'

³⁷Barnabas wanted to take John, called Mark, along with them. ³⁸But Paul reckoned that it was not a good idea to take with them someone who had left them in Pamphylia and had not gone on with them to the rest of the work. ³⁹There was a huge row, which resulted in them splitting up. Barnabas took Mark and sailed off for Cyprus. ⁴⁰Paul chose Silas, and went off, having been commended by the church to the grace of the Lord. ⁴¹They went through Syria and Cilicia, strengthening the churches.

Timothy – and new developments

16 Paul went on further, to Derbe and then Lystra. There was a disciple there by the name of Timothy, the son of a believing Jewish woman, but with a Greek father. ²The Christians in Lystra and Iconium spoke well of him. ³Paul wanted Timothy to go with them, so he took him and circumcised him because of the Jews in those regions, since they all knew that his father was Greek. ⁴When they went through the cities, they handed on to them the decisions which had been taken by the apostles and elders at Jerusalem, so that they could observe them. ⁵The churches were strengthened in faith, and grew in number every day.

⁶They went through the region of Phrygia and Galatia, since the holy spirit had forbidden

Acts 15.39–41

Acts 16.1–10

them to speak the word in the province of Asia. [7]When they came to Mysia, they tried to go into Bithynia, but the spirit of Jesus didn't allow them to do so. [8]So, passing by Mysia, they came down to Troas. [9]Then a vision appeared to Paul in the night: a man from Macedonia was standing there, pleading with him, and saying, 'Come across to Macedonia and help us!' [10]When he saw the vision, at once we set about finding a way to get across to Macedonia, concluding that God had called us to preach the good news to them.

Preaching and prison in Philippi

[11]So we sailed away from Troas and made a straight course to Samothrace, and the next day to Neapolis. [12]From there we went on to Philippi, a Roman colony which is the chief city of the district of Macedonia. We stayed in this city for some days.

[13]On the sabbath day we went outside the gate to a place by a river where we reckoned there was a place of prayer, and there we sat down. Some women had gathered, and we spoke to them. [14]There was a woman called Lydia, a godfearer, who was a seller of purple from Thyatira. The Lord opened her heart to pay attention to what Paul was saying. [15]She was baptized, with all her household.

'If you have judged me faithful to the Lord,' she begged us, 'please come and stay at my home.'

So she persuaded us.

[16]As we were going to the place of prayer we were met by a girl who had a spirit of divination. She and her oracles made a good living for her owners. [17]She followed Paul and the rest of us.

'These men are servants of God Most High!' she would shout out. 'They are declaring to you the way of salvation!'

[18]She did this for many days. Eventually, Paul got fed up with it. He turned round and addressed the spirit.

'I command you in the name of Jesus the Messiah,' he said, 'come out of her!'

And it came out then and there.

[19]When the girl's owners saw that their hope of profit had vanished, they seized Paul and Silas, dragged them into the public square before the authorities, [20]and presented them to the magistrates.

Acts 16.11–12

'These men', they said, 'are throwing our city into an uproar! They are Jews, [21]and they are teaching customs which it's illegal for us Romans to accept or practise!'

[22]The crowd joined in the attack on them, and the magistrates had their clothes torn off them and gave orders for them to be beaten with rods. [23]When they had thoroughly beaten them, they threw them into prison, and gave orders to the jailer to guard them securely. [24]With that instruction, he put them into the innermost part of the prison, and fastened their feet in the stocks.

Earthquake and salvation

[25]Around midnight, Paul and Silas were praying and singing hymns to God, and the prisoners were listening to them. [26]Suddenly there was a huge earthquake, which shook the foundations of the prison. At once all the doors flew open, and everyone's chains became loose. [27]When the jailer woke up and saw the prison doors open, he drew his sword and was about to kill himself, supposing that the prisoners had escaped. [28]But Paul shouted at the top of his voice, 'Don't harm yourself! We're all still here!'

[29]The jailer called for lights and rushed in. Trembling all over, he fell down before Paul and Silas. [30]Then he brought them outside.

'Gentlemen,' he said, 'will you please tell me how I can get out of this mess?'

[31]'Believe in the Lord Jesus,' they replied, 'and you will be rescued – you and your household.'

[32]And they spoke the word of the Lord to him, with everyone who was in his house. [33]He took them, at that very hour of the night, and washed their wounds. Then at once he was baptized, and all his household with him. [34]Then he took them into his house, put food on the table, and rejoiced with his whole house that he had believed in God.

Publicly vindicated

[35]When day broke, the magistrates sent their officers with the message, 'Let those men go.' [36]The jailer passed on what they said to Paul.

'The magistrates have sent word that you should be released,' he said. 'So now you can leave and go in peace.'

[37]But Paul objected.

'We are Roman citizens!' he said. 'They didn't put us on trial, they beat us in public, they threw us into prison, and now they are sending us away secretly? No way! Let them come themselves and take us out.'

[38] The officers reported these words to the magistrates. When they heard that they were Roman citizens, they were afraid. [39] They went and apologized, brought them out of the prison, and requested that they leave the city. [40] So when they had left the prison they went to Lydia's house. There they saw and encouraged the brothers and sisters, and then they went on their way.

Another king!

17 Paul and Silas travelled through Amphipolis and Apollonia, and came to Thessalonica, where there was a Jewish synagogue. [2] Paul went there, as he usually did, and for three sabbaths he spoke to them, expounding the scriptures, [3] interpreting and explaining that it was necessary for the Messiah to suffer and to rise from the dead, and that 'This Jesus, that I am announcing to you, is the Messiah'. [4] Some of them were persuaded, and threw in their lot with Paul and Silas, including a large crowd of godfearing Greeks, together with quite a few of the leading women.

[5] But the Jews were righteously indignant. They took some villainous men from the market-place, drew a crowd, and threw the city into an uproar. They besieged Jason's house and searched for Paul and Silas, to bring them out to the mob. [6] When they couldn't find them, they dragged Jason and some of the Christians before the town authorities.

'These are the people who are turning the world upside down!' they yelled. 'Now they've come here! [7] Jason has had them in his house! They are all acting against the decrees of Caesar – and they're saying that there is another king, Jesus!'

[8] When they heard these words, the crowd and the authorities were both greatly agitated. [9] They bound Jason and the others over, and then dismissed them.

Paul reaches Athens

[10] The Christians in Thessalonica quickly sent Paul and Silas on, by night, to Beroea. When they got there, they went to the Jewish

Acts 17.1

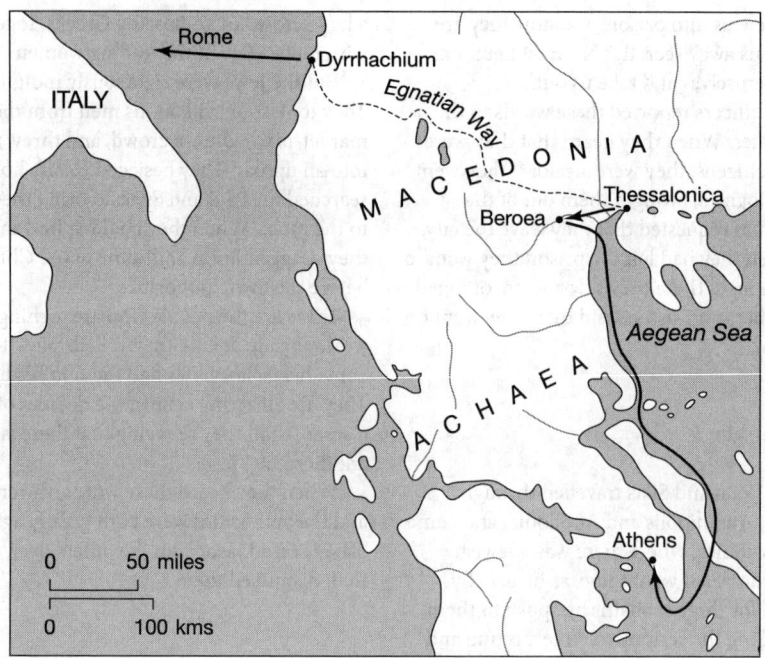

Acts 17.10–21

synagogue. ¹¹The people there were more generous in spirit than those in Thessalonica. They received the word with considerable eagerness, searching the scriptures day by day to see if what they were hearing was indeed the case. ¹²Many of them became believers, including some of the well-born Greek women, and quite a few men.

¹³But when the Jews from Thessalonica knew that the word of God had been proclaimed by Paul in Beroea, too, they came there as well, stirring up trouble and whipping up the crowd. ¹⁴So the Christians quickly sent Paul away as far as the sea-coast, while Silas and Timothy remained behind. ¹⁵Those who were conducting Paul brought him all the way to Athens, where he told them to tell Silas and Timothy to join him as soon as possible. Then they left him there.

¹⁶So Paul waited in Athens. While he was there, his spirit was stirred up as he saw the whole city simply full of idols. ¹⁷He argued in the synagogue with the Jews and the godfearers, and in the market-place every day with those who happened to be there. ¹⁸Some of the Epicurean and Stoic philosophers were disputing with him.

'What can this word-scatterer be on about?' some were saying.

'He seems to be proclaiming foreign divinities,' declared others – since he was preaching 'Jesus and Anastasis'. ('Anastasis' means 'resurrection'.) ¹⁹So they took him up to the Areopagus.

'Are we able to know', they said, 'what this new teaching really is that you are talking about? ²⁰You are putting very strange ideas into our minds. We'd like to find out what it all means.'

²¹All the Athenians, and the foreigners who live there, spend their time simply and solely in telling and hearing the latest novelty.

Paul among the philosophers

²²So Paul stood up in the midst of the Areopagus.

'Men of Athens,' he said, 'I see that you are in every way an extremely religious people. ²³For as I was going along and looking at your objects of worship, I saw an altar with the inscription, TO AN UNKNOWN GOD. Well: I'm here to tell you about what it is that you are worshipping in ignorance. ²⁴The God who made the world and everything in it, the one who is Lord of heaven and earth, doesn't live in temples made by human hands. ²⁵Nor does he need to be looked after by human hands, as though he lacked something, since he himself gives life and breath and all things to everyone. ²⁶He made from one stock every race of humans to live on the whole face of the earth, allotting them their properly ordained times and the boundaries for their dwellings. ²⁷The aim was that they would search for God, and perhaps reach out for him and find him. Indeed, he is actually not far from each one of us, ²⁸for in him we live and move and exist; as also some of your own poets have put it, "For we are his offspring".

²⁹'Well, then, if we really are God's offspring, we ought not to suppose that the divinity is like gold or silver or stone, formed by human skill and ingenuity. ³⁰That was just ignorance; but the time for it has passed, and God has drawn a veil over it. Now, instead, he commands all people everywhere to repent, ³¹because he has established a day on which he intends to call the world to account with full and proper justice by a man whom he has appointed. God has given all people his pledge of this by raising this man from the dead.'

³²When they heard about the resurrection of the dead, some of them ridiculed Paul. But others said, 'We will give you another hearing about this.' ³³So Paul went out from their presence. ³⁴But some people joined him and believed, including Dionysius, a member of the court of the Areopagus, and a woman named Damaris, and others with them.

A year in Corinth

18 After this, Paul left Athens and went to Corinth. ²There he found a Jew named Aquila, a native of Pontus, who had recently arrived from Italy with Priscilla his wife, due to Claudius' edict banishing all Jews from Rome. Paul paid them a visit ³and, because they were in the same business, he stayed with them and worked. They were, by trade, tent-makers.

⁴Paul argued every sabbath in the synagogue, and persuaded both Jews and Greeks. ⁵When Silas and Timothy arrived from Macedonia, Paul was putting great energy into the task of

Acts 18.1

Acts 18.18–28

bearing forthright witness to the Jews that the Messiah really was Jesus. [6]When they opposed him, and blasphemed, he shook out his clothes.

'Your blood be on your own heads!' he said. 'I am innocent. From now on I shall go to the Gentiles.'

[7]He moved on from the synagogue, and went in to the house of a man named Titius Justus, a godfearer who lived opposite the synagogue. [8]But Crispus, the ruler of the synagogue, believed in the Lord, with all his household, and many of the Corinthians heard about it, came to faith, and were baptized.

[9]The Lord spoke to Paul by night in a vision.

'Don't be afraid,' he said. 'Speak on, and don't be silent, [10]because I am with you, and nobody will be able to lay a finger on you to harm you. There are many of my people in this city.'

[11]He stayed there eighteen months, teaching the word of God among them.

Christianity declared legal in Achaea

[12]When Gallio was proconsul of Achaea, the Jews made a concerted attack on Paul, and led him to the official tribunal.

[13]'This man,' they said, 'is teaching people to worship God in illegal ways.'

[14]Paul was getting ready to speak when Gallio intervened.

'Look here, you Jews,' he said to them. 'If this was a matter of serious wrongdoing or some wicked villainy, I would receive your plea in the proper way. [15]But if this is a dispute about words, names and laws within your own customs, you can sort it out among yourselves. I don't intend to be a judge in such matters.'

[16]Then he dismissed them from the tribunal. [17]But the crowd seized Sosthenes, the ruler of the synagogue, and beat him right there in front of the tribunal. Gallio, however, totally ignored this.

Apollos in Ephesus and Corinth

[18]Paul stayed on for several more days with the Christians, and then said his farewells and sailed away to Syria, taking Priscilla and Aquila with him. In Cenchreae he had his hair cut off, since he was under a vow. [19]When they arrived at Ephesus he left them there, while he himself went into the synagogue and disputed with the Jews. [20]When they asked him to stay with them for a longer time, he refused, [21]and took his leave.

'I will come back to you again,' he said, 'if that's God's will.'

Then he left Ephesus, [22]and went to Caesarea. Then he went up to Jerusalem, greeted the church, and went back to Antioch. [23]When he had spent some time there, he went off again and travelled from one place to another throughout the region of Galatia and Phrygia, encouraging all the disciples.

[24]Now there arrived in Ephesus a Jew named Apollos, who came from Alexandria. He was an eloquent man, and powerful when it came to expounding scripture. [25]He had received instruction in the Way of the Lord. He was an enthusiastic speaker, and taught the things about Jesus accurately, even though he only knew the baptism of John. [26]He began to speak boldly in the synagogue. When Priscilla and Aquila heard him, they took him to one side and expounded the Way of God to him more accurately.

[27]He wanted to go across to Achaea. The Christians in Ephesus, by way of encouragement, wrote letters to the church there to welcome him. On his arrival, his work made a considerable impact, through God's grace, on the believers, [28]since he openly and powerfully refuted the Jews by demonstrating from the scriptures that the Messiah really was Jesus.

Paul in Ephesus

19 While Apollos was in Corinth, Paul travelled through the interior regions and arrived at Ephesus. There he found some disciples, [2]and said to them, 'Did you receive the holy spirit when you believed?'

'We had not heard,' they replied, 'that there *was* a "holy spirit."'

[3]'Well then,' said Paul, 'into what were you baptized?'

'Into John's baptism,' they replied.

[4]'John baptized with a baptism of repentance for the people,' said Paul, 'speaking about the one who was to come after him, and saying

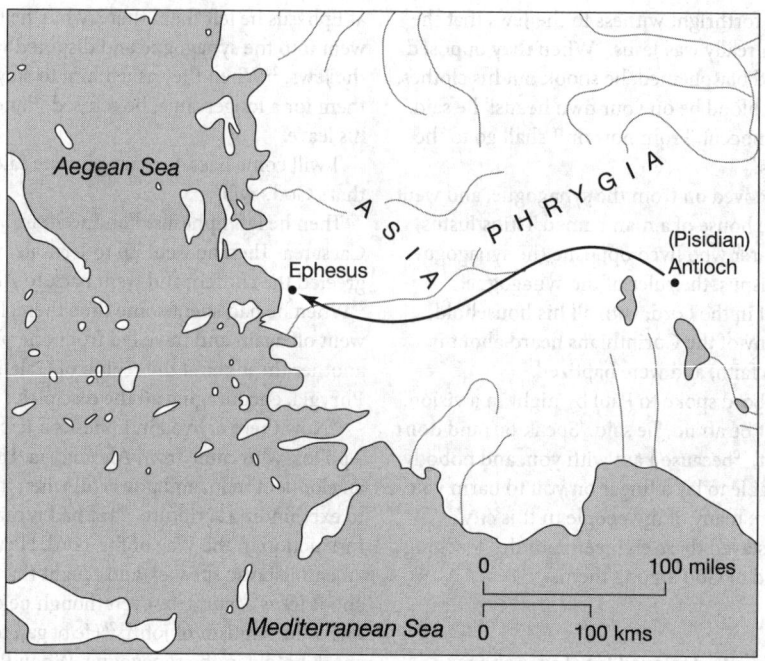

Acts 19.1–10

that that person would be the one that people should believe in – and that means Jesus.'

⁵When they heard this, they were baptized in the name of Jesus. ⁶Paul then laid his hands on them, and the holy spirit came upon them, and they spoke in tongues and prophesied. ⁷There were about twelve men in all.

⁸Paul went into the synagogue and spoke boldly there for three months, arguing and persuading them about the kingdom of God. ⁹But when some of them were hard-hearted, and wouldn't believe, and made wicked allegations about the Way in front of everybody else, Paul left them. He took the disciples with him, and argued every day in the lecture-hall of Tyrannus. ¹⁰He did this for two years, so that all the inhabitants of Asia, Jews and Greeks alike, heard the word of the Lord.

The power of God and the powers at Ephesus

¹¹God performed unusual works of power through Paul's hands. ¹²People used to take handkerchiefs or towels that had touched his skin and put them on the sick, and then their diseases would leave them and evil spirits would depart.

¹³There were some travelling Jewish exorcists who tried to use the name of the Lord Jesus on people with evil spirits.

'I command you', they used to say, 'in the name of Jesus, the one Paul proclaims!'

¹⁴There were seven of them who used to do this. They were the sons of Sceva, a Jewish high priest. ¹⁵But on one occasion the evil spirit answered them back.

'I know Jesus', it shouted, 'and I am well acquainted with Paul; but who are you?'

¹⁶The man who had the evil spirit pounced on them and, since he was much too strong for them, overpowered all of them, so that they fled out of the house naked and battered. ¹⁷This became common knowledge among both Jews and Greeks living in Ephesus. Fear came on all of them, and the name of the Lord Jesus grew greatly in prestige.

¹⁸Many people who became believers came forward to make public confession, revealing what they had been up to. ¹⁹Some who had been practising magic brought their books and burnt them in front of everyone; someone calculated how much they were all worth, and

it came to fifty thousand silver pieces. ²⁰So the word grew and was strong, in accordance with the Lord's power.

²¹Once all this had been finished, Paul decided in his spirit to go back through Macedonia and Achaea and, from there, on to Jerusalem.

'After I've been there', he said, 'I'll have to go and see Rome.'

²²He sent two of his helpers, Timothy and Erastus, on ahead to Macedonia, while he himself spent a little more time in Asia.

'Great is Ephesian Artemis!'

²³Around that time there was a major disturbance because of the Way. ²⁴There was a silversmith called Demetrius who made silver statues of Artemis, which brought the workmen a tidy income. ²⁵He got them all together, along with other workers in the same business.

'Gentlemen,' he began. 'You know that the reason we are doing rather well for ourselves is quite simply this business of ours. ²⁶And now you see, and hear, that this fellow Paul is going around not only Ephesus but pretty well the whole of Asia, persuading the masses to change their way of life, telling them that gods made with hands are not gods after all! ²⁷This not only threatens to bring our proper business into disrepute, but it looks as if it might make people disregard the temple of the great goddess Artemis. Then she – and, after all, the whole of Asia, indeed the whole world, worships her! – she might lose her great majesty.'

²⁸When they heard this, they were filled with rage.

'Great is Ephesian Artemis!' they shouted. 'Great is Ephesian Artemis!'

²⁹The whole city was filled with the uproar, and everyone rushed together into the theatre, dragging along with them the Macedonians Gaius and Aristarchus, two of Paul's companions. ³⁰Paul wanted to go in to speak to the people, but his followers wouldn't let him. ³¹Indeed, some of the local magistrates, who were friendly towards him, sent him a message urging him not to take the risk of going into the theatre. ³²Meanwhile, some people were shouting one thing, some another. In fact, the whole assembly was thoroughly confused, and most of them had no idea why they had come there in the first place. ³³The Jews pushed Alexander forward, and some of the crowd informed him what was going on. He motioned with his hand, and was going to make a statement to the people to explain things. ³⁴But when they realized he was a Jew, they all shouted together, for about two hours, 'Great is Ephesian Artemis!'

³⁵The town clerk quietened the crowd.

'Men of Ephesus,' he said, 'is there anyone who doesn't know that our city of Ephesus is the place which has the honour of being the home of Artemis the Great, and of the statue that fell from heaven? ³⁶Nobody can deny it! So you should be quiet, and not do anything rash. ³⁷You've brought these men here, but they haven't stolen from the temple, or blasphemed our goddess. ³⁸If Demetrius and his colleagues have a charge they want to bring against anyone, the courts are open and we have magistrates. People can present their cases against one another. ³⁹But if you are wanting to know anything beyond that, it must be sorted out in the authorized assembly. ⁴⁰Let me remind you that we ourselves are risking legal proceedings because of this riot today, since there is no reason we could give which would enable us to present a satisfactory explanation for this uproar.'

⁴¹With these words, he dismissed the assembly.

Round the coast and out of the window

20 After the hue and cry had died down, Paul sent for the disciples. He encouraged them, said his farewells, and set off to go to Macedonia. ²He went through those regions, encouraging them with many words and, arriving in Greece, ³stayed there three months. He was intending to set sail for Syria, but the Jews made a plot against him, and he decided to return instead through Macedonia.

⁴He was accompanied on this trip by Sopater, son of Pyrrhus of Beroea; by Aristarchus and Secundus from Thessalonica; by Gaius from Derbe; and Timothy, and Tychicus and Trophimus from Asia. ⁵They went on ahead and waited for us at Troas, ⁶while we got on board ship at Philippi, after the days of

Acts 20.1–12

Unleavened Bread, and joined them in Troas five days later. We stayed there for a week.

⁷On the first day of the week we gathered to break bread. Paul was intending to leave the following morning. He was engaged in discussion with them, and he went on talking up to midnight. ⁸There were several lamps burning in the upper room where we were gathered. ⁹A young man named Eutychus was sitting by the window, and was overcome with a deep sleep as Paul went on and on. Once sleep had got the better of him, he fell down out of the third-storey window, and was picked up dead.

¹⁰Paul went down, stooped over him and picked him up.

'Don't be alarmed,' he said. 'There is life still in him.'

¹¹He went back upstairs, broke bread and ate with them, and continued speaking until dawn. Then he left. ¹²They took up the young man alive and were very much comforted.

Paul the pastor looks back – and looks on

¹³We went on ahead to the ship and set off for Assos, with the intention of picking Paul up there (he had decided that he would walk to that point). ¹⁴When we arrived at Assos, we picked him up and went on to Mitylene, ¹⁵and from there we sailed on the next day and arrived opposite Chios. The following day we got near to Samos, and the day after that we came to Miletus. ¹⁶Paul had decided, you see, to pass by Ephesus, so that he wouldn't have to spend more time in Asia. He was eager to get to Jerusalem, if he could, in time for the day of Pentecost.

¹⁷From Miletus, Paul sent to Ephesus and called for the elders of the church, ¹⁸and they came to him.

'You know very well,' he began, 'how I have behaved with you all the time, since the first day I arrived in Asia. ¹⁹I have served the Lord with all humility, with the tears and torments that came upon me because of the plots of the Jews. ²⁰You know that I kept back nothing that would have been helpful to you, preaching to you and teaching you both in public and from house to house. ²¹I bore witness both to Jews and Greeks about repentance towards God and faith in our Lord Jesus.

²²'And now, look, I am going to Jerusalem, bound by the spirit. I have no idea what's going to happen to me there, ²³but only that the holy spirit testifies to me in city after city that

Acts 20.13–27

captivity and trouble are in store for me. ²⁴But I don't reckon my life at any value, so long as I can finish my course, and the ministry which I have received from the Lord Jesus, to bear witness to the gospel of God's grace.

²⁵'So now', he went on, 'I have gone to and fro preaching the kingdom among you, but I know that none of you will ever see my face again. ²⁶Therefore I bear witness to you this very day that I am innocent of everyone's blood, ²⁷since I did not shrink from declaring to you God's entire plan.'

Watch out for yourselves, the flock and the wolves

²⁸'Watch out for yourselves', Paul continued, 'and for the whole flock, in which the holy spirit has appointed you as guardians, to feed the church of God, which he purchased with his very own blood. ²⁹I know that fierce wolves will come in after I am gone, and they won't spare the flock. ³⁰Yes, even from among yourselves people will arise, saying things which will distort the truth, and they will draw the disciples away after them. ³¹Therefore keep watch, and remember that for three years, night and day, I didn't stop warning each of you, with tears.

³²'So now I commit you to God, and to the word of his grace, which is able to build you up and give you the inheritance among all those whom God has sanctified. ³³I never coveted anyone's silver, or gold, or clothes. ³⁴You yourselves know that these very hands worked to serve my own needs and those of the people with me. ³⁵I showed you in all such matters that this is how we should work to help the weak, remembering the words of the Lord Jesus, as he put it, "It is more blessed to give than to receive."'

³⁶When he had said this, he knelt down with them all and prayed. ³⁷There was great lamentation among them all, and they fell on Paul's neck and kissed him. ³⁸They were particularly sorry to hear the word he had spoken about never seeing his face again.

Then they brought him to the ship.

Disturbing prophecies

21 When we had left them behind and had set sail, we made a straight course to Cos, and went on the next day to Rhodes and

Acts 21.1–14

from there to Patara. ²There we found a ship heading for Phoenicia, and we got on board and set sail. ³We came in sight of Cyprus, passed it on our left side, sailed to Syria and arrived in Tyre, which was where the boat was going to unload its cargo. ⁴We found some disciples and stayed there a week – and they told Paul, by the spirit, not to go to Jerusalem. ⁵When our time there was up, we left and went on our way, with everyone, women and children included, coming with us out of the city. We knelt down on the seashore and prayed. ⁶Then we said our farewells to one another. We got on the ship and they returned home.

⁷The end of our voyage from Tyre saw us arrive at Ptolemais. There we greeted the Christians, and stayed a day with them. ⁸On the next day we left and went on to Caesarea, and went into the house of Philip the evangelist, one of the Seven, and stayed with him. ⁹He had four unmarried daughters who prophesied.

¹⁰After we'd been there several days, Agabus the prophet arrived from Jerusalem. ¹¹He came to us, took Paul's girdle, and tied himself up with it, hand and foot.

'This is what the holy spirit says,' he declared. 'The Judaeans in Jerusalem will tie up the man to whom this girdle belongs, just like this, and they will hand him over to the Gentiles.'

¹²When we heard that, we and the people of that place begged Paul not to go up to Jerusalem.

¹³Then Paul responded.

'What are you doing with all this weeping,' he said, 'breaking my heart in pieces? I am quite prepared not only to be tied up but to die in Jerusalem for the name of the Lord Jesus.'

¹⁴When we realized we couldn't dissuade him, we gave up the attempt.

'May the Lord's will be done,' was all we said.

Warding off the inevitable

¹⁵After those days we made preparations to go up to Jerusalem. ¹⁶Some of the disciples from Caesarea went with us, and took us to the house of Mnason, an elderly disciple from Cyprus. That was where we were going to be staying.

¹⁷When we came to Jerusalem, the brothers

Acts 21.15–17

and sisters welcomed us gladly. ¹⁸On the next day Paul went in with us to see James, with all the elders present. ¹⁹He greeted them and laid out before them everything which God had done through his ministry among the Gentiles, telling it all step by step. ²⁰They praised God when they heard it.

'You see, brother,' they said, 'that there are many thousands of Jews who have believed. They are all of them fiercely enthusiastic for the law. ²¹But what they have heard about you is that you teach all the Jews who live among the nations to abandon Moses, telling them not to circumcise their children and not to keep the customs. ²²Where does this leave us? They will certainly hear that you have come. ²³So do what we tell you: there are four men here who have taken a vow upon themselves. ²⁴Join in with these men. Purify yourself along with them, and pay the expenses for them as they have their heads shaved. That way everyone will know that there is no truth in the accusations against you, but rather that you too are behaving as a law-observant Jew should. ²⁵As for the Gentiles who have believed, we have written to them with our decision that they should keep themselves from what has been sacrificed to idols, from blood, from what is strangled, and from fornication.'

²⁶So Paul took the men and, the next day, underwent the ritual of purification alongside them. He went into the Temple and made the declaration, stating when the days of purification would be completed and when the time would come for sacrifice to be offered for each of them.

Riot in the Temple

²⁷When the seven days were completed, some Jews from Asia spotted Paul in the Temple. They gathered a crowd and grabbed him.

²⁸'Men of Israel,' they yelled, 'come and help us! This is the man who's been teaching everybody everywhere against our people, our law, and this place! And now, what's more, he's brought some Greeks into the Temple, and he's defiled this holy place!' ²⁹(They had previously seen Trophimus the Ephesian with Paul in the city, and they thought Paul had taken him into the Temple.)

³⁰The whole city was stirred up, and people rushed together from all around. They seized Paul and dragged him outside the Temple, and the gates were shut at once. ³¹As they were trying to kill him, word reached the tribune of the guard that all Jerusalem was in an uproar. ³²At once he took soldiers and centurions and ran down to them. When the crowd saw the tribune and the soldiers, they stopped beating Paul. ³³Then the tribune came up, arrested him, ordered him to be bound with two chains, and asked who he was and what he had done. ³⁴Some in the crowd said one thing, some said another. Since he couldn't find out what was really going on because of the uproar, he gave orders for Paul to be brought into the barracks. ³⁵When they got to the steps, the pressure of the crowd was so strong that the soldiers had to carry Paul. ³⁶The great mob of people was following, and shouting, 'Kill him! Kill him!'

Why not hear my story?

³⁷As they were about to go into the barracks, Paul turned to the tribune.

'Am I allowed to say something to you?' he asked.

'Well!' replied the tribune. 'So you know some Greek, do you? ³⁸Aren't you the Egyptian who raised a revolt some while back and led those four thousand "assassins" into the desert?'

³⁹'Actually,' replied Paul, 'I'm a Jew! I'm from Tarsus in Cilicia. That's not an insignificant place to be a citizen of. Please, please, let me speak to the people.'

⁴⁰So he gave him permission. Paul stood on the steps and motioned with his hand to the people. When, eventually, there was silence, he spoke to them in Aramaic.

22 'My brothers and fathers,' he began, 'hear me as I explain myself to you.'

²When they heard him speaking in Aramaic they became even quieter.

³'I am a Jew', he continued, 'and I was born in Tarsus in Cilicia. I received my education here, in this city, and I studied at the feet of Gamaliel. I was trained in the strictest interpretations of our ancestral laws, and became zealous for God, just as all of you are today. ⁴I persecuted this Way, right to the point of killing people, and I bound and handed over to prison both men and women – ⁵as the high priest and all the elders can testify. I received letters from them to the Jews of Damascus, where I was going in order to find the heretics who were there, tie them up, and bring them to Jerusalem to face their just deserts.

⁶'Just as I was on the way, and getting near to Damascus, suddenly a bright light shone from heaven all around me. It was about midday. ⁷I fell down on the ground and I heard a voice, saying, "Saul, Saul, why are you persecuting me?" ⁸I answered, "Who are you, Master?" And he said to me, "I am Jesus of Nazareth, and you are persecuting me!"

⁹'The people who were with me saw the light, but they didn't hear the voice of the person speaking to me. ¹⁰So I said, "What shall I do, Master?" And the Lord said to me, "Get up and go into Damascus, and there you will be informed of all the things that have been arranged for you to do."

¹¹'So, as I couldn't see because of the brightness of that light, the people with me led me by the hand, and I came to Damascus.'

Out of his own mouth

¹²'There was a man named Ananias,' Paul continued. 'He was a devout, law-keeping Jew, and all the Jews living in Damascus would testify to the fact. ¹³He came and stood beside me and said, "Brother Saul, receive your sight." In that very moment I could see, and I looked at him. ¹⁴This is what he said. "The God of our ancestors chose you to know his will, to see the Righteous One, and to hear the word from his mouth. ¹⁵This is because you are going to bear witness for him to all people, telling them what you have seen and heard. ¹⁶Now, then, what are you going to do? Get up, be baptized and wash away your sins by calling on his name."

¹⁷'After I came back to Jerusalem, and was praying in the Temple, I fell into a trance, ¹⁸and I saw him speaking to me. "Hurry up!" he said. "Leave Jerusalem as quickly as possible! They won't accept your testimony about me." ¹⁹"But, Lord," I replied, "they themselves know that in all the synagogues I used to imprison and beat those who believe in you. ²⁰And when they shed the blood of Stephen, your witness, I was

myself standing there and giving my approval. I was looking after the cloaks of those who were killing him."

²¹"'No,' he said to me. 'Go away from here! I'm sending you far away – to the Gentiles!'"

²²Up to this point the crowd listened to Paul. But now they began to shout.

'Away with him from the face of the earth!' they yelled. 'Someone like that has no right to live!'

Roman citizenship comes in useful

²³The crowd was shouting, tearing their clothes, and throwing dust in the air. ²⁴The tribune gave orders for Paul to be brought into the barracks, and he told the guards to examine him by flogging, so that he could find out just what was the reason for all the uproar against him.

²⁵As they were tying Paul up ready for the whips, Paul spoke to the centurion who was standing beside him.

'Is it lawful', he said, 'to flog a Roman citizen without first finding him guilty?'

²⁶When the centurion heard that, he went off to the tribune and spoke to him.

'What d'you think you're doing?' he said. 'This fellow's a Roman citizen!'

²⁷The tribune came and spoke to Paul.

'Tell me,' he said. 'Are you a Roman citizen?'

'Yes,' replied Paul.

²⁸'It cost me a lot of money to buy this citizenship,' said the tribune.

'Ah,' said Paul, 'but it came to me by birth.'

²⁹The people who were about to torture Paul stepped back quickly from him. As for the tribune, he was afraid, discovering that he was a Roman citizen and that he had had him tied up.

³⁰On the next day, still wanting to get to the bottom of it all, and to find out what was being alleged by the Jews, he released Paul, and ordered the chief priests to come together, with the whole Sanhedrin. He brought Paul in and presented him to them.

Paul before the Sanhedrin

23 Paul looked hard at the Sanhedrin. 'My brothers,' he said. 'I have conducted myself before God in a completely good conscience all my life up to this day.'

²Ananias, the high priest, ordered the bystanders to strike Paul on the mouth.

³'God will strike you, you whitewashed wall!' said Paul to Ananias. 'You are sitting to judge me according to the law, and yet you order me to be struck in violation of the law?'

⁴'You are insulting the high priest?' asked the bystanders.

⁵'My brothers,' replied Paul, 'I didn't know he was the high priest. Scripture says, of course, "You mustn't speak evil of the ruler of your people."'

⁶Paul knew that one part of the gathering were Sadducees, and the other part Pharisees.

'My brothers,' he shouted to the Sanhedrin, 'I am a Pharisee, the son of Pharisees. This trial is about the Hope, about the Resurrection of the Dead!'

⁷At these words, an argument broke out between the Pharisees and Sadducees, and they were split among themselves. ⁸(The Sadducees deny that there is any resurrection, or any intermediate state of 'angel' or 'spirit', but the Pharisees affirm them both.) ⁹There was quite an uproar, with some of the scribes from the Pharisees' party standing up and arguing angrily, 'We find nothing wrong in this man! What if a spirit spoke to him, or an angel for that matter?'

¹⁰Faced with another great riot, the tribune was worried that Paul was going to be pulled in pieces between them. He ordered the guard to go down and snatch him out of the midst of them and bring him back up into the barracks.

¹¹On the next night, the Lord stood by him.

'Cheer up!' he said. 'You have given your testimony about me in Jerusalem. Now you have to do it in Rome.'

The oath and the plot

¹²The next morning, the Jews made a plot together. They swore an oath, binding themselves not to eat or drink until they had killed Paul. ¹³There were more than forty of them who made this solemn vow with one another. ¹⁴They went to the high priest and the elders.

'We have sworn a solemn and binding oath', they said, 'not to taste anything until we have killed Paul. ¹⁵What you need to do is this: tell the tribune, with the Sanhedrin, to bring him down to you, as if you wanted to make a more careful examination of his case. And then, before he arrives, we'll be ready to dispatch him.'

[16]Paul's nephew (his sister's son) heard of the plot. He went off, entered the barracks, and told Paul about it. [17]Paul called one of the centurions.

'Take this young man to the tribune,' he said. 'He's got something to tell him.'

[18]So he took him off and brought him to the tribune.

'Paul the prisoner called me and asked me to bring this young man to you,' he said. 'Apparently he's got something to tell you.'

[19]So the tribune took the young man by the hand, and led him off into a private room.

'What is it you have to tell me?' he asked.

[20]'The Judaeans have agreed to ask you to bring Paul down to the Sanhedrin tomorrow,' he said. 'It will look as if they're wanting to make a more thorough investigation about him. [21]But don't do what they want! There are more than forty men who are setting an ambush for him, and they've sworn a solemn oath not to eat or drink until they've killed him. They are ready right now, waiting for the word from you!'

[22]So the tribune dismissed the lad.

'Don't tell anyone at all that you've told me about this,' he said.

We have ways of keeping you safe

[23]So the tribune summoned two of the centurions.

'Get ready a squad of two hundred,' he said. 'They're going to Caesarea. Also take seventy horsemen and two hundred light-armed guards. They leave at nine o'clock tonight. [24]Get horses ready for Paul to ride, and take him safely to Felix the governor.'

[25]He wrote a letter which went like this:

[26]'Claudius Lysias, to the most excellent governor Felix, greeting. [27]This man was seized by the Jews, who were going to kill him. When I learned that he was a Roman citizen I went with the guard and rescued him. [28]I wanted to

Acts 23.23–35

know the charge on which they were accusing him, so I took him into their Sanhedrin. ²⁹There I discovered that he was being accused in relation to disputes about their law, but that he was not being charged with anything for which he would deserve to die or to be imprisoned. ³⁰I then received information that there was to be a plot against him. So I am sending him to you at once. I have told his accusers that they must inform you of their charges against him.'

³¹So the soldiers did what they were told. They took Paul and brought him by night to Antipatris, ³²and the next day they allowed the horsemen to go on with him while they returned to barracks. ³³The company arrived at Caesarea and handed over the letter to the governor, presenting Paul at the same time. ³⁴Felix read the letter, and asked which jurisdiction Paul was from. He found out that he was from Cilicia.

³⁵'I will hear your case', he said, 'when your accusers arrive.'

He ordered that he be kept under guard in Herod's Praetorium.

Bring on the barristers

24 After five days, Ananias the high priest came down to Caesarea with some of the elders, and with a barrister named Tertullus. They told the governor what they had against Paul. ²Paul was summoned, and Tertullus began his speech of accusation.

'Most excellent Felix! We are enjoying great peace because of you! Through your wise foresight and planning things have greatly improved for this people. ³We welcome it in every way, in every place, and with every feeling of gratitude. ⁴But, so as not to keep you waiting any longer, I beg you, of your forbearance, to listen to us briefly.

⁵'We find this fellow to be a public nuisance. He stirs up civil strife among all the Jews, all over the world. He is a ringleader in the sect of the Nazoreans. ⁶He even tried to defile the Temple! But we caught him. ⁸If you examine him yourself you will be able to find out about all these things of which we're accusing him.'

⁹The Jews added their voices to this speech, agreeing that it was just as had been said.

A defence of the Hope

¹⁰The governor motioned to Paul to speak.

'I understand that you have been governor of this nation for several years', he began, 'and therefore I am all the more pleased to make my defence before you. ¹¹You will be able to discover that it is not more than twelve days since I came up to worship at Jerusalem. ¹²They didn't find me disputing with anybody in the Temple; nor was I stirring up a crowd, either in the synagogues or elsewhere in the city. ¹³They can provide no proof of any of the charges they are now bringing against me.

¹⁴'But this much I will confess to you: that it is true that I do worship the God of my ancestors according to the Way which they call a "sect". I believe everything which is written in the law and the prophets, ¹⁵and I hold to the hope in God, for which they also long, that there will be a resurrection of the righteous and the unrighteous. ¹⁶For that reason I make it my settled aim always to have a clear conscience before God and all people.

¹⁷'For several years I have been collecting alms and offerings to bring to my nation. ¹⁸That was the business I was engaged in when they found me purified in the Temple, without any crowds and without any riot. ¹⁹There were some Jews from Asia there; they are the ones who should appear before you and bring any accusations against me that they may have. ²⁰Or let these people themselves say what wrong they found in me when I stood before the Sanhedrin – ²¹unless it is about this one thing, which I shouted out as I was standing among them: "It's because of the resurrection of the dead that I am being judged before you today."'

Felix calms (and slows) things down

²²Felix was quite well informed about the Way. He adjourned the hearing.

'When Lysias the tribune comes down,' he said, 'then I will make my decision about your business.'

²³He told the centurion to keep Paul under guard, to allow him some freedom, and not to stop any of his companions from looking after him.

24After some days, Felix came with Drusilla his wife, who was Jewish. They sent for Paul and listened to him speaking about faith in the Messiah Jesus. 25As he talked about justice, self-control and the judgment to come, Felix became afraid.

'That's quite enough for now,' he said. 'You can go. When I get a good opportunity I'll call for you again another time.'

26At the same time he was hoping that Paul would give him money, and so he sent for him frequently and talked with him. 27After two years Felix handed over the reins of office to Porcius Festus. He wanted to do the Jews a favour, and so he left Paul in prison.

To Caesar you shall go

25 So Festus arrived in the province, and after three days he went up from Caesarea to Jerusalem. 2The high priests and the leading men of the Jews appeared before him, laying charges against Paul, and putting a request to him. 3They wanted him to do a special favour for them and against Paul, by sending for him to be brought up to Jerusalem. They were making a plan to kill him on the way. 4But Festus answered that he was keeping Paul at Caesarea, and that he himself would shortly be going back there.

5'So,' he said, 'your officials should come down with me. They can put any accusations of wrongdoing they may have against the man.'

6He stayed with them for a few days (about eight or ten) and then went down to Caesarea. On the next day he took his seat on the tribunal and ordered Paul to be brought to him. 7When he appeared, the Jews who had come down from Jerusalem surrounded him and hurled many serious accusations at him, which they were not able to substantiate. 8Paul made his response: 'I have offended neither against the Jews' law, nor against the Temple, nor against Caesar.'

9Festus, however, wanted to do a favour to the Jews. 'Tell me,' he said to Paul in reply, 'how would you like to go up to Jerusalem and be tried by me there about these things?'

10'I am standing before Caesar's tribunal,' said Paul, 'which is where I ought to be tried. I have done no wrong to the Jews, as you well know. 11If I have committed any wrong, or if I have done something which means I deserve to die, I'm not trying to escape death. But if I have done none of the things they are accusing me of, nobody can hand me over to them. I appeal to Caesar.'

12Festus consulted with his advisers.

'You have appealed to Caesar,' he said, 'and to Caesar you shall go.'

Agrippa and Bernice

13After some days King Agrippa came to Caesarea, with Bernice, to greet Festus. 14They spent several days there, and during that time Festus put to the king the whole matter of Paul and the case against him.

'I have a man here,' he said, 'who was left by Felix as a prisoner. 15When I was up in Jerusalem, the chief priests and the Jewish elders came before me and asked me to pass sentence on him. 16My response was that it is not our Roman custom to hand anyone over until the accused has had a chance to look his accusers in the face and make a defence against the charges. 17So they came down here, and I didn't postpone the business, but sat in court the next day and commanded the man to be brought. 18His accusers stood there and brought charges – but not of the sort of wrongdoing I had been expecting. 19It turned out to have to do with various wranglings concerning their own religion, and about some dead man called Jesus whom Paul asserted was alive. 20I simply didn't know what to do about all this dispute, and so I asked him if he would like to go up to Jerusalem and be judged there about these things. 21But Paul then appealed for his case to be sent up to His Majesty! So I gave the order that he should be kept under guard until I can send him to Caesar.'

22'I should like to hear this man for myself,' said Agrippa to Festus.

'Very well,' said Festus. 'You shall do so tomorrow.'

23On the next day, Agrippa and Bernice came with great ceremony, and entered the audience chamber. With them came the tribunes and the leading men of the city. Festus gave the order, and Paul was brought in.

24"King Agrippa', said Festus, 'and all of you assembled here, you see this man. The whole multitude of the Jews appealed to me about him, both in Jerusalem and here. They shouted that it wasn't right to let him live. 25But I found that he had done nothing to deserve death, and since he then himself appealed to His Majesty I decided to send him. 26I don't have anything definite to write to our Lord and Master about him, and so I've brought him here to you, and particularly before you, King Agrippa, so that I may know what to write once we have had a judicial hearing. 27There seems no sense to me in sending a prisoner without giving some indication of the charges against him.'

Paul before Agrippa

26 Agrippa addressed Paul. 'You are permitted', he said, 'to speak for yourself.'

Paul stretched out his hand and began his defence.

2'I consider myself blessed, King Agrippa,' he said, 'to have the chance to speak before you today in my defence concerning all the things of which the Jews have charged me, 3in particular because I know you are an expert on all matters of Jewish customs and disputes. I beg you, therefore, to give me a generous hearing.

4'All the Jews know my manner of life. I lived from my earliest days among my own people and in Jerusalem. 5They have known already for a long time (if they are willing to testify!) that I lived as a Pharisee, according to the strictest sect of our religion. 6And now I stand accused because of the hope of the promise made by God to our ancestors, 7the hope for which our twelve tribes wait with earnest longing in their worship night and day. And it is this hope, O king, for which I am now accused by the Jews! 8Why should any of you judge it unbelievable that God would raise the dead?

9'I thought I was under obligation to do many things against the name of Jesus of Nazareth, 10and that is what I did in Jerusalem. I received authority from the chief priests to shut up many of God's people in prison, and when they were condemned to death I cast my vote against them. 11I punished them many times in all the synagogues, and forced many of them to blaspheme. I became more and more furious against them, and even pursued them to cities in other lands.'

Paul's conversion (one more time)

12'While I was busy on this work', Paul continued, 'I was travelling to Damascus with authority and commission from the chief priests. 13Around midday, while I was on the road, O king, I saw a light from heaven, brighter than the light of the sun, and shining all around me and my companions on the road. 14We all fell to the ground, and I heard a voice speaking to me in Aramaic.

"'Saul, Saul," he said, "why are you persecuting me? It's hard for you, this kicking against the goads."

15"'Who are you, Lord?" I said.

"'I am Jesus", said the Lord, "and you are persecuting me. 16But get up and stand on your feet. I'm going to tell you why I have appeared to you. I am going to establish you as a servant, as a witness both of the things you have already seen and of the occasions I will appear to you in the future. 17I will rescue you from the people, and from the nations to whom I am going to send you 18so that you can open their eyes to enable them to turn from darkness to light, and from the power of the satan to God – so that they can have forgiveness of sins, and an inheritance among those who are made holy by their faith in me."

19"So then, King Agrippa, I didn't disobey this vision from heaven. 20I preached that people should repent, and turn to God, and do the works that demonstrate repentance. I preached it first to those in Damascus, then also in Jerusalem, in the whole countryside of Judaea, and among the nations. 21That is the reason the Jews seized me in the Temple and tried to slaughter me. 22But I have had help from God, right up to this very day. And so I stand here to bear witness, to small and great alike, of nothing except what the prophets, and Moses too, said would happen: 23namely, that the Messiah would suffer, that he would be the first to rise from the dead, and that he would proclaim light to the people and to the nations.'

'Paul, you're mad!'

²⁴As Paul was making his defence in this way, Festus roared out at the top of his voice, 'Paul, you're mad! All this learning of yours has driven you crazy!'

²⁵'I'm not mad, most excellent Festus,' responded Paul. 'On the contrary, I am speaking words full of truth and good sense. ²⁶The king knows about these things, and it is to him that I am speaking so boldly. I cannot believe that any of this has escaped his notice. After all, these things didn't happen in a corner. ²⁷Do you believe the prophets, King Agrippa? I know you believe them.'

²⁸'You reckon you're going to make *me* a Christian, then,' said Agrippa to Paul, 'and pretty quick, too, by the sound of it!'

²⁹'Whether quick or slow,' replied Paul, 'I pray to God that not only you but also all who hear me today will become just as I am – apart, of course, from these chains.'

³⁰The king, the governor and Bernice, and those sitting with them, got up. ³¹As they were going away, they talked to one another about it.

'This man,' they were saying, 'has done nothing to deserve death or chains.'

³²And Agrippa commented to Festus, 'This man could have been set free, if only he hadn't gone and appealed to Caesar.'

All at sea

27 When it was decided that we should sail to Italy, they handed Paul over, along with some other prisoners, to a centurion named Julius, who belonged to the Imperial Cohort. ²They got into a ship from Adramyttium, which was intending to sail to various places along the coast of Asia. So off we set. Aristarchus, a Macedonian from Thessalonica, came too.

³Next day we put in at Sidon. Julius was kind to Paul, and allowed him to go to his friends to be cared for. ⁴When we left Sidon, we sailed under the lee of Cyprus, because the winds were against us, ⁵and then crossed the sea off the coast of Cilicia and Pamphylia, arriving at Myra in Lycia. ⁶There the centurion found a ship going from Alexandria to Italy, and we got on board.

⁷After a few days we were making very heavy weather of it, and only got to the shore at Cnidus. Since the wind was not helping us, we sailed under the lee of Crete, off the coast from Salmone. ⁸Getting past that point with some difficulty, we came to a place which is called 'Fair Havens', not far from the town of Lasea.

⁹Quite a bit of time had now elapsed, and sailing was becoming dangerous. The Fast had already come and gone. Paul gave his advice.

¹⁰'Men,' he said, 'I can see we're going to have trouble on this voyage. It's going to be dangerous. We may well sustain heavy losses both to the cargo and to the ship, not to mention to human life.'

¹¹But the centurion put his faith in the helmsman and the ship-owner rather than in what Paul had said. ¹²Unfortunately, the harbour was not suitable for wintering in, so most people were in favour of going on from there to see if they could get to Phoenix, a harbour on Crete which faces both south-west and north-west. They would then be able to spend the winter there.

The storm and the angel

¹³Well, a moderate southerly breeze sprang up, and they thought they had the result they wanted. So they lifted the anchor and sailed along, hugging the shore of Crete. ¹⁴But before long a great typhoon – they call it 'Eurakylon', the Northeaster – swept down from Crete, ¹⁵and the ship was caught up by it. Since the ship couldn't turn and face into the wind, it had to give way and we were carried along.

¹⁶When we came in behind an island called Cauda, we were just able to get the ship's boat under control. ¹⁷They pulled it up, and did what was necessary to undergird the ship. Then, because they were afraid that we would crash into the Syrtis sandbanks, they lowered the sea-anchor and allowed the ship to be driven along. ¹⁸The storm was so severe that on the next day they began to throw cargo overboard, ¹⁹and on the third day they threw the ship's tackle overboard as well, with their own hands. ²⁰We then went for a good many days without seeing either the sun or the stars, with a major storm raging. All hope of safety was finally abandoned.

Acts 27.1-12

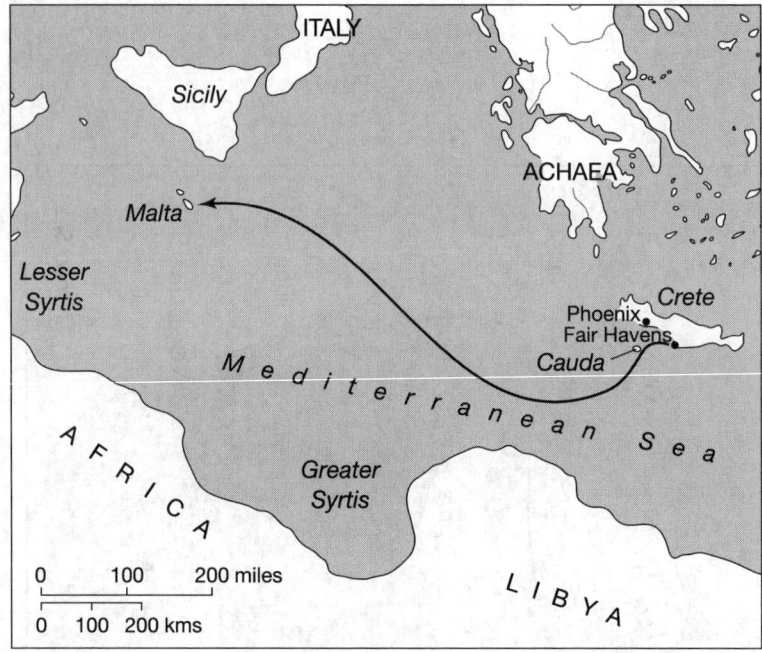

Acts 27.13–32

²¹We had gone without food a long time. Then Paul stood up in the middle of them all.

'It does seem to me, my good people,' he said, 'that you should have taken my advice not to leave Crete. We could have managed without this damage and loss. ²²But now I want to tell you: take heart! No lives will be lost – only the ship. ²³This last night, you see, an angel of the God to whom I belong, and whom I worship, stood beside me. ²⁴"Don't be afraid, Paul", he said. "You must appear before Caesar, and let me tell you this: God has granted you all your travelling companions." ²⁵So take heart, my friends. I believe God, that it will be as he said to me. ²⁶We must, however, be cast up on some island or other.'

²⁷On the fourteenth night we were being carried across the sea of Adria when, around the middle of the night, the sailors reckoned that we were getting near some land. ²⁸They took soundings and found twenty fathoms; then, a little bit further, they took soundings again and found fifteen fathoms. ²⁹They were afraid that we might crash into a rocky place, so they let down four anchors from the stern and prayed for day to come. ³⁰The sailors wanted to escape from the ship, and let down the boat into the sea under the pretence of going to put out anchors from the bow. ³¹But Paul spoke to the centurion and the soldiers.

'If these men don't stay in the ship,' he said, 'there is no chance of safety.'

³²Then the soldiers cut the ropes of the boat, and let it fall away.

Shipwreck

³³When it was nearly daytime, Paul urged all of them to eat something.

'It's now all of fourteen days,' he said, 'that you've been hanging on without food, not eating a thing. ³⁴So let me encourage you to have something to eat. This will help you get rescued. No hair of any of your heads will be lost.'

³⁵So saying, he took some bread, gave thanks to God in front of them all, broke the bread and ate it. ³⁶Then all of them cheered up and took some food. ³⁷The whole company on board was two hundred and seventy-six. ³⁸When we had eaten enough food, they threw the grain overboard to lighten the ship.

³⁹When day came, they didn't recognize the land. It appeared to have a bay with a

sandy shore, and that was where they hoped, if possible, to beach the ship. ⁴⁰They let the anchors drop away into the sea, and at the same time slackened the ropes on the rudders, hoisted the foresail, and headed for the beach. ⁴¹But they crashed into a reef and ran the ship aground. The prow stuck fast and wouldn't budge, while the strong waves were smashing the stern to bits. ⁴²The soldiers planned to kill the prisoners so that none of them would swim away and escape. ⁴³But the centurion wanted to rescue Paul, and refused permission for them to carry out their intention. Instead, he ordered all who were able to swim to leap overboard first and head for land, ⁴⁴while the rest were to come after, some on boards and some on bits and pieces of the ship. And so everyone ended up safely on land.

The snake on Malta

28 When we reached safety, we discovered that the island was called Malta. ²The local inhabitants treated us with unusual kindness: they set to and built a fire for us all, since it was cold and had started to rain. ³Paul had collected quite a bundle of brushwood, and was putting it on the fire, when a viper, escaping the heat, fastened onto his hand. ⁴The natives saw the animal clinging to his hand.

'Aha!' they said to one another. 'This man must be a murderer! He's been rescued from the sea, but Justice hasn't allowed him to live.'

⁵Paul, however, shook off the snake into the fire and suffered no harm. ⁶They kept watching him to see if he would swell up or suddenly fall down dead. But when they had waited and watched for quite some time, and nothing untoward had happened to him, they changed their minds.

'He must be a god,' they said.

⁷Publius, the leading man of the island, owned lands in the region where we were. He welcomed us, and entertained us in a most friendly fashion for three days. ⁸Publius' father was lying sick in bed with a fever and with dysentery. Paul went in to see him and prayed; then he laid his hands on him and cured him. ⁹At this, everyone else on the island who was sick came and was cured. ¹⁰They gave us many honours, and when we were getting ready to sail away they gave us everything we needed.

To Rome at last

¹¹After three months we set sail on a ship that had been spending the winter on the island. It was from Alexandria, and had the insignia of the Heavenly Twins. ¹²We arrived at Syracuse, and stayed three days. ¹³From there we raised anchor and sailed across to Rhegium. After one day there, a south wind arose, and on the second day we arrived at Puteoli, ¹⁴where we found Christians, who encouraged us to stay with them for seven days.

And so we came to Rome. ¹⁵Christians from there, hearing about us, came to meet us as far as Appian Forum and Three Taverns. When Paul saw them, he thanked God and took heart.

¹⁶When we arrived in Rome, Paul was allowed to lodge privately. He had a soldier to guard him.

¹⁷After three days, Paul called together the leading men of the Jews. When they arrived, he began to speak.

'My brothers,' he said, 'I have done nothing against our people or our ancestral customs. Yet I was made a prisoner in Jerusalem and handed over to the Romans. ¹⁸The Romans put me on trial and wanted to let me go, because they couldn't find me guilty of any capital crime. ¹⁹But the Judaeans opposed this, and forced me to appeal to Caesar. This had nothing to do with my bringing any charges against my nation! ²⁰So that's why I have asked to see you and talk with you. It is because of the hope of Israel, you see, that I am wearing this chain.'

²¹'For our part', they responded, 'we haven't received any letters about you from Judaea. Nor has anyone of our nation come here to tell us anything, or to say anything bad about you. ²²We want to hear from your own lips what you have in mind. However, as for this new sect, the one thing we know is that people everywhere are speaking out against it.'

The end is where we start from

²³So they fixed a day and came in large numbers to Paul's lodgings. He spoke to them

Acts 28.11–22

and gave his testimony about the kingdom of God. From morning to night, he explained to them the things about Jesus, from the law of Moses and the prophets.

²⁴Some were persuaded by what he said, and others did not believe. ²⁵They disagreed among themselves. So, as they were getting ready to leave, Paul said one last thing.

'The holy spirit', he said, 'spoke truly through the prophet Isaiah to your ancestors, ²⁶when he said,

Go to this people and say to them:
Listen and listen, but never hear;
look and look, but never see!

²⁷For this people's heart has grown dull,
and their ears are dim with hearing,
and they have closed their eyes –
so that they might not see with their eyes,
and hear with their ears,
and understand with their heart,
and turn, and I would heal them.

²⁸'Let it then be known to you that this salvation from God has been sent to the Gentiles. They will listen.'

³⁰Paul lived there for two whole years at his own expense, and welcomed everyone who came to see him. ³¹He announced the kingdom of God, and taught the things about the Lord Jesus the Messiah, with all boldness, and with no one stopping him.

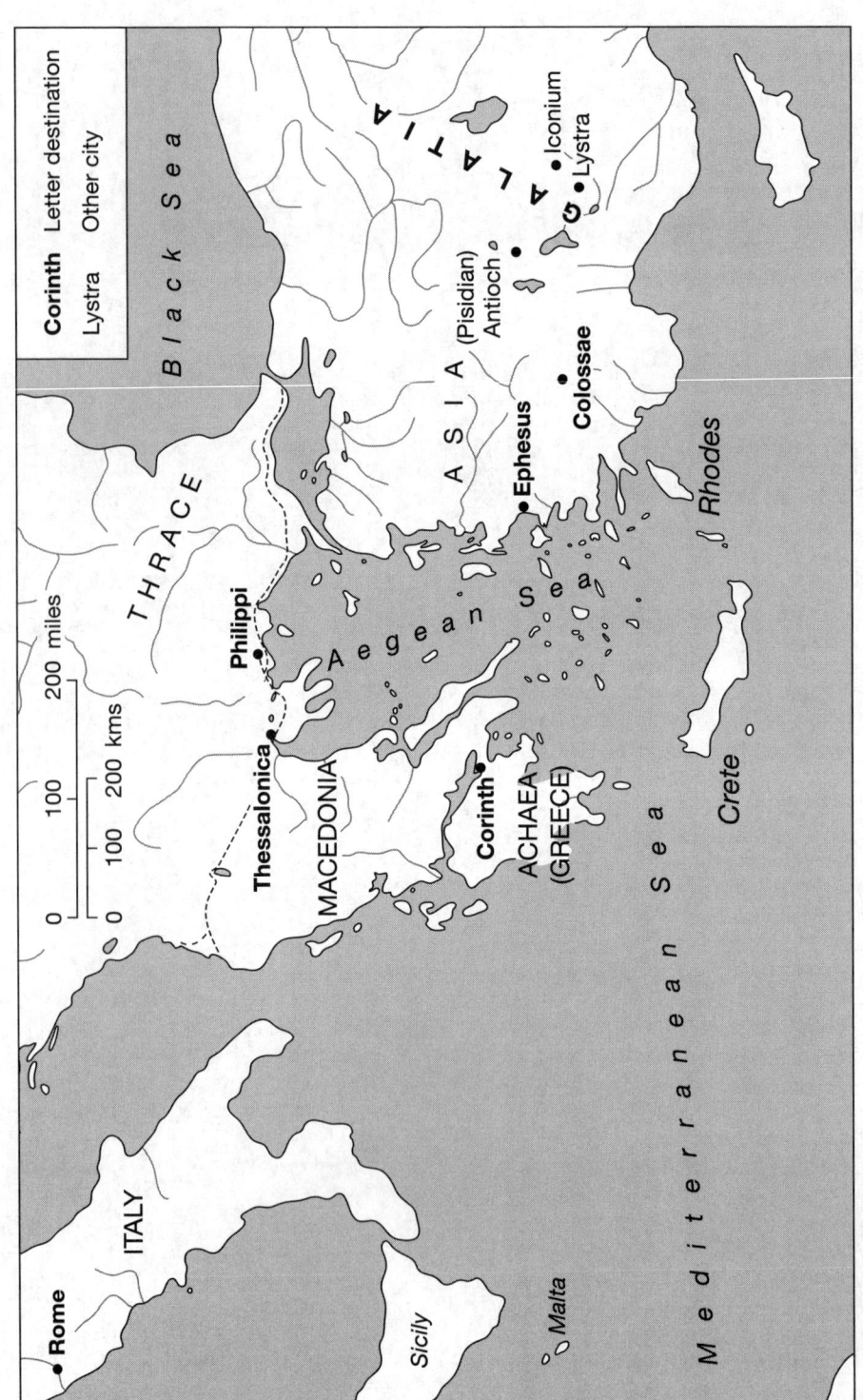

The destinations of Paul's Letters

Romans

The letter to Rome is by common consent not only Paul's masterpiece but one of the most astonishing pieces of writing on any subject from any time or culture. It is dense, fast-paced, combative and lyrical by turns. It wrestles with some of the hardest problems in philosophy or theology and ranks with anything Plato or Aristotle ever wrote – except that it is much shorter, covers more ground, and draws together the traditions of Israel while taking on the traditions of Greece. And also Rome! The letter presents – in writing to a small, disjointed group in Caesar's capital! – a picture of Jesus as the true 'son of God', the world's rightful Lord, summoning all people to believing allegiance because the 'good news' of his reign brings 'salvation', 'justice' and 'peace'. In every element of that sequence Paul is claiming that in Jesus you can see the truth of which Caesar and his rhetoric were a mere parody.

The ostensible purpose of the letter is to introduce Paul to the church in Rome ahead of his projected visit, and to solicit support for his intended trip to Spain. But there were problems in the Roman church as well. A large number of Jews had been expelled by the emperor Claudius in the late 40s, and had returned to Rome after Claudius's death in AD 54; but many ordinary Romans, including it seems some Jesus-followers, had not been happy about this, with some of the non-Jewish Christians supposing that the message of Jesus was now for Gentiles only. Tensions were in the air, too, between the different house-churches, which probably took different views on such matters as food laws, keeping of holy days, and the like. What from one point of view, then, is a general letter setting out Paul's mature view of 'the gospel', from another point of view is sharply focused on the need for Gentile Christians to understand the strange dynamic of God's dealings with Israel, and on the need for unity.

The four 'movements' of this letter (chapters 1—4, 5—8, 9—11 and 12—16) form a symphonic whole. The overarching theme is the covenant faithfulness of the one God: Paul draws on the Old Testament to stress that the one God has been faithful to his promises to, and through, Abraham, by creating from the wreck of idolatrous and sinful humankind a single forgiven family marked out by the same 'faith' or 'faithfulness' that Jesus embodied in going to his saving death. This is set out briefly in the first section (1—4), providing a platform from which Paul can survey the entire narrative of creation and humankind, from the failed vocation of the first human to the glorious promise of resurrected humankind in a newborn created order (8.18—30).

This, however, only heightens the tension left unresolved in chapters 1—4: what has God been doing with Israel? Chapters 9—11 answer the question in terms of the Messiah himself and his inauguration of the covenant renewal promised in Deuteronomy. Those who believe in his resurrection and confess him as Lord are the new covenant people. God will save 'all Israel', but only 'if they do not remain in unbelief' (11.23). His main message in chapter 11 is a sharp warning to Gentile Christians not to suppose that God has finished with his ancient people.

This then opens the way for the appeal of chapters 12—16, which is general in chapters 12 and 13 and specific in 14.1—15.13. Underlying it all is the true worship, which means being transformed by the renewal of the mind and the offering of one's whole self to God (12.1–2). This leads to a bracing and outward-facing ethic, and particularly to patterns of reconciliation, and ultimately shared worship, among Jesus-followers of all backgrounds. Paul's travel plans round off chapter 15, and chapter 16 provides a long list of greetings to Paul's many friends, and some relatives, in the different Roman house-churches.

Good news about the new king

1 Paul, a slave of King Jesus, called to be an apostle, set apart for God's good news, ²which he promised beforehand through his prophets in the sacred writings – ³the good news about his son, who was descended from David's seed in terms of flesh, ⁴and who was marked out powerfully as God's son in terms of the spirit of holiness by the resurrection of the dead: Jesus, the king, our Lord!

⁵Through him we have received grace and apostleship to bring about believing obedience among all the nations for the sake of his name. ⁶That includes you, too, who are called by Jesus the king.

⁷This letter comes to all in Rome who love God, all who are called to be his holy people. Grace and peace to you from God our father, and King Jesus, the Lord.

Paul longs to see the Roman Christians

⁸Let me say first that I thank my God for all of you, through Jesus the king, because all the world has heard the news of your faith. ⁹God is my witness – the God I worship in my spirit in the good news of his son – that I never stop remembering you ¹⁰in my prayers. I ask God again and again that somehow at last I may now be able, in his good purposes, to come to you. ¹¹I'm longing to see you! I want to share with you some spiritual blessing to give you strength; ¹²that is, I want to encourage you, and be encouraged by you, in the faith you and I share. ¹³I don't want you to be unaware, my dear family, that I've often made plans to come to you; it's just that up to now something has always got in the way. I want to bear some fruit among you, as I have been doing among the other nations.

Good news, salvation and the justice of God

¹⁴I am under obligation to barbarians as well as to Greeks, you see; both to the wise and to the foolish. ¹⁵That's why I'm eager to announce the good news to you, too, in Rome. ¹⁶I'm not ashamed of the good news; it's God's power, bringing salvation to everyone who believes – to the Jew first, and also, equally, to the Greek. ¹⁷This is because God's covenant justice is unveiled in it, from faithfulness to faithfulness. As it says in the Bible, 'the just shall live by faith'.

Humans reject God and embrace corruption

¹⁸For the anger of God is unveiled from heaven against all the ungodliness and injustice performed by people who use injustice to suppress the truth. ¹⁹What can be known of God, you see, is plain to them, since God has made it plain to them. ²⁰There are, of course, things about God which you can't see, namely, his eternal power and deity. But, ever since the world was created, they have been known and seen in the things he has made. As a result, they have no excuse: ²¹they knew God, but didn't honour him as God or thank him. Instead, they learned to think in useless ways, and their unwise heart grew dark. ²²They declared themselves to be wise, but in fact they became foolish. ²³They swapped the glory of the immortal God for the likeness of the image of mortal humans – and of birds, animals and reptiles.

Unclean desires, dishonoured bodies

²⁴So God gave them up to uncleanness in the desires of their hearts, with the result that they dishonoured their bodies among themselves. ²⁵They swapped God's truth for a lie, and worshipped and served the creature rather than the creator, who is blessed for ever, Amen.

²⁶So God gave them up to shameful desires. Even the women, you see, swapped natural sexual practice for unnatural; ²⁷and the men, too, abandoned natural sexual relations with women, and were inflamed with their lust for one another. Men performed shameless acts with men, and received in themselves the appropriate repayment for their mistaken ways.

Darkened mind, darkened behaviour

²⁸Moreover, just as they did not see fit to hold on to knowledge of God, God gave them up to an unfit mind, so that they would behave inappropriately. ²⁹They were filled with all kinds

of injustice, wickedness, greed and evil; they were full of envy, murder, enmity, deceit and cunning. They became gossips, ³⁰slanderers, God-haters, arrogant, self-important, boastful, inventors of evil, disobedient to parents, ³¹unwise, unfaithful, unfeeling, uncaring. ³²They know that God has rightly decreed that people who do things like that deserve death. But not only do they do them; they give their approval to people who practise them.

God's coming judgment will be impartial, the same for all

2 So *you* have no excuse – anyone, whoever you are, who sits in judgment! When you judge someone else, you condemn yourself, because you, who are behaving as a judge, are doing the same things. ²God's judgment falls, we know, in accordance with the truth, on those who do such things. ³But if you judge those who do them and yet do them yourself, do you really suppose that you will escape God's judgment? ⁴Or do you despise the riches of God's kindness, forbearance and patience? Don't you know that God's kindness is meant to bring you to repentance? ⁵But by your hard, unrepentant heart you are building up a store of anger for yourself on the day of anger, the day when God's just judgment will be unveiled – ⁶the God who will 'repay everyone according to their works'.

⁷When people patiently do what is good, and so pursue the quest for glory and honour and immortality, God will give them the life of the age to come. ⁸But when people act out of selfish desire, and do not obey the truth, but instead obey injustice, there will be anger and fury. ⁹There will be trouble and distress for every single person who does what is wicked, the Jew first and also, equally, the Greek – ¹⁰and there will be glory, honour and peace for everyone who does what is good, the Jew first and also, equally, the Greek. ¹¹God, you see, shows no partiality.

How God's impartial judgment will work

¹²Everyone who sinned outside the law, you see, will perish outside the law – and those who sinned from within the law will be judged by means of the law. ¹³After all, it isn't those who *hear* the law who are in the right before God. It's those who *do* the law who will be declared to be in the right!

¹⁴This is how it works out. Gentiles don't possess the law as their birthright; but whenever they do what the law says, they are a law for themselves, despite not possessing the law. ¹⁵They show that the work of the law is written on their hearts. Their conscience bears witness as well, and their thoughts will run this way and that, sometimes accusing them and sometimes excusing, ¹⁶on the day when (according to the gospel I proclaim) God judges all human secrets through King Jesus.

The claim of the Jew – and its problems

¹⁷But supposing you call yourself a 'Jew'. Supposing you rest your hope in the law. Supposing you celebrate the fact that God is your God, ¹⁸and that you know what he wants, and that by the law's instruction you can make appropriate moral distinctions. ¹⁹Supposing you believe yourself to be a guide to the blind, a light to people in darkness, ²⁰a teacher of the foolish, an instructor for children – all because, in the law, you possess the outline of knowledge and truth.

²¹Well then: if you're going to teach someone else, aren't you going to teach yourself? If you say people shouldn't steal, do you steal? ²²If you say people shouldn't commit adultery, do you commit adultery? If you loathe idols, do you rob temples? ²³If you boast in the law, do you dishonour God by breaking the law? ²⁴This is what the Bible says: 'Because of you, God's name is blasphemed among the nations'!

The badge, the name and the meaning

²⁵Circumcision, you see, has real value for people who keep the law. If, however, you break the law, your circumcision becomes uncircumcision. ²⁶Meanwhile, if uncircumcised people keep the law's requirements, their uncircumcision will be regarded as circumcision, won't it? ²⁷So people who are by nature uncircumcised, but who fulfil the law,

will pass judgment on people like you who possess the letter of the law and circumcision but who break the law.

²⁸The 'Jew' isn't the person who appears to be one, you see. Nor is 'circumcision' what it appears to be, a matter of physical flesh. ²⁹The 'Jew' is the one in secret; and 'circumcision' is a matter of the heart, in the spirit rather than the letter. Such a person gets 'praise', not from humans, but from God.

God's determined faithfulness

3 What advantage, then, does the Jew possess? What, indeed, is the point of circumcision? ²A great deal, in every way. To begin with, the Jews were entrusted with God's oracles. ³What follows from that? If some of them were unfaithful to their commission, does their unfaithfulness nullify God's faithfulness? ⁴Certainly not! Let God be true, and every human being false! As the Bible says,

> So that you may be found in the right in what you say, and may win the victory when you come to court.

⁵But if our being in the wrong proves that God is in the right, what are we going to say? That God is unjust to inflict anger on people? (I'm reducing things to a human scale!) ⁶Certainly not! How then could God judge the world? ⁷But if God's truthfulness grows all the greater and brings him glory in and through my falsehood, why am I still being condemned as a sinner? ⁸And why not 'do evil so that good may come' – as some people blasphemously say about us, and as some allege that we say? People like that, at least, deserve the judgment they get!

Jews as well as Gentiles are guilty of sin

⁹What then? Are we in fact better off? No, certainly not. I have already laid down this charge, you see: Jews as well as Greeks are all under the power of sin. ¹⁰This is what the Bible says:

> No one is in the right – nobody at all!
> ¹¹No one understands, or goes looking for God;
> ¹²all of them alike have wandered astray, together they have all become futile; none of them behaves kindly, no, not one.
> ¹³Their throat is an open grave, they use their tongues to deceive, the poison of vipers is under their lips.
> ¹⁴Their mouth is full of cursing and bitterness,
> ¹⁵their feet are quick when there's blood to be shed,
> ¹⁶disaster and wretchedness are in their paths,
> ¹⁷and they did not know the way of peace.
> ¹⁸They have no fear of God before their eyes.

¹⁹Now we know that whatever the law says, it is speaking to those who are 'in the law'. The purpose of this is that every mouth may be stopped, and the whole world may be brought to the bar of God's judgment. ²⁰No mere mortal, you see, can be declared to be in the right before God on the basis of the works of the law. What you get through the law is the knowledge of sin.

The unveiling of God's covenant justice

²¹But now, quite apart from the law (though the law and the prophets bore witness to it), God's covenant justice has been displayed. ²²God's covenant justice comes into operation through the faithfulness of Jesus the Messiah, for the benefit of all who have faith. For there is no distinction: ²³all sinned, and fell short of God's glory – ²⁴and by God's grace they are freely declared to be in the right, to be members of the covenant, through the redemption which is found in the Messiah, Jesus.

Jesus' death reveals God's covenant justice

²⁵God put Jesus forth as the place of mercy, through faithfulness, by means of his blood. He did this to demonstrate his covenant justice, because of the passing over (in divine forbearance) of sins committed beforehand. ²⁶This was to demonstrate his covenant justice in the present time: that is, that he himself is in the right, and that he declares to be in the right everyone who trusts in the faithfulness of Jesus.

The God of both Jew and Gentile

²⁷So what happens to boasting? It is ruled out! Through what sort of law? The law of works? No: through the law of faith! ²⁸We calculate, you see, that a person is declared to be in the right on the basis of faith, apart from works of the law. ²⁹Or does God belong only to Jews? Doesn't he belong to the nations as well? Yes, of course, to the nations as well, ³⁰since God is one. He will make the declaration 'in the right' over the circumcised on the basis of faith, and over the uncircumcised through faith.

³¹Do we then abolish the law through faith? Certainly not! Rather, we establish the law.

God's covenant with Abraham

4 What shall we say, then? Have we found Abraham to be our ancestor in a human, fleshly sense? ²After all, if Abraham was reckoned 'in the right' on the basis of works, he has grounds to boast – but not in God's presence!

³So what does the Bible say? 'Abraham believed God, and it was calculated in his favour, putting him in the right.' ⁴Now when someone 'works', the 'reward' they get is not calculated on the basis of generosity, but on the basis of what they are owed. ⁵But if someone doesn't 'work', but simply believes in the one who declares the ungodly to be in the right, that person's faith is calculated in their favour, putting them in the right.

⁶We see the same thing when David speaks of the blessing that comes to someone whom God calculates to be in the right apart from works:

⁷Blessed are those whose lawbreaking is forgiven
and whose sins have been covered over;
⁸Blessed is the man to whom the Lord will not calculate sin.

Abraham the father of both uncircumcised and circumcised

⁹So, then, does this blessing come on circumcised people or on uncircumcised? This is the passage we quoted: 'His faith was calculated to Abraham as indicating that he was in the right.' ¹⁰How was it calculated? When he was circumcised or when he was uncircumcised? It wasn't when he was circumcised; it was when he was uncircumcised! ¹¹He received circumcision as a sign and seal of the status of covenant membership, on the basis of faith, which he had when he was still uncircumcised. This was so that he could be the father of all who believe even when uncircumcised, so that the status of covenant membership can be calculated to their account as well. ¹²He is also, of course, the father of the circumcised who are not merely circumcised but who follow the steps of the faith which Abraham possessed while still uncircumcised.

Abraham is the father of all believers

¹³The promise, you see, didn't come to Abraham or to his family through the law – the promise, that is, that he would inherit the world. It came through the covenant justice of faith. ¹⁴For if those who belong to the law are going to inherit, then faith is empty, and the promise has been abolished. ¹⁵For the law stirs up God's anger; but where there is no law, there is no lawbreaking.

¹⁶That's why it's 'by faith': so that it can be in accordance with grace, and so that the promise can thereby be validated for the entire family – not simply those who are from the law, but those who share the faith of Abraham. He is the father of us all, ¹⁷just as the Bible says, 'I have made you the father of many nations.' This happened in the presence of the God in whom he believed, the God who gives life to the dead and calls into existence things that do not exist.

Abraham's faith – and ours

¹⁸Against all hope, but still in hope, Abraham believed that he would become the father of many nations, in line with what had been said to him: 'That's what your family will be like.' ¹⁹He didn't become weak in faith as he considered his own body (which was already as good as dead, since he was about a hundred years old), and the lifelessness of Sarah's womb.

[20]He didn't waver in unbelief when faced with God's promise. Instead, he grew strong in faith and gave glory to God, [21]being fully convinced that God had the power to accomplish what he had promised. [22]That is why 'it was calculated to him in terms of covenant justice'.

[23]But it wasn't written for him alone that 'it was calculated to him'. [24]It was written for us as well! It will be calculated to us, too, since we believe in the one who raised from the dead Jesus our Lord, [25]who was handed over because of our trespasses and raised because of our justification.

Peace and hope

5 The result is this: since we have been declared 'in the right' on the basis of faith, we have peace with God through our Lord Jesus the Messiah. [2]Through him we have been allowed to approach, by faith, into this grace in which we stand; and we celebrate the hope of the glory of God.

[3]That's not all. We also celebrate in our sufferings, because we know that suffering produces patience, [4]patience produces a well-formed character, and a character like that produces hope. [5]Hope, in its turn, does not make us ashamed, because the love of God has been poured out in our hearts through the holy spirit who has been given to us.

Jesus' death reveals God's love and guarantees final salvation

[6]This is all based on what the Messiah did: while we were still weak, at that very moment he died on behalf of the ungodly. [7]It's a rare thing to find someone who will die on behalf of an upright person – though I suppose someone might be brave enough to die for a good person. [8]But this is how God demonstrates his own love for us: the Messiah died for us while we were still sinners.

[9]How much more, in that case – since we have been declared to be in the right by his blood – are we going to be saved by him from God's coming anger! [10]When we were enemies, you see, we were reconciled to God through the death of his son; if that's so, how much more, having already been reconciled, shall we be saved by his life. [11]And that's not all. We even celebrate in God, through our Lord Jesus the Messiah, through whom we have now received this reconciliation.

The big picture in shorthand: Adam and the Messiah

[12]Therefore, just as sin came into the world through one human being, and death through sin, and in that way death spread to all humans, in that all sinned . . . [13]Sin was in the world, you see, even in the absence of the law, though sin is not calculated when there is no law. [14]But death reigned from Adam to Moses, even over the people who did not sin by breaking a command, as Adam had done – Adam, who was the imprint of the one who would come.

[15]But it isn't 'as the trespass, so also the gift'. For if many died by one person's trespass, how much more has God's grace, and the gift in grace through the one person Jesus the Messiah, abounded to the many. [16]And nor is it 'as through the sin of the one, so also the gift'. For the judgment which followed the one trespass resulted in a negative verdict, but the free gift which followed many trespasses resulted in a positive verdict. [17]For if, by the trespass of the one, death reigned through that one, how much more will those who receive the abundance of grace, and of the gift of covenant membership, of 'being in the right', reign in life through the one man Jesus the Messiah.

The triumphant reign of grace

[18]So, then, just as, through the trespass of one person, the result was condemnation for all people, even so, through the upright act of one person, the result is justification – life for all people. [19]For just as through the disobedience of one person many received the status of 'sinner', so through the obedience of one person many will receive the status of 'in the right'.

[20]The law came in alongside, so that the trespass might be filled out to its full extent. But where sin increased, grace increased all the more; [21]so that, just as sin reigned in death,

even so, through God's faithful covenant justice, grace might reign to the life of the age to come, through Jesus the Messiah, our Lord.

Leaving the state of sin through baptism

6 What are we to say, then? Shall we continue in the state of sin, so that grace may increase? ²Certainly not! We died to sin; how can we still live in it? ³Don't you know that all of us who were baptized into the Messiah, Jesus, were baptized into his death? ⁴That means that we were buried with him, through baptism, into death, so that, just as the Messiah was raised from the dead through the father's glory, we too might behave with a new quality of life. ⁵For if we have been planted together in the likeness of his death, we shall also be in the likeness of his resurrection.

Dead to sin, alive to God

⁶This is what we know: our old humanity was crucified with the Messiah, so that the bodily solidarity of sin might be abolished, and that we should no longer be enslaved to sin. ⁷A person who has died, you see, has been declared free from all charges of sin.

⁸But if we died with the Messiah, we believe that we shall live with him. ⁹We know that the Messiah, having been raised from the dead, will never die again. Death no longer has any authority over him. ¹⁰The death he died, you see, he died to sin, once and only once. But the life he lives, he lives to God. ¹¹In the same way you, too, must calculate yourselves as being dead to sin, and alive to God in the Messiah, Jesus.

The call to holy living

¹²So don't allow sin to rule in your mortal body, to make you obey its desires. ¹³Nor should you present your limbs and organs to sin to be used for its wicked purposes. Rather, present yourselves to God, as people alive from the dead, and your limbs and organs to God, to be used for the righteous purposes of his covenant. ¹⁴Sin won't actually rule over you, you see, since you are not under law but under grace.

The two types of slavery

¹⁵What then? Shall we sin, because we are not under law but under grace? Certainly not! ¹⁶Don't you know that if you present yourselves to someone as obedient slaves, you really are slaves of the one you obey, whether that happens to be sin, which leads to death, or obedience, which leads to final vindication? ¹⁷Thank God that, though you once were slaves to sin, you have become obedient from the heart to the pattern of teaching to which you were committed. ¹⁸You were freed from sin, and now you have been enslaved to God's covenant justice (¹⁹I'm using a human picture because of your natural human weakness!). For just as you presented your limbs and organs as slaves to uncleanness, and to one degree of lawlessness after another, so now present your limbs and organs as slaves to covenant justice, which leads to holiness.

Where the two roads lead

²⁰When you were slaves of sin, you see, you were free in respect of covenant justice. ²¹What fruit did you ever have from the things of which you are now ashamed? Their destination is death. ²²But now that you have been set free from sin and enslaved to God, you have fruit for holiness. Its destination is the life of the age to come. ²³The wages paid by sin, you see, are death; but God's free gift is the life of the age to come, in the Messiah, Jesus our Lord.

Dying to the law

7 Surely you know, my dear family – I am, after all, talking to people who know the law! – that the law rules a person as long as that person is alive? ²The law binds a married woman to her husband during his lifetime; but if he dies, she is free from the law as regards her husband. ³So, then, she will be called an adulteress if she goes with another man while her husband is alive; but if the husband dies, she is free from the law, so that she is not an adulteress if she goes with another man.

⁴In the same way, my dear family, you too died to the law through the body of the

Messiah, so that you could belong to someone else – to the one who was raised from the dead, in fact – so that we could bear fruit for God. ⁵For when we were living a mortal human life, the passions of sins which were through the law were at work in our limbs and organs, causing us to bear fruit for death. ⁶But now we have been cut loose from the law; we have died to the thing in which we were held tightly. The aim is that we should now be enslaved in the new life of the spirit, not in the old life of the letter.

When the law arrived: Sinai looks back to the fall

⁷What then shall we say? That the law is sin? Certainly not. But I would not have known sin except through the law. I would not have known covetousness if the law had not said, 'You shall not covet.' ⁸But sin grabbed its opportunity through the commandment, and produced all kinds of covetousness within me.

Apart from the law, sin is dead. ⁹I was once alive apart from the law; but when the commandment came, sin sprang to life ¹⁰and I died. The commandment which pointed to life turned out, in my case, to bring death. ¹¹For sin grabbed its opportunity through the commandment. It deceived me, and, through it, killed me.

¹²So, then, the law is holy; and the commandment is holy, upright and good.

Looking back on life under the law

¹³Was it that good thing, then, that brought death to me? Certainly not! On the contrary; it was sin, in order that it might appear as sin, working through the good thing and producing death in me. This was in order that sin might become very sinful indeed, through the commandment.

¹⁴We know, you see, that the law is spiritual. I, however, am made of flesh, sold as a slave under sin's authority. ¹⁵I don't understand what I do. I don't do what I want, you see, but I do what I hate. ¹⁶So if I do what I don't want to do, I am agreeing that the law is good.

¹⁷But now it is no longer I that do it; it's sin, living within me. ¹⁸I know, you see, that no good thing lives in me, that is, in my human flesh. For I can will the good, but I can't perform it. ¹⁹For I don't do the good thing I want to do, but I end up doing the evil thing I don't want to do. ²⁰So if I do what I don't want to do, it's no longer 'I' doing it; it's sin, living inside me.

The double 'law' and the miserable 'I'

²¹This, then, is what I find about the law: when I want to do what is right, evil lies close at hand! ²²I delight in God's law, you see, according to my inmost self; ²³but I see another 'law' in my limbs and organs, fighting a battle against the law of my mind, and taking me as a prisoner in the law of sin which is in my limbs and organs.

²⁴What a miserable person I am! Who is going to rescue me from the body of this death? ²⁵Thank God – through Jesus our king and Lord! So then, left to my own self I am enslaved to God's law with my mind, but to sin's law with my human flesh.

God's action in Messiah and spirit

8 So, therefore, there is no condemnation for those in the Messiah, Jesus! ²Why not? Because the law of the spirit of life in the Messiah, Jesus, released you from the law of sin and death.

³For God has done what the law (being weak because of human flesh) was incapable of doing. God sent his own son in the likeness of sinful flesh, and as a sin-offering; and, right there in the flesh, he condemned sin. ⁴This was in order that the right and proper verdict of the law could be fulfilled in us, as we live not according to the flesh but according to the spirit.

The work of the spirit

⁵Look at it like this. People whose lives are determined by human flesh focus their minds on matters to do with the flesh, but people whose lives are determined by the spirit focus their minds on matters to do with the spirit. ⁶Focus the mind on the flesh, and you'll die; but focus it on the spirit, and you'll have life, and peace. ⁷The mind focused on the flesh, you

see, is hostile to God. It doesn't submit to God's law; in fact, it can't. [8]Those who are determined by the flesh can't please God.

[9]But you're not people of flesh; you're people of the spirit (if indeed God's spirit lives within you; note that anyone who doesn't have the spirit of the Messiah doesn't belong to him). [10]But if the Messiah is in you, the body is indeed dead because of sin, but the spirit is life because of covenant justice. [11]So, then, if the spirit of the one who raised Jesus from the dead lives within you, the one who raised the Messiah from the dead will give life to your mortal bodies, too, through his spirit who lives within you.

Children of God, led by the spirit

[12]So then, my dear family, we are in debt – but not to human flesh, to live our life in that way. [13]If you live in accordance with the flesh, you will die; but if, by the spirit, you put to death the deeds of the body, you will live.

[14]All who are led by the spirit of God, you see, are God's children. [15]You didn't receive a spirit of slavery, did you, to go back again into a state of fear? But you received the spirit of sonship, in whom we call out 'Abba, father!' [16]When that happens, it is the spirit itself giving supporting witness to what our own spirit is saying, that we are God's children. [17]And if we're children, we are also heirs: heirs of God, and fellow heirs with the Messiah, as long as we suffer with him so that we may also be glorified with him.

Creation renewed and patient hope

[18]This is how I work it out. The sufferings we go through in the present time are not worth putting in the scale alongside the glory that is going to be unveiled for us. [19]Yes: creation itself is on tiptoe with expectation, eagerly awaiting the moment when God's children will be revealed. [20]Creation, you see, was subjected to pointless futility, not of its own volition, but because of the one who placed it in this subjection, in the hope [21]that creation itself would be freed from its slavery to decay, to enjoy the freedom that comes when God's children are glorified.

[22]Let me explain. We know that the entire creation is groaning together, and going through labour pains together, up until the present time. [23]Not only so: we too, we who have the first fruits of the spirit's life within us, are groaning within ourselves, as we eagerly await our adoption, the redemption of our body. [24]We were saved, you see, in hope. But hope isn't hope if you can see it! Who hopes for what they can see? [25]But if we hope for what we don't see, we wait for it eagerly – but also patiently.

Prayer, sonship and the sovereignty of God

[26]In the same way, too, the spirit comes alongside and helps us in our weakness. We don't know what to pray for as we ought to; but that same spirit pleads on our behalf, with groanings too deep for words. [27]And the Searcher of Hearts knows what the spirit is thinking, because the spirit pleads for God's people according to God's will.

[28]We know, in fact, that God works all things together for good to those who love him, who are called according to his purpose. [29]Those he foreknew, you see, he also marked out in advance to be shaped according to the model of the image of his son, so that he might be the firstborn of a large family. [30]And those he marked out in advance, he also called; those he called, he also justified; those he justified, he also glorified.

Nothing shall separate us from God's love

[31]What then shall we say to all this?
If God is for us, who is against us?
  [32]God, after all, did not spare his own son; he
  gave him up for us all!
How then will he not, with him, freely give
  all things to us?
  [33]Who will bring a charge against God's
  chosen ones?
It is God who declares them in the right.
  [34]Who is going to condemn?
It is the Messiah, Jesus, who has died, or
  rather has been raised;
who is at God's right hand, and who also
  prays on our behalf!

³⁵Who shall separate us from the Messiah's love?
Suffering, or hardship, or persecution, or famine, or nakedness, or danger, or sword? ³⁶As the Bible says,

Because of you we are being killed all day long; we are regarded as sheep destined for slaughter.

³⁷No: in all these things we are completely victorious through the one who loved us. ³⁸I am persuaded, you see, that neither death nor life, nor angels nor rulers, nor the present, nor the future, nor powers, ³⁹nor height, nor depth, nor any other creature will be able to separate us from the love of God in King Jesus our Lord.

The privileges and tragedy of Israel

9 I'm speaking the truth in the Messiah, I'm not lying. I call my conscience as witness, in the holy spirit, ²that I have great sorrow and endless pain in my heart. ³Left to my own self, I am half inclined to pray that I would be accursed, cut off from the Messiah, on behalf of my own family, my own flesh-and-blood relatives. ⁴They are Israelites; the sonship, the glory, the covenants, the giving of the law, the worship and the promises all belong to them. ⁵The patriarchs are their ancestors; and it is from them, according to the flesh, that the Messiah has come – who is God over all, blessed for ever, Amen!

Abraham's two families

⁶But it can't be the case that God's word has failed! Not all who are from Israel, you see, are in fact Israel. ⁷Nor is it the case that all the children count as 'seed of Abraham'. No: 'in Isaac shall your seed be named'. ⁸That means that it isn't the flesh-and-blood children who are God's children; rather, it is the children of the promise who will be calculated as 'seed'. ⁹This was what the promise said, you see: 'Around this time I shall return, and Sarah shall have a son.'

¹⁰And that's not all. The same thing happened when Rebecca conceived children by one man, our ancestor Isaac. ¹¹When they had not yet been born, and had done nothing either good or bad – so that what God had in mind in making his choice might come to pass, ¹²not because of works but because of the one who calls – it was said to her, 'the elder shall serve the younger'. ¹³As the Bible says, 'I loved Jacob, but I hated Esau.'

God's purpose and justice

¹⁴So what are we going to say? Is God unjust? Certainly not! ¹⁵He says to Moses, you see, 'I will have mercy on those on whom I will have mercy, and I will pity those I will pity.' ¹⁶So, then, it doesn't depend on human willing, or on human effort; it depends on God who shows mercy. ¹⁷For the Bible says to Pharaoh: 'This is why I have raised you up, to show my power in you, and so that my name may be proclaimed in all the earth.' ¹⁸So, then, he has mercy on the one he wants, and he hardens the one he wants.

¹⁹You will say to me, then, 'So why does he still blame people? Who can stand against his purpose?' ²⁰Are you, a mere human being, going to answer God back? 'Surely the clay won't say to the potter, "Why did you make me like this?"' ²¹Doesn't the potter have authority over the clay, so that he can make from the same lump one vessel for honour, and another for dishonour? ²²Supposing God wanted to demonstrate his anger and make known his power, and for that reason put up very patiently with the vessels of anger created for destruction, ²³in order to make known the riches of his glory on the vessels of mercy, the ones he prepared in advance for glory – ²⁴including us, whom he called not only from among the Jews but also from among the Gentiles?

God calls a remnant

²⁵This is what he says in Hosea,

I will call 'not my people' 'my people';
and 'not beloved' I will call 'beloved'.
²⁶And in the place where it was said to them,
'You are not my people',
there they will be called 'sons of the living God'.

²⁷Isaiah cries out, concerning Israel,

Even if the number of Israel's sons are like the sand by the sea,
only a remnant shall be saved;
²⁸for the Lord will bring judgment on the earth, complete and decisive.

²⁹As Isaiah said in an earlier passage,

If the Lord of hosts had not left us seed,
we would have become like Sodom, and been made like Gomorrah.

Israel, the nations and the Messiah

³⁰What then shall we say? That the nations, who were not aspiring towards covenant membership, have obtained covenant membership, but it is a covenant membership based on faith. ³¹Israel meanwhile, though eager for the law which defined the covenant, did not attain to the law. ³²Why not? Because they did not pursue it on the basis of faith, but as though it was on the basis of works. They have stumbled over the stumbling stone, ³³as the Bible says,

Look: I am placing in Zion
a stone that will make people stumble,
a rock that will trip people up;
and the one who believes in him
will never be put to shame.

10 My dear family, the longing of my heart, and my prayer to God on their behalf, is for their salvation. ²I can testify on their behalf that they have a zeal for God; but it is not based on knowledge. ³They were ignorant, you see, of God's covenant faithfulness, and they were trying to establish a covenant status of their own; so they didn't submit to God's faithfulness. ⁴The Messiah, you see, is the goal of the law, so that covenant membership may be available for all who believe.

The fulfilment of the covenant

⁵Moses writes, you see, about the covenant membership defined by the law, that 'the person who performs the law's commands shall live in them.' ⁶But the *faith*-based covenant membership puts it like this: 'Don't say in your heart, "Who shall go up to heaven?"' (in other words, to bring the Messiah down), ⁷or, "Who shall go down into the depths?"' (in other words, to bring the Messiah up from the dead). ⁸But what does it say? 'The word is near you, in your mouth and in your heart' (that is, the word of faith which we proclaim); ⁹because if you profess with your mouth that Jesus is Lord, and believe in your heart that God raised him from the dead, you will be saved. ¹⁰Why? Because the way to covenant membership is by believing with the heart, and the way to salvation is by professing with the mouth. ¹¹The Bible says, you see, 'Everyone who believes in him will not be put to shame.' ¹²For there is no distinction between Jew and Greek, since the same Lord is Lord of all, and is rich towards all who call upon him. ¹³'All who call upon the name of the Lord', you see, 'will be saved.'

The call to the world, and the failure of Israel

¹⁴So how are they to call on someone when they haven't believed in him? And how are they to believe if they don't hear? And how will they hear without someone announcing it to them? ¹⁵And how will people make that announcement unless they are sent? As the Bible says, 'How beautiful are the feet of the ones who bring good news of good things.'

¹⁶But not all obeyed the good news. Isaiah asks, you see, 'Lord, who has believed our report?' ¹⁷So faith comes from hearing, and hearing comes from the word of the Messiah.

¹⁸This might make us ask, did they not hear? But they certainly did:

Their sound went out into all the world,
and their words to the ends of the earth.

¹⁹But I ask, did Israel not know? To begin with, Moses says,

I will make you jealous with a non-nation;
and stir you to anger with a foolish people.

²⁰Then Isaiah, greatly daring, puts it like this:

> I was found by those who were not looking for me;
> I became visible to those who were not asking for me.

²¹But in respect of Israel he says,

> All day long I have stretched out my hands
> to a disbelieving and disagreeable people.

The remnant of grace

11 So I ask, has God abandoned his people? Certainly not! I myself am an Israelite, from the seed of Abraham and the tribe of Benjamin. ²'God has not abandoned his people', the ones he chose in advance.

Don't you know what the Bible says in the passage about Elijah, describing how he pleads with God against Israel? ³'Lord,' he says, 'they have killed your prophets, they have thrown down your altars; I'm the only one left, and they are trying to kill me!' ⁴But what is the reply from the divine word? 'I have left for myself seven thousand men who have not bowed the knee to Baal.'

⁵In the same way, at the present time there is a remnant, chosen by grace. ⁶But if it is by grace, it is no longer by works, otherwise grace would no longer be grace.

A stumble with a purpose

⁷What then? Did Israel not obtain what it was looking for? Well, the chosen ones obtained it – but the rest were hardened, ⁸as the Bible says:

> God gave them a spirit of stupor,
> eyes that wouldn't see, and ears that wouldn't hear,
> right down to this present day.

⁹And David says,

> Let their table become a snare and a trap,
> and a stumbling block and a punishment for them;
> ¹⁰let their eyes be darkened so that they can't see,
> and make their backs bend low for ever.

¹¹So I ask, then: Have they tripped up in such a way as to fall completely? Certainly not! Rather, by their trespass, salvation has come to the nations, in order to make them jealous. ¹²If their trespass means riches for the world, and their impoverishment means riches for the nations, how much more will their fullness mean!

¹³Now I am speaking to you Gentiles. Insofar as I am the apostle of the Gentiles, I celebrate my particular ministry, ¹⁴so that, if possible, I can make my 'flesh' jealous, and save some of them. ¹⁵If their casting away, you see, means reconciliation for the world, what will their acceptance mean but life from the dead?

The two olive trees

¹⁶Take another illustration: if the first fruits are holy, so is the whole lump.

And another: if the root is holy, so are the branches.

¹⁷But if some of the branches were broken off, and you – a *wild* olive tree! – were grafted in among them, and came to share in the root of the olive with its rich sap, ¹⁸don't boast over the branches. If you do boast, remember this: it isn't you that supports the root, but the root that supports you.

¹⁹I know what you'll say next: 'Branches were broken off so that I could be grafted in.' ²⁰That's all very well. They were broken off because of unbelief – but you stand firm by faith. Don't get big ideas about it; instead, be afraid. ²¹After all, if God didn't spare the natural branches, there's a strong possibility he won't spare you.

²²Note carefully, then, that God is both kind and severe. He is severe to those who have fallen, but he is kind to you, provided you continue in his kindness – otherwise you too will be cut off. ²³And they, too, if they do not remain in unbelief, will be grafted back in. God is able, you see, to graft them back in. ²⁴For if you were cut out of what is by nature a wild olive tree, and grafted, contrary to nature, into a cultivated olive tree, how much more will they, the natural branches, be grafted back into their own olive tree.

Mercy upon all

²⁵My dear brothers and sisters, you mustn't get the wrong idea and think too much of yourselves. That is why I don't want you

to remain in ignorance of this mystery: a hardening has come for a time upon Israel, until the fullness of the nations comes in. ²⁶That is how 'all Israel shall be saved', as the Bible says:

The Deliverer will come from Zion,
and will turn away ungodliness from Jacob.
²⁷And this will be my covenant with them,
whenever I take away their sins.

²⁸As regards the good news, they are enemies – for your sake! But as regards God's choice they are beloved because of the patriarchs. ²⁹God's gifts and God's call, you see, cannot be undone. ³⁰For just as *you* were once disobedient to God, but now have received mercy through *their* disobedience, ³¹so *they* have now disbelieved as well, in order that, through the mercy which has come *your* way, they too may now receive mercy. ³²For God has shut up all people in disobedience, so that he may have mercy upon all.

To God be the glory

³³O, the depth of the riches
and the wisdom and knowledge of God!
We cannot search his judgments,
we cannot fathom his ways.
³⁴For 'who has known the mind of
   the Lord?
Or who has given him counsel?
³⁵Who has given a gift to him
which needs to be repaid?'
³⁶For from him, through him and to
   him are all things.
Glory to him for ever! Amen.

The living sacrifice

12 So, my dear family, this is my appeal to you by the mercies of God: offer your bodies as a living sacrifice, holy and pleasing to God. Worship like this brings your mind into line with God's. ²What's more, don't let yourselves be squeezed into the shape dictated by the present age. Instead, be transformed by the renewing of your minds, so that you can work out what God's will is, what is good, acceptable and complete.

³Through the grace which was given to me, I have this to say to each one of you: don't think of yourselves more highly than you ought to think. Rather, think soberly, in line with faith, the true standard which God has marked out for each of you. ⁴As in one body we have many limbs and organs, you see, and all the parts have different functions, ⁵so we, many as we are, are one body in the Messiah, and individually we belong to one another.

Living together in the Messiah

⁶Well then, we have gifts that differ in accordance with the grace that has been given to us, and we must use them appropriately. If it is prophecy, we must prophesy according to the pattern of the faith. ⁷If it is serving, we must work at our serving; if teaching, at our teaching; ⁸if exhortation, at our exhortation; if giving, with generosity; if leading, with energy; if doing acts of kindness, with cheerfulness.

⁹Love must be real. Hate what is evil, stick fast to what is good. ¹⁰Be truly affectionate in showing love for one another; compete with each other in giving mutual respect. ¹¹Don't get tired of working hard. Be on fire with the spirit. Work as slaves for the Lord. ¹²Celebrate your hope; be patient in suffering; give constant energy to prayer; ¹³contribute to the needs of God's people; make sure you are hospitable to strangers.

Living alongside the world

¹⁴Bless those who persecute you; bless them, don't curse them. ¹⁵Celebrate with those who are celebrating, mourn with the mourners. ¹⁶Come to the same mind with one another. Don't give yourselves airs, but associate with the humble. Don't get too clever for yourselves.

¹⁷Never repay anyone evil for evil; think through what will seem good to everyone who is watching. ¹⁸If it's possible, as far as you can, live at peace with all people. ¹⁹Don't take revenge, my dear people, but allow God's anger room to work. The Bible says, after all, 'Vengeance is mine; I will repay, says the Lord.' ²⁰No: 'If your enemy is hungry, feed him; if he is thirsty, give him a drink. If you do this, you

will pile up burning coals on his head.' ²¹Don't let evil conquer you. Rather, conquer evil with good.

The divine purpose, and limited role, of ruling authorities

13 Every person must be subject to the ruling authorities. There is no authority, you see, except from God, and those that exist have been put in place by God. ²As a result, anyone who rebels against authority is resisting what God has set up, and those who resist will bring judgment on themselves. ³For rulers hold no terrors for people who do good, but only for people who do evil.

If you want to have no fear of the ruling power, do what is good, and it will praise you. ⁴It is God's servant, you see, for you and your good. But if you do evil, be afraid; the sword it carries is no empty gesture. It is God's servant, you see: an agent of justice to bring his anger on evildoers. ⁵That is why it is necessary to submit, not only to avoid punishment but because of conscience.

⁶That, too, is why you pay taxes. The officials in question are God's ministers, attending to this very thing. ⁷So pay each of them what is owed: tribute to those who collect it, revenue to those who collect it. Respect those who should be respected. Honour the people one ought to honour.

Love, the law and the coming day

⁸Don't owe anything to anyone, except the debt of mutual love. If you love your neighbour, you see, you have fulfilled the law. ⁹Commandments like 'don't commit adultery, don't kill, don't steal, don't covet' – and any other commandment – are summed up in this: 'Love your neighbour as yourself.' ¹⁰Love does no wrong to its neighbour; so love is the fulfilment of the law.

¹¹This is all the more important because you know what time it is. The hour has come for you to wake up from sleep. Our salvation, you see, is nearer now than it was when first we came to faith. ¹²The night is nearly over, the day is almost here. So let's put off the works of darkness, and put on the armour of light. ¹³Let's behave appropriately, as in the daytime: not in wild parties and drunkenness, not in orgies and shameless immorality, not in bad temper and jealousy. ¹⁴Instead, put on the Lord Jesus, the Messiah, and don't make any allowance for the flesh and its lusts.

The weak and the strong

14 Welcome someone who is weak in faith, but not in order to have disputes on difficult points. ²One person believes it is all right to eat anything, while the weak person eats only vegetables. ³The one who eats should not despise the one who does not, and the one who does not should not condemn the one who does – because God has welcomed them.

⁴Who do you think you are to judge someone else's servants? They stand or fall before their own master. And stand they will, because the master can make them stand.

⁵One person reckons one day more important than another. Someone else regards all days as equally important. Each person must make up their own mind. ⁶The one who celebrates the day does so in honour of the Lord. The one who eats, does so in honour of the Lord, and gives thanks to God; the one who does not eat abstains in honour of the Lord, and gives thanks to God.

The final judgment is the only one that counts

⁷None of us lives to ourselves; none of us dies to ourselves. ⁸If we live, we live to the Lord, and if we die, we die to the Lord. So, then, whether we live or whether we die, we belong to the Lord. ⁹That is why the Messiah died and came back to life, so that he might be Lord both of the dead and of the living.

¹⁰You, then: why do you condemn your fellow Christian? Or you: why do you despise a fellow Christian? We must all appear before the judgment seat of God, ¹¹as the Bible says:

As I live, says the Lord, to me every knee shall bow,
and every tongue shall give praise to God.

¹²So then, we must each give an account of ourselves to God.

The way of love and peace

¹³Do not, then, pass judgment on one another any longer. If you want to exercise your judgment, do so on this question: how to avoid placing obstacles or stumbling blocks in front of a fellow family member.

¹⁴I know, and am persuaded in the Lord Jesus, that nothing is unclean in itself, except that some things do become unclean for the person who regards them as such. ¹⁵For if your brother or sister is being harmed by what you eat, you are no longer behaving in accordance with love. Don't let your food destroy someone for whom the Messiah died!

¹⁶So don't let something that is good for you make other people blaspheme. ¹⁷God's kingdom, you see, isn't about food and drink, but about justice, peace, and joy in the holy spirit. ¹⁸Anyone who serves the Messiah like this pleases God and deserves respect from other people. ¹⁹So, then, let's find and follow the way of peace, and discover how to build each other up. ²⁰Don't pull down God's work on account of food. Everything is pure, but it becomes evil for anyone who causes offence when they eat. ²¹It is good not to eat meat, or drink wine, or anything else which makes your fellow Christian stumble.

²²Hold firmly to the faith which you have as a matter between yourself and God. When you've thought something through, and can go ahead without passing judgment on yourself, God's blessing on you! ²³But anyone who doubts is condemned even in the act of eating, because it doesn't spring from faith. Whatever is not of faith is sin.

Unity: modelled by the Messiah, encouraged by scripture

15 We, the 'strong' ones, should bear with the frailty of the 'weak', and not please ourselves. ²Each one of us should please our neighbour for his or her good, to build them up. ³The Messiah, you see, did not please himself. Instead, as the Bible says, 'the reproaches of those who reproached you are fallen on me'. ⁴Whatever was written ahead of time, you see, was written for us to learn from, so that through patience, and through the encouragement of the Bible, we might have hope. ⁵May the God of patience and encouragement grant you to come to a common mind among yourselves, in accordance with the Messiah, Jesus, ⁶so that, with one mind and one mouth, you may glorify the God and father of our Lord Jesus the Messiah.

United praise under the Messiah's universal rule

⁷Welcome one another, therefore, as the Messiah has welcomed you, to God's glory. ⁸Let me tell you why: the Messiah became a servant of the circumcised people in order to demonstrate the truthfulness of God – that is, to confirm the promises to the patriarchs, ⁹and to bring the nations to praise God for his mercy. As the Bible says:

That is why I will praise you among the nations,
and will sing to your name.

¹⁰And again it says,

Rejoice, you nations, with his people.

¹¹And again,

Praise the Lord, all nations,
and let all the peoples sing his praise.

¹²And Isaiah says once more:

There shall be the root of Jesse,
the one who rises up to rule the nations;
the nations shall hope in him.

¹³May the God of hope fill you with all joy and peace in believing, so that you may overflow with hope by the power of the holy spirit.

Coming to Rome at last

¹⁴When I think of you, my dear family, I myself am thoroughly convinced that you are full of

goodness, filled with all knowledge, and well able to give one another instruction. ¹⁵But I have written to you very boldly at some points, calling things to your mind through the grace which God has given me ¹⁶to enable me to be a minister of King Jesus for the nations, working in the priestly service of God's good news, so that the offering of the nations may be acceptable, sanctified in the holy spirit.

¹⁷This is the glad confidence I have in King Jesus, and in God's own presence. ¹⁸Far be it from me, you see, to speak about anything except what the Messiah has accomplished through me for the obedience of the nations, in word and deed, ¹⁹in the power of signs and wonders, in the power of God's spirit. I have completed announcing the good news of the Messiah from Jerusalem round as far as Illyricum. ²⁰My driving ambition has been to announce the good news in places where the Messiah has not been named, so that I can avoid building on anyone else's foundation. ²¹Instead, as the Bible says,

> People who hadn't been told about him will see;
> people who hadn't heard will understand.

²²That's why I have faced so many obstacles to stop me coming to you. ²³But now, finding myself with no more room in these regions, I have a great longing to come to you now at last after so many years, ²⁴and so to make my way to Spain. You see, I'm hoping to see you as I pass through, and to be sent on my way there by you, once I have been refreshed by you for a while.

Aid for Jerusalem

²⁵Now, though, I am going to Jerusalem to render service to God's people there. ²⁶Macedonia and Achaea, you see, have happily decided to enter into partnership with the poor believers in Jerusalem. ²⁷They were eager to do this, and indeed they owe them a debt. If the nations have shared in the Jews' spiritual blessings, it is right and proper that they should minister to their earthly needs. ²⁸So when I have completed this, and tied up all the loose ends, I will come via you to Spain. ²⁹And I know that when I come to you I shall come with the full blessing of the Messiah.

³⁰I urge you, my dear family, through our Lord Jesus the Messiah and through the love of the spirit: fight the battle for me in your prayers to God on my behalf, ³¹so that I may be rescued from the unbelievers in Judaea, and so that my service for Jerusalem may be welcomed gladly by God's people. ³²If this happens, I will come to you in joy, through the will of God, and be refreshed by being with you. ³³May the God of peace be with you all. Amen.

Commending Phoebe, greeting friends

16 Let me introduce to you our sister Phoebe. She is a deacon in the church at Cenchreae. ²I want you to welcome her in the Lord, as is proper for one of God's people. Please give her whatever practical assistance she may need from you. She has been a benefactor to many people, myself included.

³Greet Prisca and Aquila, my fellow-workers in King Jesus. ⁴They put their lives on the line for me. It isn't only me, but all the Gentile churches, that owe them a debt of gratitude. ⁵Greet the church in their house as well.

Greet my dear Epainetus; he was the first fruits of the Messiah's harvest in Asia. ⁶Greet Mary, who has worked hard for you. ⁷Greet Andronicus and Junia, my relatives and fellow prisoners, who are well known among the apostles, and who were in the Messiah before I was. ⁸Greet Ampliatus, my dear friend in the Lord. ⁹Greet Urbanus, our fellow-worker in the Messiah, and my dear Stachys. ¹⁰Greet Apelles, who has proved his worth in the Messiah. Greet the people from the Aristobulus household.

¹¹Greet my relative Herodion. Greet those in the Lord who belong to the household of Narcissus. ¹²Greet Tryphaena and Tryphosa, who have worked hard in the Lord. Greet dear Persis, who has done a great deal of work in the Lord. ¹³Greet Rufus, one of the Lord's chosen, and also his mother – my mother too, in effect! ¹⁴Greet Asyncritus, Phlegon, Hermes, Patrobas, Hermas and the family with them.

¹⁵Greet Philologus and Julia, Nereus and his sister, Olympas too, and all God's people who are with them. ¹⁶Greet one another with a holy kiss. All the Messiah's churches send you greetings.

Warnings and greetings

¹⁷I urge you, my dear family, to watch out for those who cause divisions and problems, contrary to the teaching you learned. Avoid them. ¹⁸People like that are serving their own appetites instead of our Lord the Messiah. They deceive the hearts of simple-minded people with their smooth and flattering speech. ¹⁹Your obedience, you see, is well known to all, and so I am rejoicing over you. But I want you to be wise when it comes to good, and innocent when it comes to evil. ²⁰The God of peace will quickly crush the satan under your feet. May the grace of our Lord Jesus be with you.

²¹Timothy, my fellow-worker, sends you greetings, as do Lucius, Jason and Sosipater, my relatives. ²²I, Tertius, the scribe for this letter, greet you in the Lord. ²³Gaius, who is host to me and the whole church, sends you greetings. Erastus the city treasurer sends you greetings, as does another brother, Quartus.

Final blessing

²⁵Now to him who is able to strengthen you according to my gospel, the proclamation of Jesus the Messiah, in accordance with the unveiling of the mystery kept hidden for long ages ²⁶but now revealed and made known through the prophetic writings, according to the command of the eternal God, for the obedience of faith among all the nations – ²⁷to the only wise God, through Jesus the Messiah, to whom be glory to the coming ages! Amen.

1 Corinthians

Skim through Paul's first letter to Corinth, and it reads like a shopping list of 'questions you might want to ask your apostle': what should we do about personality cults, sexual ethics, food associated with pagan temples, how to celebrate the Lord's Supper, spiritual gifts, and the question of resurrection. That is a fair impression – at one level. Paul does indeed address those issues and more. But there are five threads, silken strands of biblically rooted theological thought, which, woven tightly together, hold the entire discourse in place, like a single jeweller's rope displaying carefully arranged pearls.

The first thread is the shocking message of the crucified Messiah: a scandal to Jews, says Paul, and folly to Gentiles, but for those who are called, God's power and God's wisdom. The central fact Paul wants the status-conscious Corinthians to remember is that their very existence hangs on something their neighbours are bound to regard as sheer stupidity, and their Jewish friends down the road will see as blasphemous nonsense. The 'word of the cross' works its way through the letter, colouring ethical and practical teaching all the way: 'the Messiah died for our sins in accordance with the Bible' (15.3) is the start of the official tradition which Paul finally quotes.

The second thread is the claim that through this crazy message a different sort of 'wisdom' has been unveiled, and with it a different kind of *thinking*. 'We have the mind of the Messiah', Paul claims (2.16), though you have to work at it: 'in your thinking be grown-ups' (14.20). Ordinary ways of thinking and behaving require thorough revaluation: Jesus' death and resurrection and the gift of the spirit have introduced into the world a radically new way.

The third thread is the consequent call to *unity*. A bustling city like Corinth had many social divisions. Personality cults were a natural outgrowth of different social expectations. Divisions between rich and poor would show up embarrassingly at the Lord's Table. It is easy for different spiritual gifts to become status symbols. And so on. All such posturing must go: there is one 'body of the Messiah' (chapter 12), and each believer is a limb or an organ within that body. All have parts to play; none can do without the others. That is why Paul follows that point with the matchless short poem about love (chapter 13).

The fourth thread is the parallel call to *holiness*. Various lifestyles common in a city like Corinth ('everybody does it') are simply out of the question for those who have been 'bought with a price' from dehumanizing practices. Chapters 5 and 6 are particularly clear on this. Marriage and sex are vital areas requiring careful practical and pastoral advice (chapter 7). The question of how to stay holy in a world full of pagan worship and practice (chapters 8—10) is balanced with the challenge to avoid a dualism in which 'the world' is seen as evil: on the contrary, God made it, and it's all good – but we must not be enslaved by anything.

The fifth and final thread Paul leaves for the last, but once you see it you realize it's been there all through. The resurrection of Jesus, and the consequent revision of the ancient Jewish timetable for how God was going to put the whole world right, mean that one must live in the present in the light of that ultimate future. Your body will be raised, so what you do with it matters now! The work you do in the present is not wasted (15.58). There is continuity between the present and the future, as well as the radical discontinuity marked by a new world in which death will be no more.

Thankful for God's grace

1 Paul, called by God's will to be an apostle of King Jesus, and Sosthenes our brother; ²to God's assembly at Corinth, made holy in King Jesus, called to be holy, with everyone who calls on the name of our Lord, King Jesus, in every place – their Lord, indeed, as well as ours! ³Grace to you and peace from God our father and King Jesus the Lord.

⁴I always thank my God for you, for the grace of God that was given to you in King Jesus. ⁵You were enriched in him in everything, in every kind of speech and knowledge, ⁶just as the messianic message was established among you, ⁷so that you aren't missing out on any spiritual gift as you wait eagerly for our Lord, King Jesus, to be revealed. ⁸He will establish you right through to the end, so that you are blameless on the day of our Lord, King Jesus. ⁹God is faithful! And it is through God that you have been called into the fellowship of his son, King Jesus, our Lord.

Beware of divisions!

¹⁰Now I must appeal to you, my brothers and sisters, through the name of King Jesus our Lord, that you should all be in agreement, and that there should be no divisions among you. Instead, you should be fully equipped with the same mind and the same opinion.

¹¹You see, my dear family, Chloe's people have put me in the picture about you – about the fact that you are having quarrels. ¹²What I'm talking about is this. Each one of you is saying, 'I'm with Paul!', 'I'm with Apollos!', 'I'm with Cephas!', 'I'm with the Messiah!'

¹³Well! Has the Messiah been cut up into pieces? Was Paul crucified for you? Or were you baptized into Paul's name?! ¹⁴I'm grateful to God that I didn't baptize any of you except Crispus and Gaius, ¹⁵so that none of you could say that you were baptized into *my* name. (¹⁶All right, I did baptize Stephanas and his household as well. Apart from that, I don't know if I baptized anybody else.) ¹⁷This is the point, you see: the Messiah didn't send me to baptize; he sent me to announce the gospel! Not with words of wisdom, either, otherwise the Messiah's cross would lose its power.

God's folly

¹⁸The word of the cross, you see, is madness to people who are being destroyed. But to us – those who are being saved – it is God's power. ¹⁹This is what the Bible says, after all:

> I will destroy the wisdom of the wise;
> the shrewdness of the clever I'll abolish.

²⁰Where is the wise person? Where is the educated person? Where is the debater of this present age? Don't you see that God has turned the world's wisdom into folly? ²¹This is how it's happened: in God's wisdom, the world didn't know God through wisdom, so it gave God pleasure, through the folly of our proclamation, to save those who believe. ²²Jews look for signs, you see, and Greeks search for wisdom; ²³but we announce the crucified Messiah, a scandal to Jews and folly to Gentiles, ²⁴but to those who are called, Jews and Greeks alike, the Messiah – God's power and God's wisdom. ²⁵God's folly is wiser than humans, you see, and God's weakness is stronger than humans.

Boasting in the Lord

²⁶Think back to your own call, my brothers and sisters. Not many of you were wise in human terms. Not many of you were powerful. Not many were nobly born. ²⁷But God chose the foolish things of the world to shame the wise; God chose the weak things of the world to shame the strong; ²⁸God chose the insignificant and despised things of the world – yes, even things that don't exist! – to abolish the power of the things that do exist, ²⁹so that no creature could boast in God's presence. ³⁰Who and what you now are is a gift from God in King Jesus, who has become for us God's wisdom – and righteousness, sanctification and redemption as well; ³¹so that, as the Bible puts it, 'Anyone who boasts should boast in the Lord.'

The powerful message of the cross

2 This is how it was for me, too, my dear family. When I came to you, I didn't come and proclaim God's mystery to you by means of a superior style of speaking or wisdom. ²No: I decided to know nothing in my dealings with you except Jesus the Messiah, especially his crucifixion. ³I came to you in weakness, in great fear and trembling. ⁴My speech and my proclamation were not in persuasive words of wisdom, but in transparent proof brought home powerfully by the spirit, ⁵so that your faith might not be in human wisdom but in God's power.

God's strange wisdom

⁶We do, however, speak wisdom among the mature. But this isn't a wisdom of this present world, or of the rulers of this present world – those same rulers who are being done away with. ⁷No: we speak God's hidden wisdom in a mystery. This is the wisdom God prepared ahead of time, before the world began, for our glory.

⁸None of the rulers of this present age knew about this wisdom. If they had, you see, they wouldn't have crucified the Lord of glory. ⁹But, as the Bible says,

> Human eyes have never seen,
> human ears have never heard,
> it's never entered human hearts:
> all that God has now prepared
> for those who truly love him.

¹⁰– and that's what God has revealed to us through the spirit! The spirit, you see, searches everything, yes, even the depths of God. ¹¹Think of it this way: who knows what is really going on inside a person, except the spirit of the person which is inside them? Well, it's like that with God. Nobody knows what is going on inside God except God's spirit. ¹²And we haven't received the spirit of the world, but the spirit that comes from God, so that we can know the things that have been given to us by God.

¹³That, then, is what we speak. We don't use words we've been taught by human wisdom, but words we've been taught by the spirit, interpreting spiritual things to spiritual people.

Spiritual or merely human?

¹⁴Someone living at the merely human level doesn't accept the things of God's spirit. They are foolishness to such people, you see, and they can't understand them because they need to be discerned spiritually. ¹⁵But spiritual people discern everything, while nobody else can discern the truth about them! ¹⁶For 'Who has known the mind of the Lord, so as to instruct him?' But we have the mind of the Messiah.

3 In my own case, my dear family, I couldn't speak to you as spiritual people, but as people who were all too obviously merely human, little babies in the Messiah. ²I fed you with milk, not solid food, because you weren't able to take it – and you still can't, even now! ³You're still determined to live in the old way! Yes, wherever there is jealousy and quarrelling, doesn't that mean you're living in the old way, behaving as any merely human being might do? ⁴When someone says 'I'm with Paul!', and someone else says 'I'm with Apollos!', are you not mere humans?

God's farm, God's building

⁵So what d'you suppose Apollos actually is? What d'you think Paul is? I'll tell you: servants, through whom you came to faith, each one as the Lord gave. ⁶I planted and Apollos watered, but it was God who gave the growth. ⁷It follows that the person who plants isn't anything special, and the person who waters isn't anything special; what matters is God who gives the growth. ⁸The person who plants and the person who waters are just the same, and each will receive his own reward according to his own work. ⁹We are God's fellow-workers, you see: you are God's farm, God's building.

¹⁰According to God's grace, I laid the foundation like a wise master builder, and someone else is building on it. Everyone should take care how they build on it. ¹¹Nobody can lay any foundation, you see, except the one which is laid, which is Jesus the Messiah!

The coming day, the coming fire

¹²If anyone builds on the foundation with gold, silver, precious stones, wood, grass or straw – ¹³well, everyone's work will become visible, because the Day will show it up, since it will be revealed in fire. Then the fire will test what sort

of work everyone has done. ¹⁴If the building work that someone has done stands the test, they will receive a reward. ¹⁵If someone's work is burned up, they will be punished by bearing the loss; they themselves will be saved, however, but only as though through a fire.

¹⁶Don't you see? You are God's Temple! God's spirit lives in you! ¹⁷If anyone destroys God's Temple, God will destroy them. God's Temple is holy, you see, and that is precisely what you are.

Everything belongs to you

¹⁸Don't let anyone deceive themselves. If anyone among you supposes they are wise in the present age, let them become foolish, so that they can become wise. ¹⁹The wisdom of this world, you see, is folly with God. This is what the Bible says: 'He catches the wise in their trickery.' ²⁰And again, 'The Lord knows the thinking of the wise – and he knows that it's all a sham!'

²¹So don't let anyone boast about mere human beings. For everything belongs to you, ²²whether it's Paul or Apollos or Cephas, whether it's the world or life or death, whether it's the present or the future – everything belongs to you! ²³And you belong to the Messiah; and the Messiah belongs to God.

Judgment then rather than now

4 This is how we should be thought of: as servants of the Messiah, and household managers for God's mysteries. ²And this is what follows: the main requirement for a manager is to be trustworthy. ³Having said that, I regard it as a matter of minimal concern to think that I should be interrogated by you, or indeed by any human court. I don't even interrogate myself. ⁴I don't actually know of anything that stands against me, but that isn't what vindicates me; it's the Lord who interrogates me.

⁵So don't pass judgment on anything before the time when the Lord comes! He will bring to light the secrets of darkness, and will lay bare the intentions of the heart. Then everyone will receive praise – from God.

Apostles on display

⁶I have applied all this to myself and Apollos because of you, my dear family, so that you may learn from us, as the saying goes, not to go beyond what the Bible says – so that nobody gets puffed up in favour of one person and against another.

⁷Who is going to concede that you are special, after all? What have you got that you didn't receive? Well then, if you received it, why boast as if you didn't? ⁸Do you really suppose you've already had all the food you need? Do you think you've already become rich? Do you think you've already been crowned as royalty, leaving us behind? I wish you really were already reigning, so that we could reign alongside you!

⁹This is how I look at it, you see: God has put us apostles on display at the end of the procession, like people sentenced to death. We have become a public show for the world, for angels and humans alike. ¹⁰We are fools because of the Messiah, but you are wise in the Messiah! We are weak, but you are strong! You are celebrated, we are nobodies! ¹¹Yes, right up to the present moment we go hungry and thirsty; we are badly clothed, roughly treated, with no home to call our own. ¹²What's more, we work hard, doing manual labour. When we are insulted, we give back blessings. When we are persecuted, we put up with it. ¹³When we are slandered, we speak gently in return. To this day we have become like the rubbish of the world, fit only to be scraped off the plate and thrown away with everything else.

Puffed up or powerful?

¹⁴I'm not writing this to make you ashamed! I am simply treating you as dear children, and putting you straight. ¹⁵You've got a thousand babysitters in Christ, I know, but you haven't got many fathers – because I became your father in the Messiah, Jesus, through the gospel.

¹⁶So let me appeal to you: copy me! ¹⁷That's why I have sent Timothy to you; he's my child in the Lord, and I love him and trust him. He will remind you how I conduct myself in the Messiah Jesus, just as I teach everywhere, in each assembly.

¹⁸Some people are getting puffed up, as though I wasn't going to come to you. ¹⁹But I will come to you quickly, if the Lord wants it that way; and then I'll find out not what these puffed-up people are saying but how powerful they are. ²⁰The kingdom of God, you see, isn't about talk – it's about power. ²¹What d'you want, then? Shall I come to you with a big stick, or with love, and in a gentle spirit?

Scandal and judgment

5 Everybody's talking about the sex scandal that's going on in your community, not least because it's a kind of immorality that even the pagans don't practise! Well I never – a man taking his father's wife! ²And you're puffed up! Why aren't you in mourning? Why aren't you getting rid of the person who's done such a thing?

³Let me tell you what I've already done. I may be away from you physically, but I'm present in the spirit; and I've already passed judgment, as though I was there with you, on the person who has behaved in this way. ⁴When you are assembled together in the name of our Lord Jesus, and my spirit is there too with the power of our Lord Jesus, ⁵you must hand over such a person to the satan for the destruction of the flesh, so that his spirit may be saved on the day of the Lord Jesus.

Get rid of the 'leaven'!

⁶Your boasting is no good. Don't you know that a little yeast works its way through the whole lump of dough? ⁷Cleanse out the old yeast, so that you can be a new lump, the yeast-free lump you really are. It's Passover-time, you see, and our Passover lamb – the Messiah, I mean – has already been sacrificed! ⁸What we now have to do is to keep the festival properly: none of the yeast of the old life, and none of the yeast of depravity and wickedness, either. What we need is yeast-free bread, and that means sincerity and truth.

⁹I wrote to you in the previous letter not to become associated with immoral people. ¹⁰I didn't (of course) mean immoral people in the world at large, or greedy people, or thieves, or idolaters. To avoid them, you'd have to remove yourselves from the world altogether! ¹¹No; I was referring to people who call themselves Christians but who are immoral, or greedy, or idolaters, or blasphemers, or drunkards or robbers. You shouldn't associate with them; you shouldn't even eat with a person like that. ¹²Why should I worry about judging people outside? It's the people *in*side you should judge, isn't it? ¹³God judges the people outside. 'Drive out the wicked person from your company.'

Lawsuits in the church?

6 Can it really be the case that one of you dares to go to law against a neighbour, to be tried before unjust people, and not before God's people? ²Don't you know that God's people will judge the world? And if the world is to be judged by you, are you really incompetent to try smaller matters? ³Don't you know that we shall be judging angels? Why not then also matters to do with ordinary life? ⁴So if you have lawsuits about ordinary matters, are you actually going to appoint as judges people whom the church despises? ⁵I'm saying this to bring shame on you. Is it really true that there is no wise person among you who is able to decide between one Christian and another? ⁶But one Christian is being taken to court by another, and before unbelievers at that!

⁷Actually, to have lawsuits with one another at all represents a major setback for you. Why not rather let yourselves be wronged? Why not rather put up with loss? ⁸But you yourselves are wronging and defrauding people, and fellow Christians at that!

Inheriting God's kingdom – or not

⁹Don't you know that the unjust will not inherit God's kingdom? Don't be deceived! Neither immoral people, nor idolaters, nor adulterers, nor practising homosexuals of whichever sort, ¹⁰nor thieves, nor greedy people, nor drunkards, nor abusive talkers, nor robbers will inherit God's kingdom. ¹¹That, of course, is what some of you were! But you were washed clean; you were made holy; you were put back

to rights – in the name of the Lord, King Jesus, and in the spirit of our God.

What is the body for?

¹²'Everything is lawful for me' – but not everything is helpful! 'Everything is lawful for me' – but I'm not going to let anything give me orders! ¹³'Food for the stomach, and the stomach for food, and God will destroy the one and the other' – but the body is not meant for immorality, but for the Lord, and the Lord for the body. ¹⁴What's more, God raised the Lord; and he will raise us, too, through his power.

¹⁵Don't you know that your bodies are members of the Messiah? Shall I then take the members of the Messiah and make them members of a prostitute? Of course not! ¹⁶Or don't you know that anyone who joins himself to a prostitute is one body with her? 'The two shall become one flesh' – that's what it says. ¹⁷But the one who joins himself to the Lord becomes one spirit with him.

¹⁸Run away from immorality. Every sin that it's possible for someone to commit happens outside the body; but immorality involves sinning against your own body. ¹⁹Or don't you know that your body is a temple of the holy spirit within you, the spirit God gave you, so that you don't belong to yourselves? ²⁰You were quite an expensive purchase! So glorify God in your body.

Life within marriage

7 Let me now turn to the matters you wrote about. 'It is good for a man to have no sexual contact with a woman.' ²Well, yes; but the temptation to immorality means that every man should maintain sexual relations with his own wife, and every woman with her own husband. ³The man should give his wife her marital rights, and the woman should do the same for her husband. ⁴The woman isn't in charge of her own body; her husband is. In the same way, the man isn't in charge of his own body; his wife is. ⁵Don't deny one another, except perhaps by agreement for a period of time, so that you may have more space for prayer. But then come together again, in case the satan might tempt you because of your weakness of will.

⁶I'm not saying this as a command, but as a concession. ⁷I would be happy to see everyone be in the same situation as myself. But each person has his or her own gift from God, one this way, another that way.

Marriage and divorce

⁸To unmarried people, and to widows, I have this to say: it's perfectly all right for you to remain like me. ⁹But if you don't have power over your passions, then get married. Much better to marry than to have desire smouldering away inside you!

¹⁰I have a command, too, for married people – actually, it's not just from me, it's from the Lord: that a woman should not separate from her husband. ¹¹If she does, she should remain unmarried or return to her husband. So, too, a man should not divorce his wife.

¹²To everyone else I have this to say (this is just me, not the Lord). If a Christian has an unbelieving wife, and she is happy to live with him, he shouldn't divorce her. ¹³If a woman has an unbelieving husband, and he is happy to live with her, she shouldn't divorce him. ¹⁴The unbelieving husband, you see, is made holy by his wife, and the unbelieving wife is made holy by her husband; otherwise your children would be impure, whereas in fact they are holy. ¹⁵But if the unbelieving partner wants to separate, let them separate; a brother or sister is not bound in a case like that. God has called you in peace. ¹⁶If you're a wife, how d'you know whether or not you will save your husband? If you're a husband, how d'you know whether or not you will save your wife?

Stay the way you were called

¹⁷This is the overriding rule: everyone should conduct their lives as the Lord appointed, as God has called them. This is what I lay down in all the churches. ¹⁸If someone was circumcised when he was called, he shouldn't try to remove the marks. If someone was uncircumcised when he was called, he shouldn't get

circumcised. ⁱ⁹Circumcision is nothing; uncircumcision is nothing; what matters is keeping God's commandments!

²⁰Everyone should stay within the calling they had when they were called. ²¹Were you a slave when you were called? Don't worry about it (but if you get the chance of freedom, seize it!). ²²The one who is in the Lord and called as a slave is the Lord's freedman, just as the one who is called as a free person is the Messiah's slave. ²³You were bought at a high price; don't become the slaves of human beings. ²⁴So, brothers and sisters, let each person remain before God in the state in which they were called.

On remaining unmarried

²⁵Now when it comes to unmarried people, I have no command from the Lord, but I give my opinion as (thanks to the Lord's mercy!) a trustworthy person. ²⁶This, then, is what I think is for the best: just at the moment we are in the middle of a very difficult time, and it's best for people to remain as they are. ²⁷Are you bound to a wife? Don't try to dissolve the marriage. Have you had your marriage dissolved? Don't look for another wife. ²⁸But if you do marry, you are not sinning, and if an unmarried woman marries, she is not sinning. But people who go that way will have trouble at a human level, and I would prefer to spare you that.

²⁹This is what I mean, my brothers and sisters. The present situation won't last long; for the moment, let those who have wives live as though they weren't married, ³⁰those who weep as though they were not weeping, those who celebrate as though they were not celebrating, those who buy as though they had no possessions, ³¹those who use the world as though they were not making use of it. The pattern of this world, you see, is passing away.

Divided loyalties

³²I want you to be free from worries. The unmarried man worries about the things of the Lord, how to please the Lord; ³³but the married man worries about the things of the world, in other words, how to please his wife – ³⁴and he is pulled in both directions. So too the unmarried woman or girl worries about the things of the Lord, how to be holy both in body and spirit; but the married woman worries about the things of the world, in other words, how to please her husband.

³⁵I'm saying this for your own benefit. I'm not placing restrictions on you; my aim is that nothing will get in the way of your appropriate behaviour and steady devotion to the Lord.

³⁶If anyone thinks he is behaving improperly towards his fiancée – if he finds the situation overly stressful, and matters reach a point of necessity – then let him do as he wishes, he won't be sinning: let them marry. ³⁷But the man who settles it firmly in his heart and is not under necessity, but in control of his own will, and has made his judgment in his own heart to keep her as his fiancée, will do well. ³⁸So the one who marries his fiancée will do well; and the one who holds back from marrying will do better.

³⁹A woman is bound in marriage as long as her husband lives. But if the husband dies she is free to marry anyone she likes, only in the Lord. ⁴⁰But in my opinion she is happier if she remains as she is. And I think I too have the spirit of God.

Meat offered to idols

8 Now when it comes to meat offered to idols, we know that 'We all have knowledge'. Knowledge puffs you up, but love builds you up! ²If anybody thinks they 'know' something, they don't yet 'know' in the way they ought to know. ³But if anybody loves God, they are 'known' – by him.

⁴So when it comes to food that has been offered to idols, we know that 'idols are nothing in the world', and that 'there is no God but one'. ⁵Yes, indeed: there may be many so-called 'gods', whether in heaven or on earth, just as there are many 'gods' and many 'lords'. ⁶But for us

There is one God, the father,
from whom are all things, and we live to
   him and for him;
and one Lord, Jesus the Messiah,
through whom are all things, and we
   live through him.

Respecting weak consciences

⁷The problem is that not everybody has this 'knowledge'. Some have been accustomed up to now to eating idol-food with the assumption that it really does belong to the idol. This has left them with a weak conscience, and now that conscience will be polluted. ⁸But the food we eat won't recommend us to God. We won't be any worse off if we don't eat, and we won't be any better off if we do.

⁹But you must take care in case this official right of yours becomes a danger to the weak. ¹⁰Look at it like this: if someone with a weak conscience sees you, a person with 'knowledge', sitting down to eat in an idol-house, that conscience of theirs is likely to make up its mind actually to eat idol-food, isn't it? ¹¹And so, you see, the weak person – a brother or sister for whom the Messiah died! – is then destroyed by your 'knowledge'. ¹²That means you'll be sinning against your brother or sister, and attacking their weak conscience; and in doing this you'll be sinning against the Messiah. ¹³So, for this reason, if food causes my brother or sister to stumble, I will never ever eat meat, so that I won't make my brother or sister trip up.

The 'rights' of an apostle

9 I'm a free man, aren't I? I'm an apostle, aren't I? I've seen Jesus our Lord, haven't I? You are my work in the Lord, aren't you? ²I may not be an apostle to other people, but I certainly am to you; in fact, you are the authorized stamp of my apostleship in the Lord.

³This is the defence I make to anyone who wants to bring a charge against me. ⁴Do we not have the right to eat and drink? ⁵Do we not have the right to take a Christian wife with us on our travels, as the other apostles do, as the Lord's brothers do, as Cephas does? ⁶Or are Barnabas and I the only ones who don't have the right to be set free from the need to work? ⁷Who serves in the army at their own expense? Who plants a vineyard and doesn't eat its fruit? Who looks after animals and doesn't drink the milk?

⁸I'm not just using human illustrations to make the point; the law says the same thing, doesn't it? ⁹This is what is written in Moses's law: 'You must not muzzle a threshing ox.' God isn't concerned for oxen, is he? ¹⁰Doesn't it refer completely to us? Yes, it does – because it's written that the one who ploughs should do so in hope of the produce, and the thresher should thresh in hope of a share in the crop. ¹¹So if we have sown spiritual things among you, is it such a big thing that we should reap worldly things? ¹²If others have that kind of right over you, don't we have it even more?

Giving up rights for the gospel

But we haven't made use of this right. Instead, we put up with everything, so as to place no obstacle in the way of the Messiah's gospel.

¹³Don't you know that those who work in the Temple eat the Temple food, and those who serve at the altar share in the food from the altar? ¹⁴In the same way the Lord has laid it down that those who announce the gospel should get their living from the gospel.

¹⁵But I haven't made use of any of this. I'm not writing this in order to make it happen like this for me. It would be better for me to die than . . . Nobody's going to deprive me of my boast! ¹⁶If I announce the gospel, you see, that's no reason for me to be proud. I'm under compulsion! Woe betide me if I *don't* announce the gospel! ¹⁷If I do it willingly, I have a reward; if I do it unwillingly – well, this is the commission that's been entrusted to me! ¹⁸So what is my reward? Just this: that when I announce the gospel I should give it away free of charge; that I shouldn't make use of my rights in the gospel.

The apostle's freedom – to be enslaved to everyone

¹⁹The reason for all this is as follows. I am indeed free from everyone; but I have enslaved myself to everyone, so that I can win all the more. ²⁰I became like a Jew to the Jews, to win Jews. I became like someone under the law to the people who are under the law, even though I'm not myself under the law, so that I could win those under the law. ²¹To the lawless I became like someone lawless (even though I'm not lawless before God, but under the Messiah's law), so that I could win the lawless. ²²I became weak to the weak, to win the weak.

I have become all things to all people, so that in all ways I might save some. ²³I do it all because of the gospel, so that I can be a partner in its benefits.

The Christian athlete

²⁴Don't you know that when people run on the race-track everybody runs, but only one person gets the prize? Run in such a way that you'll win it. ²⁵Everyone who goes in for athletics exercises self-discipline in everything. They do it to gain a crown that perishes; we do it for an imperishable one. ²⁶Well then: I don't run in an aimless fashion! I don't box like someone punching the air! ²⁷No: I give my body rough treatment, and make it my slave, in case, after announcing the message to others, I myself should end up being disqualified.

The first exodus

10 I don't want you to be ignorant, my brothers and sisters, that our fathers were all under the cloud and all went through the sea. ²They were all baptized into Moses in the cloud and in the sea. ³They all ate the same spiritual food ⁴and drank the same spiritual drink. They drank, you see, from the spiritual rock that followed them, and the rock was the Messiah. ⁵But God wasn't pleased with most of them, as you can tell by the fact that he laid them low in the desert.

Don't make the same mistake again!

⁶Now these things were patterns for us, so that we should not start to crave for wicked things as they did. ⁷Nor should we commit idolatry, as some of them did – as the Bible says, 'The people sat down to eat and drink, and got up to play.' ⁸Nor should we become immoral, like some of them became immoral, and twenty-three thousand fell on a single day. ⁹Nor should we put the Messiah to the test, as some of them put him to the test, and were destroyed by serpents. ¹⁰Nor should we grumble, as some of them grumbled and were destroyed by the destroyer.

¹¹Now these things happened to them as a pattern, and they were written for our instruction, since it's upon us that the ends of the ages have now come. ¹²As a result, anyone who reckons they are standing upright should watch out in case they fall over. ¹³Every test that comes upon you is normal for human beings. But God is faithful: he won't let you be tested beyond your ability. Along with the testing, he will provide the way of escape, so that you can bear it.

The table of the Lord and the table of demons

¹⁴Therefore, my dear people, run away from idolatry. ¹⁵I'm speaking as to intelligent people: you yourselves must weigh my words. ¹⁶The cup of blessing which we bless is a sharing in the Messiah's blood, isn't it? The bread we break is a sharing in the Messiah's body, isn't it? ¹⁷There is one loaf; well, then, there may be several of us, but we are one body, because we all share the one loaf.

¹⁸Consider ethnic Israel. Those who eat from the sacrifices share in the altar, don't they? ¹⁹So what am I saying? That idol-food is real, or that an idol is a real being? ²⁰No: but when they offer sacrifices, they offer them to demons, not to God. And *I don't want you to be table-partners with demons.* ²¹You can't drink the cup of the Lord and the cup of demons. You can't share in the table of the Lord and the table of demons. ²²Surely you don't want to provoke the Lord to jealousy? We aren't stronger than him, are we?

Do everything to God's glory

²³'Everything is lawful', but not everything is helpful. 'Everything is lawful', but not everything builds you up. ²⁴Nobody should seek their own advantage, but the other person's instead.

²⁵Eat whatever is sold in the market without making any judgments on the basis of conscience. ²⁶'The earth and its fullness', after all, 'belong to the Lord'. ²⁷If one of the unbelievers invites you to dinner, and you want to go, eat whatever is put in front of

you without making any judgments on the basis of conscience. ²⁸But if someone says 'This was offered in sacrifice', then don't eat it – because of the person who told you about it, and because of conscience, ²⁹by which I don't mean your own conscience, but your neighbour's. For why should my freedom be condemned by someone else's conscience? ³⁰If I eat my share gratefully, why should someone else speak evil of me because of something I've given thanks for?

³¹So, then, whether you eat or drink or whatever you do, do everything to God's glory. ³²Be blameless before Jews and Greeks and the church of God, ³³just as I try to please everybody in everything, not pursuing my own advantage, but that of the great majority, so that they may be saved.

11 Copy me, just as I'm copying the Messiah.

Male and female in the worshipping church

²I congratulate you that you are remembering me in everything, and you are keeping the traditions as I handed them on to you. ³But I want you to know this: that the Messiah is the 'head' of every man, and the husband is the 'head' of every wife, and God is the 'head' of the Messiah. ⁴Every man who prays or prophesies while wearing something on his head brings shame on his 'head'; ⁵and every woman who prays or prophesies with her head uncovered brings shame on her 'head'. It would be just the same if she had her head shaved. ⁶For if a woman isn't covered, then she should be shaved; but if it's shameful for a woman to have her hair cut off or her head shaved, then let her be covered.

⁷A man ought not to cover his head, you see; he is the image and glory of God. But a wife is the glory of her husband. ⁸For man was not made from woman, but woman from man. ⁹And man was not created for the sake of woman, but woman for the sake of man. ¹⁰That's why the wife must have authority on her head, because of the angels. ¹¹However, woman is not apart from man, nor man apart from woman, in the Lord; ¹²for just as woman came from man, so now man comes into the world by means of woman. And everything is from God.

¹³Judge the matter for yourselves. Is it really appropriate for a woman to pray to God with her head uncovered? ¹⁴Doesn't nature itself teach you that if a man has long hair, it is shameful to him, ¹⁵but if a woman has long hair, it's her glory? Her hair is given her, you see, instead of a covering. ¹⁶If anyone wants to dispute this, we have no other custom, nor do the churches of God.

Rich and poor at the table of the Lord

¹⁷What I have to talk about now isn't a matter for praise. When you meet together, you make things worse, not better! ¹⁸What I mean is this: to begin with, I hear that when you come together in the assembly there are divisions among you. Well, I believe it – at least partly. ¹⁹There are bound to be groupings among you; that's how the genuine ones among you will stand out, I suppose! ²⁰So when you gather together into one meeting, it isn't the Lord's Supper that you eat. ²¹Everyone brings their own food to eat, and one person goes hungry while another gets drunk. ²²Haven't you got houses to eat and drink in? Or do you despise God's assembly, and shame those who have nothing? What shall I say to you? Shall I praise you? No, in this matter I shan't!

Recognizing the body

²³This, you see, is what I received from the Lord, and handed on to you. On the night when the Lord Jesus was betrayed, he took bread, ²⁴gave thanks, broke it, and said, 'This is my body; it's for you! Do this as a memorial of me.' ²⁵He did the same with the cup after supper, and said, 'This cup is the new covenant in my blood. Whenever you drink it, do this as a memorial of me.' ²⁶For whenever you eat this bread and drink the cup, you are announcing the Lord's death until he comes.

²⁷It follows from this that anyone who eats the bread or drinks the cup of the Lord in an unworthy manner will be guilty of the body and blood of the Lord. ²⁸Everyone should test themselves; that's how you should eat the bread and drink the cup. ²⁹You see, if you eat and drink without recognizing the body, you

eat and drink judgment on yourself. ³⁰That's why several of you are weak and sick, and some have died. ³¹But if we learned how to judge ourselves, we would not incur judgment. ³²But when we are judged by the Lord, we are punished, so that we won't be condemned along with the world.

³³So, my brothers and sisters, when you come together to eat, treat one another as honoured guests by waiting for each other. ³⁴If anyone is hungry, they should eat at home, so that you don't come together and find yourselves facing judgment. I will put the other matters in order when I come.

The same spirit at work

12 Now: about things relating to the spirit's work, my brothers and sisters, I don't want you to remain ignorant. ²You know that when you were still pagans you were led off, carried away again and again, after speechless idols. ³So I want to make it clear to you that nobody who is speaking by God's spirit ever says 'Jesus be cursed!'; and nobody can say 'Jesus is Lord!', except by the holy spirit.

⁴There are different types of spiritual gifts, but the same spirit; ⁵there are different types of service, but the same Lord; ⁶and there are different types of activity, but it is the same God who operates all of them in everyone. ⁷The point of the spirit being revealed in each one is so that all may benefit. ⁸One person is given a word of wisdom through the spirit; another, a word of knowledge by the same spirit; ⁹another, faith through the same spirit; another, gifts of healing by the one spirit; ¹⁰another, the working of mighty deeds; another, prophecy; another, the ability to distinguish spirits; another, various kinds of languages; another, the interpretation of languages. ¹¹It is the one spirit, the same one, whose work produces all these things, and the spirit gives different gifts to each one in accordance with the spirit's own wishes.

Many members, one body

¹²Let me explain. Just as the body is one, and has many members, and all the members of the body, though they are many, are one body, so also is the Messiah. ¹³For we all were baptized into one body, by one spirit – whether Jews or Greeks, whether slaves or free – and we were all given one spirit to drink.

¹⁴For the body, indeed, is not one member, but many. ¹⁵If the foot were to say, 'Because I'm not a hand, I'm not part of the body', that wouldn't make it any less a part of the body, would it? ¹⁶And if the ear were to say, 'Because I'm not an eye, I'm not part of the body', that wouldn't make it any less a part of the body, would it? ¹⁷If the whole body were an eye, where would the hearing be? If the whole body were the sense of hearing, what would happen to the sense of smell? ¹⁸But as it is, God has organized the members, placing each one individually in the body according to his wishes. ¹⁹If all the parts were one member, where would the body be? ²⁰So the result is this: there are many members, but one body.

The responsibilities of each member

²¹The eye can't say to the hand, 'I don't need you'; and, again, the head can't say to the feet, 'I don't need you'. ²²No: the parts of the body which seem to be weaker are all the more necessary, ²³and we give much greater honour to the parts of the body we reckon more dishonourable, so that the parts we hide in shame have a far greater dignity ²⁴which our more presentable parts don't need. In fact, God has made the body a single, organized whole; he has given greater honour to the lesser part, ²⁵so that there won't be any division in the body, but that all the members may have the same concern for one another. ²⁶If one member suffers, all the members suffer with it. If one member is exalted, all the members celebrate along with it.

Gifts and ministries

²⁷Now you together are the Messiah's body, and individually you are members of it. ²⁸In the church, God has placed apostles first, then prophets, then teachers, then powerful deeds, then gifts of healing, helpful deeds, organizational gifts, different types of languages. ²⁹Not everyone is an apostle, are they? Not

everyone is a prophet! Not everyone is a teacher! Not everyone does powerful deeds! ³⁰Not everyone has gifts of healing! Not everyone speaks with tongues! Not everyone interprets!

³¹You should be eager for the better kinds of gifts.

The need for love and the character of love

Now I'm going to show you a better way,
a much better way.

13 If I speak in human languages, or even in those of angels, but do not have love,
then I've become a clanging gong or else
a clashing cymbal. ²And if I should have
prophetic gifts, and know all mysteries,
all knowledge, too; have faith, to move the
    mountains,
but have no love – I'm nothing. ³If I give
all my possessions to the poor, and, for pride's
    sake,
my very body, but do not have love,
it's useless to me.

⁴Love's great-hearted; love is kind,
knows no jealousy, makes no fuss,
is not puffed up, ⁵no shameless ways,
doesn't force its rightful claim,
doesn't rage or bear a grudge,
⁶doesn't cheer at others' harm,
rejoices, rather, in the truth.
⁷Love bears all things, believes all things,
love hopes all things, endures all things.

Love: the bridge to God's future

⁸Love never fails. But prophecies will be abolished; tongues will stop; and knowledge, too, be done away. ⁹We know, you see, in part; we prophesy in part; ¹⁰but, with perfection, the partial is abolished. ¹¹As a child
I spoke, and thought, and reasoned like a child; when I grew up, I threw off childish ways.

¹²For at the moment all that we can see
are puzzling reflections in a mirror;
then, face to face. I know in part, for now;
but then I'll know completely, through and
    through,
even as I'm completely known. ¹³So, now,
faith, hope, and love remain, these three; and,
    of them,
love is the greatest.

Priorities in worship

14 Pursue love; and long for the spiritual gifts, especially that you may prophesy. ²Someone who speaks in a tongue, you see, isn't speaking to human beings but to God. Nobody can understand such speakers, because they speak mysteries in the spirit. ³But the one who prophesies speaks to other people, to build them up, to strengthen them, and to console them. ⁴The one who speaks in a tongue builds up himself or herself; but the one who prophesies builds up the church.

⁵I would be delighted for all of you to speak in tongues, but I would be even more delighted to have you all prophesying. The one who prophesies is greater than the one who speaks in a tongue, unless they also give an interpretation so that the church may be built up.

Speaking clearly in church

⁶Well then, my brothers and sisters, if I come to you speaking in tongues, how am I going to bring you any benefit unless I speak to you either in a revelation or in a word of knowledge or in a prophecy or in teaching? ⁷It's the same with lifeless objects that make a sound, like a flute or a lyre. If they don't give a distinct note, how will anyone know what tune is being blown or plucked? ⁸Think about it: if the trumpet doesn't make a clear sound, who will get ready to fight?

⁹It's the same with you. Unless your tongue gives a distinct message, how will anyone be able to tell what you're talking about? You will be like someone speaking into thin air. ¹⁰To be sure, there are all kinds and types of languages in the world, and none of them is meaningless. ¹¹But if I don't know the force of the words, I will remain a foreigner to the speaker, and the speaker will be a foreigner to me. ¹²It's the same with you. Since you are so eager for spiritual matters, try to specialize in doing things that will build up the church.

Praying with mind as well as spirit

¹³So the one who speaks in a tongue should pray to be able to say the same thing in clear speech. ¹⁴If I pray in a tongue, you see, my spirit prays, but my mind remains fruitless. ¹⁵Why is that important? I will pray with the spirit, and I will pray with the mind as well. I will sing with the spirit, and I will sing with the mind as well. ¹⁶You see, if you say a blessing in the spirit, how can someone who isn't one of the inner circle say the 'Amen' to your prayer? They won't know what you're talking about! ¹⁷You may well be giving thanks in fine style, but the other person isn't being built up. ¹⁸I thank God that I speak in tongues more than all of you. ¹⁹But in the assembly I would rather speak five words with my mind, to teach other people, than a thousand words in a tongue.

Signs for believers and unbelievers

²⁰Brothers and sisters, don't be children in your thinking. Be babies when it comes to evil, but in your thinking be grown-ups. ²¹This is what it says in the law: 'I will speak to this people in foreign languages and with the lips of strangers, and even so they won't listen to me, says the Lord.' ²²So tongues are not meant for believers, but are a warning for unbelievers; while prophecy is not designed for unbelievers, but for those who come to faith. ²³What I mean is this: if the whole assembly comes together and everybody speaks in tongues, and outsiders or unbelievers come in, they'll say you're crazy, won't they? ²⁴But if everyone prophesies, and outsiders or unbelievers come in, they will be called to account by everyone, judged by everyone, ²⁵the secrets of their hearts will be laid bare, and so they will fall down on their faces and worship God, declaring that 'God is truly among you'.

Final instructions for worship

²⁶So where does this leave us, my brothers and sisters? When you come together, one person has a psalm, another some teaching, another a revelation, another a tongue, and another some interpretation. Let everything be done for the general upbuilding. ²⁷If anyone speaks in a tongue, there should be two or at most three, each taking their turn, and one of them should put it into plain speech. ²⁸But if none of them can do that, let them be silent in the assembly, and speak to themselves and to God.

²⁹As for prophets, let two or three speak, and the others evaluate what is said. ³⁰If fresh revelation comes to someone sitting there, the first person should be silent. ³¹You can all prophesy one by one, so that everyone can learn, and everyone can be encouraged. ³²The spirits of prophets are under the control of prophets, ³³since God is the God, not of chaos, but of peace.

As in all the assemblies of God's people, ³⁴the women should keep silence in the assemblies. They are not permitted to speak; they should remain in submission, just as the law declares. ³⁵If they want to understand something more, they should ask their own husbands when they get home. It's shameful, you see, for a woman to speak in the assembly. ³⁶Do you suppose God's word began with you? Are you the only ones it has reached?

³⁷If anyone thinks they are a prophet, or spiritual, they should acknowledge that what I write to you is the Lord's command. ³⁸If anyone disregards this, they can be disregarded.

³⁹So, my brothers and sisters, be eager to prophesy, and don't forbid speaking in tongues. ⁴⁰But everything should be done in a seemly fashion, and in proper order.

The gospel of the Messiah, crucified, buried and risen

15 Let me remind you, brothers and sisters, about the good news which I announced to you. You received this good news, and you're standing firm on it, ²and you are saved through it, if you hold fast the message I announced to you – unless it was for nothing that you believed!

³What I handed on to you at the beginning, you see, was what I received, namely this: 'The Messiah died for our sins in accordance with the Bible; ⁴he was buried; he was raised on the third day in accordance with the Bible; ⁵he was seen by Cephas, then by the Twelve; ⁶then he was seen by over five hundred brothers and

sisters at once, most of whom are still with us, though some fell asleep; ⁷then he was seen by James, then by all the apostles; ⁸and, last of all, as to one ripped from the womb, he appeared even to me.'

⁹'I'm the least of the apostles, you see. In fact, I don't really deserve to be called 'apostle' at all, because I persecuted God's church! ¹⁰But I am what I am because of God's grace, and his grace to me wasn't wasted. On the contrary. I worked harder than all of them – though it wasn't me, but God's grace which was with me. ¹¹So whether it was me or them, that was the way we announced it, and that was the way you believed.

What if the Messiah wasn't raised?

¹²Well, then: if the royal proclamation of the Messiah is made on the basis that he's been raised from the dead, how can some of you say that there is no such thing as resurrection of the dead? ¹³If there is no such thing as resurrection of the dead, the Messiah hasn't been raised, either; ¹⁴and if the Messiah hasn't been raised, our royal proclamation is empty, and so is your faith. ¹⁵We even turn out to have been misrepresenting God, because we gave it as our evidence about God that he raised the Messiah, and he didn't! – if, that is, the dead are not raised. ¹⁶For if the dead aren't raised, the Messiah wasn't raised either; ¹⁷and if the Messiah wasn't raised, your faith is pointless, and you are still in your sins. ¹⁸What's more, people who have fallen asleep in the Messiah have perished for good. ¹⁹If it's only for this present life that we have put our hope in the Messiah, we are the most pitiable members of the human race.

The reign of the Messiah

²⁰But in fact the Messiah has been raised from the dead, as the first fruits of those who have fallen asleep. ²¹For since it was through a human that death arrived, it's through a human that the resurrection from the dead has arrived. ²²All die in Adam, you see, and all will be made alive in the Messiah.

²³Each, however, in proper order. The Messiah rises as the first fruits; then those who belong to the Messiah will rise at the time of his royal arrival. ²⁴Then comes the end, the goal, when he hands over the kingly rule to God the father, when he has destroyed all rule and all authority and power. ²⁵He has to go on ruling, you see, until 'he has put all his enemies under his feet'. ²⁶Death is the last enemy to be destroyed, ²⁷because 'he has put all things in order under his feet'. But when it says that everything is put in order under him, it's obvious that this doesn't include the one who put everything in order under him. ²⁸No: when everything is put in order under him, then the son himself will be placed in proper order under the one who placed everything in order under him, so that God may be all in all.

Resurrection gives meaning to present Christian living

²⁹Otherwise, what are people doing when they get baptized on behalf of the dead? If the dead simply aren't raised, why should people get baptized on their behalf?

³⁰And why should we face danger every hour? ³¹I die every day – yes, that's something for you to boast about, my dear family, and that's the boast I have in the Messiah, Jesus our Lord! ³²If, in human terms, I fought with wild animals at Ephesus, what use is that to me? If the dead are not raised, 'let's eat and drink, because tomorrow we're going to die'!

³³Don't be deceived: 'bad company kills off good habits'! ³⁴Sober up; straighten up; stop sinning. Yes, some of you simply don't know God! I'm saying this to bring shame on you.

The transformed resurrection body

³⁵But someone is now going to say: 'How are the dead raised? What sort of body will they come back with?' ³⁶Stupid! What you sow doesn't come to life unless it dies. ³⁷The thing you sow isn't the body that is going to come later; it's just a naked seed of, let's say, wheat, or some other plant. ³⁸God then gives it a body of the sort he wants, with each of the seeds having its own particular body.

³⁹Not all physical objects have the same kind of physicality. There is one kind of physicality

for humans, another kind for animals, another for birds, and another for fish. ⁴⁰Some bodies belong in the heavens, and some on the earth; and the kind of glory appropriate for the ones in the heavens is different from the kind of glory appropriate for the ones on the earth. ⁴¹There is one kind of glory for the sun, another for the moon, and another for the stars, since the stars themselves vary, with different degrees of glory.

⁴²That's what it's like with the resurrection of the dead. It is sown decaying, and raised undecaying. ⁴³It is sown in shame, and raised in glory. It is sown in weakness, and raised in power. ⁴⁴It is sown as the embodiment of ordinary nature, and raised as the embodiment of the spirit. If ordinary nature has its embodiment, then the spirit too has its embodiment. ⁴⁵That's what it means when the Bible says, 'The first man, Adam, became a living natural being'; the last Adam became a life-giving spirit.

⁴⁶But you don't get the spirit-animated body first; you get the nature-animated one, and you get the spirit-animated one later. ⁴⁷The first man is from the ground, and is made of earth; the second man is from heaven. ⁴⁸Earthly people are like the man of earth; heavenly people are like the man from heaven. ⁴⁹We have borne the image of the man made of earth; we shall also bear the image of the man from heaven.

The mystery and the victory

⁵⁰This is what I'm saying, my dear family. Flesh and blood can't inherit God's kingdom; decay can't inherit undecaying life. ⁵¹Look! I'm telling you a mystery. We won't all sleep; we're all going to be changed – ⁵²in a flash, at the blink of an eye, at the last trumpet. This is how it will be, you see: the trumpet's going to sound, the dead will be raised undecaying, and we're going to be changed. ⁵³This decaying body must put on the undecaying one; this dying body must put on deathlessness. ⁵⁴When the decaying puts on the undecaying, and the dying puts on the undying, then the saying that has been written will come true:

Death is swallowed up in victory!
⁵⁵Death, where's your victory gone?
Death, where's your sting gone?

⁵⁶The 'sting' of death is sin, and the power of sin is the law. ⁵⁷But thank God! He gives us the victory, through our Lord Jesus the Messiah.

⁵⁸So, my dear family, be firmly fixed, unshakeable, always full to overflowing with the Lord's work. In the Lord, as you know, the work you're doing will not be worthless.

The collection and Paul's plans

16 Now when it comes to the collection for God's people, you should do the same as I laid down for the churches in Galatia. ²On the first day of each week, every one of you should set aside and store up whatever surplus you have gained, so that when I come I won't have to take an actual collection. ³Then, when I get to you, I will write formal letters to send the people you approve, whoever they are, to Jerusalem with your gift. ⁴If it's appropriate for me to go as well, we can travel together.

⁵I shall come to you when I've been through Macedonia. I intend to pass through Macedonia, you see, ⁶and I may well end up staying with you, perhaps even through the winter. Then you will be able to send me on to wherever I shall be going to next. ⁷I don't want just to see you for a short time; I'm hoping to stay with you for a while, if the Lord allows me to. ⁸I shall be staying on in Ephesus until Pentecost. ⁹A huge and important door has opened for me here, and there is plenty of opposition.

Timothy and Apollos

¹⁰If Timothy comes, take care that he isn't fearful when he's with you. He's doing the Lord's work, after all, just as I am. ¹¹Nobody should look down on him. Send him on in peace, so that he can come to me. I'm expecting him, and so is the family here.

¹²As for our brother Apollos, I did my best to persuade him to go to you with the other family members, but it simply wasn't for the best that he should come just now. He will come when the right moment appears.

¹³Keep alert, stand firm in the faith, be brave, be strong! ¹⁴Whatever you do, do it with love.

The love that stitches it all together

¹⁵One more word of exhortation for you, my dear family. You know the household of Stephanas: they were the first fruits of Achaea, and they have set themselves to serve God's people. ¹⁶You should submit to people like that, and to everyone who is working with them and labouring hard. ¹⁷I have thoroughly enjoyed the visit of Stephanas, Fortunatus and Achaicus; they have made up for the fact that I haven't been able to see you. ¹⁸They have refreshed my spirit and yours. Give proper recognition to such people.

¹⁹The churches in Asia send you greetings. Aquila and Prisca send you many greetings in the Lord, together with the church in their house. ²⁰All the family send you greetings. Greet one another with the holy kiss.

²¹I, Paul, add my greetings in my own hand.

²²If anyone doesn't love the Lord, let them be accursed! Come, Lord, come! ²³The grace of the Lord Jesus be with you. ²⁴My love be with you all in the Messiah, Jesus.

2 Corinthians

Paul's second letter to Corinth – that is, the second letter as we now have them; there seem to have been others which have not survived – is about as different from the first one as it could be. In the first, Paul is on top of the situation: working his way through quite different topics like a skilled handyman going around the house and fixing lots of different problems. The house and its occupants will be in bad shape if these problems don't get fixed; but Paul is up for the task. Now, in the second letter, it is Paul himself who is in bad shape.

He has just suffered such a terrible time in Asia that he had despaired of life itself (1.8). Everything had gone wrong: his work had failed, his opponents in the region had got the better of him, he was facing possible execution – and the church in Corinth, called into being by God through his own preaching and tireless pastoring, had found other teachers and apostles whom they much preferred. They had told him that if he wanted to come back he'd have to produce letters of recommendation so they could see he was really up to the job. After all, who could respect a beaten-up jailbird?

It is difficult, and ultimately unnecessary, to reconstruct exactly what had passed between Corinth and Paul. What matters is Paul's response, which might be classified as the foundation charter for genuine Christian ministry. He explains what being an apostle is all about. It means having the gospel of Jesus – the shame and the pain, the horror and the death – etched into your very soul, so that the astonishing life of Jesus may shine through, perhaps in the communities you serve, perhaps in your own life as well.

That is the theme of the first main section, following the long introduction in 1.1—2.13. From 2.14 to 6.13 he gets into his stride: if you want 'letters of recommendation' for me, look in the mirror! God's spirit had worked through Paul, and that's why there is a community of the new covenant in Corinth. As always in scripture, new covenant leads to new creation (5.17). The new world has burst in upon the old one, pointing ahead to bodily resurrection (5.1–5) and for the moment working itself out through 'the ministry of reconciliation' (5.18—6.2), all rooted in the Messiah's own sin-bearing death (5.21). Having had people say he was a poor speaker, and having argued that fine words are not the point, Paul rounds off this section with a wonderful piece of ironic rhetoric (6.3–10).

A short passage on marriage (6.14—7.1) gives way to a sigh of relief when, as Paul arrives in Macedonia, his friend Titus returns from Corinth with good news. The mood has changed. This prepares the way for chapters 8 and 9, in which Paul is delicately urging them to be ready with money for the relief effort on behalf of Jerusalem.

Then he returns to the fray. Chapters 10 to 13 are a direct attack on the shadowy opponents who have been seducing the Corinthians with their 'super-apostolic' style. Here again Paul's rhetoric takes flight. *He boasts of all the wrong things*: if they want a real super-apostle, he'll show them what such a creature looks like. He's been beaten, stoned, shipwrecked, in constant danger, working night and day, putting up with terrible conditions. And when it comes to spiritual experience . . . well, the thing that really mattered was Paul's 'thorn in the flesh' (see 12.7), and the fact that, when he prayed about it three times, the word he got back was 'my grace is enough for you; my power comes to perfection in weakness' (12.9). This is the lesson of 2 Corinthians, both in what is said and in the way Paul says it. The servant will be modelled on the master. Paul carries the authority of the crucified Lord.

The God of all comfort

1 Paul, an apostle of King Jesus through God's will, and Timothy our brother; to God's assembly in Corinth, with all God's people in the whole of Achaea: ²grace and peace to you from God our father and the Lord, King Jesus!

³Let us bless God, the father of our Lord, King Jesus; he is the father of mercies and the God of all comfort. ⁴He comforts us in all our trouble, so that we can then comfort people in every kind of trouble, through the comfort with which God comforts us. ⁵Just as we have an overflowing share of the Messiah's sufferings, you see, so we have an overflowing share in comfort through the Messiah. ⁶If we are troubled, it's because of your comfort and salvation; if we are comforted, it's for the sake of your comfort, which comes about as you bear patiently with the same sufferings that we are going through. ⁷And our hope about you remains firm, because we know that, just as you've shared in our sufferings, so you will also share in our comfort.

Unbearably crushed

⁸You see, my dear family, we don't want to keep you in the dark about the suffering we went through in Asia. The load we had to carry was far too heavy for us; it got to the point where we gave up on life itself. ⁹Yes: deep inside ourselves we received the death sentence. This was to stop us relying on ourselves, and to make us rely on the God who raises the dead. ¹⁰He rescued us from such a great and deadly peril, and he'll do it again; we have placed our hope in him, that he'll do it again! ¹¹But you must cooperate with us through prayer for us, so that when God gives us this gift, answering the prayers of so many, all the more will give thanks because of what's happened to us.

¹²This is what we boast of, you see; this is what our conscience is telling us: that our conduct in the world, and in particular in relation to you, has been marked by holiness and godly sincerity, not in merely human wisdom but in God's grace. ¹³We are not writing anything to you, after all, except what you can read and understand. And I hope you will go on understanding right through to the end, ¹⁴just as you have understood us already – well, partly, at least! We are your pride and joy, just as you are ours, on the day of our Lord Jesus.

Paul's plans and God's 'Yes'

¹⁵I was quite sure of this. That's why I wanted to come to you again, so that you could have a double blessing. ¹⁶I intended to go on to Macedonia by way of you, and to come back to you from Macedonia and have you send me on to Judaea.

¹⁷Was I just fooling around when I was making plans like this? Was I concocting schemes in a merely human way, prepared to say 'Yes, yes', and 'No, no', at the same moment? ¹⁸God can bear me faithful witness that our word to you was not a mixture of Yes and No. ¹⁹The son of God, Jesus the Messiah, who was proclaimed among you by Silvanus, Timothy and myself, wasn't a Yes-and-No person; in him it's always Yes! ²⁰All God's promises, you see, find their Yes in him; and that's why we say the Yes, the Amen through him when we pray to God and give him glory. ²¹It's God who strengthens us with you into the Messiah, the anointed one; and he has anointed us, too. ²²God has stamped his seal on us, by giving us the spirit in our hearts as a first payment and guarantee of what is to come.

Painful visit, painful letter

²³For my own part, I call on God as witness, against my own life, that the reason I haven't yet come back to Corinth is because I wanted to spare you. ²⁴This isn't because I am making myself the lord and master over your faith; your faith is the reason you stand fast! Rather, it's because we are cooperating with you for your joy.

2 You see, I settled it in my mind that I wouldn't make you another sad visit. ²After all, if I make you sad, who is there to cheer *me* up except the one who is sad because of me? ³And I wrote what I did so that I wouldn't come and find sadness where I should have found joy. I have this confidence about all of you, that my joy belongs to all of you. ⁴No: I wrote to you in floods of tears, out of great trouble and anguish in my heart, not so that I could make you sad but so that you would know just how much overflowing love I have towards you.

Time to forgive

⁵But if anyone has caused sadness, it isn't me that he has saddened, but, in a measure (I don't want to emphasize this too much), all of you. ⁶The punishment that the majority has imposed is quite enough; ⁷what's needed now is rather that you should forgive and console him, in case someone like that might be swallowed up by such abundant sorrow. ⁸Let me urge you, then, to reaffirm your love for him.

⁹The reason I wrote to you, you see, was in order to know whether you would pass the test and be obedient in everything. ¹⁰If you forgive anyone anything, so do I; and whatever I have forgiven – if indeed I have forgiven anyone anything! – it's all happened under the eyes of the Messiah, and for your own sake. ¹¹The point is that we shouldn't be outsmarted by the satan. We know what he's up to!

The smell of life, the smell of death

¹²However, when I came to Troas to announce the Messiah's gospel, and found an open door waiting for me in the Lord, ¹³I couldn't get any quietness in my spirit because I didn't find my brother Titus there. So I left them and went off to Macedonia.

¹⁴But thanks be to God – the God who always leads us in his triumphal procession in the Messiah, and through us reveals everywhere the sweet smell of knowing him. ¹⁵We are the Messiah's fragrance before God, you see, to those who are being saved and to those who are being lost. ¹⁶To the latter, it's a smell which comes from death and leads to death; but to the former it's the smell of life which leads to life.

Who can rise to this challenge? ¹⁷We aren't mere pedlars of God's word, as so many people are. We speak with sincerity; we speak from God; we speak in God's presence; we speak in the Messiah.

The letter and the spirit

3 So: we're starting to 'recommend ourselves' again, are we? Or perhaps we need – as some do – official references to give to you? Or perhaps even to get from you? ²*You* are our official reference! It's written on our hearts! Everybody can know it and read it! ³It's quite plain that you are a letter from the Messiah, with us as the messengers – a letter not written with ink but with the spirit of the living God, not on tablets of stone but on the tablets of beating hearts.

⁴That's the kind of confidence we have towards God, through the Messiah. ⁵It isn't as though we are qualified in ourselves to reckon that we have anything to offer on our own account. Our qualification comes from God: ⁶God has qualified us to be stewards of a new covenant, not of the letter but of the spirit. The letter kills, you see, but the spirit gives life.

Death and glory

⁷But just think about it: when death was being distributed, carved in letters of stone, it was a glorious thing, so glorious in fact that the children of Israel couldn't look at Moses's face because of the glory of his face – a glory that was to be abolished. ⁸But in that case, when the spirit is being distributed, won't that be glorious too? ⁹If distributing condemnation is glorious, you see, how much more glorious is it to distribute vindication! ¹⁰In fact, what used to be glorious has come in this respect to have no glory at all, because of the new glory which goes so far beyond it. ¹¹For if the thing which was to be abolished came with glory, how much more glory will there be for the thing that lasts.

The veil and the glory

¹²So, because that's the kind of hope we have, we speak with great freedom. ¹³We aren't like Moses: he put a veil over his face, to stop the children of Israel from gazing at the end of what was being abolished. ¹⁴The difference is that their minds were hardened. You see, the same veil lies over the reading of the old covenant

right up to this very day. It isn't taken away, because it's in the Messiah that it is abolished. ¹⁵Yes, even to this day, whenever Moses is read, the veil lies upon their hearts; ¹⁶but 'whenever he turns back to the Lord, the veil is removed'. ¹⁷Now 'the Lord' here means the spirit; and where the spirit of the Lord is, there is freedom. ¹⁸And all of us, without any veil on our faces, gaze at the glory of the Lord as in a mirror, and so are being changed into the same image, from glory to glory, just as you'd expect from the Lord, the spirit.

Light out of darkness

4 For this reason, since we have this work entrusted to us in accordance with the mercy we have received, we don't lose heart. ²On the contrary, we have renounced the secret things that make people ashamed. We don't use tricks; we don't falsify God's word. Rather, we speak the truth openly, and recommend ourselves to everybody's conscience in the presence of God.

³However, if our gospel still remains 'veiled', it is veiled for people who are perishing. ⁴What's happening there is that the god of this world has blinded the minds of unbelievers, so that they won't see the light of the gospel of the glory of the Messiah, who is God's image. ⁵We don't proclaim ourselves, you see, but Jesus the Messiah as Lord, and ourselves as your servants because of Jesus; ⁶because the God who said 'let light shine out of darkness' has shone in our hearts, to produce the light of the knowledge of the glory of God in the face of Jesus the Messiah.

Treasure in earthenware pots

⁷But we have this treasure in earthenware pots, so that the extraordinary quality of the power may belong to God, not to us. ⁸We are under all kinds of pressure, but we are not crushed completely; we are at a loss, but not at our wits' end; ⁹we are persecuted, but not abandoned; we are cast down, but not destroyed. ¹⁰We always carry the deadness of Jesus about in the body, so that the life of Jesus may be revealed in our body. ¹¹Although we are still alive, you see, we are always being given over to death because of Jesus, so that the life of Jesus may be revealed in our mortal humanity. ¹²So this is how it is: death is at work in us – but life in you!

The God of all comfort

¹³We have the same spirit of faith as you see in what is written, 'I believed, and so I spoke.' We too believe, and so we speak, ¹⁴because we know that the God who raised the Lord Jesus will raise us with Jesus and present us with you. ¹⁵It's all because of you, you see! The aim is that, as grace abounds through the thanksgiving of more and more people, it will overflow to God's glory.

¹⁶For this reason we don't lose heart. Even if our outer humanity is decaying, our inner humanity is being renewed day by day. ¹⁷This slight momentary trouble of ours is working to produce a weight of glory, passing and surpassing everything, lasting for ever; ¹⁸for we don't look at the things that can be seen, but at the things that can't be seen. After all, the things you can see are here today and gone tomorrow; but the things you can't see are everlasting.

A house waiting in the heavens

5 For we know that if our earthly house, our present 'tent', is destroyed, we have a building from God, a house no human hands have built: it is everlasting, in the heavenly places. ²At the present moment, you see, we are groaning, as we long to put on our heavenly building, ³in the belief that by putting it on we won't turn out to be naked. ⁴Yes: in the present 'tent', we groan under a great weight. But we don't want to put it off; we want to put on something else on top, so that what is doomed to die may be swallowed up with life. ⁵It is God who has been at work in us to do this, the God who has given us the spirit as the first instalment and guarantee.

The judgment seat of the Messiah

⁶So we are always confident: we know that while we are at home in the body we are away

from the Lord. ⁷We live our lives by faith, you see, not by sight. ⁸We are confident, and we would much prefer to be away from the body and at home with the Lord. ⁹So we work hard, as a point of honour, to please him, whether we are at home or away. ¹⁰For we must all appear before the judgment seat of the Messiah, so that each may receive what has been done through the body, whether good or bad.

The Messiah's love makes us press on

¹¹So we know the fear of the Lord; and that's why we are persuading people – but we are open to God, and open as well, I hope, to your consciences. ¹²We aren't trying to recommend ourselves again! We are giving you a chance to be proud of us, to have something to say to those who take pride in appearances rather than in people's hearts.

¹³If we are beside ourselves, you see, it's for God; and if we are in our right mind, it's for you. ¹⁴For the Messiah's love makes us press on. We have come to the conviction that one died for all, and therefore all died. ¹⁵And he died for all in order that those who live should live no longer for themselves, but for him who died and was raised on their behalf.

New creation, new ministry

¹⁶From this moment on, therefore, we don't regard anybody from a merely human point of view. Even if we once regarded the Messiah that way, we don't do so any longer. ¹⁷Thus, if anyone is in the Messiah, there is a new creation! Old things have gone, and look – everything has become new!

¹⁸It all comes from God. He reconciled us to himself through the Messiah, and he gave us the ministry of reconciliation. ¹⁹This is how it came about: God was reconciling the world to himself in the Messiah, not counting their transgressions against them, and entrusting us with the message of reconciliation. ²⁰So we are ambassadors, speaking on behalf of the Messiah, as though God were making his appeal through us. We implore people on the Messiah's behalf to be reconciled to God. ²¹The Messiah did not know sin, but God made him to be sin on our behalf, so that in him we might embody God's faithfulness to the covenant.

6 So, as we work together with God, we appeal to you in particular: when you accept God's grace, don't let it go to waste! ²This is what he says:

> I listened to you when the time was right,
> I came to your aid on the day of salvation.

Look! The right time is now! Look! The day of salvation is here!

God's servants at work

³We put no obstacles in anybody's way, so that nobody will say abusive things about our ministry. ⁴Instead, we recommend ourselves as God's servants: with much patience, with sufferings, difficulties, hardships, ⁵beatings, imprisonments, riots, hard work, sleepless nights, going without food, ⁶with purity, knowledge, great-heartedness, kindness, the holy spirit, genuine love, ⁷by speaking the truth, by God's power, with weapons for God's faithful work in left and right hand alike, ⁸through glory and shame, through slander and praise; as deceivers, and yet true; ⁹as unknown, yet very well known; as dying, and look – we are alive; as punished, yet not killed; ¹⁰as sad, yet always celebrating; as poor, yet bringing riches to many; as having nothing, yet possessing everything.

¹¹We have been wide open in our speaking to you, my dear Corinthians! Our heart has been opened wide! ¹²There are no restrictions at our end; the only restrictions are in your affection! ¹³I'm speaking as though to children: you should open your hearts wide as well in return. That's fair enough, isn't it?

Don't be mismatched

¹⁴Don't be drawn into partnership with unbelievers. What kind of sharing can there be, after all, between justice and lawlessness? What partnership can there be between light and darkness? ¹⁵What kind of harmony can the Messiah have with Beliar? What has a believer

in common with an unbeliever? ⁱ⁶What kind of agreement can there be between God's temple and idols? We are the temple of the living God, you see, just as God said:

> I will live among them and walk about with them;
> I will be their God, and they will be my people.
> ¹⁷So come out from the midst of them,
> and separate yourselves, says the Lord;
> no unclean thing must you touch.
> Then I will receive you gladly,
> ¹⁸and I will be to you as a father,
> and you will be to me as sons and daughters,
> says the Lord, the Almighty.

7 So, my beloved people, with promises like these, let's make ourselves clean from everything that defiles us, outside and inside, and let's become completely holy in the fear of God.

The God who comforts the downcast

²Make room for us! We haven't wronged anybody, we haven't ruined anybody, we haven't taken advantage of anybody. ³I'm not saying this to pass judgment against you; I've already said that you are in our hearts, to die together and to live together. ⁴I speak to you freely and openly; I regularly boast about you; I am full of comfort, and fuller still of joy, over and above all our trouble.

⁵You see, even when we arrived in Macedonia, we couldn't relax or rest. We were troubled in every way; there were battles outside and fears inside. ⁶But the God who comforts the downcast comforted us by the arrival of Titus, ⁷and not only by his arrival but in the comfort he had received from you, as he told us about your longing for us, your lamenting, and your enthusiasm for me personally.

As a result, I was more inclined to celebrate; ⁸because, if I did make you sad by my letter, I don't regret it; and, if I did regret it, it was because I saw that I made you sad for a while by what I had written. ⁹Anyway, I'm celebrating now, not because you were saddened, but because your sadness brought you to repentance. It was a sadness from God, you see, and it did you no harm at all on our account; ¹⁰because God's way of sadness is designed to produce a repentance which leads to salvation, and there's nothing to regret there! But the world's way of sadness produces death.

Our boasting proved true!

¹¹Just look and see what effect God's way of sadness has had among you! It's produced eagerness, explanations, indignation, fear, longing, keenness, and punishment. You have shown yourselves faultless in the whole business. ¹²So if I'm writing to you, it's not because of the person who's done the wrong, nor because of the people who were wronged, but so that you can recognize for yourselves, in God's presence, just how eager you really have been for us. ¹³We have been comforted by all of this.

The real celebration, though, on top of all our comfort, came because Titus was so overjoyed. You really did cheer him up and set his mind at rest. ¹⁴I wasn't ashamed of the various boasts I had made to him about you. Just as I had always spoken the truth to you, so our boast to Titus turned out to be true as well. ¹⁵He is constantly yearning for you deeply as he remembers the obedience you showed, all of you, and how you welcomed him with fear and trembling. ¹⁶I am celebrating the fact that I have confidence in you in everything.

The generosity of the Macedonian churches

8 Let me tell you, my dear family, about the grace which God has given to the Macedonian churches. ²They have been sorely tested by suffering. But the abundance of grace which was given to them, and the depths of poverty they have endured, have overflowed in a wealth of sincere generosity on their part. ³I bear them witness that of their own accord, up to their ability and even beyond their ability, ⁴they begged us eagerly to let them have the privilege of sharing in the work of service for God's people. ⁵They didn't just do what we had hoped; they gave themselves, first to the Lord, and then to us as God willed it. ⁶This put us in a position where we could encourage Titus that he should complete this work of grace that he had begun among you. ⁷You have plenty of everything, after all – plenty of faith, and speech, and knowledge, and all kinds of eagerness, and plenty of love coming from us to you; so why not have plenty of this grace too?

Copying the generosity of the Lord Jesus

⁸I'm not saying this as though I was issuing an order. It's a matter of putting their enthusiasm and your own love side by side, and making sure you genuinely pass the test. ⁹For you know the grace of our Lord, King Jesus: he was rich, but because of you he became poor, so that by his poverty you might become rich. ¹⁰Let me give you my serious advice on this: you began to be keen on this idea, and to start putting it into practice, a whole year ago; it will now be greatly to your advantage ¹¹to complete your performance of it. If you do so, your finishing the job as far as you are able will be on the same scale as your eagerness in wanting to do it. ¹²If the eagerness is there, you see, the deed is acceptable, according to what you have, not according to what you don't have. ¹³The point is not, after all, that others should get off lightly and you be made to suffer, but rather that there should be equality. ¹⁴At the present time your abundance can contribute to their lack, so that their abundance can contribute to your lack. That's what makes for equality, ¹⁵just as the Bible says: 'The one who had much had nothing to spare, and the one who had little didn't go short.'

Paul's companions are on their way

¹⁶But God be thanked, since he put the same eagerness for you into Titus's heart. ¹⁷He welcomed the appeal we made, and of his own accord he was all the more eager to come to you. ¹⁸We have sent along with him the brother who is famous through all the churches because of his work for the gospel. ¹⁹Not only so, but he was formally chosen by the churches to be our travelling companion as we engage in this work of grace, both for the Lord's own glory and to show our own good faith. ²⁰We are trying to avoid the possibility that anyone would make unpleasant accusations about this splendid gift which we are administering. ²¹We are thinking ahead, you see, about what will look best, not only to the Lord, but to everybody else as well.

²²Anyway, along with the two of them we are sending our brother, who has proved to us how eager and enthusiastic he is in many situations and on many occasions; he now seems all the more eager because he is convinced about you. ²³If there's any question about Titus, he is my partner, and a fellow-worker for you. As for our brothers, they are messengers of the churches, the Messiah's glory. ²⁴So please give them a fine demonstration of your love, and of our boasting about you! Show all the churches that you mean business!

Please have the gift ready!

9 When it comes to the service you are doing for God's people, you see, I don't need to write to you. ²For I know your eagerness, and indeed I boasted about it to the Macedonians, saying that Achaea had been ready since last year. Your enthusiasm has stimulated most of them into action. ³I have sent the brothers so that our boasting about you in this respect may turn out to be true – so that you may be ready, just as I said you were. ⁴Otherwise, imagine what it would be like if people from Macedonia came with me and found you weren't ready! That would bring shame on us in this business, not to say on you. ⁵So I thought it necessary to exhort the brothers that they should go on to you in advance, and get everything about your gracious gift in order ahead of time. You've already promised it, after all. Then it really will appear as a gift of grace, not something that has had to be extorted from you.

God loves a cheerful giver

⁶This is what I mean: someone who sows sparingly will reap sparingly as well. Someone who sows generously will reap generously. ⁷Everyone should do as they have determined in their heart, not in a gloomy spirit or simply because they have to, since 'God loves a cheerful giver'. ⁸And God is well able to lavish

all his grace upon you, so that in every matter and in every way you will have enough of everything, and may be lavish in all your own good works, ⁹just as the Bible says:

> They spread their favours wide, they gave to the poor,
> their righteousness endures for ever.

¹⁰The one who supplies 'seed to be sown and bread to eat' will supply and increase your seed, and multiply the yield of your righteousness. ¹¹You will be enriched in every way in all single-hearted goodness, which is working through us to produce thanksgiving to God. ¹²The service of this ministry will not only supply what God's people so badly need, but it will also overflow with many thanksgivings to God. ¹³Through meeting the test of this service you will glorify God in two ways: first, because your confession of faith in the Messiah's gospel has brought you into proper order, and second, because you have entered into genuine and sincere partnership with them and with everyone. ¹⁴What's more, they will then pray for you and long for you because of the surpassing grace God has given to you. ¹⁵Thanks be to God for his gift, the gift we can never fully describe!

The battle for the mind

10 Think of the Messiah, meek and gentle; then think of me, Paul – yes, Paul himself! – making his appeal to you. You know what I'm like: I'm humble when I'm face to face with you, but I'm bold when I'm away from you! ²Please, please don't put me in the position of having to be bold when I'm with you, of having to show how confident I dare to be when I'm standing up to people who think we are behaving in a merely human way. ³Yes, we are mere humans, but we don't fight the war in a merely human way. ⁴The weapons we use for the fight, you see, are not merely human; they carry a power from God that can tear down fortresses! We tear down clever arguments, ⁵and every proud notion that sets itself up against the knowledge of God. We take every thought prisoner and make it obey the Messiah. ⁶We are holding ourselves in readiness to punish every disobedience, when your obedience is complete.

⁷Look at what's in front of your face. If anyone trusts that they belong to the Messiah, let them calculate it once more: just as they belong to the Messiah, so also do we! ⁸For if I do indeed boast a bit too enthusiastically about the authority which the Lord has given me – which is for building you up, not for pulling you down! – I shan't be ashamed. ⁹I wouldn't want to look as if I were trying to frighten you with my letters. ¹⁰I know what they say: 'His letters are serious and powerful, but when he arrives in person he is weak, and his words aren't worth bothering about.' ¹¹Anyone like that should reckon on this: the way we talk in letters, when we're absent, will be how we behave when we're present.

Boasting in the Lord

¹²We wouldn't dare, you see, to figure out where we belong on some scale or other, or compare ourselves with people who commend themselves. They measure themselves by one another, and compare themselves with one another. That just shows how silly they are! ¹³But when we boast, we don't go off into flights of fancy; we boast according to the measure of the rule God has given us to measure ourselves by, and that rule includes our work with you! ¹⁴We weren't going beyond our assigned limits when we reached you; we were the first to get as far as you with the gospel of the Messiah. ¹⁵We don't boast without a measuring rule in the work someone else has done. This is what we hope for: that, as your faith increases, we will be given a much larger space for work, according to our rule, ¹⁶which is to announce the gospel in the lands beyond you, not to boast in what has already been accomplished through the rule someone else has been given. ¹⁷'Anyone who boasts should boast in the Lord.' ¹⁸Who is it, after all, who gains approval? It isn't the person who commends himself. It's the person whom the Lord commends.

Super-apostles?

11 I'd be glad if you would bear with me in a little bit of foolishness. Yes: bear with me, please! ²I'm jealous over you, and it's God's own jealousy: I arranged to marry you off, like a pure virgin, to the one man I presented you to, namely the Messiah. ³But the serpent tricked Eve with its cunning, and in the same way I'm afraid that your minds may be corrupted from the single-mindedness and purity which the Messiah's people should have. ⁴For if someone comes and announces a different Jesus from the one we announced to you, or if you receive a different spirit, one you hadn't received before, or a different gospel, one you hadn't accepted before, you put up with that all right. ⁵According to my calculations, you see, I am every bit as good as these super-apostles. ⁶I may be untutored in speaking, but that certainly doesn't apply to my knowledge. Surely that's been made quite clear to you, in every way and on every point!

No, they are false apostles!

⁷Did I then commit a sin when I humbled myself in order to exalt you? When I announced the gospel of God to you without charging you for it? ⁸I robbed other churches by accepting payment from them in order to serve you; ⁹and when I was with you, and was in need of anything, I didn't lay a burden on anybody, because my needs were more than met by the brothers who came from Macedonia. That's how I stopped myself from being a burden to you – and I intend to carry on in the same way. ¹⁰As the Messiah's truthfulness is in me, this boast of mine will not be silenced in the regions of Achaea. ¹¹Why? Because I don't love you? God knows …!

¹²I'm going to continue to do what I've always done, so as to cut off any opportunity (for those who want such an opportunity!) for anyone to look as if they can match us in the things they boast about. ¹³Such people are false apostles! The only work they do is to deceive! They transform themselves so that they look like apostles of the Messiah – ¹⁴and no wonder. The satan himself transforms himself to look like an angel of light, ¹⁵so it isn't surprising if his servants transform themselves to look like servants of righteousness. They will end up where their deeds are taking them.

The boasting of a reluctant fool

¹⁶I'll say it again: don't let anyone think I'm a fool! But if they do – well, all right then, welcome me as a fool, so that I can do a little bit of boasting! ¹⁷What I'm going to say now, I'm not saying as if it came from the Lord, but as if I was a fool, as if I really did want to indulge myself in this kind of boasting. ¹⁸Plenty of people are boasting in human terms, after all, so why shouldn't I boast as well? ¹⁹After all, you put up with fools readily enough, since you are so wise yourselves. ²⁰You put up with it if someone makes you their slave, or if they eat up your property, or overpower you, or give themselves airs, or slap you in the face. ²¹Well, I'm ashamed to say it: we weren't strong enough for that!

Boasting of weaknesses

Whatever anyone else dares to boast about (I'm talking nonsense, remember), I'll boast as well. ²²Are they Hebrews? So am I. Are they Israelites? So am I. Are they the seed of Abraham? So am I. ²³Are they servants of the Messiah? – I'm talking like a raving madman – I'm a better one. I've worked harder, been in prison more often, been beaten more times than I can count, and I've often been close to death. ²⁴Five times I've had the Jewish beating, forty lashes less one. ²⁵Three times I was beaten with rods; once I was stoned; three times I was shipwrecked; I was adrift in the sea for a night and a day. ²⁶I've been constantly travelling, facing dangers from rivers, dangers from brigands, dangers from my own people, dangers from foreigners, dangers in the town, dangers in the countryside, dangers at sea, dangers from false believers. ²⁷I've toiled and laboured, I've burnt the candle at both ends, I've been hungry and thirsty, I've often gone without food altogether, I've been cold and naked.

²⁸Quite apart from all that, I have this daily pressure on me, my care for all the churches. ²⁹Who is weak and I'm not weak? Who is offended without me burning with shame?

³⁰If I must boast, I will boast of my weaknesses. ³¹The God and father of the Lord Jesus, who is blessed for ever, knows that I'm not lying: ³²in Damascus, King Aretas, the local ruler, was guarding the city of Damascus so

that he could capture me, ³³but I was let down in a basket through a window and over the wall, and I escaped his clutches.

The vision and the thorn

12 I just have to boast – not that there's anything to be gained by it; but I'll go on to visions and revelations of the Lord. ²Someone I know in the Messiah, fourteen years ago (whether in the body or out of the body I don't know, though God knows), was snatched up to the third heaven. ³I know that this particular 'Someone' (whether in the body or apart from the body I don't know, God knows) – ⁴this person was snatched up to paradise, and heard . . . words you can't pronounce, which humans aren't allowed to repeat. ⁵I will boast of Someone like that, but I won't boast of myself, except of my weaknesses. ⁶If I did want to boast, you see, I wouldn't be mad; I'd be speaking the truth. But I'm holding back, so that nobody will think anything of me except what they can see in me or hear from me, ⁷even considering how remarkable the revelations were.

As a result, so that I wouldn't become too exalted, a thorn was given to me in my flesh, a messenger from the satan, to keep stabbing away at me. ⁸I prayed to the Lord three times about this, asking that it would be taken away from me, ⁹and this is what he said to me: 'My grace is enough for you; my power comes to perfection in weakness.' So I will be all the more pleased to boast of my weaknesses, so that the Messiah's power may rest upon me. ¹⁰So I'm delighted when I'm weak, insulted, in difficulties, persecuted and facing disasters, for the Messiah's sake. When I'm weak, you see, then I am strong.

The signs of a true apostle

¹¹I've been a fool! You forced me into it. If I *was* to have received an official commendation, it ought actually to have come from you! After all, I'm not inferior to the super-apostles, even though I am nothing. ¹²The signs of a true apostle, you see, were performed among you in all patience, with signs and wonders and powers. ¹³In what way have you been worse off than all the other churches, except in the fact that I myself didn't become a burden to you? Forgive me this injustice!

¹⁴Now look: this is the third time I'm ready to come to you. And I'm not going to be a burden, because I'm not looking for what belongs to you, but you yourselves. Children, after all, shouldn't be saving up for their parents, but parents for their children! ¹⁵For my part, I will gladly spend and be spent on your behalf. If I love you all the more, am I going to be loved any the less?

¹⁶Grant me this, that I didn't lay any burden on you. But – maybe I was a trickster, and I took you by deceit! ¹⁷Did I cheat you by any of the people I sent to you? ¹⁸I urged Titus to go to you, and I sent the brother with him. Did Titus cheat you? He behaved in the same spirit as me, didn't he? He conducted himself in the same manner, didn't he?

What will happen when Paul arrives?

¹⁹You will imagine we are explaining ourselves again. Well, we're speaking in God's presence, in the Messiah! My beloved ones, it has all been intended to build you up. ²⁰I'm afraid, you see, that when I come I may find you rather different from what I would wish – and *I* may turn out to be rather different from what *you* would wish! I'm afraid there may still be fighting, jealousy, anger, selfishness, slander, gossip, arrogance and disorder. ²¹I'm afraid that perhaps, when I come once more, my God may humble me again in front of you, and I will have to go into mourning over many who sinned before, and have not repented of the uncleanness and fornication and shameless immorality that they have practised.

13 This is the third time I'm coming to you. 'Every charge must be substantiated at the mouth of two or three witnesses.' ²I said it before when I was with you the second time, and I say it now in advance while I'm away from you, to all those who had sinned previously, and all the others, that when I come back again I won't spare them – ³since you are looking for proof of the Messiah who speaks in me, the Messiah who is not weak towards you but powerful in your midst! ⁴He was crucified in weakness, you see, but he lives by God's power. For we too are weak in him, but we shall live with him, for your benefit, by God's power.

Test yourselves!

⁵Test yourselves to see if you really are in the faith! Put yourselves through the examination. Or don't you realize that Jesus the Messiah is in you? – unless, that is, you've failed the test. ⁶I hope you will discover that we didn't fail the test. ⁷But we pray to God that you will never, ever, do anything wrong; not so that we can be shown up as having passed the test, but so that you will do what is right, even if that means that we appear like people who've failed. ⁸For we cannot do anything against the truth, but only for the truth. ⁹We celebrate, you see, when we are weak but you are strong. This is what we pray for, that you may become complete and get everything in order. ¹⁰That's why I'm writing this to you while I'm away, so that when I come I won't have to use my authority to be severe with you. The Lord has given me this authority, after all, not to pull down but to build up.

Grace, love and fellowship

¹¹All that remains, my dear family, is this: celebrate, put everything in order, strengthen one another, think in the same way, be at peace; and the God of love and peace will be with you. ¹²Greet one another with the holy kiss. All God's people send you their greetings.

¹³The grace of King Jesus the Lord, the love of God, and the fellowship of the holy spirit be with you all.

Galatians

In the letter to the churches in southern Anatolia – the churches Paul and Barnabas had founded on the first missionary journey in Acts 13 and 14 – we see Paul bursting onto the literary scene like a firefighter leaping into action while still zipping up his jacket. Galatians is written in a hurry, addressing an emergency: some rival missionaries, and one in particular, have followed Paul into his new-founded churches and are telling them that Paul, as a second-order apostle, only gave them half the message. They need the other half – which is that they should get circumcised, to become part of God's covenant people.

Paul agrees with the premise that Jesus-believers are members of the Abrahamic covenant. But his point is that all who believe the gospel, who are baptized 'into the Messiah', *are already the 'seed of Abraham', heirs according to the promise* (3.29). They do not need circumcision. Indeed, if they submit to it, they are saying in effect that God has not after all launched his new world with Jesus.

That is the point of the letter: Jesus the Messiah 'gave himself for our sins, to rescue us from the present evil age, according to the will of God our father' (1.4). What matters, then, is neither circumcision nor uncircumcision: 'what matters is new creation' (6.15). God's radical act in the death of Jesus has overthrown the 'powers' that have kept the world captive, and opened up a new creation whose watchword is '[he] loved me and gave himself for me' (2.20). If keeping the Jewish law (including circumcision) was what mattered, you wouldn't have needed a crucified Messiah (2.21).

The letter proceeds in three main stages. The first two chapters explain Paul's own background, including a rare description of his initial meeting with the risen Jesus. He speaks of his own vocation in terms reminiscent of the call of the ancient prophets: he is no second-order apostle, but a primary witness, commissioned by Jesus himself. He explains how he confronted even Peter over the same issue: *all those who believe in Jesus belong at the same table, circumcised or not.*

The central section (3.1—4.11) takes the story back to Abraham. God promised the patriarch a worldwide faith-family, and that promise has now been fulfilled. But the law of Moses cannot be the means of that fulfilment, since it held out only condemnation for those who broke it (all Jews, in other words), and made a strict separation between Jew and Gentile. Here is the fundamental insight of the letter: *the Mosaic law was a temporary dispensation* until the Abrahamic promises would be fulfilled by the once-for-all divine action in the Messiah. To go back now would be like the freed slaves in Exodus wanting to go back to Egypt.

The rest of the letter (4.12–end) comes in several stages, reinforcing the message from various angles, and stressing that, though some might want to reinstate the law to regulate behaviour, that would mean going back to the old, unredeemed world of 'flesh' – the very place from which one might hope to escape. The new gift of the spirit, however, will produce 'fruit': love, joy, peace, and the rest. Paul signs off (taking the pen from the scribe) with a personal flourish: if it's marks on the body you want, he has the Messiah's marks on his. His first arrival in Galatia had been marked by severe persecution, including stoning: those wounds are enough for him, showing that he at least is part of the Jesus-shaped new creation.

Paul's distress over the Galatians

1 Paul, an apostle ... (my apostleship doesn't derive from human sources, nor did it come through a human being; it came through Jesus the Messiah, and God the father who raised him from the dead) ... ²and the family who are with me; to the churches of Galatia. ³Grace to you and peace from God our father and Jesus the Messiah, our Lord, ⁴who gave himself for our sins, to rescue us from the present evil age, according to the will of God our father, ⁵to whom be glory to the ages of ages. Amen.

⁶I'm astonished that you are turning away so quickly from the one who called you by grace, and going after another gospel – ⁷not that it is another gospel, it's just that there are some people stirring up trouble for you and wanting to pervert the gospel of the Messiah. ⁸But even if we – or an angel from heaven! – should announce a gospel other than the one we announced to you, let such a person be accursed. ⁹I said it before and I now say it again: if anyone offers you a gospel other than the one you received, let that person be accursed.

Paul's conversion and call

¹⁰Well now ... does *that* sound as though I'm trying to make up to people – or to God? Or that I'm trying to curry favour with people? If I were still pleasing people, I wouldn't be a slave of the Messiah.

¹¹You see, brothers and sisters, let me make it clear to you: the gospel announced by me is not a mere human invention. ¹²I didn't receive it from human beings, nor was I taught it; it came through an unveiling of Jesus the Messiah.

¹³You heard, didn't you, the way I behaved when I was still within 'Judaism'. I persecuted the church of God violently, and ravaged it. ¹⁴I advanced in Judaism beyond many of my own age and people; I was extremely zealous for my ancestral traditions. ¹⁵But when God, who set me apart from my mother's womb, and called me by his grace, was pleased ¹⁶to unveil his son in me, so that I might announce the good news about him among the nations – immediately I did not confer with flesh and blood. ¹⁷Nor did I go up to Jerusalem to those who were apostles before me. No; I went away to Arabia, and afterwards returned to Damascus.

Paul's first visit to Peter

¹⁸Then, after three years, I went up to Jerusalem to speak with Cephas. I stayed with him for two weeks. ¹⁹I didn't see any other of the apostles except James, the Lord's brother. ²⁰(Look, I'm not lying! The things I'm writing to you are written in God's presence.) ²¹Then I went to the regions of Syria and Cilicia. ²²I remained unknown by sight to the messianic assemblies in Judaea. ²³They simply heard that the one who had been persecuting them was now announcing the good news of the faith which he once tried to destroy. ²⁴And they glorified God because of me.

Standing firm against opposition

2 Then, after fourteen years, I went up again to Jerusalem. I took Barnabas with me, and Titus. ²I went up because of a revelation. I laid before them the gospel which I announce among the Gentiles (I did this privately, in the presence of the key people), in case somehow I might be running, or might have run, to no good effect. ³But even the Greek, Titus, who was with me, was not forced to get circumcised ... ⁴but because of some pseudo-family members who had been secretly smuggled in, who came in on the side to spy on the freedom which we have in the Messiah, Jesus, so that they might bring us into slavery ... ⁵I didn't yield authority to them, no, not for a moment, so that the truth of the gospel might be maintained for you.

Paul's agreement with Peter and James

⁶However, those who appeared to be Something – what sort of 'thing' they were makes no difference to me, God shows no partiality – those of reputation added nothing extra to me. ⁷On the contrary, they saw that I had been entrusted with the gospel for the uncircumcision, just as Peter had been with

the gospel for the circumcision ⁸(for the one who gave Peter the power to be an apostle to the circumcision gave me the power to go to the Gentiles). They knew, moreover, the grace that had been given to me. ⁹So James, Cephas and John, who were reputed to be 'pillars', gave to Barnabas and me the right hand of fellowship, that we should go to the Gentiles, and they to the circumcision. ¹⁰The only extra thing they asked was that we should continue to remember the poor – the very thing I was eager to do.

Paul confronts Peter in Antioch

¹¹But when Cephas came to Antioch, I stood up to him face to face. He was in the wrong. ¹²Before certain persons came from James, Peter was eating with the Gentiles. But when they came, he drew back and separated himself, because he was afraid of the circumcision-people. ¹³The rest of the Jews did the same, joining him in this play-acting. Even Barnabas was carried along by their sham. ¹⁴But when I saw that they weren't walking straight down the line of gospel truth, I said to Cephas in front of them all: 'Look here: you're a Jew, but you've been living like a Gentile. How can you force Gentiles to become Jews?'

Justified by faith, not works of law

¹⁵We are Jews by birth, not 'Gentile sinners'. ¹⁶But we know that a person is not declared 'righteous' by works of the Jewish law, but through the faithfulness of Jesus the Messiah.

That is why we too believed in the Messiah, Jesus: so that we might be declared 'righteous' on the basis of the Messiah's faithfulness, and not on the basis of works of the Jewish law. On that basis, you see, no creature will be declared 'righteous'.

¹⁷Well, then; if, in seeking to be declared 'righteous' in the Messiah, we ourselves are found to be 'sinners', does that make the Messiah an agent of 'sin'? Certainly not! ¹⁸If I build up once more the things which I tore down, I demonstrate that I am a lawbreaker.

¹⁹Let me explain it like this. Through the law I died to the law, so that I might live to God. I have been crucified with the Messiah. ²⁰I am, however, alive – but it isn't me any longer, it's the Messiah who lives in me. And the life I do still live in the flesh, I live within the faithfulness of the son of God, who loved me and gave himself for me.

²¹I don't set aside God's grace. If 'righteousness' comes through the law, then the Messiah died for nothing.

God's promise and Abraham's faith

3 You witless Galatians! Who has bewitched you? King Jesus was portrayed on the cross before your very eyes! ²There's just one thing I want to know from you. Did you receive the spirit by doing the works of Torah, or by hearing and believing? ³You are so witless: you began with the spirit, and now you're ending with the flesh. ⁴Did you really suffer so much for nothing – if indeed it is going to be for nothing? ⁵The one who gives you the spirit and performs powerful deeds among you – does he do this through your performance of Torah, or through hearing and believing?

⁶It's like Abraham. 'He believed God, and it was counted to him for righteousness.' ⁷So you know that it's people of faith who are children of Abraham. ⁸The Bible foresaw that God would justify the nations by faith, so it announced the gospel to Abraham in advance, when it declared that 'the nations will be blessed in you'. ⁹So you see: the people of faith are blessed along with faithful Abraham.

Redeemed from the law's curse

¹⁰Because, you see, those who belong to the 'works-of-the-law' camp are under a curse! Yes, that's what the Bible says: 'Cursed is everyone who doesn't stick fast by everything written in the book of the law, to perform it.' ¹¹But, because nobody is justified before God in the law, it's clear that 'the righteous shall live by faith'. ¹²The law, however, is not by faith: rather, 'the one who does them shall live in them'.

¹³The Messiah redeemed us from the curse of the law, by becoming a curse on our behalf, as the Bible says: 'Cursed is everyone who

hangs on a tree.' ¹⁴This was so that the blessing of Abraham could flow through to the nations in King Jesus – and so that we might receive the promise of the spirit, through faith.

Christ the seed, Christ the mediator

¹⁵My brothers and sisters, let me use a human illustration. When someone makes a covenanted will, nobody sets it aside or adds to it. ¹⁶Well, the promises were made 'to Abraham and his seed', that is, his family. It doesn't say 'his seeds', as though referring to several families, but indicates a single family by saying 'and to your seed', meaning the Messiah.

¹⁷This is what I mean. God made this covenanted will; the law, which came four hundred and thirty years later, can't undermine it and make the promise null and void. ¹⁸If the inheritance came through the law, it would no longer be by promise; but God gave it to Abraham by promise.

¹⁹Why then the law? It was added because of transgressions, until the family should come to whom it had been promised. It was laid down by angels, at the hand of a mediator. ²⁰He, however, is not the mediator of the 'one' – but God is one!

²¹Is the law then against God's promises? Of course not! No, if a law had been given that could have given life, then covenant membership really would have been by the law. ²²But the Bible shut up everything together under the power of sin, so that the promise – which comes by the faithfulness of Jesus the Messiah – might be given to those who believe.

The coming of faith

²³Before this faithfulness arrived, we were kept under guard by the law, in close confinement until the coming faithfulness should be revealed. ²⁴Thus the law was like a babysitter for us, looking after us until the coming of the Messiah, so that we might be given covenant membership on the basis of faithfulness.

²⁵But now that faithfulness has come, we are no longer under the rule of the babysitter. ²⁶For you are all children of God, through faith, in the Messiah, Jesus.

²⁷You see, every one of you who has been baptized into the Messiah has put on the Messiah. ²⁸There is no longer Jew or Greek; there is no longer slave or free; there is no 'male and female'; you are all one in the Messiah, Jesus.

²⁹And, if you belong to the Messiah, you are Abraham's family. You stand to inherit the promise.

The son and the spirit

4 Let me put it like this. As long as the heir is a child, he is no different from a slave – even if, in fact, he is master of everything! ²He is kept under guardians and stewards until the time set by his father.

³Well, it's like that with us. When we were children, we were kept in 'slavery' under the 'elements of the world'. ⁴But when the fullness of time arrived, God sent out his son, born of a woman, born under the law, ⁵so that he might redeem those under the law, so that we might receive adoption as sons.

⁶And, because you are sons, God sent out the spirit of his son into our hearts, calling out 'Abba, father!' ⁷So you are no longer a slave, but a son! And, if you're a son, you are an heir, through God.

The true God and the false gods

⁸However, at that stage you didn't know God, and so you were enslaved to beings that, in their proper nature, are not gods. ⁹But now that you've come to know God – or, better, to be known *by* God – how can you turn back again to that weak and poverty-stricken line-up of elements that you want to serve all over again? ¹⁰You are observing days, and months, and seasons, and years! ¹¹I am afraid for you; perhaps my hard work with you is all going to be wasted.

Paul's appeal to his children

¹²Become like me! – because I became like you, my dear family. This is my plea to you. You didn't wrong me: ¹³no, you know that it was

through bodily weakness that I announced the gospel to you in the first place. ¹⁴You didn't despise or scorn me, even though my condition was quite a test for you, but you welcomed me as if I were God's angel, as if I were the Messiah, Jesus! ¹⁵What's happened to the blessing you had then? Yes, I can testify that you would have torn out your eyes, if you'd been able to, and given them to me. ¹⁶So have I become your enemy by telling you the truth?

¹⁷The other lot are eager for you, but it's not in a good cause. They want to shut you out, so that you will then be eager for them. ¹⁸Well, it's always good to be eager in a good cause, and not only when I'm there with you. ¹⁹My children – I seem to be in labour with you all over again, until the Messiah is fully formed in you! ²⁰I wish I were there with you right now, and could change my tone of voice. I really am at a loss about you.

Abraham's two sons

²¹So, you want to live under the law, do you? All right, tell me this: are you prepared to hear what the law says? ²²For the Bible says that Abraham had two sons, one by the slave-girl and one by the free woman. ²³Now the child of the slave-girl was born according to the flesh, while the child of the free woman was born according to promise.

²⁴Treat this as picture-language. These two women stand for two covenants: one comes from Mount Sinai, and gives birth to slave-children; that is Hagar. ²⁵(Sinai, you see, is a mountain in Arabia, and it corresponds, in the picture, to the present Jerusalem, since she is in slavery with her children.) ²⁶But the Jerusalem which is above is free – and she is our mother. ²⁷For the Bible says,

Celebrate, childless one, who never gave birth!
Go wild and shout, girl that never had pains!
The barren woman has many more children than the one who has a husband!

²⁸Now you, my family, are children of promise, in the line of Isaac. ²⁹But things now are like they were then: the one who was born according to the flesh persecuted the one born according to the spirit. ³⁰But what does the Bible say? 'Throw out the slave-girl and her son! For the son of the slave-girl will not inherit with the son of the free.' ³¹So, my family, we are not children of the slave-girl, but of the free.

Freedom in Christ

5 The Messiah set us free so that we could enjoy freedom! So stand firm, and don't get yourselves tied down by the chains of slavery.

²Look here: I, Paul, am telling you that if you get circumcised, the Messiah will be of no use to you. ³I testify once more, against every person who gets circumcised, that he is thereby under obligation to perform the entire law. ⁴You are split off from the Messiah, you people who want to be justified by the law! You have dropped out of grace. ⁵For we are waiting eagerly, by the spirit and by faith, for the hope of righteousness. ⁶For in the Messiah, Jesus, neither circumcision nor uncircumcision has any power. What matters is faith, working through love.

Warnings against compromise

⁷You were running well. Who got in your way and stopped you being persuaded by the truth? ⁸This persuasion didn't come from the one who called you! ⁹A little yeast works its way through the whole lump. ¹⁰I am persuaded in the Lord that you won't differ from me on this. But the one who is troubling you will bear the blame, whoever he may be. ¹¹As for me, my dear family, if I am still announcing circumcision, why are people still persecuting me? If I were, the scandal of the cross would have been neutralized. ¹²If only those who are making trouble for you would cut the whole lot off!

The law and the spirit

¹³When God called you, my dear family, he called you to make you free. But you mustn't use that freedom as an opportunity for the flesh. Rather, you must become each other's

servants, through love. ⁴¹⁴For the whole law is summed up in one word, namely this: 'Love your neighbour as yourself.' ¹⁵But if you bite each other and devour each other, watch out! You may end up being destroyed by each other.

¹⁶Let me say this to you: live by the spirit, and you won't do what the flesh wants you to. ¹⁷For the flesh wants to go against the spirit, and the spirit against the flesh. They are opposed to each other, so that you can't do what you want. ¹⁸But if you are led by the spirit, you are not under the law.

¹⁹Now the works of the flesh are obvious. They are such things as fornication, uncleanness, licentiousness, ²⁰idolatry, sorcery, hostilities, strife, jealousy, bursts of rage, selfish ambition, factiousness, divisions, ²¹moods of envy, drunkenness, wild partying, and similar things. I told you before, and I tell you again: people who do such things will not inherit God's kingdom.

Fruit of the spirit

²²But the fruit of the spirit is love, joy, peace, great-heartedness, kindness, generosity, faithfulness, ²³gentleness, self-control. There is no law that opposes things like that! ²⁴And those who belong to the Messiah, Jesus, crucified the flesh with its passions and desires. ²⁵If we live by the spirit, let's line up with the spirit. ²⁶We shouldn't be conceited, vying with one another and jealous of each other.

Bearing one another's burdens

6 My dear family, if someone is found out in some trespass, then you – the 'spiritual' ones! – should set such a person right, in a spirit of gentleness. Watch out for yourselves: you too may be tested. ²Carry each other's burdens; that's the way to fulfil the Messiah's law. ³If you think you're something when you are not, you deceive yourself. ⁴Every one of you should test your own work, and then you will have a reason to boast of yourself, not of somebody else. ⁵Each of you, you see, will have to carry your own load.

Practical support in the church

⁶If someone is being taught the word, they should share with the teacher all the good things they have. ⁷Don't be misled; God won't have people turning their noses up at him. What you sow is what you'll reap. ⁸Yes: if you sow in the field of your flesh you will harvest decay from your flesh, but if you sow in the field of the spirit you will harvest eternal life from the spirit. ⁹Don't lose your enthusiasm for behaving properly. You'll bring in the harvest at the proper time, if you don't become weary. ¹⁰So, then, while we have the chance, let's do good to everyone, and particularly to the household of the faith.

Boasting in the cross

¹¹Look at the large-size letters I'm writing to you in my own hand. ¹²It's the people who want to make a fine showing in the flesh who are trying to force you into getting circumcised – for this purpose only, that they may avoid persecution for the Messiah's cross. ¹³You see, even the circumcised ones don't keep the law; rather, they want you to be circumcised, so that they may boast about your flesh.

¹⁴As for me, God forbid that I should boast – except in the cross of our Lord Jesus the Messiah, through whom the world has been crucified to me and I to the world. ¹⁵Circumcision, you see, is nothing; neither is uncircumcision! What matters is new creation. ¹⁶Peace and mercy on everyone who lines up by that standard – yes, on God's Israel.

¹⁷For the rest, let nobody make trouble for me. You see, I carry the marks of Jesus on my body.

¹⁸The grace of our Lord Jesus the Messiah be with your spirit, my dear family. Amen.

Ephesians

Ephesians is a circular; the words 'in Ephesus' in the opening address are a later addition. A good guess is that Paul wrote it from prison in Ephesus itself to the small and recently founded churches in the wider district, including those in Colossae, Hierapolis and Laodicea, up the Lycus Valley.

The letter divides easily into two. The first three chapters are framed with prayer, the long opening shout of praise (1.3–14) and the intercession and celebration to which it gives rise (1.15–23), and the prayer for the whole church to find love as its root and firm foundation (3.14–21). Paul is not only praying; he is modelling a richly Trinitarian worship, celebrating the fact that Jesus is *already* enthroned as the world's true Lord (1.20–22). Paul's imprisonment, and the fact that the letter ends with a serious warning about spiritual warfare, indicate that the church is now living in a time of 'now and not yet'; the balance looks different from different angles of vision, but nothing is gained by forgetting the 'now' just because circumstances are difficult. In between chapters 1 and 3, Paul briefly expounds the effect of the gospel: sinners are rescued by grace through faith in order to be agents of new creation (2.1-10), and Gentiles are brought in along with Jews so that there is a single family, the ultimate new Temple in which God himself dwells by the spirit (2.11–22). A community like this will be a standing sign to the powers of the world that Jesus is Lord and they are not (3.10).

The second half of the letter is a sustained appeal for *unity* and *holiness*, two of Paul's constant themes. God gives the church multiple ministries, not to pull the community apart but to enable it to grow like a single body (4.1–16). This community must live as renewed humans, avoiding the standard corruptions of surrounding paganism (4.17—5.20). This will show particularly in married life; here, indeed (5.21–33), Paul offers a glimpse of a patterned understanding of the whole scriptural narrative, rooted in the first chapters of Genesis. God's purpose was to bring heaven and earth together in the Messiah (1.10); at present he is bringing Jew and Gentile together by the spirit (2.11–22); and this is to be reflected in the mutual love and submission of husband and wife, as well as in the wider life of Jesus-shaped households.

The letter ends with a warning about the spiritual warfare to be faced by anyone who tries to pray and live in this way. He offers an extended metaphor, still used by many as an aid to daily prayer: God's complete armour. Finally, off goes Paul's messenger, his 'dear brother Tychicus', to the little churches, taking the letter (6.21), and giving news of Paul himself. He, says Paul, will 'encourage your hearts' (6.22). Ephesians has been doing that ever since.

Blessings on the sovereign God!

1 From Paul, one of King Jesus' apostles through God's purpose, to the holy ones in Ephesus who are also loyal believers in King Jesus: ²may God our father and the Lord Jesus, the king, give you grace and peace!

³Let us bless God, the father of our Lord Jesus, the king! He has blessed us in the king with every spirit-inspired blessing in the heavenly realm.

The choice and the plan

⁴He chose us in him before the world was made, so as to be holy and irreproachable before him in love. ⁵He foreordained us for himself, to be adopted as sons and daughters through Jesus the king. That's how he wanted it, and that's what gave him delight, ⁶so that the glory of his grace, the grace he poured on us in his beloved one, might receive its due praise.

⁷In the king, and through his blood, we have deliverance – that is, our sins have been forgiven – through the wealth of his grace ⁸which he lavished on us. Yes, with all wisdom and insight ⁹he has made known to us the secret of his purpose, just as he wanted it to be and set it forward in him ¹⁰as a blueprint for when the time was ripe. His plan was to sum up the whole cosmos in the king – yes, everything in heaven and on earth, in him.

The inheritance and the spirit

¹¹In him we have received the inheritance! We were foreordained to this, according to the intention of the one who does all things in accordance with the counsel of his purpose. ¹²This was so that we, we who first hoped in the king, might live for the praise of his glory. ¹³In him you too, who heard the word of truth, the gospel of your salvation, and believed it – in him you were marked out with the spirit of promise, the holy one. ¹⁴The spirit is the guarantee of our inheritance, until the time when the people who are God's special possession are finally reclaimed and freed. This, too, is for the praise of his glory.

Knowing the power of the king

¹⁵Because of all this, and because I'd heard that you are loyal and faithful to Jesus the master, and that you show love to all God's holy people, ¹⁶I never stop giving thanks for you as I remember you in my prayers. ¹⁷I pray that the God of King Jesus our Lord, the father of glory, would give you, in your spirit, the gift of being wise, of seeing things people can't normally see, because you are coming to know him ¹⁸and to have the eyes of your inmost self opened to God's light. Then you will know exactly what the hope is that goes with God's call; you will know the wealth of the glory of his inheritance in his holy people; ¹⁹and you will know the outstanding greatness of his power towards us who are loyal to him in faith, according to the working of his strength and power.

²⁰This was the power at work in the king when God raised him from the dead and sat him at his right hand in the heavenly places, ²¹above all rule and authority and power and lordship, and above every name that is invoked, both in the present age and also in the age to come. ²²Yes: God has 'put all things under his feet', and has given him to the church as the head over all. ²³The church is his body; it is the fullness of the one who fills all in all.

Warning signs on the wrong road

2 So where do you come into it all? Well, you were dead because of your offences and sins! ²That was the road you used to travel, keeping in step with this world's 'present age'; in step, too, with the ruler of the power of the air, the spirit that is, even now, at work among people whose whole lives consist of disobeying God. ³Actually, that's how all of us used to behave, conditioned by physical desires. We used to do what our flesh and our minds were urging us to do. What was the result? We too were subject to wrath in our natural state, just like everyone else.

⁴But when it comes to mercy, God is rich! He had such great love for us that ⁵he took us at the very point where we were dead through our offences, and made us alive together with the king (yes, you are saved by sheer grace!).

⁶He raised us up with him, and made us sit with him – in the heavenly places, in King Jesus! ⁷This was so that in the ages to come he could show just how unbelievably rich his grace is, the kindness he has shown us in King Jesus.

Grace, not works

⁸How has this all come about? You have been saved by grace, through faith! This doesn't happen on your own initiative; it's God's gift. ⁹It isn't on the basis of works, so no one is able to boast. ¹⁰This is the explanation: God has made us what we are. God has created us in King Jesus for the good works that he prepared, ahead of time, as the road we must travel.

Two into one will go

¹¹So then, remember this! In human terms, that is, in your 'flesh', you are 'Gentiles'. You are the people who the so-called 'circumcision' refer to as the so-called 'uncircumcision' – circumcision, of course, being something done by human hands to human flesh. ¹²Well, once upon a time you were separated from the king. You were detached from the community of Israel. You were foreigners to the covenants which contained the promise. There you were, in the world with no hope and no god!

¹³But now, in King Jesus, you have been brought near in the king's blood – yes, you, who used to be a long way away! ¹⁴He is our peace, you see. He has made the two to be one. He has pulled down the barrier, the dividing wall, that turns us into enemies of each other. He has done this in his flesh, ¹⁵by abolishing the law with its commands and instructions.

The point of doing all this was to create, in him, one new human being out of the two, so making peace. ¹⁶God was reconciling both of us to himself in a single body, through the cross, by killing the enmity in him.

Unveiling the new Temple

¹⁷So the Messiah came and gave the good news. Peace had come! Peace, that is, for those of you who were a long way away, and peace, too, for those who were close at hand. ¹⁸Through him, you see, we both have access to the father in the one spirit.

¹⁹This is the result. You are no longer foreigners or strangers. No: you are fellow-citizens with God's holy people. You are members of God's household. ²⁰You are built on the foundation of the apostles and prophets, with King Jesus himself as the cornerstone. ²¹In him the whole building is fitted together, and grows into a holy temple in the Lord. ²²You, too, are being built up together, in him, into a place where God will live by the spirit.

God's secret plan unveiled at last

3 It's because of all this that I, Paul, the prisoner of King Jesus on behalf of you Gentiles . . .

²I'm assuming, by the way, that you've heard about the plan of God's grace that was given to me to pass on to you? ³You know – the secret purpose that God revealed to me, as I wrote briefly just now? ⁴Anyway . . .

When you read this you'll be able to understand the special insight I have into the king's secret. ⁵This wasn't made known to human beings in previous generations, but now it's been revealed by the spirit to God's holy apostles and prophets. ⁶The secret is this: that, through the gospel, the Gentiles are to share Israel's inheritance. They are to become fellow members of the body, along with them, and fellow-sharers of the promise in King Jesus.

⁷This is the gospel that I was appointed to serve, in line with the free gift of God's grace that was given to me. It was backed up with the power through which God accomplishes his work.

Wisdom for the rulers

⁸I am the very least of all God's people. However, he gave me this task as a gift: that I should be the one to tell the Gentiles the good news of the king's wealth, wealth no one could begin to count. ⁹My job is to make clear to everyone just what the secret plan is, the purpose that's been hidden from the very

beginning of the world in God who created all things. ¹⁰This is it: that God's wisdom, in all its rich variety, was to be made known to the rulers and authorities in the heavenly places – through the church!

¹¹This was God's eternal purpose, and he's accomplished it in King Jesus our Lord. ¹²We have confidence, and access to God, in him, in full assurance, through his faithfulness. ¹³So, I beg you: don't lose heart because of my sufferings on your behalf! That's your glory!

God's love, God's power – in us

¹⁴Because of this, I am kneeling down before the father, ¹⁵the one who gives the name of 'family' to every family that there is, in heaven and on earth. ¹⁶My prayer is this: that he will lay out all the riches of his glory to give you strength and power, through his spirit, in your inner being; ¹⁷that the king may make his home in your hearts, through faith; that love may be your root, your firm foundation; ¹⁸and that you may be strong enough (with all God's holy ones) to grasp the breadth and length and height and depth, ¹⁹and to know the king's love – though actually it's so deep that nobody can really know it! So may God fill you with all his fullness.

²⁰So: to the one who is capable of doing far, far more than we can ask or imagine, granted the power which is working in us – ²¹to him be glory, in the church, and in King Jesus, to all generations, and to the ages of ages! Amen!

Live up to your calling!

4 So, then, this is my appeal to you – yes, it's me, the prisoner in the Lord! You must live up to the calling you received. ²Bear with one another in love; be humble, meek and patient in every way with one another. ³Make every effort to guard the unity that the spirit gives, with your lives bound together in peace.

⁴There is one body and one spirit; you were, after all, called to one hope which goes with your call. ⁵There is one Lord, one faith, one baptism; ⁶one God and father of all, who is over all, through all and in all.

⁷But grace was given to each one of us, according to the measure the king used when he was distributing gifts. ⁸That's why it says,

When he went up on high
he led bondage itself into bondage
and he gave gifts to people.

⁹When it says here that 'he went up', what this means is that he also came down into the lower place, that is, the earth. ¹⁰The one who came down is the one who also 'went up' – yes, above all the heavens! – so that he might fill all things.

Grown-up Christianity

¹¹So these were the gifts that he gave. Some were to be apostles, others prophets, others evangelists, and others pastors and teachers. ¹²Their job is to give God's people the equipment they need for their work of service, and so to build up the king's body. ¹³The purpose of this is that we should all reach unity in our belief and loyalty, and in knowing God's son. Then we shall reach the stature of the mature Man measured by the standards of the king's fullness.

¹⁴As a result, we won't be babies any longer! We won't be thrown this way and that on a stormy sea, blown about by every gust of teaching, by human tricksters, by their cunning and deceitful scheming. ¹⁵Instead, we must speak the truth in love, and so grow up in everything into him – that is, into the king, who is the head. ¹⁶He supplies the growth that the whole body needs, linked as it is and held together by every joint which supports it, with each member doing its own proper work. Then the body builds itself up in love.

Off with the old, on with the new

¹⁷So this is what I want to say; I am bearing witness to it in the Lord. You must no longer behave like the Gentiles, foolish-minded as they are. ¹⁸Their understanding is darkened; they are cut off from God's life because of their deep-seated ignorance, which springs from the fact that their hearts are hard. ¹⁹They have lost

all moral sensitivity, and have given themselves over to whatever takes their fancy. They go off greedily after every kind of uncleanness.

²⁰But that's not how you learned the king! – ²¹if indeed you did hear about him, and were taught in him, in accordance with the truth about Jesus himself. ²²That teaching stressed that you should take off your former lifestyle, the old humanity. That way of life is decaying, as a result of deceitful lusts. ²³Instead, you must be renewed in the spirit of your mind, ²⁴and you must put on the new humanity, which is being created the way God intended it, displaying justice and genuine holiness.

The kindness that imitates God himself

²⁵Put away lies, then. 'Each of you, speak the truth with your neighbour,' because we are members of one another. ²⁶'Be angry, but don't sin'; don't let the sun go down on you while you're angry, ²⁷and don't leave any loophole for the devil. ²⁸The thief shouldn't steal any longer, but should rather get on with some honest manual work, so as to be able to share with people in need.

²⁹Don't let any unwholesome words escape your lips. Instead, say whatever is good and will be useful in building people up, so that you will give grace to those who listen.

³⁰And don't disappoint God's holy spirit – the spirit who put God's mark on you to identify you on the day of freedom. ³¹All bitterness and rage, all anger and yelling, and all blasphemy – put it all away from you, with all wickedness. ³²Instead, be kind to one another, cherish tender feelings for each other, forgive one another, just as God forgave you in the king.

5 So you should be imitators of God, like dear children. ²Conduct yourselves in love, just as the Messiah loved us, and gave himself for us, as a sweet-smelling offering and sacrifice to God.

Darkness and light in matters of sex

³As for fornication, uncleanness of any kind, or greed: you shouldn't even mention them! You are, after all, God's holy people. ⁴Shameful, stupid or coarse conversations are quite out of place. Instead, there should be thanksgiving.

⁵You should know this, you see: no fornicator, nobody who practises uncleanness, no greedy person (in other words, an idolator), has any inheritance in the Messiah's kingdom, or in God's. ⁶Don't let anyone fool you with empty words. It's because of these things, you see, that God's wrath is coming on people who are disobedient.

⁷So don't share in their practices. ⁸After all, at one time you were darkness, but now, in the Lord, you are light! So behave as children of light. ⁹Light has its fruit, doesn't it, in everything that's good, and just, and true. ¹⁰Think through what's going to be pleasing to the Lord. Work it out.

Light and darkness

¹¹So don't get involved in the works of darkness, which all come to nothing. Instead, expose them! ¹²The things they do in secret, you see, are shameful even to talk about. ¹³But everything becomes visible when it's exposed to the light, ¹⁴since everything that is visible is light. That's why it says:

Wake up, you sleeper!
Rise up from the dead!
The Messiah will shine on you!

¹⁵So take special care how you conduct yourselves. Don't be unwise, but be wise. ¹⁶Make use of any opportunity you have, because these are wicked times we live in. ¹⁷So don't be foolish; rather, understand what the Lord's will is. ¹⁸And don't get drunk with wine; that way lies dissipation. Rather, be filled with the spirit! ¹⁹Speak to each other in psalms and hymns and spiritual songs, singing and chanting in your heart to the Lord, ²⁰always giving thanks for everything to God the father in the name of our Lord Jesus the Messiah.

Wives and husbands

²¹Be subject to one another out of reverence for the Messiah.

²²Wives, be subject to your own husbands, as to the Lord. ²³The man, you see, is the head of the woman, just as the Messiah, too, is head of the church. He is himself the saviour of the body. ²⁴But, just as the church is subject to the Messiah, in the same way women should be subject in everything to their husbands.

²⁵Husbands, love your wives, as the Messiah loved the church, and gave himself for it, ²⁶so that he could make it holy, cleansing it by washing it with water through the word. ²⁷He did this in order to present the church to himself in brilliant splendour, without a single spot or blemish or anything of the kind – that it might be holy and without blame. ²⁸That's how husbands ought to love their own wives, just as they love their own bodies.

Someone who loves his wife loves himself. ²⁹After all, nobody ever hates his own flesh: he feeds it and takes care of it, just as the Messiah does with the church, ³⁰because we are parts of his body. ³¹'That's why a man leaves his father and mother and is joined to his wife, and the two become one flesh.'

³²The hidden meaning in this saying is very deep; but I am reading it as referring to the Messiah and the church. ³³Anyway, each one of you must love your wife as you love yourself; and the wife must see that she respects her husband.

Children, parents, slaves and masters

6 Children, obey your parents in the Lord. This is right and proper. ²'Honour your father and your mother' – this is the first commandment that comes with a promise attached! – ³'so that things may go well with you and that you may live a long life on earth.'

⁴Fathers, don't make your children angry. Bring them up in the training and instruction of the Lord.

⁵Slaves, obey your human masters, with respect and devotion, with the same single-mindedness that you have towards the Messiah. ⁶You must get on with your work, not only when someone is watching you, as if you were just trying to please another human being, but as slaves of the Messiah. Do God's will from your heart. ⁷Get on with your tasks with a kind and ready spirit as if you were serving the master himself and not human beings. ⁸After all, you know that if anyone, slave or free, does something good, they will receive it back from the master.

⁹Masters, do the same to them! Give up using threats. You know, after all, that the master in heaven is their master and yours, and he is no respecter of persons.

God's complete armour

¹⁰What else is there to say? Just this: be strong in the Lord, and in the strength of his power. ¹¹Put on God's complete armour. Then you'll be able to stand firm against the devil's trickery. ¹²The warfare we're engaged in, you see, isn't against flesh and blood. It's against the leaders, against the authorities, against the powers that rule the world in this dark age, against the wicked spiritual elements in the heavenly places.

¹³For this reason, you must take up God's complete armour. Then, when wickedness grabs its moment, you'll be able to withstand, to do what needs to be done, and still to be on your feet when it's all over. ¹⁴So stand firm! Put the belt of truth round your waist; put on justice as your breastplate; ¹⁵for shoes on your feet, ready for battle, take the good news of peace. ¹⁶With it all, take the shield of faith; if you've got that, you'll be able to quench all the flaming arrows of the evil one. ¹⁷Take the helmet of salvation, and the sword of the spirit, which is God's word.

Prayer and peace

¹⁸Pray on every occasion in the spirit, with every type of prayer and intercession. You'll need to keep awake and alert for this, with all perseverance and intercession for all God's holy ones – ¹⁹and also for me! Please pray that God will give me his words to speak when I open my mouth, so that I can make known, loud and clear, the secret truth of the gospel. ²⁰That, after all, is why I'm a chained-up ambassador! Pray that I may announce it boldly; that's what I'm duty-bound to do.

²¹It's important that you should know how things are with me, and what I'm up to; so our

dear brother Tychicus will tell you about it. He is a loyal servant in the Lord. ²²I've sent him to you with this in mind, so that you may know how things are with us, and so that he may encourage your hearts.

²³Peace be to the whole family, and love with faith, from God the father and the Lord Jesus, the Messiah. ²⁴Grace be with all who love our Lord, King Jesus, with a love that never dies!

Philippians

The letter to Philippi celebrates a joyful 'partnership': the many-layered 'fellowship' between Paul and the first church in Europe. Sharing as they did in the Messiah's love at a deep level, they had also entered into partnership at the practical level of resources. Paul was in prison. They had sent Epaphroditus to him with a gift of money, but he had become ill on the journey and so had delayed his return (2.25–30). So Paul writes to thank them for the money and to assure them, warding off any suspicions, that their messenger has been faithful to his commission.

The letter is therefore joyful, and Paul is determined that his uncertain future in prison (will he face the death penalty?) will not detract from this. As far as he is concerned, his imprisonment has brought the gospel to public attention, and Jesus will be glorified whatever the outcome. He himself will be content, confident that if he dies he will be with the Messiah, which would be far better, but that if he remains alive it will be because he has fruitful work to do (1.21–26). All this forms a foundation for Paul to go into more detail about his hopes and prayers for the church in Philippi.

His concern, as so often, was for the church to maintain its public witness in the face of misunderstanding and hostility. Opponents will be everywhere, not least when a small group believes that 'Jesus is Lord' in a place like Philippi, a Roman colony, committed to the belief that Caesar was Lord. So trouble will come, but the church must link arms and celebrate the victory of Jesus in a hard-won unity and a costly holiness.

Paul carefully frames this appeal around what has become a famous poem. The poem itself is found in 2.6–11, with six three-line stanzas and the all-important single line in the middle. The first half tells of the descent of the one who was always 'in God's form', always 'equal with God', but who humbled himself to become human and to die the death of a disgraced slave. The five verses before the poem (2.1–5) appeal for unity; the seven verses afterwards (2.12–18) appeal for holiness. Paul can only say a little in a letter; his hearers must work out for themselves what this 'salvation' means in practice (2.12), and for that they need the Messiah's mind.

A brief paragraph about Timothy, and another about Epaphroditus, lead us to what looks as though it was going to be a conclusion; but there is more. Conditions in prison may not have favoured fluent dictation; the break between chapters 2 and 3 seems awkward to us, but that does not undermine the deeper unity of the letter as a whole. Chapter 3 is indeed closely linked to chapters 1 and 2: Paul tells his own story, as a model for what it means to have the Messiah's mind, showing how he abandoned his own apparent privileges as a loyal Jew in order to gain the ultimate Jewish prize: the Messiah himself, and resurrection! Philippians is all about learning to think messianically and to let that thinking inform every aspect of life. That is how the Philippian church, like Paul, will 'have strength for everything in the one who gives me power' (4.13).

Paul's reasons for thanks

1 From Paul and Timothy, slaves of King Jesus, to all God's holy ones in King Jesus who are in Philippi, together with the overseers and ministers: ²grace to you and peace, from God our father and King Jesus the Lord.

³I thank my God every time I think of you! ⁴I always pray with joy, whenever I pray for you all, ⁵because of your partnership in the gospel from the first day until now. ⁶Of this I'm convinced: the one who began a good work in you will thoroughly complete it by the day of King Jesus.

⁷It's right for me to think this way about all of you. You have me in your hearts, here in prison as I am, working to defend and bolster up the gospel. You are my partners in grace, all of you! ⁸Yes: God can bear witness how much I'm longing for all of you with the deep love of King Jesus.

⁹And this is what I'm praying: that your love may overflow still more and more, in knowledge and in all astute wisdom. ¹⁰Then you will be able to tell the difference between good and evil, and be sincere and faultless on the day of the Messiah, ¹¹filled to overflowing with the fruit of right living, fruit that comes through King Jesus to God's glory and praise.

The king is proclaimed

¹²Now, my dear family, I want you to know that the things I've been through have actually helped the gospel on its way. ¹³You see, everybody in the Imperial Guard, and all the rest for that matter, have heard that I am here, chained up, because of the Messiah, the king. ¹⁴My imprisonment has given new confidence to most of the Lord's family; they are now much more prepared to speak the word boldly and fearlessly.

¹⁵There are some, I should say, who are proclaiming the king because of envy and rivalry; but there are others who are doing it out of good will. ¹⁶These last are acting from love, since they know that I'm in prison because of defending the gospel; ¹⁷but the others are announcing the king out of selfishness and jealousy. They are not acting from pure motives; they imagine that they will make more trouble for me in my captivity.

¹⁸So what? Only this: the king is being announced, whether people mean it or not! I'm happy to celebrate that!

To live or to die?

Yes, and I really am going to celebrate: ¹⁹because I know that this will result in my rescue, through your prayer and the support of the spirit of King Jesus. ²⁰I'm waiting eagerly and full of hope, because nothing is going to put me to shame. I am going to be bold and outspoken, now as always, and the king is going to gain a great reputation through my body, whether in life or in death.

²¹You see, for me to live means the Messiah; to die means to make a profit. ²²If it's to be living on in the flesh, that means fruitful work for me.

Actually, I don't know which I would choose. ²³I'm pulled both ways at once: I would really love to leave all this and be with the king, because that would be far better. ²⁴But staying on here in the flesh is more vital for your sake. ²⁵Since I've become convinced of this, I know that I will remain here, and stay alongside all of you, to help you to advance and rejoice in your faith, ²⁶so that the pride you take in King Jesus may overflow because of me, when I come to visit you once again.

The gospel in public

²⁷The one thing I would stress is this: your public behaviour must match up to the gospel of the king. That way, whether I do come and see you or whether I remain elsewhere, the news that I get about you will indicate that you are standing firm with a single spirit, struggling side by side with one united intent for the faith of the gospel, ²⁸and not letting your opponents intimidate you in any way. This is a sign from God: one that signifies their destruction, but your salvation.

²⁹Yes: God has granted you that, on behalf of the king, you should not only believe in him, but also suffer for his sake. ³⁰You are engaged in the same struggle which you once watched

me go through; and, as you now hear, I'm still going through it.

Unity in everything

2 So if our shared life in the king brings you any comfort; if love still has the power to make you cheerful; if we really do have a partnership in the spirit; if your hearts are at all moved with affection and sympathy – ²then make my joy complete! Bring your thinking into line with one another.

Here's how to do it. Hold on to the same love; bring your innermost lives into harmony; fix your minds on the same object. ³Never act out of selfish ambition or vanity; instead, regard everybody else as your superior. ⁴Look after each other's best interests, not your own.

The mind of the Messiah

⁵This is how you should think among yourselves – with the mind that you have because you belong to the Messiah, Jesus:

⁶Who, though in God's form, did not
regard his equality with God
as something he ought to exploit.

⁷Instead, he emptied himself,
and received the form of a slave,
being born in the likeness of humans.

And then, having human appearance,
⁸he humbled himself, and became
obedient even to death,
yes, even the death of the cross.

⁹And so God has greatly exalted him,
and to him in his favour has given
the name which is over all names:

¹⁰That now at the name of Jesus
every knee within heaven shall bow –
on earth, too, and under the earth;

¹¹And every tongue shall confess
that Jesus, Messiah, is Lord,
to the glory of God, the father.

How salvation is worked out

¹²So, my dear people: you always did what I said, so please now carry on in the same way, not just as though I was there with you, but much more because I'm not! Your task now is to work at bringing about your own salvation; and naturally you'll be taking this with utter seriousness. ¹³After all, God himself is the one who's at work among you, who provides both the will and the energy to enable you to do what pleases him.

¹⁴There must be no grumbling and disputing in anything you do. ¹⁵That way, nobody will be able to fault you, and you'll be pure and spotless children of God in the middle of a twisted and depraved generation. You are to shine among them like lights in the world, ¹⁶clinging on to the word of life. That's what I will be proud of on the day of the Messiah. It will prove that I didn't run a useless race, or work to no purpose.

¹⁷Yes: even if I am to be poured out like a drink-offering on the sacrifice and service of your faith, I shall celebrate, and celebrate jointly with you all. ¹⁸In the same way, you should celebrate, yes, and celebrate with me.

On Timothy

¹⁹I hope in the Lord Jesus to send Timothy to you soon, so that I in turn may be encouraged by getting news about you. ²⁰I have nobody else of his quality: he will care quite genuinely about how you are. ²¹Everybody else, you see, looks after their own interests, not those of Jesus the Messiah. ²²But you know how Timothy has proved himself. Like a child with a father he has worked as a slave alongside me for the sake of the gospel. ²³So I'm hoping to send him just as soon as I see how it will turn out with me. ²⁴And I am confident in the Lord that I myself will come very soon as well.

On Epaphroditus

²⁵But I did think it was necessary to send Epaphroditus to you. He is my brother; he has worked alongside me and fought alongside me; and he's served as your agent in tending

to my needs. ²⁶He was longing for you all, you see, and he was upset because you heard that he was sick. ²⁷And he really was sick, too; he nearly died. But God took pity on him – yes, and on me as well, so that I wouldn't have one sorrow piled on top of another.

²⁸This has made me all the more eager to send him, so that you'll see him again and be glad, and my own anxieties will be laid to rest. ²⁹So give him a wonderfully happy welcome in the Lord, and hold people like him in special respect. ³⁰He came close to death through risking his life for the king's work, so that he could complete the service to me that you hadn't been able to perform.

Warning: don't trust in the flesh

3 So then, my dear family, it comes down to this: celebrate in the Lord! It's no trouble for me to write the same things to you, and it's safe for you.

²Watch out for the dogs! Watch out for the 'bad works' people! Watch out for the 'incision' party, that is, the mutilators! ³We are the 'circumcision', you see – we who worship God by the spirit, and boast in King Jesus, and refuse to trust in the flesh.

⁴Mind you, I've got good reason to trust in the flesh. If anyone else thinks they have reason to trust in the flesh, I've got more. ⁵Circumcised? On the eighth day. Race? Israelite. Tribe? Benjamin. Descent? Hebrew through and through. Torah-observance? A Pharisee. ⁶Zealous? I persecuted the church! Official status under the law? Blameless.

Gaining the Messiah

⁷Does that sound as though my account was well in credit? Well, maybe; but whatever I had written in on the profit side, I calculated it instead as a loss – because of the Messiah. ⁸Yes, I know that's weird, but there's more: I calculate everything as a loss, because knowing King Jesus as my Lord is worth far more than everything else put together! In fact, because of the Messiah I've suffered the loss of everything, and I now calculate it as trash, so that my profit may be the Messiah, ⁹and that I may be discovered in him, not having my own covenant status defined by Torah, but the status which comes through the Messiah's faithfulness: the covenant status from God which is given to faith. ¹⁰This means knowing him, knowing the power of his resurrection, and knowing the partnership of his sufferings. It means sharing the form and pattern of his death, ¹¹so that somehow I may arrive at the final resurrection from the dead.

Chasing on to the finish

¹²I'm not implying that I've already received 'resurrection', or that I've already become complete and mature! No; I'm hurrying on, eager to overtake it, because King Jesus has overtaken me. ¹³My dear family, I don't reckon that I have yet overtaken it. But this is my one aim: to forget everything that's behind, and to strain every nerve to go after what's ahead. ¹⁴I mean to chase on towards the finishing post, where the prize waiting for me is the upward call of God in King Jesus.

¹⁵Those of us who are mature should think like this! If you think differently about it, God will reveal this to you as well. ¹⁶Only let's be sure to keep in line with the position we have reached.

Citizens of heaven

¹⁷So, my dear family, I want you, all together, to watch what I do and copy me. You've got us as a pattern of behaviour; pay careful attention to people who follow it.

¹⁸You see, there are several people who behave as enemies of the cross of the Messiah. I told you about them often enough, and now I'm weeping as I say it again. ¹⁹They are on the road to destruction; their stomach is their god, and they find glory in their own shame. All they ever think about is what's on the earth.

²⁰We are citizens of heaven, you see, and we're eagerly waiting for the saviour, the Lord, King Jesus, who is going to come from there. ²¹Our present body is a shabby old thing, but he's going to transform it so that it's just like his glorious body. And he's going to do this

by the power which makes him able to bring everything into line under his authority.

4 Well then, my dear family – I miss you so much, you're my joy and crown! – this is how you must stand firm in the Lord, my beloved people.

Celebrate in the Lord!

²I have a special appeal which goes jointly to Euodia and Syntyche: please, please, come to a common mind in the Lord. ³(And here's a request for you too, my loyal comrade: please help these women. They have struggled hard in the gospel alongside me, as have Clement and my other fellow-workers, whose names are in the book of life.)

⁴Celebrate joyfully in the Lord, all the time. I'll say it again: celebrate! ⁵Let everybody know how gentle and gracious you are. The Lord is near.

⁶Don't worry about anything. Rather, in every area of life let God know what you want, as you pray and make requests, and give thanks as well. ⁷And God's peace, which is greater than we can ever understand, will keep guard over your hearts and minds in King Jesus.

⁸For the rest, my dear family, these are the things you should think through: whatever is true, whatever is holy, whatever is upright, whatever is pure, whatever is attractive, whatever has a good reputation; anything virtuous, anything praiseworthy. ⁹And these are the things you should do: what you learned, received, heard and saw in and through me. And the God of peace will be with you.

The hidden secret

¹⁰I've been having a great celebration in the Lord because your concern for me has once again burst into flower. (You were of course concerned for me before, but you didn't have an opportunity to show it.)

¹¹I'm not talking about lacking anything. I've learnt to be content with what I have. ¹²I know how to do without, and I know how to cope with plenty. In every possible situation I've learned the hidden secret of being full and hungry, of having plenty and going without, and it's this: ¹³I have strength for everything in the one who gives me power.

Closing thanks and greetings

¹⁴But you did the right thing by entering into partnership with me in my suffering. ¹⁵Indeed, as you people in Philippi know well, when the gospel was getting under way and I was moving on from Macedonia, there wasn't a single other church, except yourselves, that entered into a two-way partnership with me, giving and receiving. ¹⁶Yes: when I was in Thessalonica you sent help to me, not just once but twice.

¹⁷I stress that it isn't the gift I'm interested in. My concern is that you should have a healthy profit balance showing up on your account. ¹⁸For myself, I've received full payment, and I'm well stocked up. In fact, I'm full to overflowing, now that I have received from Epaphroditus what you sent. It's like a sacrifice with a beautiful smell, a worthy offering, giving pleasure to God. ¹⁹What's more, my God will meet all your needs, too, out of his store of glorious riches in King Jesus. ²⁰Glory be to our God and father for ever and ever, Amen!

²¹Give my greetings to all God's people in King Jesus. The family with me here send their greetings. ²²All God's people send you greetings, especially those from Caesar's household.

²³The grace of the Lord Jesus, the Messiah, be with your spirit.

Colossians

Colossians is about Wisdom: wisdom incarnate, wisdom in practice. Wisdom as God's gift to the world in Jesus the Messiah.

The church in Colossae appears to be young. Paul has only just received news of it (1.3–8). So he, in prison in Ephesus, is praying that God will fill them 'with the knowledge of what he wants in all wisdom and spiritual understanding' (1.9), and in particular that they will learn to live lives characterized by constant thanksgiving (1.12 and frequently thereafter). This thanksgiving is to be shaped by 'wisdom' itself, that is, by the Messiah himself, the 'place where you'll find all the hidden treasures of wisdom and knowledge' (2.3). To express this, Paul writes or quotes the astonishing poem of 1.15–20, celebrating the Messiah as the one through whom all things were created and through whom now all things are reconciled. John began his gospel with his own obvious echo of Genesis 1.1: 'In the beginning'. Colossians focuses on the same verse re-expressed in poetry at once both simple and highly complex.

The point, through all this, is that Jesus himself is the true 'Image'. Again as in John, he is the truly human one. Simultaneously, however, Jesus is the visible image of the invisible God. Like the image in a temple, Jesus displays the God being worshipped. Temple-imagery, in fact, occurs regularly in Colossians: 'in him . . . all the full measure of divinity has taken up bodily residence' (2.9). With his death and resurrection 'all creation under heaven' has heard the good news (1.23); Paul means that with these events a kind of shock wave went through the whole created order. A new world had been born, and Paul intends that the new little church in Colossae will realize what it means to belong to it.

This is all the more important because Paul has been aware, ever since the crisis in Galatia, that rival missionaries are likely to arrive, telling people that they need to follow the Jewish ancestral traditions. Such people will urge confused ex-pagan Messiah-followers to take on complex lists of dietary or liturgical regulations. But this is to be resisted. What matters is Jesus, not human tradition; he is the true Temple; in him you have already been circumcised; the law and all its regulations have nothing now to say to you (2.8, 9,11, 13–19).

Instead, Paul holds out the bracing picture of a genuine human existence discovered through dying and rising with the Messiah (2.20—3.17). You have already died and been raised, he says; you are part of God's new creation, and the new version of humanity which you have put on 'is being renewed in the image of the creator, bringing you into possession of new knowledge' (3.10). This means not only kindness and forbearance, but forgiveness and above all (once more) thanksgiving (3.12–17). For the rest, he offers a shorter version of the 'household code' in Ephesians and quite lengthy closing greetings, including a word about Onesimus, whose story we discover in the letter to Philemon.

Paul has not yet visited the church in Colossae, but he hopes to be released soon and to be able to come to see them. But they are already joined together in the strong bond of mutual affection and prayer. Love, he says, 'ties everything together and makes it complete' (3.14). This letter is part of the way in which Paul is putting that into practice.

Thanksgiving for the gospel's work

1 Paul, an apostle of King Jesus by God's purpose and Timothy my brother; ²to God's holy people in Colossae, the king's faithful family; grace to you and peace, from God our father.

³We always thank God, the father of our Lord, King Jesus, when we pray for you, ⁴because we've heard of your faith in King Jesus and the love you have for all God's holy people, ⁵because of the hope which is kept safe for you in the heavenly places. You heard about this before in the word of truth, the gospel ⁶which has arrived on your doorstep – just as, in fact, it's producing fruit and growing in all the world, as it has been among you, from the day you heard it and came to know the grace of God in truth. ⁷That's how you learnt it from Epaphras our beloved fellow slave. He's a loyal and faithful servant of the king on your behalf. ⁸He it was who gave us the news about your love in the spirit.

Prayer for wisdom and gratitude

⁹For this reason, from the day we heard it, we haven't stopped praying for you. We're asking God to fill you with the knowledge of what he wants in all wisdom and spiritual understanding. ¹⁰This will mean that you'll be able to conduct yourselves in a manner worthy of the Lord, and so give him real delight, as you bear fruit in every good work and grow up in the knowledge of God. ¹¹I pray that you'll be given all possible strength, according to the power of his glory, so that you'll have complete patience and become truly steadfast and joyful.

¹²And I pray that you will learn to give thanks to the father, who has made you fit to share the inheritance of God's holy ones in the light. ¹³He has delivered us from the power of darkness, and transferred us into the kingdom of his beloved son. ¹⁴He is the one in whom we have redemption, the forgiveness of sins.

In praise of Jesus Christ

¹⁵He is the image of God, the invisible one,
  the firstborn of all creation.
¹⁶For in him all things were created,
  in the heavens and here on the earth.
Things we can see and things we cannot,
  – thrones and lordships and rulers and powers –
all things were created both through him and
  for him.

¹⁷And he is ahead, prior to all else
  and in him all things hold together;
¹⁸and he himself is supreme, the head
  over the body, the church.

He is the start of it all,
  firstborn from realms of the dead;
  so in all things he might be the chief.
¹⁹For in him all the Fullness was glad to dwell
  ²⁰and through him to reconcile all to himself,
  making peace through the blood of his cross,
through him – yes, things on the earth,
  and also the things in the heavens.

Reconciled and firm in faith

²¹So what about you? Well, there was a time when you were excluded! You were enemies in your thinking, and in wicked behaviour. ²²But now he has reconciled you in the body of his flesh, through death, in order to bring you into his presence holy, blameless and without any accusation.

²³This assumes, of course, that you keep firmly on in the faith – by which I mean, solid on your foundations, and not shifting from the hope of the gospel which you heard. This gospel, after all, has been announced in all creation under heaven! And this is the gospel of which I, Paul, became a servant.

The king, living within you

²⁴Right now I'm having a celebration – a celebration of my sufferings, which are for your benefit! And I'm steadily completing, in my own flesh, what is presently lacking in the king's afflictions on behalf of his body, which is the church. ²⁵I became the church's servant, according to the terms laid down by God when he gave me my commission on your behalf, the commission to fulfil God's word.

[26]This word declares the mystery that was kept secret from past ages and generations, but now has been revealed to God's holy people. [27]God's intention was to make known to them just what rich glory this mystery contains, out there among the nations. And this is the key: the king, living within you as the hope of glory!

[28]He is the one we are proclaiming. We are instructing everybody and teaching everybody in every kind of wisdom, so that we can present everybody grown up, complete, in the king. [29]That's what I am working for, struggling with all his energy which is powerfully at work within me.

God's hidden treasure – King Jesus!

2 You see, I'd like you to know just what a struggle I am having on behalf of yourselves, and the family in Laodicea, and all the people who don't know me by sight. [2]I want their hearts to be encouraged as they're brought together in love. I want them to experience all the wealth of definite understanding, and to come to the knowledge of God's mystery – the Messiah, the king! [3]He is the place where you'll find all the hidden treasures of wisdom and knowledge.

[4]I'm saying this so that nobody will deceive you with plausible words. [5]Though I'm away from you in person, you see, I am present with you in the spirit, and I'm celebrating as I keep an eye on your good order, and the solidity of your faith in the king.

[6]So, then, just as you received King Jesus the Lord, you must continue your journey in him. [7]You must put down healthy roots in him, being built up brick by brick in him, and established strongly in the faith, just as you were taught, with overflowing thankfulness.

Beware of deceivers

[8]Watch out that nobody uses philosophy and hollow trickery to take you captive! These are in line with human tradition, and with the 'elements of the world' – not the king. [9]In him, you see, all the full measure of divinity has taken up bodily residence. [10]What's more, you are fulfilled in him, since he's the head of all rule and authority.

[11]In him, indeed, you were circumcised with a special, new type of circumcision. It isn't something that human hands can do. It is the king's version of circumcision, and it happens when you put off the 'body of flesh': [12]when you're buried with him in baptism, and indeed also raised with him, through faith in the power of the God who raised him from the dead.

The law and the cross

[13]In the same way, though you were dead in legal offences, and in the uncircumcision of your flesh, God made you alive together with Jesus, forgiving us all our offences. [14]He blotted out the handwriting that was against us, opposing us with its legal demands. He took it right out of the way, by nailing it to the cross. [15]He stripped the rulers and authorities of their armour, and displayed them contemptuously to public view, celebrating his triumph over them in him.

[16]So don't let anyone pass judgment on you in a question of food or drink, or in the matter of festivals, new moons or sabbaths. [17]These things are a shadow cast by the coming reality – and the body that casts the shadow belongs to the king! [18]Don't let anyone rule you out of order by trying to force you into a kind of fake humility, or into worshipping angels. Such people will go on and on about visions they've had; they get puffed up without good reason by merely human thinking, [19]and they don't keep hold of the Head. It's from him that the whole body grows with the growth God gives it, as it's nourished and held together by its various ligaments and joints.

Dying and rising with Christ

[20]If you died with the king, coming out from the rule of the 'worldly elements', what's the point of laying down laws as though your life was still merely worldly? [21]'Don't handle! Don't taste! Don't touch!' [22]Rules like that all have to do with things that disappear as you use them. They are the sort of regulations and teachings that mere humans invent. [23]They may give an

appearance of wisdom, since they promote a do-it-yourself religion, a kind of humility, and severe treatment of the body. But they are of no use when it comes to dealing with physical self-indulgence.

3 So if you were raised to life with the king, search for the things that are above, where the king is seated at God's right hand! ²Think about the things that are above, not the things that belong on the earth. ³Don't you see: you died, and your life has been hidden with the king, in God! ⁴When the king is revealed (and he is your life, remember), then you too will be revealed with him in glory.

Old clothes, new clothes

⁵So, then, you must kill off the parts of you that belong on the earth: illicit sexual behaviour, uncleanness, passion, evil desire and greed (which is a form of idolatry). ⁶It's because of these things that God's wrath comes on the children of disobedience. ⁷You too used to behave like that, once, when your life consisted of that sort of thing.

⁸But now you must put away the lot of them: anger, rage, wickedness, blasphemy, dirty talk coming out of your mouth. ⁹Don't tell lies to each other! You have stripped off the old human nature, complete with its patterns of behaviour, ¹⁰and you have put on the new one – which is being renewed in the image of the creator, bringing you into possession of new knowledge. ¹¹In this new humanity there is no question of 'Greek and Jew', or 'circumcised and uncircumcised', of 'barbarian, Scythian', or 'slave and free'. The king is everything and in everything!

Love, peace and thanksgiving

¹²These are the clothes you must put on, then, since God has chosen you, made you holy, and lavished his love upon you. You must be tender-hearted, kind, humble, meek, and ready to put up with anything. ¹³You must bear with one another and, if anyone has a complaint against someone else, you must forgive each other. Just as the master forgave you, you must do the same. ¹⁴On top of all this you must put on love, which ties everything together and makes it complete. ¹⁵Let the king's peace be the deciding factor in your hearts; that's what you were called to, within the one body. And be thankful.

¹⁶Let the king's word dwell richly among you, as you teach and exhort one another in all wisdom, singing psalms, hymns and spiritual songs to God with grateful hearts. ¹⁷And whatever you do, in word or action, do everything in the name of the master, Jesus, giving thanks through him to God the father.

The Christian household

¹⁸Now a word for wives: you should be subject to your husbands. This is appropriate in the Lord. ¹⁹And for husbands: you should treat your wives with love, and not be bitter with them. ²⁰And for children: obey your parents in everything; this pleases the Lord. ²¹And for fathers: don't provoke your children to anger, otherwise they might lose heart.

²²A word, too, for slaves: obey your earthly masters in everything. Don't do it simply out of show, to curry favour with human beings, but wholeheartedly, because you fear the master. ²³Whatever you do, give it your very best, as if you were working for the master and not for human beings. ²⁴After all, you know that you're going to receive the true inheritance from the master as your reward! It is the master, the king, that you are serving. ²⁵Anyone who does wrong will be paid back for wrongdoing, and there will be no favourites.

4 And a word for masters: do what is just and fair for your slaves. Remember that you too have a Master – in heaven.

The fellowship of prayer

²Devote yourselves to prayer; keep alert in it, with thanksgiving. ³While you're about it, pray for us, too, that God will open in front of us a door for the word, so that we may speak of the mystery of the king – which is why I'm here in chains. ⁴Pray that I may speak clearly about it. That's what I am duty-bound to do.

⁵Behave wisely towards outsiders; buy up every opportunity. ⁶When you speak, make

sure it's always full of grace, and well flavoured with salt! That way you'll know how to give each person an appropriate answer.

⁷Our dear brother Tychicus will tell you all my news. He is a faithful servant, indeed a fellow slave in the Lord. ⁸This is why I'm sending him to you – to let you know how things are with us, and to encourage your hearts. ⁹I'm also sending Onesimus, who is a dear and faithful brother. He is one of your own number. They will tell you everything that's going on here.

Greetings from others

¹⁰Aristarchus (who's in jail with me here) sends you greetings. So does Mark, Barnabas's nephew. You've received instructions about him; if he comes to you, do make him welcome. ¹¹Jesus Justus sends greetings as well. These three are the only fellow Jews I have among my colleagues working for God's kingdom, and they have been an encouragement to me.

¹²Epaphras, one of your own folk and also one of King Jesus' slaves, sends you greetings. He's always struggling in prayer on your behalf, praying that you will stand firm and mature, and have your minds fully settled on everything that God wants you to do. ¹³I can bear him witness that he's gone to a lot of trouble on your behalf, and also on behalf of the family in Laodicea and in Hierapolis. ¹⁴Luke, the beloved doctor, sends greetings; so too does Demas.

¹⁵Pass my greetings on to the family in Laodicea, and to Nympha and the church in her house. ¹⁶When this letter has been read to you, make sure it's read in Laodicea as well; and you, too, should read the letter that will come on to you from Laodicea. ¹⁷And say to Archippus: 'Take care to complete the service that you have received in the Lord.'

¹⁸I'm signing off in my own hand: PAUL. Remember the chains I'm wearing. Grace be with you.

1 Thessalonians

Paul's first trip to northern Greece, in Acts 16 and 17, had been exciting but troubling. Unjustly beaten and imprisoned in Philippi, he went on quickly to Thessalonica; but it wasn't long before he had to leave there in a hurry as well, heading south with a short stop in Beroea before arriving in Athens. But, having not stayed long in Thessalonica, he agonized as to whether the small group of believers he had left behind would be holding on to their new faith, or whether the trouble stirred up by the new movement would have caused them to conclude it was all a mistake and to go back to their old ways of life. So Paul sent Timothy to see how things were. To his relief and joy, Timothy returned with good news. The Thessalonian Christians were standing firm, and eager to see Paul again (3.1–10). So Paul writes this first letter in thankful relief.

The first two chapters rehearse Paul's memory of his visit to Thessalonica: his preaching, the welcome he was given, the faith, hope and love that sprang up, and his own pastoral practice among them ('like a nurse taking care of her own children', 2.7). In particular, he recalls the persecution he suffered, as well as the hostility the church members themselves encountered from their fellow citizens, angry no doubt at a new movement which no longer worshipped the local gods, including the new 'deities' of Caesar and Rome (1.9; cf Acts 17.7). The fact that the believers faced this hostility without flinching gives Paul great joy. Like a gardener planting a tree, and waiting to see if it will withstand the wind and weather, he rejoices at the signs of life which mean the roots have gone deep.

Four quick points conclude the letter. First, the new-creation code of sexual morality (faithfulness in marriage, abstinence outside) is vital (4.1–8). Second, the mutual care and financial support (known by the word *agapē*, love) which they were already practising must continue and grow: the community must live as a single family. Third, they are not to be alarmed if some of their number die before the Lord's return; when that happens, those who have died will be raised and those still alive will be transformed. This passage (4.13–18) has caused considerable difficulty through the misinterpretation of its vivid biblical imagery. The point Paul is making is substantially the same as in Philippians 3.19–21 or 1 Corinthians 15.51–52. Fourth, they are to learn how to live as daytime people in a world still asleep to the new gospel realities (5.1–11). In particular, they are to recognize that the offer of 'peace and security' – a propaganda slogan of imperial Rome – is a self-serving, dangerous lie. Instead, they are to put on the armour of the gospel and continue to celebrate.

The Gospel comes to Thessalonica

1 Paul, Silvanus and Timothy, to the assembly of Thessalonians in God the father and the Lord Jesus, the Messiah. Grace to you and peace.

²We always give thanks to God for all of you, as we make mention of you in our prayers. ³We constantly remember the accomplishment of your faith, the hard work of your love, and the patience of your hope in our Lord Jesus the Messiah, in the presence of God our father.

⁴Dear family, beloved by God, we know that God has chosen you, ⁵because our gospel didn't come to you in word only, but in power, and in the holy spirit, and in great assurance. You know what sort of people we became for your sake, when we were among you.

The Thessalonians' faith

⁶And you learned how to copy us – and the Lord! When you received the word, you had a lot to suffer, but you also had the holy spirit's joy. ⁷As a result, you became a model for all the believers in both Macedonia and Achaea. ⁸For the word of the Lord has resonated out from you, not only in Macedonia and Achaea; your faith in God has gone out to people everywhere. This means that we haven't had to say anything. ⁹They themselves tell the story of the kind of welcome we had from you, and how you turned to God from idols, to serve a living and true God, ¹⁰and to wait for his son from heaven, whom he raised from the dead – Jesus, who delivers us from the coming fury.

Paul's ministry in Thessalonica

2 For you yourselves know, my dear family, that our visit to you didn't turn out to be empty. ²On the contrary. We had already undergone awful things and been shamefully treated in Philippi, as you know; but we were open and exuberant in our God in declaring to you the gospel of God, despite a good deal of opposition.

³When we make our appeal, you see, we are not deceiving people. We don't have any impure motives; we aren't playing some kind of trick. ⁴Rather, we speak as people whom God has validated to be entrusted with the gospel; not with a view to pleasing people, but in order to please God, who validates our hearts.

⁵For we never used flattering words, as you know. Nor were we saying things insincerely, as a cover-up for greed, as God is our witness. ⁶We weren't looking for recognition from anybody, either you or anyone else – ⁷though we could have imposed on you, as the Messiah's emissaries. But we were gentle among you, like a nurse taking care of her own children. ⁸We were so devoted to you that we gladly intended to share with you not only the gospel of God but our own lives, because you became so dear to us.

Paul's fatherly concern

⁹My dear family, you will recall our hard toil, our labour. We worked night and day so as not to be a burden to any of you while we announced to you the gospel of God. ¹⁰You are witnesses, and so is God, of our holy, upright and blameless behaviour towards you believers. ¹¹You know how, like a father to his own children, ¹²we encouraged each of you, and strengthened you, and made it clear to you that you should behave in a manner worthy of the God who calls you into his own kingdom and glory.

The persecuted church

¹³So, therefore, we thank God constantly that when you received the word of God which you heard from us, you accepted it, not as the word of a mere human being but – as it really is! – the word of God which is at work in you believers. ¹⁴For, my dear family, you came to copy God's assemblies in Judaea in the Messiah, Jesus. You suffered the same things from your own people as they did from those of the Judaeans ¹⁵who killed the Lord Jesus and the prophets, and who expelled us. They displease God; they oppose all people; ¹⁶they forbid us to speak to the Gentiles so that they may be saved. This has had the effect, all along, of completing the full total of their sins. But the fury has come upon them for good.

Paul's joy and crown

[17] As for us, my dear family, we were snatched away from you for a short time, in person though not in heart. We longed eagerly, with a great desire, to see you face to face. [18] That's why we wanted to come to you – I, Paul, again and again – but the satan got in our way.

[19] Don't you see? When our Lord Jesus is present once more, what is our hope, our joy, the crown of our boasting before him? It's you! [20] Yes: you are our glory and our joy.

The sending of Timothy

3 So, when it got to the point that we couldn't bear it any longer, Silvanus and I decided to remain in Athens by ourselves, [2] and we sent Timothy – our brother, and God's fellow-worker in the gospel of the Messiah – so that he could strengthen you and bring comfort to your faith, [3] so that you wouldn't be pulled off course by these sufferings. You yourselves know, don't you, that this is what we are bound to face. [4] For when we were with you, we told you ahead of time that we would undergo suffering; that's how it has turned out, and you know about it. [5] That's why, when I too couldn't bear it any longer, I sent Timothy, so that I could find out about your faithfulness, in case somehow the tempter had put you to the test and our work would be in ruins.

Timothy's report

[6] But now Timothy has returned to us from you. He has brought us the good news of your faith – and your love; he has told us that you always have good memories of us, and that you are longing to see us, just as we are to see you. [7] So, my dear family, we are comforted about you, in all our difficulties and troubles, because of your faithfulness. [8] Now, you see, we are really alive, if you are standing firmly in the Lord. [9] For what thanks can we give back to God about you, for all the joy which we celebrate because of you in the presence of our God, [10] praying with even more fervour than you can imagine, night and day, that we may see you face to face and may put into proper order anything that is lacking in your faith?

Paul's words of blessing

[11] Now may God himself, our father, and our Lord Jesus, steer us on our way to you. [12] And may the Lord make your love for one another, and for everybody, abound and overflow, just as ours does for you. [13] That way, your hearts will be strengthened and kept blameless in holiness before God our father when our Lord Jesus is present again with all his holy ones. Amen.

Instructions on holy living

4 What remains, my dear family, is for us to ask you, and indeed to urge you in the Lord Jesus, that you should continue more and more to behave in the manner that you received from us as the appropriate way of behaving and of pleasing God. [2] You know, of course, what instructions we gave you through the Lord Jesus. [3] This is God's will, you see: he wants you to be holy, to keep well away from fornication. [4] Each of you should know how to control your own body in holiness and honour, [5] not in the madness of lust like Gentiles who don't know God. [6] Nobody should break this rule, or cheat a fellow Christian in this area; the Lord is the avenger in all such matters, just as we told you before and testified most solemnly. [7] For God did not call us to a dirty life, but in holiness. [8] Anyone who rejects this, then, is not rejecting a human command, but the God who gives his holy spirit to you.

A life of love

[9] Now, about charitable concern for the whole family: I don't really need to write to you, because you yourselves have been taught by God to show loving care for one another. [10] Indeed, you are doing this for all the Christian family in the whole of Macedonia. But we urge you, my dear family, to make this an even more prominent part of your lives. [11] You should make it your ambition to

live peacefully, to mind your own business, and to work with your own hands, just as we commanded you, ¹²so that you may behave in a way which outsiders will respect, and so that none of you may be in financial difficulties.

The Lord's coming

¹³Now concerning those who have fallen asleep: we don't want you to remain in ignorance about them, my dear family. We don't want you to have the kind of grief that other people do, people who don't have any hope. ¹⁴For, you see, if we believe that Jesus died and rose, that's the way God will also, through Jesus, bring with him those who have fallen asleep.

¹⁵Let me explain (this is the word of the Lord I'm speaking to you!). We who are alive, who remain until the Lord is present, will not find ourselves ahead of those who fell asleep. ¹⁶The Lord himself will come down from heaven with a shouted order, with the voice of an archangel and the sound of God's trumpet. The Messiah's dead will rise first; ¹⁷then we who are alive, who are left, will be snatched up with them among the clouds, to meet the Lord in the air. And in this way we shall always be with the Lord. ¹⁸So comfort each other with these words.

Children of light

5 Now when it comes to specific times and dates, my dear family, you don't need to have anyone write to you. ²You yourselves know very well that the day of the Lord will come like a midnight robber. ³When people say, 'Peace and security!', then swift ruin will arrive at their doorstep, like the pains that come over a woman in labour, and they won't have a chance of escape.

⁴But as for you, my dear family – you are not in darkness. That day won't surprise you like a robber. ⁵You are all children of light, children of the day! We don't belong to the night, or to darkness. ⁶So, then, let's not go to sleep, like the others, but let's keep awake and stay sober.

⁷People who sleep, you see, sleep at night. People who get drunk get drunk at night. ⁸But we daytime people should be self-controlled, clothing ourselves with the breastplate of faith and love, and with the helmet of the hope of salvation; ⁹because God has not placed us on the road to fury, but to gaining salvation, through our Lord Jesus the Messiah. ¹⁰He died for us, so that whether we stay awake or go to sleep we should live together with him. ¹¹So strengthen one another, and build each other up, just as you are doing.

Final exhortations

¹²This, my dear family, is the request we make of you. Take note of those who work among you and exercise leadership over you in the Lord, those who give you instruction. ¹³Give them the highest possible rank of love because of their work. Live at peace among yourselves.

¹⁴And, my dear family, we beg you to warn those who step out of line. Console the downcast; help the weak, be warm-hearted and patient towards everybody. ¹⁵Make sure nobody pays anyone back evil for evil. Instead, always find the way to do good to one another, and to everybody.

¹⁶Always celebrate,

¹⁷never stop praying;

¹⁸in everything be thankful

(this is God's will for you in the Messiah Jesus);

¹⁹don't quench the spirit,

²⁰don't look down on prophecies,

²¹test everything,

if something is good, hold it fast;

²²if something looks evil, keep well away.

Final blessings and charge

²³Now may the God of peace himself make you completely holy. May your complete spirit, soul and body be kept blameless at the coming of our Lord Jesus the Messiah. ²⁴The one who calls you is faithful; he will do it.

²⁵My dear family, pray for us.

²⁶Greet the whole family with a holy kiss. ²⁷I charge you by the Lord to have this letter read to the whole family.

²⁸The grace of our Lord Jesus the Messiah be with you.

2 Thessalonians

The second letter to Thessalonica has sometimes had its authenticity questioned, partly because the (to us) strange imagery about the Last Judgment and the events surrounding it seems so different from the Paul of the other letters. But these things were common coin in the Jewish world of Paul's day, and here as elsewhere he seems to be rethinking them in the light of the gospel.

In particular, he is aware that having explained to the Thessalonians about the coming Day of Judgment – in his original preaching and then a little in the first letter – this has not quietened speculation, but has rather increased it. Some are worried that perhaps 'the day of the Lord' might have come and gone and they might have missed it (2.2). This tells us already that 'the day of the Lord' was not thought of, as many in our own times have supposed, in terms of 'the end of the space-time universe', as though the 'heaven' of Christian imagination were so radically separate from 'earth' that if 'heaven' were to establish its kingdom this could only be by the complete abolition of 'earth'. Paul has a very different view; and at the centre of that view he sees the turbulent events of first-century Roman political life, in which in recent memory the emperor Caligula had wanted to set up a giant statue of himself in the Temple in Jerusalem. That crisis had passed (because Caligula was assassinated in the nick of time), but Paul sees it as a warning of what may yet happen. Sooner or later (he expects it to be sooner) the dark energy of latent evil, already dealt a death-blow by the cross but still awaiting final abolition, will draw itself up to its height, and then Jesus will deal with it once and for all. How much of this lurid tale Paul saw as symbolic, and how much he saw as literal, is hard to say. It points on to the similar, and more drawn-out, exposition of the defeat of evil in the book of Revelation.

Greetings and thanksgiving

1 Paul, Silvanus and Timothy, to the assembly of Thessalonians in God our father and the Lord Jesus, the Messiah: ²grace to you and peace from God our father and the Lord Jesus, the Messiah.

³We owe God a constant debt of gratitude concerning you, my dear family. It is only right and proper. Your faith is growing marvellously, and the love which every single one of you has for each other is multiplying. ⁴As a result, we ourselves can tell all the churches of God how proud we are of you – of your patience and loyalty in all your troubles, and in all the sufferings you are going through.

⁵All this is a clear sign of the just judgment of God, to make you thoroughly worthy of the kingdom of God, for which you are suffering – ⁶since it is just, on God's part, to pay back with suffering those who inflict suffering on you, ⁷and to give you, with us, respite from your sufferings.

The coming of Jesus

This will come about when the Lord Jesus is revealed from heaven with his powerful angels, ⁸in a flaming fire, meting out punishment to those who don't know God and those who don't obey the gospel of our Lord Jesus. ⁹They will pay the penalty of eternal destruction from the face of the Lord and from the glory of his power, ¹⁰when he comes to be glorified in all his holy ones, and to be marvelled at by all who believe in him, because our testimony to you was met with faith, on that day.

¹¹To that end we always pray for you, that our God may make you worthy of his call, and may complete every plan he has to do you good, and every work of faith in power, ¹²so that the name of our Lord Jesus may be glorified in you, and you in him, according to the grace of our God and of the Lord Jesus, the Messiah.

The lawless one

2 Now concerning the royal presence of our Lord Jesus the Messiah, and our gathering together around him, this is our request, my dear family. ²Please don't be suddenly blown off course in your thinking, or be unsettled, either through spiritual influence, or through a word, or through a letter supposedly from us, telling you that the day of the Lord has already arrived.

³Don't let anyone deceive you in any way. You see, it can't happen unless first the rebellion takes place, and the man of lawlessness, the son of destruction, is revealed. ⁴He is the one who sets himself against every so-called god or cult object, and usurps their role, so that he installs himself in God's temple, and makes himself out to be a god.

⁵Don't you remember that I told you this while I was with you? ⁶And now you know what is restraining him so that he will be revealed at his proper time. ⁷For the mystery of lawlessness is already at work, but the restrainer is in place – until he is taken away; ⁸and then the lawless one will be revealed. The Lord Jesus will destroy him with the breath of his mouth, and will wipe him out with the unveiling of his presence.

⁹The presence of the lawless one will be accompanied by the activity of the satan, with full power, with signs, and spurious wonders, ¹⁰with every kind of wicked deceit over those on the way to ruin, because they did not receive the love of the truth so as to be saved. ¹¹For that reason God sends upon them a strong delusion, leading them to believe the lie, ¹²so that judgment may come upon all who did not believe the truth but took pleasure in wickedness.

Exhortation to steadfastness

¹³But we always owe God a debt of gratitude for you, my family beloved by the Lord, because God chose you as the first fruits of his work of salvation, through sanctification by the spirit and belief of the truth. ¹⁴To this he called you through our gospel, so that you might obtain the glory of our Lord Jesus the Messiah.

¹⁵So then, my dear family, stand firm, and hold on tight to the traditions which you were taught, whether through what we said or through our letter. ¹⁶And may our Lord Jesus the Messiah himself, and God our father who loved us and gave us eternal comfort and

good hope by grace, ¹⁷comfort your hearts and strengthen you in every good work and word.

Requests for prayer

3 Finally, my dear family, pray for us, that the word of the Lord will go forward quickly and be glorified, as it has among you; ²and that we may be rescued from evil and wicked people. Not all, you see, have faith! ³But the Lord is faithful, and he will strengthen you and guard you from the evil one.

⁴We are confident in the Lord about you, that you are doing, and will continue to do, what we instructed you. ⁵May the Lord direct your hearts towards the love of God and the patience of the Messiah.

The dangers of idleness

⁶Here is a command we have for you, my dear family, in the name of our Lord Jesus the Messiah. Keep away from any member of the family who is stepping out of line, and not behaving according to the tradition that you received from us.

⁷You yourselves know, after all, how you should copy us. We didn't step out of line, ⁸nor did we eat anyone's food without paying for it. We worked night and day, with labour and struggle, so as not to place a burden on any of you. ⁹It wasn't that we don't have the right; it was so that we could give you an example, for you to copy us. ¹⁰And, indeed, when we were with you, we gave you this command: those who won't work shouldn't eat!

¹¹You see, we hear that there are some among you who are stepping out of line, behaving in an unruly fashion, not being busy with real work, but just busybodies. ¹²To people like that we give this commandment and exhortation in the Lord Jesus the Messiah: do your own work in peace, and eat your own bread. ¹³As for you, my dear family, don't get tired of doing what is right!

Final remarks

¹⁴If anyone doesn't obey our word in this letter, take note of them. Don't have any dealings with such a person, so that they may be ashamed. ¹⁵Don't consider a person like this an enemy: rebuke them as a member of the family. ¹⁶Now may the Lord of peace give you peace always in every way. The Lord be with you all.

¹⁷I, Paul, am sending you this greeting in my own hand. This is the sign in each letter of mine; this is how I write. ¹⁸The grace of our Lord Jesus the Messiah be with you all.

1 Timothy

The two letters to Timothy, and the letter to Titus (often referred to as the Pastoral Epistles), present us with a different kind of challenge. The style, particularly of 1 Timothy and Titus, is quite different; not different as the first and second letters to Corinth are different, but different in tone, in the use of key phrases, in the overall structure of sentences. Computers have been brought in to assess the stylistic differences but the results are uncertain (partly because the small size of the sample makes it difficult to judge). Most scholars find it difficult to see Paul as the author. A further problem is that the small personal notes, about the movements and location of Paul's associates, cannot be made to fit with Acts 13—28. It is possible, despite what Paul said about having finished work in the eastern Mediterranean, that he did in fact make another trip there after a trial in Rome. If so, then perhaps the details might be made to fit.

The two letters to Timothy are themselves very different in both style and character. The first letter moves from topic to topic (not entirely unlike 1 Corinthians). Timothy has been left behind in Ephesus as a teacher, and must give himself to that work, urging mutual love, resisting false or deluded teachings, stressing the constant duty of prayer, and in particular taking care over the selection of persons to hold leadership and teaching roles within the church.

The letter draws to a rhetorical conclusion by looking ahead with joy to the 'royal appearing' of Jesus; the language echoes things that were said about the Roman emperor (6.11–16). But the actual conclusion is yet more practical teaching: if there are rich Jesus-followers, they are not to idolize their riches but to use them for the common good. Then one more flicker of a warning: there is something called 'knowledge' (Gk. *gnōsis*) which is gaining ground in the community. It must be resisted. Paul (or whoever wrote this letter) could hardly have guessed how large a problem this was to be a hundred years later, as some of the greatest teachers of the day fought hard against the gospel-sapping theories of 'gnosticism'.

True teaching about the truth

1 Paul, an apostle of King Jesus according to the command of God our saviour and King Jesus our hope, ²to Timothy, my true child in faith: grace, mercy and peace from God the father and King Jesus our Lord.

³This is my charge to you, just as it was when I went to Macedonia: stay in Ephesus, so that you can tell the relevant people not to teach anything different, ⁴or to cling on to myths and endless genealogies. That sort of thing breeds disputes rather than the instruction in faith that comes from God. ⁵The goal of such instruction is love – the love that comes from a pure heart, a good conscience and sincere faith. ⁶Some people have wandered off from these things and turned aside to foolish talk. ⁷They want to be teachers of the law; but they don't understand either what they're talking about or the things about which they pronounce so confidently.

The purpose of the law

⁸We know, after all, that the law is good – if someone uses it lawfully! ⁹We recognize that the law is not laid down for people who are in the right, but for the lawless and disobedient, for the godless and sinners, the unholy and worldly, for people who kill their father or mother, for murderers, ¹⁰fornicators, practising homosexuals, slave traders, liars, perjurers, and those who practise any other behaviour contrary to healthy teaching, ¹¹in accordance with the gospel of the glory of God the blessed one that was entrusted to me.

Paul as an example of God's saving grace

¹²I thank King Jesus our Lord, who gave me strength. He regarded me as trustworthy by appointing me to his service – ¹³even though I used to say blasphemous things against him, and persecuted his people violently! But I received mercy, because in my unbelief I didn't know what I was doing. ¹⁴And the grace of our Lord was more than enough for me, with the faith and love that are in King Jesus. ¹⁵Here is a word you can trust, which deserves total approval: 'King Jesus came into the world to save sinners' – and I'm the worst of them! ¹⁶But this was why I received mercy: so that in me, precisely as the worst, King Jesus could demonstrate the full scale of his patience, and make me a pattern for those who were going to believe in him and so attain the life of the age to come. ¹⁷To the King of the ages, the one and only God, immortal and invisible, be honour and glory to the ages of ages, Amen!

The battle of faith

¹⁸I am giving you this command, Timothy my child, in accordance with the prophecies which were made about you before, so that, as they said, you may fight the glorious battle, ¹⁹holding on to faith and a good conscience. Some have rejected conscience, and their faith has been shipwrecked. ²⁰I include Hymenaeus and Alexander in that category. Indeed, I have handed them over to the satan, so that they may be taught not to blaspheme.

The first rule: prayer for the world

2 So, then, this is my very first command: God's people should make petitions, prayers, intercessions and thanksgivings on behalf of all people – ²on behalf of kings, and all who hold high office, so that we may lead a tranquil and peaceful life, in all godliness and holiness. ³This is good; it is acceptable with God our saviour, ⁴who wants all people to be saved and to come to know the truth. ⁵For, you see,

> There is one God,
> and also one mediator between God and humans,
> King Jesus, himself a human being.
> ⁶He gave himself as a ransom for all,
> and this was testified when the time was right.

⁷This is why I was appointed a herald and an apostle (I'm speaking the truth, I'm not lying!), a teacher of the Gentiles in faith and truth.

Women must be allowed to be learners

⁸So this is what I want: the men should pray in every place, lifting up holy hands, with no anger

or disputing. ⁹In the same way the women, too, should clothe themselves decently, being modest and sensible about it. They should not go in for elaborate hairstyles, or gold, or pearls, or expensive clothes. ¹⁰Instead, as is appropriate for women who profess to be godly, they should adorn themselves with good works. ¹¹They must study undisturbed, in full submission to God. ¹²I'm not saying that women should teach men, or try to dictate to them; rather, that they should be left undisturbed. ¹³Adam was created first, you see, and then Eve; ¹⁴and Adam was not deceived, but the woman was deceived, and fell into trespass. ¹⁵She will, however, be kept safe through the process of childbirth, if she continues in faith, love and holiness with prudence.

The character of a bishop

3 Here is a trustworthy saying: if someone is eager for the work of overseeing God's people, the task they seek is a fine one. ²The bishop must be beyond reproach. He must not have more than one wife. He must be temperate, sensible, respectable, hospitable, a good teacher. ³He must not be a heavy drinker, or violent, but must be gentle, not quarrelsome, and not in love with money. ⁴He must be good at managing his own household, with his children being subject to him with all godliness. (⁵After all, if a man doesn't know how to run his own household, how can he take care of God's church?) ⁶He must not be a recent convert, in case he gets puffed up and falls into the devil's condemnation. ⁷In addition, he must have a good reputation with outsiders, so that he may not incur reproach and fall into the devil's snare.

The character of deacons

⁸In the same way, deacons must be serious-minded, not the sort of people who say one thing today and another tomorrow, not heavy drinkers, not eager for shameful gain. ⁹They must hold on to the mystery of the faith with a pure conscience. ¹⁰They must first be tested; then, when they have been found without reproach, they may serve as deacons. ¹¹The womenfolk, too, should be serious-minded, not slanderers, but temperate and faithful in all things. ¹²Deacons should have only one wife, and should be well in charge of their children and their own households. ¹³Those who serve well as deacons, you see, gain a good platform for themselves to speak out boldly in the faith which is in King Jesus.

The mystery of godliness

¹⁴I'm writing this to you in the hope that I'll be able to come to you in the near future. ¹⁵But, if I'm delayed, this will help you to know how people should behave in God's household, which is the assembly of the living God, the pillar and firm foundation of the truth. ¹⁶Indeed, the mystery of godliness is certainly great:

He was revealed in the flesh,
and vindicated in the spirit;
he appeared to angels,
and was announced to Gentiles;
he was believed in the world,
and taken up in glory.

Beware of false teaching!

4 Now the spirit specifically declares that in the last times some people will abandon the faith, and will cling on to deceitful spirits and demonic teachings ²perpetrated by hypocritical false teachers whose consciences are branded with a hot iron. ³They will forbid marriage, and teach people to abstain from foods which God created to be received with thanksgiving by people who believe and know the truth. ⁴Every creation of God, you see, is good; nothing is to be rejected if it is received with thanksgiving, ⁵for then it is made holy by God's word and prayer.

Get into training!

⁶Set these instructions before the family. If you do this, you will be a good servant of King Jesus; you will be nourished by the words of faith and the good teaching which you

have been following. ⁷Keep well away from worthless myths, the sort of things some old women mumble on about.

Go into training in godliness! ⁸Physical exercise, you see, has a limited usefulness, but godliness is useful in every way. It carries the promise of life both now and in the future. ⁹That saying is trustworthy; it deserves to be accepted totally! ¹⁰This is what we are working and struggling for, you see, because we have set our hope on the living God, who is the saviour of all people – more especially, of believers.

Pay attention to yourself and your teaching

¹¹You must urge and teach these things. ¹²Don't let anyone look down on you because you are young, but be an example to the believers in what you say, how you behave, in love, faith and holiness. ¹³Until I come, give attention to reading, to exhortation and to teaching. ¹⁴Don't neglect the gift that is in you, which was given to you through prophecy when the elders laid hands on you. ¹⁵Work hard at these things; give yourself to them, so that everyone may see your progress. ¹⁶Pay attention to yourself and your teaching, and keep steadily on with them. If you do that, you see, you will save yourself, and those who hear you as well.

Human families and God's family

5 Don't rebuke a senior man in the church, but exhort him as you might do with your father – or, in the case of younger ones, with your brothers. ²Treat the older women as mothers, and the younger ones as sisters, with all purity.

³Pay respect to widows who really are widows. ⁴If a widow has children or grandchildren, let them first learn to respect their own family and to make some repayment to those who brought them up. This, you see, pleases God. ⁵A real widow is one who, left by herself, has set her hope on God, and continues in prayer and supplication night and day; ⁶but a self-indulgent woman is dead even while she's alive. ⁷Give these commands so that they may be beyond blame. ⁸If anyone doesn't take care of their own relatives, especially their own household, they have denied the faith; they are worse than unbelievers.

Widows

⁹Let a woman be registered as a widow if she is at least sixty years old, the wife of one husband, ¹⁰with a reputation for good works, having brought up children, shown hospitality, washed the feet of God's people, helped those who were suffering, and been steadfast in doing good wherever she can. ¹¹Refuse to register younger widows. When their desires become strong against the King, you see, they will want to marry, ¹²and they will receive condemnation because they have abandoned their earlier faith. ¹³In addition, they learn the habit of idleness, going around from one house to another, not only doing nothing but gossiping and meddling, saying things they shouldn't.

¹⁴So this is my wish: the younger ones should marry, have children, run their households and give the enemy no opportunity to slander us (¹⁵some, you see, have already gone off after the satan!). ¹⁶If any believing woman has relatives who are widowed, let her help them, so that the church won't be burdened. That way, it can help widows who really are widows.

Elders

¹⁷Elders who are good leaders ought to be paid double, particularly those who work hard in speaking and teaching. ¹⁸The Bible says, you see, 'Don't muzzle an ox when it's threshing', and 'the worker deserves his pay'.

¹⁹Don't accept an accusation against an elder, unless it is supported 'by two or three witnesses'. ²⁰When people persist in sin, rebuke them openly, so that the rest may be afraid.

²¹Before God, King Jesus and the chosen angels, I give you solemn warning to keep these commands without discrimination. Never act out of favouritism. ²²Don't be too quick to lay hands on anyone; don't share in other people's sins. Keep yourself pure.

²³You should stop confining yourself to drinking water. Use wine (in moderation!). That will be good for your digestion, and for the physical problems you often have.

²⁴Some people's sins are obvious, and walk ahead of them into the courtroom. Other people's follow them there. ²⁵In the same way, good works are obvious; but, even when they aren't, they can't stay hidden for ever.

Slaves, masters and sound teaching

6 All who live as slaves, 'under the yoke' so to speak, should consider their own masters as worthy of all respect, so that people may not say wicked things against the name of God and the teaching. ²Those who have masters who are also believers should not look down on them because they are brothers, but rather give them service, since those who receive the benefit of their work are beloved fellow believers.

Teach these things, and exhort people to do them. ³Some people teach other things, and don't hold firmly to the healthy words of our Lord King Jesus, and the teaching which goes with piety; ⁴people like that are conceited and have no understanding. They have a diseased craving for disputes and arguments about words. That just leads to envy, jealousy, evil speaking, wicked suspicions ⁵and irritating arguments among people with depraved minds who have lost their grip on the truth and imagine that godliness is a means of gain.

Godliness and contentment

⁶If it's gain you want, though, there is plenty to be had in godliness – if it's combined with contentment. ⁷We brought nothing into the world, after all, and we certainly can't take anything out. ⁸If we have food and clothing, we should be satisfied with it. ⁹People who want to be rich, by contrast, fall into temptation and a trap, into many foolish and dangerous lusts which drown people in devastation and destruction. ¹⁰The love of money, you see, is the root of all evil. Some people have been so eager to get rich that they have wandered away from the faith and have impaled themselves painfully in several ways.

The king's royal appearing

¹¹But you, man of God – you must run away from all this. Instead, chase after justice, godliness, faith, love, patience and gentleness. ¹²Fight the noble fight of the faith, get a firm grasp on the life of the coming age, the life you were called to when you made the noble public profession before many witnesses. ¹³I give you this charge before God, who gives life to all things, and King Jesus, who made the noble profession before Pontius Pilate: ¹⁴be undefiled and blameless as you keep the commandment, until the royal appearing of our Lord King Jesus, ¹⁵which the blessed and only Sovereign One, the King of kings and Lord of lords, will reveal at its proper time. ¹⁶He is the only one who possesses immortality; he lives in unapproachable light; no human being has seen him, or can see him. To him be eternal honour and power, Amen!

What to do with money

¹⁷What about people who are rich in this present world? Tell them not to think of themselves too highly, and to set their hopes, not on something so uncertain as riches, but on the God who richly provides us with everything to enjoy. ¹⁸They are to do good, to be rich in good works, generous and eager to share. ¹⁹That way, they will treasure up for themselves a good foundation for the future, and thereby come to possess the life which really is life.

²⁰Well then, Timothy: keep guard over what has been entrusted to you. Turn away from the pointless and empty talk and contradictions of what is wrongly called 'knowledge'. ²¹Some have claimed to be experts in it, but have missed the target when it comes to the faith.

Grace be with you all.

2 Timothy

The second letter to Timothy is written from prison, and it seems as though the writer knows his time is near. He reflects on his past work; he celebrates the central truths of the gospel, reflecting that though he is in chains nothing can tie up God's word (2.8–10). Bad times will come, and false teachers too; folk will listen eagerly to people who tell them what they already want to hear. But the example and teaching of the truth must be maintained. Paul – if it is he – sounds tired at the end, urging Timothy to come to him soon, and certainly before winter (4.9, 21). There is a hint of a sequence of trials (4.16–18); so far Paul has escaped being thrown to the lions (4.17; though that may be a metaphor), but this may not last much longer (4.6). It is a deeply personal letter, somewhat rambling but full of passion and faith, and deep affection for the younger man. If it is hard to fit its details into any Pauline itinerary that we know of, it is hard to imagine someone other than Paul writing in his name in so personal a fashion.

Rekindle the gift!

1 Paul, an apostle of King Jesus by God's will, according to the promise of life in King Jesus; ²to Timothy, my dear child. Grace, mercy and peace from God the father and King Jesus our Lord.

³I serve God with a clear conscience, as my forebears did, and I am grateful to him that I remember you all the time, as I pray for you night and day. ⁴I remember how you cried when I left, and I'm longing to see you and be filled with joy. ⁵I have in my mind a clear picture of your sincere faith – the faith which first came to live in Lois your grandmother and Eunice your mother, and which, I am confident, lives in you as well.

⁶That's why I now want to remind you that God gave you a gift when I laid my hands on you, and that you must bring it back into a blazing fire! ⁷After all, the spirit given to us by God isn't a fearful spirit; it's a spirit of power, love and prudence.

Don't be ashamed!

⁸So don't be ashamed of the testimony of our Lord, nor of me as his prisoner. Rather, suffer for the gospel along with us, in accordance with God's power. ⁹God saved us, and called us with a holy calling, not according to our works, but according to his own purpose and grace. He gave us this grace in King Jesus before all time and ages, ¹⁰but has now made it visible through the appearing of our saviour King Jesus, who abolished death and, through the gospel, shone a bright light on life and immortality.

¹¹I was made a herald, apostle and teacher for this gospel; ¹²that's why I suffer these things. But I am not ashamed, because I know the one I have trusted, and I'm convinced that he has the power to keep safe until that day what I have entrusted to him.

¹³Keep a firm hold on the pattern of healthy teaching which you heard from me, in the faith and love which are in King Jesus. ¹⁴You have had something very important entrusted to you, too; make sure you look after it, through the holy spirit who dwells in us.

Foes and friends

¹⁵You will know that everyone in Asia has turned away from me, including Phygelus and Hermogenes. ¹⁶May the Lord give mercy to the household of Onesiphorus; he has often refreshed me. He wasn't ashamed of my chains, ¹⁷but when he was in Rome he eagerly hunted for me and found me. ¹⁸May the Lord grant him to find mercy from the Lord on that day. And you know very well all the things he did for me in Ephesus.

Conditions of service

2 So, then, my child: you must be strong in the grace which is in King Jesus. ²You heard the teaching I gave in public; pass it on to faithful people who will be capable of instructing others as well. ³Take your share of suffering as one of King Jesus' good soldiers. ⁴No one who serves in the army gets embroiled in civilian activities, since they want to please the officer who enlisted them. ⁵If you take part in athletic events, you don't win the crown unless you compete according to the rules. ⁶The farmer who does the work deserves the first share of the crops. ⁷Think about what I say; the Lord will give you understanding in everything.

God's word is not tied up

⁸Remember Jesus the King, risen from the dead, from the seed of David, according to my gospel – ⁹for which I suffer like a criminal, even being chained up! But God's word is not tied up. ¹⁰That's why I put up with everything for the sake of God's chosen ones, so that they too may obtain, with glory that lasts for ever, the salvation which is in King Jesus. ¹¹You can rely on this saying:

If we die with him, we shall live with him;
¹²if we endure patiently, we shall reign with him;
if we deny him, he will deny us;
¹³if we are faithless, he remains faithful, for he cannot deny his own self.

Foolish words and the word of truth

¹⁴Remind them about these things; and warn them, in God's presence, not to quarrel about words. This doesn't do any good; instead, it threatens to ruin people who listen to it. ¹⁵Do your very best to present yourself before God as one who has passed the test – a workman who has no need to be ashamed, who can carve out a straight path for the word of truth. ¹⁶Avoid pointless and empty chatter. It will push people further and further towards ungodliness, ¹⁷and their talk will spread like a cancer. I'm thinking in particular of Hymenaeus and Philetus; ¹⁸they have turned aside from the truth by saying that the resurrection has already happened. They are upsetting some people's faith. ¹⁹But God's firm foundation stands, and it has this as its seal: 'The Lord knows those who belong to him', and 'Everyone who uses the name of the Lord must leave wickedness behind.'

Vessels for God's use

²⁰In a great house there are vessels not only of gold and silver, but also of wood and pottery. Some of them are given special honour in the way they're used; others are for menial purposes. ²¹So if people purify themselves from dishonourable things, they will become vessels for honour, made holy, pleasing to the master of the house, fit for every good work.

²²Run away from the passions of youth. Instead, chase after justice, faith, love and peace; you'll be in the company of all who call on the Lord from a pure heart. ²³Avoid silly and unprofitable disputes, because you know that they produce fights; ²⁴and the Lord's servant mustn't be a fighter, but must be gentle to all people, able to teach, able to bear evil without resentment, ²⁵able to correct opponents with a meek spirit. It may be that God will give them repentance so that they can arrive at a knowledge of the truth, ²⁶and, in coming to their senses, escape the devil's snare, after having been held captive by him and made to do his will.

Opponents of the truth

3 You need to know this: bad times are coming in the last days. ²People will be in love with themselves, you see, and with money too. They will be boastful, arrogant, abusive, haters of parents, ungrateful, unholy, ³unfeeling, implacable, accusing, dissolute, savage, haters of the good, ⁴traitors, reckless, puffed up, lovers of pleasure rather than lovers of God, ⁵holding on to a pattern of godliness but denying its power. Avoid people like that! ⁶This group, you see, includes those who worm their way into people's houses and ensnare foolish women who are overwhelmed with their sins and are pulled and pushed by all kinds of desires, ⁷always learning but never able to arrive at the truth. ⁸Just as Jannes and Jambres stood up against Moses, so people like this oppose the truth. In their minds they are corrupt; in their faith they are of no account. ⁹They won't get very far, though, because their foolishness will become obvious to everyone, as it was with those two.

Continue in the scriptures!

¹⁰So what about you? You have followed my teaching faithfully, and also my way of life, my aims and goals, my faith, longsuffering, love and patience, ¹¹my persecutions, my sufferings, the things I went through in Antioch, in Iconium, in Lystra, the persecutions I endured – and the Lord rescued me from all of them. ¹²Yes, everyone who wants to live a godly life in King Jesus will be persecuted, ¹³while evil people and impostors will go on to even worse things, deceiving others and being themselves deceived. ¹⁴But you, on the other hand, must stand firm in the things you learned and believed. You know who it was you received them from, ¹⁵and how from childhood you have known the holy writings which have the power to make you wise for salvation through faith in King Jesus. ¹⁶All scripture is breathed by God, and it is useful for teaching, for rebuke, for improvement, for training in righteousness, ¹⁷so that people who belong to God may be complete, fitted out and ready for every good work.

Judgment is coming – so get on with your work

4 This is my solemn charge to you, in the presence of God and King Jesus, who will judge the living and the dead, and by his appearance and his kingdom: ²announce the word; keep going whether the time is right or wrong; rebuke, warn and encourage with all patience and explanation. ³The time is coming, you see, when people won't tolerate healthy teaching. Their ears will start to itch, and they will collect for themselves teachers who will tell them what they want to hear. ⁴They will turn away from listening to the truth and will go after myths instead. ⁵But as for you, keep your balance in everything! Put up with suffering; do the work of an evangelist; complete the particular task assigned to you.

Waiting for the crown

⁶For I am already being poured out as a drink-offering; my departure time has arrived. ⁷I have fought the good fight; I have completed the course; I have kept the faith. ⁸What do I still have to look for? The crown of righteousness! The Lord, the righteous judge, will give it to me as my reward on that day – and not only to me, but also to all who have loved his appearing.

Come to me soon

⁹Make every effort to come to me soon. ¹⁰Demas, you see, has left me and gone to Thessalonica; he's in love with this present world! Crescens has gone to Galatia, and Titus to Dalmatia. ¹¹Luke is the only one with me. Get Mark and bring him with you; he's very helpful in looking after me. ¹²I sent Tychicus to Ephesus. ¹³I left a cloak at Carpus' house in Troas; please bring it with you when you come – and also the scrolls, and especially the books.

¹⁴Alexander the coppersmith did me a lot of damage. The Lord will pay him back according to what he's done! ¹⁵Watch out for him yourself. He stood out strongly against our message.

¹⁶The first time my case came to court nobody showed up to support me; they all left me alone. May it not be reckoned against them! ¹⁷But the Lord stood there beside me and gave me strength to enable me to complete my work as his royal herald, and to make sure all the Gentiles heard the proclamation; and I was snatched clear of the lion's mouth. ¹⁸The Lord will snatch me clear from every wicked deed and will save me for his heavenly kingdom. Glory to him for the ages of ages, Amen!

¹⁹Greet Prisca and Aquila, and the household of Onesiphorus.

²⁰Erastus stayed in Corinth. I left Trophimus behind in Miletus, where he was sick.

²¹Do your best to come before winter.

Eubulus sends his greetings; so do Pudens, Linus, Claudia, and all the family.

²²The Lord be with your spirit. Grace be with you all.

Titus

The short letter to Titus assumes that Paul has left him in Crete; again, this doesn't fit with the itineraries we know from Acts, so if the letter is genuine we would have to assume a substantial further period of work in the central Mediterranean region. As in 1 Timothy, one of the important things will be to appoint church leaders, particularly people who will be able to address the problems of the local culture. Church members must be reminded again and again that part of the point of the whole Christian movement is to be a family that engages in good, creative work in the wider community; this is what is meant by 'good works' (2.7, 14; 3.1, 8, 14). What matters – what will create the best impact for the gospel – is if this otherwise strange and apparently subversive 'family' is seen to be making their street, their village, their town, a better place. Disputes and divisions are inevitable, but so far as possible these are to be avoided; they will eat up energy and do nobody any good.

God's revealed plan

1 From Paul, a slave of God and an apostle of Jesus the king, in accordance with the faith of God's chosen people, and the knowledge of the truth that goes with godliness, ²in the hope of the life of the coming age. God, who never lies, promised this before the ages began, ³and has now, at the right time, unveiled his word through the proclamation entrusted to me, according to the command of our divine saviour.

⁴To Titus, my true child, according to the faith which we share.

Grace and peace from God the father and King Jesus our saviour.

Appointing elders

⁵This is why I left you in Crete: you are to set straight all the remaining matters, and appoint elders for every town, as I charged you to do. ⁶Elders must be blameless, the husband of only one wife. Their children must be believers, and must not be open to the accusation of loose living, or being rebellious. ⁷This is because an overseer, as one of God's household managers, must be blameless. He must not be stubborn, or hotheaded, or a heavy drinker, or a bully, or eager for shameful gain. ⁸He must be hospitable, a lover of goodness, sensible, just, holy and self-controlled. ⁹He must hold firmly to the reliable word which goes with the teaching, so that he may have the power both to exhort people with healthy instruction and to give a proper rebuttal to those who oppose it.

The problems in Crete

¹⁰There are many, you see, who refuse to come into line – people who speak foolishness and deceive others. This is true in particular of the circumcision party. ¹¹It's important that they should be silenced, because they are overturning whole households by teaching things that shouldn't be taught – and trying to make a shameful living out of it! ¹²One of their own, a native prophet, said, 'Cretans are always liars, evil animals, idle guzzlers.' ¹³This testimony is true! That's why you must rebuke them sternly, so that they may become healthy in the faith, ¹⁴paying no attention to Jewish myths and the commandments of people who reject the truth. ¹⁵Everything is pure to people who are pure. But if people are defiled or faithless, nothing is pure for them; even their mind and conscience are defiled. ¹⁶They declare that they know God, but they deny him by what they do. They are detestable and disobedient, and useless for any good work.

Commands to households

2 So what must you do? Just this: you must instruct people how to conduct themselves in accordance with healthy teaching.

²The older men are to be sober, dignified, sensible, and healthy in faith, love and patience. ³In the same way, older women are to be reverent in their behaviour, not slanderers or enslaved to heavy drinking, able to teach what is good. ⁴That way, they can give sensible instructions to the younger women on how to love their husbands and their children, ⁵and how to be sensible, holy, good at looking after the household, and submissive to their own husbands, so that people won't have bad things to say about the word of God. ⁶You must urge the younger men, in the same way, to be sensible ⁷in all things.

Make sure you present yourself as a pattern of good works. Your teaching must be consistent and serious, ⁸in healthy speech that is beyond reproach. That way, our opponents will be ashamed, since they won't have anything bad to say about us.

⁹Slaves must be submissive in everything to their masters. They must do what is wanted and not answer back ¹⁰or help themselves to their masters' property. They are to show good faith in everything, so that in every way they may be a good advertisement for the teaching of God our saviour.

Grace, hope and holiness

¹¹God's saving grace, you see, appeared for all people. ¹²It teaches us that we should turn our backs on ungodliness and the passions of the

world, and should live sober, just and devout lives in the present age, ¹³while we wait eagerly for the blessed hope and royal appearing of the glory of our great God and saviour, Jesus the King. ¹⁴He gave himself for us so that he could ransom us from all lawless actions and purify for himself a people as his very own who would be eager for good works.

¹⁵This is what you must say. Exhort people and rebuke them. Use full authority. Don't let anyone look down on you.

God's kindness and generosity – and ours

3 Remind them to submit to rulers and authorities, to be obedient, to be ready for every good work. ²They are not to speak evil of anyone, nor to be quarrelsome, but to be kindly. They must be completely gentle with everyone.

³We ourselves, you see, used at one time to be foolish, disobedient, deceived, and enslaved to various kinds of passions and pleasures. We spent our time in wickedness and jealousy. We were despicable in ourselves, and we hated each other. ⁴But when the kindness and generous love of God our saviour appeared, ⁵he saved us, not by works that we did in righteousness, but in accordance with his own mercy, through the washing of the new birth and the renewal of the holy spirit, ⁶which was poured out richly upon us through Jesus, our king and saviour, ⁷so that we might be justified by his grace and be made his heirs, in accordance with the hope of the life of the age to come. ⁸The saying is sure.

Watch out for disputes and divisions

I want you to insist on these things, so that those who have put their faith in God may take care to be energetic in good works. Such things are good and profitable for people. ⁹But stay well clear of foolish disputes, genealogies, quarrels and squabbles about the law; they serve no purpose, and are worthless. ¹⁰If someone is causing divisions, give them a first warning, then a second, and then avoid them. ¹¹You know that a person like that is twisted, sinful and self-condemned.

¹²When I send Artemas to you, or maybe Tychicus, do your best to come to me at Nicopolis. That's where I've decided to spend the winter. ¹³Give a really good send-off to Zenas the lawyer and Apollos; make sure they don't go short of anything. ¹⁴All our people must learn to busy themselves with good works, so that they may meet any urgent needs that arise, and not be unfruitful.

¹⁵All the people with me send you their greetings. Greet those who love us in faith. Grace be with you all.

Philemon

Paul's shortest letter is none the less profound. He writes to Philemon, a householder in Colossae. Like all householders in the ancient world, Philemon had slaves, and one of them, Onesimus, had run away. That might itself warrant the death penalty, and anyone harbouring a runaway would likewise risk criminal charges. But Onesimus had come to Paul, and under his guidance he had become a Christian. What was Paul to do?

We might prefer it if Paul had grandstanded, declaring that one should simply free all slaves at once. Instead he will put a time-bomb beside the institution (and yes, we may regret that it took so long to explode), but in the meantime he will do what he does best: reconciliation. That will be hard. Paul does hint, late in the letter, that Philemon might free Onesimus; but Onesimus must first go back to be reconciled, and Philemon must welcome him. They are brothers in the Messiah; nothing less will do.

All is summed up in the prayer of verse 6. Paul is praying that the partnership he and Philemon enjoy, the 'fellowship' in their shared faith, will have its powerful effect in bringing to realization, to a practical result, the good things that are at work in us to lead us into the King, the Messiah. Paul's prayer is that this 'work', going on secretly within each man, will lead them to reconciled unity. The fact that we still have this little gem of a letter seems to imply that the appeal was successful.

Greetings

¹Paul, a prisoner of King Jesus, and Timothy our brother: to our beloved Philemon, our colleague and partner, ²to Apphia our sister, and to Archippus our comrade-in-arms, and to God's people who meet in their house. ³May grace and peace be upon you, from God our father and King Jesus the Lord.

⁴I always thank my God when your name comes up in my prayers, ⁵because I've heard of your love and faithful loyalty towards the Lord Jesus and to all God's people. ⁶My prayer is this: that the partnership which goes with your faith may have its powerful effect, in realizing every good thing that is at work in us to lead us into the King. ⁷You see, my dear brother, your love gives me so much joy and comfort! You have refreshed the hearts of God's people.

Paul's appeal

⁸Because of all this I could be very bold in the King, and order you to do the right thing. ⁹But, because of love, I'd much rather appeal to you – yes, it's me, Paul, speaking, an old man as I am and now a prisoner of King Jesus! ¹⁰I am appealing to you about my child, the one I have fathered here in prison: Onesimus, 'Mr Useful'. ¹¹There was a time when he was use*less* to you; but now he's very useful, to you and to me.

¹²I'm sending him to you for your decision – yes, sending the man himself; and this means sending my own heart. ¹³I would have liked to keep him here with me, so that he could have been your representative in serving me in the chains of the gospel. ¹⁴But I didn't want to do anything without you knowing about it. That way, when you did the splendid thing that the situation requires, it wouldn't be under compulsion, but of your own free will.

Paul's perspective

¹⁵Look at it like this. Maybe this is the reason he was separated from you for a while, so that you could have him back for ever – ¹⁶no longer as a slave, but much more than a slave, as a beloved brother, beloved especially to me, but how much more to you, both as part of your household and in the Lord. ¹⁷So, anyway, if you reckon me a partner in your work, receive him as though he was me. ¹⁸And if he's wronged you in any way, or owes you anything, put that down on my account. ¹⁹This is me, Paul, writing with my own hand: I'll pay you back (and far be it from me to remind you that you owe me your own very self!). ²⁰Yes, my brother, I want some benefit from you in the Lord! Refresh my heart in the King.

²¹As I write this I'm confident that you'll do what I say. In fact, I know you'll do more than I say. ²²But, at the same time, get a guest room ready for me. I'm hoping, you see, that through your prayers I will be granted to you.

²³Epaphras, my fellow prisoner in King Jesus, sends you greetings. ²⁴So do Mark, Aristarchus, Demas and Luke, my colleagues here.

²⁵The grace of the Lord, King Jesus, be with your spirit.

Hebrews

The letter to the Hebrews is the most sustained 'new covenant' argument, taking passage after passage from Israel's scriptures and explaining that these texts pointed forwards to a coming fulfilment through which Israel's sacrificial system would become redundant. This message seems to be addressed to people for whom the Jewish world seemed safer, more familiar, than the strange new world of the Jesus-movement; the writer is explaining that such safety is an illusion, since through the sacrifice of Jesus God has joined heaven and earth together in the new way for which the old world, and the 'old covenant', had been longing. The letter refers to the wilderness Tabernacle rather than the Jerusalem Temple as such, so opinion has been divided as to whether it was written before or after the destruction of the latter in AD 70.

The writer (who remains anonymous) weaves his sophisticated discourse around four texts in particular. Psalm 95, he points out, was written when the Israelites were already enjoying 'rest' in the promised land, but it points on to another, further 'rest' still remaining. Psalm 110 speaks of a coming king who is also a priest, not in the line of Aaron but 'according to the order of Melchizedek', the ancient priest to whom Abraham himself paid tithes. Jeremiah 31 promised a 'new covenant' which would take the place of the original Mosaic covenant, and would accomplish what the Mosaic regulations could not, namely, forgiveness of sins. Psalm 40, read as a prophecy of the Messiah, declared that God did not ultimately want 'sacrifices and offerings' but rather the free self-offering which Jesus has now performed. Chapter 11 turns this complex argument into a single narrative, telling the story of Israel as the journey of faith, leading to Jesus himself (12.1-2) and to the promise of the new creation (12.28).

Hebrews is remarkable above all for its portrait of Jesus. Like John and Colossians, the book draws on the Jewish traditions of creation and 'wisdom' to insist that Jesus is the one through whom God created the worlds (1.2). He is massively superior to the angels (1.4-14), not least because he is the ultimate, genuine human being, seen in Genesis and in Psalm 8, to whom all things are now subject (2.5-9). The full humanness of Jesus is in fact a major theme here, both in the echo of Jesus' agony in Gethsemane (5.7) and in his resurrection and ascension through which, as the true High Priest, he 'always lives to make intercession' for his people (7.25). In his death he has defeated the devil himself (2.14), since he offered the perfect sacrifice (7.27; 9.23-28), not simply in being killed (that was only ever the prelude to the real sacrificial moment) but in the presentation of his lifeblood in the heavenly sanctuary as the cleansing agent, enabling heaven and earth to come together and sinners to be forgiven.

The letter repeatedly applies all this to people tempted to slide back into the more socially acceptable world of continuing Jewish piety. No, he says: you must press on (6.1-12; 10.19-39).

God's one and only son

1 In many ways and by many means God spoke in ancient times to our ancestors in the prophets; ²but at the end of these days he spoke to us in a son.

> He appointed this son to be heir of all things;
> through him, in addition, he created the worlds.
> ³He is the shining reflection of God's own glory,
> the precise expression of his own very being;
> he sustains all things through his powerful word.
> He accomplished the cleansing needed for sins,
> and sat down at the right of the Majesty Supreme.
> ⁴See how much greater he is than the angels:
> the name he was granted is finer than theirs.

⁵For to which angel did God ever say, 'You are my son, today I became your father'? Or, again, 'I will be his father, and he will be my son'?

The Messiah is superior to angels

⁶Again, when God brings the firstborn son into the world, he says,

> Let all God's angels worship him.

⁷In relation to the angels, this is what it says:

> God makes his angels spirits, and his servants flames of fire.

⁸In relation to the son, however, it says,

> Your throne, O God, is for ever and ever;
> the sceptre of uprightness is the sceptre of your kingdom;
> ⁹you loved justice and hated lawlessness,
> therefore God, your God, anointed you with the oil of gladness,
> as superior to your comrades.

¹⁰And, again:

> You established the earth, O Lord, from the beginning;
> and the heavens are the works of your hands;
> ¹¹they will be destroyed, but you will remain;
> all of them will grow old like clothing,
> ¹²you will roll them up like a cloak,
> and they will be changed like clothing.
> But you are the same, and your years will never give out.

¹³But to which of the angels did God ever say,

> Sit at my right hand,
> until I make your enemies a stool for your feet?

¹⁴Must we not say, then, that the angels are all servant spirits, sent to act on behalf of those who are to inherit salvation?

Don't neglect God's salvation!

2 So, then, we must pay all the closer attention to what we heard, in case we drift away from it. ²You see, if the word which was spoken through angels was reliable, with appropriate and just punishment every time anyone broke it or disobeyed it, ³how shall we escape if we ignore a rescue as great as this? It started by being declared through the Lord, and it was confirmed to us by those who heard him; ⁴and God bore witness as well, along with them, in signs and wonders and many different types of powerful deeds, and by the holy spirit, distributed in accordance with his will.

Jesus as the truly human being

⁵You see, God didn't place the world to come (which is what I'm writing about) under the control of angels. ⁶Someone has spoken of it somewhere in these terms:

> What are humans, that you should remember them?
> What is the son of man, that you should take thought for him?
> ⁷You made him a little lower than the angels,
> you crowned him with glory and honour,
> ⁸and you placed everything under his feet.

When it speaks of everything being subjected to him, it leaves nothing that is not subjected to him. As things are at present, we don't see everything subjected to him.

⁹What we do see is the one who was, for a little while, made lower than the angels – that is, Jesus – crowned with glory and honour because of the suffering of death, so that by God's grace he might taste death on behalf of everyone.

The Messiah and his brothers and sisters

¹⁰This is how it works out. Everything exists for the sake of God and because of him; and it was appropriate that, in bringing many children to glory, he should make perfect, through suffering, the one who leads the way to salvation. ¹¹For the one who makes others holy, and the ones who are made holy, all belong to a single family.

This is why he isn't ashamed to call them his brothers and sisters, ¹²when he says,

> I will announce your name to my brothers and sisters;
> I will sing your praise in the middle of the assembly,

¹³and again,

> I will place my trust in him,

and again,

> Look, here I am, with the children God has given me.

¹⁴Since the children share in blood and flesh, he too shared in them, in just the same way, so that through death he might destroy the one who has the power of death, that is, the devil, ¹⁵and set free the people who all their lives long were under the power of slavery because of the fear of death. ¹⁶It's obvious, you see, that he isn't taking special thought for angels; he's taking special thought for Abraham's family. ¹⁷That's why he had to be like his brothers and sisters in every way, so that he might become a merciful and trustworthy high priest in God's presence, to make atonement for the sins of the people. ¹⁸He himself has suffered, you see, through being put to the test, and that's why he is able to help those who are being tested right now.

Jesus and Moses

3 Well then, my brothers and sisters: you are God's holy ones, and you share the call from heaven. So think carefully about Jesus, the apostle and high priest of our confession of faith. ²He was faithful to the one who appointed him, just as Moses was faithful in all God's house. ³He deserves much more glory than Moses, you see, just as the one who builds a house deserves more glory than the house. ⁴For every house is built by someone, but the one who builds all things is God. ⁵And 'Moses was faithful, as a servant, in all his house', thereby bearing witness to the things that were yet to be spoken of; ⁶but the Messiah is over God's house as a son. What is that house? It's us – those of us who hold on tightly to the free delight and confidence of our hope.

Today's the time to listen!

⁷So listen to what the holy spirit says:

> Today, if you hear his voice,
> ⁸don't harden hearts, as in the great bitterness,
> like the day in the desert when they faced the test,
> ⁹when your fathers put me to the test, and challenged me,
> and saw my works ¹⁰for forty years.
> And so I was angry with that generation,
> and said, 'They are always straying in their hearts,
> they do not know my ways.' ¹¹As I swore
> in my anger, 'They'll never enter my rest.'

¹²Take care, my dear family, that none of you should possess an evil and unbelieving heart, leading you to withdraw from the living God. ¹³But encourage one another every day, as long as it's called 'Today', so that none of you may become hardened by the deceitfulness of sin.

Hold on tight!

¹⁴We share the life of the Messiah, you see, only if we keep a firm, tight grip on our original confidence, right through to the end. ¹⁵That's what it means when it says, 'Today, if you hear his voice, don't make your hearts hard, as in the great bitterness.'

¹⁶Who was it, after all, who heard and then became bitter? It was all those who went out of Egypt under Moses, wasn't it? ¹⁷And who was it that God was angry with for forty years? It was those who sinned, wasn't it – those whose bodies fell in the desert? ¹⁸And to whom did God swear that they would never enter his rest? Wasn't it the people who didn't believe? ¹⁹So we can see that it was their unbelief that prevented them from entering.

Getting through to the sabbath rest

4 So we are bound to worry that some of you might seem to have missed out on God's promise of entering his rest, the promise which is still open before us. ²For we certainly had the good news announced to us, just as they did; but the word which they heard didn't do them any good, because they were not united in faith with those who heard it. ³For it is we who believe who enter into the rest; as it has been said,

> As I swore in my anger,
> they will never enter my rest

– even though God's works had been complete since the foundation of the world. ⁴For it says this somewhere about the seventh day,

> And God rested on the seventh day from all his works,

⁵and again, in the present passage,

> They will never enter my rest.

⁶Therefore, since some failed to enter into it, and those who received the good news earlier on didn't enter because of unbelief, ⁷he once again appoints a day, 'Today', saying through David – after such a long interval of time! – in the words already quoted,

> Today, if you hear his voice,
> don't harden your hearts.

⁸If Joshua had given them rest, you see, he wouldn't be speaking about another subsequent 'rest'. ⁹Thus we conclude: there is still a future sabbath 'rest' for God's people. ¹⁰Anyone who enters that 'rest' will take a rest from their works, as God did from his.

Danger! God's word at work

¹¹So, then, let's make every effort to enter that 'rest', so that nobody should trip and fall through the same pattern of unbelief. ¹²God's word is alive, you see! It's powerful, and it's sharper than any double-edged sword. It can pierce right in between soul and spirit, or joints and marrow; it can go straight to the point of what the human heart is thinking, or intends to do. ¹³No creature remains hidden before God. All are naked, laid bare before the eyes of the one to whom we must present an account.

The sympathetic high priest

¹⁴Well, then, since we have a great high priest who has gone right through the heavens, Jesus, God's son, let us hold on firmly to our confession of faith. ¹⁵For we don't have a high priest who is unable to sympathize with our weaknesses, but one who has been tempted in every way just as we are, yet without sin. ¹⁶Let us then come boldly to the throne of grace, so that we may receive mercy, and may find grace to help us at the moment when we need it.

5 Every high priest, you see, is chosen from among human beings, and is placed before God on their behalf, so that he can offer gifts and sacrifices for sins. ²He is able to sympathize with people who don't know very much, or who wander off in different directions, since he too has his own share of weakness. ³That's why he has to offer sacrifices in relation to his own sins as well as those of the people.

The son becomes the priest

⁴Nobody takes the office of priesthood on himself; you have to be called by God, just as Aaron was. ⁵In the same way, the Messiah didn't exalt himself so that he might become a high priest. It came about through the one who said to him,

> You are my son; today I have become your father.

⁶As he says in another passage,

> You are a priest for ever, according to the order of Melchizedek.

⁷During the time of Jesus' earthly life, he offered up prayers and supplications, with loud shouts and tears, to the one who was able to save him from death. He was heard because of his devotion. ⁸Although he was a son, he learned obedience through what he suffered. ⁹When he had been made complete and perfect, he became the source of eternal salvation for all who obey him, ¹⁰since he has been designated by God as a high priest according to the order of Melchizedek.

Are you ready for solid food?

¹¹We have plenty to say about all this; but it may be hard to make it clear, because your capacity to take things in has become sluggish. ¹²Yes: by now you really should have become teachers, but you need someone to teach *you* the basic elementary beginnings of God's oracles. You need milk, not solid food! ¹³Everyone who drinks milk, you see, is unskilled in the word of God's justice; such people are just babies. ¹⁴Mature people need solid food – and by 'mature' I mean people whose faculties have been trained by practice, to distinguish good from evil.

No way back

6 So let's leave the basic level of teaching about the Messiah, and go on towards maturity! (Let's not repeat the performance of laying a foundation of repentance from dead works and faith towards God, ²teaching about baptisms, laying on of hands, the resurrection of the dead and eternal judgment.) ³We shall do this, if God allows us to.
⁴For once people have been enlightened – when they've tasted the heavenly gift and have had a share in the holy spirit, ⁵and have tasted the good word of God and the powers of the coming age – ⁶it's impossible to restore them again to repentance if they fall away, since they are crucifying God's son all over again, on their own account, and holding him up to contempt. ⁷You see, when rain falls frequently on the earth, and the land drinks it up and produces a crop useful to the people for whom it's being cultivated, it shares in God's blessing. ⁸But if it produces thorns and thistles, it's useless, and not far off from being cursed. What happens in the end is that it will be burned up.

Keep up the good work

⁹Even though we speak in this way, my dear people, we are confident that there are better things to be said about you, things that point to salvation. ¹⁰God is not unjust, after all – and he'd have to be if he forgot your work, and the love you showed for his name, and all the service you have rendered and are still rendering to his holy people. ¹¹I want to encourage each one of you to show the same energetic enthusiasm for the task of bringing your hope to its full, assured goal. ¹²You mustn't become lazy. There are people who are inheriting the promises through faith and patience, and you should copy them!

God's unchangeable promise

¹³When God was making his promise to Abraham, you see, he had nobody else greater than himself by whom he could swear, and so he swore by himself, ¹⁴with the words, 'I will most surely bless you, and multiply you very greatly.' ¹⁵And so in this way Abraham, after much patience, obtained the promise. ¹⁶People regularly swear by someone greater than themselves, and in all their disputes the oath confirms the matter and brings it to closure. ¹⁷So when God wanted to show all the more clearly to the heirs of the promise just how unchangeable his will was, he guaranteed it with an oath, ¹⁸so that through two unchangeable things, in which it is impossible that God should tell a lie, those of us who have come for refuge should have solid encouragement to take hold of the hope which lies before us. ¹⁹We have this hope like an anchor, secure, solid, and penetrating into the inner place behind the curtain, ²⁰where Jesus has gone in ahead of us and on our behalf,

having become a high priest for ever according to the order of Melchizedek.

Melchizedek, the great priest-king

7 For this Melchizedek, 'king of Salem, priest of the most high God, met Abraham as he was coming back after defeating the kings, and blessed him; ²and Abraham portioned out to him a tenth of everything.'

To begin with, if you translate Melchizedek's name, it means 'king of righteousness'; then he is also 'king of Salem', which means 'king of peace'. ³No mention is made of his father or mother or genealogy, nor of the beginning or end of his earthly life. He is described in a similar way to the son of God; and he continues as a priest for ever.

⁴Look and see what an exalted status he has. Abraham the patriarch gave him a tenth of the spoils! ⁵Those of Levi's sons who receive the priesthood have a command to take tithes from the people according to the law – from, that is, their own brothers and sisters, although they, too, are physical descendants of Abraham. ⁶But this man, who doesn't share their genealogy at all, received tithes from Abraham, and blessed the man who possessed the promises. ⁷It is beyond all question that the lesser is blessed by the greater. ⁸In the former case, mortal humans receive tithes; in the latter case, the one who received them was one of whom scripture declares that he is alive. ⁹And, if I can put it like this, even Levi paid tithes through Abraham – Levi, the one who receives tithes! ¹⁰He was still in his ancestor's loins, you see, when Melchizedek met him.

A new order of priesthood

¹¹So, you see, if it had been possible to arrive at complete perfection through the Levitical priesthood (for the people received the law by that means), what further need would there have been to speak of another priesthood being established 'according to the order of Melchizedek', rather than 'according to the order of Aaron'? ¹²Change the priesthood, after all, and you're bound to change the law – ¹³especially when you consider that the one of whom these things are spoken comes from another tribe altogether, one from which nobody is recruited to serve at the altar. ¹⁴It's obvious, isn't it, that our Lord was descended from Judah, and Moses never made any connection between that tribe and the priesthood.

¹⁵This is even clearer when another priest arises 'according to the order of Melchizedek', ¹⁶who attains this rank not because of a law concerning physical descent but through the power of a life that cannot be destroyed. ¹⁷What scripture says about him, after all, is, 'You are a priest for ever, according to the order of Melchizedek.' ¹⁸What is happening here is that the previous commandment is being set aside. It was, after all, weak and useless; ¹⁹the law brought nothing to perfection, did it? Instead, what appears is a better hope, through which we draw near to God.

The permanent priesthood of Jesus

²⁰This is all the more so when you consider that an oath was sworn. The Levitical priests, you see, become priests without an oath, ²¹but the Messiah attains his priesthood with an oath, through what was said to him:

The Lord has sworn and will not repent;
you are a priest for ever.

²²Jesus has thus, additionally, become the guarantee of a better covenant.

²³There needed to be a large number of Levitical priests, since they stop holding office at death. ²⁴But since he continues as a priest for ever, his priesthood is permanent. ²⁵That's why he is able to save those who come to God through him, completely and for ever – since he always lives to make intercession for them.

²⁶It was appropriate that we should have a high priest like this. He is holy, without blame or stain, separated from sinners, and elevated high above the heavens. ²⁷He doesn't need (like the ordinary high priests do) to offer sacrifices every day, first for his own sins and then for those of the people. He did this once for all, you see, when he offered himself. ²⁸For the law appoints ordinary, weak, mortal men as high priests; but the word of the oath, which comes

after the law, appoints the son, who has been made perfect for ever.

Better ministry, better covenant

8 The point of all this now appears. We have just such a high priest, who sat down at the right hand of the throne of the heavenly Majesty, ²as a minister of the holy things and of the true Tabernacle, the one set up by God rather than by humans. ³Every high priest, you see, is appointed in order to offer gifts and sacrifices, which is why this one, too, must have something to offer. ⁴If he were on earth, he wouldn't even be a priest, since there already are priests who make offerings in accordance with the law. ⁵They serve a copy and shadow of the heavenly realities, in line with what Moses was told, when he was getting ready to construct the Tabernacle: 'take care that you make everything according to the pattern that was shown you on the mountain'. ⁶Now, you see, Jesus has obtained a vastly superior ministry. In the same way, he is the mediator of a better covenant, which is established on better promises.

The promise of a new covenant

⁷If the first covenant had been faultless, you see, there wouldn't have been any reason to look for a second one. ⁸God finds fault with them when he says:

See, says the Lord, the days are coming,
when I will complete, with the house of Israel,
with Judah's house, also, a covenant that's new:
⁹not like the one which I made with their
    ancestors
on the day when I reached out and took them
    by the hand
to lead them away from the land of Egypt.
They didn't remain, after all, in my covenant,
and (says the Lord) I ceased to care for them.
¹⁰This is the covenant I will establish,
after those days with the house of Israel:
my laws will I place in their minds, says the
    Lord,
and write on their hearts; thus I shall be God
for all of them; they'll be my people indeed.

¹¹No more will they need to teach their own
    neighbours,
or their brothers and sisters, to know me, the
    Lord;
for from least unto greatest, each one shall
    know me,
¹²For I shall be merciful to their injustices
and as for their sins, I'll forget them for ever.

¹³Thus, when it speaks of a new covenant, it puts the first one out of date. And something that is out of date, and growing old, is about to disappear.

The old Tabernacle points forward to the new

9 The first Tabernacle had, of course, its own regulations for worship, and it contained the earthly sanctuary. ²A double tent was constructed. In the outer one was the lampstand, the table and the 'bread of the presence'. This is called 'the holy place'. ³After the second curtain came the inner tent, called 'the holy of holies'. ⁴This contained the golden altar, and the ark of the covenant, which was covered completely in gold. In the ark were the golden urn containing the manna, Aaron's rod that budded and the tablets of the covenant. ⁵Above it were the cherubim of glory, which overshadowed the mercy seat. There is much we could say about all this, but now is not the time.

⁶With all these things in place, the priests continually go into the first Tabernacle in the ordinary course of their duties. ⁷But only the high priest goes into the second Tabernacle, once every year, and he always takes blood, which he offers for himself and for the unintentional sins of the people. ⁸The holy spirit indicates by this that, as long as the original Tabernacle is still standing, the way is not yet open into the sanctuary. ⁹This is a picture, so to speak, of the present age. During this period, gifts and sacrifices are offered which have no power to perfect the conscience of those who come to worship. ¹⁰They only deal with foods and drinks and various kinds of washings. These are regulations for the ordering of bodily life until the appointed time, the moment when everything will be put into proper order.

The sacrifice of the Messiah

¹¹But when the Messiah arrived as high priest of the good things that were coming, he entered through the greater and much superior Tabernacle, not made with hands (that is, not of the present creation), ¹²and not with the blood of goats and calves but with his own blood. He entered, once and for all, into the holy place, accomplishing a redemption that lasts for ever.

¹³If the blood of bulls and goats, you see, and the sprinkled ashes of a heifer, make people holy (in the sense of purifying their bodies) when they had been unclean, ¹⁴how much more will the blood of the Messiah, who offered himself to God through the eternal spirit as a spotless sacrifice, cleanse our conscience from dead works to serve the living God!

The purpose of the blood

¹⁵For this reason, Jesus is the mediator of the new covenant. The purpose was that those who are called should receive the promised inheritance of the age to come, since a death has occurred which provides redemption from transgressions committed under the first covenant.

¹⁶Where there is a covenant, you see, it is vital to establish the death of the one who made it. ¹⁷A will laid down in covenant only takes effect after death; it has no validity during the lifetime of the one who made it. ¹⁸That's why even the first covenant was not inaugurated without blood. ¹⁹For when every commandment had been read out to the people by Moses, he took the blood of calves and goats, with water and scarlet wool and hyssop, and sprinkled the book itself and all the people, ²⁰saying, 'This is the blood of the covenant which God has made with you.' ²¹Then, in the same way, he sprinkled the Tabernacle, and all the vessels used in worship, with blood. ²²In fact, more or less everything is purified with blood according to the law; there's no pardon without bloodshed!

The Messiah's work in the heavenly sanctuary

²³That's why it was necessary for the copies of the heavenly objects to be purified in this way, while the heavenly things themselves require better sacrifices than these. ²⁴For the Messiah did not enter into a sanctuary made by human hands, the copy and pattern of the heavenly one, but into the heavenly one itself, where he now appears in God's presence on our behalf.

²⁵Nor did he intend to offer himself over and over again, in the same way as the high priest goes into the sanctuary year after year with blood that isn't his own. ²⁶Had that been the case, he would have had to suffer repeatedly since the foundation of the world. Instead, he has appeared once, at the close of the ages, to put away sin by the sacrifice of his own self.

²⁷Furthermore, just as it is laid down that humans have to die once, and after that comes judgment, ²⁸so the Messiah, having been offered once and for all to take away the sins of many, will appear a second time. This will no longer have anything to do with sin. It will be in order to save those who are eagerly awaiting him.

The stopping of the sacrifices

10 The law, you see, possesses a shadow of the good things that are coming, not the actual form of the things themselves. Thus it is unable to make worshippers perfect through the annual round of the same sacrifices which are continually being offered. ²If the worshippers really had been purified once and for all, they would no longer have sin on their consciences – so they would have stopped offering sacrifices, wouldn't they? ³But, as it is, the sacrifices serve as a regular annual reminder of sins, ⁴since it's impossible for the blood of bulls and goats to take sins away.

⁵That's why, when the Messiah comes into the world, this is what he says:

You didn't want sacrifices and offerings;
instead, you've given me a body.
⁶You didn't like burnt offerings and sin-offerings;
⁷then I said, 'Look! Here I am!
This is what it says about me in the scroll, the book:
I've come, O God, to do your will.'

⁸When he says, earlier, 'you didn't want, and you didn't like, sacrifices, offerings, burnt offerings and sin-offerings' (all of which are

offered in accordance with the law), ⁹then he says, 'Look! I've come to do your will!' He takes away the first so that he can establish the second. ¹⁰And it's by that 'will' that we have been sanctified through the offering of the body of Jesus the Messiah, once for all.

The finished achievement of the Messiah

¹¹Thus it comes about that every priest stands daily at his duty, offering over and over the same sacrifices, which can never take away sins. ¹²But Jesus offered a single sacrifice on behalf of sins, for all time, and then 'sat down at the right hand of God'. ¹³From that moment on he is waiting 'until his enemies are made a stool for his feet'. ¹⁴By a single sacrifice, you see, he has made perfect for ever those who are sanctified.

¹⁵The holy spirit bears witness to this too. For, after it is said,

¹⁶This is the covenant I will establish with them
after those days, says the Lord;
I will give them my laws in their hearts, and
will write them
upon their minds,

then he adds:

¹⁷And I shan't ever remember
their sins and all their lawlessness.

¹⁸Where these are put away, there is no longer a sacrifice for sin.

So – come to worship!

¹⁹So then, my brothers and sisters, we have boldness to go into the sanctuary through the blood of Jesus. ²⁰He has inaugurated a brand new, living path through the curtain (that is, his earthly body). ²¹We have a high priest who is over God's house. ²²Let us therefore come to worship, with a true heart, in complete assurance of faith, with our hearts sprinkled clean from an evil conscience and our bodies washed with pure water.

²³Let us hold on tightly to our confession of hope, without being diverted; the one who announced the message to us is trustworthy!

²⁴Let us, as well, stir up one another's minds to energetic effort in love and good works. ²⁵We mustn't do what some people have got into the habit of doing, neglecting to meet together. Instead, we must encourage one another, and all the more as you can see the great day coming closer.

Warning of judgment

²⁶For if we sin deliberately and knowingly after having received the knowledge of the truth, there is no further sacrifice for sin. ²⁷Instead, there is a fearful prospect of judgment, and a hungry fire which will consume the opponents. ²⁸If someone sets aside the law of Moses, they are to be 'put to death on the testimony of two or three witnesses', with no pity. ²⁹How much worse punishment, do you think, will be appropriate for people who trample the son of God underfoot, and profane the blood of the covenant by which they were sanctified, and scorn the spirit of grace? ³⁰We know the one who said, 'Vengeance belongs to me; I will pay everyone back', and again, 'The Lord will judge his people'. ³¹It's a terrifying thing to fall into the hands of the living God.

Suffering in hope

³²But remember the earlier times! When you were first enlightened, you went through great struggles and suffering. ³³Sometimes you were exposed to public reproach and physical abuse. Sometimes you stood alongside people who were being treated in that way. ³⁴You even shared the sufferings of those who were imprisoned. When people looted your property, you actually welcomed it joyfully, because you knew that you had a better possession, a lasting one.

³⁵So don't throw away your confidence. It carries a great reward. ³⁶What you need is patience, you see; then, when you've done what God wants, you will receive the promise.

³⁷For in just a little while from now,
the Coming One will come, and won't delay;
³⁸but my righteous one will live by faith;
and if he hesitates, my soul will not delight in
him.

⁳⁹We are not among the hesitators, who are destroyed! We are people of faith, and our lives will be kept safe.

What faith really means

11 What then is faith? It is what gives assurance to our hopes; it is what gives us conviction about things we can't see. ²It is what the men and women of old were famous for. ³It is by faith that we understand that the worlds were formed by God's word; in other words, that the visible world was not made from visible things.

⁴It was by faith that Abel offered a better sacrifice to God than Cain. That earned him the testimony that he was in the right, since God himself bore witness in relation to his gifts. Through faith, he still speaks, even though he's dead. ⁵It was by faith that Enoch was taken up so that he wouldn't see death; nobody could find him, because God took him up. Before he was taken up, you see, it had been said of him that 'he had pleased God'. ⁶And without faith it's impossible to please God; for those who come to worship God must believe that he really does exist, and that he rewards those who seek him.

Faith and the future: Noah, Abraham, Sarah

⁷It was by faith that Noah, who had been warned by God about things that were not yet seen, took the warning seriously and built an ark to save his household. He thus put the rest of the world in the wrong, and became heir to the righteous standing which accords with faith. ⁸It was by faith that Abraham, when God called him, obeyed and went out to a place where he was to receive an inheritance. Off he went, not knowing where he was going. ⁹It was by faith that he stayed in the promised land as a stranger, living in tents with Isaac and Jacob, who were joint heirs of the same promise. ¹⁰He was looking ahead, you see, to the city which has foundations, the city of which God is the designer and builder.

¹¹It was by faith that Sarah herself, who was barren, received the ability to conceive a child even when long past the right age, since she considered that God, who had promised, was trustworthy. ¹²Thus it came about that from one man, and him more or less dead, there was born a family as many as the stars of heaven in number, as uncountable as the sand on the seashore.

Faith that looks beyond death

¹³All these people died in faith. They hadn't received the promise, but they had seen it from far off, and had greeted it, and had recognized that they were strangers and wanderers in the land. ¹⁴People who say that sort of thing, you see, make it clear that they are looking for a homeland. ¹⁵Had they been thinking of the place from which they had set out, they would have had plenty of opportunity to go back to it. ¹⁶But as it was they were longing for a better place, a heavenly one. That's why God is not ashamed to be called 'their God', since he has prepared a city for them.

¹⁷It was by faith that Abraham, when he was put to the test, offered up Isaac; yes, Abraham, who had received the promise, was in the very act of offering up his only son, ¹⁸the one about whom it had been said that 'In Isaac shall your family be named'. ¹⁹He reckoned that God was capable of raising him even from the dead; and, in one sense, he did indeed receive him back from there.

²⁰It was by faith in the things that were to come that Isaac blessed Jacob and Esau. ²¹It was by faith that, when Jacob was dying, he blessed the two sons of Joseph, and 'worshipped, leaning on the top of his staff'. ²²It was by faith that, when Joseph was coming to the end, he spoke about the exodus of the children of Israel, and gave instructions concerning his own bones.

Faith and the future: Moses and the exodus

²³It was by faith that, when Moses was born, he was hidden for three months by his parents. They saw that the child was beautiful, and they weren't afraid of the king's orders. ²⁴It was by faith that Moses, when he grew up, refused

to be called the son of Pharaoh's daughter, ²⁵preferring to suffer hardship along with God's people than to enjoy the short-term pleasures of sin. ²⁶He reckoned that reproach suffered for the Messiah was worth more than all the treasures of Egypt; he was looking ahead to the reward.

²⁷It was by faith that he left Egypt, without fear of Pharaoh's anger; he kept the invisible one constantly before his eyes. ²⁸It was by faith that he kept the Passover and the sprinkling of blood, so that the destroyer of the firstborn wouldn't touch them. ²⁹It was by faith that they crossed the Red Sea as though they were on dry ground, while the Egyptians, when they tried to do the same, were drowned. ³⁰It was by faith that the walls of Jericho fell down after they had been encircled for seven days. ³¹It was by faith that the prostitute Rahab was not destroyed along with those who didn't believe; she had welcomed the spies in peace.

Faith and the future: the great crowd

³²What more can I say, then? I've run out of time to tell you about Gideon, Barak, Samson, Jephthah, David, Samuel and the prophets. ³³It was through faith that they overcame kingdoms, put justice into practice, received promises, shut the mouths of lions, ³⁴quenched the power of fire, escaped the edge of the sword, were strong where they had been weak, became powerful in battle, and sent foreign armies packing. ³⁵Women received their dead by resurrection; others were tortured, not accepting release, so that they might receive a better resurrection. ³⁶Others again experienced painful derision and flogging, and even chains and imprisonment; ³⁷they were stoned, they were sawn in two, they were put to the sword, they went about in sheepskins or goat-hides, they were destitute, they were persecuted, they were ill-treated – ³⁸the world didn't deserve them! – and they wandered in deserts and mountains, in caves and holes in the ground.

³⁹All these people gained a reputation for their faith; but they didn't receive the promise. ⁴⁰God was providing something better for us, so that they wouldn't reach perfection without our doing so as well.

Looking to Jesus

12 What about us, then? We have such a great cloud of witnesses all around us! What we must do is this: we must put aside each heavy weight, and the sin which gets in the way so easily. We must run the race that lies in front of us, and we must run it patiently. ²We must look ahead, to Jesus. He is the one who carved out the path for faith, and he's the one who brought it to completion.

He knew that there was joy spread out and waiting for him. That's why he endured the cross, making light of its shame, and has now taken his seat at the right hand of God's throne. ³He put up with enormous opposition from sinners. Weigh up in your minds just how severe it was; then you won't find yourselves getting weary and worn out.

Christian suffering is God's discipline

⁴You have been struggling against sin, but your resistance hasn't yet cost you any blood. ⁵And perhaps you have forgotten the word of exhortation which speaks to you as God's children:

> My child, don't make light of the Lord's rebuke,
> or grow weary when he takes issue with you;
> ⁶for the Lord disciplines those whom he loves,
> and chastises every child he welcomes.

⁷You must be patient with discipline. God is dealing with you as his sons and daughters. What child is there that the parent doesn't discipline? ⁸If you are left without discipline (we've all had our fair share of it!), you are illegitimate, and not true children. ⁹After all, we had earthly parents who disciplined us, and we respected them; shouldn't we much rather submit ourselves to the father of spirits, and live? ¹⁰Our earthly parents disciplined us for a little while, as they judged best; but when he disciplines us it's for our advantage. It is so that we may share his holiness. ¹¹No discipline seems to bring joy at the time, but only sorrow. Later, though, it produces fruit, the peaceful fruit of righteousness, for those who are trained by it.

Watch out for dangers!

¹²So stop letting your hands go slack, and get some energy into your sagging knees! ¹³Make straight paths for your feet. If you're lame, make sure you get healed instead of being put out of joint. ¹⁴Follow after peace with everyone, and the holiness which is necessary before you can see the Lord. ¹⁵Take good care that nobody lacks God's grace; don't let any 'root of bitterness spring up to cause trouble', defiling many people. ¹⁶No one must be immoral or worldly-minded, like Esau: he sold his birthright for a single meal! ¹⁷You know, don't you, that later on, when he wanted to inherit the blessing, he was rejected. There was no way he could change either his mind or Isaac's, even though he wept bitterly in trying to do so.

From Mount Sinai to Mount Zion

¹⁸You haven't come, after all, to something that can be touched – a blazing fire, darkness, gloom and whirlwind, ¹⁹the sound of a trumpet and a voice speaking words which the hearers begged not to have to listen to any more. ²⁰(They couldn't bear the command that 'if even a beast touches the mountain, it must be stoned'.) ²¹The sight was so terrifying that even Moses said, 'I'm trembling with fear.'

²²No: you have come to Mount Zion – to the city of the living God, the heavenly Jerusalem. You have come to where thousands and thousands of angels are gathered for a festival; ²³to the assembly of the firstborn, whose names are written in heaven. You have come to God the judge of all, to the spirits of righteous people who have been made perfect, ²⁴and to Jesus the mediator of the new covenant, and to the sprinkled blood which has better words to say than the blood of Abel.

The kingdom that cannot be shaken

²⁵Take care that you don't refuse the one who is speaking. For if people didn't escape when they rejected the one who gave them earthly warnings, how much more if we turn away from the one who speaks from heaven! ²⁶At that point, his voice shook the earth; but now he has issued a promise in the following words: 'One more time I will shake not only the earth but heaven as well.' ²⁷The phrase 'one more time' shows that the things that are to be shaken (that is, the created things) will be taken away, so that the things that cannot be shaken will remain.

²⁸Well, then: we are to receive a kingdom which cannot be shaken! This calls for gratitude! That's how to offer God true and acceptable worship, reverently and with fear. ²⁹Our God, you see, is a devouring fire.

The practical life of God's people

13 Let the family continue to care for one another. ²Don't forget to be hospitable; by that means, some people have entertained angels without realizing it. ³Remember people in prison, as though you were in prison with them. When you think of people who are having a difficult time, remember that you too live in a frail body.

⁴Let marriage be honoured by everyone; let the marriage bed remain undefiled. God will judge those who misbehave sexually or commit adultery.

⁵Keep your life free from love of money; be content with what you have. He himself has said, after all, 'I will never, ever, leave you or forsake you.' ⁶That's why we can be cheerfully confident, and say, 'The Lord is helping me; I'm not going to be afraid; what can anyone do to me?'

⁷Remember your leaders, who spoke God's word to you. Look carefully at how their lives came to complete fruition, and imitate their faith. ⁸Jesus the Messiah is the same, yesterday, today and for ever.

Outside the old city, seeking the new

⁹Don't let yourselves be carried off by strange teachings of whatever sort. The heart needs to be strengthened by grace, you see, not by rules about what to eat, which don't do any good to those who observe them.

¹⁰We have an altar from which those who minister in the Tabernacle are not allowed to eat. ¹¹For the bodies of the animals whose

blood is taken into the sanctuary by the high priest as a sin-offering are burned outside the camp. ¹²That's why Jesus too suffered outside the gate, so that he might make the people holy with his own blood. ¹³So, then, let's go out to him, outside the camp, bearing his shame. ¹⁴Here, you see, we have no city that lasts; we are looking for the one that is still to come.

¹⁵Our part, then, is this: to bring, through him, a continual sacrifice of praise to God – that is, mouths that confess his name, and do so fruitfully. ¹⁶Don't neglect to do good, and to let 'fellowship' mean what it says. God really enjoys sacrifices of that kind!

The God of peace be with you

¹⁷Obey your leaders; submit to them. They are keeping watch over your lives, you see, as people who will have to give account. Make sure they can do this with joy, not with a groan as a burden. That would be of no value to you.

¹⁸Pray for us! Our conscience is clear; we are quite sure of it. We wish to act appropriately in everything. ¹⁹I beg you especially to do this, so that I may quickly be restored to you.

²⁰May the God of peace, who led up from the dead our Lord Jesus, the great shepherd of the sheep, through the blood of the eternal covenant, ²¹make you complete in every good work so that you may do his will. May he perform, in you, whatever will be pleasing in his sight, through Jesus the Messiah. Glory be to him for ever and ever, Amen!

²²I beg you, my dear family, bear with this word of exhortation; I've written to you quite briefly, after all. ²³You should know that our brother Timothy has been released. If he comes soon, I will see you and him at the same time.

²⁴Greet all your leaders, and all God's people. Those from Italy send you greetings. ²⁵Grace be with you all.

James

'James' is the modern form of 'Jacob', and hence a popular Jewish name. The author may well be the brother of Jesus, the undisputed leader of the Jerusalem church until his death (at the hands of hardline activists) in AD 62. It urges a new standard of life on the followers of Jesus: 'the royal law' (2.8), 'the law of freedom' (1.25; 2.12), which consists of love in action, keeping the tongue under control, and looking ahead to a coming judgment in which the rich oppressors will be overthrown and the poor vindicated (1.9–11; 2.1–13; 5.1–6). James echoes Jesus' teaching at various points, particularly some elements of the Sermon on the Mount, and functions as the New Testament's rough equivalent of the book of Proverbs: short, pithy sayings which confront the hearer with a strikingly new way of life, urging a genuine 'wisdom' (1.5–8) which will enable the believer to see to the heart of reality and so live accordingly.

James is particularly concerned with putting into practice the truths to which the community gives outward assent. They are to be 'people who do the word, not merely people who hear it and deceive themselves' (1.22). This has to show up in their practice of welcoming all and sundry to worship, not discriminating in favour of the rich (2.1–7). The central statement of 'doing the word', though, comes in James's emphatic holding together of 'faith' and 'works' (2.14–26), which some have seen as a riposte to Paul's doctrine of 'justification by faith'. Closer inspection shows that what James means by 'faith' is not the rich personal 'faith' at the heart of Paul's teaching, but simply a bare intellectual assent to monotheism ('God is one') – a 'faith', as he points out, shared by the demons. And what he means by 'works' is not, as in Paul, the performance of the Jewish law, designed to bolster Jewish privilege, but the acts of love, particularly to those in need, which demonstrate a living faith in the loving God. Such 'works' are the very opposite of outward show. They display the inner reality.

That inner reality is to be displayed as well through wise, disciplined speech (3.1–12). As Jesus had warned, the mouth reveals the state of the heart. This warning opens up a wider challenge: do you want to be a friend of the world or a friend of God? You cannot be both (4.1–10), and to recognize this is a call to fresh submission and humble penitence. James ends with a call to patience and prayer: 'make your hearts strong, because the appearing of the Lord is near at hand' (5.8). The patience of Job, and the prayer of Elijah, root this appeal in scripture (5.11, 17). The severe practicality of this letter is a reminder, in almost every verse, that following Jesus is all about God's will coming true in the details of earthly life, not merely in a detached spirituality or a distant heaven.

The challenge of faith

1 James, a slave of God and of the Lord Jesus the Messiah, to the twelve dispersed tribes: greeting.

²My dear family, when you find yourselves tumbling into various trials and tribulations, learn to look at it with complete joy, ³because you know that, when your faith is put to the test, what comes out is patience. ⁴What's more, you must let patience have its complete effect, so that you may be complete and whole, not falling short in anything.

⁵If any one of you falls short in wisdom, they should ask God for it, and it will be given them. God, after all, gives generously and ungrudgingly to all people. ⁶But they should ask in faith, with no doubts. A person who doubts is like a wave of the sea which the wind blows and tosses about. ⁷Someone like that should not suppose they will receive anything from the Lord, ⁸since they are double-minded and unstable in everything they do.

The snares of the world and the gift of God

⁹Brothers and sisters who find themselves impoverished should celebrate the fact that they have risen to this height – ¹⁰and those who are rich that they are brought down low, since the rich will disappear like a wild flower. ¹¹You see, the rich will be like the grass: when the sun rises with its scorching heat, it withers the grass so that its flower droops and all its fine appearance comes to nothing. That's what it will be like when the rich wither away in the midst of their busy lives.

¹²God's blessing on the man who endures testing! When he has passed the test, he will receive the crown of life, which God has promised to those who love him. ¹³Nobody being tested should say, 'It's God that's testing me', for God cannot be tested by evil, and he himself tests nobody. ¹⁴Rather, each person is tested when they are dragged off and enticed by their own desires. ¹⁵Then desire, when it has conceived, gives birth to sin; and when sin reaches maturity it gives birth to death.

¹⁶Don't be deceived, my dear family. ¹⁷Every good gift, every perfect gift, comes down from above, from the father of lights. His steady light doesn't vary. It doesn't change and produce shadows. ¹⁸He became our father by the word of truth; that was his firm decision, and the result is that we are a kind of first fruits of his creatures.

The word that goes to work

¹⁹So, my dear brothers and sisters, get this straight. Every person should be quick to hear, slow to speak, slow to anger. ²⁰Human anger, you see, doesn't produce God's justice! ²¹So put away everything that is sordid, all that overflowing malice, and humbly receive the word which has been planted within you and which has the power to rescue your lives.

²²But be people who do the word, not merely people who hear it and deceive themselves. ²³Someone who hears the word but doesn't do it, you see, is like a man who looks at his natural face in a mirror. ²⁴He notices himself, but then he goes away and quickly forgets what he looked like. ²⁵But the person who looks into the perfect law of freedom, and goes on with it, not being a hearer who forgets but a doer who does the deed – such a person is blessed in their doing.

²⁶If anyone supposes that they are devout, and does not control their tongue, but rather deceives their heart – such a person's devotion is futile. ²⁷As far as God the father is concerned, pure, unsullied devotion works like this: you should visit orphans and widows in their sorrow, and prevent the world leaving its dirty smudge on you.

No favourites!

2 My brothers and sisters, as you practise the faith of our Lord Jesus, the anointed King of glory, you must do so without favouritism. ²What I mean is this: if someone comes into your assembly wearing gold rings, all dressed up, and a poor person comes in wearing shabby clothes, ³you cast your eyes over the person wearing fine clothes and say, 'Please! Have a seat up here!' but then you turn to the poor person and say, 'Stand there!' or, 'Get down there by my footstool!' ⁴When you do this, are you not discriminating among yourselves? Are you not turning into judges with evil thoughts? ⁵Listen, my dear brothers and sisters. Isn't it the case that God has chosen the poor (as the world sees it) to be rich in faith, and to inherit the kingdom which he has promised to those who love him? ⁶But you have dishonoured the poor man. After all, who are the rich? The rich are the ones who lord it over you and drag you into court, aren't they? ⁷The rich are the ones who blaspheme the wonderful name which has been pronounced over you, aren't they?

⁸Supposing, however, you keep the royal law, as it is written, 'You shall love your neighbour as yourself'; if you do this, you will do well. ⁹But if you show favouritism, you are committing sin, and you will be convicted by the law as a lawbreaker. ¹⁰Anyone who keeps the whole law, you see, but fails in one point, has become guilty of all of it. ¹¹For the one who said, 'Do not commit adultery', also said, 'Do not murder.' So if you do not commit adultery, but do murder, you have become a lawbreaker. ¹²Speak and act in such a way as people who are going to be judged by the law of freedom. ¹³Judgment is without mercy, you see, for those who have shown no mercy. But mercy triumphs over judgment.

Faith and works

¹⁴What use is it, my dear family, if someone says they have faith when they don't have works? Can faith save such a person? ¹⁵Supposing a brother or sister is without clothing, and is short even of daily food, ¹⁶and one of you says to them, 'Go in peace; be warm, be full!' – but doesn't give them what their bodies need – what use is that? ¹⁷In the same way, faith, all by itself and without works, is dead.

¹⁸But supposing someone says, 'Well: you have faith, and I have works.' All right: show me your faith – but without doing any works; and then I will show you *my* faith, and I'll do it by my works! ¹⁹You believe that 'God is one'? Well and good! The demons believe that, too, and they tremble! ²⁰Do you want to know, you stupid person, that faith without works is lifeless? ²¹Wasn't Abraham our father justified by his works when he offered up his son Isaac on the altar? ²²You can see from this that faith was cooperating along with the works, and the faith reached its fulfilment through the works. ²³That is how the scripture was fulfilled which says, 'Abraham believed God, and it was reckoned to him as righteousness', and he was called 'God's friend'. ²⁴So you see that a person is justified by works and not by faith alone. ²⁵In the same way, wasn't Rahab the prostitute justified by works when she gave shelter to the spies and sent them off by another road? ²⁶Just as the body without the spirit is dead, you see, so faith without works is dead.

Taming the tongue

3 Not many of you should become teachers, my brothers and sisters; you know that we will be judged more severely. ²All of us make many mistakes, after all. If anyone makes no mistakes in what they say, such a person is a fully complete human being, capable of keeping firm control over the whole body as well. ³We put bits into the mouths of horses to make them obey us, and then we can direct their whole bodies. ⁴Consider, too, the case of large ships; it takes strong winds to blow them along, but one small rudder will turn them whichever way the helmsman desires and decides. ⁵In the same way, the tongue is a little member but boasts great things. See how small a fire it takes to set a large forest ablaze! ⁶And the tongue *is* a fire. The tongue is a world of injustice, with its place established right there among our members. It defiles the whole body; it sets the wheel of nature ablaze, and is itself set ablaze by hell. ⁷Every species of beast and bird, of reptile and sea creature, you see, can be tamed, and has been tamed, by humans. ⁸But no single human is able to tame the tongue. It is an irrepressible evil, full of deadly poison. ⁹By it we bless the Lord and father; and by it we curse humans who are made in God's likeness! ¹⁰Blessing and curses come out of the same mouth! My dear family, it isn't right that it should be like that. ¹¹Does a spring put out both sweet and bitter water from the same source? ¹²Dear friends, can a fig tree bear olives, or a vine bear figs? Nor can salt water yield fresh.

True and false wisdom

¹³Who is wise and discerning among you? Such a person should, by their upright behaviour, display their works in the humility of wisdom. ¹⁴But if you have bitter jealousy and contention in your hearts, don't boast, and tell lies against the truth. ¹⁵This isn't the wisdom that comes from above. It is earthly, merely human, coming from the world of demons. ¹⁶For where there is jealousy and contention, there you will get unruly behaviour and every kind of evil practice. ¹⁷But the wisdom that comes from above is first holy, then peaceful, gentle, compliant, filled with mercy and good fruits, unbiased, sincere. ¹⁸And the fruit of righteousness is sown in peace by those who make peace.

Humility and faith

4 Where do wars come from? Why do people among you fight? It all comes from within, doesn't it – from your desires for pleasure which make war in your members. ²You want something and you haven't got it, so you murder someone. You long to possess something, but you can't get it, so you fight and wage war. The reason you don't have it is because you don't ask for it! ³And when you do ask, you don't get it, because you ask wrongly, intending to spend it on your pleasures. ⁴Adulterers! Don't you know that to be friends with the world means being enemies with God? So anyone who wants to be friends with the world is setting themselves up as God's enemy. ⁵Or do you suppose that when the Bible says, 'He yearns jealously over the spirit he has made to dwell in us', it doesn't mean what it says?

⁶But God gives more grace; so it says, 'God opposes the proud, but gives grace to the humble.' ⁷Submit to God, then; resist the devil and he will run away from you. ⁸Draw near to God, and he will draw near to you. Make your hands clean, you sinners; and make your hearts pure, you double-minded lot. ⁹Make yourselves wretched; mourn and weep. Let your laughter turn to mourning, and your joy to sorrow. ¹⁰Humble yourselves before the Lord, and he will exalt you.

Living by trust in God

¹¹Do not speak evil against one another, my dear family. Anyone who speaks evil against another family member, or passes judgment against them, speaks evil against the law and judges the law. But if you judge the law, you are not a doer of the law but a judge! ¹²There is one lawgiver, one judge who can rescue or destroy. But who are you to judge your neighbour?

¹³Now look here, you people who say, 'Today, or tomorrow, we will go to such-and-such a town and spend a year there, and trade, and make some money.' ¹⁴You have no idea what the next day will bring. What is your life? You are a mist which appears for a little while and then disappears again. ¹⁵Instead, you ought to say, 'If the Lord wills, we shall live, and we shall do this, or that.' ¹⁶But, as it is, you boast in your pride. All such boasting is evil. ¹⁷So then, if anyone knows the right thing to do, but doesn't do it, it becomes sin for them.

Warnings to the rich

5 Now look here, you rich! Weep and wail for the horrible things that are going to happen to you! ²Your riches have rotted, and your clothes have become moth-eaten, ³your gold and your silver have rusted, and their rust will bear witness against you and will eat up your flesh like fire. You have stored up riches in the last days! ⁴Look: you cheated the workers who mowed your fields by keeping back their wages, and those wages are crying out! The cries of the farm workers have reached the ears of the Lord of hosts. ⁵You have lived off the fat of the land, in the lap of luxury. You have fattened your own hearts on a day of slaughter. ⁶You have condemned the Righteous One and killed him, and he doesn't resist you.

Patience and trust

⁷So be patient, my brothers and sisters, for the appearing of the Lord. You know how the farmer waits for the valuable crop to come up from the ground. He is patient over it, waiting for it to receive the early rain and then the late rain. ⁸In the same way, you must be patient,

and make your hearts strong, because the appearing of the Lord is near at hand. ⁹Don't grumble against one another, my brothers and sisters, so that you may not be judged. Look – the judge is standing at the gates! ¹⁰Consider the prophets, my brothers and sisters, who spoke in the name of the Lord. Take them as an example of longsuffering and patience. ¹¹When people endure, we call them 'blessed by God'. Well, you have heard of the endurance of Job; and you saw the Lord's ultimate purpose. The Lord is deeply compassionate and kindly.

¹²Above all, my brothers and sisters, do not swear. Don't swear by heaven; don't swear by earth; don't use any other oaths. Let your 'Yes' be 'Yes' and your 'No' be 'No'. That way, you will not fall under judgment.

Praying in faith

¹³Are any among you suffering? Let them pray. Are any cheerful? Let them sing psalms. ¹⁴Are any among you sick? They should call for the elders of the church, and they should pray over the sick person, anointing them with oil in the name of the Lord. ¹⁵Faithful prayer will rescue the sick person, and the Lord will raise them up. If they have committed any sin, it will be forgiven them. ¹⁶So confess your sins to one another, and pray for one another, that you may be healed.

When a righteous person prays, that prayer carries great power. ¹⁷Elijah was a man with passions like ours, and he prayed and prayed that it might not rain – and it did not rain on the earth for three years and six months. ¹⁸Then he prayed again, the sky gave rain, and the earth produced its fruit.

¹⁹My dear family, if someone in your company has wandered from the truth, and someone turns them back, ²⁰know this: the one who turns back a sinner from wandering off into error will rescue that person's life from death, and cover a multitude of sins.

1 Peter

Opinion divides on the authorship of 1 Peter and 2 Peter, with many supposing that Peter himself is the author of the first letter while most cast doubt on the second.

First Peter, with many echoes of Paul, and rich exposition of scripture, addresses situations of persecution. The early Christians may have supposed that after Jesus' death and resurrection they would not themselves have to suffer, but Peter explains that the opposite is the truth: the victory won through Jesus' own suffering will now be implemented through the suffering of Jesus' people. This is coupled with the intense and glorious joy of belonging to the Jesus whom they love, and for whose final revelation they long (1.7–9). Peter introduces the later scriptural expositions by explaining that the ancient prophets had looked ahead, aware that God's purposes would be fulfilled in quite new events yet to come (1.10–12). This new age has now been inaugurated through the Messiah, the true Passover lamb, and through the powerful 'word' of the gospel which, unlike anything on offer in the rest of creation, will last for ever (1.18–25).

This leads to a classic statement of the church's identity, mixing biblically rooted metaphors: newborn babies in God's new world (2.1–3), a 'spiritual house' made of 'living stones', a 'holy priesthood, to offer spiritual sacrifices' (2.4–5), built on Jesus himself, the 'precious cornerstone' promised in Isaiah (2.5–6). The community called into existence around the Messiah thus inherits the promises of Exodus 19 ('a royal priesthood') and Hosea 1 ('once you were "no people"; now you are "God's people"', 2.9–10). The result is that the church must learn to navigate the challenges of being a new kind of community, expecting to be vilified by those who don't understand what is going on but none the less living honourably and with restraint, following the example of Jesus himself in patiently enduring the suffering that will come. Social and civic behaviour must give no extra cause for blame; the Christian refusal to worship the local gods, and to go along with the concomitant behaviour, would bring blame enough (4.1–6). They are to live as citizens of the new creation, patiently awaiting the moment when the Messiah's glory will be revealed (4.13).

The letter ends with an exhortation to leaders in the church. Here again the example of Jesus himself, the 'chief shepherd' (5.4), is paramount. All will need the combination of promise and warning in 5.7–9: we can throw all our cares upon God, who cares about us, but at the same time we must be aware that the devil 'is stalking around like a roaring lion', and must be resisted, trusting that God will 'establish and strengthen you' (5.10). The letter offers a sharp, vivid, scripturally rooted picture of what it means to live in the tension between the new world that has been launched with Jesus' death and resurrection and the old world that will fail to understand this new movement and will react with hostility. This challenge is as urgently necessary in today's world as it was in Peter's day.

Genuine faith and sure hope

1 Peter, an apostle of Jesus the Messiah, to God's chosen ones who live as foreigners among the Dispersion in Pontus, Galatia, Cappadocia, Asia and Bithynia, ²who have been set aside in advance by God the father, through the sanctification of the spirit, for obedience and for sprinkling with the blood of Jesus the Messiah. May grace and peace be poured out lavishly on you!

³May God be blessed, God the father of our Lord Jesus the Messiah! His mercy is abundant, and so he has become our father in a second birth into a living hope through the resurrection from the dead of Jesus the Messiah. ⁴This has brought us into an incorruptible inheritance, which nothing can stain or diminish. At the moment it is kept safe for you in the heavens, ⁵while you are being kept safe by God's power, through faith, for a rescue that is all ready and waiting to be revealed in the final time.

⁶That is why you celebrate! Yes, it may well be necessary that, for a while, you may have to suffer trials and tests of all sorts. ⁷But this is so that the true value of your faith may be discovered. It is worth more than gold, which is tested by fire even though it can be destroyed. The result will be praise, glory and honour when Jesus the Messiah is revealed. ⁸You love him, even though you've never seen him. And even though you don't see him, you believe in him, and celebrate with a glorified joy that goes beyond anything words can say, ⁹since you are receiving the proper goal of your faith, namely, the rescue of your lives.

Ransomed by grace

¹⁰The prophets who prophesied about the grace that was to be given to you searched and enquired about this rescue. ¹¹They asked what sort of time it would be, the time that the Messiah's spirit within them was indicating

1 Peter 1.1

when speaking of the Messiah's sufferings and subsequent glory. ¹²It was revealed to them that they were not serving themselves, but you, when they were ministering these things – things which have now been announced to you by the holy spirit who was sent from heaven, through those who preached the good news to you. The angels long to gaze on these things!

¹³So fasten your belts – the belts of your minds! Keep yourselves under control. Set your hope completely on the grace that will be given you when Jesus the Messiah is revealed. ¹⁴As children of obedience, don't be squashed into the shape of the passions you used to indulge when you were still in ignorance. ¹⁵Rather, just as the one who called you is holy, so be holy yourselves, in every aspect of behaviour. ¹⁶It is written, you see, 'Be holy, for I am holy.' ¹⁷If you call on God as 'father' – the God, that is, who judges everyone impartially according to their work – behave with holy fear throughout the time in which you are resident here.

¹⁸You know, after all, that you were ransomed from the futile practices inherited from your ancestors, and that this ransom came not through perishable things like gold or silver, ¹⁹but through the precious blood of the Messiah, like a lamb without spot or blemish. ²⁰He was destined for this from before the foundation of the world, and appeared at the end of the times for your sake, ²¹for you (that is) who through him believe in the God who raised him from the dead and gave him glory, so that your faith and hope are in God.

Newborn babies

²²Once your lives have been purified by obeying the truth, resulting in a sincere love for all your fellow believers, love one another eagerly, from a pure heart. ²³You have been born again, not from seed which decays but from seed which does not – through the living and abiding word of God. ²⁴Because, you see –

> All flesh is like grass
> and all its glory is like the flower of the field.
> The grass withers, and the flower falls
>
> ²⁵but the word of the Lord lasts for ever.

That is the word that was announced to you.

2 So put away all evil, all deceitful, hateful malice, and all ill-speaking. ²As newborn babies, long for the spiritual milk, the real stuff, not watered down. That is what will make you grow up to salvation – ³if indeed you have tasted that the Lord is gracious.

The living stone

⁴Come to him, to that living stone. Humans rejected him, but God chose him and values him very highly! ⁵Like living stones yourselves, you are being built up into a spiritual house, to be a holy priesthood, to offer spiritual sacrifices that will be well pleasing to God through Jesus the Messiah.

⁶That's why it stands in scripture:

> Look! I'm setting up in Zion
> a chosen, precious cornerstone;
> believe in him! You'll not be ashamed.

⁷He is indeed precious for you believers. But when people don't believe, 'the stone which the builders rejected has become the head cornerstone', ⁸and 'a stone of stumbling and a rock of offence'. They stumble as they disobey the word, which indeed was their destiny. ⁹But you are a 'chosen race; a royal priesthood'; a holy nation; a people for God's possession. Your purpose is to announce the virtuous deeds of the one who called you out of darkness into his amazing light. ¹⁰Once you were 'no people'; now you are 'God's people'. Once you had not received mercy; now you have received mercy.

Living in a pagan world

¹¹My beloved ones, I beg you – strangers and resident aliens as you are – to hold back from the fleshly desires that wage war against your true lives. ¹²Keep up good conduct among the pagans, so that when they speak against you as evildoers they will observe your good deeds and praise God on the day of his royal arrival.

¹³Be subject to every human institution, for the sake of the Lord: whether to the emperor as supreme, ¹⁴or to governors as sent by him to punish evildoers and praise those who do good. ¹⁵This, you see, is God's will. He wants

you to behave well and so to silence foolish and ignorant people. ¹⁶Live as free people (though don't use your freedom as a veil to hide evil!), but as slaves of God. ¹⁷Do honour to all people; love the family; reverence God; honour the emperor.

Suffering as the Messiah did

¹⁸Let slaves obey their masters with all respect, not only the good and kind ones but also the unkind ones. ¹⁹It is to your credit, you see, if because of a godly conscience you put up with unjust and painful suffering. ²⁰After all, what credit is it if you do something wrong, are beaten for it, and take it patiently? But if you do what is right, suffer for it, and bear it patiently, this is to your credit before God.

²¹This, after all, is what came with the terms of your call, because

> the Messiah, too, suffered on your behalf,
> leaving behind a pattern for you
> so that you should follow the way he walked.
> ²²He committed no sin,
> nor was there any deceit in his mouth.
> ²³When he was insulted, he didn't insult in return,
> when he suffered, he didn't threaten,
> but he gave himself up to the one who judges justly.
> ²⁴He himself bore our sins
> in his body on the cross,
> so that we might be free from sins
> and live for righteousness.
> It is by his wound that you are healed.
> ²⁵For you were going astray like sheep,
> but now you have returned to the shepherd
> and guardian of your true lives.

Marriage and its challenges

3 In the same way, let me say a word to the women. You should be subject to your husbands, so that if there should be some who disobey the word, they may be won, without a word, through the behaviour of their wives, ²as they notice you conducting yourselves with reverence and purity. ³The beauty you should strive for ought not to be the external sort – elaborate hairdressing, gold trinkets, fine clothes! ⁴Rather, true beauty is the secret beauty of the heart, of a sincere, gentle and quiet spirit. That is very precious to God. ⁵That is how the holy women of old, who hoped in God, used to make themselves beautiful in submission to their husbands. ⁶Take Sarah, for instance, who obeyed Abraham and called him 'Master'. You are her children if you do good and have no fear of intimidation.

⁷You men, in the same way, think out how to live with your wives. Yes, they are physically weaker than you, but they deserve full respect. They are heirs of the grace of life, just the same as you. That way nothing will obstruct your prayers.

The new way of life

⁸The aim of this is for you all to be like-minded, sympathetic and loving to one another, tender-hearted and humble. ⁹Don't repay evil for evil, or slander for slander, but rather say a blessing. This is what you were called to, so that you may inherit a blessing.

> ¹⁰For the one who wants to love life and see good days
> should guard the tongue from evil, and the lips from speaking deceit;
> ¹¹should turn away from evil and do good;
> should seek peace, and follow after it.
> ¹²For the Lord's eyes are upon the righteous,
> and his ears are open to their prayer,
> but the face of the Lord is against those who do evil.

¹³Who is there, then, to harm you if you are eager to do what is right? ¹⁴But if you do suffer because of your righteous behaviour, God's blessing is upon you! 'Don't fear what they fear; don't be disturbed.' ¹⁵Sanctify the Messiah as Lord in your hearts, and always be ready to make a reply to anyone who asks you to explain the hope that is in you. ¹⁶Do it, though, with gentleness and respect. Hold on to a good conscience, so that when people revile your good behaviour in the Messiah they may be ashamed.

Suffering for doing right

¹⁷It's better to suffer for good conduct (if God so wills it) than for bad. ¹⁸For the Messiah, too,

suffered once for sins, the just for the unjust, so that he might bring you to God. He was put to death in the flesh, but made alive by the spirit. [19]In the spirit, too, he went and made the proclamation to the spirits in prison [20]who had earlier on been disobedient during the days of Noah, when God waited in patience. Noah built the ark, in which a few people, eight in fact, were rescued through water. [21]That functions as a signpost for you, pointing to baptism, which now rescues you – not by washing away fleshly pollution, but by the appeal to God of a good conscience, through the resurrection of Jesus the Messiah. [22]He has gone into heaven and is at God's right hand, with angels, authorities and powers subject to him.

Transformed living

4 So, then, just as the Messiah suffered in the flesh, you too must equip yourselves with the same mental armour. Someone who suffers in the flesh has ceased from sin, [2]so as to live the rest of their mortal life no longer according to human desires but according to God's will. [3]Pagan ways of life have had quite enough of your time already, and you should put all that behind you for good – all that uncleanness, passion, drunkenness, excessive feasting, drinking-parties and lawless idolatry. [4]People are shocked that you don't now join in with the same wild and reckless behaviour, and so they call down curses on you. [5]But they will have to account for it before the one who is ready to judge the living and the dead. [6]That is why, you see, the gospel was preached even to the dead, so that, being judged in human fashion, in the flesh, they might live in God's fashion, in the spirit.

[7]The end of all things is upon us. You must keep sober, then, and self-disciplined for your prayers. [8]Above all, keep absolutely firm in your love for one another, because 'love covers a multitude of sins'. [9]Be hospitable to one another without complaining. [10]Just as each of you has received a gift, so you should use it for ministry one to another, as good stewards of God's many-sided grace. [11]If anyone speaks, they should do so as speaking God's oracles. If anyone ministers, they should do it as in the strength which God grants, so that God may be glorified in all things through Jesus the Messiah, to whom be glory and power for ever and ever. Amen.

Sharing the Messiah's sufferings

[12]Beloved, don't be surprised at the fiery ordeal which is coming upon you to test you, as though this were some strange thing that was happening to you. [13]Rather, celebrate! You are sharing the sufferings of the Messiah. Then, when his glory is revealed, you will celebrate with real, exuberant joy. [14]If you are abused because of the name of the Messiah, you are blessed by God, because the spirit of glory and of God is resting upon you. [15]None of you, of course, should suffer as a murderer or thief or evildoer, or even as a busybody. [16]But if you suffer as a Christian, don't be ashamed; rather, give God the glory for that name! [17]The time has come, you see, for judgment to begin at God's own household. And if it begins with us, what will be the end of those who do not obey the gospel? [18]And if the righteous person is scarcely saved, where will the ungodly and the sinner appear? [19]So also those who suffer according to God's will should entrust their whole lives to the faithful creator by doing what is good.

Humble shepherds

5 So, then, I appeal to the elders among you, as a fellow-elder and a witness of the sufferings of the Messiah, and as one who will share in the glory that is to be revealed. [2]Do the proper work of a shepherd as you look after God's flock which has been entrusted to you, not under compulsion, but gladly, as in God's presence, not for shameful profit but eagerly. [3]You should not lord it over those for whom you are responsible, but rather be an example to the flock. [4]And when the chief shepherd appears, you will receive the crown of glory that won't wither away. [5]In the same way, too, the younger men should submit to the elders. But let all of you clothe yourselves with humility towards one another. You see, 'God resists the proud, but gives grace to the

lowly.' ⁶Humble yourselves, then, under God's powerful hand, so that he may lift you up at the right time. ⁷Throw all your care upon him, because he cares about you.

Standing firm by God's power

⁸Stay in control of yourselves; stay awake. Your enemy, the devil, is stalking around like a roaring lion, looking for someone to devour. ⁹Resist him, staying resolute in your faith, and knowing that other family members in the rest of the world are facing identical sufferings. ¹⁰Then, after you have suffered a little while, the God of all grace, who called you in the Messiah Jesus to the glory of his new age, will himself put you in good order, and will establish and strengthen you and set you on firm foundations. ¹¹To him be the power for ever. Amen.

¹²I have written this briefly, and am sending it to you with Silvanus, whom I regard as a faithful brother. My main point is to urge and bear witness to you that this grace, in which you stand, is the true grace of God. ¹³Your chosen sister in Babylon sends you greetings; so does my son Mark. ¹⁴Greet one another with a holy kiss.

Peace to you all in the Messiah.

2 Peter

The second Petrine letter picks up the strong hope evident in the first letter, rooting it in the gospel events themselves, warning against false prophets who would lead people astray, and assuring the faithful that what seems to us like 'delay' is irrelevant in the purposes of God. The letter offers the fullest exposition in early Christian writings of the idea of sustained character development: faith must be supplemented with virtue, virtue with knowledge, knowledge with self-control, self-control with patience, patience with piety, piety with family affection, and family affection with love (1.5–7). Facing a dangerous world but holding on to the gospel hope, this is how the young church will make it clear who they truly are.

Second Peter also offers the only reference outside the gospels to the transfiguration (Mark 9.2–8; here at 1.16–21). The author links this extraordinary moment to the scriptural promises: the Bible on the one hand, and the divine revelation in Jesus on the other, are the anchors of faith. These will be needed, because false prophets will emerge in the church, just as they did in ancient Israel; and the letter gives a detailed warning against such people.

The false teachers will richly earn the condemnation they will incur (2.1–3), just as did the wicked angels and humans in ancient times (2.4–9). They will go from bad to worse; the central and detailed denunciation (2.10–22) indicates that some of these people at least have professed Christian faith but have now turned back to the corruptions of the present age, and are eager to drag others back with them, promising them 'freedom' while in fact being enslaved to corruption (2.19). It would be interesting to reflect on why warnings like this sound so unfashionable in the churches of our own time.

The warnings are the more necessary because the final day, when God will make new heavens and new earth, will surely come, even though some scoffers suggest that its present delay indicates otherwise (3.1–10). God's timetable is not the same as ours, and with his judgment 'the earth and all the works on it will be disclosed' (3.10): the veils of deceit will be stripped off and all will at last appear in their true colours. This sets the framework for the final appeal: God is being patient, and so must we, standing firm and growing in grace (3.11–18).

Confirm your call!

1 Simon Peter, a slave and apostle of Jesus the Messiah, to those who have obtained a share of faith equal to ours in the righteousness of our God and saviour Jesus the Messiah: ²may grace and peace be multiplied to you, in the knowledge of God and of Jesus our Lord.

³God has bestowed upon us, through his divine power, everything that we need for life and godliness, through the knowledge of him who called us by his own glory and virtue. ⁴The result is that he has given us, through these things, his precious and wonderful promises; and the purpose of all this is so that you may run away from the corruption of lust that is in the world, and may become partakers of the divine nature. ⁵So, because of this, you should strain every nerve to supplement your faith with virtue, and your virtue with knowledge, ⁶and your knowledge with self-control, and your self-control with patience, and your patience with piety, ⁷and your piety with family affection, and your family affection with love. ⁸If you have these things in plentiful supply, you see, you will not be wasting your time, or failing to bear fruit, in relation to your knowledge of our Lord Jesus the Messiah. ⁹Someone who doesn't have these things, in fact, is so short-sighted as to be actually blind, and has forgotten what it means to be cleansed from earlier sins. ¹⁰So, my dear family, you must make the effort all the more to confirm that God has called you and chosen you. If you do this, you will never trip up. ¹¹That is how you will have, richly laid out before you, an entrance into the kingdom of God's coming age, the kingdom of our Lord and saviour Jesus the Messiah.

Prophecy made sure

¹²So I intend to go on and on reminding you about all this – even though you know it, and have been firmly established in the truth which has come to you. ¹³But it seems right to me, as long as I am living in this present tent, to stir you up with a reminder, ¹⁴since I know that I shall shortly be putting off this tent, as our Lord Jesus the Messiah showed me. ¹⁵So I shall also be making every effort to ensure that, once I am gone, you may be able to call these things to mind at any time.

¹⁶When we made known to you the power and appearing of our Lord Jesus the Messiah, you see, we were not following cleverly devised myths. Rather, we were eyewitnesses of his grandeur. ¹⁷For when he received honour and glory from God the father, a voice spoke to him from the Wonderful Glory, 'This is my son, my beloved one, in whom I am well pleased.' ¹⁸We heard this voice, spoken from heaven, when we were with him on the holy mountain. ¹⁹And we have the prophetic word made more certain. You will do well to hold on to this, as to a lamp shining in a dark place, until the day dawns and the morning star shines in your hearts. ²⁰You must know this first of all, that no scriptural prophecy is a matter of one's own interpretation. ²¹No prophecy, you see, ever came by human will. Rather, people were moved by the holy spirit, and spoke from God.

False prophets

2 There were, however, false prophets among the people, just as there will be false teachers among yourselves, who will sneak in with their destructive false teachings, even denying the master who paid the price for them. They will earn swift destruction for themselves, ²and many will follow after their disgusting practices. The way of truth will be blasphemed because of them, ³and in their greed they will exploit you with fake prophecies. Their condemnation has not been idle for a long time now, and their destruction has not fallen asleep.

⁴God didn't spare the angels who sinned, you see, but he threw them into the pit, into dark caverns, handing them over to be guarded until the time of judgment. ⁵Similarly, he didn't spare the ancient world, but brought a flood on the world of the ungodly and rescued Noah, a herald of righteousness, with seven others. ⁶Similarly, he condemned the cities of Sodom and Gomorrah, reducing them to ashes and ruin, thus setting up an example of what would happen to the ungodly. ⁷He snatched righteous Lot out of the disaster, a man who had been deeply troubled by their shameful and unprincipled behaviour. ⁸That righteous man, you see, living in their midst, could see

and hear day after day lawless deeds which tortured his righteous soul. ⁹The Lord knows how to rescue the godly from testing, and also how to keep the unrighteous ready for the day of judgment and punishment, ¹⁰ᵃ especially those who follow after the pollution of fleshly lust and despise authority.

From bad to worse

¹⁰ᵇ Such people are arrogant and self-willed! They are not afraid to blaspheme the glorious ones, ¹¹whereas the angels, stronger and more powerful though they are, do not bring a charge of blasphemy against them before the Lord.

¹²These people are like unreasoning beasts, by nature born to be caught and destroyed. They curse at things of which they have no knowledge; they are destroyed by their own self-destructive tendencies. ¹³They commit injustice, and receive injustice as their reward. They count it pleasure to hold wild revels in the daytime. If they join you for a meal, they pollute and stain the whole thing as they wallow in their disgusting pleasures. ¹⁴Their eyes are full of adultery; they can't get enough of sin; when they find unsteady souls, they lead them astray; their hearts have been trained in greed; they are children of the curse. ¹⁵They have left the straight path and have wandered off in pursuit of Balaam son of Bosor, who loved the reward of unrighteousness, ¹⁶and was rebuked for his disobedience when a normally speechless donkey spoke in a human voice to stop the prophet's madness in its tracks.

¹⁷These people are springs without water. They are patches of fog driven along by a storm. The depth of darkness has been reserved for them! ¹⁸They utter bombastic words of folly as they entice, with licentious fleshly desires, those who have only just escaped from the company of people who behave improperly. ¹⁹They promise them freedom, but they themselves are slaves to corruption. (A person who is defeated by something, you see, is enslaved to it.) ²⁰For if they have fled the pollutions of the world through the knowledge of our Lord and saviour Jesus the Messiah, but again become entangled in them and are defeated, they have ended up in a worse state than they were before. ²¹It would have been better for them never to have known the way of righteousness than, having known it, to turn away from the holy commandment which had been given to them. ²²There is a true proverb which now applies to them: the dog returns to its own vomit, and the sow gets washed only to wallow once more in the mud.

The day of the Lord

3 My dear family, this is now the second time I am writing you a letter. Your motives are pure, and what I'm trying to do in reminding you is to stir them into action, ²so that you'll remember the words spoken earlier by the holy prophets, and by the command of the Lord and saviour which you received from your apostles. ³But you must first know this. Deceivers will come in the last days, with deceitful ways, behaving according to their own desires. ⁴This is what they will say: 'Where is the promise of his royal arrival? Ever since the previous generation died, everything has continued just as it has from the beginning of creation.' ⁵They willingly overlook this one thing, you see: the ancient heavens and earth were formed out of water and through water, by God's word – ⁶and it was by flooding the world of that time with water that it was destroyed. ⁷The heavens and earth that we now have are being preserved for fire by the same word, being kept for the day of judgment and the destruction of the wicked. ⁸So, beloved, don't forget this one thing, that a single day with the Lord is like a thousand years, and a thousand years like a single day. ⁹The Lord is not delaying his promise, in the way that some reckon delay, but he is very patient towards you. He does not want anyone to be destroyed. Rather, he wants everyone to arrive at repentance.

¹⁰But the Lord's day will come like a thief. On that day the heavens will pass away with a great rushing sound, the elements will be dissolved in fire, and the earth and all the works on it will be disclosed.

God's patience

¹¹Since everything is going to dissolve in this way, what sort of people should you be? You should live lives that are holy and godly, ¹²as

you look for God's day to appear, and indeed hurry it on its way – the day because of which the heavens will be set on fire and dissolved, and the elements will melt with heat. ¹³But we are waiting for new heavens and a new earth, in which justice will be at home. That is what he has promised.

¹⁴So, my dear family, as you wait for these things, be eager to be found without spot or blemish before him, in peace. ¹⁵And when our Lord waits patiently to act, see that for what it is – salvation! Our beloved brother Paul has written to you about all this, according to the wisdom that has been given him, ¹⁶speaking about these things as he does in all his letters. There are some things in them which are difficult to understand. Untaught and unstable people twist his words to their own destruction, as they do with the other scriptures.

¹⁷But as for you, my dear family, be on your guard, since you have been warned in advance. That way you won't be led astray through the error of lawless people and fall away from your own solid grounding. ¹⁸Instead, grow in grace and in the knowledge of our Lord and saviour Jesus the Messiah. To him be glory both now and in the day when God's new age dawns. Amen.

1 John

The three short letters of John are possibly but not certainly by the same writer as the gospel of that name. The first one moves in widening circles around the main theme of the love of God, revealed in Jesus and his death and needing to be worked out in and through the life of the community. Those who belong to Jesus have a new identity which will be fully revealed when Jesus appears, committing them in the present to the life of purity as well as love (3.1–3).

The letter opens with a passage that reminds us of the start of the gospel (the Word of life which was from the beginning), but which moves at once to the sharp challenge of discipleship. To claim that we belong to God while 'walking in the darkness' is to tell lies. But there is no need to pretend, since we have all sinned, and the good news is that the blood of Jesus will cleanse those who confess their sins and 'walk in the light' (1.5—2.2). This language of sacrifice makes sense within the biblical world of thought where 'heaven' and 'earth', designed to come together, require that everything to do with death – and sin, rooted in idolatry, is the ultimate cause of death – must be made clean if it is to come within God's presence. And, in scripture, the cleansing agent is the blood which symbolizes life. It may be easier for us today to work backwards from Jesus to an understanding of ancient biblical sacrifices: it is the life of Jesus, laid down in self-giving love for the world, that now holds heaven and earth together and enables even sinners like us to 'have fellowship' with God.

But that is only the beginning. Once we are assured of being God's people, the way we continue in this heaven-and-earth life is through the self-giving love which mirrors that of God himself (2.3–14). Many will try to deceive us, and sadly this will include some of our own number, and we will be able to recognize them because they will deny that Jesus is really Israel's Messiah (2.22). The sign of true belonging, however, is a resolute turning from sin (3.1–10), and again this means the positive challenge of self-sacrificial love modelled on that of Jesus himself (3.16).

One specific error is a further tell-tale sign of a deceitful or counterfeit faith: some will deny that Jesus the Messiah really came 'in the flesh'. This was a serious problem in parts of the early church, and John links this super-spirituality with the kind of superior attitude that thinks itself above the practical demands of love in the community (4.1–21). By contrast, the true God is known precisely in Jesus and his death; all else is, in the last analysis, a form of idolatry (5.21). The letter binds together a rich faith in Jesus with a robust call to the love which will make that faith known in the world.

The Word of Life

1 That which was from the beginning, which we have heard, which we have seen with our eyes, which we have gazed at, and our hands have handled – concerning the Word of Life! ²That life was displayed, and we have seen it, and bear witness, and we announce to you the life of God's coming age, which was with the father and was displayed to us. ³That which we have seen and heard, we announce to you too, so that you also may have fellowship with us. And our fellowship is with the father, and with his son Jesus the Messiah. ⁴We are writing these things so that our joy may be complete.

God's light and our darkness

⁵This is the message which we have heard from him, and announce to you: God is light, and there is no darkness at all in him. ⁶If we say that we have fellowship with him and walk in the dark, we are telling lies, and not doing what is true. ⁷But if we walk in the light, just as he is in the light, we have fellowship with one another, and the blood of Jesus his son makes us pure and clean from all sin. ⁸If we say that we have no sin, we deceive ourselves and the truth is not in us. ⁹If we confess our sins, he is faithful and just, and will forgive us our sins, and cleanse us from all unrighteousness. ¹⁰If we say that we have not sinned, we make him out to be a liar, and his word is not in us.

2 My children, I am writing these things to you so that you may not sin. If anyone does sin, we have one who pleads our cause before the father – namely, the Righteous One, Jesus the Messiah! ²He is the sacrifice which atones for our sins – and not ours only, either, but those of the whole world.

God's new commandment

³This is how we are sure that we have known him, if we keep his commandments. ⁴Anyone who says, 'I know him', but doesn't keep his commandments, is a liar. People like that have no truth in them. ⁵But if anyone keeps his word, God's love is truly made complete in such a person. This is how we are sure that we are in him: ⁶anyone who says, 'I abide in him', ought to behave in the same way that he behaved.

⁷My beloved ones, I am not writing a new command to you, but an old command which you have had from the very beginning. The old command is the word which you heard. ⁸Again, however, I am writing a new command to you: it is true in him and in you, because the darkness is passing away and the true light is already shining. ⁹Anyone who says, 'I am in the light', while hating another family member, is still in darkness up to this very moment. ¹⁰Anyone who loves another family member abides in the light, and there is no cause of offence in such a person. ¹¹Anyone who hates another family member is in the darkness, and walks about in the darkness. Such people have no idea where they are going, because the darkness has blinded their eyes.

¹²I am writing to you, children,
because your sins are forgiven through his name.
¹³I am writing to you, fathers,
because you have known the one who is from
    the beginning.
I am writing to you, young people,
because you have conquered the evil one.

¹⁴I have written to you, children,
because you have known the father.
I have written to you, fathers,
because you have known the one who is from
    the beginning.
I have written to you, young people,
because you are strong,
and the word of God abides in you,
and you have conquered the evil one.

People of the lie

¹⁵Do not love the world, or the things that are in the world. If anyone loves the world, the father's love is not in them. ¹⁶Everything in the world, you see – the greedy desire of the flesh, the greedy desire of the eyes, the pride of life – none of this is from the father. It is from the world. ¹⁷The world is passing away, with all its greedy desires. But anyone who does God's will abides for ever.

¹⁸Children, it is the last hour. You have heard that 'Antimessiah' is coming – and now many Antimessiahs have appeared! That's how we know that it is the last hour. ¹⁹They went out from among us, but they were not really of our number. If they had been of our number, you see, they would have remained with us. This happened so that it would be made crystal clear that none of them belonged to us. ²⁰You, however, have the anointing from the Holy One, and you all have knowledge. ²¹I am not writing to you because you don't know the truth, but because you do know it, and you know that no liar is of the truth.

²²Who is the liar? Is it not the one who denies that Jesus is the Messiah? Such a one is the Antimessiah – who denies the father and the son. ²³Nobody who denies the son has the father. One who acknowledges the son has the father too. ²⁴As for you: let what you heard from the beginning abide in you. If what you heard from the beginning abides in you, you too will abide in the son and in the father. ²⁵And this is the promise which he himself promised us: the life of the age to come.

²⁶I am writing to you about the people who are deceiving you. ²⁷You have received the anointing from him; it abides in you, and you do not need to have anyone teach you. That anointing from him teaches you about everything; it is true, it isn't a lie. So, just as he taught you, abide in him.

²⁸And now, children, abide in him, so that when he is revealed we may have boldness and may not be put to shame before him at his royal appearing. ²⁹If you know that he is righteous, you know that everyone who does what is right has been fathered by him.

Born of God

3 Look at the remarkable love the father has given us – that we should be called God's children! That indeed is what we are. That's why the world doesn't know us, because it didn't know him. ²Beloved ones, we are now, already, God's children; it hasn't yet been revealed what we are going to be. We know that when he is revealed we shall be like him, because we shall see him as he is. ³All who have this hope in him make themselves pure, just as he is pure.

⁴Everyone who goes on sinning is breaking the law; sin, in fact, is lawlessness. ⁵And you know that he was revealed so that he might take away sins, and there is no sin in him. ⁶Everyone who abides in him does not go on sinning. Everyone who goes on sinning has not seen him, or known him.

⁷Children, don't let anyone deceive you. The person who does righteousness is righteous, just as he is righteous. ⁸The person who goes on sinning is from the devil, because the devil is a sinner from the very start. The son of God was revealed for this purpose, to destroy the works of the devil. ⁹Everyone who is fathered by God does not go on sinning, because God's offspring remain in him; they cannot go on sinning, because they have been fathered by God. ¹⁰That is how it is clear who are the children of God and who are the children of the devil: everyone who does not do what is right is not of God, particularly those who do not love their brother or sister.

The challenge of love

¹¹This is the message which you heard right from the start, you see, that we should love one another. ¹²We should not be like Cain, who was of the evil one, and murdered his brother. Why did he murder him? Because his deeds were evil, while his brother's were right.

¹³Don't be surprised, my brothers and sisters, if the world hates you. ¹⁴We know that we have passed from death to life, because we love the family. Anyone who doesn't love abides in death. ¹⁵Everyone who hates their brother or sister is a murderer, and you know that no murderer has the life of the coming age abiding in them. ¹⁶This is how we know love: he laid down his life for us. And we too ought to lay down our lives for our brothers and sisters. ¹⁷Anyone who has the means of life in this world, and sees a brother or sister in need, and closes their heart against them – how can God's love be abiding in them? ¹⁸Children, let us not love in word, or in speech, but in deed and in truth.

¹⁹Because of this, we know we are of the truth, and we will persuade our hearts of this fact before him, ²⁰because if our hearts condemn us, God is greater than our

hearts. He knows everything. ²¹Beloved, if our hearts do not condemn us, we have boldness before God, ²²and we receive from him whatever we ask, because we keep his commands and give him pleasure when he sees what we are doing. ²³And this is his command, that we should believe in the name of his son Jesus the Messiah, and should love one another, just as he gave us the commandment. ²⁴Anyone who keeps his commandments abides in him, and he in them. This is how we know that he abides in us, by his spirit that he has given us.

False prophets

4 Beloved, do not believe every spirit. Rather, test the spirits to see whether they are from God. Many false prophets, you see, have gone out into the world. ²This is how we know God's spirit: every spirit that agrees that Jesus the Messiah has come in the flesh is from God, ³and every spirit that does not confess Jesus is not from God. This spirit is actually the spirit of the Antimessiah. You have heard that it was coming, and now it is already in the world.

⁴But you, children, are from God, and you have overcome them, because the one who is in you is greater than the one who is in the world. ⁵They are from the world, and that is why they speak from the world, and why the world listens to them. ⁶We are from God; people who know God listen to us, but people who are not from God do not listen to us. That is how we can tell the spirit of truth from the spirit of error.

God's love

⁷Beloved, let us love one another, because love is from God, and all who love are fathered by God and know God. ⁸The one who does not love has not known God, because God is love. ⁹This is how God's love has appeared among us: God sent his only son into the world, so that we should live through him. ¹⁰Love consists in this: not that we loved God, but that he loved us and sent his son to be the sacrifice that would atone for our sins. ¹¹Beloved, if that's how God loved us, we ought to love one another in the same way. ¹²Nobody has ever seen God. If we love one another, God abides in us and his love is completed in us. ¹³That is how we know that we abide in him, and he in us, because he has given us a portion of his spirit. ¹⁴And we have seen and bear witness that the father sent the son to be the world's saviour. ¹⁵Anyone who confesses that Jesus is God's son, God abides in them and they abide in God. ¹⁶And we have known and have believed the love which God has for us.

God is love; those who abide in love abide in God, and God abides in them. ¹⁷This is what makes love complete for us, so that we may have boldness and confidence on the day of judgment, because just as he is, so are we within this world. ¹⁸There is no fear in love; complete love drives out fear. Fear has to do with punishment, and anyone who is afraid has not been completed in love. ¹⁹We love, because he first loved us. ²⁰If someone says, 'I love God', but hates their brother or sister, that person is a liar. Someone who doesn't love a brother or sister whom they have seen, how can they love God, whom they haven't seen? ²¹This is the command we have from him: anyone who loves God should love their brother or sister too.

Faith wins the victory

5 Everyone who believes that the Messiah is Jesus has been fathered by God. Everyone who loves the parent loves the child as well. ²That is how we know that we love the children of God, because we love God and do what he commands. ³This is what loving God means: it means keeping his commandments. His commandments, what's more, are no trouble, ⁴because everything that is fathered by God conquers the world. This is the victory that conquers the world: our faith.

⁵Who is the one who conquers the world? Surely the one who believes that Jesus is God's son! ⁶It was he who came by means of water and blood, Jesus the Messiah, not by water only but by the water and the blood. The spirit is the one who bears witness, because the spirit is the truth. ⁷There are three that bear witness, you see, ⁸the spirit, the water and the blood, and these three agree together. ⁹If we have received human witness, God's

witness is greater. This is the witness of God, the testimony he has borne to his son. ¹⁰All those who believe in the son of God have the witness in themselves, but anyone who does not believe in God has made a liar of him, because they have not believed in the witness which God bore concerning his son. ¹¹This is the witness: God has given us the life of the age to come, and this life is in his son. ¹²Anyone who has the son has life. Anyone who does not have the son of God does not have life.

The true God

¹³I am writing these things to you so that you may know that you, who believe in the name of the son of God, do indeed have the life of the age to come. ¹⁴This is the bold confidence we have before him: if we ask for something according to his will, he hears us. ¹⁵And if we know that he hears us in whatever we ask, we know that we already possess the requests we have asked from him.

¹⁶If anyone sees a brother or sister committing a sin which is not deadly, they should ask, and God will give life to the people who are sinning in a way which is not deadly. There is such a thing as deadly sin; I do not say that one should pray about that. ¹⁷All sin is unrighteousness, and there is a sin which is not deadly.

¹⁸We know that everyone fathered by God does not go on sinning. The one who was fathered by God keeps them, and the evil one does not touch them. ¹⁹We know that we are from God, and the whole world is under the power of the evil one. ²⁰We know that the son of God has come and has given us understanding so that we should know the truth. And we are in the truth, in his son Jesus the Messiah.

This is the true God; this is the life of the age to come. ²¹Children, guard yourselves against idols.

2 John

The short second letter continues the same theme as the first, warning against 'deceivers'. It will be easy for followers of Jesus to be drawn away from their primary task, which is to love one another. The letter provides a quick glimpse of an early church in which different teachers are moving to and fro from place to place, so that local communities need to know who is to be trusted. The gold standard remains the coming of Jesus the Messiah in the flesh: from early days in the church this extraordinary truth, celebrated in the dramatic opening of John's gospel ('the Word became flesh', John 1.14), was under attack. While some in our own day have struggled to see how a human being could also be divine, in the early church the same problem was often seen from the other side of the coin, as to how the one God might reveal himself in and as a human being. But only the full truth, however mind-blowing, will do. Anyone who abides in 'the teaching' – the true teaching of the father and the son – is part of the fellowship of 'truth and love' (verse 3).

The letter is addressed by 'the Elder' to a particular church, seen as 'the Chosen Lady'. The author is part of a sister church, whose members he refers to as 'the children of your Chosen Sister' (verses 1, 13). It is not clear whether this was simply an elegant metaphor, or whether it was a kind of disguise at a time when churches were facing persecution.

The sign of life

¹From the Elder to the Chosen Lady and her children, whom I love in truth – as indeed, in addition to myself, do all those who know the truth, ²because of the truth that abides in us and is with us for ever. ³Grace, mercy and peace from God the father and from Jesus the Messiah, the son of the father, be with us in truth and love.

⁴I was delighted when I found some of your children walking in the truth, just as we received the commandment from the father. ⁵And now, dear Lady, I ask you, not as though I were writing you a new commandment, but the one we had from the very beginning, that we should love one another. ⁶This is love: that we should behave in accordance with his commandments. And this is the commandment, just as you heard it from the very start, that we should behave in accordance with it.

Don't be deceived!

⁷Many deceivers, you see, have gone out into the world. These are people who do not admit that Jesus the Messiah has come in the flesh. Such a person is the Deceiver – the Antimessiah! ⁸Watch out for yourselves, so that you won't lose what we have worked for, but may receive the full reward.

⁹Anyone who goes out on their own, and does not abide in the teaching of the Messiah, does not have God. One who abides in the teaching – such a one has the father and the son. ¹⁰If anyone comes to you and does not bring this teaching, don't receive them into the house; don't even give them a greeting. ¹¹Anyone who utters a greeting to such a person shares in their wicked deeds.

¹²I have many things to write to you, but I did not wish to write with pen and ink. I am hoping instead to come to you, and to speak face to face. That will complete our joy.

¹³The children of your Chosen Sister send you greetings.

3 John

The third Johannine letter is about hospitality. As the church spread, with groups of a dozen or two in a town or village, and with increasing hostility from the surrounding culture, it was vital that Jesus-followers travelling from place to place as teachers or on other business should be able to trust one another. This letter, to 'beloved Gaius', an otherwise unknown Christian, congratulates him on the hospitality that he has offered to 'family members', that is, fellow Christians, who have subsequently given glad testimony to the welcome they had received.

Unfortunately, however, not everyone is behaving in such a generous spirit. The writer warns against one Diotrephes, who is spreading false rumours about the Elder himself, and is refusing to welcome genuine fellow believers and expelling, from his community, other Jesus-followers who want to do so. The writer denounces him: he is simply trying to boost his own prestige (verses 9–10). At the same time, Demetrius is well attested (verse 12); perhaps he was the bearer of this letter.

The writer appeals to the common standard of behaviour; when things are tough, the basic things need repeating: 'don't imitate evil; imitate good!' (verse 11). This letter, like the others in this group, offers a small vignette on the challenges of living as a Jesus-follower in troubled times.

Hospitality for God's people

¹The Elder to beloved Gaius, whom I love in truth.

²Beloved, I pray that all is going well with you, and that you are every bit as healthy physically as you are spiritually. ³I was absolutely delighted, you see, when some of the family arrived and bore witness to your truthfulness, since clearly you are walking in the truth. ⁴Nothing gives me greater joy than this, to hear that my children are walking in the truth.

⁵Beloved, when you are doing all that you do for family members, even when they are strangers, you are doing a faithful work. ⁶These people have borne witness to your love in the presence of the assembly, and you will do well to send them on their way in a manner worthy of God. ⁷They went out for the sake of the Name, not accepting help from outsiders. ⁸We ought to support people like that, so that we may become fellow-workers with the truth.

Authority and example

⁹I have written something to the assembly. But Diotrephes, who wants to be the most important person there, refuses to acknowledge us. ¹⁰So, then, if I come, I will refer back to what he has done, and the slanderous words he has spoken against us. Not being satisfied with that, he doesn't welcome family members himself; and, when others want to do so, he forbids them and throws them out of the assembly.

¹¹Beloved, don't imitate evil; imitate good! Someone who does good is from God; someone who does evil has not seen God. ¹²Demetrius has been well attested by everybody, and by the truth itself. We join in this testimony, and you know that our testimony is true.

¹³I have much to write to you, but I don't want to do it with pen and ink. ¹⁴I am hoping instead to see you very soon, so that we can talk face to face.

¹⁵Peace be with you. All the friends greet you. Greet all the friends by name.

Judah

The short letter of Judah (often spelt in a modern form, 'Jude') warns against false teachers. The letter overlaps to some extent with 2 Peter. The author is the 'brother of James' (1), and he urges the hearers to work hard to defend the faith as originally given (3).

This warning is necessary because the community has been infiltrated by people who are changing the original faith into something else. They are doing two things in particular. First, they are 'transforming God's grace into licentiousness' (verse 4). As Paul saw in Romans 6, this was always going to be a danger for any who had seen the law of Moses as a strict moral code and had then heard the gospel of Jesus as a way of saying that the law didn't matter any more. Suddenly the moral brake is taken off, and the result is behavioural chaos.

Second, they are 'denying the one and only master' (verse 4), Jesus himself. They are happy to acknowledge Jesus, perhaps, but only as one teacher among others – and the others will no doubt take different views on various topics.

These two obviously go together: anything you don't like in the Mosaic law can be got around by appealing to the gospel of Jesus, and anything you don't like in the teaching of Jesus can be got around by appealing to a different teacher. To understand just how dangerous such distortions are, the writer takes his readers back to the scriptures and to some of the ways in which the ancient stories had been developed in subsequent Jewish tradition.

One must, then, stand firm. It is vital to build yourself up in faith and prayer, and to 'keep yourselves in the love of God' (verse 21). But, more importantly still, it is God himself 'who is able to keep you standing upright, and to present you before his glory, undefiled and joyful' (verse 24). When all the warnings have been duly noted, one should always return to the basic Christian activity, which is the glad celebration and praise of the God who has saved us through Jesus the Messiah (verse 25). This short letter is as bracing in its challenge today as it was to its first hearers.

Contend for the faith

¹Judah, slave of Jesus the Messiah, brother of James, to those who are called, the people whom God loves and whom Jesus, the Messiah, keeps safe! ²May mercy, peace and love be multiplied to you.

³Beloved, I was doing my best to write to you about the rescue in which we share, but I found it necessary to write to you to urge you to struggle hard for the faith which was once and for all given to God's people. ⁴Some people have sneaked in among you, it seems, who long ago were marked out for this condemnation – ungodly people, who are transforming God's grace into licentiousness, and denying the one and only master, our Lord Jesus the Messiah.

False teachers

⁵I do want to remind you, even though you know it all well, that when the Lord once and for all delivered his people out of the land of Egypt, he subsequently destroyed those who did not believe. ⁶In the same way, when some of the angels did not keep to their rightful place of authority, but abandoned their own home, he kept them under conditions of darkness and in eternal chains to await the judgment of the great day. ⁷In similar fashion, Sodom, Gomorrah and the cities round about, which had lived in gross immorality and lusted after unnatural flesh, are set before us as a pattern, undergoing the punishment of endless fire.

⁸However, these people are behaving in the same way! They are dreaming their way into defiling the flesh, rejecting authority and cursing the Glorious Ones. ⁹Even Michael the archangel, when disputing with the devil about the body of Moses, did not presume to lay against him a charge of blasphemy, but simply said, 'The Lord rebuke you.' ¹⁰These people, however, curse anything they don't know. They are like dumb animals; there are some things they understand instinctively – but it is these very things that destroy them. ¹¹A curse on them! They go off in the way of Cain; they give themselves over for money into Balaam's deceitful ways; they are destroyed in Korah's rebellion. ¹²These are the ones who pollute your love-feasts; they share your table without fear while simply looking after their own needs. They are waterless clouds blown along by the winds. They are fruitless autumn trees, doubly dead and uprooted. ¹³They are stormy waves out at sea, splashing up their own shameful ways. They are wandering stars, and the deepest everlasting darkness has been kept for them in particular.

¹⁴Enoch, the seventh in line from Adam, prophesied about these people. 'Look!' he said. 'The Lord comes with ten thousand of his holy ones, ¹⁵to perform judgment against all, and to charge every human being with all the ungodly ways in which they have done ungodly things, and with every harsh word which ungodly sinners have spoken against him.' ¹⁶These people are always grumbling and complaining, chasing off after their own desires. From their mouths come arrogant words, buttering people up for the sake of gain.

Rescued by God's power

¹⁷But you, my beloved ones, remember the words that were spoken before by the apostles of our Lord Jesus the Messiah. ¹⁸'In the last time,' they said to you, 'there will be scornful people who follow their own ungodly desires.' ¹⁹These are the people who cause divisions. They are living on the merely human level; they do not have the spirit. ²⁰But you, beloved ones, build yourselves up in your most holy faith. Pray in the holy spirit. ²¹Keep yourselves in the love of God, as you wait for our Lord Jesus the Messiah to show you the mercy which leads to the life of the age to come.

²²With some people who are wavering, you must show mercy. ²³Some you must rescue, snatching them from the fire. To others you must show mercy, but with fear, hating even the clothes that have been defiled by the flesh.

²⁴Now to the one who is able to keep you standing upright, and to present you before his glory, undefiled and joyful – ²⁵to the one and only God, our saviour through Jesus the Messiah our Lord, be glory, majesty, power and authority before all the ages, and now, and to all the ages to come. Amen.

The Revelation of John

The final book of the New Testament comes as a shock to some and a delight to others. It belongs in the genre we loosely call 'apocalyptic': that is, like the book of Daniel and several other books written in the second-Temple period, it offers a string of visions in which 'heaven' (God's realm) is visible to the seer on 'earth', unveiling the hidden realities which explain the meaning of perplexing this-worldly events. It is, in particular, a 'revelation of Jesus the Messiah' (1.1), the Lion of Judah who is also the Lamb, and of his victory over the powers of evil that would threaten the long-term purposes of the creator God whose throne he shares (5.1–5). The closing scene of the book, and of the Christian Bible, echoes Genesis 1 and 2 with its vision, not of 'saved souls' going up to 'heaven', but of the heavenly city coming to earth, so that God himself will dwell among humans. The 'new heavens and new earth' will be the ultimate cosmic Temple, and the new city will be like its inner sanctum. As in Ezekiel or Zechariah, the river of life will flow out from it, with the tree of life growing on its banks.

The author describes how his vision was granted him while he was in exile on the small Aegean island of Patmos. It was a blinding and glorious vision of Jesus himself (1.12–20), commissioning 'John' (the name was common then as now, and it is unlikely that this is the same 'John' as the author of the gospel or letters) to write to the 'seven churches' in the province of Asia (today's western Turkey): Ephesus, Smyrna, Pergamum, Thyatira, Sardis, Philadelphia and Laodicea. These specific 'letters', with relevant local colour and specific warnings and challenges, form the foundation in chapters 2 and 3 for a kind of second introduction in chapters 4 and 5, where John sees the heavenly throne-room, with all creation worshipping the true God and celebrating the victory of the 'Lamb' over the dark powers that have held back the creator's intentions for the world. Now, humans who are rescued from their sin and its consequences are to take their place as 'a kingdom and priests to our God', and 'will reign on the earth' (1.6; 5.10; 20.6). This victory is to be implemented, in a sequence of overlapping visions, through the trouble and suffering that will follow, particularly at the hands of the 'monsters' – a reference, in chapter 13, to the emperor and his local officials – who will rage against the Lamb's followers but will be overthrown in the final outworking of his victory over 'Babylon', the oppressive imperial power and the demonic powers which sustain it. Then the true 'city of God', the 'new Jerusalem', will appear (chapters 21 and 22).

The book of Revelation has always naturally appealed to artists: here above all the reader needs the disciplined imagination as well as the praying heart and the reasoning mind. Like a great piece of music that will only yield its secrets to the mature and sensitive player, the New Testament is designed not just to offer information about God, Jesus, the world and ourselves but to urge us, by inviting us to penetrate its secrets, to become the kind of people for whom, and indeed through whom, it will at last all make sense.

Look! He is coming!

1 Revelation of Jesus the Messiah! God gave it to him to show his servants what must soon take place. He signified it by sending a message through his angel to his servant John, ²who, by reporting all he saw, bore witness to the word of God and to the testimony of Jesus the Messiah. ³God's blessing on the one who reads the words of this prophecy, and on those who hear them and keep what is written in it. The time, you see, is near!

⁴John, to the seven churches in Asia: grace to you and peace from He Who Is and Who Was and Who Is To Come, and from the seven spirits that are before his throne, ⁵and from Jesus the Messiah, the faithful witness, the firstborn from the dead, and the ruler of the kings of the earth. Glory to the one who loved us, and freed us from our sins by his blood, ⁶and made us a kingdom, priests to his God and father – glory and power be to him for ever and ever. Amen.

⁷Look! He is coming with the clouds, and every eye shall see him; yes, even those who pierced him. All the tribes of the earth shall mourn because of him. Yes! Amen.

⁸'I am the Alpha and the Omega,' says the Lord God, Who Is and Who Was and Who Is To Come, the Almighty.

Jesus revealed

⁹I, John, your brother and your partner in the suffering, the kingdom, and the patient endurance in Jesus, was on the island called Patmos because of the word of God and the testimony of Jesus. ¹⁰I was in the spirit on the Lord's day, and I heard behind me a loud voice like a trumpet. ¹¹'Write down what you see in a book,' it said, 'and send it to the seven churches: to Ephesus, Smyrna, Pergamum, Thyatira, Sardis, Philadelphia and Laodicea.'

¹²So I turned to see the voice that was speaking with me. As I turned, I saw seven golden lampstands, ¹³and in the middle of the lampstands 'one like a son of man', wearing a full-length robe and with a golden belt across his chest. ¹⁴His head and his hair were white, white like wool, white like snow. His eyes were like a flame of fire, ¹⁵his feet were like exquisite brass, refined in a furnace, and his voice was like the sound of many waters. ¹⁶He was holding seven stars in his right hand, and a sharp two-edged sword was coming out of his mouth. The sight of him was like the sun when it shines with full power. ¹⁷When I saw him, I fell at his feet as though I was dead.

He touched me with his right hand. 'Don't be afraid,' he said. 'I am the first and the last ¹⁸and the living one. I was dead, and look! I am alive for ever and ever. I have the keys of death and Hades. ¹⁹Now write what you see, both the things that already are, and also the things that are going to happen afterwards. ²⁰The secret meaning of the seven stars which you saw in my right hand, by the way, and the seven golden lampstands, is this. The seven stars are the angels of the seven churches, and the seven lampstands are the seven churches themselves.

The letter to Ephesus

2 'Write this to the angel of the church in Ephesus. "These are the words of the one who holds the seven stars in his right hand, and who walks in among the seven golden lampstands. ²I know what you have done, your hard labour and patience. I know that you cannot tolerate evil people, and that you have tested those who pass themselves off as apostles, but are not, and you have demonstrated them to be frauds. ³You have patience, and you have put up with a great deal because of my name, and you haven't grown weary. ⁴I do, however, have one thing against you: you have abandoned the love you showed at the beginning. ⁵So remember the place from which you have fallen. Repent, and do the works you did at the beginning. If not – if you don't repent – I will come and remove your lampstand out of its place. ⁶You do, though, have this in your favour: you hate what the Nicolaitans are doing, and I hate it too. ⁷Let anyone who has an ear listen to what the spirit is saying to the churches. The tree of life stands in God's paradise, and I will give to anyone who conquers the right to eat from it."

The letter to Smyrna

⁸'Write this to the angel of the church in Smyrna. "These are the words of the First and

The seven churches of Asia

the Last, the one who was dead and came to life. ⁹I know your suffering and poverty (but you are rich!). I know the blasphemy of those self-styled Jews. They are nothing of the kind. They are a satan-synagogue. ¹⁰Don't be afraid of what you are going to suffer. Look: the devil is going to throw some of you into prison, so that you may be put to the test. You will have ten days of affliction. Be faithful all the way to death, and I will give you the crown of life. ¹¹Let anyone who has an ear listen to what the spirit is saying to the churches. The second death will not harm the one who conquers."

The letter to Pergamum

¹²"Write this to the angel of the church in Pergamum. "These are the words of the one who has the sharp two-edged sword. ¹³I know where you live – right there where the satan has his throne! You have clung on to my name, and have not denied my faith, even in the days of Antipas, my faithful witness, who was killed in your midst, in the dwelling-place of the satan. ¹⁴But I do have a few things against you: you have some people there who hold the teaching of Balaam, who instructed Balak to cause the children of Israel to stumble, making them eat idol-food and indulge in sexual immorality. ¹⁵So, too, you have some among you who hold the teaching of the Nicolaitans. ¹⁶So: repent! If you don't, I will come to you quickly and will fight against them with the sword of my mouth. ¹⁷Let anyone who has an ear listen to what the spirit is saying to the churches. To anyone who conquers I will give secret manna, and a white stone, with a new name written on that stone which nobody knows except the one who receives it."

The letter to Thyatira

¹⁸"Write this to the angel of the church in Thyatira. "These are the words of the son of God, whose eyes are like flaming fire and

whose feet are like exquisite brass. ¹⁹I know what you have done: I know your love, your faith, your service and your patience. I know that your works have been more impressive recently than they were before. ²⁰But I have something against you: you tolerate the woman Jezebel, who calls herself a prophet and teaches my servants (in fact, deceives my servants!) to practise fornication and to eat idol-food. ²¹I gave her time to repent, but she had no wish to repent of her immorality. ²²Look! I am going to throw her on a bed, and those who have committed fornication with her will have great distress, unless they repent of the works into which she has led them. ²³I will utterly slaughter her children, and all the churches will know that I am the one who searches minds and hearts. I will give to each of you what your deeds deserve. ²⁴For the rest of you in Thyatira, those who have not held this teaching, who haven't discovered the so-called 'satanic depths': I'm not going to put any other pressure on you. ²⁵Just hold on tightly to what you have until I come. ²⁶To anyone who conquers, who keeps my works right through to the end, I will give authority over the nations, ²⁷to rule them with a rod of iron, as when clay pots get smashed! ²⁸That is the authority I myself received from my father. What's more, I will give them the morning star. ²⁹Let anyone who has an ear listen to what the spirit says to the churches."

The letter to Sardis

3 'Write this to the angel of the church in Sardis. "These are the words of the one who has the seven spirits of God, and the seven stars. I know what you have done. You have the reputation of being alive, but you are dead. ²Wake up! Strengthen the things that remain – the things that are about to die – because I haven't found your works to be complete in the sight of my God. ³So remember how you received the message, how you heard it and kept it – and repent! So if you don't keep awake, I will come like a thief, and you won't know what time I'm coming to you. ⁴You do, however, have a few people in Sardis who haven't allowed their clothes to become dirty and polluted. They will be clothed in white and will walk with me, as they deserve. ⁵Anyone who conquers will be clothed like this in white robes, and I won't blot their name out of the book of life. I will acknowledge their name in the presence of my father and in the presence of his angels. ⁶Let anyone who has an ear listen to what the spirit is saying to the churches."

The letter to Philadelphia

⁷'Write this to the angel of the church in Philadelphia. "These are the words of the Holy One, the True One, the one who has the key of David, who opens and nobody shuts, who shuts and nobody opens. ⁸I know your works. Look! I have given you an open door, right in front of you, and nobody can shut it, since you have a little power; you have kept my word, and you haven't denied my name. ⁹Look: this is what I will do to the satan-synagogue, who call themselves Jews but who are frauds, nothing of the kind. Take note: this is what I will grant you – that I will make them come and worship before your feet, and they will know that I have loved you. ¹⁰You have kept my word about patience, and so I will keep you from the time of trial that is going to come upon the whole world, to test out all the inhabitants of the earth. ¹¹I am coming quickly! Hold on to what you have, so that nobody takes away your crown. ¹²Anyone who conquers, I will make them a pillar in the temple of my God. They will never go out of it again. I will write on that person the name of my God and the name of the city of my God, the new Jerusalem, which comes down out of heaven from my God, and my own new name. ¹³Let anyone who has an ear listen to what the spirit is saying to the churches."

The letter to Laodicea

¹⁴'Write this to the angel of the church in Laodicea. "These are the words of the Amen, the faithful and true witness, the beginning of God's creation. ¹⁵I know your works: you are neither cold nor hot. I wish you were either cold or hot! ¹⁶So, because you are lukewarm, neither cold nor hot, I am going to vomit you out of my mouth. ¹⁷You say, 'I'm rich! I've done well! I don't need anything!' – but you don't know that you are miserable, pitiful, poor, blind and

naked. ¹⁸This is my advice to you: buy from me gold refined in the fire – that'll make you rich! – and white clothes to cover yourselves and prevent your shameful nakedness being seen; and also healing ointment to put on your eyes, so that you will be able to see. ¹⁹When people are my friends, I tell them when they're in the wrong, and I punish them for it; so stir up your spirits and repent! ²⁰Look! I'm standing here, knocking at the door. If anyone hears my voice and opens the door, I will come in to them and eat with them, and they with me. ²¹This will be my gift to the one who conquers: I will sit them beside me on my throne, just as I conquered and sat with my father on his throne. ²²Let the one who has an ear listen to what the spirit is saying to the churches."'

In the throne room

4 After this I looked – and there was a door in heaven, standing open! The voice like a trumpet, which I had heard speaking with me at the beginning, spoke again. 'Come up here,' it said, 'and I will show you what must take place after these things.'

²At once I was in the spirit. There in heaven stood a throne, and someone was sitting on it. ³The seated figure had the appearance of a jasper stone or a carnelian, and there was a rainbow around the throne, looking like an emerald. ⁴Around the throne were twenty-four thrones, and sitting on the thrones were twenty-four elders, clothed in white robes, and with golden crowns on their heads. ⁵Flashes of lightning, rumblings and thunderclaps were coming from the throne, and in front of the throne seven lampstands, which are the seven spirits of God, were burning with fire. ⁶ᵃIn front of the throne there was something like a sea of glass, like crystal.

Praise to the creator

⁶ᵇIn the middle of the throne, and all around the throne, were four living creatures, full of eyes in front and behind. ⁷The first creature was like a lion, the second creature was like an ox, the third creature had a human face, and the fourth creature was like a flying eagle.

⁸Each of the four creatures had six wings, and they were full of eyes all round and inside. Day and night they take no rest, as they say,

> 'Holy, holy, holy,
> Lord God Almighty,
> Who Was and Who Is and Who Is to Come.'

⁹When the creatures give glory and honour and thanksgiving to the one who is sitting on the throne, the one who lives for ever and ever, ¹⁰the twenty-four elders fall down in front of the one who is sitting on the throne, and worship the one who lives for ever and ever. They throw down their crowns in front of the throne, saying, ¹¹'O Lord our God, you deserve to receive glory and honour and power, because you created all things; because of your will they existed and were created.'

The lion, the lamb

5 I saw that there was a scroll in the right hand of the one sitting on the throne. The scroll was written on the inside and the outside, and it was sealed with seven seals. ²I saw a strong angel announcing in a loud voice, 'Does anybody deserve to open the scroll, to undo its seals?' ³And nobody in heaven or on the earth or under the earth could open the scroll or look at it. ⁴I burst into tears because it seemed that there was nobody who was worthy to open the scroll or look inside it. ⁵One of the elders, however, spoke to me. 'Don't cry,' he said. 'Look! The lion from the tribe of Judah, the Root of David, has won the victory! He can open the scroll and its seven seals.'

⁶Then I saw in the midst of the throne and of the four living creatures, and in the midst of the elders, a lamb. It was standing there as though it had been slaughtered; it had seven horns and seven eyes, which are the seven spirits of God sent out into all the earth. ⁷The lamb came up and took the scroll from the right hand of the one who was sitting on the throne.

Worthy is the lamb!

⁸When he took the scroll, the four living creatures and the twenty-four elders fell down

in front of the lamb. They each had a harp, and they each had golden bowls full of incense, which are the prayers of God's holy people. ⁹They sing a new song, which goes like this:

> 'You are worthy to take the scroll;
> you are worthy to open its seals;
> for you were slaughtered and with your own blood
> you purchased a people for God,
> from every tribe and tongue,
> from every people and nation
> ¹⁰and made them a kingdom and priests to our God
> and they will reign on the earth.'

¹¹As I watched, I heard the voice of many angels around the throne, the living creatures and the elders. Their number was ten thousand times ten thousand, thousands upon thousands, ¹²and they were saying in full voice,

> 'The slaughtered lamb has now deserved
> to take the riches and the power,
> to take the wisdom, strength and honour,
> to take the glory, and the blessing.'

¹³Then I heard every creature in heaven, on the earth, under the earth, and in the sea, and everything that is in them, saying,

> 'To the One on the throne and the lamb
> be blessing and honour and glory
> and power for ever and ever!'

¹⁴'Amen!' cried the four living creatures. As for the elders, they fell down and worshipped.

Four horsemen

6 The next thing I saw was this. When the lamb had opened one of the seven seals, I heard one of the four living creatures say in a voice like thunder, 'Come!' ²And, as I watched, there was a white horse. Its rider was holding a bow. He was given a crown, and he went off winning victories, and to win more of them.

³When the lamb opened the second seal, I heard the second living creature say, 'Come!' ⁴And another horse went out, fiery red this time. Its rider was given permission to take peace away from the earth, so that people would kill one another. He was given a great sword.

⁵When the lamb opened the third seal, I heard the third living creature say, 'Come!' As I watched, there was a black horse. Its rider held a pair of scales in his hand. ⁶I heard something like a voice coming from the midst of the four living creatures. 'A quart of wheat for a denarius!' said the voice. 'And three quarts of barley for a denarius! But don't ruin the oil and the wine!'

⁷When the lamb opened the fourth seal, I heard the voice of the fourth living creature say, 'Come!' ⁸As I looked, there was a pale horse, and its rider's name was Death. Hades followed along behind him. They were given authority over a quarter of the earth, to kill with the sword, and with famine, and with death, and by means of earth's wild animals.

The day is coming!

⁹When the lamb opened the fifth seal, I saw under the altar the souls of those who had been killed because of the word of God and because of the witness which they had borne. ¹⁰They shouted at the tops of their voices. 'Holy and true Master!' they called. 'How much longer are you going to put off giving judgment, and avenging our blood on the earth-dwellers?' ¹¹Each of them was given a white robe, and they were told to rest for a little while yet, until the full number of those to be killed, as they had been, was reached – including both their fellow-servants and their kinsfolk.

¹²As I looked, he opened the sixth seal. There was a great earthquake, the sun turned black like sackcloth, the whole moon became like blood, ¹³and the stars were falling from heaven onto the earth as when a fig tree, shaken by a strong wind, drops its late fruit. ¹⁴The heaven disappeared like a scroll being rolled up, and every mountain and island was moved out of its place. ¹⁵The kings of the earth, the leading courtiers, the generals, the rich, the power-brokers, and everyone, slave and free, all hid themselves among the caves and rocks of the mountains. ¹⁶'Fall upon us!' they were saying to the mountains and the rocks. 'Hide us from the face of the One who sits on the throne, and

from the anger of the lamb! ⁷¹⁷The great day of their anger has come, and who can stand upright?'

Sealing God's people

7 After this I saw four angels, standing at the four corners of the earth, holding back the four winds of the earth to stop any wind from blowing on earth, or on the sea, or on any tree. ²And I saw another angel coming up from the east, holding the seal of the living God. He shouted out in a loud voice to the four angels who had responsibility for harming the earth and the sea. ³'Don't harm the earth just yet,' he shouted, 'or the sea, or the trees. Don't do it until we have sealed the servants of our God on their foreheads.'

⁴I heard the number of the people who were sealed: it was a hundred and forty-four thousand who were sealed from all the tribes of the children of Israel. ⁵Twelve thousand were sealed from the tribe of Judah, twelve thousand from the tribe of Reuben, twelve thousand from the tribe of Gad, ⁶twelve thousand from the tribe of Asher, twelve thousand from the tribe of Naphtali, twelve thousand from the tribe of Manasseh, ⁷twelve thousand from the tribe of Simeon, twelve thousand from the tribe of Levi, twelve thousand from the tribe of Issachar, ⁸twelve thousand from the tribe of Zebulun, twelve thousand from the tribe of Joseph and twelve thousand from the tribe of Benjamin. That is the number that were sealed.

The great rescue

⁹After this I looked, and lo and behold a huge gathering which nobody could possibly count, from every nation and tribe and people and language. They were standing in front of the throne, and in front of the lamb. They were dressed in white robes, holding palm branches in their hands. ¹⁰They were shouting out at the tops of their voices, 'Salvation belongs to our God, to the one who sits on the throne, and to the lamb!' ¹¹All the angels who were standing around the throne and the elders and the four creatures fell down on their faces before the throne and worshipped God. ¹²'Yes, Amen!' they were saying. 'Blessing and glory and wisdom and thanks and honour and power and strength be to our God for ever and ever! Amen!'

¹³One of the elders spoke to me. 'Who are these people dressed all in white?' he asked. 'Where have they come from?'

¹⁴'Sir,' I replied, 'you know!'

'These are the ones,' he said, 'who have come out of the great suffering. They have washed their clothes and made them white in the blood of the lamb. ¹⁵That is why they are there in front of God's throne, serving him day and night in his temple. The one who sits on the throne will shelter them with his presence. ¹⁶They will never be hungry again, or thirsty again. The sun will not scorch them, nor will any fierce heat. ¹⁷The lamb, who is in the midst of the throne, will be their shepherd. He will lead them to springs of running water, and God will wipe away every tear from their eyes.'

The golden censer

8 When the lamb opened the seventh seal, there was silence in heaven, lasting about half an hour. ²I saw the seven angels who were standing in front of God; they were given seven trumpets. ³Another angel came and stood before the altar. He was holding a golden censer, and he was given a large quantity of incense so that he could offer it, along with the prayers of all God's holy people, on the golden altar in front of the throne. ⁴The smoke of incense, with the prayers of the saints, rose up from the hand of the angel in front of God. ⁵Then the angel took the censer, filled it with fire from the altar, and threw it on the earth. There were crashes of thunder, loud rumblings, lightning, and an earthquake.

The plagues begin

⁶Then the seven angels who had the seven trumpets got ready to blow them. ⁷The first angel blew his trumpet, and hail and fire, mixed with blood, were thrown down on the earth. A third of the earth was burnt up, a third of the trees were burnt up, and so was every blade of green grass. ⁸Then the second angel

blew his trumpet, and something like a huge mountain, flaming with fire, was thrown into the sea. A third of the sea turned into blood, ⁹a third of all living sea-creatures died, and a third of the ships were destroyed. ¹⁰Then the third angel blew his trumpet, and a huge star, burning like a torch, fell from the sky, falling on a third of the rivers and on the springs of water. ¹¹The name of the star is Poisonwood: a third of the waters turned to poison, and many people died because of the waters that had become bitter. ¹²Then the fourth angel blew his trumpet, and a third of the sun was struck, and a third of the moon, and a third of the stars, so that a third of their light would be darkened, with a third of the day losing its light and a third of the night as well. ¹³Then I looked, and I heard a lone eagle flying in mid-heaven, and calling out loudly. 'Woe, woe, woe to the earth-dwellers,' it called, 'because of the sound of the other trumpets that the last three angels are going to blow!'

Locust attack

9 Then the fifth angel blew his trumpet. I saw a star falling from heaven to earth, and it was given the key to the shaft which leads down to the Abyss. ²The shaft of the Abyss was opened, and smoke came out of the pit like the smoke from a great furnace. The sun and the air became dark with the smoke from the pit. ³Then, out of that smoke, there appeared locusts on the earth, and they were given authority like the authority of scorpions on the earth. ⁴They were told not to harm the grass on the earth, nor any plant or tree, but only those people who did not have the seal of God on their foreheads. ⁵They were given instructions not to kill them, but to torture them for five months, and their torture was like the torture inflicted when a scorpion stings someone. ⁶In those days people will look for death, and won't find it. They will long to die, and death will run away from them.

⁷In appearance, the locusts looked like horses prepared for battle. They had what seemed to be crowns of gold on their heads, and their faces were like human faces. ⁸They had hair like women's hair, and their teeth were like lions' teeth. ⁹They had breastplates like iron breastplates, and the sound of their wings was like the noise of many horse-drawn chariots charging into battle. ¹⁰They have tails like scorpions' tails, and stings as well, and their tails have the power to harm people for five months. ¹¹They have as their king the angel of the Abyss, whose name in Hebrew is Abaddon, and whose name in Greek is Apollyon.

¹²The first Woe has come and gone. The next two Woes are on the way after this.

The fiery riders

¹³Then the sixth angel blew his trumpet. I heard a lone voice from the four horns of the golden altar in front of God, ¹⁴addressing the sixth angel, who had the trumpet.

'Release the four angels,' said the voice, 'the ones who are tied up by the Great River, the Euphrates.' ¹⁵So the four angels were released. They had been prepared for this hour, day, month and year, so that they would kill a third of the human race. ¹⁶The number of the troops and horsemen was two hundred million. (I heard the number.) ¹⁷As I looked, this is how the horses and their riders appeared. They had breastplates made of fire, sapphire and sulphur. Their heads were like lions' heads, and fire, smoke and brimstone came out of their mouths. ¹⁸One-third of the human race was killed by these three plagues, by the fire, smoke and sulphur that came out of their mouths. ¹⁹The power of the horses, you see, is in their mouths and their tails, since their tails are like serpents with heads. That is how they do their damage.

²⁰All the other people, the ones who had not been killed in these plagues, did not repent of the things they had made. They did not stop worshipping demons – idols made of gold, silver, bronze, stone and wood, which cannot see, hear or walk. ²¹Nor did they repent of their murders, or their magic, or their fornication, or their stealing.

A little scroll

10 Then I saw another strong angel coming down from heaven, dressed in a cloud. Over his head was a rainbow; his face was like the sun, and his feet were like fiery pillars. ²He was holding a small scroll, open, in his hand. Placing his right foot on the sea, and his left on the land, ³he shouted in a loud voice like a lion roaring. When he shouted, the seven thunders answered with their own voices. ⁴When the seven thunders spoke, I was about to write, but I heard a voice from heaven. 'Seal up what the seven thunders said,' instructed the voice. 'Don't write it down.'

⁵Then the angel whom I had seen standing on the sea and the land raised his right hand towards heaven ⁶and swore an oath by the One who lives for ever and ever, who made heaven and what it contains, the earth and what it contains, and the sea and what it contains. This was the oath: that there would be no more time, ⁷but that God's mystery would be completed in the days of the voice of the seventh angel, who was going to blow his trumpet. That is what he had announced to his servants the prophets.

⁸The voice I had heard from heaven spoke to me again. 'Go,' it said, 'and take the open scroll from the hand of the angel who is standing on the sea and on the land.' ⁹So I went up to the angel.

'Give me the little scroll,' I said.

'Take it,' he said to me, 'and eat it. It will be bitter in your stomach, but sweet as honey in your mouth.' ¹⁰So I took the little scroll from the angel's hand, and I ate it. It tasted like sweet honey in my mouth, but when I had eaten it my stomach felt bitter. ¹¹"You must prophesy again", he said to me, 'about many peoples, nations, languages and kingdoms.'

Two witnesses

11 Then a measuring rod like a staff was given to me. 'Get up,' said a voice, 'and measure God's temple, and the altar, and those who are worshipping in it. ²But leave out the outer court of the temple. Don't measure it. It is given to the nations, and they will trample the holy city for forty-two months. ³I will give my two witnesses the task of prophesying, clothed in sackcloth, for those one thousand two hundred and sixty days. ⁴These two are the two olive trees, the two lampstands, which stand before the Lord of the earth. ⁵If anyone wants to harm them, fire comes out of their mouths and devours their enemies. So if anyone wants to harm them, that is how such a person must be killed. ⁶These two have authority to shut up the sky, so that it will not rain during the days of their prophecy. They have authority over the waters, to turn them into blood, and to strike the earth with any plague, as often as they see fit. ⁷When they have completed their testimony, the monster that comes up from the Abyss will make war on them, and will defeat and kill them. ⁸Their bodies will lie in the street of the great city, which is spiritually called Sodom and Egypt, where their Lord was crucified. ⁹Their bodies will be seen by the peoples, tribes, languages and nations for three and a half days. They will not allow their bodies to be buried in a tomb. ¹⁰The inhabitants of the earth will celebrate over them, and make merry, and send presents to one another, because these two prophets tormented those who live on earth.'

¹¹After the three and a half days the spirit of life from God came in to them, and they stood up on their feet, and great fear fell on all who saw them. ¹²Then they heard a loud voice from heaven. 'Come up here!' it said. And they went up to heaven on a cloud, with their enemies looking on. ¹³At that moment there was a huge earthquake, and a tenth of the city fell, and seven thousand of the people were killed by the earthquake. The rest were very much afraid, and glorified the God of heaven.

¹⁴The second Woe has passed. The third Woe is coming very soon.

The song of triumph

¹⁵The seventh angel blew his trumpet, and loud voices were heard from heaven. 'Now the kingdom of the world has passed to our Lord and his Messiah,' said the voices, 'and he will reign for ever and ever.' ¹⁶The twenty-four elders sitting on their thrones in God's presence fell on their faces and worshipped God.

¹⁷This is what they said:

'Almighty Lord God, we give you our thanks,
Who Is and Who Was,
because you have taken your power, your great
   power,
and begun to reign.

¹⁸The nations were raging; your anger came down
and with it the time for judging the dead
to give the reward to your servants the prophets,
the holy ones, too, and the small and the great –
those who fear your name.
It is time to destroy the destroyers of earth.'

¹⁹God's temple in heaven was opened, and the ark of his covenant appeared inside his temple. There were flashes of lightning, rumblings, thunderclaps, an earthquake, and heavy hail.

The woman and the dragon

12 Then a great sign appeared in heaven: a woman clothed with the sun, with the moon under her feet, and a crown of twelve stars on her head. ²She was expecting a child, and she cried out in pain, in the agony of giving birth. ³Then another sign appeared in heaven: a great fiery-red dragon with seven heads and ten horns. On its heads were seven coronets, ⁴and its tail swept a third of the stars out of heaven and threw them down to the earth. The dragon stood opposite the woman who was about to give birth, so that he could devour her child when it was born. ⁵She gave birth to a male child, who is going to rule all the nations with a rod of iron. And the child was snatched away to God and to his throne. ⁶The woman, meanwhile, fled into the desert, where a place has been prepared for her by God, so that she could be looked after there for one thousand two hundred and sixty days.

The dragon is angry

⁷Then war broke out in heaven, with Michael and his angels fighting against the dragon, and the dragon and his angels fighting back. ⁸But they could not win, and there was no longer any place for them in heaven. ⁹So the great dragon was thrown down to the earth – the ancient serpent who is called the devil and the satan, who deceives the whole world. His angels were thrown down with him. ¹⁰Then I heard a loud voice in heaven saying, 'Now at last has come salvation and power: the kingdom of our God and the authority of his Messiah! The accuser of our family has been thrown down, the one who accuses them before God day and night. ¹¹They conquered him by the blood of the lamb and by the word of their testimony, because they did not love their lives unto death. ¹²So rejoice, you heavens and all who live there! But woe to the earth and the sea, because the devil has come down to you in great anger, knowing that he only has a short time.'

¹³When the dragon saw that he had been cast down to the earth, he set off in pursuit of the woman who had borne the baby boy. ¹⁴The woman, however, was given a pair of wings from a great eagle, so that she could fly away from the presence of the serpent into the desert, to the place where she is looked after for a time, two times and half a time. ¹⁵The serpent, for its part, spat out of its mouth a jet of water like a river after the woman, to carry her off with the force of the water. ¹⁶But the earth helped the woman by opening its mouth and swallowing up the river which the dragon had spat out of his mouth. ¹⁷Then the dragon was angry with the woman, and went off to wage war against the rest of her children, those who keep God's commands and the testimony of Jesus. ¹⁸And he stood on the sand beside the sea.

A first monster

13 Then I saw a monster coming up out of the sea. It had ten horns and seven heads. Each of the ten horns was wearing a coronet, and blasphemous names were written on the heads. ²The monster I saw was like a leopard, with bear's feet and a lion's mouth. And the dragon gave the monster its power and its throne and great authority. ³One of the heads appeared to have been slaughtered and killed, but its fatal wound had been healed. The whole earth was awed and astonished by the monster, ⁴and worshipped the dragon because it had given the monster its authority. They worshipped the monster too. 'Who is like the monster?' they were saying. 'Who can fight against it?' ⁵And the monster was given a mouth that speaks great, blasphemous words, and was given authority for forty-two months. ⁶It opened its mouth to utter blasphemies against God, to curse his name and his dwelling place – that is, those who dwell in heaven. ⁷It was granted the right to make war against God's holy people and to defeat them, and it was given authority over every tribe and people and language and nation. ⁸So everyone who lived on earth worshipped it – everyone, that is, whose name has not been written from the foundation of the world in the book of life belonging to the lamb who was slaughtered.

⁹If anyone has ears, let them hear!

¹⁰If anyone is to be taken captive, into captivity they will go. If anyone is to be killed with the sword, with the sword they will be killed. This is a summons for God's holy people to be patient and have faith.

A second monster

¹¹Then I saw another monster coming up from the earth. It had two horns like those of a lamb, and it spoke like a dragon. ¹²It acts in the presence of the first monster and with its full authority, and it makes the earth and those who live on it worship the first monster, whose fatal wound had been healed. ¹³It performs great signs, so that it even makes fire come down from heaven on the earth in the sight of people, ¹⁴and it deceives the people who live on earth by the signs which it has been allowed to perform in front of the monster, instructing the earth's inhabitants to make an image of the monster who had the sword-wound but was alive. ¹⁵It was allowed to give breath to the monster's image, so that the monster's image could speak, and it could kill anyone who didn't worship the monster's image. ¹⁶It makes everyone, small and great, rich and poor, free and slaves, receive a sign from it, marked on their right hands and on their foreheads, ¹⁷so that nobody can buy or sell unless they have the mark of the name of the monster or the number of its name.

¹⁸This calls for wisdom. Anyone with a good head on their shoulders should work out the monster's number, because it's the number of a human being. Its number is Six Hundred and Sixty-Six.

The lamb's elite warriors

14 As I watched, there was the lamb standing on Mount Zion, and with him were a hundred and forty-four thousand who had his name, and the name of his father, written on their foreheads. ²I heard a voice from heaven, like the sound of many waters, and like the sound of mighty thunder, and the voice I heard was like harpists playing on their harps. ³And they are singing a new song before the throne, and before the four creatures and the elders. Nobody can learn that song except for the hundred and forty-four thousand who have been redeemed from the earth. ⁴These are the ones who have never polluted themselves with women; they are celibate. They follow the lamb wherever he goes. They have been redeemed from the human race as first fruits for God and the lamb, ⁵and no lie has been found in their mouths. They are without blemish.

A call for endurance

⁶Then I saw another angel flying in mid-heaven, carrying an eternal gospel to announce to those who live on earth, to every nation and tribe and language and people. ⁷He spoke with a loud voice, and this is what he said: 'Fear God! Give him glory! The time has come for his judgment! Worship the one who made heaven and earth and the sea and the springs of water!'

⁸He was followed by another angel, and this is what he said: 'Babylon the great has fallen! She has fallen! She is the one who made all the nations drink the wine of the anger that comes upon her fornication.'

⁹They were followed by a third angel, who also spoke in a loud voice: 'If anyone worships the monster and its image, or receives its mark on their forehead or their hand, ¹⁰that person will drink the wine of God's anger, poured neat into the cup of his anger, and they will be tortured in fire and sulphur before the holy angels and before the lamb. ¹¹The smoke of their torture goes up for ever and ever. Those who worship the monster and its image, and those who receive the mark of its name, will have no respite, day or night.'

¹²This demands patience from God's holy people, who keep God's commands and the faith of Jesus.

¹³Then I heard a loud voice from heaven saying, 'Write this: God's blessing on the dead who from this time onward die in the Lord.'

'Yes,' says the spirit, 'so that they may rest from their works, for the deeds they have done follow after them.'

Reaping the harvest

¹⁴Then I looked, and there was a white cloud, and sitting on the cloud one like a son of man. He had a gold crown on his head, and a sharp sickle in his hand. ¹⁵And another angel came out of the temple, shouting in a loud voice to the one who was sitting on the cloud, 'It's harvest time! Put in your sickle and reap: the harvest of the earth is ripe!' ¹⁶So the one sitting on the cloud applied his sickle to the earth, and reaped the harvest of the earth.

¹⁷Then another angel came out of the temple in heaven. He, too, had a sharp sickle. ¹⁸Yet another angel came from the altar; he had authority over fire, and he spoke with a loud voice to the one who had the sharp sickle. 'Go to work with your sharp sickle,' he said, 'and gather the clusters of fruit from the vine of the earth; the grapes are there in ripe bunches!' ¹⁹So the angel went to work with his sickle on the earth, and gathered the fruit from the vine of the earth, and threw it into the great winepress of God's anger. ²⁰The winepress was trodden outside the city, and blood came out of the winepress, as high as a horse's bridle, for about two hundred miles.

Preparing the final plagues

15 Then I saw another sign – a great, amazing sight in heaven: seven angels who were bringing the seven last plagues. With them God's anger is completed. ²And I saw what looked like a sea of glass, mixed with fire. There, by that glassy sea, stood the people who had won the victory over the monster and over its image, and over the number of its name. They were holding harps of God, ³and they were singing the song of Moses the servant of God, and the song of the lamb. This is how it went:

> Great and amazing are your works,
> O Lord God, the Almighty one.
> Just and true are your ways,
> O King of the nations.
> ⁴Who will not fear you, Lord,
> and glorify your name?
> For you alone are holy.
> For all nations shall come
> and worship before you,
> because your judgments have been revealed.

⁵After this I looked, and the temple of the 'tabernacle of witness' was opened in heaven. ⁶The seven angels who had the seven plagues came out of the temple, clothed in clean, shining linen, wearing golden belts across their chests. ⁷Then one of the four living creatures gave the seven angels seven golden bowls filled with the anger of the God who lives for ever and ever. ⁸The temple was filled with smoke from the glory of God and his power. Nobody was able to go into the temple until the seven plagues of the seven angels had been completed.

The first four plagues

16 Then I heard a loud voice coming from the temple, addressing the seven angels. 'Off you go,' said the voice, 'and pour out on the earth the seven bowls of God's anger.' ²So the first one went off and poured out his bowl on the earth, and foul, painful sores came on the people who had the mark of the monster, and those who worshipped its image. ³The second one poured his bowl on the sea, and it turned into blood like that from a corpse. Every living thing in the sea died. ⁴The third one poured his bowl on the rivers and the springs of water, and they turned into blood. ⁵Then I heard the angel of the waters saying,

> 'You are the one Who Is and Who Was,
> you are the holy one, and you are just!
> you have passed the righteous sentence:
> ⁶they spilt the blood of saints and prophets
> and you have given them blood to drink.
> They deserve it.'

⁷And I heard the altar respond, 'Yes, Lord God Almighty, your judgments are true and just.'

⁸Then the fourth angel poured his bowl upon the sun, and it was allowed to burn people with its fire. ⁹People were burned up by its great heat, and they cursed the name of the God who had authority over these plagues. They did not repent or give him glory.

The last three plagues

¹⁰Then the fifth angel poured his bowl upon the throne of the monster. Its kingdom was plunged into darkness, and people chewed their tongues because of the pain ¹¹and cursed the God of heaven because of their agonies and their terrible sores. They did not repent of what they had been doing.

¹²Then the sixth angel poured his bowl on the great river Euphrates, and its water was dried up in order to prepare the way for the kings from the rising sun. ¹³Then I saw three unclean spirits coming out of the mouth of the dragon, out of the mouth of the monster, and out of the mouth of the false prophet. They were like frogs. ¹⁴These are the spirits of demons, who perform signs and go off to the kings of the whole earth, to gather them together for war on the great day of Almighty God. ¹⁵(Look – I am coming like a thief! God's blessing on the one who stays awake, and on those who keep their robes about them, so as not to go around naked and have their shame exposed!) ¹⁶And they gathered the kings together at the place which in Hebrew is called Mount Megiddo.

¹⁷Then the seventh angel poured his bowl on the air, and a loud voice came out of the temple from the throne. 'It is done!' said the voice. ¹⁸And there were lightnings and rumblings, and thunderclaps and a great earthquake, such as there had never been before, no, not such a great earthquake since the time that humans came on the earth. ¹⁹The great city was split into three parts, and the cities of the nations collapsed. Then Babylon the Great was recalled in the presence of God, so that he could give her the cup of the wine of his anger. ²⁰Every island fled away, and the mountains disappeared. ²¹Enormous hailstones, each weighing a hundred pounds, fell from the sky on people. They cursed God because of the plague of the hail, because its plague was terrible.

Babylon the Great

17 Then one of the seven angels who had the seven bowls came over and spoke to me. 'Come with me,' he said, 'and I will show you the judgment of the great whore who sits on many waters. ²She is the one with whom the kings of the earth committed fornication; she is the one whose fornication has been the wine that has made all the earth-dwellers drunk.'

³So he took me away, in the spirit, to the desert. There I saw a woman sitting on a scarlet monster. It was full of blasphemous names, and had seven heads and ten horns. ⁴The woman was wearing purple and scarlet, and was decked out with gold, precious stones and pearls. In her hand she was holding a golden goblet, full of abominations and the impurities of her fornications. ⁵On her forehead was written a name: 'Mystery! Babylon the Great, Mother of Whores and of Earth's Abominations!' ⁶I saw that the woman was drunk with the blood of God's holy people, and with the blood of the witnesses of Jesus. When I saw her, I was very greatly astonished.

⁷'Why are you so astonished?' asked the angel. 'I will explain to you the secret of the woman, and of the monster that is carrying her, the one which has the seven heads and the ten horns. ⁸The monster you saw was, and is not, and is due to come up from the Abyss and go to destruction. All the inhabitants of the earth will be amazed – all, that is, whose names are not written in the book of life from the foundation of the world – when they see the monster that was and is not and is to come.

The monster and the whore

⁹'This is a moment for a wise and discerning mind. The seven heads are seven hills, on which the woman sits. And there are seven kings; ¹⁰five have fallen, one is still there, and the other has not yet arrived, and when he does come he is destined to remain for only a short time. ¹¹And the monster, which was and is not, he is the eighth king. He is also one of the seven, and he goes to destruction. ¹²The ten horns that you saw are ten kings who have not yet received their kingdom, but will receive their authority as kings with the monster for a single hour. ¹³All of these are of one mind: they give their power and authority to the monster. ¹⁴They will make war with the lamb, and the lamb will conquer them, because he is Lord of lords and King of kings. Those with him are called and chosen and faithful.

¹⁵'As for the waters you saw,' he continued, 'where the whore was sitting, these are peoples and multitudes and nations and languages. ¹⁶The ten horns you saw, and the monster, will hate the whore and will make her desolate and naked, and will eat her flesh and then burn her in the fire. ¹⁷God has put it into their hearts to do his will and, with a single purpose, to give their kingdom to the monster, until God's words are completed. ¹⁸The woman which you saw is the great city that has royal dominion over the kings of the earth.'

Babylon's plagues

18 After this I saw another angel coming down from heaven with great authority; the earth was flooded with the light of his glory. ²He shouted out in a strong voice, and this is what he said: 'Babylon the great has fallen! She has fallen! She has become a place for demons to live, a refuge for every unclean spirit, a refuge for every unclean bird, a refuge for every unclean, hateful monster. ³All the nations drank from the wine of the wrath of her fornication; the kings of the earth committed fornication with her, and the traders of the earth became rich from the power of her luxury.'

⁴Then I heard another voice from heaven, and this is what it said: 'Come out of her, my people, so that you don't become embroiled in her sins, and so that you don't receive any of her plagues. ⁵Her sins are piled up to the sky, and God has remembered her wickedness. ⁶Pay her back as she has paid others; give her double again for all her deeds. Mix her a double dose in her own cup – the cup in which she mixed her poisons. ⁷She made herself glorious and lived in luxury; balance that by giving her torture and sorrow! She said in her heart, "I'm the queen! I'm on the throne! I'm not a widow! I'm never going to be a mourner!" ⁸Therefore her plagues will come in a single day, death, mourning and famine, and she will be burned with fire, because God the Lord, who judges her, is strong.'

Babylon's judgment

⁹The kings of the earth who committed fornication with her and shared her luxury will weep and lament over her when they see the smoke from her fire. ¹⁰They will stand far off, fearful of her tortures. 'Alas, alas,' they will say, 'the great city! Babylon the powerful city! Your judgment has come in a single hour.' ¹¹The merchants of the earth will weep and mourn over her, because nobody will buy their cargo any more, ¹²their cargo of gold and silver, of precious stones and pearls, fine linen and purple, silk and scarlet, all the sweet-smelling wood, carved ivory, vessels of expensive wood, brass, iron, marble, ¹³cinnamon, oriental spice, incense, myrrh, frankincense, wine, olive oil, fine flour, wheat, cattle, sheep, horses, chariots and bodies . . . yes, human lives.

¹⁴All the fruit for which you longed has gone from you; all your luxuries and sparkling objects have been destroyed; you won't find them any more. ¹⁵The merchants who sold these things, and who made themselves rich from her, will stand a long way off for fear of her tortures. They will weep and mourn, ¹⁶and say, 'Alas, alas! The great city! It was clothed in fine linen, purple and scarlet, decked out in gold, precious stones and pearls – ¹⁷but in a single hour such great wealth has been destroyed!'

All the master mariners, all those who ply their ships to and fro, all sailors, and all who do business on the sea, stood a long way off ¹⁸and shouted out when they saw the smoke of her fire. 'Who is like the great city?' they said. ¹⁹They threw dust on their heads and shouted out, weeping and mourning. 'Alas, alas,' they said, 'the great city! Everyone who had ships on the sea could get rich from her wealth, but in a single hour she has become a desert.'

²⁰Celebrate over her, heaven, and you holy ones, apostles and prophets, because God has passed against her the sentence she passed against you.

²¹Then a strong angel picked up a rock like a huge millstone and hurled it into the sea, with these words: 'Babylon the great city will be thrown down like that with a splash, and will never be seen again! ²²Never again will people hear the sound of harps, musicians, flute players and trumpeters in you. Never again will there be any skilled workmen plying their trade in you. Never again will people hear the sound of the mill in you. ²³Never again will anyone see the light of a lamp in you. Never again will anyone hear the voice of bridegroom and bride

in you. Your merchants were the mighty ones of the earth; all the nations were deceived by your magic.'

²⁴In her has been found the blood of prophets and God's holy ones, and all those who have been slaughtered on the earth.

God's victory

19 After this I heard something like a loud voice coming from a huge crowd in heaven. 'Alleluia!' they were saying. 'Salvation and glory and power belong to our God! ²His judgments are true and just! He has judged the great whore who corrupted the earth with her fornication, and he has avenged the blood of his servants for which she was responsible.' ³Once more they said, 'Alleluia! The smoke from her goes up for ever and ever.'

⁴Then the twenty-four elders and the four creatures fell down and worshipped God who is seated on the throne. 'Amen!' they said. 'Alleluia!' ⁵And a voice came from the throne: 'Give praise to our God, all you his servants, and you who fear him, both small and great.' ⁶Then I heard something like the sound of a great crowd, like the sound of many waters, and like the sound of strong thunder, saying, 'Alleluia! The Lord our God, the Almighty, has become king! ⁷Let us celebrate and rejoice and give him the glory, because the marriage of the lamb has come, and his bride has prepared herself. ⁸She has been given shining, pure linen to wear.' (The linen is the righteous deeds of God's holy people.)

⁹'Write this,' he said to me. 'God's blessing on those who are called to the marriage supper of the lamb.' And he added, 'These words are the true words of God.' ¹⁰I fell down at his feet to worship him, but he said to me, 'Look! Don't do that! I am a fellow-servant with you, and with your brothers and sisters who hold on to the testimony of Jesus. Worship God!' (The testimony of Jesus, you see, is the spirit of prophecy.)

The monster defeated

¹¹Then I saw heaven opened, and there was a white horse. The one who was sitting on it is called Faithful and True, and he judges and makes war justly. ¹²His eyes are like a flaming fire, and there are many coronets on his head. He has a name written there which nobody knows except himself. ¹³He is clothed in a robe dipped in blood, and he is called by the name 'God's Word'. ¹⁴The armies of heaven follow him on white horses, all wearing shining, pure linen. ¹⁵A sharp two-edged sword is coming out of his mouth, so that with it he can strike down the nations. He will rule them with a rod of iron, and he will tread the winepress of the wine of the anger of the wrath of Almighty God. ¹⁶On his robe, and on his thigh, is written a name: King of kings, and Lord of lords.

¹⁷Then I saw a single angel standing in the sun, and shouting in a loud voice, calling to all the birds that fly in mid-heaven: 'Come here! Gather round! This is God's great feast! ¹⁸Come and eat the flesh of kings, and the flesh of generals, the flesh of the strong, the flesh of horses and their riders, the flesh of all people, free and slave, small and great!' ¹⁹And I saw the monster and the kings of the earth and their armies gathered for war with the one who sits on the horse and with his army. ²⁰And the monster was captured, and with it the false prophet who had performed the signs in its presence, with which it had deceived those who received the monster's mark and those who worshipped its image. The two of them were thrown alive into the lake of fire which burns with sulphur. ²¹All the rest were killed by the sword which came out of the mouth of the one who was sitting on the horse. All the birds feasted on their flesh.

Reigning for a thousand years

20 Then I saw an angel coming down from heaven. In his hand he held the key to the Abyss, and a large chain. ²He grabbed hold of the dragon, the ancient serpent, who is the devil and the satan. He tied him up for a thousand years, ³threw him into the Abyss, and locked and sealed it over him, so that he wouldn't be able to deceive the nations any more, until the thousand years were complete. After that he must be let out for a short time.

⁴Then I saw thrones, with people sitting on them, who were given authority to judge. And

I saw the souls of those who had had their heads cut off because they had borne witness to Jesus, and because of the word of God; and also those who had not worshipped the monster or its image, and had not received the mark on their foreheads or their hands. They came to life, and reigned with the Messiah for a thousand years. ⁵The rest of the dead did not come back to life until the thousand years were complete. This is the first resurrection. ⁶Blessed and holy is the one who has a share in the first resurrection! The second death has no power over them. They will be priests to God and the Messiah, and they will reign with him for a thousand years.

Final judgment

⁷When the thousand years are complete, the satan will be released from his prison. ⁸Out he will come to deceive the nations at the four corners of the earth, Gog and Magog. He will summon them for battle, a throng like the sand of the sea in number. ⁹They came up over the full width of the earth, and closed in on the place where God's holy people are encamped, and the beloved city. Then fire came down from heaven and burnt them up. ¹⁰And the devil who had deceived them was thrown into the lake of fire and sulphur where the monster and the false prophet had already been thrown. They will be tortured day and night for ever and ever.

¹¹Then I saw a large white throne, and the one who was sitting on it. Earth and heaven fled away from his presence, and there was no room left for them. ¹²Then I saw the dead, great and small, standing in front of the throne. Books were opened; and another book was opened, which is the book of life. The dead were judged on the basis of what was written in the books, in accordance with what they had done. ¹³The sea gave back the dead that were in it; Death and Hades gave back the dead that were in them; and each was judged in accordance with what they had done. ¹⁴Then Death and Hades were thrown into the lake of fire. This is the second death, the lake of fire. ¹⁵And if anyone was not found written in the book of life, they were thrown into the lake of fire.

New heaven, new earth

21 Then I saw a new heaven and a new earth. The first heaven and the first earth had passed away, and there was no longer any sea. ²And I saw the holy city, the new Jerusalem, coming down out of heaven, from God, prepared like a bride dressed up for her husband. ³I heard a loud voice from the throne, and this is what it said: 'Look! God has come to dwell with humans! He will dwell with them, and they will be his people, and God himself will be with them and will be their God. ⁴He will wipe away every tear from their eyes. There will be no more death, or mourning or weeping or pain any more, since the first things have passed away.'

⁵The one who sat on the throne said, 'Look, I am making all things new.' And he said, 'Write, because these words are faithful and true.'

New Jerusalem

⁶Then he said to me, 'It is done! I am the Alpha and the Omega, the beginning and the end. I will freely give water to the thirsty, water from the spring of the water of life. ⁷The one who conquers will inherit these things. I will be his God and he shall be my son. ⁸But as for cowards, faithless people, the unclean, murderers, fornicators, sorcerers, idolaters and all liars – their destiny will be in the lake that burns with fire and sulphur, which is the second death.'

⁹Then one of the seven angels who had the seven bowls filled with the seven last plagues came over and spoke to me. 'Come with me,' he said, 'and I will show you the bride, the wife of the lamb.' ¹⁰Then he took me in the spirit up a great high mountain, and he showed me the holy city, Jerusalem, coming down out of heaven from God. ¹¹It has the glory of God; it is radiant, like the radiance of a rare and precious jewel, like a jasper stone, crystal-clear. ¹²It has a great high wall with twelve gates, and twelve angels at the gates, and names inscribed on the gates, which are the names of the twelve tribes of the children of Israel. ¹³There are three gates coming in from the east, three gates from the north, three gates from the south and three gates from the west. ¹⁴And the wall of the city

has twelve foundation-stones, and on them are written the twelve names of the twelve apostles of the lamb.

¹⁵The one who was talking with me had a golden measuring-rod, so that he could measure the city, its gates, and its wall. ¹⁶The city stands foursquare, with the same length and breadth. He measured the city with his rod: it was twelve thousand stadia (that is, fifteen hundred miles), with the length, the breadth and the height being equal. ¹⁷Then he measured its wall, and it was one hundred and forty-four cubits in terms of human measurement (which was what the angel was using). ¹⁸The material of which the wall is built is jasper, and the city itself is pure gold, like pure glass. ¹⁹The foundations of the city wall are decorated with every kind of precious stone: the first foundation is jasper, the second sapphire, the third agate, the fourth emerald, ²⁰the fifth onyx, the sixth carnelian, the seventh chrysolite, the eighth beryl, the ninth topaz, the tenth chrysoprase, the eleventh jacinth, the twelfth amethyst. ²¹The twelve gates are twelve pearls, with each gate consisting of a single pearl. The street of the city is pure gold, clear as glass.

God and the lamb are there

²²I saw no temple in the city, because the Lord God the Almighty is its temple, together with the lamb. ²³And the city has no need of sun or moon to shine on it, for the glory of God gives it light, and its lamp is the lamb. ²⁴The nations will walk in its light, and the kings of the earth will bring their glory into it. ²⁵Its gates will never be shut by day, for there will be no night there. ²⁶They will bring the glory and the honour of the nations into it. ²⁷Nothing that has not been made holy will ever come into it, nor will anyone who practises abomination or who tells lies, but only those who are written in the lamb's book of life.

22 Then he showed me the river of the water of life. It was sparkling like crystal, and flowing from the throne of God and of the lamb ²through the middle of the street of the city. On either bank of the river was growing the tree of life. It produces twelve kinds of fruit, bearing this fruit every month;

and the leaves of the tree are for the healing of the nations. ³Nothing accursed is there any more. Rather, the throne of God and of the lamb are in the city, and his servants will worship him; ⁴they will see his face, and his name will be on their foreheads. ⁵There will be no more night, and they will not need the light of a lamp or the light of the sun, because the Lord God will shine on them; and they will reign for ever and ever.

⁶'These words', he said to me, 'are trustworthy and true. The Lord, the God of the spirits of the prophets, has sent his angel to show his servants what must soon take place. ⁷Look, I am coming soon. God's blessing on the one who keeps the words of the prophecy of this book.'

'I am coming soon!'

⁸I, John, am the one who heard and saw these things. And when I heard them and saw them, I fell down to worship before the feet of the angel who showed them to me. ⁹'Look! Don't do that!' he said to me. 'I am a fellow-servant with you, and with the other members of your prophetic family, and with those who keep the words of this book. Worship God!

¹⁰'Don't seal up the words of the prophecy of this book,' he added. 'The time is near, you see. ¹¹Let the unjust go on being unjust, and the filthy go on being filthy – and let the just go on doing justice, and let the holy still be holy.

¹²'Look! I am coming soon. I will bring my reward with me, and I will pay everyone back according to what they have done. ¹³I am the Alpha and the Omega, the first and the last, the beginning and the end.'

¹⁴God's blessing on those who wash their clothes, so that they may have the right to eat from the tree of life and may enter the city by its gates. ¹⁵But the dogs, the sorcerers, the fornicators, the murderers, the idolaters, and everyone who loves to invent lies – they will all be outside.

¹⁶'I, Jesus, have sent my angel to give you this testimony for the churches. I am David's root and offspring; I am the bright morning star.'

¹⁷The spirit and the bride say, 'Come!' And let anyone who hears say, 'Come!' Let the

thirsty come; let anyone who wants the water of life take it freely.

¹⁸I testify to everyone who hears the words of the prophecy of this book: if anyone adds to them, God will add to that person the plagues that are written in this book. ¹⁹And if anyone takes away from the words of the book of this prophecy, God will take away that person's share in the tree of life, and in the holy city, which are described in this book.

²⁰The one who gives this testimony says, 'Yes, I am coming soon!'

Amen! Come, Lord Jesus.

²¹The grace of the Lord Jesus be with you all.

A New Testament glossary

accuser, the,
See **satan, the**.

age to come
See **present age**.

apostle, disciple, the Twelve
'Apostle' means 'one who is sent'. It could be used of an ambassador or official delegate. In the New Testament it is sometimes used specifically of Jesus' inner circle of twelve, but Paul sees not only himself but several others outside the Twelve as 'apostles', the criterion being whether the person had personally seen the risen Jesus. Jesus' own choice of twelve close associates symbolized his plan to renew God's people, Israel (who traditionally thought of themselves as having twelve tribes); after the death of Judas Iscariot (Matthew 27.5; Acts 1.18), Matthias was chosen by lot to take his place, preserving the symbolic meaning. During Jesus' lifetime they, and many other followers, were seen as his 'disciples', which means 'pupils' or 'apprentices'.

baptism
Literally, 'plunging' people into water. From within a wider Jewish tradition of ritual washings and bathings, John the Baptist undertook a vocation of baptizing people in the Jordan, not as one ritual among others but as a unique moment of **repentance**, preparing them for the coming of the **kingdom of God**. Jesus himself was baptized by John, identifying himself with this renewal movement and developing it in his own way. His followers in turn baptized others. After his **resurrection**, and the sending of the **holy spirit**, baptism became the normal sign and means of entry into the community of Jesus' people. As early as Paul, it was aligned both with the exodus from Egypt (1 Corinthians 10.2) and with Jesus' death and resurrection (Romans 6.2–11).

Christ
See **Messiah**.

circumcision
The cutting off of the foreskin. Male circumcision was a major mark of identity for Jews, following its initial commandment to Abraham (Genesis 17), reinforced by Joshua (Joshua 5.2–9). Other peoples, for example the Egyptians, also circumcised male children. A line of thought from Deuteronomy (e.g. 30.6), through Jeremiah (e.g. 31.33), to the Dead Sea Scrolls and the New Testament (e.g. Romans 2.29) speaks of 'circumcision of the heart' as God's real desire, by which one may become inwardly what the male Jew is outwardly, that is, marked out as part of God's people. At periods of Jewish assimilation into the surrounding culture, some Jews tried to remove the marks of circumcision (e.g. 1 Maccabees 1.11–15).

covenant
At the heart of Jewish belief is the conviction that the one God, YHWH, who had made the whole world, had called Abraham and his family to belong to him in a special way. The promises God made to Abraham and his family, and the requirements that were laid on them as a result, came to be seen in terms either of the agreement that a king would make with a subject people, or of the marriage bond between husband and wife. One regular way of describing this relationship was 'covenant', which can thus include both promise and **law**. The covenant was renewed at Mount Sinai with the giving of the **Torah**; in Deuteronomy before the entry to the promised land; and, in a more focused way, with David (e.g. Psalm 89). Jeremiah 31 promised that, after the punishment of **exile**, God would make a 'new covenant' with his people, forgiving them and binding them to

him more intimately. Jesus believed that this was coming true through his kingdom-proclamation and his death and **resurrection**. The early Christians developed these ideas in various ways, believing that in Jesus the promises had at last been fulfilled.

demons
See **satan, the**.

devil
See **satan, the**.

disciple
See **apostle**.

exile
Deuteronomy (27—30) warned that if Israel disobeyed YHWH, he would send his people into exile, but that if they then repented he would bring them back. When the Babylonians sacked Jerusalem and took the people into exile, prophets such as Jeremiah interpreted this as the fulfilment of this prophecy, and made further promises about how long exile would last (seventy years, according to Jeremiah 25.12; 29.10). Sure enough, exiles began to return in the late sixth century BC (Ezra 1.1). However, the post-exilic period was largely a disappointment, since the people were still enslaved to foreigners (Nehemiah 9.36); and, at the height of persecution by the Syrians, Daniel 9.2, 24 spoke of the 'real' exile lasting not for seventy years but for seventy *weeks* of years, that is, 490 years. Longing for the real 'return from exile', when the prophecies of Isaiah, Jeremiah, and so on, would be fulfilled, and **redemption** from pagan oppression accomplished, continued to characterize many Jewish movements, and was a major theme in Jesus' proclamation and his summons to **repentance**.

faith
Faith in the New Testament covers a wide area of human trust and trustworthiness, merging into love at one end of the scale and loyalty at the other. Within Jewish and Christian thinking, faith in God also includes *belief*, accepting certain things as true about God, and what he has done in the world (e.g. bringing Israel out of Egypt; raising Jesus from the dead). For Jesus, 'faith' often seems to mean 'recognizing that God is decisively at work to bring the kingdom through Jesus'. For Paul, 'faith' is both the specific belief that Jesus is Lord and that God raised him from the dead (Romans 10.9) and the response of grateful human love to sovereign divine love (Galatians 2.20). This faith is, for Paul, the solitary badge of membership in God's people in **Christ**, marking them out in a way that **Torah**, and the works it prescribes, can never do.

fellowship
The word we often translate 'fellowship' can mean a business partnership (in the ancient world, businesses were often run by families, so there's a sense of family loyalty as well), or it can mean a sense of mutual belonging and sharing in some other corporate enterprise. Within early Christianity, 'fellowship' acquired the sense not just of belonging to one another as Christians, but of a shared belonging to Jesus **Christ**, and a participation in his life through the **spirit**, expressed in such actions as the 'breaking of bread' and the sharing of property with those in need.

forgiveness
Jesus made forgiveness central to his **message** and ministry, not least because he was claiming to be launching God's long-awaited 'new **covenant**' (Jeremiah 31.31–34) in which sins would at last be forgiven (Matthew 26.28). Forgiveness doesn't mean God, or someone else, saying, of some particular fault or sin, 'It didn't really matter' or 'I didn't really mind'. The point of forgiveness is that it *did* matter, God (and/or other people) really *did* mind, but they are not going to hold

it against the offender. It isn't, in other words, the same thing as 'tolerance': to forgive is not to tolerate sin, but to see clearly that it was wrong and then to treat the offender as though it hadn't happened. The early Christian answer to the obvious question 'How could a holy and righteous God do that?' is 'Through the death of Jesus'. What's more, Jesus commanded his followers to extend the same forgiveness to one another (Matthew 6.12). Not to do so is to shut up the same door through which forgiveness is received for oneself (Matthew 18.21–35).

Gehenna, hell
Gehenna is, literally, the valley of Hinnom, on the south-west slopes of Jerusalem. From ancient times it was used as a garbage dump, smouldering with a continual fire. Already by the time of Jesus some Jews used it as an image for the place of punishment after death. Jesus' own usage blends the two meanings in his warnings both to Jerusalem itself (unless it repents, the whole city will become a smouldering heap of garbage) and to people in general (to beware of God's final judgment).

Gentiles
The Jews divided the world into Jews and non-Jews. The Hebrew word for non-Jews, *goyim*, carries overtones both of family identity (i.e. not of Jewish ancestry) and of worship (i.e. of idols, not of the one true God YHWH). Though many Jews established good relations with Gentiles, not least in the Jewish diaspora (the dispersion of Jews away from Palestine), officially there were taboos against closer contact such as intermarriage. In the New Testament the Greek word *ethne*, 'nations', carries the same meanings as *goyim*. Part of Paul's overmastering agenda was to insist that Gentiles who believed in Jesus had full rights in the Christian community alongside believing Jews, without having to become circumcised.

good news, gospel, message, word
The idea of 'good news', for which an older English word is 'gospel', had two principal meanings for first-century Jews. First, with roots in Isaiah, it meant the news of YHWH's long-awaited victory over evil and rescue of his people. Second, it was used in the Roman world of the accession, or birthday, of the emperor. Since for Jesus and Paul the announcement of God's inbreaking kingdom was both the fulfilment of prophecy and a challenge to the world's present rulers, 'gospel' became an important shorthand for both the message of Jesus himself and the apostolic message about him. Paul saw this message as itself the vehicle of God's saving power (Romans 1.16; 1 Thessalonians 2.13).

gospel
See **good news**.

heaven
Heaven is God's dimension of the created order (Genesis 1.1; Psalm 115.16; Matthew 6.9), whereas 'earth' is the world of space, time and matter that we know. 'Heaven' thus sometimes stands, reverentially, for 'God' (as in Matthew's regular '**kingdom of heaven**'). Normally hidden from human sight, heaven is occasionally revealed or unveiled so that people can see God's dimension of ordinary life (e.g. 2 Kings 6.17; Revelation 1, 4—5). Heaven in the New Testament is thus not usually seen as the place where God's people go after death; at the end, the new Jerusalem descends *from* heaven *to* earth, joining the two dimensions for ever. 'Entering the kingdom of heaven' does not mean 'going to heaven after death', but belonging in the present to the people who steer their earthly course by the standards and purposes of heaven (cf. the Lord's Prayer: 'as in heaven, so on earth', Matthew 6.10), and who are assured of membership in the **age to come**.

hell
See **Gehenna**.

high priest
See **priests**.

holy spirit
In Genesis 1.2, the spirit is God's presence and power *within* creation, without God being identified with creation. The same spirit entered people, notably the prophets, enabling them to speak and act for God. At his **baptism** by John, Jesus was specially equipped with the spirit, resulting in his remarkable public career (Acts 10.38). After his **resurrection**, his followers were themselves filled (Acts 2) by the same spirit, now identified as Jesus' own spirit; the creator God was acting afresh, remaking the world and them too. The spirit enabled them to live out a holiness which the **Torah** could not, producing 'fruit' in their lives, giving them 'gifts' with which to serve God, the world and the church, and assuring them of future resurrection (Romans 8; Galatians 4—5; 1 Corinthians 12—14). From very early in Christianity (e.g. Galatians 4.1-7), the spirit became part of the new revolutionary definition of God himself: 'the one who sends the son and the spirit of the son'.

justification
God's declaration, from his position as judge of all the world, that someone is in the right, despite universal sin. This declaration will be made on the last day on the basis of an entire life (Romans 2.1-16), but is brought forward into the present on the basis of Jesus' achievement, because sin has been dealt with through his cross (Romans 3.21—4.25); the means of this present justification is simply **faith**. This means, particularly, that Jews and **Gentiles** alike are full members of the family promised by God to Abraham (Galatians 3; Romans 4).

kingdom of God, kingdom of heaven
Best understood as the king*ship*, or sovereign and saving rule, of Israel's God YHWH as celebrated in several psalms (e.g. 99.1) and prophecies (e.g. Daniel 6.26f.). Because YHWH was the creator God, when he finally became King in the way he intended this would involve setting the world to right, and particularly rescuing Israel from its enemies. 'Kingdom of God' and various equivalents (e.g. 'No king but God!') became a revolutionary slogan around the time of Jesus. Jesus' own announcement of God's kingdom redefined these expectations around his own very different plan and vocation. His invitation to people to 'enter' the kingdom was a way of summoning them to allegiance to himself and his programme, seen as the start of God's long-awaited saving reign. For Jesus, the kingdom was coming not in a single move, but in stages, of which his own public career was one, his death and **resurrection** another, and a still future consummation another. Note that 'kingdom of heaven' is Matthew's preferred form for the same phrase, following a regular Jewish practice of saying 'heaven' rather than 'God'. It does not refer to a place ('heaven'), but to the fact of God's becoming King in and through Jesus and his achievement. Paul speaks of Jesus as **Messiah**, already in possession of his kingdom, waiting to hand it over finally to the father (1 Corinthians 15.23-28; cf. Ephesians 5.5).

last days
Ancient Jews thought of world history as divided into two periods: 'the **present age**' and 'the **age to come**'. The present age was a time when evil was still at large in its many forms; the age to come would usher in God's final reign of justice, peace, joy and love. Ancient prophets had spoken of the transition from the one age to the other in terms of the 'last days', meaning either the final moments of the 'present age' or the eventual dawning of the 'age to come'. When Peter quotes Joel in Acts 2.17, he perhaps means both: the two ages have overlapped, so that Christians live in the 'last days', the time between God's kingdom being launched in and through Jesus and it being completed at Jesus' return. The New Testament gives no encouragement to the idea that we can calculate a precise timetable for the latter event, or that the period of history immediately before Jesus' return will be significantly different (e.g. more violent) than any other (see Matthew 24.36-39).

law
See **Torah**.

life, soul, spirit
Ancient people held many different views about what made human beings the special creatures they are. Some, including many Jews, believed that to be complete, humans needed bodies as well as inner selves. Others, including many influenced by the philosophy of Plato (fourth century BC), believed that the important part of a human was the 'soul' (Gk. *psyche*), which at death would be happily freed from its bodily prison. Confusingly for us, the same word psyche is often used in the New Testament within a Jewish framework where it clearly means 'life' or 'true self', without implying a body–soul dualism that devalues the body. Human inwardness of experience and understanding can also be referred to as 'spirit'. See also **holy spirit**; **resurrection**.

message
See **good news**.

Messiah, messianic, Christ
The Hebrew word means literally 'anointed one', hence in theory either a prophet, priest or king. In Greek this translates as *Christos*; 'Christ' in early Christianity was a title, and only gradually became an alternative proper name for Jesus. In practice, 'Messiah' is mostly restricted to the notion, which took various forms in ancient Judaism, of the coming king who would be David's true heir, through whom YHWH would bring judgment to the world, and in particular would rescue Israel from pagan enemies. There was no single template of expectations. Scriptural stories and promises contributed to different ideas and movements, often focused on (a) decisive military defeat of Israel's enemies and (b) rebuilding or cleansing the **Temple**. The Dead Sea Scrolls speak of two 'Messiahs', one a priest and the other a king. The universal early Christian belief that Jesus was Messiah is only explicable, granted his crucifixion by the Romans (which would have been seen as a clear sign that he was not the Messiah), by their belief that God had raised him from the dead, so vindicating the implicit messianic claims of his earlier ministry.

miracles
Like some of the old prophets, notably Elijah and Elisha, Jesus performed many deeds of remarkable power, particularly healings. The gospels refer to these as 'deeds of power', 'signs', 'marvels' or 'paradoxes'. Our word 'miracle' tends to imply that God, normally 'outside' the closed system of the world, sometimes 'intervenes'; miracles have then frequently been denied by sceptics as a matter of principle. However, in the Bible, God is always present, however strangely, and 'deeds of power' are seen as *special* acts of a *present* God rather than *intrusive* acts of an *absent* one. Jesus' own 'mighty works' are seen particularly, following prophecy, as evidence of his messiahship.

parables
From the Old Testament onwards, prophets and other teachers used various storytelling devices as vehicles for their challenge to Israel (e.g. 2 Samuel 12.1–7). Sometimes they appeared as visions with interpretations (e.g. Daniel 7). Similar techniques were used by the **rabbis**. Jesus made his own creative adaptation of these traditions, in order to break open the world-view of his contemporaries and to invite them to share his vision of God's kingdom instead. His stories portrayed this as something that was *happening*, not just a timeless truth, and enabled his hearers to step inside the story and make it their own. As with some Old Testament visions, some of Jesus' parables have their own interpretations (e.g. the sower, Mark 4); others are thinly disguised retellings of the prophetic story of Israel (e.g. the wicked tenants, Mark 12).

Pharisees, rabbis
The Pharisees were an unofficial but powerful Jewish pressure group through most of the first centuries BC and AD. Largely lay-led, though including some of the **priests**, their aim was to purify Israel through intensified observance of the **Jewish law** (**Torah**), developing their own traditions about the precise meaning and application of scripture, their own patterns of prayer and other devotion, and their own calculations of the national hope. Though not all legal experts were Pharisees, most Pharisees were legal experts.

They effected a democratization of Israel's life, since for them the study and practice of Torah was equivalent to worshipping in the **Temple** – though they were adamant in pressing their own rules for the Temple liturgy on an unwilling (and often Saducean) priesthood. This enabled them to survive AD 70 and, merging into the early rabbinic movement, to develop new ways forward. Politically, they stood up for ancestral traditions, and were at the forefront of various movements of revolt against both pagan overlordship and compromised Jewish leaders. By Jesus' day there were two distinct schools, the stricter one of Shammai, more inclined towards armed revolt, and the more lenient one of Hillel, more ready to live and let live.

Jesus' debates with the Pharisees are at least as much a matter of agenda and policy (Jesus strongly opposed their separatist nationalism) as about details of theology and piety. Saul of Tarsus was a fervent right-wing Pharisee, presumably a Shammaite, until his conversion.

After the disastrous war of AD 66–70, these schools of Hillel and Shammai continued bitter debate on appropriate policy. Following the further disaster of AD 135 (the failed bar-Kochba revolt against Rome) their traditions were carried on by the rabbis, who, though looking to the earlier Pharisees for inspiration, developed a Torah-piety in which personal holiness and purity took the place of political agendas.

present age, age to come, eternal life
By the time of Jesus many Jewish thinkers divided history into two periods: 'the present age' and 'the age to come' – the latter being the time when YHWH would at last act decisively to judge evil, to rescue Israel, and to create a new world of justice and peace. The early Christians believed that, though the full blessings of the coming age lay still in the future, it had already begun with Jesus, particularly with his death and **resurrection**, and that by **faith** and **baptism** they were able to enter it already. 'Eternal life' does not mean simply 'existence continuing without end', but 'the life of the age to come'.

priests, high priest
Aaron, the older brother of Moses, was appointed Israel's first high priest (Exodus 28—29), and in theory his descendants were Israel's priests thereafter. Other members of his tribe (Levi) were 'Levites', performing other liturgical duties but not sacrificing. Priests lived among the people all around the country, having a local teaching role (Leviticus 10.11; Malachi 2.7), and going to Jerusalem by rotation to perform the **Temple** liturgy (e.g. Luke 1.8–9).

David appointed Zadok (whose Aaronic ancestry is sometimes questioned) as high priest, and his family remained thereafter the senior priests in Jerusalem, probably the ancestors of the **Sadducees**. One explanation of the origin of the Qumran Essenes is that they were a dissident group who believed themselves to be the rightful chief priests.

rabbis
See **Pharisees**.

redemption
Literally, 'redemption' means 'buying back', and was often used in the ancient world of slaves buying their freedom, or having it bought for them. The great 'redemption' in the Bible, which coloured the way the word was heard ever afterwards, was when God 'bought' his people Israel from slavery in Egypt to give them freedom in the promised land. When, later, the Jews

were exiled in Babylon (and even after they returned to their land), they described themselves as undergoing a new slavery and hence being in need of a new redemption. Jesus, and the early Christians, interpreted this continuing slavery in its most radical terms, as slavery to sin and death, and understood 'redemption' likewise in terms of the rescue from this multiple and tyrannous slavery, which God provided through the death of Jesus (Romans 3.24).

repentance
Literally, this means 'turning back'. It is widely used in Old Testament and subsequent Jewish literature to indicate both a personal turning away from sin and Israel's corporate turning away from idolatry and back to YHWH. Through both meanings, it is linked to the idea of 'return from **exile**'; if Israel is to 'return' in all senses, it must 'return' to YHWH. This is at the heart of the summons of both John the Baptist and Jesus. In Paul's writings it is mostly used for **Gentiles** turning away from idols to serve the true God; also for sinning Christians who need to return to Jesus.

resurrection
In most biblical thought, human bodies matter and are not merely disposable prisons for the **soul**. When ancient Israelites wrestled with the goodness and justice of YHWH, the creator, they ultimately came to insist that he must raise the dead (Isaiah 26.19; Daniel 12.2–3) – a suggestion firmly resisted by classical pagan thought. The longed-for return from **exile** was also spoken of in terms of YHWH raising dry bones to new life (Ezekiel 37.1–14). These ideas were developed in the second-**Temple** period, not least at times of martyrdom (e.g. 2 Maccabees 7). Resurrection was not just 'life after death', but a newly embodied life *after* 'life after death'; those at present dead were either 'asleep' or seen as 'souls', 'angels' or 'spirits', awaiting new embodiment.

sacrifice
Like all ancient peoples, the Israelites offered animal and vegetable sacrifices to their God. Unlike others, they possessed a highly detailed written code (mostly in Leviticus) for what to offer and how to offer it; this in turn was developed in the Mishnah (c. AD 200). The Old Testament specifies that sacrifices can only be offered in the Jerusalem **Temple**; after this was destroyed in AD 70, sacrifices ceased, and Judaism developed further the idea, already present in some teachings, of prayer, fasting and almsgiving as alternative forms of sacrifice. The early Christians used the language of sacrifice in connection with such things as holiness, evangelism and the Eucharist.

Sadducees
By Jesus' day, the Sadducees were the aristocracy of Judaism, possibly tracing their origins to the family of Zadok, David's **high priest**. Based in Jerusalem, and including most of the leading priestly families, they had their own traditions and attempted to resist the pressure of the **Pharisees** to conform to theirs. They claimed to rely only on the Pentateuch (the first five books of the Old Testament), and denied any doctrine of a future life, particularly of the **resurrection** and other ideas associated with it, presumably because of the encouragement such beliefs gave to revolutionary movements. No writings from the Sadducees have survived, unless the apocryphal book of Ben Sirach (Ecclesiasticus) comes from them. The Sadducees themselves did not survive the destruction of Jerusalem and the **Temple** in AD 70.

salvation
Salvation means 'rescue', and the meanings of the word have depended on what people thought needed rescuing, and from what. Thus, where people have imagined that the human plight was best seen in terms of an immortal **soul** being trapped in a mortal and corrupt body, 'salvation' was seen in terms of the rescue of this soul from such a prison. But for most Jews, and all early Christians, it was death itself, the ending of God-given bodily life, that was the real enemy, so that 'salvation' was bound to mean being rescued from death itself – in other words, the **resurrection**

of the body for those who had died, and the transformation of the body for those still alive at the Lord's return (e.g. 1 Corinthians 15.50–57). For Paul and others, this 'salvation' was extended to the whole of creation (Romans 8.18–25). But if 'salvation' refers to this ultimate rescue of God's created order, and our created bodies, from all that distorts, defaces and destroys them (i.e. sin, sickness, corruption and death itself), we should expect to find, and do in fact find, that often in the New Testament 'salvation' (and phrases like 'being saved') refers, not simply to people coming to **faith** and so being assured of **eternal life**, but to bodily healing and to rescue from awful plights (e.g. Acts 16.30–31; 27.44). Jesus' resurrection remains the foundation for a biblical view of salvation for the whole person and the whole creation, a salvation which, though to be completed in the future, has already begun with the mission and achievement of Jesus.

satan, the, 'the accuser', demons, devil
The Bible is never very precise about the identity of the figure known as 'the satan'. The Hebrew word means 'the accuser', and at times the satan seems to be a member of YHWH's heavenly council, with special responsibility as director of prosecutions (1 Chronicles 21.1; Job 1—2; Zechariah 3.1f.). However, it becomes identified variously with the serpent of the garden of Eden (Genesis 3.1–15) and with the rebellious daystar cast out of **heaven** (Isaiah 14.12–15), and was seen by many Jews as the quasi-personal source of evil standing behind both human wickedness and large-scale injustice, sometimes operating through semi-independent 'demons'. By Jesus' time, various words were used to denote this figure, including Beelzebul/b (lit. 'Lord of the flies') and simply 'the evil one'; Jesus warned his followers against the deceits this figure could perpetrate. His opponents accused him of being in league with the satan, but the early Christians believed that Jesus in fact defeated it in his own struggles with temptation (Matthew 4; Luke 4), his exorcism of demons, and his death (1 Corinthians 2.8; Colossians 2.15). Final victory over this ultimate enemy is thus assured (Revelation 20), though the struggle can still be fierce for Christians (Ephesians 6.10–20).

scribes
In a world where many could not write, or not very well, a trained class of writers ('scribes') performed the important function of drawing up contracts for business, marriage, and so on. Many scribes would thus be legal experts, and quite possibly **Pharisees**, though being a scribe was compatible with various political and religious standpoints. The work of Christian scribes was of initial importance in copying early Christian writings, particularly the stories about Jesus.

son of God
Originally a title for Israel (Exodus 4.22) and the Davidic king (Psalm 2.7); also used of ancient angelic figures (Genesis 6.2). By the New Testament period it was already used as a **messianic** title, for example, in the Dead Sea Scrolls. There, and when used of Jesus in the gospels (e.g. Matthew 16.16), it means, or reinforces, '**Messiah**', without the later significance of 'divine'. However, already in Paul the transition to the fuller meaning (one who was already equal with God and was sent by him to become human and to become Messiah) is apparent, without loss of the meaning 'Messiah' itself (e.g. Galatians 4.4).

son of man
In Hebrew or Aramaic, this simply means 'mortal', or 'human being'; in later Judaism, it is sometimes used to mean 'I' or 'someone like me'. In the New Testament the phrase is frequently linked to Daniel 7.13, where 'one like a son of man' is brought on the clouds of heaven to the 'Ancient of Days', being vindicated after a period of suffering, and is given kingly power. Though Daniel 7 itself interprets this as code for 'the people of the saints of the Most High', by the first century some Jews understood it as a **messianic** promise. Jesus developed this in his own way in certain key sayings which are best understood as promises that God would vindicate him, and judge those who had opposed him, after his own suffering (e.g. Mark 14.62). Jesus was thus able

to use the phrase as a cryptic self-designation, hinting at his coming suffering, his vindication and his God-given authority.

soul
See **life**.

spirit
See **life, holy spirit**.

Temple
The Temple in Jerusalem was planned by David (c. 1000 BC) and built by his son Solomon as the central sanctuary for all Israel. After reforms under Hezekiah and Josiah in the seventh century BC, it was destroyed by Babylon in 587 BC. Rebuilding by the returned exiles began in 538 BC, and was completed in 516 BC, initiating the 'second-Temple period'. Judas Maccabaeus cleansed it in 164 BC after its desecration by Antiochus Epiphanes (167 BC). Herod the Great began to rebuild and beautify it in 19 BC; the work was completed in AD 63. The Temple was destroyed by the Romans in AD 70. Many Jews believed it should and would be rebuilt; some still do. The Temple was not only the place of **sacrifice**; it was believed to be the unique dwelling of YHWH on earth, the place where **heaven** and earth met.

Torah, Jewish law
'Torah', narrowly conceived, consists of the first five books of the Old Testament, the 'five books of Moses' or 'Pentateuch'. (These contain much law, but also much narrative.) It can also be used for the whole Old Testament scriptures, though strictly these are the 'law, prophets and writings'. In a broader sense, it refers to the whole developing corpus of Jewish legal tradition, written and oral; the oral Torah was initially codified in the Mishnah around AD 200, with wider developments found in the two Talmuds, of Babylon and Jerusalem, codified around AD 400. Many Jews in the time of Jesus and Paul regarded the Torah as being so strongly God-given as to be almost itself, in some sense, divine; some (e.g. Ben Sirach 24) identified it with the figure of 'Wisdom'. Doing what Torah said was not seen as a means of earning God's favour, but rather of expressing gratitude, and as a key badge of Jewish identity.

Word
The Prologue to John's gospel (1.1–18) uses Word (Gk. *logos*) in a special sense, based on the ancient Israelite view of God's Word in creation and new creation. Here the Word is Jesus, the personal presence of the God who remains other than the world. He is the one through whom creation came into being; he is the one, now, through whom it will be healed and restored.

word
See **good news**.

YHWH
The ancient Israelite name for God, from at least the time of the exodus (Exodus 6.2f.). It may originally have been pronounced 'Yahweh', but by the time of Jesus it was considered too holy to speak out loud, except for the **high priest** once a year in the holy of holies in the **Temple**. Instead, when reading scripture, pious Jews would say *Adonai*, 'Lord', marking this usage by adding the vowels of *Adonai* to the consonants of YHWH, eventually producing the hybrid 'Jehovah'. The word YHWH is formed from the verb 'to be', combining 'I am who I am', 'I will be who I will be' and perhaps 'I am because I am', emphasizing YHWH's sovereign creative power.

Alphabetical listing of books of the Bible

1 Chronicles	391	Hosea	847
1 Corinthians	1132	Isaiah	648
1 John	1231	James	1216
1 Kings	326	Jeremiah	709
1 Peter	1221	Job	495
1 Samuel	264	Joel	858
1 Thessalonians	1182	John	1029
1 Timothy	1189	Jonah	874
2 Chronicles	422	Joshua	206
2 Corinthians	1148	Judah	1240
2 John	1236	Judges	233
2 Kings	359	Lamentations	773
2 Peter	1227	Leviticus	94
2 Samuel	297	Luke	993
2 Thessalonians	1186	Malachi	909
2 Timothy	1194	Mark	971
3 John	1238	Matthew	935
The Acts of the Apostles	1059	Micah	877
Amos	863	Nahum	884
Colossians	1177	Nehemiah	469
Daniel	831	Numbers	125
Deuteronomy	168	Obadiah	871
Ecclesiastes	631	Philemon	1201
Ephesians	1165	Philippians	1172
Esther	486	Proverbs	604
Exodus	52	Psalms	526
Ezekiel	780	The Revelation of John	1242
Ezra	457	Romans	1115
Galatians	1159	Ruth	259
Genesis	1	The Song of Songs	641
Habakkuk	888	Titus	1198
Haggai	896	Zechariah	899
Hebrews	1203	Zephaniah	892